S0-AIQ-759

WITHDRAWN FROM
MACALESTER COLLEGE
LIBRARY

THE ENCYCLOPAEDIA OF ISLAM

THE ENCYCLOPAEDIA OF ISLAM

NEW EDITION

PREPARED BY A NUMBER OF
LEADING ORIENTALISTS

EDITED BY

**P. J. BEARMAN, TH. BIANQUIS, C. E. BOSWORTH,
E. VAN DONZEL AND W. P. HEINRICHS**

ASSISTED BY C. OTT

UNDER THE PATRONAGE OF
THE INTERNATIONAL UNION OF ACADEMIES

INDEX VOLUME

BRILL

LEIDEN • BOSTON
2009

EXECUTIVE COMMITTEE:

Members: P.J. Bearman, Th. Bianquis, C.E. Bosworth, J.T.P. de Bruijn, A. Dias Farinha, E. van Donzel, J. van Ess, W.P. Heinrichs, B. Lewis, F. Rundgren, A.L. Udovitch.

Associated members: Halil İnalcik, S.H. Nasr, M. Talbi.

The preparation of this volume of the Encyclopaedia of Islam was made possible in part through grants from the Research Tools Program of the National Endowment for the Humanities, an independent Federal Agency of the United States Government; the British Academy; the Oriental Institute, Leiden; Académie des Inscriptions et Belles-Lettres; and the Royal Netherlands Academy of Sciences.

This INDEX VOLUME contains the following three indices:

ISBN 978 90 04 14448 4

© Copyright 2009 by Koninklijke Brill, Leiden, The Netherlands

All rights reserved. No part of this publication may be reproduced, translated, stored in a retrieval system, or transmitted in any form or by any means, electronic, mechanical, photocopying, recording or otherwise, without prior written permission of the publishers.

Authorization to photocopy items for internal or personal use is granted by Brill provided that the appropriate fees are paid directly to Copyright Clearance Center, 222 Rosewood Drive, Suite 910, Danvers, MA 01923, USA. Fees are subject to change.

PRINTED IN THE NETHERLANDS

THE ENCYCLOPAEDIA OF ISLAM

NEW EDITION

INDEX VOLUME

FASCICULE 1

INDEX OF SUBJECTS

COMPILED BY

P. J. BEARMAN

TABLE OF CONTENTS

LIST OF ENTRIES

For facility of *Encyclopaedia* use, since headings of entries there are generally in Arabic, Persian or Turkish, this list provides English references to either the main article in the *Encyclopaedia* or to the Index of Subjects proper, which groups all articles concerned with the subject under one heading. The main *Encyclopaedia* article is given here in bold type, the Subject Index heading is in capitals preceded by an arrow (e.g. Clove **Ḳaranful**; but Spices → CUISINE.FOOD). The Index of Subjects follows the List of Entries on p. 19. Countries and names of dynasties or caliphates, which are included *in extenso* in the Index of Subjects, are not given in the following list.

A

Abbreviations [in Suppl.] **Abbreviations**
Ablution → ABLUTION
Abridgement **Mukh̲taṣar**
Abstinence **Istibrāʾ**
Academy **Mad̲j̲maʿ ʿIlmī**
Accident **ʿAraḍ**
Accounting → FINANCE
Acquisition **Kasb**
Acrobat **D̲j̲ānbāz**
Act **ʿAmal; Fiʿl**
Addax **Mahāt**
Administration → ADMINISTRATION
Admiral **Ḳapudan Pas̲h̲a**
Adoption → ADOPTION
Adultery → ADULTERY
Advance guard **Ṭalīʿa**
Adverb **Ẓarf**
Aesthetics **ʿIlm al-D̲j̲amāl**
Agency **Wakāla**
Agriculture → AGRICULTURE
Aims (of the law) [in Suppl.] **Maḳāṣid al-S̲h̲arīʿa**
Album **Muraḳḳaʿ**
Alchemy → ALCHEMY
Alfa-grass **Ḥalfāʾ**
Algebra → MATHEMATICS
Almanac **Taḳwīm**
Alms → ALMS
Aloe **Ṣabr**
Alphabet → ALPHABET
Amazement **Taʿad̲j̲d̲j̲ub**
Amber **Kahrubā**
Ambergris **ʿAnbar**
Americas → NEW WORLD
Amplification (of poetry) **Takh̲mīs**
Amulet **Tamīma**
Analogy **Ḳiyās**
Anatomy → ANATOMY
Anecdote **Nādira**
Anemone **S̲h̲aḳīḳat al-Nuʿmān**
Angel → ANGELOLOGY
Animal → ANIMALS
Ant **Naml**
Antelope → ANIMALS
Anthology **Mukh̲tārāt**
Anthropomorphism → ANTHROPOMORPHISM
Antinomianism **Ibāḥa** (II)
Antithesis **Ṭibāḳ**
Aphrodisiacs [in Suppl.] **Muḳawwiyāt**
Apostasy → APOSTASY
Appeal **Istiʾnāf**
Apple **Tuffāḥ**
Apricot **Mis̲h̲mis̲h̲**
Aqueduct → ARCHITECTURE.MONUMENTS
Arabian peninsula → ARABIAN PENINSULA
Arabic → ALPHABET; LANGUAGES.AFRO-ASIATIC; LINGUISTICS
Arabicisation **Taʿrīb**
Arabism → PANARABISM
Arachnoids → ANIMALS
Arbitration **Taḥkīm**
Arbitrator **Ḥakam**
Archaeology → ARCHAEOLOGY
Architecture → ARCHITECTURE
Archives → ADMINISTRATION
Arithmetic → MATHEMATICS
Armour [in Suppl.] **Silāḥ**
Army → MILITARY

Arsenal **Dār al-Ṣināʿa**
Art → ART
Artemisia **Shīḥ**
Article **Maḳāla**
Articulation [in Suppl.] **Lafẓ**.1
Artisans → PROFESSIONS.CRAFTSMEN AND TRADESMEN
Ascendent **al-Ṭāliʿ**
Ascension to Heaven, Prophet's **Miʿrādj**
Ascensions **al-Maṭāliʿ**
Asceticism → ASCETICISM
Assignation **Ḥawāla**
Association **Andjuman**; **Djamʿiyya**
Associationism **Shirk**
Astrolabe **Asṭurlāb**
Astrology → ASTROLOGY
Astronomical handbook **Zīdj**
Astronomy → ASTRONOMY
Atheism **Kāfir**
Atomism **Djuzʾ**
Attributes **Ṣifa**
Autobiography → LITERATURE.AUTOBIOGRAPHICAL
Avarice **Bukhl**

B

Bābism → SECTS
Bacchism → WINE.BACCHIC POETRY
Backgammon **Nard**
Bahais → BAHAIS
Balance **al-Mīzān**
Balance of powers **Tawāzun al-Suluṭāt**
Bamboo sugar **Ṭabāshīr**
Band → MILITARY.BAND
Banking → FINANCE
Barber [in Suppl.] **Ḥallāḳ**
Bargaining **Sawm**
Barley **Shaʿīr**
Barracks **Ṭabaḳa**
Barter **Muʿāwaḍa**
Basques → BASQUES
Bat **Waṭwāṭ**
Bath → ARCHITECTURE.MONUMENTS
Battalion **Ṭabūr**
Battle → MILITARY.BATTLES
Beard, the Prophet's **Liḥya-yi Sherīf**
Beauty **ʿIlm al-Djamāl**
Bedding **Mafrūshāt**; **Mifrash**
Bedouin → BEDOUINS
Bee **Naḥl**
Beggar **Sāsān**
Belles-lettres → LITERATURE
Belomancy **Istiḳsām**
Ben-nut **Bān**
Bequest **Waṣiyya**
Berbers → BERBERS
Betrothal **Khiṭba**
Bible → BIBLE
Bibliography → LITERATURE.BIBLIOGRAPHICAL
Bier **Djanāza**
Biography → LITERATURE.BIOGRAPHICAL
Bird → ANIMALS
Birth control → LIFE STAGES.CHILDBIRTH.PREGNANCY
Bitumen **Mūmiyāʾ**
Blacksmith **Ḳayn**
Blasphemy [in Suppl.] **Shatm**
Blessing **Baraka**
Blockprinting → WRITING.MANUSCRIPTS AND BOOKS
Blood [in Suppl.] **Dam**
Blood-letter [in Suppl.] **Faṣṣād**
Blood-vengeance **Ḳiṣāṣ**; **Thaʾr**
Boar, wild **Khinzīr**
Boat **Safīna**
Body **Djism**
Book **Kitāb**
Bookbinding → WRITING.MANUSCRIPTS AND BOOKS
Bookseller **Warrāḳ**
Booktitle **ʿUnwān**.2(=3)
Boon-companion **Nadīm**
Booty → MILITARY
Botany → BOTANY
Boundaries **Takhṭīṭ al-Ḥudūd**
Bow **Ḳaws**
Bowing → PRAYER
Brand **Tamgha**; **Wasm**
Bread **Khubz**
Breadwinner [in Suppl.] **Muʿīnsiz**
Bribery → PAYMENTS
Brick **Labin**
Bridal gift *see* Dower
Bridge → ARCHITECTURE.MONUMENTS
Brigand **Ṣuʿlūk**

Broadcasting **Id̲h̲āʿa**
Broker **Dallāl**
Buddhism → Buddhism
Buffalo [in Suppl.] **D̲j̲āmūs**
Building **Bināʾ**
Butcher [in Suppl.] **D̲j̲azzār**
Butter **al-Samn**
Byzantines → Byzantine Empire

C

Calendar → Time
Caliph **K̲h̲alīfa**
Caliphate → Caliphate
Call to prayer **Ad̲h̲ān**
Calligraphy → Art; Writing.scripts
Camel → Animals
Camel-driver [in Suppl.] **D̲j̲ammāl**
Camomile [in Suppl.] **Bābūnad̲j̲**
Camphor **Kāfūr**
Canal **Ḳanāt**
Candle **S̲h̲amʿa**
Candle-maker **S̲h̲ammāʿ**
Canines → Animals
Cannon **Ṭop**
Cap [in Suppl.] **Ḳalansuwa**
Capitulations **Imtiyāzāt**
Caravan → Transport
Carmathians → Shiites.branches
Carpet → Art.tapestry; Prayer
Cart **ʿAd̲j̲ala; Araba**
Cartography → Cartography
Cattle **Baḳar**
Cause **ʿIlla**
Cedar-oil **Ḳaṭrān**
Cemetery **Maḳbara**
Ceramics → Art.pottery
Cession **Ḥawāla**
Chair **Kursī**
Chamber, underground **Sardāb**
Chamberlain **Ḥād̲j̲ib**
Chameleon **Ḥirbāʾ**
Chancellery → Documents
Charity → Alms
Charms → Charms
Cheetah **Fahd**
Cheiropters **Waṭwāṭ**
Chemistry → Alchemy
Chess **S̲h̲aṭrand̲j̲**
Chest → Anatomy
Child → Life Stages
Childbirth → Life Stages
Childhood → Life Stages
Chintz **Ḳalamkārī**
Chirognomy **al-Kaff**
Christianity → Christianity
Christians **Naṣārā**
Chronogram **Taʾrīk̲h̲.III**
Church **Kanīsa**
Cinema **Cinema**
Cinnamon [in Suppl.] **Dār Ṣīnī**
Circumcision → Circumcision
Cistern **Ḥawḍ**
Citizen **Muwāṭin**
Citrus fruits **Nārand̲j̲**
City (planning) [in Suppl.] **Madīna**
Civilisation **Medeniyyet**
Clan **Āl**
Clay **Ṭīn**
Cleanliness **Ṭahāra**
Clime **Iḳlīm**
Cloak **K̲h̲irḳa**
Cloak, the Prophet's **K̲h̲irḳa-yi S̲h̲erīf**
Clock **Sāʿa**
Clothing → Clothing
Clove **Ḳaranful**
Cock **Dīk**
Codes → Cryptography
Codification (of the law) **Tas̲h̲rīʿ**
Coffee **Ḳahwa**
Coinage → Numismatics
Coitus **Bāh**
Coitus interruptus **ʿAzl**
Colour → Colour
Column **ʿAmūd**
Comedians → Humour
Commanding right *see* Forbidding wrong
Commentary **S̲h̲arḥ**
Commentary (Qurʾanic) → Qurʾan
Commerce → Finance
Communications → Communications
Communism → Communism
Community, Muslim **Umma**
Companions (of the Prophet) → Muḥammad, the Prophet

Compass **Maghnāṭīs**.2; **al-Ṭāsa**
Concealment (of belief) **Taḳiyya**
Concubinage → WOMEN
Conference **Mu'tamar**
Confessionalism **Ṭā'ifiyya**
Confinement (of Ottoman princes) [in Suppl.] **Ḳafes**
Congress **Mu'tamar**
Conjunction **Ḳirān**
Constellation → ASTRONOMY
Constitution **Dustūr**
Consul **Consul**
Consultation **Shūrā**
Contraception **Tanẓīm al-Nasl**
Contract → LAW.LAW OF OBLIGATIONS
Cook **Ṭabbākh**
Cooking → CUISINE
Cooperatives **Taʿāwun**
Copper **Nuḥās**; *and see* Malachite
Copts → CHRISTIANITY.DENOMINATIONS
Copyist **Warrāḳ**
Coral **Mardjān**
Cornelian **ʿAḳīḳ**
Corpse **Djanāza**
Corpse-washer [in Suppl.] **Ghassāl**
Corsair → PIRACY
Corundum **Yāḳūt**
Cosmetics → COSMETICS
Cosmography → COSMOGRAPHY
Cotton **Ḳuṭn**
Country **Waṭan**
Court (of law) **Maḥkama**
Court ceremony → COURT CEREMONY
Court hierarchy [in Suppl.] **Martaba**
Courtier **Nadīm**
Couscous **Kuskusū**
Cowrie **Wadaʿ**
Craftsmanship → PROFESSIONS
Creation → CREATION
Creditor **Ghārim**
Creed **ʿAḳīda**
Crescent **Hilāl**
Criticism, literary → LITERATURE
Crocodile **Timsāḥ**
Cross **al-Ṣalīb**
Crow **Ghurāb**
Crown **Tādj**
Crucifixion **Ṣalb**
Crusades → CRUSADE(R)S
Crustaceans → ANIMALS
Cryptography → CRYPTOGRAPHY
Crystal *see* Rock-crystal
Cubit **Dhirāʿ**
Cuckoo **Wāḳwāḳ**.4
Cuisine → CUISINE
Cumin **Kammūn**
Cupper [in Suppl.] **Faṣṣād**
Currants **Zabīb**
Custody **Ḥaḍāna**
Custom → CUSTOM
Customary law → LAW
Cymbal **Ṣandj**

D

Dactylonomy **Ḥisāb al-ʿAḳd**
Dam → ARCHITECTURE.MONUMENTS
Dance **Raḳṣ**
Dandy **Ẓarīf**
Date **Nakhl**
Day **Yawm**
Death → DEATH
Debt [in Suppl.] **Dayn**
Debtor **Ghārim**
Deception (in law) **Taghrīr**
Declension **Iʿrāb**
Declination **al-Mayl**
Decoration → ARCHITECTURE; ART.DECORATIVE; MILITARY
Decree, divine **al-Ḳaḍā' wa 'l-Ḳadar**
Decree of ruler **Tawḳīʿ**
Deer **Ayyil**
Definition **Taʿrīf**
Delegations **Wufūd**
Delusion Wahm
Demography [in Suppl.] **Demography**
Demon **Djinn**
Dentistry → MEDICINE
Deposit **Wadīʿa**
Deposition [in Suppl.] **Khalʿ**
Deputisation **Wakāla**
Dervish → MYSTICISM
Description **Waṣf**
Desert → DESERTS
Devil **Iblīs**; **Shayṭān**
Devotions **Wird**
Dialect → LANGUAGES.AFRO-ASIATIC.ARABIC

Diamond **Almās**
Dictionary → DICTIONARY
Dill **Shibithth**
Diplomacy → DIPLOMACY
Disease → ILLNESS
Disputation → THEOLOGY
Dissolution **Faskh**
Ditch **Khandaḳ**
Divination → DIVINATION
Divorce → DIVORCE
Documents → DOCUMENTS
Dog **Kalb**
Donative coins **Yādgār**
Donkey **Ḥimār**
Double entendre **Tawriya**
Doubt **Shakk**
Dove **Ḥamām**
Dower → MARRIAGE
Dragoman **Tardjumān**
Dragon **al-Tinnīn**
Drama → LITERATURE
Drawing → ART
Dreams → DREAMS
Dress → CLOTHING
Dressmaker **Khayyāṭ**
Drinks → CUISINE
Dromedary → ANIMALS.CAMELS
Druggist **al-ʿAṭṭār**
Drugs → DRUGS
Drum **Darabukka**; **Ṭabl**
Drummer **Ṭabbāl**
Druze → DRUZES
Dualism → RELIGION
Dulcimer **Sanṭūr**
Duress [in Suppl.] **Ikrāh**
Dwelling **Bayt**; **Dār**
Dye → DYEING
Dyer → DYEING
Dynasty → DYNASTIES

E

Eagle **ʿUḳāb**
Earthquakes → EARTHQUAKES
Ebony **Abanūs**
Eclipse **Kusūf**
Ecliptic **Minṭaḳat al-Burūdj**
Economics → ECONOMICS
Edict **Farmān**
Education → EDUCATION
Elative **Tafḍīl**
Elegy **Marthiya**
Elephant **Fīl**
Elixir **al-Iksīr**
Eloquence **Balāgha**; **Bayān**; **Faṣāḥa**
Emancipation → EMANCIPATION
Embalming **Ḥināṭa**
Emblem of sultan **Tughra**
Emerald **Zumurrud**
Emigration → EMIGRATION
Emphatic phonemes **Tafkhīm**
Encyclopaedia **Mawsūʿa**
Endive [in Suppl.] **Hindibāʾ**
Endowment, charitable **Waḳf**
Enjambment **Taḍmīn**
Ephemeris **Taḳwīm**
Epic **Ḥamāsa**
Epidemic **Wabāʾ**
Epigraphy → EPIGRAPHY
Epistolography → LITERATURE.EPISTOLARY
Epithet → ONOMASTICS
Equation (astronomical) **al-Taʿdīl**; **Taʿdīl al-Zamān**
Equator **Istiwāʾ**
Equines → ANIMALS
Eroticism → LOVE.EROTIC
Error **Khaṭaʾ**
Error, writing *see* Mistakes
Eschatology → ESCHATOLOGY
Esoteric sense **al-Ẓāhir wa ʾl-Bāṭin**
Espionage *see* Spy
Estate **Ḍayʿa**
Eternity → ETERNITY
Ethics → ETHICS
Ethnicity → ETHNICITY
Ethnography → TRIBES
Etiquette → ETIQUETTE
Etymology **Ishtiḳāḳ**
Eulogy **Madīḥ**
Eunuch → EUNUCH
Europeanisation **Tafarnudj**
Evidence **Bayyina**
Ewer [in Suppl.] **Ibrīḳ**
Exception **Istithnāʾ**
Executor **Waṣiyya**

Exegesis **Tafsīr**
Existence **Wudjūd**
Exoteric sense **Ẓāhir**; **al-Ẓāhir wa 'l-Bāṭin**
Expedition → MILITARY
Expiation **Kaffāra**
Extremism **Taṭarruf**
Eye → ANATOMY; EVIL EYE

F

Faculty, university **Kulliyya**
Faïence **Kās̲h̲ī**
Faith → FAITH
Faith, profession of *see* Profession of faith
Falconry → FALCONRY
Family **ʿĀʾila**
Family planning **Tanẓīm al-Nasl**
Fan **Mirwaḥa**
Farming → AGRICULTURE
Fasting → FASTING
Fate → PREDESTINATION
Fauna → ANIMALS
Felines → ANIMALS
Felt **Lubūd**
Female circumcision **K̲h̲afḍ**
Fennec-fox **Fanak**
Fennel [in Suppl.] **Basbās**
Festival → FESTIVAL
Fief **Iḳṭāʿ**
Fifth, one- [in Suppl.] **K̲h̲ums**
Fig **Tīn**
Film **Cinema**
Finance → FINANCE
Fine **D̲j̲urm**
Fire **Nār**
Firefighter **Ṭulumbad̲j̲ī**
Fiscal system → TAXATION
Fish → ANIMALS
Fishing **Samak**.3
Five **K̲h̲amsa**
Flag **ʿAlam**; **Sand̲j̲aḳ**
Flamingo **Nuḥām**
Flax **Kattān**
Fleet, naval **Usṭūl**
Flora → FLORA
Flower poetry **Zahriyyāt**
Flowers → FLORA
Flute [in Suppl.] **Nāy**
Fly **D̲h̲ubāb**
Folklore → FOLKLORE
Food → CUISINE
Fools, wise [in Suppl.] **ʿUḳalāʾ al-Mad̲j̲ānīn**
Footprint, the Prophet's **Ḳadam S̲h̲arīf**
Forbidding wrong [in Suppl.] **al-Nahy ʿan al-Munkar**
Forest **G̲h̲āba**
Foreword **Muḳaddima**
Forgery (of coins) **Tazyīf**
Forgery (of writings) **Tazwīr**
Form, legal **Waṣf**.2
Form, linguistic [in Suppl.] **Lafẓ**.1
Formulas → ISLAM
Fornication **Zinā**
Fortress → ARCHITECTURE.MONUMENTS.STRONGHOLDS
Foundling **Laḳīṭ**
Fountain **S̲h̲adirwān**
Fowl **Dad̲j̲ād̲j̲a**
Fox **T̲h̲aʿlab**; *and see* Fennec-fox
Fraction **Kasr**
Frankincense **Lubān**
Fraud **Tag̲h̲rīr**
Free will → PREDESTINATION
Freedom **Ḥurriyya**; [in Suppl.] **Āzādī**
Freemasonry [in Suppl.] **Farāmūs̲h̲-k̲h̲āna**; **Farmāsūniyya**
Fruit → CUISINE.FOOD
Fundamentalism → REFORM.POLITICO-RELIGIOUS.MILITANT
Funeral **D̲j̲anāza**
Fur **Farw**
Furnishings → FURNISHINGS
Furniture [in Suppl.] **At̲h̲āt̲h̲**
Fürstenspiegel **Naṣīḥat al-Mulūk**

G

Gain **Kasb**
Gambling → Gambling
Games → Recreation
Garden → Architecture.monuments
Gate → Architecture.monuments
Gazehound **Salūḳī**
Gazelle **Ghazāl**
Gemstones → Jewelry
Gender studies → Women
Genealogy → Genealogy
Generation, spontaneous **Tawallud**
Generosity [in Suppl.] **Karam**
Geography → Geography
Geometry → Mathematics
Gesture **Ishāra**
Gift → Gifts
Giraffe **Zarāfa**
Girdle **Shadd**
Glass → Art
Gloss **Hāshiya**
Goats [in Suppl.] **Ghanam**
God **Allāh**; **Ilāh**
Gods, pre-Islamic → Pre-Islam
Gold **Dhahab**
Goldsmith **Ṣāʾigh**
Gospels **Indjīl**
Government **Ḥukūma**
Grains → Cuisine.food
Grammar **Naḥw**
Gratitude **Shukr**
Greeks **Yūnān**
Greyhound *see* Gazehound
Grocer **Baḳḳāl**
Guardianship **Ḥaḍāna**
Guild → Guilds
Gum resins **Ṣamgh**
Gunpowder **Bārūd**
Gymnasium **Zūrkhāna**
Gynaecology → Life Stages
Gypsies → Gypsies

H

Hadith → Literature.tradition-literature
Hagiography → Hagiography
Hair → Anatomy
Hair, the Prophet's **Liḥya-yi Sherīf**
Hairdresser [in Suppl.] **Ḥallāḳ**
Hamito-Semitic **Ḥām**
Hand, right **Yamīn**
Handbook **Tadhkira**
Handbook, astronomical **Zīdj**
Handicrafts → Art
Handkerchief **Mandīl**
Harbour **Mīnāʾ**
Harbourmaster **Shāh Bandar** (*and* [in Suppl.] **Shāhbandar**)
Hare [in Suppl.] **Arnab**
Headware → Clothing
Health → Medicine
Heart **Ḳalb**
Heaven **Samāʾ**
Hedgehog **Ḳunfudh**
Hell → Hell
Hemerology **Ikhtiyārāt**
Hemp **Ḥashīsh**
Hempseed **Shahdānadj**
Henbane **Bandj**
Henna **Ḥinnāʾ**
Heraldry → Heraldry
Herbs → Cuisine.food
Hereafter → Eschatology
Heresy → Heresy
Hippopotamus [in Suppl.] **Faras al-Māʾ**
Hire, contract of → Law.law of obligations
Historiography → Literature.historical
Holiness **Ḳadāsa**
Holy places → Sacred Places
Holy War **Djihād**
Homeland **Waṭan**
Homicide **Ḳatl**
Homonym **Aḍdād**
Homosexuality **Liwāṭ**
Honour **ʿIrḍ**
Hoopoe **Hudhud**
Horn **Būḳ**
Horse **Faras**
Horseback rider **Fāris**

Horseback riding **Furūsiyya**
Horticulture → ARCHITECTURE.MONUMENTS.GARDENS; FLORA
Hostelry → HOSTELRY
Houris **Ḥūr**
House *see* Dwelling
Humour → HUMOUR
Hunting → HUNTING
Hydrology → HYDROLOGY
Hydromancy **Istinzāl**
Hyena [in Suppl.] **Ḍabuʿ**
Hymn **Nas̲h̲īd**
Hyperbole **Mubālag̲h̲a**
Hypnotism **Sīmiyāʾ**.1
Hypocrisy **Riyāʾ**

I

Ice-seller **T̲h̲allād̲j̲**
Iconography → ART
Idol → IDOLATRY.IDOLS
Idolatry → IDOLATRY
Illness → ILLNESS
Illumination → ART
Image **Ṣūra**
Imagination [in Suppl.] **Wahm**.2
Impurity **D̲j̲anāba**; **Ḥadat̲h̲**
Incubation **Istik̲h̲āra**
Independence **Istiḳlāl**
Indigo **Nīl**
Individual **S̲h̲ak̲h̲ṣ**
Industry → INDUSTRY
Infanticide **Waʾd al-Banāt**
Infantryman **Yaya**
Infidel **Kāfir**
Inflection **Imāla**
Inheritance → INHERITANCE
Inimitability (of Qurʾan) **Iʿd̲j̲āz**
Injustice **Ẓulm**
Ink **Midād**
Ink-holder [in Suppl.] **Dawāt**
Inner dimension **al-Ẓāhir wa ʾl-Bāṭin**
Innovation **Bidʿa**
Inscriptions → EPIGRAPHY
Insects → ANIMALS
Insignia → MILITARY.DECORATIONS; MONARCHY.ROYAL INSIGNIA
Inspection (of troops) **Istiʿrāḍ**
Instrument **Āla**
Instrument, musical → MUSIC
Insulting the Prophet [in Suppl.] **S̲h̲atm**
Insulting verse **Hid̲j̲āʾ**
Intellect **ʿAḳl**
Intercession **S̲h̲afāʿa**
Intercourse, sexual **Bāh**
Intercourse, unlawful sexual **Zinā**
Interdiction **Ḥad̲j̲r**
Interest, bank **Ribā**
Interpolation (astronomical) **al-Taʿdīl bayn al-Saṭrayn**
Interpreter **Tard̲j̲umān**
Interrogation **Istifhām**
Interruption **Ḳaṭʿ**
Introduction **Ibtidāʾ**; **Muḳaddima**
Inventions → INVENTIONS
Invocation **Duʿāʾ**
Ipseity **Huwiyya**
Iris **Sūsan**
Iron **al-Ḥadīd**
Irrigation → IRRIGATION
Islam → ISLAM
Ivory **ʿĀd̲j̲**

J

Jackal **Ibn Āwā**
Jade **Yas̲h̲m**
Janissaries **Yeñi Čeri**
Japan(ese) **al-Yabānī**
Jasmine **Yāsamīn**
Javelin **D̲j̲erīd**
Jerboa **Yarbūʿ**
Jewelry → JEWELRY
Jews **Banū Isrāʾīl**; **Yahūd**
Journalism → PRESS
Judaism → JUDAISM
Judge **Ḳāḍī**
Jujube **ʿUnnāb**
Juncture **Waṣl**
Jurisconsult → LAW.JURIST
Jurisprudence → LAW

Jurist → LAW
Justice **ʿAdl**

K

King **Malik; Shāh**
Kingdom **Mamlaka**
Kinship **Ḳarāba**
Kitchen **Maṭbakh**
Knowledge **ʿIlm; Maʿrifa**
Kohl **al-Kuḥl**
Koran → QURʾAN
Kurdish → KURDS

L

Labour *see* Trade union
Labourers → PROFESSIONS.CRAFTSMEN AND TRADESMEN
Lakes → GEOGRAPHY.PHYSICAL GEOGRAPHY.WATERS
Lamentation → LAMENTATION
Lamp **Sirādj**
Land → LAND
Landowner **Zamīndār**
Language → LANGUAGES
Largesse coins **Yādgār**
Law → LAW
Leader **Zaʿīm**
Leasing **Kirāʾ**
Leather **Djild**
Legacy **Waṣiyya**
Legatee **Waṣī**
Legend → LEGENDS
Lemon **Nārandj**
Lemon balm **Turundjān**
Leprosy [in Suppl.] **Djudhām**
Lesbianism **Siḥāḳ**
Letter(s) **Ḥarf; Ḥurūf al-Hidjāʾ**; *and for letters of the alphabet* → ALPHABET
Lexicography → LEXICOGRAPHY
Library → EDUCATION.LIBRARIES
Lice **Ḳaml**
Licorice **Sūs**
Life → LIFE STAGES
Light **Nūr**
Lighthouse → ARCHITECTURE.MONUMENTS
Lily **Sūsan**
Linen **Kattān; Khaysh**
Linguistics → LINGUISTICS
Lion **al-Asad**
Literature → LITERATURE
Lithography **Maṭbaʿa**
Liver **Kabid**
Lizard **Ḍabb**
Locust **Djarād**
Lodge **Zāwiya**
Logic → PHILOSOPHY
Longevity **Muʿammar**
Louse *see* Lice
Love → LOVE
Lute **Sāz; ʿŪd**
Lyre **Ḳithāra**

M

Mace **Dūrbāsh**
Madman **Madjnūn**
Magic → MAGIC
Magnet **Maghnāṭīs.1**
Maintenance [in Suppl.] **Nafaḳa**
Make-up → COSMETICS
Malachite **al-Dahnadj**
Malaria **Malāryā**
Man **Insān**
Man-of-war **Usṭūl**
Mandrake **Sirādj al-Ḳuṭrub; Yabrūḥ**
Manichaeism → RELIGION.DUALISM
Manifestation **Tadjallī**
Manners → CUISINE; ETIQUETTE; VIRTUES AND VICES
Manumission → SLAVERY
Manuscript **Nuskha**
Map **Kharīṭa**
Marble [in Suppl.] **Rukhām**
Marches **al-Thughūr; Udj**

Market **Sūḳ**
Market inspector **Ḥisba**
Marquetry **Zalīdj**
Marriage → MARRIAGE
Martyr **Shahīd**
Martyrdom → MARTYRDOM
Marxism **Mārk(i)siyya**
Masonry **Binā᾽**
Mathematics → MATHEMATICS
Matter **Hayūlā**; **Ṭīna**
Mausoleum → ARCHITECTURE.MONUMENTS.TOMBS
Maxims, legal [in Suppl.] **Ḳawāʿid Fiḳhiyya**
Mayor **Ra᾽īs**
Measurements → WEIGHTS AND MEASUREMENTS
Mechanics → MECHANICS
Mediation **Shafāʿa**
Medicine → MEDICINE
Melilot [in Suppl.] **Iklīl al-Malik**
Melissa **Turundjān**
Melody [in Suppl.] **Laḥn**
Memorandum **Tadhkira**
Menstruation **Ḥayḍ**
Merchants → PROFESSIONS.CRAFTSMEN AND TRADESMEN
Mercury **Zi᾽baḳ**
Messenger **Rasūl**
Messiah **al-Masīḥ**
Metallurgy → METALLURGY
Metalware → ART
Metamorphosis → ANIMALS.TRANSFORMATION INTO
Metaphor **Istiʿāra**
Metaphysics → METAPHYSICS
Metempsychosis **Tanāsukh**
Meteorology → METEOROLOGY
Metonymy **Kināya**
Metre **Wazn**.2
Metrics → METRICS
Migration → EMIGRATION
Militancy → REFORM.POLITICO-RELIGIOUS.MILITANT
Military → MILITARY
Military rule [in Suppl.] **Niẓām ʿAskarī**
Milky Way **al-Madjarra**
Mill **Ṭāḥūn**
Miller **Ṭaḥḥān**
Millet [in Suppl.] **Djāwars**
Minaret **Manāra**
Mineralogy → MINERALOGY
Miniatures → ART.PAINTING
Mint [in Suppl.] **Fūdhandj**
Mint (money) **Dār al-Ḍarb**
Miracle → MIRACLES
Mirage **Sarāb**
Mirror **Mir᾽āt**
"Mirror for princes" *see* Fürstenspiegel
Misfortune **Shakāwa**
Misrepresentation (in law) **Tadlīs**.1
Mistakes, writing **Taṣḥīf**
Modernism → REFORM
"Moderns", the [in Suppl.] **Muḥdathūn**
Modes, musical **Maḳām**; [in Suppl.] **Laḥn**
Molluscs → ANIMALS
Monarchy → MONARCHY
Monastery → CHRISTIANITY; MYSTICISM
Monasticism **Rahbāniyya**
Money → NUMISMATICS
Money-changer [in Suppl.] **Ṣarrāf**
Money-changing [in Suppl.] **Ṣarf**
Mongols → MONGOLIA
Mongoose **Nims**
Monk **Rāhib**
Monkey **Ḳird**
Monogram, imperial **Tughra**
Monotheism **Tawḥīd**
Months → TIME
Moon **Hilāl**; **al-Ḳamar**
Morphology **Ṣarf**; **Taṣrīf**
Mosaics → ART
Mosque → ARCHITECTURE.MONUMENTS
Mountain → MOUNTAINS
Mountain goat **Ayyil**
Mulberry **Tūt**
Mule **Baghl**
Municipality **Baladiyya**
Murder **Ḳatl**
Music → MUSIC
Musk **Misk**
Mussel **Ṣadaf**
Myrobalanus [in Suppl.] **Halīladj**
Myrtle [in Suppl.] **Ās**
Mystic → MYSTICISM
Mysticism → MYSTICISM
Myths → LEGENDS

N

Name **Ism**
Narcissus **Nardjis**
Narcotics → DRUGS
Nationalisation **Ta'mīm**
Nationalism → NATIONALISM
Natron [in Suppl.] **Bawraḳ**
Natural science → NATURAL SCIENCE
Nature → AGRICULTURE; BOTANY; FLORA; LITERATURE.POETRY. NATURE
Navigation → NAVIGATION
Navy → MILITARY
Nephrite **Yashm**
New World → NEW WORLD
Newspaper **Djarīda**
Nickname **Laḳab**
Night **Layl and Nahār**
Night watch **ʿAsas**
Nightingale **Bulbul**
Nilometer **Miḳyās**
Nobility (of character) [in Suppl.] **Karam**
Nomadism → NOMADISM
Nomen unitatis *see* Noun of unity
Notables, tribal [in Suppl.] **Mala'**
Noun **Ism**
Noun of unity **Waḥda**.1
Nourishment → CUISINE
Novel **Ḳiṣṣa**
Nullity **Fāsid wa Bāṭil**
Number → NUMBER
Numerals → NUMBER
Numismatics → NUMISMATICS
Nunation **Tanwīn**

O

Oak **ʿAfṣ**
Oasis **Wāḥa**
Oath **Ḳasam**; **Yamīn**
Obedience (to God) **Ṭāʿa**
Obelisk → ARCHITECTURE.MONUMENTS
Oboe **Ghayṭa**
Obscenity → OBSCENITY
Observatory → ASTRONOMY
Obstetrics → MEDICINE
Ocean → OCEANS AND SEAS
Octagon **Muthamman**
Oil → CUISINE.FOOD; OIL
Olive **Zaytūn**
Olive oil **Zayt**
Omen **Fa'l**
Oneirocriticism [in Suppl.] **Taʿbīr al-Ru'ya**
Oneiromancy → DREAMS
Oneness **Waḥda**.2
Oneness of being **Waḥdat al-Wudjūd**
Oneness of witnessing **Waḥdat al-Shuhūd**
Onomastics → ONOMASTICS
Onomatomancy **Ḥurūf, ʿIlm al-**
Ophthalmology → MEDICINE
Opium **Afyūn**
Opposites **Aḍdād**; **Ḍidd**
Optics → OPTICS
Orange **Nārandj**
Orchestra **Mehter**; *and see* Band
Order, military → MILITARY.DECORATIONS
Order, mystical → MYSTICISM
Organ **Urghan**
Organs, body → ANATOMY
Orientalism **Mustashriḳūn**
Ornament **Zakhrafa**
Ornithomancy **ʿIyāfa**
Orphan **Yatīm**
Orthodoxy **Sunna**
Oryx **Lamṭ**; **Mahāt**
Ostentation **Riyā'**
Ostrich **Naʿām**
Ottoman Empire → OTTOMAN EMPIRE
Outward meaning **Ẓāhir**; **al-Ẓāhir wa 'l-Bāṭin**
Ownership **Milk**

P

Paediatrics → Life Stages
Paganism → Pre-Islam
Painting → Art
Palace → Architecture.monuments
Palaeography → Epigraphy; Writing
Palanquin **Maḥmal**
Paleography *see* Palaeography
Palm **Nakhl**
Palmoscopy **Ikhtilādj**
Panarabism → Panarabism
Pandore **Ṭunbūr**
Panegyric **Madīḥ**
Panislamism → Panislamism
Pantheism → Religion
Panther **Namir**
Panturkism → Panturkism
Paper **Kāghad**
Paper seller **Warrāḳ**
Papyrology → Papyrology
Papyrus **Papyrus**
Paradise → Paradise
Parakeet **Babbaghā'**
Parasol **Miẓalla**
Parchment **Raḳḳ**
Parliament **Madjlis**
Paronomasia **Muzāwadja**; **Tadjnīs**
Parrot **Babbaghā'**
Partnership **Sharika**
Party, political → Politics
Passion play **Ta'ziya**
Past **Māḍī**
Pastimes → Recreation
Pasture **Mar'ā**
Pastures, summer **Yaylaḳ**
Pastures, winter **Ḳishlaḳ**
Patriotism **Waṭaniyya**
Patronymic **Kunya**
Pauper **Faḳīr**; **Miskīn**
Pavilion → Architecture.monuments
Pay → Payments
Peace **Ṣulḥ**
Peacock **Ṭāwūs**
Peacock throne **Takht-i Ṭāwūs**
Pearl **al-Durr**; **Lu'lu'**
Pedagogy **Tarbiya**
Pediatrics *see* Paediatrics
Pen **Ḳalam**
Pen-name **Takhalluṣ**
Penal law → Law
People **Ḳawm**; **Sha'b**
Performers → Professions.craftsmen and tradesmen
Perfume → Perfume
Periodicals → Press
Persian → Languages.indo-european.iranian; Linguistics
Person **Shakhṣ**
Personal status → Law
Petroleum → Oil
Pharmacology → Pharmacology
Philately → Philately
Philology → Linguistics
Philosophy → Philosophy
Phlebotomist [in Suppl.] **Faṣṣād**
Phonetics → Linguistics
Photography → Art
Physician → Medicine
Physics [in Suppl.] **Ṭabī'iyyāt**
Physiognomancy **Ḳiyāfa**
Physiognomy → Physiognomy
Pickpocket **Ṭarrār**
Piety **Wara'**; [in Suppl.] **Taḳwā**
Pig **Khinzīr**
Pigeon **Ḥamām**
Pilgrimage → Pilgrimage
Pillar **Rukn**
Pillars of Islam → Islam
Piracy → Piracy
Pirate → Piracy
Plagiarism [in Suppl.] **Sariḳa**
Plague → Plague
Planet → Astronomy
Plants → Flora
Plaster **Djiṣṣ**
Platonic love → Love
Pleasure-garden → Architecture.monuments.gardens
Pledge **Rahn**
Plough **Miḥrāth**
Plural **Djam'**
Poem → Literature.genres.poetry
Poet **Shā'ir**
Poetry → Literature
Poison **Summ**
Pole **al-Ḳuṭb**
Police → Military
Politics → Politics

Poll-tax **Djizya**
Polytheism **Shirk**
Pomegranate blossom [in Suppl.] **Djullanār**
Porcupine **Ḳunfudh**
Port **Mīnā'**
Porter **Ḥammāl**
Portmaster **Shāh Bandar** (*and* [in Suppl.] **Shāhbandar**)
Possession (by spirits) **Zār**
Postal history → PHILATELY
Postal service → TRANSPORT
Potash **al-Ḳily**
Pottery → ART
Powers, balance of **Tawāzun al-Sulutāt**
Prayer → PRAYER
Prayer direction **Ḳibla**
Prayer niche **Miḥrāb**
Pre-emption **Shufʿa**
Pre-Islam → PRE-ISLAM
Preacher **Wāʿiẓ**
Precious stones → JEWELRY
Predestination → PREDESTINATION
Preface **Muḳaddima**
Pregnancy → LIFE STAGES.CHILDBIRTH
Presentation issues (coinage) **Yādgār**
Press → PRESS
Primary school **Kuttāb**
Principles of grammar **Uṣūl**
Principles of jurisprudence **Uṣūl al-Fiḳh**
Principles of religion **Uṣūl al-Dīn**
Printing **Maṭbaʿa**
Printing, block → WRITING.MANUSCRIPTS AND BOOKS
Prison **Sidjn**
Prisoner → MILITARY
Procedure, legal → LAW
Processions **Mawākib**
Profession of faith **Shahāda**
Professions → PROFESSIONS
Profit **Kasb**
Prologue **Ibtidā'**
Property → PROPERTY
Property owner *see* Landowner
Prophecy → PROPHETHOOD
Prophet → MUḤAMMAD, THE PROPHET; PROPHETHOOD
Prophethood → PROPHETHOOD
Prose → LITERATURE
Proselytism, Christian **Tabshīr**
Proselytism, Islamic → ISLAM
Prosody → LITERATURE.POETRY; METRICS; RHYME
Prostitution [in Suppl.] **Bighā'**
Protection **Ḥimāya**; **Idjāra**
Proverb → LITERATURE; PROVERBS
Pulpit **Minbar**
Punishment → LAW.PENAL LAW; PUNISHMENT
Punning **Tadjnīs**
Purity **Ṭahāra**
Pyramid **Haram**

Q

Qat **Ḳāt**
Quadrant **Rubʿ**
Quail **Salwā**
Queen mother **Wālide Sulṭān**
Quicksilver **Ziʾbaḳ**
Quiddity **Māhiyya**
Quotation **Taḍmīn**
Qurʾān → QURʾAN

R

Rabies *see* Dog
Radicalism **Taṭarruf**
Raid → RAIDS
Railway → TRANSPORT
Rain prayer **Istisḳā'**
Rain stone **Yada Tash**
Rainbow **Ḳaws Ḳuzaḥ**
Raisins **Zabīb**
Ransoming [in Suppl.] **Fidā'**
Reading (Qurʾanic) → QURʾAN
Rebel [in Suppl.] **Mārid**
Rebellion → REBELLION
Recitation → QURʾAN.READING
Reconnaissance force **Ṭalīʿa**
Records → ADMINISTRATION
Recreation → RECREATION

Reed **Ḳaṣab**
Reed-pen **Ḳalam**
Reed-pipe **Ghayṭa**; **Mizmār**
Reflection **Fikr**
Reform → REFORM
Register → ADMINISTRATION.RECORDS
Religion → RELIGION
Relinquishment (of a right) [in Suppl.] **Isḳāṭ**
Renewal **Tadjdīd**
Renewer **Mudjaddid**
Renunciation **Zuhd**
Repentance **Tawba**
Representation, legal **Wilāya**.1
Reptiles → ANIMALS
Republic **Djumhūriyya**
Repudiation **Ṭalāḳ**
Resemblance **Shubha**
Resettlement [in Suppl.] **Sürgün**
Resurrection **Ḳiyāma**
Retaliation **Ḳiṣāṣ**
Retreat **Khalwa**
Revelation **Ilhām**; **Waḥy**
Revolt **Thawra**
Revolution **Thawra**
Rhapsodomancy **Ḳurʿa**
Rhetoric → RHETORIC
Rhinoceros **Karkaddan**
Rhyme → RHYME
Rice **al-Ruzz**
Riddle **Lughz**
Ritual (Islamic) **ʿIbādāt**
Rituals → RITUALS
River → RIVERS
Road → TRANSPORT
Robbery, highway **Sariḳa**
Robe of honour **Khilʿa**
Rock-crystal **Billawr**
Rod **ʿAṣā**; **Ḳaḍīb**
Rodents → ANIMALS
Rooster *see* Cock
Roots **Uṣūl**; **Uṣūl al-Dīn**; **Uṣūl al-Fiḳh**
Rosary **Subḥa**
Rose **Gul**; **Ward**
Rose-water [in Suppl.] **Māʾ al-Ward**
Ruby **Yāḳūt**
Rug → ART.TAPESTRY

S

Sacred places → SACRED PLACES
Sacrifices → SACRIFICES
Saddle, horse **Sardj**
Saffron **Zaʿfarān**
Saint → SAINTHOOD
Sal-ammoniac **al-Nūshādir**
Salamander **Samandal**
Sale, contract of → LAW.LAW OF OBLIGATIONS
Salt **Milḥ**
Salt flats → GEOGRAPHY.PHYSICAL GEOGRAPHY
Sand **Raml**
Sandal, the Prophet's [in Suppl.] **al-Naʿl al-Sharīf**
Sandalwood **Ṣandal**
Sandgrouse **Ḳaṭā**
Sappan wood **Baḳḳam**
Satire **Hidjāʾ**
Saturn **Zuḥal**
Scanning **Wazn**.2
Scapulomancy **Katif**
Scholars **ʿUlamāʾ**
School, legal [in Suppl.] **Madhhab**
School, primary **Kuttāb**
Science → SCIENCE
Scorpion **ʿAḳrab**
Scribe **Kātib**; **Yazidji**; [in Suppl.] **Dabīr**
Scripts → WRITING
Scripture **Zabūr**
Scripture, tampering with **Taḥrīf**
Scrupulousness **Waraʿ**
Sea → OCEANS AND SEAS
Seafaring → NAVIGATION
Seal **Khātam**; **Muhr**
Secret [in Suppl.] **Sirr**
Secretary **Kātib**; [in Suppl.] **Dabīr**
Sectarianism **Ṭāʾifiyya**
Sects → SECTS
Sedentarisation [in Suppl.] **Iskān**
Sedentarism → SEDENTARISM
Semitic languages **Sām**.2
Sense **Ḥiss**; **Maḥsūsāt**
Sermon **Khuṭba**
Sermoniser **Ḳāṣṣ**
Servant **Khādim**

Sesame **Simsim**
Seven **Sab'**
Seveners → SHIITES.BRANCHES
Sex **Djins**
Sexuality → SEXUALITY
Shadow play **Ḳaragöz**; **Khayāl al-Ẓill**
Shawm **Zurna**
Sheep [in Suppl.] **Ghanam**
Sheep-herder **Shāwiya**
Shell **Wada'**.2
Shiism → SHIITES
Ship → NAVIGATION
Shoemaker [in Suppl.] **Iskāf**
Shoewear → CLOTHING
Shrine **Zāwiya**
Shroud [in Suppl.] **Kafan**
Sickness → ILLNESS
Siege warfare **Ḥiṣār**
Siegecraft **Ḥiṣār**; **Mandjanīḳ**
Signature of ruler **Tawḳī'**
Silk **Ḥarīr**
Silver **Fiḍḍa**
Silver coinage **Wariḳ**
Simile **Tashbīh**
Sin **Khaṭī'a**; [in Suppl.] **Ithm**; **Kabīra**
Singer → MUSIC.SONG
Singing → MUSIC.SONG
Skin blemish **Shāma**
Slander **Ḳadhf**
Slaughterer [in Suppl.] **Djazzār**
Slave **'Abd**
Slavery → SLAVERY
Snail **Ṣadaf**
Snake **Ḥayya**
Snake-charmer **Ḥāwī**
Snipe **Shunḳub**
Soap **Ṣābūn**
Socialism **Ishtirākiyya**
Society **Djam'iyya**
Soda **al-Ḳily**; *and see* Natron
Sodium **Naṭrūn**; *and see* Natron
Sodomy **Liwāṭ**
Son **Ibn**
Song → MUSIC
Sorcery → MAGIC
Soul **Nafs**
Sphere **Falak**; **al-Kura**
Spices → CUISINE.FOOD
Spider **'Ankabūt**
Spoils (of war) → MILITARY.BOOTY
Sport → ANIMALS.SPORT; RECREATION
Spouse **Zawdj**
Springs → GEOGRAPHY.PHYSICAL GEOGRAPHY
Spy **Djāsūs**
Squares, magical **Wafḳ**
Stable **Iṣṭabl**
Stamps → PHILATELY
Standard **Sandjaḳ**; **Sandjaḳ-i Sherīf**
Star → ASTRONOMY
Statecraft **Siyāsa**
Stone **Ḥadjar**
Stone, rain **Yada Tash**
Stool **Kursī**
Story **Ḥikāya**
Storyteller **Ḳāṣṣ**; **Maddāḥ**
Straits → GEOGRAPHY.PHYSICAL GEOGRAPHY.WATERS
Street **Shāri'**
Stronghold → ARCHITECTURE.MONUMENTS
Substance **Djawhar**
Succession (to the caliphate) **Walī al-'Ahd**
Successors (of the Companions) **Tābi'ūn**
Suckling → LIFE STAGES
Sufism → MYSTICISM
Sugar **Sukkar**
Sugar-cane **Ḳaṣab al-Sukkar**
Suicide **Intiḥār**
Sulphur **al-Kibrīt**
Sultan-fowl [in Suppl.] **Abū Barāḳish**.2
Summer quarters **Yaylaḳ**
Sun **Shams**
Sundial **Mizwala**
Sunshade **Miẓalla**
Superstition → SUPERSTITION
Surety-bond **Kafāla**
Surgeon **Djarrāḥ**
Swahili → KENYA
Sweeper **Kannās**
Syllable reduction **Ziḥāf**
Symbolism **Ramz**.3
Syntax **Taṣrīf**

T

Tablet **Lawḥ**
Tailor **Khayyāṭ**
Talisman **Tamīma, Tilsam**
Tambourine **Duff**
Tampering (with Scripture) *see* Scripture
Tanner [in Suppl.] **Dabbāgh**
Tapestry → ART
Tar **Mūmiyā᾽**
Tattooing **al-Washm**
Taxation → TAXATION
Tea **Čay**
Tea-house [in Suppl.] **Čāy-khāna**
Teaching → EDUCATION
Teak **Sādj**
Teeth → MEDICINE.DENTISTRY
Temperament [in Suppl.] **Mizādj**
Tent **Khayma**
Tenth *see* Tithe
Textiles → ART; CLOTHING.MATERIALS
Thankfulness **Shukr**
Theatre → LITERATURE.DRAMA
Theft **Sariḳa**
Theology → THEOLOGY
Theophany **Maẓhar**; **Tadjallī**
Thief **Liṣṣ**
Thistle **Shukāʿā**
Thought **Fikr**
Tide **al-Madd wa 'l-Djazr**
Tiles → ART
Tiller **Miḥrāth**
Time → TIME
Timekeeping → TIME
Tithe **ʿUshr**
Titulature → ONOMASTICS.TITLES
Tobacco → DRUGS.NARCOTICS
Tomb → ARCHITECTURE.MONUMENTS
Toothbrush **Miswāk**
Tooth-pick **Miswāk**
Torah **Tawrāt**
Tower **Burdj**
Town **Ḳarya**; **Ḳaṣaba**
Toys → RECREATION.GAMES
Trade → FINANCE.COMMERCE; INDUSTRY; NAVIGATION
Trade union **Niḳāba**
Tradition → LITERATURE.TRADITION-LITERATURE
Transcendentalism **Tashbīh wa-Tanzīh**
Transition (in poetry) **Takhalluṣ**
Transitivity **Taʿaddī**
Translation → LITERATURE
Transport → TRANSPORT
Travel → TRAVEL
Treasury → TREASURY
Treaty → TREATIES
Trees → FLORA
Triangle **Muthallath**
Tribal chief **Sayyid**
Tribe → TRIBES
Tribute → TREATIES
Trinity, divine **Tathlīth**
Trope **Madjāz**
Trousers **Sirwāl**
Trumpet **Būḳ**
Trust, charitable **Waḳf**
Tuareg **Ṭawāriḳ**
Turban **Tulband**
Turkic languages → LANGUAGES
Turquoise **Fīrūzadj**
Turtle **Sulaḥfā**
Twelvers → SHIITES.BRANCHES
Twilight **al-Shafaḳ**
Tyranny **Ẓulm**

U

Uncle **Khāl**
Underground chamber **Sardāb**
University **Djāmiʿa**
Uprising **Thawra**
Urban milieux → URBANISM
Usurpation **Ghaṣb**
Usury **Ribā**
Utterance [in Suppl.] **Lafẓ**.1
Utterances, mystical [in Suppl.] **Malfūẓāt**

V

Vehicle → TRANSPORT.WHEELED VEHICLES
Veil → CLOTHING.HEADWARE
Ventilation → ARCHITECTURE.URBAN
Venus **Zuhara**
Verb **Fiʿl**
Vernacular → LANGUAGES.AFRO-ASIATIC.ARABIC.ARABIC DIALECTS; LITERATURE.POETRY.VERNACULAR
Verse **Āya**
Versifying [in Suppl.] **Naẓm**.1
Veterinary science → MEDICINE
Vices → VIRTUES AND VICES
Vigils, night **Tahadjdjud**
Vikings **al-Madjūs**
Villa, seashore **Yali**
Village **Ḳarya**
Vine **Karm**
Viol **Rabāb**
Viper **Afʿā**
Virtues → VIRTUES AND VICES
Vizier Wazīr
Volcanoes → GEOGRAPHY.PHYSICAL GEOGRAPHY
Vow **Nadhr**
Voyage → TRAVEL
Vulture **Humā**; **Nasr**

W

Wadis → GEOGRAPHY.PHYSICAL GEOGRAPHY
Wagon *see* Cart
Walnut [in Suppl.] **Djawz**
War **Ḥarb**
Wardrobe → CLOTHING
Washer [in Suppl.] **Ghassāl**
Washing → ABLUTION
Washing (of the dead) **Ghusl**
Water **Māʾ**
Water-carrier **Saḳḳāʾ**
Waterhouse → ARCHITECTURE. MONUMENTS
Waterways → GEOGRAPHY.PHYSICAL GEOGRAPHY
Waterwheel **Nāʿūra**
Weapon → MILITARY
Weasel **Ibn ʿIrs**
Weather → METEOROLOGY
Weaver **al-Nassādj**; [in Suppl.] **Ḥāʾik**
Weaver-bird [in Suppl.] **Abū Barāḳish**.1
Weaving → ART.TEXTILES
Wedding **ʿUrs**
Week → TIME
Weighing (of coinage) **Wazn**.1
Weights → WEIGHTS AND MEASUREMENTS
Welfare **Maṣlaḥa**
Well → ARCHITECTURE.MONUMENTS
Werewolf **Ḳuṭrub**
Wheat **Ḳamḥ**
Wild **Waḥsh**; **Waḥshī**
Wind → METEOROLOGY
Wine → WINE
Winter quarters **Ḳishlaḳ**
Wisdom **Ḥikma**
Witness **Shāhid**
Wolf **Dhiʾb**
Women → WOMEN
Wood **Khashab**
Wool **Ṣūf**
World **ʿĀlam**
Wormwood **Afsantīn**
Wrestling **Pahlawān**; **Zūrkhāna**
Writing → WRITING

Y

Yoghourt **Yoghurt**
Young Ottomans **Yeñi ʿOthmānlilar**
Young Turks → TURKEY.OTTOMAN PERIOD

Z

Zaydis → SHIITES.BRANCHES
Zero **al-Ṣifr**
Zodiac **Minṭaḳat al-Burūdj**
Zoology → ZOOLOGY
Zoroastrianism → ZOROASTRIANS

INDEX OF SUBJECTS

The Muslim world in the Index of Subjects is the world of today. What once was the greater realm of Persia is given here under Central Asia, the Caucasus, and Afghanistan, just as part of the region once governed by the Ottoman Empire is covered by individual countries in Eastern Europe and in the Near East. States established in the past century, such as Jordan and Lebanon, are given right of place. Countries with a long history of Islam, e.g. Egypt and Syria, have a subsection "modern period", where *Encyclopaedia* articles covering the 19th and 20th centuries have been brought together.

The *mīlādī* year of death has been used for dating purposes. Thus, when an individual is listed as "15th-century", the dating refers to his/her year of death C.E. This method of dating is precise but regrettably unhelpful in some cases, as e.g. when an individual died in the very first years of a new century or when a person's major works date from the previous century.

References in regular typeface are to *Encyclopaedia* articles; those printed in boldface type indicate the main article. Entries in capitals and following an arrow refer to lemmata in the Index of Subjects itself. Thus, in the case of

> BEDOUINS **Badw**; Biʾr; Dawār; Ghanīma; Ghazw; al-Hidjar; Thaʾr
> *see also* Liṣṣ; ʿUrf.2.I; *and* → LAW.CUSTOMARY; NOMADISM; SAUDI ARABIA; TRIBES.ARABIAN PENINSULA

Badw; Biʾr; Dawār; Ghanīma; Ghazw; al-Hidjar, Thaʾr refer to articles in the *Encyclopaedia* that deal primarily with Bedouins, Badw being *the* article on Bedouins; Liṣṣ and ʿUrf.2.I refer to an article or section of an article in the *Encyclopaedia* that contains information of interest relating to Bedouins; and LAW.CUSTOMARY; NOMADISM; SAUDI ARABIA; TRIBES.ARABIAN PENINSULA refer the reader to analogous entries in the Index of Subjects.

The notation "(2x)" that follows an article—for example: Lār (2x)—indicates that there are two separate articles in the *Encyclopaedia* under the same entry that have reference to the indexed subject. Duplicate articles—on one rare occasion, triplicates—of one and the same *Encyclopaedia* entry, usually under different entry headings and thus passing through unnoticed by the Editors, as well as sections of larger articles added at a later date in the Supplement and lacking a reference in the main text, are indexed by the second occurrence of the article following the first in parentheses with the connective *and*, as, for example: Muḥammad Bey ʿUthmān Djalāl (*and* [in Suppl.] Muḥammad ʿUthmān Djalāl).

Below is the Index of Subjects proper, in which all *Encyclopaedia* articles are grouped under one or more general entries. For facility in finding an article on a specific word or topic (e.g. "abstinence" or "sports"), the reader is referred to the List of Entries on p. 1.

A

ʿABBĀSIDS → CALIPHATE

ABLUTION **Ghusl**; Istindjāʾ; Istinshāḳ; al-Masḥ ʿalā 'l-Khuffayn; Tayammum; **Wuḍūʾ**
see also Djanāba; Ḥadath; Ḥammām; Ḥawḍ; Ḥayḍ; Ṭahāra

ABYSSINIA → ETHIOPIA

Administration Barīd; Bayt al-Māl; Daftar; Diplomatic; **Dīwān**; Djizya; Kātib; [in Suppl.] Demography.I
see also al-Ḳalḳashandī.1; al-Ṣūlī; ʿUmar (I) b. al-Khaṭṭāb; *for specific caliphates or dynasties* → Caliphate; Dynasties; Ottoman Empire; *and* → Andalusia; Egypt; India; Iran
diplomatic → Diplomacy
financial ʿAṭāʾ; Bayt al-Māl; Daftar; Dār al-Ḍarb; Ḳānūn.ii *and* iii; Kasb; Khāzin; Khaznadār; Makhzan; Muṣādara.2; Mustawfī; Rūznāma; Siyāḳat; Zimām
see also Dhahab; Fiḍḍa; Ḥisba; Tadbīr.1; Waḳf; *and* → Numismatics; Ottoman Empire.administration; Payments
fiscal → Taxation
functionaries ʿĀmil; Amīn; Amīr; Amīr al-Ḥādjdj; ʿArīf; Dawādār; Djahbadh; Ḥisba; Īshīk-āḳāsī; Kalāntar; Kātib; Khāzin; Mushīr; Mushrif; Mustakhridj; Mustawfī; Parwānačī; Raʾīs; Ṣāḥib al-Madīna; Wālī; Wazīr; [in Suppl.] Dabīr
see also Barīd; Consul; Fatwā; Fuyūdj; Kōtwāl; Malik al-Tudjdjār; Mawlā; Muwāḍaʿa.2; Waẓīfa.1; *and* → Law.offices; Military.offices; Ottoman Empire
geography → Geography.administrative
legal → Law
military → Military
Mongol → Mongolia.mongols
Ottoman → Ottoman Empire
records **Daftar**.I; Ḳānūn.iii
and → Documents; Ottoman Empire.administration
archives Dār al-Maḥfūẓāt al-ʿUmūmiyya; Geniza
and → Ottoman Empire.administration

Adoption [in Suppl.] ʿĀr; [in Suppl.] ʿĀr; **Tabannin**
see also ʿĀda.iii; Yatīm.2.iii; [in Suppl.] Istilḥāḳ

Adultery Ḳadhf; Liʿān; **Zinā**
see also al-Marʾa.2
punishment of Ḥadd

Afghanistan Afghān; **Afghānistān**
architecture → Architecture.regions
dynasties Aḥmad Shāh Durrānī; Ghaznawids; Ghūrids; Kart
see also Zunbīl; *and* → Dynasties.afghanistan and india
historians of Sayfī Harawī; [in Suppl.] Isfizārī
language → Languages.indo-iranian.iranian
modern period Djāmiʿa; Dustūr.v; Khaybar; Madjlis.4.B; Maṭbaʿa.5; [in Suppl.] Ṭālibān
see also Muhādjir.3
statesmen ʿAbd al-Raḥmān Khān; Ayyūb Khān; Dūst Muḥammad; Ḥabīb Allāh Khān; Muḥammad Dāwūd Khān; Shīr ʿAlī; [in Suppl.] Amān Allāh
see also [in Suppl.] Faḳīr of Ipi
physical geography Afghānistān.i
mountains Hindū Kush; Kūh-i Bābā; Safīd Kūh
see also Afghānistān.i
waters Dehās; Hāmūn; Harī Rūd; Kābul.1; Ḳunduz.1; Kurram; Murghāb; Pandjhīr; [in Suppl.] Gūmāl
see also Afghānistān.i; Zirih
population Abdālī; Čahār Aymak; Durrānī; Ghalča; Ghalzay; Moghols; Mohmand; Türkmen.3; [in Suppl.] Demography.III; Hazāras; Kākaṛ

see also Afghān.i; Afghānistān.ii; Khaladj; Özbeg.1.d; Wazīrīs; [in Suppl.] Djirga
toponyms
ancient Būshandj; Bust; Dihistān; Djuwayn.3; Farmūl; Fīrūzkūh.1; Khōst; Khudjistān; Marw al-Rūdh; al-Rukhkhadj; Ṭālaḳān.1; Ṭukhāristān; Walwālīdj; Zābul; Zamīndāwar
present-day
districts Andarāb.1; Bādghīs; Farwān; Ḳūhistān.3; Lamghānāt
regions Badakhshān; Dardistān; Djūzdjān; Ghardjistān; Ghūr; Kāfiristān; Khōst; Nangrahār; Sīstān; Zābul; [in Suppl.] Hazāradjāt
see also Pandjhīr; Turkistān.2
towns Andkhūy; Balkh; Bāmiyān; Djām; Farāh; Faryāb.1; Gardīz; Ghazna; Girishk; Harāt; Kābul.2; Ḳandahār; Karūkh; Khulm; Ḳunduz.2; Maymana; Mazār-i Sharīf; Rūdhbār.1; Sabzawār.2; Sar-i Pul; Shibarghān; Ṭālaḳān.3; [in Suppl.] Djalālābād; Ishkāshim

AFRICA Lamlam; Zandj
Central Africa Cameroons; Congo; Gabon; [in Suppl.] Čad
see also Muḥammad Bello; al-Murdjibī; Waḳf.VIII; [in Suppl.] Demography.V
for individual countries → CHAD; CONGO; ZAIRE
literature Hausa.iii; Kano; Shāʿir.5 *and* 6; Shiʿr.7; Taʾrīkh.II.5
physical geography
deserts Sāḥil.2
population Kanuri; Kotoko; Shuwa; Ṭawāriḳ; Tubu; Zaghāwa
East Africa Djibūtī; Eritrea; Ḥabesh; Kenya; Ḳumr; Madagascar; Mafia; Somali; Sūdān; Tanzania; Uganda; Zandjibār; [in Suppl.] Malawi
see also Emīn Pasha; Muṣāḥib; Nikāḥ.II.5; al-Nudjūm; Shīrāzī; Zandj.1; Zār.1; [in Suppl.] Djarīda.viii
for individual countries → DJIBOUTI, REPUBLIC OF; ETHIOPIA; KENYA; MADAGASCAR; MALAWI; SOMALIA; SUDAN; TANZANIA
architecture Manāra.3; Masdjid.VI; Mbweni; Minbar.4
see also Shungwaya
festivals Mawlid.2; Nawrūz.2
languages Eritrea.iv; Ḥabash.iv; Kūsh; Nūba.3; Somali.5; Sūdān.2; Swahili; Yao
see also Ḳumr; Madagascar
literature Miʿrādj.3; Somali.6; Taʾrīkh.II.6 (*and* [in Suppl.] Taʾrīkh.II.8)
see also Kitābāt.6; *and* → KENYA.SWAHILI LITERATURE
mysticism Ṭarīḳa.II.3; Ziyāra.10
physical geography
waters Atbara; Baḥr al-Ghazāl.1; Shebelle
see also Baḥr al-Hind; Baḥr al-Zandj
population ʿAbābda; ʿĀmir; Antemuru; Bedja; Beleyn; Bishārīn; Danḳalī; Djaʿaliyyūn; Galla; Māryā; Mazrūʿī; Oromo; Somali.1; Yao; [in Suppl.] Demography.V
see also Diglal; Lamlam; al-Manāṣir
North Africa Algeria; Ifrīḳiya; Lībiyā; Maghāriba; al-Maghrib (2x); Mashāriḳa; Tunisia
see also al-ʿArab.v; ʿArabiyya.A.iii.3; Badw.II.d; Djaysh.iii; Ghuzz.ii; Ḥawz; Kharbga; Kitābāt.4; Lamṭ; Leo Africanus; Libās.ii; Maḥalla; Mānū; Ṣaff.3; Sipāhī.2; ʿUrf.2.I.B; Waḳf.II.3; [in Suppl.] ʿĀr; Mawlid; *and* → DYNASTIES.SPAIN AND NORTH AFRICA
for individual countries → ALGERIA; LIBYA; MOROCCO; TUNISIA; *for Egypt* → EGYPT
architecture → ARCHITECTURE.REGIONS
history [in Suppl.] **Taʾrīkh**.II.1.(e)
and → DYNASTIES.SPAIN AND NORTH AFRICA

modern period Baladiyya.3; Djamāʿa.ii; Djarīda.B; Hilāl; Ḳawmiyya.ii; Ṣiḥāfa.2

and → ALGERIA; LIBYA; MOROCCO; TUNISIA

mysticism Ṭarīḳa.II.2; Walī.2; Zāwiya.2

see also Ziyāra.4; *and* → MYSTICISM.MYSTICS

physical geography Atlas; Reg; Rīf; Sabkha; al-Ṣaḥrāʾ; Shaṭṭ; Tall; Tasili; Wādī.2

and → *the section Physical Geography under individual countries*

population Ahaggar; Berbers; Dukkāla; Khulṭ; al-Maʿḳil; Shāwiya.1; Ṭawāriḳ; Tubu; [in Suppl.] Demography.IV

see also Khumayr; Kūmiya; al-Manāṣir; Mandīl; Moors; *and* → BERBERS

Southern Africa Mozambique (*and* [in Suppl.]); South Africa

see also [in Suppl.] Djarīda.ix

for individual countries → MOZAMBIQUE

West Africa Côte d'Ivoire; Dahomey; Gambia; Ghana; Guinea; Liberia; Mali; Mūrītāniyā; Niger; Nigeria; Senegal; Sierra Leone; Togo

see also Azalay; Kitābāt.5; Ḳunbi Ṣāliḥ; al-Maghīlī; Malam; Murīdiyya; Sūdān (Bilād al-).2; Sulṭān.3; Tādmakkat; Takfīr.2; Takidda; Takrūr; ʿUlamāʾ.7; Waḳf.VIII

for individual countries → BENIN; GUINEA; IVORY COAST; MALI; MAURITANIA; NIGER; NIGERIA; SENEGAL; TOGO

architecture Ḳunbi Ṣāliḥ; Masdjid.VII

empires Mande; Oyo; Songhay.3

see also Muḥammad b. Abī Bakr; Samori Ture; Takrūr; ʿUthmān b. Fūdī

languages Hausa.ii; Nūba.3; Shuwa.2; Songhay.1; Sūdān (Bilād al-).3

see also Fulbe; Kanuri; Senegal.1; *and* → LANGUAGES.AFRO-ASIATIC.ARABIC

literature → AFRICA.CENTRAL AFRICA

mysticism Walī.9; Zāwiya.3; Ziyāra.9

and → MYSTICISM.MYSTICS.AFRICAN

physical geography

deserts Sāḥil.2

mountains Fūta Djallon; Tibesti

oases Wāḥa.2

waters Niger

population Fulbe; Ḥarṭānī; Hausa.i; Ifoghas; Kunta; Songhay.2; Ṭawāriḳ; Tukulor; Wangara; Yoruba; [in Suppl.] Demography.V

see also Lamlam; Mande; Takrūr

AGRICULTURE **Filāḥa**; Marʿā; Raʿiyya

see also Mazraʿa; Mughārasa; Musāḳāt; Muzāraʿa; Taḳdīr.2; Taḳwīm.2; [in Suppl.] Akkār; *and* → BOTANY; FLORA; IRRIGATION

agricultural cooperatives **Taʿāwun**

products Ḳahwa; Ḳamḥ; Karm; Ḳaṣab al-Sukkar; Khamr.2; Ḳuṭn; Nakhl; Nārandj; al-Ruzz; Shaʿīr; [in Suppl.] Djāwars; Hindibāʾ

see also Ḥarīr; *and* → CUISINE.FOODS

terms Āgdāl; Baʿl.2.b; Čiftlik; Ghūṭa; Maṭmūra

tools Miḥrāth

treatises on Abu 'l-Khayr al-Ishbīlī; Ibn Wāfid; Ibn Waḥshiyya; al-Ṭighnarī

ALBANIA **Arnawutluḳ**; Iskender Beg; Ḳarā Maḥmūd Pasha

see also Muslimūn.1.B.4; Sāmī; *and* → OTTOMAN EMPIRE

toponyms Aḳ Ḥiṣār.4; Awlonya; Delvina; Drač; Elbasan; Ergiri; Korča; Krujë; Lesh; Tiran; [in Suppl.] Ishkodra

ALCHEMY Dhahab; Fiḍḍa; al-Iksīr; al-Kibrīt; **al-Kīmiyā'**; Zi'baḳ
  see also Ḳārūn; Maʿdin; al-Nūs̲h̲ādir; Takwīn; *and* → METALLURGY; MINERALOGY
alchemists Dj̲ābir b. Ḥayyān; Ibn Umayl; Ibn Waḥs̲h̲iyya; al-Rāzī, Abū Bakr; al-Ṭug̲h̲rāʾī;
  [in Suppl.] Abu 'l-Ḥasan al-Anṣārī; al-Dj̲ildakī
    see also Hirmis; K̲h̲ālid b. Yazīd b. Muʿāwiya; [in Suppl.] al-Dj̲awbarī; ʿAbd al-Raḥīm;
    Findiriskī; Ibn Daḳīḳ al-ʿĪd
equipment al-Anbīḳ; al-Ut̲h̲āl
terms Rukn.2; Ṭabīʿa.3; Zuḥal; Zuhara

ALGERIA **Algeria**
  see also ʿArabiyya.A.iii.3; ʿArs̲h̲; Ḥalḳa; Zmāla.3; *and* → BERBERS; DYNASTIES.SPAIN AND
  NORTH AFRICA
architecture → ARCHITECTURE.REGIONS.NORTH AFRICA
dynasties ʿAbd al-Wādids; Fāṭimids; Ḥammādids; Rustamids
  and → DYNASTIES.SPAIN AND NORTH AFRICA
literature Ḥawfī; Malḥūn
modern period Dj̲āmiʿa; Dj̲arīda.i.B; Ḥizb.i; Ḥukūma.iv; Maʿārif.2.B; Madj̲lis.4.A.xx;
  Ṣiḥāfa.2.(i); [in Suppl.] Maḥkama.4.xi
  reform Ibn Bādīs; (al-)Ibrāhīmī; Salafiyya.1(b)
    see also Fallāḳ
Ottoman period (1518-1830) ʿAbd al-Ḳādir b. Muḥyī al-Dīn; Algeria.ii.(2); ʿArūdj̲; Ḥasan
  Ag̲h̲a; Ḥasan Baba; Ḥasan Pas̲h̲a; al-Ḥusayn; Ḥusayn Pas̲h̲a, Mezzomorto; K̲h̲ayr al-
  Dīn Pas̲h̲a
    see also Sipāhī.2
physical geography Algeria.i
  mountains ʿAmūr; Atlas; Awrās; Bībān; Dj̲urdj̲ura; Kabylia; Wans̲h̲arīs
    see also Tasili
  salt flats Tag̲h̲āza
population Ahaggar; Algeria.iii; Berbers; Zmāla.1
  see also Kabylia; *and* → BERBERS
religion Algeria.iii; S̲h̲āwiya.1
  mystical orders ʿAmmāriyya; Raḥmāniyya
    see also Darḳāwa; Ziyāniyya; *and* → MYSTICISM.MYSTICS.NORTH AFRICAN
toponyms
  ancient Ars̲h̲gūl; As̲h̲īr; al-Manṣūra; Sadrāta; [in Suppl.] Hunayn
  present day
    oases Biskra; Ḳanṭara.1; al-Ḳulayʿa.2.1; Laghouat; Sūf; Wargla; [in Suppl.] Gourara
    regions Ḥudna; Mzāb; Sāḥil.1.b; Tuwāt; Zāb
    towns Adrar.1; al-ʿAnnāba; Ārzāw; ʿAyn Temus̲h̲ent; Bidj̲āya; Biskra; Bulayda;
      Colomb-Béchar; al-Dj̲azāʾir; Djidjelli; G̲h̲ardāya; Ḳalʿat Banī ʿAbbās; Ḳalʿat
      Huwwāra; al-Ḳulayʿa.2.2; Ḳustanṭīna; Laghouat; al-Madiyya; Masīla; Milyāna;
      al-Muʿaskar; Mustag̲h̲ānim; Nadrūma; Saʿīda; S̲h̲ars̲h̲al; Sīdī Bu 'l-ʿAbbās;
      Tadallīs; Tāhart; Tanas; Tebessa; Tilimsān; Tindūf; Ṭubna; Tuggurt; Wahrān;
      Wargla

ALMS K̲h̲ayr; **Ṣadaḳa**; **Zakāt**
  see also Waḳf

ALPHABET **Abdj̲ad**; Ḥarf; Ḥisāb; **Ḥurūf al-Hidj̲āʾ**
  see also Dj̲afr; K̲h̲aṭṭ; [in Suppl.] Budūḥ; *and* → WRITING.SCRIPTS
  for the letters of the Arabic and Persian alphabets, see Ḍād; Dāl; D̲h̲āl; Dj̲īm; Fāʾ; G̲h̲ayn;

Hā᾽; Ḥā᾽; Hamza; Kāf; Ḳāf; Khā᾽; Lām; Mīm; Nūn; Pā᾽; Rā᾽; Ṣād; Sīn and Shīn; Tā᾽ and Ṭā᾽; Thā᾽; Wāw; Yā᾽; Ẓā᾽; Zāy

secret → CRYPTOGRAPHY

ANATOMY Djism; Katif; **Tashrīḥ**; [in Suppl.] Aflīmūn

see also Ishāra; Khiḍāb; Ḳiyāfa; Shāma; [in Suppl.] Dam

body

chest **Ṣadr**

eye **ʿAyn**; al-Kuḥl; Manāẓir; Ramad

see also Zaʿfarān.2; [in Suppl.] Mā᾽ al-Ward; *and* → MEDICINE.OPHTHALMOLOGY; OPTICS

hair ʿAfṣ; Afsantīn; Ḥinnā᾽; Liḥya-yi Sherīf; **Shaʿr**

see also [in Suppl.] Ḥallāḳ

limb Yamīn

organs Kabid; Ḳalb

teeth → MEDICINE.DENTISTRY

treatises on

Turkish Shānī-zāde

and → MEDICINE.MEDICAL HANDBOOKS/ENCYCLOPAEDIAS

ANDALUSIA **al-Andalus**; Gharb al-Andalus; Moriscos; Mozarab; Mudéjar; Sharḳ al-Andalus

see also Kitābāt.3; Libās.ii; Mā᾽.7; al-Madjūs; Moors; Muwallad.1; Safīr.2.b; Ṣā᾽ifa.2; al-Thughūr.2; *and* → DYNASTIES.SPAIN AND NORTH AFRICA; SPAIN

administration Dīwān.iii; Ḳūmis; Ṣāḥib al-Madīna; Ẓahīr

see also Fatā; Waḳf.II.4

architecture → ARCHITECTURE.REGIONS

art **al-Andalus**.ix

conquest of al-Andalus.vi.1; Mūsā b. Nuṣayr; Ṭāriḳ b. Ziyād

dynasties al-Murābiṭūn.4; al-Muwaḥḥidūn; Umayyads.In Spain; Zīrids.2; [in Suppl.] ʿAzafī

see also al-Andalus.vi; (Banū) Ḳasī; Ṭawīl, Banu; ʿUmar b. Ḥafṣūn; *and* → DYNASTIES.SPAIN AND NORTH AFRICA

reyes de taifas period (11th century) ʿAbbādids; Afṭasids; ʿĀmirids; Dhu ᾽l-Nūnids; Djahwarids; Ḥammūdids; Hūdids; **Mulūk al-Ṭawā᾽if**.2; Razīn, Banū; Ṭāhirids.2; Tudjīb; [in Suppl.] Ṣumādiḥ

see also Balansiya; Dāniya; Gharnāṭa; Ibn Ghalbūn; Ibn Rashīḳ, Abū Muḥammad; Ishbīliya; Ḳurṭuba; Mudjāhid, al-Muwaffaḳ; Parias; al-Sīd; Zuhayr

governors until Umayyad conquest ʿAbd al-Malik b. Ḳaṭan; ʿAbd al-Raḥmān al-Ghāfiḳī; Abu ᾽l-Khaṭṭār; al-Ḥurr b. ʿAbd al-Raḥmān al-Thaḳafī; al-Ḥusām b. Ḍirār; Tudjīb; ʿUbayd Allāh b. Ḥabḥāb; Yūsuf b. ʿAbd al-Raḥmān al-Fihrī

see also al-Andalus.vi.2; Kalb b. Wabara; Mūsā b. Nuṣayr; al-Ṣumayl

literature Aljamía; ʿArabiyya.B.Appendix; Fahrasa

and → ANDALUSIA.SCHOLARS.HISTORIANS; LITERATURE.POETRY.ANDALUSIAN

mysticism → MYSTICISM.MYSTICS.ANDALUSIAN

physical geography → SPAIN

scholars

astronomers Abu ᾽l-Ṣalt Umayya (*and* Umayya, Abu ᾽l-Ṣalt); al-Biṭrūdjī; Djābir b. Aflaḥ; Ibn al-Ṣaffār; Ibn al-Samḥ; al-Madjrīṭī; Muḥammad b. ʿUmar; al-Zarḳālī

see also Zīdj.iii.4

grammarians Abū Ḥayyān al-Gharnāṭī; al-Baṭalyawsī; Djūdī al-Mawrūrī; Ibn al-ʿArīf, al-Ḥusayn; Ibn ʿĀṣim; Ibn al-Iflīlī; Ibn Khātima; Ibn al-Ḳūṭiyya; Ibn Maḍā᾽; Ibn Mālik; Ibn Sīda; al-Rabaḥī; al-Shalawbīn; al-Shantamarī; al-Sharīf al-Gharnatī; al-

Sharīshī; al-Zubaydī; [in Suppl.] Ibn Hishām al-Lakhmī
see also al-Shāṭibī, Abū Isḥāḳ; *and* → *the section Lexicographers below*

geographers Abū ʿUbayd al-Bakrī; Ibn ʿAbd al-Munʿim al-Ḥimyarī; Ibn Ghālib; al-Idrīsī; al-ʿUdhrī; al-Warrāḳ, Muḥammad; al-Zuhrī, Muḥammad

historians al-Ḍabbī, Abū Djaʿfar; Ibn al-Abbār, Abu ʿAbd Allāh; Ibn ʿAbd al-Malik al-Marrākushī; Ibn Bashkuwāl; Ibn Burd.I; Ibn al-Faraḍī; Ibn Ghālib; Ibn Ḥayyān; Ibn ʿIdhārī; Ibn al-Khaṭīb; Ibn al-Ḳūṭiyya; Ibn Saʿīd al-Maghribī; al-Maḳḳarī; al-Rushāṭī; al-Warrāḳ, Muḥammad
see also al-Shaḳundī; al-ʿUdhrī; [in Suppl.] al-Suhaylī; *and* → DYNASTIES.SPAIN AND NORTH AFRICA

jurists al-Bādjī; al-Dānī; al-Ḥumaydī; Ibn Abī Zamanayn; Ibn ʿĀṣim; Ibn al-Faradī; Ibn Ḥabīb, Abū Marwān; Ibn Ḥazm, Abū Muḥammad; Ibn Ḳuzmān.III *and* IV (*and* [in Suppl.] Ḳuzmān.3 *and* 4); Ibn Maḍāʾ; Ibn Rushayd; ʿĪsā b. Dīnār; ʿIyāḍ b. Mūsā; al-Ḳalaṣādī; al-Ḳurṭubī, Abū ʿAbd Allāh; al-Ḳurṭubī, Yaḥyā; (al-)Mundhir b. Saʿīd; Shabṭūn; al-Ṭulayṭulī; al-Ṭurṭūshī; al-ʿUtbī, Abū ʿAbd Allāh; al-Waḳḳashī; Yaḥyā b. Yaḥyā al-Laythī; [in Suppl.] Ibn Rushd; al-Nubāhī
see also al-Khushanī; Mālikiyya; Ṣāʿid al-Andalusī; Shūrā.2; Shurṭa.2; [in Suppl.] Ibn al-Rūmiyya

lexicographers Ibn Sīda; al-Zubaydī

toponyms → SPAIN

ANGELOLOGY **Malāʾika**; [in Suppl.] Malaʾ.1
see also ʿAdhāb al-Ḳabr; Dīk; Iblīs; Ḳarīn; Rūḥāniyya; Siḥr

angels ʿAzāzīl; Djabrāʾīl; Hārūt wa-Mārūt; Isrāfīl; ʿIzrāʾīl; Mīkāl; Munkar wa-Nakīr; Riḍwān
see also al-Zabāniyya

ANIMALS Dābba; **Ḥayawān**
see also Badw; (Djazīrat) al-ʿArab.v; Farw; Hind.i.l; Khāṣī; Marbaṭ; [in Suppl.] Djazzār; *and* → ZOOLOGY

and art al-Asad; Fahd; Fīl; Ḥayawān.6; Karkaddan; Maʿdin; Namir and Nimr; [in Suppl.] Arnab
see also Zakhrafa

and proverbs Ḥayawān.2; Mathal
and see articles on individual animals, in particular Afʿā; Dhiʾb; Fahd; Ghurāb; Ḳaṭā; Khinzīr; Ḳird; Lamṭ; Naml; Yarbūʿ

animals

antelopes Ghazāl; Lamṭ; Mahāt

arachnoids ʿAḳrab; ʿAnkabūt

bats **Waṭwāṭ**

birds Babbaghāʾ; Dadjādja; Dīk; Ghurāb; Ḥamām; Hudhud; Humā; Ḳaṭā; Naʿām; Nasr; Nuḥām; al-Rukhkh; Salwā; Shunḳub; **al-Ṭāʾir**; Ṭāwūs; Ṭoghrïl; ʿUḳāb; Wāḳwāḳ.4; [in Suppl.] Abū Barāḳish
see also Bayzara; Bulbul; ʿIyāfa; al-Ramādī; Sonḳor; Timsāḥ

camels **Ibil**
see also (Djazīrat) al-ʿArab.v; Badw.II.c *and* d; Kārwān; Raḥīl; Wasm; [in Suppl.] Djammāl; *and* → TRANSPORT.CARAVANS

canines Dhiʾb; Fanak; Ibn Āwā; Kalb; Salūḳī; Thaʿlab; [in Suppl.] Ḍabuʿ

crustaceans **Saraṭān**

domesticated Baḳar; Fīl; Ibil; Kalb; Khinzīr; Nims; [in Suppl.] Djāmūs; Ghanam
see also Shāwiya.2; *and* → ANIMALS.EQUINES

equines Badw.II; Baghl; **Faras**; Ḥimār; **Khayl**
see also Fāris; Furūsiyya; Ḥazīn; Ibn Hudhayl; Ibn al-Mundhir; Iṣṭabl; Marbaṭ;

Maydān; Mīr-Āk̲h̲ūr; Sard̲j̲
felines   ʿAnāḳ; al-Asad; Fahd; Namir and Nimr; Sinnawr
fish   **Samak**
      see also al-Ṭāʾir
insects   D̲h̲ubāb; D̲j̲arād; Ḳaml; Naḥl; Naml; Nāmūs.2; **al-Ṭāʾir**
molluscs   **Ṣadaf**
reptiles   Afʿā; Ḍabb; Ḥayya; Ḥirbāʾ; Samandal; Sulaḥfā; Timsāḥ
      see also Ādam; Almās
rodents   Yarbūʿ; [in Suppl.] Faʾr
sport   Bayzara; Fahd; Furūsiyya; Ḥamām; K̲h̲inzīr; Mahāt; [in Suppl.] Ḍabuʿ
      see also Čakîrd̲j̲î-bas̲h̲î; Dog̲h̲and̲j̲î; Kurds.iv.C.5; *and* → Hunting
transformation into   Ḥayawān.3; Ḳird; **Mask̲h̲**
wild   *in addition to the above, see also* Ayyil; Fanak; Fīl; Ibn ʿIrs; Karkaddan; Ḳird; Ḳunfud̲h̲;
      Zarāfa; [in Suppl.] Arnab; Faras al-Māʾ
      see also Waḥs̲h̲; *and* → Hunting

Anthropomorphism   Has̲h̲wiyya; Karrāmiyya; **Tas̲h̲bīh wa-Tanzīh**
      see also Bayān b. Samʿān al-Tamīmī; D̲j̲ism; His̲h̲ām b. al-Ḥakam; Ḥulmāniyya; al-
      Muḳannaʿ; [in Suppl.] al-Mufaḍḍal b. Salama

Apostasy   Mulḥid; **Murtadd**
      see also Ḳatl; [in Suppl.] al-Ridda; *and* → Heresy

Arabian Peninsula   → Bahrain; Kuwait; Oman; Qatar; Saudi Arabia; United Arab
      Emirates; Yemen; *and the section Arabian Peninsula under* Architecture.regions;
      Dynasties; Pre-Islam; Tribes

Archaeology   → Architecture.regions; Epigraphy; *and the section Toponyms under in-*
      dividual countries
Turkish archaeologists   ʿOt̲h̲mān Ḥamdī

Architecture   **Architecture**; Bināʾ
      see also Kitābāt; Waḳf; *and* → Military
architects   Ḳāsim Ag̲h̲a; K̲h̲ayr al-Dīn; Sinān
decoration   Fusayfisāʾ; Kās̲h̲ī; K̲h̲aṭṭ; Parčīn-kārī; Tug̲h̲ra.2(d)
materials   D̲j̲iṣṣ; Labin; [in Suppl.] Ruk̲h̲ām
      see also Bināʾ
monuments
   aqueducts   Ḳanṭara.5 *and* 6
          see also Faḳīr; Sinān
   baths   **Ḥammām**; Ḥammām al-Ṣarak̲h̲
   bridges   **D̲j̲isr**; D̲j̲isr Banāt Yaʿḳūb; D̲j̲isr al-Ḥadīd; D̲j̲isr al-S̲h̲ug̲h̲r
          see also Dizfūl; Ḳanṭara; Sayḥān
   churches   → Christianity
   dams   **Band**
          see also Dizfūl; Sāwa.2.i; S̲h̲us̲h̲tar; [in Suppl.] Abū Sinbil; *and* → Hydrology
   gardens   **Būstān**; Ḥāʾir
          see also Bostānd̲j̲î; G̲h̲arnāṭa.B; Ḥawḍ; Māʾ.12; Srīnagar.2; Yalî; *and* → Flora;
          Literature.poetry.nature
   gates   **Bāb**; Bāb-i Humāyūn; Ḥarrān.ii.d
   granaries   [in Suppl.] Ḳaṣr.2.B

lighthouses **Manār**; al-Nāẓūr
mausolea → ARCHITECTURE.MONUMENTS.TOMBS
mills **Ṭāḥūn**
monasteries → CHRISTIANITY; MYSTICISM
mosques Ḥawḍ; Külliyye; Manāra; **Masdjid**; Miḥrāb; Minbar
see also ʿAnaza; Bāb.i; Bahw; Balāṭ; Dikka; Khaṭīb; Muṣallā.2; Zāwiya.1
individual mosques Aya Sofya; al-Azhar; Ḥarrān.ii.(b); Ḥusaynī Dālān; Kaʿba; al-Ḳarawiyyīn; Ḳubbat al-Ṣakhra; Ḳuṭb Mīnār; al-Masdjid al-Aḳṣā; al-Masdjid al-Ḥarām; Zaytūna.1
see also Anḳara; Architecture; Bahmanīs; Dhār.2; Djām; Edirne; Ḥamāt; Ḥimṣ; Kāẓimayn; Ḳazwīn; Maʿarrat al-Nuʿmān; Makka.4; Sinān
obelisks **Misalla**
palaces **Sarāy**; [in Suppl.] **Ḳaṣr**.2.A
see also Balāṭ
individual palaces Čirāghān; Ḳaṣr al-Ḥayr al-Gharbī; Ḳaṣr al-Ḥayr al-Sharḳī; Kayḳubādiyya; Khirbat al-Mafdjar; Khirbat al-Minya; Ḳubādābād; Maḥall; al-Mushattā; Ṭopḳapi̊ Sarāyi̊; al-Ukhayḍir; Yi̊ldi̊z Sarāyi̊; [in Suppl.] Djabal Says; Ḳaṣr al-Mushāsh; Ḳaṣr Ṭūbā; Ḳasṭal; al-Khuld
see also Gharnāṭa.B; Khirbat al-Bayḍāʾ; Ḳubbat al-Hawāʾ; Lashkar-i Bāzār
pavilions Köshk
see also Yali̊
strongholds Burdj; Ḥiṣār; **Ḥiṣn**; Ḳaṣaba; Sūr; [in Suppl.] **Ḳaṣr**.2
see also al-ʿAwāṣim; Bāb.ii; al-Ḳalʿa; Ribāṭ; al-Thughūr; Udj
individual strongholds Abū Safyān; Āgra; Alamūt.i.; Alindjaḳ; ʿAmādiya; Anadolu Ḥiṣāri̊; Anamur; Anapa; Asīrgarh; Atak; Bāb al-Abwāb; Bālā Ḥiṣār; Balāṭunus; Barzūya; Baynūn; Bhakkar; Čanderī; Čirmen; al-Dārūm; Djaʿbar; al-Djarbāʾ; Gaban; Gāwilgaṙh; Ghumdān; Gök Tepe; Golkonḍā; Ḥadjar al-Nasr; Hānsī; Ḥarrān.ii.(a); Ḥiṣn al-Akrād; Ḥiṣn Kayfā; Iṣṭakhr; Kakhtā; Ḳalʿat Nadjm; Ḳalʿat al-Shaḳīf; Ḳalāwdhiya; Ḳalʿe-i Sefīd; Ḳandahār; Kanizsa; al-Karak; Kawkab al-Hawāʾ; Kharāna; Khartpert; Khērla; Khotin; Khunāṣira; Kilāt-i Nādirī; Ḳoron; Ḳoyul Ḥiṣār; Lanbasar; Lüleburgaz; Mānḍū; Manōhar; al-Marḳab; Muḍgal; Narnālā; Parendā; al-Rāwandān; Rōhtās; Rūm Ḳalʿesi; Rūmeli Ḥiṣāri̊; Ṣahyūn; Shalbaṭarra; Softa; al-Ṣubayba; Umm al-Raṣāṣ; Yeñi Ḳalʿe; [in Suppl.] Bādiya; Bubashtru; al-Dīkdān; Firrīm; Nandana
see also Ashīr; Bahmanīs; Bīdar; Dawlatābād; Diyār Bakr; Ḥimṣ; Kawkabān.2; Khursābād; Maḥall; Māhūr; Thādj
tombs **Ḳabr**; **Ḳubba**; **Maḳbara**; Mashhad; **Turba**
see also Muthamman; Walī.4, 5 *and* 8; Zāwiya; Ziyāra
individual buildings Baḳīʿ al-Gharḳad; Golkonḍā; Ḥarrān.ii.(c); Maklī; Nafīsa; Rādkān; Sahsarām; Tādj Maḥall
see also Abarḳūh; Abū Ayyūb al-Anṣārī; Abū Madyan; Āgra; Aḥmad al-Badawī; Aḥmad Yasawī; Bahmanīs; Barīd Shāhīs.II; Djahāngīr; Ghāzī Miyān; Gunbadh-i Ḳābūs; Ḥimṣ; Imāmzāda; Karak Nūḥ; Karbalāʾ; Ḳazwīn; al-Khalīl; Ḳubbat al-Hawāʾ; Maʿarrat al-Nuʿmān; al-Madīna; Sulṭāniyya.2; [in Suppl.] Mamlūks.iii.a.A
water-houses **Sabīl**.2
fire-pumps Ṭulumbadji̊
fountains Shadirwān
wells Bāʾolī; **Biʾr**; Biʾr Maymūn; Zamzam
see also Ḥawḍ
regions
Afghanistan and Indian subcontinent Āgra; Bahmanīs; Barīd Shāhīs.II; Bharōč; Bīdar;

Bīdjāpūr; Bihār; Čāmpānēr; Dawlatābād; Dihlī.2; Djūnāgaṙh; Ghaznawids; Ghūrids; Golkondā; Hampī; Hānsī; Ḥaydarābād; Hind.vii; Ḥusaynī Dālān; Ḳuṭb Mīnār; Lahore; Lakhnaw; Maḥall; Mahisur; Māndū.2; Mughals.7; Multān.2; Nāgawr; Sind.4; Srīnagar.2; Tādj Maḥall; Tughluḳids.2; Uččh.2; [in Suppl.] Nandana; Ṫhaṫṫā.2
see also Burdj.iii; Bustān.ii; Imām-bārā; Lashkar-i Bāzār; Māʾ.12; Maḳbara.5; Maklī; Manāra.2; Masdjid.II; Miḥrāb; Minbar.3; Miẓalla.5; Muthamman; Parčīn-kārī; Pīshṭāḳ

Africa → Africa; *for North African architecture, see below*

Andalusia al-Andalus.ix; Burdj.II; Gharnāṭa; Ishbīliya; Ḳurṭuba; Naṣrids.2
see also al-Nāẓūr

Arabian peninsula al-Ḥidjr; Kaʿba; al-Masdjid al-Ḥarām
see also Makka.4; Ṣanʿāʾ; Ṭāhirids.3.2

Central Asia Bukhārā; Ḥiṣn.iii; Īlkhāns; Samarḳand.2; Tīmūrids.3.b
see also Miḥrāb

Egypt Abu 'l-Hawl; al-Azhar; Haram; al-Ḳāhira; Mashrabiyya.1; Nafīsa; [in Suppl.] Mamlūks
see also Miḥrāb; Misalla; Miṣr; Saʿīd al-Suʿadāʾ; al-Uḳṣur; [in Suppl.] Abū Sinbil

Fertile Crescent Baghdād; Dimashḳ; Ḥarrān.ii; Ḥimṣ; ʿIrāḳ.vii; Ḳubbat al-Ṣakhra; al-Ḳuds; Maʿarrat al-Nuʿmān; al-Marḳab.3; al-Masdjid al-Aḳṣā; al-Raḳḳa; al-Ukhayḍir; [in Suppl.] Bādiya; Dār al-Ḥadīth.I
see also Ḳaṣr al-Ḥayr al-Gharbī; Ḳaṣr al-Ḥayr al-Sharḳī; Khirbat al-Mafdjar; Miḥrāb; al-Rāwandān; [in Suppl.] Ḳaṣr al-Mushāsh; Ḳaṣr Ṭūbā; Ḳasṭal

Iran Ḥiṣn.ii; Iṣfahān.2; Iṣṭakhr; Ḳazwīn; Khursābād; Mashrabiyya.2; Rādkān; al-Rayy.2; Ṣafawids.V; Saldjūḳids.VI; Sāmānids.2(b); Sulṭāniyya.2; Tabrīz.2; Tihrān.I.3.b.ii; Ṭūs.2; Warāmīn.2; Zawāra; [in Suppl.] **Iran**.viii.(b)
see also Ḳaṣr-i Shīrīn; Miḥrāb; Ribāṭ-i Sharaf; Yazd.1; [in Suppl.] Maḳbara.4

North Africa Fās; Fāṭimid Art; Ḥiṣn.i; Ḳalʿat Banī Ḥammād; al-Ḳarawiyyīn; Zaytūna.1; [in Suppl.] Ḳaṣr.2
see also ʿAnaza; Bidjāya; Miḥrāb

Southeast Asia Ḥiṣn.iv; Indonesia.v; Masdjid.III-V

Turkey Adana; Anḳara; Aya Sofya; Diwrīgī; Diyār Bakr; Edirne; Ḥarrān.ii; Ḥiṣn Kayfā; Istanbul; Konya.2; Lāranda; ʿOthmānli̊.V; [in Suppl.] Istanbul.VIII
see also Ḳapli̊dja; Ḳāsim Agha; Khayr al-Dīn; Köshk; Miḥrāb; Rūm Ḳalʿesi; Sinān; Yali̊

terms ʿAmūd; ʿAnaza; Bahw; Balāṭ; Īwān; Muḳarbaṣ; Muḳarnas; Muthamman; Pīshṭāḳ; Riwāḳ; Sarāy; Sardāb; Shadirwān; Ṭirāz.3

urban Bāb; Dār; Funduḳ; Ḥammām; Īwān; Ḳaysāriyya; Khān.II; Madrasa.III; Masdjid; Muṣallā.2; Rabʿ; Selāmli̊ḳ; Shāriʿ; Sūḳ; Sūr
see also Kanīsa; Sarāy; [in Suppl.] Mamlūks.iii.a.B; *and* → Sedentarism; Urbanism

fountains → Architecture.monuments.water-houses

ventilation Mirwaḥa; [in Suppl.] Bādgīr
see also Khaysh; Sardāb; Sind.4

Armenia **Armīniya**; Rewān; Shimshāṭ
and → Caucasus

Art Arabesque; Fann; Fusayfisāʾ; Kāshī; Khaṭṭ; Khazaf; Kitābāt; Lawn; Maʿdin.4; Parčīn-kārī; Rasm; Taṣwīr; Ṭirāz; Zakhrafa; Zalīdj; Zudjādj
see also Architecture; Billawr; Dhahab; Fiḍḍa; ʿIlm al-Djamāl; Khātam; Muhr; Ṣūra; *and* → Animals.and art; Architecture; Writing.manuscripts and books

calligraphy **Khaṭṭ** (*and* [in Suppl.]); Tughra

see also ʿAlī; İnal; Ḳum(m)ī; Muraḳḳaʿ; Nuskha; Tazwīr; Tīmūrids.3.a; *and* → WRITING
calligraphers ʿAlī Riḍā-i ʿAbbāsī; Ḥamza al-Ḥarrānī; Ibn al-Bawwāb; Ibn Muḳla; Muḥammad Ḥusayn Tabrīzī; Müstaḳīm-zāde; Yāḳūt al-Mustaʿṣimī
ceramics → ART.POTTERY
decorative ʿĀdj; al-Asad; Djiṣṣ; Fahd; Ḥayawān.6; Hilāl.ii; Īlkhāns; al-Ḳamar.II; Mashrabiyya; Parčīn-kārī; Shams.3; Tawrīḳ; Ṭirāz; ʿUnwān.2; Yashm.2; Zakhrafa
see also Kāshī; Maʿdin.4; [in Suppl.] Mamlūks.iii.b
drawing **Rasm**
glass al-Ḳily; ʿOthmānli.VII.d; Sāmānids.2(a); **Zudjādj**; [in Suppl.] Mamlūks.iii.b.C
handicrafts Ḳalamkārī; [in Suppl.] Bisāṭ; Dawāt
see also Ḥalfāʾ
illumination **ʿUnwān**.2; [in Suppl.] Mamlūks.iii.b.D; *and* → WRITING
metalware Bīdar; Īlkhāns; **Maʿdin**.4; ʿOthmānli.VII.b; Sāmānids.2(a); Tīmūrids.3.d; [in Suppl.] Ibrīḳ; Mamlūks.iii.b.A
mosaics **Fusayfisāʾ**; Kāshī; Zalīdj
painting **Taṣwīr**.1
miniatures Īlkhāns; Mughals.9; Naḳḳāsh-khāna; ʿOthmānli.VIII
see also Fīl; Kalīla wa-Dimna.16; Māndū.3; Miʿrādj.5; al-Mīzān.3; Muraḳḳaʿ; Rustam.2; Sāḳī.3; Tīmūrids.3.a; [in Suppl.] Djawhar; *and* → ANIMALS.AND ART; ART.DRAWING
miniaturists Bihzād; Manṣūr; Maṭrāḳči; Naḳḳāsh Ḥasan (Pasha); Riḍā ʿAbbāsī; Riḍāʾī; Siyāh-ḳalem; [in Suppl.] Lewnī
see also ʿAlī; Luḳmān b. Sayyid Ḥusayn
modern painting **Taṣwīr**.3
and → ART.DRAWING
painters Djabrān Khalīl Djabrān; ʿOthmān Ḥamdī; Sipihrī; [in Suppl.] Dinet; Eyyūboghlu, Bedrī
photography **Taṣwīr**.2
pottery Anadolu.iii.6; al-Andalus.ix; **Fakhkhār**; Īlkhāns; Iznīḳ; Ḳallala; **Khazaf**; Mināʾī; ʿOthmānli.VII.a; Sāmānids.2(a); Ṣīnī; Tīmūrids.3.c; Ṭīn.2; [in Suppl.] Mamlūks.iii.b.B; Ören Ḳalʿe
regional and period al-Andalus.ix; Berbers.VI; Fāṭimid Art; Īlkhāns; ʿIrāḳ.vii; Mughals.8 and 9; ʿOthmānli.VII; Saldjūḳids.VI; Sāmānids.2(a); Tīmūrids.3.a; [in Suppl.] Iran.viii.(a); Khaṭṭ.vi; Mamlūks.iii.b
silhouette-cutting Fakhrī
tapestry Anadolu.iii.6; ʿOthmānli.VI; Sadjdjāda.2; ʿUshāḳ.2; [in Suppl.] **Bisāṭ**
see also Karkaddan; Mafrūshāt; Mifrash; Mīlās.2
textiles Ḥarīr; Ḳumāsh; Ṭirāz; [in Suppl.] Ḥāʾik
see also Ḳalamkārī; Ḳaṣab; Kattān; Ḳurḳūb; Mandīl; al-Nassādj; *and* → CLOTHING. MATERIALS
production centres al-Andalus.ix; al-Bahnasā; Dabīḳ; Tinnīs
see also Bursa; Īlkhāns; Mughals.8; ʿOthmānli.VI; al-Rayy.2; Sāmānids.2(a); Yazd.1; *and* → ART.TAPESTRY
tiles **Kāshī**
see also Anadolu.iii.6

ASCETICISM Bakkāʾ; Malāmatiyya; **Zuhd**
see also Khalwa; Manāḳib; [in Suppl.] Asad b. Mūsā b. Ibrāhīm; Ṣalāt-i Maʿkūsa; *for ascetics* → MYSTICISM.MYSTICS; SAINTHOOD
poetry **Zuhdiyya**

ASIA Almalïgh; Baikal
see also Baraba; Mogholistān
Central → CENTRAL ASIA
East Čam; Djāwī; Indochina; Indonesia; Ḳimār; Malay Peninsula; Malaysia; Patani; Philippines; al-Shīlā; al-Ṣīn; Singapore; Thailand; Tubbat; al-Yabānī; [in Suppl.] Brunei
see also Kitābāt.8; Ṣanf; Shāh Bandar.2; ʿUlamāʾ.5; Waḳf.VII.ii-vi; Wāḳwāḳ; Walī.7; Zābadj; [in Suppl.] Demography.VIII; al-Marʾa; *and* → ARCHITECTURE.REGIONS.SOUTHEAST ASIA; LAW.IN SOUTHEAST ASIA; ONOMASTICS.TITLES; PRE-ISLAM.IN SOUTHEAST ASIA
for individual countries → CHINA; INDONESIA; MALAYSIA; MONGOLIA; PHILIPPINES; THAILAND; *for Japan, see* al-Yabānī; *for Tibet, see* Tubbat
Eurasia → EUROPE
South Bangāla; Burma; Ceylon; Hind; Laccadives; Maldives; Mauritius; Minicoy; Nepal; Nicobars; Pākistān; Seychelles
see also Ruhmī; Waḳf.VII.i
for individual countries → BANGLADESH; BURMA; INDIA; NEPAL; PAKISTAN; SRI LANKA

ASSYRIA Khursābād; Nimrūd; Nīnawā.1; Zindjirli; [in Suppl.] Athūr

ASTROLOGY Ikhtiyārāt; Ḳaws Ḳuzaḥ; al-Kayd; Ḳirān; Minṭaḳat al-Burūdj; Munadjdjim; **Nudjūm (Aḥkām al-)**; al-Tasyīr
see also Khaṭṭ; Zāʾirdja; Zīdj; *and* → ASTRONOMY.CELESTIAL OBJECTS
astrologers Abū Maʿshar al-Balkhī; al-Bīrūnī; Ibn Abi ʾl-Ridjāl, Abu ʾl-Ḥasan; Ibn al-Khaṣīb, Abū Bakr; al-Ḳabīṣī; al-Khayyāṭ, Abū ʿAlī; Māshāʾ Allāh; ʿUṭārid b. Muḥammad; [in Suppl.] Yazīdjī
see also Baṭlamiyūs; *and* → ASTRONOMY; DIVINATION
terms al-Djawzahar; Ḥadd; Ḳaṭʿ; Muthallath; Saʿd wa-Naḥs (*and* al-Saʿdāni; Shaḳāwa); al-Sahm.1.b; al-Ṭāliʿ.2; al-Tinnīn

ASTRONOMY Anwāʾ; Asṭurlāb; Falak; Hayʾa; **ʿIlm al-Hayʾa**; al-Ḳamar.I; al-Kayd; Kusūf; al-Ḳuṭb; al-Madd wa ʾl-Djazr; al-Madjarra; al-Manāzil; Minṭaḳat al-Burūdj; al-Nudjūm; Zīdj
see also Djughrāfiyā; Ḳibla.ii; al-Ḳubba; al-Kura; Makka.4; Mīḳāt.2; Mizwala
astronomers ʿAbd al-Raḥmān al-Ṣūfī; Abu ʾl-Ṣalt Umayya (*and* Umayya, Abu ʾl-Ṣalt); ʿAlī al-Ḳūshdjī; al-Badīʿ al-Asṭurlābī; al-Battānī; al-Bīrūnī; al-Biṭrūdjī; Djābir b. Aflaḥ; al-Djaghmīnī; al-Farghānī; Ḥabash al-Ḥāsib al-Marwazī; Ibn Amādjūr; Ibn al-Bannāʾ al-Marrākushī; Ibn ʿIrāḳ; Ibn al-Ṣaffār; Ibn al-Samḥ; Ibn Yūnus; al-Kāshī; al-Khwārazmī, Abū Djaʿfar; al-Khāzin; al-Khazīnī; al-Khudjandī; Kushiyār b. Labān; Ḳuṭb al-Dīn Shīrāzī; al-Madjrīṭī; al-Mārdīnī; al-Marrākushī; Muḥammad b. ʿĪsā al-Māhānī; Muḥammad b. ʿUmar; al-Nayrīzī; al-Shayzarī; Taḳī al-Dīn; Thābit b. Ḳurra; al-Ṭūsī, Naṣīr al-Dīn; ʿUmar Khayyām; ʿUṭārid b. Muḥammad; al-Zarḳālī; [in Suppl.] ʿAbd al-Salām b. Muḥammad; Ḳāḍī-zāde Rūmī; al-Kūhī
see also Baṭlamiyūs; al-Falakī; Falakī Shirwānī; Ibn al-Haytham; Ḳusṭā b. Lūḳā; Sindhind; [in Suppl.] Ibn al-Adjdābī; *and* → ASTROLOGY
celestial objects
comets **al-Nudjūm**.III.b
planets al-Ḳamar.I; al-Mirrīkh; al-Mushtarī; **al-Nudjūm**.II; ʿUṭārid; Zuḥal; Zuhara
see also Minṭaḳat al-Burūdj; Ruʾyat al-Hilāl; al-Saʿdāni; Taḳwīm.1; al-ʿUzzā; Zīdj
stars and constellations ʿAḳrab; ʿAnāḳ; al-Asad; Dadjādja; Fard.e; Kalb; Ḳird; Mahāt; Minṭaḳat al-Burūdj; Muthallath; Naʿām; Nasr; **al-Nudjūm**; Radīf.1; al-Sahm.1.c; Samak.9; Saraṭān.6; Shams.2; al-Shiʿrā; Tādj; Thaʿlab; al-Tinnīn; ʿUḳāb; Zarāfa; [in Suppl.] Arnab; Ghanam

see also al-Kayd; Saʿd wa-Naḥs (*and* al-Saʿdānⁱ; S̲h̲akāwa); al-Sāk̲; Sulaḥfā; al-Ṭāʾir
chronology   **Taʾrīk̲h̲**.I.2
observatory   **Marṣad**
      see also Udjdjayn; Ulug̲h̲ Beg; ʿUmar K̲h̲ayyām
terms   al-Dj̲awzahar; Istik̲bāl; al-Maṭāliʿ; al-Maṭlaʿ; al-Mayl; Muḳābala.1; Muḳanṭarāt; Niṣf
      al-Nahār; Radīf.1; Rubʿ; Ruʾyat al-Hilāl; al-Sāk̲; al-Samt; S̲h̲akkāziyya; Ṭabīʿa.4; al-
      Taʿdīl; al-Taʿdīl bayn al-Saṭrayn; Taʿdīl al-Zamān; Taḳwīm.1; al-Ṭāliʿ.1; Zīdj̲

AUSTRIA   Beč; **Nemče**
      see also Muslimūn.2.ii

B

BĀBISM   → SECTS

BAHAIS   Bāb; Bābīs; Bahāʾ Allāh; **Bahāʾīs**; Mas̲h̲rik al-Ad̲h̲kār; Naḳd al-Mīt̲h̲āḳ; S̲h̲awḳī Efendi
      Rabbānī
      see also Lawḥ; Maẓhar; [in Suppl.] Anṣārī

BAHRAIN   **al-Baḥrayn**; āl-K̲h̲alīfa; Madj̲lis.4.A.x; Maḥkama.4.ix; Ṣiḥāfa.1.(xii)
      see also Ḳarmaṭī; ʿUṣfūrids; ʿUtūb
toponyms   al-Manāma; al-Muḥarraḳ; Yabrīn
      see also al-Mus̲h̲aḳḳar

BALKANS   **Balkan**; **Rūmeli**; al-Ṣaḳāliba
      see also Ṭarīḳa.II.6; Walī.4; Wardar; Woyvoda; *and* → EUROPE.EASTERN EUROPE
and Ottoman military   Eflāḳ; Martolos; Woynuḳ
      and → *the section* Toponyms *under Balkan states*; MILITARY.OTTOMAN

BANGLADESH   **Bangāla**; Madj̲lis.4.C
      see also Bengali; Nad̲h̲r al-Islām; Satya Pīr; [in Suppl.] Dj̲arīda.vii
literature   → LITERATURE.IN OTHER LANGUAGES
toponyms   Bāḳargandj̲; Bangāla; Bōgrā; Chittagong; D̲h̲ākā; Dīnādj̲pur; Dj̲assawr; Farīdpur;
      Sātgāʾon; Silhet; Sundarban
      see also Ruhmī; Sonārgāʾon

BASQUES   **al-Bas̲h̲kunis̲h̲**
      see also Ibn G̲h̲arsiya

BEDOUINS   **Badw**; Biʾr; Dawār; G̲h̲anīma; G̲h̲azw; al-Hidj̲ar; T̲h̲aʾr; [in Suppl.] K̲h̲uwwa
      see also Liṣṣ; ʿUrf.2.I; Wasm; *and* → LAW.CUSTOMARY; NOMADISM; SAUDI ARABIA;
      TRIBES.ARABIAN PENINSULA
writings on   Rzewuski

BENIN   Kandi; Kotonou; Kouandé

BERBERS   **Berbers**; Judaeo-Berber
      see also Ḳallala; Ḳiṣṣa.8; Libās.ii; Mafāk̲h̲ir al-Barbar; [in Suppl.] Sība; *and* → ALGERIA
customary law   ʿĀda.ii; Ḳānūn.iv
      see also ʿUrf

customs Ḥimāya.ii.II; Leff; Li<u>th</u>ām; Ṣaff.3
dynasties ʿAbd al-Wādids; ʿAmmār; Marīnids; Midrār; al-Murābiṭūn; al-Muwaḥḥidūn; Razīn, Banū; Zīrids
language → LANGUAGES.AFRO-ASIATIC
music Imẓad
religion al-Ba<u>dj</u>alī; Berbers.III; Ḥā-Mīm; Ṣāliḥ b. Ṭarīf
resistance Berbers.I.c; al-Kāhina; Kusayla; Maysara
rulers al-Ir<u>dj</u>ānī; [in Suppl.] Zīrī b. ʿAṭiyya
tribes al-Barānis; Bar<u>gh</u>awāṭa; Birzāl; al-Butr; <u>Dj</u>azūla; <u>Gh</u>āniya; <u>Gh</u>ubrīnī; <u>Gh</u>umāra; Glāwā; Gudāla; Ḥāḥā; Har<u>gh</u>a; Hawwāra; Hintāta; Ifo<u>gh</u>as; Īfran; Iraten; Kutāma; Lamṭa; Lamtūna; Lawāta; Ma<u>gh</u>īla; Ma<u>gh</u>rāwa; Malzūza; Maṣmūda; Māssa; Maṭ<u>gh</u>ara; Maṭmāṭa; Mazāta; Midyūna; Misrāta; al-Nafūsa; Nafza; Nafzāwa; Ṣanhā<u>dj</u>a; Ṭawārik; Zanāta; [in Suppl.] Awraba
see also <u>Sh</u>āwiya.1; Ṣufriyya.2

BIBLE **In<u>dj</u>īl; Tawrāt**
and → CHRISTIANITY; JUDAISM
biblical personages Ādam; ʿAmālīḳ; Ayyūb; Āzar; ʿAzāzīl; Balʿam; Bilḳīs; Binyāmīn; Bu<u>kh</u>t-naṣ(ṣ)ar; Dāniyāl; Dāwūd; <u>Dj</u>abrāʾīl; <u>Dj</u>ālūt; Firʿawn; Ḥābīl wa-Ḳābīl; Ḥām; Hāmān; Hārūn b. ʿImrān; Hārūt wa-Mārūt; Ḥawwāʾ; Ḥizḳīl; Ibrāhīm; Ilyās; ʿImrān; Irmiyā; ʿĪsā; Isḥāḳ; Ismāʿīl; Kanʿān; Ḳārūn; Ḳiṭfīr; Kū<u>sh</u>; Lamak; Lazarus; Lūṭ; Maryam; al-Masīḥ; Mūsā; Namrūd; Nūḥ; Rāḥīl; Sām.1; al-Sāmirī; Sāra; <u>Sh</u>amsūn; <u>Sh</u>amwīl; <u>Sh</u>aʿyā; <u>Sh</u>ī<u>th</u>; Sulaymān b. Dāwūd; Ṭālūt; ʿŪ<u>dj</u>; Yāfi<u>th</u>; Yaḥyā b. Zakariyyāʾ; Yaʿḳūb; Yūnus; Yū<u>sh</u>aʿ b. Nūn; Yūsuf; Zakariyyāʾ
see also <u>Dh</u>u 'l-Kifl; al-Fayyūm; Hūd; Idrīs; Yā<u>dj</u>ū<u>dj</u> wa-Mā<u>dj</u>ū<u>dj</u>; *and* → PROPHETHOOD
biblical toponyms Ṣihyawn
see also <u>Dj</u>ūdī; *and* → PALESTINE/ISRAEL
translations
into Arabic Fāris al-<u>Sh</u>idyāḳ; Saʿadyā Ben Yōsēf; al-Yāzi<u>dj</u>ī.1; [in Suppl.] al-Bustānī.2
see also ʿArabiyya.A.ii.1; Judaeo-Arabic.iii.B; Tawrāt
into Persian Abu 'l-Faḍl ʿAllāmī
see also Judaeo-Persian.i.2

BOSNIA → (former) YUGOSLAVIA

BOTANY Adwiya; al-ʿA<u>sh</u><u>sh</u>āb; Nabāt
and → AGRICULTURE; FLORA; MEDICINE; PHARMACOLOGY
botanists Abū ʿUbayd al-Bakrī; al-Dīnawarī, Abū Ḥanīfa; Ibn al-Bayṭār; al-Ṭi<u>gh</u>narī; [in Suppl.] al-<u>Gh</u>āfiḳī; Ibn al-Rūmiyya
see also Abu 'l-<u>Kh</u>ayr al-I<u>sh</u>bīlī; Filāḥa; Nīḳūlāʾūs; al-Suwaydī

BUDDHISM Ba<u>kh</u><u>sh</u>ī; Budd; **Sumaniyya**
see also Bāmiyān; al-Barāmika.1; Bilawhar wa-Yūdāsaf; Tañrï

BULGARIA **Bulgaria**; Pomaks
see also Küčük Ḳaynar<u>dj</u>a; Muhā<u>dj</u>ir.2; Muslimūn.1.B.5
physical geography
waters Merič
toponyms Burgas; Deli-Orman; Dobru<u>dj</u>a; Filibe; Hezār<u>gh</u>rad; Küstendil; Newrokop; Nīkbūlī; ʿO<u>th</u>mān Pazar; Plewna; Rusčuk; Selwi; <u>Sh</u>umnu; Ṣofya; Tatar Pazarcik; Tîrnowa; Warna; Widin; Zi<u>sh</u>towa

Burma Arakan; **Burma**; Mergui; Rangoon; Zerbadis

Byzantine Empire Biṭrīḳ; Ḳayṣar; **Rūm**
see also Anadolu.iii.1 *and* 2; Hiba.i; Iznīḳ; Ḳalāwdhiya; Ḳubrus; (al-)Ḳusṭanṭīniyya; al-Maṣṣīṣa; Mu'ta; Nauplion.1; Saracens; Umur Pasha; Wenedik; al-Ẓāhir li-Iʿzāz Dīn Allāh; *and* → Greece; Palestine/Israel; Syria; Turkey, *in particular the section Toponyms*
allies Djarādjima; Djarrāḥids; Ghassān; al-Ḥārith b. Djabala; Kinda.1; Salīḥ; [in Suppl.] Djabala b. al-Ḥārith
and → Tribes
military Alay; Lamas-ṣū; Malāzgird.2; Nafṭ.2; Tourkopo(u)loi; [in Suppl.] Dhāt al-Ṣawārī
see also al-ʿAwāṣim; Cilicia; Ṣā'ifa.1; Sayf al-Dawla; al-Thughūr.1
battles Yarmūk.2

C

Caliphate Ahl al-Ḥall wa 'l-ʿAḳd; Bayʿa; Ḥādjib.i; Ḥarb.ii; Hiba.i; Imāma; Ḳaḍīb; Kātib.i; **Khalīfa**; Libās.i; Madjlis.1; Marāsim.1; Mawākib.1; Shūrā.1; Walī al-ʿAhd; Wazīr
see also Amīr al-Mu'minīn; Ghulām.i; Khilʿa.ii; Laḳab.2; Māl al-Bayʿa; *and* → Court Ceremony
ʿAbbāsids (750-1258) **ʿAbbāsids**; Baghdād; Dīwān.i; Ḥādjib.i; Khalīfa.i.B; Marāsim.1; Mawākib.1; Muṣādara.2; Musawwida; Naḳīb.1; Naḳīb al-Ashrāf.1; Sāmarrā'; Wazīr.I.1
see also al-Abnā'.III; ʿAlī b. ʿAbd Allāh b. al-ʿAbbās; ʿAlids; Architecture.I.3; Ḍarība; Hāshimiyya; al-Hāshimiyya; Laḳab.2; Libās.i.4; Riḍā.2; al-Shuʿūbiyya; Sikka.2; Walī al-ʿAhd; [in Suppl.] al-Khuld; Shāʿir.1.B; *and* → Dynasties.persia
caliphs Abu 'l-ʿAbbās al-Saffāḥ; al-Amīn; al-Hādī ila 'l-Ḥaḳḳ; Hārūn al-Rashīd; al-Ḳādir bi 'llāh; al-Ḳāhir bi 'llāh; al-Ḳā'im bi-amr Allāh; al-Mahdī; al-Ma'mūn; al-Manṣūr; al-Muhtadī; al-Muḳtadī; al-Muḳtadir; al-Muḳtafī bi-llāh; al-Muḳtafī li-Amr Allāh; al-Muntaṣir; al-Mustaḍī'; al-Mustaʿīn (I); al-Mustaʿīn (II); al-Mustakfī; al-Mustandjid (I); al-Mustandjid (II); al-Mustanṣir (I); al-Mustanṣir (II); al-Mustarshid; al-Mustaʿṣim bi 'llāh; al-Mustaẓhir bi 'llāh; al-Muʿtaḍid bi 'llāh; al-Muʿtamid ʿalā 'llāh; al-Muʿtaṣim bi 'llāh; al-Mutawakkil ʿalā 'llāh; al-Muʿtazz bi 'llāh; al-Muṭīʿ li 'llāh; al-Muttaḳī li 'llāh; al-Nāṣir li-Dīn Allāh, Abu 'l-ʿAbbās; al-Rāḍī bi 'llāh; al-Rāshid; al-Ṭā'iʿ li-Amr Allāh; al-Wāthiḳ bi 'llāh; al-Ẓāhir bi-Amr Allāh
see also ʿAbd Allāh b. ʿAlī; Būrān; al-Khayzurān bint ʿAṭā' al-Djurashiyya; Muḥammad b. ʿAlī b. ʿAbd Allāh; al-Muwaffaḳ; al-Ruṣāfa.2
viziers Abū ʿAbd Allāh Yaʿḳūb; Abū Salāma al-Khallāl; Abū ʿUbayd Allāh; ʿAḍud al-Dīn; ʿAlī b. ʿĪsā; al-Barāmika.3; al-Barīdī; al-Djardjarā'ī.1-3; al-Faḍl b. Marwān; al-Faḍl b. al-Rabīʿ; al-Faḍl b. Sahl b. Zadhānfarūkh; al-Fayḍ b. Abī Ṣāliḥ; Ḥamīd; Hibat Allāh b. Muḥammad; Ibn al-Alḳamī; Ibn al-Baladī; Ibn al-Furāt; Ibn Hubayra; Ibn Khāḳan.2 *and* 3; Ibn Makhlad; Ibn Muḳla; Ibn al-Muslima; Ibn al-Zayyāt; al-Iskāfī, Abu 'l-Faḍl; al-Iskāfī, Abū Isḥāḳ; Ismāʿīl b. Bulbul; al-Khaṣībī; al-Rabīʿ b. Yūnus; Rabīb al-Dawla; al-Rūdhrāwarī; Wahb, Banū; al-Zaynabī
see also al-Djahshiyārī; Hilāl al-Ṣābi'; Khātam; Wazīr.I.1
secretaries Aḥmad b. Abī Khālid al-Aḥwal; Aḥmad b. Yūsuf; ʿAmr b. Masʿada; al-Ḥasan b. Sahl; Ibn al-Djarrāḥ; Ibn Khāḳan.1 *and* 4; Ibn al-Māshiṭa; al-Mūriyānī
see also Wahb, Banū; [in Suppl.] Shāʿir.1.B.ii
historians of al-Djahshiyārī; Ibn Abi 'l-Dam; Ibn Abī Ṭāhir Ṭayfūr; Ibn al-Djawzī; Ibn al-Naṭṭāḥ; Ibn al-Sāʿī; Ibn al-Ṭiḳṭaḳā; al-Madā'inī; Ṣābi'.(3).4; ʿUbayd Allāh b. Aḥmad b. Abī Ṭāhir; al-Yaʿḳūbī
see also al-Zubayr b. Bakkār

other personages   al-ʿAbbās b. ʿAmr al-G̲h̲anawī; al-ʿAbbās b. al-Maʾmūn; al-ʿAbbās b. Muḥammad; ʿAbd Allāh b. ʿAlī; ʿAbd al-Djabbār b. ʿAbd al-Raḥmān; ʿAbd al-Malik b. Ṣāliḥ; Abū ʿAwn; Abū Muslim; ʿAlī al-Riḍā; Badjkam; Badr al-K̲h̲arshanī; Bug̲h̲ā al-Kabīr; Bug̲h̲ā al-S̲h̲arābī; Dulafids; al-Fatḥ b. K̲h̲āḳān; Hart̲h̲ama b. Aʿyan; al-Ḥasan b. Zayd b. al-Ḥasan; Ḥātim b. Hart̲h̲ama; Ḥumayd b. ʿAbd al-Ḥamīd; Ibn Abi ʾl-S̲h̲awārib; Ibn Buhlūl; Ibn al-Djaṣṣāṣ.II; Ibn Ḥamdūn; Ibn Māhān; Ibn al-Mudabbir; Ibn al-Muʿtazz; Ibn Rāʾiḳ; Ibn T̲h̲awāba; Ibrāhīm b. ʿAbd Allāh; ʿĪsā b. Mūsā; ʿĪsā b. al-S̲h̲ayk̲h̲; Ḳaḥṭaba; al-Ḳāsim b. ʿĪsā; Maʿn b. Zāʾida; al-Mubarḳaʿ; Muhallabids; Muḥammad b. ʿAbd Allāh (al-Nafs al-Zakiyya); Muḥammad b. Ṭug̲h̲dj al-Ik̲h̲s̲h̲īd; Muḥammad b. Yāḳūt; Muʾnis al-Faḥl; Muʾnis al-Muẓaffar; al-Muwaffaḳ; Naṣr b. S̲h̲abat̲h̲; al-Nāṭiḳ bi ʾl-Ḥaḳḳ; al-Nūs̲h̲arī; Rāfiʿ b. Hart̲h̲ama; Rāfiʿ b. al-Layt̲h̲ b. Naṣr b. Sayyār; al-Rāwandiyya; Rawḥ b. Ḥātim; Sādjids; Ṣāliḥ b. ʿAlī; al-Sarak̲h̲sī, Abu ʾl-ʿAbbās; al-Sarī; S̲h̲abīb b. S̲h̲ayba; Sulaymān b. ʿAlī b. ʿAbd Allāh; Sunbād̲h̲; al-T̲h̲ag̲h̲rī; ʿUdjayf b. ʿAnbasa; Ustād̲h̲sīs; al-Walīd b. Ṭarīf; al-Wāt̲h̲iḳī; Yaḥyā b. ʿAbd Allāh; Yaḥyā b. Akt̲h̲am; Yūsuf al-Barm; Zawāḳīl; Ziyād b. Ṣāliḥ al-K̲h̲uzāʿī; Zubayda bt. Djaʿfar; [in Suppl.] Abū Manṣūr b. Yūsuf; Aytāk̲h̲ al-Turkī; Badr al-Muʿtaḍidī; al-Dāmag̲h̲ānī, Abū ʿAbd Allāh; al-Dāmag̲h̲ānī, Abu ʾl-Ḥasan; al-G̲h̲iṭrīf b. ʿAṭāʾ; Ibn Dirham; Sallām al-Tardjumān; Ṭug̲h̲dj

Fāṭimids (909-1171)   Dīwān.i *and* ii.(2); **Fāṭimids**; Ḥādjib.iv; Ḥidjāb.II; al-Ḳāhira; K̲h̲alīfa.i.D; Libās.i.5; Marāsim.1; Mawāḳib.1; Wazīr.I.2

    see also Laḳab.2; Ṣāḥib al-Bāb; Sitr; Wāsiṭa; al-Wazīr al-Ṣag̲h̲īr; Zimām

    caliphs   Abū ʿAbd Allāh al-S̲h̲īʿī; al-ʿĀḍid li-Dīn Allāh; al-Āmir; al-ʿAzīz bi ʾllāh; al-Ḥāfiẓ; al-Ḥākim bi-Amr Allāh; al-Ḳāʾim; al-Mahdī ʿUbayd Allāh; al-Manṣūr bi ʾllāh; al-Muʿizz li-Dīn Allāh; al-Mustaʿlī bi ʾllāh; al-Mustanṣir (bi ʾllāh); al-Ẓāfir bi-Aʿdāʾ Allāh; al-Ẓāhir li-Iʿzāz Dīn Allāh

    see also al-Walīd b. His̲h̲ām

    viziers   ʿAbbās b. Abi ʾl-Futūḥ; al-ʿĀdil b. al-Salār; al-Afḍal b. Badr al-Djamālī; al-Afḍal (Kutayfāt); Badr al-Djamālī; Bahrām; al-Baṭāʾiḥī; Dirg̲h̲ām; Djabr Ibn al-Ḳāsim; al-Djardjarāʾī.4; Ibn Killis; Ibn Maṣāl; Ruzzīk b. Ṭalāʾiʿ; S̲h̲āwar; S̲h̲īrkūh; Ṭalāʾiʿ b. Ruzzīk; Yānis; al-Yāzurī; [in Suppl.] Ibn K̲h̲alaf.2

    see also Wazīr.I.2

    secretaries   Ibn Mammātī; Ibn al-Ṣayrafī; [in Suppl.] Ibn K̲h̲alaf, Abu ʾl-Ḥasan

    historians of   Ibn al-Ṭuwayr; al-Maḳrīzī; al-Musabbiḥī

        see also Djawd̲h̲ar

    other personages   Abū Yazīd al-Nukkārī; Bardjawān; Djawd̲h̲ar; Djawhar al-Ṣiḳillī; K̲h̲alaf b. Mulāʿib al-As̲h̲habī; al-Kirmānī; Nizār b. al-Mustanṣir; al-Nuʿmān; Sitt al-Mulk; Tamīm b. al-Muʿizz li-Dīn Allāh; [in Suppl.] al-Ramlī

        see also al-Farg̲h̲ānī; Ẓāfir al-Ḥaddād

Rightly-Guided Caliphs (632-661)   K̲h̲alīfa.i.A; S̲h̲ūrā.1; [in Suppl.] **al-K̲h̲ulafāʾ al-Rās̲h̲idūn**

    caliphs   Abū Bakr; ʿAlī b. Abī Ṭālib; ʿUmar (I) b. al-K̲h̲aṭṭāb; ʿUt̲h̲mān b. ʿAffān

        see also Ḥarūrāʾ; Ibn Muldjam; K̲h̲alīfa.i.A; al-Saḳīfa; al-Ṣiddīḳ; Taḥkīm; ʿUt̲h̲māniyya; Wufūd; [in Suppl.] al-Ridda; *and* → MILITARY.BATTLES.633-660

    other personages   Abān b. ʿUt̲h̲mān; ʿAbd Allāh b. al-ʿAbbās; ʿAbd Allāh b. ʿĀmir; ʿAbd Allāh b. Saʿd; ʿAbd Allāh b. Salām; ʿAbd Allāh b. Wahb; ʿAbd al-Raḥmān b. ʿAwf; ʿAbd al-Raḥmān b. Samura; Abu ʾl-Aswad al-Duʾalī; Abū Ayyūb al-Anṣārī; Abu ʾl-Dunyā; Abū ʿUbayda al-Djarrāḥ; al-Aḥnaf b. Ḳays; al-Aḳraʿ b. Ḥābis; ʿAmr b. al-ʿĀṣ; al-As̲h̲ʿarī, Abū Mūsā; al-As̲h̲ʿat̲h̲; al-As̲h̲tar; al-Bāhilī; Ḥabīb b. Maslama; al-Ḳaʿḳāʿ b. ʿAmr; K̲h̲ālid b. al-Walīd; Muḥammad b. Abī Bakr; al-Mut̲h̲annā b. Ḥārit̲h̲a; Saʿīd b. al-ʿĀṣ; Sulaymān b. Ṣurad; Usāma b. Zayd; Yazīd b. Abī Sufyān; Zayd b. T̲h̲ābit; al-Zibriḳān b. Badr

    and → MUḤAMMAD, THE PROPHET.COMPANIONS OF *and* FAMILY OF

Umayyads (661-750) Dimashḳ; Dīwān.i; Ḥādjib.i; Khalīfa.i.A; Mawlā.2.b; **Umayyads**; [in Suppl.] Bādiya
see also Architecture.I.2; Ḳays ʿAylān; Libās.i.4; Marwānids; Sufyānids; Umayya b. ʿAbd Shams; Umayyads.In Spain; ʿUthmāniyya.4; Wufūd; *and* → DYNASTIES.SPAIN AND NORTH AFRICA.UMAYYADS
caliphs ʿAbd al-Malik b. Marwān; Hishām; Marwān I b. al-Ḥakam; Marwān II; Muʿāwiya I; Muʿāwiya II; Sulaymān b. ʿAbd al-Malik; ʿUmar (II) b. ʿAbd al-ʿAzīz; al-Walīd; Yazīd (I) b. Muʿāwiya; Yazīd (II) b. ʿAbd al-Malik; Yazīd (III) b. al-Walīd
see also Būṣīr; al-Ruṣāfa.3; al-Shām.2(a); Taḥkīm
historians of ʿAwāna b. al-Ḥakam al-Kalbī; al-Azdī
see also al-Yaʿḳūbī
secretaries ʿAbd al-Ḥamīd; Yazīd b. Abī Muslim; Ziyād b. Abīhi
other personages ʿAbbād b. Ziyād; al-ʿAbbās b. al-Walīd; ʿAbd Allāh b. ʿAbd al-Malik; ʿAbd Allāh b. Hammām; ʿAbd Allāh b. Ḥanẓala; ʿAbd Allāh b. Khāzim; ʿAbd Allāh b. Muṭīʿ; ʿAbd Allāh b. al-Zubayr; ʿAbd al-ʿAzīz b. al-Ḥadjdjādj; ʿAbd al-ʿAzīz b. Marwān; ʿAbd al-ʿAzīz b. al-Walīd; ʿAbd al-Raḥmān b. Khālid; ʿAmr b. Saʿīd; Asad b. ʿAbd Allāh; al-Aṣamm.1; Baldj b. Bishr; Bishr b. Marwān; Bishr b. al-Walīd; Bukayr b. Māhān; Bukayr b. Wishāḥ; Busr; al-Ḍaḥḥāḳ b. Ḳays al-Fihrī; al-Djarrāḥ b. ʿAbd Allāh; al-Djunayd b. ʿAbd Allāh; al-Ḥadjdjādj b. Yūsuf; Ḥanẓala b. Ṣafwān b. Zuhayr; al-Ḥārith b. Suraydj; Ḥassān b. Mālik; Ḥassān b. al-Nuʿmān al-Ghassānī; al-Ḥurr b. Yazīd; al-Ḥusayn b. Numayr; Ibn al-Ashʿath; Ibn al-Ḥaḍramī; Ibn Hubayra; Khālid b. ʿAbd Allāh al-Ḳasrī; Khālid b. Yazīd b. Muʿāwiya; Kulthūm b. ʿIyāḍ al-Ḳushayrī; Ḳurra b. Sharīk; Ḳutayba b. Muslim; Maʿn b. Zāʾida; Masāmiʿa; Maslama b. ʿAbd al-Malik b. Marwān; Maymūn b. Mihrān; Muʿāwiya b. Hishām; al-Mughīra b. Shuʿba; Muhallabids; Muḥammad b. al-Ḳāsim; Muslim b. ʿUḳba; Naṣr b. Sayyār; al-Nuʿmān b. Bashīr; Rawḥ b. Zinbāʿ; Salm b. Ziyād b. Abīhi; Shabīb b. Yazīd; Sulaymān b. Kathīr; Ṭalḥat al-Ṭalaḥāt; Tawwābūn; al-Thaḳafī, Yūsuf b. ʿUmar; ʿUbayd Allāh b. Abī Bakra; ʿUbayd Allāh b. Ḥabḥāb; ʿUbayd Allāh b. ʿUmar; ʿUbayd Allāh b. Ziyād; ʿUḳba b. Nāfiʿ; Zayd b. ʿAlī b. al-Ḥusayn; Ziyād b. Abīhi; [in Suppl.] ʿAdī b. Arṭāt; Radjaʾ b. Ḥaywa; Saʿīd b. Djubayr; Shamir b. Dhi ʾl-Djawshan
see also al-Baṭṭāl; Iyās b. Muʿāwiya; [in Suppl.] al-Sufyānī; Ṭālib al-Ḥaḳḳ
treatises on al-Ḳalḳashandī.1

CARTOGRAPHY Kharīṭa
and → GEOGRAPHY; NAVIGATION
cartographers al-Falakī; Ibn Sarābiyūn; Meḥmed Reʾīs; Pīrī Reʾīs

CAUCASUS Ādharbaydjān.ii; Armīniya; Dāghistān; **al-Ḳabḳ** (*and* [in Suppl.]); al-Kurdj
see also Djarīda.iv; Ḳarā Bāgh; Muhādjir.2; Shīrwān Shāh
mysticism Ṭarīḳa.II.5; Walī.4
physical geography
mountains al-Ḳabḳ; [in Suppl.] Shāh Dagh
waters Alindjaḳ; Gökče-tengiz; Ḳarā Deniz; Ḳïzïl-üzen; Ḳuban; Kur; al-Rass; Safīd Rūd; Terek
population Abkhāz.2; Alān; Andi; Arči; Avars; Balkar; Čečens; Čerkes; Darghin; Dido; Ingush; Kabards; Ḳapuča; Ḳaračay; Ḳarata; Ḳaytaḳ; Khaputs; Khemshin; Khinalug; Khunzal; Khvarshï; Ḳrïz; Ḳubači; Kwanadi; Laḳ; Laz; Lezgh; Noghay; Ossetians; Rūs; Rutul; Tsakhur; Ubykh; [in Suppl.] Demography.VI
see also Ḳumuḳ
resistance to Russian conquest Ḥamza Beg; Shāmil; Ushurma, Manṣūr
see also Ḥizb.iv; [in Suppl.] al-Ḳabḳ.3.d

toponyms

ancient Alindjaḳ; Arrān; Bādjarwān.1; Balandjar; Baylaḳān; Dwin; Saray; Shammākha; Shimshāṭ; Shīrwān; Shīz

present-day Akhiskha; Astrakhān; Bāb al-Abwāb; Bākū; Bardhaʿa; Batumi; Derbend; Gandja; Ḳubba; Lankoran; Makhač-ḳalʿe; Mūḳān; Nakhčiwān; Shakkī; Ṭabarsarān; Tālish; Tiflīs; [in Suppl.] Djulfā.I; Ören Ḳalʿe

CENTRAL ASIA Badakhshān; Čaghāniyān; Khʷārazm; **Mā warāʾ al-Nahr**; Mogholistān

see also Hayāṭila; Ismāʿīl b. Aḥmad; Ḳarā Khiṭāy; Ḳazaḳ; Nīzak, Ṭarkhān; Tīmūrids; Waḳf.V; [in Suppl.] Atalïḳ; Djulfā.I; Khʷādjas; *and* → DYNASTIES.MONGOLS; MONGOLIA; ONOMASTICS

for former republics of the USSR → *the section Toponyms below*

architecture → ARCHITECTURE.REGIONS

belles-lettres Tādjīkī.2; *and* → LITERATURE.DRAMA *and* POETRY.TURKISH.IN EASTERN TURKISH

former Soviet Union al-ʿArab.iii.Appendix; Basmačis; Djarīda.iv; Fiṭrat; Ḥizb.v; Khodjaev; Ṣadr al-Dīn ʿAynī; [in Suppl.] Demography.VI

and → *the section Toponyms below*

historians of ʿAbd al-Karīm Bukhārī

see also Ḥaydar b. ʿAlī

mysticism → MYSTICISM.MYSTICS; SAINTHOOD.SAINTS

physical geography

deserts Ḳaraḳum; Ḳïzïl-ḳum

mountains Ala Dagh; Altai; Balkhān; Pamirs

see also Čopan-ata

waters Aḳ Ṣu; Amū Daryā; Aral; Baḥr al-Khazar; Balkhash; Čaghān-rūd; Ču; Ili; İssïk-kul; Ḳarā-köl; Murghāb; Sïr Daryā; Ṭarāz; Turgay; Wakhsh; Zarafshān

see also Su; [in Suppl.] Māʾ.10

population Balūč; Čāwdors (*and* [in Suppl.] Čawdor); Emreli; Gagauz; Ḳaraḳalpaḳ; Khaladj; Ḳungrāt; Ḳurama; Özbeg; Tarančis; Türkmen.3; Yaghma; [in Suppl.] Demography.VI; Yomut

see also Altaians; al-ʿArab.iii.Appendix; Ghalča; Ghuzz; Ḳarluḳ; Ḳazaḳ; Ḳipčaḳ; Ḳïrgïz; Ḳumān; Kumīdjīs; Ḳun; Sārt; Tādjīk; [in Suppl.] Ersarï

reformism [in Suppl.] **Iṣlāḥ**.v

toponyms

ancient Abaskūn; Abīward; Akhsīkath; Ardjīsh; Balāsāghūn; Banākat; Fārāb; Firabr; Gurgandj; Kāth; Ḳayalïḳ; Marw al-Rudh; Marw al-Shāhidjān; Mashhad-i Miṣriyān; Nakhshab; Pishpek; Sayrām; Shūmān; Sïghnāḳ; al-Ṣughd; Sūyāb; Ṭarāz; Utrār; Yeti Su; Zamakhshar; Zamm; [in Suppl.] Dandānḳān; Djand; Īlāḳ; Isfīdjāb; Ishtīkhān

present-day

districts Atek; Ḳaratigin; Shughnān; Wakhsh; [in Suppl.] Ura-tepe

see also Ākhāl Tekke

regions Farghānā; Khʷārazm; Khuttalān; Labāb; Mangïshlak; Usrūshana; Wakhān; [in Suppl.] Dasht-i Ḳïpčaḳ

republics Tādjīkistān; Turkistān.1; Turkmenistan; Uzbekistan.2; [in Suppl.] Ḳazaḳstān; Ḳïrgïzstān

towns Aḳ Masdjid.2; Alma Ata; Āmul.2; Andidjān; ʿAshḳābād; Awliyā Ata; Bayram ʿAlī; Bukhārā; Čimkent; Djalālābād; Ghudjduwān; Hazārasp; Ḥiṣār; Kash; Khīwa; Khoḳand; Khudjand(a); Kish; Ḳubādhiyān; Marghīnān; Mayhana; Ordūbād; Özkend; Pandjdih; Samarḳand; Tashkent; Tirmidh; Toḳmaḳ; Turgay; Turkistān.3; Ürgenč; [in Suppl.] Ura-tepe

CHAD Abeshr; Bagirmi; Borkou; Kanem; Kanuri; Wadāī; Zaghāwa; [in Suppl.] **Čad**
and → AFRICA.CENTRAL AFRICA

CHARMS Afsūn; Ḥidjāb.IV; Kabid.4; Māshā᾽ Allāh; Tamīma; Tilsam; [in Suppl.] Budūḥ
see also Kahrubā; Ḳarwasha; *and* → MAGIC

CHILDHOOD → LIFE STAGES

CHINA Djarīda.v; Masdjid.V; **al-Ṣīn**
see also Bahādur; Khoḳand; Ṣīnī; Ṭibb.2; ʿUlamā᾽.6; Ziyād b. Ṣāliḥ al-Khuzāʿī
calligraphy [in Suppl.] **Khaṭṭ**.vi
dynasties Ḳarā Khiṭāy
see also Faghfūr; Gūrkhān; Yaʿḳūb Beg; [in Suppl.] Khʷādjas
literature [in Suppl.] **al-Ṣīn**.5
literary figures Liu Chih; Ma Huan; Wang Tai-yu
mysticism **Taṣawwuf**.8
see also al-Ṣīn.4; Ma Hua-lung; Ma Ming-hsin; T'ien Wu; Walī.8
personages
officials P'u Shou-keng
scholars ʿUlamā᾽.6
see also Ṭibb.2
warlords Wu Ma
for leaders in uprisings, see the section Uprisings below; *for belletrists, see the section Literature above*
physical geography
waters Aḳ Ṣu; Ili; Tarim
population Salar; Tarančis; Tungans; Yunnan.2
toponyms
ancient Bishbalïḳ; Khansā; Shūl.1; [in Suppl.] Ḳočo
present-day Aḳ Ṣu; Alti Shahr; Kansu; Kāshghar; Khānbalïḳ; Khānfū; Khotan; Ḳuldja; Ning-hsia; Shansi; Shen-si; Sinkiang; Szechuan; Tubbat; Turfan; Yārkand; Yunnan; [in Suppl.] Ḳomul
see also Sandābil; Ṣīn (Čīn) Kalān; Turkistān.1; Zaytūn
treatises on ʿAlī Akbar Khiṭā᾽ī
see also [in Suppl.] Sallām al-Tardjumān
uprisings Panthay
see also Tunganistan
leaders Ma Chung-ying; Ma Hua-lung; Ma Ming-hsin; Pai Yen-hu; T'ien Wu; Tu Wen-hsiu; Yulbārs Khān

CHRISTIANITY Ahl al-Kitāb; Dayr; Dayṣāniyya; ʿĪsā; Kanīsa; Maryam; **Naṣārā**; Rāhib; al-Ṣalīb; Tathlīth; [in Suppl.] Tabshīr
see also Dhimma; Djizya; al-Ḥākim bi-Amr Allāh; Ifrandj; Karshūnī; Ḳūmis; Lāhūt and Nāsūt.2; Maʿalthāyā; [in Suppl.] Dāwiyya and Isbitāriyya; Fidā᾽; *and* → BIBLE; CRUSADE(R)S; EUROPE; LANGUAGES.AFRO-ASIATIC.ARABIC.CHRISTIAN ARABIC; NUBIA
apologetics Ibn Zurʿa; al-Kindī, ʿAbd al-Masīḥ
churches **Kanīsa**; Ṣihyawn
see also Masdjid.I.B.3
communities Anadolu.iii.4; al-Andalus.iv; Istanbul.vii.b; Mozarab; al-Shām.2(a) (271b-2a); Ṭūr ʿAbdīn.3
see also Fener

denominations Ḳibṭ; Nasṭūriyyūn; Yaʿḳūbiyyūn; [in Suppl.] Marḳiyūniyya; Mārūniyya
see also Djarādjima; *and* → JUDAISM.JEWISH SECTS
Catholics Bas͟hīr S͟hihāb II; Isḥāḳ, Adīb; Ṣābundjī; Ṣāyig͟h, Fatḥ Allāh; S͟hayk͟hū, Luwīs; Zāk͟hir; [in Suppl.] Buṭrus Karāma; Maṭar
Copts Ibn al-ʿAssāl; Ibn Mammātī; Ibn al-Muḳaffaʿ; **Ḳibṭ**; al-Makīn b. al-ʿAmīd; Māriya; al-Mufaḍḍal b. Abi ʾl-Faḍāʾil; [in Suppl.] Ibn Kabar; Ibn al-Rāhib
see also Sullam; Taʾrīk͟h.I.1.vi; Ziyāra.3; [in Suppl.] Taʾrīk͟h.II.1.(g); *and* → EGYPT.TOPONYMS; NUBIA
Greek orthodox Gagauz
see also Paṭrīk; Zāk͟hir
Jacobites al-Ak͟hṭal; Ibn al-ʿIbrī; Ibn Zurʿa; al-Ḳuṭāmī; Yaḥyā b. ʿAdī; Yaḥyā al-Naḥwī; **Yaʿḳūbiyyūn**
see also al-Kindī, ʿAbd al-Masīḥ; Paṭrīk; Ṭūr ʿAbdīn.3
Marcionites [in Suppl.] **Marḳiyūniyya**
Maronites Farḥāt; Isṭifān al-Duwayhī; al-Rayḥānī; Salīm al-Naḳḳās͟h; Ṭanyūs, S͟hāhīn; al-Yāzidjī; Yūsuf Karam; [in Suppl.] Abū S͟habaka; al-Bustānī; **Mārūniyya**
see also Bs͟harrā; Durūz.ii; Paṭrīk; *and* → LEBANON
Melkites Abū Ḳurra; al-Antāḳī; Mīk͟hāʾīl al-Ṣabbāg͟h; al-Muḳawḳis; Saʿīd b. al-Biṭrīḳ; al-Turk, Niḳūlā; Yaḥyā b. al-Biṭrīḳ; [in Suppl.] Ibn al-Ḳuff
see also Mas͟hāḳa; Paṭrīk; [in Suppl.] Taʾrīk͟h.II.1.(g)
Monophysites → *the sections Copts, Jacobites and Nestorians under this entry*
Nestorians Buk͟htīs͟hūʿ; Ḥunayn b. Isḥāḳ al-ʿIbādī; Ibn Buṭlān; Ibn al-Ṭayyib; al-Kindī, ʿAbd al-Masīḥ; Mattā b. Yūnus; **Nasṭūriyyūn**; Sābūr b. Sahl; Yūḥannā b. Sarābiyūn; [in Suppl.] Prester John
see also al-Ṭabarī, ʿAlī b. Rabban; Ṭūr ʿAbdīn.3; Urmiya.3
Protestants Fāris al-S͟hidyāḳ; Mas͟hāḳa; Ṣarrūf; Ṣāyig͟h, Tawfīḳ; [in Suppl.] al-Bustānī.2
see also Nimr
unspecified Baḥdal; Ibn al-Tilmīd͟h; al-Masīḥī; Petrus Alfonsi; Ukaydir b. ʿAbd al-Malik; [in Suppl.] Ḥubays͟h b. al-Ḥasan al-Dimas͟hḳī; Ibn al-Ṣuḳāʿī
historiography [in Suppl.] **Taʾrīk͟h**.II.1.(g)
monasteries **Dayr**; Dayr al-Djāt͟halīḳ; Dayr Kaʿb; Dayr Ḳunnā; Dayr Murrān; Dayr Samʿān; al-Ṭūr.1
see also K͟hānḳāh; Rāhib; Ṭūr ʿAbdīn.3
writings on al-S͟hābus͟htī
persecutions G͟hiyār; al-Ḥākim bi-Amr Allāh; S͟hiʿār.4; Zunnār
polemics Ahl al-Kitāb; Taḥrīf
anti-Jewish Petrus Alfonsi
Christian-Muslim al-Suʿūdī, Abu ʾl-Faḍl; al-Ṭabarī, ʿAlī b. Rabban
see also Zaynab bt. Djaḥs͟h
pre-Islamic Abraha; ʿAdī b. Zayd; ʿAmr b. ʿAdī; ʿAmr b. Hind; Baḥīrā; Bahrām
see also G͟hassān; Lak͟hmids
saints Djirdjīs; Djuraydj
20th-century al-K͟hūrī; Ṣarrūf; S͟hayk͟hū, Luwīs; [in Suppl.] Abū S͟habaka; Abyaḍ; Maṭar
see also al-Maʿlūf; [in Suppl.] Tabs͟hīr

CIRCUMCISION K͟hafḍ; **K͟hitān**
see also ʿAbdī; ʿAlī; Kurds.iv.A.i; Mawākib.4.11; Wehbī Sayyidī

CLOTHING Banīḳa; Djallāb; Farw; Ḳumās͟h; **Libās**; Sirwāl
see also G͟hiyār; Iḥrām; K͟hayyāṭ; K͟hilʿa; Kurds.iv.C.1; S͟hiʿār.4; Ṭirāz; Zeybek; Zunnār; [in Suppl.] Kafan; *and* → MYSTICISM.DRESS

accessories Mandīl; Mirwaḥa
see also Shadd
headwear Ḳawuḳlu; Tādj; Tulband; [in Suppl.] Ḳalansuwa
see also Sharīf.(5)
veils Ḥidjāb.I; Lithām
materials Farw; Ḥarīr; Kattān; Khaysh; Ḳuṭn; Ṣūf; Tāfta
see also Fanak; Ḳalamkārī; Ḳumāsh; Lubūd; Mukhattam; *and* → ART.TEXTILES
shoewear [in Suppl.] al-Naʿl al-Sharīf
see also [in Suppl.] Iskāf

COLOUR **Lawn**; Musawwida
and → DYEING
colours Asfar
see also Sharīf.(5)

COMMONWEALTH OF INDEPENDENT STATES → CAUCASUS; CENTRAL ASIA; COMMUNISM; EUROPE.EASTERN EUROPE

COMMUNICATIONS Barīd; Ḥamām; Manār
see also Anadolu.iii.(5); *and* → TRANSPORT

COMMUNISM Ḥizb.i; **Shuyūʿiyya**
see also Lāhūtī; [in Suppl.] Sulṭān ʿAlī Ūghlī

CONGO **Congo**; al-Murdjibī

COPTS → CHRISTIANITY.DENOMINATIONS

COSMETICS Ḥinnāʾ; al-Kuḥl; al-Washm
see also Khiḍāb; *and* → PERFUME

COSMOGRAPHY ʿAdjāʾib; ʿĀlam; Falak; Ḳāf; Samāʾ.1
see also Djughrāfiyā; al-Khaḍir; Kharīṭa; al-Kura; Makka.4; *and* → ASTROLOGY; ASTRONOMY; GEOGRAPHY
treatises on al-Dimashḳī; al-Ḳazwīnī, Zakariyyāʾ; al-Kharaḳī
see also Kitāb al-Djilwa

COURT CEREMONY **Marāsim**; Mawākib (*and* [in Suppl.])
see also Miẓalla; Naḳḳāra-khāna; Sitr; Yādgār; *and* → MONARCHY.ROYAL INSIGNIA
bestowal of gifts Hiba; Khilʿa; Nithār
ranks [in Suppl.] Martaba

CREATION **Ibdāʿ**; **Khalḳ**
see also Ḥudūth al-ʿĀlam; Insān; Takwīn; Tawallud; Ṭīn.1

CRETE **Iḳrīṭish**
see also Abū Ḥafṣ ʿUmar al-Ballūṭī; Wenedik
toponyms
towns Ḳandiya

CROATIA → (former) YUGOSLAVIA

CRUSADE(R)S **Crusades**; Tourkopo(u)loi; [in Suppl.] Dāwiyya and Isbitāriyya
see also al-ʿĀdil.1; al-Afḍal b. Badr al-Djamālī; (Sīrat) ʿAntar; Ayyūbids; Balak; Baybars I; Fāṭimids.5; Ifrandj; Ḳalāwūn; Ḳilidj Arslan I; Nūr al-Dīn Maḥmūd b. Zankī; Ṣalāḥ al-Dīn; al-Shām.2(a); Ṭughtigin; Wenedik; *and* → *the section Toponyms under* PALESTINE/ISRAEL *and* SYRIA
battles al-Manṣūra; Mardj al-Ṣuffar; Nīkbūlī
castles al-Dārūm; Ḥārim; Ḥiṣn al-Akrād; Ḳalʿat al-Shaḳīf; Ṣāfītha
conquests ʿAkkā; Anadolu.iii.1; ʿĀsḳalān; Ayla; Ghazza; Ḥayfā; Ḳayṣariyya; al-Khalīl; Ḳubrus.2; al-Ḳuds.10; Ludd; Maʿarrat al-Nuʿmān
historians of Ibn al-Ḳalānisī
see also al-Nuwayrī, Muḥammad

CRYPTOGRAPHY **Muʿammā**; Ramz.2
see also Kitābāt.5; al-Sīm

CUISINE **Maṭbakh**; **Ṭabkh**
drinks Čay; Ḳahwa; Khamr; Kumis; **Mashrūbāt**; Nabīdh; Sherbet
see also Naḥl; Thallādj; Turundjān; Yoghurt; [in Suppl.] Čāy-khāna
food **Ghidhāʾ**; Kabid.5; Khubz; Kuskusū; Mishmish; Nakhl; Nārandj; al-Ruzz; al-Samn; Sawīḳ; Shaʿīr; Sikbādj; Sukkar; **Ṭaʿām**; Tīn; Tuffāḥ; Yoghurt; Zabīb; Zayt; Zaytūn [in Suppl.] Basbās; Djawz; Ḥays; Hindibāʾ
see also Filāḥa; Ḳamḥ; Maḍīra; Milḥ; Naḥl; Pist; Simsim; Ṭīn.3; [in Suppl.] Ibn Shaḳrūn al-Miknāsī
fruit Mishmish; Nakhl; Nārandj; Tīn; Tuffāḥ
see also [in Suppl.] Ḥays
dried fruit Tammām; Zabīb
grains Ḳamḥ; Kuskusū; al-Ruzz; Shaʿīr
see also Filāḥa; Khubz; Sawīḳ; *for granaries* → ARCHITECTURE.MONUMENTS
herbs Shibithth; Turundjān; [in Suppl.] Basbās
see also Shīḥ; Timsāḥ
meat Kabid.5
stews Sikbādj
oils al-Samn; Zayt
spices Kammūn; Ḳaranful; [in Suppl.] **Afāwīh**; Dār Ṣīnī
see also Kārimī; Ḳūṣ; Milḥ; Zaʿfarān.1
professions Baḳḳāl; Ṭabbākh; Ṭaḥḥān; Tammār
prohibitions Ghidhāʾ.iii *and* iv.7; Ḳahwa; Khamr; Mashrūbāt; Mayta; Nabīdh
see also Dhabīḥa.1; Ḥayawān.4; Nadjis; *and* → *individual articles under* ANIMALS
table manners **Ṭaʿām**

CUSTOM **ʿĀda**; Adab; ʿUrf
see also Abd al-Raḥmān al-Fāsī; ʿĀshūrāʾ.II; Hiba; Ḥidjāb.I; Īdjāra; Khilʿa; Mandīl; ʿUrs.2; *and* → LAW.CUSTOMARY LAW
tribal customs ʿAbābda; al-Dhunūb, Dafn; Khāwa; Muwāraba; Thaʾr; al-Washm; [in Suppl.] ʿĀr
see also Īdjāra; Taḥannuth; Zmāla.2; [in Suppl.] Malaʾ.2

CYPRUS **Ḳubrus**; Madjlis.4.A.xxiv
see also Wenedik; [in Suppl.] Mārūniyya
toponyms
towns Lefḳosha; Maghōsha

(former) CZECHOSLOVAKIA [in Suppl.] **Čeh**

D

DEATH Djanāza; Ḥināṭa; Intiḥār; Ḳabr; Maḳbara; **Mawt**; Niyāḥa; [in Suppl.] Ghassāl; Kafan
see also Ghāʾib; Ghusl; Ḳatl; Marthiya; Shahīd; Takbīr; Tasnīm.2; *and* → ARCHITECTURE.MONUMENTS.TOMBS; ESCHATOLOGY

DESERTS al-Aḥḳāf; Biyābānak; al-Dahnāʾ; Ḳaraḳum; Ḳïzïl-ḳum; Nafūd; al-Naḳb; al-Rubʿ al-Khālī; Sāḥil; al-Ṣaḥrāʾ; Sīnāʾ; al-Tīh
see also (Djazīrat) al-ʿArab.ii; Badw.II; Ḥarra; Khabrāʾ; Reg; Samūm; *and* → GEOGRAPHY.PHYSICAL GEOGRAPHY.OASES; NOMADISM

DICTIONARY **Ḳāmūs**
see also Fāris al-Shidyāḳ; Sullam; *and* → LEXICOGRAPHY

DIPLOMACY Imtiyāzāt; Mübādele; Tardjumān
see also Amān; Bālyōs; Berātlï; Daftar; Hiba; Inshāʾ; Kātib; Ḳawwās; Mandates
diplomatic accounts Aḥmad Rasmī; Ibn Faḍlān; Meḥmed Yirmisekiz; Wāṣif; [in Suppl.] al-Ghazzāl; Ibn ʿUthmān al-Miknāsī
see also Ṣubḥī Meḥmed
diplomats Consul; Elči; Safīr.2
see also Ẓahīr

DIVINATION **Kihāna**
see also Djafr; Ibn Barradjān; Malāḥim; Nudjūm (Aḥkām al-); Shāma; *and* → ASTROLOGY; DREAMS
diviners ʿArrāf; Kāhin
practices Faʾl; Firāsa; Ghurāb; Ḥisāb al-Djummal; Ḥurūf; Ikhtilādj; Istiḳsām; ʿIyāfa; al-Kaff; Katif; Khaṭṭ; Khawāṣṣ al-Ḳurʾān; Ḳiyāfa; Ḳurʿa; Māʾ.1; Riyāfa; Wadaʿ.3; Zāʾirdja
see also Būḳalā; Ikhtiyārāt; Mirʾāt
treatises on Fāl-nāma; Ibn al-Bannāʾ al-Marrākushī; Malḥama; [in Suppl.] Ibn ʿAzzūz
see also Djafr; Nudjūm (Aḥkām al-)

DIVORCE Barāʾa.I; Faskh; Suknā; al-Suraydjiyya; **Ṭalāḳ**
see also ʿAbd.3; ʿĀda; Ghāʾib; Ḥaḍāna; Ibn Suraydj; ʿIdda; ʿIwaḍ; Ḳasam; Liʿān; al-Marʾa.2; Rapak; [in Suppl.] Nafaḳa; *and* → MARRIAGE

DJIBOUTI, REPUBLIC OF **Djibūtī**; Tadjurra
and → AFRICA.EAST AFRICA

DOCUMENTS ʿAlāma; **Diplomatic**; Farmān; Inshāʾ; Kātib; Manshūr; Papyrus; **Sidjill**; Tawḳīʿ.1; Waḳf.I.2.d; Wathīḳa; Ẓahīr; [in Suppl.] Dabīr
see also Barāʾa.I; Ḳaṭʿ; Sharṭ.1; Tughra; ʿUnwān; Yarlïgh; *and* → ADMINISTRATION.RECORDS; WRITING
Ottoman ʿArḍ Ḥāl; Berāt; **Diplomatic**.iv; Farmān.ii; Irāde; Khaṭṭ-ï Humāyūn and Khaṭṭ-ï Sherīf; **Sidjill**.3; Telkhīṣ
see also Tughra.2.(b); *and* → OTTOMAN EMPIRE.ADMINISTRATION

DREAMS **Ruʾyā**; [in Suppl.] Taʿbīr al-Ruʾya

see also Isti<u>kh</u>āra; Nubuwwa
for dream interpretations, see individual articles on animals, in particular Ayyil; Ba<u>gh</u>l;
Ḍabb; Fīl; <u>Gh</u>urāb; Saraṭān.5; <u>Th</u>aʿlab; ʿUḳāb; Waṭwāṭ; Yarbūʿ
writings on   al-Dīnawarī, Abū Saʿīd; Ibn <u>Gh</u>annām; Ibn <u>Sh</u>āhīn al-Ẓāhirī; Ibn Sīrīn; al-Wahrānī

Drugs   **Adwiya**; [in Suppl.] Anzarūt
    see also Kahrubā; al-Kuḥl; Ṭibb; *and* → Medicine; Pharmacology
narcotics   Afyūn; Ban<u>dj</u>; Ḥa<u>sh</u>ī<u>sh</u>; Ḳāt; <u>Sh</u>ahdāna<u>dj</u>
    see also Filāḥa.iii; [in Suppl.] al-Zarka<u>sh</u>ī
tobacco   Bahāʾī Meḥmed Efendi; **Tutun**

Druzes   al-Darazī; **Durūz**; Ḥamza b. ʿAlī; al-Muḳtanā; <u>Sh</u>akīb Arslān; al-Tanū<u>kh</u>ī, <u>Dj</u>amāl
    al-Dīn; [in Suppl.] Binn
    see also Ḥadd; Maḥkama.4.ii, iii *and* v; Maʿn; [in Suppl.] Dawr; Ḥinn; *and* → Lebanon
historians of   Ṣāliḥ b. Yaḥyā

Dyeing   ʿAfṣ; Ḥinnāʾ; Ḳalamkārī; **Khiḍāb**; Nīl; Wars; Zaʿfarān
    see also <u>Sh</u>aʿr.1
dyer   **Ṣabbāgh**

Dynasties   **Dawla**; Ḥā<u>dj</u>ib; Mu<u>sh</u>īr; Sulṭān
    see also Čā<u>sh</u>na-gīr; <u>Kh</u>ādim al-Ḥaramayn; Laḳab; Libās.i; Malik; Marāsim; Ma<u>sh</u>wara;
    Mawākib; Pādi<u>sh</u>āh; Parda-dār; Tawḳīʿ.1; Walī al-ʿAhd; Ẓulm; [in Suppl.] <u>Kh</u>alʿ; *and* →
    Administration; Onomastics.titles
Afghanistan and India   ʿĀdil-<u>Sh</u>āhs; Ar<u>gh</u>ūn; Bahmanīs; Barīd <u>Sh</u>āhīs; Dihlī Sultanate;
    Fārūḳids; <u>Gh</u>aznawids; <u>Gh</u>ūrids; Hindū-<u>sh</u>āhīs; ʿImād <u>Sh</u>āhī; Kart; <u>Kh</u>al<u>dj</u>īs; Ḳuṭb <u>Sh</u>āhī;
    Lōdīs; Mu<u>gh</u>als; Niẓām <u>Sh</u>āhīs; Sayyids; <u>Sh</u>arḳīs; Sūrs; Tu<u>gh</u>luḳids; [in Suppl.]
    Bānī<u>dj</u>ūrids
    see also Af<u>gh</u>ānistān.v.2 *and* 3; Awadh; Dāwūdpōtrās; Dīwān.v; Hind.iv; <u>Kh</u>ʷā<u>dj</u>a-i
    <u>Dj</u>ahān; La<u>sh</u>kar; Marāsim.5; Mawākib.5; Ni<u>th</u>ār; Rānā Sāngā; Sammā; Tīpū Sulṭān;
    Zunbīl; *and* → Architecture.regions; Military.indo-muslim; Onomas-
    tics.titles.indo-muslim
ʿĀdil-<u>Sh</u>āhs (1490-1686)   **ʿĀdil-<u>Sh</u>āhs**; Bī<u>dj</u>āpūr; Hind.vii.ix
    see also Tālīḳōṭā
    rulers   Muḥammad b. Ibrāhīm II
    historians of   <u>Sh</u>īrāzī, Rafīʿ al-Dīn
Awadh Nawwābs (1722-1856)   **Awadh**
    rulers   Burhān al-Mulk; <u>Gh</u>āzi ʾl-Dīn Ḥaydar; Saʿādat ʿAlī <u>Kh</u>ān; Ṣafdar <u>Dj</u>ang;
    <u>Sh</u>u<u>dj</u>āʿ al-Dawla
    viziers   Mahdī ʿAlī <u>Kh</u>ān
Bahmanids (1347-1527)   **Bahmanīs**; Hind.vii.vii
    see also Bīdar; Gulbargā; Pē<u>sh</u>wā
    rulers   Humāyūn <u>Sh</u>āh Bahmanī; Maḥmūd <u>Sh</u>ihāb al-Dīn; Muḥammad I; Muḥam-
    mad II; Muḥammad III
    other personages   <u>Kh</u>alīl Allāh; Maḥmūd Gāwān
Bārakzays (1819-1973)   Af<u>gh</u>ānistān.v.3.B
    kings   ʿAbd al-Raḥmān <u>Kh</u>ān; Dūst Muḥammad; Ḥabīb Allāh <u>Kh</u>ān; <u>Sh</u>īr ʿAlī; [in
    Suppl.] Amān Allāh
Bengal Nawwābs
    rulers   ʿAlī Werdī <u>Kh</u>ān; <u>Dj</u>aʿfar; Sirā<u>dj</u> al-Dawla
      see also Mur<u>sh</u>idābād

Bengal Sultans (1336-1576)
sultans Dāwūd Khān Kararānī; Fakhr al-Dīn Mubārakshāh; Ḥusayn Shāh; Maḥmūd; Rādjā Ganesh; Rukn al-Dīn Bārbak Shāh; Sikandar Shāh
historians of [in Suppl.] ʿAbbās Sarwānī
Dihlī Sultans (1206-1555) Ḍarība.6.a; **Dihlī Sultanate**; Dīwān.v; Khaldjīs; Lōdīs; Nāʾib.1; Naḳīb.2; Sayyids; Sūrs; Tughluḳids
see also Burdj.III.2; Ulugh Khān
sultans Fīrūz Shāh Tughluḳ; Ghiyāth al-Dīn Tughluḳ I; Ghiyāth al-Dīn Tughluḳ Shāh II; Iltutmish; Kayḳubād; Khiḍr Khān; Ḳuṭb al-Dīn Aybak; Maḥmūd; Ibrāhīm Lōdī; Mubārak Shāh; Muḥammad b. Tughluḳ; Muḥammad Shāh I Khaldjī; Raḍiyya; Shīr Shāh Sūr; [in Suppl.] Balban; Dawlat Khān Lōdī
viziers Kāfūr (*and* Malik Kāfūr); Khān-i Djahān Maḳbūl; Miʾān Bhuʾā
historians of Baranī; al-Djuzdjānī; Niẓāmī (*and* [in Suppl.] Ḥasan Niẓāmī); Shams al-Dīn-i Sirādj ʿAfīf
other personages Mallū Iḳbāl Khān; [in Suppl.] ʿAbd al-Wahhāb Bukhārī; ʿAyn al-Mulk Multānī; Daryā Khān Noḥānī; Ikhtisān
see also ʿAlī Mardān; Hūlāgū; Khaldjīs; Sammā
Durrānīs (1747-1842) Afghānistān.v.3
kings Aḥmad Shāh Durrānī
historians of ʿAbd al-Karīm Munshī
other personages Kāmrān Shāh Durrānī
Fārūḳids (1370-1601) **Fārūḳids**
rulers Mīrān Muḥammad Shāh I
Ghaznawids (977-1186) ʿAmīd; Dīwān.v; **Ghaznawids**
see also Ḥiṣār.iii
rulers Alp Takīn; Bahrām Shāh; Ismāʿīl b. Sebüktigin; Maḥmūd b. Sebüktigin; Masʿūd b. Maḥmūd; Mawdūd b. Masʿūd; Muḥammad b. Maḥmūd b. Sebüktigin; Sebüktigin
viziers Aḥmad b. Muḥammad; Altūntāsh; al-Faḍl b. Aḥmad al-Isfarāʾinī; Ḥasanak; Maymandī
historians of Bayhaḳī; al-ʿUtbī.3
see also al-Ḳāshānī; Shabānkāraʾī; [in Suppl.] Fakhr-i Mudabbir
other personages Muḥammad Bakhtiyār Khaldjī; Shāh Malik
Ghūrids (ca. 1000-1215) **Ghūrids**
rulers Djahān-sūz; Muḥammad b. Sām; Sayf al-Dīn
see also Niẓāmī
governors Tādj al-Dīn Yildiz
Gudjarāt Sultans (1391-1583) Gudjarāt.c
see also Ulugh Khān
sultans Bahādur Shāh Gudjarātī; Maḥmūd
historians of [in Suppl.] Ḥādjdjī al-Dabīr
other personages Malik Ayāz
Kālpī Sultans Kalpī
sultans Maḥmūd Khān
Kashmīr Sultans (1346-1589) Kashmīr.i.4
sultans Sikandar (But-Shikan); Zayn al-ʿĀbidīn; [in Suppl.] Čaks
see also [in Suppl.] Gul Khātūn
historians of [in Suppl.] Ḥaydar Malik
other personages [in Suppl.] Bayhaḳī Sayyids
Khaldjīs → the section Dihlī Sultans above
Langāh dynasty of Multān (1437-1526) Multān

sultans Ḥusayn S̲h̲āh Langāh I; Ḥusayn S̲h̲āh Langāh II
Lōdīs → *the section Dihlī Sultans above*
Madura Sultans (1334-1377) [in Suppl.] Madura
  sultans Djalāl al-Dīn Aḥsan
Mālwā Sultans (1401-1531) Mālwā
  sultans Dilāwar K̲h̲ān; Hūs̲h̲ang S̲h̲āh G̲h̲ūrī; Maḥmūd
   see also Bāz Bahādur
  viziers Mēdinī Rāʾī
  other personages Malik Mug̲h̲īt̲h̲
Mug̲h̲als (1526-1858) Ḍarība.6.b *and* c; Dīwān.v; Manṣab; **Mug̲h̲als**; [in Suppl.] Ilāhī Era
  see also Fawdjdār; Kōtwāl; Maṭbak̲h̲.4; Nit̲h̲ār; Ṣadr.5; Ṣūba; Ṣūbadār; Ṣūfiyāna;
  Ṣulḥ-i kull; Suwār; Tak̲h̲t-i Ṭāwūs; Zamīndār; [in Suppl.] Dāg̲h̲ u tas̲h̲īḥa; ʿIbādat
  K̲h̲āna; Sarkār.1; Taʿalluḳ
  emperors Aḥmad S̲h̲āh.I; Akbar; Awrangzīb; Bābur; Bahādur S̲h̲āh I; Bahādur S̲h̲āh
  II; Djahāndār S̲h̲āh; Djahāngīr; Farruk̲h̲-siyar; Humāyūn; Muḥammad S̲h̲āh; S̲h̲āh
  ʿĀlam II; S̲h̲āh Djahān; [in Suppl.] Rāfiʿ al-Daradjāt
   see also Dars̲h̲an; Mumtāz Maḥall; Nūr Djahān; Tādj Maḥall; Tūzūk; [in Suppl.]
   Muḥammad Ḥākim Mīrzā
  viziers Iʿtimād al-Dawla
  secretaries Abu ʾl-Faḍl ʿAllāmī; Muḥammad Kāẓim
  historians of ʿAbd al-Ḥamīd Lāhawrī; Abu ʾl Faḍl ʿAllāmī; Bak̲h̲tāwar K̲h̲ān;
  Djawhar; G̲h̲ulām Ḥusayn K̲h̲ān Ṭabāṭabāʾī; ʿInāyat Allāh K̲h̲ān; Īsar-dās; Kh^wāfī
  K̲h̲ān; Muḥammad Kāẓim; Muḥammad S̲h̲arīf; Mustaʿidd K̲h̲ān; Muʿtamad K̲h̲ān;
  Niʿmat Allāh b. Ḥabīb Allāh Harawī; Nūr al-Ḥaḳḳ al-Dihlawī; [in Suppl.] ʿĀḳil
  K̲h̲ān Rāzī; Muḥammad Ṣāliḥ Kanbō Lāhawrī
   see also Az̲farī; Badāʾūnī; Maʾāt̲h̲ir al-Umarāʾ
  other personages ʿAbd al-Raḥīm K̲h̲ān; ʿAlī Werdī K̲h̲ān; Āṣaf K̲h̲ān; Bak̲h̲tāwar
  K̲h̲ān; Bayram K̲h̲ān; Burhān al-Mulk; Dāniyāl; G̲h̲ulām Ḳādir Rohilla; Hindāl;
  Iʿtibār K̲h̲ān; Iʿtiḳād K̲h̲ān; ʿIwaḍ Wadjīh; Kāmrān; K̲h̲ān Djahān Lōdī; K̲h̲usraw
  Sulṭān; Mahābat K̲h̲ān; Mak̲h̲dūm al-Mulk (*and* [in Suppl.] ʿAbd Allāh
  Sulṭānpūrī); Mān Singh; Mīr Djumla; Mīrzā ʿAskarī; Mīrzā ʿAzīz "Kōka"; Murād;
  Murād Bak̲h̲s̲h̲; Murs̲h̲id Ḳulī K̲h̲ān; Niẓām al-Mulk; S̲h̲afīʿā Yazdī; S̲h̲āh Manṣūr
  S̲h̲īrāzī; S̲h̲arīf Āmulī; al-Siyālkūtī; Tīpū Sulṭān; Ṭōdar Mal; Yūsuf K̲h̲ān Riḍwī;
  Yūsufī; [in Suppl.] Akbar b. Awrangzīb; ʿĀḳil K̲h̲ān Rāzī; G̲h̲āzī K̲h̲ān; Gūran;
  ʿInāyat K̲h̲ān (2x); Ḳāsim Arslān; Muḥammad Zamān Mīrzā
   see also Bāra Sayyids *(and* [in Suppl.] Bārha Sayyids); Marāt̲h̲ās
Niẓām S̲h̲āhids (1491-1633) **Niẓām S̲h̲āhīs**
  see also Aḥmadnagar; Tālīkōtā
  rulers Ḥusayn Niẓām S̲h̲āh; Malik Aḥmad Baḥrī
  other personages Malik ʿAmbar
Sayyids → *the section Dihlī Sultans above*
S̲h̲arḳī Sultans of Djawnpūr (1394-1479) **S̲h̲arḳīs**
  sultans Ḥusayn S̲h̲āh; Ibrāhīm S̲h̲āh S̲h̲arḳī; Maḥmūd S̲h̲āh S̲h̲arḳī; Malik Sarwar
Sūrīs → *the section Dihlī Sultans above*
Tug̲h̲luḳids → *the section Dihlī Sultans above*
Africa Fundj; Gwandu; S̲h̲īrāzī
  see also Bū Saʿīd; Dār Fūr; Kilwa; Songhay; Wadāī.1; Zag̲h̲āwa.(a)
Anatolia and the Turks Artuḳids; Aydîn-og̲h̲lu; Dānis̲h̲mendids; Dhu ʾl-Ḳadr; Eretna;
  Germiyān-og̲h̲ullarî; Ḥamīd Og̲h̲ullarî; Īnāl; Isfendiyār Og̲h̲lu; Ḳarāmān-og̲h̲ullarî;
  Ḳarasî; Mentes̲h̲e-og̲h̲ullarî; ʿOt̲h̲mānlî; Salṭuḳ Og̲h̲ullarî; Ṣarūk̲h̲ān; S̲h̲āh-i Arman;
  Teke-og̲h̲ullarî

see also Būrids; Derebey; Mangi̊ts; Mengüček; Ramaḍān Oghullari̊; *and* → ONOMASTICS.TITLES
Artuḳids (1102-1408) **Artuḳids**
rulers Īlghāzī; Nūr al-Dīn Muḥammad; Timurtāsh b. Il-Ghāzī
Aydi̊n-oghlu (1308-1425) **Aydi̊n-oghlu**
amīrs Djunayd
Ottomans (1281-1924) **ʿOthmānli̊**
see also ʿOthmān I; *and* → DOCUMENTS.OTTOMAN; MILITARY.OTTOMAN; OTTOMAN EMPIRE; TURKEY.OTTOMAN PERIOD
sultans ʿAbd al-ʿAzīz; ʿAbd al-Ḥamīd I; ʿAbd al-Ḥamīd II; ʿAbd al-Madjīd I; ʿAbd al-Madjīd II; Aḥmad I; Aḥmad II; Aḥmad III; Bāyazīd I; Bāyazīd II; Ibrāhīm; Maḥmūd; Meḥemmed I; Meḥemmed II; Meḥemmed III; Meḥemmed IV; Meḥemmed V Reshād; Meḥemmed VI Waḥīd al-Dīn; Murād I; Murād II; Murād III; Murād IV; Murād V; Muṣṭafā I; Muṣṭafā II; Muṣṭafā III; Muṣṭafā IV; Orkhan; ʿOthmān I; ʿOthmān II; ʿOthmān III; Selīm I; Selīm II; Selīm III; Süleymān; Süleymān II
see also Bāb-i Humāyūn; Djem; Ertoghrul; Khādim al-Ḥaramayn; Khalīfa.i.E; Mashwara; Muhr.1; Muṣṭafā.1 *and* 2; Müteferriḳa; Rikāb; Shehzāde; Ṣolaḳ; Ṭopḳapi̊ Sarāyi̊; Yeñi Čeri.3; [in Suppl.] Ḳafes; Lālā
women of Khāṣṣekī; Khurrem; Kösem Wālide; Nīlūfer Khātūn; Nūr Bānū; Ṣafiyye Wālide Sulṭān; Ṭurkhān Sulṭān; Wālide Sulṭān
grand viziers **Ṣadr-ı Aʿẓam**
see also Bāb-i ʿĀlī; Başvekil; Ḳapi̊; ʿOthmān-zāde; Telkhīṣdji; Wazīr.III
14th century ʿAlī Pasha Čandārli̊-zāde; Djandarli̊
15th century Aḥmad Pasha Gedik; Dāwūd Pasha, Ḳodja; Djandarli̊; Khalīl Pasha Djandarli̊; Maḥmūd Pasha; Meḥmed Pasha, Ḳaramānī; Meḥmed Pasha, Rūm; Sinān Pasha, Khodja.1; Zaghanos Pasha
16th century Aḥmad Pasha, Ḳara; ʿAlī Pasha Khādim; ʿAlī Pasha Semiz; Ayās Pasha; Čighāla-zāde Sinān Pāshā; Derwīsh Pasha; Ferhād Pasha; Hersek-zāde; Ibrāhīm Pasha; Ibrāhīm Pasha, Dāmād; Khādi̊m Ḥasan Pasha Ṣoḳolli̊; Khādi̊m Süleymān Pasha; Lala Meḥmed Pasha (*and* Meḥmed Pasha, Lālā, Shāhīnoghlu); Luṭfī Pasha; Meḥmed Pasha, Lālā, Melek-Nihād; Mesīḥ Meḥmed Pasha; Mesīḥ Pasha; ʿOthmān Pasha; Pīrī Meḥmed Pasha; Rüstem Pasha; Sinān Pasha, Khādi̊m; Sinān Pasha, Khodja.2; Siyāwush Pasha.1; Soḳollu Meḥmed Pasha
17th century ʿAlī Pasha ʿArabadji̊; ʿAlī Pasha Güzeldje; ʿAlī Pasha Sürmeli; Dāwūd Pasha, Ḳara; Derwīsh Meḥmed Pasha; Dilāwar Pasha; Ḥāfiẓ Aḥmed Pasha; Ḥusayn Pasha; Ibrāhīm Pasha, Kara; Ipshir Muṣṭafā Pasha; Ismāʿīl Pasha, Nishāndji̊; Ḳarā Muṣṭafā Pasha; Kemānkesh; Khalīl Pasha Ḳayṣariyyeli; Khosrew Pasha, Bosniak; Köprülü.I-III; Meḥmed Pasha, Čerkes; Meḥmed Pasha, Elmās; Meḥmed Pasha, Gürdjü, Khādi̊m; Meḥmed Pasha, Gürdjü II; Meḥmed Pasha, Öküz; Meḥmed Pasha, Sulṭān-zāde; Meḥmed Pasha, Tabani̊yassi̊; Murād Pasha, Ḳuyudju; Naṣūḥ Pasha; Redjeb Pasha; Siyāwush Pasha.2; Süleymān Pasha, Malaṭyali̊; Yemishdji Ḥasan Pasha
18th century ʿAbd Allāh Pasha; ʿAlī Pasha Čorlulu; ʿAlī Pasha Dāmād; ʿAlī Pasha Ḥakīm-oghlu; Derwīsh Meḥmed Pasha; Ḥamza Ḥāmid Pasha; Ḥamza Pasha; (Dāmād) Ḥasan Pasha; (Seyyid) Ḥasan Pasha; (Sherīf) Ḥasan Pasha; Ibrāhīm Pasha, Nevshehirli; Kaḥyā Ḥasan Pasha; Khalīl Pasha Ḥādjdjī Arnawud; Köprülü.V; Meḥmed Pasha, Balṭadji̊; Meḥmed Pasha, ʿIwaḍ; Meḥmed Pasha, Melek; Meḥmed Pasha, Muḥsin-zāde; Meḥmed Pasha Rāmī (*and* Rāmī Meḥmed Pasha); Meḥmed Pasha, Tiryāḳī; Meḥmed Pasha, Yegen, Gümrükčü; Meḥmed Pasha, Yegen, Ḥādjdjī; Rāghib Pasha; Saʿīd Efendi; Ṭopal ʿOthmān Pasha.1

19th century and on Aḥmad Wafīḳ Pasha; ʿAlī Pasha Muḥammad Amīn; Dāmād Ferīd Pasha; Derwīsh Meḥmed Pasha; Djawād Pasha; Fuʾād Pasha; Ḥusayn ʿAwnī Pasha; Ḥusayn Ḥilmī Pasha; Ibrāhīm Edhem Pasha; Ibrāhīm Ḥaḳḳī Pasha; ʿIzzet Pasha; Kečiboynuzu; Khayr al-Dīn Pasha; Khosrew Pasha, Meḥmed; Küčük Saʿīd Pasha; Maḥmūd Nedīm Pasha; Maḥmūd Shewḳat Pasha; Meḥmed Saʿīd Ghālib Pasha; Midḥat Pasha; Muṣṭafā Pasha, Bayraḳdār; Reshīd Pasha, Muṣṭafā; Ṭalʿat Bey; [in Suppl.] Esʿad Pasha

grand muftis **Shaykh al-Islām**.2

see also Bāb-i Mashīkhat; Fatwā.ii

15th century Fenārī-zāde; Gūrānī; Khosrew

16th century Abu ʾl-Suʿūd; Bostānzāde.2; Čiwi-zāde; Djamālī; Kemāl Pasha-zāde; Khōdja Efendi

17th century Bahāʾī Meḥmed Efendi; Esʿad Efendi, Meḥmed; Ḳarā-Čelebi-zāde.4; Ṣunʿ Allāh; [in Suppl.] Yaḥyā

18th century Čelebi-zāde; Dürrīzāde.1-4; Esʿad Efendi, Meḥmed (2x); Ḥayātī-zāde.2; Meḥmed Ṣāliḥ Efendi; Pīrī-zāde

19th century ʿĀrif Ḥikmet Bey; Dürrīzāde.5; Esʿad Efendi, Aḥmed; Ḥasan Fehmī Efendi

20th century Djamāl al-Dīn Efendi; Dürrīzāde,ʿAbd Allāh; Muṣṭafā Khayrī Efendi

high admirals ʿAlī Pasha Güzeldje; Čighāla-zāde Sinān Pasha; Djaʿfar Beg; Djezāʾirli Ghāzī Ḥasan Pasha; Ḥasan Pasha; Ḥusayn Pasha; Kenʿān Pasha; Khalīl Pasha Ḳayṣariyyeli; Khayr al-Dīn Pasha; Piyāle Pasha; ʿUlūdj ʿAlī; Zaghanos Pasha; [in Suppl.] Ḳaplan Muṣṭafā Pasha

see also Raʾīs.3

historians of ʿAbdī; ʿAbdī Efendi; ʿAbdī Pasha; Aḥmad Djewdet Pasha; Aḥmad Rasmī; ʿAlī; ʿAlī Amīrī; ʿĀshiḳ-pasha-zāde; ʿĀṣim; ʿAṭāʾ Bey; al-Bakrī.1; Bidlīsī; Bihishtī; Čelebi-zāde; Česhmīzāde; Djalālzāde Muṣṭafā Čelebi; Djalālzāde Ṣāliḥ Čelebi; Enwerī; Esʿad Efendi, Meḥmed; Ḥasan Bey-zāde; ʿIzzī; Ḳarā-čelebi-zāde.4; Kātib Čelebi; Kemāl, Meḥmed Nāmiḳ; Kemāl Pasha-zāde; Khayr Allāh Efendi; Luḳmān b. Sayyid Ḥusayn; Luṭfī Efendi; Maṭrāḳčī; Meḥmed Ḥākim Efendi; Meḥmed Khalīfe b. Ḥüseyn; Meḥmed Pasha, Ḳaramānī; Meḥmed Zaʿīm; Muḥyi ʾl-Dīn Meḥmed; Naʿīmā; ʿOthmān-zāde; Pečewī; Ramaḍān-zāde; Rāshid, Meḥmed; Rūḥī; Selānīkī; Shefīḳ Meḥmed Efendi; Shemʿdānī-zāde; Sheref, ʿAbd al-Raḥmān; Silāḥdār, Fîndîḳlîlî Meḥmed Agha; Ṣolaḳ-zāde; Ṣubḥī Meḥmed; Taʿlīḳī-zāde; Ṭashköprüzāde.2 *and* 3; Thüreyyā; Ṭūrsūn Beg; Urudj; ʿUshshāḳī-zāde, Ibrāhīm; Wāṣif; Wedjīhī; Yakhshī Faḳīh; [in Suppl.] Ḳantimīr, Demetrius

see also Ḥadīdī; Shāhnāmedji; Waḳaʿ-nüwīs

other personages

see also Shehzāde; Yazîdjî

13th century Sawdjî.1

14th century ʿAlāʾ al-Dīn Beg; Badr al-Dīn b. Ḳāḍī Samāwnā; Ḳāsim.1; Sawdjî.3; Shāhīn, Lala; Süleymān Pasha

see also Ṭorghud

15th century Aḥmad Pasha Khāʾin; Ewrenos; Ewrenos Oghullarî; Fenārī-zāde; Ibn ʿArabshāh; Ḳāsim.2 *and* 3; Ḳāsim Pasha, Djazarī; Mūsā Čelebi; Muṣṭafā.1 *and* 2; Suleymān Čelebi; Tīmūrtāsh Oghullarî; Turakhān Beg; [in Suppl.] Khōdjā-zāde

16th century Bostānzāde; Čiwi-zāde; Derwīsh Pasha; Djaʿfar Čelebi; Djalālzāde Muṣṭafā Čelebi; Ferīdūn Beg; Hāmōn; Ḳāsim.4; Ḳāsim Agha; Ḳāsim Pasha; Kemāl Reʾīs; Khosrew Pasha; Ḳorḳud b. Bāyazīd; Maḥmūd Pasha; Maḥmūd

Tardjumān; Meḥmed Pasha, Bïyïklï; Muṣṭafā.3; Muṣṭafā Pasha, Ḳara Shāhīn; Muṣṭafā Pasha, Lala; Muṣṭafā Pasha al-Nashshār; Özdemir Pasha; Pertew Pasha.I; Pīrī Reʾīs; Ramaḍān-zāde; Rïḍwān Pasha; Ṣarï Kürz; Selmān Reʾīs; Shāh Sulṭān; Shāhīn, Āl; Sīdī ʿAlī Reʾīs; Sinān; Ṭashköprüzāde.1; Ṭorghud Reʾīs; ʿUshshāḳī-zāde.1; Üweys; [in Suppl.] Khāʾir Beg; Yemenli Ḥasan Pasha

17th century Ābāza; Ḥaydar-oghlu, Meḥmed; Ḥusayn Pasha; Ḳāsim.5; Ḳāṭïrdjï-oghlï Meḥmed Pasha; Maʿn-zāda; Meḥmed Khalīfe b. Hüseyn; ʿOthmān Pasha, Yegen; Shāhīn, Āl; Ṭiflī; ʿUshshāḳī-zāde.1; Warwarī ʿAlī Pasha; [in Suppl.] Aḥmad Pasha Küčük; Čobān-oghullarï

18th century Ābāza; Aḥmad Pasha; Aḥmad Pasha Bonneval; Aḥmad Rasmī; Djānīkli Ḥādjdji ʿAlī Pasha; Meḥmed Ḥākim Efendi; Meḥmed Yirmisekiz; Paswan-oghlu; Patrona Khalīl; Ṣarï Meḥmed Pasha; ʿUshshāḳī-zāde.1

19th century Aḥmad Djewdet Pasha; ʿAlī Pasha Tepedelenli; Ayyūb Ṣabrī Pasha; Bahdjat Muṣṭafā Efendi; Dāwūd Pasha (2x); Djawād Pasha; Fāḍil Pasha; Ḥālet Efendi; Ḥusayn Pasha; Ibrāhīm Derwīsh Pasha; Kabakči-oghlu Muṣṭafā; Ḳōzān-oghullarï; Muṣṭafā Pasha, Bushatlï; Pertew Pasha.II; Riḍwān Begović; Ṣādïḳ Rifʿat Pasha; Shebṣefa Ḳadïn; Ṭopal ʿOthmān Pasha.2; [in Suppl.] Camondo

20th century ʿAbd al-Ḥaḳḳ Ḥāmid; Djāwīd; Djemāl Pasha; Enwer Pasha; Fehīm Pasha; Ḥasan Fehmī; ʿIzzet Pasha; Kāẓïm Ḳadrī; Kāẓïm Karabekir; Mukhtār Pasha; Münīf Pasha; [in Suppl.] Ismāʿīl Ḥaḳḳī, Manāstïrlï; ʿIzzet Hōlō

Saldjūḳs of Rūm (1077-1307) **Saldjūḳids**

rulers Kaykāʾūs; Kaykhusraw; Kayḳubād; Ḳïlïdj Arslan I; Ḳïlïdj Arslan II; Ḳïlïdj Arslan III; Ḳïlïdj Arslan IV; Malik-Shāh.4; Sulaymān b. Ḳutulmïsh; Ṭoghrïl Shāh

historians of Ibn Bībī

other personages Ashraf Oghullarï; Muʿīn al-Dīn Sulaymān Parwāna; Saʿd al-Dīn Köpek

Arabian Peninsula Bū Saʿīd; Hamdānids; Hāshimids (2x); āl-Khalīfa; Mahdids; Nadjāḥids; Rashīd, Āl; Rasūlids; Ṣabāḥ, Āl; Ṣulayḥids; Suʿūd, Āl; Ṭāhirids.3; al-Ukhayḍir, Banū; ʿUṣfūrids; ʿUyūnids; Wāḥidī; Yaʿrubids; Yuʿfirids; Ziyādids; Zurayʿids; [in Suppl.] Djabrids; Kathīrī; Ḳuʿayṭī

Āl Saʿūd (1746-) **Suʿūd, Āl**

rulers [in Suppl.] ʿAbd al-ʿAzīz; Fayṣal b. ʿAbd al-ʿAzīz

see also Muḥammad b. Suʿūd

Bū Saʿīd (1741-) **Bū Saʿīd**

sultans Barghash; Saʿīd b. Sulṭān

Carmathians (894-end 11th century) **Ḳarmaṭī**

rulers al-Djannābī, Abū Saʿīd; al-Djannābī, Abū Ṭāhir

Hāshimids (1908-1925) **Hāshimids**

rulers Ḥusayn (b. ʿAlī)

see also ʿAbd Allāh b. al-Ḥusayn; Fayṣal I; Fayṣal II

other personages Zayd b. al-Ḥusayn b. ʿAlī

Rasūlids (1229-1454) **Rasūlids**

see also Zabīd

historians of al-Khazradjī

other personages [in Suppl.] Ibn Ḥātim

see also al-Sharīf Abū Muḥammad Idrīs

Ṭāhirids (1454-1517) **Ṭāhirids**.3

rulers ʿĀmir I; ʿĀmir II

Zaydīs (860-) **Rassids**; **Zaydiyya**.3

imams al-Mahdī li-Dīn Allāh Aḥmad; al-Manṣūr bi ʾllāh, ʿAbd Allāh; al-Manṣūr bi ʾllāh, al-Ḳāsim b. ʿAlī; al-Manṣūr bi ʾllāh, al-Ḳāsim b. Muḥammad; al-Muʾayyad bi 'llāh Muḥammad; Muḥammad al-Murtaḍā li-Dīn Allāh; al-Mutawakkil ʿalā 'llāh, Ismāʿīl; al-Mutawakkil ʿalā 'llāh, Sharaf al-Dīn; al-Nāṣir li-Dīn Allāh.II; al-Nāṣir li-Dīn Allāh, Aḥmad; al-Rassī; Yaḥyā b. Ḥamza al-ʿAlawī; Yaḥyā b. Muḥammad; [in Suppl.] Abu 'l-Fatḥ al-Daylamī; al-Hādī ila 'l-Ḥakk; al-Mahdī li-Dīn Allāh, al-Ḥusayn

see also Imāma; al-Yaman.3.a

for Zaydī imams of the Caspian → SHIITES.BRANCHES.ZAYDIYYA

other personages al-Muṭahhar; al-Nāṣir li-Dīn Allāh.II; al-Sharīf Abū Muḥammad Idrīs

Zurayʿids (1080-1173) **Zurayʿids**

viziers Bilāl b. Djarīr al-Muḥammadī

Egypt and the Fertile Crescent ʿAbbāsids; ʿAnnāzids; Ayyūbids; Bābān; Būrids; Fāṭimids; Ḥamdānids; Ḥasanwayh; Mamlūks; Marwānids; Mazyad; Mirdās; Ṭūlūnids; ʿUḳaylids; Umayyads; Zangids

see also ʿAmmār; Begteginids; Djalīlī; Ṣadaḳa, Banū; *and* → EGYPT.MODERN PERIOD.MUḤAMMAD ʿALĪ'S LINE; ONOMASTICS.TITLES.ARABIC

ʿAbbāsids (750-1258) → CALIPHATE

Ayyūbids (1169-end 15th century) **Ayyūbids**

see also Rank

rulers al-ʿĀdil; al-Afḍal; Bahrām Shāh; al-Kāmil; al-Muʿaẓẓam; al-Nāṣir; Ṣalāḥ al-Dīn; (al-Malik) al-Ṣāliḥ ʿImād al-Dīn; (al-Malik) al-Ṣāliḥ Nadjm al-Dīn Ayyūb; Tūrānshāh b. Ayyūb; al-Ẓāhir Ghāzī

see also Dīwān.ii.(3)

viziers Ibn al-ʿAdīm; Ibn al-Athīr.3; Ibn Maṭrūḥ

see also Wazīr.I.3

secretaries ʿImād al-Dīn; al-Ḳāḍī al-Fāḍil

historians of Abu 'l-Fidā; Abū Shāma; Ibn Shaddād; ʿImād al-Dīn; al-Maḳrīzī; al-Manṣūr, al-Malik

see also [in Suppl.] Ḳaraṭāy

other personages Abu 'l-Fidā; Aybak; Ibn al-ʿAssāl; Ḳarāḳūsh, Bahāʾ al-Dīn; Ḳarāḳūsh, Sharaf al-Dīn; al-Muẓaffar, al-Malik

Būrids (1104-1154) **Būrids**; Dimashḳ

rulers Ṭughtigin

Fāṭimids (909-1171) → CALIPHATE

Ḥamdānids (905-1004) **Ḥamdānids**

rulers Nāṣir al-Dawla; Sayf al-Dawla; [in Suppl.] Abū Taghlib

other personages Ḥusayn b. Ḥamdān; Luʾluʾ

Ikhshīdids (935-969)

rulers Kāfūr

viziers Ibn al-Furāt.5

other personages al-Ṣayrafī

Mamluks (1250-1517) Dhu 'l-Faḳāriyya; Dīwān.ii.(4); Ḥādjib.iv; Hiba.ii; Khādim al-Ḥaramayn; Khaznadār; **Mamlūks** (*and* [in Suppl.]); Mashwara; Nāʾib.1; Ustādār

see also Ḥarfūsh; Ḳumāsh; Mamlūk; Manshūr; Rank; Zaʿīm; [in Suppl.] Mawākib; *and* → MILITARY.MAMLUK

sultans Barḳūḳ; Barsbāy; Baybars I; Baybars II; Čaḳmaḳ; Faradj; Ḥasan; Īnāl al-Adjrūd; Ḳāʾit Bāy; Ḳalāwūn; Ḳānṣawh al-Ghawrī; Khalīl; Khushḳadam; Ḳuṭuz; Lādjīn; al-Muʾayyad Shaykh; al-Nāṣir; (al-Malik) al-Ṣāliḥ; Shaʿbān; Shadjar al-Durr; Ṭūmān Bāy

administrators Faḍl Allāh; Ibn ʿAbd al-Ẓāhir; Ibn Faḍl al-ʿUmarī; Ibn Ghurāb; Ibn Ḥidjdja; Ibn al-Sadīd (Ibn al-Muzawwiḳ); Ibn al-Sadīd, Karīm al-Dīn; al-

Ḳalḳashandī.1; [in Suppl.] Ibn al-Ṣuḳāʿ; Khāʾir Beg
historians of Abu ʾl-Maḥāsin b. Taghrībirdī; Baybars al-Manṣūrī; Ibn ʿAbd al-Ẓāhir; Ibn Duḳmāḳ; Ibn Ḥabīb, Badr al-Dīn; Ibn Iyās; Ibn Shāhīn al-Ẓāhirī; al-Maḳrīzī; al-Mufaḍḍal b. Abi ʾl-Faḍāʾil; al-Nuwayrī, Shihāb al-Dīn; al-Ṣafadī, al-Ḥasan; Shāfiʿ b. ʿAlī; al-Shudjāʿī; [in Suppl.] Ḳaraṭāy
other personages Abu ʾl-Fidā; al-ʿAynī; Ibn Djamāʿa; Ibn al-Mundhir; Tankiz
Marwānids (983-1085) **Marwānids**
rulers Naṣr al-Dawla
Mazyadids (ca. 961-1150) **Mazyad**; Ṣadaḳa, Banū
rulers Ṣadaḳa b. Manṣūr
Mirdāsids (1023-1079) **Mirdās**
see also Asad al-Dawla
Ṭūlūnids (868-905) **Ṭūlūnids**
rulers Aḥmad b. Ṭūlūn; Khumārawayh
see also Ibn al-Mudabbir.1
historians of al-Balawī; Ibn al-Dāya
other personages [in Suppl.] al-ʿAbbās b. Aḥmad b. Ṭūlūn
ʿUḳaylids (ca. 990-1169) **ʿUḳaylids**
rulers Muslim b. Ḳuraysh
Umayyads (661-750) → CALIPHATE
Zangids (1127-1222) **Zangids**
rulers Masʿūd b. Mawdūd b. Zangī; Mawdūd b. ʿImād al-Dīn Zankī; Nūr al-Dīn Arslān Shāh; Nūr al-Dīn Maḥmūd b. Zankī; Zangī
viziers al-Djawād al-Iṣfahānī
see also Begteginids; Karīm Khān Zand; Luʾluʾ, Badr al-Dīn
historians of Ibn al-Athīr.2
other personages Shīrkūh

Mongols Batuʾids; Čaghatay Khānate; Čingizids; Djānids; Girāy; Īlkhāns; Ḳarā Khiṭāy; **Mongols**; Shībānids
see also Čūbānids; Ḳāzān; Ordu.2; Soyūrghāl; Tīmūrids; [in Suppl.] Āgahī; Dīwān-begi; Djamāl Ḳarshī; Yurtčī; *and* → LAW.MONGOL; MONGOLIA.MONGOLS; ONOMASTICS. TITLES.MONGOLIAN
Batuʾids (1236-1502) **Batuʾids**
see also Saray
rulers Batu; Berke; Mangū-tīmūr; Toḳtamīsh
other personages Masʿūd Beg
Čaghatayids (1227-1370) **Čaghatay Khānate**
rulers Burāḳ Khān; Čaghatay Khān; Tughluḳ Temür
historians of Ḥaydar Mīrzā
Djānids (1598-1785) **Djānids**
rulers Nadhr Muḥammad
see also Bukhārā
Girāy Khāns (ca. 1426-1792) **Girāy**
rulers Dawlat Giray; Ghāzī Girāy I; Ghāzī Girāy II; Ghāzī Girāy III; Ḥādjdjī Girāy; Islām Girāy; Ḳaplan Girāy I; Ḳaplan Girāy II; Meḥmed Girāy I; Mengli Girāy I; Ṣāḥib Girāy Khān I; Selīm Girāy I
see also Ḳalghay; Meḥmed Baghčesarāyī; Meḥmed Girāy; Thābit
Great Khāns (1206-1634) Čingizids
rulers Činghiz Khān; Ḳubilay; Möngke; Ögedey
other personages Ḳaydu; Maḥmūd Yalawač; Ṭārābī, Maḥmūd; Toluy; Töregene Khātūn

Ilkhānids (1256-1353) **Īlkhāns**
see also Ṣadr.2; Tūmān
rulers Baydu; Gaykhātū; Ghāzān; Hūlāgū; Öldjeytü; Tegüder; Togha Temür
viziers Rashīd al-Dīn Ṭabīb; Saʿd al-Dawla
historians of Djuwaynī, ʿAlāʾ al-Dīn; Ḥamd Allāh al-Mustawfī al-Ḳazwīnī; Rashīd al-Dīn Ṭabīb; Waṣṣāf
other personages Djuwaynī, ʿAlāʾ al-Dīn; Ḳutlugh-Shāh Noyan
Shaybānids (1500-1598) **Shībānids**
rulers ʿAbd Allāh b. Iskandar; Abu ʾl-Khayr; Shībānī Khān; [in Suppl.] Iskandar Khān b. Djānī Beg; ʿUbayd Allāh Sulṭān Khān
historians of Abu ʾl-Ghāzī Bahādur Khān; [in Suppl.] Ḥāfiẓ Tanïsh
Persia Afrāsiyābids; Afshār; Aḥmadīlīs; Aḳ Ḳoyunlu; Bādūsbānids; Bāwand; Buwayhids; Djalāyir; Dulafids; Faḍlawayh; Farīghūnids; Ḥasanwayh; Hazāraspids; Ildeñizids; Ilek-Khāns; Ilyāsids; Īndjū; Ḳādjār; Kākūyids; Ḳarā-ḳoyunlu; Ḳārinids; Kāwūs; Khʷārazm-shāhs; Ḳutlugh-khānids; Lur-i Buzurg; Lur-i Kūčik; Mangïts; Marʿashīs; Muḥtādjids; Musāfirids; Mushaʿshaʿ; Muẓaffarids; Rawwādids; Sādjids; Ṣafawids; Ṣaffārids; Saldjūḳids; Salghurids; Sāmānids; Sarbadārids; Sāsānids; Shaddādids; Shīrwān Shāh; Ṭāhirids.1; Tīmūrids; Zand; Ziyārids
see also Ardalān; Atabak; ʿAwfī; Čāshna-gīr; Daylam; Dīwān.iv; Djalāyir; Ghulām.ii; Ḥādjib.iii; Ḥarb.v; al-Ḥasan b. Zayd b. Muḥammad; Hiba.iv; Ḥiṣār.iii; Īlkhāns; Iran.v; Kayānids; Marāsim.3; Mawākib.3; Pīshdādids; Shāhī; Waḳf.III; Wazīr.II; *and* → LEGENDS.LEGENDARY DYNASTIES; ONOMASTICS.TITLES.PERSIAN
Afshārids (1736-1795) **Afshār**
rulers Nādir Shāh Afshār
see also Takht-i Ṭāwūs
historians of ʿAbd al-Karīm Kashmīrī; Mahdī Khān Astarābādī
Aḳ Ḳoyunlus (1378-1508) **Aḳ Ḳoyunlu**
rulers Uzun Ḥasan
Buwayhids (932-1062) **Buwayhids**
rulers Abū Kālīdjār; ʿAḍud al-Dawla; Bakhtiyār; Djalāl al-Dawla; Fakhr al-Dawla; ʿImād al-Dawla; Khusraw Fīrūz (*and* al-Malik al-Raḥīm); Madjd al-Dawla; Muʾayyid al-Dawla; Muʿizz al-Dawla; Rukn al-Dawla; Ṣamṣām al-Dawla; Shams al-Dawla; Sharaf al-Dawla; Sulṭān al-Dawla; [in Suppl.] Bahāʾ al-Dawla wa-Ḍiyāʾ al-Milla
viziers al-ʿAbbās b. al-Ḥusayn; Ibn ʿAbbād; Ibn al-ʿAmīd; Ibn Baḳiyya; Ibn Mākūlā.1 *and* 2; al-Muhallabī, Abū Muḥammad; Sābūr b. Ardashīr; [in Suppl.] ʿAbd al-ʿAzīz b. Yūsuf; Ibn Khalaf.1; Ibn Saʿdān
secretaries Hilāl al-Ṣābiʾ (*and* Ṣābiʾ.(3).9); Ibn Hindū; Ṣābiʾ.(3).7
historians of Ṣābiʾ.(3).7
other personages al-Basāsīrī; Fasandjus; Ḥasan b. Ustādh-hurmuz; Ibn Ḥādjib al-Nuʿmān; ʿImrān b. Shāhīn; al-Malik al-ʿAzīz; [in Suppl.] Ibrāhīm Shīrāzī
Dābūyids (660-760)
rulers Dābūya
Djalāyirids (1340-1432) **Djalāyir**
rulers Uways
other personages Salmān-i Sāwadjī
Ildeñizids (1137-1225) **Ildeñizids**
rulers Ildeñiz; Özbeg b. Muḥammad Pahlawān; Pahlawān
Ilek-Khāns (992-1211) **Ilek-Khāns**
see also Yaghma
Ḳādjārs (1779-1924) **Ḳādjār**; Mushīr al-Dawla

see also Ḳāʾim-maḳām-i Farāhānī; Madjlis al-S͟hūrā; *and* → IRAN.MODERN PERIOD
rulers Āg͟hā Muḥammad S͟hāh; Fatḥ ʿAlī S͟hāh; Muḥammad ʿAlī S͟hāh Ḳādjār; Muḥammad S͟hāh; Muẓaffar al-Dīn S͟hāh Ḳādjār; Nāṣir al-Dīn S͟hāh
   see also Tak͟ht-i Ṭāwūs
other personages ʿAbbās Mīrzā; [in Suppl.] Amīr Niẓām; Ḥādjdjī Ibrāhīm K͟hān Kalāntar; Mīrzā S͟hafīʿ Māzandarānī
K͟hanate of K͟hīwa K͟hīwa
   rulers Abu ʾl-G͟hāzī Bahādur K͟hān
   historians Muʾnis; [in Suppl.] Āgahī
K͟hʷārazm-S͟hāhs (ca. 995-1231) **K͟hʷārazm-shāhs**
   rulers Ats̊īz b. Anūs͟htigin; Djalāl al-Dīn K͟hʷārazm-s͟hāh; Maʾmūn b. Muḥammad; Teki͟sh
   historians of Djuwaynī; al-Nasawī
   other personages Burāḳ Ḥādjib; Terken K͟hātūn
Muẓaffarids (1314-1393) **Muẓaffarids**
   rulers S͟hāh-i S͟hudjāʿ
   historians of Muʿīn al-Dīn Yazdī
Pahlawīs (1926-1979) **Pahlawī**
   and → IRAN.MODERN PERIOD
   rulers Muḥammad Riḍā S͟hāh Pahlawī; Riḍā S͟hāh
Sādjids (ca. 856- ca. 930) **Sādjids**
   rulers Abu ʾl-Sādj; Muḥammad b. Abi ʾl-Sādj; Yūsuf b. Abi ʾl-Sādj Dīwdād
Safawids (1501-1732) Bārūd.v; Īs͟hīk-āḳāsī; Iʿtimād al-Dawla; Kūrčī; Libās.iii; **Ṣafawids**
   see also Ḥaydar; Ḳiz̊īl-bās͟h; Nuḳṭawiyya; Ṣadr.4; Ṣadr al-Dīn Ardabīlī; Ṣadr al-Dīn Mūsā; Ṣafī al-Dīn Ardabīlī; Soyūrg͟hāl; Takkalū; Tiyūl
   rulers ʿAbbās I; Ḥusayn (*and* Sulṭān Ḥusayn); Ismāʿīl I; Ismāʿīl II; Sulaymān (S͟hāh); Ṭahmāsp
   historians of Ḥasan-i Rūmlū; Iskandar Beg; Ḳum(m)ī; Ṭāhir Waḥīd
      see also [in Suppl.] Ibn al-Bazzāz al-Ardabīlī
   other personages Alḳāṣ Mīrzā; Ḥamza Mīrzā; al-Karakī; Madjlisī
      see also [in Suppl.] Lālā; Mihmān; S͟hāhbandar
Ṣaffārids (867-ca. 1495) **Ṣaffārids**
   rulers ʿAmr b. al-Layt͟h; Yaʿḳūb b. al-Layt͟h
Saldjūḳs (1038-1194) Amīr Dād; Arslan b. Saldjūḳ; Atabak; **Saldjūḳids**
   see also Sarāparda; *and* → DYNASTIES.ANATOLIA AND THE TURKS.SALDJŪḲS OF RŪM
   rulers Alp Arslan; Bahrām S͟hāh; Barkyārūḳ; Maḥmūd b. Muḥammad b. Malik-S͟hāh; Malik-S͟hāh.1-3; Masʿūd b. Muḥammad b. Malik-S͟hāh; Muḥammad b. Maḥmūd b. Muḥammad b. Malik-S͟hāh; Muḥammad b. Malik-S͟hāh; Riḍwān; Sandjar; Ṭog͟hr̊īl (II); Ṭog͟hr̊īl (III); Tutus͟h (I) b. Alp Arslan
      see also Čag͟hr̊ī-beg; Silāḥdār; Ṭog͟hr̊īl; Ṭog͟hr̊īl (I) Beg
   viziers Anūs͟hirwān b. K͟hālid; Djahīr; al-Kundurī; Madjd al-Mulk al-Balāsānī; al-Maybudī.3; Niẓām al-Mulk; Rabīb al-Dawla; [in Suppl.] Ibn Dārust
   historians of al-Bundārī; ʿImād al-Dīn; Nīs͟hāpūrī; Rāwandī; [in Suppl.] al-Ḥusaynī
   other personages Āḳ Sunḳur al-Bursuḳī; Arslan-arg͟hūn; Ayāz; al-Basāsīrī; Būrī-bars; Bursuḳ; Būz-abeh; Ḳāwurd; K͟halaf b. Mulāʿib al-As͟hhabī; K͟hāṣṣ Beg; Kurbuḳa; Niẓāmiyya; Terken K͟hātūn; al-Ṭug͟hrāʾī; [in Suppl.] Ekinči
Salg͟hurids (1148-1270) **Salg͟hurids**
   rulers Saʿd (I) b. Zangī
Sāmānids (819-1005) **Sāmānids**
   rulers Ismāʿīl b. Aḥmad; Ismāʿīl b. Nūḥ; Manṣūr b. Nūḥ; Naṣr b. Aḥmad b. Ismāʿīl; Nūḥ (I); Nūḥ (II)

viziers Balʿamī; al-Muṣʿabī; al-ʿUtbī.1 *and* 2; [in Suppl.] al-Djayhānī
historians of Narshakhī
see also al-Sallāmī
other personages Arslan b. Saldjūḳ; Sīmdjūrids; [in Suppl.] al-Djayhānī

Ṭāhirids (821-873) **Ṭāhirids**.1
rulers ʿAbd Allāh b. Ṭāhir; Muḥammad b. Ṭāhir; Ṭāhir b. al-Ḥusayn
historians of Ibn al-Daybaʿ
other personages Muḥammad b. ʿAbd Allāh (b. Ṭāhir)

Tīmūrids (1370-1506) **Tīmūrids**
see also Ṣadr.3; Soyūrghāl; Tūzūk
rulers Abū Saʿīd b. Tīmūr; Bāyḳarā; Bāysonghor; Ḥusayn; Shāh Rukh; Tīmūr Lang; Ulugh Beg
see also Khān-zāda Bēgum
historians of Ibn ʿArabshāh; Khʷāfī Khān; Shāmī, Niẓām al-Dīn; Sharaf al-Dīn ʿAlī Yazdī
other personages Mīr ʿAlī Shīr Nawāʾī; Mīrānshāh b. Tīmūr; ʿUmar-Shaykh Mīrzā

Zands (1750-1794) **Zand**
rulers Karīm Khān Zand; Luṭf ʿAlī Khān
see also Lak

Ziyārids (931-ca. 1090) **Ziyārids**
rulers Ḳābūs b. Wushmagīr b. Ziyār; Kay Kāʾūs b. Iskandar; Mardāwīdj; Wushmgīr b. Ziyār

Spain and North Africa ʿAbbādids; ʿAbd al-Wādids; Afṭasids; Aghlabids; ʿAlawīs; ʿĀmirids; ʿAmmār; Dhu 'l-Nūnids; Djahwarids; Ḥafṣids; Ḥammādids; Ḥammūdids; Hūdids; Ḥusaynids; Idrīsids; (Banū) Khurāsān; Marīnids; Midrār; al-Murābiṭūn; al-Muwaḥḥidūn; Naṣrids; Razīn, Banū; Rustamids; Saʿdids; Ṭāhirids.2; Tudjīb; Umayyads.In Spain; Waṭṭāsids; Zīrids; [in Suppl.] Ṣumādiḥ
see also ʿAlāma; Dīwān.iii; Ḥādjib.ii *and* v; Hiba.iii; Ḥiṣār.ii; al-Ḥulal al-Mawshiyya; Ḳaramānlī; Khalīfa.i.C *and* D; Laḳab.3; Marāsim.2; Mawākib.2; Parias; Shurafāʾ.1.III; Ṭawīl, Banu; Wazīr.I.4; Ẓahīr; *and* → ANDALUSIA.CONQUEST OF *and* GOVERNORS UNTIL UMAYYAD CONQUEST; CALIPHATE.FĀṬIMIDS

ʿAbbādids (1023-1091) **ʿAbbādids**; Ishbīliya
rulers al-Muʿtaḍid bi 'llāh; al-Muʿtamid ibn ʿAbbād
see also al-Rundī
viziers Ibn ʿAmmār, Abū Bakr

ʿAbd al-Wādids (1236-1550) **ʿAbd al-Wādids**
rulers Abū Ḥammū I; Abū Ḥammū II; Abū Tāshufīn I; Abū Tāshufīn II; Abū Zayyān I; Abū Zayyān II; Abū Zayyān III; Yaghmurāsan
historians of Ibn Khaldūn, Abū Zakariyyāʾ; al-Tanasī

Afṭasids (1022-1094) **Afṭasids**
rulers al-Mutawakkil ʿalā 'llāh, Ibn al-Afṭas
secretaries Ibn ʿAbdūn; Ibn Ḳabṭūrnu (*and* [in Suppl.] Ḳabṭūrnuh); Ibn Ḳuzmān.II (*and* [in Suppl.] Ḳuzmān.2)

Aghlabids (800-909) al-ʿAbbāsiyya; **Aghlabids**; Raḳḳāda
rulers Ibrāhīm I; Ibrāhīm II

ʿAlawids (1631-) **ʿAlawīs**; Ḳāʾid; Mawlāy; Shurafāʾ.1.III
rulers ʿAbd Allāh b. Ismāʿīl; ʿAbd al-ʿAzīz b. al-Ḥasan; ʿAbd al-Raḥmān b. Hishām; Ḥafīẓ (ʿAbd al-); (Mawlāy) al-Ḥasan; Mawlāy Ismāʿīl; Muḥammad III b. ʿAbd Allāh; Muḥammad IV b. ʿAbd al-Raḥmān; Muḥammad b. Yūsuf (Muḥammad V); al-Rashīd (Mawlāy); Sulaymān (Mawlāy); [in Suppl.] Muḥammad b. ʿArafa; Yūsuf b. al-Ḥasan

viziers Akanṣūs; Ibn Idrīs (I); [in Suppl.] Bā Ḥmād; Ibn ʿUthmān al-Miknāsī
historians of Akanṣūs; Ibn Zaydān; al-Kardūdī; al-Zayyānī
other personages Aḥmad al-Nāṣirī al-Salāwī (*and* al-Nāṣir al-Salāwī); Ibn Idrīs (II); Khunātha
Almohads (1130-1269) Hargha; al-ʿIḳāb; Mizwār; **al-Muwaḥḥidūn**
see also Tinmal; Ẓahīr
rulers ʿAbd al-Muʾmin; Abū Yaʿḳūb Yūsuf; Abū Yūsuf Yaʿḳūb al-Manṣūr; Ibn Tūmart; al-Maʾmūn; al-Nāṣir
historians of ʿAbd al-Wāḥid al-Marrākushī; al-Baydhaḳ; Ibn Ṣāḥib al-Ṣalāt
see also al-Ḥulal al-Mawshiyya
other personages [in Suppl.] Ibn al-Ḳaṭṭān
see also Abū Ḥafṣ ʿUmar al-Hintātī; Ibn Mardanīsh
Almoravids (1056-1147) Amīr al-Muslimīn; **al-Murābiṭūn**
see also al-Zallāḳa
rulers ʿAlī b. Yūsuf b. Tāshufīn; al-Lamtūnī; Tāshufīn b. ʿAlī; Yūsuf b. Tāshufīn
secretaries Ibn ʿAbdūn
historians of Ibn al-Ṣayrafī
see also al-Ḥulal al-Mawshiyya
other personages Ibn Bādjdja; Ibn Ḳasī
ʿĀmirids (1021-1096) **ʿĀmirids**
rulers ʿAbd al-Malik b. Abī ʿĀmir; al-Muẓaffar
viziers Ibn al-Ḳaṭṭāʿ
other personages ʿAbd al-Raḥmān b. Abī ʿĀmir
Djahwarids (1030-1070) **Djahwarids**
other personages (al-)Ḥakam ibn ʿUk(k)āsha; Ibn ʿAbdūs
Ḥafṣids (1228-1574) **Ḥafṣids**
secretaries Ḥāzim
historians of al-Ḥādjdj Ḥammūda
other personages Ibn ʿArafa
Ḥammādids (972-1152) **Ḥammādids**
rulers Bādīs; al-Manṣūr; al-Nāṣir
see also Ḳalʿat Banī Ḥammād
Ḥammūdids (1010-1057) **Ḥammūdids**
viziers Ibn Dhakwān
Hūdids (1039-1142) **Hūdids**
rulers al-Muʾtamin
Ḥusaynids (1705-1957) **Ḥusaynids**
rulers Aḥmad Bey; al-Ḥusayn (b. ʿAlī); Muḥammad Bey; Muḥammad al-Ṣādiḳ Bey
ministers Khayr al-Dīn Pasha; Muṣṭafā Khaznadār
Idrīsids (789-926) **Idrīsids**
rulers Idrīs I; Idrīs II
Marīnids (1196-1465) **Marīnids**
rulers Abu ʾl-Ḥasan; Abū ʿInān Fāris
Naṣrids (1230-1492) **Naṣrids**
viziers Ibn al-Khaṭīb
other personages [in Suppl.] Ibn al-Sarrādj; al-Nubāhī
Rustamids (777-909) **Rustamids**
historians of Ibn al-Ṣaghīr
Saʿdids (1511-1659) **Saʿdids**; Shurafāʾ.1.III
rulers ʿAbd Allāh al-Ghālib; Aḥmad al-Manṣūr; Mawlāy Maḥammad al-Shaykh

see also Mawlāy
viziers Ibn ʿĪsā
historians of ʿAbd al-ʿAzīz b. Muḥammad; al-Ifrānī
other personages al-Tamgrūtī; [in Suppl.] Abū Maḥallī
Ṭāhirids (11th-12th centuries) **Ṭāhirids**.2
Tudjībids (1019-1039) **Tudjīb**
rulers Maʿn b. Muḥammad; al-Muʿtaṣim
ʿUbaydids
historians of Ibn Ḥamādu
Umayyads (756-1031) **Umayyads.In Spain**
amīrs and caliphs ʿAbd Allāh b. Muḥammad; ʿAbd al-Raḥmān; al-Ḥakam I; al-Ḥakam II; Hishām I; Hishām II; Hishām III; al-Mahdī; al-Mundhir b. Muḥammad
see also Madīnat al-Zahrāʾ; Muʿāwiya b. Hishām; Rabaḍ; al-Ruṣāfa.4; al-Walīd b. Hishām; [in Suppl.] Bubashtru; Sulaymān b. al-Ḥakam al-Mustaʿīn
viziers Ibn ʿAlḳama.2; Ibn Shuhayd
see also Wazīr.I.4
secretaries ʿArīb b. Saʿd al-Kātib al-Ḳurṭubī; Ibn Burd.I
other personages ʿAbd al-Raḥmān b. Marwān; Ghālib b. ʿAbd al-Raḥmān; Ḥabīb b. ʿAbd al-Malik; Ḥasdāy b. Shaprūṭ; Ibn ʿAlḳama.1; Ibn Dhakwān; Ibn al-Ḥannāṭ; Ibn Ḳasī; Ibn al-Ḳiṭṭ; al-Manṣūr; Rabīʿ b. Zayd; Ṣaḳāliba.3; Ṣubḥ; ʿUmar b. Ḥafṣūn; Ziryāb; [in Suppl.] Zīrī b. ʿAṭiyya
Zīrids (972-1152) **Zīrids**.1
rulers Buluggīn b. Zīrī; al-Muʿizz b. Bādīs; Tamīm b. al-Muʿizz
historians of Umayya, Abu ʾl-Ṣalt
other personages Ibn Abi ʾl-Ridjāl
see also Ḳurhub
Zīrids of Granada (1012-1090) **Zīrids**.2
rulers ʿAbd Allāh b. Buluggīn; Zāwī b. Zīrī

E

EARTHQUAKES **Zalzala**
for accounts of earthquakes, see also Aghrī Dagh; Amasya; Anṭākiya; ʿAshḳābād; Čankiri; Cilicia; Daybul; Djidjelli; Erzindjan; Ḥarra; Ḥulwān; Istanbul.VI.f; Ḳalhāt; Kāṅgṛā; Ḳazwīn; Kilāt; Nīshāpūr; al-Ramla

ECONOMICS Bayʿ; Kasb; Māl, Tadbīr.1; Taʾmīm
see also Muḍāraba; Taʿāwun; Tidjāra.3; *and* → FINANCE

EDUCATION **Maʿārif**; **Tadrīs**; Tarbiya
see also ʿArabiyya.B.IV; Idjāza
educational reform → REFORM
institutions of learning Dār al-Ḥadīth; Djāmiʿa; Köy Enstitüleri; Kuttāb; Madrasa; Maktab; Pesantren
see also Kulliyya; Ṣadr.(c); Samāʿ.2; Shaykh; Ustādh; *and* → EDUCATION.LIBRARIES
individual establishments al-Azhar; Bayt al-Ḥikma; Dār al-Ḥikma; Dār al-ʿUlūm; Ghalaṭa-sarāyi; Ḥarbiye; al-Ḳarawiyyīn.ii; al-Khaldūniyya; Makhredj; Mulkiyya; al-Ṣādiḳiyya; Zaytūna; [in Suppl.] Institut des hautes études marocaines; Institut des hautes études de Tunis; Jamia Millia Islamia; Ṭibbiyye-i ʿAdliyye-i Shāhāne

see also Aligarh; Deoband; Filāḥa.iii; al-Ḳāhira; Laḵẖnaw; al-Madīna.ii; Makka.3; Muṣṭafā ʿAbd al-Rāziḳ; al-Mustanṣir (I); Nadwat al-ʿUlamāʾ; [in Suppl.] ʿAbd al-Bārī; ʿAbd al-Wahhāb; Farangī Maḥall

learned societies and academies Andjuman; Djamʿiyya; Djemʿiyyet-i ʿIlmiyye-i ʿOthmāniyye; Institut d'Égypte; Ḵẖalḳevi; Madjmaʿ ʿIlmī

libraries Dār al-ʿIlm; **Maktaba**
   see also ʿAlī Paṣẖa Mubārak; Ḵẖāzin; al-Madīna.ii
   collections ʿAlī Amīrī (*and* [in Suppl.] ʿAlī Emīrī); Esʿad Efendi, Meḥmed; Ḵẖudā Baḵẖṣẖ; al-Ṭūr.1; [in Suppl.] ʿAbd al-Wahhāb
     see also Geniza; *and* → LITERATURE.BIBLIOGRAPHICAL
librarians Ibn al-Fuwaṭī; Ibn Ḥadjar al-ʿAsḳalānī; Ibn al-Sāʿī; al-Kattānī
treatises on
   medieval al-Zarnūdjī
   modern-day Ergin, Osman; [in Suppl.] Tonguç

EGYPT   al-Ḳāhira (*and* [in Suppl.] Miṣr.C.2.vi); Ḳibṭ; **Miṣr**; Nūba; al-Ṣaʿīd
   see also al-ʿArab.iv; al-Fusṭāṭ; *and* → CHRISTIANITY.DENOMINATIONS.COPTS; DYNASTIES. EGYPT AND THE FERTILE CRESCENT; MUSIC.REGIONAL; NUBIA
administration Dār al-Maḥfūẓāt al-ʿUmūmiyya; Dīwān.ii; Ḳabāla; Ḵẖarādj.I; Rawk
   see also Miṣr.D.1.b; Waḳf.II.1; *and* → CALIPHATE.ʿABBĀSIDS *and* FĀṬIMIDS; DYNASTIES.EGYPT AND THE FERTILE CRESCENT.MAMLUKS; OTTOMAN EMPIRE. ADMINISTRATION
architecture → ARCHITECTURE.REGIONS
before Islam Firʿawn; Manf; Miṣr.D.1; Nūba.2; Saḳḳāra; [in Suppl.] Abū Sinbil
   see also al-Uḳṣur
dynasties ʿAbbāsids; Ayyūbids; Fāṭimids; Mamlūks; Muḥammad ʿAlī Paṣẖa; Ṭūlūnids
   and → DYNASTIES.EGYPT AND THE FERTILE CRESCENT
education al-Azhar; Dār al-ʿUlūm; Djāmiʿa; Institut d'Égypte; Maʿārif.1.ii; Madjmaʿ ʿIlmī.i.2.b; Rifāʿa Bey al-Ṭahṭāwī
   see also ʿAlī Paṣẖa Mubārak
historians of Abu 'l-Maḥāsin b. Taḡẖrābirdī; ʿAlī Paṣẖa Mubārak; al-Bakrī.2; al-Balawī; al-Damurdāṣẖī; al-Djabartī; Ibn ʿAbd al-Ḥakam.4; Ibn Duḳmāk; Ibn Iyās; Ibn Muyassar; al-Kindī, Abū ʿUmar Muḥammad; al-Maḳrīzī; al-Nuwayrī, Muḥammad; Rifāʿa Bey al-Ṭahṭāwī; al-Ṣafadī, al-Ḥasan; Salīm al-Naḳḳāṣẖ; al-Suyūṭī; al-Waṣīfī; Zaydān, Djurdjī
   see also [in Suppl.] Taʾrīḵẖ.II.1.(c); *and* → DYNASTIES.EGYPT AND THE FERTILE CRESCENT
modern period Ḍarība.4; Djarīda.i.A; Dustūr.iii; Ḥizb.i; Ḥukūma.iii; al-Iḵẖwān al-Muslimūn; Iltizām; Imtiyāzāt.iv; Madjlis.4.A.xvi; Maḥkama.4.i; Miṣr.D.7 (*and* [in Suppl.] Miṣr.D.8 *and* D.9); Salafiyya.2(a); Ṣiḥāfa.1.(i); al-Takfīr wa 'l-Hidjra; Wafd; [in Suppl.] Niẓām ʿAskarī.1.(a)
   see also Baladiyya.2; al-Bannāʾ; Madjlis al-Ṣẖūrā; Waṭaniyya
belletrists
   poets al-Bārūdī; Fikrī; Ḥāfiẓ Ibrāhīm; Ismāʿīl Ṣabrī; Ismāʿīl Ṣabrī Paṣẖa; al-Manfalūṭī; al-Māzinī; Nādjī; Nadjīb al-Ḥaddād; Nadjīb Muḥammad Surūr; Ṣalāḥ ʿAbd al-Ṣabūr; al-Ṣẖarḳāwī; Ṣẖawḳī; Ṣẖukrī; Ṭāhā, ʿAlī Maḥmūd; [in Suppl.] Abū Ṣẖādī; al-ʿAḳḳād
   writers of prose Aḥmad Amīn; Ḥāfiẓ Ibrāhīm; Maḥmūd Taymūr; al-Manfalūṭī; al-Māzinī; Muḥammad Husayn Haykal; al-Muwayliḥī; Salāma Mūsā; al-Ṣẖarḳāwī; Ṭāhā Ḥusayn; Tawfīḳ al-Ḥakīm; Yaḥyā Ḥaḳḳī; [in Suppl.] Abū Ṣẖādī; al-ʿAḳḳād; Lāṣẖīn

see also Faraḥ Anṭūn; Mayy Ziyāda; Muḥammad Bey ʿUthmān Djalāl (*and* [in Suppl.] Muḥammad ʿUthmān Djalāl)*; and* → LITERATURE.DRAMA.ARABIC *and* HISTORICAL.ARABIC; PRESS

influential persons Djamāl al-Dīn al-Afghānī; al-Marṣafī; Muḥammad ʿAbduh; Muṣṭafā Kāmil Pasha; al-Muwayliḥī.1; Rifāʿa Bey al-Ṭahṭāwī; Salāma Mūsā; al-Sanhūrī, ʿAbd al-Razzāḳ; Sayyid Ḳuṭb; Shākir, Aḥmad Muḥammad; Shaltūt, Maḥmūd; al-Subkiyyūn; Ṭāhā Ḥusayn; Umm Kulthūm; [in Suppl.] Abu ʾl-ʿAzāʾim; al-ʿAdawī; al-Bakrī; al-Biblāwī; Djawharī, Ṭanṭāwī; al-ʿIdwī al-Ḥamzāwī; ʿIllaysh

see also Rashīd Riḍā; *and* → *the section Statesmen below*

Muḥammad ʿAlī's line ʿAbbās Ḥilmī I; ʿAbbās Ḥilmī II; Fuʾād al-Awwal; Ḥusayn Kāmil; Ibrāhīm Pasha; Ismāʿīl Pasha; Muḥammad ʿAlī Pasha; Saʿīd Pasha; Tawfīḳ Pasha; [in Suppl.] Bakhīt al-Muṭīʿī al-Ḥanafī; Fārūḳ

see also ʿAzīz Miṣr; Khidīw; ʿUmar Makram; [in Suppl.] Dāʾira Saniyya; Ibʿādiyya

statesmen ʿAlī Pasha Mubārak; al-Bārūdī; Fikrī; Ismāʿīl Ṣabrī Pasha; Ismāʿīl Ṣidḳī; Luṭfī al-Sayyid; Muḥammad Farīd Bey; Muḥammad Nadjīb; al-Naḥḥās; Nūbār Pasha; Saʿd Zaghlūl; al-Sādāt; Sharīf Pasha; ʿUrābī Pasha; Yakan, ʿAdlī; [in Suppl.] ʿAbd al-Nāṣir; Māhir, ʿAlī

see also Muṣṭafā Kāmil Pasha

mystic orders Marwāniyya; Rifāʿiyya; Taṣawwuf.4; [in Suppl.] al-ʿAfīfī; Demirdāshiyya; Shaʿrāniyya

see also Bakriyya; Khalwatiyya; Zār.2; *and* → MYSTICISM

Ottoman period (1517-1798) Dhu ʾl-Faḳāriyya; Ḳāsimiyya; Ḳāzdughliyya; Miṣr.D.6; Muḥammad ʿAlī Pasha; Shaykh al-Balad

see also Ḥurriyya.ii

beys ʿAlī Bey; Muḥammad Abu ʾl-Dhahab (*and* [in Suppl.] Abu ʾl-Dhahab)

physical geography

mountains al-Ṭūr.1

oases al-Wāḥāt

waters Burullus; al-Nīl; Timsāḥ, Lake

see also Miḳyās; Rawḍa; al-Suways

population ʿAbābda; Ḳibṭ

see also [in Suppl.] Demography.IV; *and* → CHRISTIANITY.DENOMINATIONS.COPTS

toponyms

ancient Adfū; Bābalyūn; al-Bahnasā; Burullus; Dabīḳ; al-Ḳulzum; Manf; Shaṭā; Tinnīs

see also al-Sharḳiyya

present-day

regions Buḥayra; al-Fayyūm; al-Gharbiyya; Girgā; al-Sharḳiyya; Sīnāʾ

see also al-Ṣaʿīd

towns ʿAbbāsa; Abūḳīr; Akhmīm; al-ʿAllāḳī; al-ʿArīsh; Asyūṭ; Aṭfīḥ; ʿAyn Shams; Banhā; Banī Suwayf; Bilbays; Būlāḳ; Būṣīr; Dahshūr; Daḳahliyya; Damanhūr; Dimyāṭ; al-Farāfra; al-Fusṭāṭ; Girgā; Ḥulwān; al-Iskandariyya; Ismāʿīliyya; Isna; al-Ḳāhira (*and* [in Suppl.] Miṣr.C.2.vi); Ḳalyūb; Ḳanṭara.3; Ḳifṭ; Ḳunā; Ḳūṣ; Ḳuṣayr; al-Maḥalla al-Kubrā; al-Manṣūra; Manūf; Port Saʿīd; Rafaḥ; Rashīd; Saḳḳāra; Samannūd; Sīwa.1; al-Suways; al-Tall al-Kabīr; Ṭanṭā; al-Uḳṣur; al-Ushmūnayn; Uswān; al-Zaḳāzīḳ; [in Suppl.] Abū Zaʿbal

see also al-Muḳaṭṭam; Rawḍa

EMANCIPATION Ḥurriyya

for manumission → SLAVERY; *for women* → WOMEN

EMIGRATION Djāliya; **Hidjra**
see also al-Mahdjar; Muhādjir; al-Muhādjirūn; Pārsīs; Ṣiḥāfa.3; *and* → NEW WORLD

EPIGRAPHY **Kitābāt**
see also Eldem, Khalīl Edhem; Ḥisāb al-Djummal; Khaṭṭ; Musnad.1; Ṭirāz.3
sites of inscriptions Lībiyā.2; Liḥyān; Orkhon; al-Sawdāʾ; Ṣiḳilliya.4; Ṣirwāḥ.1; Ẓafār
see also Ḥaḍramawt; Sabaʾ; Ṣafaitic; Thamudic; [in Suppl.] Ḳaḥṭānite

ESCHATOLOGY ʿAdhāb al-Ḳabr; Ākhira; al-Aʿrāf; Barzakh; Baʿth; Djahannam; Djanna; Djazāʾ; Dunyā; Ḥawḍ; Ḥisāb; Isrāfīl; ʿIzrāʾīl; Ḳiyāma; Maʿād; al-Mahdī; Mawḳif.2; Munkar wa-Nakīr; Sāʿa.3; Zaḳḳūm
see also Ḳayyim; Shafāʿa; Shaḳāwa; Yawm; al-Zabāniyya; *and* → DEATH; PARADISE
hereafter Adjr.1; **Ākhira**
see also Dunyā
signs ʿAṣā; Dābba; al-Dadjdjāl; Yādjūdj wa-Mādjūdj
see also Baʿth; Sāʿa.3

ETERNITY **Abad**; Ḳidam

ETHICS Adab; **Akhlāḳ**; Ḥisba
see also Ḥurriyya; al-Maḥāsin wa ʾl-Masāwī; Miskawayh; Taḥsīn wa-Taḳbīḥ; Tanẓīm al-Nasl; Ẓarīf; *and* → VIRTUES AND VICES

ETHIOPIA Adal; Aḥmad Grāñ; Awfāt; Bāli; Dawāro; Djabart; Djimmā; **Ḥabash**; Ḥabashat
see also Ḥabesh; Kūsh; Shaykh Ḥusayn; Zār.1; *and* → AFRICA.EAST AFRICA; LANGUAGES.AFRO-ASIATIC; YEMEN.TOPONYMS
historians of ʿArabfaḳih
population ʿĀmir; Diglal; Djabart; Galla; Māryā; Oromo; Rashāʾida
toponyms Assab; Dahlak; Dire Dawa; Eritrea; Harar; Maṣawwaʿ; Ogādēn

ETHNICITY Maghāriba; Mashāriḳa; Sārt
see also Fatā; Ibn Gharsiya; Ismāʿīl b. Yasār; Mawlā; Saracens

ETIQUETTE **Adab**
see also Āʾīn; Hiba; *and* → CUISINE.TABLE MANNERS; LITERATURE.ETIQUETTE-LITERATURE

EUNUCH **Khāṣī**
see also Khādim; Mamlūk.3; Ustādh.1

EUROPE
for imitation of, see Tafarnudj; *for translations from European works* → LITERATURE.TRANSLATIONS
Eastern Europe Arnawutluḳ; Balkan; Bulgaria; Iḳrīṭish; Ḳubrus; Leh; Madjar; Yugoslavia; [in Suppl.] Čeh
see also Bulghār; Ḥizb.v; Ibrāhīm b. Yaʿḳūb; Muhādjir.2; Muslimūn.1; Rūmeli; al-Ṣaḳāliba
for individual countries → ALBANIA; BULGARIA; CRETE; CYPRUS; (former) CZECHOSLOVAKIA; GREECE; HUNGARY; POLAND; (former) YUGOSLAVIA; *the section Russia below; and* → BALKANS
waters Itil; Ṭuna; Wardar; Yayïḳ
Russia Budjāḳ; Ḳïrïm

see also Bulghār; Djadīd; Ḥizb.v; Ḳayyūm Nāṣirī; al-Ṭanṭāwī; [in Suppl.] al-Ḳabḳ.3
dynasties Girāy
Muslim Communists [in Suppl.] Sulṭān ʿAlī Ūghlī
population Bashdjirt; Besermyans; Beskesek-abaza; Bukhārlïk; Burṭās; Čeremiss; Čulïm; Čuwash; Gagauz; Ḳarapapakh; Lipḳa; Rūs; Teptyar
see also Ḳanghli; Khazar; Kimäk; Pečenegs; al-Ṣaḳāliba
toponyms
ancient Atil; Saḳsīn
present-day Aḳ Kirmān; Aḳ Masdjid.1; Azaḳ; Bāghče Sarāy; Ismāʿīl; Ḳamāniča; Ḳaraṣū-bāzār; Ḳāsimov; Ḳāzān; Kefe; Kerč; Khotin; Ḳïlburun; Sughdāḳ; Tümen
see also Yeñi Ḳalʿe
Western Europe al-Bashkunish; Burtuḳāl; Ifrandj; Īṭaliya; Malta; Nemče; Sardāniya
see also Ibn Idrīs (II); Ibrāhīm b. Yaʿḳūb; al-Madjūs; Muslimūn.2
for individual countries → AUSTRIA; FRANCE; ITALY; PORTUGAL; SPAIN; *and* → BASQUES
Arabic press in **Ṣiḥāfa**.3
Arabic printing in [in Suppl.] **Maṭbaʿa**.6
waters Ṭuna

EVIL EYE ʿ**Ayn**, Tamīma
see also Karkaddan; *and* → CHARMS; ISLAM.POPULAR BELIEFS

F

FAITH ʿAḳīda; **Īmān**; [in Suppl.] Taḳwā
and → ISLAM; RELIGION

FALCONRY **Bayzara**; Čakïrdjï-bashï; Doghandjï
see also Ṭoghrïl

FASTING ʿĀshūrāʾ; Ramaḍān; **Ṣawm**
see also ʿĪd al-Fiṭr; Ṣūfiyāna; [in Suppl.] Puasa
prayer during Ramaḍān **Tarāwīḥ**

FĀṬIMIDS → CALIPHATE

FESTIVAL **ʿĪd**; Kandūrī; Mawlid (*and* [in Suppl.]); Mawsim; Shenlik
see also Maṭbakh.2
festivals ʿAnṣāra; ʿĀshūrāʾ.II; Bārā Wafāt; ʿĪd al-Aḍḥā; ʿĪd al-Fiṭr; Khiḍr-ilyās; Mihragān; Nawrūz; Sulṭān al-Ṭalaba (*and* Ṭalaba)
see also Ghadīr Khumm; Kurds.iv.C.3; Lālish; Lĕbaran; Raʾs al-ʿĀm; Walī.9
literature on Wehbī Sayyidī

FINANCE Ribā
and → ADMINISTRATION.FINANCIAL; LAW.LAW OF OBLIGATIONS; PAYMENTS; TAXATION
accounting Muḥāsaba.2; Mustawfī
see also Daftar; *and* → ADMINISTRATION.FINANCIAL
banking Ḳirāḍ; Muḍāraba; Ribā; Suftadja; [in Suppl.] Ṣarrāf
see also Djahbadh; Sharika
commerce Bayʿ; Imtiyāzāt; Kasb; Ḳirāḍ; Shirāʾ; **Tidjāra**
see also Inshāʾ; *and* → INDUSTRY; LAW.LAW OF OBLIGATIONS

functions Dallāl; Malik al-Tud̲j̲d̲j̲ār; S̲h̲āh Bandar (*and* [in Suppl.] S̲h̲āhbandar); Tād̲j̲ir; [in Suppl.] Ṣarrāf
  see also Tard̲j̲umān
marketplace Ḥisba; Sūḳ
  see also [in Suppl.] al-Sunāmī
trade Ḳahwa; Kārimī; Ḳuṭn; Lubān; Ṭīn.3
  see also Kalah; Kārwān; Ḳaysariyya; Kirmān; Mīnāʾ; Ṣafawids.II; Szechuan; Tas̲h̲āza; Tammār; ʿUḳāẓ; Wenedik
institutions
  Arabic Bayt al-Māl; Mak̲h̲zan
  Turkish K̲h̲azīne; Māliyya
partnerships Mufāwaḍa; Mus̲h̲āraka; S̲h̲arika
terms ʿĀriyya; Bayʿ; Ḍamān; G̲h̲ārim; Ḥawāla; Hiba; Kafāla; Ḳirāḍ; Muḍāraba; Mufāwaḍa; Muḳāṭaʿa; Muk̲h̲āṭara; Mus̲h̲āraka; Ribā; Suftad̲j̲a; [in Suppl.] Dayn; Ṣakk
  and → Law.law of obligations

Flora (D̲j̲azīrat) al-ʿArab.v; Būstān; Filāḥa; Hind.i.k
  and → Architecture.monuments.gardens; Botany; Literature.poetry.nature
flowers Nard̲j̲is; S̲h̲aḳīḳat al-Nuʿmān; Sūsan; Ward; [in Suppl.] Bābūnad̲j̲; D̲j̲ullanār
  see also Filāḥa.iv; Lāle Devri; Lālezarī; Nawriyya; [in Suppl.] Māʾ al-Ward; *and* →
  Architecture.monuments.gardens; Literature.poetry.nature
plants Ad̲h̲argūn; Afsantīn; Afyūn; Ḥalfāʾ; Ḥinnāʾ; Kammūn; Ḳaranful; Karm; Ḳaṣab; Naʿām; **Nabāt**; Ṣabr; S̲h̲ibit̲h̲t̲h̲; S̲h̲īḥ; S̲h̲ukāʿā; Sidr; Simsim; Sirād̲j̲ al-Ḳuṭrub (*and* Yabrūḥ); Sūs; Turund̲j̲ān; Wars; Yāsamīn; Zaʿfarān; [in Suppl.] Aḳūnīṭun; Ās; Bābūnad̲j̲; Basbās; D̲j̲āwars; Fūd̲h̲and̲j̲; Hindibāʾ; Iklīl al-Malik
  see also Maryam; Naḥl; Namir and Nimr; Nasr; Ṣamg̲h̲; Sinnawr; Sirwāl; Timsāḥ; *and*
  → Drugs.narcotics
trees Abanūs; ʿAfṣ; Argan; Baḳḳam; Bān; Nak̲h̲l; Sād̲j̲; Ṣandal; Sidr; Tīn; Tūt; ʿUnnāba; Zaytūn.2; [in Suppl.] D̲j̲awz; D̲j̲ullanār
  see also ʿAyn S̲h̲ams; G̲h̲āba; Kāfūr; Kahrubā; Ḳaṭrān; Lubān; Ṣamg̲h̲; T̲h̲aʿlab; [in Suppl.] Halīlad̲j̲
  woods Abanūs; Baḳḳam; **K̲h̲as̲h̲ab;** Ṣandal; ʿŪd.I
    see also Lamu; *and* → *the section Trees above*; Navigation.ships *and* shipyards

Folklore [in Suppl.] **Taḳālīd**
  and → Charms; Custom; Divination; Humour; Legends; Literature.folkloric

France Arbūna; Fraxinetum
  see also Balāṭ al-S̲h̲uhadāʾ; Muslimūn.2; Rifāʿa Bey al-Ṭahṭāwī; Ṣāyig̲h̲, Fatḥ Allāh; al-S̲h̲ām.2(b)

Franks **Ifrand̲j̲**
  and → Crusade(r)s

Furnishings Mafrūs̲h̲āt; Sirād̲j̲; [in Suppl.] **At̲h̲āt̲h̲**
  see also [in Suppl.] Martaba

G

Gambling **Ḳimār**; al-Maysir

and → ANIMALS.SPORT; RECREATION.GAMES

GENEALOGY   **Ḥasab wa-Nasab**; **Nasab**; S̲h̲arīf; S̲h̲urafāʾ
   see also ʿIrḳ; Naḳīb al-As̲h̲rāf; S̲h̲araf; *and* → LITERATURE.GENEALOGICAL; ONOMASTICS

GEOGRAPHY   **Dj̲ug̲h̲rāfiyā**; Iḳlīm; Istiwāʾ; K̲h̲arīṭa; al-Ḳubba; Tak̲h̲ṭīṭ al-Ḥudūd
   see also Mag̲h̲rib; Makka.4; Mas̲h̲riḳ
   for the geography of individual areas, see Adamawa; Ād̲h̲arbaydj̲ān.i; Afg̲h̲ānistān.i; Aḳ
   Ṣu; Algeria.i; Anadolu.ii; al-Andalus.ii *and* iii.2; (Dj̲azīrat) al-ʿArab.ii; Armīniya;
   Arnawutluḳ.3; ʿAsīr; Baḥr; Dj̲azīra; Filāḥa; Ḥammāda; Indonesia; ʿIrāḳ; Iran; Lībiyā; al-
   Mag̲h̲rib; Māzandarān.2; Mūrītāniyā.1; Nadj̲d.1; Niger.1; Pākistān; Senegal.1; al-S̲h̲ām.1;
   Sīstān.2; Somali.2; Tunisia.I.a; ʿUmān.1; al-Yaman.2; Zāb.1; [in Suppl.] Ḳazaḳstān.1;
   Rādj̲asthān.1
administrative   Kūra; Mamlaka; Mik̲h̲lāf; Rustāḳ.1; S̲h̲ahr; Ṣūba; Ṭassūdj̲; Ustān
   see also Dj̲und; Iḳlīm; Wālī
geographers   Abu ʾl-Fidā; Abū ʿUbayd al-Bakrī; ʿĀs̲h̲iḳ; al-Balk̲h̲ī, Abū Zayd; al-Dimas̲h̲ḳī;
   Ibn ʿAbd al-Munʿim al-Ḥimyarī; Ibn al-Faḳīh; Ibn G̲h̲ālib; Ibn Ḥawḳal; Ibn
   K̲h̲urradād̲h̲bih; Ibn Mādj̲id; Ibn Rusta; Ibn Sarābiyūn; al-Idrīsī; al-Iṣṭak̲h̲rī; al-Ḳazwīnī;
   al-Masʿūdī; al-Muhallabī, Abu ʾl-Ḥusayn; al-Muḳaddasī; al-ʿUd̲h̲rī; al-Warrāḳ,
   Muḥammad; Yāḳūt al-Rūmī; al-Zuhrī, Muḥammad
   see also Baṭlamiyūs; Istibṣār; Ḳāsim b. Aṣbag̲h̲; al-Masālik wa ʾl-Mamālik; al-Sarak̲h̲sī,
   Abu ʾl-ʿAbbās; [in Suppl.] al-Dj̲ayhānī; Ḥudūd al-ʿĀlam
literature   Dj̲ug̲h̲rāfiyā.IV.c *and* V; Ṣurat al-Arḍ
   see also Tūrān; *and* → LITERATURE.TRAVEL-LITERATURE
physical geography
   deserts   → DESERTS
   mountains   → MOUNTAINS
   oases   **Wāḥa**
   salt flats   **Sabk̲h̲a**
      see also Azalay; Milḥ; S̲h̲aṭṭ; *for regional salt flats* → ALGERIA; OMAN
   springs   ʿAyn Dilfa; ʿAyn Mūsā; al-Ḥamma; Ḥasan Abdāl
      see also Ḳaplîdj̲a
   volcanoes   *see* ʿAdan; Ag̲h̲rî Dag̲h̲; Damāwand; Ḥarra; Ladj̲āʾ; al-Ṣafā.2; [in Suppl.] Dj̲abal
      Says
   wadis   **Wādī**
   waters
      lakes   Baikal; Bak̲h̲tigān; Balk̲h̲as̲h̲; Burullus; Gökče-tengiz; Hāmūn; al-Ḥūla; İssîk-
         kul; Ḳarā-köl; Timsāḥ, Lake; Tuz Gölü; Urmiya.1; al-ʿUtayba; Wān.1; Zirih
         see also Buḥayra; al-Ḳulzum; *and* → OCEANS AND SEAS
      oceans and seas   → OCEANS AND SEAS
      rivers   → RIVERS
      straits   Bāb al-Mandab; Bog̲h̲az-iči; Čanaḳ-ḳalʿe Bog̲h̲azî
   terms   Ḥarra; K̲h̲abrāʾ; Nahr; Reg; Rīf; Sabk̲h̲a; S̲h̲aṭṭ
      see also Ṣanf; Sarḥadd; Wālī
   urban   Ḳarya; Ḳaṣaba; K̲h̲iṭṭa; Maḥalle; Medina; Rabaḍ; S̲h̲ahr; S̲h̲ahristān
      see also Fener; Ḥayy; K̲h̲iṭaṭ; Mallāḥ; S̲h̲āriʿ; *and* → ARCHITECTURE.URBAN; SEDEN-
      TARISM; *and in particular the larger cities in the section Toponyms under each country*

GIFTS   **Hiba**; Ṣila.3
   see also Bak̲h̲s̲h̲īs̲h̲; Nit̲h̲ār; Pīs̲h̲kas̲h̲; Ras̲h̲wa; *and* → PAYMENTS

GREECE Yūnān
see also Muhādjir.2; Muslimūn.1.B.3; Pomaks
Greek authors in Arabic translation → LITERATURE.TRANSLATIONS; PHILOSOPHY.PHILOSOPHERS
toponyms
districts Karli-īli
islands Čoka Adasi; Eğriboz; Körfüz; Levkas; Limni; Midilli; Nakshe; On Iki Ada; Para; Rodos; Ṣakiz; Santurin Adasi; Semedirek; Sheytānlik; Shire; Sisām; Tashoz; Zaklise; [in Suppl.] Yedi Adalar
see also Djazā'ir-i Baḥr-i Safīd
regions Mora, Tesalya
towns Atīna; Aynabakhti; Baliabadra; Dede Aghač; Dimetoka; Karaferye; Kawāla; Kerbenesh; Kesriye; Kordos; Koron; Livadya; Menekshe; Modon; Nauplion; Navarino; Olendirek; Preveze; Selānīk; Siroz; Tirḥāla; Wodina; Yanya; Yeñi Shehir; [in Suppl.] Kuluz; Mezistre
see also [in Suppl.] Gümüldjine

GUILDS **Ṣinf**
Arabic Amīn; ʿArīf; Futuwwa.ii *and* iii; Ḥammāl; Ḥarfūsh; Khātam; Khayyāṭ; **Ṣinf**.1
see also Shadd; Shaykh; Sirwāl
Persian **Ṣinf**.2
see also Ustādh.2
Turkish Akhī; Akhī Baba; Anadolu.iii.6; Ḥarīr.ii; Ketkhudā.ii; **Ṣinf**.3; [in Suppl.] Ikhtiyāriyya; Inḥiṣār
see also Akhī Ewrān; ʿĀlima; Čā'ūsh; Kannās; Mawākib.4.4; Muhr.1

GUINEA Fūta Djallon; **Guinea**; Konakry
see also Sūdān (Bilād al-).2

GYPSIES **Čingāne**; **Lūlī**; Nūrī
see also al-Zuṭṭ

H

HADITH → LITERATURE.TRADITION-LITERATURE

HAGIOGRAPHY **Manāḳib**
see also Walī; *and* → SAINTHOOD
hagiographers Aflākī; ʿAṭā'ī; al-Bādisī.2; "Djamālī"; Ḥasan Dihlawī; Ibn ʿAskar; Ibn Maryam; al-Ifrānī; al-Kādirī al-Ḥasanī, Abū ʿAbd Allāh; al-Sharrāṭ; al-Sulamī, Abū ʿAbd al-Raḥmān
see also Aḥmad Bābā; Bākikhānli; al-Kattānī; Sinān Pasha, Khodja.1

HELL Aṣḥāb al-Ukhdūd; **Djahannam**; Saʿīr; Saḳar; Ṣirāṭ; Zaḳḳūm
see also al-Aʿrāf; Shayṭān.1; al-Waʿd wa 'l-Waʿīd; al-Zabāniyya

HEPHTHALITES Hayāṭila; Nīzak, Ṭarkhān

HERALDRY al-Asad; Rank

Heresy Bidʿa; Dahriyya; Dīn-i Ilāhī; Ghulāt; Ḳābiḍ; Kāfir; Khūbmesīḥīs; Mulḥid; Zindīḳ
see also al-Ṣalīb; Takfīr; Tanāsukh; *and* → Religion.dualism *and* pantheism
heretics Abū ʿĪsā al-Warrāḳ; Abu ʾl-Khaṭṭāb al-Asadī; Bashshār b. Burd; Bishr b. Ghiyāth al-Marīsī; Ibn Dirham; Ibn al-Rawandī; Mollā Ḳābiḍ; Muḥammad b. ʿAlī al-Shalmaghānī
see also Thābit Ḳuṭna; Wāliba b. al-Ḥubāb; *and* → Sects
refutations of Ibn al-Djawzī, ʿAbd al-Raḥmān; [in Suppl.] Afḍal al-Dīn Turka

History → Literature.historical
for the chronological history of dynastic events → Caliphate; Dynasties; *for the history of early Islam* → Caliphate.rightly-guided caliphs; Law.early religious law; Military.battles.622-632 *and* 633-660; Muḥammad, the Prophet; *for the history of regions, towns and other topographical sites, see the section Toponyms under individual countries*; *for the history of ideas* → *e.g.* Astronomy; Law; Linguistics; Mathematics; Philosophy; Theology

Hostelry **Funduḳ**; **Khān**; Manzil; [in Suppl.] Mihmān
see also Ribāṭ.1.b

Humour al-Djidd wa ʾl-Hazl; Nādira
see also Hidjāʾ.ii; Mudjūn
comic figures Djuḥā; Ibn al-Djaṣṣāṣ.II; Naṣr al-Dīn Khodja
humourists Ashʿab; al-Ghāḍirī; Ibn Abī ʿAtīḳ; Ibn Dāniyāl; Ḳaṣāb, Teodor; Sīfawayh al-Ḳāṣṣ; [in Suppl.] Abu ʾl-ʿAnbas al-Ṣaymarī

Hungary Budīn; Eğri; Esztergom; Istolnī (Istōnī) Belghrād; **Madjar**; Mohács; Pécs; Pest; Sigetwār; Szeged; Székesfehérvár; [in Suppl.] Köszeg
see also Bashdjirt; Kanizsa; Maḥmūd Tardjumān; Mezőkeresztes; Muslimūn.1.B.1; Ofen

Hunting **Ṣayd**
see also Kurds.iv.C.5; Samak; Shikārī; Zaghardji̊ Bashi̊; [in Suppl.] Segbān; *and* → Animals; Falconry
poetry **Ṭardiyya**
see also Radjaz
treatises on Kushādjim; [in Suppl.] Ibn Manglī
see also al-Shamardal
wild animals Fahd; Khinzīr; Mahāt; Naʿām; Namir and Nimr; Salūḳī; [in Suppl.] Ḍabuʿ

Hydrology Biʾr; Ḳanāt; Māʾ; Maʾṣir; Ṭāḥūn
see also Filāḥa; Ḳanṭara.5 *and* 6; Madjrīṭ; al-Mīzān.2; Sāʿa.1; *and* → Architecture.monuments.dams; Geography.waters

I

Idolatry Shirk; **Wathaniyya**
idols Nuṣub; **Ṣanam**; Ṭāghūt.1; al-Uḳayṣir
see also Shaman; Zūn; *and* → Pre-Islam.in arabian peninsula

Illness Madjnūn; Malāryā; Ramad; Saraṭān.7; [in Suppl.] Djudhām
see also Kalb; Ḳuṭrub; Summ; *and* → Plague
treatises on Ḥayātī-zāde; Ibn Buṭlān; Ibn Djazla

see also [in Suppl.] ʿUḳalāʾ al-Madjānīn; *and* → MEDICINE

INDIA **Hind**; Hindī
see also ʿĀda.iii; Balharā; Imām-bārā; Maṭbaʿa.4; Sikkat al-Ḥadīd.1; *and* → LITERATURE; MILITARY; MUSIC
administration Baladiyya.5; Ḍarība.6; Dīwān.v; Djizya.iii; Ḥisba.iv; Kātib.iii; Kharādj.IV; Pargana; Safīr.3; Taḥṣīl; Zamīndār; [in Suppl.] Taʿalluḳ
see also Kitābāt.10; Māʾ.9; Waḳf.VI; *and* → MILITARY.INDO-MUSLIM
during British rule [in Suppl.] Mufaṣṣal
agriculture Filāḥa.v
architecture → ARCHITECTURE.REGIONS
belles-lettres → LITERATURE.IN OTHER LANGUAGES *and* POETRY.INDO-PERSIAN
cuisine Maṭbakh.4
dynasties ʿĀdil-Shāhs; Bahmanīs; Barīd Shāhīs; Dihlī Sultanate; Farūḳids; Ghaznavids; Ghūrids; Hindū-Shāhīs; ʿImād Shāhī; Khaldjīs; Ḳuṭb Shāhīs; Lodīs; Mughals; Niẓām Shāhīs; Sayyids; Sharḳīs; Tughluḳids
see also Awadh; Dār al-Ḍarb; Rānā Sāngā; Tīpū Sulṭān; Vidjayanagara; *and* → DYNASTIES.AFGHANISTAN AND INDIA
education Dār al-ʿUlūm.c *and* d; Djāmiʿa; Madjmaʿ ʿIlmī.iv; Madrasa.II; Nadwat al-ʿUlamāʾ; [in Suppl.] Farangī Maḥall; Jamia Millia Islamia
see also Aḥmad Khān; Deoband; Maḥmūdābād Family; [in Suppl.] Muḥammad ʿAbd Allāh
historians of Ghulām Ḥusayn Khān Ṭabāṭabāʾī; Niẓām al-Dīn Aḥmad b. al-Harawī; Sudjān Rāy Bhandārī
see also Djaʿfar Sharīf; al-Maʿbarī; Mīr Muḥammad Maʿṣūm; *and* → DYNASTIES.AFGHANISTAN AND INDIA; LITERATURE.HISTORICAL.INDO-PERSIAN
languages Gudjarātī; Hindī; Hindustānī.i *and* ii; Lahndā; Marāṭhī; Pandjābī.1; Sind.3.a; Urdū.1; [in Suppl.] Rādjasthān.3
see also Kitābāt.10; *and* → LANGUAGES.INDO-IRANIAN
literature → LITERATURE
modern period Djamʿiyya.v; Hindustānī.iii; Ḥizb.vi; Indian National Congress; Iṣlāḥ.iv; Kashmīr.ii; Ḳawmiyya.vi; Khāksār; Khilāfa; Madjlis.4.C; al-Marʾa.5; Nikāḥ.II.3; [in Suppl.] Djarīda.vii; Maḥkama.5
see also Mahsūd; Mappila; Tablīghī Djamāʿat; [in Suppl.] Faḳīr of Ipi; Khān, ʿAbd al-Ghaffār; *and* → INDIA.EDUCATION
resistance against the British Yāghistān
Indian Mutiny Aẓim Allāh Khān; Bakht Khān; Imdād Allāh; Kānpur
Khilāfat movement **Khilāfa**; Muḥammad ʿAlī; Mushīr Ḥusayn Ḳidwāʾī; Shawkat ʿAlī; [in Suppl.] ʿAbd al-Bārī; Ḥasrat Mohānī
see also Amīr ʿAlī; [in Suppl.] Khān, ʿAbd al-Ghaffār
statesmen Nawwāb Sayyid Ṣiddīḳ Ḥasan Khān; Sālār Djang; [in Suppl.] Āzād, Abu ʾl-Kalām
see also Maḥmūdābād Family
mysticism → MYSTICISM.MYSTICS; SAINTHOOD.SAINTS
physical geography
waters Djamnā; Gangā
see also Nahr.2
population Bhaṭṭi; Bohorās; Dāwūdpōtrās; Djāṭ; Gakkhaŕ; Gandāpur; Güdjar; Ḥabshī; Hind.ii; Khaṭak; Khokars; Lambadis; Mappila; Mēd; Memon; Mēʾō; Naitias; Pārsīs; Rādjpūts; Rohillas; Shikārī; Sidi; [in Suppl.] Demography.VII
see also Khōdja; Marāṭhās; al-Zuṭṭ

Tamils Ceylon; Labbai; Marakkayar; Rawther

religion Ahl-i Ḥadīth; Barāhima; Djayn; Hindū; Ibāḥatiya; Mahdawīs; Pandj Pīr; Sikhs; Tablīghī Djamāʿat; [in Suppl.] Pīrpanthī

see also Khwādja Khiḍr; Pārsīs; Taʿziya; Yūsuf Kāndhalawī Dihlawī; Zakariyyā Kāndhalawī Sahāranpūrī; [in Suppl.] Andjuman-i Khuddām-i Kaʿba; *and* → MYSTICISM; SAINTHOOD; THEOLOGY

reform Aḥmad Brēlwī; al-Dihlawī, Shāh Walī Allāh; Ismāʿīl Shahīd; Karāmat ʿAlī; Nānak; Tītū Mīr

toponyms

ancient Arūr; Čāmpānēr; Čhat; Djāba; Djandjīra; Fatḥpūr-sikrī; Hampī; Ḥusaynābād; Kūlam; Lakhnawtī; al-Manṣūra; Mēwāṙ; Nandurbār; Nārnawl; Pānduʾā; Shikārpūr.2; Sidhpūr; Sindābūr; Sindān; Sūmanāt; Telingāna; Tonk; Tribenī; Wayhind

present-day

and → ASIA.SOUTH

regions Assam; Bihār; Bombay State; Dakhan; Djaypur; Doʾāb; Gudjarāt; Hariyānā; Ḥaydarābād.b; Kāmrūp; Kashmīr; Khāndēsh; Ḳūhistān.4; Ladākh; Lūdhiāna; Maʿbar; Mahisur; Malabar; Mēwāt; Muẓaffarpur; Nāgpur; Palamāw; Pālanpur; Pandjāb; Rādhanpūr; Rāmpur; Rohilkhand; Sundarban; Tirhut; Urīsā; [in Suppl.] Djammū; Konkan; Rādjasthān; Rohtak

see also Alwār; Banganapalle; Bāonī; Berār; Djōdhpur; Hunza and Nagir; Udaypūr; [in Suppl.] Sarkār.2

towns Adjmēr; Āgra; Aḥmadābād; Aḥmadnagar; Aligarh; Allāhābād; Ambāla; Amritsar; Anhalwāra; Arcot; Awadh; Awrangābād; Awrangābād Sayyid; Aʿẓamgarh; Badāʾūn; Bālā-ghāt; Bāndā; Bānkīpūr; Banūr; Bareilly; Barōda; Benares; Bharatpūr; Bharoč; Bhattinda; Bhōpāl; Bīdar; Bīdjāpūr; Bidjnawr; Bilgrām; Bombay City; Bulandshahr; Burhānpūr; Buxar; Calcutta; Čandērī; Dawlatābād; Deoband; Dhār; Dhārwār; Dihlī; Diū; Djālor; Djawnpur; Djūnāgaṙh; Djunnar; Dwārkā; Farīdkōṫ; Farrukhābād; Fayḍābād; Fīrūzpūr; Gulbargā; Gwāliyār; Hānsī; Ḥaydarābād.a; Ḥiṣār Fīrūza; Īdar; Islāmābād; Iṫāwā; Kalpī; Kalyāni; Kanawdj; Kāṅgṙā; Kannanūr; Kānpur; Karnāl; Karnāṫak; Katahr; Khambāyat; Khayrābād; Khuldābād; Kōṙā; Koyl; Lakhnaw; Lalitpur; Lūdhiāna; Madras; Mahīm; Māhīm; Māhūr; Mālda; Mālwā; Māndū; Manēr; Mangrōl; Mathurā; Mīraṫh; Mīrzāpur; Multān; Mungīr; Murādābad; Murshidābād; Muẓaffarpur; Nadjībābād; Nagar; Nāgawr; Nāgpur; Naldrug; Nānděṙ; Pānīpat; Parendā; Pāṫan; Paṫnā; Pūna; Rādjmahāl; Rāyčūr; Sahāranpūr; Sahsarām; Sārangpur; Sardhanā; Sarkhēdj; Shakarkhelda; Shikārpūr.3; Shōlāpur; Sirhind; Srīnagar; Śrīangapaṫṫanam; Sūrat; Tālīkōṫā; Thālnēr; Thānā; Ṫhānesar; Ṫhaṫṫā; Udgīr; Udjdjayn; Warangal; [in Suppl.] Amrōhā; Eličpur; Ghāzīpur; Irič; Kalikat; Madura; Rohtak

INDONESIA Baladiyya.7; Dustūr.xi; Ḥizb.vii; Ḥukūma.vi; **Indonesia**; Maḥkama.6; Malays; Masjumi; [in Suppl.] Ḍarība.7; Hoesein Djajadiningrat; Sukarno

see also ʿĀda.iv; Nikāḥ.II.4; Pasisir; Prang Sabīl; [in Suppl.] al-Marʾa.6

architecture → ARCHITECTURE.REGIONS

education Djāmiʿa; Pesantren

literature Indonesia.vi; Ḳiṣṣa.6; Miʿrādj.4; Shāʿir.7; Taʾrīkh.II.7; [in Suppl.] Shiʿr.5

see also Kitābāt.8; Malays; *and* → LITERATURE.POETRY.MYSTICAL

Muslim movements Padri; Sarekat Islam

see also Sulawesi

mysticism → MYSTICISM.MYSTICS

population Malays; Minangkabau; [in Suppl.] Demography.VIII
    see also Sayābidja
religion → MYSTICISM.MYSTICS; SAINTHOOD.SAINTS
    festivals Kandūrī; Lĕbaran
        see also [in Suppl.] Puasa
    recitation competitions [in Suppl.] Musābaḵa
toponyms Ambon; Atjèh; Banda Islands; Bandjarmasin; Bangka; Batjan; Billiton; Borneo
    (*and* [in Suppl.]); Djakarta; Kubu; Kutai; Lombok; Madura; Makassar; Palembang; Pasè;
    Pasir; Pontianak; Riau; Sambas; Sulawesi (*and* Celebes); Sumatra; Sunda Islands;
    Surakarta; Ternate; Tidore; [in Suppl.] Kalimantan; Mataram; Yogyakarta
    see also Zābadj

INDUSTRY Ḥarīr; Kattān; Ḵuṭn; Lubūd; Milḥ
    see also Bursa; al-Iskandariyya; Ḵayṣariyya; Zonguldak

INHERITANCE ʿĀda.iii; Akdariyya; ʿAwl; **Farāʾiḍ**; **Mīrāth**; al-Sahm.2; Waṣiyya; Yatīm.2
    see also Ḳassām; Ḵhāl; Maḵhredj; Muḵhallefāt; Tanāsuḵh
works on al-Sadjāwandī, Sirādj al-Dīn; al-Tilimsānī.2; al-ʿUkbarī

INVENTIONS ʿAbbās b. Firnās; Ibn Mādjid; Mūsā (Banū); Sāʿa.1

IRAN al-Furs; **Iran**; Kurds; Lur
    see also al-ʿArab.iii; Ḥarb.v; Kitābāt.9; Libās.iii; Zūrḵhāna; *and* → DYNASTIES.PERSIA;
    SHIITES; ZOROASTRIANS
administration Ḍarība.5; Diplomatic.iii; Dīwān.iv; Ghulām.ii; Imtiyāzāt.iii; Kātib.ii; Ḵhāliṣa;
    Ḵharādj.II; Maḥkama.3; Parwānači; [in Suppl.] Shāhbandar
    see also Kalāntar; Waḵf.III; *and* → IRAN.MODERN PERIOD
agriculture Filāḥa.iii
architecture → ARCHITECTURE.REGIONS
art → ART.REGIONAL AND PERIOD
before Islam Anūsharwān; Ardashīr; Bahrām; Dārā; Dārābdjird; Dihḵan; Djamshīd; Farīdūn;
    al-Ḥaḍr; Hayāṭila; Hurmuz; al-Hurmuzān; Ḳārinids; Kayānids; Kay Kāʾūs; Kay Ḵhusraw;
    Ḵhurshīd; Kisrā; Marzpān; Mazdak; Mulūk al-Ṭawāʾif.1; Parwīz, Ḵhusraw (II);
    Pīshdādids; Sāsānids; Shāpūr; Ṭahmūrath; Yazdadjird III; [in Suppl.] Farruḵhān
    see also Afrāsiyāb; Buzurgmihr; Hamadhān; Iḵhshīd; Iran.iv; Ispahbadh; Ḳaṣr-i Shīrīn;
    Ḳūmis; al-Madāʾin; al-Rayy; Rustam b. Farruḵh Hurmuzd; Sarpul-i Dhuhāb; Tansar;
    [in Suppl.] Dabīr; *and* → ZOROASTRIANS
cuisine [in Suppl.] Maṭbaḵh.3
dynasties → DYNASTIES.PERSIA
historians of Ḥamza al-Iṣfahānī; Ibn Manda; al-Māfarrūḵhī; al-Rāfiʿī; Ẓahīr al-Dīn Marʿashī;
    [in Suppl.] al-Ḳummī
    and → DYNASTIES.PERSIA
language → LANGUAGES.INDO-IRANIAN
literature → LITERATURE
modern period Baladiyya.4; Djāmiʿa; Djamʿiyya.iii; Djarīda.ii; Dustūr.iv; Ḥizb.iii; Ḥukūma.ii;
    Iran.v.b; Iṣlāḥ.ii; Ḳawmiyya.iii; Maʿārif.3; Madjlis.4.A.iii; Madjmaʿ ʿIlmī.ii; al-Marʾa.3;
    Shuyūʿiyya.2; Taḵrīb; [in Suppl.] Demography.III; Niẓām ʿAskarī.2; Ṣiḥāfa.4
    see also Ḵhazʿal Ḵhān; Madjlis al-Shūrā; Maḥkama.3; [in Suppl.] Amīr Niẓām; *and* →
    DYNASTIES.PERSIA.ḲĀDJĀRS *and* PAHLAWĪS; SHIITES
    activists Fidāʾiyyān-i Islām; Kāshānī, Āyatullāh; Ḵhʷānsārī, Sayyid Muḥammad; Ḵhiyābānī,
    Shayḵh Muḥammad; Ḵhurāsānī; Kūčak Ḵhān Djangalī; Lāhūtī; Maḥallātī; Ṣamṣām

al-Salṭana; Ṭālaḳānī; [in Suppl.] Āḳā Nadjafī; Ḥaydar Khān ʿAmū Ughlī; ʿIshḳī
see also Djangalī; Kurds.iii. C; Yazdī; Zayn al-ʿĀbidīn Marāghaʾī; [in Suppl.] Āzādī; Farāmūsh-khāna

influential persons Kasrawī Tabrīzī; Malkom Khān; Muṭahharī; Nāʾīnī; Nūrī, Shaykh Faḍl Allāh; Sharīʿatī, ʿAlī; Ṭihrānī; [in Suppl.] Āḳā Khān Kirmānī; Khumaynī

statesmen Muṣaddiḳ; Ṭabāṭabāʾī; Taḳīzāda; Wuthūḳ al-Dawla; [in Suppl.] Amīr Kabīr

physical geography

deserts Biyābānak

mountains Ala Dagh; Alburz; Alwand Kūh; Bīsutūn; Damāwand; Hamrīn; Hawrāmān; Zagros
see also Sarḥadd

waters Atrek; Bakhtigān, Hāmūn; Karkha; Kārūn; Mānd; Ruknābād; Safīd Rūd; Shāh Rūd.1; Shāpūr; Shaṭṭ al-ʿArab; Urmiya.1; Zāyanda-Rūd; Zirih
see also Baḥr Fāris

population Bakhtiyārī; Bāzūkiyyūn; Bilbās; Djāf; Eymir.3; Göklän; Gūrān; (Banū) Kaʿb; Ḳarā Gözlu; Ḳāshḳāy; Kurds; Lām; Lur; Shabānkāra; Shāhsewan; Shakāk; Shaḳāḳī; Sindjābī; Türkmen.3
see also Daylam; Dulafids; Eymir.2; Fīrūzānids; Iran.ii; Ḳufṣ; Shūlistān; Tat.1; [in Suppl.] Demography.III

religion Iran.vi; Ṣafawids.IV
and → Mysticism.mystics; Sainthood.saints; Shiites

toponyms

ancient Abarshahr; Ardalān; Arradjān; ʿAskar Mukram; Bādj; Bākusāyā; Bayhaḳ; Dārābdjird; Daskara; Dawraḳ; Dihistān; Dīnawar; al-Djazīra; Djibāl; Djīruft; Gurgān; Ḥafrak; Ḥulwān; Īdhadj; Iṣṭakhr; (al-)Karadj; Khargird.2; Ḳūmis; Ḳurḳūb; Mihragān.iv.1; Narmāshīr; Nasā; Nawbandadjān; al-Rayy; Rūdhbār.2; Rūdhrāwar; Ṣaymara; Shāpūr; Shūlistān; al-Sīradjān; Sīrāf; Sīsar; Suhraward; al-Sūs; Ṭālaḳān.2; Ṭārum; Tawwadj; Tūn; Ṭurshīz; Ṭūs; Tūsān; Urm; Ustuwā; Zarang; [in Suppl.] Arghiyān; Ghubayrā

present-day

islands al-Fārisiyya; Ṭunb

provinces Ādharbaydjān; Balūčistān; Fārs; Gīlān; Hamadhān; Iṣfahān; Khurāsān; Khūzistān; Kirmān; Kirmānshāh; Kurdistān; Māzandarān; Yazd
see also Astarābādh.2; Rūyān; Ṭabaristān

regions Bākharz; Hawrāmān; Ḳūhistān.1; Makrān; Sarḥadd; Sīstān; [in Suppl.] Bashkard
see also Gulistān

towns and districts Ābādah; Abarḳūh; ʿAbbādān; ʿAbbāsābād; Abhar; al-Ahwāz; Āmul.1; Ardakān; Ardistān; Asadābādh; Ashraf; Astarābādh.1; Āwa; Bam; Bampūr; Bandar ʿAbbās; Bandar Pahlawī; Bārfurūsh; Barūdjird; Barzand; Bīrdjand; Bisṭām; Būshahr; Dāmghān; Dizfūl; Djannāba; Djuwayn.1 *and* 2; Faraḥābād; Faryāb; Fasā; Fīrūzābād; Fūman; Gulpāyagān; Gunbadh-i Ḳābūs; Hurmuz; Iṣfahān; Isfarāyīn; Kāshān; Ḳaṣr-i Shīrīn; Kāzarūn; Ḳazwīn; Khʷāf; Khalkhāl; Khʷār; Khārag; Khargird.1; Khōī; Khurramābād; Khurramshahr; Kinkiwar; Ḳishm; Ḳūčān; Ḳūhistān.2; Ḳuhrūd; Ḳum; Lāhīdjān; Lār (2x); Linga; Luristān; Mahābād; Mākū; Marāgha; Marand; Mashhad; Miyāna; Narāḳ; Naṭanz; Nayrīz; Nihāwand; Nīshāpūr; Rafsandjān; Rām-hurmuz; Rasht; Rūdhbār.3; Sabzawār.1; Ṣaḥna; Ṣāʾīn Ḳalʿa; Saḳḳiz; Salmās; Sanandadj; Sarakhs; Sārī; Sarpul-i Dhuhāb; Sarwistān; Sāwa; Shāh Rūd.3; Shīrāz; Shushtar; Simnān; al-Sīradjān; Ṣōmāy; Suldūz; Sulṭānābād; Sulṭāniyya; Sunḳur; al-Sūs; Ṭabas; Tabrīz; Ṭārum; Tihrān; Turbat-i [Shaykh-i] Djām; Türkmen Čay (ı̊); Urmiya.2; Ushnū; Warāmīn;

Yazd; Zāhidān; Zandjān; Zāwa; Zawāra; Zawzan; [in Suppl.] Bashkard; Biyār; Djārdjarm; Djulfa.II; Hawsam; Ḳāʾin; Khumayn
see also Shahr; Shahristān; Tūn; *and* → Kurds.toponyms

Iraq **ʿIrāḳ**; Kurds
see also al-ʿArabiyya; Djalīlī; Lakhmids; Sawād; Shahāridja; [in Suppl.] Sūḳ.5; *and* → Caliphate.ʿAbbāsids; Dynasties.egypt and the fertile crescent

architecture → Architecture.regions

before Islam → Pre-Islam.in fertile crescent

historians of al-Azdī; Baḥshal; Ibn Abī Ṭāhir Ṭayfūr; Ibn al-Bannāʾ; Ibn al-Dubaythī; al-Khaṭīb al-Baghdādī; ʿUbayd Allāh b. Aḥmad b. Abī Ṭāhir
see also Ibn al-Nadjdjār; [in Suppl.] Taʾrīkh.II.1.(c); *and* → Caliphate.ʿAbbāsids; Dynasties.egypt and the fertile crescent

modern period Djarīda.i.A; Djāmiʿa; Dustūr.vi; Ḥizb.i; Ḥukūma.iii; Kurds.iii.C; Madjlis.4.A.iv; Madjmaʿ ʿIlmī.i.2.c; Maḥkama.4.iv; Mandates; Ṣiḥāfa.1.(vii); [in Suppl.] Niẓām ʿAskarī.1.(c)
see also Bābān; Kūt al-ʿAmāra; al-Mawṣil.2

belletrists

poets al-Akhras; al-Fārūḳī; al-Kāẓimī, ʿAbd al-Muḥsin; Maʿrūf al-Ruṣāfī; Shāʾūl; al-Zahāwī, Djamīl Ṣidḳī

writers of prose Shāʾūl

monarchy Fayṣal I; Fayṣal II; Ghāzī
see also Hāshimids

opposition leaders Ḳāsim ʿAbd al-Karīm; Muṣṭafā Barzānī

politicians al-Shahrastānī, Sayyid Muḥammad; Shīnā

prime ministers Nūrī al-Saʿīd; Rashīd ʿAlī al-Gaylānī

physical geography

mountains Sindjār

waters Abu ʾl-Khaṣīb; al-ʿAḍaym; Didjla; Diyālā; al-Furāt; Khābūr; al-Khāzir; Shaṭṭ al-ʿArab; al-Zāb

population Bādjalān; Bilbās; Djubūr; Dulaym; Lām; al-Manāṣir; Türkmen.3
see also Shammar; [in Suppl.] Demography.III; *and* → Kurds

toponyms

ancient Abarḳubādh; ʿAḳarḳūf; ʿAlth; al-Anbār; Bābil; Badjimzā; Bādjisrā; Bādūrayā; Bākhamrā; Baradān; Barāthā; Bawāzīdj; Bihḳubādh; Birs; Dayr ʿAbd al-Raḥmān; Dayr al-ʿĀḳūl; Dayr al-Aʿwar; Dayr al-Djamādjim; Diyār Rabīʿa; Djabbul; al-Djazīra; Fallūdja; Ḥadītha.I; Ḥarbāʾ; Ḥarūrāʾ; Ḥawīza; al-Ḥīra; al-Ḳādisiyya; Kalwādhā; Kaskar; Ḳaṣr ibn Hubayra; Khāniḳīn; al-Khawarnaḳ; Kūthā; Ḳuṭrabbul; al-Madāʾin; Niffar; Nimrūd; Nīnawā; al-Nukhayla; al-Ruṣāfa.1; Sāmarrāʾ; al-Ṭaff; al-Ubulla; al-Warkāʾ; Wāsiṭ; [in Suppl.] ʿUkbarā
see also al-Karkh; Nuṣratābād; Senkere

present-day

regions Bahdīnān; al-Baṭīḥa; Maysān
see also Lālish

towns Altīn Köprü; ʿAmādiya; ʿAmāra; ʿĀna; ʿAyn al-Tamr; Badra; Baghdād; Baʿḳūba; Balāwāt; Bārzān; al-Baṣra; Daḳūḳāʾ; Daltāwa; Dīwāniyya; al-Fallūdja; Ḥadītha.II; al-Ḥilla; Hīt; Irbil; Karbalāʾ; Kāẓimayn; Kirkūk; al-Kūfa; Kūt al-ʿAmāra; Maʿalthāyā; al-Mawṣil; al-Nadjaf; al-Nāṣiriyya; Nuṣratābād; Rawāndiz; Sāmarrāʾ; al-Samāwa.2; Senkere; Shahrazūr; Sindjār; Sūḳ al-Shuyūkh; Sulaymāniyya; Takrīt; Zākhū; [in Suppl.] Athūr
see also Djalūlāʾ; *and* → Kurds.toponyms

IRRIGATION Band; Ḳanāt; Māʾ; Nāʿūra
see also Filāḥa; Kārūn; al-Nahrawān; *and* → RIVERS
water **Māʾ**
see also Ḥawḍ; Sabīl.2; Saḳḳāʾ; *and* → ARCHITECTURE.MONUMENTS; HYDROLOGY; NAVIGATION; OCEANS AND SEAS; RIVERS

ISLAM ʿAḳīda; Dīn; Djamāʿa; ʿIbādāt; **Islām**; Masdjid; Muḥammad; Murtadd; Muslim; Rukn.1; Shīʿa; Taḳiyya; Tawḥīd; Umma
see also Iṣlāḥ; Iʿtikāf; Nubuwwa; Rahbāniyya; Shirk; Tawakkul; *and* → ABLUTION; ALMS; FASTING; PILGRIMAGE; PRAYER; QURʾAN; THEOLOGY
conversion to Islām.ii
early converts to → MUHAMMAD, THE PROPHET.COMPANIONS OF
European converts Pickthall
five pillars of Islam Ḥadjdj; Ṣalāt; Ṣawm; Shahāda; Zakāt
see also ʿIbādāt; al-Ḳurṭubī, Yaḥyā; Rukn.1; ʿUmra; [in Suppl.] Ramy al-Djimār
formulas Allāhumma; Basmala; Ḥamdala; In Shāʾ Allāh; Māshāʾ Allāh; Salām; Subḥān; Taʿawwudh; Tahlīl.2; Takbīr; Talbiya; Tashahhud; Taṣliya
see also Tashrīḳ; [in Suppl.] Abbreviations
popular beliefs ʿAyn; Dīw; Djinn; Ghūl; Muḥammad.2; Zār; [in Suppl.] ʿĀʾisha Ḳandīsha; Ḥinn
see also ʿAnḳāʾ; Shafāʿa.2; *and* → LAW.CUSTOMARY LAW
preaching Ḳāṣṣ; Wāʿiẓ
proselytism Daʿwa; Tablīghī Djamāʿat
Western studies of Mawsūʿa.4

ISRAEL → PALESTINE/ISRAEL

ITALY **Iṭaliya**; Ḳawṣara; Ḳillawriya; Rūmiya; Sardāniya; Ṣiḳilliya; Wenedik
and → SICILY

IVORY COAST **Côte d'Ivoire**; Kong

J

JACOBITES → CHRISTIANITY.DENOMINATIONS

JEWELRY [in Suppl.] **Djawhar**
see also Khātam
pearls and precious stones ʿAḳīḳ; al-Durr; Kūh-i Nūr; Luʾluʾ; Mardjān; Yāḳūt; Zumurrud
see also Dhahab; Fiḍḍa; Ḥadjar; Kahrubā; Maʿdin.2.3

JORDAN Dustūr.x; Ḥukūma.iii; Madjlis.4.A.vii; Maḥkama.4.vi; Mandates; Ṣiḥāfa.1.(vi); **al-Urdunn**.2
see also Taḳī al-Dīn al-Nabhānī
physical geography
mountains al-Djibāl; al-Ṭūr.5
waters al-Urdunn.1; Yarmūk.1
population al-Ḥuwayṭāt; al-Manāṣir
see also [in Suppl.] Demography.III
statesmen ʿAbd Allāh b. al-Ḥusayn; Waṣfī al-Tall

see also Hāshimids

toponyms

ancient Adhrūḥ; Ayla; al-Balḳāʾ; Djarash; al-Djarbāʾ; al-Djibāl; Faḥl; al-Ḥumayma; al-Muwaḳḳar; Umm al-Raṣāṣ; Umm al-Walīd

present-day ʿAdjlūn; al-ʿAḳaba; ʿAmmān; Bayt Rās; al-Ghawr.1; Irbid.I; Maʿān; al-Salṭ; al-Shawbak; al-Zarḳāʾ; [in Suppl.] Mafraḳ

JUDAISM Ahl al-Kitāb; Banū Isrāʾīl; Tawrāt; Yahūd

see also Filasṭīn; Hūd; Nasīʾ; al-Sāmira; *and* → BIBLE; PALESTINE/ISRAEL

communities al-Andalus.iv; al-Fāsiyyūn; Iran.ii *and* vi; Iṣfahān.1; al-Iskandariyya; Istanbul.vii.b; al-Ḳuds; Lār.2; Mallāḥ; Marrākush; Ṣufrūy

influences in Islam ʿĀshūrāʾ.I

see also Ḳibla; Muḥammad.i.I.C.2

Jewish personages in Muslim world ʿAbd Allāh b. Salām; Abū ʿĪsā al-Iṣfahānī; Abū Naḍḍāra; Dhū Nuwās; Hāmōn; Ḥasdāy b. Shaprūṭ; Ibn Abi ʾl-Bayān; Ibn Djāmiʿ; Ibn Djanāḥ; Ibn Gabirol; Ibn Kammūna; Ibn Maymūn; Ibn Yaʿīsh; Ibrāhīm b. Yaʿḳūb; Isḥāḳ b. Sulaymān al-Isrāʾīlī; Kaʿb b. al-Ashraf; al-Kōhēn al-ʿAṭṭār; Māsardjawayh; Māshāʾ Allāh; Mūsā b. ʿAzra; al-Rādhāniyya; Saʿadyā Ben Yōsēf; Saʿd al-Dawla; al-Samawʾal b. ʿĀdiyā; Shabbatay Ṣebī; Shāʾūl; Shīnā; Yaʿḳūb Pasha; [in Suppl.] Camondo; Ibn Biklārish; Nissīm b. Yaʿḳūb, Ibn Shāhīn

see also Abu ʾl-Barakāt; Kaʿb al-Aḥbār; Ḳaynuḳāʿ; Ḳurayẓa; ʿUzayr; [in Suppl.] Samawʾal b. Yaḥyā al-Maghribī, Abū Naṣr

Jewish sects ʿĀnāniyya; al-ʿĪsāwiyya; Karaites

Judaeo-Christian sects Ṣābiʾa.1

see also Naṣārā

Judaeo-Muslim sects Shabbatay Ṣebī

Jewish-Muslim relations

persecution Dhimma; Djizya; Ghiyār; al-Ḥākim bi-Amr Allāh; al-Maghīlī; Shiʿār.4; Zunnār

polemics Abū Isḥāḳ al-Ilbīrī; Ibn Ḥazm, Abū Muḥammad; al-Suʿūdī, Abu ʾl-Faḍl; ʿUzayr; [in Suppl.] Samawʾal b. Yaḥyā al-Maghribī, Abū Naṣr

see also Ahl al-Kitāb; Taḥrīf; Yahūd

with Muḥammad Fadak; Ḳaynuḳāʿ; Khaybar; Ḳurayẓa; al-Madīna.i.1; Naḍīr

see also Muḥammad.1.I.C

language and literature Judaeo-Arabic; Judaeo-Berber; Judaeo-Persian; Ḳiṣṣa.8; Risāla.1.VII

see also Geniza; Mukhtaṣar; Musammaṭ; Muwashshaḥ; Yūsuf and Zulaykhā.1; *and* → LANGUAGES.AFRO-ASIATIC.HEBREW; LEXICOGRAPHY.LEXICOGRAPHERS; LITERATURE.IN OTHER LANGUAGES

K

KENYA Gede; **Kenya**; Kilifi; Lamu; Malindi; Manda; Mazrūʿī; Mombasa; Pate; Siu

see also Nabhān; Swahili; [in Suppl.] Djarīda.viii; *and* → AFRICA.EAST AFRICA

Swahili literature Ḳiṣṣa.7; Madīḥ.5; Marthiya.5; Mathal.5; [in Suppl.] Ḥamāsa.vi; Nadira.2

see also Miʿrādj.3

poets Shaaban Robert

song Siti Binti Saad

KORAN → QURʾAN

KURDS **Kurds**

see also Kitāb al-Djilwa; *and* → IRAN; IRAQ; TURKEY
for Kurdish press in Turkey, see [in Suppl.] Ṣiḥāfa.5
dynasties ʿAnnāzids; Bābān; Faḍlawayh; Ḥasanwayh; Marwānids; Rawwādids; Shaddādids
see also Kurds.iii.B
Kurdish national movement Badrkhānī; Ḳāḍī Muḥammad; Kurds.iii.C; Muṣṭafā Barzānī
see also Bārzān; Mahābād
languages Kurds.v; Ṭūr ʿAbdīn.4.iii
sects Ṣārliyya; Shabak; Yazīdī
toponyms Ardalān; Bahdīnān; Barādūst; Bārzān; Djawānrūd; Hakkārī.2; Rawāndiz; Saḳḳiz; Sanandadj; Sāwdj-Bulāḳ; Shahrazūr; Shamdīnān; Ṣōmāy; Sulaymāniyya; Zākhū
see also Kirkūk; Kurds.ii; Orāmār; Shabānkāra; Sīsar
tribes Djāf; Hakkārī.1; Hamawand; Kurds.iii.B *and* iv.A.2; Lak.1; Shabānkāra; Shakāk; Shaḳāḳī; Sindjābī
see also Zāzā

KUWAIT Djarīda.i.A; Dustūr.xvi; **al-Kuwayt**; Madjlis.4.A.ix; Maḥkama.4.ix; Ṣabāḥ, Āl; Ṣiḥāfa.1.(ix)
see also (Djazīrat) al-ʿArab; al-ʿArabiyya; Djāmiʿa; ʿUtūb
toponyms al-Dibdiba; [in Suppl.] Aḥmadī
see also Ḳarya al-ʿUlyā

L

LAMENTATION Bakkāʾ; **Niyāḥa**; Rawḍa-khʷānī

LAND → PROPERTY; TAXATION
in the sense of agriculture, see Filāḥa; *in the sense of cooperative ownership, see* Taʿāwun; *in the sense of surveying, see* Misāḥa; Rawk

LANGUAGES **Lugha**
and → LINGUISTICS; WRITING.SCRIPTS
Afro-Asiatic Ḥām; Sām.2
see also Karshūnī; Maʿlūlā.2; Sullam
Arabic **Arabiyya**.A
see also Ibn Makkī; Ḳarwasha; Khaṭṭ; Madjmaʿ ʿIlmī.i; al-Sīm; Taʿrīb; [in Suppl.] Ḥaḍramawt.iii; *and* → ALPHABET
Arabic dialects Algeria.v; Aljamía; al-Andalus.x; Arabiyya.A.iii; ʿIrāḳ.iv; Judaeo-Arabic.i *and* ii; Lībiya.2; al-Maghrib.VII; Mahrī; Malta.2; Mūrītāniyā.6; al-Ṣaʿīd.2; al-Shām.3; Shāwiya.3; Shuwa; Siʿird; Sūdān.2; Sūdān (Bilād al-).3; Tunisia.IV; Ṭūr ʿAbdīn.4.i; ʿUmān.4; al-Yaman.5
see also Ibn al-Birr; Takrīt; al-Ṭanṭāwī; ʿUtūb; Zawdj.2 *and* [in Suppl.] 3; *and* → LITERATURE.POETRY.VERNACULAR
Christian Arabic Karshūnī; Shaykhū, Luwīs
see also ʿArabiyya.A.ii.1; Ṭūr ʿAbdīn.4
Judaeo-Arabic → JUDAISM.LANGUAGE AND LITERATURE; LITERATURE.IN OTHER LANGUAGES
Bantu Swahili; Yao
Berber **Berbers**.V; Judaeo-Berber; Mūrītāniyā.6; Sīwa.2; Taḳbaylit; Tamazight; Tarifiyt; Tashelḥīt; Ṭawāriḳ.2
see also Mzāb; Tifinagh

Berber words in Arabic Āfrāg; Agadir; Āgdāl; Aménokal; Amg̲h̲ar; Argan; Ayt; Imẓad
see also Ḳallala; Rīf.I.2(a); Tīṭ

Chadic Hausa.ii
see also Wadāī.2

Cushitic Kūs̲h̲; Somali.5

Ethiopian-Semitic Eritrea.iv; Ḥabas̲h̲.iv

Hebrew Ibn D̲j̲anāḥ

Neo-Aramaic Ṭūr ʿAbdīn.4.ii

North Arabian Liḥyān; Ṣafaitic; Thamudic
and → EPIGRAPHY

South Arabian Sabaʾ; [in Suppl.] Ḳaḥṭānite
see also Ḥaḍramawt; al-Ḥarāsīs; al-Sawdāʾ; Zabūr; *and* → EPIGRAPHY
Modern South Arabian Mahrī; S̲h̲iḥrī; Suḳuṭra.3
see also al-Baṭāḥira; al-Ḥarāsīs; [in Suppl.] Ḥaḍramawt.iii

Teda-Daza Kanuri; Tubu.3

Austronesian Atjèh; Indonesia.iii; Malays

Ibero-Caucasian Andi; Beskesek-abaza; Čerkes; Dāg̲h̲istān; Darg̲h̲in; al-Ḳabḳ; Ḳayyūm Nāṣirī
see also al-Kurd̲j̲; Tsak̲h̲ur

Indo-European Arnawutluḳ.1; [in Suppl.] South Africa.2
see also al-Ḳabḳ

Indo-Iranian

Indian Afg̲h̲ānistān.iii; Bengali.i; Ceylon; Chitral.II; Dardic and Kāfir Languages; Gud̲j̲arātī; **Hind**.iii; Hindī; Hindustānī; Kashmīrī; Lahndā; Maldives.2; Marāthī; Pand̲j̲ābī.1; Sind.3.a; Urdū.1; [in Suppl.] Rād̲j̲asthān.3
see also Mad̲j̲maʿ ʿIlmī.iv; Sidi; [in Suppl.] Burus̲h̲aski

Iranian Afg̲h̲ān.ii; Afg̲h̲ānistān.iii; Balūčistān.B; Darī; Gūrān; Hind.iii; ʿIrāḳ.iv.b; Judaeo-Persian.ii; Kurds.v; Lur; Tād̲j̲īkī.1; Tālis̲h̲.2; Tat.2; Ṭūr ʿAbdīn.4.iii; Zāzā; [in Suppl.] **Iran**.iii
see also Dāg̲h̲istān; al-Ḳabḳ; K̲h̲ʷārazm; Mad̲j̲maʿ ʿIlmī.ii; Ossetians; S̲h̲ug̲h̲nān; al-Ṣug̲h̲d; [in Suppl.] Is̲h̲kās̲h̲im
Persian dialects Simnān.3

(Niger-)Kordofanian Nūba.3

Nilo-Saharan Nūba.3; Songhay.1; Sūdān.2; Wadāī.2

Turkic Ād̲h̲arī; Balkar; Bulg̲h̲ār; Gagauz; K̲h̲alad̲j̲.2; **Turks**.II (*and* [in Suppl.])
see also Afg̲h̲ānistān.iii; Dāg̲h̲istān; al-Ḳabḳ; K̲h̲azar; Mad̲j̲maʿ ʿIlmī.iii; Sārt; [in Suppl.] Ḳazaḳstān.3

LAW ʿĀda; Dustūr; **Fiḳh**; ʿIbādāt; Id̲j̲māʿ; **Ḳānūn**.i *and* iii; Ḳiyās; Maḥkama; **S̲h̲arīʿa**; Tas̲h̲rīʿ; ʿUrf; Uṣūl al-Fiḳh; [in Suppl.] Mad̲h̲hab; Maḳāṣid al-S̲h̲arīʿa; Raʾy
see also Aṣḥāb al-Raʾy; Ḥuḳūḳ; Siyāsa.3; *and* → DIVORCE; INHERITANCE; MARRIAGE
for questions of law, see ʿAbd.3; D̲j̲āsūs; Filāḥa.i.4; Ḥarb.i; Ḥarīr; In S̲h̲āʾ Allāh; Intiḥār; Ḳabr; Kāfir; K̲h̲āliṣa; K̲h̲iṭba; Māʾ; al-Marʾa; Murtadd; Raḍāʿ; Rāḳid; Ras̲h̲wa; Safar.1; S̲h̲aʿr.2; Ṣūra; al-Surayd̲j̲iyya; ʿUrs.1.c; Waḳf.I.3; Wilāya.1

Anglo-Mohammedan law ʿĀda.iii; Amīr ʿAlī; Munṣif; [in Suppl.] Maḥkama.5
see also Ḥanafiyya

commercial law → FINANCE; *and see the section Law of Obligations below*

customary law **ʿĀda**; Dak̲h̲īl; Ḳānūn.iv; Ṭāg̲h̲ūt.2; T̲h̲aʾr; **ʿUrf**; [in Suppl.] D̲j̲irga
see also Baranta; Berbers.IV; al-Māmī; al-Marʾa.2; Mus̲h̲āʿ

early, pre-madhhab law Abū Ḥanīfa; Abū Yūsuf; al-As̲h̲ʿarī, Abū Burda; ʿAṭāʾ b. Abī Rabāḥ; al-Awzāʿī; Ibn Abī Laylā.II; Ibn S̲h̲ubruma; al-Layt̲h̲ b. Saʿd; Mālik b. Anas; Maymūn

b. Mihrān; al-Naḵẖaʿī, Ibrāhīm; al-S̲h̲aʿbī; al-S̲h̲āfiʿī; S̲h̲urayḥ; Sufyān al-T̲h̲awrī; Yaḥyā b. Ādam; [in Suppl.] Fuḳahāʾ al-Madīna al-Sabʿa; Ibn Abi ʾl-Zinād; Saʿīd b. D̲j̲ubayr
see also [in Suppl.] Raʾy

genres ʿAmal; Dustūr; Farāʾiḍ; Fatwā; Ḥisba; Ḥiyal.4; Ik̲h̲tilāf; Nāzila; S̲h̲arṭ.1; Sid̲j̲ill.3; Uṣūl al-Fiḳh; Wat̲h̲īḳa; [in Suppl.] Ḳawāʿid Fiḳhiyya
see also Ṭabaḳāt.C; Waḳf.I.2.d *and* IV

Ibāḍī law ʿAbd al-ʿAzīz b. al-Ḥād̲j̲d̲j̲ Ibrāhīm; Abū G̲h̲ānim al-K̲h̲urāsānī; Abū Muḥammad b. Baraka (*and* Ibn Baraka); Abū Zakariyyāʾ al-D̲j̲anāwunī; Ibn D̲j̲aʿfar
see also al-D̲j̲ayṭālī; Maḥkama.4.ix (Oman)

in Southeast Asia Peng̲h̲ulu; Rapak; S̲h̲arīʿa (In South-East Asia); ʿUlamāʾ.5; [in Suppl.] Maḥkama.7

inheritance → INHERITANCE

jurisprudence Fatwā; **Fiḳh**; Īd̲j̲āb; Id̲j̲māʿ; Id̲j̲tihād; Ik̲h̲tilāf; Istiḥsān; Ḳiyās; Maṣlaḥa; Nāzila; Taḳlīd
see also Sadd al-D̲h̲arāʾiʿ

jurist **Faḳīh**; Mard̲j̲aʿ-i Taḳlīd; Mud̲j̲tahid; ʿUlamāʾ
see also S̲h̲arḥ.III; [in Suppl.] Raʾy

Ḥanafī Abū Ḥanīfa al-Nuʿmān; Abu ʾl-Layt̲h̲ al-Samarḳandī; Abu ʾl-Suʿūd; al-ʿAmīdī; al-Bihārī; al-D̲j̲aṣṣāṣ; al-Ḥalabī; Ḥamza al-Ḥarrānī; Ibn ʿĀbidīn; Ibn Buhlūl; Ibn G̲h̲ānim; Ibn Ḳuṭlūbug̲h̲ā; Ibn Nud̲j̲aym; Ibn al-S̲h̲iḥna; Ḳāḍī Ḵẖān; al-Kāsānī; Ḳasṭallānī; al-Ḳudūrī, Abu ʾl-Ḥusayn Aḥmad; al-Marg̲h̲īnānī; al-Murādī.2, 3 *and* 4; al-Nasafī.4; al-Sad̲j̲āwandī, Sirād̲j̲ al-Dīn; al-Sarak̲h̲sī, Muḥammad b. Aḥmad; al-S̲h̲aybānī, Abū ʿAbd Allāh; al-S̲h̲iblī, Abū Ḥafṣ; al-Ṭaḥāwī; al-Ūs̲h̲ī; Wānkulī; [in Suppl.] Abū ʿAbd Allāh al-Baṣrī; Abu ʾl-Barakāt; al-Dāmag̲h̲ānī, Abū ʿAbd Allāh Muḥammad b. ʿAlī; al-Dāmag̲h̲ānī, Abu ʾl-Ḥasan ʿAlī b. Muḥammad; al-Ḵẖaṣṣāf; al-Sunāmī; Yaḥyā
see also ʿAbd al-Ḳādir al-Ḳuras̲h̲ī; al-Fatāwā al-ʿĀlamgīriyya; Ibn Dukmāḳ; al-Ṣayrafī; al-Taftāzānī; Ẓāhir

Ḥanbalī Aḥmad b. Ḥanbal; al-Bahūtī; al-Barbahārī; G̲h̲ulām al-K̲h̲allāl; Ibn ʿAḳīl; Ibn al-Bannāʾ; Ibn Baṭṭa al-ʿUkbarī; Ibn al-D̲j̲awzī; Ibn al-Farrāʾ; Ibn Ḥāmid; Ibn Ḳayyim al-D̲j̲awziyya; Ibn Ḳudāma al-Maḳdisī; Ibn Mufliḥ; Ibn Rad̲j̲ab; Ibn Taymiyya; al-Kalwad̲h̲ānī; al-K̲h̲allāl; al-K̲h̲iraḳī; al-Marwazī; al-Ṭūfī; al-ʿUkbarī; al-Yūnīnī; Yūsuf b. ʿAbd al-Hādī
see also ʿUt̲h̲mān b. Marzūḳ; *and* → THEOLOGY

Mālikī Aḥmad Bābā; Asad b. al-Furāt; al-Bād̲j̲ī; al-Bāḳillānī; Bannānī; al-Burzulī; al-Dānī; al-Fāsī; Ibn ʿAbd al-Ḥakam; Ibn Abī Zamanayn; Ibn Abī Zayd al-Ḳayrawānī; Ibn ʿAmmār, Abu ʾl-ʿAbbās; Ibn ʿArafa; Ibn ʿĀṣim; Ibn al-Faraḍī; Ibn Farḥūn; Ibn Ḥabīb, Abū Marwān; Ibn al-Ḥād̲j̲d̲j̲; Ibn al-Ḥād̲j̲ib; Ibn al-Ḳāsim; Ibn Ḳuzmān.III *and* IV (*and* [in Suppl.] Ḳuzmān.3 *and* 4); Ibn Madāʾ; Ibn Rus̲h̲ayd; Ibn Sūda; al-Ibs̲h̲īhī(1); ʿĪsā b. Dīnār; ʿIyāḍ b. Mūsā; al-Ḳābisī; al-Ḳalaṣādī; al-Kardūdī; Ḳaṣṣāra; K̲h̲alīl b. Isḥāḳ; al-K̲h̲us̲h̲anī; al-Ḳurṭubī, Abū ʿAbd Allāh; al-Ḳurṭubī, Yaḥyā; Mālik b. Anas; al-Manūfī.4 *and* 5; al-Māzarī; Muḥammad b. Saḥnūn; Saḥnūn; Sālim b. Muḥammad; al-Sanhūrī, Abu ʾl-Ḥasan; S̲h̲abṭūn; al-S̲h̲āṭibī, Abū Isḥāḳ; S̲h̲ihāb al-Dīn al-Ḳarāfī; al-Ṭulayṭulī; al-Ṭurṭus̲h̲ī; al-ʿUtbī, Abū ʿAbd Allāh; al-Wans̲h̲arīsī; Yaḥyā b. Yaḥyā al-Layt̲h̲ī; al-Zaḳḳāḳ; al-Zuhrī, Hārūn; al-Zurḳānī; [in Suppl.] Abū ʿImrān al-Fāsī; al-Azdī; Ibn Daḳīḳ al-ʿĪd; Ibn Dirham; Ibn Rus̲h̲d; al-Nubāhī
see also Ibn ʿAbd al-Barr; al-Ḳaṣṣār; Laḳīṭ; al-S̲h̲arīf al-Tilimsānī; al-Tilimsānī.1; *and* → ANDALUSIA.JURISTS

S̲h̲āfiʿī al-ʿAbbādī; Abū S̲h̲ud̲j̲āʿ; Bād̲j̲ūrī; al-Bag̲h̲awī; al-Bulḳīnī; Daḥlān; al-D̲j̲anadī; al-D̲j̲īzī; al-D̲j̲uwaynī; Ibn Abī ʿAṣrūn; Ibn Abi ʾl-Dam; Ibn ʿAḳīl; Ibn ʿAsākir; Ibn D̲j̲amāʿa; Ibn Ḥabīb, Badr al-Dīn; Ibn Ḥad̲j̲ar al-Haytamī; Ibn Ḳāḍī S̲h̲uhba.1; Ibn

Ḳāsim al-Ghazzī; Ibn al-Ṣalāḥ; Ibn Suraydj; al-Ḳalḳashandī; al-Ḳalyūbī; al-Ḳazwīnī, Abū Ḥātim; al-Ḳazwīnī, Djalāl al-Dīn; al-Ḳazwīnī, Nadjm al-Dīn; al-Kiyā al-Harrāsī; Makhrama; al-Māwardī; al-Mutawallī; al-Muzanī; al-Nawawī; al-Rāfiʿī; al-Ramlī; al-Shāfiʿī; al-Shahrazūrī; al-Shīrāzī, Abū Isḥāḳ; al-Subkī; al-Sulamī, ʿIzz al-Dīn; al-Suʿlūkī; al-Ṭabarī, Abū ʾl-Ṭayyib; al-Ṭabarī, Aḥmad b. ʿAbd Allāh; Zakariyyāʾ al-Anṣārī; [in Suppl.] Abū Zurʿa; Ibn Daḳīḳ al-ʿĪd; al-Zarkashī

    see also Abū Thawr; Dāwūd b. Khalaf; al-Isfarāyīnī; al-Ṭabarī, Abū Djaʿfar; al-Taftāzānī; al-Ziyādī

Shiite → SHIITES

Ẓāhirī Dāwūd b. Khalaf; al-Ḥumaydī; Ibn Dāwūd; Ibn Ḥazm, Abū Muḥammad; (al-)Mundhir b. Saʿīd

    see also Ṣāʿid al-Andalusī; [in Suppl.] Ibn al-Rūmiyya

law of obligations ʿAḳd; ʿĀriyya; Bayʿ; Ḍamān; Dhimma; Fāsid wa Bāṭil; Faskh; Hiba; Īdjāb; Īdjār; Inkār; ʿIwaḍ; Kafāla; Khiyār; Ḳirāḍ; Muʿāmalāt; Muʿāwaḍa.3; Muḍāraba; Mufāwaḍa; Mughārasa; Mushāraka; Rahn; Ṣulḥ; Wadīʿa; Wakāla; [in Suppl.] Dayn; Ghārūḳa

    see also ʿAmal.4; Djāʾiz; Ghasb; Ḳabḍ.i; Ḳasam; Maḍmūn; Suftadja; Wathīḳa; Yamīn; [in Suppl.] Ikrāh

    contract of hire and lease Adjr; **Īdjār**; Kirāʾ; Musāḳāt; Muzāraʿa; [in Suppl.] Ḥikr; Inzāl

    contract of sale Barāʾa.I; **Bayʿ**; Iḳāla; ʿIwaḍ; Muʿāwaḍa.1; Muwāḍaʿa.1; Salam; Shirāʾ; Tadlīs.1; Taghrīr; [in Suppl.] Darak; Ṣarf

       see also Ḍarūra; Ildjāʾ; Mukhātara; Ṣafḳa; Salaf; Sawm; Tidjāra; [in Suppl.] Ṣarrāf

law of personal status Ḥaḍāna; Hiba; ʿIdda; Mahr; Mīrāth; Nikāḥ; Riḍāʿ; Ṭalāḳ; Waḳf; Yatīm; [in Suppl.] Nafaḳa; Tabannin

    see also Wilāya.1; *and* → DIVORCE; INHERITANCE; MARRIAGE

law of procedure ʿAdl; Amīn; Bayyina; Daʿwā; Ghāʾib; Ḥakam; Iḳrār; Ḳaḍāʾ; Maẓālim; Shāhid; Sidjill.2

Mongol Ṣadr.2; Yarghu; Yāsā

offices Faḳīh; Ḥakam; Ḥisba; Ḳāḍī; Ḳāḍī ʿAskar; Ḳassām; Mardjaʿ-i Taḳlīd; Nāʾib.1; Shaykh al-Islām

    see also Amīn; Fatwā; Khalīfa.ii; Maḥkama; Shurṭa

Ottoman Bāb-i Mashīkhat; Djazāʾ.ii; Djurm; Fatwā.ii; ʿIlmiyye; Ḳānūn.iii; Ḳānūnnāme; Ḳassām; Maḥkama.2; Makhredj; Medjelle; Medjlis-i Wālā; Mewlewiyyet; Narkh; Shaykh al-Islām.2; Sidjill.3; [in Suppl.] Müfettish

    see also Ḥanafiyya; al-Ḥaramayn; ʿUlamāʾ.3; Waḳf.IV (*and* [in Suppl.] Waḳf.II.2); *and* → DYNASTIES.ANATOLIA AND THE TURKS.OTTOMANS.GRAND MUFTIS

penal law ʿĀḳila; Diya; Ḥadd; Ḳadhf; Ḳatl; Khaṭaʾ; Ḳiṣāṣ.5; Murtadd; Ṣalb; Sariḳa; Taʿzīr; ʿUḳūba; [in Suppl.] Shatm

    see also Djazāʾ.ii; Muḥṣan; al-Ṣalīb; Shubha; Sidjn; Ṭarrār; Thaʾr; ʿUrf.2.II; Zinā; [in Suppl.] Ikrāh

reform → REFORM

schools Ḥanābila; Ḥanafiyya; Mālikiyya; al-Shāfiʿiyya; Uṣūliyya.1; al-Ẓāhiriyya; [in Suppl.] Akhbāriyya

    see also Ibn Abī Laylā; Sufyān al-Thawrī; al-Ṭabarī, Abū Djaʿfar; Wahhābiyya; Zaydiyya; [in Suppl.] Madhhab

terms Adāʾ; Adjr.2; ʿAdl; Aḥkām; Ahl al-Ḥall wa ʾl-ʿAḳd; ʿAḳd; Akdariyya; ʿAḳīḳa; ʿĀḳila; ʿAmal.3 *and* 4; Amān; ʿĀmil; Amīn; ʿĀriyya; ʿArsh; ʿAwl; ʿAzīma.1; Baʿl.2.b; Bāligh; Barāʾa.I; Bayʿ; Bayʿa; Bayyina; Burhān; Ḍamān; Dār al-ʿAhd; Dār al-Ḥarb; Dār al-Islām; Dār al-Ṣulḥ; Ḍarūra; Daʿwā; Dhabīḥa; Dhimma; Diya; Djāʾiz; Djanāba; Djazāʾ.ii; Djihād; Djizya; Djurm; Faḳīh; Farāʾiḍ; Farḍ; Fāsid wa Bāṭil; Fāsiḳ; Faskh; Fatwā; Fayʾ; Fiḳh; Ghāʾib; Ghanīma; Ghārim; Ghasb; Ghusl; Ḥaḍāna; Ḥadath; Ḥadd; Ḥadjr; Hady; Ḥakam;

Ḥaḳḳ; Ḥawāla; Ḥayḍ; Hiba; Ḥiyal.4; Ḥuḳūḳ; Ḥulūl; ʿIbādāt; Ibāḥa.I; ʿIdda; Idhn; Īdjāb; Īdjār; Idjmāʿ; Idjtihād; Iḥrām; Iḥyāʾ; Iḳāla; Ikhtilāf; Iḳrār; Ildjāʾ; Inkār; Inṣāf; Istibrāʾ; Istiḥsān; Istiʾnāf; Istiṣḥāb; ʿIwaḍ; Ḳabāla; Ḳabḍ.i; Ḳaḍāʾ; Ḳadhf; Kafāʾa; Kafāla; Ḳānūn; Ḳānūnnāme; Ḳasam; Ḳatl; Khaṭaʾ; Khiyār; Kirāʾ; Ḳirāḍ; Ḳiṣāṣ; Ḳiyās; Liʿān; Liṣṣ; Luḳaṭa; Maḍmūn; Mafṣūl; Mahr; Maṣlaḥa; Mawāt; Mawlā.5; Maẓālim; Milk; Muʿāmalāt; Muʿāwaḍa; Muḍāraba; Mudjtahid; Mufāwaḍa; Mughārasa; Muḥṣan; Mukhāṭara; Munāṣafa; Musāḳāt; Mushāraka; Mutʿa; Muṭlaḳ; Muwāḍaʿa.1; Muzāraʿa; Nadjis; Nāfila; Naṣṣ; Nāzila; Niyya; Rahn; Ribā; Rukhṣa.1; Sabab.2; Ṣadaḳa; Sadd al-Dharāʾiʿ; Ṣafḳa; Ṣaḥīḥ.2; al-Sahm.2; Salaf; Salam; Sariḳa; Sawm; Shāhid; Shakhṣ; Shakk.1; Sharika; Sharṭ.1; Shirāʾ; Shubha; Shufʿa; Sidjn; Suftadja; Suknā; Sukūt; Ṣulḥ; Sunna.2; Tadlīs.1; Taghrīr; Ṭahāra; Taḳlīd; Taklīf; Ṭalāḳ; Talfīḳ; Tashrīʿ; Tasʿīr; Taʿzīr; Umm al-Walad; ʿUmūm wa-Khuṣūṣ; ʿUrf; Uṣūl al-Fiḳh; Wadīʿa; Wakāla; Waḳf; Waṣf.2; Waṣiyya; Wathīḳa; Wilāya.1; Wuḍūʾ; Yamīn; Ẓāhir; Zaʿīm; Zakāt; Zinā; [in Suppl.] ʿAḳār; Darak; Dayn; Djabr; Ghārūḳa; Ḥikr; Ikrāh; Inzāl; Isḳāṭ; Ḳawāʿid Fiḳhiyya; Khalʿ; Madhhab; Maḳāṣid al-Sharīʿa; Muʿāhid; Muḥallil; Nafaḳa; al-Nahy ʿan al-Munkar; Raʾy; Ṣakk; Sanad; Ṣarf
see also Bayt al-Māl; Hudna; Ṣaghīr; Shukr.2; Shūrā.2; Siyāsa.3; Taḥkīm

LEBANON Djarīda.i.A; Dustūr.ix; Ḥizb.i; Ḥukūma.iii; **Lubnān**; Madjlis.4.A.vi; Maḥkama.4.iii; Mandates; Mutawālī; Ṣiḥāfa.1.(iii); Ṭāʾifiyya
see also Baladiyya.2; Djāliya; Ḳays ʿAylān; al-Maʿlūf; Ṭanyūs, Shāhīn; Türkmen.3; Yūsuf Karam; Zaʿīm; [in Suppl.] Aḥmad Pasha Küčük; al-Bustānī; Demography.III; *and* → CHRISTIANITY.DENOMINATIONS.MARONITES; DRUZES
belletrists
poets Fāris al-Shidyāḳ; Khalīl Muṭrān; al-Maʿlūf; Ṭuʿma, Ilyās; al-Yāzidjī; [in Suppl.] Abū Māḍī; al-Bustānī.4 *and* 8
see also al-Bustānī.7; Nuʿayma, Mīkhāʾīl; al-Rayḥānī
writers of prose al-Maʿlūf; Nuʿayma, Mīkhāʾīl; al-Yāzidjī; [in Suppl.] al-Bustānī.6
see also Faraḥ Anṭūn; Mayy Ziyāda; *and* → PRESS
education Djāmiʿa; Maʿārif.1.iii
governors Bashīr Shihāb II; Dāwūd Pasha; Djānbulāt; Fakhr al-Dīn; Ḥarfūsh; Shihāb
see also Maʿn; Maʿn-zāda
historians of Iskandar Agha
see also [in Suppl.] Taʾrīkh.II.1.(c)
religious leaders Sharaf al-Dīn; Yūsuf Karam; [in Suppl.] Mūsā al-Ṣadr
see also Mutawālī
toponyms
ancient ʿAyn al-Djarr
present-day
regions al-Biḳāʿ; al-Shūf
towns Baʿlabakk; Batrūn; Bayrūt; Bsharrā; Bteddīn; Djubayl; Karak Nūḥ; Ṣaydā; Ṣūr; Ṭarābulus al-Shām

LEGENDS Ḥikāya
and → BIBLE.BIBLICAL PERSONAGES; ESCHATOLOGY; QURʾAN.STORIES
legendary beings ʿAnḳāʾ; al-Burāḳ; Dīw; al-Djassāsa; Djinn; Ghūl; Hātif; ʿIfrīt; Ḳuṭrub; Parī; Sīmurgh; ʿŪdj; Zuhāk
see also al-Rukhkh
legendary dynasties Kayānids; Pīshdādids
see also Firdawsī; Ḥamāsa.ii
legendary locations Damāwand; Djūdī; Ergenekon; Ḥūsh; Ḳïzïl-elma; Sāwa.3; Wabār

see also Tūrān; Wāḳwāḳ

legendary people Abū Rig͟hāl; Abū Safyān; Abū Zayd; ʿAdnān; Afrāsiyāb; Ahl al-Ṣuffa; Amīna; Āṣāf b. Barak͟hyā; Aṣḥāb al-Kahf; Barṣīṣā; al-Basūs; Bilḳīs; al-Dad͟jd͟jāl; D͟jams͟hīd; Ḥabīb al-Nad͟jd͟jār; Ḥanẓala b. Ṣafwān; Hind bint al-K͟huss; Hirmis; Hūs͟hang; Ibn Buḳayla; al-Kāhina; Ḳaḥṭān; Kāwah; al-K͟haḍir; Luḳmān; Masʿūd; Naṣr al-Dīn K͟hod͟ja; Sām; Saṭīḥ b. Rabīʿa; S͟hiḳḳ; Siyāwus͟h; Sulaymān b. Dāwūd; Ṭahmūrat͟h; Yād͟jūd͟j wa-Mād͟jūd͟j; [in Suppl.] al-D͟jarādatān[i]; Salmān al-Fārisī; al-Sufyānī

see also Ak͟hī Ewrān; ʿAmr b. ʿAdī; ʿAmr b. Luḥayy; Aṣḥāb al-Rass; Ḳuss b. Sāʿida; Muʿammar; Ṣarı̊ Ṣalṭūḳ Dede; Ṭursun Faḳīh; Zarḳāʾ al-Yamāma; Zuhayr b. D͟janāb; *and* → QURʾAN.STORIES

legendary stories ʿAbd Allāh b. D͟judʿān; Akt͟ham b. Ṣayfī; Almās; al-Baṭṭāl; Buhlūl; Damāwand; D͟jird͟jīs; D͟jūdī; al-Durr; Fāṭima; al-G͟hazāl; al-Ḥaḍr; Ḥāʾiṭ al-ʿAd͟jūz; Haram; Hārūt wa-Mārūt; Hudhud; Isrāʾīliyyāt; K͟hālid b. Yazīd b. Muʿāwiya; Ḳiṣaṣ al-Anbiyāʾ; Nūḥ

see also Wāḳwāḳ

LEXICOGRAPHY **Ḳāmūs**; Laḥn al-ʿĀmma

see also S͟harḥ.I; Sullam; *and* → LINGUISTICS

lexicographers

for Andalusian lexicographers → ANDALUSIA

Arabic Abū Zayd al-Anṣārī; al-Azharī; al-D͟jawālīḳī; al-D͟jawharī; Farḥāt; al-Fīrūzābādī; Ibn al-Birr; Ibn Durayd; Ibn Fāris; Ibn Makkī; Ibn Manẓūr; Ibn Sīda; Ibn al-Sikkīt; al-Ḳazzāz; al-K͟halīl b. Aḥmad; Muḥammad Murtaḍā; Nas͟hwān b. Saʿīd; al-Ṣag͟hānī, Raḍiyy al-Dīn; al-S͟haybānī, Abū ʿAmr (*and* [in Suppl.] Abū ʿAmr al-S͟haybānī); al-Tahānawī; Tammām b. G͟hālib; al-Yāzid͟jī.2 *and* 3; al-Zamak͟hs͟harī; al-Zubaydī; [in Suppl.] Abū Isḥāḳ al-Fārisī; al-Bustānī.1 *and* 2; al-Fārābī; al-S͟hartūnī

see also Abū Ḥātim al-Rāzī; Ak͟htarī; al-Rāg͟hib al-Iṣfahānī; al-Tanūk͟hī, D͟jamāl al-Dīn; al-T͟haʿālibī, Abū Manṣūr ʿAbd al-Malik; [in Suppl.] Ibn Kabar

Hebrew Ibn D͟janāḥ

see also Judaeo-Arabic.iii.B

Persian ʿAbd al-Ras͟hīd al-Tattawī; Aḥmad Wafīḳ Pas͟ha; Burhān; Surūrī Kās͟hānī; Taḳī Awḥadī; [in Suppl.] Dehk͟hudā

see also Ārzū K͟hān; Mahdī K͟hān Astarābādī; Riḍā Ḳulī K͟hān; al-Tahānawī

Turkish Ak͟htarī; al-Kās͟hg͟harī; Kāẓı̊m Ḳadrī; Niʿmat Allāh b. Aḥmad; Sāmī

see also Esʿad Efendi, Meḥmed; Luṭfī Efendi; Riyāḍī; S͟hināsī; Wānḳulı̊

terms Fard.b

LIBYA D͟jāmiʿa; D͟jarīda.i.B; Dustūr.xii; **Lībiyā**; Mad͟jlis.4.A.xviii; Ṣiḥāfa.2.(iv)

see also ʿArabiyya.A.iii.3; al-Bārūnī; Ḳaramānlī; K͟halīfa b. ʿAskar; Sanūsiyya; *and* → DYNASTIES.SPAIN AND NORTH AFRICA

population → AFRICA.NORTH AFRICA; BERBERS

toponyms

ancient Ṣabra; Surt; Zawīla

present-day

oases Awd͟jila; Baḥriyya; al-D͟jag͟hbūb; D͟jawf Kufra; al-D͟jufra; Ghadamès; Kufra

regions Barḳa; al-D͟jufra; Fazzān

see also Nafūsa

towns Ad͟jdābiya; Beng͟hāzī; Darna; D͟jādū; Murzuḳ; Ṭarābulus al-G͟harb

see also G͟hāt

LIFE STAGES **Ḥayāt**

childbirth ʿAḳīḳa; Āl; Liʿān; al-Marʾa.2.c; Mawākib.4.2
see also Raḍāʿ; Waʾd al-Banāt; *and* → MEDICINE.OBSTETRICS
pregnancy Rāḳid; Waḥam
birth control **Tanẓīm al-Nasl**
suckling **Raḍāʿ**
treatises on ʿArīb b. Saʿd al-Kātib al-Ḳurṭubī
childhood Bālig͟h; **Ṣag͟hīr**; Yatīm
see also Ḥaḍāna; al-S͟hayb wa ʾl-S͟habāb; [in Suppl.] Nafaḳa; *and* → CIRCUMCISION; EDUCATION; MARRIAGE
old age **Muʿammar**
see also al-S͟hayb wa ʾl-S͟habāb; S͟hayk͟h; *and* → DEATH

LINGUISTICS **Lug͟ha**; Naḥw; Taṣrīf; Uṣūl
see also Balāg͟ha; Bayān; Laḥn al-ʿĀmma; S͟harḥ.I; *and* → LANGUAGES; LEXICOGRAPHY
grammarians/philologists
biographies of al-Zubaydī
8th century ʿAbd Allāh b. Abī Isḥāḳ; Abū ʿAmr al-ʿAlāʾ; al-Ak͟hfas͟h.I; ʿĪsā b. ʿUmar; al-K͟halīl b. Aḥmad; Ḳuṭrub; al-Mufaḍḍal al-Ḍabbī; Sībawayhi; al-S͟haybānī, Abū ʿAmr (*and* [in Suppl.] Abū ʿAmr al-S͟haybānī); Yūnus b. Ḥabīb
see also [in Suppl.] Abu ʾl-Bayḍāʾ al-Riyāḥī
9th century Abū Ḥātim al-Sid͟jistānī; Abū ʿUbayd al-Ḳāsim b. Sallām; Abū ʿUbayda; Abū Zayd al-Anṣārī; al-Ak͟hfas͟h.II; al-Aṣmaʿī; al-Bāhilī, Abū Naṣr; D͟jūdī al-Mawrūrī; al-Farrāʾ; Ibn al-Aʿrābī, Muḥammad; Ibn Sallām al-D͟jumaḥī; Ibn al-Sikkīt; al-Kisāʾī, Abu ʾl-Ḥasan; al-Layt͟h b. al-Muẓaffar; al-Māzinī, Abū ʿUt͟hmān; al-Mubarrad; Muḥammad b. Ḥabīb; al-Ruʾāsī; al-Yazīdī.2; [in Suppl.] Abu ʾl-ʿAmayt͟hal
10th century al-Ak͟hfas͟h.III; al-Anbārī, Abū Bakr; al-Anbārī, Abū Muḥammad; al-ʿAskarī.i; D͟jaḥẓa; al-Fārisī; G͟hulām T͟haʿlab; Ḥamza al-Iṣfahānī; Ibn al-ʿArīf, al-Ḥusayn; Ibn D͟jinnī; Ibn Durayd; Ibn Durustawayh; Ibn Kaysān; Ibn K͟hālawayh; Ibn al-K͟hayyāṭ, Abū Bakr; Ibn al-Ḳūṭiyya; Ibn al-Naḥḥās; Ibn al-Sarrād͟j; al-Ḳālī; Ḳudāma; Nifṭawayh; al-Rummānī; al-Sīrāfī; al-Ṭayālisī, D͟jaʿfar; T͟haʿlab; al-Zad͟jd͟jād͟j; al-Zad͟jd͟jād͟jī; al-Zubaydī; [in Suppl.] Abū Isḥāḳ al-Fārisī; Abū Riyās͟h al-Ḳaysī; Abu ʾl-Ṭayyib al-Lug͟hawī; al-Ḥātimī; Ibn Kaysān; Ibn Miḳsam
11th century al-Ad͟jdābī; al-ʿAskarī. ii; Ibn al-Birr; Ibn Fāris; Ibn al-Ḥād͟jd͟j; Ibn al-Iflīlī; Ibn Makkī; Ibn Sīda; al-Ḳazzāz; al-Marzūḳī; al-Rabaḥī; al-Rabaʿī; al-S͟hantamarī; Ṭāhir b. Aḥmad b. Bābas͟hād͟h; al-Wāḥidī; [in Suppl.] Abū Usāma al-Harawī; al-D͟jurd͟jānī
12th century al-Anbārī, Abu ʾl-Barakāt; al-Baṭalyawsī; al-D͟jawālīḳī; al-D͟jazūlī, Abū Mūsā; al-Ḥarīrī; Ibn Barrī, Abū Muḥammad; Ibn Maḍāʾ; Ibn al-S͟had͟jarī al-Bag͟hdādī; al-Maydānī; al-Tibrīzī; al-Zamak͟hs͟harī; [in Suppl.] Abu ʾl-Barakāt; Ibn His͟hām al-Lak͟hmī
13th century al-Astarābād͟hī, Raḍī al-Dīn; Ibn al-Ad͟jdābī; Ibn al-At͟hīr.1; Ibn al-Ḥād͟jd͟j; Ibn al-Ḥād͟jib; Ibn Mālik; Ibn Muʿṭī; al-Muṭarrizī; al-S͟halawbīn; al-S͟harīs͟hī; al-ʿUkbarī; [in Suppl.] al-Balaṭī, Abu ʾl-Fatḥ ʿUt͟hmān; Ibn al-Ad͟jdābī; al-Zand͟jānī
14th century Abū Ḥayyān al-G͟harnāṭī; al-Astarābād͟hī, Rukn al-Dīn; Fak͟hrī; Ibn Ād͟jurrūm; Ibn ʿAḳīl, ʿAbd Allāh; Ibn Barrī, Abu ʾl-Ḥasan; Ibn His͟hām, D͟jamāl al-Dīn; Ibn K͟hātima; Ibn al-Ṣāʾig͟h; al-S͟harīf al-G͟harnaṭī; Yaḥyā b. Ḥamza al-ʿAlawī
15th century al-Azharī, K͟hālid; Ibn ʿĀṣim; al-Sanhūrī, Abu ʾl-Ḥasan; al-Suyūṭī
17th century ʿAbd al-Ḳādir al-Bag͟hdādī
18th century Farḥāt
19th century Fāris al-S͟hidyāḳ; Ibn al-Ḥād͟jd͟j; al-Nabarāwī; al-Yāzid͟jī.1
see also Fuʾād Pas͟ha

20th century [in Suppl.] Arat; al-Shartūnī
phonetics Ḥurūf al-Hidjāʾ.II; Makhāridj al-Ḥurūf; Mushtarik; Ṣawtiyya; Tafkhīm
see also Hāwī; Ḥurūf al-Hidjāʾ; Imāla; Uṣūl
for Arabic and Persian dialects → LANGUAGES; *for the letters of the alphabet* → ALPHABET
terms Aḍdād; Āla.i.; ʿĀmil; ʿAṭf; Dakhīl; Djāmʿ; Fard.c; Fiʿl; Gharīb; Ḥaraka wa-Sukūn.ii; Ḥarf; Hāwī; Ḥikāya.I; Ḥukm.II; Ḥulūl; Ibdāl; Iḍāfa; Idghām; Iḍmār; ʿIlla.i; Imāla; Iʿrāb; Ishtiḳāḳ; Ism; Istifhām; Istithnāʾ; Kasra; Ḳaṭʿ; Khabar; Ḳiyās.2; Māḍī; Maʿnā.1; Muʿarrab; Mubālagha.a; Mubtadaʾ.1; Muḍāriʿ; Mudhakkar; Muḍmar; Musnad.2; Muṭlaḳ; Muwallad.2; Muzdawidj; Nafy; Naṣb; Naʿt; Nisba.1; Rafʿ.1; Sabab.4; Ṣaḥīḥ.3; Sālim.2; Ṣarf; Sharṭ.3; Ṣifa.1; Ṣila.1; Taʿaddī; Tafḍīl; Tafkhīm; Taḳdīr.1; Tamthīl.1; Tanwīn; Taʿrīb; Taʿrīf.2; Taṣrīf; Waḍʿ al-Lugha; Waḥda.1; Waṣl; Wazn.2; Ẓarf; [in Suppl.] Ḥāl; Lafẓ
see also Basīṭ wa-Murakkab; Ghalaṭāt-i Meshhūre; Ḥurūf al-Hidjāʾ; Taʿlīḳ

LITERATURE **Adab**; ʿArabiyya.B; ʿIrāḳ.v; Iran.vii; ʿOthmānli̊.III; Tunisia.V; Turks.III; Urdū.2
autobiographical Ibn Ṭūlūn; Nuʿayma, Mīkhāʾīl; Sālim; Shāʾūl; Zaydān, Djurdjī
see also Shaybānī; Tardjama.1; Tūzūk
bibliographical **Bibliography**; Fahrasa
compilers Ibn Khayr al-Ishbīlī; Ibn al-Nadīm; Kātib Čelebi; al-Ruʿaynī; al-Ṭihrānī; [in Suppl.] Ismāʿīl Pasha Baghdādli̊
biographical Faḍīla; **Manāḳib**; Mathālib; **Ṭabaḳāt**; Tadhkira.2 *and* 3; Tardjama.1; Tūzūk
see also ʿIlm al-Ridjāl; Maʾāthir al-Umarāʾ; Mughals.10; Shurafāʾ.2; Ṣila.2.II.c; *and* → HAGIOGRAPHY; LITERATURE.HISTORICAL *and* POETRY; MEDICINE.PHYSICIANS.BIOGRAPHIES OF; MUḤAMMAD, THE PROPHET
criticism [in Suppl.] **Naḳd**
classical Ibn ʿAbbād; Ibn al-Athīr.3; Ibn al-Muʿtazz; Ibn Rashīḳ; Ibn Sharaf al-Ḳayrawānī; Ḳudāma; al-Sidjilmāsī; [in Suppl.] al-Djurdjānī; al-Ḥātimī
and → RHETORIC.TREATISES ON
modern Kemāl, Meḥmed Nāmi̊ḳ; Köprülü; Kurd ʿAlī; al-Māzinī; Olghun, Meḥmed Ṭāhir; [in Suppl.] Alangu; Atač
terms Mubālagha.b; Waḥshī
drama **Masraḥ**; Taʿziya
Arabic Khayāl al-Ẓill; **Masraḥ**.1 *and* 2
see also ʿArabiyya.B.V
playwrights Abū Naḍḍāra; Faraḥ Anṭūn; Ibn Dāniyāl; al-Ḳusanṭīnī; al-Maʿlūf; Nadjīb al-Ḥaddād; Nadjīb Muḥammad Surūr; al-Naḳḳāsh; Ṣalāḥ ʿAbd al-Ṣabūr; Salīm al-Naḳḳāsh; al-Sharḳāwī; Shawḳī; al-Yāzidjī.3; [in Suppl.] al-Bustānī.1
see also Isḥāḳ, Adīb; Ismāʿīl Ṣabrī; Khalīl Muṭrān; Muḥammad Bey ʿUthmān Djalāl (*and* [in Suppl.] Muḥammad ʿUthmān Djalāl); Shumayyil, Shiblī; Ṭuʿma, Ilyās
Central Asian **Masraḥ**.5
Persian **Masraḥ**.4; Taʿziya
playwrights Muḥammad Djaʿfar Ḳaradja-dāghī; [in Suppl.] Amīrī; ʿIshḳī
Turkish Ḳaragöz; Ḳawuḳlu; **Masraḥ**.3; Orta Oyunu
playwrights ʿAbd al-Ḥaḳḳ Ḥāmid; Aḥmad Wafīḳ Pasha; Ākhund-zāda; Djewdet; Karay, Refīḳ Khālid; Ḳaṣāb, Teodor; Kemāl, Meḥmed Nāmi̊ḳ; Khayr Allāh Efendi; Manāṣti̊rli̊ Meḥmed Rifʿat; Meḥmed Raʾūf; Mīzāndji̊ Meḥmed Murād; Muḥibb Aḥmed "Diranas"; Muṣāḥib-zāde Djelāl; Oktay Rifat; Shināsī; [in Suppl.] Alus; Bashḳut; Čamli̊bel; Ḥasan Bedr al-Dīn
see also Djanāb Shihāb al-Dīn; Ebüzziya Tevfik; Ekrem Bey; Kaygi̊li̊, ʿOthmān Djemāl; Khālide Edīb; Muʿallim Nādjī

Urdu **Masraḥ**.6

playwrights Amānat; [in Suppl.] Āg͟hā Ḥas͟har Kas͟hmīrī

epistolary **Ins͟hā'**; Kātib; **Risāla**; [in Suppl.] **Maktūbāt**

see also Ṣadr.(b)

letter-writers ʿAbd al-Ḥamīd; Aḥmad Sirhindī; ʿAmr b. Masʿada; al-Babbag͟hā'; G͟hālib; Ḥāletī; al-Hamad͟hānī; Harkarn; Ibn ʿAmīra; Ibn al-At͟hīr.3; Ibn Idrīs.I; Ibn Ḳalāḳis; Ibn al-K͟haṣīb; Ibn al-Ṣayrafī; al-Ḳabtawrī; al-Ḳāḍī al-Fāḍil; Kānī; K͟halīfa S͟hāh Muḥammad; K͟hʷāndamīr; al-K͟hʷārazmī; al-Maʿarrī; Mak͟hdūm al-Mulk Manīrī; Meḥmed Pas͟ha Rāmī (*and* Rāmī Meḥmed Pas͟ha); Muḥammad b. Hindū-S͟hāh; Oḳču-zāde; Ras͟hīd al-Dīn (Waṭwāṭ); Saʿīd b. Ḥumayd; al-S͟haybānī, Ibrāhīm; Ṭāhir b. Muḥammad; Ṭāhir Waḥīd; al-ʿUtbī, Abū ʿAbd al-Raḥmān; al-Wahrānī; Yūsufī; [in Suppl.] ʿAbd al-ʿAzīz b. Yūsuf; Amīr Niẓām; Ibn K͟halaf; Muḥammad Ṣāliḥ Kanbō Lāhawrī; al-S͟hartūnī

see also Aljamía; al-D͟junayd; Ibn al-ʿAmīd.1; Ibn al-K͟haṭīb; Mug͟hals.10; Sud͟jān Rāy Bhandārī; al-Was͟hs͟hā'; [in Suppl.] Isfizārī; Mans͟hūrāt

etiquette-literature **Adab**; al-Maḥāsin wa 'l-Masāwī

see also al-D͟jidd wa 'l-Hazl; D͟jins; Ḥiyal; Iyās b. Muʿāwiya; Kalīla wa-Dimna; Kātib; Marzban-nāma; Nadīm; Sulūk.1; Ṭufaylī; Ẓarīf

authors Abū Ḥayyān al-Tawḥīdī; al-Bayhaḳī; D͟jāḥiẓ; al-G͟huzūlī; Hilāl al-Ṣābi'; al-Ḥuṣrī.I; Ibn ʿAbd Rabbih; Ibn Abi 'l-Dunyā; Ibn al-Muḳaffaʿ; al-Ḳalyūbī; al-Ḳās͟hānī; al-Kisrawī; al-Marzubānī; Merd͟jümek; al-Nīsābūrī; al-Rāg͟hib al-Iṣfahānī; al-S͟hims͟hāṭī; al-Ṣūlī; al-Tanūk͟hī, al-Muḥassin; al-Was͟hs͟hā'

see also al-D͟jahs͟hiyārī; al-Ḳalḳas͟handī.1; S͟habīb b. S͟hayba; al-Zarnūd͟jī

folkloric Bilmed͟je; Ḥikāya; Nādira; [in Suppl.] Taḳālīd

see also Yahūd.5; *and* → *the section Poetry.vernacular below*; PROVERBS

genealogical Mat͟hālib

see also Ṭabaḳāt

genealogists al-Abīwardī; al-D͟jawwānī; al-Hamdānī; al-Kalbī.II; al-Ḳalḳas͟handī.1; Ḳāsim b. Aṣbag͟h; al-Marwazī; Muṣʿab; al-Rus͟hāṭī; al-Zubayr b. Bakkār; [in Suppl.] Fak͟hr-i Mudabbir

see also Ibn Da'b; al-Ḳādirī al-Ḥasanī; al-K͟hʷārazmī; Mihmindār

genres

for the genres of non-literary disciplines → ASTRONOMY; LAW; THEOLOGY; *etc.*

poetry G͟hazal; Ḥamāsa; Hid͟jā'; Kān wa-Kān; Ḳaṣīda; K͟hamriyya; al-Ḳūmā; Madīḥ; Malḥūn; Mart͟hiya; Mat͟hnawī; Mufāk͟hara; Munṣifa; Musammaṭ; Muwas͟hs͟haḥ; Naḳā'iḍ; Nawriyya; S͟hahrangīz; S͟harḳī; Ṣuʿlūḳ.II.4 *and* III.2; Tad͟hkira.2 *and* 3; Ṭardiyya; Tard͟jīʿ-band; Waṣf.1; Zad͟jal; Zahriyyāt; Zuhdiyya; [in Suppl.] Ḥabsiyya; Ḳiṭʿa; Naẓm.1

see also ʿArabiyya.B; Iran.vii; Rabīʿiyyāt; Sāḳī.2; S͟hawāhid; Tak͟hmīs; Wā-sēk͟ht

prose Adab; Ad͟jā'ib; Awā'il; Badīʿ; Bilmed͟je; D͟jafr; Faḍīla; Fahrasa; Ḥikāya; Ilāhī; Ins͟hā'; Isrā'īliyyāt; K͟hiṭaṭ; Ḳiṣṣa; Laḥn al-ʿĀmma; Lug͟hz; al-Mag͟hāzī; al-Maḥāsin wa 'l-Masāwī; Maḳāla; Maḳāma; Manāḳib; Masā'il wa-Ad͟jwiba; al-Masālik wa 'l-Mamālik; Masraḥ; Mat͟hālib; Mawsūʿa; Muḳaddima; Muk͟htaṣar; Munāẓara; Nādira (*and* [in Suppl.]); Naṣīḥat al-Mulūk; Riḥla; Risāla; S͟harḥ; Ṣila.2; Sīra; Sunan; Ṭabaḳāt; Tad͟hkira.1; Tafsīr; Tard͟jama; Uḳṣūṣa; [in Suppl.] Arbaʿūn Ḥadīt͟h; Malfūẓāt; Taḳrīẓ

see also Alf Layla wa-Layla (363b); ʿArabiyya.B; Bibliography; D͟jug͟hrāfiyā; Fatḥnāme; Ḥayawān; Ḥiyal; Iran.vii; Malāḥim; Mat͟hal; S͟hāhnāmed͟ji; Zuhd; *and* → CHRISTIANITY.MONASTERIES.WRITINGS ON; LITERATURE.TRADITION-LITERATURE; PILGRIMAGE

historical Isrā'īliyyāt; al-Mag͟hāzī; Tard͟jama.1; **Ta'rīk͟h**.II

see also Fatḥnāme; Ṣaḥāba; Ṣila.2.II; *and* → *the sections Biographical, Mag͟hāzī-litera-*

ture and Tradition-literature under this entry
Andalusian → ANDALUSIA
Arabic **Ta'rīkh**.II.1
on countries/cities → *individual countries*
on dynasties/caliphs → *individual dynasties under* DYNASTIES
universal histories Abu 'l-Fidā; Abū Mikhnaf; Akanṣūs; al-Antāķī; ʿArīb b. Saʿd al-Kātib al-Ķurṭubī; al-ʿAynī; al-Bakrī.1 *and* 2; al-Balādhurī; Baybars al-Manṣūrī; al-Birzālī; Daḥlān; al-Dhahabī; al-Diyārbakrī; al-Djannābī; al-Djazarī; al-Farghānī; Ḥamza al-Iṣfahānī; Ḥasan-i Rūmlū; al-Haytham b. ʿAdī; Ibn Abī Shayba; Ibn Abī Ṭayyiʾ; Ibn Aʿtham al-Kūfī; Ibn al-Athīr.2; Ibn al-Dawādārī; Ibn al-Djawzī (Sibṭ); Ibn al-Furāt; Ibn Kathīr; Ibn Khaldūn; Ibn Khayyāṭ al-ʿUṣfurī; Ibn al-Sāʿī; al-Kalbī.II; Kātib Čelebi; al-Kutubī; al-Makīn b. al-ʿAmīd; al-Masʿūdī; Miskawayh; Münedjdjim Bashi; al-Muṭahhar b. Ṭāhir al-Maķdisī; al-Nuwayrī, Shihāb al-Dīn; Saʿīd b. al-Biṭrīķ; al-Ṭabarī, Abū Djaʿfar; al-Thaʿālibī, Abū Manṣūr (*and* al-Thaʿālibī, Abū Manṣūr ʿAbd al-Malik); al-Thaķafī, Ibrāhīm; Wathīma b. Mūsā; al-Yaʿķūbī; al-Yūnīnī
see also Akhbār Madjmūʿa
8th-century authors Abū Mikhnaf; ʿAwāna b. al-Ḥakam al-Kalbī; Sayf b. ʿUmar
9th-century authors al-Balādhurī; al-Fāķihī; al-Farghānī; al-Haytham b. ʿAdī; Ibn ʿAbd al-Ḥakam.4; Ibn Abī Shayba; Ibn Abī Ṭāhir Ṭayfūr; Ibn Aʿtham al-Kūfī; Ibn Khayyāṭ al-ʿUṣfurī; Ibn al-Naṭṭāḥ; al-Kalbī.II; al-Madāʾinī; Naṣr b. Muzāḥim; al-Wāķidī; Wathīma b. Mūsā; al-Yaʿķūbī; al-Ziyādī
10th-century authors ʿArīb b. Saʿd al-Kātib al-Ķurṭubī; al-Azdī; Baḥshal; al-Balawī; al-Djahshiyārī; Ḥamza al-Iṣfahānī; Ibn al-Dāya; Ibn al-Ķūṭiyya; Ibn Manda; Ibn al-Ṣaghīr; al-Kindī, Abū ʿUmar Muḥammad; al-Masʿūdī; al-Muṭahhar b. Ṭāhir al-Maķdisī; Saʿīd b. al-Biṭrīķ; al-Ṭabarī, Abū Djaʿfar; Wakīʿ; al-Waṣīfī
11th-century authors al-Antāķī, Abu 'l-Faradj; Ibn al-Bannāʾ; Ibn Burd.I; Ibn Ḥayyān; Ibn al-Raķīķ; al-Māfarrūkhī; al-Rāzī, Aḥmad b. ʿAbd Allāh; al-Thaʿālibī, Abū Manṣūr
12th-century authors al-ʿAẓīmī; Ibn al-Djawzī; Ibn Ghālib; Ibn al-Ķalānisī; Ibn Ṣāḥib al-Ṣalāt; Ibn al-Ṣayrafī, Abū Bakr; Ibn Shaddād, Abū Muḥammad; ʿImād al-Dīn; Shīrawayh; ʿUmāra al-Yamanī
see also al-Baydhaķ; Ibn Manda
13th-century authors ʿAbd al-Wāḥid al-Marrākushī; Abū Shāma; al-Bundārī; al-Djanadī; Ibn Abi 'l-Dam; Ibn Abī Ṭayyiʾ; Ibn al-ʿAdīm; Ibn al-Athīr.2; Ibn al-Djawzī (Sibṭ); Ibn Ḥamādu; Ibn Khallikān; Ibn al-Mudjāwir; Ibn Muyassar; Ibn al-Nadjdjār; Ibn al-Sāʿī; Ibn Saʿīd al-Maghribī; Ibn Shaddād, ʿIzz al-Dīn; Ibn Shaddād, Bahāʾ al-Dīn; Ibn al-Ṭuwayr; al-Makīn b. al-ʿAmīd; al-Manṣūr, al-Malik; al-Rāfiʿī; [in Suppl.] Ibn ʿAskar; Ibn Ḥātim
14th-century authors Abu 'l-Fidā; Baybars al-Manṣūrī; al-Birzālī; al-Dhahabī; al-Djazarī; Ibn Abī Zarʿ; Ibn al-Dawādārī; Ibn Duķmāķ; Ibn al-Furāt, Nāṣir al-Dīn; Ibn Ḥabīb, Badr al-Dīn; Ibn ʿIdhārī; Ibn Kathīr, ʿImād al-Dīn; Ibn Khaldūn; Ibn al-Khaṭīb; Ibn al-Ṭiķṭaķā; al-Khazradjī, Muwaffaķ al-Dīn; al-Kutubī; al-Mufaḍḍal b. Abi 'l-Faḍāʾil; al-Nuwayrī, Shihāb al-Dīn; al-Ṣafadī, Ṣalāḥ al-Dīn; Shāfiʿ b. ʿAlī; al-Sharīf Abū Muḥammad Idrīs; al-Wādīʾāshī; al-Yūnīnī
15th-century authors Abu 'l-Maḥāsin b. Taghrībirdī; ʿArabfaķih; al-ʿAynī; al-Fāsī; Ibn ʿArabshāh; Ibn Shāhīn al-Ẓāhirī; al-Maķrīzī; al-Sakhāwī
16th-century authors al-Diyārbakrī; al-Djannābī, Abū Muḥammad; Ḥasan-i Rūmlū; Ibn al-Daybaʿ; Ibn Iyās; Ibn Ṭūlūn; Mudjīr al-Dīn al-ʿUlaymī; al-Nahrawālī; al-Suyūṭī
17th-century authors ʿAbd al-ʿAzīz b. Muḥammad; al-Bakrī (b. Abi 'l-Surūr); Ibn

Abī Dīnār; Kātib Čelebi; al-Makkarī; al-Mawzaʿī; al-Shillī

18th-century authors al-Damurdāshī; al-Ḥādjdj Ḥammūda; al-Ifrānī; Münedjdjim Bashî; al-Murādī.3

19th-century authors Aḥmad al-Nāṣirī al-Salāwī (*and* al-Nāṣir al-Salāwī); Akanṣūs; ʿAlī Pasha Mubārak; Daḥlān; al-Djabartī; Ghulām Ḥusayn Khān Ṭabāṭabāʾī; Ibn Abi ʾl-Ḍiyāf; al-Turk, Nikūlā; al-Zayyānī

see also al-Kardūdī

20th-century authors Ibn Zaydān; Kurd ʿAlī; [in Suppl.] Maṭar

Indo-Persian Mughals.10; **Taʾrīkh**.II.4

on countries/cities → INDIA

on dynasties/caliphs → *individual dynasties under* DYNASTIES.AFGHANISTAN AND INDIA

13th-century authors al-Djuzdjānī

14th-century authors Baranī; Shams al-Dīn-i Sirādj ʿAfīf

16th-century authors Abu ʾl-Faḍl ʿAllāmī; Djawhar; Gulbadan Bēgam; Niẓām al-Dīn Aḥmad al-Harawī; [in Suppl.] ʿAbbās Sarwānī

17th-century authors ʿAbd al-Ḥamīd Lāhawrī; Bakhtāwar Khān; Firishta; Ināyat Allāh Kańbū; Mīr Muḥammad Maʿṣūm; Niʿmat Allāh b. Ḥabīb Allāh Harawī; Nūr al-Ḥakk al-Dihlawī; Shīrāzī, Rafīʿ al-Dīn; [in Suppl.] ʿĀkil Khān Rāzī; Ḥādjdjī al-Dabīr; Ḥaydar Malik; Muḥammad Ṣāliḥ Kanbō Lāhawrī

see also Badāʾūnī

18th-century authors ʿAbd al-Karīm Kashmīrī; Ḳāniʿ; Khʷāfī Khān; Niʿmat Khān; Sudjān Rāy Bhandārī

19th-century authors ʿAbd al-Karīm Munshī; Ghulām Ḥusayn Khān Ṭabāṭabāʾī; Ghulām Ḥusayn "Salīm"

see also Aẓfarī

Persian **Taʾrīkh**.II.2; [in Suppl.] Čač-nāma

on Afghanistan → AFGHANISTAN

on Iran → IRAN

on dynasties/caliphs → *individual dynasties under* DYNASTIES.PERSIA

universal histories Mīrkhʷānd; Niẓām-shāhī; Sipihr

10th-century authors Balʿamī.2; Ḥamza al-Iṣfahānīʾ [in Suppl.] al-Ḳummī

11th-century authors Bayhaḳī; Gardīzī; al-Māfarrūkhī

12th-century authors Anūshirwān b. Khālid; al-Bayhaḳī, Ẓahīr al-Dīn; Ibn Manda; [in Suppl.] Ibn al-Balkhī

13th-century authors Djuwaynī, ʿAlāʾ al-Dīn; Ibn Bībī; Ibn-i Isfandiyār; [in Suppl.] Ḥasan Niẓāmī; al-Ḥusaynī

see also al-Rāfiʿī

14th-century authors Banākitī; Ḥamd Allāh al-Mustawfī al-Ḳazwīnī; Shabānkāraʾī; Waṣṣāf; [in Suppl.] al-Aḳsarāyī

15th-century authors ʿAbd al-Razzāḳ al-Samarḳandī; Ḥāfiẓ-i Abrū; Ẓahīr al-Dīn Marʿashī

16th-century authors Bidlīsī, Sharaf al-Dīn; Djamāl al-Ḥusaynī; Ghaffārī; Ḥaydar Mīrzā; Khʷāndamīr; Ḳum(m)ī; al-Lārī; Shāmī, Niẓām al-Dīn; [in Suppl.] Ḥāfiẓ Tanîsh

see also ʿAlī b. Shams al-Dīn

17th-century authors ʿAbd al-Fattāh Fūmanī; Ḥaydar b. ʿAlī; Iskandar Beg; Rāzī, Amīn Aḥmad; Ṭāhir Waḥīd

18th-century authors Mahdī Khān Astarābādī

see also Īsar-dās

19th-century authors ʿAbd al-Karīm Bukhārī; [in Suppl.] Fasāʾī

Turkish   Sh̲āhnāmed̲j̲i; **Ta'rīk̲h̲**.II.3; Waḳaʿ-nüwīs
    on the Ottoman Empire → DYNASTIES.ANATOLIA AND THE TURKS.OTTO-
    MANS.HISTORIANS OF
    universal histories   Sh̲ārih̲ ül-Menār-zāde
       see also Nesh̲rī
    15th-century authors   ʿĀsh̲ik̲-pas̲h̲a-zāde; Meḥmed Pas̲h̲a, Ḳaramānī; Yak̲h̲sh̲ī Faḳīh
    16th-century authors   ʿĀlī; Bihis̲h̲tī; D̲j̲alālzāde Muṣṭafā Čelebi; D̲j̲alālzāde Ṣāliḥ
       Čelebi; Kemāl Pas̲h̲a-zāde; Luḳmān b. Sayyid Ḥusayn; Maṭrāḳčī; Meḥmed Zaʿīm;
       Nesh̲rī; Selānīkī; Seyfī
       see also Ḥadīdī; Med̲j̲dī
    17th-century authors   ʿAbdī; ʿAbdī Pas̲h̲a; Ḥasan Bey-zāde; Ḥibrī; Ḳarā-čelebi-
       zāde.4; Kātib Čelebi; Meḥmed K̲h̲alīfe b. Hüseyn; Sh̲ārih̲ ül-Menār-zāde;
       Ṭas̲h̲köprüzāde.2; Wed̲j̲īhī
    18th-century authors   ʿAbdī Efendi; Aḥmad Rasmī; Čelebi-zāde; Čes̲h̲mīzāde;
       Enwerī; ʿIzzī; Müned̲j̲d̲j̲im Bas̲h̲ī; ʿOt̲h̲mān-zāde; ʿUs̲h̲s̲h̲āḳī-zāde, Ibrāhīm
       see also [in Suppl.] Ḳantimīr, Demetrius
    19th-century authors   Aḥmad D̲j̲ewdet Pas̲h̲a; ʿĀṣim; ʿAṭāʾ Bey, Ṭayyārzāda; Esʿad
       Efendi, Meḥmed; Kemāl, Meḥmed Nāmîḳ; K̲h̲ayr Allāh Efendi; Wāṣif
    20th-century authors   Aḥmad Rafīḳ; ʿAlī Amīrī; (Meḥmed) ʿAṭāʾ Beg; Luṭfī Efendi;
       Mīzānd̲j̲î Meḥmed Murād; S̲h̲ems al-Dīn Günaltay; S̲h̲eref, ʿAbd al-Raḥmān;
       T̲h̲üreyyā
       see also Ḥilmī
    in Eastern Turkish   Abu 'l-G̲h̲āzī Bahādur K̲h̲ān; Bāk̲î k̲h̲ānlî; Muʾnis; [in Suppl.]
       Āgahī
hunting   → HUNTING.POETRY
imagery   → *the section Topoi and imagery below*
in other languages   Afg̲h̲ān.iii; Aljamía; Bengali.ii; Berbers.VI; Beskesek-abaza; Bosna.3;
    Hausa.iii; Hindī; Indonesia.vi; Judaeo-Arabic.iii; Judaeo-Persian.i; Kano; Ḳiṣṣa.8;
    Lahndā.2; Laḳ; Masrah̲.6; Pand̲j̲ābī.2; S̲h̲iʿr.7; Sind.3.b; Somali.6; Tād̲j̲īkī.2; Tas̲h̲elḥīt.3;
    [in Suppl.] S̲h̲iʿr.5
    for Chinese → CHINA; *for Swahili* → KENYA; *for Malaysian* → MALAYSIA; *for Eastern*
    Turkish languages → *the sections* LITERATURE.HISTORY.TURKISH, POETRY.TURKISH *and*
    PROSE.TURKISH; *and* → LITERATURE.POETRY.MYSTICAL *and* TRANSLATIONS
    Bengali authors   Nad̲h̲r al-Islām; Nūr Ḳuṭb al-ʿĀlam
    Bosnian authors   [in Suppl.] Ḳāʾimī
    Hindi authors   Malik Muḥammad D̲j̲āyasī; Nihāl Čand Lāhawrī; Prēm Čand; Sud̲j̲ān Rāy
       Bhandārī; [in Suppl.] Kabīr
       see also ʿAbd al-Raḥīm K̲h̲ān; Ins̲h̲āʾ; Lallūd̲j̲ī Lāl
    Judaeo-Arabic authors   Mūsā b. ʿAzra; al-Samawʾal b. ʿĀdiyā; [in Suppl.] Nissīm b. Yaʿḳūb,
       Ibn Sh̲āhīn
       and → JUDAISM.LANGUAGE AND LITERATURE
    Judaeo-Persian authors   Sh̲āhīn-i S̲h̲īrāzī
       and → JUDAISM.LANGUAGE AND LITERATURE
    Pashto authors   K̲h̲us̲h̲ḥāl K̲h̲ān K̲h̲aṭak
    Tatar authors   G̲h̲afūrī, Med̲j̲īd
mag̲h̲āzī-literature   Abū Maʿs̲h̲ar al-Sindī; Ibn ʿĀʾid̲h̲; al-Kalāʿī; **al-Mag̲h̲āzī**; Mūsā b. ʿUḳba
    see also al-Baṭṭāl; Sīra
personages in literature   Abū Ḍamḍam; Abu 'l-Ḳāsim; Abū Zayd; Ali Baba; Ayāz; Aywaz.2;
    al-Basūs; al-Baṭṭāl; Bekrī Muṣṭafā Ag̲h̲a; Buzurgmihr; D̲h̲u 'l-Himma; D̲j̲ams̲h̲īd; D̲j̲uḥā;
    al-G̲h̲ādirī; Ḥamza b. ʿAbd al-Muṭṭalib; Ḥātim al-Ṭāʾī; Ḥayy b. Yaḳẓān; Körog̲h̲lu; Manas;
    Naṣr al-Dīn K̲h̲od̲j̲a; Rustam; Sām; Ṣarî Ṣaltūḳ Dede; S̲h̲ahrazād; al-Sīd; Sindbād; Siyāwus̲h̲

see also Ṭufaylī; Yūsuf and Zulaykhā

picaresque Maḳāma; Mukaddī

pilgrimage-literature → PILGRIMAGE

poetry Arūḍ; Ḥamāsa; Ḳāfiya; Lughz; Maʿnā.3; Mukhtārāt; Muzdawidj; Shāʿir; **Shiʿr**; Wazn.2; [in Suppl.] Naẓm.1

see also Rāwī; Sharḥ.II; Takhalluṣ.1; Taʾrīkh.III; [in Suppl.] Sariḳa; *for poetical genres* → LITERATURE.GENRES.POETRY; *and* → METRICS

Andalusian ʿArabiyya.B.Appendix; Khamriyya.vi; Muwashshaḥ; Nawriyya; Shāʿir.1.D; Zadjal; Zahriyyāt.1

anthologies al-Fatḥ b. Khāḳān; al-Fihrī; Ibn Bassām; Ibn Diḥya; Ibn Faradj al-Djayyānī; al-Shaḳundī

8th-century poets Ghirbīb b. ʿAbd Allāh

9th-century poets ʿAbbās b. Firnās; ʿAbbās b. Nāṣih; al-Ghazāl

see also Ibn ʿAlḳama.2

10th-century poets Ibn ʿAbd Rabbih; Ibn Abī Zamanayn; Ibn Faradj al-Djayyānī; Ibn Ḳuzmān.I (*and* [in Suppl.] Ḳuzmān.1); Muḳaddam b. Muʿāfā; al-Ramādī; al-Sharīf al-Ṭalīḳ

11th-century poets Abū Isḥāḳ al-Ilbīrī; Ibn al-Abbār; Ibn ʿAbd al-Ṣamad; Ibn ʿAmmār; Ibn Burd.II; Ibn Darrādj al-Ḳasṭallī; Ibn Gharsiya; Ibn al-Ḥaddād; Ibn al-Ḥannāṭ; Ibn al-Labbāna; Ibn Māʾ al-Samāʾ; Ibn al-Shahīd; Ibn Shuhayd; Ibn Zaydūn; al-Muʿtamid ibn ʿAbbād; Wallāda

see also Ṣāʿid al-Baghdādī; al-Waḳḳashī

12th-century poets al-Aʿmā al-Tuṭīlī; Ḥafṣa bint al-Ḥādjdj; Ibn ʿAbdūn; Ibn Baḳī; Ibn Ḳabṭūrnu (*and* [in Suppl.] Ḳabṭūrnuh); Ibn Khafādja; Ibn Ḳuzmān.II *and* V (*and* [in Suppl.] Ḳuzmān.2); Ibn al-Ṣayrafī; al-Ḳurṭubī; al-Ruṣāfī; Ṣafwān b. Idrīs

see also Mūsā b. ʿAzra

13th-century poets Ḥāzim; Ibn al-Abbār; Ibn ʿAmīra; Ibn Sahl; Ibn Saʿīd al-Maghribī; al-Ḳabtawrī; al-Shushtarī

14th-century poets Ibn al-Ḥādjdj; Ibn Khātima; Ibn Luyūn; Ibn al-Murābiʿ; al-Sharīf al-Gharnāṭī

see also [in Suppl.] al-Ruʿaynī

Arabic Atāba; Ghazal.i; Ḥamāsa.i; Hidjāʾ; Kān wa-Kān; Ḳaṣīda.1; al-Ḳūmā; Madīḥ.1; Maḳṣūra; Malḥūn; Marthiya.1; Mawāliyā; Mawlidiyya; Mukhtārāt.1; Musammaṭ.1; Muwashshaḥ; Naḳāʾiḍ; Nasīb; Rubāʿī.3; Shāʿir.1; **Shiʿr**.1; Takhmīs; Ṭardiyya; Ṭayf al-Khayāl; ʿUdhrī; Zahriyyāt.1; Zuhdiyya; [in Suppl.] Ḳiṭʿa.1; Muḥdathūn

see also ʿArabiyya.B.II; ʿIlm al-Djamāl; Ḳalb.II; Mawlid; Muwallad.2; Ṣuʿlūk; *and* → LITERATURE.POETRY.ANDALUSIAN *and* POETRY.MYSTICAL

anthologies al-Muʿallaḳāt; al-Mufaḍḍaliyyāt; **Mukhtārāt**.1

anthologists Abu ʾl-Faradj al-Iṣbahānī; Abū Tammām; al-ʿAlamī; al-Bākharzī; al-Buḥturī; Diʿbil; al-Hamdānī; Ḥammād al-Rāwiya; Ibn Abī Ṭāhir Ṭayfūr; Ibn Dāwūd; Ibn al-Ḳutayba; Ibn al-Muʿtazz; Ibn al-Ṣayrafī; ʿImād al-Dīn; al-Nawādjī; al-Sarī al-Raffāʾ; al-Shayzarī; al-Shimshāṭī; al-Thaʿālibī, Abū Manṣūr ʿAbd al-Malik; [in Suppl.] Abū Zayd al-Ḳurashī; al-Bustānī.3; Muḥammad b. Sayf al-Dīn, Ibn Aydamir; al-Zandjānī

see also al-Ṭayālisī, Djaʿfar

works Bānat Suʿād; Burda.2; Madjnūn Laylā.1; al-Muʿallaḳāt

pre-Islamic poets ʿAbīd b. al-Abraṣ; Abū Dhuʾayb al-Hudhalī; Abū Duʾād al-Iyādī; Abū Kabīr al-Hudhalī; ʿAdī b. Zayd; al-Afwah al-Awdī; al-Aghlab al-ʿIdjlī; ʿAlḳama; ʿĀmir b. al-Ṭufayl; ʿAmr b. al-Ahtam; ʿAmr b. Ḳamīʾa; ʿAmr b. Kulthūm; ʿAntara; al-Aʿshā; al-Aswad b. Yaʿfur; Aws b. Ḥadjar; Bishr b. Abī Khāzim; Bisṭām b. Ḳays; Durayd b. al-Ṣimma; al-Ḥādira; al-Ḥārith b. Ḥilliza; Ḥassān b.

Thābit; Ḥātim al-Ṭā'ī; Ibn al-Iṭnāba al-Khazradjī; Imru' al-Ḳays b. Ḥudjr; Ḳays b. al-Khaṭīm; al-Khansā'; Laḳīṭ al-Iyādī; Laḳīṭ b. Zurāra; al-Munakhkhal al-Yashkurī; Muraḳḳish; al-Mutalammis; al-Nābigha al-Dhubyānī; Salāma b. Djandal; al-Samaw'al b. ʿĀdiyā; al-Shanfarā; Ta'abbaṭa Sharran; Ṭarafa; Ṭufayl b. ʿAwf; Uḥayḥa b. al-Djulāḥ; Umayya b. ʿAbi 'l-Ṣalt; ʿUrwa b. al-Ward; Zuhayr *see also* ʿArabiyya.B.I; Ghazal; Hudhayl; al-Muʿallaḳāt; al-Mufaḍḍaliyyāt; Mufākhara.2; Nasīb.2.a; Shāʿir.1A; al-Shantamarī; Ṣuʿlūk.II.4

mukhaḍramūn poets (6th-7th centuries) al-ʿAbbās b. Mirdās; ʿAbd Allāh b. Rawāḥa; Abū Khirāsh; Abū Miḥdjān; ʿAmr b. Maʿdīkarib; Ḍirār b. al-Khaṭṭāb; Ḥassān b. Thābit; al-Ḥuṭay'a; Ibn (al-)Aḥmar; Kaʿb b. Mālik; Kaʿb b. Zuhayr; Khidāsh b. Zuhayr al-Aṣghar; Labīd b. Rabīʿa; Maʿn b. Aws al-Muzanī; **Mukhaḍram**; Mutammim b. Nuwayra; al-Nābigha al-Djaʿdī; al-Namir b. Tawlab al-ʿUklī; al-Shammākh b. Ḍirār; Suḥaym; [in Suppl.] Abu 'l-Ṭamaḥān al-Ḳaynī; Ibn Muḳbil *see also* Hudhayl; Nasīb.2.b; [in Suppl.] Muḥdathūn

7th and 8th-century poets al-ʿAbbās b. al-Aḥnaf; ʿAbd Allāh b. Hammān; Abū ʿAṭā' al-Sindī; Abū Dahbal al-Djumaḥī; Abū Dulāma; Abu 'l-Nadjm al-ʿIdjlī; Abū Ṣakhr al-Hudhalī; Abu 'l-Shamaḳmaḳ; Adī b. al-Riḳāʿ; al-ʿAdjdjādj; al-Aḥwaṣ; al-Akhṭal; al-ʿArdjī; Aʿshā Hamdān; al-Ashdjaʿ b. ʿAmr al-Sulamī; Ayman b. Khuraym; al-Baʿīth; Bashshār b. Burd; Dhu 'l-Rumma; Djamīl; Djarīr; Dukayn al-Rādjiz; al-Farazdaḳ; al-Ḥakam b. ʿAbdal; al-Ḥakam b. Ḳanbar; Ḥammād ʿAdjrad; Ḥamza b. Bīḍ; Ḥāritha b. Badr al-Ghudānī; al-Ḥuḍayn; Ḥumayd b. Thawr; Ḥumayd al-Arḳaṭ; Ibn Abī ʿUyayna; Ibn al-Dumayna; Ibn Harma; Ibn Ḳays al-Ruḳayyāt; Ibn Ladja'; Ibn al-Mawlā; Ibn Mayyāda; Ibn Mufarrigh; Ibn Muṭayr; Ibn Sayḥān; ʿImrān b. Ḥiṭṭān; ʿInān; Ismāʿīl b. Yasār; Kaʿb b. Djuʿayl al-Taghlabī; Ḳaṭarī b. al-Fudjā'a; al-Kumayt b. Zayd al-Asadī; al-Ḳuṭāmī; Kuthayyir b. ʿAbd al-Raḥmān; Laylā al-Akhyaliyya; Manṣūr al-Namarī; Marwān b. Abī Ḥafṣa and Marwān b. Abi 'l-Djanūb; Miskīn al-Dārimī; Mūsā Shahawātin; Musāwir al-Warrāḳ; Muṭīʿ b. Iyās; Nubāta b. ʿAbd Allāh; Nuṣayb; Nuṣayb b. Rabāḥ; al-Rāʿī; Ru'ba b. al-ʿAdjdjādj; Ṣafī al-Dīn al-Ḥillī; Ṣafwān al-Anṣārī; Saḥbān Wā'il; Ṣāliḥ b. ʿAbd al-Ḳuddūs; Salm al-Khāsir; al-Sayyid al-Ḥimyarī; al-Shamardal; Sudayf b. Maymūn; Sufyān al-ʿAbdī; Sulaymān b. Yaḥyā; Surāḳa b. Mirdās al-Aṣghar; Ṭahmān b. ʿAmr al-Kilābī; Tawba b. al-Ḥumayyir; Thābit Ḳuṭna; al-Ṭirimmāḥ; al-Uḳayshir; ʿUmar b. Abī Rabīʿa; ʿUrwa b. Ḥizām; ʿUrwa b. Udhayna; Waḍḍāḥ al-Yaman; Wāliba b. al-Ḥubāb; al-Walīd.2; al-Walīd b. Ṭarīf; al-Walīd b. ʿUḳba; Yazīd Ibn Ḍabba; al-Zafayān; al-Zibriḳān b. Badr; Ziyād al-Aʿdjam; [in Suppl.] ʿAbd al-Raḥmān b. Ḥassān; Abū ʿAmr al-Shaybānī (*and* al-Shaybānī, Abū ʿAmr); Abū Ḥayyā al-Numayrī; Abū Ḥuzāba; Abū Nukhayla; Bakr b. al-Naṭṭāḥ; al-Nadjāshī

see also Nasīb.2.c *and* d; Ṣuʿlūk.III.2; [in Suppl.] Muḥdathūn

9th and 10th-century poets Abān b. ʿAbd al-Ḥamīd; ʿAbd Allāh b. Ṭāhir; Abu 'l-ʿAtāhiya; Abu 'l-ʿAynā'; Abū Dulaf; Abu 'l-Faradj al-Iṣbahānī; Abū Firās; Abū Nuwās; Abu 'l-Shīṣ; Abū Tammām; Abū Yaʿḳūb al-Khuraymī; al-ʿAkawwak; ʿAlī b. al-Djahm; al-ʿAttābī; al-Babbaghā'; al-Baṣīr; al-Buḥturī; al-Bustī; Diʿbil; Dīk al-Djinn; al-Ḥimṣī; al-Djammāz; al-Hamdānī; (al-)Ḥusayn b. al-Ḍaḥḥāk; Ibn al-ʿAllāf; Ibn Bassām; Ibn al-Ḥadjdjādj; Ibn Kunāsa; Ibn Lankak; Ibn al-Muʿadhdhal; Ibn Munādhir; Ibn al-Muʿtazz; Ibn al-Rūmī; al-Ḳāsim b. ʿĪsā; Khālid b. Yazīd al-Kātib al-Tamīmī; al-Khālidiyyāni; al-Khaṭṭābī; al-Khubza'aruzzī; al-Kisrawī; Kushādjim; al-Ma'mūnī; Muḥammad b. ʿAbd al-Raḥmān al-ʿAṭawī; Muḥammad b. Ḥāzim al-Bāhilī; Muḥammad b. Umayya; Muḥammad b. Yasīr al-Riyāshī; al-Muṣʿabī; Muslim b. al-Walīd; al-Mutanabbī; Naṣr b. Nuṣayr; Sahl b. Hārūn b. Rāhawayh; Saʿīd b. Ḥumayd; al-Ṣanawbarī; al-Sarī al-Raffā'; al-

S̲h̲ims̲h̲āṭī; Ṭāhir b. Muḥammad; Tamīm b. al-Muʿizz li-Dīn Allāh; ʿUlayya; al-ʿUtbī, Abū ʿAbd al-Raḥmān; al-Warrāḳ, Maḥmūd; al-Waʾwāʾ al-Dimas̲h̲ḳī; Yamūt b. al-Muzarraʿ; [in Suppl.] Abu ʾl-ʿAmayt̲h̲al; Abu ʾl-Asad al-Ḥimmānī; Abu ʾl-Ḥasan al-Mag̲h̲ribī; Abū Hiffān; Abu ʾl-ʿIbar; Abū Riyās̲h̲ al-Ḳaysī; Abū Saʿd al-Mak̲h̲zūmī; Abū S̲h̲urāʿa; ʿAlī b. Muḥammad al-Tūnīsī al-Iyādī; Faḍl al-S̲h̲āʿira; al-Fazārī; al-Ḥamdawī

see also al-Hamad̲h̲ānī; Ibn Abī Zamanayn; Nasīb.2.d; S̲h̲ahīd; al-Ṣūlī; al-Ṭufaylī; al-Yazīdī.2

11th-13th-century poets al-Abīwardī; ʿAmīd al-Dīn al-Abzārī; al-Arrad̲j̲ānī; al-Badīʿ al-Asṭurlābī; Bahāʾ al-Dīn Zuhayr; al-Bāk̲h̲arzī; Ḥayṣa Bayṣa; al-Ḥuṣrī.II; Ibn Abi ʾl-Ḥadīd; Ibn Abī Ḥaṣīna; Ibn al-ʿAfīf al-Tilimsānī; Ibn al-Habbāriyya; Ibn Ḥamdīs; Ibn Ḥayyūs; Ibn Hindū; Ibn al-Ḳaṭṭān; Ibn al-Ḳaysarānī.2; Ibn K̲h̲amīs; Ibn Maṭrūḥ; Ibn al-Nabīh; Ibn Ras̲h̲īḳ; Ibn Sanāʾ al-Mulk; Ibn al-S̲h̲ad̲j̲arī al-Bag̲h̲dādī; Ibn S̲h̲araf al-Ḳayrawānī; Ibn S̲h̲ibl; Ibn al-Taʿāwīd̲h̲ī; al-Kammūnī; Ḳurhub; al-Maʿarrī; al-Marwazī; Mihyār; Muḥammad b. ʿAlī b. ʿUmar; al-Rūd̲h̲rāwarī; al-Ṣag̲h̲ānī; ʿAbd al-Muʾmin; Ṣāʿid al-Bag̲h̲dādī; al-S̲h̲arīf al-ʿAḳīlī; al-S̲h̲arīf al-Raḍī; S̲h̲umaym; al-Tallaʿfarī; Tamīm b. al-Muʿizz; al-Ṭarābulusī al-Raffāʾ; al-Tihāmī; al-Tilimsānī.3; al-Ṭug̲h̲rāʾī; ʿUmāra al-Yamanī; al-Wāsānī; Ẓāfir al-Ḥaddād; [in Suppl.] Abu ʾl-Ḥasan al-Anṣārī; al-Balaṭī, Abu ʾl-Fatḥ ʿUt̲h̲mān; al-Būṣīrī; al-G̲h̲azzī; al-Isʿirdī

see also al-K̲h̲azrad̲j̲ī; Nasīb.2.d; al-Wāt̲h̲iḳī; Yāḳūt al-Rūmī

14th-18th-century poets ʿAbd al-ʿAzīz b. Muḥammad; ʿAbd al-G̲h̲anī; al-Bakrī; al-Būrīnī; Farḥāt; Ibn Abī Ḥad̲j̲ala; Ibn ʿAmmār; Ibn Ḥid̲j̲d̲j̲a; Ibn Nubāta; Ibn al-Ṣāʾig̲h̲; Ibn al-Wannān; al-Ṣanʿānī, Ḍiyāʾ al-Dīn; Suʿūdī; al-Warg̲h̲ī; al-Yadālī; al-Yūsī

see also K̲h̲iḍr Beg; al-S̲h̲irbīnī; al-Wādīʾās̲h̲ī

19th and 20th-century poets al-Ak̲h̲ras; al-Bārūdī; Fāris al-S̲h̲idyāḳ; al-Fārūḳī; Fikrī; Ḥāfiẓ Ibrāhīm; Ibn Idrīs (I); Ismāʿīl Ṣabrī; Ismāʿīl Ṣabrī Pas̲h̲a; Ḳaddūr al-ʿAlamī; al-Kāẓimī; ʿAbd al-Muḥsin; K̲h̲alīl Muṭrān; al-K̲h̲ūrī; al-Maʿlūf; al-Manfalūṭī; Mardam.2; Maʿrūf al-Ruṣāfī; al-Māzinī; Nād̲j̲ī; Nad̲j̲īb al-Ḥaddād; Nad̲j̲īb Muḥammad Surūr; Saʿīd Abū Bakr; Ṣalāḥ ʿAbd al-Ṣabūr; Ṣāyig̲h̲, Tawfīḳ; al-S̲h̲ābbī; al-S̲h̲arḳāwī; S̲h̲āʾūl; S̲h̲awḳī; S̲h̲ukrī; Ṭāhā, ʿAlī Maḥmūd; Ṭuʿma, Ilyās; al-Tūnisī, Maḥmūd Bayram; al-Turk, Niḳūlā; Yakan, Muḥammad Walī al-Dīn; al-Yāzid̲j̲ī.1-4; al-Zahāwī, D̲j̲amīl Ṣidḳī; [in Suppl.] Abū Māḍī; Abū S̲h̲ādī; al-ʿAḳḳād; al-Bustānī; Buṭrus Karāma; Ibn ʿAmr al-Ribāṭī; Ibn al-Ḥād̲j̲d̲j̲; Ḳabbānī

see also S̲h̲āʿir.1.C; S̲h̲iʿr.1.b

transmission of **Rāwī**

transmitters Ḥammād al-Rāwiya; Ibn Daʾb; Ibn Kunāsa; K̲h̲alaf b. Ḥayyān al-Aḥmar; K̲h̲ālid b. Ṣafwān b. al-Ahtam; al-Kisrawī; al-Mufaḍḍal al-Ḍabbī; Muḥammad b. al-Ḥasan b. Dīnār; al-S̲h̲arḳī b. al-Ḳuṭāmī; al-Sukkarī; al-Ṣūlī; [in Suppl.] Abū ʿAmr al-S̲h̲aybānī (*and* al-S̲h̲aybānī, Abū ʿAmr)

and → LINGUISTICS.GRAMMARIANS.8TH *and* 9TH CENTURY

bacchic → WINE

Indo-Persian Mug̲h̲als.10; Sabk-i Hindī; S̲h̲āʿir.4

see also Pand̲j̲ābī.2; *and →* LITERATURE.POETRY.MYSTICAL *and* PERSIAN

11th-century poets Masʿūd-i Saʿd-i Salmān; [in Suppl.] Abu ʾl-Farad̲j̲ b. Masʿūd Rūnī

14th-century poets Amīr K̲h̲usraw; Ḥasan Dihlawī; [in Suppl.] Ḥamīd Ḳalandar

16th-century poets Fayḍī; T̲h̲anāʾī; [in Suppl.] Kāhī; Ḳāsim Arslān

see also ʿAbd al-Raḥīm K̲h̲ān

17th-century poets G̲h̲anī; G̲h̲anīmat; Idrākī Bēglārī; Ḳudsī, Muḥammad D̲j̲ān;

Malik Ḳummi; Munīr Lāhawrī; Nāṣir ʿAlī Sirhindī; Naẓīrī; Salīm, Muḥammad Ḳulī; S̲h̲aydā, Mullā; Ṭālib Āmulī; Tug̲h̲rā, Mullā; [in Suppl.] G̲h̲anīmat Kund̲j̲āhī

18th-century poets Ārzū K̲h̲ān; As̲h̲raf ʿAlī K̲h̲ān; Bīdil; Dard; Ḥazīn; Ḳāniʿ; Mak̲h̲fī; Wafā.1

see also Taḥsīn

19th-century poets Aẓfarī; G̲h̲ālib; Rangīn; [in Suppl.] Adīb Pīs̲h̲āwarī

see also Afsūs

love **G̲h̲azal**; **Nasīb**; Raḳīb; S̲h̲ahrangīz; Turks.III.4; ʿUd̲h̲rī

see also al-Marzubānī; Nard̲j̲is; S̲h̲awḳ.1(a); S̲h̲awḳ, Taṣadduḳ Ḥusayn; *and* → LOVE

Arabic poets al-ʿAbbās b. al-Aḥnaf; Abū D̲h̲uʾayb al-Hud̲h̲alī; Abū Nuwās; al-Aḥwaṣ; al-ʿArd̲j̲ī; Bas̲h̲s̲h̲ār b. Burd; D̲j̲amīl al-ʿUd̲h̲rī; Ibn Dāwūd; Ibn al-Dumayna; Ibn Mayyāda; Ibn al-Nabīh; Ibn Sahl; Ibn Zaydūn; Imruʾ al-Ḳays; Kut̲h̲ayyir b. ʿAbd al-Raḥmān; Laylā al-Ak̲h̲yaliyya; Manṣūr al-Namarī; Muraḳḳis̲h̲.1; Nād̲j̲ī; Nuṣayb b. Rabāḥ; al-Ramādī; Saʿīd b. Ḥumayd; Suḥaym; ʿUmar b. Abī Rabīʿa; ʿUrwa b. Ḥizām; ʿUrwa b. Ud̲h̲ayna; al-Walīd.2

see also ʿInān; Mad̲j̲nūn Laylā.1; *and* → LOVE.EROTIC

Persian poets Ḥāfiẓ; Muḥtas̲h̲am-i Kās̲h̲ānī; Saʿdī; Ṣāʾib; S̲h̲ahriyār; Zulālī-yi K̲h̲ʷānsārī

see also Farhād wa-S̲h̲īrīn; Mad̲j̲nūn Laylā.2; S̲h̲ahīd; Wāmiḳ wa ʿAd̲h̲rāʾ; Wīs u Rāmīn

Turkish poets

see also Farhād wa-S̲h̲īrīn; Mad̲j̲nūn Laylā.3

Urdu poets Dāg̲h̲; Mīr Muḥammad Taḳī; S̲h̲awḳ

see also Mad̲j̲nūn Laylā.4; *and* → LOVE.EROTIC

mystical

Arabic ʿAbd al-G̲h̲anī; al-Bakrī, Muḥammad; al-Bakrī, Muṣṭafā; al-Dimyāṭī; al-Ḥallād̲j̲; Ibn ʿAd̲j̲ība; Ibn ʿAlīwa; Ibn al-ʿArabī; al-Mad̲j̲d̲h̲ūb; Mak̲h̲rama.3; al-S̲h̲us̲h̲tarī

see also ʿAbd al-Ḳādir al-D̲j̲īlānī; Abū Madyan; al-Ḳādirī al-Ḥasanī; al-Yāfiʿī; [in Suppl.] al-Hilālī

Central Asian Aḥmad Yasawī

Indian Bāḳī bi ʾllāh; Bīdil; Dard; "D̲j̲amālī"; Hānsawī; Ḥusaynī Sādāt Amīr; Imdād Allāh; Malik Muḥammad D̲j̲āyasī; [in Suppl.] Ḥamīd Ḳalandar; Kabīr

see also Bhitāʾī; Pand̲j̲ābī.2; S̲h̲āʾir.4

Indonesian Ḥamza Fanṣūrī

Persian Aḥmad-i D̲j̲ām; ʿAṭṭār; Bābā-Ṭāhir; D̲j̲alāl al-Dīn Rūmī; Faḍl Allāh Ḥurūfī; G̲h̲ud̲j̲duwānī; Humām al-Dīn b. ʿAlāʾ Tabrīzī; ʿIrāḳī; Kamāl K̲h̲ud̲j̲andī; Ḳāsim-i Anwār; Kirmānī; Lāhid̲j̲ī; Maḥmūd S̲h̲abistarī; Sanāʾī; S̲h̲īrīn Mag̲h̲ribī, Muḥammad; Sulṭān Walad; [in Suppl.] ʿĀrif Čelebī; ʿImād al-Dīn ʿAlī, Faḳīh-i Kirmānī

see also Abū Saʿīd b. Abi ʾl-K̲h̲ayr; K̲h̲araḳānī; S̲h̲awḳ; [in Suppl.] Aḥmad-i Rūmī

Turkish ʿĀs̲h̲iḳ Pas̲h̲a; Faṣīḥ Dede; Guls̲h̲anī; Güls̲h̲ehrī; Hüdāʾī; Müned̲j̲d̲j̲im Bas̲h̲i̊; Nefes; Nesīmī; Refīʿī; S̲arī̊ ʿAbd Allāh Efendi; Sezāʾī, Ḥasan Dede; S̲h̲eyyād Ḥamza; Yūnus Emre; [in Suppl.] Es̲h̲refog̲h̲lu; Esrār Dede; Rūs̲h̲anī, Dede ʿUmar; Süleymān Dhātī

see also Ḥusām al-Dīn Čelebi; Ismāʿīl al-Anḳarawī; Ismāʿīl Ḥaḳḳī; Ḳayg̲h̲usuz Abdāl; K̲h̲alīlī; Sulṭān Walad; Yazīd̲j̲i-og̲h̲lu

nature Ibn K̲h̲afād̲j̲a; Nawriyya; Rabīʿiyyāt; al-Ṣanawbarī; Zahriyyāt

see also al-Walīd.2; [in Suppl.] Ward

Persian G̲h̲azal.ii; Ḥamāsa.ii; Hid̲j̲āʾ.ii; Ḳaṣīda.2; K̲h̲amsa; Madīḥ.2; Malik al-S̲h̲uʿarāʾ;

Marthiya.2; Mathnawī.2; Mukhtārāt.2; Musammaṭ; Mustazād; Rubāʿī.1; Shahrangīz.1; Shāʿir.2; **Shiʿr**.2; Takhalluṣ.2; Tardjīʿ-band; Zahriyyāt.2; [in Suppl.] Ḥabsiyya; Ḳiṭʿa.2

see also Radīf.2; Ṣafawids.III; Sāḳī.2; Shaman; Shaʿr.3; Sharīf; Wā-sēkht; Yaghmā Djandaḳī; [in Suppl.] Miʿrādj.6; Ṣawladjān; *and* → LITERATURE.POETRY.INDO-PERSIAN *and* POETRY.MYSTICAL

anthologies **Mukhtārāt**.2; **Tadhkira**.2

anthologists ʿAwfī; Dawlat-Shāh; Luṭf ʿAlī Beg; Taḳī Awḥadī; Taḳī al-Dīn; [in Suppl.] Djādjarmī.2

biographies Dawlat-Shāh; Sām Mīrzā; **Tadhkira**.2; Taḳī al-Dīn; Wafā.4

stories Barzū-nāma; Farhād wa-Shirīn; Iskandar Nāma.ii; Kalīla wa-Dimna; Madjnūn Laylā.2; Wāmiḳ wa ʿAdhrāʾ; Wīs u Rāmīn; Yūsuf and Zulaykhā.1

9th-century poets Muḥammad b. Waṣīf

see also Sahl b. Hārūn b. Rāhawayh

10th-century poets Bābā-Ṭāhir; Daḳīḳī; Kisāʾī; al-Muṣʿabī; Rūdakī; Shahīd; [in Suppl.] Abū Shakūr Balkhī; Maʿrūf Balkhī

11th-century poets Asadī; Azraḳī; Farrukhī; Firdawsī; Gurgānī; Ḳaṭrān; Lāmiʿī, Abu ʾl-Ḥasan; Manūčihrī; ʿUnṣurī

12th-century poets ʿAbd al-Wāsiʿ Djabalī; Anwarī; Falakī Shirwānī; ʿImādī (*and* [in Suppl.]); Khāḳānī; Labībī; Mahsatī; Muʿizzī; Mukhtārī; Ṣābir; Sanāʾī; Sayyid Ḥasan Ghaznawī; Shufurwa; Sūzanī; ʿUmar Khayyām; Ẓahīr-i Fāryābī; [in Suppl.] ʿAmʿaḳ; Djamāl al-Dīn Iṣfahānī; Mudjīr al-Dīn Baylaḳānī

13th-century poets ʿAṭṭār; Bābā Afḍal; Djalāl al-Dīn Rūmī; ʿIrāḳī; Kamāl al-Dīn Ismāʿīl; Niẓāmī Gandjawī; Pūr-i Bahāʾ; Saʿdī; [in Suppl.] Djādjarmī.1

see also Shams-i Ḳays; Sūdī

14th-century poets ʿAṣṣār; Awḥadī; Banākitī; Ḥāfiẓ; Humām al-Dīn b. ʿAlāʾ Tabrīzī; Ibn-i Yamīn; ʿIṣāmī; Khʷādjū; Nizārī Ḳuhistānī; Rāmī Tabrīzī; Salmān-i Sāwadjī; ʿUbayd-i Zākānī; [in Suppl.] Badr-i Čāčī; Djādjarmī.2; ʿImād al-Dīn ʿAlī, Faḳīh-i Kirmānī

see also Faḍl Allāh Ḥurūfī; Ḥamd Allāh al-Mustawfī al-Ḳazwīnī; Sūdī

15th-century poets Busḥāḳ; Djāmī; Fattāḥī; Ḥāmidī; Kātibī; Sayfī ʿArūḍī Bukhārī; Sharaf al-Dīn ʿAlī Yazdī; Shīrīn Maghribī, Muḥammad; [in Suppl.] ʿĀrifī

see also Djem

16th-century poets Bannāʾī; Baṣīrī; Fighānī; Hātifī; Hilālī; Muḥtasham-i Kāshānī; Mushfiḳī; Nawʿī; Saḥābī Astarābādī; Sām Mīrzā; ʿUrfī Shīrāzī; Waḥshī Bāfḳī

see also Luḳmān b. Sayyid Ḥusayn

17th-century poets Asīr; al-Dāmād; Ḳadrī; Ḳalīm Abū Ṭālib; Kāshif; Lāhīdjī.2; Nāẓim Farrukh Ḥusayn; Ṣāʾib; Saʿīdā Gīlānī; Shawkat Bukhārī; Shifāʾī Iṣfahānī; Ṭāhir Waḥīd; Taḳī Awḥadī; ʿUnwān, Muḥammad Riḍā; Ẓuhūrī Turshīzī; Zulālī-yi Khʷānsārī

see also al-ʿĀmilī; Ghanīmat; Khushḥāl Khān Khaṭak; [in Suppl.] Findiriskī; *and* → LITERATURE.POETRY.INDO-PERSIAN

18th-century poets Hātif; Ḥazīn; Luṭf ʿAlī Beg; Nadjāt; Shihāb Turshīzī; Wafā.2 *and* 3

see also Āzād Bilgrāmī

19th-century poets Furūgh; Furūghī.1 *and* 2; Ḳāʾānī; Ḳurrat al-ʿAyn; Nashāṭ; Riḍā Ḳulī Khān; Ṣabā; Sabzawārī; Shaybānī; Shihāb Iṣfahānī; Surūsh; Wafā.5-9; Waḳār; Yaghmā Djandaḳī; [in Suppl.] Wiṣāl

see also Iḳbāl; Ḳāʾim-maḳām-i Farāhānī; Sipihr; Wafā.4

20th-century poets Bahār; Furūghī.3; Lāhūtī; Nafīsī, Saʿīd; Nīmā Yūshīdj; Parwīn Iʿtiṣāmī; Pūr-i Dāwūd; Rashīd Yāsimī; Shahriyār; Shūrīda, Muḥammad Taḳī;

Sipihrī; Wuthūḳ al-Dawla; Yaghmā'ī; Yazdī; [in Suppl.] ʿĀrif, Mīrzā; Ashraf al-Dīn Gīlānī; Dehkhudā; ʿIshḳī
see also Iḳbāl

Turkish Ḥamāsa.iii; Hidjā'.iii; Ḳaṣīda.3; Khamsa; Ḳoshma; Madīḥ.3; Māni; Marthiya.3; Mathnawī.3; Mukhtārāt.3; Musammaṭ.1; Rabīʿiyyāt; Rubāʿī.2; Shahrangīz.2; Sharḳi; **Shiʿr**.3; Turks.III (*and* [in Suppl.]); [in Suppl.] Ghazal.iii
see also Alpamish; ʿĀshiḳ; Ilāhī; Karadja Oghlan; Ozan; Shāhnāmedji; Shāʿir.3; Tardjīʿ-band; Therwet-i Fünūn; *and* → LITERATURE.POETRY.MYSTICAL

anthologies **Mukhtārāt**.3; **Tadhkira**.3

anthologists Żiyā Pasha

biographies ʿĀshiḳ Čelebi; Laṭīfī; Riḍā; Riyāḍī; Sālim; Sehī Bey; **Tadhkira**.3; [in Suppl.] Meḥmed Ṭāhir, Bursali

stories Farhād wa-Shirīn; Iskandar Nāma.iii; Madjnūn Laylā.3; Yūsuf and Zulaykhā.2

12th-century poets Aḥmad Yuknakī; Ḥakīm Ata

13th-century poets Dehhānī; Sheyyād Ḥamza

14th-century poets Aḥmadī; ʿĀshiḳ Pasha; Burhān al-Dīn; Gülshehrī; Sheykh-oghlu; Yūnus Emre

15th-century poets Āhī; Aḥmad Pasha Bursali; Dāʿī; Firdewsī; Gulshanī; Ḥamdī, Ḥamd Allāh; Ḳāsim Pasha; Ḳayghusuz Abdāl; Khalīlī; Khiḍr Beg; Süleymān Čelebi, Dede; Yazidji-oghlu
see also Djem; Ḥāmidī

16th-century poets Āgehī; ʿAzīzī; Bāḳī; Baṣīrī; Bihishtī; Dhātī; Djaʿfar Čelebi; Djalāl Ḥusayn Čelebi; Djalālzāde Muṣṭafā Čelebi; Djalālzāde Ṣāliḥ Čelebi; Faḍlī; Faḳīrī; Fawrī; Ferdī; Fighānī; Fuḍūlī; Ghazālī; Gulshanī; Ḥadīdī; Ḳarā-čelebi-zāde; Kemāl Pasha-zāde; Khāḳānī; Khayālī; Ḳorḳud b. Bāyazīd; Lāmiʿī, Shaykh Maḥmūd; Laṭīfī; Luḳmān b. Sayyid Ḥusayn; Me'alī; Medjdī; Mesīḥī; Mihrī Khātūn; Naẓmī, Edirneli; Nedjātī Bey; Newʿī; Rewānī; Sehī Bey; Surūrī.1; Sūzī Čelebi; Tashlidjali Yaḥyā; Wālihi
see also Ṭashköprüzāde.1

17th-century poets ʿAṭā'ī; ʿAzmī-zāde; Bahā'ī Meḥmed Efendi; Faṣīḥ Dede; Fehīm, Undjuzāde Muṣṭafā; Ḥāletī; Ḳarā-čelebi-zāde; Ḳul Muṣṭafā; Ḳuloghlu; Nā'ilī; Nāẓim, Muṣṭafā; Naẓmī, Sheykh Meḥmed; Nefʿī; Niyāzī; ʿÖmer ʿĀshiḳ; Riyāḍī; Ṣari ʿAbd Allāh Efendī; Ṭiflī; Wedjīhī; Weysī; Yaḥyā
see also Ṭashköprüzāde.3; [in Suppl.] Ḳā'imī

18th-century poets Belīgh, Ismāʿīl; Belīgh, Meḥmed Emīn; Čelebi-zāde; Česhmīzāde; Fiṭnat; Gevherī; Ghālib; Ḥāmī-i Āmidī; Ḥashmet; Kānī; Meḥmed Pasha Rāmī (*and* Rāmī Meḥmed Pasha); Nābī; Naḥīfī; Naẓīm; Nedīm; Nesh'et; Newres.1; ʿOthmān-zāde; Rāghib Pasha; Sezā'ī, Ḥasan Dede; Thābit; Wehbī Sayyidī
see also ʿUshshāḳī-zāde, Ibrāhīm

19th-century poets ʿĀrif Hikmet Bey; ʿAynī; Dadaloghlu; Derdli; Dhihnī; Fāḍil Bey; Faṭīn; Fehīm, Süleymān; Ismāʿīl Ṣafā; ʿIzzet Molla; Kemāl, Meḥmed Nāmiḳ; Laylā Khānim; Menemenli-zāde Meḥmed Ṭāhir; Muʿallim Nādjī; Newres.2; Pertew Pasha.II; Redjā'ī-zāde; Shināsī; Sünbül-zāde Wehbī; Surūrī.2; Wāṣif Enderūnī; Żiyā Pasha

20th-century poets ʿAbd al-Ḥaḳḳ Ḥāmid; Djanāb Shihāb al-Dīn; Djewdet; Ekrem Bey; Hāshim; Kanık; Köprülü (Meḥmed Fuad); Ḳoryürek; Laylā Khānim; Meḥmed ʿĀkif; Meḥmed Emīn; Muḥibb Aḥmed "Diranas"; Nāẓim Ḥikmet; Oktay Rifat; Orkhan Seyfī; Ortač, Yūsuf Ḍiyā; Sāhir, Djelāl; Tanpinar, Aḥmed Ḥamdī; Tewfīḳ Fikret; Yaḥyā Kemāl; Yücel, Ḥasan ʿAlī; [in Suppl.] ʿĀshik Weysel;

Bölükbashî; Čamlîbel; Eshref; Eyyūboghlu; Gövsa; Kisakürek
see also Therwet-i Fünūn; [in Suppl.] Ergun; Fîndîḳoghlu

in Eastern Turkish Ādharī.ii; Bābur; Bāḳîkhānlî; Burhān al-Dīn; Dhākir; Djambul Djabaev; Ghāzī Girāy II; Ḥamāsa.iv; Hidjā᾽.iii; Iskandar Nāma.iii; Ismā῾īl I; Ḳayyūm Nāṣirī; Ḳutadghu Bilig; Luṭfī; Mīr ῾Alī Shīr Nawā᾽ī; Mu᾽nis; Sakkākī; Shahriyār; Yūsuf Khāṣṣ Ḥādjib; [in Suppl.] Mīrzā Shafī῾ Wāḍiḥ Tabrīzī

translations from Western langs. Ismā῾īl Ḥaḳḳi ῾Ālīshān; Kanık; Shināsī; Tewfīḳ Fikret

Urdu Ghazal.iv; Ḥamāsa.v; Hidjā᾽.iv; Ḳaṣīda.4; Madīḥ.4; Madjnūn Laylā.4; Marthiya.4; Mathnawī.4; Mukhtārāt.4; Musammaṭ.2; Mushā῾ara; Shahrangīz.3; **Shi῾r**.4; Urdū.2
see also Tardjī῾-band; Wā-sōkht

17th-century poets Nuṣratī

18th-century poets Ashraf ῾Alī Khān; Dard; Djur᾽at; Maẓhar; Sawdā; Sūz; Walī; [in Suppl.] Ḥasan, Mīr Ghulām
see also Ārzū Khān; Taḥsīn

19th-century poets Amānat; Anīs; Aẓfarī; Dabīr, Salāmat ῾Alī; Dāgh; Dhawḳ; Ghālib; Faḳīr Muḥammad Khān; Ḥālī; Ilāhī Bakhsh "Ma῾rūf"; Inshā᾽; Mīr Muḥammad Taḳī; Muḥsin ῾Alī Muḥsin; Mu᾽min; Muṣḥafī; Nāsikh; Nasīm; Rangīn; Shawḳ, Taṣadduḳ Ḥusayn; [in Suppl.] Ātish
see also [in Suppl.] Āzād

20th-century poets Akbar, Ḥusayn Allāhābādī; Āzād; Djawān; Iḳbāl; Muḥammad ῾Alī; Rāshid, N.M.; Ruswā; Shabbīr Ḥasan Khān Djosh; Shiblī Nu῾mānī; [in Suppl.] Ḥasrat Mohānī
see also Āzurda

vernacular Ḥawfī; Malḥūn; Mawāliyā; Nabaṭī; Zadjal
see also Būḳalā; al-Shām.3

prose Adab; Ḥikāya; Ḳiṣṣa; Maḳāma; Mawsū῾a; Muḳaddima; Naṣīḥat al-Mulūk; Risāla; Sharḥ; Tafsīr; Uḳṣūṣa; [in Suppl.] **Nathr**
and → *the sections Etiquette-literature, Historical, and Travel-literature under this entry*; PRESS
for authors in fields other than belles-lettres, see the respective entries

Arabic ῾Arabiyya.B.V; Ḥikāya.i; Ḳiṣṣa.2; Maḳāla.1; Maḳāma; Mawsū῾a.1; Mi῾rādj.2; Nahḍa; Naṣīḥat al-Mulūk.1; Risāla.1; Sadj῾.3; Sīra Sha῾biyya; Uḳṣūṣa; [in Suppl.] **Nathr**
and → LITERATURE.DRAMA; PRESS

works Alf Layla wa-Layla; ῾Antar; Baybars; Bilawhar wa-Yūdāsaf; Dhu 'l-Himma; Kalīla wa-Dimna; Luḳmān.3; Sayf Ibn Dhī Yazan; Sindbād al-Ḥakīm; ῾Umar al-Nu῾mān
see also Sindbād; Tawaddud; [in Suppl.] Madīnat al-Nuḥās

8th-century authors Ibn al-Muḳaffa῾

9th-century authors al-Djāḥiẓ; al-Tha῾labī, Muḥammad; [in Suppl.] Abu 'l-῾Anbas al-Ṣaymarī

10th-century authors al-Hamadhānī

11th-century authors Ibn Nāḳiyā; [in Suppl.] Abu 'l-Muṭahhar al-Azdī
see also al-Tha῾ālibī, Abū Manṣūr ῾Abd al-Malik

12th-century authors al-Ḥarīrī; al-Ṣaymarī; al-Wahrānī; [in Suppl.] al-Djazarī

13th-century authors
see also al-Sharīshī

14th-century authors Ibn Abī Ḥadjala

15th-century authors
see also al-Ibshīhī

17th-century authors al-Shirbīnī; al-Yūsī

18th-century authors al-Warghī

19th-century authors al-Maʿlūf; al-Yāzidjī.1; [in Suppl.] al-Bustānī.6

20th-century authors Aḥmad Amīn; Faraḥ Anṭūn; Ḥāfiẓ Ibrāhīm; Maḥmūd Taymūr; al-Maʿlūf; al-Manfalūṭī; Mayy Ziyāda; al-Māzinī, Ibrāhīm; Muḥammad Ḥusayn Haykal; al-Muwayliḥī; Nuʿayma, Mīkhāʾīl; al-Rayḥānī; Salāma Mūsā; Sayyid Ḳuṭb; al-Sharḳāwī; Shāʾūl; Ṭāhā Ḥusayn; Tawfīḳ al-Ḥakīm; Ṭuʿma, Ilyās; al-Tūnisī, Maḥmūd Bayram; Yaḥyā Ḥaḳḳī; Zaydān, Djurdjī; [in Suppl.] Abū Shādī; al-ʿAḳḳād; Lāshīn; al-Shartūnī

see also Djamīl al-Mudawwar; al-Khālidī; Kurd ʿAlī; Shumayyil, Shiblī

Persian Ḥikāya.ii; Iran.vii; Ḳiṣṣa.4; Maḳāla.2; Mawsūʿa.2; Naṣīḥat al-Mulūk.2; Risāla.2; [in Suppl.] Miʿrādj.6

see also Ṣafawids.III; *and* → LITERATURE.DRAMA; PRESS

works Bakhtiyār-nāma; Dabistān al-Madhāhib; Ḳahramān-nāma; Kalīla wa-Dimna; Madjnūn Laylā.2; Marzbān-nāma; Wāmiḳ wa ʿAdhrāʾ

see also Niẓām al-Mulk; Niẓāmī ʿArūḍī Samarḳandī

11th-century authors Kay Kāʾūs b. Iskandar; Nāṣir-i Khusraw

12th-century authors Ḥamīdī; al-Ḳāshānī; Naṣr Allāh b. Muḥammad; Niẓāmī ʿArūḍī Samarḳandī; Rashīd al-Dīn (Waṭwāṭ); al-Samʿānī, Abu ʾl-Ḳāsim

13th-century authors Saʿdī

14th-century authors Nakhshabī

15th-century authors Kāshifī

16th-century authors

see also Shemʿī

17th-century authors ʿInāyat Allāh Kańbū

18th-century authors Mumtāz

19th-century authors Shaybānī

see also Furūgh.2

20th-century authors Bahār; Hidāyat, Ṣādiḳ; Nafīsī, Saʿīd; Shaykh Mūsā Nathrī; Ṭālibūf; Zayn al-ʿĀbidīn Marāghaʾī; [in Suppl.] Āl-i Aḥmad; Bihrangī; Dehkhudā

Turkish Ḥikāya.iii; Ḳiṣṣa.3; Maddāḥ; Maḳāla.3; Risāla.3; Turks.III; [in Suppl.] Mawsūʿa.3

see also Bilmedje; Therwet-i Fünūn; *and* → LITERATURE.DRAMA; PRESS

works Alpamïsh; Billur Köshk; Dede Ḳorḳut; Ḳahramān-nāma; Oghuz-nāma; Yūsuf and Zulaykhā.2

see also Merdjümek; Ṣarï Ṣalṭuḳ Dede

14th-century authors Sheykh-oghlu

15th-century authors Sheykh-zāde.3

16th-century authors Wāsiʿ ʿAlīsi

see also Shemʿī

17th-century authors Nergisī; Weysī

18th-century authors ʿAlī ʿAzīz, Giridli; Nābī

19th-century authors Ḳaṣāb, Teodor; Kemāl, Meḥmed Nāmïḳ; Sāmī; Shināsī; Żiyā Pasha; [in Suppl.] Čaylaḳ Tewfīḳ

see also Ḳiṣṣa.3(b); Therwet-i Fünūn

20th-century authors Aḥmad Ḥikmet; Aḥmad Midḥat; Aḥmad Rāsim; Djanāb Shihāb al-Dīn; Ebüzziya Tevfik; Ekrem Bey; Fiṭrat; Hïsar; Ḥusayn Djāhid; Ḥusayn Raḥmī; Karay, Refīḳ Khālid; Kaygïlï, ʿOthmān Djemāl; Kemāl; Kemal Tahir; Khālid Ḍiyāʾ; Khālide Edīb; Laylā Khānïm; Meḥmed Raʾūf; Oktay Rifat; ʿÖmer Seyf ül-Dīn; Orkhan Kemāl; Reshād Nūrī; Sabahattin Ali; Sezāʾī, Sāmī; Tanpinar, Aḥmed Ḥamdī; Yaḥyā Kemāl; Yaʿḳūb Ḳadrī; [in Suppl.] Atač; Atay; Esendal; Haliḳarnas Balïḳčïsï; Meḥmed Ṭāhir, Bursalï

see also Aḥmad Iḥsān; Ileri, Djelāl Nūrī; İnal; Ismāʿīl Ḥaḳḳi ʿĀlīshān; Ḳiṣṣa.3(b); [in Suppl.] Eyyūboghlu

in Eastern Turkish   Bābur; Rabg͟hūzī; [in Suppl.] Āgahī
      see also Tīmūrids.2; Turks.III.6
  Urdu Ḥikāya.iv; Ḳiṣṣa.5; Urdū.2; [in Suppl.] Mawsūʿa.5
      and → LITERATURE.DRAMA; PRESS
      18th-century authors Taḥsīn
      19th-century authors Amān, Mīr; D̲j̲awān; Faḳīr Muḥammad K͟hān; Surūr
      20th-century authors Iḳbāl; Nad̲h̲īr Aḥmad Dihlawī; Prēm Čand; Ruswā; S̲h̲abbīr
        Ḥasan K͟hān D̲j̲os̲h̲; S̲h̲iblī Nuʿmānī; [in Suppl.] Āzād
proverbs in Mat̲h̲al.4
    and → PROVERBS.COLLECTIONS OF
terms ʿArūḍ; ʿAtāba; Badīʿ; Balāg͟ha; Bayān; Dak͟hīl; Fard.a; Faṣāḥa; Fāṣila; Ibtidāʾ; Id̲j̲āza;
    Iḍmār; Iḳtibās; Intihāʾ; Irtid̲j̲āl; Istiʿāra; Ḳabḍ.iii; Ḳāfiya; Ḳaṭʿ; Kināya; Luzūm mā lā
    yalzam; al-Maʿānī wa ʾl-Bayān; Mad̲j̲āz; Maʿnā.3; Muʿāraḍa; Muzāwad̲j̲a; Radīf.2;
    Rad̲j̲az.4; S̲h̲awāhid; Ṣila.2; Taʿad̲j̲d̲j̲ub; Tad̲j̲nīs; Taḍmīn; Tak̲h̲alluṣ; Tak̲h̲mīs;
    Tak͟hyīl.1; Taʾrīk͟h.III; Tas̲h̲bīh; Tawriya; Ṭayf al-K͟hayāl; Waḥs̲h̲ī; Waṣf.1; [in Suppl.]
    Sariḳa
    and → LITERATURE.GENRES; METRICS; RHETORIC
topoi and imagery Buk͟hl; Bulbul; G͟hurāb; Gul; Ḥamām; Ḥayawān.5; Inṣāf; al-Ḳamar.II;
    Ḳaṭā; Nard̲j̲is; Raḥīl; Sāḳī; S̲h̲amʿa; S̲h̲aʿr.3; al-S̲h̲ayb wa ʾl-S̲h̲abāb; [in Suppl.] Ward
    see also G͟hazal.ii; ʿIs̲h̲ḳ; K͟hamriyya; Rabīʿiyyāt; Zahriyyāt
tradition-literature At̲h̲ar; **Ḥadīt̲h̲**; Ḥadīt̲h̲ Ḳudsī; Hind.v.e; Sunan; Sunna; Uṣūl al-Ḥadīt̲h̲;
    [in Suppl.] Arbaʿūn Ḥadīt̲h̲
    see also Ahl al-Ḥadīt̲h̲; Has̲h̲wiyya; K͟habar; Mustamlī; Nask͟h; Riwāya; S̲h̲arḥ.III;
    ʿUlamāʾ
  authoritative collections Abū Dāʾūd al-Sid̲j̲istānī; Aḥmad b. Ḥanbal; Anas b. Mālik; al-
    Bayhaḳī; al-Buk͟hārī, Muḥammad b. Ismāʿīl; al-Dāraḳuṭnī; al-Dārimī; Ibn Ḥibbān;
    Ibn Mād̲j̲a; Muslim b. al-Ḥad̲j̲d̲j̲ād̲j̲; al-Nasāʾī; al-Ṭayālisī, Abū Dāwūd; al-Tirmid̲h̲ī,
    Abū ʿĪsā
    see also al-ʿAynī; Ibn Hubayra
  terms al-D̲j̲arḥ wa ʾl-Taʿdīl; Fard.d; G͟harīb; Ḥikāya.I; Id̲j̲āza; Isnād; K͟habar al-Wāḥid;
    Mas̲h̲hūr; Matn; Muʿanʿan; Munkar; Mursal; Muṣannaf; Musnad.3; Mustamlī;
    Mutawātir.(a); Rafʿ.2; Rid̲j̲āl; Ṣaḥīḥ.1; Ṣāliḥ; Sunan; Tadlīs.2; Tadwīn; Tawātur;
    T̲h̲iḳa; Umma.2
    see also Ḥadīt̲h̲; Taʿlīḳ
  traditionists Rāwī; Rid̲j̲āl; Ṣāliḥ; T̲h̲iḳa
    see also al-Rāmahurmuzī
    7th century ʿAbd Allāh b. ʿUmar b. al-K͟haṭṭāb; Abū Bakra; Abū Hurayra; al-
      Aʿmas̲h̲; Ibn Abī Laylā.I; Ibn Masʿūd; Kaʿb al-Aḥbār; al-K͟hawlānī, Abū Idrīs;
      al-K͟hawlānī, Abū Muslim; [in Suppl.] D̲j̲ābir b. ʿAbd Allāh
      see also ʿĀʾis̲h̲a bint Abī Bakr; Umm Salama Hind
    8th century Abu ʾl-ʿĀliya al-Riyāḥī; Abū Mik͟hnaf; al-As̲h̲ʿarī, Abū Burda; D̲j̲ābir
      b. Zayd; al-Fuḍayl b. ʿIyāḍ; G͟hundjār; al-Ḥasan b. Ṣāliḥ b. Ḥayy al-Kūfī; al-
      Ḥasan al-Baṣrī; Ibn Abī Laylā.II; Ibn Daʾb; Ibn Isḥāḳ; Ibn al-Naṭṭāḥ; Ibn
      S̲h̲ubruma; Ibn Sīrīn; ʿIkrima; al-Layt̲h̲ b. Saʿd; Maymūn b. Mihrān; Muḳātil b.
      Sulaymān; Nāfiʿ; al-Nak͟haʿī, Ibrāhīm; Saʿīd b. Abī ʿArūba; al-S̲h̲aʿbī; S̲h̲uʿba b.
      al-Ḥad̲j̲d̲j̲ād̲j̲; al-Suddī; ʿUrwa b. al-Zubayr; Warḳāʾ b. ʿUmar; Yazīd b. Zurayʿ;
      al-Zuhrī, Ibn S̲h̲ihāb; [in Suppl.] Abū ʿAmr al-S̲h̲aybānī (*and* al-S̲h̲aybānī, Abū
      ʿAmr); Ibn D̲j̲uraydj
    9th century Abū Nuʿaym al-Mulāʾī; Baḳī b. Mak͟hlad; Ibn Abī K͟haythama; Ibn
      Abi ʾl-S̲h̲awārib; Ibn Abī S̲h̲ayba; Ibn ʿĀʾis̲h̲a.IV; Ibn Rāhwayh; Ibn Saʿd; Ibn
      Sallām al-D̲j̲umaḥī; Ibrāhīm al-Ḥarbī; al-Karābīsī.2; al-Marwazī; Muslim b. al-

Ḥadjdjādj; Nuʿaym b. Ḥammād; al-Ṣanʿānī, ʿAbd al-Razzāḳ; Sufyān b. ʿUyayna; al-Ṭayālisī, Abū Dāwūd; ʿUmar b. Shabba; Wakīʿ b. al-Djarrāḥ; al-Wāḳidī; Yaḥyā b. Maʿīn; al-Ziyādī; Zuhayr b. Ḥarb; [in Suppl.] Abū ʿĀṣim al-Nabīl; Asad b. Mūsā b. Ibrāhīm

see also Ibn Khayyāṭ al-ʿUṣfurī; Ibn Ḳuṭlūbughā; Yamūt b. al-Muzarraʿ

10th century Abū ʿArūba; al-Anbārī, Abū Bakr; al-Anbārī, Abū Muḥammad; Ghulām Thaʿlab; Ibn al-ʿAllāf; Ḳāsim b. Aṣbagh; al-Khaṭṭābī; al-Saraḳusṭī; al-Sidjistānī; al-Ṭabarānī; [in Suppl.] Ibn ʿUḳda; al-Ramlī

11th century al-Ḥākim al-Naysābūrī; Ibn ʿAbd al-Barr; Ibn al-Bannāʾ; Ibn Fūrak; Ibn Mākūlā.3; al-Ḳābisī; al-Khaṭīb al-Baghdādī; al-Sahmī; al-ʿUdhrī

12th century al-Baghawī; Ibn al-ʿArabī; Ibn ʿAsākir; Ibn Ḥubaysh; Ibn al-Ḳaysarānī.1; Ibn al-Nadjdjār; al-Lawātī; Razīn b. Muʿāwiya; al-Rushāṭī; al-Ṣadafī; al-Sarrādj, Abū Muḥammad; Shīrawayh; al-Silafī; [in Suppl.] al-Zamakhsharī.2

see also al-Samʿānī, Abū Saʿd

13th century al-Dimyāṭī al-Shāfiʿī; Ibn al-Athīr.1; Ibn Diḥya; Ibn Faraḥ al-Ishbīlī; al-Ṣaghānī, Raḍiyy al-Dīn; al-Ṭabarī, Aḥmad b. ʿAbd Allāh; [in Suppl.] Ibn Daḳīḳ al-ʿĪd

14th century al-Dhahabī; Ibn Kathīr; al-Mizzī; al-Wādīʾāshī

15th century Ibn Ḥadjar al-ʿAskalānī; al-Ibshīhī.2; al-Ḳasṭallānī; Muʿīn al-Miskīn; al-Suyūṭī

see also Ibn Ḳuṭlūbughā

20th century Shākir, Aḥmad Muḥammad

Shiite ʿAbd Allāh b. Maymūn; Dindān; Djaʿfar al-Ṣādiḳ; Ibn Bābawayh(i); al-Kashshī; al-Kāẓimī, ʿAbd al-Nabī; al-Kulaynī, Abū Djaʿfar Muḥammad; Madjlisī; Muḥammad b. Makkī; Shāh ʿAbd al-ʿAẓīm al-Ḥasanī; [in Suppl.] Akhbāriyya; al-Barḳī; Djābir al-Djuʿfī

see also Asmāʾ; al-Ṭihrānī

translation

from Greek and Syriac **Tardjama**.2

and → MEDICINE.PHYSICIANS.GREEK; PHILOSOPHY.PHILOSOPHERS.GREEK

from Middle Persian Ibn al-Muḳaffaʿ; Tansar; **Tardjama**.3

from Western languages

into Arabic Muḥammad Bey ʿUthmān Djalāl (*and* [in Suppl.] Muḥammad ʿUthmān Djalāl); Shāʾūl; Shumayyil, Shiblī; **Tardjama**.4; al-Yāzidjī.5

into Persian Muḥammad Ḥasan Khān; Nafīsī, Saʿīd; Sharīʿatī, ʿAlī; **Tardjama**.5

into Turkish Ismāʿīl Ḥaḳḳi ʿĀlīshān; Kanık; Khālide Edīb; Shināsī; **Tardjama**.6; Żiyā Pasha

travel-literature Djughrāfiyā.(d); **Riḥla**

authors ʿAbd al-Ghanī; al-ʿAbdarī; Abū Dulaf; Abū Ṭālib Khān; Aḥmad Iḥsān; ʿAlī Bey al-ʿAbbāsī; ʿAlī Khān; al-ʿAyyāshī; Ewliyā Čelebi; Fāris al-Shidyāḳ; al-Ghassānī; Ghiyāth al-Dīn Naḳḳāsh; Ibn Baṭṭūṭa; Ibn Djubayr; Ibn Idrīs(II); Kurd ʿAlī; Ma Huan; Meḥmed Yirmisekiz; Nāṣir-i Khusraw; Shiblī Nuʿmānī; Sīdī ʿAlī Reʾīs; al-Tamgrūtī; Tamīm b. Baḥr al-Muṭṭawwiʿ; al-Tidjānī, Abū Muḥammad; al-Tudjībī; al-Tūnisī, Muḥammad; al-Tūnisī, Shaykh Zayn al-ʿĀbidīn; Yāḳūt al-Rūmī; al-Zayyānī; [in Suppl.] al-Ghazzāl; Ibn Nāṣir.3; Iʿtiṣām al-Dīn; Maḥammad b. Aḥmad al-Huḍīgī

see also Hārūn b. Yaḥyā; Ibn Djuzayy; Ibn Rushayd; Ibn Saʿīd al-Maghribī; Ibrāhīm b. Yaʿḳūb; Khayr Allāh Efendi; Leo Africanus; Zayn al-ʿĀbidīn Marāghaʾī; Zayn al-ʿĀbidīn Shīrwānī; [in Suppl.] Sallām al-Tardjumān

narratives [in Suppl.] Akhbār al-Ṣīn wa ʾl-Hind

wisdom-literature al-Aḥnaf b. Ḳays; ʿAlī b. Abī Ṭālib; Buzurgmihr; Hūshang; Luḳmān; Sahl b. Hārūn b. Rāhawayh; [in Suppl.] Djāwīdhān Khirad

see also Aktham b. Ṣayfī; Buhlūl; al-Ibs̲h̲īhī; [in Suppl.] ʿUḳalāʾ al-Madjānīn
wondrous literature   Abū Ḥāmid al-G̲h̲arnāṭī; **ʿAdjāʾib**; Buzurg b. S̲h̲ahriyār; al-Ḳazwīnī
   see also Ibn Sarābiyūn; Ḳiṣaṣ al-Anbiyāʾ; Sindbād; [in Suppl.] Madīnat al-Nuḥās

LOVE   **ʿIs̲h̲ḳ**
   see also Is̲h̲āra; Ḳalb.II; *and* → LITERATURE.POETRY.LOVE
erotic   Djins; G̲h̲azal; Nasīb; [in Suppl.] Muḳawwiyāt
   see also Abū Dahbal al-Djumaḥī; Abū Nuwās; Abū Ṣak̲h̲r al-Hud̲h̲alī; al-ʿArdjī; Dayr;
   Dīk al-Djinn al-Ḥimṣī; Djurʿat; Fāḍil Bey; Ḥammād ʿAdjrad; Ibn ʿAbd Rabbih; Ibn Faradj
   al-Djayyānī; Ibn Ḳays al-Ruḳayyāt; Ibn Maṭrūḥ; K̲h̲amriyya; Wāliba b. al-Ḥubāb
mystical   ʿĀs̲h̲iḳ; ʿIs̲h̲ḳ; S̲h̲awḳ
   and → LITERATURE.POETRY.MYSTICAL; MYSTICISM
platonic   G̲h̲azal.i.3; **ʿUd̲h̲rī**
   see also Djamīl al-ʿUd̲h̲rī; Ibn Dāwūd; Kut̲h̲ayyir b. ʿAbd al-Raḥmān; Laylā al-
   Ak̲h̲yaliyya; Murakk̲is̲h̲.1; Nuṣayb b. Rabāḥ; al-Ramādī; ʿUmar b. Abī Rabīʿa; ʿUrwa b.
   Ḥizām; al-Walīd.2
poetry   → LITERATURE.POETRY.LOVE
treatises on   al-Antāḳī, Dāʾūd; Ibn Ḥazm, Abū Muḥammad; Rafīʿ al-Dīn; al-Tidjānī, Abū
   Muḥammad
   see also Buk̲h̲tīs̲h̲ūʿ

M

MACEDONIA   → (former) YUGOSLAVIA

MADAGASCAR   **Madagascar**; Massalajem
   and → AFRICA.EAST AFRICA

MAGIC   ʿAzīma.2; Djadwal; Istinzāl; K̲h̲āṣṣa; Nīrandj; Ruḳya; **Siḥr**; Sīmiyāʾ; Wafḳ; Yada
   Tas̲h̲; [in Suppl.] Budūḥ
   see also Djinn.III; Ḥadjar; Ḥurūf; Istik̲h̲āra; Istiḳsām; Istisḳāʾ; Kabid.4; al-Ḳamar.II; Ḳatl.ii.2;
   K̲h̲awāṣṣ al-Ḳurʾān; Kihāna; Kitābāt.5; Rūḥāniyya; Sidr; Zār; *and* → CHARMS; DIVINATION
magicians   ʿAbd Allāh b. Hilāl; S̲h̲aʿbad̲h̲a
   see also Antemuru
treatises on   al-Makḳarī; al-Zarḳālī; [in Suppl.] Ibn ʿAzzūz; al-Būnī

MALAWI   Kota Kota; [in Suppl.] **Malawi**
   and → AFRICA.EAST AFRICA

MALAYSIA   Malacca; **Malay Peninsula**; Malays; **Malaysia**
   see also Baladiyya.6; Djāmiʿa; Indonesia; Kandūrī; Kitābāt.8; Partai Islam se Malaysia
   (Pas); Rembau; [in Suppl.] Maḥkama.7.ii; al-Marʾa
architecture   → ARCHITECTURE.REGIONS
literature   ʿAbd Allāh b. ʿAbd al-Ḳādir; Dāwūd al-Faṭānī; Ḥikāya.v; Ḳiṣṣa.6; Malays; S̲h̲āʿir.7;
   Taʾrīk̲h̲.II.7; [in Suppl.] S̲h̲iʿr.5
   see also Indonesia.vi
states   Penang; Perak; Sabah; Sarawak; Terengganu; [in Suppl.] Kelantan
   see also [in Suppl.] Kalimantan

MALI   Adrar.2; Aḥmad al-S̲h̲ayk̲h̲; Aḥmadu Lobbo; Ḥamāliyya; Kaʿti; **Mali**; Mansa Mūsā
   see also Mande; Sūdān (Bilād al-).2

historians of al-Saʿdī
toponyms
ancient Tādmakkat
present-day
regions Kaarta
towns Bamako; Dienné; Gao; Segu; Timbuktu

MAMLUKS **Mamlūks** (*and* [in Suppl.])
see also Ḥarfūsh; Manshūr; Mihmindār; Rank; Yāsā.2; *and* → DYNASTIES.EGYPT AND THE FERTILE CRESCENT; MILITARY.MAMLUK

MARONITES → CHRISTIANITY.DENOMINATIONS; LEBANON

MARRIAGE Djilwa; Khiṭba; Mutʿa; **Nikāḥ**; ʿUrs; [in Suppl.] Djabr
see also ʿAbd.3.e; ʿĀda.iii *and* iv.4; ʿArūs Resmi; Fāsid wa Bāṭil.III; Ghāʾib; Ḥaḍāna; Kafāʾa; Kurds.iv.A.1; al-Marʾa.2; Mawākib.4.3 *and* 5; Raḍāʿ; Shawwāl; Suknā; Sukūt; Wilāya.1; [in Suppl.] Nafaḳa; *and* → DIVORCE
dower **Mahr**; Ṣadāḳ

MARTYRDOM Fidāʾī; Maẓlūm; **Shahīd**
see also Ḥabīb al-Nadjdjār; (al-)Ḥusayn b. ʿAlī b. Abī Ṭālib; Khubayb; Madjlis.3; Mashhad; Masʿūd; Ziyāra.5; [in Suppl.] ʿAbd Allāh b. Abī Bakr al-Miyānadjī

MATHEMATICS Algorithmus; al-Djabr wa ʾl-Muḳābala; Ḥisāb al-ʿAḳd; Ḥisāb al-Ghubār; **ʿIlm al-Ḥisāb**; Misāḥa; **al-Riyāḍiyyāt**; [in Suppl.] ʿIlm al-Handasa
and → NUMBER
algebra **al-Djabr wa ʾl-Muḳābala**
geometry **Misāḥa**; [in Suppl.] **ʿIlm al-Handasa**
mathematicians
Greek Uḳlīdis
see also Balīnūs
Islamic Abū Kāmil Shudjāʿ; Abu ʾl-Wafāʾ al-Būzadjānī; ʿAlī al-Ḳūshdjī; al-Bīrūnī; Ibn al-Bannāʾ al-Marrākushī; Ibn al-Haytham; Ibn ʿIrāḳ; Isḥāḳ Efendi; al-Ḳalaṣādī; al-Karābīsī.1; al-Karadjī; al-Kāshī; al-Khʷārazmī; al-Khāzin; al-Khudjandī; Kushiyār b. Labān; al-Madjrīṭī; al-Mārdīnī; Muḥammad b. ʿĪsā al-Māhānī; Muḥammad b. ʿUmar; al-Shīrāzī, Abu ʾl-Ḥusayn; Thābit b. Ḳurra; al-Ṭūsī, Naṣīr al-Dīn; ʿUmar Khayyām; ʿUṭārid b. Muḥammad; [in Suppl.] Ḳāḍī-zāde Rūmī; al-Kūhī; Samawʾal b. Yaḥyā al-Maghribī, Abū Naṣr
see also Ḳusṭā b. Lūḳā
terms Fard.f; Kasr; Ḳaṭʿ; Ḳuṭr; Māl; Manshūr; Muḳaddam; Muṣādara.1; Muthallath; al-Sahm.1.a; al-Taʿdīl bayn al-Saṭrayn
see also al-Mīzān; [in Suppl.] Halīladj

MAURITANIA Adrar.3; Atar; Ḥawḍ; Māʾ al-ʿAynayn al-Ḳalḳamī; Madjlis.4.A.xxii; **Mūrītāniyā**; Ṣiḥāfa.2.(iii)
see also Dustūr.xv; Lamtūna; al-Māmī; Sūdān (Bilād al-).2
historians of al-Shinḳīṭī; al-Yadālī
toponyms
ancient Awdaghost; Ghāna; Ḳunbi Ṣāliḥ; Shinḳīṭ
present-day Nouakchott; Walāta

MECHANICS Ḥiyal.2; al-Ḳarasṭūn; [in Suppl.] al-Djazarī; **Ḥiyal**
see also Ibn al-Sāʿātī; ʿUmar Khayyām; Urghan; *and* → HYDROLOGY

MEDICINE **Ṭibb**
and → ANATOMY; DRUGS; ILLNESS; PHARMACOLOGY
centres of Bīmāristān; Gondēshāpūr; Ḳalāwūn; [in Suppl.] Abū Zaʿbal
see also Baghdād; Dimashḳ; al-Madīna; [in Suppl.] Ṭibbiyye-i ʿAdliyye-i Shāhāne
dentistry
dental care Miswāk
see also ʿAḳīḳ; Mardjān
treatises on Hāmōn
see also Ibn Abi ʾl-Bayān
diseases → ILLNESS; PLAGUE
medical handbooks/encyclopaedias ʿAlī b. al-ʿAbbās; al-Djurdjānī, Ismāʿīl b. al-Ḥusayn; Ibn al-Nafīs; Ibn Sīnā; al-Masīḥī; Shānī-zāde; al-Ṭabarī, ʿAlī b. Rabban; Yūḥannā b. Sarābiyūn; al-Zahrāwī, Abu ʾl-Ḳāsim
medicines Almās; ʿAnbar; al-Dahnadj; Dhahab; al-Durr; Fiḍḍa; Kāfūr; Ḳaṭrān; al-Ḳily; al-Kuḥl; Lubān; Maghnāṭīs.1; Mardjān; Milḥ.2; Misk; Mūmiyāʾ; Ṣābūn; Ṣamgh; Ṭabāshīr; Zaʿfarān.2; [in Suppl.] Bawraḳ; Halīladj
see also Bāzahr; al-Iksīr; Kabid.3; Ziʾbaḳ; [in Suppl.] Afāwīh; Dam; *for medicinal use of animal parts, food and plants or flowers, see specific articles under* ANIMALS, CUISINE *and* FLORA, *respectively*
obstetrics ʿArīb b. Saʿd al-Kātib al-Ḳurṭubī
and → LIFE STAGES.CHILDBIRTH
ophthalmology ʿAyn; Ramad; Ṭibb
see also [in Suppl.] Māʾ al-Ward; *and* → ANATOMY.EYE; OPTICS
ophthalmologists ʿAlī b. ʿĪsā; ʿAmmār al-Mawṣilī; al-Ghāfiḳī; Ibn Dāniyāl; Khalīfa b. Abi ʾl-Maḥāsin
see also Ḥunayn b. Isḥāḳ al-ʿIbādī; Ibn al-Nafīs; Ibn Zuhr.V
physicians Djarrāḥ; Ḥāwī; [in Suppl.] Faṣṣād
see also ʿAyn; Constantinus Africanus; Ḥikma; Kabid.3; Masāʾil wa-Adjwiba; *and* → MEDICINE.OPHTHALMOLOGY.OPHTHALMOLOGISTS; PHARMACOLOGY
biographies of Ibn Abī Uṣaybiʿa; Ibn Djuldjul; Ibn al-Ḳāḍī; Isḥāḳ b. Ḥunayn
see also Ibn al-Ḳifṭī
7th century [in Suppl.] Ahrun; al-Ḥārith b. Kalada
and → *the section Physicians.Greek below*
9th century Bukhtīshūʿ; Ḥunayn b. Isḥāḳ al-ʿIbādī; Ibn Māsawayh; Sābūr b. Sahl; Yūḥannā b. Sarābiyūn
see also Māsardjawayh; al-Ṭabarī, ʿAlī
10th century ʿAlī b. al-ʿAbbās; ʿArīb b. Saʿd al-Kātib al-Ḳurṭubī; Ibn Djuldjul; Isḥāḳ b. Ḥunayn; Isḥāḳ b. Sulaymān al-Isrāʾīlī; Ḳusṭā b. Lūḳā; al-Rāzī, Abū Bakr; Ṣābiʾ.(3); Saʿīd al-Dimashḳī; [in Suppl.] Ibn Abi ʾl-Ashʿath
11th century al-Anṭākī, Abu ʾl-Faradj; Ibn Buṭlān; Ibn Djanāḥ; Ibn Djazla; Ibn al-Djazzār; Ibn Riḍwān; Ibn Sīnā; Ibn al-Ṭayyib; Ibn Wāfid; Ibn Zuhr.II; al-Masīḥī; al-Zahrāwī, Abu ʾl-Ḳāsim
12th century Abu ʾl-Barakāt; al-Djurdjānī, Ismāʿīl b. al-Ḥusayn; Ibn Djāmiʿ; Ibn al-Tilmīdh; Ibn Zuhr.III *and* IV; al-Marwazī, Sharaf al-Zamān; Umayya, Abu ʾl-Ṣalt; [in Suppl.] Ibn Biklārish; Samawʾal b. Yaḥyā al-Maghribī, Abū Naṣr
see also Ibn Rushd
13th century Ibn Abi ʾl-Bayān; Ibn Abī Uṣaybiʿa; Ibn Hubal; Ibn al-Nafīs; Ibn Ṭumlūs; Saʿd al-Dawla; al-Suwaydī; [in Suppl.] Ibn al-Ḳuff

14th century Ḥādjdjī Pasha; Ibn al-Khaṭīb; Isḥāḳ b. Murād; Ḳuṭb al-Dīn Shīrāzī
15th century Bashīr Čelebi; Yaʿḳūb Pasha
16th century al-Anṭākī, Dāʾūd; Hāmōn; Yūsufī
17th century Ḥayātī-zāde
18th century al-Ṣanʿānī, Ḍiyāʾ al-Dīn; [in Suppl.] Ādarrāḳ; Ibn Shaḳrūn al-Miknāsī
19th century and on Bahdjat Muṣṭafā Efendi; Muḥammad b. Aḥmad al-Iskandarānī; Shānī-zāde; Shumayyil, Shiblī; [in Suppl.] ʿAbd al-Salām b. Muḥammad
Christian Bukhtīshūʿ; Ḥunayn b. Isḥāḳ al-ʿIbādī; Ibn Buṭlān; Ibn Māsawayh; Ibn al-Ṭayyib; Isḥāḳ b. Ḥunayn; Ḳusṭā b. Lūḳā; Ṣābiʾ.(3); Sābūr b. Sahl; al-Ṭabarī, ʿAlī; Yūḥannā b. Sarābiyūn; [in Suppl.] Ahrun; Ḥubaysh b. al-Ḥasan al-Dimashḳī; Ibn al-Ḳuff
Greek Diyusḳuridīs; Djālīnūs; Rūfus al-Afsīsī; [in Suppl.] Ahrun; Buḳrāṭ
see also Ḥunayn b. Isḥāḳ al-ʿIbādī; Ibn Riḍwān; Ibn al-Ṭayyib; Isḥāḳ b. Ḥunayn; Iṣṭifān b. Basīl; Usṭāth; Yaḥyā b. al-Biṭrīḳ; Yūnān; [in Suppl.] Ḥubaysh b. al-Ḥasan al-Dimashḳī; Ibn Abi ʾl-Ashʿath
Jewish Hāmōn; Ibn Abi ʾl-Bayān; Ibn Djāmiʿ; Ibn Djanāḥ; Isḥāḳ b. Sulaymān al-Isrāʾīlī; Māsardjawayh; Saʿd al-Dawla; Yaʿḳūb Pasha; [in Suppl.] Ibn Biklārish
see also Abu ʾl-Barakāt; Ḥayātī-zāde.1; Ibn Maymūn
Ottoman Bahdjat Muṣṭafā Efendi; Bashīr Čelebi; Ḥādjdjī Pasha; Hāmōn; Ḥayātī-zāde; Isḥāḳ b. Murād; Shānī-zāde; Yaʿḳūb Pasha
see also Ḥekīm-bashi̊; [in Suppl.] Ṭibbiyye-i ʿAdliyye-i Shāhāne
surgery al-Zahrāwī, Abu ʾl-Ḳāsim
terms Bīmāristān; Djarrāḥ; Ḥidjāb; Ḳuwwa.5; Sabab.1; [in Suppl.] Mizādj; Muḳawwiyāt
see also Ḥāl
veterinary Bayṭār; Ibn Hudhayl; Ibn al-Mundhir

MELKITES → CHRISTIANITY.DENOMINATIONS

MESOPOTAMIA → IRAQ

METALLURGY Ḳalʿī; Khārṣīnī; **Maʿdin**
see also Kalah; al-Mīzān.1; *and* → MINERALOGY.MINES
metals Dhahab; Fiḍḍa; al-Ḥadīd; Nuḥās; Ziʾbaḳ
and → MINERALOGY.MINERALS; PROFESSIONS.CRAFTSMEN AND TRADESMEN.ARTISANS

METAPHYSICS **Mā baʿd al-Ṭabīʿa**
see also ʿAbd al-Laṭīf al-Baghdādī; Māhiyya; Muṭlaḳ

METEOROLOGY al-Āthār al-ʿUlwiyya
see also Anwāʾ; Sadjʿ.2; [in Suppl.] Ibn al-Adjdābī
weather magic Yada Tash
winds **Rīḥ**; Samūm

METRICS **ʿArūḍ**, Wazn.2
and → LITERATURE.POETRY
metres Mudjtathth; Mutadārik; Mutaḳārib; Mutawātir.(b); Radjaz; Ramal.1; Sarīʿ; Ṭawīl; Wāfir
terms Dakhīl; Fard.a; Ḳaṭʿ; Sabab.3; Ṣadr.(a); Sālim.3; Watid; Ziḥāf
treatises on Bābur; al-Djawharī; al-Khalīl b. Aḥmad; al-Khazradjī, Ḍiyāʾ al-Dīn; Mīr ʿAlī Shīr Nawāʾī; Shams-i Ḳays; al-Tibrīzī

MILITARY Baḥriyya; Djaysh; **Ḥarb**; [in Suppl.] Niẓām ʿAskarī
see also Dār al-Ḥarb; Djihād; Fatḥnāme; Ghazw

architecture Ribāṭ
see also Ṭabaḳa; *and* → ARCHITECTURE.MONUMENTS.STRONGHOLDS
army **Djaysh**; Istiʿrāḍ (ʿArḍ); **Lashkar**; Radīf.3
see also Djāsūs; Ṣaff.2; *and* → MILITARY.MAMLUK *and* OTTOMAN
contingents Bāzinḳir; Djāndār; Djaysh.iii.2; Djund; Ghulām; Gūm; Ḳūrčī; Maḥalla; Mamlūk; Mutaṭawwiʿa; Sipāhī.2; Ṭabūr; Ṭalīʿa; Ṭulb; Tūmān.1; [in Suppl.] Shālīsh.1
see also Almogávares; Fāris; *and* → MILITARY.OTTOMAN.ARMY CONTINGENTS
band Naḳḳāra-khāna; Ṭabl-khāna
see also Mehter
battles
see also Shiʿār.1; Tugh; *and* → MILITARY.EXPEDITIONS; TREATIES
before 622 Buʿāth; Dhū Ḳār; Djabala; Fidjār; Ḥalīma; Shiʿb Djabala; Ubāgh; [in Suppl.] Dāḥis
see also Ayyām al-ʿArab; Ḥanẓala b. Mālik; [in Suppl.] Silāḥ.1
622-632 Badr; Biʾr Maʿūna; Buzākha; Ḥunayn; Khandaḳ; Khaybar; Muʾta; Uḥud
see also Mālik b. ʿAwf; [in Suppl.] al-Ridda; Salmān al-Fārisī
633-660 Adjnādayn; ʿAḳrabāʾ; al-Djamal; Djisr; Faḥl; Ḥarūrāʾ; al-Ḳādisiyya.2; Mardj al-Ṣuffar; Ṣiffīn; Yarmūk.2; [in Suppl.] Dhāt al-Ṣawārī
see also ʿAbd Allāh b. Saʿd; ʿĀʾisha bint Abī Bakr; ʿAlī b. Abī Ṭālib; al-Hurmuzān; Musaylima; al-Nahrawān; Rustam b. Farrukh Hurmuzd; Taḥkīm; [in Suppl.] al-Ridda
661-750 ʿAyn al-Warda; Balāṭ al-Shuhadāʾ; Baldj b. Bishr; al-Bishr; Dayr al-Djamādjim; Dayr al-Djāthalīḳ; al-Ḥarra; al-Khāzir; Mardj Rāhiṭ; [in Suppl.] Wādī Lakku
see also (al-)Ḥusayn b. ʿAlī b. Abī Ṭālib; Kulthūm b. ʿIyāḍ al-Ḳushayrī; (al-)Ḳusṭanṭīniyya
751-1258 al-Arak; Bākhamrā; Dayr al-ʿĀḳūl; Fakhkh; Ḥaydarān; Hazārasp; Ḥiṭṭīn; al-ʿIḳāb; Köse Dāgh; Malāzgird.2; Shant Mānkash; Ṭarāz; Ubbadha; al-Zallāḳa; [in Suppl.] Dandānḳān
see also Ḥadjar al-Nasr; al-Madjūs; al-Manṣūr bi ʾllāh, Ismāʿīl; Mardj Dābiḳ
1258-18th century ʿAyn Djālūt; Čāldirān; Dābiḳ; Djarba; Ḥimṣ; Ḳoṣowa; Mardj Dābiḳ; Mardj Rāhiṭ; Mardj al-Ṣuffar; Mezőkeresztes; Mohács.a *and* b; Nīkbūlī; Pānīpat; Tālīkōṭā; Tukarōʾī; Wādī ʾl-Khaznadār; Zenta; [in Suppl.] Kőszeg
see also Aynabakhtī; Baḥriyya.iii; Fatḥnāme; Ḥarb; Nahr Abī Fuṭrus; ʿOthmān Pasha; Wenedik.2; Zsitvatorok
after 18th century Abuklea; Atjèh; Česhme; Farwān; Gök Tepe; Isly; Kūt al-ʿAmāra; Maysalūn; Nizīb; Rīf.II; al-Tall al-Kabīr; [in Suppl.] al-Ḳabḳ.3.f *and* j
see also al-ʿAḳaba; Gulistān
bodies ʿAyyār; Dawāʾir; Djaysh.iii.1; Futuwwa; Ghāzī; al-Shākiriyya
see also ʿAlī b. Muḥammad al-Zandjī; al-Ikhwān; Khashabiyya; Sarhang; *and* → MILITARY.ARMY.CONTINGENTS
booty Fayʾ; **Ghanīma**; [in Suppl.] Khums
see also Baranta; Ghazw; Khāliṣa; Pendjik; *and* → MILITARY.PRISONERS
Byzantine → BYZANTINE EMPIRE; *for battles fought between the Arabs and Byzantines* → BYZANTINE EMPIRE.MILITARY
decorations **Nishān**; **Wisām**
expeditions Ghāzī; **Ṣāʾifa**
see also Ghazw
Indo-Muslim Bārūd.vi; Ghulām.iii; Ḥarb.vi; Ḥiṣār.vi; Lashkar; Sipāhī.3; Suwār
see also Istiʿrāḍ (Arḍ)
Mamluk al-Baḥriyya; Baḥriyya.II; Bārūd.iii; Burdjiyya; Ḥalḳa; Ḥarb.iii; Ḥiṣār.iv; **Mamlūk**; Ṭabaḳa; Wāfidiyya; [in Suppl.] Shālīsh
see also Amīr Ākhūr; al-Amīr al-Kabīr; Atābak al-ʿAsākir; Čerkes.ii; ʿĪsā b. Muhannā;

Khāṣṣakiyya; Ḳumāsh; Rikābdār; Silāḥdār; Ṭulb
battles ʿAyn Djālūt; Dābiḳ; Ḥimṣ; Mardj Rāhiṭ; Wādī ʾl-Khaznadār
navy **Baḥriyya**; Dār al-Ṣināʿa; Daryā-begi; Ḳapudan Pasha; Lewend.1; Nassads; Raʾīs.3; Riyāla; Usṭūl
see also ʿAzab; Gelibolu; Kātib Çelebi; [in Suppl.] Dhāt al-Ṣawārī; *and* → NAVIGATION.SHIPS; PIRACY; *for Ottoman maritime topics* → DYNASTIES.ANATOLIA AND THE TURKS.OTTOMANS.HIGH ADMIRALS; MILITARY.OTTOMAN
offices Amīr; ʿArīf; Atābak al-ʿAsākir; Fawdjdār; Ispahbadh; Ispahsālār; Istiʿrāḍ (ʿArḍ); Ḳāʾid; Manṣab; Sālār; Sardār; Sarhang; Shiḥna; Silāḥdār
see also Amīr al-Umarāʾ; Dārūgha; Ḳāḍī ʿAskar; Ḳūrčī; *and* → MILITARY.OTTOMAN
Ottoman Bāb-i Serʿaskeri; Baḥriyya.iii; Balyemez; Bārūd.iv; Devshirme; Djebeli; Ghulām.iv; Ḥarb.iv; Ḥarbiye; Ḥiṣār.v; Müsellem; Radīf.3; Sandjaḳ; Sipāhī.1; Tersāne; Tugh.2; ʿUlūfe; Yeñi Čeri; [in Suppl.] Djebedji; Muʿīnsiz; Niẓām ʿAskarī.3
see also ʿAskarī; Ḍabṭiyya; Gelibolu; Gūm; Ḥareket Ordusu; Istiʿrāḍ (Arḍ); Ḳapïdji; Karakol; Martolos; Mensūkhāt; Mondros; Nefīr; Ordu; Pendjik; Tīmār; Ziʿāmet; *and* → MILITARY.NAVY
army contingents al-Abnāʾ.V; ʿAdjamī Oghlān; Akïndjï; Alay; ʿAzab; Bashï-bozuḳ; Bölük; Deli; Devedji; Djānbāzān; Eshkindji; Ghurabāʾ; Gönüllü; Khāṣṣekī; Khumbaradjï; Lewend; Niẓām-ï Djedīd; Odjaḳ; Orta; Woynuḳ; Yaya; Yeñi Čeri; Yerliyya; Zeybek; [in Suppl.] Djebedji; Segbān
see also Akhī; Eflāḳ; Martolos; Nefīr; Sipāhī.1
battles Čaldirān; Dābiḳ; Ḳoṣowa; Mezőkeresztes; Mohács.a *and* b; Nīkbūlī; [in Suppl.] al-Ḳabḳ.3.f *and* j
see also Wenedik
officers Bayraḳdār; Biñbashï; Bölük-bashï; Čāʾūsh; Čorbadjï.1; Ḍābiṭ; Daryā-begi; Ḳapudan Pasha; Mushīr; Rikābdār; Riyāla; Zaghardjï Bashï; [in Suppl.] Yüzbashï
see also Sandjaḳ; Silāḥdār
pay ʿAṭāʾ; Inʿām; Māl al-Bayʿa; Rizḳ.3; ʿUlūfe
police Aḥdāth; ʿAsas; Ḍabṭiyya; Karakol; **Shurṭa**
see also Dawāʾir; Futuwwa; Kōtwāl; Martolos; Naḳīb.2
prisoners Lamas-ṣū; Mübādele.ii; [in Suppl.] Fidāʾ
see also Sidjn; *and* → MILITARY.BOOTY
reform → REFORM.MILITARY
tactics Ḥarb; Ḥiṣār; Ḥiyal.1
see also al-ʿAwāṣim; Fīl; al-Thughūr; *and* → ARCHITECTURE.MONUMENTS.STRONGHOLDS
terms Tadjmīr; Zaʿīm
treatises on Ibn Hudhayl; al-Ṭarsūsī; [in Suppl.] Fakhr-i Mudabbir
see also Ḥarb.ii; Ḥiyal.1
weapons ʿAnaza; ʿArrāda; Balyemez; Bārūd; Dūrbāsh; Ḳaws; Mandjanīḳ; Nafṭ.2; Ṭop; [in Suppl.] **Silāḥ**
see also ʿAlam; Asad Allāh Iṣfahānī; Hilāl.ii; Ḥiṣār; Ḳalʿī; Lamṭ; Marātib

MINERALOGY **Maʿdin**
see also al-Mīzān.1
minerals Abū Ḳalamūn; ʿAḳīḳ; Almās; Bārūd; Billawr; al-Dahnadj; Fīrūzadj; al-Kibrīt; al-Kuḥl; Maghnāṭīs.1; Milḥ; Mūmiyāʾ; Naṭrūn; Yāḳūt; Yashm; [in Suppl.] Bawraḳ
see also al-Andalus.v; Damāwand; Golkondā; Ḥadjar; Kirmān; Maʿdin; Malindi; *and* → JEWELRY; METALLURGY
mines al-ʿAllāḳī; Anadolu.iii.6; al-Andalus.v.2; ʿAraba; Armīniya.III; Badakhshān; Billiton; Bilma; Čankïrï; al-Djabbūl; Djayzān; al-Durūʿ; Farghānā; Firrīsh; Gümüsh-khāne; Kalah; Ḳarā Ḥiṣār.2 *and* 3; Ḳayṣariyya; al-Ḳily; Ḳishm; Maʿdin.2; al-Maʿdin; Sofāla; Zonguldak

see also Fāzūghlī; Filasṭīn; Milḥ
treatises on al-Suwaydī; al-Tīfāshī
see also ʿUṭārid b. Muḥammad

MIRACLES **Karāma**; **Muʿdjiza**
see also Āya; Dawsa; Māʾ al-ʿAynayn al-Ḳalḳamī; Miʿrādj (*and* [in Suppl.]); *and* → SAINTHOOD

MONARCHY Malik; Mamlaka
see also Darshan; Naṣīḥat al-Mulūk; Shāh; Tigin; *and* → COURT CEREMONY
royal insignia Miẓalla; Sandjaḳ; Sarāparda; Shamsa; Tādj; Takht-i Ṭāwūs; Tughra
see also Shams.3; Tamgha; Tugh

MONASTICISM **Rahbāniyya**
and → CHRISTIANITY.MONASTERIES

MONGOLIA Ḳaraḳorum; Khalkha; **Mongolia**; Mongols
Mongols Batuʾids; Čaghatay Khānate; Čūbānids; Djalāyir; Djānids; Giray; Hayāṭila; Ilkhāns; Kalmuk; Ḳarā Khiṭāy; Ḳūrīltāy; Mangït; **Mongols**
see also Dūghlāt; Ergenekon; Khānbalïḳ; Ḳïshlaḳ; Ḳūbčūr; Ḳungrāt; Libās.iii; Ötüken; Tīmūrids; Tūmān.1; Ulus; Yaylaḳ; *and* → DYNASTIES.MONGOLS; LAW.MONGOL; TRIBES.CENTRAL ASIA, MONGOLIA AND POINTS FURTHER NORTH
administration Soyūrghāl; Yām; Yarlïgh; [in Suppl.] Dīwān-begi; Yurtčï
and → LAW.MONGOL
battles ʿAyn Djālūt; Ḥimṣ; Mardj Rāhiṭ; Wādī ʾl-Khaznadār
historians of Djuwaynī, ʿAlāʾ al-Dīn; Ḥamd Allāh al-Mustawfī al-Ḳazwīnī; Ḥaydar Mīrzā; Rashīd al-Dīn Ṭabīb; Waṣṣāf
see also Tamīm b. Baḥr al-Muṭṭawwiʿ; *and* → DYNASTIES.MONGOLS; *and the section Historians Of under individual dynasties*
physical geography
waters Orkhon

MONOPHYSITES → CHRISTIANITY.DENOMINATIONS

MOROCCO **al-Maghrib**
see also ʿArabiyya.A.iii.3; Ḥimāya.ii; Mallāḥ; Rīf.II; Sulṭān al-Ṭalaba (*and* Ṭalaba)
architecture → ARCHITECTURE.REGIONS.NORTH AFRICA
dynasties ʿAlawīs; Idrīsids; Marīnids; Saʿdids; Waṭṭāsids
see also Bū Ḥmāra; Ḥasanī; Shurafāʾ.1.III; Ẓahīr; [in Suppl.] Aḥmad al-Hība; *and* → DYNASTIES.SPAIN AND NORTH AFRICA
historians of Aḥmad al-Nāṣirī al-Salāwī (*and* al-Nāṣir al-Salāwī); Akanṣūs; Ibn Abī Zarʿ; Ibn al-Ḳāḍī; al-Zayyānī
see also Ibn al-Raḳīḳ; al-Kattānī; [in Suppl.] ʿAllāl al-Fāsī; Maḥammad b. Aḥmad al-Huḍīgī; *and* → DYNASTIES.SPAIN AND NORTH AFRICA
modern period Baladiyya.3; Djarīda.i.B; Djaysh.iii.2; Dustūr.xvii; Ḥizb.i; Ḥukūma.iv; Madjlis.4.A.xxi; Maḥkama.4.x; Makhzan; Ṣiḥāfa.2.(ii); [in Suppl.] Sība
belletrists
poets Ibn Idrīs (I); Ḳaddūr al-ʿAlamī; [in Suppl.] Ibn ʿAmr al-Ribāṭī; Ibn al-Ḥādjdj
education Djāmiʿa; Maʿārif.2.C; Madjmaʿ ʿIlmī.i.2.d; [in Suppl.] Institut des hautes études marocaines
reform Salafiyya.1(c); Tartīb

see also [in Suppl.] Muḥammad b. ʿAbd al-Karīm
scholars al-Tādilī
statesmen [in Suppl.] ʿAllāl al-Fāsī
for sultans → DYNASTIES.SPAIN AND NORTH AFRICA.ʿALAWIDS
physical geography al-Maghrib.I
deserts al-Ṣaḥrāʾ
see also Reg
mountains Atlas; Rīf.I.2
plateaux Ḥammāda
population Dukkāla; Glāwā; Ḥarṭānī; Khulṭ; Shāwiya.1; [in Suppl.] Awraba
see also al-Fāsiyyūn; al-Maʿḳil; *and* → BERBERS
religion al-Maghrib.VI
mystical orders Darḳāwa; Hansaliyya; Hazmīriyyūn; ʿIsāwā; al-Nāṣiriyya; Shādhiliyya; Wazzāniyya; [in Suppl.] Ḥamādisha
for Djazūliyya, *see* al-Djazūlī, Abū ʿAbd Allāh
see also Sharḳāwa; Ziyāniyya; [in Suppl.] ʿĀʾisha Ḳandīsha; *and* → MYSTICISM; SAINTHOOD
toponyms
ancient Anfā; Bādis; al-Baṣra; Fāzāz; al-Ḳaṣr al-Ṣaghīr; Nakūr; Shalla; Sidjilmāsa; Tāmasna; Tinmal; Tīṭ; Walīlī
present-day
districts Tafīlālt; Tāzarwālt
islands [in Suppl.] al-Ḥusayma
regions Darʿa; Figuig; Gharb; Ḥawz; Ifni; Rīf.I.2; Spartel; al-Sūs al-Aḳṣā; Tādlā; Wādī Nūn; [in Suppl.] al-Sāḳiya al-Ḥamraʾ
towns Agadir-ighir; Āghmāt; al-ʿArāʾish; Aṣfī; Aṣīla; Azammūr; Damnāt; (al-)Dār al-Bayḍāʾ; al-Djadīda; Dubdū; Faḍāla; Fās; Garsīf; al-Ḳaṣr al-Kabīr; al-Mahdiyya; Marrākush; Mawlāy Idrīs; Melilla; Miknās; Ribāṭ al-Fatḥ; Sabta; Salā; Shafshāwan; Ṣufrūy; al-Suwayra; Tamgrūt; Ṭandja; Tārūdānt; Tāzā; Tīṭṭāwīn; Tīznīt; Wadjda; Wazzān; [in Suppl.] Azrū; Benī Mellāl
see also al-Ḥamrāʾ; Tīṭ

MOUNTAINS Adjaʾ and Salmā; Adrar.2; Aghrī Dagh; Aïr; Ala Dagh; Aladja Dagh; Alburz; Altai; Alwand Kūh; ʿAmūr; Atlas; Awrās; Balkhān; Beshparmaḳ; Bībān; Bingöl Dagh; Bīsutūn; Čopan-ata; Damāwand; Deve Boynu; Djabala; al-Djibāl; Djūdī; Djurdjura; Elma Daghī; Erdjiyas Daghī; Fūta Djallon; Gāwur Daghlarī; Ḥaḍūr; Ḥamrīn; Ḥarāz; Hawrāmān; Hindū Kush; Ḥirāʾ; Ḥiṣn al-Ghurāb; Ḥufāsh; al-Ḳabḳ; Kabylia; Ḳaraḳorum; Ḳāsiyūn; Khumayr; Kūh-i Bābā; al-Lukkām; Nafūsa; Pamirs; Safīd Kūh; al-Sarāt; al-Sharāt; Sindjār; Sulaymān; Tibesti; Toros Dağları; al-Ṭūr; Ulu Dāgh; Wansharīs; Zagros; [in Suppl.] Shāh Dagh; al-Sharaf
see also Hind.i.i; Ḳarā Bāgh; Tasili; Thabīr; *and* → *the section Physical Geography under individual countries*

MOZAMBIQUE Kerimba; Makua; **Mozambique** (*and* [in Suppl.]); Pemba; Sofāla

MUḤAMMAD, THE PROPHET Hidjra; Ḥirāʾ; al-Ḥudaybiya; Khaybar; Khuzāʿa; Ḳudāʿa; Ḳuraysh; al-Madīna.i.2; Mawlid; Miʿrādj (*and* [in Suppl.]); **Muḥammad**; Ṣaḥāba; Sunna; Tābiʿūn; Ṭulaḳāʾ; Ummī.2; Wufūd
see also al-Ḳurʾān; Muʾākhāt; al-Muʾallafa Ḳulūbuhum; Nubuwwa; Nūr Muḥammadī; Sayyid; Sharaf; Sharīf; Taḥannuth; Taṣliya; Waḥy; [in Suppl.] Bayʿat al-Riḍwān; Mawlid.3; Shatm; *and* → MILITARY.BATTLES.622-632

belongings of Athar; al-Burāḳ; Burda.1; Dhu 'l-Faḳār; Duldul; Emānet-i Muḳaddese; Ḳadam Sharīf; Khirḳa-yi Sherīf; Liḥya-yi Sherīf; [in Suppl.] al-Naʿl al-Sharīf

biographies of **al-Maghāzī**; **Sīra**

biographers Abd al-Ḥaḳḳ b. Sayf al-Dīn; al-Bakrī, Abu 'l-Ḥasan; Daḥlān; al-Diyārbakrī; al-Djawwānī; al-Ḥalabī, Nūr al-Dīn; Ibn Hishām; Ibn Isḥāḳ; Ibn Sayyid al-Nās; ʿIyāḍ b. Mūsā; Ḳarā-čelebi-zāde.4; al-Ḳasṭallānī; Liu Chih; Mughulṭāy; Muḥammad Ḥusayn Haykal; Muʿīn al-Miskīn; al-Ṭabrisī, Amīn al-Dīn; al-Tanūkhī, Djamāl al-Dīn; Wahb b. Munabbih; Weysī; [in Suppl.] Dinet

see also Hind.v.e; Ibn Saʿd; al-Khargūshī; [in Suppl.] al-Suhaylī

companions of **Ṣaḥāba**

see also Ahl al-Ṣuffa; al-Salaf wa 'l-Khalaf; Tābiʿūn; [in Suppl.] Shatm

individual companions Abū Ayyūb al-Anṣārī; Abū Bakra; Abu 'l-Dardāʾ; Abū Dharr; Abū Hurayra; ʿAdī b. Ḥātim; ʿAmmār b. Yāsir; Anas b. Mālik; al-Arḳam; al-Ashʿarī, Abū Mūsā; ʿAttāb; al-Barāʾ (b. ʿĀzib); al-Barāʾ (b. Maʿrūr); Bashīr b. Saʿd; Bilāl b. Rabāḥ; Bishr b. al-Barāʾ; Burayda b. al-Ḥuṣayb; Diḥya; Djāriya b. Ḳudāma; Ghasīl al-Malāʾika; Hāshim b. ʿUtba; Ḥurḳūṣ b. Zuhayr al-Saʿdī; Ibn Masʿūd; Kaʿb b. Mālik; Khabbāb b. al-Aratt; Khālid b. Saʿīd; Ḳutham b. al-ʿAbbās; Maslama b. Mukhallad; al-Miḳdād b. ʿAmr; Muʿāwiya b. Ḥudaydj; al-Mughīra b. Shuʿba; Muḥammad b. Abī Ḥudhayfa; Muṣʿab b. ʿUmayr; al-Nābigha al-Djaʿdī; al-Nuʿmān b. Bashīr; Saʿd b. Abī Waḳḳāṣ; Ṣafwān b. al-Muʿaṭṭal; Saʿīd b. Zayd; Shaddād b. ʿAmr; Shuraḥbīl b. Ḥasana; Ṭalḥa; Tamīm al-Dārī; ʿUbayd Allāh b. al-ʿAbbās; ʿUbayd Allāh b. ʿUmar; ʿUḳba b. Nāfiʿ; ʿUrwa b. Masʿūd; ʿUtba b. Ghazwān; ʿUthmān b. Maẓʿūn; al-Walīd b. ʿUḳba; Zayd b. Thābit; al-Zibriḳān b. Badr; al-Zubayr b. al-ʿAwwām; Zuhayr b. Ḳays; [in Suppl.] Djābir b. ʿAbd Allāh; Ibn Mītham

see also al-Ḳaʿḳāʿ; Khawlān.2; Ḳuss b. Sāʿida; Rawḥ b. Zinbāʿ; Ubayy b. Kaʿb; Usāma b. Zayd; Uways al-Ḳaranī; ʿUyayna b. Ḥiṣn; Waraḳa b. Nawfal; Zayd b. ʿAmr; [in Suppl.] Khawla bt. Ḥakīm

family of al-ʿAbbās b. ʿAbd al-Muṭṭalib; ʿAbd Allāh b. ʿAbd al-Muṭṭalib; ʿAbd al-Muṭṭalib b. Hāshim; Abū Lahab; Abū Ṭālib; ʿAḳīl b. Abī Ṭālib; ʿAlī b. Abī Ṭālib; Āmina; Djaʿfar b. Abī Ṭālib; Fāṭima; Ḥalīma bint Abī Dhuʾayb; Ḥamza b. ʿAbd al-Muṭṭalib; (al-)Ḥasan b. ʿAlī b. Abī Ṭālib; al-Ḥasan b. Zayd b. al-Ḥasan; Hāshim b. ʿAbd Manāf; (al-)Ḥusayn b. ʿAlī b. Abī Ṭālib; Ruḳayya; ʿUbayd Allāh b. al-ʿAbbās; Umm Kulthūm; Zayd b. Ḥāritha

see also Ahl al-Bayt; Sharīf; Shurafāʾ; *and → the section Wives below*

daughters Fāṭima; Ruḳayya; Umm Kulthūm; Zaynab bt. Muḥammad

wives ʿĀʾisha bint Abī Bakr; Ḥafṣa; Khadīdja; Māriya; Maymūna bint al-Ḥārith; Ṣafiyya; Sawda bt. Zamʿa; Umm Salama Hind; Zaynab bt. Djaḥsh; Zaynab bt. Khuzayma

opponents of Abū Djahl; Kaʿb b. al-Ashraf; Umayya b. Khalaf; ʿUtba b. Rabīʿa; al-Walīd b. al-Mughīra

see also Zuhra; [in Suppl.] Malaʾ.2

MUSIC Ghināʾ; Ḳayna; Maḳām; Malāhī; **Mūsīḳī**; Ramal.2; Shashmaḳom; [in Suppl.] Īḳāʿ; Laḥn

see also Lamak; al-Rashīdiyya; Samāʿ.1

composers → *the section Musicians below*

instruments Būḳ; Darabukka; Duff; Ghayṭa; Imẓad; Ḳithāra; Miʿzaf; Mizmār; Nefīr; Rabāb; Ṣandj; Sanṭūr; Saz; Ṭabl; Ṭunbūr; ʿŪd.II; Urghan; Zurna; [in Suppl.] Nāy

see also Mehter; Mūrisṭus; Naḳḳāra-khāna; Ṭabbāl

military → MILITARY.BAND

musicians

composers

first centuries Ibn Muḥriz; Ibrāhīm al-Mawṣilī; Isḥāḳ b. Ibrāhīm al-Mawṣilī; Maʿbad

b. Wahb; Yaḥyā al-Makkī; Yūnus al-Kātib al-Mughannī; Ziryāb; [in Suppl.] ʿAllawayh al-Aʿsar; al-Dalāl; Faḍl al-Shāʿira

see also al-Ḳāsim b. ʿĪsā

13th to 16th centuries Ṣafī al-Dīn al-Urmawī; Tānsin; [in Suppl.] Ḥabba Khātūn

17th and 18th centuries Ismāʿīl Ḥaḳḳi; Ṣolaḳ-zāde

19th and 20th centuries al-Ḳusanṭīnī; Lāhūtī; Laylā Khānîm; Shewḳī Beg; Zekāʾī Dede

flautists [in Suppl.] Barṣawmā al-Zāmir

lute players ʿAzza al-Maylāʾ; Djaḥẓa; Ṣafī al-Dīn al-Urmawī; Sāʾib Khāthir; Zalzal; Ziryāb; [in Suppl.] ʿAllawayh al-Aʿsar

regional

Andalusian al-Ḥāʾik; Umayya, Abu ʾl-Ṣalt

Egyptian Ṭaḳṭūḳa

Indian **Hind**.viii; Khayāl

see also Bāyazīd Anṣārī; Tānsin; [in Suppl.] Ḥabba Khātūn

Kurdish Kurds.iv.C.4

Persian Mihragān.iv.3

see also Lāhūtī; Naḳḳāra-khāna

Turkish Ilāhī; Ḳoshma; Mehter; Sharḳî; Taḳsīm; Turks.IV; Türkü

see also Laylā Khānîm; Māni; Nefīr; Shewḳī Beg; Zekāʾī Dede; [in Suppl.] Ḳantimīr, Demetrius

song **Ghināʾ**; Khayāl; Nashīd; Nawba; Shashmaḳom; Türkü

see also Abu ʾl-Faradj al-Iṣbahānī; Ḥawfī; Ilāhī; Mawāliyā.3; Shāʿir.1.E

singers ʿĀlima; Ḳayna

see also ʿĀshiḳ; al-Barāmika.5

legendary [in Suppl.] al-Djarādatānⁱ

see also [in Suppl.] Ḥabba Khātūn

early Islamic period ʿAzza al-Maylāʾ; Djamīla; al-Gharīḍ; Ḥabāba; Ibn ʿĀʾisha.I; Ibn Misdjaḥ; Ibn Muḥriz; Ibn Suraydj; Maʿbad b. Wahb; Mālik b. Abi ʾl-Samḥ; Nashīṭ; Rāʾiḳa; Sāʾib Khāthir; Ṭuways; [in Suppl.] al-Dalāl

during the ʿAbbāsid caliphate Ibn Bāna; Ibn Djāmiʿ; Ibrāhīm al-Mawṣilī; Isḥāḳ b. Ibrāhīm al-Mawṣilī; Mukhāriḳ; Sallāma al-Zarḳāʾ; Shāriya; ʿUlayya; Yaḥyā al-Makkī; Yūnus al-Kātib al-Mughannī; [in Suppl.] Badhl al-Kubrā

mid-13th to 19th centuries [in Suppl.] Ḥabba Khātūn

20th century Siti Binti Saad; Umm Kulthūm

songwriters → MUSIC.MUSICIANS.COMPOSERS

terms Ṭarab; Taḳsīm; Tik wa-tum; [in Suppl.] Īḳāʿ; Laḥn

see also Ustādh.1; Wadjd

treatises on ʿAbd al-Ḳādir b. Ghaybī; Abu ʾl-Faradj al-Iṣbahānī; al-Ḥāʾik; Ibn Bāna; Ibn Khurradādhbih; Mashāḳa; (Banu ʾl-) Munadjdjim.4; Mūrisṭus; Mushāḳa; Ṣafī al-Dīn al-Urmawī; al-Ṣaydāwī; al-Tādilī; ʿUmar Khayyām; Yūnus al-Kātib al-Mughannī; [in Suppl.] al-Mufaḍḍal b. Salama

see also Abu ʾl-Maḥāsin b. Taghrībirdī; İnal; Malāhī; [in Suppl.] Ḳantimīr, Demetrius

MYSTICISM Allāh.III.4; Darwīsh; Dhikr; Ibāḥa.II; Karāma; Murīd; Murshid; Pīr; Samāʿ.1; Shaykh; Ṭarīḳa; **Taṣawwuf**; Zuhd

see also Sadjdjāda.3; Saʿīd al-Suʿadāʾ; Ṭāʾifa; *and* → DYNASTIES.PERSIA.ṢAFAWIDS

architecture → *the section Monasteries below*

concepts Baḳāʾ wa-Fanāʾ; al-Insān al-Kāmil; Ishrāḳ; Lāhūt and Nāsūt; Tawakkul; Zāʾirdja.2

see also Allāh.III.4; al-Ḥallādj.IV; Ibn al-ʿArabī; al-Niffarī; Uwaysiyya

dervishes **Darwīsh**; Raḳṣ

see also Tādj; [in Suppl.] Buḳʿa; *and* → MYSTICISM.ORDERS

dress Khirḳa; Pālāhang; Shadd.1

early ascetics ʿĀmir b. ʿAbd al-Ḳays al-ʿAnbarī; al-Ḥasan al-Baṣrī; al-Fuḍayl b. ʿIyāḍ; Ibrāhīm b. Adham; Maʿrūf al-Karkhī; Sarī al-Saḳaṭī

see also Bakkāʾ

literature [in Suppl.] Maktūbāt; Malfūẓāt; *and* → LITERATURE.POETRY.MYSTICAL

see also Zuhdiyya

monasteries Khānḳāh; Ribāṭ.1.b; Tekke; Zāwiya

mystics Darwīsh; Murīd; Murshid; Pīr; Shaykh

see also Pist; Walī; *and* → HAGIOGRAPHY

African (excluding North Africa and Egypt) ʿUmar b. Saʿīd al-Fūtī; [in Suppl.] al-Duwayḥī

see also Ṣāliḥiyya; Sūdān (Bilād al-).2; Ṭarīḳa.II.3; Taṣawwuf.9; Walī.9 *and* 10; Zāwiya.3; Ziyāra.9 *and* 10; [in Suppl.] al-Madjādhīb; Mozambique

Andalusian Abū Madyan; Ibn al-ʿArabī; Ibn al-ʿArīf, Abu ʾl-ʿAbbās; Ibn ʿĀshir; Ibn Barradjān; Ibn Ḳasī; Ibn Masarra; al-Shushtarī

see also al-Ṭalamankī

Arabic (excluding Andalusian and North African) ʿAbd al-Ghanī; ʿAbd al-Ḳādir al-Djīlānī; ʿAbd al-Karīm al-Djīlī; ʿAdī b. Musāfir; Aḥmad al-Badawī; ʿAydarūs; al-Bakrī, Muḥammad; al-Bakrī, Muṣṭafā; Bishr al-Ḥāfī; al-Bisṭāmī, ʿAbd al-Raḥmān; al-Damīrī; al-Dasūḳī, Ibrāhīm b. ʿAbd al-ʿAzīz; al-Dasūḳī, Ibrāhīm b. Muḥammad; Dhu ʾl-Nūn, Abu ʾl-Fayḍ; al-Dimyāṭī, al-Bannāʾ; al-Dimyāṭī, Nūr al-Dīn; al-Djunayd; al-Ghazālī, Abū Ḥāmid; al-Ghazālī, Aḥmad; al-Ḥallādj; al-Harawī al-Mawṣilī; Ibn ʿAṭāʾ Allāh; al-Ḳazwīnī, Nadjm al-Dīn; al-Kharrāz; al-Kurdī; al-Ḳushashī; Makhrama; al-Manūfī; al-Muḥāsibī; al-Munāwī; al-Murādī.1 *and* 2; al-Niffarī; al-Nūrī; Rābiʿa al-ʿAdawiyya al-Ḳaysiyya; al-Rifāʿī; Sahl al-Tustarī; al-Sarrādj, Abū Naṣr; al-Shaʿrānī; al-Shiblī, Abū Bakr; Sumnūn; ʿUthmān b. Marzūḳ; al-Yāfiʿī; Yūsuf b. ʿĀbid al-Idrīsī; Zakariyyāʾ al-Anṣārī; [in Suppl.] Abu ʾl-ʿAzāʾim; al-ʿAdawī; al-ʿAfīfī; al-Ḥiṣāfī

see also Abū Nuʿaym al-Iṣfahānī; Abū Ṭālib al-Makkī; Bā ʿAlawī; Baḥraḳ; Bakriyya; Bayyūmiyya; Faḍl, Bā; Faḳīh, Bā; Faḳīh, Bal; Hurmuz, Bā; Ḳādiriyya; Marwāniyya; Saʿdiyya; Shādhiliyya; al-Ṣiddīḳī; Yashruṭiyya; [in Suppl.] al-Bakrī; Demirdāshiyya; Shaʿrāniyya; *and* → MYSTICISM.EARLY ASCETICS

Central Asian Aḥmad Yasawī; Ḥakīm Ata; Naḳshband; al-Tirmidhī, Abū ʿAbd Allāh; Tirmidhī; Zangī Ātā; [in Suppl.] Aḥrār

see also Ḳalandariyya; Pārsāʾiyya; Ṭarīḳa.II.5; Uwaysiyya; Walī.5; Yasawiyya; [in Suppl.] Khʷādjagān

Chinese → CHINA

Indian Abū ʿAlī Ḳalandar; Aḥmad Sirhindī; Ashraf ʿAlī; Bahāʾ al-Dīn Zakariyyā; Bāḳī bi ʾllāh (*and* [in Suppl.]); al-Banūrī; Budhan; Burhān al-Dīn Gharīb; Burhān al-Dīn Ḳuṭb-i ʿĀlam; Čirāgh-i Dihlī; Čishtī; Djahānārā Bēgam; Djalāl al-Dīn Ḥusayn al-Bukhārī; "Djamālī"; Farīd al-Dīn Masʿūd "Gandj-i-Shakar"; Gīsū Darāz; Hānsawī; Ḥusaynī Sādāt Amīr; Imdād Allāh; Kalīm Allāh al-Djahānābādī; Ḳuṭb al-Dīn Bakhtiyār Kākī; Malik Muḥammad Djāyasī; Miyān Mīr, Miyādjī; Mubārak Ghāzī; Muḥammad Ghawth Gwāliyārī; al-Muttaḳī al-Hindī; Muẓaffar Shams Balkhī; Niẓām al-Dīn Awliyāʾ; Niẓām al-Dīn, Mullā Muḥammad; Nūr Ḳuṭb al-ʿĀlam; Shāh Muḥammad b. ʿAbd Aḥmad; Thānesarī; [in Suppl.] ʿAbd al-Bārī; ʿAbd al-Wahhāb Bukhārī; Bulbul Shāh; Farangī Maḥall; Gadāʾī Kambō; Ḥamīd Ḳalandar; Ḥamīd al-Dīn Ḳāḍī Nāgawrī; Ḥamīd al-Dīn Ṣūfī Nāgawrī Siwālī; Ḥamza Makhdūm; Kabīr; Kanbō

see also ʿAydarūs; Čishtiyya; Dārā Shukōh; Dard; Djīwan; Hind.v; Khalīl Allāh (*and* Khalīl Allāh But-shikan); Malang; Mughals.6; Naḳshbandiyya.3; Shaṭṭāriyya;

Suhrawardiyya.2; Ṭarīḳa.II.7; Taṣawwuf.7; Walī.6; Ziyāra.7; [in Suppl.] Maktūbāt; Malfūẓāt; Tabrīzī, Djalāl al-Dīn

Indonesian ʿAbd al-Raʾūf al-Sinkilī; ʿAbd al-Ṣamad al-Palimbānī; Ḥamza Fanṣūrī; Shams al-Dīn al-Samaṭrānī
see also Ṭarīḳa.II.8; Walī.7; Ziyāra.8

North African ʿAbd al-Ḳādir al-Fāsī; ʿAbd al-Salām b. Mashīsh; Abu 'l-Maḥāsin al-Fāsī; Abū Muḥammad Ṣāliḥ; Aḥmad b. Idrīs; ʿAlī b. Maymūn; al-ʿAyyāshī; al-Daḳḳāḳ; al-Djazūlī; al-Hāshimī; Ḥmād u-Mūsā; Ibn ʿAbbād; Ibn ʿAdjība; Ibn ʿAlīwa; Ibn ʿArūs; Ibn Ḥirzihim; al-Ḳādirī al-Ḥasanī; al-Kūhin; al-Lamaṭī; Māʾ al-ʿAynayn al-Ḳalḳamī; al-Madjdhūb; al-Sanūsī, Abū ʿAbd Allāh; al-Sanūsī, Muḥammad b. ʿAlī; al-Sanūsī, Shaykh Sayyid Aḥmad; al-Shādhilī; al-Tidjānī, Aḥmad; [in Suppl.] al-Asmar; al-Dilāʾ; al-Fāsī; Ibn ʿAzzūz; Maḥammad b. Aḥmad al-Huḍīgī
see also ʿAmmāriyya; ʿArūsiyya; Darḳāwa; Hansaliyya; Hazmīriyyūn; al-Ifrānī; ʿĪsāwā; Madaniyya; al-Nāṣiriyya; Raḥmāniyya; Shādhiliyya; Tidjāniyya; Walī.2; Wazzāniyya; Zāwiya.2; Ziyāniyya; [in Suppl.] Ḥamādisha; Ṭayyibiyya

Persian ʿAbd al-Razzāḳ al-Ḳāshānī; Abū Saʿīd b. Abi 'l-Khayr; Abū Yazīd al-Bisṭāmī; Aḥmad-i Djām; ʿAlāʾ al-Dawla al-Simnānī; ʿAlī al-Hamadānī; al-Anṣārī al-Harawī; Ashraf Djahāngīr; Bābā-Ṭāhir; Djalāl al-Dīn Rūmī; Faḍl Allāh Ḥurūfī; Ghudjduwānī; Ḥamdūn al-Ḳaṣṣār; Hudjwīrī; Ibn Khafīf; ʿIrāḳī; al-Kalābādhī; Kamāl Khudjandī; Ḳāsim-i Anwār; Kāzarūnī; Khalīl Allāh (*and* Khalīl Allāh But-shikan); Kharaḳānī; al-Khargūshī; Kirmānī; Kubrā; al-Ḳushayrī.1; Lāhīdjī.1; Maḥmūd Shabistarī; Nadjm al-Dīn Rāzī Dāya; Naḳshband; Rūzbihān; Saʿd al-Dīn al-Ḥammūʾī; Saʿd al-Dīn Kāshgharī; Ṣadr al-Dīn Ardabīlī; Ṣadr al-Dīn Mūsā; Ṣafī; Saʿīd al-Dīn Farghānī; Sayf al-Dīn Bākharzī; Shams-i Tabrīz(ī); al-Suhrawardī, Abu 'l-Nadjīb; al-Suhrawardī, Shihāb al-Dīn Abū Ḥafṣ; Sulṭān Walad; Tirmidhī; Zayn al-ʿĀbidīn Shīrwānī; [in Suppl.] ʿAbd Allāh b. Abī Bakr al-Miyānadjī; Abū ʿAlī; Aḥmad-i Rūmī; ʿAyn al-Ḳuḍāt al-Hamadhānī; Ibn al-Bazzāz al-Ardabīlī; al-Sindī; Tabrīzī, Djalāl al-Dīn
see also Djāmī; Madjlisī-yi Awwal; Naḳshbandiyya.1; Niʿmat-Allāhiyya; Ṣafawids.I.ii; Taṣawwuf.5

Turkish Aḳ Shams al-Dīn; Altï Parmak; ʿĀshïḳ Pasha; Badr al-Dīn b. Ḳāḍī Samāwnā; Baraḳ Baba; Bīdjān; Emīr Sulṭān; Faṣīḥ Dede; Fehmī; Gulshanī; Gülshehrī; Ḥādjdjī Bayrām Walī; Hüdāʾī; Ḥusām al-Dīn Čelebi; Ismāʿīl al-Anḳarawī; Ismāʿīl Ḥaḳḳī; Ḳaygusuz Abdāl; Khalīlī; Ḳuṭb al-Dīn-zāde; Merkez; Niyāzī; Sezāʾī, Ḥasan Dede; ʿUshshāḳī-zāde.1; [in Suppl.] ʿĀrif Čelebī; Eshrefoghlu; Esrār Dede; Rūshanī, Dede ʿUmar; Süleymān Dhātī
see also Ashrafiyya; Bakriyya; Bayrāmiyya; Bektāshiyya; Djilwatiyya; Gülbaba; Ilāhī; Khalwatiyya; Mawlawiyya; Naḳshbandiyya.2; Shaʿbāniyya; Shamsiyya; Sunbuliyya; Ṭarīḳa.II.5; Taṣawwuf.6; ʿUshshāḳiyya; Walī.4

orders **Ṭarīḳa**.II

individual orders ʿAmmāriyya; ʿArūsiyya; Ashrafiyya; Bakriyya; Bayrāmiyya; Bayyūmiyya; Bektāshiyya; Čishtiyya; Darḳāwa; Djilwatiyya; Hansaliyya; Hazmīriyyūn; ʿĪsāwā; Ḳādiriyya; Ḳalandariyya; Khalwatiyya; Madaniyya; Marwāniyya; Mawlawiyya; Mīrghaniyya; Murīdiyya; Naḳshbandiyya; al-Nāṣiriyya; Niʿmat-Allāhiyya; Pārsāʾiyya; Raḥmāniyya; Rifāʿiyya; Saʿdiyya; Ṣāliḥiyya; Sanūsiyya; Shaʿbāniyya; Shādhiliyya; Shamsiyya; Shaṭṭāriyya; Suhrawardiyya; Sunbuliyya; Tidjāniyya; ʿUshshāḳiyya; Wazzāniyya; Yasawiyya; Yashruṭiyya; Ziyāniyya; [in Suppl.] Demirdāshiyya; Ḥamādisha; Khʷādjagān; Shaʿrāniyya
for ʿAdawiyya, *see* ʿAdī b. Musāfir; *for* ʿAfīfiyya, *see* [in Suppl.] al-ʿAfīfī; *for* Aḥmadiyya (Badawiyya), *see* Aḥmad al-Badawī; *for* Dasūḳiyya (Burhāmiyya), *see* al-Dasūḳī, Ibrāhīm b. ʿAbd al-ʿAzīz; *for* al-Djazūliyya, *see* al-Djazūlī; *for*

Gulshaniyya, *see* Gulshanī; for Idrīsiyya, *see* Aḥmad b. Idrīs; *for* Kāzarūniyya (Murshidiyya, Isḥāḳiyya), *see* Kāzarūnī; *for* Kubrawiyya, *see* Kubrā; *for* Yāfiʿiyya, *see* al-Yāfiʿī
see also Nūrbakhshiyya; Ṣafawids.I.ii; Uwaysiyya; [in Suppl.] al-Madjādhīb; Ṭayyibiyya

terms Abdāl; ʿĀshiḳ; Awtād; Baḳāʾ wa-Fanāʾ; Basṭ; Bīsharʿ; Čāʾūsh; Darwīsh; Dawsa; Dede; Dhawḳ; Dhikr; Djilwa; Faḳīr; Fikr; al-Ghayb; Ghayba; Ghufrān; Ḥaḍra; Ḥaḳīḳa.3; Ḥaḳḳ; Ḥāl; Ḥidjāb.III; Ḥuḳūḳ; Ḥulūl; Ḥurriyya; Huwa huwa; Ikhlāṣ; Ilhām; ʿInāya; al-Insān al-Kāmil; Ishān; Ishāra; ʿIshḳ; Ishrāḳ; Ithbāt; Ittiḥād; Ḳabḍ.ii; Kāfir; Ḳalb.I; Kalima; Karāma; Kashf; Khalīfa.iii; Khalwa; Khānḳāh; Khirḳa; al-Ḳuṭb; Lāhūt and Nāsūt; Madjdhūb; Manzil; Maʿrifa; Muḥāsaba.1; Munādjāt; Murīd; Murshid; Nafs; Odjaḳ; Pālāhang; Pīr; Pūst; Pūst-neshīn; Rābiṭa; Ramz.3; Rātib; Ribāṭ; Riḍā.1; Rind; Rūḥāniyya; Rukhṣa.2; Ṣabr; Ṣadr; Shaṭḥ; Shawḳ; Shaykh; Shukr.1; Ṣidḳ; Silsila; Sulṭān.4; Sulūk.2; Tadjallī; Ṭāʾifa; Ṭarīḳa.I; Tekke; Terdjümān; Wadjd; Waḥdat al-Shuhūd; Waraʿ; Waẓīfa.2; Wird; Wudjūd.2; [in Suppl.] Buḳʿa; Ghawth; Mawḳif; Sirr; Taḳwā.4 *and* 5; Wahm.2
see also Čelebī; Futuwwa; Gülbaba; Gulbāng; Lawḥ; Lawn; Waṭan

N

NATIONALISM Istiḳlāl; **Ḳawmiyya; Waṭaniyya**; [in Suppl.] Taʿrīb.2
see also Djangalī; Khilāfa; Pāshtūnistān; al-Shuʿūbiyya; ʿUrūba; Waṭan; *and* → PANARABISM; PANISLAMISM; PANTURKISM; POLITICS.MOVEMENTS

NATURAL SCIENCE **al-Āthār al-ʿUlwiyya**; **Ḥikma**; Masāʾil wa-Adjwiba; Ṭabīʿa; [in Suppl.] **Ṭabīʿiyyāt**
see also Nūr.1
natural scientists al-Bīrūnī; al-Dimashḳī; Ibn Bādjdja; Ibn al-Haytham; Ibn Rushd; Ibn Sīnā; Ikhwān al-Ṣafāʾ; al-Ḳazwīnī; al-Marwazī, Sharaf al-Zamān
and → ALCHEMY; ASTRONOMY; BOTANY; METAPHYSICS; ZOOLOGY

NATURE → AGRICULTURE; BOTANY; FLORA; LITERATURE.POETRY.NATURE

NAVIGATION Djughrāfiyā; Iṣbaʿ; Kharīṭa; Maghnāṭīs.2; Manār; **Milāḥa**; Mīnāʾ
see also al-Khashabāt; Rīḥ; al-Ṭāsa
ships Milāḥa (esp. 4); Nassads; **Safīna**; Shīnī; Usṭūl
see also Baḥriyya.2; Kelek; *and* → MILITARY.NAVY
shipyards Dār al-Ṣināʿa; Tersāne
treatises on Ibn Mādjid; Sīdī ʿAlī Reʾīs; Sulaymān al-Mahrī; al-Tādilī
see also Djughrāfiyā.IV.d; Milāḥa.1 *and* 3

NEPAL **Nepal**

NESTORIANS → CHRISTIANITY.DENOMINATIONS

NEW WORLD Djāliya; Djarīda.i.C.; **al-Mahdjar**
immigrants Djabrān Khalīl Djabrān; al-Maʿlūf; Nuʿayma, Mīkhāʾīl; al-Rayḥānī; [in Suppl.] Abū Māḍī; Abū Shādī
see also Pārsīs; Ṭuʿma, Ilyās

NIGER **Niger**
see also Sūdān (Bilād al-).2
physical geography Niger.1
toponyms Bilma; Djādū; Kawār

NIGERIA Hausa; **Nigeria**; Yoruba
see also Djarīda.vi; Fulbe; al-Kānemī; Kanuri; Nikāḥ.II.6; Sūdān (Bilād al-).2; *and* → AFRICA.CENTRAL AFRICA *and* WEST AFRICA
leaders Muḥammad Bello; ʿUthmān b. Fūdī
see also Gwandu; [in Suppl.] Mai Tatsine
toponyms
provinces Adamawa; Bornū
towns Ibadan; Kano; Katsina; Kūkawa; Sokoto

NOMADISM **Badw**; Horde; Īlāt; Khāwa; Khayma; Marʿā; Yörük
see also Baḳḳāra; Baranta; Dakhīl; Dawār; Ḥayy; Ḳayn; *and* → BEDOUINS; GYPSIES; TRIBES
nomadic ideology **Taʿarrub**
nomadic possessions Khayma; Mifrash
see also Khayl; Zmāla.2
residences Ḳîshlaḳ; Yaylaḳ

NUBIA ʿAlwa; Barābra; Dongola; al-Marīs; **Nūba**
see also Baḳṭ; Dār al-Ṣulḥ; Ibn Sulaym al-Aswānī; al-Muḳurra; Sōba; *and* → EGYPT.TOPONYMS; SUDAN.TOPONYMS
languages Nūba.3
peoples Nūba.4

NUMBER Abdjad; Ḥisāb al-ʿAḳd; Ḥisāb al-Djummal; Ḥurūf; ʿIlm al-Ḥisāb
and → MATHEMATICS
numbers Khamsa; Sabʿ
see also al-Ṣifr

NUMISMATICS Dār al-Ḍarb; Sikka; Tazyīf; Wazn.1
see also ʿAlī Pasha Mubārak; Ismāʿīl Ghālib; Makāyil; Nithār
coinage Aḳče; Bālish; Čao; Čeyrek; Dīnār; Dirham.2; Fals; Ḥasanī; Larin; Mohur; Pāʾī; Pāra; Pawlā; Paysā; Riyāl; Rūpiyya; Ṣadīḳī; Ṣāḥib Ḳirān; Shāhī; Tanga; Ṭarī; Wariḳ
see also Dhahab; Fidda; Filori; Hilāl.ii; Sanadjāt; Tamgha; Wadaʿ.1; Yādgār; *and* → DYNASTIES; WEIGHTS AND MEASUREMENTS
for coinage in the name of rulers, see al-Afḍal (Kutayfāt); ʿAlī Bey; Ghāzi ʾl-Dīn Ḥaydar; Ḳaṭarī b. al-Fudjāʾa; Khurshīd; al-Manṣūr, al-Malik Muḥammad; Muṣṭafā.1; [in Suppl.] Farrukhān.2; *for coinage under dynasties, see in particular* Artuḳids; Barīd Shāhīs; Khwārazm-shāhs; Lōdīs.5; Mughals.10; al-Muwaḥḥidūn; ʿOthmānlî.IX; Rasūlids.2; Ṣafawids.VI; Saldjūḳids.VIII; Ṣiḳilliya.3; Ṣulayḥids.2; Tīmūrids.4; Yādgār; [in Suppl.] Mamlūks.iv
shell currency Wadaʿ.1
special issues Yādgār
mint localities Abarshahr; al-Abbāsiyya; Andarāb.1; Ānī; Bāghče Sarāy; Islāmābād; Iṣṭakhr; al-Kurdj; Māh al-Baṣra; Mawlāy Idrīs; Māzandarān.7; Wāsiṭ.4; [in Suppl.] Biyār; Firrīm
reform ʿAbd al-Malik b. Marwān; [in Suppl.] al-Ghiṭrīf b. ʿAṭāʾ
see also Tūmān.2
terms ʿAdl.2; Salām (*and* Sālim.1); Tūmān.2; Wazn.1

O

OBSCENITY **Mudjūn**; **Sukhf**

OCEANS AND SEAS **Baḥr**; al-Madd wa 'l-Djazr
see also Kharīṭa; *and* → CARTOGRAPHY; NAVIGATION
waters Aral; Baḥr Adriyās; Baḥr Bunṭus; Baḥr Fāris; Baḥr al-Hind; Baḥr al-Khazar; Baḥr al-Ḳulzum; Baḥr Lūṭ; Baḥr Māyuṭis; al-Baḥr al-Muḥīṭ; Baḥr al-Rūm; Baḥr al-Zandj; Marmara Deñizi

OIL **Nafṭ**.3
see also Ta'mīm
for cooking oil → CUISINE.FOOD
oilfields ʿAbbādān; Abḳayḳ; Altîn Köprü; al-Baḥrayn; al-Dahnā'; al-Ghawār; al-Ḥasā; al-Ḳaṭīf; Khārag; Khūzistān; Kirkūk; Kirmānshāh; al-Kuwayt; Lībiyā; Nadjd.3; Rām-hurmuz; Ra's (al-)Tannūra; (al-)Ẓahrān; [in Suppl.] Aḥmadī
see also Djannāba; Fārs; al-Khubar; Yanbuʿ

OMAN al-Ibāḍiyya.g; Madjlis.4.A.xiii; Maḥkama.4.ix; Nabhān; Ṣiḥāfa.1.(xiii); **ʿUmān**
see also [in Suppl.] al-Ḥārithī
dynasties Bū Saʿīd; Yaʿrubids
physical geography ʿUmān.1
salt flats Umm al-Samīm
population ʿAwāmir; al-Baṭāḥira; al-Djanaba; al-Durūʿ; Hinā; al-Ḥubūs; al-ʿIfār; (Banū) Kharūṣ; Mahra; Mazrūʿī; Nabhān; Wahība; [in Suppl.] **ʿUmān**.iii
and → TRIBES.ARABIAN PENINSULA
toponyms
islands Khūryān-mūryān; Maṣīra
regions al-Bāṭina; Ra's Musandam; al-Rustāḳ; al-Sharḳiyya; Ẓafār; al-Ẓāhira
towns al-Buraymī; Ḥāsik; ʿIbrī; Ḳalhāt; Masḳaṭ; Maṭraḥ; al-Mirbāṭ; Nizwa; al-Rustāḳ; Ṣalāla; Ṣuḥār
see also (Djazīrat) al-ʿArab; Wabār.2; [in Suppl.] Gwādar

ONOMASTICS Bā; Ibn; **Ism**; Kisrā; Kunya; Laḳab; Nisba.2
see also al-Asmā' al-Ḥusnā; Oghul; Ṣiḳilliya.2
epithets Ata; Baba; Ghufrān; Humāyūn; al-Ṣiddīḳ; Tādj
in form of address Agha; Ākhūnd; Beg; Begum; Čelebī; Efendi; Khʷādja; Khātūn; Khudāwand; Shaykh; Ustādh
see also Akhī; Sharīf.(3)
proper names Aḥmad; Dhu 'l-Faḳār; Humā; Marzpān; Meḥemmed; Mihragān. iv.2; Sonḳor; Thaʿlaba; Ṭoghrîl
see also al-Asad; Payghū; Yaylaḳ
titles
African Diglal; Sulṭān.3; [in Suppl.] Mai
Arabic ʿAmīd; Amīr al-Mu'minīn; Amīr al-Muslimīn; Asad al-Dawla; ʿAzīz Miṣr; ʿIzz al-Dawla; ʿIzz al-Dīn; Khādim al-Ḥaramayn; Khidīw; Malik; Mihmindār; Mushīr; Sardār; Sayyid; Shaykh al-Balad; Shaykh al-Islām.1; Sulṭān.1; Tubbaʿ
see also Dawla.2
Central Asian Afshīn; Ikhshīd; Ḳosh-begi; Shār; [in Suppl.] Atalîḳ; Dīwān-begi; İnaḳ
Indo-Muslim Āṣāf-Djāh; Khʷādja-i Djahān; Khān Khānān; Nawwāb; Niẓām; Pēshwā; Ṣāḥib Ḳirān; Sardār; Shār; Ulugh Khān

Mongolian Noyan; Ṣāḥib Ḳirān; Ṭarkhān
Persian Agha Khān; Ispahbadh; Ispahsālār; Iʿtimād al-Dawla; Khʷādja; Marzpān; Mīr; Mīrzā; Mollā; Pādishāh; Ṣadr; Sālār; Sardār; Sarkār Āḳā; Shāh; Tekfur; Ustāndār
Southeast Asian Penghulu; Sulṭān.2
Turkish Alp; Beglerbegi; Dāmād; Daryā-begi; Dayi̊; Gülbaba; Khʷādjegān-i Dīwān-i Humāyūn; Khāḳān; Khān; Khudāwendigār; Mīr-i Mīrān; Mushīr; Pasha; Payghū; Ṣadr-i Aʿẓam; Shaykh al-Islām.2; Ṣu Bashi̊; Tekfur; Tigin; Yabghu
see also Čorbadji̊; Terken Khātūn; Tughra

Optics Ḳaws Ḳuzaḥ; **Manāẓir**
see also Mirʾāt; Sarāb
works on Ibn al-Haytham; Kamāl al-Dīn al-Fārisī; Uḳlīdis
see also Ḳuṭb al-Dīn Shīrāzī

Ottoman Empire Anadolu.iii.2 *and* 3; Ertoghrul.1; Istanbul; Lāle Devri; **ʿOthmānli̊**; Tanẓīmāt
see also Bāb-i ʿĀlī; Ḥidjāz Railway; Pasha Ḳapusu; Shenlik; Ṭursun Faḳīh; [in Suppl.] Sürgün; *and* → Dynasties.anatolia and the turks; Europe.eastern; Law.ottoman; Military.ottoman; *and the section Ottoman Period under individual countries*
administration Berātli̊; Ḍabṭiyya; Dīwān-i Humāyūn; Eyālet; Imtiyāzāt.ii; Khāṣṣ; Khazīne; Mashwara; Millet.3; Mukhtār; Mülāzemet; Mulāzim; Mulkiyya; Nāḥiye; Nishāndji̊; Reʾīs ül-Küttāb; Sandjaḳ; Tīmār; Ulaḳ; Ziʿāmet; [in Suppl.] Dāʾira Saniyya
see also Ḳaḍāʾ; Maʾmūr; Odjaḳ; Waḳf.IV (*and* [in Suppl.] Waḳf.II.2); [in Suppl.] Niẓām ʿAskarī.3; *and* → Documents.ottoman; Law.ottoman; Military.ottoman
archives and registers Başvekalet Arşivi; Daftar-i Khāḳānī; Ḳānūn.iii; Maṣraf Defteri; Mühimme Defterleri; Sāl-nāme; **Sidjill**.3; Taḥrīr
see also Daftar.III; Ferīdūn Beg; Maḥlūl
financial Arpali̊ḳ; Ashām; Bayt al-Māl.II; Daftardār; Dār al-Ḍarb; Dirlik; Djayb-i Humāyūn; Duyūn-i ʿUmūmiyye; Irsāliyye; Ḳāʾime; Khazīne; Māliyye; Muḥāsaba.2; Mukhallefāt; Muṣādara.3; Rūznāmedji; Sāliyāne; Siyāḳat; ʿUlūfe; [in Suppl.] Sanad
see also Bakhshīsh; Ṣurra
fiscal Ḍarība.3; Djizya.ii; Ḥisba.ii; Kharādj.III; Muḥaṣṣil; Mültezim; ʿOthmānli̊.II; Resm; Taḥrīr; Ṭapu; Tekālīf; Tīmār; Ziʿāmet
see also Mutaṣarrif; Shehir Ketkhüdāsi̊
agriculture Filāḥa.iv; Māʾ.8; Raʿiyya.2
and → Agriculture
architecture → Architecture.regions.turkey
court ceremony Čāʾūsh; Khirḳa-yi Sherīf; Marāsim.4; Mawākib.4; Mehter; Selāmli̊ḳ
cuisine Maṭbakh.2
diplomacy Bālyōs; Consul; Elči; Hiba.v; Penče
see also Berātli̊; Imtiyāzāt.ii; Ḳawwās; *and* → Diplomacy
education Ghalaṭa-sarāyi̊; Külliyye; Maʿārif.I.i; Makhredj; Mulkiyya; Ṣaḥn-i Thamān; Ṣofta; [in Suppl.] Ṭibbiyye-i ʿAdliyye-i Shāhāne
see also Ḥarbiye; *and* → Education; Reform.educational
functionaries Āmeddji; Aʿyān; Bazi̊rgan; Bostāndji̊; Bostāndji̊-bashi̊; Čaki̊rdji̊-bashi̊; Čāshnagīr-bashi̊; Ḍābiṭ; Ḍabṭiyya; Daftardār; Dilsiz; Doghandji̊; Elči; Emīn; Ghulām.iv; Ḥekīm-bashi̊; Ič-oghlani̊; ʿIlmiyye; Ḳāʾim-maḳām; Ḳapu Aghasi̊; Ḳawwās; Ketkhudā.1; Khaznadār; Khʷādjegān-i Dīwān-i Humāyūn; Maʾmūr; Mewḳūfātči̊; Mīr-Ākhūr; Mushīr; Mustashār; Mutaṣarrif; Nishāndji̊; Reʾīs ül-Küttāb; Rūznāmedji; Ṣadr-ı Aʿẓam; Shāhnāmedji; Shehir Emāneti; Shehir Ketkhüdāsi̊; Tardjumān.2; Telkhīṣdji; Ṭulumbadji̊; ʿUlamāʾ.3; Waḳaʿ-nüwīs; Wālī; Wazīr.III; Yazi̊dji̊; [in Suppl.] Segbān

see also ʿAdjamī Oghlān; ʿAsas; Bālā; Baltadjī; Bālyōs; Bīrūn; Enderūn; al-Ḥaramayn; Khāṣī.III; Khāṣṣ Oda; Khāṣṣekī; Mābeyn; *and* → LAW.OTTOMAN; MILITARY.OTTOMAN

history ʿOthmānlī.I; [in Suppl.] Taʾrīkh.II.1

and → DYNASTIES.ANATOLIA AND THE TURKS.OTTOMANS; LITERATURE.HISTORICAL.TURKISH; TURKEY.OTTOMAN PERIOD; *and the section Toponyms in the countries once falling within the Ottoman Empire*

industry and trade Ḥarīr.ii; Kārwān; Ḳuṭn.2; Milḥ.3; ʿOthmānlī.II; Sūḳ.7

see also Maʿdin.3; [in Suppl.] Ṣarrāf

law → LAW.OTTOMAN

literature → LITERATURE

military → MILITARY.OTTOMAN

modernisation of Baladiyya.1; Ḥukūma.i; Ḥurriyya.ii; Iṣlāḥ.iii; Ittiḥād we Teraḳḳī Djemʿiyyeti; Madjlis.4.A.i; Madjlis al-Shūrā; Tanẓīmāt

and → TURKEY.OTTOMAN PERIOD

mysticism → MYSTICISM.MYSTICS.TURKISH

reform of **Tanẓīmāt**; Yeñi ʿOthmānlīlar

P

PAKISTAN Djināḥ; Dustūr.xiv; Ḥizb.vi; Ḥukūma.v; Madjlis.4.C; al-Marʾa.5; **Pākistān**; Urdū.1; Ziyāʾ al-Ḥaḳḳ; [in Suppl.] Djarīda.vii; Maḥkama.5; Niẓām ʿAskarī.4

see also Ahl-i Ḥadīth; Dār al-ʿUlūm.c; Djamʿiyya.v; Djūnāgaṙh; Hind.ii *and* iv; Kashmīr.ii; Ḳawmiyya.vi; Khaybar; Muhādjir.3; Pashtūnistān; Sind.2; *and* → INDIA

architecture → ARCHITECTURE.REGIONS

education Djāmiʿa

language Urdū.1

see also Pākistān; *and* → LANGUAGE.INDO-EUROPEAN.INDO-IRANIAN.INDIAN

literature Urdū.2

and → *the subsection Urdu under* LITERATURE.POETRY *and* PROSE

physical geography

see also Pākistān

mountains Sulaymān

waters Kurram; Mihrān; Zhōb

population Afrīdī; Dāwūdpōtrās; Mahsūd; Mohmand; Mullagorī; Wazīrīs; Yūsufzay; [in Suppl.] Demography.VII; Gurčānī

see also Djirga

statesmen Djināḥ; Liyāḳat ʿAlī Khān; Ziyāʾ al-Ḥaḳḳ

see also Mawdūdī

toponyms

ancient Čīnīōt; Daybul; Ḳandābīl; Khayrābād.ii; Ṭūrān

present-day

districts Chitral; Ḥāfiẓābād; Hazāra; Khārān; Khayrpūr; Kilāt.2; Kōhāt; Kwaṫṫa; Mastūdj; Sībī

regions Balūčistān; Dardistān; Dēradjāt; Dīr; Djahlāwān; Kaččhī; Las Bēla; Makrān; Pandjāb; Sind; Swāt; Wazīrīs

towns Amarkot; Bādjawr; Bahāwalpūr; Bakkār; Bannū; Bhakkar; Gūdjrāṅwāla; Gudjrāt; Ḥasan Abdāl; Ḥaydarābād; Islāmābād; Karāčī; Kilāt.1; Ḳuṣdār; Kwaṫṫa; Lāhawr; Mastūdj; Peshāwar; Rāwalpindi; Shikārpūr.1; Sībī; Siyālkūt; Uččh; Zhōb; [in Suppl.] Gilgit; Gwādar

PALESTINE/ISRAEL Djarīda.i.A; **Filasṭīn**; Ḥizb.i; Madjlis.4.A.xxiii; Maḥkama.4.v; Mandates; Ṣiḥāfa.1.(v)
see also Djarrāḥids; Ḳays ʿAylān; al-Khālidī; al-Sāmira; Shāhīn, Āl; Yashruṭiyya; [in Suppl.] Demography.III; Waḳf.II.2; *and* → CRUSADE(R)S
architecture Ḳubbat al-Ṣakhra; al-Ḳuds; al-Masdjid al-Aḳṣā
see also Kawkab al-Hawāʾ
belletrists Ṣāyigh, Tawfīḳ
historians of Mudjīr al-Dīn al-ʿUlaymī
Ottoman period Ẓāhir al-ʿUmar al-Zaydānī
physical geography
deserts al-Naḳb; Sīnāʾ
see also al-Tīh
mountains/hills al-Ṭūr.2, 3 *and* 4
waters Baḥr Lūṭ; al-Ḥūla; Nahr Abī Fuṭrus; al-Urdunn.1; Yarmūk.1
toponyms
ancient Arsūf; ʿAthlīth; ʿAyn Djālūt; Bayt Djibrīn; al-Dārūm; Irbid.II; Sabasṭiyya.1; Subayta
present-day
regions al-Ghawr.1; Mardj Banī ʿĀmir; al-Naḳb
towns ʿAkkā; ʿAmwās; ʿĀsḳalān; Baysān; Bayt Laḥm; Bīr al-Sabʿ; Ghazza; Ḥayfā; Ḥiṭṭīn; al-Khalīl; al-Ḳuds; Ladjdjūn; Ludd; Nābulus; al-Nāṣira; Rafaḥ; al-Ramla; Rīḥā.1; Ṣafad; Ṭabariyya; Ṭulkarm; Yāfā
see also Ḳayṣariyya; Ṣihyawn
under British mandate Filasṭīn.2; Muḥammad ʿIzzat Darwaza; [in Suppl.] Amīn al-Ḥusaynī
see also Mandates

PANARABISM Ḳawmiyya; **Pan-Arabism**; **ʿUrūba**; [in Suppl.] al-Djāmiʿa al-ʿArabiyya; Taʿrīb.2
see also Waṭaniyya
partisans of al-Kawākibī; Nūrī al-Saʿīd; Rashīd Riḍā; al-Zahrāwī, ʿAbd al-Ḥamīd; [in Suppl.] ʿAbd al-Nāṣir; Muḥibb al-Dīn al-Khaṭīb; Sāṭiʿ al-Ḥuṣrī
see also al-Kāẓimī, ʿAbd al-Muḥsin

PANISLAMISM Ḳawmiyya; **Pan-Islamism**; **al-Rābiṭa al-Islāmiyya**
see also Dustūr.xviii; Iṣlāḥ.ii; Khilāfa; Muʾtamar; Taḳrīb
partisans of ʿAbd al-Ḥamīd II; Djamāl al-Dīn al-Afghānī; Fiṭrat; Gasprali (Gasprinski), Ismāʿīl; Ḥālī; Kūčak Khān Djangalī; Māʾ al-ʿAynayn al-Ḳalḳamī; Meḥmed ʿĀkif; Rashīd Riḍā; Ṣafar; [in Suppl.] Andjuman-i Khuddām-i Kaʿba; al-Bakrī
see also Djadīd

PANTURKISM Ḳawmiyya.iv; **Pan-Turkism**
partisans of Gasprali (Gasprinski), Ismāʿīl; Gökalp, Ziya; Riḍā Nūr; Suʿāwī, ʿAlī; Yūsuf Aḳčura
see also Türk Odjaghî

PAPYROLOGY Ḳirṭās; Papyrus
see also Diplomatic.i.15; *and* → DOCUMENTS

PARADISE al-ʿAshara al-Mubashshara; Dār al-Salām; **Djanna**; Ḥūr; Kawthar; Riḍwān; Salsabīl; Tasnīm.1
see also al-Aʿrāf

PAYMENTS Adjr.2; ʿAṭāʾ; Djāmakiyya; Ḥawāla; Inʿām; Māl al-Bayʿa; Maʿūna; Rizḳ.3; Ṣila.3;

Soyūrg̲h̲āl; Ṣurra; ʿUlūfe
  see also Waẓīfa.1; [in Suppl.] Ṣakk; *and* → Treaties.tributes
bribery   Marāfiḳ; **Ras̲h̲wa**

Perfume   Bān; Ḥinnāʾ; Kāfūr; Misk
  see also al-ʿAṭṭār; Maʿdin.4; ʿŪd.I.1; [in Suppl.] Tug̲h̲dj

Persia   → Iran

Pharmacology   Adwiya; Aḳrābād̲h̲īn; **al-Ṣaydana**; Ṭibb
  see also Diyusḳuridīs; D̲j̲ālīnūs; Nabāt; *and* → Botany; Drugs; Medicine
pharmacologists   Ibn al-Bayṭār; Ibn Samad̲j̲ūn; Ibn al-Tilmīd̲h̲; Ibn Wāfid; al-Kōhēn al-ʿAṭṭār;
    Sābūr b. Sahl; [in Suppl.] al-G̲h̲āfiḳī; Ibn Biklāris̲h̲; Ibn al-Rūmiyya
  see also al-ʿAs̲h̲s̲h̲āb; al-ʿAṭṭār; al-Bīrūnī; al-Suwaydī; Yaḥyā b. al-Biṭrīḳ

Philately   **Posta**
  and → Transport.postal service

Philippines   **Philippines**
  see also [in Suppl.] al-Marʾa; *and* → Asia.east

Philosophy   Falāsifa; **Falsafa**; Ḥikma; Mā baʿd al-Ṭabīʿa; Manṭiḳ; Naẓar
  see also ʿĀlam.1; Allāh.iii.2; al-Maḳūlāt; Muk̲h̲taṣar; S̲h̲arḥ.IV
logic   **Manṭiḳ**
  terms   Āla.iii; ʿAraḍ; Dalīl; Faṣl; Fiʿl; Ḥadd; Ḥaḳīḳa.2; Ḥud̲j̲d̲j̲a; Ḥukm.I; Huwa huwa.A;
      Muḳaddam; Natīd̲j̲a; S̲h̲arṭ.2; Taʿrīf.1
    see also Ḳaṭʿ; al-Sūfisṭāʾiyyūn
philosophers   **Falāsifa**; [in Suppl.] Mas̲h̲s̲h̲āʾiyya
  Christian   Ibn al-Ṭayyib; Ibn Zurʿa; Mattā b. Yūnus; Yaḥyā b. ʿAdī; Yaḥyā al-Naḥwī
  Greek   Aflāṭūn; Anbaduḳlīs; Arisṭūṭālīs; Balīnūs; Baṭlamiyūs; Buruḳlus; D̲j̲ālīnūs;
      Fīthāg̲h̲ūras; Furfūriyūs; al-Iskandar al-Afrūdīsī; al-Sūfisṭāʾiyyūn; Suḳrāṭ;
      T̲h̲amisṭiyus
    see also Ḥunayn b. Isḥāḳ al-ʿIbādī; Īsāg̲h̲ūd̲j̲ī; Isḥāḳ b. Ḥunayn; Lawn; al-Maḳūlāt;
      Mattā b. Yūnus; Nīḳūlāʾūs; al-S̲h̲ayk̲h̲ al-Yūnānī; Usṭāth̲; Ut̲h̲ūlūd̲j̲iyā; Yaḥyā b. al-
      Biṭrīḳ; Yaḥyā al-Naḥwī; Yūnān; [in Suppl.] Mas̲h̲s̲h̲āʾiyya
  Islamic
      biographers of   al-S̲h̲ahrazūrī, S̲h̲ams al-Dīn
      9th century   Abu ʾl-Hud̲h̲ayl al-ʿAllāf; al-Kindī, Abū Yūsuf; al-Sarak̲h̲sī, Abu ʾl-
          ʿAbbās
        see also Dahriyya; Falāsifa; Lawn
      10th century   Abū Sulaymān al-Manṭiḳī; al-Fārābī; Ibn Masarra; al-Mawṣilī; al-
          Rāzī, Abū Bakr; [in Suppl.] al-ʿĀmirī
      11th century   Abū Ḥayyān al-Tawḥīdī; Bahmanyār; Ibn Ḥazm; Ibn Sīnā; Miskawayh
      12th century   Abu ʾl-Barakāt; al-Baṭalyawsī; Ibn Bād̲j̲d̲j̲a; Ibn Rus̲h̲d; Ibn Ṭufayl;
          al-Suhrawardī, S̲h̲ihāb al-Dīn Yaḥyā; ʿUmar K̲h̲ayyām
        see also al-G̲h̲azālī; Ḥayy b. Yaḳẓān; Is̲h̲rāḳiyyūn; al-S̲h̲ahrastānī, Abu ʾl-Fatḥ
      13th century   al-Abharī; Ibn Sabʿīn; al-Kātibī; Ṣadr al-Dīn al-Ḳūnawī; al-S̲h̲ahrazūrī,
          S̲h̲ams al-Dīn; al-Ṭūsī, Naṣīr al-Dīn
        see also Fak̲h̲r al-Dīn al-Rāzī
      14th century   D̲j̲amāl al-Dīn Aḳsarayī
      16th century   al-Maybudī.2

17th century al-Dāmād; al-Fārūḳī, Mullā; Lāhīdjī.2; [in Suppl.] Findiriskī
19th century Sabzawārī; [in Suppl.] Abu 'l-Ḥasan Djilwa
Jewish Ibn Gabirol; Ibn Kammūna; Isḥāḳ b. Sulaymān al-Isrā'īlī; Judaeo-Arabic.iii; Saʿadyā Ben Yōsēf
see also Abu 'l-Barakāt
terms Abad; ʿAdam; ʿAḳl; ʿAmal.1 *and* 2; Anniyya; Awwal; Basīṭ wa-Murakkab; Dhāt; Dhawḳ; Ḍidd; Djawhar; Djins; Djism; Djuz'; Farḍ.g; Ḥadd; Ḥaraka wa-Sukūn.I.1; Hay'a; Ḥayāt; Hayūlā; Ḥiss; Ḥudūth al-ʿĀlam; Ḥulūl; Huwiyya; Ibdāʿ; Idrāk; Iḥdāth; Ikhtiyār; ʿIlla.ii; ʿInāya; Inṣāf; ʿIshḳ; Ishrāḳ; al-Ḳaḍā' wa 'l-Ḳadar.A.3; Kawn wa-Fasād; Ḳidam; Ḳuwwa.4, 6 *and* 7; Maʿād; Māhiyya; Maḥsūsāt; Malaka; Maʿnā.2; Nafs; Nihāya; Nūr.2; Saʿāda; Sabab.1; Shakhṣ; Shakk.2; Shay'; Shubha; Ṭafra; Takhyīl.2; Tawallud; Ṭīna; ʿUnṣur; Waḥda.2; Wahm; Wudjūd.1; al-Ẓāhir wa 'l-Bāṭin; Zamān.1; [in Suppl.] Mashshā'iyya
see also Athar.3; ʿAyn; Dahriyya; Insān; Ḳaṭʿ; Ḳiyāma; Siyāsa.2; Takwīn; *and* → PHILOSOPHY.LOGIC.TERMS

PHYSIOGNOMY **Firāsa**; Ḳiyāfa; Shāma; [in Suppl.] Aflīmūn
and → ANATOMY; DIVINATION

PILGRIMAGE ʿArafa; al-Djamra; **Ḥadjdj**; Hady; Iḥrām; Kaʿba; Minā; Muṭawwif; al-Muzdalifa; Radjm; al-Ṣafā.1; Saʿy; Shiʿār.1; Talbiya; Tarwiya; Tashrīḳ; Ṭawāf; **ʿUmra**; al-Wuḳūf; Zamzam; **Ziyāra**
see also Amīr al-Ḥādjdj; Ḥidjāz Railway; Kārwān; Kāẓimayn; Makka; Thabīr; al-Thaʿlabiyya; [in Suppl.] ʿAtabāt; Darb Zubayda; Fayd; *and* → ISLAM; SACRED PLACES
pilgrimage literature Ziyāra.1.d *and* e

PIRACY **Ḳurṣān**
see also al-ʿAnnāba; Djarba; Ḥusayn Pasha (Küčük); Lewend; [in Suppl.] Küčük ʿAlī Oghullarï
corsairs ʿArūdj; Ḥasan Baba; Ḥusayn Pasha, Mezzomorto; Kemāl Re'īs; Khayr al-Dīn Pasha; Selmān Re'īs; Ṭorghud Re'īs; ʿUlūdj ʿAlī; Umur Pasha

PLAGUE ʿAmwās; **Wabā'**
see also Ibn Khaldūn, Walī al-Dīn; *and* → DEATH; ILLNESS
treatises on Ibn Khātima; Ibn Riḍwān; al-Masīḥī

POLAND **Leh**
see also Islām Girāy; Ḳamāniča; Köprülü; Lipḳa; Muslimūn.1.A.1; *and* → OTTOMAN EMPIRE

POLITICS Baladiyya; Dawla; Djumhūriyya; Dustūr; Ḥimāya.2; Ḥizb; Ḥukūma; Ḥurriyya.ii; Istiḳlāl; Ḳawmiyya; Madjlis; Makhzan; Mandates; Mashyakha; Medeniyyet; Musāwāt; Muwāṭin; Nā'ib.2; Shūrā.3; Siyāsa; Takhṭīṭ al-Ḥudūd; Tawāzun al-Sulutāt; Thawra; Waṭaniyya; Ẓulm.2; [in Suppl.] Āzādī; al-Djāmiʿa al-ʿArabiyya; Niẓām ʿAskarī; Taʿrīb.2
see also Ahl al-Ḥall wa 'l-ʿAḳd; Imtiyāzāt; Mashwara; Salṭana; *and* → ADMINISTRATION; DIPLOMACY; OTTOMAN EMPIRE
doctrines Ḥizb.i; Ishtirākiyya; Mārk(i)siyya; Shuyūʿiyya; Ta'mīm; [in Suppl.] Hidjra; Taʿrīb.2
see also Musāwāt; Muslimūn.4; Radjʿiyya; Tawāzun al-Sulutāt; *and* → PANARABISM; PANISLAMISM; PANTURKISM
movements Djadīd; Djangalī; Istiḳlāl; Ittiḥād we Teraḳḳī Djemʿiyyeti; Khāksār; Khilāfa; al-Rābiṭa al-Islāmiyya

see also Fiṭrat; Ḥamza Beg; Ḥizb; Ḥurriyya.ii; Kūčak K̲h̲ān D̲jangalī; Taṭarruf; T̲hawra; ʿUrābī Pas̲ha; [in Suppl.] ʿAbd al-Bārī; *and* → PANARABISM; PANISLAMISM; PANTURKISM; REFORM.POLITICO-RELIGIOUS

parties Demokrat Parti; **Ḥizb**; Ḥürriyet we Iʾtilāf Fīrḳasî; Partai Islam se Malaysia (Pas); S̲h̲uyūʿiyya.1.2; Teraḳḳī-perver D̲jumhūriyyet Fīrḳasî; Wafd
    see also And̲juman; D̲jamʿiyya; (Tunalî) Ḥilmī; Ḥizb.i; Is̲h̲tirākiyya; K̲h̲īyābānī, S̲h̲ayk̲h̲ Muḥammad; Leff; Luṭfī al-Sayyid; Mārk(i)siyya; Muṣṭafā Kāmil Pas̲ha; Sarekat Islam; [in Suppl.] ʿAbd al-Nāṣir; *and* → COMMUNISM; REFORM
reform → REFORM
terms S̲haʿb.2; Taṭarruf; T̲hawra; Zaʿīm; Ẓulm.2; [in Suppl.] K̲halʿ

PORTUGAL **Burtuḳāl**; G̲harb al-Andalus
    see also Ḥabes̲h; *and* → ANDALUSIA; SPAIN
toponyms Bād̲ja; Ḳulumriya; al-Maʿdin; Mīrtula; S̲hantamariyyat al-G̲harb; S̲hantarīn; S̲hilb; S̲hintara; Uks̲hūnuba; (al-)Us̲hbūna; Yābura; [in Suppl.] Ḳaṣr Abī Dānis

PRAYER Ad̲hān; D̲hikr; D̲jumʿa; **Duʿāʾ**; Fātiḥa; Iḳāma; K̲haṭīb; K̲huṭba; Ḳibla; Ḳunūt; Ḳuʿūd; Maḥyā; Masd̲jid; Miḥrāb; Mīḳāt; Muṣallā; Rakʿa; Rātib; **Ṣalāt**; Ṣalāt al-K̲hawf; Subḥa; Sutra; Tahad̲jd̲jud; Tarāwīḥ; Waẓīfa.2; Wird; Witr
    see also Amīn; Dikka; G̲hāʾib; Gulbāng; Istiʾnāf; Maḳām Ibrāhīm; al-Mas̲ḥ ʿalā ʾl-K̲huffayn; Namāzgāh; Takbīr; Tas̲hahhud; *and* → ABLUTION; ARCHITECTURE.MOSQUES; ISLAM
bowing Sad̲jda
carpet Sad̲jd̲jāda
collections of
  shiite Zayn al-ʿĀbidīn
of petition Istisḳāʾ; Munās̲hada

PRE-ISLAM al-ʿArab.i; (D̲jazīrat) al-ʿArab.vii; Armīniya.II.1; Badw.III; D̲jāhiliyya; G̲hassān; Kinda.1 *and* Appendix; Lak̲hmids; Liḥyān; Maʿin; Makka.1; Nabaṭ; Rūm
    see also Ḥayawān.2; Ilāh; al-Kalbī.II; Lībiyā.2; *and* → ASSYRIA; BYZANTINE EMPIRE; IDOLATRY; MILITARY.BATTLES; ZOROASTRIANS
customs/institutions ʿAtīra; Baliyya; G̲hid̲hāʾ.i *and* ii; Ḥad̲jd̲j.i; Ḥilf; Ḥimā; Ḥimāya; Istisḳāʾ; Kāhin; K̲hafāra; Mawlā; Nuṣub; Radāʿ.2; Sādin; Ṭawāf; ʿUkāẓ; ʿUmra; ʿUrs; Waʾd al-Banāt; [in Suppl.] al-Was̲hm.1
    see also Fayʾ; G̲hanīma; Īlāf; Karkūr; Nār; Ṣadā; S̲hayba; Taḥannuth; T̲habīr
gods Dhu ʾl-K̲halaṣa; D̲hu ʾl-S̲harā; Hubal; Isāf wa-Nāʾila; Ḳaws Ḳuzaḥ; al-Lāt; Manāf; Manāt; Nasr; S̲hams.1; S̲hayʿ al-Ḳawm; Suʿayr; al-Sud̲jd̲ja; Suwāʿ; Ṭāg̲hūt.1; Tañrî; al-Uḳayṣir; al-ʿUzzā; [in Suppl.] Wadd; Yag̲hūth; Yaʿūk
    see also Ag̲hāt̲hūd̲hīmūn; ʿAmr b. Luḥayy; D̲jāhiliyya; Hirmis; Hurmuz; Ilāh; Kaʿba.V; al-Ḳamar.II; Mawḳif.3; Rabb; Ṣanam; S̲hayṭān; Zūn
in Arabian peninsula Abraha; (D̲jazīrat) al-ʿArab.i *and* vi; Bakr b. Wāʾil; D̲jadhīma al-Abras̲h; G̲humdān; Ḥabas̲hat; Ḥād̲jib b. Zurāra; Ḥaḍramawt; Hās̲him b. ʿAbd Manāf; Hind bint al-K̲huss; Ḥums; Ḳatabān; Ḳayl; Ḳusayy; Ḳuss b. Sāʿida; Mārib; Nuṣub; Sabaʾ; Sad̲jʿ.1; Salhīn; Taʾrīk̲h.I.1.iv; T̲hād̲j; Tubbaʿ; ʿUkāẓ Yahūd.1; [in Suppl.] Ḥaḍramawt.i
    see also Badw.III; Dār al-Nadwa; Ḥanīf.4; Kinda.Appendix; T̲habīr; Zabūr; *and* → IDOLATRY; LITERATURE.POETRY.ARABIC; MILITARY.BATTLES; OMAN.TOPONYMS; SAUDIA ARABIA.TOPONYMS; TRIBES.ARABIAN PENINSULA; UNITED ARAB EMIRATES.TOPONYMS; YEMEN.TOPONYMS
in Egypt → EGYPT.BEFORE ISLAM
in Fertile Crescent K̲hursābād; Manbid̲j; Maysān; Nabaṭ; al-Zabbāʾ; [in Suppl.] At̲hūr
    see also Biṭrīḳ.I; Ḥarrān; S̲hahārid̲ja; S̲hahrazūr; Tadmur; [in Suppl.] Iyās b. Ḳabīṣa;

and → MILITARY.BATTLES
Ghassānids Djabala b. al-Ayham; Djillik; **Ghassān**; al-Ḥārith b. Djabala; [in Suppl.] Djabala b. al-Ḥārith
Lakhmids ʿAmr b. ʿAdī; ʿAmr b. Hind; al-Ḥīra; **Lakhmids**; al-Mundhir IV; al-Nuʿmān (III) b. al-Mundhir
in Iran → IRAN.BEFORE ISLAM
in Southeast Asia [in Suppl.] Mataram.1
in Turkey Tañri; Turks.I.1

PREDESTINATION Adjal; Allāh.II.B; Iḍṭirār; Ikhtiyār; Istiṭāʿa; **al-Ḳaḍāʾ wa ʾl-Ḳadar**; Ḳadariyya; Kasb; Ḳisma
see also ʿAbd al-Razzāḳ al-Ḳāshānī; Badāʾ; Dahr; Duʿāʾ.II.b; Ḳaḍāʾ; Shaḳāwa
advocates of Djabriyya; Djahmiyya; al-Karābīsī.2; Sulaymān b. Djarīr al-Raḳḳī; Zayd b. ʿAlī b. al-Ḥusayn
opponents of Ghaylān b. Muslim; **Ḳadariyya**; Ḳatāda b. Diʿāma; Maʿbad al-Djuhanī

PRESS **Djarīda**; Maḳāla; **Maṭbaʿa** (*and* [in Suppl.]); **Ṣiḥāfa**
Arabic ʿArabiyya.B.V.a; Baghdād (906b); Būlāḳ; **Djarīda**.i; Ḳiṣṣa.2; Maḳāla.1; al-Manār; **Maṭbaʿa**.1; al-Rāʾid al-Tūnusī; **Ṣiḥāfa**
see also Nahḍa; Zākhir
journalism Abū Naḍḍāra; al-Bārūnī; Djabrān Khalīl Djabrān; Djamāl al-Dīn al-Afghānī; Djamīl; Fāris al-Shidyāḳ; Ibn Bādīs; Isḥāḳ, Adīb; al-Kawākibī; al-Khaḍir; Khalīl Ghānim; Khalīl Muṭrān; Kurd ʿAlī; Luṭfī al-Sayyid; al-Maʿlūf; Mandūr; al-Manūfī.7; al-Māzinī; Muṣṭafā ʿAbd al-Rāziḳ; al-Muwayliḥī; al-Nadīm, ʿAbd Allāh; Nadjīb al-Ḥaddād; Nimr; Rashīd Riḍā; Ṣafar; Saʿīd Abū Bakr; Salāma Mūsā; Salīm al-Naḳḳāsh; Ṣarrūf; Shāʾūl; Shaykhū, Luwīs; Shīnā; Shumayyil, Shiblī; Ṭāhā Ḥusayn; Yaḥyā Ḥaḳḳī; al-Yāzidjī.2 *and* 3; Yūsuf, ʿAlī; al-Zahrāwī, ʿAbd al-Ḥamīd; Zaydān, Djurdjī; [in Suppl.] Abū Shādī; al-Bustānī; Muḥibb al-Dīn al-Khaṭīb
see also al-Mahdjar
Indian **Maṭbaʿa**.4; [in Suppl.] **Djarīda**.vii
journalism Muḥammad ʿAlī; Ruswā; Shabbīr Ḥasan Khān Djosh; [in Suppl.] Āzād; Ḥasrat Mohānī
see also Nadwat al-ʿUlamāʾ
Persian **Djarīda**.ii; Maḳāla; **Maṭbaʿa**.3; [in Suppl.] **Ṣiḥāfa**.4
journalism Furūghī.3; Lāhūtī; Malkom Khān; Rashīd Yāsimī; Yaghmāʾī; Yazdī; [in Suppl.] Amīrī
Turkish **Djarīda**.iii; Djemʿiyyet-i ʿIlmiyye-i ʿOthmāniyye; Ibrāhīm Müteferriḳa; Maḳāla; **Maṭbaʿa**.2; Meshʿale; Mīzān; [in Suppl.] **Ṣiḥāfa**.5
see also Ādharī.ii
journalism Aḥmad Iḥsān; Aḥmad Midḥat; Djewdet; Ebüzziya Tevfik; Gasprali (Gasprinski), Ismāʿīl; Ḥasan Fehmī; (Aḥmed) Ḥilmī; Hisar; Ḥusayn Djāhid; Ileri, Djelāl Nūrī; İnal; Ḳaṣāb, Teodor; al-Kāẓimī, Meḥmed Sālim; Kemāl; Kemāl, Meḥmed Nāmiḳ; Khālid Ḍiyāʾ; Köprülü (Meḥmed Fuad); Manāṣtirli Meḥmed Rifʿat; Meḥmed ʿĀkif; Mīzāndji Meḥmed Murād; Örik, Nahīd Ṣirrī; Orkhan Seyfī; Ortač, Yūsuf Ḍiyā; Riḍā Nūr; Sāhir, Djelāl; Sāmī; Shināsī; Suʿāwī, ʿAlī; Tewfīḳ Fikret; Yūsuf Aḳčura; Żiyā Pasha; [in Suppl.] Aghaoghlu; Atay; Čaylaḳ Tewfīḳ; Eshref; Ṭāhir Beg
see also Badrkhānī; Fedjr-i Ātī; Khalīl Ghānim; Saʿīd Efendi

PROFESSIONS al-ʿAṭṭār; Baḳḳāl; Bayṭār; Dallāl; Djānbāz; Djarrāḥ; Ḥammāl; Kannās; Kātib; Ḳayn; Ḳayna; Khayyāṭ; Mukārī; Munādī; Munadjdjim; al-Nassādj; Ṣabbāgh; Ṣāʾigh; Saḳḳāʾ; Sāsān; Shaʿbadha; Shāʿir; Shammāʿ; Ṭabbākh; Ṭabbāl; Tādjir; Ṭaḥḥān; Tardjumān; Ṭarrār;

Thallādj; Ṭulumbadjī̆; ʿUlamāʾ; Warrāḳ; [in Suppl.] Dabbāg̲h̲; Djammāl; Djazzār; Faṣṣād; G̲h̲assāl; Ḥāʾik; Ḥallāḳ; Iskāf; Ṣarrāf
    see also Asad Allāh Iṣfahānī; Aywaz.1; K̲h̲ādim; S̲h̲āwiya; Ṣinf; Ustād̲h̲; and → LAW.OFFICES; MILITARY.OFFICES
craftsmanship   Ṣināʿa
craftsmen and tradesmen
    artisans   Ṣabbāg̲h̲; Ṣāʾig̲h̲; Warrāḳ; [in Suppl.] Ḥāʾik; Iskāf
    labourers   Ḥammāl; Kannās; Ḳayn; K̲h̲ayyāṭ; S̲h̲ammāʿ; Ṭaḥḥān; [in Suppl.] Dabbāg̲h̲; Djazzār; G̲h̲assāl; Ḥallāḳ
    merchants   al-ʿAṭṭār; Baḳḳāl; Mukārī; **Tādjir**; Tammām; Thallādj; [in Suppl.] Djammāl
        see also Tidjāra; and → FINANCE.COMMERCE.FUNCTIONS
    performers   Djānbāz; Ḳayna; S̲h̲āʿir.1.E; Ṭabbāl
        see also al-Sīm

PROPERTY   **Māl**; Milk; Taʿāwun; Waḳf; Zamīndār; [in Suppl.] ʿAḳār
    see also Munāṣafa; S̲h̲ufʿa; Soyūrg̲h̲āl; Tiyūl; and → TAXATION.TAXES and TITHE-LANDS

PROPHETHOOD   **Nubuwwa**; Rasūl; Waḥy
    and → MUḤAMMAD, THE PROPHET
prophets   Ādam; Alīsaʿ; Ayyūb; Hārūn b. ʿImrān; Ḥizḳīl; Hūd; Ibrāhīm; Idrīs; Ilyās; Irmiyā; ʿĪsā; Isḥāḳ; Ismāʿīl; Lūṭ; Muḥammad; Mūsā; Nūḥ; Ṣāliḥ; S̲h̲amwīl; S̲h̲aʿyā; S̲h̲īth; S̲h̲uʿayb; Yaḥyā b. Zakariyyāʾ; Yaʿḳūb; Yūnus; Yūs̲h̲aʿ b. Nūn; Yūsuf; Zakariyyāʾ
    see also Fatra; Ḥanẓala b. Ṣafwān; ʿIṣma; K̲h̲ālid b. Sinān; Luḳmān; Mubtadaʾ.2; Zayd b. ʿAmr; and → MUḤAMMAD, THE PROPHET
false prophets   Ḥā-Mīm; Musaylima; Sadjāḥ; Ṭulayḥa
lives of   al-Kisāʾī; **Ḳiṣaṣ al-Anbiyāʾ**; al-T̲h̲aʿlabī, Aḥmad b. Muḥammad; ʿUmāra b. Wathīma; Wahb b. Munabbih; Wat̲h̲īma b. Mūsā

PROVERBS   **Mathal**; Tamt̲h̲īl.2
    see also Iyās b. Muʿāwiya; Nār; and → ANIMALS.AND PROVERBS; LITERATURE.PROVERBS IN
collections of   Abū ʿUbayd al-Ḳāsim b. Sallām; al-ʿAskarī.ii; Ḥamza al-Iṣfahānī; al-Maydānī; Ras̲h̲īd al-Dīn (Waṭwāṭ); S̲h̲ināsī; al-T̲h̲aʿālibī, Abū Manṣūr ʿAbd al-Malik; al-Yūsī; al-Zamak̲h̲s̲h̲arī; [in Suppl.] al-Mufaḍḍal b. Salama

PUNISHMENT   **ʿAd̲h̲āb**; **ʿUḳūba**
in law   Diya; Djazāʾ.ii; Ḥadd; Ḳatl.ii; Ḳiṣāṣ; Ṣalb; Taʿzīr; **ʿUḳūba**
    see also ʿAbd.3.i; Kaffāra; Siyāsa.1; and → LAW.PENAL LAW
in theology   ʿAd̲h̲āb; ʿAd̲h̲āb al-Ḳabr; Djazāʾ; Munkar wa-Nakīr
    see also Ḳiyāma; Mas̲h̲
physical   Falaḳa; Ṣalb
    see also Radjm

Q

QATAR   Ḳaṭar; Madjlis.4.A.xi; Maḥkama.4.ix; Ṣiḥāfa.1.(xi)
toponyms   al-Dawḥa; Hādjir; al-Zubāra
    see also al-ʿUdayd

QURʾAN   Allāh.i; Āya; Fāṣila; Iʿdjāz; Ḳirāʾa; **al-Ḳurʾān**; Muḳaṭṭaʿāt; Muṣḥaf; Nask̲h̲; Sūra; Tafsīr; Umm al-Kitāb; [in Suppl.] Naẓm.2
    see also ʿArabiyya.A.ii; Basmala; Faḍīla; Hamza; Indjīl; Iṣlāḥ.i.B.1; K̲h̲alḳ.II; K̲h̲awāṣṣ al-

Ḳur'ān; ʿUmūm wa-Khuṣūṣ; Zayd b. Thābit
commentaries Mukhtaṣar; Sharḥ.III; **Tafsīr**; Ta'wīl
see also al-Ẓāhir wa 'l-Bāṭin
in Arabic ʿAbd al-Razzāḳ al-Ḳāshānī; Abu 'l-Faḍl ʿAllāmī; Abū Ḥayyān al-Gharnāṭī; Abu 'l-Layth al-Samarḳandī; Abu 'l-Suʿūd; Abū ʿUbayda; al-ʿAskarī.ii; al-Baghawī; Baḳī b. Makhlad; al-Bayḍāwī; al-Bulḳīnī.4; al-Dāmād; al-Dārimī; Djīwan; Fakhr al-Dīn al-Rāzī; Fayḍī; Ghulām Ḥusayn Khān Ṭabāṭabā'ī; Gīsū Darāz; Gūrānī; Ibn Abi 'l-Ridjāl; Ibn ʿAdjība; Ibn Barradjān; Ibn Kathīr, ʿImād al-Dīn; Ismāʿīl Ḥaḳḳi; al-Kalbī.I; Kalīm Allāh al-Djahānābādī; Kemāl Pasha-zāde; al-Ḳurṭubī, Abū ʿAbd Allāh; al-Ḳushayrī.1; al-Maḥallī; al-Māturīdī; Mudjāhid b. Djabr al-Makkī; Mudjīr al-Dīn al-ʿUlaymī; Muḥsin-i Fayḍ-i Kāshānī; Muḳātil b. Sulaymān; al-Nīsābūrī; al-Rāghib al-Iṣfahānī; al-Rummānī; Sahl al-Tustarī; al-Shaḥḥām; al-Shahrastānī, Abu 'l-Fatḥ; al-Sharīf al-Raḍī; al-Suhrawardī, Shihāb al-Dīn Abū Ḥafṣ; al-Sulamī, Abū ʿAbd al-Raḥmān; al-Suyūṭī; al-Ṭabarī, Abū Djaʿfar; al-Ṭabrisī, Amīn al-Dīn; al-Thaʿālibī, ʿAbd al-Raḥmān; al-Thaʿlabī, Aḥmad b. Muḥammad; al-Wāḥidī; al-Yadālī; [in Suppl.] ʿAbd al-Wahhāb Bukhārī; Abu 'l-Fatḥ al-Daylamī; al-Aṣamm; al-Zamakhsharī.2; al-Zarkashī
see also ʿAbd Allāh b. al-ʿAbbās; Abū Nuʿaym al-Mulā'ī; Aḥmadiyya; al-ʿAlamī; al-Dihlawī, Shāh Walī Allāh; Djafr; Djilwatiyya; Ḥādjdjī Pasha; Hind.v.e; Ibn Masʿūd; Ḳuṭb al-Dīn Shīrāzī; al-Manār; al-Suddī; Sufyān b. ʿUyayna; al-Sulamī, ʿIzz al-Dīn; Thānesarī.3; al-Ṭūfī; Warḳā' b. ʿUmar; [in Suppl.] Saʿīd b. Djubayr
late 19th and 20th centuries al-Ālūsī.2; Aṭfiyāsh; Mawdūdī; Muḥammad b. Aḥmad al-Iskandarānī; Muḥammad Abū Zayd; Muḥammad Farīd Wadjdī; Sayyid Ḳuṭb; Shaltūt, Maḥmūd; [in Suppl.] Djawharī, Ṭanṭāwī
in Persian Abu 'l-Futūḥ al-Rāzī; al-Dawlatābādī; Djāmī; Kāshifī; al-Maybudī.1; Muṣannifak; al-Taftāzānī
in Turkish Aḳ Ḥiṣārī.b
in Urdu Ashraf ʿAlī
createdness of Miḥna
see also Djahmiyya; al-Zuhrī, Hārūn
readers ʿAbd Allāh b. Abī Isḥāḳ; Abū ʿAmr b. al-ʿAlā'; al-Aʿmash; ʿĀṣim; al-Dānī; Ḥamza b. Ḥabīb; Ibn ʿĀmir; Ibn Kathīr; ʿĪsā b. ʿUmar; al-Kisā'ī; Nāfiʿ al-Laythī; al-Sadjāwandī, Abū ʿAbd Allāh
see also Abu 'l-ʿĀliya al-Riyāḥī; al-Dāraḳuṭnī; Ḥafṣ b. Sulaymān; Ibn al-Djazarī; Ibn al-Faḥḥām; Ibn Mudjāhid; Ibn Shanabūdh; al-Ḳasṭallānī; Makkī; al-Malaṭī; Mudjāhid b. Djabr al-Makkī; [in Suppl.] Ibn Miḳsam
transmitters al-Yazīdī.1
reading Adā'; Ḥarf; Ḳaṭʿ; Khatma; **Ḳirā'a**; **Tadjwīd**
see also al-Shāṭibī, Abu 'l-Ḳāsim; al-Sidjistānī; Taʿawwudh; Tahadjdjud; Waṣl; Yaḥyā b. Ādam; [in Suppl.] Lafẓ.2
recitation competition [in Suppl.] Musābaḳa
recensions ʿAbd Allāh b. al-Zubayr; ʿAbd al-Malik b. Marwān; Abu 'l-Dardā'; ʿĀ'isha bint Abī Bakr; al-Ashʿarī, Abū Mūsā; ʿĀṣim; al-Dimyāṭī; al-Ḥadjdjādj b. Yūsuf; Ibn Masʿūd; Nāfiʿ al-Laythī; Ubayy b. Kaʿb
see also Abu 'l-Aswad al-Du'alī; ʿArabiyya.ii.1 *and* 2; al-Ḥuṣrī.II; Warsh; Zayd b. Thābit
stories ʿĀd; Ādam; Aṣḥāb al-Kahf; Ayyūb; Bilḳīs; Dāwūd; Djālūt; Firʿawn; Ḥābīl wa Ḳābīl; Ḥawwā'; Ibrāhīm; ʿĪsā; al-Iskandar; al-Khaḍir; Lūṭ; Maryam; Mūsā; Nūḥ; Sulaymān b. Dāwūd; Yūnus; Yūsuf; Zakariyyā'
see also Ḳiṣaṣ al-Anbiyā'; Shayṭān.2; al-Thaʿlabī, Aḥmad b. Muḥammad; Yāfith; *and* → BIBLE.BIBLICAL PERSONAGES
suras al-Aḥḳāf; Aṣḥāb al-Kahf; Fātiḥa; al-Fīl; Ghāshiya; Kawthar; Luḳmān; al-Muʿaw-

widhatān[i]; al-Muddaththir and al-Muzzammil; al-Musabbiḥāt; Sadjda; al-Ṣāffāt; Ṭā-Hā
see also Ḥayawān.3; **Sūra**

terms Adjr.1; Aḥkām; ʿĀlam; Amr; al-Aʿrāf; ʿAṣā; Aṣḥāb al-Kahf; Aṣḥāb al-Rass; Aṣḥāb al-Ukhdūd; Āya; Baḥīra; al-Baḥrayn; Baʿl; Barāʾa; Baraka; Barzakh; Birr; Dābba; Daʿwa; Dharra; Dīn; Djahannam; Djāhiliyya; Djanna; Djinn; Dunyā; Faḳīr; Farāʾiḍ; Fitna; Fiṭra; Furḳān; al-Ghayb; Ḥadd; Ḥaḳḳ; Ḥanīf; Hātif; Ḥawārī; Ḥayāt; Ḥidjāb; Ḥisāb; Ḥizb; Ḥudjdja; Ḥūr; Iblīs; Īlāf; Ilhām; ʿIlliyyūn; Kaffāra; Kāfir; Kalima; Ḳarīn; Ḳarya; Ḳawm; Ḳayyim; Khalḳ; Khaṭīʾa; Ḳiyāma; Kursī; Ḳuwwa.2; Lawḥ; Madjnūn; Maḳām Ibrāhīm; Milla; Millet; Miskīn; Mīthāḳ; al-Munāfiḳūn.1; Nadhīr; Nafs.I; Nār; Raḥma; Rizḳ; Rudjūʿ; Rukn; Ṣabr; Ṣadr; al-Ṣāffāt; Ṣaḥīfa; Sakīna; Salām; al-Ṣāliḥūn; Shaḳāwa; Shakk.1; Shirk; al-Ṣiddīḳ; Sidjdjīl; Sidjdjīn; Sidrat al-Muntahā; Sirādj; Ṣirāṭ; Subḥān; Sulṭān; Takhyīl.3; Umm al-Kitāb; Umm al-Ḳurā; Umma.1; Ummī.1; Waḥy; Yatīm.1; al-Zabāniyya; Zabūr; Ẓulm; [in Suppl.] Asāṭīr al-Awwalīn; Lafẓ.2; Malaʾ.1
see also Ḥikāya.I; Sabab.1; Samāʾ.1

translations Ḳurʾān.9
see also Aljamía
into English Aḥmadiyya; Pickthall
into Malay ʿAbd al-Raʾūf al-Sinkilī
into Persian al-Dihlawī, Shāh Walī Allāh
see also Khaṭṭ.ii
into Swahili Kenya (891a)
into Urdu ʿAbd al-Ḳādir Dihlawī; Djawān; Rafīʿ al-Dīn

R

RAIDS Baranta; Ghanīma; **Ghazw**
and → BEDOUINS; MILITARY.EXPEDITIONS

REBELLION **Fitna**; **Thawra**; [in Suppl.] Mārid

RECREATION Cinema; Ḳaragöz; Khayāl al-Ẓill; Masraḥ; Orta Oyunu
games Djerīd; Kharbga; Ḳimār; **Laʿib**; al-Maysir; Mukhāradja; Nard; Shaṭrandj
see also Ishāra; Kurds.iv.C.5; Maydān; *and* → ANIMALS.SPORT
sports Čawgān; Pahlawān; Zūrkhāna

REFORM Djamʿiyya; **Iṣlāḥ**
see also Baladiyya; Ḥukūma; al-Manār; *and* → WOMEN.EMANCIPATION
educational Aḥmad Djewdet Pasha; Aḥmad Khān; al-Azhar.IV; Ḥabīb Allāh Khān; Maʿārif; Münīf Pasha; Nadwat al-ʿUlamāʾ; Yücel, Ḥasan ʿAlī; [in Suppl.] al-ʿAdawī; Muḥammad ʿAbd Allāh; Sāṭiʿ al-Ḥuṣrī
see also al-Marṣafī
financial Muḥaṣṣil
land Taʿāwun
legal Medjelle; Mīrāth.2; Nikāḥ.II; Ṭalāḳ.II; Talfīḳ; Tashrīʿ; Waḳf.II.5
see also Djazāʾ.ii; Imtiyāzāt.iv; Maḥkama; [in Suppl.] Maḳāṣid al-Sharīʿa
reformers Abu 'l-Suʿūd; Aḥmad Djewdet Pasha; Küčük Saʿīd Pasha; al-Sanhūrī, ʿAbd al-Razzāḳ
see also Ileri, Djelāl Nūrī; Khayr al-Dīn Pasha
military Niẓām-i Djedīd

numismatic → NUMISMATICS
Ottoman Tanẓīmāt
politico-religious Atatürk; Djamāl al-Dīn al-Afghānī; Ileri, Djelāl Nūrī; Ibn Bādīs; (al-)Ibrāhīmī; Ismāʿīl Ṣidķī; Ķāsim Amīn; Khayr al-Dīn Pasha; Midḥat Pasha; Muḥammad ʿAbduh; Muḥammad Bayram al-Khāmis; Nurculuk; Padri; Rashīd Riḍā; Shaltūt, Maḥmūd; al-Subkiyyūn; Ṭāhā, Maḥmūd Muḥammad; Taķī al-Dīn al-Nabhānī; [in Suppl.] ʿAbd al-Nāṣir
see also Baladiyya; Bast; Djamʿiyya; Dustūr; Ḥarbiye; Ibrāhīm Müteferriķa; al-Ikhwān al-Muslimūn; Iṣlāḥ; Mappila.5.ii; Salafiyya; Shaʿb; al-Shawkānī; Tadjdīd; Taķrīb; [in Suppl.] Abu 'l-ʿAzāʾim; *and* → POLITICS
militant al-Bannāʾ; Fidāʾiyyān-i Islām; Ḥamāliyya; Ibn Bādīs; al-Ikhwān al-Muslimūn; Mawdūdī; Sayyid Ķuṭb; al-Takfīr wa 'l-Hidjra; Taṭarruf; **Uṣūliyya**.2; ʿUthmān b. Fūdī
see also Ibn al-Muwaķķit; Mudjāhid; [in Suppl.] al-Djanbīhī

RELIGION ʿAķīda; **Dīn**; al-Milal wa'l-Niḥal; Milla; Millet.1
see also Ḥanīf; Tawḥīd; Umma; *and* → BAHAIS; BUDDHISM; CHRISTIANITY; DRUZES; ISLAM; JUDAISM; ZOROASTRIANS
dualism Dayṣāniyya; Mānī; Mazdak; **Thanawiyya**; Zindīķ
see also Īrān.vi; Kumūn; al-Nazzām
pantheism ʿAmr b. Luḥayy; Djāhiliyya; Hindū; Kaʿba.V
see also Ḥarīriyya; Ḥadjdj.i; Ibn al-ʿArabī; Ibn al-ʿArīf; Kāfiristān; Kamāl Khudjandī; *and* → IDOLATRY; PRE-ISLAM.GODS
popular → ISLAM.POPULAR BELIEFS
religious communities Bābīs; Bahāʾīs; Djayn; Durūz; Hindū; Islām; Madjūs; Naṣārā; Ṣābiʾ; Ṣābiʾa; al-Sāmira; Sikhs; Sumaniyya; Yahūd; Yazīdī; Zindīķ
see also al-Barāmika.1; Ibāḥatiya; Kitāb al-Djilwa; al-Milal wa'l-Niḥal; Millet; Nānak; al-Shahrastānī, Abu 'l-Fatḥ; *and* → BAHAIS; BUDDHISM; CHRISTIANITY; DRUZES; INDIA.RELIGION; ISLAM; JUDAISM; SECTS; ZOROASTRIANS

RHETORIC Badīʿ; **Balāgha**; **Bayān**; Faṣāḥa; Ḥaķīķa.1; Ibtidāʾ; Idjāza; Iķtibās; Intihāʾ; Istiʿāra; Kināya; al-Maʿānī wa 'l-Bayān; Madjāz; Mubālagha; Muķābala.3; Muwāraba; Muzāwadja; Muzdawidj; Ramz.1; Taʿadjdjub; Tadjnīs; Taḍmīn; Takhyīl.4; Tamthīl.2; Tarṣīʿ; Tashbīh; Tawriya; Ṭibāķ
see also Ishāra
treatises on al-ʿAskarī.ii; Ḥāzim; Ibn al-Muʿtazz; al-Ķazwīnī (Khaṭīb Dimashķ); al-Rādūyānī; Rashīd al-Dīn Waṭwāṭ; al-Sakkākī; al-Sidjilmāsī; Yaḥyā b. Ḥamza al-ʿAlawī; [in Suppl.] al-Djurdjānī; Ibn Wahb; al-Zandjānī

RHYME **Ķāfiya**; Luzūm mā lā yalzam
and → LITERATURE.POETRY; METRICS

RITUALS ʿAķīķa; ʿAnṣāra; ʿĀshūrāʾ; Khitān; Rawḍa-khʷānī; [in Suppl.] Ramy al-Djimār
see also Bakkāʾ; Ḥammām; al-Maghrib.VI; Zār; [in Suppl.] Dam; *and* → CUSTOMS; ISLAM.FIVE PILLARS OF ISLAM *and* POPULAR BELIEFS

RIVERS **Nahr**
see also Maʾṣir; *and* → NAVIGATION
waters al-ʿAḍaym; ʿAfrīn; Alindjaķ; al-ʿAlķamī; Amū Daryā; al-ʿĀṣī; Atbara; Atrek; Baḥr al-Ghazāl.1; Baradā; Čaghān-rūd; Congo; Čoruh; Ču; Darʿa; Dawʿan; Dehās; Didjla; Diyālā; Djamnā; Djayḥān; al-Furāt; Gangā; Gediz Čayi̊; Göksu; al-Ḥamma; Harī Rūd;

Ibruh; Ili; Isly; Itil; Kābul.1; Karkha; Kārūn; Khābūr; Khalkha; al-Khāzir; Ḳïzïl-irmāḳ; Ḳïzïl-üzen; Ḳuban; Ḳunduz; Kur; Kurram; Lamas-ṣū; Mānd; Menderes; Merič; Mihrān; al-Mudawwar; Nahr Abī Fuṭrus; Niger; al-Nīl; Ob; Orkhon; Özi; al-Rass; Safīd Rūd; Sakarya; Sandja; Sayḥān; Shaṭṭ al-ʿArab; Shebelle; Sïr Daryā; Tādjuh; Ṭarāz; Tarim; Terek; Ṭuna; Turgay; al-Urdunn.1; (al-)Wādī al-Kabīr; Wādī Yāna; Wakhsh; Wardar; Yarmūk.1; Yayïḳ; Yeshil İrmak; al-Zāb; Zarafshān; Zāyanda-Rūd; Zhōb; [in Suppl.] Gūmāl; Irtish

see also Hind.i.j; ʿĪsā, Nahr; Urmiya.2; Zabadānī; *and* → *the section Physical Geography under individual countries*

ROMANIA Boghdān; Dobrudja; Eflāḳ; Erdel; Isakča

see also Budjāḳ; Muslimūn.1.B.2; [in Suppl.] Ḳantimīr, Demetrius

toponyms

districts Deli-Orman

islands Ada Ḳalʿe

towns Babadaghï; Bender; Bükresh; Ibrail; Köstendje; Medjidiyye; Nagyvárad; Temeshwār; [in Suppl.] Yash

RUSSIA → EUROPE.EASTERN EUROPE

S

SACRED PLACES Abū Ḳubays; al-Ḥaram al-Sharīf; Ḥudjra; Kaʿba; Karbalāʾ; Kāẓimayn; al-Khalīl; al-Ḳuds.II; al-Madīna; Makka; al-Muḳaṭṭam; al-Nadjaf; Ṭūbā; Zamzam; [in Suppl.] Ḳadamgāh

see also Ḥawṭa; Ḥimā; Ḳāsiyūn; Mawlāy Idrīs; Mudjāwir; Shāh ʿAbd al-ʿAẓīm al-Ḥasanī; Shayba; Walī; *and* → ARCHITECTURE.MONUMENTS; SAINTHOOD

for Hindus, see Allāhābād; Buxar; Djūnāgaṛh; Dwārkā; Ganga; Ḥasan Abdāl; Sūrat; Udjdjayn

pilgrimage to **Ziyāra**

SACRIFICES ʿAḳīḳa; ʿAtīra; Baliyya; Dhabīḥa; Fidya; Hady; Ḳurbān; Shiʿār.2 *and* 3

see also Ibil; ʿĪd al-Aḍḥā; Kaffāra; Nadhr; [in Suppl.] Dam

SAINTHOOD Mawlid

see also ʿAbābda; Mawlā.I; Ziyāra; *and* → CHRISTIANITY; HAGIOGRAPHY; MYSTICISM

saints **Walī**

see also Karāma; Ziyāra; *and* → SACRED PLACES

African Shaykh Ḥusayn

see also Ziyāra.9

Arabic Aḥmad b. ʿĪsā; Aḥmad al-Badawī; Nafīsa

see also Ḳunā; Ziyāra.1 *and* 2; *and* → MYSTICISM.MYSTICS

North African Abū Muḥammad Ṣāliḥ; Abū Yaʿazzā; ʿĀʾisha al-Mannūbiyya; al-Bādisī.1; al-Daḳḳāḳ; al-Djazūlī, Abū ʿAbd Allāh; Ḥmād u-Mūsā; Ibn ʿArūs; al-Ḳabbāb; Ḳaddūr al-ʿAlamī; al-Khaṣāṣī; Muḥriz b. Khalaf; al-Sabtī; al-Shāwī; [in Suppl.] Ḥamādisha

see also al-Maghrib.VI; Sabʿatu Ridjāl; Walī.2; Ziyāra.4; *and* → MYSTICISM.MYSTICS

Central Asian Aḥmad Yasawī; Uways al-Ḳaranī; Zangī Āta

see also Walī.5; Ziyāra.6; *and* → MYSTICISM.MYSTICS

Indian Abū ʿAlī Ḳalandar; Ashraf Djahāngīr; Badīʿ al-Dīn; Badr; Bahāʾ al-Dīn Zakariyyā;

Čishtī; Farīd al-Dīn Masʿūd "Gandj-i Shakar"; Ghāzī Miyān; Gīsū Darāz; Imām Shāh; Khwādja Khiḍr; Maghribī; Makhdūm al-Mulk Manīrī; Masʿūd; Niẓām al-Dīn Awliyāʾ; Nūr Ḳuṭb al-ʿĀlam; Ratan; Shāh Muḥammad b. ʿAbd Aḥmad; [in Suppl.] Bābā Nūr al-Dīn Rishī; Gadāʾī Kambō; Gangōhī; Ḥamīd al-Dīn Ḳāḍī Nāgawrī; Ḥamīd al-Dīn Ṣūfī Nāgawrī Siwālī; Kanbō

see also Ḥasan Abdāl; Pāk Pāṭan; Walī.6; Ziyāra.7; *and* → MYSTICISM.MYSTICS

Indonesian Ziyāra.8

and → MYSTICISM.MYSTICS

Persian ʿAlī al-Hamadānī; Bābā-Ṭāhir

see also Ziyāra.5; *and* → MYSTICISM.MYSTICS

Southeast Asian and Chinese Walī.7 *and* 8

Turkish Akhī Ewrān; Emīr Sulṭān; Ḥādjdjī Bayrām Walī; Ḥakīm Ata; Ḳoyun Baba; Merkez; Ṣarı̊ Ṣalṭūḳ Dede

see also Walī.4; Ziyāra.6; *and* → MYSTICISM.MYSTICS

terms Abdāl; Ilhām

SAUDI ARABIA (Djazīrat) al-ʿArab; Djarīda.i.A; Djāmiʿa; Dustūr.vii; al-Hidjar; al-Ikhwān; Madjlis.4.A.viii; Maḥkama.4.vii; Ṣiḥāfa.1.(viii); **al-Suʿūdiyya, al-Mamlaka al-ʿArabiyya**; Wahhābiyya

see also Bā ʿAlawī; Badw; Baladiyya.2; Barakāt; Makka; [in Suppl.] Demography.III; *and* → PRE-ISLAM.IN ARABIAN PENINSULA; TRIBES.ARABIAN PENINSULA

before Islam → PRE-ISLAM.IN ARABIAN PENINSULA

dynasties Hāshimids (2x); Rashīd, Āl; Suʿūd, Āl

and → DYNASTIES.ARABIAN PENINSULA

historians of al-Azraḳī; Daḥlān; al-Fāḳihī; al-Fāsī; Ibn Fahd; Ibn Manda; Ibn al-Mudjāwir; Ibn al-Nadjdjār; al-Samhūdī

see also al-Diyārbakrī

physical geography Nadjd.1

deserts al-Aḥḳāf; al-Dahnāʾ; Nafūd; al-Rubʿ al-Khālī

see also Badw.II; Ḥarra

mountains Djabala; Ḥirāʾ; Ḥufāsh; Raḍwā; al-Sarāt; Thabīr; al-Ṭuwayḳ

see also Adjaʾ and Salmā

plains ʿArafa; al-Dibdiba; al-Ṣammān

wadis al-ʿAtk; al-Bāṭin; Bayḥān; Bayḥān al-Ḳaṣāb; Djayzān; Fāʾw; Ḥamḍ, Wādī al-; al-Rumma; al-Sahbāʾ; Sirḥān; Tabāla; Turaba.1; Wādī Ḥanīfa

waters Dawʿan

population → TRIBES.ARABIAN PENINSULA

toponyms

and → *the section Physical Geography above*

ancient Badr; al-Djār; Fadak; al-Ḥidjr; al-Ḥudaybiya; Ḳurḥ; Madyan Shuʿayb; al-Rabadha; al-Thaʿlabiyya; Wādī 'l-Ḳurā

see also Fāʾw

present-day

districts al-Aflādj; al-Djawf; al-Ḳaṣīm; al-Khardj

islands Farasān

oases al-Dirʿiyya; Dūmat al-Djandal; al-Ḥasā; al-Khurma; al-ʿUyayna

regions ʿAsīr; Bayḥān; al-Ḥāḍina; Ḥaly; al-Ḥawṭa; al-Ḥidjāz; Ḳurayyāt al-Milḥ; Nadjd; Nafūd; Raʾs (al-)Tannūra; al-Rubʿ al-Khālī; Tihāma

towns Abhā; Abḳayḳ; Abū ʿArīsh; Burayda; al-Dammām; al-Djawf; Djayzān; al-Djubayl; al-Djubayla; Djudda; Fakhkh; Ghāmid; Ḥāyil; al-Hufūf; Ḥuraymilā; Ḳarya al-Suflā; Ḳarya al-ʿUlyā; al-Ḳaṣāb; al-Ḳaṭīf; Khamīs Mushayṭ; Khaybar;

al-Khubar; al-Kunfudha; al-Madīna; Makka; Minā; al-Mubarraz; Nadjrān; Rābigh; al-Riyāḍ; Tabāla; Tabūk; al-Ṭāʾif; Taymāʾ; Turaba.2 *and* 3; al-ʿUlā; ʿUnayza; al-Yamāma; Yanbuʿ; (al-)Ẓahrān; [in Suppl.] Fayd; Ṣabyā
see also (Djazīrat) al-ʿArab; al-ʿĀriḍ; Bīsha; Ḍariyya

SCIENCE **ʿIlm**; Mawsūʿa
see also Ibn Abī Uṣaybiʿa; Shumayyil, Shiblī; [in Suppl.] al-Bustānī; Ibn al-Akfānī.3; Ibn Farīghūn; *and* → ALCHEMY; ASTROLOGY; ASTRONOMY; BOTANY; MATHEMATICS; MECHANICS; MEDICINE; OPTICS; PHARMACOLOGY; ZOOLOGY

SECTS ʿAdjārida; Ahl-i Ḥadīth; Ahl-i Ḥakk; Aḥmadiyya; ʿAlids; Azāriḳa; al-Badjalī; Baḳliyya; Bihʾāfrīd b. Farwardīn; Bohorās; Burghūthiyya; Djabriyya; Djahmiyya; al-Djanāḥiyya; al-Djārūdiyya; Durūz; Farāʾiḍiyya; Ghurābiyya; Ḥarīriyya; Ḥashīshiyya; Ḥulmāniyya; Ḥurūfiyya; al-Ibāḍiyya; Ḳarmaṭī; Karrāmiyya; Kaysāniyya; al-Khalafiyya; Khāridjites; Khashabiyya; Khaṭṭābiyya; Khōdja; Khūbmesīḥīs; Khurramiyya; Kuraybiyya; Mahdawīs; Manṣūriyya; al-Mughīriyya; Muḥammadiyya; Mukhammisa; Muṭarrifiyya; al-Muʿtazila; Nadjadāt; Nāwūsiyya; al-Nukkār; Nuḳṭawiyya; Nūrbakhshiyya; Nuṣayriyya; al-Rāwandiyya; Rawshaniyya; Salmāniyya; Ṣārliyya; Satpanthīs; Shabak; Shābāshiyya; Shaykhiyya; Shumayṭiyya; Ṣufriyya; Tablīghī Djamāʿat; ʿUlyāʾiyya; ʿUthmāniyya; Yazīdī; [in Suppl.] Dhikrīs; Pīrpanthī
see also Abu ʾl-Maʿālī; ʿAlī Ilāhī; Bābāʾī; Bābīs; Bāyazīd Anṣārī; Bishārʿ; Dahriyya; al-Dhammiyya; Dīn-i Ilāhī; Ghassāniyya; Ghulāt; Ḥā-Mīm; Imām Shāh; ʿIrāḳ.vi; Kasrawī Tabrīzī; al-Kayyāl; Kāẓim Rashtī; Ḳîzîl-bāsh; al-Malaṭī; Mazdak; Mudjtahid.III; Sālimiyya; Sulṭān Sehāk; *and* → MYSTICISM.ORDERS

Alids ʿAbd Allāh b. Muʿāwiya; Abū ʿAbd Allāh Yaʿḳūb; Abu ʾl-Aswad al-Duʾalī; Abū Hāshim; Abū Nuʿaym al-Mulāʾī; Abū Salāma al-Khallāl; Abu ʾl-Sarāyā al-Shaybānī; ʿAlī b. Muḥammad al-Zandjī; ʿ**Alids**; al-Djawwānī; Hāniʾ b. ʿUrwa al-Murādī; al-Ḥasan b. Zayd b. Muḥammad; Ḥasan al-Uṭrūsh; Ḥudjr; al-Ḥusayn b. ʿAlī, Ṣāḥib Fakhkh; Ibrāhīm b. al-Ashtar; Khidāsh; Muḥammad b. ʿAbd Allāh (al-Nafs al-Zakiyya); al-Mukhtār b. Abī ʿUbayd; Muslim b. ʿAḳīl b. Abī Ṭālib; Sulaym b. Ḳays; Sulaymān b. Ṣurad; al-Ukhayḍir, Banū; Yaḥyā b. ʿAbd Allāh; Yaḥyā b. Zayd; Zayd b. ʿAlī b. al-Ḥusayn
see also Dhu ʾl-Faḳār; al-Djanāḥiyya; al-Djārūdiyya; Ghadīr Khumm; al-Maʾmūn; Sharīf; Zaynab bt. ʿAbd Allāh al-Maḥḍ; [in Suppl.] al-Nadjāshī; *and* → SHIITES

Bābism Bāb; **Bābīs**; Kāshānī; Ḳurrat al-ʿAyn; Maẓhar; Muḥammad ʿAlī Bārfurūshī; Muḥammad ʿAlī Zandjānī; Muḥammad Ḥusayn Bushrūʾī; Ṣubḥ-i Azal
see also al-Aḥsāʾī; Mudjtahid.III; Nuḳṭat al-Kāf; al-Sābiḳūn

Druzes → DRUZES

Hindu Barāhima; Ibāḥatiya; Nānak; [in Suppl.] Pīrpanthī

Ibāḍīs ʿAbd al-ʿAzīz b. al-Ḥādjdj Ibrāhīm; Abū Ghānim al-Khurāsānī; Abū Ḥafṣ ʿUmar b. Djamīʿ; Abū Ḥātim al-Malzūzī (*and* al-Malzūzī); Abu ʾl-Khaṭṭāb al-Maʿāfirī; Abū Muḥammad b. Baraka; Abu ʾl-Muʾthir al-Bahlawī; Abū Zakariyyāʾ al-Djanāwunī; Abū Zakariyyāʾ al-Wardjlānī; Aṭfiyāsh; al-Barrādī; al-Bughṭūrī; al-Dardjīnī; Djābir b. Zayd; al-Djayṭālī; al-Djulandā; **al-Ibāḍiyya**; Ibn Baraka; Ibn Djaʿfar; al-Irdjānī; al-Lawātī; Maḥbūb b. al-Raḥīl al-ʿAbdī; al-Mazātī; al-Nafūsī; al-Shammākhī al-Īfranī; al-Tanāwutī; al-Wisyānī; [in Suppl.] Abū ʿAmmār; al-Ḥārithī; Ṭālib al-Ḥaḳḳ
see also ʿAwāmir; Azd; Ḥalḳa; al-Khalafiyya; (Banū) Kharūṣ; *and* → DYNASTIES.SPAIN AND NORTH AFRICA.RUSTAMIDS; LAW; SECTS.KHARIDJITES

historians of Abu ʾl-Muʾthir al-Bahlawī; Abū Zakariyyāʾ al-Wardjlānī; al-Barrādī; al-Bughṭūrī; al-Dardjīnī; Ibn al-Ṣaghīr; Ibn Salām; al-Lawātī; Maḥbūb b. al-Raḥīl al-ʿAbdī; al-Mazātī; al-Sālimī
see also al-Nafūsī

Jewish → JUDAISM
Kharidjites Abū Bayhas; Abū Fudayk; Abū Yazīd al-Nukkārī; al-Ḍaḥḥāḳ b. Ḳays al-Shaybānī; Ḥurḳūṣ b. Zuhayr al-Saʿdī; ʿImrān b. Ḥiṭṭān; Ḳaṭarī b. al-Fudjāʾa; **Khāridjites**; Ḳurrāʾ; Ḳuʿūd; Mirdās b. Udayya; Nāfiʿ b. al-Azraḳ; al-Nukkār; Shabīb b. Yazīd; ʿUbayd Allāh b. Bashīr; al-Walīd b. Ṭarīf
see also ʿAdjārida; Azāriḳa; Ḥarūrāʾ; al-Ibāḍiyya; Ibn Muldjam; Imāma; Istiʿrāḍ; al-Manṣūr bi ʾllāh; Nadjadāt; Ṣufriyya; al-Ṭirimmāḥ; ʿUbayd Allāh b. Ziyād; [in Suppl.] al-Kaff
Shiite → SHIITES

SEDENTARISM Sārt; [in Suppl.] **Iskān**
see also Shaʿb.1; *and* → ARCHITECTURE.URBAN; GEOGRAPHY.URBAN

SENEGAL Djolof; **Senegal**
see also Murīdiyya
physical geography Senegal.1
toponyms Ṭūbā; [in Suppl.] Dakar

SEXUALITY ʿAzl; Bāh; Djins; Khitān; Liwāṭ; Siḥāḳ; [in Suppl.] Bighāʾ; Muḳawwiyāt
see also Djanāba; Khāṣī; Tanẓīm al-Nasl; *and* → ADULTERY; CIRCUMCISION; LOVE.EROTIC
treatises on al-Tīfāshī

SHIITES ʿAbd Allāh b. Sabaʾ; ʿAlids; Ghulāt; Imāma; Ismāʿīliyya; Ithnā ʿAshariyya; Sabʿiyya; **Shīʿa**; Taḳiyya; Wilāya.2; Zaydiyya
see also Abu ʾl-Sarāyā al-Shaybānī; ʿAlī b. Abī Ṭālib; ʿAlī Mardān; Madjlis.3; Taʿziya; [in Suppl.] Batriyya; *and* → SHIITES.SECTS
branches Ismāʿīliyya; Ithnā ʿAshariyya; Ḳarmaṭī; Nizāriyya; Zaydiyya
see also Hind.v.d; Imāma; Sabʿiyya; *and* → SHIITES.SECTS
Carmathians (Djazīrat) al-ʿArab.vii.2; al-Djannābī, Abū Saʿīd; al-Djannābī, Abū Ṭāhir; Ḥamdān Ḳarmaṭ; al-Ḥasan al-Aʿṣam; **Ḳarmaṭī**
see also ʿAbdān; al-Baḥrayn; Baḳliyya; Daʿwa; Shābāshiyya
Ismāʿīliyya ʿAbd Allāh b. Maymūn; Abū ʿAbd Allāh al-Shīʿī; Abu ʾl-Khaṭṭāb al-Asadī; Allāh.iii.1; (Djazīrat) al-ʿArab.vii.2; Bāb; Bāṭiniyya; Dāʿī; Daʿwa; Fāṭimids; Ḥaḳāʾiḳ; Hind.v.d; Ibn ʿAṭṭāsh; Ikhwān al-Ṣafāʾ; Imāma; **Ismāʿīliyya**; Lanbasar; Madjlis.2; al-Mahdī ʿUbayd Allāh; Malāʾika.2; Manṣūr al-Yaman; Maymūn-diz; Sabʿiyya; Shahriyār b. al-Ḥasan; al-Ṭayyibiyya; Yām; Zakarawayh b. Mihrawayh; [in Suppl.] Dawr; Satr
see also Ḥawwāʾ; Ikhlāṣ; Maṣyād; Sabʿ; Salamiyya; Ṣulayḥids; Umm al-Kitāb.2; al-Ẓāhir wa ʾl-Bāṭin; [in Suppl.] Pīrpanthī; *and* → CALIPHATE.FĀṬIMIDS; SHIITES.IMAMS
authors Abū Ḥātim al-Rāzī; Abū Yaʿḳūb al-Sidjzī; al-Kirmānī; al-Muʾayyad fi ʾl-Dīn; al-Nasafī.1; Nāṣir-i Khusraw; [in Suppl.] Djaʿfar b. Manṣūr al-Yaman
and → *the sections Mustaʿlī-Ṭayyibīs and Nizārīs below*
Mustaʿlī-Ṭayyibīs Bohorās; al-Ḥāmidī; Luḳmāndjī; al-Makramī; Makramids; Muḥammad b. Ṭāhir al-Ḥārithī; Shaykh Ādam; Sulaymān b. Ḥasan; Sulaymānīs; Ṭāhir Sayf al-Dīn; al-Ṭayyibiyya; [in Suppl.] ʿAlī b. Ḥanẓala b. Abī Sālim; ʿAlī b. Muḥammad b. Djaʿfar; Amīndjī b. Djalāl b. Ḥasan; Ḥasan b. Nūḥ; Idrīs b. al-Ḥasan
see also Ismāʿīliyya
Nizārīs Agha Khān; Fidāʾī; Khōdja; Maḥallātī; Nizār b. al-Mustanṣir; **Nizāriyya**; Pīr Ṣadr al-Dīn; Pīr Shams; Rāshid al-Dīn Sinān; Sabz ʿAlī; Shāh Ṭāhir; al-Shahrastānī, Abu ʾl-Fatḥ; Shams-al-Dīn Muḥammad; Shihāb al-Dīn al-Ḥusaynī;

al-Ṭūsī, Naṣīr al-Dīn; [in Suppl.] Khayrkhʷāh-i Harātī
see also Sarkār Āḳā; Satpanthīs
of Alamūt Alamūt.ii; Buzurg-ummīd; Ḥasan-i Ṣabbāḥ; Ḥashīshiyya; Nūr al-Dīn Muḥammad II; Rukn al-Dīn Khurshāh; [in Suppl.] Muḥammad III b. Ḥasan
see also Fidāʾī

Sevener **Sabʿiyya**
see also Sabʿ

Twelver Imāma; **Ithnā ʿAshariyya**; Mudjtahid.II; Mutawālī; al-Rāfiḍa; Uṣūliyya.1; [in Suppl.] Akhbāriyya
see also Buwayhids; al-Ẓāhir wa ʾl-Bāṭin; *and* → *the sections Imams, Jurists and Theologians below*

Zaydiyya al-Djārūdiyya; Muṭarrifiyya; **Zaydiyya**; [in Suppl.] Batriyya
see also Imāma; Rassids; *and* → DYNASTIES.ARABIAN PENINSULA.ZAYDĪS
scholars al-Ḥasan b. Ṣāliḥ b. Ḥayy al-Kūfī; Ibn Abi ʾl-Ridjāl; al-Rassī; Sulaymān b. Djarīr al-Raḳḳī; Yaḥyā b. Ḥamza al-ʿAlawī; Zayd b. ʿAlī b. al-Ḥusayn; [in Suppl.] Abu ʾl-Barakāt; Abu ʾl-Fatḥ al-Daylamī; Aḥmad b. ʿĪsā; Djaʿfar b. Abī Yaḥyā; al-Ḥākim al-Djushamī
for Zaydī imams of Yemen → DYNASTIES.ARABIAN PENINSULA.ZAYDĪS
for Zaydī imams of the Caspian, see al-Ḥasan b. Zayd b. Muḥammad; Ḥasan al-Uṭrūsh; Muḥammad b. Zayd; al-Nāṣir li-Dīn Allāh.I; al-Thāʾir fi ʾllāh; Yaḥyā b. ʿAbd Allāh; Yaḥyā b. Zayd; **Zaydiyya**.2
for others, see Ibn Ṭabāṭabā

doctrines and institutions Bāṭiniyya; Djafr; Ḳāʾim Āl Muḥammad; Khalḳ.VII; Madjlis.2 *and* 3; al-Mahdī; Malāʾika.2; Mardjaʿ-i Taḳlīd; Maẓhar; Maẓlūm; Mudjtahid.II; Mutʿa.V; Radjʿa; Safīr.1; Tanāsukh.2; Taʾwīl; al-Ẓāhir wa ʾl-Bāṭin; [in Suppl.] Āyatullāh
see also Adhān; Ahl al-Bayt; ʿAḳīda; Bāb; Ghayba; Ḥudjdja; Imāma; ʿIlm al-Ridjāl; Imām-bārā; Imāmzāda; Mollā; Umm al-Kitāb.2; Ziyāra.1.a *and* 5; *and* → THEOLOGY.TERMS.SHIITE

dynasties Buwayhids; Fāṭimids; Ṣafawids; Zaydiyya.3
see also Mushaʿshaʿ; al-Ukhayḍir, Banū

imams ʿAlī b. Abī Ṭālib; ʿAlī al-Riḍā; al-ʿAskarī; Djaʿfar al-Ṣādiḳ; (al-)Ḥasan b. ʿAlī b. Abī Ṭālib; (al-)Ḥusayn b. ʿAlī b. Abī Ṭālib; Muḥammad b. ʿAlī al-Riḍā; Muḥammad b. ʿAlī (al-Bāḳir); Muḥammad al-Ḳāʾim; Mūsā al-Kāẓim; Zayn al-ʿĀbidīn; [in Suppl.] Muḥammad b. Ismāʿīl al-Maymūn
see also Bāb; Ghayba; Imāmzāda; Malāʾika.2; Maẓlūm; Riḍā.2; Safīr.1

jurists al-ʿĀmilī; al-Dāmād; al-Ḥillī.1 *and* 2; al-Ḥurr al-ʿĀmilī; Ibn Bābawayh(i); Ibn Shahrāshūb; al-Karakī; Kāshānī, Āyatullāh; Kāshif al-Ghiṭāʾ; Khʷānsārī, Sayyid Mīrzā; Khʷānsārī, Sayyid Muḥammad; Khiyābānī, Shaykh Muḥammad; Khurāsānī; al-Kulaynī, Abū Djaʿfar Muḥammad; Madjlisī; Madjlisī-yi Awwal; al-Māmaḳānī; al-Mufīd; Muḥammad b. Makkī; al-Murtaḍā; Muṭahharī; Nāʾīnī; al-Shahīd al-Thānī; Sharaf al-Dīn; Sharīʿatmadārī; Shīrāzī; al-Ṭabrisī, Abū Manṣūr; al-Ṭabrisī, Amīn al-Dīn; Ṭabrisī; al-Ṭūsī, Muḥammad b. al-Ḥasan; [in Suppl.] Āḳā Nadjafī; Anṣārī; Bihbihānī; Burūdjirdī; Fayḍ-i Kāshānī; Ḥāʾirī; Ibn Abī Djumhūr al-Aḥsāʾī; al-Ḳaṭīfī; Khumaynī; Mūsā al-Ṣadr
see also ʿĀḳila; Mardjaʿ-i Taḳlīd; Mollā; Mudjtahid.II; Mutʿa.V; Uṣūliyya.1; [in Suppl.] Akhbāriyya

places of pilgrimage Karbalāʾ; Kāẓimayn; al-Nadjaf; Sāmarrāʾ; [in Suppl.] ʿAtabāt; Ḳadamgāh; Mashhad.3
see also Shāh ʿAbd al-ʿAẓīm al-Ḥasanī; Ziyāra.1.a *and* 5

rituals Rawḍa-khʷānī

sects Ahl-i Ḥaḳḳ; ʿAlids; Baḳliyya; Bohorās; Djābir b. Ḥayyān; al-Djanāḥiyya; al-Djārūdiyya; Ghurābiyya; Ḥurūfiyya; Ibāḥa.II; Kaysāniyya; Khashabiyya; Khaṭṭābiyya; Khōdja;

Khurramiyya; Kuraybiyya; Manṣūriyya; al-Mughīriyya; Muḥammadiyya; Mukhammisa; Muṭarrifiyya; al-Muʿtazila; Nāwūsiyya; Nūrbakhshiyya; Nuṣayriyya; al-Rāfiḍa; al-Rāwandiyya; Salmāniyya; Satpanthīs; Shaykhiyya; Shumayṭiyya; Ṭāwūsiyya; ʿUlyāʾiyya; al-Wāḳifa; [in Suppl.] Kāmiliyya

see also ʿAbd Allāh b. Sabaʾ; Bāṭiniyya; Bayān b. Samʿān al-Tamīmī; Bektāshiyya; Ghulāt; Hind.v.d; Imām Shāh; Ḳaṭʿ; al-Kayyāl; Kāẓim Rashtī; Ḳîzîl-bāsh; Mudjtahid.III; Mushaʿshaʿ; Tawwābūn; [in Suppl.] Ibn Warsand; *and* → BAHAIS; DRUZES; SECTS.ʿALIDS

Kaysāniyya Abū Hāshim; Kaysān; **Kaysāniyya**

see also al-Sayyid al-Ḥimyarī

Khaṭṭābiyya Abu ʾl-Khaṭṭāb al-Asadī; Bashshār al-Shaʿīrī; Bazīgh b. Mūsā; **Khaṭṭābiyya**

see also Mukhammisa; al-Ṣāmit

Khurramiyya Bābak; [in Suppl.] Bādhām

Mukhammisa **Mukhammisa**

see also al-Muḥassin b. ʿAlī

Shaykhism al-Aḥsāʾī; Rashtī, Sayyid Kāẓim; **Shaykhiyya**

terms → THEOLOGY.TERMS.SHIITE

theologians al-Dāmād; al-Ḥillī; Hishām b. al-Ḥakam; al-Ḥurr al-ʿĀmilī; Ibn Bābawayh(i); Ibn Shahrāshūb; al-Karakī; Kāshif al-Ghiṭāʾ; Khwānsārī, Sayyid Mīrzā; al-Kulaynī, Abū Djaʿfar Muḥammad; Lāhīdjī.2; Mīr Lawḥī; al-Mufīd; Mullā Ṣadrā Shīrāzī; al-Nasafī.1; Shayṭān al-Ṭāḳ; Ṭabrisī; al-Thaḳafī, Ibrāhīm; al-Ṭūsī, Muḥammad b. al-Ḥasan; al-Ṭūsī, Naṣīr al-Dīn; [in Suppl.] Akhbāriyya; Ibn Abī Djumhūr al-Aḥsāʾī; Ibn Mītham

see also al-ʿAyyāshī; Ḥudjdja; Imāma; Khalḳ.VII; Mollā; Sharīʿatī, ʿAlī; *and* → *the section Jurists above*

traditionists → LITERATURE.TRADITION-LITERATURE.TRADITIONISTS.SHIITES

SIBERIA **Sibīr**

physical geography

waters Ob; [in Suppl.] Irtish

see also Tobol

population Bukhārlîk; Tobol

toponyms → EUROPE.EASTERN EUROPE

SICILY Benavert; Kalbids; **Ṣiḳilliya**

see also Aghlabids.iii; Asad b. al-Furāt; Fāṭimids; Ṭarī

local rulers Ibn al-Ḥawwās; Ibn al-Thumna

poets Ibn Ḥamdīs; Ibn al-Khayyāṭ

scholars Ibn al-Birr; Ibn al-Ḳaṭṭāʿ; Ibn Makkī

see also al-Idrīsī

toponyms Balarm; Benavent; Djirdjent; Ḳaṣryānnih; Siraḳūsa

see also al-Khāliṣa

SLAVERY **ʿAbd**; Ghulām; Ḳayna; Khāṣī; Mamlūk; Mawlā; al-Ṣaḳāliba; Umm al-Walad

see also Ḥabash.i; Ḥabshī; Hausa; ʿIdda.5; Istibrāʾ; Khādim; Ḳul; Maṭmūra; Sidi; [in Suppl.] Nafaḳa; *and* → MUSIC.SONG.SINGERS

manumission ʿAbd.3.j; ʿİtḳnāme; Tadbīr.2

slave revolt Zandj.2

SOMALIA Ṣiḥāfa.1.(xv); **Somali**

see also Ḥabesh; Muḥammad b. ʿAbd Allāh Ḥassān; Ogādēn; *and* → AFRICA.EAST AFRICA

physical geography Somali.2

religious orders Ṣāliḥiyya
  see also Somali.4
toponyms
  regions Guardafui
    see also Ogādēn
  towns Barawa; Berberā; Hargeisa; Maḳdishū; Merka; Shungwaya; Zaylaʿ

SOUTH(-EAST) ASIA → ASIA

SOVIET UNION → CAUCASUS; CENTRAL ASIA.FORMER SOVIET UNION; COMMUNISM; EUROPE.EASTERN EUROPE; SIBERIA

SPAIN Aljamía; Almogávares; al-Burt; al-Bushārrāt; Moriscos
  see also Ibn al-Ḳiṭṭ; Ifni; al-ʿIḳāb; *and* → ANDALUSIA; DYNASTIES.SPAIN AND NORTH AFRICA
physical geography al-Andalus.ii *and* iii.2
  see also Wādī.3
  mountains al-Shārāt
  waters al-Ḥamma; Ibruh; al-Mudawwar; Shaḳūra; Tādjuh; (al-)Wādī al-Kabīr; Wādī Yāna; [in Suppl.] Araghūn; Wādī Lakku
toponyms
  ancient Barbashturu; Bulāy; Ḳasṭīliya.1; al-Madīna al-Zāhira; Shadūna; Shaḳunda; Shaḳūra; Shantabariyya; Tākurunnā; Ṭalabīra; Tudmīr; [in Suppl.] Āfrāg; Balyūnash
    see also Rayya
  present-day
    islands al-Djazāʾir al-Khālida; Mayūrḳa; Minūrḳa; Yābisa
    regions Ālaba wa ʾl-Ḳilāʿ; Djillīḳiyya; Faḥṣ al-Ballūṭ; Firrīsh; Ḳanbāniya; Ḳashtāla; Navarra; Wādī ʾl-Ḥidjāra; Walba; [in Suppl.] Araghūn; al-Sharaf
    towns Alsh; Arkush; Arnīṭ; Badjdjāna; Balansiya; Bālish; Banbalūna; Barshalūna; al-Basīt; Basta; Baṭalyaws; Bayyāna; Bayyāsa; Biṭrawsh; al-Bunt; Burghush; Dāniya; Djarunda; Djayyān; al-Djazīra al-Khaḍrāʾ; Djazīrat Shuḳr; Finyāna; Gharnāṭa; Ifrāgha; Ilbīra; Ishbīliya; Istidja; Ḳabra; Ḳādis; Ḳalʿat Ayyūb; Ḳalʿat Rabāḥ; Ḳanṭara.2; Ḳarmūna; Ḳarṭādjanna; al-Ḳulayʿa; Ḳūnka; Ḳūriya; Ḳurṭuba; Labla; Laḳant; Lārida; Lawsha; Liyūn; Lūrḳa; al-Maʿdin; Madīnat Sālim; Madīnat al-Zahrāʾ; Madjrīṭ; Mālaḳa; Mārida; al-Mariyya; Mawrūr; al-Munakkab; Mursiya; Runda; Saraḳusṭa; Shaḳūbiya; Shalamanḳa; Shalṭīsh; Shant Mānkash; Shant Yāḳub; Shantamariyyat al-Sharḳ; Sharīsh; Shāṭiba; Ṭarīfa; Ṭarrakūna; Ṭulayṭula; Ṭurṭūsha; Tuṭīla; Ubbadha; Uḳlīsh; Urdjudhūna; Uryūla; Wādī Āsh; Washḳa; [in Suppl.] Ashturḳa
      see also al-Andalus.iii.3; Balāṭ; Djabal Ṭāriḳ; al-Ḳalʿa; *and* → PORTUGAL

SRI LANKA **Ceylon**; Sarandīb
  and → INDIA.POPULATION.TAMILS

SUDAN Dār Fūr; Dustūr.xiii; Ḥizb.i; Madjlis.4.A.xvii; al-Mahdiyya; Ṣiḥāfa.1.(ii); **Sūdān**; [in Suppl.] Niẓām ʿAskarī.1.(d)
  see also Baladiyya.2; Fundj; Ḥabesh; Nūba; *and* → AFRICA.EAST AFRICA
history [in Suppl.] **Taʾrīkh**.II.8
Mahdist period ʿAbd Allāh b. Muḥammad al-Taʿāʾishī; Khalīfa.iv; **al-Mahdiyya**; ʿUthmān Diḳna; [in Suppl.] Manshūrāt
  see also Awlād al-Balad; Dār Fūr; Emīn Pasha; Rābiḥ b. Faḍl Allāh; Taʿāʾisha; [in Suppl.] al-Madjādhīb

modern period
influential persons Ṭāhā, Maḥmūd Muḥammad
see also al-Tūnisī, Muḥammad; al-Tūnisī, Shaykh Zayn al-ʿĀbidīn
physical geography
waters al-Nīl
population ʿAbābda; ʿAlwa; (Banū) ʿĀmir; Baḳḳāra; Barābra; Djaʿaliyyūn; Ghuzz.iii; Nūba.4; Rashāʾida; Shāyḳiyya; Taʿāʾisha; Zaghāwa
see also Bedja; Fallāta
religious orders Mīrghaniyya
see also [in Suppl.] al-Madjādhīb
toponyms
ancient ʿAydhāb; Sōba
present-day
provinces Baḥr al-Ghazāl.3; Berber.2; Dār Fūr; Fāshōda; Kasala
regions Fāzūghlī; Kordofān
towns Atbara; Berber.3; Dongola; al-Fāshir; Kasala; Ḳerrī; al-Khurṭūm; Omdurman; Sawākin; Shandī; Sinnār; al-Ubayyiḍ; Wad Madanī; Wādī Ḥalfā

SUPERSTITION ʿAyn; Faʾl; Ghurāb; Ḥinnāʾ; Khamsa; Ṣadā
see also ʿAḳīḳ; Bāriḥ; Laḳab

SYRIA Dimashḳ; **al-Shām**
see also [in Suppl.] Waḳf.II.2; *and* → LEBANON
architecture → ARCHITECTURE.REGIONS
before Islam → PRE-ISLAM.IN FERTILE CRESCENT
dynasties ʿAmmār; Ayyūbids; Būrids; Fāṭimids; Ḥamdānids; Mamlūks; Umayyads; Zangids
see also [in Suppl.] al-Djazzār Pasha; *and* → DYNASTIES.EGYPT AND THE FERTILE CRESCENT; LEBANON
historians of al-ʿAẓīmī; Ibn Abī Ṭayyiʾ; Ibn al-ʿAdīm; Ibn ʿAsākir; Ibn al-Ḳalānisī; Ibn Kathīr; Ibn Shaddād; Ibn Ṭūlūn; Kurd ʿAlī; al-Kutubī; al-Yūnīnī; Yūsuf b. ʿAbd al-Hādī; [in Suppl.] Maṭar
see also [in Suppl.] Taʾrīkh.II.1.(c); *and* → DYNASTIES.EGYPT AND THE FERTILE CRESCENT
modern period Djarīda.i.A; Djāmiʿa; Dustūr.ix; Ḥizb.i; Ḥukūma.iii; Madjlis.4.A.v; Madjmaʿ ʿIlmī.i.2.a; Maḥkama.4.ii; Mandates; Maysalūn; Salafiyya.2(b); al-Shām.2, esp. (b) *and* (c); Ṣiḥāfa.1.(iv); [in Suppl.] Niẓām ʿAskarī.1.(b)
see also Baladiyya.2; Kurd ʿAlī; Mardam.2; [in Suppl.] Demography.III
belletrists
poets al-Khūrī; Mardam.2; [in Suppl.] Buṭrus Karāma; Ḳabbānī
historians [in Suppl.] Maṭar
statesmen al-Khūrī; Mardam.1; al-Zahrāwī, ʿAbd al-Ḥamīd; al-Zaʿīm
physical geography al-Shām.1
mountains Ḳāsiyūn; al-Lukkām
waters ʿAfrīn; al-ʿĀṣī; Baradā; al-ʿUtayba; Yarmūk.1; Zabadānī; [in Suppl.] Ḳuwayḳ
toponyms
ancient Afāmiya; ʿArbān; al-Bakhrāʾ; al-Bāra; Barḳaʿīd; Dābiḳ; Diyār Muḍar; Diyār Rabīʿa; al-Djābiya; al-Djazīra; Djilliḳ; Manbidj; Namāra.1; al-Raḥba; Raʾs al-ʿAyn; Rīḥā.2; al-Ruṣāfa.3; Shayzar; [in Suppl.] Ḳūrus
present-day
districts al-Bathaniyya; al-Djawlān
regions al-Ghāb; Ḥawrān; Ḳinnasrīn.2; Ladjāʾ; al-Ṣafā.2

see also G̲h̲ūṭa
towns Ad̲h̲ri'āt; Bāniyās; Boṣrā; Buzā'ā; Dayr al-Zōr; Dimas̲h̲ḳ; Djabala; al-
Djabbūl; Djisr al-S̲h̲ug̲h̲r; Ḥalab; Ḥamāt; Ḥārim; Ḥimṣ; Ḥuwwārīn; Ḳanawāt;
Ḳarḳīsiyā; K̲h̲awlān.2; Ḳinnasrīn.1; al-Lād̲h̲iḳiyya; Ma'arrat Maṣrīn; Ma'arrat
al-Nu'mān; Ma'lūlā; Maskana; Maṣyād; al-Mizza; Namāra.2 *and* 3; al-Raḳḳa;
Ṣāfīt̲h̲a; Salamiyya; Ṣalk̲h̲ad; Tadmur; Ṭarṭūs; Zabadānī
see also al-Marḳab

T

TANZANIA   Dar-es-Salaam; Kilwa; Mikindani; Mkwaja; Mtambwe Mkuu; **Tanzania**
see also Swahili; *and* → AFRICA.EAST AFRICA
Zanzibar   Barg̲h̲as̲h̲; Bū Sa'īd; Kizimkazi; **Zandjibār**
see also Tumbatu

TAXATION   Bād̲j̲; **Bayt al-Māl**; Ḍarība; D̲j̲izya; Ḳānūn.ii *and* iii; K̲h̲arād̲j̲; Taḥrīr; Taḥṣīl; Taḳsīṭ;
'Us̲h̲r; [in Suppl.] Ḍarība.7
see also Ḍabṭ; D̲j̲ahbad̲h̲; Mā'; Ma'ṣir; Ra'iyya; Taḳdīr.2; Ta'rīk̲h̲.I.1.viii; Zakāt
collectors   'Āmil; Dihḳan; Muḥaṣṣil; Mültezim; Mustak̲h̲rid̲j̲
see also Amīr; Taḥṣīl
taxes   'Arūs Resmi; 'Awāriḍ; Bād-i Hawā; Badal; Bād̲j̲; Bas̲h̲maḳlîḳ; Bennāk; Čift-resmi;
D̲j̲awālī; D̲j̲izya; Filori; Furḍa; Ispend̲j̲e; K̲h̲arād̲j̲; Ḳūbčūr; Maks; Mālikāne; Mīrī;
Muḳāsama; Muḳāṭa'a; Pīs̲h̲kas̲h̲; Resm; Tamg̲h̲a; Tekālīf; 'Us̲h̲r
see also Ḥisba.ii; Ḳaṭī'a; Waẓīfa.1
land taxes   Bas̲h̲maḳlîḳ; Bennāk; Čift-resmi; **K̲h̲arād̲j̲**; Mīrī; Muḳāsama; 'Us̲h̲r; [in Suppl.]
Ta'alluḳ
see also Daftar; Daftar-i K̲h̲āḳānī; Ḳabāla; Ḳānūn.iii.1; Rawk; Ustān
tithe-lands   Ḍay'a; Īg̲h̲ār; Iḳṭā'; Iltizām; K̲h̲āliṣa; K̲h̲āṣṣ; Ṣafi; Tīmār; Zamīndār; Zi'āmet
see also Ba'l.2.b; Dār al-'Ahd; Fay'; Filāḥa.iv; Za'īm
treatises on   Abū Yūsuf; al-Mak̲h̲zūmī; al-Tahānawī; Yaḥyā b. Ādam
see also Abū 'Ubayd al-Ḳāsim b. Sallām

THAILAND   Patani; **Thailand**
see also [in Suppl.] al-Mar'a

THEOLOGY   'Aḳīda; Allāh; Dīn; D̲j̲anna; **'Ilm al-Kalām**; Imāma; Īmān; Kalām; al-Mahdī;
Uṣūl al-Dīn
see also 'Ālam.1; Hilāl.i; *and* → ISLAM
disputation   Masā'il wa-Ad̲j̲wiba; Munāẓara; Radd; [in Suppl.] 'Ibādat K̲h̲āna
see also Mubāhala
treatises on   al-Samarḳandī, S̲h̲ams al-Dīn
schools
Shiite   Ismā'īliyya; It̲h̲nā 'As̲h̲ariyya; Ḳarmaṭī; Uṣūliyya.1; [in Suppl.] Ak̲h̲bāriyya
see also Mu'tazila
Sunni   As̲h̲'ariyya; Ḥanābila; Māturīdiyya; Mu'tazila
see also 'Ilm al-Kalām.II; Ḳadariyya; Karāmat 'Alī; Murd̲j̲i'a; al-Nad̲j̲d̲j̲āriyya
terms   Ad̲j̲al; Ad̲j̲r; 'Adl; 'Ahd; Ahl al-ahwā'; Ahl al-kitāb; Āk̲h̲ira; 'Aḳīda; 'Aḳl; 'Aḳliyyāt;
'Ālam.2.; 'Amal.2; Amr; al-Aṣlaḥ; Ba't̲h̲; Bāṭiniyya; Bid'a; Birr; Da'wa; Dīn; D̲j̲amā'a;
D̲j̲azā'; D̲j̲ism; Du'ā'; Fard.g; Fāsiḳ; Fi'l; Fitna; Fiṭra; al-G̲h̲ayb; G̲h̲ayba; G̲h̲ufrān; Ḥadd;
Ḥaḳḳ; Ḥaraka wa-Sukūn.I.2 *and* 3; Ḥisāb; Ḥud̲j̲d̲j̲a; Ḥudūt̲h̲ al-'Ālam; Ḥulūl; I'd̲j̲āz;

Iḍṭirār; Ikhlāṣ; Ikhtiyār; ʿIlla.ii.III; Imāma; Īmān; Islām; ʿIṣma; Istiṭāʿa; Ittiḥād; al-Ḳaḍāʾ wa ʾl-Ḳadar; Kaffāra; Kāfir; Kalima; Karāma; Kasb; Kashf; Khalḳ; Khaṭīʾa; Khidhlān; Ḳidam; Kumūn; Ḳunūt; Ḳuwwa.3; Luṭf; Maʿād; al-Mahdī; al-Manzila bayn al-Manzilatayn; al-Mughayyabāt al-Khams; al-Munāfiḳūn.2; Murtadd; Muṭlaḳ; Nāfila; Nafs; Nāmūs.1; Nūr Muḥammadī; Riyāʾ; Rizḳ; Rudjūʿ; Ruʾyat Allāh; Sabīl.1; Shubha; Ṣifa.2; Ṭāʿa; Taḥsīn wa-Taḳbīḥ; Taḳlīd; Taklīf; Tanāsukh; Tashbīh wa-Tanzīh; Tawallud; Tawba; Tawfīḳ; Waraʿ; al-Ẓāhir wa ʾl-Bāṭin; Ẓulm; [in Suppl.] Ḥāl; Ithm; Kabīra; al-Nahy ʿan al-Munkar; Taḳwā

see also Abad; Allāh.ii; In Shāʾ Allāh; ʿInāya; Ṣūra; *and* → Eschatology; Qurʾan.terms

Shiite Badāʾ; Ghayba; Ibdāʿ; Kashf; Lāhūt and Nāsūt.5; Maẓhar; Maẓlūm; al-Munāfiḳūn.2; Naḳḍ al-Mīthāḳ; Radjʿa; al-Sābiḳūn; Safīr.1; al-Ṣāmit; Sarkār Āḳā; Tabarruʾ; Tanāsukh.2; Waṣī

and → Shiites.doctrines and institutions

theologians ʿUlamāʾ

see also Sharḥ.III

in early Islam Djahm b. Ṣafwān; al-Ḥasan al-Baṣrī; Wāṣil b. ʿAṭāʾ; [in Suppl.] al-Aṣamm; al-Ḥasan b. Muḥammad b. al-Ḥanafiyya; Ibn Kullāb

Ashʿarī al-Āmidī; al-Ashʿarī, Abu ʾl-Ḥasan; al-Baghdādī; al-Bāḳillānī; al-Bayhaḳī; al-Djuwaynī; al-Faḍālī; Fakhr al-Dīn al-Rāzī; al-Ghazālī, Abū Ḥāmid; Ibn Fūrak; al-Īdjī; al-Isfarāyīnī; al-Kiyā al-Harrāsī; al-Ḳushayrī; al-Sanūsī, Abū ʿAbd Allāh; al-Simnānī; [in Suppl.] al-Ṭūsī

see also Allāh.ii; ʿIlm al-Kalām.II.C; Imāma; Īmān; [in Suppl.] Ḥāl

Ḥanbalī ʿAbd al-Ḳādir al-Djīlānī; Aḥmad b. Ḥanbal; al-Anṣārī al-Harawī; al-Barbahārī; Ibn ʿAbd al-Wahhāb; Ibn ʿAḳīl; Ibn Baṭṭa al-ʿUkbarī; Ibn al-Djawzī; Ibn Ḳayyim al-Djawziyya; Ibn Ḳudāma al-Maḳdisī; Ibn Taymiyya; al-Khallāl

see also Īmān; *and* → Law

Māturīdī ʿAbd al-Ḥayy; Bishr b. Ghiyāth; al-Māturīdī

see also Allāh.ii; ʿIlm al-Kalām.II.D; Imāma; Īmān

Muʿtazilī ʿAbbād b. Sulaymān; ʿAbd al-Djabbār b. Aḥmad; Abu ʾl-Hudhayl al-ʿAllāf; Aḥmad b. Abī Duʾād; Aḥmad b. Ḥābiṭ; ʿAmr b. ʿUbayd; al-Balkhī; Bishr b. al-Muʿtamir; Djaʿfar b. Ḥarb; Djaʿfar b. Mubashshir; Djāḥiẓ; al-Djubbāʾī; Hishām b. ʿAmr al-Fuwaṭī; Ibn al-Ikhshīd; Ibn Khallād; al-Iskāfī; al-Khayyāṭ; Muʿammar b. ʿAbbād; al-Murdār; al-Nāshiʾ al-Akbar; al-Naẓẓām; al-Shaḥḥām; Thumāma b. Ashras; al-Zamakhsharī; [in Suppl.] Abū ʿAbd Allāh al-Baṣrī; Abu ʾl-Ḥusayn al-Baṣrī; Abū Rashīd al-Nīsābūrī; Ḍirār b. ʿAmr; al-Ḥākim al-Djushamī; Ibn Mattawayh

see also Ahl al-Naẓar; Allāh.ii; Ḥafṣ al-Fard; Ibn ʿAbbād, Abu ʾl-Ḳāsim; Ibn Abi ʾl-Ḥadīd; Ibn al-Rāwandī; ʿIlm al-Kalām.II.B; Imāma; Khalḳ.V; Lawn; Luṭf; al-Maʾmūn; al-Manzila bayn al-Manzilatayn; al-Waʿd wa ʾl-Waʿīd; [in Suppl.] al-Aṣamm; Ḥāl; Muḥammad Ibn Shabīb

Shiite → Shiites

Wahhābī Ibn ʿAbd al-Wahhāb; Ibn Ghannām

Indo-Muslim ʿAbd al-ʿAzīz al-Dihlawī; ʿAbd al-Ḳādir Dihlawī; Ashraf ʿAlī; Baḥr al-ʿUlūm; al-Dihlawī, Shāh Walī Allāh; al-ʿImrānī; ʿIwaḍ Wadjīh; [in Suppl.] ʿAbd Allāh Sulṭānpūrī; Farangī Maḥall

see also Hind.v.b; al-Maʿbarī; Mappila; Ṣulḥ-i kull; Tablīghī Djamāʿat; ʿUlamāʾ.4

Christian Ibn Zurʿa; Yaḥyā b. ʿAdī; Yaḥyā al-Naḥwī

and → Christianity.denominations

Jewish Ibn Maymūn; Saʿadyā Ben Yōsēf

19th and 20th centuries Muḥammad ʿAbduh; Muḥammad Abū Zayd

see also Sunna.3

TIME Abad; Dahr; Ḳidam; **Zamān**
see also Ibn al-Sāʿātī
calendars Djalālī; Hidjra; Nasīʾ; **Taʾrīkh**.I; [in Suppl.] Ilāhī Era
see also Nawrūz; Rabīʿ b. Zayd; Sulaymān al-Mahrī; Taḳwīm; ʿUmar Khayyām
day and night ʿAṣr; ʿAtama; **Layl and Nahār**; al-Shafaḳ; **Yawm**
see also Taʾrīkh.I.1.iii; Zīdj
days of the week Djumʿa; Sabt
months
see also al-Ḳamar
Islamic al-Muḥarram; Rabīʿ; Radjab; Ramaḍān; Ṣafar; Shaʿbān; Shawwāl
see also Taʾrīkh.I.1.iii
Syrian Nīsān; Tammūz; Tishrīn
Turkish Odjaḳ
timekeeping Anwāʾ; al-Ḳamar; Mīḳāt; Mizwala; Sāʿa.1
see also Asṭurlāb; Ayyām al-ʿAdjūz; Hilāl.i; Rubʿ; Taʿdīl al-Zamān

TOGO Kabou; Kubafolo; **Togo**

TRANSPORT **Naḳl** (*and* [in Suppl.])
and → ANIMALS.CAMELS *and* EQUINES; HOSTELRY; NAVIGATION
caravans Azalay; **Kārwān**; Maḥmal; ʿUḳayl.2; [in Suppl.] Djammāl
see also Anadolu.iii.5; Darb al-Arbaʿīn; Khān
mountain passes Bāb al-Lān; Bībān; Dār-i Āhanīn; Deve Boynu; Khaybar
see also Chitral
postal service **Barīd**; Fuyūdj; Ḥamām; Posta; Raḳḳāṣ; Ulaḳ; Yām
see also Anadolu.iii.5
stamps **Posta**
railways Ḥidjāz Railway; **Sikkat al-Ḥadīd**
see also Anadolu.iii.5; al-Ḳāhira (442a); Khurramshahr; Zāhidān
roads **Shāriʿ**; [in Suppl.] **Ṭarīḳ**
wheeled vehicles ʿAdjala; Araba

TRAVEL **Riḥla**; Safar
and → LITERATURE.TRAVEL-LITERATURE
supplies Mifrash
and → NOMADISM

TREASURY **Bayt al-Māl**; Khazīne; Makhzān
and → ADMINISTRATION.FINANCIAL

TREATIES Baḳṭ; Küčük Ḳaynardja; Mandates; Mondros; **Muʿāhada**; Türkmen Čay (i); Zsitvatorok
see also Dār al-ʿAhd; Ḥilf al-Fuḍūl; Mīthāḳ-i Millī; Tudmīr
tributes Baḳṭ; Parias; [in Suppl.] Khuwwa
and → TAXATION

TRIBES ʿĀʾila; ʿAshīra; Ḥayy; **Ḳabīla**; Sayyid
see also ʿAṣabiyya; Ḥilf; Khaṭīb; Sharīf.(1); Shaykh; [in Suppl.] Bisāṭ.iii; Iskān; al-Ridda; Sürgün; *and* → CUSTOM.TRIBAL CUSTOMS; LAW.CUSTOMARY LAW; NOMADISM; *and the section Population under entries of countries*
Afghanistan, India and Pakistan Abdālī; Afrīdī; Bhaṭṭi; Čahar Aymaḳ; Dāwūdpōtrās; Djāt;

Durrānī; Gakkhaŕ; Gandāpur; Ghalzay; Güdjar; Khaṭak; Khokars; Lambadis; Mahsūd; Mē'ō; Mohmand; Mullagorī; Sammā; Sumerā; Wazīrīs; Yūsufzay; [in Suppl.] Gurčānī; Kākaṛ; Sulaymān Khēl

see also Afghān.i; Afghānistān.ii

Africa ʿAbābda; ʿĀmir; Antemuru; Bedja; Beleyn; Bishārīn; Danķalī; Djaʿaliyyūn; Kunta; Makua; Māryā; Mazrūʿī; Shāyķiyya; Zaghāwa

see also Diglal; Fulbe; al-Manāṣir; Mande; *for North Africa, see the section Egypt and North Africa below*

Arabian peninsula

ancient ʿAbd al-Ķays; al-Abnā'.I; ʿĀd; ʿAkk; ʿĀmila; ʿĀmir b. Ṣaʿṣaʿa; al-Aws; Azd; Badjīla; Bāhila; Bakr b. Wā'il; Ḍabba; Djadhīma b. ʿĀmir; Djurhum; Fazāra; Ghanī b. Aʿṣur; Ghassān; Ghaṭafān; Ghifār; Hamdān; Ḥanīfa b. Ludjaym; Ḥanẓala b. Mālik; Ḥārith b. Kaʿb; Hawāzin; Hilāl; ʿIdjl; Iram; Iyād; Kalb b. Wabara; al-Ķayn; Khafādja; Khathʿam; al-Khazradj; Kilāb b. Rabīʿa; Kināna; Kinda; Khuzāʿa; Ķuraysh; Ķushayr; Laʿaķat al-Dam; Liḥyān.2; Maʿadd; Maʿāfir; Māzin; Muḥārib; Murād; Murra; Naḍīr; Nawfal; Riyām; Saʿd b. Bakr; Saʿd b. Zayd Manāt al-Fizr; Salīḥ; Salūl; Shaybān; Sulaym; Taghlib b. Wā'il; Tamīm b. Murr; Tanūkh; Ṭasm; Taym Allāh; Taym b. Murra; Thaķīf; Thamūd; ʿUdhra; ʿUķayl.1; Yāfiʿ; Yarbūʿ; Yās; [in Suppl.] Kathīrī; Ķuʿayṭī

see also Asad (Banū); Ḥabash (Aḥābīsh); al-Ḥidjāz; Makhzūm; Mustaʿriba; Mutaʿarriba; Nizār b. Maʿadd; Numayr; Rabīʿa (and Muḍar); Shayba; Thaʿlaba; al-Uķayṣir; Wabār; Wufūd; Zarķā' al-Yamāma; Zuhayr b. Djanāb; Zuhra; [in Suppl.] Aʿyāṣ; al-Ridda

present-day ʿAbdalī; ʿAķrabī; ʿAwāmir; ʿAwāzim; Banyar; al-Baṭāḥira; Buķūm; al-Dawāsir; al-Dhī'āb; Djaʿda (ʿĀmir); al-Djanaba; al-Durūʿ; Ghāmid; Hādjir; Ḥakam b. Saʿd; Hamdān; al-Ḥarāsīs; Ḥarb; Ḥāshid wa-Bakīl; Ḥassān, Bā; Ḥawshabī; Hinā; al-Ḥubūs; Hudhayl; Ḥudjriyya; Hutaym; al-Ḥuwayṭāt; al-ʿIfār; Ķaḥṭān; Khālid; (Banū) Kharūṣ; Khawlān; Ķudāʿa; Madhḥidj; Mahra; al-Manāṣir; Mazrūʿī; Murra; Muṭayr; Muzayna; Nabhān; Ruwala; Shammar; Shararāt; Subayʿ; Ṣubayḥī; Sudayri; Ṣulayb; Thaķīf; ʿUtayba; Wahība; Yām

see also (Djazīrat) al-ʿArab.vi; Badw; al-Ḥidjāz; Shāwiya.2; ʿUtūb; al-Yaman.4

Central Asia, Mongolia and points further north Čāwdors; Dūghlāt; Emreli; Gagauz; Göklän; Ķarluķ; Ķungrāt; Mangit; Mongols; Özbeg; Pečenegs; Salur; Sulduz; Tatar; Tobol; Toghuzghuz; Türkmen; Turks.I.2; Yaghma; [in Suppl.] Sariķ; Yomut

see also Ghuzz; Īlāt; Ķāyi; Khaladj; Ķishlaķ; Yaylaķ

Egypt and North Africa ʿAbābda; Ahaggar; al-Butr; Djazūla; Dukkāla; Ifoghas; Khulṭ; Kūmiya; al-Maʿķil; Mandīl; Riyāḥ; Zmāla

see also Khumayr; *and* → BERBERS

Fertile Crescent

ancient Asad; Bahrā'; Djarrāḥids; Djudhām; Lakhm; Muhannā; al-Muntafiķ.1; Taghlib b. Wā'il; Ṭayyi'; Waththāb b. Sābiķ al-Numayrī; [in Suppl.] al-Namir b. Ķāsiṭ

see also Tanūkh.2; al-Uķayṣir; Unayf

present-day ʿAnaza; Asad (Banū); Bādjalān; Bilbās; Ḍafīr; Djāf; Djubūr; Dulaym; Hamawand; al-Ḥuwayṭāt; Kurds.iv.A; Lām; al-Manāṣir; al-Muntafiķ.2; Ṣakhr; Shammar

see also al-Baṭīḥa; Shāwiya.2

Iran Bāzūkiyyūn; Bilbās; Djāf; Eymir.2 *and* 3; (Banū) Kaʿb; Ķarā Gözlū; Kurds.iv.A; Lak; Lām; Shāhsewan; Shakāk; Shaķāķī; Sindjābī

see also Daylam; Dulafids; Fīrūzānids; Göklän; Īlāt; Shūlistān

Turkey Afshār; Bayat; Bayindir; Begdili; Čepni; Döger; Eymir.1; Ķādjār; Ķāyi; Takhtadji; Takkalū; Ṭorghud; Yörük; [in Suppl.] Čawdor *see also* Shakāk; Shaḳāḳī; Tamgha

TUNISIA Baladiyya.3; Djāmiʿa; Djamʿiyya.iv; Djarīda.i.B; Dustūr.i; Ḥizb.i; Ḥukūma.iv; Istiḳlāl; al-Khaldūniyya; Maʿārif.2.A; Madjlis.4.A.xix; Salafiyya.1(a); **Tunisia;** [in Suppl.] Demography.IV; Maḥkama.4.xii
see also Fallāḳ; Ḥimāya.ii; Khalīfa b. ʿAskar; Ṣafar; [in Suppl.] Inzāl; *and* → BERBERS; DYNASTIES.SPAIN AND NORTH AFRICA
historians of Ibn Abī Dīnār; Ibn Abi ʾl-Ḍiyāf; Ibn ʿIdhārī; [in Suppl.] ʿAbd al-Wahhāb
see also Ibn al-Raḳīḳ; al-Tidjānī, Abū Muḥammad; *and* → DYNASTIES.SPAIN AND NORTH AFRICA
institutions
educational al-Ṣādiḳiyya; Zaytūna; [in Suppl.] Institut des hautes études de Tunis
see also [in Suppl.] ʿAbd al-Wahhāb; Ḳābādū
musical al-Rashīdiyya
press al-Rāʾid al-Tūnusī; **Ṣiḥāfa**.2.(v)
language ʿArabiyya.A.iii.3; Tunisia.IV
literature Malḥūn; Tunisia.V; *and* → LITERATURE
belletrists Saʿīd Abū Bakr; al-Shābbī; al-Tūnisī, Maḥmūd Bayram; al-Tūnisī, Muḥammad; al-Warghī
nationalists al-Thaʿālibī, ʿAbd al-ʿAzīz; [in Suppl.] al-Ḥaddād, al-Ṭāhir
Ottoman period (1574-1881) Aḥmad Bey; al-Ḥusayn (b. ʿAlī); Ḥusaynids; Khayr al-Dīn Pasha; Muḥammad Bayram al-Khāmis; Muḥammad Bey; Muḥammad al-Ṣādiḳ Bey; Muṣṭafā Khaznadār; Tunisia.II.c; [in Suppl.] Ibn Ghidhāhum
physical geography Tunisia.I.a
pre-Ottoman period ʿAbd al-Raḥmān al-Fihrī; Aghlabids; Ḥafṣids; Ḥassān b. al-Nuʿmān al-Ghassānī; (Banū) Khurāsān; Tunisia.II.b
and → BERBERS; DYNASTIES.SPAIN AND NORTH AFRICA
toponyms
ancient al-ʿAbbāsiyya; Ḥaydarān; Ḳalʿat Banī Ḥammād; Manzil Bashshū; Raḳḳāda; Ṣabra (al-Manṣūriyya); Subayṭila
present-day
districts Djarīd
islands Djarba; Ḳarḳana
regions Djazīrat Sharīk; Ḳasṭīliya.2; Nafzāwa; Sāḥil.1
towns Bādja; Banzart; Ḥalḳ al-Wādī; Ḳābis; al-Kāf; Ḳafsa; Ḳallala; al-Ḳayrawān; al-Mahdiyya; Monastir; Nafṭa; Safāḳus; Sūsa; Ṭabarḳa; Takrūna; Tūnis; Tūzar; Üsküdār

TURKEY Anadolu; Armīniya; Istanbul; Ḳarā Deniz; **Turks**.I.5
see also Libās.iv; *and* → OTTOMAN EMPIRE
architecture → ARCHITECTURE.REGIONS
dynasties → DYNASTIES.ANATOLIA AND THE TURKS; OTTOMAN EMPIRE
language → LANGUAGES.TURKIC
literature → LITERATURE
modern period (1920-) Baladiyya.1; Demokrat Parti; Djāmiʿa; Djarīda.iii; Djümhūriyyet Khalḳ Fîrḳasî; Dustūr.ii; Ḥizb.ii; Ishtirākiyya; Khalḳevi; Köy Enstitüleri; Kurds.iii.C; Madjlis.4.A.ii; Mīthāḳ-i Millī; Shuyūʿiyya.3; Teraḳḳī-perver Djumhūriyyet Fîrḳasî; Turks.I.5; [in Suppl.] Demography.III; Niẓām ʿAskarī.3; Ṣiḥāfa.5
see also Djamʿiyya.ii; Iskandarūn; Iṣlāḥ.iii; Ittiḥād we Teraḳḳī Djemʿiyyeti; Karakol Djemʿîyyetî; Ḳawmiyya.iv; Kemāl; Kirkūk; Maʿārif.1.i; Māliyye; Nurculuk; Yüzellilikler; *and* → LITERATURE; PRESS

educators [in Suppl.] Ismāʿīl Ḥakkī Balṭadjîoghlu; Tonguç
religious leaders Nursî
statesmen/women Atatürk; Çakmak; Ḥusayn Djāhid; Ileri, Djelāl Nūrī; Kāẓim Karabekir; Khālide Edīb; Köprülü (Mehmed Fuad); Meḥmed ʿĀkif; Menderes; Okyar; Orbay, Ḥüseyin Raʾūf; Shems al-Dīn Günaltay; Sheref, ʿAbd al-Raḥmān; Yeğana, ʿAlī Münīf; Yücel, Ḥasan ʿAlī; [in Suppl.] Adîvar; Aghaoghlu; Atay; Esendal; İsmet İnönü; Özal
see also Čerkes Edhem; Gökalp, Ziya; Hîsar; *and* → Turkey.ottoman period.young turks

mysticism → Mysticism.mystics; Sainthood.saints

Ottoman period (1342-1924) Ḥizb.ii; Istanbul; Ittiḥād-i Muḥammedī Djemʿiyyeti; Ittiḥād we Teraḳḳī Djemʿiyyeti; Maʿārif.1.i; Madjlis.4.A.i; Madjlis al-Shūrā; Maṭbakh.2; **ʿOthmānlî**; Türk Odjaghî; Yeñi ʿOthmānlîlar; [in Suppl.] Niẓām ʿAskarī.3
see also Aywaz.1; Derebey; Djamʿiyya.ii; Khalīfa.i.E; [in Suppl.] Demography.II; Djalālī; *and* → Ottoman Empire
Young Ottomans and Young Turks **Yeñi ʿOthmānlîlar**
see also Djamʿiyya; Djewdet; Dustūr.ii; Fāḍil Pasha; Ḥukūma.i; Ḥurriyya.ii; Ittiḥād we Teraḳḳī Djemʿiyyeti
individuals Djawīd; Djemāl Pasha; Enwer Pasha; (Tunalî) Ḥilmī; Isḥāḳ Sükutī; Kemāl, Meḥmed Nāmîḳ; Mīzāndjî Meḥmed Murād; Niyāzī Bey; Ṣabāḥ al-Dīn; Shükrü Bey; Suʿāwī, ʿAlī; Ṭalʿat Bey; Yeğana, ʿAlī Münīf; Yūsuf Aḳčura; Żiyā Pasha

physical geography
mountains Aghrî Dagh; Ala Dagh; Aladja Dagh; Beshparmaḳ; Bingöl Dagh; Deve Boynu; Elma Daghî; Erdjiyas Daghî; Gāwur Daghlarî; Toros Dağları; Ulu Dāgh
see also Ṭūr ʿAbdīn
waters Boghaz-iči; Čanaḳ-ḳalʿe Boghazî; Čoruh.I; Djayḥān; Gediz Čayî; Göksu; Ḳîzîl-irmāḳ; Lamas-ṣū; Marmara Deñizi; Menderes; al-Rass; Sakarya; Sayḥān; Tuz Gölü; Wān.1; Yeshil İrmak

population Yörük; Zāzā; Zeybek; [in Suppl.] Demography.II
see also Muhādjir.2; Türkmen.3

pre-Islamic period → Pre-Islam; Turkey.toponyms

pre-Ottoman period Mengüček
see also Kitābāt.7; *and* → Dynasties.anatolia and the turks; Turkey.toponyms

toponyms
ancient ʿAmmūriya; Ānī; Arzan; ʿAyn Zarba; Baghrās; Bālis; Beshike; Būḳa; al-Djazīra; Dulūk; Dunaysir; Ḥarrān; Lādhiḳ.1; Shabakhtān; Sīs; Sulṭān Öñü; Ṭorghud Eli
see also Diyār Bakr; Shimshāṭ
present-day
districts Shamdīnān; Terdjān; Yalowa
islands Bozdja-ada; Imroz
provinces Aghrî; Čoruh; Diyar Bakr; Hakkārī; Ičil; Kars; Ḳasṭamūnī; Khanzīt; Ḳodja Eli; Mūsh; Newshehir; Tundjeli
regions al-ʿAmḳ; Cilicia; Dersim; Diyār Muḍar; Djānīk; Menteshe-eli; Teke-eli; Ṭūr ʿAbdīn; Tutak
towns Ada Pāzārî; Adana; Adiyaman; Afyūn Ḳara Ḥiṣār; Aḳ Ḥiṣār.1 *and* 2; Aḳ Shehr; Akhlāṭ; Ala Shehir; Alanya; Altîntash; Amasya; Anadolu; Anamur; Anḳara; Anṭākiya; Antalya; ʿArabkīr; Ardahān; Artvin; Aya Solūk; Āyās; Aydîn; ʿAynṭāb; Aywalîk; Babaeski; Bālā; Bālā Ḥiṣār; Balāṭ; Bālikesrī; Bālṭa Līmānī; Bandirma; Bāyazīd; Bāybūrd; Baylān; Bergama; Besni; Beyshehir; Bidlīs; Bīgha; Biledjik; Bingöl; Bīredjik; Birge; Bodrum; Bolu; Bolwadin; Bozanti; Burdur; Bursa; Čankîrî; Čatāldja; Česhme; Čölemerik; Čorlu; Čorum; Deñizli; Diwrīgī;

Diyār Bakr; Edirne; Edremit; Eğin; Eğridir; Elbistan; Elmalî; Enos; Ereğli; Ergani; Ermenak; Erzindjan; Erzurum; Eskishehir; Gebze; Gelibolu; Gemlik; Giresun; Göksun; Gördes; Gümüsh-khāne; al-Hārūniyya; Ḥiṣn Kayfā; Iskandarūn; Isparta; Istanbul (*and* [in Suppl.]); Iznīḳ; Ḳarā Ḥiṣār; Ḳaradja Ḥiṣār; Kars; Ḳasṭamūnī; Ḳayṣariyya; Kemākh; Killiz; Ḳîrḳ Kilise; Kirmāstī; Ḳîrshehir; Ḳoč Ḥiṣār; Konya; Köprü Ḥiṣārî; Ḳoylu Ḥiṣār; Ḳōzān; Ḳūla; Kutāhiya; Lādhiḳ.2 *and* 3; Lāranda; Lüleburgaz; Maghnisa; Malaṭya; Malāzgird.1; Malkara; Maʿmūrat al-ʿAzīz; Marʿash; Mārdīn; al-Maṣṣīṣa; Mayyāfāriḳīn; Menemen; Mersin; Merzifūn; Mīlās; Mudanya; Mughla; Mūsh; Naṣībīn; Newshehir; Nīgde; Nīksār; Nizīb; Orāmār; ʿOthmāndjîḳ; Payās; Rize; al-Ruhā; Ṣabandja; Ṣāmsūn; Ṣart; Sarūdj; Siʿird; Silifke; Simaw; Sīnūb; Sīwās; Siwri Ḥiṣār; Sögüd; Sumaysāṭ; al-Suwaydiyya; Tall Bāshir; Ṭarabzun; Ṭarsūs; Tekirdagh; Tīre; Tirebolu; Toḳat; Tundjeli; ʿUshāḳ; Wān.2; Wezīr Köprü; Wize; Yalowa; Yeñi Shehir; Yeshilköy; Yozgat; Zaytūn; Zindjirli; Zonguldak; [in Suppl.] Ghalaṭa; Izmīd; Izmīr; Kaysūm
see also Fener; Ḳarasî.2; (al-)Ḳusṭanṭīniyya

U

Umayyads → Caliphate; Dynasties.spain and north africa

United Arab Emirates al-Ḳawāsim; Madjlis.4.A.xii; Maḥkama.4.ix; Ṣiḥāfa.1.(x); [in Suppl.] **al-Imārāt al-ʿArabiyya al-Muttaḥida**
population Mazrūʿī
see also Yās; *and* → Tribes.arabian peninsula
toponyms Abū Ẓabī; al-Djiwāʾ; Dubayy; al-Fudjayra; Raʾs al-Khayma; al-Shāriḳa; Ṣīr Banī Yās; Umm al-Ḳaywayn; al-Ẓafra; [in Suppl.] ʿAdjmān
see also (Djazīrat) al-ʿArab; al-Khaṭṭ; Ṭunb; al-ʿUdayd

Urbanism → Architecture.urban; Geography.urban; Sedentarism
for city planning, see [in Suppl.] Madīna; *for rowdy urban groups, see* Zuʿʿār; *for urban militia, see* Aḥdāth

(former) USSR → Caucasus; Central Asia.former soviet union; Communism; Europe.eastern europe; Siberia

V

Virtues and Vices
virtues ʿAdl; Ḍayf; Futuwwa; Ḥasab wa-Nasab; Ḥilm; ʿIrḍ; Murūʾa; Ṣabr; Ẓarīf; [in Suppl.] Karam
see also Sharaf; Sharīf *and* → Ethics; Humour
vices Bukhl
see also Kaffāra; *and* → Adultery; Drugs.narcotics; Gambling; Law.penal law; Obscenity; Wine

W

Weights and Measurements Aghač; Arpa; Dhirāʿ; Dirham.1; Farsakh; Ḥabba; Iṣbaʿ; Istār;

Makāyil; Marḥala; Miḳyās; **Misāḥa**; al-Mīzān; Ṣāʿ; Sanadjāt; Tōlā; Tūmān.2; **Wazn**.1; [in Suppl.] Gaz
see also al-Ḳarasṭūn

WINE **Khamr**; Sāḳī
see also Karm
bacchic poetry **Khamriyya**
Arabic Abū Nuwās; Abū Miḥdjan; Abu 'l-Shīṣ; ʿAdī b. Zayd; Ḥāritha b. Badr al-Ghudānī; (al-)Ḥusayn b. al-Ḍaḥḥāk; Ibn al-ʿAfīf al-Tilimsānī; Ibn Sayḥān; Tamīm b. al-Muʿizz li-Dīn Allāh; Tamīm b. al-Muʿizz; al-Walīd.2
see also al-Babbaghāʾ; Ibn al-Fāriḍ; Ibn Harma; al-Nawādjī; Yamūt b. al-Muzarraʿ
Turkish Rewānī; Riyāḍī
boon companions Ibn Ḥamdūn; al-Ḳāshānī; Khālid b. Yazīd al-Kātib al-Tamīmī
see also Abu 'l-Shīṣ; ʿAlī b. al-Djahm

WOMEN ʿAbd; Ḥarīm; Ḥayḍ; Ḥidjāb.I; ʿIdda; Istibrāʾ; Khafḍ; **al-Marʾa**; Nikāḥ; Siḥāḳ; [in Suppl.] Bighāʾ
see also ʿArūs Resmi; Bashmaḳlîḳ; Khayr; Khiḍr-ilyās; Lithām; Tunisia.VI; ʿUrf.2.II; Zanāna; *and* → DIVORCE; LIFE STAGES.CHILDBIRTH *and* CHILDHOOD; MARRIAGE
and beauty al-Washm
and → COSMETICS
and literature al-Marʾa.1
see also Ḳiṣṣa; Shahrazād
Arabic authors al-Bāʿūni.6; Ḥafṣa bint al-Ḥādjdj; ʿInān; al-Khansāʾ; Laylā al-Akhyaliyya; Mayy Ziyāda; ʿUlayya; Wallāda; al-Yāzidjī.4; [in Suppl.] Faḍl al-Shāʿira
see also ʿAbbāsa; ʿĀtika; Khunātha; Ḳiṣṣa.2; Shilb; Uḳṣūṣa
Persian authors Ḳurrat al-ʿAyn; Mahsatī; Parwīn Iʿtiṣāmī
see also Gulbadan Bēgam; Makhfī
Turkish authors Fiṭnat; Khālide Edīb; Laylā Khānîm (2x); Mihrī Khātūn
see also Ḳiṣṣa.3(b)
and religion Zār
mystics ʿĀʾisha al-Mannūbiyya; Djahānārā Bēgam; Nafīsa; Rābiʿa al-ʿAdawiyya al-Ḳaysiyya
see also Walī.5
concubinage ʿAbd.3.f; Khaṣṣekī; Umm al-Walad
emancipation Ḳāsim Amīn; Malak Ḥifnī Nāṣif; Saʿīd Abū Bakr; Salāma Mūsā; Ṭalāḳ.II.3; [in Suppl.] al-Ḥaddād, al-Ṭāhir
see also Ḥidjāb; Ileri, Djelāl Nūrī; al-Marʾa; Wuthūḳ al-Dawla; al-Zahāwī, Djamīl Ṣidḳī; [in Suppl.] Ashraf al-Dīn Gīlānī
influential women
Arabic ʿĀʾisha bint Ṭalḥa; Asmāʾ; Barīra; Būrān; Hind bint ʿUtba; al-Khayzurān bint ʿAṭāʾ al-Djurashiyya; Khunātha; Shadjar al-Durr; Sitt al-Mulk; Ṣubḥ; Sukayna bt. al-Ḥusayn; Zubayda bt. Djaʿfar; [in Suppl.] Asmāʾ
see also al-Maʿāfirī; Zumurrud Khātūn; *and* → MUḤAMMAD, THE PROPHET.FAMILY OF.DAUGHTERS *and* WIVES
Indo-Muslim Nūr Djahān; Samrū
Mongolian Baghdād Khātūn; Khān-zāda Bēgum; Töregene Khātūn
Ottoman ʿĀdila Khātūn; Khurrem; Kösem Wālide; Mihr-i Māh Sulṭān; Nīlūfer Khātūn; Nūr Bānū; Ṣafiyye Wālide Sulṭān; Shāh Sulṭān; Shebṣefa Ḳadîn; Ṭurkhān Sulṭān
see also Wālide Sulṭān
Turkish Terken Khātūn; Zumurrud Khātūn

legendary women al-Basūs; Bilḳīs; Hind bint al-Khuss
see also Āsiya; Zarḳāʾ al-Yamāma
musicians/singers ʿAzza al-Maylāʾ; Djamīla; Ḥabāba; Rāʾiḳa; Sallāma al-Zarḳāʾ; Shāriya; Siti Binti Saad; ʿUlayya; Umm Kulthūm; [in Suppl.] Badhl al-Kubrā; al-Djarādatān[i]; Faḍl al-Shāʿira; Ḥabba Khātūn
see also ʿĀlima; Ḳayna; Ṭaḳṭūḳa
mystics → *the section And Religion above*

WRITING **Khaṭṭ** (*and* [in Suppl.])
see also Ibn Muḳla; Kitābāt; *and* → ART.CALLIGRAPHY; EPIGRAPHY
manuscripts and books Daftar; Ḥāshiya; **Kitāb**; Muḳābala.2; **Nuskha**; Tadhkira; Taʿlīḳ; Taṣḥīf; Taṣnīf; Tazwīr; ʿUnwān; Warrāḳ; [in Suppl.] Abbreviations
see also Ḳaṭʿ; Maktaba
blockprinting **Ṭarsh**
bookbinding Īlkhāns; Kitāb; Nuskha; ʿOthmānli.VII.c; [in Suppl.] Mamlūks.iii.b.D.iii
booktitles **ʿUnwān**.2(=3); Zubda
materials Djild; Kāghad; Ḳalam; Khātam; Ḳirṭās; Midād; Papyrus; Raḳḳ; [in Suppl.] Dawāt
see also ʿAfṣ; Afsantīn; Diplomatic; Īlkhāns; Maʿdin.4
scripts Khaṭṭ; Siyāḳat; Tawḳīʿ.2; Tifinagh; Tughra.2(d)
see also Nuskha; Swahili; Taʿlīḳ; Warrāḳ; Zabūr; *and* → ART.CALLIGRAPHY; EPIGRAPHY
for Persian scripts, see [in Suppl.] Iran.iii.f.ii.V
for non-Arabic, non-Latin scripts, see [in Suppl.] Turks.II.(vi)

Y

YEMEN Djarīda.i.A; Dustūr.viii; Madjlis.4.A.xiv *and* xv; Maḥkama.4.viii; Ṣiḥāfa.1.(xiv); Yaḥyā b. Muḥammad; **al-Yaman**; [in Suppl.] Niẓām ʿAskarī.1.(e)
see also ʿAsīr; Ismāʿīliyya; Mahrī; Makramids; Ṭāghūt.2; ʿUrf.2.I.A.2; [in Suppl.] Abū Mismār; *and* → DYNASTIES.ARABIAN PENINSULA
architecture → ARCHITECTURE.REGIONS
before Islam al-Abnāʾ.II; Abraha; Dhū Nuwās; (Djazīrat) al-ʿArab; Ḥabashat; Ḥaḍramawt; Ḳatabān; Ḳayl; Mārib; al-Mathāmina; Sabaʾ; al-Sawdāʾ; Wahriz; Yazan; [in Suppl.] Ḥaḍramawt
see also [in Suppl.] Bādhām
British protectorate of Ḥaḍramawt period (1839-1967) ʿAdan; Wāḥidī
see also [in Suppl.] Ḥaḍramawt.ii.1; Kathīrī; Ḳuʿayṭī
dynasties Hamdānids; Mahdids; Rasūlids; Ṣulayḥids; Ṭāhirids.3; Yuʿfirids; Zaydiyya.3; Ziyādids; Zurayʿids; [in Suppl.] Kathīrī; Ḳuʿayṭī
see also Rassids; *and* → DYNASTIES.ARABIAN PENINSULA
historians of al-Djanadī; al-Khazradjī; al-Mawzaʿī; al-Nahrawālī; al-Rāzī, Aḥmad b. ʿAbd Allāh; al-Sharīf Abū Muḥammad Idrīs; al-Shillī; ʿUmāra al-Yamanī
see also Ibn al-Mudjāwir
language al-Yaman.5; [in Suppl.] Ḥaḍramawt.iii
and → LANGUAGES.AFRO-ASIATIC.ARABIC *and* SOUTH ARABIAN
Ottoman periods (1517-1635 and 1872-1918) Maḥmūd Pasha; al-Muṭahhar; Özdemir Pasha; Riḍwān Pasha; [in Suppl.] Yemenli Ḥasan Pasha
see also Baladiyya.2; Khādim Süleymān Pasha
physical geography
mountains Ḥaḍūr; Ḥarāz; Ḥiṣn al-Ghurāb; al-Sarāt; Shahāra; Shibām.4; [in Suppl.] al-Sharaf

see also al-Yaman.2
wadis Barhūt; al-Khārid; al-Saḥūl; Turaba.1
population ʿAbdalī; ʿAḳrabī; Banyar; Hamdān; Ḥāshid wa-Bakīl; Ḥawshabī; Ḥudjriyya; Ḳaḥṭān; Khawlān; Madhhidj; Mahra; Yāfiʿ
see also Yām; al-Yaman.4; Yazan; *and* → TRIBES.ARABIAN PENINSULA
toponyms
ancient al-ʿĀra; Shabwa; Ṣirwāḥ; Ẓafār
see also Nadjrān
present-day
districts Abyan; ʿAlawī; ʿĀmiri; ʿAwdhalī; Dathīna; Faḍlī; Ḥarāz; Ḥarīb; al-Ḥayma; Ḥudjriyya
islands Ḳamarān; Mayyūn; Suḳuṭra
regions ʿAwlaḳī; Ḥaḍramawt; Laḥdj; al-Shiḥr; Tihāma; [in Suppl.] Ḥaḍramawt.ii
towns ʿAdan; ʿAthr; Bayt al-Faḳīh; Dhamār; Ghalāfiḳa; Ḥabbān; Hadjarayn; Ḥāmī; Ḥawra; al-Ḥawṭa; al-Ḥudayda; Ibb; ʿIrḳa; Ḳaʿṭaba; Kawkabān; Ḳishn; Laḥdj; al-Luḥayya; Mārib; al-Mukallā; al-Mukhā; Rayda; Ṣaʿda; al-Saḥūl; Ṣanʿāʾ; Sayʾūn; Shahāra; al-Shaykh Saʿīd; Shibām; al-Shiḥr; Taʿizz; Tarīm; al-Ṭawīla; Thulā; Zabīd; Ẓafār; [in Suppl.] ʿĪnāt
see also (Djazīrat) al-ʿArab

(former) YUGOSLAVIA Džabić; Khosrew Beg; Muslimūn.1.B.6; Pomaks; Riḍwān Begović; **Yugoslavia**; [in Suppl.] Handžić; Malḳoč-oghulları̊
see also ʿÖmer Efendi; Ṭopal ʿOthmān Pasha.2
literature → LITERATURE.IN OTHER LANGUAGES
toponyms
provinces [in Suppl.] Dalmatia
regions Yeñi Bāzār.1
republics Bosna; Ḳaradagh; Ḳoṣowa; Māḳadūnyā; Ṣı̊rb
towns Aḳ Ḥiṣār.3; Aladja Ḥiṣār; Banjaluka; Belgrade; Eszék; Ishtib; Ḳarlofča; Livno; Manāṣtı̊r; Mostar; Nish; Okhrī; Pasarofča; Pirlepe; Prishtina; Prizren; Raghūsa; Sarajevo; Sisḳa; Travnik; Üsküb; Waradīn; Yeñi Bāzār.2; [in Suppl.] Semendire
see also Zenta

Z

ZAIRE Katanga; Kisangani

ZANZIBAR → TANZANIA

ZOOLOGY **Ḥayawān**.7
and → ANIMALS
writers on al-Damīrī; al-Marwazī, Sharaf al-Zamān
see also al-Djāḥiẓ

ZOROASTRIANS Gabr; Iran.vi; **Madjūs**; Mōbadh; Zamzama
see also Bihʾāfrīd b. Farwardīn; Ghazal.ii; Gudjarāt.a; Pārsīs; Pūr-i Dāwūd; Sarwistān; Shīz; al-Ṣughd; Sunbādh; Taʾrīkh.I.1.vii; Ustādhsīs; Yazd.1; Zamzam; Zindīḳ
dynasties Maṣmughān
gods Bahrām

THE ENCYCLOPAEDIA OF ISLAM

NEW EDITION

INDEX VOLUME

FASCICULE 2

GLOSSARY AND INDEX OF TERMS

TABLE OF CONTENTS

LIST OF ABBREVIATIONS

A	Arabic	Ott	Ottoman
Akk	Akkadian	P	Persian
Alg	Algerian Arabic	Pah	Pahlavi
Alt	Altaic languages	Pash	Pashto
Ar	Aramaic	Ph	Phoenician
Arm	Armenian	Por	Portuguese
Ass	Assyrian	Pu	Punjabi
B	Berber	Rus	Russian
Bed	Bedouin	San	Sanskrit
C	Coptic	Sem	Semitic languages
Cau	Caucasian	Serb	Serbo-Croatian
Ch	Chinese	Sic	Sicilian Arabic
Dem	Demotic	Sin	Sindhi
Egy	Egyptian Arabic	Sl	Slavic
Eng	English	Sp	Spanish
Eth	Ethiopic	SpA	Spanish Arabic
Fr	French	Sun	Sundalese
Ger	German	Sw	Swahili
Gk	Greek	Syr	Syriac
Goth	Gothic	T	Turkish
H	Hindi	Taj	Tajiki
Hau	Hausa	Tun	Tunisian Arabic
Heb	Hebrew	U	Urdu
Hun	Hungarian	Uy	Uyghur
Ind	Indonesian	Yem	Yemeni Arabic
IndP	Indo-Persian		
Ir	Iraqi Arabic	anc.	ancient
It	Italian	ant.	antonym
J	Javanese	dim.	diminutive
K	Kurdish	fem.	feminine
Kash	Kashmiri	f. / ff.	and following page(s)
Kaz	Kazakh	g	gram
L	Latin	lit.	literally
Leb	Lebanese Arabic	pl.	plural
Mal	Malay	pop.	popular
MidP	Middle Persian	s.	singular
Mon	Mongolian	syn.	synonym
Mor	Moroccan Arabic	ult.	ultimately
N.Afr	North African	var.	variant
O.Fr	Old French	→	see

GLOSSARY AND INDEX OF TERMS

The entries in this Glossary are listed alphabetically following the Roman alphabet. The entry appears where possible under the singular form of the word, with the plural form, provided it was found in the *Encyclopaedia*, following in parentheses. If the plural form has the more important technical meaning, or the singular was not specified in the *Encyclopaedia*, the plural form will have an entry of its own.

Although the root system common to Semitic languages is for the most part ignored, some terms, such as adjectives, plurals, adjectival plurals, etc. of a word, will be included under that word's entry, e.g. *ʿaskarī* is included under *ʿaskar*, *ʿaḳliyyāt* is included under *ʿaḳl*, etc. Where it might not be obvious to someone searching alphabetically, and for facility of use, a cross-reference in the Glossary is provided, e.g.

furūʿ → FARʿ

Entries marked in bold refer to articles in the *Encyclopaedia*. All cross-references to entries within the Glossary are given in small capitals. A term made up of more than one component, as e.g. *ahl al-ʿahd*, is generally listed under the first element; thus *ahl al-ʿahd* is found under *ahl*.

Where found in the *Encyclopaedia*, the term's etymological origin has been noted; see the List of Abbreviations on p. 139. The transcription in the Glossary follows for the most part that of the *Encyclopaedia*. Certain words such as Baghdad and sultan, which are now part and parcel of the English language, have not been transcribed, and for easy recognition, Qurʾān is written thus and not as Ḳurʾān. In words of Berber or North African origin, a schwa has been used to reproduce a neutral vowel.

The index is not comprehensive; multiple page references are given only for pages that note a significantly different definition or translation from one already listed, or for those pages that treat the term more than just in passing.

A

aʿaban (Mor) : a large outer wrap for Berber men. V 745b

āb (P) : water; and → ĀBDĀR-BĀSHĪ; ĀBSHĀR

♦ āb-anbar → MIṢNAʿA

♦ āb-i gus̲h̲t (P) : a stew on the basis of mutton stock, which seems to have become the staple of the poor in the course of the 19th century. XII 611a

aba : roughly-spun cloth. X 371b

ʿabāʾ (A), or *ʿabāʾa* : a coat, shoulder mantle, worn by both sexes in the Arab East. V 740a

ʿabāʾa → ʿABĀʾ

abad (A) : time in an absolute sense. I 2a

In philosophy, ~ or *abadiyya* is a technical term corresponding to ἀφθαρτός, meaning incorruptible, eternal *a parte post*, in opposition to AZAL or *azaliyya*. I 2a; V 95a

♦ abadī (A) : 'having no end'. I 333a

♦ abadiyya → ABAD

abʿādiyya (A, pl. *abāʿid*), or **ibʿādiyya** : uncultivated or uncultivable land in Egypt under Muḥammad ʿAlī; estates reclaimed from lands uncultivated at the time of the 1813-14 cadaster and granted on favourable terms. II 149a; XII 379a

abad̲j̲ad → ABD̲J̲ĀD

abanūs (A, P, T, < Gk) : ebony wood. I 3a

abardī → BARDĪ

ʿabāya (Alg) : a sleeveless, long overblouse for men; a sleeveless, flowing dress for women. V 745b

abayān (A) : in zoology, the prawn and the shrimp. IX 40a, where many more synonyms are given

ʿabayt̲h̲arān (A) : in botany, a type of artemisia, also called *rayḥān al-t̲h̲aʿālib* 'the foxes' basilicum'. IX 435a

ʿabbādiyya → S̲H̲AKKĀZIYYA

abbāla : camel nomads in the central Sudan belt of Africa. IX 516a

ʿabbas (Alg) : a verb signifying in Algeria 'to go among the peasants to levy contributions of grain, butter, dried fruits, etc.' in the name of Abu 'l-ʿAbbās al-Sabtī, a renowned Moroccan saint of the 12th century. VIII 692a

ʿabbāsī (P) : in numismatics, a Ṣafawid coin introduced by Shāh ʿAbbās I, the value of which was 4 S̲H̲ĀHĪ, 200 dīnārs, 50 per TŪMĀN. It remained the normal Persian denomination for most of the remainder of the dynasty. VIII 790a; IX 203b

♦ ʿabbāsiyya (Mor) : in Morocco, charitable gifts of grain, fritters, fruit, meat or fish, made to the poor in the name of Abu 'l-ʿAbbās al-Sabtī, a renowned Moroccan saint of the 12th century. VIII 692a

ʿabd (A, pl. *ʿabīd*) : a slave, in particular a male slave, a female slave being termed *ama* (pl. *imāʾ*). I 24b

In theology, ~ means 'the creature'. In the Qur'ān, the angels are also called ~. IV 82b

♦ ʿabd ḳinn (A) : a slave born in his master's house; later applied to the slave over whom one has full and complete rights of ownership. I 25a

♦ ʿabd mamlūka (A) : a purchased slave. I 25a

♦ ʿabīd al-buk̲h̲ārī (A) : descendants of the black slaves who had been imported in large numbers by the Saʿdids into Morocco. I 34b; I 47a; I 356a

♦ ʿabīd al-s̲h̲irāʾ (A) : black Sudanese slaves bought for the army under the Fāṭimids. II 858b

abda'a → ITHT̲H̲AG̲H̲ARA

abdāl (A, s. BADAL) : in mysticism, the highest rank in the ṣūfī hierarchical order of saints (syn. G̲H̲AWT̲H̲). I 69b; generally accepted as the fifth place descending from the ḲUṬB. I 94b; ascetic or pietistic persons who are regarded as intercessors and dispensers of BARAKA. VIII 498a

In the Ottoman empire, ~ was used for the dervishes in various dervish orders. I 95a; later, when the esteem enjoyed by the dervishes declined, ~ (and *budalāʾ*, s. *badīl*, both used as a singular) came to mean 'fool' in Turkish. I 95a

ābdār-bās̲h̲ī (P) : in Ṣafawid times, an official in the royal kitchen in charge of drinks. XII 609b

abd̲j̲ad (A), or *abad̲j̲ad, abū d̲j̲ad* : the first of the mnemotechnical terms into which the twenty-eight consonants of the Arabic alphabet are divided. I 97a

ābiḳ (A) : a runaway slave. I 26b

ʿabḳarī (A) : a genie of great intelligence. IX 406b

abnāʾ (A, s. IBN) : sons

As a denomination, it is applied to two tribes, viz. the descendants of Saʿd b. Zayd Manāt b. Tamīm, and the descendants born in Yaman of Persian immigrants. I 102a; X 173a; XII 115b

♦ abnāʾ al-atrāk (A) : a term sometimes used in the Mamlūk sultanate to designate the Egyptian or Syrian-born descendants of the Mamlūks. I 102a; and → AWLAD AL-NĀS
♦ abnāʾ al-daraza (A) : lit. sons of sewing, a proverbial expression current in the ʿAbbāsid period to refer to the tailors of Kūfa, who had taken part in the revolt of Zayd b. ʿAlī against the Umayyads (120-2/738-40). IV 1161a
♦ abnāʾ al-dawla (A) : a term applied in the early centuries of the ʿAbbāsid caliphate to the members of the ʿAbbāsid house, and by extension to patrons (*mawālī*, s. MAWLA) who entered its service and became adoptive members. I 102a; Khurāsānian guards and officials in the ʿAbbāsid caliphate. V 57b
♦ abnā-yi sipāhīyān (T) : a term sometimes used in formal Ottoman usage, in place of the more common *sipāhī oghlanlari̊* (→ DÖRT BÖLÜK), to denote the first of the six regiments of cavalry of the standing army. I 102a
♦ abnāʾ al-waṭan (A) : inhabitants, natives, compatriots. XI 175b
abraḳ → BARḲĀʾ
abrāmīs (A) : in zoology, the bream. VIII 1023a
ābshār (P) : in Muslim India, large water chutes, made of inclined and carved marble slabs, which intercepted the flow of water in the long channels that ran the entire length of gardens, providing the transition from one level to another. IX 175a
abū (A) : father
♦ **abū barāḳish** (A) : a name, no longer in use, given to two birds with brilliant plumage: the Franciscan or Grenadier weaver-bird, or Durra-bird (*Euplectes oryx franciscana*), and the Porphyrion or Blue Taleva/Purple Gallinule (*Porphyrio porphyrio*), better known as the Sultan-fowl. In the Ḥidjāz, ~ was used in place of *birḳish* to denote the chaffinch (*Fringilla coelebs*), also called *shurshur*. XII 19a; and → ḤIRBĀʾ
♦ abu ʾl-bayḍ → SALḲAʿ
♦ abū būz (A) : 'having a snout', a simple but functional transport vessel, driven by a motor, with a prow which resembles that of a schooner and with a square stern, built in Oman. VII 53b
♦ abū dhaḳan (A) : in zoology, the goat fish or mullet (*Mullus barbatus*). VIII 1021a
♦ abū djād → ABDJĀD
♦ **abu ʾl-hawl** (A) : lit. father of terror; Arabic name for the sfinx of Giza. I 125b
♦ abū isḥāḳī → FĪRŪZADJ
♦ **abū ḳalamūn** (A) : originally, a certain textile of a peculiar sheen, then a precious stone, a bird, and a mollusc. In Persian, ~ is said to have the meaning of chameleon. I 131a
♦ abū ḳarn (A) : in zoology, the unicorn fish (*Naseus unicornis*). VIII 1021a; and → KARKADDAN
♦ abū marīna (A) : in zoology, the monk seal. VIII 1022b
♦ abū mihmāz (A) : in zoology, the ray or skate. VIII 1022b
♦ abū minḳar (A) : in zoology, the half-beak (*Hemiramphus*). VIII 1021a
♦ abū minshar (A) : in zoology, the sawfish (*Pristis pristis*). VIII 1021a
♦ abū miṭraḳa (A) : in zoology, the hammer-head shark (*Sphyrna zygaena*). Other designations are *baḳra*, *miṭrāḳ al-baḥr*, and *samakat al-Iskandar*. VIII 1021a; VIII 1022b
♦ (a)bū mnīr (A) : in zoology, the seal. VIII 1022b
♦ (a)bū nawwāra (A) : lit. the one with the flower; in zoology, a Saharan name which is used for the hare as well as for the fox. XII 85b
♦ abu ʾl-rakhwa → SALWĀ
♦ abū ṣanṣūn (A) : in zoology, the sansun kingfish. VIII 1021b
♦ abū sayf (A) : in zoology, the swordfish (*Xiphias gladius*). VIII 1021a
♦ abū shinthiyā → SHĪḤ

♦ abū ṣundūḳ (A) : in zoology, the coffer fish (*Ostracion nasus*). VIII 1021a

♦ abū thalāthīn → SALḲAʿ

abyaḍ (A) : the colour white; also, saliva, a sword, money, and paradoxically, in Africa, coal. In the Qurʾān, ~ and *aswad* express the contrast between light and dark rather than white and black. V 700a, where are listed many other terms to denote white; and → ZAHR

ʿād (A) : from the expression *min al-ʿād*, it has been suggested that ~ means 'the ancient time' and that the tribe ʿĀd arose from a misinterpretation of this. I 169b

♦ ʿādī : very ancient. I 169b

ʿāda (A), or *ʿurf* : a (pre-Islamic) custom; customary law. I 170a; I 744b; I 1179a; IV 155a ff.; VIII 486a

adāʾ (A) : lit. payment, accomplishment.

In law, ~ is a technical term to designate the accomplishment of a religious duty in the time prescribed by the law, a distinction being drawn between the perfect accomplishment, *al-adāʾ al-kāmil*, and the imperfect, *al-adāʾ al-nāḳis*. I 169b

In the reading of the Qurʾān, the traditional pronunciation of the letters (syn. ḲIRĀʾA). I 169b

adab (A, pl. *ādāb*) : originally, a habit, a practical norm of conduct, equivalent to SUNNA; during the evolution of its sense, ~ came to mean an ethical 'high quality of soul, good upbringing, urbanity and courtesy', in contrast to Bedouin uncouthness. From the first century of the HIDJRA, it came to imply the sum of intellectual knowledge which makes a man courteous and 'urbane', based in the first place on poetry, the art of oratory, the historical and tribal traditions of the ancient Arabs, and also on the corresponding sciences: rhetoric, grammar, lexicography, metrics. As a result of contact with foreign cultures, this national concept of ~ gradually came to include a knowledge of those sections of non-Arab literature with which Arab Muslim civilisation became familiar from the early ʿAbbāsid period; it widened its Arab content into *humanitas* without qualification. In the modern age ~ and its plural *ādāb* are synonyms of literature. I 175b

In mysticism, the norms of conduct which govern relations between master and disciples, and those between the disciples themselves. IV 94b

In military science, the plural form *ādāb* is a synonym of ḤIYAL, strategems in war. III 510b

♦ adab al-djadal : in theology and law, a method of debating in which were discussed questions that were controversial. It was not a matter of finding the truth, but of convincing the opponent of the greatest possible probability which one believes to have found. VII 566a

adak → NADHR-NIYĀZMANLIK

ʿadāla (A) : the quality of ʿADL; the state of a person who in general obeys the moral and religious law. I 209b

In public law, ~ is one of the principal conditions for carrying out public functions, while in private law, ~ belongs to the theory of evidence. I 209b

ʿadam (A) : the absence of existence or being, used by the Muslim philosophers as the equivalent of Aristotle's στέρησις. I 178b; V 578b

adan (J, Sun) : the Javanese and Sundanese form of ADHĀN. VI 675b

ʿadas (A) : in botany, lentils, one of the winter crops in mediaeval Egypt. V 863a

adat (Mal, < A ʿĀDA) : a custom, usage, practice; customary law, the juridical customs of Indonesia. I 173a; for taxes and tolls having to do with *adat*, e.g. *adat cap, adat ḥaḳḳ al-ḳalam, adat hariya, adat kain*, etc., XII 200b

aḍāt (A, N.Afr *ḍāya*) : in the Sahara of southern Morocco and Algeria, small basins where the limestone of the ḤAMMĀDAS has dissolved. III 136b

aḍdād (A, s. ḌIDD) : lit. opposites; in linguistics, words which have two meanings that are opposite to each other. I 184b

ʿaddān (A) : in Syria, a conventional rotation, according to which the distribution of the separate sections of water in the irrigation of the GHŪṬA is carried out. II 1105b

ʿādet-i aghnām → ḲOYUN RESMI

ʿadhaba (A, Egy *dhuʾāba*) : the loose end of the turban, which usually hangs behind from the turban. The usual length is four fingers long between the shoulders. X 611b; X 612a; in mysticism, one of the initiatory rites is the practice of letting the ~ hang down (*irkhāʾ al-~*). X 246a

ʿadhāb (A) : 'torment, suffering, affliction', inflicted by God or a human ruler. I 186b

♦ **ʿadhāb al-ḳabr** (A) : in eschatology, the punishment in the tomb. I 186b; V 236b

adhān (A, T *ezan*) : 'announcement'; as technical term, ~ indicates the call to the divine service of Friday and to the five daily prayers. I 187b; II 593b; VI 361b; VIII 927b

♦ ezan adı̊ (T) : the regular name of a child, chosen at leisure by the family and bestowed, with a recitation of the ADHĀN, a few days after birth. IV 181a

adhargūn (P, A *adharyūn*) : lit. flame-coloured; a plant about 2-3 feet high with finger-long elongated leaves, of a red-yellow colour, and malodorous blossoms with a black kernel, thought to be either the *Buphthalmos* or the *Calendula officinalis* 'marigold'. I 191b

ʿadhrāʾ → SUNBULA

ʿādj (A) : ivory, exported in the Islamic period in all probability solely from East Africa. I 200a

ʿadjāʾib (A) : 'marvels', especially the marvels of Antiquity, e.g. the Pharos of Alexandria. I 203b

In the Qurʾān, the ~ denote the marvels of God's creation. I 203b; II 583b

In geographical literature, the ~ form a peculiar literary genre, reaching its full development in the cosmographies of the 8th/14th century. I 203b

adjal (A) : the appointed term of a man's life or the date of his death; the duration of existence. I 204a

ʿadjala (A) : the generic term for wheeled vehicles drawn by animals; carriage. In Mamlūk Egypt, ~ was supplanted by ʿARABA as a generic term. In modern Egypt, ~ is now the word for bicycle. I 205a

ʿadjam (A) : people qualified by *ʿudjma*, a confused and obscure way of speaking, as regards pronunciation and language, i.e. non-Arabs, primarily the Persians. I 206a

♦ **ʿadjamī oghlān** (T) : 'foreign boy', the term applied to Christian youths enrolled for service in the Ottoman sultan's palace troops. I 206b; II 1087a; IV 242b

♦ **ʿadjamiyya** (A) : the term used for the writing of non-Arabic languages in Arabic characters. I 207a; I 404b; and → ALJAMÍA

adjārib → MAZRŪʿĀN

adjdhāʿ (A), or *al-djidhāʿ* : the name for the group formed by four children of ʿAwf b. Kaʿb, one of whose families held an office related to the Meccan pilgrimage which in later times was considered one of the greatest merits of the Tamīm. X 173a

adjīr (A) : in the hierarchy of guilds, an apprentice (syn. *mubtadiʾ*). Other levels were worker, *ṣāniʿ*, and master, MUʿALLIM or *usṭā*. IX 644b; IX 794a

adjlāf → AṬRĀF

adjnād → DJUND

adjsād → DJASAD

adjr (A, < Akk) : reward, wages, rent.

In theology, the reward, in the world to come, for pious deeds. I 209a

In law, ~ denoted in Mecca, in the time of the Prophet, any payment for services rendered. Later, the term was restricted to wages or rent payable under a contract of hire, IDJĀRA. I 209a

♦ adjr al-mithl (A) : in law, the remuneration in a contract to hire that is determined by the judge. III 1017a

♦ adjr musamma^{n} (A) : in law, the remuneration in a contract to hire that is fixed in the contract. III 1017a

ādjurr (A, < P *agūr* ?) : baked brick, used notably in public baths; of varying dimensions, and sometimes cut on an angle or partly rounded off, ~ is used in parts of buildings where accuracy of line is important (pillars, pedestals, stairways, etc.) and functions as horizontal tying material alternating with courses of rubble to maintain regularity of construction. I 1226b; V 585b

ʿadjuz (A) : in prosody, the name for the second hemistich of an Arabic poem. I 668b; VIII 747b; the name of the last foot of a verse. VIII 747b; another meaning of ~ in prosody occurs in the context of MUʿĀḲABA, to describe the case of e.g. in the RAMAL metre, the foot *fāʿilātun* having its last cord *-tun* shortened, thus *fāʿilātu*, when the first cord *fā-* of the following foot is not shortened. VIII 747b

♦ ʿadjuz hawāzin (A), or *aʿdjāz hawāzin* : 'the rear part of the Hawāzin'; in early Islam, those tribes, viz. the Naṣr b. Muʿāwiya, Djusham b. Muʿāwiya and Saʿd b. Bakr, that did not rebel in the ridda. XII 693a

ʿadjwa → TAMR

ʿadjz (A) : in medicine, impotence. XII 641a

ʿadl (A) : justice; rectilinear, just.

In Muʿtazilite doctrine, ~ means the justice of God and constitutes one of the five fundamental dogmas. I 209a; I 334b; I 410a; III 1143b

In law, ~ (pl. *ʿudūl*) is a person of good morals, the *ʿudūl* being the scriveners or notaries in the judiciary administration. In public law, ~ is one of the principal conditions for carrying out public functions, and in private law, it is a principal condition of a witness for the bringing of evidence. I 209a ff.; IX 207a; professional witness in the law courts. VIII 126a; IX 208a

In numismatics, ~ means 'of full weight'. I 210a

adrama (al-ṣabiyy) → ITHTHAGHARA

adrar (B) : 'mountain', Berber geographical term applied to a number of mountainous regions of the Sahara. I 210b

adwiya → DAWĀʾ

afʿā (A) : in zoology, the viper; also other similar kinds of snakes. Most sources state that ~ denotes the female, with the male being called *ufʿuwān*, but ~ is always employed in a generic sense. I 214b

afādhān → KŪNIYA

afāriḳa : the descendants of the Graeco-Romans and the latinised Berbers, mostly Christians, living in Gabès in Tunisia in the 3rd/9th century. They were no longer mentioned as a separate ethnic group by the 7th/13th century. IV 338b ff.; X657b

afāwih (A, pl. of *afwāh*, s. *fūh*) : spices, aromatic substances added to food and beverages to increase pleasant flavour and promote digestion (syn. *maṣāliḥ*). The meaning of ~ is not sharply marked off from *ʿiṭr, ṭīb* 'scents' and *ʿaḳḳār* 'drugs'. XII 42a, where many spices are listed

afghānī (A) : in numismatics, a coin introduced in Afghanistan by Shīr ʿAlī in place of the rupee. IX 446b

ʿafiṣ (A) : the quality of food being pungent. II 1071b

āfrāg (B 'enclosure') : in Morocco, an enclosure of cloth, which isolates the encampment of the sovereign and his suite from the rest of the camp. ~ corresponds to the Persian *sarāča* or SARĀPARDA. I 236a; V 1206a

ʿafṣ (A) : in botany, the gall, an excrescence which forms on certain kinds of trees and shrubs as the result of the sting of various insects. The Arabic term was probably applied to the oak-gall in particular, but also denotes the fruit of the oak or a similar tree and the tree itself. I 239a; X 665b

afsantīn (A, < Gk), or *afsintīn, ifsintīn* : in botany, the common wormwood (*Artemisia absinthium*); other similar kinds of plants. In medicine, ~ is often called *kas͟hūt͟h rūmī*. I 239b; IX 434b; and → S͟HĪḤ

afs͟hīn : a pre-Islamic title borne by princes in Central Asia. I 241a

afsūn (P) : charm, incantation; now used in Iran to designate especially a charm against the biting of poisonous animals. I 241b

ʿāfūr (A) : a sand devil; the word has an echo of ʿIFRĪT in it. III 1038a

ʿafw → G͟HUFRĀN

afwāh → AFĀWĪH

afyūn (A, < Gk) : opium; in Iran and Turkey often called TIRYĀḲ ‘antidote’. I 243a

agadir (B, < Ph *gadir*) : in North Africa, one of the names of a fortified enclosure among the Berbers, also called *ḳaṣr* (*gasr*), *temidelt, g͟hurfa, ḳalʿa* (*gelâa*), and *ig͟herm* (pl. *ig͟herman*). I 244b; XII 512b

āgdāl (A, < B) : pasturage reserved for the exclusive use of the landowner. I 245b

In Morocco, ~ has acquired the sense of a wide expanse of pasture lands, surrounded by high walls and adjoining the sultan’s palace, reserved for the exclusive use of his cavalry and livestock. I 245b; I 1346b; V 1206a; gardens. IV 685b

ag͟ha (T, P *āḳā*) : in Eastern Turkish, ‘elder brother’, ‘grandfather’, ‘uncle’, ‘elder sister’. I 245b; in Persian, ~ sometimes signifies eunuch. I 246a

In Ottoman times, ~ meant ‘chief’, ‘master’, and sometimes ‘landowner’. As a title ~ was given to many persons of varying importance employed in government service, usually of a military or non-secretarial character, and came to be also used for eunuchs in the harems of the sultans of Constantinople. I 245b; V 472b

ag͟hač (T) : in Ottoman Turkish, a ‘tree’, ‘wood’. In Eastern Turkish, ~ means both ‘the male member’ and a measure of distance, a parasang, three times the distance at which a man standing between two others can make himself heard by them. I 247a

ag͟hānī → MAG͟HĀNĪ

ag͟hi̊t (T) : in Turkish folklore, lyrical compositions expressive of grief. They commemorate the deceased and treat of general aspects of death or express sorrow over collective calamities. VI 610a

ag͟hlaf, ag͟hral → ALK͟HAN

ag͟hrem (B) : ‘settlement’. X 78a

ag͟hriba (A), or *ag͟hribat al-ʿarab* : lit. the crows [of the Bedouin]; a designation in early Islam for poets of negroid maternal ancestry. IX 864a; an outcast [from a tribe]. X 910a

ag͟hrum (B) : bread. V 41b

ag͟ht͟ham → S͟HAYB

agurram (B) : among the Berbers of Morocco, the name for a saint. V 1201a

aḥābīs͟h (A) : Abyssinians (→ ḤABAS͟H); companies or bodies of men, not all of one tribe. III 7b; possibly the Meccan militia of slaves of Ethiopian origin in the period immediately before the HID͟JRA. I 24b, but see III 8a

The word is also applied to men who formed a confederacy either at a mountain called al-Ḥubs͟hī or at a WĀDĪ called Aḥbas͟h. III 7b

āḥād (A, s. *aḥad*) : in the science of Tradition, ~ are Traditions from a relatively small number of transmitters, not enough to make them MUTAWĀTIR. III 25b; an isolated report. X 932a; and → FARD

ahal (Touareg), or *tende* : grand parties held by unmarried young people in Touareg society. X 380a

aḥbār → ḲISSĪS

ʿahd (A, pl. *ʿuhūd*) : 'joining together'; a contract. I 255a; a written designation of succession left by a caliph from the time of the Umayyad caliph ʿAbd al-Malik onwards. I 255b; IV 938b; XI 126a; and → AHL AL-ʿAHD; WALĪ AL-ʿAHD

As a Qurʾānic term, ~ denotes God's covenant with men and His commands, the religious engagement into which the believers have entered, political agreements and undertakings of believers and unbelievers towards the Prophet and amongst each other, and ordinary civil agreements and contracts. I 255a

In law, ~ is generally restricted to political enactments and treaties. I 255a; land which had capitulated before conquest was known as ~ land. IV 14b

In mysticism, ~ is the covenant, consisting of religious professions and vows which vary in the different orders, with which the dervish is introduced into the fraternity. II 164b

In the science of diplomatic, ~ was a supreme grade of appointment, which concerned only the highest officials. It has fallen into disuse since the time of the Fāṭimids. II 302b

In Christian Arabic, *al-ʿahd al-ʿatīḳ* is the term for the Old Testament, and *al-ʿahd al-djadīd* the term for the New Testament. I 255a

♦ ʿahdnāme (T) : in the Ottoman empire, the document drawn up to embody the covenant, *ʿahd*, made with a ḤARBĪ. The items in an ~ are called *ʿuhūd*, or *shurūṭ* (s. SHARṬ). III 1179b; treaty of dependence. IX 483b

aḥdab (A) : hunchback. I 161a

aḥdāth (A) : lit. young men; a kind of urban militia, whose function was that of a police, which played a considerable role in the cities of Syria and Upper Mesopotamia from the 4th/10th to the 6th/12th centuries. I 256a; I 1332b; II 963a; VIII 402a; arbitrary actions at odds with the divine Law. I 384a

In Ṣafawid Persia, the ~ were the night patrols in the cities, also called *gezme* and ʿASAS. I 687a

aḥfara → ITHTHAGHARA

ʿāhira (pl. *ʿawāhir*) → BAGHIYY

aḥḳāf (A) : the title of SŪRA xlvi of the Qurʾān; in geography, a term variously translated as 'curved sand dunes', the name of a sand desert in Southern Arabia, and the whole of al-Ramla or just its western half. I 257a

aḥkām (A, s. ḤUKM) : judicial decisions. I 257a; juridical and moral rules. IV 151b; astrological signs. VII 558a

♦ al-aḥkām al-khamsa (A) : in law, the 'five qualifications' (obligatory, recommended, indifferent, reprehensible, forbidden), by one or the other of which every act of man is qualified. I 257b; IX 324b; X 932a

♦ aḥkām al-nudjūm (A) : astrology (→ NADJM). VII 558a

♦ aḥkāmī (A), or *munadjdjim* : an astrologer who interprets the astrological signs. VII 558a

ahl (A, pl. *ahāl*) : family, inmates, people, meaning those dwelling in a defined area but not specifically a nation. I 257b; IV 785b; in the tribal structure of the Bedouin, ~ (syn. ĀL) denotes offspring up to the fifth degree. I 700b; in combinations, ~ often means 'sharing in a thing, belonging to it' or 'owner of the same'. I 257b; in its plural form, *al-ahālī* means the indigenous, autochthonous peoples. XI 175a

♦ ahl al-ʿabāʾ → AHL AL-BAYT

♦ ahl al-ʿahd (A) : non-Muslims living outside the Islamic state. The term was extended occasionally to both the MUSTAʾMIN, the foreigner granted the right of living in Islamic territory for a limited period of time, and the DHIMMĪ. I 255b

♦ **ahl al-ahwāʾ** (A) : term applied by orthodox theologians to those followers of Islam whose religious tenets in certain details deviate from the general ordinances of the sunnī confession. I 257b

◆ **ahl al-**(baḥt̲h̲ wa 'l-)**naẓar**   (A) : 'those who apply reasoning', a term probably coined by the Muʿtazila to denote themselves; later, it came to mean careful scholars who held a sound, well-reasoned opinion on any particular question. I 266a

◆ **ahl al-bayt**   (A) : lit. the people of the house, viz. the family of the Prophet. The term has been interpreted variously; the current orthodox view is based on a harmonising opinion, according to which the term includes the *ahl al-ʿabāʾ* (the Prophet, ʿAlī, Fāṭima, al-Ḥasan and al-Ḥusayn) together with the wives of the Prophet. I 257b; II 843b; IX 331a; among the s̲h̲īʿa, the ~ (which they call by preference *ʿitra*) is limited to the AHL AL-KISĀʾ and their descendants. I 258a; IX 331a

◆ **ahl al-buyūtāt**   (A) : those who belong to Persian families of the highest nobility; later, the nobles in general. I 258b

◆ **ahl al-dār**   (A) : lit. the people of the house; the sixth order in the Almohad hierarchy. I 258b

◆ ahl al-daʿwa   → MADHHAB

◆ ahl al-d̲h̲ikr   (A) : 'possessors of edification', a Qurʾānic term signifying witnesses of previous revelations. I 264a

◆ ahl al-d̲h̲imma   → DHIMMA

◆ ahl al-d̲j̲amāʿa   (A) : lit. the people of the community, an alternative of the appellative *ahl al-sunna wa 'l-d̲j̲amāʿa*, an early designation of one of the warring parties at Ṣiffīn, and one of the 73 factions into which the Islamic community will be divided and the only one which will eventually attain salvation. IX 880b

◆ ahl al-faḍl   (A) : aristocrats, in contrast to the rude and untutored masses (*arād̲h̲il, sufahāʾ, ak̲h̲issāʾ*). IX 330a

◆ **ahl al-ḥadīt̲h̲**   (A), and *aṣḥāb al-ḥadīt̲h̲* : the partisans of Traditions, ḤADĪT̲H̲; traditionists, as opposed to the AHL AL-RAʾY. I 258b

◆ **ahl al-ḥall wa 'l-ʿaḳd**   (A) : 'those who are qualified to unbind and to bind'; term for the representatives of the Muslim community who act on its behalf in appointing and deposing a caliph or another ruler. I 263b

◆ ahl al-ḥarb   → ḤARBĪ

◆ ahl al-ik̲h̲tiyār   → IKHTIYĀR

◆ ahl al-it̲h̲bāt   (A) : 'people of the firm proof'; an appellation for Ḍirār b. ʿAmr and his school by al-As̲h̲ʿarī. III 1037a; III 1144a

◆ ahl al-it̲h̲nayn   → THANAWIYYA

◆ ahl al-kanīf   (A) : the poor and needy members of a tribe. X 910a

◆ **ahl al-ḳibla**   (A) : the people of the ḲIBLA, viz. the Muslims. I 264a

◆ **ahl al-kisāʾ**   (A) : the people of the cloak, viz. the Prophet and his daughter Fāṭima, his son-in-law ʿAlī, and his grandsons al-Ḥasan and al-Ḥusayn, whom the Prophet sheltered under his cloak. I 264a; IX 331a

◆ **ahl al-kitāb**   (A) : lit. the people of the Book, viz. Jews and Christians, and later also extended to Sabeans, Zoroastrians and, in India, even idolaters. I 264b; IV 408b

◆ ahl al-ḳiyās   (A) : the name given to the Muʿtazila by their adversaries. II 102b

◆ ahl al-kudya   (A) : 'vagabonds', one of the numerous terms for 'rascals, scoundrels' in the mediaeval and modern periods. XI 546a

◆ ahl al-madar   (A) : people who lived in mud-brick houses in Arabia at the rise of Islam. I 608b; V 585a

◆ ahl al-mad̲h̲hab   → MADHHAB

◆ ahl al-milla   → MILLA

◆ ahl al-naṣṣ   → IKHTIYĀR

◆ ahl al-naẓar   → AHL AL-(BAḤT̲H̲ WA 'L-)NAẒAR

◆ ahl al-raʾy   (A), and *aṣḥāb al-raʾy* : partisans of personal opinion, as opposed to the traditionists, AHL AL-ḤADĪT̲H̲. I 692a

♦ **ahl al-ṣuffa** (A) : a group of the Prophet's Companions who typify the ideal of poverty and piety. I 266a

♦ **ahl al-sunna** (A) : the sunnīs, i.e. the orthodox Muslims. I 267a; III 846a; IV 142a; party of the orthodox traditionists. I 694a; I 1039b; and → AHL AL-DJAMĀʿA

♦ ahl al-ṭaraf → ḲABĪLĪ

♦ ahl al-taswiya (A) : in early Islam, advocates of equality between non-Arabs and Arabs. IX 514a

♦ ahl al-tathniya → THANAWIYYA

♦ ahl al-tawḥīd (A) : 'monotheists', the definition used by certain authors for the totality of Muslims, and by other groups, such as the Muʿtazila and the Almohads, for themselves. X 389a

♦ ahl al-wabar (A) : Bedouin living in tents of camel's-hair cloth in Arabia at the rise of Islam. I 608b; V 585a

♦ **ahl-i ḥadīth** (A) : a designation used in India and Pakistan for the members of a Muslim sect, who profess to hold the same views as the early AHL AL-ḤADĪTH and not be bound by any of the four sunnī legal schools. I 259a

♦ **ahl-i ḥaḳḳ** (A) : 'men of God', a secret religion prevalent mainly in western Persia. They are also called ʿAlī Ilāhī, but this is an unsuitable title. The central point in their dogma is the belief in the successive manifestations of God, the number of these being seven. I 260a

♦ **ahl-i wāris** (Mal, < P, < A) : inheritors, used among the Muslims of Indonesia. I 267a

♦ ahlī → WAḲF KHAYRĪ

♦ ahliyya (A) : a diploma from al-Azhar after a minimum of 8 years of study. I 818a; primary education, with *taḥṣīl* (secondary) and *ʿālimiyya* (higher) following. XI 490a

In law, the legal capacity of an individual to be a subject of the law, either a right-acquiring capacity, *ahliyyat wudjūb*, or an execution capacity, *ahliyyat idāʾ*. IX 248a; XI 208a; in Persian modern legal language, *ahliyyat* is used to mean nationality. IV 785b

aḥlāf (A, s. ḤILF) : a group formed by all but one of Zayd b. ʿAbd Allāh's descendants. X 173b

ahlīladj → HALĪLADJ

ahliyya(t) → AHL

aḥmāl (A) : one of two groups (*al-aḥmāl*) formed by the sons of Yarbūʿ b. Ḥanẓala, which was made up of four sons born by the same mother; three other sons formed a group called *al-ʿuḳad* (or *al-ʿuḳadāʾ*). X 173b

aḥmar (A) : the colour red, the colour for which Arabic terminology is the richest. V 700b, where many synonyms are given; and → ZAHR

aḥmas, aḥmasī, aḥmasiyya → ḤUMS

aḥnāf (A) : the characteristic of having misshapen feet. I 303b

āhū : gazelles, or deer, on the island of Samos. IX 679b

aḥwāḍ (A) : in agriculture, the small squares into which a field is divided, which the water reaches by channels. IV 683b

ʿāʾid → WUṢLA

ʿāʾila (A) : family, given way today mostly to *usra*. I 305b

āʾīn (P) : 'law, rite, institution', found in a title translated from Pahlawī into Arabic by Ibn Muḳaffaʿ in the middle of the 2nd/8th century, and in later titles on Persian Islamic history. I 306b

āḳ birčak → ĀḲ SAḲĀL

aḳ daryā → AḲ ṢU

āḳ sāḳāl (P) : 'grey-beard', the elder of a Shāhsewan group. Women elders were known as *āḳ birčak* 'grey hairs'. IX 224a

aḳ ṣu (T) : white water; as a technical term, ~ denotes the original bed of a river (syn. *aḳ daryā*). I 313b

āḳā → AGHA

ʿaḳaba (A, pl. *ʿiḳāb*) : a mountain road, or a place difficult of ascent on a hill or acclivity. The best-known place of this name is *al-ʿaḳaba*, between Minā and Mecca, where the ritual stone-throwing of the pilgrimage takes place. I 314b

ʿaḳāl (A), or *brīm* : ringed cord or rope to go over the headscarf worn by men. V 740b; X 611b

ʿaḳār (A) : in law, ~ denotes immovable property, such as houses, shops and land, and as such is identical with 'realty' or 'real property' (ant. *māl manḳūl*). The owner of ~ is also deemed to be the owner of anything on it, over it or under it, to any height or depth. XII 55a

ʿakawwak (A) : thick-set. I 315b

akbaba → NASR

aḳče (T) : 'small white', in numismatics, the name for the Ottoman silver coin referred to by European authors as *aspre* or *asper*. I 317b; II 119a; V 974a; VIII 978a

In Ottoman administration, taxes and dues (*rüsūm*, → RASM) which were paid in cash were often called ~. VIII 486a

ʿaḳd (A) : the legal act, especially that which involves a bi-lateral declaration, viz. the offer and the acceptance. I 318a

In the science of diplomatic, ~ is used for contract (syn. ʿAHD, **mithāḳ**), in particular a civil contract, often more clearly defined by an additional genitive, such as *ʿaḳd al-nikāḥ, ʿaḳd al-ṣulḥ*, etc. II 303a

In rhetoric, ~ 'binding' denotes the IḲTIBĀS when it is put into verse and its source is indicated. III 1091b

In archery, ~, or *ḳafla*, denotes the lock, locking, sc. the position on the bow-string of the fingers of the right hand, and especially that of the thumb in the 'Mongolian' technique of locking. IV 800b

In grammar, the nexus linking the two terms of the nominal and verbal phrases. IV 895b

In astronomy, ~ means node (syn. *ʿuḳda*), and it is often used, in combination with *raʾs* and *dhanab*, instead of DJAWZAHAR to indicate the two opposite points in which the apparent path of the moon, or all planets, cuts the ecliptic. V 536a

akdar (A) : troubled, obscure; for some Muslim scholars, the origin of the name AKDARIYYA for a difficult question of law. I 320b

♦ **akdariyya** (A) : in law, the name of a well-known difficult question about inheritance, viz. whether a grandfather can exclude a sister from her inheritance in the case of a woman leaving behind as her heirs her husband, her mother, her grandfather, and her sister. I 320a

ʿakf (A) : a word used in the Qurʾān to designate the ceremonial worship of the cult and also the ritual stay in the sanctuary, which was done, for example, in the Meccan temple. VI 658a

akhawi (Touareg) : a woman's camel saddle, provided with semi-circular hoops attached to the side, used by the Touareg of the Sahara. III 667a

akhbār → KHABAR

♦ akhbārī (A) : an historian. XI 280b

♦ **akhbāriyya** (A) : in Twelver shīʿism, those who rely primarily on the Traditions, *akhbār*, of the IMĀMs as a source of religious knowledge, in contrast to the *uṣūliyya*, who admit a larger share of speculative reason in the principles of theology and religious law. XII 56b

akhḍar (A) : the colour green, an adjective also associated with the notion of darkness, since it sometimes denotes black, dark, grey. V 700b; and → ZAHR

akfānī → KAFAN

akhfash (A) : nyctalope, or devoid of eyelashes. I 321a

akhī (T < *aḳi̊* 'generous') : a designation of the leaders of associations of young men organised as guilds in Anatolia in the 7th-8th/13th-14th centuries, who adopted the ideals of the FUTUWWA. I 321a; II 966b ff.; a Turkish trade guild. IX 646a; one of three grades in the ~ organisation, denoting the president of a corporation of *fityān* (s. FATĀ) and owner of a meeting-house, ZĀWIYA. I 322b; II 967b; one of nine categories in the trade guild, itself divided into six divisions: the first three divisions were *aṣḥāb-tark*, the experienced, and the last three, *naḳībler*, the inexperienced. IX 646a

ākhira (A) : the life to come, the condition of bliss or misery in the hereafter. I 325a

akhissāʾ → AHL AL-FAḌL

akhlafa (A) : a verb conveying the notion 'he [the child] passed the time when he had nearly attained to puberty'. VIII 822a

akhlāḳ (A, s. *khulūḳ* 'innate disposition') : in philosophy, ethics. I 325b

akhmās → TAKHMĪS

akhnif (A), or *khnīf* : a short Berber cape of black wool, woven in one piece, with a large red or orange medallion on the back, hooded for men, unhooded for women. II 1116a; V 745b

akhras (A) : mute. I 330b

akhriyān (< Gk *'agarīnós* 'Hagarene') : the self-designation, documented from 835/1432, by the Muslim Bulgarians living in the central Rhodoe between Nevrokop and Pazardžik, but having been adopted by the Ottomans to describe somewhat dubious converts in the Balkans in a pejorative sense, it fell out of use, to survive only as a Rumelian term. X 698b

ākhtabēgī → ĀKHŪRBEG

akhṭal (A) : loquacious. I 331a

akhtām (A, s. *khatm*) : in Tunisia, a ceremony stemming from Ḥafsid days of the 'closing' of public readings of the canonical collections of al-Bukhārī and Muslim and of the *Shifāʾ* of al-Ḳāḍī ʿIyāḍ, readings which finish on 27 Ramaḍān in the Great Mosque in the presence of the head of state himself. X 657a

ākhūnd (T, P) : a title given to scholars; in Persian it is current since Tīmūrid times in the sense of 'schoolmaster, tutor'. I 331b

ākhūr-sālār → SĀLĀR

ākhūrbeg (IndP) : under the Dihlī sultanate, the superintendent of the royal horses, there being one for each wing of the army. Under the Mughals, this officer was known as the *ātbēgī* or *ākhtabēgī*. V 689b

ʿaḳib (A) : in law, a descendant. A charitable endowment that was characterised as *muʿaḳḳab* 'for a descent group' was understood to apply to two or more generations of lineal descendants who qualified as beneficiaries simultaneously. XI 70b

In anatomy, the heel. XI 254b

ʿaḳīd (A) : a leader of a Bedouin raid. II 1055a; among the Jordanian tribes, in early modern times, a specific leader of raids at the side of the chief, known in full as ~ *al-ghazw*. IX 115b

In 19th-century Sudan, an imperial proconsul, a category of functionaries that differed from the older royal courtiers not only in the great diversity of their ethnic origin but also in that they were allowed to absent themselves for extended periods from the presence of the king. XI 11a

ʿaḳīda (A, pl. *ʿaḳāʾid*) : in theology, creed; doctrine, dogma or article of faith. I 332b; IV 279b

ʿaḳīḳ (A) : cornelian; the name has been transferred to any kind of necklace which is of a red colour. I 336a; VIII 269a

ʿaḳīḳa (A) : the name of the sacrifice on the seventh day after the birth of a child; also, the shorn hair of the child, which is part of the seventh-day ritual. I 337a; IV 488a; VIII 824b

ʿāḳil (A, pl. *ʿuḳḳāl*) : 'sage'; in law, *compos mentis*. IX 63a; and → ʿUḲALĀʾ AL-MADJĀNĪN

Among the Druze, a member initiated into the truths of the faith; those not yet initiated, yet members of the community, are called *djuhhāl* (→ DJĀHIL). II 633a

akila → IKLA

ʿāḳila (A, pl. *ʿawāḳil*) : in penal law, the group of persons upon whom devolves, as the result of a natural joint liability with the person who has committed homicide or inflicted bodily harm, the payment of compensation in cash or in kind, the DIYA. I 29a; I 337b

aḳi̊n → ZHIRAW

♦ **aḳi̊ndji̊** (T) : irregular cavalry during the first centuries of the Ottoman empire, based on and primarily for service in Europe. I 340a

aḳiṭ (A) : sour-milk cheese, made by pre-Islamic Arabs. II 1057b; X 901a

akkār (A, < Ar; pl. *akara*) : lit. tiller, cultivator of the ground; term applied to the peasantry of Aramaean stock in Syria and Iraq with a pejorative sense. XII 58b

ʿaḳḳār → AFĀWĪH

ʿaḳl (A) : reason; intellect or intelligence. I 341b; IV 157a

In neoplatonic speculation, ~ is the first, sometimes the second, entity which emanates from the divinity as the first cause, or proceeds from it by means of intellectual creation. I 341b

In scholastic theology, ~ is a natural way of knowing, independently of the authority of the revelation, what is right and wrong. I 341b

To the philosophers of Islam, who followed Aristotle and his Greek commentators, more especially Alexander of Aphrodisias, ~ is that part of the soul by which it 'thinks' or 'knows' and as such is the antithesis of perception. The Muslim philosophers recognised a hierarchy of separate intelligences (*ʿuḳūl mufāriḳa*), usually ten in number, each lower one emanating from the higher. I 341b

In penal law, ~ (pl. *ʿuḳūl*) is the compensation in cash or in kind required by the ʿĀḲILA in cases of homicide or instances of bodily harm. I 338a; and → DIYA

In prosody, a deviation from the proper metre, in particular a missing *la* in the foot *mufāʿa[la]tun*. I 672a; a case of ZIḤĀF where the fifth vowel is elided. XI 508b

In Druze hierarchy, the highest of the five cosmic ranks in the organisation. II 632a

♦ al-ʿaḳl al-awwal (A) : in ʿAbd al-Razzāḳ al-Ḳāshānī's mystical thought, the Universal Reason, which proceeds by a dynamic emanation from God. This is a spiritual substance and the first of the properties which the divine essence implies. I 89b

♦ **ʿaḳliyyāt** (A) : a technical term in scholastic theology, signifying the rational (and natural) knowledge which the reason can acquire by itself. According to the Muʿtazilī tradition and Saʿadya al-Fayyūmī, ~ denotes that which is accessible to the reason and especially, on the ethical level, the natural values of law and morals. The term also denotes a genus of theological dissertations, going back to the 6th/12th century. I 342b

aḳlaf → ALKHAN

aḳlām → ḲALAM

aklat al-maḥabba (A) : a feast-day meal among the Ṣārliyya in northern Iraq, once every lunar year, to which everyone contributed a cock boiled with rice or wheat. IX 64a

aḳligh → MUṢAFFAḤĀT

aḳraʿ (A) : bald. I 343a
ʿaḳrab (A, pl. *ʿaḳārib*) : in zoology, the scorpion. I 343b
In astronomy, *al-~* is the term for Scorpius, one of the twelve zodiacal constellations. I 343b; VII 83b
aḳrābādhīn (A, < Syr) : a title of treatises on the composition of drugs; pharmacopoeias. I 344a
aḳsaḳal : in traditional Özbeg society, the respected older headman of a village, who mediated disputes. VIII 233b
aḳsimā : a term usually translated as 'liquid, syrup', but, since one of the recipes mentions the presence of yeast among the ingredients of this drink, it must presumably be a variety of sweetened beer such as FUḲḲĀʿ. VI 721b; IX 225a
aḳūniṭun (A, < Gk) : in medicine, a particularly deadly poison originating from a plant root. Synonyms are *khāniḳ al-nimr, khāniḳ al-dhiʾb, ḳātil al-nimr, nabbāl*, and *bīsh*. XII 59b
aḳwāl (A, B *agwāl, gullāl*) : a goblet-shaped drum, about 60 cm long, still to be found in the Maghrib. In Tripolitania, a similar instrument called the *tabdaba* is used. X 33a
āl (A) : a clan, a genealogical group between the family and the tribe. Later, ~ came to mean the dynasty of a ruler. I 345b; a demon who attacks women in childbed, a personification of puerperal fever. I 345b; in Persian administration, a royal seal. XI 192b; and → AHL; SARĀB
āla (A, pl. *ālāt*) : an instrument, utensil.
In grammar, ~ is found in expressions as *ālat al-*TAʿRĪF, instrument of determination, and *ālat al-tashbīh*, instrument of comparison. I 345b
In the classification of sciences, *ālāt* is the name of such attainments as are acquired not for their own sake, but 'as a means to something else'. I 345b
In philosophy, ~ is another term for logic, following the peripatetic view that it is an instrument, not a part, of philosophy. I 345a
For ~ in Moroccan music, → GHINĀʾ
aʿlā (A) : higher; *al-aʿlā* is used as an epithet to differentiate between the patron and the client, when both are referred to as MAWLĀ. I 30b
alaaqad (Somali) : in Somali society, a woman specialist who relieves people of spirits through the performance of a ritual. IX 723b
ālaba (A) : a geographical term used to denote the northern part of the Iberian peninsula beyond the left bank of the upper valley of the Ebro. I 348b
♦ **ālaba wa 'l-ḳilāʿ** (A) : a geographical expression used in the 2nd-3rd/8th-9th centuries to denote that part of Christian Spain which was most exposed to the attacks of summer expeditions sent from Cordoba by the Umayyad AMĪRS. I 348b
alābālghā (A) : the trout. VIII 1021a
ālāčigh (P) : the dwelling of the Shāhsewan in Persia, which is hemispherical and felt-covered; within each one lives a household of on average seven or eight people. IX 223b
aladja (T) : chintz with coloured stripes; used in many geographical names. I 348b; V 560a ff.
ʿalaf (A) : fodder. XI 412a; and → ʿULŪFE
ʿalam (A, pl. *aʿlām*) : signpost, flag (syn. LIWĀʾ, RĀYA). I 349a
♦ ʿalamdār → SANDJAḲDĀR
♦ ʿalem-i nebewī → SANDJAḲ-I SHERĪF
ʿālam (A, pl. *ʿālamūn, ʿawālim*) : world. I 349b
♦ ʿālam al-djabarūt (A) : 'the world of (divine) omnipotence', BARZAKH, to which belong, according to al-Ghazālī, the impressionable and imaginative faculties of the human soul. I 351a

♦ ʿālam al-malakūt (A) : a Qurʾānic term for 'the world of Kingdom, of Sovereignty', the world of immutable spiritual truths, and hence of the angelic beings, to which are added all of Islamic tradition, the Preserved Table, the Pen, the Scales, and often the Qurʾān. I 351a

♦ ʿālam al-mulk (A) : a Qurʾānic term meaning 'the world of kingship', i.e. the world of becoming, the world here below. I 351a

ʿalāma (A, T *ʿalāmet*) : emblem, presented by early Islamic rulers to their close pages as a sign of honour. VIII 432b

In the science of diplomatic, the signature of the person drawing up the document, part of the concluding protocol in the classical period. II 302a; X 392b

In the Muslim West, a mark of ratification or initialling, on all official chancery documents. I 352a; the formula of authorisation (*wa 'l-ḥamdu li-llāhi waḥdah*), written in large lettering at the head of despatches and commissions. II 331b

For ~ in dating, → MADKHAL

ālāp (H) : the introductory improvisation, the first part in a performance of classical or art music of India. III 454a

ʿalas (A) : in agriculture, a variety of wheat. II 1060b

ālāt → ĀLA

ʿalath (A) : in botany, the wild endive (*hindibāʾ barrī*), known under a variety of names: *ghalath, yaʿḍīd, bakla murra*, ṬARKHASHḲŪḲ and variants. XII 370b

alay (T, prob. < Gk *allagion*) : in Ottoman usage, a troop, a parade, and hence a crowd, a large quantity. It was used from the time of the 19th-century military reforms to denote a regiment. I 358a

♦ alay-beyi → ZAʿĪM

ʿalāya (A) : in Oman, the upper quarter of a wadi or water channel, frequently occupied by a tribe in traditional rivalry with another tribe occupying the lower quarter, *sifāla*. XII 818a

albasti : in Özbeg folk tradition, a witch-like DJINN. VIII 234b

ʿalem → ʿALAM

alif → HAMZA

♦ alif al-ḳaṭʿ → ḲAṬʿ

♦ alif maḳṣūra (A) : a long *ā* not followed by HAMZA. XI 222a

ʿālim → FAḲĪH; ʿULAMĀʾ

♦ **ʿālima** (A, pl. *ʿawālim*) : lit. a learned, expert woman, ~ is the name of a class of Egyptian female singers forming a sort of guild, according to sources of the 18th and 19th centuries. I 403b

♦ ʿālimiyya → AHLIYYA

ʿāliya (A, pl. *ʿawālī*) : grand master, the highest rank in the game of chess. IX 367a

aljamía (Sp, < A *al-ʿadjamiyya* 'non-Arabic') : the name used by the Muslims of Muslim Spain to denote the Romance dialects of their neighbours in the north of the Iberian peninsula. In the later Middle Ages, ~ acquired the particular meaning which is attributed to it today: a Hispanic Romance language written in Arabic characters. The literature in ~ is termed *aljamiada*. I 404b

alkhan (A) : a term for 'uncircumcised' in the ancient language (syn. *aḳlaf, aghlaf, aghral*). V 20a

allāh (A) : God, the Unique One, the Creator; already to the pre-Islamic Arabs, ~ was one of the Meccan deities, possibly the supreme deity. I 406a

♦ **allāhumma** (A) : an old formula of invocation, used in praying, offering, concluding a treaty and blessing or cursing. I 418a

ʿalma → GHĀZIYA

almās (A, < Gk) : in mineralogy, the diamond. I 419a

almogávares (Sp, < A *al-mughāwir*) : the name given at the end of the Middle Ages to certain contingents of mercenaries levied from among the mountaineers of Aragon. I 419b

alp (T) : 'hero', a figure which played a great role in the warlike ancient Turkish society (syn. *batur* (→ BAHĀDUR), *sökmen, čapar*); used also as an element in compound proper names or as a title by Saldjūḳ and subsequent rulers. I 419b

altin (T), or *altun* : in mineralogy, gold, also used of gold coins. I 423b

ālū-yi malkum (P) : lit. plums of Malcolm; potatoes, introduced into Persia in the 18th century, called after Sir John Malcolm the British envoy, who is commonly but probably erroneously thought to have brought them. XII 610b

aluka → MAʾLUKA

āluwī (A, < Gk) : the aloe drug, i.e. the juice pressed from the leaves of the aloe. VIII 687b

alwān (A) : in music, a lute with a long neck and plucked strings. VI 215b

alya (A) : the fat tail of a sheep. II 1057b; XII 318a

ama → ʿABD

ʿamā (A) : in the mystical thought of ʿAbd al-Karīm al-Djīlī, the simple hidden pure Essence before its manifestation, one of the important scales or 'descents' in which Absolute Being develops. I 71a

āmad (U) : in Urdu poetry, the part of the elegy, MARTHIYA, where the army's preparation for battle is described, sometimes including a detailed description of the hero's horse. VI 611b

ʿamal (A) : performance, action. I 427a; II 898a; 'that which is practised', the moral action in its practical context and, secondarily, the practical domain of 'acting'. I 427b

In law, ~ is judicial practice. I 427b

As a legal and economic term, ~ denotes labour, as opposed to capital. I 428a

In later Muslim administration, ~ means 'fief'. IX 153b; region. IX 739a

♦ ʿamal bi 'l-yad (A), or *ʿamal al-yad* : in medicine, the early expression for surgery, later replaced by *djirāḥa*. II 481b

♦ ʿilm ʿamalī → ʿILM

♦ ʿamaliyya (A) : the practical sciences, viz. ethics, economics and politics, as determined by the philosophers. I 427b

ʿamāla (A) : an administrative allowance, e.g. that given to an AMĪR. I 439a

ʿamāma → ʿIMĀMA

amān (A) : safety, protection.

In law, a safe conduct or pledge of security by which a non-Muslim not living in Muslim territory becomes protected by the sanctions of the law in his life and property for a limited period. I 429a; II 303b; III 1181b; and → IDHN

ʿamār al-dam (A) : among the Bedouin of Cyrenaica and the Western Desert of Egypt, the vengeance group, which also functions as a blood-money group. Among the Aḥaywāt Bedouin of central Sinai and their neighbours, the vengeance and blood-money group is called a *damawiyya* or *khamsih*. X 442b f.

amarg → ṬARAB

ʿamārī → HAWDA

amazzal (B), and *amzyad, amḥaz, amḥars, awrith* : an institution concerning an individual, occurring in the case of a stranger to the group who, usually after committing some offence in his own clan, has imposed the ʿĀR 'transfer of responsibility', and obtained the protection of another group which he makes henceforward the beneficiary of his work. The stranger becomes ~ when his protector has given to him in marriage his own daughter or another woman over whom he holds the right of DJABR. XII 79b

ʿamd (A) : in law, an intentional act; one that is quasi-deliberate is called *shibh* (→ SHUBHA) *ʿamd*. II 341a; IV 768b; IV 1101b

āmeddji (T, < P *āmad*) : an official of the central administration of the Ottoman empire, who headed the personal staff of the REʾĪS ÜL-KÜTTĀB ʻchief Secretaryʼ. The office seems to have come into being later than the 17th century and increased in importance after the reforms. I 433a; II 339a; referendar or reporter of the Imperial Dīwān. VIII 481b

aménokal (B) : any political leader not subordinate to anyone else. The title is applied to foreign rulers, to high-ranking European leaders, and to the male members of certain noble families; in some regions of the Sahara, ~ is also given to the chiefs of small tribal groups. I 433b; X 379a

amghar (B) : an elder (by virtue of age or authority); ~ is used for different functions among the various Berber tribes. I 433b; X 379a

amḥars → AMAZZAL

amḥaz → AMAZZAL

ʿamīd (A) : lit. pillar, support; a title of high officials of the Sāmānid-Ghaznawid administration, denoting the rank of the class of officials from whom the civil governors were recruited. I 434a; under the Saldjūḳs, an official in charge of civil and financial matters. VI 275a; a designation for the tribal chief (syn. *ʿimād*). IX 115b

ʿāmil (A, pl. *ʿummāl, ʿawāmil*) : a Muslim who performs the works demanded by his faith; as technical term, it came to denote tax-collector, government agent; (provincial) governor [in North Africa and Spain] in charge of the general administration and finance. I 435a; financial administrator. I 19b

In law, the active partner in a MUḌĀRABA partnership. I 435a

Among the Bohorās sect in India, ~ denotes a local officiant appointed by the head of the sect to serve the community in respect of marriage and death ceremonies, and ritual prayer. I 1255a

In grammar, ~ signifies a *regens*, a word which, by the syntactical influence which it exercises on a word that follows, causes a grammatical alteration of the last syllable of the latter. I 436a; IX 360a; IX 527b

♦ ʿawāmil al-asmāʾ (A) : in grammar, the particles governing nouns. III 550a

amīn (A) : safe, secure; with the more frequent form *āmīn*, a confirmation or corroboration of prayers, Amen. I 436b; (pl. *umanāʾ*) trustworthy; an overseer, administrator. I 437a; VIII 270b

As a technical term, ~ denotes the holders of various positions ʻof trustʼ, particularly those whose functions entail economic or financial responsibility. I 437a; and → EMĪN

In law, ~ denotes legal representatives. I 437a

In the Muslim West, ~ carried the technical meaning of head of a trade guild, which in the East was called ʿARĪF. I 437a

♦ amīn al-ʿāṣima (A) : the chairmen of the municipalities of Damascus, Beirut, Baghdad and Amman, thus called in order to emphasise their particular importance in relation to the seat of the government; elsewhere in the Arab East, the original designation, *raʾīs al-baladiyya*, is retained. I 975b

♦ amīn al-ḥukm (A) : the officer in charge of the administration of the effects of orphan minors (under the early ʿAbbāsids). I 437a

amīr (A, pl. *umarāʾ*; T *emīr*) : commander, governor, prince. I 438b; a person invested with command (AMR), and more especially military command. I 445a; III 45b; IV 941 ff.

♦ **amīr āḵhūr** (A) : the supervisor of the royal stables. I 442b; IV 217b; and → MĪR-ĀKHŪR

♦ **amīr dād** (P) : the minister of justice under the Saldjūḳs. I 443b

♦ amīr djāndār (< P) : in Mamlūk Egypt, 'Marshal of the Court', under whose command the RIKĀBDĀR 'groom' was. VIII 530a
♦ amīr al-djuyūsh (A) : the commander-in-chief of the army. XI 188a
♦ **amīr al-ḥādjdj** (A) : the leader of the caravan of pilgrims to Mecca. I 443b
♦ **al-amīr al-kabīr**, or amīr kabīr → ATABAK
♦ **amīr madjlis** (A) : the master of audiences or ceremonies. Under the Saldjūḳs of Asia Minor, the ~ was one of the highest dignitaries. Under the Mamlūks, the ~ had charge of the physicians, oculists and the like. I 445a
♦ **amīr al-muʾminīn** (A) : lit. the commander of the believers; adopted by ʿUmar b. al-Khaṭṭāb on his election as caliph, the title ~ was employed exclusively as the protocollary title of a caliph until the end of the caliphate as an institution. I 445a
♦ **amīr al-muslimīn** (A) : lit. commander of the Muslims; title which the Almoravids first assumed. I 445b
♦ amīr shikār (A) : an institution, first known as *amīr al-ṣayd* 'master of the chases', established by the Umayyads. I 1152a
♦ **amīr silāḥ** (A) : the grand master of the armour. Under the Mamlūks, the ~ was in charge of the armour-bearers and supervised the arsenal. I 445b
♦ **amīr al-umarāʾ** (A) : the commander-in-chief of the army. I 446a; II 507b
♦ amīrī (A) : a cotton product from Khʷārazm that enjoyed a great reputation. V 555a
♦ al-umarāʾ al-muṭawwaḳūn → ṢĀḤIB AL-BĀB
ʿāmir → DĀYMAN
amladj (A) : in botany, the fruit of the *Phyllanthus emblica*, which was useful against haemorrhoids. The Arabs and Europeans in the Middle Ages mistook it for a myrobalanus. XII 349b
ʿamlūḳ (A) : the offspring of a DJINN and a woman. III 454b
ʿamm (A, pl. *aʿmām*) : paternal uncle. IV 916b
♦ ʿamm waḍḍāḥ (A) : a child's game described as searching (in the dark) for a very white bone tossed far away, with the finder being allowed to ride upon his playmates. The Prophet is said to have engaged in this as a child. V 615b
āmma (A), or *maʾmūma* : a wound penetrating the brain; a determining factor in the prescription of compensation following upon physical injury, DIYA. II 341b
ʿāmma (A, pl. *ʿawāmm*) : the plebs, common people. I 491a; I 900a ff.; IV 1098a; V 605b; and → KHĀṢṢ
♦ ʿāmmī (A) : one who is secular in religious matters. IX 185b; among the Twelver Uṣūliyya, a lay believer. VIII 777b; one not trained in the law. IX 324b
♦ ʿāmmiyya (A) : a revolt among the common people. IX 270b
amr (A) : as Qurʾānic and religious term, divine command. I 449a
For ~ in Ottoman Turkish, → EMR
amrad (A) : a handsome, beardless youth. XI 126b; XII 598a
ʿamūd (A, pl. *ʿumdān*) : a tent pole; a monolithic column and capital; a constructed pillar. I 457b; IV 1148a; the main stream of a river, in particular the Nile, as distinguished from the minor branches and the canals. VIII 38a
♦ ʿamūd al-ḳaṣīda → MUSAMMAṬ
amzwār → MIZWĀR
amzyad → AMAZZAL
ānā : originally, an Indian money of account, a sixteenth share, one rupee being 16 ~. Later, the name was given to an actual coin. VI 121b
ʿāna → ISTIḤDĀD
ʿanāʾ → DJALSA; KIRĀʾ MUʾABBAD
ʿanāḍīl (A) : a despised class of workmen, including such professions as barber, butcher, cupper, etc. IV 819b

ʿanāḳ (A) : in zoology, ~ or *ʿanāḳ al-arḍ* denotes a kind of lynx, the caracal (< T *ḳaraḳulaḳ*). I 481a; II 739b; IX 98b; X 224a; and → SAKHLA

In astronomy, *ʿanāḳ al-arḍ* is γ Andromedae and *ʿanāḳ al-banāt* is the ζ of the Great Bear. I 481a

anayasa → ḲĀNŪN-I ESĀSĪ

ʿanaza (A) : a short spear or staff, syn. *ḥarba*. I 482a; XII 735b; and → KARKADDAN

In North Africa, ~ survives as an architectural term signifying an external MIḤRĀB for those praying in the court of the mosque. I 482a

anbā (A) : in al-Buraymī in Arabia, the term for mangoe (syn. *hanb*). I 540b; in India, a kind of sweet lemon, the fruit of which is salted while still green. VII 962b

ʿanbar (A) : ambergris (*ambra grisea*), a substance of sweet musk-like smell, easily fusible and burning with a bright flame, highly valued in the East as a perfume and medicine. I 484a; a large fish, also called *bāl*, which swallows a form of ambergris called *al-mablūʿ* 'swallowed ambergris' or 'fish-ambergris', which floats on the sea; the sperm-whale. I 484a; VIII 1022b

♦ ʿanbar shiḥrī (A) : ambergris. IX 439a

anbata (A) : a verb which conveys the meaning 'his [a boy's] hair of the pubes grew forth, he having nearly attained the age of puberty'. VIII 822a

anbīḳ (A, < Gk) : in alchemy, the part known as the 'head' or 'cap' of the distilling apparatus (syn. *raʾs*); also, the additional faucet-pipe which fits onto the 'cap'. I 486a

ʿandam → BAḲḲAM

andargāh (P, A *mustaraḳa* 'stolen') : epagomenae, the five odd days added at the end of the Persian year as intercalary days. II 398a; generally known in Persian as the 'five Gāthās (*pandj gāh*) or 'stolen' (*duzdīdha*) days. X 261b; also known as *lawāḥiḳ* 'appendages'. X 267a

andarz (P) : wisdom literature. X 231a

andjudhān → ḤILTĪT

andjuman (P, T *endjümen*) : meeting, assembly, army. I 505a; for its modern use → DJAMʿIYYA

anf (A) : in music, the nut of the ʿŪD. X 769b

anfiya → SUʿŪṬ

anflūs → MIZWĀR

anghām (A, s. *naghm*) : in music, musical modes. IX 101a

angusht (P) : fingerbreadth; a unit of measurement under the Mughals which was standardised at 2.032 cm by the emperor Akbar at the end of the 10th/16th century. II 232a

angusṭ : in zoology, the crawfish, spiny lobster (*Palinarus vulgaris*), also known as *ankūsh*. IX 40a, where many more synonyms are given

angūza (Pash), or *hing* : in botany, term for the *Ferula assafoetida*, very abundant in Afghanistan. I 223a

ʿanḳāʾ (A) : a fabulous bird approximating the phoenix, in all likelihood a type of heron. I 509a

In music, an ancient instrument described as having open strings of different lengths but identically situated bridges. The name suggests a long-necked instrument, probably a trapezoidal psaltery, one species of which was known later as the ḲĀNŪN. VII 191a

ʿankabūt (A) : spider. I 509a; and → SAMAK ʿANKABŪT

In astronomy, a movable part on the front of the astrolabe. I 723a

anḳad (A) : a generic name for the tortoise and the hedgehog. V 389b

anḳalīs (A, L *Anquilla*) : the eel. VIII 1021a

ankūsh → ANGUSṬ

anmāṭ (A) : large carpets with fringes, said in a Tradition to have been the subject of considerable expenditure by the Prophet for a wedding. X 900a

anniyya (A) : an abstract term formed to translate the Aristotelian term τὸ ὅτι 'thatness' of a thing (syn. *al-anna*); ~ is also used for non-existential being. I 513b

anṣāb → NUṢUB

anṣār (A) : 'helpers'; those men of Medina who supported Muḥammad. I 514a

ʿansāra (A) : the name of a festival. Among the Copts, ~ is the name for Pentecost, while in North Africa, ~ denotes the festival of the summer solstice. I 515a

anshūyah (A, < Sp *anchoa*), or *andjūyah* : in zoology, the anchovy (*Engraulis boelema*). VIII 1021a, where many synonyms are found

ʿantarī (A) : in Egypt, a story-teller who narrates the Romance of ʿAntar. I 522a; (< T) a short garment worn under the ḲAFṬĀN; a lined vest ranging from short to knee length, worn by women. I 522a; V 740b

anwāʾ (A, s. *nawʾ*) : a system of computation based on the acronychal setting and helical rising of a series of stars or constellations. I 523a; VIII 98a; VIII 734a

ʿanz (A), or *ṣafiyya* : a one-year old female goat, called thereafter, progressively, *thanī, rabāʿī, sadīs* and, after seven years, *sāligh*. XII 319a

anzarūt (A) : in botany, a gum-resin from a thorn-bush which cannot be identified with certainty. It was used for medical purposes. XII 77b, where synonyms are found

āpa : 'older sister', an important term in Özbeg kinship terminologies. VIII 234a

apadāna (MidP) : in architecture, a hypostile audience-hall of the Persian kings. I 609b f.

ʿār (A) : shame, opprobrium, dishonour. XII 78a

In North Africa, ~ presupposes a transfer of responsibility and of obligation, arriving at a sense of 'protection' for the suppliant, in default of which dishonour falls on the supplicatee, who is obliged to give satisfaction to the suppliant. The most simple transfer is by saying *ʿār ʿalīk* 'the ~ on you', and making a material contact with the person to whom the appeal is made, for example touching the edge of his turban or laying one's hand on him or his mount. ~ is also used towards saints, to whom sacrifices are offered to obtain their intercession. III 396a; XII 78a

ʿarab (A) : Bedouins; Arabs. The tribes that were the first to speak Arabic after the confusion of the tongues at Babel are known as *al-ʿarab al-ʿāriba*, in contradistinction to *al-ʿarab al-*MUTAʿARRIBA (sometimes *al-mustaʿriba*), referring to the descendants of Ismāʿīl who learned Arabic by settling among the 'true' Arabs. X 359b

♦ al-ʿarab al-bāʾida (A) : the legendary extinct tribes of the Arabs. X 359a; XI 5a; XI 461a

♦ ʿarabī → ḲAṬĀ; for ~ (ḥaḍramī), → SUḲUṬRĪ

♦ **ʿarabiyya** (A) : the Arabic language. I 561b; and → ʿARABA

ʿaraba (T, < A ʿARRĀDA), or *ʿarabiyya* : a cart, introduced into Mamlūk Egypt. Its name supplanted ʿADJALA in popular use as a generic term for carriage. I 205b; I 556b

♦ ʿaraba pāzārï (T) : in certain Rumelian towns under the Ottomans, a market presumably located on the outskirts of the town or along a major road. IX 797a

♦ ʿarabiyyat ḥanṭūr (Egy, < Hun *hintó*), and *ʿarabiyyat kārrō* (< It *carro*) : a cab. I 206a

ʿaraḍ (A, pl. *aʿrāḍ*) : the translation of the Aristotelian term συμβεβηκός 'accident', denoting 1) that which cannot subsist by itself but only in a substance of which it is both the opposite and the complement, and 2) an attribute which is not a constituent element of an essence. I 128b; I 603b

arādhil → AHL AL-FAḌL

aʿradj → ʿARDJĀ

aʿrāf (A, s. *ʿurf*) : 'elevated places'; a term used in the Qurʾān, in an eschatological judgement scene, and interpreted as 'Limbo'. I 603b

ʿarāʾish (A) : brushwood huts, in Western Arabia. I 106b; trellises of grape vines. I 604b

araḳ (A) : in medicine, insomnia. XI 563a

arāk → KABĀTH

ʿaraḳ (A) : wine made from the grape. VI 814b
ʿaraḳčīn → ʿARAḲIYYA
ʿaraḳiyya (A) : a skull cap, often embroidered, worn by both sexes by itself or under the head-dress in the Arab East; called *ʿaraḳčīn* in ʿIrāḳ. A synonym on the Arabian peninsula is *maʿraḳa*. V 740b ff.; X 611b; in the Turkish Ḳādirī dervish order, a small felt cap which the candidate for admission to the order brought after a year and to which the SHAYKH attached a rose of 18 sections; the cap is then called *tādj*. IV 382b; in earlier times in Syria ~ was a sugar cone-shaped cap adorned with pearls worn by women. X 611b
arandj (A) : a cotton product from Khʷārazm that enjoyed a great reputation. V 555a
ʿaraṣa (A) : in Mamlūk times, an open unroofed space used e.g. for storing cereals. IX 793b
ārāsta → PASAZH
arbaʿīniyya → ČILLA
arbaʿūn (A) : forty.
arbaʿūn ḥadīthan (A, T *ḳirḳ ḥadīth*, P *čihil ḥadīth*) : a genre of literary and religious works centred around 40 Traditions of the Prophet. XII 82b
arḍ (A) : earth, land.

♦ arḍ amīriyya (A) : in law, land to which the original title belongs to the State, while its exploitation can be conceded to individuals. II 900b

♦ arḍ madhūna (A) : an expression occasionally heard in Saudi Arabia which is used to distinguish the sands of al-Dahnāʾ from those of al-Nafūd, the colour of which is said to be a lighter shade of red; ~ is also equated with *arḍ mundahina* 'land only lightly or superficially moistened by rain'. II 93a

♦ arḍ mamlūka (A) : in law, land to which there is a right of ownership. II 900b

♦ arḍ matrūka → MATRŪK

♦ arḍ mawāt → MAWĀT

♦ arḍ mawḳūfa (A) : in law, land set aside for the benefit of a religious endowment. II 900b

♦ arḍ mundahina → ARḌ MADHŪNA

ʿarḍ (A) : review of an army or troops. I 24a; petition. IX 209a; and → ISTIʿRĀḌ
In astronomy, planetary latitude. XI 504a

♦ **ʿarḍ ḥāl** (T) : petition, used in the Ottoman empire. I 625a

♦ ʿarḍ odasi̊ (T) : in Ottoman palace architecture, the audience hall. IX 46b

ʿardjā (A) : lame; in prosody, ~ is used to designate the unrhymed line inserted between the third line and the last line of a monorhyme quatrain, RUBĀʿĪ. The composition is then called *aʿradj*. VI 868a
ardjawān (< P ?) : a loan-word in Arabic, the colour purple. V 699b
arəḳḳas (Kabyle, < A RAḲḲĀṢ) : a simple contrivance of a water-mill made from a pin fixed on a small stick floating above the moving mill-stone; this pin, fixed to the trough containing grain, transmits a vibration to it which ensures the regular feeding of the grain into the mouth of the mill. VIII 415b
argan (B) : in botany, the argan-tree (*argania spinosa* or *argania sideroxylon*), growing on the southern coast of Morocco. I 627b
arghūl (A) : a type of double reed-pipe which has only one pipe pierced with finger-holes, while the other serves as a drone. The drone pipe is normally longer than the chanter pipe. When the two pipes are of equal length, it is known as the ZUMMĀRA. The ~ is played with single beating reeds. The drone pipe is furnished with additional tubes which are fixed to lower the pitch. In Syria, the smaller type of ~ is called the *mashūra*. VII 208a
ʿāriḍ (A, pl. *ʿurrāḍ*) : the official charged with the mustering, passing in review and inspection of troops. III 196a; IV 265a ff.

♦ 'āriḍ-i mamālik (IndP) : the head of the military administration in Muslim India. He was also known as *ṣāḥib-i dīwān-i 'arḍ*. The Mughal name was *mīr bakhshī*. As a minister, he was second only to the WAZĪR. He was the principal recruiting officer for the sultan's standing army; he inspected the armaments and horses of the cavalry at least once a year, kept their descriptive rolls, and recommended promotions or punishments accordingly. The ~ was also responsible for the internal organisation and the discipline of the standing army and the commissariat. V 685b

'arīḍ → 'ATŪD

♦ 'arīḍa (A) : a subtraction register, for those categories where the difference between two figures needs to be shown. It is arranged in three columns, with the result in the third. II 78b

'ārif → ṢŪFĪ

'arif (A, pl. *'urafā'*) : lit. one who knows; a gnostic. IV 326a; as a technical term, applied to holders of certain military or civil offices in the early and mediaeval periods, based on competence in customary matters, *'urf*. I 629a

In education, a senior pupil, monitor, who aided the teacher in primary schools. V 568a

In the Muslim East, ~ was used for the head of the guild. I 629b

In Oman and trucial Oman, ~ is the official in charge of the water distribution. IV 532a

Among the Ibāḍiyya, the plural form *'urafā'* are experts (inspectors, ushers) appointed by the assistant of the SHAYKH, *khalīfa*. One of them supervised the collective recitation of the Qur'ān, another took charge of the communal meals, and others were responsible for the students' education, etc. III 96a

arīka → MINAṢṢA

'arīsh (A), and *'arsh* : in pre-Islamic Arabia, a simple shelter. IV 1147a

'ariyya (A, pl. *'arāyā*) : in law, fresh dates on trees intended to be eaten, which it is permitted to exchange in small quantities for dried dates. VIII 492a

'āriyya (A) : in law, the loan of non-fungible objects, distinguished as a separate contract from the loan of money or other fungible objects. ~ is defined as putting someone temporarily and gratuitously in possession of the use of a thing, the substance of which is not consumed by its use. I 633a; VIII 900a

ark (P) : citadel. X 484b

arkān → RUKN

arkh → FAZZ

arma (Songhay, < A *rumāt* 'arquebusiers') : a social class made up of the descendants of the BĀSHĀs who in the early 19th century maintained a weak state around the Niger river with their headquarters at Timbuktu. X 508b

armatolik (T) : an autonomous enclave, institutionalised on Greek territories in the Ottoman empire due to gradually deteriorating conditions of banditry. X 421a

arnab (A, pl. *arānib*) : in zoology, the hare. XII 85b

In astronomy, ~ is the Hare constellation found beneath the left foot of Orion, the legendary hunter. XII 85b

For in anatomy, → ARNABA

♦ arnab baḥrī (A) : in zoology, the term for *aplysia depilans*, a nudibranch mollusc of the order of *isthobranchia*, found widely in the sea. XII 85b

♦ arnaba (A) : in anatomy, the tip (e.g. of the nose, *arnabat al-anf*). V 769a

In music, ~, or *rabāb turkī*, is a pear-shaped viol with three strings, which in Turkey appears to have been adopted from the Greeks, possibly in the 17th century, and which plays a prominent part in concert music today. VIII 348a

arpa (T) : barley. I 658a

♦ arpa tanesi (T) : a barley grain, used under the Ottomans to denote both a weight (approximately 35.3 milligrams) and a measure (less than a quarter of an inch). I 658a

♦ **arpalik̤** (T) : barley money, used under the Ottomans up to the beginning of the 19th century to denote an allowance made to the principal civil, military and religious officers of state, either in addition to their salary when in office, or as a pension on retirement, or as an indemnity for unemployment. In the beginning it corresponded to an indemnity for fodder of animals, paid to those who maintained forces of cavalry or had to look after the horses. I 658a

ʿarrāda (A) : a light mediaeval artillery siege engine, from which the projectile was discharged by the impact of a shaft forcibly impelled by the release of a rope. I 556b; I 658b; III 469b ff.; and → MAND̲J̲ANĪK̤

ʿarrāf (A) : eminent in knowledge, a professional knower; a diviner, generally occupying a lower rank than the KĀHIN in the hierarchy of seers. I 659b; IV 421b

arrang (A, < Sp *arenque*), or *ranga, ranka* : in zoology, the herring. VIII 1021a

ars̲h̲ (A) : in law, the compensation payable in the case of offences against the body; compensation in cases of homicide is termed DIYA. II 340b

ʿars̲h̲ (A) : throne of God. V 509a; in North African dialects, 'tribe', 'agnatic group', 'federation'. I 661a; IV 362a; and → ʿARS̲H̲

In Algerian law, the term given, during about the last hundred years, to some of the lands under collective ownership. I 661a

ars̲h̲īn (P) : roughly 'yards', a unit of measurement. X 487a

ʿarsī (A) : in mediaeval ʿIrāk̤, a beggar who stops the circulation of blood in an arm or leg so that people think the limb is gangrenous. VII 494a

arsusa → URṢŪṢA

aru (B, pl. *irwan*) : the Berber equivalent of *ṭālib*, student, from whom the Ibāḍiyya of the Mzāb recruit their ʿAZZĀBA for the religious council. III 98b

ʿarūḍ (A) : in prosody, the last foot of the first hemistich, as opposed to the last foot of the second hemistich, the ḌARB. I 667b; IV 714b; VIII 747b

♦ ʿilm al-ʿarūḍ (A) : the science of metrics, said to have been developed by al-K̲h̲alīl of Mecca. I 667b; IV 57a; VIII 894a

ʿarūs (A) : the term for both bridegroom and bride, though in modern usage, ~ has been supplanted by *ʿarīs* for bridegroom and *ʿarūsa* for bride. X 899b; and → SĀBIʿ AL-ʿARŪS

♦ **ʿarūs resmi** (T) : an Ottoman tax on brides. The rate varied depending on whether the bride was a girl, widow, divorcee, non-Muslim, Muslim, rich or poor. In some areas, it was assessed in kind. The tax, which seems to be of feudal origin, is already established in the K̤ĀNŪNs of the 15th century in Anatolia and Rumelia, and was introduced into Egypt, Syria and ʿIrāk̤ after the Ottoman conquest. It was abolished in the 19th century and replaced by a fee for permission to marry. I 679a

aruzz → RUZZ

♦ aruzz mufalfal (A) : a very popular mediaeval dish which resembled a type of Turkish *pilaw*. Made with spiced meat and/or chickpeas or pistachio nuts, the dish may contain rice coloured with saffron, white rice alone, or a combination of both. A variation of this dish, made from lentils and plain rice, was called *al-mud̲j̲addara* and is similar to the modern preparation of the same name. VIII 653a

♦ al-aruzziyya (A) : a mediaeval dish containing meat and seasonings (pepper, dried coriander and dill), into which a small amount of powdered rice was added during cooking, and washed (whole) rice towards the end of the preparation. VIII 653a

arwāḥ → RŪḤ

ary (A) : honey (> T *arı* 'bee'). VII 906b

arzal → AṬRĀF

ās (A, < Akk) : in botany, the myrtle (*Myrtus communis*). IX 653a; XII 87a

ʿaṣā (A) : a rod, stick, staff (syn. K̤AḌĪB). Among the ancient Arabs, ~ was in common use for the camel herdsman's staff. In the Qurʾān, it is used a number of times, in particular for Moses' stick. I 680b; and → S̲H̲AG̲H̲ABA

♦ s̲h̲āḳḳ al-ʿaṣā (A) : 'splitter of the ranks of the faithful'; under the Umayyads, a term used to characterise one who deserted the community of the faithful and rebelled against the legitimate caliphs. VII 546a

ʿaṣaba (A) : male relations in the male line, corresponding to the agnates. I 681a; IV 595b; VII 106b

♦ **ʿaṣabiyya** (A) : spirit of kinship in the family or tribe. Ibn K̲h̲aldūn used the concept of this term as the basis of his interpretation of history and his doctrine of the state; for him it is the fundamental bond of human society and the basic motive force of history. I 681a; II 962b; III 830b; factional strife. IV 668b; affiliation to a tribal faction (syn. *naʿra, s̲h̲ahwa, niḥla*). IV 835a

asad (A, pl. *usūd, usud, usd*) : in zoology, the lion; in astronomy, *al-~* is the term for Leo, one of the twelve zodiacal constellations. I 681a; VII 83a

āṣaf (Ott) : in the Ottoman empire, a synonym for *wezīr* (→ WAZĪR). XI 194b

ʿaṣāʾib (A) : the 'troops', 500 in number, the eighth degree in the ṣūfī hierarchical order of saints. I 95a; and → ʿIṢĀBA

ʿasal → ʿIKBIR

ʿaṣal (A) : in botany, the rhododendron. VII 1014b

aṣāla (A) : authenticity. X 365b

asaliyya → D̲H̲AWLAḲIYYA

aṣamm (A) : deaf; in mathematics, the term used for the fractions, such as 1/11 or 1/13, which cannot be reduced to fractions called by words derived from names of their denominators, such as 1/12, which is half one sixth, 'sixth' being derived from six. III 1140b

āsārāk (A, < B *asarag*) : in urban geography, great main squares enclosed in the walls of the ḳaṣaba in the Mag̲h̲rib, where the people could assemble for the festivals and the army participate in ceremonies. IV 685a

ʿasas (A) : the night patrol or watch in Muslim cities. Under the Ottomans, the ~ was in charge of the public prisons, exercised a kind of supervision over public executions, and played an important role in public processions. He received one tenth of the fines imposed for minor crimes committed at night. I 687a; IV 103b
In North Africa, the ~ assured not only public security but also possessed a secret and almost absolute authority in the important affairs of the community. He kept guard at night in the central market, at warehouses and on the ramparts till the advent of the French. I 687b

asāṭīr → USṬŪRA

ʿasb (A) : the semen of a stallion. IV 1146a

ʿaṣb (A) : in early Islam, a Yemenite fabric with threads dyed prior to weaving. V 735b
In prosody, a deviation from the proper metre, in particular a missing FATḤA in the foot *mufāʿal[a]tun*. I 672a; a case of ZIḤĀF where the fifth vowelled letter of the foot is rendered vowelless. XI 508b

♦ ʿaṣba (A) : a folded scarf worn by women in the Arab East. V 740b

aṣbaʿ → IṢBAʿ

asbāb → SABAB

asefru (B, pl. *isefra*) : a genre of oral poetry popular in Kabylia, a Berberophone area of Algeria, consisting of a sonnet of nine verses grouped in three strophes rhyming according to the scheme a a b. Another poetic genre is the so-called *izli*, a song of two or three couplets in rhyme, whose production is anonymous. X 119a

asfal (A) : lower; *al-asfal* is used as an epithet to differentiate between the patron and the client, when both are referred to as MAWLĀ. I 30b

aṣfar (A) : yellow; also, in distinction from black, simply light-coloured. I 687b; V 700b

♦ banu 'l-aṣfar (A) : the Greeks; later, applied to Europeans in general, especially in Spain. I 687b; V 700b

as̲h̲ → TOY

aṣḥāb (A, s. **ṣāḥib**) : followed by the name of a locality in the genitive, ~ serves to refer to people who are companions in that particular place. Followed by a personal name in the genitive, ~ is, alongside the NISBA formation, the normal way of expressing the 'adherents of so-and-so' or the 'members of his school'. When followed by an abstract noun in the genitive, ~ denotes adherents of a specific concept. VIII 830b; and → ṢAḤABA; ṢĀḤIB

♦ aṣḥāb al-arbāʿ (A) : in Mamlūk times, night patrols coming under the authority of the chief of police, *wālī*. I 687a

♦ aṣḥāb al-as̲h̲āʾir (A) : the four mystical orders of the Burhāmiyya, Rifāʿiyya, Ḳādiriyya and Aḥmadiyya, according to D̲j̲abartī. II 167a

♦ aṣḥāb al-ḥadīt̲h̲ → AHL AL-ḤADĪT̲H̲

♦ aṣḥāb al-it̲h̲nayn → T̲H̲ANAWIYYA

♦ **aṣḥāb al-kahf** (A) : 'those of the cave', the name given in the Qurʾān for the youths who in the Christian West are usually called the 'Seven Sleepers of Ephesus'. I 691a; IV 724a

♦ aṣḥāb al-naḳb → NAḲB

♦ **aṣḥāb al-rass** (A) : 'the people of the ditch' or 'of the well'; a Qurʾānic term, possibly alluding to unbelievers. I 692a; III 169a

♦ **aṣḥāb al-raʾy** → AHL AL-RAʾY

♦ aṣḥāb al-saṭḥ (A), or *suṭūḥiyya* : 'the roof men', designation for the followers and disciples of the 7th/13th-century Egyptian saint Aḥmad al-Badawī. I 280b

♦ aṣḥāb al-s̲h̲ad̲j̲ara (A) : 'the men of the tree'; those who took the oath of allegiance to the Prophet under the tree in the oasis of al-Ḥudaybiya, as mentioned in Q 48:18. VIII 828a; XII 131a

♦ **aṣḥāb al-uk̲h̲dūd** (A) : 'those of the trench'; a Qurʾānic term, possibly alluding to unbelievers. I 692b

♦ aṣḥāb-tark → AK̲H̲Ī

asḥam → SALḲAʿ

ashām → ESHĀM

aṣḥar → ṢAḤRĀʾ

as̲h̲āra → AWMAʾA

ʿas̲h̲ara (A, pl. *ʿas̲h̲r*) : ten.

♦ **al-ʿas̲h̲ara al-mubas̲h̲s̲h̲ara** (A) : the ten to whom Paradise is promised. The term does not occur in canonical Traditions and the list of names differs, Muḥammad appearing in only some. I 693a

♦ al-ʿas̲h̲r al-uwal (A) : the first ten nights of a month, each month being divided into three segments of ten. The other segments are respectively *al-ʿas̲h̲r al-wusaṭ* and *al-ʿas̲h̲r al-uk̲h̲ar*, with the latter sometimes only nine nights in 'defective' months. X 259b

as̲h̲bāh (A, s. *s̲h̲ibh*) : component of a book title, *al-As̲h̲bāh wa'l-naẓāʾir*, of some of the most influential ḲAWĀʿID works of the later period, ~ referring to cases that are alike in appearance and legal status, with *naẓāʾir* (s. *naẓīr*) denoting cases that are alike in appearance but not in legal status. XII 517a

ās̲h̲d̲j̲i̊ (T) : lit. cook; an officer's rank in an ORTA, subordinate to that of the ČORBAD̲J̲I̊, or 'soup purveyor'. VIII 178b

as̲h̲hada (A) : a technical term of childhood, said of a boy (or girl: *as̲h̲hadat*) who has attained to puberty. VIII 822a

ʿāshiķ (A) : lover; a term originally applied to popular mystic poets of dervish orders. It was later taken over by wandering poet-minstrels. Their presence at public gatherings, where they entertained the audience with their religious and erotic songs, elegies and heroic narratives, can be traced back to the late 9th/15th century. I 697b; III 374a; IV 599a; V 275a ff.

ʿāshikh (Azerī Turkish, < ʿĀSHIĶ) : in Azerī literature, a genre of folk-literature comprising romantic poems, which made great advances in Ādharbaydjān in the 17th and 18th centuries and formed a bridge between the classical literary language and the local dialects. I 193b

ʿāshir (A, pl. *ʿushshār*) : in early Islam, a collector of ZAKĀT from Muslim merchants as well as imposts on the merchandise of non-Muslim traders. The institution is attributed to ʿUmar, but in the course of time, the ~ acquired an exceedingly unavory reputation for venality. XI 409a

ʿashīra (A) : usually a synonym of ĶABĪLA 'tribe', ~ can also denote a subdivision of the latter. I 700a; IV 334a

ʿashiyya (A), and variants : a word loosely taken in the sense of evening, although it used to designate more precisely the end of the day, NAHĀR. In this sense it was the opposite of ḌUḤĀ. V 709b

ashl (A, P *ṭanāb*) : rope; a unit of measurement equalling 39.9 metres. II 232b

ashlḥi (B, pl. *ishlḥiyen*), or *ashlḥiy* : a native speaker of Tashelḥīt. X 344b

āshpazkhāna (P, A MAṬBAKH) : kitchen (P *āsh* 'soup', *āshpaz* 'cook'), which term was not in general used before the 19th century, *maṭbakh* being the common term. XII 608b

ʿashr → ʿASHARA

ʿashraf → WAṬWĀṬ

ashrāf (A, s. SHARĪF) : in India, ~ denoted Muslims of foreign ancestry. They were further divided into *sayyid* (those reckoning descent from the Prophet through his daughter Fāṭima), *shaykh* (descendants of the early Muslims of Mecca and Medina), *mughal* (those who entered the subcontinent in the armies of the Mughal dynasty), and *paṭhān* (members of Pashtō-speaking tribes in north-west Pakistan and Afghanistan). III 411a; IX 330b; and → SHARĪF

ashrafī (A) : in numismatics, a Burdjī Mamlūk gold coin, the coinage of which was continued by the Ottomans after their conquest of Egypt and Syria. VIII 228b; an Ottoman gold coinage, introduced under Muṣṭafā II to replace the discredited SULṬĀNĪ. VIII 229b; an Aķ Ķoyunlu gold coin, copied exactly on the Burdjī Mamlūk ~. Its weight was ca. 3.45 g. VIII 790a; in Ṣafawid Persia, all the gold coins were popularly called ~ , but there were actually several different varieties to which the name was given, which were distinguished from one another by their weights rather than by their designs or legends. The true ~, used by Ismāʿīl as a standard for his gold coinage, weighed 18 *nukhūd*s (approximately 3.45 g), and had its origin in the weight of the Venetian gold ducat. VIII 790b

ʿashshāb (A) : from *ʿushb*, a fresh annual herb which is afterwards dried and, in medical literature, denotes simples, ~ means a gatherer or vendor of herbs; a vendor or authority on medicinal herbs. I 704a

ʿāshūrāʾ (A, < Heb) : the name of a voluntary fast-day, observed on the 10th of Muḥarram. I 265a; I 705a; XII 190a; in South Africa, a festival commemorating the martyrdom of al-Ḥusayn, the grandson of the Prophet. IX 731a

ʿaṣīda (A) : a meal of barley and fat. X 901b

aṣīl (A) : a term used in reference to the time which elapses between the afternoon, ʿAṢR, and sunset; in the contemporary language this word tends to be employed for the evening twilight. V 709b; and → KAFĀLA

ʿasīr (A) : lit. captive, term also sometimes used for slave. I 24b āsitāne   → TEKKE

'askar   (A) : army, in particular one possessing siege artillery. II 507a; 'garrison settlements' (syn. *mu'askar, ma'askar*) founded in the Arab East during the caliphate period. IV 1144a

♦ 'askarī   (A, < 'ASKAR; T *'askerī*) : in Ottoman technical usage a member of the ruling military caste, as distinct from the peasants and townspeople; ~ denoted caste rather than function, and included the retired or unemployed ~, his wives and children, manumitted slaves of the sultan and of the ~, and also the families of the holders of religious public offices in attendance on the sultan. I 712a; IV 242a; IV 563a; IX 540a

'askerī   → 'ASKARĪ

askiya   (Songhay) : a dynastic title of the Songhay empire of West Africa, first adopted in 898/1493 by Muḥammad b. Abī Bakr. IX 729b

aṣl   (A, pl. **uṣūl**) : root, base. III 550a; ancestry. XI 276b

In grammar, a basic form, concept or structure, with a wide range of meanings extending over phonology, morphology and syntax, e.g. a standard phoneme in contrast with an allophone; a root-letter in the derivational system; a radical consonant opposed to an augment; etc. When used in the plural, the fundamental principles of grammar as a science. X 928b, where more definitions of ~ are found

In classical Muslim administration, ~ is the estimated figure, as opposed to the amount actually received, ISTIḴHRĀDJ. II 78b

In dating, ~ is the number of days in a given number of completed years. X 268b

In military science, *uṣūl* were the theoretical divisions of the army into five elements: the centre (*ḳalb*), the right wing (*maymana*), the left wing (*maysara*), the vanguard (*muḳaddama*), and the rear guard (*sāḳa*). III 182a

In music, the *uṣūl* are the basic notes which, with the pause, make up the cycles of an ĪḴĀ'. XII 408b; metres. IX 418a

In astronomy, the epoch position (L *radix*). XI 503b

In law, because early ḴAWĀ'ID were collected under the title of *uṣūl*, ~ acquires, minimally, a fourfold meaning: an act that has already been legally determined and now serves as a 'model' for similar cases; a scriptural pronouncement considered decisive for the legal determination of a given act; a legal principle; and a source of the law. XII 517a; and → WAṢF

For *uṣūl* in prosody, → FAR'

♦ **uṣūl al-dīn**   (A) : the bases (or principles) of the religion. If *uṣūl* meant the same here as in *uṣūl al-fiḳh*, the two expressions would be synonymous, for the theologian goes back to the same authorities as the jurist to justify his interpretation of dogma; instead in ordinary usage ~ represent not the sources of theological judgement but, in some way, the judgement itself, thus the science of ~ is another way of designating *'ilm al*-KALĀM. X 930b

♦ **uṣūl al-fiḳh**   (A) : the 'roots' or sources of legal knowledge, viz. the Qur'ān, *sunna*, consensus and analogy. II 887b; X 323b; X 931b; legal theory. II 182b

♦ **uṣūl al-ḥadīth**   (A) : the principles of ḤADĪTH; the disparate disciplines the mastery of which distinguished a true scholar of *ḥadīth* from a mere transmitter. The term ~ was never satisfactorily defined nor differentiated from similar ones like *'ulūm* (or *'ilm) al-ḥadīth, iṣṭilāḥ al-ḥadīth*, etc. There are instances of *'ilm al-riwāya* being used as a synonym. X 934a

♦ uṣūliyya   → AḴHBĀRIYYA

aṣlaḥ   (A) : most suitable or fitting; in theology, the 'upholders of the *aṣlaḥ*' were a group of the Mu'tazila who held that God did what was best for mankind. I 713b

aslamī   (A) : a term used to designate first-generation Spanish converts, who were formerly Christians, whereas the term *islāmī* was reserved for the former Jews. VII 807b asmāʾ → ISM

asmānḏjūnī → YĀḲŪT AKHAB

asmar (A) : in physiognomy, a dark brown, or black, complexion. XI 356a

asmār → KH̲URAFĀʾ

asp-i dāg̲h̲ī (IndP) : under the Mug̲h̲als, a payment in accordance with the actual number of horsemen and horses presented at muster, unlike the BAR-ĀWARDĪ, a payment based on an estimate. IX 909a

asparez : a race-course. X 479a

ʿaṣr (A) : time, age; the (early part of the) afternoon. This period of day follows that of the midday prayer, ẒUHR, and extends between limits determined by the length of the shadow, but is variable, according to the jurists. I 719a; V 709b

♦ ṣalāt al-ʿaṣr (A) : the afternoon prayer which is to be performed, according to the books of religious law, in between the last time allowed for the midday prayer, ẒUHR, and before sunset, or the time when the light of the sun turns yellow. According to Mālik, the first term begins somewhat later. I 719a; VII 27b; VIII 928b

ʿassālāt → ʿIKBIR

ʿassās (A) : night-watchman. This term is used particularly in North Africa; at Fez at the beginning of the 20th century, ~ also was used for policemen in general. I 687b
In the Mzāb, ~ is used for the minaret of the Abāḍī mosques. I 687a

astān (P) : in mediaeval administration, a province. I 2b; a district. I 3a

asṭurlāb (A, < Gk), or *asṭurlāb* : astrolabe. The name of several astronomical instruments serving various theoretical and practical purposes, such as demonstration and graphical solution of many problems of spherical astronomy, the measuring of altitudes, the determination of the hour of the day and the night, and the casting of horoscopes. When used alone ~ always means the flat or planispheric astrolabe based on the principle of stereographic projection; it is the most important instrument of mediaeval, Islamic and Western, astronomy. I 722b

asṭūrū (A, < Gr) : in zoology, the oyster. VIII 707a

aswad (A) : the colour black. V 705b; and → ABYAḌ

ata (T) : father, ancestor; among the Og̲h̲uz, ~ was appended to the names of people who had acquired great prestige. ~ can also mean 'wise', or even 'holy', 'venerated'. I 729a; XI 114a

ʿaṭāʾ (A) : lit. gift; the term most commonly employed to denote, in the early days of Islam, the pension of Muslims, and, later, the pay of the troops. I 729a

ʿataba (A, pl. **ʿatabāt**) : doorstep.
In (folk) poetry, ~ (or *fars̲h̲a* 'spread, mat') is used to designate the first three lines of a monorhyme quatrain (*a a a a*), or each of the three lines, when insertions have been made between the third line and the last, e.g. as in *a a a x a*. The last line is then called the *g̲h̲aṭā* 'cover' or, in longer compositions, the *ṭāḳiyya* 'skull-cap'. VI 868a
In its plural form, more fully *ʿatabāt-i ʿāliya* or *ʿatabāt-i muḳaddasa, ʿatabāt* designates the s̲h̲īʿī shrine cities of ʿIrāḳ (Nad̲j̲af, Karbalāʾ, Kāẓimayn and Sāmarrā) comprising the tombs of six of the IMĀMS as well as a number of secondary shrines and places of visitation. XII 94a

ʿatāba (A) : a modern Arabic four line verse, common in Syria, Palestine, Mesopotamia and ʿIrāḳ, in a sort of WĀFIR metre. The first three lines not only rhyme, but generally repeat the same rhyming word with a different meaning. The last line rhymes with the paradigm ~ 'lovers' reproach', the last syllable of which is often supplied without making sense. I 730b

atabak (T *atabeg*) : the title of a high dignitary under the Sald̲j̲ūḳs and their successors; under the Turks, a military chief. I 731a; commander-in-chief of an army (syn. *amīr kabīr*). I 138a; I 444a

♦ **atābak al-ʿasākir** (T, A) : commander-in-chief of the Mamlūk army, who after the decline of the office of the viceroy, *nāʾib al-salṭana*, became the most important AMĪR in the Sultanate. I 732b

ʿatala (A) : in archery, a powerful Persian bow which is very curved. IV 798a

atalïḳ (T) : a title which existed in Central Asia in the post-Mongol period meaning in the first place a guardian and tutor of a young prince, then a close counsellor and confidant of the sovereign. It was synonymous with *atabeg* (→ ATABAK). I 733b; XII 96b

atalikat (Cau) : a custom among the Čerkes tribes of the Caucasus, which consisted of having children raised from birth (boys until 17-18 years) in the families of strangers, often vassals. This created a sort of foster brotherhood which served to tighten the feudal bonds and unite the various tribes. II 23a

aṭam (A) : a fabulous marine creature mentioned by mediaeval Arab authors. It lurks in the Sea of China, has the head of a pig, is covered with a hairy fleece instead of scales, and shows female sexual organs. VIII 1023a

ʿatama (A) : the first third of the night from the time of waning of the red colour of the sky after sunset, SHAFAḲ. I 733b; a variant name given to the *ṣalāt al-ʿishāʾ* (→ ʿISHĀʾ). VII 27a

atān → ḤIMĀR

ātāy → ČAY

ātbēgī → ĀKHŪRBEG

ʿaṭf (A) : connection; in grammar, ~ denotes a connection with the preceding word. There are two kinds of ~ : the simple co-ordinative connection, *ʿaṭf al-nasaḳ*, and the explicative connection, *ʿaṭf al-bayān*. In both kinds, the second word is called *al-maʿṭūf*, and the preceding *al-maʿṭūf ʿalayhi*. I 735b

In rhetoric, ~ as used by al-ʿAdjdjādj, in the sense of 'folding back' or 'adding on', may have meant paronomasia. ~ seems to be take up again in the term *taʿaṭṭuf* of Abū Hilāl al-ʿAskarī. X 68b

♦ ʿaṭfa → SHĀRIʿ

athar (A) : trace; as a technical term, it denotes a relic of the Prophet, e.g. his hair, teeth, autograph, utensils alleged to have belonged to him, and especially impressions of his footprints, *ḳadam*. I 736a

In the science of Tradition, ~ usually refers to a Tradition from Companions or Successors, but is sometimes used of Traditions from the Prophet. I 1199a; III 23a

In astrology, ~ is also used as a technical term in the theory of causality, with reference to the influence of the stars (considered as higher beings possessing a soul) on the terrestrial world and on men. I 736b

athāth (A) : lit. belongings, ~ means various household objects and, especially in modern Arabic, furniture. XII 99a

athmān (A) : gold and silver (on which ZAKĀT is due), also *ʿayn, naḳd, nāḍḍ*. XI 413a

ʿaththarī (A, < the name of the deity ʿAthtar) : a term equivalent to *baʿl* 'unwatered cultivated land'. I 969a

ʿāṭif → MUSALLĪ

ʿatīḳ (A) : a pure-bred horse, as opposed to a work horse, *birdhawn*. XI 412b; and → ʿITḲ

ʿātiḳa (A) : in archery, an old bow whose wood has become red. IV 798a

ʿātikī (A, < *Ḳabr ʿĀtika*, a concentration of textile workshops in Damascus) : in the 11th/17th century, a Syrian fabric, sufficiently renowned to be exhibited in the markets of Cairo. IX 793b

ʿatīra (A) : among the Arabs of the DJĀHILIYYA, a ewe offered as a sacrifice to a pagan divinity, as a thanksgiving following the fulfillment of a prayer concerning in particular the increase of flocks. Also called *radjabiyya*, since these sacrifices took place in the month of Radjab. I 739b; XII 317a

ātishak : in medicine, syphilis. VIII 783a; X 457b

aṭlāl (A) : the remains or traces of former encampments; in literature, a trope in the NASĪB section of the ḲAṢĪDA. XII

atmadja → ČAKÎR

aṭrāf (IndP, < A) : a term used to designate the higher stratum of the non-ASHRĀF population of India, which consists for the most part of converts from Hinduism, embracing people of many statuses and occupations. The terms *adjlāf* and *arzal* (or *ardhāl*) are used to designate the lower stratum. III 411a; IX 330b

In the science of Tradition, a so-called ~ compilation is an alphabetically-arranged collection of the Companions' MUSNADs, with every Tradition ascribed to each of them shortened to its salient feature (→ ṬARAF), accompanied by all the ISNAD strands supporting it which occur in the Six Books and a few other revered collections. VIII 518b

ʿattābī (A) : a kind of silk-cotton cloth, woven around 580/1184 in ʿAttābiyya, one of the quarters of Baghdad. I 901b

ʿaṭṭār (A) : a perfume merchant or druggist; later, as most scents and drugs were credited with some healing properties, ~ came to mean chemist and homeopath; sometimes dyers and dye merchants are also known by this term. I 751b

In India, ~ denotes an alcohol-free perfume-oil produced by the distillation of sandal-wood-oil through flowers. I 752b

attūn (A) : a kiln used for firing bricks, similar to that of the potters, consisting of a furnace with a firing-room on top. V 585b

ʿatūd (A), or *ʿarīḍ* : a one-year old male goat, called, progressively, *djadhaʿ* or *tays* when two years old, then *thanī, rabāʿī, sadīs* and, after seven years, *sāligh*. XII 319a

aṭūm (A) : in zoology, the dugong, one of the sirenian mammals or 'sea cows'. Other designations are *maliṣa, nāḳa al-baḥr, zālikha*, and *ḥanfāʾ*. VIII 1022b; the caret or caouane turtle (*Caretta caretta*) (syn. *ḥanfāʾ*). IX 811a

awāʾil (A, s. AWWAL 'first') : a term used to denote e.g. the 'primary data' of philosophical or physical phenomena; the 'ancients' of either pre-Islamic or early Islamic times; and the 'first inventors' of things (or the things invented or done first), thus giving its name to a minor branch of Muslim literature with affinities to ADAB, historical, and theological literature. I 758a

♦ awāʾil al-suwar → FAWĀTIḤ AL-SUWAR

awāradj (A) : in classical Muslim administration, a register showing the debts owed by individual persons and the instalments paid until they are settled. II 78b; VIII 652a

ʿawāriḍ (A) : a term used under the Ottomans down to the second quarter of the 19th century to denote contributions of various types exacted by the central government in the sultan's name. The Ottoman fief-system and the institution of the WAḲF deprived the government to a great extent of the vast revenues. Therefore it resorted, at first in emergencies and later annually, to the imposition of the ~, either in cash or in kind. I 760a; IV 234b; VIII 486b

awārik (A) : 'eaters of *arāk* leaves', the name of a famous breed of white camels raised by the Bedouin living near the oasis of Bīsha, in western Arabia. I 541a; I 1239b

ʿawāṣim (A, s. *ʿāṣima*) : lit. protectresses; strongholds in the frontier zone extended between the Byzantine empire and the empire of the caliphs in the north and north-east of Syria. Those situated more to the front were called *al-thughūr*. I 465b; I 761a; X 446b; a separate government founded by Hārūn al-Rashīd in 170/786-87, made up of the frontier strongholds which he detached from the Djazīra and DJUND of Ḳinnasrīn. I 761a; II 36a

āwāz → BAḤR

ʿawbar (A), or *hawbar* : in zoology, the whelp of the cheetah. II 740b

awbās͟h (A) : 'riff-raff', the name given to groups of young men who were considered elements of disorder in mediaeval Baghdad. II 961b

awd̲j̲ (A, < San *ucča*; pl. *awd̲j̲āt*) : in astronomy, the apogee, the farthest point in a planet's orbit. The lowest point, the perigee, is called *ḥaḍīḍ*. VIII 101b; IX 292a; XI 503b

awhāz (A) : attendants (who, al-Hamdānī writes, stood at the gates of the ancient town of Ẓafār in Yemen and acted as guards). XI 380a

awḳā → WUḲĀ

awḳaʿa → WAḲAʿA

awḳāf → WAḲF

ʿawl (A) : lit. deviation by excess; in law, the method of increasing the common denominator of the fractional shares in an inheritance, if their sum would amount to more than one unit. I 764b

awlād (A, s. *walad* 'child') : sons, children; for the many other designations for childhood and its subdivisions, VIII 821b ff.

♦ **awlād al-balad** (A) : the term used during the Sudanese Mahdi period (1881-98) to designate persons originating from the northern riverain tribes. Under the Mahdi Muḥammad Aḥmad, they became the ruling class but gradually lost their status under his successors. I 765a; V 1250a

♦ **awlād al-nās** (A) : lit. children of the people; the term used among the Mamlūks for the sons of mamlūks who could not join the exclusive society of the Mamlūk upper class. Only those who were born an infidel and brought as a child-slave from abroad, were converted to Islam and set free after completing military training, and bore a non-Arab name, could belong to that society. The ~ were joined to a unit of non-mamlūks called the ḤALḲA, which was socially inferior to the pure mamlūk units, and formed there the upper stratum. The term ABNĀʾ AL-ATRĀK was sometimes used as an alternative. I 102a; I 765a; III 99b

awmaʾa (A) : to notify with a gesture, syn. *as͟hāra*. XII 601a

awrit͟h → AMAZZAL

awtād (A, s. **watid** 'tent peg') : in prosody, one of two pairs of metrical components distinguished by al-K͟halīl. The ~ consist of three consonants each and are called *watid mad̲j̲mūʿ* (when the first two consonants are 'moving', i.e. have a short vowel, and the last 'quiescent') and *watid mafrūḳ* (when the first and the third consonants are 'moving' and the middle one 'quiescent'). I 670b; XI 181b; two other types are defined by al-Fārābī and al-Ḳarṭād̲j̲annī as, respectively, ~ *mufrad* (a SABAB *k͟hafīf* + one vowelless letter) and ~ *mutaḍāʿif* (two vowelled + two vowelless letters), both outside traditional ʿARŪḌ. XI 181b

In mysticism, ~ (s. *watad*; syn. *ʿumud*) 'stakes' is the third category of the hierarchy of the RID̲J̲ĀL AL-G͟HAYB, comprising four holy persons. I 95a; I 772a

awtār (A, s. *watar*) : in music, the strings of a musical instrument. VI 215b; X 769b

ʿawwāʾ (A) : in mediaeval ʿIrāḳ, a vagabond who begs between sunset and the evening worship, at times singing. VII 494a

awwal (A, pl. AWĀʾIL) : first.

In philosophy, ~ was brought into Muslim thought by the Arab translators of Aristotle and Plotinus to indicate either the First Being or the First Created. I 772a

♦ awwaliyya (A) : an abstract noun derived from *awwal* indicating the essence of 'that which is first'. Its plural *awwaliyyāt* means the First Principles in the order of knowledge, i.e. the propositions and judgements immediately evident by themselves. I 772b

awzān (A, s. WAZN) : in music, a Turkish instrument popular with the Mamlūk sultans of Egypt. Ibn Ghaybī places it among the lutes of three strings and says that it was played with a wooden plectrum by Turkish minstrels. X 769b

♦ awzān al-shiʿr (A) : in prosody, deviations in the metrical forms, e.g. shortening of the metre. I 671a; VIII 667b

āya (A, pl. *āyāt*) : sign, token; miracle; a verse of the Qurʾān. I 773b; V 401b; miracle of the prophet, as opposed to miracle of God's friends, or saints, KARĀMA. XI 110a

♦ **āyatullāh** (A, < *āyat Allāh*) : lit. miraculous sign of God; a title with a hierarchical significance used by the Twelver shīʿīs, indicating one at the top of the hierarchy, amongst the elite of the great MUDJTAHIDs. XII 103b

aʿyān (A, s. ʿAYN) : notables, the eminent under the caliphate and subsequent Muslim regimes. I 778a; II 640b

Under the Ottomans in the eighteenth century, ~ acquired a more precise significance and came to be applied to those accorded official recognition as the chosen representatives of the people vis-à-vis the government, later to become local magnates and despots. I 778a ff.; II 724a; III 1187b

In philosophy, ~ is used for the particular things that are perceived in the exterior world, as opposed to those things that exist in the mind. I 784a

♦ aʿyāniyye (T) : in the Ottoman period, a fee paid by the AʿYĀN to obtain documents from the provincial governors according them official recognition as the chosen representatives of the people vis-à-vis the government. I 778b

ʿayb (A) : a fault in a person. IV 1100b; and → KABĀRA

ayfd → SHAWKA

ayhuḳān (A) : in botany, wild rocket. VII 831a

ayḳash (A) : a system according to which the *ṭālib*s 'students' of North Africa use the numerical value of letters for certain magical operations; a specialist in this technique is called in the vernacular *yaḳḳāsh*. I 97b

aym (A) : in zoology, a large snake, called *yaym* on the Arabian peninsula. I 541b

ʿayn (A) : eye; evil eye; the thing viewed; source. I 784b; a flowing spring. I 538b; observer, spy. II 486b

In Algeria, in the region of Oued Righ, and in Libya, in the eastern parts of the Shāti, ~ is an artesian well, formerly dug by specialists and very fragile, but now drilled and harnessed according to modern techniques. I 1232a

In the mediaeval kitchen, ~ is the top of an oven which could be opened or closed to adjust the oven's temperature. A synonym is *fam*. VI 808a

In mysticism, ~ is used to indicate the super-existence of God's deepest essence. I 785a

In music, the sound-hole of an ʿŪD. X 769b

In law, physical goods. XI 60b; and → ATHMĀN

For ~ in numismatics, → WARIḲ

♦ ʿayn al-ḳiṭṭ (A) : 'cat's eye', in botany, applied to five plants: the Corn camomile (*Anthemis arvensis*), Camomile (*A. nobilis*), Wild camomile (*Matricaria chamomilla*), Water speedwell (*Veronica anagallis aquatica*), and Minor phalaris (*Phalaris minor*). IX 653a

♦ ʿayn al-yaḳīn (A) : 'the contemplation of the evident'; a mystical term which can be used in the double sense of intuition, i.e. the pre-rational sense of intuitive understanding of the philosophical first principles, and the post-rational sense of the intuitive understanding of super-rational mystical truth. I 785a

♦ ʿaynāʾ (A) : 'with big, black eyes', used in poetry to describe the oryx and addax antelope. V 1227b

ayran (T) : a cool refreshing drink made from YOGHURT and water, called *dūgh* in Persian and *lassi* in India. XI 337b

ʿaysh → KUSKUSŪ

ayt (B) : 'sons of', used either in compounds, or before a proper noun to indicate a tribe. I 792a

aywaz (T, < A *ʿiwaḍ*) : a term applied to the footmen employed in great households in the later Ottoman empire. They were generally Armenians of Van, sometimes Kurds; Greeks are also said to have been among them. Their duties included waiting at table, filling and cleaning the lamps and doing the shopping for the household. I 792a

ayyām → YAWM

ʿayyār (A) : lit. rascal, tramp, vagabond; a term applied to certain warriors who were grouped together under the FUTUWWA in ʿIrāḳ and Persia from the 9th to the 12th centuries, on occasions appearing as fighters for the faith in the inner Asian border regions, on others forming the opposition party in towns and coming into power, indulging in a rule of terror against the wealthy part of the population. I 794a; I 900b ff.; II 961b; VIII 402a; VIII 795b; VIII 956a

ayyil (A) : in zoology, the mountain goat. The descriptions given by the zoologists, however, apply rather more to the deer, but in pre-Islamic and early Islamic poetry, ~ may actually mean the mountain-goat, since the deer probably never existed on the Arabian peninsula. I 795a

ʿazab (A, T *ʿazeb*) : lit. an unmarried man or woman, a virgin; the term applied to several types of fighting men under the Ottoman and other Turkish regimes between the 13th and the 19th centuries, who were forbidden to marry before retirement. I 807a; Ottoman light infantry. IX 128b

ʿazāba (A, < ʿIṢĀBA ?) : a headdress with pearls and gold worn in Morocco and Egypt. X 611b

azal (A) : eternity; in philosophy, ~ or *azaliyya* is a technical term corresponding to ἀγένητος, meaning ungenerated, eternal *a parte ante*; Ibn Rus̲h̲d used *azaliyya* for 'incorruptible'. I 2a; V 95a; and → DAHRIYYA

azala (A) : a special unit of 100 cubic cubits 'of balance', used in mediaeval ʿIrāḳ to count the volume of earth, reeds and brushwood which had to be transported when constructing and upkeeping raised canal banks. V 865a

aʿẓam → MUʿAẒẒAM

azalay (B) : a term for the great caravans made up of several thousand dromedaries which carry the salt from the salt deposits of the Southern Sahara to the tropical regions of the Sahel in spring and autumn. I 808b; I 1222a

azaliyya → AZAL

ʿaẓāliyyāt (A) : in zoology, the order of saurians. X 510a

azharī → FĪRŪZAD̲J̲

ʿazīb (A), or *ʿazl, hans̲h̲īr* : 'latifundium', a form of land tenure in ancient North Africa. I 661a; lands owned by a ZĀWIYA which are let out and whose profits are shared with the tenants (*ʿazzāb*). V 1201b

ʿazīma (A) : determination, resolution, fixed purpose; in religious law, ~ is an ordinance as interpreted strictly, the opposite of RUK̲H̲ṢA, an exemption or dispensation. I 823a In magic, ~ is an adjuration, or the application of a formula of which magical effects are expected. I 823a

ʿazīz (A) : powerful, respected; in the science of Tradition, a Tradition coming from one man of sufficient authority to have his Traditions collected when two or three people share in transmitting them. III 25b

ʿazl (A) : *coitus interruptus*. I 826a; X 198b; and → ʿAZĪB

azr → IZĀR

azraḳ (A) : the colour blue, also having the sense of 'livid, haggard'. Its plural, *zarāḳīm*, designates snakes. V 700a

azyab (A) : in Yemen, the southeast wind. I 180b; the north-east wind. VII 52a

ʿazzāba   (A, s. ʿazzābī) : 'recluses', 'clerks'.

Among the Ibāḍiyya, members of a special council, ḤALḲA, presided over by a SHAYKH, who were distinguished from the laity by their tonsure (they had to shave their heads completely) and by their simple white habits. Their lives were subject to a severe discipline; they were governed by a strict moral code and any misdemeanour was punished immediately. III 95a

B

bā   (A) : a genealogical term used in South Arabia to form individual and (secondarily) collective proper names. I 828a

♦ **bā-sharʿ**   (P) : lit. with law, i.e. following the law of Islam; one of the two categories into which dervishes in Persia are divided. The other is BĪ-SHARʿ. II 164b

bāʿ   (A), or ḳāma : a basic measure of length consisting of the width of the two arms outstretched, i.e. a fathom, canonically equal to four ḎHIRĀʿs (199.5 cm) or approximately 2 metres, and thus the thousandth part of a mile. In Egypt, the ~ is four 'carpenter's' cubits, or 3 metres. I 535b; II 232b; VII 137b

baʿʿādjūn   (A) : 'cleavers', according to e.g. Ibn Ḵhaldūn, magicians who had only to point their finger at a piece of clothing or a skin, while mumbling certain words, for that object to fall into shreds; with the same gestures, fixing upon sheep, they could instantaneously cleave them. VIII 52b

bāb   (A) : gate. I 830a

In early shīʿism, ~ denotes the senior authorised disciple of the IMĀM, and among the Ismāʿīliyya, ~ is a rank in the hierarchy, denoting the head of the DAʿWA and thus the equivalent in Ismāʿīlī terminology of the dāʿī al-duʿāt. I 832b; and → SAFĪR

Among the Bābīs, ~ is the appellation of the founder, Sayyid ʿAlī Muḥammad of Shīrāz. I 833a

♦ **bāb-i ʿālī**   (T) : the (Ottoman) Sublime Porte, the name for the Ottoman government. I 836a

♦ **bāb-i humāyūn**   (T) : lit. Imperial Gate, the principal entrance in the outer wall of the sultan's New Serail. I 836b

♦ **bāb al-ʿilm**   (A) : 'the gate of knowledge', the title given to the Mustaʿlī-Ṭayyibī Ismāʿīlī savant of India Luḵmandji b. Ḥabīb (d. 1173/1760) by the thirty-ninth DĀʿĪ. V 814b

♦ **bāb marzūḵ**   (A) : 'lucky door', the term used for the hyena by the Arab nomads of the Sahara regions. XII 173b

♦ **bāb-i mashikhat**   (T) : the name for the office or department of the SHAYKH AL-ISLĀM under the Ottomans in the 19th century. I 837b

♦ **bāb al-saʿādet**   (T) : lit. the Gate of Felicity, the gate leading from the second into the third court, proceeding inward, of the imperial palace of the Ottomans. II 697b

♦ **bāb-i serʿaskeri**   (T) : the name for the War Department in the Ottoman empire during the 19th century. I 838a

baba   → MURSHID

babbaghāʾ   (A), or babghāʾ : in zoology, both parakeet and parrot. The term represents both female and male, singular and collective. I 845b

babghāʾ   → BABBAGHĀʾ

babr   (A, pl. bubūr) : in zoology, the tiger. II 739a

bābūnadj   (A, < P bābūna) : in botany, the common camomile, primarily Anthemis nobilis, also called Roman camomile, but also Matricaria chamomilla and other varieties. XII 114b

bād-i hawā (T), or *ṭayyārāt* : lit. wind of the air; a general term in Ottoman fiscal usage for irregular and occasional revenues from fines, fees, registration, charges, and other casual sources of income which appeared for the first time in the first quarter of the 10th/16th century and continued through the 18th century. I 850a; II 147a; VIII 487b; IX 474a

badāʾ (A) : appearance, emergence.

In theology, the alteration of God's purpose. I 265b; the emergence of new circumstances which cause a change in an earlier ruling. I 850a

bādahandj → BĀDGĪR; MALḲAF

badal (A, T *bedel*) : substitute; and → ABDĀL; ʿIWAḌ

In the Ottoman empire, a term used to denote a contribution made by a tax-payer in lieu of his performing some service for the government or furnishing it with some commodity. These special 'substitute' cash contributions were exacted when either the subjects failed to fulfil their obligations or the government forwent its rights in this regard. I 760b; I 855a; II 147a

In Afghanistan, ~ means revenge by retaliation, vendetta, and is one of the three main pillars of the special social code of the Afghans. I 217a

In grammar, a variant. V 804a

♦ bedel-i ʿaskerī (T) : an exemption tax in the place of enrollment in the national service. VIII 201a

badan (A) : body, in particular the human body, often only the torso. II 555a; in mediaeval Islam, a short, sleeveless tunic from cotton or silk, worn by both sexes and usually associated with the Arabian peninsula, but it has been shown to have also been a fairly common article of feminine attire in mediaeval Egypt. V 739a; as *badana*, a seamless robe made from linen and gold thread, recorded as having been made for the Fāṭimid caliphs. X 532a

In seafaring, ~ is used to designate a kind of boat typical of Northern Oman which is constructed according to two models: one for fishing, the other for the transportation of goods and for cabotage. This is the typical boat with an entirely sewn hull in order to avoid damage in case of a collision with reefs at water level. VII 53b

As zoological term, → WAʿL

♦ badana → BADAN

bādandj → BĀDGĪR

baddāʿ (Bed) : among the Sinai Bedouin, a composer adept at spontaneous improvisation. IX 234b

bādgīr (P), or *bād-gīr* : lit. wind-catcher; an architectural term used in Persia for the towers containing ventilation shafts and projecting high above the roofs of domestic houses. In mediaeval Arabic, the device was known as *bādahandj* or *bādandj*. V 665b; IX 49b; XII 115a

badhadj → SAKHLA

bādhāward → SHAWKA

bādhiḳ (A) : in early Islam, a prohibited product prepared by means of grapes. IV 996b

bādhindjān (A) : in botany, the aubergine, one of the summer crops in mediaeval Egypt. V 863a

badhr al-kattān (A) : in botany, linseed. IX 615a

badhrundjubūya → TURUNDJĀN

badīʿ (A) : innovator, creator, thus, one of the attributes of God. I 857b; III 663b

In literature, ~ is the name for the innovations of the ʿAbbāsid poets in literary figures, and later for trope in general. I 857b; IV 248b; V 900a; XII 650a

♦ badīʿiyya (A) : in literature, a poem in which the poet uses all kinds of figures of speech. I 858a; I 982b

♦ ʿilm al-badīʿ (A) : the branch of rhetorical science which deals with the beautification of literary style, the artifices of the ornamentation and embellishment of speech. I 857b; I 982b

badīha → IRTIDJĀL

bādiya (A) : in the Umayyad period, a residence in the countryside, an estate in the environs of a settlement or a rural landed property in the Syro-Jordanian steppeland. XII 116b

baʿdiyya → IFTITĀḤ

bādj (A, < P *bāzh*) : a fiscal technical term among the Turks, ~ was applied to various forms of tax as well as being used for 'tax' in general. I 860b; II 147a

♦ bādj-i buzurg (T, < P) : in the Īlkhānid and Djalāʾirid periods, the customs-duty levied on goods in transit through or imported into the country. I 861b

♦ bādj-i tamgha (T, < P) : in the Īlkhānid and Djalāʾirid periods, the tax levied on all kinds of goods bought and sold in cities, on woven stuffs and slaughtered animals; it is normally referred to as *tamgha-i siyāh* 'black tamgha'. I 861b

♦ bādjdār (T, < P) : in the Īlkhānid and Djalāʾirid periods, a tax collector, who collected tolls at certain places according to a tariff fixed by the central government. I 861a

badjdja → SUDJDJA

badjrā : the common Indian river-boat, a sort of barge without a keel, propelled by poles or by oars, on the deck of which cabins might be mounted. VII 933a

badr → ḲAMAR

♦ badra (A) : the skin of a lamb or goat capacious enough to contain a large sum of money. In numismatics, the usual amount reckoned as a ~ was 10,000 dirhams (this figure was considered by the Arabs to represent both the perfection and the ultimate limit of numeration). It was thus analogous to the TŪMĀN. X 620a

bādrundjubūya → TURUNDJĀN

badw (A) : pastoral nomads of Arabian blood, speech and culture, the Bedouin. I 872a

bāgh (P) : term for a suburban palace in Tīmūrid times, meaning a park or estate with building and gardens. IX 46a

baghbūr → FAGHFŪR

baghdādī → SABʿĀNĪ

baghghāl (A) : a muleteer, also known as MUḲĀRĪ or *ḥammāra*, who emerged as a distinct group of transport workers during the ʿAbbāsid period. XII 659a

bāghī → BUGHĀT; MULḤID

baghiyy (A, pl. *baghāyā*), and *mūmis, ʿāhira, zāniya* : prostitute. A more vulgar word was *ḳaḥba*, from the verb 'to cough', because professional prostitutes used to cough to attract clients. XII 133a

baghl (A, fem. *baghla*, pl. *bighāl*) : mule; hinny (offspring of a stallion and she-ass). I 909a

In Egypt, the feminine form *baghla* (pl. *baghalāt*) also denoted a female slave born of unions between ṢAḲĀLIBA and another race. I 909a

♦ baghl al-sammān → SALWĀ

♦ baghla (< Sp/Por *bajel/baxel*) : in the Gulf area, a large sailing ship used in the Gulf of Oman and the Indian waters. VIII 811b; and → BAGHL

♦ baghlī (A) : the earliest Arab DIRHAMS which were imitations of the late Sasanian *drahms* of Yezdigird III, Hormuzd IV and (chiefly) Khusraw II; ʿAbd al-Malik's monetary reforms in 79/698-9 drastically altered the style. II 319a

bağlama → SĀZ

bagsı → OZAN

bagtal : a word used in Laḳ society to designate the KHĀN's family and the nobility. V 618a bag͟hy (A) : encroachment, abuse. XI 567b

bāh (A), and *waṭʾ* : coitus. I 910b; and → DJIMĀʿ

bahādur (Alt) : courageous, brave; hero. Borrowed into many languages, ~ also frequently appears as a surname and an honorific title. I 913a; and → SARDĀR

bahaḳ (A) : in medicine, vitiligo. V 107a; and → DJUDHĀM

bahār → NARDJIS

baḥīra (A) : the name in the pre-Islamic period for a she-camel or ewe with slit ears. I 922a

bāhit → SHĀDHANA

bahlawān → PAHLAWĀN

bahlūlī → TANKA

bahma → SAKHLA

baḥr (A, pl. *buḥūr*) : a place where a great amount of water is found. Accordingly, ~ is not only applied to the seas and oceans but also, uniquely, because of its outstanding size, to the Nile. I 926b; VII 909b; VIII 38a

The plural *buḥūr* means, in prosody, the ideal metric forms as given in the circles devised by al-K͟halīl. I 671a; VIII 667b; XI 200b; in music, secondary modes, alongside main modes (*ang͟hām*) and *āwāz* modes. IX 101a

♦ ʿilm al-baḥr (A) : the art of navigation, also known as *ʿulūm al-baḥriyya*. VII 51a

♦ **al-baḥrayn** (A) : lit. the two seas; a cosmographical and cosmological concept appearing five times in the Qurʾān. I 940b

♦ **baḥriyya** (A) : the navy. I 945b; XII 119b

bahrad͟j (A) : in numismatics, counterfeit money. X 409b

bahramānī (A) : the deep red colour (Rubicelle, Escarboucle) of the ruby, also called *rummānī* (defined at the present time as 'carmine' or 'pigeon's blood'). XI 262b

baht (A) : in the *Arabian Nights*, the name of a city, made up of ~ stone, whose effect is mad laughter leading to death. XII 552b

baḥt͟h (A) : study, examination, inquiry. I 949a; and → AHL AL-(BAḤTH WA 'L-) NAẒAR

bahw (A) : an empty and spacious place extending between two objects which confine it; the axial nave in a mosque, ~ is a term primarily belonging to the vocabulary of Western Muslim architecture. It also is defined as a tent or pavilion chamber situated beyond the rest. I 949b

baḥzad͟j (A), or *barg͟haz* : in zoology, the calf of the oryx or addax antelope at birth. If it is completely white, it is called *mārī*. V 1227b

bāʿid͟j → KHANNĀḲ

bāʾika → ḤĀṢIL

bāʾin (A) : in law, an irrevocably divorced woman. III 1011b

baʾīn → BĀʾOLĪ

baʿīr (A) : the individual camel, regardless of sex, as opposed to *ibil*, the species and the group. III 666a

baḳʿa (A) : a term applied especially to a place where water remains stagnant. I 1292b; and → BUḲʿA

baḳāʾ wa-fanāʾ (A) : 'subsistence' and 'effacement', ṣūfī terms referring to the stages of the development of the mystic in the path of gnosis. I 951a; IV 1083b; VIII 306b; VIII 416a

bāḳālāw (A, < Sp *bacallao*), with var. *bāḳālyū, baḳala, baḳlāwa* : the stockfish. VIII 1022b

baḳar (A) : cattle; mediaeval Arab authors distinguished between the domestic ~ *ahlī* and the wild ~ *waḥs͟hī*, meaning either the *mahā* (*Oryx beatrix*) or the AYYIL, or even the *yaḥmūr* 'roedeer' and the *t͟haytal* 'bubale antelope'. I 951b

bak͟hīl → BUKHL

bakhnūḳ (Tun) : an embroidered head shawl for women, worn in Tunisia. V 745b

bakhshi (< Ch *po-che* ?) : a Buddhist priest, monk; later 'writer, secretary', a term stemming from Mongol administrative usage. In the 15th and 16th centuries, it came to mean a wandering minstrel among the Turkomans and the Anatolian Turks. I 953a; bard. I 422a; X 733a f.; and → BĀKHSHĪ

In Persia, a subdistrict or county. VIII 154a; VIII 586a

♦ bakhshī al-mamālik (IndP), or MĪR-BAKHSHĪ : in Mughal India, more or less the equivalent of the classical ʿĀRIḌ, the official charged with the mustering, passing in review and inspection of troops. IV 268b; V 686a; IX 738b

bākhshī : in traditional Özbeg society, a practitioner of shamanistic healing, especially the removal of spirits. He often was a MOLLĀ learned in the Qurʾān. Synonyms are *parīkhʷān* or *duʿākhʷān*. VIII 234b; as *bakhshi̊*, a shaman in Ḳazakh, Ḳi̊rghi̊z, Ozbeg and Tādjīk society. X 733b

bakhshīsh (P) : a gratuity bestowed by a superior on an inferior, a tip or 'consideration' thrown into a bargain, and a bribe, particularly one offered to judges or officials. Under the Ottomans, ~ came to mean the gratuity bestowed by a sultan upon his accession on the chief personages of state, the Janissaries and other troops of the standing army. I 953a

baḳḳ (A) : in zoology, a bug. II 248a; IV 522a

bakkāʾ (A) : lit. weepers; in early Islam, ascetics who during their devotional exercises shed many tears. I 959a

baḳḳāl (A) : retailer of vegetables; grocer (syn. *khaḍḍār*). I 961a, where many synonyms used regionally are listed

baḳḳam (A, < San) : sappan wood, an Indian dye wood obtained from the *Caesalpinia Sappan L.* The Arabic equivalent frequently given by Arab philologists is *ʿandam*, which, however, denotes the dragon's blood, a red gum exuding from certain trees. I 961b

baḳḳāra : cattle nomads in the central Sudan belt of Africa. IX 516a

baḳla → ʿALATH

bakradj (A) : the traditional coffee pot (syn. *dalla*), one of a number of traditional kitchen utensils used still in rural regions, along with the coffee cup, *findjān*, and many more articles. Terms for these items vary from one area to another. XII 776b

baḳṭ (A, < Lat *pactum*, Gk) : an annual tribute yielded by Christian Nubia to the Muslims. I 32a; I 966a

bāl → ʿANBAR

baʿl (A) : master, owner, husband; in law, ~ denotes unwatered tillage and unwatered cultivated land. I 968a

♦ baʿlī (A) : as an adjective, frequently attached to the name of a vegetable or fruit; in such cases, it stresses the good quality. At Fez, ~ describes a man, avaricious, dry and hard, while the feminine *baʿliyya* is applied to a succulent fig. I 969b

bāla (Yem) : a folk poetry genre for men in northern Yemen tribal areas, usually improvised and sung at weddings and other celebrations. IX 234a f.

bālā (P) : height, high; since 1262/1846 the term for a grade in the former Ottoman Civil Service, to which the Secretary of State and other senior officials belonged. I 969b

balad → SHAYKH

♦ **baladiyya** (A) : municipality; the term used to denote modern municipal institutions of European type, as against earlier Islamic forms of urban organisation. I 972b

♦ baladiyyūn → SHĀMIYYŪN

balāgha (A) : eloquence. I 858a; I 981b; I 1114a; II 824a; to Ḳazwīnī (d. 1338), ~ was the term for the science of rhetoric as a whole. I 1116a

balam (A) : a typically ʿIrāḳī term for a barque which has both bows and stern pointed in shape, with a flat deck and a capacity of transporting from 5 to 10 tons, and is used on the Euphrates river. VII 53b
In zoology, a term for anchovy, found again in the Latinised term to specify a subspecies limited to a particular region (*Engraulis boelema*), and for the sand-smelt, both small fish. VIII 1021b; VIII 1023a

balamīda (A, < *Pelamys*) : in zoology, the pelamid, also called *būnīt*, the bonito. VIII 1021a

balāṭ (A, < L or Gk *palatium*) : a paved way; flagging; the term most usually applied to the naves of a mosque. I 950a; I 987b; I 988a; palace. IX 44a
♦ balāṭa (A) : a 'flag-stone' of any kind of material serving to pave the ground or to bear a monumental or memorial inscription. I 987b

balg͟ham (A, < Gk) : phlegm, one of the four cardinal humours. XII 188b

bālig͟h (A) : in law, major, of full age. I 993a

balīlad͟j (P) : in botany, a variety of myrobalanus (*Terminalia bellerica*). XII 349b

bālis͟h (P 'cushion') : a 13th-century Mongolian monetary unit, coined both in gold and silver. It was in use particularly in the eastern part of the empire. Its value was assessed at 6,192 gold marks. I 996b

baliyya (A, pl. *balāyā*) : a name given, in pre-Islamic times, to a camel (more rarely a mare) tethered at the grave of his master and allowed to die of starvation, or sometimes burnt alive. Muslim tradition sees in this practice proof of the pre-Islamic Arabs' belief in resurrection, because the animal thus sacrificed was thought to serve as a mount for its master at the resurrection. I 997a

baʿliyya → BAʿL

ballūṭ (A, pl. *balāliṭa*) : in botany, acorn, fruit of the oaktree. II 744a

bals͟hūn (A) : in zoology, the heron. I 1152b

balṭad͟ji̊ (T) : a name given to men composing various companies of palace guards under the Ottomans down to the beginning of the nineteenth century. The ~ was originally employed in connection with the army in the felling of trees, the levelling of roads and the filling of swamps. The term was used alternatively with the Persian equivalent, *tabardār*, both meaning 'axe-man', and hence 'woodcutter', 'pioneer', 'halberdier'. I 1003b

balyemez (T, < Ger *Faule Metze*) : lit. that eats no honey; a large caliber gun, which name (probably a jesting and popular transformation of the famous German cannon 'Faule Metze' of the year 1411) came to the Ottomans through the numerous German gun-founders in the Turkish services; the ~ was first introduced into the Ottoman army in the time of sultan Murād II. I 1007b; I 1062b

bālyōs (T, < It *bailo*) : the Turkish name for the Venetian ambassador to the Sublime Porte. With the generalised meaning of European diplomatic or consular agent, the word is also encountered in some Arabic dialects and Swahili. I 1008a; II 60b

bamm → ZĪR

bān (A, P) : the ben-nut tree (*Moringa aptera Gaertn.*), the wood of which was used for tent-poles. Its fruit, called *s͟hūʿ*, was a commodity and greatly in demand. The ~ was used as a simile by poets for a tender woman of tall stature. I 1010b

bāna → İLİD͟JA

banafsad͟j (A) : in botany, the violet (> *banafsad͟jī* 'violet-coloured'). V 699a

banāt naʿs͟h → BINT

band (P) : anything which is used to bind, attach, close or limit; a dam built for irrigation purposes. I 1012a; in Persian literature, each of the single separating verses of a TARD͟JĪʿ-BAND; also loosely used to designate each complete stanza, which usage is more common. X 235b

bandar (P) : a seaport or port on a large river. The word ~ passed into the Arabic of Syria and Egypt where it is used in the sense of market-place, place of commerce, banking exchange and even workshop. I 1013a

bandayr (Alg, < Goth *pandero*), or *bandīr* : in Algeria, a round tambourine with snares stretched across the inside of the head, probably called GHIRBĀL in the early days of Islam. II 620b

bandish : the composition, the second part in a performance of classical or art music of India, which in vocal music may be KHAYĀL, *dhrupad*, TARĀNA or one of several more modern forms; in instrumental music, as played on the stringed instruments, *sitār* and *sarod*, it is generally called *gat*. III 454a

bandj (A, P *bang*, < San) : henbane, a narcotic drug. In the popular dialect of Egypt, ~ is used for every kind of narcotic. I 1014b; III 266b

bandjārā : a term used in India to designate dealers rather than mere commissariat carriers, who travelled all over the country with large droves of laden cattle and regularly supplied the Indian armies and hunting camps. VII 932b

bang → BANDJ

banīḳa (A, pl. *banāʾiḳ*) : originally, in early Arabic, any piece inserted to widen a tunic or a leather bucket; in the Arab West, ~ was used for a kind of man's tunic and, more frequently, for an element of women's hair-covering. In Algiers, ~ is still used for a kind of square headdress, provided with a back flap, which women use to cover their heads to protect themselves against the cold when leaving the baths. I 1016a

In Morocco, ~ means a dark padded cell; a closet serving as an office for a 'minister'. I 1016b

banish (A), or *banīsh* : a wide-sleeved man's coat, worn in the Arab East. V 740b

bannāʾī → HAZĀR-BĀF

banoyta → DARDAR

bānuwānī : in mediaeval ʿIrāḳ, a vagrant who stands before a door, rattles the bolt and cries 'O Master', in order to get alms. VII 494a

bāʾolī (U, H), and *baʾīn* : a step-well in Muslim India, usually found at the principal shrines associated with Čishtī *pīrs* (→ MURSHID). They are meant for the use of men and animals. I 1024a; V 884b; V 888b

bar-āwardī (IndP) : lit. by estimate; under the Mughal emperor Akbar, the payment at a rather low rate made in advance for a contingent of a size less than the titular rank, ultimately coming to define the number of the second or *sawār* (→ SUWĀR) rank. IX 909a

bārā wafāt (U) : a term used in the subcontinent of India for the twelfth day of Rabīʿ I, observed as a holy day to commemorate the death of the Prophet Muḥammad. I 1026a

barāʾa (A) : release, exemption; freedom from disease, cure; in law, ~ is the absence of obligation; *barāʾat (al-dhimma)* means freedom from obligation. I 1026b

As a Qurʾānic term, ~ also means the breaking of ties, a kind of dissociation or excommunication, which theme was developed by the Khāridjites as being the duty to repudiate all those who did not deserve the title of Muslim. I 207a; I 811a; I 1027b

In classical Muslim administration, a receipt given by the DJAHBADH or KHĀZIN to taxpayers. II 78b; XI 409b; ~ has been increasingly employed in a concrete sense to denote written documents of various kinds: licence, certificate, diploma, demand for payment, passport, a label to be attached to a piece of merchandise, a request or petition to the sovereign. I 1027a

In the science of diplomatic, ~ (syn. *risāla*) in Morocco was a letter addressed to a community, in order to announce an important event, or in order to exhort or to admonish. It was generally read from the MINBAR in the mosque on Friday. II 308a

♦ barāʾat al-dhimma → BARĀʾA

♦ barāʾat al-tanfīdh (A) : the consular *exequatur*. I 1027b

♦ barāʾat al-thiḳa (A) : diplomatic 'credentials'. I 1027b

barāʿa (A) : in prosody, 'virtuosity', the ability to make intricate conceits appear natural, one of a tripartite typology of poets, the other two being *ṭabʿ* 'natural talent' and *ṣināʿa* 'artfulness'. XII 654a

♦ barāʿat al-istihlāl (A) : in rhetoric, the 'skilful opening', an introduction that contains an allusion to the main theme of the work. III 1006a

bāradarī (H) : a term, also applied to Muslim buildings in India, for a hall with twelve adjacent bays or doors, three on each side; ~ was figuratively used to designate 'summer house' as well. V 1214b

baraka (A) : (divine) blessing; in practice, ~ has the meaning of 'very adequate quantity'. I 1032a

In the vocabulary of the Almohads, ~ was used in the sense of 'gratuity which is added to a soldier's pay'. I 1032a

baramis (A, < L *Abramis brama*) : in zoology, the bream. VIII 1021a

bārandj : 'coloured', melons from Khʷārazm. X 435b

baranta (T) : an Eastern Turkish term, though now regarded as old-fashioned, for 'foray, robbery, plunder', 'cattle-lifting'. I 1037b

Among the nomad Turkish peoples, ~ once represented a specific legal concept involving a notion of 'pledge, surety', e.g. the appropriation of a quantity of his adversary's property by a man who has been wronged, in order to recover his due. I 1037b

baraṣ (A, pl. *abraṣ*) : in medicine, a term used for leprosy, but could be applied to other skin diseases as well. V 107a; XII 271a; and → DJUDHĀM

barastūk → BARASŪDJ

barasūdj (A, < P *parastūg*) : in zoology, the mullet. Variants are *barastūk* and *ṭarastudj*. VIII 1021a

barāt (K) : in the YAZĪDĪ tradition, little balls of dust from the Lālish area made with water from the Zamzam spring, which have great religious significance. XI 315a

barata (T) : a special type of headdress, KÜLĀH, of woollen cloth in the shape of a sleeve whose rear part fell on the back, worn by palace domestics in Ottoman Turkey. V 751b

barbā (A, < C *p'erpé* 'temple') : name given by the Egyptians to solidly constructed ancient buildings of pagan times. I 1038b

barbaṭ (P, < *bar* 'breast' and *baṭ* 'duck') : in music, a lute whose sound-chest and neck were constructed in one graduated piece, unlike the ʿŪD, whose sound-chest and neck were separate. Arabic authors generally do not discriminate between the two instruments. X 768b

barbūsha (B) : a variety of couscous, made with barley semolina. This is called *ṣīkūk* in Morocco. V 528a

barda (A) : in zoology, the pink sea-bream, whose Arabic term is found again in the Latinised nomenclature to specify a sub-species limited to a particular region (*Chrysophrys berda*). VIII 1021a

bardī (A), *waraḳ al-~* and *abardī* : the term for papyrus. VIII 261b; VIII 407b

bardjīs → MUSHTARĪ

bārgāh : guy ropes, used to support the Mongol ruler's large tent. IX 45b

bārgīr-suwār → SUWĀR

bāriʾ (A) : creator; one of the names of God (syn. *khāliḳ*). According to the *Lisān al-ʿArab*, ~ is he who creates without imitating a model, and is nearly always used for the creation of living beings in particular. IV 980b

barīd (Ass, < L *veredus* / Gk *beredos*) : postal service; post horse, courier, and post 'stage'. I 1045a; II 487a; III 109b

bāriḥ (A) : a term applied to a wild animal or bird which passes from right to left before a traveller or hunter; it is generally interpreted as a bad omen. I 1048a; 'that which travels from right to left', one of the technical terms designating the directions of a bird's flight, or an animal's steps, which play an important part in the application of divination known as FA'L, ṬĪRA and ZADJR. II 760a

bariyya → KHALḲ

bāriz (A) : visible; in grammar, often contrasted at a syntactical level with *mustatir* 'the concealed', for the pronouns in particular. XII 546a

barḳ (A) : lightning; telegraph. I 573a

barḳā' (A), and *abraḳ* : a Bedouin term from the Arabian peninsula denoting a hill whose sides are mottled with patches of sand. I 536b

barmā'iyyūn (A), or *ḳawāzib* : the amphibian mammals, such as the seal, the walrus, the sea lion etc. VIII 1022b

barnāmadj → FAHRASA

barnī (A) : a variety of dates. XII 366b

baro (Oromo) : a hymn with alternate verses. IX 399a

barrakān (N.Afr) : a heavy wrap worn by men in Tunisia in mediaeval times. V 745a; a large enveloping outer wrap for both sexes in present-day Libya. V 745b

barrānī (A), or *muḍāf* : one of the three main sources of revenue for the Egyptian government in the years immediately preceding the Napoleonic invasion of 1798, ~ were extraordinary taxes, the payment of which was demanded by the *multazims* (→ MÜLTEZIM) to increase their profits; they were collected regularly despite their illegality. II 148a; newly-arrived rural immigrant, in Oran contrasted with the oldest immigrants, the Oulad el-bled. XI 51a

barrāz → MUBĀRIZ

barsha (A) : a term, used round the South Arabian coasts, for a long, covered boat; also applied to large warships (cf. Ott *barča*, < It *bargia, barza*). VIII 811b

barsīm → ḲATT

bārūd (A, < Ar ?) : saltpetre; gunpowder. I 1055b

barzakh (A, P) : obstacle, hindrance, separation.

In eschatology, the boundary of the world of human beings, which consists of the heavens, the earth and the nether regions, and its separation from the world of pure spirits and God; Limbo. I 1072a

baṣal (A) : in botany, onions, one of the winter crops in mediaeval Egypt. V 863a

basbās (A), or *rāziyānadj* : in botany, the fennel (*Foeniculum vulgare*), in North Africa termed *bisbās*, which in the Eastern countries means the red seed-shell of the nutmeg (*Myristica frangrans*). I 214b; XII 128b

♦ basbāsa (A) : in botany, nutmeg. XII 128b

bash (T) : head, chief.

♦ bash ḳara ḳulluḳdju (T) : lit. head scullion; in Ottoman times, an officer's rank in an ORTA, subordinate to that of the ČORBADJÎ, or 'soup purveyor'. VIII 178b

♦ **bashî-bozuḳ** (T) : lit. leaderless, unattached; in the Ottoman period, ~ was applied to both homeless vagabonds from the province seeking a livelihood in Istanbul and male Muslim subjects of the sultan not affiliated to any military corps; from this last usage, ~ came to signify 'civilian'. I 1077b; IX 406b

basha (T) : a Turkish title, not to be confused with PASHA, nor with the Arabic or old eastern pronunciation of it. Put after the proper name, it was applied to soldiers and the lower grades of officers (especially Janissaries), and, it seems, also to notables in the provinces. VIII 281b

basharūsh → NUḤĀM
bashi-bozuḳ → BASH
bashīr (A) : in zoology, the polypterus Bichir. VIII 1021a; and → NADHĪR
bashmaḳlïḳ (T) : a term applied in 16th and 17th-century Ottoman Turkey to fief revenues assigned to certain ranks of ladies of the sultan's harem for the purchase of their personal requirements, particularly clothes and slippers. I 1079b
bashtarda (T, < It *bastarda*) : the term for the great galley of the commander-in-chief of the Ottoman navy. The principal types of Ottoman ships in the period of the oared vessels were the *ḳādïrgha* (< Gk *katergon*) 'galley', the *ḳālīte* 'galliot', and the *fïrḳate* 'frigate'. Although the ~ was not the largest unit of the fleet, it was a galley larger than the *galea sensile* (T *ḳādïrgha* or *čektiri*), but smaller than the galeazza or galiass (T *mawna*). I 948a ff.; VIII 565a; VIII 810b
bashtina → ČIFTLIK
bashwekīl → ṢADR-I AʿẒAM
basīṭ (wa murakkab) (A) : simple (and composite), the translation of Gk απλοῦς and συνθετος. Used as such in pharmacology, in grammar, philosophy and medicine, MUFRAD is found for *basīṭ*, and in logic, mathematics and music, *muʾallaf* is more commonly used for *murakkab*. I 1083b; and → MURAKKAB
In prosody, the name of the second Arabic metre, formed by the two feet *mustafʿilun fāʿilun*. I 670a; I 675a
♦ basīṭa → MIZWALA
basḳaḳ (T) : governor, chief of police. VIII 281a
Among the Mongols, an official whose main duty was to collect taxes and tribute; the commissioners and high commissioners sent to the conquered provinces (or the West only?), notably in Russia. Its Mongol equivalent was DĀRŪGHA or *darogha*. VIII 281a; IX 438a
basmala (A) : the formula *biʾsm*ⁱ *llāh*ⁱ *l-raḥmān*ⁱ *l-raḥīm*ⁱ, also called *tasmiya*. I 1084a; III 122b; V 411b
bast (P) : sanctuary, asylum; a term applied to certain places (mosques and other sacred buildings, especially the tombs of saints; the royal stables and horses; the neighborhood of artillery) which were regarded as affording inviolable sanctuary to any malefactor, however grave his crime; once within the protection of the ~, the malefactor could negotiate with his pursuers, and settle the ransom which would purchase his immunity when he left it. I 1088a
basṭ (A) : in mysticism, a term explained as applying to a spiritual state corresponding with the station of hope, 'expansion'. I 1088b; III 361a; IV 326a
In mathematics, the part or the numerator of a fraction (syn. *ṣūra, makhradj*). IV 725b
bāsūr (A, pl. *bawāsīr*) : in medicine, haemorrhoids. X 784a
baṭāʾin (P) : a cotton cloth, produced in Zarand in Iran, which appears to have been used as lining for clothes. Called al-Zarandiyya it was taken to Egypt and the most distant parts of the Maghrib. V 151a
baṭāna → DJARF
baʿth (A) : lit. to send, set in motion; in theology, ~ denotes either the sending of prophets or the resurrection. I 1092b
bathn (A) : on the Arabian peninsula, a small, deadly but innocent-appearing snake living in the sands. I 541b
baṭīḥa (A, pl. *baṭāʾiḥ*) : marshland, the name applied to a meadowlike depression which is exposed to more or less regular inundation and is therefore swampy. In particular, it was applied in the ʿAbbāsid period to the very extensive swampy area on the lower course of the Euphrates and Tigris, also called *al-baṭāʾiḥ*. I 1093b
bāṭil → FĀSID; RADHĪ

bāṭin (A) : in Ismāʿīlī theology, the inner meaning of sacred texts, as contrasted with the literal meaning, ẒĀHIR. I 1099a

♦ **bāṭiniyya** (A) : the name given to the Ismāʿīlīs in mediaeval times, referring to their stress on the BĀṬIN, and to anyone accused of rejecting the literal meaning of such texts in favour of the *bāṭin*. I 1098b; XI 389b

batman (P) : a measure of capacity introduced in Persia in the 15th century, equal to 5.76 kg. This was apparently the standard weight in most Persian provinces under the rule of the Ṣafawids. VI 120a

baṭn (A, < Sem 'stomach', cf. Heb 'uterus'; pl. *buṭūn*) : in Arabic 'a fraction of a tribe', designating a uterine relationship; in geography, ~ is used in geographical names with the meaning of 'depression, basin'. I 1102a; the plural form *al-buṭūn* was used to refer to the two sons of Saʿd b. Zayd Manāt, Kaʿb and ʿAmr, who were not among the group called *al-*ABNĀʾ. X 173a; sub-tribe. XI 101b

batr → BAṬṬ

batrāʾ (A) : in early Islam, a term for a Friday sermon, *khuṭba*, lacking the ḤAMDALA. III 123a; as *al-batrāʿ*, or *al-butayrāʾ*, 'the truncated speech', the name for Ziyād b. Abīhi's inaugural speech as governor, which though considered a masterpiece of eloquence, did not praise God and did not bless the Prophet. XI 520b

baṭrakh : botargo, a fish delicacy like caviar, *khibyāra*, not widely consumed in Arab countries. VIII 1023a

baṭṭ (A), or *batr* : in medicine, an incision (for the removal of morbid matter). II 481b In zoology, a duck. IX 98b

baṭṭāl (A) : idle, inactive, in particular, a discharged, dismissed or exiled member of the Mamlūk military nobility. V 332b

batur → ALP

baʿūḍ (A) : in zoology, the gnat. II 248a; mosquitos. IV 522a

bavik (K), or *mal* : a Kurdish extended family, consisting of a group of houses or household or family in the strict sense of father, mother and children. The union of many *bavik*s constitutes the clan, or *ber*. V 472a

bawārid (A) : cooked green vegetables preserved in vinegar or other acid liquids. II 1064a; cold vegetable dishes, prepared also from meat, fowl and fish; frequent ingredients were vinegar and a sweetening agent, sugar or honey. X 31b

♦ bawāridiyyūn : makers and sellers of *bawārid*. II 1064a

bawraḳ (A, < P *būra*), and *būraḳ* : natron, sesqui-carbonate of soda. It was found either as a liquid in water or as a solid on the surface of the soil. XII 130b; borax. VIII 111b

bay (A, T *beg*) : name applied to the ruler of Tunisia until 26 July 1957, when a Republic was proclaimed in Tunisia. I 1110b; and → BEY

♦ bay al-amḥāl : in Tunisia, the heir apparent to the Bey and head of the army until the advent of the Protectorate. I 1111a

bayʿ (A) : in law, a contract of sale, which is concluded by an offer, **idjāb**, and acceptance, *ḳabūl*, which must correspond to each other exactly and must take place in the same meeting. I 1111a

♦ bayʿ al-ʿarāyā → BAYʿ AL-MUZĀBANA

♦ bayʿ al-barāʾa (A) : in law, a sale without guarantee wherein the seller is freed from any obligation in the event of the existence, in the sale-object, of such a defect as would normally allow the sale to be rescinded. I 1026b

♦ bayʿ al-gharar (A) : 'dangerous or hazardous trading', in law, a prohibited transaction, an example of which is *bayʿ ḥabal al-ḥabala*, namely, the sale of a pregnant she-camel for slaughter with the prospect that it may produce a female young one, which will again bear young. X 468a

♦ bayʿ ḥabal al-ḥabala → BAYʿ AL-GHARAR

♦ bayʿ al-ḥaṣāt → BAYʿ AL-MUNĀBADHA
♦ bayʿ ilḳāʾ al-ḥadjar → BAYʿ AL-MUNĀBADHA
♦ bayʿ al-ʿīna (A), or *ʿīna* : in law, a ‘sale on credit’, also known as MUKHĀṬARA. VII 518b; VIII 493a
♦ bayʿ al-muʿāwama (A) : in law, the purchase of the yield of palm-trees for two or three years in advance, an example of the sale of things which are not yet in existence at the time of the contract and thus prohibited. X 467b
♦ bayʿ al-mulāmasa (A) : in law, a prohibited transaction concluded without the goods being seen or examined beforehand, the covered goods being simply touched with the hand. X 468a
♦ bayʿ al-munābadha (A) : in law, a prohibited sale in which the exchange is irrevocably concluded by the two parties handing over the goods without seeing or testing them beforehand. Another form of this transaction is bayʿ al-ḥaṣāt or bayʿ ilḳāʾ al-ḥadjar, when as a sign of the conclusion of the agreement, a small stone is handed over in place of the goods. X 468a
♦ bayʿ al-muzābana (A) : in law, a transaction during which any goods the weight, size or number of which is not known is sold in bulk for a definite measure, weight or number of another commodity. It is a prohibited sale but according to Tradition, one exception was allowed, when a poor man who does not possess a palm-tree of his own, in order to procure for his family fresh dates, purchases for dried dates the fruit of a palm on the tree, but it has to be valued. Such a sale is termed *bayʿ al-ʿarāyā*. X 467b
♦ bayʿ al-muzāyada (A) : in law, an auction, which is only permitted in three cases: in direst poverty, in sickness or when deeply in debt. X 467b
♦ bayʿ al-ʿurbān (A), or *bayʿ al-ʿurbūn* : in law, a form of prohibited sale in which an earnest-money is given which belongs to the vendor if the transaction is not carried through. X 467b
♦ bayʿ bi'l-istighlāl → GHĀRŪḲA
♦ al-bayʿ bi'l-wafāʾ (A) : in law, a ‘conditional sale’ of part of the plot of a debtor to the lender, to be nullified as soon as the debt is redeemed. XII 322b
♦ bayʿatān fī bayʿa (A) : in law, a double sale, which is a legal device to get around the prohibition of interest. An example is the transaction called MUKHĀṬARA, where e.g. the (prospective) debtor sells to the (prospective) creditor a slave for cash, and immediately buys the slave back from him for a greater amount payable at a future date; this amounts to a loan with the slave as security, and the difference between the two prices represents the interest. III 511b; VII 518b

bayʿa (A) : a term denoting, in a very broad sense, the act by which a certain number of persons, acting individually or collectively, recognise the authority of another person. I 1113a; II 302b; VI 205b
♦ bayʿat al-ḥarb (A) : ‘the pledge of war’, the name of a promise given to the Prophet at ‘the second ʿAḳaba’ in 622 by seventy-three men and two women who promised to defend Muḥammad, if necessary, by arms. I 314b; V 995b
♦ bayʿat al-nisāʾ (A) : ‘the pledge of the women’, the name of a meeting between the Prophet and twelve men from Medina at ‘the first ʿAḳaba’ in 621 where the latter formally accepted Islam and made certain promises. I 314b; V 995b
♦ **bayʿat al-riḍwān** (A) : the name given to an oath of allegiance exacted by the Prophet from some of his followers during the Medinan period. XII 131a

bayāḍ (A) : ‘blank book’, a technical term in literature referring to a sort of anthology in the form of an informal notebook with poetical fragments. VII 529a
In medicine, the affected skin of the leper. X 510a

bayaḍ (A), or *bayyāḍ* : a silurus of the Nile, whose Arabic term is found again in the Latinised nomenclature to specify a sub-species limited to a particular region (*Bagrus bajad*). VIII 1021a

bayān (A) : lucidity, distinctness, clarity.
In rhetoric, a near syn. of BALĀGHA 'eloquence'; *ḥusn al-bayān* means distinctiveness (of expression). I 1114a; VIII 614b; and → AL-MAʿĀNĪ WA 'L-BAYĀN

bayāt (A) : a night-attack (of a raiding group of Bedouin). II 1055b

bayḍ al-ḳiṭṭ (A) : 'cat's testicles', in botany, the variety *Astragalus sieberi* of the genus Milk vetch. IX 653b

bayḍa (A) : in clothing, properly an iron helmet (also *khūdha*, < P *khūd*) from their resemblance in shape to an ostrich egg, but, according to al-Kattānī, also a turban. X 611b; XII 735b; and → MIGHFAR

baydaḳ → SHAṬRANDJ

bāyina (A) : a bow which uses too long an arrow, this being considered a fault because it reduces the draw and consequently makes the shot less powerful. IV 798a

bāyirāt (A) : in law, lands that have been abandoned, which raised the question whether such lands should pay land tax. IV 1036a

bayn (U) : in Urdu poetry, the part of the elegy, *marthiya*, where the martyr's family, the poet himself and all believers are lamented. VI 611b

♦ bayniyya (A) : 'intermediary'; in grammar, a division of consonants in between the occlusive and the constrictive, designating the letters *ʿ, l, m, n, r, w, y, alif*. The term ~ is recent, from 1305/1887; the ancient practice was to say e.g. 'those which are between the SHADĪDA 'occlusive' and the RIKHWA 'constrictive''. III 599a

bayraḳdār (T *bayraḳ*, P *dār*) : 'standard-bearer', under the Ottomans, applied to various officers of both the 'feudal' and the 'standing' army and to certain hereditary chieftains of Albania. I 1134b

bayt (A, pl. *buyūt*) : dwelling; covered shelter where one may spend the night. In pre-Islamic Arabia, the ~, or *bayt shaʿar*, was a tent of goat's hair and of average size. It served as a dwelling for breeders of small livestock (that is to say, of numerous Bedouin). I 1139b; II 113b; IV 1147a; and → DĀR; ~ may sometimes designate a 'sanctuary'; thus, when used with the definite article, *al-bayt*, or *al-bayt al-ḥarām, al-bayt al-ʿatīḳ*, it signifies the holy place at Mecca. I 1139b
In prosody, ~ (pl. *abyāt)* is a line of poetry consisting of two clearly distinct halves called MIṢRĀʿ. I 668a; two hemistichs with between 16 and 30 syllables and a caesura. VIII 583a
In the game of chess or backgammon, the term for a field on which a piece stands. VII 963a; IX 366b
In archery, a sector or 'house' of the bow, thus the upper limb is called *bayt aʿlā*, also called *bayt al-ramy* 'house of shooting' because the shot is made according to this plan. The lower limb is the 'lower house' (*bayt asfal*) or 'house of perpendicularity' (*bayt al-isḳāṭ*), i.e. that which falls away towards the ground. IV 799a

♦ bayt al-ibra → IBRA

♦ bayt maftūḥ (A) : in architecture, a multi-courtyard house. VI 809a

♦ **bayt al-māl** (A) : the 'fiscus' or treasury of the Muslim state. The notion of public as distinct from private ownership and the idea of properties and monies designed to serve the interests of the communities is said to have been introduced first by ʿUmar b. al-Khaṭṭāb; coupled with the institution of the DĪWĀN, it marks the starting point of the ~ as the state treasury. Previously the term designated the depository where money and goods were temporarily lodged pending distribution to their individual owners. In the administration of the later caliphate, the term MAKHZAN seems to have almost replaced the ~, which reflects the proportionate increase of presentations in kind and the diminution of fiscal receipts in hard cash. I 1141b

♦ bayt al-māldjī (Alg) : the trustee of vacant estates, a member of the council governed by the DEY. I 368a

♦ bayt al-sadjdjāda (A) : in modern Egyptian usage, the central office of a ṣūfī order, serving as the residence and the office of the order's SHAYKH or his senior aide, *wakīl*. VIII 744a

♦ bayt al-ṭāʿa (A) : in Egypt and Sudan, the institution of police-executed enforced obedience of rebellious wives, abolished since the late 1960s. VIII 32a

♦ al-abyāt al-mushadjdjara (A) : in prosody, verses which can be read from beginning to end and from end to beginning. IX 461a

bayṭār (A, < Gk) : veterinary surgeon. I 1149b

bayyāra (A) : a cesspool. V 1007a

bayyāz (A), and *bayyāzī, biyāz, bāziyy, bayzārī* : Spanish-Maghribī terms for hawker, which frequently gave way to *ṭayyār*, or *ṣakkār* 'falconer'. I 1152b

bayyina (A, pl. *bayyināt*) : clear, evident.

In the Qurʾān, ~ appears as a substantive, meaning 'manifest proof'. I 1150b

In law, ~ denotes the proof *per excellentiam*—that established by oral testimony—, although from the classical era the term came to be applied not only to the fact of giving testimony at law but also to the witnesses themselves. I 1150b

bayzara (A, < P *bāzyār* 'ostringer') : the art of the flying-hunt; falconry. I 1152a

bäz (T) : a common word for coarse cotton cloth in various Turkish dialects. V 557a

bāz (P) : in zoology, goshawk. I 1152a

bāzahr (A, < P *pā(d)-zahr* 'against poison') : bezoar, a remedy against all kinds of poisons, highly esteemed and paid for up to the 18th century. The bezoar-stone, a gall stone, is obtained from the bezoar-goat (*Capra aegagrus Gm.*). I 1155b

bazand (A) : a pre-Islamic word for raised canal banks in mediaeval ʿIrāḳ. V 865a

bāzār (P, T *pāzār*) : syn. of SŪḲ, in some villages in Afghanistan, ~ is used for the town itself, in its entirety. IX 789a

♦ bāzār-i khāṣṣ (IndP) : in Muslim India, the market on the principal streets of the city. IX 800b

♦ mīnā bāzār (IndP) : in Muslim India during the Mughal period, a market in the nature of a fête, arranged in the palace, in which the ladies of the nobles set up shops and the Emperor, along with his queens, made purchases. IX 801a

bāzinḳir (T or P) : slave-troops equipped with fire-arms; a term current during the late Khedivial and Mahdist periods in the Sudan. I 1156b

bazirgan (T, < P 'merchant') : under the Ottomans, ~ was applied to Christian and especially Jewish merchants, some of whom held official appointments in the Ottoman palace or armed forces. I 1157a

♦ bazirgan-bashi (T) : under the Ottomans, the chief purveyor of textiles to the Imperial household. I 1155b

baẓr (A, pl. *buẓūr*) : in anatomy, the clitoris. IV 913a

♦ baẓrāʾ (A) : a woman who is affected by clitorism, or is believed to be so. An uncircumcised woman is called *lakhnāʾ*. Expressions such as *ibn al-~* or *ibn al-lakhnāʾ* meaning in effect 'son of the uncumcised woman' are considered injurious. IV 913a

bāzūband → SĀʿID

bazz → ḲUMĀSH

bazzāz (A, T *bezzāz*) : a textile dealer, cloth merchant. V 559b; XII 756b

bedestān (T), or *bedesten, bezzāzistān* : the centre of a city's economic life as the place of business of the leading merchants, and the centre for financial transactions, where valuable imported wares were sold. IV 227a; X 414a

bədʿiyya (B) : in North Africa, a sleeveless vest for men; in Morocco, a sleeveless KHAFṬĀN for women. V 745b

beg (T) : a title, 'lord', used in a number of different ways. Under the Īlkhāns, ~ was sometimes used for women, and under the Mughals the feminine form, *begam* (→

BEGUM), was common. Under the Ottomans, ~ was in wide use for tribal leaders, high civil and military functionaries, and the sons of the great, particularly PASHAS. I 1159a; and → BEY; ULU BEG

♦ **begum** (IndP), and *begam* : feminine of BEG, and an honorific title of the royal princesses under the Mughals. I 1161a

♦ **beglerbegi** (T), or *beylerbeyi* : a title, 'beg of the begs', 'commander of the commanders'. Originally designating 'commander-in-chief of the army', ~ came to mean provincial governor and finally was no more than an honorary rank. I 1159b; II 722a ff.

♦ beglerbegilik (T) : a term used for an administrative division in the Ottoman empire until it was replaced by EYĀLET. Thereafter, ~ continued to be used for the office of a BEGLERBEGI. II 722a

bekči (T) : a watchman who, by a decree of 1107/1695, patrolled the quarters, *maḥalle* (→ MAḤALLA), in Ottoman Istanbul with a lantern in his hands and arrested any strangers found there after the bed-time prayer. The ~ became a characteristic figure in the folklore of Istanbul. IV 234b

beledī → ḲASSĀM

bəlgha (B) : flat slippers, usually pointed at the toe, but sometimes rounded, worn by both sexes in North Africa. V 745b

belūk : a vocal art in West Java which marks religious, family and agrarian rites, and which is in the course of disappearing. VIII 153b

belwo (Somali) : in Somali literature, a genre of poetry dealing specifically with the theme of love, developed during the late 1940s and 1950s, which grew into an important vehicle for the expression of nationalist, anti-colonial feeling. A similar genre is *heello*. IX 726a

ben-ʿamma (A) : among the Arabs of Transjordania, a form of agreement, the object of which is to establish a state of peace between tribes. III 389a

bendahara (Mal) : the Chief Minister in Malay sultanates, the highest dignitary after the sultan. He is followed by the PENGHULU *bendahari*, who is responsible for maintaining the sacred traditions, the *temenggung*, responsible for security, and the *laksamana*, the supervisor of the fleet. IX 852a

bender (A) : in music, a sort of big tambourine without bells. IV 382b

benlāk → BENNĀK

bennāk (T, < A *banaka* ?), or *benlāk* : an Ottoman poll tax paid by married peasants possessing a piece of land less than half a *čift* (→ ČIFTLIK) or no land. The former were also called simply ~, or in full *ekinlü bennāk*. I 1169b; II 32b; and → DJABĀ

ber (K) : the Kurdish clan, formed by the union of many extended families, BAVIK. A collection of ~ constitutes the tribe. V 472a

berāt (T, < A BARĀʾA) : a term in Ottoman Turkish denoting a type of order issued by the sultan. In its more limited sense, ~ meant also 'a deed of grant', 'a writ for the appointment to hold an office'. All appointments throughout the empire whether that of a high-ranking pasha, even that of the Syrian Church bishops, or that of a low-ranking employee of a mosque, were effected by a ~. Its constant attribute was *sherif* or *humāyūn* 'imperial'. I 1170a

♦ **berātli** (T) : holder of a BERĀT; a term applied in the late 18th and early 19th centuries to certain non-Muslim subjects of the Ottoman empire, who held *berāt*s conferring upon them important commercial and fiscal privileges. These *berāt*s were distributed by the European diplomatic missions in abusive extension of their rights under capitulation. I 1171b

bərbūkh (Alg) : a variety of couscous, with fine grain, eaten cold, without butter, and moistened with a little milk. V 528a

beshlik → ČEYREK

beste (T) : a vocal composition in four verses each followed by the same melodic passage. IX 876a

bey (T) : var. of BEG, title given to the sons of pashas, and of a few of the highest civil functionaries, to military and naval officers of the rank of colonel or lieutenant colonel, and popularly, to any persons of wealth, or supposed distinction. I 1159a; II 507b; V 631a; the name applied to the ruler of Tunisia until 26 July 1957 when Bey Lamine was deposed and the Republic was proclaimed. I 1110b

♦ beylerbeyi → BEGLERBEGI

♦ **beylik** (T) : a term denoting both the title and post (or function) of a BEY, and the territory (or domain) under his rule. Later, by extension, it came to mean also 'state, government', and, at the same time, a political and administrative entity sometimes enjoying a certain autonomy. In North Africa, the term is used in the former Ottoman possessions, but not in Morocco or in the Sahara, and refers to government and administrative authority at every stage. I 1191a; II 338b

In Ottoman administration, the most important of three offices into which the Ottoman chancellery was divided, the ~ saw to the despatch of imperial rescripts, orders of the viziers, and in general all ordinances other than those of the department of finance. VIII 482a

beza : a type of salt in the salt works near Bilma, in Niger, ~ is in the form of crystals and, not treated in any way, is used for human consumption. I 1221b

bezzāzistān → BEDESTĀN

bhakti (H) : a north Indian movement, sometimes seen incorrectly as a Hindu reaction seeking to strengthen Hinduism against the advancing pressure of conversions to Islam. III 456b

bhāng (< San *bhaṅga*, A BAN<u>DJ</u>, P *bang*) : in India, a product of the dried leaves of hemp reduced to powder and mixed with flour and spices, originally eaten but later more commonly smoked. III 266b; VI 814b

bi-lā kayf (A) : lit. without how, i.e. without specifying manner or modality; in theology, a doctrine taking a central position between those who interpreted the anthropomorphic expressions in the Qur'ān literally and those who interpreted them metaphorically. I 333b

bī-<u>sh</u>arʿ (**bi<u>sh</u>arʿ**) (P) : lit. without law, i.e. rejecting not only the ritual but also the moral law of Islam; one of the two categories into which dervishes in Persia are divided. The other is BĀ-<u>SH</u>ARʿ. The term seems primarily to denote the adepts of the Malāmatiyya ṣūfī sect. I 1239b; II 164b

bīʿa → KANĪSA

bībī (T) : originally, 'little old mother', 'grandmother', 'woman of high rank', ~ was used in Ottoman Turkish in the sense of 'woman of consequence', 'lady', and in 13th-century <u>Kh</u>urāsān as a title for women of distinction. I 1197b

bidʿa (A) : innovation, a belief or practice for which there is no precedent in the time of the Prophet. I 1199a; IV 141b

♦ bidʿat (T) : dues in contradiction to the <u>sh</u>arīʿa or to Ottoman administrative principles, which nevertheless continued to be levied either by the State or TĪMĀR-holders, e.g. the *bidʿat-i <u>kh</u>inzīr* 'pig-tax' which provided the treasury with a large revenue. II 147a; VIII 486b

♦ bidʿat marfūʿe (T) : in Ottoman administration, pre-conquest taxes and dues that were abolished by the sultan's specific order. VIII 486b

♦ bidʿat maʿrūfe (T) : in Ottoman administration, pre-conquest taxes and dues that were customarily recognized. VIII 486b

bīdār (A) : in Oman and Trucial Oman the official subordinate to the ʿARĪF, the latter being in charge of the water distribution. IV 532a

bīgār → ḤA<u>SH</u>AR

bīghā : a standard measure of area in Muslim India, divided into twenty BĪSWĀ. The ~ varied considerably by region, with a distinction between a larger (*pakkā*) and a smaller (*kaččā*) measure. VII 140a
bighā' (A) : the Qur'ānic term for prostitution. XII 133a
bikāsīn → SHUNKUB
bikr (A) : a virgin girl. III 17a; X 901b
billawr (A, < Gk ?) : in mineralogy, rock-crystal. I 1220b
bilmedje (T) : the name given to popular riddles among the Ottoman Turks. I 1222a
bilyūn (Mor), or *gersh* : a coin with the value of a twentieth of a douro or RIYĀL. III 256a
bīmāristān (P) : a hospital; in modern usage, a lunatic asylum. I 1222b
binā' (A) : building, the art of the builder or mason. I 1226a
In grammar, the state of a word that is fixed to one final short vowel or to none at all, and thus the opposite of IʿRĀB. III 1249b; and → WAZN
biñbashi (T) : 'head of a thousand'; a Turkish military rank. It appears as early as 729/1328-29 among the Western Turks. Although it was not much used in the regular Ottoman forces of the classical period, it reappeared in the 18th century when it designated the officers of the newly raised treasury-paid force of infantry and cavalry. From the end of the 18th century, it became a regular rank in the new European-style armies. I 1229a; VIII 370b
binish (T) : a kind of very full caftan with wide sleeves, worn most frequently as a travelling or riding garment in the Ottoman period. V 752a; all public appearances of the sultan, whether on horseback or in a boat. VIII 529a
binn : a Druze term denoting one of a number of earlier races or sects, said to have been a group of inhabitants of Hadjar in the Yemen who believed in the message of Shaṭnīl, the incarnation of Ḥamza in the Age of Adam. XII 135b
bint (A, pl. *banāt*) : daughter.
♦ bint labūn (A) : a female camel in its third year. XI 412a
♦ bint makhaḍ (A) : a female camel in its second year. XI 412a
♦ banāt naʿsh (A) : in astronomy, the Plough (δεζη Ursae Majoris). VII 51a
bi'r (A, pl. *abyār*) : well; cistern, reservoir; even any hole or cavity dug in the ground, whether containing water or not. I 538b; I 1230a
birdhawn (A, pl. *barādhīn*) : in zoology, 'of common parentage', one of four classifications of a horse, usually used for the draught-horse or pack-horse. II 785b; nag of non-Arab stock. IV 1143b; IV 1146a
birdjāṣ (A) : during the early ʿAbbāsid period, a kind of equestrian game, in which the contestant had to get his lance-point through a metal ring fixed to the top of a wooden column, thus revealing his skill or otherwise in controlling his horse and aiming his weapon. IV 265b
bīrindj → SHABAH
birindjāsaf → SHĪḤ
birka (A) : an external cistern; fish pond. VIII 816a; VIII 1022a
At Fez and Rabat and in Tunisia, a special (slave) market, existing until well into the 20th century. I 35a
birḳish → ABŪ BARĀḲISH
birr (A) : a Qur'ānic term meaning 'pious goodness'. I 1235b; charitable gift. VIII 712a
birsām : in medicine, pleurisy. IX 9b
birsīm (A) : in botany, Egyptian clover. VI 163a
bīrūn (P) : outside; in Ottoman Turkish, the name given to the outer departments and services of the Ottoman imperial household, in contrast to the inner departments, known as ENDERŪN. The ~ was thus the meeting-point of the court and the state and,

besides palace functionaries, included a number of high officers and dignitaries concerned with the administrative, military, and religious affairs of the empire. I 1236a; II 1089a

bisāṭ (A, pl. *busṭ, busuṭ, absiṭa*) : a generic term for carpet. XII 136a

bisbās → BASBĀS

bīsh → AĶŪNĪṬUN

bīshar' → BĪ-SHAR'

bishāra (A) : equivalent used for Greek *evangelium* 'announcement of good news', found for the first time in Freytag's Arabic-Latin dictionary. XII 772a

bishṭ (A) : a mantle, jacket, worn by both sexes in Syria and Palestine. V 740b

bissasfaltus → MŪMIYĀ'

bīswā : a standard measure of area used in Muslim India, divided into twenty *bīswānsā*. In turn, twenty ~ was one BĪGHĀ. The ~ varied considerably by region. VII 140a

bit' (A) : mead, an alcoholic drink consisting of a mixture of honey and wine. The Egyptians used to be very fond of it in mediaeval times. VI 720a; VII 907b; hydromel. IV 998a

biti (T) : an Ottoman sultan's order, more or less obsolete after 1500. I 1170a

bitikči (T) : secretaries in Mongolian Persia, especially in the military administration, who were especially knowledgeable in Turkish or Mongolian. It was their task to translate into these two languages original documents probably written in Persian, and in 'Irāķ also in Arabic. I 1248b; IV 757a

biṭriķ (A, < L *Patricius*) : patriciate; an honorary dignity, not connected with any office, and conferred for exceptional services to the state. In the history of the Arabs before Islam, only two Ghassānid dynasts, viz. al-Ḥārith b. Djabala and his son al-Mundhir, are known to have received this much coveted Roman honour. The term found its way into Muslim literature, and in the military annals of Arab-Byzantine relations, it became the regular term for a Byzantine commander. I 1249b; V 620a

biṭṭīkh ('ayn) al-nims → NIMS

bīwe resmī (T) : under the Ottomans, the ISPENDJE tax paid by widows at the rate of 6 AĶČES per person. II 146b

bocca : a mini-community, specific to the Wansharīs massif in central Algeria, whose administrative coverage often corresponds to a cleared area. XI 139a

bölük (T) : in Eastern Turkish and in Persian, ~ designated a province or region. I 1256a

In Ottoman Turkey, from the time of the reforms on, ~ designated units of infantry or cavalry of the standing army. I 102a; I 1256a; II 1097b; II 1121a; and → DÖRT BÖLÜK

♦ **bölük-bashi̊** (T) : the title given to the commanders of the BÖLÜKs of the AGHA. The ~ was mounted and had an iron mace and a shield tied to his saddle; when the sultan left the Palace for the mosque, the ~ was present wearing ornate clothes and holding in his hand a reed instead of a spear. I 1256b

börk (T) : the most widespread Turkish head-gear in Ottoman Turkey, the ~ was in a cone or helmet shape, raised in front and decorated at the base with gold braid; officers wore it decorated in addition with a plume. V 751b

boru (T), and NEFĪR : a trumpet without holes which could produce five notes within an ambitus of one and a half octaves. Older *boru*s were apparently made of bronze, but by the 10th/16th century brass was in use. VI 1007b

bostāndji̊ (T, < P **būstān** 'garden') : a term applied in the old Ottoman state organisation to people employed in the flower and vegetable gardens, as well as in the boathouses and rowing-boats of the sultan's palaces. The ~s formed two ODJAĶs 'army units'. I 1277b; IV 1100b; soldier-gardener. X 568b

♦ **bostāndji̊-bashi̊** (T) : the senior officer of the ODJAĶ of the BOSTĀNDJĪs. As the person responsible for the maintenance of law and order on the shores of the Golden Horn, the Sea of Marmora and the Bosphorus, he used to patrol the shores in a boat with a retinue of 30 men, as well as inspect the countryside and forests around Istanbul. He was very close to the sultan. I 1278b

brīm → ʿAḲĀL; ḤAKW

budalāʾ → ABDĀL

budd (A, P *but*; pl. *bidada*) : a temple, pagoda; Buddha; an idol. I 1283b

būdjādī (A, < *abdjād*) : in North Africa, used for 'beginner', literally, 'one still at the abecedarian stage'. I 98a

budna → SINĀM

budūḥ (A) : an artificial talismanic word formed from the elements of the simple three-fold magic square. The uses of the word are most various, to invoke both good and bad fortune, but by far the most common use is to ensure the arrival of letters and packages. II 370a; XII 153a

bughāt (A, s. *bāghī*) : 'rebels'; in law, sectarian-minded Muslims who reject the authority of the ruler, considered by the Zaydīs and Imāmīs as unbelievers, but by the Sunnīs as erring Muslims. IV 772a; IX 205a

bughtāḳ : a bonnet worn by Īlkhānid princesses. It consisted of a light wood frame covered with silk, from the top of which protruded a long feather. The ~ could be ornamented with gold and precious stones and sometimes had a long train which hung down behind. V 748b; X 611b

buhār (A) : in zoology, the diacope, whose Arabic term is found again in the Latinised nomenclature to specify a sub-species limited to a particular region (*Diacope bohar*). VIII 1021a

buḥayra (A, dim. of *baḥra*) : lake. In North Africa, ~ (*bḥēra*) denotes a low-lying plain; its most common meaning, however, is 'vegetable garden, field for market gardening'. I 1288a

In Almohad times, ~ meant an irrigated garden. I 1288a

buḥūr → BAḤR

būḳ (A) : in music, the generic name for any instrument of the horn or trumpet family. I 1290b; a kind of reed-pipe that became quite famous in Western Europe. The original ~ was a horn or clarion, and was made of horn or metal. Pierced with holes for fingering, and played with a reed, the ~ evolved into a new type of instrument, somewhat similar to the modern saxophone. VII 207b

buḳʿa (A), or *baḳʿa* : a region which is distinguishable from its surroundings, more particularly a depression between mountains. I 1292b; a patch of ground marked out from adjoining land by a difference in colour, etc. or a low-lying region with stagnant water. XII 154a

In the central and eastern parts of the Islamic world, ~ acquired the sense of 'dervish convent', 'mausoleum' or in general 'a building for pious, educational or charitable purposes'. IX 474b; XII 154a

būḳalā (Alg) : a two-handled pottery vase used by women in the course of the divinatory practices to which it gave its name. I 1292b; III 290a

būḳalamūn (A) : a coloured (violet, red and green) cloth, with a moiré, watered-silk effect, produced in the Tinnīs workshops and especially prized by the Fāṭimid court in Cairo. X 532a

bukhl (A) : avarice, the person who practices it being called *bakhīl* or, less often, *bākhil*. I 1297b

bukht (A, s. *bukhtī*, pl. *bakhātī*) : in zoology, the species produced as a result of the crossing of two-humped stallions with Arab female camels; it did not breed and was mainly used as a beast of burden. III 665b

būḳīr (A) : in zoology, a kind of bird. I 168b
bukra → GHUDWA
buku (Sw?) : in zoology, the Zanzibar Pouched Rat (*cricetomys gambianus* Cosensi), reported to be nearly three feet long from snout to the end of the tail. XI 448b
bukubulbīs (A) : in zoology, the barbel. VIII 1021a
bularghuči̊ → YURTČI̊
bulbul (A) : in zoology, the Syrian nightingale. I 541b; I 1301a
♦ bulbula → IBRĪḲ
bulḳa (A) : in mineralogy, piebaldness, uneven colouring which is a defect or impurity in a gem. XI 263a
bullayḳ (A) : in prosody, term used by Ṣafī al-Dīn al-Ḥillī for a ZADJAL that is jocular or obscene. XI 373b
bulūk (P, pl. *bulūḳāt*) : a district, in particular a district watered by river water. V 873b f.
būmī → ZAMĪNDĀR
bunbuk → KHINZĪR AL-BAḤR
bunduḳ (A) : in botany, the parasol pine. V 50b; and → KAWS AL-BUNDUḲ
bunīča (P) : in Persia, a group assessment, on the basis of which taxes were levied on the craft guilds. The tax based on this assessment was subsequently allocated among the individual members of the guild. This form of tax was abolished in 1926. II 151b; the right to exercise a trade, given to some guilds, was called *ḥaḳḳ al-~*. IX 645b
būnīt → BALAMĪDA
bunn (A) : in zoology, the carp. VIII 1023a; and → ḲAHWA
♦ bunnī al-Nīl (A) : in zoology, the Nile barbel, whose Arabic term is found again in the Latinised nomenclature to specify a sub-species limited to a particular region (*Barbus bynni*). VIII 1021b
būraḳ → BAWRAḲ
burd → BURDA
burda (A), or *burd* : a wrap of striped woollen cloth produced in the Yemen, before and during the Prophet's time, usually worn by men. I 1314b; III 316a; V 734a
burdj (A, pl. *burūdj*) : a square or round tower, whether adjacent to a rampart or isolated and serving as a bastion or dungeon; masonry pier of a bridge. I 1315a; a moveable tower, used as a siege instrument. III 473a; a pigeon-house. III 109a
In astronomy, each of the twelve signs of the zodiac. I 1315a; and → MINṬAḲAT AL-BURŪDJ
In music, ~ denotes a mode. I 1315a
♦ burdj-i kabūtar (P) : pigeon towers, the construction of which on the fertile plain around Iṣfahān was encouraged by Shāh ʿAbbās so that he could heavily tax the guano harvest. XII 457a
burdjās (A) : a chivalrous duel with lances, an equestrian sport regularly practised in the 6th-7th/12th-13th centuries. II 954a
burdjīn (A) : in botany, the name of one of five varieties of the red jujube; it has small fruits with a violent astringency, spreads on the ground and grows to the height of sitting. X 868b
burdjuma (A) : 'knuckle'; in its plural form, *barādjim*, was the term for five (or six or four) components of the Ḥanẓala b. Mālik group, the less numerous ones, against their brothers, three other sons of Ḥanẓala, X 173b
burghul (A, T *bulgur*) : crushed wheat, considered a dish of the poor. II 1067a
burghūth (A) : in zoology, fleas, diptera of the *pulex* family. IV 522a
♦ burghūth al-māʾ (A) : in zoology, the water-beetle (*Daphnia pulex*). VIII 1022a
burhān (A) : decisive proof, clear demonstration; a Qurʾānic term signifying a brilliant manifestation, a shining light from God. In correlation, ~ is also the decisive proof

which the infidels are called upon to furnish as justification of their false beliefs. I 1326b

In law, ~ refers to the quality of certitude (based upon an argument of authority, which can be either a scriptual text or the eye-witnessing of an obvious fact) which is proper to reasoning 'in two terms', in order to prove the radical distinction between or the identity of two comparable 'things'; it is found especially in al-Shāfiʿī, Ibn Ḥanbal and Dāwūd. I 1326b

In logic, ~ came to designate syllogistic demonstration. I 1327a

būrī (A) : in zoology, the grey mullet. I 168b; VIII 1023a

burḳuʿ (A) : in early Islam, a woman's face veil consisting of a fabric suspended from the centre front of the headband by a string creating a mask-like effect. It is still worn by married women among the Sinai Bedouin. V 735a

In military science, a chamfron or armour for the horse's head (syn. *kashka, sarī, tishtaniyya*). XII 739a

burnus (A) : a sort of high cap or bonnet, worn in the Prophet's time. Already this early, the ~ must also have designated by extension a woollen hooded cloak. V 734b; X 612a

burt (A, < L *portus*) : 'gate', the northeastern border of Muslim Spain, called as such by the geographers, although they differed as to where it lay. I 1337a

burtuḳāl, burtuḳāliyyāt → NĀRANDJ

burṭul[la] (A; P *pertele*) : in clothing, a high cap; with the pronunciation barṭala, a low skullcap. In modern parlance, it means the TĀDJ of a bishop. X 612a

bürüme (T) : 'one with a coat of mail', in the Ottoman army, a DJEBELI who held a TĪMĀR of above 2,000 AḲČEs. II 528b; a coat of mail consisting of linked steel rings that a djebelü who enjoyed a *tīmār* above 3,000 *aḳčes*. X 503a

būs (A) : a term used in addition to the general term LAWN 'colour' for a notion of brightness, of clear colour. V 699b

būsh (A) : a variety of ʿABĀʾ made in North Syria. V 740b

♦ būshī (A), or *pūshī* : a black face veil worn by women in Iraq. V 740b

būsḥāḳī → FĪRŪZADJ

busht (A) : woollen wraps. IX 765a

busr → TAMR

bussadh → MARDJĀN

būstān → BOSTĀNDJİ

būtaḳ (A, pl. *bawātiḳ*) : in chemistry, a melting-pot. V 114b

buṭṭa (A) : a measure used in Egypt for weighing flour. The ~ was equal to 50 Egyptian RAṬLs, i.e. 22.245 kg. VI 119a

büyük kirpi → ḲUNFUDH

buyuruldu (T) : an order of an Ottoman grand vizier, vizier, BEGLERBEGI, *defterdār* (→ DAFTARDĀR), or other high official to a subordinate. A ~ is of two main types: a decision written in the margin of an incoming petition or report, or an order issued independently. It deals with various administrative matters, especially appointments, grants of fiefs, economic regulations, safe-passage, etc. I 1357b

buyūtāt (P) : under the Ṣafawids, the Royal Household, which was divided into a number of offices and workshops. II 335a; in Muslim Spain, the most influential families. XI 191b

būz (A) : snout.

♦ abū būz → ABŪ BŪZ

buz-kashī (P) : in Afghanistan, the equestrian sport of 'goat-dragging'. IV 1144b

buzuk → ṬUNBŪR

buzurg → BĀDJ-I BUZURG; SHASHMAḲOM

C

čabūtra (P) : in Mughal architecture, a platform. X 59b

čadirkhäyal (T) : one of two varieties of puppet theatre in Central Asia, a marionette show with full-bodied miniature marionettes suspended and activated from above on strings. VI 765a

čādur → RŪ BAND; SHAWDAR

čaghāna (T) : in music, the 'Jingling Johnny' (Fr *chapeau chinois*, Ger *Schellenbaum*), now superseded by the portable glockenspiel. X 37b

čahār (P) : four.

♦ čahār bāgh (P) → BĀGH

♦ čahār sūķ → SŪĶ

♦ čahār tāķ (P) : the mostly diminutive Sasanian fire temple with four axial arched openings. Set in the midst of a large open space, it served to house the sacred fire. This layout obviously lent itself to Muslim prayer, and literary sources recount how such fire temples were taken over and converted into mosques. The domed chamber, characteristic of Iranian mosques, derives from the ~. VI 684a

♦ čahārtār → TĀR

čaki̊r (T) : a merlin and falcon, one of the birds of prey making up the traditional sport of hawking at the Ottoman court. The others were the *shāhīn* 'peregrine falcon' and the *atmadja* 'sparrow-hawk'. II 614b

♦ **čaki̊rdji̊-bashi̊** (T) : chief falconer, a high official of the Ottoman court and head of the whole organisation of hawking. II 6a; II 614b

čaķshīr (T, A *shaķshīr*) : Turkish-style pantaloons, underdrawers, worn by both sexes in Egypt, Syria and Palestine. V 740b

čālīsh → SHĀLĪSH

čālpāra → MUṢAFFAḤĀT

čandi : a temple of either Hindu or Buddhist intention, ultimately of Indian origin but modified by Indonesian religious concepts. The ~ has been proposed as one of the origins of the basic Indonesian mosque. VI 701b

canķri : a word used in Laķ society to designate children of marriages between BAGTALS and women of lower social orders. V 618a

čao (P, < Ch *ṭṣʿau*) : the name given to paper currency in circulation in Iran for about two months in 693/1294. It was made of the bark of the mulberry tree, was oblong in shape, and bore the SHAHĀDA. II 14a

čapar → ALP

čapūķ → TUTUN

čarkh → SANG

♦ čarkh-kamān (P) : a multiple-firing arbalest, borrowed from the Mongols. IV 798a

čarkhadji̊ → ĶARĀGHUL

čarpāra → MUṢAFFAḤĀT

čarshi̊ (T) : in Ottoman times, common term for both individual business locales and covered markets, which may encompass over a hundred shops, contrasting with *pāzār*, an open-air market held once or several times a week. IX 796b

čārtār → TĀR

čāshna-gīr (P, A *dhawwāķ*) : 'taster', the title of an official, generally an AMĪR, at the court of the Muslim sovereigns from the time of the Saldjūķs. The title does not appear to be found under previous dynasties, although caliphs and princes did undoubtedly have overseers for their food. The term ~ is also found as the name of a kind of crystal decanter. II 15a

♦ **čāshnagīr-bāshī** (T) : 'chief taster', a high official at the Ottoman court. A document dated 883/1478-9 lists 12 tasters as subordinate to the ~. Later, the number employed rose considerably, reaching as high as 117. By the 18th century, the ~ had clearly fallen in status and had responsibilities more related to the preparation of food. II 15a; an Ottoman court dignitary, whose duty it was to assist the sultan in mounting his horse by holding him under the arm or under the armpit. VIII 529b

čatr (P), or *čitr* : a term used in the Iranian cultural sphere to designate a parasol held over the sovereign and considered as one of the insignia of rank. In this, it is the synonym of the Arabic MIẒALLA. VII 192b; the variant *čitr* gave rise to the Arabicised forms *djitr* and *shitr* which were used in the Mamlūk sultanate. VII 192a

čā'ūsh (T) : officials staffing the various Ottoman Palace departments; low-ranking military personnel. In Uygur, ~ refers to a Tou-kiu ambassador. In North Africa, it is still seen in its Arabic form of *shā'ūsh*, where it means a court usher or mace-bearer. II 16a Under the ancient Turks, the Saldjūḳs, the Ayyūbids and the Mamlūks, the ~ formed a privileged body under the direct command of the ruler; under the Ottomans, they were part of the official ceremonial escort of the sultan on his departure from the palace or when he had an audience with foreign dignitaries. Their services were also used as ambassadors or envoys by the sultan or his grand vizier. The ranks of ~ and *čā'ūsh wekīlī* were used in the cavalry and the navy at the beginning of the 19th century. After the army reorganisation in 1241/1826, a ~ held the equivalent rank of a sergeant. II 16a

In certain religious sects, the term designates a grade in the hierarchy of the sect. II 16a

čawgān (P) : the stick used in polo. The term is also used in a wider sense for the game itself, which originated in Persia and was generally played on horseback, though sometimes on foot; ~ was also used for any stick with the end bent back, particularly those for beating drums. II 16b

čawk : in Muslim India, a market usually located at places where four roads met. IX 800b

čay (P) : tea, introduced to sultan Mawlay Ismāʿīl in Morocco in ca. 1700; ~ is variously termed *ātāy, tāy, shāy* and *shāhī*, in different parts of the Islamic world. II 17b

♦ **čāy-khāna** (P) : lit. tea-house, ~ covers a range of establishments in Iran serving tea and light refreshments. The term *ḳahwa-khāna* 'coffee-house' is used synonymously, although coffee is never served. XII 169a

čebken → ČEPKEN

čedik (T) : an indoor shoe with a low leg, worn in the Ottoman period. It was most often made in yellow Moroccan leather, with a supple sole. V 752b

čektiri → BASHTARDA

čelebī (T) : a term of unknown origin applied to men of the upper classes in Turkey between the end of the 13th and the beginning of the 18th century, as a title primarily given to poets and men of letters, but also to princes and heads of a ṣūfī order; ~ is the most general title of the head of the Mawlawī order of dervishes. II 19a; VI 883a; its Syrian and Egyptian variant, *shalabī* or *djalabī*, has the meaning of 'barbarian'. II 19a

čeltükdji (T) : in the Ottoman empire, a rice grower with a special status as labourer of the sultan on the state's rice fields. They are also listed in the surveys as *kürekdji* or *ortaḳdji*. The condition of a ~ was quite onerous, since apart from the hardships borne by him in irrigating and cultivating the rice, he had to surrender half of his production to the state treasury. V 880a

čepken (T), or *čebken, sallama* : a short caftan with sleeves, buckled and bordered, worn as an outer garment in the Ottoman period. V 752a; XI 494a

česhme (T, < P) : one of two kinds of water fountains (→ SABĪL) in Istanbul. The ~ is self-service, the water being received from a tap above a basin, while the other, called *sebīl*, is served by an attendant behind a grill. The ~s of Istanbul are mural fountains which consist of a recessed niche framed by a rectangle with a protruding basin, made of carved white marble. II 26a; VIII 682a

čewgān (T) : a crescent-shaped, jingling rattle with bells, one of two types of brass percussion supporting the drum of the musical ensemble MEHTER. VI 1008a

čeyrek (T, < P *čahāryak*) : a quarter of an hour; a coin, also known as *beshlik*, or five piastre piece. The silver ~ had a fineness of 830, weighed 6.13 grams and measured 24 mm in diameter. II 28b

čhadjdjā : an architectural feature found in Indian mosques, namely, the eaves pent to throw off monsoon water and increase shade. VI 690b

čhatrī (H, < San, dim. of *čhattra*) : lit. umbrella; an Indo-Muslim architectural form of the *čhattra*, sc. small, canopied structures placed at the junctions of the *chemin de ronde* of a fortification, or as decorative elements at roof level on mosque, tomb or other building, or as simple cover of an inhumation less imposing than a tomb proper. The characteristic form is that of a domed canopy supported on four strong pillars, with heavy protecting eaves. III 442b ff.; VII 195a

čhattra → ČHATRĪ

chêng (Ch) : a Chinese musical instrument which was probably not used by Islamic peoples, although known to them. The ~ was made of tubes of reed joined together. It was blown through a tube and the notes were obtained by fingerholes. VII 208b

chiao-chu → TAO-CHANG

chundawand (H) : a custom among Indian Muslims by which the group, being the sons of each wife, is entitled to its allotted portion of the inheritance until the extinction of its last member. I 172a

čift-resmi (T) : the basic land tax in the Ottoman empire paid in principle by every Muslim peasant possessing one *čift* (→ ČIFTLIK). Depending upon the fertility of the soil, it was originally levied in the lands conquered from the Byzantines in Western Anatolia and Thrace, on both Muslim and Christian peasants alike, although in other parts of the empire, the Christians were subjected to a different tax. The *Ḳānūnnāme* of Meḥemmed II specifies that the rate of the tax was 22 AKČES, the equivalent of seven services for the TĪMĀR-holder. II 32a; VII 507b; VIII 486b

čifte naḳḳāre → NAḲḲĀRA

čiftlik (T, < P *djuft* 'pair' + Turkish suffix *lik*), or *čift* : farm.

In Ottoman times it designated, at first, a certain unit of agricultural land in the landholding system, and then, later on, a large estate. Originally, it was thought of as the amount of land that could be ploughed by a pair of oxen; it applied to a holding of agricultural land comprising 60 or 80 to 150 DÖNÜMS, the size depending upon the fertility of the soil. In the Slav areas of the Ottoman empire, the term *bashtina* was often substituted for ~. II 32b

čihra (U) : descriptive rolls for the soldiers of the Indian army, introduced by Akbar to check evasions of military obligations. XII 176b

In Urdu poetry, ~ denotes the introductory verses of the elegy, *marthiya*, setting the tone with no restrictions as to details. VI 611b

čile → DEDE

čilim → NARDJĪLA

čilla (P, A *al-arbaʿīniyya*) : a quadragesimal fast. I 1122a; forty days of spiritual confinement in a lonely corner or cell for prayer and contemplation; one of the five main Čishtī ṣūfī practices adopted in order to harness all feelings and emotions in establishing communion with God. II 55b; IV 991a

♦ čilla-i maʿkūs (P) : the inverted ČILLA, performed by tying a rope to one's feet and having one's body lowered into a well, and by offering prayers in this posture for forty days. II 55b

čimshīrlik → ḲAFES

čirāgh (T, pl. **čirāghān**) : a means of illumination, such as candle, torch or lamp. *Čirāghān* festivities, in which tulip gardens were illuminated with lamps and candles, were held at a palace on the European side of the Bosphorus of the same name. II 49a

čīt (P, T, H *čhint*) : chintz, a popular British imitation of Indian muslin that enjoyed demand in the Ottoman empire after 1780. V 564a

čitak (Serb 'coarse', pl. *čitaci*) : in some parts of southern Serbia and Bulgaria, designation of Bulgarian Muslims, said sometimes to be only given to Serbs converted to Islam; ~ seems to be, however, limited to Turks in the two countries. VIII 320a; in former Yugoslavia, the designation of Muslims speaking Serbo-Croat, Macedonian or Albanian, who are largely of South Slavonic stock converted to Islam under the Ottomans from the 9th/15th century onwards. An alternative, *gadjal*, was used less often by also pejoratively. X 697b ff.

čitr → ČATR

čizme (T) : the most widespread shoes in Turkey during the Ottoman period, with a high leg reaching up as far as the knee and a supple sole. V 752b

çöğür → ČŪGŪR

čorbadjî (T) : lit. soup-provider; the commander of eight units of infantry or cavalry, BÖLÜK, in the Galipoli ODJAḲ. I 1256a; the title applied among the Janissaries to commanders of the ORTAs and the *agha bölükleri*. The title of ~ was also given to the village notables who entertained travellers. Later, until a half-century ago, it became an appellation of merchants and rich Christians. II 61b; VIII 178b

♦ čorbadjî kečesi (T) : the crested headdress generally worn on ceremonial occasions by the ČORBADJÎ, also called *ḳalafat*. Its crest was made either of cranes' feathers or of herons' feathers. II 61b

♦ čorbadjî yamaghî (T) : the aide to the ČORBADJÎ. II 61b

cot (P) : the pair of oxen used for labour; the work carried out by the peasant in one day. V 473a

čūb (P) : wood; and → TUTUN

♦ čūb-i čīnī (P) : the china root, considered a universal cure, and which the Ṣafawid physician ʿImād al-Dīn stated cured infertility, opium addiction, baldness, rheumatism and haemorrhoids. VIII 783b; X 457b

čūgūr (T) : a musical instrument of the pandore type, with five strings and a wooden belly. It was invented by Yaʿḳūb Germiyānī of Kütāhiya, and was used by the Janissaries. X 626a; as *çöğür*, a variant of the SĀZ 'lute', originally from eastern Turkey and Ādharbaydjān, characterised by a shorter neck and with a total length of about 100 cm. IX 120a

čuḳadār (T) : in the Ottoman empire, a valet-de-chambre at the palace. IX 706b

čūl : loess dune. IX 431a

čumāk (T) : the club or mace. X 595a

čūpān (P) : 'herdsman, shepherd', a term adopted by Turkish peoples in close contact with the Iranian language-area. II 69a, where also can be found many words, chiefly plant names, in which *čoban* forms a compound

♦ čūpānbegī (P) : a tax on flocks and herds, levied in 9th/15th-century Persia. It was possibly synonomous with ḲŪBČŪR. IV 1042a

čupūḳ → TUTUN

D

ḍabb (A) : in zoology, the thorn-tail lizard (*Uromastix spinipes*). II 70a

dābba (A, pl. *dawābb*) : in zoology, any living creature which keeps its body horizontal as it moves, generally a quadruped, in particular, a beast of burden or pack animal: horse, donkey, mule, or camel. II 71a

dabbāba (A) : penthouse, a siege instrument, mainly a Frankish weapon. III 473a ff.; testudine. III 472a

dabbāg͟h (A) : the profession of a tanner. XII 172a

dabbūs : in music, a wooden sceptre, to the head of which is attached a number of chains with jingling pieces of metal fixed loosely in the links, used by the dervish. IX 11a

In Mamlūk terminology, *fann al-dabbūs* is the mace game, one of the branches of horse-riding. II 955a

dabdāb, dabdaba → ṬABL AL-MARKAB

dabīb (A) : 'crawling', in literature, a theme originating in pre-Islamic poetry where it was possible to crawl under the tent in order to approach a woman but became purely conventional with later urban poets. V 778b

dabīḳī : a type of material, manufactured more or less everywhere but stemming originally from a locality in the outer suburbs of Damietta called Dabīḳ. II 72b; cloth made essentially from linen and often stitched with gold or silk. X 532a

dabīr (P) : scribe, secretary, used as the equivalent in the Persian cultural world, including the Indo-Muslim one during the sultanate period, of the Arabic KĀTIB. The head of the Correspondence ministry in the Dihlī sultanate was called *dabīr-i k͟hāṣṣ*. IV 758b; XII 173a; and → ʿUMDAT AL-MULK

♦ dabīr-i sarā (IndP) : in the Dihlī sultanate, the registrar of the palace. IV 759a

ḍābiṭ (A, T *zabit*) : an Ottoman term for certain functionaries and officers; later, officers in the armed forces. Originally, ~ designated a person in charge or in control of a matter or of (? the revenues of) a place. By the 11th/17th century, it was already acquiring the technical meaning of army officer, and in the 12th/18th century, it was in common use in this sense. II 74a

In Persia, in the smaller ports, a tribal chief or goverment official who managed the port's customs. XII 717a

For ~ in the science of Tradition, → ṢAḤĪḤ

dabr → NAḤL

ḍabṭ (A) : the assessment of taxable land by measurement, applied under the later Dihlī Sultanate and the Mug͟hals. II 74b; II 155b

♦ **ḍabṭiyya** (A, T *zabtiyye*) : a late Ottoman term for the police and gendarmerie. II 74b

ḍabuʿ (A, < Sem; P *kaftār*, T *ṣirtlan*, B *ifis*), and *ḍabʿ* : in zoology, the hyena. From this generic term, other terms have been derived to differentiate the male, *ḍibʿān* (alongside *d͟hīk͟h*), and female, *ḍibʿāna*. The cub is called *furʿul*. XII 173b, where can be found other synonyms

dabūr (A) : in meteorology, the west wind. VIII 526b

ḍād (A) : the fifteenth letter of the Arabic alphabet, transcribed *ḍ*, with the numerical value 800. Its definition presents difficulties but the most probable is: voiced lateralized velarized interdental fricative (in Arabic: *rik͟hwa mad͟jhūra muṭbaḳa*). II 75a

dad͟jād͟ja (A) : in zoology, the domestic fowl. II 76a

In astronomy, the constellation of the Swan, also called *al-Ṭāʾir*. II 76a

♦ dadjādjat al-baḥr (A), *dadjādjat al-ḳubba* : (in local pronunciation, *didjādja*), certain kinds of fish. II 76a

♦ dadjādjat al-māʾ → SHUNḲUB

dadjdjāl (A, < Syr) : lit. deceiver; the personage endowed with miraculous powers who will arrive before the end of time and, for a limited period of either 40 days or 40 years, will let impurity and tyranny rule the world. His appearance is one of the proofs of the end of time. II 76a; IV 408b

dādjin (A) : among the pre-Islamic Arabs, a sheep kept near the house and especially fattened for the table. II 1057b

♦ dādjina → ḲAYNA

dadjr (A), or *dudjr, dudjūr* : in mediaeval agriculture, the wooden cross-beam of the ancient tiller to which the ploughshare was fixed by means of a strap of iron; sometimes the dual (*dadjrān*) can be found, because it was in two parts with one joined to the other by another strap and/or a cord. VII 22a

dafʿ (A) : in law, the reply, and, by extension, every reply made by a party in contradiction of a plea raised by his opponent. II 171b

ḍafāʾir (A, s. *ḍafīra*), or *ghadāʾir* : locks of hair. IX 312a

dafn al-dhunūb (A) : burial of offences; a nomadic practice which consists of a make-believe burial of the offences or crimes of which an Arab is accused. II 248a; IV 407a

daftar (A, < Gk; T *defter*) : a stitched or bound booklet, or register, more especially an account or letter-book used in administrative offices. According to the administrative tradition, Khālid b. Barmak introduced the register into the central administration during the reign of al-Ṣaffāḥ; until that time, records were kept on papyrus, *ṣuḥuf*. I 1090a; II 77b

♦ daftar-i awāridja : a cash-book, showing the balance of moneys in hand, one of the seven main registers on which the Īlkhānid system of book-keeping was based. II 81a

♦ daftar-i derdest : one of the auxiliary registers used in the Ottoman period alongside the DAFTAR-I KHĀḲĀNĪ to note changes, the ~ was a list of the villages or towns constituting the nucleus of the military fiefs and showing the successive changes which each fief had undergone. II 82b

♦ daftar-i idjmāl : one of the auxiliary registers used in the Ottoman period alongside the DAFTAR-I KHĀḲĀNĪ to note changes, the ~ was a summary based on the detailed register, omitting the names of the inhabitants and giving the revenues only as lump sums for each unit. II 82a; X 113a

♦ **daftar-i khāḳānī** : the collection of registers in which were entered, during the Ottoman period, the results of the surveys made every 30 or 40 years until the beginning of the 11th/17th century, containing primarily lists of the adult males in the villages and towns, their legal status, their obligations and privileges, and the extent of the lands which they possessed, information on the way in which the land was used, and fiscal information with regard to revenues of the country. The ~ cannot be called a land-register; the land-register, in the modern sense of the term, was established in Turkey only from the second half of the 19th century. II 81b

♦ daftar-i mufradāt : a budget register showing the income and expenditure by cities, districts and provinces under the Īlkhānids, one of the seven main registers on which their system of book-keeping was based. II 81a

♦ daftar-i rūznāmče : one of the auxiliary registers used in the Ottoman period alongside the DAFTAR-I KHĀḲĀNĪ to note changes, the ~ was a 'day-book', into which the deeds of grants issued to new fief-holders were copied as they occurred. II 82b

♦ daftar-i taḥwīlāt : an off-shoot of the DAFTAR-I TAWDJĪHĀT, a register dealing with disbursements for stocks and running expenses in state establishments and enterprises under the Īlkhānids, one of the seven main registers on which their system of book-keeping was based. II 81a

♦ daftar-i taʿlīḳ → RŪZNĀMADJ

♦ daftar-i tawdjīhāt : a register of disbursements under the Īlkhānids, one of the seven main registers on which their system of book-keeping was based. II 81a

♦ **daftardār** (P, T *defterdār*) : keeper of the DAFTAR; an Ottoman term for the chief finance officer, corresponding to the MUSTAWFĪ in the eastern Islamic world. The title ~ seems to originate with the Īlkhānids who appointed persons to make and keep the registers. The office of ~ was renamed MĀLIYYE (Ministry of Finance) in 1253/1838, although the term remained in use for provincial directors of finances. II 83a

♦ daftarkhāne (T) : under the Ottomans, the archives of the register-office to which the old registers were consigned each time a new survey was made. II 82b

♦ defter-i mufaṣṣal → TAḤRĪR

dāgh u taṣḥīḥa (IndP) : a term used in Muslim India for the branding of horses and compilation of muster rolls for soldiers, introduced by Akbar in order to check all evasions of military obligations. V 685b; XII 176b

ḍaghṭa (A) : pressure; in the religious sense, the pressure applied in the tomb by the questioning asked of one's religion. I 187a

ḍaḥāʾ (A) : the period corresponding to the sun's progress over the second quarter of the diurnal arc. It comes to an end at midday. V 709b

dahān band (P) : a face veil consisting of a small, white mask covering only the mouth and chin. It was worn in the Tīmūrid period. V 749a

daḥi : a title in Serbia under the Ottomans, derived from DAYİ. IX 671b

ḍāḥik (A) : *risibile.* V 1261b

In anatomy, the pre-molar. VI 130a

dāhiya (A, pl. *duhāt*) : statesman. XI 521b

ḍaḥiyya (A) : the name for the animal sacrificed on the occasion of the feast of the 10th day of Dhu 'l-Ḥidjdja. II 213a; in the Negev and other parts of former Palestine, ~ is used synonymously with *fidya* to designate a blood sacrifice made in the interests of the living for purposes of atonement. II 884a

dahnadj (A, P *dahna, dahāna*, T *dehne-i frengī*) : in mineralogy, malachite, green copper-ore. II 92a

dahol : a Kurdish bass drum which is beaten on both sides. V 478a

dahr (A) : time in an absolute sense. I 2a; infinitely extended time. II 94b

♦ **dahriyya** : holders of materialistic opinions of various kinds, often vaguely defined; philosophers of Greek inspiration. They were called the *azaliyya* by the Ikhwān al-Ṣafāʾ. I 128a; II 95a; II 770b

ḍahūl (A) : oviparous, like the female ostrich, who scratches and flattens in the sand a shallow hole (*udḥī*) in which to lay her eggs. VII 829a

daḥya → ḲISHSHA

dāʿī (A) : 'he who summons' to the true faith, a title used among several dissenting Muslim groups for their chief propagandists; it became especially important in the Ismāʿīlī and associated movements, where it designated generically the chief authorised representatives of the IMĀM. The title ~ came to mean something different in each of the sects which issued from the classical Fāṭimid Ismāʿīlism. II 97b

ḍaʿīf (A, pl. *ḍuʿafāʾ*) : weak (syn. *waḍīʿ*); unable to bear arms, as opposed to SHARĪF. IX 330a

In the science of Tradition, the term for a weak Tradition, along with *saḳīm*, infirm. III 25a; Traditions without any claim to reliability. VIII 983b

In modern South Arabia, the plural form *ḍuʿafāʾ* denotes non-arms bearers, a group comprising builders, potters and field workers. VII 145a; and → MISKĪN dāʾir (A) : in astronomy, the time since rising, *faḍl al-~* being the 'hour-angle'. XI 505b; and → DĀʾIRAT AL-ẒILL

♦ dāʾira (A) : in music, with DUFF, a generic name for tambourine, but reserved for a round type; a round tambourine with small bells attached to the inside of the shell or body, sometimes attached to a metal or wooden rod fixed across the inside of the head. This instrument is popular in Persia and Central Asia. II 621a; and → DAWĀʾIR; ZMĀLA

♦ dāʾirat al-maʿārif (A) : an expression with the double meaning 'Department of Education' and 'encyclopaedia'. As of the 1960s Arab countries of the former Ottoman empire had replaced MAʿĀRIF with *tarbiya* for 'education'. V 903a

♦ **dāʾira saniyya** (T) : the term used in the Ottoman empire during the last quarter of the 19th century for the administration of crown lands. XII 179a

♦ dāʾirat al-ẓill (A) : in astronomy, the cross-section of the shadow of the earth during an eclipse of the sun or moon. V 536a

dāk͟hil (A) : in the Ottoman empire, one of two categories of viziers, the ~ sitting in the imperial DĪWĀN in Istanbul and the *k͟hāridj* who sat in the provinces. XI 197a; and → MUḤALLIL

dak͟hīl (A) : interior, inward, intimate; hence 'guest, to whom protection should be assured' and, 'stranger, passing traveller, person of another race'. II 100a; XII 78b

In philology, ~ denotes a foreign word borrowed by the Arabic language. II 100a; VII 261b

In metrics, ~ is a term denoting the consonant preceding the rhyming consonant, the ~ itself being preceded by an *alif*. II 100a; IV 412a

daḳīḳ (A) : in culinary matters, meal. X 788b

dakka → DIKKA

daḳḳāḳ (A) : a miller. XII 758a

daḳḳūr (A, pl. *daḳāḳira*), or *dakkūr* (pl. *dakākīr*) : fetish. XI 177a

dāl (A) : the eighth letter of the Arabic alphabet, transcribed *d*, with the numerical value 4. It is defined as voiced dental occlusive. II 101a

For ~ in Persian zoology, → NASR

dalang (Mal, Ind) : puppetmasters. IX 245a

dalāl (A) : in rhetoric, the plural *dalālāt* can mean semantics of individual words and sentences. V 901a; and → TAS͟HARRUF

dālāy (Mon), or *dala* : a term applied in Īlk͟hānid Persia originally to the subjects of the Great K͟hān came to be applied to land which belonged immediately to the ruler. The term rapidly went out of use. IV 975b

dalīl (A, pl. *dalāʾil*) : sign or indication; proof. II 101b; the demonstration of that which is not immediately and necessarily known. III 544a

In Medina, the ~ (pl. *adillāʾ*) is a guide who is responsible for the physical needs of the pilgrim, such as food, lodging and local transport. V 1004a

dāliya (A) : a kind of draw-well still in use in Egypt and other eastern countries for raising water for irrigation. It usually consists of two posts about five feet in height. These posts are coated with mud and clay and then placed less than three feet apart. They are joined at the top by a horizontal piece of wood, in the centre of which a lever is balanced. The shorter arm of the lever is weighted, while at the end of the longer arm hangs a rope carrying a leather pail. The peasant stands on a platform on the river bank and pulls down the balanced pole until the pail dips into the water and is filled. A slight upward push, which is helped by the counterweight, raises the bucket above the irrigation canal, into which it is emptied. V 863b

dalḳ (A) : a ritual ceremony of appeasing the DJINN in Iraq, carried out by pouring water mixed with sugar and salt. XII 777a dalla → BAKRADJ

dallāl (A), or *simsār* : lit. guide; in law, ~ indicates a broker, an agent, 'the man who shows the purchaser where to find the goods he requires, and the seller how to exact his price'. Women are also found taking the part of agents. Known as *dallāla*, they act as intermediaries for harems of a superior sort. II 102b

In the Muslim West, the ~ is exclusively an intermediary who, in return for remuneration, sells by public auction objects entrusted to him by third parties. In the large towns, they are grouped in specialised guilds. II 102b

dallāla → DALLĀL

dallīna → DILLĪNA

dalw (A) : a 'water bucket', in ancient Arabia, said to be made mostly from the hides of two young camels, in which case the bucket may be called *ibn adīmayn*. I 1230a; I 1231b

In astronomy, *al-~* is the term for Aquarius, one of the twelve zodiacal constellations. VII 84a

dam (A, pl. *dimā'*) : blood; blood-guilt. XII 188b

In botany, ~ *al-akhawayn* 'the blood of the two brothers' is used for dragon's-blood. IX 808b

♦ damawiyya → ʿAMĀR AL-DAM

dām → PAYSĀ; WALĪ 'L-DAM

dāmād (P) : son-in-law, title used by sons-in-law of the Ottoman sultans. II 103a

damāma : a kettle-drum, probably of a smaller size than the KŪRGĀ. X 34a

ḍamān (A) : in law, ~ is the civil liability in the widest meaning of the term, whether it arises from the non-performance of a contract or from tort or negligence. In the sense of suretyship, guarantee, ~ is a liability specially created by contract. In a wider sense, it is used of the risk or responsibility that one bears with regard to property of which one enjoys the profit. II 105a; and → ḲABḌ ḌAMĀN

In a financial sense, ~ stands for 'farming' (of taxes). The tax-farmer, *ḍāmin*, pays annually to the State a contracted sum, less than the calculated revenue from the tax, and afterwards undertakes its recovery on his own account. The State is assured of a precise and immediate return from the pockets of rich individuals but loses a portion of the money paid by the tax-payer and the control of operations. I 1144b; II 105b; III 323b; and → ḲABĀLA

♦ ḍamān al-adjīr (A), or *ḍamān al-ṣunnāʿ* : in law, the liability for the loss or damage caused by artisans. II 105a

♦ ḍamān al-**darak** (A) : in law, the liability for eviction. II 105a; the guarantee against a fault in ownership. XII 198a

♦ ḍamān al-ghaṣb (A) : in law, the liability for the loss of an object taken by usurpation. II 105a

♦ ḍamān al-mabīʿ (A) : in law, the liability for the loss of an object sold before the buyer has taken possession. II 105a

♦ ḍamān al-rahn (A) : in law, the liability for the loss of a pledge in the possession of the pledgee. II 105a

♦ ḍamān al-ṣunnāʿ → ḌAMĀN AL-ADJĪR

dāmānī (A) : a variety of apple (from Dāmān in Mesopotamia), said to be proverbial because of its redness, one of a number of varieties praised by the geographers, most named, as the ~ apple, after their provenance, e.g. *al-isfahānī, al-ḳūfānī*, etc. X 587b; and → GHALḲ

ḍāmin → ḌAMĀN

dāmir (A) : a woman's jacket with short sleeves, worn in Syria and Palestine. V 740b

ḍamīr (A) : in grammar, as ~ *muttaṣil* 'bound pronoun' and its opposite, ~ *munfaṣil* 'separate, independent pronoun'. XI 173a; and → MUḌMAR
ḍamma (A) : in grammar, ~ denotes the short vowel *u*. III 172a
dammūsa (A) : on the Arabian peninsula, the slippery sand-swimming skink. I 541b
damūs, dāmūs : a brick vault. I 207b; crypt. XI 488b
ḍa'n (A) : in zoology, sheep. XI 411b
dāna-farang (H, < P) : malachite. VIII 269a
danānīr → DĪNĀR
dandī : a (West-African) locally-woven cloth. XI 8a
dandī (H) : a simple kind of litter used in India for transporting people. It was essentially a hammock slung from a pole. VII 932a
dāni<u>sh</u>kada → KULLIYYA
dann (A, pl. *dinān*) : an amphora with tapered base, in which the fermentation of grapes takes place. IV 997b

♦ danniyya → ḲALANSUWA

dār (A) : (dwelling place), house. The two words most commonly used to designate a dwelling place, BAYT and ~, have etymologically quite different meanings. *Bayt* is, properly speaking, the covered shelter where one may spend the night; ~ (from *dāra* 'to surround') is a space surrounded by walls, buildings, or nomadic tents, placed more or less in a circle. II 113b; palace, large dwelling complex. IV 1016b; VIII 344a

In the 5th/11th and 6th/12th centuries in Baghdad and Damascus, ~ was the name borne by the large depots with the name of the commodity for which the establishment was noted. IV 1015a

♦ **dār al-ʿahd** (A) : 'the land of the covenant'; considered by some Muslim jurists as a temporary and often intermediate territory between the DĀR AL-ISLĀM and the DĀR AL-ḤARB. II 116a

♦ dār al-ḍamāna (A) : among the Wazzāniyya, a Moroccan ṣūfī order, the 'house of warranty', which the founder's eldest son Sīdī Muḥammad made the order's ZĀWIYA, meaning that the BARAKA of the *<u>sh</u>urafāʾ* (→ <u>SH</u>ARĪF) was sufficient to save any sinner from the Last Judgement. XI 201b

♦ **dār al-ḍarb** (A) : the mint, the primary function of which was to supply coins for the needs of government and of the general public. At times of monetary reforms, the ~ also served as a place where obliterated coins could be exchanged for the new issues. The large quantities of precious metals which were stored in the ~ helped to make it serve as an ancillary treasury. I 24a; II 117b; and → ḌARB<u>KH</u>ĀNE-I ʿĀMIRE

♦ **dār al-ḥadī<u>th</u>** (A) : a term first applied to institutions reserved for the teaching of ḤADĪ<u>TH</u> in the 6th/12th century. Until these special institutions were set up, the teaching of *ḥadī<u>th</u>*, as of other branches of religious learning, was carried out in the mosques. II 125b; V 1129a; XII 195a

♦ **dār al-ḥarb** (A) : the territories under perpetual threat of a missionary war, <u>DJ</u>IHĀD. The classical practice of regarding the territories immediately adjoining the lands of Islam as the ~ and inviting their princes to adopt Islam under the pain of invasion, is reputed to date back to the Prophet. Classically, the ~ includes those countries where the Muslim law is not in force, in the matter of worship and the protection of the faithful and the <u>DH</u>IMMĪs. I 26a; II 126a; II 131b

♦ **dār al-ḥikma** (A) : 'the house of wisdom', a term used by Arab authors to denote in a general sense the academies which, before Islamic times, spread knowledge of the Greek sciences, and in a particular sense the institute founded in Cairo in 395/1005 by the Fāṭimid caliph al-Ḥākim. II 126b; II 859b; V 1125b

♦ **dār al-ʿilm** (A) : 'the house of science', the name given to several libraries or scientific institutes established in eastern Islam in the 3rd/9th and 4th/10th centuries.

The most important ~ was the one founded in Baghdad by the vizier Abū Naṣr Sābūr b. Ardas̲h̲īr in the last quarter of the 4th/10th century, with more than 10,000 books on all scientific subjects. It was burnt down when the Ald̲j̲ūḳs reached Baghdad in 447/1055-56. II 127a

♦ **dār al-islām** (A) : 'the land of Islam', the whole territory in which the law of Islam prevails. Its unity resides in the community, the unity of the law, and the guarantees assured to members of the UMMA. In the classical doctrine, everything outside ~ is DĀR AL-ḤARB. II 127b

♦ dār al-k̲h̲arād̲j̲ (A) : a brothel, in the Muslim West. XII 134a

♦ dār al-maʿārif (A) : schools founded by the Ottoman sultan ʿAbd al-Mad̲j̲īd I in 1849. I 75a

♦ dār al-mulk (A) : the private quarters of the caliph and his close associates in Muslim Spain. IX 45a

♦ **dār al-nadwa** (A) : the name of a town hall in Mecca in the time of the Prophet. II 128b

♦ **dār al-salām** (A) : 'the abode of peace', a name of Paradise in the Qurʾān; also a name for the city of Baghdad. II 128b

♦ **dār al-ṣināʿa** (A), or *dār al-ṣanʿa* : an industrial establishment, workshop; the term is always applied to a state workshop, e.g. under the Umayyads in Spain to establishments for gold and silver work intended for the sovereign, and for the manufacture and stock-piling of arms. The most widely-used sense is that of an establishment for the construction and equipment of warships, giving rise to the word 'arsenal' in the Mediterranean languages. II 129b; XII 120a

♦ dār ṣīnī → DĀRṢĪNĪ

♦ **dār al-ṣulḥ** (A) : 'the house of truce', territories not conquered by Muslim troops but by buying peace by the giving of tribute, the payment of which guarantees a truce or armistice. The Prophet himself concluded such a treaty with the Christian population of Nad̲j̲rān. II 131a

♦ **dār al-ʿulūm** (A) : 'the house of sciences', an establishment for higher instruction founded in 1872 by ʿAlī Pas̲h̲a Mubārak, whose aim was to introduce students of al-Azhar to modern branches of learning; the religious institutions at Deoband and Lucknow. I 817b; II 131b

♦ dār al-wakāla (A) : 'the house of procuration or agency', term for the urban caravanserai before this became a synonym for FUNDUḲ, which itself at the end of the 7th/13th century began to be replaced by K̲H̲ĀN as a designation for suburban hostelries. IV 1015a

darabukka : in music, a vase-shaped drum, the wider aperture being covered by a membrane, with the lower aperture open. In performance it is carried under the arm horizontally and played with the fingers. II 135b; the ~ has come to have a variety of names east of Morocco, e.g. the *dirrīd̲j̲, darbūka, dirbakka, ḍarābukka* and even *ṭabla*. In Persia ~ is known as the *dunbak* or *tanbak*. X 33a

darad̲j̲ (A) : in zoology, the courser, nearly ubiquitous in the Arabian desert. I 541b

darāʾib, or *ʿawāʾid* : the customary law of the Bedouin of the Western Desert and Cyrenaica. X 889b

darak → ḌAMĀN AL-DARAK

daraḳa (A, > *adarga*) : in military science, a shield, probably made from hide stretched over a wooden frame (syn. *turs, d̲j̲unna, mid̲j̲ann*). V 651b; XII 736a

darara bashu : in Ethiopia, at the tomb of S̲h̲ayk̲h̲ Nūr Ḥusayn, a black stone that the s̲h̲ayk̲h̲ is believed to have brought back with him from Mecca, which is kissed and touched as part of the ceremony of ZIYĀRA. XI 539b

darāy, hindī : in music, the Indian bell. X 35a

darb → SHĀRIʿ

ḍarb (A) : in prosody, the last foot of the second hemistich, as opposed to the last foot of the first hemistich, the *ʿarūḍ*. I 672b; IV 714b; VIII 747; and → IṢBAʿ

In mathematics, ~ is the term used for multiplication. III 1139b

In the art of the book, a cancellation. X 408b

For ~ as lithomancy, → ṬARḲ

♦ ḍarb khāne, ḍarrābkhāne → ḌARBKHĀNE-I ʿĀMIRE

♦ ḍarb al-raml → RAML

♦ ḍarb al-sadʿa (A) : shell-divination. VIII 138b

♦ ḍarb al-ṣilāḥ (A) : 'body piercing', one of the deeds transcending the natural order, *khawāriḳ al-ʿādāt*, practiced by the Saʿdiyya order. VIII 728b

♦ ḍarbkhāne-i ʿāmire (T), or *ḍarrābkhāne, nuḳrakhāne, dār al-ḍarb* : the Ottoman mint. II 118a

darbazīn (A) : a balustrade. VI 662a

dardar (< SARDĀR) : 'sultan' in Tagorri, an ʿAfar dialect in Tadjura. The ~ is assisted by a *banoyta* 'vizier', which two functions alternate within two clans, the Burhanto and Diinite. X 72b

dargāh (P) : lit. place of a door; royal court, palace in Persia; in Muslim India, ~ is used to designate a tomb or shrine of a *pīr* (→ MURSHID). II 141b; IV 26a; VI 125b; VIII 954a

darī (P) : the court language, and language of government and literature, in pre-Islamic Persia. II 142a; IV 55a; XII 429b

In India, ~ is used to designate the normal floor-mat, a flat-woven pile-less rug of thick cotton. VIII 742a

dārī (A) : in the mediaeval eastern Muslim world, the perfume merchant. IX 100b

darība : in Muslim India, a short lane or street, usually one where betel leaves were sold. IX 800b

ḍarība (A) : a tax, applied in particular to the whole category of taxes which in practice were added to the basic taxes, ZAKĀT, DJIZYA and KHARĀDJ. Apart from *djizya*, these taxes form the basis of the official fiscal system of Islam and are essentially concerned with agriculture and stock-breeding. II 142b; XII 199b; an urban tax on buildings. V 1199a

dāridja (A) : the colloquial Arabic language (syn. *al-lugha al-ʿāmmiyya*). I 561b

ḍarīḥ → ḲABR

ḍarim → HAYTHAM

ḍarrāb (A) : a minter, one of the craftsmen employed as staff in the mint who carried out the actual coining operation. II 118a

In Muslim Spain, ~ was the term used for night-watchman. I 687b

♦ ḍarrābkhāne → ḌARBKHĀNE-I ʿĀMIRE

dars (A, pl. *durūs*) : lesson, lecture; in mediaeval usage, ~ meant 'a lesson or lecture on law'. V 1124b; a class, consisting of lecture and dictation. X 80b

darshan (San) : the (Hindu) ceremonial appearance of a king to his subjects, adopted by the Mughal emperor Akbar and his immediate successors. It was abandoned by Awrangīb in 1078/1668. II 162a

dārṣīnī (A, < P *dār čīnī*) : Chinese cinnamon, *Cinnamomum cassia*, although it cannot be established with certainty with what original plant ~ is to be associated. In pharmacognostic texts *Cinn. cassia* is also rendered by *salīkha*, which allegedly is not identical with ~ . XII 197a

dārūgha (P, < Mon) : originally a chief in the Mongol feudal hierarchy, ~ is first met in Persia in the Īlkhānid period. In his main capacities he belonged to the military hierarchy. In Ṣafawid Persia, his functions were sometimes those of a governor of town, but more commonly those of a police officer, his duties to prevent misdeeds, tyranny, brawls, and actions contrary to the sharīʿa. In the 12th/18th and 13th/19th centuries, his function at times superseded even that of the *muḥtasib* (→ ḤISBA). At the beginning of the Constitutional period, most of his duties were taken over by the municipalities and the police force. In some cases, the ~ was appointed to collect taxes or to control certain ethnic minorities; ~ was also used to denote a kind of head clerk controlling the staff of the larger government departments in Ṣafawid Persia. II 162a

In Muslim India, ~ denoted an official in the royal stables; the British used it to designate the native head of various departments and, later, the local chief of police. II 162b

ḍarūra (A), and *iḍṭirār* : necessity; in law, ~ has a narrow meaning: what may be called the technical state of necessity (resulting from certain factual circumstances which may oblige an individual to do some action forbidden by the law), and a wider sense: to describe the necessities or demands of social and economic life, which the jurists had to take into account in their elaboration of the law which was otherwise independent of these factors. The legal schools agree that prohibitions of a religious character may be disregarded in cases of necessity and danger, while most of the offences committed under the rule of necessity are excused without any form of punishment. However, murder, the amputation of a limb, and serious wounding likely to cause death, irrespective of the circumstances, are never excused. The term in its wider sense signifies practical necessity, the exigencies of social and economic life. It takes into consideration the existence of rules and whole institutions in Muslim law which reasoning by strict analogy would have condemned. II 163b

darwa (A) : a typical style of hairdressing used by an Arabic-speaking tribe of Bedja origin in Upper Egypt with branches in the northern Sudan. I 1b

darwāza (P) : in architecture, a gatehouse. X 59a

darwīsh (P) : a mendicant, dervish; a member of a religious fraternity. II 164a

daryā-begi (T), or *deryā-beyi* : 'sea-lord', a title given in the Ottoman empire to certain officers of the fleet, who usually held their appointments for life and transmitted them to their sons. II 165b

dasātīn (A) : in music, the frets of an ʿŪD. X 769b

dashīsha → SIMĀṬ

♦ dashīsha kubrā (A) : the endowments made for the Holy Cities by the Mamlūk sultans Djaḳmaḳ and Ḳāʾitbāy; under the Ottomans, Murād III made a new endowment called the *dashīsha ṣughrā*. XI 66b

dasht : steppe, e.g. *dasht-i Ḳipčaḳ*, the Ḳipčaḳ Steppe, the great plains of Southern Russia and western Kazakhstan. IX 61a; XII 203b

dasim (A) : the quality of foods being oily and greasy, similarly *samīn* 'rich in fats'. II 1071b

dāsinī → YAZĪDĪ

dāsitān (Ott) : in literature, the brief verse section in praise of the dynasty appended to the longer didactic poem *Iskender-nāme* by the poet Aḥmedī. X 291a

dastabān (P, N.Afr *ḳuffāz*) : the glove used by a falconer during the hunt. I 1152b

dastaḳ → MIḲWAM

dāstān (U, P *destān*) : in Urdu literature, a collection of short stories within a 'frame', recited to general audiences as well as to royal courts and rich households. They are the Urdu equivalents of Arab collections like *Alf layla wa-layla* and *Sīrat ʿAntar* and can be considered precursors of modern Urdu fiction. III 119a; III 375b; V 201b

In Turkish literature, the Persian term *destān* is used for the ancient popular epics in syllabic verse, transmitted orally, as well as the first verse chronicles of epic type. III 114b; IX 844a; X 733b

♦ destāndjï (T) : one of two groups of Türkmen bards, a relater of epics; the other group is made up of the *tirmedji*, who sings poems (*tirme*) on various themes.

dastār (P) : the turban cloth, also known as *mayzar*. X 611a

dastūr (P, A DUSTŪR) : a Persian term which in the period of the classical caliphate came to be used as a synonym of ḲĀNŪN in the sense of 'tax-list'. IV 558a; in the Ṣafawid period, ~ is defined as a Zoroastrian priest who knows the Avesta and the Zand, the Middle Persian literature, and has the authority to command laymen (*behdīns*) to do religious works. VII 215b

In classical Muslim administration, ~ is a copy of the *djamāʿa* made from the draft. II 79a

In East Africa, ~ is the term used for custom and customary law, synonymous with ʿĀDA. I 170a

♦ dastūr al-ʿamal (P) : a detailed assessment of revenue, prepared and sent annually by the MUSTAWFĪs of the central government in Persia to the provinces, on the basis of which the provincial *mustawfī*s allocated the tax demand among the provincial population. II 151a

ḍawʾ → NŪR

daʿwa (A) : call, invitation; propaganda. II 168a; pretension. IX 432a; and → DAʿWET

In the Qurʾān, ~ is the call to the dead to rise from the tomb on the day of Judgement. II 168a

In the religious sense, ~ is the invitation addressed to men by God and the prophets, to believe in the true religion, Islam. The concept that the religion of all the prophets is Islam and that each prophet has his own ~, was developed by the Ismāʿīlīs. II 168a

In its politico-religious sense, the ~ denotes the invitation to adopt the cause of some individual or family claiming the right to the imamate over the Muslims, thus the ʿAbbāsid ~, which was, strictly speaking, propaganda for a member of the Prophet's family, and Ismāʿīlī ~, propaganda for the IMĀM, who alone could give mankind good guidance. II 168a

Among the Ismāʿīlīs, ~ is one of nine periods of instruction which completed the initiation of Ismāʿīlī neophytes. II 169b; IV 203b

♦ al-daʿwa al-djadīda (A), or *daʿwa djadīda* : the branch of Ismāʿīlīs, known as the Nizārīs, who refused to recognise Mustaʿlī after the death of al-Mustanṣir in 487/1094. They are now represented by the Khodjas. II 170b; III 254a

♦ al-daʿwa al-ḳadīma (A) : the branch of Ismāʿīlīs, known as the Mustaʿlīs or Ṭayyibīs, who followed Mustaʿlī after the death of al-Mustanṣir in 487/1094. They are now represented by the Bohoras in India. II 170b

♦ daʿwat (IndP) : the communal administration of the Yemeni Sulaymānī sect, which split off from the Bohoras in the 10th/16th century. I 1255a

♦ daʿwat-i samāʾ (IndP) : in the Shaṭṭārī mystic ideology, the control of heavenly bodies which influenced human destiny. IX 370a

daʿwā (A) : action at law, case, lawsuit. II 170b

In hunting, a live calling bird. IV 745a

dawāʾ (A, pl. **adwiya**) : every substance which may affect the constitution of the human body; every drug used as a remedy or a poison. I 212b; gunpowder. I 1056a

♦ adwiya mufrada (A) : simple drugs. I 212b; V 251b; and → ṢAYDANA

♦ adwiya murakkaba (A) : composite drugs. I 212b; V 251b; and → ṢAYDANA

dawādār (P) : the bearer and keeper of the royal inkwell, which post was created by the Saldjūḳs. It was held by civilians. II 172b; secretary. VIII 432a; and → DĀWĀTDĀR

ḍawāḥī (A), or *ḍawāḥī 'l-Rūm* : 'outer lands' (of the land of the Greeks), constituting a kind of no-man's land in the Arab-Byzantine frontier regions. X 446b

dawāʾir (A, s. DĀʾIRA) : circles.
In the science of metrics, the ~ are the five metric circles used by al-Kh̲alīl for the graphic presentation of the sixteen metres. They are arranged according to the number of consonants in the mnemonic words of the metres which compose them. I 669b
In Algeria, a group of families attached to the service and person of a native chief. Before the French conquest, ~ denoted especially four tribal groups encamped to the south-west of Oran and attached to the service of the BEY of that city. They were organised as a militia. II 172b

dawār (A) : an encampment of the Arab Bedouin in which the tents are arranged in a circle or an ellipse around the open space in the middle where the cattle pass the night. In North Africa, this arrangement is called *dūwār* or *dawwār*. II 174b; XII 318b
In Algeria, *douar* has lost its original meaning, and is employed to designate an administrative area, either nomad or sedentary, placed under the authority of the same chief. II 175a
According to Ibn al-Kalbī, ~ is the procession that the Arabs made around the *anṣāb* 'sacred stones', which served as replicas of the Black Stone of the Kaʿba. VIII 155b

dawāt (A) : ink-holder, inkwell (syn. *miḥbara*); ~ is also used for *miḳlama* 'the place for keeping the pen', and for *ḳalamdān* 'penbox'. IV 471b; V 988b; XII 203b
♦ dāwātdār (IndP) : the keeper of the sultan of Delhi's inkpot or inkhorn. IV 759a; and → DAWĀDĀR

daʿwet (T, < A *daʿwa*) : in the science of Turkish diplomatic, the invocation composed of the formula containing the name of governor (the Bey's name), ranging from the simplest *huwa* to the longest titles. II 314b

dāwiyya (A, O.Fr *devot*) : the Knights Templars, one of the Frankish military orders, known to the Arabs from their experiences with the Crusaders. The Knights Hospitallers, known to the Arabs as *Isbitāriyya*, was another such order. XII 204b

dawla (A) : turn, reversal (especially in battle); victory; the reign of the Mahdī. From the middle of the 3rd/9th century, ~ attained the meaning of 'dynasty, state', still in force today. *Al-dawla* is used as the second element in titles; its earliest usage was noted at the end of the 3rd/9th century. II 177b; IV 293b; V 621b ff.

dawm (A) : in botany, the gingerbread tree, a palm which on occasion replaces the date palm in the Gulf. I 540a; the edible fruit of the jujube, called ~ by the Bedouin of Arabia and KUNĀR by the townsmen. I 540b

dawr (A, pl. *adwār*) : lit. revolution, period; the periodic movement of the stars.
In sh̲īʿism, ~ is for the extreme sects the period of manifestation or concealment of God or the secret wisdom. XII 206b
In music, ~ denotes one of two cycles which make up an ĪḲĀʿ, each of which is composed of several basic notes and a pause. XII 408b
♦ dawr al-kash̲f (A) : 'period of manifestation', the period for the Ismāʿīliyya before the DAWR AL-SATR, during which the twelve angels of the zodiac kept the unadulterated pure unity of God, TAWḤĪD. At the end of time, the ḲĀʾIM will bring forth a new ~. XII 206b
♦ dawr al-satr (A) : 'period of concealment', the period for the Ismāʿīliyya from Adam to the ḲĀʾIM, the last speaking prophet. A synonym is *al-dawr al-kabīr*. XII 206b

dawsa (A) : lit. trampling; a ceremony formerly performed in Cairo by the SH̲AYKH̲ of the Saʿdī order, consisting of the *sh̲ayk̲h̲* riding over the members of the order on horseback. It was believed that by such physical contact, the BARAKA of the *sh̲ayk̲h̲* was communicated to his followers. II 181b; VIII 525b; VIII 728b

dawsh̲ān (A) : in the context of Yemen, a sort of tribal herald, considered a menial job. XI 277a dawudu : a land-leasing system in Kurdish Iran, in which the landowner, in return for supplying earth and seed, takes two-tenths of the harvest. V 473b

dawul → ṬABL

dawwār → DAWĀR

ḍayʿa (A, pl. *diyāʿ*) : estate.

In its fiscal context, ~ denotes an estate subject to tithes. The holder of the ~ was not usually its cultivator, and the peasant rents went for the greater part to the holder of the ~ . II 187b

♦ ḍiyāʿ al-khāṣṣa (A), *ḍiyāʿ al-sulṭān* and *ḍiyāʿ al-khulafāʾ* : the private estates of the caliph in early Islamic times. IV 972b

daydabān (A, < P *dīdebān*) : a term applied at different times to certain categories of sentinels, watchmen, inspectors, etc. II 189a

ḍayf (A) : guest; host, which meaning, however, occurred later. II 189a

dayi̊ (T) : lit. maternal uncle; an honorific title used to designate official functions in the Regencies of Algiers and Tunis. II 189a; title of the Janissary rulers of Algiers, Tunis and Tripoli in North Africa. IX 671b

dāyman (A) : lit. always; said after finishing a cup of coffee to thank the host, one of several customs associated with coffee drinking, another being the saying of *ʿāmir* (lit. fully inhabited) when finishing drinking coffee in a house of a bereaved person. XII 756a

dayn (A, pl. *duyūn*) : debt; claim; in law, an obligation, arising out of a contract (loan, sale, transaction or marriage) or out of a tort requiring reparation. I 29a; XII 207a

♦ dayn fī dhimma (A) : in law, an obligation which has as its object a personal action. XII 207a

♦ dayn fi ʾl-ʿayn (A) : in law, an obligation which has as its object a non-fungible, determinate thing. XII 207a

♦ **duyūn-i ʿumūmiyye** (T) : the Ottoman public debt; more particularly the debt administration set up in 1881. II 677a

dayr (A, < Syr) : a Christian monastery, which continued functioning after the Arab conquest of the Middle East. They were often named after a patron saint or founder but also occasionally after the nearest town or village or a feature of the locality. II 194b

For its meaning in Somalia, → GUʾ

♦ (A) : in prosody, a poem describing evenings spent in a convent or monastery. IV 1005a

dāyra → ZMĀLA

daysam (A) : the first swarm that leaves with the young queen bee (syn. *lūth, riḍʿ, ṭard*). VII 907a

ḍaywan (A) : in zoology, the Fettered cat (*Felis ocreata*), and also used for the European wild cat (*Felis sylvestris lybica*) and the Sand cat (*Felis margarita*). IX 651b, where are listed synonyms

ḍayzan (A) : a man who marries his father's widow (the marriage is called *nikāḥ al-maḳt*), a practice which the Qurʾān disapproves of. VI 476b

dede (T) : lit. grandfather, ancestor; a term of reverence given to the heads of DARWĪSH communities. II 199b; a member of a religious order resident in one of the cells of the DARGĀH or ZĀWIYA, who has fulfilled his *čile* (period of trial) and been elevated to the rank of dervish. VI 884a

In western Turkish heroic tales, ~ is used for the rhapsodes. II 199b

In Istanbul and Anatolia, ~ was also used as a term of respect for various wonder-working holy men. II 200a

In the terminology of the Ṣafawid order, ~ denoted one of the small group of officers in constant attendance on the MURSHID. II 200a

defter → DAFTAR
deglet nūr → GHARS
deli (T) : 'mad, heedless, brave, fiery', a class of cavalry in the Ottoman empire, formed in the Balkans at the end of the 9th/15th century or the beginning of the 10th/16th century. Later, they were officially styled as *delīl* (guides) but continued to be popularly known by the their original name. Called ~ on account of their extraordinary courage and recklessness, they were recruited partly from the Turks and partly from the Balkan nations. They became brigands in the 12th/18th century and were disbanded in the 13th/19th century by sultan Maḥmūd II. II 201a
demirbash (T) : lit. iron-head; the movable stock and equipment, belonging to an office, shop, farm, etc. In Ottoman usage ~ was commonly applied to articles belonging to the state and, more especially, to the furniture, equipment, and fittings in government offices, forming part of their permanent establishment. II 203b; ~ also means stubborn or persistent, and was applied by the Turks to King Charles XII of Sweden, possibly in this sense or to indicate his long frequentation of Turkish government offices. II 203b
derbend (T) : a mountain pass, defile. XI 114b
derebey (T) : 'valley lord', the Turkish designation of certain rulers in Asia Minor who, from the early 12th/18th century, made themselves virtually independent of the Ottoman central government in Istanbul. Ottoman historians usually call them *mutaghallibe* 'usurpers', or *khānedān* 'great families'. The best known ~ families are the Ḳara ʿOthmān-oghlu of Aydin, Manisa and Bergama in western Anatolia, the Čapan-oghlu of Bozok in central Anatolia, and the family of ʿAlī Pāshā of Djānīk in eastern Anatolia or Trebizond and its neighbourhood. II 206b
dergāh → TEKKE
deryā-beyi → DARYĀ-BEGI
destān(dji) → DĀSTĀN
destimal (T) : lit. napkin; in relation to relics of Islam, the gauze with inscriptions printed on it in which some objects holy to Islam are kept at the Istanbul University Library. The ~ was specially made for the visits to the Holy Mantle organised by the Sultan-Caliph on 15 Ramaḍān. V 761b
devedji (T, P *shuturbān*) : 'cameleer', the name given to certain regiments of the corps of Janissaries. II 210b
devekushu → NAʿĀM
devshirme (T) : the term in the Ottoman period for the periodical levy of Christian children for training to fill the ranks of the Janissaries and to occupy posts in the Palace service and in the administration. The earliest reference to the term appears to be contained in a sermon delivered by Isidore Glabas, metropolitan of Thessalonica, in 1395. By the end of the 10th/16th century, the system began to show signs of corrupt practices by the recruiting officers. By the beginning of the 11th/17th century, the ranks of the Janissaries had become so swollen with Muslim-born 'intruders' that frequent recruitments were no longer necessary. The system, however, continued at least till 1150/1738, but sporadically. I 36a; I 268b ff.; II 210b; II 1086a ff.
dey (Alg, < T DAYI) : a ruling power in Algeria, who succeeded the AGHAS of the army corps and ruled until the capture of Algiers by France. I 368a; and → DAYI
♦ deynek (T) : a commander's baton or cane, carried by a number of high Ottoman navy officers. It was also called *ṣadafkārī ʿaṣā*, because it was encrusted with mother of pearl of different colours. VIII 565b
dhabḥ (A) : one of the two methods of slaughtering animals according to Muslim law by which the animal concerned becomes permissible as food. It consists of slitting the throat, including the trachea and the oesophagus (there are divergencies between the schools in respect of the two jugular veins); the head is not to be severed. At the

moment of slaughter, it is obligatory to have the necessary intention and to invoke the name of God. Preferably the victim should be laid upon its left side facing in the direction of the ḲIBLA. II 213b

dhabīḥa (A) : in law, a victim (animal) destined for immolation in fulfilment of a vow, for the sacrifice of ʿAḲĪḲA, on the occasion of the feast of the 10th day of Dhu 'l-Ḥidjdja, or in order to make atonement for certain transgressions committed during the ḤADJDJ. II 213a; XII 221b

dhabl (A) : in botany, the shell of the tortoise, highly valued for the manufacture of combs and bracelets, *masak*. IX 811a

dhahab (A) : in mineralogy, gold. II 214a

♦ dhahabiyya (A) : a Nile vessel, especially known in the 19th century. VIII 42b

dhakāʾa (A) : the strict ritual of slaughtering the DHABĪḤA which must be followed and which does not differ in form from the ritual slaughter of animals permitted as food. II 213a

dhāl (A) : the ninth letter of the Arabic alphabet, with the numerical value 700, representing the voiced interdental fricative (*rikhwa madjhūra*). II 217b

dhanab (A) : tail.

In astronomy, ~ or *dhanab al-tinnīn* 'the dragon's tail' refers to the waning node, one of the points where the moon passes through the ecliptic during an eclipse of the moon. V 536a; VIII 101b; X 531a; and → KAWKAB AL-DHANAB

♦ dhanab al-dadjādja → RADĪF

♦ dhanab al-ḳiṭṭ (A) : 'cat's tail', in botany, the Bugloss (*Anchusa italica*) and the Goldylocks (*Chrysocoma*). IX 653a

♦ dhanab al-sirḥān → AL-FADJR AL-KĀDHIB

dhanb (A, pl. *dhunūb*) : sin. Synonyms are KHAṬĪʾA, *sayyiʾa*, which is an evil action, and *ithm*, a very grave sin, a crime against God. IV 1106b; and → DAFN AL-DHUNŪB

dharāʾiʿ (A) : a method of reasoning to the effect that, when a command or prohibition has been decreed by God, everything that is indispensable to the execution of that order or leads to infringement of that prohibition must also, as a consequence, be commanded or prohibited. I 276a

dharāriḥī (A) : in mediaeval ʿIrāḳ, a vagrant feigning serious wounds for begging purposes. VII 494b

dharīḥ (A) : in architecture, a silver enclosure, which surrounds a shīʿī shrine. XI 533a

dharr → NAML

♦ **dharra** (A) : a term denoting in the Qurʾān the smallest possible appreciable quantity, interpreted by the commentators of the Qurʾān as: dust which remains clinging to the hand after the rest has been blown off, or weightless dust, seen when sunlight shines through a window; the weight of the head of a red ant; the hundredth part of a grain of barley; or atom. ~ was not generally used to denote the philosophical atomism of Democritus, Epicurus and the Muslim 'atomists'. In its stead, the two technical terms DJUZʾ and DJAWHAR *fard* were preferred. Modern Arabic does render atom with ~. II 219b

dhāt (A) : thing; being, self, ego.

In philosophy, ~ is most commonly employed in two different meanings of substance and essence, a translation of the Greek οὐσία. When used in the sense of 'substance', it is the equivalent of the subject or substratum and is contrasted with qualities or predicates attributed to it and inhering in it. In the second sense of 'essence', it signifies the essential or constitutive qualities of a thing as a member of a species, and is contrasted with its accidental attributes (→ ʿARAḌ). Some Muslim philosophers distinguish, within the essence, its prior parts from the rest. II 220a; V 1262a

In Muslim India, ~ was one of the two ranks into which the *manṣabdār* (→ MANṢAB)

was divided, the other being *suwār*. The rank of ~ was meant for calculating one's salary according to the sanctioned pay scale. V 686a

♦ dhāt al-anwāṭ (A) : 'that of the suspended things', among early Muslims, the name for the SIDR tree. IX 549b

♦ dhāt al-ḥalaḳ (A) : an armillary sphere, constructed by ʿAbbās b. Firnās in 9th-century Muslim Spain. I 11b

♦ dhāt al-niṭāḳayn (A) : 'she of the two girdles', the nickname of Asmāʾ, elder half-sister of ʿĀʾisha and wife of al-Zubayr. XI 550b

♦ dhātī (A) : essential; the conceptually and ontologically prior part of the essence of a thing. II 220b; V 1262a

dhawḳ (A) : taste; insight or intuitive appreciation. II 221a; direct experience. II 1041a
In philosophy, ~ is the name for the gustatory sense-perception which, according to Aristotle, is a kind of sub-species of the tactual sense, localised in the gustatory organ, the tongue. It differs, however, from tactual sense because mere contact with skin is not sufficient for gustation to occur. II 221a
In aesthetics, ~ is the name for the power of aesthetic appreciation, something that 'moves the heart'. II 221a
In mysticism, ~ denotes the direct quality of the mystic experience. The metaphor of 'sight' is also often used, but ~ has more qualitative overtones of enjoyment. II 221a

dhawlaḳ (A) : tip (of the tongue). VI 130a; VIII 343a

♦ dhawlaḳī (A) : 'pointed'; in grammar, for al-Khalīl, those consonants that are produced with the tip of the tongue, such as the *r*. VIII 343a

♦ dhawlaḳiyya (A), and *asaliyya* : in grammar, two terms used by al-Khalīl to indicate articulation with the tip of the tongue but specifying only the form of the tongue. III 598a

dhawu 'l-arḥām (A) : relatives in the maternal line; in law, a third class of heirs recognised only by the Ḥanafī and Ḥanbalī schools of law, who can only succeed to an inheritance in the total absence of any representative of the fixed-shares heirs and the ʿAṢABA. IV 916b

dhawwāḳ → ČĀSHNA-GĪR

dhayl (A, pl. *dhuyūl, adhyāl*) : 'tail', a continuation of a text, simultaneously attached to the work of which it is the 'appendix' and detached from it. IX 158b; IX 603b f.; X 277a; and → MUDHAYYAL

♦ dhayl al-ḳiṭṭ (A) : 'long cat's tail', in botany, either the Cat's tailgrass (*Phleum pratense*) or Alfagrass (*Lygeum spartum*). IX 653a

dhiʾb (A) : in zoology, the wolf, and, in local usage, the jackal. II 223a

dhīkh → ḌABUʿ

dhikr (A) : 'remembering' God, reciting the names of God; the tireless repetition of an ejaculatory litany; a religious service common to all the mystical fraternities, performed either solitarily or collectively, also known as *ḥaḍra, ʿimāra*, or simply *madjlis*. II 164b; II 223b; II 891b; IV 94b; X 245a; a discourse. IX 112a; the revelation sent down to Muḥammad. V 402a

♦ dhikr-i ʿalāniyya → DHIKR-I DIL

♦ dhikr al-ʿawāmm (A) : the collective DHIKR sessions. II 224a

♦ dhikr-i dil (P) : the DHIKR of the heart, as opposed to a public one (*dhikr-i ʿalāniyya*, or *dhikr-i tan*). As practiced by al-Hamadānī, the first figure of the Khʷādjagān ṣūfī movement, it was accompanied by the prolonged holding of the breath. XII 521a

♦ dhikr-i djahr (< A) : a practice of reciting the names of God loudly while sitting in the prescribed posture at prescribed times, adopted by the Čishtī mystics. II 55b; as ~ *djahrī*, repetitive oral prayer, called '~ of the saw' (T *arra*) (in Arabic, ~ *al-minshār*), which practice gave the Yasawiyya the name of Djahriyya. XI 295a

♦ dhikr-i khafī (< A) : a practice of reciting the names of God silently, adopted by the Čishtī mystics. II 55b

♦ dhikr al-khawāṣṣ (A) : the DHIKR of the privileged (mystics who are well advanced along the spiritual path). II 224a

dhimma (A) : the term used to designate the sort of indefinitely renewed contract through which the Muslim community accords hospitality and protection to members of other revealed religions, on condition of their acknowledging the domination of Islam; the beneficiaries of the ~ are also collectively referred to as the ~, or *ahl al-dhimma*. Originally only Jews and Christians were involved; soon, however, it became necessary to consider the Zoroastrians, and later, especially in Central Asia, other minor faiths not mentioned in the Qur'ān. II 227a

In law, ~ is a legal term with two meanings: in legal theory, ~ is the legal quality which makes the individual a proper subject of law, that is, a proper addressee of the rule which provides him with rights or charges him with obligations. In this sense, it may be identified with legal personality (*fi 'l-dhimma* 'in personam'). The second meaning is that of the legal practitioners and goes back to the root of the notion of obligation. It is the *fides* which binds the debtor to his creditor. II 231a; XII 207a; abstract financial responsibility. I 27a

♦ dhimmī (A) : the beneficiary of the DHIMMA. A ~ is defined as against the Muslim and the idolater; and also as against the *ḥarbī* who is of the same faith but lives in territories not yet under Islam; and finally as against the *musta'min*, the foreigner who is granted the right of living in an Islamic territory for a short time (one year at most). II 227a

dhirā' (A) : cubit, a basic measure of length, being originally the length of the arm from the elbow to the top of the middle finger. The name ~ is also given to the instrument used for measuring it. One ~ was 24 IṢBA', although the cubit was not always used with great precision and a considerable number of different cubits were in common use in Islam, e.g. the legal cubit, the black cubit, the king's cubit, and the cloth cubit. II 231b; VII 137b

A minor branch of a river, also called *khalīdj*, as distinguished from the main stream (*'amūd*). VIII 38a

In anatomy, the arm. XII 830b

dhrupad → BANDISH; KHAYĀL

dhu'āba → 'ADHABA

dhubāb (A) : in zoology, the fly. II 247b

♦ dhubābī (A0 : a variety of emerald, which when drawn near a snake's eyes, make them bulge out of their sockets and burst. Other types of emeralds were experimented with but did not have the same effect. XI 570a

dhubbān (A) : the term used in navigation to designate the standard angular distance of four fingers, IṢBA's, wide, i.e. a handbreadth. IV 96b; VII 51a

dhura (A) : in botany, the great sorghum (*Sorghum vulgare*), also called Indian millet, *djāwars hindī*. IV 520a; XII 249b

dhurr → ḲAMḤ

dhurriyya (A) : the descendants of 'Alī, one of a class of noble blood, *sharaf*, that existed in Egyptian terminology of the 9th/15th century. IX 332a

dībāča (P) : in prosody, a conventional introduction. IV 1009b

dībādj (A, < P) : silk brocade. III 209b

♦ dībādja → 'UNWĀN

ḍib'ān → ḌABU'

dibdiba (A) : any flat, firm-surfaced area; the term is related to the classical *dabdaba*, referring to the drumming sounds of hooves on hard earth. II 248b dibs (A) : syrup, molasses; a treacle of grapes, carob, etc. I 69a; II 1062b; IX 804b

dibs͟hī → DJIḤḤ

ḍidd (A, pl. *aḍdād*) : contrary; one of the four Aristotelian classes of opposites, viz. relative terms, contraries, privation and possession, and affirmation and negation. II 249a; and → AḌDĀD

diffiyya (A) : a heavy winter cloak for men, worn in Egypt. V 740b

diflā (A) : in botany, the oleander. IX 872b

dīg-i d̲j̲ūs͟h → TAS͟HARRUF

dīh → TIK WA-TUM

dihḳān (A, < P *dehkān*) : the head of a village and a member of the lesser feudal nobility of Sasanian Persia. They were an immensely important class, although the actual area of land they cultivated was often quite small. Their principal function was to collect taxes. In Transoxania, the term was applied to the local rulers as well as the landowners. The spread of the IḲṬĀʿ system in the 5th/11th century and the depression of the landowning classes diminished the position and influence of the ~, and the term acquired the sense of peasant, which is its meaning in modern Iran. I 15b; II 253b; V 853b

dihlīz (A) : the palace vestibule where the ruler appeared for public audience. VIII 313b

dīk (A) : in zoology, the cock, of which several kinds (*hindī, nabaṭī, zand̲j̲ī*, etc.) are mentioned in the sources. II 275a

diḳḳ → KATTĀN

dikka (A), or *dakka* : a platform in a mosque near the MINBAR to which a staircase leads up. This platform is used as a seat for the muezzin when pronouncing the call to prayer in the mosque at the Friday service. Mosques of the Ottoman period have their ~ in the form of a rostrum against the wall opposite the MIḤRĀB. II 276a; VI 663a; and → FŪṬA

♦ dikkat al-muballig͟h → MUBALLIG͟H

ḍilʿ → D̲J̲ABAL; SĀḲ; S͟HAYʾ

dilḳ (A) : the patched garment of ṣūfīs, also worn by clowns. V 740b

dillīna (A, < Gk), or *dallīna* : the flat mussel (*Tellina planata*). VIII 707a; its export as pickled mussels from Rosetta, in Egypt, was mentioned by the mediaeval geographer al-Idrīsī. VIII 438a

dilsiz (T, P *bīzabān*) : lit. tongueless; the name given to the deaf mutes employed in the inside service of the Ottoman palace, and for a while at the Sublime Porte. Established in the palace from the time of Meḥemmed II to the end of the sultanate, they served as guards and attendants, and as messengers and emissaries in highly confidential matters, including executions. II 277a

dīmak (A, < P *dīma* 'cheek'), or *daymak* : in archery, the 'arrow-pass', sc. the side of the handle continuous with the the part facing the archer as he shoots (*wad̲j̲h*). IV 799a

dīn (A, pl. *adyān*) : religion; the obligations which God imposes on man; the domain of divine prescriptions concerning acts of worship and everything involved in it. II 293b; IV 171b

For ~ as second element in titles, V 621b ff.

♦ dīn al-ḥaḳḳ (A) : a Qurʾānic expression denoting 'the religion of Truth'; the revealed religion; the religion of the golden mean. II 294b

♦ **dīn-i ilāhī** : the heresy promulgated by the Indian Mug͟hal emperor Akbar in 989/1581, as a result of his discussions with learned men of all religions, which he vainly hoped would prove acceptable to his subjects. The new religion was related to earlier *alfī* heretical movements in Indian Islam of the 10th/16th century, implying the need for the reorientation of faith at the end of the first millennium of the advent of the Prophet. I 317a; II 296a

dīnār (A, < Gk; pl. *danānīr*) : Muslim gold coin issued by the Umayyad caliph ʿAbd al-Malik b. Marwān, to replace the Byzantine *denarius*. There are earlier types of *dīnār*s dating from ca. 72/691-2, but the coinage reform of ʿAbd al-Malik drastically affected the style which it would henceforth have. I 77b; II 297a; V 964a ff.

♦ dīnār d̲h̲ahabī (A) : a double DĪNĀR, of a weight of 4.57 gr, struck first by the Almohads. The traditional *dīnār* was called *dīnār fiḍḍī* or *ʿas̲h̲rī* in the Marīnid sources. VI 573a

♦ danānīr al-ṣila (A) : special coins, presentation issues, struck for non-currency purposes. XI 228b

dirʿ (A), or *sard, zarad, muzarrad* (< P *zard*) : in military science, protective body armour in the shape of coats of mail, which were considered valuable in desert fighting in the pre-Islamic period. XII 735b

dirāya (A) : the term used by al-Rāmahurmuzī to distinguish transmissions of Traditions by people who have learned to discern between all transmission minutiae, from those by people who merely transmit without paying proper heed to all sorts of crucial details in ISNĀD as well as contents of Tradition, which he terms *riwāya*. VIII 421a; X 934a

dirham (A, < Gk) : the name indicates both a weight and the silver unit of the Arab monetary system, used from the rise of Islam down to the Mongol period. II 319a; V 964a ff.; VI 118a

In early mathematics, ~ was the term used for the absolute number. II 361a

♦ dirham warak̲ (A), or *dirham aswad* : in numismatics, so-called black dirhams, which were described as 'rough, uneven, small rectangles or squares of low silver content, the weight of which depended on the haphazard way the cold chisel of the flan cutter fell'. XI 199b

dirlik (T) : living, livelihood; a term used in the Ottoman empire to denote an income provided by the state, directly or indirectly, for the support of persons in its service. It is used principally of the military fiefs, but also applies to pay, salaries, and grants in lieu of pay. II 322a; IX 656a

dirra (A) : a whip of ox-hide, or of strips of hide on which date-stones have been stitched. X 406b

dirrīd̲j̲ (A), or *durrayd̲j̲* : a drum. II 135b; X 33a; a lute with a long neck and plucked strings. VI 215b; and → DARABUKKA

dirṣ (A, pl. *adrāṣ, durūṣ*), and *s̲h̲ibrik̲* (pl. *s̲h̲abārik̲*) : in zoology, the kitten of both wild and domestic cats. IX 651b; the young of the jerboa. XI 283b

dirwa (A) : a typical style of hairdressing, which has given rise to the nickname Fuzzy-wuzzy, practised by the ʿAbābda tribe of Upper Egypt. I 1b

dīw (P) : the name of the spirits of evil and of darkness, creatures of Ahriman, the personification of sins, whose number is legion. II 322b

diʿwa → ISTILḤĀḲ

dīwān (A) : a register; an office. I 801b; I 1145b; II 323a; IV 937b

In literature, a collection of poetry or prose. II 323a

For a list of *dīwān*s not listed below, II 328b ff.

♦ dīwān al-badal : under the Mamlūks, a special department established to facilitate the exchange of feudal estates of the members of the ḤALḲA against payment or compensation which had become usual after the death of the Mamlūk al-Nāṣir Muḥammad. III 99b

♦ **dīwān-begi** : the title of high officials in the Central Asian k̲h̲ānates in the 16th-19th centuries. XII 227b; among the Tīmūrids, the office of secretary of the DĪWĀN or chief of the secretariat of the *dīwān*. VIII 481b

♦ dīwān efendi : in the Ottoman empire, chancellor of the Admiralty. VIII 422a; in the Ottoman provinces, an important official attached to the *wālī*. In Egypt, under

Muḥammad ʿAlī, the ~ became a kind of president of the council of ministers. VIII 481b

♦ dīwān raḳamlari̊ (T) : term for the SIYĀḲAT numerals, in effect the 'written out' shapes of the numerals in Arabic, reduced to a skeletal and schematised form. IX 693a

♦ **dīwān-i humāyūn** (T) : the name given to the Ottoman imperial council founded by Meḥemmed II after the conquest of Istanbul, which, until the mid-11th/17th century, was the central organ of the government of the empire. II 337b

♦ dīwānī (A) : in land management, land held by the ruler as head of state as opposed to crown land. IV 974b

In calligraphy, a form of Arabic script which consisted of letters and particular signs devised from abbreviations of the names of numbers. It was already in use during the ʿAbbāsid caliphate by the army of scribes and accountants working in the Treasury, although according to Turkish sources, the ~ script was allegedly invented for writing official documents and registers of the DĪWĀN-İ-HUMĀYŪN. *D̲j̲alī dīwānī* is a variant type of ~ with the letters written within each other. It flourished from the 9th/15th century onwards. I 1145b; II 315b; IV 1125b; VIII 151b; and → TAWḲĪʿ

diya (A), or *ʿaḳl, maʿḳūla* : in law, a specified amount of money or goods due in cases of homicide or other injuries to physical health unjustly committed upon the person of another. It is a substitute for the law of private vengeance. In its restricted and most usual sense in law, it means the compensation which is payable in cases of homicide. I 29a; I 171b; I 338a; II 340b; V 180a

diyāmīrūn : in medicine, a robb, made from mulberry juice for swellings of the mouth and for angina. X 752a

diyānay (P) : an ancient type of double reed-pipe. Its two pipes have been described as being of equal length, each of which is pierced by five finger-holes, which gave an octave between them. According to al-Fārābī, the ~ was also called the *mizmār al-mut̲h̲annā* or *muzāwad̲j̲*. VII 208a

d̲j̲aʿāla → D̲J̲UʿL

d̲j̲aʿba (A) : in archery, a fairly large, leather quiver having a lid fixed by means of a cord, *mik̲h̲d̲h̲af*. IV 799b

d̲j̲abā (T), or *d̲j̲abā bennāk* : in Ottoman times, married peasants possessing no land. I 1169b

d̲j̲ābāḍūli (Mor), or *d̲j̲ābāḍūr* : a full-length, caftan-like garment with either no buttons or a single button in front. V 745b; a short tunic worn over a waistcoat. XI 543b

d̲j̲ābāḍūr → D̲J̲ĀBĀḌŪLI

d̲j̲abal (A, pl. **d̲j̲ibāl**) : a massive mountain, rocky hillock; other synonyms in common use among the Bedouin in Arabia are *ḍilʿ* (pl. *ḍulūʿ*, *ḍilʿān*), *ḥazm*, which is usually lower than a ~, *abraḳ* (pl. *burḳān*) and BARḲĀʾ (pl. *burḳ*). Promontories jutting out from the island escarpments are called *k̲h̲as̲h̲m* 'nose' (pl. *k̲h̲us̲h̲ūm*). I 536b; II 534b; the name for a very large ruby, of which three were known to have been bought by the ʿAbbāsid caliphs al-Manṣūr, al-Mahdī and al-Mutawakkil. XI 263b

d̲j̲abbād̲h̲a → SARAFSĀR

d̲j̲abbāna (A, pl. *d̲j̲abbānāt*) : a piece of unbuilt land serving, i.a., as a meeting place and a cemetery. V 23a; V 347a; and → MAḲBARA

d̲j̲abbār → D̲J̲AWZĀʾ

d̲j̲abha → SUD̲J̲D̲J̲A

d̲j̲ābī (A) : a collector of the *ṣadaḳa* tax. X 50b

d̲j̲ābih (A) : 'that which comes from in front', one of the technical terms designating the directions of a bird's flight, or an animal's steps, which play an important part in the application of divination known as FAʾL, ṬĪRA and ZAD̲J̲R. II 760a; and → NĀTIḤ

djabr (A) : compulsion. I 27b; and → DJABRIYYA

In law, ~ is compulsion in marriage exercised upon one or other of the prospective partners. XII 233a

In medicine, minor or simple surgery. II 481b

♦ **al-djabr wa 'l-muḳābala** (A) : originally two methods of transforming equations, later, the name given to algebra, the theory of equations. II 360b

♦ **djabriyya** (A), or *mudjbira* : the name given by opponents to those whom they alleged to hold the doctrine of DJABR 'compulsion', viz. that man does not really act but only God. It was also used by later heresiographers to describe a group of sects. The Muʿtazila applied it to traditionists, Ashʿarite theologians and others who denied their doctrine of ḲADAR 'free will'. II 365a; III 1142b

♦ djabriyyūn (A) : in the writings of the Ikhwān al-Ṣafāʾ (4th/10th century), the name of the representatives of the branch of mathematics called *al*-DJABR WA 'L-MUḲĀBALA. II 361b

djadal → ADAB

♦ djadaliyyūn (A) : controversialists. X 440b; and → ADAB

djadhaʿ → ʿATŪD

♦ djadhaʿa (A) : a female camel in its fifth year. XI 412a

djadhba (A) : in mysticism, divine attraction. VIII 306b; IX 863a

djādhī → ZAʿFARĀN

djadhīdha (A) : in agriculture, wheat husked and crushed. II 1060b

djadhr (A) : in mathematics, ~ is the term used for the square root. III 1139b

djādī → ZAʿFARĀN

djadīd (A, T *djedīd*) : new, modern. II 366a

In Persian prosody, the name of a metre of rare occurrence, said to have been invented by the Persians. I 677b

In Central Asia and among the Muslims of Russia, the name of a reform movement (followers of the *uṣūl-i djedīd[e]* 'the new methods') in the 19th and 20th centuries. II 366a; XII 466b

djadwal (A), or *khātim* : a scientific table. XI 497b

In sorcery, quadrangular or other geometrical figures into which names and signs possessing magic powers are inserted. These are usually certain mysterious characters, Arabic letters and numerals, magic words, the Names of God, the angels and demons, as well as of the planets, the days of the week, and the elements, and lastly pieces from the Qurʾān. II 370a

For ~ in the Ottoman context, → KHARḲ

♦ al-djadwal al-mudjarrad (A) : in dating, a double-argument table used for the calculation of *madākhil* (→ MADKHAL) from which the initial week day can be read off directly for every month of every year within the respective cycles. X 270b

djady (A) : lit. kid; in astronomy, *al-* ~ is the term for Capricorn, one of the twelve zodiacal constellations. VII 84a; and → SAKHLA

djaʿfarī → KĀGHAD

djafīr (A) : in archery, one of the terms for quiver. IV 800a

djafna → MIʿDJAN

djafr (A) : the generic name for an esoteric literature of apocalyptic character which arose as a result of the persecution which the descendants of ʿAlī and Fāṭima had suffered. Later, deviating from its original form of esoteric knowledge, reserved for the successors and heirs of ʿAlī, it became assimilated to a divinatory technique accessible to the wise whatever their origin, particularly mystics, consisting of speculations based on the numerical value of the Arabic letters. II 375b; IV 1129a; and → SAKHLA

dj͟ag͟hāna (A, < P *čag͟hāna*) : in music, a jingling instrument of small cymbals attached to a frame, in Europe given the name Chapeau Chinois or the Jingling Johnny. Another name for it is *zillī mās͟ha*. IX 10a ff.

djāgīr : land given or assigned by governments in India to individuals as a pension or as a reward for immediate services. The holder of such land was called *djāgīrdār*. II 378b; IX 581a

♦ djāgīrdār → DJĀGĪR

djāh (P) : in astronomy, the north pole, used by Islamic navigators of the Indian Ocean. The term was also used for the Pole Star. V 543a; VII 51a

djahannam (A) : hell. I 334b; II 381b; and → SAʿĪR

djahārdah → S͟HAHĀRDAH

djahbad͟h (P, pl. *djahābid͟ha*) : a financial clerk, expert in matters of coins, skilled money examiner, treasury receiver, government cashier, money changer or collector. I 1144b; II 382b; the functionary in the Treasury whose task it was to prepare the monthly statement of income and expenditure. II 79b

djaḥfal → ḲURDŪS

djāhil (A, pl. *djuhhāl*) : 'ignorant'. Among the Druze, members of the community not yet initiated into the truths of the faith; the initiated are the *ʿuḳḳāl*. II 633a

♦ djāhilī (A) : 'pre-Islamic'; in Sayyid Ḳuṭb's book *Maʿālim fi 'l-ṭarīḳ*, ~ means 'barbaric', 'anti-Islamic', 'wicked', and implies apostasy from Islam, punishable by death. IX 117b

♦ **djāhiliyya** (A) : the term for the state of affairs in Arabia before the mission of the Prophet; paganism; the pre-Islamic period and the men of that time. II 383b

djaḥmaris͟h (A) : a term used for a female hare while suckling. XII 84b

djahr → D͟HIKR-I DJAHR

djaḥwas͟h (A) : a child who has passed the stage of weaning. VIII 822a

djāʾifa (A) : a wound penetrating the interior of the body; a determining factor in the prescription of compensation following upon physical injury, DIYA. II 341b

djaʿīla → DJUʿL

djāʾiz (A) : permissable; in law, the term preferred by Ḥanafī authors to specify that the juridical act was legitimate or licit, in point of law, apart from its being valid, ṢAḤĪḤ, or not. Other schools also use it to denote the revocability of e.g. a contract. II 389b
In logic, ~ means what is not unthinkable. II 390a
In the vocabulary of tents, ~ is the main ridge piece, which was of considerable importance. IV 1147b

♦ djāʾiza → ṢILA

djalabī → ČELEBĪ

djalālī (P) : the name of an era founded by the Saldjūḳ sultan Maliks͟hāh b. Alp Arslan, called after his title Djalāl al-Dawla, although it is sometimes termed *malikī*; a calendar used often in Persia from the last part of the 5th/11th century onwards. II 397b; VI 275b; X 267b
In Ottoman Turkish, a term used to describe companies of brigands, led usually by idle or dissident Ottoman army officers, widely spread throughout Anatolia from about 999/1590 but diminishing by 1030/1620. IV 499a; IV 594a; XII 238a

djalam (A) : shears. XII 319a; a strain of sheep in the time of Djāḥiẓ found in Ṭāʾif, which was very high on its hooves and had a fleece so smooth that it appeared bald. XII 318a

djalba (A, < Por/Sp *gelba/gelva*) : a large type of barque used by Arabs on the Arabian Sea and Indian Ocean shores. Ibn Djubayr observed that they were stitched together with coir, i.e. coconut palm fibres. VIII 811a

d̲j̲alī (A), or *d̲j̲alīl* : a name given to every large type of script, but more specifically used for the large type of THULUT̲H̲. It was used for large-sized frames and also for public buildings and their inscriptions. IV 1123b; V 224a

♦ d̲j̲alī dīwānī → DĪWĀNĪ

d̲j̲alīl → D̲J̲ALĪ

d̲j̲ālis̲h̲ (A, < T *čalis̲h̲* 'battle'), also written **s̲h̲ālīs̲h̲** : in military science, the vanguard of an army, as described during the battle of Ḥiṭṭīn in 584/1187, syn. ṬALĪʿA, *muḳaddama*; also during the Mamlūk period, a special flag hoisted over the *ṭablk̲h̲āna* to make known the decision to dispatch a large expedition against a strong enemy. III 184a; XII 722a

d̲j̲āliya (A, pl. D̲J̲AWĀLĪ) : the term used for the Arabic-speaking communities with special reference to North and South America. II 403b; II 470b

d̲j̲allāb (A) : 'importer', slave-trader. I 32b; I 929a; an outer garment used in certain parts of North Africa, variant of D̲J̲ALLĀBIYYA. II 404b; sheep merchant. XII 316b

♦ d̲j̲allābiyya (A) : in Morocco and the west of Algeria, a hooded outer robe with long sleeves, originally worn by men only, now by both sexes. II 404b; V 745b; in Egypt, the loose body shirt still commonly worn by men, pronounced *gallābiyya.* V 741a

d̲j̲allāla (A) : a 'scatophagous animal', mentioned in Tradition and developed in FIḲH with regard to the prohibition of certain foods. II 1069b; V 8b

d̲j̲alsa (A), and *ʿanā', zīna* : in Morocco, the prevalent system of perpetual lease by WAḲF of dilapidated shops and workshops, whereby the tenant makes the necessary repairs, pays an annual rent and thus acquires the perpetual usufruct of the property. XII 369a

♦ d̲j̲alsat al-istirāḥa (A) : in the Islamic ritual prayer, the return to the sitting position after the second inclination, RAKʿA, which practice is common among the Ḥanbalīs and the S̲h̲āfiʿīs, and now also widespread among Mālikī worshippers. VIII 929b

d̲j̲alṭīṭa → FALṬĪṬA

d̲j̲alwa → D̲J̲ILWA

d̲j̲amʿ (A), or *d̲j̲amāʿa* : in grammar, the plural for units numbering three or more. II 406b; VIII 990b

In mysticism, ~ is contrasted with *farḳ* 'separation', and denotes seeing all things as brought together through God's reality. XI 38a

d̲j̲āma-dār → D̲J̲AMDĀR

d̲j̲amāʿa (A, T *d̲j̲emāʿa*) : meeting, assembly.

In religion, the community (of believers). II 411a; the common practices and beliefs of the Companions. II 295a

In North Africa, as *djemaa*, ~ denoted local administrative assemblies, which owned property collectively. II 412b; IV 362a

In Morocco, a tribal assembly of men able to bear arms, which dealt with all the business of the tribe, civil, criminal, financial and political. V 1198b

In the Ottoman empire, as *d̲j̲emāʿat* or *piyādegān*, one of three principal subdivisions of the Janissary corps, later expanded to 101 regiments, for those created before Meḥemmed's time. The other two were the *segbān*, a small corps of keepers of the palace hounds, and the BOLÜK or *ag̲h̲a bölükleri*. XI 323b

For ~ in grammar, → D̲J̲AMʿ

d̲j̲amād → MAʿDIN

d̲j̲āmāhāt (P, < A *d̲j̲amāʿa*) : among the S̲h̲āhsewan in Persia, a community which moved and camped as a unit during the autumn migration in October and the spring migration in May, performing many religious ceremonies jointly. IX 224a

d̲j̲āmakān (T) : a disrobing chamber in the Ottoman sultan's palace. X 567a

djāmakiyya (A, < P) : salary; originally, that part of the regular salary given in dress or cloth; under the Mamlūks, ~ denoted the part of the salary given in money. II 413b; a grant. IX 269a

djamal (A, Heb *gimel*) : in zoology, the male camel, sometimes used equally with *ibil* for the species. III 666a

♦ djamal al-baḥr (A), or *ḳuba*ʿ : in zoology, the humpbacked whale. VIII 1022b

djamalūn (A) : in architecture, a gable roof. I 616a

djamdār (A, < P *djāma-dār* 'clothes-keeper') : 'platoon commander', the lowest commissioned rank in the Indian Army. It also denotes junior officials in the police, customs, etc., or the foreman of a group of guides, sweepers. II 421b

♦ djamdāriyya (A) : under the Mamlūks, the keepers of the sultan's wardrobe. II 421b; VIII 432a

djāmedān (T) : a short, trimmed waistcoat without sleeves, worn as an outer garment in the Ottoman period. V 752a

djāmiʿ (A, pl. *djawāmi*ʿ) : mosque; and → MASDJID DJĀMIʿ

In philosophy and science, the plural form, *djawāmi*ʿ, is used to denote the compendium or handbook. VII 536b; *djawāmi*ʿ is also used for the 'short' recension of Ibn Rushd's commentary on Aristotle's works. VII 539a; summaries. X 454b

♦ djāmiʿ al-ḥisāb (A) : the master-ledger of the Īlkhānids, from which the annual financial reports were prepared, one of the seven main registers on which their system of book-keeping was based. II 81b

♦ djāmiʿ al-ṣadaḳa (A) : an alms collector, one of the 'representatives' despatched to Yemen under the early regimes. XI 272a

djāmiʿa (A) : an ideal, a bond or an institution which unites individuals or groups; university. II 422b; in modern usage, ~ has also been used to characterise a political, united movement; more specifically, ~ signifies the political unification of Muslim states. VIII 359b ff.

djamʿiyya (A, T *djemʿiyyet*; P *andjuman*) : society; association. This term was perhaps first used to refer to the organised monastic communities or congregations which appeared in the Uniate Churches in Syria and Lebanon. In the middle of the 19th century, ~ came into more general use, first in Lebanon and then in other Arabic-speaking countries, to refer to voluntary associations for scientific, literary, benevolent or political purposes. By the middle of the 20th century, ḤIZB had replaced ~ to refer to political movements and organisations. II 428b; III 514b ff.

djammāl (A) : camel-driver or cameleer; also an owner and hirer of camels, and a dealer in camels. XII 241b

djamra (A, pl. *djimār*) : pebble. II 438a; tribe. VIII 381a; ~ is the name given to the three places (*al-djamra al-ūlā, al-djamra al-wusṭā, djamrat al-ʿaḳaba*) where pilgrims returning from ʿArafat during the pilgrimage stop to partake in the ritual throwing of stones. II 438a; III 36a; VIII 379a

♦ djamarāt al-ʿarab (A) : tribes that never allied themselves with others. VIII 120a; X 173b; the groups of Bedouin tribes. VIII 379a

djamūḥ (A) : in the terminology of horse-riding, a horse that checks its head to escape from control by the hands. II 953b

djamulyān → GÖNÜLLÜ

djāmūs (A, < P *gāv-i mīsh* 'bull-sheep') : in zoology, the Indian buffalo or water buffalo (*Bubalus bubalis*). XII 242b

In Algeria, ~ designates women's bracelets carved from the horns of the water buffalo. XII 244a

♦ djāmūs al-baḥr (A) : in zoology, the hippopotamus, to some writers. XII 244a

♦ djāmūs al-khalāʾ (A) : in zoology, the African buffalo (*Syncerus caffer*), called thus by the Sudanese. It was unknown to the Arab writers. XII 242b

djanāba (A) : in law, the state of major ritual impurity, caused by marital intercourse, to which the religious law assimilates any *effusio seminis.* II 440b; VIII 929a

djanāḥ (A) : wing; in botany, ~ *al-nasr* 'vulture's wing' is the Cardoon (*Cynara cardunculus*). VII 1014b

djanāza (A) : corpse, bier, or corpse and bier, and then, funeral. II 441b

djānbāz (P, Egy *ganbādhiya*) : an acrobat, especially 'rope-dancer'; soldier; horse-dealer. II 442b

♦ **djānbāzān** : the name of a military corps in the Ottoman empire, serving only in time of war, in the vanguard, and charged with dangerous tasks. It was abolished towards the end of the 16th century. II 443a

djāndār (P) : the name of certain guards regiments who provided the sovereign's bodyguard from the Saldjūḳs on. II 444a; V 685a

djandji dalem (J) : 'the royal promise', a term in Java for the TAʿLĪḲ-ṬALĀḲ institution. I 173b

djang (U) : in Urdu poetry, the part of the elegy, MARTHIYA, where the battle is described, with stress on the hero's valour and often including a description of his sword. VI 611b

djanīn (A) : the term for the child in its mother's womb; foetus. VIII 821b

djank (A) : in music, the harp. II 1073b; IX 10a

djānḳī (P) : council of state. XI 194a

djanna (A) : garden; Paradise. II 447a

♦ djannat al-khuld (A) : 'the garden of eternity', i.e. Paradise. XII 529b

djanṭīṭa → FALṬĪṬA

djanūb (A) : in meteorology, the south wind. VIII 526b

djār → IDJĀRA

djarab (A) : in medicine, scabies. V 107a; VIII 783a; IX 902b; X433a

♦ djarab al-ʿayn → RAMAD ḤUBAYBĪ

djarād (A, s. *djarāda*) : in zoology, locusts. For the different stages of the locust's development, Arabic has special names, such as *sirwa, dabā, ghawghāʾ, khayfān*, etc., which, however, are variously defined. II 455a; and → ḲAYNA

djarāʾid (Tun) : a pair of men's leather leggings. V 745b

djaras (A, pl. *adjrās*) : in music, the cup, bowl or cone-shape bell; the sphere-shaped bell was called the *djuldjul.* ~ also stood for a large bell, *djuldjul* meaning a small bell. A collection of these bells, on a board or chain, is known as a *ṭabla.* IX 10b f.

djardaḳ, djardhaḳ → RAGHĪF

djarf (A) : one of a number of terms for a seine or drag-net, i.e. a large pouched net used for fishing on the high seas, also called *djārūf, djarrāfa, ḳaṭṭāʿa* and *baṭāna.* VIII 1021b

djarḥ (A) : in law, the contestation that a witness is ʿADL. I 209b

♦ **al-djarḥ wa 'l-taʿdīl** (A) : lit. disparaging and declaring trustworthy; in the science of Tradition, a technical phrase used regarding the reliability or otherwise of traditionists. II 462a; VIII 515a

djarīb (A) : the basic measure of area in earlier Islamic times, which, as well as being a measure of capacity for grain, etc., equal to four ḲAFĪZS, became a measure of surface area, originally the amount of agricultural land which could be sown with a *djarīb*'s measure of seed. The extent of the ~ of area varied widely. Canonically, it was made up of 100 ḲAṢABAS, hence approx. 1600 m^2. VII 138a

djarīd (A) : the firm central stem of the palm which, when stripped of the leaf, is used for different purposes. Used in the manner of a javelin, the ~ gave its name to DJERĪD, the well-known equestrian sport so popular in Abyssinia, the Near East and Turkey. VII 923a

♦ **djarīda** (A, pl. *djarāʾid*) : lit. leaf; a usual term in modern Arabic for a newspaper, the adoption of which is attributed to Fāris al-Shidyāḳ (syn. ṢAḤĪFA, usually used in the pl. *ṣuḥuf*). II 464b; XII 247a; in Sicily, a document which set out the different legal and social levels, defining the status on the one hand of the people of the countryside, having limited rights, and on the other that of the urban classes. IX 585b

♦ al-djarīda al-musadjdjala (A) : in classical Muslim administration, the sealed register. II 79a

♦ al-djarīda al-sawdāʾ (A) : in classical Muslim administration, the central register of the army office prepared annually for each command, showing the names of the soldiers, with their pedigree, ethnic origin, physical descriptions, rations, pay, etc. II 78b

djāriḥ (A, pl. *djawāriḥ*) : a 'beast of prey', used in hawking. I 1152a

djarīma (A), or **djurm** : a sin, fault, offence; in modern law, the technical term for crime. II 479b

In Ottoman usage, in the forms *djerīme* and *djereme*, fines and penalties. Other prescribed fines were called *ḳînlîḳ* and *gharāmet*. II 479b; II 604a

djāriya (A) : maidservant, female slave. I 24b

djarkh (A, < P *čarkh*) : a crossbow. II 506b; an individual arbalest whose bow is drawn back by means of a wheel (whence its name); by this, very long arrows, approaching the length of javelins, could be fired. IV 798a

djarm → GARMSĪR

djarr (A), or *khafḍ* : in grammar, the genitive case. III 1008a

In mediaeval agriculture, the trace, which attached the beam of the ploughshare to the centre of the yoke (*nīr*). VII 22b

♦ djarr al-djiwār (A) : in grammar, a term denoting 'attraction of the indirect case'. II 558b

djarrāḥ (A) : in medicine, surgeon. II 481b

djarrār (A) : 'he who drags (someone) along'; in military terminology, the commander of 1,000 men. X 91a; an army corps. IV 1144b

In the context of the pilgrimage, ~ is the name given to the few *muṭawwifūn* (→ MUṬAWWIF) who worked outside the special guild. They dealt primarily with pilgrims too poor to hire the services of a bona fide *muṭawwif*. VI 171a

djars (A, pl. *adjrās*) : in grammar, the result of the application of the articulatory organs to the place of the 'cutting', MAḲṬAʿ. III 597b

djarūsha (A) : the ancient *tribulum*, a technique using animal power motivating sharp stones and iron blades for threshing corn. X 411a

djasad (A, pl. *adjsād*) : body, in particular that of a higher being such as an angel. II 555a

♦ adjsād (A) : in alchemy, the metals, corresponding to Gk τὰ σώματα. V 111a

djaʾsh (A) : in archery, a light and weak bow which, contrary to the KATŪM, vibrates when loosed. IV 798a

djāshankīriyya → USTĀDĀR

djaṣṣ (A) : gypsum manufactured in the town of Siʿird, which was used in the building of local houses. IX 574b

♦ djaṣṣāṣ (A) : a seller of gypsum. XII 759a

djāsūs (A) : spy; in particular, a spy sent among the enemy. II 486b

djāti (H) : an Indian musical term for modes, constructed on heptatonic series of notes, *mūrččhanā*. III 452b; caste. III 459b

djawāb → SHARṬ

djawād (A) : in zoology, the 'excellent runner', one of the more precise terms for a horse. IV 1143b

djawālī (A, s. *djālī*) : lit. émigrés; and → DJĀLIYA

As a fiscal term, ~ came to mean the poll-tax levied on non-Muslims, DJIZYA. II 490a; II 561a

djawāmiʿ → DJĀMIʿ

djāwars (A, < P *gāwars*) : in botany, millet (*Panicum miliaceum*). XII 249b

djawarsh (A, pl. *djawārish*) : in medicine, a stomachic. IX 805a; XI 381b

djawarshin (A) : in medicine, an electuary. XII 641a

djawf (A) : in geography, a depressed plain, sometimes replaced by *djaww*, a basin with a spring well. II 491b; VIII 1048b

djawlakh (P) : sack-cloth, probably the origin for the name, arising from the founder's distinctive garb, of the Djawlaḳiyya movement that penetrated into Anatolia in the first half of the 7th/13th century. IV 473b

djawhar (A, < P) : jewel; atom. II 494b; XII 250b

In philosophy, the technical term for οὐσία 'substance'. I 784b; II 493a

djawḳa (A, pl. *djawḳāt*) : in Lebanon, a troupe accompanying the ZADJAL poet, with whome they engage in poetic duelling at festivals. XI 376a

djawr (A) : oppression. XI 567b

djawshan (A, P) : in military science, a lamellar armour, popular throughout most Islamic countries but the Islamic West by the 12th century. XII 737b

djāwun → ḤĀWŪN

djaww → DJAWF

djawwāla (A) : globetrotter. I 116a

djawz (A, < P *gawz*) : the nut in general, and the walnut (*Juglans regia*) in particular. XII 264a; the walnut tree. VIII 732b; for many fruits combined with ~, XII 264b

♦ **djawzahar** (A, < P *djawz čihr* 'nut-shape'), *tinnīn*, or *ʿuḳda* (< Gk) : in astronomy, the two opposite points in which the apparent path of the moon, or all planets, cuts the ecliptic. In course of time, these points come to move on to the ecliptic. In texts dating from the 5th/11th century, ~ also indicates the *circulus pareclipticus* of the moon; and the nodes of the orbit of any of the five planets. II 501b; V 536a; VIII 101b; and → FALAK AL-DJAWZAHAR

djawzāʾ (A) : in astronomy, *al-~* is the term for Orion, the stellar figure, replaced by the translators with *al-djabbār*, and Gemini, one of the twelve zodiacal constellations, also called *al-tawʾamān*. VII 83a

djawzal (A, pl. *djawāzil*) : the chick of a sandgrouse, ḲAṬĀ. IX 744b

djayb → DJĪB

♦ al-djayb al-maʿkūs → SAHM

♦ al-djayb al-mustawī → SAHM

♦ **djayb-i humāyūn** (T) : the privy purse of the Ottoman sultans, which contents provided for the immediate needs and expenses of the sovereign. II 502b

djaysh (A) : army. II 504a

In the south of Algeria and Morocco, *djīsh* means an armed band to go out on an ambush, GHAZW, against a caravan or a body of troops. When the ~ consisted of several hundred men, it was called a *ḥarka*. II 509b

In Morocco, *djīsh* (pronounced *gīsh*), denotes a kind of feudal organisation in the Moroccan army. II 509b

djazāʾ (A) : recompense both in a good and in a bad sense, especially with reference to the next world. II 518a

In Ottoman usage, ~ means punishment. II 518a; and → ḲĀNŪN-I DJAZĀʾĪ

For ~ in grammar, → SHARṬ

♦ djazāʾilči : tribal levy, as e.g. that known as the Khyber Rifles, paid by the government of India for the protection of the Khyber in the late 19th century. I 238a; and → KHĀṢṢADĀR

djazīra (A) : island; peninsula; territories situated between great rivers or separated from the rest of a continent by an expanse of desert; a maritime country. II 523a
Among the Ismāʿīlīs, ~ is the name of a propaganda district. II 523a

djazīza → DJAZZĀZ

djazm (A) : in grammar, quiescence of the final ḤARF of the MUḌĀRIʿ. III 173a

djazz → IḤFĀʾ

djazzār (A) : a slaughterer of camels, sheep, goats and other animals. Today, ~ is synonymous with *ḳaṣṣāb* and *laḥḥām*, the two terms for butcher, but in mediaeval times, they formed a distinct group of workers. XII 267a

djazzāz (A) : a shearer of wool-bearers. The shears he uses are called *djalam* and the wool obtained *djazīza*. XII 319a

djebedji (T) : the name given to a member of the corps of 'Armourers of the Sublime Porte', which had charge of the weapons and munitions of the Janissaries. The corps was closely associated with the Janissaries, and was abolished together with the latter in 1241/1826. I 1061b; XII 269b

djebe (T) : in Ottoman army usage, a simple armour perhaps made of metal plates, which a DJEBELI who enjoyed a small TĪMĀR as low as 730 AḲČEs had to wear. X 503a
♦ **djebeli** (T), or *djebelü* : an auxiliary soldier in the Ottoman empire, mostly of slave origin. II 528b; man-at-arms. IX 656b; a fully-armed auxiliary horseman. X 503a

djedhba → ḤĀL

djerīd (A) : a wooden dart or javelin used in the game of the same name, popular in the Ottoman empire from the 10th-13th/16th-19th centuries. The game consisted of a mock battle in the course of which horsemen threw darts at one another. II 532a

djiʿāl → DJUʿL

djīb (A, < San *jīva* 'bow-string, half chord') : in mathematics, often misread as *djayb* 'breast-pocket', this transcription from Sanskrit led to Eng 'sine' (< L *sinus* 'breast'). X 232a

djibāya (A) : the collection of taxes. X 307b; XI 532b

djidār → LUʾAMA

djidd (A) : a common ancestor (which links different sections of a tribe). XI 276b

djiddāba (A) : in zoology, the djeddaba kingfish, whose Arabic term is found again in the Latinised nomenclature to specify a sub-species limited to a particular region (*Caranx djeddaba*). VIII 1021b

djidhāʿ → ADJDHĀʿ

djidhr (A) : root; in mathematics, ~ is represented by the area of a rectangle having the side of the square as its length and the unit as its width. II 360b

djiflik (T, pl. *djafālik*) : land given by Muḥammad ʿAlī and his successors to themselves or to members of their family. XII 179a

djihād (A) : an effort directed towards a determined objective; a military action with the object of the expansion of Islam and, if need be, of its defence. II 64a; II 126a; II 538a; III 180a ff.; IV 772a; VIII 495a ff.; IX 845b

djiḥḥ (Nadjdī A) : in botany, the term for watermelon in Nadjd (*ḥabḥab* in the Ḥidjāz, *dibshī* in the south). I 540b

djiḳa (P) : a plume, for a headdress. XI 192b

djild (A), or *adīm* : leather; parchment. Synonyms of the latter meaning are *waraḳ*, ḲIRṬĀS, RAḲḲ or *riḳḳ*. II 540a; VIII 407b

djilfa (A) : the nib of a reed-pen. IV 471a

djillāya (A) : an embroidered coat-like outer garment, a wedding costume, worn by women in Syria and Palestine; in Yemen, a man's marriage caftan. V 741a

djilwa (A) : the ceremony of raising the bride's veil, and the present made by the husband to the wife on this occasion. II 542b

In mysticism, ~ (or *djalwa*) is the name of the state in which the mystic is on coming out of seclusion, KHALWA. II 542b

djīm (A) : the fifth letter of the Arabic alphabet, with the numerical value 3, representing the *g* (occlusive, postpalatal, voiced, *shadīda madjhūra*). II 543b

djimāʿ (A) : coitus (syn. *bāh*). XII 641a

djimat (Mal) : an amulet, in particular a written one. II 545a

djinās (A) : paronomasia; → TADJNĪS

♦ djinās al-ḳalb (A) : in literary theory, an imperfect paronomasia whereby there is difference in the arrangement of the letters, e.g. the juxtaposition of *fatḥ* and *ḥatf*. When the two words occur at the beginning and the end of the verse, it is called *mudjannaḥ*. X 69b

♦ djinās al-khaṭṭ → MUṢAḤḤAF

djindār (T) : the second animal in the row of mules forming the caravans that used to operate in Anatolia. IV 678b

djinn (A) : a Qurʾānic term applied to bodies composed of vapour and flame, who came to play a large role in folklore. II 546b; III 669a; V 1101a; and → ʿAMLŪḲ; ḤINN; KHUSS

djins (A, < Gk) : genus; race. II 550a; sex. II 550b

Under the Circassian rule in the Mamlūk period, *al-djins*, meaning the Race, denoted the Circassian race. II 24b

In music, ~ denotes the 'form' of the ĪḲĀʿ, whose metrical patterns were chosen by the musician by modifying the basic notes. The early music schools knew seven or eight forms. XII 408b

djirāḥa → ʿAMAL BI ʾL-YAD

djirāya (A) : salary, in the terminology of the Azharīs during the Ottoman period; originally, a number of loaves of bread sent daily by the Ottoman sultan to someone. II 413b

djirdjir (A) : in botany, rocket (*Eruca sativa*). IX 653a

djirga (Pash) : an informal tribal assembly of the Pathans in what are now Afghanistan and Pakistan, with competence to intervene and to adjudicate in practically all aspects of private and public life among the Pathans. I 217a; V 1079a; XII 270a

djirm (A) : body, in particular the heavenly bodies. II 554b

djirrat (A) : in Čishtī mysticism, a ~ is a mystic who visits kings and their courts and asks people for money. This was considered an abuse, along with the status of a *muḳallid* (a mystic who has no master), as contact with the state in any form was not permitted. II 55b

djisān → ZAʿFARĀN

djīsh → DJAYSH

djism (A) : body. II 553b; for synonyms, → BADAN; DJASAD; DJIRM

♦ djism taʿlīmī (A) : mathematical body; a term used by Aristotle in contrast to *djism ṭabīʿī* 'physical body'. II 555a

♦ djismiyyāt (A) : a term employed by Abu 'l-Hudhayl to denote the corporeal pleasures of Paradise. II 449b

djisr (A, pl. *djusūr*) : a bridge of wood or of boats. II 555a; IV 555a

In mediaeval Egypt, the plural *djusūr* is used for 'irrigation dams', of which there were two types: the small irrigation dams (*al-djusūr al-baladiyya*), important for conveying water from one field to another in the village, and the great irrigation dams (*al-djusūr al-sulṭāniyya*), constructed for the provinces. V 862b

djiṣṣ (A) : plaster. II 556b

djitr → MIẒALLA

djiwār (A) : protection of another tribe; neighbourhood. I 429b; I 890b; II 558a; IX 864b; and → DJARR AL-DJIWĀR

dji̱zya (A) : the poll-tax levied on non-Muslims in Muslim states. II 490a; II 559a
dji̱önk (T) : a manuscript collection of folk poetry. VIII 171b
dji̱ūʿ (P) : hunger; in mysticism, voluntary hunger was one of the foundations of the Khalwatiyya order. IV 992a
dji̱uʿaydī → ḤARFŪSH
♦ dji̱uʿaydiyya (A) : the populace. XI 546a
dji̱ubba (A) : a woollen tunic with rather narrow sleeves, worn over the shirt, ḲAMĪṢ, by both sexes in the time of the Prophet. V 733b; a coat-like outer garment worn by both sexes today in the Arab East. V 741a; in Tunisia, ~ denotes a full-length, sack-like chemise without sleeves. V 745b; a gown. IX 765a
dji̱ubn (A) : a mild cheese; its residual whey is termed *māʾ al-dji̱ubn*. XII 318b
dji̱udhām (A) : in medicine, leprosy. Other terms for the disease, depending on the symptoms, were *baraṣ, bahaḳ, waḍaḥ* and *ḳawābī*. XII 270b; for more euphemisms, XII 271a; elephantiasis. V89b; X 433a; impetigo. VII 1014a
dji̱ūdī (A) : a large, sea-going ship. III 324b
dji̱uʾdji̱uʾ → ṢADR
dji̱ughrāfiyā (A, < Gk) : geography; in mediaeval Arabic, geography was termed *ṣūrat al-arḍ* or *ḳaṭʿ al-arḍ*, with ~ being explained as 'map of the world and the climes'. The Arabs did not conceive of geography as a science, and the use of ~ for geography is a comparatively modern practice. II 575b
dji̱uhhāl → DJĀHIL
dji̱uhlūl → SHUNḲUB
dji̱uḥūd (A) : in theology, denial of God. XI 478a
dji̱ūkāndār (P) : an official responsible for the care of the ČAWGĀNs and for the conduct of the game of polo. II 17a
dji̱ūkh (A), or *dji̱ūkha* : a wide-sleeved coat worn by men in the Arab East. V 741a; a long, woollen outer robe without sleeves or collar which is closed by a single button at the neck worn by men in North Africa. V 745b
dji̱uʿl (A), or *dji̱ʿāl, dji̱aʿāla, dji̱aʿīla* : in early Islamic warfare, a kind of contract, regarded as degrading, received by mercenary irregulars often drawn from tribal splinter-groups and led by their own chieftains; ~ also served to designate the sum, levied in advance, as insurance against failure to participate in an obligatory razzia. VIII 496b
dji̱ulāb (P) : rose julep. XII 550b
dji̱ulāha : in India, a low Muslim weaver caste. XII 483a
dji̱ulāhiḳ → KAWS AL-BUNDUḲ
dji̱ulandji̱ubīn (P) : rose honey. XII 550b
dji̱ulbān (A) : in botany, bitter-vetch, one of the winter crops in mediaeval Egypt. V 863a
dji̱uldji̱ul → DJARAS
♦ dji̱uldji̱ulān → SIMSIM
dji̱ull → WARD
dji̱ulla → KABŪSH
dji̱ullanār (A, < P *gul-i anār*) : in botany, the blossom of the wild pomegranate tree, also called *al-maẓẓ*. XII 277a
♦ dji̱ullanārī (A) : the deeply saturated yellow colour of the yellow sapphire. XI 262b
dji̱ulūs (A, T *dji̱ülūs*) : accession to the throne. XII 504a
dji̱umʿa → YAWM AL-DJUMʿA
dji̱umhūriyya → MASHYAKHA
dji̱umla (A, pl. *dji̱umal*) : in law, a term meaning a general Qurʾānic statement made more specific only by a ḤADĪTH which supplies a more precise definition, as opposed to NAṢṢ. VII 1029a

In grammar, a sentence. IX 526a

Its plural form *dju̲mal* denotes a compendium or handbook, especially in grammar. VII 536b

dju̲mmār (A) : the pith of the palm-tree, eaten by pre-Islamic Arabs. II 1058b

dju̲mmayz → TĪN

dju̲nd (A, pl. *adju̲nād*) : an armed troop. Under the Umayyads, ~ was applied especially to (Syrian) military settlements and districts in which were quartered Arab soldiers who could be mobilised for seasonal campaigns or more protracted expeditions. Later, ~ took on the wider meaning of armed forces. II 601a; IX 263b

Under the Mamlūks, ~ is sometimes applied to a category of soldiers in the sultan's service, but distinct from the personal guard. II 601b

For geographers of the 3rd/9th and 4th/10th centuries, the plural *adju̲nād* denoted the large towns. II 601b; V 125a

dju̲ndub (A) : in zoology, the locust. V 566b

dju̲ng (P) : lit. boat; an informal notebook with poetical fragments. VII 529a; VII 602a

djū̲nī → ḲAṬĀ

dju̲nna → DARAḲA

dju̲nub (A) : in law, a person who is in a state of major ritual impurity. II 440b

dju̲ra → ṬUNBŪR

dju̲rad̲h̲ (A, pl. *dji̲rd̲h̲ān, dju̲rd̲h̲ān*) : in zoology, a term defining all rats of a large size without distinction of species. XII 285b

♦ dju̲rad̲h̲ān (A) : 'the two rats', the name of the two symmetrical dorsal muscles of the horse. XII 286b

♦ dju̲rd̲h̲āna (A) : the name of a variety of date, on the Arabian peninsula. XII 286b

dju̲raydī 'l-nak̲h̲l (Ir) : 'palm-tree rat', a term used in ʿIrāḳ to designate the ichneumon or Egyptian mongoose, sub-species *persicus* or *auropunctatus*. VIII 49b

dju̲rdju̲nadji̊ (T) : a comic dancer. VIII 178b

dju̲rm → DJARĪMA

dju̲rn → HĀWIN

dju̲rnal (A) : under Muḥammad ʿAlī of Egypt, a 'daily administrative report'; the term was borrowed during the reign of Ottoman sultan ʿAbd al-Ḥamīd I to denote written denunciations. I 64a

dju̲rūf (A) : in Yemen, caves hewn out of the rock. X 449b

dju̲sūr → DJISR

dju̲zʾ (A, pl. *adju̲zāʾ*) : part, particle; a technical term used in scholastic theology (*kalām*) and philosophy to describe the philosophical atom in the sense of the ultimate (substantial) part that cannot be divided further, sometimes also called *al-dju̲zʾ al-wāḥid*. II 220a; II 607b

In prosody, the eight rhythmic feet which recur in definite distribution and sequence in all metres. I 669b

In the science of the Qurʾān, ~ is a division of the Qurʾān for purposes of recitation. II 607b

In literature, a booklet. XI 354b

djū̲z s̲h̲ikastan (P) : 'breaking the nut', a rite performed by the superior of the ʿAlī-Ilāhīs. X 398a

dju̲zāf (A) : in law, buying or selling provisions wholesale without fixing weights and measures. X 467b; unascertained quantities. XII 703b

dju̲zāzāt (A) : index cards, as for example the collection in the Egyptian Academy of Science that was prepared for the historical dictionary and for the dictionary of technical and scientific terms. V 1092b

do'āb (P) : lit. two waters; in the subcontinent of India, ~ is generally applied to the land lying between two confluent rivers, and more particularly to the fertile plain between the Jamna and the Ganges in present Uttar Pradesh in India. II 609b; XI 1a

dogāh → SHASHMAḲOM

doghandji (T) : falconer. Hawking was a favourite traditional sport at the Ottoman court. II 614a

dohā : in Indo-Persian poetry, couplet. XII 483a

dokkali (B) : woollen and cotton wall covers, once a major craftsmanship in Adrar, Algeria. I 210b

dolāb (T) : a swivel-box, through which servant in Ottoman Turkish houses of the upper class communicated with the women's apartments. IV 899a

dolama (T) : a caftan worn by the least important Ottoman palace servants, which had a long robe, fastened in front, with narrow sleeves. V 752a

dōlī (H) : a litter used in India for transporting people. It is a simple rectangular frame or bedstead, usually suspended by the four corners from a bamboo pole and carried by two or four men; when used by women there are usually curtains hanging from the bamboo. The ~ was much used for the transport of sick persons, and in war to carry casualties off the battlefield. A form where the frame is supported on two poles is used as the bier to transport a corpse to the burial-ground. VII 932a

dombra : a lute used in Kazakhstan, with two or three strings. X 733b

donādon (K), or *kirās gihorrīn* 'changing one's shirt' : reincarnation, a belief of the YAZĪDĪ religion. XI 314a

donanma (T) : a fleet of ships, navy; the decoration of the streets of a city for a Muslim festival or on a secular occasion of public rejoicing such as a victory, and, more particularly, the illumination of the city by night and the firework displays which formed part of these celebrations. II 615a

dönüm (T, A *dūnam*) : the standard measure of area in the Turkish lands of the Ottoman empire and the Arabic lands of ʿIrāḳ, Syria and Palestine directly under Ottoman rule until 1918, originally considered to equal one day's ploughing. In Turkey it equalled 939 m^2 (approx. 1,000 sq. yards), but in the 19th century the new ~ was equated with the hectare; in 1934 the metric system of weights and measures was officially adopted by the Turkish Republic. In Syria and Palestine in recent times, the ~ is 1,000 m^2 = 0.247 acres, while in Iraq a larger ~ of 2,500 m^2 is used, despite the official adoption of the metric system in 1931. II 32b; V 474a; VII 138a

dört (T) : four.

♦ dört bölük (T), or *bölükat-i erbaʿa* : a collective name for the four lowest cavalry regiments of the ḲAPÎ ḲULLARÎ. They were regarded as inferior in comparison to the remaining two higher divisions, the *sipāhī oghlanlarî* and the *silāḥdārlar*. II 1097b

♦ dört ḳapî (T) : 'four doors', a doctrine of the Bektāshiyya, comprising *ṭarīḳa, ḥaḳīḳa, maʿrifa* and *sharīʿa*. X 332b

♦ dörtlük (T) : in Turkish prosody, a strophe consisting of four lines, hence synonymous with the term RUBĀʿĪ in its broader sense. VIII 580b

doston (Taj) : a lyrical epic poem. X 65b

drafsh-i kāwiyān (P) : the Iranian national flag; according to legend, it was the apron of the blacksmith Kāwah, who brought about the fall of the tyrant Zohak. IV 775a

duʿā' (A, pl. *adʿiya*) : appeal, invocation (addressed to God) either on behalf of another or for oneself, or against someone; hence, prayer of invocation. II 617a

In the science of diplomatic, ~ is the formula of benediction for the addressee. II 302a; II 314b

In prosody, ~ is the sixth and final section of a ḲAṢĪDA, wherein the poet implores God for the prosperity of the sultan or person to whom the poem is addressed and expresses his thanks for the completion of the work. IV 715b; V 956b; V 960a

♦ du'ā' al-wasīla → TAṢLIYA

♦ du'ākh^w^ān → BĀKHSHĪ

dūbaytī → RUBĀ'Ī

dubb al-baḥr (A) : in zoology, the sea lion, also called *asad al-baḥr* and *baḳrat al-baḥr*. VIII 1022b

dubbā' → ḲUTHTHĀ'

dūd al-ḳazz (A) : in zoology, the silkworm. X 752a

dudjr → DADJR

dudjūr → DADJR

duff (A) : in music, the generic term for any instrument of the tambourine family. II 620a

dūgh → AYRAN

dügün → TOY

ḍuḥā (A) : 'forenoon', the first part of the day, up to the moment when the sun has traversed a quarter of the diurnal arc. II 622b; V 709b

♦ ṣalāt al-ḍuḥā (A) : a sixth prayer performed in some circles, on top of the five compulsory prayers, at the same time before midday as the 'AṢR was performed after midday. VII 28a

duhn (A, pl. *adhān*) : oil extracted from any plant other than the olive. XI 486a

♦ duhn al-ḥall (A), or *ṣalīṭ djuldjulān, shīradj* (P *shīra*) : the oil of sesame. IX 615a; XI 486a

duhul (A, P *dohol*) : a drum with a shorter body than the long-bodied cylindrical drum, mentioned by Nāṣir-i Khusraw as one of the martial instruments of the Fāṭimids. In Egypt of modern times it is known as *ṭabl al-baladī*. X 33b

dūka (Tun) : a pointed bonnet for women. V 745b

dukhān → TUTUN

dukhla (A) : 'entering', consummation of a marriage. The wedding night was known as *laylat al-~*. X 903a; X 905b

dukhn (A) : in botany, the small sorghum (*Pennisetum spicatum*) widespread in the Sudan and also called Moorish millet. XII 249b

duḳmaḳ (A) : in zoology, a silurus of the Nile, the Euphrates and the Niger, whose Arabic term is found again in the Latinised nomenclature to specify a sub-species limited to a particular region (*Bagrus docmac*). VIII 1021b

dūlāb (P, pl. *dawālīb*) : a water-wheel. Al-Muḳaddasī (4th/10th century) noted that there were many alongside the banks of the Nile for irrigating orchards during the low waters. According to him, the *ḳādūs* was the bucket. V 863b f.

dulband → TULBAND

dūm (A) : in botany, jujube-like fruits of the *Ziziphus* trees, highly valued for food. IX 549a

du'mūṣ (A) : the maggot. VIII 1022a

dūnam → DÖNÜM

dunbak, or *tanbak* → DARABUKKA

dundj → 'IKBIR

dunyā (A) : lit. nearer, nearest; in theology, this (base) world, as opposed to DĪN and the correlative ĀKHIRA. II 295a; II 626b

durāb (A) : in zoology, the chirocentrus, whose Arabic term is found again in the Latinised nomenclature to specify a sub-species limited to a particular region (*Chirocentrus dorab*). VIII 1021b

durāda (A, < Sp *dorado*) : in zoology, the goldfish (*Sparus aurata*). VIII 1021a

durar → DURR

dūrbāsh (P) : lit. be distant; the mace or club used as an emblem of military dignity, and in Persian and Turkish usage, the functionary who carries the mace. II 627b durḳāʿa → ḲĀʿA

durr (A), or *durar* : pearl. II 628a; artistic poetry of high quality. IX 448b; and → LUʾLUʾ

durrāʿa (A) : the gown worn by a secretary (*kātib*) in mediaeval times. IV 756a; in Syria and Palestine, a woman's outer coat, open in front, sometimes synonymous with DJUBBA. V 741a; in North Africa, a long robe with sleeves for both sexes. V 746a

durūd → TAṢLIYA

dūṣ : in metallugry, cast iron. V 971b

dūshāb (P) : in the mediaeval Near East, a drink from syrup or from preserves of fruit which is sometimes non-alcoholic, but which is frequently mentioned in the context of drinks which can ferment and become alcoholic. VI 720b

dūshākh (P) : a crown-like hat with a pointed rim on either side, worn by men of high rank in Saldjūḳ Persia and of Inner Asian, Turkish origin. V 748a

dustūr (A) : originally from Persian, ~ seems originally to have meant a person exercising authority, whether religious or political. Later, ~ acquired a specialised meaning, designating members of the Zoroastrian priesthood. The word occurs in *Kalīla wa-dimna* in the sense of 'counsellor'. More commonly it was used in the sense of rule or regulation, and in particular the code of rules and conduct of the guilds. In Arabic, ~ was employed in a variety of meanings, notably 'army pay-list', 'model or formulary', 'leave', and also, addressed to a human being or to invisible DJINN, 'permission'. In modern Arabic, ~ means constitution. II 638a; and → DASTŪR

Under the Ayyūbids, ~ meant a legal release from a campaign. The term gradually died out in the period of the Mamlūks. III 186b

In astronomy, a circular instrument, known also as *al*-SHAKKĀZIYYA. V 84a

♦ düstūr (T) : principle, precedent, code or register of rules; applied in particular to the great series of volumes, containing the texts of new laws, published in Istanbul (and later Ankara) from 1279/1863 onwards. II 640a

♦ dustūr-i mükerrem (T) : one of the honorific titles of the grand vizier of the Ottoman empire. II 638a

dutār (T), variants *dotar, dūtār* : in music, a lute with two strings. VIII 234b; X 733b f.

dūwār → DAWĀR

duwwāma (A) : the game of tops (syn. *khudhrūf*). V 616b

duyūn → DAYN

duzale : a Kurdish flute with two pipes of reed or bird bone, pierced with holes and whose mouthpiece has a kind of vibratory tongue. The sound resembles that of the Scottish bagpipes. V 478a

duzdīdha → ANDARGĀH

düzen (T) : in music, the tunings [of the lute]. IX 120b

E

efe (T) : the chief of the Zeybek or Turkish mountaineers in Western Anatolia. His word was law, even to the extent of whether one could marry another. His assistant was called *kızan*. XI 493b

efendi (T, < Gk) : an Ottoman title, already in use in the 7th/13th and 8th/14th centuries in Turkish Anatolia. A 16th-century FATWĀ applied the term to the owner of slaves and slave-girls. Later, ~ became increasingly common in Ottoman usage as a designation of members of the scribal and religious, as opposed to the military, classes, in particular of certain important functionaries. During the 13th/19th century, although the Ottoman government made attempts to regulate the use of the term by law, ~ was used, following the personal name, as a form of address or reference for persons possessing a certain standard of literacy, and not styled BEY or PA<u>SH</u>A; ~ thus became an approximate equivalent of the English mister or French monsieur. In 1934 it was finally abolished, but has remained in common use as a form of address for both men and women. I 75a; II 687a

eflāḳ (T, < Ger *Wallach*) : under the Ottomans, ~ denoted the Balkan Rumanians and those north of the Danube. II 687b; II 915a

efsane (T, < P *afsāna*) : legend; completely fantastic story, fabricated or superstitious. III 373b

eklan → IMG<u>H</u>AD

elči (T) : envoy, messenger; in Ottoman diplomacy, the normal word for ambassador, although *sefīr* (< A SAFĪR) was used. II 694a; and → MAṢLAḤATGÜZĀR; SAFĪR
In eastern Turkish, ruler of a land or people. II 694a

elifi nemed (T) : a woollen initiatic girdle, worn by the Mewlewīs, so called because with its tapering end when laid out flat, it resembled the letter *alif*. They also wore a second type of woollen girdle, the *tīg<u>h</u>bend*, during their dance, in order to hold in place the ample skirt of the garment known as the TENNŪRE. IX 167b

emānet (T) : the function or office of an EMĪN. II 695b; the system of collection of MUḲĀṬAʿA revenues directly by the *emīn*. II 147b

♦ **emānet-i muḳadesse** (T) : the name given to a collection of relics preserved in the treasury of the Topkapı palace in Istanbul. II 695b

♦ emāneten (T) : one of three principal ways in which mining activity was organised in the Ottoman empire, the others being ILTIZĀMEN and IḤĀLE; ~ meant the direct administration of mines or mining districts through state-appointed superintendents. V 974b

emīn (T, < A AMĪN) : an Ottoman administrative title usually translated intendant or commissioner. Primarily, an ~ was a salaried officer appointed by or in the name of the sultan, to administer, supervise or control a department, function or source of revenue. The term is used also of agents and commissioners appointed by authorities other than the sultan, and at times, by abuse, the ~ appears as tax-farmer. II 695b

emr (T, < A AMR) : a term denoting a general order issued in the name of the Ottoman sultan, as well as a special order which decreed the issue of a BERĀT. I 1170a

enderūn (T) : inside.
Under the Ottomans, ~ was used to designate the inside service (as opposed to BĪRŪN, the outside service) of the imperial household of the Ottoman sultan, comprising four departments, viz. the Privy Chamber, the Treasury, the Privy Larder, and the Great and Little Chambers. II 697b; IV 1097a

entārī (T) : a kind of caftan, worn in the Ottoman period under the real caftan and fur, descending as far as the ankle or covering the knee. V 752a

enzel (Tun, < A **inzāl**) : in law, a perpetual lease system found not only on 'habous' (inalienable property, the yield of which is devoted to pious purposes) but also on private, *mulk*, properties, peculiar to Tunisia. XII 369a; XII 423a

eren → ERMI<u>SH</u>

ermi<u>sh</u> (T, < 'to reach, attain') : with *baba, ata, eren* and *yatir*, a term for saint in the Turkish world.

eshām (T, < A **ashām**, s. *sahm* 'share') : the word used in Turkey to designate certain treasury issues, variously described as bonds, assignats and annuities. Although the ~ reverted to the state on the death of the holder, they could be sold, the state claiming a duty of one year's income on each such transfer. The ~ were introduced in the early years of the reign of Muṣṭafā III and the practice was continued by later sultans; their purpose and names varied from time to time. I 692b

eshkindji (T), or *eshkündji* : a term in the Ottoman army denoting in general a soldier who joined the army on an expedition. As a special term, ~ designated auxiliary soldiers whose expenses were provided by the people of peasant, *reʿāyā* (→ RAʿIYYA), status. From the mid-10th/16th century, the ~ lost importance and gradually disappeared. II 714b; cavalry participating in the campaigns. X 503a

esrār : a pandore viol from India, with the TĀWŪS one of the two best-known examples. The ~ has a membrane on its face and has five strings played with the bow together with a number of sympathetic strings. VIII 348b

eyālet (T, < A *iyāla*) : in the Ottoman empire, the largest administrative division under a governor-general, BEGLERBEGI. An ~ was composed of SANDJAKS, which was the basic administrative unit. The ~ system was replaced by that of *wilāyet* in 1281/1864. I 468b; I 906b; II 721b

ezan → ADHĀN

F

fāʾ (A) : the twentieth letter of the Arabic alphabet, transcribed *f*, with the numerical value 80. It is defined as fricative, labio-dental, unvoiced. II 725a

faḍāʾil (A, s. **faḍīla**) : lit. virtues, a genre of literature exposing the excellences of things, individuals, groups, places, regions and such for the purpose of a *laudatio*. II 728b; VI 350a

In Mamlūk terminology, ~, or *kamālāt*, was often applied to the exercises necessary for the mastery of horse-riding. II 954b

♦ faḍāʾil al-afʿāl (A) : in the science of Tradition, a genre consisting of Traditions that list human actions which are believed to be particularly pleasing to God. VIII 983a

fadān (A) : a word that seems to have been applied at the same time to the yoke, to the pair of oxen and to the implement that they pull to till the land, i.e. the tiller. An evolved form, FADDĀN, came to designate also the area that a pair of oxen could till in a given time. VII 21b

faddān (A) : a yoke of oxen; the standard measure of land in Egypt in former times. It was defined by al-Ḳalḳashandī (9th/15th century) as equalling 400 square ḲAṢABAS, i.e. 6,368 m^2. Since 1830, the ~ has corresponded to 4200.833 m^2. VII 138a

fadhlaka (A, < *fa-dhālika*) : in mathematics, the sum, total. Besides being placed at the bottom of an addition to introduce the result, ~ is also employed for the summing up of a petition, report, or other document. By extension, ~ acquired the meaning of compendium. II 727b

faḍīkh (A) : a kind of date, from which wine was made. IV 995b; a drink composed of fruits (dates, etc.) mixed in water. VI 720b; an intoxicating drink made from different kinds of dates. VII 840a

faḍīla → FAḌĀʾIL

fadjdjāʾ → FARʿ

fadjr (A) : dawn, daybreak.

♦ al-fadjr al-kādhib (A), or *al-ṣubḥ al-kādhib* : lit. the false dawn; the Arabic term for the column of zodiacal light which is a symmetrically converse phenomenon in the circadian cycle (syn. *dhanab al-sirḥān* 'the wolf's tail') during which prayers are forbidden. It is followed by the 'true dawn', *al-ṣubḥ al-ṣādiḳ*. VIII 928b; IX 179b

♦ ṣalāt al-fadjr (A) : the morning prayer which is to be performed in the period from daybreak, or 'the true dawn', when faces can still not yet be recognised, until before sunrise. VII 27b; VIII 928b faḍl → DĀʾIR; RAḤMA; ṢILA

fāfīr (Egy) : in Egypt, the term used for papyrus. VIII 261a

fag̲h̲fūr (P), or *bag̲h̲būr* : title of the emperor of China in the Muslim sources. II 738a

♦ fag̲h̲fūrī : Chinese (porcelain). The term has entered Modern Greek in the sense of porcelain, and also Slav languages, through the Russian *farfor*. II 738a; III 345b

fāg̲h̲iya, fag̲h̲w → ḤINNĀʾ

fahd (A, < Gk or L *pardus* ?; P *yūz*) : in zoology, the cheetah (*Acinonyx jubatus*). II 738b

fāḥis̲h̲a (A) : a sin. XI 509a

faḥl (A, pl. *fuḥūl*) : lit. stallion; in literature, a term given to a powerful poet. I 405b; XII 648b

fahm → IDRĀK

faḥm (A) : in mineralogy, coal, used in early Islam as fuel for ovens while its ashes were utilised as a cleaning agent. V 118a; V 965a; a sort of charcoal. VII 886a

fahrasa (A, < P *fihrist*) : the name given in Muslim Spain to kinds of catalogues, in which scholars enumerated their masters and the subjects or works studied under their direction. Synonyms of this term are: *barnāmad̲j̲, t̲h̲abat, mas̲h̲īk̲h̲a* (*mas̲h̲yak̲h̲a*) and *muʿd̲j̲am*. The genre, which appears to be a particular speciality of the Andalusians, should be associated with the transmission of ḤADĪT̲H̲. I 96b; II 743b

fāʿil (A) : in grammar, the agent. VIII 384a

fāʾit (A), or *fawāt* : continuation of a work (syn. *ṣila*), but connoting discontinuity in relation to the original work. IX 604a

fāʾiẓ → AL-MĀL AL-ḤURR

faḳʿ (A) : on the Arabian peninsula, truffles. I 540b

fak̲h̲k̲h̲ār (A) : earthenware vase, pottery, ceramics, produced by practically every country in the Islamic world. II 745a

fak̲h̲r (A) : self-praise. VIII 376b

♦ fak̲h̲riyya (T, < A) : in Turkish prosody, ~ is the last but one section of a ḲAṢĪDA, wherein the poet praises himself. IV 715b

fāḳiʿ (A) : said of the child who has become active, and has started to grow. VIII 822a

faḳīh (A, pl. *fuḳahāʾ*) : in its non-technical meaning ~ denotes anyone possessing knowledge, *fiḳh,* of a thing (syn. *ʿālim*, pl. *ʿulamāʾ*). II 756a

In law, ~ became the technical term for a specialist in religious law and in particular its derivative details, *furūʿ*. In older terminology, however, ~ as opposed to *ʿālim* denotes the speculative, systematic lawyer as opposed to the specialist in the traditional elements of religious law. II 756a; and → MUTAFAḲḲIH

In several Arabic dialects, forms like *fiḳī* have come to denote a schoolmaster in a KUTTĀB or a professional reciter of the Qurʾān. II 756a

faḳīr (A, pl. *fuḳarāʾ*) : a needy person, a pauper; its etymological meaning is 'one whose backbone is broken'.

In mysticism, a ~ is a person 'who lives for God alone'. Total rejection of private property and resignation to the will of God were considered essential for the ~ who aspired to gnosis. II 757b

In irrigation terminology (pl. *fuḳur*), the water outlet of a canal, ḲANĀT; a well or group of wells linked by a gallery. IV 532b

fakk → ĪWĀN

fakkāk (A) : the individual who devotes himself totally or episodically to the ransoming of Muslims held captive by infidels; in the Muslim West by the 13th century, ~ came to denote the man who liberates a captive, whether Muslim or not, as an extension of the equivalent appearing in a Christian context, called *alfaqueque* in Castillian. XII 307a faḳḳūs (A) : in botany, unripe melons, one of the summer crops in mediaeval Egypt. V 863a

faḳr (A) : poverty. XI 141b

fa'l (A) : an omen, appearing in varied forms, ranging from simple sneezing, certain peculiarities of persons and things that one encounters, to the interpretation of the names of persons and things which present themselves spontaneously to the sight, hearing and mind of man. II 758b

♦ **fāl-nāme** (P) : book of divination, consulted in the Muslim East (especially in Iranian and Turkish countries) in order to know the signs or circumstances that are auspicious for some decision. II 761b

falad̲j̲ (A, pl. *aflād̲j̲*) : the term used in Oman, Trucial Oman, and Bahrain to designate an underground aqueduct with surface apertures to facilitate cleaning. This type of aqueduct, which may be of Persian origin, is now called SĀḲĪ (pronounced *sād̲j̲ī*, pl. *sawād̲j̲ī*) in al-Aflād̲j̲, the district in Nad̲j̲d which takes its name from ~. I 233a; I 539a; IV 531b

falak (A, pl. *aflāk*) : sphere, in particular the Celestial Sphere. II 761b; VIII 101b

♦ falak al-awd̲j̲ → AL-FALAK AL-K̲H̲ĀRID̲J̲ AL-MARKAZ

♦ falak al-burūd̲j̲ (A) : in astronomy, the term for L. *ecliptica*. II 762b

♦ falak al-d̲j̲awzahar (A) : in astronomy, the massive ball into which, according to Ibn al-Hayt̲h̲am, the moon is inserted, and which carries it along as it moves. V 536a

♦ al-falak al-ḥāmil (A) : in astronomy, the deferent. II 762b; IX 292b

♦ al-falak al-k̲h̲ārid̲j̲ al-markaz (A), or *falak al-awd̲j̲* : in astronomy, the term for L. *excentricus*. II 762b

♦ al-falak al-māʾil (A) : in astronomy, the term for L. *circulus obliquus* (or *deflectens*). II 762b

♦ al-aflāk al-māʾila ʿan falak muʿaddil al-nahār (A) : in astronomy, the term for the circles parallel to the equator. II 762b

♦ falak muʿaddil al-nahār (A) : in astronomy, the term for L. *circulus aequinoctialis* (the celestial equator). II 762b

♦ al-falak al-mumat̲h̲t̲h̲al li-falak al-burūd̲j̲ (A) : in astronomy, the term for L. *circulus pareclipticus*. II 762b

♦ al-falak al-mustaḳīm (A) : the astronomical term for L. *sphaera recta*, the celestial sphere as appearing to the inhabitants of the equatorial region, where the celestial equator passes through the zenith. II 762b

♦ falak al-tadwīr (A) : in astronomy, the epicycle. II 762b; IX 292b

falaḳa (A) : an apparatus used for immobilising the feet in order to apply a bastinado on the soles of the feet. The ~ existed in three different forms: a plank with two holes in it, of the pillory type; two poles joined at one end; or a single, fairly stout pole with a cord fixed at the two ends. In the Muslim East, especially among the Turks, the ~ was used as an instrument of torture, while in North Africa its use was confined to the schoolmaster. II 763b

falāsifa (A, < Gk; s. *faylasūf*) : the Greek thinkers; philosophers. II 764b

fālid̲j̲ (A, pl. *fawālid̲j̲*) : the *camelus bactrianus*, or camel proper, with two humps. III 665b

In medicine, hemiplegia. V 89b; VIII 111a; IX 8a

falīd̲j̲a (A), and *s̲h̲uḳḳa* : bands of hair or wool forming the awning of an Arab tent. They were sewn side-by-side and formed a rectangle. Those that were placed at the two edges, that is, those that form the larger side of the rectangle, were called *kisr* or *kasr*. IV 1147b

fallāḥ (A, pl. *fallāḥīn*) : ploughman; member of the sedentary rural population. I 575a; II 899a

fallāḳ (A, B *fellāga*) : brigands and subsequently rebels in Tunisia and Algeria. Originally the term was applied to individuals who wished to escape punishment, to deserters, and to fugitive offenders, who eventually formed bands supporting themselves by brigandage. The uprising brought about by Khalīfa b. ʿAskar in southern Tunisia in 1915 gave new meaning to the word. Later, the incidents which occurred in Tunisia between 1952 and 1954, as well as the Algerian rebellion in 1954, made the term popular again. II 767b

fallāta : term, strictly signifying the Fulānī, used in the Nilotic Sudan for Muslim immigrants from the western *bilād al-sūdān*, and in particular those from northern Nigeria, many of whom are primarily pilgrims en route to Mecca. ~ has largely superseded the older *takārir* or *takārna*. II 767b

fals (A, pl. *fulūs*) : the name of the copper or bronze coin, regardless of its size or weight. II 768a

In astronomy, a small ring placed under the wedge at the front of the astrolabe to protect one of the movable parts of the instrument, the 'spider', and ensure a smooth turning. I 723a

falsafa (A, < Gk) : Greek thought; philosophy. ~ began as a search by Muslims with shīʿī leanings for a coherence in their intellectual and spiritual life, evolving later to grow closer to orthodox KALĀM and finally fusing with it. II 769b

falta (A) : a precipitate, arbitrary act, excusable only because God had bestowed success on it. IX 422a

falṭīṭa (A), or *djalṭīṭa, djanṭīṭa* : a skirt of Spanish origin worn mainly by Jewish and Andalusian women in the Muslim West. V 746a

fam → ʿAYN

fanāʾ → BAḲĀʾ WA-FANĀʾ

fanak (A, < P; pl. *afnāk*) : in zoology, the fennec-fox (*Fennecus zerda*), in the Muslim West, and the Corsac or Karagan Fox (*Vulpes corsac*, < T *ḳūrsāḳ*), in the Muslim East. However, in the imagination of all the authors who used the word, ~ must have meant the mink (*Mustela lutreola*), whose pelt was greatly esteemed in the luxury fur-trade. II 775a

fānī → PĪR

fānīd → SUKKAR

fann (A) : the modern name for art. II 775b

♦ fann al-multazim (A) : committed art, that is, art that shows social concern, first examples of which are to be found after the Suez crisis in Egypt. X 365b

faʾr (A, pl. *fiʾrān, fiʾara, fuʾar*) : in zoology, the majority of types and species of the sub-order of the Myomorphs; the family of Soricids. XII 285b, where can be found many synonyms and varieties

♦ faʾr firʿawn (A) : lit. Pharaoh's rat; in Egypt, with the geographical sub-species *pharaonis*, the ichneumon or Egyptian mongoose, sometimes called *ḳiṭṭ firʿawn* 'Pharaoh's cat'. VIII 49b

farʿ (A, pl. *furūʿ*) : a branch; in archery, a self-bow (syn. *fadjdjāʾ, fidjw, munfadjā*). IV 798a

In fiscal law, ~ was a supplementary increase, discovered or invented in the course of history, upon the official taxes for the defrayal of attendant expenses or any other reason. I 1144a; IV 1041a; and → FURŪʿ AL-FIḲH

In military science, *furūʿ* are the operations by the irregulars, who do not form part of the army proper but who may play a part in the preliminaries and on the fringes of the battle. III 182a

In prosody, the *furūʿ* are the modifications in the feet of the metres, due to deviations, e.g. *mu[s]tafʿilun* becomes *mutafʿilun* when its *sīn* is lost, the 'normal' foot being part

of the *uṣūl* (→ AṢL) form of the feet, and the altered foot, one of the *furūʿ*. I 671b
As a literary topos, ~ denoted thick, soft and fragrant hair. IX 313a

♦ furūʿ al-fiḳh (A) : in law, the body of positive rules derived from the sources of legal knowledge, *uṣūl al-fiḳh* (→ AṢL). I 257b; II 889b; IX 323b

faraʿa (A, pl. *furuʿ*) : the firstling of a flock or herd, sacrificed in the pre-Islamic period during the month of Radjab as an invocation to the deities to increase the number of flocks. VIII 373b

faradjiyya (A) : a long-sleeved man's robe in Egypt. V 741a; a green robe. XII 612b; the Moroccan variant *faradjiyya* (B *tafaradjit*) is a very light gown with a deep slit at the breast which may or may not have sleeves and is worn under the KHAFTĀN or garment by both sexes. It also comes in a half-length version called *nuṣṣ faradjiyya*. V 746a

farāʾiḍ (A, s. *farīḍa*) : lit. appointed or obligatory portions; as a technical term, ~ means the fixed shares in an estate which are given to certain heirs according to the provisions of Muslim law. The whole of the Islamic law of inheritance is called *ʿilm al-farāʾiḍ*. II 783a; VII 106b

farakh (P) : a type of cloth brocade, which along with a type called *mushtī* was manufactured especially in Yazd. XI 304a

farāmush-khāna (P) : in Iran, a centre of masonic activities, freemasonry seemingly having come over from India where the first lodge was founded by the British in 1730. XII 290a

faras (A) : in zoology, the horse (*Equus caballus*) in the sense of saddle-horse, the rider of which is termed FĀRIS. II 784b; II 800a; IV 1143b; the chesspiece. IX 366b
In astronomy, a wedge which is fitted into a slit in the narrow end of the broadheaded pin at the front of the astrolabe to prevent the pin from coming out. I 723a; a 'cavallo'. X 367b

♦ faras al-baḥr (A) : in zoology, the bellows fish (*Centriscus*). VIII 1021a

♦ **faras al-māʾ** (A) : in zoology, the hippopotamus. XII 294a

farāsha (A, P *parwāna*) : in zoology, the moth. IX 282a

faraṭ (A) : lit. dying before one's parents; a child who dies before reaching maturity. VIII 821b

fard (A, pl. *afrād*) : 'only, solitary, unique, incomplete, incomparable'; in prosody, ~ denotes a line of verse taken in isolation (intact or reduced to a single hemistich). II 789b
In lexicography, *afrād* are the words handed down by one single lexicographer, as distinct from *āḥād* and *mafārīd*. II 790a
In the science of Tradition, ~ is synonomous with *gharīb muṭlaḳ* and means a Tradition in which the second link of the chain of those who have transmitted it is only represented by a single transmitter. II 790a; ~ is used of an ISNĀD with only one transmitter at each stage, or of a Tradition transmitted only by people of one district. III 25b
In astronomy, ~ denotes the star alpha in Hydra, *al-shudjāʿ*, and hence the most brilliant. II 790a
In arithmetic, *al-ʿadad al-fard* is the odd number (from 3 upwards, inclusive), as opposed to the even number, *al-ʿadad al-zawdj*. II 790a
In theology and philosophy, ~ denotes the species, as restricted by the bond of individuation. II 790a
In mysticism, *al-afrād* are seven in number and occupy the fourth category in the hierarchy of the saints. I 95a

farḍ (A), or *farīḍa* : lit. something which has been apportioned, or made obligatory; as a technical term in religious law, ~ is a religious duty or obligation, the omission of which will be punished and the performance of which will be rewarded. It is one of the so-called *al-aḥkām al-khamsa*, the five qualifications by which every act of man is qualified. II 790a; VIII 486b

♦ farḍ ʿayn (A) : the individual duty such as ritual prayer, fasting, etc. II 790a; VIII 497b

♦ farḍ kifāya (A) : the collective duty, the fulfilment of which by a sufficient number of individuals excuses others from fulfilling it, such as funeral prayer, holy war, etc. II 539a; II 790a; VIII 497b

farhang (P) : politeness, knowledge, education; dictionary.

In recent decades, ~ has come to be used also in the sense of culture, while *farhangistān* has been adopted for 'academy'. V 1095b

farhangistān → FARHANG

farīḍa → FARĀʾIḌ; FARḌ

fāridj → KATŪM

farīḳ → ṢAFF

fārīna (A) : a soft variety of wheat, grown in Algeria. The indigenous hard variety, *triticum durum*, was known as *gemḥ*. IX 537b

farīr → FAZZ; SAKHLA

fāris (A, (pl. *fursān*, *fawāris*) : the rider on horseback (and thus not applicable to a man riding a camel or mule), implying, in contrast to *rākib* 'horseman', the valiant, the champion, the intrepid warrior. II 800a

farḳ (A, (pl. *furūḳ*) : like FAṢL, separation, difference; in law, the decisive difference that brings about a different legal determination, ḤUKM, that is, that indicates the difference between outwardly similar cases. XII 517a

farḳad (A) : in astronomy, the star 'the oryx calf' (= Phercad), γ *Ursae minoris*, and with the associated β *Ursae minoris* together form *al-farḳadayn* (= Elfarcadin) 'the two calves', the 'guardians' of the North Pole. V 1230a; VII 51a; and → FAZZ

farmān (P, T *fermān*) : originally command, but by the 9th/15th century, ~ had come to denote the edict or document, as issued by the ruler, itself. There were many synonyms, such as *ḥukm*, *mithāl* and *raḳam*, which later came to designate a document issued by authorities of lower rank. II 309a; II 803a

♦ farmān-i bayāḍī : in the Mughal period, a confidential and important FARMĀN, not involving a sum of money, which received only a royal seal and was folded and dispatched in such a way that its contents remained private to the recipient. II 806a

farmāsūniyya (A) : freemasonry. XII 296a; and → FARĀMUSH-KHĀNA

farrān (A) : an oven-worker. V 41b

In Morocco, a communal oven. V 41b

farrāsh (A) : lit. spreader of the carpets; a servant who looks after the beds and the house generally. IV 899a; an attendant in a library. VI 199a; and → YURTČÏ

farrūdj (A) : a robe similar to the ḲABĀʾ, but slit in the back, worn in the Prophet's time. V 733b

farsakh (P), and *farsang* : a measure of distance on a time basis, originally the distance which could be covered on foot in an hour: approx. 5.94 km for cavalry, and 4 km for foot-soldiers. In present-day Iran, the ~ is now fixed at precisely 6 km. II 812b

farsang → FARSAKH

farsha → ʿATABA

fārsī (P, A), also *pārsī* : in linguistics, the name for modern Persian, the official language of Iran. *~-i darī* or simply DARĪ is also used in native sources, referring to the oldest and most respected variety of (Classical) literary Persian or simply as an equivalent of ~. XII 427a ff.

♦ fārsī-nigārī (P) : a simple Persian style of writing, with a minimum of Arabic loan words. XI 238b

♦ fārsī-i ʿāmiyāna (P) : Persian as it is written and spoken in Tehran, which is becoming the common spoken standard all over Iran. XII 433b

♦ fārsī-i bāstānī (P) : denomination for 'old archaic' modern Persian vs. *fārsī-i naw*, a 'new' variety, sometimes found in scholarly publications. XII 428b

♦ fārsī-i naw → FĀRSĪ-I BĀSTĀNĪ

farūdiyya (A) : a square kerchief bound around the cap by women in Egypt. V 741a; X 612a

farw (A), or *farwa* : a fur; a garment made of, or trimmed with, fur. Although *farwa* can mean also a cloak of camel-hair, it is likely that this term in ancient poetry refers to sheepskins with the wool left on (in Morocco called *haydūra*), used as carpets, to cover seats, or for protection against the cold. II 816b

fa's → ḤAKMA

faṣāḥa (A) : clarity, purity; in rhetoric, ~ is the term for the purity and euphony of language, and can be divided into three kinds: *faṣāḥat al-mufrad*, with respect to a single word when it is not difficult to pronounce, is not a foreign or rare word and its form is not an exception to the usual; *faṣāḥat al-kalām*, with respect to a whole sentence, when it does not contain an objectionable construction, a discord, an obscurity (through a confusion in the arrangement of the words) or a metaphor too far-fetched and therefore incomprehensible; and *faṣāḥat al-mutakallim*, with respect to a person whose style conforms to the above conditions. I 981b; II 824a

faṣd (A) : in medicine, bleeding. II 481b; XII 303b; and → FAṢṢĀD

fas̲h̲t (A, pl. *fus̲h̲ūt*), or *ḳuṭʿa, nad̲j̲wa* : the term for reef in the Persian Gulf. I 535b

fāsid (A) : in law, a legal act which does not observe the conditions of validity *stricto sensu* required for its perfection; vitiated and therefore null. Only in the Ḥanafī school of law is ~ distinct from *bāṭil* 'null and void', where it denotes a legal act which lacks one of the elements essential for the existence of any legal activity. I 319a; II 829b; VIII 836a; IX 324b

fāsiḳ (A) : in theology, one who has committed one or several 'great sins'. According to the Muʿtazila, who elaborated the thesis of the so-called intermediary status, the ~ is not entirely a believer nor entirely an infidel, but 'in a position between the two' (*fī manzila bayna 'l-manzilatayn*). Al-As̲h̲ʿarī maintained the same opinion, but added that if the ~ was a believer before becoming a sinner, the 'great sin' committed will not invalidate his standing as a believer; this position was adopted by the sunnīs as a whole. II 833a

In law, ~ is the opposite of ʿADL, a person of good morals. I 209b; II 834a

faṣi̊l (T) : a term in Ottoman music which in its classical form can be defined as a variable selection of pieces, usually by different composers, fitting into a series of prescribed slots organised in such a way as to emphasise, within the overall unity of mode, contrast and variety. It thus alternates between instrumental and vocal, unmeasured and measured, and juxtaposes vocal pieces using contrasting rhythmic cycles. VII 1043a; X 143b

fasīl → T̲H̲AʿLAB

faṣīl (A) : in architecture, an *intervallum*. I 616a

♦ **faṣīla** (A) : an object which is separated, like a young animal when weaned, and a palmtree sucker when transplanted; also the smallest 'section' of a tribe, the closest relatives. II 835a

fāṣila (A, pl. *fawāṣil*) : a separative; in prosody, ~ denotes a division in the primitive feet, meaning three or four moving consonants followed by one quiescent, e.g. *ḳatalat, ḳatalahum*. II 834b; VIII 667b; and → SAD̲J̲ʿ

In Qurʾānic terminology, ~ signifies the rhymes of the Qurʾānic text. II 834b; VIII 614b

In music, ~ denotes the pause which, with the basic notes, makes up the rhythm, ĪḲĀʿ. XII 408b

faskh (A) : in law, the dissolution of any contractual bond whatever, effected, as a rule, by means of a declaration of intention pronounced in the presence of the other contracting party, or by judicial process. The term is to be distinguished from *infisākh* which comes about without the need of any declaration or judicial decree. Dissolution of marriage open to the wife or her relatives is by way of ~, while the dissolution of marriage by the man is ṬALĀḲ. II 836a; III 1056b; and → NASKH

♦ faskha : in Mauritania, the dowry supplied by the family of the bride when she joins the conjugal home. VI 313a

faskiyya → SAHRĪDJ

faṣl (A, pl. *fuṣūl*) : separation, disjunction; in logic, ~ is 'difference', and, in particular, 'specific difference', the third of the five predicables of Porphyry. For logicians, ~ stands both for every attribute by which one thing is distinguished from another, whether it be individual or universal, and, in transposition, for that by which a thing is essentially distinguished. II 836b; and → SHAʿĪRA

In its plural form, *fuṣūl* is employed in philosophy and science to denote aphorisms or short chapters. VII 536b; in literature, brief sentences or paragraphs in rhymed prose. X 427a; in shadow-play terminology, the acts into which plays are divided. IV 1136b

♦ al-faṣl al-ʿāmm (A) : 'common difference', a term in logic for what allows a thing to differ from another and that other to differ from the former; equally it is what allows a thing to differ from itself at another time. This is the case of separable accidents. II 837a

♦ al-faṣl al-khāṣṣ (A) : 'particular difference', a term in logic for the predicate which is necessarily associated with accidents. II 837a

♦ faṣl al-suluṭāt → TAWĀZUN AL-SULUṬĀT

♦ faṣlī (A) : 'seasonal', the term employed by Muslim rulers in India to designate a variety of indigenous calendars. X 263b

faṣṣ → ḲAṢAB(A)

faṣṣād (A) : lit. phlebotomist; in mediaeval Islamic society, the practitioner of *faṣd* who bled veins of the human body and performed circumcisions for men and women. A similar profession was cupping, *ḥidjāma*, which was performed by a *ḥadjdjām* but was less popular and enjoyed less status: the cupper was a much-satirised character in Arabic tales. XII 303b

fatā (A, pl. *fityān*) : a boy, manservant; slave. I 24b; and → FUTUWWA

In the mediaeval Muslim East, the *fityān* (syn. *ʿayyārūn*; → ʿAYYĀR) were private groups, recruited from the depressed classes, which played the role of 'active wing' of the popular oppositions to the official authorities. I 256b; VIII 402a

In Muslim Spain, ~ was the slave employed in the service of the prince and his household, or of the ḤĀDJIB, who held an elevated rank in the palace hierarchy. II 837a

♦ al-fatayān al-kabīrān (A) : the two majordomos under whose control the entire management of the princely household in Muslim Spain was placed. II 837a

fatḥ al-kitāb (A) : bibliomancy, a form of sorcery. VIII 138b

fatḥa (A) : in grammar, ~ denotes the short vowel *a*. III 172a

In North Africa, ~ is a slit in the DJALLĀBIYYA at the top of the armlets through which the bare forearm can be thrust. II 405a

For ~ in prayer, → FĀTIḤA

fatḥnāme (T) : an Ottoman official announcement of a victory; a versified narrative of exploits, written by private persons as a literary exercise. II 839a

fātiḥa (A, pl. *fawātiḥ*) : the opening (*sūra*); designation of the first SŪRA of the Qur'ān; (or *fatḥa*) a prayer ceremony in certain Arab countries, particularly in North Africa, in which the arms are stretched out with the palms upwards, but without any recitation of the first sūra. II 841a; V 409b; V 425a

♦ fawātiḥ al-suwar (A), and *awā'il al-suwar, al-ḥurūf al-muḳaṭṭaʿāt* : 'the openers of the SŪRAS', a letter or group of letters standing just after the BASMALA at the beginning of 29 sūras and recited as letters of the alphabet. They are generally referred to in European languages as 'the mysterious letters'. V 412a

fātik (A, pl. *futtāk*) : a killer, a syn. of ṢUʿLŪK, or category into which the *ṣuʿlūk* fell. IX 864a

faṭīm (A) : a child weaned or ablactated. VIII 822a

faṭīr → KHAMĪR

fatra (A) : a relaxing; an interval of time, more particularly with respect to the period separating two prophets or two successive messengers. In its more current usage, ~ is applied to the period without prophets from the time of Jesus Christ to Muḥammad. In later times, ~ was also applied, by analogy, to periods of political interregnum. II 865a; a suspension of (Qur'ānic) revelation. XI 143a

faṭṭāma → SHAMLA

faṭūr (A) : the meal marking the end of the fast of Ramaḍān. IX 94b

fāṭūs (A), or *ḥūt al-ḥayḍ* : a fabulous marine creature mentioned by mediaeval Arab authors. It shatters the ships which it encounters, but is put to flight when the sailors hang from the peripheral points of the vessel rags stained with menstrual blood, *ḥayḍ*. VIII 1023a

fatwā (A) : in law, an opinion on a point of law. II 866a; II 890a

fawāt → FĀ'IT

fawātiḥ → FĀTIḤA; IFTITĀḤ

fawdjār : under the Dihlī sultanate, the superintendant of elephants, who, among other things, was ordered to train them to stand firm at the sight of fire and in the noise of artillery. V 690a

fawdjdār (IndP) : an executive and military officer, the administrative head of a district, *sarkār*, in the Mughal administration of India. I 317a; II 868a

fay' (A) : in pre-Islamic times, chattels taken as booty. II 869a; in early Islam, ~ were the immoveable properties acquired by conquest, a foundation in perpetuity for the benefit of successive generations of the community, in contrast to the moveable booty, *ghanīma*, which was distributed immediately. I 1144a; IV 1031a; spoils of war. VIII 130b

In the terminology of time, ~ denotes the shade in the east which, when it moves from the west (where it is called *ẓill*) to the east, marks midday. V 709b

fayḍ → IFĀḌA

fayḍa → RAWḌA; ṢĀḤIB AL-FAYḌA

faydj (A, < P; pl. **fuyūdj**) : a courier of the government postal service and also commercial mail serving the population at large. It was a common term all over North Africa and Egypt during the 5th/11th and 6th/12th centuries, while on the Egypt-Syria route the word *kutubī*, letter-bearer, was used. I 1044b; II 969b

♦ faydj ṭayyār (A) : express courier. II 970b

faylaḳ → ḲURDŪS

faylasūf (A) : a philosopher; in popular language, ~ is applied in an uncomplimentary sense to freethinkers or unbelievers. II 872a

fayruzadj → FĪRŪZADJ

fāza : in Arabia, the name the Tiyāha give to a tent whose ridge-pole rests on a row of two poles. The Sbāʿ use *mgawren* or *garneyn*. IV 1148a

fazʿa (A) : a counter-attack (of a raiding group of Bedouin). II 1055b

fazz (A), *farīr, farḳad, djawdhar* : in zoology, the calf of the oryx or addax antelope from birth until its weaning. A male bull calf has the *arkh* (and variants) and the adult male *shāt*. The old bull is termed *ḳarhab*. V 1227b faẓẓ (A) : water which is still drinkable, found in the stomach of camels. III 666b; and → FĪL AL-BAḤR

fellāga → FALLĀḲ

fermān → FARMĀN

fərmla (Alg) : a vest for elderly men in Algeria. V 746a

fidā' (A) : the redemption, repurchase, or ransoming of Muslim prisoners or slaves held by unbelievers. III 183a; VIII 502a; XII 306b

fidām (A) : a piece of linen cloth which protected the mouth, worn by Zoroastrian priests, but often also by the cup-bearer, SĀḲĪ, for whom it served as a filter for tasting the drink and to help him know the precise taste. VIII 883b; X 612a

fidāwī (A, < **fidā'ī**) : one who offers up his life for another. Among the Nizārī Ismāʿīlīs, ~ was used of those who risked their lives to assassinate the enemies of the sect. II 882a; VIII 442a

In Algeria, ~ means a narrator of heroic deeds. II 882a

During the Persian revolution of 1906-7, the term was applied in the first place to the adherents of the republican party, later to the defenders of liberal ideas and the constitution. II 882a

♦ fidāwiyya (Alg) : a tale or song of heroic deeds. II 882a

fiḍḍa (A) : in mineralogy, silver. II 883a

fidjār (A) : sacrilege; known particularly in the name *ḥarb al-fidjār* 'the sacrilegious war', a war waged towards the end of the 6th century AD during the holy months between the Ḳuraysh and Kināna on the one side and the Ḳays-ʿAylān on the other. II 883b

fidjw → FARʿ

fidya (A) : a general designation among Syro-Palestinians for a blood sacrifice made for purposes of atonement, practised in the interests of the living. II 884a; a Qur'ānic term to denote the fast which compensates for the days of Ramaḍān in which fasting has not been practised, or to denote the impossibility of purchasing a place in Paradise. XII 306b; a minor KAFFĀRA or compensation, to be paid when one has taken advantage of one of five dispensations. IX 94b

♦ fidyat al-mulk (P, < A) : in taxation matters, an additional levy of one-tenth from landed estates, decreed, and later abolished, by the Salghurid ruler Saʿd b. Zangī. IV 1041a

fiḳh (A) : understanding, knowledge, intelligence, and thus applied to any branch of knowledge (as in *fiḳh al-lugha*, the science of lexicography); the technical term for jurisprudence, the science of religious law in Islam. In addition to the laws regulating ritual and religious observances, containing orders and prohibitions, ~ includes the whole field of family law, the law of inheritance, of property and of contracts and obligations, criminal law and procedure, and, finally, constitutional law and laws regulating the administration of the state and the conduct of war. II 886a; IX 322b

In older theological language, ~ was used in opposition to ʿILM, the accurate knowledge of legal decisions handed down from the Prophet and his Companions, and was applied to the independent exercise of the intelligence, the decision of legal points by one's own judgement in the absence or ignorance of a traditional ruling bearing on the case in question. II 886a

fikr (A, pl. *afkār*) : thought, reflection; in mysticism, ~ is used habitually in contrast to DHIKR: in the performance of ~, the ṣūfī, concentrating on a religious subject, meditates according to a certain progression of ideas or a series of evocations which he assimilates and experiences, while in *dhikr*, concentrating on the object recollected, he allows his field of consciousness to lose itself in this object. II 891b

fiḳra (T) : a kind of short news item generally of entertaining nature, combining anecdote with comment on some matter of contemporary importance. VI 94b

fīl (A, < P *pīl*) : in zoology, the elephant. II 892b; the bishop in chess. IX 366b

♦ fīl al-baḥr (A) : in zoology, the elephant seal; the walrus, also called *faẓẓ*. IV 648b; VIII 1022b

fiʿl (A) : act, action, opposed in noetics and metaphysics to *ḳuwwa* 'potentiality, power'. II 898a; V 578a

In grammar, the verb. II 895b; and → ISM AL-FIʿL

In logic, ~ is one of the ten categories, *actio* as opposed to *passio*. II 898a

In theology, ~ designates the action of God *ad extra*, 'what is possible (not necessary) for God to do'. II 898b

♦ fiʿl al-taʿadjdjub (A) : in grammar, the verb of surprise. IX 528a

filāḥa (A) : lit. ploughing; the occupation of husbandry, agriculture. II 899a

♦ filāḥat al-araḍīn (A) : agronomy. II 902a

♦ filāḥat al-ḥayawānāt (A) : zootechny. II 902a

filawr (A), or *ḥādjūr* : in mediaeval ʿIrāḳ, a beggar or vagrant who simulates a hernia or ulcer or tumour or some similar affliction with his testicles or anus, or with her vulva, in the case of a woman. VII 494a

filḳ (A), also *sharīdj* : in archery, a bow consisting of a single stave split length-wise and spliced with glue. IV 797b

filori (T) : the Ottoman name for the standard gold coins of Europe; a local Balkan tax amounting to one ~, imposed on the semi-nomadic Vlachs of the Balkans, in which sense it is usually referred to as *resm-i filori*. II 914b ff.; VIII 487a

filw (A) : a foal between birth and one year of age. II 785a

fiʿma : transversal associations, in ʿAfar society, which counterbalance tribal divisions. X 71b

findjān (A) : in clothing, a headdress worn by women in Cairo and Syria, gilt below and decked with pieces of silver. X 612a; and → BAKRADJ

firandj → IFRANDJ

firāsa (A) : physiognomancy, a technique of inductive divination which permits the foretelling of moral conditions and psychological behaviour from external indications and physical states, such as colours, forms, and limbs. II 916a; V 100a; clairvoyance. XI 110b

firʿawnī → KĀGHAD

firda → FURḌA

firdjardāt (A, < MidP *fragard* 'chapter, section') : a type of poems, as defined by Ḥamza al-Iṣfahānī in a commentary on a verse by Abū Nuwās. XI 210a

firfīr (< G ?) : a loan-word in Arabic for the colour violet. V 699b

firind (A, < P) : damascening, or a pattern drawn on a sword. V 972a; VIII 237a

firḳ → WAKĪR

firḳa (A) : sect. The ~ *nādjiya* is the sect that alone will be saved out of the 73 into which the community will be divided, according to a Tradition. VIII 990a; XI 103a

firḳate → BASHTARDA

firṣād → TŪT

fīrūzadj (P), or *fayruzadj* : in mineralogy, turquoise, mined in the Sāsānid period and even earlier around Nīshāpūr. There are different kinds, distinguished by colour; the best kind was considered to be the *būsḥāḳī* (i.e. *Abū Isḥāḳī*) and the finest variety of this, the sky-blue *azharī*. ~ is explained as 'stone of victory' whence it is also called *ḥadjar al-ghalaba*. II 927b; VIII 112a

firz, or *firzān* → SHAṬRANDJ

fisḳ (A) : moral deficiency. XI 567b

fisḳiyya (A, pl. *fasāḳī*) : a small basin which collected water from the SHADIRWĀN. IX 175b

fiṭām → SAKHLA

fitna (A) : putting to the proof, discriminatory test; revolt, disturbance; civil war; a Qur'ānic term with the sense of temptation or trial of faith, and most frequently as a test which is in itself a punishment inflicted by God upon the sinful, the unrighteous. The great struggles of the early period of Muslim history were called ~. II 930b

fiṭra (A) : a Qur'ānic term meaning 'a kind or way of creating or of being created', which posed serious theological and legal difficulties for the commentators. II 931b; 'common to all the prophets' or 'part of the general SUNNA or religion'. IX 312b

In law, the amount of ZAKĀT paid. XI 418a

fityān → FATĀ

♦ fityānī (A) : a variety of couscous which is prepared by cooking grain in gravy and which is sprinkled with cinnamon. V 528a

fizr → ḲAṬĪʿ

foggara (Alg, < A *faḳḳara*; pl. *fgāgīr*) : a term used in southern Algeria to designate a *ḳanāt*, a mining installation or technique for extracting water from the depths of the earth. IV 529a; a subterranean drainage channel. XII 328b

frenk-khāne (T) : in 19th-century Ottoman cities, a building in a European style, intended to house European merchants during their more or less extended stays. IX 799b

frīmla (N.Afr) : a corselet for women in Algeria; an embroidered bolero in Libya. V 746a

fūdhandj (A, < P, < H *pūdana*) : in botany, mint. The Arabic nomenclature for mint is abundant; other names are *ḥabaḳ, nammām*, for water-mint, and *naʿnaʿ* or *nuʿnuʿ*, peppermint. XII 309b

fudjl (A) : in botany, the radish, one of the summer crops in mediaeval Egypt. V 863a

fuḍūlī (A) : in law, an unauthorised agent. VIII 836a; XI 208a

fūh → AFĀWĪH

fuḥsh → SUKHF

fuḥūl → FAḤL

fūḳ → TAFWĪḲ

fuḳaysha → ṢANDJ

fūḳiyya : a body shirt for men worn under the DJALLĀBIYYA in Morocco. V 746a

fuḳḳāʿ (A) : a sparkling fermented drink, almost a 'beer'. It was frequently sweetened and flavoured with fruit, so that one might call ~ the mediaeval equivalent of shandy or almost so. VI 721a; IX 225a; X 32a; XI 369b

fūl (A) : in botany, beans, one of the winter crops in mediaeval Egypt. V 863a

♦ fūl mudammas → ṬAʿMIYYA

fūlādh → ḤADĪD

fulk (A) : a Qur'ānic term for ship, used *inter alia* of Noah's ark and the ship from which Jonah was thrown. IV 870b; VIII 808a

full → YĀSAMĪN

funduḳ (A, < Gk) : a term used, particularly in North Africa, to denote hostelries at which animals and humans can lodge, on the lines of caravanserais or KHĀNs of the Muslim East. II 945a; IV 1015a; IX 788b

In numismatics, an Ottoman gold coin. VIII 229b

furāniḳ : messengers in the postal service in the ʿAbbāsid period. I 1045b

furār → SAKHLA

furḍa (A) : a term used interchangeably in Ottoman documents and Arabic texts with *firda*, with reference to personal taxes; the ~ was attested in Ottoman Egypt after 1775 as one of the many illegal charges imposed on peasants by soldiers of the provincial governors. II 948a; an emporium. XII 507a; and → MĪNĀʾ

♦ furdat (firdat) al-ruʾūs (A) : a personal tax in Egypt under Muḥammad ʿAlī amounting to 3 per cent on known or supposed revenue of all the inhabitants, paid by all government employees, including foreigners, by employees of non-government establishments, by the *fallāḥīn* (→ FALLĀḤ), and by artisans and merchants. II 149a; II 948a

♦ firdat al-taḥrīr (A) : in Ottoman Egypt, the name for the comprehensive levy which in 1792 replaced all the illegal charges imposed on peasants by soldiers of the provincial governors. II 948a

furdj → KATŪM

furfur → SAKHLA

furḳān (A, < Ar) : a Qurʾānic term, which poses problems of interpretation, and has been variously translated as 'discrimination', 'criterion', 'separation', 'deliverance', or 'salvation'. II 949b; X 318a

furn (A) : a communal oven, in technical usage corresponding to *kūsha* 'lime-kiln'. V 41b; X 30b

furs (A) : one of two terms, the other being ʿADJAM, to denote the Persians. II 950b

furūʿ → FARʿ

furʿul → ḌABUʿ

furūsiyya (A) : the whole field of equestrian knowledge, both theoretical and practical. Treatises on ~ by actual horsemen, veterinary surgeons or riders appeared at a late stage in Arabic literature, many repeating passages from earlier works written by philologists, but also with added pages on riding, describing various methods and principles co-existing in the Muslim world. II 953b

fusayfisāʾ (A, < Gk) : in art, mosaic. I 610b; II 955a

fustān (A) : in dress, the term for the European dress worn by women; a European suit (*taḳm*) might also be worn by women who eschew the traditional *milāya*. XII 776a

fusṭāṭ (A, < Gk) : a small hair tent used by travellers. II 957b; IV 1147a

fuṣūl → FAṢL

fūṭa : in mediaeval Islam, a long piece of sari-like cloth originating in India and serving a variety of functions: as a loincloth, apron, and a variety of headdress. V 737b; a simple cloth with a seam, fastened in front and behind to the girdle, *tikka* (modern *dikka*). IX 676b

futurifu : in Gāo, in West Africa, a horn, invented by the *Askiya* Muḥammad Bunkan (d. 1537). X 36b

futuwwa (A, T *fütüwwet*) : a term invented in about the 2nd/8th century as the counterpart of *muruwwa* (→ MURŪʾA), the qualities of the mature man, to signify that which is regarded as characteristic of the FATĀ, young man; by this term it has become customary to denote various movements and organisations which until the beginning of the modern era were widespread throughout all the urban communities of the Muslim East. I 520a; II 961a

futyā (A), or *iftāʾ* : the act of giving an opinion on a point of law, FATWĀ; the profession of the adviser. II 866a

fuwwa (A) : in botony, madder. X 118a

fuyūdj → FAYDJ

G

gabr (P) : a term of doubtful etymology, denoting Zoroastrians, and used generally in Persian literature. II 970b

♦ gabrī : in art, ceramic ware developed in Persia. The ornamentation of this ware, produced by means of larger or smaller scratches in the slip that covers the body under the transparent partly coloured glaze, consists of schematic representations, recalling the ancient culture of Persia, notably of fire altars, as well as of men and beasts, birds, lions and dragons depicted in a curiously stylised manner. II 746a

gad̲j̲al → ČITAK

gām : a pace, a unit of measurement. X 43b

gand̲j̲ : in Muslim India, a grain market. IX 800b

gandu (Hau) : the Hausa extended family, a largely self-supporting unit based on agriculture and formerly dependent on slave labour. III 277b

gandūra (N.Afr) : a full-length tunic with short sleeves, worn by men in southern Morocco and by both sexes in Algeria. V 746a

gāra → ḲĀRA

gargad̲j̲ (IndP) : in Mug̲h̲al India, a movable tower used in sieges. These towers were very strong structures with solid beams covered by raw hides, tiles, or earth to protect them from the liquid combustibles thrown by the garrison; they could be destroyed only by hurling heavy stones or by a sortie. III 482a

garmsīr (P, A *d̲j̲arm*) : in geography, a term used to denote hot, desert-type or subtropical lowland climates; in Arabic, ~ is particularly used for the hot, coastal region of the Persian Gulf shores and the regions bordering on the great central desert. V 183a

garneyn → FĀZA

gat → BANDIS̲H̲

gaṭṭāya (B) : a kind of mat of plaited hair, which is worn very long and grown only from the top of the cranium, the remainder of the head being shaved. The wearing of the ~ is a local custom absorbed by the ʿĪsāwī order. IV 95a

gāw-band (P) : the person who worked draft oxen. XI 305a

gawd (P) : a usually octagonal pit in the centre of a traditional gymnasium, ZŪRK̲H̲ĀNA, about a metre deep, in which the exercises take place. The ~ is surrounded by spectator stands, of particular importance being the *sardam*, an elevated and decorated seat reserved for the director, MURS̲H̲ID, whose function is to accompany the exercises with rhythmic drumming and the chanting of verse from classical Persian poetry. XI 573a

gāwdār (P) : cattle-raiser. IX 682b

gaytan : corduroy. X 371b

gaz (P) : a measure of length in use in Iran and Muslim India, the Persian cubit, D̲H̲IRĀʿ, of the Middle Ages, either the legal cubit of 49.8 cm or the Isfahan cubit of 79.8 cm. Until recently, a ~ of 104 cm was in use in Iran. II 232a; XII 313b; in 1926 an attempt was made to equate the traditional Persian measures with the metric system, so that the ~ was fixed at 1 m; after 1933 the metric system was introduced but the older measures nevertheless remained in popular use. VII 138a

In Muslim India, sixty ~ formed the side of the square BĪGHĀ, a traditional measure of area. Five thousand ~ made the length of a *kuroh* (Persian) or KROŚA (Sanskrit), the traditional measure of road-length. XII 313b

In botany, tamarisk. XI 303a; a very hard and solid wood, used for cabinet-making and for timber framing. V 669b

♦ gaz-i ilāhī : a measure introduced by the Mug̲h̲al emperor Akbar in 994/1586, equal to ca. 32 inches. IV 1055b; XII 313b

♦ gaz-i mukassar (P) : the 'shortened' cubit of 68 cm, used for measuring cloth. II 232a

♦ gaz-i shāhī (P) : the 'royal' cubit of 95 cm, in use in 17th-century Persia. II 232a

gečid resmi (T) : tolls levied in the Ottoman empire at mountain passes and river fords. II 147a

gedik (T) : lit. breach; in law, a form of long-term lease arrangement of WAḲF property in Egypt, which involved, in addition to perpetual lease, the ownership and use of tools and installations of shops and workshops. XII 369a; in the Ottoman period, the right to exercise a craft or a trade, either in general or, more frequently, at a special place or in a specific shop. They were inheritable if the heir fulfilled all other conditions for becoming a master in the craft. VIII 207a; IX 542a; IX 798a; XII 421a

geguritan → SINGIR

gemḥ → FĀRĪNA

geniza (Heb) : a place where Hebrew writings were deposited in order to prevent the desecration of the name of God which might be found in them. As a term of scholarship, ~ or Cairo *geniza*, refers to writings coming from the store-room of the 'Synagogue of the Palestinians' in the ancient city of Fusṭāṭ. II 987b

gerebeg (J) : a grand parade that takes place in certain areas in Java after the ʿĪD prayers at the end of Ramaḍān, with as its centerpiece a magical 'mount of blessing' that conveys some of the sultan's mystical power. XII 682b

gersh → BILYŪN

gezme → AḤDĀTH

ghāba (A) : forest. II 991a

ghabānī (A), or *ghabāniyya* : a head scarf with an embroidered pattern of lozenges, worn by both sexes in the Arab East. V 741a

ghabghab (A) : in zoology, an animal's dewlap. VII 22b

ghabn fāḥish (A) : in law, the concept of excessive loss, which is the only means by which a contract can be challenged in the case of fraud. I 319a

ghaḍaf → ḲAṬĀ

ghadāʾir → ḌAFĀʾIR

ghadāt (A) : a variant name for the *ṣalāt al-fadjr* (→ FADJR). VII 27a

ghaddār (A) : a traitor. XII 830a

ghadjar (A) : gypsies. IX 235b

ghādus (A, < L *Gadus*) : in zoology, the cod. VIII 1021a

ghafāra → KHUWWA

ghaffār, ghafūr → GHUFRĀN

ghāʾib (A) : absent; in law, usually the person who, at a given moment, is not present at the place where he should be. But, in certain special cases, the term is applied also to the person who is at a distance from the court before which he was to bring an action or who does not appear at the court after being summoned. II 995b

♦ ṣalāt al-ghāʾib (A) : the name given to the prayer said for a dead person whose body cannot be produced. II 996a

ghāʾira → ẒĀHIRA

ghalath → ʿALATH

ghalča (P) : an imprecise designation of those mountain peoples of the Pamirs who speak Iranian languages; a term used in English for the Iranian Pamir languages. The word, though of uncertain origin, has different meanings in different languages: 'peasant' or 'ruffian' in New Persian, 'squat, stupid' in Tādjikī; in old Yaghnābi, 'slave'. II 997b

ghālī → GHULĀT; ḲĀLĪ

gh̲alḳ (A) : in meteorology, a closed period during the middle of the ~ season; before this was *awwal al-~* and after it the *dāmānī* seasons. VII 52a

gh̲alla (A) : income. XI 414b

gh̲alṭa (A, pl. *gh̲alaṭāt*) : error.

♦ **gh̲alaṭāt-i mesh̲hūre** (T) : lit. well-known errors; solecisms brought about by phonetic changes, characteristic of Turkish, producing (drastic) modifications in Arabic and Persian loan-words and branded by the purists, e.g. *bēdāwā* < *bād-i hawā*. II 997a

gh̲ammāz (A) : he who screws up his eyes, intriguer, one of the numerous terms in the mediaeval and modern periods for 'rascal, scoundrel'. XI 546a

gh̲anam (A, pl. *agh̲nām, gh̲unūm, agh̲ānīm*) : the class of small livestock with a predominance of either sheep or goats, according to country. Also, understood in the sense of 'sheep-goat patrimony'. XII 316b

gh̲anīma (A), or *gh̲unm* : booty, in particular moveable booty, which was distributed immediately, as opposed to FAY'. I 1144a; II 1005a; XII 316b

gh̲arāmet → DJARĪMA

gh̲arānīḳ (A) : cranes; in the Qur'ān, 'the exalted ones', referring to the Arabian goddesses, al-Lāt, al-ʿUzza and Manāt, the origin of the Satanic verses, or those which Satan inserted into the revelation, later abrogated by LIII, 21-7. V 404a

gh̲arar → BAYʿ AL-GH̲ARAR

gh̲arāsa (A) : the act of planting. I 135b

gh̲araza (A) : the act of pricking, as with a tattooing needle (*mīsh̲am*, pl. *mawāsh̲im*). XII 830b

gh̲ārib → ṬĀLIʿ

gh̲arīb (A, pl. GH̲URABĀ') : lit. strange, uncommon; in philology, ~ means rare, unfamiliar (and consequently obscure) expressions (syn. *waḥsh̲ī, ḥūsh̲ī*), and frequently occurs in the titles of books, mostly such as deal with unfamiliar expressions in the Qur'ān and ḤADĪTH̲. I 157b; II 1011a

In the science of Tradition, ~ means a Tradition from only one Companion, or from a single man at a later stage, to be distinguished from *gh̲arīb al-ḥadīth̲*, which applies to uncommon words in the text, MATN, of Traditions. III 25b

♦ gh̲arīb muṭlaḳ → FARD

gh̲ārim (A), or *gh̲arīm* : in law, a debtor or creditor. II 1011b; XII 207b

gh̲arḳad (A) : a kind of bramble. I 957b

gh̲ārr → TAGH̲RĪR

gh̲arrā' (A) : in zoology, the spotted dogfish. VIII 1022b

gh̲ars (Alg) : soft dates produced in the Sūf, along with the variety known as *deglet nūr*, which are harvested for export only. IX 763b

gh̲ārūḳa (A) : in law, a system whereby a debtor landowner transfers part of his plot, and the right to cultivate it, as security on a loan until redemption. Other Arabic terms for the same system were *rahn ḥiyāzī* and *bayʿ bi 'l-istigh̲lāl*, and in Ottoman Turkish *istigh̲lāl*. ~ is a form of usury, and as such prohibited by Islamic law. XII 322b

gh̲aṣb (A) : in civil law, usurpation, the illegal appropriation of something belonging to another or the unlawful use of the rights of another. II 1020a

gh̲āsh̲iya (A) : a covering, particularly, a covering for a saddle; one of the insignia of royal rank carried before the Mamlūk and Saldjūḳ rulers in public processions. II 1020a; VI 854a

In the Qur'ān, ~ is used metaphorically of a great misfortune that overwhelms someone. II 1020b

gh̲āsil → GH̲ASSĀL

gh̲asīl al-malā'ika (A) : 'washed by the angels', a term by which Ḥanzala b. Abī ʿĀmir is known, referring to the fact that he died without having performed the GH̲USL following sexual intercourse. IX 204b

ghassāl (A) : a washer of clothes and also of the dead, the latter more often known as *ghāsil*. The social position of the corpse-washer was higher than that of the washer of clothes. XII 322b

ghaṭā → ʿATABA

ghaṭaṭ → ḲAṬĀ

ghatmāʾ → ḲAṬĀ

ghawghāʾ (A) : those who swarm like tiny beasts, one of the numerous terms in the mediaeval and modern periods for 'rascals, scoundrels'. XI 546a

ghawr (A) : in geography, a depression, plain encircled by higher ground. II 1024b

ghawṭ (Alg, pl. *ghīṭān*) : a funnel-like excavation, in which date palms are planted in the Sūf. IX 763b

ghawth (A) : lit. succour, deliverance; an epithet of the head of the ṣūfī hierarchy of saints (syn. *badal*). Some say that it is a rank immediately below the head, ḲUṬB, in the hierarchy. V 543b; XII 323b

ghawwāṣ (A) : a diver. XII 550a

ghayb (A) : absence; what is hidden, inaccessible to the senses and to reason; in Qurʾānic usage, with rare exceptions, ~ stands for mystery. I 406b ff.; II 1025a

In mysticism, ~ means, according to context, the reality of the world beyond discursive reason which gnosis experiences. II 1026a

♦ **ghayba** (A) : absence, occultation; and → NĀʾIB AL-GHAYBA

In mysticism, ~ is also used for the condition of anyone who has been withdrawn by God from the eyes of men and whose life during that period may have been miraculously prolonged. II 1026a; III 51b

Among the Twelvers, ~ became a major historical period, divided into two parts: the lesser ~ (from 260/874 to c. 329/941) and the greater ~ (from the death of the fourth IMĀM onwards). II 1026a; IV 277b

In law, ~ is the state of being not present at the place where one should be. II 995b

♦ ghayba munḳaṭiʿa (A) : in law, an absence not interrupted by information on a person's existence; the continuous absence of a plaintiff. II 995b

ghaydāḳ (A) : lit. soft or tender; a term applied to a youth or young man; when applied to a boy, ~ signifies that he has not attained to puberty. VIII 822a

ghayhab → SALḲAʿ

ghaylam → SULAḤFĀ

ghaym (A) : in mineralogy, cloudiness, a defect or impurity in a gem. XI 263a

ghayn (A) : the nineteenth letter of the Arabic alphabet, transcribed gh, with the numerical value 1,000. It is defined as a voiced postvelar fricative. II 1026b

ghayṭa (< Fr *guetter*), or *ghāʾita*, *ghāyṭa* : in music, a reed-pipe of two kinds, popular in Muslim Spain and North Africa. One is a cylindrical tube blown with a single reed, and the other is a conical tube blown with a double reed. The cylindrical tube instrument is known in Egypt as the *ghīṭa*. II 1027b; VII 207b

ghazā-nāme → MENĀḲİB-NĀME

ghazal (A, T *ghazel*) : lit. flirtation; in prosody, an elegy of love; the erotic-elegiac genre. It has the rhyme scheme *aa xa xa xa*, etc. I 586a; II 1028a; X 719b; XII 323b

♦ ghazel-i mülemmaʿ (T) : in Ottoman poetry, a variant of the *ghazal*, which is written in alternating Turkish and Persian and/or Arabic hemistichs. X 917a; and → MULAMMAʿĀT

♦ ghazel-i musammaṭ (T) : in Ottoman poetry, a *ghazal* the verses of which, with the exception of the MAṬLAʿ, have 'inner rhyme' in that the middle and end of their first hemistich rhymes with the middle of their second hemistich. X 719a

ghāzī (A, pl. *ghuzāt*) : a fighter for the faith, a person who took part in a razzia, or raid against the infidels, GHAZW; later, a title of honour, becoming part of the title of certain Muslim princes, such as the AMĪRs of Anatolia and more particularly the first

Ottoman sultans; soldiers of fortune, who in times of peace became a danger to the government which employed them. I 322b; II 1043b; VIII 497a

♦ ghuzāt al-baḥr (A) : pirates. II 526a

♦ **ghāziya** (A, pl. *ghawāzī*) : an Egyptian dancing-girl who sang and danced primarily in the streets, making a speciality of lascivious dances and often becoming a prostitute. Today both the dancing-girl and the singer are called *ʿalma* in the cities but in the rural areas the dancer is still known as ~. I 404a; II 1048a; in the past, the term for belly-dancer, today usually called *raḳḳāṣa*. XII 778a

ghazw (A, pl. *ghizwān*) : an expedition, raid, usually of limited scope, conducted with the aim of gaining plunder. I 892a; II 509b; II 1055a

♦ ghazwa (A, pl. *ghazawāt*) : a term used in particular of the Prophet's expeditions against the infidels. II 1055a; VIII 497a

ghidhāʾ (A, pl. *aghdhiya*) : feeding; food. II 1057a

ghidjak : one of a type of viol used in Central Asia to accompany the bard, the others being *ḳil ḳobuz*, in Kazakhstan, and the *kiak*. X 733b

ghifāra (A, pl. *ghafāʾir*) : in clothing, in early times a red cloth with which women protected their veil from the oil on the hair. In Muslim Spain, the name of a similar cap for men, who usually wore not turbans but *ghafāʾir* of red or green wool, whilst Jews wore a yellow one. X 612a; and → MIGHFAR

ghīla (A) : a nursing woman. VIII 824a

ghilāf (A) : a sheath. IV 518b

ghilmān → GHULĀM

ghīnā → ḲĪNĀ

ghināʾ (A) : song, singing; music in its generic sense. In Morocco, the song is divided into folk or popular song, *ḳarīḥa*, and the art song, *āla* or *ṣanʿa*, while in Algeria ~ is grouped under *kalām al-hazl* and *kalām al-djidd*. II 1072b f.

ghirāra (A) : a measure of capacity for grain in central Syria and Palestine in the mediaeval period, of different size in every province, e.g. the ~ of Damascus contained 208.74 kg of wheat, whereas the ~ of Jerusalem, at least at the end of the Middle Ages, weighed three times as much. IV 520a; VI 118b

ghirbāl (A) : a parchment-bottom sieve, which in the pre-Islamic period sometimes took the place of tambourines to supply rhythm. II 1073b; X 900b; and → BANDAYR

ghirnīḳ (A), and *kurkī* : in zoology, the crane. I 1152b

ghirr (A) : an inexperienced person. X 93a

ghīṭa → GHAYṬA

ghiyār (A) : the compulsory distinctive mark in the garb of DHIMMĪ subjects under Muslim rule, described as a piece of cloth placed over the shoulder; the garment which bears the ~. II 1075b; V 744b

ghižak → KAMĀNDJA

ghlāla (Mor) : a sleeveless outer robe for women in Morocco. V 746a

ghubār (A) : dust; in mathematics, ~ was the name for the immediate parents of the modern European numerals, while what are now called 'Arabic' numerals were known as 'Indian'. Sometimes the names were reversed, however, or both forms were called Indian or both called ~. III 1140a; and → ḤISĀB AL-GHUBĀR

In calligraphy, ~ or *ghubārī* is a name given to every type of very small script difficult to read with the naked eye, but often found in the NASKH script. IV 1124a

ghubba (A, pl. *ghabīb*) : a term in the Persian Gulf for an area of deep water, of 15 fathoms or more. I 535b

ghubbān (A) : in zoology, the green scarus, whose Arabic term is found again in the Latinised nomenclature to specify a sub-species limited to a particular region (*Scarus ghobban*). VIII 1021b

ghudfa (A) : a large head shawl for women, worn in the Hebron area. V 741a

ghudwa (A), or *bukra* : in lexicography, a term used to denote the time which elapses between the morning twilight prayer, FADJR, and the sunrise. V 709b

ghufrān (A) : the verbal noun of 'to forgive', ~ refers to the two divine names, *al-ghafūr* and *al-ghaffār* 'the All-Pardoning One whose power to pardon is endless'. A frequent synonym is *ʿafw*. II 1078b; IV 1107a

ghūl (A, pl. *ghīlān, aghwāl*) : a fabulous being believed by the ancient Arabs to inhabit desert places and, assuming different forms, to lead travellers astray, to fall upon them unawares and devour them. Generally, a ~ is considered a male as well as a female being in the early sources. II 1078b

ghulām (A, pl. *ghilmān*; P pl. *ghulāmān*) : a young man or boy; by extension, either a servant, sometimes elderly and very often, but not necessarily, a slave servant; or a bodyguard, slave or freedman, bound to his master by personal ties; or sometimes an artisan working in the workshop of a master whose name he used along with his own in his signature. Rulers owned an often impressive number of slave boys who served as attendants or guards and could rise to fairly high office in the hierarchy of the palace service, as well as others who formed a component of varying importance in the armed forces. I 24b; II 1079b; VIII 821b

In falconry, a technical term for the hawker's assistant, who kept the aviary well provided with pigeons and other game-birds and was responsible for the nourishment and training of the hawks. I 1152b

♦ al-ghilmān al-khāṣṣa (A) : the personal guard of certain ʿAbbāsid caliphs. II 1080a

♦ ghulāmān-i khāṣṣa-yi sharīfa (P) : 'slaves of the royal household', a cavalry regiment formed from the ranks of the Georgians and Circassians under the Ṣafawids. II 1083b; IV 36a; VIII 769a

ghulāmān → GHULĀM

ghulāt (A, s. *ghālī*) : 'extremists', those individuals accused of exaggeration, *ghulū*, in religion; in practice, ~ has covered all early speculative shīʿīs except those later accepted by the Twelver tradition, as well as all later shīʿī groups except Zaydīs, orthodox Twelvers, and sometimes Ismāʿīlīs. II 1093b

ghulūw (A) : in literary criticism, overblown hyperbole. XII 655b

ghumūḍ (A) : in literary criticism, the 'obscurity' of poetry, in contrast to the 'clarity', *wuḍūḥ*, of prose. XII 655b

ghunča (P) : in botany, the rosebud, a recurring image in eastern Islamic literature. II 1133a

ghunna (A) : in Qurʾānic recitation, the nasal sound of certain letters in excess of ordinary speech. X 73b

ghūra → TURSHĪ

ghurāb (A, < L *corvus*) : in zoology, the crow. II 1096b

In navigation, a large type of mediaeval Muslim galley (< Sp *caraba*), frequently mentioned in accounts of the naval warfare between the Muslims and the Franks during Crusading and Mamlūk times. In archaic Anglo-Indian usage, it yielded the term *grab*, a type of ship often mentioned, in the Indian Ocean context, from the arrival of the Portuguese to the 18th century. VIII 810a

ghurabāʾ (A, T *ghurebā*) : an Ottoman term for the two lowest of the six cavalry regiments of the ḲAPÏ ḲULLARÏ. The regiment riding on the sultan's right side was known as *ghurebāʾ-i yemīn* and that riding on his left as *ghurebāʾ-i yesār*. II 1097b

ghurfa → AGADIR

ghurra (A) : the first day of the month, in historical works and correspondence. V 708a; a term used in Bedouin society for the young girl, who must be a virgin, white and free, given by the family of a murderer to a member of the injured family as compensation. In turn the latter forgoes his right of vengeance. VI 479b

In law, ~ is a special indemnity to be paid for causing an abortion. I 29a; VIII 823b

ghurūb → ṬĀLIʿ

ghuruḳ (? Mon) : in mediaeval Transoxania, a royal hunting ground. V 857b

ghusl (A) : general ablution, uninterrupted washing, in ritually pure water, of the whole of the human body, including the hair. ~ applies also to the washing of the corpse of a Muslim. For the living, the essential ~ is that which is obligatory before performing the ritual daily prayers. II 1104a; VIII 929a

ghuṣn (A) : in prosody, separate-rhyme lines in each stanza of a MUWASHSHAḤ. VII 809b

ghūṭa (A) : the name given in Syria to abundantly irrigated areas of intense cultivation surrounded by arid land. It is produced by the co-operative activity of a rural community settled near to one or several perennial springs, whose water is used in a system of canalisation to irrigate several dozen or hundred acres. II 541a; II 1104b

ghuzāt → GHĀZĪ

ginān (H, < San *jñāna*) : in Nizārī Ismāʿīlism, a poetical composition in an Indian vernacular, ascribed to various PĪRS who were active in preaching and propagating the DAʿWA. The ~ resembles didactic and mystical poetry and is often anachronistic and legendary in nature. VIII 126a

girebān, girīvān → SHUTIK

girīz (T), or *girīzgāh* : in Turkish prosody, ~ is the passage marking the transition from the NASĪB to the main part of the ḲAṢĪDA. IV 715b; and → MAKHLAṢ

gīṭūn (N.Afr) : the name given to shelters in North Africa made of sackcloth or pieces of material or of canvas produced in Europe. The name derives from the classical *ḳayṭūn* 'room in a BAYT'. IV 1149b

gīwa : characteristic foot-gear of the Bakhtiyārī tribeswomen. I 956a

gnīdra (Alg) : a light, lacy chemisette for women in Algeria. V 746a

göbak (P) : among the Shāhsewan in Persia, a 'navel' or descent group. IX 224a

♦ göbek adî (T) : 'navel name'; in Turkey, a name given to a new-born child by the midwife as she cuts the umbilical cord. IV 181a

göčmen → MUHĀDJIR

goni (Kanuri) : one who has memorised the Qurʾān, a term for saint in Chad and the Nilotic Sudan. XI 124a

gönüllü (T) : volunteer; in the Ottoman empire, ~ was used as a term (sometimes with the pseudo-Persian pl. *gönüllüyān*, in Arabic sources usually rendered *djamulyān* or *kamulyān*) with the following meanings: volunteers coming to take part in the fighting; a 10th/16th-century organised body stationed in most of the fortresses of the empire, in Europe, Asia and Egypt; and an 11th/17th-century body among the paid auxiliaries who were recruited in the provinces to serve on a campaign. II 1120b

gorani → POTURI

goruta → YODJANA

göstermelik (T) : inanimate objects, without any direct connection with the shadow play, which are shown on the screen before the actual play in order to attract the interest of spectators and fire their imagination. IV 601b

göt-tikme (T) : a type of tent possessed by the Türkmen Yomut and Göklen tribes. The ~ essentially is an ÖY 'tent-house', but without the trellis walls, and regarded as inferior, though more portable. IV 1150b

gotba → ʿUDIYA

gourbi (Alg) : a shack, a fixed dwelling used in the Algerian sedentarisation of nomads in the 20th century. IX 537b

grab → GHURĀB
gu' (Somali) : the season from April to June which is the 'season of plenty' in Somalia. The other seasons are *xagaa* (July-August), *dayr* (September-November) and *jiilaal* (December-March). IX 714b
guban (Somali) : lit. burnt; a hot, dry region. IX 714a
gudhār (P) : a restricted area of a guild in which it practised its trade. IX 645b; also *gudhar*, a passage. X 488a
gul (P, T *gül*) : in botany, the rose, a recurring image in eastern Islamic literature. II 1133a
Among the dervishes, *gül* signifies a particular ornament, fashioned from wedge-shaped pieces of cloth, on the top of a dervish cap, which distinguishes the head of a house of the order; in various contexts ~ is the badge of different dervish orders and of distinct grades within the orders. II 1134a
♦ **gülbaba** (T) : a title, with the sense of head of a Muslim cloister, TEKKE, of the Bektāshī order. II 1133b
♦ **gulbāng** (P) : lit. song of the nightingale; in Turkish usage, *gülbāng* is applied to the call of the muezzin and to the Muslim war-cry. Under the Ottomans, ~ was used of certain ceremonial and public prayers and acclamations, more specifically those of the Janissary corps. II 1135a; and → TERDJÜMĀN
guldasta : in architecture, a shaft-like pinnacle, introduced in Tughluḳid work as a prolongation of the angle turret. VIII 315b
gūm (N.Afr, < A *ḳawm*) : the name given in the Arab countries of North Africa to a group of armed horsemen or fighting men from a tribe. They were given an official existence by the Turks in the former Regencies of Algiers and Tunis, who made them the basis of their occupation of the country, and were later used by the French to pacify the country. II 1138b
♦ gūma : a levy of GŪMS, troops; a plundering foray; sedition, revolt. II 1138b
gunbad (P) : a domed mausoleum. XI 114a
gunbrī (N.Afr, dim. *gunībrī*) : in its most primitive form, with a gourd, shell, or wooden sound-chest, a skin or leather belly, and horsehair strings wihtout tuning pegs, the earliest form of the pandore, or ṬUNBŪR, a long-necked lute-like instrument, known to us. It is to be found among the rural populations of North Africa from the Atlantic to the Nile. The North African name carries in its consonants *n-b-r* a trace of the old Egyptian word *nefer*. X 625a
güregen : 'royal son-in-law', a Činggisid title that Tīmūr Lang assumed after taking Saray Malik as his wife. X 511a
gürīzgāh (T, < P) : in Turkish prosody, the device in which the real purpose of the ḲAṢĪDA was revealed, either by openly naming the patron who was to be the subject of the encomium that followed immediately or by a clever allusion that rarely left any doubt as to the identity of the patron. V 957b; and → MAKHLAṢ
guru (J) : in Malaysia and Thailand, a mystical teacher. VIII 294a; VIII 296b ff.
gzîdan (K) : a Kurdish dance performed at the occasion of a festival celebrating the gathering of the mulberry harvest, which consists of sweeping the soil under the trees before the children climb them to shake them so as to allow the women to gather the berries. V 477b

H

hāʾ (A) : the twenty-sixth letter of the Arabic alphabet, transcribed *h*, with numerical value 5. It is an unvoiced glottal spirant (in Arabic: *rik̲h̲wa mahmūsa*). III 1a

ḥāʾ (A) : the sixth letter of the Arabic alphabet, transcribed *ḥ*, with numerical value 8. It is an unvoiced pharyngeal spirant (in Arabic: *rik̲h̲wa mahmūsa*). III 2a

ḥababawar → S̲H̲AḲĪḲAT AL-NUʿMĀN

ḥabaḳ → FŪD̲H̲AND̲J̲

ḥabal → BAYʿ AL-G̲H̲ARAR

ḥaballaḳ → NAḲAD

ḥabara (A) : a dark, silky enveloping outer wrap for women, worn in the Arab East. V 741a

ḥabas̲h̲ (A), or *ḥabas̲h̲a* : a name said to be of south Arabian origin, applied in Arabic usage to the land and peoples of Ethiopia, and at times to the adjoining areas in the Horn of Africa. III 2b

♦ **ḥabas̲h̲at** : a term found in several Sabaean inscriptions with apparent reference to Aksumite Abbyssinia, it has generally been assumed to apply not only to the territory and people of the Aksumite empire but also to a south Arabian tribe related to the former and in close contact with them; incense-collectors, applicable to all the peoples of the incense regions, that is, of the Mahra and Somali coasts and Abyssinia proper. III 9a

ḥabaṭ → ḤAWṬA

ḥabb (A) : grains, seeds.

♦ ḥabb al-naʿām (A) : in botany, 'ostrich berries', the red fruit of the sarsaparilla or thorny bindweed (*Smilax bona nox*) of the liliaceae family. VII 830b

♦ habb al-zalīm → YĀSAMĪN

ḥabba (A) : lit. grain or kernel; as a unit of weight, a ~ was a fraction in the Troy weight system of the Arabs, of undefined weight. The most probable weight of the ~ in the early days of Islam was about 70-71 milligrammes (1.1 grains). III 10b

ḥabḥab → D̲J̲IḤḤ

habbār → RUBĀḤ

ḥabīb (A) : lit. beloved; *al-Ḥabīb* is the usual Ḥaḍramī title of a SAYYID. IX 115a; IX 333a

ḥabīs (A) : an anchorite, recluse. IX 574a

habiz (SpA) : assumed to have been derived from *aḥbās* pronounced with a variation in timbre, i.e. *aḥbīs*, a term denoting property intended for charitable use and converted into a non-transferable right, but one that is not recognised in the Andalusī juridical texts concerning mortmain. XI 75a

ḥabḳa → TIMSĀḤ

ḥabs → MAWḲŪF; SID̲J̲N; ʿURWA; WAḲF

♦ **ḥabsiyya** (P, < A) : in Persian literature, a poem dealing with the theme of imprisonment. The genre can also be found in Urdu poetry and in the Indian tradition of Persian poetry. XII 333b

ḥabs̲h̲ī : a term applied in India for those African communities whose ancestors originally came to the country as slaves, in most cases from the Horn of Africa, although some doubtless sprang from the slave troops of the neighbouring Muslim countries. The majority, at least in the earlier periods, may well have been Abyssinian (→ ḤABAS̲H̲), but the name was used indiscriminately for all Africans. In modern India, ~ is often heard applied in a pejorative sense to an Indian of dark skin, and also frequently to a man of Gargantuan appetite. III 14a hād (A) : in botany, *cornucala monacantha*, which grows in dried-out basins in the Libyan Desert and provides excellent food for camels. V 352a

ḥadaba (A) : on the Arabian peninsula, a plain with a mantle of gravel. I 536b

ḥadaḳ (A) : the black pupil (of the oryx and addax), which in contrast to the white of the eye was an image dear to the poets. V 1229b

ḥaḍāna (A), or *ḥiḍāna* : in law, ~ is the right to custody of the child. I 28b; III 16b

ḥadat͟h (A) : in law, minor ritual impurity, as opposed to major impurity, DJANĀBA. A person who is in a state of ~ is called a *muḥdit͟h* and he can regain ritual purity by means of simple ablution, WUḌŪʾ. III 19b; VIII 929a; ~ in its plural form, *aḥdāt͟h*, means arbitrary actions at odds with the divine Law. I 384a

ḥadd (A, pl. *ḥudūd*) : hindrance, impediment, limit, boundary, frontier; in the Qurʾān, ~ is used (always in the pl.) to denote the restrictive ordinances or statutes of God. III 20b

In law, ~ has become the technical term for the punishments of certain acts which have been forbidden or sanctioned by punishments in the Qurʾān and have thereby become crimes against religion. The punishments are the death penalty, either by stoning or by crucifixion or with the sword; the cutting off of the hand and/or the foot; and flogging with various numbers of lashes, their intensity depending on the severity of the crime. III 20b

In theology, ~ in the meaning of limit, limitation, is an indication of finiteness, a necessary attribute of all created beings but incompatible with God. III 20b

In scholastic theology, philosophy and metaphysics, ~ is a technical term for definition, e.g. *ḥadd ḥaḳīḳī*, that which defines the essence of a thing, and *ḥadd lafẓī*, that which defines the meaning of a word. III 21a

In logic, ~ means the term of a syllogism. III 21a

In astrology, ~ denotes the term of a planet or the unequal portion, of which there are five, each belonging to a planet, into which the degree of each sign of the zodiac is divided. III 21a

Among the Druze, the main officers of the religious hierarchy are called *ḥudūd*. The five great *ḥudūd* 'cosmic ranks', adopted in a modified form from Ismāʿīlī lore, consist of the *ʿaḳl*, the *nafs al-kulliyya*, the *kalima*, the *sābiḳ*, and the *tālī*. II 632a; III 21a

ḥaddād (A, pl. *ḥaddādīn*) : a blacksmith. IV 819a; XII 756b

ḥaddūta → UḤDŪT͟HA

ḥad͟had͟h (A) : in prosody, a deviation in the metre because of the suppression of a whole *watid mad͟jmūʿ* (→ AWTĀD), as in *mutafā[ʿilun]*. I 672a

ḥad͟haf (A) : a strain of sheep in the time of al-D͟jāḥiẓ, with a black fleece and almost without a tail and ears, found in the Ḥid͟jāz and Yemen. Similar to the ~ was the *ḳahd*, with a russet-coloured fleece. XII 318a; a teal, or wild duck. IX 98b

ḥad͟hāfa (A) : a missile, recommended to throw between the legs of the galloping animal in hunting manuals in order to hamstring an animal. V 1229b

ḥad͟hd͟hāʾ (A) : a sandal-maker, whose profession in pre-modern times had a low social status because working with leather was regarded as unclean. XII 463b

ḥad͟hf (A) : in prosody, a deviation in the metre because of the suppression of a moving and a quiescent consonant, a *sabab k͟hafīf* (→ SABAB), e.g. *mafāʿī[lun]*. I 672a

In rhetoric, the truncation of words. VIII 427a; ellipsis. XII 669a

ḥad͟hw (A) : in prosody, the vowel immediately before the RIDF. IV 412a

hadī (A) : the name for the animal sacrificed in order to make atonement for certain transgressions committed during the ḤADJDJ. II 213a

hādī (A, pl. *huddāʾ*) : the sporting pigeon; the sport of pigeon-flying (*zad͟jl, zid͟jāl*) was very popular from the 2nd-7th/8th-13th centuries, among all the Muslim peoples. III 109a hadia langgar (Ind, < A HADIYYA) : a gift for the permission to cast the anchor, one of the tolls and taxes known in Atjèh in relation to sea trade. XII 200b

ḥadīd (A) : in metallurgy, iron; three kinds of iron were distinguished: natural iron, *al-sābūrḳān*, and artificial iron, of which there were two kinds, the weak or female, i.e. malleable or wrought iron (P *narmāhan* 'soft iron') and hard or male, i.e. manufactured steel (*fūlādh*). III 22b; V 971a

♦ ḥadīd ṣīnī → ṬALIḲŪN

ḥadīḍ → AWDJ

ḥāḍira (A) : in administrative geography, 'regional capital'. IX 36b

ḥadīth (A) : narrative, talk; *al-ḥadīth* is used for Tradition, being an account of what the Prophet said or did, or of his tacit approval of something said or done in his presence. III 23b; and → AHL AL-ḤADĪTH; DĀR AL-ḤADĪTH; KHABAR

♦ **ḥadīth ḳudsī** (A), and *ḥadīth ilāhī*, *ḥadīth rabbānī* : a class of Traditions which give words spoken by God, as distinguished from *ḥadīth nabawī* 'prophetical Tradition', which gives the words of the Prophet. III 28b

♦ ḥadīth ilāhī → ḤADĪTH ḲUDSĪ

♦ ḥadīth nabawī → ḤADĪTH ḲUDSĪ

♦ ḥadīth rabbānī → ḤADĪTH ḲUDSĪ

♦ ḥadīth al-thaḳalayn (A) : a Tradition which refers to the two sources of guidance that Muḥammad says he is leaving behind for the Muslims: the Qur'ān and AHL AL-BAYT. IX 331b; XI 389a

hadiyya (A) : a gift which in the Muslim East frequently implied an effort on the part of a person on a lower level of society to get into the good graces of a recipient of a higher social status, as opposed to HIBA. In the Muslim West ~ is commonly used with the restricted meaning of a sumptuous gift offered to a sovereign, either by another sovereign or by a group of some kind, while in Morocco especially, ~ was an obligatory gift made to the sultan by his subjects, later becoming a supplementary tax. III 343a; III 346b; in Persia, ~ is a gift to an equal, and the normal expression for the exchange of presents on diplomatic missions. III 347b

ḥadjal (A) : in zoology, the partridge. IX 98b

ḥadjar (A) : stone; also applied to any solid inorganic body occurring anywhere in Nature. III 29b; and → BAYʿ AL-MUNĀBADHA

♦ ḥadjar al-maṭar → YADA TASH

♦ ḥadjar al-ʿuḳāb (A) : 'eagle's stone', a stone-like substance found in the eagle's eyrie, which, when sucked, cures stammering. X 784a; also called *ḥadjar al-nasr* 'vulture's stone' and *ḥadjar al-ṭalḳ* 'stone of confinement'. VII 1013b

hadjar (A, Eth *hagar* 'town') : the normal word for 'town' in the epigraphic dialects of pre-Islamic South Arabia, now an element in place-names given to pre-Islamic town ruins in South Arabia. III 29b

ḥadjdj (A) : the pilgrimage to Mecca, ʿArafāt and Minā, one of the five pillars of Islam. It is also called the Great Pilgrimage in contrast to the ʿUMRA, or Little Pilgrimage. One who has performed the pilgrimage is called *ḥādjdj* or *ḥādjdjī*. III 31b; III 38b; and → AMĪR AL-ḤĀDJDJ

♦ ḥadjdj al-wadāʿ (A) : the last pilgrimage of the Prophet, in the year 10/632. III 37a

ḥadjdjām → FAṢṢĀD

ḥādjib (A) : the person responsible for guarding the door of access to the ruler, hence 'chamberlain'; a title corresponding to a position in the court and to an office the exact nature of which varied considerably in different regions and in different periods: superintendent of the palace, chief of the guard, chief minister, a head of government. III 45a; VIII 728a; XII 336b

Among the Būyids, ~ was known as a military rank in the army, with the meaning of general. III 46b

In Persian prosody, the internal RADĪF, which precedes the rhyme rather than following it. VIII 369a

♦ ḥādjib al-ḥudjdjāb (A), or *al-ḥādjib al-kabīr* : the equivalent of the Persian *sipah-sālār* (→ ISPAHSĀLĀR) or the Arabic AMĪR AL-UMARĀʾ found among dynasties like the Sāmānids, Būyids, G̲h̲aznawids and Great Saldjūḳs. VIII 924a

♦ al-ḥādjib al-kabīr → ḤĀDJIB AL-ḤUDJDJĀB

hadjin (A), or *s̲h̲ihrī* : the 'mixed breed', whose sire is better bred than the dam, one of four classifications of a horse. II 785b

ḥādjira → ẒĀHIRA

ḥādjis (A) : in Yemen, term for poetic inspiration. IX 235b

hadjm (A) : in medicine, cupping without or after the scarification, S̲H̲ARṬ. II 481b

hadjr → WIṢĀL

ḥadjr (A) : prevention, inhibition; in law, the interdiction, the restriction of the capacity to dispose; ~ expresses both the act of imposing this restriction and the resulting status. A person in this status is called *maḥdjūr* (*maḥdjūr ʿalayh*). I 27b; III 50a

♦ ḥadjra (A), or *kuffa, ṭawḳ* : in astronomy, the outer rim on the front of the astrolabe, which encloses the inner surface and into which a number of thin discs are fitted. I 723a

ḥādjūr → FILAWR

ḥadr → TAḤḲĪḲ

ḥaḍra (A) : presence; a title of respect; in mysticism, ~ is a synonym of *ḥuḍūr* 'being in the presence of God'. III 51a; a communal DHIKR exercise. IV 992b

The regular Friday service of the dervishes is called ~. III 51; in North Africa, the DHIKR recitation session. XI 468a

hady (A) : oblation; a pre-Islamic sacrificial offering which survived in Islam under the name ḌAḤIYYA. III 53b

haff → ḲUS̲H̲ḲUS̲H̲

ḥaffāra (A) : in zoology, the wrasse, whose Arabic term is found again in the Latinised nomenclature to specify a sub-species limited to a particular region (*Chrysophrys haffara*). VIII 1021a

ḥaffī (A) : a cotton material stemming from Nīs̲h̲āpūr. V 555a

ḥāfir (A) : a horse, as used in Tradition prohibiting competitions of animals. V 109a; 'horseshoe', a crescent-shaped ruby affixed to a piece of silk and attached to the top of the sovereign's turban, one of the caliph's insignia. VI 850a; hoof. IV 249b

ḥāfiẓ (A) : a designation for one who knows the Qurʾān by heart. VIII 171a; a great traditionist. IX 608a; and → ḤIRZ

hafr (A) : a dried-up well. X 788a

ḥafs̲h̲rūsī → KALB AL-BAḤR

haft-band (P) : in literature, a variety of TARDJĪʿ- or TARKĪB-BAND, particularly common in MART̲H̲IYAS, where each ḲAṢĪDA part, *k̲h̲āna*, comprises seven verses. X 235b

haft-rangī (P) : in art, a glazed tile technique similar to *cuerda seca* in which the design is incised and/or drawn with a greasy substance to separate colours. X 520a

ḥāgūza (Mor) : the name of a festival celebrated in Morocco, especially in the country, at the beginning of the solar year. V 1202a

ḥāʾik (A, pl. *ḥāka*), or *ḥayyāk* : weaver (syn. *nassādj*). XII 340b

In North Africa, ~, or *ḥayk, taḥaykt*, is a large outer wrap, usually white, worn by both sexes. V 746a

ḥāʾir (A) : a park or pleasure-garden, or zoological garden. III 71a

ḥakam (A) : in law, an arbitrator who settles a dispute (syn. *muḥakkam*). III 72a

♦ ḥakama → SARAFSĀR

ḥakawātī (A) : the professional storyteller of folktales. XII 775a

hā**kh**ām-ba**sh**ï (T) : in the Ottoman period, a chief rabbi, sent from Istanbul and having access to the central government. V 335b

ḥaḳīḳa (A, pl. ḤAḲĀʾIḲ) : reality; essence, truth; in rhetoric and exegesis, *al-ḥaḳīḳa* is the basic meaning of a word or an expression, and is distinguished from MADJĀZ, metaphor, and *kayfiyya*, analogy. III 75a; XII 653a

In philosophy, ~ has an ontological and a logical meaning. The ontological meaning (*ḥaḳīḳat al-shayʾ*) is best translated by 'nature' or 'essential reality'; the logical meaning (*al-ḥaḳīḳa al-ʿaḳliyya*) is the truth which 'the exact conception of the thing' establishes in the intelligence. III 75a ff.; V 1262a

In mysticism, ~ is the profound reality to which only experience of union with God opens the way. III 75b

♦ al-ḥaḳīḳa al-muḥammadiyya (A) : in the mystical thought of Ibn ʿArabī, the universal rational principle through which the Divine knowledge is transmitted to all prophets and saints, also called *rūḥ Muḥammad*. V 544a

♦ **ḥaḳāʾiḳ** (A) : the Ismāʿīlī term for their secret philosophical doctrines. I 1255b; III 71b

ḥākim → WĀLĪ

ḥakīm (A, pl. *ḥukamāʾ*; T *ḥekīm*) : sage; physician.

♦ al-ḥukamāʾ (A) : the ninth degree in the ṣūfī hierarchical order of saints. I 95a

♦ **ḥekīm-ba**sh**ï** (T) : in the Ottoman empire, the title of the chief palace physician, who was at the same time head of the health services of the state. III 339b

ḥaḳḳ (A, pl. **ḥuḳūḳ**) : something right, true, just, real; established fact; reality. I 275a; III 82b; and → AHL-I ḤAḲḲ; DĪN AL-ḤAḲḲ; RASM

In law, ~ is a claim or right, as a legal obligation. Religious law distinguishes *ḥaḳḳ Allāh*, God's penal ordinances, with *ḥaḳḳ al-ādamī*, the civil right or claim of a human. III 82b; III 551b; *ḥuḳūḳ*, when used of things in law, signifies the accessories necessarily belonging to them, such as the privy and the kitchen of a house, and servitudes in general. III 551b

In mysticism, ~ *al-yaḳīn* is the real certainty which comes after the acquisition of visual certainty and intellectual certainty. *Ḥuḳūḳ al-nafs* are such things as are necessary for the support and continuance of life, as opposed to the *ḥuẓūẓ*, things desired but not necessary. III 82a-b; III 551b

♦ ḥaḳḳ ʿaynī (A) : in law, a real right, as opposed to *ḥaḳḳ shakhṣī* 'personal right'. IX 495a

♦ ḥaḳḳ al-djahābidha → MĀL AL-DJAHĀBIDHA

♦ ḥaḳḳ-i ḳapan → ḲAPAN

♦ ḥaḳḳ-i ḳarār (T) : a fixed charge in the Ottoman empire on parcels of land known as ČIFTLIK, which a peasant had to pay in order to obtain permission to sell or give up his land. II 907a; VIII 486a

♦ ḥaḳḳ shakhṣī → ḤAḲḲ ʿAYNĪ

♦ ḥaḳḳ al-shurb → SHURB

♦ ḥuḳūḳ bayt al-māl (A) : assets of the Treasury; those monies or properties which belong to the Muslim community as a whole, the purpose to which they are devoted being dependent upon the discretion of the IMĀM or his delegate. I 1142a

ḥakma (A) : in the terminology of horse-riding, the curb-chain of the bit, which is also composed of branches, *shākima*, and a mouthpiece, *faʾs*. II 954a

ḥākūra (A) : a type of garden. XI 89a; in Sahelian Africa, an estate granted by the sultan to religious scholars or notables. XI 99b

ḥakw (A) : a binding for a waist wrapper, worn by both sexes on the Arabian peninsula (syn. *brīm*). V 741a

ḥāl (A, pl. *aḥwāl*) : state, condition; in mysticism, a spiritual state; the actualisation of a divine 'encounter'. III 83b; trance; among the Ḥmādsha in North Africa, ~ is used for a light, somnambulistic trance, while a deeper, wilder trance is called *djedhba*. XII 350b; and → ṬARAB

In medicine, ~ denotes 'the actual functional (physiological) equilibrium' of a being endowed with NAFS. III 83b

In grammar, ~ is the state of the verb in relation to the agent, its 'subjective' state. III 83b; circumstantial qualifier. IX 527b

In scholastic theology, ~ is the intermediate modality between being and non-being. III 83b; a technical term employed by some 4th-5th/10th-11th century Baṣran scholastic theologians, *mutakallimūn*, to signify certain 'attributes' that are predicated of beings. I 411a; II 570b; XII 343b

♦ ʿilm-i ḥāl (T) : a genre in Ottoman literature, forming a kind of catechism of the basic principles of worship and of behaviour within the family and the community. VIII 211b

ḥāla (A, pl. *ḥuwal*) : a term in the Persian Gulf for a low sandy islet which may be covered at high tide. I 535b

ḥalaḳ → DHĀT AL-ḤALAḲ

ḥalāl (A) : in law, everything that is not forbidden. III 660b

♦ ḥalāl al-dam (A) : in law, one who can be killed with impunity. IV 772a

ḥalam(a) → ḲIRDĀN

ḥalāwī (A) : in zoology, the guitar fish, whose Arabic term is found again in the Latinised nomenclature to specify a sub-species limited to a particular region (*Rhinobatus halavi*). VII 1021b

ḥalazūn (A) : in zoology, the general term for snail. VIII 707a

ḥalf → ḲASAM; MUSALSAL AL-ḤALF

ḥalfāʾ (A) : in botany, alfa-grass (*Stipa tenacissima*) and esparto-grass (*Lygoeum spartum*), two similar plants found in North Africa. The former is called in Tunisia ~ *rūsiyya* or *geddīm*. A field of alfa is sometimes called *zemla*. III 92a, where can also be found dialectal terms used in the harvesting of both plants

ḥalīb (A) : fresh milk, straight from the animal. XII 318b

halīladj (P, San), or *ahlīladj, ihlīladj* : in botany, myrobalanus, the plum-like fruit of the *Terminalia chebula*-tree, found in South Asia and the Malayan archipelago. The Arabs knew five kinds of myrobalanus. XII 349a

In mathematics, ~, but especially its variant *ihlīladj*, was used to designate an ellipse. XII 349b

ḥālim (A) : a boy who has attained to puberty, or virility. VIII 822a

ḥalḳ → ISTIḤDĀD

ḥalḳa (A) : a circle; gathering of people seated in a circle; gathering of students around a teacher, hence 'course'. I 817a; III 95a; V 1129a

Among the Ibāḍī-Wahbīs of the Mzāb, ~ was a religious council made up of twelve recluses, *ʿazzāba*, presided over by a SHAYKH. III 95a

Under the Ayyūbids and Mamlūks, a term for a socio-military unit which, during most of the period of Mamlūk rule, was composed of non-Mamlūks. Under Ṣalāḥ al-Dīn it seems to have constituted the elite of his army. I 765b; III 99a; and → AWLĀD AL-NĀS

In military science, ~ was the term used for the encirclement of the enemy in an increasingly tightening ring, a strategy employed by the Turkish and Mongol tribes in the field of battle. The same tactics were also very common in hunting, especially in the early decades of Mamlūk rule. III 187b

In astronomy, part of the suspensory apparatus of the astrolabe, the ~ is the ring which passes through the handle, ʿURWA, moving freely. I 723a

ḥalḳiyya (A) : in grammar, a term used by al-Khalīl to denote the laryngeals. III 598a
ḥall al-manẓūm (A) : lit. dissolving the versified; in literature, turning poetry into prose. XII 649b
ḥallādj (A) : cotton carder; the carder separated the fibre from the seed by beating the cotton with a bow-like instrument called *kemān* or *yay*. V 559a, where also can be found many names of artisans working with cotton in the Ottoman period
ḥallāḳ (A) : a barber, hairdresser (syn. *muzayyin*). XII 350a
ḥallām (A) : a mediaeval dish made from kid or calf, boiled in vinegar until cooked, then soused overnight in a mixture of vinegar, cinnamon, galingal, thyme, celery, quince, citron and salt, and stored in glass or earthenware vessels. X 31b
ḥālūsh → KALB AL-MAYY
hām, hāma → ṢADĀ
hama ūst (P) : 'All is He', in mystical thought on the subcontinent, the equivalent of WAḤDAT AL-WUDJŪD. The opposite, WAḤDAT AL-SHUHŪD, was said to maintain that 'All was from Him' (*hama az ūst*) or 'All is through Him' (*hama bidūst*). X 318a
hamada (Alg) : silicified limestone. XII 328a
ḥamal (A) : lamb; in astronomy, *al-~* is the term for Aries, one of the twelve zodiacal constellations, also called *al-kabsh* 'the ram' because of its 'horns'. VII 83a; XII 319a
♦ ḥamalat al-ʿilm (A), or *naḳalat al-ʿilm* : lit. bearers of learning; among the Ibāḍiyya, the ~ were teams of missionaries who were sent out after completion of their training to spread propaganda in the various provinces of the Umayyad caliphate. III 650b
ḥamām (A, pl. *ḥamāʾim, ḥamāmāt*) : in zoology, any bird 'which drinks with one gulp and coos', that is, any of the family of the Columbidae: pigeons and turtle-doves. In the restricted sense, ~ denotes the domestic pigeons. III 108b, where are found many terms, in the different countries, for the many different types of birds; for *ḥamām ḳawwāl*, → WĀḲWĀḲ
ḥamāsa (A) : bravery, valour; in literature, the title of a certain number of poetic anthologies which generally include brief extracts chosen for their literary value. III 110b; the boasting of courage, a subject of occasional verse. I 584b; the genre of the epic poem, although ~ has been replaced today by MALḤAMA in this sense. III 111b
In Persian literature, ~ has come to denote a literary genre, the heroic and martial epic. III 112a
♦ ḥamāsiyya : in Turkish literature, ~ indicates an epic poem. III 114b
hamasāla (P) : allocations on the revenue of specific villages or districts, according to which the taxpayers paid their taxes, up to the amount stipulated, to the holder of the ~ instead of to the government tax-collector. IV 1045a
ḥamd (A) : praise; in Urdu religious literature, specifically praise of God. V 958a
♦ **ḥamdala** (A) : the saying of the formula *al-ḥamdu li 'llāh* 'Praise belongs to God'. III 122b
ḥamḍ (A) : in botany, on the Arabian peninsula, a bush and a prime source of salt needed by camels. I 540b; IV 1143b
♦ ḥamḍiyyāt → NĀRANDJ
ḥāmiḍ → ḲĀRIṢ
ḥāmil (A) : in astronomy, an eccentric deferent for the epicycle nested within the pareclipic, one of three postulated solid rotating orbs to bring about a planet's observed motions. XI 555a
ḥamla (A) : in the Ottoman empire, the term used to designate the group of people at the rear of the Baghdad-Aleppo caravan. IV 679a; the charge of a wild animal. V 9a
ḥammāda (N.Afr) : large areas which are the outcrops of horizontal beds of secondary or tertiary limestone or sandstone (or calcareous or gypso-calcareous crusts of the quaternary era). III 136b

ḥammāl (A) : street-porter, bearer, who transports packages, cases, furniture, etc. on his back in towns and cities. In Istanbul, if two or more porters are required, a long pole, called *sırık* in Turkish, is used to carry the heavy load. In Fās, the ~ mostly carries cereals; the Berber word for porter, of which there is a special guild, is *žrzāya*. III 139a

♦ ḥammālbā<u>sh</u>ī (P) : in Ṣafawid Persia, beginning in ca. 1850, the collector of a port's customs fees. XII 717b

ḥammām → MUKAYYIS; WAḲḲĀD; ZABBĀL

ḥammāra → BA<u>GH</u>GHĀL

hamsāya (Pash) : in Afghanistan, a client attached to and living under the protection of a tribe. I 217a

ḥamūla (A) : a group of people who claim descent from a common ancestor, usually five to seven generations removed from the living. III 149b

hāmūr (A) : in the Persian Gulf, term for the grouper. I 541b

hamza (A) : the orthographical sign *alif*, which is the first letter of the Arabic alphabet, with numerical value 1. It is an unvoiced glottal occlusive. III 150a

♦ hamzat al-waṣl → ḲAṬʿ

ḥanak (A), or *taḥnīk al-ʿimāma* : a turban which was distinctively wound under the chin. Originally, the ~ was worn by the chief eunuchs of the Fāṭimid court, who were the AMĪRs of the palace. The caliph al-ʿAzīz was the first ruler to appear in the ~. This fashion was introduced into the East by the Fāṭimids from North Africa, where it still may be seen, especially in southern Algeria and Morocco. V 738a; for *taḥnīḳ*, the way of pulling it under the chin, X 610a; X 614b; and → IḲTIʿĀṬ

In anatomy, the palate. VI 130a

hanb → ANBĀ

ḥanbal (A) : a rug made of coarse wool. IX 764b

hanbala (A), or *hunbuʿa* : the swaying and limping gait of the hyena, as described in pre-Islamic poetry. XII 174a

handasa → ʿILM

ḥanfāʾ → AṬŪM

ḥanīf (A, pl. *ḥunafāʾ*) : in Islamic writings, one who follows the original and true (monotheistic) religion. In the Qurʾān, ~ is used especially of Abraham. III 165a; later Islamic usage occasionally uses ~ as the equivalent of MUSLIM. III 165b

♦ ḥanīfiyya (A) : the religion of Abraham, or Islam, especially when used by Christian writers. III 165b

ḥanīnī (A) : a headdress, borrowed (both name and object) by the ladies of France and Spain in the 14th-16th centuries (*hen[n]in*), and which is worn up to the present day by women among the Druse of the Lebanon and in Algeria and Tunis. X 58a

ḥāniṭ (A) : the child who has reached the age of reason. VIII 822a

ḥāni<u>th</u> → TAḤANNU<u>TH</u>

ḥannāt (A) : a wheat merchant. XII 757b

ḥan<u>sh</u>al (A, s. *ḥan<u>sh</u>ūlī*) : small parties of Bedouin on foot. II 1055a

han<u>sh</u>īr → ʿAZĪB

ḥantam → IKLĪL AL-MALIK

ḥanūṭ (A) : a perfume or scented unguent used for embalming (**ḥināṭa**), consisting of sweet rush or some mixture (*<u>dh</u>arīra*), musk, ʿANBAR, camphor, Indian reed and powdered sandal wood. III 403b f.

ḥānūṭ (A, < Ar) : a tent. IV 994b

ḥanẓal (A) : in botany, colocynth (*Citrullus colocynthis*), also called *ḳi<u>thth</u>āʾ al-naʿām* 'the ostrich's cucumber'. V 1229a; VII 830b

ḥāra (A) : a quarter or ward of a town; in Morocco, used as a synonym of MALLĀḤ, a special quarter for Jews. II 230a; III 169b; and → <u>SH</u>ĀRIʿ

ḥarāba (A) : a one-day battle among tribal factions; if it lasted longer than one day, it was called a *kawn*. IV 835a

ḥaraka (A) : motion; in philosophy, ~ is used for the Aristotelian notion of motion. III 170a

In grammar, ~ is a state of motion in which a ḤARF 'letter' exists when not in a state of rest, *sukūn*. It implies the existence of a short vowel, *a*, *i*, or *u*, following the letter. III 172a

♦ ḥarakī (A) : in modern-day terminology, 'activist', as in *tafsīr* ~ 'activist exegesis'. IX 118a

ḥaram (A) : among the Bedouin, a sacred area around a shrine; a place where a holy power manifests itself. I 892b; III 294b; III 1018a; the sacred territory of Mecca. I 604a; IV 322a; V 1003a

♦ **al-ḥaramayn** (A) : the two holy places, usually Mecca and Medina, but occasionally, in Mamlūk and Ottoman usage, Jerusalem and Hebron. III 175a

♦ ḥaramgāh → ḤARĪM

haram (A, pl. *ahrām, ahrāmāt*) : pyramid, pre-eminently the pyramid of Cheops and Chephren. III 173a

ḥarām (A) : a term representing everything that is forbidden to the profane and separated from the rest of the world. The cause of this prohibition could be either impurity (temporary or intrinsic) or holiness, which is a permanent state of sublime purity. IV 372b

♦ ḥarāmiyya (A) : 'bastards', currently 'highway bandits', one of the numerous terms in the mediaeval and modern periods for 'rascal, scoundrel'. XI 546a

ḥarb (A) : war. III 180a

♦ ḥarba → ʿANAZA

♦ ḥarbī (A), or *ahl al-ḥarb* : a non-Muslim from the DĀR AL-ḤARB. I 429b; II 126b; III 547a; VII 108b; IX 846a

ḥareket ordusu (T) : 'investing' or 'marching' army. I 64a; the name usually given to the striking force sent from Salonica on 17 April 1909 to quell the counter-revolutionary mutiny in the First Army Corps in Istanbul. III 204a

ḥarf (A, pl. *ḥurūf, aḥruf*) : letter of the alphabet; word. III 204b; in grammar, articulation of the Arabic language, a phoneme. III 597a; a Qur'ānic reading; dialect. III 205b

♦ ḥarf ʿilla (A), or *muʿtalla* : in grammar, a 'weak' consonant, viz. the semi-vowels *alif, wāw, yā'*. III 1129b; VIII 836b; VIII 990b

♦ ḥarf mutaḥarrik (A) : in grammar, an individual 'moving' consonant; a consonant with a vowel, as opposed to *ḥarf sākin*; a short syllable. I 669b

♦ ḥarf sākin → ḤARF MUTAḤARRIK

♦ ḥarfiyya (A) : a name for the cap of the turban. X 612a

♦ **ḥurūf al-hidjā'** (A) : the letters of the alphabet. III 596b

♦ ḥurūf al-muʿdjam (A) : in grammar, properly, those letters with diacritical points, but in practice ~ has become a synonym for *ḥurūf al-hidjā'*, the letters of the alphabet, but referring solely to writing. III 597a

♦ al-ḥurūf al-muḳaṭṭaʿāt → FAWĀTIḤ AL-SUWAR

♦ al-ḥurūf al-muṭbaḳa → IṬBĀḲ

♦ ʿilm al-**ḥurūf** (A) : onomatomancy, a magical practice based on the occult properties of the letters of the alphabet and of the divine and angelic names which they form. III 595b

♦ ḥurūfiyya (A) : in art, a movement of abstract art using Arabic calligraphy. X 366a

ḥarfūsh (A, pl. *ḥarāfīsh, ḥarāfīsha*), sometimes *kharfūsh* : vagabond, ne'er-do-well, often used in the sense of ruffians, rascals, scamps. The term frequently appears from the

7th/13th to the 10th/16th century in chronicles and other works dealing with the Mamlūk domains of Egypt and Syria, where it denotes the lowest element in the strata of Mamlūk society. During the Ottoman period ~ was replaced by *dju*ʿ*aydī* as a general term for vagabond, beggar. III 206a; XI 546a

ḥarīd (A) : in zoology, the parrot fish, whose Arabic term is found again in the Latinised nomenclature to specify a sub-species limited to a particular region (*Scarus harid*). VIII 1021b

harim → PĪR

hārim (A, pl. *hawārim*) : a (female) camel which feeds from the *harm* bush. I 541a

ḥarīm (A), also *ḥaramgāh*, **zanāna** : a term applied to those parts of the house to which access is forbidden; hence more particularly to the women's quarters. III 209a

ḥarīr (A, Ott *ipek*) : silk (syn. *ibrīsam, ḳazz*); ~ occurs in the Qur'ān, where it is said that the raiment of the people of Paradise will be silk, but Tradition and the schools of law traditionally forbid the wearing of silk to men, allowing it to women. III 209b

♦ ḥarīra (A) : a gruel made from flour cooked with milk, eaten by pre-Islamic Arabs. II 1059a

harīr → KHURŪR

harīsa (A) : the term for a dish of meat and bulgur, but in Egypt a sweet pastry made of flour, melted butter and sugar. V 234b; XII 775b

ḥarīsh → KARKADDAN

ḥarka → DJAYSH

ḥarḳāniyya (A) : a type of black turban, which the Prophet is said to have worn on his campaigns. The derivation of the term is uncertain: according to al-Suyūṭī, ~ stems from *ḥ-r-ḳ* 'to burn'. X 610a

ḥarmaliyyāt (A) : in mineralogy, inclusion or patches looking like African rye, a defect in a gem. XI 570a

ḥārr → ḲĀRIṢ

ḥarra (A, pl. *ḥirār*) : a basalt desert in Arabia, which owes its origin to subterranean volcanoes which have repeatedly covered the undulating desert with a bed of lava. I 535a; III 226a; III 362a; IX 817a

ḥarrāḳa (A) : 'fire ship'; ~ presumably denoted in origin a warship from which fire could be hurled at the enemy, but was soon used for passenger-carrying craft in Mesopotamia and also on the Nile. VIII 811a

ḥarrāthā → KALB AL-MAYY

ḥarṭānī (A, < B ?; pl. *ḥarāṭīn*) : name given in northwest Africa to a sedentary population of the oases in the Saharan zone; ~ is not applied in dialect exclusively to human beings, but is variously used for a horse of mixed breed, an ungrafted tree, a wilding, or a holding of land that is not free. III 230b

ḥarth (A) : crops. XI 412b

ḥarūn (A) : in the terminology of horse-riding, a horse that refuses to walk forward. II 953b

harwala (A), or *khabab* : a more rapid pace than *ramal*. X 864b

ḥarz → ʿIBRA

ḥasab (A) : nobility, possessed by one (*ḥasīb*) either with noble ancestry or acquired by the performance of memorable deeds of prowess or the display of outstanding virtues. III 238b

ḥasan (A) : good; in the science of Tradition, one of three kinds of Traditions, in between ṢAḤĪḤ 'sound' and ḌAʿĪF 'weak' or *saḳīm* 'infirm'. ~ Traditions are not considered as strong as *ṣaḥīḥ* Traditions, but are necessary for establishing points of law. III 25a; a 'fair' Tradition, a genuine euphemism for mostly poorly authenticated Traditions. VIII 983a

♦ **ḥasanī** (A) : the name given in Morocco to the money minted on the orders of Mawlay al-Ḥasan from 1299/1881-2 onwards. A ~, or *dirham ḥasanī*, is a coin with the value of a tenth of a douro. III 256a

ḥaṣāt → BAYʿ AL-MUNĀBA<u>DH</u>A

ḥa<u>sh</u>ar : corvée labour, syn. *bīgār*. XII 550a

ḥa<u>sh</u>arāt (A) : in zoology, insects; and → HAWĀMM WA-ḤA<u>SH</u>ARĀT

♦ ḥa<u>sh</u>arāt al-arḍ (A), or *<u>kh</u>a<u>sh</u>ā<u>sh</u>* : in zoology, small animals which live on the ground. III 307b

hā<u>sh</u>ima (A) : a fracture of a bone; a determining factor in the prescription of compensation following upon physical injury, DIYA. II 341b

hā<u>sh</u>imiyya (A) : a term commonly applied in the 2nd-3rd/8th-9th centuries to members of the ʿAbbāsid house and occasionally to their followers and supporters. III 265a

ḥa<u>sh</u>ī<u>sh</u> (A) : a narcotic product of *Cannabis sativa*, hemp. III 266a

♦ ḥa<u>sh</u>ī<u>sh</u>at al-naḥl → TURUN<u>DJ</u>ĀN

♦ ḥa<u>sh</u>ī<u>sh</u>at al-sanānīr (A) : 'herb for cats', in botany, the labiate Balm (*Melissa officinalis*). IX 653a

♦ **ḥa<u>sh</u>ī<u>sh</u>iyya** (A) : the name given in mediaeval times to the followers in Syria of the Nizārī branch of the Ismāʿīlī sect. Carried by the Crusaders from Syria to Europe, the name appeared in a variety of forms in Western literature, and eventually found its way in the form of 'assassin' into French and English usage with corresponding forms in Italian, Spanish and other languages, used at first in the sense of devotee or zealot. III 267b

ḥā<u>sh</u>iya (A, pl. *ḥawā<u>sh</u>ī*) : margin; marginal note, super-commentary on the commentary, <u>SH</u>ARḤ; gloss. I 593a; I 816b; III 268b; the entourage of a ruler. III 269a

ḥa<u>sh</u>m (A, P), or *ḥa<u>sh</u>m-i ḳalb, afwā<u>dj</u>-i ḳalb, ḳalb-i sulṭānī* : a term used in the 7th/13th century to denote the Dihlī cavalry, or the standing army at the capital. III 199a; V 685a; and → KABĀRA

♦ ḥa<u>sh</u>m-i aṭrāf : in India during the Dihli sultanate, a term denoting the cavalry which the IḲṬĀʿ-holders recruited from the regions in which they were posted, or from the garrisons under their command. Later, it was called the *ḥa<u>sh</u>m-i bilād-i mamālik*. V 685a

ḥa<u>sh</u>r (A) : in eschatology, the gathering. V 236a

♦ ḥa<u>sh</u>r ʿāmm → ḤA<u>SH</u>R <u>KH</u>ĀṢṢ

♦ ḥa<u>sh</u>r <u>kh</u>āṣṣ (A) : 'specific resurrection'; among the Imāmīs, the resurrection that will involve believers and unbelievers only from Muḥammad's community, and not from earlier communities, in contradistinction to the Resurrection, *ḥa<u>sh</u>r ʿāmm*. VIII 372a

ha<u>sh</u>t bihi<u>sh</u>t (P) : lit. eight paradises; a technical term in Mu<u>gh</u>al architecture used for a special nine-fold plan of eight rooms (four oblong [open] axial porches and four usually double-storeyed corner rooms) arranged around a central (often octagonal) domed hall. VII 795a; IX 46b

ḥa<u>sh</u>w (A) : 'stuffing'; 'farce', hence 'prolix and useless discourse'. I 671b; III 269b; and → ṢILA

In prosody, ~ is a collective name for the feet of a verse other than the last foot of the first hemistich and the last foot of the second hemistich. I 671b

♦ **ḥa<u>sh</u>wiyya** (A) : lit. those that stuff; a contemptuous term with the general meaning of 'scholars' of little worth, particularly traditionists. It is used of the *aṣḥāb al-ḥadī<u>th</u>* (→ AHL AL-ḤADĪ<u>TH</u>) who recognise as genuine and interpret literally the crudely anthropomorphic Traditions. I 410b; III 269b; IX 879b

ḥāṣil (A), or *bāʾika* : in mediaeval Islam, a warehouse. IX 788b; IX 793b; a shop. IV 1015b

In administration, revenue. IV 1055b; X 503b

ḥaṣūr (A) : one who leads a celibate life. X 12a
ḥatār (A), or *ḥitr, hutra* : a band placed vertically around the awning of an Arab tent, in order to fill the space which separates it from the ground. IV 1147b; and → ṬARĪḲA
hātif (A) : an invisible being whose cry rends the night, transmitting a message; a prophetic voice which announces in an oracular style a future happening. III 273a; in modern Arabic, a telephone. III 273b
ḥaṭīm (A) : a semi-circular wall of white marble, opposite the north-west wall of the Kaʿba. The semi-circular space between the ~ and the Kaʿba, which for a time belonged to the Kaʿba, is not entered during the perambulation. IV 318a
hawāʾiyya → HĀWĪ
ḥawāla (A) : lit. draft, bill; ~ is the cession, i.e. the payment of a debt through the transfer of a claim. III 283a; IV 405b; IX 770a
In finance, ~ is an assignation on a MUḲĀṬAʿA, tax payment, effected by order of the ruler in favour of a third party. The term is used both for the mandate and for the sum paid. III 283b
In Ottoman Turkish, ~ has the sense of a tower placed at a vantage-point; these towers were sometimes built for blockading purposes near castles which were likely to put up a long resistance. III 285a
ḥawāmīm (A), or *ḥawāmīmāt* : a name for the SŪRAs that begin with the initials *ḥā-mīm*: xl-xlvi. IX 887b
hawāmm wa-ḥasharāt (A) : in biology, crawling and swarming creatures, usually also including mice, rats, hedgehogs, lizards and snakes. X 378b
ḥawāntī (A) : in Muslim Spain, a shopkeeper in the SŪḲ, as opposed to the major trader, TĀDJIR. IX 789a
ḥawārī (A, < Eth) : apostle; a bird in Sumatra, 'smaller than a pigeon, with a white belly, black wings, red claws and a yellow beak', mentioned by al-Ḳazwīnī. IX 699b f.
♦ ḥawāriyyūn (A) : a collective term denoting twelve persons who at the time of the 'second ʿAḳaba' are said to have been named by Muḥammad (or those present) as leaders of the inhabitants of Mecca. III 285a
hawāy : a bird, which 'speaks better than a parrot', recorded in Mozambique by al-Ḳazwīnī in the 13th century. Presumably a mynah bird is meant. IX 699b
hawbar → ʿAWBAR; RUBĀḤ
ḥawḍ (A, pl. *aḥwāḍ, ḥiyāḍ*) : a cistern or artificial tank for storing water; drinking trough, wash-basin. III 286b; V 888a
In eschatology, the ~ is the basin at which on the day of the resurrection Muḥammad will meet his community. III 286a
♦ ḥawḍ al-sabīl → SABĪL
♦ ḥawḍ-i sulṭānī (IndP), or *ḥawḍ-i shamsī* : the first lake built outside the capital city of Dihlī, in the 7th/13th century, as a reservoir constructed for supplying drinking water to the city, but used for irrigation also. V 883b
hawda : a term used in India to designate the litter on working and processional elephants, either a long platform from which the passengers' legs hang over each side, or a more elaborate boxed-in structure with flat cushions which afforded more protection during tiger and lion hunts. The seat on the back of processional elephants has the ~ covered by a canopy, often jewelled, and is known as *ʿamārī*. VII 932b
ḥawdal → RUBĀḤ
ḥawdjam → WARD
ḥawfī (A) : a type of popular poetry peculiar to Algeria, consisting of short poems of between two and eight verses which are sung by girls or young women. The genre is more commonly called *taḥwīf*, which means the act of singing the ~. III 289b; IX 234a
ḥāwī (A, pl. *ḥāwiyyūn, ḥuwā*) : a snake-charmer or itinerant mountebank. III 291a

hāwī (A) : 'pertaining to air'; in grammar, an attribute of the letter *alif* which according to Sībawayh 'has some [exhaled] air'. For al-Khalīl, the *alif, wāw*, and *yā'* were *hawā'iyya*, that is to say *fī 'l-hawā'* 'in the air [exhaled]', which could be said to be slightly different. III 291a

ḥawidjār-bāshī (P) : in Ṣafawid times, an official in charge of supervising the poultry yard and scullery of the royal kitchen. XII 609b

hāwin (A) : the traditional mortar used for grinding coffee and spices (syn. *djurn*). XII 776b

ḥawīr (A) : in botany, the indigo tree, whose dye is called NĪL. I 540b

ḥawḳal (A) : a jealous, impotent old man. V 552a

ḥawl (A) : in law, a one-year holding period, a condition that applies in the obligation of ZAKĀT. XI 408a; XI 414a; and → ṬARAB

♦ ḥawlī (A) : a foal between one and two years of age. II 785a

♦ ḥawliyya (A) : a term used in the Sudan and the horn of Africa to denote a feast held in honour of a saint. VI 896b;

♦ ḥawliyyāt (A) : in literature, the genre of annals. X 298b

ḥawma : a district. IX 473a

ḥawrā' (A, pl. *ḥūr*) : white, applied in particular to the very large eye of the gazelle or oryx; by extension, ~ signifies a woman whose big black eyes are in contrast to their 'whites' and to the whiteness of the skin. III 581b

In eschatology, the plural **ḥūr** 'houris' is used in the Qur'ān for the virgins of Paradise promised to the believers. II 447b; III 581b

ḥawsh (A) : an unroofed burial enclosure, typically Cairene. IV 429b; in mediaeval Islam, an enclosed area, urban or suburban, of rural aspect, a yard of beaten earth, where cattle or poor immigrants could be accommodated. IX 788b

ḥawshab → KHUZAZ

ḥawṭ (A) : in southern Arabia, a red and black twisted cord which a woman wears round her hips to protect her from the evil eye. III 294a

♦ **ḥawṭa** (A), or *ḥabaṭ* : enclave, enclosure; in southern Arabia the name given to a territory placed under the protection of a saint and thus considered sacred. III 294a

ḥāwūn (A) : in the mediaeval kitchen, a mortar to crush e.g. spices. A similar larger mortar (*djāwūn*) was used for pounding meat and vegetables. VI 808b; X 114b

ḥawz (A, > Sp *alfoz* 'district'; pl. *aḥwāz*) : in North Africa, particularly Morocco, the territory, suburb, environs of a large town; in Tunisia, ~ had a fiscal sense. With *al-*, ~ denotes exclusively the region of Marrakesh, the Haouz, a wide embanked plain drained by two wadis. III 300b

hay'a (A) : shape, form, state, quality; configuration; in philosophy, predisposition, disposition. III 301a

♦ **ʿilm al-hay'a** (A) : in astronomy, (a branch of) astronomy, dealing with the geometrical structure of the heavens. III 302a; III 1135a; VIII 105b; VIII 785b

ḥayʿala (A) : the shīʿī formula of the call to prayer. XI 479b

ḥayāt (A) : life. III 302a

ḥayawān (A) : the animal kingdom; an animal or animals in general, including man, who is more precisely called *al-ḥayawān al-nāṭiḳ*. III 304b

ḥayḍ (A) : menstruation; menstrual blood. A discharge which exceeds the legal duration fixed for the menses is called *istiḥāḍa*. III 315b; VIII 1023a

ḥaydar (A) : 'lion'; by-name given to ʿAlī b. Abī Ṭālib. III 315b

ḥayderī (T) : a short dervishes' garment without sleeves, stopping at the waist. V 752a

haydūra → FARW

ḥayk → ḤĀ'IK

haykal (A, pl. *hayākil*) : in mysticism, the physical world as a whole as well as the planets. II 555a; as a Qur'ānic term, an entity in the story of the Creation that encloses the seas which surround the heavens and the earth and is itself enveloped by the KURSĪ. IV 984a

haylādj (A), or *mutaḳaddim* : 'significator', in astronomy, the 'advancing' planet or place. Along with the promissor, the succeeding or second (*al-thānī*) planet or place, it is used to calculate the TASYĪR arc. X 366b

haylala (A) : the formula *lā ilāha illā 'llāh.* X 465b

hayr (A, pl. *hayarāt*) : the name for the Great Pearl Banks, which stretch along nearly the entire length of the Arabian side of the Persian Gulf. I 535b

ḥayra → TAḤAYYUR

ḥays (A) : a mixture of dates, butter and milk, associated with the tribal tradition of the Ḳuraysh and said to be among the favourite dishes of the Prophet. II 1059a; X 901a; XII 366b

hays → SILB

haytham (A) : in zoology, the young eaglet, male and female (syn. *ḍarim, tuladj* and *tulad*). X 783b

ḥaythūthiyya → KAYFŪFIYYA

hayūlā (A, < Gk) : substance, primary matter; ~ is sometimes substituted for *mādda* and sometimes distinguished from it, but frequently the two terms are considered virtually synonymous. II 554a; III 328a; X 530a

ḥayy (A) : clan, i.e. the primary grouping in nomadic life. I 306a; III 330a; in certain modern dialects, a quarter in a town or settlement, in particular that inhabited by the same ethnic or tribal element. III 330b

ḥayya (A) : in zoology, snake, a generic name of the ophidians, embracing all kinds of reptiles from the most poisonous to the most harmless. III 334b

ḥayyāk → ḤĀ'IK

hazadj (A) : in prosody, the name of the sixth Arabic metre. I 670a; a metre of quantitative rhythm composed of a foot of one short and three longs repeated three times, hence four equal feet. VIII 579a

hazār-bāf (P) : lit. thousand-weave; in architecture, a glazing tile technique, also known as *bannā'ī* 'mason-like', simulating the pattern of masonry, consisting of glazed bricks or ends of bricks, set into a matrix of unglazed bricks to form geometric and epigraphic patterns to cover large surfaces. X 520a

hazārāt : millenary cycles, a theory of Indian astronomy. I 139b

ḥazawwar (A) : said of a boy who has become strong, and has served, or one who has nearly attained the age of puberty. VIII 822a

ḥāzī (A, < Ar) : an observer of omens; a generic term covering different divinatory and magical practices. IV 421b; one who divines from the shape of the limbs or moles on the face. I 659b

ḥāzir (A) : sour milk, despised by pre-Islamic Arabs. II 1057b

ḥaẓīra : in architecture, a funerary enclosure. X 520b

hazliyya (A) : in prosody, a satirical, slanderous and obscene poem. XI 238b

ḥazm → DJABAL

ḥazzāb (A) : a person attached to certain mosques in Algeria, who had to recite a defined portion of the Qur'ān, ḤIZB, twice a day so as to achieve a complete recitation of the Qur'ān in one month. III 513b

ḥazzūra (A, pl. *ḥazzūrāt, hazāzīr*) : a riddle, which with story-telling and jokes, *nukat* (s. *nukta*), are the most common and basic forms of entertainment among the Bedouin and the inhabitants of rural areas around the Middle East. XII 775a hedje (T) : in Turkish prosody, syllabic metre, usually of 11 syllables divided 6-5 with no caesura. VIII 2b

heello → BELWO

hees → MAANSO

ḥekīm → ḤAKĪM

hēl (A) : cardamom, frequently used to flavor coffee. XII 775b

herbed (P) : a Zoroastrian who knows the Avesta and has been initiated as a priest. VII 215b

hiba (A) : a gift, especially that from a more highly placed person to one on a lower level of society, in contrast to HADIYYA. III 342b

In law, ~ is a gift *inter vivos*, a transfer of the ownership of a thing during the lifetime of the donor, and with no consideration payable by the donee. III 350a

♦ hiba bi-sharṭ al-ʿiwaḍ (A) : a gift with consideration, whereby the donee undertakes to compensate the donor. III 351a

ḥibāla (A, pl. *ḥabāyil*), or *uḥbūla* : in hunting, a snare with a draw-net. IX 98b

ḥibāra (A) : in early Islam, a striped garment similar to the BURDA and said to be the favourite garment of the Prophet; also, a fabric. V 734a

ḥibn → RUBĀḤ

ḥibr → MIDĀD

ḥidāʾ (A) : in zoology, the kite. I 1152b

ḥidd (A, pl. *ḥudūd*) : a term in the Persian Gulf for a sand bank. I 535b

hidjāʾ (A) : a curse; an invective diatribe or insult in verse, an insulting poem; an epigram; a satire in prose or verse. III 352b; a trivial mocking verse of an erotic and obscene content. VIII 376b; and → ḤURŪF AL-HIDJĀʾ

ḥidjāb (A) : the veil. I 306b; III 359a; the curtain behind which caliphs and rulers concealed themselves from the sight of their household, also known as *sitāra, sitr*. III 360a; an amulet which renders its wearer invulnerable and ensures success for his enterprises. III 361a

In medicine, ~ is a membrane which separates certain parts of the organism, e.g. *ḥidjāb al-bukūriyya* 'hymen', *al-ḥidjāb al-ḥādjiz* or *ḥidjāb al-djawf* 'diaphragm', *al-ḥidjāb al-mustabṭin* 'pleura'. III 359a

In mysticism, ~ represents everything that veils the true end, all that makes man insensitive to the Divine Reality. III 361a

ḥidjāma → FAṢṢĀD

hidjar → HIDJRA

ḥidjāzī → ʿUDHRĪ

ḥidjr → ḤIṢĀN

hidjra (A) : the emigration of Muḥammad from Mecca to Medina in September 622; the era of the ~, distinguished by the initials A.H., beginning on the first day of the lunar year in which that event took place, which is reckoned to coincide with 16 July 622. III 366a; ~ implies not only change of residence but also the ending of ties of kinship and the replacement of these by new relationships. VII 356a

In the context of Saudi Arabia, ~ (pl. **hidjar**) is a Bedouin settlement, many of which were established by ʿAbd al-ʿAzīz b. ʿAbd al-Raḥmān Āl Suʿūd to promote the sedentarisation of the Bedouin of Saudi Arabia during the first quarter of the 20th century. III 361b; III 1064b; IX 904b

In Yemen, an inviolable sanctuary recognized by the tribes that are linked to it, often by a formal agreement, and used by them as neutral territory. XI 276b

In law, emigration to the DĀR AL-ISLĀM, by Muslims residing in the DĀR AL-ḤARB. XII 368a

hidjrān → WIṢĀL

hidjris → RUBĀḤ; THAʿLAB

hidjwiyya (T, < A) : in Turkish literature, a satirical ḲAṢĪDA attacking an enemy or someone of whom the poet disapproves. IV 715b

ḥikāya (A) : 'imitation', hence tale, narrative, story, legend. III 367a; in the *Fihrist*, ~ is used in the sense of a textual copy as well as an account of the facts, equivalent to RIWĀYA. III 368b; and → KHABAR

In the science of Tradition, ~ implies a literal quotation, a verbatim reproduction, as in the expression *ḥakaytu ʿanhu 'l-ḥadītha ḥikāyatan*. III 368b

In grammar, ~ means the use in a narrative of the verbal form which would have been used at the time when the event narrated took place. III 368b

♦ ḥikāyat iʿrāb (A) : in grammar, the exact repetition of a word used by a speaker with a vowel of declension no longer appropriate to its function in the new context. III 368b

♦ ḥikāyat ṣawṭ (A) : onomatopoeia. III 368b

ḥiḳḳa (A) : a female camel in its fourth year. XI 412a

ḥikma (A) : wisdom; science and philosophy. III 377b; IX 879b; and → DĀR AL-ḤIKMA

In the Qurʾān, ~ is used in several Medinan passages for the revelation or part of it. V 402b

ḥikr (A) : in law, one of the various forms of long-term lease of WAḲF property, common in Egypt and Syria. Similar forms were called DJALSA, ENZEL, GEDIK, IDJĀRATAYN, KHULUWW AL-INTIFĀʿ and NAṢBA. XI 67b; XII 368b

hilāl (A) : the new moon, the crescent. III 379a; and → TAHLĪL

ḥilf (A) : a covenant, compact, especially that between quite separate tribes, conducing to the amalgamation of these tribes; friendship, and, by extension, oath. III 388b

In pre-Islamic Arabia, the ~ was an institution which merged with that of WALĀʾ, the admission of an individual to a clan; a second type of ~ consisted of the agreement between the clans within one tribe through which they settled on a common line of conduct; a third type of ~ could also be arranged between opposing clans within one group, or between different groups, for the accomplishment of a particular object. III 388b

ḥill (A) : in law, freedom of action in sexual matters. I 27a; the unconsecrated area outside of the ḤARAM of Mecca. X 864b

ḥilla (A, pl. *ḥilal*) : in Saudi Arabia, a shanty town that grew up around the main urban centres. X 944a

ḥilm (A) : justice and moderation, forbearance and leniency, self-mastery and dignity of bearing, as contrasted with *djahl*, the fundamental characteristic of the DJĀHILIYYA, and *safah* or *safāha*. III 390b; V 435a; discretion. IX 332b

ḥiltīt (A) : 'devil's dirt'; the latex of the asafoetida (*andjudhān*) which, when exposed to the air, hardens into a dirty-yellow gum resin. VIII 1042b

ḥimā (A) : lit. protected, forbidden place; in Arabia, an expanse of ground, with some vegetation, access to and use of which are declared forbidden by the man or men who have arrogated possession of it to themselves. II 1005b; III 294b; III 393a; IV 1143b; VIII 495a; IX 817a

ḥimāla → ḤIRZ

ḥimār (A) : in zoology, the donkey (fem. *atān, ḥimāra*). III 393b

♦ ḥimār hindī (A) : 'white donkey', a term used by al-Djāḥiẓ for the rhinoceros, translated from the Greek. IV 647b

♦ ḥimār al-waḥsh (A) : in zoology, the onager. V 1228a

ḥimāya (A) : 'protection', from the pre-Islamic period given, in return for financial compensation, by a nomadic tribe to the settled inhabitants (syn. KHAFĀRA), or the protection by a superior of the property of the inferior, from whose point of view it is called

TALDJIʾA. The institution of ~ is almost unrecognised by Islamic law, but was in fact important in classical Islamic society. III 394a
In the context of mediaeval Islamic taxation, a supplementary tax levied by the police for their services. I 1144a; II 143b; III 394b
In politics, ~ refers to various bilateral treaty agreements, particularly those contracted between Great Britain and the sheikhly rulers of states on the western seaboard of the Persian Gulf. III 395a
In North Africa, ~ has been used officially of the protection exercised by a foreign Christian power over certain individuals, then over states. III 395a

ḥiml (A) : lit. load, a measure of capacity used in mediaeval Egypt for great quantities of various commodities. The ~ was reckoned at 600 Egyptian RAṬLS, i.e. 266 kg, but as far as spices were concerned it consisted of 500 *raṭl*s only, i.e. 222.45 kg. VI 119b

ḥināḍ (A) : horses thinned down for horse-racing by being covered with blankets so that excessive weight was sweated off. II 953a

ḥināṭa → ḤANŪṬ

hind (A) : in geography, ~ denoted regions east of the Indus as well as practically all the countries of Southeast Asia; only when used together with *sind*, which referred to Sind, Makran, Baluchistan, portions of the Panjab and the North-West Frontier Province, was the whole of mediaeval India meant. III 404b

hindibāʾ (A) : in botany, cultivated endive (*Cichorium endivia*), particularly widespread in the Muslim West and known there under its Mozarabic name *sharrāliya* or its arabicised form *sarrākh*; in Morocco, the Berber term *tīfāf* is mainly used. XII 370b; chicory, one of the Prophet's preferred vegetables. II 1058a

hindū (A) : name given to the largest religious community of India. III 458b

hing → ANGŪZA

ḥinn (A) : an inferior species of DJINN, belief in which is accepted by the Druze. XII 371a

ḥinnāʾ (A) : in botany, henna (*Lawsonia alba*), the whitish flower of which was called *fāghiya* or *faghw*. III 461a

ḥinṭa → ḲAMḤ

ḥinth (A) : in law, perjury. IV 687b; X 99a

ḥirbāʾ (A) : in zoology, the chameleon. The female is most often called *umm ḥubayn*, while the male is referred to by a number of KUNYAS, the most frequent in Muslim Spain being *abū barāḳish*. The idea of 'chameleonism', i.e. the ability to become invisible by turning the same colour as that of any object on which it happens to be, is termed *talawwun*. II 1059b; III 463a

ḥirfa → ṢINF

hirkūl (A), or *manāra* : in zoology, the finback. VIII 1022b

hirmīs → KARKADDAN

hirr → SINNAWR

ḥirz (A) : a talismanic charm (pl. *aḥrāz*), pronounced *ḥurz* in the Maghrib today. Other words for 'amulet' are *ḥidjāb* in Egypt, *ḥimāla, ḥāfiẓ, ʿūdha, miʿw adha* amongst the Arabs of the Mashriḳ, *yafta, nuskha* and *ḥimāla* amongst the Turks, and *tilism* amongst the Persians. X 500b
In law, safe keeping, either by the guarding by a watchman or by the nature of the place, e.g. a private house. IX 62b

ḥisāb (A) : computation; in the Qurʾān, the 'reckoning' which God will require on the Day of Judgement, YAWM AL-ḤISĀB. III 465a
♦ **ḥisāb al-ʿaḳd** (A), or *ḥisāb al-ʿuḳad* or *al-ʿuḳūd, ḥisāb al-yad*, and *ḥisāb al-ḳabḍa bi 'l-yad* : dactylonomy, digital computation, the art of expressing numbers by the position of the fingers. III 466a

♦ **ḥisāb al-djummal** (A) : a method of recording dates by chronogram, consisting of grouping together, in a word or a short phrase, a group of letters whose numerical equivalents, added together, provide the date of a past or future event. III 468a

♦ **ḥisāb al-ghubār** (A) : calculation by means of dust, a Persian method which owes its name to the use of a small board on which the calculator spread a fine layer of dust in which he drew GHUBĀR numerals. III 468b

♦ ḥisāb hawāʾī → ḤISĀB MAFTŪḤ

♦ ḥisāb al-hind (A) : calculation by means of the Indian numerals. III 466b

♦ ḥisāb maftūḥ (A), or *ḥisāb hawāʾī* : mental calculation. III 469a

♦ ḥisāb al-nīm (A) : a divinatory procedure based upon the process of adding the numerical value of all the letters forming a word (in this case a proper name), by which it can be predicted which of the two rulers at war will be the victor and which the vanquished. III 468b

♦ **ʿilm al-ḥisāb** (A) : arithmetic. III 1138a

ḥiṣān (A) : a term used to distinguish the pure-bred stallion from the pedigree brood-mare, which is called *ḥidjr*, since the word for horse, FARAS, is not specific. II 785a; IV 1143b

ḥiṣār (A) : in military science, siege. III 469a

In Turkish use, a castle, fortress, citadel, stronghold, a common component of place-names in Turkey. III 483a

♦ ḥiṣār-eri (T) : in the Ottoman empire, guards in the fortresses. X 503a

ḥisba (A) : the duty of every Muslim to 'promote good and forbid evil'; the function of the person, *muḥtasib*, who is effectively entrusted in a town with the application of this rule in the supervision of moral behaviour and more particularly of the markets. III 485b; VIII 402b; religious magistrature, judgeship. I 27b

For the Ottoman empire, → IḤTISĀB

ḥiṣn (A) : fortress, a fairly common element in place-names. III 498a

ḥiss (A) : in philosophy, sense-perception, sometimes used with the meaning of (individual) sense. III 509a

ḥitr → ḤATĀR

ḥiyal (A, s. *ḥīla*) : artifices, devices, expedients, stratagems; the means of evading a thing, or of effecting an object; mechanical artifices, automata; tricks of beggars and conjurors, etc. III 510b; XII 371b

In law, circumventions of the law. I 28a; legal devices; the use of legal means for extra-legal ends. I 123b; III 159b; III 511a

In military science, ~ (with synonyms *makāʾid* and *ādāb*) is a technical term for strategems of war. III 510b

ḥiyāṣa (A) : a cloth belt with a silver plaque in the centre, worn by men in the Arab East. V 741a; a bridal girdle. X 904a

ḥiyāza → ḲABḌ

ḥizām (A) : a belt or sash worn about the waist by both sexes in the Arab East. V 741a

ḥizb (A, pl. *aḥzāb*) : a group, faction, a group of supporters; part, portion. III 513a; in modern Arabic, a political party. III 514a

In Qurʾānic studies, ~ indicates a definite portion of the Qurʾān which a believer binds himself to recite. In certain countries, e.g. Egypt and those of North Africa, the Qurʾān is divided into 60 *ḥizb*s, which are half the length of the 30 DJUZʾs attested from a very early period. III 513b

In mysticism, ~ or **wird** (pl. *awrād*) denotes the recitation of Qurʾānic verses and prayers composed by the founder of the order at the beginning of the DHIKR session. II 224a; X 245a; in Egypt, ~ denotes a religious fraternity, as well as the 'office' of each fraternity, consisting of the above-mentioned recital during the Friday service.

From this meaning, ~ has come to mean formulae of 'supererogatory liturgy'. III 513b; ejaculatory prayer. XI 113a

hoca → KHĀWDJA

ḥol (Mal) : a term used in Malaysia to denote a feast held in honour of a saint. VI 896b

horde (Eng, < T ORDU) : name given to the administrative centre of great nomad empires, particularly also to the highly adorned tent of the ruler; then to such nomad confederacies themselves, insofar as they formed a tenuous association linked to no particular place, substantially different in their way of life and government from the settled population, and inflicting considerable damage on this population by their marauding attacks. III 536a

hoz → TIRA

ḥubāra (A), or *ḥubārā* : in zoology, the bustard. I 541b; II 1058b; IX 98b

ḥubus → WAḲF

hubūṭ → ṬĀLIʿ

ḥudāʾ (A), or *ḥidāʾ* : the camel driver's song. II 1073a

hūdabarī (P) : in the time of the Tīmūrids, term used in conjunction with SOYŪRGHĀL if the latter was on a permanent basis and not renewed annually. IX 732a

hudhud (A) : in zoology, the hoopoe. III 541b

ḥudjariyya (A, < *ḥudjra* 'room') : a term used in Egypt for the slaves who were lodged in barracks near to the royal residence. Under the Fāṭimids, they were organised into a sort of military bodyguard. II 507a; II 1080a; III 545b

ḥudjdja (A) : a Qurʾānic term meaning both proof and the presentation of proof, ~ is applied to a conclusive argument attempting to prove what is false as well as what is true; dialectical proof. III 543b

In shīʿī theology, the ~ refers to that person through whom the inaccessible God becomes accessible, and sometimes to any figure in a religious hierarchy through whom an inaccessible higher figure became accessible to those below. In its more specialised meaning, ~ referred to a particular function within the process of revelation, sometimes identified with the role of Salmān as witness to ʿAlī's status as IMĀM. III 544b

Among the Ismāʿīliyya, ~ is a rank in the hierarchy, coming under the BĀB. The ~ conducted the DAʿWA, and was one of the greater DĀʿĪs, of whom there were twelve, or occasionally twenty-four. Each seems to have been in charge of a district. In some works, the ~ is also called the *lāḥiḳ*. I 832b; II 97b; III 544b

Among the Nizārīs, ~ was used for Ḥasan-i Ṣabbāḥ as visible head of the movement when the IMĀM was hidden; later, it developed into one ~ who alone, by divine inspiration, could fully perceive the reality of the *imām*; eventually the ~ became simply the *imām*'s heir-apparent. III 544b

ḥudjra (A) : room, apartment; with *al-*, especially the room of ʿĀʾisha where the Prophet, Abū Bakr and ʿUmar were buried, now one of the holiest places of Islam. III 545b

hudna (A) : peace agreement; truce. I 24a; III 546b

In law, ~ is equivalent to 'international treaty', whose object is to suspend the legal effects of hostilities and to provide the prerequisite conditions of peace between Muslims and non-Muslims, without the latter's territory becoming part of the DĀR AL-ISLĀM. III 547a

ḥudūd → ḤADD

ḥuḍūr → ḤAḌRA

ḥudūth (A) : the verbal noun of *ḥadatha*, which means 'to appear, to arise, to take place'. III 548a

♦ **ḥudūth al-ʿālam** (A) : in philosophy, both the existence of a thing, after its non-existence, in a temporal extension; and contingency, i.e. the fact of a being's existing after not having existed, but in an ontological or essential extension, which does not necessarily involve time. III 548a

ḥufra → WAḲʿA

hūhū → WĀḲWĀḲ

ḥukamāʾ → ḤAKĪM

ḥuḳḳ → MAGHNĀṬĪS

♦ ḥuḳḳa → IBRA; NARDJĪLA

ḥukm (A, pl. *aḥkām*) : decision, judgement. I 257a; effect. I 318b; injunction. VIII 667a; and → FARMĀN

For ~ in law, → AḤKĀM

In philosophy, ~ means the judgement or act by which the mind affirms or denies one thing with regard to another, and thus unites or separates them. III 549a; also, sensory intuition, where assent of the mind immediately follows perception. III 549b

In grammar, ~ means the specific activity of a word, the proper function which the word performs at its basic position, *martaba*, in which it is placed. III 550a

In Ottoman Turkish, ~ is also used in the sense of a special type of order, the documents of which were to be dealt with separately by the administration and which, at present, are registered in the Turkish archives as a separate archival item, *aḥkām defterleri*. I 1170b

♦ ḥukm-i ḥāṣil : the sharing of the harvest; one of three methods of collecting land revenue under the Dihlī sultanate. II 273a

♦ ḥukm-i misāḥat : the measurement of the area under cultivation and assessment according to a standard rate of demand per unit area according to the crop sown; one of three methods of collecting land revenue under the Dihlī sultanate. II 273a

♦ ḥukm-i mushāhada : the estimating of the probable yield of the harvest; one of three methods of collecting land revenue under the Dihlī sultanate. II 273a

ḥuḳna (A) : in hunting, the covered-over pit-trap, also called *ughwiyya, mughawwāt, wadjra* and *dafīna*. V 9a; IX 98b

ḥukr (A) : a tax on the lands used for pasture, paid by shepherds in Morocco during the Marīnid period. VI 573b

ḥuḳra → SHĀWĪ

ḥuḳūḳ → ḤAḲḲ

ḥukūma (A) : the act or office of adjudication by a sovereign, a judge or an arbitrator. I 384a; III 551b

Under the Saldjūḳs, and in the Ottoman period, ~ denoted the office or function of governorship, usually provincial or local. III 552a

In the Kurdish lands, the term *ḥukūmet* stood for a number of regions listed among the components of certain Ottoman EYĀLETs. III 552a

In modern Arabic, ~ means government, which sense seems to have been first used in 19th-century Turkey. In Persia, *ḥukūmat* still has the more general sense of political authority. III 552a

♦ ḥukūmat, ḥukūmet → ḤUKŪMA

ḥükümdār (T, A) : a governor-general. IV 686b

ḥulā (A) : ornaments, personal jewellery. III 568b

ḥulalliyya : a large dark wrap wound around the body with the upper parts pulled down over the shoulders and secured with pins, worn in Egypt. V 741a

ḥulla (A) : a word which in the mediaeval period used to refer to a suit consisting of two or more garments. Today, it means 'a western suit of clothes'. V 737a

ḥullān (A), or *ḥullām* : the lamb or kid born of a Caesarian section. XII 319a

ḥulm → RUʾYĀ

ḥulūl (A) : the act of loosing, unfastening, untying; resolving a difficulty; in scholastic theology and mysticism, an infusion of substance, the incarnation of God in a creature. In the thought of al-Ḥallādj, ~ means an intentional complete union (in love), in which the intelligence and the will of the subject are acted upon by divine grace. III 102b; III 571a,b; IV 283a
In grammar, ~ denotes the occurrence of the accident of inflection, IʿRĀB. III 571b
In law, ~ denotes the application of a prescription. III 571b
In philosophy, ~ denotes both the inhesion of an accident in an object and the substantial union of soul and body. III 571b

ḥulwān (A) : a succession tax paid by those heirs of the tax farmers (→ MÜLTEZIM) who desired to inherit tax farms. It was one of the taxes which formed an additional source of revenue for the Egyptian government in the years immediately preceding the Napoleonic invasion of 1798. II 148b; 'douceur', 'donative'. III 572a

humā (P) : in zoology, the bearded vulture (*Gypaetus barbatus*), the largest of the birds of prey in the Old World. III 572a

humāyūn (P) : 'fortunate, glorious, royal'; used as an epithet of the ruler, but has in recent years become obsolete. III 574a

ḥummuṣ (A) : in botany, chick peas, one of the winter crops in mediaeval Egypt. V 863a

ḥumra (A) : in medicine, erysipelas. IX 9b

ḥums (A) : in pre-Islamic times, the holy families serving the local sanctuaries. II 1059a; people observing rigorous religious taboos, especially Ḳuraysh and certain neighbouring tribes. Although ~ is the plural of *aḥmas* 'hard, strong (in fighting or in religion)', one of the ~ is called *aḥmasī*, fem. *aḥmasiyya*. The observance of the taboos was called *taḥammus*. III 577b

hunbuʿa → HANBALA

ḥunṭūz (A) : in Morocco, a headdress worn by women, triangular in shape, made of linen, three inches long and broad and a span high, with silk and silver, the whole thing looking like a camel's hump. X 612a

ḥūr → ḤAWRĀʾ

ḥurḍa (A) : the archer in a game of MAYSIR. VI 924a

hurmizd → MUSHTARĪ

ḥurrās (A) : a guard. XII 549b

ḥurriyya (A, T *ḥurriyyet*) : an abstract formation derived from *ḥurr* 'free'. In a legal sense, ~ denotes freedom as opposed to slavery; through mysticism, where ~ appears as one of the guide-posts on the mystical path, and denotes basically the freedom of the mystic from everything except God and the devotion to Him, ~ came to occupy a significant position in Muslim metaphysical speculation. III 589a

ḥurūf, ḥurūfiyya → ḤARF

ḥurūḳ → ṬĀLIʿ

ḥurz → ḤIRZ

ḥusayniyya → TAKIYA

ḥūsh (A) : the country of the DJINN, into which no human ventures; a fabulous kind of camels, which are the issue of a cross between ordinary camels and *djinn* stallions. III 637b
♦ ḥūshī → GHARĪB; WAḤSHĪ

ḥusn (A) : loveliness, excellence; and → BAYĀN; TAKHALLUṢ

ḥūt (A, pl. *aḥwāt, ḥītān*, in dialect, *ḥiyūta*) : a term often used to designate fish in general, but applied primarily to very large fish and cetaceans. VIII 1020b; and → SAMAK
In astronomy, *al-* ~ is the term for Pisces, one of the twelve zodiacal constellations. VII 84a

♦ ḥūt al-ḥayḍ → FĀṬŪS
♦ ḥūt mūsā (A), or *ḥūt mūsā wa-yūsha*ʿ : lit. the fish of Moses [and of Joshua], in zoology, a name for the common sole (*Solea vulgaris*). VIII 1020b
♦ ḥūt sīdnā sulaymān (A) : lit. the fish of our master Solomon, in zoology, a name for the common sole (*Solea vulgaris*). VIII 1021a
♦ ḥūt sulaymān (A) : lit. the fish of Solomon, in zoology, a name for the salmon. VIII 1023a
♦ ḥūt Yūnus (A) : lit. the fish of Jonah, in zoology, a name for the whale. VIII 1022b
♦ ḥūtiyyāt (A) : in zoology, the marine mammals or cetaceans. VIII 1022b
ḥutra → ḤATĀR
huwa huwa (A) : lit. he is he, or it is it; in logic, ~ means what is represented as entirely identical; modern logicians express this equation with ≡. III 642b
In mysticism, ~ is the state of the saint whose perfect personal unity testifies to divine unity in the world. III 642b
ḥuwārāt (A) : in mysticism, female attendants who received the donations of the female devotees. X 249b
huwayriyya → WARDJIYYA
huwiyya (A) : ipseity, an abstract term formed to translate the Plotinian category of identity, ταὐτότης, and the Aristotelian ὄν 'being', although for the latter ~ is used interchangeably with ANNIYYA and *wudjūd*. I 514a; III 644a
In modern Arabic, ~ means 'identity'. III 644a
hūwiyya (A) : the most characteristic part of the ritual surrounding the yearly occasion of retreat of the Demirdāshiyya order, in which the head of the order, a number of leaders and some members form a circle turning anti-clockwise while calling *hū, hū*. XII 208b
ḥuwwārā (A) : the whitest flour, for baking bread. V 41b
ḥuẓūẓ → ḤAKK

I

ʿibādāt (A, s. *ʿibāda*) : submissive obedience to a master, and therefore religious practice, corresponding, in law, approximately to the ritual of Muslim law. III 647a; 'the religious acts which bring the creature into contact with his creator', while its counterpart, MUʿĀMALĀT, signifies relations between individuals. VI 467a; acts of worship. IX 323b
♦ **ʿibādat-khāna** (IndP) : a house of worship built by the Mughal emperor Akbar (1542-1605) where learned men of all religions assembled to discuss theological problems. I 317a; XII 378a
ʿibādī (A) : Christian. I 196a
ibʿādiyya → ABʿĀDIYYA
ibāḥa (A) : originally, 'making a thing apparent or manifest', hence 'making a thing allowable or free to him who desires it'; in law, ~ was first used with regard to those things which every one is permitted to use or appropriate (and → MUBĀḤ); in a narrower sense, ~ denotes the authorisation, given by the owner, to consume (part of) the produce of his property. III 660b
In theology, ~ is a term that is commonly applied to antinomian teachings (or actions) of certain shīʿī and ṣūfī groups, as in the accusation *ibāḥat al-maḥārim* 'allowing the forbidden'. II 136b; III 662a; VIII 146a
♦ ibāḥiyya → SHUYŪʿIYYA

ʿibāra (A) : in mysticism, the ‘literal language’, which is unsuitable for exoteric topics, in contrast to the coded language of ISHĀRA. XII 753a

ibdāʿ (A) : absolute creation; primordial innovation; the bringing into existence with nothing preceding, as opposed to KHALḲ, the bringing into existence from an existing thing. III 663b

ibdāl (A) : replacement, mutation; in grammar, a term indicating both morphological features involving a mutation of a phonetic character, and doublets, e.g. *madaḥa* and *madaha*, which have the same meaning but differ from each other by a single consonant. III 665a; VIII 836b

ibhām (A) : in literary theory, amphibology. X 395b

ibil (A) : in zoology, the collective noun for the dromedary (*camelus dromedarius*) and the camel proper (*camelus bactrianus*). III 665b; and → BAʿĪR; DJAMAL

ibn (A, pl. ABNĀʾ) : son. III 669b; descendant. VIII 163a

♦ ibn adīmayn → DALW

♦ ibn awbar (A) : in botany, the sand truffle. III 670a

♦ ibn ʿirs (A) : in zoology, the ferret (*Mustela putorius furo*). II 739b; weasel. III 670a; X 224a

♦ ibn al-khiyāratayn (A) : ‘the son of the elect’, a designation by shīʿīs to the fourth IMĀM of the Twelver shīʿa since, according to a tradition of the Prophet, the Ḳuraysh are the elect of the Arabs and the Persians are the elect of the non-Arabs. XI 482a

♦ ibn yaʿḳūb (A) : lit. the son of Jacob; in zoology, a name for the common sargo (*Diplodus sargus*). VIII 1021a

ibra (A) : a term used in navigation denoting the needle of a compass, *ḥuḳḳa*. The rose of the compass was known as *bayt al-ibra* and consisted of a circle divided into thirty-two rhumbs (*akhnān*) which were named after prominent stars whose risings and settings were approximately on these rhumbs. VII 51b

♦ ibrat al-rāʿī, or *ibrat al-rāhib* → SHAWKA

ibrāʾ → ṢULḤ AL-IBRĀʾ

ʿibra (A) : the assessed value of the revenue on an estate. III 1088b; IV 557a; ~ may have originated simply as an extension of MASĀḤA and MUḲĀSAMA, the average annual value of the crop over a number of years, usually three, assessed by whatever method, being taken as the basis on which the tax was calculated. The term ~ is not met with after the early centuries and appears to have been replaced by *ḥarz*, which, in the later centuries, seems usually to have meant not an average calculation made on the basis of three or more years, but an arbitrary valuation arrived at by the tax-collector, sometimes, but not always, after an inspection of the crop during growth or harvest time. IV 1031b; IV 10388a

ibrīḳ (A) : in art, a term used for any kind of ewer, irrespective of function or material, but generally a vessel for pouring water or wine. Other terms for specific kinds of ewers are *bulbula* or *kubra*. V 989a; XII 406a

In music, the neck (syn. *ʿunḳ*) of the ʿŪD. X 769b

ibrīsam → ḤARĪR

ibrīz (A) : in numismatics, purified gold. Other laudatory terms for coins are *djayyid* ‘good, excellent’, *khāliṣ, khāṣṣ, ṣafī, ṣurāḥ* ‘pure (unmixed) metal’, and *ṣaḥḥ*, the paraph or official mark on an ʿOthmānli gold coin testifying to its authenticity. X409b

ibrīzim (P) : a type of silk from Khurāsān. V 329a

ibtidāʾ (A) : introduction, prologue; in rhetoric, the ~ is one of the three sections of the poem or composition which should receive particular attention and should conform to certain criteria of style and content. The other two sections are TAKHALLUṢ ‘transition’, and the **intihāʾ** ‘conclusion’. III 1006a; III 1246a

In law, ~ is used as a technical term in the expression *ibtidāʾan*, meaning ‘per se’. I 339a; and → ISTIʾNĀF

ič oghlānï (T), or *ič agha* : lit. lad of the interior; the name given to the ʿADJAMĪ OGHLĀN after he was appointed to the sultan's household. I 206b; Ottoman term for those boys and youths, at first slaves, recruits and occasionally hostages, later free-born Muslims, who were selected for training in the palaces in Edirne and Istanbul in order to occupy the higher executive offices of the state. I 394a; III 1006b

icazetname → IDJĀZA

ʿīd (A, < Ar) : festival. III 1007a

♦ **ʿīd al-aḍḥā** (A), and *ʿīd al-ḳurbān*, *ʿīd al-naḥr* : the 'sacrificial festival' during the yearly pilgrimage on 10 Dhu 'l-Ḥidjdja. This festival is also known as *al-ʿīd al-kabīr* 'the major festival' as opposed to *al-ʿīd al-ṣaghīr* 'the minor festival, another name for ʿĪD AL-FIṬR. III 1007b; XII 317a; and → LEBARAN

♦ **ʿīd al-fiṭr** (A) : the 'festival of breaking the fast' of Ramaḍān on 1 Shawwāl. III 1008a; and → ʿĪD AL-AḌḤĀ; LEBARAN

♦ ʿīd al-ḳurbān → ʿĪD AL-AḌḤĀ

♦ ʿīd al-naḥr → ʿĪD AL-AḌḤĀ

īdāʿ → TAḌMĪN; WADĪʿA

iʿdādī (T) : 'military preparatory' schools, founded by the Ottoman sultan ʿAbd al-Madjīd I in 1845. I 75a

iḍāfa (A, P *ezāfe*, T *izâfet*) : in grammar, the uniting of one term with another, the determinative complement or 'construct state', by which possession, material, etc. is expressed. The first term is called *al-muḍāf*, the second *al-muḍāf ilayhi*. III 1008a; for Persian *ezāfe*, XII 441a

idāra (A) : common name in the modern Islamic languages for administration, acquiring its technical significance during the period of European influence. III 1010b

idbār → IḲBĀL

ʿidda (A) : in law, the duration of widowhood, or the legal period of abstention from sexual relations imposed on widows or divorced women, or women whose marriages have been annulled, providing the marriage was consummated, before remarriage. I 28a; I 172b; III 1010b; VIII 28a; VIII 836a

iddighām → IDGHĀM

ʿīdgāh → NAMĀZGĀH

idghām (A), or *iddighām* : in grammar, the contraction of two similar consonants in a geminate. III 1013a; assimilation. VIII 121a; VIII 344a; VIII 836b; X 73b

īdhāʾ → SHATM

idhāʿa (A) : broadcasting (*mudhīʿ* 'broadcaster', *midhyāʿ* 'microphone'), inaugurated in the Islamic world in Turkey in 1925. III 1014a

idhār → LIDJĀM

ʿidhār (A), or *khaṭṭ* : the down of a young man. IX 313b

idhkhir (A) : in botany, a fragrant plant used to decorate houses and tombs, but also used by blacksmiths. IV 819b; and → KHAMĪL

idhn (A) : authorisation, in particular, in law, the authorisation necessary to enable certain types of incapable persons to conclude isolated legal transactions, and the general authorisation to carry out commercial transactions in a normal way. III 1016a

In religious law, a safe conduct given by non-Muslims to a Muslim in their territory. For its opposite, → AMĀN. I 429b

īdjāb → BAYʿ

idjāba (A) : 'answer-poem', a genre of Arabic poetry. VIII 805a

idjār (A), and *idjāra* : in law, a contract to hire, in particular the hiring out of a service and of movable objects, with the exception of ships and beasts which are used for transportation. III 1017a; V 126b; XII 691b

idjāra (A) : the granting of protection to a stranger according to ancient Arab practice; to ask for protection is *istadjāra*, and the *djār* (pl. *djirān*) is mostly the person protected, but may also be the protector. III 1017b; and → ĪDJĀR; IDJĀZA

♦ idjāratayn (A, T *idjāreteyn*) : a form of long-term leasing of WAḲF property, common in Anatolia and all countries formerly part of the Ottoman empire since the 16th or 17th century. ~ contracts involved immediate payment of a lump sum as well as yearly, variable, rather low rents. XII 368b; a 'double rent' agreement, whereby a relatively high entry fine was paid, in exchange for which the tenant was allowed a lease which his heirs might inherit. IX 542a

iʿdjāz (A) : lit. the rendering incapable, powerless; since the second half of the 3rd/9th century, the technical term for the inimitability or uniqueness of the Qurʾān in content and form. III 1018a; V 426b; IX 887a

īdjāz (A) : in rhetoric, terseness. VIII 614b; X 79a

idjāza (A) : authorisation, licence; and → RIḲĀʿ

In the science of Tradition, ~ means, in the strict sense, one of the methods of receiving the transmission of a Tradition, whereby an authorised guarantor of a text or of a whole book gives a person the authorisation to transmit it in his turn so that the person authorised can avail himself of this transmission. III 27a; III 1020b

In law, the qualification, upon culmination of one's legal education, to teach the law (~ *li 'l-tadrīs*), issue a fatwā (~ *li 'l-fatwā*), or both. X 80b

In modern Persian and in Ottoman Turkish, as *icazetname*, the term has come into modern use to mean 'certificate of fitness' (to teach). III 1021a

In prosody, ~ (or *idjāra*) is used for the substitution of an unrelated letter for the RAWĪ, the rhyme letter. IV 412b

In rhetoric, ~ is used both when a poet builds some lines or even a whole poem on a single line or hemistich suggested by somebody else, often a ruler, and when two poets compose alternately a hemistich or one or more lines of the same poem. When this is done in the form of a contest, the term *tamlīṭ* (*mumālaṭa, imlāṭ*) is found. III 1022a

idjdhāb → TAḤAYYUR

idjhāb (A) : abortion, which is prohibited after quickening (*nafkh al-rūḥ*), usually at the end of the fourth month. X 199a

idjmāʿ (A) : in law, the third, and in practice the most important, of the sources of legal knowledge, being the unanimous agreement of the community on a regulation imposed by God. Technically, ~ is the unanimous doctrine and opinion of the recognised religious authorities at any given time. I 259b; II 182b; II 887b; III 1023a; V 239a; IX 324b

idjmāl (A) : a summary register. IX 123b f.

idjtihād (A) : lit. effort; in law, the use of individual reasoning; exerting oneself to form an opinion in a case or as to a rule of law, achieved by applying analogy to the Qurʾān and the custom of the Prophet. The opposite is called TAḲLĪD, the unquestioning acceptance of the doctrines of established schools and authorities. I 259b; III 1026a; IX 324b

♦ idjtihād fi 'l-madhhab (A) : the creative development of the law within the broad structures of the *madhhab*. X 138a

♦ idjtihād muṭlaḳ (A) : in law, the creative act of *idjtihād* through which the founding IMĀMs derived from the revealed sources a systematic structure of law. X 137b

idjtimāʿ (A) : in astronomy, the conjunction (mean or 'true') of the sun and moon. In astrology, ~ is sometimes employed to refer to the conjunction of the planets, although *ḳirān* is preferred. IV 259a

In human psychology, ~ is the intermediary between the faculty of desire and the active power, the decision which follows after a hesitation between action and no-action, as a result of which one of the two prevails. According to others, ~ is the desire to act at its maximum intensity. V 577b

idjtizāʾ (A) : in metrics, the shortening of vowels. XI 374a
idmāʾ → SHIʿĀR
iḍmār (A) : concealing; in grammar, ~ is used in the sense of 'imply'; it is used by grammarians when speaking about an unexpressed grammatical element, supposedly existent and active (ant. *iẓhār*). With Sībawayh, ~ refers to the personal pronoun, which later became *al*-MUḌMAR, which was preferred over *al-maknī*, the Kūfan term. III 1027b
In prosody, ~ has taken on a technical meaning, denoting 'the quiescence of the *tāʾ* of *mutafāʿilun* in the *Kāmil*'. I 672a; III 1028a; a case of ZIḤĀF where the second vowelled letter of the foot is rendered vowelless. XI 508b
idrādj (A) : in prosody, ignoring the caesura between hemistichs (syn. *tadwīr*). X 79a
idrāk (A, P *dar-yāftan*) : sensory perception; comprehension (syn. *fahm*); in philosophy, ~ implies an *adaequatio rei et intellectus*. The whole philosophical problem of ~ is to find out what this adequation is, and how and where it is achieved. III 1028a
idrār (A) : pension. XI 84b
iḍṭirāb → ṬARAB
iḍṭirār (A) : compulsion, coercion, as opposed to IKHTIYĀR, freedom of choice.
In theology, human actions carried out under compulsion were distinguished from those carried out of free choice; the latter were voluntary and the results of an acquisition, *iktisāb* (→ KASB). With al-Ashʿarī, the opposite correlatives became no longer *iḍṭirār-ikhtiyār*, but *iḍṭirār-iktisāb*. In later Ashʿarite theology, ~ is reserved for an action that, of itself, cannot take place. III 1037b; and → ḌARŪRA
ifāḍa (A) : a term used for the running of the pilgrims from ʿArafāt on the evening of the 9th of Dhu 'l-Ḥidjdja after sunset in which they trace the road by which they had come from Mecca. III 36a; along with *fayḍ* 'course made in an enthusiastic manner', ~ is used for the other courses than SAʿY. IX 97b; and → ṬAWĀF AL-IFĀḌA
iflās (A) : in law, bankruptcy. V 717b
iflāt → IṬLĀḲ
ʿifr → KHANZUWĀN
ifrād (A) : in the context of the pilgrimage, one of three methods of performing it, consisting of making the ḤADJDJ alone, at the prescribed time, the ʿUMRA being performed outside the month of the pilgrimage or simply neglected. III 35a; III 53b; X 865b
ifrandj (A), or *firandj* : the Franks. The name was originally used of the inhabitants of the empire of Charlemagne, and later extended to Europeans in general. In mediaeval times, ~ was not normally applied to the Spanish Christians, the Slavs or the Vikings, but otherwise it was used fairly broadly of continental Europe and the British Isles. Between the 16th and the 19th centuries, ~ came to designate European Catholics and Protestants. III 1044a
ifrāṭ (A) : among the shīʿīs, exaggeration in religion. IX 163b
ifrīḳiya (A, < L) : the eastern part of the Maghrib, whence the name adopted by some modern historians for Eastern Barbary. It was sometimes confused with the whole of the Maghrib and sometimes considered as a geographically separate region. III 1047a
ʿifrīt (A, pl. *ʿafārīt*) : an epithet expressing power, cunning and insubordination, ~ occurs only once in the Qurʾān, in the sense of rebellious. Later, in its substantive form, it came to mean a class of particularly powerful chthonian forces, formidable and cunning. In the popular tales, the ~ is a DJINN of enormous size, formed basically of smoke; it has wings, haunts ruins and lives under the ground. ~ may be used of humans and even animals, and then expresses cunning, ingenuity and strength. In Egyptian Arabic, ~ also has the meaning of the ghost or spirit of a person deceased. III 1050a; IX 406b
ifsintīn → AFSANTĪN
iftāʾ → FUTYĀ

iftitāḥ (A) : in the science of diplomatic, the introduction or introductory protocol of documents, whose individual parts (*fawātiḥ*), according to al-Ḳalḳas͟handī, are the *basmala, ḥamdala, tas͟hahhud, ṣalwala* (*taṣliya*), *salām*, and *baʿdiyya* (*ammā baʿdu*). II 302a; and → ṬIRĀZ

īg͟hāl (A) : in rhetoric, epiphrasis. V 898a; and → MUBĀLAG͟HA

īg͟hār (A) : in classical Muslim administration, both an exemption or a privilege with respect to taxes, and the land which was covered by this privilege. The term became absorbed in that of IḲṬĀʿ in later centuries. III 1051a

♦ ig͟hāra (A) : lit. raiding; in literature, the rather archaic procedure of a famous poet forcing a less famous one to give up a flawless line, because the more famous poet has a greater right to it. XII 647a; XII 707b

ig͟herm → AGADIR

ig͟hrāb → ISTIG͟HRĀB

ig͟hrīḳiyya → YŪNĀN

ig͟htāla → TAḌABBABA

iğretileme → ISTIʿĀRA

iḥāle (T) : one of three principal ways in which mining activity was organised in the Ottoman empire, the others being EMĀNETEN and ILTIZĀMEN. ~ meant the long-term concessionary leasing of state lands for purposes of mining exploration to licensed individuals or mining companies. V 974b

īhām (P) : in prosody, *double entendre*. IX 90b; X 395a; and → TAWRIYA

iḥāṭa (A) : in law and theology, integral truth. V 239b

iḥāza → USTĀN

iḥdāt͟h (A) : an innovation in time; the act of bringing into existence a thing that is preceded by a time. III 1051a

iḥfāʾ (A), or *d̲jazz* : moustache. The verb used in cutting the ~ is *ḳaṣṣ*. IX 312a f.

ihlīlad̲j → HALĪLAD̲J

iḥrām (A) : the state of temporary consecration of someone who is performing the pilgrimage, ḤAD̲JD̲J or ʿUMRA. The entering into this holy state is accomplished by the statement of intention, accompanied by certain rites, and for men, by the donning of the ritual garment. A person in this state is called *muḥrim*. III 1052b

iḥrans͟hafa (A) : to prepare to fight (said of a cock); to begin to pay a forfeit (said of a man). XI 546a

iḥṣāʾ (A) : 'enumeration'; among the Nuḳtawiyya sect, ~ is used to designate the process of how, when a being rises or descends from one level of existence to another, the traces of his former existence are still visible and can be discerned by the insightful. VIII 115a; population census. X 307b

iḥsān (A) : in Mauritania, a contract for the loan of a lactiferous animal, the hiring of a young camel for the purpose of following a she-camel so that she continues to give milk. VI 313a; and → IKHLĀṢ

iḥṣān → MUḤṢAN

ihtidāʾ (A) : orientation, e.g. as given by the stars (in nightly travel). VIII 97b

iḥtikār (A) : the holding up of or speculation in foodstuffs, condemmed by Tradition. X 467b

iḥtisāb (A, T) : an official term in the administration of the Ottoman empire, its basic meaning being the levying of dues and taxes, both on traders and artisans and also on certain imports, but it came to denote the whole aggregate of functions that had devolved upon the *muḥtasib* (→ ḤISBA). III 489a; licenses, providing part of the revenue of the tax system of the Ottoman period. V 334a

iḥtiyāṭ (A) : in Turkish military usage, reserve of the regular army, to be contrasted with the *redīf* (→ RADĪF) 'reserve army' or militia, created in 1834. VIII 370a

In law, prudence in legal matters, characteristic of the S͟hāfiʿī school. IX 812b

iḥyāʾ → MAWĀT

īḳāʿ (A) : a term denoting musical metrics or rhythm in the sense of measuring the quantity of notes. The early Islamic ~ can be considered as a forerunner of mediaeval European mensura. XII 408b

īḳāb (A) : penetration from sexual intercourse. XI 510a

iḳāla (A) : in law, *mutuus dissensus*, a mutual agreement between the parties to put an end to a contract. I 319b; III 1056b

iḳāma (A) : the second call to the ṢALĀT, pronounced by the muezzin in the mosque before each of the five prescribed daily *ṣalāt*s and that of the Friday service. I 188b; III 1057a; VIII 927b; XI 269b

iḳbāl (A) : in astronomy, in the expression *al-iḳbāl wa 'l-idbār*, trepidation, the presumed oscillation of the equinoxes. XI 504a

ʿikbir (A) : the bee-glue (syn. *khatm, dundj*), which with wax (*shamʿ*) and honey (*ʿasal*) is produced by the workers (*ʿassālāt*) among the bees. VII 907a

iḳdāda (A) : a white KĀFIYYA worn in summer in the Arab East. V 741a

ikerzī (B) : a Berber turban consisting of a white cloth wound about the head leaving the crown uncovered. V 746a

ikfāʾ (A) : in prosody, the substitution of a cognate letter for the rhyme letter, RAWĪ, e.g. *nūn* for *mīm*. IV 412b

ikhāwa → KHĀWA

ikhlāṣ (A) : 'dedicating, devoting or consecrating oneself' to something; ~ is pre-eminently an interior virtue of the faithful Muslim, whose perfection of adherence, and witness, to his faith is gauged by ~ and *iḥsān* 'uprightness in good'. The opposites of ~ are *nifāḳ* 'hypocrisy' and *shirk* 'associating others, or other things, with God'. III 1059b; VIII 547a

ikhshīd (P) : a title given to local Iranian rulers of Soghdia and Farghāna in the pre-Islamic and early Islamic periods. III 1060b

ikhtilādj (A) : spontaneous pulsations, tremblings or convulsions of the body, particularly the limbs, eyelids and eyebrows, which provide omens the interpretation of which is known as *ʿilm al-ikhtilādj* 'palmoscopy'. III 1061a; V 100b

ikhtilāf (A) : 'difference, inconsistency'; in law, the differences of opinion among the authorities of law, both between schools and within each of them. III 1061b

ikhtirāʿ (A) : in literary criticism, 'original invention', as differing from crude plagiarism. XII 656b

ikhtiyār (A) : choice; and → IḌṬIRĀR

In philosophy, ~ means free preference or choice, option, whence power of choice, free will. III 1037a; III 1062a

In law, ~ has the meaning of opinion freely stated. III 1062a

In treatises on the IMĀMA, where ~ has the meaning of choice or election, it is customary to contrast the *ahl al-ikhtiyār* with the *ahl al-naṣṣ*, the supporters of free election with the supporters of textual determination. III 1063a

In astrology, the auspicious days. X 366b

♦ **ikhtiyārāt** (A) : 'hemerologies and menologies' (L. *electiones*); in divination, hemerology, an astrological procedure whose aim is to ascertain the auspicious or inauspicious character of the future, dealing with years, months, days and hours. III 1063b; VIII 107b

In literature, ~ is a synonym of MUKHTĀRĀT 'anthologies'. III 1064a; VII 528b

♦ **ikhtiyāriyya** (T, < A) : the elite or veterans of an Ottoman guild or army unit. XII 409b

ikhwān (A) : brethren; the term most commonly used for DARWĪSH in Morocco and Algeria. II 164a; a religious and military movement of Arab tribesmen which had its heyday from 1912-1930 in Arabia. III 1064a

♦ ikhwāniyya (A) : in prosody, a versified letter, in which protestations of friendship are found integrated with the theme of youth and of old age. IV 1005a; IX 387a

ikindi dīwānî (Ott) : in the Ottoman empire, the afternoon DĪWĀN, held in the Grand Vizier's own residence to take care of lesser affairs. XI 196b

ikla (A), or *akila* : in medicine, either gangrene or cancer. X 911b

iḳlāb (A) : in Qurʾānic recitation, the 'alteration' of a letter's sound. X 73b

♦ iḳlāba (A) : in modern Mecca, the ceremony held to celebrate when a boy has read through the whole of the Qurʾān (the ceremony after the half or one-third is called *iṣrāfa*). IV 1113a

iklīl al-malik (A) : in botany, the melilot (*Melilotus officinalis*) (infrequent syn. *nafal, ḥantam, shadjarat al-ḥubb*). In Muslim Spain, ~ was known under the Romance name *ḳurunīlla*. XII 410a

iḳlīm (A, < Gk) : in geography, clime, climate; region. I 658a; III 1079b; V 398a

In administrative geography, ~ was used for province or canton, the equivalent or a subdivision of a KŪRA. This usage is peculiar to Syria and Upper Mesopotamia. III 1077b; V 398a; zone. IX 36b

In al-Masʿūdī, ~ is used for the Persian *keshwar*, which refers to the seven great kingdoms of the world. III 1077b

ikrāh (A) : in law, duress, of which there are two kinds: unlawful (*ikrāh ghayr mashrūʿ*) and lawful (*ikrāh bi-ḥaḳḳ*). Only the former is recognised by the Qurʾān and has legal effects. I 319a; XII 410b

iḳrār (A) : in law, affirmation, acknowledgement; recognition of rights. The declarant is called *al-muḳirr*, the beneficiary *al-maḳarr lahu*, and the object of the recognition *al-muḳarr bihi*. I 28b; III 511b; III 1078a; IX 845b

Among the Bektāshīs, the ceremony of initiation. IX 168a

iksīr (A, < Gk; pl. *akāsīr*) : originally the term for externally applied dry-powder or sprinkling-powder used in medicine, ~ came to be used for the elixir, the substance with which the alchemists believed it possible to effect the transformation of base metals into precious ones. III 1087b

♦ iksīrīn (A) : in medicine, an eye-powder. III 1087b

iḳṭāʿ (A) : in fiscal administration, a form of grant, often (wrongly) translated as 'fief'; the delegation of the fiscal rights of the state over lands to the military. I 1353a; II 508a; III 1088a; IV 975a; IV 1043b

iḳtiʿāṭ (A), or *iʿtidjār* : the opposite of *taḥnīk* (→ ḤANAK), or the way the turban-cloth is brought under the chin. X 614b

iḳtibās (A) : 'to take a live coal (*ḳabas*) or a light from another's fire', hence to seek knowledge; in rhetoric, ~ means to quote specific words from the Qurʾān or from Traditions without indicating these as quoted, found both in poetry and prose. III 1091b; XII 664a

iḳtirān (A) : in astronomy, conjunction. VIII 105a

iktisāb → KASB

iḳwāʾ (A) : in prosody, faulty rhyme. II 1073b; the change of the vowel MADJRĀ, e.g. *u* with *i*. IV 412b

īl (A, T *il*; pl. ĪLĀT) : in Turkish, empire; district over which authority is exercised, territory; people; peace. III 1092a; in the Republican period, *il* was introduced to replace *vilāyet* for province. III 1092b; VIII 189a

In Persian, ~ was used of 'tribesfolk' (syn. *ulus*), and by the 7th/13th century had become current with the meaning 'submissive, obedient'. III 1092b

īlāʾ (A) : in law, an 'oath of continence', the husband swearing in the name of God not to have sexual relations with his wife for at least four months. When this time had passed without a resumption of conjugal relations, the marriage was not automatically broken up except in Ḥanafī law, the other schools allowing the wife to judge the occasion for the severance, which would take place by a repudiation that the husband would pronounce, or that the ḲĀḌĪ would formulate in his place. IV 689a; VI 478a; VIII 28a

īlāf (A) : a Qurʾānic term which probably refers to economic relations entered into by the Ḳurays͟hīs well before the advent of Islam; the lexicographers define ~ as 'pact guaranteeing safety, safe conduct, undertaking to protect'. III 1093a

ilāh (A, pl. *āliha*) : deity; in pre-Islamic poetry, *al-* ~ was an impersonal divine name although for Christians and monotheists, it denoted God; by frequency of usage, *al-* ~ became Allāh. III 1093b

♦ **ilāhī** (A) : in Turkish literature, a genre of popular poetry of religious inspiration, consisting of poems sung, without instrumental accompaniment, in chorus or solo during certain ceremonies, and distinguished from other types of popular religious poetry by its melody and use in ritual. III 1094a; 'divine [hymn]'. VIII 2b; and → TAʾRĪK͟H-I ILĀHĪ

♦ ilāhiyyāt (A) : in philosophy, ~ gained currency as denoting the whole mass of questions concerning God. I 415a

ʿilal (A, s. **ʿilla** 'cause') : diseases, defects; in poetry, one of two groups of metrical deviations (the other being ZIḤĀF), ~ appear only in the last feet of the two halves of the lines, where they alter the rhythmic end of the line considerably, and are thus clearly distinct from the ḤAS͟HW feet. As rhythmically determined deviations, ~ do not just appear occasionally but have to appear regularly, always in the same form, and in the same position in all the lines of the poem. I 671b

In the science of ḤADĪT͟H, ~, usually rendered 'hidden defects', is a main approach of ISNĀD criticism; it highlights links between certain pairs of transmitters which are subject to dispute. VIII 515a

īlāt (P) : nomadic or semi-nomadic tribes, term first used in Īlk͟hānid times. Early Islamic geographers and historians refer to these tribes by the generic term *al-akrād*, by which they mean not necessarily people of Kurdish race but non-Arab and non-Turkish tent dwellers and herdsmen. III 1095b f.

ʿilb → SIDR

ilçe (T) : district. VIII 189a

ild͟jāʾ → TALD͟JIʾA

ilḥād → MULḤID

ilhām (A) : lit. to cause to swallow or gulp down; a Qurʾānic term denoting God's revelation to men individually, as opposed to His revelation to men generally by messages sent through the prophets, WAḤY. III 1119b

ilid͟ja (T) : 'hot spring'; a bath served by a hot spring. Other synonyms are ḲAPLÎD͟JA, used primarily of the baths served by thermal springs in Bursa, and *bāna*. II20b

ilḳa → ḲIS͟HS͟HA

ilḳāʾ → ṬARḤ

ʿilla (A, pl. *ʿilal*) : cause. III 1127b; in law, explanatory principle, the raison d'être of the law. V 239a ff.; and → ḤARF ʿILLA; SABAB

ʿilliyyūn (A, < Heb *ʿelyōn*) : a Qurʾānic term meaning both the 'place in the book where the deeds of the pious are listed' and 'an inscribed book'. III 1132b

ʿilm (A) : knowledge; the result of laborious study. III 1133a; and → ḤAMALAT AL-ʿILM

♦ ʿilm al-aktāf → KATIF

♦ ʿilm al-asārīr (A) : in divination, chiromancy. V 100a

♦ ʿilm ʿamalī (A) : in philosophy, practical knowledge, which comprises, according to al-K͟hʷārazmī, ethics, domestic economy and politics. I 427b; in theology, the knowledge of religious obligations, complete only when these obligations are fulfilled, as opposed to *ʿilm naẓarī* 'the knowledge of things'. III 1133b

♦ ʿilm al-ʿazāʾim (A) : the talismanic art, consisting of calling upon DJINNS and angels for the performance of some project. IV 264b; V 100b

♦ **ʿilm al-djamāl** (A) : aesthetics. III 1134a

♦ **ʿilm al-handasa** (A) : in mathematics, geometry. XII 411b

♦ ʿilm al-ḳāfiya (A) : rhyme theory. VIII 894a

♦ ʿilm naẓarī → ʿILM ʿAMALĪ

♦ ʿilm sharʿī (A) : revealed knowledge. I 427b

For other expressions with *ʿilm*, → the final component.

♦ **ʿilmiyye** (T) : the body of the higher Muslim religious functionaries in the Ottoman empire, especially those administering justice and teaching in the religious colleges. III 1152a; X 805a

iltibās → SABAB

iltifāt (A) : in rhetoric, apostrophe, a stylistic device. V 898a

iltizām (A) : a form of tax-farm used in the Ottoman empire. III 1154a; and → MÜLTEZIM

For ~ in prosody, → LUZŪM MĀ LĀ YALZAM; TAḌAMMUN

iltizāmen (T) : one of three principal ways in which mining activity was organised in the Ottoman empire, the others being EMĀNETEN and IḤĀLE. ~ meant the farming out of mining revenues to investors on a short-term contract basis. The usual term for these contracts in the mining context was six years. V 974b

īmāʾ → ISHĀRA

ʿimād → ʿAMĪD

imāla (A) : in the science of phonetics, ~ stands for inflection, a palatalisation, produced by a rising movement of the tongue towards the prepalatal region. III 1162a; the inclination of the vowel *a* towards *i*. VIII 343b

imām (A) : leader of the official prayer rituals, the ṢALĀT. From the earliest days of Islam, the ruler was ~ as leader in war, head of the government and leader of the common *ṣalāt*. Later, as the ruler's representatives, the governors of the provinces became leaders of the *ṣalāt*, just as they were heads of the KHARĀDJ. They had to conduct ritual prayer, especially the Friday *ṣalāt*, on which occasion they also delivered the sermon, KHUṬBA. Starting from ʿAbbāsid times, the office devaluated; the ~ no longer represented a political office, but came to belong to the personnel of the mosque. Each mosque regularly had one. He had to maintain order and was in general in charge of the divine services in the mosque. VI 674b; VIII 927b

In religious practice, the ~ is the transveral bead of a larger size on a rosary that separates the groups of beads. IX 741b

In the science of the Qurʾān, *al-imām* is the Median standard codex. V 408a

In mathematics, the number with which the numerator of a fraction is in relationship (syn. *maḳām*, *mukhradj*). IV 725b

♦ imām al-difāʿ (A) : among the Ibāḍiyya, an IMĀM invested by the people living in a state of secrecy, *ahl al-kitmān*, to defend them in misfortune. III 658a

♦ **imām-bārā** (U) : lit. enclosure of the IMĀMs; a term used in Muslim India for the buildings where the shīʿis assemble during Muḥarram and recite elegies on the martyrdom of Ḥasan and Ḥusayn. III 1163a

♦ **imāma** (A) : the imamate, 'supreme leadership' of the Muslim community. III 1163b

♦ imāmān (A) : in mysticism, the two assistants of the ḲUṬB, the second category in the hierarchy of the saints. I 95a

♦ **imāmzāda** (P) : the designation for both the descendant of a shīʿī IMĀM and the shrine of such a person. III 1169b

ʿimāma (A, pl. *ʿamāʾim*) : in Arab dress, the cloth wound round the cap, which term came to be used also for the whole headdress. In Algiers, it was pronounced *ʿamāma* and was there an unwound turban, often given as a present to the walī of the woman one wished to marry. X 608b; X 611b; X 612b

īmān (A) : in theology, faith (in God). III 1170b; IV 171b ff.

ʿimāra → DHIKR

♦ ʿimāret (T, < A *ʿimāra* 'foundation') : soup kitchen, erected as a public convenience in Ottoman times. IV 1152a; V 333b; XI 88b; an oven. X 533a

imazīghən (B, s. *amazigh*) : 'proud ones' or 'proud ones of the West', the term the Berbers use to call themselves. X 644a; and → IMGHAD

imḍā (T), or *tewḳīʿ-i ḳāḍī* : in Turkish diplomatic, the legal formula which was usually placed on the right side close to the first lines of the text of a copy stating (usually in Arabic) the conformity of the copy with the original. II 315b; and → PENČE

imghad (Touareg) : in the Touareg strongly-classed society, vassals who have had to accept the supremacy of the nobles, *imazhəghăn*, who are the uppermost class. Between the nobles and the vassals, although almost equal to the latter, are the maraboutic tribes who by virtue of their religious status do not participate in warfare and depend on the nobles for their defence. In the fourth place come the artisans, traditionally called blacksmiths (*inăḍăn*) and the lowest-ranking of all are the negro slaves (*eklan*), owned by all four of the above-mentioned castes. X 379a

imlāṭ → IDJĀZA

ʿimma (A) : properly, the style or form of winding the turban, then the turban itself. X 612b

immar, immara → SAKHLA

imsāk (A) : in religious law, abstinence, e.g. from things which break the fast. IX 94b; and → IMSĀKIYYA

♦ imsākiyya (A) : modern religious time tables distributed for the whole month of Ramaḍān. They indicate in addition to the times of prayer, the time of the early morning meal, *suḥūr*, and the time before daybreak (called the *imsāk*) when the fast should begin. VII 30b

imtilākh → KHIṢĀʾ

imtiyāzāt (A) : commercial privileges, (Ottoman) capitulations granted to non-Muslims living outside the DĀR AL-ISLĀM. III 1178b

imẓad (B) : hair, fur; ~ denotes a musical instrument once in use among the Touareg noblewomen, generally compared to a violin, but held by the player on her thighs as she sat low down, just above the ground, with her legs tucked back. III 1195b

in shāʾ allāh → ISTITHNĀʾ

ʿīna → BAYʿ AL-ʿĪNA

inaḍan → IMGHAD

inaḳ (T) : a title which existed in various Turkic and Mongol states, belonging to the close retinue of the ruler. XII 419a

inʿām (A) : lit. favour, beneficence; applied more specifically to donatives, largesse, given to troops. III 1200b; VIII 398b

In Persia, ~ was a present, usually of money, given from superiors to inferiors. III 347b

ʿinān (A) : in law, ~ is best rendered as a limited investment partnership in which relations between the partners are based on mutual agency alone and not mutual suretyship; one of the two classes of commercial partnership among the Ḥanafīs, the other being MUFĀWAḌA. VII 310a; *sharikat ʿinān* means partnership in traffic, contracted when each party contributes capital. IX 348b; and → LIDJĀM

♦ dhuʾl-ʿinān (A) : in astronomy, the constellation of the Waggoner, also known as *mumsik al-aʿinna*. XI 458a i'nāt → LUZŪM MĀ LĀ YALZAM

'ināya (A) : providence. III 1203a

In 'Abd al-Razzāḳ al-Ḳās̲h̲ānī's mystical thought, ~ covers ḲAḌĀ' and ḲADAR both, just as they contain everything that is actual; it is the divine knowledge, embracing everything as it is, universally and absolutely. I 90a

In mysticism, ~ is used with the more precise meaning of divine 'benefaction' or of a 'gift granted' by God. III 1203a

in'āẓ → INTIS̲H̲ĀR

indjīl (A, < Gk) : gospel; in the Qur'ān, ~ is used to refer to the Revelation transmitted by Jesus as well as the scripture possessed and read by the Christian contemporaries of Muḥammad, i.e. the four Gospels; in current usage extended to mean the whole of the New Testament. III 1205a

īndjū (Mon) : under the Mongols, royal estates granted as apanages to the Great K̲h̲ān's relatives. Gradually the concept of ~ land became assimilated to existing concepts of crown lands and came to signify land over which the ruler had full rights of disposal and which he granted on a heriditary title to his family and others. Whether the grantees then had full rights of disposal themselves is not clear. III 1208a; IV 975b

infaḥa (A) : rennet used to make cheese. XII 318b

infāḳ (A) : a type of olive oil made from green unripe olives. XI 486a

infisāk̲h̲ → FASK̲H̲

infitāḥ (A) : lit. opening, in particular the 'Opening' of Egypt under Sādāt to Western investment and expertise, to oil country investment, and to the previously-marginalised private sector of the country. XII 626a

inḥirāf (A) : in the moral sense, deviation. XI 567b; and → SAMT

inḥiṣār (T, < A), and *ḥaṣîr* : monopolies and restrictive practices of Ottoman guilds, the full term being *inḥiṣār-i bey'i ve s̲h̲irā*. These monopolies included restrictions concerning the number or kind of people allowed to perform a trade or profession, as well as limitations imposed on production or on commerce. XII 421a

inī lit. younger brother (pl. *iniyyāt*), term for the younger *mamlūk*. X 7b

inkār (A) : in law, denial, as when a person who is summoned by law to acknowledge a debt denies that he owes it. The transaction which puts an end to the legal conflict is called *ṣulḥ 'alā inkār*. III 1236b; IX 845b; and → NAHY

inḳilāb, inkilap → S̲H̲AG̲H̲ABA; T̲H̲AWRA

inṣāf (A) : equity; in poetry, a genre, or at least a theme, also called *as̲h̲'ār al-naṣaf* or *as̲h̲'ār munṣifa*, indicating verses in which the poets praise the fervour and the valour in war of the rival clan and acknowledge that victory has been hard-won. III 1236b

In ethics, ~ came to mean impartiality, objectivity, integrity, in short a complete ethical code for the activity of the man of learning; also, a method of argument in which, instead of immediately asserting the inferiority or error of that which is being attacked in comparison with that being defended, both are placed on a fictitious equal footing although it is granted that one or the other is inferior or wrong. III 1237a

insān (A) : man. III 1237a

♦ **al-insān al-kāmil** (A) : in mysticism, the concept of the Perfect Man. I 117b; III 1239a

ins̲h̲ā' (A) : the composition of letters, documents or state papers; later, a form of literature in which were included style-books for chancery scribes, copy-books and letter manuals. II 306b; III 1241b; VIII 749b; and → MUNS̲H̲Ī

insī (A) : the part of the point of the nib of a reed-pen to the left of the incision, called thus, 'human', because it is turned towards the writer. IV 471a

intidāb → MANDATES

intaḍat (al-sinn) → IT̲H̲T̲H̲AG̲H̲ARA

intihāʾ → IBTIDĀʾ

intiḥāl (A) : in literary criticism, the ascription of others' verses to oneself. XII 707b

intiḥār (A) : suicide. In Tradition literature, ~ is used to designate suicide by piercing or cutting one's throat. III 1246b

intiḳāl → TANĀSU<u>KH</u>

intiḳāl-i ʿādī (T) : in the Ottoman empire before the 11th/16th century, ṬAPU land that was passed to sons and brothers. X 209b

inti<u>sh</u>ār (A) : in medicine, the erection of the penis (syn. *inʿāẓ*), functional problems of which are generally known by the term *istir<u>kh</u>āʾ al-ḳaḍīb*, paralysis or slackening of the penis. XII 641a

inzāl → ENZEL; ṢĀḤIB AL-INZĀL

ʿīr → KĀRWĀN

iʿrāb (A) : a technical term in grammar, sometimes translated as inflexion; however, there is no adequate term directly to translate ~. By ~ Arab grammarians denoted the use of the three short vowels at the end of the singular noun. I 569b; III 1248b

īrād-i̊ <u>d</u>jedīd → NIẒĀM-I̊ <u>D</u>JEDĪD

irāda (A) : 'willingness'; in mysticism, a choice of affiliation with an order, whereby the aspirant (*murīd*) puts himself under total obedience to a master who takes charge of his spiritual education. X 245b

♦ **irāde** (T) : lit. will; a term adopted in Ottoman official usage from 1832 to designate decrees and orders issued in the name of the sultan. Later, under the constitution, the sultan's function was limited to giving his assent to the decisions of the government and ~ remained in use for this assent. III 1250a

ʿirāfa (A) : in divination, the knowledge of things unseen or of things to come, on the basis of things visible or present. IV 421b; V 100b

In administrative terminology, a unit headed by an ʿARĪF. I 629a; a small group of tribesmen massed together for the purpose of the distribution of the stipends. XI 520b

ʿirāḳ → <u>SH</u>A<u>SH</u>MAḲOM

♦ ʿirāḳ ʿa<u>d</u>jamī (A) : from the late mediaeval period on, ~ indicated Iranian Media (called *al-<u>d</u>jibāl* by the ancient geographers), to distinguish it from *ʿirāḳ ʿarabī*, ʿIrāḳ proper. I 206b

♦ ʿirāḳiyya (A), or *ʿirāḳya* : a kind of reed-pipe which may have been the forerunner of the European rackett. It has a cylindrical pipe and is played with a double reed. VII 208a

iram (A) : in geography, a pile of stones erected as a way-mark. III 1270a

ʿirār (A) : the cry of the male ostrich, which has a different tone than that of the female, *zimār*. VII 829a

ʿirḍ (A, pl. *aʿrāḍ*) : a term corresponding approximately to the idea of honour, but somewhat ambiguous and imprecise; a strong army; a valley covered with palm trees. At the present day, ~ has become restricted to the woman and her virtue. IV 77a; VI 475a; among the Bedouin, a man's ~ is pledged when he extends his protection, e.g. to a guest, a protégé or when he acts as a travelling companion. In this context, ~ or the protection to which the protector pledges his ~ is often referred to in North Africa as *wa<u>d</u>jh*. X 890a

In Tradition literature and poetry, ~ also has the meaning of the body of animals, or even of men; the parts of the body which sweat; the smell of a man or a woman. IV 77a

irdabb (A) : a measure of capacity for grain. Originally a Persian measure, the ~ was used in Egypt for a long time under the Ptolemies and the Byzantines, and is still in use today. The actual weight of the ~ varied depending on time and place. VI 119a irdāf (A) : in rhetoric, a term denoting implication, e.g. *ṭawīl al-nid̲j̲ād* 'with long cross-belt', meaning 'tall in stature', because the one cannot go without the other. V 117a

ʿirḳ (A, pl. *ʿurūḳ*) : vein; root; race, stock. IV 78b

In Tradition literature, ~ is found with the indiscriminate sense of artery and vein, blood; certain anomalies of birth. IV 78b

In geography, ~ is used to describe the form masses of sand can take in Saudi Arabia. I 537a; in sub-Saharan Africa, ~ (Eng *erg*) designates great stretches of dunes, clothed with a herbaceous vegetation which stabilises the sands. VIII 837a

♦ ʿirḳ al-ḥayya (A) : 'serpent's root', a root of the melilot introduced from Syria into the Arab West and used there as an antidote against poisonous snakebites. XII 410a

♦ ʿirḳ (ʿurūḳ) al-luʾluʾ (A) : 'the veins of the pearl', designation for the mother-of-pearl. VIII 707a

irṣād (A) : in law, the use of public funds, excluding a private involvement in the transaction, to sustain public or philanthropic services. XI 64b; XII 826a

irsāl (A) : the legislative function of prophecy. IX 812b; and → ḲABḌ

♦ **irsāliyye** (T), or *māl-i irsāliyye* : an Ottoman financial term applied to the annual 'remittances' of cash and kind sent to the personal treasury of the sultan in Istanbul by the holders of the non-feudal SAND̲J̲AḲS as well as by the governors of the non-feudal Arab provinces. The latter consisted of the balance left in each provincial treasury after the provincial expenditures and governor's salary were paid. IV 79b

irtiʿās̲h̲ (A) : in medicine, trembling. V 89b

irtidād → MURTADD

irtid̲j̲āʿ → RAD̲J̲ʿIYYA

irtid̲j̲āl (A) : in pre- and early Islam, the improvising, extemporising of a poem or a speech. A synonym is *badīha*, with the slight difference being that in the case of *badīha*, the poet allows himself a few moments of thought. IV 80b

iryāla → RIYĀLA

ʿiṣāb → LID̲J̲ĀM

♦ ʿiṣāba (A, pl. *ʿaṣāʾib*), also *ʿaṣb[a]* : a headband worn by women in the Arab East. V 741a; among the Mamlūks, the double camel hump-like erection on the *ṭurṭūr* worn by men or women. X 611b; the cross or long bar in the Mamlūk coat of arms. X 611a; under the Ayyūbids and Mamlūks in Egypt, the *ʿaṣāʾib sulṭāniyya* were the flags of the sultan in the public processions, for the flags enveloped the head of the lance like a turban. X 612b; and → ṢAFF

ʿīsāwiyya (A) : in Morocco, a simple, wide tunic consisting of a hole in the centre for the head and one at each side for the arms, made of striped wool and worn by men; also, a very ample blouse of strong cotton worn over other clothing. V 746a

iṣbaʿ (A), or *aṣbaʿ* : in anatomy, the finger; as a measurement of length, ~ is the breadth of the middle joint of the middle finger, conventionally 1/24 of the cubit, D̲H̲IRĀʿ. IV 96b; a fingerbreadth and subdivision of the ḲABḌA, which is made up of four ~. II 232a

In Arab navigational texts, ~ is the unit of measurement of star altitude. It was considered to be the angle subtended by the width of a finger held at arm's length against the horizon. IV 96b

In astronomy, ~ or *iṣbaʿ al-kusūf* refers to the twelve equal parts, called fingers, which divided the diameter of the sun or of the moon in order to obtain a standard for measuring the amount of an eclipse. In the West one spoke of 'digits'. V 537a

In music, ~ denotes the tonal mode; the rhythmic mode is called *ḍarb*. II 1074a

iṣbahbad̲h̲ → ISPAHBAD̲H̲

iṣbahsalār → ISPAHSĀLĀR

isbitāriyya → DĀWIYYA
isfādrūḥ → ṢAFR
iṣfahsalār → ISPAHSĀLĀR
isfānākhiyya a spinach and meat dish. X 31b
isfīdrūy → ṢAFR
isfirnī (A, < Gk *Sphyraena*), or *safarna*, *safarnāya* : in zoology, the spet or barracuda. VIII 1021a
ʿishāʾ (A) : evening or beginning of the night; a variant name given to the *ṣalāt al-maghrib*. VII 26b
♦ ṣalāt al-ʿishāʾ (A) : the evening prayer which is to be performed, according to the law books, from the last term mentioned for the *ṣalāt al-maghrib* (→ MAGHRIB) till when a third, or half of the night has passed, or till daybreak. VII 27b; VIII 928b

ishān (P) : in mysticism, ~ was formerly used in Central Asia in the sense of SHAYKH or MURSHID, teacher or guide, in contrast to MURĪD, disciple or pupil. Since the very existence of *ishāns* was strongly disapproved of by the Soviet and Chinese authorities, the term is now obsolescent, if not obsolete. IV 113a

ishʿār (A) : in pre-Islamic times, the custom of making an incision in the side of the hump of the camel marked for the sacrifice during the pilgrimage and letting blood flow from it. III 32b

ishāra (A) : gesture, sign, indication; in rhetoric, ~ acquired the technical meaning of allusion. IV 113b
In mysticism, ~ is the esoteric language of the inexpressible mystical experience. IV 114b; XII 752b; symbolic expression. VIII 139b; a silent gesture or sign (syn. *īmāʾ*, *ramz*). VIII 428b
For ~ in grammar, → ISM AL-ISHĀRA

ishbāʿ (A) : in metrics, one of the six vowels of the rhyme, to wit, the vowel of the DAKHĪL. IV 412a; the lengthening of vowels. XI 374a
In poetry, the lengthening of short syllables, and the shortening of long syllables, especially in end position. VII 811a
In mineralogy, uniform, intense and deeply saturated colour (of a gem). XI 263a

ishdād (A) : a woven, woollen belt, worn by both sexes in the Arab East. V 741a

īshīk-āķāsī (P) : a Ṣafawid administrative term meaning ‘usher’. The ~ was a minor court official who operated in two different branches of the administrative system, namely, the DĪWĀN and the ḤARAM. IV 118b

ʿishķ (A) : love, passion; the irresistable desire to obtain possession of a loved object or being. III 103a; IV 118b; X 776a

ishķīl (A) : in botany, the sea onion, a plant whose leaves are wide and thick, bent back, covered with a sticky liquid and whose ends are thorny. VIII 687b

ishrāf → ṬĀLIʿ

ishrāķ (A) : illumination; the name given to illuminative Wisdom, advocated by Shihāb al-Dīn Suhrawardī. IV 119b
♦ **ishrāķiyyūn** (A) : adepts of Shihāb al-Dīn Suhrawardī's illuminative Wisdom, ISHRĀĶ, used first, however, in a text by Ibn Waḥshiyya in the 4th/10th century to denote followers of a hermetic tradition who had received some illumination which had placed their works above those of the Peripatetics, *mashaʾiyya*. The term can be applied without hesitation, however, to all of Suhrawardī's followers, who still exist in Iran today. IV 120b

ishtiķāķ (A) : in grammar, translated approximately as etymology or derivation by means of analogy, ĶIYĀS. In its general sense, ~ signifies ‘taking one word from another’, under certain defined conditions. IV 122a; IX 528a

is͟htirākiyya (A) : socialism. The word seems to have been first used in this sense in 19th-century Turkish, but fell into disuse, and was replaced by *sosyalist*. Adopted in Arabic, it soon gained universal currency in the Arab lands. IV 123b

īs͟hūrūni → LĀS͟HŌN

iskāf (A, pl. *asākifa*), or *iskāfī* : a shoemaker, who like other artisans who worked with leather, had a low social status in pre-modern times because his work was regarded as unclean. XII 463a

iskān (A) : lit. coming into a peaceful state, settlement, the allocation of living quarters as space; in modern usage, 'sedentarisation' as a stage after a migratory or nomadic existence. XII 463b

isḳāṭ (A) : in law, relinquishment, specifically of a right, divided into true relinquishment (~ *maḥḍ*) and quasi-relinquishment (~ *g͟hayr maḥḍ*). XII 466a

iskemle (T) : stool.

♦ iskemle ag͟hasi̊ (T), or *iskemled͟jiler bas͟hi* : in Ottoman court life, an officer chosen from among the oldest grooms, whose duty was to carry a stool plated with silver which the sultan used in mounting his horse, when he did not prefer the assistance of a mute who went on his hands and knees on the ground. VIII 530b

isḳumrī (A, < Gk *Scomber*) : in zoology, the mackerel. VIII 1021a

iṣlāḥ (A) : reform, reformism; in modern Arabic, ~ is used for 'reform' in the general sense; in contemporary Islamic literature it denotes more specifically orthodox reformism of the type that emerges in the doctrinal teachings of Muḥammad ʿAbduh, in the writings of Ras͟hīd Riḍā, and in the numerous Muslim authors who are influenced by these two and, like them, consider themselves disciples of the Salafiyya. IV 141a

islām (A) : submission, total surrender (to God). IV 171b

In European languages, it has become customary to speak of Islam to denote the whole body of Muslim peoples, countries, and states, in their socio-cultural or political as well as their religious sphere. Modern Arabic often uses *al-islām* in a similar sense. IV 173b

♦ islāmī → ASLAMĪ; MUSLIM

ism (A, pl. *asmāʾ*), also *ʿalam, ism ʿalam* : name; in Arabic-Islamic usage the full name of a person is usually made up of the following elements: the *kunya*, usually a name compound with *abū* 'father of', or *umm* 'mother of'; the ~ ; the *nasab*, or pedigree, a list of ancestors, each being introduced by the word *ibn* 'son of' (the second name of the series is preceded by *bint* 'daughter of', if the first name is that of a woman); and the *nisba*, an adjective ending in *ī*, formed originally from the name of the individual's tribe or clan, then from his place of birth, origin or residence, sometimes from a school of law or sect, and occasionally from a trade or profession. A certain number of persons are also known by a nickname, *laḳab*, or a pejorative sobriquet, *nabaz*, which when the name is stated in full, comes after the *nisba*. IV 179a

In grammar, ~ is the technical term used to signify the noun. IV 181b

♦ ism ʿayn (A) : in grammar, the term used for a word denoting a concrete individual, as opposed to an *ism d͟jins*, a generic word. I 785a

♦ ism d͟jins → ISM ʿAYN

♦ ism al-fiʿl (A) : in grammar, the nominal verb. IX 528a

♦ ism al-is͟hāra (A), or *al-ism al-mubham* : in grammar, the demonstrative noun. IX 527b

♦ ism mawṣūl (A) : in grammar, a relative noun. IX 528a

♦ **al-asmāʾ al-ḥusnā** (A) : lit. the most beautiful names, being the 99 names of God. I 714a

ʿiṣma (A) : in theology, a term meaning immunity from error and sin, attributed by sunnīs to the prophets and by s͟hīʿis also to the IMĀMS. IV 182b; IX 423a; ~ denotes also infallibility, in sunnism in respect of the community and in shīʿism in respect of the *imāms*. IV 184a; VIII 95a

ismākiyya (A) : systematic ichthyology. VIII 1020b

isnād (A) : in the science of Tradition, the chain of authorities (syn. *sanad*) going back to the source of the Tradition, an essential part of the transmission of a Tradition. III 24a; IV 207a; VIII 514b

In grammar, ~ denotes the relationship between the *musnad* 'that which is supported by (the subject)', and the *musnad ilayhi* 'that which supports (the subject)', the relationship of attribution or predication. IV 895b; VII 705a

In the science of diplomatic, ~ means the decisive words *an yuʿhada ilayhi*, etc. in letters of appointment. II 302a

♦ isnād ʿālī (A) : lit. a high *isnād*, when there are very few links between the transmitter and the Prophet, or between him and a certain authority. Such a Tradition, the quality of which is known as *ʿuluww*, is considered a valuable type on the ground that the fewer the links, the fewer the possible chances of error. III 26a; IX 607b

♦ isnād nāzil (A) : lit. a low *isnād*, when there are many links between the transmitter and the Prophet, or between him and a certain authority. The quality of such Traditions is called *nuzūl*. III 26a

ispahbadh (P, A *iṣbahbadh*) : army chief; the Islamic form of a military title used in the pre-Islamic Persian empires and surviving in the Caspian provinces of Persia down to the Mongol invasions. IV 207a

ispahsālār (P, A *iṣbahsalar, isfahsalar*), and *sipahsālār* : army commander; the title given to commanders-in-chief and general officers in the armies of many states of the central and eastern mediaeval Islamic world. II 210b; IV 208a; VIII 769b; VIII 924a; in Muslim India, governor or viceroy. IX 738b

ispendje (T, < Sl *yupanitsa*), or *ispenče* : the Ottoman name of a poll tax levied on adult non-Muslim subjects and amounting usually to 25 AḲČES a year. Originally, ~ was a feudal peasant household tax in the pre-Ottoman Balkans; it extended into eastern Anatolia from 1540 onwards. II 146b; IV 211a; VIII 487a

isrāʾ → MIʿRĀDJ

iṣrāfa → IḲLĀBA

israʾīliyyāt (A) : a term covering three kinds of narratives: those regarded as historical, which served to complement the often summary information provided by the Qurʾān in respect of the personages in the Bible, particularly the prophets; edifying narratives placed within the chronological (but entirely undefined) framework of 'the period of the (ancient) Israelites'; and fables belonging to folklore, allegedly (but sometimes actually) borrowed from Jewish sources. IV 211b

ist (A) : in anatomy, the arm. XII 830b

iṣṭabl (A, < Gk; pl. *iṣṭablāt*, rarely *aṣābil*) : stable, i.e. the building in which mounts and baggage animals are kept tethered; the actual stock of such animals belonging to one single owner. IV 213b

istakhr (P) : a small cistern, used to irrigate the land in mediaeval Persia. V 869b

iṣṭām (A) : in the mediaeval kitchen, a utensil used for stirring. Another utensil for the same purpose was the *ḳasba fārisiyya*. VI 808b

istār (A) : a weight in the apothecary's or troy system, taken over from the Greeks and usually estimated according to two different scales. On the one hand are the equations: 1 *istār* = 6 DIRHAM and 2 *dānaḳ* = 4 MITHḲĀL (an apothecary's stater); on the other, 1 *istār* = 6 $^1/_2$ *dirham* = 4 $^1/_2$ *mithḳāl* (commercial ~ in the East). IV 248b

istiʿādha (A) : the practice for protecting oneself from the evil influence of Satan, by pronouncing *aʿūdhu bi 'llāhi min al-shayṭān al-radjīm*. IX 408b

istiʿāna → TAḌMĪN

istiʿāra (A, T *iğretileme*) : in rhetoric, the term commonly used in the sense of metaphor. In the early period, ~ is used occasionally in the sense of ‘borrowing of a theme by one author from another’. IV 248b; XII 650a; in Turkish literature, ~ is a class of trope in which the comparative elements of the relationship between objects are stressed in various degrees. V 1028a

♦ istiʿāra-i makniyya (Ott, mod.T *kapalı iğretileme*) : in Turkish literature, an implicit metaphor, in which the comparison is achieved by reference to an attribute of an object without mentioning the object itself, ‘a cool stream *sang lullabies*’. V 1028a

♦ istiʿāra-i muṣarraḥa (Ott, mod.T *açık iğretileme*) : in Turkish literature, an explicit metaphor, in which the comparison is achieved by direct reference to an object, ‘our *lions* are off to the battlefield’. V 1028a

♦ istiʿāra ta<u>kh</u>yīliyya (A) : in rhetoric, a specific type of metaphor, characterised by the lack of a substratum, as in ‘the claws of Death’, where the metaphor ‘claws’ is not tied by an underlying simile to a part of death since death does not have any part that could be likened to claws. X 129b

istibḍāʿ (A) : a form of intercourse forbidden by the Prophet, consisting of a man who, fearing that he himself could not sire a robust offspring, placed his wife in the hands of a better progenitor. XII 133a

istibdād (A) : absolutism. I 64a; XI 569b

istibdāl (A) : in law, dation in payment. XII 207b

In WAḲF administration, a case in which the *waḳf* administrator is authorised to divest the foundation of properties which are no longer useful and to acquire others in their stead. IX 542a; XI 62b ff.

istibrāʾ (A) : confirmation of emptiness; in law, ~ is a) the temporary abstention from sexual relations with an unmarried female slave, in order to verify that she is not pregnant, on the occasion of her transfer to a new master or a change in her circumstances; and b) an action of the left hand designed to empty completely the urethra, before the cleaning of the orifices which must follow satisfaction of the natural needs. I 28a; I 1027a; IV 252b

istidlāl (A) : in logic, proof by circumstantial evidence. VII 1051a

In law, inductive reasoning. I 1326b; V 238b

In theology, inference. I 410b

In linguistic analysis, argumentation. VIII 894a

In rhetoric, demonstration. V 898a

istīfāʾ (A) : in law, taking possession of goods (syn. ḲABḌ). X 467a

istifhām (A) : in grammar, interrogation, indicated simply by the intonation of the sentence or by two interrogative particles. IV 255a

isti<u>gh</u>lāl → <u>GH</u>ĀRŪḲA

isti<u>gh</u>rāb (A) : in rhetoric, with *i<u>gh</u>rāb*, the concept of ‘evoking wonder’, related to ‘feigned amazement’ or TAʿA<u>DJDJ</u>UB. X 4a

istiṣḥāb al-ḥāl (A) : in law, a presumption of continuity, a source of law that was accepted by al-<u>Gh</u>azālī. X 932a

istiḥāḍa → ḤAYḌ

istiḥdād (A) : shaving the pubis, *ʿāna*. The syn. *ḥalḳ* is used for shaving the buttocks (*ḥalḳat al-dubur*). IX 312b

istiḥḍār (A) : the invocation of <u>DJ</u>INNS and angels and making them perceptible to the senses; spiritism. IV 264b; V 100b; and → ISTI<u>KH</u>DĀM

istiḥḳāḳ (A) : in eschatology, ‘merit’ which, in Muʿtazilī thinking, is attached to human deeds, bringing reward. III 465b

In literary criticism, ‘greater claim’, one of the three ways a poet can avoid the charge of plagiarism. XII 708b

istiḥsān (A) : in law, arbitrary personal opinion. I 730a; a method of finding the law which for any reason is contradictory to the usual ḲIYĀS, reasoning by analogy. III 1237a; IV 255b; juristic preference. IX 324b

istiḳāma → ṬĀLIʿ

istiḳbāl (A) : in astronomy, the opposition of sun and moon, that is, the situation wherein their elongation from each other amounts to 180 degrees. IV 259a
In astrology, ~ is sometimes employed to refer to the diametric aspect of the planets, although in general MUḲĀBALA is preferred. IV 259a

istik̲h̲āra (A) : the concept which consists of entrusting God with the choice between two or more possible options, either through piety and submission to His will, or else through inability to decide oneself, on account of not knowing which choice is the most advantageous one. The divine voice expresses itself either by means of a dream or by rhapsodomancy, ḲURʿA. IV 259b
In literary texts, ~ is merely a pious formula for a request to God for aid and advice, with no ritual character. IV 260a

istik̲h̲bār → TAḲSĪM

istik̲h̲dām (A) : making a spirit do a certain thing, one of three procedures of spiritism. The other two are *istinzāl* 'making a spirit descend in the form of a phantom' and *istiḥḍār* 'making a spirit descend into a body'. IX 570b; and → TAWRIYA

istik̲h̲fāf (A) : in law, blasphemy. VII 248a

istik̲h̲rād̲j̲ (A) : in classical Muslim administration, the amount actually received, as opposed to the estimate, AṢL. II 78b; extracting money by force or violence. VII 724a

istiḳlāl (A) : separate, detached, unrestricted, not shared, or sometimes even arbitrary; in Ottoman official usage, ~ acquired the meaning of unlimited powers, e.g. in the terms of appointment of a provincial governor or military commander. In both Turkish and Arabic in the late 18th and early 19th centuries, ~ is commonly used in the sense of the independence of the holder of power from the restraints by either subjects or suzerain. IV 260b
During the same period, under the influence of European political thought and practice, ~ began to acquire the modern meaning of political sovereignty for a country or nation and, in Arabic, became primarily associated with the national independence movements among the Arabs. IV 260b

istiḳrār (A) : in classical Muslim administration, an inventory of the army supplies remaining in hand after issues and payments have been made. II 79a

istiḳsām (A) : in divination, belomancy, consultation of the throw of darts, three types of which were practised by the ancient Arabs. IV 263b; V 101a

isṭīl (A) : in mediaeval ʿIrāḳ, a vagabond who pretends to be blind for begging purposes. VII 494a

istiʾlāf (A) : (gracious) remission. XI 75b

iṣṭilāḥ (A, pl. *iṣṭilāḥāt*) : in the works of early grammarians, in the discussion on language, ~ was used in the sense of a social institution tacitly accepted by its users; when opposed to *aṣl al-lug̲h̲a* 'language', ~ denoted metalanguage. V 805b; Arabic words or calques from the Greek which have assumed a technical meaning. II 765b; IV 696b

istilḥāḳ (A), also *diʿwa* : in law, the affiliation of an illegitimate child, as occurred in 44/665 when Ziyād b. Abīhi was officially recognised as the son of Abū Sufyān. XI 520a; XII 475a

istimālet (T, < A) : conciliation; an Ottoman policy in the conquered lands. X 505a

istiʿmār (A) : colonisation. XII 722b

istimnāʾ (A) : masturbation. IX 566a

istimṭār → ISTISḲĀʾ

isti'nāf (A) : lit. recommencement, renewal; in law, in modern Arabic, appeal; in classical law, ~ is used with its sense of recommencement with regard to the ʿIBĀDĀT, the religious duties, especially prayer, i.e. when the entire prayer, which has been interrupted by the occurrence of a ritual impurity, has to be begun again. In Mālikī law, ~ is called *ibtidā'*. IV 264a

istinbāṭ (A) : in law, deduction (syn. *istikhrādj al-ḥakk*). V 238b

istindjā' (A) : in law, the purification incumbent upon the Muslim after the fulfilment of his natural needs. IV 264b

istinshāk (A) : in law, the inhaling of water through the nostrils at the time of the ablutions, WUḌŪ' and GHUSL. IV 264b

istinzāl (A) : in divination, hydromancy. IV 264b; V 860a; and → ISTIKHDĀM
In metallurgy, the smelting of ores to obtain metals. V 973a

istiʿrāḍ (A) : the mustering, passing in review and inspecting of troops, also known as *ʿarḍ*, the official charged with this duty being known as the ʿARĪḌ. IV 265a
Among the Khāridjites, ~ is a technical term meaning the interrogation to which the enemies of these sectarians were subjected on falling into their hands; used, in a general sense, of religious murder, the putting to death of Muslims and pagans who objected to their still rudimentary doctrine. IV 269a; IV 1076b

istirkhā' → INTISHĀR

istiṣḥāb (A) : in law, the principle by which a given judicial situation that had existed previously was held to continue to exist as long as it could not be proved that it had ceased to exist or had been modified. I 276a; IV 269b; IX 324b

istishrāk (A) : orientalism. XII 722b

istiskā' (A), or *istimṭār* : a supplication for rain during periods of great droughts, a rogatory rite still practised at the present day (notably in Jordan and Morocco) and dating back to the earliest Arab times. I 109a; IV 269b; VIII 931a

istiṣlāḥ (A) : in law, like ISTIḤSĀN, a method by which the otherwise usual method of deduction, analogy, is to be excluded in the preparation of legal decisions. IV 256b

istiṣnāʿ (A) : in finance, a manufacturing or 'made-to-order' contract, which, like MUḌĀRABA, MUSHĀRAKA, *idjāra* (→ IDJĀR), and MURĀBAḤA, was designed by sharīʿa advisors to newly-created Islamic finance institutions as part of the profit and loss sharing of modern-day banking. XII 691b

istiṭāʿa (A) : in theology and scholastic theology, the term for the 'capacity' to act created by God in the human subject. I 413b; III 1063a; IV 271a

istiṭāla → ṢIFĀT AL-ḤURŪF

istitār → MUKĀSHAFA

istithnā' (A) : in a religious context, ~ refers to the saying of the formula 'if God wills', *in shā' Allāh*. III 1196a; VII 607a
In grammar, ~ signifies 'exception', i.e. that one or more beings are excepted from the functions exercised in a complete sentence, as in 'everyone came except Zayd'. IV 272b

istiwā' (*khaṭṭ al-*) (A) : the line of equality, of equilibrium, that is to say, the equator, which divides the earth into two hemispheres, the northern and the southern, and joins together all those points of the globe where day and night are equal. IV 273a

īṭā' (A) : in prosody, a defect of the rhyme occurring when the same word in the same meaning is repeated in the rhymes of lines belonging to the same poem. It is permissable under certain circumstances. IV 413a

ītār (A) : in archery, the act of stringing or bracing the bow. IV 800a

itāwa (A, < *atā*) : lit. gift; a general term met with, especially in pre- and proto-Islamic times, meaning a vague tribute or lump payment made, for example, to or by a tribe or other group; later, the word describes, sometimes in a denigrating way, a tip or bribe. IV 276a

itb (A) : a loose gown worn by women on the Arabian peninsula. V 741a

itbāʿ (A) : a particular form of paronomasia, constituted by the repetition of a qualifying term to which there is added a metaplasm, i.e. the deliberate alternation of a radical consonant, usually the first, but never the third, e.g. *ḥasan basan* 'wonderfully attractive'. The first element is called *matbūʿ* or *mutbaʿ*, and the second *tābiʿ*. VII 823a

iṭbāḳ (A) : in grammar, velarisation; the *ḥurūf al-muṭbaḳa* are 'the emphatic consonants', that is, *ṣād, ẓāʾ, ṭāʾ* and *ḍād*. III 598b; X 83a

ithbāt (A) : to witness, to show, to point to, to demonstrate, to prove, to establish, to verify and to establish the truth, to establish (the existence of something); in mysticism, ~ is the opposite of *maḥw*, the effacement of the 'qualities of habit', and denotes the fact of performing one's religious obligations. IV 277a; and → TASHBĪH

ithm (A) : in theology, sin (→ DHANB). XII 475a

ithmid → KUḤL

ithnayn (A) : (of the) two; and → THANAWIYYA

♦ ithnayniyya (A) : in religion, duality. X 441a

iththaghara (A) : a verb which means '[a boy] bred his central milk teeth or front teeth, or he bred his teeth after the former ones had fallen out' (Lane). Several terms refer to different stages of this process: *shakka, ṭalaʿa, nadjama, nasaʿa, intaḍat (al-sinn), adrama (al-ṣabiyy), aḥfara, abdaʾa*. VIII 822a

iʿtibār (A) : in the science of Tradition, the consideration of whether a transmitter who is alone in transmitting a Tradition is well known, or whether, if the Tradition is solitary by one authority, someone in the chain has another authority, or whether another Companion transmits it. III 26b

iʿtidāl → TAṬARRUF

iʿtidjār → IḲTIʿĀṬ

iʿtiḳād (A) : the act of adhering firmly to something, hence a firmly established act of faith. In its technical sense, the term denotes firm adherence to the Word of God. It may be translated in European languages by the words 'croyance', 'belief', 'Glauben', with the proviso that this 'belief' is not a simple opinion or thought, but is the result of deep conviction. IV 279a

iʿtikāf (A) : a period of retreat in a mosque, a particularly commended pious practice which can be undertaken at any time. IV 280a

iʿtimād (A) : in archery, the holding firmly in the left hand the grip or handle of the bow while the right-hand fingers make a good locking of the string, the two hands exerting equal force. IV 800b

♦ **iʿtimād al-dawla** (A) : lit. trusty support of the state, a title of Persian viziers during the Ṣafawid period and subsequently. IV 281b

ʿitḳ (A) : emancipation (of slave). The freedman is called *ʿatīḳ* or *muʿtaḳ*. I 29b; the special ceremony of release from servitude of a *mamlūk*, who then became a member of the Mamlūk household of the Sultan at the Cairo citadel. X 7b

♦ ʿitḳ al-sāʾiba (A) : in Mālikī and Ḥanbalī law, an ancient type of enfranchisement of the slave without patronage, which term refers to the pre-Islamic custom of turning loose in complete freedom one particular she-camel of the herd, protected by taboos. I 30b

♦ **ʿitḳnāme** (T), *ʿitîḳnāme, ʿitāḳnāme* : an Ottoman term for a certificate of manumission, given to a liberated slave. IV 282b

iṭlāḳ (A) : in archery, the loose, loosing, the last and most important phase of shooting. There are three basic kinds of loosing: the MUKHTALAS, SĀKIN and MAFRŪḲ. IV 800b

♦ iṭlāḳāt (A) : in the science of diplomatic, the name given to documents reaffirming decisions of former rulers; sometimes, however, they were simply called TAWḲĪʿ. II 303b; II 306b

♦ iṭlāḳiyya (A) : one of two main headings in the monthly and yearly accounting registers of the Īl<u>kh</u>ānids, under which fell payments by provincial tax-farmers made to members of the court, palace servants, and the military. III 284a; and → MUḲARRARIYYA

ʿiṭr → AFĀWĪH

ʿitra → AHL AL-BAYT

ittibāʿ (A) : 'active fidelity' to the Traditions of both the Prophet and the SALAF, a term preferred by reformists to *taḳlīd*, which denoted the servile dependence on traditional doctrinal authorities that they rejected. IV 152a

ittiḥād (A) : unity, association, joining together; in theology, the Christian incarnation of the Word in the person of Jesus, which concept is rejected by Muslims as being contradictory. IV 283a

In mysticism, the mystic union of the soul with God. IV 283a

ittiṣāl (A), or **wiṣāl** : in mysticism, a union of man and God which excludes the idea of an identity of the soul and God. IV 283a; the act of forming an amorous relationship, the equivalent of *wuṣla*. XI 210b; and → ṬĀLIʿ

ityān al-mayta (A) : necrophilia. IX 566a

ʿiwaḍ (A) : exchange value, compensation, that which is given in exchange for something; in law, ~ is used in a very broad sense to denote the counterpart of the obligation of each of the contracting parties in onerous contracts which are called 'commutative', that is, contracts which necessarily give rise to obligations incumbent on both parties. Thus in a sale, the price and the thing sold are each the ~ of the other. IV 286a

In unilateral contracts, ~ (*badal* and *<u>th</u>awāb* are also used) is employed in a more restricted sense: it is applied to the compensation offered by one of the two parties who is not absolutely obliged to give any. IV 286a

īwān (P, T *eyvān*) : in architecture, a chamber or a hall which is open to the outside at one end, either directly or through a portico; an estrade or a raised part of a floor; a palace or at least some sort of very formal and official building; any one of the halls in a religious building, MADRASA or mosque, which opens onto a courtyard. Art historians and archaeologists have given ~ a technically precise meaning, that of a single large vaulted hall walled on three sides and opening directly to the outside on the fourth. IV 287a; a room enclosed by three walls, opening out in the whole width of the fourth side, like an enormous gaping flat-based ledge, and generally roofed by a cradle vault (semi-cylindrical). Although not without similarity to the Greek *prostas*, the ~ does seem to be a genuinely Iranian creation. It became a characteristic theme of Sāsānid architecture. II 114a; and → LĪWĀN

In the terminology of horse-riding, a light bit. Two other types of bit were used: the *fakk*, a snaffle bit, and the *nāzikī*, seemingly the equivalent of the modern bit used by the Spahis. II 954a

iwazz (A) : in zoology, wild geese. IX 98b

iyād → NUʾY

ʿiyāfa (A) : animal omens (zoomancy) and, in the strict sense, ornithomancy, that is to say, the art of divining omens in the names of birds, their cries, their flight and their posture. IV 290b

iyāla → EYĀLET

ʿiyān (A) : observation (*bi 'l-~* 'first-hand'). III 736a; XII 801a

In the vocabulary of mediaeval agriculture, a strap of iron that attached the ploughshare to the crossbeam. VII 22a

izār (A), *azr, miʾzar, īzār* : a large sheet-like wrap worn both as a mantle and as a long loin cloth or waist cloth by pre-Islamic Arabs. III 1053a; V 732b; a large, enveloping body wrap for women in the Arab East or for both sexes in North Africa. V 741a; V 746a; a fringed shawl worn by Jewish women in Morocco. V 746a; and → RIDĀʾ

iẓhār → IḌMĀR
izli → ASEFRU
ʿiẓlim → NĪL
izran (B) : in Tarifiyt, the genre of short songs, a part of the traditional oral literature. X 242a

J

jawi → PEGON
jiilaal → GU'
juru kunci (J) : 'key bearers'; in Java, the custodians of a holy tomb, who guard the proper rituals performed during a pilgrimage to the tomb. XI 537a

K

ḳāʿ (A) : in topography, a depression on the fringes of the volcanic fields south of Syria, free of stones, with a diameter of several hundreds of metres. Such depressions probably originated from volcanic eruptions of gas. V 593a
ḳāʿa (A) : in modern dwellings in Egypt, the principal room in the ḤARĪM, with a central space and lateral extensions. The walls surrounding the central space rise to the level of the terraces and carry a lantern which lights the interior. II 114b; an elongated hall with two axial ĪWĀNs and a sunken central area, usually square, known as the *durḳāʿa*. IV 428b; VIII 545b

♦ ḳāʿa muʿallaḳa (A) : in architecture, a raised hall, a living unit located on the second floor. VIII 545b

ḳaʿada (A) : 'those who sit down', term for the designation of the quietists in early Islam who abstained from overt rebellion and warfare against the ruling authority. I 207a; V 572a; XII 505a
ḳaʾan → KHĀḲĀN
kaʿb (A) : in mathematics, ~, or *mukaʿʿab*, denotes the third power of the unknown quantity. II 362a; the cube root. III 1139b

In anatomy, a knucklebone (pl. *kiʿāb*), used in very early Islam as dice. V 616b

♦ kaʿb kaʿb (A) : in mathematics, the term for the sixth power. III 1140b

kaʿba (A) : the most famous sanctuary of Islam, called the temple or house of God, and situated in the centre of the great mosque in Mecca. The name ~ is connected with the cube-like appearance of the building. In former times the word also used to designate other similarly shaped sanctuaries. IV 317a
ḳaba zurna → ZURNA
ḳabā → ḲABĀʾ
ḳabāʾ (A, < Sp *capo* or *capa*), or *ḳabā* : a cloak or cape worn by soldiers. III 100a; V 739b; V 743b; a luxurious, sleeved robe, slit in front, with buttons, made of fabrics such as brocade. V 733b; V 748a ff.
kabāʾir (A, s. *kabīra*) : the 'grave sins', mentioned in the Qurʾān, the exact definition of which remained variable. The ~ are distinguished from the *ṣaghāʾir* 'lesser sins'. IV 1107b
kabaḳ (A, < T 'gourd'), or *ḳabaḳ* : in archery, a small target. II 954a; in Mamlūk terminology, a 'gourd' game (*ramy al-ḳabaḳ*), one of the branches of horse-riding. II 955a; IV 801a

ḳabāla (A) : in law, a guarantee, used mainly in connection with fiscal practice. It concerns the levying of the land-tax, KHARĀDJ, and that of special taxes, *mukūs* (→ MAKS). Local communities were held jointly responsible by the Treasury for the payment at the required time of the full amount of land-tax demanded. When individuals had difficulty in finding the necessary ready money immediately, an application was made to a notable to advance the sum required. The matter having generally been agreed in advance, this notable acted as a guarantor for the debt of the locality in question. This procedure constitutes the contract of ~, the offer being called *taḳbīl* and the person named *mutaḳabbil.* I 1144a; IV 323a; XI 75b
Alongside its use with regard to taxation on land, ~, as well as ḌAMĀN in this context, occurs in a more permanent sense to signify the farming of special revenues, generally of *mukūs* (→ MAKS), especially in towns, such as the sale of salt or the management of baths or even of a local customs office. IV 324a

kabar (A, < Eth *kabaro*) : an early term for a cylindrical drum with a single membrane.

kabāra (A), or *maʿtab* : among the Bedouin in the Western Desert and Cyrenaica, amends for offences against honour. They are known as *ḥashm* in ʿIrāḳ, *ḥashm* and *ʿayb* in Northern Yemen, *manshad* in parts of the Central Region (the Sinai, Jordan and Palestine). X 890b

ḳabas → IḲTIBĀS

kabāth (A) : the ripe fruit of the thorn tree *arāk* (*Capparis sedata*). II 1058b

kabbāda → SANG

ḳabbūs → MIʿZAF

kabd → KABID

ḳabḍ (A) : lit. seizure, grasping, contraction, abstention, etc., and used in the special vocabulary of various disciplines.
In law, ~ signifies taking possession of, handing over. In Mālikī law *ḥiyāza* is more frequently used. *Tasallum* is also employed to mean the act of handing over. Taking possession is accomplished by the material transfer of the thing when movable goods are involved; by occupation when it is a question of real estate, but also symbolically by the handing over of the keys or title deeds of the property. III 350a; IV 325b
In mysticism, ~ is a technical term used to denote a spiritual state of 'contraction' as opposed to 'expansion', BASṬ. I 1088b; IV 326a
In prosody, ~ is the suppression of the fifth quiescent letter in the feet *faʿūlun* and *mafāʿīlun* which occurs in the metres *ṭawīl, hazadj, muḍāriʿ* and *mutaḳārib*, so that these feet are reduced to *faʿūlu* and *mafāʿilun* respectively. A foot suffering this alteration is called *maḳbūḍ.* I 672a; IV 326b; XI 508b
In the Islamic ritual prayer, ~ is the position assumed after the saying of the words '*allāhu akbar*'. The hands are placed on the base of the chest, the right hand over the left. The Imāmīs and the Mālikīs let the arms fall at this point: the position of *sadl* or *irsāl.* VIII 929a

♦ ḳabḍ amāna (A) : in law, the term used for when the trustee, in regard to contracts which involve the temporary transfer of something from one contracting party to the other, is only held responsible if he has been at fault or in transgression, TAʿADDĪ, of the rules of the contract or of the customary dealings in such matters. IV 326a

♦ ḳabḍ ḍamān (A) : in law, the term used for when the trustee, in regard to contracts which involve the temporary transfer of something from one contracting party to the other, is held responsible for any loss arising in respect of the object, even through chance or circumstances over which he has no control. IV 326a

♦ ḳabḍa (A) : a measure of length, equalling a handsbreadth, or one-sixth, of the cubit, DHIRĀʿ. The ~ , in turn, consisted of four IṢBAʿs. II 232a; VII 137b
In archery, the grasp, sc. the position of the left hand (for a right-handed person) on

the grip or handle of the bow. In order to distinguish this technique from that of the ʿAḲD, the authors sometimes call this more precisely *al-ḳabḍa bi ʾl-shamāl*. IV 800b

kabid (A, according to lexicographers the only correct form), or *kabd, kibd* : in anatomy, the liver; through contiguity of meaning, ~ is also used to designate the parts of the body in the vicinity of the liver. Thus, for instance, in classical Arabic ~ can denote the surfaces of the body more or less close to the liver as well as the chest and even the belly. In the same way ~ is also frequently used to cover the middle, centre, interior (we would say heart) of something. IV 327a

ḳābiḍ (A) : the quality of food being astringent. II 1071b

ḳābila (A) : in alchemy, the part known as the 'receiver' of the distilling apparatus. I 486a

ḳabīla (A) : a large agnatic group, the members of which claim to be descended from one common ancestor; this word is generally understood in the sense of tribe. IV 334a

♦ ḳabīlat Suʿaydiyyīn (A) : a Türkmen community near Baʿlabakk in Lebanon, which speaks a Turkish idiom and preserves a narrative of its origins that relates it vaguely to the Saldjūḳs and Ottomans. X 685a

♦ ḳabīlī (A, pl. *ḳabāʾil*) : a tribesman; in Yemen, one of various status groups which include the city dweller of tribal origin, ʿarabī, and, at the bottom of the social order, those with menial occupations without tribal origin, called either *banu ʾl-khums* 'sons of the fifth' or *ahl al-ṭaraf* 'people of the extremity'. XI 277a

ḳabīlī → ḲABĪLA

kabīr (A) : lit. large; designation for a tribal chief. IX 115b; an attorney under customary law proceedings among the Bedouin in the Central Region of the Sinai, Jordan and Palestine. X 888b; and → ṢAGHĪR

♦ **kabīra** (A, pl. *kabāʾir*) : in theology, a grave sin.

ḳabr (A) : tomb; ~ was first applied to the pit used as a burial place for a corpse (as was the term *ḍarīḥ*), giving rise to its habitual use in the text of numerous epitaphs containing the expression *hādhā ḳabru* . . . 'this is the grave of . . .'. Originally distinguished from the term *ṣandūḳ* 'cenotaph', ~ had the more general meaning of the tumulus or construction covering the grave to bring it to notice, a custom current in Islamic countries from early times. IV 352a; ~ is used almost exclusively as a term that refers to the location of a tomb or to describe a simple grave with no architectural features attached to it.

kabīsa (A, < Ar) : intercalation, which compensates for the difference between the lunar and solar years. The plural form *kabāʾis* was used for 'leap years'. X 258a,b

kabsh → ḤAMAL; SINNAWR

ḳabūl → BAYʿ; KAWS

ḳabūs → MIʿZAF

kabūsh (A), and *shalīl* : in the terminology of horse-riding, a cloth worn by the horse. The terms *tashāhir* and *djulla* are confined to stable-cloths. II 954a

ḳačḳun → YAWA

ḳaḍāʾ (A, T *ḳażāʾ*) : originally meaning 'decision', ~ has in the Qurʾān different meanings according to the different contexts, e.g., doomsday, jurisdiction, revelation of the truth, and predestination, determination, decree. IV 364b

In theology, ~ means God's eternal decision or decree concerning all beings, that must be fulfilled in all circumstances, and the execution and declaration of a decree at the appointed time; sudden death. IV 364b

In a religious context, ~ is the technical term for the neglected performance of religious duties, e.g. repeating prayers to make up for having omitted them at the appointed time, as opposed to ADĀʾ. I 169b; IV 365a; IX 94b

In law, ~ stands for both the office and the sentence of a ḲĀḌĪ 'judge'; ~ is also found in legal terminology with the meaning 'payment of a debt'. IV 364b ff.

In ʿAbd al-Razzāḳ al-Ḳas̲h̲ānī's mystical thought, ~ means the existence of the universal types of all things in the world of the Universal Reason. I 89b

In the Ottoman empire, *ḳażāʾ* meant not only the judgement of the ḲĀḌĪ but also the district which his administrative authority covered. The term ~, denoting an administrative district, has remained in use in the Turkish republic. IV 365a

♦ **al-ḳaḍāʾ wa ʾl-ḳadar** (A) : when combined into one expression, these two words have the overall meaning of the Decree of God, both the eternal Decree (the most frequent meaning of ḲAḌĀʾ) and the Decree given existence in time (the most frequent sense of ḲADAR). Other translations are possible, for example, *ḳaḍāʾ*, predetermination; *ḳadar*, decree or fate, destiny, in the sense of determined or fixed. It is also possible to use *ḳaḍāʾ* alone for decree in its broadest sense and define *ḳadar* more precisely as existential determination. The expression combining them is in general use and has become a kind of technical term of scholastic theology. I 413a; II 618a; IV 365a

In Persian literature, *ḳaḍāʾ u ḳadar* is a genre of poetry devoted to stories about the working of fate, fashionable in the 10th-11th/16th-17th centuries. VI 834b; VIII 776a

♦ ḳaḍāʾ u ḳadar → AL-ḲAḌĀʾ WA ʾL-ḲADAR

ḳadam (A) : in mysticism, 'priority', a principle arising in the second half of the 19th century in Egypt that implied the exclusive right of a ṣūfī order to proselytise and to appear in public in an area if it could be proved that it had been the first to do so, i.e. that it had seniority (*ḳidam*). X 324a; and → ATHAR

♦ ḳadamgāh (A *ḳadam* 'foot', P *gāh* 'place') : lit. place of the [imprint of the Prophet's] foot, syn. **ḳadam s̲h̲arīf**; there are many such places all over the Arab lands and in Turkey, and they are especial objects of veneration in Muslim India, along with *pand̲j̲agāh*s 'places of the [imprint of the] palm of the hand', impressions of the hands of holy men. XII 501b

ḳadar (A) : measure, evaluation, fixed limit; in its technical sense, ~ designates determination, the divine decree in so far as it sets the fixed limits for each thing, or the measure of its being. III 1142b; IV 365b; and → AL-ḲAḌĀʾ WA ʾL- ḲADAR

In ʿAbd al-Razzāḳ al-Ḳas̲h̲ānī's mystical thought, ~ is the arrival in the world of the Universal Soul of the types of existing things; after being individualised in order to be adapted to matter, these are joined to their causes, produced by them, and appear at their fixed times. I 89b

ḳadāsa (A) : holiness; beings that are pure, wholly unsullied or in touch with the divine. IV 372a

ḳaḍb → ḲATT

♦ ḳaḍba (A) : in archery, a quiver made from the *nabʿ* wood (*Grewia tenax*). IV 800a

kaddād (A, pl. *kawādīd*) : a tiller of the soil. I 233b

kaddāḥ (A) : a flint-maker. XII 757a

ḳadḥ (A) : in medicine, the operation for cataract. II 481b; X 456a

kad̲h̲d̲h̲āb → ṢĀLIḤ

ḳad̲h̲d̲h̲āf (A) : oarsman, part of the crew of the warships in the Muslim navy. XII 120a

ḳad̲h̲f (A) : in law, a slanderous accusation of fornication, ZINĀʾ, or of illegitimate descent; in the latter case, it amounts to accusing the mother of fornication. I 29b; IV 373a

ḳāḍī (A) : in law, a judge, a representative of authority, invested with the power of jurisdiction. In theory, the head of the community, the caliph, is the holder of all powers; like all other state officials, the ~ is therefore a direct or indirect delegate, NĀʾIB, the delegate retaining the power to do justice in person. The objective being the application of the law, which is essentially religious, the function of the judge is a religious one. In theory, his competence embraces both civil and penal cases, and includes the administration of mosques and pious endowments. His competence in penal matters, however, is restricted to the very few crimes envisaged by the law, their repression being currently undertaken by the police. II 890b; IV 373b

♦ **ḳāḍī ʿaskar** (A) : judge of the army; an institution dating from the 2nd/8th century. Under Saladin, this institution was called *ḳāḍī les͟hker*. The position began to lose its importance after the middle of the 10th/16th century, when power passed into the hands of the grand MUFTĪ of Istanbul. It was finally abolished under the Turkish republic. IV 375a

♦ ḳāḍi ʾl-d͟jamāʿa (A) : ḲĀḌĪ of the community of Muslims; a title which ʿAbd al-Raḥmān gave, between 138/755 and 141/758, to the *ḳāḍī* of the Spanish territory already conquered, until then known as *ḳāḍi ʾl-d͟jund* ʻḳāḍī of the military districtʼ. Later, ~ became an institution similar to that of the ḲĀḌI ʾL-ḲUḌĀT. IV 374b; VI 2a

♦ ḳāḍi ʾl-d͟jund → ḲĀḌĪ ʾL-D͟JAMĀʿA

♦ ḳāḍi ʾl-ḳuḍāt (A) : ʻthe judge of judgesʼ; the highest position in the system of judicial organization of the Islamic state, which, when combined with the institution of the *wizāra* (→ WAZĪR), was the highest step under the authority of the caliph. The institution of ~ was an adaptation of the Persian *mōbedān-mōbed*. I 164b; IV 374a; VI 2a

♦ ḳāḍī les͟hker → ḲĀḌĪ ʿASKAR

ḳaḍīb (A) : rod (syn. *ʿaṣā*), one of the insignia of the sovereignty of the caliph. IV 377b
In archery, a bow made of a stave all of a piece and unspliced, sc. a self-bow. IV 798a
In music, a wand which supplied rhythm. II 1073b; a percussion stick. VIII 852b; IX 10b
In anatomy, the penis. XII 641a

ḳadīd (A) : in pre-Islamic Arabia, meat cut into thin strips and left to dry in the sun. II 1059a

ḳādima (A) : a quill feather. XI 517a

ḳadi̊n → K͟HĀṢṢEKĪ

♦ ḳaḍi̊nlar salṭanati̊ (T) : ʻthe rule of the womenʼ, the period from the mid-10th/16th to the mid-11th/17th centuries, when royal women enjoyed a large measure of influence in the Ottoman empire. XI 130b

ḳādi̊rg͟ha → BAS͟HTARDA

kadk͟hudā : a giver of years. X 367b; and → KETK͟HUDĀ

ḳadriya (A) : cedar-oil, extracted from cedarwood. IV 772b

ḳādūs (A, pl. *ḳawādīs*) : the bucket used in the water wheel (DŪLĀB) on the banks of the Nile in mediaeval Egypt. V 863b
In Fās, a pipe of a water channel, taking the water to individual houses; the special workers for the upkeep of the water channels were called *ḳwādsiyya* (< ~). V 877b

kāf (A) : the twenty-second letter of the Arabic alphabet, transcribed *k*, with the numerical value 20. It is defined as occlusive, postpalatal, surd. IV 399a

ḳāf (A) : the twenty-first letter of the Arabic alphabet, transcribed *ḳ*, with the numerical value 100. It is defined as occlusive, uvulovelar, surd. IV 400a

ḳafā (A) : nape of the neck. IX 312b

kafāʾa (A) : equality, parity and aptitude; in law, ~ denotes the equivalence of social status, fortune and profession (those followed by the husband and by the father-in-law), as well as parity of birth, which should exist between husband and wife, in default of which the marriage is considered ill-matched and, in consequence, liable to break up. I 27b; IV 404a; IV 1116b; and → KUFU

kafāla (A) : in law, an institution corresponding to some extent to the surety-bond, with the difference that the jurists distinguished two types of surety-bond: that for which the surety, *kafīl*, is binding to secure only the appearance in court of the debtor, *aṣīl* or *makfūl*; known as the *kafāla bi 'l-nafs*, it is an institution peculiar to Islamic law. And, secondly, the *kafāla bi 'l-māl*, by means of which the surety stands as a pledge to the creditor, *makfūl lahu*, that the obligation of the principal debtor will be fulfilled. IV 404b

kafan (A) : shroud, a cloth or cloths woven by an *akfānī*, which the deceased's body is wrapped in, by a professional enshrouder, *kaffān*, and then buried. Sometimes the corpse was borne without a bier or it could be carried in an open wooden coffin *(ṣandūḳ, tābūt)*. XII 502b

ḳafes (T) : lit. cage; the late but popular term for the area of the harem of the Topkapı Palace in which Ottoman princes of the blood (*sheh-zādeler*) were confined from the early 17th century onwards. In a more abstract sense, ~ is applied to the system whereby the rights of claimants to the Ottoman throne were determined. Of earlier usage is the appellation *shimshīrlik* or *čimshīrlik* 'the box shrub', a reference to the little courtyard planted with boxwood, at the northeast corner of the sultan's mother's courtyard. XII 503b

♦ ḳafesī (T) : a dome-shaped ḲAVUḲ 'cap', worn with a long turban forming folds fastened towards the base with a fine thread or pin. It was worn in Ottoman Turkey from the 17th century by the functionaries of the Defter (→ DAFTAR). V 751b

kaff (A) : palm, paw; in divination, *ʿilm al-~* is a process which belongs to the realm of physiognomy, designating more specifically chirognomy or the art of deducing the character of a person according to the shape and appearance of the hands. But the use of the term has become general. It also covers both chiromancy (the study of the lines of the hand), dactylomancy (prognostications drawn from the observation of the finger joints), and onychomancy (divination from the finger nails). IV 405b

In prosody, ~ is a deviation in the metre because of the suppression of the 7th consonant, e.g. the *nūn* of *fāʿilātu[n]*. I 672a; XI 508b

For ~ in military science, → SĀʿID

♦ kaff al-ʿadhrāʾ (A) : in botany, *Anastatica hierochuntia, Cruciferae*, the dried seed-heads of which can last for years and are blown around the desert, the seeds germinating when water is available. The plant, used as a birth charm, is also called *kaff Fāṭima bint al-nabī* or *kaff Maryam*. VI 631b

♦ kaff al-hirr (A) : in botany, the Corn crowfoot (*Ranunculus arvensis*) and the Asiatic crowfoot (*R. asiaticus*). IX 653a

♦ kaff al-nasr (A) : 'vulture's foot', in botany, the Scolopender or Hart's tongue (*Scolopendrium vulgare*), and also the Water milfoil (*Myriophyllum verticillatum*). VII 1014b

ḳaffāl (A) : a locksmith. XII 757a

kaffāra (A) : Qurʾānic term for an expiatory and propitiatory act which grants remission for faults of some gravity. IV 406b; IX 94b

kāfī (Pu) : a genre of Muslim Punjabi literature, comprising a lyric consisting of rhymed couplets or short stanzas having a refrain repeated after each verse, and normally following the usual Indian poetic convention whereby the poet assumes a female persona, typically that of a young girl yearning to be united with her husband/love, allegorically to be understood as an expression of the soul's yearning for God. VIII 256a

kafīl → KAFĀLA

ḳāfila → KĀRWĀN

kāfir (A) : originally, 'obliterating, covering', then, 'concealing benefits received', i.e. ungrateful, which meaning is found even in the old Arab poetry and in the Qurʾān; the development of meaning to 'infidel, unbeliever' probably took place under the influence of Syriac and Aramaic. IV 407b

♦ kāfir niʿma (A) : in theology, an unbeliever by ingratitude. XI 478a

♦ **kāfirkūb** (A, < *kāfir* + P *kūbīdan*) : lit. heathen-basher, i.e. a club; the term is testified, only in the plural *kāfirkūbāt*, in ʿIrāḳ from the end of the 2nd/8th century, although al-Ṭabarī cites it when describing the incidents arising in 66/685 during the revolt of al-Mukhtār. It seems to be a term born of a particular period and in a relatively circumscribed area which swiftly became obsolete. IV 44b; IV 411a

ḳāfiya (A, pl. *ḳawāfin*) : in prosody, rhyme. Originally, the word meant 'lampoon', then 'line of poetry', 'poem'. These earlier senses survived in Islamic times after the word had also come to be used in the technical sense of 'rhyme'. The native lexicographers believe that 'rhyme' is the original and that 'line of poetry', 'poem' are secondary. IV 411b; and → SADJʿ

♦ ḳāfiya muḳayyada (A) : fettered *ḳāfiya*, a rhyme in which the rhyme consonant is not followed by a letter of prolongation. IV 412a

♦ ḳāfiya muṭlaḳa (A) : loose *ḳāfiya*, a rhyme in which the rhyme consonant is followed by a letter of prolongation or by a short vowel and a vowelled or quiescent *hāʾ*. IV 412a

kāfiyya (A, < It *[s]cuffia*; pl. *kawāfī*), or *kūfiyya* : a head scarf, a rectangular piece of cloth of linen or silk in various colors, almost a yard square, worn by both sexes in the Arab East. The cloth is folded diagonally, the ends hang down or are tied below the chin, and above it the Bedouin sometimes and townsmen usually wind a turban. This form, which is known in Egypt since Mamlūk times and is mentioned in the *Arabian Nights*, came into prominence again as part of the dress of the Wahhābīs. V 741a; X 613a

ḳafīz (A) : a measure of capacity used in ʿIrāḳ and caliphal Persia for weighing small quantities of grain. Its actual weight varied. VI 119b f.

kaff (A) : in a religio-political context, the quiescent attitude of some Khāridjite groups in early Islam (→ ḲAʿADA). XII 505a

kaffān → KAFAN

kāfī (P) : in Western Indian literature, a sung ṣūfī lyric poem with a refrain repeated after each verse, first brought to perfection by Saččal Sarmast (d. 1242/1827) of Khayrpūr in Upper Sind. V 611a

ḳafla → ʿAḲD

ḳaftān → KHAFTĀN

kāfūr (A, < H *karpūra, kappūra*, Mal *kapur*) or *ḳāfūr, ḳa(f)ūr* : in botany, camphor, the white, translucent substance which is distilled together with camphor oil from the wood of the camphor tree (*Cinnamomum camphora*) indigenous to east Asia (China, Formosa, Japan). IV 417b; VIII 1042b

The same word ~ (variants *kufurrā, kifirrā, djufurrā* etc.) also designates the integument of the palm leaf or of the grapevine. IV 418a

kāghad (A, < P), or *kāghid* : paper. After its introduction in Samarḳand by Chinese prisoners in 134/751, various kinds of paper were then made and it must be supposed that paper achieved some importance as early as the second half of the 2nd/8th century. Names for the different kinds of paper are: *firʿawnī, sulaymānī, djaʿfarī, ṭāhirī*, and *nūḥī*. IV 419b

ḳaghan → KHĀḲĀN

kāghān (A) : in mediaeval ʿIrāḳ, a boy who acts as a male prostitute. VII 494a

♦ kāghānī (A) : in mediaeval ʿIrāḳ, a vagrant who gives out that he is demoniacally possessed or an epileptic. VII 494a

kāghid → KĀGHAD

kaghnı̊ (T) : a Byzantine wagon, used in mediaeval Turkicised Anatolia. I 205b

kahār (IndP) : in the Mughal period, a bearer of different kinds of litters, classed as infantry. V 687a

ḳaḥba (pl. *ḳiḥāb*) → BAGHIYY
ḳahd → ḤADHAF
kaḥḥāl (A) : in medicine, an oculist. I 388a; an ophthalmist. V 357a

kāhin (A) : a term of controversial origin. It appears to have been used by the 'Western Semites' to designate the possessor of a single function with related prerogatives: the offering of sacrifices in the name of the group, the representing of this group before the deity, the interpretation of the will of the deity, and the anticipation and communication of his wishes. The Arab ~ combined the functions of sacrificer and guardian of the sanctuary, and those of the *mantis* and the *augur*; hence, it is possible to render ~ by 'priest', in the sense of agent of the official cult. But the predominance of nomadism, where it was usually the head of the family or tribe who offered sacrifices and in which frequent migrations prevented the establishment of an official form of worship and fixed places of worship, weakened the first role of the ~ while favouring the development of the second, more in keeping with the expectations of most of his fellow-tribesmen. Thus it is virtually necessary to translate ~ as 'diviner' with the dual meaning of the Latin *divinus*, that is to say, 'one inspired' and 'prophet', without excluding his strictly priestly role in places where social conditions allowed it, such as at Mecca. IV 420b; and → ʿARRĀF

ḳāhiriyya (A) : omnipotence (of God). I 89b
kāhiya → KETKHUDĀ
kahramān → KĀRIM

kahrubā (P), also *kāhrabāʾ* : yellow amber; today, ~ also used for electricity. IV 445b
kahūr (P) : in botany, a spiny shrub, enjoyed by camels. V 669b

ḳahwa (A) : coffee; originally a name for wine, ~ was transferred towards the end of the 8th/14th century to the beverage made from the berry of the coffee tree; the word for coffee in Ethiopia, *būn*, has passed into Arabic in the form *bunn*, as a name of the coffee tree and berry. IV 449a; XII 775b

♦ ḳahwači-bāshī (P) : in Ṣafawid times, an official in the royal kitchen who headed the department of coffee making. XII 609b

♦ ḳahwa-khāna → ČĀY-KHĀNA

kahya → KETKHUDĀ

ḳāʾid (A, pl. *ḳuwwād*) : an imprecise term, but one always used to designate a military leader whose rank might vary from captain to general. II 507b; IV 456a; designation for a tribal chief (referring to the chief's leadership in war). IX 115b

♦ ḳāʾid raʾsih (A) : 'governor of himself', a powerful ḲĀʾID who was removed from office and compelled to live at court, with the honour due to his rank. IV 456b

ḳāʿid (A) : lit. sitter; in shīʿī terminology, the 'sitting' members of the family of the Prophet, who refused to be drawn into ventures of armed revolt, in contrast to the ḲĀʾIM. IV 456b

♦ ḳāʿida → ḲAWĀʿID

ḳaʿīd (A), and *khafīf* : a term applied to a wild animal or bird which approaches a traveller or hunter from the rear, one of the technical terms designating the directions of a bird's flight, or an animal's steps, which play an important part in the application of divination known as FAʾL, ṬĪRA and ZADJR. I 1048a; II 760a

ḳāʾif (A, pl. *ḳāfa*) : a physiognomist. I 28b
ḳāʾila → ẒĀHIRA

ḳāʾim (A) : lit. riser, the shīʿī MAHDĪ, referring both to the member of the family of the Prophet who was expected to rise against the illegitimate regime and restore justice on earth, and to the eschatological Mahdī. Synonyms in shīʿī terminology are: *ḳāʾim āl Muḥammad, al-ḳāʾim bi 'l-sayf, al-ḳāʾim bi-amr Allāh, ḳāʾim al-ḳiyāma*. IV 456b; V 1235b

Among the Ismāʿīliyya, ~ is the name of the seventh 'speaking' prophet who will abrogate Muḥammad's sharīʿa and restore the pure unity, *tawḥīd*, of the times before Adam's fall. IV 203b; IV 457a; XII 206b

♦ ḳā'im bi-aʿmāl (A) : in the science of diplomacy, the term for *chargé d'affaires*. VIII 813a; and → MAṢLAḤATGÜZĀR

♦ **ḳā'im-maḳām** (T) : the title borne by a number of different officials in the Ottoman empire. The most important of them was the *ṣadāret ḳā'im-maḳāmî* or *ḳā'im-maḳāmî pasha* who stayed in the capital as deputy when the grand vizier had to leave for a military campaign. The ~ enjoyed almost all the authority of the grand vizier, issuing *fermān*s (→ FARMĀN) and nominating functionaries, but he was not allowed to intervene in the area where the army was operating. IV 461b; colonel. X 872a

In 1864 the ~ became the governor of an administrative district, and under the Republican regime he continued to be administrator of such a distict. IV 461b

In Ottoman Egypt, ~ was applied to the acting viceroy before Muḥammad ʿAlī Pasha, and under the latter to specific grades in the military and administrative hierarchies. IV 461b

ḳā'ime (T, < A) : the name formerly used for paper money in Turkey, an abbreviation for *ḳā'ime-i muʿtebere*. Originally, the word was used of official documents written on one large, long sheet of paper. IV 460a; debt certificate, issued in the summer of 1840 by the Porte, that was acceptable in government offices in payment of obligations. X 203a

kā'in (A, pl. *kā'ināt*) : in speculative theology and philosophy, the existent thing. IV 795a

kaʿk (A) : in the mediaeval Middle East, a pastry, to which dough SAWĪḲ was added. IX 93b

ḳāḳum (A) : in zoology, the ermine. II 817a

ḳaʿḳāʿ (A) : a man whose foot-joints can be heard cracking as he walks; often found as a proper name in the early days of Islam. IV 463b

ḳalʿa (A) : castle, fortress. IV 467a; citadel. IX 411a; and → AGADIR

kalab (A) : in medicine, rabies. IV 490a; XII 189b

ḳālab (A, pl. *ḳawālib*) : in the mediaeval kitchen, a mould. VI 808b

In the religious terminology of metempsychosis, one of the terms for the body in which the spirit is incarnated. V 893b; X 182a

ḳalaba → SHAGHABA

ḳalafat → ČORBADJÎ KEČESI

ḳalāḳil (A) : a name for the SŪRAs that begin with *ḳul* 'say:': lxxii, cix and cxii-cxiv. IX 887b

ḳalam (A, < Gk κάλαμος 'reed'; pl. *aḳlām*) : the reed-pen used for writing in Arabic script. It is a tube of reed cut between two knots, sliced obliquely (or concave) at the thicker end and with the point slit, in similar fashion to the European quill and later the steel-pen. IV 471a

In Ottoman usage, ~ (pronounced *ḳalem)* was used figuratively to designate the secretariat of an official department or service; it then came to be the normal term for an administrative office. This usage has survived in modern Turkish, and is also current in Arabic. IV 471b

♦ ḳalam al-ṭūmār → MUKHTAṢAR AL-ṬŪMĀR

♦ ḳalamdān → DAWĀT

♦ **ḳalamkārī** (< P *ḳalam* 'pen' + *kār* 'work') : the hand-painted and resist-dyed cottons of India, known as chintz. IV 471b

♦ aḳlām-i sitta (P) : 'six [calligraphic] styles', the main Islamic scripts, viz. *muḥaḳḳaḳ*, *rīḥān*, *thuluth*, *naskh*, *tawḳīʿ*, *riḳāʿ*. IV 1123a

kalām (A) : a word; in the Qur'ān, ~ is found in the expression *kalām allāh* 'the Word of God'. IV 468b; ~, or **ʿilm al-kalām**, is also the term for 'theology', one of the religious sciences of Islam and the discipline which brings to the service of religious beliefs discursive arguments. III 1141b ff.; a rational argument, defensive apologetics, or the science of discourse (on God). I 694a; IV 468b

For ~ in music, → GHINĀ'

ḳalān : a Mongolian tax, apparently a general term for occasional exactions of a specifically Mongol rather than Islamic character, imposed on the sedentary population by the Mongols and including some kind of corvée. VII 233b

ḳalandar (T, < P ?) : 'a vagabond of scandously offensive behaviour'; the name given to the members of a class of wandering dervishes which existed formerly, especially in the 7th/13th century, in the Islamic world, within the area extending from Almaliḳ in Turkestan in the east to Morocco in the west, practising in its extreme form the antinomian way of life of Malāmatiyya mysticism. ~ passed into Arabic also in the form *karandal*. IV 58b; IV 472b; VI 225b

♦ ḳalandariyyāt (P) : in Persian literature, a genre of poetry, named after the ḲALANDAR. Poems of this genre can be quatrains or may have a form intermediate between the ḲAṢĪDA and the GHAZAL. They are characterised by the use of antinomian motives referring to the debauchery of beggars and drunks. IV 58b; IX 4b

ḳalansuwa (P, A, pl. *ḳalānis*), and *ḳalansuwa ṭawīla, ṭawīla* or *danniyya* : the name for a cap worn by men either under the turban proper or alone on the head. Caps of different shapes were called ~; varieties of ~ are *ṭurṭūr, burnus, urṣūṣa*, etc. X 609a; XII 508a; a distinctive, tall, conical Persian hat, resembling a long amphora-like wine jar known as *dann*, worn in the mediaeval Islamic period. Its top was pointed. IV 940a; V 737b; X 612b; a pointed bonnet for men in Algeria and Tunisia. V 746a

♦ ḳalansuwa buḳrāṭ (A) : in medicine, a particular kind of head bandage. XII 508b

♦ ḳalansuwa nuhās (A) : the metal cap of the obelisk near Heliopolis. XII 508b

♦ ḳalansuwa turāb (A) : in modern Arabic, a chemical sublimating vessel. XI 508b

kalāntar (P) : a term used in the 8th/14th and 9th/15th centuries to mean 'leader', occurring especially with reference to the tribal and military classes. From the late 9th/15th century onwards, ~ designates (i) an official belonging to 'civil' hierarchy in charge of a town or district or the ward of a town, (ii) the head of a guild, and (iii) the head of a tribe or sub-tribe. In its first sense, which is now obsolete, ~ sometimes overlapped or was synonymous with RA'ĪS, DĀRŪGHA, and KETKHUDĀ. IV 474a

kalawta (A), or *kalūta* : a kind of cap which is first mentioned in the Fāṭimid period. It was to become a standard item in Ayyūbid and Mamlūk times. V 738a; X 612b; in Persian, pronounced *kulōta*, a veil worn by women or a child's cap. X 613a

kalb (A) : in zoology, the domestic dog (*Canis familiaris*). IV 489b; wood-eating worms. IV 491b

In the game of backgammon, the piece played with (P *muhra*). VII 963a

For ~ in astronomy, IV 492a; IX 471b

♦ kalb al-baḥr (A), or *ḥafshrūsī* : in zoology, the white whale. VIII 1022b; the dog-fish, also called the *kawsadj* or *lakhm*. IV 491b

♦ kalb al-mā' (A) : in zoology, the otter; in the western Islamic world, ~ is the name for the beaver. IV 491b

♦ kalb al-mayy (A) : in zoology, the mole-cricket (*gryllotalpa vulgaris*), also called *ḥālūsh* or *ḥarrāthā*. IV 491b

ḳalb (A, pl. *ḳulūb*) : heart. IV 486a; (A, P, T) false, base, impure. X 409a; and → AṢL, ḤASHM

♦ kalpazan (< P *ḳalb-zan*) : in numismatics, a counterfeiter of coins. X 409b kalba (P) : in Iran, a sausage, a popular food item introduced in the 20th century. XII 611b

kaldāniyyūn (A) : the 'Chaldaeans', one of seven ancient nations according to al-Masʿūdī, and consisting of several smaller nations whose common kingdom, in the Fertile Crescent and the Arabian peninsula, preceded that of the Persians and whose common language is Syriac. VIII 1007b

ḳāldjiyān (T) : in Ottoman times, the worker in the mint who prepared the standard ingots by melting the metal. II 119a

ḳalemiyye (T) : in the Ottoman empire, one division of the ruling elite, the men of the pen, later referred to as *mülkiyye* 'bureaucrats'. XII 675b

ḳalewī → ḲALLĀVĪ

ḳalghay : a title best known as indicating the deputy or heir apparent of the KHĀNs of the Crimean Khānate. Its linguistic origins are uncertain. IV 499b

ḳālī (T) : a type of carpet (variants *ghālī, khālī*) manufactured at Ḳālīḳalā (now Erzerum). Although ~ is generally considered to be Turkish in origin, it is unattested in ancient Turkish texts. It may therefore be of Iranian origin. XII 136a

ḳalʿī (A), or *ḳalaʿī* : in metallurgy, tin; the Arabic name, either after Kalah, a well known port on the peninsula of Malacca, or *kaling*, the Malayan word for tin, bears witness to the fact that tin had to be imported. IV 502a; V 964b; and → RAṢĀṢ ḲALʿĪ
~ is also used for a type of sword which is often mentioned, especially in early Arabic poetry. This kind of sword is generally considered to be of Indian origin. IV 502b

ḳalīb (A) : in early Islam, the common ditch, into which e.g. ʿUtba b. Rabīʿa was thrown when mortally wounded in the battle of Badr. X 944b

kalima (A, pl. *kalimāt*) : the spoken word, utterance; ~ can also be extended to mean 'discourse' and 'poem'. IV 508a; VIII 532a
In Druze hierarchy, ~ is the third of the five cosmic ranks in the organisation. II 632a
♦ kalimat al-tawḥīd (A) : the first article of the SHAHĀDA (*lā ilāha illā llāh*). X 389a
♦ kalimāt-i ḳudsiyya (P) : 'holy sayings', eight adages or rules that are the essentials of Khʷādjagān doctrine and thought. XII 521b

ḳāliṣ (A) : in botany, the name of a plant, which seemed to represent a human head with a high cap. XII 508b

ḳālīte → BASHTARDA

ḳalḳala → ṢIFĀT AL-ḤURŪF

ḳallāb (A) : in numismatics, a counterfeiter of coins. X 409b

kallābazī : the master of the hawking-pack, assisting the falconer or hawker, who sets his greyhounds on the gazelle or the hare. I 1152b

ḳallāvī (T), *ḳalewī*, or *kal[l]ewī* : a headdress reserved for dignitaries with the rank of pasha which, from the 18th century, became official head-gear in Ottoman Turkey. It was a ḲAVUḲ with the body of a cone, worn with a white turban rolled around, draped and bulging in four places, decorated with a gold band. V 751b;

ḳalpaḳ (T) : busby, a kind of bonnet of lamb's fleece or woollen cloth decorated with lamb's fleece, worn by men and women in Ottoman Turkey. V 751b

ḳalūḳ (A) : in the terminology of horse-riding, a horse of uncertain temper. II 954a

kalūta → KALAWTA

ḳalyān → NARDJĪLA
♦ ḳalyandār : a water pipe carrier, employed by people of rank. X 754a

kalym : the purchase of the fiancée, a custom among the Čerkes tribes of the Caucasus which could only be avoided by resorting to abduction in case of refusal by the parents. The pretence of forcible abduction remains an essential rite in the marriage ceremony. II 23a

ḳāma → BĀʿ
kāma<u>kh</u> (A, pl. *kawāmi<u>kh</u>*) : a variety of relish or condiment, served, several at a time, in small bowls into which bread or morsels of food could be dipped. X32a
kamāla (A) : a renewable seasonal contract covering two seasons, either summer-autumn or winter-spring, which engages a shepherd or goatherd. XII 319b; and → FAḌĀʾIL
kamān (P) : bow; in music, a violin bow. VIII 346b; VIII 348a
♦ kamāna : in India, a bamboo bow, used to cut marble. VIII 269a
♦ kamān<u>dj</u>a (A, < P *kamānča*, dim. of *kamān*), or more rarely *<u>sh</u>ī<u>sh</u>ak* (A, < P, T *<u>gh</u>ičak, <u>gh</u>i<u>dj</u>ak*, etc., < San *<u>gh</u>o<u>sh</u>aka* ?) : in music, the hemispherical viol, perhaps the best known form of viol in the Islamic east. The body consists of a hemisphere of wood, coconut, or a gourd, over the aperture of which a membrane is stretched. The neck is of wood, generally cylindrical, and there is a foot of iron, although sometimes there is no foot. In texts where both the *<u>gh</u>i<u>dj</u>ak* and the ~ are described, the former is a larger type of the latter, having, in addition to its two ordinary strings, eight sympathetic strings. In Egypt, the hemispherical viol is nowadays called *rabāb miṣrī*. VIII 348a
kamar (P) : a broad belt often red in colour, worn by men in the Arab East. V 741a; IX 167b
ḳamar (A) : in astronomy, the moon; the full moon is termed *badr*. IV 518a
ḳamḥ (A) : in botany, wheat; in Iraq ~ is called *ḥinṭa* and in Arabia *<u>dh</u>urr*. IV 519b; V 863a
ḳamil → ḲAML
kāmil (A) : in prosody, the name of the fifth Arabic metre. I 670a
kamīn (A) : the rear-guard (of a raiding group of Bedouin). II 1055b; in military science, an ambuscade by a detachment of the army drawn up in a carefully chosen position near the rear-guard. III 202b
ḳamīṣ (A, < late L *camisia*), or *ḳamīṣa* : a shirt-like dress worn by both sexes all over the Arab world. V 733b ff.
ḳamī<u>sh</u> → LÜLE
ḳaml (A) : lice; some maintain that ~ applies only to females and that for males the term is *ṣuʾāb* (pl. *ṣiʾbān*, which actually designates nits). All species of lice, including head-lice and body-lice, fall within this term. A man more prone than others to give rise to lice is called *ḳamil*. IV 521b
kammūn (A) : in botany, cumin (*Cuminum Cyminum*); ~ was also used as a generic term for other plants which bore aromatic or medicinal seeds: *kammūn armanī* or *rūmī* was in fact caraway (*Carum Carvi*), also called *kammūn barrī* 'wild cumin'. ~ *ḥulw* was one of the names for aniseed, while ~ *aswad* was fennel-flower, properly called *<u>sh</u>ūnīz*. IV 522a, where can be found more variants; *kammūn kirmānī* is wild cumin (*Lagoecia cuminoides*). IX 653a
ḳamṭa (A) : a red cloth, adorned with pearls, which Egyptian women twisted around their ṬARBŪ<u>SH</u>. X 612b
kamulyān → GÖNÜLLÜ
ḳāmūs (A, < Gk) : dictionary; during the time of the Prophet, ~ was used for 'the bottom, the very deepest part of the sea', and later, following Ptolemy, geographers applied the term, in the form *uḳiyānūs*, to 'the mass of water surrounding the earth', more particularly the Atlantic Ocean. Al-Fīrūzābādī used ~ metaphorically as the title of his great dictionary, which name stuck, still carrying the sense of 'fullness, exhaustiveness' in contrast to *muʿ<u>dj</u>am* 'lexicon'. IV 524a
kān wa-kān (A) : in literature, one of the seven post-classical genres of poetry. The genre was devised by the Bag<u>h</u>dādī poets and its name derives from the formula used by story-tellers to open their narratives: 'there was and there was', i.e. 'once upon a time'. A ~ poem is in monorhyme with a long vowel after the rhyme letter. IV 528a

ḳanāʿa (A) : contentment with little, one of the components of asceticism, ZUHD. XI 560a
kanʿad (A) : in the Persian Gulf, term for the king mackerel. I 541b
ḳanāt (A, pl. *ḳanawāt, ḳanā, ḳunī, aḳniya*) : a canal, irrigation system, water-pipe. Used also for a baton, a lance, etc., ~ originally meant reed. IV 528b; XII 735b
In Persian, ~ is used today especially for underground water pipes, a mining installation or technique using galleries or cross-cuts to extract water from the depths of the earth. By means of a gently sloping tunnel, which cuts through alluvial soil and passes under the water-table into the aquifer, water is brought by gravity flow from its upper end, where it seeps into the gallery, to a ground surface outlet and irrigation canal at its lower end. IV 529a
ḳanbal → MIḲNAB
kanbiyaṭūr (A) : Campeador (< L *campeator*), a title in Castilian Spain given to el-Cid. IX 533a
ḳanbūs → MIʿZAF
kanbūsh → ḲUMĀSH
kandjifa (A) : playing cards, attested since Mamlūk times. V 109a
kandūrī (P), or *kandūra* : a leather or linen table-cloth; in India, ~ means also a religious feast held in honour of a venerated person like Fāṭima, and as such was imported into the Indonesian archipelago, where it has become a feast given with a religious purpose, or at least in conformity with religious law. IV 540a; religious meal. IX 154a
kanib (A, P *kanab*) : the hemp seed. III 266b
kanīsa (A, < Ar; pl. *kanāʾis*) : synagogue, church, temple; syn. *bīʿa*, which unlike ~ is found once in the Qurʾān. IV 545a
ḳannād-khāna (P) : a confectioner's shop. XI 307a
kannās (A) : lit. sweeper; a sanitary worker in the mediaeval Near East who swept public squares and other places such as prisons, dungeons and latrines, and transported garbage in boats or by other means to places outside the cities. The term is synonymous with *kassāḥ*; other terms used for the same occupation are *sammād* and *zabbāl* 'dung collectors'. IV 547b
kannis → SHUNḲUB
ḳanṭara (A, pl. *ḳanāṭir*) : a bridge, particularly one of masonry or stone; an aqueduct (especially in the plural), dam; high building, castle. IV 555a
kantawiyya (A) : the Kantaeans, a Mandaean sect. X 440a
kantu : a type of salt in the salt works near Bilma, in Niger, ~ is moulded into loaves in hollowed out palm-trunks and used chiefly for the feeding of animals. I 1222a
kānūn (A) : a brazier. V 42b
ḳānūn (A, < Gk; pl. *ḳawānīn*) : a financial term belonging to the field of land-taxes; a code of regulations, state-law (of non-Muslim origin). IV 556a
In fiscal administration, ~ refers both to the principles on which was based the assessment of taxes and to the resulting sum due from the taxpayer, either in the case of a single property or all the properties in one district taken together. In those provinces where many lands were assessed by the procedure of ~, this word came to mean a kind of fiscal cadaster. II 79a; IV 557a
In Mongol administration, the 'Domesday Book of the Empire', the survey and assessment book. II 81b
In law, *ḳawānīn* were at first regulations issued by the guardians of public order (especially the governors) in the fields of common law and penal law where the sharīʿa was silent. Under the Ottoman sultans, ~ came to be applied mainly to acts in the domain of administrative and financial law and of penal law. Nowadays, in all Middle Eastern countries, ~ denotes not only those codes and laws which are directly inspired by western legislation, such as civil and commercial law, administrative and penal law,

but also those laws and codes which are confined to reproducing, albeit simplifying, the provisions of the s̲h̲arīʿa. The word ~, however, has been replaced by *lāʾiḥa* (pl. *lawāʾiḥ*) in Egypt and by NIẒĀM or *tartīb* elsewhere. IV 556b
In organisations, e.g. guilds in Ottoman times, ~ was used also for the statutes, which were drawn up by the guildsmen and registered with the ḲĀḌĪ. IV 558b
Among the Berbers, especially in Kabylia and the Aurès, ~ was adopted to mean the customs, mainly as regards penal matters, pertaining to a particular village. IV 562a
In music, the ~ is the present-day psaltery of the Arabs and Turks, a stringed musical instrument with a shallow, flat, trapezoidal sound-chest. It has fallen into disuse in Spain and Persia, where it was once very popular. It is, however, still a great favourite in North Africa, Egypt, Syria and Turkey, where it is to be found strung trichordally with from 51 to 75 strings. VII 191a
♦ al-ḳānūn al-asāsī (A, T *ḳānūn-i esāsī*, P *ḳānūn-i asāsī*) : 'basic law', the constitution. II 651b; II 659b; in Turkey, *ḳānūn-i esāsī* was replaced by *anayasa* during the linguistic reforms in the Republic. II 640a ff.; IV 558b
♦ ḳānūn-i d̲j̲azāʾī (T) : in Ottoman usage, a penal code. II 518b
♦ ḳānūn al-hayʾa (A) : 'the astronomical law', term used by al-K̲h̲ud̲j̲andī for the sine law, because of its frequent use in astronomy. V 46a
♦ ḳānūn al-k̲h̲arād̲j̲ (A) : in fiscal administration, the basic survey in accordance with which the K̲H̲ARĀD̲J̲ is collected. II 78b
♦ **ḳānūnnāme** (T) : in Ottoman usage, ~ generally referred to a decree of the sultan containing legal clauses on a particular topic. In the 9th/15th century the term *yasaḳnāme* had the same meaning. ~ was occasionally extended to refer to regulations which viziers and pashas had enacted, to laws which a competent authority had formulated or to reform projects. However, a ~ was like any normal ḲĀNŪN in that only a sultan's decree could give it official authority. IV 562a; Ottoman tax register. VIII 203b

ḳānungo : in the Mug̲h̲al empire, one of the three chief PARGANA officials, the others being the *amīn* and the *s̲h̲iḳdār* (→ S̲H̲IḲḲDĀR), who were responsible for the *pargana* accounts, the rates of assessment, the survey of lands, and the protection of the rights of the cultivators. VIII 271a

ḳapan (T, < A *ḳabbān* 'a public balance', 'a steelyard') : an Ottoman term used to designate the central 'markets' for basic commodities, which were established in Istanbul in order to ensure the authorities' control of the importation and distribution of the raw materials needed by the craftsmen and of the foodstuffs to provision the people, and in order to facilitate the collection of the tolls and taxes due to the state. IV 226b
In Ottoman fiscal administration, ~ (or *ḥaḳḳ-i ḳapan, resm-i ḳapan*) was also the name for weighing duties levied at the public scales, paid in kind on cereals and dried vegetables, and in cash on other produce. II 147a; III 489b

ḳapanid̲j̲a (T) : a sumptuous fur worn by the Ottoman sultan, with a large fur collar, narrow or short sleeves, decorated with fur below the shoulders, with straight supplementary sleeves, laced with frogs and loops in front. V 752a

ḳapï (T) : lit. gate; by extension the Ottoman Porte, that is, the sultan's palace; ~ is also used for the grand vizier's palace and the seat of government. IV 568a
♦ ḳapï ag̲h̲asï → ḲAPU AG̲H̲ASÏ
♦ ḳapï kāhyasï → ḲAPÏ KETHÜDASÏ
♦ ḳapï kethüdasï (T), or *ḳapï kāhyasï* : an agent, 'close to the Porte', of a high dignitary of an Ottoman subject or vassal. IV 568a
♦ ḳapï ḳullarï (T) : lit. slaves of the Porte; the sultan's troops. I 35b; IV 568a
♦ **ḳapïd̲j̲i** (T) : the guard placed at the main gates of the Ottoman sultan's palace in Istanbul. IV 568a
♦ ḳapïya čïkma (T) : the appointment of ʿAD̲J̲AMĪ OG̲H̲LĀNs to the palace service. I 206b

ḳapli<u>dj</u>a (T), or *îlî<u>dj</u>a, kaplu<u>dj</u>a, ḳablu<u>dj</u>a* : the general term used in Turkey for a place where a hot spring is roofed over, as in a bath house. III 1120b; IV 569b, where are listed many more synonyms; and → ÎLÎ<u>DJ</u>A

ḳaptan   → ḲAPUDAN; ḲAPUDAN PA<u>SH</u>A

ḳapu a<u>gh</u>asî (T), or *kapî a<u>gh</u>asî* : the chief white eunuch and the senior officer in the Ottoman sultan's palace, until the late 10th/16th century. He was the sole mediator between the sultan and the world outside the palace, and had the authority to petition the sultan for the appointment, promotion and transfer of palace servants, A<u>GH</u>AS and IČ O<u>GH</u>LANS. II 1088a; IV 570b; IV 1093a

ḳapudan   (T, < It *capitano*), or *ḳaptan* : any commander of a ship, small or large, foreign or Turkish. VIII 564b

♦ **ḳapudan pa<u>sh</u>a** (T), or *ḳaptan pasha, ḳapudan-i deryā* : the title of the commander-in-chief of the Ottoman navy, becoming current only ca. 975/1567. Earlier titles were *deryā begi* and *ḳapudan-i deryā*. The squadron-commander was known as *ḳaptan*, and the individual commander as *re'îs* (→ RA'ĪS). I 948a; IV 571b; VIII 564b
In the 10th/16th century, the ~ became as well the governor of an EYĀLET, which consisted of a group of ports and islands. II 165

♦ ḳapudan-i deryā   → ḲAPUDAN PA<u>SH</u>A

♦ ḳapudana bey   (T) : one of three grades of admiral, instituted when the naval hierarchy was organised under 'Abd al-Ḥamīd I, or later under his successor Selīm III. The other two were *patrona bey* 'vice-admiral' and *riyāla bey* 'rear-admiral'. VIII 566b ff.

kār   (A, T) : a form of music known in Turkey (*kʲār*). I 67a; and → ṢINF

ḳar'   → ḲU<u>THTH</u>Ā'

♦ ḳar'a   (A) : in alchemy, the part known as 'cucurbit' of the distilling apparatus, the lower part of the alembic. I 486a; XII 550b

ḳāra   (A, pl. *ḳūr*) : in geography, a small, isolated flat-topped hill, known as *ḡāra* in North Africa. V 361b

ḳarā (T) : black, dark colour; strong, powerful. The former meaning is commonly meant when ~ is a first component of geographical names; the latter with personal names, although it may refer to the black or dark brown colour of hair or to a dark complexion. IV 572b

ḳarāba (A) : kinship; as a technical term, ~ seems to be of post-HI<u>DJ</u>RA usage. In the Qur'ān, and pre-Islamic poetry, the preferred term is *ḳurba*. The superlative *al-aḳrabūn* is also found, with the meaning of the closest relatives, those who have a claim to inherit from a man. IV 595a

ḳarabataḳ   (T) : a performance practice associated exclusively with the Ottoman music ensemble, MEHTER, consisting of the alternation of soft passages played by a partial ensemble with thunderous tutti passages. VI 1008a

karābīsī   (A) : clothes-seller. IV 596a

ḳarā<u>gh</u>ul   (Ott, < Mon; mod.T **karakol**) : lit. black arm; in Ottoman times, a patrol during military campaigns, sent out apart from the vanguard forces, *čar<u>kh</u>a<u>dj</u>î*, by the Ottoman army. The maintenance of security and order in different quarters in Istanbul was carried out by Janissary orders called *ḳulluḳ*. In modern Turkish, ~ became *karakol*, which is the common term for police station or patrol. IV 611a

ḳarā<u>gh</u>ulām   : in the Ayyūbid army under Ṣalāḥ al-Dīn, a second grade cavalryman. I 797b; VIII 468a

ḳaragöz (T) : lit. black eye; in literature, ~ is the principal character in the Turkish shadow play, and also the shadow play itself, which is played with flat, two-dimensional figures, manipulated by the shadow player, which represent inanimate objects, animals, fantastic beasts and beings, and human characters. IV 601a

karakol   → ḲARĀ<u>GH</u>UL

ḳaraḳul : lambskin. I 506a

karam (A) : the qualities of nobility of character, magnanimity, generosity, all the virtues making up the noble and virtuous man. XII 511b; and → SHARAF

karāma (A, pl. *karāmāt*) : a marvel wrought by a saint, mostly consisting of miraculous happenings in the corporeal world, or else of predictions of the future, or else of interpretation of the secrets of hearts, etc. IV 615a

ḳaran (A) : in archery, a quiver made from pieces of leather put together in such a way that the air can circulate through interstices left so that the fletchings of the arrows do not deteriorate. IV 800a; and → ḲIRĀN

karandal → ḲALANDAR

ḳaranful (A) : in botany, the clove. IV 626b

ḳarārīṭ → ḲARRĪṬA

ḳarasṭūn (P ?) : an instrument made up of a long beam which has at one of its ends a stone as a weight. If the Armeno-Persian origin of the word is correct, the ~ must be a kind of lever or balance, very similar to the SHĀDŪF, the contrivance used for raising water and still in use in certain eastern countries. IV 629a; the Roman balance or steelyard. IV 629a; V 529b; VII 195b

ḳaraẓ (A) : in botany, the acacia tree or fruit. VIII 1042b; XII 172a

kārbānsālār → KĀRWĀN

karbās (P) : a kind of coarse cotton weave, woven in many parts of the province of Kirmān. V 152a

ḳarbūṣ (A, pl. *ḳarābīṣ*) : the pommel of a horse saddle, the cantel, or back pommel, being called *muʾakhkhara* or *ḳarbūṣ muʾakhkhar*. II 954a; IX 51a; the saddle rested on a pad, *mirshaḥa*, held in position by girths, *ḥizām*, and a breast-strap, *labab*. II 954a

ḳarḍ (A), or *salaf* : in law, the loan of money or other fungible objects. I 633a; VIII 899b; the loan of consummation. I 26b

In numismatics, clipping coins with scissors. X 409b

♦ ḳarḍ ḥasan (A) : in law, an interest-free loan. VII 671b; VIII 899b

kardūs (A, pl. *karādīs*) : in military science, a squadron, an innovation which is said to have been introduced by Marwān II. III 182b; VIII 794a

ḳarḥab → FAZZ

kārī → KIRĀʾ

ḳāriʾ → ḲURRĀʾ; MUḲRIʾ

ḳarīb (A) : lit. near; in Persian prosody, the name of a metre, of rare occurrence, said to have been invented by the Persians. I 677b

karīf (K) : in the YAZĪDĪ tradition, an unrelated male on whose knees one has been circumcised and with whom a life-long bond exists. XI 315b

ḳāriḥ (A) : a foal between four and five years of age. II 785a

ḳarīḥa → GHINĀʾ

kārim (A) : yellow amber, in Egypt (syn. *kahramān*); also, a fleet, especially a merchant fleet. IV 640b

♦ **kārimī** (A, < KĀRIM ?) : the name of a group of Muslim merchants operating from the major centres of trade in the Ayyūbid and Mamlūk empires, above all in spices. IV 640a

ḳarīn (A) : a companion; in pre-Islamic usage, and in the Qurʾān, a term for a man's spirit-companion or familiar. IV 643b; IX 407a

♦ ḳarīna (A) : in Arabic literary theory, one of the terms used to indicate SADJʿ rhyme. VIII 737b; and → ḲAYNA

In Persian literature, ~ , or *ḳarīna-yi ṣārifa*, was used for a clue required to express the relationship between a MADJĀZ 'trope', and the corresponding ḤAḲĪḲA 'literal speech'. Such a clue is either implied in the context or specifically added, e.g. in *shīr-i* shamshīrzan, where the adjective points to the actual meaning of 'valiant warrior'. V 1027a

ḳāriṣ (A) : the quality of food being piquant, not always interchangeable with *ḥārr* 'hot' or *ḥāmiḍ* 'sour'. II 1071b

kārīz : a term used in eastern and south-eastern Persia, Afghanistan, and Balūčistān to designate a *ḳanāt*, a mining-installation or technique for extracting water from the depths of the earth. IV 529a

♦ kārīzkan → MUḲANNĪ

karkaddan (A, < P *kargadān*) : in zoology, the rhinoceros; ~ is the term for three varieties: the Indian rhinoceros, also called *mirmīs, ziba'rā/zib'arā* and *sinād*; the rhinoceros of Java; and the rhinoceros of Sumatra (P *nishān*). The African species was known to the Arabs well before Islam: the Black rhinoceros was called *ḥarīsh* or *khirtīt* (also one of the many terms for the rhinoceros' horn), and Burchell's rhinoceros, *hirmīs, abū ḳarn, umm ḳarn* and *'anaza*. IV 647a

♦ karkaddan al-baḥr (A), or *ḥarīsh al-baḥr* : in zoology, the narwhal (*Monodon monoceros*). IV 648b; VIII 1022b

ḳarḳal (A) : in Mamlūk times, the small receptacle in which water falls before flowing over the SHADIRWĀN; the channel itself was called *silsal*. IX 175b

ḳarḳas (A) : in mediaeval times, a special kind of clay, appended by a cord to documents and into which a seal ring was impressed. IV 1103b

karkh (A, < Ar *karka* 'fortified city') : a word associated with various towns in areas of Aramaic culture before the Islamic conquest; in Baghdād, a specific area and more generally the whole of the west side below the Round City was called al-~. IV 652a

kārkhāna (P) : a workshop. V 312a

ḳarḳī (A) : in prosody, term used by Ṣafī al-Dīn al-Ḥillī for a ZADJAL that contains lampoons. XI 373b

karkūr (N.Afr, B *aḳkur*), more exactly *ḳarkūr* : a heap of stones, and, more especially, a sacred heap of stones. The cult of heaps of stones seems to come from a rite of transference or expulsion of evil; the individual, picking up a stone, causes the evil of whatever kind that afflicts him to pass onto it and gets rid of it by throwing it or depositing it with the stone on a place suitable for absorbing it. The accumulation of these expiatory pebbles forms the sacred piles of stones which rise all along the roads, at difficult passes and at the entrances to sanctuaries. IV 655b

karm (A) : in botany, the vine, grapevine. IV 659a; in art, *karma* is a vine-scroll frieze. I 611b

ḳarmāṭī → KŪFĪ

karnā : in music, a six- to eight-foot long piece of hollow bamboo with a cow's horn at the end. X 407a

karōh → KROŚA

karr (A) : attack.

♦ karr wa-farr (A) : in military science, the tactic of withdrawal and counter-attack. VIII 131a; XI 542a

karrām (A) : a vine-tender. IV 667a

karranāy in music, an instrument of the horn and trumpet type. X 35a

ḳarrīṭa (Alg, < It *carretta*) : a cart and wagon; in the 16th century, its plural *ḳarārīṭ* was used to designate Portuguese wagons. I 206a

ḳarṣana → ḲURṢĀN

ḳarshi (anc.T and Uy) : castle. IV 671b; Mongolian term for palace. V 858b

karshūnī (A, < Syr) : the name of the Syriac script used by the Christians of Syria and Mesopotamia for writing Arabic. IV 671b

In India, ~ is applied to the Syriac script used for writing Malayalam, the vernacular language of the Malabar Christians. IV 671b

kārvān-kesh → KĀRWĀN

kārwān (A, < P) : a caravan, composed of horses, mules, donkeys, and especially camels; in India, caravans for the bulk transport of grain were pulled by oxen. In the pre-Islamic period, the Arabs had for long used the word *ʿīr*, and later the more usual word *ḳāfila*, which at the beginning of the 1st/7th century was current for gatherings of traders, as the equivalent of ~ . IV 676b

In the Ottoman period, the leader responsible for organising the ~ was called *kervān-bashi̊* (in Persia and India, *kārvān-kesh* or *kārbānsālār*). IV 677b

♦ kārwānsarāy (P) : caravanserai. IX 44; and → ĶAYSĀRIYYA

ḳarwasha (A) : originally, the name of the argot of the Moroccans practising the trades of sorcerer and treasure-seeker in Egypt, today applied to the secret language of the Dakārna (s. Dakrūnī) of Sudanese origin installed in the Village of the Sudanese close to Madāmūd in Upper Egypt and elsewhere. A part of the vocabulary is of Moroccan origin, while the grammar is that of the spoken language of the region of Luxor. IV 679b

ḳarya (A, T *ḳarye*; pl. *ḳurā*) : a town, village; and → NĀḤIYE

As a Qurʾānic term, ~ indicates an important town. Mecca, Medina, Sodom, Nineveh, and the coastal town are so called. IV 680a

♦ al-ḳaryatayn (A) : a Qurʾānic term for Mecca and Medina. IV 680a

♦ umm al-ḳurā → UMM AL-ĶURĀ

kās → ṢANDJ

♦ kāsatān → MUṢAFFAḤĀT

ḳaṣʿa in music, a small shallow kettledrum. X 35b

ḳaṣab (A) : in botany, any plant with a long and hollow stem like the reed (*Arundo donax*), to which the term is especially applied. IV 682a; a coloured linen cloth manufactured at Tinnīs, or a white one made at Damietta, or sometimes a cotton cloth made at Kāzarūn, out of which women's fine veils were woven, some set with precious stones. It can also mean a silken material, as well as a kind of brocade encrusted with little strips of gold or silver. IV 682b; X 532a

In mineralogy, in the singular (*ḳaṣaba*), the best emeralds, which are extracted from the vein as one piece. The small ones extracted from the earth by sieving are called *faṣṣ* 'cabochon'. The beads cut from the latter are 'lentil-like', *ʿadasiyya*. XI 570a f.

♦ ḳaṣab al-bardī (A), or *al-bardī* : the papyrus reed. IV 682a

♦ ḳaṣab al-djarīra (A) : the sweet flag (or fragrant rush). IV 682a

♦ ḳaṣab ḥulw → ĶAṢAB AL-SUKKAR

♦ ḳaṣab al-maṣṣ → ĶAṢAB AL-SUKKAR

♦ **ḳaṣab al-sukkar** (A), also *ḳaṣab al-maṣṣ* or *ḳaṣab ḥulw* : in botany, the sugar cane. IV 682b; V 863a

ḳaṣaba (A, mod. T *kasaba*) : originally, the essential part of a country or a town, its heart. This usage occurs especially in the Muslim West, where it is also applied to the most ancient part of a town (syn. *al-madīna*); later, a fortified castle, residence of an authority in the centre of a country or a town; principal town. III 498b; IV 684b; chef-lieu. V 311b

In North Africa, ~ occurs in the sense of fortress-citadel (dialect: *ḳaṣba*). IV 685a

In the Turkish Republic, a *kasaba* is a town with from 2000 to 20,000 inhabitants. I 974b; and → KÖY

As a basic measure of length, ~ equalled a number of cubits varying between five and eight, but giving an average length of four metres. VII 137b; the ~ was predominantly used in surveying. In 1830 the ~ was established at 3.55 metres. II 232b

ḳasam (A), and *yamīn, ḥalf* : an oath. IV 687b
In the Qur'ān, ~ or its verb *aḳsama* apply, in general, to the oaths pronounced by God himself. IV 687b
In law, ~ is the extrajudiciary oath by which a person binds himself to do or not to do a certain specific physical or juridicial act, by invoking the name of God or one of the divine attributes. IV 687b

ḳasama (A, < ḲASAM) : in law, an oath by which is asserted the guilt or innocence of an individual presumed to have killed someone, repeated fifty times, either by the ʿAṢABA of the victim of a murder (Mālikī school of law, where it is a procedure of accusation), or by the inhabitants of the place of the crime (Ḥanafī school of law, where it is a procedure for the defence of the one presumed guilty). IV 689b

kasb (A) : in economic life, gain. IV 690b
In theology, ~ means acquisition, appropriation. The verb *kasaba* is frequently found in the Qur'ān, mainly with the sense of acquiring those rewards or punishments which are the fruit of moral acts. ~ has had a long history in the scholastic theology, especially in the Ashʿarī school, where ~ and *iktisāb* were employed to define that which reverted to man in a 'freely' accomplished and morally qualified act. III 1063a; IV 692a

ḳasba fārisiyya → IṢṬĀM

ḳaṣba → ḲAṢABA

ḳaṣdīr → RAṢĀṢ ḲALʿĪ

kash → YASHM

ḳashaʿrīr (A) : in medicine, the shivers. X 510a

kashf (A) : in mysticism, the act of lifting and tearing away the veil (which comes between man and the extra-phenomenal world). IV 696b; VIII 429a; X 318b
Under the Mamlūks, the term ~ was used to designate a mission of AMĪRs from Cairo to Upper Egypt that consisted in guaranteeing security during harvests, inspecting the condition of the canals, and, to a growing extent, controlling the Bedouin. VIII 865a

kāshī (P, T, < *Kāshānī*) : in art, the tiles or trimmed pieces of faïence serving to cover completely or partially the main fabric of buildings in a design principally decorative but also, at times, to protect them against humidity. IV 701a
♦ kāshī-kārī (P) : a process of tile-decorating, whereby the design is reproduced on tiles of baked earth which are then painted, generally with different metal oxides, to become polychromatic, then rebaked. IV 702a
♦ kāshī-yi muʿarraḳ-kārī (P), or simply *muʿarraḳ-kārī* : a technique of tile-decorating, which consists of cutting, according to precise forms, pieces of monochrome ~ of different colours to compose a polychrome design. IV 701b

kāshif (A) : under the Ottomans, a district prefect. VIII 235a; ~ is still in use today in Egypt. VIII 865b

ḳāshiḳ : in music, a rattle instrument, made up of two wooden spoons attached to each other, in the hollow of which are a number of small bells, used in Persia and Turkey. IX 11b

kashk (P) : a kind of whey. V 152b; a type of yoghurt. XII 608b

ḳashḳa (T) : in western Turkish, the name given to a blaze on the forehead of animals such as horses, sheep and cattle; in Čaghatay the word also means 'brilliant', 'gallant'. It is probable that *ḳashḳāy*, the name of a Turkish people living in the Fārs province of Iran, is related to one of these meanings. IV 705b

kashkūl (P) : an oval bowl of metal, wood or coconut (calabash), worn suspended by a chain from the shoulder, in which the dervishes put the alms they receive and the food which is given them. IV 706b

In modern Arabic, ~ is sometimes used for a kind of album or collection of press cuttings, as well as denoting a 'beggar's bowl'. IV 706b

ḳashshāba (Mor) : a long sleeveless outer gown for men, and a long-sleeved flowing tunic with a deep slit down the breast for women, worn in Morocco. V 746a

kashshāfa → ṬALĪʿA

kashṭ (A) : an erasure on a written document. X 408b

kashūth rūmī → AFSANTĪN

kāsib (A, pl. *kawāsib*) : a carnivore. II 739b

ḳaṣīda (A) : in poetry, a polythematic ode which numbers at least seven verses, but generally comprises far more. It consists essentially of three parts of variable length: (1) an amatory prologue (NASĪB) in which the poet sheds some tears over what was once the camping place of his beloved now far off; (2) the poet's narration of his journey (*raḥīl*) to the person to whom the poem is addressed; (3) the central theme, constituted by the panegyric of a tribe, a protector or a patron, or in satire of their enemies. The Arabic ~ is a very conventional piece of verse, with one rhyme and in a uniform metre. From the end of the 2nd/8th century onwards, the classical ~ gave birth to a whole series of autonomous poetic genres. All these genres are represented in independent pieces, to which the name of ~ continues often to be given, even though incorrectly. I 583b; I 668a; IV 713b

The Persian ~ is a lyric poem, most frequently panegyric. Quantitatively, a poem cannot be a ~ unless the number of its distichs exceeds fifteen and does not exceed thirty. The ~ comprises three parts: the exordium, the eulogy, and the petition. It is first and foremost a poem composed for a princely festival, especially the spring festival and the autumn one, and was connected with courtly life in Persia. IV 57b; IV 714a

The Turkish ~ has the same rhyme scheme and metric patterns as the ~ in Arabic and Persian. The usual length of a Turkish ~ is between 15 and 99 couplets, but in fact, some longer ones exist. Theoretically, a complete Turkish ~ should contain six sections: NASĪB, TAGHAZZUL, GIRĪZGĀH, MADḤIYYA, FAKHRIYYA and DUʿĀʾ, but invariably do not contain all of them. Very often, one or more are left out, the most frequent omissions being the *taghazzul, fakhriyya* and *duʿāʾ* sections. IV 715b

In Swahili, ~ normally refers to a poem praising the Prophet. V 963a

♦ ḳaṣīda bahāriyya (A *ḳaṣīda* and P *bahār*) : in Urdu prosody, an ode with a prelude that was a description of spring. V 958b

♦ ḳaṣīda simṭiyya → MUSAMMAṬ

♦ ḳaṣīda zadjaliyya → MALḤŪN

♦ ḳaṣīda-yi madīḥa → MADĪḤ

ḳaṣīm (A) : in geography, the sandy area where the *ghaḍā* bush abounds. IV 717a

kāsir (A, pl. *kawāsir*) : a rapacious predator, used in hawking. I 1152a; a day-hunting raptor. X 783b

ḳāṣir (A) : in law, a person under guardianship. XI 208b

ḳaṣīr (A) : in North Africa, a refugee, like the ṬANĪB, but one entitled to make use of his prestige among his former group with which he has not severed all relations. XII 78b; among contemporary nomads like the Ruwalāʾ, ~ indicates a mutual relationship between members of different tribes by which each grants protection against his fellow-tribesmen. III 1018a

ḳasm (A) : a term for a land tax, in Syria and Palestine in the 10th/16th century, coming to a fifth, sometimes as much as a third, of the produce. VII 507b

kasr (A) : in mathematics, a fraction. From the time of Ibn al-Bannāʾ onwards, the Arab mathematicians distinguished five kinds of fractions: *mufrad* (simple), *muntasib* (fraction of relationship), *mukhtalif* (disjunct), *mubaʿʿaḍ* (subdivided), and *mustathnā* (excepted). IV 725a

In medicine, a fracture. II 481b
In grammar, the sound of the vowel *i*. IV 731a
For ~ in Bedouin culture, → FALĪDJA

ḳaṣr (A, pl. *ḳuṣūr*) : residence of a ruler, palace, or any building on a larger scale than a mere home, used in particular for Umayyad desert palaces and frontier forts. In the Maghrib, pronounced *ḳṣar*, also a collective granary or store house. IX 44a; XII 512a; and → AGADIR
In medicine, torticollis. X 788b
♦ ḳaṣra (A) : in anatomy, the base of the neck. X 788b
♦ ḳaṣriyya (A) : the palace guard of the Fāṭimids. IX 685b

kasra (A) : in grammar, ~ denotes the vowel *i*, more specifically the written sign itself, KASR denoting the sound in question. III 172a; IV 731a

ḳāṣṣ (A, pl. *ḳuṣṣāṣ*) : a popular story-teller or preacher, deliverer of sermons whose activity considerably varied over the centuries, from preaching in the mosques with a form of Qurʾānic exegesis to downright charlatanism. IV 733b; X 274b; an older, if not the primary meaning of ~ is 'a kind of detective responsible for examining and interpreting tracks and marks on the ground'; thus is it found twice in the Qurʾān. V 186a; jester. IX 552b

ḳaṣṣāb → DJAZZĀR
♦ ḳaṣṣābči-bāshī (P), or *sallākhči-bāshī* : in Ṣafawid times, the butcher in the royal kitchen. XII 609b

kassāḥ → KANNĀS

ḳassām (T, < A) : in Ottoman law, the title given to the trustee who divided an estate between the heirs of a deceased person. Ottoman law recognised two types of ~ , those under the *ḳāḍī ʿasker* 'judge of the army', and the others employed locally in each ḲĀḌĪ's court. The local ~ was called *shehrī* or *beledī*. IV 735b; VI 4b
♦ ḳassāmlïḳ → ḲISMA

ḳaṣṣār (A) : a fuller; bleacher. IV 1161a; V 89b; laundryman. XII 757b; a term in the Persian Gulf for a projecting rock. I 535b

ḳaṣṣāṣ (A) : in parts of the Central Region (the Sinai, Jordan and Palestine), an expert who determines the amount due for a particular injury, as payment for amends in place of retaliation for homicide or bodily injury, known as *muʾarrish* in Yemen and *naẓẓār* in the Western Desert. X 890b; and → ḲIṢṢA-KHʷĀN

ḳassī (A) : a striped fabric from Egypt containing silk, one of seven things forbidden by Muḥammad in a Tradition. V 735b

ḳasṭ → TAḲSĪṬ

ḳāt (A) : in botany, a smooth-stemmed shrub (*Catha edulis, Methyscophyllum glaucum*) that grows in East Africa and southwestern Arabia. Its leaves and young shoots (*kalāwīt*, s. *kilwāt*) contain an alkaloid, katin, which produces a euphoric, stimulating, exciting but finally depressing effect when chewed or drunk in a decoction; it is widely used in Ethiopia, Djibouti, East Africa and Yemen. IV 741a

ḳaṭʿ (A) : lit. cutting off; in the science of Qurʾānic reading, ~ or *waḳf* was the pause in reading, based on the sense or otherwise. Later, a distinction was made between the short pause for breath, and the other pauses, based on the sense; according to some, ~ indicated only the first; according to others only the second. IV 741b
In grammar, ~ is used in the term *alif al-ḳaṭʿ* for the disjunctive *hamza* which, opposed to the *hamzat al-waṣl*, cannot be elided. ~ further indicates the deliberate cutting, for a special purpose, between elements of a sentence which syntactically are closely connected. IV 742a; XI 172b
In prosody, ~ indicates cutting short the ending of certain metrical feet, e.g., the shortening of the metrical *fāʿilun* to *fāʿil*. This shortened form is then called *maḳṭūʿ*. IV 742a

In mathematics, ~ is used in many terms: *ḳaṭʿ zāʾid* 'hyperbola', *ḳaṭʿ nāḳiṣ* 'ellipse', *ḳaṭʿ mukāfī* 'parabola', and *ḳaṭʿ mukāfī mudjassam* 'paraboloid'. IV 742a
In astrology, ~ indicates scission. IV 742a
In the science of diplomatic, ~ refers to the format of paper. *Al-ḳaṭʿ al-kāmil* was an in-folio format used for treaties, *al-ḳaṭʿ al-ʿāda*, a small ordinary format used for decrees and appointments of the lowest rank. IV 742b
In logic, ~ means 'to assert something decisively or refute someone completely'. IV 743a
In medicine, the excision of soft diseased substance. II 481b
In art, *ṣanʿat-i ḳaṭʿ* was the art of cutting silhouette, brought from Persia to Turkey in the 10th/16th century, and to the west in the 11th/17th century, where at first, as in the east, light paper on a dark gound was always used. II 755b
♦ ḳaṭʿ al-ṭarīḳ (A), or *muḥāraba* : highway robbery or robbery with violence (syn. *al-sirḳa al-kubrā*), which in certain circumstances is punished with death. IV 770a; V 768a; IX 63a

ḳaṭā (A, pl. *ḳaṭawāt, ḳaṭayāt*) : in zoology, the ornithological family of Pteroclididae or sandgrouse. The term is onomatopaeic for their cry. Three species are distinguished: the *kudrī* or *ʿarabī* (*Pterocles Lichtensteini*), corresponding to the Lichtenstein's or Close-barred sandgrouse; the *djūnī* or *ghaḍaf, ghatmāʾ* (*Pterocles orientalis*), the Black-bellied sandgrouse; and the *ghaṭaṭ* (*Pterocles alchata*), the Large Pintailed sandgrouse. IV 743a

kataba 'l-kitāb (A) : lit. he has written the book; a fabulous marine creature mentioned by mediaeval Arab authors. It lives in the Indian Ocean, and its juice produces an invisible ink legible only at night. VIII 1023a

ḳaṭānī (A) : legumes. XI 413a

katar (P) : a type of levelling board used in central Iran for the preparation of irrigation check banks, and operated by two men, one pulling and the other pushing. II 905b

ḳaṭf (A) : in prosody, a deviation in the metre because of the suppression of a *sabab khafīf*, a moving and a quiescent consonant, and the preceding vowel, e.g. in *mufāʿal[atun]*. I 672a

ḳaṭīʿ (A) : a family flock of ten to forty animals, called *fizr* if there are only sheep, and *ṣubba* if there are only goats. XII 319a
♦ **ḳaṭīʿa** (A, pl. *ḳaṭāʾiʿ*) : a Muslim administrative term designating, on the one hand, those concessions made to private individuals on state lands in the first centuries of the HIDJRA, and, on the other hand, the fixed sum of a tax or tribute, in contradistinction to taxation by proportional method or some variable means. III 1088a; IV 754b; IV 973a
In early Islam, ~ was a unit of land, often a sizable estate, allotted to prominent individuals in the garrison cities founded at the time of the conquests. V 23a

kātib (A, pl. *kuttāb*) : a secretary, a term which was used in the Arab-Islamic world for every person whose role or function consisted of writing or drafting official letters or administrative documents. In the mediaeval period, ~ denoted neither a scribe in the literary sense of the word nor a copyist, but it could be applied to private secretaries as well as to the employees of the administrative service. It can denote merely a book-keeper as well as the chief clerk or a Secretary of State, directly responsible to the sovereign or to his vizier. IV 754b; XII 720a
In law, an author or compiler of legally-watertight formulae for use in *shurūṭ* (→ SHARṬ). IX 359a
In Western and Spanish Arabic, ~ is an alternative name for ʿUṭārid, the planet Mercury. VIII 101a; XI 555a
♦ kātib al-sirr (A) : in Muslim administration, the private secretary. X 392b

katība (A) : in military terminology, a squadron. IV 1144b

katif (A, pl. *aktāf*) : in anatomy, the shoulder. IV 763a

♦ ʿilm al-katif (A), or *ʿilm al-aktāf* : scapulomancy or omoplatoscopy, i.e. divination by the use of the shoulder-bones. This art forms a part of the practices of physiognomy. It is universal in scope, inasmuch as it provides for the foretelling of what will happen in the different regions of the earth towards which the four sides of the scopula are pointed according to the signs revealed by it. IV 763a; V 100a

ḳaṭīfa (P) : a fabric made in Yazd, which was renowned for its excellence. XI 304a

katih (P) : quickly prepared rice with clarified butter, eaten by the inhabitants of the Caspian provinces and especially Gīlān. XII 611a

ḳātil al-nimr → AḲŪNĪṬUN

ḳatīl al-raʿd (A) : lit. victim of the thunder; a name for the quail, as ancient belief held that the quail would be inevitably struck down by stormy weather. VIII 1006b

ḳātir (P) : in tribal Persia of the 19th century, a sum of money, which was increased or diminished according to the prosperity or otherwise of the tribes and the power of the government to exercise authority over them. III 1105b

ḳātı̊rdjı̊ (T) : a muleteer. IV 766a

ḳaṭirān → ḲAṬRĀN

katkhudā → KETKHUDĀ

ḳatl (A) : killing, putting to death, used in the two principal meanings of the word, sc. the crime of murder and the punishment of execution. IV 766b

katm (A) : a black dye which masks the red of the henna. IX 383b

ḳatma (T) : in the Ottoman empire, a device that brought water added to the main water conduits of the state waḳfs to the city at certain specified points. The sultan gave his formal permission for this ~ water upon application and recognised ownership rights over this water. V 882b

katra : in Muslim India, a term for a market, usually known after the commodity sold there. IX 800b

ḳaṭrān (A), or *ḳiṭrān, ḳaṭirān* : tar obtained by dry distillation of organic substances; the residuum left after the distillation of tar, i.e. liquid pitch; cedar-oil extracted from cedarwood. The substance is obtained from several kinds of coniferous trees, especially the *Cedrus Libani*, and was used as a medicine. IV 772b

kātriya (Tun) : a lieutenant in the army in the Regency of Tunis. IX 657a

ḳatt (A), and *ḳaḍb, barsīm* : in botany, alfalfa, a common crop raised in the shade of date palms in the Gulf. I 540a

ḳaṭṭaʿa → DJARF

ḳattāb (A) : in the mediaeval period, a seller of saddles stuffed with straw. XII 759a

kattān (A) : both flax and linen, in the early period usually called *ḳubāṭī* 'Coptic [stuff]' since they were imported from Egypt. White and coloured linen, ḲAṢAB and *sharb*, and brocaded linen, *diḳḳ*, were produced and exported to Muslim and non-Muslim countries until the industry began to decline in the first half of the 7th/13th century, probably the consequence of the increasing import of European fabrics. IV 774a; V 863a

katūm (A), and *fāridj, furdj* : in archery, a bow made from a single stave, hence it does not vibrate when loosed. IV 798a

katun : in Ottoman Greece, a semi-permanent settlement of Albanian or Vlach cattle breeders. VIII 169b

ḳaṭwa → NAṬṬĀLA

ḳavuḳ (T) : a rather high, variously-shaped cap, with a headband wound round it, worn by officers of the Janissaries; other professions had their own special ~, some with specific names. IV 806a ff.; the ~, whose height varied, normally had the form of a contracted or enlarged cylinder, flat or bulging; but there were also those which resembled a truncated cone or a cupola. The highest *ḳavuḳs* (40 to 60 cm) were kept rigid by means of a construction of metal bars or a kind of basket. They had a smooth or quilted surface and were trimmed with cotton to give the effect of relief or a dome shape with the quilting. V 751a

ḳawābī → DJUDHĀM

ḳawad → ḲIṢĀṢ

ḳawā'id (A, s. *ḳā'ida*) : rules. X 929a; in law, **ḳawā'id fiḳhiyya** are the *madhhab*-internal legal principles, legal maxims, general legal rules that are applicable to a number of particular cases in various fields of the law, whereby the legal determination (*aḥkām*) of these cases can be derived from these principles. XII 517a

♦ ḳawā'id aghlabiyya (A), also ~ *aktharіyya* : in law, 'preponderant' rules, which outnumber the generally valid rules (*ḳawā'id kulliyya*), and are couched not in maxims but in questions, e.g. "Can a presumption be canceled by another presumption or not?" XII 517a

♦ ḳawā'id istiḳrā'iyya (A) : in law, legal principles that were arrived at by induction from *furū'* (→ FAR') decisions. XII 517b

♦ al-ḳawā'id al-khams (A), also *al-ḳawā'id al-kubrā* : in law, five principles that were accepted by all schools, attested since the 8th/14th century. XII 517b, where they can be found

♦ al-ḳawā'id al-kubrā → AL-ḲAWĀ'ID AL-KHAMS

♦ ḳawā'id kulliyya → ḲAWĀ'ID AGHLABIYYA

♦ ḳawā'id uṣūliyya (A) : in law, hermeneutic principles formulated by the legal theorists, which at times were not carefully separated from the ḲAWĀ'ID FIḲHIYYA, XII 517b

kawāmikh → KĀMAKH

kawārīr → ZUDJĀDJ

ḳawāzib → BARMĀ'IYYŪN

kawda → WADA'

ḳawī (A) : a description of a man who is strong in himself, with *muḳwī* used when he owns a robust mount. V 576a

kawkab (A, pl. *kawākib*) : in astronomy, star; according to context, ~ can mean 'planet' specifically. VIII 97b; and → MURĀHIḲ

♦ kawkab al-dhanab (A), or (*kawkab*) *dhū dhanab* : in astronomy, 'star with a tail', a comet. VIII 102b

♦ (al-kawākib) al-mutaḥayyira (A) : in the 'scientific' period of Arabic-Islamic astronomy which was based on translations from Greek, the common term in astronomy for the five planets (Mercury, Venus, Mars, Jupiter, and Saturn) without the Sun and Moon. VIII 101a; XI 555a

♦ (al-kawākib) al-sayyāra (A) : in the 'scientific' period of Arabic-Islamic astronomy which was based on translations from Greek, the common term in astronomy for the five planets plus the Sun and Moon. VIII 101a; XI 555a

♦ al-kawākib al-sufliyya (A) : in astronomy, the lower planets (below the Sun), Moon, Mercury and Venus. VIII 101b

♦ al-kawākib al-thābita (A) : in astronomy, the fixed stars, known as simply *al-thawābit*. VIII 98a

♦ al-kawākib al-'ulwiyya (A) : in astronomy, the upper planets (beyond the Sun), Mars, Jupiter and Saturn. VIII 101b

♦ kawkaba (A, pl. *kawkabāt*), or *ṣūra*, pl. *ṣuwar* : in astronomy, constellation. VIII 98b

ḳawḳal → WĀḲWĀḲ

ḳawḳan (A) : in Hispano-Arabic, the usual term for snail. VIII 707a kawlī (P) : in modern times, the general term for the gipsy in Iran, but a wide variety of names are used locally. V 818b

ḳawl (A) : in music, a vocal form, at present in India a form of religious song. III 453a
Among the Yazīdīs, a sacred hymn, which together form a large corpus of texts representing the Yazīdī counterpart to both the sacred and the learned traditions of other cultures. XI 314b

♦ ḳawlī (T, < A) : the 'word-member', one of two classes of the ordinary members of the AKHĪ organization, YIGIT, who made a general profession only, as opposed to the active 'sword-member', *sayfī*. I 323a

ḳawm (A, pl. *akwām, aḳāwim, aḳāyim*) : people; in literature sometimes applied to 'men', used in opposition to *nisā'* 'women'. IV 780b; a term of tribal provenance used to denote a group of people having or claiming a common ancestor, or a tribe descended from a single ancestor. IV 781a; VIII 234a
In Atjeh, ~ has acquired a peculiar form, *kawōm*, and is used to mean 'all those who descend from one man in the male line'. IV 781a
In North Africa, the ~ (goum) means a contingent of cavalry levied from a tribe, a practice continued by the French. IV 784b
Under the Circassian rule in the Mamlūk period, *al-ḳawm*, meaning the People, was applied only to the Circassians. II 24b
In India, a term for the social division among the non-Muslim population, denoting different groups such as the Bhaṭṭī, Tarkhān, Pindjārā; it is debatable whether these should be called castes or not. III 411a

♦ **ḳawmiyya** (A) : nationalism. IV 781a

♦ ḳawmiyyāt (A) : ethnic groups, the study of whihc is differentiated from folklore, *khalḳiyyāt*, or studies at the popular level. X 734b

ḳawmā → ḲŪMĀ

ḳawmānī (A) : in tribal organisation, a member of an enemy faction. IV 835a

kawn (A, pl. *akwān*) : in philosophy, generation, especially in the phrase **kawn wafasād**, generation and corruption, which renders Aristotle's *De generatione et corruptione*. IV 794b
In scholastic theology, ~ is the advent in nature of the existent thing, the existentialisation of all corporal beings. IV 795a
As tribal term, → ḤARĀBA

kawōm → ḲAWM

kaws (A) : in meteorology, the south-west monsoon. VII 52a; the west wind (or *dabūr*), which, with the east wind (*ḳabūl*, also called *azyab*), was the most important of the prevailing winds of the three periods in which navigation was possible during the monsoons. VIII 527a

ḳaws (A) : the bow, as used in archery. IV 795b, where are found many terms for the names of various kinds of bows and for the components of the bow
In music, the bow of a stringed instrument. VIII 346a
In astronomy, *al-~* is the term used for the bow of Sagittarius (cross-bow), one of the twelve zodiacal constellations. VII 83b; VIII 842a

♦ ḳaws al-bunduḳ (A) : 'pellet- or stone-bow', the archetype of the arbalest used solely for shooting birds and already known in the Prophet's time. The projectile used was a ball of hardened clay (*djulāhiḳ* or *bunduḳ*). IV 797b; in Mamlūk terminology, one of the branches of horse-riding. II 955a

♦ ḳaws ḥidjāzī (A) : a simple, wooden bow, either short or long, used by the pre-Islamic Arabs. IV 797b

♦ ḳaws al-ḥusbān (A) : a hand bow adapted to shoot short arrows; it had therefore an arrow guide but no nut or locking mechanism. IV 798a

♦ **ḳaws ḳuzaḥ** (A) : in meteorology, the rainbow (syn. *ḳaws Allāh, ḳaws rasūl Allāh, ḳaws al-samāʾ, ḳaws al-g͟hamām*, etc.). IV 803a f.

♦ ḳaws al-rikāb → ḲAWS AL-RID͟JL

♦ ḳaws al-rid͟jl (wa ʾl-rikāb) (A) : the most common name in the Mamlūk period for the cross-bow type of weapon; it seems to have been given to cross-bows of various sizes, including those employed in sieges. The *ḳaws al-rikāb* had a stirrup in which the foot was placed. III 476a; IV 798a

♦ ḳaws wāsiṭiyya (A) : the Arab composite bow; the adjective does not stem from Wāsiṭ but from its proper sense of median, intermediate, probably with reference to the components of this bow. IV 797b

♦ ḳaws al-ziyār (A) : the ‘wheel cross-bow’, which was operated like the ordinary cross-bow to shoot a powerful arrow, but requiring several men to operate it. III 469b; IV 798a

kawsad͟j → KALB AL-BAḤR

ḳawṭ → ḲĪNĀ

kawt͟har (A) : a Qurʾānic word for the name of a river in Paradise or a pond which was shown to the Prophet at the time of his ascension to the Throne of God. IV 805b

ḳawuḳlu (T) : lit. the man with the ḲAVUḲ; a character of the Turkish ORTA OYUNU theatre. IV 806a

kawwāk͟h (A) : in hunting, a stalker at a hut for the capture of sandgrouse. IV 745a

ḳawwāl → ZAD͟JD͟JĀL

♦ ḳawwālī : a type of (sung) poetry known on the subcontinent. X 320a; mystical chants. XI 119a

ḳawwās (A), or occasionally *ḳawwāṣ* : bow-maker. IV 796b; a bowman, later, musketeer, ‘policeman-soldier’, especially the one in the service of high-placed Turkish officials and foreign ambassadors. From this term is derived the French *cawas* and the German *Kawasse*. IV 808b

In colloquial usage, both in Turkey and in other Islamic states, ~ denotes the servants and guards of foreign embassies. IV 808b

kayd (A) : in astronomy, *al-~* is the name of a fictitious star, whose earliest mention so far known is in Ibn Hibintā’s *al-Mug͟hnī* where it is listed as ‘one of the stars with a tail’. IV 809b

ḳayḍ (A) : in astrology, ‘the clutch [of the ostriches]’, the numerous small stars surrounding the star group *udḥī al-naʿām* ‘the nesting place of the ostriches’. VII 830b

kayf (A) : state; discretion.

♦ bi-lā kayf (A) : in theological writings, when referring to *ṣifāt k͟habariyya*, attributes of God based on the evidence of Qurʾān and Tradition which should be understood ~, ~ was taken to mean ‘without further comment’ by the Ḥanbalīs and other Tradition proponents close to them. Theologians, however, used ~ in the sense of ‘without qualifying God in a way only to be applied to His creation’, presenting it as a middle course between a literal acceptance of the anthropological statements in Scripture (TAS͟HBĪH) and the metaphorical interpretation in the Muʿtazilī sense (TAʿṬĪL). X 344a

♦ kayfiyya → ḤAḲĪḲA

kayfūfiyya (A) : philosophical-theological term used by the Karrāmiyya for ‘the quality of God’. Another one of their terms, called by al-Bag͟hdādī *ʿibārāt sak͟hīfa* ‘ridiculous expression’, was *ḥayt͟hūt͟hiyya* ‘the ubiquitousness of God’. IV 668b

ḳayḳab (A) : a wooden saddle-bow, on which the horse’s saddle was built. IV 1145a

ḳayl (A) : among the Sabaeans, in the pre-Islamic period, the leader of the S͟HAʿB, the grouping in their social organisation constituted of a number of clans; the ~ came from the dominant clan, but was himself subordinate to the king. IV 818b; a kinglet. IX 162b

ḳayn (A) : an artisan, workman; current usage reserves it above all for blacksmith. Since the men working at this trade usually belonged to the lowest stratum of the population, ~ became a deprecatory term applied to slaves and was used as an insult in the desert. IV 819a

♦ **ḳayna** (A, pl. *ḳaynāt, ḳiyān*) : female singing slave. I 32b; IV 820b; other terms for the professional singing girl were *dād̲j̲ina, mudd̲j̲ina, musmiʿa, karīna, ṣadūḥ* (and *ṣādiḥa*), and *d̲j̲arāda*. II 1073a; IV 820b

ḳayṣar (A, < Gk) : the usual name in early Islam for the Roman and Byzantine emperor. It is always used without the article, like a proper name. IV 839a

ḳaysāriyya (A, < Gk; pl. *ḳayāsīr*), also *ḳayṣāriyya* : the name of a large system of public buildings laid out in the form of cloisters with shops, workshops, warehouses and frequently also living-rooms, originally distinguished from the SŪḲ 'market' probably only by its greater extent, and by having several covered galleries around an open court, while the *sūḳ* consists only of a single gallery. At the present day, ~ is not infrequently quite or almost identical in meaning with the Persian word *kārwānsarāy*. IV 840a; IX 796b; in mediaeval Islam, an imperial establishment for the protection of stages on major commercial routes. IX 788b

In Algiers at the present day, ~ means barracks; after the first half of the 17th century it was used to denote the Janissaries' barracks. IV 841a

ḳayṣūm → S̲H̲ĪḤ

ḳayṭūn → GĪṬŪN

kayy (A) : in medicine, cauterization by fire with the object of surgical incision. II 481b

ḳayyān (A), or *muḳayyin* : a profession in mediaeval Islam, consisting of acquiring young slaves fit to become *ḳiyān* 'female singing slaves', in forming them under strict rules and in hiring out their services to private persons. IV 822b

For ~ in botany, → YĀSAMĪN

kayyās → MUKAYYIS

ḳayyim (A, pl. *ḳawama*) : lit. he who stands upright; with *bi, ʿalā, li* or the genitive alone, 'he who takes something upon himself, takes care of something or someone and hence also has authority over them'. This meaning of supervisor is found in all possible applications: administrator of a pious foundation, of baths, superintendent of a temple, caretaker of a saint's grave, etc. IV 847b; VI 677b; XI 63a; lessee of the steam bath. III 140b

In eschatological literature, ~ denotes a provider, a husband, of a woman. IV 847b

As adjective, 'commanding' or 'correct, right' (*al-dīn al-ḳayyim*). IV 847b

ḳayyūm (A) : the title of the topmost saint, in the thought of Aḥmad al-Sirhindī, of an invisible hierarchy of saints. V 545b; XI 118b

ḳażāʾ → ḲAḌĀʾ

kazāg̲h̲and (A,P) : in miitary science, a protective mail hauberk which had its own padded lining and a decorative outer layer of cloth. XII 737b

ḳazaḳ (T) : independent; vagabond. IV 848a

Under the Tīmūrids, ~ signified the pretenders in contrast to the actual rulers, and also their supporters, who led the life of an adventurer or a robber at the head of their men. At the same time, ~ began also to be applied to nomad groups which separated from their prince and kinsmen and so came into conflict with the state; later, ~ had also the meaning of nomad, in contrast to the sedentary Sart population in Central Asia. IV 848b

The status of ~ is also regarded as a very old social institution of the nomad Turkic peoples. The word became the name of a political unit and later an ethnic designation by having been applied in the former meanings to those groups of the Özbek tribal confederacy that had abandoned the K̲H̲ĀN Abu 'l-K̲h̲ayr and migrated to the north-east steppes of Turkistān, where they formed the core of the population of the present Kazakhstan. IV 848b

ḳazanlïḳ (T) : a cauldron, as e.g. found in the mausoleum of Aḥmad Yasawī, used for preparing food for pilgrims and ṣūfīs. X 681a

ḳazmaḳ → ḲĀZŪ

ḳāzū : the dredging of a canal, apparently from *ḳazmaḳ* 'to dig'. XII 550a

ḳazz → ḤARĪR

ḳeblī → SAMŪM

kehledān (T) : in Ottoman times, the worker in the mint who made the ingots into plates to be minted. II 119a

kelek (T, A, < Akk *kalakku*), or *kellek, kelik* : a curious raft made of bags of goat's hair, which is already known from the sculptures of Nineveh and has hardly changed in the course of centuries. Particularly mentioned by travellers in Mesopotamia and Persia, ~ is said to be typical for the upper part of the Tigris. IV 870a; VIII 810b

kelle push : a small white or red cloth cap, around which the turban can be twisted. X 612b

kemān (T), or *yay* : a bow-like instrument used by Ottoman carders to separate the cotton fibre from the seed by beating with it, in order to make the cotton clean and fluffy. V 559a

kenīz (P) : a female slave. I 24b

kēris (Mal) : in the East Indies, a double-edged dagger or short sword, retained from pre-Islamic times and having an almost magical and pagan significance amongst a population sometimes only superficially converted to Islam. XII 736b

kervān-bashï → KĀRWĀN

keshif (T) : in Ottoman administration, a detailed protocol compiled after damages to WAḲF-owned buildings, e.g. a BEDESTĀN, due to fire, determining the expenses involved in reparation. IX 542b

keshwar → IḲLĪM

kəskās (N.Afr) : a conical vessel made of earthenware or plaited alfalfa, used in North Africa for the preparation of couscous. V 528a

kəswa kbīra (Mor) : an elegant wedding and festivity dress of Jewish women consisting of several parts, derived from the 15th-century Spanish dress style. V 746a

ketkhudā (P, > T *kʾahya*), or *katkhudā* : master of the house, head of the family; husband, chief of a tribe, headman of a village; tithe-officer in a town. IV 8b; IV 893b; steward. I 278a; and → KALĀNTAR

In Ottoman administration, ~ designated someone who looked after the affairs of an important government official or influential person, i.e. an authorised deputy official. IV 893b

In Ottoman and Persian guilds, the head of a guild, who dealt with the material and administrative aspects of guild life. He was chosen by the guild nobles and his appointment was confirmed by the ḲĀḌĪ. IV 894a; IX 645b

In North Africa, the form *kāhiya* was current in Tunisia until recent times to designate the subordinates of the caïds, governors at the head of particular administrative divisions. In a more general way, *kāhiya* was in general use with the sense of 'assistant to a high official, president or director'. In Algeria, the *kahya* was a bey's lieutenant, but also a police superintendent and even a simple corporal in the army of AMĪR ʿAbd al-Ḳādir. The use of the term for a subordinate endowed it with the pejorative meaning of 'inferior quality'. IV 894b

khāʾ (A) : the seventh letter of the Arabic alphabet, transcribed *kh*, with the numerical value 600. It is defined as a voiceless post-velar fricative. IV 894b

khabab → HARWALA

khabal (A) : in medicine, possession, as in being possessed. XII 189b

khabar (A, pl. *akhbār, akhābir*) : a report, piece of information, especially of a historical, biographical or even anecdotal nature. IV 895a; VI 350a; X 272b; from the 8th/14th century onwards, ~ is used interchangeably with ḤADĪTH and ḤIKĀYA in the sense of 'story'. III 369a; and → ṢĀḤIB AL-KHABAR; SHIʿR

In the science of Tradition, ~ refers both to Traditions that go back to Muḥammad and to Traditions that go back to the Companions or Successors. III 23b; IV 895a

In Arabic grammar, the constituent parts of the nominal phrase, e.g. *zayd*[un] *karīm*[un], where *zayd*, the first term, is MUBTADAʾ, and *karīm*, the second one, is ~. IV 895b; predicate. VIII 384a

♦ **khabar al-wāḥid** (A) : in the science of Tradition, a Tradition going back to a single authority. Synonyms are *khabar al-āḥād* (→ ĀḤĀD, and III 25b), *khabar al-infirād* and *khabar al-khāṣṣa*. IV 896a

khabbāz (A) : a baker. V 41b; XII 756b

khabl (A) : in prosody, a type of double deviation (ZIḤĀF), whereby there are two cases per foot, combining KHABN and ṬAYY. XI 508b

khabn (A) : in prosody, a deviation in the metre because of the loss of the second consonant of a foot, e.g. the *sīn* in *mu[s]tafʿilun*. I 672a; XI 508b

khabrāʾ (A, pl. *khabārī*) : in geography, a silt flat, as is common in the Syrian desert, which comprises part of Syria, Jordan and northern Saudi Arabia and is mostly composed of highly dissected terrain. The rainfall, which usually occurs in the form of sudden cloudbursts, picks up a large amount of material from the erosion remnants and carries it inland downstream at high velocities. When such a stream reaches a gently sloping and wide open area, the ensuing loss in the velocity of the water stream causes the silts to be deposited. A ~ is the resulting silt flat. II 248b; IV 897b

In Arabia, a hollow with an impervious bottom holding water for a while after rain. I 538a; a small pond formed by rain. V 40a

khabūṭ (A) : in the terminology of horse-riding, a horse that stamps its fore-feet. II 953b

khadam (A, pl. *khuddām*) : collective noun for 'free servants'; further used, often linked in paronomasia with *ḥasham*, to denote the partisans and entourage of a great man, above all, of a military leader or ruler. IV 899a,b

khadang : a wood, probably birch, native to Čāč (now Tashkent) in Central Asia. X 348b

khadd al-ʿadhrāʾ (A) : lit. virgin's cheek; the name for the anemone in mediaeval ʿIrāḳ. IX 248b

khaḍḍār → BAḲḲĀL

khādim (A, pl. *khuddām*) : a (free) servant, domestic; eunuch. I 33a; IV 899a; IV 1087a; a female slave. I 24b

In North Africa, ~ has acquired the specialised meaning of negress, while *khdīm* is used for a domestic servant. I 24b; IV 899a

♦ **khādim al-ḥaramayn** (A) : lit. servant of the two holy places (that is, Mecca and Medina), a title used by a number of Mamlūk and Ottoman sultans. IV 899b

khaḍīr, banū (A, s. *khaḍīrī*) : a generic term in Nadjd for Arabs of dubious ancestry, i.e. not recognised as descendants of either ʿAdnān or Ḳaḥṭān, not to be taken as the name of a tribe. IV 905b

khadīra (A) : in botany, a productive palm tree which has lost its dates when they were still green. VII 923b

khwādja (P, pl. *khwādjagān*) : a title used in many different senses in Islamic lands. In earlier times it was variously used of scholars, teachers, merchants, ministers and eunuchs. In mediaeval Egypt it was a title for important Persian and other foreign merchants. In Sāmānid times, with the epithet *buzurg* 'great', it designated the head of the administration; later, ~ was a title frequently accorded to viziers, teachers, writers, rich men, and merchants. In the Ottoman empire it was used of the *ulema*, and in the plural form *khwādjegān* designated certain classes of civilian officials (→ KHWĀDJEGĀN-I DĪWĀN-I HUMĀYŪN). In modern Turkey, pronounced *hodja* (modern orthography *hoca*) it designates the professional men of religion, but is used as a form of address for teachers in general. In Egypt and the Levant (pronounced *khawāga* or *khawādja*), it was used for merchants, then more particularly for non-Muslim merchants, and then as a more or less polite form of address for non-Muslims in general. IV 907a; IV 1092b In India, ~ designates those Ismāʿīlīs who follow the Agha Khān. IV 907a; as **khōdja**, the name of an Indian caste consisting mostly of Nizārī Ismāʿīlīs and some sunnīs and Twelver shīʿīs split off from the Ismāʿīlī community; in a looser sense, *khōdja* refers to the Indian Nizārīs in general. V 25b

♦ **khwādja-i djahān** : a title of high dignitaries in various sultanates of India, notably the sultanate of Dihlī, the Bahmanids, and the sultanate of Madura. IV 907b

♦ **khwādjas**, or *khōdjas* : the designation of two lineages of spiritual and political leaders in Eastern Turkistan, where they played a decisive role from the late 10th/16th century to the last quarter of the 19th century. XII 522b

♦ **khwādjegān-i dīwān-i humāyūn** (Ott) : under the Ottomans, a title given to the heads of the imperial chancery. From the mid-11th/17th century, ~ was also given to various officials additional to the chief clerks of the dīwān, whereby a century later, the numbers of people holding this rank grew to several times more than the holders of the actual office. IV 908b

khafāra (A) : 'protection', used, often together with ḤIMĀYA, to designate certain social practices. Orginally, it primarily denoted the protection which Arab tribes extended to merchants, travellers and pilgrims crossing their territories, often in return for payment or as part of an agreement. Later, the word's usage became extended to the 'protection' in return for an obligatory payment exacted by various social groups from other groups or from richer individuals. IV 913a; and → KHUWWA

khafḍ (A), or *khifāḍ* : female excision, corresponding to *khatn* or KHITĀN, the circumcision of boys. Under Islam, ~ has never been regarded as obligatory, but has been considered as recommended. IV 913a; VIII 824b

For ~ in grammar, → DJARR

khafīf (A) : in prosody, the name of the eleventh Arabic metre. I 670a; and → ḲAʿĪD

khafiyye (T, < A) : lit. secret (police); under the Ottoman sultan ʿAbd al-Ḥamīd II, ~ came to mean a network of espionage and informing, and included the whole range of informers and spies from the highest social levels to the lowest. I 64a

khaftān (P), or *ḳaftān, ḳuftān* : an ample, full-length robe with sleeves that buttons down the front. This originally Persian garment became extremely popular throughout the Arab world. V 737b

khāk (P) : earth; an inconspicuous grave with no solid shelter attached to it, ~ is known only from literary sources and plays no role in epigraphy or funerary architecture similar to that of TURBA, of which it is a translation. X 674a

In Ṣafawid administration, ~ *āb* is the first water given to wheat, *dūn āb* the water given to wheat when it was nearly ripe, both requiring dues to be paid by the district to the MĪRĀB. V 874a

♦ khāḳ-sār (IndP) : 'humble as dust', the name of a 20th century Indian movement for national regeneration. IV 916b

khāḳān (T, < Mon *ḳaghan* or *khaghan*) : (supreme) ruler; ~ was applied by the Turks and the mediaeval Muslim geographers and historians to the heads of the various Turkish confederations, but also to other non-Muslim rulers such as the Emperor of China. IV 915a; VIII 621b; in the form *ḳaʾan* it was borne by the successors of Čingiz-Khān, the Mongol Great Khāns in Ḳaraḳorum and Peking. IV 915a

♦ khāḳānī (A) : a beggar in the time of al-Djāḥiẓ, who painted over his face in order to make it swell up; possibly a male prostitute. VII 494b

khāl (A, pl. *akhwāl*) : maternal uncle, whether a full, consanguineous or uterine one. The paternal uncle is *ʿamm* (pl. *aʿmām*). IV 916a; and → SHĀMA

khalʿ (A) : in political science, deposition, forced abdication; in modern Arabic *khalaʿa min al-ʿarsh* or *rafaʿa min al-manṣab* is used. XII 524b

In early Islam, exclusion of a tribe-member from his tribe by his kinsmen. IX 864b; X 3a; and → KHALĪʿ

In medicine, luxation. II 481b

khalaf → AL-SALAF WA ʾL-KHALAF

khalandj (A) : in botany, the high-growing poplar, greatly prized for bows. IV 1085b

khālī (A) : 'empty'; in the Ottoman empire, a term for uncultivated land. X 503b; and → ḲĀLĪ

khalīʿ (A, pl. *khulaʿāʾ*) : in early Islam, one who has been disowned by his kinsmen for fear of accepting the consequences of his crimes, acquiring soon the meaning of SHĀṬIR 'a rebel who makes a conscious decision to practise evil'. IX 864a

al-khālidāt (A) : the 'Fortunate Isles', the Canaries. VII 962a

khalīdj (A) : a canal from a river. V 533b; IX 659a; and → DHIRĀʿ

khalīfa (A, pl. *khulafāʾ, khalāʾif*) : caliph. As a title, after the first four caliphs (**al-khulafāʾ al-rāshidūn**), Abū Bakr, ʿUmar, ʿUthmān and ʿAlī, ~ passed to the Umayyads, then to the ʿAbbāsids. But it was also assumed by the Spanish Umayyad ʿAbd al-Raḥmān III and his successors as well as by shīʿī Fāṭimids, the Ḥafṣids and the Marinids. ~ was never officially transferred to the Ottoman sultans. IV 937a; ~ was also used as a title during the Sudanese Mahdist period (1881-1898). IV 952b

In political theory, ~ is the title of the leader of the Muslim community. The full title is *khalīfat rasūl Allāh* 'successor of the messenger of God'. IV 947b

In mysticism, ~ may have any of the following meanings, all carrying the idea of vicarship: the ḲUTB or perfect man, *al-insān al-kāmil*, around whom the spheres of being evolve, upon whom the Muḥammadan Reality, which is the hidden side of his own reality, irradiates; the successor of the (alleged) founder of an order or of the deceased leader of a group of mystics; a MURĪD who, after having reached a certain stage of mystical perfection, is granted permission by his spiritual master to initiate novices and to guide them on the mystical path; the deputy of the head of an order in a particular area; the pre-eminent representative and principal propagator of an order in a particular area acting independently. IV 950a; X 246a

Among the Bektāshiyya, ~ refers to a rank of spiritual achievement which could be attained only by those who had been ordained as *bābā*, head of a TEKKE. IV 951b

Among the Sanūsiyya, ~ may denote the representative of the head of the order who has been sent on a mission to a ZĀWIYA. IV 952a

Among the Nizārī Ismāʿīlīs, a plenipotentiary of the long-hidden IMĀM. I 353b

♦ khalīfat al-balad (A) : in the Khatmiyya order, the term for the local KHALĪFA (syn. *khalīfat al-nāḥiya*). X 249b

♦ al-khulafāʾ al-rāshidūn → KHALĪFA

khalīlī (A) : name of highly esteemed grapes in the region of Samarḳand. IX 110b

khālis → ṬARRĀR

khāliṣ → IBRĪZ

♦ **khāliṣa** (P, < A; pl. *khāliṣadjāt*) : in Persia, crown lands, and lesser rivers, ḲANĀTs and wells belonging to the crown. IV 972b

Under the Dihlī sultanate, ~ land was an area under direct revenue administration from which the troops could be paid in cash. II 272b

khaliyya (A) : the hive of bees. VII 906b, where variants are found

khalūḳ (A) : a perfume that is said to have left yellow stains. X 900b

khalḳ (A) : creation, the act of creating (syn. *bariyya*); Creation. IV 980a; and → IBDĀʿ

♦ khalḳdjilik (T) : democracy. VIII 219a

♦ khalḳ al-insān (A) : human anatomy. IX 394b

♦ khalḳiyyāt → ḲAWMIYYĀT

khalwa (A) : privacy, seclusion.

In mysticism, ~ means 'retirement, seclusion, retreat', and, more specifically, 'isolation in a solitary place or cell', involving spiritual exercises. IV 990a; IX 300a; X 245a; XII 522a

In law, the theory of ~ is that consummation between husband and wife is presumed to have occurred if they have been alone together in a place where it would have been possible for them to have had sexual intercourse. III 1011a

In North Africa, ~ is used for a heap of stones where women, for purposes of a mystical nature, attach rags to reeds planted between the stones and where they burn benzoin and styrax in potsherds. IV 381b; V 1201b

In Chad and the Nilotic Sudan, a Qurʾānic school. XI 124b

khalwātiyya (A) : a variety of ʿABĀʾ made in Ḥasbaya. V 741a

khamīl (A) : a silken robe with fringes, said to be part of Fāṭima's trousseau, along with a water-skin, *ḳirba*, and a cushion filled with rushes, *idhkhir*. X 900a

khamīr (A) : a leavened bread, an elided expression for *khubz khamīr*, as is the term for an unleavened bread, *faṭīr*, for *khubz faṭīr*. V 41b

♦ khamīra (A) : yeast. III 1087b

khamīs (A) : Thursday. IV 994a; IV 1009a

In military science, the five elements into which the army is divided: the centre, right wing, left wing, vanguard, and rear guard. III 182a; IV 1144b; and → KHAMSA WA-KHAMĪS

khamīṣa (A) : a black garment with edging. IX 313a

khammār → TIDJĀRA

khamr (A, < Ar) : wine. IV 994b

♦ **khamriyya** (A) : in prosody, a Bacchic or wine poem. This name does not seem to be attested in the mediaeval nomenclature of the genres. The usual expressions *al-ḳawl fī 'l-khamr, lahu maʿānī fī 'l-khamr, waṣṣāf li 'l-khamr*, indicate the existence of themes, but do not include any willingness to organise them into an independent poem. IV 998a

khamsa (A) : five; also, a piece of jewellery called 'the hand of Fatma' which is used as an amulet. I 786a; IV 1009a; XII 775b

In Persian and Turkish literature, a set of five MATHNAWĪ poems, e.g. the five epic poems of Niẓāmī of Gandja. Occasionally the term *sitta*, a set of six poems, is used for collections of the mathnawī poems of ʿAṭṭār and Sanāʾī. IV 1009b

♦ khamsa wa-khamīs (A) : a formula said against the evil eye. IV 1009a

khamsih → ʿAMĀR AL-DAM

khān (T, P) : in Turkish, a title first used by the Tʿu-chüeh apparently as a synonym of *ḳaghan*, the later KHĀḲĀN, with which its relationship is obscure; ~ was afterwards normally applied to subordinate rulers. The term was applied to various ranks throughout Islamic history, surviving into modern times in much the sense of the English 'esquire'. IV 1010b; and → SULṬĀN

In military science, a commander of ten thousand soldiers. IV 1019b

In India today, a common affix to the names of Muslims of all classes and is often regarded as a surname. IV 1010b

Of Persian origin, ~ designates both a staging-post and lodging on the main communication routes, and a warehouse, later a hostelry in the more important urban centres. IV 228a; IV 1010b; sometimes the urban ~ would be not a structure, but a group of several specialised markets, like the Khān al-Khalīlī in Cairo, a collection of shops enclosed by two large gateways. IV 1015b

♦ **khān khānān** (IndP) : a high military title in mediaeval Indo-Muslim usage, the highest title conferred on an officer of the state. IV 1019b; V 629b

♦ khānazād : under the Mughals, a noble belonging to families previously connected with imperial service. VII 322a

♦ khānedān → DEREBEY

♦ **khānḳāh** (A, < P *khānagāh*; pl. *khawāniḳ, khānḳāhāt*) : a building usually reserved for Muslim mystics belonging to a dervish order. The terms RIBĀṬ, TEKKE and ZĀWIYA refer to establishments with similar aims. The usual translation of 'monastery' does not convey the complexity of the institution. IV 433a; IV 1025a; VIII 494a; X 415b

khāna (P) : in literature, each single ḲAṢĪDA part of a TARDJĪʿ-BAND or TARḲĪB-BAND. X 235b

khanāzir → KHINZĪR

khandaḳ (A, < P) : ditch, trench, moat. Its most famous use is in the 'expedition of the ~ ', in which Muḥammad foiled a Meccan attempt to storm Medina in 5/627. IV 1020b; another expedition involving a ~ was in 327/939 in Muslim Spain before Simancas at the river of Alhándega (< *al-khandaḳ*). IX 304a

khandjal → ZALZŪM

khandjar (A) : in military science, a heavy dagger or short stabbing sword, which appears to have been of eastern Iranian or Turkish origin. XII 736b

khāniḳ (A) : choking.

♦ khāniḳ al-dhiʾb → AḲŪNĪṬUN

♦ khāniḳ al-fuhūd (A) : in botany, a variety of aconite (*Doronicum pardalianches*), also called *khāniḳ al-namir* (→ AḲŪNĪṬUN); by metonymy, ~ has been extended to mean the effects of poisoning induced by this plant. II 740b

♦ khāniḳ al-nimr → AḲŪNĪṬUN

khannāḳ (A) : in mediaeval Islam, a category of thieves, the strangler or assassin, who may have worked by suffocating his victim but may also have been a disembowler, *bāʿidj*, or one who pounded his victim's head with a stone, *rādikh*. V 769a

khansāʾ (A) : 'with a flat muzzle', in poetry, a description used for the oryx and addax antelope. V 1227b

khʷānsālār (P) : the overseer of the food at the court of the Muslim sovereigns. II 15a; VIII 954a; steward. VIII 924b

khanzuwān (A) : in zoology, the male pig, boar; the wild boar, whether under three years old, a three-year old, a four-year old or an old boar is called *ratt* (pl. *rutūt*), and *ʿufr/ʿifr* (pl. *ʿifār, aʿfār*). V8a

khār čīnī → ṬĀLIḲŪN

khār pusht → ḲUNFUDH

kharā (A) : human excrement, used as fuel in the public baths of Ṣanʿāʾ. IX 2b

kharadj (A), and *khaṣaf, naṣīf* : a term in the vocabulary of colour meaning a mixture, a combination of two colours sometimes regarded as opposites. V 699b

kharādj (A, < Gk) : tax, more specifically, land tax. IV 1030b; in mediaeval Persian usage and in the Ottoman empire, ~ also meant a tribute, taken from e.g. the peace agreements made after the victories of the Ottomans in the West. IV 1034a; IV 1055a

In Ottoman usage, ~ denoted both the land tax and the poll-tax on the state's non-Muslim subjects. IV 1053b

In the Muslim West, ~ was the tax imposed upon prostitutes, who were called *kharādjiyyāt* or *kharādjayrāt*. XII 134a; and → DĀR

For ~ in India, → MUWAẒẒAF

khăraz (A) : in Mecca, the local name for the system of man-made underground channels bringing sweet water to houses. VI 179a; and → WADAʿ

kharbāg → KHARBGA

kharbaḳ (A) : in botany, the hellebore. IX 434b; IX 872b

kharbasha (A) : to botch something, do untidy work. XI 546a

kharbga (N.Afr) : in North Africa, a type of the game of draughts, played on a square board made up of holes marked out in the ground or in rock and having 49 component squares or 'houses'. According to the number of holes along each side, the game is called either *khamūsiyya* (5 holes) or *sabūʿiyya* (7 holes). A player is known as *kharbāg* or *kharbāgī*. A different game called ~ uses a rectangle on which diagonals are traced. IV 1071b

khardal (A) : a mustard sauce, containing saffron and other dried spice s. When mixed with brown vinegar, it was used to prevent the 'transformation' of fish. XI 381b

khardj : an age group. X 7b

khardja (A) : in prosody, the last line of a stanza; as used by Ṣafī al-Dīn al-Ḥillī, all the lines with common rhyme. XI 373b

khardjlïk (T) : in the Ottoman period, a sum (usually 50 AKČE per person) collected annually by the ESHKINDJI 'auxiliary soldier', from an assistant, YAMAḲ, to join the sultan's army on an expedition. II 714b

kharfūsh → ḤARFŪSH

khargāh : a trellis tent, serving as a private chamber for the Mongol ruler. IX 45b

khārib (A, pl. *khurrāb*) : a camel thief. V 768b; IX 864b

khāridj (A) : in mathematics, a quotient. IV 725b; and → DĀKHIL

♦ khāridjī (A) : the epithet for a member of the sectarian group Khāridjites but, equally, a rebel in general, without any religious connotation. XII 598b

kharīdj (A) : in early Islam, a guessing game. V 616b

kharīf (A) : in India, the harvest collected after the end of the rains. II 909a; autumn crop. V 579b

kharīr → KHURŪR

kharīṭa (A, < Fr), or khāriṭa : in modern Arabic, a map, for which several terms were used in mediaeval Arabic, e.g. *djughrāfiyā, ṣūrat al-arḍ, rasm al-arḍ*, etc. IV 1077b

kharḳ (A, pl. *khurūḳ*) : in mineralogy, cavity, either filled with water, air, mud, *raym*, or sometimes worms, a defect or impurity in a gem. XI 263a

In the vocabulary of Ottoman irrigation, a water-channel (syn. *djadwal*). V 878b

kharkhara → KHURŪR

kharm (A) : in prosody, the absence of the initial short syllable in the first line of a poem. X 389b; XI 27b

kharrāz (A) : a leather bag maker, whose profession in pre-modern times had a low social status because working with leather was regarded as unclean. XII 463b

kharrūba (Sic) : a small-sized stellate coin introduced in Sicily by the Fāṭimids, whose weight was theoretically 0.195 gr but which in practice varied between 0.65 and 1.25 gr. IX 590a

kharṣ (A) : assessment of taxes. X 307b

khārṣīnī (A, < P *khār čīnī* 'hard substance from China), also *ḥadīd ṣīnī* : in metallurgy, a hard, highly-esteemed alloy, the constituents of which have not been established with certainty, but it is not zinc, as often assumed. According to the physcial qualities attributed to it, ~ best corresponds to hard lead, i.e. an alloy consisting of a mixture of lead, antimony and small quantities of copper, iron and tin. IV 1084a

khartāwī (T) : a high, pointed ḲAVUḲ, worn with a turban rolled around, whose end was often left free. It was worn in Turkey from the 17th century on. V 751b kharūf → SAKHLA

♦ kharūf al-baḥr (A), or *umm zubayba* : the manatee, one of the sirenian mammals or 'sea cows'. VIII 1022b

kharwār (P) : a donkey's load, a unit of weight which was widespread in the Persian lands in all periods. The Būyid ruler ʿAḍud al-Dawla fixed it at 96.35 kg, but in later times a heavier ~ was introduced, weighing 288 kg; at present a ~ of 297 kg is widespread, although others are used. VI 120b

khas → YASHM

khaṣaf → KHARADJ

khasf (A) : 'swallowing up', as e.g. in the apocalyptic prophecy figuring the Sufyānī, an opponent of the Mahdī, of what would happen to a Syrian army by the desert between Mecca and Medina. XII 755a

khashab (A) : in botany, wood. IV 1085a; the word used by the ʿUtūb for their boats. X 956a

♦ khashaba (A, pl. *khashabāt*; T *lawḥ*) : 'club', 'wooden beam'; a plate of wood through which a knotted string was threaded, the only instrument for measurement used in mediaeval Islamic navigation. The ~ was used for measuring the altitude of a star above the horizon. It was held at fixed distances from the eye using the knots placed on the string, and this enabled the height of the plate to measure different angular altitudes. The ~ originally represented the hand of the navigator held at arm's length. VII 51a; and → KHASHABIYYA

In the plural, **khashabāt** was the name given to wooden pillars which in mediaeval times were driven into the seabed at the place where the Shaṭṭ al-ʿArab empties into the Gulf, to guide sailors in danger of being drawn into a dangerous whirlpool and also on occasion to signal the approach of pirates. IV 1086a; and → KHISHĀB

♦ **khashabiyya** (A, < *khashab*, s. *khashaba* 'club') : 'men armed with clubs', an appellation for the *mawālī* of Kūfa who formed the main part of the followers of al-Mukhtār and took the field under his generals. IV 1086a

khashāsh → ḤASHARĀT

khashkhāsh (A) : in botany, the oppyx, or poppy (*Papaver somniferum*). I 243a; IX 249a; IX 615a

khashm → DJABAL

khashshāb (A) : a wood-seller. XII 758b

khaṣī (A, pl. *khiṣyān*) : castrated man, the man or animal who has undergone the ablation of the testicles; the complete eunuch, deprived of all his sexual organs, is a *madjbūb* (pl. *madjābīb*). I 33a; IV 1087a

khaṣmān (A, s. *khaṣm*, pl. *khuṣūm* or *khuṣamāʾ*) : in law, the (two) parties to a lawsuit, whereby each party is the *khaṣm* of the other. II 171a

khaṣr → AL-NAʿL AL-SHARĪF

khaṣṣ (A) : in botany, lettuce, one of the summer crops in mediaeval Egypt. V 863a

khāṣṣ (A, fem. *khāṣṣa*, pl. *khawāṣṣ*) : 'personal, private, pertaining to the state or ruler', a term used in Ottoman administration. At first used interchangeably, later, *khāṣṣa* came to be used for the services and matters concerning the ruler and his palace, while ~ was used rather for the private estates of the ruler. IV 972b; IV 1094a; and → MAMLAKA

In magic, **khāṣṣa** (pl. *khawāṣṣ*), also *khāṣṣiyya* (pl. *khāṣṣiyyāt*), in the meaning of 'sympathetic quality', is a recurring theme, indicating the unaccountable, esoteric forces in animate and inanimate Nature. It was believed that all objects were in relation to one another through sympathy and antipathy and that diseases could be caused and cured, good and ill fortune be brought about as a result of the relations of these tensions. IV 1097b

Al-khāṣṣa also denotes the elite, the notables, or the aristocracy, and is frequently mentioned in one breath with its counterpart *al-ʿāmma*, which signifies commonalty, the plebs, or the masses. I 82b; I 491a; IV 1098a; IX 232a; in Ismāʿīlī usage, the *khāṣṣ* were the elite who knew the BĀṬIN, and the *ʿāmm*, the ignorant generality. I 1099a

Among the Yazīdīs, ~ is a holy figure (also *mēr*; → MĪR). XI 314a

For ~ in numismatics, → IBRĪZ

For ~ in Indian administration, → DABĪR; KHĀṢṢA-NIWĪS

♦ khāṣṣ al-khāṣṣ (A) : 'specific difference' or 'the particular of the particular', a term in logic for what constitutes the species. It is the simple universal attributed to the species in reply to the question: what is it in its essence in relation to its genus. II 837a

♦ khāṣṣa → KHĀṢṢ

♦ khāṣṣa-niwīs (IndP) : in the Dihlī sultanate, the secretary attached to the court or on court duty. IV 759a

♦ **al-khāṣṣa wa 'l-ʿāmma** → KHĀṢṢ

♦ khāṣṣat al-shams (A) : in astronomy, the mean solar anomaly. IX 292a

♦ -khawāṣṣ-i hümāyūn (T) : in Ottoman administration, one of two types of *khāṣṣ*-TĪMĀR, viz. imperial revenues, belonging theoretically to the sultan but actually within the public treasury. The other type, *khawāṣṣ-i wuzerā'* and *umerā'*, was reserved for the members of the government and provincial governors. X 503a

♦ **khawāṣṣ al-ḳur'ān** (A) : the art of drawing prognostications from verses of the Qur'ān to which beneficial effects are attributed. IV 1133b

♦ khawāṣṣ-i wuzerā' → KHAWĀṢṢ-I HÜMĀYŪN

♦ ʿilm al-khawāṣṣ (A) : the knowledge of the natural properties of the letters, based on alchemy. III 595b

khāṣṣadār : a tribal levy; in the 1920s paid by the government of India to replace the Khyber Rifles, to ensure safety of the Khyber Pass. I 238b; and → DJAZĀ'ILČĪ

khaṣṣāf (A) : a cobbler. XII 526b

khāṣṣakiyya (A) : under the Mamlūks, the sultan's bodyguard and select retinue, considered to be the most prestigious body within the Mamlūk military aristocracy. IV 1100a

khāṣṣekī (T, < P *khāṣṣagī*, < A *khāṣṣ* 'private, special, confidential') : a term applied to persons in the personal service of Ottoman rulers, both in the palace from the 10th/16th to the 13th/19th centuries, e.g. the sultan's concubines, whose number varied between four and seven. The favourites were honoured by the title of *ḳadîn*. Those who bore him a child were called *khāṣṣekī sulṭān*; and in the military organisation, where the 14th, 49th, 66th, and 67th companies or *orta*s of the Janissary corps were called *khāṣṣekī ortalarî*. IV 1100a; XI 130b

♦ khāṣṣekī sulṭān → KHĀṢṢEKĪ

khaṭ' → KHAṬA'

khaṭa' (A) : a mistake, which is made in thought, speech or action (ant. *ṣawāb* 'what is correct'); hence in the field of knowledge, error; in that of action, omission, failure, all this, of course, unintentional. IV 1100b

In logic, ~ denotes an error (ant. *ṣawāb*). IV 1101a

In law, ~ or *khaṭ'* is an unintentional action, an act contrary to law, in which the intention of committing an illegal act is lacking, while the action itself may be deliberate (ant. *ʿamd*). IV 768b; IV 1101b

khātam (A, P *muhr*), or *khātim* : a seal, signet, signet-ring; the impression (also *khatm*) as well as the actual seal-matrix. ~ is applied not only to seals proper, engraved in incuse characters with retrograde inscriptions, but also to the very common seal-like objects with regular inscriptions of a pious or auspicious character; indeed, anything with an inscription stamped upon it may be called ~. II 306a; IV 1102b

In Morocco, at the present time, ~ denotes also any kind of ring worn on the finger. IV 1105b

♦ khātam al-waṣiyyīn (A) : a title among the Imāmīs referring to the Twelfth Imām, but also found as an epithet of ʿAlī. XI 161b

khaṭīʾa (A, pl. *khaṭāyā, khaṭīʾāt*) : in theology, a moral lapse, sin, syn. of DHANB. IV 1106b

khaṭīb (A, pl. *khuṭabāʾ*) : among the ancient Arabs, the name for the spokesman of the tribe, often mentioned along with the *shāʿir*, the poet. The distinction between the two is not absolutely definite, but essentially is that the *shāʿir* uses the poetic form while the ~ expresses himself in prose, often, however, also in SADJʿ 'rhymed prose'. IV 1109b; designation for a tribal chief. IX 115b

In early Islam, with the advent of the *khuṭba*, the address from the MINBAR in the mosque, the ~ was given a specifically religious character. IV 1110a; preacher of the Friday sermon. VIII 955a

khātim → DJADWAL; KHĀTAM

khātina (A) : a female circumciser, cutter of clitorises. Tradition attributes to the Prophet the expression *muḳaṭṭiʿat al-buẓūr* (s. BAẒR) which has a pejorative sense, but ~ and its syn. *mubaẓẓira* do not seem to have a contemptuous connotation. IV 913a

khatm → AKHTĀM; ʿIKBIR; KHĀTAM

khatma (A, pl. *khitām*), or *khitma* : the technical name for the recitation of the whole of the Qurʾān from the beginning to end. IV 1112b; X 74b

In classical Muslim administration, ~ is the statement of income and expenditure prepared and presented monthly by the DJAHBADH to the DĪWĀN. II 78b

♦ al-khatma al-djāmiʿa (A) : in classical Muslim administration, the annual statement. II 78b

khaṭṭ (A, pl. *khuṭūṭ*) : writing, script. IV 1113a; the black or white lines on the hooves of wild cattle or on the flanks and the backs of stags (syn. *raml*). IV 1128b; and → ʿIDHĀR

In divination, ~ (or *raml*) is the line which the geomancer traces on the sand when he is practising psammomancy. IV 1128b

♦ khaṭṭ al-idjāza → RIḲĀʿ

♦ khaṭṭ al-istiwāʾ → ISTIWĀʾ

♦ **khaṭṭ-i humāyūn** (Ott), and *khaṭṭ-i̊ sherīf* : in Ottoman administration, the decrees and rescripts of the Ottoman sultans, and written by them personally. From the reign of Murād III onwards, the decrease in the power of the Grand Viziers to act independently in state affairs led to a system of obtaining a ~ for almost anything except trivial matters. IV 1131a

♦ khaṭṭ-i muʿammāʾī (P, T) : an artificial script used in both Persia and Turkey, ~ is the rearrangement of a ḤADĪTH or some other important saying in a way which is difficult to read. IV 1126b

♦ khaṭṭ-i shadjarī (P, T) : 'tree-like writing', a name given by western scholars to an artificial script, applied to THULUTH and used both in Persia and Turkey for writing book titles, in which the letters bear a resemblance to the branches of a tree. IV 1126b

♦ khaṭṭ-i sherīf → KHAṬṬ-I̊ HUMĀYŪN

♦ khaṭṭ-i sünbülī (T) : 'hyacinth script', a script invented by the Turkish calligrapher ʿĀrif Ḥikmet (d. 1337/1918), in which the letters resemble a hyacinth and are also reminiscent of DĪWĀNĪ letters. IV 1126b

♦ al-khaṭṭ bi-raml (A) : in divination, geomancy. IV 1128b

khaṭṭāra (Mor, pop. *khettara* or *rhettara*) : a term used to designate the underground draining system, existing especially in Marrakesh, with wells sunk to a depth of 40 m. IV 532b

khaṭṭī (A) : 'from al-Khaṭṭ' in Baḥrayn or Hadjar, a description for a spear with a bamboo or strong reed shaft, often made by a certain expert named Samhar, whence the appellation samharī. XII 735b

khātūn (T) : a title of Soghdian origin borne by the wives and female relations of the T'u-chüeh and subsequent Turkish rulers. It was employed by the Saldjūḳs and Kh^W^ārazm-Shāhs and even by the various Čingizid dynasties. It was displaced in Central Asia in the Tīmūrid period by *begüm*, which passed into India and is still used in Pakistan as the title of a lady of rank (→ BEGAM). IV 1133a; X 419a

khaul (J) : a celebration in Java, similar to the MAWLID in the Middle East, held once a year to honour the day a saint passed away or was born. XI 537a

khāwa (A, < *ikhāwa* 'brotherliness') : a term formerly used on the Arabian peninsula for payments made in return for the right to enter alien territory and for protection while staying there. Similar payments made by pilgrim caravans on the way to the Holy Cities were called *ṣurra*. IV 1133a

khawāriḳ al-ʿādāt (A) : among the Saʿdiyya Ṣūfi order, deeds transcending the natural order, such as healing, spectacles involving body piercing, *ḍarb al-ṣilāḥ*, and, best known, the DAWSA. VIII 728b

khawāṣṣ al-ḳurʾān → KHĀṢṢA

khawātim (A, s. *khātima*) : in the science of diplomatic, the concluding protocal of documents, consisting of the ISTITHNĀʾ, the *taʾrīkh* (dating), and the *ʿalāma* (signature). II 302a

khawf → ṢALĀT AL-KHAWF

khawkha (A) : private entrance to the mosque. IX 49b

khawr (A) : on the Arabian peninsula, a term for an inlet in the Arabian shores of the Persian Gulf; a submarine valley. I 536a; XI 292b; also, a desert well with water too salty for humans to drink from. I 538b

khawtaʿ → KHIRNIḲ

khayāl (A) : figure. IV 602b; also **ṭayf al-~** or ~ *al-ṭayf*, phantasm of the beloved, a standard amatory topic of poetry. X 220a; X 400a

In Ibn al-ʿArabī's thought, an important term used as a corrective to ʿAḲL. X 318b

In Indian music, the most important song form in the classical repertoire. It arose as a reaction to the traditional rigid and austere composition *dhrupad*. Its content deals primarily with religious and amorous themes, and consists of a relatively short set piece employed as the basis for improvisation. III 453b; IV 1136a

♦ **khayāl al-ẓill** (A) : 'the shadow fantasy', popular name for the shadow-play, possibly brought over from south-east Asia or India and performed in Muslim lands from the 6th/12th to the present century. IV 602b; IV 1136b

♦ khayāla (A) : equitation, the art of horseback riding. IV 1143b

khayāshīm (A, s. *khayshūm*) : the nasal cavities. VI 130a; VIII 121a

khayl (A, pl. *khuyūl, akhyāl*) : in zoology, the equine species. The term has no singular, and like *ibil* 'camels' and *ghanam* 'sheep', is included in the category of collectives for domestic animals forming the basis of nomadic life. IV 1143a

khaylāniyyāt (A), or *banāt al-māʾ* : in zoology, the sirenian mammals or 'sea cows'. VIII 1022b

khayma (A) : a tent; ~ was originally used to denote a rudimentary shelter, circular in construction, erected on three or four stakes driven into the ground with supporting cross-members covered with branches or grass. IV 1147a

♦ khaymānegān (T) : lit. people living in tents; in Ottoman administration, any wandering subject who might come and exploit the land on a temporary basis, paying rents or tithes to the owner. VI 960a

khayr (A) : charity, gifts in money or kind from individuals or voluntary associations to needy persons. In Islam, to make such gifts is a religious act. The word has the sense of freely choosing something, i.e. virtue or goodness, a service to others beyond one's kin. It also means goods such as property or things that have material value. IV 1151a

♦ khayr wa-khidmat (A) : among the AHL-I ḤAḲḲ, an offering of cooked or prepared victuals, like sugar, bread etc., which with raw offerings of male animals (→ NADHR WA-NIYĀZ) is an indispensable feature of a DHIKR session. I 261b

♦ khayrī → WAḲF KHAYRĪ

khaysh (A, pl. *khuyūsh, akhyāsh*, n. of unity, *khaysha*) : a coarse, loose linen made with flax of poor quality and used in the manufacture of sacks, wrappings and rudimentary tents; also, a kind of fan, still used in ʿIrāḳ, where it is now called by the Indian name *pānka*. IV 1160b

khayyāṭ (A) : a tailor, dressmaker. IV 1161a

khayzurān (A) : a rod, one of the insignia of sovereignty of the Umayyad caliphs in Muslim Spain. IV 377b; bamboo. IV 682a; VIII 1022a

khazaf (A) : in art, ceramics. IV 1164b

khāzin (A, pl. *khuzzān, khazana*) : lit. he who keeps safe, stores something away; a term for a quite menial and lowly member of the ʿAbbāsid caliphal household. IV 1181b; a keeper of books or librarian. IV 1182a; VI 199a

As a term of mediaeval Islamic administration, ~ stands for certain members of the financial departments and also of the chancery; an archivist. III 304b; IV 1181b

The plural *khazana* is found in the Qurʾān and denotes the angels who guard Paradise and Hell. IV 1181b

♦ khāzindār, **khaznadār** (T) : in Mamluk usage, keeper of the treasury (var. of *khizānadār*), an office originally given to an amīr of forty but later upgraded and filled by an amīr of 100. IV 186b; in Ottoman administration, a treasurer. XII 511b

khazīne (T, < A *khazīna*) : the Ottoman state treasury. IV 1183b; the annual income of a province sent to Istanbul. IV 1184b

In popular language, ~ gradually took the form of *khazne*, and came to be used as a place for storing any kind of goods or for storing water. IV 1183b; and → KHZĀNA

khazīr (A), or *khazīra* : a gruel generally made from bran and meat cut up into small pieces and cooked in water, eaten by pre-Islamic Arabs. II 1059a

khazl (A) : in prosody, a type of double deviation (ZIḤĀF), whereby there are two cases per foot, combining IḌMĀR and ṬAYY. XI 508b

khazna (A) : in music, the uppermost internode (of a flute). XII 667a

khaznadār → KHĀZINDĀR

khazne → KHAZĪNE

khazz (A) : a term for a mixture of silk and wool, but sometimes also used for silk. III 209b; poplin. VII 17b; floss silk. XII 341a; black silk. X 609b

In zoology, beaver (syn. *ḳunduz*). II 817a

khazzān (A) : a type of sedentary merchant in mediaeval Islam, who, by means of stocking or de-stocking, plays on variations of price as influenced by space, time and the quantities of the commodities traded. IX 789a; a wholesaler. X 469a

khel → TIRA

khettara → KHAṬṬĀRA

khibāʾ (A) : a kind of tent, probably similar to the BAYT in size, but distinguished from it by the camel hair (*wabar*) or wool that was used to make the awning. Apparently, it was the usual dwelling of the cameleer nomads. It is impossible to be certain whether the distinction between ~ and *bayt* corresponds to a different geographical distribution, to a contrast between two large categories of nomads in Arabia, or simply to different levels of life within one tribe. IV 1147a

khibyāra → BAṬRAKH

khidāʿ (A) : trickery. IX 567b

khiḍāb (A) : the dyeing of certain parts of the body (and especially, in regard to men, the beard and hair) by means of henna or some similar substance. V 1b; IX 312a; IX 383b

khidhlān (A) : in theology, a term applied exclusively to God when He withdraws His grace or help from man (ant. LUṬF). I 413b; V 3b

khidīw (A, < P) : khedive, the title of the rulers of Egypt in the later 19th and early 20th centuries. In a way, ~ was a unique title among the vassals of the Ottoman sultan, which the ambitious viceroy of Egypt sought precisely in order to set himself apart and above so many other governors and viceroys of Ottoman dominions. V 4a

khidmatiyya (IndP) : in the Mughal infantry, the name given by Akbar to a caste of Hindu highway robbers, called *māwī*s, whom he recruited to guard the palace and control highway robbery. V 686b

khidmet (T) : one of seven services to be rendered by the RAʿIYYA to the TĪMĀR-holder such as the provision of hay, straw, wood, etc. II 32a; and → KHAYR WA-KHIDMET

♦ khidmet aḳčesi (T), or *maʿīshet* 'livelihood' : in the Ottoman tax system, service-money which government agents were allowed to collect for themselves as a small fee for their services. VIII 487b

khidr (A, pl. *khudūr*) : the section inside the Arab tent reserved for women. The term derives from the name of the curtain which separated this section from the rest of the tent. IV 1148a

khifāḍ → KHAFḌ

khilʿa (A, pl. *khilaʿ*) : a robe of honour, also called *tashrīf*. Throughout much of the mediaeval period, the term did not designate a single item of clothing, but rather a variety of fine garments and ensembles which were presented by rulers to subjects whom they wished to reward or to single out for distinction. These robes were normally embellished with embroidered bands with inscriptions known as ṬIRĀZ and were produced in the royal factories. I 24a; V 6a; V 737a

♦ khilʿet behā (T) : lit. the price of a KHILʿA, a sum of money given in place of the robe of honour to Janissary officers upon the accession of a sultan in the Ottoman empire. V 6b

khilāfa (A) : caliphate; the name of a politico-religious movement in British India, manifesting itself in the years after the First World War. V 7a

khilfa → RAʾS

khīmī (A, < Gk) : a kind of edible mussel, probably the *Chana Lazarus* L., the juice of which is said to get the digestion going. VIII 707a

khinnaws (A, pl. *khanānīs*) : in zoology, a piglet. V 8a

khinzīr (A, pl. *khanāzir*), or *khinzīr barrī* : in zoology, all suidae or porcines belonging to the palaearctic zone, without any distinction between the pig (~ *ahlī*) and the wild boar, *Sus scrofa* (~ *waḥshī*). In North Africa, *ḥallūf* is preferred, while the Touaregs use *aẓubara*, or *taẓubarat*. V 8a

In medicine, the plural form *khanāzir* denotes scrofulous growths on the neck. V 9b; X 433a

♦ khinzīr abū ḳarnayn (A) : in zoology, the African phacocherus (*Phacochoerus aethiopicus*) and hylocherus (*Hylochoerus meinertzhageni*). V 9b

♦ khinzīr al-arḍ (A) : in zoology, the orycterops (Orycteropus afer). V 9b

♦ khinzīr al-baḥr (A) : 'sea-pig', in zoology, the dolphin and porpoise, also called *bunbuk*. V 9b; VIII 1022b

♦ khinzīr al-māʾ → KHINZĪR AL-NAHR

♦ khinzīr al-nahr (A), or *khinzīr al-māʾ* : in zoology, the potamocherus (*Potamochoerus porcus*) of Africa. V 9b

khīrī (A) : in botany, the stock. IX 435a

khirḳa (A) : rough cloak, scapular, coarse gown, a symbol of embarking on the mystical path. V 17b; the patched robe of the ṣūfīs, synonymous with *dilḳ*. V 737a; V 741a; a veil, head scarf, worn by women in the Arab East. V 741a; in Turkey, a full, short caftan with sleeves. V 752a; and → MANDĪL

In mysticism, from the original meaning of cloak, ~ has been broadened to designate the initiation as such. V 17b; followed by a noun complement, it may serve to define various categories or degrees of initiation to the mystical path, e.g. *khirḳat al-irāda, khirḳat al-tabarruk*. V 18a

♦ khirḳat al-futuwwa (A) : the act of investiture originally conferred by the ʿAbbāsid caliphs and later by the Ayyūbid sultans, which was one of the features marking out the chivalric orders of the Islamic world before they spread into Christendom. V 18a

♦ khirḳa khiḍriyya (A) : 'investiture by al-Khiḍr', an expression describing those cases in which some contemplatives are said to have received spiritual direction directly from the powerful and mysterious person who, in the Qurʾān, shows a wisdom superior to the prophetic law. V 17b

♦ khirḳa-yi saʿādet (T) : under the Ottomans, the annual ceremony held on 15 Ramaḍān of honouring the collection of relics preserved in the treasury of the Topkapı Palace in Istanbul. II 695b; and → KHIRḲA-YI SHERĪF

♦ **khirḳa-yi sherīf** (T), or KHIRḲA-YI SAʿĀDET : one of the mantles attributed to the Prophet, preserved at the Topkapı Palace in Istanbul. II 695b; V 18a

khirniḳ (A, pl. *kharāniḳ*), or *khawtaʿ* : in zoology, the leveret, a young hare. XII 84b

khirtīt → KARKADDAN

khiṣāʾ (A) : in medicine, the ablation of the testicles, an operation consisting of incising and at the same time cauterizing the scrotum by means of a red-hot blade of iron and removing (*sall, salb* or *imtilākh*) the testicles. IV 1087a,b

khishāb (A), or *al-khashabāt* : a group of Mālik b. Ḥanẓala's descendants, which included the offspring of Mālik's sons, Rabīʿa, Rizām and Kaʿb. X 173b

khitān (A) : (male) circumcision. V 20a; VIII 824b

♦ khitānān (A) : the two circumcised parts, i.e. that of the male and the female. V 20a

khiṭaṭ (A, s. *khiṭṭa*) : in literature, a genre consisting of description of the historical topography of town quarters (→ KHIṬṬA).

khiṭba (A) : in law, 'demand in marriage', betrothal, not involving any legal obligation, but certain effects nevertheless follow from it, although the law schools differ: the right of seeing the woman, and the right of priority, in that once a woman is betrothed to a man, that woman cannot be sought in marriage by another man. V 22b; VIII 27b

khitma → KHATMA

khiṭr (A) : a flock of two hundred sheep or goats. XII 319b; and → NĪL

khiṭṭa (A, pl. KHIṬAṬ) : a piece of land marked out for building upon, a term used of the lands allotted to tribal groups and individuals in the garrison cities founded by the Arabs at the time of the conquests. V 23a; X 645a

khiwān (A, < P) : a wooden surface or table. IV 1025a; VI 808b; X 4b

khiyāna (A) : in law, embezzlement. IX 62b

khiyār (A) : in law, the option or right of withdrawal, i.e. the right for the parties involved to terminate the legal act unilaterally. V 25a

♦ khiyār al-ʿayb (A), or *khiyār al-naḳīṣa* : in law, the option in the case of a latent defect making the agreement void. V 25b

♦ khiyār al-madjlis (A) : in law, a Meccan doctrine, later taken up by al-Shāfiʿī, whereby an offer in a transaction can be withdrawn after it has been accepted, as long as the two parties have not separated. I 1111b; III 1017a

♦ khiyār al-ruʾya (A) : in law, the option of sight, rejected by the Shāfiʿīs. V 25b

♦ khiyār al-sharṭ (A) : in law, *jus paenitandi*, a clause by means of which, in certain legal acts (in particular, contracts), one of the parties, or both of them, reserve the right to annul or to confirm, within a specified time, the legal act which they have just drawn up. I 319b; V 25a; IX 359a

♦ khiyār al-taʿyīn (A) : in law, a clause allowing the one making the stipulation to make his final choice between the different objects of one and the same obligation. V 25b

khnīf → AKHNIF

khō shāb → SHERBET

khōdja → KHWĀDJA

khöömei (Mon) : a raucous, guttural voice, very rich in harmonics, sometimes approaching diphony, as used in nomadic music. X 733b

khoṭoz (T) : a popular feminine head-gear in the form of a conical KÜLĀH or hood decorated with a fine scarf or shawl and trimmed with feathers, precious stones and ribbons, worn in Ottoman Turkey. V 751b

khubz (A) : generic term for bread, whatever the cereal employed and whatever the quality, shape and method of preparation. V 41b

khudāwand (P) : God, lord, master, used in Ghaznawid times in the sense of lord or master, as a term of address to the sultan in documents and letters belonging to the Saldjūḳs and Khwarazmshāhs, and also as a form of address to government officials (civil and miltary) and patrons in general. There is no established etymology for this word and no Middle or Old Persian antecedent. V 44a

♦ **khudāwendigār** (P) : a title used for commanders and viziers during the Saldjūḳ period. As an attribute, the term was also used for mystics like Djalāl al-Dīn Rūmī. V 44b

In Ottoman usage, the term was used as the title of Murād I, and as the name of the SANDJAḲ and province of Bursa. V 44b

khūdha → BAYḌA

khudhrūf → DUWWĀMA

khūdja (Tun) : a secretary in the army in the Regency of Tunis. IX 657a

khuff (A, pl. *khifāf*) : a sort of shoe or boot made of leather, worn in early Islamic times. V 735b; XII 463a; a leather outer sock, still worn in the Arab East. V 741a

In zoology, a camel, as used in Tradition prohibiting competitions with animals. V 109a

In anatomy, a flat sole, as that of a camel or ostrich. VII 828b

khuffāsh → WAṬWĀṬ

khulʿ (A) : in law, a negotiated divorce. III 19a; IV 286a; X 151b; a divorce at the instance of the wife, who must pay compensation to the husband. VI 477b

khulaʿāʾ (A) : ‘outlaws’, in early Islam, those expelled from their tribe to a life of brigandage. X 910a

khulafāʾ → KHALĪFA

khulāṣa (A) : in literature, a technical term referring to a selection made from an extensive work. VII 528b

khuld (A, < Ar; pl. *khildān*) : in zoology, the Mole rat or Blind rat (*Spalax typhlus*). XII 287b

khulla (A) : in botany, graminaceous and herbaceous vegetation. IV 1143b

khulṭa (A) : in business, partnership, *~t shuyūʿ* denoting a joint undivided co-ownership and *~t al-djiwār* a jointly managed partnership. XI 414b khuluww (al-intifāʿ) (A) : in law, a system in Egypt and Palestine for repairs and setting up of installations, whose main features were a loan made to the WAḲF and the right of the *waḳf* at any time to repurchase the property and repay the tenant the added value. XII 368b; a form of rent that gave the tenant the right to act like a proprietor, i.e. in selling, bequeathing and alienating his rights in the property. XI 67b

In Algeria and Tunis, ~ was rather like *ḥikr*, long-term leasing of WAḲF property, and involved perpetual usufruct or even 'co-proprietorship' with the *waḳf*. XII 368b

khumāsiyy (A) : 'a boy five spans in height, said of him who is increasing in height' (Lane). VIII 822a

khumbara (P), or *ḳumbara* : bombs, used in Ottoman warfare. There is mention in the sources of bombs made of glass and of bronze: *shīshe khumbara, tundj khumbara*. I 1063a

♦ **khumbaradji** (T, < P) : in the Ottoman military, a bombardier, grenadier. I 1062a; V 52b

khums (A) : lit. one-fifth; a one-fifth share of the spoils of war, and, according to the majority of Muslim jurists, of other specified income. I 1142a; II 869b; IX 420a; XII 531a; one of five tribal departments into which Baṣra was divided under the Umayyads. I 1085b

khumūl (A) : the effacement of self, one of the components of asceticism, ZUHD. XI 560a khunyāgar (P) : pre-Islamic Persian minstrels (*gōsān* in the Parthian period, *huniyāgar* in Middle Persian) who performed as storytellers, singers and musicians as well as improvising poets. From the 5th/11th century on, the performing artist became increasingly referred to by *rāmishgar* or *muṭrib*. IX 236b

khurāfa (A) : a fabulous story; superstition, fairy tale, legend. III 369b

khurafāʾ (A), or *asmār* : in literature, a genre of Sāsānid literature translated into Arabic consisting of prose narratives without ostensible didactic pretences, often of erotic content. X 231b

khurāsānī (A) : in Ottoman Turkey, the round turban worn by viziers and other officials who were no longer in active service and therefore did not wear the *müdjewweze*, a barrel- or cylindrical-shaped cap, worn with the turban cloth from the time of Süleymān's dress edict, as the proper court and state headdress. Also, a cap of red material, worn by ʿOthmān I and the Tatars and Čaghatay Turks, called *tādj-i* ~. X 612b

khurrem (P) : cheerful, smiling; a name for both men and women. V 66a

khurūdj (A) : armed rising. XI 478a

In prosody, the letter of prolongation following the *hāʾ* as WAṢL (as in *yaḳtuluhū*). IV 412a

khurūr (A), or *kharīr, kharkhara, harīr* : the purring of a cat. IX 651b

khuṣā (A) : in medicine, testicles. Those of the fox (~ *al-thaʿlab*), cock and ram were used in the preparation of aphrodisiacs. XII 641b

khushdāsh (A) : among the Mamlūks, a brother-in-arms. VI 325b

khushdāshiyya (A) : comradeship, as existed in the Mamlūk household. VI 325b; manumission [of a Mamlūk]. VI 318b

khushkār (A) : a coarse-ground flour, used for baking bread consumed in the classical period by people of less means. V 42a

khushshāf → WAṬWĀṬ

khushūna (A) : in medicine, hoarseness of the bronchial tubes. X 868b

khusrawānī (A, < P *kisrā*) : a kind of drink or a very fine, royal silk used for clothing and used to cover the Kaʿba in the late 1st/7th century, V 185a

khuss (A) : the son of a man and of a *djinniyya*. III 454b

♦ khussān (A) : according to Ibn Durayd, the stars around the (North) Pole that never set, i.e. the circumpolar stars. VIII 101a khusūf → KUSŪF

khuṭba (A) : sermon, address by the *khaṭīb*, especially during the Friday service, on the celebration of the two festivals, in services held at particular occasions such as an eclipse or excessive drought. V 74a; a pious address, such as may be delivered by the WALĪ of the bride on the marriage occasion. VIII 27b

In the vocabulary of colour, ~ is applied to a dirty colour, a mixture of two blended colours, alongside the more general term for colour, LAWN. V 699b

khuṭṭāf → WAṬWĀṬ

khuwān (A) : a solid, low 'table', synonymous with *mā'ida*. XII 99b

khuwwa (A), also KHĀWA : in the Syrian desert, its borderlands and northern Arabia, protection-money, paid to Bedouin in order to pass through regions safely or to protect property. In North Africa, the terms KHAFĀRA or *ghafāra* are most widely used. I 483b; IX 316b; XII 305a; XII 535a

khuzām al-ḳiṭṭ (A) : 'cat's mignonette', in botany, the varieties *Astragalus Forskallii* and *Astragalus cruciatus* of the genus Milk vetch. IX 653b

khuzāmā (A) : in botany, lavender. V 80a

khuzaz (A, pl. *khizzān, akhizza*), or *ḥawshab, ḳuffa* : in zoology, the male hare, or buck. XII 84b

khzāna (Mor) : the official tent of state authorities, of conical design and made of unbleached cloth decorated with black patterns. IV 1149

kiai → KYAHI

kiak → GHIDJAK

ḳibāl → AL-NAʿL AL-SHARĪF

kibd → KABID

ḳibla (A) : the direction of Mecca (or, to be exact, of the Kaʿba or the point between the *mīzāb* 'water-spout' and the western corner of it), towards which the worshipper must direct himself for prayer. IV 318a; V 82a; V 323b; VIII 1054a

In many Muslim lands, ~ has become the name of a point of the compass, according to the direction in which Mecca lies; thus ~ (pronounced *ibla*) means in Egypt and Palestine, south, whereas in North Africa, east. V 82b; V 1169a

♦ ḳiblat al-kuttāb (A) : 'model of calligraphers', the name for Yāḳūt al-Mustaʿṣimī. XI 264a

kibrīt (A, < Akk) : in mineralogy, sulphur, brimstone. V 88b; alchemists invented many pseudonyms for sulphur, such as 'the yellow bride' (*al-ʿarūs al-ṣafrā'*), 'the red soil' (*al-turba al-ḥamrā'*), 'the colouring spirit' (*al-rūḥ al-ṣābigh*), 'the divine secret' (*al-sirr al-ilāhī*), etc. V 90a

ḳibṭ (A, < Gk) : a Copt, or native Christian of Egypt. V 90a

ḳidam (A) : in philosophy and theology, the term for eternity. V 95a; and → ḲADAM

ḳidḥ (A) : in archery, the shaft of an arrow, the forepart (towards the head) being called *ṣadr* and the rear part the *matn*. The forepart includes a socket (*ruʿz*) meant to take the head (*naṣl* or *zudjdj*). IV 799b

ḳidr (A, pl. *ḳudūr*) : in the mediaeval kitchen, a cooking pot or casserole, made of stone, earthenware, copper or lead and of various sizes. VI 808a

ḳighadj (A, < T *kiğaç* 'slope, incline') : in archery, a term denoting either an exercise in which an archer, shooting parallel with his left thigh, shoots at a ground target, or else any kind of downwards shot made from horseback. Possibly, it also means shooting rearwards by a group of cavalrymen at full gallop. IV 801b

kihāna (A) : divination, the art of knowing that which cannot be spontaneously known. V 99b

kikha (K) : an elected chief of a Kurdish village. V 472a

ḳil ḳobuz → GHIDJAK

ḳilāda (A) : in the terminology of horse-riding, a collar worn by a horse. II 954a
ḳi̊li̊d̲j̲ (T) : in Ottoman administration, a term for a TĪMĀR registered in the ID̲J̲MĀL register constituting an indivisible fiscal and military unit. X 503b ff.
ḳilid̲j̲ūrī (T ?) : a double-edged sabre, recommended for hunting the wild boar. V 9a
kilīm (T, < P *gilīm*) : a woolen rug generally long and narrow in shape. XII 136a
kilwāt → ḲĀT
ḳily (A, < Ar), or *ḳilā* : in mineralogy, potash, potassium carbonate [K_2CO_3], but also soda, sodium carbonate [NA_2CO_3]; ~ thus indicates the salt which is won from the ashes of alkaline plants, but is also confusingly used for the ashes themselves and the lye. Synonyms are *shabb al-ʿuṣfūr* and *shabb al-asākifa*. V 107a
ḳīma (A) : in law, the market value (of the victim of bloodshed). I 29b
ḳimar (A) : gambling, strictly prohibited according to Islamic law. V 108b
ḳīmī (A) : in law, non-fungible. XII 55a
kīmiyāʾ (A, < Syr) : alchemy (syn. *ṣanʿa*), abbreviated *al-kāf*, which serves also as a pseudonym. V 110a
ḳīn → YĀSAMĪN
ḳīnā (A) : a flock of one to two hundred sheep; such a flock for goats is called *g̲h̲īnā* or *ḳawṭ*. XII 319b
ḳināʿ (A, pl. *aḳniʿa*; > Sp *al-quinal*), also *miḳnaʿ(a)* : a cloth that men and women wound on the head, like the ʿIṢĀBA and the KŪFIYYA. Sometimes it also seems to mean a woman's veil of silk embroidered with gold, then again to be the same as ṬAYLASĀN. X 612b
kinana (A) : in archery, a quiver made from skins; some lexicographers note that the ~ can be made from skin or wood. IV 800a
kināya (A) : in rhetoric, a term corresponding approximately to metonomy and meaning the replacement, under certain conditions, of a word by another which has a logical connection with it (from cause to effect, from containing to contained, from physical to moral, by apposition etc.); ~ constitutes a particular type of metaphor. V 116b
In law, indirect. XI 61b
ḳinbār (A) : coconut palm fibre. VIII 811a
ḳindīl (A, < Gk) : in archery, a cylindrical quiver in which the arrows are placed with their heads downwards, as opposed to the procedure with the D̲J̲AʿBA. IV 799b; (oil) lamp. IX 282a; IX 288a; IX 665a
ḳi̊nli̊ḳ → D̲J̲ARĪMA
ḳinna (A) : in botany, galbanum, the desiccated latex of *Ferula galbaniflua*, used as a spice and medicine. VIII 1042b
ḳinnīna (A) : in chemistry, a phial, one of the many apparatuses in a lab described in the 5th/11th century. V 114b
kirāʾ (A) : in law, the leasing or hiring out of things, in particular immovable property and ships and beasts which are used for transportation. The contracting parties are the *kārī*, the lessor, and the *muktarī*, the lessee. V 126b
♦ kirāʾ muʾabbad (A) : in law, *conductio perpetua*, the lease in return for a quit-rent of ancient French law, the equivalent of emphyteusis or emphyteutic lease. In Egypt, ~ is known as *mudda ṭawīla*, in Algeria as *ʿanāʾ*, and in Morocco as *kirāʾ ʿalā ʾl-tabḳiya*. V 127a
ḳirāʾa (A, pl. *ḳirāʾāt*) : reading; in the science of the Qurʾān, recitation; a special reading of a word or of a single passage of the Qurʾān; a particular reading, or redaction, of the entire Qurʾān. V 127a; V 406a; X 73a
ḳirab (A) : a water-bag, which nomadic peoples of Arabia made out of the skins of animals. XII 659a

ḳirāḍ (A) : in law, a commercial arrangement in which an investor or group of investors entrusts capital or merchandise to an agent-manager who is to trade with it and then return it to the investor with the principal and previously agreed-upon share of the profits (syn. MUḌĀRABA, *muḳārada*). The ~ combines the advantages of a loan with those of a partnership. Its introduction in the form of the *commenda* in the Italian seaports of the late 10th and early 11th centuries AD was germinal to the expansion of mediaeval European trade. V 129b

kirad̲j̲i (T) : in the Ottoman empire, a purveyor of caravan transport. X 533b

kirān (A) : in music, a lute like the ʿŪD. X 768b

ḳirān (A) : in astrology, the conjunction; without further qualification, this refers to the mean or true conjunction of Saturn and Jupiter. V 130b; VIII 833a

In astronomy, ~ is sometimes used in place of *id̲j̲timāʿ*, the conjunction of the sun and moon. IV 259a

In the context of the pilgrimage, ~ denotes one of three methods of performing the pilgrimage, viz. when the *ʿumra* 'Little Pilgrimage' and the *ḥad̲j̲d̲j̲* 'Great Pilgrimage' are performed together. The other two methods are IFRĀD and TAMATTUʿ. III 35a; III 53b; X 865b

In the terminology of ploughmen, ~ (or *ḳaran*) refers to a rope passing over the oxen's head and attached to the beam of the tiller. VII 22b

For ~ in numismatics, → ṢĀḤIB ḲIRĀN

kirās → S̲H̲UTIK

ḳīrāṭ (A, < Gk) : a unit of weight. 24 *ḳīrāṭ*s made up a *mit̲h̲ḳāl*, which was equal to 60 barley grains. VI 118a; on the other hand, sometimes 4 barley grains made a ~. III 10b; V 11b

ḳirba → K̲H̲AMĪL

ḳird (A) : in zoology, a substantive having the general sense of monkey, but representing in fact only the members of two families, the colobids and the cercopithecids, the only primates known in ancient Arabia. V 131a, where can be found many regional synonyms

In astronomy, the asterism ζ, λ *Canis majoris* and ὺ, κ, θ, γ, λ, μ, ε *columbae* is wrongly called *al-ḳurūd* 'the Apes' in some treatises, a mistake arising from a misspelling of *al-Furūd* 'the Hermits'. V 133a

ḳirdān (A), and *ḥalam* : in zoology, a sort of moth. IV 522a; XI 9a

ḳirḳ (A) : merels, a recreational board game, which could involve stakes. V 109a

kirkira → ṢADR

ḳirmid (A, < Gr; pl. *ḳarāmid*) : in contemporary Arabic, tile; in mediaeval Syria, the fired brick of the baths. V 585b

ḳirmiz (A) : in botany, cochineal, used for dying leather and skins. V 586a

kirpi → ḲUNFUD̲H̲

ḳirṣ → ḲURṢ

ḳirs̲h̲ (A, < It *grosso*; pl. *ḳurūs̲h̲*) : in numismatics, a piastre. IX 269b; a silver coin, called *thaler* upon its first issue in Europe. IX 599a

In zoology, a shark. V 434a; fish of cartilaginous skeleton (pl. *ḳirs̲h̲iyyāt*), in other words the selachians or squalidae. VIII 1022b

ḳirṭās (A, < Gk; pl. *ḳarāṭīs*) : papyrus, papyrus roll; parchment; rag paper. IV 742a; V 173b; VIII 261b; VIII 407b; bag. V 174a

In medicine, ~ refers to a dressing, and a kind of absorbent gauze. V 174a

kīs → MUKAYYIS

kisāʾ (A) : a general word for garment; in North Africa, a piece of flannel worn by learned men around the body and head. In earlier times everyone wore it and it was called *ḥayk* (→ ḤĀʾIK). X 613a

ḳiṣāṣ (A) : in law, retaliation (syn. *ḳawad*), which is applied in cases of killing (*ḳiṣāṣ fī 'l-nafs*), and of wounding which do not prove fatal (*ḳiṣāṣ fī-mā dūn al-nafs*). I 29a; IV 770a; V 177a

♦ ḳiṣaṣ al-anbiyāʾ → ḲIṢṢA

ki<u>sh</u>k (A) : a preparation of barley and milk, used in medicine as an antidote to fever and, when the body was washed with it, as a treatment for exhaustion as it opened the pores. IX 225a

ḳi̊<u>sh</u>laḳ (T, < *ḳi̊<u>sh</u>* 'winter') : winter quarters, originally applied to the winter quarters, often in warmer, low-lying areas, of pastoral nomads in Inner Asia, and thence to those in regions like Persia and Anatolia (ant. YAYLAḲ 'summer quarters'). The Arabic equivalent is *ma<u>sh</u>tā*, and approximate Persian equivalent *sardsīr*. V 182b

In Čag<u>h</u>atay Turkish of Central Asia, the sense of ~ evolved from that of 'the <u>kh</u>ān's residence, winter quarters of the tribe' into the additional one of 'village'. V 182b

In Ottoman usage, ~ meant 'barracks' and it spread thus with the form *ḳi̊<u>sh</u>la* into the Balkan languages. This meaning has in fact passed into the Arabic colloquials of Syria and Egypt, as has also that of 'hospital, infirmary', so that in Egyptian Arabic we have both *ḳu<u>sh</u>lāḳ* 'barracks' and *ḳa<u>sh</u>la* 'hospital'. V 182b

ḳi<u>sh</u>r (A) : a decoction of coffee husks, which when drunk alleviates the state of anxiety that follows the state of euphoria induced by ḲĀT. IV 741a

ḳi<u>sh</u>riyyāt → SARAṬĀN

ḳi<u>sh</u><u>sh</u>a (A) : in zoology, the name for the female baboon and the young monkey, also called *daḥya* and *ilḳa*, according to different places and people. V 131b

ki<u>sh</u>t<u>kh</u>ʷān (P) : a cultivated field. XI 303b

ḳisma (A, T *ḳismet*) : fate, destiny; in this final sense, and especially via Turkish, *ḳismet* has become familiar in the West as a term for the fatalism popularly attributed to the oriental. V 184a

In mathematics, ~ is the term used for division of a number. III 1139b

In Ottoman usage, *ḳismet* was also a technical term of the *ḳassāmli̊ḳ*, the official department of state responsible for the division of estates between the various heirs, *resm-i ḳismet* denoting the payment which the ḲASSĀM received from the heirs of a deceased person in payment for the trusteeship of the estate. IV 735b; V 184b

ḳismet → ḲISMA

kisr → FALĪ<u>DJ</u>A

ḳiṣṣa (A, pl. *ḳiṣaṣ*) : the term which, after a long evolution, is now generally employed in Arabic for the novel, while its diminutive UḲṢŪṢA (pl. *aḳāṣīṣ*) has sometimes been adopted as the equivalent of novella, short story, before being ineptly replaced by a calque from the English 'short story', *ḳiṣṣa ḳaṣīra*. V 185b; used of every kind of story, but applied particularly, as in the title **ḳiṣaṣ al-anbiyā**ʾ, to edifying tales and stories of the prophets. III 369a; V 180a

In the science of diplomatic, ~ was the term for petition. II 306a

♦ ḳiṣṣa-<u>kh</u>ʷān (T) : the Turkish equivalent of Arabic *ḳaṣṣāṣ*, a teller of stories about the pre-Islamic prophets, the champions of Islam or the great mystic figures. III 374a; V 951a; IX 409a; and → <u>SH</u>AYYĀD

ḳissīs (A) : in the Qurʾān, with the RĀHIB and sometimes also the *aḥbār*, a religious leader of the Christians.

ḳisṭ (A) : a measure of weight used for olive oil in Egypt during the period of the Umayyad and ʿAbbāsid caliphs. Its actual weight varied. VI 119a

ḳisṭās (A, < Gk or Ar) : the Qurʾānic word for the common balance. VII 195b

kiswa (A) : the veil or covering of the Kaʿba. X 532a

ḳiṭʿa (U, < A; pl. *ḳiṭaʿ*), or *muḳaṭṭaʿa* : lit. piece, part cut off from the whole, segment; in literature, a short monothematic poem, or a piece of a longer poem. IX 470a; XII 538b

kitāb (A, pl. *kutub*) : something written, notes, list, letter; book. The beginnings of the Arabic book go back to the early Islamic period. V 207a;V 401b

In the Qur'ān, the transaction of contractual enfranchisement, consisting of the master's granting the slave his freedom in return for the payment of sums (*kitāba*) agreed between them. In law, ~ became later known as *mukātaba* or *kitāba*. The slave freed thus is called *mukātab*. I 30a

♦ **kitāb al-dj̲ilwa** (A) : 'the Book of Revelation', one of the two sacred books of the Yazīdīs, which contain the fundamentals of their religion, the other being the Maṣḥaf-räs̲h̲. V 208b

♦ kitāba → KITĀB

♦ **kitābāt** (A) : inscriptions, the first dated Arabic one going back to the year 31/652. V 210b

ḳitār, ḳitarā → ḲIT̲H̲ĀRA

ḳiṭār (A) : in classical Arabic, a train of camels drawn up one behind the other, now used with modified meaning to designate a railway train. I 572b

ḳit̲h̲āra (A), or *ḳitarā* : in music, an instrument of the lyre family. It first appears in Arabic literature on music in the 3rd/9th century to denote a Byzantine or Greek instrument of this type. It was made up of a richly-decorated rectangular sound box, two vertical struts fastened together by a yoke and (twelve) strings which were left free at their greatest width. The ~ and the *lūrā* were variants of the same instrument, but the ~ was the instrument for professionals, while the *lūrā* was a smaller instrument played by beginners and amateurs. At a later period, the term, as *ḳitār*, was used to denote a different instrument, the guitar. V 234a

ḳit̲h̲t̲h̲ā' al-ḥimār (A) : in botany, *Ecballium elaterium*. IX 872b

kitmān (A) : secret; among the Ibāḍiyya, a state of secrecy, the condition in which they were to do without an imamate, because of unfavourable circumstances. III 658a

ḳiṭmīr : the name of the dog in SŪRA xviii in the Qur'ān; among the Turks of East Turkistan, as in Indonesia, it was still customary in recent times to inscribe letters which it was desired to protect from loss, with ~ instead of 'registered'. I 691b

ḳiṭr → NUḤĀS

♦ ḳiṭrān → ḲAṬRĀN

♦ ḳiṭriyya (A) : a type of red turban, worn by the Prophet. X 610a

ḳiṭṭ → SINNAWR

♦ ḳiṭṭ-namir → WAS̲H̲AḲ

ḳiyāda (A) : the command of an army in time of war. X 838a

ḳiyāfa (A) : in divination, the science of physiognomancy (*ḳiyāfat al-bas̲h̲ar*), and the examination of traces on the ground (*ḳiyāfat al-at̲h̲ar*). V 100a; V 234b; VIII 562a

ḳiyāma (A) : in theology, the action of raising oneself, of rising, and of resurrection. V 235b

♦ yawm al-ḳiyāma (A) : the Day of Resurrection, which with the Last Hour (*al-sā'a*) and the Day of Judgement (*yawm al-dīn*) constitute one of the necessary beliefs of Islam. V 235b

ḳiyās (A) : in law, judicial reasoning by analogy, the fourth source of Islamic law. It is the method adopted by the jurisconsults to define a rule which has not been the object of an explicit formulation. III 1026a; V 238b

In grammar, ~ indicates the 'norm', meaning the instrument which enables the grammarian to 'regulate' the morphological or syntactical behaviour of a word, where this is not known through transmission or audition, on the basis of the known behaviour of another word, by means of a certain kind of analogy. It is synonymous with *miḳyās*. V 242a

In logic, ~ is the general name for syllogism. I 1327a; II 102b; IX 359b

♦ ḳiyās ḥamlī (A) : in logic, the attributive or predicative syllogism, as opposed to *ḳiyās sharṭī*, the conditional or hypothetical syllogism. IX 359b

♦ ḳiyās al-maʿnā → SHABAH

♦ ḳiyās al-shabah → SHABAH

kiyūniyā (A, < Gk) : 'columella', the interior of the Purpura and of the trumpet-snail, which used to be burned for its etching power. VIII 707a

ḳiz (T) : 'girl, unmarried female', but often used with the more restricted meanings of 'daughter, slave girl, concubine'. In mediaeval usage, one of its denotations was 'Christian woman', doubtless influenced by the meanings 'slave girl, concubine'. V 242b

♦ ḳizlar aghasi (T) : the chief black eunuch, guardian of the ḤARĪM and the third most important palace royal after the sultan and the grand vizier in the middle period of the Ottoman empire. XI 130b

kiẓāma (A, pl. *kaẓāʾim*) : in the Ḥidjāz, an underground canal used for extracting water from the depths of the earth; especially a series of wells sunk at a certain distance from one another and linked by a gallery laid out at a level that does not tap the underground water. IV 532b

kızan → EFE

ḳizil-bāsh (T) : lit. red-head; in its general sense, ~ is used loosely to denote a wide variety of extremist shīʿī sects, which flourished in Anatolia and Kurdistān from the late 7th/13th century onwards. The common characteristic was the wearing of red headgear. In its specific sense, ~ was a term of opprobrium applied by the Ottoman Turks to the supporters of the Ṣafawid house, and adopted by the latter as a mark of pride. I 262a; III 316a; IV 34b ff.; V 243a; V 437b

kneze (Serb) : lit. prince; under the Ottomans, a local strongman. IX 671a

kočak (K) : among the Yazīdīs, a visionary, diviner and miracle-worker, who is thought to communicate with the 'World of the Unseen' by means of dreams and trances. XI 315b

ḳol (T) : one of three 'arms' of a postal route; also a technical term in administrative language. I 475a; an actor's guild. IX 646b

♦ ḳol aghasi (T) : a military rank intermediate between those of YÜZBASHI and BIÑBASHI; commander of a wing. I 246a

♦ ḳolčaḳ (T) : in military science, a rigid tube-like iron vambrace for the lower arms, known also as *ḳulluḳ*, which appeared in the second half of the 13th or early 14th century and was almost certainly of Sino-Mongol origin. XII 738b

köle → KUL

ḳolu (P) : in pre-Tīmūrid Persia, a headman of a craft, appointed as such by the members. IX 645b

konfil : a cap worn by women in Algiers and Tunis. X 613a

kontosh (T) : a fur (or caftan) with straight sleeves and a collar, worn in Ottoman Turkey. V 752a

ḳopi : a salt-bed. IX 832a

köprü ḥaḳḳi (T) : a bridge-toll levied in the Ottoman empire. II 147a

kopuz, or *ḳopuz*: the lute of the Oghuz, which they brought into Asia Minor, the ancestor of the present SĀZ. It seems to have had three strings, a long neck and a soundboard of hide. IX 120a; X 733b

ḳorazin (T) : in military science, a mail-and-plate armour, made of pieces of iron plate of various shapes and sizes designed to protect different parts of the body were linked by pieces of mail of varying widths depending on the degree of flexibility required. First appearing in ʿIrāḳ or western Persia in the 14th century, it spread to become the most typical 15th to 18th-century form of Islamic armour for both men and horses. XII 737b

kōs → KROŚA

kös (T) : a large copper kettledrum, which could measure one-and-a-half metres at the top. It was taken on Ottoman military campaigns and played at official occasions. VI 1008a

ḳosh-begi (T) : the title of high officials in the Central Asian khānates in the 16th to 19th centuries, probably with the meaning 'commander of the (royal) camp, quarter-master'. V 273a; XII 419b

köshk (T, < P *kūshk*) : in architecture, a pavilion in a pleasance which could be merely a modest shelter or have several rooms. It was rarely a substantial building. The term gave rise to the English 'kiosk'. V 274a

In Ottoman naval terminology, ~ was the name given to the after-deck or poop cabin. V 274a

ḳoshma (T) : originally a general term for poetry among the Turkish peoples, later, applied to the native Turkish popular poetry, in contrast to the classical poetry taken from the Persian and based on the laws of Arabic metrics. V 274b; VIII 2b; X 736b; a folk-musical form, which varies in different parts of Anatolia and Azerbaijan, but which contains typically an instrumental introduction, followed by a vocal recitative and melody. V 275b

kotel (K) : a funeral cortège. V 476b

kōtwāl (H) : a commander of a fortress, town, etc. V 279b; IX 438b; in India, before and under the Mughals, and in British India for approximately a century more, ~ was used in the sense of 'official responsible for public order and the maintenance of public services in a town'. V 280a

k'ou-t'ou → TAO-T'ANG

köy (T) : village, in Ottoman and Crimean Tatar usage; many placenames in the Ottoman empire are compounded with ~. In the sense of an open village, ~ is opposed to *ḳaṣaba*, meaning a small town. V 281b

ḳoyun resmi (T), or *ʿādet-i aghnām* : the most important tax levied on livestock in the Ottoman empire at the rate of 1 AKČE for two sheep, collected directly for the central treasury. II 146b

ḳozaḳ (T) : in agriculture, cotton bolls. V 558b

ḳozbekči (T) : in the Ottoman empire, a body of officials performing various services on the sultan's behalf. X 564b

krośa (H, later *kōs*, P *karōh*) : lit. earshot, this term later became the standard term for describing distance. It has been differently reckoned at different periods and in different regions, and has almost everywhere a distinction between a larger and a smaller measure. VII 138b

kü : an instrumental piece evoking nature, among the Ḳazakhs and the Ḳirghiz, inspired by the circumstances of the performance and dependent on interaction with the audience. X 733b

ḳubʿ (A, pl. *aḳbāʿ*) : in Egypt, the name for the innermost cap of the turban, which could be kept on, even when sleeping, while the turban proper was taken off and put on a special turban stand (*kursī al-ʿimāma*). The ~ thus corresponds in a way to the later ṬĀḲIYYA and ʿARAḲIYYA. X 613a

ḳūba (A) : in medicine, eczema. III 291a; in music, a double-membrane drum shaped like an hour-glass. X 33a

ḳubaʿ (A) : in zoology, one of the multiple names for the ray or skate (→ RĀYA). VIII 1022b; and → DJAMAL AL-BAḤR

ḳubāṭī → KATTĀN

ḳubba (A, T *ḳubbe*) : a hide tent, in pre-Islamic Arabia. IV 1147a; a tomb surmounted by a dome. IV 352b; V 289a; the general name for the sanctuary of a saint. VI 651b

In the construction of scales and balances, the ~ was the housing for the pointer (*lisān*), often used also as a carrying handle. V 295b

In geography and astronomy, ~ , *ḳubbat al-ʿālam, ḳ. al-arḍ, ḳ. Arīn* are expressions used to denote the geographical centre of the earth at the zenith of which exists the dome of the heavens, *ḳubbat al-samāʾ* or *wasaṭ al-samāʾ*. The ~ is defined as being equidistant from the four cardinal points, and thus situated on the equator. V 297a

♦ **ḳubbat al-hawāʾ** (A) : 'the Dome of the Winds', a popular appellation for isolated monuments situated on rocky spurs. V 297b

♦ ḳubbat al-k͟haḍrāʾ (A) : term best translated as 'Dome of Heaven', ~ was the name of the palace erected at Damascus by Muʿāwiya and recurs frequently in early Islamic times for other palaces. IX 44b

♦ **ḳubbe wezīri** (T) : lit. vizier of the dome, the name given, under the Ottomans, to the members of the *dīwān-i humāyūn* who came together on several mornings each week around the grand vizier in the chambers of the Topkapı Palace called *ḳubbe altı̂* because it was crowned by a dome. This institution was abandoned under Aḥmed III. V 299b

ḳubbaʿa (A) : in architecture, the capital of a column; in Arab dress, a kind of cap or turban. X 613a

ḳūbčūr (Mon) : a tax of Mongolian origin. Originally, a tax on flocks and herds, payable by the Mongol nomads to their ruler, and later, a poll-tax to be paid by the subject population. The animal-levy continued to be paid by the Mongols until it was abolished by G͟hāzān; it is sometimes referred to as *ḳūbčūr-i mawāshī* to distinguish it from the poll-tax. IV 1050a; V 299b

kubra   → IBRĪḲ

kūdiya   → ZĀR

kūdj (A) : a headdress worn by women, along with an ʿIṢĀBA. The word is perhaps a corruption of *serag͟hūdj* or *serakūdj*, which is said to mean a Tatar cap. X 613a

kudrī   → ḲAṬĀ

ḳudsī   → ḤADĪT͟H ḲUDSĪ

kudya (A) : begging. XI 546a; and → AHL AL-KUDYA

kuffa   → ḤADJRA

ḳuffa   → K͟HUZAZ

ḳuffāz   → DASTABĀN

kūfī (A) : a term used to designate the angular form of Arabic script, as opposed to the flexible *naskhī* script. It continued to be in use for some five centuries after the advent of Islam, especially for writing Ḳurʾāns. Moreover, it was used for writing the titles of manuscripts and their sections and the BASMALAs at their beginnings until almost the end of the 7th/13th century, often as an element of decoration. IV 1121a ff.; V 217a ff. The best distinguished types of ~ styles of writing are *māʾil* (used in the Ḥidjāz in the 2nd/8th century), *mashḳ* (used in the Ḥidjāz and Syria), western (with round shapes), and eastern ~ (also called *ḳarmāṭī*, characterised by its edgy forms). Later direct developments of these ~ script styles are *mag͟hribī* (used in al-Andalus and till the present day in the MAG͟HRIB) and *sūdānī* (used in sub-Saharan West Africa). VIII 151a

kūfiyya   → KĀFIYYA

ḳufl (A) : in prosody, a line with separate rhyme; used by Ṣafī al-Dīn al-Ḥillī, however, for a single line, irrespective of whether it has common, SIMṬ, or separate rhyme. XI 373b

In archery, the catch of the stock or arrow-guide (*midjrāt*) of a cross-bow. IV 798a

kufr (A) : unbelief; the following kinds of unbelief are distinguished: *kufr al-inkār* (neither recognising nor acknowledging God); *kufr al-djuḥūd* (recognising God, but not acknowledging Him with words, that is remaining an unbeliever in spite of one's better knowledge); *kufr al-muʿānada* (recognising God and acknowledging him with words but remaining an unbeliever (obdurate) out of envy or hatred); *kufr al-nifāḳ* (outwardly acknowledging, but at heart not recognising God and thus remaining an unbeliever, that is a hypocrite). IV 408a

♦ kufriyyāt (A) : in literature, a genre of blasphemous or heretical poems. III 355b

kufu (Sw, < A *kafāʾa*) : in East Africa, a husband of equal socio-economic class. VIII 34a

kūh-i nūr (P) : the name of a diamond, now weighing 106 $^{1}/_{16}$ carats but originally much larger, possibly the diamond mentioned by Bābur in his Memoirs and now incorporated in the state crown used by Queen Elizabeth, consort of King George VI, at their coronation in 1937. V 353b

kuḥl (A pl. *akḥāl*) : in mineralogy, traditionally translated as antimony sulphide (stibnite), the Arabic word, the origin of our word alcohol, was used in mediaeval Arabic and Persian texts to indicate both an eye cosmetic, an eye ungent and a lead mineral found at Isfahan (syn. *ithmid, surma*). From the fine powder used to stain the eyelids, the word was applied to an essence obtained by distillation. The process needed for the production of alcohol itself was probably introduced into the Islamic world from Europe, where it was first discovered in the 7th/13th century. I 1089a; V 356a; also used in a much wider sense for the 'science and art of caring for the eyes', the equivalent of the ophthalmology of the West at the present day. I 785a

♦ kuḥlī → YĀḲŪT AKHAB

kuhūla (A) : the period of age following that of SHABĀB. IX 383a

ḳūḳa (P) : applied in Turkish to the plumed headdress worn by the princes of Moldavia and Wallachia and by the Aghas of the Janissaries. X 613a

ḳūḳī (A) : in numismatics, the term for the early DĪNĀR in North Africa and Spain. II 297b

kūkra (A) : in zoology, the talitrus, a small leaping crustacean, also known as the sand-flea (*Talitrus saltator*), and often used as bait in fishing. VIII 1021b

kukum → WĀḲWĀḲ

kukur → WĀḲWĀḲ

kül irkin (T) : an old Turkic title held by tribal chiefs. X 556a

ḳul (T, pl. *ḳullar*), or *köle* : an old Turkish word which came, in Islamic times, to mean 'slave boy, male slave', also in a religious sense 'slave of God'. However, the original meaning of ~ was that of 'servant, vassal, dependent', slavery in the Islamic juridical sense not existing among the ancient Turks. I 24b; V 359a

Under the Ottomans, the plural *ḳullar* became the standard designation for the Janissaries. V 359a

♦ ḳullar aghasi̊ (T) : the title given to the commander-in-chief of the sovereign's slave forces under the Ottomans and the Persian Ṣafawids alike. V 359b; VIII 770a

♦ **ḳul-oghlu** (T) : lit. son of a slave, in Ottoman usage, more specifically the son of a Janissary, admitted to the pay-roll of the corps. In the period of Turkish domination in Algeria and Tunisia, ~ (as *ḳulughlī, kulughlī* and, with dissimilation, *ḳurughlī, kurughlī* : the French *koulougli* and variants) denoted those elements of the population resulting from marriages of Turks with local women. I 371a; V 366b

ḳula (A) : a children's game mentioned in ancient poetry and described as played with two small wooden boards, one twice as long as the other and the one being hit with the other. The Prophet's uncle al-ʿAbbās is described as having played ~ as a boy, this being in an anecdote intended to show his innate decency. V 615b; and → MIḲLĀ

külāh (T) : a cap, hat, a very widespread masculine and feminine head-gear in Ottoman Turkey, of which several dozen variants existed. They could be made from felt or woollen cloth combined with other materials such as cotton, fur, small turbans, scarves and trimmings. As to their shape, the most common were caps, head-dresses in the shape of a dome, cone, cylinder broadening towards the top, tube, helmet, brimmed hats with flaps and straps. V 751b; X 613a

ḳulḳās (A) : in botany, *colocasia antiquorum*, one of the summer crops in mediaeval Egypt. V 863a

ḳulla (A) : a jar. V 386a

In architecture, a crown to a minaret which replaced the MABKHARA, so-called because of its resemblance to the upper half of the typical Egyptian water container, pear-shaped and with at least two bronze finials whose crescents are orientated towards the ḲIBLA. VI 367b

kullāb → MIHMĀZ

kulliyya (A, T *fakülte*, P *dānishkada*) : lit. completeness. In the 19th century ~ acquired the technical meaning of faculty as a unit of teaching and learning, mostly at the university level, according to branches of learning. II 423a; V 364a

külliyye (T) : in Ottoman usage, the complex of buildings with varying purposes centred round a mosque. The concept of a ~ was inherent in the earliest form of the mosque where one building housed the place of prayer and teaching as well as serving as a hostel. Later, other services were incorporated under one foundation document, and each was housed in its own building within an enclosure. V 366a

ḳulluḳ (T) : one of seven services, to be rendered by the RAʿIYYA to the TĪMĀR-holder, such as the provision of hay, straw, wood, etc. II 32a; and → ḲARĀGHUL; ḲOLČAḲ

ḳulughlī, kulughlī → ḲUL-OGHLU

ḳūmā (A), or *ḳawmā* : the name of one of the seven types of post-classical poetry. It was invented by the people of Baghdad, and it is connected with the *saḥūr*, the last part of the night when, during the month of Ramaḍān, it is still permitted to eat and drink and to take meals at that time. The ~, which is always in Arabic colloquial, has only been cultivated in ʿIrāḳ, where it has been used to express various themes, such as those of love, wine-drinking, of flower-description, etc. Technically, there are two types: the first is made up of strophes of four hemistichs, of which three (the first, second and fourth) are the same in length and rhyme with each other, while the third is longer and does not rhyme with the rest; and the second is made up of three hemistichs of the same rhyme, but of increasing length. V 372b

ḳumanya (T) : in the Ottoman military, special campaign allowances, used, with sultanic largesse, *bakhshīsh*, to mark times of celebration such as accessions to the throne or campaign victories. X 811b

ḳumāsh (A, pl. *aḳmisha*) : cloth, any woven stuff, synonymous with the classical words *bazz* and *thiyāb*. V 373b

Under the Mamlūks, ~ took on the specialised meaning of ‘dress uniform’ although this sense is not found in any dictionary. The Mamlūk ~ must have been a heavy garment, as Mamlūk soldiers threw off their armour and ~ when fleeing the battlefield. V 373b; ~ (pl. *ḳumāshāt*) was also sometimes used in Mamlūk terminology as a synonym for *kanbūsh* or ‘caparison’ of a horse. V 374b

ḳumbara → KHUMBARA

ḳumbāz (A) : an overgarment, gown, made of striped silk, worn by both sexes in the Arab East. V 741a

kümbed → TURBA

kumis (Rus, < T *ḳimiz*) : koumiss, fermented mare’s milk, the staple drink of the steppe peoples of Eurasia from the earliest time. V 375b

ḳūmis (A, < L *comes* pl. *ḳawāmis*) : a title which in al-Andalus denoted the Christian responsible to the state for the *muʿāhidūn* or Scriptuaries, or at least, for the Christian

Mozarabs. I 491a; V 376a; VIII 834a; ~ was also applied to the counts of the Christian kingdoms. V 377a

kumma (A, pl. *kumām*), or *kimma* : a little tight-fitting cap. X 613a

ḳummal (A) : a Qur'ānic term usually translated as 'lice', but commentators define it as either crickets or a sort of moth. IV 522a

kumūn (A) : in theology, 'latency', a key-notion of speculative physics, especially in the system of al-Naẓẓām, where all natural qualities, with the exception of movement, were 'bodies' inherent in other bodies: e.g. fire is not hot and luminous, but is composed of heat and luminosity; as such fire is itself an ingredient of wood where it is latent until the wood is burnt. V 384a

kunak : the swearing of brotherhood, a custom among the Čerkes tribes of the Caucasus by which a man became a member of another clan. II 23a

kunār (A) : in botany, a tree (*ziziphus spina Christi*) found in the upland districts of Kirmān. V 148a; the jujube tree. V 669b; and → DAWM

kunbūsh (A) : a large and richly decorated cloth that was hung over the hindquarters of a horse, to display the saddle. IV 1145a

kündekārī (T) : a woodwork technique consisting of tongue-and-groove panelling of polygons and stars set in a strapwork skeleton. VIII 968a

kundur → LUBĀN

ḳundus → ḲUNDUZ

ḳunduz (A), or *ḳundus* : in zoology, the beaver (syn. *khazz*). II 817a

ḳunfudh (A, pl. *ḳanāfidh*) : in zoology, the hedgehog (P *khār pusht*, T *kirpi*) and the porcupine (P *tashī*, T *büyük kirpi*). V 389b, where many bynames can be found; and → LAYLAT AL-ḲUNFUDH

♦ ḳunfudh al-baḥr (A) : in zoology, the edible sea-urchin. V 390b; VIII 1021a

♦ ḳunfudh baḥrī (A) : in zoology, the beaver. V 390b

kūniya (A), or *ḳūniyā* : the wooden setsquare (syn. *afādhān*) and level used by carpenters and land surveyors in mediaeval times. VII 198b; VII 202a

kunkur → WĀḲWĀḲ

ḳunnāḥa (A) : a polo-stick and, in general, a curved piece of wood.

In the terminology of mediaeval agriculture, ~ refers to a kind of joining pin used to connect the ploughshare (or rather the cross-beam) to the beam, SILB. VII 22b

kunnāsh (A) : a compendium. X 226a

ḳunūt (A) : 'standing', 'a prayer during the ṢALĀT'; a term in religion with various meanings, regarding the fundamental signification of which there is no unanimity among the lexicographers. V 395a; VIII 930b; and → TAṢLIYA

kunya (A) : patronymic, an onomastic element composed of *abū* 'father' or *umm* 'mother' plus a name, in principle, the eldest son's name, but the ~ can also be composed of the name of a younger son or even of a daughter. IV 179a; V 395b

ḳūpūz (T) : in music, an open chest viol with two strings, which is very popular in Turkestan. VIII 348b; as *ḳūbūz*, a rather primitive bowed instrument in Central Asia. X 769a; and → MIʿZAF

♦ ḳūpūz rūmī : in music, an instrument with five double strings, according to Ibn Ghaybī. X 769a

ḳur' (A, pl. *ḳurū'*) : a Qur'ānic word which is defined both as the inter-menstrual period and as synonymous with *ḥayḍ* 'menstrual indisposition' by the Qur'ān commentators. III 1011a; IV 253a

kura (A) : in astronomy, the sphere, globe. V 397a

♦ al-kura al-muḥarriḳa (A) : in physics, the burning-glass. V 397b

♦ laʿb al-kura (A) : the game of polo, also called *laʿb al-ṣawladjān* or *al-ḍarb bi 'l-kura*, one of the branches of horse-riding. II 955a

kūra (A, < Gk) : in geography and mediaeval administration, an administrative unit within a province, a district. V 397b; IX 308b; a pagarchy. I 330a; I 1340b; a province. VIII 636a; IX 305b

ḳurʿa (A) : the drawing of lots, whatever form this may take. V 398a

In divination, rhapsodomancy, the interpretation of verses or parts of verses or prophetic words encountered by chance on opening the Qurʾān or the *Ṣaḥīḥ* of al-Bukhārī. IV 1133b; V 100b; V 398b

kūrakān, or *küreken* : lit. son-in-law; in onomastics, a title used by Tīmūr and successors, indicating that the ruler had married a princess of the royal Čaghatayid house. X 525b

ḳurʾān (A) : the Muslim scripture, containing the revelations recited by Muḥammad and preserved in a fixed, written form. V 400a

kurāsa (A) : in the early ʿAbbāsid period, a booklet of bound papyrus sheets. V 173b

ḳurba (A) : an act performed as a means of coming closer to God. VIII 712a; and → ḲARĀBA

ḳurbān (A, < Heb) : a sacrifice, a sacrificial victim; in Muslim ritual, the killing of an animal on the 10th Dhu ʾl-Ḥidjdja. Also used once in the Qurʾān as more or less synonymous with 'gods', possibly connected to the genuinely Arabic word ~ (pl. *ḳarābīn*), from *ḳ-r-b* 'to be near', meaning the courtiers and councillors in immediate attendance on a king. V 436b

In Christian Arabic, ~ means the eucharist. V 437a

ḳūrči (T, < Mon *ḳorči* 'archer') : a military term with a variety of different meanings: he who bears arms, the sword, chief huntsman; armourer, sword-cutler, troop of cavalry, captain of the watch; leader of a patrol, commandant of a fort, gendarmerie in charge of a city's security; sentry, sentinel, inspector. V 437a

In Ṣafawid usage, ~ denoted a member of the Turcoman tribal cavalry which formed the basis of Ṣafawid military power, and in this sense was therefore synonymous with ḲÏZÏL-BĀSH. V 437b

ḳurduḥ, ḳurdūḥ → RUBĀḤ

ḳurdūs (A) : among the nomadic stockbreeders in early Islam, a term for a herd of mounts numbering 100 and above into the thousands (syn. *djaḥfal, faylaḳ*). IV 1144b

kürekdji → ČELTÜKDJI

küreken → KŪRAKĀN

kūrgā the largest of the kettledrums, greatly favoured by the Mongols; nearly the height of a man, it is probably the *ṭabl al-kabīr* mentioned by Ibn Baṭṭūṭa. X 34a

ḳūrīltāy (Mon *ḳurilta*) : an assembly of the Mongol princes summoned to discuss and deal with some important questions such as the election of a new KHĀN. IV 499b; V 498a

ḳurḳ (N.Afr, pl. *aḳrāḳ*) : cork-soled sandals, distinctly Maghribī. V 743b

kurki → POTURI

kurkī → GHIRNĪḲ

kurkum (A) : in botany, curcuma, *Curcuma longa* L. III 461a; XI 381b

kurkūr (A, < Gk, pl. *karākīr*) : a type of large ship used especially for freight, known to the pre-Islamic poets and mentioned still in mediaeval Mesopotamia. VIII 811a

ḳurmūṣ → TIMRĀD

kurr (A) : a measure of capacity used in ʿIrāḳ and Persia in the classical period for weighing great quantities of grains. Its actual weight varied. VI 119b

ḳurra (A) : in pre-Islamic times, a mixture of flour mixed with hair, obtained from spreading the flour on the head and then shaving it, which people in times of famine ate. IV 521b

ḳurrāʾ (A, s. *ḳāriʾ*) : usually rendered as 'reciters of the Qurʾān', a group of Iraqians who rose against ʿUthmān and later on against ʿAlī, after he had accepted the arbitration. A new interpretation for the term is 'villagers' (*ahl al-ḳurā*) but this remains speculative. V 499a

kurradj (A) : a hobbyhorse. V 616b

kurrāsa (A, pl. *karārīs*) : in bookmaking, a quire, usually consisting of five double sheets. V 207a ff.

ḳurṣ (A), or *ḳirṣ* : a metallic cap or crown, often studded with jewels, worn on top of a woman's headdress in the Arab East. V 741a; X 58a; a pancake of barley-flour, pure or mixed with a little wheat-flour, known in North Africa as *kesra* V 42a

ḳurṣāl (A, < It *corsale*; pl. *ḳarāṣil, ḳarāṣīl*) : a synonym for ḲURṢĀN 'corsair, pirate', but less commonly found. V 502b

kursālī (A, < It *corsale*; pl. *kursāliyya*) : a synonym for ḲURṢĀN 'corsair, pirate', but less commonly found. V 502b

ḳurṣān (A, < It *corsale*; pl. *ḳarāṣina, ḳarāṣin, ḳarāṣīn*) : corsair, pirate, whence the abstract noun *ḳarṣana* 'privateering, piracy'. Although Arabic had *liṣṣ al-baḥr* for 'sea robber', privateering, the attacking of enemy ships with the more or less explicit connivance of the authorities, had to Arabs clearly a different character from piracy, a private enterprise involving the capture and pillaging of any vessels encountered, which nevertheless they conflated in ~. V 502b

In Andalusia, ~ had a double sense of 'corsair' and 'boat'. V 502b

kursī (A, < Ar) : a seat, in a very general sense (chair, couch, throne, stool, even bench). In the daily life of mediaeval Muslims, it refers more specifically to a stool, i.e. a seat without back or arm-rests. V 509a; XII 601b; a wooden stand with a seat and a desk, the desk for the Qurʾān and the seat for the reader. VI 663b

Among the other objects designated by ~, the following are examples: a support (stool) on which the turban is deposited during the night; a chair of particular design used by women in childbirth; a stool for daily ablutions; in mediaeval Egypt, a seat for flour-sellers; an astrolabe-stand; a slab into which a pointed instrument is implanted, through the base; in Mecca, a kind of moving ladder (or staircase) near the Kaʿba; among the Persians, a kind of stove (a low 'table', under which a fire is lit. Blankets are laid on this table and then wrapped round the knees to provide warmth); the base of a column, pedestal; a plate supporting the powder compartment and percussion mechanism of the flint-lock rifle; in Spain, small pieces of silver or gold worn by women in their collars and known in Spanish as *corci*; the seat of the bishop, his see, diocese etc. V 509b; in Mughal architecture, a terrace. X 58b

In the Qurʾān, ~ tends to be accorded the sense of throne by the commentators, since its function is to bestow a particular majesty on the one who sits there. Nevertheless, ~ need not indicate a seat in the usual sense of the word. There are other interpretations of the term, some allegorical, e.g. the absolute knowledge of God, or his kingdom, some literal, e.g. footstool, a bench set before the throne. V 509a

In astronomy, ~ denotes a triangular piece of metal which is firmly attached to the body of the astrolabe. I 723a

In orthography, ~ signifies each of the characters (*alif, wāw, yāʾ*) on (or under) which the *hamza* is placed; in calligraphy, a kind of embellishment in square form. V 509b

♦ kursī al-sūra (A) : the place where the ritual reader of the Qurʾān sits cross-legged in the mosque, not to be confused with DIKKA. II 276a

ḳurṭ (A) : in botany, clover, one of the winter crops in mediaeval Egypt. V 863a

ḳurṭum (A), and *ʿuṣfur* : in botany, safflower. III 461a; bastard saffron, *Carthamus tinctorius* L. V 586a; XI 382a ḳurūʾ (A) : a woman's menstrual periods or periods of purity, as used in Q 2:228 with regard to the amount of time after a divorce the woman must wait before remarrying. X 151b ff.

ḳurug̲h̲lī, kurug̲h̲lī → ḲUL

ḳuruḳ (P) : the prohibition of men and boys from any place where the king's wives were to pass. The consequences to those who failed to get out of the way were sometimes fatal. Though probably not a new practice, it was rigorously enforced in Persia under the Ṣafawids. VI 856b

ḳurūn al-sunbul (A) : in botany, ergot. IX 872b

kurunb (A) : in botany, cabbage, one of the summer crops in mediaeval Egypt. V 863a

kurūr (A) : the reincarnation of souls, a doctrine professed by the Muʿtazilī Aḥmad b. Ḥābiṭ, which, although differing from Muʿtazilī teachings, found with him justification in the Qurʾān. Its corollary, also professed by him, was the doctrine of the TAKLĪF of animals. I 272a

kurziyya (N.Afr, < P) : a simple winding cloth of white wool or strips of wool for the head, distinctly Mag̲h̲ribī. V 743b; 613a

kūs in music, the great kettledrum (pl. *kūsāt*). X 35a

ḳuṣʿa → NĀFIḲĀʾ

kūs̲h̲a → FURN

ḳus̲h̲aḳ (T) : the ceremony of the girding, carried out during the initiation of apprentices to Turkish tanners' guilds in Anatolia, Rumelia and Bosnia. I 323b

ḳūs̲h̲d̲j̲i (T) : the profession of falconer, in Ottoman times. I 393a

kūs̲h̲k : mud-brick buildings with a central court or domed hall surrounded by living quarters and used as residences of the feudal aristocracy of Central Asia. IX 44b

ḳus̲h̲k̲h̲āne (T) : in Ottoman Turkey, a special kitchen reserved exclusively for the sultan himself, one of many separate kitchens serving a special group in the sultan's palace. VI 810b

ḳus̲h̲ḳus̲h̲ (A) : the sand-smelt, a small fish, also called *balam* and *haff*. VIII 1023a

kus̲h̲tī (P) : traditional Iranian wrestling, until the 1940s the crowning event of a ZŪRK̲H̲ĀNA session, but since overtaken by international freestyle and graeco-roman wrestling. ~ survived in a modernised form under the name of *~-yi pahlawānī* but lost its organic link with the *zūrk̲h̲āna*. XI 573a

kuskusū (A, < B) : couscous, a culinary preparation containing semolina which is the national dish of the peoples of North Africa. The equivalent term among the majority of the Bedouin tribes of Algeria and at Tlemcen is *ṭʿām* used alone, elsewhere it is *ʿays̲h̲, mʿās̲h̲*, or *noʿma*. V 527b

kust (P) : quadrant. IX 682b

kustī → S̲H̲UTIK

kusūf (A), or *k̲h̲usūf* : in astronomy, the eclipse of the sun or of the moon. *Al-kusūf* is used alike for the eclipse of the moon (*kusūf al-ḳamar*) and for that of the sun (*kusūf al-s̲h̲ams*), but they are often distinguished as *al-k̲h̲usūf*, eclipse of the moon, and *al-kusūf*, of the sun. V 535b; VIII 931b

♦ ṣalāt al-kusūf (A) : a communal prayer held in the mosque in the event of an eclipse (of the sun or the moon). VIII 931b

ḳut (T) : glory, fortune. XI 359b

ḳuṭʿa → FAS̲H̲T

ḳuṭāmī (A) : in zoology, the falcon. V 540b

ḳuṭb (A, pl. *aḳṭab*) : a pole, a pivot around which something revolves, e.g. the pivot for mill stones. V 542b

In astronomy, ~ designates the axis of the celestial east-west movement and, more specifically, its two poles. In modern terminology, the terrestrial poles are also called

~ (with adjective *ḳuṭbī* 'polar'). Apart from this, in the construction of the astrolabe ~ (also *miḥwar, watad*) signifies the central pivot, or axis, which keeps together its different discs, the spider, and the rule. I 723a; V 542b

In mysticism, ~ denotes either the most perfect human being, *al-insān al-kāmil,* who heads the saintly hierarchy, or else the universal rational principle, *al-ḥaḳīḳa al-muḥammadiyya*, through which divine knowledge is transmitted to all prophets and saints, and which manifests itself in *al-insān al-kāmil*. Each of the various ranks in the saintly hierarchy has also been conceived of as being headed by a ~ . IV 950a; V 543b

♦ ḳuṭb suhayl (A) : in astronomy, the south pole, a term used by Islamic navigators. V 543a

♦ ḳuṭbiyya (A, P) : in mysticism, the office of ḲUṬB. X 328b

ḳuththā' (A) : (a kind of) cucumber, one of the Prophet's preferred vegetables, along with some other gourds: *dubbā'* 'a kind of marrow' and *ḳar'* 'marrow'. II 1058a,b

ḳuṭn (A), or *ḳuṭun* : cotton, cultivated everywhere and a flourishing industry from the period of the Arab conquests on. V 554b; V 863a

ḳuṭr (A) : in mathematics, the diameter of a circle or of any section of a cone and the diameter of a cone; the diagonal of a parallelogram or of any quadrilateral; the hypotenuse of the so-called umbra triangle. V 566b

♦ ḳuṭr al-ẓill (A) : in astronomy, the cosecant function. XI 503a

ḳuṭrub (A, < Syr) : the werewolf. V 566b; the male of the SI'LĀT, considered thus by those sources who do not consider the *si'lāt* to be the female of the GHŪL, a fabulous being. II 1078b

kuttāb (A, pl. *katātīb*) : a type of beginners' or primary school; an appellation for the Islamic traditional school, also known as *maktab*. V 567b; VI 196b; and → KĀTIB

kuṭṭaka (H) : 'dispersion'; in mathematics, a method of continued fractions, referred to as early as the 5th century by Āryabhaṭa. I 133a

kutubī → FAYDJ

ḳu'ūd (A) : sitting; the sitting posture in prayer which is the penultimate component of a *rak'a*. V 572a

In early Islamic history, the designation of the political attitude of a faction of the Khāridjīs, the *ḳa'ada*, which is sometimes taken to refer to 'self-declared non-rebels' although the generally accepted notion is 'quietism'. V 572a

ḳuwīthra (A, dim. of ḲITHĀRA), or *ḳuwitra* : in music, a lute with a smaller and shallower sound-chest than the 'ūd, its head being fixed obliquely rather than at a right angle. It is common to the whole of the Maghrib and has four double strings. X 769b

ḳuwwa (A) : 'strength, power'; also, a thread which is part of a rope. In its sense of power, ~ plays a role in the discipline of Qur'ānic studies, theology, philosophy, medicine, and human psychology. V 576a; and → LĀ-ḲUWWA

kūz (A, pl. *akwāz, kīzān*) : a jug or pitcher, fashioned with a squat globular body, low foot short neck and a curved handle. V 989b; VIII 892a; a long and narrow vessel, often fitted with a handle, which, among its other functions, was used for the preparation or storage of FUḲḲĀ', a sparkling drink. VI 721a; in the plural *kīzān*, translated by Goitein as 'bowls'. VI 721b

kuzbara : in botany, coriander. IX 615a

ḳwādsiyya → ḲĀDŪS

kyahi (J), or *kiai, kyai* : in Indonesia, a religious teacher, respected old man. VIII 294a; VIII 296b; originator of PESANTREN. XI 536b

L

lā-ḳuwwa (A) : in philosophy, inability or weakness, a translation of Aristotle's ἀδυναμία; ~ predisposes to undergo something easily and quickly, the opposite of ḲUWWA. V 577b

laashin (Somali, pl. *laashinno*) : in the southern, mainly agriculturalist clans of Somalia, specific reciters of poetry who often recite in an extemporised manner. IX 725b

labab → ḲARBŪṢ

labābīdī → LUBŪD

labad → ṢŪF

laban (A) : milk. In certain dialects, the distinction has arisen between ḤALĪB, milk, and ~, fully or partially curdled milk. II 1057b; VI 722a; buttermilk. XII 318b; and → YOG͟HURT

♦ al-labaniyya (A) : a mediaeval dish containing meat and leeks or onion, cooked in milk together with a little powdered rice. VIII 653a

labān → ṢADR

labbād → LUBŪD

labbāda → LIBDA

labda → LIBD

labin (A), or *libn* : unfired brick whose use in building dates back to the earliest antiquity. The ~ generally has a geometric, fairly regular shape, that of a parallel-sided rectangle. The wooden mould into which the dampened clay is put is called *milban*. V 584b

lad̲j̲ʾa (A) : in botany, ~ *k̲h̲aḍrāʾ* is the green turtle or true chelon (*Chelonia mydas*) and ~ *sahfiyya* is the imbricated chelon (*Chelonia imbricata*). IX 811a

lād̲j̲ward : lapis lazuli. VIII 269a

laffa (A) : a man's turban cloth in the Arab East. V 741a

laffāf → YATĪMA

lafīf (A) : in law, an 'unsifted' witness, neither a virtuous man nor a professional, more a 'man in the street'. I 428a; and → S̲H̲AHĀDAT AL-LAFĪF

lafūt (A) : in zoology, a term used for two different types of fish: the lophot (*Lophotes*) and the unicorn fish (*Lophotes cepedianus*). VIII 1021a; VIII 1021b

lafẓ (A) : lit. to spit out; in grammar, the actual expression of a sound or series of sounds, hence 'articulation', and, more broadly, the resulting 'linguistic form'. It has always been distinct from ṢAWT 'individual sound'. In morphological contexts, will typically contrast with MAʿNĀ 'meaning' while at the syntactical level, the formal realisation (*lafẓī*) is contrasted with the implied (*muḳaddar*). XII 545b

In theology, a term introduced by Ḥusayn b. ʿAlī al-Karābīsī in the 3rd century to replace *ḳirāʾa*, the recitation of the Qurʾān which occurs in time (as opposed to *kalām Allāh*, which is eternal), which gave it a broader meaning as any quoting from the Qurʾān including beyond formal recitation. XII 546b

♦ lafẓī → LAFẒ

lag̲h̲ïm (T) : explosive mines of various types and sizes, an instrument of war used in the Ottoman empire. I 1063a

♦ lag̲h̲ïmd̲j̲ïlar (T) : in Ottoman military, the sappers who, with the aid of the large labour forces set at their disposal, prepared the trenches, earthworks, gun-emplacements and subterranean mines indispensable in siege warfare. I 1062a

lag̲h̲w → ṢILA

♦ lag̲h̲w al-yamīn → YAMĪN

lāgmī : 'palm-wine', a drink in Arabia, extracted from the sap rising in the palm trunk.

This very sweet and refreshing liquid ferments quite quickly, becoming charged with alcohol which renders it intoxicating. VII 923b

lahāt (A) : in anatomy, the uvula. VI 129b

laḥḥām → DJAZZĀR

lāḥib (A) : 'clearly marked'. XI 155a

lahīb : in medicine, congestion (there is question as to its exact meaning). IX 9b

lāḥiḳ → ḤUDJDJA; MUḌĀRIʿ

laḥn (A) : a manner of speaking; in grammar, dialectical or regional variation, which was judged contrary to the grammarians' instinctive conception of the norm. Thus, ~ takes on the sense of 'deed of committing faults of language', then of 'perverted use (solecism, barbarism, malapropism, etc.)', and becomes a synonym of KHAṬAʾ. V 606b; V 804a

In music, in its early sense, a musical mode, comparable to *naghma* (pl. *anghām*) and MAḲĀM; more generally and more commonly, melody (pl. *alḥān, luḥūn*). XII 546b

In rhetoric, ~ 'letter riddle' is seen as one of the different types of *taʿmiya* 'mystification'. VIII 427a

♦ **laḥn al-ʿāmma** (A) : lit. errors of language made by the common people; in lexicography, a branch designed to correct deviations by reference to the contemporary linguistic norm, as determined by the purists. The treatises which could be classed under this heading, correspond, broadly speaking, to our 'do not say . . . but say . . .', the incorrect form generally being introduced by 'you say' or 'they say', and the correct form by *wa 'l-ṣawāb* 'whereas the norm is . . .'. V 605b; XII 388a

lāhūt (A) : divinity, the antithesis of *nāsūt*, humanity. V 611b

In the mystical thought of al-Ḥallādj, ~ means the incommunicable world of the divine essence, the world of absolute divine transcendence, and therefore absolutely superior to all other 'spheres of existence'. I 351a; V 613a

lahw (A) : amusement. V 615a

laʿib (A) : play(ing), which came in Islam to be considered the exclusive prerogative of children, bracketed at times with women also in this respect. V 615a

lāʾiḥa → ḲĀNŪN

lāʾiṭ → LŪṬĪ

laḳab (A, pl. *alḳab*) : in onomastics, nickname or sobriquet, and at a later date under Islam and with more specific use, honorific title. It is usually placed after the NISBA. IV 180a; IV 293b; V 618b; VIII 56a

laḳāniḳ (A, < L), or *naḳāniḳ* : mutton sausages, containing little semolina and sold by *naḳāniḳiyyūn*. II 1063b

lakhm → KALB AL-BAḤR

lakhnāʾ → BAẒRĀʾ

laḳīṭ (A) : in law, a foundling; according to Mālikī doctrine, a human child whose parentage and whose status (free or slave) is unknown. I 26a; V 639a; VIII 826b

laksamana → BENDAHARA

laḳṭ (A) : in medicine, the (surgical) removal of a thing. X 456a

laḳwa (A) : facial paralysis. VIII 111b; in zoology, the female eagle (var. *liḳwa*). X 783b

laʿl (A) : in mineralogy, a kind of ruby, according to al-Bīrūnī. V 968a

lāla → SHAḲĪḲAT AL-NUʿMĀN

lālā (P), or *lala* : a preceptor or tutor, especially of royal princes, becoming a more common usage after the advent of the Ṣafawids and passing to the Ottomans. IV 37a; VIII 770b; IX 211a; XII 547a; in the Ottoman empire, a synonym for *wezīr* (→ WAZĪR). XI 194b lālaka (A, pl. *lawālik*) : a nailed boot used by common people in pre-modern times. XII 463a

lalamiko (Sw) : in Swahili literature, an elegy. VI 612b

lāle devri (T) : 'the Tulip Period', the name given to one of the most colourful periods of the Ottoman empire, corresponding to the second half of the reign of Aḥmed III (1703-30) and more precisely to the thirteen years of the vizierate of Nevs͟hehirli Ibrāhīm Pas͟ha. V 641a

lālla (Mor) : the name for women saints of Berber origin in Morocco. V 1201a

lām (A) : the twenty-third letter of the Arabic alphabet, transcribed *l*, with the numerical value 30. It is defined as fricative, lateral and voiced. V 644b

lamṭ (A) : in mediaeval Islam, the oryx of the Sahara. The term is now obsolete. V 651b; antelope. XI 20a; XII 844a

laʿn → S͟HATM

lanḍaī → MIṢRĀʿ

land͟j (A, < Eng 'launch'), or *lans͟h* : in Kuwayt, a motor launch provided with one or two sails, and employed, though not a great deal, along the Bāṭina, whereas in the Red Sea, the term is found from ʿAḳaba to as far as G͟hardaḳa and Port Sudan. VII 53b

langgar (J) : in Indonesia, a small mosque serving for the daily cult and religious instruction alone. VI 700a; the little prayer-cabin near the house. VII 103b

lans͟h → LAND͟J

lārī → LARIN

larin (P *lārī*) : the larin, a silver coin current in the Persian Gulf and Indian Ocean in the 16th and 17th centuries. It takes its name from the town of Lār, the capital of Lāristān at which it was first struck. It weighed about 74 grains, and its shape was a thin silver rod about 4 inches long, doubled back and then stamped on either side. II 120b; V 683b

lāsa (A) : a woman's head scarf of white silk or cotton net into which flat metal strips have been decoratively hammered, worn in Syria and Palestine. V 741b

las͟hkar (P) : the term normally used by the Indian Muslim rulers for army. V 685a

♦ **las͟hkar-i bāzār** (P) : a complex of military encampments, settlements and royal palaces in southern Afg͟hānistān, which apparently flourished in the 5th/11th and 6th/12th centuries. V 690b

lās͟hōn (< Heb 'tongue, language') : a form of slang used by Jewish traders and artisans. Occasionally it was called *īs͟hūrūni*. This slang was based on the utilisation of a basically Hebrew vocabulary in accordance with completely Arabic morphology and syntax. IV 301b

lassi → AYRAN

lāṭī → LŪṬĪ

lāṭiʾa (A) : a small, tight-fitting cap, but probably not the proper name for it. X 613a

laṭīfa (A, pl. *laṭāʾif*) : in mysticism, the 'subtle organ' (syn. *ṭūr*, pl. *aṭwār*), a theory of levels developed from the time of Nad͟jm al-Dīn Kubrā (d. 617/1220-1) and the mystics of his school. V 300b; XII 753b

laṭīm (A) : 'knocked out of the enclosure by a blow', the name for the ninth horse in a race, according to the order of finishing. II 953a; and → YATĪM

♦ laṭīma (A) : silk. IX 865a

lāṭiniyya (A) : Romance [language]. V 318b

lāṭis (A), or *lūṭis* : in zoology, the Nile perch (*Lates nilotica*). VIII 1021a

lawāḥiḳ → ANDARGĀH

lawāṭa-kār → LŪṬĪ

lawḥ (A, pl. *alwāḥ*) : board, plank; tablet, table; school-child's slate; blackboard. V 698a; and → K͟HAS͟HABA

In the Qur'ān and the pseudoepigraphical literature, ~ has the specific meaning of the tablet as the record of the decisions of the divine will, which is kept in heaven. It can also mean the tablet as the original copy of the Qur'ān. V 698a

Among the Bahā'īs, ~ is the name for a letter sent by Bahā' Allāh. I 911b

lawn (A) : the general term used to express the concept of colour. Besides this precise sense, it also denotes 'shade', 'aspect', 'type', 'dish (of food)', etc. V 698b, where a host of terms for colours, too numerous to list in this Glossary, are given

lawṭa (A) : in music, an instrument of the lute type, with four double strings and is very popular in Turkey. It appears to have been borrowed, together with its name, from Italy and is certainly of comparatively modern adoption since it is not mentioned by Ewliyā Čelebi. X 769b

lawth (A) : in law, the notion of serious presumption. IV 690a

layālī → LAYL

layḳ (A) : ink well. VIII 52a

layl (A, pl. *layālin*) : nighttime, night (ant. NAHĀR). V 707b; and → ṢĀḤIB AL-LAYL

♦ laylat al-barā'a (A) : 'the night of quittancy', i.e. forgiveness of sins, a religious festival, marking the night of mid-Sha'bān. I 1027b; IX 154a

♦ laylat al-dukhla → DUKHLA

♦ laylat al-ḥanna (A), or *ḥenna gedjesi* : the principal ceremony of the adornment of the bride before a wedding, when in the presence of her female relations and friends, the bride's eyelids were blackened with kohl and the hands and feet coloured with henna. In earlier times, yellow patches, nuḳaṭ al-'arūs, used to be put on the cheeks. X 904a

♦ laylat al-harīr (A) : 'the night of clamour', the name of a violent conflict, on 10 Ṣafar 37/28 July 657, between 'Alī and Mu'āwiya after a week of combat. I 383b

♦ laylat al-kashfa (A) : in early literature on the Shabak and Ṣarlīs, term referring to the three annual nightly celebrations, in which both sexes take part. IX 153b

♦ laylat al-ḳunfudh (A), or *laylat al-anḳad* : 'the hedgehog's night', a night racked by insomnia. V 390a

♦ laylat al-maḥyā (A) : a night made alive by devotional activity, MAḤYĀ, which came to denote: 1) the night of 27 Radjab, when religious gatherings were held at the shrine of 'Alī, in early 8th/14th-century al-Nadjaf, 2) the night of 27 Ramaḍān, when the Ḥarīriyya order commemorated the death of the order's founder, and 3) the night of mid-Sha'bān in several parts of the Islamic world. VI 88a

♦ layālī (A) : in music, a solo melodic modal improvisation entrusted to the human voice without written music. VI 97a

♦ al-layālī al-bulḳ (A), or *al-ayyām al-bulḳ* : the forty 'mottled' days, which, in two series of twenty, immediately precede and follow AL-LAYĀLĪ AL-SŪD and during which the cold is less severe. V 708a

♦ al-layālī al-sūd (A) : lit. the black nights, e.g. the very cold period which begins in December and ends forty days later. V 708a

lāzim (A) : in law, 'binding'. I 319b; VIII 836a

♦ lāzima (A, pl. *lawāzim*) : in music, a short melodic formula. XII 667b

lazma (A) : a curb-bit, part of the horse's bridle. IV 1145a

lebaran (Ind) : 'end, close'; the name generally used in Indonesia for the 'ĪD AL-FIṬR, the 'minor festival'. The expression *lebaran haji* is sometimes used for the 'ĪD AL-AḌḤĀ, the 'major festival'. V 714b

leff (A) : a term used in the Berber-speaking regions of central and southern Morocco (a different term is used in a similar way in Berberophone regions of northern Morocco, and *ṣoff* appears to be its equivalent in Kabylia) to denote a kind of political alliance or party, which were invoked, like military alliances, when violent conflict occurred: members of the same ~ were expected to give support to each other, when any one of them became involved in conflict with opponents from the other ~. V 715a

leh (Ott, < Polish) : the ancient Ottoman Turkish term for the Poles and Poland. From the 12th/18th century, the Turks also called the country Lehistān. V 719a

lewend (T, < ? It *levantino*) : in the Ottoman period, two kinds of daily-wage irregular militia, one sea-going (*deñiz*), the other land-based (*ḳarā*), both existing from early times. The land-based ~ were further divided into *ḳapîlî lewend, ḳapîsîz lewend*, and *mīrī lewend*. V 728a

liʿān (A) : 'cursing', 'oath of imprecation'; in law, the oath which gives a husband the possibility of accusing his wife of adultery without legal proof and without his becoming liable to the punishment prescribed for this, and the possibility also of denying the paternity of a child borne by the wife. It frees the husband and wife from the legal punishment for respectively ḲADHF and incontinence. I 1150b; IV 689a; V 730a

liban → YOGHURT

libās (A, pl. *lubus, albisa*) : clothing, apparel. V 732a; in Egypt, ~ acquired the general meaning of 'drawers' for men. IX 677b

For glossaries of terms for articles of clothing, V 740a, V 745b

libd (A, pl. **lubūd**), or *labad* : felt; a pad of felt (pl. *albād*), used. e.g. to cushion the chamfered ends of the vertical posts of a tent. IV 1147b; moquette saddle, or a piece of felt put under the saddle. V 798a

♦ labda : in Morocco, a small felt carpet, favoured by the middle classes for performing the *sudjūd*. ~s are especially used by FAḲĪHS and have almost beome one of their distinctive marks. VIII 741a

♦ libda (A), or *labbāda* : a brown or white felt cap worn by men in the Arab East, either under the ṬARBŪSH or alone. V 741b; X 613a

libn → LABIN

libna (A) : in astronomy, a large mural quadrant. VIII 574a

lidjādja (A) : obstinacy, of obstinate character. X 828a

lidjām (A, < P *likām*) : the harness of the horse, which includes the reins, *ʿinān*, the cheek straps, *idhār*, and the browband, *ʿiṣāb*. II 954a; IV 1144b; also, the curb bit, used to rein horses suddenly or make swift turns. II 953a

līf (A) : fiber. X 900a

lift (A) : in botany, the turnip, one of the summer crops in mediaeval Egypt. V 863a

liḥya-yi sherīf (T) : the hairs of the Prophet. According to al-Bukhārī, Muḥammad permitted people to get his hair when he was being shaved; the hairs of his head and beard, thus obtained, were preserved and later circulated in all Islamic countries. They are today kept in a silver box at the Topkapı Palace. V 761a

līḳ (A) : the black powder of collyrium. VIII 52a

liḳwa → LAḲWA

liman reʾīsi (T) : 'captain of the port', an admiral in the Ottoman navy. He was also commander of the midshipmen (*mandedji*). VIII 565b

līmanda (A) : in zoology, the dab, the nomenclature of which was drawn directly from Greco-Roman (*Limanda*). VIII 1021a

līmī (A) : in zoology, the umbra limi, whose Arabic term is found again in the Latinised nomenclature to specify a sub-species limited to a particular region (*Umbra limi*). VIII 1021b

limma (A) : in zoology, the limma ray, whose Arabic term is found again in the Latinised nomenclature to specify a sub-species limited to a particular region (*Raia lymma*). VIII 1021b; and → ṢUDGH

lipḳa (< Polish), or *lubḳa, lupḳa* : the name given to the Tatars who since the 14th century inhabited Lithuania. V 765b

lisān (A) : tongue; language. V 805a; an oral message. VIII 532a; and → LUGHA
In the language of scales and balances, ~ is the pointer (on a scale). V 295b
♦ lisān al-ghayb (A, P) : 'the tongue of the unseen', the title given to Ḥāfiẓ. X 320a
♦ ʿilm al-lisān (A), or *lisāniyyāt* : linguistics. V 806b

liṣṣ (A, P *duzd*, Ott *khayrsïz*, T *hırsız*; pl. *luṣūṣ*) : thief, robber (syn. *sāriḳ*). V 767b; IX 866a
♦ liṣṣ al-baḥr → ḲURṢĀN

litha (A) : in anatomy, the gums. VI 129b; X 423b
♦ lithawī (A) : in linguistics, gingival or alveolar, although the early grammarians seemed to use ~ to describe an interdental. X 423b

lithām (A, Touareg *tegulmust, shāsh*) : the mouth-veil, a piece of material with which the Bedouin concealed the lower part of the face, the mouth and sometimes also part of the nose. It served the practical purpose of protecting the organs of respiration from heat and cold as well as against the penetration of dust. It also made the face unrecognisable, and thus formed a protection against the avenger of blood. The ~ has no considerable importance for Islam from the purely religious point of view. V 744a; V 769a

liwā → LIWĀʾ

liwāʾ (A, T *liwā*) : a banner, flag, standard. I 349a; an army brigade, both under the Ottomans and in the Iraqi army, *amīr al-liwāʾ* being a brigadier (as in Egypt until 1939). V 776a; VIII 370b
Under the Ottomans, *liwā* indicated a province, several of which were at a certain moment joined into an EYĀLET, later *wilāyet*. Synonymous with *sandjaḳ*, ~ was mainly used in official documents. Accordingly, *mīr liwā* (< A *amīr al-liwāʾ*) stood for *sandjaḳ begi*, the governor and military commander of a ~. Of all the states issued from the Ottoman empire, only Iraq kept the term ~ (up till 1974) to indicate a province. V 776a
♦ liwāʾ-i sherīf → SANDJAḲ-I SHERĪF

līwān (A) : at times the spoken Arabic form of ĪWĀN, generally furnished with carpets and divans. II 114b; in India, ~ is the usual name for the western end of a mosque, directed towards Mecca. VI 689b

liwāṭ (A) : sodomy. V 776b

lol (Kash) : a love lyric in Kashmiri poetry. XII 333a

lōrī → LŪLĪ, NŪRĪ

luʾama (A) : in mediaeval agriculture, a rather imprecise term which would designate on the one hand all the parts of the tiller, whether of wood or iron, and on the other hand only the ploughshare, which is not very likely, or, more probably, like *silb*, the beam tied to the cross-beam at a point called *djidār*. VII 22b

lubad (A), and *al-libad* : the name for all of ʿUnayd b. Muḳāʿis's children but Minḳar. X 173a

lubān (A), and *kundur* : in botany, frankincense, a gum resin from various Boswellia varieties, indigenous in South Arabia and Somalia. V 786a; VIII 1042b
♦ lubān djāwī (A) : in botany, the Javanese (in fact, Sumatran) frankincense, i.e. benzoin, obtained from various kinds of styrax-trees whose fumes are said to remove a cold in the head. V 786b

lubb al-bardī (A) : the pulp of the papyrus. V 173b

lūbiya (A) : in botany, kidney beans, one of the summer crops in mediaeval Egypt. V 863a

lubūd (A, s. LIBD, *labad*) : felt, one of the less expensive products among the woollen articles manufactured in the mediaeval world. The felt-maker was called *labbād, lubūdī* and *labābīdī*. V 798a
♦ lubūdī → LUBŪD

lūd (Tun) : a boat devised by the islanders of Ḳarḳana, an archipelago lying off the eastern coast of Tunisia, where the shallows extend very far out to sea. The ~ is broad, without a keel and therefore well adapted to the contours of the sea-bed. IV 651b

luffāḥ → SIRĀDJ AL-ḲUṬRUB; YABRŪḤ

lugha (A) : speech, language, in current usage; in the Qur'ān, *lisān* is used to express the concept of 'language', ~ being completely absent. IV 122a; V 803a

♦ ('ilm al-)lugha (A) : lexicology or, more exactly, the science of the datum of the language. IV 524a; V 806a; lexicography. VIII 614a

♦ fiḳh al-lugha (A) : a synonym of *'ilm al-lugha*, but it seems likely that this was a more specialised branch of the same discipline, that is, the study of the semiological distinctions and affinities which exist between the elements of vocabulary. IV 524a; V 806a

♦ al-lugha al-makhzaniyya (A) : the language of the Moroccan government, a correct Arabic intermediate between the literary and the spoken Arabic, composed of official formulae, regular clichés, courteous, concise and binding to nothing. VI 136b

lughz (A, pl. *alghāz*) : enigma, a literary play on words. The ~ is generally in verse, and characteristically is in an interrogative form. Thus, for *falak* 'heavenly firmament' : 'What is the thing which in reality has no existence, but nevertheless you see it in existence wherever you confront it [. . .] and if we cut off its head (= *fa*), it will be yours (= *lak*)?'. V 806b

luḥma → SADĀ

lukāṭ (A) : in art, a mosaic of coloured tiles, as found in the Alhambra. I 500a

luḳaṭa (A) : in law, an article found, or more precisely, picked up. V 809b

lüle (T) : a measure of capacity traditionally defined as the amount of water passing through a pipe of given dimensions in 24 hours, or approximately 60 m^3. One-fourth of a ~ was a *ḳamīsh*, one-eighth was a *masura*. V 882a f.

lūlī (P, pl. *lūliyān*) : one of the names for gypsies in Persia, with *lūrī, lōrī*. V 816b; and → NŪRĪ

lu'lu' (A, pl. *la'āli', la'ālī*), and *durr* : pearl. The difference between the two synonyms cannot be defined with precision, although some say that the ~ is a pierced pearl and the *durr* the unpierced one. V 819a; the word for pearl-trader can only be derived from ~ : *la''āl* or *la''ā'*. V 820a

In onomastics, a proper name for a person of servile origin, a guard or an officer or a leader of a special body of GHULĀMS in the service of a prince. V 820a

lung (P) : a cloth wrapped around the loins and passed between the legs of wrestlers when exercising; when wrestling, leather breeches, *tunbān*, are worn. XI 573a

lūra (A), or *lūrā* : a wooden, pear-shaped instrument of five strings, played by the Byzantines and identical with the *rabāb* of the Arabs. VIII 347b; and → ḲITHĀRA

lūrī → LŪLĪ, NŪRĪ

luṭf (A) : a Qur'ānic term, derivatives of which are used in the two senses of 'kind' and 'subtle', the opposite of KHIDHLĀN. V 833b

In theology, ~ is applied to the notion of divine grace, favour or help, being developed by the Mu'tazila to deal with an aspect of human freedom and its relation to divine omnipotence. Divine favour makes it possible for man to act well and avoid evil. V 833b

lūth → DAYSAM

luthgha (A) : in grammar, a deviation in the pronunciation of a number of phonemes (not exclusively *ghayn*, as is often believed). V 804a

lūṭī (P) : in current Persian, ~ (also *lāṭī, lawāṭa-kār*) denotes an itinerant entertainer accompanied by a monkey, bear or goat, which dances to the sound of a drum and coarse songs. This, however, appears to have been a late restriction of the meaning of the term, deriving perhaps from its earlier use to describe a jester attached to a royal or princely court. In other contexts, it is equivalent to a loose liver, gambler, and winebibber. V 839a

In Arabic sexual terminology, a homosexual (syn. *lāʾiṭ*; pl. *lāṭa*) playing the active part in the act of sodomy, LIWĀṬ, as opposed to the *maʾbūn*, the passive partner, who practices *ubna*. V 776b

lūṭis → LĀṬIS

luṭṭ (A) : in zoology, the burbot (*Lota lota*). VIII 1021a

luzūm mā lā yalzam (A) : 'observing rules that are not prescribed'; in prosody, the term commonly used for the adoption of a second, or even a third or fourth, invariable consonant preceding the rhyme consonant, *rawī*, which, at least in classical poetry, remains itself invariable (syn. *iʿnāt, iltizām*). The term is also used in dealing with rhymed prose, *sadj̲ʿ*. In later Arabic and Persian literary theory the term also covers a variety of other devices which have nothing to do with the end rhyme. V 839b

In Persian rhetoric and prosody, the terms ~ and *iʿnāt* are used, as in Arabic, for the adoption of a second invariable consonant in prose and in poetry, and the reduplication of the rhyme consonant. In addition, however, the two terms are used for the repetition of two or more words in each hemistich or line of poetry, and for the use of internal rhyme. V 841a

M

mā baʿd al-ṭabīʿa (A, < trans. Gk τὰ μετὰ τὰ φυσικά), or *mā baʿd al-ṭabīʿiyyāt* : metaphysics, an expression which denotes either the discipline which one embarks upon after physics, utilising the results of the natural sciences, or else it can be one whose goal lies beyond the apprehendable objects which are the concern of physics. V 841a

māʾ (A) : water. V 859b; and → DJ̲UBN

In medicine, ~ is used as a technical term for cataract: *māʾ nāzil fi ʾl-ʿayn*. I 785b

In mineralogy, full 'éclat' or transparency (of a gem). XI 263a

♦ māʾ ḥiṣrim (A) : a drink made from verjuice, known from the 4th/10th century. VI 723a

♦ māʾ laymūn (A) : lemonade, probably made from green lemons/limes, a drink known from the 4th/10th century. VI 723a

♦ māʾ s̲h̲aʿīr → S̲H̲AʿĪR

♦ **māʾ al-ward** (A), and *māward* : rose water, an essential preparation in pharmacology, extracted from the petals of the damask rose (*Rosa damascena*) (*ward dj̲ūrī, ward gūrī, ward baladī, ward s̲h̲āmī*). XII 550a

♦ māʾ zaʿfarān (A) : a clear liquid distilled from saffron, used to scent clothing without leaving a trace of its colour. XI 381b

♦ māʾzahr (A) : orange blossom water, one of the major scented waters obtained by distillation. VII 962b

maʿād (A) : lit. place of return, a technical term in religious and philosophical vocabulary, bringing together the two senses of return and recommencement: return to the source of being which is God, and a second creation which is the Resurrection. V 892b; a synonym of ĀK̲H̲IRA, the Hereafter. I 325a; eschatology. V 235b; IX 208b

maʿāhira (A) : bells (which, al-Hamdānī writes, were attached to the gates of the ancient town of Ẓafār in Yemen). XI 380a

maʿānī (A, s. MAʿNĀ) : meanings; contents. I 784b; V 320b ff.

♦ **al-maʿānī wa ʾl-bayān** (A) : two of the three categories into which, since the time of al-Sakkākī (d. 626/1229), the study of rhetoric has often been divided, the other being BADĪʿ. *ʿIlm al-bayān* can be best translated with 'science of figurative speech', as it only deals with the simile (as an introduction to the discussion of metaphor), the metaphor, the analogy, the metonymy and the allusion, and statement by implication. *ʿIlm al-maʿānī* indicates a set of rather strict rules governing the art of correct sentence structure, the purpose of which was to demonstrate that changes in word order almost invariably lead to changes in meaning. I 858a; I 1114a; V 898a; VIII 894a

♦ al-maʿānī al-t͟hāniya → MAʿNĀ

maanso (Somali) : a genre of poetry, handling serious themes, sometimes referred to as 'classical poetry' by English-speaking scholars. Less 'serious' poetry, such as work and dance songs, is called *hees*. ~ is composed by named individuals. IX 725b

maʿārif (A, s. MAʿRIFA) : education, public instruction. The term was already used in mediaeval times to denote the secular subjects of knowledge or culture in general, in opposition to the religious sciences, *ʿulūm* (→ ʿILM). Starting from the 19th century, ~ came into use in Egypt and Iran to denote public education and kept this notion until the 1950s; ~ in the sense of education has died out in official usage, steadily being replaced by *tarbiya*. It seems that the same process is taking place in non-official usage. V 902b

maʾāṣir → MARĀṢID; MAʾṢIR

maʿaskar → ʿASKAR

maʾāt͟hir → MAT͟HĀLIB

mābeyn (T, < A *mā bayn* 'what is between') : the intermediate apartments of the Ottoman palace, lying between the inner courts of the palace and the harem, a place where only the sultan, the eunuchs and the womenfolk could penetrate and where the corps of select pages known as *mābeynd͟ji*s waited on the monarch for such intimate services as dressing and shaving him. V 938b

mabīt (A) : a place where one halts for the night. V 498a

mabk͟hara (A), or *mibk͟hara* : an incense burner. V 987b; in architecture, a two-storey octagonal pavilion crowning the minaret (so-called because it resembled the top of an incense burner). IV 429a; VI 367a

mablūʿ → ʿANBAR

mabsūṭ (A) : a literary type which multiplies detail and argument, in contrast to MUK͟HTAṢAR, which synthesises and compresses. IX 324a

maʾbūn → LŪṬĪ

madad-ī maʿās͟h (IndP) : in Mug͟hal India, a common prebend. XI 96a

maḍāfa → MANZIL

madāfin (A) : in Yemen, granaries, cone-shaped structures made out of sandstone and about six or seven metres deep. X 449b

madar (A) : the term designating in classical Arabic the mortar used to point unfired brick. It is made of earth with an admixture of lime or ash. ~ also refers to the construction of earth and *labin*, unfired brick. V 585a; and → AHL AL-MADAR

♦ madara (A) : a village built of *labin*, unfired brick. V 585a

madār (A) : in the science of Tradition, a term used to indicate that certain MATNs, or *matn* clusters, are due to one particular transmitter who is held responsible for disseminating these to a number of pupils. VIII 517a; the 'pivot' or 'common link'. X 382a

maḍbūṭ (A) : coffee with sugar (ant. *sāda*). XII 775b

madd (A), and *nazʿ al-watar* : in archery, the draw, drawing of a bow. This consists of bringing the bow-string back towards oneself. This technique has variants in terms of the anchor-point selected, which can be at different levels: eyebrow, earlobe, moustache, chin, sternum. IV 800b

In music, the sustaining of notes. IX 101a

♦ **al-madd wa ʾl-d͟jazr** (A) : lit. the ebb and the flow, the name given to the phenomenon of the tide. V 949b mādda → HAYŪLĀ

maddāḥ (A, T *meddāḥ*) : lit. panegyrist; in Ottoman usage, the professional story-tellers of the urban milieux. The Persians used ~ in the same way, but more rarely; as for the Arabs, they used it, in a fairly late period, to designate the 'begging singers of the streets'. III 367b; V 951a; in Egypt, a folk poet, associated primarily with a religious repertory. IX 235b

In North Africa, the *maddāḥ* is a kind of religious minstrel who goes to festivals to sing the praises of saints and of God, and holy war, and who is accompanied on the tambourine and flute. V 951a

maddūḥ (A) : a drink made by Bedouin, when dying of thirst in the desert, from a slaughtered camel's blood, which had been beaten carefully so as to separate the sediment from the serum, which was then drunk. XII 189b

madfan → MAḲBARA

madḥ → MADĪḤ

ma<u>dh</u>hab (A, pl. *ma<u>dh</u>āhib*) : a way of thinking, persuasion; the five schools of law in orthodox Islam, viz. the Ḥanafī, Mālikī, <u>Sh</u>āfiʿī, Ḥanbalī, and <u>D</u>jaʿfarī. Some other later schools, such as the Ẓāhiriyya founded by Dāwūd b. <u>Kh</u>alaf al-Ẓāhirī, the traditionists and a short-lived one founded by al-Ṭabarī, were also called ~. II 890a; IX 323a; XII 551a

Among the Wahbi Ibāḍiyya, who call themselves *ahl al-ma<u>dh</u>hab* or *ahl al-daʿwa*, ~ is the equivalent of DAʿWA. II 170a

♦ ma<u>dh</u>hab al-ḥaḍarāt (A) : the name for the Plotinian scheme of dynamic emanation. III 51b

madḥiyya (T, < A) : in Turkish prosody, the ~ or eulogy is the couplet which comprises the central part of the ḲAṢĪDA. IV 715b; ~ also is used to designate any poem composed for the purpose of extolling an individual, including the *nefes* or *ilāhī* types of poems written or uttered by members of the mystic orders to eulogise God or leading personalities of these religious brotherhoods, and the secular poems circulated by the literary innovators of the last century. V 957a

maʾ<u>dh</u>ūn (A) : in law, a slave authorised by his master either to conclude an individual sale, or generally to engage in trade. I 29a; I 1112a; III 50b

Among the Ismāʿīlīs, ~ was the name for subordinates to a DĀʿĪ who were licensed to preach. II 97b

In mysticism, ~ was used, with *muḳaddam* 'one sent in advance' and <u>KH</u>ALĪFA, for a representative appointed by a <u>SH</u>AY<u>KH</u> to a region where the latter's authority was established, in order to initiate others. X 246a

māḍī (A) : in grammar, the preterite, a technical term used to denote the verbal form that normally, but not solely, is devoted to the expression of past time. V 954b

māḍī-sālār (P) : in administration, the official in charge of the major canals leading off from the river. XI 473a

madīd (A) : in prosody, the name of the third Arabic metre. I 670a

madīḥ (A, P *ḳaṣīda-yi madīḥa*), or *madḥ* : the genre of the panegyric poetry in Arabic and other Islamic literatures, the individual poem being usually referred to as *umdūḥa* (pl. *amādīḥ*) or *madīḥa* (pl. *madāʾiḥ*). A panegyric can be an independent unit as well as a component of a larger literary work, usually the ḲAṢĪDA. In the latter case, ~ is the technical term used to refer to the section of the poem devoted to the praise of God, the Prophet, the sultan, the grand vizier, etc. IV 714b; V 931a; V 955a

In Urdu poetry, the specifically secular eulogy, addressed to rulers, governors, nobles, and other rich or influential lay persons, was usually termed *madḥ* rather than ~ . Other terms were *taʿrīf* and *sitāʾi<u>sh</u>*. ~ could also refer to a eulogy of religious persons, living or dead, although praise of God, the Prophet, ʿAlī and subsequent <u>sh</u>īʿī IMĀMS had their own terminology. V 958a maḍīḳ (A) : shallows or a ford. I 215a

maʿdin (A, pl. *maʿādin*) : mine, ore, mineral, metal. In modern Arabic, however, ~ is mostly used for metal, *mandjam* meaning mine, *muʿaddin*, miner, and *djamād*, mineral. V 963b

madīna (A) : the Arabic town and city, the lower town (L *suburbium, pars inferior civitatis*). IX 411a; XII 551a; and → ḲAṢABA

maḍīra (A) : a dish of meat cooked in sour milk, sometimes with fresh milk added, and with spices thrown in to enhance the flavour. This dish seems to have been quite well sought-after in mediaeval times. V 1010a; X 31b

madjalla (A) : a scroll. V 812a; a legal code. X 655b

madjānīḳ (A) : catapults. X 842a

madjarra (A) : in astronomy, the galaxy or Milky Way. V 1024b; the movable cursor of a sine quadrant. XI 461b

madjāz (A) : in rhetoric, a term meaning trope and, more generally, the use of a word deviating from its original meaning and use, its opposite being ḤAḲĪḲA. III 898b; V 1025b; interpretation, paraphrase. I 158b

♦ madjāz-i mursal (P, T) : free trope, or the trope that is not based on a similarity of form but on abstract relationships (between a condition and the place where it manifests itself, a whole and its parts, a cause and its effects, etc.). V 1027a ff.

madjbūb → KHĀṢĪ

madjbūr (A) : in later Ashʿarite theology, the term for when human free choice, which is only acquisition, also remains without true ontological freedom, and is thus compulsory. III 1037b

madjd → SHARAF

madjdhūb (A) : lit. the attracted one, a term in mysticism for the name for the representative of a type of piety which is chiefly of a passive nature, in contradistinction to the more active 'striding one', *sālik*, a characteristic which is expressed in numerous pairs of oppositions. While the ~, on the way to God, may abandon himself to be drawn by divine attraction, the *sālik* depends on his own exertions, which is, however, in the same way as the attraction, a gift of God. Usually, mixed forms occur, as in 'the strider who is attracted' and the 'attracted one who is striding'. In more recent literature in particular, ~ is a frequently used extenuating and exculpating designation of eccentric ecstatics, love-maddened persons, holy fools, and despisers of the law. V 1029a

madjdūḥ (A) : the blood of a sacrificed camel. III 666b

madjhūl (A) : in the science of Tradition, a traditionist who is unknown either as regards his person, or his reliability. III 26b; VIII 516b

In grammar, the ~ is the verb whose agent is not known or, if known, remains unexpressed and cannot be expressed. II 897a

madjhūr (A) : 'voiced'; in grammar, ~ signifies the manner of articulation of the letters of the alphabet (ant. *mahmūs* 'unvoiced'). III 598a, X 1a

mādjin (A) : a debauchee. IV 1005b

madjlis (A, T *medjlis*; pl. *madjālis*) : a term meaning a meeting place, meeting assembly, a reception hall (of a caliph, high dignitary or other personage) and a session which is held there, a hall in which a professor's courses are given or a judge's sentences delivered (hence 'praetorium, tribunal'), or further where the debates of an assembly take place (hence 'council'). V 1031a; ~ assumed the modern connotation of parliament in the 19th century, as the concept of parliamentarism became widespread, thanks to the impact of Western influence on the Middle East. V 1033b

In literature, *amālī* 'dictations', but also at times *madjālis*, are the lessons recorded by the pupils of a professor and published; one of the most famous works of this category is *Kitāb al-madjālis* or *al-Amālī* by Thaʿlab. V 1033a

Among the Ismāʿīlīs, ~ referred to a formal session of religious instruction, the place of it, and also to the lecture or sermon read in it by a DĀʿĪ to the faithful. V 1033a Among the Indian shīʿīs, ~ is especially used for the shīʿī mourning assemblies held during Muḥarram to commemorate the tragedy of Karbalāʾ. V 1033a; the collective term for the stationary shīʿī commemorative rituals is *madjālis al-ʿazāʾ*. VIII 465a

♦ madjlis al-ʿaḳd (A) : in law, the contractual meeting, in which and at which time the contract must be concluded. I 319a

♦ madjlis ḥīrī (A) : in architecture, the T-shaped reception hall common in ʿAbbāsid residences from Sāmarrā to Egypt, called after the city of al-Ḥīra. VIII 545a

♦ madjlis-niwīs (P) : under ʿAbbās I of the Ṣafawids, the head of a special chancellery set up to administer the newly-created royal administration, taking over some of the duties of the MUNSHĪ AL-MAMĀLIK and in the course of the 11th/17th century surpassing the latter in rank and sphere of competence (syn. *wāḳiʿa-niwīs*). IV 758a

♦ madjlis al-shaʿb (A) : the People's Assembly, the name for the legislative body in a number of Arab countries, e.g. Syria. V 1049a

♦ **madjlis al-shūrā** (A) : the name given to extraordinary, ad hoc consultative assemblies in the Ottoman empire, taking place between the Russo-Ottoman war of 1768-74 and, roughly, the abolition of the Janissaries in 1826. Such assemblies appeared in other Islamic political centres as well later on; in Egypt under the Khedive Ismāʿīl the parliament was known as the *madjlis shūrā al-nuwwāb*. V 1082b

♦ **medjlis-i wālā** (T) : in the Ottoman empire, the Supreme Council of Judicial Ordinances, in full *medjlis-i wālā-yi aḥkām-i ʿadliyye*, created in 1838 for the purpose of taking over the legislative duties of the old DĪWĀN-I HÜMĀYŪN. VI 972b

madjmaʿ (A, pl. *madjmāmiʿ*) : lit. a place of collecting, a place in which people collect, assemble, congregate. Whereas *madjlis* had been the current term in earlier Arab civilisation for [the place of] an informal literary gathering and developed the meaning of 'council', ~ came to be used in the second half of the 19th century for private academies and clubs which met to discuss language and literature as well as other problems. Although they were short-lived, they eventually gave rise to the founding of still-existing official academies all over the Middle East. V 1090a

♦ **madjmaʿ ʿilmī** (A) : a technical term for Academy of Science, taking hold in the second half of the 19th century. V 1090a

madjmūʿa (A, T *medjmūʿa*) : in Persian literature, a technical term most often referring to a volume of prose texts by more than one author. VII 528b; in Turkish literature, *medjmūʿa* was used until the Tanẓīmāt period to represent the genre of anthology, as well as a collection of either verse or prose or a mixture of both. After the Tanẓīmāt, ~ meant a periodical or journal, but now *dergi* is used for this purpose. VII 531a

madjnūn (A, pl. *madjānīn*) : possessed, mad, madman; DJINN-possessed. V 1101a

madjrā (A), or *mudjrā* : in prosody, the vowel of the *rawī*, rhyme letter. IV 412a
A measure of distance, ~ measures at the most 150 km/100 miles. II 1121b

maʿdjūn (A) : in medicine, an electuary. IX 805a; XI 369b; a confection. XII 641a

madjūs (A) : originally an ancient Iranian priestly caste, ~ is used in Arabic primarily for Zoroastrians. V 1110a; as *al-~*, used by Arabic historians and geographers writing about the Maghrib and Northern Spain with the sense of Northmen, Vikings, denoting the participants in the great Viking raids on Spain. V 1118a

madjzūʾ (A) : in prosody, a deviation consisting of one DJUZʾ missing in each of the two hemistiches. I 671a; VIII 421a

madkhal (A, pl. *madākhil*) : lit. entrance; in dating, a rule for calculating the week day. X 264b; the week day of the first day of a year or month or of a particular date, represented by a number (sometimes given a separate name, *ʿalāma* 'indicator') from 1 (Sunday) till 7 (Saturday). X 270a; XI 502b

maḍmūn (A) : in law, the thing for which one is liable or responsible, occurring in the following connections: *maḍmūn bihi* 'thing pawned', *maḍmūn ʿanhu* 'debtor', *maḍmūn lahu* or *ʿalayhi* 'creditor'. V 1121b; and → ḌAMĀN

maḍrab (A) : in music, a wooden stick covered with tow or cotton and held by the musician between thumb and index finger, used with the SANṬŪR 'dulcimer'. IX 19b

madraḳa (A) : a variety of tunic, TH̲AWB, worn by Jordanian women. V 741b

madrasa (A) : a school, in the sense of both institution and place of learning; in modern usage, ~ is specifically the name of an institution and place of learning where the Islamic sciences are taught, i.e. a college for higher studies, as opposed to an elementary school of traditional type, *kuttāb*. In mediaeval usage, ~ was essentially a college of law in which the other Islamic sciences, including literary and philosophical ones, were ancillary subjects only. I 593a; V 1123a; in Persia in the 5th/11th century, ~ could mean a centre for ṣūfīs. IV 1025b

In Indonesia, ~ is also used for the traditional boarding school, *pesantren*. III 1227b

maʿdūm → SH̲AYʾIYYA

mafāk̲h̲ir → MATH̲ĀLIB

mafārīd → FARD

mafḳūd (A) : in law, a person who at a given moment is not present at the place where he should be and concerning whose existence there is uncertainty. Without the uncertainty, he is called *g̲h̲āʾib*. If his absence extends to a period when persons of the same generation as him are dead, the judge declares him dead; his estate then goes to his heirs and his marriage or marriages are dissolved. II 995b

mafrad̲j̲ (A) : in Yemeni architecture, the top storey of a multi-storey tower house, used as a second reception room and for the daily afternoon ḲĀT-chewing ritual. IX 2b

mafras̲h̲ → MIFRAS̲H̲

mafrūḍ al-ḳalem (T) : under the Ottomans, an autonomous status of prebends whereby their taxes were 'excluded from the registers'. Another category was *maḳṭūʿ al-ḳadem* 'the interference of the local authorities are cut'. X 505b

mafrūk (A) : lit. twisted; in archery, ~ denotes a way of loosing an arrow, involving a light, partial draw, a brief moment at rest, and then a sudden end to the draw followed immediately by the loose. IV 800b

mafrūs̲h̲ (A) : furnished, provided with furnishings, from *fars̲h̲*, which in mediaeval times came to mean the more solid domestic objects that filled the role of 'furniture', according to western concepts. V 1158a

♦ **mafrūs̲h̲āt** (A) : in mediaeval times, that which is spread out (on the ground or on a bed), bedding. Carpets, mats and cushions played an important part in domestic interiors. V 1158a

mafṣūl (A, < *vassal* ?) : in law, a term used to denote certain categories of landed estates in Syria in the time of the Mamlūks. V 1159a

maftūḥ → MUNTAḲ

mafʿūl bihi (A) : in grammar, the direct object. VIII 384a

mag (Somali) : in Somali society, the payment of blood money, traditionally in livestock. IX 713b

mag̲h̲ānī (A), or *ag̲h̲ānī* : a pair of loggias that flank a reception hall on both sides and which were intended for the singers and musicians, who traditionally performed behind curtains or screens. VI 719a

mag̲h̲āriba (A) : the Arab-speakers of the Muslim West, as opposed to the *mas̲h̲āriḳa*, those of the East. The frontier between the two major groupings, which includes Muslim Spain, in spite of its special circumstances and its separate destiny, was, and still is, located to the east of Tripoli, at Lebda. V 1159a

maghāzī (A), also *maghāzī 'l-nabī, maghāzī rasūl allāh* : a term which signifies in particular the expeditions and raids organised by the Prophet Muḥammad in the Medinan period. In a broader sense, it refers to the Prophet's general biography and background. V 1161b; VIII 53a

maghnam (A) : either the mass of the booty or that part of it which goes to the central government. II 1005a; VIII 496b

maghnāṭis (A, < Gk) : magnetite (lodestone, magnetic iron ore, Fe_3O_4); compass, also called *ḥuḳḳ al-ḳibla* (box for the *ḳibla*), *bayt al-ibra* (house of the needle), and the modern *ḥikk*. V 1166b

maghrib (A) : that part of Africa which Europeans have called Barbary or Africa Minor and then North Africa, including Tripolitania, Tunisia, Algeria and Morocco; the west, the setting sun. V 1183b; Morocco, which name is a deformation of the southern metropolis of the kingdom, Marrākush. The country's full name is *al-mamlaka al-maghribiyya*. V 1184a; and → MAṬLAʿ

♦ ṣalāt al-maghrib (A) : the sunset prayer which is to be performed, according to the law books, in between the time after sunset and the time when the red twilight, *shafaḳ*, has disappeared. There are small deviations only, in connection with a predilection for the first term. VII 27b; VIII 928b

♦ maghribī → KŪFĪ

maghrūr A) : a person who is self-deceived. X 93a

maghshūsh A) : in numismatics, an adulterated, alloyed, base coin. X 409b

magnahuli : a kind of WAḲF, in favour of women only, existing on the island of Great Comore. I 170a

mahā → BAḲAR

maḥabba (A) : love of the soul and of God. III 84a; IV 94b; and → AKLAT AL-MAḤABBA

In the Čishtī mystical doctrine, the following kinds of ~ are distinguished: *maḥabbat-i islāmī* 'love which a new convert to Islam develops with God on account of his conversion to the new faith', *maḥabbat-i khāṣṣ* 'love which is the result of cosmic emotion, and which should be developed by the mystic', and *maḥabbat-i muwahhibī* 'love which a man develops as a result of his 'effort' in the way of following the Prophet'. II 55b

maḥāla (A, pl. *maḥāl*) : the huge pulley which is used for raising water from wells. In Egypt, the word is also used to denote a wooden water-wheel for irrigation, comparable to the NĀʿŪRA. V 863b f.

maḥall (A) : lit. place of alighting, settling, abode. V 1214b; in philosophy, the thing qualified. III 571a

In the Mughal empire, a subdivision (syn. PARGANA) of a *sarkār* 'district' and the lowest fiscal unit. I 317a; also in the context of Islamic India, ~ is widely used in the sense of 'palace pavilion' or 'hall', and more particularly of private apartments in the palace, the *maḥall-sarā*; hence also a queen or consort. V 1214b; IX 46b; small hunting lodge. X 594a

♦ **maḥalla** (A, T *maḥalle*) : a place where one makes a halt, where one settles (for a longer or shorter time); a quarter of a town, especially in Turkish, Persian and Urdu. IV 229b; V 1220b; characteristically, the Ottoman **maḥalle** consisted of a religious community grouped around its mosque (or church or synagogue) and headed by its religious chief. V 1222b

In North Africa, ~ designates a movable camp, then, by extension, the troops on campaign within the territory at least nominally dependent on the sovereign who commands them or entrusts the command to the heir apparent, another member of the royal family or, exceptionally, to a confirmed war commander. V 1220b

māhāniyya (A) : the Māhānians, a sect of the Marcionites. X 440a

maḥāra → SARAṬĀN
maḥāris → MANĀẒIR
al-maḥāsin wa 'l-masāwī (A) : lit. merits and faults. A literary genre which developed in the course of the first centuries of the Islamic period, having originated within the Arabo-Muslim heritage, although some scholars have concluded, ill-advisedly, that it was inspired by an ancient Iranian model. Two categories of ~ may be distinguished: MUNĀẒARA 'theological debate' and MUFĀKHARA, MUNĀẒARA 'secular debate'. V 1223b
mahāt (A, pl. *mahā^n, mahawāt, mahayāt*) : in zoology, the large oryz and the addax antelope. The root *m-h-w* suggests sparkling whiteness, and *al-mahā* is applied to rock crystal, the spearl, and any bright star. The almost immaculate coat of these beautiful, desert antelopes certainly warrants the description. V 1227a, where many regional variations are given
mahawī → YĀḲŪT ABYAḌ
maḥḍar (A) : decree. I 117a; XII 636b; and → SIDJILL
mahdī (A) : lit. the rightly guided one. The name of the restorer of religion and justice who, according to a widely-held Muslim belief, will rule before the end of the world. Throughout Islamic history there has been a recurrence of Mahdī movements. In early days, the best known Mahdī was Ibn Tumart, the founder of the Almohad movement; in modern times, the Sudanese Muḥammad al-Mahdī. In radical shī'ism, belief in the coming of the Mahdī of the family of the Prophet became a central aspect of the faith. V 1230b; V 1247b
mahdjar (A) : the name given to places in Northern, Central and Southern America to which Lebanese, Syrians, Palestinians and other Arabs have emigrated. V 1253a
maḥdjūr → ḤADJR
maḥfil (A) : the term for a freemason lodge. XII 286a
maḥfūr (A, pl. *maḥāfīr*) : common to the Syrian desert, an open, ring-shaped storage dam built along the edges of a silt flat, KHABRĀ', with an up-stream opening, where, after the central hollowed-out depression has been coated with silt, the water can be naturally stored for a long time, occasionally lasting throughout the entire dry summer season. IV 897b

♦ maḥfūra (A) : a carpet that is decorated with a relief design. XII 136a

maḥfūẓ (A) : lit. committed to memory; in the science of Tradition, an acceptable Tradition which, when compared with one which is SHĀDHDH, a Tradition from a single authority which differs from what others report, is considered of greater weight. III 26b

In mysticism, preserved from sin. XI 110b

māhī zahrah (P) : lit. fish poison; in botany, *Anamirta cocculus* or *Menospirmum cocculus*. IX 872b
māhin → MIḤNA
māhiyya (A) : quiddity; in logic, that which replies to the question: what is this? I 513b; V 1261a

In theology and metaphysics, ~ is that through which a thing is what it is. In this sense, the term is synonymous with essence, *dhāt*, and with reality, *ḥaḳīḳa*. V 1261a

maḥkama (A) : in law, a court of justice. VI 1a
maḥlūl (A) : vacant. In Ottoman administration, ~ is used in the registers of a grant or office which has been vacated by the previous holder, by death, dismissal, or transfer, and not yet re-allocated. The term is also used more generally for land and other assets left without heir. VI 44b
maḥmal (A) : a type of richly decorated palanquin, perched on a camel and serving in the past to transport people, especially noble ladies, to Mecca. VI 44b

In a more restricted and precise, political sense, ~ designates palanquins of this same type which became political symbols and were sent from the 7th/13th century by sovereigns with their caravans of pilgrims to Mecca (or the principal caravan when it was split up) in order to bolster their prestige. VI 44b

mahmūsa → MAD̲J̲HŪRA

mahr (A) : in law, the gift which the bridegroom has to give the bride when the contract of marriage is made and which becomes the property of the wife. I 209a; VI 78b; VIII 27b

In the pre-Islamic period, the ~ was the purchase price of the bride and was handed over to her legal guardian; the bride received none of it. She was given the **ṣadāḳ**, a voluntary gift, not as a result of the contract. In the period shortly before Muḥammad, however, the ~, or at least a part of it, seems already to have been given to the women. According to the Qur'ān, this is already the prevailing custom. By this amalgamation of ~ and *ṣadāḳ*, the original significance of the ~ as the purchase price was weakened and became quite lost in the natural course of events. VI 79a

♦ mahr al-mit̲h̲l (A) : a bridal gift fixed by the ḲĀḌĪ according to the circumstances of the bridegroom, when the *mahr* is not fixed at the conclusion of the marriage contract and when the parties cannot agree upon it. VIII 27b

maḥras → MAS̲H̲LAḤ

maḥrem (A), or *mḥarram* : the compartment in a Bedouin tent reserved for the womenfolk. Here, the cooking is done and the provisions stored. The other compartment is for receiving menfolk. IV 1148b

mahriyya (A) : the méhara, a species of camel famed for its speed and the slimness of its limbs and body. III 666a

maḥsūsāt (A) : in philosophy, sensibilia, frequently contrasted with *maʿḳūlāt* 'intelligibilia'. III 509a; VI 87a

māḥūz (A) : 'space between two armies'; ~ could be applied to a maritime forward post in relation to the city by which it was controlled and was used to describe the port of two small cities on the Palestinian coast, G̲h̲azza and Azdūd. VIII 502a

maḥw → IT̲H̲BĀT

maḥyā (A) : in mysticism, a communal nightly liturgical ritual in which the recital of supplications for divine grace for the Prophet is central. VI 87b; the name among the Demirdās̲h̲iyya order for their ḤAḌRA. XII 208b; and → LAYLAT AL-MAḤYĀ

mai (Kanuri) : official title of the Sefawa (or Sayfuwa) rulers in Central Africa, the first of whom was probably from the 5th/11th century. IV 567a; V 357b; XII 569a

♦ mai wallafa wakoki, or *mai waka* (Hau) : a Muslim poet. IX 244a

māʾida → K̲H̲UWĀN

māʾil → KŪFĪ

maʿīs̲h̲et → K̲H̲IDMET AḲČESĪ

māʿiza (A) : in zoology, the goat, with *s̲h̲iyāh al-maʿz*. XII 316b

makāʾid → ḤIYAL

maḳāla (A, pl. *maḳālāt*) : an article, published in a newspaper or periodical, in Arabic, Persian and Turkish. V 90a; originally, an oral message. VIII 532a

In Persian, ~ has been used to denote a collection of discourses, spoken or written, on a given subject; it was used in reference to spoken discourses and sermons up to the late 19th century. ~ has also been used to designate a book's inner divisions, while its plural, *maḳālāt*, has also been used for the utterances, statements and dictations of ṣūfī S̲H̲AYK̲H̲S. VI 91b

maḳām (A, pl. *maḳāmāt*) : lit. place, position, rank; in music, ~ began to appear in Islamic musical treatises at the end of the ʿAbbāsid period, to designate Arabo-Irano-Turkish and assimilated musical modes, and is still predominantly used today. VI 96b; VIII 2b; X 734a

In mysticism, *maḳāmāt* are the progressive stations that the soul has to attain in its search for God. III 83b

In architecture, ~ can denote a little chapel and a saint's tomb. VI 651b

♦ **maḳām ibrāhīm** (A) : in Qur'ānic usage, a place of prayer, established at the location of a stone in the sanctuary of Mecca known as ~. Some scholars say ~ denotes the whole place of the pilgrimage, others say ʿArafa, Muzdalifa and the Djimār are meant; a third group maintains that ~ refers to ʿArafa only, while the fourth view identifies it with the Ḥaram of Mecca. VI 104b

♦ al-maḳām al-ʿirāḳī (A) : a typically ʿIrāḳī genre whose poem is entrusted to a solo singer and the accompaniment to an instrumental quartet from the beginning to the finale. VI 101b

maḳāma (A, pl. *maḳāmāt*) : an Arabic literary genre of rhymed prose, created by al-Hamadhānī (358-98/968-1008). Translation of ~ with 'assembly' or 'session' does not convey exactly the complex nature of the term. The structure of the ~ is characterised by the existence of a hero, whose adventures and eloquent speeches are related by a narrator to the author who, in turn, conveys them to his readers. Many later imitators of al-Hamadhānī, however, were to dispense with the hero, if not with both characters. VI 107a

maḳāṣid al-sharīʿa (A) : lit. the aims or purposes of the law; in legal theory, the idea that the sharīʿa is a system that encompasses aims or purposes, not merely a collection of inscrutable rulings. XII 569b

makāyil (A, s. *miḳyal*) : measures of capacity, a non-uniform system in the Muslim countries and thus of a bewildering diversity. VI 117a

maḳbara (A) : cemetery (syn. *djabbāna, madfan, turba*). VI 122a

maḳbūḍ → ḲABḌ

maḳbūl (A) : in the science of Tradition, an acceptable Tradition which fulfils the requirements, and is either *ṣaḥīḥ* 'sound' or *ḥasan* 'good'. III 26b

makfūl → KAFĀLA

maʾkhadh (A) : in music, the initial note. The final note is termed *rakz*. IX 101a

makhāridj al-ḥurūf → MAKHRADJ

makhāṣir (A) : in early Islam, the insignia of the KHAṬĪB, lance, staff, or bow. IV 1110a

makhazza → MUʾARNIBA

makhbaz (A, pl. *makhābiz*) : bakery. VI 807b

makhlaṣ (P, < A) : the transitional distich between the prologue and the panegyric of a Persian ḲAṢĪDA, which must skilfully introduce the name of the person being eulogised. IV 57b; IV 714b; nom-de-plume. VIII 3a; IX 354a

In Urdu prosody, the second section of the prelude of a ḲAṢĪDA, the crucial link between the prelude and the actual praise, was usually called *gurēz* (P 'deviation, flight') but ~, *talkhīṣ* and even *takhalluṣ* are given as alternatives. V 959b

makhmal (A) : velvet, for which e.g. Kāshān was well known during the Ṣafawid period. IV 695a

makhradj (A, T *makhredj*; pl. *makhāridj*) : place of exit.

♦ **makhāridj al-ḥurūf** (A) : lit. the place of emission of the letters; in grammar, the points of articulation of the 29 phonemes of Arabic. III 598a; VI 129b; X 73b

♦ **makhredj** (T) : an Ottoman term used in education and law.

In Ottoman education, ~ was used in reference to two schools in the 19th century, of which one prepared students for employment in Ottoman administrative offices (*makhredj-i aḳlām*), the other for military schools (*makhredj-i mekātib-i ʿaskeriyye*). VI 133a

In Ottoman law, ~ had two meanings. Certain judicial districts in the empire were referred to as *makhredj mewlewiyyeti*. The name derived from a common attribute of the judges appointed to these districts. All were judges 'going out' to their first appointment after teaching in schools. The judges who had completed this appointment and were awaiting assignment to a higher ranking judicial district were called *makhredj mewālīsi*. VI 133b; in Ottoman inheritance law, ~ was the term for the denominator which was used to divide an inheritance among heirs. VI 133b

makhrūṭ (A) : cone; in astronomy, the shadow of the earth during an eclipse of the moon. V 536a

makhzan (A) : in Morocco, the government; at first ~ was applied more particularly only to the financial department, the Treasury. VI 133b; and → AL-LUGHA AL-MAKHZANIYYA; SĪBA

makhzen (Mor) : a garrison placed in a stronghold. II 510a

makkārī : 'for hire', a term used in the Ottoman empire to designate small caravans operating between cities, which would transport merchants and travellers for a fare. IV 678b

makkās (A) : probably a tax-farmer under the Ḥafṣids; collector of the MAKS. II 146a

makkī (A) : in the mediaeval Near East, a beggar who pretends to be a rich merchant who has been robbed of his goods. VII 494b

makkūk (A) : a measure used for weighing grains in northern Syria and Upper Mesopotamia. Its actual weight varied, e.g. that of Aleppo and Tripoli contained 83.5 kg of wheat and that of Ḥamāt 92.77 kg. IV 520a; VI 118b

maḳlūb (A) : 'transposed'; in the science of Tradition, a term used when a Tradition is attributed to someone other than the real authority to make it an acceptable GHARĪB Tradition, or when two Traditions have the ISNĀD of the one with the MATN of the other. III 26a

maknī → IḌMĀR

makrūh (A) : in law, a reprehensible action, an action disapproved of; one of the five juridical qualifications of human actions. VI 194b

maḳrūn, maḳrūna → ZUMMĀRA

makrūna (A) : a head scarf worn by Bedouin women on the Arabian peninsula. V 741b

makrūs (Alg, pl. *makārīs*) : an adolescent of 12-14 years; in the Mzāb, ~ means an adult fit to carry arms. III 98a

maks (A, < Ar; pl. *mukūs*) : a toll, custom duty; in old law books, used in the sense of *ʿushr* the tenth levied by the merchants, more properly the equivalent of an excise duty than of a custom. VI 194b; octroi duties. II 146a; tax unsanctioned by the sharīʿa; non-canonical tax. VIII 71b; VIII 955a

maḳṣūra (A, pl. *maḳāṣir*) : in poetry, the name given to a poem whose rhyme is constituted by an *alif maḳṣūra*. VI 195b

In architecture, a box or compartment for the ruler built in a mosque, near the MIḤRĀB, introduced at the beginning of the Umayyad period either to protect the ruler from hostile attacks or for the purpose of teaching and performing the ṢALĀT. VI 661b ff.; antechamber. XI 488b

maḳṭaʿ (A) : in Persian prosody, the term for the last distich, BAYT, which in the GHAZAL contains the nom-de-plume of the author. II 1033b; IV 715a

In grammar, a 'cutting' in the resonance emitted from the chest as it rises in the throat to produce the ḤARF. III 597b

maktab (A, pl. *makātib*) : originally, an appellation for the Islamic traditional school frequently known also as *kuttāb*. In Egypt, the Copts too used ~ to denote their own traditional schools; a school; bureau, department; office; agency. VI 196b

In modern Persian usage, in addition to its basic meaning of 'school', ~ has acquired also the connotation of an 'instructing manual'. VI 197a

♦ maktab al-sabīl → SABĪL

♦ **maktaba** (A, P *kitāb-khāna*) : a library. VI 197b

maḳtal (A) : a genre in Turkish narrative literature denoting works commemorating miracles and happenings around the martyrs of the house of the Prophet, particularly his grandson Ḥusayn. III 374a; V 193b

makth (A) : stop, stay; in astronomy, ~ means the phase in which the moon is eclipsed. For the case of total eclipse, the place where it begins is called *awwal al-makth* and where the moon begins to emerge from the shadow, *ākhir al-makth*. V 536b

maḳṭūʿ (A) : in the science of Tradition, a Tradition going back to a Successor regarding words or deeds of his. III 25b; an ISNĀD which is 'cut off' at the level of the Successor, thus without mention of either the Prophet or a Companion. VII 631a

In Ottoman Turkey, a form of poll-tax, DJIZYA, which was fixed by agreement, and which amount thus could not be altered. It was extensively applied. II 563b

For ~ in prosody, → ḲAṬʿ

♦ maḳṭūʿ al-ḳadem → → MAFRŪḌ AL-ḲALEM

maktūbāt (A) : lit. letters; term used especially in Muslim India for the epistles of ṣūfī leaders. XII 571b

maḳūlāt (A) : in philosophy, the (ten) Aristotelian categories, and the translation of the title of the work of Aristotle on that subject. VI 203b

maʿḳūla, maʿḳūlāt → DIYA; MAḤSŪSĀT

mal → BAVIK

māl (A, pl. *amwāl*) : possession, property, referring among the Bedouin particularly to camels, but also to estates and money, and in any case to concrete things. The word is formed from *mā* and *li* and means properly anything that belongs to anyone. VI 205a; taxes. II 148a; IV 1034a; VI 205a; capital. II 361a; and → SHARIKAT AMWĀL

In mathematics, ~ was used for the unknown quantity in an equation; in this meaning it was afterwards replaced by *shayʾ*. Used for the unknown in quadratic equations, it became the word for the square of a number. The fourth power is called *māl al-māl*, the fifth *māl^u kaʿb^in*, the square of the cube. II 361a; VI 205b

In law, *fīʾl māl* or *fī ʿayn al-māl* means 'in rem'. XI 410b

♦ **māl al-bayʿa** (A), also *ḥaḳḳ al-bayʿa, rasm al-bayʿa* and *ṣilat al-bayʿa* : a term used for the payments made to army officers at the time of the swearing of the oath of allegiance, BAYʿA, to a new ruler. VI 205b

♦ māl al-djahābidha (P), or *ḥaḳḳ al-djahābidha* : the fee of the DJAHBADH for his services to the government, levied as a charge on the taxpayer. II 382b

♦ al-māl al-ḥurr (A) : one of the three main sources of revenue for the Egyptian government in the years immediately preceding the Napoleonic invasion of 1798, ~ was composed of the MĪRĪ, a fixed tax, and the *fāʾiẓ*, a tax which went to the concessionaries of tax farms and was fixed by the terms of the concession. All the land taxes were farmed out by the government to *multazim*s (→ MÜLTEZIM), who collected them through their agents. II 148a

♦ māl al-kushūfiyya (A) : one of the three main sources of revenue for the Egyptian government in the years immediately preceding the Napoleonic invasion of 1798, ~ were taxes which paid for the military and administrative expenses within the Egyptian provinces. II 148a

♦ māl manḳūl → ʿAḲĀR

♦ māl nāṭiḳ → MĀL ṢĀMIT

♦ māl ribawī (A) : in law, goods capable of usury and interest, RIBĀ. VIII 492b

♦ māl ṣāmit (A) : dumb property, in contrast to *māl nāṭiḳ* 'speaking money', applied to slaves and cattle. VI 205a

♦ māl-i ādharūy (P) : rent paid for fire-temple premises or land by Zoroastrians in 4th/10th-century eastern Persia. IX 683a

♦ māl-i khāṣṣa (P) : in Persia, the funds controlled by the royal court, *dargāh*, in contradistinction to *māl-i maṣāliḥ*, the funds controlled by the *dīwān*. IV 972b

♦ māl-i maṣāliḥ → MĀL-I KHĀṢṢA

♦ māl-î muḳātele (T) : 'fighting money', revenue from land grants, DIRLIK. IX 656a

mala' (A) : lit. a group of people, a host, crowd, and more generally, the public, hence *fī mala', fi 'l-mala'* 'publicly'. The term also denotes decisions taken as a result of collective consultation, and since collective decisions are usually taken by the leaders of the group, ~ often denotes the notables and leaders of the community (syn. *wudjūh, ashrāf, ru'asā'*). XII 573a

♦ al-mala' al-a'lā (A) : 'the upper host', Qur'ānic term explained either as the angels who thus been named because they dwell in heaven, which differentiates them from the earthly ones, the sons of Adam. As used in Tradition, ~ is explained as though standing for the Ḳuraysh. XII 573a

malāḥa (A) : in law, as interpreted by shī'ī jurists, a category of taxable wealth, along with booty, produce of the sea, buried treasure, and minerals, that refers to profit (from trade, agriculture and craft), DHIMMĪ land bought by a Muslim and '*ḥalāl* goods mixed with *ḥarām* ones'. XII 533b

malāhī (A, s. *malhā*) : a term which, in a figurative sense, is used as the equivalent of 'musical instruments', sometimes being replaced by *ālat al-lahw* or linked with the word *lahw* 'game, pastime, amusement'. VI 214a

malāḥim → MALḤAMA

malā'ika (A, s. *malak*) : angels, a concept so frequently used in the Qur'ān, Muḥammad's audience was obviously familiar with it; it must have been a pre-Islamic borrowing. VI 216b

mālaḳ (A), or *mimlaḳa* : in mediaeval agriculture, a wide board that the ploughman presses on with all his weight and is pulled along by two oxen, the ~ is a rudimentary implement for levelling the earth after ploughing and burying completely the seed which was sown there before the ploughshare turned over the soil. The word is an equivalent of the Egyptian *zaḥḥāfa*. VII 22b

malaka (A) : in philosophy, ~ is used to translate the Greek *hexis* 'a being in a certain state or habit'. It is contrasted with privation, 'ADAM, in translations and commentaries on Aristotle. VI 220a

malakī (A) : in numismatics, a variety of DĪNĀR instituted in 479/1086 under the Ṣulayḥids in Yemen. IX 816b

malam (Hau, < A *mu'allim*; pl. *malamai*) : ~ was formerly used to designate a man versed in the Arabic language and Islamic sciences to whatever extent. Nowadays, although the traditional ~ remains a familiar feature of Hausa society, the term itself has been debased to the point where (like the Arabic term *al-sayyid*) it merely serves the function of the English 'Mr'. In the phrase *shehu malami*, it is used as an epithet for a distinguished exponent of the Islamic sciences. VI 223a; IX 244a

malāmiyya (A) : in Ibn al-'Arabī's tripartite division of the Men of God, the Blameworthy, also called the Realisers (*muḥaḳḳiḳūn*), viz. the Prophet and the greatest friends of God, who are above the ascetics, on the lowest rung, and the ṣūfīs. The basic activity of the Realisers is *taḥḳīḳ* 'giving everything that has a ḤAḲḲ its *ḥaḳḳ*'. X 317b

malang (P ?) : a term with uncertain etymology, used in Muslim India, to denote wandering dervishes of the Ḳalandarī, BĪ-SHAR' or antinomian type. VI 228b

malāryā (A) : in medicine, a neologism for malaria. VI 229a

malāsa (A) : extreme smoothness (of a gem). XI 570a

malfūf → TĀMM

malfūẓāt (A, s. *malfūẓ*) : lit. utterances; in mysticism, the conversations of a mystic teacher. When given literary form by Ḥasan Sidjzī of Delhi in 707/1307, it became a type of mystical genre, developing mainly in India. XII 577a

malḥama (A, pl. *malāḥim*) : an epic; in the Islamic Middle Ages, ~ meant a writing of a divinatory character, specifically the *Malḥamat Dāniyāl*, a collection of meteorological signs with their divinatory meanings. VI 247a; VIII 106a

In its plural form, **malāḥim**, it is applied to a literature consisting of predictions of a historical character. II 377a; VI 216a

malḥūn (A), or *ḳaṣīda zadjaliyya* : a term designating a language which sprang from the local North African dialects which served for the expression of certain forms of dialectal poetry, as well as this poetry itself. I 571b; VI 247b; XI 375a

malik (A, pl. *mulūk*) : king; as a kingly title, the term appears repeatedly in pre-Islamic inscriptions from southern Arabia and the Syrian desert fringes. Islam, however, presented a new order in which God alone was the King. Considered to be a term of abuse, ~ was not officially assumed by Muslim rulers in the early centuries of Islam, but towards the middle of the 4th/10th century, the Būyids began adopting the title, as did Sāmānid, Khʷārazmī, Ghaznawid, Saldjūḳ, Fāṭimid, Ayyūbid and Mamlūk rulers after them. ~ was also freely applied to princes, viziers and provincial governors, which rendered the term less majestic, the title *sulṭān* being considered superior as it conveyed a sense of independent sovereignty. VI 261a

♦ **malik al-shuʿarāʾ** (A) : 'king of the poets', an honorific title of a Persian poet laureate. It was the highest distinction which could be given to a poet by a royal patron. Like other honorifics, it confirmed the status of its holder within his profession and was regarded as a permanent addition to his name which sometimes even became a hereditary title. VI 276a; IX 241b

♦ **malik al-tudjdjār** (A) : 'king of the big merchants', an office and a title which existed in Iran from Ṣafawid times, and probably earlier, until the end of the Ḳādjār period. The ~ was chosen by the prominent merchants of each big town and nominated by the authorities to be the link between the trading community and the authorities. He also settled disputes between the Iranian merchants and their customers, between the merchants themselves, and between local and foreign merchants and trading-firms. VI 276b

♦ malikī → DJALĀLĪ

♦ **mulūk al-ṭawāʾif** (A) : 'the kings of the territorial divisions', the Arabic phrase used by Muslim historians originally for the regional rulers of the Parthian or Arsacid period in pre-Islamic Persia; the rulers of the principalities which arose on the ruins of the Umayyad empire of al-Andalus at the end of the 5th/11th century. VII 551a

mālik (A) : in law, owner (of a slave). I 24b

♦ **mālikāne** (< A *mālik* and P *-āne*) : in law, intangible property, i.e. fiscal revenues, whenever the enjoyment of them is connected with full ownership. The term's content has nonetheless changed over the centuries. VI 277b; VIII 405b

♦ mālikiyyat al-māl (A) : in law, patrimonial ownership. I 27a

malīkh (A), or *masīkh* : 'completely insipid'; in the terminology of food, one of the degrees of insipidity, along with *tafih* 'without either real sweetness, acidity or bitterness'. II 1071a

malīl → MALLA

maliṣa → AṬŪM

māliyye (T, < A) : a term used in the 19th and 20th centuries, in Arabic and Turkish, to refer to financial affairs and financial administration. In the Ottoman empire, and in various of its successor states, the term has also acquired a more specific reference to the Ministry of Finance. VI 283b

malḳaf (Egy) : (wind) catcher; the usual term for the ventilation shaft known as *bādahandj* in mediaeval Arabic. XII 115b

Malkāyē (Syr) : Melkites, a nickname of members of the Jacobites who supported the resolutions of Chalcedon that branded the Jacobites as heretics for their monophysite christology. XI 259a

malla (A), or *malīl* : 'hot ash', a loaf of bread cooked under ashes, eaten in ancient Arabia by Bedouin. V 41b; X 30b

mallāḥ (A) : the name given to the place of residence, quarter, assigned to the Jews of Morocco. There is a difference between the urban ~ and the rural ~. The former is a quarter adjacent to the Muslim city, integrated within it or shifted to the nearby periphery, yet enclosed within a separate enclave defended by a wall and a fortified gateway. The latter is an 'open' village exclusively inhabited by Jews, situated some distance from the nearest *ḳṣar* or fortress of the protector. VI 292b; a boatman, who during the ʿAbbāsid period hired out boards for transporting passengers or goods. XII 659b

mals → MATN

ma'luka (A) : an oral message. According to the Arab lexicographers, ~ derives from the root *aluka* which signifies 'to champ the bit' when used in reference to a horse. VIII 532a

malūsa (A) : a large Turkish-style turban worn by religious dignitaries in Tunisia. V 746a

mamālik → MAMLAKA

mamlaka (A, pl. *mamālik*) : absolute power over things and especially over beings: to begin with, that of God over creation as a whole, and then, that of any individual, in certain circumstances; ~ is also applied to the place either in origin or by application, of the power under consideration. In this latter sense, the most current denotation of ~ is a piece of territory under the control of some authority; a kingdom. VI 313b

In geographical literature, ~ refers to the Islamic world. VI 313b

In Ṣafawid Persia, the plural *mamālik* referred to provinces and regions alienated from the direct control of the central government, in contrast to KHĀṢṢA, provinces and districts under its direct administration. VI 16b; VIII 751a; state lands. IV 36a

mamlūk (A) : lit. thing possessed, hence 'slave', especially used in the sense of military slave. The term is especially known in relation to the Mamlūk sultanate established and maintained by *mamlūk*s in Egypt (1250-1517) and in Syria (1260-1516); and in relation to the role of their sucessors, the neo-Mamlūks, in Ottoman Egypt. I 24b; VI 314a

For ~ in land law, → ARḌ

mamsūkh → MASKH

maʾmūma → ĀMMA

ma'mūr (A) : in the late Ottoman empire and Turkish republic, a civil official. VI 340b

man (H) : the maund, a weight in Brtish India equalling 3,200 TŌLĀS. X 564a

manʿ (Yem) : 'protection' of those to whom the tribesman has special obligations; in Yemen, the customary law, consistent with the sharīʿa, in opposition to ṬĀGHŪT, customary tribal law in contradiction to the sharīʿa. X 94a

maʿnā (A, pl. MAʿĀNĪ) : 'meaning, what the speaker intends to say'; in grammar, ~ indicates the semantic counterpart of *lafẓ*, the linguistic expression. VI 346a

In philosophy, ~ is used to translate a number of Greek expressions, to denote e.g. concept, thought, idea, meaning, entity. VI 347a

In poetry, ~ meant both the meaning of a word or proposition in a certain given verse, and the meaning of a trope. VI 347b

In Nuṣayriyya terminology, ~ is 'the Essence', a name for God. VIII 148a

♦ al-maʿānī al-thāniya : in philosophy, the five predicables (genus, species, difference, property, accident), also known as *al-alfāẓ al-khamsa*. II 550a

manākh (A) : war for territory, one of the Bedouin's warlike activities. II 1055a

manāḳib (A, s. MANḲABA) : a plural substantive, rendered approximately by 'qualities, virtues, talents, praiseworthy actions', featuring in the titles of a quite considerable number of biographical works of a laudatory nature, which have eventually become a part of hagiographical literature in Arabic, in Persian and in Turkish. Immediately following the development of mysticism and the cult of saints, the subjects preferred are the marvellous aspects of the life, the miracles or at least the prodigies of a ṣūfī or of a saint believed to have been endowed with miraculous powers; hence, ~ ultimately acquires the sense of 'miracles' or 'prodigies'. VI 349a

♦ menāḳib-nāme (Ott) : in literature, the often semi-legendary tales of the worthy exploits of significant political or religious figures. A similar type of exemplary tale, the *ghazā-nāme*, dealt more specifically with military exploits in frontier regions. X 291a

manāḳirī (A) : 'beak-ambergris', according to mediaeval authors, the term for a variety of ambergris which contains the claws and beak of a bird which alights on the lumps and being unable to get away perishes on them. In actuality, ambergris frequently contains the hard mandibles of a cuttle-fish which serves as food to the spermwhale. I 484a

manām → RUʾYĀ

manāniyya → MĀNAWIYYA

manār (A), or *manāra* : lighthouse; an elevated place where a light or beacon is established; the means of marking (with fire, originally) routes for caravans or for the army in war; lampstand; certain kinds of 'arms' (arm-rests of seats, thrones, etc.); minaret, i.e. the tower alongside (or on top of) a mosque, used to call the faithful to prayer (in this sense normally **manāra**). VI 358b; VI 361b

In East Africa, ~ (Sw *mnara*, pl. *minara*) also refers to the pillar tombs which are an architectural peculiarity of the eastern African coast. VI 370a

For ~ in zoology, → HIRKŪL

mānawiyya (A), or *manāniyya* : the Manichaeans. X 439b f.

manāzil → MANZIL

manāẓir (A), or *ʿilm al-manāẓir* : the science of optics. VI 376a

In travel, ~ was used to designate the fires and their sites, near the sea, which guided ships and gave warning of the arrival of an enemy (by lighting the fire in the direction of the town), syn. *nīrān, mawāḳīd, maḥāris*. Some fires were lit on the Mediterranean coast from Alexandria as far as the regions of North Africa. It is even recorded that opposite the Palestinian coast an exchange of signals of this kind was made between ships and the coast. VI 359a

manda → MANDATES

mandala (J) : in East and Central Java, a rural Hindu-Buddhist type of school, where ascetical *gurus* imparted religious doctrine and mystical wisdom to students residing together in a communal setting. It is thought by some scholars to be the precursor of the PESANTREN. VIII 296b

mandara (A) : a large room in an Egyptian house, whose central part, a substitute for the courtyard, is paved, adorned with a fountain and surrounded by two or three ĪWĀNS. II 114b

mandates (Eng, A *intidāb*, T *manda*) : a system of trusteeship, instituted by the League of Nations after the end of the First World War, for the administration of certain territories. VI 385b

mandedji → LIMAN REʾĪSI

mandī : in Muslim India, a market where different commodities, particularly corn, were brought from outside and sold in bulk. During the Dihlī sultanate, the officer who looked after the market in general was called *shaḥna-i mandī*. IX 800b f.

mandīl (A, < L *mantellum*), normalised *mindīl* : handkerchief, napkin, towel; piece of cloth, used for many other purposes, such as covering or carrying something or serving, attached to the body, as an untailored part of dress. Syn. *mas̲h̲ūs̲h̲, mins̲h̲afa, k̲h̲irḳa*. VI 402b; X 613a
In Syria and Palestine, ~ is the name for a woman's head scarf, veil. V 741b
In Iraq, ~ denotes an embroidered kerchief hung from the waist sash by men. V 741b

mand̲j̲ālī (Telugu) : a measure of weight in South India, being the equivalent of a seed notionally used, of about 260 mg. VI 122a

mand̲j̲am → MAʿDIN

mand̲j̲anīḳ (A, < Gk) : mangonel; a general term for any kind of stone-throwing siege-engine. The expressions ~ and *ʿarrāda* are both used for this kind of machine, and although the *ʿarrāda* may have been the smaller of the two, the expressions often seem to be interchangeable. III 469b; III 472b; VI 405a

mandūb (A) : in law, a meritorious and recommended action. VI 408a

mandrāg̲h̲ūras → SIRĀD̲J̲ AL-ḲUṬRUB

mangh (Sin), or *mungh* : in Sind, wind catchers, from around 1 m square and up to 2 m high, which rise above the flat roofs of houses to catch the summer wind. IX 638a

mang̲h̲ir (T) : an Ottoman copper coin. II 118a; VIII 229a

manhad̲j̲ (A, pl. *manāhid̲j̲*) : in mediaeval times, an avenue separating tribal lots, as in in the establishment of the town of al-Kūfa where there were 15, each forty cubits wide, radiating from the central area. V 346a

manhal (A, pl. manāhil) : in Medina, a public watering place, about 10 m below ground and reached by steps. V 1007a

manhūk (A) : in prosody, a deviation in the metre consisting of a line being 'weakened to exhaustion', i.e. when it is reduced to a third of its size. I 671a

manḥūl (A) : in literary criticism, an existing piece of poetry that is falsely attributed. XII 648a

māni (T, < A *maʿnā*) : a form of Turkish popular poetry, most usually a piece of poetry made up of heptasyllabic verses rhymed on the pattern *a a b a*, but there are also some rhymed *b a c a*; each quatrain may be sufficient to fulfil a certain function or to transmit a certain message. VI 420b
♦ kesik māni : 'truncated *māni*', a MĀNI reduced to the schema *a b a* by the disappearance of the first verse. VI 420b

manḳaba (A, pl. MANĀḲIB) : a narrow street between two houses; a difficult path on the mountain; a noble action. VI 349b
♦ manḳabat (U) : in Urdu poetry, praise of the fourth caliph, ʿAlī, and of subsequent s̲h̲īʿī IMĀMs. V 958a; VIII 776a

manḳāna (A) : a clock, constructed in the 9th century in Muslim Spain by ʿAbbās b. Firnās. I 11b

manḳūl (A) : 'moveable', in its plural form *manḳūlāt* 'moveable properties'. XI 89a

mann (A) : the standard weight for small quantities of dry (and even liquid) commodities in most provinces of Persia. VI 120a; in Egypt, the ~ was used to weigh spices such as cinnamon, nutmeg, mace, cloves, cubeb and borax. VI 119a; one ~ equals approximately two pounds. XI 269b

manṣab (IndP) : a term of the military system of the Mug̲h̲als in India, denoting a rank, the holder of which was termed *manṣabdār*. Personal or D̲H̲ĀT rank was expressed numerically in even-numbered decimal increments and could vary from as low as 20 *d̲h̲āt* to a maximum of 7000 *d̲h̲āt* for the highest nobles. *D̲h̲āt* determined the *manṣabdār*'s relative status and his pay. *Manṣabdārs* could simultaneously hold trooper, or SUWĀR, ranks. VI 422b
♦ manṣabdārī (IndP) : in the Mug̲h̲al period, the monolithic military and civil service organisation introduced by Akbar. V 685b

manṣabdār → MANṢAB
man<u>sh</u>ad → KABĀRA
man<u>sh</u>ūr (A, pl. *man<u>sh</u>ūrāt, manā<u>sh</u>īr*) : lit. spread out, ~ has come to mean a certificate, an edict, a diploma of appointment, and particularly, a patent granting an appanage. VI 423a
In Egypt in the early Arab period, ~ was a pass which the government compelled the peasants to have, designed to curb increasing movement away from the land. II 303a; VI 423a
In ʿAbbāsid times, ~ was given to grants of fiefs, while under the Fāṭimids (and Ayyūbids) it denoted certain letters of appointment. Under the Mamlūks, ~ became restricted to feudal grants, in different grades according to size and writing. II 303a; VI 423b; VIII 814b
In modern Egypt, edicts of the government are called ~. In many Arabic states, serial publications now are called *man<u>sh</u>ūrāt*. VI 424b
In mathematics, ~ means prism. VI 424b
In astronomy, *man<u>sh</u>ūrāt* denotes spherical prisms; according to Ptolemy, 'sawn pieces' or 'disks' comprised between two circles parallel to and equidistant from the equator of a sphere. II 763a
♦ **man<u>sh</u>ūrāt** (A) : term for the letters, responsa and edicts of Muḥammad b. ʿAbd Allāh, the Sudanese Mahdī (d. 1885), which were transcribed by his followers in numerous manuscript collections. XII 594a; and → MAN<u>SH</u>ŪR
mansir → MIḲNAB
manṣūb (A) : the chief agent in India of the Yemeni Sulaymānī sect, which split from the Bohorās in the 10th/16th century. I 1255a; IX 829b
For ~ in grammar, → NAṢB
In its plural form, *manṣūbāt*, lit. set-ups, was the term for the numerous problems in the game of chess. IX 366b
manṭal (A) : in Yemeni architecture, the 'long drop', where the fuel, human excrement, for heating the bath is kept. IX 2b
manṭiḳ (A) : in philosophy, logic. VI 442a
mantū : a steamed dumpling, one of the Özbeg noodle dishes for which their cuisine is known. VIII 234b
manzil (A, T *menzil*; pl. *manāzil*) : a halt; a temporary stay; stage of a journey. VI 454b; hospice or night lodging intended for travellers; a stopping place for caravans. I 1225a; IV 1011a; VI 455a; at the present time, ~ denotes a lodging, a house and even an apartment. V 455a
At the end of the Ottoman period, ~ signified a private hostelry, as opposed to the *maḍāfa*, which was communal. VI 455a
In Iran and, especially, in Hindūstān, ~ came to designate a camp, characteristically the royal camp. VI 456a
In astronomy, **manāzil**, or, more fully, *manāzil al-ḳamar*, are the lunar mansions, or stations of the moon, a system of 28 stars, groups of stars, or spots in the sky near which the moon is found in each of the 28 nights of her monthly revolution. I 523a; VI 374a
In mysticism, ~ is the stage in the spiritual journey of the soul. III 84a; VI 454b
♦ manzila → MAWḌIʿ
♦ **al-manzila bayn al-manzilatayn** (A) : a theological term used by Wāṣil b. ʿAṭāʾ and the later Muʿtazila for designating the salvational status of the mortal sinner. They held that any Muslim guilty of a serious sin is neither believer nor non-believer, and is liable to punishment in the Fire. I 694b; VI 457b; XI 165a
♦ menzil-<u>kh</u>āne → ULAḲ
manẓūm → ḤALL AL-MANẒŪM

mar'a (A) : a woman. VI 466a
marʿā (A) : pasture. VI 490a
♦ marāʿī (P) : a pasture tax in Īlkhān Persia (syn. *ʿalafkh*ʷ*ār, ʿalafčar*). IV 1042a; VI 491b; in 19th-century usage in Kāshān, ~ was a tax on sheep and goats levied at so much per animal which bore young and was in milk. IV 1042b
maraḍ (A) : illness, with ~ *al-mawt* being the last illness. XI 172b
marāfiḳ (A, s. *marfiḳ*) : lit. benefits, favours, one of several terms used for bribes, douceurs. This form of bribery became institutionalised in the ʿAbbāsid caliphate with the establishment of a special office, the *dīwān al-marāfiḳ*, in which were placed bribes and money from commissions collected from aspiring candidates for office. II 325a; VI 498a
marāʿī → MARʿĀ
maraḳ (A), or *maraḳa* : in the terminology of food, a broth. II 1059a
maʿraḳa → ʿARAḲIYYA
marāṣid (A), or *ma'āṣir* : customs, dues and tolls which exist on the frontiers, on the international trade routes, and the ports. II 143a; and → MA'ṢIR
marāsim (A) : official court ceremonies, both processional and non-processional. Synonyms are *rusūm*, especially for the whole range of ceremonial, including protocol and etiquette, MAWSIM and *mawkib* (→ MAWĀKIB). VI 518a
marātib (A, s. **martaba**) : lit. ranks, degrees, a term applied especially in Muslim India to the drums and standards, *aṭbāl wa ʿalamāt*, borne by the sultan or conferred by him on the great AMĪRs, later elaborated as 'standards, kettledrums, trumpets, bugles and reedpipe' as carried by two ships among the fifteen of the governor of Lāharī Bandar. The ~ could function as battle ensigns. VI 536b; XII 600b
marbaṭ (A, pl. *marābiṭ*), or *marbiṭ* : the place where domestic animals are tethered. Among the nomads, the ~ simply involves tying the animal's halter to some bush or a large stone buried in the sand. For sedentary and urban populations, the ~ takes the form of a kind of shelter, beneath which animals can shelter from the sun. By extension, ~ very soon took on the general sense of stables. VI 537b
In Saudi Arabia and the United Arab Emirates, ~ and *mirsal* are also the names of the 'leash' which holds the falcon down to its perching-block or on the falconer's gauntlet. VI 537b
marḍī (N.Afr, pl. *marāḍī*) : in the customary law of the Bedouin of the Western Desert and Cyrenaica, a mediator, although glossed in some sources as a judge. X 889b
mardjaʿ-i taḳlīd (P) : a title and function of a hierarchical nature denoting a Twelver jurisconsult who is to be considered during his lifetime, by virtue of his qualities and his wisdom, a model for reference, for 'imitation' or 'emulation' by every observant Imāmī shīʿī (with the exception of other MUDJTAHIDs) on all aspects of religious practice and law. VI 548b; XII 103b
mardjān (A) : in mineralogy, coral. As a rule, red coral (*Corallium rubrum*) is used as a piece of jewelry; in medicine, ~ is used above all in collyria against eye diseases. The Persian *bussadh*, often employed as a synonym, is strictly speaking the root of the coral, as well as the subsoil to which it is stuck. VI 556a
mardjūḥa → URDJŪḤA
mardūd (A) : in the science of Tradition, a 'rejected' Tradition, more particularly a Tradition from a weak transmitter which contradicts what authorities transmit. III 26b
mardūf → RIDFA
marfa' → MĪNĀ'
marfiḳ → MARĀFIḲ
marfūʿ (A, pl. *marfūʿāt*) : lit. lifted up.

In the science of Tradition, a Tradition traced back to the Prophet whether or not the ISNĀD is complete. Transmitters who developed the habit of frequently 'raising' ISNĀD strands 'to the level' of *marfūʿāt* were called *raffāʿūn*. III 25b; VIII 384a; and → MUTTAṢIL; RAFʿ

marfūw → TĀMM

marḥala (A, pl. *marāḥil*) : in mediaeval Islamic usage, a stage of travel, normally the distance which a traveller can cover in one day; it was, therefore, obviously a variable measurement of length, dependent on the ease or difficulty of the terrain to be crossed. VI 558b

marham (A) : in medicine, a pomade, prescribed among others as an aphrodisiac. XII 641b

mārī → BAḤZAD̲J̲

mārid (A) : a term found once in the Qurʾān, meaning rebel, someone practicing *murūd* or *tamarrud* 'resistance to the established order', but, with ʿIFRĪT, ended by being used of one particular class of fantastic beings from the nether regions. The popular tales represent the ~ as being superior to the *ʿifrīt*: he is forty times stronger and has at his command a thousand auxiliaries. III 1050a; IX 406b; XII 598a

maʿriḍ (A) : 'place of display', term in some countries for a public slave market which every big town had in the mediaeval period. I 32b

maʿrifa (A) : knowledge, cognition. III 1133a; VI 568b

In grammar, ~ designates the definite noun, as opposed to *nakira*, indefinite noun. VI 569a

In onomastics, ~ is the appellative formed of Ibn followed by the ISM, LAḲAB or NISBA of the father or of an ancestor, sometimes celebrated but more often obscure. This is also called *s̲h̲uhra*. III 670a

māristān (A) : a lunatic asylum. I 500b

māriyya (A) : a pearl-grey tone of e.g. the plumage of sandgrouse. IV 744a

markab (A) : lit. conveyance; in early Arabic usage, the most general word for 'ship' . The term was, however, used in the first place for travel by land, with such specific meanings as 'riding-beast', 'conveyance drawn by animals'. VIII 808a

marḳab (A) : observatory; an elevated site from which it is possible to see and observe, such as the summit of a mountain, of a fortified castle or of a watch-tower. VI 577a

♦ marḳaba (A) : the mountain refuge of a brigand-poet. IX 865b

markaz → MUWAS̲H̲S̲H̲AḤ

mārk(i)siyya (A, < Ger Marx) : Marxism, the doctrine developed by Karl Marx and Friedrich Engels in the 19th century. VI 583a

marḳiyūniyya (A) : in religion, the Marcionites, an important non-monotheistic tendency in early Christianity. XII 599b

markūb (A) : pointed men's shoes of thick red morocco, worn in Egypt. V 741b

marmar → RUK̲H̲ĀM

marnab (A) : in zoology, the Brown rat (*Mus decumanus*) or 'Sewer rat'. XII 285b

marsā → MĪNĀʾ

marṣad (A) : a place where one keeps watch; in astronomy, an observatory (syn. *raṣad*). VI 599b

marsūm (A) : in the science of diplomatic, a grade of appointment used for military personnel in Mamlūk times only. Distinction is made between major and minor appointments: *mukabbara* is the appointment of the commander of a fortress and military persons of medium rank, and *muṣag̲h̲g̲h̲ara* is the appointment for the lower ranks. II 303a

In Saudi Arabia, an administrative order issued by the King (rather than ḲANŪN). X 353b

martaba (A) : a term with a variety of meanings: class, rank, degree assigned by etiquette, rank, hierarchy, arrangement of places in an audience, sofa, an upholstered piece of furniture. XII 600b; and → ḤUKM; MARĀTIB

martak (A) : in mineralogy, yellow lead. IX 872b

mar<u>th</u>āt → MAR<u>TH</u>IYA

mar<u>th</u>iya (A, pl. *marā<u>th</u>ī*), or *mar<u>th</u>āt* : elegy, a poem composed in Arabic (or in an Islamic language following the Arabic tradition) to lament the passing of a beloved person and to celebrate his merits. IV 1027a; VI 602b

In Urdu poetry, the ~ is almost always religious and usually about the Karbalāʾ martyrs, although a secular type exists. V 635b; VI 610b

martolos (T, < Gk) : a salaried member of the Ottoman internal security forces, recruited predominantly in the Balkans from among chosen land-owning Orthodox Christians who, retaining their religion, became members of the Ottoman ʿASKARĪ caste. By 1722 the institution was merged with the Muslim local security police. VI 613a

maʿrūf (A) : in the science of Tradition, a weak Tradition confirmed by another weak one, or a Tradition superior in MATN or ISNĀD to one called MUNKAR; also, a traditionist when two or more transmit from him. III 26b

marumakkatyam : in southern India, a law of inheritance whereby the children of the sister inherit, practiced by the Moplas. I 172a

mārūniyya (A, < Syr), or *mawārina* : in religion, the name of the Syrian Christian sect of the Maronites, which first entered into union with the Roman Catholic Church in ca. A.D. 1180. XII 602a

maryamiyya (A) : in botany, *Salvia triloba*. VI 631b

maryūl (N.Afr) : a short, embroidered shift for women in Libya. V 746a

marzpān (P, A *marzubān*) : warden of the march, markgrave; the title of a military governor of a frontier province under the Sāsānids in the 4th or 5th centuries AD. By mid-6th century, the ~ had become a high-ranking military and administrative official. After the decline of the Sāsānid empire, *marzubān* survived at Marw and Marw al-Rūd as the title of local Iranian officials under Muslim rule. It came to be used as a proper name and was also used metaphorically in poetry for a ruler or master, or for a leader of the Magians. VI 633a

masāʾ (A) : originally, 'evening twilight', but today applied to the evening, as opposed to *ṣabāḥ* 'morning'. It also comes to designate the period which begins at noon and encroaches upon the night. V 709b

maṣāff (A) : a line of troops. II 1080a

♦ maṣāffiyya : a corps of slaves, probably originating from those employed to form a line of troops in the reception rooms of the ʿAbbāsid court, under the command of the Chamberlain and numbering 10,000 men. In 317/929, the ~ forced the caliph al-Ḳāhir to flee. They were massacred in 318/930. II 1080b

masāḥa (A) : one of three ways of assessing land tax, <u>KH</u>ARĀ<u>DJ</u>, the other two being MUḲĀSAMA and MUḲĀṬAʿA. The amount due was based on the measurement of the land, but ~ did not, however, involve a comprehensive cadastral survey. Usually only the land sown was taken into account. It differed from the *muḳāsama* system in that the tax demand did not vary in a good year or a bad year. Known in the early centuries, it continued to be used down to modern times. IV 1037b

masāʾil → MASʾALA

masak → <u>DH</u>ABL

masʾala (A, pl. *masāʾil*) : question, problem.

♦ al-masʾala al-minbariyya : in law, a particular problem of inheritance, which ʿAlī is reported to have solved off-hand when it was submitted to him while he was on the MINBAR. I 765a

♦ al-mas'ala al-**suraydjiyya** : in law, a hotly debated problem of repudiation to which Ibn Suraydj, the S̲h̲āfiʿī jurist, gave his name. III 949b; IX 893b

♦ **masā'il wa-adjwiba** : lit. questions and answers, a technique of argumentation in mediaeval Islam which has strongly influenced, both in form and content, numerous Arabic writings in virtually all fields of knowledge. Unsolved problems, or questions and objections propounded by a third person, are followed by answers or explanations and refutations. Sometimes the author, at the request of a third person, composed a monograph on a group of themes, and even dedicated it to him. The pattern of questions and answers often became a literary topos, and, finally, the pattern also turned into a technique of scientific research or presentation, without any dialogue between teacher and pupil or between two opponents. VI 636a

♦ masā'il mulak̲h̲k̲h̲aba : in law, a category of questions 'called by special names', to which e.g. the AKDARIYYA belongs. I 320a

masāliḥ → AFĀWIH; MAṢLAḤA

masālik wa-mamālik (A) : 'routes and kingdoms', in geographical literature, the name given by R. Blachère to what he saw as a sub-genre. VI 639b

maʿṣara (A) : in early Islam, a shallow vat, in which, for example, grapes were trodden. IV 997b

maṣdar (A) : in grammar, the verbal noun. IX 528a

masdjid (A) : mosque. The modern Western European words (Eng *mosque*, Fr *mosquée*, Ger *Moschee*, It *moschea*) come ultimately from the Arabic via Spanish *mezquita*. VI 644b

The word is used in the Qur'ān for sanctuary, especially the Meccan sanctuary; ~ is also applied to pre-Islamic sanctuaries. Even as late as Ibn K̲h̲aldūn, ~ is used in the general meaning of a temple or place of worship of any religion. VI 644b

♦ **al-masdjid al-akṣā** : lit. the remotest sanctuary; in the Qur'ān, ~ is opposed to 'the sacred [pagan] sanctuary' of Mecca, but in the context of the time it is not clear whether ~ meant an actual physical sanctuary or a spiritual one. There was very early consensus, perhaps as early as 15 AH, that ~ meant Jerusalem. Today, the most common use of ~ is for the large building located on the south side of the Ḥaram platform and next to the Dome of the Rock in Jerusalem. VI 707a

♦ masdjid djāmiʿ : in early Islam, the common name used for the chief (Friday) mosque in a certain place, but by the time of al-Maḳrīzī (9th/15th century), the word *djāmiʿ* meant any mosque of some size. VI 656a

♦ **al-masdjid al-ḥarām** : the name of the Mosque of Mecca, already found in the pre-Islamic period. IV 708a

♦ **masdjidī** (A, pl. *masdjidiyyūn*) : an adjective specifically concerning the Friday mosque of Baṣra in the time of al-D̲j̲āḥiẓ and used to designate groups of adults or young people who were accustomed to meet together in that building, near the gate of the Banū Sulaym, as well as of poets, popular story-tellers, and transmitters of religious, historical and literary Traditions, in particular those regarding poetic verses. VI 709a

māsh : the mungo bean. X 31b

mʿās̲h̲ → KUSKUSŪ

al-masḥ ʿalā 'l-k̲h̲uffayn (A) : lit. the act of passing the hand over the boots; a term designating the right whereby sunnī Muslims may, in certain circumstances, pass the hand over their shoes instead of washing their feet as a means of preparing themselves for the saying of the ritual prayer. VI 709b

mās̲h̲ā' allāh (A) : a phrase occurring in the Qur'ān and widely used in the Islamic lands of the Middle East with the general meaning of 'what God does, is well done'. The formula denotes that things happen according to God's will and should therefore be accepted with humility and resignation. In a cognate signification, the phrase is often used to indicate a vague, generally a great or considerable, but sometimes a small, number or quantity of time. The phrase is also the equivalent of the English 'God knows what', and, as signifying 'what God has willed', expressing admiration or surprise. VI 710b

mashādjin (A) : water-driven trip-hammers, i.e. stones fitted to axles which are installed on running water for pounding e.g. ores or flax for paper. V 969b

mashaffa → SHAFFĀFIYYA

mashaʾiyya → ISHRĀḲIYYŪN

mashʿal (A) : torches, e.g. that accompanied the bridegroom to the bath. X 905a

mashʿar (A, pl. *mashāʿir*) : a place or thing which puts one in the presence or gives a feeling of the sacred or of a divinity; a place where the rites of sacrifice were performed. The journey between ʿArafa and Minā and that between al-Ṣafā and al-Marwa is called *al-mashʿar al-ḥarām*. IX 424b, where are found synonyms

mashāriḳa (A) : the Arabs and Arabised peoples of the East in contrast to those of the West called MAGHĀRIBA. VI 712a

mashāyikh → SHAYKH

mashdūd → SHADD

mashhad (A) : any sacred place, not necessarily having a construction associated with it; a tomb in general, the burial place of an earlier prophet, saint or forerunner of Muḥammad or of any Muslim who had had pronounced over him the profession of faith; a martyrium; any small building with obvious religious features like a MIḤRĀB. V 289a; VI 713b

♦ mashhadī (A, P) : a pilgrim to the shrine of the eighth IMĀM ʿAlī al-Riḍā who has performed all the rites in the prescribed fashion. XII 605b

mashhūr (A) : in the science of Tradition, a well-known Tradition transmitted via a minimum of three different ISNĀDs. III 25b; VI 717a

In law, the 'predominant' opinion, as opposed to the isolated or 'anomalous' opinion, SHĀDHDH. I 428a

mashīkha → FAHRASA; MASHYAKHA

mashḳ → KŪFĪ

mashla (A) : a variety of ʿABĀʾ made in Baghdad. V 741b

mashlaḥ (A), or *mushallaḥ, mashlakh, maḥras* : an undressing and rest room found in the steam bath. III 141a

mashlakh → MASHLAḤ

mashraba (A) : a niche attached to lattice wooden windows known as MASHRABIYYA where the water jars were kept cool and fresh for drinking. VI 717b

mashrabiyya (A) : a technique of turned wood used to produce lattice-like panels, like those which were used in the past to adorn the windows in traditional domestic architecture. The ~ technique is a speciality of Cairo, where it was used with a latitude of patterns and combinations. The panels are composed of small pieces of wood which are turned in various forms and are fixed together without glue or nails, but simply by being inserted into each other, thus giving the panel more resistance towards the flexibility of the wood with the change of temperature. V 1153a; VI 717b

mashriḳ (A) : the East; for the Arab world, all the lands to the east of Egypt. VI 720a; and → MAṬLAʿ

♦ **mashriḳ al-adhkār** (A) : a term used in the Bahāʾī movement for four related concepts: a). In Iran (loosely) to describe early morning gatherings for reading of prayers and sacred writings. b). Generally of any house erected for the purpose of prayer. c). Most widely, to refer to Bahāʾī temples. d). In its widest application, to refer to a central temple in conjunction with various dependencies regarded as intrinsic to the overall institution. These include a school for orphans, hospital and dispensary for the poor, home for the aged, home for the infirm, college of higher education, and traveller's hospice. With the exception of a home for the aged in Wilmette, Illinois, no dependencies have as yet been established. I 918a; VI 720a

mashrūʿ (A) : in law, the lawful act, as a term sometimes used in place of DJĀʾIZ as e.g. in the contract of crop-sharing and in the contract of association. II 390a

mashrūbāt (A) : drinks, which in law are a subject of particular interest due to those that are permitted and those that are forbidden. VI 720b

mashrūṭ (A) : inferior marriage, a legal institution characteristic of North Africa, called AMAZZAL among the Zemmur in Morocco. I 171b

♦ mashrūṭiyyat (P) : a constitution. X 493a

mashshāʾiyya (A, < Gk *peripatētikoi*) : the Peripatetic or Aristotelian school of Greek philosophy and its Arabo-Islamic followers. While in the Greek sources, the designation is restricted to Aristotle's personal disciples, the Arabic equivalent is used for the Hellenistic tradition of his philosophy in general. Synonyms are *mashshāʾūn, mashshāʾiyyūn, mushāt*. XII 605b

mashtā → ḲĪSHLAḲ

mashtūm → SHATM

mashṭūr (A) : in prosody, a deviation in the metre consisting of the suppression of a complete half, *shaṭr*, as e.g. when the RADJAZ is reduced to one hemistich. I 671a

maṣḥūb → ṢĀḤIB

masḥūra → ARGHŪL

mashūra → MASHWARA

mashūsh → MANDĪL

mashwara (A, T *meshweret*), or *mashūra* : consultation, in particular by the ruler of his advisers, the latter being variously defined. The term sometimes also appears to mean some kind of deliberative gathering or assembly. Among Ottoman historians, ~ was commonly used to denote ad hoc meetings and councils of military and other dignitaries to consider problems as they arose. The sultan was not normally present at such gatherings. In the course of the 19th century, ~ or *meshweret* was much used by Turkish and Arabic authors, first to describe European representative institutions, and then to justify their introduction to the Islamic lands. VI 724a

mashyakha (A, s. *shaykh*), or *mashīkha* : a plural of SHAYKH and an abstract noun denoting a *shaykh*'s position or authority. VI 725b

In the Muslim West ~ was used to designate the collectivity of urban elders and notables often wielding considerable political influence in the cities and hence carrying the sense of a 'municipal council'. VI 725b

During Bonaparte's Egyptian expedition, ~ acquired a new meaning. Seeking an Arabic expression for 'republic', Bonaparte's orientalist experts came to use ~. This was apparently an intended allusion to the Directoire of five who were governing France at the time. In the second half of the 19th century, ~ in the sense of republic gave ground to **djumhūriyya**. II 594a; VI 725b; and → FAHRASA

maṣīf → YAYLAḲ

masīḥ (A, < Ar) : with the definitve article, the Messiah. The root word in Arabic has the meanings of 'to measure' and 'to wipe, stroke'. VI 726a

masika (Sw) : in Zanzibar, the Long Rains, which last with decreasing vigour for about three months starting in March. The Short Rains, *mvuli*, fall in October and November. XI 447a

masīkh → MALĪKH; MASKH

maʾṣir (Akk ?) : a technical term of fiscal practice in the hydraulic civilisation of early Islamic ʿIrāḳ, doubtless going back to earlier periods there. From being a barrier across the river to halt shipping, ~ soon acquired the meaning of 'customs house where tolls are collected' and then the actual tolls themselves. VI 728b

♦ ma'āṣiriyyūn : a body of officials attached to the police guard of Baghdad in the caliphate of al-Muʿtaḍid (279-89/892-902) who collected tolls from river traffic on the Tigris. VI 729a; and → MARĀṢID

maʿṣiya (A, pl. *maʿṣiyāt*) : in theology, an act of disobedience; when used in reference to the prescriptions of the divine law, often becoming a syn. of KHAṬĪʾA or DHANB. IV 1107b; and → ṬĀʿA

maskh (A) : the metamorphosis of men into animals. The product of the metamorphosis is called ~ (*miskh*) or *masīkh* (*mamsūkh*). II 95b; III 305b; VI 736b; X 182a

maskūk (A, pl. *maskūkāt*) : coined money. IX 592a

maṣl (A) : dried curd cheese. X 31b

♦ maṣliyya : a dish of lamb (or kid), with finely-chopped dried curd cheese, *maṣl*, sprinkled on top. of traditional Arab provenance. X 31b

maṣlaḥa (A, pl. *maṣāliḥ*) : the concept in Islam of public interest or welfare. II 254b; VI 738b

In law, ~ in the sense of 'general good' and 'public interest' is used as a basis for legal decisions. I 276a; VI 738b; IX 324b

In Ibn Rusta, 'fort'. X 82b; garrison. X 306a

♦ maṣlaḥatgüzār (T) : in Ottoman diplomacy, the term for *chargé d'affaires*. II 694a; and → ḲĀʾIM BI-AʿMĀL

maslaka (A) : with ṬARĪḲ, a term for road, but figuring prominently in Arabic geographical literature in the name of a sub-genre, the 'road books', e.g. AL-MASĀLIK WA 'L-MAMĀLIK, an important element of which was the fixing of the geographical coordinates of places. XII 794b

maṣliyya → MAṢL

maslūb (A) : in medicine, castrated by evulsion. IV 1087a

maṣnaʿa (A, pl. *maṣāniʿ*) : a Qurʾānic word meaning 'notable palaces, fortresses and edifices in which special endeavours are invested'. IX 626a

maṣnūʿ (A) : 'artful', as contrasted with 'natural'. XII650b; in literary criticism, a forged piece of poetry (syn. *mawḍūʿ*, *muftaʿal*). XII 648a

masraba (A) : beginning of the stomach. IX 312a

maṣraf defteri (T) : in Ottoman administration, the household account book of viziers and governors, or of palace personnel such as waterbearers, which covered for time periods of a month up to several years detailed monthly inventories of household economic transactions. VI 745b

masraḥ (A) : 'scene', increasingly employed as 'theatre' (frequently synonymous with *tiyātrō* (< It); in Arabic literature, primarily a phenomenon of the last two centuries. VI 746a

mast (A), or *mazz, mazd, mizz* : a long stocking of soft, yellow leather; inner shoe worn by both sexes in the Arab East. V 741b; and → ṬARAB

māst → YOGHURT

maṣṭaba (A) : in topography, an elevated piece of land in the north of Palestine, used for pitching the Mamlūk sultan's pavilion on top when he travelled through. V 594a

In architecture, a seat of stone, e.g. alongside a fountain. V 681b

mastaka (J), or *mustaka* : an ornament on top of a sphere on the roof of a Javanese mosque. In later times, this ornament was crowned by a crescent as the decisive symbol of Islam. VI 700b

maʿṣūm (A) : in theology, sinless, like the Prophet. XI 110b; immune from error and sin. XI 478a

masūmi (A) : a fine ʿABĀʾ of white wool for men, produced in Baghdad. V 741b

masura → LÜLE
maʿtab → KABĀRA
maṭāf (A) : the term for the pavement on which the circumambulation of the Kaʿba is performed. IV 318a
maṭāliʿ → MAṬLAʿ
maṭar (A) : a measure of capacity for liquids, e.g. olive oil, used in mediaeval Egypt. According to a Venetian source, the ~ contained, in the later Middle Ages, about 17 kg of olive oil. VI 119b
maṭbaʿa (A) : printing, printing-house, printing-press; the Arabic verb *ṭabaʿa* in the sense of printing a book is a neologism probably inspired by the Italian or the French. VI 794b
maṭbakh (A, pl. *maṭābikh*) : kitchen, cookhouse, also in mediaeval times, undoubtedly also slaughterhouse. VI 807a
maṭārif (A) : items of streaked silk originating from Yemen. IX 866a
matbūʿ (A) : in prosody, a natural poet, 'poète de génie', as opposed to a painstaking poet, 'poète d'étude', *mutakallif*. XII 648b; and → ITBĀʿ
maṭfara (A, pl. *maṭāfira*) : in music, a place of 'jumping' towards higher notes. IX 101a
mathal (A, pl. *amthāl*) : a proverb, popular saying, also comprising the extensive group of comparisons involving a comparative in the form *afʿal^u min*; adages (gnomes, dicta); set turns of speech; parable, fable. III 369b; VI 815b; a figurative expression. IV 248b
mathālib (A, s. *mathlaba, mathluba*) : lit. faults, vices, defects; disgrace; in early Islam, ~ was broadly applied to what were regarded as subjects of shame for the tribes, the ethnic groups or even clans, rather than separate individuals; ~ was used in poetry in connection with themes in satire to denigrate or revile an enemy. Later, ~ appeared in the titles of a number of works usually written by genealogists and collectors of historical Traditions and can be contrasted with *maʾāthir* or *mafākhir* 'exploits, feats, glorious titles' and MANĀḲIB. I 892a; VI 828a
mathānī (A) : a technical term used in the Qurʾān, the precise meaning of which is unclear. It refers to the revelation sent down to Muḥammad and commentators have usually understood it to refer to the (seven) verses of the Fātiḥa, the first chapter of the Qurʾān. Another interpretation is that ~ refers to the punishment-stories, which may have once formed a collection separate from the Qurʾān. V 402a
mathlath → ZĪR
mathnā → ZĪR
mathnāt (A) : an expression, mentioned by al-Djawharī, that may refer to the quatrain. It is said to be equivalent to 'what is called in Persian DŪBAYTĪ, which is singing (*al-ghināʾ*)'. VIII 583b
mathnawī (A, P, T, U) : in literature, a poem written in rhyming couplets. In Arabic such a poem is called MUZDAWIDJ. The single characteristic which separates the ~ from all other classical verse forms is its rhyming scheme *aa bb cc*, etc. Otherwise, the name is given to poems differing greatly in genre as well as in length and composition; this form is eminently suitable for epic and didactic verse because of the freedom allowed in rhyming. I 677a; IV 58a ff.; V 201a; VI 832a
maṭlaʿ (A, pl. *maṭāliʿ*) : in astrology, the rising point of a celestial body, usually a star, on the local horizon. This concept was important in Islamic folk astronomy, as distinct from mathematical astronomy, because it was by the risings and settings of the sun and stars that the ḲIBLA, the direction of Mecca, was usually determined in popular practice. The terms used for the rising and setting points of the sun were usually *mashriḳ* and *maghrib*, ~ being generally reserved for stars. The term ~ was also used to denote the 'time of rising' in the expression *maṭlaʿ al-fadjr*, daybreak or the beginning of morning twilight. VI 839a

In poetry, ~ refers to the first distich of a poem, which opens the poem and signals all the areas of expression. IV 714b

In shadow-play terminology, the prologue with which it starts. IV 1136b

Its plural, **maṭāliʿ**, denoted ascensions, an important concept in mediaeval spherical astronomy and astronomical timekeeping. ~ represent a measure of the amount of apparent rotation of the celestial sphere, and are usually measured from the eastern horizon. Two kinds were used: (1) right ascensions, or ascensions in *sphaera recta*; and (2) oblique ascensions, or ascensions in *sphaera obliqua*. Right ascensions refer to the risings of arcs of the ecliptic over the horizon of a locality with latitude zero, and were called in mediaeval scientific Arabic *maṭāliʿ fi 'l-falak al-mustaḳīm*. Oblique ascensions, associated with a specific latitude, were called *maṭāliʿ al-balad* or *al-maṭāliʿ al-baladiyya*. VI 792b

maṭlūb → ṬĀLIB

maṭmūra (A, pl. *maṭāmīr*) : a natural or man-made cavity used for the concealment of victuals or of riches; a silo. VI 842a; a cave, large or small and very deep, in which prisoners or Christian slaves were confined; subterranean prison. VI 843a

Al-Djāḥiẓ calls the (subterranean ?) cells of monks by the plural form, *maṭāmīr*. VI 842b

matn (A) : text, especially the text of a book as distinguished from its oral explanation or its written or printed commentary. VI 843a

In medicine, castration by incising and at the same time cauterising the scrotum by means of a red-hot blade of iron and removing the testicles (syn. *mals, khiṣāʾ*). IV 1088a

In the science of Tradition, ~ denotes the content or text itself, as distinct from the chain of traditionists who have handed it down, ISNĀD. VI 843a; VIII 514b

For ~ in archery, → ḲIDḤ

maṭrāḳ (A) : a contest with a stick, cudgel or rapier for the purpose of training and knight-errantry. VI 843b

maṭrūḥ (A) : in the science of Tradition, a rejected Tradition, held by some to be synonymous with a Tradition that is MATRŪK, by others to be a separate class of Traditions less acceptable than ḌAʿĪF, but not so bad as *mawḍūʿ* 'fictitious', the worst type of all. III 26b

matrūk (A) : in law, land placed at the disposal of corporate bodies. II 900b; in Ottoman land law, a category of land called *arāḍī-yi matrūka* 'assigned lands', e.g. roads, rivers, village commons, etc. V 473a; VI 844b

In the science of Tradition, ~ is a Tradition from a single transmitter who is suspected of falsehood in Tradition, or is openly wicked in deed or word, or is guilty of much carelessness or frequent wrong notions. III 26b

maʿṭūf → ʿAṬF

maʿūna (A, pl. *maʿūnāt, maʿāwin*) : lit. assistance; an administrative term of early Islamic history with several meanings. In texts relating to the pre-ʿAbbāsid period, it refers to allocations comparable with, but distinct from, stipends and rations. ~ was sometimes a gratuity paid to those who were not in receipt of stipends, sometimes a bonus supplementary to stipends, and sometimes a regular (more precisely, annual) payment made to those in receipt of stipends and rations alike; *maʿūnāt* was even used as a global term for private income from public funds. From the 3rd/9th century onwards, the leader of the ~ was charged with police duties. The actual police building was called ~ too, at least by the time of the Geniza documents. VI 848b

mawākib (A, s. *mawkib*) : processions, specifically solemn processions; audience. VI 518a; VI 849b; XII 612b; in Turkish usage, *mawkib*, or *mewkib-i hümāyūn*, was used for the prince's procession while for the sultan either *rikāb* or *binish* were common. VIII 529a

mawāḳīd → MANĀẒIR
mawālid → MAWLID
mawāliyā (A, pl. *mawāliyāt*), or *mawāliyyā, mawālī* and *muwālayāt* : in poetry, a non-classical Arabic verse form which was well established by the 6th/12th century, when it always occurs as four hemistichs of BASĪṬ, all with the same rhyme. Later, it was elaborated into a variety of multi-rhyme compositions. VI 867b
As folk-verse, ~ is a favourite in Arab lands. In common parlance the composition itself is almost always called a *mawwāl*, although ~ is still used, especially in writing. III 289b; VI 868a
In music, *mawwāl* also stands for an interpretative freesong, with no set tune. VI 868b
māward → MĀʾ AL-WARD
mawārina → MĀRŪNIYYA
mawā<u>sh</u>ī (P), and *mawā<u>sh</u>* : a tax in Īl<u>kh</u>ān Persia levied on flocks and herds. IV 1042a,b
mawāt (A) : in law, dead lands, land which is uncultivated or merely lying fallow, which belongs to nobody and which is, in general, far from centres of population. Legal scholars use **iḥyāʾ** 'bringing to life' to mean putting such a piece of land to use. II 900b; III 1053b; IV 1036a; V 871b; VI 869b
mawāzin (A, s. *mīzān*) : weights, a non-uniform system in the Muslim countries and thus of bewildering diversity. VI 117a
mawḍiʿ (A) : place; in ethics, the 'place' of an act as determining its goodness or badness. IX 527a
In the grammar of Sībawayhi, ~ *fi 'l-kalām* 'place in speech' denotes the position in which a speech element is used. The correlative of ~ is *manzila*, which represents status on the paradigmatic axis, and a third term in this set, *mawḳiʿ*, denotes simply the occurrence of an element in the string without regard to its function. IX 527a
♦ mawḍiʿ al-<u>sh</u>ams : in astronomy, the true solar longitude. IX 292a
mawḍūʿ → MAṢNŪʿ; MAṬRŪḤ
māwī → <u>KH</u>IDMATIYYA
mawʿiẓa → WĀʿIẒ
mawḳiʿ → MAWḌIʿ
mawkib → MAWĀKIB
mawḳif (A) : place of standing; specifically the place where the WUḲŪF, the halt, is held during the pilgrimage, viz. ʿArafāt and Muzdalifa or <u>D</u>jamʿ. VI 874a
In eschatology, the ~ is the place where, on the day of resurrection, several scenes of the last judgment will take place. V 236a; VI 874a
In pre-Islamic times, ~ was one of the terms used to designate the religious shrines, usually in the form of stones, to be found along tracks and at camping sites, of the nomadic tribes. VI 874a
In mysticism, the intermediate moment between two 'spiritual stations', MAḲĀM, represented as a halting and described as a state of stupor and of the loss of reference points acquired since the preceding stage. XII 613a
mawḳūf (A) : in the science of Tradition, a Tradition going back only to a Companion. III 25b; VII 631a; VIII 384a
In law, a state of suspense between parties and equally as regards any third party; a category of contract which is neither valid nor invalid. I 319b; III 1016b; VIII 836a; 'made into a WAḲF', as in the term *ḥabs* ~ or *ṣadaḳa mawḳūfa*, an early legal institution of a temporary endowment for a limited number of people that reverted to the founder or his heirs after their extinction, which has survived in Mālikī doctrine. XI 59b; the object of the WAḲF. XI 60a; and → ARḌ
mawlā (A, pl. *mawālī*) : a person linked by proximity to another person; patron; client; freedman; a party to an egalitarian relationship of mutual help, that is, a kinsman, confederate, ally or friend. IV 44a; VI 874a

In the Qur'ān and in Traditions, ~ is applied to God with the meaning of tutor, trustee and lord. VI 874a

♦ **mawlāy** : lit. my lord, an honorific title borne by the Moroccan sultans of the Sharīfian dynasties (Sa'dids and 'Alawids) who were descended from al-Ḥasan b. 'Alī, with the exception of those who were called Muḥammad and whose title was therefore SAYYIDĪ or *sīdī*. VI 888b

In mysticism, ~ is a title frequently used in connection with saints, especially in North Africa. VI 874b

mawlid (A, pl. *mawālid*), or *mawlūd* : the time, place or celebration of the birth of a person, especially that of the Prophet Muḥammad or of a saint; a panegyric poem in honour of the Prophet. VI 895a; XII 613a; a great festival, of which there are three in Egypt: on the 17th or 18th of January, on or about the vernal equinox, and about a month after the summer solstice. I 281a

♦ **mawālid** : genethlialogy, i.e. the art of deducing portents from the position of the stars at the time of birth, an area of judicial astrology. VIII 106a

♦ **mawlidiyya** or *mīlādiyya* : a poem composed in honour of the Prophet on the occasion of the anniversary of his birth and recited as a rule before the sovereign and court after ceremonies marking the *laylat al-mawlid*. VI 897b; X 657a

mawlūd → MAWLID

mawna → BASHTARDA

mawsim (A) : market, especially in connection with the markets of early Arabia; festival, generally with a religious basis. When such a festival signifies the birthday of a prophet or local saint, the term more generally used is MAWLID, but often some other event in a holy man's life, or even his death, may be celebrated, often at a date which shows continuity with some ancient nature festival or other rite; also, season. Thus in Lebanon, ~ denotes the season of the preparation of silk, while in India and in European terminology referring to these parts of the world, it has required the meaning of 'season' in connection with the weather conditions special to those regions, such as the regularly returning winds and rain periods. *Monsoon, mousson, moesson* and other corruptions of the term are found in this literature. VI 903a; pilgrimage. I 159b

mawsū'a (A) : in literature, an encyclopaedia, a neologism that emerged in the 20th century, though the tendency to encylopaedic writing was not absent. VI 903b; XII 614a

mawṣūl → ṢILA

mawt (A) : death. Its synonym *wafāt*, more exactly 'accomplishment, fulfilment', i.e. of a man's term of life, is Qur'ānic and carries the sense of God's predetermining a man's lifespan or executing His decree concerning a man's term of life. In modern Arabic, ~ is considered stark, unlike the euphemistic and delicate sense of 'demise, decease' that *wafāt* carries. VI 910b

mawthiḳ (A) : a Qur'ānic term used for the assurance from God taken by Jacob upon his sons for their safely bringing back Joseph. VII 188a

mawṭin → WAṬAN

mawwāl → MAWĀLIYĀ

mawz (A) : in botany, the banana (tree). VIII 732b

maydān (A, pl. *mayādīn*) : a large, open, demarcated area, flat and generally rectangular, designed for all kinds of equestrian activity; the exercises of mounted formations; in figurative usage, the confrontation of two parties; like the English 'field', ~ is extended to the broad sense of 'domain of activity', physical, intellectual or spiritual. VI 912b; hippodrome. II 954b

♦ maydānī : in archery, an arrow of a specified pattern. VI 912b

maykhān (Mon) : a low tent requiring little wood for its construction and in recent times covered with cotton cloth purchased from Chinese traders. IV 1151a

mayl (A) : in spherical astronomy, declination, the measure of the distance of a celestial body from the celestial equator. Muslim astronomers tabulated either the declination and right ascensions of stars or their ecliptic coordinates. Also of concern to them was the solar declination, *mayl al-shams*, of which there were two kinds, *al-mayl al-awwal* and *al-mayl al-thānī*. VI 914b

In philosophy, 'inclination', a development by Ibn Sīnā and his school of Philoponos's idea of impressed force, against Aristotle's explanation of motion. XII 769b

♦ al-mayl al-aʿẓam, or *al-mayl al-kullī* : the obliquity of the ecliptic, the basic parameter of spherical astronomy. VI 914b

♦ mayl ṭabīʿī : in physics, natural inclination; also a current philosophical term. I 112a

maymana → AṢL

maysara → AṢL

maysir (A) : an ancient game of chance, using arrows to win parts of a slaughtered beast. It was forbidden by the Qurʾān. VI 923b

mayta (A) : dead (used of irrational beings); as a substantive, ~ means an animal that has died in any way other than by slaughter. In later terminology, the word means firstly an animal that has not been slain in the ritually prescribed fashion, the flesh of which therefore cannot be eaten, and secondly all parts of animals whose flesh cannot be eaten, whether because not properly slaughtered or as a result of a general prohibition against eating them. II 1069a; VI 924b

mayzar → DASTĀR

maʿz (A) : in zoology, goats. XI 411b

maẓāhir → MAẒHAR

māʾzahr → MĀʾ

maẓālim → MAẒLIMA

mazar (A), or *mizr* : the word for various fermented drinks; beer. II 1061a; VI 721a; and → NABĪDH

mazār : in Muslim India, a term used for signifying a *pīr*'s (→ MURSHID) tomb, especially for the smaller wayside shrine. VI 125b

mazd → MAST

mazhar (A), or *mizhar* : in music, a round tambourine with or without jingling rings. The former in Persia was called the DĀʾIRA. ~ is also said to be the term for a lute, but this is doubtful. II 620b f.; a lute that appears to have been identical with a BARBAṬ but with a skin belly. Arabic lexicographers unanimously identify the ~ with the ʿŪD. The modern ~ is a tambourine. X 768b

maẓhar (A, pl. *maẓāhir*) : lit. place of outward appearance, hence 'manifestation, theophany', a technical term used in a wide variety of contexts in shīʿism, ṣūfism, Bābism, and, in particular, Bahāʾism, where it is of central theological importance. At its broadest, the term may be applied to any visible appearance or expression of an invisible reality, reflecting the popular contrast between the exoteric (ẒĀHIR) and the esoteric (BĀṬIN). In its more limited application, however, it refers to a type of theophany in which the divinity or its attributes are made visible in human form. VI 952a

♦ maẓhar ilāhī, or *maẓāhir-i ilāhiyya* : the Bahāʾī technical term for manifestations of God which feature through the prophets, never cease and are successive. I 916a; VI 953a

mazīdī (A) : in mediaeval ʿIrāḳ, a beggar who gives out that he just needs a little more money to purchase what he needs. VII 494a

maẓlima (A, pl. *maẓālim*) : an unjust or oppressive action, an antonym of ʿADL; its plural form, **maẓālim**, came to denote the structure through which the temporal authorities took direct responsibility for dispensing justice. *Maẓālim* sessions were held regularly under the ʿAbbāsid caliphs al-Mahdī and al-Hādī. VI 933b; IX 325a; the name of a tax under the Aghlabids. II 145b

maẓlūm (A, P) : someone or something treated or used wrongfully, unjustly, injuriously, or tyrannically. In Persian, ~ also means 'mild, gentle, modest'. VI 958b
In s̲h̲īʿī, especially Twelver, Islam, ~ is an attribute characterising the IMĀMs, especially al-Ḥusayn b. ʿAlī and ʿAlī al-Riḍā, who are ready for martyrdom. VI 958b

mazraʿa (A) : arable land, a field, for grain production as opposed to pasture, vineyard, orchard, etc.; in Ottoman administration, ~ designates a periodic settlement or a deserted village and its fields. To register a piece of land as ~, it was required that it be checked whether the place had a village site in ruins, its own water supply and a cemetery. VI 959a

mazraba (A) : the net which is used, especially in Tunisia, for tunny fishing. It involves a huge enclosure formed of meshed cloth with which the tunny bed is surrounded. VIII 1021b

mazrūʿān (A) : the term, properly al-mazrūʿānⁱ, used to refer to two of Kaʿb b. Saʿd's sons (probably ʿAmr and ʿAwf), while the rest of his sons were called al-ad̲j̲ārib 'the scabby ones'. X 173a

mazz → MAST

maẓẓ → DJULLANĀR

mazzār (A) : a brewer. VI 721a

mḍamma (Mor) : a leather belt worn by men, women and children in Morocco. V 746a

meddāḥ, m[ddāḥ → MADDĀḤ

medeniyyet (T, < A madīna) : in political science, civilisation, introduced into Ottoman Turkish towards the middle of the 19th century, meaning the secular political system believed to be common in Europe and contrasted with the traditional oriental dynastic despotism. VI 968a

medin : a silver coin, based on the half-dirham, struck by the Burd̲j̲ī Mamlūks and continued by the Ottomans after their conquest of Egypt and Syria. VIII 228b

medina (Fr, < A madīna) : in the Mag̲h̲rib, used by the French to designate the ancient part of the great Islamic cities, beyond which have been constructed the modern quarters of the city. VI 969b

medjelle (T, < A mad̲j̲alla) : originally, a book or other writing containing wisdom; in its best-known application, ~ refers to the civil code in force in the Ottoman empire and briefly in the Turkish Republic from 1869-1926. Known in full as the Med̲j̲elle-yi Aḥkām-î ʿAdliyye, it covers contracts, torts and some principles of civil procedure. VI 971a

med̲j̲idiyye (T) : in numismatics, Ottoman coins of 20 piastres. I 75a

med̲j̲lis-i wālā → MAD̲J̲LIS

med̲j̲mūʿa → MAD̲J̲MŪʿA

mehter (P 'greater') : in music, an Ottoman ensemble consisting of combinations of double-reed shawms (zurna), trumpets (boru), double-headed drum (ṭabl), kettle-drums (naḳḳāre, kös) and metallic percussion instruments. The ~ was an analogue of the wind, brass and percussion ensembles used for official, municipal and military purposes in other Islamic states. The Ottoman ~ was outlawed in 1826. VI 1007a

mela → PETH

melayu → PEGON

mēlmastyā → PAS̲H̲TŪNWALĪ

men-huan (Ch) : in Chinese mysticism, the hereditary line of a S̲H̲AYK̲H̲, the group of faithful under the domination of that line, the considerable ensemble of goods and lands owned by it, and, finally, the holy places that bear its charisma. X 338b; XI 122a

menāḳib → MANĀḲIB

mensūkhāt (A, s. *mensūkh* 'annulled') : an expression used in the Ottoman empire, after the abolition of certain early Ottoman army units, in the 11th/17th century, for the fiefs and other grants these units had previously held. These were referred to as *mensūkhāt tîmarî* 'annulled fiefs'. VI 1017a

məntān (N.Afr), or *məntāl* : a man's waistcoat with long, straight sleeves, worn in Morocco, Algeria and Tunisia. V 746b

menzil → MANZIL

meshweret → MASHWARA

mewḳūfātči (T), or *mewḳūfātī* : in Ottoman administration, the title given to the director of the 'Bureau of Retained Revenues', whose task was to manage the *mewḳūf aḳče*, money accruing from unused sstate expense allocations, and from vacant fiefs and other grants. VI 1029a

mewlewiyyet (T), or *mollalîḳ* : a title given to certain judicial districts in the Ottoman empire. VI 1029b; a generic term used in the Ottoman empire to designate the positions held by the MOLLĀs in civil and religious administration, which embraces simultaneously the rank, the duties or jurisdiction and the tutorial functions of the *mollā*. VII 222a

mgawren → FĀZA

mḥarram → MAḤREM

miʾa (A) : hundred; in the plural, *al-miʾūn* refers to all SŪRAs other than the 'seven long ones', AL-SABʿ AL-ṬIWĀL, with over 100 verses: x-xii, xvi-xviii, xx, xxi, xxiii, xxvi and xxxvii. IX 887b

mīʿād (A) : in the customary law of the Bedouin of the Central Region of the Sinai, Jordan and Palestine, as well as Yemen, a trial; for the Bedouin of the Western Desert and Cyrenaica 'a gathering of all interested parties and anyone else who wishes to attend, in which the agreement reached behind the scenes by means of negotiations is announced'. X 889b

mibkhara → MABKHARA

mīḍaʾa (A) : a basin for ablutions. X 647a

midād (A) : ink. In Middle Eastern manuscripts, two types of black ink were generally used, both of which date from pre-Islamic times. One was prepared on the basis of carbon and oil, and the other one from gall-nuts and ferrous components, the former originally being designated as ~, the latter as *ḥibr*. Later, the two words were used as synonyms. VI 1031b

midhyāʿ → IDHĀʿA

miʿdjan (A) : 'the trough', a depression in the pavement on which the circling of the Kaʿba is performed, just opposite the door. According to legend, Ibrāhīm and Ismāʿīl mixed the mortar used in building the Kaʿba here. IV 318a

In the mediaeval kitchen, a wooden bowl in which the dough for bread was mixed, also called *djafna*. VI 808a

midjann → DARAḲA

midjmara (P) : a censer; in the anthology of Luṭf ʿAlī Beg, the term for each of the parts it is divided into. V 834a

In astronomy, the Arabic version of the Greek constellation name for the Altar, *Ara*. V 1024b

midjrāt → ḲUFL

midjwāl (A) : a piece of white fabric, used in the game of MAYSIR, which was held over the archer's hands so that he could not see the arrows in the quiver. VI 924a

midraʿa (A) : a woolen, sleeved tunic worn only by the very poor in mediaeval times. V 737a

miḍrab (A) : among the pre-Islamic Bedouin, a tent under which important people camped when travelling. IV 1147a
In the mediaeval kitchen, a mallet. VI 808b

miḍrāb → NĀY ṬUNBŪR

mifrāṣ (A) : a broad iron instrument. XI 476b

mifrash (A, P *mafrash*, T *mifresh*) : a travelling pack for bedding. The term is now generally applied to the woven rectangular bedding packs still used by nomads, and normally made in pairs to balance on either side of the camel carrying them. VII 1a

mifresh → MIFRASH

mighfar (A), or *ghifāra* : a cap or headcloth of mail worn on military expeditions in early Islam. Over it a ḲALANSUWA or a helmet known as *bayḍa* (so-called because of its resemblance to an ostrich egg) was worn. The Prophet wore a ~ on the day Mecca surrendered. V 735a; X 613b; XII 737b

mighrafa (A) : in the mediaeval kitchen, a ladle. VI 808b

miḥakk (A) : in mineralogy, the touchstone, which measured the specific gravities of gold and noted the speed of solidification after it had been removed from the furnace. V 970a
In the mediaeval kitchen, a metal scraper used to clean bowls. VI 808a

miḥashsh (A) : in the mediaeval kitchen, a large copper rod-like instrument for stuffing intestines. V 808b

miḥāya : in the mysticism of Chad and the Nilotic Sudan, erasures, sc. verses that are washed off the writing-board and drunk, one of the regular activities of the saint. XI 124b

miḥbara → DAWĀT

miḥlab (A) : a wooden container in which yeast was kept, used in the mediaeval kitchen. VI 808a

miḥmal (A) : scales for gold. VII 195b

mihmān (P) : lit. guest, occurring in various compounds such as *mihmāndār*, an official in Ṣafawid Persia appointed to receive and to provide hospitality for guests, *mihmāndār-bāshī*, the official who superintended the *mihmāndār*, and the *mihmān-khāna*, a rest house instituted by the Ḳādjār shāh Nāṣir al-Dīn after his first trip to Europe in 1873. XII 618a

- ♦ mihmāndār → MIHMĀN; MIHMINDĀR
- ♦ mihmāndār-bāshī → MIHMĀN
- ♦ mihmān-khāna → MIHMĀN

mihmāz (A, pl. *mahāmiz*) : the spurs in a horse's riding equipment (syn. *kullāb*, pl. *kalālīb*; N.Afr *shabūr, shābīr*), more in vogue in the Muslim West than the East. IV 1145b

mihmindār (P) : the title of the 18th dignity, out of the 25 at the Mamlūk sultan's court; part of his duties was to receive ambassadors and delegations of Bedouin. VII 2a; and → MIHMĀN

mihna (A, pl. *mihan*) : a profession, service and handiness, mostly domestic (syn. ṢINĀʿA); *aṣḥāb al-mihan* are artisans, *māhin* is one who serves others skilfully, a servant. IX 626b

miḥna (A, pl. *miḥan*) : a testing, trial. More particularly, it signifies the procedure adopted by the caliph al-Maʾmūn in 218/833, and officially applied under his two immediate successors, for the purpose of imposing the view that the Qurʾān had been created. V 1124a; VII 2b

miḥrāb (A, pl. *maḥārīb*) : the prayer niche in the mosque, indicating the direction of prayer. It is made up of an arch, the supporting columns and capitals, and the space between them. Whether in a flat or recessed form, it gives the impression of a door or a doorway. VII 7a

mihragān (P, A *mihrdjān*) : the name of an Iranian Mazdaean festival, traditionally celebrated in Iran around the autumn equinox. VII 15a; ~ and NAWRŪZ are celebrated by the Nuṣayrīs as the days when the divinity of ʿAlī is manifested in the sun. VIII 146b; XI 401b
In music, the name of some musical themes whose origin goes back to the Sāsānid period. VII 19b

miḥrak (A) : in the mediaeval kitchen, a metal instrument used for raking out the embers and ash from the oven when baking was finished. VI 808a

miḥrāth (A, pl. *maḥārīth*), and *miḥrath* (pl. *maḥārith*) : a plough. In mediaeval times, however, ~ was more specifically applied to the tiller, which is not equipped with wheels or a mould-board or a coulter, but consists essentially of a ploughshare, a cross-beam, a handle and a pole (or beam). Although it goes back to the earliest antiquity, this agricultural implement is still in use, without modification of note, throughout the Islamic world. VII 21b

mihrdjān → MIHRAGĀN

mihtar (A) : in Mamlūk Egypt, the head of the *rikāb-khāna*, the depot for harness and in general for all the material required for horses and stables. VIII 530a

miḥwar → ḲUṬB; ẒILL

mīḳāt (A, pl. *mawāḳīt*) : appointed or exact time; in law, ~ is applied to the times of prayer and to the places where those who enter the ḤARAM are bound to put on the IḤRĀM. VII 26b
In astronomy, *ʿilm al-mīḳāt* is the science of astronomical timekeeping by the sun and stars and the determination of the times of the five prayers. VII 27b; and → MUWAḲḲIT
♦ mīḳātī (A) : an astronomer who specialised in spherical astronomy and astronomical timekeeping, but unlike the MUWAḲḲIT, was not necessarily associated with any religious institution. Mention of such astronomers appeared for the first time in Egypt in the 7th/13th century. VII 29b

mikhadda (A) : properly, pillow, but might be used as a cushion for sitting upon. V 1158b; XII99a

mikhdhaf → DJAʿBA

mikhlāf (A, pl. *makhālīf*) : in mediaeval administrative geography, an 'administrative province' or 'rural area', a term used particularly in Yemen. In the early 6th/13th century, ~ is defined with the restricted sense of the settled and cultivated lands around a fortress. From the period of Ayyūbid rule in Yemen onwards, ~ gradually falls out of use there and it is no longer used at the present time. VII 35a; IX 166a

miḳlā (A), and *miḳlāt* : a pan generally used for frying fish and the like, made of iron and used in the mediaeval kitchen. A stone-made ~ was used for other purposes, although the distinction between the two is unclear. VI 808a,b
In hunting, a radial trap (syn. *ḳula*). II 1037a

miḳlāʿ (A) : in the vocabulary of arms, a sling (syn. *mikhdhaf[a]*). XII 85a; XII 741b

miḳlama → DAWĀT

miḳnaʿ(a) → ḲINĀʿ

miḳnab (A) : among the nomadic stockbreeders in early Islam, a term for a herd of mounts of up to 50 (syn. *mansir* or *minsar, raʿīl, ḳanbal*). IV 1144b

miḳran (A) : in mediaeval agriculture, a piece of wood fixed on the oxen's head, when they plough, by means of a rope called *tawthīḳ*. VII 22b

miḳṭara (A) : the occasional name for an apparatus, more often called a FALAḲA, used for immobilising the feet in order to apply a bastinado on the soles of the feet. II 763b

miḳwam (A) : in the terminology of mediaeval agriculture, the handle of the ploughshare (syn. *dastaḳ*, < P *dastah*). VII 22b

mikwar(a) (A), or *mikwāra* : a word for turban. He who wore one was called *mukawwir*, which like *mutaʿammim*, came to mean a theologian, a man of learning, while in

Muslim Spain also an official and jurist, because they alone wore the turban there. X 613b

miḳyās (A) : measurement, means of measuring; any simple measuring instrument; in Egypt the name of the Nilometer, i.e. the gauge in which the annual rise of the river can be measured. VII 39b; the gnomon of the sundial, also called *s̲h̲aḵẖṣ* or *s̲h̲āḵẖiṣ*. VII 210a; and → ḲIYĀS

mīl → SANG

mīlād (A) : time of birth, in contradistinction to MAWLID, which may denote also 'place of birth'; Christmas. VII 40b; in South Africa, festival celebrating the birthday of the Prophet. IX 731a

mīlādiyya → MAWLIDIYYA

milāḥa (A) : navigation, seamanship; seafaring. VII 40b

milal → MILLA

milban (A) : a wooden mould used to fabricate unfired brick, composed essentially of dampened, shaped clay, which is then turned into the ~ without a bottom or cover, packed tight and finally dried in the sun; the clay is fined down with sand, gravel, chopped straw or potsherds in fixed proportions to prevent its crumbling and cracking. Once taken out of the ~ , the brick is left for a while longer in the sun. V 585a

milḥafa (N.Afr), and *mlaḥfa, tamǝlḥaft* : a large, enveloping outer wrap worn by women in the Arab East and by both sexes in North Africa. V 741b; V 746a

milḥ (A) : salt, which was already familiar to the ancient Arabs of pre-Islamic times, using it not only as seasoning but also in certain rites, e.g. for the oath that cemented an alliance, made around a fire. The two types of salt that were known were sea salt (~ *baḥrī*) and rock salt (~ *barrī*; and → MILḤ ANDARĀNĪ). VII 57a

♦ milḥ andarānī (A) : the probable correspondence for rock salt. considered to be the most valuable. VII 57b

♦ milḥ al-bawl (A) : uric salt. VII 58a

milk (A, pl. *amlāk*) : private property; in law, ~ denotes ownership, which is distinguished from possession, *yad*. The characteristic feature of ~ is its perpetual nature. I 28b; VII 60b

♦ amlāk-i salṭanatī (P) : a term used under the Ḳād̲j̲ārs in contradistinction to *amlāk-i ḵẖāṣṣa*, private estates. IV 973a; after the grant of the Persian Constitution, the ~ were the personal estates of the ruler, also referred to as *amlāk-i s̲h̲āhī*. IV 979b

♦ amlāk-i s̲h̲āhī → AMLĀK-I SALṬANATĪ

milla (A, pl. *milal*, P *millat*, T *millet*) : religion, sect; with the article, *al-milla* means the true religion revealed by Muḥammad and is occasionally used elliptically for *ahl al-milla*, the followers of the Islamic religion. II 294b; VII 61a

In the Qurʾān, ~ always means 'religion', e.g. the religion of the Christians and Jews, the religion of Abraham. II 294b; VII 61a

In Ottoman Turkish, **millet** came to denote the internally-autonomous religious groups within the Ottoman empire (Jews, Armenians, Greek Orthodox, etc.). VII 61b

In modern Persian and Turkish, ~ means 'nation, people'. VII 61a

♦ **al-milal wa 'l-niḥal** (A) : one of the stock phrases employed, in the heresiographical literature, to denote an enumeration of religious and occasionally philosophical doctrines, as well as the various groups or schools which profess them. VII 54a

millat → MILLA

millet → MILLA

mīm (A) : the twenty-fourth letter of the Arabic alphabet, transcribed *m*, with the numerical value 40. It is defined as occlusive, bilabial, voiced and nasal. VII 64b

mimʿār-bas̲h̲ī (T) : a local master-builder, not to be confused with the Ottoman's Chief Architect officiating in Istanbul. IX 540b

mimlaḳa → MĀLAḲ
mīnā → BĀZĀR
mīnā' (A, P *bandar*, T *liman*) : port, harbour; ~ became the comprehensive term for both of these meanings at the expense of the classical terms *marsā* (referring more specifically to the maritime aspect implied by 'harbour'), *furḍa* (referring more to the economic function implied by 'port), and *marfa'*. VII 66a
mīnā'ī (P ?) : in art, a type of ceramics with polychrome under- and over-glaze painting produced during the late 6th/12th and early 7th/13th centuries. The precise mediaeval name of this ware is uncertain. Iranian authors of the 11th/14th centuries link the term to translucent or luminous substances such as the sky or wine vessels; ~ is also used by them to describe a type of glass. Later authors use the term to describe glass vessels that had been painted and gilded. VII 72b; enamel. IV 1167a
minaṣṣa (A) : the throne, or high chair, on which the bride was raised and unveiled in her new home (syn. SARĪR, used in *Sīrat Sayf*, described as having been made of juniper wood and decorated with plates of gold and shining jewels). In late 19th-century Mecca, the throne was called *rīka* (< *arīka*). X 905a
minbar (A) : the raised structure or pulpit from which solemn announcements to the Muslim community were made and from which sermons were preached. VII 73b
mindīl → MANDĪL
min<u>dj</u>al → ZABR
min<u>dj</u>am (A) : the tongs and the beam of the common balance. VII 195b
minhā<u>dj</u> → <u>SH</u>ARĪʿA
minḳār (A), or *ṣāḳūr* : in mineralogy, a pickaxe, which was the main tool of the miner. It had a sharp end to peck the stone and a flat end to hammer or to drive wedges. V 968b
minsar (A) : in zoology, the beak of a vulture. VII 1013a; and → MIḲNAB
min<u>sh</u>afa (A) : a large, white head veil for women in the Arab East. V 741b; and → MANDĪL
min<u>sh</u>ār → <u>DH</u>IKR-I <u>DJ</u>AHR
minṭaḳat al-burū<u>dj</u> (A), and *minṭaḳat falak al-burū<u>dj</u>* : the zodiac; the ecliptic circle. VII 81b
mintān (T) : a short caftan without sleeves, stopping at the waist, worn in Ottoman Turkey. V 752a
mīr (P, < A AMĪR) : a Persian title applied to princes, but also borne by poets and other men of letters. In India and Pakistan, SAYYIDs sometimes call themselves by the title. It also occurs in official titles in both the Dihlī sultanate and in Mu<u>gh</u>al administration, e.g. *mīr baḥr* 'naval commander'. VII 87b; IX 333a

♦ mīr-āb → MĪRĀB

♦ **mīr-ā<u>kh</u>ūr** (T) : under the Ottomans, the master of the stables, the official given charge of all aspects relating to the supply and maintenance of the Ottoman sultan's stables. VII 88a; VIII 529a and → AMĪR Ā<u>KH</u>ŪR

♦ mīr-ʿalem (T) : under the Ottomans, the 'standard-bearer'. VIII 529a

♦ mīr ba<u>kh</u><u>sh</u>ī : quartermaster-general. Under the Mu<u>gh</u>al emperor Akbar, the ~ was administrative head of the military department and responsible for all transport arrangements during campaigns. He could be placed in command of an army in the field. I 316b

♦ mīr mun<u>sh</u>ī : under the Mu<u>gh</u>als, one of the terms for the head of the chancellery, along with MUN<u>SH</u>Ī AL-MAMĀLIK. IV 760

♦ mīr sāmān : under the Mu<u>gh</u>al emperor Akbar, the ~ was in charge of the BUYŪTĀT department and was responsible for the organisation of the factories, workshops and stores maintained by the emperor. I 316b

♦ mīr-zāda → MĪRZĀ

♦ mīr-i far<u>sh</u> : the term usually applied to stone weights, often of marble carved and inlaid with semi-precious stones, used to hold down a pall over a grave. VII 88a

♦ **mīr-i mīrān** (T) : 'supreme commander', a military and political term used in 18th-century Ottoman Turkish administrative practice as being virtually synonymous with BEGLERBEGI 'provincial governor', and then increasingly used to denote the honorary rank of *beglerbegi*, although this last title was considered as somewhat superior to that of ~. In the 19th century, ~ also became a civil service rank. VII 95b; VIII 280b

♦ **mīrī** (T, < A *amīrī*) : 'belonging to the government'. Under the Ottomans, ~ was singled out to designate assets that belong of right to the highest Muslim authority, the sultan. Throughout Ottoman history, it was used as a noun meaning 'lands belonging to the government', 'land tax' levied from them, as well as 'the public treasury'. II 148a; V 792b; VII 125a

♦ al-mīrī (Ir) : the government. VII 88a

♦ mīrzā → MĪRZĀ

mīrāb (P), and *mīr-āb* : an official of the state responsible for the distribution of the water of a ḲANĀT. IV 531a; V 872b; an official in charge of the construction and upkeep of the channels and dams. XII 550a

mirabbaʿ → RUBĀʿĪ

miʿrā<u>dj</u> (A), and *isrāʾ* : originally, a ladder, then 'ascent'; in particular, the Prophet's ascension to Heaven. VII 97b; XII 618a

♦ miʿrā<u>dj</u>-nāma (P) : in literature, a genre of accounts of the Prophet's celestial journey. XII 618a

mirʾāt (A, pl. *marāʾī*) : mirror. VII 105b

mīrā<u>th</u> (A, pl. *mawārī<u>th</u>*) : inheritance, *wāri<u>th</u>* being the heir and *mūri<u>th</u>* the person leaving the estate. This branch of Islamic law is called *ʿilm al-farāʾiḍ* 'the science of the ordained quotas'. VII 106b

mirbāʿ → RĀBIʿ

mirfaʿ (A) : a footstool, an ink-stand and the base of the small oriental table. In certain texts it may be replaced by KURSĪ. V 509a

mirfaḳa → WISĀDA

mīrī → MĪR

mirʿizz (A) : flock, tuft of wool. XII 317a

mirkās (A), or *mirḳās* : 'merguez', a North African kind of fried sausage made from minced leg of mutton with the addition of various spices and ingredients, such as pickle, pimento, dried coriander, nard and cinnamon. VII 126a

mirkaz (A, pl. *marākiz*) : a rammer used by masons in Ibn <u>Kh</u>aldūn's time to beat earth mixed with lime and gravel, etc. V 585b

mirmīs → KARKADDAN

mirrī<u>kh</u> (A) : in astronomy, the planet Mars, called by astrologers *al-naḥs al-aṣ<u>gh</u>ar* 'the minor misfortune' because it is credited with the most ominous omens and effects. VII 127a

mirsal → MARBAṬ

mir<u>sh</u>aḥa → ḲARBŪṢ

mirwad (A) : a small probe or stick with a rounded end used by women to apply cosmetic to their eyebrows, eyelashes or the edges of their eyelids. In mediaeval times, the sticks were commonly of bronze. V 356b

mirwaḥa (A) : fan, vane. Large fans are called *mirwaḥat al-*<u>KH</u>AY<u>SH</u>, hand fans *mirwaḥat al-<u>kh</u>ūṣ* 'palm-leaf fan'. VII 127b

In music, a jingling instrument used by Christians. IX 11a

mīrzā (P < *mīr-zāda* or *amīr-zāda*), and *mirzā* : 'born of a prince', a title given to noblemen and others of good birth. Since the time of Nādir S̲h̲āh's conquest of India, it has been further applied to educated men outside of the class of *mullā*s or *ʿulamāʾ* (→ MOLLĀ). In modern times, but not formerly, the title is placed after the name of a prince; when placed before the name of other persons bearing it, it is equivalent to 'Mr'. VII 129a

In Indian usage, it is given, from Mug̲h̲al times onwards, to kinsmen of the Mug̲h̲als, the Tīmūrids, the Ṣafawids, members of other royal houses and to certain Mug̲h̲al nobles. In modern times in India and Pakistan, the prefixed ~ is particularly used by men of the Mug̲h̲al division of AS̲H̲RĀF Muslims. VII 129b

♦ **mīrzāʾī** (IndP) : in India, an appellation, somewhat contemptuous, given to a follower of Mīrzā G̲h̲ulām Aḥmad of Ḳādiyān. VII 132b

mirzam (A) : in astronomy, *al-~* designated β Canis Maioris, β Canis Minoris and γ Orionis; in modern times in Central Arabia, *el-mirzem* is used for Sirius. IX 471b; and → NUḤĀM

misabbaʿ → SABʿĀNĪ

misāḥa (A) : the measurement of plane surfaces; survey, the technique of surveying. VII 137b; and → MUḲĀSAMA

♦ **ʿilm al-misāḥa** (A) : the science of measurement, plane and solid geometry. VII 135a

misalla (A, pl. *masāll*) : lit. large needle; an obelisk. VII 140b

miʿṣam (A) : in anatomy, the wrist. XII 830b

miṣbāḥ → SIRĀD̲J̲

misbaḥa (A) : the traditional rosary, commonly used by men, associated with a ritual based on the custom of mentioning on every occasion God's Most Beautiful Names. XII 775b

miṣfāt (A) : in the mediaeval kitchen, a strainer, made of wood or metal. VI 808b

misḥ (A, pl. *amsāḥ, musūḥ*) : felt, used e.g. as a saddle felt. IV 1146a; a coarse cloth. IX 677a

mīs̲h̲am → G̲H̲ARAZA

mis̲h̲far (A) : a camel's lip. IV 249b

mis̲h̲mis̲h̲ (A) : in botany, the apricot-tree and its fruit (*Prunus armeniaca*). VII 141b

mis̲h̲ṭāḥ (A) : a place where flour is sifted by shaking. IX 361b

misk (A) : musk. VII 142a

misk̲h̲ → MASK̲H̲

miskīn (A, pl. *masākīn, miskīnūn*) : poor, destitute; miserable, humble. II 757b; VII 144b

In modern South Arabia, ~ denotes the top layer of the population subject to the tribesmen, comprising the petty traders and artisans, constituting the layer above the *ḍuʿafāʾ* (→ ḌAʿĪF). VII 145a

In ʿIrāḳī Kurdistan, *miskēn* denotes villagers who do not claim tribal origin, a class of lowly social status and often oppressed by tribal neighbours. VII 145a

miṣnaʿa (A, P *āb-anbār*) : a water storage cistern. V 875b; XI 302a

miṣr (A, pl. *amṣār*) : in earliest Islam, the settlements developing out of the armed encampments established by the Arabs in the conquered provinces outside Arabia and then, subsequently, the capital towns or metropolises of the conquered provinces; the land of Egypt and its capital city. VII 146a

As a geographical term, ~ is defined as an administrative unit, a large urban centre where a ruler or governor resides and which has located there the administrative organs, treasury, etc. of the province. VII 146b

miṣrāʿ (A) : in poetry, one of two clearly distinct halves of a line of poetry. I 668a; VIII 579a; in Afghan poetry, a lyrical distich in a peculiar metre, also called *landaī*. I 221a
misrā<u>kh</u> (A) : in Yemen, tribal assembly places. XI 276b
miss → NUḤĀS
misṭara (A) : a ruler. VII 198b; XI 150b
miswāk (A) : toothbrush; tooth-pick; the more usual word is *siwāk* (pl. *suwuk*), which denotes also the act of cleansing the teeth. The instrument consists of a piece of smooth wood, the end of which is incised so as to make it similar to a brush to some extent. VII 187a
miswara → WISĀDA
mītad → ṬARĪḲA
mī<u>th</u>āḳ (A) : covenant, agreement, used 25 times in the Qurʾān and often linked with its synonym ʿAḲD. The majority of the Qurʾānic usages relate to compacts between God and various members of His human creation, the unilateral imposition of a covenant by God upon Man. In modern Arabic, ~ denotes a treaty, pact or agreement. VII 187b
♦ **mī<u>th</u>āḳ-i millī** (T) : "the National Pact", a proclamation voted by the last Ottoman Parliament which met in Istanbul in January 1920, proclaiming the territorial integrity of the remaining non-Arab heartlands of the Ottoman empire. VII 188a
mi<u>th</u>āl → FARMĀN
mi<u>th</u>ḳāl (A) : the oldest Arab unit of Troy weight. III 10b; an apothecary's stater equalling two *dānaḳ*; a gold DĪNĀR. IV 248b; a standard weight unit, which was not everywhere the same. VI 118a
miʾūn → MIʾA
miyāḳis (A, < Gr) : in zoology, the common mussel (*Mytilus edulis* L.), a popular foodstuff. VIII 707a
miyān (T), or *miyān-<u>kh</u>āne* : in Turkish poetry, the third line of each stanza of the <u>SH</u>ARḲI̊. IX 354a
miyāna (H) : 'middle-sized'; a litter used in India, provided with side-curtains rather than the box enclosure of the PALKĪ. VII 932a
mīyāndār (P) : in traditional Iranian wrestling, KU<u>SH</u>TĪ, the most accomplished and senior member, who conducted the proceedings. Under him in seniority came the PAHLAWĀN 'athlete', *naw<u>kh</u>ʷāsta* 'beginner', and *nawča* 'novice'. XI 573a
mīzāb → ḲIBLA
mizā<u>dj</u> (A, pl. *amzi<u>dj</u>a*) : lit. mixture; in mediaeval medicine, temperament, balance of elements within the body, corresponding to the *krasis* of Ancient Greek physicians. VIII 100a; XII 627b
In metaphysics, the final qualitative pattern resulting from definite proportions of the constituents of a given mixture, i.e. hot, cold, moist and dry. I 1084a
miʿzaf (A, pl. *maʿāzif*), and *miʿzafa* : in music, a term denoting today any string or wind instrument or even, more restrictedly, a piano, but one which was employed in mediaeval Islamic times to instruments with 'open strings', which were played with the fingers or a plectrum. VII 189b; according to the author of the *Tā<u>dj</u> al-ʿarūs*, the ~ was the instrument now known as the *ḳabūs*, a very old instrument (var. *ḳabbūs, ḳanbūs, ḳupūz* or ḲŪPŪZ), described by Ewliyā Čelebi as having been invented by a vizier of Muḥammad II named Aḥmed Pa<u>sh</u>a Hersek O<u>gh</u>lu and being a hollow instrument, smaller than the *<u>sh</u>a<u>sh</u>tār* (→ TĀR) and mounted with three strings. It has survived in Poland, Russia, and the Balkans where it is a lute proper. X 769a; and → ḲŪPŪZ
mizaffa (A) : a litter, e.g. for carrying a bride. X 900a
miẓall (A) : a canopy, a portable but firm construction, serving as well as the general's tent, insignia of command, rallying point and headquarters on campaign. In the Muslim West, much confusion is caused because of the resemblance in both form and meaning between ~ and MIẒALLA. VII 192a

miẓalla (A) : lit. an instrument or apparatus for providing shade, *ẓill*, apparently synonymous with the SHAMSA, *shamsiyya*, lit. an instrument or apparatus for providing shelter for the sun, probably therefore referring to the sunshade or parasol borne on ceremonial occasions and processions over early Islamic rulers. In Mamlūk sources this appears as *djitr, shitr* (< P *čitr*, → ČATR) denoting the parasol as one of the insignia of royalty; VII 191b; among the pre-Islamic Bedouin, a large tent, often made of goat's hair. V 1147a; VII 192b

mīzān (A) : balance, scales; in eschatology, the Qur'ānic 'balance' which weighs the deeds of an individual. III 465b

In the scientific thought of Djābir b. Ḥayyān, ~ forms a fundamental principle meaning a.o. specific gravity, the metaphysical principle *par excellence*, and a speculation on the letters of the Arabic alphabet. II 358b

In mathematics, ~ means, among other things, testing the correctness of any calculation. VII 198b

In divination, in magic squares, ~ stands for the sum of the largest and smallest figures; it is half the total of the vertical row, horizontal row or of the diagonals. VII 198b

In astronomy, *al-~* is the term for Libra, one of the twelve zodiacal constellations. VII 83b

♦ 'ilm al-mīzān : alchemy. VII 198b

mi'zar → IZĀR

mizhar → MAZHAR

mizmār (A) : lit. an instrument of piping. In the generic meaning, it refers to any instrument of the wood-wind family, i.e. a reed-pipe or a flute. In the specific sense, ~ refers to a reed-pipe (i.e. a pipe played with a reed) as distinct from a flute. In Persian, the equivalent of ~ in this sense is NĀY. VII 206b

♦ mizmār al-muthannā → DIYĀNAY

mizr → MAZAR; NABĪDH

mizwad (A, pl. *mazāwid*) : a food-bag, made by the Touaregs from cheetah skin if they can catch the animal. II 740a

mizwala (A), and *sā'a shamsiyya* : in modern Arabic, a sundial. In mediaeval Islam, horizontal sundials were called *rukhāma* or *basīṭa*, vertical sundials *munḥarifa*. VII 210a

mizwār (A, < B *amzwaru* 'he who precedes, he who is placed at the head') : in North Africa, chief of a religious brotherhood, the superintendent of a ZĀWIYA or the chief of a body of *shorfā* (→ SHARĪF), equivalent to the Arabic MUḲADDAM. In those districts of Morocco where the old Berber organisation has survived, mainly in the Great Atlas and Central Atlas, *amzwār* is sometimes the equivalent of *anflūs*, the political adviser to a body. VII 211b

mizz → MAST

mōbadh (P) : chief of the Madjūs, a title for a type of Zoroastrian priest which in the Sāsānid state had a variety of ritual, judicial and administrative responsibilities. By the 4th or 5th century, a three-level hierarchy had developed of local *mōbadh*s, grand *mōbadh*s of provinces or regions and a supreme *mōbadh* over the entire state. The function of ~ continued to exist in Islamic times but it is not always clear whether ~ is used as a generic term for any priest or is used in a specifically technical sense in sources referring to Islamic Iran; this term is also used somewhat loosely in modern scholarship for Zoroastrian priests in early Islamic times. VII 213b

mōbedān-mōbed → ḲĀḌI 'L-ḲUḌĀT

mofussil → MUFAṢṢAL

mohur (Eng, < P *muhr*, < San *mudrā*) : in numismatics, an Indian gold coin. VII 221a

mollā (P, < A MAWLĀ), or *mullā* : a title of function, of dignity or profession, and of rank, limited, with a few exceptions, to the Turco-Iranian and Indian world, ~ indicates in the first instance any Muslim scholar who has acquired a certain degree of religious education and the aptitude to communicate it. In current usage, ~ is most often applied to the *ʿulamāʾ*, the religious scholars. Distinguished by his clothing and physical appearance, his prestige and claim to knowledge, the ~ in Iran today has succeeded in occupying a wide range of functions at many different levels. Exercising the basic prerogatives in matters of education, ritual functions (prayers, marriages, funerals etc.) and judicial functions, the *mollā*s constitute the basis of what has been called, erroneously in the view of some, a veritable clergy. VII 221a; and → MEWLEWIYYET

♦ mollalïḳ → MEWLEWIYYET

mozarab (Sp) : a word of uncertain origin, denoting 'arabised' Christians living under Muslim rule in Andalusia after the conquest of 711 AD. VII 246b

mposa (Sw) : in East Africa, the proposer of a marriage, a senior member of the family who is usually but not necessarily from the groom's family. VIII 33b

muʿabbad (A) : 'worn down by traffic'. XI 155a

muʾaddib (A) : a later appellation than MUDARRIS or MUʿALLIM for teacher in the Arab lands; in some cases, the ~ was a higher rank, namely, the more learned or the private tutor. V 568a

muʿaddin → MAʿDIN

muʾa<u>dh</u><u>dh</u>in (A), and *munādī* : originally, among the Arab tribes and in the towns, the crier making important proclamations and invitations to general assemblies. From the beginning of Islam, ~ and *munādī* have been used to designate the official whose main function is to summon the believers to public worship on Friday and to the five daily prayers. Both terms are used quite indiscriminately. VI 675b

muʾa<u>dj</u><u>dj</u>al (A) : in law, yearly, variable, rather low rents. XII 368b; in India, 'deferred dower', the remainder of the MAHR after a token amount has been paid at the time of marriage, becoming payable when the wife is divorced or widowed. I 172b

muʿa<u>dj</u><u>dj</u>al (A) : in law, a lump sum paid immediately. XII 368b; in India, 'prompt dower', a token amount of the MAHR paid at the time of marriage. I 172b

muʾā<u>dj</u>ir (A) : a deviant, in the sexual sense. V 778a

muʿāf (A) : one of five classes, that of 700 men-at-arms excepted from taxation, into which the population of Eastern Transcaucasia was divided in the late 18th century under Muḥammad Ḥasan. IX 255a

♦ muʿāfī (P) : under the Ṣafawids, a temporary (but renewable) grant of immunity. Another similar grant was called the *musallamī*. IX 732b

♦ muʿāf-nāme (T) : in the Ottoman empire, a letter of exemption. X 801a

muʿāhad (A) : a non-Muslim under the protection of the Islamic state, syn. MUʿĀHID. IV 768a; an unbeliever connected with the Muslim state by a treaty. V 178b

♦ **muʿāhada** (A) : treaty, agreement. VII 250a

muʿāhid (A) : lit. one who enters into a covenant or agreement with someone; in mediaeval times, those People of the Book who submitted to the Arab conquerors of the Middle East on conditions of an ʿAHD 'agreement' or of <u>DH</u>IMMA 'protection'. Syn. MUʿĀHAD. XII 630b

muʿāḳaba (A) : in prosody, the obligatory alternation of the shortening of two adjacent cords. This phenomenon occurs in the *madīd, ramal, <u>kh</u>afīf*, and *mu<u>dj</u>ta<u>th</u><u>th</u>* metres. The apparent reason for the existence of this phenomenon is to avoid a sequence of four moving letters. VIII 747b

muʿākama (A) : a term denoting a scantily dressed woman, var. *mukāʿama*, which also means pressing one's lips on the lips of a person of the same sex. IX 566b

muʿāḳara (A) : a term denoting the action of two or more friends who drink together; also, a meal taken with friends. VII 850a

mu'ākhāt (A) : brothering, a practice found in the early days of Islam by which two men became 'brothers'. VII 253b

muʿaḳḳab → ʿAḲIB

muʿālidj (A) : lit. treating, developing; in Muslim Spain, ~ had the sense of 'retailer of fruit and vegetables'. I 961b

mu'allaf → BASĪṬ

♦ **al-mu'allafa ḳulūbuhum** (A) : lit. those whose hearts are won over; the term applied to those former opponents of the Prophet Muḥammad who are said to have been reconciled to the cause of Islam by presents of 100 or 50 camels from Muḥammad's share of the spoils of the battle of al-Ḥunayn after Muḥammad's forces had defeated the Hawāzin confederation. VII 254a

muʿallaḳ (A) : suspended.

In the science of Tradition, ~ is used when there is an omission of one or more names at the beginning of the ISNĀD, or when the whole *isnād* is omitted. III 26a

al-muʿallaḳāt (A) : in literature, the name of a collection of pre-Islamic Arabic poems, generally numbered at seven. VII 254a

muʿallal (A) : in the science of Tradition, ~ applies to a Tradition with some weakness in ISNĀD or MATN. Al-Ḥākim calls it a Tradition mixed with another, or containing some false notion of the transmitter, or given as MUTTAṢIL when it is MURSAL. III 26a

muʿallim (A) : teacher, syn. MUDARRIS, and later MU'ADDIB. V 568a; a primary school instructor or Qur'ān teacher. X 80a; in guild terminology, master-craftsman. VIII 871b; IX 168b; an ocean pilot. VII 51a

♦ al-muʿallim al-thālith (A) : lit. the third teacher; an appellation for Mīr Muḥammad Bāḳir b. Shams al-Din Muḥammad al-Ḥusaynī al-Astarābādī, known as (Ibn) al-Dāmād. II 103b; an appellation for Naṣīr al-Dīn al-Ṭūsī, also called Muḥaḳḳiḳ-Ṭūsī. X 746a

♦ al-muʿallim al-thānī (A) : lit. the second teacher; an appellation for Abū Naṣr al-Fārābī. I 631a

muʿāmalāt (A) : in law, transactions concerning credit granted by a donor to a beneficiary; also, the bilateral contracts, as opposed to the ʿIBĀDĀT which constitute the 'ritual of Islamic law'. In this general sense, the ~ define juridico-human relations and ensure that the Muslim's behaviour conforms to juridico-moral theories. VII 255b; interpersonal acts. IX 323b

mu'āmara (A) : in classical Muslim administration, an inventory of orders issued during the period of the general issue of pay, *ṭamaʿ*, bearing at its end a signed authorisation by the sultan. II 79a

muʿammā (A) : lit. something made obscure, hidden; a word puzzle, verbal charade, a kind of literary play upon words (syn. LUGHZ and UḤDJIYYA); the ~ is distinguished by the absence of the interrogatory element and by the fact that the sense of the passage had been made 'blind' by various procedures; also, secret writing, code. V 806b; VII 257a; VIII 217a; an enigmatic anagram of a name. X 516a

muʿammar (A) : an appellative of legendary and historical people who are alleged to have lived to an exceptionally great age. VII 258a

muʿanʿan (A) : in the science of Tradition, an ISNĀD where *ʿan* ('on the authority of') is used with no clear indication of how the Tradition was received. III 26a; *isnāds* omitting the established transmission methods and with only one or more times the preposition *ʿan* between two transmitters are called ~. Closely connected with this is the *isnād* which is *mu'annan*, which introduces the information transmitted by an older to a younger authority simply by means of the conjunction *anna* 'that'. VII 260a

mu'annan → MUʿANʿAN

mu'annath   → MUDHAKKAR

mu'āraḍa   (A) : opposition; in literary theory, ~ indicates imitation or emulation (syn. *naẓīra*); the poet composes his work in the same rhyme and metre, and in doing so, often tries to surpass the original. The imitating of someone's work was also used sometimes as a deliberate act of homage. VII 261a; IX 463b; X 124a; 'counter-poem'. VIII 805a; and → NAḲĀ'IḌ

As a technique in manuscript production, ~ has the meaning of collation, i.e. the textual comparison of a manuscript with another of the same work, preferably with one from which it was copied; syn. MUḲĀBALA. VII 490b

mu'arniba   (A, < *arnab*), or *murniba* : regions where (adult) hares are plentiful; the regions where young hares are predominant are called *makhazza* or *mukharniḳa*. XII 85a

mu'arrab   (A) : an arabicised loan or foreign word, in theory, only those which were integrated into the Arabic of pre- and early Islamic times; those of the post-classical period are called MUWALLAD. However, *muwallad* does not only refer to loan words, but to all kinds of linguistic neologisms which came up in post-classical Arabic. The difference between ~ and *muwallad* is not taken into consideration by all philologists, and so ~ often is the general term for 'loan word, foreign word'. VII 261b; X 240b

mu'arrish   → ḲAṢṢĀṢ

mu'āṣir   (A) : contemporary. XII 637b; and → RASM

mu'askar   → 'ASKAR

mu'āṭāt   (A) : in law, a mutual delivery of the object of sale and of the sale price. I 318b; XII 706a

mu'āwaḍa   (A) : barter, exchange; in law, ~ stands for a contract which is based on a mutual obligation, in opposition to a contract with a one-sided obligation. Examples are contracts of sale, lease and marriage. VII 263b; and → ṢULḤ AL-IBRĀ'

mu'āwama   → BAY' AL-MU'ĀWAMA

mu'awwidhatān[i]   (A), and *mu'awwidhāt* : the name given to the last two SŪRAS of the Qur'ān, because they both begin with the words 'Say: I seek refuge in the Lord'. V 409b; VII 269b; IX 887b

mu'ayyidī   (A) : in numismatics, the half-dirham coin, later known as the medin. XII 592b

mu'aẓẓam   (A) : 'highly venerated', the epithet (also *a'ẓam*) of Abū Ḥanīfa, the eponymous founder of the Ḥanafī school of law, giving rise to the name of the suburb of Baghdad where his supulchral mosque is found. IV 855b

muba''aḍ   (A) : 'partial', a term for a slave held in joint ownership and enfranchised by one of the owners, who, however, is not wealthy enough to compensate his fellow-owners for the value of their shares. I 30a

In mathematics, ~ is a subdivided fraction, or a fraction of a fraction. IV 725b

mübādele   (T, < A *mubādala*) : exchange, used in Ottoman Turkish for the exchange of commodities and of values, the exchange of prisoners of war, the exchange of ambassadors, and the exchange of populations. VII 275a

mubāḥ   (A) : 'licit, authorised', one of the five juridical qualifications of human acts. VII 276a; 'indifferent', neither obligatory or recommended, nor forbidden or reprehensible. III 660b

mubāhala   (A) : a term indicating both the spontaneous swearing of a curse in order to strengthen an assertion or to find the truth, and a kind of ordeal, invoked for the same purpose, between disputing individuals or parties, in which the instigation or call to the ordeal is more important than the execution; also, ~ is the name of a 'historical' ordeal which is said to have been proposed in 10/632-3 by the Prophet to a deputation of the Christian Nadjrānīs. VII 276a

mubālag͟ha (A) : in grammar, ~ is used to denote the intensive meaning of a number of morphemes and syntagmas. Most consistently it is applied to the intensive participles of the forms *faʿūl, faʿʿāl*, etc. VII 277a
In literary theory, ~ came to mean hyperbole, intensification. Ḳudāma (d. 337/948) uses ~ to denote a very specialised type of emphasising (*īg͟hāl* with later authors) in which a poetic idea is rounded out by a pertinent little exaggeration at the end of the line. VII 277a; emphasis. VIII 614b

muballig͟h (A) : a participant in the Friday or feast-day prayers with a loud voice. While saying his prayer, he has to repeat aloud certain invocations to the IMĀM, for all to hear. In mosques of any importance, he stands on a platform, DIKKA, and is therefore called *dikkat al-muballig͟h*. II 276a

mubāraʾa (A) : in law, a form of divorce by mutual agreement by which husband and wife free themselves by a reciprocal renunciation of all rights. I 1027a

mubāriz (SpA), or *barrāz* : 'the champion who comes out of the ranks, when two armies are ranged against one another, to challenge an enemy to single combat'. IX 533a

mubas͟hs͟hir → NAD͟HĪR; TABS͟HĪR

mubayyiḍa (A) : 'those clothed in white', i.e. ʿAlids and their supporters at the battle at Fak͟hk͟h in 169/786, as opposed to their opponents, *al-musawwida* 'those clothed in black', ʿAbbāsids and their supporters. III 617a; (< P *safīd-d̲jāmagān*) followers of a semi-secret organisation devoted to the cult of Abū Muslim who proclaimed the imminent return of Zoroaster and wore white garments. They were involved in a number of revolts in eastern Iran and Transoxania in the 2nd/8th century. IV 16b; VII 500a

mubham (A) : 'obscure'; in the science of Tradition, ~ is used of an ISNĀD when a transmitter is named vaguely, e.g., *rad̲jul* (a man), or *ibn fulān* (son of so and so). III 26a; and → ISM

mūbiḳāt (A) : deadly sins, the term used in a Tradition for the 'seven capital sins' of Christian morality. IV 1107b

mubtadaʾ (A) : beginning, start; in grammar, ~ is generally translated as 'inchoative'. It designates the first component part with which one begins the nominal phrase, whose second component is the predicate, K͟HABAR. VII 283a
In history, ~ is employed in particular with regard to the beginning of the creation and also to biblical history in general. VII 283b

mubtadiʾ → AD̲JĪR

mūdaʿ → WADĪʿA

mudabbad̲j (A) : 'variegated, embellished'; in the science of Tradition, the term used when two contemporaries transmit Traditions from one another. III 26a

mudabbar → TADBĪR

mudabbir → ṬĀLIʿ

muḍāf → BARRĀNĪ; IḌĀFA; MUFRAD

mudallas (A) : in the science of Tradition, a Tradition with a concealed defect, TADLĪS, in the ISNĀD. III 26a

muḍāraba (A), and, in S͟hāfiʿī and Mālikī sources, **ḳirāḍ**, *muḳāraḍa* : in law, a commercial association whereby an investor entrusts capital to an agent who trades with it and shares with the investor a pre-determined proportion of the profits. Losses incurred in the venture are the responsibility of the investor; the agent loses his time and effort, and any profit he would have gained were it successful. VII 284b; profit-sharing. IX 348b

mudārāt (A) : in Imāmī tradition, a practice of treating others in a friendly manner while concealing your true attitude towards them. IX 206a; diplomacy. X 824b

muḍāriʿ (A) : similar; in grammar, ~ is the verbal form characterised by the prefixing of one of four augments, marks of the person, *hamza, tāʾ, yāʾ* and *nūn*. It is devoted to the expression of the present and future, and is the opposite of MĀḌĪ, characterised by the suffixing of personal markings and allocated to the expression of the past. V 954b; VII 285b

In prosody, ~ is the name of the twelfth Arabic metre, said to be invented by Abu 'l-ʿAtāhiya. I 108a; I 670a

In literary theory, ~ is used of an imperfect paronomasia whereby the two juxtaposed words have a divergent consonant but are homorganic, i.e. of a similar articulation area, as in *dāmis* and *ṭāmis*. Non-homorganic use is termed *lāḥiḳ*. X 69b

mudarris (A) : a teacher, instructor; in mediaeval usage, when used without a complement, a professor of law at a MADRASA. The same term with a complement was sometimes used to designate other professors. V 1124b; V 1131a; in the hierarchy of modern Egyptian universities, ~ is an instructor holding the Ph.D. but ranking below an *ustādh* and *ustādh musāʿid*, roughly analogous to an assistant professor in an American university. X 80a

mudawwara (A) : lit. something circular; a term used in the central and western parts of the Arab world in the later Middle Ages to denote a large tent of rulers and great men, used especially when the army was on the march. VII 286a

During the Fāṭimid caliphate, the silver table that was set up after the procession on the ʿĪDs and covered with magnificent foods for a banquet. VI 851a

mudd (A) : a measure (of various weights) of capacity. The ~ was (about) 1.05 litres in ʿIrāḳ, 3.673 litres in Syria, and 2.5 litres in Egypt. VI 117b

♦ mudd al-nabī (A) : the MUDD of Medina, forming the basis for establishing the value of the ṢĀʿ (4 ~ is 1 *ṣāʿ*). VIII 654a

muddaʿī (A) : in law, the plaintiff in a lawsuit. II 170b

♦ muddaʿā ʿalayh (A) : in law, the defendant in a lawsuit. II 170b

♦ muddaʿā bihi (A) : in law, the object of the claim in a lawsuit. II 171a

muddakhir → MUDĪR

muddaththir (A) : the title of the 74th SŪRA of the Qurʾān, derived from the first verse which may be translated 'O you covered in a cloak'. VII 286a; and → MUZZAMMIL

muddjina → ḲAYNA

mudéjar (Sp, < A *mudadjdjan*) : a term, first appearing in Spanish texts ca. 1462, to designate the Muslim who, in return for the payment of tribute, continued to live in territories conquered by the Christians; it is also used to characterise the manifrestations relative to this culture, thus mudéjar architecture, literature, etc. VII 286a

mudhahhib (A) : in manuscript production, a gilder, or decorator. V 208a

mudhākara (A) : in the context of the mystical order of the Yashruṭiyya, a lesson on the Qurʾān and the order. XI 298b

mudhakk (A) : a term for a foal older than five years of age. II 785a

mudhakkar (A) : masculine; in grammar, a technical term for one of the two states of a noun, whose opposite is *muʾannath* 'feminine'. VII 289b

♦ mudhakkarāt (A) : in poetry, poems composed about boys. IX 8b

mudhayyal (A) : a complex chronogram, whereby the principal chronogram is completed by a supplementary chronogram, *dhayl*, the sum of the two providing the date. III 468a

In literary theory, ~ is used for an imperfect paronomasia whereby several letters are appended to one of the two words, e.g. *djawā* and *djawānih*. X 69b

mudhīʿ → IDHĀʿA

mūdiʿ → WADĪʿA

mūḍiḥa (A) : a wound laying bare the bone, a determining factor in the prescription of compensation following upon physical injury, DIYA. II 341b

muʿḍila (A, pl. *muʿḍilāt*) : a difficult question of law, an abstruse legal case which the proponents of RAʾY used, and the anti-*raʾy* sources decried, to expand Islamic law beyond the resources of the traditionists (syn. *ughlūṭa*, pl. *ughlūṭāt*). XII 688a

mudīr (A, T *müdīr*) : the title of governors of the provinces of Egypt, an office created by Muḥammad ʿAlī shortly after 1813. The chief task of the ~ is the controlling of the industrial and agricultural administration and of the irrigation, as executed by his subordinates. At the present time, Egypt comprises 25 *mudīriyyas* or governorates. VII 290a; and → SĀḲĪ

In astronomy, the 'director', a small circle, on which the centre of Mercury's deferent rotates, in the Ptolemaic model. X 941a

In law, an active trader, distinguished (by the Mālikīs) from an investor (*muḥtakir, muddakhir*) as concerns the payment of ZAKĀT. XI 414a

♦ mudīriyya (A) : administrative district. IX 166b; and → MUDĪR

mudjabbir (A) : in medicine, a bone-setter, bone-healer. II 481b

mudjaddara → ARUZZ MUFALFAL

mudjaddid (A) : renewer (of the century), a term used for the renovator whom God will send to the Muslim community at the turn of each century, in order to explain matters of religion. VII 290a

mudjahhiz (A) : a type of merchant in mediaeval Islam, the purveyor who supplies travellers with all that they need. IX 789a; an exporting merchant. X 469a

mudjāhid (A, pl. *mudjāhidūn*) : a fighter for the faith, one who wages war against the unbelievers. VII 290b

In Muslim India, the *mudjāhidīn* were the rebellious forces of Aḥmad Brēlwī (d. 1831), who fought the Sikhs to oust them from the Pandjab. I 282b; IV 196b; VII 290b

In Saudi Arabia, the *mudjāhidūn* is the popular name for the National Guard, made up of detachments of the Ikhwān. III 1068a

mudjallī (A), or *muḳaffī* : a name for the third horse in a horse-race, according to the order of finishing. II 953a

muʿdjam → FAHRASA; ḤURŪF AL-MUʿDJAM; ḲĀMŪS

mudjannaḥ → DJINĀS AL-ḲALB

mudjarrad → DJADWAL; RABBĀNĪ

mudjāwara (A) : 'proximity, association'; in rhetoric, one of three types of metaphor as defined by al-Sakkākī, as e.g. the container for the contained: *zudjādja* 'bottle' = 'wine'. V 117a

mudjāwir (A) : neighbour; a person, who, for a shorter or longer period of time, settles in a holy place in order to lead a life of asceticism and religious contemplation and to receive the BARAKA 'blessing' of that place. VII 293b; VIII 495b; the permanently-appointed personnel of places of pilgrimage (guards, cleaners, guides, etc.) who in general belong to the local population. VII 294b

In Egypt until today, ~ may indicate any student of the Azhar who comes from outside and lives in the premises of al-Azhar. VII 293b

mudjawwaza (A, T *müdjewweze*) : apparently only found in Turkish, a barrel- or cylindrical-shaped cap, worn with the turban cloth from the time of Süleymān's dress edict, as the proper court and state headdress. Süleymān is said to have been the first sultan to wear it; it was previously the military cap, the red top of which peeped out from the turban cloth. X 613b

mudjāzāt → SHARṬ

mudjbira → DJABRIYYA

mudjdiba (A) : in geography, a term applied to terrain covered with moving sands and totally waterless. VIII 845b

muʿdjiza (A) : lit. that by means of which (the Prophet) confounds, overwhelms his opponents; the technical term for miracle. It does not occur in the Qurʾān, which denies miracles in connection with Muḥammad, whereas it emphasises his 'signs', *āyāt*, later taken to mean the verses of the Qurʾān. ~ and ĀYA have become synonyms; they denote the miracles performed by God in order to prove the sincerity of His apostles. The term

KARĀMA is used in connection with the saints; it differs from ~ in so far as it denotes nothing but a personal distinction granted by God to a saint. VII 295b

mudjrā → MADJRĀ

mudjtahid (A) : in law, one who possesses the aptitude to form his own judgement on questions concerning the sharīʿa, using personal effort, IDJTIHĀD, in the interpretation of the fundamental principles of the law. III 1026b; VII 295b; and → MUṬLAḲ

♦ mudjtahid al-fatwā (A) : in law, someone who can issue a legal opinion on the basis of the legal principles (ḲAWĀʿID) of his school. XII 517b

mudjtathth (A) : in prosody, the name of the fourteenth Arabic metre. Theoretically, it comprises three feet: *mustafʿilun / fāʿilātun / fāʿilātun* to each hemistich, but in practice there is just one single *fāʿilātun*. This metre is not used by the ancient poets. I 670a; VII 304a

mudjūn (A) : a word whose meaning ranges from jest and frivolity to the most shameless debauchery, including vulgarity, coarseness, impudence, libertinage, obscenity and everything that may provoke coarse laughter, such as scatological humour, ~ nourished, from a literary viewpoint, entertaining works full of more or less obscene anecdotes. VII 304a

♦ mudjūniyyāt (A) : poetry of sexual perversion. IX 453b

muḍmar (A) : implicit; in grammar, ~ (syn. *ḍamīr*) designates a noun in which the person is disguised by means of a mark. This term is the converse of *muẓhar* 'explicit', designating a noun in which the person is revealed in a clear manner. The category of the implicit noun corresponds to that of the personal pronoun in Western grammar. VII 304b; IX 527b; and → TAḲDĪR; ẒĀHIR

mudradj (A) : 'inserted'; in the science of Tradition, ~ is used of a gloss in the MATN, or of giving with one ISNĀD texts which differ with different *isnād*s, or of mentioning a number of transmitters who differ in their *isnād* without indicating this. Generally, ~ is used of inserting something in the *isnād* or the *matn* of one Tradition from another to make this appear part of it. III 26a

muḍṭarib (A) : 'incongruous'; in the science of Tradition, ~ is used when two or more people of similar standing differ with one another in their version of a Tradition. The difference may affect ISNĀD or MATN. III 26a

♦ muḍṭarib al-ḥadīth (A) : a man whose Traditions are confused. III 26a

mufādana (A) : in mediaeval Egypt, taxation by FADDĀN, a system of payment in kind. IV 1032a

al-mufaḍḍaliyyāt (A) : in literature, the title of an anthology of early Arabic poems, mainly pre-Islamic, some dating to the beginning of the 6th century. VII 306b

mufākhara (A, pl. *mufākharāt*) : in poetry, a genre consisting of self-praise, but hardly ever separated from HIDJĀʾ, taunting and deriding the rival. VII 308b; a contest for precedence and glory, usually taking place between groups, tribes and clans in pre-Islamic Arabia, although in post-Islamic times, there were caliphs who were not ashamed to take part in them. VII 309b

mufakhkham → TAFKHĪM

mufalfil (A) : in the mediaeval Near East, a beggar who pretends to have been the victim of a robbery. The ~ works together with a confederate. VII 494b

mufarridj (A) : in medicine, a cordial made from saffron. XI 381b

mufaṣṣal (A) : lit. separated, hived off; in administrative usage of British India, whence the form *Mofussil*, the provinces, the rural districts and stations, as opposed to the administrative headquarters of a Presidency, District or region (*ṣadr*, or in Anglo-Indian usage, *Sudder*). XII 561a; XII 632a

mufāwaḍa (A) : in law, a form of commercial partnership, most prominently associated with the Ḥanafī school, and in a lesser degree with the Mālikīs. For the Ḥanafīs, the

~ is one of two classes of commercial partnership, ʿINĀN being the other, and is perhaps best translated as a universal, or unlimited, investment partnership. VII 310a

In the context of Mālikī law, ~ denotes a partnership in which each of the contracting parties confers on the other an unqualified mandate to dispose of their joint capital in any acceptable manner designed to benefit their common enterprise. VII 311a

müfettis͟h (T, A *mufattis͟h*) : in the Ottoman legal system of the 12th/18th century, a level of five judges, three in Istanbul and one each in Bursa and Edirne, whose duties were to oversee and inquire into the conducting of the Imperial pious foundations; in the 19th century under the Tanẓīmāt reforms, ~ became an overseer and inspector of various new administrative mechanisms. In modern Turkish, ~ (*müfettiş*) is a standard word for 'inspector'. XII 632a

mufrad (A, pl. *mufradāt*) : in grammar, ~ denotes the singular, usually when applied to the 'simple' noun, in opposition to the dual and plural forms. II 406b; VII 313a; in morphology, ~ means 'simple', as opposed to MURAKKAB 'compound', and designates a noun made up of a single element. In syntax, ~ means 'in isolation', as opposed to *muḍāf* 'in annexation' and designates a noun which is not followed by a determinating complement. VII 313b

In lexicography, more often used in the plural *mufradāt*, ~ denotes the words taken in isolation in the lexicon. I 1083a; VII 313b

In mathematics, ~ denotes simple or ordinary fractions. IV 725b

♦ al-mufradūn (A) : the ninth degree in the ṣūfī hierarchical order of saints. I 95a

muftaʿal → MAṢNŪʿ

muftī (A) : the person who gives an opinion on a point of law, FATWĀ, or is engaged in that profession. II 866a; IX 325a

mug͟haffal (A) : in early Islam, an 'irresponsible wit'. IX 552b

mug͟hālaṭa maʿnawiyya → TAWRIYA

mug͟hārasa (A) : in law, a lease for agricultural planting, one of the most-used forms of contract. Under its terms, the owner of a piece of land charges a person with the planting of trees on it under a co-ownership basis, and in return, he agrees to grant the planter ownership of a predetermined proportion of the whole crop. The lessee thus becomes an owner; and he can put an end to the common ownership by demanding a division of the land. VII 346b

mug͟harrir (A) : an adventurer. X 915a

al-mug͟hayyabāt al-k͟hams (A) : lit. the five mysteries, things concealed in the unseen; in theology, ~ are regarded as known to God alone as part of His prescience and foreknowledge of all aspects of nature and human activity. They are usually identified with the five things known to God as expounded in Q 31:34 : the hour of the Last Judgement; when rain will be sent down; what it is in the womb (i.e. the sex and number of children); what a man will gain, of his sustenance, on the morrow; and when a man shall die. VII 346b

mug͟hnam → WAKĪR

mug͟hnī (A), or *mūg͟hnī* : in music, a sort of arch-lute, said to have been invented by Ṣafī al-Dīn al-Urmawī. X 770a

muḥabbar (A) : fabric of high quality manufactured in Yemen; artistic poetry of high quality. IX 448b

muḥabbat-i kull (IndP) : absolute love, the highest station of spiritual attainment in the religious thought of the Mug͟hal emperor Akbar. IX 846b

muḥabbis → WĀḲIF

muhādana → MUWĀDAʿA

muḥāḍara (A, pl. *muḥāḍarāt*) : a gathering in the course of which the participants converse and exchange information, quotations and stories. VII 851b; a lecture. XI 57a

In the mystical thought of al-Ḳus̲h̲ayrī, ~ is getting oneself into position vis-à-vis the objective sought, the first of three stages in the progression towards Reality. This stage remains 'behind the veil', the lifting of which belongs to the second stage. IV 697a

muḥaddab → MUMAT̲H̲T̲H̲AL

muḥaddit̲h̲ (A) : the usual term for a technical specialist in Traditions. I 259a

muḥad̲j̲d̲j̲ar (P) : balustrade. IX 191b

muhād̲j̲ir (A, pl. *muhād̲j̲irūn*) : lit. one who migrates; in Turkey and Ottoman lands, ~ was used for refugees and the victims of the population exchanges in the early years of the Republic; by 1933 the term was replaced by the neologism *göčmen*. VII 350b

In India, ~ has been used to describe those Muslims from the Indo-Pakistan subcontinent who migrated from their homes in order to protect their religion and to safeguard their interests as Muslims, the first group leaving in the early decades of the 20th century and the second group in 1947. VII 354b

In early Islam, the plural **muhād̲j̲irūn** stands for the Emigrants, those Meccan Muslims who emigrated from Mecca to Medina either just before Muḥammad himself or in the period up to the conquest of Mecca in 8/630. VII 356a; members of Arab tribes, who settled at Medina after their conversion to Islam and thus renounced returning to their tribes, are also designated as ~. VIII 828a

muḥāfaẓa (A) : governorate. IX 166b

muḥākāt (A) : in the poetics of the philosophers, symbols, mimeses, enigmas. IX 459a; imitative, i.e. figurative, language which presents one thing by means of another in the way of similes and metaphors, sometimes used as a synonym of TAK̲H̲YĪL. X 130a,b; XII 654b

muḥaḳḳaḳ (A) : 'strongly expressed (word); tightly-woven (cloth)'; ~ is a form of Arabic script, whose main characteristic is the feature that the left corner of twenty-one letters are angled. This script was used for long-page format Qurʾāns and also for frames. After the end of the 11th/17th century, ~ yielded place to T̲H̲ULUT̲H̲. IV 1123a; VIII 151b

muḥakkam → ḤAKAM

muḥakkima (A) : the phrase *al-muḥakkima al-ūlā* stands for the cry *lā ḥukm illā li 'llāh*, raised at Ṣiffīn by those who protested against arbitration. I 384a

muḥallabiyya (A) : a popular rice pudding dish; the mediaeval version of it was made with meat or chicken, sweetened with honey and seasoned with spices to which saffron-coloured rice is added. VIII 653a

muḥallil (A) : lit. someone who makes a thing legal, legaliser, legitimator; in law, the figure who acts as a 'man of straw' in order to authenticate or make permissible some legal process otherwise of doubtful legality or in fact prohibited. XII 632a

In early Islam, a horse entered into a competition, whose owner made no wager and gained the whole amount staked by all the other entrants if his horse won (syn. *dāk̲h̲il*). II 953b; in gambling, a 'legaliser', i.e. someone who did not contribute to the stakes, which made the gambling legal, although the law schools differ as to the legality of this procedure. V 109b; and → TAḤLĪL

muḥammaḍa (A, pl. *muḥammaḍāt*) : citrus fruits. IV 740b

muḥammadī (A) : in numismatics, the name given in the reign of the Ṣafawid Muḥammad K̲h̲udābanda to the double) :

muḥammadī (A) : in numismatics, the name given in the reign of the Ṣafawid Muḥammad K̲h̲udābanda to the double *s̲h̲āhī*, or 100 dīnārs. In 1888 it was renamed *dō s̲h̲āhī*. VIII 790a; IX 203b

muḥammira (A, P *surk̲h̲-d̲j̲āmagān*) : 'wearers of red', the name for the K̲h̲urramiyya, a religious movement founded in the late 5th century AD by Mazdak and the various Iranian sects which developed out of it. VII 664a muḥannak (A) : in the Fāṭimid court, a eunuch in private service who wore a turban passing under the chin. IV 1092a

muḥāraba → KAṬʿ AL-ṬARĪḲ

muḥarraf (A) : 'altered'; in the science of Tradition, ~ is used of a change occurring in the letters of a word. III 26a

In literary theory, ~ is used for an imperfect paronomasia whereby there is difference in vocalisation between the two words, e.g. *al-dayn* and *al-dīn*. X 69b

muḥarram (A) : the first month of the Muslim year. The name was originally not a proper name but an adjectival epithet qualifying Ṣafar I, the first month of the pre-Islamic Meccan year. VII 464a

muharridj (A) : a clown, popular as entertainment, especially in North Africa. XII 778a

muḥarrir → MUNSHĪ AL-MAMĀLIK

muḥāsaba (A) : lit. accounting; in classical Muslim administration, ~ is the term given to the comprehensive accounting presented by an ʿĀMIL on relinquishing his appointment when it is not approved by the authority to whom he presents it. When it is approved, it is called MUWĀFAḲA. II 78b

In Ottoman finance, ~ referred to financial accounting. VII 465b

In mysticism, ~, more precisely *muḥāsabat al-nafs*, denotes 'inward accounting, spiritual accounting'. VII 465a

muḥāsib (A) : accountant. XI 88b

muḥaṣṣil (A) : a term used under the Anatolian Saldjūḳs and Ottomans for various types of revenue collectors. It acquired special significance amid extensive Ottoman financial reforms of 1838-9. VII 467b

muḥāwarāt (A) : in literature, correspondence in the form of letters; as used by Yūsufī, author of an INSHĀʾ collection, ~ are divided into three kinds: letters to persons of higher rank, *murāḳaʿāt*; letters to persons of the same rank, *murāsalāt*; and letters to persons of lower rank, *riḳāʿ*. XI 362b; characteristic modes of expression, set turns of speech, turns of phrases. VI 816a; XII 631a,b

muḥdathūn (A) : lit. the Moderns; in literature, those poets who came after the ancient poets (called *ḳudamāʾ, mutaḳaddimūn* or AWĀʾIL) of the pre-Islamic and early Islamic periods. No formal end of the ~ movement is recognised, but mostly the term applies to poets of the first few centuries of the ʿAbbāsid period. XII 637b

muḥdith → ḤADATH

muḥīl (A) : in law, the transferor, i.e. one who has a debt to A and a claim against B, and settles his debt by transferring his claim against B to the benefit of A. In this case, A is the creditor, *al-muḥtāl*, and B is the cessionary, *al-muḥtāl ʿalayhi*. III 283a

muḥillūn (A) : lit. those who make lawful (what is unlawful); an expression used in early Islamic historical texts to denote those who had shed the blood of al-Ḥusayn b. ʿAlī. VII 470a

mühimme defterleri (T) : in Ottoman administration, the 'Registers of Important Affairs', a collection of 263 registers, continued until 1905, containing copies of sultans' rescripts, for the most part addressed to governors and ḲĀḌĪs but also to foreign rulers. VII 470a

muḥkam → MUTASHĀBIH

muhmala (A) : a gloss signifying the unpointed ḤARF, e.g. *ʿayn muhmala*. III 597a

muhr (P) : a seal, signet or signet-ring. VII 472a

In Arabic, the term for a foal at birth; from then on, it is given different names, determined by the stage of development of the teeth. II 785a

♦ muhrdār (T *mühürdār*) : the keeper of the seals, 'private secretary', in Persian and Ottoman administration. IV 1104a; VII 473a

muhra → KALB

muḥrim (A) : the pilgrim who has entered the state of ritual purity. II 1069a; III 1052b

muḥṣan (A) : in law, a term denoting a certain personal status: married (and the marriage has been duly consummated), free, and Muslim. The quality of *iḥṣān* resides in each spouse when both satisfy all three criteria. VII 474b; XI 509b

muḥtakir → MUDĪR

muḥtāl (A) : in mediaeval Islam, a category of thieves, one who worked by stratagems and who did not kill in the course of his crimes and was therefore looked down on by his more desperate and violent confrères. V 769a; and → MUḤĪL

muḥtalim (A) : dreaming, and particularly dreaming of copulation and experiencing an emission of the seminal fluid in dreaming. VIII 822a

muḥtasib → ḤISBA

mühürdār (T) : in the Ottoman empire, a private secretary. XI 202a

muʿīd (A, T) : lit. repeater; in the primary school system, an assistant. V 568a; IX 702b

muʿīnsiz (A *muʿīn* 'supporter', T *siz* 'without') : in the Ottoman military, someone who had nobody to look after his family and other dependents if he was drafted, i.e. a breadwinner, and thus was exempted from military service, but served as reservist (RADĪF, MUSTAḤFIẒ). XII 640b

mukaʿʿab → KAʿB

mukāʿama → MUʿĀKAMA

muḳābal (A) : a pair of complimentary opposites, e.g. absence and presence. III 84a

♦ **muḳābala** (A) : in astronomy, ~ is used as the term for the opposition of a planet and the sun or of two planets with one another. In opposition, the difference in longitude between the heavenly bodies is 180 degrees. ~ may be used to refer to the opposition of sun and moon, although the usual technical expression for this phenomenon is *al-istiḳbāl*. VII 490a

In astrology, the diametric aspect of the planets. IV 259a

As a technique in manuscript production, ~ has the meaning of 'collation', i.e. the textual comparison of a manuscript with another of the same work, preferably with one from which it was copied. A synonym is *muʿāraḍa*. VII 490b

In literary theory, ~ refers to a type of antithesis, in which both sides of the opposition consist of two or more terms. VII 491b

♦ muḳābeled̲j̲i (T) : clerk. VIII 291a

mukabbara → MARSŪM

muḳābeled̲j̲i → MUḲĀBAL

mukābir (A) : in mediaeval Islam, a category of thieves, the robber with violence. V 769a

muḳaddam (A) : lit. placed in front; the chief, the one in command, e.g. of a body of troops or of a ship (captain). In the dervish orders, ~ is used for the head of the order or the head of a monastery. VII 492a; in North Africa, the official who administers individual local ZĀWIYAs and initiates, instructs and supervises members. XI 468a; the administrator in the middle of the Mamlūk hierarchy, who stood at the head of a barracks, *ṭabaḳa*. The highest member of the hierarchy was known as *muḳaddam al-mamālīk al-sulṭāniyya*. X 7b; and → MAʾD̲H̲ŪN

In logic, ~ means the protasis in a premise in the form of a conditional sentence. VII 492a

In mathematics, ~ means the first of two numbers in a proportion, or in other words, the divided number in a simple division. VII 492a; and → TĀLĪ

♦ muḳaddama → AṢL, ṬALĪʿA

muḳaddar → LAFẒ; TAḲDĪR

mukaddī (A, pl. *mukaddūn*, ? < P *gadā*) : in mediaeval Islam, a wandering beggar or vagrant, who, with a remarkable talent for plausible lying and a knowledge of certain effective dodges, succeeds in opening up the purses of those simple persons who allow themselves to be taken in by his eloquent but mendacious words. IV 735a; VII 493b

muḳaddim (A) : the shadow-play master, who manipulated the figurines with sticks. IV 1136b

muḳaddima (A) : the foreword, preface or introduction to prose works; as a literary genre, the independent development of the preface, which had a stereotyped form consisting of initial commendations, a middle part and closing praises, was developed in particular by al-Djāḥiẓ and Ibn Ḳutayba. VII 495b

mukaddis (A) : in mediaeval ʿIrāḳ, a beggar who makes a collection for buying a shroud. VII 494a

mukāfaʾa (A) : according to al-Khwārazmī, the term preferred by scribes for what critics of poetry called MUṬĀBAḲA 'antithesis'. X 451a

muḳaffī → MUDJALLĪ

mukaffir (A) : in poetry, term used by Ṣafī al-Dīn al-Ḥillī for a ZADJAL that contains admonitions and wisdom. XI 373b

mukallaf (A) : in law, one who is obliged to fulfil the religious duties. I 993b; and → TAKLĪF

♦ mukallafa (A) : in Egypt, the term used to designate the land survey registers. II 79b

muḳallid → DJIRRAT; TAḲLĪD

muḳannī (A) : a specialist in constructing a ḲANĀT, a mining installation for extracting water from the depths of the earth, called *kārīzkan* in Afghanistan. IV 529b; in Yazd, ~s were also known as *čāhkhūyān*; they were highly rated for their skill and often employed outside of Yazd. XI 305a

muḳanṭarāt (A) : in astronomy, the parallel circles at the horizon, normally called circles of height or parallels of height. This term was borrowed in the Middle Ages by Western astronomers, under the term *almícantarat*. VII 500b

muḳaʿʿr → MUMATHTHAL

muḳāraʿa → MUKHĀRADJA

muḳāraḍa → MUḌĀRABA

muḳārana (A) : a rhetorical figure introduced by Ibn Abi ʾl Iṣbaʿ, consistiing of a 'combination of figures' made up of metaphorical antitheses. X 451a

muḳarbaṣ (A), or *muḳarbas* : in architecture, a term denoting a technique of craftmanship used in the mediaeval Muslim West, yielding Sp. *mocárabe*. It can be defined as 'work formed by a geometric combination of interlocking prisms, externally cut in concave surfaces and used as decoration in vaults, cornices etc.' It forms a counterpart to, but is different in execution from the MUḲARNAS technique of the Muslim central and eastern lands. The ~ was carved in jesso, brick, wood, marble or stone and was frequently coloured. VII 500b

mukārī (A) : lit. hirer; a dealer in riding beasts and beasts of burden, usage being extended from the person buying and selling and hiring to the muleteer or other person accompanying a loaded beast. VII 501b

muḳarnas (A, < Gk) : in architecture, 'stalactites', a type of decoration typical for Islamic architecture all over the central and eastern parts of the Muslim world, composed of a series of niches embedded within an architectural frame, geometrically connected and forming a three-dimensional composition around a few basic axes of symmetry. The essential function of the ~ is ornamental. Its counterpart in the Muslim West is MUḲARBAṢ. I 1229a; II 863b; VII 501b

muḳarr → IḲRĀR

muḳarrabūn → TASNĪM

muḳarrariyya : one of two main headings in the monthly and yearly accounting registers of the Īlkẖānids, under which fell the regular (*muḳarrar*) payments made every year by order of the sovereign from the *dīwān-i aʿlā* to ḲĀḌĪs, SHAYKHs, SAYYIDs, students, financial officials, etc. III 284a; and → IṬLĀḲIYYA

mukarrib (A) : lit. unifier; in ancient Yemen, a sovereign superior to the kings. IX 91a; IX 675b

muḳāsama (A) : lit. dividing out; a system of raising the land tax, involving the levy, by agreement, of a percentage or share of the crops, usually taken when these last had ripened. The early sources on law and finance distinguished it from the system of MISĀḤA, the assessment of a fixed lump sum on the land according to its fertility, location, etc., and from the system of MUḲĀṬAʿA, which implied a fixed annual sum payable without regard to the variations of prosperity and harvest and often the subject of a tax-farming contract. Known in the early centuries, it continued to be used down to modern times. IV 1032a ff.; VII 506b

In the Ottoman empire and in India, ~ is one of two terms describing the land tax (the other is MUWAẒẒAFA); the *kẖarādj muḳāsama* refers to a certain proportion of the produce accruing to the state from every field. II 158a; IV 1055b; VII 507a

mukāshafa (A) : in mysticism, ~ means illumination, epiphany (ant. *satr* 'veiling', *istitār* 'occultation). In the mystical thought of al-Ḳushayrī, ~ is the lifting of the veil, a 'raising of the curtain' on to the world of mystery, the second of three stages in the progression towards Reality. IV 697a

mukāsir (A) : among the Ismāʿīlīs, the name of one of the subordinates who assists the DĀʿĪ. II 97b

mukassar (A) : in geometry, the square of a unit of linear measure. IV 725b

muḳāṭaʿa (A) : in the mediaeval taxation system, ~ was used for the sum handed over by a tax farmer in return for the collection and management of the revenue from a given province or district. IV 1038a; VII 508a

In the Ottoman empire, ~ denoted tax farm, especially used by the Ottomans in connection with taxation imposed on the traffic in commodities in and out of the empire or at the entry to the big towns. VII 508a; and → MUḲĀṬAʿADJĪ

♦ muḳāṭaʿadjī (T, A) : in Lebanon under Ottoman rule, the title borne by members of families responsible for the levying of a contractual tax on a district, *muḳāṭaʿa*. V 792a

mukātab(a) → KITĀB

muḳātil (A) : in Western and Spanish Arabic, *al-* ~ is an alternative name for the planet Saturn. VIII 101a; XI 555a

muḳaṭṭaʿāt (A) : one of the names given to the mysterious letters placed at the head of 26 SŪRAs of the Qurʾān. VII 509a

In poetry, ~ are fragmentary pieces, very often topical poems, such as elegies, chronograms and satires. III 58a

mukawwir → MIKWAR(A)

muḳawwiyāt (A, s. *muḳawwī*) : in medicine, originally stimulants but gradually taking on the meaning of aphrodisiacs. XII 640b

muḳayyin → ḲAYYĀN

mukayyis (A), or *kayyās* : the 'masseur', one who wields the *kīs*, a bag of tow used to massage the clients, in a **ḥammām** 'steam bath'. III 140b

muḳbulā (A) : a term for a fish stew, also known as *munazzalat al-samak*, based on eel or carp. VIII 1023a

mukẖābarāt (A) : the intelligence and police services in Arab countries. XII 670b

mukẖaḍram (A, pl. *mukẖaḍramūn*) : a person who lived in the DJĀHILIYYA and in the time of Islam, applied in particular to poets; *al-mukẖaḍramūn* constitute the class of pagan poets who died after the proclamation of Islam, although the meaning has been extended to poets living in the Umayyad and the ʿAbbāsid period. VII 516a

In the science of Tradition, ~ signifies a transmitter who accepted Islam but had not seen the Prophet. VII 516a

♦ mukhaḍramū 'l-dawlatayn (A) : 'the poets of the two dynasties', a term for poets living in the Umayyad and the ʿAbbāsid period. VII 516a

mukhallefāt (T, < A) : 'things left behind (at death)', an Ottoman financial-judicial term alluding to the property of deceased officials and of those who died without heirs that the Ottoman treasury confiscated. The inheritances of the minors or the mentally handicapped who could not oversee their shares were also seized and kept until they reached puberty; the treasury also approved the expenditure of the money for them. I 1147b; VII 517a; for compound terms having to do with clerks, departments, etc. of Ottoman administration involved in ~, VII 517a

mukhammas (A) : in Arabic, early Persian and Turkish poetry, a five-line MUSAMMAṬ, a stanzaic form of poetry, with either four lines of separate rhyme and one line with common rhyme, or blocks of five rhyming lines, e.g. *aaaaa bbbbb* etc. VII 660a ff.; and → TAKHMĪS

mukhammisa (A) : in religion, the Pentadists, a name applied to a doctrinal current among the shīʿī extremists which espoused the divinity of Muḥammad, ʿAlī, Fāṭima, al-Ḥasan and al-Ḥusayn. VII 517a

mukhannath (A) : effeminate, used as a synonym for a homosexual although in normal usage refers to the genuine hermaphrodite. V 776b

In mediaeval Spain, a (male) singer disguised as a woman. V 778a

mukhāradja (A) : the game of mora, morra, or mication (L *micatio*, It *mora*), played all around the shores of the Mediterranean, and also in Arabia and Iraq. It is a game of chance and is in principle forbidden by Islam. Synonyms are *muḳāraʿa, munāhada* and *musāhama*, followed by *bi 'l-aṣābiʿ* 'with the fingers'. VII 518a

mukharnika → MUʾARNIBA

mukhaṣṣiṣ → TAKHṢĪṢ

mukhāṭara (A) : a legal device, familiar in mediaeval European mercantile circles in its Latin garb *mohatra*, which is a form of 'a double sale', *bayʿatān fī bayʿa*. Its purpose was to circumvent the prohibition of any form of interest on a capital loan. VII 518b; and → BAYʿATĀN FĪ BAYʿA

mukhattam (A) : a pattern of lines in cloth, from silks to woolen materials, forming quadrangular compartments, i.e. checks. Such cloths seem to have been woven almost everywhere in the Islamic lands. VII 519a

mukhtalas (A) : 'snatched'; in archery, a way of loosing an arrow, by drawing rapidly and loosing immediately without any break in time. IV 800b

mukhtalif (A) : in mathematics, disjunct fractions which do not have the same denominator. IV 725b

mukhtalis (A) : in law, a thief who comes secretly but goes away openly. IX 63a; and → ṬARRĀR

mukhtār (A) : lit. chosen person; in the late Ottoman empire and some of its successor states, the headman of a quarter or village, appointed by the central government and charged with a variety of duties. VII 519a

In law, (an act done) by choice, not under compulsion. VII 635b

♦ **mukhtārāt** (A) : in literature, an anthology, selection of poetry, the oldest of which in Arabic is the *al-Muʿallaḳāt*. VII 526b

mukhtaṣar (A) : a handbook or an abridged manual, usually condensed from a longer work. VII 536a, where is also found a list of approximately equivalent terms; an epitome, a concise exposition. IX 324a

♦ mukhtaṣar al-ṭūmār (A) : in calligraphy, a larger type of script, used for the TUGHRA when there were few strokes; a large script was called *ḳalam al-ṭūmār*. X 596a

mukhtaṣṣ (A) : in Mālikī law, an intermediate category between GHANĪMA and FAY᾿, which includes property taken out of enemy territory by stealth. XII 532a

mukḥula (A) : a small narrow-necked vessel, in mediaeval times commonly of glass, used to keep the eye cosmetic KUḤL in. A special object known in Khurāsān as *wasma-djūsh* was used for grinding the substance and pouring it into the ~. V 356b f.; and → NAFFĀṬ

muḳīm (A) : a term denoting 'a person domiciled in the place and satisfying the stipulations of the law'; in Indonesia, the Friday communal prayer is only valid, according to the Shāfiʿī school of law, if 40 *muḳīms* are present, and since the population was rarely numerous enough to allow this, ~ acquired the meaning of 'department, circle' because of the custom of grouping several villages together. I 741a

muḳla (A) : a very wide turban worn by *ʿulamā᾿* (→ FAKĪH) in Egypt. V 741b; also the headdress of Coptic priests with a long narrow band. X 613b

muḳri᾿ (A) : the teacher of Qur᾿ānic readings and recitation, a member of a relatively small professional elite. Every ~ must be a *ḳāri᾿* (pl. ḲURRĀ᾿), a reciter of the Qur᾿ān and a much more common performer. X 73a

muḳrif (A) : the 'approacher', whose dam is of better breeding than the sire, one of the four classifications of a horse. II 785b

muḳṭaʿ (A) : holder of a fief, IḲṬĀʿ. V 862b; a provincial governor under the Dihlī sultanate, transferable at will, who commanded the local military forces and was paid personally by the grant of a revenue assignment or by a percentage of the provinical revenues. II 272b

muḳtaḍab (A) : 'untrained' or 'extemporised'. IX 10b

In prosody, the name of the thirteenth Arabic metre, in fact little used. I 670a; VII 540

muktarī → KIRĀ᾿

muḳwiī → ḲAWĪ

mulā᾿a (A) : a large, enveloping outer wrap worn by women in the Arab East. V 741b

mulaffaḳ → TĀMM

mulaḥḥin (A) : composer. XII 547a; in the northern Yemeni tribal system, a composer or singer of folk poetry. IX 234b

mulāmasa → BAYʿ AL-MULĀMASA

mulammaʿāt (A) : in Persian literature, ~ are macaronic verses, a mixed composition of Arabic, Persian and sometimes Turkish elements used to obtain a humorous effect. III 355b

mulassan → AL-NAʿL AL-SHARĪF

mulaththam (A) : 'wearing a veil', a description of Berber nomadic tribes like the Touareg. V 652a

mülāzemet (T, < A *mulāzama*) : in Ottoman administration, the certificate of eligibility for office. VII 545a; and → MULĀZIM

mulāzim (A, T *mülāzîm*) : in Ottoman administration and military, a candidate for office in the Ottoman learned hierarchy (the ʿILMIYYE). VII 545b; also, a tax-farmer, part of a special corps to collect the poll-tax in certain districts; one of 300 special mounted bodyguards whom sultan Süleymān I selected from among his household to accompany him on campaigns, so-called because they were preparing for important administrative posts which came by way of reward for their services to the sultan. VII 545a; the personal bodyguard to the Ṣafawīd shāh. I 8a; reserves for posts in the Ottoman palace and guild system. VII 545b

In the Ottoman military, ~ applied to the lowest two ranks of officers after the reorganisation of the army in the 19th century, corresponding to the rank of lieutenant. VII 545b mulḥam (A) : a cotton and silk fabric. V 554b; a fabric with a silk warp and a woof of some other stuff. V 737a; as *mulḥam ṭirāzī*, a combination fabric of silk warp and woof of another material with embroidered bands. X 536a

mulḥid (A, pl. *malāḥida*) : a deviator, apostate, heretic, atheist. There is no evidence of pre-Islamic usage in a religious meaning, which arose in the ʿAbbāsid period on the basis of Qurʾānic verses. Under the Umayyads, ~ had been synonymous with *bāgh̲ī* 'rebel' and *sh̲āḳḳ al-ʿaṣā* 'splitter of the ranks of the faithful', denoting the desertion (*ilḥād*) of the community of the faithful and rebellion against the legitimate caliphs. VII 546a

In Sald̲jūḳ times, the appellation *al-malāḥida al-ḳūhiyya* was used for the Ismāʿīlī heretics who took refuge in Ḳūhistān. V 355a

In Ottoman usage, ~ and *ilḥād* were commonly employed to describe subversive doctrines among the sh̲īʿīs and ṣūfīs. VII 546b

mulimm → MUTARAʿRIʿ

mulk (A) : royal power, a term used in the Qurʾān with reference to God and to certain pre-Islamic personages, who all appear in the Old Testament, and in the former case is synonymous with *malakūt*. VII 546b

mulkiyya (A, T *mülkiyye*) : a title to property (→ MILK). VII 547a

Under the Ottomans, *mülkiyye*, or more precisely *idāre-i mülkiyye*, had by roughly the 1830s become the customary Ottoman term for civil administration. VII 547a; and → ḲALEMIYYE

mullā → MOLLĀ

multazam (A) : the name for the part of the wall of the Kaʿba between the Black Stone and the door of the Kaʿba, so-called because the visitors press their breasts against it while praying fervently. IV 318a

mültezim (T, < A *multazim*) : in Ottoman administration, a tax-farmer who, from the mid-16th century on, collected taxes and dues on behalf of the Ottoman treasury. The ~ could either deliver all the proceeds while drawing a salary, or he could buy the right to retain the proceeds himself by paying the treasury an agreed sum in advance; this latter system was known as *iltizām*, which differed from the other term used for a tax-farm, *muḳāṭaʿa*, in that it referred to the collection of revenues from the imperial domains. *Muḳāṭaʿa* was applied to the collection by contract of other revenues. VII 550b

mulūk al-ṭawāʾif → MALIK

mulūk̲h̲iyya → ṬAʿMIYYA

mumālaṭa → ID̲JĀZA

mumāt̲h̲ala (A) : in rhetoric, total or nearly total equivalency of the two phrases that form a TARṢĪʿ. X 304b

mumāt̲h̲il → TĀMM

mumat̲h̲t̲h̲al (A) : in astronomy, a parecliptic orb, centred on the Earth and in the plane of the ecliptic, whose convex surface, *muḥaddab*, was contiguous with the eighth orb of the fixed stars while its parallel concave surface, *muḳaʿʿar*, was contiguous with the convex survace of Jupiter's parecliptic. This is one of three postulated solid rotating orbs to bring about a planet's observed motions. XI 555a

mumayyiz (A) : in law, the 'discerning minor', a stage in the transition from the status of minor to that of major. I 993b; VIII 836a

♦ mümeyyiz (T) : in the Ottoman empire, a clerk who examined every matter to be put before the SH̲AYK̲H̲ AL-ISLĀM as to correctness of presentation. II 867a

muʾmin (A) : lit. believer; one of the names of God. VII 554b

mūmis → BAG̲H̲IYY

mūmiyāʾ (A, P *mūmiyāʾī*) : bitumen, mineral tar (L *Mumia naturalis persica*), a solid, black, shining mineral liquid which trickles from rock-caves. In ancient medicine, it was mainly used against lesions and fractures. It is to be distinguished from the *Mumia factitia var. humana*, the bituminous substance of the Egyptian mummies, which is called *biṣṣasfalṭus* (and variants). VII 556a

mumsika (A) : a bit of metal, projecting from the outer rim of the astrolabe and fitting into an exactly corresponding indentation on the edge of each disc, which prevents the discs from turning. I 723a

muʾna (A) : in law, an impost. XI 410b; in North Africa, a special allowance for food, to which members of a GŪM were entitled when on active service. II 1138b

munābadha → BAYʿ AL-MUNĀBADHA

munabbat-kārī (P) : in architecture, lime plaster. V 600b; in art, filigree. X 518b

munādī (A) : town crier, herald; in the Qurʾān, ~ is used for the one who will proclaim the Last Day and give the summons to Judgement, in popular Islam usually identified with the angel Isrāfīl. VII 557a

munādjāt (A) : a whispering to, talking confidentially with someone; in religion, 'extempore prayer', as opposed to the corporate addressing of the deity in the ṢALĀT. VII 557b; a doxological supplication. IX 213a; 'whispered prayers'. XI 482b

In mysticism, the ṣūfīs' communion with God. VII 557b

♦ munādjāt Mūsā (A) : a synonym for TAWRĀT, the Torah. X 394a

munadjdjim (A) : in astrology, an astrologer, he who knows the lot of humans and their destiny from the positions of the stars (syn. AḤKĀMĪ). VII 557b

munaffidh → ṢĀḤIB AL-ASHGHĀL

munāfiḳūn (A) : a Qurʾānic term usually translated with 'hypocrites', to refer to dissenters within the community, whether openly or in secret. VII 561a

munāghāt (A) : term for the beggars' jargon of the Banū Sāsān. IX 70b

munāhada → MUKHĀRADJA

munāḳaḍāt → NAḲĀʾIḌ

munʿaḳid (A) : in law, a contract which fulfils all the conditions necessary to its formation. II 836a

munaḳḳila (A) : a fracture with displacement of a bone, a determining factor in the prescription of compensation following upon physical injury, DIYA. II 341b

munakkis (A) : in the terminology of horse-riding, a horse with bad head carriage. II 954a

munāsaba (A), or *tanāsub* : in rhetoric, correspondence between words in regard either to their pattern or to their meaning. II 825b

In law, the means of identifying or verifying the ratio (*ʿilla*) of a ruling. XII 570a

munāṣafa (A) : in law, reciprocal property-sharing by two co-owners, each of them holding the half of a one and undivided object, a special form of co-ownership. VII 564a

In the context of Muslim-non-Muslim relations, ~ historically became particularly important in the juridicial, fiscal and administrative organisation of border regions between Islamic and Frankish Crusader states in 12th and 13th-century Syria. The *raison d'être* of a ~ was to arrange a compromise on disputed border territories which neither the Frankish nor the Muslim neighbouring states were able to control completely. VII 564a

munāshada (A) : a set form of oath, at the beginning of a prayer of petition, sometimes involving a threat or coercion, directed at God. VII 564b

munaṣṣaf (A) : in early Islam, a prohibited product prepared by means of grapes. IV 996b

munāẓara (A, pl. *munāẓarāt*) : a scientific, in particular theological-juridical, dispute between Muslims and adherents of the AHL AL-KITĀB, and between Muslims themselves. V 1130b; V 1223b; VII 565b; VIII 363b

In literature, a literary genre in which two or more living or inanimate beings appear talking and competing for the honour which of them possesses the best qualities. VII 566b

munāziʿ (A) : in the terminology of horse-riding, a horse that takes the bit in its teeth and jerks the hands. II 953b

munazzalat al-samak → MUḲBULĀ

munfad̲j̲ā → FARʿ

munfaṣil (A) : in the science of Tradition, ~ is applied to a Tradition with several breaks in the ISNĀD, to distinguish it from MUNḲAṬIʿ. III 26a

munfatiḥa (A) : open, disengaged; in grammar, a term meaning non-velar, indicating all the letters of the Arabic alphabet except for *ṣād, ẓāʾ, ṭāʾ*, and *ḍād*. III 596b

mungh → MANGH

munḥarifa → MIZWALA; SAMT

munḳalib (A) : in the science of Tradition, a term used by some to indicate a Tradition which has a slight transposition in the wording. III 26a

munkar (A, pl. *munkarāt, manākīr*) : 'unknown, objectionable'; in the science of Tradition, a Tradition whose transmitter is alone in transmitting it and differs from one who is reliable, or is one who has not the standing to be accepted when alone. When one says of a transmitter *yarwi 'l-manākīr* 'he transmits ~ Traditions', this does not involve the rejection of all his Traditions; but if he is called *munkar al-ḥadīt̲h̲*, they are all to be rejected. III 26b; VII 575b; and → NAHY

munkasir → NĀḲIṢ

munḳaṭiʿ (A) : in the science of Tradition, applied commonly when there is a break in the ISNĀD at any stage later than the Successor; ~ has also been used of an *isnād* including unspecified people, or one later than a Successor who claims to have heard someone he did not hear. III 25b; and → YATĪM

munk̲h̲afiḍa (A) : 'lowered'; in grammar, those letters whose pronunciation does not require the elevation of the back of the tongue, i.e. all but the emphatic consonants, *ḥurūf al-muṭbaḳa*, and *ḳāf, g̲h̲ayn*, and *k̲h̲āʾ*. III 596b

munsalak̲h̲ (A), or *sarār* : the last day of the month, in historical works and correspondence. V 708a

munṣarif → MUTAMAKKIN

munsariḥ (A) : in prosody, the name of the tenth Arabic metre. I 670a

muns̲h̲ī (A), or more correctly *muns̲h̲iʾ* : in the Persian and Indo-Muslim worlds, a secretary in the ruler's chancery, an exponent of the high-flown epistolary style general in mediaeval Islamic chanceries from the 2nd/8th century onwards known as INS̲H̲Āʾ. IV 757b; VII 580b; VIII 481b

♦ muns̲h̲ī al-mamālik (A) : under the Mongols, the top position of the secretary class, in charge of the state chancellery; under him came the *muns̲h̲ī*, who drafted documents, and the *muḥarrir*, who prepared fair copies. IV 757b

muns̲h̲id (A) : a reciter of poems. IX 229a; in Egypt, a folk poet, associated primarily with a religious repertory. IX 235b; an improvisator. X 36a

munṣif (A) : lit. one who metes out justice; a term used in Indo-Muslim administration, and then in that of British India, to denote a legal official or judge of subordinate grade. VII 580b; sub-judge. I 287b

♦ **munṣifa** (A) : the name given by mediaeval Arabic critics and anthologists to those poems in which a description of the fights between tribes is accompanied by a recognition, with equity, of the opponent's valour and the sufferings endured by the poet's own side. VII 580b

muntahib (A) : in law, a robber who falls upon someone and robs him at a place where help is available. IX 63b muntaḳ (A) : 'pronounceable'; in mathematics, the term for the category of fractions whose denominator lies between 3 and 10 (syn. *maftūḥ*); the rest are called *aṣamm* 'deaf' and are expressed by *dj̲uzʾ min* 'a part of'. IV 725b

muntasib (A) : in mathematics, a fraction of relationship. IV 725b, where an example in modern notation is given

muntaṣib (A) : in calligraphy, a highly-prolonged upright stroke. X 596a

murābaḥa (A) : in law, a mark-up contract, a permissible form of sale that allows a purchaser to buy with the intention of subsequently reselling to a designated buyer with a fixed profit rate. IX 471a; XII 691b

murābaṭa → MURĀBIṬ

murabbaʿ (A) : a lute with a quadrangular sound box. V 234a

In poetry, a four-line MUSAMMAṬ, a stanzaic form of poetry, composed of three lines with separate rhyme and one line with common rhyme. VII 660b; VIII 584b; IX 353b

In mathematics, ~, or MĀL, denotes the second power of the unknown quantity. II 362a

In astronomy, the Southern Cross. VII 51a

In Persian cooking, jam. XII 610a

♦ murabbaʿa (A) : in urban architecture, a square in the city. XII 759a

♦ murabbacılık (T) : a land-leasing system in Turkey, in which, in exchange for his work, the farmer only touches one-fourth of the harvest. V 473b

murābiṭ (A, pl. *murābiṭūn*) : marabout. Originally, a warrior in the holy war, DJIHĀD or RIBĀṬ, who was slain fighting against the infidel. V 1200b; a type of warrior-monk who inhabited a *ribāṭ*, a fortified convent on the frontiers of Islam. VII 583b; hence a saint, who never took part in a *dj̲ihād* in his lifetime. Of the words used for saint in Morocco: *walī, sayyid, ṣāliḥ*, ~ is the only one applied to the descendants of a saint, who possess the BARAKA, miraculous powers, of their ancestor. V 1200b

♦ **al-murābiṭūn** (A) : the Almoravids, a dynasty of Berber origin which ruled in North Africa and then Spain during the second half of the 5th/11th century and the first half of the 6th/12th century. VII 583b

♦ murābaṭa (A) : 'measures of vigilance', in al-G̲h̲azālī's mystical thought, a fundamental concept made up of six degrees, outlined in his exposition 'On spiritual surveillance and inward accounting' in Book 38 of his *Iḥyāʾ*. VII 465a

muraddaf (A) : in Persian prosody, a poem with RADĪF, a word or whole phrase that follows the rhyme letter, not to be confused with the term *murdaf*, which means 'provided with a RIDF', a letter of prolongation immediately preceding the rhyme letter. VIII 369a

murag̲h̲g̲h̲abāt (A) : in s̲h̲īʿī law, the daily and non-daily supererogatory prayers. VII 879a

murāhiḳ (A) : in law, the minor on the point of reaching puberty, a stage in the transition from the status of minor to that of major. I 993b; as a term connected with a child's development, 'he was, or became, near to attaining puberty or virility' (Lane) (syn. *kawkab*). VIII 822a

murāḳaʿāt → MUḤĀWARĀT

murāḳaba (A) : 'spiritual surveillance', in al-G̲h̲azālī's mystical thought, the second of the six degrees making up the 'measures of vigilance', *murābaṭa* (→ MURĀBIṬ). It is an examination of the motives of the action and the soul's hidden intentions, in order to reject everything that would serve to satisfy egoism or any passion and that is not performed with a view to God alone. VII 465a; a practice of absorption in mystic contemplation, adopted by the Čis̲h̲tī mystics in order to harnass all feelings and emotions in establishing communion with God. II 55b

muraḳḳaʿ (A) : an album, in which paintings and drawings, alternating with specimens of calligraphy, were mounted. No actual examples earlier than the 16th century have survived, but the period of the ~ would appear to be coterminous with that of classical Persian painting. VII 602b; VIII 787b; X 363a

In mysticism, the patched mantle worn by ṣūfīs. VIII 742b

murakkab (A) : composite; and → BASĪṬ

In grammar, the construct state of the noun. I 1083b; the singular, when applied to the 'compound' noun. II 406b; and → MUFRAD

In medicine, the compound of the constituents. I 1083b

murāsalāt → MUḤĀWARĀT

muraṣṣaʿ (A) : in the Ottoman empire, a very prestigious, high-degree order or decoration, NISHĀN, that was elaborately adorned with diamonds or brilliants, usually worn with a sash across the breast. VIII 58b

murattab (A, pl. *murattabūn*) : in mediaeval Islam, an official in the postal service. I 1044b

For the Turkish *müretteb*, → NIẒĀM

murdaf → MURADDAF

murdjān (A) : the smaller of two sizes of pearls, the larger being DURR. V 819b; and → ṬAYRA

murdji'a (A) : the name of a politico-religious movement in early Islam, in later times referring to all those who identified faith with belief, or confession of belief, to the exclusion of acts. VII 605b

murdjif (A) : agitator, one of the numerous terms in the mediaeval and modern periods for 'rascal, scoundrel'. XI 546a

murdjiḳāl (A) : 'bat'; an apparatus for ascertaining differences of level. It consists of an equilateral triangle with a plumb-line which hangs from the middle of one side. The triangle is suspended by this side. Two rods, an ell in length, are erected to ten ells apart; a rope is passed from the top of one to the top of the other and the ~ is suspended in its centre by two threads. If the plumb-line goes through the triangle, both places are on the same level. VII 203a

murīd (A, P *shāgird*) : lit. he who seeks; in mysticism, the novice or postulant or seeker after spiritual enlightenment by means of traversing the ṣūfī path in obedience to a spiritual director. VII 608b

mūrith → MĪRĀTH

murniba → MU'ARNIBA

murr (A) : in botany, myrrh, a gum resin from the bark of several varieties of thorny scrubs of *Commiphora abyssinica*. VIII 1042b

♦ murrī (A) : a condiment, made with barley flour. IX 225a; X 32a

mursal (A, pl. *mursalūn*) : envoy. V 423b; without a specific textual basis. IX 364b; in the science of Tradition, a Tradition in which a Successor quotes the Prophet directly, that is, the name of the Companion is lacking in the ISNĀD. III 26a; VII 631a; VIII 384a

♦ mursal al-ṣaḥābī (A) : a Tradition in which a Companion describes some event involving the Prophet at which he/she could not possibly have been present. VII 631a

murshid (A), and **baba** (T 'father'), PĪR, SHAYKH : lit. one who gives right guidance; in mysticism, the spiritual director and initiator into the order of the novice who is following the ṣūfī path. VII 631b

♦ murshid-i kāmil (P) : 'perfect spiritual director', a title assumed by the SHAYKHs of the Ṣafawiyya ṣūfī order in the 8th/14th century, demanding complete obedience from all their adherents. The title was adopted by the Ṣafawid shāhs, the temporal monarchs in Persia during the 10th-early 12th/16th-early 18th centuries. VII 632a

♦ murshida (A) : in theology, a breviary. XII 802b

murtadd (A) : 'one who turns back', especially from Islam, an apostate. Apostasy is called *irtidād* or *ridda*; it may be committed verbally by denying a principle of belief or by an action, e.g. treating a copy of the Qur'ān with disrespect. IV 771a; VII 635a

murtāḥ (A) : a name for the seventh horse in a horse-race, according to the order of finishing. II 953a

murtahis͟ha → RAHĪS͟H

murtat͟ht͟h (A) : lit. he who is worn out, a warrior of the type that is not allowed special burial rites because his death is not a direct and immediate result of his wounds. IX 205a

murtaziḳa → RIZḲ

murū'a (A), or *muruwwa* : a term used especially in pre-Islamic and early Islamic usage, the meaning of which is imprecise. There is reason to believe that ~ originally describes the sum of the physical qualities of man and then by a process of spiritualisation and abstraction his moral qualities. After Islam, its meaning was extended thanks to the now pre-dominating moral focus. Broadly speaking, with the rightly-guided caliphs, ~ means chastity, good nature and observance of Qur'ānic laws, with the Umayyads, ~ implies politics, diplomacy, work, dignity and compassion, and with the early ʿAbbāsids, ~ implies merit and is contrasted with abjectness; with the moralists, ~ is identified with ADAB in the meaning of good conduct. Becoming more and more abstract, ~ finally came to mean virtue. VII 636a

In law, ~ indicates the fact of abstaining from any act capable of offending religion although not constituting an illicit act. VII 637b

In the spoken language of today, ~ means 'energy' in Egypt (*miriwwa*) and Syria (*muruwwa*), as in the expression 'so-and-so has not the ~ to accomplish such a thing'. VII 637b

murūd → MĀRID

mürurnāme (T) : in the Ottoman period, a special authorisation from the sultan given to the MUSTA'MIN proposing to travel. This document was obtained through the intermediary of his ambassador. III 1181b

muruwwa → MURŪ'A

musāʿadat (IndP) : 'assistance', a rate of interest that doubled the original loan given to officers in the Mug͟hal army in ten years. V 689b

musābaḳa (A, pl. *musābaḳāt*) : race, competition, contest, especially a contest in the recitation of the Qur'ān, ~ *tilāwat al-Ḳur'ān*, held in many contemporary Muslim countries. XII 642a

musabbiḥāt (A) : the name given to SŪRAS lvii, lix, lxi, lxii and lxiv, because they begin with the phrase *sabbaḥa* or *yusabbiḥu li 'llāh*. VII 650b; IX 887b

muṣādara (A) : in mediaeval administration, ~ is firstly 'an agreement with someone over the payment of taxation due'. The most frequently found meaning is, however, 'the mulcting of an official of his (usually) ill-gotten gains or spoils of office'. The latter meaning was also found in the Ottoman empire, but here ~ was extended to the property of non-officials as well as to deceased persons. II 152b; VII 652b

In mathematics, ~ are premisses or postulates. VII 652b

muṣaddar → ṢADR

musaddas (A) : in Arabic, early Persian and Turkish poetry, a six-line MUSAMMAṬ, a stanzaic form of poetry, with either five lines of separate rhyme and one line with common rhyme, or blocks of six rhyming lines, e.g. *aaaaaa bbbbbb* etc. VII 660a ff.

In later Persian and Indo-Muslim poetry, a type in which the first four lines rhyme with one another, while the remaining two lines rhyme among themselves, e.g. *aaaa bb, cccc dd, eeee ff* etc. This type is often called a TARKĪB-BAND. VII 662a; X 236a

muṣaffaḥāt (A) : in music, 'clappers', known in Persia and Turkey as *čarpāra* (lit. four pieces') or *čālpāra*, in Egypt as *aḳlig͟h*, and in Spain as *kāsatān* (whence perhaps castanet). IX 10b

musāfiḳ → ṢANDJ
musāfir (A) : a traveller. XII 642b
muṣaghghara → MARSŪM
musāhama → MUKHĀRADJA
muṣaḥḥaf (A) : 'mistaken'; in the science of Tradition, ~ is used of a slight error in the ISNĀD or MATN, commonly confined to an error in the dots. III 26a
In literary theory, ~ (also *djinās al-khaṭṭ*) is used for an imperfect paronomasia whereby there is difference in diacritics between the two words. X 69b
muṣāḥib (A, Ott) :
musahibu (Sw, < A **muṣāḥib**) : a term of East African Muslim court life. It is possible that the literary word *musahibu* is simply *ṣāḥib* with the *mu*-prefix (in Swahili morphology to be placed before all words denoting persons and also trees), but in some of the Swahili chronicles and the older epics, *musahibu* occurs in a special meaning, that of the close companion of the sultan. He is usually a half-brother or cousin. He has, among other things, to accompany the ruler wherever he goes and to protect him against treason. VII 657b
musāhim → SAHM
musāḳāt (A) : in law, a lease of a plantation for one crop period, with profit-sharing. The contract for such a lease is between the owner of the plantation and a husbandman, who undertakes to tend the trees or vines of the plantation for one season, at the end of which the proceeds of the crop are divided in agreed portions between the two contracting parties. The landowner's portion constitutes his rent. V 871b; VII 658b
muṣālata (A) : the wholesale lifting of other people's poems, as distinguished from the other kind of plagiarism: taking up, and playing with, existing and attributable motifs. IX 56a; XII 707b
musālima (A) : the term used for Spanish converts adopting Islam in the first generation. Thereafter, they were called *muwalladūn* (→ MUWALLAD). VI 881a
muṣallā (A) : any place of prayer, therefore also mosque. VI 653b; the place where the ṢALĀT is performed on certain occasions; VII 658b; the sanctuary or covered area in a mosque; the open space, usually outside a settlement, used during the two festivals (ʿĪD AL-AḌḤĀ and ʿĪD AL-FIṬR) by the entire Muslim community; a directional indicator either entirely isolated in a huge open space, or set in a long wall. VII 659b
In North Africa, the ~ is a large threshing floor, with a wall provided with a MIḤRĀB and an elevated place for the speaker, used for the rites of 10 Dhu 'l-Ḥidjdja. VII 659a
musallam → SALAM
♦ musallamī → MUʿĀFĪ
musallī (A), or *ʿāṭif* : the name for the fifth horse in a horse-race, according to the order of finishing. II 953a
muṣallī (A) : the name for the fourth horse in a horse-race, according to the order of finishing. II 953a
musallim → SALAM
musalsal (A) : lit. strung together.
In the science of Tradition, ~ is applied when the transmitters in an ISNĀD use the same words, or are of the same type, or come from the same place. III 26a
In calligraphy, ~ is a term for the letters of the THULUTH script when joined to each other. It was sometimes practised by calligraphers to show off their skill. IV 1124a
♦ musalsal al-ḥalf (A) : in the science of Tradition, a Tradition in which each transmitter swears an oath. III 26a
♦ musalsal al-yad (A), and *al-musalsal fi 'l-akhdh bi 'l-yad* : in the science of Tradition, a Tradition in which each transmitter gives his hand to the one to whom he transmits the Tradition. III 26a; III 977a

musāmaḥāt (A) : in the science of diplomacy, documents of a primarily business nature concerning tax-relief, probably only in Mamlūk times, divided into large, issued in the name of the sultan, and small, in the name of the governor. II 303a

musammaṭ (A), also *ḳaṣīda simṭiyya* : an originally Arabic (then also Hebrew, Persian, Turkish) stanzaic form of poetry, whose single stanzas, normally all of the same structure, consist of two elements: first, a fixed number of lines that rhyme with each other, the rhyme, however, changing from one stanza to the next (separate rhymes), followed by a stanza-closing line that rhymes with the end lines in all other stanzas of the poem. This rhyme that runs through the whole poem (common rhyme) is called *ʿamūd al-ḳaṣīda* by the Arab authorities. The lines correspond to the hemistichs in normal poetry. The rhyme scheme of a simple ~ is thus e.g. *bbb a, ccc a, ddd a*, etc. VII 660a; XI 374b

muṣannaf (A, pl. *muṣannafāt*) : in Arabic literature, an early technical term applied to a collection of religious learning organised upon an abstract, structured subdivision in chapters, hence the opposite of MUSNAD, a collection arranged according to the first or oldest transmitter. III 24a; VII 662b; X 360a

musannam → TASNĪM

muṣāriʿ → ṢURʿA

musarwal (A) : a pigeon with feathered legs, a horse with white legs, or a tree with branches down on the trunk. IX 677b

musāwāt (A) : equality. In modern times, ~ has been used for the political concept of human equality. VII 663a

musawwad (A) : a term found in pre-Islamic South Arabian inscriptions to indicate an aristocratic group in Ḥaḍramawt; ~ is used to this day to denote the SAYYIDS, the descendants of the Prophet. XII 338b

musawwida (A) : lit. the wearers, or bearers, of black; the name given to the partisans of the ʿAbbāsids at the time of the DAʿWAS of Abū Muslim al-Khurāsānī and Abū Salama al-Khallāl against the Umayyads, apparently from the black banners these rebels wore. VII 664a; and → MUBAYYIḌA

muṣawwir (A) : in Q 59:24, applied to God as the fashioner of forms, but normally used as the equivalent of ‘painter, draughtsman’ when applied to a person. In Persian, ~ is used as a professional epithet, as in Mīr Muṣawwir, the term NAḲḲĀSH being more often used, as in Ottoman Turkish, for ‘painter’. X 361b

musayyaḥa (A) : a silk KĀFIYYA worn in the Arabic East. V 741b

müsellem (A) : ‘exempt’; in the Ottoman military, provincial landed cavalrymen, excused from any dues or taxes on land initially granted them, who later became transformed into auxiliary forces no longer employed in actual fighting but in discharging duties such as dragging guns, levelling roads, digging trenches, carrying provisions and casting cannon balls. Then, as the Ottoman state required them to pay taxes rather than serve in the army, they lost their privileged status and dissolved into the tax-paying populace. VII 665a; VIII 404b

mushāʿ (A) : in law, common and repartitional ownership by the entire village community of all agricultural lands of the village. I 661a; VII 666b

mushāʿara (A) : in Muslim India, a poetical contest; in Urdu usually pronounced *mushāʿira*, ~ has come to be applied in its wider aspect to denote an assembly where Urdu poets come together to recite their compositions. VII 667b; IX 434a

mushaʿbidh → SHAʿBADHA

mushadjdjara → BAYT

muṣḥaf (A, pl. *maṣāḥif*) : codex, a complete text of the Qurʾān considered as a physical object. The term ~ is not always consistently used to refer to the Qurʾānic text said to be completed in the time of ʿUthmān, while *ṣuḥuf* was reserved, again not consistently, for the first collection, said to be undertaken in the time of Abū Bakr. V 406a; VII 668b; a collection of written leaves placed between two covers, or a collection of a complete assemblage of leaves, each leaf being called a *ṣaḥīfa*, or a collection of pieces, of documents, a corpus, or vulgate. VIII 835a

mu<u>sh</u>āhada (A) : in the mystical thought of al-Ḳu<u>sh</u>ayrī, ~ is direct vision, the 'presence of the reality', the third of three stages in the progression towards Reality. IV 697a

mu<u>sh</u>a‘‘ib (A) : in mediaeval ‘Irāḳ, a person who maims a child at birth in order to make use of it at a future time for begging purposes. VII 494a

mu<u>sh</u>ākil (A) : in Persian prosody, the name of a metre, of rare occurrence, said to have been invented by the Persians. I 677b

mu<u>sh</u>allaḥ → MA<u>SH</u>LAḤ

mu<u>sh</u>āraka (A) : in law, 'participation financing', a contractual partnership. Its essence is joint exploitation of capital (or, in full or in part, of the work and skills of the partners or of the credit for partnership investment) with joint participation in profits and losses. Unlike the MUFĀWAḌA, the ~ is a limited investment partnership in which the core of the investment is money. VII 671b

mu<u>sh</u>āraṭa (A) : agreement, arrangement; in al-<u>Gh</u>azālī's mystical thought, the first of the six degrees making up the 'measures of vigilance', *murābaṭa* (→ MURĀBIṬ). It is the anticipatory accounting of the soul made in the morning every day, which consists of instructing it in the engagements that it is to fulfill. VII 465a

mu<u>sh</u>āt → MA<u>SH</u><u>SH</u>ĀʾIYYA

mu<u>sh</u>āwar (A) : an adviser, in Muslim Spain especially used for an adviser of judges. IX 505b; consultant *faḳīh*. X 945b

♦ mü<u>sh</u>āwir (T) : a technical adviser, whether a foreigner or not, synonym of *müste<u>sh</u>ār* (→ MUSTA<u>SH</u>ĀR). VII 733a

mu<u>sh</u>īr (A) : lit. one who points out, advises, hence 'counsellor, adviser' in administrative usage, in recent times also acquiring in military usage the connotation of 'field-marshal' in both the Arab and Turkish worlds. According to some authorities, ~ was at first (before the ‘Abbāsids) the title of the ministers (later WAZĪR) or secretaries of state (KĀTIB). However, with a few exceptions, this older and broader conception did not survive. VII 677a

mu<u>sh</u>rif (A) : lit. overseer, supervisor, controller; the title of an official, whose office seems basically to have been a financial one, and who appears at various times and with various duties in the history of the ‘Abbāsid caliphate and its successor states, from North Africa to the eastern Islamic lands. I 389b; VII 678b; VIII 702b

In the early <u>Gh</u>aznawid sultanate, the ~ was, next to the financial officer, also spy and internal intelligence agent. VII 679a

In Egypt and Syria of the Ayyūbids and Mamlūks, ~ was used for the official in charge of the royal kitchens, watching over the food cooked there. VII 679b

Under the Ḥafṣids, the ~ was head of the maritime customs. II 146a

mu<u>sh</u>ṭ (A) : in music, the bridge-tailpiece of an ‘ŪD. X 769b

♦ mu<u>sh</u>ṭī → FARA<u>KH</u>

mu<u>sh</u>tarī (A, P *hurmizd*) : in astronomy, the planet Jupiter. A synonym is *bar<u>dj</u>īs*. VII 680a; VIII 101a

mu<u>sh</u>tarik (A), or *mu<u>sh</u>tarik* : in grammar, homonym. I 184b; as used by modern linguists, ~ denotes 'polysemy', i.e. it qualifies a noun which can have several meanings. VII 680b

mūsīḳī (A), later *mūsīḳā* : music, strictly speaking, the theory of music, contrasting therefore with <u>GH</u>INĀʾ 'song' or musical practice. VII 681a

musinna (A), or *<u>th</u>aniyya* : a cow in its third year. XI 412a

muslim (A, pl. **muslimūn**) : the person who professes Islam, *islāmī* being exclusively used today for what is relative to Islam. VII 688b; VII 695a

musmiʿa → ḲAYNA

musnad (A) : in early Islam, any inscription in the pre-Islamic South Arabian script. VII 704b

In grammar, ~ is defined by later classical Arabic grammarians as 'that which is leant upon (or propped against) (the headword or subject), is supported by (it)'. They define *musnad ilayhi* as 'that which supports', i.e. the headword or subject. The relationship between them is termed ISNĀD 'the act of leaning (one thing against another)', 'the relationship of attribution or prediction'. However, the terms have a different, almost reversed, meaning in Sībawayh. VII 705a

In the science of Tradition, ~ indicates a work in which each Companion's Traditions were collected together, an arrangement that was not very convenient since the Traditions were not arranged by subject. III 24a; VII 705b; ~ is also applied to an ISNĀD that goes back all the way to the Prophet without a link missing. VII 705b; VIII 384b

mustaḍʿafūn (A) : in early Islam, the social group of the weakest Meccans. X 839b

mustadrak (A) : a continuation of a work, characterised by both continuity and discontinuity: it follows the line of the original work but amends it by means of reflection on the basis of the constitutive principles of the latter; omissions of the author of the original work are corrected. IX 604a

mustafād (A) : a collective name for indirect taxes under the ʿAlawīs. II 146a

mustafī (A) : in law, the person who asks for an opinion on a point of law, FATWĀ. II 866a

mustafīḍ (A) : in the science of Tradition, a Tradition which is treated by most as an intermediate class between Traditions with two transmitters, MAS͟HHŪR, and Traditions with many transmitters, MUTAWĀTIR, although some treat a ~ Tradition as being equivalent to either the one or the other. III 25b

mustag͟hallāt (A) : objects that provide income. XI 413b

mustaḥabb (A) : in law, a recommendable action, corresponding largely to MANDŪB. VII 722b

mustaḥfiẓ (A) : in Turkish military usage, the territorial army. VIII 371a

mustaka → MASTAKA

mustaḳarr (A) : lit. permanent; among the Fāṭimids, ~ denotes IMĀMS descended from ʿAlī and Fāṭima. II 851b

mustaḳfī (A) : in mediaeval Islam, a cut-purse who follows and steals up behind a person to rob him. V 768b

mustak͟hrid͟j (A) : in mediaeval administration, the person responsible for collecting money, such as that of the poor-tax or land-tax. VII 724a; and → ISTIK͟HRĀD͟J

In Muslim Spain, the ~ was the official who collected on behalf of the Muslim state the taxation due from the Mozarabs, a possible translation from the Latin *exceptor*. V 376a; VII 724a

mustakraha (A) : a woman who has been raped. XI 509b

mustakris͟h (A) : a child who has become large in his stomach or hard in his palate, and has begun to eat. A syn. to the verb *istakras͟ha* is *tazakkara*.VIII 822a

muṣṭalaḥa (A) : the term for a technical term. I 572a

mustaʿliya (A) : 'raised'; in grammar, those letters whose pronunciation requires the elevation of the back of the tongue, i.e. the emphatic consonants, *ḥurūf al-muṭbaḳa*, and *ḳāf*, *g͟hayn*, and *k͟hā'*. III 596b; VIII 343b; X 83a

mustaʾmin (A) : a non-Muslim, not living on Muslim territory, who has been given a safe conduct or pledge of security and thereby becomes protected by the sanctions of the law in his life and property for a limited period. I 429b; II 341b; V 178b

mustamlī (A) : a Tradition transmitter's clerk, the earliest representatives of this professional class emerging in the course of the first half of the 2nd/8th century. His function was to write the Tradition down from dictation and to reiterate the Tradition in a way audible to the audience. V 1133b; VII 725b

mustaraḳa → ANDARGĀH; ṬABAḲA

mustaʿriba (A) : lit. arabicised; in genealogy, the name of one of the three groups into which the population of Arabia is divided, the other groups being the *ʿarab ʿāriba* (the, for the most part, extinct original Arabs of pure stock) and the MUTAʿARRIBA. Like the latter, ~ is applied to tribes who were not originally Arabs. They trace their descent from Maʿadd b. ʿAdnān, a descendant of Ismāʿīl. All the north Arabian tribes are included among the ~, so that the Ḳuraysh, to which Muḥammad belonged, are one of them. VII 732b

In Muslim Spain, ~ was applied to the Christian Spaniards who retained their religion under Islam (Eng Mozarab). VII 732b

mustashār (A, T *müsteshār*) : counsellor; under the Ottomans, the general secretary to a ministry or the under-secretary of state. The function was retained under the Turkish Republic and each ministry has its ~; also, the name given to the 'counsellors' of Turkish or foreign embassies or legations. VII 732b

mustashriḳ (A, pl. **mustashriḳūn**) : an orientalist, one who studies the Orient; one becoming like the Oriental. VII 735b

mustathnā (A) : lit. excepted, separated; in mathematics, excepted fractions, separated by the subtraction sign. IV 725b

♦ **müstethna eyāletler** (T) : in Ottoman administration, those provinces of the Ottoman empire separated from the 'normally-administered' ones of the Anatolian and Rumelian heartland. VII 756a

mustatir → BĀRIZ

mustawdaʿ (A) : under the Fāṭimids, a trustee or guardian of the imamate, whose function was to 'veil' the true IMĀM, MUSTAḲARR, in order to protect him, and who acted by right of an assignment which so to speak allowed him to enter the family of the true *imām*s. II 851b; XI 482b

mustawfā → TĀMM

mustawfī (A) : in mediaeval administration, an official who was in charge of official accounts and thus acted as an accountant-general. IV 977b; VII 753b

For the Ottoman empire, → DAFTARDĀR

mustawḳad (A) : 'fire-place', a major cooking contrivance found in the mediaeval kitchen. It was designed to accommodate several cooking pots and/or pans side-by-side at the same time. It was erected to about half-a-person's height, giving easy access to the cooking food and was provided with vents allowing for an intake of air over the coals and for the expulsion of smoke. VI 808a

mustawshima → WASHM

mustazād (A) : lit. additional; in Persian and kindred literature, principally Turkish and Urdu, a poem of which each second hemistich is followed by a short metrical line which has some bearing on the sense of the first hemistich without altering the meaning. All these lines rhyme together throughout the poem. I 677b; VII 754b

müsteshār → MUSTASHĀR

müstethna eyāletler → MUSTATHNĀ

müsweddedji (T) : a clerk in the Ottoman empire who drafted in hypothetical terms every matter for the SHAYKH AL-ISLĀM, who had no contact with litigants nor their advocates. II 867a

mutʿa (A) : lit. enjoyment; in law, temporary marriage, also called *nikāḥ al-mutʿa*, a marriage which is contracted for a fixed period. It was authorised at the beginning of

Islam but forbidden later by the SUNNA; shīʿism tolerates it, however. VI 476a; VII 757a; VIII 28b; also, the indemnity payable to a divorced wife when no dowry has been stipulated. VII 759a; X 154a

muṭāʿ (A) : as *al-* ~, a term mentioned in al-Ghazālī the meaning of which is unclear: R.A. Nicholson tentatively suggested it should be read as identical with ḲUṬB as *al-ḥaḳīḳa al-muḥammadiyya*, but this was rejected by W.H.T. Gairdner, who had earlier questioned L. Massignon's suggestion that al-~ is an obscure allusion to the doctrine of the *ḳuṭb* as the head of the saintly hierarchy. V 544a

mutaʿadd → TAʿADDĪ

mutaʿammim → MIKWAR(A)

mutaʿarriba (A) : 'those who seek to become Arabs'; in genealogy, the term applied to the descendants of Ḳaḥṭān who were regarded as 'having become Arabs' in contrast to the supposedly indigenous 'pure' Arab tribes. They settled in southern Arabia. VII 759b

mutaʿashshā (A) : in mediaeval Islam, the name for the places where pilgrims stopped for the evening meal on the pilgrim highway running from ʿIrāḳ to the Holy Cities. XII 198b

mutaʿaṣṣib (A) : narrow-minded. X 552a

muṭābaḳ (A) : in literary theory, the repetition of the same word with a different meaning, according to the early theorist Thaʿlab, which later became subsumed under the term TARDĪD. Ḳudāma assigned the meaning of 'pun' to ~. X 69a; and → ṬIBĀḲ

♦ muṭābaḳa (A) : in literary theory, a contrast between two single contraries; antithesis. VII 491b; X 450b; and → TAḌAMMUN

mutabarriz (A) : the name for the second horse in a horse-race, according to the order of finishing. II 953a

muṭabbikh (A) : said of a young man who is full (or plump). VIII 822a

mutaḍādd → ṬIBĀḲ

mutadārik (A) : in prosody, the name of the sixteenth Arabic metre. It does not seem to have been used by the poets before Islam or the first century AH. It is made up, in each hemistich, of four *fāʿilun*, which may be reduced to *faʿilun* or even *faʿlun*. I 670a; IV 412b; VII 759b

muʿtadil (A) : temperate, as in climate. XI 303a

mutadjabbir (A) : a tyrant. V 521b

mutafaḳḳih (A) : a student of FIḲH 'undergraduate', as opposed to FAḲĪH 'doctor of the law' or 'graduate student'. V 1124b

muʾtafikāt (A, < Heb *mahpeka*) : in the Qurʾān, the 'subverted [cities]', referring most likely to Sodom and Gomorrah, the cities of Lot. V 424a; V 832b

mutaghallibe → DEREBEY

mutaḥayyir → KAWKAB

muʿtaḳ → ʿITḲ

mutaḳabbil → ḲABĀLA

mutaḳaddim → HAYLĀDJ

mutakallaf (A) : artificial, as poetry, not springing from sound talent. XII 649b

mutakallif → MAṬBŪʿ

mutakallim → ḤĀL

mutaḳārib (A) : in prosody, the name of the fifteenth Arabic metre, comprising in each hemistich, four feet made up of one short and two longs (*faʿūlun*). A certain number of licences are possible, in particular, the omission of the fourth foot, the shortening or even the cutting out of the third syllable of a foot, etc. I 670a; VII 763a

mutakāwis (A) : in prosody, the situation in which the two quiescent consonants of the rhyme letter, *rawī*, are separated by four vowelled consonants (as in *faw[ḳa ḳadami]h*). IV 412b

mutak͟hayyila (A) : in the poetics of the philosophers, a faculty responsible for the re-actualisation of images which have been perceived in the past. IX 458b
muṭālaba (A) : in law, the 'exaction of payment' (Ger *Haftung*). I 29a
muʿtalla → ḤARF ʿILLA
mutamakkin (A) : in grammar, 'having full freedom of movement', i.e. a masculine noun declinable in three cases, a synonym of *munṣarif*. IX 53a; X 193b
muʾtamar (A) : conference or congress; in the modern Islamic context, the convening of Muslims from throughout the world in order to deliberate over common concerns. VII 764b
muʿtamir (A) : a pilgrim performing the ʿUMRA 'lesser pilgrimage'. X 864b
mutammima (A, pl. *mutammimāt*) : the generic term for the genre of complements in Arabic literature. IX 603b
mutanad͟jd͟jis → NAD͟JIS
mutarādif (A) : in prosody, the situation in which the two quiescent consonants of the rhyme letter, *rawī*, come in immediate succession (as in *ḳāl*). IV 412b
mutarad͟jd͟jila (A) : a woman who tries to resemble men in clothing habits and ornaments. IX 566b
mutāraka → MUWĀḌAʿA
mutarākib (A) : in prosody, the situation in which three vowelled consonants stand between the two quiescent consonants of the rhyme letter, *rawī* (as in *fī[d͟jabali]y*). IV 412b
mutaraʿriʿ (A), or *mulimm* : a child 'almost or quite past the age of ten years, or active' (Lane). VIII 822a
mutarassil (A) : in the mediaeval period, chancery clerk, secretary (syn. KĀTIB). XII 662b
mutaṣaddī : in Muslim India, the functionary in the Dihlī sultanate who issued both permits to merchants who brought their merchandise into the market for sale and passes for goods which were taken out of the city. IX 801a
mutaṣaddir → ṢADR
mutasallik → ṢĀḤIB AL-LAYL
mutasalṭin (A) : a petty prince. IX 849a
mutaṣarrif (A, T *müteṣarrif*) : in Ottoman administration, the chief administrative official of the SAND͟JAḲ or LIWĀʾ, the second highest in the hierarchy of administrative districts, as defined by the provincial administration laws of 23 Rabīʿ I 1284/25 July 1867 and S͟hawwāl 1287/1871. With the transformation of the old *sand͟jaḳ*s into *wilāyet*s (→ EYĀLET) in 1921, ~ passed out of use as a designation for a type of local official. VII 774a; IX 13b; governor. VIII 1b

♦ mutaṣarrifiyya (A) : a synonym of SAND͟JAḲ, an (administrative) regime, as e.g. created in Lebanon in 1861. V 794a; V 1253a

mutas͟hābih (A) : in Qurʾānic science, the term for the 'ambiguous' verses, whose picturesque style, if taken literally, would seem to ascribe human attributes or acts to God, distinct from the *muḥkam* verses, whose sense is clearly established. I 409a ff.
mutaṭawwiʿa (A), or *muṭṭawwiʿa* : lit. those who perform supererogatory deeds of piety, those over and above the duties laid upon them by the s͟harīʿa; in military contexts, ~ was used as a designation for volunteer fighters, especially to be found on the frontiers of the Islamic world, where there were great opportunities to fight a holy war against the pagans. From around the 5th/11th century, ~ was replaced more and more by G͟HĀZĪ and MUD͟JĀHID for the concept of volunteer warriors for the faith. VII 776b; VIII 795b; volunteers who served in the early Islamic armies without regular stipends, but who shared in the plunder. VIII 568b

In present-day Bedouin society, elders responsible for order and decency. V 768a

In contemporary Saudi Arabia, *muṭawwiʿ* (a modern formation from the same root) is used to designate the religious police who enforce the closure of shops during the times of public prayer, oversee morals, etc. VII 777b

mutawakkil → TAWAKKUL

♦ mutawakkiliyya (A) : a plant, or dish, forbidden by al-Ḥākim in addition to the classical food prohibitions. II 1070a

mutawālī (A, Leb *mtawleh*; pl. *matāwila, mutāwila*) : the name for the Twelver shīʿīs in Lebanon, and for those who emigrated from there to Damascus (but not, generally speaking, for those resident in other parts of Syria). VII 780a

mutawallī (A) : in Mughal India, a manager of land-grants. VIII 751b; and → NĀẒIR

mutawaṣṣī → WAṢĪ

mutawātir (A) : 'uninterrupted'. IX 371a; in the science of Tradition, a Tradition (or, in general, any report) with so many transmitters that there could be no collusion, all being known to be reliable and not being under any compulsion to lie. III 25b; VII 781b

In prosody, ~ is applied to the rhyme in which only one moving letter intervenes between the last two quiescents. VII 781b

♦ mutawātir bi 'l-lafẓ (A) : in the science of Tradition, a Tradition in which the texts appended to the various chains are identical in wording. VII 781b

♦ mutawātir bi 'l-maʿnā (A) : in the science of Tradition, a Tradition in which the texts are identical in meaning only, as opposed to *mutawātir bi 'l-lafẓ*. VII 781b

muṭawwiʿ → MUTAṬAWWIʿA

muṭawwif (A, pl. *muṭawwifūn*) : the pilgrim's guide in Mecca. His task is to assist the pilgrim by supplying his material needs and in performing the rites of the pilgrimage. The *muṭawwifūn* are organised in a special guild, which is divided in sub-guilds. An alternative term sometimes encountered is *shaykh al-ḥadjdj*. VI 170b; VII 782a

muṭayyin (A) : in the mediaeval Near East, a beggar who smears himself with mud and feigns madness. VII 495a

mutaẓarrif → ẒARĪF

mutazawwidja (A) : an appellative for women in early Islam who have had several husbands. I 308b

muʿtazila (A) : 'those who separate themselves, who stand aside', name of a religious movement founded at Baṣra in the first half of the 2nd/8th century by Wāṣil b. ʿAṭāʾ, subsequently becoming one of the most important theological schools of Islam. VII 783a; also the name given by al-Masʿūdī to a group of four extremist shīʿī sub-sects. VII 793b

mutbaʿ → ITBĀʿ

muṭbaḳa → IṬBĀḲ

müteferriḳa (T) : under the Ottomans, a corps of mounted guards, or member of the guard, who were especially attached to the person of the sultan. VII 794a

muthaʿlib (A) : the term for a country where foxes abound. X 433a

muthallath (A) : in mathematics, a triangle. VII 794b

In astronomy, *kawkab al-muthallath* is the constellation of the (northern) Triangle. The star at the apex is an astrolabe star and is called *raʾs al-muthallath*. VII 794b

In astrology, *muthallatha* is used for each of the four divisions of the zodiacal circle, each of which includes three signs 120 degrees apart. VII 84b; VII 794b

muthamman (A) : in mathematics, an octagon, octagonal. VII 795a

In architecture, plan figures and buildings of eight equal sides. VII 795a

♦ muthamman baghdādī (A) : in Mughal architecture, the irregular octagon with four longer and four shorter sides, which may assume the shape of a square or rectangle with chamfered corners. VII 795a

muthannā (A) : in grammar, the dual. II 406b
In prosody, *muthannayāt*, or *thunāʾiyyāt*, are used for short-lined quatrains with rhyme scheme *a b a b*. VIII 584b
In calligraphy, 'facing each other', not a special script on its own but possible to apply to any type of script; also called 'mirror-like writing' (Ott *ʿaynalï yazï*). IV 1124b
mutḳin (A) : 'exact'; in the science of Tradition, a quality of a reliable transmitter of Tradition. II 462a
muṭlaḳ (A) : 'absolute', as opposed to restricted, *muḳayyad*; 'general', as opposed to KHĀṢṢ. VII 799b
In grammar, *mafʿūl muṭlaḳ* denotes the absolute object (cognate accusative), i.e. a verbal noun derived, mostly, from the verb of a sentence and put in the accusative to serve as an object, even if the verb is intransitive. VII 799b
In law, ~ is applied to the MUDJTAHIDs of the heroic age, the founders of the schools, who are called *mudjtahid muṭlaḳ*, an epithet which none after them has borne. VII 799b
In dogmatics, ~ is applied to existence, so that *al-wudjūd al-muṭlaḳ* denotes God as opposed to His creation, which does not possess existence in the deepest sense. VII 799b
muṭrib → KHUNYĀGAR
muttarid (A) : in grammar, 'perfectly uniform, recurrent or general', the highest end of the scale used to assess geographical recurrence of a LUGHA, or the frequence of an element or linguistic form within one grouping. V 804b
muttaṣil (A) : contiguous; in the science of Tradition, an unbroken ISNĀD traced back to the source. III 25b; VIII 384b
♦ muttaṣil marfūʿ (A) : in the science of Tradition, an unbroken ISNĀD going back to the Prophet. III 25b
♦ muttaṣil mawḳūf (A) : in the science of Tradition, an unbroken ISNĀD going back to a Companion. III 25b; VIII 384b
muṭṭawwiʿa → MUTAṬAWWIʿA
muwādaʿa (A) : a truce of friendship. IX 373b; peace between Muslim and non-Muslim communities, also called *muhādana*, for a specific period of time. IX 845a f.
In Mālikī law, a system for ensuring that a female slave observe the period of sexual abstinence, ISTIBRĀʾ, by giving the slave into the hands of a trustworthy person, preferably a woman, who forbade the new owner to come near her until the period had elapsed. IV 253b
muwāḍaʿa (A) : understanding; in law, ~ means the rescission of a sale or transaction. A synonym is *mutāraka*. VII 801a; a covering document in a transaction which sets out the real relationship of the parties to each other and the real purport of their agreement, intended to prevent one party from using a document on which the transaction is recorded to its exclusive advantage and for a purpose contrary to the aim of the whole of the agreement. III 511b
In mediaeval administration, ~ denotes the contract of service of officials. VII 801a
muwāfaḳa (A) : connivance, in religion. X 135a
In administration, a term for the comprehensive accounting presented by an ʿĀMIL on relinquishing his appointment when it is approved by the authority to whom he presents it. If they differ, it is called *muḥāsaba*. II 78b
♦ al-muwāfaḳa wa 'l-djamāʿa (A) : in administration, the comprehensive accounting presented by an ʿĀMIL on relinquishing his appointment, one of the many records and registers of a Muslim administrative office of the 4th/10th century. II 78b
muwaffad → WĀFID
muwaḥḥidūn (A, s. *muwaḥḥid*) : 'unitarians'; a name by which the Druze call themselves. II 631b; the name given to the adherents of the reformist movement of which

the principal element was the divine unicity, TAWḤĪD, which ruled during the 6th/12th and 7th/13th centuries in North Africa and Spain, known in the West as the Almohads. VII 801b

muwaḳḳit (A) : a professional astronomer associated with a religious institution, whose task it was to ascertain the ḲIBLA and the times of prayer. Mention of such astronomers appeared for the first time in Egypt in the 7th/13th century. VI 677b; VII 29b

muwālāt → WALĀʾ

muwālayāt → MAWĀLIYĀ

muwallad (A) : a hybrid, of mixed blood, a word originally belonging to the vocabulary of stock-breeders; hence, a cross-breed, half-caste or even 'one who, without being of Arab origin, has been born among the Arabs and received an Arabic education'. VII 807a; originally meaning home-born slaves. VI 881a

In Muslim Spain, the descendants of non-Arab neo-Muslims, brought up in the Islamic religion by their recently-converted parents, thus the members of the second generation, the sons, and, by extension, those of the third generation, the grandsons. The sons of an Arab father and indigenous mother were not regarded as ~. I 85b; I 491a; VII 807b; X 823b; original population of Spain. IX 232a; convert. X 605a

In grammar and literary theory, ~ refers to a word, linguistic phenomenon, or literary feature not found in classical Arabic of pre- and early Islamic times, thus 'post-classical'. VII 808b; X 240b; XII 638a; and → MUʿARRAB

muwāraba (A) : ambiguity; in rhetoric, ~ denotes the ability to remedy a gaffe or an offensive phrase by repeating the expression in an attenuated form, if not radically modified, or else by trying to make the person addressed believe that he has not properly understood what has been said to him. VII 808b

Among the G͟humāra, a Berber tribe of northwestern Morocco, a 5th/11th-century custom consisting of a recently-married bride, still a virgin, being carried off clandestinely by the young men of the locality and held far from her husband for a month or even more, sometimes several times in succession if very beautiful. This custom was flattering to the woman. VII 809a

muwāṣafa (A) : in mediaeval administration, a list showing the circumstances and causes of any changes occurring in the army. II 79a

muwāṣala → WIṢĀL

muwas͟hs͟haḥ (A), or *muwas͟hs͟haḥa* : in literature, a genre of stanzaic poetry, which, according to indigenous tradition, developed in al-Andalus towards the end of the 3rd/9th century. It is reckoned among the seven post-classical genres of poetry in Arabic. Its fundamental characteristics were the arrangement in strophes and the addition of a final part, K͟HARD͟JA (also called *markaz*), in vernacular Arabic or Romance mixed with the vernacular. I 595b; I 601a; VII 809a

muwat͟ht͟hiḳ (A), or *s͟hurūṭī* : in law, the profession of drafting deeds. IX 208a

muwāṭin (A) : citizen, a modern word coined around the turn of the 20th century. VII 812b; compatriot, fellow-citizen. XI 175a

muwattar (A) : in music, a lute like the ʿŪD. X 768b

muwāzana (A) : in rhetoric, metrical or word-formational equivalency between the final words of both phrases that form a TARṢĪʿ. X 304b

muwaẓẓaf(a) (A), or *waẓīfa* : in mediaeval administration, a form of land tax depending on the return that the land was capable of yielding, and being due whether the land was tilled or not. For Muslim writers or historians of India, the ~ is always meant when K͟HARĀD͟J is mentioned. IV 1055b; VII 507b

For the Turkish *muwaẓẓafe*, → NIẒĀM

muzābana → BAYʿ AL-MUZĀBANA

muzammilātī (A) : in mediaeval Cairo, the attendant of the waterhouse, SABĪL, who was in charge of cleaning its premises and its utensils, and of raising the water from the cistern and serving it to the thirsty. VIII 679b ff.

muzamzim → ZAMZAMA

muzannam (A) : in poetry, term used by Ṣafī al-Dīn al- Ḥillī for a ZADJAL in which, contrary to rule, the classical language is proponderant. XI 373b

muzāraʿa (A) : in law, a lease of agricultural land with profit-sharing, in which contract the owner of the land arranges with a husbandman for the latter to have the use of his land for a specified period, during which the husbandman sows, tends and harvests an agricultural crop. When the crop is harvested, the two parties to the contract divide the proceeds in agreed shares, the share of the landowner constituting the rent for the lease of his land. II 905b; V 871b; VII 822b

muzarrad → DIRʿ

muzāwadj → DIYĀNAY

♦ **muzāwadja** (A) : coupling; in literary theory, paranomasia, a play on words consisting in the coupling of two terms which are similar in external form or in meaning and linked by the conjuction *wa-*, e.g. (*bayna-hum*) *hardj wa-mardj* 'between them there are disagreements', where the two elements have an independent existence. VII 823a

In rhetoric, the 'coupling' of two themes conveying comparable effects by means of two parallel expressions. VII 823b

muzāyada → BAYʿ AL-MUZĀYADA

muzayyin → ḤALLĀḲ

muzdawidj (A) : double; in grammar, the use of two terms in which the form of one is changed to make it resemble that of the other. VII 825b

In rhetoric, ~ consists in establishing a kind of alliteration between two adjacent words having the same form, the same metrical quantity and the same rhyme. VII 825b

In prosody, a poem with rhyming couplets, usually written in the RADJAZ metre which has either eleven or twelve syllables. In Persian and Turkish, it is called MATHNAWĪ. I 2b; I 108a; VI 832b; VII 825b; VIII 376a

♦ muzdawidjāt (A) : a poem in the RADJAZ metre consisting of strophes of five hemistichs in which the first four hemistichs rhyme together and the fifth ones have a common rhyme. Sometimes the strophe has only four hemistichs, the first three rhyming together and the fourth rhyming jointly. VII 825b

muzayyif (A) : in numismatics, a forger of coins (*zāʾif* or *zayf*, pl. *zuyūf*, 'false coin'). X 409b

muẓhar → MUḌMAR

muzzammil (A) : the title of the 73rd SŪRA of the Qurʾān, derived from the first verse which may be translated 'O you covered in a cloak'. VII 286a; and → MUDDATHTHIR

mvuli → MASIKA

myron : sacred oil, in the Cilician-Armenian kingdom. IX 679a

N

naʿām (A, P *ushturmugh*, T *devekushu*, both 'camel-bird') : in zoology, a collective noun denoting the ostrich (*Struthio camelus*) without any distinction of sex. VII 828a, where many variant names are found

In botany, the pellitory of Judaea (*Parietaria judaïca*). VII 830b

In astronomy, the twentieth lunar house bears the plural form *al-naʿāʾim* and is divided into two groups: *al-naʿāʾim al-wārida* 'the incoming ostriches' and *al-naʿāʾim al-ṣādira* 'the outgoing ostriches'. VII 830b

nāb (A, pl. *niyāb*) : in anatomy, the canine tooth. III 1162b; VI 130a

In Persian, a measuring rod. II 232b

nabʿ (A) : in botany, *Grewia tenax*, a wood from which the pre-Islamic Arabs made their bows, still used today in Somalia. IV 797b

nabaʾ (A) : a Qurʾānic term for 'news, announcement', which meaning ~ has retained until today; also, an edifying tale, a story of a prophet. III 369a

nabaʿ (A) : a shallow water source. I 100a

nabāt (A) : plants. VII 831a; and → SUKKAR

♦ nabātī : a strong yellow-coloured paper preferred by Cairo printers. IV 420a

nabaṭī (A) : in literature, the name given to the popular vernacular poetry of Arabia. VII 838a

nabaz (A, pl. *anbāz*) : in onomastics, an unpleasant sobriquet, LAḲAB, such as that of Marwān I (*al-ḥimār* 'the ass'). IV 180a; V 618b

nabbāl → AḲŪNĪṬUN

nabbās̲h̲ (A) : lit. burrower, excavator; in mediaeval Islam, a category of thieves, said to be well-known and presumably a man who dug up a people's buried treasure hoards. V 769a

nabī (A, pl. *nabiyyūn*) : prophet. When used in the Qurʾān, ~ seems to occur only in Medinan passages and is applied specifically only to Muḥammad and certain other 'messengers'. V 423b

nabīd̲h̲ (A) : intoxicating drinks, several kinds of which were produced in early Arabia, such as *mizr* (from barley; and → MAZAR), BITʿ (from honey or spelt) or FAḌĪK̲H̲ (from different kinds of dates). These ingredients were steeped in water until they were fermented, and the result of the procedure was a slightly intoxicating drink. Sometimes ~ was consumed mixed with strong intoxicating ingredients like cannabis. IV 996a; VI 721a; VII 840a; and → S̲H̲ARĀB

nābita (A) : a term of classical Arabic meaning 'rising generation', but one which today has acquired the pejorative sense of 'bad lot, rogue'. VII 843b

nabḳ (A) : in botany, the fruit of the SIDR tree. IX 549b

nabl (A) : in archery, a wooden or Arab arrow, one of the three main words denoting the arrow, the others being SAHM and *nus̲h̲s̲h̲āb* 'Persian arrow'. IV 799a

nāḍḍ → AT̲H̲MĀN

nad̲h̲īr (A, pl. *nud̲h̲ur*) : 'warner'; a Qurʾānic term, whose opposite is *bas̲h̲īr*, *mubas̲h̲s̲h̲ir*. Both ~ and *bas̲h̲īr* are applied to the prophets, the former when they are represented as warners, the latter as announcers of good tidings. ~ is used as an epithet of Noah, the great warner before the Deluge, and of Muḥammad himself. VII 845a

nad̲h̲r (A, pl. *nud̲h̲ūr*) : 'vow', a procedure which was taken over into Islam from the pre-Islamic Arabs, for whom the vow always had more or less the character of a self-dedication, and underwent modification. In Islam the vow and the oath are treated together. VII 846a

♦ nad̲h̲r wa-niyāz (A) : among the AHL AL-ḤAḲḲ, raw offerings, including animals of the male sex, oxen, sheep, cocks, intended for sacrifice, which with cooked or prepared victuals (→ K̲H̲AYR WA-K̲H̲IDMAT) is an indispensable feature of a D̲H̲IKR session. I 261a; X 398a

♦ nad̲h̲r-niyāzmanlik (T) : a composite term denoting offerings of money, cereals or beasts given to the custodians of saints' tombs in Central Asia. A synonym is ṢADAḲA, while in the Western Turkish world, *adak, nad̲h̲r* and *niyāz* are used. XI 115a; XI 534b

nadīm (A, pl. *nidām, nudamāʾ, nudmān*) : drinking companion, and, by extension, friend, courtier (or confidant) of kings or of wealthy persons; his function is to entertain them, eat and drink in their company, play chess with them, accompany them in hunting and participate in their pastimes and recreations. VII 849b; XII 719b

nādira (A), pl. *nawādir* : lit. rare thing, rarity; a pleasing anecdote containing wit, humour, jocularity and lively repartee, of the type which has never ceased to be an integral feature of all social gatherings, whether intimate or official. VII 856b

In grammar, the plural form *nawādir* also denotes compounds containing *abū, umm, ibn* etc., and dual forms. VI 823a

naʿdja (A) : a reproductive ewe. XII 319a

nadjama → ITHTHAGHARA

nadjāsāt → NADJIS

nadjdjār (A) : a carpenter. XII 758b

nadjis (A) : impure (ant. *ṭāhir*). In law, *nadjāsāt* are things impure in themselves and cannot be purified; *mutanadjdjis* is applied to those things which are defiled only. The law schools differ in their definitions of what is impure. VII 870a

nadjl (A) : progeny. VIII 821b

nadjm (A, pl. **nudjūm**) : star (syn. *kawkab*, also 'planet'); an alternative name for the Pleiades, otherwise called *al-thurayyā*. VIII 97b

♦ **nudjūm (aḥkām al-)** (A) : 'decrees of the stars', astrology. VIII 105b; the art of drawing omens from the position of the stars at a person's birth. VIII 705b

nadjr → LAYṬ

nadjsh (A) : the raising of prices, condemmed by Tradition. X 467b

nadjwa → FASHT

nadjwā (A) : under the Fāṭimids, a tax which had to be paid by those who were present at the Ismāʿīlī learned meetings which were held at the palace, abolished by al-Ḥākim. III 81a

nadra (A) : in minerology, a pure or virtually pure piece of gold and silver. XII 533a

nafādh (A) : in prosody, the vowel of the *hāʾ* serving as WAṢL. IV 412a

nafaḳa (A) : in law, maintenance, i.e. of the necessities of life, consisting of food, clothing and shelter, which obligation arises from kinship, ownership and marriage. III 1011b; VIII 433a; XII 643b

nafal (A, pl. *anfāl*) : in early Islam, a bonus share given to those warriors who distinguished themselves (in the battle). II 1005b; VIII 800b; XII 352a; and → IKLĪL AL-MALIK

naffādh (A) : a seller of amulets and images, listed by the 8th/14th-century poet Ṣafī al-Dīn al-Ḥillī as a well-known figure amongst the swindlers who preyed on the credulous. X 500b

naffāsh (A) : in botany, the Seville orange (*Citrus aurantium amara* or *vulgaris* or *bigaradia*), also called NĀRANDJ. VII 962a

naffāṭ, naffāṭa → NAFṬ

nāfidh (A), or *sālik* : through-way, e.g. *shāriʿ nāfidh* or *ghayr nāfidh* 'cul-de-sac'. IX 320b

nāfiḳāʾ (A, pl. *nawāfiḳ*) : the burrow of the jerboa (syn. *ḳuṣʿa* and variants). XI 283b

nāfila (A, pl. *nawāfil*) : in theology, supererogatory work; those works which are supererogatory in the plain sense, in contradistinction to other works which have become a regular practice, *sunna muʾakkada*. VII 878a

In law, ~ is used for the supererogatory ṢALĀT as well as for the whole class of supererogatory *ṣalāt*s. VII 878b; VIII 931a

nafīr → NEFĪR

nafs (A, pl. *anfus, nufūs*) : soul; self, person. VII 880a; and → RŪḤ

In divination, ~ is a term of geomancy, being the first 'house' of the *ummahāt*, because it guides to problems concerning the soul and spirit of the inquirer, and to the beginning of affairs. VII 883a

♦ al-nafs al-kulliyya (A) : in Druze hierarchy, the second of the five cosmic ranks in the organisation. II 632a; in Abū Bakr al-Rāzī's thought, ~ is the Universal Soul, the 'second Eternal' of five, which shook and agitated Matter in order to produce the world, without success. III 328a

nafṭ (A, P *naft*) : the purest form of Mesopotamian bitumen. I 1055b; a generic, vague appellation for a substance which is basically petroleum. VII 884a; 'Greek fire', a liquid incendiary compound which was hurled at people, the various siege weapons which were made of wood, and ships. I 1055b; VII 884a; fireworks; gunpowder. I 1056a; oil, in the modern sense of the word. VII 886b

♦ naffāṭ, or *zarrāḳ* : a specialist in discharging 'Greek fire' in the form of a jet, by means of a special copper tube, called the *naffāṭa, zarrāḳa*, or *mukḥula*. I 1055b

nafūd (A) : a sandy area, in the north of the Arabian peninsula; in the south it is called a *ramla*. I 537a; II 91b; VII 891a

nafūr (A) : in the terminology of horse-riding, a horse that swerves and shies. II 954a

nafy (A) : in grammar, negation (ant. *īdjāb* 'affirmation'). VII 895b; and → NEFY

naga (J) : a Hindu serpent guardian spirit, which sculpture frequently graces the entrance to a saint's tomb chamber. XI 121a

naghma → LAḤN

nahār (A) : a day, which extends from sunrise to sunset. V 707b; the ~ begins at the moment that the upper edge of the sun appears on the horizon, just as the night and the official day begin when the opposite edge, now uppermost, disappears. V 709b

nahḍa (A) : 'awakening', the Arab renaissance, the rebirth of Arabic literature and thought under Western influence since the second half of the 19th century. VII 900a; XII 772a

nahdj → SHĀRIʿ

naḥīta (A, pl. *nuḥut*) : the 'moving section', a bee hive that is not welded to the wall of a dwelling, being the modern apiarist technique known as 'mobilist'. VII 907a

nāḥiye (T, < A *nāḥiya* 'district, vicinity') : in Ottoman administration, the subdivisions of a *wilāyet* 'province' (→ EYĀLET); the rural subdivision of a ḲAḌĀʾ. The subdivisions of a ~ are called *ḳarye* 'village'. In the Turkish Republic, the ~ is a subdivision of the *ilçe* or district. VII 906a

naḥl (A, P) : in zoology, domestic or social bees (apid family). A swarm is called *dabr*, which is grouped around the 'chief', *yaʿsūb*. VII 906a

nahr (A, pl. *anhār, anhur*) : running water, hence a perennial watercourse, river, stream of any size, thus opposed to a *wādī* 'a watercourse filled only at certain times of the year' or a *sayl* 'periodic torrent', 'flood'; artificially-contrived running water-courses, i.e. canals and navigations. VII 909b

naḥr (A) : in law, one of the two methods of slaughtering animals, by which the animal concerned becomes permissible as food. The term applies to camels only, and consists of driving the knife in by the throat without it being necessary to cut in the manner prescribed for the DHABḤ, the camel remaining upright but at the same time facing the ḲIBLA. II 213b; and → YAWM AL-NAḤR

naḥs → SAʿD WA-NAḤS

naḥw (A, pl. *anḥāʾ*) : path, way; fashion, manner. V 913a

In grammar, the term for 'grammar' (to be contrasted with LUGHA 'lexical studies') and, more specifically, 'syntax' (the counterpart of ṢARF or TAṢRĪF 'morphology', so that for 'grammar' one also finds the phrase *naḥw wa-ṣarf*). VII 913a; VIII 894a; initially, ~ signified 'type of expression'. V 804a

♦ naḥwī (A, pl. *naḥwiyyūn*) : grammarian. V 804a; V 1133b; in its plural form ~ refers to an (anonymous ?) group of participants in the grammatical debate in which Sībawayhi was involved. IX 525b

nahy (A) : prohibition; in religion, the phrase **al-nahy ʿan al-munkar** ‘forbidding wrong’ (in full, preceded by *al-amr bi ’l-maʿrūf* ‘commanding right’) is used to refer to the exercise of legitimate authority, either by holders of public office or by individual Muslims, with the purpose of encouraging or enforcing adherence to the requirements of the s̲h̲arīʿa (syn. *tag̲h̲yīr al-munkar, inkār al-munkar*). XII 644b

nāʾib (A) : substitute, delegate, any person appointed as deputy of another in an official position; VII 915a; and → SAFĪR

In the Mamlūk and Dihlī sultanates, the ~ is the deputy or lieutenant of the sultan; the governor of the chief provinces. VII 915a

In law, a judge-substitute, or delegate of the ḲĀḌĪ in the administration of law. VII 915b

In politics, a parliamentary deputy. VII 915b

♦ nāʾib bārbeg (IndP) : in the Dihlī sultanate, a chamberlain. X 591b

♦ nāʾib al-g̲h̲ayba (A) : under the Mamlūks, the temporary governor of Cairo (or Egypt) during the absence of the sultan. II 996a; VII 915a

♦ nāʾib k̲h̲āṣṣ → SAFĪR

♦ nāʾib al-salṭana (A) : under the Mamlūks, a sort of Prefect of Upper Egypt, a post created in 780/1378 and inaugurated at Asyūṭ. VIII 865a; a viceroy. I 138a

♦ al-nāʾib al-ʿumūmī (A) : in modern legal usage, the public prosecutor. VII 915b

nāʾiba (A) : an occasional tax in kind, levied by the first Saʿdīs; it later became more or less permanent and payable in cash. II 146a

nāḳa (A) : the female camel, a term also found in the Qurʾān, where it appears in the edifying stories of Ṣāliḥ, the T̲h̲amūd, etc. III 666a

♦ nāḳa al-baḥr → AṬŪM

♦ ṣāḥib al-nāḳa (A) : ‘the man with the she-camel’; a popular nickname for Yaḥyā b. Zikrawayh, an Ismāʿīlī agitator. VIII 831a

naḳā (A) : a term connected with *nuḳāwā*, a generic noun denoting alkaline plants utilised for washing linen and whitening cloths; a ‘rite of reconciliation’, used in the Ḥid̲j̲āz for righting injuries, whereby an offender pronounces a formula on the doorstep of the aggrieved person, who then appears, covers the former’s hand with a cloth, and kills a sheep to celebrate the reconciliation. VII 920a

On the Arabian peninsula, ~ or *naḳā* (pl. *niḳyān*) denotes a large dune bare of vegetation. II 537a; and → ṬIʿS

naḳad (A) : a strain of sheep in Bahrain in the time of al-D̲j̲āḥiẓ, which was stunted but a good wool producer. Other small-sized sheep were the *ḥaballaḳ*, which is still bred, and the *ṭimṭim*, with shorn ears and a woolly dewlap under the throat, found in Yemen. XII 318a

naḳāʾiḍ (A, s. *naḳīḍa*) : in prosody, a form of poetic duelling in which tribal or personal insults are exchanged in poems, usually coming in pairs, employing the same metre and rhyme, synonymous with *munāḳaḍāt*. Sometimes *naḳīḍa* is used for what is more properly termed a *muʿāraḍa*, a poem with the same metre and rhyme as another, made by way of emulation or in order to surpass, without the invective element. VII 920a

naḳāniḳ → LAḲĀNIḲ

naḳarāt (T) : lit. peckings; in Turkish poetry, the refrain, that is, the ultimate line or ultimate and penultimate lines of each stanza of the S̲H̲ARḲI̊. IX 354a

naḳb (A, pl. *nuḳūb*) : an underground tunnel; in military science, mining, a system of siege warfare which reached the peak of its success in the late 6th/12th and the 7th/13th centuries. After the Crusades, mining declined considerably. III 473b

In mediaeval Islam, ~ gave rise to the designation *aṣḥāb al-naḳb* or *naḳḳābūn*, thieves who burrowed into cellars and vaults from the outside or from adjacent houses. V 768b

naḳd (A) : in law, the portion of the dowry handed over at the conclusion of a marriage.

In modern Arabic, ~ signifies 'money'. VII 921a; and → ATHMĀN
In literature, the genre of literary criticism, in modern Arabic *al-~ al-adabī* but in mediaeval times most commonly ~ *al-shiʿr* 'criticism of poetry' (syn. *intiḳād*). The critic is *nāḳid* (pl. *nuḳḳād, naḳada*), more rarely *naḳḳād*. XII 646b

naḳḍ (A) : 'refutation', in particular when used in reference to a book. VIII 363a; and → RADD

♦ **naḳḍ al-mīthāḳ** (A) : in shīʿism and, more commonly, Bahāʾism, the act of violating a religious covenant. VII 921a

nakhkhās (A) : 'cattle-dealer', a term in the mediaeval period for a slave merchant. I 32b; XII 757a; in Muslim India, a market where slaves as well as animals were sold. IX 800b

nakhl (A, s. *nakhla*) : in botany, the date palm (*Phoenix dactylifera*). I 540a; VII 923a

nākhudāh (A, < H *nāo* and P *khudā*) : in navigation, a term for 'captain'. VII 41b

naḳīʿ (A) : drinks composed of fruits (dates, etc.) mixed in water. VI 720b; X 901a

naḳīb (A, pl. *nuḳabāʾ*) : chief, leader, of a tribe or other group; in early Islam, the Medinans negotiating with Muḥammad about the HIDJRA were asked to appoint 12 *nuḳabāʾ* as representatives. Both the number 12 and the sense of ~ as representative were repeated in the preparatory stages of the ʿAbbāsid revolution. VII 926a
During the Dihlī sultanate, the ~ was an official of lower rank than the *ḥādjib*, chamberlain, probably best translated 'usher'. VII 926a
Under the Mamlūks, the *nuḳabāʾ* were the military police, responsible for seeing that the members of the expeditionary force, despatched against a strong enemy, presented themselves on time and in the appointed place. III 184a
In mysticism, *al-nuḳabāʾ* are the 300 'chiefs', the seventh degree in the ṣūfī hierarchical order of saints. I 95a; for the Demirdāshiyya order, XII 208b; in modern Egyptian usage, the *nukabāʾ* are ṣūfīs who run the brotherhood's regional cells on behalf of the regional deputy, KHALĪFA. The *shaykh*'s closest associate is called *naḳīb al-sadjdjāda*. VIII 744a; in North Africa, the ~ or *nāʾib* is another term for the *khalīfa* or deputy of a ZĀWIYA. XI 468a
In guild terminology, the ~ was the master's assistant and the master of ceremonies. IX 168b; and → AKHĪ

♦ **naḳīb al-ashrāf** (A) : lit. the marshal of the nobility; under the ʿAbbāsids, the office of head of the community of ʿAlid descendants. VII 926b; IX 333b; his function was to investigate all claims to descent from the Prophet's family and to keep rolls of the legitimate descendants of the Prophet, for they were entitled to a lifetime pension. The ~ for the sunnīs was called the *naḳīb al-hāshimiyyīn*, for the shīʿīs, the *naḳīb al-ṭālibiyyīn*. V 1131b; IX 333b

♦ naḳīb al-hāshimiyyīn → NAḲĪB AL-ASHRĀF

♦ naḳīb al-riwāḳ (A) : at al-Azhar, the superintendent of the [Maghribī] students. X 640a

♦ naḳīb al-sadjdjāda → NAḲĪB

♦ naḳīb al-ṭālibiyyīn → NAḲĪB AL-ASHRĀF

naḳīḍa → NAḲĀʾIḌ

naḳīr (A) : in early Islam, a palmtrunk which is hollowed out and into which small dates and water are poured and allowed to ferment. IV 995b

nakira → MAʿRIFA

nāḳiṣ (A) : in literary theory, an imperfect paronomasia whereby one term is incomplete by one or two letters, which may be at the beginning or end or in the middle of the term. X 69b
In dating, the current year (syn. *munkasir* 'broken') as opposed to the completed (*tāmm*) year. X 268b

naḳḳāb(ūn) → NAḲB

naḳḳāra (A, T *naḳḳāre*) : a medium-sized kettle-drum made of copper, one of the instruments of the military band, NAḲḲĀRA-KHĀNA. The two parts of the ~ were tuned differently to produce bass and treble tones, and were struck with sticks of uniform shape. VI 1008a; VII 927b

♦ čifte naḳḳāre (T) : a 'double drum'. VIII 178b

♦ **naḳḳāra-khāna** (P) : a kind of military band, composed of various instruments, kettle-drums, horns, trumpets, and reed-pipes. VII 927b; X 34b

naḳḳāsh (A) : die-sinker, one of the craftsmen employed as staff in the mediaeval mint, whose professional activity was restricted to engraving only. II 118a; an artist who embellishes surfaces; an illuminator of manuscripts; an embroiderer; a wall decorator. VII 931a

♦ naḳḳāshī (A) : a term which covers drawing and painting, whether representational or decorative. VIII 451b

♦ **naḳḳāsh-khāna** (T, < A and P) : the name of the Ottoman royal painting atelier. VII 931a

naḳl (A) : transport. VII 932a; XII 658b; and → TARDJAMA

naḳra (A) : in music, a beat. X 498a

naḳṣ (A) : in prosody, a type of double deviation (ZIḤĀF), whereby there are two cases per foot, combining ʿAṢB and KAFF. XI 508b

naḳsh → TAṢWĪR

♦ naḳsh ḥadīda (N.Afr) : the name given to the sculpturing of plaster applied, with an iron tool, more or less thickly on the wall. II 556b

nāḳūs (A, < Syr; pl. *nawāḳīs*) : a kind of rattle once used and in some places still used by Eastern Christians to summon the community to divine service. It is a board pierced with holes which is beaten with a rod. I 188a; VII 943a; a percussion slab. IX 10b

naʿl (A) : in early Islam, a sandal which could be of palm fibre, smooth leather, or leather with animal hair. V 735b; a general word for shoe used throughout the Middle East today. V 741b; and → SIKKA

♦ **al-naʿl al-sharif** (A) : the sandal of the Prophet Muḥammad, which, according to Tradition, had two leather thongs (*ḳibāl, zimām, shisʿ*) which passed between the toes and were attached to the sole. The other end of the pair of thongs pased through two loops to which were also attached the two arms of the *shirāk*, the folded strap that passed behind the wearer's ankle. At the forepart of the sandal there was an extension shaped like a tongue (*mulassan*) and the middle part of the sole waas narrow, with hollows (*khaṣrān*) cut on each side. XII 660a

nāla → SHATM

nalam (Mal) : a genre of Acehnese poetry, using partly the *urdjūza* (→ RADJAZ), partly the ḲAṢĪDA as model, but remaining closely tied to indigenous conventions. According to the demands of its metre, *sanja* (< A SADJʿ), it usually comprises two hemistiches and numbers sixteen metric units of one to three syllables each, the latter being arranged to form eight feet of a sort. XII 727b

nāma (P) : a letter; royal edict or diploma; a register, and in many ways the equivalent of the Arabic KITĀB 'book'. In present-day Persian, ~ is productively used to form neologisms, such as *asās-nāma* 'statute', *shinās-nāma* 'identity card'. VII 943b

namāʾ (A) : growth. XI 410b

namash (A) : in mineralogy, freckles or inclusions, a defect or impurity in a gem. XI 263a

namāzgāh (P) : 'place of prayer', in India, an alternative name for *ʿīdgāh*, the open structure built usually to the west of a town, consisting solely of what in a mosque would be the western wall, with MIḤRĀB(S) and MINBAR and, essentially, within a spacious enclosure which should be capable of accommodating the entire adult male Muslim population. The structure is used only for the celebration of the two ʿĪD festivals, and no special sanctity attaches to it. VII 947a

namir (A), or *nimr* : in zoology, the panther (*Panthera pardus*), better known, in Africa, by the name of 'leopard'. VII 947b; VIII 120a

♦ namira : in early Islam, a man's wrap with strips of varying colours which give it the appearance of a tiger's skin. V 734a; the black ink of the writing contrasting with the white of the page. VII 950a

naml (A) : in zoology, ants (s. *namla*). In law, small ants (*dharr*) are permitted to be killed when they intrude upon the human domain and cause damage or when they display aggression. VII 951a

nammām → FŪDHANDJ; ṢANDAL

nāmūs (A) : originally, a transcription of the Greek νόμος, which was left untranslated in Ibn Hishām. It is also a true Arabic word, with such varied meanings that only some can be considered old and original. In the modern vernacular, ~ has survived as 'midge', with *nāmūsiyya* as 'mosquito net'. VII 953b; the bearer of a favourable secret. II 486b

In religion and philosophy, ~, from the Greek loanword, is used frequently for 'divine law', revealed through the prophets. VII 954a; for the Ikhwān al-Ṣafāʾ, ~ meant a kind of divine being. VII 954b; 'law,' interpreted as the angel Gabriel, in Waraḳa's confirmation of the authenticity of Muḥammad's first revelation. XI 143a

In magic, ~ is used for magical formulae, particularly those which are based on illusions of the senses. VII 955a

In zoology, ~ is a noun used in the collective sense denoting the totality of dipterous, nematoceratous insects or mosquitos. VII 955b

♦ nāmūsiyya → NĀMŪS

naʿnaʿ → FŪDHANDJ

nanawātai → PASHTŪNWALĪ

nānkār (P) : under the Mughals, an allowance paid out of the land revenue by the holder of rights over the land, ZAMĪNDĀR. XI 438b

nār (A, pl. *nīrān*) : fire. VII 957b; for ~ in compounds, VII 958a ff.; and → MANĀẒIR

nārandj (A, < P *narang*) : in botany, the hesperideous or aurantiaceous fruits, including oranges and lemons (modern Arabic *ḥamḍiyyāt*). The term ~ passed at a relatively late stage, along with the introduction of these fruits, into the majority of European languages, thus Fr. *orange*, Sp. *naranja*. It is believed that the Portuguese brought the orange from the Indies to Spain and Portugal, whence its current name *burtuḳāl* (T *portakal*), which has supplanted ~ in numerous local dialects; modern botanical science has created *burtuḳāliyyāt* to define these fruits. VII 961b, where many local names for the orange can be found

naʿra → ʿAṢABIYYA

nard (P) : the game of backgammon (trictrac); any kind of dicing. V 109a; VII 963a

nardjīla (A, < P *nāgīl* 'coconut, water pipe'), or *shīsha* : the water pipe, constructed from a coconut shell or gourd and traditionally smoked by the poor, whereas the rich used a *ḳalyān* made of porcelain and painted glass, and encrusted with precious stones. When Lane visited Egypt, the lowest orders smoked the *gōza* (< *djawza* 'coconut'), which differed from the ~ in having a short, fixed cane for a mouthpiece. Popular in all of Muslim Asia, the ~ is called a *ḥuḳḳa* in India (or *hookah*, which denotes the vessel containing the water), *čilim* (the bowl on top of the pipe) in Afghanistan, and *ḳalyān* in Persia. X 754a

nardjis (A, T *nergis*, P *nargis* and *ʿabhar*) : in botany, the narcissus. In al-Andalus, three terms were used: *nardjis ḳādūsī* (the meadow narcissus), *nardjis aṣfar* (jonquil) and *bahār* (< *ʿabhar* ?). VII 963b

narkh (P) : in the Ottoman empire, the prices determined by official authorities for various goods, especially food, shoes and some other basic goods. VII 964a
narmāhan, narmāhin → ḤADĪD
nasaʿa → ITHTHAGHARA
nasab (A) : kinship, the relationship, particularly ancestral, i.e. the genealogy of an individual or a tribe. The list of ancestors is introduced either by *ibn* 'son of' or by *bint* 'daughter of', if the first name is that of a woman. III 238b; IV 179b; VII 967a; VIII 56a
naṣārā (A, s. *naṣrānī*) : Christians in the Muslim Arab world. In the Qur'ān, where it is found fifteen times, ~ denotes Christians in general, in the eastern groups known to the Muslims of the Nestorians, Melkites and Jacobites. Other words for Christians are *masīḥī, rūm* (specifically, the Byzantine Christians) and *ifrandj* (the western Christians). VII 970a
naṣb (A) : setting up, raising; in grammar, the accusative and subjunctive cases, because both take *-a* and are thus *manṣūb* 'raised'. III 1249a; VII 974b
In music, a secular song, which in pre-Islamic Arabia found expression on all occasions of joy, and would include wedding songs, children's songs and lullabies, although it is said to be no more than a refined camel driver's song, ḤUDĀʾ. II 1073a
♦ naṣba (A) : a form of long-term lease arrangement of WAḲF property in Tunis, which involved, in addition to perpetual lease, the ownership and use of tools and installations of shops and workshops. XII 369a
nasham (A) : in botany, *Chadara velutina*, used in the construction of pre-Islamic Arab bows. IV 797b
nashīd (A, pl. *anāshīd, nashāʾid, anshād*) : in music, a piece of oratory, a chant, a hymn and a form of vocal music. This type of ~ is always placed at the head of a vocal composition, or at the start of a musical performance in the guise of a prelude leading to the main theme, borrowing from it the fragment of text which is essential to its development; the sources assign different lengths to it. II 1073a ff.; VII 975b; in the contemporary period, ~ is employed as the equivalent of 'hymn', e.g. *nashīd waṭanī* 'national anthem'. VII 976a; with *inshād, unshūda*, the measured (*mīzān al-shiʿr*) type of solo, chorus or antiphon, the unmeasured (*ghayr mawzūn*) being called *tartīl*. II 1073a
nashīṭa (A) : casual plunder obtained while journeying to meet the enemy. II 1005a
nāshiz (A) : in law, a recalcitrant wife. X 406a; XII 644a
nashshāl → ṬARRĀR
nasīʾ (A) : intercalary month, intercalation, or person (pl. *nasaʾa*) charged, in pre-Islamic Mecca, with the duty of deciding on intercalation. The Arabic system of ~ can only have been intended to move the ḤADJDJ and the fairs associated with it in the vicinity of Mecca to a suitable season of the year. It was not intended to establish a fixed calendar to be generally observed. VII 977a; X 260b
In Judaeo-Islamic societies, ~ (Heb) is an honorific title used to designate descendants of the house of David, who were accorded particular respect. VII 977b
nasīb (A) : in literature, a generic term applied in mediaeval sources to love poetry. In its modern understanding it denotes the amatory prologue of the ḲAṢĪDA, the polythematic ode. Disregarding individual attempts to change the character of the ~, and innovations limited to a particular period, the generic features are to be defined as follows: an elegiac concept of love, the evocation of memories, and a Bedouin setting alluded to by generic signals. IV 715b; VII 978a
naṣīf → KHARADJ
naṣīḥāt al-mulūk (A) : lit. advice for rulers; in pre-modern Islamic literature, the genre which consists of advice to rulers and their executives in politics and statecraft, the

ruler's comportment towards God and towards his subjects, the conduct of warfare, diplomacy and espionage, etc., corresponding to the genre of mediaeval European literature known as that of 'mirrors for princes' or *Fürstenspiegel*. VII 984b

nāsik (A, pl. *nussāk*) : in early Islam, a representative of the ascetic movement, who wore rough woollen cloth in order to react against the people wearing more luxurious dress, and possibly also in imitation of the dress of Christian monks and ascetics. X 313b

nāsikh (A) : a copyist. II 304a; VI 199a; VIII 149a; an abrogator. VII 988b

♦ al-nāsikh wa 'l-mansūkh → NASKH

naskh (A) : the act of cancellation, abrogation; in Qurʾānic exegesis, in the science of Tradition, and in law, ~ (syn. *al-nāsikh wa 'l-mansūkh*) is the generic label for a range of theories concerning verses and Traditions which, when compared, suggest frequent, serious conflict; abrogation VII 1009b

In calligraphy, ~, or *naskhī*, is used to designate the flexible, rounded script which in the post-Umayyad period was a favourite script of the scribes. It is sometimes called 'broken' kūfic, and in the far Iranian provinces was used especially for personal inscriptions on pottery. IV 1122a; V 221a; VIII 151a ff.

In religion, ~ is a type of metempsychosis; according to al-Īdjī, ~ refers to the passage from one human body to another human body, MASKH to passage from human to animal, *raskh* to transformation into a vegetal state, and *faskh* to that into mineral form. X 182a

♦ naskh-i taʿlīḳ, naskh-taʿlīḳ → NASTAʿLĪḲ

♦ naskhī → NASKH

naṣl → ḲIDḤ

nasnās (A, pl. *nasānis*), or *nisnās* : in mediaeval Arabic literature, a 'demi-man' with human face and vertical stance, without a tail and possessing the faculty of speech, but also covered with a thick fleece, usually russet-coloured; in all likelihood, the ~ was nothing other than an anthropomorphic ape observed by seafaring Arab merchants of the Indian Ocean. V 133a

nasr (A, P *dāl*, T *akbaba*; pl. *ansur, nusūr, nisār*) : in zoology, the vulture, of which eight species are known in the lands of Islam. VII 1012b, where many variants are found; and → DJANĀḤ AL-NASR; ḤADJAR AL-ʿUḲĀB; KAFF AL-NASR; ẒUFR AL-NASR

In astronomy, ~ is in the names of two well-known stars: Altair (alpha *Aquilae*) derived from *al- ~ al-ṭāʾir* 'the vulture flying', in the 17th Boreal constellation of the Eagle, and Vega (alpha *Lyrae*) derived from *al- ~ al-wāḳiʿ* 'the vulture perched', in the 19th Boreal constellation of the Lyre. VII 1014b

naṣrānī → NAṢĀRĀ

naṣrī (A) : in numismatics, a square silver coin of Ḥafṣid Tunisia, which remained in use after the Ottomans conquered the Maghrib. VIII 228b

naṣṣ (A) : in law, a text whose presence in either Qurʾān or Tradition must be demonstrated to justify an alleged ruling. III 1062b; VII 1029a

In the science of Tradition, ~ is the 'raising' of a Tradition, i.e. its attribution to its originator, not necessarily the Prophet. VII 1029a

In shīʿism, designation, e.g. of the imamate. IX 423a; among the Bohorās sect in India, the appointment of the head of the sect. I 1254b; and → IKHTIYĀR

♦ naṣṣ wa-taʿyīn (A) : the shīʿī principle that the Prophet had designated ʿAlī to be his successor. VII 1029a

nassādj (A) : weaver, textile worker, synonymous with *ḥāʾik* although less derogatory. VII 1029b; and → TANAWWUṬ NASSĀDJ

♦ nassādjī (P) : a Persian tax levied on every man or woman living in the village who had a loom. IV 1042b nastaʿlīḳ (P), or *nas̲k̲h̲-i taʿlīḳ, nas̲k̲h̲-taʿlīḳ* : a script, which is said in the works on calligraphy to have been formed by joining NASK̲H̲ and TAʿLĪḲ, which compound gradually came to be pronounced as ~. The invention of this script goes back as far as the 7th/13th century. In Turkey and in Arabic countries it is erroneously called *taʿlīḳ*. IV 1124a; VIII 151b; and → S̲H̲IKASTA TAʿLĪḲ

nasṭūriyyūn (A, s. *nasṭūrī*), also *nasāṭira* : the Nestorian or East Syrian, later called Assyrian, Christians, whose practitioners under ʿAbbasid rule were prominent in the fields of medicine, science and philosophy. VII 1030a

nāsūk̲h̲iyya → TANĀSUK̲H̲

nāsūr, nāṣūr (A) : in medicine, anal fistulas. X 784a

nāsūt → LĀHŪT

naswar → SUʿŪṬ

naʿt (A) : qualification, in grammar, a technical term used to designate a qualifying adjective and its function as an epithet, synonymous with ṢIFA and *waṣf*. VII 1034a; IX 527b

In poetry, ~ denotes a ḲAṢĪDA praising and expressing devotion to the Prophet Muḥammad. IV 715b; an encomium of the Prophet. IX 213a

In onomastics, ~ means a personal name. The Umayyads considered an ISM and KUNYA sufficient, but the use of LAḲAB and ~ became current under the ʿAbbāsids. II 302a

naṭʿ → SUFRA

nat̲h̲r (A) : prose, whose opposite is NAẒM, poetry. XII 662b

♦ al-nat̲h̲r al-mursal (A) : prose that does not keep to the rules of SAD̲J̲ʿ. XII 665b

natīd̲j̲a (A) : an almanac, also called RUZ-NĀMA and TAḲWĪM. X 146b

In logic, the conclusion resulting from the combination of the two premisses, *muḳaddimāt*, in the syllogism, ḲIYĀS. In place of the usual ~ we also find RIDF or *radf* ʻdeductionʼ. VII 1034b

nātiḥ (A) : a term applied to a wild animal or bird which approaches a traveller or hunter from the front. I 1048a

nāṭiḳ (A) : among the Ismāʿīliyya, one of seven ʻspeakingʼ prophets, each of whom reveals a new religious law. The seventh ~, the ḲĀʾIM, will abrogate Muḥammad's s̲h̲arīʿa and restore the pure unit, *tawḥīd*, of the times before Adam's fall. IV 203a; XI 161b; XII 206b; and → ṢĀMIT

In poetry, a didactic poem in which each verse is sung to another mode, popular in the 16th and 17th centuries. IX 101a

naṭrūn (A) : in mineralogy and pharmacology, a compound of sodium carbonate ($NaCO_3$) and sodium bicarbonate ($NaHCO_3$) with several impurities, obtained partly from natural crystallisations occurring in sodium-containing lakes and partly artificially. VII 1035a; XII 130b

In modern Morocco, ~ (var. *litrūn, liṭrūn*) indicates a mixture of gypsum and rock salt. VII 1035a

naṭṭāla (A) : an artificial irrigation contrivance, still in use in Egypt, as well as in many African countries. Two men stand face to face, each holding two cords of palm-fibre ropes to which is attached a wide, shallow waterproof basket. This basket, made from twisted palm leaves or leather, is known in Egypt by the name *ḳaṭwa*. The two men holding the ropes bend slightly toward the water, dip the basket and fill it. Then they straighten while turning to the field, thus raising the basket which is emptied into the mouth of the irrigation canal. V 863b

naʾūr (A) : soot, as used in filling the trace left by a tattooing needle. Other materials used were antimony (*kuḥl*) or indigo (*nīl*). XII 830b

nāʿūra (A, pl. *nawāʿīr*) : ʻnoriaʼ, a current-driven, water-raising wheel, sometimes confused with SĀḲIYA. It is mounted on a horizontal axle over a flowing stream so that the water strikes the paddles that are set around its perimeter. The water is raised in pots attached to its rim or in bucket-like compartments set into the rim. The large norias at Ḥamāt in Syria can still be seen today. I 1232a; V 861a ff.; VII 1037a

nawā → S̲H̲AS̲H̲MAḲOM

nawāb → NAWWĀB

nawādir → NĀDIRA

nāward (P) : a training-routine of a horse. IV 1146a

nawba (A) : 'turn'; in its non-technical meaning, appearing in the *Ag̲h̲ānī* by al-Iṣbahānī of the 4th/10th century, ~ refers to the practice of having a given musician perform regularly at court on a particular day of the week, or to several musicians taking turns to sing during a single sitting; in the art-music of the Islamic Middle East and North Africa, ~ denotes a complex form made up of a number of individual pieces arranged in a standard sequence. VII 1042a; X 34b

♦ nawbat : in Muslim India, a large orchestra consisting of wind and percussion instruments. These usually played at regular periods in the gateways of palaces and shrines. III 452b

nawča → MĪYĀNDĀR

nawḥ (A) : in music, the elegy. II 1073a

♦ nawḥa (A) : in Persian literature, a genre of strophic poems in classical metres which are sung on occasions involving breast-beating or self-flagellation with chains. They often have unconventional rhyme-schemes and arrangements of lines and refrains within the stanza. The number and placement of stresses in each line are important, those for breast-beating having a more rapid rhythm than those for chain-flagellation. VI 609b

In Urdu literature, a short elegy on the theme of the Karbalāʾ martyrs, also called SALĀM. VI 610b

nawkar (P) : an official. X 488a

nawk̲h̲ʷāsta → MĪYĀNDĀR

nawr → NAWRIYYA

nawriyya (A, < *nawr* 'flower') : in literature, a genre of poetry devoted to the description of flowers, which, however, is practically impossible to separate, as a genre, from the *rawḍiyya* or *rabīʿiyya* (descriptions of gardens or of the spring, respectively). VII 1046a; VIII 357a, where *rabīʿiyyāt* in Ottoman literature is treated

nawrūz (P, A *nayrūz*) : the first day of the Persian solar year, marked by popular festivities. It begins at the vernal equinox. VI 523a ff.; VII 1047a; VIII 146b

nawwāb (P, < A *nuwwāb*), or *nawāb* : in Muslim India, a title originally granted by the Mug̲h̲al emperors to denote a viceroy or governor of a province, certainly current by the 18th century. A ~ might be subordinate to another governor and the title tended to become a designation of rank without necessarily having any office attached to it. In the later 18th century, the term was imported into English usage in the form Nabob, applied in a somewhat derogatory manner to Anglo-Indians who had returned from the subcontinent laden with wealth. It eventually passed into other languages, including French. VII 1048a

nāy (P, T *ney*) : in music, a rim-blown flute made of reed, a term used by the Persians in early days to designate the reed-pipe (A *mizmār*). The flute was called *nāy narm* 'soft *nāy*'. Later, they called the reed-pipe the *nāy siyāh* 'black *nāy*', and the flute the *nāy safīd* 'white *nāy*', because of the colour of the instruments. VII 207a; XII 667a; and → RUWĪN NĀY

♦ nāy ṭunbūr : in music, a pandore mounted with two strings, which was played with a plectrum, *miḍrāb*, instead of the fingers. X 625a

nayrūz → NAYRŪZ

nayzak (A, < P *nīza*) : in miliary science, a javelin. XII 735b; and → SHIHĀB
naz' al-watar → MADD
nazam (M, < A *naẓm*) : a genre of Malay poetry, consisting of a long sequence of couplets comprising two hemistiches, each usually numbering from nine or ten up to twelve syllables, that rhyme with each other on one of the following patterns: *aa, bb, cc, . . .; aa, aa, aa, . . .; aa, ba, ca, ...* XII 727b
naẓar (A) : theory, philosophical speculation; and → 'ILM NAẒĀRĪ
In philosophy, a term which probably not until the 9th century AD received the meaning of research in the sense of scientific investigation as translation of the Greek θεωρία. VII 1050a
In dialectical theology, ~ meant 'reflection', 'rational, discursive thinking'. VII 1051a
In archery, the aim. IV 800b
♦ naẓariyya (A) : the theoretical sciences, as determined by the philosophers. I 427b
naẓarāna (IndP) : in numismatics, beginning in the reign of Shāh Djahān I, blanks that were of full weight and standard alloy but smaller than the dies with which they were struck, so that frequently a third or more of the legends were 'off flan'. The resulting coins, known as ~ mohurs or rupiya, did not do justice to the die-sinker's work, but on occasion special efforts were made to cut blanks to their correct size so that they could receive the full impression of the dies. XI 230b
nāzikī → ĪWĀN
nāzila (A, pl. *nawāzil*) : in law, especially Mālikī law, a specific case, case in question, distinguished from the FATWĀ by the fact that it is not, properly speaking, a juridical consultation but a case which is set forth as a real case. VII 1052a
nāẓim → ṢŪBADĀR
nāẓir (A), *mutawallī* or *ḳayyim* : the administrator of a charitable endowment. XI 63a; inspector of finance. XI 191a; in the Ottoman empire, a synonym for *wezīr* (→ WAZĪR). XI 194b
naẓīr (A) : in astronomy, ~ denotes the nadir, the bottom, the pole of the horizon (invisible) under the observer in the direction of the vertical; also, the deepest (lowest) point in the sphere of heaven; originally (and generally), the point diametrically opposite a point on the circumference of a circle or the surface of a sphere. VII 1054a
For ~ in law, → ASHBĀH
♦ naẓīra → MU'ĀRAḌA
nāẓūr (A) : in mediaeval Muslim Spain and parts of the Maghrib (where *nāḍūr*), a look-out or watch-tower of one kind or another, and in parts of the 19th-century Maghrib, a lighthouse. Ibn Baṭṭūṭa uses it in its original sense of the 'man whose business it was to keep watch'. VII 1056a
naẓm (A) : the arrangement of pearls in a necklace; in literature, poetry with perfect order and symmetry; composition; versification. IX 449a; IX 458a; XII 668a; in western and central Sudanic prosody, the versifying of an existing prose text. IX 243b; in Urdu poetry, a thematic poem. IX 162a
♦ naẓm al-manthūr (A) : in literature, the setting of prose into verse, opposite of ḤALL AL-MANẒŪM. XII 662b
nāẓūr (A) : a term used in Muslim Spain and certain parts of North Africa in mediaeval times to denote a look-out or watch-tower of one kind or another, and, in parts of 19th-century North Africa at least, a lighthouse; originally, the man whose business it was to keep watch. VII 1056a
naẓẓār → ḲAṢṢĀṢ
nefer (Egy) : in Egypt, the pandore, or ṬUNBŪR, a long-necked lute-like instrument. X 624b; and → GUNBRĪ

nefes (T, < A *nafas* 'breath') : a type of poem written or uttered by members of Turkish mystic orders to eulogise God or leading personalities of the orders. V 275a; V 957a; VIII 2b

nefīr (T, < A *nafīr*) : in Ottoman usage, a term alluding to a musical instrument similar to a horn. The person playing the instrument was referred to as *nefīrī*. VIII 3b; as *nafīr*, a trumpet, chief instrument of the cylindrical tube type. I 1291b; X 35a; and → BORU

In military usage, ~ alludes to a body of men assembled for a common purpose. VIII 3b

♦ nefīr-i ʿāmm (T) : in the Ottoman empire, the recruitment of volunteers by a general call to arms, in contrast with *nefīr-i khāṣṣ*, the mobilisation of a certain well-defined group of people. VIII 3b

♦ nefīr-i khāṣṣ → NEFĪR-I ʿĀMM

nefy (T, < A *nafy*) : under the Ottomans, banishment, internal exile, a temporary punishment imposed on individual members of the ruling elite who had incurred the sultan's disfavour. XII 767a

nemče (T, < A *al-nimsā*) : 'mute', a term borrowed from the Slavonic used by the Ottomans to indicate the Germans. In a broader sense, they also used it for the territory of the Holy Roman Empire, which lasted until 1806, and in a restricted sense for the territories under Habsburg rule within the boundaries of modern Austria. VIII 4a

nezik (T) : in music, a fork-shaped 'spool' in the head of the folk shawm, ZURNA, which allows the instrument maker to fit the body of the instrument, in the region of the seven fingerholes and the thumbhole, with an easily made cylindrical bore instead of the traditional conical bore. XI 574a

ngano (Sw) : in Swahili literature, the word for invented tales including fables, as opposed to *hadithi*, legends about the Prophet Muḥammad although today they contain some of the most fantastic adventure tales. XII 643a

nidāl (A) : in archery, a long bow. II 954a

nifāḳ → IKHLĀṢ

nīfuk (N.Afr) : a slit for the elbow at the lower extremity of the armlets in the DJALLĀBIYYA. II 405a

nigār → TAṢWĪR

nihāya (A) : in philosophy, a term denoting that which forbids access to something beyond a certain limit. The concept of ~ applies to such realities as time, space, and the division of bodies. VIII 24a

niḥla → ʿAṢABIYYA

niḳāba (A) : 'trade union', i.e. association for defending the interests of and promoting the rights of wage and salary earners; ~ can also denote the liberal professions and even those of employers. The term's usage became general after the First World War. VIII 25b

♦ niḳābiyya (A) : syndicalism. VIII 25b

nikāḥ (A) : marriage (properly, sexual intercourse), used both for stable and temporary unions. VI 475b; VIII 26b

♦ nikāḥ al-khidn (A) : concubinage, which is prohibited by the Qurʾān. VI 476a

♦ nikāḥ al-maḳt (A) : marriage to the father's widow, which is prohibited by the Qurʾān. VI 476a

♦ nikāḥ al-mutʿa → MUTʿA

♦ nikāḥ al-raḥt (A) : a form of polyandry forbidden by the Prophet, whereby a woman takes a group of husbands (less than ten) and, if she has a child, attributes the paternity to one of this group, who is unable to refuse it. XII 133a

niḳris (A) : in medicine, gout. X 433a

♦ al-niḳris al-ḥārr (A) : in medicine, feverish gout. IX 9b

nīl (P, < San *nīla* 'blue'), or *nīlādj* : the oldest known organic dye, *Indigo tinctoria* L., *Indigoferae*; the main component of natural indigo, which can be obtained from various kinds of indigofera (*Isatis tinctoria, Cruciferae*) and from the knotweed (*Polygonum tinctorium, Polygonaceae*). VIII 37b
In the Middle Ages, the Arabs used ~, actually indigo, to indicate woad (Dioscurides' ἰσάτις). The constant confusion between the two plants led to a series of Arabic synonyms, like *ʿiẓlim, wasma* (*wāsima*), *khiṭr, nīla, tīn akhḍar* etc. which were used indifferently for the two plants. VIII 37b

nīlādj → NĪL

nīlūfar (A, P 'water lily', < Gr Νειλόφερον) : in botany, lotus seeds. IX 615a; in Turkish, *nīlūfer* are water-lily flowers. IX 417a

nīm-fatḥa (P) : in Persian prosody, an extra short vowel, added to words ending in two consonants (*nūn* excepted) preceded by a short vowel, or one consonant preceded by a long vowel. I 677a

nim-ling (P) : in archery, a quiver made of various skins sewn together. IV 799b

niʿma → KĀFIR NIʿMA

nimʿa → RAḤMA

nimekare (P) : a land-leasing system in Kurdish Iran, in which the landowner leases out the irrigated lands and supplies the seed, and the peasant supplies the work, with the landowner taking three-fifths of the harvest and the peasant two-fifths. V 473b

nimr → NAMIR

nims (A, pl. *numūs, numūsa*) : in zoology, the ichneumon or Egyptian mongoose (*Herpestes ichneumon*). In some parts of the Islamic world such as the Maghrib and Lebanon, ~ has been erroneously applied to the weasel (*Mustela nivalis*). As a result of similar confusion, some Arabic dialects employ ~ to identify various other members of the sub-family Mustelidae such as the stone-marten (*Martes foina*), the polecat (*Mustela putorius*) and the ferret (*Mustela putorius furo*); the term is even found erroneously applied to the civet (*Genetta genetta*). VIII 49b
In botany, ~ is given to two plants: *al-nims* is, in the Maghrib, Downy koelaria (*Koelaria pubescens*); *biṭṭīkh nims* 'ichneumon melon' or *biṭṭīkh ʿayn al-nims* 'ichneumon's eye melon' is a nickname given to the watermelon (*Citrullus vulgaris*, of the variety *ennemis*). VIII 50b

nīr → DJARR

nīrān → MANĀẒIR

nīrandj (A, < P *nayrang, nīrang*) : the operations of white magic, comprising prestidigitation, fakery and counter-fakery, the creating of illusions and other feats of sleight-of-hand, ḤIYAL. V 100b; VIII 51b; amulets which have an extraordinary power over men and over natural phenomena; acts done by magicians. VIII 52b

niṣāb (A, pl. *nuṣub, anṣiba*) : lit. base; in law, a minimum quantity. XI 408a; the definite minimum value. IX 62b

nīsān (A, < Heb) : the seventh month in the Syrian calendar, which corresponds to April of the Roman year and like it has 30 days. VIII 53b

nisba (A) : in grammar, the adjective of relation. VIII 53b
In onomastics, the element of a person's name, consisting of an adjective ending in *ī*, formed originally from the name of the individual's tribe or clan, then from his place of birth, origin or residence, sometimes from a MADHHAB or sect, and occasionally from a trade or profession. In Arabic, the ~ is always preceded by the definite article, which in Persian disappears. IV 180a; VIII 54a
In geometry, ~ 'relationship' (or *tasmiya* 'denomination') conveys the idea of a fraction, as opposed to *kasr*, the common term. IV 725b

niṣf (A) : half, in numismatics, the term for the half DĪNĀR, or *semissis*, struck in North Africa and Spain during the transitional period and in the early years of the 2nd/8th century. The third *dīnār, thulth*, or *tremissis*, was also struck, while the quarter *dīnār, rubʿ*, was introduced by the Aghlabids in North Africa early in the third quarter of the 2nd/8th century. II 297b

♦ **niṣf al-nahār** (A) : 'half of the day', 'midday'; in astronomy, used in the expression which denotes the 'meridian circle' (*dāʾirat* ~). VIII 56b

nishān (P) : under the Ottomans, ~ basically denoted a sign or a mark and also designated the sultan's signature, *ṭughra*, and, by extension, a document bearing it. Since the 10th/16th century, this category denoted especially those orders, concerning financial matters, which were drawn up by the highest financial department of the empire; also, the standards of the Janissaries; the insignia on military, naval and other uniforms; and, later, decorations bestowed by the sultan. In 19th and 20th-century literary Arabic, ~ had essentially the same connotations. The ~ are to be distinguished clearly from medals. I 1170b; VIII 57b; the ruler's sign manual. X 595a; and → KARKADDAN

♦ nishān-i humāyūn → TUGHRA

♦ **nishāndji** (T) : under the Ottomans, secretary of state for the sultan's signature, TUGHRA; chancellor. VIII 62a; under the Saldjūḳs and Mamlūks, an official for drawing the sultan's signature, also called *tewḳīʿī*. VIII 62a; X 597b

nisnās → NASNĀS

nisrīn → WARD

niṭʿ (A), or *niṭaʿ* : in anatomy, the anterior part of the palate. II 101a; the alveoles of the palate. VI 129b

nitādj (A) : the parturition of pregnant sheep. XII 319a

niṭāḳayn → DHĀT AL-NIṬĀḲAYN

nithār (A) : in the pre-modern Middle East, the showering of money, jewels and other valuables on occasions of rejoicing, such as a wedding, a circumcision, the accession of a ruler, the victorious return from a military campaign etc. VIII 64a

In numismatics, the Mughal silver (sometimes also gold) coin scattered at weddings, processions and other public spectacles. VII 345a; other terms for largesse-coins were *nūr afshān* and *khayr ḳabūl*. VIII 64b

♦ nithārī : in numismatics, for a short time the name of the quarter-rupee during the reign of the Mughal ruler Djahāngīr. VIII 64b

niṭʿiyya (A) : in grammar, a term used by al-Khalīl for the prepalatals. III 598a

niyāba → WILĀYA

niyāḥa (A) : lamentation; the term is used to designate the activity of professional mourners who play a great role in funeral ceremonies all around the Mediterranean. VIII 64b

niyāz → NADHR WA-NIYĀZ

niyya (A) : intention. Acts prescribed by Islamic law, obligatory or not, require to be preceded by a declaration by the performer that he intends to perform such an act. This declaration, pronounced audibly or mentally, is called ~. Without it, the act would be null, *bāṭil*. VIII 66a

niẓām (A) : in Muslim India, an honorific title which became characteristic of the rulers of the state of Ḥaydarābād, derived in the first place from the fuller title ~ *al-mulk*. VIII 67a; and → ḲĀNŪN

In Turkish military usage, ~ or *niẓāmiyye, ʿasākir-i niẓāmiyye, ʿasākir-i muwaẓẓafe* was used in the strict sense for an active or regular army (standing army) and in the wider sense for regular or disciplined troops (syn. *müretteb*). IV 1185a; VIII 370a

♦ **niẓām ʿaskarī** (A) : military organisation, the system of military rule in modern Islamic lands. XII 670a

♦ **niẓām-i̊ d̲j̲edīd** (T) : lit. new system; in the Ottoman empire, the new military units, the 'New Order', created by the sultan Selīm III in 1793 to be a corps of troops properly trained in the European manner. To finance these he initiated a special fund, the 'New Revenue' (*īrād-i̊ d̲j̲edīd*), from taxes on brandy, tobacco, coffee, silk, wool, sheep and the yields from the fiefs of TĪMĀR-holders in Anatolia who had neglected their duties in war. VIII 75a

♦ **niẓāmiyya** (A) : in Sald̲j̲ūḳ historical sources, the term often used for the partisans and protégés of the vizier Niẓām al-Mulk. VIII 81b
In the Ottoman legal context, the *niẓāmiyye* courts, or 'secular' courts, were instituted in the Tanẓīmāt period and restricted the jurisdiction of the religious (*s̲h̲arʿī*) courts to the area of personal law. III 1153b; VI 6b

niẓāmiyye → NIẒĀM; NIẒĀMIYYA

nḳāb (N.Afr) : a face veil for married women in Morocco and Algeria, often synonymous with LIT̲H̲ĀM. V 746b

nnṣaḥt (B, < A *naṣīḥa*) : in Tas̲h̲elḥīt literature, a genre whose purpose it is to provide the illiterate population with information on orthodox Islamic practice. X 346a

noʿma → KUSKUSŪ

noyan (Mon, pl. *noyad*) : a Mongolian title, rendered in the Muslim chronicles of the Mongol and Tīmūrid periods in the Arabic script as *nūyān, nūyīn, nuyīn* etc. In the pre-Čīnggisid period the *noyad* were the hereditary clan chieftains. Under Čīnggis K̲h̲ān and his successors, the title was granted initially as a military rank, and it came to mean 'commander'. Under the Yüan regime in China, ~ was used to refer to all officials serving in public posts. VIII 87a

nubuwwa (A) : prophecy, in the first instance the precognition given by the divinity to the prophet and the prediction made by the latter of future contingencies, and in the second instance 'revelation' (syn. WAHY). VIII 93b

nud̲j̲abāʾ (A) : in mysticism, the seventy 'pre-eminents', the sixth degree in the ṣūfī hierarchical order of saints. I 95a

nud̲j̲ūm (A, s. NAD̲J̲M) : in astronomy, the stars. The term for astrology was *aḥkām al-nud̲j̲ūm* (→ NAD̲J̲M) 'decrees of the stars'. VIII 97b

nuffār (A) : a term for those who took part in the siege of the house of the caliph ʿUt̲h̲mān b. ʿAffān in 35/655, which culminated in his assassination. I 382b; II 415a

nuḥāf → NUḤĀM

nuḥām (A) : in zoology, the Greater Flamingo, *Phoenicopterus ruber roseus* or *antiquorum* of the order of the Phoenicopteridae (*nuḥāmiyāt*), which resemble waders with their long legs and palmipeds with their webbed feet. Other mediaeval names for the flamingo were *mirzam* and *turund̲j̲ān*, which refers to its striking colour, while in Egypt, it is called *bas̲h̲arūs̲h̲* (< O.Fr *becharu*), becoming in Tunisia *s̲h̲abrūs̲h̲*. Also found are the terms *nuḥāf, niḥāf, surk̲h̲āb* and *rahū 'l-māʾ* 'aquatic crane'. VIII 110b

nuḥās (A) : in metallurgy, the term most often used in Arabic for copper (Cu). Other terms, according to al-Bīrūnī, were *al-miss* (in ʿIrāḳ and K̲h̲urāsān) and *al-ḳiṭr* (i.e. brass). VIII 111b; brass. XII 552b

nūḥī → KĀG̲H̲AD

nuḳabāʾ → NAḲĪB

nuḳāwā → NAḲĀʾ

nuk̲h̲ab (A) : in literature, 'selections'. X 482b

nuk̲h̲ūd → ʿAS̲H̲RAFĪ; TŪMĀN

nuḳl → ṬĪN

♦ nuḳla → TANĀSUK̲H̲

nuḳra (A) : in numismatics, refined silver in bars or ingots. XI 147b; and → WARIḲ

In the mediaeval kitchen, a copper basin for washing smaller containers and vessels in hot water. V 808b

♦ nuḳrakhāne → ḌARBKHĀNE-I ʿĀMIRE

nuḳṣān (A) : in mathematics, the term used for subtraction. III 1139b

As a Persian term in linguistics, *nuḳsānī* means 'deficiency'. XII 430b

nukat → ḤAZZŪRA

nuḳta (A) : in mathematics, the term for the geometrical point. II 220a

nuʿmān → SHAḲĪḲAT AL-NUʿMĀN

♦ nuʿmānī → SABʿĀNĪ

numruḳ → WISĀDA

nūn (A) : the twenty-fifth letter of the Arabic alphabet, transcribed *n*, with the numerical value 50. VIII 120b

♦ nūn ghunna : in Indian phonetics, the final form of *nūn* written without its diacritical point, used when a nasalised long vowel stands finally in a word, or even morpheme. VIII 121b

♦ ṣāghir nūn (T) : in Ottoman Turkish, the term for the Persian *gāf*, which was used in writing to convey the gutterally pronounced /ñ/. VIII 121a

nūr (A) : light (syn. *ḍawʾ*, also *ḍūʾ* and *ḍiyāʾ*). VIII 121b

♦ **nūr Allāh** → NŪR MUḤAMMADĪ

♦ **nūr muḥammadī** (A) : 'the Muḥammadan light', in theology, the concept of Muḥammad's pre-existence, which preceded the creation of Ādam. In early ḤADĪTH material, ~ is identified with the spermatic substance of Muḥammad's ancestors. Another kind of divine pre-existent light is referred to as nūr Allāh, said to have reached Muḥammad and the shīʿī imāms through the previous prophets. VIII 125a

♦ nūra (A) : lime, used to make a depilatory paste. IX 312a

♦ **nūrī** (A) : a member of certain gipsy tribes, a more correct vocalisation being nawārī. In Persian, the current name for gipsy is *lūrī, lōrī*, or LŪLĪ. VIII138a

nurcular → NURCULUK

nurculuk (T) : the name given by the modern Turkish press and authorities to the entire body of the teachings of Saʿīd Nursī, a religious leader in late Ottoman and Republican Turkey. His followers were called *Nurcular*. VIII 136b

nūshādir (A, < ? Pah) : sal-ammoniac. In the earliest Latin translations (*nesciador, mizadir*), the transliteration of the Arabic name is still used; in the Latin forms *aliocab, alocaph* is also found the general term *al-ʿuḳāb*. VIII 148a

nushshāb → NABL

nushūḳ → SUʿŪṬ

nuskha (A) : 'transcript', 'copy'; in the manuscript era, 'manuscript'. VIII 149a; a certified verbatim copy of an original document. IX 359a; both the original and the copy are called ~ since each 'replaces' the other. X 181b; and → ḤIRZ

nuṣṣ raʾs (N.Afr) : lit. half the head; a small helmet or cap worn by seamen in the Maghrib. X 613b

nuṣūb (A, pl. *anṣāb*) : in the plural (more often used), the blocks of stone on which the blood of the victims sacrificed for idols was poured, as well as sepulchral stones and those marking out the sacred enclosure of the sanctuary. Among sedentary populations, the ~, a rough stone, has become the ṢANAM, a stone carved with the image of the idols of the Kaʿba. VIII 154b

nūtī (A, pl. *nawātiya*) : a sailor; on a mediaeval Islamic warship, the ~ made up the crew, along with the oarsmen (ḲADHDHĀF), craftsmen and workmen (*dhawu 'l-ṣināʿa wa 'l-mihan*), fighting men (e.g. NAFFĀṬ) and the marines. XII 120a

nuwwāla (Mor) : a conical roof of a hut with branches, found increasingly alongside the tent in the plains of Morocco as dwelling. V 1197b nuwayḵsa → ṢANDJ

nuʾy (A) : a drain, edged with mounded earth, *iyād*, surrounding a tent to prevent water from penetrating underneath. IV 1148a

nuzha (A) : in music, a rectangular type of psaltery of greater compass than the ḴĀNŪN. It was invented in the 7th/13th century; 108 strings were mounted in the instrument. VII 191a

nuzūl → ISNĀD NĀZIL

O

oba (K), or *obā* : among the Kurds, a temporary association of stock-breeders from different villages, formed in the spring to lead the herds to the pastures and to return at the end of the autumn. Neither kinship nor tribal relations are necessary to be a member of the ~, which system is particular to the semi-nomadic tribes and makes its appearance towards the end of the 19th and the beginning of the 20th century. V 472a; among the S̲h̲āhsewan in Persia, a herding unit of three to five households. IX 224a; in eastern Anatolia, the grazing area of a nomadic household. VI 961b; in the Turco-Mongol tribal scheme, a clan, lineage or local segment of a clan. VIII 608a; X 126a

ocak-zāde → ODJAḴ

ōda (Ir) : in modern Iraqi architecture, two small rooms flanking the ĪWĀN. II 114a

odjaḵ (T, > A *wud̲j̲āḵ*) : fireplace, hearth, chimney; in modern Turkish, *ocak* replaced the traditional name for the month of January by law in 1945. VIII 161a

Under the Ottomans, an army unit. I 368a; VIII 161b; IX 657a; XII 409b; family. I 1267a; VIII 161a; a TĪMĀR-holding family. X 505b

In mysticism, a religious order. IV 167b; among the Bektās̲h̲iyya, and the Mawlawiyya, ~ had a special place in their TEKKEs. VIII 161b

♦ ocak-zāde : among the Alevis of Anatolia, an ~ is a spiritual guide who belonged to one of the lineages stemming from the twelve IMĀMs. VIII 161b; as *odjaḵ-zāde*, under the Ottomans, sons of established military families. X 505a

♦ odjaḵ-zāde → OCAK-ZĀDE

♦ odjaḵ og̲h̲lu (T) : 'son of a good house'. VIII 163a

♦ odjaḵlı̊ḵ (T) : in the Ottoman empire, a system whereby a given region was responsible for supplying an arsenal with one particular ship-building commodity. I 947b; an accounting system applied for securing gunpowder supplies, a special fund allocated for purchases and requisitions of essential supplies such as sulphur and saltpetre. V 979a; a special sort of TĪMĀR. VIII 161a; family succession. I 1267a

og̲h̲lan → OG̲H̲UL

og̲h̲ul (T, pl. OG̲H̲LAN) : 'offspring, child', with a strong implication of 'male child', as opposed to Ḵı̊z 'girl'; ~ is very frequently found in Turkic family names where it takes the place of the Persian *zāde* or the Arabic IBN. VIII 163a

♦ og̲h̲lan (T) : an original plural of OG̲H̲UL, which evolved into an independent singular, meaning 'youth', 'servant', 'page', 'bodyguard'. From ~ comes the German *Uhlan*, the name for light cavalry. VIII 163a

okka (T) : in the Ottoman empire, a measure of weight equal to 1.283 kg. VI 120b

ordu (T, Mon *orda*) : 'the royal tent or residence', 'the royal encampment', a term which became widespread in the mediaeval Turco-Mongol and then in the Persian worlds, acquiring from the second meaning that of 'army camp'. VIII 174a; in Turkish military usage, army corps. VIII 370b

For Indo-Persian usage, → URDU

♦ ordu-yu hümāyūn (T) : under the Ottomans, a general term for the imperial army. VIII 174b

♦ ordudju bashi̊/aghasi̊ (T) : the chief of a staff of tradesmen and technicians who accompanied the Janissaries on their campaigns away from the capital. VIII 174b

ʿörf (T), or *ʿörfī* : under the Ottomans, a large, dome-shaped headdress, ḲAVUḲ, worn with a white turban rolled around and which, draped, forms harmonious folds. It was worn from the 18th century by the religious classes. V 751b; and → TEKĀLĪF-I FEWḲALʿĀDE

orta (T) : lit. centre; in Ottoman military terminology, the equivalent of a company of fighting men in the three divisions of which the Janissary corps was eventually composed. VIII 178b

♦ **orta oyunu** (T) : 'entertainment staged in the middle place', a form of popular Turkish entertainment so-called because it takes place in the open air, *palanka*, around which the spectators form a circle. VIII 178b

ortaḳdji → ČELTÜKDJI

ʿösher → ʿUSHR

otlaḳ resmi → YAYLAḲ RESMI

öy (T) : among the Türkmen Yomut and Göklen tribes, a type of tent, either *aḳ öy* 'white house' (taken from the colour of the covering felts when new) or *ḳara öy* 'black house' (from the colour of the felts when old and blackened by smoke). The ~ has a trellis wall, with a doorway in it, circular in plan, with a roof wheel supported by struts from the top of the trellis wall. IV 1150b

ozan (T) : a Turkish bard; the term ~ was replaced in the late 9th/15th century by ʿĀSHIḲ, nevertheless, in certain contemporary dialects of Anatolia, ~ has survived with the meaning 'poet', 'singer', as also as an element of the terms *ozanlama* 'assonantal sayings, proverbs', *ozancı* 'garrulous person', *ozanlık* 'pleasantry' and *ozannama* improvised story, song'. In Turkmen, ~ is archaic and is replaced by *bagsı* 'popular poet', but at the present day, in modern Turkish, ~ has replaced the Arabic term *shāʿir* (*şair*). I 697b; VIII 232a; IX 239a

♦ ozancı → OZAN

♦ ozanlama → OZAN

♦ ozanlık → OZAN

♦ ozannama → OZAN

P

pāʾ (P), or *bāʾ-i fārsī* : the BĀʾ with three points subscript, invented for Persian as supplement to the second Arabic letter, *bāʾ*, and to represent the unvoiced, as opposed to the voiced, bilabial plosive. VIII 237a

paččī-kārī → PARČĪN-KĀRĪ

pād-zahr → YADA TASH

pada : in India, song. XII 483a

pādishāh (P) : the name for Muslim rulers, especially emperors. VIII 237a

In Turkish folklore, the chief of the DJINN. II 548a

pahlawān (P, < *pahlaw* 'Parthian'; A *bahlawān*) : in pre-modern Persian and thence in Turkish, 'wrestler', 'one who engages in hand-to-hand physical combat', subsequently 'hero', 'warrior', 'champion in battle'. VIII 238b

In Arabic, *bahlawān* is clearly a secondary development, and has in more recent times acquired the meaning of 'acrobat', 'tightrope walker in a circus', etc. In the most recent colloquial of Cairo, it has become a pejorative term for 'tricky person'. VIII 239a

♦ pahlawānī (P), or *pahlawī* : lit. Parthian; in linguistics, term at one time for Parthian and Middle Persian, as well as for the local dialect of the northern region called Fahla in an Arabicised form. XII 428a

pāʾī (H 'quarter', > Eng 'pie') : in numismatics, the smallest copper coin of British India = one-twelfth of an anna. Originally, the ~ was the quarter of an anna or pice (→ PAYSĀ); after the Acts of 1835, 1844 and 1870, the pie was one-third of a pice. VIII 239b

paisā → PAYSĀ

pāiza (Mon) : during the Mongol empire, an imperial tablet, given e.g. to postal couriers along with a decree, YARLÎGH, marked with a seal, which gave them absolute powers of requisition. XI 268a

pālāhang (P, Ott *pālāheng*) : lit. string, rope, halter, cord; ~ is applied to the belt worn around the waist by dervishes, especially the Bektāshīs, and on which is fixed a disc of stone with twelve flutings at the edge. VIII 244a

palanka → ORTA

palkī (H ?) : 'palanquin', an enclosed variety of litter used in India for transporting people, its central pole having an upward curve to afford more head-room for the passenger. In its common form it was in use for considerable journeys. A more elaborate form, with its carriage and pole covered with plates of silver, was in use in royal processions. VII 932a

pān (H ?) : in Mughal cuisine, a heart-shaped green leaf smeared with lime and catechu, to which is added slices or granules of betel-nut with aromatic spices, sometimes camphor, musk, or costly perfumes. A ~ was often presented to a courtier as a mark of royal favour. VI 814b

♦ pāndān : betel-boxes. I 299b

panbuḳ (T) : cotton, in western Turkish. V 557a, where other variants are found as well as terms in eastern Turkish

pandjagāh → ḲADAMGĀH

pandūl, or *pandūr* : in the Ottoman period, a militia recruited in the Balkans among the free peasants and entrusted with duties of local security. X 564b

panghulu → PENGHULU

pānka → KHAYSH

papyrus (Eng, < Gr) : one of the world's oldest writing materials, ~ was used in Egypt, the land of is provenance, since the 6th dynasty, ca. 2470-2270 BC. The Arabs, after their conquest of Egypt, used *bardī, abardī* or *waraḳ al-bardī*, although the term employed in Egypt was *fāfīr*.

pāra (P) : 'piece', 'fragment'; in numismatics, a Turkish coin of the Ottoman and early Republican periods. The ~ was originally a silver piece of 4 AḲČEs, first issued early in the 18th century; it soon replaced the *aḳče* as the monetary unit. With the post-World War II inflation, the ~ eventually disappeared from use; in present-day Turkey, *para* has acquired the general meaning of money. VIII 266b

parčīn-kārī (P, U *paččī-kārī*) : in architecture, a technique of inlay-work, usually set in marble, used on the Indo-Pakistan subcontinent. VIII 267a

parda-dār (P) : lit. the person who draws the curtain; 'court chamberlain', a term used among the dynasties of the eastern Islamic world from the Saldjūḳ period onwards as the equivalent of Arabic ḤĀDJIB. III 48b; VIII 270b

pargana (H, < San) : in Indo-Muslim administrative usage, a term denoting an aggregate of villages, a subdivision of a district (syn. MAḤALL). In later Anglo-Indian usage, the term was often rendered as *pergunnah*. VIII 270b

parī (P, T *peri*) : in folklore, a fairy, belonging to the realm of supernatural tales; in Turkish everyday speech as well as in stories of fantastic adventures and tales of the supernatural, *peri* is often taken as a synonym of DJINN. II 547b; VIII 271a

♦ parīkhʷān   → BĀKHSHĪ

♦ parīs̲h̲ānī   (P) : 'untidy turban', the name of the turban worn by the common people in the reign of Süleymān I. X 613b

parias   (< L) : in the mediaeval Iberian peninsula, a tribute paid by one ruler to another in recognition of his superior status. VIII 272a

parmaḳ   (T) : under the Ottomans, a measure of length equivalent to one and a quarter inches. I 658a

♦ parmaḳ ḥisābi̊   (T) : the original Turkish method of versification, wherein the verses are based not on quantity but on the number and stress of the syllables. IX 353b

pārsī   (P) : lit. inhabitant of Fārs, the name given to those descendants of the Zoroastrians who migrated to India, mostly to Gudjarāt, from the 4th/10th century onwards. VIII 273a; and → FĀRSĪ

parwāna   (P), or *parwānača* : in mediaeval Persian administration, the term used for the document 'related' by the official to the chancery, PARWĀNAČĪ. VIII 277a; and → FARĀS̲H̲A

♦ **parwānači**   (P) : 'relater', in mediaeval Persian administration, a term used for the official who noted down the instructions for the promulgation of deeds, and who forwarded them to the chancery. The function is recorded for the first time under Tīmūr. VIII 276b

pās-i anfās   (P) : a practice of regulating the breath, adopted by the Čis̲h̲tī mystics in order to harnass all feelings and emotions in establishing communion with God. II 55b

pasazh   (T) : in 19th-century Ottoman cities, a shop-lined covered street, a modern version of the *ārāsta*. IX 799b

pasha   (T, < P *pādis̲h̲āh*) : under the Ottomans, the highest official title of honour, used in Turkey until the advent of the Republic and surviving for sometime after that in certain Muslim countries originally part of the Turkish empire (Egypt, ʿIrāḳ, Syria); ~ was military rather than feudal in character, although it was not reserved solely for soldiers but was also given to certain high civil (not religious) officials. VIII 279b; in the Ottoman empire, a synonym for *wezīr* (→ WAZĪR). XI 194b

♦ **pashaliḳ**   (T) : the office or title of a PASHA; the territory under the authority of a *pasha* (in the provinces). VIII 282a

pās̲h̲īb   (IndP) : in Mug̲h̲al siegecraft, a raised platform constructed by filling the space between the top of the fort wall and the base of the besieger's camp below, with bags of sand and earth. III 482a

pas̲h̲tūnwalī   (Pash) : the special social code of the Afghans, the main pillars of which are *nanawātai* 'right of asylum', BADAL 'revenge by retaliation, vendetta', and *mēlmastyā* 'hospitality'. I 217a

pasisir   (J) : originally an administrative unit of the Central Javanese kingdom of Mataram. VIII 284a

pathān   → AS̲H̲RĀF

paṭrīk   (Ott, < A BIṬRĪḲ 'patricius') : in the Ottoman empire, the term for the patriarch of the Greek Orthodox and Eastern Christian Church, of whom by the 19th century there were seven. VIII 287b

patrona   (T, < It) : in the Ottoman navy, a 'galley carrying the lieutenant-general or the next in command to the chief of the squadron'; the term is also applied to Christian ships. VIII 565a;

♦ patrona bey : in the Ottoman navy, 'vice-admiral'. VIII 566b

patuḳ   (P) : a habitual location for a guild. IX 646a; as *pātuḳ*, the place where s̲h̲īʿī funeral flags are stored. X 488a

patwāri   : in the Mug̲h̲al empire, the village accountant, whose functions resembled those of the ḲĀNUNGO in the administrative unit PARGANA. VIII 271a

pawlā : in numismatics, the name given in the Mug̲h̲al emperor Akbar's monetary system to the quarter-*dām* (quarter-PAYSĀ). VIII 288a

pāyak (IndP) : in the Dihlī sultanate, the footsoldiers who were maintained within the infantry contingents and who were mostly Hindūs. They were good archers and were generally arrayed in front of the lines of horses, or around the elephants in order to prevent them from fleeing. V 686b

payg̲h̲ū (T) : a Turkish name or title found among the early Saldjūḳs, usually written *P.y.g̲h̲ū* or *B.y.g̲h̲ū*. These orthographies seem to reflect the old Turkish title YABG̲H̲U. VIII 288b

paysā (H, Eng 'pice'), or *paisā* : in numismatics, a copper coin of British India, equalling 3 pies or $^1/_4$ anna. Under the Mug̲h̲als, ~ became applied to the older *dām*, introduced by S̲h̲īr S̲h̲āh, 40 of which went to the rupee, as the unit of copper currency. In the currencies of modern India and Pakistan, 100 ~s equals one rupee, and in that of Bangladesh, one taka. VIII 288b

pāzār → BĀZĀR; ČARS̲H̲Ī

pegon (Mal), *jawi* or *melayu* : in Indonesia, the name for Arabic characters that were adapted for the vernaculars. III 1217a; VIII 153a

penbe ḳabbānī (T) : in the Ottoman period, a special building into which all cotton imported for sale in the large cities had to be brought. There cotton was to be weighed, taxed, and distributed. To accommodate caravan merchants with their cotton goods, special caravanserais called *penbe-k̲h̲ānī* (in Egypt, *wakālat al-ḳuṭn*) were built. V 559a

♦ penbe-k̲h̲ānī → PENBE ḲABBĀNĪ

penče (T, < P *pand̲j̲a* 'palm of the hand') : in the science of diplomatic, a sign placed on a document issued by higher Ottoman officials, used instead of the TUG̲H̲RA. It was usually placed not at the beginning but on the left hand or right hand margin or at the foot of the scroll. Sometimes it was called *imḍā* or erroneously *ṭug̲h̲ra*. II 314b; VIII 293b

pend̲j̲ik (T, < P *pand̲j̲ yak* 'fifth') : in Ottoman financial and administrative usage, a term denoting the fifth which the sultan drew as the ruler's right (equivalent to the Arabic *k̲h̲ums*) from booty captured in the DĀR AL-ḤARB. VIII 293b

♦ pend̲j̲ikči bas̲h̲ī (T) : the official in charge of the process of extracting the sultan's fifth. VIII 293b

penghulu (Ind, Mal; Sun *panghulu*) : lit. headman, chief, director; used in southeast Asia as a title for secular and religious leaders. VIII 294a; IX 852a; the highest official in a mosque in Java, often a learned man who has studied theology and is a pupil of the *pesantren*, the Indonesian religious school, or of the modern MADRASA; he may even have studied in Mecca. VI 701a

penyair → S̲H̲ĀʿIR

pergunnah → PARGANA

peri → PARĪ

pertaapan → PONDOK

pesantren (J) : in Indonesia, the educational institution where students, *santri*, study classical Islamic subjects and pursue an orthoprax communal life. PONDOK is an alternative term, preferred in Malaysia and the Patani region of southern Thailand. Sometimes the two terms are combined in Indonesia, when the speaker means to make clear that a traditional Islamic boarding school, a '*pondok pesantren*', and not merely a religious day school (such as the more modern *madrasa*), is meant. VIII 296a

pes̲h̲dār (T) : in the Ottoman empire, the term for the third animal of a mule caravan operating in Anatolia. IV 678b

pes̲h̲ek (T) : in the Ottoman empire, the term for the leading animal of a mule caravan operating in Anatolia, which kept some way ahead of the others and carried a smaller load. IV 678b

pēshwā (P) : 'leader'; in onomastics, a title for one of the ministers of the Bahmanī sultans of the Dakhan and, more specifically, the hereditary ministers of the Marāthā kings of Satara. VIII 300b

peth, or *mela* : in Muslim India, an occasional or seasonal market. IX 800b

peyk (T) : in the Ottoman military organisation, a messenger. IX 712b

pīpā : in music, the so-called 'balloon guitar' of the Chinese, who are said to have possessed it since the days of the Han dynasty. It was introduced into ʿIrāḳ by the Mongols in the 13th century. X 769a

pīr (P) : lit. old person, elder; in Islamic law, used for people in their fifties or even in their forties, while those even older are often qualified as *harim, fānī* 'decrepit, worn out'. VIII 306a

In general Persian usage, ~ is often, as with Arabic SHAYKH, used in compound expressions by metonomy, e.g. *pīr-i dihḳān* 'well-matured wine'. VIII 306a

For ~ in mysticism, → MURSHID

♦ pīr awtār (IndP) : the daily allowance paid to FĀḲIRs from collective village sources. VIII 306b

♦ pīr bahn (IndP) : a woman owing spiritual allegiance to the same spiritual mentor and therefore a sister. VIII 306b

♦ pīr bhāi (IndP) : a disciple of the same spiritual mentor and therefore a brother. VIII 306b

♦ pīr kā nayza (IndP) : a standard carried in procession to the grave of some saint. VIII 306b

♦ pīr-i kharābāt (IndP) : in popular Indo-Muslim usage, a *pīr* free from the bonds of sharīʿa law; owner of a tavern. VIII 307a

♦ pīr-i mughān (IndP) : lit. chief priest of the Magi, but generally the term used for a tavern keeper. VIII 306b

♦ pīr pāl (IndP) : land endowed for assistance of the *pīr* or for maintenance of some mausoleum. VIII 306b

♦ pīr-i ṣuḥbat (IndP) : a saint from whose company one derives spiritual benefit. VIII 306b

♦ pīr-i ṭarīḳat (IndP) : a saint to whom one owes spiritual allegiance. VIII 306b

♦ pīr zāda (IndP) : the son of the *pīr*. VIII 306b

♦ pīrān (IndP) : charity lands bestowed on the poor in honour of a saint. VIII 306b

♦ **pīrpanthī** (IndP, < P *pīr* + *panth* 'way of the spiritual master') : the name given in Pakistan and Western India to Hindus who follow Muslim pīrs, whether living or dead; more precisely, to the disciples of Imām Shāh, a dissident Ismāʿīlī, and to the Hindu disciples of ṣūfī masters originating from Sindh, Pandjāb or Rādjasthān. XII 681a

pīrāhan (P) : a close-fitting, long-sleeved robe, covering the entire body down to the feet, worn by women in Tīmūrid Persia. V 749a

pīrāmūz (P) : a style of calligraphy, used for writing copies of the Qurʾān. IV 1123a

pīrān → PĪR

pīrpanthī → PĪR

pishkāsh (P) : a present from an inferior to a superior; from the Mongol period onwards, ~ denoted a form of tribute to the Persian sovereign from the governors. III 347b; as a technical term, ~ denotes a 'regular' tax and an *ad hoc* tax levied by rulers on provincial governors and others, and an *ad hoc* impost laid by governors and officials in position of power on the population under their control. VIII 312b

♦ pīshkāsh-niwīs (P) : 'registrar of presents'; under the Ṣafawids, the official of the royal secretariat who recorded their number and value. This official is found until the second half of the 19th century. VIII 312b

pīshtāḳ (P) : lit. the arch in front; in architecture, a portal in the form of a monumental arched niche in a rectangular frame. VI 683a; VIII 313b; XII 455a
pīshwā (P) : chief. IX 499b
pist (P) : a kind of food compounded of the liver of gazelles or almonds, etc. A daily portion of the size of a pistachio, *pista*, is taken by derwishes and others who undertake long fasts and is sufficient to maintain life. VIII 316b
piştmala (K) : a kind of praetorian guard of the Kurdish chiefs who are recruited in all the fractions, TIRA, of the tribe and who, in the past, had almost the status of slave. V 472
piyādegān → DJAMĀʿA
pomaks : the name given to a Bulgarian-speaking group of Muslims in Bulgaria and Thrace, now divided amongst Bulgaria, Greece and Macedonia. This name, which is usually given them by their Christian fellow-countrymen, used also to be given occasionally by Bulgarians to Muslims speaking Serbian in western Macedonia, who are usually called *torbeši* (s. *torbeš*), sometimes also POTURI. VIII 320a; X 698b
pondok (Mal, < A *funduḳ*), or *pertaapan* : hut, cottage; lodgings; by extension, an Islamic religious boarding school. VIII 294a; VIII 296a; and → PESANTREN
portakal → NĀRANDJ
post : in India, the decoction of the poppy-husks to make opium. I 243a
pōst → PŪST
posta (T, A, < It *posta*) : a term borrowed in the 19th century to designate the new conception of European-style postal services in the Near East. In more recent times, it has been replaced at the formal level by BARĪD, but *būsta* and *būstadjī* 'postman' continue in use in the Arab Levant at the informal level, and *posta* remains the standard term in Modern Turkish. In modern Persian, also *post*, from the French *poste*, is used. VIII 325b
For postage stamps (A *ṭābiʿ* [*barīdī*], P *tambr*, T *pul*), VIII 325b
pōstakī → PŪST
potur (T) : a pair of trousers, full as far as the knee and straight from the knee to the ankle, worn in Ottoman Turkey. V 752b; converted peasantry of Bosnia (< Serb *poturčiti*). X 697b; and → POTURNĀK
♦ potur oghullarï (T) : in the Ottoman period, Bosnian Muslim lads recruited for the Janissaries. A document dating from 998/1589 defines them as 'circumcised but ignorant of Turkish'. II 211b
♦ potur ṭāʾifesi → POTURNĀK
♦ poturi (Serb) : in former Yugoslavia, the designation, with *torbeš* (pl. *torbeši*) and occasionally *kurki*, of Serbian Muslims by the neighbouring Christian population in West Macedonia. In the Reka region of Serbia, they were known as *gorani*. X 697b
♦ poturnāk (Serb) : the name for Bosnians who converted to Islam. The reference occurs as early as 921/1515; in a separate document dated 981/1573, they are called *potur ṭāʾifesi*. II 211b
poya (SpA) : in Andalus, a bread the dough of which was made at home to be picked up by a journeyman baker and baked in a communal oven. The term has survived under the forms *pīwa, pūya, būya* in some regions of Morocco and Algeria to designate the salary of the baker, which in the mediaeval period consisted of a piece of the bread which the baker sold at a profit. V 42b
prang sabil (Mal, *prang* 'war') : the name of the holy war, DJIHĀD, in East Asia. VIII 333a
prem-gāthā (H) : lit. love song; a school of writing in Awadhi (Eastern Hindi), of ṣūfī inspiration, comprising narrative love stories. III 456b
puasa (Ind) : the Indonesian term for Ramaḍān, the month of fasting. XII 682a

pul → POSTA
pū<u>sh</u>ī → BŪ<u>SH</u>Ī
pūst (P, T *pōst* or *pōstakī*) : 'skin'; a tanned sheepskin, used as the ceremonial seat or throne of the head, *pīr* or *<u>sh</u>ay<u>kh</u>*, of a dervish order. VIII 343b
♦ **pūst-ne<u>sh</u>īn** (P) : lit. the one sitting on the (sheep's) skin; the title given to the *baba* or head of a dervish TEKKE in Persian and Ottoman Turkish ṣūfī practice. VIII 343b

R

rā' (A) : the tenth letter of the Arabic alphabet, transcribed as *r*, with the numerical value 200. It is defined as vibrant, apical, alveolar and voiced. VIII 343a
raʿāʿ (A) : a mob, thieves, one of the numerous terms in the mediaeval and modern periods for 'rascal, scoundrel'. XI 546a
raʿʿād (A) : in zoology, the electric ray ναρκε. V 1168a
rabʿ (A, pl. *ribāʿ*) : home, domicile, home town or home country; in Cairene architecture, ~ designates a type of urban dwelling which is a rental multi-unit building founded for investment; ~ can also refer to the living quarters belonging to a religious institution. VIII 344a
In mediaeval Islam, facilities for temporary accommodation in cities concentrated in a single building. IX 788b
rabāʿ (A) : a name for a foal between three and four years old. II 785a
rabāʿa (A), or *magʿad al-ri<u>dj</u>āl* : the compartment in a Bedouin tent reserved for receiving menfolk. In the middle, a hearth is scraped out and used for making coffee. IV 1148b
rabāb (A) : in music, the generic name for the viol, or any stringed instrument played with a bow. VIII 346a; the instrument known as rebeck. I 1124a; in Egypt, a two-string spike-fiddle. IX 235b
♦ rabāb miṣrī → KAMĀN<u>DJ</u>A
♦ rabāb turkī → ARNABA
♦ rabāba (A) : in music, the small viol. V 547b; the Arabian one-string spike-fiddle. IX 235a
rabaḍ (A, pl. *arbāḍ*) : district or quarter of a town situated outside the central part. This term lies at the origin of the Spanish word *arrabal*, which has the same meaning. VIII 348b
In Muslim Spain, ~ was given to the civil quarter situated below the strictly military quarter; ~ was also applied to the quarters of the lepers and of prostitutes, while among the Spanish Christians it designated a parish. VIII 348b
rabāʿī → ʿATŪD
rabb (A, pl. *arbāb*) : lord, God, master of a slave. Pre-Islamic Arabia probably applied this term to its gods or to some of them. In pre-Islamic times, ~ also was one of the titles given to certain of the KĀHINs. VIII 350a
♦ rabbānī (A) : among the mystical order ʿĪsāwā, the slow introductory section of their ecstatic dancing, a form of invocation, during which the dancers, standing in line, hold hands and perform vertical bending movements together with lateral motions. It is followed by a more rapid section, the *mu<u>dj</u>arrad*, and the dance often ends in displays of fakirism. IV 95a
♦ arbāb al-sa<u>dj</u>ā<u>dj</u>īd, and *ma<u>sh</u>āyi<u>kh</u> al-sa<u>dj</u><u>dj</u>āda* (A) : in Egypt, from the end of the 11th/17th century, applied to the leaders of Egypt's major ṣūfī *ṭuruḳ* (→ ṬARĪḲA)

and *ṭuruḳ*-linked institutions. ~, however, seems to have been reserved for the four family-based *ṭuruḳ* which traced themselves back to the Rightly-Guided Caliphs and the Companions, namely, *al-Bakriyya, al-ʿInāniyya, al-Khuḍayriyya*, and *al-Wafāʾiyya*. VIII 743b

rābiʿ (A), or *sayyid al-mirbāʿ* : a designation for tribal chief (from the chief's entitlement to a quarter of captured booty). IX 115b

rabīʿ (A) : the name of the third and fourth months of the Muslim calendar. Originally, ~ means the season in which, as a result of the rains, the earth is covered with green; this later led to the name ~ being given to spring. VIII 350b; in Muslim India, ~ is the harvest collected at the end of the winter. II 909a; spring crop. V 579b

♦ rabīʿiyya (A, pl. **rabīʿiyyāt**) → NAWRIYYA

rābiṭ(a) → WUṢLA

rābiṭa (A, > Sp *rábida* 'monastery') : 'bond'; in mysticism, ~ originally meant the relationship of a MURĪD to his master, and hence a close friendship; a hermitage which was a place of retreat for persons considered to be saints, accompanied by their disciples. VIII 359b; VIII 503b; liaison of the disciple's heart, in imagination, with that of his SHAYKH. IX 156a

In Muslim Spain, a fortified enclosure, a bastion constructed on the coast to deter enemy attacks from the sea; ~ sometimes served as a substitute for RIBĀṬ. VIII 359a

In 19th-century Ottoman usage, ~ became a political notion in the sense of 'league' and with *islāmiyya* attached to it, ~ soon rendered the European word Pan-Islam. VIII 359b

♦ **al-rābiṭa al-islāmiyya** (A) : lit. the Islamic league. VIII 359b

rabṭ (A) : in medicine, ligature (of veins). II 481

♦ rabṭa (A) : in women's dress, a kind of turban, consisting of the ṬĀḲIYYA, ṬARBŪSH, and the FARŪDIYYA. X 613b

raḍāʿ (A), *riḍāʿ* or *raḍāʿa* : suckling; in law, the suckling which produces the legal impediment to marriage of foster-kinship. VIII 361a; the suckling is called *raḍīʿ*. VIII 822a

♦ raḍāʿ al-kabīr (A) : the suckling of non-infants. VIII 361b

radd (A) : 'return'; in literature, a response to an adversary, intended to refute his statements or opinions. Another term in frequent use is *naḳḍ* 'refutation', although *naḳḍ* is principally employed in reference to a book. VIII 362b

In mathematics, ~ denotes reduction and refers to the operation (division) by which an integral coefficient is reduced to unity. II 361a

♦ radd al-ʿadjuz ʿalā 'l-ṣadr (A) : in prosody, the rhetorical figure of anticipating the rhyme word in the first half (at times even the beginning of the second half) of the line. VIII 747b

radf → NATĪDJA

radhī (A) : in numismatics, bad, corrupt (coin), with *bāṭil* 'false, unsound, currency cancelled or withdrawn from circulation, one of the pejorative terms for coins. X 409b

raḍīʿ → RAḌĀʿ

radīf (A, T *redīf*) : lit. one who rides behind, 'pillion rider'; in its plural form *rawādif*, immigrants. V 346a

In grammar, the plural *rawādif* signified the last two groups of the ABDJAD terms, which consisted of the consonants peculiar to Arabic, as opposed to the first six groups which preserve faithfully the order of the 'Phoenician' alphabet. I 97b

In astronomy, *al-~*, or *al-ridf*, is the ancient Arabic name for *dhanab al-dadjādja*, the star Deneb (α Cygni); ~ also refers to a star or constellation that is rising at sunrise, while its opposite (*raḳīb*) is setting. VIII 368b

In Persian prosody, the adjunction of a word or a short phrase, always shorter than a hemistich, to the rhyme letter and its repetition thoughout the poem. It is very frequently used in GHAZALs. IV 57a; VIII 368b
In Turkish military usage, *redīf* was the name given by Maḥmūd II to the reserve army, 'militia', created in 1834. The *redīf* was made up of battalions (*tabur*, → ṬABŪR). VIII 370a
♦ radīf mutadjānis (A) : in Persian prosody, a special artifice with complete paronomasia between RADĪFs, resulting from the fact that the *radīf* does not have the same meaning throughout the poem (which it is supposed to have). VIII 369a

rāḍikh → KHANNĀḲ

radjʿa (A) : return; in shīʿī theology, the return to life, which will precede the universal resurrection and gathering; only the virtuous will take part in it under the guidance of the Mahdī of the last times. I 334b; IV 457a; V 236a; VIII 372b; the passing of the soul into another body either human or animal; the transmigration of the spirit of holiness from one IMĀM to the next, more usually known as *tanāsukh*; return of power to the shīʿa; return from concealment, usually of a particular *imām* at the end of his occultation. VIII 371b; X 182a,b
In classical Muslim administration, a requisition issued by the paymaster for certain troops stationed in outlying areas, for one issue of pay. II 79a
♦ al-radjʿa al-djāmiʿa (A) : in classical Muslim administration, a global requisition issued by the head of the army office for each general issue of arm pay, rations, etc. II 79a

radjab (A) : the seventh month of the Islamic calendar, observed in the DJĀHILIYYA as a holy month in spring. VIII 373b
♦ radjabiyya (A) : a special pilgrim caravan which set off from Cairo in the month of RADJAB, mentioned from time to time in the 8th/14th century chronicles. III 35a; and → ʿATĪRA
♦ al-radjabiyyūn (A) : in mysticism, the tenth degree in the ṣūfī hierarchical order of saints. I 95a

rādjaputra (San) : 'king's son'. XII 684a

radjaz (A) : tremor, spasm, convulsion (as may occur in the behind of a camel when it wants to rise); thunder, rumble, making a noise. VIII 375b; the oracular utterance of war. VIII 733a
In prosody, the name of the seventh Arabic metre, the simplest, and according to tradition, the oldest metre. It has a rising rhythm and is dipodically bound. This metre is most often used for short poems and improvisations in pre-Islamic and early Islamic times. A poem composed in this metre is called *urdjūza*. I 670a; I 673b; IV 80b; VIII 375b; poetry defined by 'halved', i.e. three-foot, lines without caesura. VIII 378b
In Urdu poetry, ~ refers to the hero's battle oration which forms part of the MARTHIYA. VI 611b

radjfa (A) : in the Qurʾānic story of Shuʿayb, commonly glossed as 'earthquake'. IX 491a; X 436a

rādjiʿ → WUṢLA

radjīm (A) : lit. stoned; for explaining the Qurʾānic expression *al-shayṭān al-radjīm*, it has been suggested that ~ is an Ethiopic loan word meaning 'accursed'. IX 408b

radjʿiyya (A), or *irtidjāʿ* : the term coined in modern Arabic for reaction in the political sense. VIII 379a; with *aṣḥāb al-radjʿa*, adherents of any of the shīʿī doctrines described under RADJʿA. VIII 372b

radjm (A) : stoning; the casting of stones at Minā, one of the pre-Islamic rites preserved by Muḥammad and inserted among the ceremonies of the pilgrimage. VIII 379a
In law, a ḤADD punishment of death by stoning which occurs in certain cases of immorality. IV 770a; VIII 379a

raḍkh (A) : a bonus share (of the booty given at the discretion of the IMĀM to those bondmen, women, and DHIMMĪs who may in some way have contributed to victory). II 1006b; XII 532b

rafʿ (A) : elevation, the act of raising something; in grammar, the nominative and indicative cases, because both take *-u* and are thus *marfūʿ* 'raised'. III 1249a; IV 895b; VIII 383b

For ~ in the science of Tradition, → MARFŪʿ

raʾfa → RAḤMA

rāfiḍa (A), or *al-rawāfiḍ* : a term that refers to the proto-Imāmiyya (and, subsequently, the Twelver shīʿa) as well as any of a number of shīʿī sects. The origin of *al-~* is a matter of dispute, but is variously said to recall the desertion of Zayd b. ʿAlī, the rejection of the first two caliphs, or both. VIII 386b

rafīḳ (A) : companion; in Tradition, the phrase *al-rafīḳ al-aʿlā* is closely associated with AL-MALAʾ AL-AʿLĀ and to be placed with them is said to be the Prophet's last wish. XII 573b

rafraf (A) : the tail of a turban hanging behind. X 610b

rāged → RĀḲID

raghīf (A) : a round bread, quite thick and cooked in an oven, also called *djardaḳ* or *djardhaḳ* (from Persian). V 42b; VI 808a

raḥā (A) : in Muslim Spain, a water mill. I 492a; a mill. V 548a

rahbāniyya (A) : monasticism. VIII 396b

rāhdār (P), or *tutḳavul* : the 'guardian of the roads' in the Īlkhānid and Djalāʾirid periods, paid by the central government and under the orders of a senior military commander. I 861a

♦ rāhdārī (P) : road tolls. IV 977b

raḥḥāl (A), or *raḥḥāla* : the person endowed with skill in the saddling of a camel, or one who travelled much. The form *raḥḥāla* neatly translates as 'globetrotter'. VIII 528a

rāhib (A, pl. *ruhbān, rahābīn, rahābina*) : a monk, known to pre-Islamic poetry and to the Qurʾān and Tradition. VIII 397a

raḥīl (A) : 'travelling by camel', in Arabic poetry applied to themes involving a desert journey. In its specific meaning ~ denotes a section of the polythematic ḲAṢĪDA, following the NASĪB, where the poet describes his camel and his travels. IV 713b; VIII 397b

raḥim (A) : in medicine, the uterus. The expressions *bard al-~* or *ṣalābat al-~* seem to indicate frigidity or anorgasm in the medical literature. XII 641a

rahīsh (A), or *murtahisha* : in archery, a bow whose string, at the moment of loosing, strikes the part called the *ṭāʾif*, the torus; such a bow, usually slim and light, vibrates when loosed. IV 798a

raḥma (A) : a Qurʾānic term, denoting either kindness, benevolence (syn. *raʾfa*) or, more frequently, an act of kindness, a favour (syn. *niʿma* or *faḍl*). Almost invariably, ~ is applied to God. VIII 398a

rahn (A) : in law, pledge, security; *rāhin* is the giver, and *murtahin* the taker of the pledge. VIII 400a

♦ rahn ḥiyāzī → GHĀRŪḲA

rahū 'l-māʾ → NUḤĀM

raʾī → ṢĀḤIB

rāʾib (A) : clotting, as does milk when it curdles. VI 722a; and → YOGHURT

raʿīl → MIḲNAB

raʾīs (A, pl. *ruʾasāʾ*, T *reʾīs*) : head, chief, leader of a recognisable group (political, religious, juridical, tribal, or other). The term goes back to pre-Islamic times and was used in various senses at different periods of Islamic history, either to circumscribe specific functions of the holder of the office of 'leadership' or as an honorific title. VIII 402a; IX 115b

In the scholastic community, ~ was applied to any scholar who had reached the summit of his field in his locality. V 1131b; and → KALĀNTAR

In the Ottoman navy, the term *reʾīs* was used for an individual commander. I 948a; VIII 403b; in modern Turkish, *reis* means 'captain of a small merchant vessel, skipper; able-bodied seaman'. VIII 403b

♦ raʾīs al-balad (A) : in the mediaeval Near East, a kind of mayor, whose influence counterbalanced, and sometimes exceeded, that of the ḲĀḌĪ 'judge'. I 256a

♦ raʾīs al-baladiyya → AMĪN AL-ʿĀṢIMA

♦ reʾīs efendi → REʾĪS ÜL-KÜTTĀB

♦ reʾīs kesedāri̊ (T) : in the Ottoman empire, pursebearer to the REʾĪS EFENDI. VIII 422a

♦ **reʾīs ül-küttāb** (T, < A), or *reʾīs efendi* : properly, 'chief of the men of the pen', a high Ottoman dignitary, directly under the grand vizier, originally head of the chancery of the Imperial Dīwān, later secretary of state or chancellor and Minister of Foreign Affairs. VIII 481b

♦ reʾīs al-ʿulemāʾ (T) : the supreme religious head of Bosno-Herzegovinian Muslims, as well as the highest religious authoritative body; an Ottoman office created in 1882 in order to gain control over Muslim religious institutions. I 1274a

rāʿiyat al-s̲h̲ayb (A) : the first white hair which appears on the head. IX 383a

raʿiyya (A, pl. *raʿāyā*; T pl. *reʿāyā*) : lit. pasturing herd of cattle, sheep, etc., a term which in later Islam came to designate the mass of subjects, the tax-paying common people, as opposed to the ruling military and learned classes. I 712a; VIII 403b

♦ raʿiyyatī : under the Mug̲h̲als, land that was purely peasant-held, paralleling the land held by ZAMĪNDĀRs. XI 439a

rakʿa (A) : lit. the act of bowing, bending; in the act of worship, a sequence of utterances and actions performed during the prayer. VIII 406b; VIII 929a,b

raḳāʿa (A) : burlesque, a genre of literature, closely akin to SUK̲H̲F, practiced a.o. by al-Ṣaymarī. XII 16b

raḳaba (A, T *raḳabe*) : lit. neck, nape of the neck; term frequently used in the Qurʾān for 'slave'. I 24b

In Ottoman land law, the original title to land. II 900b; V 473a; the freehold ownership of agricultural lands in the Ottoman empire. II 906b

In law, the 'physical person'. I 29a

raḳam → FARMĀN

rak̲h̲āwa (A) : softness. XI 570a

raḳīb (A) : 'guardian, vigilant one who knows everything that takes place'; one of the names of God. VIII 406b

In Arabic love poetry, the person who, by watching or simply being present, prevents the lovers from communicating with each other. VIII 406b

For ~ in astronomy, → RADĪF

rākib (A, pl. *rukkāb*) : in some brotherhoods in North Africa, a courier who served to link the local ZĀWIYAs with the 'mother' *zāwiya*. XI 468a; and → FĀRIS

rāḳid (A, N.Afr *rāged* or *bū mergūd*) : lit. sleeping child; in law, a foetus which is considered to have stopped its development, continuing to stay in the womb in an unchanged condition for an indefinite period of time, after which it may 'wake up' again and resume its development until it is born. VIII 407a

raḳīḳ (A) : the generic term for slave. I 24b

♦ raḳīḳa (A, pl. *raḳāʾiḳ*) : an action that elevates man (in the eyes of God). XI 560a

raḳḳ (A), or *riḳḳ* : parchment, used alongside other terms used in a less specific manner, such as ḲIRṬĀS, denoting papyrus, *waraḳ*, later reserved for paper, and DJILD, leather. VIII 407b

rakkāḍ (A) : a type of merchant in mediaeval Islam, the itinerant trader who owes his profits to his knowledge of the differences in purchase and sale prices according to the places where the transactions take place. IX 789a; X 469a

raḳḳāṣ (A, Fr *rekkas*) : in the Muslim West, a messenger who travels on foot long distances in order to carry official or private mail; nowadays, an occasional messenger, above all in time of war. I 1046a; VIII 415a

Other technical senses are: pendulum; hand of a watch; trigger of a fire-arm; part of a mill which produces a noise through the movement of the millstone. VIII 415a

♦ raḳḳāṣa → GHĀZIYA

raḳḳī (A, < *Raḳḳa*) : in the mediaeval Muslim world, a well-known kind of coarse soap, similar to date-palm paste, from which lozenges were made in Damascus. VIII 693a

raḳṣ (A) : dance, generally frowned upon in Islam for it is connected with ecstasy. VIII 415

♦ raḳṣ-i bismil (P) : 'the dance of the ritually slaughtered [bird]'; a literary expression for the convulsions of the lover who resembles 'a headless chicken'. VIII 416a

rakwa (A) : a leather bowl, one of the ṣūfī paraphernalia. VIII 742b; a waterbottle. XI 129a

rakz → MAʾKHADH

raʿla → SIRB

ramad (A) : in medicine, ophthalmitis, inflammation of the eye, or ophthalmia (conjunctivitis), inflammation of the conjunctiva. VIII 417a

♦ ramad ḥubaybī (A), or *djarab al-ʿayn* : one of the medical terms for trachoma. I 785b

♦ ʿilm al-ramad (A) : originally only meaning the study of 'conjunctivitis', ~ now embraces the study of eye diseases of all types. I 785a

ramād (A) : ordinary ashes; ashes for washing. VIII 419b

ramaḍān (A) : name of the ninth month of the Muslim calendar, the only month to be mentioned in the Qurʾān. VIII 417b

ramadiyya (A) : tramps, vagabonds, one of the numerous terms in the mediaeval and modern periods for 'rascal, scoundrel'. XI 546a

ramaka (A) : in zoology, a mare of mixed breed. II 785a; IV 1143b

ramal (A) : a rapid pace. X 864b

In prosody, the name of the eighth Arabic metre. I 670a; VIII 421a

In music, a rhythmic mode said to have been invented by Ibn Muḥriz, a famous Meccan musician of the 1st-2nd/7th-8th centuries. III 883a; VIII 421b

♦ ʿilm al-ramal (A) : geomancy, i.e. divination from points formed in sand. X 501b

ramas, ramaṣ → RAMATH

ramath (A) : in the Gulf area, a raft or a sort of raft made of tree trunks or lengthy pieces of wood tied together by coconut fibre. It has variant names in other parts of the Middle East: *ramaṣ, ramas*, and SAFĪNA, which is the classical term for ship in general. VII 53b

rāmishgar → KHUNYĀGAR

raml (A, pl. *rimāl, armul*) : sand; also, the black or white lines on the hooves of wild cattle or on the flanks and the backs of stags (syn. khaṭṭ). IV 1128b; VIII 423b

In divination, ~ , and *ḍarb al-raml* mean geomancy (→ KHAṬṬ); also, in Persian usage, divination by means of dice. II 761b; IV 1128b; VIII 138b; VIII 423b

♦ ramla → NAFŪD

ramm (A, pl. *rumūm*) : a geographical term employed by al-Iṣṭakhrī to denote a tribal district in Persia in the early centuries. III 1096b; V 451b

ramūḥ (A) : in the terminology of horse-riding, a horse that kicks. II 953b

ramy al-djimār (A) : lit. the throwing of pebbles', a practice that probably goes back to early Arabia and whose most celebrated survival is in the ritual throwing of stones in the valley of Minā by the pilgrims returning from ʿArafāt in the course of the pilgrimage. XII 687b

ramz (A, pl. *rumūz*) : winking, signalling with your eyes and eyebrows; allusion, symbol, cypher. VIII 426b; and → TAʾRĪKH

In rhetoric, ~ 'circumlocution' denotes a specific subcategory of KINĀYA. VIII 427a

For ~ in mysticism, → ISHĀRA

In modern Arabic literature, ~ became an exact equivalent of the Western term 'symbol'. VIII 430a; according to al-Ṭabarī, ~ in pre-Islamic poetry also meant an unintelligible murmur or whisper. VIII 428b

rannaḳ (A) : 'feeble', used to describe the sun in a poem by Ibn Rūmī. XI 157a

rank (P) : lit. colour, dye, a term used in mediaeval Arabic sources primarily to designate the emblems and insignia of AMĪRs and sultans in Egypt, Syria, and al-Djazīra. Mamlūk historians occasionally also use it as a generic term for emblem in general, such as e.g. the ~s of merchants' guilds and those of Bedouin chieftains in Tunisia. VIII 431b

rapak (J) : a technical term for the charge made by the wife, at the court for matters of religion, that the husband has not fulfilled the obligations which he took upon himself at the TAʿLĪḲ of divorce. VIII 433a

raʾs (A, pl. *ruʾūs, arʾus*) : head; in geography, ~ is the common word for 'cape', but it also used with the meaning of 'headland, promontory'. VIII 433b In astronomy, ~ , or ~ *al-tinnīn* 'the dragon's head', refers to the crescent node, one of the points where the moon passes through the ecliptic, during an eclipse of the moon. V 536a; VIII 101b; the plural *ruʾūs* denotes 'the direction of the zenith'. X 163b; and → MUTHALLATH

In agriculture, the first of two successive harvests [of sugar cane], the second being termed *khilfa*, which usually gives better sugar then the first. IV 683b

♦ **raʾs al-ʿām** (A) : New Year's Day, lit. beginning of the year, i.e. 1 al-Muḥarram. VIII 433b

♦ raʾs al-hirr (A) : 'cat's head', in botany, the Hemp nettle (*Galeopsis*). IX 653a

♦ raʾs al-māl → SALAM

♦ raʾs al-rubʿ (A), or *raʾs al-khums* : in early Islam, the officially appointed leader of a town's division into quarters or fifths, selected from among the chiefs of the larger tribal groups represented in the division. V 23b

raṣad → MARṢAD

rasan (A) : the bozal, a bit preferred to the curb bit by Arab horsemen in the East. II 953a

raṣāṣ (A), or *usrub* : in mineralogy, lead, which was mostly obtained from galena (lead sulphide). V 967a

♦ raṣāṣ ḳalʿī (A) : in metallurgy, tin (syn. ḲALʿĪ, *ḳaṣdīr*). V 964b ff.

♦ raṣāṣa (A) : a gauge, used before the Nilometer was built to measure the rising of the Nile. VII 39

rashād (A) : in botany, cress or rocket, forbidden by al-Ḥākim in addition to the classical food prohibitions. II 1070a

rāshidūn (A, s. *rāshid*) : orthodox, or rightly-guided. For the first four caliphs, → AL-KHULAFĀʾ AL-RĀSHIDŪN

rashwa (A, pl. *rushā*) : in law, 'bribe', which is strictly forbidden by law. VIII 451a

raskh → NASKH

rasm (A, T *resm*) : the act of drawing, a drawing, not always distinguished from painting. VIII 451b; *al-~ al-ḥadīth* 'modern painting', a Western-influenced form of art, which practice began at the end of the 19th century, eventually replacing Islamic art (syn. *taṣwīr, muʿāṣir*). X 365a

In Ottoman usage, **resm** (pl. *rüsūm*) means state practices and organisations as distinguished from those based on Islamic principles and traditions, specifically taxes and dues introduced by the state called *rüsūm-i ʿurfiyye*. ~ was sometimes called *ḥaḳḳ* in the sense of legal right, as in the term *ḥaḳḳ-î ḳarār*, a fee which feudal cavalryman took when vacant MĪRĪ land was assigned to a peasant. The term ~ is also used synonymously with ḲANŪN, *teklīf* and ʿADĀT. A ~ is called *ʿadāt* whenever it originates from a locally-established custom. VIII 486a; for specific taxes, → BĀD-I HAWĀ; ČIFT-RESMI; FILORI; ḲAPAN; ḲISMA; YAYLAḲ RESMI

♦ rasm al-ṣadārat (P) : in Tīmūrid Persia, a specific tax which was raised as a percentage on WAḲF-revenues, and which made up the financial support for the ṢADR, also called *sahm al-ṣadārat*. VIII 750a

rass (A) : in prosody, the vowel (always *a*) immediately before the *alif* of the TAʾSĪS, the *alif* of prolongation placed before the rhyme letter. IV 412a; and → AṢḤĀB AL-RASS

rāst → SHASHMAḲOM

rasūl (A, pl. *rusul*) : messenger, apostle; in the secular sense, diplomatic envoy, ambassador. V 423b; VIII 454b

ratha : in Muslim India, the bullock-cart with a domed canopy used particularly by women on journeys; their escorts may walk on foot beside them. VII 932b

rātib (A, pl. *rawātib*) : a word meaning what is fixed and hence applied to certain non-obligatory ṢALĀTS or certain litanies, such as the DHIKR. VIII 459a

rātīnadj → ṢAMGH

raṭl (A, < Ar) : in the mediaeval Near East, the most common weight of capacity, used for small quantities of various commodities. The actual weight of a ~ varied depending on time, place and type of commodity. The ~ of Baghdad, which was equal to 401.674 g (according to others, 397.26 g), was considered the 'canonical' ~ of the Muslims, because it was used from the days of the first caliphs. VI 117a ff.; VIII 654a

ratt → KHANZUWĀN

rattī (< San *raktikā*) : 'red one', in Muslim India, a measure of weight used for small quantities of various commodities, e.g. jewels. Its name derives from the seed of a small red-flowered leguminous creeper, *Abrus precatorius*; the actual weight of such a ~ seed varies from 80 to 130 mg, its notional weight, at least up to the 8th/14th century, being 116.6 mg. Abu 'l-Faḍl calls the ~ *surkh*. VI 122a

rawādif → RADĪF

rawḍ (A) : meadow. XI 399b

♦ rawḍa (A, pl. *riyāḍ*) : lit. garden; in Arabia, a basin or hollow whose bottom does not hold water, so that wild vegetation may be fairly abundant there. In the north it is called *fayḍa*. I 538a

In Muslim India, a monumental tomb within an enclosure, not necessarily of a *pīr* (→ MURSHID). VI 125b; X 59a

♦ **rawḍa-khwānī** (P) : a shīʿī Persian mourning ritual commemorating the suffering and martyrdom of Ḥusayn, the grandson of the Prophet Muḥammad, and other shīʿī martyrs. VIII 465a

♦ rawḍiyya → NAWRIYYA

rawghan (P) : clarified butter. V 152b

rawī (A) : in prosody, the rhyme letter which, since it occurs in every type of rhyme, is considered its principal consonant after which famous poems are often named, e.g. the *Lāmiyya* of al-Shanfarā. IV 412a; VIII 368b

rāwī (A, pl. *ruwāt*) : reciter and transmitter of poetry, as also of narrative Traditions and ḤADĪTH. There is an intensive form *rāwiya*, explained as 'copious transmitter', used in mediaeval sources as a synonym to *rāwī*. In modern research ~ is applied, as a rule, to the learned collectors of Bedouin poetry in the 8th century. VIII 466b; IX 236a

rāwiya → RĀWĪ

rawk (? < Dem *ruwkh* 'land distribution') : in Egyptian administration, ~ means a kind of cadastral survey which is followed by a redistribution of the arable land. III 99a; VIII 467b

rawnaḳ (A) : glittering brightness, splendour. XI 263a

rawwāgh (A) : in the terminology of horse-riding, a horse that shies. II 953b

ra'y (A, pl. *ārā'*) : personal opinion; in law, the decision of legal points by one's own judgement in the absence or ignorance of a traditional ruling bearing on the case in question, although for an opinion on a specific question of law, ḳawl is most commonly used, ~ being more often used for the body of such opinions held by a particular jurist. I 730a; II 886a; IX 878b; XII 687b; and → AHL AL-RA'Y

In theology, adherence to a body of theological doctrine, i.e. ~ *al-Djahmiyya*. XII 687b

rāya (A) : a term for flag, used during the Prophet's lifetime along with LIWĀ' and, less commonly, *ʿalam*. Some Traditions contrast the ~, the Prophet's black flag, with his *liwā'*, which was white. The use of the ~ does not seem to be confined to Muslims, since at Badr, Ṭalḥa carried the ~ of the idolaters. I 349a

In zoology, ~ (< *Raia*) or *radja* means 'ray' or 'skate'. VIII 1021a; for other synonyms, VIII 1022b

♦ rāyat-i aʿlā (U) : title used by the Sayyid kings of Dihlī. IX 119b

rayb → SHAKK

rayd (A, pl. *aryād, ruyūd*) : a ledge of a mountain, resembling a wall, or a resting upon ledges of mountains. At least in the Ḥaḍramawt, ~ is the term for the centre of the territory of a Bedouin tribe, which is generally a depression in the rocky plateau. VIII 470a

rayhaḳān → ZAʿFARĀN

rayḥān, rayḥānī → RĪḤĀN; ZUMURRUD

raym → KHARḲ

rayya (SpA, < L *regio*) : in Muslim Spain, the name given to the administrative circle comprising the south of the peninsula, the capital of which was successively Archidona and Málaga. VIII 473b

rāziyānadj → BASBĀS

razḳa → RIZḲ

reʿāyā → RAʿIYYA

redīf → RADĪF

reg (Eng, < A *riḳḳ*) : a stony flat or almost flat surface, commonly found in the deserts where deposits of sand are lacking, ~ has become a scientific word in French used in reference to any part of the globe. VIII 481a; and → RIḲḲ

re'īs → RA'ĪS

resimcılık (T) : a land-leasing system in Turkey, in which the amount of the rent depends on the situation and fertility of the soil, the rentability of the cultivation and the degree of the dependence of the peasant. V 473b

resm → RASM

rezza (Mor) : a small, rather flat turban, worn in Morocco. V 746b

ribā (A) : lit. increase; in law, usury and interest, and in general any unjustified increase of capital for which no compensation is given. The exact meaning of ~ is unknown, but it entailed, evidently, a condemnation, from a moral point of view, of those who grew rich through the misery of others, without the loan granted helping the borrower in any way to retrieve his fortunes, such as lending dates to a starving man, etc. I 111b; IV 691b; VIII 491a; VIII 915a; XII 690b

ribāṭ (A) : in Qur'ānic usage, the preparations made with the mustering of cavalry, with a view to battle; after the great conquests, ~ was used to denote a fortified edifice, normally situated in hazardous regions. VIII 493b

In music, intercalation. X 498a

In mystical terminology, the urban residence of ṣūfīs, in the East and in Egypt more commonly known as *khānḳāh*. VIII 493b; and → KHĀNḲĀH; MURĀBIṬ; SIKKA

riḍʿ → DAYSAM

riḍā (A) : lit. the fact of being pleased or contented; contentment, approval; a term found in mysticism and also in early Islamic history. VIII 509a; X 377b; in mysticism, submission to and agreement with the divine will. XI 141b

In early Islamic history, ~ has a special role in the events leading up to the ʿAbbāsid revolution, when the Umayyad proponents made their propaganda in the name of *al-riḍā min āl Muḥammad* 'a member of the House of the Prophet who shall be acceptable to everybody', which allowed partisans of both ʿAlī's family and those of al-ʿAbbās to claim that they were the intended new leaders. VIII 509a

In shīʿism, ~ is the LAḲAB of the eighth imām, ʿAlī al-Riḍā b. Mūsā al-Kāẓim. VIII 509b

ridā' (A) : a piece of white seamless cloth, draped around the upper half of the wearer's chest, which, with the IZĀR, makes up the garment worn by men during the pilgrimage. I 1053a

riḍāʿ → RAḌĀʿ

ridāfa (A) : in pre- and early Islam, the institution of viceroyship. X 175a

ridda (A) : lit. apostasy; in early Islam, the name given for the series of battles against tribes, both nomadic and sedentary, which began shortly before the death of the Prophet and continued throughout Abū Bakr's caliphate. XII 692b

ridf (A) : in prosody, the *wāw* and *yā'* immediately preceding the rhyme letter as letters of prolongation or to mark the diphthongs *aw* en *ay*, and the *alif* as letter of prolongation in the same position. IV 412a; VIII 369a; and → NATĪDJA; RADĪF

♦ ridfa (A), or *shadjara* : alternate.

In prosody, with regard to the MAWĀLIYĀ as folk-verse, the sestet of alternating rhymes which are added, as a form of elaboration, after the *farsha* (→ ʿATABA), the first three lines; ~ is also used for each of the two rhymes. The verse is then said to be *mardūf* or *ṣaʿīdī* 'Upper Egyptian'. VI 868a

♦ ridf-i zā'id (P) : in Persian prosody, a consonant intervening between the RIDF and the rhyme letter. VIII 369b

ridjāl (A, s. *radjul*) : men; as a technical term, the transmitters of ḤADĪTH 'Muslim Tradition'. VIII 514b

♦ ridjāl al-ghayb (A) : 'the men of the mystery', the hierarchy of saints, in which there are ten categories, crowned by the ḲUṬB. I 94b; II 1025b

♦ **ʿilm al-ridjāl** (A) : the science devoted to the study of the persons figuring in ISNĀDs, with the purpose of establishing their moral qualities, the bibliographical details which will provide the necessary checks on either the materials transmitted or the *isnād*s themselves, and the exact identification of the names, to prevent confusion between persons of the same name. III 1150b

ridjl (A) : foot; and → SĀḲ

♦ ridjl ghurāb (A) : 'crow's foot'; in the science of diplomatic, the popular term for the signature, ʿALĀMA, of the person drawing up the document, used with great lack of respect. II 302a

♦ ri**dj**l al-ḳiṭṭ, or *ri**dj**l al-hirr, ẓufr al-ḳiṭṭ* : in botany, the Cat's foot (*Antennaria dioica*). IX 653a

riḍwān (A) : in the Qur'ān, God's grace, favour, which believers will meet in the hereafter. VIII 509a; VIII 519a

rīf (A, pl. *aryāf*) : countryside; a food-producing fringe of a river traversing arid country. VIII 521b; VIII 562a

In Morocco, ~ denotes, in the circle of tents, those which are on the periphery. By extension (?), certain Berberophone groups of the Middle Atlas use it to define a group of tents held together by a close relationship in the male line. VIII 521b

rifāda (A) : the institution of providing food for the pilgrims in Mecca. I 9a; I 80a

rīḥ (A) : wind. VIII 526b; in music, a musical phrase. XII 351a

♦ rīḥ al-sabal (A) : in medicine, an eye complaint, to be cured by the roasted flesh of the scorpion. I 344a

riḥāla (A) : in early Islam, a camel saddle made of wooden bows joined together with leather thongs and adorned with skins. III 667a

rīḥān (A), or *rīḥānī, rayḥān, rayḥānī* : basil; and → ʿABAYTHARĀN

In Persian calligraphy, ~ is a smaller version of the Arabic script called MUḤAḲḲAḲ, used for copying Qur'āns, and like *muḥaḳḳaḳ*, starting to go out of circulation after the 11th/17th century in favour of NASKH. IV 1123a; VIII 151b

riḥiyyāt (N.Afr) : flat, leather slippers worn by both sexes in North Africa. V 746b

riḥla (A) : a journey, voyage, travel; a travelogue; originally, the word ~ connoted the act of saddling one or more camels. VIII 528a

rīka → MINAṢṢA

riḳʿa (T), *riḳʿī* or *ruḳʿa* : in Turkish calligraphy, a script probably invented during the second half of the 12th/18th century. The main characteristics of ~ are that its letters are less rounded and more straight than in the DĪWĀNĪ script; ~ was used along with *dīwānī* in the DĪWĀN-Ï HUMĀYŪN, and like Persian SHIKASTA *nastaʿlīḳ*, it also became a standard form of hand-writing among Turks, used for letters and every kind of correspondence. When written rapidly and without adhering to the rules, ~ is called *riḳʿa ḳirmasi*. IV 1126a; a more common variant of this script has now become the cursive for daily use throughout the Middle East. VIII 151b

riḳāʿ (A) : in Persian calligraphy, a smaller version of the TAWḲĪʿ script. Formerly used for writing letters, epics and stories, ~ later came to be used for writing the final pages of Qur'āns and especially those of learned books. The Ottoman calligraphers called this script *idjāza* or *khaṭṭ al-idjāza*. IV 1123b; VIII 151b; and → MUḤĀWARĀT

rikāb (A) : lit. stirrup; in Persian and Turkish usage at Muslim courts, 'the sovereign himself or his presence, the foot of the throne'. VIII 528b

In Turkish usage, ~ was also applied to the imperial cavalcade and the procession formed on this occasion; the audience given by the sultan, whether or not he was in procession; and the service of the sultan or simply his presence, which was not necessarily immediate. ~ and *rikāb-ï hümāyūn* were also used in the sense of interim or substitute. VIII 529a

♦ rikāb aghalarï (T) : name applied to a certain number of important officers or dignitaries of the Ottoman palace (from 4 to 11, according to the different sources). VIII 529a

♦ rikāb ḳāʾimmaḳāmï (T) : the substitute for the grand vizier, who was appointed to the Ottoman sovereign when the grand vizier moved from place to place. VIII 529a

♦ rikāb solaghï (T) : the name given to the eight *solaḳ* lieutenants who walked by the Ottoman sultan's stirrup in the great procession. VIII 529a

♦ **rikābdār** (P, < A RIKĀB), or *rikībdār* : 'one put in charge of the stirrup, one who holds the stirrup, when his master mounts'; in a wider sense, ~ meant a kind of squire, groom or riding attendant who had charge of the care and maintenance of harness and saddlery and of everything required for mounting on horseback. The term was used especially in Egypt and Turkey. In Persia it was replaced by its Turkish synonym *üzengi* (or *zengü*) *ḳurčisi*. Synonyms in Arabic were *rikābī* and *ṣāḥib al-rikāb*. VIII 529b ff.

In 19th and early 20th-century Egyptian usage, *rikib-dār* or *rakbdār* means 'jockey groom'. VIII 530a

♦ rikābī (A) : according to al-Zahrāwī, a type of olive oil made when the oil is washed in water; also, a Syrian olive, one of the best varieties, so-called because it was exported from Syria on camelback. XI 486a; XI 487a; and → RIKĀBDĀR

♦ rikāb-i̊ hümāyūn → RIKĀB

♦ rikāb-i̊ hümāyūnde (T) : 'with the (Ottoman) sultan', a term used in speaking of the troops of the capital or of the grand vizier insofar as he was endowed with the full powers of the sultan. VIII 529a

♦ rikāb-khāna (A) : in Mamlūk Egypt, the depot for harness and in general for all the material required for horses and stables. VIII 530a

riḳāḳ → SHAWBAḲ

rikāz (A) : buried treasure. XI 413b

rikhl → SAKHLA

rīkhta : in Bengali literature, half-Persian, half-Bengali poetry, introduced by Nūr Ḳuṭb al-ʿĀlam. VIII 125a

rikhwa (A) : 'relaxed'; in grammar, a division equivalent in modern phonetics with 'constrictive', designating the letters *h, ḥ, gh, kh, sh, ṣ, ḍ, z, s, ẓ, th, dh, f*. III 599a

riḳḳ (A) : an abstract term for 'slavery'. I 24b; and → RAḲḲ

In geography (Eng **reg**), 'dessicated terrain, terrain where water has disappeared, at least on the surface'. VIII 481a

rimāya (A) : archery. IV 795b

rind (P, pl. *runūd, rindān*) : 'scamp, knave, rogue, drunkard' or 'a debauchee', a name given to groups of young men who were considered elements of disorder in mediaeval Baghdad from the time of the Saldjūḳs. In the terminology of poetry and mysticism, ~ acquired the positive meaning of 'one whose exterior is liable to censure, but who at heart is sound'. II 961b; VIII 531a

risāla (A) : originally, the oral transmission of a message; message, mission; missive, letter, epistle, monograph; from the 5th/11th century onwards ~ could also be a synonym of MAḲĀMA. VIII 532a; and → BARĀʾA; PARWĀNAČI

In Ottoman Turkish, ~ also denoted 'a piece of cloth fixed to the front of a dervish's *tādj* or cap' and, by the 19th century, 'a booklet or a weekly or monthly journal'. VIII 544a

ristik → SHUTIK

rithāʾ (A) : 'lamentation'; in prosody, the corresponding literary genre. VI 603a

riwāḳ (A, < P; pl. *arwiḳa, riwāḳāt*), or *ruwāḳ* : in architecture, that part of a structure that forms its front. Depending on the type of structure, a ~ could be a gallery, an ambulatory, a portico, a colonnade, a porch, or a balcony. ~ was also used to indicate the Greek stoa, such as the stoa attributed to Aristotle in Alexandria. VIII 544b; the space between two rows of pillars. VI 661b; the moveable screen of the nomadic tent. II 113b; an entire tent of a certain type similar to a FUSṬĀṬ. VIII 545a; ~ was later used for 'student lodgings', because of the many students living in the halls of mosques. VI 662b; and → NAḲĪB AL-RIWĀḲ

♦ al-riwāḳiyyūn (A) : the Stoics. VIII 545a

riwāya (A) : in literature, the oral transmission of a Tradition, a poem or a story; also the authorised transmission of books. In modern Arabic, ~ has been adopted to mean a story, a novel, a play or a film. III 369b; VIII 545b; and → DIRĀYA; ḤIKĀYA

riyāʾ (A) : ostentation, hypocrisy. In ṣūfism, ~ stands in opposition to *ikhlāṣ* ‘sincerity’. V 513a; VIII 547a

riyāḍiyyāt (A), or *riyāḍa* : mathematics. VIII 549b

riyāfa (A, < RĪF) : in divination, the water-diviner’s art which estimates the depth of water under the earth through the smell of the earth, its vegetation and the instinctive reactions of certain creatures, in particular, the hoopoe. VIII 562a

riyāl (A, < Sp *real*) : in numismatics, a name used for a silver coin in a number of Islamic countries, first recorded in the East in Persia in 1609. The ~ is still in use today in Yemen, Saudi Arabia, Oman, the United Arab Emirates, Dubai and Qatar. III 256a; VIII 563b

♦ **riyāla** (T, < It *reale*), *riyāle, riyāla bey*, or *iryāla* : a general officer of the Ottoman navy who commanded the galley of the same name, later ‘rear-admiral’; the rank of ~ was at first known among the Turks only as applied to officers of the navies of Christendom, coming into use among the Turkish sailors in the time of Meḥemmed IV, 1058-99/1648-87. VIII 564a

rizḳ (A, pl. *arzāḳ*) : lit. anything granted by someone to someone else as a benefit, hence in theology and the Qurʾān, ‘bounty, sustenance, nourishment’. I 204a; VIII 567b In military terminology, ~ is used to designate the regular payments, in cash and in kind, made to those soldiers registered on the DĪWĀN of earliest Islamic times and, by the ʿAbbāsid period, on the more elaborate *dīwān al-djaysh*, hence equivalent to ʿAṬĀʾ or ṬAMAʿ. Those soldiers drawing regular allowances were called *murtaziḳa*. A single pay allotment was termed *razḳa* (pl. *razaḳāt*). VIII 568b

♦ rizḳa (pl. *rizaḳ*) → AWḲĀF AHLIYYA

rōk (Dem) : a kind of cadastral revision, under Ṣalāḥ al-Dīn, of which the object was to measure the surface area of all the lands in Egypt, to assess their value in terms of land tax, *kharādj*, and to distribute them to officers and soldiers as a substitute to salaries. VII 164b

rū band (P) : a rectangular white veil fastened over the *čādur*, the all-enveloping wrap worn outside, and falling over the face. The ~, an innovation in the Ṣafawid period, had a small slit covered with netting over the eyes to permit vision. V 749b

rubʿ (A) : lit. quarter; in astronomy, quadrant. VIII 574a; and → NIṢF; ṬARĪ

♦ rubʿ āfāḳī (A) : in astronomy, the universal horary quadrant, known in mediaeval Europe as *quadrans vetus*. VIII 574b

♦ **al-rubʿ al-khālī** (A) : ‘the Empty Quarter’, a vast and inhospitable sand-sea occupying much of the south and southeast of the Arabian peninsula. VIII 575b

♦ rubʿ mudjayyab (A) : in astronomy, the sine quadrant (syn. *rubʿ al-shakkāziyya*), with markings resembling modern graph-paper, developed from the *rubʿ al-sāʿāt*. V 84a; VIII 574b

♦ rubʿ al-muḳanṭarāt (A) : in astronomy, a quadrant in the form of one-half of the markings on an astrolabe plate, the rete being replaced with a thread with movable bead attached at the centre. VIII 575a

♦ rubʿ al-sāʿāt (A) : in astronomy, the horary quadrant, marked with a radial solar scale and curves for the hours. VIII 574b

♦ rubʿ al-shakkāziyya → RUBʿ MUDJAYYAB

rubāb (P) : in music, a Persian and Eastern Turkish instrument of the lute family, with a vaulted sound-chest and incurvations at the waist. As described by Ibn Ghaybī, the lower part of the belly was of skin and three double strings were mounted on it. In Persia it has fallen into disuse but in Turkestan it still continues to be favoured, although here it is strung with three single strings together with twelve sympathetic strings. It has found its way into India and China. It is to be distinguished from the RABĀB. VIII 346a; X 770a

rubaḥ (A), and *rubbāḥ* : in zoology, the large male baboon, also known as *ḳurduḥ, ḳurdūḥ, ḥawdal, ḥibn*. His thick fur hood earned him the epithets *habbār, hawbar*. In the Hidjāz he was known as *hidjris*, a name for the fox in other countries. V 131b

rubāʿī (A, pl. *rubāʿiyyāt*), and *mirabbaʿ, du-baytī, tarāna* : a verse form; in Persian prosody, the shortest type of formulaic poem, usually but inaccurately called 'quatrain', said to have been the earliest of the verse forms invented by the Persians. It is derived from no less than twenty-four varieties of the HAZADJ metre. The ~ is defined not only by the number of lines but also by its pattern of rhyme (*a a b a*, less commonly *a a a a*) and its metre. In Arabic, this verse form is called *rubāʿiyya*. I 677a; IV 58a; VI 868a; VIII 578b

In numismatics, a quarter-dīnār. X 239a

♦ rubāʿiyya (A) : in literary theory, a literary work in four parts, translating both tetralogy and quartet. VIII 585a; and → RUBĀʿĪ

rūd : 'string'; in music, an instrument of the lute family, of Persian origin. X 769b

rūdhbār (P), or *rūdbār* : lit. a district along a river, or a district intersected by rivers. VIII 586a

rudjūʿ (A) : in theology, return (to God). VIII 587a; and → ṬĀLIʿ

rughām (A) : mucus (of sheep). XII 317b

rūḥ (A, pl. *arwāḥ*) : in early Arabic poetry, 'breath', 'wind'; in the Qurʾān, ~ denotes a special angel messenger and a special divine quality. In post-Qurʾānic literature, ~ is equated with NAFS and both are applied to the human spirit, angels and DJINN. VII 880a

♦ rūḥ afzā (A) : in music, an instrument of the lute family with a hemispherical sound-chest and six double strings of silk and metal. X 770a

♦ rūḥ Muḥammad → AL-ḤAḲĪḲA AL-MUḤAMMADIYYA

♦ arwāḥ (A) : in alchemy, quicksilver and sulphur, corresponding to Gk τὰ πνεύματα. V 111a

rūḥāniyya (A) : 'spirituality', 'spiritual being'; in angelology, the *spiritus rector*, the angel who rules each of the celestial spheres. VIII 593b

ruḥla (A) : the destination of a journey; a rarer meaning is that of a noble or learned man to whom one may travel. VIII 528a

ruḳʿa (A) : a piece of clothing; an administrative document; a sealed, personal message. VIII 835a; and → RIḲʿA

ruḳāḳ (A) : a very thin bread, cooked on a slab of iron, called *ṭābaḳ* or *ṭābil* in the mediaeval period and now *ṣādj*, heated on a hearth or a brazier. V 42b

rukh (A) : redistribution of land. VII 164b

rukhām (A) : in mineralogy, marble, often used interchangeably with *marmar* (< Gk) to refer to a wide variety of hard stones, including marble, granite and diorite. Where the two terms were distinguished, it usually had to do with colour, *marmar* referring to white marble or alabaster, ~ assuming various shades and hues. XII 695b

♦ rukhāma → MIZWALA

rukhkh (A) : in zoology, a huge ostrich-like bird (*Aepyornis maximus*), now extinct, probably existing well into historical times as a peculiar species in Madagascar. Though early Arab seafarers could conceivably have seen the bird face-to-face, Arabic tradition soon turned the ~ into a fabulous creature embellishing it with all kinds of strange details. VIII 595a

In chess, the term for rook, castle. IX 366b

rukhṣa (A, pl. *rukhaṣ*) : lit. permission, dispensation; in law, ~ is a legal ruling relaxing or suspending by way of exception under certain circumstances an injunction of a primary and general nature. Its counterpart is ʿAZĪMA. VIII 595a; IX 778a

♦ rukhṣat (U, < A) : in Urdu poetry, the part of the elegy where the martyr-hero bids farewell to his nearest and dearest. VI 611b ruḳḳ (A) : a term in the Persian Gulf for a shoal. I 535b

rukn (A, pl. *arkān*) : lit. corner, support, pillar; the eastern corner of the Ka'ba where the stone was. X 376a

In religious usage, the plural *arkān* is commonly found in the expression *arkān al-dīn* or *arkān al-'ibāda*, denoting the basic 'pillars' of religion and religious observance. These so-called 'pillars of Islam' are usually enumerated as: profession of faith (SHAHĀDA); the pilgrimage (ḤADJDJ); the worship (ṢALĀT); fasting (ṢAWM); and alms-giving (ZAKĀT, ṢADAḲA). To these some authorities add a sixth, perpetual warfare against infidels (DJIHĀD). VIII 596b

In law, a condition in a contract. I 319a

In natural science and alchemy, ~ denotes cardinal point, part, direction, and, in particular, element. VIII 596b

ruḳya (A) : enchantment, magical spell, permitted in exceptional cases, on condition that it brings benefit to people and does not harm anyone. VIII 600a

rūm (A) : name for the Romans, the Byzantines, and the Christian Melkites interchangeably. VIII 601a

♦ **rūmī** (A) : a designation for the Turks from Byzantium, *al-rūm*, which was once under the Eastern Roman Empire. VIII 612a

In Ottoman art and architectural ornamentation, ~ also indicated a special motif in the form of a leaf or stylised animal designs. VIII 612b

♦ rūmiyya (A) : a tribute paid by some groups of the Banū 'Āmir to the Spanish in the 16th century. IX 537a

rumāt → ARMA

rumḥ (A) : the game of lance, also called *thaḳāfa* or *thiḳāf*, one of the branches of horse-riding. II 955a; in military science, the long bamboo-hafted spear or lance, used as a thrusting weapon in close fighting. XII 735b; XII 736b

rummānī → BAHRAMĀNĪ

rūpiyya (< San *rūpya*) : in numismatics, an Indian coin, a rupee. VIII 618a

rūsakhtadj (P) : in chemistry, antimony. VIII 111b; golden marcasite stone. V 972a, where transcribed as *rusukhtadj*

rushd (A) : in law, discretion or responsibility in acting. I 993b; mental maturity. VIII 821b

♦ rüshdiyye (T) : under the Ottomans, the secondary school of six grades (ages 11 to 16), created during the reign of Maḥmūd II (1801-39). I 75a; V 904a

russa → URṢŪṢA

rustāḳ (A, pl. *rasātīḳ*; < MidP *rōstāg*) : lit. rural district, countryside; in mediaeval administrative usage, ~ designated a district or canton centred on a town. VIII 636a

In wider literary usage, ~, or *rustā*, was contrasted with the urban centres, and its populations regarded as country bumpkins compared with the more sophisticated town-dwellers. VIII 636a

rusukhtadj → RŪSAKHTADJ

rusūm → MARĀSIM; RASM

ruṭab → TAMR

rutaylā' (A) : in zoology, the tarantula. IX 873a

ruṭūbāt (A) : in medicine, dyscratic juice in the stomach. IX 432a

ruwīn nāy in music, a brazen-pipe. X 35a

ru'yā (A) : lit. vision, nocturnal vision, dream. Muslim tradition distinguishes between ~, the true dream, the dream inspired by God, and *ḥulm*, the false dream, resulting from the passions and preoccupations of the soul, or inspired by Satan. VIII 645a

In its philosophical-mystical meaning, the term, like *manām*, describes the dream as a means to transmit fictitious observations or, in the best instances, information and knowledge which convey another, higher reality. VIII 647a

♦ **ru'yat al-hilāl** (A) : in astronomy, the sighting of the lunar crescent, of particular importance for the fixing of the beginning and end of Ramaḍān and the festivals. VIII 649b

ruʿz → ḲIDḤ

ruzdjārī (A, < P) : in the mediaeval period, a day-labourer. XII 758a

rūznāma (P) : lit. record of the day, hence acquiring meanings like 'almanac, calendar, daily journal' etc; in mediaeval administration, the daily record or day-book of payments and receipts of the treasury; also called *daftar-i taʿlīḳ* under the Īlkhānids. The form *rūznāmadj* points to an origin in Sāsānid administration. The keeper of the ~ under the Ottomans was called **rūznāmedji**. II 78b; VIII 652a; X 146b
In Fāṭimid and early Ayyūbid Egypt, ~ was used in a sense contrary to its etymological meaning and its usage in the eastern Islamic world, sc. for the rendering of accounts every ten days. VIII 652a

♦ rūznāmedji → RŪZNĀMA

ruzz (A), or *aruzz, uruzz* : in botany, rice, *Oryza sativa* L., one of two major cultivated species, the other being the indigenous African variety *O. glaberrima*, both of which spring from perennial rice. VIII 652b; and → ARUZZ

♦ ruzza (A) : a small turban for young people in Morocco. X 613b

S

ṣāʿ (A) : a measure of capacity which was used in the Ḥidjāz in the days of Muḥammad, equal to 4 MUDDS. The ~ did not spread to other countries, except perhaps in Algeria and Tunisia where it is still used, with varying equivalences. V 118a; VIII 654a

sāʿa (A) : lit. hour, hence 'clock'. For the ancient Arabs, ~ meant nothing more than 'a moment, a brief lapse of time' since they apparently did not divide the day in 24 hours. This meaning is retained in the classical language in such expressions as *summ sāʿa* 'instantly fatal poison'. V 708b; VIII 654a
For the ancient Arabs, ~ meant nothing more than 'a moment, a brief lapse of time', as they did not divide the day into 24 hours. V 708b
In eschatology, *al-sāʿa* is the Last Hour, which, with the Day of Resurrection and the Day of Judgement, constitutes one of the 'necessary beliefs' which determine the content of the Muslim faith. V 235b; VIII 656a

♦ sāʿa shamsiyya → MIZWALA

saʿāda (A) : happiness, bliss; in Islamic philosophy, a central concept to describe the highest aim of human striving, which can be reached through ethical perfection and increasing knowledge. VIII 657b

sabʿ (A), or *sabʿa* : the number seven. VIII 662b

♦ al-sabʿ al-ṭiwāl (A) : lit. the seven long ones; a designation for SŪRAS ii-vii and ix. IX 887b

♦ **sabʿatu ridjāl** (Mor) : in Morocco, the collective designation of seven patron saints, venerated in certain towns and tribal areas, as well as in some parts of Algeria. VIII 671b

♦ **sabʿiyya** (A) : the Seveners, a designation for those shīʿī sects which recognise a series of seven IMĀMS. VIII 683b

sabab (A, pl. *asbāb*) : lit. rope, coming to designate anything which binds or connects; hence also 'bond, alliance; a means of arriving at, or achieving, something; way of access'. VIII 666b
In philosophy, ~ is used as a synonym of *ʿilla* cause, reason'. The ~ is also called *mabdaʾ* 'principle'; it is 'that which a thing needs, whether in its quiddity or in its existence'. III 1129b; VIII 666b

In medicine, ~ denoted the efficient cause, exclusively that which has an effect within the human body, whether it produces illness or restores or preserves health. VIII 667a

In law, ~ is the designation given by the law maker for an injunction (ḤUKM). The ~ may not be the actual cause but merely serves as a mark (*ʿalāma*) to indicate that a certain *ḥukm* should apply. VIII 667a

In prosody, one of two pairs of metrical components distinguished by al-Khalīl, consisting of two consonants each. One is called *sabab khafīf* (when the first consonant is 'moving', i.e. has a short vowel, and the second is 'quiescent') and the other *sabab thaḳīl* (when both consonants are 'moving'). I 670b; XI 508b; a third type was introduced into Persian prosody, the *sabab-i mutawassiṭ*, consisting of an overlong syllable (e.g. *yār*). VIII 667b

In grammar, ~ is used by Sībawayhi to denote a 'semantic link' between words that bring about a change in the expected case ending. In addition to the direct ~, he recognized an indirect link which he calls *iltibās* 'involvement'. VIII 668a

♦ sabab khafīf → SABAB

♦ sabab thaḳīl → SABAB

♦ sabab-i mutawassiṭ → SABAB

sabad (A) : smooth, as e.g. in describing goats' hair. XII 317a

sabal (A) : in medicine, the pathological eye condition of pannus. 456a

sabʿānī (A), or *misabbaʿ, nuʿmānī, baghdādī* : in folk-verse, a composition with the rhyme scheme *a a a z z z a*, which is an elaboration of the monorhyme quatrain. VI 868a

sābāṭ (A) : in Indian siegecraft, a word used to express two walls, the foundations of which were laid at a distance of about one musket-shot (from the fort). They were protected by planks, fastened together by raw hides and made strong, and thus formed something like a lane which was then carried to the wall of the fort during an assault. III 482a; a covered passage. V 510b

sabʿatu ridjāl → SABʿ

sabb → SHATM

ṣabbāgh (A) : a dyer, a skilled artisan in the mediaeval Near East. IV 1161a; VIII 671b

sabbāk (A) : a melter, one of the craftsmen employed as staff in the mint who carried out the actual coining operation. II 118a

sabbāla → SABĪL

sābiʿ al-arūs (A) : the first seven days of marriage, which play a special part in the marriage ceremony. According to a usage sanctioned by the Prophet, the husband is meant to spend them with his wife if she is a virgin. A very old custom in Morocco had the husband buying fish on the seventh day, which his mother or other women then threw over the wife's feet. probably an old magical practice to secure fertility. X 906a

ṣabīb (A) : a term used in addition to the general term LAWN 'colour' for a notion of liquid colour or tincture, also applied to the object which it colours. V 699b

sābiḳ (A) : the name for the first horse in a horse-race, according to the order of finishing. II 953a

In Druze hierarchy, the right wing, the fourth of the five cosmic ranks in the organisation. II 632a

♦ sābiḳa (A) : in early Islam, the principle of precedence in Islam (length of adherence to the cause), observed in the division of revenues. X 819b

♦ **al-sābiḳūn** (A), or *al-sābiḳūn al-awwalūn* : lit. foregoers; in shīʿism, occasionally applied to the Prophet, imāms, and Fāṭima in recognition of their status as pre-existent beings and the first of God's creatures to respond to the demand 'Am I not your Lord?'. VIII 678b

In early Bābism, ~ was applied with what seems deliberate ambiguity to the group of eighteen disciples who, with the Bāb, formed the primary cadre of the sect's hierarchy. These early believers were ~ in the double sense of having preceded the rest of mankind in recognition of the new cause and in being actual incarnations of the Prophet and imāms. VIII 679a

In early Islam, the circle of early Muslims consisting of those who accepted Islam before the Prophet entered the house of al-Arḳam b. Abi 'l-Arḳam. VIII 828a

In Qur'ānic exegesis, those Muslims who prayed in both directions, viz. Jerusalem and Mecca, who emigrated with Muḥammad to Medina, and who took part in the battle of Badr and in the treaty of al-Ḥudaybiya. VIII 828a

sabīl (A, pl. *subul*; T *sebīl*) : lit. way, road, path; in the Qur'ān, ~ is also used figuratively in e.g. the expressions *sabīl Allāh*, the idea of fighting in the way of God, and *ibn al-sabīl* 'son of the road', later taken as 'traveller, wayfarer', and therefore as a fit object of charity or compassion. VIII 679a

In architecture, ~ designates water-houses which provide water for free public use; less common is also *sabbāla* 'public fountain, drinking basin'. The term ~ is also used to designate other charitable objects, such as *ḥawḍ al-sabīl*, i.e. a drinking trough for the animals, or *maktab al-sabīl* which is a charitable elementary school for boys. VIII 679b

For ~ in Turkey and Iran, → ČESHME and SAḲḲĀ-KHĀNA, respectively

ṣabir (A) : aloes or some other bitter vegetable substance. III 404a

ṣabiyy (A) : a youth, boy, or male child; one that has not yet been weaned, so called from the time of his birth. The fem. counterpart is *ṣabiyya*. VIII 821b

In law, a minor (also *ṣaghīr*), who has the capacity to conclude purely beneficial transactions and to accept donations and charitable gifts. An intelligent (*ṣabiyy yaʿḳilu*), discriminating (MUMAYYIZ) minor, moreover, can adopt Islam, enter into a contract of manumission by *mukātaba*, if he is a slave, and carry out a procuration. VIII 826a; and → ṬIFL

sabʿiyya → SABʿ

sābīzak → YABRŪḤ

sabḳ (A), or *sibāḳ* : the sport of horse-racing. II 953a

sabk-i hindī (P) : 'the Indian style'; the third term of a classification of Persian literature into three stylistic periods, the other two being *sabk-i khurāsānī* (also called *sabk-i turkistānī*) and *sabk-i ʿirāḳī*, referring respectively to the eastern and the western parts of mediaeval Persia. VIII 683b

sabkha (A, pl. *sibākh*; N.Afr. *sebkha*) : in geography, salt marshes or lagoons and the salt flats left by the evaporation of the water from such areas. VII 57b; VIII 685a; XII 328a

sabla (A) : a loose gown worn by women in Egypt, synonymous with THAWB. V 741b

sabr (A, pl. *subūr*) : an advance party of a raiding group of Bedouin. II 1055b

ṣabr (A) : patience, endurance; resignation; the cardinal virtue in mysticism. VIII 685b; endurance of adversity. XI 141b

In botany, ~ denotes the aloe, a species of the *Liliaceae*. Three varieties of the aloe are generally mentioned: *suḳuṭrī, ʿarabī* (*ḥaḍramī*) and *simindjānī* (→ SUḲUṬRĪ). VIII 687b

♦ ṣabra (A) : a very hard stone. VIII 688b

sabt (A) : the sabbath, and thus Saturday (*yawm al-~*, technically, Friday evening to Saturday evening); it is also suggested to mean 'a week', that is, from ~ to ~, as well as a more general sense of a long period of time. VIII 689a

sabuʿ al-baḥr (A) : 'beast of the sea', in zoology, the sea wolf (*Anarhichas lupus*). VIII 1021a

ṣābūn (A, < Gk) : soap, a mixture of fat or tallow and vegetable ashes, used to dye the hair red, and brought on the market in solid or liquid form. In Spain, ~ also indicates the lye obtained by leaving the ashes to soak in water. VIII 693a

sābūrḳān → ḤADĪD

sabziči-bāshī (P) : in Ṣafawid times, an official in the royal kitchen responsible for green salads. XII 609b

ṣād (A) : the fourteenth letter of the Arabic alphabet, transcribed *ṣ*, with the numerical value 90. It is defined as an alveolar sibilant, voiceless and velarised in articulation. VIII 695b

saʿd wa-naḥs (A) : lit. the fortunate and the unfortunate; in astrology, terms used to describe the stars, based on the influence exerted by the planets and the signs of the zodiac on earthly events. VIII 705a; *saʿd*, followed by a noun, is given to some stars and constellations. VIII 705b

♦ **al-saʿdān**[i] (A) : lit. the two lucky (planets); in astrology, the two beneficent planets Jupiter and Venus, contrasting with Saturn and Mars, *al-naḥsān*[i] 'the two unlucky, maleficent (planets)'. VIII 716b

sāda → MAḌBŪṬ

sadā (A) : the warp of a fabric; the weft is called *luḥma*. XII 341a

ṣadā (A) : a term with many meanings, including those of thirst, voice, echo, and screech-owl, in the sense of *hāma* (or *hām*, the male owl), which denotes a bird charged with taking shape in the skull of someone who has been murdered, to return to the tomb of the dead man until vengeance was exacted. VIII 706b

ṣadaf (A, s. *ṣadafa*) : in zoology, two classes of molluscs: mussels (*Lamellibranchiata*) and snails (*Gastropoda*), both including the mother-of-pearl. VIII 707a

♦ ṣadaf al-durr (A), or *al-sadaf al-luʾluʾī* : in zoology, the pearl mussel. VIII 707a

♦ ṣadaf al-firfir (A), or *ṣadaf furfūra* : in zoology, the snail family of the Purpura. VIII 707a

♦ ṣadaf ḳīrūkis (A) : in zoology, the trumpet-snail (*Tritonium nodiferum* L). VIII 707a

♦ ṣadafkārī ʿaṣā → DEYNEK

ṣadāḳ (A) : dowry (syn. MAHR).

ṣadaḳa (A) : voluntary alms, a charitable donation which does not require offer and acceptance and which is moreover always irrevocable; obligatory alms are also frequently termed ~ but are commonly known as ZAKĀT. III 350a; V 424b; VIII 495a; VIII 708b

In law, ~ is also used to refer to the tax on livestock, as well as to expiatory penalties. VIII 711b

♦ ṣadaḳa mawḳūfa → MAWḲŪF

♦ ṣadaḳa muḥarrama (A) : in law, the term used by the early Shāfiʿīs for a permanent WAḲF in favour of the poor or of certain classes of relatives or descendants or even clients, and then, after their distinction, to the poor. XI 59b

ṣadāret ḳāʾim-maḳāmī → ḲĀʾIM-MAḲĀM

sadd al-dharāʾiʿ (A) : lit. closing off the means that can lead to evil; in law, a mechanism devised by Mālikī jurists to resolve loopholes in the law, probably the only source of Islamic law to be presented in a negative form. VIII 718a

ṣadḥat al-maṭar (A) : 'rain bead', utilised by Arab tribes accounted of South Arabian or Yemeni genealogy, which could direct rain away from a particular spot. XI 227a

sadhāb (A) : in botany, the rue plant. II 1071b

ṣadīgh (A) : 'an epithet applied to a child, in the stage extending to his completion of seven days, because his temple becomes firm only to this period' (Lane). VIII 821b

ṣādiḥa → ḲAYNA

ṣadīḳī (IndP), correctly *ṣiddīḳī* : in numismatics, a gold coin of the value of two pagodas, weighing 106 grains (= 6.87 g), named thus by Tīpū Sultan of Mysore. VIII 726b

sādin (A) : in early Arabia, the guardian of a shrine. VIII 728a; X 774a

ṣādirāt (P, < A, s. *ṣādir*), or *ṣādiriyyāt* : one of the unfixed taxes in Persia, comprising levies made to meet special expenditure such as that occasioned by a military expedition, the construction or repair of a royal building, or some special festivity, or simply to make good a deficit in the revenue. According to the nature of the occasion, the whole country or a district or section of the community only was subjected to the levy. II 152a; IV 1041a f.

sadīs → ʿATŪD

sādj (A) : in botany, the teak tree, *Tectona grandis* L., of the family of the *Verbenaceae*. VIII 732b

In Arab dress, a green or black ṬAYLASĀN. X 613b

ṣādj (A) : a concave metal plate. V 42b; X 30b

sadjʿ (A) : in pre-Islamic times, the rhythmic, rhymed utterance of the soothsayer, which does not have a fixed metre or proper rhyme and is thus distinct from both poetry and prose. V 420a; VIII 732b

In literature of the Islamic period, rhymed prose, and the basis of the *stylus ornatus*, a characteristic feature of the later INSHĀʾ literature, but also of various other genres. III 1242b; VIII 734a; along with *fāṣila, ḳarīna* and *sadjʿa*, ~ also refers to its rhyme, as opposed to the rhyme of verse, *ḳāfiya*. VIII 737b

♦ sadjʿa → SADJʿ

sadjda (A) : 'bowing down', the name of two Qurʾānic SŪRAS. VIII 740a

♦ sadjdat al-tilāwa (A) : a technical term referring to the 14 Qurʾānic passages which require a ritual of bowing to be formed at the end of their recitation. VIII 740a

sadjdja, or *sādjdja* → ṢANDJ

sadjdjāda (A) : a prayer carpet. VIII 740b; XII 136a

In mysticism, ~ may refer to the mystical path initiated by a founding saint, hence a synonym of *ṭarīḳa, silsila* and *khilāfa*. IV 950a; VIII 743b; and → BAYT AL-SADJDJĀDA; NAḲĪB AL-SADJDJĀDA; SHAYKH AL-SADJDJĀDA

sādjisī (A) : a strain of sheep in the time of al-Djāḥiẓ, which was very large and had wool of a pure white. XII 318a

sadl → ḲABḌ

ṣadr (A, pl. *ṣudūr*) : lit. chest, breast, bosom, of all animals or of humans only. When used for only the breast of humans, ~ is contrasted with e.g. the *kirkira* of the camel-stallion, the *labān* of the horse, the *zawr* of the lion, the *djuʾdjuʾ* of the bird, etc. VIII 746b

In a figurative sense, ~ means any 'first, front, or upper part' of a thing. VIII 747b

In prosody, the first foot of a verse, as opposed to *ʿadjuz*, the last foot; often also loosely applied to the entire first hemistich. VIII 747b; another meaning of ~ in prosody occurs in the context of MUʿĀḲABA, to describe the case of e.g. in the RAMAL metre, the foot *fāʿilātun* having its first cord *fā-* shortened, thus *faʿilātun*, when the last cord *-tun* of the preceding foot is not shortened. VIII 747b

In architecture, the niche in the centre of the ĪWĀN's back wall. IX 176a

In epistolography, ~ refers to the introductory formulae of letters and prefaces in books (the latter also *taṣdīr*); exordium, proem. VIII 748

In music, the chest of a stringed instrument. VIII 347b

In a personal sense, an eminent or superior person or *primus inter pares*, whence its use for a chief, president or minister; in the academic sense, ~ is mostly applied to a professor in ADAB and mostly in the derived forms *muṣaddar* and *mutaṣaddir*. The title was especially used in the Persian world for a high religious dignitary whose function was concerned essentially with the administration of religious affairs. VIII 748a; IX 738b; and → ṢADR-I AʿẒAM

In Mug̲h̲al India, a provincial level officer in charge of land-grants. VIII 751a

For ~ in archery, → ḲIDḤ

♦ ṣadr al-ṣudūr : the more exalted title of *ṣadr*, borne by the Būrhānī *ṣadr*s of Transoxania in Ḳarak̲h̲ānid and Sald̲j̲ūḳ times. VIII 748b; in Mug̲h̲al India, a central minister, who controlled land-grants and cash-grants, and recommended appointments of *ḳāḍī*s 'judges' and *muftī*s 'interpreters of law and customs'. The local *ṣadr*s were his subordinates. VIII 751a

♦ **ṣadr-i aʿẓam** (T), commonly *ṣadr aʿẓam* : 'the greatest of the high dignitaries', the grand vizier, a title which, in the Ottoman empire, was used synonymously with *wezīr-i aʿẓam* from the mid-10th/16th century. In the 19th century, there were some unsuccessful attempts to convert ~ to *bas̲h̲wekīl* 'chief minister'. VIII 751b

sadra → S̲H̲UTIK

ṣadūḥ → ḲAYNA

ṣadūḳ (A) : 'truthful'; in the science of Tradition, a quality of a reliable transmitter of Tradition, although not as authoritative as T̲H̲IḲA or MUTḲIN. II 462a; VIII 983a

sadūs → SUDŪS

ṣafā (A) : lit. hard, smooth stone, whence also 'tract of stony ground'. VIII 756a

safah, safāha → ḤILM

safan (A) : in zoology, the sephen skate, whose Arabic term is found again in the Latinised nomenclature to specify a sub-species limited to a particular region (*Raia sephen*). VIII 1021b

ṣafan (A) : in anatomy, the scrotal sheath. IV 1087b

safar (A) : journey, travel. VIII 764b; 'journeying' often to visit the graves of the dead, syn. ZIYĀRA. XI 524b

ṣafar (A) : name of the second month of the Islamic year, also called ~ *al-k̲h̲ayr* or ~ *al-muẓaffar* because of its being considered to be unlucky. VIII 764b

safarna, safarnāya → ISFIRNĪ

ṣaff (A, pl. *ṣufūf*, B *ṣoff*) : lit. rank, row or line, company of men standing in a rank, row or line; in religious practice, ~ is used for the lines of worshippers assembled in the mosque or elsewhere for the prescribed worship. VIII 793b; a long rug with a row of MIḤRĀB decorations side by side, which may be used for communal family prayers. VIII 741b

In military terminology, the rank in an army formation. VIII 794a

In political organisation, not limited to but mostly in certain parts of North Africa, chiefly Algeria, southern Tunisia and Libya, a league, alliance, faction or party (syn. *ʿiṣāba, farīḳ, ṭāʾifa, ḥizb*), a diffuse system of two (or more) mutually opposing or rivalling leagues dividing villages or desert towns, clans and families, or comprising whole tribes, whose league members had a strict obligation of mutual assistance. In Morocco, the term *leff* is used with the same meaning throughout. IV 835a; VIII 794a; X 758a

♦ ṣaffa (A) : a small embroidered bonnet trimmed with coins, worn by women in the Arab East. V 741b

♦ **al-ṣāffāt** (A, < *ṣaffa* 'to be lined up in a row') : title of SŪRA xxxvii and used three times in text, where generally understood to mean '(angels) standing in ranks'; in sūras xxiv and lxvii, however, ~ is glossed as 'outspread wings' of birds. VIII 798a

saffāḥ (A) : bloodthirsty; generous. Al-Saffāḥ was the surname of the first ʿAbbāsid caliph. I 103a

ṣaffāḳatān → ṢAND̲J̲

saffūd (A) : in the mediaeval kitchen, a roasting skewer. VI 808b

ṣafī (A, pl. *ṣafāyā*) : in early Islam, special items consisting of immoveable property selected from booty by the leader. VIII 798a; XII 532a; and → IBRĪZ

♦ ṣafiyya (A, pl. *ṣafāyā*) : any special object of the booty which attracted the leader of a foray, and which he had the right to reserve for himself. The term appears as ṢAWĀFĪ in respect to state domains. II 869b; and → ʿANZ

♦ **ṣawāfī** (A, s. *ṣafī*) : in early Islam, the land which the IMĀM selects from the conquered territories for the treasury with the consent of those who had a share in the booty. VIII 798b; crown lands in general, the private estates of the caliph being known as *ḍiyāʿ al-khāṣṣa*, *ḍiyāʿ al-sulṭān* and *ḍiyāʿ al-khulafāʾ*. IV 972b

safīh (A) : a spendthrift. XI 299b

ṣafīḥa (A) : plate. IX 251b

♦ ṣafīḥa shakkāziyya → SHAKKĀZIYYA

♦ ṣafīḥa zarḳālliyya (A) : in astronomy, an astrolabic plate serving the latitude of the equator, developed by two Andalusian astronomers in the 5th/11th century, Ibn al-Zarḳāllu and ʿAlī b. Khalaf. It differs from the *ṣafīḥa shakkāziyya* by its set of markings. IX 251b; XI 461b

♦ ṣafīḥa zīdjiyya (A) : in astronomy, the equatorium, called thus by al-Zarḳālī. His equatorium is totally independent and represents all the planetary deferents and related circles on both sides of a single plate, while a second plate bears all the epicycles. XI 461b

safila (A) : scum. IV 1132b

safīna (A, pl. *sufun, safāʾin, safīn*) : ship, used from pre-Islamic times. VIII 808a; and → RAMATH

In codicology, a specific kind of shape in use for notebooks. Its architecture is that of an oblong-shaped book, but it is used in a vertical position, the sewing of the leaves being in the top edge, very much as present-day noteblocks. VIII 150a

In astronomy, ~ represents Argus, one of the eastern constellations made up of 45 stars, the brightest of which is *suhayl* or Canopus. The term *safīnat nūḥ* denotes the Great Bear. VIII 811b

♦ safīnat nūḥ → SAFĪNA

safīr (A, pl. *sufarāʾ*, T *sefīr*) : ambassador, messenger; in Twelver shīʿism, ~ refers to the four deputies of the twelfth IMĀM during the Lesser Occultation (260-329/874-941). The office they held was called *sifāra*. Synonyms of ~ are BĀB and NĀʾIB or *nāʾib khāṣṣ*. VIII 811b; X 935b

In diplomacy, ~, initially meaning envoy as well as mediator and conciliator, becomes ambassador or diplomatic agent, the post or embassy being *sifāra*. VIII 812b; and → ELČI

♦ safīr fawḳa 'l-ʿāda (A) : in diplomacy, ambassador extraordinary. VIII 813a

♦ safīr mufawwaḍ (A) : in diplomacy, ambassador plenipotentiary. VIII 813a; the Ottoman term was *orta elči* or simply *sefīr*. II 694a; and → ELČI

♦ safīra (A) : ambassadress, or an ambassador's wife. VIII 813a

ṣafiyya → ʿANZ; ṢAFĪ

ṣafḳa (A) : lit. striking hands together; in law, the ratification of a commercial contract; ~, unlike *bayʿ*, contains the meaning of a bargain that is achieved swiftly and profitably. VIII 818a; the *negotium*. I 318b

ṣafr (A), or *isfīdrūy, isfādrūḥ* (< P *sapīd rūy*) : in metallurgy, bronze, much used in early Islam for plain kitchen wares and implements, and as the alloy upon which coppersmiths based most of their work. V 970b; V 985b

ṣafrāʾ (A) : yellow; in mediaeval texts, yellow bile, one of the four cardinal humours, the others being black bile, phlegm and blood. XII 188b

safsāri (N.Afr) : a large outer wrap for women, worn in Tunisia and Libya. V 746b

safūf (A) : in medicine, a medicinal powder. IX 805a
ṣag͟hāʾir → KABĀʾIR
ṣag͟hāna → DJAG͟HĀNA
ṣāg͟hir nūn → NŪN
ṣag͟hīr (A) : infant, child; one who has not attained to puberty (opp. *kabīr*). VIII 821b
In law, a minor, as opposed to BĀLIG͟H. Fifteen was generally regarded as the age that divided between majority and minority for males and females alike. I 993a; VIII 821b; and → ṢABIYY
ṣaḥāb → ṢUḤBA
ṣaḥāba (A, s. *ṣaḥābī*, or ṢĀḤIB), or AṢḤĀB : the Companions of the Prophet, dating from the first conversions (at Mecca in 610 and Medina in June 621) until the death of Anas b. Mālik (91/710 or 93/712). In earlier times the term was restricted to those who had been close to the Prophet. Later, it also included those who had met him during his lifetime, or who had seen him even if only for quite a short time. After the Qurʾān, the Companions were the sources of authentic religious doctrine. S͟hīʿism in general holds a different attitude towards the Companions, because with their approval the first three caliphs took away the rights of ʿAlī and his family. IV 149a; VIII 827b
ṣaḥābī → ṢAḤĀBA
ṣaḥāfī → ṢIḤĀFA
saḥara (A) : agents of fallen angels. IX 569b
saḥarī (A) : in the mediaeval Near East, a beggar who begins to ply his 'trade' before the dawn. VII 494b
saḥāt → WAṬWĀṬ
ṣaḥḥ → IBRĪZ
ṣāḥib (A, pl. AṢḤĀB, ṢAḤĀBA) : 'companion'; the counsellor of a ruler; in compounds, partner, match (sometimes 'adversary'), someone (or something) endowed with s.th. or characterised by s.th. (syn. *d͟hū*), adherent of a specific concept, owner, possessor, lord, chief. VIII 830b; in the Ottoman empire, a synonym for *wezīr* (→ WAZĪR). XI 194b; and → AṢḤĀB
In literature, the poet's, soothsayer's, or orator's alter ego among the DJINN, from whom he receives (some of) his inspiration (syn. *s͟hayṭān, raʾī*, and *tābiʿ*). VIII 830b; IX 407a
In mysticism, the 'adept', as opposed to the *maṣḥūb* 'master', their relationship being called *ṣuḥba*. VIII 830b
In tribal organisation, a member of the same faction. IV 835a
♦ ṣāḥib al-aḥbās (A) : in al-Andalus, a curator or administrator general of mortmain property, whose mission was to prevent the disappearance of real estate or the alteration of its status. XI 77a
♦ ṣāḥib al-as͟hg͟hāl (A) : an important official in charge of finance under the Almohads, of whom there seemed to be only one at any given time. He was always mentioned among the high officers of the state. The Ḥafṣids took over the title of ~ , and presumably his office, from the Almohads; later, this official is referred to as *munaffid͟h*. II 145b
♦ **ṣāḥib al-bāb** (A) : 'high chamberlain', a title borne in Fātimid Egypt by a man of the sword counted among the first rank of AMĪRS (*al-umarāʾ al-muṭawwakūn* '*amīr*s bearing a collar'). The ~ (syn. **al-wazīr al-ṣag͟hīr**) ranked next after the vizier. VIII 831b
♦ ṣāḥib dīwān (P, < A) : a title under the Īlk͟hāns, and sometimes in later times also, for the vizier. XI 192b
♦ ṣāḥib al-fayḍa (A) : in the Tid͟jāniyya brotherhood, the description of the person

who ‘channels the infusion of grace’ which the Tidjānīs receive from their master. In 1929 the Senegalese Ibrāhīm Niasse declared that Aḥmad al-Tidjānī had told him in a vision that he was ~ and thereafter Niasse referred to his followers as Djamāʿat al-Fayḍa ‘Community of Grace’. X 465a

♦ ṣāḥib ḥadīth → ṢĀḤIB SUNNA

♦ ṣāḥib al-inzāl (A) : in Muslim Spain, the functionary at court who had the responsibility of arranging accommodation for the sovereign’s guests and for itinerant poets in the precincts of the palace. IX 232b

♦ ṣāḥib al-khabar (A) : the title of one of a ruler’s officers in provincial capitals whose duty it was to report to his master all new happenings, the arrival of strangers, etc. This post was often given to the director of the postal service. IV 895b; intelligence agent. X 787a

♦ **ṣāḥib ḳirān** (A, P) : ‘Lord of the (auspicious) conjunction’, a title first assumed by Tīmūr, and after his death occasionally applied to lesser sovereigns, but officially assumed by the Mughal emperor Shāh Djahān, who styled himself *ṣāḥib ḳirān-i thānī* ‘the second Lord of the conjunction’. VIII 833a

In numismatics, the name of a Persian coin of 1000 dīnārs, the tenth part of a TŪMĀN; it has since been corrupted into *ḳirān* or *ḳrān*. VIII 833b; a coin standard introduced in 1241/1825 in Persia. IX 203b

♦ ṣāḥib al-layl (A) : ‘worker by night’, in mediaeval Islam, the nocturnal housebreaker who got in either by boring or by scaling walls, *mutasallik*. V 769a

♦ **ṣāḥib al-madīna** (A) : in Muslim Spain, an administrative official. The duties entrusted to the holders of this title were diverse, and could involve policing and public order, justice, the levying of taxes and even leading armies, all of which leads one to think that there were no strictly determined duties but rather a nexus of functions varying in extent according to the confidence placed in the holder. VIII 833b

♦ ṣāḥib al-naẓar fi ’l-maẓālim (A) : an official in early Islam appointed to consider complaints about injustices of the government officials, including the AMĪRs. I 439a

♦ ṣāḥib al-rikāb → RIKĀBDĀR

♦ ṣāḥib al-shārib → SĀḲĪ

♦ ṣāḥib sunna (A) : an individual from among the AHL AL-SUNNA, a MUḤADDITH well-known for his travelling in search of Traditions containing SUNNAs all over the eastern Islamic world. The appellative *ṣāḥib ḥadīth* is not a synonym for ~ , as the latter frequently had his handling of Traditions frowned upon and the former was known for his support of one or more BIDʿAs ‘innovations’. IX 880a f.

♦ ṣāḥib al-waḳt (A) : in the Tidjāniyya brotherhood, a term used for the ḲUṬB, meaning he who dominates the universe during his lifetime. X 464a

♦ ṣāḥib al-yad (A) : in law, the person in possession of the object in dispute, thus the defendant. II 171a

♦ ṣāḥib-dīwān (A) : under the Īlkhāns, the chief financial administrator, on a par with the vizier. VIII 831a

♦ ṣāḥib-i dīwān-i ʿarḍ → ʿARĪḌ

♦ al-ṣāḥibān (A) : in Ḥanafi legal sources, the ‘two disciples’ of Abū Ḥanīfa, i.e. Abū Yūsuf and Muḥammad al-Shaybānī. VIII 830b

ṣaḥīfa (A, pl. *ṣuḥuf*) : lit. a flat object, a plaque, a leaf, whence, a surface or material on which one can write, applied especially to fragments of the Qurʾān or Tradition or any other document of a solemn nature; the written texts themselves. VIII 834b; according to Ibn Manẓūr, a ~ can be opened out, fixed on a wall or attached to something, differing from a *ruḳʿa*, which is necessarily sealed. VIII 835a; and → MUṢḤAF; RISĀLA

ṣaḥīḥ (A) : lit. sound, healthy; in the science of Tradition, a sound Tradition, i.e. one supported by a chain of transmitters going back to the Prophet in an uninterrupted manner. Each pair of two transmitters in that chain must both be considered ʿADL 'upright' or 'honest' to the point that their testimonies are admissible in a court of law, and ḌĀBIṬ 'painstakingly accurate', and they should be known to have met each other. A whole collection of such Traditions is also termed ~ . III 25b; VIII 835b

In law, a valid act, i.e. an act carried out in conformity with the prescriptions of the law, and which must in principle produce all its effects. II 389b; VIII 836a; IX 324b

In grammar, ~ refers to the 'sound' letters, loosely the consonants of Arabic, defined by default as being neither 'weak' letters (→ ḤARF ʿILLA) nor vowels; in later grammar, ~ may also denote a 'correct' utterance. VIII 836b

sāḥil (A, pl. *sawāḥil*) : in geography, 'edge, border zone'; in English, the Sahel, the region to the south of the Sahara (→ ṢAḤRĀʾ) characterised by periodic drought. VIII 836b; coast, whence Swahili. X 194a

sāḥir (A) : magician. XI 129b

saḥḳ → SIḤĀḲ

sahla (A) : lit. level, smooth place. XII 697b

sahm (A) : in archery, an arrow made from a reed, or of hard solid wood. IV 799a

In geometry, the versed sine (*al-djayb al-maʿkūs*) of the arc *a b*, if one erects a perpendicular *c b* in the middle of a chord of an arc, which reaches to the arc; the sine (*al-djayb al-mustawī*) which corresponds to our sine is *a c*. VIII 841b

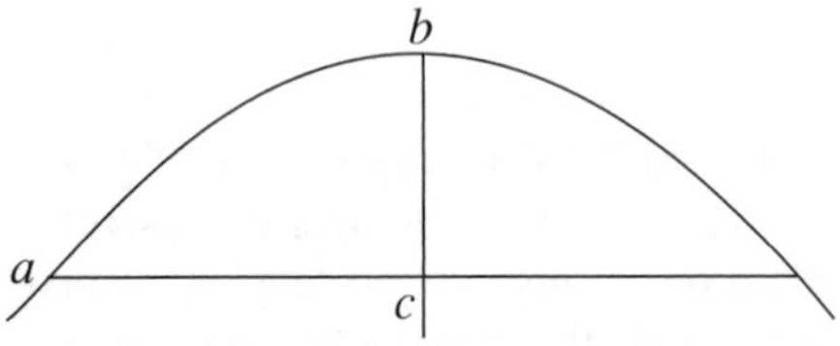

In law, ~ (pl. *ashum*) is found in the context of inheritance where it denotes the fixed share of an heir, and in the context of partnership and profit-sharing, where as a term used in modern share companies, ~ is defined as a partial ownership of a large capital. The holder is called *musāhim*. VIII 842a; and → ESHĀM

♦ sahm al-ghayb (A) : in astrology, the arrow, the hitting of the secret of the future. VIII 842a

♦ sahm al-ṣadārat → RASM AL-ṢADĀRAT

ṣaḥn (A) : lit. plate; a flat, stony terrain. IX 763b

In architecture, a courtyard. V 510b; VI 661b

In music, a cup-shape instrument, made up of a bronze cup, *ṭusayt*, which was struck against another of its kind, favoured in martial music. IX 10a

ṣaḥrāʾ (A) : fem. of *aṣḥar* 'fawn, tawny coloured'; in geography, an ensemble of stony terrain, steppelands and sands; desert. In English, the Sahara, the desert in the northern part of Africa. VIII 845b

sahrīdj (A), or *fasḳiyya* : a reservoir of water. I 24a

saḥūr (A) : the last part of the night when, during the month of Ramaḍān, it is still permitted to eat and drink. V 372b; meal taken after midnight during the fast. IX 94b

sāʾiba (A) : a beast brought out of the herd for offering to the gods of ancient Arabia; a freed slave, but one foot-loose and without a patron in early Islam; by extension, a woman left to herself, a rebel or a prostitute; the breaking of allegiance to a sovereign; and from the latter, the territory where this dissidence was rife. XII 729b

sāʿid (A) : in military science, an arm protection consisting of segmented vambraces for the lower arms, probably of iron or bronze but perhaps also of hardened leather, while the upper arms were protected by the sleeves of a mail hauberk or by flaps of lamellar armour attached to the body of a lamellar cuiras. Other arm protections were termed *bāzūband* and *kaff*. XII 738b

ṣaʿīdī → RIDFA

ṣāʾifa (A, < *ṣayf* summer'; pl. *ṣawāʾif*) : summer raid or military expedition. The term is used in the contexts of Arabo-Byzantine warfare and Muslim-Christian warfare in Spain. I 82b; VIII 869b

ṣāʾigh (A, pl. *ṣāgha, ṣawwāghūn*) : a goldsmith, a skilled craftsman in the mediaeval Near East. VIII 871a

ṣāʿiḳa (A) : a thunderbolt, used in the Qurʾān with reference to the Thamūd when they hamstrung the 'camel of God'. X 436a

saʿīr (A) : one of various words used in the Qurʾān for hell fire, occurring 16 times. Other terms used are *djahannam* and *saḳar*; unlike them, ~ seems to be a native Arabic formation with the meaning '[place of] fiercely kindled flame'. VIII 872a

sāʾis (A) : under the Mamlūks, a stage groom in the postal service. Other personnel were couriers, *barīdī*, and 'outriders', *sawwāḳ*. I 1046a

sāḳ (A) : lit. leg or thigh; the foot of a compass (syn. *ridjl*); in mathematics, the perpendicular of a right-angled triangle with horizontal base, or the equal sides of an isosceles triangle (*ḍilʿ* is also used for any side of any triangle). VIII 872a

In astronomy, ~ may refer to a star that is in a leg of a constellation figure representing a person or an animal, e.g. ~ *al-asad* or *sāḳā 'l-asad* (dual) for either or both of α Bootis and α Virginis. VIII 872a

♦ sāk al-asad → SĀḲ

♦ sāk al-djarāda (A) : lit. the locust's leg, in astronomy, the name given to a variety of vertical sundial in which the horizontal gnomon is moved along a groove at the top of the rectangular sundial according to the season (since the shadow-lengths at the hours depend on the solar longitude). VIII 872b

♦ sāka → AṢL

ṣaḳāla (A) : lustre (of a gem). XI 570a

ṣaḳāliba (A, s. *ṣaḳlabī, ṣiḳlabī*) : the Slavs and other fair-haired, ruddy-complexioned peoples of northern Europe; ethnic groups of central or eastern Europe; white slaves of European origin; Germanic tribes. I 490b; IV 1088b; V 1120b; VIII 872b; its singular was often used in the mediaeval period in the sense of 'eunuch'. I 33a

sakandjabīn : a drink, the classical oxymel. X 529b

saḳanḳūr (A) : a Nile creature, said to be the result of a cross between a crocodile and a fish. VIII 42b; an Egyptian skink, *Scincus officinarum*, a variety of lizard which when dried and salted is credited with remarkable aphrodisiac qualities. XII 641b

sakar (A) : wine. X 903b

saḳar (A) : one of the terms in the Qurʾān for 'hell' or, more precisely, one of the gates of hell, or else one of the 'stages'. VIII 881a; and → SAʿĪR

saḳaṭ (A, pl. *asḳāṭ*) : lit. refuse; a term used by Abu 'l-Faḍl Djaʿfar al-Dimashḳī (6th/12th century) for spice. XII 42b

♦ saḳaṭī (A) : pedlar. IX 57a

sakbīnadj (A) : in botany, sagapenum, the yellow translucent resin from *Ferula Scowitziana* which causes irritation of the skin and whose smell resembles that of asafoetida. VIII 1042b

sakhīf → SUKHF

sakhla (A, pl. *sakhl, sikhāl, sukhlān*), and *bahma* (pl. *baham, bihām*) : names for newborn lambs and kids, called thus indiscriminately. In ancient terminology, the distinction between lamb and kid only appeared clearly at the age of weaning (*fiṭām*), around four or five months. Until then, the young lamb-kid is called *badhadj, farīr, furār* or *furfur*. After weaning, the kid becomes a *djafr* and the lamb *kharūf*, and when the sex is determined, before it is one year old, *djady* and *ʿutʿut* for the he-kid, *ʿanāḳ* for the she-kid, *ḥamal* and *immar* for the he-lamb and *rikhl* and *immara* for the she-lamb. XII 319a

sāḳī (A) : cup-bearer, the person charged with pouring wine, to be distinguished from the chief butler or sommelier (*s̲h̲arābī* or *ṣāḥib al-s̲h̲arāb*). Synonyms or quasi-synonyms that are attested are *mudīr, k̲h̲ādim*, and the paraphrase *d̲h̲ū zud̲j̲ād̲j̲āt* 'the one who holds the glasses'. VIII 883b

In Saudi Arabia, a term used for an underground aqueduct with surface apertures to facilitate cleaning of the channel in the district al-Aflād̲j̲, in southern Nad̲j̲d, which itself was named after the term for the same aqueduct, FALAD̲J̲ (pl. *aflād̲j̲*), still used in Oman. I 233a

♦ sāḳī-nāma (P) : in Persian poetry, a genre in the MUTAḲĀRIB metre wherein the speaker calls to the SĀḲĪ for wine and complains of the instability of the world, the fickleness of destiny, and the inconstancy of his beloved. VIII 885b

saḳīfa (A) : a covered communal place appropriate for conversation and discussion, any type of covered forum or public courtyard; an approximate syn. is ṢUFFA, which seems rather to be applied to the space covered with palm foliage which constituted the primitive mosque. VIII 887b; and → RIWĀḲ; S̲H̲ARAʿA

In historical texts, ~ is applied virtually exclusively to the prolonged and acerbic negotiations which preceded the nomination of Abū Bakr as successor to the Prophet. The expression *saḳīfat Banī Sāʿida*, usually shortened to *al-~* or *yawm al-~*, is invariably applied to this specific historical episode. VIII 887b

saḳīm → ḌAʿĪF

sākin (A) : quiescent; in grammar, ~ denotes a letter not followed by FATḤA, KASRA or ḌAMMA. III 172a

In archery, ~ denotes a way of loosing an arrow. The archer draws slowly, holding the draw in order to verify that the position of the shot is good, and then looses calmly. IV 800b

sakīna (A) : in the Qurʾān, ~ denotes God's presence, a presence shown in the divine aid vouchsafed to the Prophet and the believers in battle, giving them the victory. VIII 888b

sāḳiya (A, pl. *sawāḳī*) : a complex hydraulic machine with over two hundred component parts, still in use today. It consists essentially of a large vertical wheel erected over the water supply on a horizontal axle. This wheel carries a chain-of-pots or a bucket chain. On the other end of its axle is a gear-wheel that engages a horizontal gear-wheel to which the driving bar is attached. The animal is harnessed to the free end of this bar, and as it walks in a circular path, the gears and the wheel carrying the chain-of-pots rotate. The pots dip in succession into the water and when they reach the top, they empty into a channel. V 861a ff.

ṣaḳīz (T, P *saḳḳiz*) : in botany, gum mastic, a product for which Chios, the Greek island off the Turkish coast called ~ in Ottoman Turkish, is famous. V 168a; VIII 889b

ṣakk (A, pl. *ṣikāk*) : in finance and law, document, contract of sale, suggested for want of any other etymology through Persian *čak* as the origin of Eng. 'cheque'. XII 699a; a mandate for payment. III 283b; a medium by which funds were remitted from place to place. III 382b

In classical Muslim administration, an inventory required for every issue of pay showing the names of the payees, with numbers and amounts, and bearing the signed authority to pay of the sultan. The ~ was also required for the hire of muleteers and camel-drivers. II 79a; and → ẒAHĪR

saḳḳāʾ (A, T *saḳḳā* or *saḳa*) : lit. water-carrier, a term denoting manual workers who carried water in a leather-bottle (*ḳirba*) or jar (KŪZ) on their shoulders or on a mule. V 882b; VIII 892a

♦ saḳḳā-k̲h̲āna (P) : a drinking fountain in the Persian bazaar or street, often constituted into WAḲF. V 876a

ṣaḳḳār → BAYYĀZ
saḳḳiz → ṢAḲİZ
ṣaḳr (A) : in zoology, the falcon. I 541b
ṣāḳūr → MINḲĀR
sākw (A) : a woollen or velvet coat worn by women in the Arab East. V 741b
saḳy (A) : irrigated land, distinct from dry land, BAʿL, which was reserved for the cultivation of cereals. I 491b

sāl-nāme (T) : in Ottoman Turkish administration, official yearbooks issued by the Ottoman central government, by provincial authorities and a number of civil (ministries) and military (army, fleet) institutions, appearing between 1263/1847 and the end of the empire (1918); semi-official and non-governmental annuals. I 75a; I 975a; VIII 898a

salab (A) : spoils of the war, such as clothes, weapons and, occasionally, the mount of an adversary killed in battle. II 1005b; XII 532a

salaf (A) : in law, a purchaser's payment for goods due for deliver by the recipient of such payment at the end of a specified period (syn. SALAM); also, the loan of fungible commodities (syn. ḲARḌ). VIII 899b

The 'pious ancients', the main witnesses of early Islam. I 416b; IV 142a; VIII 900a

♦ **al-salaf wa 'l-khalaf** (A) : lit. the predecessors and the successors, names given to the first three generations and to the following generations of the Muslim community respectively. VIII 900a

♦ **salafiyya** (A) : a neo-orthodox brand of Islamic reformism, originating in the late 19th century and centred on Egypt, aiming to regenerate Islam by a return to the tradition represented by the 'pious forefathers' (*al-salaf al-ṣāliḥ*). VIII 900b

salaḥa (A) : to defecate. XII 734b

salam (A), or *salaf* : in law, a forward sale, one of two contracts (the other is ṢARF) which become invalid if the material transfer does not take place at the time of the agreement. In this contract, the price is to be paid at the time of the contract. IV 326a; ~ has as its fundamental principle prepayment by a purchaser, *al-musallim*, for an object of sale, *al-musallam fīhi*, to be delivered to him by the vendor, *al-musallam ilayhi*, on a date at the end of a specified period. In such a transaction, the price agreed upon at the contracting parties' meeting for delivery of the merchandise is termed *ra's al-māl*. V 559a; VIII 493a; VIII 914b

salām (A) : safety, salvation; peace (in the sense of quietness); salutation, greeting; a formula of salutation or benediction (containing the word ~). VIII 915b; and → IFTITĀḤ

In Islamic prayer, ~ denotes a *ṣalawāt* (s. ṢALĀT) litany, pronounced from the minarets every Friday about half an hour before the beginning of the midday service before the call to prayer, *adhān*. This part of the liturgy is repeated inside the mosque before the beginning of the regular ceremonies by several people with good voices standing on a DIKKA. The same name is given to the benedictions on the Prophet which are sung during the month of Ramaḍān about half an hour after midnight from the minarets. VIII 917b

In Urdu prosody, a short poem on the theme of the Karbalāʾ martyrs, normally containing a word such as *salām, salāmī, mudjrā* or *mudjrāʾī* in the first few verses. VI 610b

In numismatics, ~ (sometimes abbreviated to *s*) on coins means 'of full weight, complete'. VIII 918a

salāmūra (A), or *sanamūra* : the pickling or maceration of fish with spices in brine. VIII 1023a

sālār (P) : commander; essentially a military term, as e.g. in ISPAHSĀLĀR 'supreme army commander', ~ by itself was also often used for the commander of a particular group, such as the Muslim fighters of the faith centred on Lahore in the Gh̲aznawid period. VIII 924a; and → MĀDĪ-SĀLĀR

♦ āk̲h̲ur-sālār (P) : 'head of the stables', a term found as far west as Mamlūk Egypt and Syria. VIII 924b; and → AMĪR ĀK̲H̲ŪR

salāriyye (T), or *salārlïk* : one of the local taxes in the Ottoman empire which was added to the ʿUS̲H̲R to raise it from one-tenth to one-eighth. II 146b; VIII 203b; VIII 486b

salārlïk → SALĀRIYYE

ṣalāṣil (A, s. *ṣalṣal*) : in music, term applied to all high-sounding clashed metal instruments. IX 10a

ṣalāt (A, pl. *ṣalawāt*) : the ritual prayer, one of the five pillars of Islam. Every Muslim who has attained his majority is bound to observe the five daily prayers (→ ʿAṢR, FAD̲J̲R, ʿIS̲H̲Āʾ, MAG̲H̲RIB, ẒUHR). In some circles, a sixth prayer is performed (→ ḌUḤĀ). IV 771b; V 74a ff.; V 424b; VII 27a; VIII 925a

♦ ṣalāt ʿalā ʾl-mayyit (A), or *ṣalāt al-d̲j̲anāza* (or *d̲j̲ināza*) : the prayer over a dead person. VIII 931b

♦ ṣalāt al-ʿaẓīmiyya (A) : in the Sanūsiyya brotherhood, a prayer for the Prophet inherited from Aḥmad b. Idrīs, which takes its title from the repetition of *Allāh al-ʿAẓīm*. IX 24b

♦ ṣalāt al-d̲j̲anāza (or *d̲j̲ināza*) → ṢALĀT ʿALĀ ʾL-MAYYIT

♦ ṣalāt al-d̲j̲umʿa → YAWM AL-D̲J̲UMʿA

♦ ṣalāt al-g̲h̲āʾib → G̲H̲ĀʾIB

♦ ṣalāt al-ḥād̲j̲a (Ind) : in Ačeh, the *ṣalāt*s during the night of the middle of S̲h̲aʿbān. IX 154a

♦ ṣalāt al-ʿīd (A) : the festival of public prayer of the whole community, common to both of the two canonical festivals (→ ʿĪD). It has preserved older forms of the *ṣalāt* than the daily or even the Friday *ṣalāt*. It should be celebrated in the open air, which is still often done, though now mosques are preferred. The time for its performance is between sunset and the moment when the sun has reached its zenith. III 1007a; VIII 930b

♦ ṣalāt al-istisḳāʾ → ISTISḲĀʾ

♦ **ṣalāt al-k̲h̲awf** (A) : lit. the prayer of fear, an alternative ritual prayer in the context of warfare. When a Muslim army is close to the enemy, and it fears an attack, one group will perform the ritual prayer while the other stands guard, then the roles are reversed. This prayer, with its special measures and regulations, is called ~. VIII 934a

♦ ṣalāt al-kusūf → KUSŪF

♦ ṣalāt maḳlūba (A) : an ascetic practice that consists of reciting the Qurʾān and praying while suspended by the feet in a dark place. XI 561b

♦ **ṣalāt-i maʿkūsa** (P, A) : lit. the act of worship performed upside-down; one of the extreme ascetic practices found among extravagant members of the dervish orders, such as in mediaeval Muslim India among the Čis̲h̲tiyya. XII 699a

♦ ṣalāt al-nāfila → NĀFILA

♦ ṣalāt al-sahw (A) : 'prayer of negligence', to be added immediately after the regular prayer by someone who has inadvertently omitted or misplaced one of its elements. The ~ consists of performing two prostrations with their TAKBĪR, then sitting for the TAS̲H̲AHHUD and the final salutation. VIII 928a

♦ ṣalāt al-**witr** (A) : a prayer performed between the evening prayer and the dawn prayer (preferably towards the end of the night). *Witr* signifies 'uneven' and denotes a special RAKʿA which is performed in isolation or which is added to one or more pairs of *rakʿa*s. VIII 930a; XI 213a

♦ al-ṣalawāt al-ibrāhīmiyya (A) : a formula pronounced during the TAS̲H̲AHHUD inspired in part by Q 33:56 and Q 11:73 ('O God, bless Muḥammad and the family of Muḥammad as You blessed Abraham and the family of Abraham, and bless Muḥammad and the family of Muḥammad as You blessed Abraham and the family of Abraham in the worlds. You are worthy of praise and of glory'). VIII 929b

ṣalawāt → ṢALĀT

salb → KHIṢĀʾ

ṣalb (A) : crucifixion, a ḤADD punishment of death. In Abū Ḥanīfa and Mālik, ~ consists in the criminal being tied alive to a cross or a tree and his body ripped up with a spear so that he dies; this is the more original form. According to al-Shāfiʿī and Ibn Ḥanbal, the criminal is first killed with a sword and then his corpse is ignominiously exposed on a tree or cross. IV 770b; VIII 935a; in later Persian and Turkish usage, ~ meant 'hanging'. VIII 935b

saldjamiyya a mediaeval dish of turnip, chicken, onion, cheese and seasonings. X 31b

salghun (T) : an Ottoman emergency levy, collected by the state in kind, cash or services rendered. VIII 486b

ṣalīb (A, pl. *ṣulub, ṣulbān*) : a cross, and, particularly, the object of Christian veneration. The term is used for cross-shaped marks, e.g. brands on camels and designs woven into cloth, and in legal contexts for the instrument of execution. VIII 980a

sāligh → ʿATŪD

ṣāliḥ (A, pl. **ṣāliḥūn**) : righteous, virtuous, incorrupt. VIII 982b; VIII 990a; a Qurʾānic epithet applied to prophets, who are considered to be 'men of goodness'. VIII 498a; and → MURĀBIṬ

In the science of Tradition, ~ indicates a transmitter who, although otherwise praised for his upright conduct, is known to have brought into circulation one or more Traditions spuriously ascribed to the Prophet. The contents of such Traditions, as well as their underlying meaning, characterise their recognised inventor as ~ rather than as *waḍḍaʿ* 'forger' or *kadhdhāb* 'liar'. Although ~ Traditions can theoretically be found among those labelled ṢAḤĪḤ, the majority fall under the categories of *ḥasan* 'fair' or *ḍaʿīf* 'weak'. VIII 982b; ~ is used by Abū Dāʾūd for Traditions about which he has made no remark, some being sounder than others. III 25b

sālik → MADJDHŪB; NĀFIDH; SULŪK

salīkha → DĀRṢĪNĪ

salīl (A) : a child or male offspring; a child, specifically at the time of his birth and (from then) until its weaning. VIII 821b

sālim (A) : intact, sound, i.e. free of damage or blemish, thus 'well' as opposed to 'ill' (syn. ṢĀḤĪḤ). VIII 900b

In numismatics, unclipped coins of full weight, or a sum of money free from charges and deductions. VIII 990a

In grammar, ~ is used to denote a) a 'sound' root, i.e. one in which none of the radicals is a 'weak' letter (*ḥarf ʿilla*), nor a hamza, nor a geminate; b) a word with a 'sound' ending, no matter whether the preceding radicals are weak or not; and c) the 'sound' plural as opposed to the broken plural. VIII 990a

In prosody, ~ denotes a regular foot, which has not undergone any of the changes called ZIḤĀFĀT or ʿILAL, or a line of poetry consisting of such feet. VIII 990a

salīmī → YŪSUFĪ

salīt (A) : in popular Arabic usage, ~ means 'oil', in Yemen, 'sesame oil'. VIII 1000b

sāliyāne (T, < P *sāl* 'year'), or *sālyāne* : in Ottoman administration, the yearly income allotted to some categories of provincial rulers and governors (16th-19th centuries). VIII 994a

salḳaʿ (A) : in zoology, the male ostrich, commonly called ẓalīm 'very dark' (rather than 'oppressed'), similarly with other adjectives used to define him: *asḥam* and *ghayhab*. It is surnamed *abu 'l-bayḍ* 'father of the eggs' and *abū thalāthīn* 'father of thirty [eggs]' as it takes its turn sitting on the eggs. VII 828a, where many variants are found

salkh (A) : in dating, 'the thirtieth day' in the month. X 259b

sall → KHIṢĀʾ

sallākhči-bāshī → ḲAṢṢĀBČI-BĀSHĪ

sallama → CEPKEN

sallār (A) : under the Saldjūḳs, a military governor, with SHIḤNA. I 434a

salsabīl (A) : in the Qurʾān, the name of a fountain in Paradise. VIII 999a; and → SHĀDIRWĀN; UḤDJIYYA

ṣalṣāl (A) : dry clay. I 177b

salṭana (A) : sovereignty, ruling power. VIII 1000b

salūḳī (A) : in zoology, the name given to a member of the gazehound family, so-called because it pursues its quarry by sight and not by scent. The ~ has often been mistaken for the greyhound by travellers to the Middle East. VIII 1001b

şalvar (T) : baggy trousers made out of two metres of silk cloth and with black braids embroidered around the leg openings and on the borders of the pockets, worn by the Zeybek of Western Anatolia as part of their folk costume. XI 494a

salwā (A, pl. *salāwā*) : in zoology, both the quail (*Coturnix coturnix*, of the order of Galliformae, family of Phasianidae), also called *sumānā* (pl. *sumānayāt*); and the corncrake or landrail (*Crex crex*, *Crex pratensis*, of the Rallidae family), whose mode of life is quite similar to that of the quail. In North Africa, the corncrake is known as the 'quails' mule', *baghl al-sammān*, and the 'slow, lazy one', *abu 'l-rakhwa*, because of its clumsy flight. VIII 1006a

ṣalwala → IFTITĀḤ

samʿ (A) : scriptural or Traditional authority; according to the Muʿtazila, reflection, *fikr*, must precede recourse to ~ . II 891b

♦ samʿī (A) : authoritarian. I 410a

samāʾ (A, pl. *samāwāt*) : lit. the upper part of anything, the sky, the heavens; for the ancient Arabs, ~ , in the most common meaning of 'heaven', was not primarily associated with the stars, but it was first the location for the 'high-flying clouds'. VIII 1014a

samāʿ (A) : hearing'; song, musical performance; in mysticism, the 'spiritual oratorio' which often accompanies the DHIKR session. II 224a; VIII 1018a; X 245a

In lexicology and grammar, ~ signifies 'that which is founded on authority', as opposed to *ḳiyāsī* 'founded on reason'. VIII 1018a

In education, ~ (pl. *samāʿāt*) means [certificate of] hearing, audition; authorisation; licence. VIII 1019b

♦ samaʿ-khāna (A) : a place for religious music-making and dancing. VIII 240b; VIII 415b

ṣamagh → ṢAMGH

samak (A, pl. *asmāk, sumūk, simāk*) : in zoology, fish, whether of fresh water or of the sea, often replaced by one of its two synonyms ḤŪT and *nūn* (< Akk). VIII 1020b

♦ samak ʿankabūt (A) : in zoology, the spider crab (*Maia squinado*). IX 40a

♦ samakat al-Iskandar (A) : lit. the fish of Alexander [the Great]; in zoology, the hammer-head shark (*Sphyrna zygaena*). VIII 1021a

samandal (A, < Gk) : in zoology, the salamander, which many early Arabic authors identified as a bird. VIII 1023b

samānghūnī (< P ?) : a loan-word in Arabic for the colour sky-blue. V 699b

samar (A, pl. *asmār*) : a conversation, an evening gossip; stories told at an evening gathering (especially with Ibn al-Nadīm) or stories in general; tales of the supernatural; reports. III 369b samāwa (A) : in architecture, the space above the first level (syn. RIWĀḲ). VIII 544b

samawī → YĀḲŪT AKHAB

ṣamgh (A, pl. *ṣumūgh*), or *ṣamagh* : in botany, gum resins, the desiccated latexes of several plants and the mixtures of natural resins (*rātīnadj*) with gum-like substances; ~ is usually used alone for ~ *ʿarabī*, gum arabic, the viscous secretion gained from the bark of the acacia tree (*ḳaraẓ*) and so called because it was exported from Arab ports and spread by the Arabs. V 798a; VIII 1042b; XI 150b

sāmī (A, < *Sām* 'Shem') : the relative adjective 'Semitic', as in *al-lughāt al-sāmiyya* 'the Semitic languages'. VIII 1007b

samīd, samīdh (A) : a semolina bread. V 42a

samīḳān (A, s. *samīḳ*) : two yokelets, a form of the yoke consisting of two pieces of wood, each encircling the neck of the ox like a collar and joining under the animal's dewlap, attached to each other by means of a rope. VII 22b

samīn → DASIM

sāmira (A, s. *sāmirī*) : the Samaritans, that part of the people of Israel which does not identify itself with Judaism. VIII 1044a

ṣāmit (A) : 'the Silent One', among several extremist shīʿī groups, the designation of a messenger of God who does not reveal a new Law, as opposed to AL-NĀṬIḲ, a speaking prophet. VIII 1046b

samm → SUMM

sāmm (A), or *al-sāmma* : a term for 'death', derived from *samm* 'poison' (→ SUMM). IX 872a

sammād → KANNĀS

ṣammān (A) : in geography, hard stony ground by the side of sands. VIII 1048a

sammūr (A) : in zoology, the sable. II 817a

samn (A) : butter, made from cows', goats' and ewes' milk, heated over the fire to extract its impurities, and hence called clarified butter (as distinct from *zubd* which is butter made from churned milk). VIII 1048b; XII 318b

samt (A, pl. *sumūt*) : in astronomy, azimuth or direction, usually applied to the direction of a celestial object measured on the horizon, determined by the arc of the horizon between the east- or west-points and the foot of the vertical arc through the celestial object. The complementary arc measured from the meridian was called *inḥirāf*, *munḥarifa* being applied to a vertical sundial inclined at a specific angle to the meridian. V 83; VIII 1054a

♦ samt al-raʾs (A) : lit. direction of the head; in astronomy, a term used to denote the point of the celestial sphere directly above the observer. VIII 1054a

samūm (A, > Eng *simoom*) : a hot wind of the desert accompanied by whirlwinds of dust and sand, and set in motion by moving depressions which form within the trade winds or calm zones of the high, subtropical depressions. This wind is especially characteristic of the Sahara, in Egypt, in Arabia and in Mesopotamia. VIII 1056a; ~ is hardly used in North Africa, where the hot wind is called, after its direction of origin, and according to the various regions, *ḳeblī* or *sharḳī*. VIII 1056b

samurāt (A) : in the pre-Islamic period, three sacred trees that stood before the sanctuary of al-ʿUzza at Nakhla, and were assimilated to the three divinities. V 692b

ṣanʿa (A) : in grammar, a formal process effected on an element of the language. V 804a; and → GHINĀʾ

♦ ṣanʿat-i ḳaṭʿ → ḲAṬʿ

sanad (A, T *sened*; pl. *asnād*) : lit. support, stay, rest; in administrative usage, a document on whch reliance can formally be placed (*masnūd*), hence an authenticated document. In Ottoman practice, a document with e.g. a seal attached. XII 703a; and → ISNĀD; SILSILA

sanadjāt, or *ṣanadjāt* (< P *sang*; s. *sandja* or *ṣandja*) : the weights of a balance, steel-yard; weights of a clock. IX 3a; counterweights or pellets discharged from the mouths of falcons in water-clocks. IX 3b

ṣanam (A) : image, representation; idol. ~ progressively replaced NUṢUB; from being the rough stone making up the *nuṣub*, the idol became 'a carved stone'. IX 5b; IX 282a; syn. *wathan*. XI 176B

sanamūra → SALĀMŪRA

ṣanawbar (A) : pine nut, pine-cone; in astronomy, the shadow of the earth during an eclipse of the moon. V 536a; IX 8b

ṣandal (A) : in botany, sandalwood. IX 9a

In the Maghrib, ~ indicates thyme (*nammām*) and the wild cultivated mint. IX 9b

ṣandj, or *ṣindj* (A) : in music, the generic term for any kind of cymbal. Other terms for the cymbal are *zīl* (< T *zill*), *kās*, *kāsa* or *ka'ṣ*, *sadjdja* or *sādjdja*, *fuḳaysha* (in Syria), *nuwayḳsa* (in Morocco), *ṣaffāḳatān*, and *musāfiḳ(a)*. IX 9b ff.; as *ṣandj ṣīnī* (Chinese ~), this musical instrument with 'open strings' and played on with beating rods was described by Ibn Sīnā and Ibn Zayla. It later became known as the SANṬŪR, and is clearly the dulcimer. VII 191a

sandjaḳ (T) : a flag, standard; ensign, cornet. I 4b; IX 11b

In Ottoman administration, ~ was a political region, a district of the feudal cavalry, and an administrative unit. I 468b; II 723b; IX 13a; and → LIWĀ'

Among the Yazīdīs, a sacred effigy of the Peacock Angel, the leader of the seven archangels to whom God entrusted the world. There were originally seven of these images, two of which are still known to exist. XI 315a

♦ sandjaḳdār : 'royal standard-bearer', distinguished in Mamlūk times from the ordinary *ʿalamdār*. IX 12b

♦ **sandjaḳ-i sherīf**, *liwā'-i sherīf*, or *ʿalem-i nebewī* (T) : the sacred standard of the Prophet, kept in the palace of Topkapı at Istanbul. IX 13b

ṣandūḳ → ḲABR; KAFAN

ṣanf : in geography, an island; a kingdom of the mainland, bordering on the sea; or a sea, apparently referring in travel accounts to Čampā or Champa, situated between Cambodia and the delta of the Song Coi in Vietnam. IX 17a

sang (P) : a (heavy) wooden board, the lifting of which while lying on one's back makes up one of the exercises done by wrestlers in a traditional gymnasium; others are push-ups, *shinā*, swinging Indian clubs, *mīl*, whirling at speed, *čarkh*, and stepping forth to swing above their heads a heavy iron bow, *kabbāda*, on the cord of which are strung heavy rings. XI 573a

♦ sang-i mūṣā (IndP) : black onyx. VIII 269a

sanga → WALI SANGA

ṣāniʿ → ADJĪR

sāniḥ (A) : a term applied to a wild animal or bird which passes from left to right before a traveller or hunter; it is generally interpreted as a good omen. I 1048a; 'that which travels from right to left', one of the technical terms designating the directions of a bird's flight, or an animal's steps, which play an important part in the application of divination known as FA'L, ṬĪRA and ZADJR. II 760a; IV 290b

sāniya (A) : in Muslim Spain, a type of pumping machine to irrigate land, along with the NĀʿŪRA. I 492a

saniyya (A) : in the Ottoman empire, lands which were the private freehold of the sultan, administered by a well-organised establishment called the *dā'ira saniyya*. After the revolution of 1908, ~ lands were ceded to the state and were transferred to the newly-formed department of *al-amlāk al-mudawwara*. XII 179a

sanja → NALAM
sant : in India, poet-saint. XII 483b
sanṭ (A) : in botany, acacia. IV 1085b
sanṭūr (A, < Ar), or *sinṭīr* : the dulcimer, a stringed musical instrument of similar structure to the psaltery, ḲĀNŪN, but with two of its sides oblique instead of one. The strings, which are mounted dichordally in Egypt, are of metal and are beaten with sticks instead of plectra as in the *ḳānūn*. In the time of Ibn Sīnā, it was called *ṣandj ṣīnī*. VII 191a; IX 19b
♦ sanṭūr turkī (A) : a dulcimer which is very popular in present-day Turkey. It has 160 strings, grouped in fives, giving 32 notes, and a two octave chromatic scale. VII 191b
♦ sanṭūr fransiz (A) : a dulcimer which is very popular in present-day Turkey. It is mounted with 105 strings, grouped in fives, which are placed on the sound-chest in the Occidental way. VII 191b
sar čarkhī (P) : in 19th-century southern Persia, a wheel tax paid for water wells by some districts. V 872a
ṣarʿ (A) : in medicine, epilepsy. X 510a
sarāb (A) : mirage, specifically the illusion of water seen at midday which appears to be on the ground, as opposed to *āl*, which is seen early and late in the day and makes things appear to float in mid-air and quiver. IX 27a
sarafsār (P, A *ḥakama*, N.Afr *djabbādha*) : a fixed martingale, attached to the horse's bridle. It was Persian in origin, appearing ca. the 5th/11th century in miniature paintings.. IV 1145a
saraḳusṭiyya (A) : a type of fur produced in Saraḳusṭa, in Muslim Spain. IX 37a
sarāna (P) : beginning with the Mongol conquest, a poll-tax. IV 1042b
sarāparda (P) : lit. palace curtain, term applied to the great tent carried round by the sultans of the Saldjūḳs. IX 39b; and → ĀFRĀG
sarāpāy (P) : in Persian literature, a genre of poetry devoted to the description of an ideal human body 'from top to toe', fashionable in the 10th-11th/16th-17th centuries. VI 834b
sarār → MUNSALAKH
saraṭān (A, pl. *sarāṭīn*) : in zoology, crustaceans (*ḳishriyyāt*) in general and, more specifically, those which are collected for human consumption (*maḥāra*). IX 40a
In astronomy, *al-~* is the term for Cancer, one of the twelve zodiacal constellations. VII 83a; IX 40b
♦ saraṭān al-baḥr : in zoology, the lobster (*Homarus vulgaris*), the crab (*Carcinus*). IX 40a, where many synonyms are found
♦ saraṭān nahrī : in zoology, the crayfish, river lobster. IX 40a
♦ saraṭān nāsik : in zoology, the hermit crab, soldier crab, also known as *ḳaṭā*. IX 40a
sarāy (P) : dwelling, habitation, house, palace; compounded with another substantive ~ indicates a particular kind of building, as in KĀRWĀN SARĀY. IX 44a
sarb (A) : in zoology, the grey gilthead, whose Arabic term is found again in the Latinised nomenclature to specify a sub-species limited to a particular region (*Chrysophrys sarba*). VIII 1021a
sārbān → YURTČÎ
sard → DIRʿ
ṣard → SARDSĪR
sardāb (P, pl. *sarādīb*; A *sirdāb*) : lit. cool water; in architecture, an underground recess in a dwelling, motivated by the fierce sun and hot summer of ʿIrāḳ and Persia. II 114a; IX 49b; any kind of underground room or passage. IX 49b; semi-underground chamber. XI 302a; a small room supplied with cool water. V 12b

sardam → GAWD

sardār (P, A *sirdār*, T *serdār*) : lit. holding or possessing the head; supreme military commander, whose post or office is called *sardāriyyat*. ~ *bahādur* was a title of honour in British India, given to Indian commissioned officers. IX 50b; in the Ottoman army, *serdār-i ekrem* was the term for the commander-in-chief. IX 14a

♦ sardāriyyat → SARDĀR

sardsīr (P, A *ṣard*) : lit. cold region; a geographical term used to denote cool, temperate highland regions. It also serves as a synonym to the Turkish ḲI̊SHLAḲ, i.e. the winter pasture grounds of nomads. In Arabic, ~ or *ṣard* is particularly used for the mountainous Zagros hinterland of Fārs and Kirmān. V 183a

sardj (A, pl. *surūdj*) : horse saddle. IX 51a

♦ sarīdja : mule or camel saddle. IX 51a

ṣarf (A) : in law, the contract of exchange of gold for gold, silver for silver, and gold and silver for each other. This is one of two contracts which become invalid if the material transfer does not take place at the time of the agreement, the other being SALAM. IV 326a; XII 703a

In early Arabic grammar, full declination, said of a noun; also, as used by al-Farrāʾ in particular, the divergence or non-identity between two constituents of the sentence. In later grammer ~ came to indicate the science of 'morphology'. IX 53a,b; X 360b; and → NAḤW; TAṢRĪF

♦ ṣarfa (A) : lit. turning away; in the science of the Qurʾān, a concept that God prevented the competent from taking up the challenge of producing even one SŪRA like those Muḥammad recited, thus proving that it was impossible. V 426b

sarhang (P) : in mediaeval Persian (para)military, a rank of officer or commander. In modern Persian, the rank of colonel. IX 54a

ṣari̊ (T) : 'pale-faced'. IV 884b

sarī → BURḲUʿ

sariʿ (A) : in prosody, the name of the ninth Arabic metre. I 670a; IX 54b

sārīfūn → SHĪḤ

sāriḳ → LIṢṢ

ṣari̊ḳ (T) : a headband, used to wind around a ḲAVUḲ. IV 806a; X 614a

♦ ṣari̊ḳdji̊ : under the Ottomans, a turban-maker. X 609b

sariḳa (A) : in law, theft, for which the Qurʾān prescribes cutting off the right hand. Islamic legal theory distinguishes between two types: *al-sariḳa al-ṣughrā* 'theft' and *al-sariḳa al-kubrā* 'highway robbery or brigandage'. V 768a; IX 62b

In literary criticism, plagiarism. XII 707a

sārindā : in music, an Indian open chest viol with three strings. VIII 348b

sarīr (A), and *takht* : a throne-like seat, not used at mealtimes, however. In the case of ~, two people could sit on it, hence it was quite a long seat; *takht* could mean any of the following: board, seat, throne, sofa, bed, calculating tablet, chest or box. V 509a; XII 99a,b; and → MINAṢṢA

In the geography of the Libyan Desert, a plain of compressed gravel. V 352a

sariyya (A) : in military science, a detachment of the army. XII 532b

sarkār (P) : lit. head of affairs; in Mughal Indian administration, a district in hierarchy under the *ṣūba* 'province' and above the PARGANA or MAḤALL 'subdistrict'; in informal Anglo-Indian usage through British Indian times, often written 'Sircar', the state or the government, the British domination in India, 'the Raj' being a neologism of the post-1947 period in modern India; in modern-day India, anglicised as 'the (northern) Circars', specifically the coastal territory north of Madras and the Coromandel coast in penisular South India. XII 710a

♦ **sarkār āḳā** (P) : 'lord and chief', a term used for a number of heterodox religious leaders within the broad s͟hīʿī tradition. IX 63b

sarlawḥ → ʿUNWĀN

ṣarmātiyya (A) : shoemakers. IX 168b

ṣarrāf (A) : lit. money-changer, a banker in pre-modern Islam. XII 710a

sarrāk͟h → HINDIBĀʾ

sārt (T, < San) : merchant; all sedentary Muslims, irrespective of language or ethnicity; later, ~ came to mean the Persian-speaking sedentary population, in contrast to *türk*, which was used for the Turkic-speaking nomadic or semi-nomadic population; even later, among the Uzbeks in the 19th century, ~ was chiefly used for Turkic-speaking or bilingual town-dwellers, while TĀD͟JĪK, earlier synonymous, was reserved for Persian-speakers only. IX 66b ff.; X 63b

sārūd͟j (P) : mortar. V 868b

sarw (A) : in botany, a cypress. IX 70a

sāsānī (A, P, < A *banū sāsān*) : beggar, trickster; pertaining to magic or sleight-of-hand. IX 70a

saʿtar (A) : in botany, thyme bushes. V 390a

satr (A) : 'concealment'; among the Ismāʿīliyya, ~ denotes the periods of absence of an IMĀM. II 1026b; XII 712a

Among the Druze, ~ refers to the period of absence of al-Ḥakim and Ḥamza. II 1026b

sattūk͟ (A), or *suttūk͟* : in numismatics, base coins coated with gold or silver. X 409b

saʾuri, or *tuzg͟hü* : under the Īlk͟hāns, an *ad hoc* impost laid by governors and officials in position of power on the population under their control. VIII 312b

ṣawāb → K͟HAṬĀʾ

sawād (A) : rural district, environs of town. VIII 636a; IX 87a; 'black land', the oldest Arabic name for the alluvial land on the Euphrates and Tigris, now Iraq. IX 87a; agricultural settlement. V 345b

ṣawāfī → ṢAFĪ

sawār → SUWĀR

sawgand-nāma (P) : in literature, an oath-poem. IX 116b

sawīk͟ (A) : in pre-Islamic times, a kind of dried barley meal to which was added water, butter or fat from the tails of sheep. II 1059a; IX 93b; X 901a; also, a fermented beverage with a basis of barley and honey. II 1060a; and → S͟HARĀB

ṣawlad͟jān (A, < P *čawgān* 'polo stick'): in literature, used as a trope for the curving eyebrows and locks or tresses of hair of a beuatiful girl. XII 713a; and → KURA

In music, a drumstick. X 33b

sawm (A) : in law, the bargaining involving both vendor and purchaser that occurs before a sale. ~ differs from BAYʿ in that the former is no more than an offer to enter into the latter after the manifest approval of the vendor. IX 93b; pasture (to which animals are sent). XI 412a

ṣawm (A), or *ṣiyām* : fasting, one of the five pillars of Islam. V 424b; IX 94a

In zoology, the dung of an ostrich. VII 829a

♦ ṣawm al-taṭawwuʿ : in religious law, voluntary or supererogatory fasting. IX 95a

ṣawmaʿa (A, > Sp *zoma*; pl. *ṣawāmiʿ*) : the minaret, other terms for the minaret being MANĀRA and *miʾd͟hana*. Originally, ~ means the cell in which a person (usually a monk) secludes himself, with the particular gloss that the cell has a slender pointed apex; later, ~ came to designate the entire structure of which the cell was a small part. VI 362b

In North Africa, ~ is the standard term for minaret, and is also used more generally to mean 'a higher place' and 'a high building'. VI 362b sawsan → SŪSAN

ṣawt (A) : in grammar, the resonance (emitted from the chest), which the Arab grammarians contrast with *nafas*, the expiratory breath. III 597a; sound or speech sound. IX 96a

♦ ṣawtiyya (A) : in grammar, the modern phonetical description of Arabic. IX 95b

sawwāk̲ (A) : in mediaeval times, a seller of roast meat. XII 757b; and → SĀʾIS

saʿy (A) : during the pilgrimage, the ritual of traversing seven times (four times going
and three times returning) the distance between al-Ṣafā and al-Marwa. III 35a; IX 97b

ṣayd (A) : the pursuit and capture of wild animals; wild game. IX 98b

ṣaydana (A), or *ṣaydala* : in the eastern Muslim world, pharmacology, in the meaning
of pharmacognosy; the druggist's actual store of drugs; the handbook of drugs, the
pharmacopeia. The druggist is called *al-ṣaydanālī* or *al-ṣaydanānī*, and is practically
synonymous with ʿAṬṬĀR. In the West, the corresponding terms are *[ʿilm] al-adwiya al-
mufrada* or *al-murakkaba*, or *[ʿilm] al-ʿuṭūr/ʿaṭṭār*. IX 100a

♦ ṣaydanānī, or *ṣaydanālī* → ṢAYDANA

ṣaydjān (A) : in zoology, the sidjan scarus, whose Arabic term is found again in the Latinised
nomenclature to specify a sub-species limited to a particular region (*Scarus siganus*).
VIII 1021b

sāyebān (Ott) : in the Ottoman empire, the so-called shadow-hanging, a large tent of
three poles, carried by a vizier on campaign. XI 196b

sayf (A, pl. *suyūf*) : in military science, the broad-bladed, short sword, the weapon most
frequently mentioned in the ancient literary sources, probably stabbing swords for
close, hand-to-hand combat rather than cavalry swords. The ~ of Indian steel (*hindī,
muhannad*) were particularly prized. XII 735a; XII 736b

In mediaeval agriculture, the dual (*sayfān*) is used for the holding bar of the ploughshare. VII 22b

♦ sayfī (A) : the 'sword-member', one of two classes of the ordinary members of
the AK̲H̲Ī organisation, YIGIT, who probably were the active members. The other class
was made up of *k̲awlī*s 'word-members'. I 323a

ṣayf → ṢĀʾIFA

ṣayḥa (Yem) : a declaimer of tribal poetry. IX 234b; a cry, used in the Qurʾān with reference to the T̲h̲amūd when they hamstrung the 'camel of God'. X 436a

saykarān (A, < Syr *s̲h̲ak̲h̲rōnā*), or *sīkrān, s̲h̲ukrān* : in botany, henbane (*hyoscyamus*) to
the early physicians of western Islam. Later Arab botanists used ~ for another henbane
(*hyoscyamus muticus*) which drives the taker mad, and also for the hemlock. I 1014b

sayl → NAHR

sayr (A) : in mysticism, a visionary voyage, a degree of the mystical journey. IX 863a

ṣayr (A) : small fish, preserved by salting and smoking. VIII 1023a

ṣayyād → TŪTIN

ṣayyāg̲h̲ (A) : a goldsmith. XII 757b

sayyāra → KAWKAB

sayyiʾa → D̲H̲ANB

sayyid (A, pl. *asyād, sāda, sādāt*) : originally chief, e.g. of an Arabian tribe; later, in
Islamic times, a title of honour for descendants of the Prophet. IX 115a; IX 333a;
master; the equivalent of Mr or Esquire. I 24b; II 687b; IX 332a ff; and → AS̲H̲RĀF;
MAWLĀY; MURĀBIṬ

♦ sayyid al-s̲h̲uhadāʾ : appellation of the Prophet's paternal uncle, Ḥamza b. ʿAbd al-
Muṭṭalib. IX 204b

♦ sayyid al-tumūr → ṢUFRĪ

♦ sayyida : the title of Madam, in contemporary Arabic usage. IX 332b

♦ sayyidī, or *sīdī* : originally the term used by a slave to address his/her master, came
to be applied to persons regarded as holy, especially mystical masters or ṣūfīs in general. IX 332b f.

sāz (T), or *bağlama* : in music, the Turkish lute; used in Persian for a musical instrument in general, stringed instruments, wind instruments, and the musical band itself. IX 120a; a stringed instrument, which frequently accompanied Turkish folk religious poetry, NEFES. VIII 2b; for names in our time corresponding to the different lute sizes, IX 120a

In Balūčistān, ~ also means the tuning of instruments. IX 120a

♦ sāz-i kāsāt (P) : lit. musical bowls, earthenware bowls, the notes of which were determined by the amount of water with which each was filled. IX 11b

♦ sāz-i alwāḥ-i fūlād (P) : 'instrument of slabs of steel', a glockenspiel, comprising 35 slabs, each giving a particular note. IX 11b

sebkha → SABKHA

sefīr → SAFĪR

segāh → SHASHMAḲOM

segbān (T, Ott *sekbān, segmen,* < P *sagbān* 'servant in charge of dogs') : in the Ottoman military, first used for the guardians of the sultan's hunting dogs, then applied to member of various salaried infantry units within the Janissaries, and finally as the name of groups of infantry auxiliaries or militias. In present-day provincial Turkish, *seğmen* refers to an armed ceremonial escort in national dress. II 1121a; III 317b; XII 713a

sekbān → SEGBĀN

sekkīn (Mor) : a sword with an almost straight blade, carried by the horsemen making up the *djīsh* (→ DJAYSH). II 511a

selāmlïḳ (T), or *selāmlïḳ dā'iresi* : under the Ottomans, the outer, more public rooms of a traditionally-arranged house, used e.g. for the reception of guests and non-family members. IX 123a; the men's part of a house. IX 540b

♦ selāmlïḳ ālāyï : the Ottoman sultan's ceremonial procession from the palace to the mosque for Friday worship. IX 123a

selīmī → YŪSUFĪ

semedi (J) : with *tapa*, ascetic feats and a form of Javanese meditation. XI 537a

semer (T) : a kind of padded saddle, worn on the back of a street-porter in Istanbul, *ḥammāl*, on which the weight of the burden rests. III 139a

sêqut : a land-leasing system in Kurdish Iran, in which the landowner supplies soil and water and receives two-thirds of the harvest. V 473b

seraghūdj, seraḳūdj → KŪDJ

serambi : in Indonesia, the front veranda of a mosque, often the place of the religious court; by extension, Islamic judge. VIII 294a

ser'asker (T) : under the Ottomans, an army commander; after the destruction of the Janissaries in 1241/1826, ~ denoted a commanding officer who combined the functions of commander-in-chief and minister of war, inheriting also the responsibility for public security, police, firefighting etc. in the capital. I 838a; II 513a; III 552b

serbest (T) : an Ottoman term connoting the absence of limitations or restrictions. III 589b

♦ serbest tīmār : under the Ottomans, a fief in which all the revenues go to the timariot, as against an ordinary TĪMĀR in which certain revenues are reserved for the imperial exchequer. III 589b; a category of TĪMĀR that enjoyed certain immunities. X 505b

serčeshme (T) : under the Ottomans, the title for the leader of all irregular militia, LEWENDS. VIII 185a

serdār → SARDĀR

sere (T 'palm') : lit. spreading-out; in calligraphy a geometrical figure appearing from the crowded group of intersecting lines formed by the names of the sultan and his father, placed at the bottom of the verticals of the TUGHRA. X 596b

sergüdhesht-nāme (T) : in Turkish literature, a genre of the tale of adventure, where the poet tells the story of an affair with one beautiful person or stories of four people. IX 213a

sesajen (J) : the bringing of offerings in the form of a blessed ceremonial meal, *slamatan*, during a visit to a holy place in Java. XI 537a

setre (T) : a military garment covering the knee and fastened at the front, worn in Turkey up to the 13th/19th century. V 752a; VIII 371a

sêykbar : a land-leasing system in Kurdish Iran, in which the landowner supplies the land, the water, the seed and the beasts of labour, and takes a portion of the harvest. V 473b

shā' al-ḍa'n (A), and *shiyāh al-ḍa'n, ḍā'ina* : sheep. XII 316b

shab-niwīs (IndP) : in the Dihlī sultanate, the secretarial officer on night duty in the palace. IV 759a

shaʿb (A, pl. *shuʿūb*) : in the Sabaean social organisation of pre-Islamic southwest Arabia, a social unit consisting of a number of clans, one of which occupied a dominating position. IV 746a; IV 819a; IX 150b

In geography, ~ (pl. *shiʿbān*) is the coral reef, in particular those off the Arabian coast southwards to the Red Sea. The term ~ is not used for the reef on the Arabian side of the Persian Gulf, where e.g. FASHT is used. I 535a

In politics, ~ evolved from 'a people' to 'the people', i.e. the ruled, later to signify the common people, the deprived lower classes, those who were previously outside the circle of power (also often simply called *djamāhīr* 'masses'). IX 151a ff.

shabāb (A) : young manhood, one of the terms designating a specific period within childhood. VIII 821b; this period extends from puberty to the end of the thirties, or from 15 to 32 years of age. IX 383a

Among the Yazīdīs, a flute. XI 315a

♦ shabābiyya, or *shabība* : with *shabāb*, youth and the beginnings of adulthood, as well as the vigour of this age. IX 383a

shabāblikiyya (A, < Ar ?) : a variety of outer garment, ʿABĀ', made in Ḥasbaya and worn in Syria and Palestine. V 741b

shaʿbadha (A), or *shaʿwadha* : in divination, prestidigitation, sleight of hand, hence *mushaʿbidh* (*mushaʿwidh*) 'magician, trickster'. IX 152b

shabah (A) : similarity. V 240a; in law, *ḳiyās al-~* 'analogy of resemblance' is the less authoritative type of analogical reasoning distinguished by al-Shāfiʿī, the other being *ḳiyās al-maʿnā*. III 1129b ; IX 184a

In mineralogy, ~ (syn. *bīrindj*) is brass, an alloy of copper and zinc. V 971a

shabala (A) : a technical term of childhood, said of someone who has become a youth or young man. VIII 822a

shaʿbān (A) : name of the eighth month of the Islamic lunar year, called *shab-i barāt* in Indian Islam. IX 154a

♦ shaʿbāna (Mor) : in Morocco, a festival resembling a carnival celebrated on the last day of SHAʿBĀN. IX 154b

shabb (A) : in metallurgy, alum. V 965a ff.; and → ḲILY

shābb (A) : youth, young man.

♦ al-shābb al-ẓarīf : 'the elegant, witty youth', nickname for the poet Ibn al-ʿAfīf al-Tilimsānī. X 500a

shabbāba (A) : in music, a flute. VI 214b; XII 667a

shabbūṭ (A) : in botany, a certain kind of fish. X 769a; a round and flat fish. XI 427b

shabība → SHABĀBIYYA

shābīr → MIHMĀZ

shābīzadj → YABRŪḤ

shabrūsh → NUḤĀM

shabshaba (A) : a ritual mostly current in Egypt in which a woman casts a spell by beating her genitals with a slipper while pronouncing a magic formula to jinx and inattentive husband or a female rival. XII 776b

shabūb (A) : in the terminology of horse-riding, a horse that rears. II 954a

shabūr → MIHMĀZ

shabūrḳān : in metallurgy, meteoric steel, often mentioned in early Arabic literature, with the comment that it was a rare material. V 971b

shadd (A), or *shadd al-wasṭ* 'binding up the waist' : the act of girding with an initiatic belt or girdle; in certain mystical orders, the belt or girdle itself. The origin of the act of girding is attributed to the *kustī*, the sacred girdle of the Zoroastrians, the girding of which was a rite of passage into manhood. The novice girded with the ~ was known as *mashdūd* or, more fully, *mashdūd al-wasṭ*. IX 167a; the official appointed by the Fāṭimids to wind the caliph's turban, later called *laffāf*. X 57b; X 614a; the turban-cloth, then the whole turban, used as such particularly in North Africa and Egypt. Sometimes ~ was particularly the white-and-blue striped turban of the Copts, while that of the Muslim world was called SHĀSH. X 614a

♦ shadd al-walad : in guild terminology, the ceremony whereby the apprentice entered into his profession. IX 168b

♦ shadda (A), or *tashdīd* : in orthography, the special sign for marking the doubling of a consonant. IV 1120a

shadh (T) : a rank given to senior members of the princely family below the Ḳaghan. III 1060b

shādhana (A) : in mineralogy, haematite, which results from converting magnetite or other minerals (syn. *bāhit* or *ḥadjar al-bahta*). V 1166b f.

shādhdh (A) : in the science of Tradition, a Tradition from a single authority which differs from what others report. If it differs from what people of greater authority transmit, or if its transmitter is not of sufficient reliability to have his unsupported Traditions accepted, it is rejected. III 25b; VII 576a; irregular. IX 371a

shadīda (A) : 'energetic'; in grammar, a division equivalent in modern phonetics to 'occlusive', designating the letters *hamza, ḳ, dj, ṭ, t, d, b*. III 599a

shādirwān (A, < P) : originally, a precious curtain or drapery suspended on tents of sovereigns and leaders and from balconies of palaces; in architecture, a wall fountain surmounted by a decorative niche, usually made of painted and gilded wood with MUḲARNAS, and connected to a sloping marble panel, *salsabīl*, which led the water from the wall down into a stone or marble basin. The function of the ~ , which faced the SABĪL window, was not only decorative but it served also to air the water coming from the cistern. VIII 680a; IX 175a

shadjara (A) : in botany, a tree; and → RIDFA

♦ shadjarat al-ḥubb → IKLĪL AL-MALIK

♦ shadjarat al-ṣanam → SIRĀDJ AL-ḲUṬRUB

shadjawī (A) : in the mediaeval Near East, a beggar who pretends to have been imprisoned and loaded with chains for fifty years. VII 494b

shadjr (A) : in anatomy, the corner, or commissure, of the lips. II 75a; III 598a; the side of the mouth. VI 129b

♦ shadjriyya (A) : in grammar, a term used by al-Khalīl possibly denoting lateral, for use in phonetics, but its meaning remains obscure. III 598a

shādūf (A) : the contrivance used for raising water, still in use in certain eastern countries. It is a simple machine consisting of a wooden beam pivoted on a raised fulcrum. At one end of the beam is a bucket, at the other end a counterweight. The bucket is dipped into the water, then the beam is rotated by means of the counterweight and the contents of the bucket are emptied into a cistern or supply channel. IV 629a; V 861a

shafʿ (A) : a prayer consisting of an even number of RAKʿAS. X 97b

shafāʿa (A) : in eschatology, the intercession or mediation by certain persons, and notably Muḥammad, for others on the Last Day. He who makes the intercession is called both *shāfiʿ* and *shafīʿ*. I 334b; IX 177b
In law, intercession for a debtor. IX 177b
Also, the laying of a petition before a king. IX 177b

shafaḳ (A) : the red colour of the sky after sunset. I 733b; the evening twilight, the time at which the MAGHRIB prayer should be performed. V 709a; VIII 928b; morning or evening twilight, the periods between daybreak and sunrise and between sunset and nightfall. IX 179b
♦ al-shafaḳ al-aḥmar (A) : 'the red dawn', which follows upon the 'true dawn' (→ AL-FADJR AL-KĀDHIB). IX 179b

shaghaba (A) : 'to wander away from the road, excite people against each other, kick up a row', one of a number of verbs to describe rebellion, as *ʿaṣā* 'to rebel', *thāra* 'to raise dust by galloping through the sands like a bull, to assault', and *ḳalaba* 'to overturn, be reversed' (whence *inḳilāb*, used in the 20th century for a coup d'état fomented by a small number of individuals, often military men). XII 598a

shāgird → MURĪD

shāh (P) : king; in set phrases ~ means 'pre-eminent, principal'. IX 190b f.
In chess, the chesspiece king. A game was won by ~ *māt* 'checkmate'. IX 366b
In the Indian subcontinent, ~ is appended to the names of persons claiming descent from the Prophet and has today become a surname. IX 191a
♦ **shāhanshāh** (P) : king of kings. IX 190b
♦ **shāhī** (P) : lit. royal, kingly; in numismatics, a Ṣafawid principal coin, valued at 50 dīnārs. VIII 790a; IX 203a
♦ shāhī safīd (P) : the 'white *shāhī*', term used to distinguish the silver coin from the copper or 'black' *shāhī*. IX 203b
♦ shāhmurk (A, < P *shāhmurgh* 'kingbird') : in zoology, one of the arabicised forms for the Sultan-fowl, whose splendid plumage earned him the title of 'king' of the birds. XII 20a
♦ shāhzāde (P, T **shehzāde**) : prince, one of the titles used for the male children born to a reigning Ottoman sultan, gradually superseding the earlier term ČELEBI. IX 414a

shahāda (A) : the Islamic confession of faith, one of the five pillars of Islam. I 332b; IX 201a
In law, testimony, witnessing. I 28b; IX 201a
In Urdu poetry, the *shahādat* is the part of the elegy, MARTHIYA, where the death of the martyr is described, either al-Ḥusayn or some member of his family. VI 611b
♦ shahādat al-lafīf (A) : in law, the testimony of a group of at least twelve men, who need not be ʿADL, a practice which came into existence during the 16th and 17th centuries in North Africa. IX 208a
♦ al-shahāda bi 'l-tasāmuʿ (A) : in law, testimony on the strength of public knowledge, i.e. without having witnessed the event or the legal act that is at the basis of it. IX 208a
♦ al-shahāda ʿalā 'l-shahāda (A) : in law, the testimony of a witness which is transmitted by two other witnesses. IX 208a

shahārdah, or *djahārdah, arbaʿata ʿashara*: 'fourteen', a recreational board game, which could involve stakes. V 109a

shāhbandar (P) : lit. harbour, port master; a term for a customs officer, collector of taxes; in Turkish usage, a consul and, formerly, a merchant's syndic. I 1013a; IX 193b; XII 716a
In Indonesia, ~ denotes the harbour master, appointed by the local ruler or sultan and

chosen from among the foreign traders who had settled in the port. In big harbours, more than one ~ were sometimes active. He supervised the merchandise, took care of the transport and storage, inspected the markets and guaranteed the security of the ships and the well-being of their crew, passengers and tradesmen. Tolls were fixed on his estimate of the value of the goods carried by the ship. VI 209b; IX 194b; XII 199b

shāhdānadj (P) : hemp; in modern-day Persian, the hemp seed. III 267a; IX 202a

shāhī → ČAY; MUḤAMMADĪ

shāhid (A, pl. **shawāhid**) : witness, one who gives testimony, *shahāda,* which in Islamic law is the paramount medium of legal evidence, alongside *iḳrār* 'acknowledgement' and *yamīn* 'oath'. IX 207a; and → SHĀHID ʿADL

In literary theory, a probative quotation, most often testimony in verse, which serves to establish a rule in the 'literary sciences'. IX 370b; proof text. IX 459a

♦ shāhid ʿadl (A), or, briefly, *shāhid* or *ʿadl* : in law, a professional witness whose ʿADĀLA has been established by the court, first appearing in Egypt at the beginning of the 8th century AD. IX 208a

shahīd (A, pl. *shuhadāʾ*) : witness; martyr, of which there are two types: *shuhadāʾ al-maʿraka* 'battlefield martyrs', who have special burial rites, and *shuhadāʾ al-ākhira* 'martyrs in the next world only'. IX 203b ff.

♦ shuhadāʾ al-dunyā (A) : 'martyrs in this world only', martyrs accorded the burial rights of the battlefield martyrs, *shuhadāʾ al-maʿraka*, but not the rewards in the next world, because they went into battle without the right intention. IX 206b

♦ shuhadāʾ al-ghurba (A) : 'martyrs who died far from home', those who leave their homes, e.g. in order to preserve their faith in times of persecution, and die in a foreign land. IX 206a

♦ shuhadāʾ al-ḥubb (A) : 'martyrs of love', according to a prophetic Tradition, those who love, remain chaste, conceal their secret and die. IX 206a

shāhidjānī (A) : term for fine cotton materials originating from Khurāsān, called after Marw, which full name is Marw al-Shāhidjān 'Royal Marw'. V 554b

shāhīn : a musical instrument which would appear to have been a small three-holed recorder such as was common with pipe and tabor players in mediaeval Western Europe. It was played with the fingers of one hand, the other hand being used for beating the drum. VII 209b; and → ČAKÎR

In the Mughal infantry, a swivel-gun or wall-piece, one of the light artillery. V 687a

shahmurk : in zoology, the Purple Gallinule. V 8b

shaḥna-i mandī → MANDĪ

shāhnāmedji → SHEHNĀMEDJI

shahr (P, T *shehir*) : town; kingdom. IX 212a

♦ **shahrangīz** (P), and *shahrāshūb* 'upsetting the town' : in Persian literature, a genre of short poetical witticisms or love poems on young artisans, usually quatrains but also occurring as ḲAṢĪDAs, fashionable in the 10th-11th/16th-17th centuries. IV 59a; VI 834a; VIII 776b; IX 212a

♦ shahr-āshob (U, < P *shahrāshūb*) : in Urdu literature, a socially-motivated poem, whose main purpose is the portrayal of a city in disarray, by naming a series of professions and describing the state of affairs governing the individuals associated with each of them. IX 213b

♦ shahrāshūb → SHAHRANGĪZ

♦ **shehir emāneti** (T) : in the Ottoman empire, the term for two successive institutions, filled by the *shehir emīni*. The first involved the construction, repair, provisioning and payment of salaries of the personnel of the imperial palaces, and the functionary was in rank one of the four great civilian dignitaries of the outside administration of the palace. This institution died out to appear again in the latter half of the 19th century whereby the functionary, who was more of a town prefect, had duties as that of cleansing and keeping tidy the city and touring the markets and bazaars. IX 413a

♦ **shehir ketkhüdasi** (T) : in the Ottoman empire, an official whose primary function was to collect the specified taxation from a town or its quarters. IX 414a

shahristān (P) : lit. place of kingship; province, provincial capital, (large) town; in modern Iran, a sub-provincial administrative district. I 2b; IX 220a

shahrūd, or *shāhrūdh* : in music, an instrument of the lute family allegedly invented in 299/912 by Ḥakīm b. Aḥwaṣ al-Ṣughdī, which in al-Fārābī's day had a compass of three octaves. According to Ibn Ghaybī, it had ten double strings and was twice the length of the ordinary ʿŪD. X 769b

shāhrūdh → SHAHRŪD

shāhrukhī → TANGA-YI NUḲRA

shahwa (A) : longing, appetite; also the term for a birthmark on a child (in the shape of the food the pregnant mother craved but was not given). XI 32b; and → ʿAṢABIYYA

shāʿir (A) : poet. IX 225a; XII 717b; in northern Egypt, ~ has come to mean Gypsy poets who perform on the Egyptian two-string spike-fiddle, *rabāb*. IX 235b; and → KHAṬĪB

♦ shāʿir al-balāṭ (A) : poet laureate. IX 229b

♦ syair (Mal, Ind, < A *shāʿir*) : an extended verse form, which may run to hundreds of stanzas, each of which consists of four lines with the same end rhyme. The composer of ~ is called a *penyair*. IX 244a; XII 727B

♦ shāʿira (A, pl. *shaʿāʾir*) : term denoting the *budna* (→ SINĀM), extended in the plural to all the rites of the pilgrimage. IX 424b

shaʿīr (A) : in botany, barley. V 863a; IX 225a

♦ māʾ shaʿīr (A) : lit. barley water; the name for 'barley beer', of which a special variety was drunk in mediaeval Islam during the nights of the month of Ramaḍān. VI 721b

♦ shaʿīra (A) : in music, the cylinder inserted into the head of a reed-pipe which lowered the pitch when required. Later, this device was called *ṭawḳ* or *faṣl*. VII 207a

shaḳāʾ → SHAḲĀWA

shaḳāʾiḳ → SHAḲĪḲAT AL-NUʿMĀN

shaḳāwa (A), or *shaḳwa*, *shaḳāʾ* : misfortune, misery, used both in the meaning of a situation in this world and in the hereafter. IX 246b

In astrology, the concept of ~ is described by the term *naḥs* (→ SAʿD WA-NAḤS). IX 247a

shākhiṣ → MIḲYĀS

shakhṣ (A) : lit. bodily form, shape; in philosophy, an individual, a person. I 409b; IX 247b f.; and → MIḲYĀS

In modern law, ~ is found in the compounds *shakhṣ ṭabīʿī* 'natural person' and *shakhṣ iʿtibārī* 'assumed person', coined under the influence of western legal systems. IX 247b

♦ shakhṣiyya (A) : legal personality, a concept that does not exist in Islamic law, at least historically, and is subsumed by AHLIYYA. IX 248a

shakhshīkha : in music, the general term for the rattle. IX 11b

shakhtūr (Ir) : a wooden raft, used on the Euphrates since it is not navigable by steamers. I 461a

shaḳīḳa (A) : a full sister, in the law of inheritance, as opposed to a half-sister on the father's side, *ukht li 'l-ab*. I 320a

♦ **shaḳīḳat al-nuʿmān** (A, P *lāla*, Ber *ṭīkūk*, SpA *ḥababawar*), or *shaḳāʾiḳ al-nuʿmān, shaḳir* : in botany, the anemone. Both *shaḳāʾiḳ* and *nuʿmān* can be used separately as synonyms. IX 248b

shākila (A) : in calligraphy, the upper horizontal stroke of the letter *kāf*. X 598a

shākima → ḤAKMA

shaḳir → SHAḲĪḲAT AL-NUʿMĀN

shākiriyya (A, < P *čākir*) : a term denoting private militias fighting under the patronage of princes from the ruling dynasty, or commanders belonging to the class of military nobility, during Umayyad and ʿAbbāsid rule. IX 249b; among the Turkic Oghuz tribes, a guard corps (termed *shākirī* by al-Marwazī). X 556b

shakk (A) : perplexity, uncertainty, doubt. There is some suggestion that ~ refers to the objective fact of uncertainty and another word, *rayb*, to the state of perplexity consequent to that fact. IX 250a

In mineralogy, arsenic. IX 872b

♦ shakka → ITHTHAGHARA

shākk → ʿAṢĀ

shakkāziyya (A) : in astronomy, the term for the markings, consisting of two families of orthogonal circles, of a universal stereographic projection which underlies a family of astronomical instruments serving all terrestrial latitudes. IX 251b; an instrument that is apparently a simplified version of the *ʿabbādiyya* type, with only one complete grid of equatorial coordinates and an ecliptical grid limited to the great circles of longitude for the beginnings of the zodiacal signs on its face, while its back resembles that of a standard astrolabe. XI 461b

shakl (A, pl. *ashkāl*) : 'figure'; in geomancy, 'squill'. IV 1128b

In prosody, a type of double deviation (ZIḤĀF), whereby there are two cases per foot, combining KHABN and KAFF. XI 508b

♦ shakl al-ḳaṭṭāʿ (A) : in spherical trigonometry, the principle of the transversal. V 397a

♦ al-shakl al-mughnī (A) : in spherical trigonometry, the principle of the four magnitudes. V 397a

♦ al-shakl al-ẓillī (A) : in spherical trigonometry, the principle of the tangent. V 397a

shakshāk (N.Afr) : in North Africa, a round tambourine with both snares and jingling implements, called in other parts *ṭabīla*. II 621b

shaḳshīr → ČAḲSHĪR

shakwa (A) : a goatskin container, in which fresh milk is churned by swinging on posts. XII 318b

shaḳwa → SHAḲĀWA

shāl (A, > Eng 'shawl') : the turban-cloth or whole turban, especially in Egypt, sometimes also kerchiefs worn by women, e.g., in Arabia and North Africa. X 614a

shalabī → ČELEBĪ

shalba (A) : in zoology, a silurus of the Nile and the Niger, whose Arabic term is found again in the Latinised nomenclature to specify a sub-species limited to a particular region (*Schilbe mystus*). VIII 1021b

shalīl → KABŪSH

shālish → DJĀLISH

shālīsh (P), also *čālīsh* : in military science, a vanguard (A syn. *muḳaddama*). X 164b

shām (A) : Syria; the north; 'the left-hand region', because in ancient Arab usage, the speaker in western or central Arabia was considered to face the rising sun and to have Syria on his left and the Arabian peninsula, with Yaman ('the right-hand region') on his right. IX 261b

♦ shāmiyyūn (A) : in Muslim Spain, the viziers of eastern origin, the others being called *baladiyyūn*. XI 192a

shāma (A, pl. *shāmāt*) : naevus, skin blemish, mole. Originally ~ denoted the coloured marks on a horse's body, but is now, with *khāl* (pl. *khīlān*), applied to all marks of a colour different from the main body, including accidental marks, abcesses or freckles caused by an illness and presaging death. IX 281a

shamʿa (A) : candle. IX 281b

♦ sham'adān (A) : candelabrum, candlestick. IX 282a

♦ sham'ī (A), or **shammā'** : candlemaker. IX 288a

shamāl (A) : in meteorology, the north wind. VIII 526b

shaman (P) : idolator, an unspecified type of non-Muslim religious person (syn. *but-parast*). IX 282a

shambar (A) : a large veil common to the Hebron area and southern Palestine. V 741b

shamla (A), or *shimāl* : a bag, perhaps made of hedgehog skin, which is used to enclose the maternal mammaries of small livestock in order to wean their young. Another method, also used, is applying a gag (*faṭṭāma*) to the muzzle of the young. XII 319a

shammās (A) : lit. deacon, a title in Catholicism denoting someone who lives a life of asceticism and service to others. XI 423as

shams (A) : the sun. IX 291a

♦ **shamsa** (A), or *shamsiyya* : a jewel used by the 'Abbāsid and Fāṭimid caliphs as one of the insignia of kingship; not a sunshade but a kind of suspended crown, made out of gold and silver, studded with pearls and precious stones, and hoisted up by the aid of a chain. IX 298b; and → MIẒALLA; 'UNWĀN

♦ shamsī (A) : an alcoholic drink made of honey and dry raisins, of which the mediaeval Egyptians were very fond. VII 907b

♦ shamsiyya → SHAMSA

shamṭā' → SHAYB

shamūs (A) : in the terminology of horse-riding, a horse that is difficult to mount. II 954a

shamushk (A, pl. *shamushkāt*) : a type of boot of Coptic Arab origin. XII 463a

shanaḳ → WAḲṢ

shānī → SHĪNĪ

shanīn (A) : a drink make of whey or milk diluted with water. II 1061a

shapḳa (T) : the modern European hat, which in 1925 replaced the fez in Turkey. X 611a; X 614a

sha'r (A) : hair, pelt. IX 311b; the wool of goats. IX 764b; the hair of camels and dromedaries is usually called ~ and occasionally WABAR. IX 312a

sha'ra → TASH'ĪR

shara'a (A) : verb relating to watering animals at a permanent water-hole, implying lapping at or drinking water; to drive (or lead) animals to water; as noun (pl. *ashru'*) ~ means a projecting, covered area, syn. SAḲĪFA. IX 326a

sharāb (A) : a beverage, known also as *nabīdh* or *sawīḳ*, prepared by macerating raisins and subsequently dates, doubtless to improve the taste of the water, yielding a fermented liquor. XI 441a

♦ sharābī → SĀḲĪ

sharaf (A) : elevation, nobility, pre-eminence, in the physical and moral sense (cf. *madjd* 'illustriousness on account of birth', *ḥasab* 'individual quality, merit', and KARAM 'illustriousness acquired by oneself'). IX 313b

In astrology, 'exaltation' (ant. *hubūṭ* 'dejection'). X 942a; X 556a

♦ sharaf al-nisba (A) : the descendants of al-Ḥasan and al-Ḥusayn, one of a class of noble blood, *sharaf*, that existed in Egyptian terminology of the 9th/15th century. IX 332a

sharak (A, pl. *ashrāk*) : a noose, used in hunting small-sized birds by placing them in line on a taut cord. IX 98b

sharaḳraḳ → ṬAYR AL-'ARĀḲIB

sharb (A) : a fine linen, which with DABĪḲĪ, often formed the ground fabric for ṬIRĀZ. X 537b

♦ sharba → SHERBET

sharbūsh (A, < P *sarpūsh*; pl. *sharābīsh, sharābish*), or *sharbush* : the headdress of the AMĪRS under the Mamlūks in Egypt. According to al-Maķrīzī, it resembled the TĀDJ, was three-cornered, worn without a turban, and formed part of a set of robes of honour. It had a markedly military character, contrasting to the turban of the jurists. Under the Circassian Mamlūks, the ~ fell into disuse. X 614a

sharḥ (A, pl. *shurūḥ*) : a commentary on a text. I 593a; IX 317a

♦ al-sharḥ al-mazdjī (A) : in literature, a method of interweaving the text with its commentary in such a way that the two together form a smooth and coherent whole. IX 209b

shārī → SHIRĀʾ

shāriʿ (A, pl. *shawāriʿ*) : clearly-defined way, main road, highway; situated on a main road, at the side of a road. ~ was generally the term for a main arterial road, lesser roads in the vocabulary of urban patterning being *sikka* (pl. *sikak*), *ḥāra, darb* (pl. *durūb*), *ʿatfa* and *zuķāķ*, in Cairo, and *nahdj* and *zanķa*, in Tunis. IX 320b; law-giver, characteristically Muḥammad in his function as model and exemplar of the law, but in a rare extension of meaning, sometimes transferred to the jurists. IX 322a f.

sharīʿa (A, pl. *sharāʾiʿ*) : a prophetic religion in its totality; within Muslim discourse, the rules and regulations governing the lives of Muslims. IX 321a; Islamic jurisprudence. VIII 249b; the area around a water-hole, or the point of entry to it, the place at which the animals drink; the seashore, with special reference to animals which come there. IX 326a

In the Qurʾān, where it appears once, and in Tradition literature, ~ designates a way or path, divinely appointed. Its cognate *shirʿa* and synonym *minhādj* are also used once. IX 321a

sharīdj → FILĶ

sharīf (A, pl. *ashrāf*, **shurafāʾ**, N.Afr *shorfā*) : 'noble', 'exalted', 'eminent', among the pre-Islamic Arab tribes a free man who could claim a distinguished rank because of his descent from illustrious ancestors. In Islamic times, ~ was especially applied to the descendant of Muḥammad's family, AHL AL-BAYT, and with time to the ʿAlids alone. VII 926b; IX 329b ff.; and → ḌAʿĪF

In North Africa, a person who traces his origin to the Prophet's family through ʿAlī and Fāṭima. I 371b

sharika (A), or *shirka* : in law, partnership. VII 671b; IX 348a

♦ sharikat al-ʿaķd (A) : in law, a contractual partnership. VII 671b

♦ sharikat amwāl (A) : in law, partnership of capital, contracted when two partners put their capital in one project and agree on certain conditions for administration, profit and loss. IX 348b

♦ sharikat ʿinān → ʿINĀN

♦ sharikat al-milk (A) : in law, a proprietary partnership. VII 671b

♦ sharikat al-ṣanāʾiʿ (A) : in law, partnership in crafts or trades. IX 348b

♦ sharikat wudjūh (A) : in law, partnership of personal credit, contracted when two well-known persons ask others to sell to them goods without payment on the basis of their reputation, and then sell the goods for cash. IX 348b

shaʿriyya (A) : a black face veil of goat's wool or horse hair, worn by women in the Arab East. V 741b

sharkh (A) : in the terminology of childhood, 'a youth or young man; the offspring of a man' (Lane). VIII 821b

sharķi̊ (T) : lit. oriental, eastern; in Turkish music, a certain form of classical Turkish song. IX 353b

In Turkish literature, a genre of Turkish strophic poem composed on literary lines with the aim of being set to music. IX 353b; a type of folk-poetry of Anatolia. I 677b

sharrāliya → HINDIBĀʾ

sharṭ (A, pl. *shurūṭ*, *sharāʾiṭ*) : lit. condition; in law, condition, term, stipulation. IX 358b; and → KHIYĀR AL-SHARṬ

In logic, hypothesis, condition. IX 359b; and → ḲIYĀS ḤAMLĪ

In grammar, ~ denotes the protasis of a conditional sentence, the apodisis being variously referred to as *djawāb, djazāʾ* or *mudjāzāt*. IX 360a

In its plural form, *shurūṭ* refers in law to a wide variety of prescribed model documents used in transactions. IX 359a; and → MUWATHTHIḲ

In medicine, scarification. II 481b

shāsh (A, > Eng 'sash') : the winding cloth of a turban in Syria and Palestine. V 741b; from 780/1378 the ~ was part of a woman's dress, as the cloth embroidered with gold and pearls, thrown over the double ṬURṬŪR. X 614a; and → LITHĀM

♦ shāsha (A) : in Oman and the United Arab Emirates, the local open boat made from palm fibres. VII 53b

♦ shāshiyya (A) : originally the turban-cloth made of *shāsh* muslin. In Egypt, a cap, around which the turban-cloth was wound; it was of silk and might be trimmed with pearls and gold. Also the name given to the paper cap put on criminals, and also to iron helmet-like caps. In early 20th-century Morocco, a black cap for young people in the form of the ṬARBŪSH; also a headdress in the form of a sugar-loaf, which the Darḳāwa dervishes wore. X 614a

shash (P) : six

♦ **shashmaḳom** (Tadzhik, < P *shash*, A *maḳām*) : the modal and formal concept of art music played in the urban centres of Uzbekistan. The six *maḳom* cycles are called *buzruk* (< *buzurg*), *rost* (< *rāst*), *navo* (< *nawā*), *dugokh* (< *dogāh*), *segosh* (< *segāh*) and *iroḳ* (< *ʿirāḳ*), based on four of the former twelve main modes and two former 'derived' modes. IX 360b f.

♦ shashtār → TĀR

shaṣna (A) : a mole or barrier built in the water for protection. I 180b

shāt → FAZZ

shatar (A) : in medicine, an infection of the eyelid. IX 9b

shaṭawī (A) : textile goods from Shaṭā, in Egypt, highly praised by travellers. IX 361a

shatfa (A) : a horizontal strip on an emblem or insignia, RANK, introduced onto the shield in the early 14th century. VIII 431b

shaṭḥ (A, pl. *shaṭaḥāt*), or *shaṭḥiyya* : in mysticism, ecstatic expression, commonly used for mystical sayings that are frequently outrageous in character. I 60b; IX 361b

shātim, shatīm → SHATM

shāṭir (A, pl. *shuṭṭār*) : 'artful (ones)', the name given to groups of young men who were considered elements of disorder in mediaeval Baghdad. II 961b; an outcast. IV 1132b; and → KHALĪʿ

shātiya (A) : a winter (military) expedition (ant. ṢĀʾIFA). VII 816a

shatm (A) : an act of insult, vilification, defamation, abuse or revilement, the person doing thus is termed *shātim* or *shattāma* and the one who is vilified *mashtūm* or *shatīm*. If it is directed against God, the Prophet, or other historical personalities or objects venerated by the Muslim community, ~ is considered an act of blasphemy, syn. *sabb*, *laʿn* (cursing, malediction), *ṭaʿn* (accusing, attacking), *īdhāʾ* (harming, hurting) or the verb *nāla min* (to do harm to someone, to defame). XII 725b

shaṭr (A) : in prosody, a single hemistich, of 15 or less syllables. VIII 583a

shaṭrandj (P, < San) : the game of chess. The chesspieces were called: *shāh* 'king', *firzān* (*firz*) 'queen', lit. adviser, *fīl* 'bishop', lit. elephant, *baydaḳ* 'pawn', lit. footman, *rukhkh* 'rook', *faras* 'horse'. IX 366a f.

♦ shaṭrandjiyya : a meat pie containing bones with no meat on them. IX 367a

shaṭṭ (A) : originally, one side of a camel's hump; eventually ~ came to mean a stream's bank, and occasionally it was extended to mean a plot of land, close to the bank of a stream. In modern-day Iraq, ~ can describe a stream, as also in ~ *al-ʿarab*, the tidal estuary formed by the united stream of the Tigris and the Euphrates; river. VIII 13a; IX 368a

In geography, ~ is used in the high plains of North Africa and the northern Sahara for the saline pasturages surrounding a salt flat, *sabkha*, often confused with the latter. IX 368a

shattāma → SHATM

shaṭwa (A) : a Bethlehem married woman's hat. V 741b

shāʾūsh → ČĀʾŪSH

shaʿwadha → SHAʿBADHA

♦ shaʿwadhī (A) : express courier. IX 152b

shawādhdh (A) : in the science of the Qurʾān, uncanonical 'deviant' readings. V 128a

shawāhid → SHĀHID

shawbaḳ (A) : in the mediaeval kitchen, a small rolling pin used to bake an ordinary loaf of bread (*raghīf*). For the thin *riḳāḳ*, a large one was used. VI 808a

shawdar (A, P *čādur*), or *shawdhar* : a black, enveloping outer wrap for women worn in the Arab East. V 741b

shāwī (A, pl. **shāwiya**) : sheep-breeder or herder. In Syria and the Arabian peninsula, *shāwiya* is the urban term, *ḥuḳra* being the desert term, for tribes specialising in herding flocks. IX 374b ff.; and → ṬABBĀKH

♦ shāwiya → SHĀWĪ

shawḳ (A) : desire, longing, yearning, craving, much used as a technical term in Islamic religious thought and mysticism. IX 376b

shawka (A) : in botany, *al-shawka al-bayḍāʾ* is the whitethorn, the white acanthus, mostly rendered with *bādhāward*, which is actually the Arabic acanthus, *al-shawka al-ʿarabiyya*. Synonyms or other types of the thistle are *ṭūb(a)* (< L *tubus*), *ibrat al-rāʿī, ibrat al-rāhib, ayfd* and *tāfrūt* (both Berber). IX 496b

♦ shawkī (A) : 'thorny one'. in botany, the name of one of five varieties of the red jujube; it has fruits the size of peas, with large seeds and little flesh, is found frequently in Toledo, is effective against chronic diarrhoea originating from a weak stomach, and staunches the loss of blood. X 868b

shawna → SHĪNĪ

shāy → ČAY

shayʾ (A) : a thing, entity (L *res*). IX 380b

In the Qurʾān, ~ assumed the meaning of 'belongings' or 'property'. II 361a

In mathematics, ~ is another word for absolute number, especially to denote the unknown quantity in linear problems (syn. *ḍilʿ*). It also serves as a general expression for auxiliary quantities and often takes the place of *al-djidhr*, the root. II 361a ff.; and → MĀL

♦ shayʾiyya (A) : 'thingness' of e.g. the non-being, *maʿdūm*, a philosophical concept. IX 381a

shayb (A) : lit. white hair; old age, senescence (syn. *aghtham* 'grey which is white rather than black'); in poetry, ~ is frequently found in the expression *al-shayb wa 'l-shabāb* 'old age and youth'. Although not restricted to males, the term *shamṭāʾ* is cited by lexicographers for feminine old age. IX 313a; IX 383a

shayka (T) : in the Ottoman military, a small, flat-bottomed gunboat. X 624a

shayham (A) : in zoology, the porcupine. X 432b

shaykh (A, pl. *shuyūkh, mashāyikh*) : lit. an elder, someone whose age appears advanced and whose hair has gone white, used for a man over fifty years old. ~ carries the idea of authority and prestige and is thus applied to the chief of any human group: family, tribe, guild, etc., as well as to the head of a religious establishment and to any Muslim scholar of a certain level of attainment. IV 335a; VI 725b; VIII 207a; IX 115b; IX 397a; when used with a complement, the term designated the master of various fields. V 1131a; and → MASHYAKHA; MURSHID

In mysticism, the ~ is the spiritual master, the novice's 'educator', ~ *al-tarbiya*. IX 397b

One of three grades of the AKHĪ organisation, which seems to have played practically no active role, but probably refers to the leader of a dervish settlement, to which the members of the organization felt themselves attached. I 323a

In Ḥaḍramawt, ~ denotes class distinction, not a tribal chief; the *mashāyikh* are those noble families with the right to the hereditary title of ~ . XII 339a

In Muslim India, ~ is one of the four divisions among the ASHRĀF, Muslims of foreign ancestry; the ~ is said to be descended from the early Muslims of Mecca and Medina. III 411a; IX 397b

♦ shaykh al-akbar (A) : 'the Greatest Master', a title given to Ibn al-ʿArabī. X 317a

♦ shaykh al-baḥr (A) : in zoology, the seal. Other designations are *ʿīdj al-baḥr, fuḳma, fuḳḳama*, and *bū mnīr*. VIII 1022b

♦ **shaykh al-balad** (A) : the mayor of a town, or an employee looking after the good management of the town. IX 397b; in 18th-century Ottoman Egypt, the title given to the most powerful BEY in Cairo, superseding the titles *amīr miṣr, kabīr al-ḳawm*, and *kabīr al-balad*. IX 398b

♦ shaykh al-ḥadjdj → MUṬAWWIF

♦ **shaykh al-islām** (A) : an honorific title applied essentially to religious dignitaries in the Islamic world up to the early 20th century. Under the Ottomans, ~ was given to the individual in the Ottoman empire in whom the right to issue an opinion on a point of law, FATWĀ, was vested exclusively. The office of the ~ was abolished in 1924 and was replaced by a department for religious affairs, attached to the Prime Minister. I 837b; II 867a; III 552b; III 1152a; VI 19a; IX 399b f.

♦ shaykh al-sadjdjāda (A), or *walī 'l-sadjdjāda* : 'the prayer-rug sitter', a term normally applied to leaders of ṣūfī communities or heads of holy lineages who fell heir to the spiritual authority and blessing of a revered saintly founder. VIII 743b; IX 398a

♦ shaykh al-shuyūkh (A) : during Ayyūbid and Mamlūk rule, the holder of the office of controlling the practice of ṣūfism, whose role was more political than spiritual. The Ottomans later introduced the *shaykh al-ṭuruḳ* 'head of the mystical paths' with the same function. IX 397b

♦ shaykh al-yahūdī (A), or *abū marīna* : in zoology, the monk seal. VIII 1022b

♦ shaykha (A) : a woman in whom is recognised the quality of a spiritual master, above all vis-à-vis other women. IX 398a; commune. I 863a

shaypūr an instrument of the horn and trumpet type. X 35a

shayṭān (A, pl. *shayāṭīn*) : evil spirit, demon, devil, either human or DJINN. IX 406b ff.; and → RADJĪM; ṢĀḤIB

shayyād (A) : a speaker, or one who recited or sang stories or poems in a loud voice, term used in Persian and Turkish between the 7th/13th and 10th/16th centuries, and replaced in the following century by e.g. the Persian *ḳiṣṣakhān*. Its etymology is unclear, Arabic lexicographers equating it with Persian *shayd* 'deceit' which brought about its equation with 'liar' or 'trickster'. Later 19th-century European writers added the meaning 'dervish'. IX 409b f.

shehīlī (Alg) : the sirocco, which brings temperatures of 104° F and higher several times a year. I 366a

shehir emāneti, ~ emīni, ~ ketkhüdasi̊ → SHAHR

shehnāmedji (T), or **shāhnāmedji** : in Ottoman literature, the term for a writer of literary-historical works in a style inspired by the *Shāh-nāma* of Firdawsī. IX 211b

shehrī → ḲASSĀM

shehu (Hau, < A SHAYKH) : once the coveted title of a great scholar and teacher, ~ is nowadays commonly used as a personal name. In the phrase *shehu malami* (→ MALAM), it is used as an epithet for a distinguished exponent of the Islamic sciences. VI 223a

shehzāde → SHĀHZĀDE

shemle (T) : in the reign of Süleymān I, a carelessly wound turban-cloth, worn by the common people. In North Africa it was a cloth, still sometimes wound over the turban. X 614a

shenlik (T) : an Ottoman term for public festivities which marked special occasions, involving the participation of the entire populace. IX 416b

sherbet (T, < A *sharba*) : a sweet, cold drink, made of various fruit juices. Another fruit-based drink, possibly of alcoholic content, was *khō shāb*. VI 864b; IX 417a

♦ sharbatči-bāshī (P) : in Ṣafawid times, an official in the royal kitchen who supervised the sherbets and syrups. XII 609b

shewādān (P) : cellars in houses in Shushtar, in which the inhabitants shelter in the excessive heat of summer; syn. SARDĀB. IX 512b

shiʿār (A) : a term with various significations: the rallying signal for war or for a travel expedition, war cry, standard, mark indicating the place of standing of soldiers in battle or pilgrims in the pilgrimage; a syn. of *idmāʾ* 'to draw blood'; the distinctive clothing, etc. which the DHIMMĪs were required to wear in ʿAbbāsid and later times. IX 424a

shiʿb (A) : a ravine. IX 425a

shibaʿ (A) : in mineralogy, intensity of colour (of a gem). XI 263a

shibiththth (A, pop. *shibitt, shabath*, B *aslīlī*) : in botany, dill. IX 431b

shibr (A) : 'span', that is, the span of the hand from the thumb to the little finger, a premodern basic measure of length. VII 137b

shibriḳ → DIRṢ

shibuk→ TUTUN

shidirghū : in music, as written and described by Ibn Ghaybī, a long instrument with half of its belly covered with skin. It had four strings and was mostly used in China. X 770a

shifā (A) : in anatomy, the lips. VI 130a

shighār (A) : the exchange of a girl for a wife by her brother or father without any money being spent. This type of union is also applied to married women, whereby a man repudiates his wife and exchanges her for another man's. Although forbidden in Islam, marriage by exchange is nonetheless practised even to the present day. VI 475b

shīḥ (A, < Ar *sīḥā*) : in botany, the plant species Artemisia (*Compositae*), as well as the specific *Artemisia iudaica L.* Other specific types of ~ are *sārīfūn* (probably *A. maritima*), *ṭarkhūn* (*A. dracunculus* 'tarragon'), *ḳayṣūm* (*A. abrotanum* 'southernwood'), *birindjāsaf* (*A. vulgaris* 'mugwort'), and AFSANTĪN or *abū shinthiyā* 'wormwood'. IX 434b

shihāb (A, pl. *shuhub*) : in astronomy, a shooting star. A synonym, of Persian origin, was *nayzak* (pl. *nayāzik*). VIII 103a

shiḥna (A) : a body of armed men, sufficing for the guarding and control of a town or district on the part of the sultan; used by Abu 'l-Faḍl Bayhaḳī in the sense of the commander of such an armed body. IX 437a; under the Saldjūḳs and their successors, a military commander installed at the head of each city, who exercised military, political, and administrative functions; ~ was later superseded by the term DĀRŪGHA. VIII 402b; IX 15a; IX 437a

♦ shiḥnagī (P) : the office of a SHIḤNA. IX 437b

shiḥra (A) : a narrow tract of land. IX 439a

shihrī → HADJĪN

shikārī (P, < *shikār* 'game, prey; the chase, hunting') : a native hunter or stalker, who accompanied European hunters and sportsmen, term current in Muslim India, passing into Urdu and Hindi. IX 439b; *shikargāh* is the game reserve. IX 638a

shikasta (P), *shikasta nastaʿlīḳ*, or *khaṭṭ-i shikasta* : a script which came into existence at the beginning of the 11th/17th century under the Ṣafawids, as a result of writing NASTAʿLĪḲ rapidly and of the calligraphers being under the influence of SHIKASTA TAʿLĪḲ. ~ was used mostly in writing letters and sometimes for official correspondence. Nowadays it is sometimes used in writing poetry in an artistic fashion. IV 1124b; a highly cursive style developed from TAʿLĪḲ and NASTAʿLĪḲ, and now mostly in use in Iran, where it has become a means of expression of the new Islamic Iranian identity. VIII 151b

♦ shikasta taʿlīḳ (P), or *taʿlīḳ* : 'broken' TAʿLĪḲ, the result of writing *taʿlīḳ* rapidly. The letters are written in a more intricate style. It started to appear in the 8th/14th century but declined in use when NASTAʿLĪḲ started to spread in the 10th/16th century. IV 1124a

shīkha (Mor, pl. *shīkhāt*) : a free female singer in Morocco, who participates, in a company of *shīkhāt*, in family feasts or solemn ceremonies. IV 823b

shiḳḳ (A) : in Muslim India, a word sometimes used to denote a province in the 9th/15th century. II 273a

In mediaeval literature, a half-human monster, like the NASNĀS. V 133b

♦ shiḳḳa (A, pl. *shiḳaḳ*) : an oblong band or panel, many of which, when sewn together, make up the roof of a tent; their number depends on the importance one wishes to accord to the tent. IV 1148a

♦ shiḳḳdār (IndP) : in Muslim India, the functionary in charge of the general administration and civil affairs during the Dihlī sultanate. Later, he was replaced by the FAWDJDĀR under the Mughals. II 273a; II 868a; and → ḲĀNUNGO

shimāl → SHAMLA

shimrīr (N.Afr, > Sp *sombrero*) : in Morocco, the name given to the Euopean hat, sometimes also called *ṭarṭūr*. X 614b

shimshīrlik → ḲAFES

shīn → SĪN

shinā → SANG

shīnī (A) : the average mediaeval Muslim warship. It was a two-banked galley, with a special officer in charge of each bank. The ~ carried a crew of about 140 to 180 oarsmen. VII 44b; IX 444a; other transcriptions are *shawna, shīniyya, shānī* (pl. *shawānī*). VIII 810a

shinḳāb → SHUNḲUB

shintiyān (Egy) : in Egypt, 'drawers' for women. IX 677b

shipship (T) : an Ottoman Turkish shoe, mule, without heels, but with the end slightly raised and a supple sole. V 752b

shiʿr (A) : poetry. IX 448b; XII 727a; injurious poetry, *hidjāʾ*, especially for the archaic and Umayyad periods. IX 449a; collections of poetry, also called *khabar*. IX 318a; in Urdu, alongside the general meaning of poetry (syn. *shāʿirī*), ~ also means a verse or couplet. IX 469b

♦ al-shiʿr al-ḥurr (A) : free verse. IX 464a; XII 34b

♦ al-shiʿr al-mursal (A) : blank verse. VIII 909a; IX 464a; XII 34b

shiʿrā (A) : in astronomy, Sirius, the brightest fixed star in the sky; the dual *al-shiʿrayān* designated both Sirius and Procyon. IX 471b, where also can be found the specifying adjectives, which were sometimes used on their own

shirʿa (A) : a fine string, as stretched on a bow, or a lute. IX 326a; and → SHARĪʿA

shirāʾ (A) : buying and selling, a term used in both early Islamic theology, especially associated with the Khāridjites, who were known as *shārī* (pl. *shurāt*), and in (commercial) law, where it had the predominant meaning of buying rather than selling. IX 470a

shirāʿ (A) : in seafaring, the sail of a ship, stretched above it to catch the wind; the neck of a camel. IX 326a

shīradj → DUHN AL-ḤALL

shirāḥa (A) : in agriculture, palm-protection. VI 832a

shirāk → AL-NAʿL AL-SHARĪF

shirk (A) : polytheism, the giving of partners to God. I 333a; III 1059b; IX 484b; the idolatry of self and of creaturely things. I 70a; and → IKHLĀṢ

♦ shirka → SHARIKA

shisʿ → AL-NAʿL AL-SHARĪF

shīsh (A) : a drink or sauce. VI 721b

♦ shīsha → NARDJĪLA; ZUDJĀDJ

shīshak → KAMĀNDJA

shīsham (Sin) : in botany, Indian rosewood. IX 638a

shitr → MIẒALLA

shiyāh al-ḍaʾn → SHĀʾ AL-ḌAʾN

shiyāh al-maʿz → MĀʿIZA

shölen → TOY

shorfā → SHARĪF

shūʿ → BĀN

shuʿāʿ (A) : used in the literature of scholastic theology for both the light rays emanating, for example, from the sun, and the visual rays (i.e. rays emanating from the eye). VI 376a; double refraction. XI 263a

shubbāk (A) : one of the caliphal insignia, a lattice screen or grill, which with a curtain (*sitr*) separated the caliph from those attending the public sittings. I 1074b; V 1032a; a grilled loge in which the ʿAbbāsid caliph sat on the 29th of Dhu ʾl-Ḥidjdja to review the horses and constumes chosen for the New Year's procession. VI 850b

shubha (A, pl. *shubah*, *shubuhāt*) : lit. resemblance; in theology and philosophy, ~ is a false or specious argument which 'resembles' a valid one; a counter-argument in later scholastic theology. IX 492b

In penal law, semblance, an illicit act which nevertheless 'resembles' a licit one, one of the grounds for avoidance of the fixed penalties. II 831b; III 20b; IX 492b

♦ shubhat al-ʿaḳd (A) : in penal law, a case where the act has been done as the result of a contract which observed merely the conditions of formation. II 832a; IX 493a

♦ shubhat al-fāʿil (A) : in Shāfiʿī law, a case of SHUBHA, as when another woman is substituted for the bride on the wedding night. IX 493a

♦ shubhat al-ṭarīḳ (A), or *shubhat al-djiha* : in Shāfiʿī law, a case of SHUBHA, applied in cases where the schools of law disagree. IX 493a

♦ shubha fi ʾl-fiʿl (A), or *shubhat ishtibāh*, *shubhat mushābaha* : in penal law, a case where the action with which the accused is charged resembles an action which is normally permissable. II 832a; IX 492b

♦ shubha fi ʾl-maḥall (A), or *shubhat mulk*, *shubha ḥukmiyya* : in penal law, a case where the illegality founded upon a proof text may appear dubious because of the existence of another, ambiguous text. II 832a; IX 492b

shuddi (H) : in India, a 20th-century movement launched by the reformist Arya Samaj that sought to 'reclaim' descendants of former converts to Islam to the true faith of their more ancient ancestors. XII 564a

shudjāʿ → FARD

shufʿa (A) : in law, the right of pre-emption, the right of the co-owner to buy out his partner's share which is for sale. I 172b; III 513a; V 878b; IX 494b

shufārī → YARBŪʿ

shuhadāʾ → SHAHĪD

shuhra → MAʿRIFA

shukāʿā (A), or *shukāʿ* : in botany, the thistle. IX 496b

shukka (A, pl. *shikāk*) : on the Arabian peninsula, an area of gravel and limestone. VIII 575b; and → FALĪDJA

shukkub → SHUNKUB

shukr (A) : thankfulness, gratitude; achnowledgment; praise. When used on the part of God, ~ means recompense, reward. IX 496b

shūkrān → SAYKARĀN

shumrūkh (A, pl. *shamārīkh*) : a cult of demons that, according to al-Bakrī (11th century), existed among the Banū Warsifān, one of the Berber tribes of Tripolitania. V 1183a

shün ay (T, < Ch *rùn*) : in dating, the early Turkish name for the intercalary month. X 263b

shūnīz → KAMMŪN

shunkub (A, pl. *shanākib*), or *shukkub, shinkāb* : in zoology, the common snipe (*Capella gallinago gallinago*), known in the Maghrib and Egypt as *kannis, dadjādjat al-māʾ* and *bikāsīn* (< Fr *bécassine*) and in Iraq as *djuhlūl*, the same term as for the sandpiper (*Tringa*); also, with *shunkub al-bahr*, the trumpet fish (*Centriscus*). IX 504b

♦ shunkub kabīr (A) : in zoology, the great or solitary snipe (*Capella major* or *media*). IX 504b

♦ shunkub muzawwak (A), or *shunkub khawlī* (Egy) : in zoology, the painted snipe (*Rostratula benghalensis*). IX 504b

♦ shunkub ṣaghīr (A) : in zoology, the Jack snipe (*Limnocryptes minimus*). IX 504b

shūrā (A) : the council; consultative assembly; consultation. I 110a; V 1084a; IX 504b; from the early 19th century, ~ was applied to every type of Western governmental body, including elective and representative parliaments. IX 506a

♦ shūrā-yi dewlet (T) : in the Ottoman empire, a council of justice composed of Muslims and Christians, set up in 1868 under ʿAbd al-ʿAzīz. This was a court of review in administrative cases; it also had certain consultative functions, and was supposed to prepare the drafts of new laws. I 56b; II 641b

shurafāʾ (A, Mor *shorfā*, s. *sharīf*) → SHARĪF

shurāʿiyya (A) : a long-necked camel. IX 326a

shurb (A) : drinking, drink; salted water, drunk e.g. at the ceremony of girding the initiatic belt among the *fityān* (→ FATĀ). IX 167a

♦ hakk al-shurb (A, Ott *hakk-i̊ shurb*) : in law, the right to make use of water from a water-channel at a given interval to irrigate one's land. V 879a

shurshur → ABŪ BARĀKISH

shurṭa (A, pl. *shuraṭ*, pop. pl. *shurṭiyya*) : a special corps, which came into being in early Islam and which was more closely linked to the caliph or governor than the army. This corps was basically concerned less with war than with the maintenance of internal order and, little by little, became a kind of police force. An individual in such a corps is a *shurṭī*. II 505a; IV 373b; VIII 402b; IX 510a

♦ shurṭa ṣughrā (A) : in Muslim Spain, one of three categories of the *shurṭa*, whose jurisdiction, according to Ibn Khaldūn, was applied to the ʿĀMMA, as opposed to the *shurṭa ʿulyā*, whose jurisdiction concerned the misdemeanours of people belonging to the KHĀṢṢA. The third category, *shurṭa wusṭā*, is not mentioned by Ibn Khaldūn. IX 510b

♦ shurṭa ʿulyā → SHURṬA ṢUGHRĀ
♦ shurṭa wusṭā → SHURṬA ṢUGHRĀ
shurūṭ → ʿAHDNĀME; SHARṬ
♦ shurūṭī → MUWATHTHIḲ
shuṭfa (A) : a badge; under the Mamlūks a green badge that the male SHARĪF had to wear fastened to his turban to distinguish him from others. IX 334a
shutik (K) : in the YAZĪDĪ tradition, a girdle, one of several garments with religious significance; others include a shirt (*kirās*, whose neckline is called *girīvān*), and a cord, *ristik*, worn by a few religious dignitaries. Another sacred shirt (*sadra*, which has a pocket called *girebān*) and a sacred girdle or cord, *kustī*, are also known in Zoroastrianism. XI 315a
shuturbān → DEVEDJÎ
shuʿūbiyya (A, < *shuʿūb*, s. SHAʿB) : a movement in early Islam which denied any privileged position of the Arabs. IX 513b
shuʿūr (A) : in philosophy, the notion of consciousness or apperception. I 112b
shuwayḥī (A), or *shuwayḥiyya* : a woman's belt, usually woven of goat's hair and quite ornate, worn mainly in southern Palestine. V 741b
shuwwāsh (A) : servants, also *khuddām* (→ KHĀDIM) especially for the day-to-day operations of the zāwiya. XI 468a
shuyūʿiyya (A) : communism (syn. *ibāḥiyya*). IX 517a
sība (A) : a term borrowed from local speech by the French to designate the absence of control by the sultan of Morocco over a considerable part of his territory at the end of the 19th century. In dichotomy with the *bilād al-makhzan*, the *bilād al-~* was a land outside the authority of the sultan, hence free from taxes and conscription, whose people lived in an insolent, free fashion impervious to all outside influences. XII 729a
sibāḥa (A) : swimming. V 109a
sibāḥī → SIPĀHĪ
sibāḳ → SABḲ
sibākh (A) : topsoil. XI 446a
ṣiʾbān → ḲAML
sibizghi : an Uzbeki flute, related to the Persian NĀY, which with the *tüdük*, used in Turkmenistan, accompanies the nomadic bard and is remarkable for its technique. X 733b
sīdāra (A) : a skull cap like the ṬĀḲIYYA worn under MIKNAʿA and ʿIṢĀBA. X 614b
ṣiddīḳ (A) : 'eminently veracious', 'believing', in Qurʾānic usage, applied to the prophets Abraham and Idrīs, and to Mary and Joseph. As an epithet, *al-ṣiddīḳ* is applied to the first caliph Abū Bakr. IX 534b
♦ ṣiddīḳī → ṢADĪḲĪ
sīdī → MAWLĀY; SAYYIDĪ
sidjdjīl (A, < Akk) : one of the mysterious words of the Qurʾān, together with SIDJDJĪN, denoting a hard, flint-like stone. IX 538a
sidjdjīn (A) : one of the mysterious words of the Qurʾān, still interpreted in various ways as either the seventh and lowest earth, a rock or well in hell, the home of Iblīs, hell fire, something painful, hard, durable or eternal (influenced by its resemblance to SIDJDJĪL), or the name of the record in which all human acts are set down. IX 538a
sidjill (A, < Ar, < L *sigillum*; pl. *sidjillāt*) : lit. seal, in early Arabic referring to a document, or to a scroll on which documents are written. II 302b; IX 538b; also, the judicial verdict prepared by a judge. II 79a; IX 538b; during the Mamlūk period, the judicial court registers kept by official witnesses. IX 538b

In classical Muslim administration, ~ is the letter given to an envoy or messenger, authorising him, on arrival, to recover the expenses of his journey from any ʿĀMIL. II 79a; IX 538b

In notarial usage, ~ referred to an official record of a case, based on and including the *maḥḍar* 'the minutes of the case or transaction conducted before a judge' and the judge's decision or verdict. IX 539a

In Ottoman administrative usage, ~ was a general term used for 'register'. IX 539a

sidjillāt → YĀSAMĪN

sidjn (A), and *ḥabs* : prison. IX 547a

ṣidḳ (A) : 'truthfulness, sincerity', a term in mysticism, where it is defined as the complete agreement of one's inner convictions and outward acts. IX 548b

sidr (A, n. of unity *sidra*) : in botany, the jujube, a shrub or tree of the various Rhammaceae belonging to the genus *Ziziphus*, called *ʿilb* in the south of Arabia. I 540b; IX 549a; X 868b

♦ **sidrat al-muntahā** (A) : 'the lote tree on the boundary', a Qurʾānic phrase describing where Muḥammad met Gabriel for the second time. IX 550a

ṣidriyya (A) : a sleeveless vest worn by both sexes in the Arab East. V 741b

ṣifa (A, pl. *ṣifāt*) : attribute, lit. description; in its plural form, *ṣifāt*, used in theology in particular for the divine attributes. I 333b; I 411a; IX 551b; XII 344b

In grammar, ~ (syn. NAʿT) denotes any general or descriptive predicate term, a qualifying adjective. IV 182a; IX 551a; XII 344a

♦ ṣifāt al-ḥurūf (A) : the manners of articulation of the letters, important in Qurʾānic recitation. Some fine points include *ḳalḳala*, the strong pronunciation of certain letters when they are quiet (*sākin*), *takrīr*, the trilling of the *rāʾ* at certain times, and *istiṭāla*, the stretching of the sound from one side of the tongue to the other when pronouncing *ḍād*. X 73b

sifāla → ʿAYĀLA

sifāra (A) : in Fāṭimid administration, an office in which the ethnic factions of the palace and the army were represented, filling a gap, along with the office of the WASĀṬA, in the vizierate created by al-Ḥākim in 409/1018. The vizierate was later re-established during the reign of his son al-Ẓāhir, but the offices of the ~ and *wasāṭa* continued to be filled irregularly till the end of the dynasty by persons with a lower rank than the vizier. XI 189a; and → SAFĪR

ṣifr (A) : 'empty'; in mathematics, the small circle indicating the absence of number, i.e. the zero. III 1139b; IX 556b

ṣīgha (A) : lit. form. I 318b

In Persia, a designation for a second temporary marriage, MUTʿA, with the same man after the expiry of the first, in order to evade the period of abstention, ʿIDDA, which in such a case is considered to be unnecessary. The woman in such an arrangement is also called ~ . VII 759a

sïghnaḳ (T) : place of refuge. IX 557b

ṣiḥāfa (A), or *ṣaḥāfa* : the written press, profession of the journalist, *ṣaḥāfī*. IX 558a; XII 730a

siḥāḳ (A), or *saḥḳ, tasāḥuḳ* : lesbianism. Lesbians are called *sāḥiḳāt, saḥḥāḳāt* or *musāḥiḳāt*. II 551a; IX 565b

siḥr (A) : lawful, 'white magic', also called *al-ukhdha* 'charm, incantation', and sorcery, 'black magic'. I 1084b; IV 770a; V 100b; IX 567b

sīkāh (A) : in music, a three-quarter-tone. XII 667b; and → WUSṬĀ ZALZAL

siḳāya (A) : the institution of providing water for the pilgrims in Mecca. I 9a; I 80a; VI 144b; XI 441a; the name of the building, close to Zamzam, where the distribution took place. VII 840a

In Fās, the popular term for public fountain. VIII 680b

sikbādj (A, < P *sik* 'vinegar' and *bādj* 'type [of meat]'), or ZIRBĀDJ : a vinegar- and flour-based meat stew or broth cooked with vegetables, fruit, spices and date-juice, originally from the Sāsānid court and later popular under the ʿAbbāsids. IX 576a; XI 369b

sikka (A) : lit. an iron ploughshare; an iron stamp or die used for stamping coins. From this latter meaning, ~ came to denote the result of the stamping, i.e. the legends on the coins, and then the whole operation of minting coins; coinage. I 117b; IX 591b; a post 'stage', also called *ribāṭ* in Persia, of which there were no less than 930 in the ʿAbbāsid empire. I 1044b; VIII 500a; a ploughshare, also called *sinn, sinna, naʿl.* VII 22a; the name for the Turkish dervish cap. X 614b; and → SHĀRIʿ

♦ **sikkat al-ḥadīd** (A, P *rāh-i āhan*, T *demiryolu*) : lit. iron line; the railway. IX 600b

sikke-zen (T), or *sikke-kün* : in Ottoman times, the worker who, under strict supervision, prepared the steel moulds in the mints. II 119a

ṣiḳlabī → ṢAḲĀLIBA

sīkrān → SAYKARĀN

ṣīkūk → BARBŪSHA

ṣila (A) : lit. connection, what is connected; also, a gift, reward, remuneration (syn. *djāʾiza*). IX 607b; and → WAṢL

In grammar 'adjunct' (syn. *ḥashw, zāʾid, faḍl, laghw*), a syntactical term which denotes the clause which complements such word classes termed *mawṣūl*, e.g. the relative pronouns *alladhī, man, mā, ayy-* and the subordinative *an, anna.* IX 603a; appended clause, especially relative clause, with the occasional synonym *waṣl.* XI 173a

In literature, ~ denotes the continuation, the complement of a work (for syn., IX 603b). In certain cases, e.g. historiography, a ~ can be both a kind of summary or partial rewriting, with additions of the original work, and a continuation of the latter. IX 603b f.; and → FĀʾIT

silāḥ (A, pl. *asliḥa, suluḥ, sulḥān, silāḥāt*) : in military science, general term for both offensive weapons and protective armour and equipment, the collective sense also often included in the term *ʿudda*, lit. equipment, gear, tackle. XII 734b, at the end of which article a large glossary of weaponry terms can be found

♦ **silāḥdār** (P, A *amīr silāḥ*) : lit. armsbearer, a military-administrative title and function gong back to the days of the Great Saldjūḳs. Chief of the army's arsenal where the armour and weapons were stored, the ~ was one of the most trusted personnel in the sultan's palace, directly responsible to the sultan. Among the Mamlūks, the ~ was one of the nine most important office holders. IX 609b

♦ silāḥdārlar → DÖRT BÖLÜK

♦ silāḥdāriyya (P, A) : under the Mamlūks, a royal unit with a number of horsemen ranging from 110 to 120, commanded by a SILĀḤDĀR. IX 610a

siʿlāt (A, pl. *saʿālī*) : the female of the GHŪL, a fabulous being, although the sources do not all agree on the distinction. II 1078b

silb (A) : in mediaeval agriculture, a term for the piece of wood whose end joins on to the ploughshare, clearly the same pole or beam called *waydj* and *hays* in Yemen or in Oman. VII 22a

silḳ (A) : beets, one of the Prophet's preferred vegetables. II 1058a

silḳī → ZUMURRUD

sillawr (A) : in zoology, the sheat fish. VIII 1021a

silsal → ḲARḲAL

silsila (A) : lit. chain, in particular the chain of saints of a mystical order leading back to the historic founder. II 164b; IX 611a; the chain of initiation and transmission of mystical knowledge also known as *sanad.* IV 950b

sīm (A, var. *sīn*) : argot; *lughat al-~* is a secret vocabulary or argot employed by criminals, beggars, gypsies and other groups for communication among themselves. It is still found in the contemporary Arabic world, notably the ~ *al-ṣāgha* 'argot of gold and silversmiths', based largely on Hebrew and recorded so far in Cairo and Damascus. IX 611b

sīmā (A), or *sīmā'* : a mark of recognition of the believer, either physical or moral; the distinctive mark of Muslims in relation to other peoples. IX 613a

ṣimāda (A) : a bonnet-like hat trimmed with coins most common to women of Ramallah; a man's headcloth in Iraq; a cloth used for covering the head underneath the turban in the Ḥidjāz. V 741b; VII 920a

simāṭ (A) : a low oblong table. XII 99a; a mat. X 4b

♦ al-simāṭ al-Khalīlī (A), or *ʿadas al-Khalīl* : in mediaeval times, a meal consisting of lentils cooked in olive oil that was distributed daily to everybody in the town of Hebron, meant to honour Abraham's generosity and hospitality. This practice, which was peculiar to Hebron, was at its height during the Mamlūk period; the meal consisted then of a certain recipe called *dashīsha* and bread and was distributed three times a day. IV 957a

simindjānī → SUḲUṬRĪ

sīmiyā' (A, < Gk) : a name for certain genres of magic, a.o. hypnotism and letter magic (also *sīmiyya*), mastered in particular by Aḥmad al-Būnī (d. 622/1225). VIII 430a; IX 612a

simsār → DALLĀL

simsim (A) : in botany, sesame (syn. *djuldjulān*). V 863a; IX 614a

simṭ (A, pl. *sumūṭ*) : a necklace of pearls; an entire poem. IX 449a; the term for the common-rhyme lines in a MUWASHSHAḤ poem. VII 809b

sīmurgh (P) : a mythical giant bird of Persian epic tradition. IX 615a

sīn and **shīn** (A) : the twelfth and thirteenth letter of the Arabic alphabet. In the Eastern form of the ABDJAD, *sīn* has the numerical value 60 and *shīn* that of 300. IX 615a

ṣināʿa (A, pl. *ṣināʿāt*) : the occupation of and production by artisans; craft, industry; the action of shipbuilding. IX 625a; in prosody, titivation. IX 455a

sinād (A) : in music, one of three kinds of song, which, according to Ibn al-Kalbī, had a slow refrain but was full of notes. II 1073b

In prosody, a violation of rules applying to vowels and consonants that precede the rhyme letter, *rawī*, namely, the *sinād al-tawdjīh*, the changing of the vowel immediately preceding the quiescent *rawī*; the *sinād al-ishbāʿ*, the changing of the vowel of the DAKHĪL; the *sinād al-ḥadhw*, the changing of the vowel immediately preceding the RIDF; the *sinād al-ridf*, the rhyming of a line that has a *ridf* with one that has not; and the *sinād al-ta'sīs*, the rhyming of a line that has TA'SĪS with one that has not. IV 412b

For ~ in zoology, → KARKADDAN

sinām (A) : a knife-cut on the two sides of the back, which marked a victim, *budna*, intended to be slaughtered in sacrifice at the time of the pilgrimage. IX 424b

sinān (A) : in military science, the head or blade of a spear, its foot of iron, stuck into the ground when the weapon was not being carried, being called *zudjdj*. XII 735b

sindhind (A calque 'Sind and Hind', < San *siddhānta* 'perfected') : a term applied to a class of Sanskrit astronomical texts. IX 640b

ṣindj → ṢANDJ

sindjāb (A) : in zoology, the grey squirrel. II 817a

sinet (K) : circumcision, in Kurd society practised a few days after birth by a specialist, *sinetker*, or by a simple barber. V 471a

ṣinf (A, pl. *aṣnāf, ṣunūf*) : lit. sort, kind; a group of something; various crafts and trades, profession (syn. *ḥirfa, kār*); (erroneously) guild. II 967a; IX 626b; IX 644a

singir (J), or *geguritan* : in Java, a form of Islamic poetry that treats themes similar to those of religious SYAIRs, consisting of verse lines of between eight to ten syllables in length, which can be grouped into rhyming couplets, quatrains, or groups of variable lengths. XII 728b

ṣīnī (A, P *čīnī*) : a generic term for Chinese ceramics including porcelain. IX 647a

sinn, sinna → SIKKA

ṣinnāra (A) : in the mediaeval kitchen, a poker used to remove a loaf of bread from the oven if it fell upon the floor inside. VI 808a

sinnawr (A, pl. *sanānīr*), or *sunnār, sunār* : in zoology, the cat (syn. *hirr, ḳiṭṭ*), both wild and domestic. Of the latter, ~ *miṣrī* 'Egyptian cat' (*Felis maniculata*) and ~ *shīrāzī* 'Persian cat' (*Felis angorensis*) are typical. IX 651b, where are listed many synonyms

In military science, a battering-ram (syn. *kabsh*). III 469b

♦ sinnawr al-zabād → ZABĀD

sīp (P) : mother of pearl. VIII 269a

sipāh (P), or *sipah* : army.

♦ **sipāhī** (P, > Eng *sepoy*, Fr *spahi*) : soldier; in the Ottoman empire, a TĪMĀR-holder. VIII 203b; cavalryman. IX 656a

In North Africa, a *sbāʾiḥiyya* (s. *sibāḥī*) denoted a corps of mounted gendarmerie. In the 19th and early 20th centuries, it was used for troopers of the corps of locally-raised cavalry organised by the French army there. IX 657a

♦ sipāhī oghlanlarï → DÖRT BÖLÜK

♦ sipāhīlik (T) : the SIPĀHĪ profession and class, prevalent with the Ottomans until the use of handguns made it necessary to resort to mercenaries during the war against the Habsburgs in 1593-1606. X 502b

♦ sipahsālār → ISPAHSĀLĀR

siʿr → TASʿĪR

sīra (A, pl. *siyar*) : way of going, way of acting, conduct; memorable action, record of such an action; in its pl. form, ~ is also used for 'rules of war and of dealings with non-Muslims'. IX 660b

As a Qurʾānic term, ~ is found with the meaning 'state' or 'appearance'. III 369b

In literature, ~ is used for biography, especially that of the Prophet, and for the genre of romantic biographies of famous characters of antiquity or of the Islamic era. III 369b; V 1161b; IX 660b

♦ **sīra shaʿbiyya** (A) : modern designation for a genre of lengthy Arabic heroic narratives called in western languages either popular epics or popular romances. IX 664a

ṣirāʿ → ṢURʿA

sirādj (A, < P *čirāgh*) : lamp, beacon (syn. *miṣbāḥ*, ḲINDĪL). IX 665a

♦ **sirādj al-ḳuṭrub** (A, < Syr) : lit. the werewolf's lamp; in botany, the name for the mandrake, the plant species of *Mandragora officinarum* L, and more specifically for its forked root (syn. *mandrāghūras*, **yabrūḥ**, *shadjarat al-ṣanam, luffāḥ*). IX 667a

sirāḥ (A) : the sweat lost by horses covered by blankets in a thinning-down process for horse-racing. II 953a

ṣirāṭ (A, < ult. L *strata*) : 'way'; in the Qurʾān, ~ is almost always introduced by the verb *hadā* 'to guide' or the verbal noun *hudā* 'guidance', and qualified by *mustaḳīm* 'right'. IX 670b

As a proper name, al-Ṣirāṭ is the bridge which dominates hell. IX 670b

sirb (A, pl. *asrāb*) : a flock of birds (syn. *raʿla*, pl. *riʿāl*). IV 744a

sirbāl (A) : a tunic. VIII 883b; a garment in general. IX 676b

sirdāb → SARDĀB

sirī → ṢUFRĪ

sırık → ḤAMMĀL

sirḳa (A) : in law, theft, *al-~ al-ṣughrā* being used for simple theft and *al-~ al-kubrā*, or ḲAṬʿ AL-ṬARĪḲ, used for brigandage and highway robbery. V 768a

sirr (A) : lit. secret; in mysticism, the notion of mystery, arcana, in the sense of a teaching, a reality or even a doctrinal point, hidden by nature or which is kept hidden from persons considered unworthy of knowing it; also the notion of a 'subtle organ', one of the layers of the 'heart', making up the human spiritual anatomy, which may be translated as 'inner consciousness'. XII 752b

sirwāl (A, P *s͟halwar*; pl. *sarāwīl*) : trousers. IX 676a

ṣīṣa (A, pl. *ṣayāṣī*), or *ṣīṣiyya* : in zoology, the very long, straight with a slight backward slope and a two-and-a-half turn spiral, horns of the addax (*Addax nasomaculatus*). V 1228b

sisāmuwīdā (A, < Gk) : in botany, sesame-like plants, considered as classes of a wild sesame. IX 615a

sitāʾis͟h → MADĪḤ

sitār → TĀR

sitāra (A) : in Muslim Spain, an orchestra formed by female singing slaves, named after the curtain which separated in theory the caliph from the singers and musicians. IV 823b; and → ḤID͟JĀB

sitr (A) : veil, a curtain behind which the Fāṭimid caliph was concealed at the opening of the audience session. IX 685a; the name given to the curtain by which Muḥammad concealed his women from the gaze of the world. IX 902b; and → ḤID͟JĀB

sitta → K͟HAMSA

siwāk → MISWĀK

ṣiwis͟h (Ott) : in Ottoman administration, the omission of one year in every 33, to keep the financial year in line with the religious year. X 263a

siyāḳat (T, A *siyāḳa*), or *siyāḳ* : in ʿAbbāsid financial administration, 'accounting practice', 'revenue bookkeeping practice'. IX 692b

In calligraphy, a script considered to have been used from the Umayyad period onwards, which has no artistic appearance and was used in financial registers and suchlike. II 332b; IV 1124a; IX 692b; a curious stenographic-like Arabic script in which diacritics are not used. VIII 151b

ṣiyām → ṢAWM

siyar (A) : in jurisprudence, the area concerned with the rules of war and of dealings of non-Muslims, apostates and rebels. V 1162b; VIII 495b; and → SĪRA

siyāsa (A) : statecraft, management of affairs of state; from mid-19th century onwards, politics and political policy. IX 693b; punishment, extending as far as capital punishment; the violence the ruler has to use to preserve his authority, specifically punishment beyond the ḤADD penalties. IX 694a

♦ siyāsa s͟harʿiyya (A) : the concept of 'juridical policy', methodically taken up by Ibn ʿAḳīl, Ibn Taymiyya and Ibn Ḳayyim al-D͟jawziyya, or 'governance in accordance with the s͟harīʿa', a sunnī doctrine calling for harmonisation between FIḲH and SIYĀSA. In modern times, a recognition of authority in the state to take legal acts as needed for the public good when the s͟harīʿa has no text, NAṢṢ, on the matter, provided the s͟harīʿa is not infringed thereby. I 276b; IX 694b f.

♦ siyāsat-gāh (P) : a place of torture and execution. IX 694a

♦ siyāset (T) : (corporal) punishment in Ottoman penal law. II 518b

slamatan → SESAJEN

smala → ZMĀLA

ṣoff → LEFF; ṢAFF

ṣofra : term for a design in the centre of a carpet from ʿUs͟hāḳ, which would seem to indicate the medallion ʿUs͟hāḳ of modern terminology. X 914a

ṣofta (T) : under the Ottomans, a student of the theological, legal or other sciences (var. *sūk͟hte*). VIII 221b; IX 702b

sökmen → ALP

ṣolaḳ (T 'left-handed') : in the Ottoman military organisation, the name of part of the sultan's bodyguard, comprising four infantry companies of the Janissaries, originally archers. IX 712a

sonḳor (T), or *sunḳur* : one of many words denoting birds of prey, specifically the gerfalcon (*falco gyrfalco*). IX 730a

soyūrg͟hāl (Mon, P, or *suyūrg͟hāl*) : favour, reward granted by the ruler to someone, sometimes of a hereditary nature; in the course of time, ~ came to mean various grants formerly known as IḲṬĀʿ. IX 731b; in Persia, in post-Tīmūrid times, designation for a grant of immunity, often hereditary, from the payment of taxation, frequently, though not by any means always, granted to members of the religious classes. III 1089b; IV 1043b

sowar (Anglo-Eng, < P **suwār**) : in the Indian Army of British India, the designation for troopers in cavalry regiments. IX 909b

stribant : in India, a custom whereby the sons of each wife are regarded as one group and each group is awarded an equal share in the inheritance. Another custom called *chundawand*, similar in effect, entitles the group to its allotted portion until the extinction of its last member. I 172a

su bas͟hi̊ (T) : in Turkish tribal usage, 'commander of the army, troops'; in the Ottoman empire, a common military and police title. IX 736b

ṣuʾāb → ḲAML

suʿāt (A) : 'runners' in the postal service, first appearing during the Buwayhid dynasty. I 1044b; 'the dregs of the people, one of the numerous terms in the mediaeval and modern periods for 'rascal, scoundrel'. XI 546a

ṣūba (< ? A *ṣawb* 'patch, track') : in the Mug͟hal empire from Akbar onwards, the term for 'province', which was divided into SARKĀRs and PARGANAs. VIII 271a; IX 738a

♦ **ṣūbadār** : in the Mug͟hal empire, the governor of a province, ṢŪBA, also known as *sipāhsālār* (→ ISPAHSĀLĀR), *nāẓim* and *ṣāḥib ṣūba*. IX 738b

ṣubas͟hi̊ (Ott) : constable. X 413b; person in charge of a *subas͟hi̊liḳ*, a division of a SAND̲JAḲ. X 502b

ṣubba → ḲAṬĪʿ

subḥa (A, P *tasbīḥ*, T *tesbīḥ*, modT *tespih*) : rosary, consisting of three groups of beads made of wood, bone, mother of pearl, etc. and used by nearly all classes of Muslims except the Wahhābīs. IX 741b; in classical Tradition, ~ is used in the sense of supererogatory ṢALĀT. IX 742b

subḥān (A) : a Qurʾānic term, recorded solely in the form of an exclamative and annexed to *allāh* or some substitute, e.g. *rabb*, and translated most commonly 'Glory be to God'. IX 742b

sūbiyya (Egy) : an Egyptian spiced beverage, made with either wheat or rice, in either an intoxicating or a legal, non-alcoholic, version. VIII 653a

sūdānī → KŪFĪ

ṣudayra (A) : a short, sleeveless vest, worn by men in Egypt. V 741b

sudda (A) : threshold. IX 762a

ṣudg͟h (A, P *zulf*) : love locks of hair, one of a number of female hairstyles in pre- and early Islam, along with *ṭurra* 'fore locks' and *limma* 'shoulder locks'. IX 313a

sud̲jd̲ja (A) : horses; the name of an idol in pre-Islamic Arabia, as are *bad̲jd̲ja* 'blood drawn from an incision of a camel's vein' and *d̲jabha* 'forehead; a lunar mansion, the moon; horses; humiliation; the leading men of a tribe; the persons responsible for levying money for a ransom or debt'. IX 763a

al-suds al-fak͟hrī (A) : in astronomy, a sextant made by al-K͟hud̲jandī and dedicated to Fak͟hr al-Dawla that determines the obliquity of the ecliptic. V 46b

sudūs (A), or *sadūs* : a green ṬAYLASĀN worn by women, especially in winter time as a protection from the cold. X 614b

ṣūf (A) : the wool of camel (syn. *wabar*). IV 1148a; wool of sheep (syn. *labad*). IX 764b; XII 317a

♦ ṣūfa (A) : a woollen tampon. IX 249a

♦ ṣūfī (A) : in the 2nd/8th century, still an expression for a somewhat disreputable fringe movement of ascetics, in the course of the 3rd/9th century ~ was adopted for reasons which are not clear for the entire mystical movement. It never succeeded in imposing itself universally, however: in the East, in Khurāsān and in Transozania, a mystic was for a long time called ḤAKĪM and 'knower of God' (*ʿārif*) was often used. X 314a

sufahā' → AHL AL-FAḌL

ṣuffa (A), or *ẓulla* : in architecture, a colonnade, and according to Lane, a long, covered portico or vestibule, which formed part of the mosque at Medina. I 266a; I 610a; and → SAḲĪFA

ṣūfiyāna (P) : in the Mughal empire, the days of abstinence from eating meat, introduced by Akbar. IX 766b

ṣufr (A), or *bīrindj* : yellow; in mineralogy, brass. VIII 111b; IX 766a; bronze. XII 552b

♦ ṣufrī (A) : a variety of date, in particular from the al-Aflādj district in southern Nadjd, called by al-Hamdānī *sayyid al-tumūr*, although present-day inhabitants regard the *sirī* variety as the *sayyid*. I 233b

sufra (A), and *naṭʿ* : a table (syn. KHULWĀN and *mā'ida*), whereby ~ is a skin stretched out on the ground and serving, not only among the early Bedouin, but also in circles of sedentary Arabic civilisation, various functions in the home and in the country. In dialect, ~ is an ordinary table and *sufradjī* is a waiter in a restaurant or cafe. XII 99b; a mat. X 4b

♦ sufrači-bāshī (P) : in Ṣafawid times, an official in charge of arranging the floor cloth on which food was consumed. XII 609b

♦ sufradjī → SUFRA

suftadja (A, < P *sufta* 'pierced') : in finance, a negotiable instrument in the form of a written bill of credit similar to the modern drawing of a cheque; like ṢAKK, a medium through which funds were remitted. II 382b; VIII 493a; IX 769b

suhayl → SAFĪNA

ṣuḥba (A), or *ṣaḥāb* : in Yemen, an alliance among the Arab tribes of the desert based on a kind of fraternal relationship. It is an agreement, both defensive and offensive, by which two tribes undertake to take up arms on one another's behalf and henceforth may go to live on the territories of the other and also take advantage of its pastures. Excluded from this treaty are the fornicator and the thief. VI 491a; and → ṢĀḤIB

♦ ṣuḥbatiyya → YAZĪDĪ

suḥla (A) : the weanling hare. XII 84b

suḥna (A) : a term applied to the colour of the complexion, used in addition to the general term LAWN 'colour'. V 699b

ṣuḥuf → DAFTAR; DJARĪDA; MUṢḤAF

suḥūr → IMSĀKIYYA

sūḳ (A, < Ar; pl. *aswāḳ*) : market, in the sense of both the commercial exchange of goods or services and the place in which this exchange is normally conducted. IX 786b; XII 756a

♦ čahār sūḳ (P) : 'cruciform market'; in architecture, a type of bazaar with four streets for merchants and artisans, or four sides. V 665b; IX 796b

ṣuḳʿ (A) : region. X 896a

sūḳa (A) : lit. those led to pasture, one of the numerous terms in the mediaeval and modern periods for 'rascal, scoundrel'. XI 546a

suḳaṭ (A) : second-hand goods. XII 757b

sukhaymānī → UMMA

sukhf (A) : lack of substance; indecency, obscenity (more properly, *fuḥsh*); in literature, a genre of poetry of which the basis is sexuality and scatology, although MUDJŪN was preferred among early mediaeval literati. The adjectival form is *sakhīf*, meaning either shallow-witted or obscene. IV 780b; IX 804a; XII 16b

sūkhte → ṢOFTA

sukkar (A, < P) : the sap crushed from the sugar-cane, solid sugar. Some common types of sugar are *ṭabarzad* 'sugar set hard in moulds', *nabāt* 'sugar, also produced from other substances such as rose syrup or violet syrup, set on palm sticks placed in the recipient where it was being prepared', *fānīd* 'sugar made in elongated moulds produced by adding the oil of sweet almonds or finely-ground white flour to the process of decoction', and *sulaymānī* 'sugar made from hardened 'red sugar' broken into pieces and further cooked'. IX 804b

sukkayt (A) : 'silenced by shame at finishing last', the name for the tenth horse in a horse-race, according to the order of finishing. II 953a

suknā (A) : lit. abode; a Qur'ānic term referring to a woman's right upon her husband to provide shelter for her; also her right to stay in the matrimonial house during her waiting period following divorce or death. IX 805a

sukr (A) : in mysticism, 'intoxication', especially in the vocabulary of al-Ḥallādj. III 102b

suku : in Malaysia, matrilineal descent groups. VIII 483b

sukūn → ḤARAKA

sukurrudja (A) : in chemistry, a pan, one of the many apparatuses in a lab described in the 5th/11th century. V 114b

sukūt (A) : lit. silence; in law, an individual's action of not actively expressing an opinion when involved in an action or contract that requires acceptance or rejection, which 'answer' is clarified by circumstance. IX 806b; IX 845b

suķūṭ (A), or *suķūṭ al-kusūf* : falling, the ἔμπτωσις of Ptolemy; in astronomy, the phase from the beginning (*badʾ*) of an eclipse to the beginning of totality. V 536b

suķuṭrī (A, < *suķuṭra*) : one of a variety of the aloe, considered to be the best and probably corresponding with the *Aloe Parryi* Baker, the *Aloe Socotrina*, which thrives in great quantities on the island of Socotra. The other frequently mentioned varieties are *ʿarabī (ḥaḍramī)* and *simindjānī*. VIII 687b

sulāḥ (A) : in zoology, the particularly vile-smelling droppings of the fox. X 432b

sulaḥfā (A, pl. *salāḥif*), or *sulaḥfāʾ*, *sulaḥfiyya* : in zoology, the tortoise or turtle in general, terrestrial as well as aquatic. The male is also called *ghaylam*, the female also *ṭuwama*. IX 811a, where dialectal names are also found

In astronomy, *al-sulaḥfā*^{h} is one of several names for the nineteenth boreal constellation of the Lyre situated between Hercules and the Swan. IX 811a

sulaṭān (A) : in Muslim Spain, a designation for Alfonso VII of Castile after he had come to the throne as a child. IX 849a

sulaymānī → KĀGHAD; SUKKAR

ṣulb (A) : in geography, hard, stony ground. VIII 1048a

ṣulḥ (A) : truce, armistice; peace and reconciliation. II 131a; IX 845a

♦ ṣulḥ al-ibrāʾ (A) : in Shāfiʿī law, a peace settlement by virtue of which the claimed object would be a HIBA 'donation', as opposed to a *ṣulḥ al-muʿāwaḍa*, when the object is replaced by another. IX 845b

♦ ṣulḥ ʿalā inkār → INKĀR

♦ **ṣulḥ-i kull** (IndP) : universal toleration, a policy of the Mughal emperor Akbar. I 317a; IX 846a

sullam (A) : a bilingual Coptic-Arabic vocabulary. IX 848b

sulṭān (A, < Syr; pl. *salāṭīn*) : holder of power, authority; sultan. VIII 1000b; IX 849a

In the Shībānid realm, ~ denoted an individual eligible to succeed to the khānate. The sovereign had the title *khān*. IX 429b

♦ sulṭān Ibrāhīm (A) : lit. the sultan Abraham; in zoology, the red mullet (*Mullus barbatus*). VIII 1021a

♦ sulṭān al-sawāḥil (A) : the title of Meḥmed, who also used the title Teke Bey, of the Teke-oghullari̊, a Türkmen dynasty. X 413a

♦ **sulṭān al-ṭalaba** (A, pop. *al-ṭolba*) : a traditional Moroccan spring festival, celebrated annually in the second half of April, primarily at Fās. A central feature of the feast was the election of a mock sultan. IX 857b; X 148b

♦ sulṭānī (A, T) : in numismatics, the first Ottoman gold coin, which, when it was introduced in 882 AH, adopted the weight standard of the Venetian ducat, *ca.* 3.52 g. VIII 228b

♦ sulṭānli̊ḳ (T) : in the Ottoman empire, a fief for which one has received investiture. IX 727b

suluk : in Javanese literature, a poetical genre of short mystical poems. VIII 294a

sulūk (A) : in political theory, conduct or comportment of leaders. IX 861b

In mysticism, ~ is the Islamic version of the archetypal motif of the 'journey' which mystics of different religious traditions have used to describe the various steps to realise union with the divine; the progress which the mystic makes on the *via mystica*; also 'spiritual correctness', the 'travelling-manners' which the mystic must possess to traverse the stations of the Way. The ṣūfī wayfarer is called a *sālik*. IX 862a

ṣuʿlūk (A, pl. *ṣaʿālīk*) : in pre- and early Islam, the knight-errant of the desert, brigand of the highways; brigand-poet. II 963b; VIII 496b; IX 863b; XII 122a

sulūḳī (A, pl. *sulūḳiyya*) : the greyhound, used in hawking and falconry. I 1152b

sumʿa wa-riyāʾ (A) : ostentation, i.e. done in order that people may 'hear and see' it. X 900b

sumānā → SALWĀ

sumaniyya (A, < Skr) : the Buddhists. IX 869a

sumayrī (A, pl. *sumayriyyāt*) : a type of ship mentioned as a troop-carrying craft in the historical accounts of the Zandj rebellion in the later 3rd/9th century, and used in 315/927 in order to prevent the Carmathians from crossing the Euphrates. VIII 811a

summ (A, P *zahr*; pl. *sumūm*), or *samm* : poison, venom. IX 872a

sūmūlak : a pudding-like food made of sprouted wheat, which Özbegs distribute to family and friends during the celebration of the New Year. VIII 234b

sunan → SUNNA

sunār → SINNAWR

sunbula (A) : 'the ear of the corn'; in astronomy, *al-~* is the term for Virgo, one of the twelve zodiacal constellations. Some philologists explain ~ to be Coma Berenices. The constellation is also known as *al-ʿadhrāʾ*, while ~ stands for the star α Virginis. VII 83b

sūndar : a Kurdish musical instrument of the pandore type, resembling the ČŪGŪR but with twelve metal strings. X 626a

sundus (P) : a type of green brocade, made in Yazd. XI 304a

sunna (A, pl. **sunan**) : habit, hereditary norm of conduct, custom; a normative custom of the Prophet or of the early community; orthodoxy. I 175b; II 888b; III 23b; IV 147b ff.; IX 878a

In its plural form, *sunan* refers to several important collections of Traditions and legal pronouncements, becoming the generic book title of such works. IX 874a

♦ sunna muʾakkida → NĀFILA

sunnār → SINNAWR

sūr (A, pl. *aswār, sīrān*) : the wall of a town or other enclosed urban or built-up space. IX 881b

♦ sūr-nāme (Ott) : in literature, a work describing imperial weddings and circumcision feasts. X 293a

sūra (A, < Syr *ṣūrṭā, sūrthā*; pl. *suwar*) : a Qurʾānic term, ~ refers to a unit of revelation. The Qurʾān gives no indication as to how long these units of revelation were. They were most likely only parts of the present sūras, of which there are 114 of widely varying length and form, divided into a number of verses. V 402a; V 409b ff.; IX 885b

ṣūra (A) : image, form, shape; face, countenance. IX 889a; and → KAWKABA; TAṢWĪR

♦ **ṣūrat al-arḍ** (A) : lit. the form or shape of the earth; title for two early Islamic geographical works covering the world as it was then known. IX 893b; and → DJUGHRĀFIYĀ; KHARĪṬA

♦ ṣūrat al-rāmī (A) : in astronomy, the constellation of Sagittarius. VIII 842a

ṣurʿa (A), or *ṣirāʿ* : 'wrestling', with the basic idea of hurling one's opponent to the ground. In mediaeval times, it may have been a popular sport; in 251/865 citizens hired *muṣāriʿūn* (s. *muṣāriʿ*) to defend their houses against the violence of the Turkish soldiery. VIII 239a

ṣurad (A) : in zoology, the shrike, mentioned in Tradition. VII 906b

surādiḳ (A) : among the pre-Islamic Bedouin, a cloth tent of quite large dimensions. IV 1147a

ṣurāḥ → IBRĪZ

süratdji̊ (T) : in the Ottoman army, a rapid-fire artilleryman. XI 328b

surau : in Sumatra, a centre for religious studies; a religious school. VIII 237b; VIII 296b

suraydjiyya → MASʾALA

surghūs (A) : in zoology, the common sargo. VIII 1021a

sürgün (T) : lit. expulsion; under the Ottomans, the compulsory re-settlement of people from various parts of the empire. IV 225a; IV 238a; IX 655a; XII 767a

surkh → RATTĪ

surkhāb → NUḤĀM

surkhadja (P) : in medicine, measles. IX 474b

surma → KUḤL

surnāy (P), and *suryānāy* : in music, the Persian reed-pipe. X 35a

ṣurra (A, T *ṣurre*) : lit. bag, purse; a sealed purse containing coins. IX 894a

Under the Mamlūks, a purse of money distributed as a gift by the ruler. IX 894a

Under the Ottomans, payment made by pilgrim caravans on the way to the Holy Cities, in return for the right to enter alien territory and for protection while staying there. I 483b; IV 1133b; VIII 489b; IX 894a

♦ ṣurrat al-ḥaramayn (A) : the sum once sent by Islamic countries such as Egypt and Tunisia for distribution to the poor of Mecca and Medina during the pilgrimage. IV 1133b

surriyya (A) : a concubine. I 28a; V 553b

sūs (A, P *mahak, mathak*) : in botany, licorice, both the root and the decoction from the root (syn. *ʿūd al-sūs, shadjarat al-furs*). IX 897b; a cavity in wood. XI 263a

sūsan (P, < MidP), or more often *sawsan* : in botany, the iris or lily (*Iris florentina* L., or *Lilium sp.*). The blue iris was called *sūsan asmāndjūnī*; other colours were white and yellow. IX 902b

sutra (A) : initially, a veil or screen, covering, protection, shelter; in Islamic prayer, a technical term for any object placed by the worshipper some distance before him, in front of which no person should pass while the prayer is being performed. VIII 928a; IX 902b

suttūḳ → SATTŪḲ

suʿūṭ (A, Egy *nushūḳ*, P *anfiya*) : snuff, which was adopted in places like Yemen and in the Ottoman empire at times when regular smoking was proscribed. It has long been common in Afghanistan, where it is called *naswar*. X 754a

suwār (P, IndP *sawār*) : horseman; in Muslim India, a rank in the Mug̲h̲al military indicating the number of troopers (*tābīnān*) and horses the *manṣabdār* (→ MANṢAB) was ordered to maintain. VI 422b; IX 909a

♦ bārgīr-suwār : a category of horsemen in the Mug̲h̲al army, who neither owned horses nor were enrolled as troopers of the *manṣabdārs* (→ MANṢAB), the *ṭābīnān*. However, as they were fit for cavalry service, in times of emergency they were provided with horses and went into action. They were not, however, part of the regular cavalry. V 686b

suyūrg̲h̲āl → SOYŪRG̲H̲ĀL

suyūrsāt (P) : purveyance; one of the unfixed taxes in Persia, consisting of levies made for the keep and expenses of military forces, government officials, and foreign envoys passing through the country, and like the ṢĀDIRĀT bore heavily upon the peasantry. II 152a; IV 1043a

sūz-u gudāz (P) : in Persian literature, a genre of short poems devoted to the description of painful experiences, fashionable in the 10th-11th/16th-17th centuries. VI 834b

syair → S̲H̲ĀʿIR

T

tā' (A) : the third letter of the Arabic alphabet, with the numerical value 400, representing a voiceless, slightly aspirated, dental (or dento-alveolar) stop. X 1a

ṭā' (A) : the sixteenth letter of the Arabic alphabet, with the numerical value 9, representing a voiceless, unaspirated, dental (dento-alveolar) stop with simultaneous velarisation. X 1a

For ~ in music, → TIK WA-TUM

ṭāʿa (A, pl. *ṭāʿāt*) : in theology, an act of obedience to God, contrasted with *maʿṣiya*, an act of disobedience to God, hence a sin. X 1b

taʿaddī (A) : lit. transgression; in law, tort or negligence. II 105a; XI 22a

In grammar, transitivity. Verbs that are *mutaʿadd* cause the agents to be in the nominative and the verb complements to be in the accusative. X 3b

taʿad̲j̲d̲j̲ub (A) : lit. amazement; in rhetoric, one of the basic effects or aims of the poetic process, especially of imagery. X 4a

taʿāḳul (A) : in law, joint liability by the ʿĀḲILA. I 338a

taʿalluḳ (A), or more often, *taʿalluḳa* : lit. dependence, being related to, dependent on; in late Mug̲h̲al Indian administration, a jurisdiction, fiscal area, from which a fixed amount of taxes was to be collected by a revenue official called TAʿALLUḲDĀR or *taʿalluḳadār*. Distinguished from the older term *zamīndārī*, the ~ did not give its holder feudal rights, and thus the *taʿalluḳdār* ranked lower than the ZAMĪNDĀR. XII 767b

♦ taʿalluḳdār : under the Mug̲h̲als, a term from the late 11th/17th century onwards for a ZAMĪNDĀR who paid revenue not only on his own jurisdiction but also on those of others. XI 439a

ṭaʿām (A) : food, nourishment. X 4b

taʿammul (A) : in rhetoric, artificiality. X 304b

taʿarrub (A) : in earliest Islam, the return (syn. *tabaddā*) to the Arabian desert after emigration, *hid̲j̲ra*, to the garrison towns and participation in the warfare to expand the Islamic empire. X 5a

taʿāruḍ (A) : in law, conflicting possibilities. IX 324b

taʿaṣṣub (A), or *tanaṭṭuʿ*, *tazammut*, *tas̲h̲addud* : fanaticism, rigorism, synonyms of TAṬARRUF. X 372a taʿaṭṭuf → ʿAṬF

taʿāwun (A) : mutual aid; in the 20th century, ~ took on the meaning of co-operation in all modern senses of the term, with *taʿāwunī* (co-operative), *mutaʿāwin* (co-operator), and *taʿāwuniyya* (co-operativism, principally agricultural), and was applied to the activities and institutions of international co-operation. X 5b

taʿawwudh (A) : the use of the phrase *aʿūdhu bi 'llāhi min* . . . ('I take refuge from God against . . .'), syn. *istiʿādha*, and, more specifically, the formula *aʿūdhu bi 'allāhi mina 'l-shayṭāni 'l-radjīm* which is a safeguard against misspeaking, omission of words, and other such mistakes when preceding a Qurʾānic recitation or prayer. Its counterpart is *ṣadaḳa 'llāhu 'l-ʿaẓīm*, which follows any formal recitation. X 5a

taʿayyuf → TAṬAYYUR

tāb-khāne (T) : lodgings for dervishes added on both sides of the prayer hall of a mosque. XII 471a

ṭābaʿ (Mor) : the seal, either on a seal ring or mounted on a stem, until recent times serving for the authentication of official documents. IV 1105b

tabaddā → TAʿARRUB

ṭabāhidja : a dish, one of whose stages of preparation calls for a combination of saffron with honey, nuts, corn starch, pepper and various spices mixed together and added to the pot. XI 381b

ṭabaḳ al-manāṭiḳ (A) : in astronomy, an equatorium designed to determine the position of the planets by manual means; the first reference to such an instrument appears in the work of the Hispano-Arab Azarquiel. IV 703a

ṭābaḳ → RUḲĀḲ

ṭabaḳa (A, pl. *ṭibāḳ*) : in Mamlūk times, the barracks in the Cairo citadel where the Royal Mamlūks were quartered. X 5a; Mamlūk tiered accommodation. IX 792b

In architecture, the most common type of living-unit in a Cairene RABʿ, a kind of duplex with a vestibule, a recess for water jars, a latrine and a main room consisting of a slightly raised ĪWĀN and a DŪRḲĀʿA. An inner staircase led up to a mezzanine, *mustaraḳa*, used for sleeping. Each unit had its own enclosed private roof. A ~ may also be a triplex with an additional room above the mezzanine. VIII 344a; and → ṬABAḲĀT

♦ **ṭabaḳāt** (A, s. *ṭabaḳa*) : in literature, a genre of biographical works arranged according to generation, *ṭabaḳa*; ultimately applied to those which follow alphabetical order. VI 109b; X 7b

tabakkala → TAHASHSHADA

tabannin (A) : adoption, the giving of one's name to another who does not belong within his 'natural' descendance, which is strictly prohibited in the Qurʾān. XII 768a

ṭabar axe. X 18b

tabardār → BALṬADJĪ

ṭabarī (A) : a green silk brocade, known after their place of production, Ṭabaristān. XII 448b

tabarruʾ (A, P *tabarrā*) : in Islamic religious polemics, the doctrine of exemption or of disengagement, in particular exemption from responsibility. It developed under the Khāridjites to mean 'to regard as an enemy', and in Ṣafawid Persian of the 10th/16th century it was widely expanded to become an euphemism for insult or execration. X 21a

tabarruk (A) : in mysticism, a casual method of affiliation with an order, little exacting in terms of initiation, which consists of the simple reception of BARAKA conveyed by an initiatory lineage. The modality of ~ allows and explains the practice of multiple affiliation. X 245b

ṭabarzad → SUKKAR

ṭabāshīr (A) : a medicament from the crystalline concretions in the internodes of the bamboo, known as 'bamboo sugar', and consisting of silicic acid, silicates, and carbonate of calcium. X 23a

tabattul (A) : in mysticism, 'consecration to God'. IV 697a; celibacy. IV 1089a

ṭabbākh (A) : professional cook, unlike *ṭāhī* or *shāwī* 'roaster', who was probably a slave and not a professional. X 23b

ṭabbāl (A) : drummer; owner of a drum. X 24a

tabbān (A) : a straw seller. XII 757a

tabdaba → AḲWĀL

tabdīl → TAḤRĪF

tabīʿ (A) : a cow or bull in its second year. XI 412a

tābiʿ (A, pl. TĀBIʿŪN) : follower; and → ITBĀʿ; POSTA; ṢĀḤIB

♦ **tābiʿūn** (A) : the Followers, or Successors, of the Prophet's Companions. A large number of these were contemporaries of the Companions, ṢAḤĀBA; some might even have been alive during the Prophet's lifetime but without satisfying the conditions which would have permitted them to be classed among the *ṣaḥāba*. The last of the ~ died around 180/796. IV 149a; VIII 900a; X 28b

♦ atbāʿ al-tābiʿūn (A) : the Successors of the TĀBIʿŪN. There are no sufficiently precise criteria enabling us to define exactly this group of men. They are essentially the most eminent disciples of the great *tābiʿūn*. The middle of the 3rd/9th century can be taken as their *terminus ad quem*. IV 149a; VIII 900a

ṭābiʿ → TAMGHA

ṭabīʿa (A) : lit. nature, a term of Islamic science, philosophy and theology, usually translated in the context of Aristotle's φύσις and defined as 'the essential first principle of motion and rest'. X 25b

♦ ṭabīʿī (A) : natural (ant. *maṣnūʿ*), XII 769a

♦ **ṭabīʿiyyāt** (A, < *ṭabīʿī*) : the science of physics, or natural sciences. VIII 105b; XII 769a

ṭābil → RUḲĀḲ

ṭabīla → SHAKSHĀK

ṭābīnān → (BĀRGĪR-)SUWĀR

taʿbīr (A) : 'the passage of one thing to another, one sense to another', hence 'explanation', like *tafsīr*, lit. commenting, explaining. In current usage, ~ is confined to the sense of 'interpretation of dreams' (→ TAʿBĪR AL-RUʾYA) while TAFSĪR is used for commentaries on e.g. the Bible and the Qurʾān. XII 770a

♦ **taʿbīr al-ruʾya** (A) : the interpretation of dreams, oneiromancy. XII 770a

tabīra : in music, a drum. X 35a

ṭabkh (A) : the action of cooking either in a pot, by boiling or stewing, or by roasting, broiling, frying or baking. X 30a

ṭabl (A) : the generic name for any member of the drum family. X 32b; or *dawul*, a rather large wooden double-headed drum held slantwise by a strap and beaten with two sticks of uneven dimensions and shape. It was the basic percussion instrument of the Ottoman ensemble, MEHTER. VI 1007b

♦ ṭabl al-baladī → DUHUL

♦ ṭabl al-markab : in music, the mounted drum, probably identical with the *dabdāb*, *dabdaba*, and NAḲḲĀRA. X 35a

♦ **ṭabl-khāna** : lit. drum house; the name given in Islamic lands to the military band and its quarters in camp or town. X 34b

♦ ṭabla → DJARAS

tablīgh (A) : propagating the faith. X 38a

tabriʾa (A) : an Ibāḍī penal sanction (*tebriya*), viz. 'an indemnity paid by the parents of the murderer to those of the victim for continuing to live within the tribe'; a term used for all sorts of declaratory or constitutive acts which absolve from responsibility. I 1026b

tab<u>sh</u>īr (A) : lit. proclamation, spreading of the good news; in modern works, term for Christian proselytism and the work of missionaries (*mubashshirūn*) within the Islamic world. XII 772a

♦ tab<u>sh</u>īriyya (A) : missionary activities. XII 772b

ṭabū (T) : in Ottoman administration, a land register. V 336a

ṭābūn (A), or *ṭābūna* : originally, the cavity in which a fire was made to shelter it from the wind; an oven. II 1059a; a small jar-shaped oven used for baking bread. In Jordan it consists of a small construction in which is placed a sort of cooking-pot, surrounded by embers to cook the dough in the interior. V 42b

ṭabūr (T) : in military usage, a pallisade formed of waggons arranged in a circle or square; a body of troops sent out for reconnaissance; a battalion; a body of about 1,000 men commanded by a BIÑBA<u>SH</u>Ī. X 51a

tābūt (A) : coffin. I 200a; XII 503a; the Ark in biblical times. X 168b; 'water-screw', a kind of hydraulic machine for irrigating the fields, in use in Egypt from the times of the Ptolemys until the present. It consists of a wooden cylinder (about 6-9 feet in length) hooped with iron. While the spiral pipe is fixed between the inside wall of the ~ and an iron axis, its upper extremity is bent into a crank and its lower end turns on a stake set under the water. One or two peasants crouch at the water's edge, endlessly turning the crank handle. The water rises from bend to bend in the spiral pipe until it flows out at the mouth of the canal. V 864a

In law, the orphan's property deposited in the <u>sh</u>arīʿa court. XI 300a

tabwīb (A) : in the science of Tradition, the bringing together of material in chapters under certain subject headings. X 80a

ṭābya (A) : in architecture, 'cobwork', a technique by which earth with which chalk and crushed baked earth or broken stones are often mixed is rammed between two boards, kept parallel by beams. The wall is plastered over, often in such a way as to simulate joints of heavy bond-work beneath. When this plaster falls, the regularly spaced holes left by the beams become visible. Cobwork was general in the Muslim West in the 5th/11th and 6th/12th centuries. I 1226b

tabyīt (A) : in religious law, each day of fasting. IX 94b

taḍabbaba (A), also *taḥallama, ig<u>h</u>tāla* : in the terminology of childhood, a verb which expresses the stage when a child becomes fat. VIII 822a

taḍādd → ṬIBĀḲ

taḍammun (A) : in literary criticism, 'implication', that is, 'house' denotes a ceiling, one of a threefold system of denotation outlined by al-Zan<u>dj</u>ānī, along with MUṬĀBAḲA 'congruence' and *iltizām* 'concomitance'. XII 655a

tadāris → TADRĪS

tadāwul (A) : a mode of transmission. IX 455b

tadbī<u>dj</u> (A) : 'brocading', in rhetoric, a subcategory of ṬIBĀḲ 'antithesis', a separate figure based on the use of various colours in one line. X 451a

tadbīr (A) : when used synonymously with SIYĀSA, ~ means government, administration; in the phrase ~ *al-manzil*, ~ is used to mean administration or management of a household. ~ *al-manzil* 'economics' is one of the three subdivisions of practical philosophy in the Hellenistic tradition. X 52b

In law, a grant of enfranchisement which takes effect upon the master's death. The <u>Sh</u>āfiʿī school also applies it to an enfranchisement to take effect from a date after the master's death. A slave freed thus is *mudabbar*. I 30a; X 53a tad̲h̲iya   (A) : the act of displaying; in the Qurʾānic story of the creation, the spreading out of the earth. IV 984b

tad̲h̲kira   (A, pl. *tad̲h̲ākīr*) : memorandum, or aide-mémoire. I 80a; X 53b
In the science of diplomatic, orders laid down for the higher officials, ambassadors, and commanders of fortresses, chiefly concerned with income and expenditure. I 304a
In Arabic literature, ~ represents two different genres of text presentation: handbooks and notebooks. X 53b
In Persian literature, a 'memorial' of the poets, a genre characterised by a combination of biography and anthology. VII 529b; X 53b
In older Turkish literature, a genre of works treating the lives of holy men and great ṣūfīs. V 193a; X 54b

tad̲h̲yīl   (A) : in prosody, a deviation in the metre because of the addition of a quiescent consonant to the *watid mad̲jmūʿ* (→ AWTĀD), thus *mustafʿilun* becomes *mustafʿilān*. I 672a

taḍʿīf   (A) : in mathematics, the term for duplation. III 1139b

taʿdīl   (A) : in law, the attestation of the ʿADĀLA of a witness; the procedure for substantiating the *ʿadāla* is also known as ~ , or TAZKIYA. I 209b
In the science of Tradition, the testing and verification procedure traditionally required at the outset of all transmitters. VIII 900b
In astronomy, correction or equation (pl. *taʿādīl*), applied to mean positions of the sun, moon and planets to derive the true positions, as in *taʿdīl al-s̲h̲ams* 'the solar equation' and **taʿdīl al-zamān** (or *taʿdīl al-ayyām bi-layālīhā*) 'the equation of time'. IX 292a ff.; X 55a,b; XI 503b
   ♦ **al-taʿdīl bayn al-saṭrayn**   (A) : lit. correcting between the two lines, an expression used in mathematics and mathematical astronomy for interpolation. X 55b

tād̲j   (A, < P; pl. *tīd̲jān*) : crown, an object, like the name, that came from old Persia. X 57b; during the caliphate, one of the caliphal insignia, not a crown per se but an elaborate turban wound in a particuar fashion. VI 850a; and → ʿARAḲIYYA
In zoology, the name given to the comb of a cock and similar birds; X 58b
In astronomy, ~ *al-saʿdān* is used for Saturn (*zuḥal*) and ~ *al-d̲jabbā*r is a star near Orion. X 58a,b

tad̲ja   → TAʿZIYA

tad̲jaʿfara   (A) : to convert to Imāmism. IX 116b

tad̲jallī   (A) : in mysticism, the manifestation of God to a person at the time of Judgement and then in Paradise, used first ca. 180/796 by Rabāḥ b. ʿAmr al-Ḳaysī. The ~ consists of MUKĀS̲H̲AFA 'unveiling', which allows divine light to 'irradiate' the heart. X 60b

tad̲jānus   (A) : in rhetoric, paronomasia. VIII 614b

tad̲jdīd   (A) : renewal, both in terms of renewal of the religion and of the Arab Muslim world in its confrontation with the West. X 61b

tād̲jik   (P) : term used to designate the Persians, as opposed to the Turks. By the 19th century, ~ was sometimes used to denote the Eastern Iranian peoples, as distinct from the Persians proper of central and western Persia; hence its usage in the designation of Tajikistan set up in 1924. X 62a; in China, ~ almost exclusively means speakers of Iranian Pamir languages in Xinjiang, in particular, speakers of Sarikulī. X 64a

tād̲jir   (A) : a merchant, trader; the cognomen of *al-Tād̲jir* was known for merchants who traded outside their own towns or lands on a large scale. X 67a; and → ḤAWĀNTĪ

taʿd̲jīra   (Tun) : a large embroidered shawl, worn by women in Tunisia. V 746b

tad̲jmīr   (A) : in early military and administrative usage, 'keeping the troops quartered on distant frontiers, far away from their families'. X 67a

tadjnīs (A) : in prosody, paronomasia. IX 462b; X 67b

♦ tadjnīs ishtiḳāḳ (A) : 'figura etymologica', in prosody, the accumulation of a number of forms from the same verbal root in the same line of a poem. VIII 577b; X 67bff.

♦ tadjnīs tāmm (A) : in rhetoric, a pair of utterances within a line or colon, which are semantically different but phonetically identical. X 67b; and → TĀMM

tadjrīd (A) : abstraction. X 365b; X 932b

tadjwīd (A) : lit. to make better; the art of reciting the Qur'ān; the orthoepic rules of Qur'ān reading (ḲIRĀ'A; *tilāwa*), concerning pausal location (*waḳf*) and division of verses. IX 365b; X 72b

tadjzi'a (A) : specialisation. X 935b

tadlīs (A, < L *dolus*) : 'concealing defects', a term of Islamic law used in both the law of sale and contract ('misrepresentation' in English common law, syn. TAGHRĪR) and in the science of Tradition, where the defect may consist in pretending to have heard a Tradition from a contemporary when that is not so (*tadlīs al-isnād*), or in calling one's authority by an unfamiliar ISM, KUNYA or NISBA (*tadlīs al-shuyūkh*), or in omitting a weak transmitter who comes between two sound ones (*tadlīs al-taswiya*). III 26a; VIII 421a, X 77a,b

taḍmīn (A) : lit. inclusion; in prosody, 'quotation', a rhetorical figure where a poem by another author is taken as the basis and inserted in one's own poem to obtain humorous effects (related terms are *isti'āna* 'seeking help' and *īdā'* 'depositing'). III 355a; V 960b; X 78b; also 'enjambement', a defect of the rhyme, occurring when one line runs into another in such a way that the end of the line only makes complete sense when we add the beginning of the next. IV 413a; X 79a

In rhetoric, implication. VIII 614b; X 79a

tadrīs (A) : in classical and mediaeval periods, the teaching of the religious law, *fiḳh*; when combined with a qualifying phrase, ~ could be used with regard to instruction in other subjects, e.g. ~ *al-tafsīr* 'teaching Qur'ānic exegesis'. ~ came to signify the office of professorship, not merely a profession, a reification that is reflected in the use of the plural *tadāris* indicating separate professorships in different fields. Other terms for the transmission of knowledge were the relatively uncommon *taṣdīr* for instruction generally and *ta'līm*, which usually referred to instruction at a basic level. In contemporary usage, ~ is less specified (→ MUDARRIS). X 80a,b

tadwīn (A) : in the science of Tradition, the collecting of traditions in writing in order to derive legal precepts from them and not as a mere memory aid, for which *kitābat al-'ilm* or *kitābat al-ḥadīth* was used. X 81a

In administration, the drawing up of lists. X 81a

In literature, the gathering of poetry of a certain poet or tribe. X 81a

tadwīr (A) : in astronomy, an epicycle, embedded within the deferent, that contained the actual planet, one of three postulated solid rotating orbs to bring about a planet's observed motions. XI 555a; and → IDRĀDJ; TAḤḲĪḲ

taḍyīḳ (A): in literary theory, a term invented by al-Suyūṭī, according to his own testimony, for devices and artifices such as the avoidance of pointed or unpointed letters or alternating such letters from word to word, the avoidance of labials, the inclusion of a certain letter in every word of the line, the use of all letters of the alphabet in one line, etc. V 841a

tafarnudj (A, P *gharbzada[gī]*, T *alafranga[lik]* 'West-struck[ness]) : lit. adopting, imitating or aping the manners and customs of Europeans, used by the journalist Khalīl al-Khūrī in 1860 but may be older. X 81b

tafarrudj (A, T *teferrüdj*) : in Ottoman guilds, a ceremony, wherein the master awarded his pupil with an apron, once he was qualified in his craft. IX 646a

tafāwut-i ʿamal (P) : under the Ḳādjārs, a sum levied by the provincial governors in addition to the regular tax assessment, for the expenses of the administration; it was abolished by the newly convened National Assembly in 1907. II 152b

tafḍīl (A) : lit. superiority, the act of raising something to a higher level or degree.
In grammar, the elative, the raising of a quality to a degree combining both the comparative and the superlative functions of European adjectives. X 82a

ṭaff (A) : an area raised above the surrounding country or fringe, edge, bank. X 82a

tafih → MALĪKH

tafʿīl → WAZN

♦ tafʿīla (A) : in metrics, the constituent metrical foot. XII 482b

taʿfīn → TAKWĪN

tafkhīm (A) : in grammar, velarisation. A letter that is velarised is called *mufakhkham*. VIII 343a; IX 96a; X 83a

ṭafra (A) : lit. leap or impulsive movement; in philosophy, a term in the anti-atomistic theory of al-Naẓẓām, who argued that it is possible to move over a distance without going through all the parts of the distance, by leaping over those parts. V 385a; X 83b

tāfrūt → SHAWKA

tafsīr (A) : exegetic interpretation; commentary on the Qurʾān. I 410a; IV 147a; VII 361a; IX 320a; X 83a; also used for commentaries on Greek scientific and philosophical works, being equivalent to SHARḤ, while Jews and Christians writing in Arabic also use ~ in the context of translations and commentaries on the Bible. X 83b

tāfta (P, > It *taffeta*, Ger *Taft*) : a silk cloth of technically simple plain or tabby weave, usually dyed in one colour only with a soft shimmering appearance, used mainly in dress in Persia and Turkey from the 16th century onwards. X 88a

tafwīḍ (A) : a theological doctrine, according to which God had entrusted the care of the worldly creation to the IMĀMs. I 304b; the principle of 'leaving it to God' to elucidate through scripture. I 411a
In the science of diplomatic, ~ was the grade of appointment applied to supreme ḲĀḌĪs, used in Mamlūk times only. II 303a

tafwīḳ (A) : in archery, nocking. This consists of bracing the arrow's nock (*fūḳ*) on the binding of the bow-string. There must be no play there, so that when the archer draws back the arrow, together with the bow-string, he accompanies the latter in its rearwards path to the chosen anchorage-point. IV 800b

tagg → ṬAḲṬŪḲA

taggalt (Touareg) : in Touareg society, the bride-price, paid by the groom-to-be's father to the bride's father. X 380a

taghazzul (T) : in Turkish prosody, the section of the ḲAṢĪDA which embraces subjects more often found in a GHAZAL, such as love or wine. IV 715b

taghbīr (A) : cantillation (of the Qurʾān). II 1073b

ṭāghiya (A) : a tyrant. IV 839b

taghrīr (A) : fraud, deception; in law, a fraudulent action (by a *ghārr*) that takes place against a second person who buys or enters into a contract. X 77b, X 93a

ṭāghūt (A, pl. *ṭawāghīt*) : in pre- and early Islamic usage, the pre-Islamic deities like al-Lāt and al-ʿUzzā, later applied to Satan, sorcerer and rebel, and to any power opposed to that of Islam. X 93b
As a legal term in Yemen, ~ was used to refer to the customary law of the tribes, at times in distinction to *sharʿ al-manʿ*, customary tribal law that was compatible with the sharīʿa. VI 473b; X 94a

ṭaghw (A) : mountain peak, any high place. X 93a

taghyīr → NAHY

tagor → TAGRA

tagra : a leather bucket for drawing water in Tagorri, the ʿAfar dialect of Tadjura, which name is derived from the plural, *tagor*. X 71b

tāgulmust (Touareg) : the famous headveil with which the Touareg man covers his entire face except for the eyes. X 379b

ṭā-ḥā (A) : two isolated letters at the head of sura xx in the Qurʾān, taken to mean either an imperative (from the root *w-ṭ-ʾ*) or from a proper name. Muslim Tradition has from the 3rd/9th century made Ṭā-ḥā one of the names of the Prophet, and from the 4th/10th century mystics see in Ṭā-ḥā the purity (*ṭahāra*) and rectitude (*ihtidāʾ*) of the heart of the Prophet. X 1b

tahadjdjud (A) : sleep; to be awake, to keep a vigil, to perform the night ṢALĀT or the nightly recitation of the Qurʾān. X 97b

taḥallama → TAḌABBABA

taham (A), and *tihāma* : 'land descending to the sea'. X 481b

tahammul (A) : in law, the 'acceptance of responsibility'. I 339a

taḥammus → ḤUMS

taḥannuth (A, < Heb) : a form of religious devotion, in which Muḥammad is said to have been engaged one month each year in a cave on Ḥirāʾ. III 166a; III 462a, X 98b; it has been hypothesised also that ~ is the condition one assumes in law when one is liable (*ḥānith*) to fulfill a binding vow, and thus that ~ when referring to the Prophet reflects the idea that he had made a vow to enter a period of retreat. X 99a

ṭahār (A) : the name in Mecca for the rite of circumcision. V 20b

ṭahāra (A) : ritual purity, a necessary condition for the valid performance of prayer. III 647a; X 99a

♦ ṭahāra ḥaķīķiyya (A) : 'real' ritual purity, attained by the elimination of any blemish from the body, the clothing and the place. VIII 929a

♦ ṭahāra ḥukmiyya (A) : 'prescribed' ritual purity, attained by WUḌŪʾ or by GHUSL. VIII 929a

taḥashshada (A) : a term used by al-Hamdānī in the 4th/10th century for members of the tribal group of Bakīl transferring their allegiance to the tribal group of Ḥāshid (ant. *tabakkala*). III 259b

taḥaykt → ḤĀʾIK

taḥayyur (A) : 'ravishment', the name given by the mystical order ʿĪsāwā to the ecstatic dancing practiced as a form of invoking God. It is also called *ḥayra* or *idjdhāb*. IV 95a; and → RABBĀNĪ

taḥbīs (A) : in law, the process by means of which during his lifetime someone renounces ownership of property and such property remains permanently withdrawn from any commercial transaction and is converted from an item of personal estate to the real estate of a family or an institution. XI 75a

taḥdjīr (A) : 'delimitation'; in law, the defining of the limits of MAWĀT land by e.g. setting stones along the length of each boundary in order to fix the extreme limits of the area to be brought into use. III 1054a

ṭaḥḥān (A) : miller, owner and operator of a mill (→ ṬĀḤŪN) to grind wheat and other grains to produce flour. X 102a

♦ ṭaḥḥāna (A) : an animal-powered mill. In contemporary Egyptian usage, a grinder (~ *filfil* 'pepper grinder'). X 114b

ṭāhī → ṬABBĀKH

ṭāhir → NADJIS

♦ ṭāhirī → KĀGHAD

taḥķīķ (A) : in Qurʾānic recitation, the term for slow recitation, slower than *tartīl*, which is the ideal form, and used principally in learning and practising. Medium-paced recitation is known as *tadwīr*, whereas rapid recitation is called *ḥadr*, generally reserved for private use. V 128a; X 73b; and → MALĀMIYYA

taḥkīm (A) : in law, arbitration (→ ḤAKAM). Historically, ~ refers to the arbitration that took place between ʿAlī b. Abī Ṭālib and Muʿāwiya. X 107a

tahlīl (A) : the saying of the formula *lā ilāha illā ʾllāh*, the first element of the SHAHĀDA. X 108a; jubilation at seeing the new moon (*hilāl*). X 108a

taḥlīl (A) : the process by which something is made ḤALĀL 'permissible', e.g. in law, the intervening marriage, frequently for a reward, made for the sole purpose of allowing a thrice-divorced couple to remarry. The man who undertakes ~ is called *muḥallil*. X 154b

ṭahmal (A) : in zoology, a silurus, whose Arabic term is found again in the Latinised nomenclature to specify a sub-species limited to a particular region (*Pimelopterus tahmel*). VIII 1021b

taḥmīd (A) : : the saying of the praise formula *al-ḥamdu-li ʾllāh*. V 425b

taḥnīḳ → ḤANAK

taḥnīṭ (A) : to prepare a corpse for burial with embalming substances. X 111a

taḥrīf (A) : change, alteration, forgery; used with regard to words and more specifically with regard to what Jews and Christians are supposed to have done to their respective scriptures (syn. *tabdīl*). X 111a

taḥrīr (A) : land census; survey. VIII 291a; VIII 419a; revision of a text, even 'edition', ~ refers to the elements of a text or commentary which have been chosen for comment, clarification or correction. IX 320a

In Ottoman administration, a technical term for the tax registers for the most part compiled during the 15th-16th centuries, mainly designed to keep track of that part of Ottoman state revenue which did not reach the central treasury, but was assigned locally. The most extensive form of ~ was the *defter-i mufaṣṣal*, which contained an enumeration of taxpayers listed by settlement and taxes due. X 112b

♦ taḥrīrī (A) : 'epistolary'; in calligraphy, a name given to a more simple form of the SHIKASTA *nastaʿlīḳ* script and used for writing letters and taking notes. IV 1124b

taḥrīsh (A) : inciting (animals) against each other, forbidden by the Prophet as gambling. V 109a

taḥṣīl (A) : in Indo-Muslim usage, in the British Indian provinces of Bombay, Madras and the United Provinces, the collection of revenue and, thence, the administrative area from which this taxation was collected. The official in charge was the *taḥṣīldār*. X 113a; and → AHLIYYA

taḥsīn wa-taḳbīḥ (A) : 'determining something to be good or repellent'; in theology, a phrase referring to the controversy over the sources of the moral assessment of acts. X 114a

ṭāḥūn (A) : mill; a small domestic grinding mill for use in a kitchen, though *ḥāwūn* 'mortar' was more commonly used. X 114b

♦ ṭāḥūna (A) : general word for mill, as well as watermill. In contemporary Egyptian usage, variously grist mill, windmill, and, in the expression *ṭaḥūnit bunn*, coffee grinder. X 114b; in Muslim Spain, a horse-driven mill. I 492a

taḥwīf → ḤAWFĪ

taḥwīl (A) : in Ottoman administration, the annual renewal of the diplomas of the governors of provinces, of the brevets of the MOLLĀs or judges in towns of the first class (~), and of the brevets of the timariots or holders of military fiefs. This task was carried out by an office in the chancellery. VIII 482a

In dating, the 'changing' of one tax year to another. X 263

tahyast (Touareg) : a simple camel saddle, with a pommel in the form of a rectangular batten, used by the Touareg of the Sahara. III 667a

ṭāʾif → RAHĪSH

♦ **ṭā'ifa** (A, pl. *ṭawā'if*), or *ṭāyfā* : a group, party, company of men; a professional or trade group, corporation (syn. *ṣinf*); a religious or sectarian group, whence ṬĀ'IFIYYA 'confessionalism'. X 116a; a tribe, tribal section. IX 221b; IX 245b; and → ṢAFF

♦ ṭā'ifat al-ḳawm (A), or in short *al-ṭā'ifa* or *al-ḳawm* : 'the group of the men of God', a designation favoured by ṣūfīs for themselves. X 114b

♦ ṭā'ifat al-ru'asā (A) : a guild of corsair captains which, for three centuries, furnished the Algerian treasury with the greater part of its resources. I 368a

ṭā'ifiyya (A) : confessionalism, sectarianism; the system of proportional political power-sharing between different religious groups practiced in Lebanon since the French mandate. X 115a

ṭā'ir (A), or *al-ṭayr* : any being or thing which is able to live or to fly above the ground level. X 117b; in astronomy, al-Ṭā'ir denotes the Swan, the 20th northern constellation (syn. DAḎJĀḎJA), and the star Altaïr, sc. α *Aquilae*. X 117b

♦ ṭayr al-abābīl (A) : mentioned in Q 105:3 as having pelted the army of Abraha when it was attacking Mecca, thought to be either swifts (*Apus apus*), swallows (*Hirundo rustica*) or bats. X 117b

♦ ṭayr al-ʿarāḳib (A) : in zoology, all birds of bad omen, such as the green woodpecker, *s͟harakrak* (*Picus viridis*). X 117b

♦ ṭayr al-d͟jamal (A) : in zoology, the ostrich. X 117b

♦ ṭayr al-ḥarrāt͟h (A) : in zoology, the lapwing, seagull. X 117b

♦ ṭayr al-layl (A) : in zoology, the screech-owl. X 117b; and → WAṬWĀṬ

♦ ṭayr al-mā' (A) : in zoology, the waterfowl. I 1152b; X 117b

♦ ṭayr al-Sulaymān (A) : in zoology, the hoopoe (*Upupa epops*). X 117b

♦ ṭayr al-timsāḥ (A) : in zoology, the Egyptian plover (*Plavianus aegyptius*), also known as *saḳsāḳ, zaḳzāḳ* or *tawram*. X 117b; X 510a

♦ ṭayra (A), or *murd͟jān* : in ichthyology, the *Myripristis*, a small fish of the Mediterranean and Red Sea. X 117b

ṭāḳ (A) : arcade. IX 409a; arch. XII 757a; a green *ṭaylasān*, a name of very rare occurrence. X 614b

taḳaddum (A) : in philosophy, the absolute anteriority of God. IX 382a

takāfu' (A) : 'balancing', the term used by Ḳudāma for antithesis (ṬIBĀḲ), a rather idiosyncratic usage and much talked about in later sources. Strangely, however, ~ was revitalised later by some to denote a specific type of *ṭibāḳ*, one in which one term or both terms of the antithesis are figurative. X 450b

takāful (A) : in finance, insurance. XII 691b

taḳālīd (A, s. TAḲLĪD) : the ensemble of inherited folk traditions and practices, popular customs and manners, and folklore in general, although the loanword from English *fulklūr* is often used, especially for the discipline and its study at large. In recent years also, the term al-turāt͟h al-s͟haʿbī 'folk inheritance' is being used to denote the common Arabic heritage of popular culture. XII 774b

takalluf (A) : in rhetoric, constraint. X 304b

taḳammuṣ → TANĀSUK͟H

takārir → FALLĀTA

takārna → FALLĀTA

taḳas͟hs͟huf (A) : the mortification of the flesh. XI 560a

taḳāwī (Egy) : seed (for sowing). IV 1032b

takayda (Tun) : a pointed woman's bonnet in Tunisia. V 746b

taḳāzīḥ (A) : 'showing the colours of the rainbow'. IV 804b

taḳbīl (A) : kissing or touching (*istilām*) the Black Stone of the Kaʿba, part of the ancient pagan custom. X 376a; the kissing of the carpet on coming face-to-face with the sovereign. IV 940b; and → ḲABĀLA

takbīr (A) : the saying of the formula *allāhu akbar*. X 119b

♦ takbīr al-iḥrām : the TAKBĪR with which the ritual prayer begins, and which puts the worshipper into a temporary state of special relationship with God. III 1053a; VIII 929a, X 119b

taḳdīr (A) : predestination. VIII 125b

In grammar, the imaginary utterance a speaker intends when he says something else, e.g. when saying 'Zayd is in the house' (*Zayd fī' l-dār*) the speaker intends 'Zayd has made his abode in the house' (*Zayd istaḳarra fi 'l-dār*); the latter is termed ~ , also *muḍmar (fi 'l-niyya)* 'concealed (in the mind)' or *muḳaddar* 'intended'. X 119b

In land management and taxation, the process of estimating the amount or value of a crop (syn. *takhmīn*). X 122a

takfīr (A) : the act of identifying someone as a KĀFIR 'unbeliever' or, when born a Muslim, 'apostate'. IX 118a; X 122a

takfīt (A) : in art, inlay in metal (syn. *taṭʿīm*), a technique by which the artist enriches a metal object by overlaying parts of its surface with patterns formed from wires or sheets of a different metal, popular after the 6th/12th century. V 986a

takhalkhul (A) : brittleness (of a gem). XI 570a

takhalluṣ (A) : in onomastics, and particularly in Persian literature, the pen-name adopted by a poet or writer. IV 181a; X 123a

In prosody, the section of the ḲAṢĪDA, in Persian prosody also called *gurīzgāh* and *makhlaṣ*, where the poet turns from the prologue to subsequent themes, esp. the panegyric. It is often called the *khurūdj* 'exit'. IV 57b; X 123a

♦ ḥusn al-takhalluṣ : 'good transition', an artifice used in poetry to effect a formal fusion of heterogeneous motifs. IX 452a

takhathʿama (A) : 'to smear oneself with blood', as on the occasion of a pact of alliance among tribes. IV 1106a

takhayyur (A) : in law, an 'eclectic' expedient used as a basis for reform. X 155a; X 161b

takhfīf (A) : lit. weakening; in grammar, ~ *al*-HAMZA are all the accidents that can befall the *hamza*, such as the *hamza bayna bayna*; the phonetic change of *hamza* into another articulation; and the suppression of *hamza*. III 151a

takhmīn → TAḲDĪR

takhmīs (A, pl. *takhāmīs*) : in prosody, the amplification of poetry that involves the addition of three hemistichs to each BAYT of a given poem; the rhyme letter of the added hemistichs is determined by the first hemistich of each successive *bayt*. This extra material usually precedes the original *bayt*; less commonly the *bayt* may be split and filled, which process is called *tashṭīr*. If the number of added hemistichs is more or less than three, the term for the poem is variously *tarbīʿ* (2 added hemistichs), *tasbīʿ* (5 added hemistichs), etc. VII 661a; IX 243b; X 123b

In North Africa, the taking of Berber captives for the service of the state, such slaves being termed *akhmās*. XII 533a

takhṣiṣ (A) : the principle in which a particular prescription is preferred to a general prescription. The 'particulariser' was called *mukhaṣṣiṣ* or *dalīl al-~* . IV 256a; X 867a

takht (P) : in the Tīmūrid period, a pavilion with a view. IX 46a; and → SARĪR

♦ **takht-i ṭāwūs** (P) : the Peacock Throne, a name given to various highly-decorated and much bejewelled royal thrones in the Eastern Islamic world. X 125a

takhtadji (T, < *takhta* 'wood') : lit. one who works in woods and forests, woodcutter, sawyer; the name of one of the Turkish nomadic groups of Anatolia. X 125b

takhṭīṭ al-ḥudūd (A) : lit. delimiting boundaries or frontiers, in modern Arabic usage. X 126b

takhyīl (A) : lit. creating an image or an illusion; in literary theory, ~ is a kind of make-believe in the form of giving, to a fact stated in the poem, a fantastic interpretive twist which on the surface explains and supports that fact, but on closer inspection turns out to be an illusion. It was first identified by ʿAbd al-Ḳāhir al-Djurdjānī, who contrasted these phantasmagorical poetic notions (*maʿānī takhyīliyya*) with realistic commonsensical ones (*maʿānī ʿaḳliyya*). X 129a; XII 653a; and → ISTIʿĀRA; TAWRITA
In logic, the 'evocation of images of things in the minds of listeners by means of figurative language'. X 129b; and → MUḤĀKĀT
In rhetoric, 'giving the impression of praising while one is lampooning and vice versa', as used by Abū Hilāl al-ʿAskarī. X 132a

taʿḳīd (A) : in rhetoric, obscurity. V 898b

takīn → TIGIN

takiya (P), or *Ḥusayniyya* : a special, usually temporary, structure built for the staging of shīʿī passion plays. The ~ is a theatre-in-the-round with a stark, curtainless, raised platform as a stage, which is surrounded by a broad circular strip covered by sand, used for battles of foot and on horseback among other uses. X 406b

takiyya (A) : a hospice. X 635a

taḳiyya (A) : the precautionary dissimulation of one's faith, characteristic of shīʿism, and dispensing with the ordinances of religion in cases of constraint and when there is a possibility of harm. I 1099a; IX 422b; X 134b

ṭāḳiyya (A, < P; pl. *ṭawāḳī*) : the common skull cap worn, in the Arab East, by both sexes alone or under the headdress. Originally a round cap with flat top in various colours, worn without the turban-cloth, under al-Nāṣir Faradj it was extended in height and swollen out like a cupola. In more recent times ~ has been used as a synonym for ʿARAḲIYYA. V 741b; X 614b; and → ʿATABA

taḳlīd (A) : 'imitation'; in law, the unquestioning acceptance of the doctrines of established schools and authorities. A person bound to practise ~ is called *muḳallid*. II 890a; III 1026b; IX 324b; X 137a
In theology, imitation of the Prophet, of his Companions and their pious successors. I 1039a; III 1173b
In the science of diplomatic, ~ was a grade of appointment for high officials such as WAZĪRS and ḲĀḌĪS, although under the Mamlūks it was restricted to very special high officials such as the confidential secretary, *kātib al-sirr*. II 303a
In numismatics, counterfeit (with *muḳallad* 'counterfeited'). X 409b
♦ taḳlīd-i sayf (A, T *ḳilïc kushatmasï*) : in Ottoman ceremonial, the girding of the sword, which signified the actual accession to rule of the sultan, in lieu of a coronation in Western style. According to tradition, this took place for the first time in 1421 when Murād II was girded. VI 530b

taklīf (A, pl. *takālīf*) : in theology, the fact of an imposition on the part of God of obligations on his creatures. The person who is governed by this is *mukallaf*. X 138b; the doctrine of individual responsibility. I 272a
In law, every individual who has at his disposal the full and entire scope of the law. X 138b
In Ottoman administration, *teklīf* (pl. **tekālīf**) was used synonymously with RESM 'taxes and dues introduced by the state'. VIII 486a; X 412b
♦ tekālīf-i fewḳalʿāde : 'extraordinary taxes', distinguished from *tekālīf-i sherʿiyye*, canonical taxes in accordance with the sharīʿa. The former could include *ʿörfī* taxes, those imposed by the sultan and his servants according to custom, also called ʿAWĀRIḌ. X 412b
♦ tekālīf-i shāḳḳa : 'onerous exactions', in Ottoman administration, exactions taken illegally by local authorities. VIII 486b; X 412b

ṭaḳm (A) : in music, a set of flutes. XII 667a; and → FUSTĀN
takmīl (A) : lit. completion; among the *fityān* (→ FATĀ), full initiation, symbolised by the putting on of ritual trousers (*sirwāl*, P *shalwar*). IX 167a
♦ takmila (A) : the continuation of an original work, expressing the idea of completion, becoming the latter's perfection. Works bearing this title are fairly late. IX 604a
taḳnīn (A) : in law, the codification of the sharīʿa. X 353a
taḳrīb (A) : 'rapprochement', a term widely used to designate an ecumenical trend within modern Islam in general and a movement towards reconciliation between sunnī and shīʿī Muslims in particular. X 139b
takrīr → ṢIFĀT AL-ḤURŪF
taḳrīr (A) : remarks on a text. IX 320a
In the science of diplomatic, the documents (diplomatic notes) presented to the Ottoman government by members of the foreign diplomatic corps. II 314a
In Ottoman administration, reports, e.g. those presented to the sultan by the grand vizier acting as representative of the government. VIII 481b
In taxation matters, liability. IV 1038b
taḳrīẓ (A) : lit. the act of praising; in mediaeval literature, a minor genre, tending to be formulaic in form and style, which consisted of statements praising the virtues of a particular work, some composed after the death of the author of the work in question but probably for the most part composed at the time of the work's appearance with the aim of advertising it. XII 781a
taḳsīm (A, pl. *taḳāsīm*) : in music, a solo melodic modal improvisation entrusted to an instrumentalist, played in the eastern Arab countries and Turkey. The corresponding North African genre is called *istikhbār*. In Ottoman court music of the 15th and 16th centuries, ~ was given to the initial section of vocal forms of the NAWBA repertoire. VI 97a; X 143a; XII 667b
taḳsīra (A) : a short-sleeved jacket worn by both sexes in Syria and Palestine. V 742a
taḳsīṭ (A) : in early Islamic financial administration, the allocation or distribution amongst the taxpayers of the global amount of taxation due (syn. *ḳasṭ, ḳisṭ*), or the instalments by which it was paid. X 144a
ṭaḳṭaḳa → ṬAḲṬŪḲA
taḳṭīʿ → WAZN
taḳṭīr (A) : in pharmacology, distillation. XII 550b
ṭaḳṭūḳa (A) : in music, a form of strophic song in Egyptian colloquial Arabic. It is unclear whether it has anything to do with *ṭaḳṭaḳa*, a manner of singing to accompaniment of a wand in the 11th and 12th centuries, or to a traditional Egyptian Bedouin song called *tagg*, which is accompanied by the beating of two sticks. X 144a
ṭakūk → WĀḲWĀḲ
taḳwā (A) : in religion and mysticism, fear of God, or godliness, devoutness, piety, pious abstinence, etc. XI 141b; XII 781b
taḳwīm (A, pl. *taḳāwīm*) : tabular form of almanac data. X 146b; a retrospective calendar of events. X 291a; in astronomy, annual ephemeris, with information of the true positions of the sun, planets and moon, from which one could determine the position of the seven celestial bodies relative to each other. X 145a
takwīn (A) : 'bringing into being', the artificial generation of minerals, plants and animals; in the case of plants and animals, the process is often called *tawlīd*, and Ibn Waḥshiyya also gives *taʿfīn* 'putrefaction'. X 147a
In Ibn Sīnā, ~ is the production, with an intermediary, of corruptible beings. III 664b
tāl (H) : in Indian music, a cyclic time-measure punctuated by a stress pattern which is marked on a pair of drums. III 454a
ṭalā (A) : in the terminology of childhood, 'the youngling of any kind; an infant until a month old or more' (Lane). VIII 821b

ṭalaʿa → ITHTHAGHARA
talaḥḥī (A) : with *iltiḥā*, a rare synonym for the *taḥnīk*, or way the turban-cloth is brought under the chin (→ ḤANAK). X 614b
ṭalāḳ (A) : in law, repudiation of the wife by the husband, by way of the simple unilateral declaration *anti ṭāliḳ*. I 27b; II 836b; III 949b; IV 689a; X 151a; and → TAʿLIḲ-ṬALĀḲ
- ♦ ṭalāḳ al-bidʿa : in law, the triple repudiation of the wife in one saying. XI 478b
- ♦ ṭalāḳ radjʿī : in law, a revocable repudiation. XII 644a
- ♦ ṭalāḳ al-tafwīḍ : in law, the right of the wife to divorce the husband. I 172b

tālār (P) : in architecture, a flat-roofed portico. I 616a; (*ṭālār*) a colonnaded verandah associated with private dwellings, where it usually provided an open and sheltered vista toward an enclosed garden, pool, or courtyard that served as the physical centre of domestic space. VIII 789a; a pillared hall known from Achmaenid times and adopted during the Ṣafawid period for audience halls. XII 457b
talāthama (A) : to kiss one another. V 770a
talāʾum (A) : in rhetoric, euphony. VIII 614b
talawwun → ḤIRBĀʾ
talbīna (A) : a dish similar to *ḥarīra*, a gruel made from flour cooked with milk, but eaten at funeral meals by pre-Islamic Arabs. II 1059a; VII 908b
talbīs (A) : in mysticism, the practice of 'concealing, changing the guise of something to make it appear other than it is'. XII 752b
talbiya (A) : the invocation made in a loud voice and repeatedly by the pilgrim upon entering the state of ritual taboo for the Pilgrimage at Mecca. X 160a
taldjiʾa (A), or **ildjāʾ** : lit. putting under protection; in the first three or four centuries of Islam, the practice of the 'commending' by an inferior to a superior of a possession of which the former remains the legal owner but for which, by virtue of a tacit agreement, the latter is to be responsible vis-à-vis the administrative authority and more particularly the tax authorities. III 394a; III 1113a
In law, a fictitious sale resorted to by a person who wishes to protect his possessions from possible confiscation. III 394a; III 1113a
talfīḳ (A) : in law, a patchwork approach to the juristic tradition, by bringing together certain elements of two or more doctrines in such a manner as to create therefrom yet another, different doctrine. IX 325b; X 161a
In literary criticism, the knitting together of two independent motifs. XII 709a
ṭalḥ (A) : in botany, a variety of acacia (*Acacia seyal*). I 168b; X 757b
ṭalī (A, pl. *ṭulyān*) : a young lamb. I 541a
tālī (A) : lit. follower; in Druze hierarchy, the Left Wing, the fifth of the five cosmic ranks in the organisation. II 632a
In horse-racing, the name for the sixth horse in a horse-race, according to the order of finishing. II 953a
In logic and arithmetic, the portion following the MUḲADDAM, i.e. the second of two numbers in a proportion. VII 492a
ṭāliʿ (A) : lit. that which rises; in astronomy, that point of the ecliptic which is rising over the horizon at a given moment, called the ascendent or horoscopus. The determining of the ascendent was necessary in mathematical astrology. The opposite point of the ecliptic is *al-ghārib* 'descendent'. X 163a
In astrology, *al-~* is the 'zodiacal sign which rises on the horizon at the first moment of a man or woman's birth'. Other terms used to describe positions are ḲIRĀN 'conjunction' in regard to the relationships between stars, *mumāzadj* 'coincidence' of planets between stars, *ittiṣāl* for the relation of planets between themselves, *ishrāf* 'apogee' of a planet, *hubūṭ* 'declension' of a planet; RAʾS (L *caput*), the ascendent node, in opposition to DHANAB (L. *cauda*), the descendant node, *ghurūb* 'setting' of the planets,

rudjūʿ for their retrograde motion, *istiḳāma* for their 'direct course', MUḲĀBALA 'opposition' of the planets in the signs of the zodiac, *ḥurūḳ* 'fire, which springs into flame on the planets when they find themselves in the signs of the zodiac, *mudabbir* 'regent', said of a planet whose ascendent is in one of the signs of the zodiac, and *ṭulūʿ al-shaʿrā al-ʿabūr* 'heliacal rising of Sirius'. X 163b

ṭalīʿa (A, pl. *ṭalāʾiʿ*) : in military science, an advance guard or reconnaissance force (syn. *kashshāfa* 'scouts'), either an individual or a small group of three or four men, although descriptions of battles in the later Middle Ages evidence much larger bodies of soldiers. Sometimes translated as 'vanguard', this should be reserved for *muḳaddama*, which represents a separate corps of the regular army. X 164a; XII 722a

ṭālib (A) : student; in law, the plaintiff in a lawsuit. The defendant is called *maṭlūb*. II 171a; X 888b; and → ARU; AYḲASH; ṬOLBA

♦ **ṭālibān** (P, < A ṬĀLIB) : a Persian plural, as term ~ 'religious students' came into use in the last years of the 20th century for a radical Islamist group in Afghanistan. XII 786a

taʿlīḳ (A), also *taʿlīḳa* : in scholarly activity, the 'appending upon (*ʿalā*)' a text or the 'deriving from (*ʿan*)' an author and then to the resulting notes, glosses, comments, excerpts and appendices. Similar to ḤĀSHIYA, ~ is much less firmly anchored in manuscripts; in later centuries, ~ came to be used quite frequently in titles of essays. X 165a
In calligraphy, a script which is said to have got its name from its letters being connected to each other. According to Persian scholars, ~ is a compound of TAWḲĪʿ, RIḲĀʿ and NASKH scripts. It was used for writing books and letters, and in the DĪWĀNS for official correspondence. It gave place to SHIKASTA TAʿLĪḲ. IV 1124a; there are two variants, Persian ~ and Ottoman ~ . VIII 151b
In the science of Tradition, a tradition derived from (*muʿallaḳ ʿan*) an authority without the indication of a complete ISNĀD or the complete text. X 165b

♦ taʿlīḳ-ṭalāḳ (J) : a Javanese legal institution by which the husband declares to his wife's guardian and the witnesses, immediately after contracting his marriage, that, if he leaves his wife for a certain time without providing for her and without sending her tidings, if he severely illtreats her or commits another unseemly act, then his wife is free to complain before the Muslim authority concerned. If there is evidence of her husband's failing in these respects, the authority states that a ṬALĀḲ has taken place. I 174a; VIII 433a; X 154b

ṭāliḳ (A) : an untethered camel, or a repudiated wife (→ ṬALĀḲ). X 151b

♦ ṭāliḳa (T, < Sl *taliga*) : a carriage, widely used in the 19th century and still in use in Turkey, with no door, but a footboard, surmounted by a small platform. I 558a

ṭalīḳ → ṬULAḲĀʾ

ṭāliḳūn : a copper alloy, which equals μεταλλικόν, and is probably identical with 'Chinese iron' (*khār čīnī, ḥadīd ṣīnī*). Hot ~ dipped in water is said to drive flies off and to prevent eyelashes from growing again after they have been depilated with a pair of tweezers. VIII 111b

taʿlīm → TADRĪS

ṭalḳ (A) : in metallurgy, asbestos, from Badakhshān, out of which wicks and fire-resistant cloths were made in early Islam. V 965a

tall (A) : a hill, mound, tumulus (Eng. tell); in the Maghrib, ~ is said to be 'marly, grey or darkish soil', and by extension, the whole region where this type of soil is found, that part of the Maghrib, from the Moroccan Gharb to northern Tunisia, still under a marked Mediterranean influence. X 167a

talmīḥ (A) : in rhetoric, allusion, which consists of alluding to famous passages in the Qurʾān or Traditions, or in profane literature. A related figure is IḲTIBĀS. III 1091b

talthīma (A) : a woman's veil. V 769b

♦ tal<u>th</u>īmat al-bayāḍ : under the Fāṭimids, the distinctive dress of the chief ḲĀḌĪs, who wore it along with the turban and ṬAYLASĀN. V 769b

talwīn → TAMKĪN

ṭʿām → KUSKUSŪ

ṭamaʿ (A) : in classical Muslim administration, an issue of pay. II 79a

tamānuʿ (A) : in theology, 'reciprocal hindrance', a major argument for TAWḤĪD, the oneness of God. X 389a; 'mutual prevention'. X 441a

tamarrud → MĀRID

tama<u>thth</u>ul (A) : in rhetoric, the activity of one who quotes a line or two of poetry to encapsulate the gist of the situation in which he finds himself, a very popular literary technique in the *Arabian Nights*. X 180a

tamattuʿ (A) : 'enjoyment'; one of three methods of performing the pilgrimage, viz. by accomplishing the ʿUMRA at the same time as the pilgrimage, resuming secular life and dedicating oneself once again to the pilgrimage. III 53b; X 865b

tambākū → TUTUN

tambr → POSTA

tam<u>dj</u>īd (A) : among Copts, songs of praise about a saint. XI 530a

tam[lḥaft → MILḤAFA

tam<u>gh</u>a (T) : brand or sign placed on livestock or personal property; seal [of the king or other] (A syn. *ṭābiʿ*); and, by extension, tariff or commercial tax; in the Ottoman empire, ~ refers to market dues, the tax levied on all kinds of goods bought and sold in cities, on woven stuffs and slaughtered animals, and normally referred to as *tam<u>gh</u>a-i siyāh* 'black *tam<u>gh</u>a*'. I 861b; II 147a; X 170a; also *ṭam<u>gh</u>ā* or *tam<u>gh</u>ā*, a Mongolian tax on trade and urban crafts, possibly originally a poll-tax on urban dwellers and merchants. IV 31a; IV 1050a; X 170a; and → BĀ<u>DJ</u>-I TAM<u>GH</u>A

♦ tam<u>gh</u>a<u>dj</u>î (T) : title of 'keeper of the seal', appearing in the earliest Turkish inscriptions from the 8th century, and was later used as term for tax collector. X 170a,b

tamhīd → TA<u>SH</u>BĪB

taʾmīm (A, P *millī kardan*, T *devletleştirme*) : nationalisation, that is, the state's assumption of control or ownership of natural resources, services or economic enterprises, from private individuals or corporations. X 176b

tamīma (A, pl. *tamāʾim*) : amulet, talisman. In origin, ~ means a stone with white speckles on a black field or vice versa, threaded on a thong or cord and word around the neck to avert danger (syn. *taʿwī<u>dh</u>, ʿū<u>dh</u>a*). X 177b; X 500b; XII 775b

taʿmiya (A) : cryptography. VII 257b

In rhetoric, mystification. VIII 427a

ṭaʿmiyya (Egy) : the national food of Egypt, Egyptian beans, *fūl mudammas* 'Jew's marrow' or *mulū<u>kh</u>iyya*. II 1065a

tamkīn (A) : 'strengthening, stability'; in mysticism, the spiritual act of endurance and stability, contrasted, according to al-Hu<u>dj</u>wīrī, with *talwīn* which indicates a change, an alternating transition from one state to another. III 84b

tamlīṭ → I<u>DJ</u>ĀZA

tāmm (A) : in literary theory, complete agreement in nature, number, and arrangement of consonants and vowels between two words of different meaning. This category can be further divided into *mumā<u>th</u>il*, where both words belong to the same word class (*zāʾir*: 'visiting' from *z-w-r* and 'roaring' from *z-ʾ-r*), *mustawfā*, where both words belong to different word classes (*yaḥyā*: verb and proper name), *malfūf*, where one of the words is a composite and the composite term consists of two independent words (*<u>dh</u>ā hibah* and *<u>dh</u>āhibah*), and *marfūw*, where one of the words is a composite and the composite term consists of one word and a fragment of another. When both terms are composites, it is called *mulaffaḳ*. X 69a tamma (Mon), or *tanma* : in the Mongolian army, contingents selected from the total available Mongol power. Their purpose was to maintain and extend Mongol rule, and they were initially stationed on the steppe-sedentary borders. Some ~ units later formed the bases of the permanent armies of the subsidiary khānates into which the Mongol empire was divided. VII 233a

tammār (A) : a seller of dates. X 179a

tammūz : the tenth month in the Syriac calendar, corresponding to July in the Roman calendar. X 179b

tamr (A) : dried dates. A basic, and sometimes the only food for Arabs in early times, dates were eaten also fresh (*ruṭab*) or when they were beginning to ripen (*busr*); a special variety called *ʿadjwa* were considered to be a sovereign remedy against poisons and sorcery. II 1058a; IV 995b

♦ tamr ḥinnāʾ : in Cairo, the mignonette plant. III 461a

tamthīl (A) : lit. the adducing of a likeness, example; representation. In grammar, ~ denotes the citing of examples and the technique of definition by exemplification; also, the creation or use of such expressions. In morphology, synonomous with WAZN, and syntactically, 'a systematic recourse to paradigm and to a relation of equivalence between an utterance and a sequence that is not said', later replaced by TAKDĪR. X 179b

In rhetoric, the assimilation of one thing to another, e.g. *naḳī al-thawb* 'clean of clothing' meaning 'exempt from moral vice'. IV 249a ff.; V 117a; X 180a; a simile. II 825b; X 180a

♦ tamthīliyya shāʿirī (U) : in Urdu poetry, 'gnomic verse', in which the thought expressed in the first hemistich of a verse is followed by an illustrative metaphor or simile in the second. IX 90b

ṭamūḥ (A) : in the terminology of horse-riding, a horse that is regarded as impossible to ride. II 954a

tamyīz (A) : the faculty of 'discernment'; in the terminology of childhood, the faculty which enables the child to grasp ideas and thus to distinguish between good and evil. VIII 822b

In the context of the Almohad movement, the methodical and stringent elimination of real or suspected dissidents, which took place in 523 or 524/1128-9. III 959b

tamzak (Touareg) : among the Touareg, a camel's saddle, more luxurious than the TARIK. III 667a

ṭaʿn → SHATM

ṭanāb → ASHL

tanaḳḳul → TANĀSUKH

tanāsub → MUNĀSABA

tanāsukh (A), or *nāsūkhiyya* : in theology, the doctrine of reincarnation, metempsychosis (syn. *nuḳla, tanaḳḳul, intiḳāl, taḳammuṣ*). I 178b; II 136b; IV 45a; VIII 146a; VIII 147b; X 182a; and → RADJʿA

In law, in the context of the laws of succession, ~ is evoked in reference to the fact that 'heirs die after other heirs in such a way that the initial heritage remains undivided'. X 182a

tanaṭṭuʿ → TAʿAṢṢUB

tanawwuṭ nassādj (A) : in zoology, the weaver-bird. XII 19b

tandjīr (A) : a vessel in which sweetmeats were commonly made, used in the mediaeval kitchen. A special type of MUSTAWḲAD 'fire-place' was recommended for the preparation of sweetmeats, which required long cooking over low heat with much stirring, for the shape and position of this *mustawḳad* made it easier to hold the pan and control the heat. VI 808a

tandjīz (A) : in law, the immediate effect of the act of founding a WAḲF. XI 61b
tanfal → THAʿLAB
tanfīdha (A) : a land grant. XI 388a
tanga, and TANKA : in numismatics, terms spelled the same in Arabic but pronounced differently and with uncertain etymology, for coinage in the subcontinent. IX 203a; X 185a

♦ tanga-yi nuḳra : in numismatics, a coin introduced by Tīmūr in 792/1390, weighing 5.38 g. It was later reduced to that of the MITHḲĀL, 4.72 g, and became known as the *shāhrukhī*. IX 203a

tängrikän : a wise man; also, an old Turkī title 'ruler'. X 186b
ṭanīb (A) : in North Africa, a man who, to safeguard his rights, to escape from justice or to save his life, leaves the clan of his birth, alone or with his family, and goes to establish himself in a different tribe which promises to assist him. The term is linked with *ṭunub* 'tent-cord', the suppliant being obliged, originally, to touch at least a cord of the tent of the one to whom he appeals. XII 78b
tanka : in numismatics, the generic name for coined money under Maḥmūd of Ghazna and the name of a specific denomination when Shams al-Dīn Iltutmish regularised the currency as part of his administrative reforms in the 13th century. The Mughal ruler Akbar applied ~ to his 2-*dām* copper coin weighing around 41.5 g. The tenth part of the ~ , which weighed 4.15 g, was named the *tankī*. VIII 618a; X 185a; under Bahlūl, a billion issue of 9.2 to 9.4 gms, of traditional north Indian standard, but issued in sufficient quantity for the sobriquet of *bahlūlī* to be applied to it. V 785a

♦ tankī → TANKA

tanma → TAMMA
tannūr (A, < Ar) : a domestic baking oven of Mesopotamian origin. Cylindrical and beehive shaped, it gave the appearance of a large, inverted pot, from which it probably evolved. II 1059a; V 42b; VI 807b; X 30b; also, the large stove-shaped candelabra made in Egypt, frequently found in mosques, and made of gold, silver or copper. VI 665b; any place from which water pours forth. VIII 437b
tañrı (T) : heaven, God. X 186b
tanṣīr (A) : conversion, or more precisely, Christianisation (< NAṢĀRĀ). XII 772a
ṭanṭūr (A), or *ṭarṭūr* : a high conical cap resembling a mitre, worn by ṣūfīs in the Arab East. V 742a; X 58a

In Algeria, a high brimless hat which was part of the uniform of the Turkish military élite. V 745b

Among the Druze, a high pointed woman's headdress of wood, horn, or metal, once very common. V 742a

tanwīn (A) : in grammar, nunation. VIII 121a; X 193b

♦ tanwīn al-tarannum (A) : a special usage of *tanwīn* connected with poetic declamation. X 193b

tanzīh (A) : 'withdrawal'; in theology, denying God any resemblance to anything. I 410b; X 318a; transcendentalism. The negative equivalent of ~ is *taʿṭīl*, divesting God of his attributes. X 341b f.
tanzīl (A) : a revelation to be proclaimed publicly to mankind. I 1099a; a term for the Qurʾān. XI 389a

Among the Ismāʿīliyya, the outward revelation, represented by the Prophet, as opposed to the TAʾWĪL 'inner truth', represented by the IMĀM. II 631a; X 391b; XI 389a

tanẓīm (A) : 'ordering, setting in order, regulating. X 201a

♦ **tanẓīm al-nasl** (A), also *tanẓīm al-ʿusra* : family planning, that is, the conscious planning of the occurrence of a pregnancy, including decisions on the interval between pregnancies. X 197a

♦ **tanẓīmāt** (A) : in Ottoman history, the sum of reforms from 1839 till some time between 1871 and 1881, and by extension Ottoman history in its entirety during those years. Also, more specifically, the edict of 3 November 1839 called the Khaṭṭ-i Humāyūn often called the ~ *fermānî*. X 201a

tao (Ch) : way.

♦ tao-chang (Ch), or *daozhang* : lit. Head of the Way, the term in Chinese mysticism for SHAYKH, also called 'Master of the Faith' *chiao-chu* or *jiaozhu*. XI 122a

♦ tao-t'ang (Ch), or *daotang* : lit. Hall of the Way; in Chinese mysticism, the centre of the master's KHĀNAḲĀH to where once in his life the adept must make pilgrimage as the first of his obligations and to pay homage to him by the *k'ou-t'ou* 'great prostration' (> Eng kowtow) and by offering a present (*hai-ti-yeh*, < A *hadiyya*). XI 122a

tapa → SEMEDI

ṭapu (T) : in Ottoman fiscal administration, the holding of state-owned lands by a subject of the sultan; also, short for *resm-i ṭapu*, the tax payable when ~ land was leased by the cultivator. X 209b; and → ṬAPU RESMI

♦ ṭapu resmi (T) : in the Ottoman empire, an occasional (BĀD-I HAWĀ) tax paid on entering into possession of a ČIFTLIK. II 147a

♦ ṭapu senedi (T) : the document issued to legalise the possession of ṬAPU land. X 210a

tār (P 'string') : a weaver's warp. XI 496b

In music, a long-necked pandore with an elongated vault-shaped sound-chest and curvatures at the waist. Europe has borrowed the type in the *chitarra battente*. Quite a number of differently strung instruments bear this word: *yaktār*, a one-stringed instrument, better known in India; DŪTĀR, a two-stringed ṬUNBŪR with a pear-shaped sound-chest in Central Asia; *sitār*, originally a three-stringed instrument but now more generally mounted with four strings. In India it has even more strings, and is distinguished from the ṬUNBŪR by its being fretted and played with a plectrum; *čārtār* or *čahārtār*, a four-stringed instrument, still in use in India; *pančtār*, a five-stringed instrument known in Afghanistan; and *shashtār* or *shashtā*, a six-stringed instrument, of which there were three different types, one of which had fifteen double-sympathetic strings in addition. X 625b

ṭār (A) : in music, a round tambourine with jingling plates fixed in openings in the shell or body of the instrument. II 621a

ṭarab (A) : a term denoting poetic and musical emotion, evoking a broad spectrum of sentiments, from the most private to the most violent. Al-Ghazālī called an uncontrollable trance *iḍṭirāb*. ~ came ultimately to denote music, in particular the music of entertainment, with a negative nuance that has gradually diminished but never disappeared completely. Equivalents are *ḥawl* in Mauritania, *amarg* among the Berbers of Morocco, *ḥāl* among the Persians, and *mast* in Afghanistan. VI 214a; X 210b

In music, the ~ was probably the original of the European *tiorba*; the name is still to be found in an instrument of India. Ibn Ghaybī describes a ~ *al-futūḥ*, which had six double strings, and a ~ *zūr*. X 769b

ṭaradiyya → ṬARDIYYA

ṭaraf (A, pl. AṬRĀF) : province. I 924b; point, cape. X 241b; and → ḲABĪLĪ

In the science of Tradition, the ~ is the gist, or most salient feature, of a Tradition. VII 706b; and → AṬRĀF

♦ ṭarafdār (IndP) : under the Bahmanīs, the governor of a province originally responsible for both the civil and military administration of the province, and under whom the commanders of the forts were placed. During the century that followed the establishment of the dynasty, the power of the ~ was greatly curtailed. I 924b

♦ ṭarafān (A), or *dhu 'l-ṭarafayn* : in prosody, in the context of MUʿĀĶABA, to describe the case e.g. in the RAMAL metre, of both the first and the last cord of the foot *fāʿilātun* being shortened, thus *faʿilatu*, when the preceding and following cords are not shortened. VIII 747b

taraffuḍ (A) : the harbouring of moderate (?) Rāfiḍī ideas. IX 492a

tarāna (P) : in Indian music, a song composed of meaningless syllables. III 453a; a term of pre-Islamic origin which denoted songs intended for feasting and wine. VIII 579b; and → RUBĀʿĪ

tarannum (A) : in singing, the lengthening of the final vowel in the ĶĀFIYA MUṬLAĶA. IV 413b

tarassul (A) : 'correspondence'; in calligraphy, the name given by the DĪWĀN secretaries to a plainer form of the SHIKASTA TAʿLĪĶ. IV 1124a

ṭarastudj → BARASŪDJ

tarāwīḥ (A, s. *tarwīḥa*) : lit. pauses; the term for ṢALĀTs that are performed in the nights of the month of Ramaḍān. X 222a

taraza (N.Afr), or *tarazala, tarazal* : a wide-brimmed straw hat for both sexes, worn in Morocco and Algeria. V 746b

tarazal, tarazala → TARAZA

tarbīʿ (A) : in astrology, the quartile aspect. IV 259b
In prosody, the addition of two hemistichs after each pair of hemistichs of the original poem. IX 243b; X 124a

tarbiya (A) : general term in more recent Arabic for education, pedagogy; and → MAʿĀRIF; SHAYKH

ṭarbūsh (A) : hats of various types for men, worn in North Africa. V 746b; in Egypt, a tight-fitting cap, usually of red wool, with a tassel of black or blue silk. In Syria and ʿIrāķ, the ~ had sometimes a peak, which hung behind or at the side and kept in position by a piece of cloth. This cap used to be called *shāshiyya* in Egypt. X 614b

ṭard → DAYSAM

tardīd (A) : in rhetoric, a term referring to a repetition of the same word with the same meaning in different syntactic contexts to create a contrast. X 69a

tarḍiya (A) : the eulogy *raḍiya 'llāhu ʿanhu*, which it is a duty to pronounce when one mentions the name of a Companion of the Prophet. VIII 828b

ṭardiyya (A), or *ṭaradiyya* : in literature, the hunting poem. I 1154b; X 223a

tardjahār (A) : a bowl with a graduated orifice in its underside that submerges in a given period, an ancient device for measuring time. XII 373a

tardjama (A, pl. *tarādjim*) : a translation from one language to another. Two other terms used in this sense, in the first few centuries of Islam, are *naķl* and, to a lesser extent, TAFSĪR. X 225b; XII 788a
In literature, a term in titles introducing a biography, or, especially in North Africa, the biography or autobiography itself; *ʿilm al-tarādjim* is a branch of historical research, sometimes confused by the Twelver shīʿīs with *ʿilm al-ridjāl* (→ RIDJĀL). III 1151a; VI 349b; X 224b
In the science of diplomatic, the designation of the sender in the address, ʿUNWĀN, which developed from the simple *akhūhu* or *waladuhu* to *al-mamlūk al-Nāṣirī*, etc. II 302a; and → ʿUNWĀN

♦ ʿilm al-tarādjim → TARDJAMA

tardjīʿ (A, pl. *tardjīʿāt*) : in music, the refrain of a song. II 1073b
In Persian literature, a refrain poem, also called **tardjīʿ-band** (or *tarkīb-band*, T *tercî-bent* and *terkîb-bent*), a variation of the ĶAṢĪDA written in a single metre composed of parts which each have their own rhyme and are separated by a distich (*tardjīʿ band*) that often serves as a refrain, *wāsiṭa*. I 677b; IV 715a; X 235b

♦ tardjīʿ-band → TARDJĪʿ

tardjīḥ (A) : in law, the exercise of preference. IX 324b
tardjumān (A, < Ar; Ott *terdjümān*, > It *drog(o)man*), or *turdjumān* : interpreter. X 236b; and → *terdjümān*
ṭarfāʾ (A) : a type of tamarisk. X 219a
tarfīl (A) : in prosody, a deviation in the metre consisting of the addition of a moving and a quiescent consonant, a *sabab khafīf* (→ SABAB); thus *mutafāʿilun* becomes *mutafāʿilātun*. I 672a
ṭarḥ (A), and *ilḳāʾ* : in alchemy, an inert or molten substance. III 1087b
♦ ṭarḥa : a large, dark head veil that hangs all the way down the back, worn by women in Egypt. V 742a; a neck-veil. X 610b
ṭarī (A, < *tarì*) : 'fresh, new'; a gold coin (A *rubʿ, rubāʿī* 'quarter-dīnār') struck in Sicily by the Fāṭimids and Kalbids. Under the later Normans, the ~ was approximately one gram in weight, with the SHAHĀDA engraved on one side and the cross of St. Antony, in the form of T, on the other. X 213a; X 238b
taʿrīb (A) : lit. Arabisation or Arabicisation; in grammar, the method or process by which foreign words are incorporated into Arabic, becoming MUʿARRABĀT. More broadly, ~ is the translation of foreign scientific, literary and scholarly works into Arabic. X 240a
For ~ as political policy, XII 790b
taʾrīdj (A) : in classical Muslim administration, an addition register, showing those categories which need to be seen globally, arranged for easy addition, with totals. Receipts for payments made are also registered in the ~ . II 78b
taʿrīf (A) : lit. making known; in logic, a word or a statement that is a definition, *ḥadd*, or a statement that is a descriptive definition, *rasm*. 'Man is a rational animal' is an example of the first, and 'man is an animal capable of laughter' is an example of the second. X 241a
In grammar, the fact or process of making a word grammatically definite (→ MAʿRIFA). X 241a
In literature, a term for biography, appearing in the title of lives of saints, possibly for reasons of discretion, in a period where MANĀḲIB seems to be confined to the hagiographical sphere. This term seems to be particularly common in Morocco. VI 349b For its use in Urdu prosody, → MADĪḤ
tarik (Touareg) : among the Touareg, a camel's saddle with a pommel in the form of a cross. VI 667a
ṭarīḳ (A, pl. *ṭuruḳ, ṭuruḳāt*) : 'road, route, way, path', ~ shares a common field of geographical reference with similar terms like ṢIRĀṬ, *darb*, MASLAKA and SHĀRIʿ, though each is to be distinguished in its usage. XII 794b
♦ **ṭarīḳa** (A, pl. *ṭuruḳ, ṭarāʾiḳ*) : path (syn. *ṭarīḳ*); method of instruction, initiation and religious exercise; also, a religious brotherhood which forms the organised expression of religious life in Islam. II 164a; X 243b; in the science of Tradition, the plural form *ṭuruḳ* refers to ISNĀD strands. X 381b
In the terminology of tents, one or several bands of hair or wool, about twenty cm wide at the most, attached to the sewing of the awning band, *falīdja*. Each ~ was equipped at each of its extremities with a device for anchoring it called *ḥatār* and it was to this that the rope (*ṭunub*, pl. *aṭnāb*) was attached and tied to a peg (*watid*) driven into the ground some distance away with a mallet (*mītad*). IV 1147b
In zoology, the empty shell of an (ostrich) egg after the hatching of the chicks. VII 829b
♦ ṭarīḳa ḥallādjiyya (A) : a phrase referring to the beneficial effect of a spiritual influence, here al-Ḥallādj, traversing time, since *ṭarīḳa* is not invariably indicative of a materialised order. X 246b

♦ ṭarīḳa k̲h̲iṭābiyya (A) : 'way of eloquence'; a form employed in Ḳur'ānic preachings. II 447

♦ ṭarīḳa al-muḥammadiyya (A) : the proper terminology for 'mystical brotherhood', since in the final analysis, ṭarīḳa has meaning for the ṣūfīs only in terms of the relationship wich it establishes with the Prophet. This modality is correctly called 'the Muḥammadan Way', sometimes also al-ṭarīḳa al-muṣṭafawī. X 246b

♦ ṭarīḳat al-k̲h̲awādjagān: 'way of the masters', a line of 7th/13th-century Central Asian S̲H̲AYḴHs, not a constituted order, reckoned to be the initiators of the Naḵsh-bandiyya. X 245a

♦ ṭuruḳ ḥurra (A) : 'free ṣūfī orders', term for the orders functioning in Egypt in the latter half of the 20th century outside the formal administrative framework of the Ṣūfī Council and more numerous than those who de facto recognised its jurisdiction and were known as ṭuruḳ rasmiyya 'official ṣūfī orders'. X 325a

ta'rīk̲h̲ (A, < Sem; pl. tawārīk̲h̲) : date, dating, chronology, era. X 257b; history, historiography. X 271a; XII 795a

In the science of diplomatic, ~ 'dating' is one of the parts of a Turkish document; it is marked by means of an Arabic formula, e.g. taḥrīr^{an} fī and is followed by the decade of the month, the name of the month, and the year. II 307a; II 315a

In Turkish and Persian poetry, a chronogram, consisting of a a group of letters whose numerical equivalents, added together, provide the date of a past or future event, known in Arabic as RAMZ. III 468a; X 302a

♦ ta'rīk̲h̲-i Ilāhī (P 'Ilāhī Era') : the 'divine era', introduced by the Mug̲h̲al emperor Akbar in 992/1584. The first year of this solar year was the year of Akbar's accession, 963/1555-6. XII 410b

ṭarḳ (A), also ḍarb : lithomancy. The technicalities of this cleromantic rite are unknown to us, but it is supposed to have consisted of casting pebbles (ḥaṣā) on the sand and of interpreting the patterns they made, or the signs which are given by the way they fell on top of each other. Instead of pebbles, grain or nuts could be used. From the marks made by the pebbles on the ground, lines were traced in the sand, and from this there has been a gradual development which ultimately results in making ṭarḳ bi 'l-ḥaṣā the synonym of k̲h̲aṭṭ bi 'l-raml, i.e. geomancy (→ K̲H̲AṬṬ). IV 1128b

ṭark̲h̲ān (A, < M.Per), or tark̲h̲ān : a high-ranking Inner Asian title of considerable antiquity; also a personal name. By the Činggisid era, ~ had come to mean 'those who are exempt from compulsory contributions, and to whom the booty taken on every campaign is surrendered'. X 303a; under the Ilk̲h̲āns, personal immunities granted to Mongol princes and princesses and tho members of the religious classes and scribes. IV 1045a

♦ tark̲h̲āniyyāt (A) : in the science of diplomatic, concessions granting aged officials exemption from taxes, and possibly also a fixed salary, in the classical period. II 303b

ṭark̲h̲ash̲ḵūḳ (A) : in botany, taraxacum, the dandelion used in popular medicine because of its bitter substance. XII 370b; and → ʿALAT̲H̲

tark̲h̲īm (A) : in grammar, phonetic reduction. IX 528a

ṭark̲h̲ūn → S̲H̲ĪḤ tarkīb (A) : a composition. IV 981a

♦ tarkib-band (P) : in Persian literature, a refrain poem like the TARDJĪʿ, but called a ~ if the refrain differs in each instance where it occurs. I 677b; VII 662a; X 235b and → MUSADDAS

tarma (A) : a gallery, or wide room, giving on to the courtyard of a house through three bays. II 114a

ṭarrāḥī (A) : in art, designing; in the context of pictures, the production of the under-drawing. VIII 451b

ṭarrār (A) : pickpocket, also called *k̲h̲ālis*, MUK̲H̲TALIS or *nas̲h̲s̲h̲āl*, each of which indicates acquisition of other people's property in a public place, with *muk̲h̲talis* placing greater emphasis on secrecy and *nas̲h̲s̲h̲āl* indicating swiftness. X 304a

ṭars̲h̲ (A) : in art, an engraved block used for printing. X 304b

tarṣīʿ (A) : in rhetoric, a stylistic feature of word combination based on the principle of equivalence of sound. X 304b

tarsīm (A) : in Mamlūk times, perhaps predominantly, the detaining of a person in one place or putting him under guard. IX 547a

tartīb (A) : in Moroccan usage, the term employed by the MAK̲H̲ZAN to denote the reforms (*tartībāt*) it was obliged to undertake during the second half of the 19th century under European pressure, with connotations similar to those of TANẒĪMĀT in the Ottoman empire. ~ is still applied to the fiscal reforms initiated ineffectively by Mawlāy al-Ḥasan (1873-94) and revived by his successor Mawlāy ʿAbd al-ʿAzīz (1894-1907) in the least favourable of circumstances and only brought to a conclusion by the Protectorate. X 307b; in Morocco, a single tax, which merged the ZAKĀT and ʿUS̲H̲R. V 1199a; and → ḲĀNŪN

♦ bi 'l-tartīb : lit. step by step; in music, slow motion. IX 101a

tartīl (A) : in the science of the Qur'ān, an incantatory mode of recitation (syn. *taḥḳīḳ*). V 128a; and → NAS̲H̲ĪD

ṭarṭūr → TAḤḲĪḲ; ṬANṬŪR; ṬURṬŪR

tarwiya (A) : the 'day of watering', the name for the 8th day of D̲h̲u 'l-Ḥid̲j̲d̲j̲a (*yawm al-~*), on which day the pilgrimage begins. Arabic authors explain this as the day on which the pilgrims water their animals and provide themselves with water for the following days, but some Western scholars see in this name traces of an ancient rain rite. III 35b; X 312b: the name given to the first day of the pilgrimage, possibly because of the rite of drinking a fermented beverage on the occasion. II 1060a

ṭāsa (A) : in astronomy, the magentic compass. X 312b

taṣābī (A) : in the expression ~ *'l-s̲h̲ayk̲h̲*, a collection of motifs given in poetic dialogues warning the old man not to cavort like a young man. IX 385b

tasāḥuḳ → SIḤĀḲ

tasāk̲h̲īnī (A) : a kind of neck-veil, *ṭaylasān*. X 615a

tasallum → ḲABḌ

taṣarruf (A) : in Ottoman land law, property in the form of usufruct. V 473a

taṣawwuf (A) : 'the wearing of woolen clothes (*ṣūf*)'; the phenomenon of mysticism within Islam. X 313b

tasbīʿ → TAK̲H̲MĪS

tasbīḥ (A) : the saying of the formula *subḥāna 'llāh*. V 425b; and → SUBḤA

taṣdīr → ṢADR; TADRĪS

tasdīs (A) : in astrology, the sextile aspect. IV 259b

tasekkurt (B) : the partridge. IX 536b

tasfīr (A) : the art of bookbinding. VIII 150b

tas̲h̲addud → TAʿAṢṢUB

tas̲h̲ahhud (A) : the recitation of the Islamic affirmation of faith, especially in the ṢALĀT. VIII 929b; X 340b

tas̲h̲āhir → KABŪS̲H̲

tas̲h̲arruf (A) : the ceremony of initiation in the heterodox Ṭāwūsī ritual, whereby the initiate, in the presence of the initiator, *dalāl*, contracts several obligations and is presented with the *dīg-i d̲j̲ūs̲h̲* 'boiling pot'. X 397b

tas̲h̲bīb (A) : in literature, ~ is frequently used as a simple synonym for G̲H̲AZAL and NASĪB. II 1028a; IV 714b; in Urdu literature, ~ is the prelude of the ḲAṢĪDA, also, but less frequently, called *tamhīd*. V 958b

In rhetoric, ~ is synonymous with *ibtidāʾ* 'introduction, prologue', in its widest sense. III 1006a

tashbīh (A) : 'the act of comparing, comparison'; in rhetoric, a simile. IV 249b; VIII 614b

In theology, the comparing of God to the created; anthropomorphism. I 410b; III 160a; X 318a; X 341b; used in polemical language, the positive pendant to ~ is *ithbāt*, the affirmation of the divine attributes by analogy. X 342a

In prosody, description of the beloved, a standard amatory topic of poetry. X 220a

For ~ in grammar, → ĀLA

tashdīd → SHADDA

tashī → ḲUNFUDH

taṣḥīf (A) : a mistake in writing (syn. TAḤRĪF, without the specialised used of the latter). One who commits mistakes in writing is *ṣaḥafī* or *ṣuḥufī*. X 347a; in prosody, forgery. IX 455b

In rhetoric, paronomasia based on modifications of the graphic representations of two words and not on sound. II 825b

tashʿīr (A), or *shaʿra* : in mineralogy, cleavage, a defect or impurity in a gem. XI 263a

tashlama (T) : in Turkish folk poetry, a satirical genre, which has social injustices as one of its main targets. III 358a

tashrīʿ (A) : in law, statutory legislation incorporating elements from the sharīʿa, in an attempt to adapt it to the changing requirements of a modern society. X 353a

tashrīf → KHILʿA

tashrīḥ (A) : in medicine, anatomy, both as a description of the human body and as the empirical science of dissection. X 354b

tashrīḳ (A), and *ayyām al-~* : a special name for 11–13 Dhu 'l-Ḥidjdja, the last three days of the Muslim pilgrimage, during which the pilgrims stay in Minā and throw seven stones daily on each of the three piles of stones there. Traditionally they are called *al-ayyām al-maʿdūdāt* 'the numbered, i.e. few, days'. III 32a; X 356b; in early Islam, ~ was also given to the solemn ṢALĀT on the morning of 10 Dhu 'l-Ḥidjdja. X 357a

tasht-dār (P) : the 'keeper of the washing vessels'; a palace officer under the Ghaznavids and the Saldjūḳs. II 1082a

tashṭīr (A) : in prosody, the intercalation of two hemistichs between the first two of an existing poem. IX 243b; IX 462b; X 124a

taʿṣīb (A) : in law, the male relationship. XI 208b

taṣʿīd (A) : in pharmacology, the procedure of sublimation (rudimentary distillation). XII 550b

tasili (Touareg), conventionally *tassili* : used by the Touareg as a generic term for the sandy and rocky ensemble of plateaux of the central Saharan massif. X 357b

ṭā-sīn (A) : the two letters found at the head of sura xxvii that have been taken by early mystics to designate Iblīs. X 1b

tasʿīr (A) : in law, the fixing of a commodity's price, which requires a political decision. *Tathmīn* refers to estimating the value, *ḳīma*, of the subject-matter. A comparison of the two verbal nouns makes the distinction between *siʿr* and *thaman*, both 'price', appear less subtle. X 358b

taʾsīs (A) : in prosody, an *alif* of prolongation placed before the rhyme letter, *rawī*, and separated from it by a consonant which may be changed at will. IV 412a

taslīm (A) : submission. X 377b

taṣliya (A) : the invocation of God's blessing upon the Prophet Muḥammad, commonly referring to the section of the TASHAHHUD in which the worshipper recites the *ṣalāt ʿalā 'l-nabī*. A ~ is also a part of the response to the ADHĀN, also known as the *duʿāʾ*

al-wasīla. More broadly, ~ is understood as the repetition of the phrase *ṣallā 'llāhu ʿalayhi wa-sallama* 'May the prayers and peace of God be upon him'. In India and Pakistan especially, *durūd* is used to refer to the ~ , while *ḳunūt* also overlaps with it. X 358b

tasmīr (A) : shoeing a horse with nails, a Gallo-Roman invention in the 6th century, unknown in early Islam, where tribes used a sandal of iron or leather, *naʿl*. IV 1144b

tasmiya → BASMALA; NISBA

taṣnīf (A) : lit. sorting out, distinguishing, classifying something, whence 'putting in order, composing a book, etc.' and then as a common noun 'orderly presentation or classification'. X 360a

tasnīm (A) : the name of a fountain in Paradise, occurring in Q 83:27, whose water will be drunk by the *muḳarrabūn* 'those who are admitted to the divine presence'; also, the verbal noun of form II of *s-n-m* 'raising graves above the level of the earth'. It is said the Muḥammad's grave is *musannam*. X 360a

taṣrīʿ (A) : in prosody, internal rhyme, a shortening or lengthening of the last foot of a rhyme appearing at the end of the first hemistich, in order to make it conform to the pattern of the last foot of the second hemistich. II 825b; IV 413b

taṣrīf (A) : in grammar, one of the two main divisions of linguistic theory, 'morphology', the other being NAḤW 'syntax'. In later grammar, ṢARF is used and in modern Arabic it has become the usual term for 'morphology'. X 360b

In rhetoric, the transformation of a root (into various *awzān*). VIII 614b

taṣrīḥ (A) : in mysticism, an unequivocal declaration of one's feelings and intentions, seen as the opposite of *ramz* (→ IS͟HĀRA). VIII 428b

ṭassūd͟j (A, pl. *ṭasāsīd͟j*; < MidP *tasōk* 'one quarter') : in Sāsānid and early Islamic ʿIrāḳ, a sub-province, subdivision of a KŪRA 'province'. The ~ was in turn divided into RUSTĀḲS 'district'. I 3a; VIII 636a; X 361a

taṣwīr (A) : the constitution of a shape. IV 981a; in art, the representational arts (painting, drawing, sketching, engraving and photography) and the process of their creation (syn. ṢŪRA, pl. *ṣuwar*, and the rarer *taṣwīra*, pl. *taṣāwīr*, or in Persian texts *naḳs͟h* and *nigār*), often contrasted with *timt͟hāl* 'sculpture'. X 361b

♦ taṣwīr s͟hamsī, or *taṣwīr ḍawʾī* : along with the more simple TAṢWĪR and the borrowed *fūtūg͟hrāfiyā*, terms for photography, introduced in Muslim lands soon after its invention in 1839. X 363b

taswiya (A) : the act of leveling; in the Qurʾānic story of the creation, the 'leveling' of the sky. IV 984b

tasyīr (A) : in astrology, a procedure of artificial continuation of a planet or of an astrological house or any other definite part of the heavens to another star or its aspects, or other houses with the object of ascertaining the equatorial degree situated between these two places, the figure of which is used to prognosticate the date of a future happening, either good or evil. X 366a

tat (T) : a term used in earliest Turkish with the general meaning of 'alien, non-Turk', but speedily coming to be applied to the Persians as opposed to the Turks, with a somewhat contemptuous nuance of meaning as with the term TĀD͟JĪḲ. X 368a; in Arabic and Ottoman Turkish sources for the military and social history of Syria after its conquest by Selīm I in 922/1516, foreign troops in Syria, those neither Arab nor Rūmī, distinguished from the *yerlü*, locally-recruited toops. X 369b; XI 333b

♦ tātī : the name given to New Western Iranian dialects surviving in language islands in the eastern Caucasus region. X 369b

taṭabbub (A) : medical practice. IX 8a

taṭarruf (A) : extremism, radicalism, the opposite of moderation, *tawassuṭ*, *iʿtidāl*. X 372a

ṭāṭawī → WĀḲWĀḲ
taṭawwuʿ → ṢAWM
taṭayyur (A) : in divination, an augury based on the flight of birds (syn. *taʿayyuf*). XII 777b
taṭfīl → ṬUFAYLĪ
taṭhīr (A) : in law, a purifying punishment. X 406a
ta<u>th</u>lī<u>th</u> (A) : lit. to make or call three; in theology, the doctrine of the divine Trinity. X 373b
In astrology, the trine aspect. IV 259b; VII 794b
ta<u>th</u>mīn → TASʿĪR
ta<u>th</u>wīb (A) : repetition; the term for the formula *al-ṣalāt <u>kh</u>ayr min al-nawm*, pronounced twice in the morning prayer. I 188a
taʿṭīl (A) : 'stripping'; in theology, ~ is applied to the denial of attributes, that is, the assertion that God does not possess attributes of power, knowledge, speech etc. which are distinct from His essence. I 334a; I 411a; III 953b; X 342b
taṭʿīm → TAKFĪT
taṭwīʿ (Tun) : the diploma of secondary education from the Zaytūna of Tunis. IX 160b
ṭāʿūn (A) : in medicine, the plague. VIII 783a; IX 477a; both the bubonic plague and the swellings of the lymph glands so characteristic of this disease. XI 2b; and → WABĀʾ
ṭāʾūs → ṬĀWŪS
ṭawāf (A) : the circumambulation of a sacred object (syn. *dawār*), specifically the Kaʿba during the pilgrimage. The pavement surrounding the Kaʿba on which the course is run is called al-*maṭāf*. The ~ itself is obligatory, but two other circumambulations, that of greeting or arrival (~ *al-tahiyya* or ~ *al-ḳudūm*) and that of departure (~ *al-wadāʿ*) are not. I 610b; III 35a; X 376a,b
♦ ṭawāf al-ifāḍa : the circumambulation of the Kaʿba on 10 <u>Dh</u>u ʾl-Ḥi<u>dj</u>dja, after the sacrifice. III 35b; VII 169b
tawakkul (A) : in religion and especially mysticism, trust in God to such an extent that one does not support oneself; submission to the divine will. He who trusts in God is called *mutawakkil*. VIII 596a; VIII 691b; X 376b
tawallud (A) : 'engendered act'; according to the Muʿtazilite Bi<u>sh</u>r b. al-Muʿtamir, ~ is an act prompted by a cause which is itself the effect of another cause. Thus, in the act of opening a door with a key, there is first a voluntary act, then the movement of the hand which turns the key, and lastly that of the key which turns the tongue of the lock. This last movement is an engendered act for it does not emanate directly from a voluntary decision. I 413b; I 1243b; X 378a
In biology and philosophy, spontaneous generation, that is, the generation of plants and animals directly from inanimate matter, as opposed to sexual generation or procreation, *tawālud*. X 378a
tawālud → TAWALLUD
tawʾamān → AWZĀʾ
ṭawā<u>sh</u>ī (A) : in the Ayyūbid army under Ṣalāḥ al-Dīn, fully-equipped cavalrymen. I 797b; II 507a; VIII 468a; a eunuch. I 33a; IV 1087a; the bottom member in the hierarchy of the Mamlūk barracks, responsible for training small groups of *mamlūk*s only. X 7b
ṭawāsīn (A) : a name for the SŪRAs that begin with the letters *ṭā-sīn*: xxvi-xxviii. IX 887b
tawassuṭ → TAṬARRUF
tawātur (A) : roughly 'broad authentication'; in the science of Tradition, ~ indicates that a historical report or a prophetic tradition is supported by such a large number of ISNĀD strands, each beginning with a different Companion or other ancient authority, that its authenticity or truthfulness is thereby assumed to be guaranteed. X 381b

In law, a form of testimony which consists of the affirmation of a fact by a number of persons so large (a minimum of twenty-five is generally accepted) as logically to exclude any possibility of fraud or lying. The ~ is superior to all other modes of proof with the exception of confession. II 171b

♦ tawātur lafẓī   (A) : in the science of Tradition, the verbatim MUTAWĀTIR transmission of a text, distinguished from tawātur maʿnawī, transmission according only to the gist or one salient feature of a given text. The latter far outnumbers the former. X 381b

♦ tawātur maʿnawī   → TAWĀTUR LAFẒĪ

tawāzun al-suluṭāt   (A) : in political science, the balance of powers. The notion of 'separation of powers' (faṣl al-suluṭāt), originally introduced as faṣl al-ḥukm or infiṣāl al-ḳuwwa al-ḥākima by al-Ṭaḥṭāwī, was taken up in the Muslim world from the second third of the 19th century. Classically this concept is unknown. X 382a

ṭawb   (A) : unbaked brick. I 1226b

tawba   (A) : in religion, repentance. X 385a; XI 141b

tawbīkh   (A) : verbal reprimand. X 406a

tawbīr   (A) : an instinctive attempt by a hare to blur its tracks by placing its body weight on the back foot only. The back foot has a pad which is covered with hair and thus prevents the toes and claws from marking the ground. XII 85a

tawdjīh   (A) : in prosody, the vowel before the quiescent rhyme letter; according to others, also before the vowelled rhyme letter. IV 412a; and → TAWRIYA

ṭawf   (A, pl. aṭwāf) : a raft of early ʿAbbāsid Mesopotamia, similar to the KELEK. IV 870b; VIII 810b

tawfīḳ   (A) : in theology, 'facilitating, helpfulness, predisposing towards', used especially of God's grace and help towards mankind, and seen as the opposite of KHIDHLĀN. X 386b

tawḥīd   (A) : the assertion of God's unity, in a word, monotheism. X 317b; X 389a; in current usage, ~ , or ʿilm al-tawḥīd, is the modern equivalent of ʿilm al-kalām, theology. X 389b; a kind of dates. I 126b; and → NĀṬIḲ

tawhīm   → TAWRIYA

taʿwīdh   → TAMĪMA

ṭawīl   (A) : lit. long; in prosody, the name of the first Arabic metre. The ~ forms, with the metres basīṭ and madīd, the group of metres whose hemistichs consist of 24 consonants each. I 670a; X 389b

In numismatics, the name of a coin in Ḥasā, on the Arabian peninsula, which is only an inch long and of very base silver, if not copper, without any trace of inscription. V 684a; and → ḲALANSUWA

taʾwīl   (A) : explanation, exposition, or interpretation of the Ḳurʾān. IV 147a; X 390b; and → TANZĪL

ṭawḳ   → ḤADJRA; SHAʿĪRA

tawḳīʿ   (A, T tewḳīʿ) : an extended table of memorable events; a tabular almanac providing seasonal information. X 146b; edict, decree of the ruler. X 392b

In calligraphy, a variety of the THULUTH script, with its letters somewhat more compressed and rounded. This script was used in Persia for the final page, sc. that with the colophon showing the date and place of copying and the scribe's name, of elongated format Ḳurʾāns. IV 1123b; for Turkish diplomatic practice, a specific technique for writing more formal and solemn documents. The script used was the DĪWĀNĪ, also known as tewḳīʿ in its various forms. II 315b; VIII 151b; X 393b

In the science of diplomatic, ~ seems originally to have been the ruler's signature, which was appended in the chancellery. Later on, ~ was also used for letters of appointment, quite generally to begin with, but later only for the lesser officials. II

303a; X 392b; into the 10/16th century, ~ in the *corroboratio* refers to the seal; not until the 11th/17th century was ~ replaced by the (long overdue) expression MUHR. II 311b; and → IMḌĀ; IṬLĀḲĀT

♦ tawḳīʿ ʿalā ʾl-ḳiṣaṣ (A) : in the science of diplomatic, the decision of petitions in open court, said to have been the custom even in Sāsānid times. II 303b; X 392b

tawḳīr (A) : respect. XI 388a

tawlīd → TAKWĪN

tawrāt (A) : the Pentateuch. IX 321b; X 393b

tawrīḳ (A) : in art, arabesque, mostly of the sort restricted to foliage. The term is preserved in Spanish *ataurique*, commonly used by Spanish authors to designate the genuine arabesque. I 498b; I 560b; X 395a

tawriya (A) : in rhetoric, mispointing information for secrecy. VIII 427a; in prosody, double-meaning. IX 460b; a one-term pun (*double entendre*), also known by a confusing number of other names, e.g. *īhām, tawhīm, ta<u>kh</u>yīl, taw<u>dj</u>īh, mu<u>gh</u>ālaṭa maʿnawiyya*, etc. A related figure is the *isti<u>kh</u>dām*, based on a compound sentence where the main clause and the subordinate each 'make use of' one of the double meanings of the term on which the figure depends. X 67b; X 395a

taw<u>th</u>īḳ → MIḲRAN

ṭāwūs (A, < Gk; pl. *ṭawāwīs, aṭwās*), or *ṭāʾūs* : in zoology, the peacock (*Pavo*), nicknamed *Abu ʾl-wa<u>sh</u>y* 'he of the splendid coat', of the family of the Phasianidae, comprising four species: the blue peacock, the spiciferous peacock, the Congo peacock and the black peacock. I 177b; X 396a

In music, a pandore viol from India, with the ESRĀR one of the two best-known examples. The ~ is practically identical with the *esrār*, but is adorned with the figure of a peacock at the bottom of the body of the instrument. VIII 348b

♦ ṭāwūsiyya (A) : in zoology, the greater peacock moth (*Saturnia pyri*) and the lesser peacock moth (*Saturnia pavonia*), from the family of Saturnidae, and the peacock butterfly (*Vanessa io*), from the family of Nymphalidae. X 396b

tawwāb (A, pl. **tawwābūn**) : 'penitent', in its plural form, the self-imposed title of an early <u>sh</u>īʿī movement. X 398a

ṭawwāb (A) : a mason who builds a wall in clay. V 585b

tawakkul (A) : in mysticism, confidence in God. XI 141b

tawwaziyya (A) : textiles from the mediaeval city of Tawwa<u>dj</u> (Tawwaz) in southern Persia. IX 310b

tāy → ČAY

tayammum (A) : ritual purification with sand, soil, or dust, allowed when water is unavailable. II 1104a; VI 709b; VIII 926b; X 399b

tay<u>dj</u>ï <u>dj</u>emāʿatï (T) : in the Ottoman empire, a special category of MÜSELLEM which enjoyed exemption from taxes in exchange for breeding horses for the royal stables. IX 855a

ṭayf al-<u>kh</u>ayāl → <u>KH</u>AYĀL

ṭaylasān (P, pl. *ṭayālisa*) : a headshawl worn over the turban, worn in mediaeval Islam particularly by religious scholars and notables in the northern and eastern parts of Iran and even by the common folk in Fārs. V 747b; X 398b; insignum of rank. X 375b

ṭayr (A) : in mysticism, spiritual flight, one of the degrees of the mystical journey. IX 863a; for ~ in zoology, → ṬĀʾIR

tays → ʿATŪD; TAYYĀS

ṭayy (A) : in prosody, a deviation in the metre due to the suppression of the fourth consonant of a foot. I 672a; XI 508b

ṭayyār → BAYYĀZ

♦ ṭayyāra (A) : 'flyer', a name describing a kind of skiff used in mediaeval Mesopotamia. VIII 811a; and → BĀD-I HAWĀ

tayyās (A), or *tays* : a goat-herd. XII 317a

ṭayyibāt : 'jocose poems', a genre in Persian literature, defined by classical Persian literary critics according to its contents rather than to its form. III 355

tazakkara → MUSTAKRISH

tazammut → TAʿAṢṢUB

taẓarruf (A) : in mediaeval Islamic social and literary life, an intensification of certain features, intellectual, literary, social, and personal, that are held to characterise the man of ADAB. XI 460a

taʿzīr (A, pl. *taʿāzir*) : in law, discretionary punishment by the ḲĀḌĪ in the form of corporal chastisement, generally the bastinado, for offences for which no ḤADD punishment is laid down. The term means both showing respect and disrespect. I 29b; II 519a; X 406a; X 799b

taʿziya (A) : in Persian literature, the shīʿī passion play, the occurrence of which is not documented before the late 12th/18th century. IV 50b; X 406b; in Muḥarram processions on the Indian subcontinent, ~ signifies the bier on which al-Ḥusayn's headless body was carried from the battlefield to its final resting place; it also stands for his tomb. It is called *tadja*, due to phonetic transformation, on the island of Trinidad, where they are still being built. X 408a

In literature, a letter of condolence addressed to the parents of the deceased, becoming frequent from the 2nd/8th century onwards. When it is in verse, it is virtually indistinguishable from the MARTHIYA. VI 605a

tazkiya (A) : in law, the procedure for substantiating the ʿADĀLA of witnesses, also called *taʿdīl*. I 209b

♦ al-tazkiya al-ʿalāniyya : the second stage of the procedure known as TAZKIYA, in which the persons who received a sealed envelope in the first stage (→ AL-TAZKIYYA AL-SIRRIYYA) appear at the public hearing to confirm their former attestation. I 209b

♦ al-tazkiya al-sirriyya : the first stage of the procedure known as TAZKIYA, in which the judge proceeds to a secret investigation, by sending a question in a sealed envelope to qualified persons. I 209b

tazwīr (A) : the falsification or forgery of a document or piece of writing. X 408b

tazyīf (A) : in numismatics, the forgery of coins. X 409b, where are found many terms associated with counterfeit coins.

tebriya → TABRIʾA

teferrüdj → TAFARRUDJ

tegulmust → LITHĀM

tekālīf → TAKLĪF

tekaṭkaṭ (Touareg) : a large, loose tunic with sleeves, often dark indigo-coloured, worn by both sexes among the Touareg. Under it men wear large trousers with a low crotch, women a skirt. X 379b

tekfur (P, T, < Arm *taghavor* 'crown bearer'), or *tekvur* : a title used in late Rūm Saldjūḳ and early Ottoman times by Persian and Turkish historians to denote Byzantine lords or governors of towns and fortresses in Anatolia and Thrace. X 413b

tekke (T, < A *takiyya*, pl. *takāyā*; P *takiya*), *tekiyye* or *tekye* : an establishment belonging to a group of ṣūfīs, where they gather around a SHAYKH and perform their ritual and their devotions, etc. It is thus similar to RIBĀṬ, KHĀNḲĀH, *dergāh*, ZĀWIYA and *āsitāne*, but it has not yet been determined how ~ is employed in preference to these other terms. It seems that its use was first developed in an Ottoman context from the 10th/16th century onwards, with the rise of an organized Ottoman network of brotherhoods. X 415a

teklīf → TAKLĪF
telkh̲is̲ (T, < A) : in Ottoman administration, a document in which the most important matters are summed up for presentation to the sultan. X 416b; memoirs, e.g. those presented to the sultan by the grand vizier acting as representative of the government. The officer to whom they were given was called the **telkh̲īṣdji**. VIII 481b ff.; X 415b
♦ telkh̲īṣdji → TELKH̲ĪṢ
temenggung → BENDAHARA
temidelt → AGADIR
temlīk-nāme (T) : in the Ottoman empire, a special diploma issued by the sultans, recognising proprietary rights on waste land as well as on running water and springs within the area delimited by the document. V 878b
tende → aHAL
tennūre (T) : in Ottoman Turkey, a long dervish's robe without sleeves. V 752a; IX 168a
teptyar (Rus, < A *daftar*) : 'people of the register', a social term and subsequently ethnonym, used to denote populations of Volga Tatar, Mish̲är, Bash̲kir, Čuvash̲ and Volga Finnic origins, all of whom spoke a Tatar dialect in Bash̲kiria. X 417b
teraḳḳī (T) : 'advancement', a bonus granted to cavalrymen in the Ottoman empire. IX 656a; a pay raise in the Ottoman military. X 811b; XI 324b
terdjümān (T) : in mysticism, a term used by the members of FUTUWWA groups and by the Turkish dervish orders of the Mawlawiyya and Bektāsh̲iyya for speech utterances, generally in verse, recited during the ritual or, outside this, during the accomplishment of some piece of work or some particular act. These formulae, which are made up of a prayer, are pronounced in order to seek pardon for some offence. ~ can also denote a sum of money or a sacrifice made in order to secure pardon for an offence. In practice, ~ is often mixed up with *gül-bank* (→ GULBĀNG), which is reserved for longer prayers in prose. X 418b; and → TARDJUMĀN
terken (T) : in old Turkish, a royal title, often but not invariably applied to females, and in these cases roughly equivalent to 'queen'. X 419a
terlik (T) : in Ottoman Turkey, the most popular shoes, worn by men and women, without heels or quarters slightly raised at the end, in leather or material and often decorated. V 752b
tersāne (T, < Genoese *tersana*) : 'dockyard, maritime arsenal'; in the Ottoman period, it was applied in particular to the Ottoman Imperial Arsenal on the eastern side of the Golden Horn, at Galata, opposite Istanbul. X 420a
tesbīḥ → SUBḤA
teslīm tash̲i̊ (T) : 'stone of submission', the name given to a small, twelve-fluted disc worn on a cord, sometimes with smaller stones strung along the cord, around the neck, and given to the young Bektāsh̲ī dervish at the end of his novitiate. VIII 244b
təstmal (N.Afr) : a fringed head scarf for women worn in Libya. V 746b
tewḳiʿ → TAWḲĪʿ; TUGH̲RA
♦ tewḳīʿī → NISH̲ĀNDJI̊
th̲āʾ (A) : the fourth letter in the Arabic alphabet, with the numerical value 500, representing the voiceless member of the apico-interdental triad of fricatives, as opposed to the voiced DH̲ĀL and the velarised ẒĀʾ. X 423b
th̲abat → FAHRASA
th̲ābit (A) : having the characteristic of 'positive', as e.g. the non-entity in Muʿtazilī thought. I 178b
th̲aḳāfa → RUMḤ
th̲aḳalayn → ḤADĪTH̲ AL-TH̲AḲALAYN
thākur (H) : an honorary title, used to address the Hindus of the Lohaga caste. VIII 307a

thaʿlab (A, pl. *thaʿālib*; P *wāwi, rūbāh*, T *tilki*) : in zoology, the fox (*Vulpes vulpes*), which bears the nicknames of Abu ʾl-Ḥusayn, Abu ʾl-Nadjm, Abu ʾl-Nawfal, Abu ʾl-Wathab and Abū Ḥinbiṣ. The vixen is called *thaʿlaba, thuʿala, thurmula* and *thuʿlubān*, with the nickname Umm ʿUwayl, and the fox-cub is known as *hidjris* and *tanfal*. X 432a
In botany, ~ is secondary growth on the date-palm, which needs to be pruned away (syn. *fasīl*). X 433a
♦ thaʿlaba → THAʿLAB
♦ thaʿlabiyyāt (A) : in astronomy, several stars of the Great Bear. X 433a
♦ dāʾ al-thaʿlab (A) : 'fox disease', in medicine, alopecia and baldness. X 433a
♦ ʿinab al-thaʿlab (A) : 'fox grape', in botany, the current. X 433a
thaldj (A) : snow or ice. X 435a
♦ **thallādj** (A) : the seller of snow or ice. The NISBA al-Thaldjī relates to the Banū Thaldj, however. X 435a
♦ thaldjiyyāt : in poetry, snow poems. IX 8b
thalweg : main navigation channel. IX, 369a; X 127a
thaman → TASʿĪR
thanawiyya (A) : in heresiography, the term for dualists, becoming current in the 4th/10th century, covering a number of different sectarian groups, in particular the Manichaeans, the Bardesanites, and the Marcionites. It seems to have been preceded by *aṣḥāb al-ithnayn*, while the expressions *ahl al-ithnayn* and *ahl al-tathniya* are also found. X 439b
thanāyā (A) : in anatomy, the incisors. VIII 695b
thanī (A) : the name for a foal between two and three years old. II 785a; and → ʿATŪD; MUSINNA
thaʾr (A) : blood revenge, which by law could settle most homicide disputes among Bedouin in modern times but in actuality only settles a small minority of cases. X 442b; punitive raids of retaliation, one of the Bedouin's activities. II 1055a
thāra → SHAGHABA
tharīd (A) : a dish consisting of bread crumbled into a broth of meat and vegetables, associated with the tribal tradition of the Ḳuraysh and said to be among the favourite dishes of the Prophet. II 1059a; V 41b; X 31a
thawāb (A) : in theology, recompense, especially with reference to the next world, usually only in a good sense. II 518a; and → ʿIWAḌ
thawābit → AL-KAWĀKIB AL-THĀBITA
thawb (A, pl. *thiyāb, athwāb* 'clothes') : in early Islam, a general word for garment and fabric. V 733b; in modern times, a basic tunic worn by both sexes throughout the Middle East; a woman's dress. V 742a
thawr (A, < Gk) : in astronomy, *al-~* is the term for Taurus, one of the twelve zodiacal constellations. VII 83a
thawra (A, P *inḳilāb*, T *inkilap*) : uprising, revolt or revolution. The term has undergone a change over the centuries, from implying an undesirable development to a desirable one, even in the latter part of the 20th century being employed in a juxtaposition with Islam that was previously inconceivable: ~ *islāmiyya*, meaning revolution designed to restore the good old order of early Islam. X 444a f.
thaytal → BAḲAR
thayyib (A) : a girl over the age of puberty who is no longer virgin, being either widowed or repudiated. III 17a; X 901b
therwet-i fünūn (T) : lit. riches of the arts; the name of a late Ottoman Turkish literary movement, named after the journal with the same title which ran from 1896 till its closure in 1901. The movement has also been referred to as *Edebiyyāt-i̊ djedīde*. X 445b

thiḳa (A, pl. *thiḳāt*) : 'trustworthy'; in the science of Tradition, the highest quality of a reliable transmitter of Tradition, although through over-use it gradually lost its positive meaning, becoming more often than not a meaningless epithet. I 104b; II 462a; VIII 900b; VIII 983a; X 446a

thiḳāf → RUMḤ

thikhan (A) : thickness. XI 556b

thiyāb → ḲUMĀSH

thuʿala → THAʿLAB

thughūr (A, s. *thaghr*) : lit. gaps, used for ports of entry between the DĀR AL-ISLĀM and the DĀR AL-ḤARB, in particular the forward strongholds in the frontier zone which extended between the Byzantine empire and the empire of the caliphs in the north and north-east of Syria, and the march lands, 'the Marches', in al-Andalus between the Arabs and the Christian kingdoms to the north. I 761a; II 503a; VIII 603a; VIII 869b; X 446b; and → ʿAWĀṢIM

In naval science, strategic ports. X 446b; XII 120a

thulth → NIṢF

thuʿlubān → THAʿLAB

thulūl (A) : in medicine, a wart. XII 350a

thuluth (A) : lit. one-third; in calligraphy, a script which is generally said to have derived its name from being based on the principle of a third of each letter being sloping. It was and is still used for every kind of frame and for book titles in all Muslim countries. IV 1123b; VIII 151b

thūm (A) : in botany, garlic, one of the winter crops in mediaeval Egypt. V 863a

thumān (A) : in botany, a grass. IV 1147a

thumn (A) : a measure used in Muslim Spain for weighing olive oil. A ~ contained $2^1/_4$ Spanish raṭls (503.68 g), i.e. 1.12 kg. VI 121a

thunāʾiyyāt → MUTHANNAYĀT

thurayyā → NADJM

thurmula → THAʿLAB

ṭīb → AFĀWĪH

ṭibāḳ (A) : 'antithesis', in rhetoric, a figure consisting in the inclusion, in a verse or colon, of words of opposite meaning (syn. *muṭābaḳa* and *muṭābaḳ*, and in later writings, *taḍādd* and *mutaḍādd*). X 450b

tibāra (H) : a Hindī term also applied to Muslim buildings in India, for a hall with three adjacent bays or doors. V 1214b

ṭibb (A) : medicine. X 452a

♦ al-ṭibb al-nabawī (A) : 'prophetic medicine', a genre of medical writing arising in the 3rd/9th century, intended as an alternative to the exclusively Greek-based medical systems and authored by clerics rather than physicians. X 453a

tibgh → TUTUN

tibnī (A) : the designation for the colour of the palest, straw-coloured yellow sapphire. XI 262b

tibr (A) : gold dust. X 915a; raw ore. XII 704a

tidjāra (A) : trafficking, trade, commerce; a trader is known as TĀDJIR (pl. *tudjdjār*, *tidjār*, *tudjur*, *tadjr*, and in Ibn al-Athīr, *tudjār*), which early on was synonomous with *khammār* 'wine-seller'. X 466a

tidyanin → TIQSIḌIN

tifā(wa) → TUFFA

tīfāf → HINDIBĀʾ

tifinagh (Touareg, s. *tafinekḳ*) : 'Phoenician letters', the alphabet of the Touareg, consisting of geometrical consonantal characters. X 380b; X 476b ṭifl (A) : child; according to Lane, 'a child until he discriminates . . . after which he is called *ṣabiyy*' or 'a child from the time of his birth . . . until he attains to puberty'. VIII 821b

tiftik (T) : the silky hair of the white long-haired goats in central Anatolia. I 511a

tīghbend (T) : among the Bektāshīs, a girdle fashioned from ram's wool, the girding on of which is the second element in their ceremony of initiation, *iḳrār*. IX 168a; and → ELIFI NEMED

tigin (T), or *takīn* : an ancient Turkish title with the original meaning of 'prince'. In the early Türk empire it denoted the legitimate son or grandson of the Supreme Ḳaghan, but since royal princes in the Türk empire usually held high military and administrative office, ~ gradually became detached from the necessity of royal descent and became a title of function. Among eastern Turks, ~ retained its meaning, but further west, it decreased in status and could be applied to any military leader. By the time of the Mongol invasions, it seems to have fallen out of use. X 480b

tihāma → TAHAM

ṯiḥuža (B) : in Tarifiyt, the genre of fairy tales, a part of the traditional oral literature. X 242a

tik wa-tum (A) : in music, a technical term corresponding to the learned term *ṭāʾ*, meaning the note struck, sharp and heavy, on the edge of the tambourine, sometimes of the little cymbal that is fixed there; or on the back of the closed left hand when the hands are beaten; or with the left foot on the ground when dancing. It is one of the two terms of the fundamental metrical dualism of the MUWASHSHAḤ: *ṭāʾ* (usually *tik*) and *dīh* (usually *tum*). The latter is struck on the stretched skin at the centre of the tambourine; on the centre of the open left palm if the hands are beaten; or with the right foot on the ground when dancing. X 498a

tikka → FŪṬA

ṭīkūk → SHAḲĪḲAT AL-NUʿMĀN

ṭilāʾ (A) : the pitch with which a camel's skin was smeared; also, a kind of syrup made from grapes that was cooked till two-thirds was evaporated, losing its inebriating power. IV 995b

tilasm, tilism → ḤIRZ; TILSAM

tilāwa → TADJWĪD

tillīs (A) : a measure of capacity which was used in Egypt in the caliphal period for measuring grain. VI 119a

tilmas (B) : 'spring, water-hole', which plural *tilmisān* is a plausible, if not certain, etymology for the Tlemcen, a town of western Algeria. X 498b

tilsam (A, Gk τέλεσμα), also *tilsim, tilism, tilasm* : a talisman, that is, an inscription with astrological and other magic signs or an object covered with such inscriptions, especially also with figures from the zodiacal circle or the constellations and animals that were used as magic charms to protect and avert the evil eye. X 500a

tīm (P) : term used by Nāṣir-i Khusraw for caravanserai, still used in its diminutive form *tīmča* in parts of the Iranian world. IX 796a; XII 457a

tīmār (P, T equivalent *dirilik*, DIRLIK) : lit. care, attention; in the Ottoman empire, a system of non-hereditary prebends, divided into three categories: KHĀṢṢ, ZIʿĀMET and ~ , used to sustain a cavalry army and a military-administrative hierarchy in the core provinces. X 502a; and → SERBEST

tīmča → TĪM

timrād (A, pl. *tamārid*) : narrow pierced pigeon hole in the loft (*ḳurmūṣ*, < Gk) of a pigeon. When placed at the foot of the loft, it forced the pigeon to climb up a ladder inside its nesting-place, which strengthened its muscles, thus becoming an indoor pigeon as distinct from an outside one which returned to the loft through pigeon-holes at the top. III 109b

timsāḥ (A, < C *ʾimsaḥ*; pl. *tamāsīḥ*) : in zoology, the Nile crocodile (*Crocodilus vulgaris*), the only crocodile known in the Arabophone countries. X 510

♦ ḥabḳa al-timsāḥ : in botany, the common calamint (*Clinopodium vulgare* or *Calamintha clinopodium*), a labiat member of the Melissa genus. X 505b

timt͟hāl → TAṢWĪR

ṭimṭim → NAḲAD

timucuha → TIQSIḌIN

tīn (A) : in botany, the common fig (*ficus carica*), widespread throughout the Mediterranean. A tree and fruit resembling ~ is *d̲jummayz*, the sycamore fig. X 529a

♦ tīn ak͟hḍar → NĪL

ṭīn (A) : mud, clay; in the Qurʾān, the material from which man was made, and the substance from which Jesus will create a live bird. X 529b; edible clay or earth, a diatomaceous earth or kieselguhr, made up of the siliceous remains of minute marine organisms, found in various parts of Persia in mediaeval Islamic times (also called *nuḳl, ṭīn nad̲jāḥī* 'successful, auspicious, valued clay'. X 530b

♦ ṭīn-i mak͟htūm (A) : *terra limnia*, a sort of volcanic earth that had reputedly medicinal power and a famous export product from Lemnos, an island in the northern part of the Aegean Sea, which used to be dug once yearly with some ceremony. V 763b

♦ **ṭīna** (A) : in philosophy, matter, rendering the basic meaning of Gk ὕλη, Ar. HAYŪLĀ, in early Arabic translations from the Greek and in the first period of Arabic philosophical writings. X 530a

ṭinfisa (A) : a kind of carpet with a pile. XII 136a

tinmal (B), or *tinmallal* : a Berber term for terraces for agriculture on a mountain side. X 530b

tinnīn (A) : lit. dragon; in folklore, an enormous serpent. III 335a; X 531a

In astronomy and astrology, the Arabic name for the constellation Draco (the third of the 21 northern constellations according to Ptolemy); also the figure of a mythological dragon, or serpent, which was assumed to cause solar and lunar eclipses. X 531a; and → D͟HANAB; D̲JAWZAHAR

♦ d͟hanab (al-tinnīn) → D͟HANAB

♦ raʾs (al-tinnīn) → RAʾS

tiqsiḍin (B) : a narrative genre popular in Kabylia, a Berberophone area of Algeria, consisting of long narratives in verse recounting the adventures of Muslim heroes and saints. Other narrative genres are the *tidyanin*, aetiological legends about animals, and the *timucuha*, which narrate the adventures of heroes and heroines who assert the moral and symbolic organisation of the conventional Kabyle society. X 119a

tira (P) : a subdivision of a tribe; among the Kurdish, ~ can be best described as a political group, not to be confused with the *hoz*, a group of the same lineage. The ~ is subdivided into many *k͟hel*, each *k͟hel* composed of twenty to thirty tents or households united by economic links as well as by family links. V 472a; among the S͟hāhsewan in Persia, a tribal section, formed by two or three winter camps of 10-15 households. IX 224a

ṭīra (A) : originally, the observation and interpretation of the spontaneous flight, cries and perching activities of certain birds, used in divination; evil presentiments aroused by the contents of a phrase or a song are generally also grouped under this head. A whole literature, essentially of poetry and proverbs, created to dissuade man from following the ideas inspired in him by ~ , and to which all men are subject, is derived from the term. II 758b ff.; IV 290b; V 101a

ṭirāz (A, pl. *ṭuruz*; < P) : textiles. I 24a; silken fabrics and brocades designed for ceremonial robes. I 501a; embroidery, especially embroidered bands with writing in them; an elaborately embroidered robe, such as might be worn by a ruler or his entourage. ~

garments were bestowed as tokens of royal favour and were among the standard gifts brought by diplomatic embassies to other rulers as part of foreign policy. III 219a; V 736b; X 534b; XII 341b; ~ , or *dār al-ṭirāz*, also came to designate the workshop in which such fabrics or robes were manufactured. X 534b

In art, from the meaning 'embroidered strip of writing' ~ came to mean 'strip of writing', border or braid in general, applied not only to material but also to any inscriptions on a band, whether hewn out of stone, done in mosaic, glass or faience, or carved in wood. X 534b; X 538b

In relation to papyrus, until the middle of the 4th/10th century, ~ could designate the inscriptions officially stamped with ink upon the rolls of papyrus in the factories. ~ in turn extended to indicate the factories themselves. X 534b

In the science of diplomatic, ~ was the term for the introductory protocol in diplomatic documents, with considerable variety in the wording. The purpose seems to have been to endow the document with a certain authenticity. From the 4th/10th century, the ~ was omitted altogether. It is also called *iftitāḥ*. II 301b

tirbāl (A) : in architecture, an Iranian square-shafted tower with an external ramp winding round it, the remains of which still stand in Fīrūzābād. VI 365a

ṭirimmāḥ (A) : tall, proud. X 541a

tīrkas͟h (P) : in archery, a quiver made of horse-hair, used by archers from the province of Gīlān. IV 799b

tirme(d͟ji) → DESTĀND͟JI̊

ṭirs (A) : parchment from which the original text had been washed off and which then was written on again. II 540b; VIII 408a

tiryāḳ (A) : in medicine, a remedy which could be used as a prophylactic against poison. IX 873a; and → AFYŪN

ṭiʿs (A, pl. *ṭuʿūs*) : on the Arabian peninsula, a dune bare of vegetation. A larger dune is called *naḳāʾ*. II 537a

tis͟hrīn (Syr) : the name of the first two months of the Syrian calendar. X 548a

tis͟htaniyya → BURḲUʿ

ṭisḳ → WAḌĪʿA

tīṭ (B) : a Berber word for 'sacred spring'. X 548a; X 757a

tiwala (A) : 'spells by means of which a woman seeks to gain a man's love'. X 177b

tiyūl (T) : a grant of money or land in pre-modern Persian lands. X 550b; a type of appanage in the Turcoman states of eastern Anatolia. X 502a

♦ tiyūldār : the holder of a TIYŪL. X 550b

ṭog͟hri̊l (T) : a designation in Old Turkish for a bird of prey, a possibility being the Crested Goshawk (*Astur trivirgatus*). It was certainly used for hunting purposes. The Turkish word may have given Magyar *turul* 'a kind of falcon or eagle'. From Uyg͟hur times onwards, ~ was a common personal name. X 552b

tōlā (H 'balance, scales') : a Mug͟hal measurement of weight for both gold and silver. In British India, by a regulation of 1833, the ~ of 180 grains, being also the weight of the rupee, was extablished as unit of the system of weights. II 121a; X 563b

ṭolba (Mor, s. *ṭālib* 'student') : in Morocco, a colloquial plural that denotes the students at madrasas or at universities. For their spring festival, → SULṬĀN AL-ṬALABA. X 148b

ton : 'group', in Mali, *ton jon* 'group of slaves' being the basic social institution of the Bambara empire of Segu, making up the army and a good part of the bureaucracy. IX 121b

ṭop (T) : in the Ottoman military, the term used for cannon. It originally denoted 'ball', hence cannon-ball; it appears in almost all the Turkic languages and passed into the usage of Persian, the Caucasian and the Balkan languages, etc. X 564b

♦ ṭopdju : in the Ottoman military, a member of the corps of artillerymen. X 564b

♦ ṭopkhāne : in the Ottoman military, the name for the central arsenal in Istanbul. X 564b

ṭopal (T) : lame; as 'the lame' a nickname given to two prominent Ottoman figures on account of their walking with a limp. IV 884b; X 564b

torbeš → POTURI

toy (T) : a public feast given by the ruler, a practice that was apparently introduced into the Islamic world by the Saldjūḳs from the custom among the pastoral nomads of Eurasia. The institution was also known as *shölen* or *ash*. VI 809b; the festival of marriage or of circumcision throughout the Türk world, called *dügün* in Turkey. X 733b

tozluḳ (T) : breeches worn by men as an outer garment in Ottoman Turkey. V 752b

trīmūlīn (A) : in zoology, the arenicol, a small beach worm (*Arenicola marina*), often used as bait in fishing. VIII 1022a

tuan (M 'master') : term preferred for 'saint' instead of WALĪ in Aceh. XI 121b

ṭūb (A) : in the Muslim West, a lump of earth or an unfired brick, whence Sp. *adobe*. In Egypt, ~ is used as a synonym of *ādjurr* 'fired brick'. V 585b; and → SHAWKA

tubbaʿ : a term (pl. *tabābiʿa*) used by Muslim writers as a dynastic title for those Ḥimyarite rulers who, between the late 3rd and early 6th centuries A.D., controlled the whole of Southwest Arabia. It is not clear how the Muslim writers came to envisage ~ as a title; it was not used by the rulers themselves. X 575b

tubbān (A) : very short drawers, made of hair, reportedly worn by the men who bore ʿĀʾisha's litter on the pilgrimage, and worn under trousers by Umayyad soldiers. V 733b; IX 677a

tuc (Mon) : according to Marco Polo, a corps of 100,000 of the Great Khān's troops. X 590a

tudhrī (A) : in music, a trill. II 1073b

tüdük → SIBIZGHI

tufah → TUFFA

tufangčī (T) : in the Ṣafawid and Ottoman military, a musketeer. I 8a; I 1068a; VIII 786a; IX 477a

ṭufaylī (A) : in mediaeval Arabic literature, an uninvited guest and/or a social parasite, whose behaviour constitutes *taṭfīl*, which covers a variety of actions ranging from coming uninvited to social functions to consuming more than one's share of food or drink to overstaying one's welcome. The ~ was one of the most popular character types in the Arabic ADAB genre. The lexicographers distinguished between a ~ who comes uninvited while people are eating (*wārish*) and one who comes uninvited while people are drinking (*wāghil*). X 586b; cadgers. X 4b

tuffa (A), or *tufah, tifā, tifāwa* : in zoology, the Jungle Cat (*Felis chaus*), trained to hunt game. II 739b

tuffāḥ (A) : in botany, the apple (*Pyrus malus, Rosaceae*). Some preparations made from the ~ were fruit purée (*djawārish al-tuffāḥ*), apple juice (*sharab al-tuffāḥ*) and apple sauce (*rubb al-tuffāḥ*). X 587a

♦ tuffāḥ al-djinn → YABRŪḤ

♦ tuffāḥ indjān (A) : in botany, the berries of the mandrake, called thus in one Palestinian village in the 1970s, said to encourage broodiness in chickens. XI 225b

♦ tuffāḥiyya (A) : a mediaeval meat dish with apple. X 31b

tugh (T, < Ch *tu* 'banner') : among the early Turks and Ottomans, an emblem of royal authority, a standard, traditionally a horse's tail or a bunch of horse hair on a pole, or a drum. A great ruler would be described as having nine ~s, the maximum. Under the Ottomans, those to whom royal authority had been delegated had a lesser number of ~s. X 590a

tughra (T, A *ṭughrā*, pl. *ṭughrāwāt*) : in the science of Turkish diplomatic, a calligraphic emblem of Turkish rulers, from the time of the chiefs of the Oghuz; the device or the sign of the sultan, also called *nishān-i humāyūn, tewḳiʿ* (→ TAWḲĪʿ) and *ʿalāmet*, and of different design for each sultan. It contains the name of the sultan and all his titles and other distinctions with the formula *muẓaffar dāʾima*, encased in an ornamental design, always with the same motifs and shape. II 314b; IV 1104b; V 232b; VIII 62a; X 595a; and → ʿUNWĀN

In Ottoman administration, chancellor. VIII 62a

♦ ṭughra-kesh (T) : in late Ottoman administration, a clerk especially assigned to drawing and painting the TUGHRA; in the earlier period NISHĀNDJI, also *tughra čekmek*, and in Persian *tughra kashīdan*. II 314b, X 597b

♦ ṭughrāʾī (A) : in Turkish administration, dating from the Saldjūḳ and Khwārazm-Shāhī periods, the official charged with drawing the TUGHRA. X 595b

ṭughyān (A) : tyranny. XI 567b

ṭuḥayḥī (A) : on the Arabian peninsula, a small, fierce-looking lizard. I 541b

tuḥfat al-ʿūd (A) : in music, according to Ibn Ghaybī, a half-sized lute. X 769b

tukʾa → WISĀDA

tuku (J) : the remnant of a bride-price in Java. I 174a

tulad, tuladj → HAYTHAM

ṭulaḳāʾ (A, s. *ṭalīḳ* 'a person set free [from imprisonment or slavery]') : in early Islam, a technical term denoting the Meccans of Ḳuraysh who, at the time when Muḥammad entered Mecca in triumph, were theoretically the Prophet's lawful booty but whom he in fact released. It was subsequently used opprobriously by opponents of the Meccan late converts. X 603a; a derogatory name, sometimes applied to the Umayyads by their opponents, explained as a reference to the fact that as a result of Muḥammad's conquest of Mecca, they had become his property but he had then magnanimously chosen to set them free. X 841b

ṭulb (A, pl. *aṭlāb*) : in the military of the Ayyūbid and Mamlūk periods, a squadron or battalion of cavalrymen. In the Ayyūbid army, ~ was the basic parade and field unit, although it appears to have been an ad hoc formation; under the Mamlūks, ~ is used both for an AMĪR's entourage of personal MAMLŪKs and for the larger unit under his command. IX 610a; X 608a

tulband (T, < P *dulband*) : a sash or wrapper for the head, thence turban, the typical form of traditional headdress in the eastern Islamic lands, the Iranian world, and the Muslim and Sikh parts of the Indian subcontinent. X 608a

ṭulma (A) : 'flat bread'; in ancient Arabia, a kind of pancake cooked on a heated stone. V 41b

ṭulumba (T, < It *tromba*) : water pump for firefighting; these appeared first in Italy in the 15th century and spread around the Mediterranean shores. They are mentioned as ~ already in the 1560s, but the firefighting pump was introduced into the Ottoman empire by a renegade Frenchman in 1718. X 616a

♦ **ṭulumbadji** (T) : fireman, firefighter; Ewliya Čelebi mentions a guild of *~yān* who had the task of pumping water out of ships in the 16th century. After 1720, the ~s comprised a company of the Janissaries until the latter was abolished in 1826. The personage of the ~ was a major figure in Istanbul folklore of the 19th and early 20th centuries. X 616a

tūmān (P) : in numismatics, the unit of account which formed the basis of the Persian currency system during the period of Ṣafawid rule; its value was fixed at the currently-established weight of 10,000 silver dīnārs. The weight of the ~ was customarily expressed as a fixed number of MITHḲĀLs or *nukhūd*s of refined silver which could then be converted into coin with the value of 10,000 dīnārs. One *mithḳāl*, weighing approximately 4.60 g, was equal to 24 *nukhūd*s which each weighed about 0.192 g. VIII 790a; X 619b

In the Mongol empire, ~ refers to a division of the army numbering 10,000 men, which was further broken up into units of 1,000, 100 and 10. It is frequently mentioned in Persian and Arabic sources as the standard formation of the Mongol army in battle, but whether ~s actually had a full complement of 10,000 troops remains an open question. The ~ also is used to refer to an administrative district within the Ilkhānate. X 619a

tumāntōḳ : in Muslim India, a standard appearing in Mughal court ceremony, resembling the common ʿALAM but with its shaft adorned with Tibetan yak-tails. VI 533b

ṭūmār (A, < Gk) : a sixth of a papyrus roll, the smallest piece used in the trade. IV 742a; V 173b; and → MUKHTAṢAR AL-ṬŪMĀR

ṭumrūḳ → WAṬWĀṬ

tunbāk → TUTUN

tunbān → LUNG

ṭunbūr (A, < P *dum* or *dunba* 'tail' and *bara* 'lamb'; pl. *ṭanābīr*) : in music, the classical name for the pandore and various types of long-necked instruments in the East. It is generally to be distinguished from the lute, ʿŪD, by its smaller sound-chest and longer neck. A wire strung instrument, the *tel* ~, was smaller than the others and was popular with the women-folk. Synonymous terms for the instrument are *buzuk, djura*, SĀZ, etc. V 234a; X 624b, where variants and many other terms can be found

♦ ṭunbūr khurāsānī (A) : the pandore favoured in Khurāsān and to the north and east of it, generally found with two strings although sometimes mounted with three. X 625a

♦ ṭunbūr mīzānī (A), or ~ baghdādī : the pandore attributed to the Ṣabians, which retained in its frets the scale of pagan times, was used in ʿIrāḳ and to the south and west of it. It was generally found with two strings. X 625a

♦ ṭunbūr-i shīrwānī (P) : a pandore with a deep pear-shaped sound-chest and two strings, favoured by the people of Tabrīz. It was played with the fingers. X 625a

♦ ṭunbūra-yi turkī (P) : a pandore with sometimes three strings, but generally two, whose sound-chest was smaller than the *ṭunbūr-i shīrwānī*, although it had a longer neck. It was played with the fingers. X 625a

tunḳus (A) : in zoology, the tench. VIII 1021a

ṭunub → ṬANĪB; ṬARĪḲA

tūp-khāna (P) : in the Ṣafawid military, artillery. VIII 786a; artillery park. IX 476b

ṭūr (A, < Ar *ṭūrā* 'mountain') : mountain, with *djabal al-~* being the name for Mount Sinai, and, with *djabal zaytā* or ~ *zaytā*, also for the Mount of Olives. X 663a ff. For ~ in mysticism, → LAṬĪFA

turʿa (A) : a canal of a river, distinguised from minor branches and the main stream. VIII 38a

turandj → ʿUNWĀN

turba (A, T *türbe*; pl. *turab*) : an Islamic funerary building or complete funerary complex of various forms, or, in a more generic sense, denoting only the funerary aspect of the building. When used as the only term in a funerary inscription, ~ suggests the meaning 'mausoleum'. X 674b; with *kümbed*, a tomb surmounted by a dome, ~ is the classical word which was driven out of use by ḲUBBA, until it was again popularised by the Turks. V 289a; VI 652b; VIII 964b

In its basic meaning, ~ is 'earth', 'dust' and 'soil', the material from which the earth and mankind were formed. X 674a

türk → SĀRT

türkü (T, < *türkī*) : in Ottoman Turkish music, both the folksong in general, as opposed to the song belonging to Turkish art music, SHARḲĪ, and a genre of folksong, primarily identified by the melodies proper to it. X 736a; a type of folk-poetry of Anatolia. I 677b; VIII 2b

türkmen (T, A *al-turkumān, al-tarākima*) : 'resembling the Turks, Turk-like', a term used collectively for Turkic tribes distributed over much of the Near and Middle East and Central Asia from mediaeval to modern times. X 682a

ṭurmūḳ → WAṬWĀṬ

turmus (A) : in botany, lupin, one of the winter crops in mediaeval Egypt. V 863a

ṭurra (A) : lit. border of a piece of cloth, upper border of a document; confused with TUG͟HRA in 13th-century Arabic literary and popular usage, arising from the part of the document where the *ṭug͟hrā* was normally affixed. X 595b; *al-~ al-sukayniyya* 'Sukayna-style curls', a particular hair-style made famous by Sukayna bt. al-Ḥusayn, a granddaughter of ʿAlī b. Abī Ṭālib. IX 803a; and → ṢUDG͟H; ʿUNWĀN

turs (A) : in military science, shield. IX 891a; XII 736a

turs͟hī (P) : pickled vegetables, which condiment, along with sour grapes, *g͟hūra*, dried lemons and walnuts, remain essential to Persian cooking. XII 609a

♦ turs͟hīči-bās͟hī (P) : in Ṣafawid times, an official in the royal kitchen who supervised the preparation of pickled vegetables. XII 609b

ṭurṭūr (A) : a high cap around which the turban can be wound. In the 8th/14th century, the pointed ~ , with or without the turban, was the headdress of the common people in Egypt and the countries adjoining it. X 615a; and → S͟HIMRĪR

turud͟jān → TURUND͟JĀN

ṭuruḳ → S͟HAYK͟H AL-S͟HUYŪK͟H; ṬARĪḲA

turund͟jān (A), more commonly *bādrund͟jubūya* : in botany, balm (*Melissa officinalis* L.) of the Labiatae, the lemon balm or bee plant, its synonyms being *bad͟hrund͟jubūya, turud͟jān, ḥabaḳ al-turund͟jānī*, and *ḥas͟hīs͟hat al-naḥl*. It has been cultivated since Antiquity, was known in Spain in the 10th century AD and was possibly introduced further north by Benedictine monks. X 740b; and → ḤAS͟HĪS͟HAT AL-SANĀNĪR; NUḤĀM

ṭusayt → ṢAḤN

tūs͟hmāl-bās͟hī (P) : in Ṣafawid times, supervisor of the royal kitchen, a subordinate to the steward of the royal household, *nāẓir al-buyūtāt*, and responsible for the quantity and quality of the meat served at the court, also acting as the royal taster. XII 609b

ṭusūt (A) : in music, the general term for harmonica, played with sticks, *ḳuḍbān*. An author of the 9th/15th century refers to the harmonica as the *kīzān* 'cups' and *k͟hawābiʾ* 'jars'. IX 11b

tūt (A), also *tūt͟h* : in botany, the mulberry, *Morus* spp., of the Moraceae, known for its fruit and leaves. A synonym is *firṣād*. X 752a

♦ tūt al-arḍ (A) : in botany, the strawberry. X 752a

♦ tūt al-ʿullayḳ (A) : in botany, the raspberry. X 752a

tūtin (P) : a cigar-shaped raft of reeds, found among the population of hunters (*ṣayyād*s) in Sīstān, on which they travel to fish and hunt waterfowl. IX 682b; XI 516b

tūtiyā (A) : in mineralogy, calamine or tutty, used to denote the natural zinc ores, especially zinc carbonate, or the white zinc oxide which was obtained during the treatment of the ores. V 149b; V 356b; V 965a

tutun (A) : in botany, tobacco, more specifically, pipe tobacco. Other terms used are the Arabic *duk͟hān* and *tibg͟h*, and, for water-pipe tobacco, the Persian *tunbāk* and *tambākū*. While in much of the Western world smoking was long deemed unbecoming for women of polite society, no such social stigma seems to have existed in the Middle East. Until the 20th century, a smoking device that was widely used was the regular tobacco pipe. Originally made of clay, and later also of wood, these pipes were known as *čupūḳ* or *čapūḳ* in Turkish and Persian (< P *čūb* 'wood'). Lane observed similar pipes, known as *s͟hibuk* or *ʿūd*, in early 19th-century Egypt. X 753a

tutḳavul → RĀHDĀR
ṭuwama → SULAḤFĀ
tuyugh (T), or *tuyuğ* : in Turkish literature, a type of quatrain, similar to the RUBĀʿĪ. I 677b
tuyūl : in mediaeval Persia, temporary grants in return for services. They frequently carried with them the right to collect (as well as to receive) the taxes, and rights of jurisdiction. III 1089b; IV 1043 ff.; IX 733a
tuzghü → SAʾURI
tūzūk (T, < P) : in military science, a ruler's or military commander's 'arrangement', or the order in which he keeps his soldiers and establishment. ~ is often coupled with *ḳāʿida, maḍbūṭ*, and *ḍabṭ u rabṭ*, all of which are synonymous in these contexts. X 760b
From the post-Tīmūrid period on, a generic title for memoirs and biographies of rulers. X 760b

U

ubna → LŪṬĪ
ʿūd (A, pl. *aʿwād, ʿīdān*) : 'wood, piece of wood, plank, spar', in botany, agallocha wood, which is the better term for ~, often incorrectly defined as aloe wood (ṢABR). ~ has to do with certain kinds of resinous, dark-coloured woods with a high specific weight and a strong aromatic scent, used in medicine as perfume and incense. The designation derived from the place of origin was also usual, e.g. *al-ʿūd al-mandalī, al-ʿūd al-samandūrī, al-ʿūd al-ḳimārī*, etc. X 767b
In music, the lute, whose player is an *ʿūdī*. I 66b; X 768a, where many different terms for lutes and the names of the various parts of the ~ are found; and → TUTUN
♦ al-ʿūd al-hindī : a wood mostly synonymous with agollocha. X 767b
♦ ʿūd ḳadīm → ʿŪD KĀMIL
♦ ʿūd kāmil : a larger ʿŪD than the classical one (*ʿūd ḳadīm*), with five strings, which was common by the time of Ṣafī al-Dīn al-Urmawī (d. 692/1293). X 769b
♦ ʿūd al-ḳarḥ : in botany, *Anacyclus pyrethrum* D.C., *Compositae*. X 767b
♦ ʿūd al-rīḥ : lit. fragrant wood; in botany, *Berberia vulgaris* L., *Berberidaceae*. X 767b
♦ ʿūd al-ṣalīb : lit. cross wood; in botany, *Paeonia officinalis* L., *Ranunculaceae*. X 767b
♦ ʿūd al-shabbūṭ : in music, a lute whose shape resembles the round and flat fish of that name, invented by Zalzal. XI 427b
♦ ʿūd al-ʿuṭās : 'sneezing wood'; in botany, *Schoenocaulon officinale, Liliaceae*. X 767b
♦ al-ʿūdāni : 'the two things of wood' of the KHAṬĪB, viz. the minbar and the staff or wooden sword which he has to hold in his hand during the sermon. IV 1110b
ʿudār (A) : part of the ancient Arabs' repertoire of fabulous animals, the ~ was a male whose habit was to make men submit to assaults, which proved mortal if worms developed in the anus of the victim. II 1078b
ʿudda → SILĀḤ
ʿūdha → ḤIRZ; TAMĪMA
udhī → ḌAHŪL
ʿudhr (A) : in law, a plea. I 319b

ʿudhrī (A) : the NISBA of the Arabian tribe ʿUdhra, ~ came to mean an elegiac amatory genre among the poets of the tribe, who expressed passionate desire for an unattainable beloved, chastity and faithfulness until death. *Al-ḥubb al-* ~ is a favourite theme in classical Arabic poetry and prose, often identified with 'platonic' or 'courtly' love. The opposite, performative, physical love, is known as Ḥidjāzī. X 774b; X 822b

udhun (A) : ear.

♦ iltihāb al-udhun (A) : in medicine, otitis. X 433a

ʿudiya (A) : 'having a single tent-pole'; among the Tiyāha on the Arabian peninsula, a tent whose ridge-pole rests on a row of three poles. The Sbāʿ call it a *gotba*. IV 1148a

udj (T) : frontier. II 1044b; under the Ottomans, a military post. VIII 608b; the frontier districts or marches. X 777a

♦ udj-bey (T) : the military lord of a district zone carrying out war against the neighbouring Christians. X 777b

ʿudjra (A) : protuberance, knot. X 508a

ʿudjma → ʿADJAM

udm (A), or *idām* : a condiment, eaten with bread by pre-Islamic Arabs. II 1058a; V 42a

ʿudūl → ʿADL

ufk (A) : falsehood. IX 567b

ʿufr → KHANZUWĀN

ufʿuwān → AFʿĀ

ughlūṭa → MUʿḌILA

uḥbūla → ḤIBĀLA

ʿuhda (A) : in Egypt under Muḥammad ʿAlī, an estate consisting of bankrupt villages whose taxes were collected by their new landholders rather than by members of the government. II 149a

uḥdjiyya (A, pl. *aḥādjⁱⁿ*) : 'riddle, conundrum', one of three kinds of literary plays upon words, the others being LUGHZ and MUʿAMMĀ. The term denotes a simple guessing game, e.g. 'guess what I have in my hand', but can also mean a type of enigma fairly close to the *lughz*. Thus for *salsabīl* 'wine' : 'What is the alternative sense meant by the person setting forth a riddle when he says: ask (= *sal*) the way (= *sabīl*)?'. V 807a

uḥdūtha (A) : 'speech, tale', giving rise to *ḥaddūta* 'folktale' in colloquial Arabic. XII 775a

ʿuhūd → ʿAHD; ʿAHDNĀME

ʿuḳāb (A) : the Prophet's flag, according to the traditional literature. I 349a; the black banner used in the battles against Ḳuraysh. IX 14a; and → NŪSHĀDIR

In zoology, the eagle (pl. *aʿḳub, ʿiḳbān, ʿuḳbān, ʿaḳābīn*), which has the tecnonyms of *Abu 'l-ashyam* 'father of the one with the mole or beauty spot', *Abu 'l-ḥudjdjādj* 'the man with the pilgrims', i.e. of Mecca, *Abu 'l-ḥasan* 'the fine one', *Abu 'l-dahr* 'the long-lived one', *Abu 'l-haytham* 'the eaglet's father', and *Abu 'l-kāsir* 'the breaker of ones'. Out of the nine species of Aquilae, seven are known in the Arab-speaking lands. I 1152b; X 783b, where numerous terms for the various eagles are found

In astrology, al-~ is the name of the 17th boreal constellation, yielding in ancient Latin texts such deformations as *alaocab, aloocab, alaucab*, etc. X 784a

ʿuḳad, or *al-ʿuḳadāʾ* → AḤMĀL

ʿuḳalāʾ al-madjānīn (A) : 'wise fools', a general denomination for individuals whose actions contradict social norms, while their utterances are regarded as wisdom. Several authors of classical Arabic literature have treated the phenomenon in specific works that belong to the literary genre dealing with unusual classes of people, such as the blind or misers. XII 816b

ʿuḳda → ʿAḲD; DJAWZAHAR

ukhdha → SIḤR

ukhrūf → UḲRŪF

uḳhuwān (A) : in botany, the chrysanthemum; ~ is also used to render the παρθένιον of Dioscorides, by which we should probably understand the medical *Matricaria chamomilla*, still in use today. XII 114b

uḳiyānūs → ḲĀMŪS

ūḳiyya (A) : in numismatics, a piece of 40 dirhams. XI 413a

ʿuḳḳāl → ʿĀḲIL; DJĀHIL

ukla (A) : an itch. IX 435a

uḳnūm (A, < Syr; pl. *aḳānīm*) : hypostasis. X 374a

uḳrūf (A), or *ukhrūf* : a high cap common in the Maghrib, which could be made either quite simply or of valuable material. X 615a

uḳṣūṣa (A) : in modern Arabic literary terminology, the fictional genre of the short story. The term enjoys less currency than *ḳiṣṣa ḳaṣīra*, the Artabic literal translation of the English term. X 796b

ʿuḳūba (A) : in law, punishment in all its forms, encompassing both discretionary punishments and those designated as ḤADD. ~ is frequently confused with DJAZĀʾ, which can be both punishment and reward. X 799a

ulači (Mon) : during the Mongol empire, both a postal courier and an ostler, the functionary responsible for the welfare of the post horses. XI 268a

ulaḳ (T) : the official courier service in the Ottoman empire, which origin, with some reason, the Ottomans traced to the Mongols. The state couriers are also termed ~ . From the middle years of Süleymān's reign, a network of staffed posting stations, *menzil-khāne*, was introduced along the major routes. X 800a

ūlaḳ : an Özbeg sport in which men on horseback battle to carry the carcass of a cow to a goal, played at the celebration of weddings and circumcisions. VIII 234b

ʿulamāʾ (A, s. *ʿālim*) : the term denoting scholars of almost all disciplines, although referring more specifically to the scholars of the religious sciences. In Sunni Islam, the ~ are regarded as the guardians, transmitters and interpreters of religious knowledge, and of Islamic doctrine and law, embracing those who fulfil religious functions in the community that require a certain level of expertise in religious and judicial issues. The *ʿālim* is often seen as opposed to the *adīb*, he of 'profane knowledge', ADAB. X 801b; XII 720b

ulee (Oromo) : a long, forked stick, carried by pilgrims to the tomb of Shaykh Ḥusayn, having a practical use but being above all a sign of their status as pilgrims. IX 399a

ulkā : in the Ṣafawid period, a district or region held by a tribal group. X 550b; and → YURD

ulu beg (T) : 'senior lord'; in Saldjūḳ and early Ottoman administration, the designation for the father of the ruling family in his capacity as ruler of the state. It was he who concluded treaties, struck coins and was apparently commemorated in the Friday public prayer. VIII 192b

ʿulūfe (A, T; < *ʿalaf* 'provender or grain rations for mounts') : in Ottoman financial and military organisation, the wages of members of the imperial household. This basic pay for members of standing military regiments at the Porte was continuous in both peace and war. Use of the term ~ for salary also separated military from administrative personnel, since the latters' wages were usually termed *waẓīfe* (pl. *waẓāʾif*). X 811b

ulugh khān (T 'great khan') : a title borne by various of the ethnically Turkish Dihlī Sultans in 7th-8th/13th-14th-century Muslim India. X 814a

ulus (Mon) : a Turkic term meaning 'country' or 'district' (→ ĪL), which when it came into Mongolian acquired the meaning of 'people', and as such is found referring to both the Mongol peoples themselves and neighbouring nations who were absorbed by them. It was also applied to the various appanages given to the sons of Čingiz Khān, and can often be translated henceforth as 'state'. X 814a

ʿuluww → ISNĀD ʿĀLĪ

ʿumda (A, pl. *ʿumad*) : in 19th-century Egypt, the term for veteran masters in the guilds. XII 409b

♦ ʿumdat al-mulk (IndP) : in the Dihlī sultanate, the title for the chief secretary, DABĪR, also called *ʿalāʾ dabīr* and *dabīr-i khāṣṣ*. IV 758b

umdūḥa → MADĪḤ

umm (A) : mother.

In astronomy, the inner surface, usually depressed, on the front of the astrolabe, enclosed by the outer rim, ḤADJRA. I 723a

♦ umm al-banīn → UMM AL-WALAD

♦ umm ḥubayn → ḤIRBĀʾ

♦ umm ḳarn : in zoology, the trigger fish (*Balistes*). VIII 1021a; and → KARKADDAN

♦ **umm al-kitāb** : lit. the mother of the book, an experssion that appears three times in the Qurʾān and some forty Prophetic traditions, but has no equivalent in the earlier Semitic languages. It most often denotes the heavenly prototype of the Qurʾān, identified with *al-lawḥ al-maḥfūẓ*. In an extension of this, certain authors, particularly the mystics, define ~ as the first intellect or the Supreme Pen, which writes down the destinies on the tablet. Some authors see in ~ the celestial 'matrix' of all the revealed books. X 854a

In shīʿism, ~ is also the title of an enigmatic book associated with the early shīʿī GHULĀT of southern ʿIrāḳ. Originally produced in Arabic, only a later enlarged version, written in archaic Persian, has been preserved by the Central Asian Nizārī Ismāʿīlī communities in present-day Tajikistan, Afghanistan and northern areas of Pakistan. X 854b

♦ **umm al-ḳurā** : lit. the mother of settlements, or villages, a Qurʾānic expression that has been taken to mean Mecca, although Bell pointed out that the idea of a cluster of settlements or hamlets fits much better the topography of the Medinan oasis in Muḥammad's day, whereas Mecca was from early times a necleated town, and moreover, all three of the passages in which ~ appears in the Qurʾān are Medinan. IV 680a; X 856a

♦ umm sālim : in zoology, the bifasciated lark. I 541b

♦ umm al-shabābīṭ : in zoology, the barbel (*Barbus sharpeyi*). VIII 1021a

♦ umm thalāth: in zoology, the nickname given to the female sandgrouse, because she lays two or three eggs. IV 744a

♦ **umm walad** : in law, the title given to a concubine, or slave-girl, who has a child by her master. In contrast, the name for a free woman was *umm al-banīn* 'mother of sons'. I 28a; X 857a

♦ umm zubayba → KHARŪF AL-BAḤR

♦ **ummī** (A, pl. *ummiyyūn*) : 'belonging to a people without a revealed book', this term appears four times in the Qurʾān in the plural, and once in the singular in regard to the Prophet. There is no basis in the Qurʾān for the traditional view that ~ means 'illiterate'. V 403b; X 863b

umma (A, pl. *umam*) : as a Qurʾānic term, ~ denotes the nation of the Prophet, the Community. II 411a; in the Qurʾān, ~ usually refers to communities sharing a common religion, while in later history it almost always means the Muslim community as a whole. In modern usage, the plural *umam* means 'nations' and is therefore distinct from the Islamic meaning normally associated with ~ . X 861b

In geography, a term on the Arabian peninsula for the Tihāma fogs, also called *sukhaymānī*. IX 39b

ʿumra (A) : the Little or Lesser Pilgrimage, in contrast to the ḤADJDJ, the Great Pilgrimage. It consists of walking seven times around the Kaʿba, praying two *rakʿa*s, a sequence of actions performed in the ṢALĀT, facing the *maḳām Ibrāhīm* and the Kaʿba, and finally traversing seven times the distance between Ṣafā and Marwa. III 31b; III 35a; X 864b; and → ʿURS

ʿumrā (A) : as defined by the Ḥanafī, Shāfiʿī and Ḥanbalī schools of law, a gift with full ownership but as a life interest, the donee undertaking to restore the property on his death, at the latest. In the Mālikī school, ~ is a gift of the usufruct and as such valid; it thus becomes very hard to distinguish it from *ʿāriyya* 'loan for use'. III 351a

ʿumūm wa-khuṣūṣ (A) : lit. generality and specificity, a term of legal theory that bears upon the scope of applicability of rules of law. According to the majority view, whenever an interpreter came across a general expression in a text (e.g. *muslimūn* 'Muslims', *al-darāhim* 'the dirhams'), he had grounds for an initial presumption to the effect that the author of the text intended an all-inclusive reference. If he subsequently discovered a contextual clue indicating that specificity rather than all-inclusiveness was intended, he would have grounds for setting aside this initial presumption. Otherwise the initial presumption would stand. X 866b

ūniḳs (A, < Gk) : in zoology, a kind of water-snail, valued because of its aroma. VIII 707a

ʿunḳ → IBRĪḲ

ʿunnāb (A) : in botany, the jujube tree (*Ziziphus jujuba*), syn. *zafzūf* (dim. *zufayzif*). IX 549b; X 868a

ʿunṣur (A, pl. *ʿanāṣir*) : 'origin', 'family', 'race', 'constituent'; in modern Arabic, the plural *ʿanāṣir* may also be rendered as 'nationalities'. X 868b

In philosophy, elementary body, material cause; element, matter. X 530a; X 868b

ʿunwān (A, pl. *ʿanāwīn*) : the address or superscription at the head of a document. In manuscript production, ~ is used for the title of a composition and is thus one of the terms used for an illuminated frontispiece or headpiece, with or without the title of the book inscribed in it. The other technical terms are *tardjama, ṭurra, ṭughrā, sarlawḥ, dībādja, shamsa* and *turandj*, although there is no consensus as to their exact meaning. Apart from the last two, which are medallions of round or oval shape, the other terms may refer to any type of illumination preceding the main text. X 870b

In the science of diplomacy, the ~ is part of the introduction of documents, denoting the direction or address. Al-Ḳalḳashandī collected fifteen different forms of the ~ . II 302a; X 870b

ʿurafāʾ → ʿARĪF

ʿurāt (A) : the 'naked', name for turbulent social elements who grouped themselves around the caliph and barred the path of the besiegers of Baghdad in 196/812 until their resistance was overcome. I 437b

ʿurbān → BAYʿ AL-ʿURBĀN

urdjūḥa (A), or *mardjūḥa* : a seesaw, according to tradition where Muḥammad first saw ʿĀʾisha. V 616a

urdjūza → RADJAZ

urdu (U, < T ORDU), and *zabān-i urdu* : in South Asia, the term used to designate the mixed Hindustani-Persian-Turkish language of the court and the army; now the Urdu language of a large proportion of the Muslims in the subcontinent. VIII 174b; X 873b

ʿurf (A, P) : custom, customary law, administrative regulations on matters of penal law, obligations and contracts, issued by Muslim rulers, called ḲĀNŪN in Turkey. I 170a; X 887b; and → ʿĀDA; AʿRĀF; ʿARĪF

In Ottoman dress, a large globe- or pad-shaped turban worn by learned men, corresponding to the Arabic *danniyya* and the Persian *kulāhī-ḳāḍī*. Meḥemmed II was fond of wearing the ~ embroidered with gold. X 615a

urfī (A) : in zoology, the braize orphe, whose Arabic term is found again in the Latinised nomenclature to specify a sub-species limited to a particular region (*Pagrus orphus*). VIII 1021b

ʿurfuṭ (A) : in botany, the name of a thorny shrub which exudes an evil-smelling resin. III 587a

urg͟han, urg͟hanūn : in music, the artifically wind-blown instrument known as the organ. It also stood for a certain stringed instrument of the Greeks, and was used by the Persians to denote a species of vocal composition somewhat similar to the mediaeval European *organum.* At no period in Muslim history, however, was the organ considered an instrument of music in the same sense as e.g. the NĀY or ʿŪD. It was probably accepted as an interesting mechanical device. X 34b; X 893a

♦ urg͟hanūn al-būḳī : in music, the flue-pipe organ. X 893b

♦ urg͟hanūn al-zamrī : in music, the reed-pipe organ, a very primitive type in which the bellows are inflated by the mouth. X 893b

ūriyā (Syr) : teacher. IX 490a

urka (A), or *ḳattal* : in zoology, the orc or grampus, one of the marine mammals or cetaceans. VIII 1022b

ʿurs (A, pl. *aʿrās*), or *ʿurus* (pl. *ʿurusāt*) : originally the leading of the bride to her bridegroom, marriage, also the wedding feast simply, ~ is the wedding performed in the tribe or the house of the man, whereas *ʿumra* is the wedding performed in the house of tribe of the woman. X 899b; in the Indo-Pakistan subcontinent, a feast held in honour of a saint. VI 896b; XI 535b; a death anniversary. X 59b; among the dervishes, a celebration to commemorate a dead saint. VIII 416a; in South Africa, festival commemorating death anniversaries of ṣūfī saints. IX 731a

urṣūṣa (A), *arsusa*, or *russa* : in dress, said to be a melon-shaped hat. X 615a

ʿurūb : water-mills. X 479a

ʿurūba (A) : lit. the quality or nature of Arabness; in modern political parlance, the doctrine of Arabism or pan-Arabism. X 907b

ʿurwa (A), or *ḥabs* : part of the suspensory apparatus of the astrolabe, ~ is the handle, which is affixed to the point of the KURSĪ so that it can be turned to either side in the plane of the latter. I 723a

usbūʿ (A) : a week; also the term for a wedding in early Islam, since a wedding lasted a week. X 900a

usbūr (A) : in zoology, the sparid fish. VIII 1021a

ʿuṣfur → ḲURṬUM

ʿus͟har (A) : in botany, a tree of the Middle East and Africa (*Calotropis syriaca*). XI 107b

ʿus͟hb → ʿAS͟HS͟HĀB

us͟hnān (A) : a perfumed (powdered, pasty?) mixture for washing and scenting the clothes and hands, used in mediaeval times. VIII 653a

ʿus͟hr (A, T *ʿös͟her*; pl. *aʿs͟hār, ʿus͟hūr*) : in law, the tenth or tithe; generally a tax on the land owned by Muslims, or a tax on the commercial goods to be paid by all merchants, Muslim or non-Muslim. X 917a; in the Ottoman empire, the main land tax for Muslims, a tithe of the produce. VII 507b

us͟hturbān (P) : the Persian equivalent of the Arabic *d͟jummāl* ‘camel-driver’, ‘owner and hirer of camels’, ‘a dealer in camels’. XII 241b

us͟hturmurg͟h → NAʿĀM

üsküf (T) : in the Ottoman empire, a high KÜLĀH ‘cap’ worn by the Janissaries. Its rear part fell in the form of a covering on the back, a ribbon ornamenting it at the base where a metal case for the officer’s spoon or plume was also fixed. V 751b; also called usḳūfiyya (< It scuffia; = A kūfiyya), a peaked cap embroidered with gold, which the officials of the Janissaries and some Palace officials like the Baltad͟jis wore, also called ḳūḳa. Süleymān Pas͟ha is said to have invented it; it came into general use in the reign of Murād I and became a kind of ruler’s crown. X 615a

usra → CĀʾILA
usrub → RAṢĀṢ
usṭā → ADJĪR

ustādār (P) : in the Mamlūk sultanate, the title of one of the senior AMĪRs, who headed the *dīwān al-ustādāriyya*, which was responsible for managing expenditure on the sultan's household supplies. The ~ was in charge of the food tasters, *al-ḏjashankīriyya*, as well as for the court retinue and the servants in the sultan's palace. X 925a; (< *ustādh al-dār*). X 926a

ustādh (A, < Pah; pl. *ustādhūn, asātidha*), or *ustād* : an intelligent and hightly-esteemed person; a master, in the sense of professor, or maestro in music; a master craftsman; eunuch. I 33a; X 925b; as an honorific among the S̲h̲āfiʿīs, al-~ denoted Abū Isḥāḳ al-Isfarāyīnī. X 926a

♦ ustādhiyya : a neologism meaning professorate. X 926a

ustān (P), or *istān* : in administrative geography, province, with its subdivisions being S̲H̲AHR or KŪRA; state domains, administered by an *ustāndār*; in high ʿAbbāsid times, ~ acquired a special connotation regarding taxation, explained either as *iḥāza*, land taken over by the state, or MUḲĀSAMA, land from which taxation was taken as a fixed proportion of its produce. X 926a

♦ **ustāndār** (P) : an administrative term for the governor of a province or for the official in charge of state domains. X 927b

usṭukussāt (A, < Gk στοιχεῖα), or *ʿanāṣir* : in philosophy, the primary bodies. X 530a

usṭūl (A, < Gk στόλος; pl. *aṣāṭīl*) : in the Arab navy, the term for a fleet, and secondarily, an individual 'galley' or 'man-of-war'. X 928a; XII 120a

usṭūra (A, pl. *asāṭīr*) : legend, myth. III 369a

♦ **asāṭīr al-awwalīn** (A) : a Qurʾānic phrase meaning 'stories of the ancients', suggesting a set expression that had been long in use. Its meaning hardly in doubt, most of the discussion has concerned its derivation, for *asāṭīr* was a plural without singular. Nowadays the term has been reinstated in the singular form *usṭura*. III 369a; XII 90b

ustuwā : uplands. X 928b

uṣūl → AṢL

♦ uṣūlī (A) : a specialist in **uṣūl al-fiḳh**. X 930b

♦ **uṣūliyya** (A) : lit. those who go back to first principles; in law, the doctrine of going back to first principles, and more specifically, within the Twelver s̲h̲īʿī tradition, those of its adherents commonly identified as supporting application of the rationalist principles of jurisprudence. The term does not appear to have been used until the 6th/12th century. X 935a; and → AKHBĀRIYYA

In modern theologico-political parlance, ~ is used as the equivalent of 'fundamentalism', but in less formal Egyptian Arabic, Islamic fundamentalists are often called *islāmiyyīn, al-sunniyya*, or, in the singular, *ikhwāngī* or *rāgil sunnī*. X 937a

ʿuṭārid (A, P *tīr*) : in astronomy, the planet Mercury, also called *al-kātib* in Andalusian and Maghribī sources. X 940a

utenzi (Sw), or *utendi* : in Swahili literature, the verse epic. IV 886b

uthāl (A, > Lat *aludel*), or *athāl* : in chemistry, a pot used in the sublimation process for causing bodies to pass from the solid state to that of gaseous aggregation by means of steam pressure. X 946a

utrudj, utrudjdja (A) : in botany, the citron, thought to be found in the Qurʾān under the name of *mitk, matk*. II 1058b; IV 740b; one of the names for the Cedrate tree or Adam's apple (*Citrus medica Risso*). V 962a, where many variant names are found

ʿutūb (A, s. *ʿutbī*) : in its most strict sense, communities of Nadjdī origin, probably from tribal stocks, who in the 17th century moved to the Gulf coast and settled in Kuwayt and Bahrain.

uṭum (A, pl. *āṭām*) : in early Islam, a fort. V 436a
ʿuṭʿuṭ → SAK͟HLA
uwaysiyya (A) : in mysticism, a class of mystics who look for instruction from the spirit of a dead or physically absent person, derived from Uways al-Ḳaranī, who is supposed to have communicated with Muḥammad by telepathy. X 958a
üzengi ḳurčisi → RIKĀBDĀR, kept often either by one of the royal ladies or by a trusted official. II 806a; a small round seal for decrees relating to titles, high appointments, DJĀGIRS and the sanction of large sums. VII 473b
ʿuzla (A) : isolation, one of the components of asceticism, ZUHD. XI 560a
uzuk, or *ūzuk* : in Muslim India, a royal seal (a 'privy' seal), kept often either by one of the royal ladies or by a trusted official. II 806a; VII 473b; a simple seal with his name in *nastaʿlīḳ* characters, owned by Akbar. IV 1104b

V

vār : in Muslim Pand̲jābī literature, an historical ballad. VIII 256b
vāv : in Gud̲jarāt, an analogous structure to the BĀʾOLĪ 'step-well', with the entire well being covered at surface level. V 888b

W

wā-sōk͟ht (U, P) : in Perso-Urdu literary criticism, a theme intrinsic to Persian love poetry that came to be exploited for its own sake in the 10th/16th-century G͟HAZAL; in Urdu poetry of the 18th and 19th centuries, a stanzaic poem devoted to the theme of repudiating the beloved, which genre seems to have originated with Sawdā. Variously transcribed as WĀSŌK͟H and WĀ-SŪK͟HT. VIII 776a; IX 378a; XI 2a
wā-sūk͟ht → WĀ-SŌK͟HT
wabāʾ (A, P *wabā*) : in medicine, an epidemic, pestilence, and theoretically distinguished from *ṭāʿūn* in the more specific sense of 'plague' (a mediaeval Arabic expression found in medical treatises is 'every *ṭāʿūn* is a ~ but not every ~ is a *ṭāʿūn*') although with later Muslim writers it is doubtful whether the precise distinction existed. IX 477a; XI 2a; cholera. VIII 783a
wabāl (A) : in astrology, 'detriment'. X 942a
wabar (A) : camel's hair. IX 764b
♦ ahl al-wabar : 'the people of the camel skin', a designation for nomads, as opposed to *ahl al-madar*, i.e. the sedentaries. V 585a
waʾd (A) : infanticide, in pre-Islamic times generally of newborn daughters, who were buried alive (**waʾd al-banāt**), prohibited by Q 81:8. X 199a; X 6a
al-waʾd al-k͟hāfī : 'the hidden burying alive', i.e. coitus interruptus. XI 6b
waʿd (A) : in eschatology, part of the dogma of **al-waʿd wa ʾl-waʿīd**, promises and threats in the life beyond, one of the five fundamental principles dear to the Muʿtazilīs. With this slogan, the Muʿtazila expressed their conviction that not only the unbelievers had to face damnation on the Day of Judgement but that Muslims who had committed a grave sin without repentance also were threatened by eternal hellfire. III 465a; IX 341b; X 6b
wadʿ → WADAʿ
waḍʿ al-lug͟ha (A) : lit. the establishment of language; in linguistics and legal theory, a view of the nature of language, which is understood to be a code made up of patterned

vocal sounds or vocables and their meanings and this code was seen to have emerged out of a primordial establishment of the vocables *for* their meaning. V 805b; X 7a

waʿda (A) : a communal meal. IX 20b

wadaʿ (A, s. *wadaʿa*), or *wadʿ* : cowrie shells, *Cypraea moneta* or *Cypraea annulus*, used in India and widely in West Africa as money down to the early 20th century. They were also known in Egypt as *kawda*, or *kūda*, reflecting its Hindi and Sanskrit origin as *kauri* (> cowrie). XI 7b; ~ could also be called *kharaz*, and the term was used also for shells in general. XI 9b

wadaad (Somali) : in Somali society, a man of religion, who also mediates in disputes between lineages. This term is used in contrast to *waranle* 'warrior', the other class of Somali men. IX 723a

waḍaḥ → DJUDHĀM

waḍḍaʿ → ṢĀLIḤ

wadhārī : an expensive cloth of cotton woven on cotton made in the Transoxianan village of Wadhār, which was made into a light resistant type of yellow overcoat, very popular in winter. VIII 1030b; XII 176b

wādī (A, pl. *widyān, awdiya*) : a watercourse filled only at certain times of the year; stream channel. I 538a; VII 909b; XI 13b; in the Maghrib, all watercourses, including the great perennial rivers; it can equally designate, in very arid regions, low-lying areas where there is a total lack of any flow. XI 14a

waḍīʿ → ḌAʿĪF

wadīʿa (A, pl. *wadāʾiʿ*) : in law, the legal contract that regulates depositing an object with another person, whether real or supposed. The actual act of depositing is *īdāʿ*, ~ is in reality the noun for the object of the contract, and *mūdiʿ* is the person who deposits an object or property with the *mūdaʿ* 'depositary'. The ~ is a depositing process which produces no benefit or ownership for the depositary vis-à-vis the object. XI 21b

waḍīʿa (P, < A) : in taxation matters, a tax schedule (syn. *ṭisḳ*) drawn up to meet the variety of physical conditions placed on land for the payment of land tax. IV 1037b

wadjd (A) : in mysticism, a technical term meaning 'ecstasy, rapture', feelings which dissociated the mystic from his personal qualities. The highest state of ecstasy was called *wudjūd* 'existence'. XI 23a

wadjh (A, pl. *wudjūh*) : face; variant. I 155a; in music, the belly of the ʿŪD. X 769b; and → ʿIRḌ

wādjib (A) : in theology, a synonym of FARḌ 'a religious duty or obligation', the omission of which will be punished and the performance of which will be rewarded. The Ḥanafī school, however, makes a distinction between these two terms, applying *farḍ* to those religious duties which are explicitly mentioned as such in the Qurʾān and the SUNNA, or based on consensus, and ~ to those the obligatory character of which has been deduced by reasoning. II 790a

wafāt → MAWT

wafaya (A, pl. *wafayāt*) : obituary. XI 345b

wafd (A) : lit. delegation; the name of a nationalist political party in modern Egypt. XI 25b

wafḍa (A) : originally, a shepherd's leather bag; in archery, a quiver made from skin entirely, with no wood in its construction. IV 800a

wāfid (A) : 'one who comes, makes his way, in a delegation or group' (syn. *muwaffad*); used in the collective, **wāfidiyya**, for Mamlūk troops of varying ethnic origins who came to Egypt and Syria to join the Sultanate's military forces. XI 26b; XI 220a

wāfir (A) : in prosody, the name of the fourth Arabic metre. I 670a; XI 27b

wafķ (A, pl. *awfāķ*) : lit. harmonious arrangement; in sorcery, a square, in the field of which certain figures are so arranged that the addition of horizontal, vertical and diagonal lines gives in every case the same total (e.g. 15 or 34). II 370a; X 501b; XI 28a

wāg̲h̲il → ṬUFAYLĪ

wāḥa (A, pl. *wāḥāt*) : oasis. XI 31a

waḥam (A), also *waḥām, wiḥām* : pregnancy craving; little noted in the medical literature, in popular Islam, ~ was considered very important to attend to, cf. the verb *waḥḥama* 'to slaughter a camel in order to satisfy a woman's craving'. XI 32a

waḥda (A) : oneness; unit, unity, used as a technical term in philosophy and theology with these meanings, though not occurring in the Ḳurʾān. XI 37a

In grammar, the genitive construct *ism al-* ~ 'noun of unity' forms the counterpart to *ism al-d̲j̲ins* 'generic noun'. XI 36a

♦ **waḥdat al-s̲h̲uhūd** : 'the oneness of witnessing', a doctrine established by S̲h̲ayk̲h̲ Aḥmad Sirhindī. I 416a; III 102a; XI 37b; monotheism. I 297b

♦ **waḥdat al-wud̲j̲ūd** : 'the oneness of existence', a main line of mysticism which came to dominate from Ibn al-ʿArabī onwards. I 416b; III 102b; X 318a; XI 37a; pantheism. I 297b

waḥf (A) : a woman's exuberant hair. IX 313a

wahhābiyya (A) : in law, both the doctrine and the followers of Muḥammad b. ʿAbd al-Wahhāb. XI 39b

wāḥid (A), or *fard, mufrad* : in grammar, the singular. II 406b

wahm (A, pl. *awhām*) : lit. notion, supposition, in particular false notion, delusion; in philosophy, estimative faculty (also *al-ķuwwa al-wahmiyya*); imagination. I 112a; III 509b; XI 48b; XII 822b; 'whim'. VIII 953a

♦ **wahmiyyāt** : the science of *fantasmagorica*. VIII 105b

waḥs̲h̲ (A, pl. *wuḥūs̲h̲*) : wild, desolate, uninhabited; a collective noun meaning 'wild animals'. XI 52a

♦ **waḥs̲h̲ī** (A) : wild; the singulative of WAḤS̲H̲. ~ has two opposites: *ahlī* 'domesticated' and *insī* 'the side that points toward the human body'. A synonym is *ḥūs̲h̲ī* (< *wuḥūs̲h̲ī* ?), said to be a relative adjective derived from AL-ḤŪS̲H̲, a land of the d̲j̲inn, whence come the *ḥūs̲h̲ī* camels, jinn-owned stallions that allegedly sire offspring among herds belonging to men. XI 52a; the part of the point of the nib of a reed-pen to the right of the incision. IV 471b; XI 52b

In literary criticism, ~ and *ḥūs̲h̲ī* denote words that are uncouth and jarring to the ear due to their being archaic and/or Bedouinic. XI 52b; and → G̲H̲ARĪB

♦ **waḥs̲h̲iyya** : bestiality. II 551a

waḥy (A) : a Ḳurʾānic term primarily denoting revelation in the form of communication with speech. XI 53b; and → ILHĀM

waʿīd (A) : the K̲h̲ārid̲j̲ite and Muʿtazilī doctrine of unconditional punishment of the unrepentant sinner in the hereafter. VII 607a; IX 341b; and → WAʿD

waʿil (A) : in zoology, the ibex. V 1228b

wāʿiẓ (A, pl. *wuʿʿāẓ*) : a preacher, mostly a preacher who gives sermons conveying admonishments (*waʿẓ, mawʿiẓa*), the public performance of which is called *mad̲j̲lis al-waʿẓ* or *mad̲j̲lis al-d̲h̲ikr*. In the Ḳurʾān, the root *w-ʿ-ẓ* in most cases contains a warning; however, the root can also indicate 'good advice' and 'right guidance'. ~ can also mean WAṢIYYA, the spiritual testament that a father gives his son. XI 56a

waķʿa (A) : part of the expression *waķʿat al-ḥufra* 'day of the ditch', sometimes considered a literary topos, but referring to a trap in which the notables of Toledo fell and were all slain, in either 181/797-8 or 191/806-7. X 605a

♦ **waķʿa-nüwīs** (T) : 'events/event-writer', the post of the late Ottoman official historian who with his predecessors compiled a continuous, approved narrative of recent

Ottoman history as a formal historical record, dating from the early 18th century. The post was early on called *weḳāyiʿ-nüwīs* and it is known to have been held on an ad hoc basis by individual historians from the early 17th century, who recorded the events of a military campaign or an embassy. XI 57a

waḳaʿa (A), or *awḳaʿa* : in grammar, the nearest thing to 'transitive'. IX 528a

wakāla (A) : in law, power of attorney or deputyship. X 376b; XI 57b

In mediaeval Islam, a meeting-place in cities for commercial agents. IX 788b

♦ waḳālat al-ḳuṭn → PENBE ḲABBĀNÎ

♦ waḳāla muḳayyada : an authorisation that is limited by its modus operandi, its opposite being *waḳāla muṭlāḳa*. XI 58a

♦ waḳāla muwaḳḳata : an authorisation that is restricted by a time designated in the contract setting it up. XI 58a

waḳaṣ → WAḲṢ

waḳf (A, pl. *awḳāf*), or *ḥubus, ḥabs* : in law, the act of found a charitable trust and hence the trust itself. The Imāmī shīʿīs distinguish between ~ and *ḥabs*, the latter being a precarious type of ~ in which the founder reserves the right to dispose of the ~ property. I 661a; VIII 512b; XI 59a; XII 823a; and → ḲAṬʿ

♦ waḳf ʿāmm : an endowment designated for the Muslim community as a whole or groups of an undetermined number of people being in need of charity that are supposed to exist continually till the end of time. Its opposite is *waḳf khāṣṣ*, an endowment for a limited number of people who would eventually die out. XII 824a

♦ waḳf khāṣṣ → WAḲF ʿĀMM

♦ waḳf khayrī : charitable WAḲFS dedicated to pious causes, as opposed to family *waḳf*s, *waḳf ahlī*, made in favour of one's relatives and descendants. XI 60b

♦ waḳf al-nuḳūd : 'cash waḳf', cash holdings possessed by WAḲFS, whose foundation administrators lent out at interest, with the purpose of creating liquid assets for the endowment. XI 89a

♦ waḳf-i awlād : a family WAḲF, also known as *waḳf ahlī* (→ WAḲF KHAYRĪ). XI 92b

♦ waḳfiyya, or *rasm al-taḥbīs* : the document recording the WAḲF's founder's declaration. XI 61b

♦ awḳāf ahliyya : one of three divisions of the *waḳf* system among the Mamlūks, the ~ included the great foundations of sulatans and AMĪRS, supported by urban and agricultural estates, whose revenues served combined charitable and private purposes. The other two divisions were the *awḳāf ḥukmiyya*, which were supervised by the Shāfiʿī chief judge and included urban buildings in Cairo and Fusṭāṭ, and whose revenues served purely philanthropic functions such as the support of the Holy Cities; and the *rizaḳ* (s. *rizḳa*) *aḥbāsiyya*, a special kind of endowment based on the alienation of treasury land for the benefit of individuals rather than institutions. XI 65a

♦ awḳāf-i tafwīḍī (P) : WAḲF's constituted by the reigning shāh. XI 86a

wāḳiʿa-niwīs → MADJLIS-NIWĪS

wāḳif (A), or *muḥabbis* : the founder of a WAḲF. XI 60a

♦ al-wāḳifa, or *al-wāḳifiyya* : lit. the ones who stand still, or who stop, put an end to; the name of a shīʿī sect given to them by their Twelver opponents because they let the succession of IMĀMS end with the seventh *imām* Mūsā al-Kāẓim. XI 103a

♦ wāḳifiyya : in theology, term for the 'Abstentionists'. I 275a; and → WĀḲIFA

wakīl (A, pl. *wukalāʾ*; T *wekīl*) : agent; in the context of the pilgrimage, the ~ is especially used to designate an agent of the *muṭawwifūn* (→ MUṬAWWIF). His task is to meet pilgrims arriving in Djudda, help them choose a *muṭawwif*, be responsible for them in Djudda until they depart for Mecca and again when they return to Djudda. Like the *muṭawwifūn*, the *wukalāʾ* are organised in a special guild. VI 170b

In law, the representative of a party. I 319b; an agent or trustee. X 377a

In hydraulics, ~ is known in Oman and the United Arab Emirates to be the name for the official in charge of the upkeep of the *falaḏj*, a mining installation for extracting water from the depths of the earth. IV 532a

In the Ottoman empire, a synonym for *wezīr* (→ WAZĪR). XI 194b

♦ wakīl-i dār : under the Salḏjūḳs, the intendant, an influential official of the sultan's court entourage. VIII 954a

♦ wekīl-i kharḏj : under the Ottomans, the paymaster-general, an officer in each regiment who oversaw the distribution of funds held in trust for use by those in special need as well as the collection of contributions for each regiment's independent campaign provisions fund, ḲUMANYA. XI 325a

♦ wakīl-i nafs-i nafīs-i humāyūn : in Ṣafawid Persia, an office created by Shāh Ismāʿīl, whose functionary was to be the *alter ego* of the shāh, superior in rank both to the WAZĪR, the head of the bureaucracy, and the AMĪR AL-UMARĀʾ, the commander in chief of the ḲĬZĬLBĀSH forces. VIII 768b

wakīr (A) : a flock of more than two hundred sheep or goats. When several ~ are joined together with their dogs and carrier donkeys, the large entity ensuing, sometimes numbering several thousand head, is called a *firḳ* or *mughnam*. XII 319b

waḳḳād (A, Tun *sakhkhān*) : the 'stoker' of the furnace of a **ḥammām** 'steam bath'. III 140a

waḳs (A) : in prosody, a deviation in the metre because of the loss of both the second consonant of a foot and its vowel. I 672a; a case of ZIḤĀF where the second vowelled letter is elided. XI 508b

In law, ~ (or *waḳaṣ*, also *shanaḳ*) is the amount of property below the minimum quantity on which ZAKĀT is due, *niṣāb*, and between each subsequent *niṣāb*. XI 411b

waḳt (A) : time; and → ṢĀḤIB AL-WAḲT

wāḳwāḳ (A) : a name, possibly onomatopoeic, of uncertain origin, found in mediaeval literature to mean variously an island or group of islands inhabited by a dark-skinned population who speak a distinct language; a people or race; and a tree producing human fruit. XI 103b

In zoology, a member of the Cuculides family of birds (Eng. cuckoo). Local names include *ḥamām ḳawwāl, ṭāṭawī, ṭakūk, ḳawḳal, kukur, kukum, kunkur* and *hūhū*. XI 108a

waʿl (A) : in zoology, the ibex, on the Arabian peninsula also called *badan*. I 541b; IX 98b

walāʾ (A) : proximity.

In law, contractual clientage (syn. *muwālāt*), a solution in early Islam to the problem of affiliating non-tribesman to a tribal society; though most such tribesmen were clearly converts, conversion was not necessary for the legal validity of the tie. The persons linked to one another by ~ were known as MAWLĀ. In pre-Islamic poetry, ~ usually denoted an egalitarian relationship of mutual help, but in later literature, it more commonly designates an unequal relationship of assistance, *mawlā* being a master, manumitter, benefactor or patron on the one hand, and a freedman, protégé or client on the other. I 30b; III 388b; VI 874b ff.

♦ walāʾ al-muwālāt : in Ḥanafī law, an institution between free men. I 30b

walad → AWLĀD

walāya (A) : in theology, a term often taken as the equivalent or simply an alternative vocalisation of WILĀYA, but which has in shīʿī usage the specific meaning of 'devotion', denoting the loyalty and support that is due the IMĀM from his followers. In shīʿism, ~ is one of the pillars of Islam. XI 209a

wālī (A, pl. *wulāt*) : person in authority, governor, prefect, administrator manager. A near-synonym is *ḥākim* 'one who exercises power, jurisdiction, etc.'. Under the Ottomans, the ~ , also termed PASHA, was the governor of a province. XI 109b; local ruler. IX 6b; and → AṢḤĀB AL-ARBĀʿ

♦ wāli 'l-ḥarb (A) : the name for the governor of a province, who was still essentially the general of an army of occupation, in the first generations following the Arab conquest. III 184a

walī (A, pl. *awliyā'*) : in mysticism, a saint, friend of God, often a mystic in general. I 137b; VIII 742b; XI 109b; and → MURĀBIṬ; WILĀYA

In law, a guardian for matrimonial purposes. I 27b; VIII 27a; curator of the *maḥdjūr* 'a person who is restricted of the capacity to dispose'. III 50a

♦ **walī al-ʿahd** (A) : the title granted to the heir presumptive, in the sense of beneficiary of a contract (ʿAHD) concluded between him and his community. An heir to the caliphate was more formally entitled *walī ʿahd al-muslimīn.* IV 938b; XI 125b

♦ walī 'l-dam (A) : in law, the next of kin who has the right to demand retaliation. IV 689b; V 178b; IX 547b

♦ walī ḥaḳḳ Allāh (A) : in al-Tirmidhī's thought, one of two classes of friends of God, with *walī Allāh.* The first comes near to God on the mystical path by observing the obligations of the divine legal order with all his inner power, while the second reaches his aim through divine grace. XI 110a

♦ walī mudjbir (A) : '*walī* with power of coercion', the father or grandfather who has the right to marry his daughter or granddaughter against her will, so long as she is a virgin. VIII 27b

♦ walī 'l-sadjdjāda → SHAYKH AL-SADJDJĀDA

♦ wali sanga (Ind) : lit. nine saints; the legendary founders of Islam in Java. XI 120b; XI 536b

wālide sulṭān (A, T) : in the Ottoman empire, mother of the reigning sultan, used only for the duration of the son's reign. IX 709a; XI 130a

walīma (A) : a wedding dinner-party. III 210a; X 900b

wangala : in Mauritania, the custom of slaughtering and sharing, each day, a sheep within a given group. VI 313a

wansharīs (B) : 'nothing higher', a reference by local people to a mountain massif in Central Algeria. XI 138b

waraʿ (A) : in mysticism, the 'spirit of scruple', advocated in so-called 'sober' ṣūfism. IX 812b; XI 141a; for Dhu 'l-Nūn al-Miṣrī, 'total abstinence'. XI 141a

waraḳ (A) : one of the terms for parchment, later to be reserved for paper. VIII 407b; with *waraḳa*, the leaf of a tree or of a manuscript. VIII 835a; and → DJILD; RAḲḲ; WARRĀḲ

In contemporary Arabic usage, 'money'. XI 148a; and → DIRHAM WARAḲ

♦ waraḳ al-bardī → BARDĪ

warashān (A) : in zoology, a type of bird. XI 152a

ward (A, s. *warda*; P *djull* or GUL) : in botany, *Rosa sp., Rosaceae*, any flower but generally the rose. According to Maimonides, it was known to physicians as *djull*, but the Arabs used this only for the white rose; *nisrīn* was the wild rose or Chinese rose. According to Ibn al-Bayṭār, the red variety is called *ḥawdjam* and the white *watīr*. XI 144b; XII 550a; and → MĀ' AL-WARD

For ~ in literature, XII 828a

♦ wardī (A) : the pale rose-pink colour of the ruby. XI 262b

wardjiyya (A), and *wariyya, huwayriyya* : in Kuwayt, the local open boat made from palm fibres. VII 53b

wariḳ (A) : in numismatics, silver money, distinguished from gold money, *ʿayn*, and refined silver in bars or ingots, *nuḳra*. The meanings of *nuḳra* and *wariḳ* changed as a result of Ṣalāḥ al-Dīn's introduction of pure silver coins, which he called *nuḳra* dirhams while the term ~ was reserved for the debased coins. In 815/1412-13, the last *nuḳra* dirhams were demonetised and ~ resumed its significance of silver coinage in general. XI 147b

wāris̲h̲ → ṬUFAYLĪ
wārit̲h̲ → MĪRĀT̲H̲
wariyya → WARD̲J̲IYYA
warrāḳ (A) : lit. producer or seller of leaves, WARAḲ; in mediaeval Islam, the copyist of manuscripts, paper seller, and also bookseller. The earliest known person with this designation seems to be a man of Wāsiṭ who died in 195/811. XI 150a
wars (A) : a yellow dye from a perennial plant cultivated in Yemen, identified as *curcuma*. V 786a; or as *Memecylon tinctorium, Melastomaceae*, or sometimes *Flemmingia rhodocarpus* BAK, *Leguminosae*. Al-Dīnawarī describes the best ~ as *bādira*, from a young plant, the other sort being called *ḥabas̲h̲ī* because of some blackness in it. Dyestuffs are not always so easily identified and it may have been at times confused with *Carthamus tinctorius, Compositae*, the safflower. XI 152a; the sap of the Ceylon cornel tree. VII 1014b
wasaḳ (A, pl. *awsuḳ*) : a measure of volume, reportedly equivalent to 300 ṢĀʿ according to the *ṣāʿ* of the Prophet, or in weight, 609.84 kg. XI 412b
wasaṭ (A, pl. *awsāṭ*) : in astronomy, the mean motion. XI 503b
♦ wasaṭ al-s̲h̲ams (A) : in astronomy, the mean solar longitude. IX 292b
wasāṭa (A) : in Fāṭimid administration, a function which involved interposing and interceding between the Imām and the ethnic factions of the palace and the army, filling a gap, along with the office of the SIFĀRA, in the vizierate created by al-Ḥākim in 409/1018. The vizierate was later re-established during the reign of his son al-Ẓāhir, but the offices of the ~ and *sifāra* continued to be filled irregularly till the end of the dynasty by persons with a lower rank than the vizier. XI 189a
wasé kuala : in Aceh in Indonesia, a tax demanded by the *shahbandar* 'harbour master' for disembarking or loading certain goods, for preserving the water supply for departing ships, and for help for those stranded. XII 200b
waṣf (A) : lit. description; in poetry, a literary genre of flattering or embellished description. XI 153a
In law, form, external aspects, or incident, each of which is opposed to substance, *aṣl*. XI 158b
For ~ in grammar, → NAʿT
was̲h̲aḳ (A), or *kiṭṭ-namir* : in zoology, the Serval or Tiger-Cat (*Leptailurus serval*). II 739b; lynx. II 817a
was̲h̲īd̲j̲ (A) : in botany, a tree (ash ?) mentioned as providing wood for spear shafts. XII 735b
wās̲h̲ima → WAS̲H̲M
was̲h̲m (A) : tattooing; a woman who tattoos other is *wās̲h̲ima* and a woman who asks to be tattooed is *mustaws̲h̲ima*, both of whom are said to have been cursed by the Prophet. XI 160a; XII 830b
waṣī (A, pl. *awṣiyāʾ, waṣiyyūn*) : in law, the executor of a will. I 28b; XI 63a
In s̲h̲īʿī theology, variously rendered as legatee, executor, successor or inheritor, first used to designate ʿAlī as the inheritor of Muḥammad's worldly possessions and of his political and spiritual authority. Early Ismāʿīlī doctrine held that each of the first six speaking prophets (→ NĀṬIḲ) was succeeded by a legatee; while the *nāṭiḳ* brought the scripture in its generally accepted meaning, the ~ introduced a systematic interpretation of its inner, esoteric aspects. One who falsely claims to be a ~ is a *mutawaṣṣī*. XI 161a; and → K̲H̲ĀTAM AL-WAṢIYYĪN
♦ **waṣiyya** (A, pl. *waṣāyā*) : lit. inheritance; in s̲h̲īʿī theology, the utterance by which a WAṢĪ is appointed and, more generally, an instruction of a legal or moral nature. XI 161b

In law, bequest or legacy (defined as the transfer of the corpus or the usufruct of a thing after one's death without a consideration), and last will and testament. I 137b; IX 115b; IX 781b; XI 171b

In the science of diplomatic, that part of the text of a (state) document in which the duties of the nominee are specified in detail. II 302a

waṣīf (A) : in the terminology of childhood, '[a boy] who has become of full stature and fit for service' (Lane). VIII 822a; a male slave; negro. I 24b

wāṣil (A) : lit. reaching; in grammar, used by Ibn al-Sarrādj to refer to a level of interaction between the action denoted by the verb, the doer, and the semantic object covering the semantic side of verb intransitivity which the term TAʿADDĪ does not. X 4a

wāsima → NĪL

wāsiṭa (A) : mediator. IX 779b; under the Fāṭimids, a minister who was given neither the title nor the office of vizier but only the duty of acting as intermediary between the caliph and his officials and subjects. II 857b; XI 171a; and → TARDJĪʿ

waṣiyya → WAṢĪ

wasḳ (A) : a measure of capacity which was used in the Ḥidjāz in the days of Muḥammad, equal to 60 MUDDs. The ~ did not spread to other countries. VI 118a

waṣl (A), or *ṣila* : in prosody, a letter of prolongation following the *rawī* 'rhyme letter'. It can also consist of a vowelless *hāʾ* followed by a short vowel or a *hāʾ* followed by a letter of prolongation and preceded by a short vowel. IV 412a

In grammar, broadly denotes juncture, i.e. a syntactic or phonological 'connecting'; thus the antonym of both interruption (ḲAṬʿ) and pause (*waḳf*, → ḲAṬʿ). XI 172b; and → ṢILA

waṣla (A) : Egyptian musical composition, which combined elements of the earlier local NAWBA and the Turkish FAṢĪL. X 143b

wasm (A, pl. *wusūm*) : brand, as in camel brands by which Bedouin identify their camels. Brands are sometimes placed on things other than animals, e.g. tombs, rocks, wells or trees, to indicate whose territory they are or are protected by. XI 173b

♦ wasma → NĪL

♦ wasma-djūsh : in mediaeval times, a word used in Khurāsān to designate a special object for grinding KUḤL 'eye cosmetic' and pouring it into narrow-necked vessels. V 357a

wāsōkh → WĀ-SŌKHT

wasūṭ (A) : among the pre-Islamic Bedouin, a tent made of hair, generally said to be smaller than the MIẒALLA, but larger than the BAYT or the KHIBĀʾ, but sometimes described as the smallest tent. IV 1147a

waswās (A) : satanic whispering in the heart, inciting evil. III 1119b

waṭʾ → BĀH

watad → AWTĀD; ḲUṬB

waṭan (A) : homeland, fatherland, syn. *mawṭin*. I 64a; IV 785b; XI 174b; in early usage, the locality from which a person came. IV 785b; XI 174b

In mediaeval mysticism, used in the sense of 'the heavenly kingdom'. IV 785b

♦ waṭaniyya (A) : nationalism, patriotism, civic pride, in all the modern applications of these terms. XI 175a

watar → AWTĀR

wathaniyya (A) : idolatry, a later term. In classical Arabic, idolatry is given by the phrase *ʿibādat al-aṣnām* (or *al-awthān*).

wathīḳa (A, pl. *wathāʾiḳ*) : a document that certifies the commission of a promise or legal act; a general term for an official or legal document or formulary. In modern Arabic the plural is often used in the sense of 'official records, archives', housed in a *dār al-wathāʾiḳ*. IX 733a; XI 178b

watid → AWTĀD
watīr → WARD
waṭwāṭ (A, pl. *waṭāwīṭ, waṭāyīṭ*) : in zoology, all cheiropters or bats, without distinction of families or species, syn. *khuffāsh* (pl. *khafāfīsh*). The bat is also called *ṭā'ir al-layl, khushshāf* and *khuṭṭāf* by comparison with the swallow, *saḥāt, ṭurmūḳ, ṭumrūḳ*, and *ʿashraf*. XI 183a
wāw (A) : the twenty-seventh letter of the Arabic alphabet, with the numerical value 6. It stands either for the semivowel *w* or for the long vowel *ū*. XI 183a
wāwī (A) : in zoology, the jackal. I 541b
wayang (Ind) : a shadow play performance. XII 759b
waydj → SILB
waʿẓ → WĀʿIẒ
wazagh (A) : a kind of lizard, the killing of which, preferably with one blow, is prescribed by SUNNA. IV 768a
waẓīfa (A, pl. *waẓā'if*) : lit. task, charge, impose obligation; an administrative fiscal term meaning an extra, fixed payment, made by the tax collector, on top of the land tax collected; it subsequently also came to mean the financial allowance or stipend paid to an official or as a reward for someone who had pleased a ruler or governor, and by extension, the official post or function itself. XI 184b; and → MUWAẒẒAF; ʿULŪFE
In mysticism, a devotional text or litany, normally consisting of a sequence of prayer formulas, invocations, and verses from the Qur'ān, recited by the members of some ṣūfī orders as one of the elements of their assignment of daily devotions, and also as part of the liturgy of a ḤAḌRA or communal DHIKR ritual. XI 184b
wazīr (A, T *wezīr*) : vizier or chief minister; head of the bureaucracy. From its original Qur'ānic meaning as 'helper' it acquired the sense of 'representative' or 'deputy', and under the ʿAbbāsids came to designate the highest-ranking civil functionary of the state next to the caliph. VIII 768b; XI 185a
♦ **al-wazīr al-ṣaghīr** (A) : head chamberlain, a term of Fāṭimid administrative usage, also called *ṣāḥib al-bāb*, who was equal in status to the commander-in-chief of the army. XI 197b
♦ wazīr al-tafwīḍ (A) : 'vizier with delegated powers'; a term employed by al-Māwardī for the minister who was entrusted with full powers. II 857b; XI 186b
♦ wazīr al-tanfīdh (A) : a designation by al-Māwardī for the ministers who, notwithstanding their power and influence over the caliphs, were considered as agents for the execution of the sovereign's will. II 857b; XI 187a
♦ wazīr-i čap (P) : a title sometimes given to the official historiographer during the Ṣafawid rule. XI 194a
♦ wezīr-i aʿẓam → ṢADR-I AʿẒAM
wazn (A, pl. AWZĀN) : lit. the act of weighing; in eschatology, the 'weighing' of deeds on the Last Day, with good deeds being heavy and bad deeds light. III 465a
In numismatics, the weight at which the gold and silver coinage was struck. XI 198b
In language and literature, the establishing of a pattern in morphology or in prosody, which resulted in a word form or metre. A morphological ~ is also called BINĀ' (pl. *abniya*) and prosodical weighing or scanning is also *taḳṭīʿ* or *tafʿīl*. XI 200a
wēsh (Pash) : in Afghanistan, the ancient custom of periodical redistribution of land. I 217a
wezīr → WAZĪR
widjā' (A) : in medicine, a form of castration consisting of binding the cord supporting the testicles and making them gush out. IV 1088a
wilāya (A) : in law, representation, the power of an individual to personally initiate an action. When a person acts on behalf of others, ~ is more often termed *niyāba*. XI

208a; the power of a WALĪ to represent his ward. III 50b; guardianship over a child, involving guardianship over property (*wilāyat al-māl*) and over the person (*wilāyat al-nafs*). To these should be added the father's duty to marry his child off when the latter comes of age (*wilāyat al-tazwīdj*). VIII 824a

In s͟hīʿism, the position of ʿAlī b. Abī Ṭālib as the single, explicitly designated heir and successor to Muḥammad; the guardianship of ʿAlī of the community, as expressed in the doctrinal creed pronounced by s͟hīʿīs: *lā ilāh illā Allāh, Muḥammad rasūl Allāh, ʿAlī walī Allāh.* XI 208b

In mysticism, sainthood. VIII 742a

Among the K͟hāridjites, the dogmatic duty of solidarity and assistance to the Muslim. I 1027b

♦ wilāyat al-faḳīh (A) : 'the guardianship of the jurist', in modern Iran the mandate of the jurist to rule, promulgated by K͟humaynī. XII 530a; the position of the supreme leader in modern Iran. XI 209b

♦ wilāyat al-māl → WILĀYA

♦ wilāyat al-nafs → WILĀYA

♦ wilāyat al-tazwīdj → WILĀYA

wilāyet → EYĀLET

wird (A, pl. *awrād*) : in mysticism, set, supererogatory personal devotions observed at specific times, usually at least once during the day and once again at night; a distinctive aspect of ~ when compared to ḤIZB and D͟HIKR is its close association with a particular spiritual guide to whom it is attributed as well as the set times for its observance. XI 209b; and → ḤIZB

wisāda (A) : in mediaeval times, a large cushion often used for supporting the back (syn. *mirfaḳa, tukʾa, miswara, numruḳ,* MIK͟HADDA); a pillow. V 1158b; XII 99a

wiṣāl (A), less frequently *muwāṣala* : in mysticism, 'maintaining an amorous relationship, chaste or otherwise' (syn. *waṣl*; ant. *hadjr* or *hidjrān*). XI 210b; and → ITTIṢĀL

wisām (A) : in Morocco, a term applied to each of the nine orders, decorations, that were regulated in a document (*ẓahīr*) of 14 December 1966. VIII 61b; in modern Arabic usage, a decoration, order, medal or badge of honour. When European-type orders were first imitated in 19th-century Persia and the Ottoman empire, the term used was NIS͟HĀN. XI 212a

wis͟hāḥ (A) : according to Lane, an ornament worn by women (consisting of) two series of pearls and jewels strung or put together in regular order, which two series are disposed contrariwise, one of them being turned over the other. VII 809b

witr → ṢALĀT AL-WITR

woynuḳ (T, < Sl) : in Ottoman military and administrative usage, a particular category of troops amongst other Balkan Christian landholding or tax-exempt groups employed by the sultans to perform specific combat and other militarily-related tasks. XI 214b

woywoda (Ott, < Sl) : in mediaeval Serbia, a high-ranking commander and, on the eve of the Ottoman conquest, the governor of a military district. In early Ottoman sources, the term refers to former Christian lords, and soon it began to designate agents in charge of revenues from domains which enjoyed full immunity. XI 215a

wudjāḳ → ODJAḲ

wudjūd (A) : in philosophy, being. XI 216a; and → MUṬLAḲ

In mysticism, a verbal noun derived from *wadjada* 'to find' or 'to experience'. XI 217a; and → WADJD

wuḍūʾ (A) : lit. cleansing; the simple ablution, which is sufficient for cleansing after a minor ritual impurity, ḤADAT͟H. III 19b; VIII 764b; VIII 929a; XI 218a

wuḍūḥ → G͟HUMŪḌ

wufūd (A, s. **wafd**) : delegations; in the time of the Prophet, the mainly tribal deputations which came to him in Medina, mainly during the ninth year of the Islamic era. XI 219a

wuḳā (A), and *wuḳāya, awḳā* : a variety of women's bonnets, usually decorated with coins, worn in Syria and Palestine. V 742a

wuḳūʿ-gūʾī (P), or *zabān-i wuḳūʿ* : in Persian poetry, a new style, developed in the 16th century, of introducing in the GHAZAL references to actual experiences of love and incidents occurring in the relationship of lovers and their beloved. The ~ in turn generated a number of subsidiary genres. VIII 776a

wuḳūf (A) : lit. place of standing, station; in the context of the pilgrimage, the ~ is the culminating ceremony, on 9 Dhu 'l-Ḥidjdja, in the plain of ʿArafat in front of the *Djabal al-raḥma*, a small rocky eminence. The ceremony begins at noon with the joint recital of the prayers of ẒUHR and of ʿAṢR brought forward, and lasts until sunset. A second ~, in the morning of 10 Dhu 'l-Ḥidjdja, is not obligatory. III 35b; XI 220b

wushmgīr (P) : 'quail-catcher', according to al-Masʿūdī. XI 221a

wushshaḳ (A) : ammoniac, a gum resin, the product of the ammoniac gum tree. VIII 1042b

wuṣla (A) : in grammar, one of a group of terms for referential and copulative elements mostly called *ʿāʾid* but also *rābiṭ(a)* and *rādjiʿ*. XI 173a

wusṭā Zalzal (A) : in music, the middle, or neutral, third among the frets of the lute, named after the famous lute-player at the early ʿAbbāsid court. Al-Fārābī first described it and placed it at the ratio of 27:22 between the nut and the bridge of the lute, which corresponds to the modern note *sīkāh*. XI 427b

X

xagaa → GUʾ

xeer (Somali) : Somali customary law, which exists alongside the SHARĪʿA. IX 713b; IX 723b

Y

yāʾ (A) : the twenty-eighth letter of the Arabic alphabet, with the numerical value 10. It stands for the semivowel *y* and for the long vowel *ī*. XI 222a

yābānī (A) : in modern Arabic, a person of Japanese descent. XI 223a

yabghu (T) : an ancient Turkish title, found in the Orkhon inscriptions to denote an office or rank in the administrative hierarchy below the Ḳaghan, thus analogous to the title *shadh*, whom the ~ preceded in the early Turk empire. XI 224a

yabrūḥ (A) : in botany, the Mandragora or mandrake (*Mandragora officinarum, Solanaceae*, also called *Atropa mandragora L.* and *M. officinarum*), a perennial herbaceous plant common in the Mediterranean region. Its root is often forked and is the part known as ~ , while the plant itself is generally called *luffāḥ*. Other names for the ~ are *sābīzak*, *shābīzadj*, and *tuffāḥ al-djinn* (by which it is still known today). XI 225a; and → SIRĀDJ AL-ḲUṬRUB

yad (A) : lit. hand, ~ covers a vast semantic range: power, help, strength, sufficiency, ability to act, etc. XI 280a; the very large bead on a rosary that serves as a kind of handle. IX 741b; and → ʿAMAL; ḤISĀB; MILK; MUSALSAL AL-YAD; ṢĀḤIB AL-YAD

yada ta<u>sh</u> (T) : lit. rain stone, appearing in Arabic texts as *ḥad<u>j</u>ar al-maṭar*, a magical stone by means of which rain, snow, fog, etc., could be conjured up by its holder(s). Knowledge and use of such stones has been widespread until very recent times in Inner Asia. Originally identified as nephrite, it seems more likely that the original ~ was the bezoar (P *pād-zahr*), which is a calculus or concretion formed in the alimentary tract of certain animals, mainly ruminants. XI 226b

yādgār (P) : lit. souvenir, keepsake; in numismatics, any special issue of coins struck for a variety of non-currency purposes. XI 228a

yaʿḍid → ʿALA<u>TH</u>

yāfiʿ (A) : in the terminology of childhood, 'a boy grown up . . . grown tall' (Lane). VIII 822a

yafta → ḤIRZ

ya<u>gh</u>mā (P) : plunder. XI 238a

yaḥmūr → BAḲAR

yahūd (A, < Ar, s. *yahūdī*) : the common collective singular for 'Jews'. A less common plural *hūd* is also used. XI 239b

ya<u>kh</u>čāl (P) : in architecture, a mud-brick structure built in Iran to make and store ice. XII 457a

ya<u>kh</u><u>sh</u>a (Pah) : a pearl. IX 659a

yaḳīn (A) : in law, a certainty. XI 219a

yaḳḳā<u>sh</u> → AYḲA<u>SH</u>

yaktār → TĀR

yaḳṭīn (A) : a plant mentioned in the Qurʾān, probably a kind of *Cucurbitacea*. VI 651a; VI 901a; VII 831a

yaʿḳūbī (A, pl. **yaʿḳūbiyyūn**, *yaʿāḳiba, yaʿḳūbiyya*) : a Jacobite Christian, the designation for a member of the Syrian Orthodox Church, whose dogmatical position of monophysitism was thought to be at variance with the moderate dyophysite christology formulated by the Fourth Ecumenical Council of Chalcedon and consequently was branded as heresy. XI 258b

yāḳūt (A, < Gk) : in mineralogy, corundum, a crystallised form of alumina [$A1_2O_3$] which occurs in many colours, among which ~ *aḥmar* 'red corundum' or 'ruby' is the finest. According to al-Tīfā<u>sh</u>ī, the second best is the ~ *aṣfar* 'yellow sapphire' or 'oriental topaz'. XI 262a

♦ yāḳūt akhab (A), or *azraḳ* : the blue sapphire, the third-ranked corundum, below the ruby and yellow sapphire. Gradations in its colour ranges from ink blue, *kuḥlī*, to the lighter sky-blue, *samāwī* or *asmān<u>dj</u>ūnī*. XI 262b

♦ yāḳūt abyaḍ (A) : the leuco-sapphire, the fourth and last-ranked corundum, after the ruby, yellow sapphire, and blue sapphire. It has two shades, the more prized of which is the *mahawī* or *billawrī* (rock crystal-like). XI 262b

yali̊ (T, < Gk) : lit. bank, shore; in Ottoman times, a residence, villa built on the edge of the water. V 642a; XI 266b

yaltuma (T) : a musical instrument of the pandore type, but smaller with three strings and a waisted sound-chest like the TĀR. It was invented by <u>Sh</u>amsī Čelebi, the son of the Turkish poet Ḥamdī Čelebi. X 626a

yām (A, P; < Mon *ḳam*) : the effective network of communications established by the Mongols to control the vast extent of their empire. It was designed to facilitate the travels of envoys going to and from the Mongol courts; for the transportation of goods; for the speedy transmission of royal orders; and to provide a framework whereby the Mongol rulers could receive intelligence. VII 234a; in the 13th century, ~ also signifies the postal service of the Mongol <u>Kh</u>āns and sometimes a postal relay. XI 267b

♦ yāmči (Mon) : postal courier; also a functionary charged with the postal relay. XI 268a

yamaḳ (T) : 'adjunct'; in the Ottoman army, an assistant to an auxiliary soldier, ESHKINDJI. II 714b; IX 543a; in Serbia, a self-appointed local Janissary leader outside the regular Ottoman hierarchy. IX 671a

yamāma (A) : in zoology, wild pigeon, as opposed to the domesticated pigeon, ḤAMĀM. XI 269a

yamīn (A, pl. *aymān, aymun*) : lit. the right hand, but often used in Arabic with the transferred sense of 'oath'. IV 687b; XI 280a; and → ḲASAM

♦ yamīn al-ghamūs (A) : in law, an oath to perform a deed that one knows to have been already performed. Expiation is not required, except in the Shāfiʿī school. IV 688b

♦ yamīn al-munkir (A) : in law, an oath taken by a debtor who refuses to recognise his debt or his obligation, used by a petitioner as a method of proof. In former times many Muslims preferred to avoid pronouncing the oath, even though they did not admit to being debtors. III 1236b

♦ yamīnu ṣabr^{in} (A) : an oath imposed by the public authorities and therefore taken unwillingly. VIII 685b

♦ laghw al-yamīn (A) : in law, an oath taken by mistake (through a slip of the tongue) or in a thoughtless manner, which does not require expiation. IV 688b

yamkhūr (A, pl. *yamākhīr*) : in zoology, the drone bee. VII 907a

yanbūʿ (A) : well. XI 281a

yār (T) : eroded, vertical bank or gorge of a river, cliff. XI 287b

yarāʿ (A) : in music, a flute, blown into from a hole as distinct from the MIZMĀR, a reed pipe. VI 214b; VII 206b

yarbūʿ (A, < Ar) : in zoology, the jerboa. jumping mouse or jumping hare (*Jaculus*) of the class of rodents and family of dipodids (*Dipus*). Arabic authorities mention three kinds of jerboa: *al-shufārī* 'big and elongated'; *al-tadmurī* 'that of Palmyra'; and *dhu 'l-rumayḥ* 'bearing a short lance'. XI 283a; also the gerbil and jird. XII 287b, where many technical terms relating to these animals can be found

yarghu (T) : trial, interrogation, the Mongolian tribunal or court of justice, hence *yarghuči*, a judge. According to al-Djuwaynī, the ~ held at the court of the Great Khān was called the Great ~. XI 284b

♦ yarghuči → YARGHU

yarıcılık (T) : a land-leasing system in Turkey, in which the peasant uses his own tools, plough and livestock and gives half of the harvest to the landowner. V 473a

yarlïgh (T), or *yarlïḳ* : under the Mongols and their successor states, a decree, edict, command, contextually equivalent in Islamic chancery practice to the more specific documentary forms of FARMĀN, ḤUKM or BERĀT. IX 43a; XI 288b

yāsā (Mon) : law, decree, order; in the phrase 'the Great ~ of Čingiz Khān', a comprehensive legal code laid down by the founder of the Mongol empire. XI 293a

yasaḳ : a tribute. X 417b

♦ yasaḳ-ḳulu (T) : under the Ottomans, a special agent who was authorised to inspect any person for bullion or old AḲČE; Ottoman law required that all bullion produced in the country or imported from abroad be brought directly to the mints to be coined, and upon the issue of a new *aḳče*, those possessing the old were to bring it to the mint. II 118b

♦ yasaḳčï (T) : under the Ottomans, Janissaries whose function it was to protect foreign embassies and consulates and to escort diplomats leaving their residences, whether officially or unofficially. IV 808b

♦ yasaḳnāme → ḲĀNŪNNĀME

yāsamīn (A), *yāsimīn, yāsamūn* : in botany, the jasmine shrub. Several sub-species are found in the Arabic-speaking lands: *Jasminum floribundum*, called *habb al-zalīm* 'male ostrich seeds'; *Jasminum fructicans*, called *yāsamīn al-barr* 'country jasmine'; *Jasminum grasissimum*, called *ḳayyān* 'flourishing, blooming' and *suwayd* 'blackish', proper to Yemen; *Jasminum officinale*, called *ḳīn, sidjillāṭ*; and *Jasminum sambac*, called *full*. XI 294a

yasar (A, pl. *aysār*) : a player of MAYSIR; those who presided over the division of the parts were called *al-yāsirūn*. VI 924a

yashm (P) : in mineralogy, jade, known to Eastern Turkic peoples as *kash* and to the Mongols as *khas*. XI 296b

yāsidj (T ?) : an arrow with a flat-edged head, recommended for hunting the wild boar. V 9a

yaʿsūb → NAḤL

yatīm (A, *yatāmā*) : a child, below the age of puberty, who has lost his father (after puberty ~ is not used). In the animal world, ~ denotes a young one that has lost its mother. A child who has lost its mother is called *munḳaṭiʿ*, and a child who has lost both its parents is called *laṭīm*. XI 299a; XII 531b

yatīma (A) : known as *al-yatīma*, a large white gem, weighing seven dirhams, one of the many gems in the turban worn by the Fāṭimid caliph of Egypt. X 57b

yati̊r → ERMISH

yattūʿ (A) : in botany, wolfs' milk, of the class of Euphorbia, a gum resin. VIII 1042b; IX 872b

yawa (T), or *ḳačḳun* : one of the occasional (BĀD-I HAWĀ) taxes paid in the Ottoman empire while recovering runaway cattle or slaves. II 147a

yawm (A, pl. *ayyām*) : day, the whole 24-hour cycle making up a day, with NAHĀR meaning 'the daylight period', i.e. from sunrise to sunset. In a specialised sense, ~ means 'day of battle' (→ AYYĀM AL-ʿARAB). The plural *ayyām* occurs, especially in early Arabic poetry, in a similar sense to its apparent antonym *layālī* 'nights', referring to the passage of time, or 'destiny, fate'. XI 300b

♦ yawm al-aḍāḥī (A) : lit. day of the morning sacrifices; a name for 10 Dhu 'l-Ḥidjdja which can be traced back to the pre-Islamic pilgrimage. III 32b

♦ yawm al-ʿarūba → YAWM AL-DJUMʿA

♦ yawm al-dīn → ḲIYĀMA

♦ yawm al-**djumʿa** (A) : Friday, which in modern times most Muslim states have made an official day of rest. The term is clearly pre-Islamic, when it was known as *yawm al-ʿarūba* or *yawm ʿarūba*, and designated the market day which was held in al-Madīna on Friday. It is the weekly day of communal worship in Islam, when the *ṣalāt al-djumʿa* 'Friday prayer', is performed at the time of the midday prayer, which it replaces. II 592b; VIII 930a

♦ yawm al-ḥisāb (A) : a Qurʾānic expression for the Day of Judgement, synonymous with *yawm al-dīn*. III 465a

♦ yawm al-ḳiyāma → ḲIYĀMA

♦ yawm al-naḥr (A) : 'the day of sacrifice'; the 10th of the month of Dhu 'l-Ḥidjdja. III 36a

♦ yawm al-tarwiya → TARWIYA

♦ **ayyām al-ʿadjūz** (A) : lit. the days of the old woman; an old expression used in the Islamic countries bordering on or near to the Mediterranean to denote certain days of recurrent bad weather usually towards the end of winter. The duration of this period varies from one to ten days; more frequently it lasts one, five or seven days. This yearly cycle varies from country to country, involving the last four (or three) days of February and the first three (or four) days of March of the Julian calendar. I 792b

♦ **ayyām al-ʿarab** (A) : lit. days of the Arabs; a name given in Arabian legend to the combats which the Arabian tribes fought among themselves in the pre-Islamic and also early Islamic era. I 793a

♦ al-ayyām al-bulḳ → AL-LAYĀLĪ AL-BULḲ

♦ ayyām al-maʿdūdāt → TASHRĪḲ

♦ ayyām al-tashrīḳ → TASHRĪḲ

yay → KEMĀN

yaya (T) : lit. pedestrian; in the Ottoman military of the 14th-16th centuries, infantryman. IX 13a; XI 301a; a special corps consisting of *reʿāyā* (→ RAʿIYYA) soldiers. VIII 404b

♦ yayabashi̊ (T) : chief infantryman, commander of the infantry or cavalry unit, BÖLÜK, in the Janissary ODJAḲS. I 1256a

yaylaḳ (T, < *yay* 'spring', later 'summer') : summer quarters, the upland pastures favoured by the nomads of Central Asia for fattening their herds after the harsh steppe or plateau winters. Its Persian synonym is GARMSĪR. The Arabic equivalent is *maṣīf.* V 182b; XI 301b

♦ yaylaḳ resmi (T), or *otlaḳ resmi, resm-i čerāghah* : under the Ottomans, the pasturage dues charged usually at the rate of one sheep or its money equivalent for each flock of sheep of 300 which crossed into another district. It was paid to the person who held the land. I 146b

♦ yaylaḳiyya (Ott) : a later Ottoman term with a pseudo-Arabic ending for 'rent paid for summer pastures or lodgings'. XI 301b

yaym → AYM

yazak (P) : in military science, an advanced guard (syn. ṬALĪʿA). X 164b

yazīdī (A, K *ēzdī, ēzdīdī*) : member of a mainly Kurdish-speaking group, *yazīdiyya*, whose communal identity is defined by its distinctive religious tradition. In the ~ hymns, the community is occasionally referred to as the *sunna, ṣuḥbatiyya* 'those who claim discipleship' or *dāsinī.* XI 313a

yazi̊dji̊ (T) : lit. writer, secretary, used in Ottoman times for the clerks in the various government departments, such as the treasury; ~ could also be used for the secretary of high court and military officials. XI 317a

yelek (T, A) : a woman's long coat, tightly fitting, worn in the Arab East; a long vest worn by both sexes in Iraq. V 742a; in Turkey, a waistcoat without sleeves formerly worn as an outer garment. V 752a

yemeni (T) : light shoes worn by the Zeybek in Western Anatolia as part of their folk costume. XI 494a

yeni čeri (T) : lit. new troop; the Janissary corps, a body of professional, that is, salaried, infantrymen of the Ottoman empire in its heyday, called 'new troop' not so much because of the novelty of the idea as because at the time of its introduction by the vizier Khayr al-Dīn Pasha in the 14th century, it opposed then-prevailing military traditions cherished by the frontier warriors. XI 322b

yerliyya (T, A, < T *yerlü* 'local') : during the Ottoman empire, term used by Damascene sources for the local Janissary corps. XI 333b

yerlü → TAT

yigit (T) : one of three grades in the AKHĪ organization, designating the ordinary unmarried member of the organisation. I 322b

yi̊ldi̊z (T) : star. XI 336b

yodjana (San 'league') : a Hindu unit of distance equalling four *goruta* 'cow-roar', the length at which a cow's lowing can be heard, or KROŚA 'earshot'. VII 138b

yoghurt (T) : yogurt, a preparation of soured milk made in the pastoralist, more temperate northern tier of the Middle East, Central Asia, and the Balkans. The product is called *māst* in Persia, *laban* in Syria and Palestinian Arabic, *zabādī* in Egyptian Arabic, *liban* in Iraqi Arabic, *rā'ib, laban, labne*, etc. on the Arabian peninsula. XI 337b

yörük (Ott) : in the Ottoman empire, a term denoting a particular class of nomads obliged to serve in the Ottoman army; in modern ethnological and anthropological literature, a term for and also a self-designation of nomadic pastoralists, as opposed to Türkmen, Kurdish or other pastoralist tribal groups of Anatolia. IX 674a; XI 338b

yughrush (T) : in the Ḳarakhānid period, the term for vizier. XI 224a

yük (T) : an Ottoman weight, being the two bales slung across a beast of burden, the equivalent of ca. 154 kg. III 212b; IV 678b

yūnān (A, s. *yūnānī*) : the ancient Greeks, reflecting the name 'Ionians'. XI 343b

♦ yūnāniyya (A) : the ancient Greek language. In Western Islam, *ighrīḳiyya* is occasionally mentioned as the correct designation of ancient Greek. XI 343b

yūnkār (T) : a musical instrument of the pandore type, but smaller with three strings. It was invented by Shamsī Čelebi, the son of the Turkish poet Ḥamdī Čelebi. X 626a

yurd : a type of appanage, which with the term *ulka* (or *ulkā*) survived in the Turcoman states of eastern Anatolia under the Ottomans in the sense of hereditary appanage. X 502a

yurt : the domed, felt-covered tent of Turkmen nomads; originally 'homeland, encampment or camping place', and in Orkhon and early Turkish, 'an abandoned campsite'. IV 1150b; VIII 233b; XII 838b

♦ **yurtči** (T) : under the Mongols, a salaried officer responsible for choosing camp sites for the army or court, organising them, and supervising their use. Besides the ~ , three other officials were responsible for the management of the camp: the *farrāsh* or tent-pitcher; the *bularghucï* or keeper of lost property; and the *sārbān* or cameleer. XII 838b f.

yūsufī (T) : in full, *ʿimāme-i yūsufī*, an old name for the Turkish turban, said to have been originally invented by Joseph and called after him. Selīm I and II wore these, which were then called *selīmī*s (A *salīmī*) after them. X 615a

yūz → FAHD

yüzbashï (T, > A *yūzbashī*) : lit. head of a hundred [men]; in the later Ottoman and now Turkish and Arab military, the rank of captain. XII 840b

In Muslim India, an engraver of coin dies. XII 840b

yüzellïlïkler (T) : lit. the 150 [undesirables]; term for those whom the Turkish government wished to exclude from the general amnesty demanded by the Allies during the peace negotiations at Lausanne in 1923, but whose names it was at that time undecided about. XI 363b

Z

ẓāʾ (A) : the seventeenth letter of the Arabic alphabet, with the numerical value 900. Its transliteration *ẓ* reflects an urban/sedentary pronunciation as 'emphatic' (pharyngealised) *z*. XI 363a

zabād (A), or *sinnawr al-zabād* : in zoology, the civet cat (*Viverra civetta*). IX 653b

♦ zabādī → YOGHURT

zabān-i urdu → URDU

zabān-i wuḳūʿ → WUḲŪʿ-GŪʾĪ

zabāniyya (A) : Qurʾānic term usually interpreted as the guardians of Hell or else the angels who carry off the souls at death. XI 369a

zabardjad : in mineralogy, the chrysolith. II 93b; and → ZAMURRUD zabbāl   (A, Tun g̲h̲abbār) : 'superintendent of the supply of dung-fuel for the furnace' of a ḥammām 'steam bath'. III 140a; and → KANNĀS

zabīb   (A) : dried grapes, raisins or currents. XI 369b; or zbīb, a non-alcoholic drink made from dried grapes. VI 723b

♦   zabībiyya   (A) : a dish, probably of Egyptian provenance, prepared from fresh fish with a sweet and sour spiced sauce poured over it. XI 369b

zabit   → ḌĀBIṬ

zabr   (A) : the act of pruning, practised in Andalusia on the grapevine to increase the vine's productivity with an iron pruning knife, mind̲j̲al. IV 659b

zabtiyye   → ḌABṬIYYA

zabūr   (A) : term found in pre-Islamic poetry for a written text, and in the Qurʾān referring to a divine scripture, in some contexts specifically to a scripture of David, probably the Psalms. With the discovery of South Arabian cursive writing on palm ribs and wooden sticks, it has become evident that ~ refers to this particular way of writing. XI 372a; term found in poetry for pre-Islamic Holy Scriptures. X 394a

zaʿbūt   (A) : a woollen garment. IX 765a

zabzab   (A) : in zoology, the badger. II 739b

zāde   → OG̲H̲UL

zād̲j̲   (A) : in metallurgy, vitriol. VIII 111b

zad̲j̲ad̲j̲   (A) : in zoology, the flight of the ostrich. VII 828b

zad̲j̲al   (A) : in its non-technical meaning, 'voice, sound or cry, trilling or quavering of the voice' (Lane). XI 373a

In poetry, a genre in Muslim Spain, written only in the Arabic dialect of Spain. Its most frequent rhyme scheme is aa bbb a ccc a, that is, the rhyme scheme of a MUSAMMAṬ with introductory lines. III 849b; V 1207a; VII 661b XI 373a; in present-day Arabic, ~ may denote various types of dialect poems, even those with monorhyme. XI 373a; XI 376a

zad̲j̲d̲j̲āl   (Leb) : in Lebanese colloquial poetry, a composer of ZAD̲J̲AL vernacular poetry. When contrasted to a ḳawwāl 'a performer or 'speaker' of zad̲j̲al' or S̲H̲ĀʿIR, ~ implies a lack of ability to spontaneously or extemporaneously compose. IX 234b

zad̲j̲l   (A), or zid̲j̲āl : the sport of pigeon-flying, popular from the 2nd-7th/8th-13th centuries. The homing pigeon, zād̲j̲il (pl. zawād̲j̲il), received the closest attention from its owner. III 109a,b

zad̲j̲r   (A) : often used as the equivalent of ṬĪRA, ~ originally consisted of the deliberate instigation of the flight and cries of birds, but has now come to stand for evil omen or divination in general. I 659b; II 758b; IV 290b

zaʿfarān   (A) : in botany, saffron, Crocus sativus L. or Crocus officinalis Pers. III 461a; XI 381a; and → MĀʾ ZAʿFARĀN

In medicine, one of the simple medicaments, appearing under various names besides ~ : rayhaḳān, d̲j̲ādī, d̲j̲ādhī and d̲j̲isān. XI 381b

zaffa   (A) : the procession of bride or bridegroom to their wedding. X 904a ff.

zafzūf   → ʿUNNĀB

zag̲h̲al   (A) : in numismatics, a counterfeit coin. X 409b

zag̲h̲ar   (T), zag̲h̲ārī   (A) : a hunting dog, hound. IV 745a; XI 384b

♦   zag̲h̲ard̲j̲i̇   (T) : keeper of the hounds, which company in the Ottoman empire was probably in origin part of the hunting force of the early Ottoman sultans. XI 384b

♦   zag̲h̲ard̲j̲i bas̲h̲i   (T) : in the Ottoman military, the title of one of the three commanders who formed the administrative focus of the Janissary corps of the Ottoman army, the other two being the S̲h̲amsund̲j̲i̇ Bas̲h̲i̇ and the Turnad̲j̲i̇ Bas̲h̲i̇. XI 384b

zag̲h̲rada   (A, pl. zag̲h̲radāt) : a trilling ululation, as uttered in joy. VI 160a zaḥḥāfa → MĀLAḲ

♦ zaḥḥāfāt (A) : in zoology, the class of reptiles. X 510a

zāhid (A, pl. *zuhhād*) : an ascetic, pious person who has given up all worldly goods. V 1124b; VIII 498a

ẓāhir (A, pl. *ẓawāhir*) : lit. the outward meaning of a word, language or event; in legal theory, the meaning first comprehended by the mind upon hearing a particular term or expression that potentially has two or more meanings. VII 1029a; XI 388b; and → BĀṬIN

In law, ~ *al-riwāya* or ~ *al-madhhab* is the most authoritative doctrine, that which is transmitted from Abū Ḥanīfa, Abū Yūsuf and al-Shaybānī through a large number of channels by trustworthy and highly qualified jurists. XI 388b

In theology, **al-ẓāhir wa ʾl-bāṭin** are paired, in Qurʾānic and shīʿī usage as opposites protraying both the inside and outside of a thing, the inner and outer dimension. XI 389a

In grammar, the opposition ~ 'explicit' versus MUḌMAR 'the suppressed' is recognised for the contrast between overt and implicit elements generally. XII 546a

♦ ẓāhira (A) : the heat that reigns during the ẒUHR 'midday prayer'. Other terms used are *hādjira*, *ḳāʾila*, *ghāʾira*. V 709b

♦ **ẓāhiriyya** (A) : name of a a theologico-juridical school, thus called because it relied exclusively on the literal sense (ẒĀHIR) of the Qurʾān and of Tradition. XI 394a

ẓahīr (A) : lit. help, support; in the administration of the Muslim West, a royal decree issued by the sovereign and conferring an administrative prerogative, such as a nomination to a political or religious post, or granting a privilege, either moral or material, upon the beneficiary. The term first appeared under the Almohad dynasty, replacing another term, *ṣakk*, used earlier by the Almoravids and the Taifa kingdoms with the same meaning. XI 387b

zahr (A) : flower, blossom, more precisely, yellow flower, yellow blossom. XI 399b

In prosody, in particular associated with the folk MAWWĀL, ~ is the expansion of the rhymes into polysyllabic paronomasias, achieved by deliberate distortion of the normal pronunciation. A *mawwāl* devoid of ~ is described as *abyaḍ* 'white'; if so ornamented, it is either *aḥmar* 'red' or *akhḍar* 'green'. VI 868a ff.

♦ **zahriyyāt** (A, s. *zahriyya*) : in literature, poetry dedicated to the description of flowers. XI 399b

ẓahr (A), or *ẓahriyya* : in manuscript production, the recto of the first folio. X 870b

zahw (A) : a kind of date, from which wine was made. IV 995b

zāʾid (A, pl. *zawāʾid*) : in grammar, an auxiliary consonant. XI 200a; in Persian lexicography, ~ came to be used to denote any letter added to or removed from the base form (*aṣlī*) without changing its meaning. XII 430b; and → ṢILA

zāʾif → MUZAYYIF

zaʿīm (A, pl. *zuʿamāʾ*) : chief, leader; a tribal chief. IX 115b; XI 402b

In the Ottoman empire, a person in charge of a ZIʿĀMET, a division of a SANDJAḲ. A ~ who was given the title of *alay-beyi* would be chosen to be responsible for all matters concerning the SIPĀHĪs in the *sandjaḳ*. X 502b; XI 403a; XI 495a

In law, guarantor, trustee. XI 402b

In modern-day Lebanon, a political entrepreneur whose function is to serve as intermediary between his community and the state and to keep the inter-community game in balance. XI 403a

zāʿir → ZUʿʿĀR

zāʾirdja (A), or *zāʾiradja* : in divination, a technique that involved a mechanical means of calculating portents with the aid of a series of concentric circles combining the letters of the alphabet, geomancy and astrology. V 101a; XI 404a

♦ zāʾiradja al-ʿālam (A) : a circular divinatory table. VIII 691a

zakāt (A) : obligatory payment by Muslims of a determinate portion of specified categories of their lawful property for the benefit of the poor and other enumerated classes, one of the five pillars of Islam. IV 1151b; V 424b; VIII 708b; VIII 925b; XI 406b; the tax levied on both landed and moveable property. I 1144a; the prescribed tithe on agricultural produce. I 968b; II 142b; and → ṢADAḲA

♦ zakāt al-dawlaba (A) : under the Mamlūks, a tax which was payable by Muslim shopkeepers on their merchandise, abolished by Ḳalāwūn who realised that it tended to impoverish the merchants. IV 485b

♦ zakāt al-fiṭr (A) : a payment due on behalf of all Muslims in connection with the termination of the fast of Ramaḍān. As a ZAKĀT for persons, not property, it is also termed *zakāt al-badan* and *zakāt al-ra's*. I 27a; XI 418a

zak͟hrafa (A) : in art, ornament, ornamentation. XI 423a

zaḳḳūm (A) : in eschatology, a tree growing in Hell with bitter fruit which the damned are condemned to eat, mentioned in the Qur'ān three times. XI 425b

zakūrī (A) : in mediaeval ʿIrāḳ, bread collected as alms and intended for prisoners and beggars. VII 494a

zaḳzaḳa (A) : the twittering of large numbers of birds in trees. XI 422b

zaḳzūḳ (A, pl. *zaḳāzīḳ*) : in zoology, the carp. XI 422b

zalīd͟j (A, pl. *zalā'id͟j*), also *zallīd͟j* : in art, a mosaic composed of fragments of pottery squares with a coloured enamelled surface, first attested in ancient Persian and Mesopotamia but foremost popular in the Muslim West. II 748a; VIII 682a; XI 426a

zālik͟ha → AṬŪM

ẓalīm (A) : in astronomy, two constellations (*al-ẓalīmān*[i]), one *al-* ~ *al-s͟himālī* 'the northern male' or μ Sagittarii, and *al-* ~ *al-d͟janūbī* 'the southern male' or λ Sagittarii, also called *rāʿī al-naʿā'im* 'the ostrich herder'. VII 830b; and → NAʿĀM

In astrology, the star α Eridani. VII 830b

zallād͟j (A) : a term used for a Nile boat. VIII 42b

zallīd͟j → ZALĪD͟J

zalzala (A, pl. *zalāzil*), also *zilzāl* : earthquake. XI 428a

zalzūm, zalẓūm (A) : in zoology, the tusks of the wild boar (syn. *k͟hand͟jal*). V 8b

zām : a unit of measurement, equal to three FARSAK͟Hs. IV 1083a

zamān (A) : time. XI 434a

♦ zamāniyya (A) : mean time. X 367a

zamāzima (A) : according to al-ʿAynī, precious 'bridles' that the eponymous ancestor of the Sāsānids is supposed to have donated to the Zamzam well. XI 440b; in al-Ṭabarī, the Magians. XI 442b; and → ZAMZAMĪ

zamīn-būs (P) : in Čis͟htī mystical practice, the practice of prostration before the S͟HAYK͟H. IX 786a

zamīndār (P) : lit. land-holder, master of the land; under the Mug͟hals, a class of holders of rights over land (syn. *būmī*), also comprising the various tributary chiefs and autonomous Rād͟jas, who were called thus by the Mug͟hal chancery. VII 322a; XI 438b; XII 768a

♦ zamīndārī → TAʿALLUḲ

zammāra (A) : 'joined'; the name in the mediaeval period for a double reed-pipe. Since the 18th century, it was known in the East as ZUMMĀRA, a vulgarisation of ~. VII 208a; in southern Tunisia, the name for the G͟HAYṬA, a reed-pipe of cylindrical bore or an oboe of conical bore. II 1027b

zamzam (A) : an onomatopoeic qualifier, with *zumāzim*, denoting an 'abundant supply of water'; the name of the sacred well located at the perimeter of the sacred complex of Mecca. XI 440a

♦ **zamzama** (A) : in early Arabic, 'the confused noise of distant thunder' (Lane), but widely used in sources of early history for the priests of the Magians reciting and intoning the Zoroastrian prayers and scriptures. Also, in al-Ṭabarī, the Zoroastrian rites (with *muzamzim* for the adherent of Zoroastrianism). XI 442b

♦ zamzamī (A, pl. *zamāzima*) : part of the pilgrimage service industry, the function of the ~ in Mecca is to distribute the sacred water of Zamzam to those who desire it, whether in the mosque precincts or at home. VI 171a; XI 442a

♦ zamzamiyyāt (A) : small phials (of clay or metal) sealed and sold as containing water from the sacred well of Zamzam. XI 442a

zanāna → ḤARĪM

zanbaḳ (A) : in botany, lilac. XI 183a

zandaḳa → ZINDĪḲ

zandj (A) : term for the peoples of Black Africa, especially those whom the Arabs came into contact with through their voyages nad trade in the western part of the Indian Ocean and living in the eastern parts of Africa. XI 444b
In botany, the black rhubarb, according to Ibn al-Bayṭār. XI 445a

zang : in music, the sonette. X 35a

zangī : black. XI 452a

zānī (A) : a male fornicator, with *zāniya* (pl. *zawānī*), his female counterpart. XI 509a; and → BAGHIYY

zāniya → ZĀNĪ

zanḳa → SHĀRIʿ

zār (A, Somali *saar*) : name for a popular cult of spirits found in northeastern Africa and such adjacent regions as the Arabian peninsula, and an exorcism ritual for those same spirits. The possessed person is called 'bride' (*ʿarūsa*), the chief celebrant either *kūdiya* or *shaykha*. I 35b; IX 723b; XI 455b

zar-i maḥbūb : in numismatics, a three-quarter's weight Ottoman gold coin, 2.64 g, introduced in the last years of Aḥmed III's reign (1115-43/1703-30). VIII 229b

zarad → DIRʿ

zaradkāshiyya (A) : under the Mamlūks, the AMĪRs of the arsenal, whose duty was to guard the arsenal. IX 610a

zarāfa (A, pl. *zarāfāt, zarāfī, zarāʾif, zurāfa*; P *ushtur-gāw-palang* 'camel-cow-leopard') : in zoology, the giraffe. XI 457b; an Abyssinian hybrid beast. X 946a
In astronomy, a secondary boreal constellation situated between that of the Waggoner and that of the Little Bear. XI 458a

zarāḳīm → AZRAḲ

zarbiyya (A, pl. *zarābī*), or *zirbiyya, zurbiyya* : a carpet decorated with multicoloured bands. XII 136a

zardjūn (P ?) : a loan-word in Arabic for the colours red and gilt. V 699b

ẓarf (A, pl. *ẓurūf*) : lit. vessel, container; courtesy, elegance. I 175b; refinement. XI 160b
In grammar, a subset of nouns of place or time in the dependent (*naṣb*) form indicating when or where the event occurs. IX 527b; IX 551a; XI 459b; temporal adjunct. IX 53b

zarī (P), or *zar baft* : a gold brocade, for which e.g. Kāshān was well known during the Ṣafawid period. IV 695a

ẓarībān (A), or ẓarbān : in zoology, the zoril. V 389b

ẓarīf (A, pl. *ẓurafāʾ*) : in mediaeval Islamic social and literary life, a person endowed with elegance, refinement (ẒARF), syn. *mutaẓarrif*, also translatable as 'man of the world', 'dandy', or in the plural, 'refined people'. XI 460a

zarnīkh (A) : in mineralogy, orpiment. X 946a

zarrāḳ, zarrāḳa → NAFFĀṬ

zâviyeli (T) : a term used by Turkish scholars to refer to a type of 'Convent Mosque' with a domed or vaulted central hall flanked by side rooms. XI 467b

zawāl (A) : 'midday', marked for the astronomers by the sun crossing the meridian, and for the simple faithful by the displacement of the shade which moves from the west to the east. V 709b

zawāḳīl (A) : a shadowy group of Arab brigands and mercenaries active during the ʿAbbāsid period. The etymology of the designation is unclear; the verb *zawḳala* means 'to let the two ends of a turban hang down from one's shoulders'. XI 463b

zawdj (A, < Gk *zeugos*; pl. *azwādj*) : basically 'two draught animals yoked together', ~ has come to mean 'couple, pair'. In the Qurʾān, the dominant meaning is 'spouse', that is, 'wife, woman'. In the Maghrib, the form is *djawz* (thus becoming also a homonym for the Persian 'nut'; → DJAWZ). XI 464b; XII 842b; and → ZAWW

zawīla (A) : a special leather produced in Zawīla, the mediaeval Islamic capital of the Fazzān. XI 466a

zāwiya (A, pl. *zawāyā*) : lit. corner, nook; a religious foundation of a quasi-monastic type. In Mamlūk Cairo, the ~ was generally a small construction housing a SHAYKH, with room for students to group informally around him; in the Near East, ~ denoted small rooms of a mosque shut off by wooden lattices, sometimes also called MAḲṢŪRA. In 6th/12th-century Baghdad, a ~ was a place where an ascetic lived in solitude and by the 8th/14th century, it had come to be used also in the sense of RIBĀṬ, a '*coenobium*'. In Morocco, the ~ is the chapel which contains the tomb of a saint and the buildings attached to it, an oratory and guest-house. Some *zāwiya*s are centres of mysticism and they are always centres of religious instruction. IV 380a; IV 433a; V 1129b; V 1201b; VI 662a; VIII 503b; X 415b; XI 466b; XII 223b; in the Maghrib, ~ is used not only for the actual building but also to denote the ṬARĪḲA itself and is synonomous for the *ṭarīḳa*'s collective membership. XI 467b

zawḳala → ZAWĀḲĪL

zawr → ṢADR

zawrāʾ (A) : in archery, probably a bow with a strong bend made from *nasham* wood (*Chadara velutina*). It was also called *ḳaws munḥaniya*. IV 798a

zawraḳ (A, pl. *zawāriḳ*, < ? P) : in mediaeval Mesopotamia, a skiff or dinghy used for local traffic; larger, sea-going *zawraḳ*s are recorded in the Mediterranean. VIII 811a

zāwuḳ → ZIʾBAḲ

zaww (A, < ? P *zūd*) : in mediaeval Mesopotamia, a swift type of vessel, often mentioned as used by caliphs and great men of state, which could be a luxuriously-appointed gondola. VIII 811a; a kind of catamaran. XII 659b

zāy (A), also, more rarely, *zāʾ* : the eleventh letter of the Arabic alphabet, transcribed *z*, with numerical value 8. It represents a voiced sibilant. For the 'emphatic' variant, → ẒĀʾ. XI 471a

zaybaḳ → ZIʾBAḲ

zayf → MUZAYYIF

zayt (A) : the oil or expressed juice of the olive, although it could be applied today to any oil. The term ~ *maghsūl* 'washed oil', or alternatively ~ *al-māʾ*, might refer either to the Roman technique of removing a bitter glucoside from the fruit by first soaking it in a solution of lye followed by a thorough washing, or by crushing the olives and then purifying the liquid by floating it on water. XI 485b

zaytūn (A) : in botany, the olive and olive tree (*Olea europaea* L is the cultivated olive; *Olea oleaster*, the wild one). IX 435a; XI 486a

zhiraw (Kaz) : a reciter of epic poetry; repressed by Soviet ideology as symbolic of a feudal culture, the ~ has been replaced by the *zhirshi*, who creates only minor epics, and by the *aḳïn*, who, as in Ḳirghizia also, sings for his clan and whose repertoire consists of extracts from epics arranged as songs, or poems adapted to the social circumstances of the performance. X 733b

zhirshi → ZHIRAW

ziʿāmet (T, < A *ziʿāma*) : in Ottoman military and land tenure organisation, a larger-size TĪMĀR, although before the 10th/16th century the limits were less clearly defined, whose holder was a ZAʿĪM, serving in the Ottoman army when called upon. XI 495a

ziʾbaḳ (A) : in metallurgy and alchemy, mercury, also called quicksilver (*argentum vivum*). Variant forms include *zaybaḳ, zība/iḳ* and *zāwuḳ*. V 967b; X 946a; XI 495b

zibaʿrā → KARKADDAN

zibbūn (A) : in Libya, a man's jacket with long sleeves. V 746b

zīdj (A, < MidP *zīg* 'rope, towline'; pl. *zīdjāt*) : in astronomy, a handbook with tables and explanatory text. A typical one might contain a hundred folios of text and tables, though some are substantially larger. I 139b; III 1136a; VIII 101b; X 264b; XI 496b

zidjāl → ZADJL

ziḥāf (A, pl. *ziḥāfāt*) : in prosody, the optional reduction of a long to a short syllable or of two short syllables to one, one of two groups of metrical deviations (the other being ʿILAL). In Persian, ~ is not an element of variation within the same poem, but is used to distinguish one metre from the other. I 671b; VIII 667b; XI 508a

ẓihār (A, < *ẓahr* 'back') : in law, an oath, which may be translated very vaguely as 'incestuous comparison'. Presumably the husband says to his wife: 'You are for me like my mother's back', *ka-ẓahri ummī*, or any other comparison of a part of the body of his wife with that of a woman he could not marry without committing incest. IV 688a; a vow of continence. VIII 28a

zikrāna : a special hut which is not orientated towards the ḲIBLA, in which the DHIKR is recited six times daily by the Dhikrī sect in Baluchistan. XII 222b

zīl → ṢANDJ

ẓill (A) : the central theme or aim of a SŪRA (syn. *miḥwar*). IX 887b; and → FAYʾ
In astronomy, the cotangent. XI 502b; and → ḲUṬR AL-ẒILL

zillī māsha → DJAGHĀNA

zilzāl → ZALZALA

zimām (A, pl. *azimma*) : lit. rein, halter; in mediaeval administration, a department of control and audit (*dīwān al-azimma*) in the central administration; under the Fāṭimids, a person in control, one holding the reins of power, viz. director of the treasury and major domo. XI 509a; and → AL-NAʿL AL-SHARĪF

zimār → ʿIRĀR

zīna → DJALSA

zināʾ (A) : unlawful fornication, punishable by penal law if the partners are not married to each other or united by the bond of ownership. I 29b; I 910b; III 20b; XI 509a

zindāna (A) : a song form among women in western Algeria. IX 234a

zindīḳ (A, < MidP; pl. *zanādiḳa*) : anyone who, professing to be a Muslim, is really an unbeliever or anyone who belongs to no religion. He is then accused of *zandaḳa* 'heresy, unbelief'. The term ~ had in Middle Persian, along with the meaning of 'heretic' in a broad sense, the very precise one of 'Manichaean' and the Arabic word retains this ambivalence. Synonyms are *mulḥid*, *murtadd* or *kāfir*. IV 771b; VI 421b; X 440b; XI 510b

zindjār : in mineralogy, verdigris. VIII 111b; IX 872b

ziʿnufiyyāt al-aḳdam (A) : in zoology, the class of pinnipeds, which include the seal, the walrus, and the sea lion. VIII 1022b

zīr (A) : in music, one of the four strings of the ʿŪD, which have special names. The others are *mathnā*, *mathlath* and *bamm*. VI 215b

♦ zīr al-baḥr (A) : in zoology, the squill-fish (*Scyllarus latus*) and the mantis-shrimp (*Squilla mantis*), also called *istākūzā al-raml*. IX 40a

zīr-i zamīn (P) : lit. subterranean; a chamber under the ground in southern Persia where people would spend the hottest time of the day. IX 49b

zirbādj (P) : a mediaeval meat dish with vegetables and seasoning. X 31a; XI 369b

ziryāb (A) : in zoology, a black bird. XI 516b; a loan-word in Arabic for the colour yellow. V 699b

ziyāda (A) : in architecture, a term used to designate the broad open enclosure on three of the four sides of a mosque, which illusionistically increases its scale. I 620b; VI 679b

In mathematics, ~ is the term used for addition. III 1139b

♦ ziyādāt al-thiḳāt (A) : in the science of Tradition, additions by authorities in ISNĀD or MATN which are not found in other transmissions. III 26a

ziyāra (A, pl. *ziyārāt*; T *ziyāret*) : pious visitation, pilgrimage to a holy place, tomb or shrine. In Turkish, *ziyāret* can be applied as well to the holy place itself. XI 524a; the dues levied in the Independence Party of ʿAllāl al-Fāsī in Morocco. XI 468b

♦ ziyāra-nāma (P) : special salutations pronounced by a pilgrim, even one who cannot undertake the journey to a saint's shrine, for various special occasions. XI 534a

ziyāret → ZIYĀRA

zmāla (Alg) : popularised during the French invasion of Algeria under the form *smala*, that which a person or tribe carries when in motion, i.e. all one's goods, with nothing left behind. These ~s were formed at a time of movement in an unsafe region or in a period of conflict. ʿAbd al-Ḳādir used the concept of ~ in his resistance against the French, forming thus a mobile city, which at the time of its dispersal in May 1843 was estimated at between 25,000 and 60,000 persons. A smaller structure called *dāyra* (< *dāʾira*) was established in Morocco at the end of 1843, surving as his base, but surrendering in December 1847. XI 540b

zolota (T) : in numismatics, a large-sized silver coin, 18.5-19.7 g, introduced under Süleymān II on the European pattern. A half- ~, 8.65-9.85 g, was also struck. VIII 229a

zorba (T, pl. *zorbāwāt*, *zorab*) : 'insolent one', 'rebel', a group of native Damascene Janissaries that went on the rampage in Damascus in 1746, many of whom were then killed by the governor's private troops. XI 334a

zorṭalbī (U) : in India, a tribute exacted by force due from the feudatory states, a relic of Muslim supremacy. II 597b

zozān (K) : (summer) pasturing camps. V 445a; V 451b

zuʿʿār (A, s. *zāʿir*) : lit. rowdy, ill-behaved lads, notably in the Egyptian and Syrian urban milieux during the Mamlūk and Ottoman periods, and often connected with the mystical orders; also used for 'gypsies' outside of the urban area. XI 546a, where can be found many synonyms for 'rascals, scoundrels'

zubānayān (A) : lit. the two pincers; in astronomy, the two stars known as the Two Pincers in the constellation of Cancer. IX 40b

zubb al-ḳiṭṭ (A) : 'cat's penis', in botany, the variety *Astragalus cahiricus* of the genus Milk vetch. IX 653b

zubda (A, pl. *zubad*) : primary meaning is 'cream (of milk), (fresh) butter' (for which → SAMN), secondary meaning is 'best part, essence, selection', in which meaning ~ became a popular leading word of book titles, indicating that the work in question either encompasses the most important facts of its subject-matter or that it is an abridged version of some lengthier treatise. XI 552a

zubra (A) : a piece of iron. XI 372a

zudjādj (A, s. *zudjādja*; P *ābgīna* or *shīsha*), also *zadjādj*, *zidjādj* : glass, syn. *kawārīr* 'glass vessels, pieces of glass'. XI 552a zudjdj → ḲIDḤ; SINĀN

zufayzif → ʿUNNĀB

ẓufr (A) : claw; in botany, ~ *al-nasr* 'vulture's claw' is the Greek Catananche (*Hymenonema Tournefortii* or *Catananche graeca*). VII 1014b

♦ ẓufr al-ḳiṭṭ → RIDJL AL-ḲIṬṬ

zuḥal (A) : in astronomy, the planet Saturn. XI 555a; and → MUḲĀTIL
In alchemy, lead. XI 556a

zuhara (A, P *[a]nāhīd*) : in astronomy, the planet Venus. XI 556a
In alchemy, copper. XI 556b

zuhd (A) : in religion, the material and spiritual asceticism facilitating closer association with the divine. Its practitioner is a *zāhid*. X 377b; XI 141b; XI 559b

♦ **zuhdiyya** (A, pl. *zuhdiyyāt*) : in literature, a pious, homiletic or ascetic poem. IX 4b; IX 453b; XI 562a

ẓuhr (A) : noon, midday.

♦ ṣalāt al-ẓuhr (A) : the midday prayer which is to be performed from the time when the sun begins to decline till the time when shadows are of equal length with the objects by which they are cast, apart from their shadows at noon. VII 27b; VIII 928b

zuhūmāt (A) : people who avoid 'fatty meats', like the Marcionites, presumably meaning they did eat fish. XII 600a

zuḳāḳ → SHĀRIʿ

zukaym

♦ zukaym al-Ḥabasha (A) : in the mediaeval Near East, a fraudulent warrior engaged in DJIHĀD 'holy war'. VII 495a

♦ zukaym al-marḥūma (A) : in the mediaeval Near East, a band of blind men led by an *isṭīl*, a beggar who pretends to be blind. VII 495a

♦ zukaym al-mughālaṭa (A) : in the mediaeval Near East, a beggar who feigns inability to speak. VII 494b

zukhruf (A) : a Qurʾānic term meaning 'gold' (> 'ornamental work'), the origin of which seems to be a deformation, via Syriac, of Gk. *zōgrapheō* 'to paint'. XI 423a

zulf → ṢUDGH

ẓulla (A) : in pre-Islamic Arabia, a simple shelter in the form of a sort of canopy. IV 1147a,b; VIII 545a; and → ṢUFFA

zullāmī (A) : in the Muslim West, the vulgarisation of *zunāmī*, a reed-pipe invented about the beginning of the 3rd/9th century at the ʿAbbāsid court by a musician named Zunām. The word *zunāmī* was accorded little recognition in the East, but in Spain (Sp. *xelami*) and North Africa, as ~, it became the most important reed-pipe. VII 207a

ẓulm (A) : wrongdoing, evil, injustice, oppression and tyranny, particularly by persons who have power and authority, frequently used as the antonym to ʿADL 'justice'. XI 567b

zumāzim → ZAMZAM

zummāra (A, < *zammāra*) : a vulgarisation of ZAMMĀRA, but since the 18th century, the name for a double-reed pipe in the East. It has cylindrical tubes and is played with single beating reeds. It is to be found with a varying number of finger-holes and is named accordingly. In the MAGHRIB, it is called *maḳrūn* and *maḳrūna*. Another type of double reed-pipe, which has only one pipe pierced with finger holes, while the other serves as a drone, is also called ~ when the two pipes are of the same length. When the drone pipe is longer than the chanter pipe, it is known as ARGHŪL. VII 208a

zumurrud (A), also *zumurrudh* : in mineralogy, the emerald, the most valuable of the beryl family, often confused with *zabardjad* (< Gk *smaragdos* 'emerald'), the peridot. The next in value is known as *rayḥānī*, i.e. of basil leaf colour, followed by the *silḳī*, of chard green colour. XI 569b

zunāmī → ZULLĀMĪ

zunbūʿ (A) : in botany, the grapefruit tree. VII 962a

zunbūr (A) : in zoology, the hornet. IX 873a

zunnār (A, < Gk) : a distinctive girdle DHIMMĪs were required to wear in the mediaeval period, wider than the *minṭaḳa*, the general word for 'girdle'. IX 167a; XI 571b; a belt, usually made of folded scarf, worn by both men and women in Syria and Palestine. V 742a

In Persian ṣūfī poetry, locks of the beloved. XI 572a

zurdānī (N.Afr) : in zoology, the Striped rat, or 'Barbarian rat' (*Arvicanthus barbarus*). XII 286a

zūrkhāna (P), or *zūr-khāna* : lit. house of strength; the traditional gymnasium of Iran, in the centre of which lies the *gawd*, a usually octagonal pit in which the exercises take place. IV 8b; VIII 239a; XI 572b

zurna (T, P *surnā*) : in music, a double-reed shawm with seven holes (6 in front and 1 behind), the basic melody instrument of the Ottoman *mehter* 'ensemble'. VI 1007b; XI 574a; oboe. VIII 178b

♦ ḳaba zurna (T) : in music, a large instrument used by the official Ottoman palace *mehter* 'ensemble' in the capital. It had a range of over two octaves and could produce all the notes needed for pre-19th century Ottoman music. VI 1007

THE ENCYCLOPAEDIA OF ISLAM

NEW EDITION

INDEX VOLUME

FASCICULE 3

INDEX OF PROPER NAMES

COMPILED BY

EMERI van DONZEL

ASSISTED BY

NATHALIE van DONZEL

EDITED BY

RONALD E. KON

WITH ASSISTANCE OF

JELLE BRUNING, JOEP LAMEER, HANS van der MEULEN, ABDURRAOUF OUESLATI

TABLE OF CONTENTS

PREFACE TO THE
INDEX OF PROPER NAMES

The Index of the *Encyclopaedia of Islam, New Edition* (12 vols., 1960-2005) consists of three parts: the *Index of Subjects* (Index Volume, pp. 1-135), *Glossary and Index of Terms* (Index Volume, pp. 139-592), and the present *Index of Proper Names*, which completes the trilogy.

In the trilingual EI1 (German, English, French, 1913-1939), the keywords were given in Arabic, Persian, and Turkish. Using the same keyword in the three editions was considered preferable to three different terms. Another reason was that translating an Islamic concept into a western language can lead to confusion and misunderstanding as to its exact meaning. "Alms" for the Arabic *zakāt* is a case in point. This system required an index for optimal use, however.

Although an index to the first edition was compiled by W. Heffening before the outbreak of World War II and survived the war, it was never published. It is now part of the collection of the Leiden University Library. The Editors of the second edition also opted for an index, to be published even before the *Encyclopaedia* was completed because of the extended size of the EI2 and its slow progress. After initial hesitation, the publisher agreed to the idea, provided it would be cumulative and published in one fascicule for both the English and French editions.

The first *Index* to EI2 was compiled by Mrs. Hilda Pearson, assisted by her husband, the renowned bibliographer J.D. Pearson. Edited by the undersigned, it covered volumes I-III and was published in 1979, jointly by E.J. Brill and G.-P. Maisonneuve and Larose, Paris, with financial support by UNESCO on the recommendation of the International Council for Philosophy and Humanistic Studies. The initial compilation immediately evidenced the problems an indexer is confronted with: inconsistent spellings and dates; variant names of the same person or of peoples and places; printing errors.

The second edition of the *Index*, also compiled by H. and J.D. Pearson, was published ten years later, in 1989, with grants from the National Endowment for the Humanities (NEH), an independent Federal Agency of the United States.

With the third edition of the *Index*, published in 1991 and covering Volumes I-VII, a separate *Index of Subjects* was announced as from Volume VIII in order to facilitate the use of EI2. It appeared in 1993. Consequently, the fourth edition of the *Index* (1993) was renamed *Index of Proper Names*. The *Glossary and Index of Terms* appeared, only in English, in 1995, covering Volumes I-VIII.

The seventh and to date last *Index of Proper Names*, still bilingual, appeared in 2002 with the data of Volume X and that part of the Supplement that had already been published.

In pre-computer times, the production of the *Index of Proper Names* was made on index cards listing the proper name and the reference to volume, page and column (a or b), each different for the English and French editions. These cards were then set on tape in magnetic codes, which themselves were transformed into legible text on sheets of photographic paper. Xeroxes of these sheets served as proofs and corrections were made on them. It was a laborious process, especially with the proofreading of the manual typesetting.

In the *Index of Proper Names* the Arabic article *al-* is ignored in the alphabetization. A year or a Roman numeral behind a person's name indicates the year or century of his death according to the Roman calendar. Rulers and other royalty are further specified by the name of the dynasty to which they belong. Titles such as Mollā (Mullā), al-Ẓāhir etc. do not appear before the name except, for instance, in the case of the Ayyūbid rulers who are known by their title *al-Malik*.

Banū behind a name indicates a tribe, even if it is not Arabic. *Umm* after the name indicates the mother of a better-known son or daughter. Unless a person is better known by his *kunya, ism* or *laḳab*, he is referred to by his *nisba*. Under *masdjid* one finds an alphabetical list of mosques with their locality and, if known, their date of construction.

I would like to express my gratitude to Ronald E. Kon and his collaborators Jelle Bruning, Joep Lameer, Hans van der Meulen, and Abdurraouf Oueslati. They accomplished the painstaking and ungrateful task of correcting the mistakes that had slipped into the *Index of Proper Names* over the many years of its preparation. I thank my daughter Nathalie who has assisted me in going through the English and French texts in order to establish the cards. She also separated the English Index from the French for this last *Index of Proper Names*.

E. van Donzel Wassenaar, May 2008

A

Aʿara → Dhu 'l-Sharā; Ghidhā
Aʿarrāṣ, al-Rashīd (Mawlāy) b. al-Sharīf viii, 440a
Aaron → Hārūn b. ʿImrān
Aaron b. Elijah (the Younger) (1369) iv, 605b
Aaron b. Jeshuah → Hārūn b. al-Faradj
Aaron b. Joseph (the Elder) (XIV) iv, 605b, 607a
al-Aʿazz, amīr (XII) i, 440a
Āb-i Diz (Luristān) → Dizfūl
Āb-i Gargar → Shushtar
Abā al-Khayl, Āl (Burayda) i, 1313a
Aba 'l-Ḳiʿdān → Abḳayḳ I,100a
ʿAbābda (Bedja) i, **1a**, 1157b; 1172a; vii, 124b; viii, 866a
Ābādah i, **2b**
Ābādān → ʿAbbādān
Ābādeh → ii, 811a; Ābādah
Ābādī Begum Umm Muḥammad ʿAlī (Rāmpūr, 1924) vii, 421a
ʿAbādila → ʿAbdalī
ʿAbādila, Banū (Makka) iii, 263a; vi, 150a, 151a
Abāḍites → Ibāḍiyya
Abʿādiyya → Ibʿādiyya
Abāʾir s, 117b
Abāḳā (Īl-Khān, ĪlKhān) (1282) i, 860b, 1110a, 1188b, 1295a; ii, 606b, 607b, 1122a, 1125a; iv, 30b, 31a, 88a, 620b, 817a; v, 162a, 827a, 828b; vi, 16a, 231a, 231a, 322a, b, 420a, 482b; vii, 479b; viii, 342b, 443a; x, 896b; xi, 285b
ʿAbalāt (VII) ii, 1011b
Aban, Ramdan (XX) iv, 362b
Ābān → Taʾrīkh
Abān b. ʿAbd Allāh al-Marwānī (Umayyad), al-Andalus) (X) s, 153a
Abān b. ʿAbd al-Ḥamīd al-Lāḥiḳī (815) i, **2b**, 108a, 587a, 1216b; iii, 73a, 135b, 309a, 878b, 879a, 890b; iv, 54b, 504a, 822b; vi, 276a, 949a; vii, 798b, 825b; viii, 376b, 839a; ix, 451a, 526b, 660b; xi, 127a
Abān b. Abī ʿAyyāsh (VIII) ix, 491b, 818b
Abān b. Ṣadaḳa (VIII) i, 1034a
Abān b. Saʿīd b. al-ʿĀṣī b. Umayya (VII) vii, 571a
Abān b. Taghlib al-Bakrī (758-9) ix, 555b
Abān b. ʿUthmān b. ʿAffān (723) i, **2b**; x, 29a; xi, 473b; s, 230b
Abān b. al-Walīd al-Badjalī (VIII) viii, 577a
Abanūs i, **3a**
Abarḳubādh i, **3a**; vi, 920a
Abarḳūh i, **3b**; vi, 366a; viii, 315a; ix, 199a; x, 553b, 674b, 675a
Abarshahr (Nīshāpūr) i, **3b**; v, 354b
Abarwīz b. al-Maṣmughān (758) vi, 744b
Abas (953) i, 637b; ii, 679b; iv, 669b
Abaskūn i, **3b**; i, 720b; ii, 1111b; vii, 71a; viii, 625b
Abaza i, **4a**, 100b, 1000a, b, 1189a; viii, 566b; s, 524a
Abaza Ḥasan Agha (XVII) iv, 766a
Abaẓa vi, 316b
Abāẓa, Fikrī (XX) ix, 558b
Abāzā, Köprülü Dāmādî (1088) ix, 697b
Ābāza (Georgians) i, **4a**, 100b, 1189a, 1190a; x, 218a
Ābāza Aḥmed Pasha → Ābāza Meḥmed Pasha
Ābāza Ḥasan Pasha (1658) i, **4a**; iii, 88a, 318a, 1001b, 1248b; iv, 843b, 885a; v, 33a, b, 258a, b, 729a; vii, 707b
Ābāza Meḥmed Pasha (1634) i, **4a**, ii, 712b, 724a, 1090b; iii, 1248a; iv, 869b, 970a, 971b; v, 257a, b; 720a; vi, 994a; vii, 598a, 600b; viii, 197a
Abāẓa Muḥammad Katkhudā (XVIII) s, 44a
Ābāza Muḥammad Pasha (1771) i, **4b**; iv, 869b
Abazeed, Shaykh (Abū Yazīd) Al-Bistāmī (874) x, 71b
Abb → Ibb
ʿAbba → Libās
Abbā Djifār (XIX) ii, 545a-b; iii, 6a, 49a; x, 249a
ʿAbbād ii, 570a
ʿAbbād, Banū → ʿAbbādids
ʿAbbād b. Akhdār al-Tamīmī (681) vii, 123b
ʿAbbād b. Djulanda (ʿUmān) (VII) i, 451a; 812b; s, 693b

ʿAbbād b. Ḥusayn al-Ḥibatī (780) vi, 920b
ʿAbbād b. Muḥammad → al-Muʿtadid bi-'llāh
ʿAbbād b. Sulaymān al-Ṣaymarī (864) i, **4b**; iv, 985b, 1162b; v, 97a, 576b, 806a; vii, 784b; ix, 202b, 382a; x, 343b; xi, 7a-b; s, 226b, 391b
ʿAbbād b. Ziyād (VII) i, **5a**; iii, 882a; iv, 536a; vi, 545a; s, 508a
ʿAbbād Ibn D̲j̲amāʿa (XIV) vii, 407b
ʿAbbādān i, **5a**, 927b, 1244b; ii, 250b; iii, 1015a; iv, 1b, 6a, 7b, 674b, 906a, 1038b, 1057a, 1086a, 1171b; v, 65b, 80a; v, 573a, 865b; vi, 664b, 919b, 920b, 921b; vii, 887b; viii, 840a; ix, 57a, 369a, 523a; x, 173b, 766a; xi, 446a; s, 32a, 48b, 57a, 291a
al-ʿAbbādī, Abū ʿĀṣim (1066) i, **5b**
ʿAbbādids/ʿAbbād, Banū (XI) i, **5b**, 862a, 1238a, 1338b; ii, 243a; iii, 791a; v, 632b; vi, 606b; vii, 292b; viii, 617b
ʿAbbās, amīr (1146) ix, 437b
ʿAbbās, Banū (Kabylia) iv, 361a, b, 478a
ʿAbbās I, S̲h̲āh (Ṣafawid) (1629) i, **7b**, 15a, 95a, 190a, 228b, 240b, 267b, 553b, 625b, 643a, 685b, 701a, 707b, 904a, 942b, 1013a, 1066a, 1067a, 1068a, 1117a; ii, 16b, 104a, 283a, 976a, 1083b; iii, 157b, 210b, 214a, 348a,b, 1101b, 1190a; iv, 36a, 50a, 98a, 103a, 695a, 976b, 1041a, 1044a; v, 245a, 371a, 457b, 493a, 663b, 829b, 908b, 1113b; vi, 714b, 715a, b, 762b, 939a; vii, 224a, 317a, 600b, 928b;viii, 115b, 116a,b, 769a; s, 63a, 94b, 139a, b, 140a, b, 238a, 239a, 274b, 275a, 308a
ʿAbbās II, S̲h̲āh (Ṣafawid) (1666) i, 228b, 243a, 1068a; iii, 1102b; iv, 977a; v, 493b, 869a, 1089b, 1114a; vii, 61b, 224a, 318a, 476a; viii, 770b; s, 139a, 276a
ʿAbbās III, S̲h̲āh (Ṣafawid) (1749) ii, 310b; viii, 771b
al-ʿAbbās (al-Kūfa) (817) vi, 335b
al-ʿAbbās b. ʿAbd al-Muṭṭalib (653) i, **8b**, 15a, 80a, 152b; ii, 726a; iii, 328a; iv, 320a; vi, 335a, 660a; vii, 369b, 371b; s, 92b
ʿAbbās b. Abi 'l-Futūḥ (1154) i, **9a**, 196b, 198b; ii, 318a
al-ʿAbbās b. Aḥmad b. Ṭūlūn (Ṭūlūnid) (IX) i, 250b; v, 49a; vi, 452b; s, **1a**
al-ʿAbbās b. al-Aḥnaf (808) i, **9b**, 587a, 1081b; ii, 1031b; iii, 1202b, 1262a; iv, 489a; vi, 253a, 468b; vii, 566b, 694b
al-ʿAbbās b. ʿAlī b. Abī Ṭālib (680) iii, 609b, 610a, 611a; v, 823a; s, 95a
al-ʿAbbās b. ʿAmr al-G̲h̲anawī (917) i, **11a**; vii, 760b
al-ʿAbbās b. D̲j̲aʿfar (VIII) s, 326b
al-ʿAbbās b. al-Faḍl, amīr (861) iv, 733a
ʿAbbās b. Firnās (887) i, **11a**, 83a; ii, 1038a; viii, 616a, 632a,b
al-ʿAbbās b. al-Ḥasan al-D̲j̲ard̲j̲arāʾī → al-D̲j̲ard̲j̲arāʾī
al-ʿAbbās b. al-Ḥusayn al-S̲h̲īrāzī (973) i, **11b**; ii, 827a; iii, 730a
al-ʿAbbās b. ʿĪsā b. Mūsā (IX) vi, 332b
al-ʿAbbās b. al-Maʾmūn (838) i, **11b**; vi, 337b, 338a, b, 379a; vii, 776b
al-ʿAbbās b. Mandīl (XIII) vi, 404a
al-ʿAbbās b. Mirdās al-Sulaymī (VII) i, **12a**, 343b; ii, 1023b; iv, 832a; ix, 388b, 817a, 865a
al-ʿAbbās b. Muḥammad b. ʿAlī (802) i, **12b**; iv, 871a
al-ʿAbbās b. Mūsā b. ʿĪsā (813) vi, 334a
al-ʿAbbās b. al-Musayyib (811) vi, 333a
ʿAbbās b. Nāṣiḥ al-T̲h̲aḳafī (852) i, **12b**
al-ʿAbbās b. Saʿīd (Saʿd) (VIII) vii, 629b
al-ʿAbbās b. Saʿīd al-D̲j̲awharī (828) vi, 600a; x, 368a; s, 411b, 412b, 414a
ʿAbbās b. S̲h̲īt̲h̲ (G̲h̲ūrid) (XI) ii, 1100a
al-ʿAbbās b. al-Walīd I (Umayyad) (750) i, **12b**, 57b, 1244a; ii, 715a; vi, 506a, 740a
ʿAbbās Ag̲h̲a (XVIII) vii, 653a
ʿAbbās Āḳā Ṣarrāf (XX) s, 365a
ʿAbbās Efendī → ʿAbd al-Bahāʾ / Bahāʾīs
ʿAbbās Ḥamāda (XX) vi, 170a
ʿAbbās Ḥilmī I Pas̲h̲a, viceroy (1854) i, **13a**, 396a, 815a; ii, 149a, 423b; iv, 775b; vi, 75a; vii, 182b, 428b, 429b
ʿAbbās Ḥilmī II, K̲h̲edive (1944) i, **13a**, 817b; iii, 515a; vii, 438a, 715a; s, 39b, 123a, 300a
ʿAbbās Huwaydā (amīr) (XX) vii, 450a
ʿAbbās al-Ḳaṣṣāb, S̲h̲ayk̲h̲ (XX) vi, 614a
ʿAbbās al-Ḳaṭṭān (XX) vi, 165b, 175b
ʿAbbās K̲h̲ān (Trākāne) (1822) s, 327b
ʿAbbās-ḳulī K̲h̲ān Ādamiyyat (XX) s, 291a
ʿAbbās Ḳulī K̲h̲ān Lārīd̲j̲ānī Sartīp (XIX) v, 664a
al-ʿAbbās al-Mag̲h̲rāwī (XIII) vi, 404a
ʿAbbās Mīrzā (Ḳād̲j̲ār) (1833) i, **13b**, 15a, 626a; ii, 839a, 952a; iii, 1103b, 1109a; iv,

163b, 391b, 392a, b, 462a, 861b, 1047b; v, 919a; vi, 484a, 502b, 551b, 715a
ʿAbbās Mīrzā III (Ḳād̲j̲ār) (1735) vi, 56a
ʿAbbās Mīrzā Mulk-ārā (Ḳād̲j̲ār) (XIX) iv, 393b
ʿAbbās Sarwānī (XVI) s, **1b**
ʿAbbās al-S̲h̲ihābī, amīr (XIX) ii, 444a, 636a
ʿAbbāsa (town) i, **14b**
ʿAbbāsa bint Aḥmad b. Ṭūlūn (IX) i, 14b
ʿAbbāsa bint al-Mahdī (VIII) i, **14a**; s, 263a
ʿAbbāsābād i, **14b**
ʿAbbāsī → Sikka
al-ʿAbbāsī, ʿAbd al-Laṭīf (XVII) ix, 4b
al-ʿAbbāsī, Muḥammad al-Mahdī (XIX) i, 819b; s, 411b
ʿAbbāsids i, **15a**, 33a, 34a, 43a, 59a, 102a, 103b, 124b, 125a, 141a, 149a, 381a, 386b, 402b, 530a, 550b, 1352a; ii, 74b, 168b, 281a, 551b, 951a; iii, 265a, 984b; iv, 15b-17b, 44b-45b, 939a; v, 326a, 347b, 620b, 736a, 1233a; vi, 1b, 2a, 11a, 118b, 194a, 261a, 352a, 434a, 518a, b, 519a, b, 549b, 665a, 668b, 669b, 670a, 674b, 676a, 849b, 880b; vii, 43b, 160a, 191b; ix, 265a, b, 593b; xi, 185a; s, 31b
– administration ii, 78a, 143a, 144a, 304b, 305a, 324a, 890b; iv, 755a, b, 939a-943a, 973b
– art, architecture i, 561a, 616a; ii, 745b, 1054b; v, 216b
– history i, 118a; iii, 899b, 925b; v, 488a
ʿAbbāsiyya (Cairo) s, 208b
al-ʿAbbāsiyya (Ifrīḳiya) i, **24a**, 248a, 815b; iv, 829a; s, 144a
ʿAbbāsiyya (military academy) s, 5b
Abbottābād iii, 336a
Abbreviations s, **2a**
ʿAbbūd, Ibrāhīm (Sūdān) (XX) v, 1064b; ix, 749a
ʿAbd/ʿabīd i, **24b**, 47a, 371a, 490b, 1060a; ii, 133b, 858b, 1079b, 1081a; iii, 3a, 277a, 345b; iv, 82b, 83a, 282b, 567a, 738a, 1116a; v, 58a, 358b, 359a, 856b, 942a, 1248b; viii, 879b
ʿAbd b. Ḥumayd (863) vii, 691b
ʿAbd al-Aḥad Abū Aḥmad Sirhindī (1578) s, 313a
ʿAbd al-Aḥad K̲h̲ān Mangït al-Buk̲h̲ārī, Amīr (1910) i, 1296a; vi, 419a, 765a
ʿAbd al-ʿĀl (1332) i, 280b; x, 189a
ʿAbd al-ʿAlī al-Lakhnawī → Baḥr al-ʿUlūm, ʿAbd al-ʿAlī al-Lakhnawī
ʿAbd al-ʿAlī Niẓām al-Dīn b. Muḥammad Bīrd̲j̲andī (1527) x, 146a
ʿAbd Allāh, ʿA.H. (1973) v, 190a
ʿAbd Allāh, (king) → ʿAbd Allāh b. al-Ḥusayn
ʿAbd Allāh, Mawlāy → ʿAbd Allāh b. Ismāʿīl
ʿAbd Allāh, S̲h̲arīf (1877) vi, 151a
ʿAbd Allāh I (Ag̲h̲labid) (817) i, 248a, **250a**; iii, 982a; ix, 584a
ʿAbd Allāh II (Ag̲h̲labid) (903) i, **250b**, 986b; iii, 982b
ʿAbd Allāh II (ʿAbd al-Wādid) → ʿAbd al-Wādids
ʿAbd Allāh III (Āl Ṣabāḥ) (1965) viii, 669a
ʿAbd Allāh III b. ʿAd̲j̲īb III (Ḳerrī) (1747) iv, 893a
ʿAbd Allāh (Umayyad) → ʿAbd Allāh b. Muḥammad b. ʿAbd al-Raḥmān
ʿAbd Allāh b. al-ʿAbbās (686) i, **40a**, 55b, 107a, 567b; ii, 219b, 359b, 416a, 480b, 888b, 1071a; iii, 235b, 241a, 242a, 370b, 608b, 649a, 1081b; iv, 767b; v, 406b; vi, 218a, 636a, 657b, 661a, 666b, 668b, 669b, 738a; vii, 75a, 100a, 262a, 293a, 758a; ix, 422a; s, 311a, b, 358a
ʿAbd Allāh b. ʿAbbō (XVI) i, 1343a
ʿAbd Allāh b. ʿAbd al-ʿAzīz b. ʿAbd al-Ḥaḳḳ (1159) v, 60b, 61a
ʿAbd Allāh b. ʿAbd al-ʿAzīz b. Musāʿad (XX) i, 1313a
ʿAbd Allāh b. ʿAbd al-D̲j̲alīl vi, 264b
ʿAbd Allāh b. ʿAbd al-Ḥakam → Ibn ʿAbd al-Ḥakam, ʿAbd Allāh
ʿAbd Allāh b. ʿAbd al-Ḳādir (1854) i, **41b**
ʿAbd Allāh b. ʿAbd al-Karīm (Marʿas̲h̲ī) (1467) vi, 513b
ʿAbd Allāh b. ʿAbd al-Malik (Umayyad) (703) i, **42a**; v, 500a; vi, 774b; vii, 408b
ʿAbd Allāh b. ʿAbd al-Muʾmin (XII) i, 160b; iii, 138b; s, 113b
ʿAbd Allāh b. ʿAbd al-Muṭṭalib (570) i, **42b**, 80a, 438b
ʿAbd Allāh b. ʿAbd al-Raḥmān I (IX) iii, 74a, 495a; iv, 254b, 672b
ʿAbd Allāh b. ʿAbd al-Raḥmān b. Abī Bakr (1513) ii, 730a
ʿAbd Allāh b. ʿAbd al-Ẓāhir → Ibn ʿAbd al-Ẓāhir

ʿAbd Allāh b. Abī ʿAmr b. Ḥafs b. al-Mug͟hīra (680) vi, 140a
ʿAbd Allāh b. Abī Bakr (VII) i, 109b, 110a, 738a
ʿAbd Allāh b. Abī Bakr al-Miyānad͟jī (1131) i, 840a, 841a; x, 322b; s, **2b**, **104b**
ʿAbd Allāh b. Abi ʾl-D͟jawād (IX) i, 249b
ʿAbd Allāh b. Abī Isḥāḳ (735) i, **42b**; iii, 1262a
ʿAbd Allāh b. Abī Rabīʿa b. al-Mug͟hīra Mak͟hzūmī (631) vi, 138b, 140b; vii, 862b
ʿAbd Allāh b. Abī Sarḥ → ʿAbd Allāh b. Saʿd
ʿAbd Allāh b. Abī Yūsuf, Amīr (Marīnid) (1262) vi, 593a
ʿAbd Allāh b. ʿAdī (976) vii, 576b; viii, 516b
ʿAbd Allāh b. Aḥmad b. Ḥanbal (903) i, 273b; iii, 158b; s, 16a
ʿAbd Allāh b. Aḥmad b. K͟halīfa (1849) ii, 108b; iv, 953a
ʿAbd Allāh b. ʿAlawī al-Haddād (1720) i, 829b
ʿAbd Allāh b. ʿAlī (ʿAbbāsid) (764) i, 16a, 17a, **43a**, 103a, 108b, 773a; ii, 281a; iii, 292b, 398a, 991a; vi, 333b, 427b, 921b; vii, 910b
ʿAbd Allāh b. ʿAlī al-ʿAbs͟hamī (VII) s, 26a
ʿAbdallāh bin Alī bin Nassir, Sayid (1820) iv, 886b, 887a; vi, 612b
ʿAbd Allāh b. ʿAlī al-ʿUyūnī (XI) iv, 664a
ʿAbd Allāh b. ʿAlī b. Zannūn (1229) vi, 222b
ʿAbd Allāh b. al-Amīn (IX) s, 116b
ʿAbd Allāh b. ʿĀmir (680) i, **43b**, 47b, 107a, 304a, 441a, 695b, 1130a; ii, 811b; iii, 304a; iv, 14b, 220a; v, 56b; vi, 620a; viii, 62b; ix, 34a
ʿAbd Allāh b. ʿAmr b. al-ʿĀṣ viii, 41a
ʿAbd Allāh b. ʿAmr al-Kindī (VIII) i, 48b; iv, 837b, 838a
ʿAbd Allāh b. Asad → al-Yāfiʿī
ʿAbd Allāh b. ʿAṣim (1013) vii, 82b
ʿAbd Allāh b. ʿAṭāʾ al-Makkī (VIII) vii, 398a
ʿAbd Allāh b. ʿAwn (767) ix, 771a
ʿAbd Allāh b. ʿAwn b. Arṭabān (639) vi, 920a
ʿAbd Allāh b. Abī Bakr al-Miyāmid͟jī (ʿAyn al-ḳuḍāt al-Hamad͟hānī) ix, 862b
ʿAbd Allāh b. Barrī → Ibn Barrī, Abū Muḥammad
ʿAbd Allāh b. Bū G͟hāba (XIX) vi, 251a
ʿAbd Allāh b. Budayl (VII) iv, 99b; v, 354b
ʿAbd Allāh b. Bulayhid (XX) v, 998b; vi, 156b
ʿAbd Allāh b. Buluggīn (Zīrid) (1082) i, **43b**, 251a, 600a; ii, 1013a, 1016b; vi, 222b; vii, 553a
ʿAbd Allāh b. Burayda (733) vii, 576a
ʿAbd Allāh b. Dīnār vi, 263a
ʿAbd Allāh b. D͟jabala b. Ḥayyān al-Kinānī (834) iii, 1151a
ʿAbd Allāh b. D͟jaʿfar b. Abī Ṭālib (699) i, **44a**; ii, 372b; iii, 608b, 819b, 889b; vi, 344b; s, 92b
ʿAbd Allāh b. D͟jaʿfar al-Ṣādiḳ (VIII) vii, 645b
ʿAbd Allāh b. D͟jahm (IX) viii, 89b
ʿAbd Allāh b. D͟jaḥs͟h (VII) i, **44b**; v, 316a
ʿAbd Allāh b. D͟jalwī Āl Suʿūd (XX) i, 1313a
ʿAbd Allāh b. D͟jarīr al-Bad͟jalī (VII) iv, 1106b
ʿAbd Allāh b. D͟judʿān (VI) i, **44b**, 115b; iii, 389b, 739a; iv, 821a; s, 247a, 380b
ʿAbd Allāh b. Fayṣal b. ʿAbd al-ʿAzīz (Āl Suʿūd) (XX) vi, 156a; s, 305b
ʿAbd Allāh b. Fayṣal b. Turkī (Āl Suʿūd) (1887) ii, 176b; ix, 904a
ʿAbd Allāh b. Fūdī (1828) v, 222b; vii, 435b
ʿAbd Allāh b. G͟haṭafān, Banū s, 225b
ʿAbd Allāh b. al-Ḥaḍramī → Ibn al-Ḥaḍramī
ʿAbd Allāh b. Ḥamdān (Ḥamdānid) (902) ii, 453a; iii, 126b; v, 451b; vi, 900a
ʿAbd Allāh b. Hammām b. al-Salūlī (715) i, **45a**
ʿAbd Allāh b. Ḥamza → al-Manṣūr bi-ʾllāh
ʿAbd Allāh b. Ḥanẓala (683) i, **45a**, 50a, 55a; iii, 226b, 227a; v, 997a
ʿAbd Allāh b. Ḥarb → ʿAbd Allāh b. ʿAmr al-Kindī
ʿAbd Allāh b. al-Ḥārit͟h (VIII) s, 233a
ʿAbd Allāh b. al-Ḥārit͟h b. Nawfal al-Hās͟himī (Babba) (VIII) vii, 877b, 1045b
ʿAbd Allāh b. al-Ḥasan b. al-Ḥasan (ʿAlid) (762) i, **45b**; iii, 615b, 786b, 984a; vi, 334b; vii, 348a
ʿAbd Allāh b. Ḥasan b. Ḥusayn b. ʿAlī b. Ḥusayn b. Muḥammad b. ʿAbd al-Wahhāb (XX) vi, 156b

ʿAbd Allāh b. Ḥasan Āl al-Shaykh (XX) vi, 157a
ʿAbd Allāh b. Ḥātim (Ḥamdānid) (1110) iii, 125b
ʿAbd Allāh b. Ḥaydara (XIX) i, 345a
ʿAbd Allāh b. Hilāl al-Ḥimyarī al-Kūfī (VIII) i, **45b**
ʿAbd Allāh b. Ḥumayd b. Ḳaḥtaba (811) v, 855b; vi, 333b; x, 348b
ʿAbd Allāh b. Ḥumayyid al-Sālimī (1944) i, 736a; s, 356a
ʿAbd Allāh b. Hurmuz (Baṣra) (780) vi, 878b
ʿAbd Allāh b. Ḥusayn (Marāgha) (893) vi, 499a
ʿAbd Allāh b. al-Ḥusayn, Amīr (Hāshimite) (1951) i, **46a**, 447b; ii, 662b; iii, 264b, 605a, 606b, 1065b, 1066a; iv, 262a; v, 337b, 1053b, 1054b; vi, 31b, 262a; viii, 246a; x, 885b, 886b; s, 70a, 301a
ʿAbd Allāh b. al-Ḥusayn Rawāḥī (1166) viii, 459b
ʿAbd Allāh b. ʿIbāḍ (VII) i, 810a; iii, 648a, 651b; vii, 858b; s, 337b
ʿAbd Allāh b. Ibrāhīm al-Aghlab → ʿAbd Allāh I/II (Aghlabid)
ʿAbd Allāh b. Ibrāhīm b. Shāhrukh (Tīmūrid) (1451) i, 91a, 135a, 147b, 227b; iii, 989b; s, 51a
ʿAbd Allāh b. Ibrāhīm al-Mismaʿī (X) iii, 1015b, iv, 100a
ʿAbd Allāh b. Ibrāhīm al-Nadjdī (XVII) iii, 677b
ʿAbd Allāh b. Idrīs II (Idrīsid) (IX) vi, 742b
ʿAbd Allāh b. Idrīs al-Djaʿfarī (XI) i, 784a
ʿAbd Allāh b. Iskandar (Shaybānid) (1598) i, **46b**, 1295b; ii, 45a, 446a; vi, 621a; ix, 429a; s, 340a, b
ʿAbd Allāh b. Ismāʿīl, Mawlāy (ʿAlawid) (1757) i, **47a**, 356a; ii, 510b, 820a; v, 1192a; vi, 595a; vii, 39a, 387a
ʿAbd Allāh b. ʿItbān (VII) iv, 99b
ʿAbd Allāh b. Ḳaḥṭān (Yaʿfurid) (X) ii, 854a; iv, 199b
ʿAbd Allāh b. Ḳāsim al-Fihrī (al-Bunt) (XI) i, 1309b; iii, 496a
ʿAbd Allāh b. Ḳāsim al-Ẓāhirī (885) i, 600a
ʿAbd Allāh b. Ḳawām al-Dīn (Marʿashī) (1360) vi, 511b
ʿAbd Allāh b. Kerrīw al-Laghwāṭī (1921) vi, 251a
ʿAbd Allāh b. Khālid b. Asīd (VII) s, 26a
ʿAbd Allāh b. Khaṭal (VII) iv, 821a
ʿAbd Allāh b. Khāzim al-Sulamī (692) i, 3b, **47b**, 86a, 1293a; viii, 62b
ʿAbd Allāh b. Khurdhādhbah (IX) iv, 645b
ʿAbd Allāh b. Kulayb b. Thaʿlaba (IX) vi, 568a
ʿAbd Allāh b. Lahīʿa (790) xi, 179b; s, 87b
ʿAbd Allāh b. Maḥfūf al-Munadjdjim (1265) iv, 1130a
ʿAbd Allāh b. Maḥmūd al-Shāshī i, 147a
ʿAbd Allāh b. Mālik (XI) iv, 1127a
ʿAbd Allāh b. al-Maʾmūn (ʿAbbāsid) (808) vi, 331b, 332b
ʿAbd Allāh (ʿUbayd Allāh) b. Marwān II (Umayyad) (746) i, 16a; ii, 90b, 234b; vi, 624a, 641b
ʿAbd Allāh b. Masʿūd → Ibn Masʿūd, ʿAbd Allāh
ʿAbd Allāh b. Maṭar (Abū Rayḥāna) (VII) vii, 564b
ʿAbd Allāh b. Maymūn (VIII) i, **48a**; ii, 170a, 301a, 850b, 851b; iii, 1072a
ʿAbd Allāh b. Mazdalī (XII) ii, 1013a
ʿAbd Allāh b. Muʿāwiya (748) i, **48b**, 53b; ii, 441a; iii, 1266a; iv, 44b, 99b, 837a, 838a; v, 63b; vi, 427b, 624b; vii, 359b, 1016a; s, 233a
ʿAbd Allāh b. al-Mubārak → Ibn al-Mubārak, ʿAbd Allāh
ʿAbd Allāh b. al-Mughīra b. Saʿīd al-Badj alī vii, 348a
ʿAbd Allāh b. Muḥammad, Sharīf → Makka
ʿAbd Allāh b. Muḥammad (Mīkālī) (915) vii, 26a
ʿAbd Allāh b. Muḥammad b. ʿAbd Allāh (VIII) vii, 389a
ʿAbd Allāh b. Muḥammad b. ʿAbd al-Laṭīf, Shaykh (XX) iii, 1065a
ʿAbd Allāh b. Muḥammad b. Lubb (X) s, 80a
ʿAbd Allāh b. Muḥammad b. ʿAbd al-Raḥmān al-Marwānī (Umayyad, al-Andalus) (912) i, **49a**, 83b, 85b, 634a; iv, 665b; vi, 222a, 520b, 568a, 852a; vii, 569a; s, 153a
ʿAbd Allāh b. Muḥammad b. ʿAbd al-Salām (Abdullahi Sikka) iv, 550a
ʿAbd Allāh b. Muḥammad b. ʿAbd al-Wahhāb (1827) iii, 678b; xi, 41a

ʿAbd Allāh b. Muḥammad b. Maslama → Ibn al-Afṭas
ʿAbd Allāh b. Muḥammad b. Saʿd (ṣāḥib al-basīṭ) (1146) i, 1083a
ʿAbd Allāh b. Muḥammad Āl Muʿammar (1726) ii, 321a
ʿAbd Allāh b. Muḥammad Fūdī (XIX) ii, 942a, 1145a, b, 1146a, b; iii, 276b; vii, 435b; viii, 17a
ʿAbd Allāh b. Muḥammad Ghāzī (XX) vi, 175b
ʿAbd Allāh b. Muḥammad al-Kātib (X) i, 1309a; iv, 830a
ʿAbd Allāh b. Muḥammad Ḳuṭb Shāhī (1672) vii, 93b; s, 302a
ʿAbd Allāh b. Muḥammad al-Māzandarānī (1363) ii, 81a; iv, 1035a
ʿAbd Allāh b. Muḥammad al-Nāshiʾ al-Akbar (906) viii, 378a
ʿAbd Allāh b. Muḥammad al-Taʿāʾishī (Abdullāhi) (Khalīfa) (1899) i, **49b**, 765a, 962a; ii, 124a; iv, 687a, 952b, 953a; v, 268a, 1249a-1251b; viii, 170b
ʿAbd Allāh b. al-Muʿizz (Zīride) (XI) vii, 483b
ʿAbd Allāh b. al-Muḳaffaʿ → Ibn al-Muḳaffaʿ, ʿAbd Allāh
ʿAbd Allāh b. Mūsā b. Nuṣayr (720) i, **50a**; vi, 221b, 926b
ʿAbd Allāh b. Musʿab b. Thābit (800) xi, 243a
ʿAbd Allāh b. Muslim (VIII) i, 1033b
ʿAbd Allāh b. al-Muʿtazz → Ibn al-Muʿtazz
ʿAbd Allāh b. Muṭīʿ (692) i, 45a, **50a**; iii, 226b, 227b; vii, 522a
ʿAbd Allāh b. Nāfiʿ al-Azraḳ (VIII) vii, 398b
ʿAbd Allāh b. Nawf i, 850b
ʿAbd Allāh b. Nawfal, ḳāḍī (VII) vi, 671a
ʿAbd Allāh b. Rabīʿ (VIII) iii, 650b
ʿAbd Allāh b. Rabīʿa b. Riyāḥ al-Hilālī (VII) s, 92b
ʿAbd Allāh b. al-Rand (XII) ii, 463b; iv, 415b; v, 1181b
ʿAbd Allāh b. Rashīd → Rashīd, Āl
ʿAbd Allāh b. Rawāḥa (629) i, **50b**, 968b; ii, 372a; iii, 354a; iv, 835b, 1187b; v, 398b; vi, 604a; vii, 756b; viii, 118b, 459b
ʿAbd Allāh b. Sabaʾ (VIII) i, **51a**, 382b; ii, 1094a; iii, 1164a; vii, 399a; viii, 387a; ix, 420b
ʿAbd Allāh b. Saʿd b. Abī Sarḥ (656) i, **51b**, 115a, 451b, 966a, 1029a, 1157b; ii, 131a, 327b, 525b, 615a; iv, 825b; v, 90b; vii, 154a, 156b, 393a, 394b; viii, 38a, 84b, 862b
ʿAbd Allāh b. Salām (663) i, **52a**, 1020b; ii, 363a; iii, 1232b; iv, 212a, 824b; vi, 636b
ʿAbd Allāh b. Ṣāliḥ (XII) ix, 9b; s, 397a
ʿAbd Allāh b. Salīm (VIII) vii, 807a
ʿAbd Allāh b. Sālim (Āl Ṣabāḥ) (XX) v, 575a
ʿAbd Allāh b. Sayf al-Dawla (Ḥamdānid) (949) vi, 930a
ʿAbd Allāh b. Shaykh ʿAydarūs (1662) i, **781b**
ʿAbd Allāh b. al-Shaykh (Marrākush) (1607) vi, 594b
ʿAbd Allāh b. al-Ṣimma ix, 777a
ʿAbd Allāh b. Sinān (IX) iv, 117a
ʿAbd Allāh b. Sulṭān Maḥmūd (Marʿashī) (1561) vi, 514b, 515a
ʿAbd Allāh b. Suʿūd (Āl Suʿūd) (1818) ii, 321a; iii, 362b, 999a; ix, 903b
ʿAbd Allāh b. Ṭāhir I b. al-Ḥusayn (Ṭāhirid) (844) i, **52b**, 99b, 121b, 154a, 157b, 241a, 619a, 685a, 789b; ii, 524a; iii, 1083a; iv, 17a, 20b, 531a, 646a, b; v, 57b, 872b, 923a; vi, 336b, 337a, b, 707b, 775a; vii, 18b, 160b, 1016b; viii, 62b; x, 104b, 227b; s, 15a
ʿAbd Allāh b. Ṭarīf (VIII) iii, 659b
ʿAbd Allāh b. Thawr → Abū Fudayk, ʿAbd Allāh b. Thawr
ʿAbd Allāh b. Thunayyan (1841) ix, 904a
ʿAbd Allāh b. Ubayy b. Salūl al-Khazradjī (631) i, **53a**, 307b, 514b, 1283a; iv, 824b, 1187b; v, 996b; vii, 356b, 367a, 373b, 561b, 852b; s, 133b
ʿAbd Allāh b. ʿUfayṣān (XIX) iv, 751a
ʿAbd Allāh b. ʿUmar I b. al-Khaṭṭāb (693) i, 40a, 50b, **53b**, 382b; iii, 65a; vi, 263a, 278b, 658a; vii, 522a, 783b; x, 33a
ʿAbd Allāh b. ʿUmar II b. ʿAbd al-ʿAzīz (749) i, 49a, **53b**, 257b; ii, 90a, 744b; v, 731a; vi, 624a
ʿAbd Allāh b. ʿUmar al-ʿArdjī → al-ʿArdjī
ʿAbd Allāh b. ʿUmāra (921) s, 223a
ʿAbd Allāh b. Unays al-Anṣārī (VII) v, 315b; vi, 658b
ʿAbd Allāh b. Unays al-Djuhanī (VII) iii, 540b; v, 315b
ʿAbd Allāh b. ʿUthmān Faḍlī (XX) ii, 737a
ʿAbd Allāh b. Wahb al-Ḳurashī → Ibn Wahb, ʿAbd Allāh al-Ḳurashī

ʿAbd Allāh b. Wahb al-Rāsibī (658) i, **54b**; iii, 235a; iv, 1074b, 1075a; vi, 280b; vii, 912b
ʿAbd Allāh b. Yaḥyā al-Kindī → Ṭālib al-Haḳḳ
ʿAbd Allāh b. Yāsīn al-Gazūlī (or Djazūlī) (Almoravid) (1057) i, 762a, 864a, 1044b, 1176a; ii, 527a, 1121b; v, 653b, 654a, b; vi, 742b, 744a; vii, 584b, 613a; s, 27a
ʿAbd Allāh b. Yazīd (Ibāḍī) (VIII) viii, 387b; s, 225b
ʿAbd Allāh b. Zaynab (Medina) (796) vi, 263b
ʿAbd Allāh b. al-Ziʿbarā (mukhaḍram) s, 91a
ʿAbd Allāh b. al-Zubayr (692) i, 41a, 45a, 50b, **54b**, 76b, 77a, 107a, 113b, 115a, 148b, 443b, 453b, 482a, 550a, 704a, b, 713b, 784b, 810a; ii, 89b, 197a, 360a, 415a; iii, 40a, 226b, 270b, 573b, 607b, 608b, 620b, 970a, 1254b; iv, 319a, 493a, 938a, 1075b; v, 997a, 1231a, 1232a; vi, 139a, 140a, b, 147a, 149a, 344a, 544b, 545a, 622a, 660b, 669a, 708b; vii, 97b, 267b, 268a, b, 357a, 358b, 400b, 403a, 521a, b, 546a, 649b, 694a, 858b; viii, 119a, 997a; ix, 901b; x, 843a; s, 26a, 230b, 311a, b, 357b
ʿAbd Allāh al-ʿAbdalkānī vii, 26a
ʿAbd Allāh Abū Djābir b. ʿAbd Allāh (625) s, 230a
ʿAbd Allāh Abu 'l-Djimāl, Sīdī v, 51a
ʿAbd Allāh Abū Yaʿḳūb b. Dāwūd (VIII) viii, 351a
ʿAbd Allāh Āl Khalīfa → ʿAbd Allāh b. Aḥmad b. Khalīfa
ʿAbd Allāh Āl Sulaymān Āl Ḥamdān (XX) vi, 156a
ʿAbd Allāh Āl Thānī (Ḳatar) (XX) ii, 177b
ʿAbd al-Allāh al-ʿAnbarī → ʿĀmir b. ʿAbd al-Ḳays
ʿAbd Allāh al-Ashʿarī (VIII) vi, 493a
ʿAbd Allāh al-Ashtar (VIII) vii, 389a
ʿAbd Allāh Awwal al-Islām, Sulṭān (Makassar) (VII) vi, 116b
ʿAbd Allāh al-Azraḳ b. al-Mughīra (VIII) vi, 140a
ʿAbd Allāh al-Balʿamī → Balʿamī
ʿAbd Allāh al-Balansī → ʿAbd Allāh b. ʿAbd al-Raḥmān I
ʿAbd Allāh al-Bayyāsī (1226) i, 1150b; ii, 516a
ʿAbd Allāh Bey (XVIII) s, 268a
ʿAbd Allāh Bosnevī (1644) i, 1271b
ʿAbd Allāh Djammāʿ al-Ḳāsimī (XVI) iv, 892b
ʿAbd Allāh Djewdet → Djewdet, ʿAbd Allāh
ʿAbd Allāh Dürri-zāde, Shaykh al-Islām (XX) vi, 984b
ʿAbd Allāh Efendi, Shaykh al-Islām (XVIII) vi, 800b
ʿAbd Allāh al-Ghālib bi-'llāh (Saʿdid) (1574) i, **55b**, 245a, 859b, 1224b; ii, 619b; vi, 591b, 594b, 596a, b, 597a, b; s, 377b
ʿAbd Allāh al-Ḥas, Shaykh (XX) s, 248a
ʿAbd Allāh Ilāhī, Mollā→ Ilāhī
ʿAbd Allāh Ḳādirī (XX) x, 961a
ʿAbd Allāh Ḳarshe (Abdullahi Qarshe) ix, 726a
ʿAbd Allāh al-Kātib → ʿAbd Allāh b. Muḥammad al-Kātib
ʿAbd Allāh al-Kāzarūnī (ʿālim) (1063) vi, 626b
ʿAbd Allāh Khān → Ḥasan ʿAlī Bārha
ʿAbd Allāh Khān (Ghazīpūr) (XVIII) s, 325b
ʿAbd Allāh Khān, Özbeg (Khīwā) (1598) vi, 310a; vii, 317a, 677a, 925a; viii, 749b
ʿAbd Allāh Khān, Özbeg (Khīwa) (1855) s, 46a
ʿAbd Allāh Khān, Özbeg (Khīwa) (1920) iv, 1065b
ʿAbd Allāh Khān b. Iskandar (Shaybānid) s, 340a, b
ʿAbd Allāh Khān Amīn al-Dawla (1847) vii, 453b, 454a
ʿAbd Allāh Khān Brahoi (XVII) i, 1005b
ʿAbd Allāh Khān-Ḳalʿa (town) vi, 619a, 621a
ʿAbd Allāh Khān Rohilla (XVIII) iii, 60a, b
ʿAbd Allāh Ḳuṭb al-Mulk → Ḥasan ʿAlī Bārha
ʿAbd Allāh Ḳuṭb Shāh (1672) iii, 318b, 319a, 427a; v, 549b; vi, 837b
ʿAbd Allāh al-Maghrāwī → Sīrat Baybars
ʿAbd Allāh Marwārīd iii, 490b
ʿAbd Allāh Menou (Miṣr) (XIX) vii, 180b
ʿAbd Allāh Mīrzā (Tīmūrid) → ʿAbd Allāh b. Ibrāhīm b. Shāhrukh
ʿAbd Allāh Niyāzī Sirhindī (XVI) ii, 500a, b; iii, 492b

ʿAbd Allāh Pas͟ha → Fikrī, ʿAbd Allāh Pas͟ha
ʿAbd Allāh Pas͟ha (ʿAkkā) (XIX) i, 1078b; ii, 210a, 636a; vii, 426b
ʿAbd Allāh Pas͟ha Muḥsin-Zāde Čelebi (1749) i, **56a**, 292a; iii, 132b
ʿAbd Allāh Reʾfet (poet) (XVIII) vi, 1000a
ʿAbd Allāh al-Riḍā → ʿAbd Allāh al-S͟hayk͟h al-Ṣāliḥ
ʿAbd Allāh Saʿd D͟jaʿalī (XIX) i, 765a; ii, 351b
ʿAbd Allāh al-Saksīwī (1350) vi, 593b
ʿAbd Allāh Ṣāliḥ Fārsī (1982) x, 195b
ʿAbd Allāh Sari → Sari ʿAbd Allāh Efendī
ʿAbd Allāh Sarrād͟j (XX) vi, 152b
ʿAbd Allāh Sulṭānpūrī, Mak͟hdūm al-Mulk, b. S͟hams al-Dīn (1582) s, **3a**
ʿAbd Allāh S͟haḳrūn (XX) vi, 755b
ʿAbd Allāh S͟haṭṭārī, S͟hayk͟h (1485) i, 1284a
ʿAbd Allāh al-S͟haybī (XX) vi, 156b
ʿAbd Allāh al-S͟hayk͟h al-Ṣāliḥ iii, 262b
ʿAbd Allāh ʿUmar Balk͟hayr (XX) vi, 177b, 179a
ʿAbd Allāh ʿUrayf (XX) vi, 176b
ʿAbd Allāh Zāk͟hir, S͟hammās (1734) vi, 796b
ʿAbd Allāh al-Wazīr (XX) vi, 566b
ʿAbd al-ʿAllām Fayẓ K͟hān Og͟hlu (XIX) iv, 505a
ʿAbd ʿAmr → ʿAbd al-Raḥmān b. ʿAwf
ʿAbd al-As͟hhal (Āl ʿAbd al-As͟hhal) i, 771b; viii, 897b
ʿAbd al-ʿAẓīm b. Zayn al-ʿĀbidīn (Marʿas͟hī) (1400) vi, 512b
ʿAbd al-ʿAẓīm Mīrzā, Sayyid i, 262b
ʿAbd al-ʿAzīz → ʿAbd al-ʿAzīz b. al-Ḥasan
ʿAbd al-ʿAzīz (Banū ʿAbbās) (XVI) iv, 478a
ʿAbd al-ʿAzīz (G͟halzay) (1715) i, 229a; iii, 603b
ʿAbd al-ʿAzīz I (Marīnid) → Abū Farīs ʿAbd al-ʿAzīz I
ʿAbd al-ʿAzīz (Ottoman) (1876) i, **56b**, 285b, 286b, 397b, 836b, 948a; ii, 49a, 935b; iii, 250a, 621b; iv, 876a; vi, 68a, b, 69a, 342a, 372b, 758a; viii, 59b s, 281b
ʿAbd al-ʿAzīz (amīr) (Marrākūs͟h) (1353) vi, 593b
ʿAbd al-ʿAzīz, Mawlāy → ʿAbd al-ʿAzīz b. al-Ḥasan
ʿAbd al-ʿAzīz (Mountains) vi, 539b
ʿAbd al-ʿAzīz, Özbeg K͟hān (1670) vi, 856a
ʿAbd al-ʿAzīz b. ʿAbd al-Ḥaḳḳ (K͟hurāsān, Banū) (1105) v, 60a
ʿAbd al-ʿAzīz b. ʿAbd al-Ḳādir b. G͟haybī (XV) i, 67a
ʿAbd al-ʿAzīz b. ʿAbd al-Muṭṭalib, ḳādī (VIII) vi, 140a
ʿAbd al-ʿAzīz b. ʿAbd al-Raḥmān b. al-Fayṣal (Āl Suʿūd) (1953) i, 39a, 233b, 443b, 555b, 709b, 762a, 885b, 958a, 1299a, 1313a; ii, 77a, 108b, 175b, 176b, 354a, 569a, 573a, 626a, 660a; iii, 238a, 263b, 326b, 361b, 365a, 643b, 1062a, 1064b, 1066a, b; iv, 680b, 703b, 765b, 925b, 1073a; v, 63a, 574b, 575a, 998a, 999a; vi, 33a, 34a, 45b, 151b, 152b, 153a, 154b, 155a, 169b, 262a, 306b; vii, 422a, 782b; viii, 246a; ix, 904a; s, **3b**, 4b, 293b, 305b
ʿAbd al-ʿAzīz b. ʿAbd al-Raḥmān al-Azdī (817) vi, 335b
ʿAbd al-ʿAzīz b. ʿAbd al-Raḥmān b. Abī ʿĀmir (Balansiya, ʿĀmirid) (1041) i, 446a, 985b; vi, 344b, 576b
ʿAbd al-ʿAzīz b. ʿAbd al-Salām (1262) ix, 436a
ʿAbd al-ʿAzīz b. Abī Dulaf (873) ii, 623b; iv, 100a
ʿAbd al-ʿAzīz b. Abī Ḥāzim (VIII) vi, 280b
ʿAbd al-ʿAzīz b. D͟jaʿfar → G͟hulām al-K͟hallāl
ʿAbd al-ʿAzīz b. Fayṣal al-Dawīs͟h → ʿUzayyiz b. Fayṣal
ʿAbd al-ʿAzīz b. al-Ḥād͟jd͟j Ibrāhīm (1808) i, **57a**
ʿAbd al-ʿAzīz b. al-Ḥad͟jd͟jād͟j (744) i, **57a**; iii, 990b
ʿAbd al-ʿAzīz b. al-Ḥasan (ʿAlawid, Sultan of Morocco) (1943) i, **57b**, 357a, 1281b; ii, 820a; iii, 62a, 240a, 562a; v, 890a, 1193a, b; vi, 595b; s, 114a
ʿAbd al-ʿAzīz b. Ḥātim i, 1041a; ii, 679a
ʿAbd al-ʿAzīz b. Marwān I (Umayyad) (674) i, 42b, **58a**, 76b, 77b, 148b, 1242b; ii, 327b, 427b, 788a, 958a; iii, 271b, 572a, 819b; v, 552a, b; vi, 621b, 622a, b, 659a, 664a; s, 273a
ʿAbd al-ʿAzīz b. Marwān (Miṣr) (704) vii, 159b; x, 821a
ʿAbd al-ʿAzīz (II) b. Muḥammad (Ṣadr) (1196) viii, 749a

ʿAbd al-ʿAzīz b. Muḥammad b. al-Nuʿmān, ḳāḍī (XI) ii, 169b; iii, 78b, 79a
ʿAbd al-ʿAzīz b. Muḥammad b. Suʿūd (Āl Suʿūd) (1803) i, 554a; ii, 321a, 492b; iii, 678b; iv, 925a, b; vii, 410b; ix, 903n
ʿAbd al-ʿAzīz b. Muḥammad al-Fishtālī (1621) i, **58a**, 289a
ʿAbd al-ʿAzīz b. Mūsā b. Nuṣayr (718) i, 50a, **58b**, 608b, 1054b, 1338b; ii, 485b. 1009a, 1012b; iii, 587b; iv, 115a, 672b; v, 367b; vii, 643b; x, 585a, 848a
ʿAbd al-ʿAzīz b. Shuʿayb al-Ballūtī (961) i, 121b; iii, 1085a
ʿAbd al-ʿAzīz b. ʿUmar Māza (Ṣadr) (XII) viii, 749a
ʿAbd al-ʿAzīz b. al-Walīd (728) i, **58b**
ʿAbd al-ʿAzīz b. Yūsuf, Abu ʾl-Ḳāsim (X) s, **4a**, 398a
ʿAbd al-ʿAzīz al-Bakrī (Walba) (XI) i, 155b; ii, 1009a; xi, 109a
ʿAbd al-ʿAzīz al-Bawandī, Shaykh (XX) ii, 436a
ʿAbd al-ʿAzīz al-Dabbāgh (XIX) i, 277b; v, 647b; ix, 24b
ʿAbd al-ʿAzīz al-Dihlawī b. Walī Allāh, Mawlānā Shāh (1824) i, **59a**, 282a, 827b, 1193a; ii, 254b; iii, 431a; iv, 196a, 625b; vii, 442a; viii, 69a; s, 293a
ʿAbd al-ʿAzīz Fahmī (XX) iii, 516a, 518b
ʿAbd al-ʿAzīz al-ʿIrāḳī (XX) vi, 110a
ʿAbd al-ʿAzīz Khān (Bukhārā) (1680) i, 1295b; ii, 446a
ʿAbd al-ʿAzīz al-Mālik al-Manṣūr (Mamlūk) (1405) ii, 781b
ʿAbd al-ʿAzīz al-Manṣūr → ʿAbd al-ʿAzīz b. ʿAbd al-Raḥmān
ʿAbd al-ʿAzīz Pasha (1725) vi, 502b
ʿAbd al-ʿAzīz al-Shāwīsh, Shaykh (XX) vii, 439a
ʿAbd al-ʿAzīz Āl Suʿūd (1953) xi, 45b
ʿAbd al-ʿAzīz al-Tabbāʿ, Sīdī (1508) vi, 591a, b
ʿAbd al-ʿAzīz University vi, 174a
ʿAbd al-Bahāʾ (1920) i, 915b, 916b, 917a, 918a; s, 77a
ʿAbd al-Bāḳī (1821) vii, 685b
ʿAbd al-Bāḳī (Farangī Maḥall) (XIX) s, 4b, 292a
ʿAbd al-Bāḳī, Maḥmūd → Bāḳī, Maḥmūd ʿAbd al-
ʿAbd al-Bāḳī al-Fārūḳī → al-Fārūḳī, ʿAbd al-Bāḳī
ʿAbd al-Bāḳī al-Ḥanbalī (1661) iii, 677b
ʿAbd al-Bāḳī Khān (1736) vi, 56a
ʿAbd al-Bāḳī, Mīr Niẓām al-Dīn (Niʿmat-Allāhī) (XVI) viii, 46a
ʿAbd al-Bāḳī Nahāwandī (XVII) i, 857a
ʿAbd al-Bāḳī Naḳshbandī → Bāḳī bi-ʾllāh, Khwādja
ʿAbd al-Bārī, Ḳiyām al-Dīn Muḥammad (Farangī Maḥall) (1926) vii, 354b; s, **4b**, 74a, b, 292a, b, 293b, 360b
ʿAbd al-Bārī, Mawlānā (XX) vii, 354b
ʿAbd al-Barr b. ʿAnbasa (al-Ḳabḳ) (X) iv, 346b
ʿAbd al-Bāsiṭ ʿAbd al-Ṣamad, Shaykh (XX) x, 74a
ʿAbd al-Dār, Banū iv, 320a; v, 581a, b; vi, 137b, 145a
ʿAbd al-Dār b. Ḳuṣayy (VI) vi, 145a
ʿAbd al-Djabbār, Shaykh (XII) ii, 964a
ʿAbd al-Djabbār b. ʿAbd al-Raḥmān al-Azdī (759) i, **59a**; vi, 428a; vii, 360a
ʿAbd al-Djabbār b. Aḥmad (1025) i, **59b**, 343a; iii, 832a, 905b, 1019a, 1023a, 1071b, 1072a, 1144a, 1165b, 1171a; iv, 615b, 985b; v, 96a, 97a, 237a, 240a, 833b; vi, 376a; vii, 312a, 634a; viii, 534a, 981a; s, 13a, b, 14a, 25a, b, 31b, 225b, 343a, b, 346a, 348a, 392a, 393a
ʿAbd al-Djabbār b. al-Ḥusayn b. Muʿayya, Sayyid (XI) s, 19a
ʿAbd al-Djabbār b. Ḳays al-Murādī (Ibāḍī) (VIII) iii, 653b
ʿAbd al-Djalīl b. Ḥāfiẓ Abū Isḥāḳ (XVII) vii, 574a
ʿAbd al-Djalīl Abu ʾl-Maḥāsin → al-Dihistānī
ʿAbd al-Djalīl Djalīlī (XVII) ii, 402a
ʿAbd al-Djalīl al-Ḳazwīnī al-Rāzī (1170) vi, 549a
ʿAbd al-Fattāḥ ʿAmr (XX) s, 301a
ʿAbd al-Fattāḥ Fūmanī (XVII) i, **60a**
ʿAbd al-Fattāḥ Ismāʿīl (Yemen) (XX) xi, 275b
ʿAbd al-Ghaffār b. ʿAbd al-Karīm → al-Ḳazwīnī
ʿAbd al-Ghaffār al-Akhras → al-Akhras
ʿAbd al-Ghaffār al-Dasūḳī → al-Dasūḳī, Ibrāhīm b. Ibrāhīm
ʿAbd al-Ghaffār al-Ḥimṣī (VIII) iv, 115b

ʿAbd al-Ghaffār Khān (Kōhāt) → Khān, ʿAbd al-Ghaffār
ʿAbd al-Ghāfir (Ghaffār) b. Husayn al-Kāshgharī (XI) iv, 699a
ʿAbd al-Ghanī b. Ismāʿīl al-Nābulūsī (1731) i, **60a**, 596a, 795b, 1109b, 1235b; ii, 900a; iii, 935a; iv, 1006b; vi, 215a; vii, 724b, 812a
ʿAbd al-Ghanī b. Saʿīd al-Miṣrī (X) s, 38a
ʿAbd al-Ghanī Maḥmūd (1875) vi, 614a
ʿAbd al-Ghanī al-Maḳdisī → al-Maḳdisī, ʿAbd al-Ghanī
ʿAbd Ḥadad (IV B.C.) vi, 378b
ʿAbd al-Hādī, Banū iv, 834b
ʿAbd al-Ḥāfiẓ, Mawlāy → Ḥāfiẓ, ʿAbd al-
ʿAbd al-Ḥakam, Banū → Ibn ʿAbd al-Ḥakam
ʿAbd al-Ḥakīm ʿĀmir (XX) s, 5b, 8b, 9a
ʿAbd al-Hakīm al-Siyālkōtī → al-Siyālkōtī
ʿAbd al-Ḥaḳḳ, Shaykh (Dihlī) (1642) vii, 938a; s, 10b
ʿAbd al-Ḥaḳḳ b. ʿAbd al-ʿAzīz b. Khurāsān (XI) iii, 137b; v, 60a
ʿAbd al-Ḥaḳḳ b. Faḍl-i Ḥaḳḳ (XIX) ii, 735b, 736b
ʿAbd al-Ḥaḳḳ b. Sayf al-Dīn al-Dihlawī (1642) i, **60b**, 702b, 957a; ii, 296b ; vi, 131b, 354a; vii, 988a
ʿAbd al-Ḥaḳḳ Abū Muḥammad → Marīnids
ʿAbd al-Ḥaḳḳ Ḥāmid (1937) i, **61a**, 1302a; ii, 692b; iii, 1199b; iv, 1153a; vi, 759a; s, 149b
ʿAbd al-Ḥaḳḳ al-Hindī, Shaykh (XX) vi, 175b
ʿAbd al-Ḥaḳḳ al-Ishbīlī s, 389b
ʿAbd al-Ḥaḳḳ Mollā (XIX) i, 61a, 921a; iv, 1153a
ʿAbd al-Ḥaḳḳ Muḥaddith Shaykh i, 260a; iii, 430a, 435a
ʿAbd al-Ḥalīm Maḥmūd, Shaykh (XX) s, 225a
ʿAbd al-Ḥalīm Pasha b. Muḥammad ʿAlī Pasha (XIX) iii, 515a
ʿAbd al-Ḥalīm Sharar (1926) x, 879a
ʿAbd al-Ḥamīd I (Ottoman) (1789) i, **62b**, 481b, 1004a; ii, 209b, 534a; iv, 946a; v, 314a; vi, 58a; vii, 387b; s, 401b
ʿAbd al-Ḥamīd II (Ottoman) (1918) i, **63b**, 286b, 289b, 294b, 298b, 431a, 657a, 736a, 776a, 948a, 958a, 1090a; ii, 104b, 289a, 354b, 418b, 430b, 474b, 489b, 513b, 532a, 533b, 642a, 682a, 878b; iii, 357b, 364a, 993a, 994a, 1199a, 1257b; iv, 168b, 681b, 872a, 876b, 946a; v, 61b, 905a, 949a, 1035a; vi, 8b, 89a, b, 92b, 93a, 286a, 304b, 531a, b, 614b, 733b, 758a, 759b, 760a; vii, 184b, 205b, 434b, 525b, 547a, 573b; viii, 59b, 248a; s, 100b, 161b, 179a, 211b, 282b, 296b, 330b, 359b
ʿAbd al-Ḥamīd b. Bādīs → Ibn Bādīs
ʿAbd al-Ḥamīd b. Yaḥyā b. Saʿd (750) i, **65b**, 588a; ii, 304b; iii, 494b, 1242b, 1263a; iv, 755b; vii, 985a; viii, 533a
ʿAbd al-Ḥamīd Efendi (XIX) ii, 878b
ʿAbd al-Ḥamīd Khān (Kashmīr) (XX) iv, 711a
ʿAbd al-Ḥamīd Lāhawrī (1654) i, **66a**; vii, 139b, 342b
ʿAbd al-Ḥamīd al-Manāzī (940) vi, 242b
ʿAbd al-Ḥayy, Mawlawī (XIX) iv, 196a; s, 4b
ʿAbd al-Ḥayy, Shaykh (XVI) s, 312a
ʿAbd al-Hayy al-Lakhnawī (1886) i, **66a**, 282b; iii, 164a; s, 292b, 293a
ʿAbd al-Ḥusayn, Mīrzā (XIX) iv, 979a
ʿAbd al-Ḥusayn Hazhīr (1949) ii, 882b; vii, 447a
ʿAbd al-Ḥusayn Nūshīn (1970) vi, 764a
ʿAbd al-Ilāh (Hāshimid) (1882) ii, 872b; iii, 264a; vi, 151a, b, 615a, 616a
ʿAbd al-Kaʿba → ʿAbd al-Raḥmān b. Abī Bakr;ʿAbd al-Raḥmān b. ʿAwf; ʿAbd al-Raḥmān b. Samura
ʿAbdelkader → ʿAbd al-Ḳādir
ʿAbd el-Kader → ʿAbd al-Ḳādir b. Muḥyī al-Dīn
ʿAbd al-Ḳādir (peninsula) vi, 641b
ʿAbd al-Ḳādir b. ʿAlī → al-Fāsī, ʿAbd al-Ḳādir
ʿAbd al-Ḳādir b. ʿAmāra (Fundj) (1557) ii, 944a
ʿAbd al-Ḳādir b. Burhān Shāh (Niẓām Shāhī) (XVI) iii, 625b, 1161a
ʿAbd al-Ḳādir b. Ghaybī (1435) i, **66b**; ii, 1074a
ʿAbd al-Ḳādir b. Muḥammad al-Maḳrīzī (1332) vi, 193b
ʿAbd al-Ḳādir b. Muḥyī al-Dīn, Amīr (1883) i, **67a**, 85a, 357a, 369a, 789a, 1177b, 1197b, 1247a; ii, 160b, 173a, 288b;

iii, 561b, 806b; iv, 362a, 383a; v, 1160b, 1192b; vi, 252a; vii, 64b, 263a, 391a, 671a, 722a; s, 296a
ʿAbd al-Ḳādir Badāʾūnī → Badāʾūnī
ʿAbd al-Ḳādir al-Baghdādī (1682) i, **68a**, 712b; vi, 196a, 635a; vii, 580b; s, 388a, 407b
ʿAbd al-Ḳādir Dihlawī (1813) i, **68b**, 282b, 827b; ii, 735b; iii, 431a; iv, 196a; v, 803a
ʿAbd al-Ḳādir al-Djīlānī (al-Djīlī) (1166) i, **69a**, 91b, 137b, 595b, 903b, 904a, 1173a; ii, 535b; iii, 160b, 842b; iv, 380a-383a, 1134a; v, 475a, 1201a; vi, 178b, 251b, 280a, 354a, 463a, 644a; vii,189a, 726b; s, 182b, 223b, 323b
ʿAbd al-Ḳādir al-Fāsī → al-Fāsī, ʿAbd al-Ḳādir
ʿAbd al-Ḳādir Ghiyāth al-Dīn b. Maḥmūd Khaldjī (1500) vi, 309b
ʿAbd al-Ḳādir al-Gīlānī → ʿAbd al-Ḳādir al-Djīlānī
ʿAbd al-Ḳādir Khwādja Sawda (1873) x, 65a
ʿAbd al-Ḳādir al-Ḳurashī (1373) i, **70b**; ix, 36a; s, 191b
ʿAbd al-Ḳādir al-Maghribī (XX) ii, 451b; iv, 159a; x, 240b
ʿAbd al-Ḳādir al-mawsūm ba-Ḳādir Shāh → Ikhtiyār al-Dīn Abu ʾl-Mudjāhid Ḳādir Khān
ʿAbd al-Ḳādir al-Shaybī, Shaykh (XX) vi, 153b
ʿAbd al-Ḳādir al-Ṭubdjī (XIX) vi, 251b
ʿAbd al-Ḳāhir b. Ṭāhir al-Baghdādī → al-Baghdādī
ʿAbd al-Ḳāhir al-Djurdjānī → al-Djurdjanī
ʿAbd al-Karīm (Bulfī) (1626) ix, 637a
ʿAbd al-Karīm (ḳāʾid, Marrākūsh) (1659) vi, 142b, 595a
ʿAbd al-Karīm (Wadāī) xi, 11a
ʿAbd al-Karīm, Mawlānā (1450) vi, 70a
ʿAbd al-Karīm, Mīr (XVII) i, 254a
ʿAbd al-Karīm b. ʿAbd Allāh (Marʿashī) (1467) vi, 514a, 516a
ʿAbd al-Karīm b. ʿAdjarrad → Ibn ʿAdj arrad
ʿAbd al-Karīm b. ʿAlī Pérez (XVII) i, 405a
ʿAbd al-Karīm b. Mughīth (VIII) s, 92a
ʿAbd al-Karīm b. Muḥammad (Marʿashī) (1452) vi, 513b, 514b
ʿAbd al-Karīm b. Muḥibb al-Dīn (1606) vii, 912a
ʿAbd al-Karīm Bukhārī (1830) i, **71a**
ʿAbd al-Karīm al-Djazārī, Banū iii, 961a
ʿAbd al-Karīm al-Djīlī (1428) i, **71a**, 596a; iii, 329a, 709a, 1240b; v, 525b; vi, 211a
ʿAbd al-Karīm Kashmīrī (1784) i, **71b**
ʿAbd al-Karīm Ḳāsim al-Khalīl (1915) iii, 519b, 1259a
ʿAbd al-Karīm Khān (Ḳarakhānid) (955) iii, 1113b; iv, 698b; v, 856b
ʿAbd al-Karīm Khān (Noghay) (1504) i, 721b
ʿAbd al-Karīm Khān b. Shāhrukh (1746) v, 29a
ʿAbd al-Karīm (XX) vii, 416b
ʿAbd al-Karīm Lāhurī, Shaykh ii, 55a
ʿAbd al-Karīm Maʿmūr Khān (XVII) vii, 332a
ʿAbd al-Karīm Munshī (1851) i, **72a**
ʿAbd al-Karīm al-Sammān (1775) x, 257a
ʿAbd al-Ḳawī (XVII) vii, 452b
ʿAbd al-Ḳays, Banū i, **72b**, 529a, 545a, 942a; iv, 764a; v, 346a; vi, 441b, 649a; vii, 671a; s, 24b
ʿAbd al-Kerīm Pasha (XVIII) vii, 275b
ʿAbd al-Khāliḳ Ḥassūna (1972) s, 240b
ʿAbd al-Khāliḳ b. Abi ʾl-Ṭalḥ al-Shihābī iii, 124b
ʿAbd al-Khāliḳ Ghudjduwānī (1220) xi, 116a
ʿAbd al-Khāliḳ al-Sharḳī (XVIII) vi, 356b
ʿAbd al-Khallāḳ Torres (Morocco) (XX) vii, 416a
ʿAbd al-Krīm (XX) vii, 416b
ʿAbd al-Ḳuddūs al-Anṣārī (1983) v, 1005b; vi, 175b, 176b
ʿAbd al-Laṭīf b. Ulugh Beg (Tīmūrid) (1449) vi, 601b; x, 813a
ʿAbd al-Laṭīf al-Baghdādī (1231) i, **74a**, 595a; iii, 877a, 956b; v, 862a, 1129b, 1130a; vi, 204b, 367a, 410b, 412b, 413a, 637b, 845a, 1016b; vii, 140b, 141b, 165a; s, 115b, 408a
ʿAbd al-Laṭīf Čelebī → Laṭīfī
ʿAbd al-Laṭīf Ḳastamunilī → Laṭīfī
ʿAbd al-Laṭīf al-Ḳayātī (1842) vi, 355a
ʿAbd al-Laṭīf Khān (Ḳazān) (XVI) iv, 849a
ʿAbd al-Laṭīf Khān (Samarḳand) (XVI) i, 46b

ʿAbd al-Laṭīf Mīrzā (Tīmūrid) (1450) i, 91a, 227b
ʿAbd al-Madān b. al-Dayyān (Balḥārith Āl) iii, 223a, b
ʿAbd al-Madjīd I (Abdülmecid) (Ottoman) (1861) i, 37a, **74b**, 216b, 284b, 298a, 776a; 1226a; ii, 49a, 613a, 801a, 912a, 935a; iv, 143a; vi, 175a, 757a, b; vii, 428a; viii, 58b, 59a
ʿAbd al-Madjīd II (Abdülmecid) (Ottoman) (1944) i, **75b**, ii, 119b; iv, 946b
ʿAbd al-Madjīd (Fāṭimid) → al-Ḥāfiẓ
ʿAbd al-Madjīd Salīm, muftī (1954) x, 140a; s, 208b
ʿAbd al-Malik, Amīr (Sindjār) (1149) vi, 870b
ʿAbd al-Malik I b. Nūḥ (Sāmānid) (961) i, 421b, 984b; iii, 46b; v, 325a, 1162b; vi, 432b; viii, 1027b; s, 230b, 357b, 358a
ʿAbd al-Malik II (Sāmānid) (1000) iii, 196b
ʿAbd al-Malik b. ʿAbd al-ʿAzīz → Ibn Djuraydj al-Makkī
ʿAbd al-Malik b. Abī ʿĀmir al-Maʿāfirī al-Muẓaffar (1008) i, 6a, **75b**, 242a, 446a, 494b, 1040b, 1096a; iii, 495b, 674a; 819a; iv, 632b; vii, 815b; x, 853a
ʿAbd al-Malik b. Abī Muḥammad Hudhayl (1103) ix, 307b
ʿAbd al-Malik b. Aḥmad II b. Hūd → ʿImād al-Dawla b. Hūd
ʿAbd al-Malik b. ʿAlī b. ʿAbd al-Malik b. Abī Shayba (1210) vi, 381a
ʿAbd al-Malik b. ʿAttāsh → Ibn ʿAttāsh
ʿAbd al-Malik b. Bishr b. Marwān al-Baṣra s, 52a
ʿAbd al-Malik b. Ghiṭrīf (faḳīh) (XI) vi, 436a
ʿAbd al-Malik b. Ḥabīb (852) iv, 87a, b; vi, 374b; vii, 539b; viii, 515b; ix, 38a
ʿAbd al-Malik b. Hishām → Ibn Hishām, ʿAbd al-Malik
ʿAbd al-Malik b. Ḳaṭan al-Fihrī (741) i, **76a**, 991a; iv, 494b, 672b, 805a
ʿAbd al-Malik b. Muḥammad al-Shaykh al-Mahdī (Saʿdid) (XVI) i, 55b, 288b
ʿAbd al-Malik b. Makkī (XIII) iv, 338a
ʿAbd al-Malik b. al-Manṣūr → ʿAbd al-Malik b. Abī ʿĀmir; ʿAbd al-Malik al-Muẓaffar
ʿAbd al-Malik b. Marwān (Umayyad) (705) i, 2b, 45a, 47b, 55b, 58a, **76a**, 120a, 142a, 148b, 320b, 453b, 482a, 550a, 610a, 710b, 1038a, 1143b, 1242b, 1293a, 1349a; ii, 117b, 297b, 319b, 324a, 360a, 456b, 480a, 768b, 911a; iii, 40a, 648b, 717a; iv, 654b, 929b; vi, 139a, 140a, 147a, 230b, 336b, 338b, 428a, 505b, 621b, 622b, 623a, 625a, 626a, 640b, 659b, 660b, 665a, 669a, 676a, 677b, 774b; vii, 159b, 225b, 357a, 650a; x, 844b; s, 103b, 311a, b
ʿAbd al-Malik b. Marwān, vizier (749) vii, 75a, 269b
ʿAbd al-Malik b. Mughīth (VIII) i, 608b; ii, 485b; v, 1121a
ʿAbd al-Malik b. al-Muhallab (VIII) vii, 359b
ʿAbd al-Malik b. Muḥammad b. Djawhar (XI) ii, 389a
ʿAbd al-Malik b. Mundhir b. Saʿīd (979) vii, 570a
ʿAbd al-Malik b. Mūsā b. Nuṣayr (720) i, 50a
ʿAbd al-Malik b. Nūḥ (Sāmānid) (X) viii, 110a
ʿAbd al-Malik b. Sakardid (768) vi, 312a
ʿAbd al-Malik b. Ṣāliḥ b. ʿAlī (811) i, **77b**, 761b; vi, 331a, 332a, 333b, 334a, 379a
ʿAbd al-Malik b. Shihāb al-Mismaʿī (780) vi, 640b
ʿAbd al-Malik b. Yazīd (777) vi, 618a
ʿAbd al-Malik b. Zaydān (Saʿdid) (1631) vi, 594b
ʿAbd al-Malik b. Zuhr → Ibn Zuhr
ʿAbd al-Malik al-Ḥārithī s, 649b
ʿAbd al-Malik Murād (XX) vi, 155a
ʿAbd al-Malik al-Muẓaffar (1008) → ʿAbd al-Malik b. Abī ʿĀmir
ʿAbd al-Malik al-Muẓaffar (Afṭasid) (1065) i, 6a, 242a. 446a, 985b, 1096a; ii, 1012a; iii, 674a
ʿAbd Manāf, Banū i, 681a; iv, 320a; v, 435a, 581a; vi, 145a, 168b, 349a
ʿAbd al-Masīḥ (VI) vi, 726a; vii, 307b
ʿAbd al-Masīḥ b. ʿAmr → Ibn Buḳayla
ʿAbd al-Masīḥ b. Nāʿima al-Ḥimṣī x, 228a
ʿAbd al-Matīn Khān (Dīr) (XX) ii, 317a
ʿAbd al-Medjīd (Ottoman) (1861) x, 201a
ʿAbd al-Muḥsin Saʿdūn (XX) vi, 616a; vii, 468b
ʿAbd al-Muʾmin b. ʿAbd Allāh Khān (Shaybānid) (1589) i, 8a, 46b, 1001b; vi, 715a; s, 340b

ʿAbd al-Muʾmin b. Abi ʾl-Fayḍ (Djāhīd) (1748) vi, 418b
ʿAbd al-Muʾmin b. ʿAlī b. ʿAlwī (Almohad) (1163) i, **78a**, 680a, 1044b, 1129b, 1148b, 1176a, 1205b; ii, 145b, 307b, 331b, 352b, 353a, 459a, 516a, 537a, 818b, 1009a; iii, 138b, 207b, 386b, 470b, 910a, 958b, 978b; iv, 415b, 479b, 827b, 943b; v, 61a, 379a, 626a, 1189b, 1245b; vi, 134a, 404a, 592a, 597a, 742b; vii, 247b, 585b, 802a; s, 113b, 376b
ʿAbd al-Munʿim b. Idrīs (842) vii, 283b
ʿAbd al-Munʿim Ayyūb II (Muḳaddam) (XV) i, 1280b
ʿAbd al-Muṭṭalib, Sharīf (XIX) vi, 151a
ʿAbd al-Muṭṭalib b. Ghālib, Sharīf (1886) vi, 175a
ʿAbd al-Muṭṭalib b. Hāshim (VII) i, 42b, **80a**, 115b, 136b, 851a; iii, 203b, 260a, 1093a; iv, 260a, 264a, 270b; vi, 168b
ʿAbd al-Muṭṭalib b. Riḍā al-Dīn (Marʿashī) (1400) vi, 512b
ʿAbd al-Nabī (Mathurā) (1660) vi, 839a
ʿAbd al-Nabī b. Aḥmad Sirhindī (1582) s, 313a
ʿAbd al-Nabī b. ʿAlī (XII) ii, 517a; v, 1244b, 1245a
ʿAbd al-Nabī Fakhr al-Zamānī Ḳazwīnī (1619) vi, 834a; vii, 530a
ʿAbd al-Nāṣir, Djamāl (1970) ii, 649a, 674a; iii, 518a, 1069b, 1259a; iv, 125a, b, 719a, 781a, 783b; v, 1061b; vi, 24a; vii, 765a; viii, 247a, 717a; s, **5a**, 70a, 306a
ʿAbd al-Nāṣir Ḥusayn → ʿAbd al-Nāṣir, Djamāl
ʿAbd Rabbih al-Kabīr (698) i, 810b; iv, 753a; vii, 357b
ʿAbd Rabbih al-Ṣaghīr (VII) i, 810b
ʿAbd al-Raḥīm b. Aḥmad (Yemen) (IX) i, 402b
ʿAbd al-Raḥīm b. Aḥmad b. Ḥadjdjūn Ḳūnā (1196) v, 386b
ʿAbd al-Raḥīm b. ʿAlī → al-Ḳāḍī al-Fāḍil
ʿAbd al-Raḥīm b. Ilyās (X) ii, 857a; iii, 80a
ʿAbd al-Raḥīm b. Muḥammad → Ibn Nubāta
ʿAbd al-Raḥīm al-ʿAbbāsī (XVI) i, 1109b
ʿAbd al-Raḥīm, Khān-i Khānān (1627) i, **80b**, 431a, 628a, 1136a, b, 1331a; ii, 597b; iii, 457b; iv, 1018a, 1127b; vi, 128a, 271b; vii, 129b, 328a, 331b, 332a, 343a, 458a, 478a, 938a, 1055a; ix, 396b
ʿAbd al-Raḥīm al-Mutawakkil ʿalā ʾllāh (Karūkh) (IX) iv, 673a
ʿAbd al-Raḥmān, Sharīf (Pontianak) (XVIII) s, 150b
ʿAbd al-Raḥmān I b. Muʿāwiya, al-Dākhil (Umayyad, al-Andalus) (788) i, **81b**, 86b, 493b, 497b, 618b, 1079b; ii, 1009a; iii, 12a, 702a; iv, 665b; v, 510b, 1160a, 1164b; vi, 221b, 428b, 520b, 568a; vii, 269a, 563b, 941b; x, 848a; s, 82a
ʿAbd al-Raḥmān II b. al-Ḥakam al-Mutawassiṭ (Umayyad, al-Andalus) (852) i, 11a, **82b**, 121b, 494a, 498a, 864b, 1012a, 1319b; ii, 515b, 1009a, 1038a; iii, 74a, 816a; iv, 672b, 822a; v, 510b, 1118b, 1119b; vi, 132a, 520b, 568a; vii, 275a, 633a; x, 850a
ʿAbd al-Raḥmān III al-Nāṣir (Umayyad, al-Andalus) (961) i, **83b**, 439b, 494a, 498a, 628b, 658a, 864b, 997a, 1012a, 1092a, 1150a, 1326a, 1343a; ii, 297b, 525a, 821b, 915b, 1009a; iii, 46a, 1042a; iv, 254b, 632b, 943a; v, 510b, 625b, 777b, 1008b; vi, 222a, 431b, 435a, 520b, 568a, 576a; vii, 45a, 248b, 486a, 569b, 641b; x, 849a, 851a; s, 80a, 153a
ʿAbd al-Raḥmān IV al-Murtaḍā (Umayyad, al-Andalus) (1018) i, **84a**; ii, 1012b; iii, 147a, 496a, 791a; vi, 141b
ʿAbd al-Raḥmān V al-Mustaẓhir (Umayyad) (1024) i, **84a**; iii, 791a, 938b
ʿAbd al-Raḥmān, Mawlāy → ʿAbd al-Raḥmān b. Hishām
ʿAbd al-Raḥmān b. ʿAbbās b. Rabīʾa Hāshimī (VII) iii, 716b, 717b
ʿAbd al-Raḥmān b. ʿAbd Allāh → Ibn ʿAbd al-Ḥakam, Abu ʾl-Ḳāsim
ʿAbd al-Raḥmān b. ʿAbd Allāh b. ʿAbd al-Wahhāb (1869) xi, 43a
ʿAbd al-Raḥmān b. Abī ʿAlī (Marīnid) (1353) vi, 593b
ʿAbd al-Raḥmān b. Abī Bakr (VII) i, 109b, 110a, 145b; ii, 625b; s, 351b
ʿAbd al-Raḥmān b. Abī Ifellūsen (1382) vi, 593b, 594a
ʿAbd al-Raḥmān b. Abī Nās Mandīl (XIII) vi, 404a
ʿAbd al-Raḥmān b. Abī Nuʿaym al-Mulāʾī (IX) i, 143a

ʿAbd al-Raḥmān b. Aḥmad (822) vi, 337b
ʿAbd al-Raḥmān b. ʿAlī → Ibn al-Daybaʿ
ʿAbd al-Raḥmān b. ʿAlī b. Bā Ḥassān (1415) iii, 270a
ʿAbd al-Raḥmān b. al-Ashʿath → Ibn al-Ashʿath
ʿAbd al-Raḥmān b. ʿAwf al-Zuhrī (652) i, **84b**, 382a, 687a; ii, 366a, 625a, 846a; iii, 209b, 586b; iv, 521b; v, 110b; vi, 79a; vii, 254a, 364a; ix, 38a; s, 89b
ʿAbd al-Raḥmān b. al-Ḍaḥḥāk (VII) ii, 90a
ʿAbd al-Raḥmān b. Djabala (812) vi, 333b
ʿAbd al-Raḥmān b. Djābir b. ʿAbd Allāh (VIII) s, 231a
ʿAbd al-Raḥmān b. Fayṣal (Āl Suʿūd) (1889) iv, 925b; ix, 904a
ʿAbd al-Raḥmān b. Fayṣal b. ʿAbd al-ʿAzīz (Āl Suʿūd) (XX) s, 305b
ʿAbd al-Raḥmān b. Ḥabīb al-Fihrī (755) i, 81b, **86a**; iii, 654a; iv, 336b; viii, 688a; ix, 753b
ʿAbd al-Raḥmān b. Ḥabīb al-Ṣiklabī (778) i, 86b
ʿAbd al-Raḥmān b. al-Ḥakam (VII) s, 10a
ʿAbd al-Raḥmān b. al-Ḥakam II al-Mustanṣir (969) ix, 740b
ʿAbd al-Raḥmān b. al-Ḥārith b. Hishām al-Makhzūmī (640) vi, 139a, 140b; viii, 853b
ʿAbd al-Raḥmān b. Ḥassān b. Thābit (722) s, **9b**
ʿAbd al-Raḥmān b. Hishām, Mawlāy (ʿAlawid) (1859) i, 67b, **84b**, 315b, 356b, 357a, 1224b, 1346b; ii, 117a, 160a, 173a, 510b, 823a; iii, 806a; iv, 634a; vi, 136a, 250b, 595b, 597a; vii, 39a, 391a
ʿAbd al-Raḥmān b. Ḥusayn Āl Suʿūd (XIX) iv, 1073a
ʿAbd al-Raḥmān b. ʿĪsā b. Dāʾūd (X) i, 387b; iv, 1094a
ʿAbd al-Raḥmān b. ʿĪsā al-Murshidī i, 867b
ʿAbd al-Raḥmān b. Isḥāḳ b. Haytham i, 214a
ʿAbd al-Raḥmān b. Kaʿb al-Aṣamm (VII) i, 266b
ʿAbd al-Raḥmān b. al-Ḳāḍī vii, 622a
ʿAbd al-Raḥmān b. al-Ḳāsim → Ibn al-Ḳāsim
ʿAbd al-Raḥmān b. Kaysān s, 88b, 90b
ʿAbd al-Raḥmān b. Khālid b. al-Walīd b. al-Mughīra (666) i, **85a**, 449b; iv, 928b; vi, 139a, b
ʿAbd al-Raḥmān b. Mahdī al-Baṣrī (813) i, 272b; viii, 515a
ʿAbd al-Raḥmān b. Mahdī (Sudan) (1959) v, 1252b
ʿAbd al-Raḥmān b. al-Manṣūr b. Abī ʿĀmir (XI) vi, 842a
ʿAbd al-Raḥmān b. Marwān b. Yūnus, Ibn al-Djillīḳī (889) i, **85b**, 494a, 1092a, 1339a; ii, 1009a; vi, 568a
ʿAbd al-Raḥmān b. Mishkam al-Khawlānī (VII) iv, 1135a
ʿAbd al-Raḥmān b. Muʿāwiya → ʿAbd al-Raḥmān I
ʿAbd al-Raḥmān b. Muḥammad b. Abī ʿĀmir (Sanchuelo) (1009) i, 76a, **84a**, 446a, 494b; iii, 495b, 739b, 746b, 819a; v, 743b, 1239a, b; x, 853a
ʿAbd al-Raḥmān b. Muḥammad b. al-Ashʿath → Ibn al-Ashʿath
ʿAbd al-Raḥmān b. Muḥammad b. ʿAlī al-Barḳī (VIII) s, 127a
ʿAbd al-Raḥmān b. Muḥammad b. Murshid (Munḳidh, Banū) (1204) vii, 579b
ʿAbd al-Raḥmān b. Muslim (VIII) viii, 67a
ʿAbd al-Raḥmān b. Muṣṭafā al-ʿAydarūsī i, 280b, 782a
ʿAbd al-Raḥmān b. Nāṣir (Safi) (XVIII) s, 401b
ʿAbd al-Raḥmān b. Rabīʿa → al-Bāhilī
ʿAbd al-Raḥmān b. Rustam b. Bahrām (768) i, 125a, 134b, 1175b; iii, 297a, 654a, b, 655a, 1041b; iv, 827a; v, 696a; vi, 312a; viii, 638a
ʿAbd al-Raḥmān b. Samura (670) i, 47b, **86a**, 1001a, 1344a; iv, 14b, 356b; v, 57a; viii, 595b; ix, 682b
ʿAbd al-Raḥmān b. Shāshū (XVII) vii, 470a
ʿAbd al-Raḥmān b. Ṣubḥ (VIII) s, 425b
ʿAbd al-Raḥmān b. Sulaymān al-Ahdal (1835) i, **255b**, 782a
ʿAbd al-Raḥmān b. ʿUdays al-Balawī (VII) v, 318b
ʿAbd al-Raḥmān b. Umm al-Ḥakam (al-Kūfa) (VII) iii, 970a; vii, 269b
ʿAbd al-Raḥmān b. ʿUtba al-Fihrī, Ibn Djaḥdam (685) v, 121b; vi, 622a
ʿAbd al-Raḥmān b. Yazīd b. al-Muhallab (VII) vii, 359b
ʿAbd al-Raḥmān ʿAbdī Pasha → ʿAbdī Pasha

ʿAbd al-Raḥmān al-ʿAmr (Dūra) (XIX) iv, 961a
ʿAbd al-Raḥmān ʿAzzām Pasha (XX) s, 240b
ʿAbd al-Raḥmān al-Barḳūḳī (XX) vi, 955b
ʿAbd al-Raḥmān al-Fāsī (1685) i, **86a**; vi, 255b, 350a; s, **302b**
ʿAbd al-Raḥmān al-Ghāfikī (732) i, **86b**, 493a, 988b
ʿAbd al-Raḥmān Ghāzī (XI) s, 280a
ʿAbd al-Raḥmān Harawī, Mīrzā (XIX) ii, 433b
ʿAbd al-Raḥmān Ismāʿīl (XX) vii, 903a
ʿAbd al-Raḥmān Kahyā → ʿAbd al-Raḥman Katkhudā
ʿAbd al-Raḥmān Ḳaramānī, Shaykh (XVI) i, 1235a
ʿAbd al-Raḥmān Katkhudā (Kiḥya) (1776) i, 815a; iv, 438a, 439b, 852b, 853a
ʿAbd al-Raḥmān Khān (Bārakzay) (1901) i, **87a**, 223b, 224b, 232a, 796b; ii, 1001b; iv, 411a; v, 1079a; vi, 765b, 807a; s, 237b, 368a
ʿAbd al-Raḥmān Khān (Noghay) (1538) i, 721b
ʿAbd al-Raḥmān al-Madjdhūb (1569) xi, 112b
ʿAbd al-Raḥmān Maẓhar, Shaykh (XX) vi, 171b
ʿAbd al-Raḥmān Mushfiḳī → Mushfiḳī
ʿAbd al-Raḥmān al-Nadjūmī (XIX) i, 49b, 765a; v, 1250a, b
ʿAbd al-Raḥmān al-Nāṣir → ʿAbd al-Raḥmān III
ʿAbd al-Raḥmān Pasha (1684) i, 905a, 1284b
ʿAbd al-Raḥmān Pasha Bābān (1812) i, 845a
ʿAbd al-Raḥmān al-Rashīd (Dār Fūr) (1800) ii, 123a
ʿAbd al-Raḥmān Rushdī Pashā, Būlāḳ (XIX) i, 1299b
ʿAbd al-Raḥmān Sanchuelo → ʿAbd al-Raḥmān b. Muḥammad b. Abī ʿĀmir
ʿAbd al-Raḥmān Sheref (XX) i, 1089b; iv, 297b; vi, 94a
ʿAbd al-Raḥmān al-Ṣūfī (986) i, **86b**; ii, 300a; vi, 374b, 600b; s, 251a, 449a
ʿAbd al-Raḥmān al-Sūr (Ṣaydā) (XIX) i, 63b
ʿAbd al-Rashīd b. Maḥmūd (Ghaznawid) (1051) i, 1130b, 1344b; ii, 1052a
ʿAbd al-Rashīd b. Ṣālih al-Bākuwī (XV) i, 967a
ʿAbd al-Rashīd Daylamī (XVII) iv, 1128a
ʿAbd al-Rashīd Khān Sulṭānī (Dihlī) (XIV) ii, 622b; iii, 317a; vi, 49a
ʿAbd al-Rashīd al-Tattawī (1658) i, **88a**, iv, 526a
ʿAbd al-Raʾūf al-Sinkilī (1693) i, **88a**, 742a; iii, 1220a, 1233b; v, 433a, 525b; vi, 235b
ʿAbd al-Rāziḳ, ʿAlī (XX) iii, 1168b; iv, 161a, 906b, 947a; s, 121b
ʿAbd al-Rāziḳ, Muṣṭafā (1947) i, 820a
ʿAbd al-Razzāḳ, vizier (XI) i, 1192a
ʿAbd al-Razzāḳ (Ṣufrī) (IX) iii, 1036a
ʿAbd al-Razzāḳ (Sabzawār) (1338) ix, 47b
ʿAbd al-Razzāḳ, Shihāb al-Islām (vizier) (1122) ix, 16b
ʿAbd al-Razzāḳ b. ʿAbd al-Ḳādir (1206) iv, 380b, 381a
ʿAbd al-Razzāḳ b. Ḥammām al-Ṣanʿānī (827) → al-Ṣanʿānī
ʿAbd al-Razzāḳ b. Ḥasanwayh (X) iii, 258a
ʿAbd al-Razzāḳ, Abū Manṣūr Muḥammad (Ṭūs) (X) ii, 918b; x, 741b
ʿAbd al-Razzāḳ (Bānsa) Sayyid (1724) vi, 354b; viii, 69a; s, 292b, 293a
ʿAbd al-Razzāḳ Karabaka (XX) vi, 751a
ʿAbd al-Razzāḳ al-Ḳāshānī (al-Ḳāshī) (1329) i, **88b**, 347a, 351a; vi, 638a
ʿAbd al-Razzāḳ al-Lāhidjī → Lāhidjī
ʿAbd al-Razzāḳ al-Samarḳandī (1482) i, **90b**; iii, 58a; xi, 1b; s, 51a
ʿAbd al-Razzāḳ al-Sanhūrī (XX) vi, 24a, 37a
ʿAbd al-Reshīd ʿIṣmet Allāh (X) s, 82a
ʿAbd al-Saʿīd Mir ʿĀlim → Mir ʿĀlim
ʿAbd al-Salām (Sokoto) (XIX) vii, 435b
ʿAbd al-Salām II, Shaykh (1915) i, 1072a
ʿAbd al-Salām, al-Ḥādjdj (XIX) iii, 395b
ʿAbd al-Salām b. Aḥmad → Ibn Ghānim
ʿAbd al-Salām b. Mashīsh al-Ḥasanī (1227) i, **91a**, 353a; v, 1201a; vi, 249b, 280a, 355a, 356a; s, 350b
ʿAbd al-Salām b. Muḥammad b. Aḥmad al-Ḥasanī al-ʿAlamī al-Fāsī (1895) s, **10a**
ʿAbd al-Salām ʿĀrif → ʿĀrif, ʿAbd al-Salām
ʿAbd al-Salām al-Ḳādirī (1698) vi, 356b
ʿAbd al-Salām Khundjī, Shaykh (Ḳuṭb al-Awliyāʾ) (1345) v, 671a

ʿAbd al-Salām ʿUmar (XX) vi, 177b
ʿAbd al-Salām Yazbak ʿAmād (XVIII) ii, 444a
ʿAbd al-Ṣamad b. al-Muʿaḏẖḏẖal → Ibn al-Muʿaḏẖḏẖal
ʿAbd al-Ṣamad Ibn Ḵẖazar (XII) v, 1179b
ʿAbd al-Ṣamad al-Palimbānī (1776) i, **92a**; ii, 183a; iii, 1233b; vi, 235b; viii, 245a
ʿAbd al-Ṣamad Zayn al-Dīn (1634) vi, 354b
ʿAbd al-Sattār al-Bāsil (XX) vi, 219b
ʿAbd S̲h̲ams, Banū i, 9a, 55b, 136b, 151a; v, 435a; vi, 137b, 138a, 145a, 560a, 565b; x, 841a; s, 103b
ʿAbd al-ʿUzza → ʿAbd al-Raḥmān b. Abī Bakr; Abū Lahab b. ʿAbd al-Muṭṭalib
ʿAbd al-Wādids (Banū ʿAbd al-Wād, Zayyānids, Banū Zayyān) i, **92a**, 129b, 168a, 367a, 1176b, 1205b; iii, 67b, 68b, 499a, 832a, 833b; v, 531a, 1180a, b, 1190a; vi, 142a, 404a, b, 405a, 440b, 441a, 572b, 728b; vii, 263a, 1022a; viii, 723b; xi, 239a; s, 113a, 144b, 376b
ʿAbd al-Wahhāb (ḳāḍī) (1030) vi, 279a
ʿAbd al-Wahhāb, Mawlānā (1903) s, 360b
ʿAbd al-Wahhāb, Muḥammad b. Ḥasanayn al-Ḥiṣāfī (1949) s, 371a
ʿAbd al-Wahhāb b. ʿAbd al-Raḥmān b. Rustum (ʿIbāḍī Imām) (811) i, 250a; ii, 441b; iii, 297b, 651a, 655a, 1041b; iv, 415b, 919b; vi, 840b, 946a; viii, 112b
ʿAbd al-Wahhāb b. Abi ʾl-Faraḏj̲ (1141) iii, 161a
ʿAbd al-Wahhāb b. Aḥmad, Nāʾib al-Ḥaram (XX) vi, 157a, 166a
ʿAbd al-Wahhāb b. Buḵẖt (731) i, 1103a, b; ii, 234b, 236a
ʿAbd al-Wahhāb b. Dāwūd (Ṭāhirid) (XV) i, 181b; vii, 996a
ʿAbd al-Wahhāb b. D̲h̲u ʾl-Himma ii, 234b
ʿAbd al-Wahhāb b. Faḍl Allāh (1317) ii, 732a
ʿAbd al-Wahhāb b. Ibrāhīm b. Muḥammad (750) vi, 230b
ʿAbd al-Wahhāb b. Makkī (XIII) iv, 338a
ʿAbd al-Wahhāb b. Muḥammad b. G̲h̲ālib b. Numayr al-Anṣārī (XII) s, 15b
ʿAbd al-Wahhāb b. Yūsuf al-Tuḏj̲ībī (XX) s, 11a
ʿAbd al-Wahhāb Ās̲h̲ī (XX) vi, 176b, 177b
ʿAbd al-Wahhāb Buḵẖārī, S̲h̲ayḵẖ (1525) s, **10b**
ʿAbd al-Wahhāb al-Hamadānī (1540) i, 234a
ʿAbd al-Wahhāb al-Ḳazzāz (XX) vi, 165b
ʿAbd al-Wahhāb al-Makkī iv, 338a
ʿAbd al-Wahhāb al-Subkī → al-Subkī, Tāḏj̲ al-Dīn
ʿAbd al-Wahhāb al-Sumādiḥī al-Tuḏj̲ībī (1968) s, **11a**
ʿAbd al-Wāḥid II al-Ras̲h̲īd (Almohad) (1241) iii, 338a, 705a, 921b, 1055a; v, 48b; xi, 239a; s, 389a
ʿAbd al-Wāḥid b. Ayman (VII) s, 357b
ʿAbd al-Wāḥid b. al-Muḳtadir bi-ʾllāh (X) vii, 414a
ʿAbd al-Waḥīd b. al-Muwaffaḳ vii, 543a
ʿAbd al-Wāḥid b. Sulaymān b. ʿAbd al-Malik (VIII) iii, 878a; v, 1156a
ʿAbd al-Wāḥid b. Yazīd al-Hawwārī (VIII) iii, 169b, 297b, 1040b
ʿAbd al-Wāḥid b. Zayd (793) viii, 354b
ʿAbd al-Wāḥid b. Ziyād b. al-Muhallab (VIII) vii, 359b
ʿAbd al-Wāḥid al-Hās̲h̲imī (VII) s, 400b
ʿAbd al-Wāḥid al-Liḥyānī → Abū Darba al-Liḥyānī
ʿAbd al-Wāḥid al-Marrākus̲h̲ī (XIII) i, **94a**, 389b, ii, 72a; v, 1160b; s, 388a
ʿAbd al-Wāsiʿ D̲j̲abalī b.ʿAbd al-D̲j̲āmiʿ (1160) i, **94b**; viii, 971a
ʿAbd al-Wāsiʿ al-Niẓāmī i, 91a
ʿAbd Yag̲h̲ūt̲h̲ b. Ṣalāt iii, 223a
ʿAbd al-Ẓāhir, Banū ii, 305b
ʿAbda, Banū vi, 595a, 741b
ʿAbda b. al-Ṭabīb (VII) iv, 833a, 998b; vii, 308a
Abdāl i, **94b**; s, 168b
Abdāl, S̲h̲ayḵẖ → Bābā Walī
Abdāl Mūsā (XIV) iv, 811b
Abdālān-i Rūm i, 1162a; iv, 473b
Abdālī (Durrānī), Banū i, 72b, **95a**, 229a, b, 295a; ii, 628b; iii, 177b, 604a; iv, 537b; vi, 714a; vii, 853a; viii, 771a
ʿAbdalī, ʿAbdiliyyūn (Laḥḏj̲) i, **95b**, 345a
ʿAbdallāb ii, 351b, 944a; iv, 892b
ʿAbdallah → ʿAbd Allāh
ʿAbdallāhī → ʿAbdullāhi
ʿAbdān (Ḳarmaṭī) (IX) i, **95b**; ii, 851a; iii, 123b; iv, 198a, b, 660b; vi, 438b; viii, 922a
al-ʿAbdarī, Abū ʿAbd Allāh b. al-Ḥāḏj̲ḏj̲ → Ibn al-Ḥāḏj̲ḏj̲
al-ʿAbdarī, al-Ḥasan b. Muḥammad al-Iskandarī al-Kūs̲h̲ī viii, 51b

al-ʿAbdarī, Muḥammad b. Muḥammad (XIV) i, **96a**, 602b; iii, 736b; vii, 186a
Ābdast → Wuḍūʾ
Abdelkader → ʿAbd al-Ḳādir b. Muḥyī al-Dīn al-Ḥasanī
Abderrahmane El-Mejdoub (XVI) vi, 254b
ʿAbdī (XVII) i, **96b**
al-ʿAbdī → Abu ʾl-Hudhayl; Djaʿfar b. al-Sammāk; al-Walīd
al-ʿAbdī, Abū Muḥammad vi, 633a
ʿAbdī, Mawlawī ʿAbd Allāh (1664) v, 611a; viii, 256a
ʿAbdī Beg Nawīdī (1580) viii, 775b
ʿAbdī Čelebi Čiwi-zāde (1552) ii, 56b
ʿAbdī Efendi (XVIII) i, **97a**
Abdī Ipekçi (XX) vi, 95b
ʿAbdī Pasha (1692) i, **97a**; iv, 438a, 569a; vi, 990b
ʿAbdillāh, Banū → Muṭayr, Banū
ʿAbdīn (palace) s, 301a
Abdjad i, **97a**
Abdjar b. Djābir (641) i, 964a
ʿAbdū al-Ḥammūlī (1901) vi, 103a; x, 144a
Abdul Ghafoor, P.K. (XX) vi, 461a
ʿAbdülḥaḳḳ Ḥāmid Tarhan (XIX) vi, 610a
Abdul Kadiri (Gwandu) (XIX) ii, 1146a
Abdullah → ʿAbd Allāh
Abdullah bin Abdul Kadir Munshi → Munshi Abdullah
Abdullah Awlaniy (1934) vi, 769a, b
Abdullah Badriy vi, 769b
Abdullah Cevdet → Djewdet, ʿAbd Allāh
Abdullahi dan Fodio → ʿAbd Allāh b. Muḥammad Fūdī
Abdullah Haron, Imām (1995) ix, 731a
Abdullah Kadi Abdus Salaam, Imām (1807) ix, 730b
Abdullah Ḳadiriy (1839) vi, 767a, 769b
Abdullahi Sikka (XVII) iv, 550a
ʿAbdullāhi al-Taʿāʾishī → ʿAbd Allāh b. Muḥammad al-Taʿāʾishī
Abdullay Ba Demba (Fūta Djallon) (XVIII) ii, 960a, 1132b
Abdur Ghafur Breshna (1974) vi, 768a
Abdurähim Tiläsh Ötkür (XX) vi, 768a
Abdurrahiman Bafaki Tangal, Syed (1973) vi, 460a
Abdurrauf Abdurahim-oghlî Fiṭrat (1937) vi, 767b
Abdurrauf Shahidi (Shashudilin) (XX) vi, 767a
Abéché → Abeshr
Ābeh → Āwa
Abel → Hābīl
Abencerages → Ibn al-Sarrādj
Abenguefith → Ibn Wāfid
Abenragel → Ibn Abi ʾl-Ridjāl
Abeshr (Abeche) i, **98a**; s, 164a, 165b
Abhā i, **98a**, 707b, 709b; vi, 192a
Abhar i, **98b**; s, 22a
al-Abharī (985) vi, 279a, 280b
al-Abharī, Athīr al-Dīn Mufaḍḍal b. ʿUmar (1264) i, **98b**, 321a; ii, 949a; iii, 805a; iv, 92a; s, 414a
Abhay Singh (XVIII) i, 1053a; iii, 1010b
al-Ābī (1030) ii, 590b; vi, 820b; viii, 595a
Abi ʾl-ʿĀfiya, Banū ii, 979a
Abi ʾl-Ḥasan, Banū → Kalbids
Āb-i Istāda (lake) s, 329b
Āb-i Mashhad → Kashaf Rūd
Abi ʾl-Shawārib, Banū iii, 691a; s, 386a
Abīb → Taʾrīkh
ʿAbīd → ʿAbd; Makhzan
ʿĀbid, Banū (Meknes) iv, 416a; v, 379a; vi, 595a
ʿAbīd b. al-Abraṣ (VI) i, **99a**, 1241b; iii, 1177b; vii, 254b; s, 272b
ʿAbid b. ʿAlī (970) vi, 193a
ʿAbīd b. Sharya → Ibn Sharya
ʿAbīd al-Bukhārī (Morocco) i, 47a, 356a; v, 1191b, 1192a; vi, 891b
ʿĀbid al-Mutaʿāl b. ʿAbd al-Mutaʿāl (1881) vi, 627a
ʿAbīda, Banū vi, 566a
ʿAbīdā b. Hilāl (698) i, 811a; iv, 753a; v, 378a
ʿĀbidīn Pasha (1908) iii, 1117a; s, 63a
ʿAbidin Tadia Tjoessoep (South Africa) (1699) ix, 730b
ʿĀbidiyya iv, 668a
Abidjan ii, 63a
Abīduḳlīs → Anbaduḳlīs
Ābiḳ → ʿAbd
Ābinūs → Abanūs
Ābish Khātūn (1286) ii, 812a; iv, 975b, 1046b, 1047a; vi, 482a
Abīward (Bāward) i, **99b**
al-Abīwardī, Abu ʾl-Muẓaffar Muḥammad (1113) i, **100a**; s, 326b
Abkarius → Iskandar Agha
Abḳayḳ (Buḳayḳ) i, **100a**

Abkhāz i, **100b**, 1189b; iv, 351a; v, 488a, b, 496a
ʿAbla i, 518b, 521b
al-Ablaḳ → Samawʾal
al-Ablaḳ al-Asadī i, 659b
al-Abnāʾ i, **102a**; v, 1111a; s, 115b, 116a
Abnāʾ al-Atrāk i, 102a
Abnāʾ al-dawla i, 102a; v, 57b
Abnā-yi sipāhīyān i, 102a
Abnūs → Abanūs
Abomey ii, 93b, 94a
Abou Chabakeh, Elias → Abū Shabaka, Ilyās
Aboukir → Abūḳīr
ʿAbr Muḥarram vi, 438b
Abraha (VI) i, **102a**, 144b, 549a; ii, 895a; iv, 318b; vi, 145b, 358b, 561b, 563b; ix, 817b
Abraham → Ibrāhīm al-Khalīl
Abraham ben Ezra (1168) vii, 568a
Abrash al-Kalbī (745) iii, 494b; vi, 624a
al-ʿAbrī, Mādjid b. Khāmis (ʿUmān) (1927) viii, 993b
ʿAbs, Banū i, 518b, 521b; ii, 71b, 873b, 1023a; iv, 1144a; s, 177a
ʿAbsīs, Banū vi, 649a
al-Abshīhī → al-Ibshīhī
al-Abṭaḥ (al-Muʿābada) vi, 154a, b
Abtariyya iii, 244a; s, 129b
Abū → Kunya
Abu ʾl-ʿAbbās, amīr → Aḥmad II (Ḥafṣid)
Abu ʾl-ʿAbbās b. Abī Sālim (1387) vi, 593b, 594a
Abu ʾl-ʿAbbās b. Wāsil (1006) s, 119a
Abu ʾl-ʿAbbās ʿAbd Allāh → ʿAbd Allāh I (Aghlabid)
Abu ʾl-ʿAbbās ʿAbd Allāh b. Ibrāhīm → ʿAbd Allāh II (Aghlabid)
Abu ʾl-ʿAbbās Aḥmad (Ḥafṣid) → Aḥmad I, II
Abu ʾl-ʿAbbās Aḥmad (Marīnid) (XIV) i, 167b; iii, 836a
Abu ʾl-ʿAbbās Aḥmad (Sharīf, Ceuta) s, 112b
Abu ʾl-ʿAbbās Aḥmad b. ʿAbd Allāh → Abū Maḥallī al-Sidjilmāsī
Abu ʾl-ʿAbbās Aḥmad b. al-ʿArūs → Ibn ʿArūs
Abu ʾl-ʿAbbās al-Aʿmā → al-Aʿmā al-Tuṭīlī
Abu ʾl-ʿAbbās al-Īrānshahrī i, 1031b
Abu ʾl-ʿAbbās al-Ḳaṣṣāb (XI) i, 146a; iv, 1057b
Abu ʾl-ʿAbbās al-Maghribī (XII) ii, 528a
Abu ʾl-ʿAbbās Maʾmūn b. Maʾmūn (Khwārazmshāh) (1017) vi, 726b
Abu ʾl-ʿAbbās Muḥammad b. al-Aghlab → Muḥammad I (Aghlabid)
Abu ʾl-ʿAbbās al-Nabātī (1240) i, 214b; iii, 737a; s, 114b
Abu ʾl-ʿAbbās Rabindjānī (942) vi, 608b
Abu ʾl-ʿAbbās al-Saffāḥ (ʿAbbāsid) (754) i, 12b, 16a, 17a, 42b, 43a, 45b, **103a**, 107b, 116b, 149a, 485a, 895a, 1033b; ii, 178a, 324a; iii, 265b, 988b; iv, 446b, 729a; v, 1233a; vi, 139b, 262b, 334b, 345a, 427b, 428a; vii, 396a; s, 31b, 198b
Abu ʾl-ʿAbbās Ṣuʿlūk (X) s, 356b
Abu ʾl-ʿAbbās al-Ṭabīkhī (963) vii, 694b
Abū ʿAbd al-ʿĀl → Aḥmad al-Badawī
Abū ʿAbd Allāh → Djaʿfar al-Ṣādiḳ
Abū ʿAbd Allāh b. al-Djannān (kātib) (XIII) viii, 573b
Abū ʿAbd Allāh b. Djarāda (XI) iii, 730b, 766a; s, 30a
Abū ʿAbd Allāh b. Manda → Ibn Manda
Abū ʿAbd Allāh b. Mardanīsh (Martinez) (1172) iii, **864b**; vi, 339b
Abū ʿAbd Allāh b. Muʿādh → Ibn Muʿādh
Abū ʿAbd Allāh b. Muḥsin al-Bashīr (XII) iii, 207b
Abū ʿAbd Allāh al-Andalusī (X) vi, 727b
Abū ʿAbd Allāh Aṣbagh b. al-Faradj al-Faḳīh vii, 400b
Abū ʿAbd Allāh Aṣbagh al-Warrāḳ (811) xi, 150a
Abū ʿAbd Allāh al-Baṣrī al-Djuʿal (980) iii, 832a,b; vii, 312a; s, **12b**
Abū ʿAbd Allāh al-Dāmaghānī (Ḳāḍī) → Dāmaghānī
Abū ʿAbd Allāh al-Djayhānī → al-Djayhānī
Abū ʿAbd Allāh Ḥusayn (X) iii, 128b
Abū ʿAbd Allāh al-Ḥuṣrī (XI) i, 146a
Abū ʿAbd Allāh al-Māhānī → al-Māhānī
Abū ʿAbd Allāh al-Mahdī li-Dīn Allāh (X) s, 363a, b
Abū ʿAbd Allāh Muḥammad (amīr) (XIV) iii, 68b, 826a, b
Abū ʿAbd Allāh Muḥammad I → al-Mustanṣir
Abū ʿAbd Allāh Muḥammad II → Abū ʿAṣīda

Abū ʿAbd Allāh Muḥammad III → al-Mustanṣir
Abū ʿAbd Allāh Muḥammad V (Ḥafṣid) (1526) i, 678a; iii, 69a; iv, 1156a
Abū ʿAbd Allāh Muḥammad b. al-ʿAbbās b. ʿĪsā al-ʿUbbādī (1467) s, 403a
Abū ʿAbd Allāh Muḥammad b. Muḥammad b. al-ʿAbbās (1513) s, 403a
Abū ʿAbd Allāh Muḥammad b. Abi ʿUmar Ibn ʿAbd al-Barr (XII) ix, 308b
Abū ʿAbd Allāh Muḥammad b. Aḥmad Djayhānī (IX) iv, 22a
Abū ʿAbd Allāh Muḥammad b. ʿAlī al-ʿAlawī, Sayyid (1053) s, 19a, 401a
Abū ʿAbd Allāh Muḥammad b. ʿAnbasa (X) i, 159a
Abū ʿAbd Allāh Muḥammad b. Bakr al-Nafūsī, Shaykh (1048) ii, 141a; iii, 95b; vi, 948a
Abū ʿAbd Allāh Muḥammad b. Ḥamawiya al-Djuwaynī (1135) i, 765b
Abū ʿAbd Allāh Muḥammad b. al-Ḥasan (970) s, 13a, b
Abū ʿAbd Allāh Muḥammad b. al-Ḥasan (Tripoli) (1022) vii, 482a, b
Abū ʿAbd Allāh Muḥammad b. Ibrāhīm b. al-Sarrādj → Ibn al-Sarrādj
Abū ʿAbd Allāh Muḥammad b. Khālid al-Barkī (IX) s, 127b
Abū ʿAbd Allāh Muḥammad b. Muḥammad b. Yūsuf al-Sarrādj → Ibn al-Sarrādj
Abū ʿAbd Allāh Muḥammad Ādarrāḳ (1658) s, 40a
Abū ʿAbd Allāh Muḥammad al-Andalusī (1573) i, 56a
Abū ʿAbd Allāh Muḥammad al-Fāsī → Ibn al-Ḥādjdj
Abū ʿAbd Allāh Muḥammad al-Gharnāṭī → Ibn al-Sarrādj
Abū ʿAbd Allāh Muḥammad al-Ḥādjdj (Dilāʾī) (1729) s, 223b
Abū ʿAbd Allāh Muḥammad al-Ḥasan → al-Ḥasan
Abū ʿAbd Allāh Muḥammad al-Hazmīrī (XIV) iii, 339a, b
Abū ʿAbd Allāh Muḥammad Ibn ʿAbd al-Munʿim → Ibn ʿAbd al-Munʿim
Abū ʿAbd Allāh Muḥammad al-Mālaḳī → Ibn al-Sarrādj
Abū ʿAbd Allāh al-Shīʿī (911) i, **103b**, 249a, 863b, 1175b; ii, 98a, 852a, b; iii, 655b; iv, 198a, 361a; v, 540b, 1242b, 1243a; vi, 439a, 727b
Abū ʿAbd Allāh al-Tamīmi (X) iv, 1134a
Abū ʿAbd Allāh Yaʿḳūb b. Dāʾūd (802) i, **103b**, 157b; ii, 870a; v, 1238b; vii, 646b
Abū ʿAdnān (VIII) s, 20a
Abu ʾl-Aghlab Ibrāhīm (Aghlabid) (851) ix, 584b
Abū Aḥmad b. Djaʿfar (ʿAbbāsid) (IX) vii, 390b
Abū Aḥmad b. al-Mutawakkil → al-Muwaffaḳ (ʿAbbāsid)
Abū Aḥmad ʿAbd al-Salām (1014) ii, 127b; v, 928b
Abū Aḥmad al-ʿAskarī → al-ʿAskarī
Abū Aḥmad al-Ḥusayn b. Isḥāḳ Ibn Karnīb (X) vi, 844b
Abū Aḥmad Khalaf (Ṣaffārid) (1003) viii, 797b
Abū Aḥmad Muḥammad b. Maḥmūd b. Sebüktigin (Ghaznawid) (1030) vi, 780a
Abū Aḥmad al-Mūsawī (1004) iv, 378a
Abu ʾl-Aḥwas Maʿn b. Sumādiḥ al-Tudjībī (1052) vi, 576b
Abu ʾl-ʿAlāʾ b. Karnīb (X) i, 159a
Abu ʾl-ʿAlāʾ Ibn Ḥassūl (1058) viii, 938a
Abu ʾl-ʿAlāʾ al-Maʿarrī → al-Maʿarrī
Abu ʾl-ʿAlāʾ Mawdūdī, Mawlānā (1979) ii, 437a; iii, 433b; vi, 461b, **872a**
Abu ʾl-ʿAlāʾ al-Rabaʿī → Ṣāʿid al-Baghdādī
Abū ʿAlī b. Khalāṣ (XIII) s, 111b
Abū ʿAlī b. Marwān (Diyār Bakr) (X) ii, 344a; iii, 128b; v, 453a
Abū ʿAlī b. Muḥammad b. Sūrī (XI) ii, 1099b, 1100a
Abū ʿAlī b. al-Samḥ (XI) vi, 845b; s, 25a
Abū ʿAlī b. ʿUthmān II, Abū Saʿīd (XIV) s, 112b
Abū ʿAlī b. al-Walīd (XI) s, 30a
Abū ʿAlī Aḥmad b. Muḥammad b. al-Muẓaffar (955) s, 386b
Abū ʿAlī al-Baghdādī → al-Ḳālī, Abū ʿAlī
Abū ʿAlī al-Balʿamī → al-Balʿamī
Abū ʿAlī al-Baṣīr s, 25a
Abū ʿAlī Čaghānī (X) iv, 22b, 23a, 100b; v, 76a; s, 125b
Abū ʿAlī al-Djuzdjānī (IX) vi, 569b
Abū ʿAlī al-Fārisī → al-Fārisī
Abū ʿAlī al-Fārmadī (1080) ii, 1038b; iii, 103a; iv, 1058a; s, **14b**

Abū ʿAlī al-Ḥākim → Muḥammad b. Aḥmad Abu ʾl-Shalaʿlaʿ
Abū ʿAlī al-Ḥasan b. ʿAlī al-Djīlī i, 1237a; ii, 496a
Abū ʿAlī al-Ḥasan b. Ismāʿīl b. Ḥammād (Ibn Dirham) (X) s, 385a
Abū ʿAlī al-Ḥasan b. Marwān (Diyār Bakr) (997) vi, 626a
Abū ʿAlī Ḥasan b. Muḥammad (Mīkālī) (1032) → Ḥasanak
Abu ʿAlī al-Ḥasan b. Muḥammad b. Bāṣo (1275) ix, 252b
Abū ʿAlī al-Ḥasan b. Yaḥyā (XI) ix, 582b
Abū ʿAlī al-Ḥasan al-Yūsī, Shaykh (XVII) vi, 591a
Abū ʿAlī Ḥusayn b. Abi ʾl-Ḥusayn (927) i, 688a; iii, 255a
Abū ʿAlī al-Ḥusaynī (1003) ii, 125b; v, 1126b
Abū ʿAlī Ḳalandar Pānīpatī (1324) i, **104b**; iv, 666a
Abū ʿAlī al-Ḳālī → al-Ḳālī
Abū ʿAlī al-Masīlī (XII) vi, 728b
Abū ʿAlī Muḥammad b. Aḥmad al-Balkhī ii, 918b
Abū ʿAlī Muḥammad b. Arslān, Muntadjab al-Mulk (kātib) (1139) vi, 913b
Abū ʿAlī Muḥammad b. Ilyās (955) ii, 1b; iii, 1156b; v, 158a, b, 352b
Abū ʿAlī Muḥammad al-Khuzāʿī → Diʿbil
Abū ʿAlī al-Muḥassin (Ṣābiʾ) (1010) viii, 674b
Abū ʿAlī Ṣāliḥ b. ʿAbd al-Ḥalīm (XIV) v, 1157a
Abū ʿAlī Shādhān (1040) vi, 914b
Abū ʿAlī Shatrandj (XII) iii, 355b
Abū ʿAlī Simdjūrī → Simdjūrī
Abū ʿAlī al-Sindī (IX) i, 162b
Abū ʿAlī Ṭāhir al-Mazdaḳānī (XII) ii, 282a
Abū ʿAlī Ṭarsūsī (X) i, 146b
Abu ʿAlī al-Yūsī → al-Yūsī
Abū ʿAlī Zāhir (998) i, 146a
Abu ʾl-ʿĀliya al-Riyāḥī (708) i, **104b**
Abu ʾl-ʿAmaythal (854) ix, 454a; s, **15a**
Abū ʿĀmir b. Abī Yaʿḳūb Yūsuf (Marīnid) (1288) vi, 593a
Abū ʿĀmir Ibn Arḳam (vizier) (XII) vi, 110b
Abū ʿĀmir al-Kinānī al-Laythī → ʿUrwa b. Udhayna
Abū ʿĀmir al-Rāhib (VII) vi, 647a
Abū ʿAmmār ʿAbd al-Kāfī al-Wardjlānī (XIII) iii, 96b; s, **15a**
Abū ʿAmmār al-Aʿmā Nukkārī (X) i, 163a, 164a; iii, 95b, 659b
Abū ʿAmr b. al-ʿAlāʾ al-Māzinī → al-Māzinī
Abū ʿAmr ʿAbbād b. Muḥammad → al-Muʿtaḍid b. ʿAbbād
Abū ʿAmr Ismāʿīl b. Nudjayd (976) ix, 811b
Abū ʿAmr al-Iṣṭakhrī iii, 823b
Abū ʿAmr al-Mughāzilī (X) i, 159a
Abū ʿAmr al-Shaybānī, Isḥāḳ b. Mirār → al-Shaybānī, Abū ʿAmr Isḥāḳ b. Mirār
Abū ʿAmr Zabbān b. al-ʿAlāʾ (770) i, 42b, 104b, **105a**, 158a, 167a, 717b; iii, 136a, 742a; iv, 249a; v, 805a; vii, 114a; s, 24b
Abū ʿAmr al-Zāhid (X) s, 37b
Abū ʿAmra Kaysān → Kaysān
Abu ʾl-ʿAnbas al-Ṣaymarī (888) iv, 1099b; ix, 453b s, **16a**
Abu ʾl-ʿArab Muḥammad al-Tamīmī (945) i, 24a, **106a**; vi, 352b, 353b
Abū ʿArīsh i, **106b**; v, 808a; vi, 191b; s, 30a
Abū ʿArūba (930) i, **106b**
Abu ʾl-ʿĀṣ, Banū vi, 621b, 622a
Abu ʾl-Asad al-Ḥimmānī (VIII) s, **17b**
Abu ʾl-ʿAsākir Sulṭān b. Sadīd al-Mulk ʿAlī (Munḳidh, Banū) (1154) vii, 578a
Abu ʾl-ʿAshāʾir (Ḥamdānid) (956) vi, 506b
Abū ʿAṣīda (Ḥafṣid) (1309) iii, 67b
Abū ʿĀṣim al-Nabīl (828) iii, 25a; s, **17b**
Abu ʾl-ʿAskar b. Maʿdān (1030) vi, 193a
Abu ʾl-Aswad al-Duʾalī (Dīlī) (688) i, **106b**, 565a, 566b, 1297b; iii, 173a; iv, 731b; v, 116b; vii, 280a, 913a; ix, 525a
Abu ʾl-Aswār Shāwur (Shaddādid) i, 638a, 660b; ii, 680b; iv, 347b, 348a, 815a
Abū ʿAṭāʾ al-Sindī (VI) i, **107a**
Abu ʾl-ʿAtāhiya (825) i, **107b**, 569b, 587a, 751b, 1081b; iii, 618a, 996a, 1019b, 1262b; vi, 253a; vii, 694b; viii, 376b; xi, 126b; s, 122b, 304a
Abu ʾl-ʿAtāhiya (Ṭarīf, Āl) (Yemen) s, 335a
Abu ʾl-Aṭbāḳ → Mubārak Abu ʾl-Aṭbāḳ
Abu ʾl-Aʿwar al-Sulamī (VII) i, **108a**; ix, 818a; s, 221b
Abū ʿAwn ʿAbd al-Malik b. Yazīd al-Khurasānī (766) i, 16a, **108b**; iv, 447b; x, 926b

Abu 'l-ʿAynāʾ (896) i, **108b**, 1082b; iii, 672b; s, 25a
Abu 'l-ʿAysh Aḥmad (Idrīside) (954) iii, 1036b
Abū Ayyūb al-Anṣārī (672) i, **108b**, 312b; iv, 270b; v, 533a; vi, 354a, 645b, 646b, 862a
Abū Ayyūb al-Madīnī ii, 1011b; iii, 682a, 698b
Abu 'l-ʿAzāʾim (1937) s, **18a**
Abu 'l-Badr b. Nuṣrat Shāh (Bengal) → Fīrūz Shāh, ʿAlāʾ al-Dīn (Bengal)
Abū Baghla (Kabylia) (XIX) iv, 362a
Abu 'l-Bahār b. Khalūf (XI) vii, 482a
Abū Baḥr Ṣakhr → al-Aḥnaf b. Ḳays
Abu 'l-Baḳāʾ (Runda) (1285) viii, 616a
Abu 'l-Baḳāʾ, Shaykh (XV) i, 841b
Abu 'l-Baḳāʾ b. Abī Zakariyyāʾ (Ḥafṣid) (1311) iii, 67b; v, 531a; vi, 404b
Abu Bakari b. Mwengo (XVIII) s, 351b
Abū Bakr (Ildeñizid) (1208) vi, 500b
Abū Bakr (Manding Bori, Mali) (XIII) vi, 421b
Abū Bakr (al-Ṣiddīḳ) (634) i, **109b**, 114b, 127b, 158b, 381b, 382a, 443b, 549b, 697a, 1113b; ii, 601a, 725a, 842b, 844a, 845b; iii, 33a, 64a, b; iv, 927b, 937a; v, 404b, 777a; vi, 138b, 139a, 152b, 168b, 266b, 350b, 546b, 575a, 604a, 645b, 647a, b, 650a, 652a, 659a, 668b, 671a, 675a; ix, **534b**; s, 89b, 129b, 130a, 343a, 692b, 693a, b
Abū Bakr (Ḥafṣid) → Abū Yaḥyā Abū Bakr
Abū Bakr (Salghūrid) → Abū Bakr b. Saʿd b. Zangī
Abū Bakr Sayf al-Dīn (Mamlūk) (1341) ii, 285b
Abū Bakr b. ʿAbd Allāh → Ibn Abī 'l-Dunyā
Abū Bakr b. ʿAbd al-ʿAzīz (Balansiya) (1085) i, 446a, 986a
Abū Bakr b. ʿAbd al-Karīm (ḳāʾid) (1668) vi, 595a
Abū Bakr b. ʿAbd al-Raḥmān b. al-Mughīra (711) vi, 140a
Abū Bakr b. ʿAbd al-Raḥmān ʿUbayd Allāh (716) s, 311b
Abū Bakr b. ʿAbd al-Ṣamad → ʿAbd al-Ṣamad
Abū Bakr b. Abī Djamra (1202) viii, 635b
Abū Bakr b. Abī Saʿīd (XV) i, 852b
Abū Bakr b. Abī Shayba → Ibn Abī Shayba
Abū Bakr b. Aḥmad → Ibn Ḳāḍī Shuhba
Abū Bakr b. Aḥmad b. Muḥammad b. Zayd Ṭūsī i, 423b
Abū Bakr b. ʿAlī al-Ḥamawī → Ibn Ḥidjdja
Abū Bakr b. ʿAlī al-Ṣinhādjī → al-Baydhāk
Abū Bakr b. al-ʿArabī → Ibn al-ʿArabī
Abū Bakr b. ʿAyyāsh (809) i, 707a; xi, 243b
Abū Bakr b. Bahrām al-Dimashḳī (1691) i, 698a; ii, 589a
Abū Bakr b. Eldiguz → Abū Bakr b. Pahlawān
Abū Bakr b. Fakhr al-Dīn (Maḳdishū) (XII) vi, 128b
Abū Bakr b. Ḥammād (X) iv, 662b
Abū Bakr b. Ibrāhīm al-Ṣaḥrāwī → Ibn Tifalwīt
Abū Bakr b. Ismāʿil b. ʿAbd al-Haḳḳ (XII) v, 60b
Abū Bakr b. Kīrān (1851) s, 390b
Abū Bakr b. al-Khamīs (XIII) s, 382a
Abū Bakr b. al-Maḳbūl al-Zaylaʿī (XVI) v, 807b
Abū Bakr b. Mīrānshāh b. Tīmūr (Timūrid) (XV) vii, 105b
Abū Bakr b. Mudjāhid → Ibn Mudjāhid, Aḥmad
Abū Bakr b. al-Mughīra al-Makhzūmī (712) s, **311a**
Abū Bakr b. Muḥammad b.ʿAmr b. Ḥazm (ca. 730) x, 81a
Abū Bakr b. Muḥammad (Maḳdishū) (XIV) vi, 128b
Abū Bakr b. Muḥammad, Shaykh s, 223a
Abū Bakr b. Muḥammad, Sultan (Adal) (XVI) i, 286b; iii, 4a
Abū Bakr b. al-Nāṣir Muḥammad (Mamlūk) (1341) vi, 323b
Abū Bakr b. Pahlawān Muḥammad (Ildeñizid) (1210) i, 300b, 301a; iii, 1111b, 1112a; iv, 349a; vi, 501a; viii, 235a
Abū Bakr b. Saʿd (I) b. Zangī (Salghurid) (1260) i, 434a, 942b; iv, 498a, 764b; v, 671a; vi, 609a; viii, 701b, 720a, 978b
Abū Bakr b. Shādhān (X) ix, 847b
Abū Bakr b. Shāhūya (Ḳarmaṭī) iv, 664b
Abū Bakr b. ʿUmar (Maḳdishū) (XIV) vi, 128b
Abū Bakr b. ʿUmar al-Lamtūnī → al-Lamtūnī

Abū Bakr b. Ẓafar Khān (XIV) ii, 1077a
Abū Bakr b. Zahr iv, 1007b
Abū Bakr b. Zayd al-Djirāʿī (1478) i, 759a
Abū Bakr al-Ādjurrī → al-Ādjurrī
Abū Bakr Aḥmad b. ʿAbd al-Raḥmān (1040) vi, 353b
Abū Bakr Aḥmad b. ʿAlī b. Thābit → al-Khaṭīb al-Baghdādī
Abū Bakr Aḥmad b. Isḥāḳ b. Zayd b. Ṭāhir (Ṭāhirid, al-Andalus) (1063) x, 105b
Abū Bakr Aḥmad b. Kāmil (961) x, 11a
Abū Bakr al-Aṣamm → al-Aṣamm
Abū Bakr al-ʿAtīḳ (Sokoto) (1842) vii, 435b
Abū Bakr al-ʿ Aydarus → al-ʿAydarus, Abū Bakr
Abū Bakr al-Bayṭār → Ibn al-Mundhir
Abū Bakr Djamālī Yazdī (1185) vi, 908a
Abū Bakr Dughlat → Abū Bakr Mīrzā b. Sāniz
Abū Bakr al-Hirawī (1199) vi, 691b
Abū Bakr Hishām → Hishām III
Abū Bakr Ibn Zaydūn b. al-Muʿtamid Ibn ʿAbbād (1091) vii, 766b
Abū Bakr al-Ḳaffāl (1026) i, 146a
Abū Bakr al-Ḳaṭīʿī (978) i, 273b; iii, 158b
Abū Bakr al-Khallāl → al-Khallāl
Abū Bakr al-Kharāʾiṭī → al-Kharāʾiṭī
Abū Bakr al-Khwārizmī → al-Khwārizmī
Abū Bakr al-Marwāzī → al-Marwāzī, Abū Bakr
Abū Bakr al-Mayūrḳī → al-Mayūrḳī, Abū Bakr
Abū Bakr Mīrzā (Tīmūrid) (XV) iv, 586a, b
Abū Bakr Mīrzā b. Sāniz (1514) ii, 622a; iv, 699a
Abū Bakr Muḥammad b. Ayyūb → al-Malik al-ʿĀdil I
Abū Bakr Muḥammad b. Hāshim (Khālidī) (990) iii, 111a; iv, 936b
Abū Bakr Muḥammad b. Isḥāḳ (Karrāmī) (XI) viii, 63b
Abū Bakr al-Rāzī → al-Rāzī
Abū Bakr Saʿd b. Zangī Rashīd al-Dīn (atabeg) (XIV) vi, 524a
Abū Bakr Sayf al-Dīn b. Kāmil → al-Malik al-ʿĀdil II
Abū Bakr al-Shāshī (X) i, 126b; s, 194b, 384a
Abū Bakr al-Sidjistānī (928) iii, 158b
Abū Bakr Tādj al-Dīn, Sultan (XIX) viii, 1042a
Abū Bakr Wafāʾī, Pīr (1496) i, 966a
Abū Bakr Yaʿḳūb b. Nāṣir al-Dīn, ḳāḍī (XIV) iv, 1127b
Abū Bakr al-Zubaydī → al-Zubaydī
Abū Bakra (671) i, **111a**; vi, 710a; s, 354b
Abū Barāʾ (VII) i, 1232b
Abu 'l-Barakāt al-ʿAlawī al-Zaydī (1145) s, **19a**
Abu 'l-Barakāt Hibat Allāh al-Baghdādī (1164) i, **111b**; ii, 774a; iv, 306a; vi, 450b; s, 273b
Abu 'l-Barakāt al-Barbarī al-Maghribī (Maldives) vi, 245b
Abu 'l-Barakāt Muḥammad al-Balāfiḳī → Ibn al-Ḥādjdj
Abū Barāḳish (1145) i, 131b; s, **19a**
Abū Baṣīr (627) vi, 651b
Abū Baṭṭa → al-Irdjānī
Abu 'l-Bayḍāʾ al-Riyāḥī (VIII) s, **20a**, 73b
Abū Bayhas al-Hayṣam b. Djābir (713) i, **113a**; IX, 766b
Abu Bekr Musaliar, T.K. (XX) vi, 462a
Abū Bilal → Mirdās b. Udayya
Abū Bishr Mattā b. Yūnus → Mattā b. Yūnus
Abū Budjayr Yaḥyā al-Nadjashī (IX) xi, 126b
Abū Bukayr (1179) x, 303a
Abū Burda → al-Ashʿarī
Abū Dabbūs → Idrīs al-Maʾmūn
Abū Ḍabī → Abū Ẓabī
Abū Dahbal al-Djumaḥī (715) i, **113b**
Abu 'l-Daḳḳāḳ (XI) vi, 569b
Abū Ḍamḍam i, **113b**
Abū Ḍarba al-Liḥyānī (Ḥafṣid) (1317) iii, 67b; iv, 338a; v, 1247a
Abu 'l-Dardāʾ (652) i, **113b**, 959b
Abū Dāʾūd, Zayn al-Dīn al-Ḳurashī (XIII) viii, 156b
Abū Dāʾūd al-Bakrī (VIII) i, 141b, 1001a
Abū Dāʾūd al-Sidjistānī (889) i, **114a**; iii, 24a, 158b; vi, 346b, 634a, 658a; s, 232b
Abu 'l-Dawāniḳ → al-Manṣūr, Abū Djaʿfar ʿAbd Allāh (ʿAbbāsid)
Abū Dāwūd Muḥammad b. Aḥmad (IX) s, 125b
Abū Dāwūdids → Bānīdjūrids
Abū Dhabī → Abū Ẓabī
Abu 'l-Dhahab → Muḥammad Abu 'l-Dhahab
Abu 'l-Dhahab, Muḥammad Bey (1775) i,

391b, 392a, 1033a; iii, 992a, iv, 853a; vii, 179a; s, **20b**, 44a
Abū Dharr al-Ghifārī (652) i, **114b**, 266b, 382a, 549b; ii, 846b; vii, 264b, 517b, 780a; ix, 819b
Abū Dharr al-Harawī (XI) i, 864b
Abu 'l-Dhawwād Muḥammad, amīr b. al-Musayyab (996) (ʿUḳaylid) x, 786b; s, 119a
Abū Dhuʾayb al-Hudhalī (649) i, **115a**; iii, 273a; iv, 252a; vi, 603b; vii, 308a, 843b, 980b, 981a; x, 2b
Abu 'l-Ḍiyāʾ Tewfīk → Ebüzziya Tevfik
Abū Djad → Abdjad
Abū Djaʿfar b. Aḥmad b. ʿAbd Allāh b. Ḥabash (al-ḥāsib) iii, 9a
Abū Djaʿfar Aḥmad (Ifrīḳiyya) (IX) viii, 844b
Abū Djaʿfar Aḥmad b. ʿAṭiyya (vizier) (XII) ii, 1014a
Abū Djaʿfar Aḥmad b. Muḥammad (Sīstān) (963) i, 116a
Abū Djaʿfar Aḥmad b. Muḥammad b. Khalaf (Ṣaffārid) (X) viii, 797a
Abū Djaʿfar Aḥmad b. Muḥammad al-Barḳī → al-Barḳī
Abū Djaʿfar al-Andalūsī → al-Ruʿaynī
Abū Djaʿfar al-Ḥadhdhāʾ (X) iii, 823b
Abū Djaʿfar Ḥamdīn → ʿAlī b. Aḍḥā
Abū Djaʿfar al-Hāshimī (1078) i, 1040a; iii, 160a, 699b, 700a, 766b
Abū Djaʿfar Ibn Saʿīd (1165) iii, 66a
Abū Djaʿfar al-Khāzin → al-Khāzin
Abū Djaʿfar al-Manṣūr → al-Manṣūr (ʿAbbāsid)
Abū Djaʿfar Muḥammad b. ʿAbd Kān → Ibn ʿAbd Kān
Abū Djaʿfar Muḥammad b. Abi 'l-Ḥusayn Aḥmad (X) s, 357a
Abū Djaʿfar Muḥammad b. Abi 'l-Ḥasan al-ʿAskarī (IX) vii, 459b
Abū Djaʿfar Muḥammad b. al-Zubayr → Ibn al-Zubayr
Abū Djaʿfar al-Ruʾāsī → al-Ruʾāsī
Abū Djaʿfar al-Ṭūsī → al-Ṭūsī
Abū Djaʿfar Ustādh-Hurmuz → Ustādh-Hurmuz
Abū Djahl ʿAmr b. Hishām b. al-Mughīra (624) i, **115a**, 136b, 151a, 868a; ii, 843b; iii, 152b; vi, 138a, 145b, 146b, 603b; vii, 369b
Abu 'l-Djārūd → al-Djārūdiyya
Abu 'l-Djārūd Ziyād b. al-Mundhir (VIII) ii, 485a; vii, 399a; s, 48b
Abu 'l-Djaysh Mudjāhid → Mudjāhid al-Āmirī
Abu Djisrā (ʿIrāḳ) i, 865b
Abū Djubayla → Djabala b. al-Ḥārith
Abu 'l-Djūd Muḥammad b. al-Layth (X) iv, 1182b
Abū Djummayza (1889) ii, 124a; iv, 953a; v, 1250b
Abu 'l-Djunayd → Abū Nukhayla
Abū Duʿāba ʿAṭiyya (1063) vi, 379b
Abū Duʾād al-Iyādī (VI) i, **115b**; iv, 289a, 919a
Abū Dulaf (Sāmarrā) i, 621a, 624a
Abū Dulaf al-Khazradjī (X) i, **116a**, 570b, 967a; iii, 106a; vi, 364b, 365a, 624b; vii, 495a; ix, 70b, 611b; x, 304b; s, 116a, 363a
Abū Dulaf al-Ḳāsim al-ʿIdjlī → al-Ḳāsim b. ʿIsā
Abū Dulāma Zand b. al-Djawn (776) i, **116b**, 909b; iv, 1003b; vi, 475b
Abu 'l-Dunyā Abu 'l Ḥasan ʿAlī (928) i, **117a**
Abū Duwād → Abū Duʾād
Abu 'l-Faḍāʾil → Ḥamdānids
Abu 'l-Faḍāʾil al-Sayyid Rukn al-Dīn → al-Astarābādhī, Rukn al-Dīn
Abu 'l-Faḍl b. Abī Sālim (Marīnid) (XIV) vi, 593b
Abu 'l-Faḍl b. al-ʿAmīd (vizier) (970) vi, 199a, 637b
Abu 'l-Faḍl b. Idrīs Bidlīsī → Bidlīsī
Abu 'l-Faḍl b. Mubārak Nāgawrī → Abu 'l-Faḍl ʿAllāmī
Abū Faḍl b. al-Naḥwī → Ibn al-Naḥwī
Abu 'l-Faḍl al-ʿAbbās b. ʿĪsā (faḳīh) (943) iv, 683b
Abu 'l-Faḍl al-ʿAbbās al-Shīrāzī → al-ʿAbbās b. al-Ḥusayn
Abu 'l-Faḍl ʿAllāmī (1602) i, **117a**, 297a, 1331a; ii, 296a, 380a, 871a, b; iii, 423b; iv, 704a,759b, 1127b; vi, 131a, 456b; vii, 199b, 221a, 321b, 342b, 898a, 925a; s, 3b, 142b, 280a, 325a, 410b
Abu 'l-Faḍl Djaʿfar b. ʿAlī al-Dimashḳī (XII) vi, 205a; s, 42b
Abu 'l-Faḍl Djaʿfar b. Ḥalwān (XII) v, 60b
Abu 'l-Faḍl Djaʿfar b. Muḥammad, al-Thāʾir fi-'llāh (961) iii, 255a; vi, 941b; x, **430b**; s, 363a

Abu 'l-Faḍl Djaʿfar b. al-Muḳtadī (XI) vii, 540b
Abu 'l-Faḍl Djamāl al-Dīn Muḥammad → Djamāl Ḳarshī
Abu 'l-Faḍl al-Djārūdī (XI) i, 515b
Abu 'l-Faḍl Ismāʿīl → Ismāʿīl, Abu 'l-Faḍl
Abu 'l-Faḍl ʿIyāḍ → ʿIyāḍ
Abu 'l-Faḍl Maʾmūrī vii, 322a
Abu 'l-Faḍl Mīrzā (Ḳādjār) (XX) vii, 432b
Abu 'l-Faḍl Muḥammad → Ibn al-ʿAmīd
Abu 'l-Faḍl Muḥammad al-Baghdādī, vizier (XI) v, 929b
Abu 'l-Faḍl Mūsā al-Iznīḳī → al-Iznīḳī
Abu 'l-Faḍl Raydān → Raydān al-Saḳlabī
Abu 'l-Faḍl ʿUbayd Allāh (Mīkālī) (1044) vii, 26a
Abu 'l-Faradj → Babbaghāʾ; Ibn al-Djawzī; Ibn al-ʿIbrī; Ibn al-Nadīm; Ibn al-Ṭayyib; al-Shīrāzī
Abu 'l-Faradj b. Amarī (al-kabīr al-ḥilw) ix, 30a, 199b
Abu 'l-Faradj b. Masʿūd Rūnī (1106) iv, 61b; s, **21a**
Abu 'l-Faradj b. al-Ṭayyib → Ibn al-Ṭayyib
Abu 'l-Faradj Furḳān → Jeshuah b. Judah
Abu 'l-Faradj Hārūn → Hārūn b. al-Faradj
Abu 'l-Faradj al-Iṣbahānī (967) i, 10a, **118a**, 590a, 1354a; iii, 928a; v, 936b; vi, 99a, 604b; vii, 306b, 358b, 771a; viii, 14b; s, 24a, 35b, 64a, 116b, 183a, 310b, 311b, 401a, 409a
Abu 'l-Faradj Muḥammad Fasāndjus → Ibn Fasāndjus
Abu 'l-Faradj Muḥammad al-Waʾwāʾ (X) iv, 1005b
Abu 'l-Faradj Sidjzī s, 21a
Abu 'l-Faraḥ (Bārha) (XIV) s, 126b
Abū Fāris b. Abī Isḥāḳ (Ḥafṣid) (1283) iii, 67a
Abū Fāris b. Aḥmad al-Manṣūr (Saʿdid) (1603) vi, 591a, 594b
Abū Fāris ʿAbd al-ʿAzīz al-Mutawakkil (Ḥafṣid) (1434) i, 93a, 448b, 1225a, 1247a; ii, 459a; iii, **68b**, 778a, 843b; iv, 416a, 739b; v, 531a; s, 399a
Abu Fāris ʿAbd al-ʿAzīz I (Marīnid) (1372) iii, 832a, 836a
Abū Farrādj → Aḥmad al-Badawī
Abu 'l-Fatḥ → Ibn al-ʿAmīd; Ibn al-Furāt; al-Muẓaffar
Abu 'l-Fatḥ b. Abi 'l-Shawk (ʿAnnāzid) (XI) i, 512b
Abu 'l-Fatḥ al-Balaṭī → al-Balaṭī
Abu 'l-Fatḥ Beg Bayāndur (1502) ii, 174a; s, 280b
Abu 'l-Fatḥ al-Bustī → al-Bustī
Abu 'l-Fatḥ Dāwūd b. Naṣr (Multān) (1010) vi, 65b
Abu 'l-Fatḥ al-Daylamī, al-Nāṣir li-Dīn Allāh (1052) s, **22a**
Abu 'l-Fatḥ al-Ḥarrānī (1083) iii, 766b
Abu 'l-Fatḥ al-Ḥulwānī (1112) iii, 766b
Abu 'l-Fatḥ al-Ḥusaynī (XVI) s, 383a
Abu 'l-Fatḥ Ibrāhīm → Ibrāhīm b. Shāhrukh
Abu 'l-Fatḥ al-Iskandarī → al-Hamadhānī
Abu 'l-Fatḥ Khān Bakhtiyārī (XVIII) iv, 104a, b
Abu 'l-Fatḥ Marzbān al-Sharḳ b. Ḳumādj vi, 14b
Abu 'l-Fatḥ Muḥammad b. ʿAnnāz → Muḥammad b. ʿAnnāz
Abu 'l-Fatḥ Muḥammad Shāh → Maḥmūd I, Sayf al-Dīn, Begarhā
Abu 'l-Fatḥ al-Muẓaffar (X) vii, 414a
Abu 'l-Fatḥ al-Nāṣir al-Daylamī (Imām, Yemen) (1055) vii, 996a
Abu 'l-Fatḥ Naṣr b. Ibrāhīm (al-Ḳuds) (X) v, 330a
Abu 'l-Fatḥ Yūsuf b. Khwārazm-Shāh vi, 14b
Abu 'l-Fawāris (Ayyūbid) (Kirmān) (1028) i, 131b
Abu 'l-Fawāris Fanārūzī (1027) x, 232a
Abu 'l-Fayḍ Khān (Djānid), (Bukhārā) (1747) ii, 446a; vi, 418b; vii, 854b
Abu 'l-Fayyāḍ Sawwār (IX) s, 35b
Abu 'l-Fidāʾ, al-Malik al-Muʾayyad ʿImād al-Dīn (Ayyūbid) (1331) i, **118b**, 595a, 804b; ii, 585a; iii, 120a, 900b, 966b; iv, 485a; v, 925a, 1011b; vi, 231a, 283a, 377b, 381b, 429a, 439b, 544a, 580a; vii, 167b, 186a, 537a, 992a
Abū Firās al-Ḥamdānī (968) i, **119b**, 592a, 1249b; iii, 129b, 398a, 825a; iv, 55b; v, 647b; vi, 379a, b, 506b; vii, 577b, 770b
Abu 'l-Fityān → Aḥmad al-Badawī
Abū Fudayk ʿAbd Allāh b. Thawr (693) i, **120a**, 550a, 942a; iv, 764a, 1076a; vii, 671a
Abū Fuṭrus → Nahr Abī Fuṭrus

Abu 'l-Futūḥ Dāwūd b. Naṣr (XI) vii, 549a
Abu 'l-Futūḥ al-Ḥasan (Mūsāwī) (1039) i, 552a; iii, 262b; vi, 148b
Abu 'l-Futūḥ al-Rāzī (1131) i, **120a**; vii, 103a
Abu 'l-Futūḥ Yūsuf → Buluggīn b. Zīrī
Abu 'l-Futūḥ Yūsuf b. ʿAbd Allāh (Kalbid) (998) iv, 497a
Abu 'l-Ghaḍanfar (1157) vi, 367a
Abu 'l-Ghanāʾim Saʿd (Fasandjus) (XI) ii, 827a
Abū Ghānim Bishr b. Ghānim al-Khurāsānī (IX) i, **120b**, iii, 653b, 656b
Abū Ghānim Naṣr (Ḳarmaṭī) (VIII) iv, 494a, 661a
Abu 'l-Gharānik → Muḥammad II (Aghlabid)
Abu 'l-Ghayth b. ʿAbda (ʿIdjl) (Ḳarmaṭī) (X) iv, 662a
Abu 'l-Ghāzī Bahādur Khān (Khīwa) (1663) i, **120b**, 607b, 45a; ii, 1109b; iv, 1064a; v, 24a, 273b; vi, 416a, 418a, b; viii, 164a; s, 97b, 168b, 228a, 245b, 280b, 419b, 420a
Abū Ghosh, Banū v, 334a
Abū Ghubshān (Makka) (IX) v, 78a; viii, 1003a
Abū Ghufayl (Barghawāṭa) (913) i, 1044a
Abū Ḥabasha vi, 1039b
Abū Ḥadīd, Muḥammad Farīd Wadjdī (XX) i, 598a; s, 244b
Abu 'l-Ḥadjdjādj b. al-Shaykh (1207) s, 381b
Abu 'l-Ḥadjdjādj Yūsuf b. Abi 'l-Ḳāsim → Ibn al-Sarrādj
Abu 'l-Ḥadjdjādj Yūsuf b. al-Sarrādj → Ibn al-Sarrādj
Abū Ḥafṣ, Shaykh (1163) vi, 521a
Abū Ḥafṣ ʿAmrūs b. Fatḥ, Shaykh → ʿAmrūs b. Fatḥ
Abū Ḥafṣ al-Ḥaddād → Malāmatiyya (Nīshāpūr)
Abū Ḥafṣ al-Shiṭrandjī → al-Shiṭrandjī
Abū Ḥafṣ Sughdī iv, 55a, 525b
Abū Ḥafṣ al-ʿUkbarī (998) v, 10a
Abū Ḥafṣ (ʿUmar b. Maslama al-Ḥaddād) (874) vi, 569b
Abū Ḥafṣ ʿUmar I (Ḥafṣid) (1285) iii, 67a
Abū Ḥafṣ ʿUmar b. Djamīʿ (XIV) i, **121a**
Abū Ḥafṣ ʿUmar al-Ballūṭī (IX) i, 83a, **121b**, 1249a; ii, 744b; iii, 1083a
Abū Ḥafṣ ʿUmar b. al-Ḥādjdj (XII) iv, 116a
Abū Ḥafṣ ʿUmar al-Hintātī (Īntī) (1175) i, 78b-79b, **121b**, 161a; ii, 526b; iii, 66a, 461b; vi, 742b
Abū Ḥafṣa Yazīd (684) vi, 625a
Abu 'l-Hakam b. al-Mughīra → Abū Djahl
Abū Ḥāla al-Tamīmī (VII) iv, 898b
Abū Ḥāmid al-Gharnāṭī (al-Andalūsī) (1169) i, **122a**, 203b, 204a, 593b, 602b; v, 1012a, 1016a, 1018a; vi, 413b; vii, 140b, 474a; viii, 896b; ix, 582a
Abū Ḥāmid al-Marw al-Rūdhī (X) i, 126b
Abū Ḥammū I Mūsa b. Abī Saʿīd (ʿAbd al-Wādid) (1318) i, 93a, 94a, **122b**; v, 1180a; vi, 728b
Abū Ḥammū II (1389) i, 93a, **122b**, 155a; ii, 979a; iii, 826b, 831b, 832a
Abū Ḥamza al-Khurasānī x, 377a
Abū Ḥamza → al-Mukhtār b. ʿAwf
Abū Ḥamza Madjmaʿ b. Samʿān al-Ḥāʾik s, 341b
Abū Ḥanīfa al-Dīnawarī → al-Dīnawarī
Abū Ḥanīfa al-Nuʿmān (Fāṭimid) → al-Nuʿmān
Abū Ḥanīfa al-Nuʿmān b. Thābit (767) i, 70b, **123a**, 164a, 481b, 692a, 730b, 904a; ii, 489a, 1022a; iii, 512a, 687b, 984b; iv, 855b; v, 239b, 731b; vi, 24a, 123b, 263b, 264b, 265b, 352b, 634b; vii, 606b, 663b; s, 232b, 303b, 304a, 401a
– doctrine i, 164b, 332b; ii, 116a, 832a; iii, 162b, 209b, 1164b
Abū Ḥanẓala → Abū Sufyān b. Ḥarb b. Umayya
Abū Ḥarb (Kākūyid) (XI) iv, 465b
Abū Ḥarb b. Manučihr (XII) v, 662a
Abū Ḥarb Bakhtiyār (XI) ix, 613b, 614a
Abū Ḥarb al-Mubarḳaʿ (IX) v, 326b
Abū Ḥarb al-Ṣaffār (IX) vi, 605a
Abū Ḥarb al-Yamanī → Abū Ḥarb al-Mubarḳaʿ
Abu 'l-Ḥārith Djummayn vii, 857a
Abu 'l-Ḥārith Muḥammad b. Farīghūn (X) ii, 799a
Abu 'l-Ḥasan b. Āḳā Riḍā (painter) (XVII) vi, 425b, 426a, 534a; vii, 339a
Abu 'l-Ḥasan b. Bahlūl i, 737b
Abu 'l-Ḥasan b. Bandār (X) vi, 224a
Abu 'l-Ḥasan al-Aḥmar (810) s, **22b**
Abu 'l-Ḥasan al-Akhfash (IX) i, 167b, 321b
Abu 'l-Ḥasan ʿAlī → ʿAzafī, Banū 'l-

Abu 'l-Ḥasan ʿAlī (Marīnid) (1352) i, 93a, **124b**, 129b, 138a, 155a, 496a, 506b, 634a, 1149a, 1339b; ii, 146a, 525a, 822b; iii, 67b, 68a, 135a, 867b; iv, 828a; v, 531a, 1190a; vi, 124a, 258a, 356a, 404b, 422a, 441a, 572a, b, 573b, 593a, b, 597a; s, 45b, 376b, 377a

Abu 'l-Ḥasan ʿAlī (Muley Hacén) (Naṣrid) (1485) vii, 1020b, 1026b

Abu 'l-Ḥasan ʿAlī b. ʿAbd Allāh (1067) s, 343a

Abu 'l-Ḥasan ʿAlī b. Abī Fāris (Ḥafṣid) (XV) iii, 69a

Abu 'l-Ḥasan ʿAlī b. Kaʿb al-Anṣārī (X) s, 13b

Abu 'l-Ḥasan ʿAlī b. Khalaf al-Zayyāt (1063) s, 390b

Abu 'l-Ḥasan ʿAlī b. al-Khalīl (VIII) iv, 1004a

Abu 'l-Ḥasan ʿAlī b. Maʾmūn b. Muḥammad (Khwārazm-Shāh) (XI) vi, 340a

Abu 'l-Ḥasan ʿAlī b. Muḥammad al-Ṣūfī al-Muzayyin (X) s, 350a

Abu 'l-Ḥasan ʿAlī b. Saʿīd al-Dawla (Ḥamdānid) (X) iii, 130b

Abu 'l-Ḥasan ʿAlī b. Yūsuf al-Ḥakīm (XIV) viii, 818b

Abū Ḥassan (Abū Ḥassūn) ʿAlī al-Bādisī (Waṭṭāsid) (1549) i, 859b, **860a**; ii, 819b; vi, 1009b

Abu 'l-Ḥasan ʿAlī al-Ḥuṣrī → al-Ḥuṣrī

Abu 'l-Ḥasan ʿAlī al-Maghribī → al-Maghribī

Abu 'l-Ḥasan ʿAlī al-Shādhilī → al-Shādhilī

Abu 'l-Ḥasan al-Anṣārī (1197) s, **23a**

Abu 'l-Ḥasan Ardistānī (XIX) s, 23b

Abu 'l-Ḥasan al-Awwal (al-Māḍī) → Mūsā al-Kāẓim

Abu 'l-Ḥasan al-Battī (1015) s, **23a**

Abu 'l-Ḥasan Djilwa, Mīrzā (1897) s, **23b**

Abu 'l-Ḥasan Fihr vi, 263a

Abu 'l-Ḥasan Hilāl (Ṣābiʾ) viii, 674a

Abu 'l-Ḥasan Kharaḳānī → Kharaḳānī

Abu 'l-Ḥasan (Tānā) Ḳuṭb Shāhī (1686) i, 1210a; ii, 180b; iii, 427a; v, 549b; vi, 837b

Abu 'l-Ḥasan Lārī (XVII) vii, 224a

Abu 'l-Ḥasan Muḥammad b. Hilāl (Ṣābiʾ) (1088) iii, 752b; vi, 198b, 243a; vii, 857b; viii, 674b

Abu 'l-Ḥasan Muḥammad b. Ibrāhīm b. Sīmdjūr → Sīmdjūr, Banū

Abu 'l-Ḥasan al-Maghribī (X) s, **24a**

Abu 'l-Ḥasan al-Rabaʿī → al-Rabaʿī

Abu 'l-Ḥasan al-Rummānī → al-Rummānī

Abu 'l-Ḥasan Shāh, Imām (1791) iv, 201b

Abu 'l-Ḥasan al-Samlālī (XVII) i, 355b

Abu 'l-Ḥasan Shīrāzī → al-Shīrāzī, Abu 'l-Ḥasan

Abu 'l-Ḥasan al-Tamgrūtī (XVI) i, 593b

Abu 'l-Ḥasan Thābit b. Abī Saʿīd Sinān (Ṣābiʾ) (976) vii, 542a; viii, 673b

Abu 'l-Ḥasan Thābit b. Ibrāhīm b. Hārūn (Zahrūn) (Ṣābiʾ) (980) viii, 673b; xi, 343a

Abu 'l-Ḥasanāt Muḥammad → ʿAbd al-Ḥayy

Abū Ḥāshid b. Yaḥyā b. Abī Ḥāshid (1052) s, 22b

Abū Hāshim (Sharīf) → Makka

Abū Hāshim b. al-Djubbāʾī (933) i, 4b, 411a; ii, 218b, 569b, 570a; iii, 171b, 832a, 1143a, 1165b; v, 702a; s, 12b, 13b, 25b, 32a, 226b, 343b, 346b, 348a

Abū Hāshim ʿAbd Allāh b. Muḥammad b. al-Ḥanafiyya (717) i, 15a, 48b, **124b**, 402a; ii, 441a; iii, 265a, 574a, 1265b; iv, 837a; vi, 332b; vii, 396a, 524a; ix, 412b; s, 357b

Abū Hāshim al-Bāwardī iv, 797a, 800b

Abū Hāshim Muḥammad, Sharīf (Hāshimid) (1094) vi, 148b

Abū Ḥassūn ʿAlī al-Bādisī (Waṭṭāsid) → Abū Ḥassan ʿAlī al-Bādisī

Abū Ḥātim Aḥmad → ʿAzafī, Banū

Abū Ḥātim ʿAnbasa b. Isḥāḳ (856) ii, 72a

Abū Ḥātim al-Malzūzī, Yaʿḳūb b. Labīd (772) i, **125a**; iii, 297a, 654b; vi, 310b, 311a

Abū Ḥātim al-Rāzī (890) iii, 158b

Abū Ḥātim al-Rāzī (933) i, **125a**, 160b, 694a; iii, 158b; iv, 661b; vii, 517a, 652a, 968b, 1006b; x, 391a

Abū Ḥātim al-Sidjistānī (869) i, **125b**, 158b, 167b, 718b; iii, 641b, 844b; vii, 258a, 279b, 281a

Abū Ḥātim al-Warsinānī (X) v, 167a

Abū Ḥātim Yaʿḳūb b. Ḥabīb → al-Ibāḍiyya

Abū Ḥātim Yūsuf b. Muḥammad (Rustumid) (907) vii, 895b

Abū Ḥātim al-Zuṭṭī (X) iv, 661a

Abu 'l-Hawl (Hōl) i, **125b**; vi, 414a; s, 408a
Abu 'l-Haydjā' ʿAbd Allāh b. Ḥamdān → ʿAbd Allāh b. Ḥamdān
Abu 'l-Haydjā' b. Rabīb al-Dawla (XI) x, 897b
Abu 'l-Haydjā' b. Saʿd al-Dawla (Ḥamdānid) (1011) iii, 130b; vii, 116a, 860a; s, 94a
Abu 'l-Haydjā' Hadhbānī (XII) v, 454a, 455a
Abu 'l-Haydja' Ḥusayn b. Muḥammad (Rawwādid) (988) ii, 680a; viii, 460b
Abu 'l-Haydjā' al-Rawwādī al-Kurdī, amīr (X) ii, 680a
Abū Ḥayyā al-Numayrī (760) viii, 120b; s, **24a**
Abū Ḥayyān al-Gharnāṭī (1344) i, **126a**, 445b, 593a, 602b; iii, 698b, 801a, 861b; vii, 262a, 400a
Abū Ḥayyān al-Tawḥīdī (1023) i, **126b**, 130a, 151b, 159a, 176a, 427a, 590a, 1354a; ii, 387b, 766b, 774b; iii, 355a, 672b, 754b, 1071b, 1263b; v, 320a; vi, 443b, 845b; vii, 143b, 144a, 304b; viii, 615a; x, 67a; s, 13a, b, 72b, 88b, 119b, 289b, 389b, 398b
Abu 'l-Ḥazm b. Djahwar (vizier) (1031) ii, 389a; iii, 496a, 786a, 973bl vi, 189a
Abū Hiffān, ʿAbd Allāh b. Aḥmad al-Mihzamī (869) iv, 1005a; vii, 660b; s, **24b**
Abū Hilāl al-ʿAskarī → al-ʿAskarī
Abū Ḥimāra → Bū Ḥmāra
Abu 'l-Hindī al-Riyāḥī iv, 1004a; viii, 884a
Abū Hubayra b. Rabīʿa b. Riyāḥ al-Hilālī (VII) s, 92b
Abu 'l-Hudā (XIX) i, 63b; ii, 418b, 419a; v, 949a
Abū Ḥudhayfa b. al-Mughīra (VII) vi, 139b
Abu 'l-Hudhayl al-ʿAllāf (840) i, 2a, 4b, 10a, **127b**, 204b, 713b; ii, 449b; iii, 63b, 172a, 1143a, 1266a; v, 384a, 576b; vi, 335a, 336b, 458a, 468b, 636b; vii, 259a, 260a, 401a, 546b, 604a, 1031b, 1057a; s, 88b, 225b, 226a, 227a, 392a, 393b
Abū Ḥulmān al-Fārisī (988) iii, 570b
Abū Hurayra al-Dawsī al-Yamānī (678) i, 52a, **129a**, 266b, 714a; iii, 242b; v, 1010a; vi, 79a, 674b; vii, 570b; s, 230b, 311a, b
Abū Hurayra al-Rāwandī (VIII) iv, 838a
Abū Ḥusayn, Banū → Kalbids
Abu 'l-Ḥusayn b. Abī Yaʿlā (1131) i, 274a, b, 1039a; iii, 766b; iv, 990a
Abu 'l-Ḥusayn b. Samʿūn (997) iii, 159b; v, 10a
Abu 'l-Ḥusayn Aḥmad b. al-Ḥasan al-Uṭrūsh (X) i, 688a; iii, 255a; s, 356b
Abu 'l-Ḥusayn al-Baṣrī (1044) iii, 1023b, 1025b, 1144a; s, 14a, **25a**
Abū Ḥuzāba, al-Walīd b. Ḥunayfa (704) s, **26a**
Abu 'l-ʿIbar, Abu 'l-ʿAbbās Muḥammad (866) vii, 857a; s, 16b, **26a**
Abū Ibrāhīm Aḥmad b. Muḥammad (Aghlabid) (863) i, 24a, 248b, 250b, 621a; iii, 287b; iv, 829b
Abū Ibrāhīm Isḥāḳ al-Fārābī → al-Fārābī
Abū ʿIḳāl al-Aghlab (Aghlabid) (841) i, 248b, 250b; iv, 415b
Abū ʿIkrima ʿĀmir b. ʿImrān al-Ḍabbī → al-Ḍabbī
Abū ʿIkrisha → Ḥādjib b. Zurāra
Abū ʿImrān Faḍl b. al-Djarrāḥ (XII) ii, 484b
Abū ʿImrān al-Fāsī (1039) vi, 744a, 942b; vii, 483b; s, **26b**
Abū ʿImrān Mūsā b. Muḥammad vi, 709b
Abū ʿImrān Mūsā al-Ḥasan Muḥammad, Shaykh (1106) v, 247b
Abū ʿInān Fāris b. Abi 'l-Ḥasan ʿAlī (Marīnid) (1359) i, 93a, 124b, **129b**, 155a; ii, 822a, 979a; iii, 68a, 462a, 736a, 756a, 826a, 867a; iv, 635a, 729b; v, 531a, 626b, 1190a; vi, 142a, 572b, 593b; vii, 37a, 1024a
Abu 'l-ʿIrmās → Abū Nukhayla
Abū ʿĪsā (Zandjī) (IX) vii, 526b
Abū ʿĪsā al-Iṣfahānī (VII) i, **130a**; iv, 96a, 603b, 604b, 606b
Abū ʿĪsā Muḥammad b. Hārūn al-Warrāḳ (861) i, **130a**; 905a; iv, 1132a; vi, 949a; vii, 459b; viii, 980b
Abū Isḥāḳ → al-Shāṭibī
Abū Isḥāḳ I (Ḥafṣid) (1283) iii, 48b, 67a
Abū Isḥāḳ II (Ḥafṣid) (1369) iii, 68a, 867a
Abū Isḥāḳ, Sayyid (1207) vi, 840b
Abū Isḥāḳ b. al-Rashīd (ʿAbbāsid) (IX) i, 439b
Abū Isḥāḳ Čishtī (VII) ii, 50b
Abū Isḥāḳ Djamāl al-Dīn Īndjū (1350) iii, 1022a, 1208b; iv, 102b, 498b, 909b; v, 163a; vi, 908a; s, 415a
Abū Isḥāḳ al-Fārisī → al-Iṣṭakhrī

Abū Isḥāḳ al-Fārisī, Ibrāhīm b. ʿAlī (987) s, **27b**
Abū Isḥāḳ al-Ḥuṣrī → al-Ḥuṣrī
Abū Isḥāḳ Ibrāhīm → Isḥāḳ b. Alp Takīn (Ghaznawid)
Abū Isḥāḳ Ibrāhīm b. Abī ʿAbd Allāh b. al-Sarrādj → Ibn al-Sarrādj
Abū Isḥāḳ Ibrāhīm b. Abī 'l-Ḥasan Hilāl → al-Ṣābiʾ
Abū Isḥāk Ibrāhīm b. Abī Saʿīd Sinān (Ṣābiʾ) viii, 673a
Abū Isḥāḳ Ibrāhīm al-Adjdābī → al-Adj dābī
Abū Isḥāḳ Ibrāhīm al-Harawī (IX) i, 162b
Abū Isḥāḳ Ibrāhīm Ḳuwayrā (X) vi, 844b
Abū Isḥāḳ Ibrāhīm al-Sāḥilī (1346) vi, 258b, 421b, 422a
Abū Isḥāḳ al-Ilbīrī (1067) i, **130b**, 602a
Abū Isḥāḳ Īndjū (1357) iii, 1208b; viii, 806b
Abū Isḥāḳ Ismāʿīl b. al-Ḳāsim → Abu 'l-Atāhiya
Abū Isḥāḳ al-Kāzarūnī → al-Kāzarūnī
Abū Isḥāḳ Muḥammad b. Maʾmūn → al-Muʿtaṣim
Abū ʿIṣma (Zaydī) (805) vi, 438a
Abū Kabīr al-Hudhalī (VII) i, **130b**; vii, 309a
Abū Kabrayn → Bū Ḳabrīn
Abū Kadr/Akdar (1179) x, 303a
Abu 'l-Kalām Āzād → Āzād
Abū Ḳalammas → Ḳalammas
Abū Ḳalamūn i, **131a**
Abū Kalb → Sikka
Abū Kālīdjar al-Marzubān, ʿImād al-Dīn (Būyid) (1048) i, **131b**, 512b, 1355a, b; ii, 194a, 391a, 856a, 962a; iii, 860a; iv, 294b, 379a, 457b, 911b; vi, 270b, 272b; vii, 270b, 731b, 1018a; viii, 945b
Abū Kālīdjār Garshāsp → Garshāsp
Abu 'l-Kamāl Tamīm b. Zīrī (Īfranid) (1054) i, 1044b; iii, 1043a; v, 1177b
Abū Kāmil Shudjāʿ b. Aslam (X) i, **132b**; ii, 361b; viii, 555b
Abū Karib Asʿad → Asʿad Kāmil
Abū Ḳarib Budayr b. Abī Ṣakhr (VII) s, 357b
Abū (Ibn) Karib (Kurayb, Karnab) al-Ḍarīr (VIII) i, 1116b; iv, 837a; v, 433b; viii, 371b
Abu 'l-Ḳāsim i, **133b**
Abu 'l-Ḳāsim → al-Zahrawī
Abu 'l-Ḳāsim b. al-ʿAbbād vi, 204b
Abu 'l-Ḳāsim b. Abi 'l-Zinād (VIII) s, 380b
Abu 'l-Ḳāsim b. ʿAddū vii, 585a
Abu 'l-Ḳāsim b. Manda → Ibn Manda, ʿAbd al-Raḥmān
Abu 'l-Ḳāsim b. Maḥfūẓ, Djamāl al-Dīn iv, 810b
Abu 'l-Ḳāsim b. ʿUbayd Allāh al-Mahdī (Fāṭimid) (X) i, 207b; iii, 297b; v, 1175a, 1243b
Abu 'l-Ḳāsim b. Yūsuf b. al-Sarrādj → Ibn al-Sarrādj
Abu 'l-Ḳāsim ʿAlī (Mīkālī) (986) vii, 26a
Abu 'l-Ḳāsim ʿAlī, Khwādja (Mīkālī) (1032) vii, 26a
Abu 'l-Ḳāsim Anūdjūr (Unūdjūr) → Unūdjūr
Abu 'l-Ḳāsim ʿĀrif (Ḳazwīn) (1934) iv, 71a
Abu 'l-Ḳāsim Bābur b. Baysunghur (Tīmūrid) (1457) i, 91a, 147b, 701a; iii, 603a; iv, 523b; vi, 513b; vii, 90a
Abu 'l-Ḳāsim al-Barrādī → al-Barrādī
Abu 'l-Ḳāsim Bishr-i Yāsīn (990) i, 146a
Abu 'l-Ḳāsim Djaʿfar b. al-Uṭrūsh (925) i, 688a; iii, 255a; s, 356b
Abu 'l-Ḳāsim al-Djardjarāʾī → al-Djardj arāʾī
Abu 'l-Ḳāsim Farāhānī → Ḳāʾim-Maḳām, Abū l'-Ḳāsim
Abu 'l-Ḳāsim al-Fazarī → al-Fazarī
Abu 'l-Ḳāsim al-Ḥakkār → ʿAbd al-ʿAzīz b. Yūsuf
Abu 'l-Ḳāsim Ḥasan al-Shaddād (XIV) vii, 210b
Abu 'l-Ḳāsim al-Ḥusayn b. ʿAlī al-Maghribī (vizier) → al-Maghribī
Abu 'l-Ḳāsim al-Ḥusayn b. Rawḥ al-Nawbakhtī (938) viii, **812a**
Abu 'l-Ḳāsim al-Kaʿbī al-Balkhī → al-Balkhī
Abu 'l-Ḳāsim Ḳāʾimmaḳām (Irān) (XIX) s, 70b
Abu 'l-Ḳāsim Khalaf → al-Zahrāwī
Abu 'l-Ḳāsim Khān (Ḳaʾim Maḳām) (1835) vii, 454a
Abu 'l-Ḳāsim al-Ḳushayrī → al-Ḳushayrī
Abu 'l-Ḳāsim al-Madjriṭī → al-Madjriṭī
Abu 'l-Ḳāsim Maḥmūd → Maḥmūd b. Sebüktigin
Abu 'l-Ḳāsim al-Makkī (faḳīh) (XI) vii, 294b

Abu 'l-Ḳāsim Muḥammad b. Yaḥyā → ʿAzafī, Banū
Abu 'l-Ḳāsim Muḥammad al-Sīmāwī al-ʿIrāḳī (XIII) v,112a; s, 270a
Abu 'l-Ḳāsim Rabīb al-Dīn (vizier) (1220) vi, 632a
Abu ʿl-Ḳāsim Rāmis̲h̲t (1140) ix, 668a
Abu 'l-Ḳāsim Samd̲j̲ū al-Miknāsī (VIII) vi, 1038a
Abu 'l-Ḳāsim S̲h̲ayk̲h̲ al-Raʾīs (Ḳād̲j̲ār) (XIX) iv, 164b
Abu 'l-Ḳāsim al-Wāsānī → al-Wāsānī
Abu 'l-Ḳāsim Yazīd b. Mak̲h̲lad, S̲h̲ayk̲h̲ (X) iii, 95a, b, 656a; s, 48b
Abu 'l-Ḳāsim al-Zayyānī → al-Zayyānī
Abū Ḳatāda, Anṣārī vi, 267b
Abū Ḳays b. Abī Anas vii, 361b
Abū Ḳays b. al-Aslat (wāʾil) (VI) i, 771b
Abū Ḳays b. al-Aslat (poet) (VI) ix, 227a
Abū K̲h̲alaf al-Ḳuḍāʿī (XI) vi, 198a
Abū K̲h̲ālid ʿAbd al-ʿAzīz (Asīd, Banū) i, 148b
Abū K̲h̲ālid Yazīd al-Wāsiṭī (al-D̲j̲ārūdiyya) ii, 485a; s, 48b
Abu K̲h̲alīfa al-D̲j̲umaḥī → al-Faḍl b. al-Ḥubāb
Abu 'l-K̲h̲aṣīb (VIII) i, **133b**
Abu 'l-K̲h̲aṣīb Wuhayb b. ʿAbd Allāh (802) ix, 34a
Abu 'l-K̲h̲aṭṭāb al-Asadī (762) i, **134a**, 1156a; iv, 203a, 1132a; vi, 917b; vii, 517a
Abu 'l-K̲h̲aṭṭāb al-Kalwad̲h̲ānī → al-Kalwad̲h̲ānī
Abu 'l-K̲h̲aṭṭāb al-Maʿāfirī (Ibāḍī Imām) (757) i, **134a**, 1099a, 1175a; ii, 374b; iii, 296a, 297a, 654a, 1040b; iv, 827a; v, 696a; vi, 841a; viii, 638a
Abu 'l-K̲h̲aṭṭār al-Ḥuṣām b. Dirār al-Kalbī (745) i, **134b**, 490a; ii, 1012b; iii, 601b; iv, 494b, 672b; vi, 221b
Abu 'l-K̲h̲ayr (Yemen) s, 354b
Abu 'l-K̲h̲ayr ʿAbd al-Raḥmān (1786) vi, 112b
Abu 'l-K̲h̲ayr Abū Āzād (1868) i, 827b; s, 354b
Abu 'l-K̲h̲ayr Ḥammād al-Dabbās (1131) i, 69a
Abu 'l-K̲h̲ayr al-Ḥusayn al-Bag̲h̲dādī (XI) i, 1236b
Abu 'l-K̲h̲ayr al-Is̲h̲bīlī (XI) i, **135b**; ii, 901b
Abu 'l-K̲h̲ayr K̲h̲ān Özbeg (1469) i, 46b, **135a**, 147b, 148a; ii, 44b; vi, 417b; ix, 426a; s, 51a
Abu 'l-K̲h̲ayrāt b. Ibrāhīm (XIX) ii, 124a
Abu 'l-K̲h̲ayrid → S̲h̲ībānids
Abū K̲h̲ayt̲h̲ama Zuhayr b. Ḥarb (857) iii, 687a; vii, 691b
Abū K̲h̲azar Yag̲h̲lā b. Zaltāf, S̲h̲ayk̲h̲ (X) iii, 95a, b, 656a
Abū K̲h̲āzim Ibn Abī Yaʿlā (1133) iii, 766b
Abū K̲h̲āzim Ibn al-Farrāʾ (1039) iii, 766b
Abū K̲h̲irās̲h̲ K̲h̲uwaylid (VII) i, **136a**
Abu 'l-K̲h̲uḍayb (Ṭabaristān) (VIII) ix, 54b
Abuḳraṭ(īs) → Buḳrāṭ
Abū Ḳubays, D̲j̲abal i, **136a**, 178a; vi, 162a, 168b, 578b, 791b
Abū Ḳudāma Yazīd b. Fandīn al-Īfranī (803) iii, 1041b
Abū Ḳuḥāfa (ʿUt̲h̲mān) b. ʿĀmir (VI) i, 109b, 110a
Abū Kurayb Muḥammad b. al-ʿAlāʾ (862) vii, 691a; x, 11b
Abū Ḳurays̲h̲ (VIII) i, 1298a
Abū Ḳurrā al-Īfranī al-Mag̲h̲īlī (Ṣufrī) (765) i, 367a, 1175b; iii, 1040b, 1041a; v, 1164b; vi, 311b, 312a; ix,768a
Abū Ḳurra, Theodore (820) i, **136b**
Abū Lahab b. ʿAbd al-Muṭṭalib (624) i, 9a, 80a, 115b, **136b**, 152b; iii, 366b; vi, 146b
Abū Layla → al-Hārit̲h̲ b. ʿAbd al-ʿAzīz; Sulaymān Pas̲h̲a Misrāklî
Abū Layla Isḥāḳ b. Muḥammad (Awraba) (VIII) s, 103a
Abu 'l-Layt̲h̲ Naṣr → al-Ḥāfiẓ al-Samarḳandī
Abu 'l-Layt̲h̲ al-Samarḳandī (983) i, 123b, **137a**; ii, 98b; iii, 163a; vii, 1052b; ix, 535a
Abū Layt̲h̲ al-Siḳillī (XII) iv, 118a
Abū Leylī S̲h̲ayk̲h̲ Süleymān (Malāmī) (XVI) vi, 228a
Abū Lubāba i, 266b
Abū Luʾluʾa (VII) iii, 586b; vii, 347a; x, 820a
Abu 'l-Maʿālī → Muḥammad b. ʿAbd al-Bāḳī
Abu 'l-Maʿālī (Mug̲h̲al) (XVI) s, 324b
Abu 'l-Maʿālī b. Sayyid Mubārak (Bayhaḳī) (XVI) s, 132a
Abu 'l-Maʿālī ʿAbd al-Malik → al-D̲j̲uwaynī
Abu 'l-Maʿālī al-K̲h̲aṭīrī vii, 397a

Abu 'l-Maʿālī Muḥammad b. ʿUbayd Allāh (XI) i, **137a**
Abu 'l-Maʿālī al-Musharraf b. al-Muradjdjā vii, 295a
Abu 'l-Maʿālī Naṣr Allāh iv, 704a
Abu 'l-Maʿālī Saʿd al-Dawla → Saʿd al-Dawla Sharīf
Abu 'l-Maʿālī Sharīf I → Saʿd al-Dawla Sharīf
Abu 'l-Maʿālī Sharīf II (Ḥamdānid) (XI) iii, 130b
Abū Māḍī, Īliyyā (1957) v, 1254b, 1255a, b; s, **27b**
Abū Madyan Hawwārī (Boumedienne, Houari) b. Muḥammad b. Sahla (1978) iii, 564a; iv, 363a; v, 1071a; vi, 250b
Abū Madyan Shuʿayb al-Andalusī (1197) i, 91b, **137b**, 141a, 159b, 1205a; ii, 100b, 183a; iii, 339a, 701b, 800a, 844a, 866a; iv, 1006b; vi, 196b, 280a, 356a; ix, 316a; x, 124b; xi, 112a; s, 403a
Abu 'l-Mafākhir Yaḥyā (1335) ix, 111a
Abu 'l-Maghrāʾ b. Mūsā b. Zurāra (IX) iv, 89a, b, 90a
Abū Maḥallī al-Sidjilmāsī (1613) vi, 594b; s, **28b**
Abu 'l-Maḥāsin b. Taghrībirdī (1470) i, **138a**, 595a; ii, 782a, 954a; iii, 188b, 775b; iv, 294b; vi, 194a; vii, 172b; s, 386b, 389a
Abu 'l-Maḥāsin al-Fāsī (1604) i, **138b**
See also al-Fāsī, Abu 'l-Maḥāsin
Abu 'l-Maḥāsin al-Shaybī (1433) vi, 824a
Abū Maḥdhūra (VII) vi, 677a
Abū Maḥmūd b. Djaʿfar b. Falāḥ al-Kutāmī (X) vii, 488b
Abu 'l-Makārim b. Muḥammad al-Abharī (XI) v, 930a
Abu 'l-Makārim Aḥmad b. al-ʿAbbās, Tādj al-Dīn (XII) ii, 333b; vi, 14b
Abū Makārim Hibat Allāh (Rabīʿa, Banū) viii, 90b
Abū Makhrama → Makhrama, Bā
Abu 'l-Malāḥim (dāʿī) (885) vi, 438b
Abu 'l-Malīḥ b. Mammati → Ibn Mammatī
Abū Manṣūr → al-Thaʿālibī
Abū Manṣūr b. Bahāʾ al-Dawla (1008) s, 119a
Abū Manṣūr b. Sāliḥān (X) viii, 694a
Abū Manṣūr b. Yūsuf (1067) iii, 699b, 766a; s, **29b**, 192a
Abū Manṣūr al-Azdī (XI) i, 515b
Abū Manṣūr Farāmurz (Kākūyid) (1051) iii, 471b; iv, 101a, 465b
Abū Manṣūr Ilyās al-Nafūsī (IX) i, **139a**; ii, 369a; iv, 920a; vi, 452b
Abū Manṣūr Kumrī s, 271b
Abū Manṣūr al-Maʿmarī (Muʿammarī) (X) iv, 63b
Abū Manṣūr Muḥammad b. ʿAbd al-Razzāḳ (X) (Ṭūs) x, 425b
Abū Manṣūr Muḥammad b. ʿAlī (1027) ii, 127b; v, 928b
Abū Manṣūr Ṭalḥa b. Ruzayḳ (808) vi, 333a
Abū Marwān, Sīdī (1111) i, 512a
Abū Marwān b. Ḥayyān → Ibn Ḥayyān
Abū Marwān b. Razīn s, 81b
Abū Marwān ʿAbd al-Malik b. ʿAbd al-ʿAzīz (XIII) s, 81b
Abū Marwān ʿAbd al-Malik b. Djawhar (vizier) (IX) vii, 569a
Abū Maʿshar Djaʿfar b. Muḥammad al-Balkhī (886) i, **139a**, 589b; iii, 463b, 1072b, 1136b, 1137a; iv, 1182b; v, 130b, 297a, 950a; vii, 85b, 559a, 977a; viii, 100a, 103b, 106b, 107a, 108a; s, 17a
Abū Maʿshar Nadjīḥ al-Sindī (787) i, **140a**
Abū Maslama, Shaykh (XI) i, 755a
Abū Masʿūd al-Anṣārī (720) vii, 27a
Abū Matallī (Marabout) (XVII) ix, 545b
Abu 'l-Mawāhib (Kilwa) → al-Ḥasan b. Sulaymān
Abu 'l-Mawāhib (1628) viii, 425a
Abū Midfaʿ → Sikka
Abū Miḥdjān ʿAbd Allāh Mālik (ʿAmr) b. Ḥabīb al-Thaḳīfī (637) i, **140a**; iii, 850b; iv, 385b, 1002a; vi, 641b
Abū Miḥdjān Nuṣayb b. Rabāḥ → Nuṣayb
Abū Mikhnaf (774) i, **140b**; iii, 608a, 610a; v, 947b
Abū Mismār, al-Sharīf Ḥammūd (1818) s, **30a**
Abu 'l-Muʿaskar al-Ḥusayn b. Maʿdān (Makrān) (XI) iii, 906a
Abu 'l-Muʾayyad Balkhī (X) ii, 918b; xi, 360b
Abū Muḍar Ziyādat Allāh → Ziyādat Allāh III
Abū Mudjālid al-Baghdādī (882) iv, 1162a
Abu 'l-Mughīra b. Ḥazm → Ibn Ḥazm
Abu 'l-Mughīra ʿAmr b. Sharaḥīl al-ʿAnsī (Ḳadarī) iv, 370a

Abu 'l-Mughīth al-Rāfiḳī (IX) i, 153b
Abu 'l-Muhādjir Dīnār al-Anṣārī (681) ii, 525b; iv, 826a; v, 518a; vi, 878a; x, 790a
Abū Muḥammad (Sufyānid) (744) vi, 624a
Abū Muḥammad b. Abī Hafṣ (XIII) ii, 1007b, 1008a
Abū Muḥammad b. Baraka (X) i, **140b**; iii, 731b
Abū Muḥammad b. Djiyār al-Djayyānī (XII) ii, 516a
Abū Muḥammad b. ʿUbayd Allāh (1195) viii, 635b
Abū Muḥammad ʿAbd Allāh b. ʿAbd al-Muʾmin (Almohad) (XII) iii, 386b; v, 61a
Abū Muḥammad ʿAbd Allāh b. ʿAbd al-Wāḥid (1228) iii, 66a
Abū Muḥammad ʿAbd Allāh b. Barrī → Ibn Barrī
Abū Muḥammad ʿAbd Allāh b. Manṣūr → Ibn Ṣulayḥa
Abū Muḥammad ʿAbd Allāh b. ʿUmar Tādj al-Dīn (Awlād al-Shaykh) (1244) i, 766a, b
Abū Muḥammad ʿAbd Allāh al-ʿĀdil (Almohad) (1227) vi, 339b
Abū Muḥammad ʿAbd al-Wahhāb b. Aḥmad → Ādarrāḳ
Abū Muḥammad ʿAbd al-Wāḥid (Almohad) (1224) vi, 592b
Abū Muḥammad ʿAbd al-Wāḥid b. Abī Ḥafṣ, Shaykh (1221) iii, 66a
Abū Muḥammad al-Ḥasan b. Ḥamdān, Nāṣir al-Dawla (1048) vii, 118b
Abū Muḥammad Ḳāsim → ʿAzafī
Abū Muḥammad Ṣāliḥ b. Yanṣāran (1234) i, **141a**; iii, 339a
Abū Muḥammad Ṭalḥa b. ʿAbd Allāh b. Khalaf al-Khuzāʿi → Ṭalḥat al-Ṭalaḥāt
Abū Muḥammad al-Tamīmī (1095) iii, 766b
Abū Muḥammad Wīslān b. Yaʿḳūb (X) iii, 95b
Abū Muḥammad Ziyādat Allāh → Ziyādat Allāh I
Abū Muḥammad al-Zubayr b. ʿUmar (1143) ii, 1013b
Abū Muḥriz (ḳāḍī) (818) i, 685a
Abū Muḳātil Ḥafṣ b. Salm al-Samarḳandī (VIII) vi, 457b; vii, 606b
Abu 'l-Mulūk → Bāwand
Abu 'l-Munadjdjā (X) iv, 663b
Abū Mūsā (island) i, 535b; iv, 778a, b; vii, 449b; s, 417b, 418a
Abū Mūsā al-Ashʿarī → al-Ashʿarī
Abū Mūsā al-Dabīlī → al-Dabīlī
Abū Mūsā I ʿĪsā b. Ādam (IX) i, 162a
Abū Mūsā ʿĪsā b. Ṣabīḥ → al-Murdār
Abū Mūsā al-Kharrāz iv, 801a
Abū Muṣʿab Muḥammad b. Ayyūb → Muḥammad b. Ayyūb
Abu 'l-Musāfir al-Fatḥ (Sādjid) (929) vi, 499a
Abū Musallam Musharraf b. ʿUbayd Allāh (XI) vii, 651a
Abū Muslim al-Khurāsānī (754) i, 15b, 16a, 16b, 43a, 49a, 103a, 116b, **141a**, 149a, 755a, 1293a; ii, 78a, 86b, 110a, 505a, 739b, 966b; iii, 802b, 988a; iv, 15b, 16a, 45a, 411b, 446b, 718a, 838a; v, 57a, b, 63b, 64a, 69a, 618a, 855a; vi, 332a, 427b, 619b, 620a, b, 661a, 677a, 744b; vii, 94b, 500a, 664a, 1016a; ix, 423b, 874b; x, 845a
Abū Muslim b. Ḥammād (Ḳarmaṭī) (X) iv, 662b
Abu 'l-Muṭāʿ Dhu 'l-Ḳarnayn (Ḥamdānid) (XI) iii, 128b
Abu 'l-Muṭahhar al-Azdī (XI) i, 133b; iii, 368a, 1264a; vii, 495a; s, **31a**
Abu 'l-Muṭarrif b. ʿAmīra → Ibn ʿAmīra
Abu 'l-Muṭarrif ʿAbd al-Raḥmān (917) vii, 941b
Abu 'l-Muthannā → al-Sharḳī b. al-Kutāmī
Abu 'l-Muʾthir al-Bahlawī (IX) i, **141b**
Abu 'l-Muẓaffar (amīr) (1021) iii, 799a
Abu 'l-Muẓaffar b. Yūnus (1197) iii, 751b
Abu 'l-Muẓaffar ʿAbd Allāh (Muḥtādjid) (951) vii, 477b
Abu 'l-Muẓaffar Ḥamdān b. Nāṣir al-Dawla (Ḥamdānid) (X) vii, 983b; s, 36a
Abu 'l-Muẓaffar Ḳāsim b. Djihāngīr (Aḳ-Ḳoyunlu) (1498) vi, 541a
Abu 'l-Muẓaffar Naṣr b. Sebüktigin (1021) x, 425b, 426a, 869a
Abū Naḍḍāra, Yaʿḳūb b. Rafāʾīl Ṣanūʿ (1912) i, **141b**, 597a; ii, 466b; vi, 746b
Abū Nadjāḥ b. Ḳannāʾ (1129) i, 440a
Abu 'l-Nadjīb → ʿAmʿaḳ
Abu 'l-Nadjm → Badr b. Ḥasanwayh
Abu 'l-Nadjm al-ʿIdjlī (724) i, **142a**, 207b; viii, 377a; s, 259a

Abū Nahshal b. Ḥumayd al-Ṭūsī (IX) i, 154a, 1289b; iii, 573a
Abū Nās (Mandīl) (XIII) vi, 404a
Abū Naṣr (vizier) (Bukhārā) (X) vi, 340a
Abū Naṣr b. al-Ṣabbāgh (1085) vii, 781a
Abū Naṣr Aḥmad b. Muḥammad (Farīghūnid) (1010) ii, 799b, 1011a; vii, 407a
Abū Naṣr Aḥmad al-Munāzī → al-Munāzī
Abū Naṣr Hārūn b. Saʿīd al-Tustarī (Ṣābīʾ) (1052) vii, 730a; viii, 674b
Abū Naṣr Manṣūr b. ʿIrāḳ (XI) s, 544a
Abū Naṣr al-Miṣrī s, 267a
Abū Naṣr Mushkān (XI) i, 1130b; iv, 758b
Abū Naṣr Sābūr → Sābūr b. Ardashīr
Abū Naṣr Saʿd, al-Mustaʿīn bi-'llāh (Ciriza/ Muley Zad) (Naṣrid) (1463) vii, 1020b, 1026a
Abū Naṣr Shāh-Fīrūz (X) s, 118b
Abū Naṣr-i Fārsī (XI) vi, 783a
Abū Nātiḥ → al-Maʿlūf, Ibrāhīm
Abū Nuʿaym al-Faḍl b. Dukayn al-Mulāʾī (834) i, **143a**; viii, 515a
Abū Nuʿaym al-Iṣfahānī (1038) i, **142b**; ii, 359b; iv, 212a; v, 1234b, 1235a; vi, 263a, b, 266b, 352b, 353a, 354a, 821a; vii, 95b; viii, 498a, 518a
Abū Nūḥ (800) vi, 204a
Abū Nukhayla al-Ḥimmānī (754) s, **31a**
Abū Nuḳṭa (Wahhābī) (1809) s, 30b
Abū Numayy I, Muḥammad (Sharīf) (1301) i, 21a, 553a; iii, 262b; vi, 149b
Abū Numayy II, Muḥammad (Sharīf) (1566) i, 1032b; ii, 517b, 572a, 788a; iii, 262b; v, 18a
Abū Numayy b. Abi 'l-Barakāt (Makka) (XVI) ix, 14a
Abū Nūr b. Abī Ḳurra (Īfrānid) (1058) iii, 1043b
Abū Nuwās (813) i, 2b, 10b, 14a, 108a, 116b, 118b, **143b**, 150b, 158b, 196b, 438a, 587b, 751b, 1081b; ii, 437b, 591b, 1032a; iii, 156b, 328a, 618a, b, 745b, 1202b, 1262b; iv, 54b, 252a, 919a, 1004a, b, 1008b; v, 133a, 778b; vi, 253a, 468b, 604b, 641a; vii, 114a, 261b, 414b, 694b, 982a; viii, 884b; xi, 126b, 127a; s, 25a, 58b, 253a, 352b
Abu 'l-Rabīʿ (Marīnid) (1310) s, 112b
Abu 'l-Rabīʿ b. Sālim → al-Kalāʿī
Abu 'l-Raddād (860) vii, 40a
Abū Radjāʾ b. Ashhab (IX) vii, 409a
Abū Rakwa Walīd b. Hishām (1007) ii, 858b; iii, 78b, 79b; xi, **129a**
Abū Rās (1823) ix, 20b
Abū Rashīd al-Nīsābūrī (XI) s, **31b**, 345a, 346a, 393a
Abu 'l-Rawāʾīn (ʿĪsāwā) (1556) iv, 94a
Abu 'l-Rayḥān al-Bīrūnī → al-Bīrūnī
Abū Rayyāsh (Aḥmad b. Abī Hāshim) vi, 267b, 268a
Abū Ridjāʾ Muḥammad Zamān Khān (1872) ii, 500b
Abu 'l-Ridjāl b. Abī Bakkār (904) vi, 775b
Abū Righāl (VI) i, **144b**
Abū Riyāḥ Kaysānī iv, 837a
Abū Riyāsh al-Ḳaysī (950) v, 374b; s, **32a**
Abū Ruʾba (VII) vii, 606a
Abū Ruḳayba → Bourguiba
Abū Rudaynī ʿUmar b. ʿAlī (IX) viii, 53a
Abu 'l-Saʿādāt Muḥammad → al-Nāṣir Abu 'l-Saʿādāt
Abu 'l-Ṣabbāḥ b. Yaḥyā al-Yaḥṣubī (VIII) iv, 115a
Abū Saʿd al-Ḥasan b. Ḥamdūn (1211) iii, 784a
Abū Saʿd b. Muḥammad b. Mamā, Shabānkāra (XI) ix, 311a
Abū Saʿd al-ʿAlāʾ b. Sahl (X) viii, 122a
Abū Saʿd al-Makhzūmī s, **32b**
Abū Saʿd al-Mubārak al-Mukharrimī, ḳāḍī (XII) i, 69a
Abū Saʿd Saʿīd b. Abi 'l-Faḍl al-Maydānī (1145) vi, 914a
Abū Saʿd al-Tustarī (1048) vii, 118b, 730a
Abu 'l-Sādj Dīwdād b. Dīwdast (Sādjid) (879) i, **145a**; vii, 395a; viii, 745a
Abū Safyān (VII) i, **145b**
Abū Sahl b. Nawbakht (VIII) x, 226b
Abū Sahl Dūnash b. Tāmīm (X) iv, 304a
Abū Sahl al-Harawī (X) s, 38a
Abū Sahl al-Ḳūhī (982) vi, 600b; s, 412a
Abū Saʿīd (Īl-Khān) (1335) i, 91a, 510b, 764b, 908b, 1011a; ii, 68a, 401a, 706a; iii, 57b, 1122b; iv, 860a; vii, 170a, 189b, 404b, 462a, 820a, 928a; viii, 541b; s, 363b, 415a
Abū Saʿīd (Marīnid) (1331) i, 859b; ii, 146a, 822a, 979a; s, 45b
Abū Saʿīd b. Abi 'l-Khayr (1049) i, **145b**, 162b; iii, 103a; iv, 63b, 1025b, 1057b; vi, 638a, 914b; vii, 550a, viii, 505a

Abū Saʿīd b. al-Aʿrābī i, 114b
Abū Saʿīd b. Ḳarā Yūsuf, amīr (XV) iv, 587b
Abū Saʿīd b. Muʿāwiya b. Yazīd b. al-Muhallab (VIII) vii, 359b
Abū Saʿīd b. Sulṭān Muḥammad b. Mīrānshāh (Tīmūrid) (1469) i, 135a, **147b**, 227b, 311b, 852b; iii, 603a, 1100b; iv, 34a, 588a; vi, 54a, 193b, 309b, 456a, 482a, b, 501b, 505a; vii, 105b; x, 964b; s, 50b, 51a
Abū Saʿīd al-Aflaḥ → al-Aflaḥ b. ʿAbd al-Wahhāb
Abū Saʿīd Āḳ-Sunḳur ʿAbd Allāh Ḳasīm al-Dawla (al-Ḥadjib) (1094) vi, 379b
Abū Saʿīd Bahādur (1335) iv, 860a, 909b; ix, 211a; x, 413a, 525b
Abū Saʿīd al-Djannābī → al-Djannābī
Abū Saʿīd Efendi (shaykh al-Islām) (XVII) vi, 969a
Abū Saʿīd Gurgān, Sultan (1469) vii, 78b
Abū Saʿīd al-Ḳarmātī → al-Djannābī
Abū Saʿīd Khalafa al-Badjī → Sayyidī Abū Saʿīd
Abū Saʿīd al-Kharrāz → al-Kharrāz
Abū Saʿīd al-Khaṭṭābī → al-Khaṭṭābī
Abū Saʿīd al-Marwazī (IX) i, 153b
Abū Saʿīd Muḥammad b. Yūsuf (amīr) (841) vi, 506a
Abū Saʿīd Sandjar al-Djāwulī → ʿAlam al-Dīn Sandjar
Abū Saʿīd Sinān b. Thābit b. Ḳurra (Ṣābiʾ) (943) viii, 673a
Abū Saʿīd al-Sīrāfī → al-Sīrāfī
Abū Saʿīd ʿUthmān I (ʿAbd al-Wādid) (1303) i, 93a; iii, 833a
Abū Saʿīd ʿUthmān II (ʿAbd al-Wādid) (1352) i, 93a; iii, 867a
Abū Saʿīd ʿUthmān (Marīnid) → ʿUthmān II (Marīnid)
Abū Saʿīd ʿUthmān b. ʿAbd al-Muʾmin, Sayyid (Gharnāṭa) (XII) ii, 1013b, 1014a; iii, 66a, 755a, 772a
Abū Saʿīd-zāde Feyḍ Allāh Efendi, Shaykh al-Islām (XVII) i, 394a
Abū Saʿīd Zayd (XI) i, 1310a
Abū Ṣakhr al-Hudhalī (VII) i, **148b**
Abu ʾl-Saḳr b. Bulbul, vizier (890) xi, 498b
Abū Salama b. ʿAbd al-Asad Makhzūmī (624) vi, 138a
Abū Salama Ḥafṣ b. Sulaymān al-Khallāl (vizier) (744) i, 15b, 16a, 16b, 103b, **149a**, 1293a; iii, 988a; vi, 334b, 620b; vii, 664a; ix, 423b
Abū Ṣāliḥ al-Armanī (XIII) vi, 411a, b; viii, 91a
Abū Ṣāliḥ Mufliḥ, Shaykh (941) iii, 161a, 735a
Abū Sālim ʿAlī (Marīnid) iii, 826a, 867a
Abu ʾl-Ṣalt Umayya al-Andalusī (1134) i, **149a**; vi, 450 b; viii, 42b
Abū Sammāl (Asad, Banū) vii, 564b
Abu ʾl-Sarāyā al-Ḥamdānī → Ḥamdānids
Abu ʾl-Sarāyā al-Sarī b. Manṣūr al-Shaybānī (815) i, **149b**, 402b; iii, 243b, 950b; iv, 17a; vi, 334b
Abu ʾl-Ṣaydāʾ al-Dabbī → al-Dabbī abu ʾl-Ṣaydāʾ
Abu ʾl-Ṣaydāʾ Ṣāliḥ b. Ṭārif (VIII) iii, 224a; iv, 15b, 44b; vii, 606a
Abū Sayyāra, ʿUmayla b. al-Aʿzal s, **33a**
Abū Sekkine (Bagirmi) (XIX) i, 910b
Abū Seray → Ḳarḳīsiyā
Abū Shabaka, Ilyās (1947) s, **33b**
Abū Shādī, Aḥmad Zakī (1955) i, 598b; vii, 869a; s, **34a**
Abū Shaḥma (VII) s, 230a
Abū Shākir al-Dayṣanī (zindīḳ) i, 48b; iii, 496b
Abū Shakūr Balkhī (X) iv, 63a; viii, 885a; s, **35a**
Abu ʾl-Shalaʿlaʿ Muḥammad → Muḥammad b. Aḥmad
Abū Shāma, Shihāb al-Dīn al-Maḳdisī (1268) i, **150a**, 1314b; iii, 268a, 693b, 753a, 934a, 1158a; vi, 430a; vii, 167a
Abu ʾl-Shamaḳmaḳ (796) i, **150a**; iii, 966a
Abū Shamir al-Ḥanafī (IX) vii, 606b; s, 88b
Abū Shantūf (Hintāta) (XVI) vi, 743a
Abu ʾl-Shawk Fāris (ʿAnnāzid) (1045) i, 512b; iii, 258b, 571b; v, 453b, 454a
Abu ʾl-Shaykh (979) vi, 821a
Abu ʾl-Shibl ʿĀṣim al-Burdjūmī (IX) iv, 1005a
Abu ʾl-Shīṣ al-Khuzāʿī (915) i, **150b**; iv, 1004b; vii, 694b; s, 33a
Abū Shuʿayb (island) → Lār (island)
Abū Shuʿayb Ayyūb al-Ṣinhādjī (XII) i, 159b, 809b; iii, 339a
Abū Shudjāʿ Aḥmad b. Ḥasan (XII) i, **150b**, 867b; iii, 817a
Abū Shudjāʿ Bādh b. Dustāk → Bādh

Abū Shudjāʿ Fātik b. ʿAbd Allāh al-Rūmī, ʿAzīz al-Dawla (1022) v, 929b, 933a,b; vii, 116b, 770b
Abū Shudjāʿ Rudhrawārī (XI) ii, 384b; iii, 258b; s, 398a
Abū Shudjāʿ Shīrawayh (1115) → Shīrawayh, Abū Shudjāʿ
Abū Shurāʿa (255) s, **35a**
Abu Simbil → Abū Sinbil
Abu 'l-Simṭ Marwān b. Abi 'l-Djanūb (X) vi, 625b
Abu 'l-Simṭ Marwān b. Sulaymān (X) vi, 625a
Abū Sinbil s, **35b**
Abū Ṣufra Abu 'l-Muhallab (VII) iv, 1056b; vii, 357a
Abū Sufyān b. Ḥarb b. Umayya (653) i, 9a, 115b, **151a**, 381b, 868a, 1283b; ii, 375b, 843b, 1020b; iii, 455a; vi, 138a, 145b, 146b; vii, 254a, 264a, 369b, 370a; x, 841a; s, 103b, 133b, 350a
Abū Sufyān Maḥbūb b. al-Raḥīl → Maḥbūb b. al-Raḥīl
Abū Sulaymān Dāʾūd b. Ibrāhīm al-Thalātī (1559) i, 121b
Abū Sulaymān al-Sidjistānī al-Manṭiḳī (985) i, 127a, **151b**, 235b; ii, 359a; vi, 641a; s, 13b, 398b
Abū Sulaymān Muḥammad b. Maʿshar → al-Maḳdisī, Abū Sulaymān
Abu 'l-Surrī → Sahl b. Maṣlīaḥ
Abu 'l-Surūr al-Mufarridj → Ibn al-Sarrādj
Abu 'l-Suʿūd, ʿAbd Allāh (XIX) ii, 466b
Abu 'l-Suʿūd Muḥammad b. Muḥyi 'l-Dīn al-ʿImādī (Khodja Čelebi) (1574) i, **152a**, 1235a; ii, 32b, 56b, 687a; iii, 163b; iv, 375a, 376a, 557a, 560a, 881b; v, 682a; vi, 3b, 226b, 227a; vii, 546a, 912a; viii, 486b; ix, 401b
Abū Taghlib Faḍl Allāh al-Ghaḍanfar (Ḥamdānid) (979) i, 211b, 824b, 954b; ii, 344a, 483a; iii, 127b, 128a, b, 246a, 841a; iv, 663b, 1084a; vi, 540a, 930a; vii, 910b, 911a, 995b; s, **36a**
Abū Ṭāhir b. ʿAlī, Atābeg (Lūr-i Buzurg) (XII) v, 826b
Abū Ṭāhir b. Ḥassūl (XI) vi, 638a
Abū Ṭāhir ʿAbd al-Raḥmān b. Aḥmad (Imām) (1091) ix, 86b
Abū Ṭāhir b. ʿAwf (1185) iv, 137a; vi, 279a, 429a
Abū Ṭāhir Ibrāhīm al-Ḥamdānī (1010) iii, 128a, b
Abū Ṭāhir al-Khātūnī vi, 351b
Abū Ṭāhir Saʿīd (1087) i, 147a
Abū Ṭāhir Sulaymān al-Ḳarmaṭī → al-Djannābī
Abu 'l-Ṭāhir Tamīm → Tamīm b. Yūsuf
Abū Ṭāhir Ṭarsūsī i, **152b**; iv, 63b, 445a
Abū Ṭāḳa → Sikka
Abū Ṭālib b. ʿAbd al-Muṭṭalib (619) i, 9a, 80a, 118b, **152b**, 381b; vi, 139b, 146a, b
Abū Ṭālib ʿAbd Allāh → ʿAzafī (Banū)
Abū Ṭālib Aḥmad b. al-Ḳāsim (1656) vii, 779a
Abū Ṭālib al-Akhīr (1128) s, 363a
Abū Ṭālib b. al-Ḥusayn, Sharīf (XVII) s, 407b
Abū Ṭālib b. Muḥammad Khudābanda (XVII) i, 8b; iii, 157b
Abū Ṭālib Fandaruskī (XVIII) iii, 114b
Abū Ṭālib Iṣfahānī, Mīrzā (XIX) s, 290a
Abū Ṭālib Kalīm → Kalīm
Abū Ṭālib Khān (1806) i, **153a**; iii, 1046a
Abū Ṭālib al-Makkī (996) i, **153a**, 274a, 351a; iii, 570b; iv, 470a, 486b; vii, 465a; viii, 993b; x, 9a
Abū Ṭālib al-Nāṭiḳ (1033) s, 335b
Abū Ṭālūt (Khāridjī) (VII) iv, 1076a
Abū Ṭālūt Sālim b. Maṭar (VII) iv, 1076a; vii, 858b
Abu 'l-Ṭamaḥān al-Ḳaynī (634) i, 115b; iv, 820a; s, **37a**
Abū Tamīm Anṣārī (VII) vi, 837a
Abū Tammām Ḥabīb b. ʿAws (845) i, 53a, 118b, **153a**, 331a, 386b, 449b, 592a, 822a, 857b, 1114b, 1289a, 1290a; ii, 248b; iii, 110b, 111b, 879a; v, 935a; vi, 107b, 625b, 635b; vii, 307b, 527a, 694b, 982a; viii, 892a; s, 15a, 26a, 32b, 33a, 277b, 650b
Abū Tāshufīn I (1337) i, 122b, **155a**
Abū Tāshufīn II (1393) i, 122b, 123a, **155a**; iii, 832a
Abū Tawwāma (XIII) vi, 131a
Abū Tāyih (Tawāyihī) → ʿAwda b. Ḥarb
Abū Ṭayyib → al-Mutanabbī; al-Ṭabarī
Abu 'l-Ṭayyib al-Lughawī (962) iii, 665a; s, **37b**, 361b
Abu 'l-Ṭayyib Muḥammad al-Numayrī (X) iv, 1005b
Abū Ṭayyib al-Shawwā (X) vii, 492b
Abū Ṭayyiba (cupper) (VII) s, 304a

Abū Thābit (ʿAbd al-Wādid) (XIV) i, 93a; iii, 867a; s, 377a
Abū Thābit ʿĀmir (Marīnid) (1308) v, 48b; vi, 441a, 593b; s, 103a
Abu ʾl-Thanāʾ Maḥmūd b. Ādjā i, 1109b
Abū Thumāma (VII) iv, 472a
Abū Thawr (854) i, **155a**
Abū Ṭulayḥ → Abuklea
Abū Turāb → ʿAlī b. Abī Ṭālib
Abū Turāb al-Athīrī (vizier) (XI) s, 29b
Abū Turāb Ḥaydar al-Din "Kāmil" (XVIII) iv, 544b
Abū Turāb Mīrzā → Ismāʿīl (III) (Ṣafawid)
Abū Turāb Nakhshabī (859) x, 377a
Abū Ṭuwayriḳ Badr (1570) ix, 425a
Abū ʿUbayd b. Masʿūd (VII) x, 819a
Abū ʿUbayd al-Bakrī (1094) i, 96a, **155b**, 345a, 488a, 511b, 600b, 862b; ii, 584b; iii, 991b; iv, 339a; v, 1011a, 1017b; vi, 257b, 258a, 359b, 639b, 640a, 822a; vii, 228a, b, 584a, 761a; viii, 17a; x, 346a; s, 304b, 376b
Abū ʿUbayd al-Ḳāsim b. Sallām (838) i, 156a, **157b**, 158b, 718b; iv, 547b; v, 175a; vi, 194b, 344b, 654b, 816a, 822a; vii, 262a; viii, 150b, 672a; ix, 318a, 662a; x, 918a; s, 15b, 317b
Abū ʿUbayd Allāh (786) i, 103b, **157b**, 1033b
Abū ʿUbayd al-Thaḳafī (634) ii, 555a
Abū ʿUbayda ʿĀmir b. al-Djarrāḥ (639) i, 110a, **158b**, 460b, 970b, 996a, 1137b, 1139a, 1215b; ii, 279b, 280a; iii, 397b; v, 923a; vi, 379a, 505b, 544b, 774a; vii, 570b; viii, 989b; ix, 263a; x, 820a
Abū ʿUbayda al-Djanāwanī → al-Djanāwanī
Abū ʿUbayda Maʿmar b. al-Muthannā (824) i, 105b, 108b, 125b, 143b, **158a**, 167b, 588b, 717b, 718b, 794a; ii, 241a; iv, 1077a; vi, 786a, 828b; vii, 254b, 262a, 402a, 841a; s, 15b, 73b, 177a
Abū ʿUbayda Muslim b. Abī Karīma al-Tamīmī (Ibāḍī) (VIII) i, 120b, 134a; iii, 649b, 650b, 651b, 654a, 658a; vii, 524b; viii, 638a; ix, 766a
Abū ʿUdhba (1713) vi, 847b
Abu ʾl-ʿUḳūl (1300) vii, 30a; x, 163a
Abu ʾl-ʿUlāʾ b. ʿAbd al-Muʾmin (Almohad) (XII) ii, 1072a
Abu ʾl-ʿUlāʾ Idrīs → Idrīs al-Maʾmūn
Abū ʿUlāmā al-Mashdjaʿī (1750) vi, 191b
Abū Umāma Asʿad (VII) vi, 645b
Abū ʿUmar b. Kawthar (XII) ix, 308b
Abū ʿUmar al-Djarmī → al-Djarmī, Abū ʿUmar
Abū ʿUmar Ibn Yūsuf (ḳāḍī ʾl-ḳuḍāt) (922) iii, 101a, 692a; vi, 279b
Abū ʿUmar Inālū (XII) ii, 1013a
Abū ʿUmar Tāshufīn b. Abi ʾl-Ḥasan (Marīnid) (XIV) iii, 867a
Abū Umayma → Ismāʿīl Ṣabrī
Abū Usāma al-Harawī (1009) s, **38a**
Abū ʿUtba → Abū Lahab b. ʿAbd al-Muṭṭalib
Abū ʿUthmān b. Saʿīd b. al-Ḥakam (Minūrḳa) (XIII) vii, 87a
Abū ʿUthmān Saʿīd (1620) vi, 187a
Abū ʿUthmān Saʿīd b. ʿAbd Allāh al-Tilimsānī → al-Tilimsānī, Abū ʿUthmān
Abū ʿUthmān Saʿīd b. Hāshim (1009) iii, 111a; iv, 936b
Abū ʿUthmān Saʿīd b. Muḥammad b. al-Ḥaddād (914) i, 249b
Abū ʿUthmān Saʿīd b. Yaʿḳūb al-Dimashḳī (950) i, 1223b, 1340a; ii, 948b; vi, 902b
Abū ʿUzaiyyiz → Ḳatāda b. Idrīs
Abu ʾl-Wafāʾ (vizier) (978) vi, 930a
Abu ʾl-Wafāʾ, Shaykh (1491) iv, 230b
Abu ʾl-Wafāʾ b. al-ʿAḳīl → Ibn al-ʿAḳīl
Abu ʾl-Wafāʾ al-Būz(a)djānī (998) i, 127a, **159a**, 1354a; iii, 1140a; vi, 119b, 600b; s, 398b, 412a, b, 413b, 414a
Abu ʾl-Wafāʾ Ibrāhīm (1756) viii, 730a
Abu ʾl-Walīd b. al-Dabbāgh (1151) viii, 635b
Abu ʾl-Walīd b. al-Aḥmar (XV) i, 352a
Abu ʾl-Walīd al-Azraḳī → al-Azraḳī
Abu ʾl-Walīd al-Bādjī → al-Bādjī
Abu ʾl-Walīd Ḳurṭubī → Ibn Rushd, al-Djadd
Abu ʾl-Walīd Muḥammad b. Aḥmad b. Abī Duʾād i, 271b
Abu ʾl-Walīd Muḥammad b. Djahwar → Ibn Djahwar, Abu ʾl-Walīd
Abu ʾl-Ward b. al-Kawthar (750) i, 43a; iv, 493b
Abū Yaʿazzā Yalannūr b. Maynūn al-Hazmīrī (1177) i, 137b, **159b**; vi, 356b; s, 38b
Abū Yaddās b. Dūnās (Īfrānid) (1009) iii, 1043b
Abū Yaḥyā b. al-Sakkāk (1413) ix, 347a

Abū Yaḥyā Abū Bakr I al-S͟hahīd (Ḥafṣid) (1309) iii, 67b
Abū Yaḥyā Abū Bakr II al-Mutawakkil (Ḥafṣid) (1346) iii, 49a, 67b; iv, 416a; v, 531a
Abū Yaḥyā al-Marwazī (X) i, 159a; vi, 844b
Abū Yaḥyā al-Zad̲j̲d̲j̲ālī (1294) vi, 824b
Abū Yaḥyā Zakariyyāʾ → Ibn al-Liḥyānī
Abū Yaḥyā Zakariyyāʾ → al-Ird̲j̲ānī
Abū Yaknī (amīr) (Ḥammādids) (1088) iii, 138a; vi, 427a
Abū Yaʿḳūb b. ʿAbd al-Muʾmin (1163) vi, 521a
Abū Yaʿḳūb al-Aḳṭaʿ (X) iii, 100a
Abū Yaʿḳūb Ḳādī al-K͟handaḳ (X) i, 816a
Abū Yaʿḳūb al-K͟huraymī, Isḥāḳ b. Ḥassān b. Ḳūhī (821) i, **159b**; vi, 437b, 606a; s, 25a
Abū Yaʿḳūb al-S͟haḥḥām (871) vii, 784b
Abū Yaʿḳūb al-Sid̲j̲zī (Sid̲j̲istānī) (X) i, **160a**; iii, 328b; iv, 199a, 508b, 662b; vii, 968b; s, 52b
Abū Yaʿḳūb al-Sūsī (900) iv, 990b
Abū Yaʿḳūb Yūsuf I b. ʿAbd al-Muʾmin (Almohad) (1184) i, **160b**, 1288a, 1339b; ii, 352b, 525a, 744b, 1014a; iii, 771b, 910a, 957a; iv, 116a; vii, 803b; ix, 308b; s, 307a
Abū Yaʿḳūb Yūsuf II al-Mustanṣir (Almohad) (1224) vii, 1020b
Abū Yaʿḳūb Yūsuf I b. ʿAbd al-Ḥaḳḳ (Marīnid) (1307) i, 92b; iii, 470b; vi, 142a, 356a, 440b, 441a, 521b, 572a, 593b, 596b; vii, 1022a; s, 112b, 377a
Abū Yaʿḳūb Yūsuf b. Abī Saʿīd (Ḳarmaṭī) (977) iv, 664a
Abū Yaʿḳūb Yūsuf b. Ibrāhīm al-Sadrātī al-Ward̲j̲ilānī (1174) viii, 756a; s, 15b
Abū Yaʿḳūb Yūsif b. Nūḥ → Yūsuf b. Nūḥ
Abū Yaʿḳūb Yūsuf al-Bādisī (XIV) i, **860a**
Abū Yaʿḳūb Yūsuf al-Baṣīr → Yūsuf al-Baṣīr
Abu ʾl-Yaḳẓān Muḥammad b. Aflaḥ (894) i, 139a; vii, 402a
Abū Yaʿla b. al-Farrāʾ → Ibn al-Farrāʾ
Abū Yaʿla b. Zurʿa (871) ix, 317b
Abū Yasār ʿAbd Allāh al-T͟haḳafī (748) iv, 371a
Abū Yaʿzā (Yaʿazzā) Hazmīrī (1177) iii, 339a, 800b; xi, 112a
Abū Yazīd → Mak͟hdūm S͟hāh Dawlat
Abū Yazīd al-Bisṭāmī (874) i, **162a**, 1168a; ii, 32a; iv, 321a, 1057b; vi, 225a, b, 569b; vii, 95b; ix, 65b; x, 250a
Abū Yazīd Mak͟hlad al-Nukkārī (947) i, **163a**, 699b, 770b, 863a, 1238a; ii, 852b, 977a; iii, 95b, 297b, 656a, 657b, 659b, 1040b, 1042a; iv, 459b, 479a, 740b, 827b; v, 696a, 1175a, b, 1246a, b; vi, 353b, 434a, b, 435a, 727b, 945a; vii, 485b; viii, 113b; s, 236b, 306b
Abū Yazīd al-Sulamī → Yazīd b. Usayd al-Sulamī
Abu ʾl-Yumn al-ʿUlaymī → Mud̲j̲īr al-Dīn
Abū Yūsuf (Almohad) → Abū Yaʿḳūb Yūsuf I
Abū Yūsuf Hamadānī (1140) xi, 294b
Abū Yūsuf Yaʿḳūb (Marīnid) (1286) ii, 819a, 822a, b; vii, 1021b, 1022a; viii, 808b; s, 112a
Abū Yūsuf Yaʿḳūb (Rustamid) (908) iii, 655b
Abū Yūsuf Yaʿḳūb b. Ibrāhīm al-Anṣārī al-Kūfī (798) i, 28a, 123a, 124a, **164a**, 588b, 773a; ii, 231b, 890b; iii, 162b, 512b; iv, 949a; vi, 2a, 24a, 264b, 352b, 495b, 659a; vii, 646a, 662b; viii, 497b; x, 917b
Abū Yūsuf Yaʿḳūb al-Ḳirḳisānī (Ḳarḳasānī) (Karaite) (X) iv, 605a
Abū Yūsuf Yaʿḳūb al-Manṣūr (Almohad) (1199) i, 137b, **165a**, 495b, 499b, 533b, 604b, 605b, 634a, 1224b; ii, 307b, 331b, 510a, 525a, 1007b; iii, 748b, 910b, 978b; iv, 118a, 461a, 614a, 729b; vi, 134a, 596b, 597a; vii, 211b, 579b, 802b; viii, 507a; s, 274a
Abū Zaʿbal s, **38a**
Abū Ẓabī i, **166a**, 539b, 1313b, 1314a; ii, 557b, 619a; iv, 751b, 778a; v, 1058b; vi, 37b, 961b; s, 42a, 416b
Abu ʾl-Zād̲j̲ir Ismāʿīl → Ismāʿīl b. Ziyād al-Nafūsī
Abū Ẓafar → Bāhadur S͟hāh II
Abu ʾl-Ẓafar al-Hindī al-Sayyāḥ vi, 112b
Abū Zakariyyāʾ (Ḥafṣid) (1279) vi, 404a
Abū Zakariyyāʾ b. K͟haldūn → Ibn K͟haldūn
Abū Zakariyyāʾ al-D̲j̲anāwunī (XII) i, **166b**, 1028a
Abū Zakariyyāʾ al-Farrāʾ → al-Farrāʾ
Abū Zakariyyāʾ al-Mag͟hribī, S͟hayk͟h (XII) ii, 198a; v, 924b, 926b

Abū Zakariyyāʾ Yaḥyā b. al-Khayr al-Wardj(a)lānī (XII) i, 125a, **167a**; ii, 141a; iii, 95a; vi, 311a, b, 449a, 945a, 948b; viii, 112b; s, 15b
Abū Zakariyyāʾ Yaḥyā I (Ḥafṣid) (1249) i, 121b, 605b; ii, 1008a, 1014b; iii, 66a, 296b, 338a, 461b, 673a; iv, 337b; v, 1150a; s, 111b
Abū Zakariyyāʾ Yaḥyā II (Ḥafṣid) (1279) → al-Wāthiḳ
Abū Zakariyyāʾ Yaḥyā III (Ḥafṣid) (1295) iii, 67a; iv, 338a
Abū Zakariyyāʾ Yaḥyā IV (Ḥafṣid) (1489) iii, 69a
Abū Zakariyyāʾ al-Ẓamāmī, dāʿī (X) iv, 661a
Abū Zayd → al-Balkhī
Abū Zayd (Banū Hilāl) i, **167b**; iii, 387a, b
Abū Zayd b. Yūsuf al-Ḥarḍānī (Almohad) (XII) iii, 231a
Abū Zayd ʿAbd al-Raḥmān b. Igit → Ibn Igit
Abū Zayd ʿAbd al-Raḥmān b. Maʿlā, Shaykh (XII) iii, 96a
Abū Zayd ʿAbd al-Raḥman al-Hazmīrī (XIV) iii, 339a, b, 731a
Abū Zayd al-Anṣārī, Saʿīd b. Aws (830) i, 108b, 125b, 143b, **167b**, 717b, 1098a; s, 38b, 73b, 317b
Abū Zayd al-Fāzārī (XIII) iv, 541a
Abū Zayd al-Ḥasan al-Sīrāfī (X) ii, 583b; s, 56a
Abū Zayd al-Ḳayrāwānī (996) vi, 279a
Abū Zayd al-Ḳurashī (X) iv, 835b; vii, 254b; s, **38b**
Abū Zayd al-Manāṭiḳī vi, 354a
Abū Zayd Muḥammad b. Abi ʾl-Khaṭṭāb al-Ḳurashī (X) vii, 254b, 527a; s, **38b**
Abū Zayd al-Naḥwī s, 286b
Abū Zayd al-Sarūdjī → al-Ḥarīrī
Abū Zayd al-Sīrāfī → Akhbār al-Ṣīn wa ʾl-Hind
Abū Zayyān I (ʿAbd al-Wādid) (1308) i, **167b**; v, 1180a
Abū Zayyān II (1398) i, **167b**
Abū Zayyān III (1550) i, **168a**
Abū Zayyān Muḥammad → Muḥammad IV (Marīnid)
Abū Zḥūr al-Markab, Banū vi, 46a
Abu ʾl-Zift al-Ḥasan (VIII) iii, 616a
Abu ʾl-Zinād (751) iii, 494b; vi, 263a; viii, 973b; s, 380a
Abū Ẓiyā Tewfīḳ Bey → Tewfīḳ Bey
Abū Ziyād b. Salmā (718) iv, 54a
Abu ʾl-Zubayr vi, 263a
Abū Zurʿa (1423) s, **39a**
Abū Zurʿa al-Rāzī iii, 158b
Abuʿam → Tāfīlālt
Abubacer → Ibn Ṭufayl
Abubakar Atiku (Kano) iv, 550b
Abubakar Imam (XX) iii, 282b
Abūkārib Asʿad (ca. 400) x, 575b
Abūḳīr i, **168a**
Abuklea i, **168b**
Abulcasis → al-Zahrāwī
Abulelizor, Albuleizor → Ibn Zuhr, Abu ʾl-ʿAlāʾ
Abulpharagius Benattibus → Ibn al-Ṭayyib
Abumeron → Ibn Zuhr
al-ʿAbūr → Nudjūm
Aburdja, Mudjīr al-Dīn (XIV) s, 105b
Abūshahr → Būshahr
Abushka → Nawāʾī, ʿAlī Shīr
Abūṣīr → Būṣīr
al-Abwāʾ i, **169a**; iii, 362b; vii, 645b; s, 312a
Abwāb → Darband
Abyaḍ, Georges (1959) vi, 746b, 750b, 751b, 755a; s, **39b**
Abyaḍ b. Ḥammāl al-Māribī (VII) vi, 566a, b
Abyan i, **169a**, 538a; vi, 562b, 563a, b; s, 338a
al-Abyārī, Shaykh ʿAbd al-Hādī (1888) s, **40a**
Abyssinians (Ḥimyar) xi, 379b
al-Abzārī → ʿAmīd al-Dīn
Ačalpur → Eličpur
Ačakzay s, 507b
Accra (Ghana) ii, 1003b
Acheh → Atjèh
Achehnese → Malay
Achir → Ashīr
Acier (fr.: Steel) → Fūlādh
Açores → al-Djazāʾir al-Khālida
Acre → ʿAkkā
ʿĀd, Banū i, **169a**, 257a, iii, 537b, 1270a; iv, 820b; v, 497b, 811a; vi, 82a; ix, 91a
ʿĀd b. ʿŪs b. Iram b. Sām b. Nūḥ ix, 775a
ʿĀd Shaykh vi, 628b
ʿĀd Te-Mikāʾēl vi, 628b
Adāʾ i, **169b**
ʿĀda i, **170a**, 173a, 277a, 741b, 744b,

746b, 980b, 1179a; ii, 22b, 890b; iv, 154b-156a
Ada Ḳalʿe i, **174b**
Ada Pāzārì i, **175a**
Adab i, 23a, 66a, 133b, **175b**, 326a, 328b, 345b, 588a; ii, 951b; iii, 884b, 893a, 1262a; iv, 510a; s, 93b
ʿAdad → Ḥisāb
Adal i, **176b**, 763b, 1172b; iii, 3b, 4a
ʿAdāla → ʿAdl
Adalar → Kìzìl Adalar
ʿAdalī ii, 120b
Adʿali, Banū x, 72a
Adalya → Antalya
Ādam (Abu 'l-Bas̲h̲ar) i, **176b**; iv, 947b; v, 210a; vi, 218b
Ādam al-Ilūrī (1992) xi, 338a
Ādam, Mawlānā (XIV) s, 353a
Adam, sultan (Banjarmasin) (1857) s, 150b
ʿAdam i, **178b**; v, 578b
Adama → Modibbo Adama
Adamiyyat, Ḥusayn Ruknzāda iv, 72b; v, 198b
Adamawa i, **179a**; ii, 9b, 10b, 941b, 942b
ʿAdan i, 106b, 169a, **180b**, 536a, 539a, 552a, 554b, 781a, 976a; ii, 469a, 675a, 737a; iii, 881b; iv, 519a, 746a, 901b, 1188b; v, 71a, 1059b, 1244b; vi, 36a, 354b, 438b; vii, 66b; s, 338a
ʿAdan Lāʿa vi, 438b
Adana i, **182a**; v, 558a; vi, 59b, 69a; s, 138b
Adareñña → Harari
Adārisa → Idrīsids
Ādarrāḳ s, **40a**, 399b
Adāt → Naḥw
ʿĀdat → ʿĀda
al-ʿAdawī, Abu 'l-Baḳāʾ vi, 106b
al-ʿAdawī, Muḥammad Ḥasanayn Mak̲h̲lūf (1936) vi, 279a; s, **40b**
Aday, Banū vi, 416b, 417a
al-ʿAḍaym i, **184a**
Aḍḍād i, **184b**; v, 705a
ʿAddās (Niniveh) viii, 677a
Addax → Mahāt
ʿAḍēm → al-ʿAḍaym
Aden → ʿAdan
Adfūū i, **186a**; vi, 672a
al-Adfūwī i, 186b; vi, 214b
Aḍḥāʾ → ʿĪd al-aḍḥāʾ
ʿAd̲h̲āb i, **186b**
ʿAd̲h̲āb al-Ḳabr i, **186b**; iv, 667b; v, 236b
Adham K̲h̲ān (amīr) (1561) i, 1155a; vi, 310a, 407a
Adhamiyya → Ibrāhīm b. Adham
Ad̲h̲ān i, **187b**; ii, 432b, 593b; iv, 181a; vi, 361b
Ād̲h̲ār → Taʾrīk̲h̲
Ād̲h̲arbāyd̲j̲ān i, 8a, 13b, **188b**, 300b, 420b, 639a, 642b, 644a, 660a, 731b, 1052a, 1107b; ii, 680b, 903b; iii, 530a, 1099b; iv, 3a, 19b-20a, 347b, 392a; v, 496b, 497a, 729b, 730a, 1213b; vi, 15b, 56a, 64a, b, 120a, 130b, 200b, 202b, 274a, 334a, 335a, 337a, b, 338a, b, 420b, 438a, 482a, 492b, 495a, 498a, b, 499a, b, 500a, 501a, b, 502b, 504a, 512b, 514a, 516b, 539a, 541a, 553b, 623a, 670b; vii, 432a, 655b, 656a; viii, 642b; x, 41b; s, 23b, 47a, 70b, 71b, 116a, 135a, 147b, 170a, 239b, 274b, 282a, 326a, 366a, 378a
Ād̲h̲arbāyd̲j̲ān (Russia) → Azerbayd̲j̲ān
Ad̲h̲argūn i, **191b**
Ād̲h̲arī (Azerī) i, 191a, **192a**, 756a, 1072b; ii, 89a, 938b; iv, 351a, 627b, 732a; v, 8a; vii, 352a, 353a; x, 710a; s, 415b
Ād̲h̲arī literature x, **726b**
Ad̲h̲aryūn → Ad̲h̲argūn
ʿAd̲h̲aym (river) v, 442a
ʿAd̲h̲rāʾ → Nud̲j̲ūm
ʿAd̲h̲rāʾ (Mard̲j̲ Rāhiṭ) vi, 545b
Ad̲h̲rāma x, 92b
Ad̲h̲riʿāt i, **194a**; vi, 546a, 548a, 742a, b, 743a
Ad̲h̲ruḥ i, 55a, 108b, **194b**, 384a, b, 451b; ii, 535a; iv, 938a; vii, 373b; x, 883a; s, 230a
Ad̲h̲ur-Walās̲h̲ (VII) iv, 644b
al-Ad̲h̲wāʾ i, **194b**
ʿAdī, Banū iii, 386a, b; v, 1183a; vi, 137b, 145a, 649a
ʿAdī, Banū (village) s, 40b
ʿAdī b. ʿAmr, Banū v, 78b, 79a
ʿAdī b. Arṭāt (820) iv, 291a; s, **41a**
ʿAdī b. Ḥātim (687) i, **195a**; iii, 241a, 274b; v, 499b
ʿAdī b. Musāfir al-Hakkārī (1162) i, **195a**; v, 209a, 475b, 644a
ʿAdī b. al-Riḳāʿ (VIII) i, **196a**, 436a; ii, 480a
ʿAdī b. Zayd al-ʿIrādī (VI) i, 115b, **196a**, 565a, 584b; iii, 462b, 1261a; iv, 1002a; vii, 568b; viii, 119b, 884a

Ādi Granth iii, 456b
al-Adīb, Abu ʾl-Ḥasan (X) ix, 8b
Adīb Isḥāḳ → Isḥāḳ, Adīb
Adīb al-Mamālik → Amīrī, Muḥammad Ṣādiḳ
Adīb Pīshāwarī (1930) s, **41a**
Adīb Ṣābir → Ṣābir b. Ismāʿīl al-Tirmidhī
al-ʿĀḍid li-Dīn Allāh (Fāṭimid) (1171) i, **196b**, 797a; ii, 318a, 856b, 857a; vi, 198a; vii, 163b; viii, 131b
Adïghe i, 1000a; ii, 21b, 22a
Adighes → Čerkes
al-ʿĀdil (vizier) (1041) vii, 270b
al-ʿĀdil, Abū Muḥammad (Almohad) → Abū Muḥammad ʿAbd Allāh
al-ʿĀdil I, al-Malik, Sayf al-Dīn (Ayyūbid) → al-Malik al-ʿĀdil I
al-ʿĀdil II, al-Malik, Abū Bakr (Ayyūbid) → al-Malik al-ʿĀdil II
ʿĀdil, Amīr ii, 401b; iv, 584b
al-ʿĀdil b. al-Salār (vizier) (1153) i, 9a, **198b**; ii, 318a, 856b; iii, 868a; iv, 137a; vii, 579a
ʿĀdil Djabr (XX) vi, 615b
ʿĀdil Girāy Khān (Crimea) (1671) i, 311a; ii, 88a, 1113b; v, 140a
ʿĀdil Khān (Lāhawr) (1395) vi, 49b
ʿĀdil Khān I (Fārūḳid) (1441) ii, 814b
ʿĀdil Khān II (Fārūḳid) (1501) ii, 814b; vi, 51a
ʿĀdil Khān III (Fārūḳid) (1520) ii, 815a, 1127b; iii, 422a; vi, 51a, 67b; vii, 105a
ʿĀdil Pasha (Bahdīnān) (1808) i, 920a
ʿAdil Shāh (Afshārid) (1748) i, 246b; iii, 177b; iv, 104a; vii, 674b
ʿĀdil-Shāhs (Bīdjāpur) i, **199a**, 1048a, 1202b, 1203a, 1323a; ii, 220a, 1135a; iii, 425a, 426a, 447b, 1161a; vi, 68a, 269b, 369a, b, 536b, 610b, 695b; vii, 80a, 289a, 300a, 325b, 943a; ix, 483a
ʿĀdila Khātūn (XVIII) i, **199a**
ʿĀdilābād district i, 1322a; ii, 257b, 258a; iii, 481b; vi, 87a
Adilcevaz vi, 242b
ʿĀdilī → Bāysonghor
Adīnā Beg Khān (XVIII) i, 296a; iii, 1158b; v, 598b
Adivar, Adnan Bey (1955) i, 836b; iv, 933b, 934a, b; s, **41b**
Adiyaman i, **199b**; vi, 231a, 507a
ʿĀdj i, **200a**, 501a
Adjaʾ wa-Salmā i, **203a**, 536b; s, 304b
ʿAdjabshīr vi, 502b
ʿAdjāʾib i, 122a, 157a, **203b**; ii, 77a, 583b, 586b
Adjal i, **204a**
ʿAdjala i, **205a**
Adjall Shams al-Dīn ʿUmar Bukhārī, Sayyid (XIV) vi, 702b, 703a; viii, 159b
ʿAdjam i, **206a**; iii, 212b; iv, 338b
ʿAdjamī oghlān i, **206b**, 1004a, 1256b, 1278a; ii, 986a, 996b, 1087a; iv, 242b
al-ʿAdjamiyya → Aljamía
ʿAdjārida i, **207a**
Adjaristān i, 468b, 1108b
al-Adjdābī, Abū Isḥāḳ i, **207a**
al-Adjdābī, al-Ḥusayn b. ʿAbd Allāh (1040) vi, 353b
Adjdābiya i, **207a**; v, 695b; s, 380b
Adjdir s, 377b
Adjdanaḳān i, 796b
al-ʿAdjdjādj, Abu ʾl-Shaʿthāʾ (715) i, 142a, **207b**, 1154b, 1310b; iii, 1262a; viii, 377a; x, 68b; s, 31b
ʿAdjīb s, 22a
ʿAdjīb al-Māndjilak (Fundj) (1607) ii, 944a; iv, 893a
ʿAdjību b. ʿUmar Tal i, 297a
Adjirlū vi, 17a
ʿAdjīsa vi, 727b
ʿAdjlān b. Rumaytha, Sharīf (1375) i, 553a; vi, 149b
ʿAdjlān Beg b. Ḳarasï (1335) iv, 628a
ʿAdjlān al-Hamdānī (VII) s, 400b
ʿAdjlūn i, **208a**; vi, 345a, 547b; s, 391a
al-ʿAdjlūnī (1749) vi, 352b
ʿAdjmān vi, 38a; vii, 782b; s, **42a**, 416b
Adjmēr i, **208a**; ii, 50a, 274b; iii, 441a; v, 1218b, 1219b; vi, 53b, 369a, 691b; s, 5a, 55b, 293b, 353b, 420b
al-Adjnādayn i, **208b**; v, 323b, 800a; vi, 138b, 544b; s, 37a
Adjōdhān vi, 49b, 294b; s, 73b, 353a
Adjr i, **209a**; iii, 1017a
ʿAdjrūd vi, 455b
Adjūdānbāshī s, 108b, 290b
Adjurān (Sōmālī) vi, 128b
al-Ādjurrī, Abū Bakr (971) iii, 159a, 735a; s, 83a
al-Adjurrī, Abū ʿUbayd (913) viii, 516a
Ādjurrūmiyya → Ibn Ādjurrūm
ʿAdjūz → Ayyām al-ʿAdjūz

al-ʿAdjūz al-Djurashiyya → Asmāʾ bint ʿUmays
Adjwad b. Zāmil al-Djabrī i, 553a, 942b; ii, 159b, 176a; iv, 764b; s, 234a
Adjwaf → Taṣrīf
Adjyād vi, 155a, 160b, 167a, 178a
ʿAdl i, **209a**, 334b, 410a, 415b; ii, 834a; iii, 1143b
ʿAdlī i, **210a**
ʿAdn → Djanna
ʿAdnān i, **210a**, 544b; iv, 448a; vi, 472b
Adowa → Adua
Adrar i, **210b**; v, 654a
Adrār n-Deren (Atlas) i, 748a
Adrar Ifoghas i, **210b**; iii, 1038b
Adrar Tmar i, **210b**, 733b
Adrianople → Edirne
Adriatique → Baḥr Adriyas
al-Adrīzī, Abu 'l-ʿAbbās Aḥmad b. Ibrāhīm (1754) vi, 357a
Adua vi, 643b
ʿAḍud al-Dawla Fannā-Khusraw (Būyid) (983) i, 87a, 151b, **211b**, 381a, 824a, 899b, 900a, 955a, 1005b, 1223b, 1350b, 1353a, 1354a, 1355b; ii, 127a, 144b, 344a, 487a, 748b, 802b, 812a, 856a, 893b, 905a, 925b; iii, 128a, 258a, 344b, 671a, 703a, 704a, 730a, 823b, 1157a, 1176a; iv, 24a, 222a, 358a, 675a, 859b, 975a; v, 153a, 158b, 229b, 353a, 452b, 867b, 873a, 896b, 1125a; vi, 117b, 120b, 193a, 198b, 199a, 261b, 519a, 521b, 522a, 600b, 626a, 634b, 637b, 658a, 676a; vii, 272b, 312b, 535b, 560b, 771a, 860a; s, 4a, 36b, 94a, b, 118a, 119a, 127a, 263b, 304b, 390a
ʿAḍud al-Dawla Shīrzād (XII) vi, 783a
ʿAḍud al-Dīn → al-Īdjī
ʿAḍud al-Dīn Muḥammad b. ʿAbd Allāh (vizier) (1178) i, **212b**; iii, 891b; vii, 707a, 726b
ʿAḍudī Hospital i, 900a, 901a, 1223b, 1224a
Adulis vi, 641b, 643b
al-ʿAdwa s, 305a
ʿAdwān, Banū iii, 363b; ix, 763b; s, 33a
Adwiya i, **212b**, 1056a, 1057a; v, 251b
Aegean Sea i, 464a; v, 505b, 506a, b
Aelius Gallus vi, 561a
Afʿā i, **214b**
Āfāḳ Pārsā (XX) vi, 486a
Āfāḳīs (Gharībīs) (XV) iv, 908a; v, 1258a; vi, 62b, 63a, 67b
Āfāḳiyya (White Mountain) x, 250b; xi, 288a; s, 522a, 523a
Afʿāluhu taʿālā i, 343a, 412b
Afāmiya (Apamea) i, **215a**; iv, 919b; vi, 578b; vii, 578a; viii, 128a
ʿAfar, Banū (Somali) ii, 113b, 535b; iii, 1053a; v, 522a, 524a; x, 71b
ʿAfar (ʿUmān) → al-ʿIfār
ʿAfārīt → ʿIfrīt
Afāriḳa iv, 338b, 339a, b
Afāwīh s, **42a**
al-Afḍal → Rasūlids
al-Afḍal b. Amīr al-Djuyūsh (Fāṭimid vizier) (1100) vi, 519b
al-Afḍal b. Badr al-Djamālī (1121) i, 149a, **215a**, 440a, 711a, 870b, 1091b; ii, 127a, 305a, 329a, 855b, 856b, 858a, 861b; iii, 545b, 932a; v, 290a, 328a; vii, 148a, 163a, 725a; s, 408a
al-Afḍal, al-Malik, b. Ṣalāḥ al-Dīn (Ayyūbid) (1225) → al-Malik al-Afḍal b. Ṣalāḥ al-Dīn
al-Afḍal al-ʿAbbās (Rasūlid) (1377) viii, 457a, x, 146b
Afḍal al-Dawla Ḥaydarābād (1869) iii, 322b
Afḍal al-Dīn Kirmānī (XII) vi, 493b
Afḍal al-Dīn Turka (1446) s, **43b**
Afḍal Khān (Bīdjāpūr) (1659) i, 199b, 1204a; vi, 126b, 534b
Afḍal Khān Bārakzay (Afghānistān) (1867) i, 87a, 232a; ii, 638a
al-Afḍal Kutayfāt (1131) i, **216a**; ii, 857b; iii, 54b; iv, 200a
al-Afḍal Muḥammad b. Abi 'l-Fidāʾ (XIV) i, 119a; iii, 120a, 900b
al-Afḍal al-Rasūlī → al-Afḍal al-ʿAbbās
Afḍal-i Ṣadr, Khwādja → Afḍal al-Dīn Turka
al-Afḍal Shāhinshāh (vizier) vii, 510b
Afendopolo, Caleb (1522) iv, 605b
Āferīn → Taʾrīkh
ʿAffān Abū ʿUthmān (VII) s, 103b
ʿAffān b. Muslim iv, 683a
Afghān/Afghan i, **216b**, 1068a; iv, 1b, 37a-b; v, 72a, 461a, 782a; vi, 47b, 62a, 342b, 343a; vii, 674a; viii, 257b; s, 1b, 142a, 143b, 147a, 206b, 312a, 325a

– literature i, 1123a; v, 72a
– wars 1st: i, 72a, 962a; iv, 1143a; v, 102a, 580a; 2nd: i, 87b, 238a; v, 580b; 3rd: i, 238b; ii, 30b
al-Afghānī → Djamāl al-Dīn
Afghānī, ʿAlī Muḥammad (XX) iv, 73b
Afghānistān i, **221a**, 853a, 676a; iii, 13a; iv, 535b; v, 501a; vi, 86a, b, 365b, 764b, 771b, 806a; vii, 12a; viii, 282a, b; ix, 446b; x, 685b; s, 214b, 237a, 329b, 332b, 367a
– demography s, 214b
– ethnography i, 95a, 216-220, 224a, b; v, 245b
– geography i, 71a, 221-223
– history i, 39a, 77a, 87a, b, 225b-233a, 295b; ii, 3a, 638a, 657a, 1100b; iii, 13a; iv, 357b, 917b; s, 270a
– institutions ii, 426a; iii, 13b; v, 1079a
– languages i, 220a, b, 225a
– religion i, 225b, 1123-4
ʿAfīf, Shaykh (Ṭāḳa) vi, 83b
ʿAfīf al-Dīn → Bodufenvalugē Sīdī (Maldives)
ʿAfīf al-Dīn al-Tilimsānī → al-Tilimsānī
Afīfan vi, 743b
ʿAfīfī, Banū vi, 128b
al-ʿAfīfī, ʿAbd al-Wahhāb (1758) s, **44a**, 408a
al-ʿAfīfiyya s, 44a, 408a
ʿAfis (Aleppo) vi, 230b
Afkhāz → Abkhāz
al-Aflādj i, **233a**, 538b, 546b; ii, 175b
Aflaḥ b. ʿAbd al-Wahhāb b. Rustam (Rustumid) (871) iii, 657a, 659b, 1041b; vi, 841a; vii, 895a; viii, 639a
Aflaḥ (Marzūḳ) b. Yasār → Abū ʿAṭāʾ al-Sindī
Aflaḥ al-Nāshib (Barka) (X) ii, 495a
ʿAflaḳ, Michel (XX) iv, 125a, b, 126a, 783a
Aflākī, Shams al-Dīn Aḥmad (XIV) i, **234a**; vi, 354b; viii, 972b; s, 83b
Aflāṭūn i, **234a**, 350a, 631a; ii, 493a, 779b; iv, 329a
Aflīmūn (144) iv, 406a; s, **44b**
ʿAfrāʾ iii, 1038a
Āfrāg i, **236a**
Āfrāg (al-Manṣūra) s, **45b**
Afrāgha → Ifrāgha
Afrāʾīm b. al-Zaffān iii, 906b
Afrandj Aḥmad (Miṣr) (1711) vi, 325a; vii, 179a
ʿAfrār, Banū vi, 82b, 83b
Afrāsiyāb (Baṣra) (XVII) i, **236b**, 1087a; iii, 1257a; iv, 813b, 816a; vi, 511a, b, 764b
Afrāsiyāb II, Muẓaffar al-Dīn (XIV) v, 827a
Afrāsiyāb (Tūrānian) i, **236a**, 1072b; iii, 112b, 813b, 816a; ix, 696b
Afrāsiyāb b. Kiyā Ḥasan (XIV) i, 237a
Afrāsiyāb I b. Yūsufshāh (1296) iii, 337a, b; v, 827a
Afrāsiyābids (Kiyā-i Čulāb) (XIV) i, **237a**; vi, 938b
Afrīdī, Banū i, 217a, 219b, **237b**, 769a; ii, 1066a; iv, 1143a; vii, 548b
Afrīdūn → Farīdūn
Afrīdūn b. Farīburz (XI) iv, 348a
Afrīghids iv, 753b, 754a, 1062a, 1063b, 1065b
Āfrīghūnids → Farīghūnids
ʿAfrīn i, **239a**; viii, 128b
Afrīnūh, Alexandra (XX) vii, 903a
ʿAfrīt → ʿIfrīt
ʿAfṣ i, **239a**
Afsantīn i, **239b**
Afshār, Banū (Oghuz) i, **239b**; ii, 75b; iii, 1100a, 1102b, 1107a, 1109b; v, 154a, 825a; vi, 18a, 483b, 522b, 526a; vii, 673a; ix, 597b; s, 71a, 147b
Afshār Urūmī Ḳulī Khān (Imām) (XIX) vi, 484a
Afshāri-Zand (1763) vi, 551a
Afshīn (1080) vii, 122a
al-Afshīn Ḥaydar (Khaydar) b. Ḳāwūs (Ushrūsana) (841) i, 52b, 145a, 154a, **241a**, 637a, 844a, 1072b, 1104a; iii, 471a; iv, 20b, 646a, 647a, 718b; v, 856a; vi, 337b, 338b, 499a; vii, 395a, 664a, 776a; viii, 501a; x, 925a; s, 116a
Afşin (Kaza) vi, 509a
Afsūn i, **241b**
Afsūs (Afsōs) (1809) i, **241b**
Afṣūs (Ephesus) → Aya Solūk
Aftakīn, Naṣr al-Dawla (XI) viii, 83a
Aftakīn al-Turkī (X) vii, 488b, 910b, 911a; viii, 832a
Afṭasids (Banu ʼl-Afṭas) (XI) i, 6a, **242a**, 1092a, 1338b; iii, 680b; vi, 568a
Afughal vi, 591a

al-Afwah al-Awdī (VI) i, **242b**
Afyūn i, **243a**; ii, 904b
Afyūn Ḳarā Ḥiṣār i, **243b**; iv, 578a; vi, 71b; s, 268b, 348b
Afzar vi, 384b
al-Afzārī, Asʿad b. Naṣr → ʿAmīd al-Dīn al-Abzārī al-Anṣārī
Aga → Agha
Agadès i, 307a; vi, 364b
Agadir i, **244b**
Agadir-Ighir i, 56a, **244b**, 357b, 1321a; iii, 62b; vi, 142b; ix, 900b
Āgāh Efendi (XIX) iv, 875b, 876b; vi, 92a
Āgāh Efendī → Čapanzāde Agāh Efendī
Āgahī, Muḥammad Riḍā (1874) vii, 574b; s, **46a**
Agarsif → Garsīf
Agathodaemon → Aghāthūdhīmūn
Agau i, 1163a; v, 522a
Agdāl (Marrākush) i, 85a, **245b**, 1346b; vi, 595b, 596b; s, 114a
Āgehī (1577) i, **245b**
Agēl → ʿUḳayl
Agha i, 35b, **245b**, 368a, 1256a; ii, 1121a; v, 472b
Agha Faḍl Allāh (XVIII) vii, 444a
Aghā Furṣat Shīrāzī, Mīrzā (XX) iv, 397b, 789a
Āghā Ḥashar Kashmīrī (1935) i, 1166a; s, **46b**
Agha Ḥusayn Pasha → Ḥusayn Pasha, Agha
Agha Khān (title) i, **246a**; ii, 140a; v, 942b
Agha Khān I → Maḥallatī, Āghā Khān (1881)
Agha Khān II (1885) i, 246b; ix, 435b
Agha Khān III (1957) i, 1196b; iii, 532b
Agha Khān IV, Shāh Karīm (XX) ii, 129a; iv, 201b; viii, 84a
Aghā Khān Kirmānī, Mīrzā ʿAbd al-Ḥusayn → Aḳā Khān Kirmānī
Āghā Khān Nūrī, Mīrzā (1855) iii, 554b; iv, 394a, 978b; vi, 20a; s, 71a
Aghā Mīr → Sayyid Muḥammad Khān (Awadh)
Aghā Mīrak (Aḳa Mīrak) (XV) i, 1211b, 1213a
Aghā Muḥammad Ḳāẓim Tunbākū-furūsh (XIX) x, 397b
Āghā Muḥammad Shāh → Aghā Ḥashar Kashmīrī
Āghā Muḥammad Shāh (Ḳādjār) (1797) i, 230a, b, **246b**, 701b, 720b, 1008b; ii, 335b, 812a, 838b; iii, 106a, 1103a; iv, 38a-b, 390a, b, 391a, 638a, 855b, 978b, 1091b; v, 156a, 164b, 495a, 663b, 825b, 835a; vi, 483b, 484a, 493a, 495a, 528a, 715a; s, 94b, 336a, 405b
Aghā Muṭahhar (XVIII) vii, 444a
Aghā Sayyid Djamāl ii, 651a
Aghač i, **247a**
Aghānī → Awghānī
al-Aghānī → Abu 'l-Faradj al-Iṣbahānī
Aghaoghlu, Aḥmed (1939) s, **47a**
Aghāthūdhīmūn i, **247a**; v, 111b
al-Aghlab al-ʿIdjlī (641) i, **247b**; iii, 1262a; viii, 377a
Aghlabids (Banū 'l-Aghlab) i, 18a, 24a, 104a, **247b**, 439b, 532b, 862b, 986a, 1148b, 1175b, 1246b, 1319a, 1346a; ii, 145b; iii, 655b, 981b, 1041b; v, 220b; vi, 280b, 331a, 334a, 336b, 337b, 338a, 364a, 452b, 453a, 457a, 712b; x, 213a; s, 103a, 120b, 144b
Āghmāt Aylān i, 7b, **250b**; v, 654b, 1178b; vi, 293b, 356a, 591b, 592a, 741a, b, 742b, 743b
Aghri̊ i, **251a**, 1117b; vi, 200b
Aghri̊ Dagh i, **251b**; v, 441a, 465a; vi, 200b, 201b
Aghsartʿan → Akhsitān
al-Aghwāṭ → Laghouat
al-Aghzāz → Ghuzz
Āgrā i, **252b**, 757b, 1323a, 1324a, 1347b; ii, 271a; iii, 449b, 450a, 575b; v, 1135a, 1217a, 1218b, 1219a; vi, 53b, 128a, 343a, 369b; vii, 314a; s, 10b, 142b
Agrigento → Djirdjent
Aguedal → Āgdāl
Agung, Sultan (Mataram) (Susuhunan 1646) ii, 390b; iii, 1221b; ix, 852b; s, 150b, 607a
Aḥābīsh i, 24b, 891b; iii, 7b; vi, 266a
Aḥadīs v, 686b; vii, 446a
Ahaggar i, **254b**, 433b; iii, 298a
Ahangarān ii, 1096b, 1099b; s, 411a
Ahar → Ḳaradja-Dagh
ʿAhd i, **255a**, 429b, 439b, 1143b; ii, 164b, 302b, 303a; iii, 396b; iv, 14b, 938b
al-Aḥdab → Ibrāhīm al-Aḥdab
al-Aḥdab, Muḥammad b. Wāsil (XIV) viii, 987a

al-Ahdal (Sayyids) i, **255b**; vi, 352a
al-Ahdal, Abū Bakr b. Abi ’l-Ḳāsim (1626) i, **255b**
al-Ahdal, Abū Bakr b. ʿAlī, Ḳuṭb al-Yaman (1300) i, 255b
al-Ahdal, Ḥusayn b. al-Ṣiddīḳ (1497) i, **255b**; vi, 354b
Aḥdāth i, **256a**, 687a, 1332b; ii, 963a; v, 329b
ʿAḥdī (Aḥmed of Baghdād) (1593) x, 55a
Āhī (1517) i, **257a**
Aḥiḳar → al-Ḥayḳar
Āhinsa Bāʾī (1587) vi, 190a
al-Aḥḳāf i, 169a, **257a**; vii, 496a; viii, 576a
Aḥkām i, **257a**; iii, 551b; iv, 151b; v, 870b, 878b
Ahl i, **257b**, 700b; iv, 785b
Ahl al-ahwāʾ i, **257b**
Ahl Bārikalla v, 891b
Ahl al-bayt i, **257b**, 957b; ii, 169b, 843b; vi, 604b
Ahl al-buyūtāt i, **258b**
Ahl al-dār i, **258b**
Ahl al-dhimma i, **258b**, 338a, 855b; ii, 126b, 127b, 131b, 142b, 154a, 211a, 324a, 341b, 487b, 559b, 565a, 657b, 1075b; iii, 233b, 1180a, 1187a; iv, 240b; v, 179a, 736b
Ahl al-farḍ → Mīrāth
Ahl al-ḥadīth i, **258b**, 692a, 1242a; ii, 889a; iii, 163a, 269b, 512b; s, 293a
Ahl-i ḥadīth i, **259a**
Ahl-i Ḥaḳḳ i, **260a**, 840a, 841b; ii, 96a, 850a, 1140b; iv, 49a, 187b; v, 475b, 823a; vi, 201a, 502b; ix, 7a, 64a, 855a; x, 326a
Ahl al-ḥall wa ’l-ʿaḳd i, **263b**
Ahl al-kahf → Aṣḥāb al-kahf
Ahl al-kalām → Ahl al-naẓar
Ahl al-ḳibla i, **264a**
Ahl al-kisāʾ i, **264a**; ii, 844a
Ahl al-kitāb i, **264a**; ii, 227a, 1065b; iv, 408a, b
Ahl al-naẓar i, **266a**
Ahl al-raʾy → Aṣḥāb al-raʾy
Ahl al-Saḳīfa → Saḳīfa
Ahl al-ṣuffa i, 114a, 129a, **266a**
Ahl al-sunna i, **267a**, 694a, 1039b; ii, 412a; iii, 248a, 846a; iv, 142a
Ahlī (Shirāz) (1535) iv, 67a
Ahl-i wāris i, **267a**
Aḥlāf → Ḥilf
Aḥlāf, Banū (ʿAmārna) vi, 142b
Aḥlāf, Banū (Ḳurashī) vi, 137b
Ahlī (Shirāz) (1535) viii, 775a
Aḥmad (Aghlabid) → Abū Ibrāhīm Aḥmad
Aḥmad I (Āl Ṣabāḥ) (1950) viii, 669a
Aḥmad (Bahmanī) → Aḥmad Shāh
Aḥmad (Brunei XV) s, 152a
Aḥmad (Djalāyirid) → Aḥmad b. Uways
Aḥmad (Ilkhānid) → Aḥmad Takudār
Aḥmad I (Ḥafṣid) (1350) iii, 68a; iv, 416a
Aḥmad II (Ḥafsid) (1394) iii, 68b, 826b, 827b, 831b; v, 531a
Aḥmad III (Ḥafṣid) (1569) iii, 69b
Aḥmad I (Ḳarakhānid) → Aḥmad Khān b. Khiḍr
Aḥmad (Muḥammad) i, **267a**
Aḥmad I al-Muḳtadir b. Hūd (Hūdid) (1081) i, 499a, 865a, 1040b; ii, 112a; iii, 542a; iv, 478a; v, 683a; vii, 768a
Aḥmad II al-Mustaʿīn (Hūdid) (1110) i, 495b; iii, 542b; s, 383a
Aḥmad III al-Mustanṣir (Hūdid) (1142) i, 1083a; ii, 1013b; iii, 543a
Aḥmad I (Ottoman) (1617) i, **267b**, 510b, 954b, 1226a, 1267a; ii, 208b, 543a, 684a; iii, 1185a; v, 18a, b, 272a; vi, 508b, 799a; s, 257b, 330b
Aḥmad II (Ottoman) (1695) ii, **268a**; v, 262a
Aḥmad III (Ottoman) (1736) i, **268b**, 394b, 395a, 776a, 836b, 1076b; ii, 212b, 684a; iii, 1002a; iv, 874a, 969b; v, 18b, 19a, 641b, 642b, 643b; vi, 55a, 57a, 198b
Aḥmad, Shaykh (Bārzān) (XX) i, 1072a; v, 467a
Aḥmad b. al-ʿAbbās b. ʿĪsā b. Shaykh (X) iv, 90b
Aḥmad b. ʿAbd Allāh (ʿAbd al-Wādid) → Abū Zayyān III
Aḥmad b. ʿAbd Allāh, Sulṭān (Faḍlī) (XX) ii, 737a
Aḥmad b. ʿAbd Allāh (Dilāʾī) (1680) vi, 891b; s, 223b
Aḥmad b. ʿAbd Allāh b. Abi ’l-ʿAlāʾ (IX) vii, 518b
Aḥmad b. ʿAbd Allāh al-Khūdjistānī (892) i, 452b; iii, 245a; v, 47a, 48a; vii, 76b; x, 741b
Aḥmad b. ʿAbd Allāh Maʿn al-Andalusī (XVII) iv, 380a

Aḥmad b. ʿAbd al-ʿAzīz b. Abī Dulaf (IX) i, 452b; ii, 301a, 623b; iv, 100a
Aḥmad b. ʿAbd al-ʿAzīz al-Khurāsānī (XII) iii, 138b; v, 60b
Aḥmad b. ʿAbd al-Raḥīm → Abū Zurʿa
Aḥmad b. ʿAbd al-Raḥmān b. ʿAbd Allāh Rawāḥī (1312) viii, 459b
Aḥmad b. ʿAbd al-Raḥmān b. Nafāda (1204) viii, 376a
Aḥmad b. ʿAbd al-Raḥmān al-Djazāʾirī ii, 183a
Aḥmad b. ʿAbd al-Ṣamad Shīrazī (vizier) (1040) vi, 453a; vii, 26b, 801a
Aḥmad b. Abi 'l-ʿAzāʾim (1970) s, 18b
Aḥmad b. Abī Bakr → Muḥtādjids
Aḥmad b. Abī Duʾād (854) i, 153b, **271a**, 273a; ii, 385b; iii, 707a, 974b, 994b; iv, 289b, 718b; v, 647a; vi, 336a, 338b; vii, 4a, 392b, 401a, 776b, 777b; s, 17b, 25a, 90b
Aḥmad b. Abi 'l-Ḳāsim al-Ṣawmaʿī (1604) i, 159b
Aḥmad b. Abī Khālid al-Aḥwal (826) i, 241a, **271b**; vi, 334a, 336a, 337b
Aḥmad b. Abī Mismār (Abū ʿArīsh) (XIX) s, 30b
Aḥmad b. Abī Rabīʿa (X) ix, 208b
Aḥmad b. Abi 'l-Saʿīd (al-Ḳarawiyyīn) (X) iv, 632b
Aḥmad b. Abī Saʿīd b. Tīmūr (Aḥrār) (XV) s, 51a
Aḥmad b. Abī Ṭāhir Ṭayfūr → Ibn Abī Ṭāhir
Aḥmad b. Abī ʿUmāra → Ibn Abī ʿUmāra
Aḥmad b. ʿAdjlān, Sharīf (1396) vi, 149b
Aḥmad b. ʿAlāʾ al-Dīn (Marāgha) (XII) vi, 500b
Aḥmad b. ʿAlī (Rayy) (924) i, 125b; iv, 661b
Aḥmad b. ʿAlī (Mai, Bornu) (XIX) i, 1260a
Aḥmad b. ʿAlī b. Khayrān (1039) ii, 127b
Aḥmad b. ʿAlī b. Thābit → al-Khaṭīb al-Baghdādī
Aḥmad b. ʿAlī al-Hāshimī ii, 276a
Aḥmad b. ʿAlī, Sayyid, Karkiyā (1592) v, 603b
Aḥmad b. ʿAlī al-Ikhshīd (X) iv, 418b
Aḥmad b. ʿAlī Zunbul (1653) iv, 1130a
Aḥmad b. ʿAmr al-Sulamī i, 697a
Aḥmad b. ʿAṭāʾ (922) x, 314b
Aḥmad b. al-Aṭrābulusī (IX) iii, 660a
Aḥmad b. Aṭṭāsh (Alamūt) (XII) i, 353a; iii, 725a; iv, 101b, 102a
Aḥmad b. al-ʿAynī (XV) s, 38a
Aḥmad b. Bā Ḥmād (XIX) s, **114a**
Aḥmad b. Baṣo (XII) iv, 118a
Aḥmad b. Bāyazīd II (Ottoman) (XVI) i, 396a, 1120b; iv, 1159a; v, 677b; vii, 272b
Aḥmad b. Buwayh (Būya) → Muʿizz al-Dawla Aḥmad
Aḥmad b. Djābir → Aḥmad Āl Djābir
Aḥmad b. Djaʿfar, Amīr s, 125b
Aḥmad b. Djaʿfar al-Kattānī → al-Kattānī, Muḥammad b. Djaʿfar
Aḥmad b. Djamīl (1182) vi, 110b
Aḥmad b. Faḍlān → Ibn Faḍlān
Aḥmad b. Fahd (1436) vii, 672a
Aḥmad b. Faradj → Ibn Faradj al-Djayyānī
Aḥmad b. Farīghūn ii, 798b
Aḥmad b. al-Furāt → Ibn al-Furāt, Abu 'l-ʿAbbās Aḥmad
Aḥmad b. Ghālib (Djayzān) (XVII) ii, 517b
Aḥmad b. Ḥābiṭ (IX) i, **272a**
Aḥmad b. al-Ḥādjdj (1697) s, 403b
Aḥmad b. al-Ḥādjdj ʿUmar (XIX) ix, 122a
Aḥmad b. Ḥanbal (855) i, 114a, 155a, 259a, 271a, **272b**, 589b, 694b, 1242a, 1244b, 1245b; ii, 182b, 294b, 889b, 890a, 1093a; iii, 24a, 158a, 1266a; iv, 142a, 469b, 470a, 735a; v, 426a, 731b; vi, 123b, 351b, 352b, 353a, 627b, 636a; vii, 3a, 361b, 467a, 691b, 706a; s, 16a, 392a
Aḥmad b. Ḥarb (849) iv, 667a, 668a; vi, 728b
Aḥmad b. al-Ḥasan, al-Mahdī li-Dīn Allāh, Imām → al-Mahdī li-Dīn Allāh Aḥmad b. al-Ḥasan b. al-Ḳāsim
Aḥmad b. Ḥasan al-Kalbī (969) iv, 496b
Aḥmad b. al-Ḥusayn, al-Mahdī li-Dīn Allāh, Imām → al-Mahdī li-Dīn Allāh Aḥmad b. al-Ḥusayn
Aḥmad b. Ḥusayn, Sulṭān (Faḍlī) (XIX) ii, 737a
Aḥmad b. Ibrāhīm b. Ḥamdūn → Ibn Ḥamdūn
Aḥmad b. Ibrāhīm al-Uḳlīdisī → al-Uḳlīdisī
Aḥmad b. Idrīs, Sharīf (1837) i, **277b**, 709b; vi, 354b; viii, 990a; ix, 22b; x, 249a; s, 278b
Aḥmad b. al-Imām al-Manṣūr bi-'llāh al-Ḳāsim (Zaydī) (1650) vii, 270a
Aḥmad b. ʿImrān, ḳāḍī (XII) iii, 125b
Aḥmad b. ʿĪsā b. Muḥammad b. ʿAlī al-Muhādjir (956) i, **277b**, 551b

Aḥmad b. ʿIsā b. Shaykh al-Shaybānī (IX) vi, 540a; vii, 760a
Aḥmad b. ʿIsā b. Zayd (861) s, **48a**
Aḥmad b. Isḥāḳ, Khwādja Pīr (XV) s, 84b
Aḥmad b. Ismāʿīl (Rasūlid) (1424) i, 553a; iv, 642b
Aḥmad II b. Ismāʿīl (Samānid) (914) ii, 1082a; iii, 254b, 757b; iv, 22a, b; vi, 853a; viii, 797a, 1037a
Aḥmad b. Isrāʾīl (vizier) (IX) vii, 793b
Aḥmad b. al-Ḳāḍī (Kabyle) (1611) i, 428b; ii, 537b; iv, 361b, 1155b, 1156a
Aḥmad b. Ḳāsim, Sīdī s, 132b
Aḥmad b. Kayghulugh (X) iv, 100a
Aḥmad b. Khālid → Aḥmad al-Nāṣirī
Aḥmad b. Khalīfa (Baḥrayn) (1796) i, 942b; iv, 751a, 953a
Aḥmad b. Khalīfa, Pasha (1694) x, 36b
Aḥmad b. al-Khaṣīb, Abū ʿAlī Aḥmad → Ibn al-Khaṣīb
Aḥmad b. al-Khaṣīb al-Djardjarāʾī → al-Djardjarāʾī
Aḥmad b. Khiḍr Khān b. Ibrāhīm (Ḳarakhānid) (1095) vi, 274a
Aḥmad b. Khiḍrōya (ṣūfī) (IX) i, 162b
Aḥmad b. Khūdja (XIX) vi, 251a
Aḥmad b. Kurhub (916) ix, 585a
Aḥmad b. Mādjid → Ibn Mādjid
Aḥmad b. Maḥmūd (XIII) iii, 1116a
Aḥmad b. Makki (Ḳābis) (XIV) iv, 338a; x, 213b
Aḥmad b. Maʿn (Duruz) (1697) ii, 635a
Aḥmad b. Marwān → Naṣr al-Dawla b. Marwān
Aḥmad b. Marzūḳ → Ibn Marzūḳ
Aḥmad b. Mīrānshāh b. Tīmūr (Tīmūrid) (XV) vii, 105b
Aḥmad b. al-Muʿadhdhal → Ibn al-Muʿadhdhal
Aḥmad b. Muʿāwiya → Ibn al-Ḳiṭṭ
Aḥmad b. al-Mubārak b. al-Walīd, (dāʿī muṭlaḳ) (XIII) s, 62a
Aḥmad b. Muḥammad (Maḥmūd) (XV) s, **49a**
Aḥmad b. Muḥammad (Mūrītāniyā) (1891) vii, 614b
Aḥmad b. Muḥammad (Sharwān-Shāh) (981) iv, 346a, 347a
Aḥmad b. Muḥammad b. ʿAbd al-Ṣamad (XI) i, **278a**
Aḥmad b. Muḥammad b. Ḥabīb Allāh → Ahmad(u) Bamba Mbacké
Aḥmad b. Muḥammad b. Ilyās (Araghūn) (X) s, 80a
Aḥmad b. Muḥammad b. al-Ḳāsim (XII) ix, 899b
Aḥmad b. Muḥammad b. Khayrāt (Djayzān) (XVIII) ii, 517b
Aḥmad b. Muḥammad Ādarrāḳ → Ādarrāḳ
Aḥmad b. Muḥammad al-Aghlab → Abū Ibrāhīm Aḥmad
Aḥmad b. Muḥammad al-Barḳī → al-Barḳī
Aḥmad b. Muḥammad al-Ḥabūḍī (1230) s, 338b
Aḥmad b. Muḥammad ʿIrfān → Aḥmad Brēlwī
Aḥmad b. Muḥammad al-Manṣūr → Aḥmad al-Manṣūr
Aḥmad b. Muḥammad al-Ṣāḥib (1386) vii, 537a
Aḥmad b. Muḥammad b. Sālim al-Baṣrī (967) ix, 65b
Aḥmad b. Muḥammad Zayn (1906) viii, 286a
Aḥmad b. Muḥriz (Marrākush) (1668) vi, 595a, 891b
Aḥmad b. Muḥsin, Sharīf (XX) i, 1133a
Aḥmad b. Mulḥim Maʿn (1697) vi, 343b, 344a
Aḥmad b. Mūsā (1893) vi, 251a
Aḥmad b. Mūsā b. Aḥmad al-Bukhārī → Bā Aḥmad
Aḥmad b. Mūsā b. Djaʿfar (IX) vii, 396b
Aḥmad b. Mūsā b. Shākir (869) vi, 600a; s, 412a
Aḥmad b. Mūsā al-Samlālī → Ḥmad u-Mūsā
Aḥmad b. Nāṣīr (Nāṣiriyya, Morocco) i, 290a; vii, 1007a
Aḥmad b. Naṣr (Saḥnūn) (846) viii, 844b
Aḥmad b. Naṣr (Samānid) (X) s, 357a
Aḥmad b. Niẓām al-Mulk (vizier) (XII) vii, 735a
Aḥmad b. Rusta → Ibn Rusta
Aḥmad b. Ṣadaḳa iv, 929a
Aḥmad b. Sahl b. Hāshim (919) i, **278a**
Aḥmad b. Saʿīd (Āl Bū Saʿīd) (1783) vii, 227a; ix, 776a; x, 816b; xi, 292b
Aḥmad b. Saʿīd, Imām (Āl Bū Saʿīd) (1741) vi, 735a, 843a, 963a
Aḥmad b. Saʿīd (961) i, 600a
Aḥmad b. Saʿīd (1783) i, 554a, 1098a, 1281b

Aḥmad b. Sālim (Aḥlāf) (XIX) v, 596b
Aḥmad b. Shādgeldi (Amasya) (XIV) i, 432a, 1117b, 1118a
Aḥmad b. Shāhīn (XVII) vi, 187a
Aḥmad b. Sharḳāwī al-Khalifī (1898) s, 40b
Aḥmad b. Shaykh Merkez (XVI) vi, 1023a
Aḥmad b. Sīdī Aḥmad (Mūrītāniyā) (1899) vii, 614b
Aḥmad b. Sulaymān, Zaydī Imām (1171) i, 552b; v, 954a
Aḥmad b. Sumayt al-Nakhlī (686) vi, 920a
Aḥmad b. Tabarūya (1009) vii, 43b
Aḥmad b. Ṭāhir vi, 438a
Aḥmad b. Taymiyya → Ibn Taymiyya, Taḳī al-Dīn Aḥmad
Aḥmad b. al-Ṭayyib (899) vi, 204b
Aḥmad b. al-Ṭayyib wad al-Bashīr (1824) x, 248b
Aḥmad b. al-Trīkī (XVIII) vi, 250a
Aḥmad b. Ṭūlūn (Ṭulūnid) (884) i, 139a, 205a, **278a**, 341a, 517a, 551a, 621a, 990a, b, 1224a; ii, 36b, 129b, 130a, 281b, 305a, 328a, 958b, 1080b; iii, 86a, 398a, 745b, 880a; iv, 134a, 655a, 841b; v, 49a, 91a, b, 327a, 624a; vi, 195a, 365a, 379a, 413a, 455a, 654a, 657a, 669b, 672b, 676b, 677a; vii, 147b, 161a, 766a; viii, 91a, 464a; x, 616b; s, 120b
Aḥmad b. ʿUbayd Allāh b. al-Khaṣīb → al-Khaṣībī, Aḥmad b. ʿUbayd Allāh
Aḥmad b. ʿUbayda (941) ix, 819a
Aḥmad b. ʿUḳba al-Ḥadramī (1489) s, 208a
Aḥmad (Ḥabashī) b. ʿUmar b. ʿAbd Allāh b. Ibrāhīm b. al-Aghlab (870) vi, 295a
Aḥmad b. Uways (Djalāyirid) (1410) i, 401b, 903b, 1051a, 1119a; ii, 401b; iv, 33b, 584b, 586a, b; vi, 324a; vii, 171b, 602b
Aḥmad b. Yaḥyā, Imām (1948) i, 555a
Aḥmad b. Yaḥyā b. Abī 'l-Baghl (X) vii, 653a
Aḥmad b. Yaḥyā b. al-Murtaḍā, al-Mahdī li-Dīn Allāh → al-Mahdī li-Dīn Allāh Aḥmad b. Yaḥyā
Aḥmad b. Yaḥyā al-Yaḥṣubī → Tādj al-Dawla (Labla)
Aḥmad b. Yūsuf (828) i, **279a**
Aḥmad b. Yūsuf, Sīdī (XVII) i, 374b, 1300b; iv, 481b; vii, 64a
Aḥmad b. Yūsuf al-Miṣrī → Ibn al-Dāya
Aḥmad b. Zaynī Daḥlān → Daḥlān
Aḥmad al-ʿAbbās b. Muḥammad al-Shaykh al-Aṣghar (Saʿdid) (1659) vi, 595a
Aḥmad ʿAbd al-Ḥaḳḳ, Shaykh (Ṣābiriyya) (XV) ii, 54a, 56a; s, 293a
Aḥmad Abu 'l-ʿAbbās b. al-ʿArūs (1463) xi, 112b
Aḥmad Abu 'l-Fatḥ (XX) s, 6a
Aḥmad Agha Ḳarā ʿOthmān-oghlu (XVIII) iv, 593a
Aḥmad al-Aḥṣāʾī → al-Aḥṣāʾī
Aḥmad Āl Djābir Āl Ṣabāḥ (XX) iii, 1066a; v, 575a; s, 50a
Aḥmad ʿAlī (ḳāḍī) (al-Mahdiyya) (XIX) v, 1252a, b
Aḥmad ʿAlī Khān Sulṭān Dulhā (Bhōpāl) (XIX) i, 1196a, 1197a
Aḥmad ʿAlī Khān, Nawwāb (XIX) iv, 666b; v, 779b
Aḥmad ʿAlī Shawḳ Ḳidwāʾī (1925) vi, 838b
Aḥmad Allāh, Mawlawī (Fayḍabād) (XIX) ii, 870b
Aḥmad Amīn (1954) i, **279b**; iv, 159b; vi, 408b; vii, 786b
Aḥmad al-ʿArabī (XX) v, 1005a
Aḥmad al-Aʿradj al-Saʿdī (1523) ii, 527b; v, 119a; vi, 591a, 594a, b, 893a, b
Aḥmad Ashraf, Shāh (XX) s, 74a
Aḥmad Bā Djābir al-Ḥaḍramī (1592) i, 781b
Aḥmad Bābā (1523) vii, 625a
Aḥmad Bābā al-Massūfī (1627) i, 96b, **279b**, 289a, 594b; iii, 763b, 844a; iv, 476b; vi, 187a, 258b, 280a; ix, 20b
Aḥmad al-Badawī, Abu 'l-Fityān (1276) i, **280a**, 404a, 1127a; ii, 1009b; iii, 90b; vi, 87b, 354b, 454a, 652b; vii, 175b; x, 189a
Aḥmad Bakr b. Mūsā (Dār Fūr) ii, 123a
Aḥmad Bamba → Ahmad(u) Bamba Mbacké
Aḥmad Barēlawī → Aḥmad Brēlwī
Aḥmad Beg (Ḳarāmān-oghlu) → Fakhr al-Dīn Aḥmad
Aḥmad Bey (Ḳusṭanṭīna) v, 532a
Aḥmad Bey (Tunis) (1855) i, 37a, **281b**; ii, 461b; iii, 94b, 561b, 636a, 684a, 720b; vi, 251a, 798a; vii, 436b, 717b
Aḥmad Bey (1942) iii, 636b
Aḥmad Bey Bosniak (1662) iv, 723a; vi, 325a

Aḥmad Bīdjān → Bīdjān Aḥmad
Aḥmad Brēlwī al-Mudjaddid, Sayyid (1831) i, **282a**, 432b; ii, 140a, 254b, 316b, 437a; iii, 119b, 335b, 431a; iv, 196a, b, 625b, 626a; vii, 290b, 442a, 555a, 939a
Aḥmad al-Burnusī Zarrūḳ (1493) ii, 293a
Aḥmad Bushnāḳ Pasha (XVII) i, 904b, 905a
Aḥmad the Cameleer (1545) vi, 226a, 227b, 228a, b
Aḥmad Dghughī, Sīdī vi, 891a; s, 53a, 350b
Aḥmad al-Dhahabī (ʿAlawid) (XVIII) i, 47a, 356a
Aḥmad Djaʿfar Shīrāzī, Sayyid (XV) i, 1255a
Aḥmad Djalāʾir → Djalāʾir
Aḥmad Djalāʾīr → Aḥmad b. Uways
Aḥmad Djalāl al-Dīn Pasha (XIX) vii, 206a
Aḥmad-ı Djām (1141) i, **283a**
Aḥmad Djazzār → Djazzār Pasha
Aḥmad Djewdet Pasha (1895) i, **284b**, 397a, 505a; ii, 474b, 702b, 935a; iii, 250a, b, 993a; iv, 168b, 872a; v, 837a, 1083a, 1084b; vi, 6b, 614b, 971b; vii, 546b
Aḥmad Emīn Yalman (XX) ii, 475a, b; vi, 93a, b
Aḥmad Faḍīl (Kasala) (1899) iv, 687a
Aḥmad Fahmī Abu ʾl-Khayr (1960) s, 263a
Aḥmad Fāris al-Shidyāḳ → Fāris al-Shidyāḳ
Aḥmad al-Fayḍ Abādī (XX) vi, 176a
Aḥmad Fuʿād b. Fārūḳ (XX) s, 299b, 301b
Aḥmad al-Ganduz (XIX) vi, 250b
Aḥmad Ghulām Khalīl → Ghulām Khalīl
Aḥmad Grāñ b. Ibrāhīm (1543) i, **286b**, 932b, 1172b; ii, 91a; iii, 4a, 176a; vi, 642a
Aḥmad Ḥādjdjī Beg (1467) vii, 90b
Aḥmad al-Hība (1919) v, 890b, 891a; vi, 595b; s, **47b**
Aḥmad Ḥikmet (1927) i, **287a**; iii, 260b
Aḥmad Ibrāhīm al-Ghāzī → Aḥmad Grāñ
Aḥmad Ibrāhīm al-Ghazzāwī (XX) vi, 176b, 177a
Aḥmad Iḥsān (1942) i, **287a**; ii, 474b; s, 773b
Aḥmad, Imām (Zaydī) (1962) ix, 2a; xi, 274a
Aḥmad Inaltigin (1033) vi, 780a
Aḥmad ʿIzzet Pasha Furgaç → ʿIzzet Pasha, Aḥmed Furgaç
Aḥmad Kamal Bāshāzāda vii, 262a
Aḥmad Ḳānṣawḥ (XVII) vii, 514b
Aḥmad-i Ḳarāḥiṣārī (1556) iv, 1125a, b
Aḥmad Ḳaramānlī (Tarāblus al-Gharb) x, 214a
Aḥmad Katkhudā Mustaḥfiẓān Kharpūṭlū (1735) iv, 438a
Aḥmad Ḳawām (XX) vii, 655a
Aḥmad Khān, Sayyid (Batuʾid) (1505) iii, 44b
Aḥmad Khān, Sir Sayyid (1898) i, 38b, **287b**, 403b, 443a, 505b, 827b; ii, 27b, 97a, 426b, 549b; iii, 93b, 358b, 431a, b, 433a, 458a, 1204b; iv, 170a, b; v, 202a; vi, 461b, 488b, 872a; vii, 534a, b; viii, 241a; ix, 433b; s, 74a, 106b, 107b, 247a
Aḥmad Khān b. Ḥasan Hārūn (Ilek-khān) (XII) iii, 1114b; iv, 581a
Aḥmad Khān b. Hūlāgū → Aḥmad Takūdār
Aḥmad Khān b. Hushang Shāh Ghūrī (1438) vi, 52b
Aḥmad Khān b. Khiḍr Khān (Ilek-khān) (XI) iii, 1114b, 1115b
Aḥmad Khān b. Muḥammad Zamān Khān → Aḥmad Shāh Durrānī
Aḥmad Khān ʿAlāʾ al-Dawla, Mīrzā (XX) s, 365a
Aḥmad Khān Bangash (Farrukhābād) (XVIII) ii, 808b; iii, 60a, 1158b
Aḥmad Khān Nāṣir Djang (XVIII) vii, 446a
Aḥmad Khān Sūr → Sikandar Shāh III Sūr
Aḥmad Khān Ūsmī (Dāghistān) (1587) ii, 87a
Aḥmad al-Khaṣībī (X) iv, 424a
Aḥmad Khattū Maghribī → Maghribī, Aḥmad Khattū
Aḥmad Khayr al-Dīn (XX) vi, 751a, b
Aḥmad al-Khudjistānī (IX) ix, 613b
Aḥmad al-Ḳlībī (XIX) vi, 607a
Aḥmad Köprülü → Köprülü
Aḥmad Lobo → Ahmadu Lobbo
Aḥmad Māhir (XX) iii, 515b, 516b, 518b; x, 366a; s, 58a
Aḥmad Maḥmūdī (1930) vi, 763b
Aḥmad al-Maʿḳūr (Dār Fūr) ii, 122b
Aḥmad Mallāk (Sfax) (XIX) vi, 251a
Aḥmad Maniklī Pasha (Kasala) (XIX) iv, 686b
Aḥmad al-Manīnī (1759) viii, 728b

Aḥmad Manṣūr b. Aḥmad, Shaykh (Manda) vi, 385b
Aḥmad al-Manṣūr al-Dhahabī, Mawlāy (Saʿdid) (1603) i, 58b, 279, **288b**, 1347a; ii, 134a, 308a, 510a, 819b; iii, 70a, 339b, 814a, 1047a; iv, 635a, b; v, 1119a; vi, 124a, 142b, 248b, 259a, 351a, 589b, 591a, 594b, 596b, 597b, 743a; viii, 724a; s, 28b, 223a
Aḥmad al-Masīlī (XIV) vi, 728b
Aḥmad Midḥat Pasha (1913) i, **289a**, 975a; ii, 473b, 474a, b; iii, 357b, 375a, 622a, 630a, 1200a; iv, 602a, 682a, 930a, 931b; v, 194a, 195b; vii, 205b; s, 64b
Aḥmad Mīrẓā ʿAḍud al-Dawla b. Fatḥ ʿAlī Shah (XIX) vi, 481b
Aḥmad Mukhtār Pasha (1912) iv, 201a; v, 314a; vi, 192a, 983b; ix, 2a; s, 64b
Aḥmad al-Muḳtadir → Aḥmad I (Hūdid)
Aḥmad Mumtāz Pasha (Sawākin) (XIX) iv, 687a
Aḥmad Mürshidī i, 1202a
Aḥmad Mūsā (painter) iii, 1127a, b
Aḥmad Nadā (Filāḥa) (XIX) ii, 900b
Aḥmad al-Naḥḥās (X) i, 321b
Aḥmad Narāghī, Mullā (1829) vii, 298b
Aḥmad al-Nāṣir b. al-Hādī ilā ʾl-Ḥaḳḳ (Zaydī Imām) (934) iii, 124b; vi, 436a; vii, 444b, 773a; s, 335b
Aḥmad al-Nāṣirī al-Salāwī (1897) i, **290a**, 315b; v, 1209b; vii, 1007a; s, 395a, b
Aḥmad Nayrīzī (Khaṭṭ) (XVIII) iv, 1123b
Aḥmad Niyāzī → Niyāzī Bey
Aḥmad Niẓām Shāh Baḥrī → Malik Aḥmad Baḥrī (Niẓām Shāhī)
Aḥmad-oghlu Shukr Allāh (XII) vii, 207b; viii, 806b
Aḥmad Pasha → al-Djazzār; Hersek-zāde; Miḳdād
Aḥmad Pasha (Ḳars) (1741) vi, 56b
Aḥmad Pasha, Ḳara (1555) i, **291b**; ii, 704a; v, 67a
Aḥmad Pasha (Ṣūfī) s, 49b
Aḥmad Pasha b. Ḥasan Pasha (Baghdād) (1747) i, 270a, **291a**, 905a; iii, 106a, 252a, 1257b; vi, 541b; vii, 853b
Aḥmad Pasha Abū Widān (Dār Fūr) (1843) ii, 123b; iv, 686b
Aḥmad Pasha Bonneval (1747) i, **291b**, 395b, 1064b; ii, 511b; iii, 203b, 253a; iv, 738b; v, 52b
Aḥmad Pasha Bursalỉ (1496) i, **292a**; vi, 609b
Aḥmad Pasha Gedik (1482) i, **292b**, 354b, 767b; ii, 337b, 530a; iii, 341b; iv, 656a, 868b, 892a; v, 726a, 764a
Aḥmad Pasha Khāʾin (1524) i, **293a**; iii, 998a; vii, 177b, 721a
Aḥmad Pasha Küčük s, **49a** (See also S.V.) Küčük Aḥmad Pasha
Aḥmad Rafīḳ Altỉnay (1937) i, **293b**; vi, 94a
Aḥmad al-Raḳḳī i, 758b
Aḥmad Rāsim (1932) i, 287b, **293b**; v, 196a; vi, 94b; s, 64b
Aḥmad Rasmī (1783) i, **294b**; iii, 157a
Aḥmad Rātib Pasha (XIX) vi, 151b
Aḥmad al-Rāzī → al-Rāzī
Aḥmad Riḍwān (XVI) iv, 129a
Aḥmad al-Rīfī Pasha (Tangier) (XVIII) i, 47b
Aḥmad Rỉzā (Riḍā) (XX) ii, 430b, 474b; iv, 285a; vii, 206a
Aḥmad Ṣābir (XX) vi, 153a
Aḥmad Ṣaʿlūk (923) iv, 100a
Aḥmad al-Ṣāwī (1825) vi, 354b, 355a
Aḥmad Shāh I, Shihāb al-Dīn (Bahmānid) (1436) i, 923b, 924a, 925a, b, 1200a, b, 1323a; ii, 981a, 1115a, 1125b; iii, 15a, 417b, 420b, 638b; iv, 961b; v, 1215b; xi, 1b
Aḥmad Shāh II, ʿAlāʾ al-Dīn (Bahmānid) (1458) i, 923b; ii, 814b; iii, 421a, 577a; iv, 962a; vi, 53b, 66b
Aḥmad Shāh III Niẓām al-Dīn (Bahmānid) (1463) i, 923b; vi, 66b, 67a
Aḥmad Shāh I (Gudjarāt) (1442) i, 295a, 299b, 506b; ii, 11a, 1125a; iii, 418b, 445a, 638a, 1010a; vi, 52b; vii, 957a
Aḥmad Shāh II (Gudjarāt) (1458) i, 295a; ii, 1125b
Aḥmad Shāh III (Gudjarāt) (1561) ii, 1129a; vi, 52b
Aḥmad Shāh (Turcoman) (1074) vii, 121a
Aḥmad Shāh, ʿAlāʾ al-Dīn (Atjèh) (1735) i, 743b
Aḥmad Shāh b. Muḥammad ʿAlī Shāh (Ḳādjār) (XX) ii, 652b; iv, 392a, 398b; v, 61b; vii, 432a; s, 342a
Aḥmad Shāh b. Muḥammad Shāh Shams al-Dīn (Bengal) → Rādjā Ganesh
Aḥmad Shāh Bahādur (Mughal) (1775) i,

295a; iii, 60a, 1158b; vi, 535b; vii, 316a, 457b, 869b
Aḥmad <u>Sh</u>āh Durrānī (Abdālī, Af<u>gh</u>ān) (1773) i, 72b, 95b, 218b, 226b, 229b, 230a, 238a, **295a**, 432b, 454b, 970b, 1001b, 1005b, 1020a; ii, 488b, 628b, 1049b, 1131b; iii, 60b, 335b, 427b, 1158b; iv, 390a, 537b, 709b; v, 29a, 102a, 598b, 1079a; vi, 535b, 715a; vii, 220a, 290b, 316a, 457b, 549a, 869b; viii, 253b
Aḥmad <u>Sh</u>āh Ganesh, <u>Sh</u>ams al-Dīn (Bengal) (1442) i, 295a; iii, 419a
Aḥmad <u>Sh</u>āh Masʿūd (2001) s, 786b
Aḥmad al-<u>Sh</u>ahīd Bā Faḍl (1523) ii, 730a
Aḥmad <u>Sh</u>ahīd, Sayyid (XIX) ii, 54b
Aḥmad <u>Sh</u>āhīs (Gu<u>d</u>jarāt) vi, 126a, 368b, 369a
Aḥmad <u>Sh</u>āhs (India) i, 295a, 1193a, 1329b; vi, 126a, 368b, 369a
Aḥmad <u>Sh</u>ākir al-Karamī (XX) vi, 176a
Aḥmad <u>Sh</u>arīf (Sanūsī) (XX) i, 277b, 1071a; v, 758a
Aḥmad <u>Sh</u>awḳī → <u>Sh</u>awḳī Aḥmad
Aḥmad al-<u>Sh</u>ay<u>kh</u> (Amadu Sēku) (1898) i, **297a**; ii, 567b; iii, 39b
Aḥmad al-Sibāʿī (XX) vi, 176a, b, 177a
Aḥmad Ṣiddīḳ, <u>Kh</u>wā<u>d</u>ja (1259) ii, 1078a
Aḥmad al-Si<u>d</u>jzī (1009) i, 725a; s, 412b
Aḥmad Sirhindī, <u>Sh</u>ay<u>kh</u> (1624) i, **297a**, 347a, 957a, 1022b; ii, 30a, 55a, 296b, 380b, 871b, 1144a; iii, 430a, 432b, 435b; vii, 290b, 297a, 327a, b, 432b; ix, 296a; x, 256a, 321a, 958b; xi, 118b; s, 313a
Aḥmad al-Subaḥī (XX) vi, 153b
Aḥmad Sulṭān Bayat (XIX) vi, 202b
Aḥmad al-Tābiʿī (XX) vi, 722b
Aḥmad Tāʾib → ʿU<u>th</u>mān-zāde
Aḥmad Takūdār (Il<u>kh</u>ān) (1284) i, 903a; ii, 606b, 607b; iii, 1122a; iv, 31a, 620b, 817b, 975b; v, 827a
Aḥmad Taymūr (XX) vi, 75a, b
Aḥmad al-Ṭayyib al-ʿAl<u>d</u>j (XX) vi, 755b
Aḥmad Ṭūsūn → Ṭūsūn b. Muḥammad ʿAlī
Aḥmad ū-Mūsā, Awlād Sīdī (Tazerwalt) vi, 589b, 743a, 744a
Aḥmad Wafīḳ Pa<u>sh</u>a (1891) i, 61b, 63b, 285b, **298a**, 473b; iii, 249b; iv, 791a; vi, 373a, 759a
Aḥmad Wāṣif → Wāṣif
Aḥmad al-Waṭṭāsī (1545) vi, 594a, 893b
Aḥmad Wehbī → Pīr Meḥmed Wehbī <u>Kh</u>ayyāṭ
Aḥmad Wuld ʿAyda (amīr) (1932) vii, 627a
Aḥmad Yasawī (1166) i, **298b**, 1162a; iii, 76b, 1115a, 1116a; v, 264a, 859a; vii, 933b; x, 250a, 681a, 962b; xi, 116a; s, 51a, 521a
Aḥmad Yuknakī, Adīb (XII) i, **299a**
Aḥmad al-Zarrūḳ (1494) xi, 112b
Aḥmad Zayn al-Dīn, <u>Sh</u>ay<u>kh</u> (1581) vi, 458b, 459a, 462a, 463a
Aḥmad Zekī Welīdī → Togan, Zekī
Aḥmad Ziwar Pa<u>sh</u>a (1926) ii, 934b; iii, 516b
Ahmad Ziyaʾi (XX) vi, 768b
Aḥmad Zog → Zog, King
Aḥmadābād i, **299b**; ii, 1125b; iii, 16a, 445a, b; v, 1210a; vi, 50b, 51b, 52a, 53b, 126a, 131a; s, 10b, 23b, 70b, 335b
Aḥmadī → Sikka
Aḥmadī (town) s, **50a**
Aḥmad-i Rūmī (XIV) s, **49b**
Aḥmadī, Tā<u>d</u>j al-Dīn Ibrāhīm b. <u>Kh</u>iḍr (1413) i, **299b**, 325a; ii, 98a; iii, 115a; iv, 128b; vi, 609b; vii, 567b; ix, 418a
Aḥmadīl b. Ibrāhīm b. Wahsūdān al-Rawwādī al-Kurdī (amīr) (1111) i, 300a; v, 454a; vi, 499b; viii, 470a
Aḥmadīlīs i, 190a, **300a**; iii, 1112a; vi, 499b
Aḥmadiyya i, 225b, **301a**; ii, 58b, 63b, 129a, 535b, 538b, 1004a; iii, 411b, 433b, 1228b; iv, 84b, 890a, 891a, 951a; s, 248b, 278b
Aḥmadiyya (Derw(v)ish) i, 281a; ii, 164b
al-Aḥmadiyya (<u>Kh</u>alwatiyya) iv, 992a, 993a
Aḥmadnagar i, 81a, **303a**; ii, 99b, 158b; iii, 15b, 425b, 426b, 626a; iv, 202a; vi, 63a, b, 67a, 121b, 269a, b, 271b, 488b, 534b, 535b; viii, 73b; s, 246a
Aḥmadnagar (Gu<u>d</u>jarāt) ii, 1125a; iii, 625b
Aḥmadnagar (Uttar Pradesh) → Farrū<u>kh</u>ābād
Aḥmaddu I (Mūrītāniyā (1841) vii, 614b
Aḥmadu (Ḥamadu) II (1852) i, 303b; ii, 941b; iii, 39a
Aḥmadu III (1862) i, 303b; ii, 941b
Ahmad(u) Bamba Mbacké (1927) ii, 63b, 568a; vii, 609a; x, 575a; xi, 123a, 469a; s, 182a

Aḥmadu Bello, Sir → Bello, Alhaji Aḥmadu
Aḥmadu Lobbo, Seku (1844) i, **303a**; ii, 251b, 252a, 941b; iii, 38b; v, 394b
Aḥmadu Sheykhu → Aḥmad al-Shaykh
Aḥmadzay, Banū → Wazīrīs
Aḥmadzay Khāns (Kilāt) v, 102a
al-Aḥmar → Abu 'l-Ḥasan al-Aḥmar
Aḥmar, Banu 'l- → Naṣrids
Aḥmed → Aḥmad
Aḥmed Aghaoghlu (XIX) vi, 94a
Aḥmed Beg b. Ibrāhīm Beg (Menteshe) (1380) vi, 1018b
Aḥmed Čelebi, Zurnazen Edirneli Daghī (XVII) vi, 1007b
Aḥmed of Edirne, Pīr (1591) vi, 228a
Aḥmed Esʿad Efendi, Shaykh al-Islām (XVIII) vi, 1004b
Aḥmed Faḳīh (Ḳonya) (XIII) viii, 972b; s, **50a**
Aḥmed Fewzī Pasha (XIX) viii, 84b
Aḥmed Hāshim (XX) vi, 94b
Aḥmed Iḥsān Bey (XX) vi, 93a
Aḥmed ʿIṣām al-Dīn (1561) s, 614a
Ahmed Kabaklî (XX) vi, 95b
Aḥmed Khalīl → Fîndîḳoghlu
Aḥmed Midḥat Efendi (XIX) vi, 93a, b
Ahmed Moulavi C.N. (XX) vi, 462b
Aḥmed Nazīf (XIX) vii, 532a
Aḥmed Pasha (mamlūk) (1747) vi, 1002a
Aḥmed Riḍā Bey (1895) vi, 93a; vii, 206a
Aḥmed-i dāʿī (1421) viii, 211a, 212a, 544b
Aḥmed-oghlu Shükrullāh (XV) vii, 207b; viii, 806b
al-Aḥnaf b. Ḳays (VII) i, **303b**, 343b, 1001a; ii, 415a, b; iii, 391b, 583a, 782a; iv, 14b; v, 56b; ix, 34a
al-Ahnūm (Yemen) vi, 436b
Aḥrām → Ḥaram
Aḥrār, Khwādja ʿUbayd Allāh (1490) i, 147b, 148a, 849a; iv, 113a; v, 859a; vii, 934a, 935a; viii, 800b; x, 250b; s, **50b**, 121b
Aḥrār al-Dustūriyyīn s, 18a
Aḥrārs v, 803a; viii, 242a, 254b
Aḥruf → Ḳirāʾa
Ahrun b. Aʿyān al-Ḳass (VII) i, 213a; vi, 641a; s, **52a**
al-Aḥsāʾ → al-Ḥasā; Hufhūf
al-Aḥsāʾ (Shiʿites) ix, 904b, 905a
al-Aḥsāʾī, Shaykh Aḥmad (1826) i, **304b**, 596a; iv, 51a, 854b; vi, 551b; ix, 403b; s, 305a
Aḥsan → Djalāl al-Dīn
Aḥsanābād → Gulbargā
al-Ahtam iv, 832a, b
Ahūsar vi, 514b
Aḥwāḍ → Ḥawḍ
Aḥwāl → Ḥāl
al-Aḥwal → Yaḥyā b. Ādam
al-Aḥwal, Muḥammad b. al-Ḥasan (873) vii, 282a; viii, 918b
al-Ahwānī, ʿAbd al-ʿAzīz ii, 743b; v, 605b, 608b
al-Aḥwaṣ al-Ashʿarī (VIII) vi, 493a
al-Aḥwaṣ al-Anṣārī (728) i, 10b, **305a**; ii, 91a, 428b, 1029b; iii, 2b; iv, 1002a; s, 10a
al-Ahwāz i, 145a, 211b, **305b**, 695a, 1046b; ii, 383a, 426a; iii, 244b; iv, 6a, 7b, 675b; v, 80a, b, 81b, 867b; vi, 117b, 119b, 333b, 539a, 660b; vii, 26a, 271a; s, 35a, 118b, 119a
Aḥzāb → Ḥizb
ʿĀʾīḍ, Āl i, 555a, 709b
ʿĀʾiḍ b. al-ʿAbbās b. Mandīl (1269) vi, 404a
ʿĀʾiḍ b. Marʿī al-Mughaydī (XIX) i, 709b
ʿĀʾidh b. Saʿīd (657) vii, 463b
ʿĀʾidh, Banū (Makhzūm) vi, 633b
ʿĀʾila i, **305b**, 700a
Āʾīn i, **306b**
Āʾīn al-Mulk (Khaldjī amīr) (1303) vi, 406b
Aïr (Ayr) i, **307a**; viii, 17b
ʿĀʾisha bint Abī Bakr (678) i, 107a, 109b, 110a, **307b**, 383a, 1048a; ii, 414a, 415b, 416a, 845b, 1059a; iii, 64a, 65a, 242b, 359b; v, 616a; vi, 467a, 475b, 575b, 621b, 640b, 646a, 652a, 659a, 669a; vii, 371a, 393a; s, 133a, 230a, 311a
ʿĀʾisha bint ʿImrān → ʿĀʾisha al-Mannūbiyya
ʿĀʾisha bint Muʿāwiya b. al-Mughīra (VII) i, 76a; s, 103b
ʿĀʾisha bint Ṭalḥa (VII) i, **308b**; vi, 478a; vii, 650b
ʿĀʾisha bint Yūsuf al-Bāʿūnī (XVI) i, 1109b
ʿĀʾisha Ḳandīsha s, **52b**, 351a
ʿĀʾisha al-Mannūbiyya (1257) i, **308b**; vi, 251a, 355a
ʿĀʾishe Sulṭān bint Murād III (Ottoman) (1586) vi, 865a

Aïssaoua → ʿĪsāwa
Aït Aḥmad (Kabylia) (XX) iv, 363a
Ajarafe → al-Sharaf
Ajjer (Touareg) ii, 368b, 875a, 992a, 1022a
Aḳ Deniz → Baḥr al-Rūm
Aḳ Ḥiṣār i, **309a**; v, 284b
Aḳ Ḥiṣārī i, **309b**
Aḳ Kirmān i, **310a**, 1119b, 1252b; iv, 239a
Aḳ Ḳoyunlū i, 148b, 190a, 240a, 292b, **311a**, 639b, 666b, 861a, 903b, 1067a, 1117a, 1128b, 1133b, 1234a, 1328a; ii, 20b, 174a, 344b, 348a, 614a, 711b; iii, 198b, 315b, 507a, 1100b, 1257a; iv, 34a-35a, 267b, 475a; v, 54a, 457a, 492a; vi, 483a, 493a, 495a, 515b, 541a, 901a; x, 45b, 963b; s, 208a, 227b, 419b
Aḳ Masdjid i, **312a**
Aḳ Sarāy (town) i, **312a**; iv, 578b; vi, 55b, 120b, 226b, 275b
Aḳ Sarāy (palace) i, **312b**; s, 59a, 146a
Aḳ Shams al-Dīn (1459) i, 109a, **312b**, 777a, 869b; iii, 43b, 131a; vi, 226a, 978b
Aḳ Shams al-Dīn, al-Mawlā (XVI) vi, 913b
Aḳ Shehr i, **313a**
Aḳ Ṣu (river) i, 184a, **313b**, 454b; vi, 56a, 505b, 506a
Aḳ Ṣu (town) i, **313b**
Aḳ Ṣu (village) i, **314a**
Aḳ Sunḳūr b. ʿAbd Allāh al-Ḥādjib (1094) i, **314a**, 1117a
Aḳ Sunḳūr I al-Bursuḳī, Ḳasīm al-Dawla (1133) i, 300a, **314a**, 664a, 1337a; iii, 86b, 87a, 1118b; iv, 201a; v, 921b; vi, 64a, 380a, 500a, 506b; vii, 408a, 733a, b, 983b; viii, 944a
Aḳ Sunḳūr II Nuṣrat al-Dīn (Aḥmadīlī) (XII) i, 300b; vi, 500a; viii, 239b
Aḳ-Sunḳūr al-ʿĀdilī al-Sāḳī (1249) iv, 484a
Aḳ Sunḳūr al-Aḥmadīlī (1133) i, 300b
Aḳ Sunḳur al-Ṣalārī viii, 986a
Āḳā → Āghā
Aḳā Khān Kirmānī, Mīrzā ʿAbd al-Ḥusayn (1896) iv, 70b, 72a, 397b, 787b, 788b, 789a; vi, 292b, 834b; s, **53a**, 76b, 109b
Āḳā Mīrak (XVI) viii, 788a
Āḳā Muḥammad ʿAlī Khān Ḥādjdj Muḥammad (Niʿmat Allāhī) (1884) viii, 47b
Āḳā Muḥammad Khān (Ḳādjār) (1848) vi, 551b
Āḳā Nadjafī, Muḥammad Taḳī Iṣfahānī (1931) v, 1087b; vii, 918b; s, **54a**
Āḳā Riḍā (painter) (XVII) vi, 426a; vii, 339a
Āḳā Rustam (XVI) vi, 515a
Āḳā Ṣādiḳ, Ḥādjdjī (XIX) s, 53a
al-ʿAḳaba (mountain road) i, **314b**; viii. 379b
al-ʿAḳaba (port/Gulf) i, 9a, 50b, 64b, **314b**, 534a, 548b, 783b; iii, 36a; v, 995b; vi, 151b, 154a; vii, 65a; s, 8b, 198b, 230a
ʿAḳaba b. Muḥammad (Khuzāʿī) (IX) vi, 900a
ʿAḳabat al-Ḳibliyya vi, 545b
ʿAḳabat al-Nisāʾ i, **315a**
ʿAḳabi, Banū vi, 128b
Akaev, Askar (XXI) s, 537b
Āḳāʾī iv, 51b
ʿAḳāʾid → ʿAḳīda
Akagündüz (1958) s, **55a**
ʿAḳāl → ʿImāma
Akanṣūs, Abū ʿAbd Allāh (1877) i, **315a**; iii, 948b; vi, 113a; vii, 392a
ʿAḳār s, **55a**
Akara (Mālwā) vi, 309a
ʿAkārib → ʿAḳrabī
ʿAḳarḳūf i, **315b**
Aḳāsī Beg → Wafā, Mīrzā Sharaf al-Dīn
Āḳāsī, Ḥādjdjī Mīrzā (XIX) v, 1222a
al-ʿAkawwak, ʿAlī b. Djabala (828) i, **315b**; iv, 718b; s, 17b
Akbar (Mākū) (1642) vi, 202b
Akbar I, Abu ʾl-Fatḥ Djalāl al-Dīn Muḥammad b. Humāyūn (Mughal) (1605) i, 8b, 80b, 117a, b, 208b, 228b, 229a, 238a, 252b, 253a, **316a**, 417b, 710b, 733a, 807b, 856b, 864b, 1069a, 1135a, b, 1136a, b, 1194a, 1323a, 1324a, 1331a, 1347b; ii, 50a, 121a, 155b, 156b, 162a, 271b, 272a, 296a, 336b, 379b, 503b, 814a, 840a, 871a, 973b, 1048a, 1085a, 1122b, 1129a, 1131a, 1144a; iii, 201b, 245b, 318b, 348a, 423b, 430a, 449b, 457a, 482b; iv, 219a, 523b, 709a, 910a, 922a, 1104a, 1159b; v, 598a, b, 599b, 635a, 686a, 689b, 1135b, 1217a; vi, 52b, 67a, 127a, 131a, 269b, 271b, 342b, 369b, 407a, 410a, 424b, 425a, 456b, 488b, 516b, 533b, 534a; vii, 133b, 134a, b, 139a, 195a, 221a, 314a, b, 317a, 320a, 327a, 329b, 337b, 345a, 573b,

932a; viii, 67b, 116b, 253b, 368a; ix, 846a; s, 1b, 3a, b, 107b, 126b, 132a, 142b, 167a, 176b, 210b, 237b, 242b, 258a, 259b, 292a, 312a, 313a, 324b, 366b, 378a, 410b, 636b
Akbar II (Mughal) (1837) ii, 221b; vii, 316b
Akbar b. Awrangzīb (1688) i, 769a; vi, 132a, 534b, 856a; s, **55b**
Akbar, Sayyid Ḥusayn Allāhābādī (1921) i, **317b**; iii, 358b
Akbarnagar → Rādjmahal
Akbar Shāh II ii, 221b; iv, 1102b
Aḳbughā ʿAbd al-Wāḥid, amīr (XIV) i, 814b
Aḳče i, **317b**; ii, 118a, 119a, b; v, 974a
Aḳče Ḳodja (XIV) i, 468b
ʿAḳd i, **318a**; ii, 303a, b; iii, 1091b
Akdariyya i, **320a**
al-Akfānī i, 1220b; iii, 1088a
al-Aḳfahsī (1405) vi, 720b; x, 586b
Akh → ʿĀʾila; Ikhwān; Muʾakhāt
al-Akhal (Sicily) (IX) vii, 483b
Ākhāl Tekke i, **320b**
Akhalčikh → Akhiskha
Akhalkhalaki (Armenia) i, 643a; v, 495a, b
Akharnar → Nudjūm
Akh(w)āsh, Banū v, 153b
Akhaweyn, Mullā i, 323a
Akhbār → Khabar; Taʾrīkh
Akhbār al-ʿAbbās iv, 446a
Akhbār Madjmūʿa i, **320b**, 600b
Akhbār al-Ṣīn wa ʾl-Hind i, 991b; ii, 583b; iv, 648a; s, **55b**
al-Akhbārī, Muḥammad b. ʿAbd al-Nabī al-Nīshābūrī (XIX) iv, 703b; vi, 551a; s, 57a
Akhbāriyya iv, 50a, 51a; vi, 549a, 550b, 551a; vii, 300b; viii, 779b; s, **56b**, 95b, 103b, 134b
Akh-čay (Mākū) vi, 200b, 201a, b
al-Akhḍar i, **321a**; v, 700b, 706a
Akhḍar, Djabal i, 207b, 1048b, 1049a, b; v, 759b, 760a
al-Akhḍarī, Abū Zayd (XVI) i, **321a**, 1019b
al-Akhfash i, **321a**; s, 22b, 361b
al-Akhfash al-Akbar (793) i, **321b**
al-Akhfash al-Aṣghar, Abu ʾl-Ḥasan (927) i, **321b**; vii, 279b, 280a, 526b
al-Akhfash al-Awsaṭ (825) i, **321b**; iii, 758a; viii, 379a; x, 86a; s, 317b
Akhī i, **321b**, 347b, 468a, 510a, 510b; ii, 966b, 967b; iv, 621a, b; v, 254a; viii, 175a
Akhī Baba i, 323a, **323b**; ii, 968a; v, 173a
Akhī Čelebi (XV) iii, 340a
Akhī Ewrān i, 323a, **324a**, 510b; ii, 968a, 1138a; v, 173a
Akhī Faradj Zandjānī, Shaykh (1065) i, 322a; ii, 966b
Akhī Khazzām b. Ghālib (IX) iv, 215a, 216a
Akhī Sirādj al-Dīn ʿUthmān, Shaykh (XIV) ii, 51b; v, 639a
Akhīdjūḳ (1359) i, 323b, **325a**; ii, 401a, 967a; vii, 820b
Ākhir → al-Asmāʾ al-Ḥusnā
Ākhir-i Čārshamba → Ṣafar
Ākhira i, **325a**
Akhiskha i, 4a, **325a**; vi, 59b
Akhī-zāde, Āl i, 323a
Akhī-zāde Hüseyin Efendi, Shaykh al-Islām (1634) v, 272b; vii, 598a
Akhī-zāde ʿAbdülḥalīm Efendi (XVII) i, 732b; iv, 900b
Akhlāḳ i, **325b**
Akhlāṭ (Khilāṭ) i, **329a**, 627a, 639a, 799a, 1206b; ii, 393a; iv, 354b, 817b; v, 455a; vi, 124b, 243b, 244a, 505a, 626a
Akhmīm/Ikhmīm i, **330a**, 1038b; vi, 119a, 413a, 912b
al-Akhnas b. Sharīḳ i, 891a
Akhnūkh → Idrīs
al-Akhras (1874) i, **330a**
Akhsatān b. Manūčihr b. Afrīdūn (Sharwān-shāh) (1159) iv, 348b, 915a
al-Akhshabān i, 136a
Akhshām → Ṣalāt
Akhsīkath i, **330b**; ii, 791a; vi, 557b; s, 406b
Akhsitān (Aghsartʿan) b. Gagik (XI) v, 489a, b
Ākhtabēgī → Atabak
al-Akhṭal (710) i, **331a**, 586a, 1241a; ii, 480a, 789a; iii, 354a; iv, 315b, 744b, 819a, 1002b, 1008b; vi, 379a, 475a, 545a, 671a; vii, 843a, 920b, 981a; viii, 110a, 130b; s, 10a, 394a, b
Akhtarī (1561) i, **331b**; iv, 365a
Akhū Muḥsin (985) i, 95b, 96a, 403a; vi, 917b
Akh Ṣu → Aḳ Ṣu
Akhū Ṭāz → Djardamur

Ākhūnd i, **331b**
Akhund Bābā (Mullā Ilyās) (XVII) ii, 316b
Akhund Darwīza → Darwīza
Ākhund-zāda, Mīrzā Fatḥ ʿAlī (1878) i, **331b**; ii, 217a; iii, 358a; iv, 73b; v, 919b; vi, 291b, 758a, b, 763a, b; vii, 438b; viii, 116a; s, 53b, 76b, 109a, 290b
Ākhūr → Amīr Ākhūr
Ākhūremīrizāde Ḥāshimī (XVI) iii, 153b
Akhwakh i, 504a; iv, 631a
al-ʿĀḳib b. ʿAbd Allāh (1550) viii, 18b
ʿĀḳib al-Anuṣammanī of Takidda x, 122a
ʿAḳīda i, 121a, 195a, 310a, **332b**; iv, 279b
ʿĀkif Pasha → Muḥammad ʿĀkif Pasha
ʿAḳīḳ i, **336a**
al-ʿAḳīḳ i, **336b**; iii, 121b; s, 199b
ʿAḳīḳ al-Yamāma (Tamra) i, 336b
ʿAḳīḳ Dhāt ʿIrḳ i, 336b
ʿAḳīḳa i, **337a**; iv, 488a
al-ʿAḳīḳī, al-Ḥasan b. Muḥammad b. Djaʿfar (IX) vii, 418a
ʿAḳīl b. Abī Ṭālib (670) i, **337b**; vi, 650b, 828b; vii, 689a; ix, 715a
ʿAḳīl b. Djābir b. ʿAbd Allāh (VIII) s, 231a
ʿAḳīl b. ʿUllafa al-Murrī vii, 629b
ʿAḳīl Khān Rāzī, Mīr Muḥammad (1696) vi, 132a; s, **57b**
Āḳil al-Murār → Ḥudjr Āḳil al-Murār
ʿĀḳila i, **337b**; ii, 342a; iv, 334b
Aḳi̊ndji̊ i, **340a**, 1302b; ii, 611b
Aḳīt, Āl vi, 259b
ʿAkk, Banū i, **340b**; vi, 652b
ʿAkkā (Acre) i, 216a, **341a**, 946b, 1078a, b; ii, 63b, 129b; iii, 188a, 325a, b, 473a, 474b; iv, 485b, 965a; v, 594a, 595a; vi, 322a, b, 406a, 579a, 652a, b; vii, 168b, 817a, 998a; xi, 393b; s, 20b, 120b, 121a, 162b, 205a, b, 268a, b
al-ʿAḳḳād, ʿAbbās Maḥmūd (1964) i, 598a; iii, 1207b; iv, 85b, 159b; v, 189a; vi, 91a, 409b, 414b; vii, 441a; viii, 88a; s, **57b**
ʿAkkār vi, 345a, 579a; s, **58b**
ʿAkkāsbāshī (XX) s, 109b
Akkerman → Aḳ Kirmān
Aḳḳūsh al-Afram (Damascus) vii, 991b
ʿAḳl i, **341b**, 1116a; iv, 157a, 487a, b
ʿAḳliyyāt i, **342b**; iv, 469b
Aklub, Banū iv, 1106a
Aḳlūḳiyā vi, 420a
Akmal al-Dīn al-Bābartī (XIV) i, 299b
Aḳmesdjid iv, 500a
ʿAḳr (Wāsiṭ) (720) vi, 740a
al-Aḳraʿ b. Ḥābis (VII) i, **343a**, 1247b; ii, 608b; iii, 169a; v, 109a; viii, 82b
ʿAḳrab i, **343b**
ʿAḳrabāʾ i, **344a**, 628b; ii, 569a; vii, 402b
Aḳrābādhīn i, **344a**
ʿAḳrabī i, **345a**
Akrād → Kurds
Aḳrā-Rūdh vi, 498b
ʿAks → Balāgha
al-Aḳṣā → Masdjid al-Aḳṣā
Aḳsarā → Aḳ Sarāy
al-Aḳsarāʾī, ʿIsā b. Ismāʿīl iii, 181a
Aḳsarayī → Djamāl al-Dīn
al-Aḳsarāyī, Karīm al-Dīn (1320) s, **59a**
Aḳshehirli → Ḥasan Fehmī Efendi
Aḳ-Shehr vii, 1018a
Akstafa s, 146a
Aksu (Bug) vi, 56a
Aḳsu (Khotan) s, 98a
Aksum ii, 895b; iii, 9a, b, 10a; vii, 862a, b, 863a
Aḳṭāʿ v, 152a
al-Aḳṭaʿ → Abū Yaʿḳūb; ʿAmr b. ʿUbayd Allāh
Aktau (Mangi̊stau mts) vi, 415a
Aḳtaw (XIV) ii, 612b
Aḳṭāy (Mamlūk) (XIII) i, 944b
Aktham b. Ṣayfī i, **345a**; vi, 267a
al-ʿAḳūla → Dayr al-ʿĀḳūl
al-ʿĀkūl i, 336b
Aḳūnīṭun s, **59b**
Aḳūr → Athūr
Āḳūsh (Āḳ-ḳūsh) al-Burunlī (al-Barlī) (1261) vi, 322a; vii, 729b
Akūsha ii, 141b, 142a
Al (the definite article) → Taʿrīf
al-Aḳwās → Arkush
Āl (clan) i, 258b, **345b**, 700b
Āl followed by a family name, see also under that name
Āl (demon) i, **345b**
Āl → Sarāb
Āl Shaykh ix, 905a
Āl Sulaymān, ʿAbd Allāh (XX) vi, 153a, 155b, 161a, 163b, 165b, 166a, b
Āl-i Aḥmad, Sayyid Djalāl (1969) iv, 73b; v, 200b; s, **60a**, 135b
Āl-i Burhān (Bukhārā) i, 1295a; iii, 1115a; iv, 582a; v, 858a; viii, 403b, 748b, 942b; x, 211b

Āla i, **345b**
al-ʿAlāʾ b. al-Ḥaḍramī (VII) i, 942a; ii, 811b; iv, 220a, 764a, 832b; vii, 570b
Ala Dagh i, **346a**
ʿAlāʾ al-Dawla (Kākūyid) → ʿAlāʾ al-Dawla Muḥammad b. Dushmanziyār
ʿAlāʾ al-Dawla (Timūrid) (1459) i, 147b
ʿAlāʾ al-Dawla b. Sulaymān Beg (XV) i, 324a; ii, 240a; iv, 553a
ʿAlāʾ al-Dawla ʿAlī b. Farāmurz → ʿAlī b. Farāmurz
ʿAlāʾ al-Dawla Ata-Khān (Kākūyid) (1227) iv, 466b
ʿAlāʾ al-Dawla Bozḳurd (Dhu ʾl-Ḳadr) (1515) vi, 509b, 510a, 541a
ʿAlāʾ al-Dawla Farāmarz b. ʿAlī (XII) i, 113a
ʿAlāʾ al-Dawla Ḥasan Bāwandī (1171) v, 662a
ʿAlāʾ al-Dawla Muḥammad b. Dushmanziyār (Kākūyid) (1041) i, 132a, 512b; iii, 331a, 942b; iv, 100b, 465a, b, 466b, 1103b; vi, 600b, 907a
ʿAlāʾ al-Dawla al-Simnānī (1336) i, 88b, **346b**, 702b; v, 301a; viii, 408b; s, 122a
ʿAlāʾ al-Dīn → Djahān-Sūz; Djuwaynī; Ghūrids; Ḳayḳubād I; Khwārazmshāhs; Saldjūḳs
ʿAlāʾ al-Dīn (Vize) (1562) vi, 228a
ʿAlāʾ al-Dīn (engineer) (XIII) vi, 406a
ʿAlāʾ al-Dīn (Marāgha) (XII) vi, 500b
ʿAlāʾ al-Dīn, Sulṭān (Makassar) (XVII) vi, 116b
ʿAlāʾ al-Dīn b. Maḥmūd I Khaldjī (Mālwā) (1462) vi, 54a,
ʿAlāʾ al-Dīn b. Muḥammad Shāh IV (Sayyid, Dihlī) (1442) vi, 53a
ʿAlāʾ al-Dīn Aḥmad Bahmanī → Aḥmad Shāh II
ʿAlāʾ al-Dīn ʿĀlam Shāh → ʿĀlam Shāh
ʿAlāʾ al-Dīn ʿAlī b. Faḍl Allāh → Faḍl Allāh
ʿAlāʾ al-Dīn ʿAlī b. Yūsuf Bālī (1497) ii, 879b
ʿAlāʾ al-Dīn ʿAlī Eretna → Eretna
ʿAlāʾ al-Dīn ʿAlī Karamān-Oghlu (XIV) vii, 593b
ʿAlāʾ al-Dīn Beg (1333) i, **348a**
ʿAlāʾ al-Dīn Dāwūd (Mengüček, Erzincan) (XIII) vii, 871a
ʿAlāʾ al-Dīn Fīrūz → Fīrūz Shāh (Bengal)
ʿAlāʾ al-Dīn Ḥasan Bahman Shāh (1347) i, 923b, 924b, 1200a; ii, 51b, 99b, 180a, 270a, 1124b; vi, 67a; vii, 289a, 458a
ʿAlāʾ al-Dīn Ḥusayn → Djahān-Sūz; Ḥusayn Shāh
ʿAlāʾ al-Dīn ʿImād Shāh (Berar) (1532) i, 914b; iii, 425a, 1159b, 1160a
ʿAlāʾ al-Din Ḳara Sonḳor (1207) i, 300b; iii, 1112a
ʿAlāʾ al-Dīn Karāba (Atabeg) (XII) vi, 501a
ʿAlāʾ al-Dīn Khaldjī (Dihlī Sultanate) (1315) i, 444b, iv, 921a; vi, 271a, 309b, 691b, 1027a; vii, 957a; viii, 5b
ʿAlāʾ al-Dīn Mudjāhid (Bahmānid) (1378) vii, 458b
ʿAlāʾ al-Dīn Muḥammad III Nizārī (1255) vii, 974a; viii, 598b
ʿAlāʾ (Ḍiyāʾ) al-Dīn Muḥammad (Ghūrid) (1215) ii, 1101b, 1103a
ʿAlāʾ al-Dīn Muḥammad (Khaldjī) → Muḥammad Shāh I Khaldjī (Dihlī)
ʿAlāʾ al-Dīn Muḥammad b. Ḥasan → Alamūt
ʿAlāʾ al-Dīn Muḥammad b. Tekish (Khwārazm-Shāh) (1220) i, 4a, 1001b, 1010a, 1311a; ii, 43a, 329b, 393b, 571a, 606a, 752a, 894a, 1101b; iii, 114a, 195b, 196b, 197a, 198a; iv, 502b, 583a; v, 662b; vi, 77a, 482a, 717a, 939a; vii, 410a; viii, 63b, 432a; ix, 558a; s, 246a
ʿAlāʾ al-Dīn Muḥammad (vizier, Sabzawār) (1342) ix, 47b, 48a
ʿAlāʾ al-Dīn Pasha → ʿAlāʾ al-Dīn Beg
ʿAlāʾ al-Dīn Riʿāyat Shāh al-Ḳahhār (Atjèh) (1604) i, 743a; iii, 1220a; vii, 71b
ʿAlāʾ al-Dīn Ṣāḥib Andavār, Shaykh (Marakkayar) vi, 503b
ʿAlāʾ al-Dīn (Sihālī) (XIV) i, 936b; s, 292a
ʿAlāʾ al-Dīn Tekish → Tekesh
ʿAlāʾ al-Mulk Ḥusaynī Shūshtarī Marʿashī (XVII) vi, 516b
Ala Shehir i, **346a**
Ālā Singh (Patiala) (XVIII) i, 1022b, 1194b; ii, 488b; iii, 485a
ʿAlā-yi Tabrīzī, ʿAbd Allāh (XIII) iv, 1045b, 1047b
Ālaba wa ʾl-ḳilāʿ i, **348b**
Alaca (Čorum) ii, 62b
Alačik iv, 1150b
Alacuas → Arkush
Aladdin → Alf Layla wa-Layla

Aladja i, **348b**
Aladja Dagh i, **348b**
Aladja Ḥiṣār i, **348b**; vi, 69b
Älägän (Mākū) vi, 201a
Alaham, Banū s, 145a
Alahort → al-Ḥurr b. ʿAbd al-Raḥmān al-Thaḳafī
al-ʿAlāʾī s, 251b
ʿAlāʾī, Shaykh (XVI) ii, 500a; iii, 492b
ʿAlāʾiyya → Alanya
ʿAlāḳa → Nisba
ʿAlam i, **349a**; iii, 197a
ʿĀlam i, **349b**
ʿĀlam (poet) (Hind) (XVIII) iii, 457b
ʿAlam, Queen (Nadjāhid) (1150) i, 552b; v, 1244a
ʿAlam al-Dīn, Āl ii, 749b, 751a; iv, 834b
ʿAlam al-Dīn Ḳayṣar (Mamlūk) (XIII) i, 780b; iii, 967a
ʿAlam al-Dīn al-Sakhāwī (1245) i, 150a
ʿAlam al-Dīn Sulaymān Maʿn (XVI) vi, 343a, b
ʿAlam Khān → ʿAyn al-Mulk Multānī
ʿAlam Khān (Gudjārāt) (1545) vi, 52a
ʿAlam Khān Fārūḳī (I) → Farūḳids
ʿAlam Khān Fārūḳī (II) → Farūḳids
ʿĀlam Shāh ʿAlāʾ al-Dīn (Sayyidid) (Dihlī) (1478) i, 855b, 856a; ii, 270b; iii, 418a; v, 783b; vi, 62a; ix, 118b, 110a
al-Aʿlam al-Shantamarī → al-Shantamarī
ʿAlāma i, **352a**; ii, 302a, 303a, 307b, 331b
Alamak → Nudjūm
ʿAlambardār (1004) vii, 550a
Alambic → al-Anbīḳ
ʿĀlamgīr I → Awrangzīb
ʿĀlamgīr II, ʿAzīz al-Dīn (Mughal) (1759) iii, 1158b; vi, 535b; vii, 316a, 869b
al-ʿAlamī, Āl i, **352a**
al-ʿAlamī, ʿAbd al-Ḳādir → Ḳaddūr al-ʿAlamī
al-ʿAlamī, Muḥammad b. al-Ṭayyib (1721) i, **352b**
ʿĀlamiyān, Mīrzā, nazīr (XVII) iv, 1039b, 1044b
ʿĀlamshāh Begum (XV) viii, 766b
Alamūt i, **352b**, 688b, 1359b; ii, 191a, 192a, 194a; iii, 253b, 254a, 501b; iv, 199b, 201b, 202a, 859b; v, 656b; vi, 64b, 494a, 512a, 789b; vii, 657a, 974a; viii, 72a; s, 356b
Alān (Alans) i, **354a**, 837a; ii, 86a; iv, 344a, 345a, b, 349a, b; v, 288a; vi, 420a; viii, 180a; x, 690a
Äländ (Adharbāydjān) vi, 200b, 201a, 202a
Aland (Djāgīr) vi, 63a, 369a
Alangu, Tahir (1973) s, **61b**
Alanya i, **354b**, 476b; iv, 817b
Alarcos → al-Arak
Alas (Atjèh) i, 740a
Alashehir ii, 989b; iii, 211b
Ālāt → Āla
Alauddin, Sultan (Malacca) (XV) vi, 211b, 212a
Alava → Ālaba wa ʾl-ḳilāʿ
Alavi of Mambram, Syed (1843) vi, 463a
ʿAlawī (ʿAdan) i, **355a**
ʿAlawī, Bā → Bā ʿAlawī
ʿAlawī, Buzurg (XX) iv, 73a; v, 199b, 200a
al-ʿAlawī, al-Ḥasan b. Djaʿfar (XI) vii, 461a
al-ʿAlawī, Muḥammad b. ʿUbayd Allāh (X) vii, 769b
ʿAlawids, Alawites → ʿAlawīs; Nuṣayrīs
Alawites → Nuṣayrī
ʿAlawīs (ʿAlawiyya) i, 47a, 315b, **355a**, 689a, 1058a, 1149a; ii, 134a, 146a, 308a, 823a; iii, 256b, 536a, 973a; iv, 634a; v, 592a, 656a; vi, 135a, 248b, 743a, 791b, 888b; viii, 147b; x, 698b; s, 48a, 336b, 339a
ʿAlawiyya (Mamlūks) iii, 992a
Alay i, **358a**
Alāy (river) vi, 618b
al-Alāya (ʿUmān) vi, 961b
ʿAlāyā → Alanya
al-ʿAlāyilī, ʿAbd Allāh (XX) iv, 783a
Alay-beyi-zāde → Muḥammad Emīn b. Hadjdjī Meḥmed
Albacete → al-Basīṭ
Albania → Arnawutluḳ; Awlonya
Albaicin → Gharnāṭa
Albarracin → Shantamariyyat al-Sharḳ
Albatenius, Albategni → al-Battānī
Albistān → Elbistān
Alboacen/Albohazen → (Abu ʾl-Ḥasan) Ibn Abī ʾl-Ridjāl al-Ḳayrawānī
Albohali → al-Khayyāṭ, Abū ʿAlī
Albū Muḥammad → Bū Muḥammad, Āl
Albubather → Ibn al-Khaṣīb, Abū Bakr
Albucasis → al-Zahrāwī
Albufera (lake) → Balansiya

Album → Murakkaʿ
Albumasar → Abū Maʿshar al-Balkhī
Albuquerque, Alfonso de i, 181b, 553b, 1038b; iii, 585a; vi, 51a, 459a; s, 234b
Alburz i, **358b**; iv, 1a, 4b-5a, 6b, 9b, 400b; v, 657b; vi, 337b, 492b, 494b; s, 309a
Alcacer do Sal → Ḳaṣr Abī Dānis
Alcala → al-Ḳalʿa
Alcantara → al-Ḳanṭara
Alcaraz s, 143a
Alcazar i, **358b**
Alcazarquivir → al-Ḳaṣr al-Kabīr
Alchabitius → al-Ḳabīṣī, ʿAbd al-ʿAzīz Abu ʾl Ṣaḳr
Alchemy → al-Kīmiyāʾ
Alcira → Djazīrat Shuḳr
Alcolea → al-Ḳulayʿa
Alcoran → al-Ḳurʾān
Aldamov → ʿAlibek Aldamov
Aldebaran → Nudjūm
Aledo → Alīṭ
Alekper ʿAlī Akbar Ṣābir
Alembic → al-Anbīḳ
ʿAlemdār Muṣṭafā Pasha (XIX) v, 1083a, 1084a
ʿAlem-i Nebewī → Sandjaḳ-i Sherīf
Aleppo → Ḥalab
Alessio → Lesh
Alexander of Aphrodisias → al-Iskandar al-Afrūdīsī
Alexander the Great → al-Iskandar, dhu ʾl-Ḳarnayn
Alexander of Damascus → al-Iskandar al-Dimashḳī
Alexander romance → Iskandar-nāma
Alexandretta → Hatay; Iskandarūn
Alexandria → al-Iskandariyya
Alexandropolis → Dede Aghač
Alf layla wa-layla i, 144b, **358b**, 359a, 574b, 595b, 1127a; ii, 356b, 547b; iii, 81a, 281b, 371a, 1050a; v, 951a
Alfa-grass → Ḥalfāʾ
Alfarabius → al-Fārābī
Alfard → Nudjūm
Alfraganus → al-Farghānī
Alfonso → Alfūnsho
Alfūnsho i, **364b**
Alfūnsho (the Warrior) (XII) i, 390a, 495b, 1150a; ii, 526b, 1007a, 1013a; iii, 543a, 771a; s, 81a, 397b
Alfūnsho III (IX) i, 85b, 1338b; ii, 1009a, b; iii, 842a; v, 498b, 1107b; s, 92a
Alfūnsho V (Naples) (XV) iv, 139b, 730a
Alfūnsho VI (XI) i, 6b, 7a, 43b, 242b, 390a, 495a; ii, 243b, 1013a; iii, 706a; v, 392b, 498b, 1107b
Alfūnsho VII (XII) i, 1083a, 1150a; ii, 1009b, 1013b; iii, 771b; v, 498b
Alfūnsho VIII (XII) i, 161b, 165b, 495b, 605b, 1150a; iii, 1055a; iv, 482b; v, 392b
Alfūnsho XI (XIV) ii, 525a
Algarve → Gharb al-Andalus
Algazel → al-Ghazālī
Algebra → al-Djabr wa ʾl-muḳābala
Algeciras → al-Djazīra al-Khaḍrāʾ
Algedi → Nudjūm
Alger → al-Djazāʾir
Algeria i, **364b**, 661a, 1321a; ii, 172b; iii, 297b, 385a; iv, 1155b; v, 696a; vi, 248a, 250b, 789b, 947a, 1043a; viii, 901b; x, 155a; s, 215b
– demography s, 215b
– geography i, 364b-366b
– history i, 37a, 85a, 356a, 366b-370b; iii, 524b, 561b, 562b, 564a, 727b, 1003b; iv, 362b; vi, 841a
– institutions i, 373a, 374a, 413a, 978a; ii, 425b; iii, 524b, 727b, 1003b; v, 916a
– languages, literature i, 374a-379b; ii, 469a; iii, 727b
– population i, 171a, 370b-373a, 1177a, b; v, 1164b
Algeziras → al-Djazīra al-Khaḍrāʾ
Algiers → al-Djazāʾir
Algol → Nudjūm
Algomaiza → Nudjūm
Algorithmus i, **379b**; iv, 1070b
Alhabor → Nudjūm
Alhagiag bin Thalmus → Ibn Ṭumlūs
Alhaiot → Nudjūm
Alhama → al-Ḥamma
Alhambra → Gharnāṭa
Alhān (Yemen) vi, 436a
Alhazen → Ibn al-Haytham
Alhichante i, 405a
Alhidade → Asṭurlāb
Alhucemas → al-Ḥusayma; al-Khuzāmā
al-ʿAlī (province) vi, 574b
ʿAlī I b. Ibrāhīm (ʿĀdil Shāh) (1580) viii, 74a

ʿAlī II b. Muḥammad (ʿĀdil Shāh) (1672) viii, 154b
ʿAlī I b. Muḥammad (Idrīsid) (849) iii, 1035b; s, 103a
ʿAlī II b. ʿUmar (Idrīsid) (IX) iii, 1035b, 1036a; s, 103a
Alī, Mai (Bornū) (1684) i, 1259b
ʿAlī, Muṣṭafā b. Aḥmad Čelebī (1600) i, **380a**; ii, 895a; iii, 1200b; iv, 704a; vi, 351b, 412b; vii, 721a; viii, 3b; ix, 410a; s, 83a
ʿAlī, Shaykh (Ḳāḍī al-Ḳuḍāt) vi, 15b
ʿAlī b. al-ʿAbbās al-Madjūsī (982) i, **381a**; ii, 60a, 481b; iv, 330a; s, 52b, 271b
ʿAlī b. ʿAbd Allāh, Sharīf (1908) iii, 605b; vi, 151b, 154a
ʿAlī b. ʿAbd Allāh b. al-ʿAbbās (735) i, **381a**; iii, 574a
ʿAlī b. ʿAbd Allāh (dāʿī) (XV) s, 407a
ʿAlī b. ʿAbd Allāh al-Ṭūsī (IX) i, 718b; s, 394b
ʿAlī b. ʿAbd al-ʿAzīz Umm al-Walad-zāde (1514) iv, 471b
ʿAlī b. ʿAbd al-Muʾmin (XII) i, 160b
ʿAlī b. ʿAbd al-Raḥmān (astronomer) (XI) iii, 81a
ʿAlī b. ʿAbd al-Raḥmān b. Hudhayl al-Andalusī i, 1149b
ʿAlī b. ʿAbd al-Raḥmān al-Djamal (Idrīsī Sharīf) (XIX) ii, 160a
ʿAlī b. Abī Bakr (Harāt) (1214) i, 593b
ʿAlī b. Abi ʾl-Faradj al-Baṣrī (1261) iii, 111b; vii, 527b
ʿAlī b. Abi ʾl-Gharāt (Masʿūdid) (1138) i, 1214b
ʿAlī b. Abī Ḥafṣ Iṣfahānī (XIII) s, 35a
ʿAlī b. Abi ʾl-Ridjāl vi, 374b
ʿAlī b. Abī Ṭālib (661) i, 44a, 152b, 181b, 212b, 260b, 337b, **381b**, 400b, 549b, 765a; ii, 218a, 414a, 625b, 725a, 726a, 842b, 846a, 848a, 993a; iii, 33a, 241a, 583b, 887a, 1254b, 1265a; iv, 277b, 836b, 1035a, 1074b, 1140a; v, 406b, 499a, 777a, 996b; vi, 11b, 107b, 139b, 267b, 279b, 337a, 350b, 351b, 374a, 604a, 605b, 621b, 645a, 650b, 652a, 657b, 659b, 664a, 669a, b; vii, 265a, 364a, 393a, 581b, 672b, 903b, 912b; ix, 410a; s, 89b, 92b, 94a, 119a, 130a, 157a, 270a, 351b, 357b, 358b, 401a
– antagonists i, 52a, 54a, 108a, 308a, 1343b; iii, 235a, 583a, 887a
– doctrines i, 263a, 275b; ii, 889a, 961a, 1098b; iii, 1163b
– supporters i, 51a, 107a, 109a, 117a, 195a, 431b, 704a; ii, 480b; iii, 123b, 235a, 583a
ʿAlī b. Abī Zayd (1122) ii, 490a
ʿAlī b. Aḍḥā al-Hamdānī (XII) ii, 1013b; iii, 850a, b
ʿAlī b. Afrāsiyāb → ʿAlī Pasha Afrāsiyāb
ʿAlī b. Aḥmad b. Abī Saʿīd (Tīmūrid) (1546) i, 1019a
ʿAlī b. Aḥmad al-Ḍayf (XI) ii, 484a; vii, 544a
ʿAlī b. Aḥmad al-Ḥabbāl ii, 137a
ʿAlī b. Aḥmad al-ʿAḳīḳ (911) ix, 819a
ʿAlī b. Amādjūr (IX) vii, 28b
ʿAlī b. ʿAsākir → Ibn ʿAsākir
ʿAlī b. Aybak al-Turkumānī (1259) vi, 321b, 327a
ʿAlī b. Bakkār (823) viii, 498a
ʿAlī b. Burhān Niẓām Shāh (XVI) iii, 1161a
ʿAlī b. Buwayh → ʿImād al-Dawla ʿAlī b. Būya
ʿAlī b. Dāʾūd (VIII) i, 103b
ʿAlī b. Dāwūd, Kurd (892) vi, 900a
ʿAlī b. Djabala → al-ʿAkawwak
ʿAlī b. Djaʿfar b. Falāḥ (XI) viii, 922b
ʿAlī b. al-Djahm (863) i, 153b, 154a, **386a**; iv, 491a; vi, 539a, 625b; viii, 376b
ʿAlī b. Djānbulāṭ (XVII) x, 215b
ʿAlī b. Djinnī (1065) x, 461b
ʿAlī b. Djūdayʿ al-Kirmānī, Azdī (VIII) x, 845a
ʿAlī b. Dubays (Mazyadid) (XII) vii, 406b
ʿAlī-i Dūstī (XIII) i, 347b
ʿAlī Ben ʿAyād (XX) vi, 751a, b
ʿAlī b. al-Faḍl al-Djayshānī (881) i, 551b; iv, 198a, b, 661a; vi, 438b, 439a; s, 335a
ʿAlī b. Fakhr al-Dīn b. Ḳurḳumāz Maʿn (1633) vi, 343b
ʿAlī b. Farāmurz (Kākūyid) (1095) iv, 466a, b; vii, 489a
ʿAlī b. al-Furāt → Ibn al-Furāt, Abu ʾl-Ḥasan ʿAlī
ʿAlī b. Ghadhāhum (Ḳābis) (XIX) iv, 338b, 403b
ʿAlī b. Ghāniya (1187) i, 165a, 1150a; ii, 463b, 1007a; iv, 337b, 614a, b

ʿAlī b. al-Ḥaddād (XII) iv, 381a
ʿAlī b. Ḥamdūn (927) iv, 459a; vi, 727b
ʿAlī b. Ḥamdūsh, Sīdī (1722) vi, 891a; xi, 113a; s, 53a, 350b
ʿAlī b. Ḥammūd (Ḥammūdid) (1016) iii, 147a, 743a, 786a; vi, 222a, 852b; vii, 563b
ʿAlī b. Ḥamūd (Bū Saʿīd) (1918) i, 1283a
ʿAlī b. Ḥamza al-Iṣfahānī (X) i, 154b; iii, 156b
ʿAlī b. Ḥanẓala b. Abī Sālim (1229) s, **61b**
ʿAlī b. al-Ḥasan (Kilwa) (XII) v, 106b; vii, 250a s
ʿAlī b. al-Ḥasan al-Hāshimī (XIX) vi, 106a
ʿAlī b. al-Ḥasan b. al- Muslima → Ibn al-Muslima
ʿAlī b. Ḥasan Bughra Khān → ʿAlī Tegīn
ʿAlī b. al-Ḥasan al-Mubārak → Abu 'l-Ḥasan al-Aḥmar
ʿAlī b. Ḥātim → al-Ḥāmidī, ʿAlī b. Ḥātim
ʿAlī b. Haydar (Ṣafawid) (1494) iii, 316a; iv, 34b; viii, 237b, 766b
ʿAlī b. Ḥazm → Ibn Ḥazm, Abū Muḥammad ʿAlī
ʿAlī b. Ḥirzihim → Ibn Ḥirzihim, ʿAlī
ʿAlī b. Hishām (829) i, 400a; vi, 337b, 338a; s, 116b, 252b
ʿAlī b. Hudhayfa b. Māniʿ (XIII) iv, 87b
ʿAlī b. Ḥudjr (858) vii, 691b
ʿAlī b. Ḥumayd b. ʿAbd Allāh (Tanga) (XX) vi, 963b
ʿAlī b. Ḥusām al-Dīn → al-Muttaḳī
ʿAlī b. Ḥusayn → Sīdī ʿAlī Reʾīs, Sīdī Raʾīs
ʿAlī b. al-Ḥusayn (Kilwa) v, 106b, 1157b
ʿAlī b. al-Ḥusayn, Bey (XVIII) vi, 113a
ʿAlī b. al-Ḥusayn b. Djaʿfar b. Ibrāhīm al-Walīd (1159) vii, 411a
ʿAlī b. al-Ḥusayn b. al-Muslima → Ibn al-Muslima
ʿAlī b. Ḥusayn Zayn al-ʿĀbidīn → Zayn al-ʿĀbidīn
ʿAlī b. al-Ḥusayn b. ʿAbd al-ʿAlī al-Karakī → al-Muḥaḳḳiḳ al-Thānī
ʿAlī b. al-Ḥusayn b. ʿAlī (Hāshimid) (XX) ii, 572b; iii, 263b, 606b, 1067a
ʿAlī b. al-Ḥusayn b. ʿAlī b. Abī Ṭālib (VII) iii, 227b, 610a, b
ʿAlī b. Ḥusayn b. Ḥusayn b. ʿAlī al-Ḳurashī (1284) s, **62a**
ʿAlī b. Ḥusayn b. Idrīs (dāʿī muṭlaḳ) (XVI) s, 358b
ʿAlī b. al-Ikhshīd (X) iv, 418a
ʿAlī b. ʿĪsā b. Dāʾūd b. al-Djarrāḥ (vizier) (946) i, **386b**, 1046b, 1223b; ii, 79b, 195a, 197b, 325a, b, 383a, 388b, 453a, 1080b; iii, 100b, 133a, 153a, 619b, 692a, 739a, 886b, 949a; v, 319b, 953a; vi, 498a; vii, 542b, 1031a; s, 199a, 400b, 402a
ʿAlī b. ʿĪsā b. Māhān → Ibn Māhān
ʿAlī b. ʿĪsā b. Maymūn (Ḳādis) iv, 383b
ʿAlī b. ʿĪsā al-Ḥarrānī (843) vi, 600a
ʿAlī b. ʿĪsā al-Kaḥḥāl (XI) i, **388a**, 449a, 785b
ʿAlī b. Isḥāḳ b. Ghāniya (1188) ii, 1007a, b; iv, 614a; vi, 457a
ʿAlī b. al-Ḳāḍī al-Nuʿmān (al-Azhar) (X) i, 816a
ʿAlī b. Kamāl al-Dīn, Sayyid (Marʿashī) (1400) vi, 512b, 513a, 516a
ʿAlī b. Ḳara ʿUthmān (Aḳ-Ḳirmān) (XV) i, 311b, 312a
ʿAlī b. Karmākh (XII) vii, 549b
ʿAlī b. al-Karmānī (VIII) iii, 988b
ʿAlī b. Ḳawām al-Dīn al-Marʿashī (1405) vi, 512b, 513a
ʿAlī b. Khalaf (1063) vi, 423b, 543a; viii, 537b
ʿAlī b. Khalīl (XV) iv, 221b
ʿAlī b. Khashram (872) i, 1244a
ʿAlī b. Khurshīd (Daylamī) (X) i, 688a
ʿAlī b. Mahdī → Mahdids
ʿAlī b. Masʿūd I (Ghaznawid) (1049) ii, 1051b
ʿAlī b. Maʿṣūm → ʿAlī Khān
ʿAlī b. Maymūn (1511) i, **388b**; v, 625a
ʿAlī b. Mazyad (XI) i, 684a; vii, 497a; s, 119a
ʿAlī b. Muʾayyid (1384) vi, 13a
ʿAlī b. Mubārakshāh (XV) x, 53b
ʿAlī b. Mudjāhid al-ʿĀmirī Iḳbāl al-Dawla (1076) i, 1055a; ii, 112a; iii, 542b, 773a; vi, 926b; vii, 292b, 293a; viii, 880b
ʿAlī b. Mudjaththil al-Mughaydī (XIX) i, 709b
ʿAlī b. Muḥammad → Ṣulayḥids
ʿAlī b. Muḥammad b. ʿAbd Allāh b. al-Ḥasan (VIII) vii, 389a
ʿAlī b. Muḥammad b. Barrī (1339) vii, 622a
ʿAlī b. Muḥammad b. Djaʿfar al-Ḳurashī (1215) s, **62a**
ʿAlī b. Muḥammad b. Tawba, ḳāḍī (XI) i, 130b

ʿAlī b. Muḥammad b. al-Walīd (dāʿī muṭlaḳ) (1215) iv, 200b; s, 61b
ʿAlī b. Muḥammad al-Ḳūshdjī (1474) i, **393a**; vi, 601b, 980a
ʿAlī b. Muḥammad al-Sāmarrī (IX) vii, 443b
ʿAlī b. Muḥammad Sharīf (Wadāī) (1874) xi, 11b
ʿAlī b. Muḥammad al-Ṣulayḥī (dāʿī) (XI) i, 181b; ii, 517a; iii, 862b; vii, 732a
ʿAlī b. Muḥammad al-Tūnisī al-Iyādī (976) s, **62b**
ʿAlī b. Muḥammad al-Zandjī (883) i, **388b**, 551a, 942a, 1096a; vii, 526a; s, 49a
ʿAlī b. Muḳarrab (ʿUyūnid) i, 74a
ʿAlī b. Mūsā iii, 1114a
ʿAlī b. Mūsā al-Kāẓim (al-Riḍā) (816) vi, 334b, 335a
ʿAlī b. Mūsā al-Riḍā → ʿAlī al-Riḍā
ʿAlī b. Nāṣir Abu ʾl-Ḥārithī (XIX) s, 355b
ʿAlī b. Rabāḥ b. Djanbulāt (1712) ii, 443b
ʿAlī b. Rabban al-Ṭabarī → al-Ṭabarī
ʿAlī b. Rashīd b. Muḥammad (Mandīl) (1351) vi, 404b
ʿAlī b. Rayṭa (760) vi, 745a
ʿAlī b. Riḍwān viii, 103a
ʿAlī b. Ṣalāḥ al-Dīn (Imām al-Djihād, Yemen) (1436) vii, 996a
ʿAlī b. Ṣāliḥ iv, 505a
ʿAlī b. Ṣāliḥ → Wāsiʿ ʿAlīsi
ʿAlī b. Salmān al-Dāʿī iv, 78a
ʿAlī b. Sayyid Muḥammad b. ʿAlī (XX) i, 277b
ʿAlī b. al-Shāh al-Fārisī iv, 503b
ʿAlī b. Shams al-Dīn (XVI) i, 60a, **389a**
ʿAlī b. Sulaymān al-ʿAnṭakī (X) s, 38a
ʿAlī b. Sulaymān al-Damnātī (XX) ii, 109b
ʿAlī b. Ṭāhir (ʿAdan) (1497) vi, 132b
ʿAlī b. al-Ṭāhir (Djelfa) vi, 254b
ʿAlī b. Ṭaybughā al-Biklimishī (XIV) vi, 543a
ʿAlī b. ʿUbayd Allāh b. Abī Rāfiʿ iii, 1151a
ʿAlī b. ʿUbayd Allāh b. al-Ḥasan (IX) iii, 951a
ʿAlī b. ʿUmar (ḥādjib) (XII) iii, 47a
ʿAlī b. ʿUmrān (Ispahbad) (XI) iv, 100b
ʿAlī b. Wafā iv, 283b
ʿAlī b. Wahsūdān (919) ii, 191b, 192a; iv, 100a; viii, 472a; s, 356b
ʿAlī b. Waṣīf (dāʿī) (X) iv, 662b
ʿAlī b. Yaddar (al-Sūs al-Aḳṣā) ix, 899b
ʿAlī b. Yaḥyā b. Tamīm, amīr (XII) i, 149a; ii, 459a
ʿAlī b. Yaḥyā al-Armanī ix, 678a
ʿAlī b. Yaḥyā al-Munadjdjim (888) ii, 127a; iv, 111a, 1005a; v, 1125a; vi, 625b; s, 17b, 25a
ʿAlī b. Yaḥyā al-Ṣūfī (XV) iv, 1125b
ʿAlī b. Yakhlaf al-Nafūsī (ʿIbāḍī) (XII) iii, 657a
ʿAlī b. Yaḳṭīn (798) vii, 646b
ʿAlī b. Yedder (Idder) (1254) vi, 141b
ʿAlī II b. Yūsuf Pasha (XIX) x, 214b
ʿAlī b. Yūsuf b. Tāshufīn (Almoravid) (1143) i, 78b, **389a**, 495b, 499b, 1347a; ii, 818b, 821b, 838a, 1007a, 1013a; iii, 542b, 712b, 771a, 959a, 977b; iv, 633a; vi, 590b, 591b, 592a, 596b; vii, 247b, 584a, 585b; viii, 690a; s, 397b
ʿAlī b. Yūsuf al-Tūnisī s, 62b
ʿAlī b. Ẓāfir → Ibn Ẓāfir
ʿAlī b. al-Zandjī (X) v, 352b
ʿAlī b. Ziyād (799) viii, 843b
ʿAlī-Ābād vi, 384a
ʿAlī ʿAbd al-Raḥmān al-Ḥusaynī (XX) s, 18a
ʿAlī ʿAbd al-Rāziḳ → ʿAbd al-Rāziḳ
ʿAlī Abū ʿAbbās Sarwānī → ʿAbbās Sarwānī
ʿAlī Abū Ḥassūn (Īligh) (XVII) viii, 440a
ʿAlī ʿAdil-Shāh I (1579) i, 199a, 1047a, 1202b, 1203b, 1323b; iii, 426a, 1161a; v, 938a
ʿAlī ʿAdil-Shāh II (1637) i, 199b; ii, 120b; iii, 119a, 426b; vi, 837a
ʿAlī Agha (Modon) (XIX) vii, 217b
ʿAlī Agha (Pinarhisar) (XIX) iv, 322b
ʿAlī Agha b. Fatḥ ʿAlī Khān, Shaykh (XIX) v, 296b
ʿAlī al-Akbar → ʿAlī b. al-Ḥusayn b. ʿAlī
ʿAlī Akbar Dihkhudā (1956) iv, 71a
ʿAlī Akbar Ḳawām al-Mulk (XIX) s, 336a
ʿAlī Akbar Khān Bahmān (XX) vi, 154b
ʿAlī Akbar Khiṭāʾī (XVI) i, **390b**; ii, 588a
ʿAlī Akbar Ṣābir (1911) i, 194a; iii, 358a
ʿAlī al-Aʿlā, Sayyid (1419) iii, 600b; viii, 8b
ʿAlī al-Amīn (XV) s, 399a
ʿAlī Amīrī (1923) i, **391a**
ʿAlī Āmulī → ʿAlī b. Ḳawām al-Dīn al-Marʿashī
ʿAlī al-ʿArabī Ilyās (XVI) i, 776b

ʿAlī al-Aʿradj (XVIII) i, 47b
ʿAli Ardobus Ibrahim (1959) vi, 768b
ʿAlī al-Asʿad, Pasha (XIX) s, 162b
ʿAlī al-Armanī, amīr (863) i, 638b; ii, 235a
ʿAlī Aṣghar Khān Amīn al-Sulṭān, Mīrzā (1907) ii, 418a, 435a, 652a; iv, 394a, 979b; vii, 1004b; s, 365a
ʿAlī al-Ashrafī al-Akhlāṭī, Ḥādjib (1226) vi, 505a
ʿAli Askar Askar-Oghlï (XX) vi, 769a
ʿAlī al-Aswārī (1193) vi, 636b
ʿAlī ʿAzīz Efendi Giridli (1798) i, **391a**; iii, 375a
Ali Baba → Alf Layla wa-Layla
ʿAlī al-Baghdādī (XVIII) vi, 249b
ʿAlī Bār, Ḥādjib (1119) vi, 64a
ʿAlī Barīd Shāh (1579) i, 1047a, 1200a, b; iii, 426a; v, 1215b
ʿAlī Beg (Aḳ-Ḳoyunlu) (1439) vi, 541a
ʿAlī Beg (Turkman) (XIII) i, 243b; ii, 204b
ʿAlī Beg, Ḥādjdjī → Idrīs (the hidden)
ʿAlī Beg b. ʿAlāʾ al-Dīn (Ḳarāmānid) (XIV) iv, 623a, b
ʿAlī Beg b. Shahsuwār (Dhu ʾl-Ḳadrlï) (1515) ii, 240a; vi, 508a, 510a
ʿAlī Beg Hersek-zāde (XVI) iii, 342a
ʿAlī Beg Ḳarāmān-oghlu (XIII) iv, 620a
ʿAlī Ber → Sonni ʿAlī
ʿAlī Bey (Bulūṭ Ḳāpān) (1773) i, **391b**, 728b; ii, 233b; iii, 158a, 300a; iv, 723a, 852b, 853a; vi, 325b; vii, 420b, 709b; s, 20b, 268a
ʿAlī Bey (Ḥusaynid) (1756) iii, 605a, 635b
ʿAlī Bey (Ḥusaynid) (1782) iii, 636a
ʿAlī Bey (Ḥusaynid) (1902) iii, 636b
ʿAlī Bey (Miṣr) (1773) vii, 179a
ʿAlī Bey (Trabzon) (1878) vi, 373a, 759a
ʿAlī Bey, Amīr (Mombasa) (1589) v, 105a; vi, 128b, 129a; vii, 226a
ʿAlī Bey al-ʿAbbāsī (1818) i, **392a**
ʿAlī Bey Eretna-oghlu → Eretna
ʿAlī Bey Evrenos-zāde (XV) ii, 703a, 721a
ʿAlī Bey Mikhāl-oghlu (XVII) i, 340b
ʿAlī Birādarān (XX) vii, 421b
ʿAlī al-Bisṭāmī (1462) vi, 71a
ʿAlī Burghul (Bulghūr) (XVIII) ii, 460a; iv, 617b
ʿAlī Čelebī → Wāsiʿ ʿAlīsi
ʿAlī Čelebī → ʿAlī, Muṣṭafā b. Aḥmad Čelebī; Ḳinalizāde ʿAlāʾ ʾl-Dīn ʿAlī
ʿAlī Dāya (1033) vi, 522b, 523a
ʿAlī Dede, Pīr (1528) vi, 226b, 228a
ʿAlī Dede al-Bosnawī (1598) i, 759a
ʿAlī Diara (XIX) iii, 39a
ʿAlī Dīnār (1916) ii, 124a, 125a
ʿAlī Djāh, Niẓām (Ḥaydarābād) (1803) iii, 322a
ʿAlī Djamālī → Djamālī
ʿAlī Djānbūlād (1605) vi, 343b
ʿAlī Djanbulāṭ (1778) ii, 443b
ʿAlī Djānib (XX) vi, 93b, 94a
ʿĀlī Efendi → ʿĀlī ʿAzīz
ʿAlī Ekber → ʿAlī Akbar Ṣābir
ʿAlī Emīrī (1924) vi, 542b; s, **63a**
ʿAlī Fethi (Okyar) → Okyar, ʿAlī Fethi
ʿAlī Fuʾād Cebesoy (XX) ii, 700b
ʿAlī al-Hādī → al-ʿAskarī, Abu ʾl-Ḥasan ʿAlī al-Naḳī / al-Hādī
ʿAlī Ḥāfiẓ (XX) v, 1005b
ʿAli Haji ibni Raja Ahmad (1870) vi, 237a
ʿAlī Ḥakīm-Ilāhī, Āḳā (XIX) s, 24a
ʿAlī al-Hamadānī (1385) i, 347b, **392b**, 1004b; ii, 967a; iv, 708a; v, 301a; vii, 988a; x, 251a; s, 364b
ʿAlī Ḥarāzim b. al-ʿArabī Barāda (XVIII) x, 464a
ʿAlī Ḥarfūsh (XVI) ii, 750a
ʿAlī Ḥazīn, Shaykh → Ḥazīn, Muḥammad ʿAlī b. Abī Ṭālib
ʿAlī Hüseynzāde (XX) vi, 94a
ʿAlī Ibn Ashkīlūlā (XIII) vii, 1021a
ʿAlī-Ilāhī i, 225b, 260a, **392b**; ii, 106b
ʿAlī Ḳapu (Iṣfahān) vi, 17a
ʿAlī Ḳarabāsh (1685) i, 965b; iv, 991b
ʿAlī al-Karakī (1534) x, 936a
ʿAlī al-Ḳārī (1605) i, 1235b; ii, 500b; iii, 29a, 711a; v, 1235a, b; x, 916a
ʿAlī Ḳarīb b. Il-Arslan, ḥādjib (XI) iii, 47a; vii, 407a
ʿAlī al-Kassār ii, 39b
ʿAlī Kathīr, Banū ix, 898b
ʿAlī Kemāl Bey (XX) ii, 474b; iii, 595a; iv, 636a; vi, 94b
ʿAlī Khwādja (Djand) (XIII) s, 246a
ʿAlī Khān → Mahdī ʿAlī Khān; Sayyid ʿAlī Khān
ʿAlī Khān (Oghuzz) (XI) vi, 416a
ʿAlī Khān, Ḥādjdjī Mīrzā (1936) vi, 86b
ʿAlī Khān, Nawwāb (1858) vi, 77b
ʿAlī Khān, Shaykh (1666) vi, 526a

ʿAlī Khān b. Agha Khān (XX) i, 246b
ʿAlī Khān b. Dawlat Khān (Pandjāb) (XVI) ii, 47b
ʿAlī Khān b. Ḥusayn Khān Bayat (1865) vi, 203a
ʿAlī Khān Amīn al-Dawla, Mīrzā (1848) vi, 291b
ʿAlī Khān Amīn al-Dawla, Mīrzā (1904) vii, 1004b
ʿAlī Khān al-Madanī (1705) i, **392b**
ʿAlī Khān al-Marāghī, Ḥādjdjī (XIX) vii, 440a
ʿAlī Khān Nuṣrat al-Mulk Ḳara Güzlü (1797) vi, 484a
ʿAlī Khān Türe (1947) ix, 650a
ʿAlī Khān Ẓahīr al-Dawla → Ẓahīr al-Dawla
ʿAlī Khān Zangana, Shaykh (XVII) v, 169b
ʿAlī al-Khaznī (1909) vi, 750a
ʿAlī Khūrshīd, Fāshōda (XIX) ii, 828a
ʿAlī Khwīshāwand → ʿAlī Ḳarīb
ʿAlī Kiyā b. Iskandar-i Shaykhī (Marʿashī) (1402) i, 237b; v, 603a; vi, 512b
ʿAlī Kiyā b. Sayyid Muḥammad (Marʿashī) (1476) vi, 514a, b, 515b
ʿAlī Kolen Sonnī (Gao) (XIV) ii, 977a
ʿAlī Kücük, Zayn al-Dīn b. Begtegin (XII) i, 1160b; ii, 347b; iv, 76a
ʿAlī Ḳulī Khān (Bareilly) (XVII) i, 1042b
ʿAlī Ḳulī Khān Afshār → ʿĀdil Shāh Afshār
ʿAlī-ḳulī Khān Bakhtīyārī s, 291a
ʿAlī Ḳulī Khān Istadjlū (Shīr Afkan) (1607) ii, 380b; s, 366b
ʿAlī Ḳulī Khān Khān-i Zamān (XVI) ii, 498b; s, 325a
ʿAlī Ḳulī Khān Shāmlū (XVI) i, 7b
ʿAlī Ḳulī Khān Wālih (XVIII) vii, 530b
ʿAlī Ḳulī Ṣafarov → Ṣafarov, ʿAlī Ḳulī
ʿAlī Kūra (XVIII) vi, 249b
ʿAlī Kurdī Ḳazwīnī, Mawlānā vii, 935a; s, 51b
ʿAlī al-Ḳūshdjī (1474) i, **393a**, 776b; ii, 588a; viii, 541b, 542a
ʿAlī Mahdī Muḥammad (Somalia) ix, 721a
ʿAlī Māhir (XX) iii, 516a; s, 6b, 300a, b, 301a, b, **557b**
ʿAlī Mardān i, **393b**
ʿAlī Mardān Khaldjī (1213) i, **393b**; vi, 244b; vii, 433a
ʿAlī Mardān Khān (Ḳandahār) (1657) i, 228b, 1347b; iv, 666a; v, 886a; vii, 318a, b, 333a, 632a; s, **63a**
ʿAlī Mardān Khān Bakhtiyarī (XVIII) i, **393b**; ii, 311a; iii, 1103a; iv, 104b, 639b; v, 825b
ʿAlī Mardān Khān Faylī (XVIII) v, 825a
ʿAlī Mardān Khān Shāmlū (XVIII) i, 393b
ʿAlī Mīkālī (1032) vi, 522b
ʿAlī Mīrzā Ẓill al-Sulṭān (Ḳādjār) (XIX) vii, 453b
ʿAlī Mubārak Pasha vi, 412a
ʿAlī al-Mudjāhid (Rasūlid) i, 181b
ʿAlī al-Mudjāshiʿī al-Farazdaḳī (1086) vi, 913a
ʿAlī Muftī (XX) vi, 165b
ʿAlī Mughāyat Shāh (Atjèh) (1530) i, 742b; ii, 1220a
ʿAlī Muḥammad Khān (Rohilla) (1749) i, 1042b; iii, 59b, 60a; vii, 316a, 457b; viii, 426a, 572a, b
ʿAlī Muḥammad Mukhliṣ i, 1123b
ʿAlī Muḥammad Shīrāzī → Bābī, ʿAlī Muḥammad
ʿAlī Murād Khān (Zand) (XVIII) vii, 674b
ʿAlī Murād Mamīwand Khān (XVIII) v, 825a, b
ʿAlī Murād, Mīr (1894) iv, 1160a
ʿAlī Mushtāḳ, Mīr Sayyid (1757) v, 834b
ʿAlī al-Muttaḳī → al-Muttaḳī al-Hindī
ʿAlī al-Naḳī → al-ʿAskarī, Abu 'l-Ḥasan ʿAlī
ʿAlīNāṣirMuḥammad(Yemen)(XX) xi,275b
ʿAlī Nawrūz → Ḥasan Muḳaddam
ʿAlī Nūr al-Dīn al-Yashruṭī (1891) xi, 298b
ʿAlī Nūrī, Mullā (1830) viii, 695a
ʿAlī Pasha → Djanbulāt-oghlū; Djānīkli; Ferah; Hādjdji; Kemānkesh; Muʿadhdhinzāde
ʿAlī Pasha (Baghdād) (1764) i, 199a, 905a
ʿAlī Pasha I (Ḥusaynid) xi, 145b
ʿAlī Pasha b. Afrāsiyāb (Baṣra) (1652) i, 236b, 1087a; vi, 112a; vii, 673b
ʿAlī Pasha ʿArabadji (1693) i, 268a, **394a**, 558a
ʿAlī Pasha Čāndārli-zāde (1407) i, **394a**, 1303a; ii, 444b, 611a; vii, 594a; viii, 35b
ʿAlī Pasha Čorlulu (1711) i, 56a, 268b, 269a, **394b**; ii, 1091a; iv, 233b
ʿAlī Pasha Dāmād (1716) i, 268b, 269a, **395a**; iii, 1002a; iv, 969a; vii, 905b

ʿAlī Pasha Güzeldje (1621) i, **395a**; iv, 572a; viii, 182a
ʿAlī Pasha Ḥakīm-oghlu (1758) i, 174b, **395b**, 1018a, 1267b; iv, 437b, 544a, 861b; s, 268a
ʿAlī Pasha Ḳaramānlì (1793) iv, 617b, 618a
ʿAlī Pasha Khādim (1511) i, **396a**, 1120b, 1207b; iv, 231a, 1093a; v, 269a, b; vi, 72b, 1026a
ʿAlī Pasha Moldowandji (XVIII) vii, 709a
ʿAlī Pasha Mubārak (1893) i, 168a, **396a**, 596b; ii, 131b, 167a, 892a; v, 22b, 909a; vi, 602a, b; s, 369a
ʿAlī Pasha Muḥammad Amīn (1870) i, 298b, **396b**; ii, 642a, 934b, 996b; iii, 357a, 1187b, 1188a; vi, 758a, 759a
ʿAlī Pasha Rizvanbegovič → Riḍwān Begovič
ʿAlī Pasha Semiz (1565) i, 291b, **398a**, 843b
ʿAlī Pasha Silāḥdār (XIX) iii, 628b
ʿAlī Pasha Sürmeli (1695) i, 268a, **398a**
ʿAlī Pasha Tepedelenlì (1822) i, **398b**, 653a, 657a; ii, 708b; iii, 91a, 628a; iv, 588b, 589a, 656b; v, 727b, 773b; vi, 58b; vii, 240b, 719b
Āli Rādjās Kannanūr iv, 547a
ʿAlī Razmārā (XX) vii, 654b; s, 158a
ʿAlī Reʾīs b. Ḥüseyn ii, 588b, 589a
ʿAlī al-Riḍā, Abu 'l-Ḥasan b. Mūsā b. Djaʿfar (Imām) (818) i, **399b**, 402b, 551a, 1250a; ii, 248b, 731b; iii, 1169b; iv, 17a, 45b; v, 59a; vi, 510b, 613b, 713b, 714a, 958b; vii, 396b, 450b, 605a; s, 127b, 604b
ʿAlī Riḍā b. Ḥādjdjī Ibrāhīm Khān (XIX) s, 336a
ʿAlī Riḍā b. Riḍā Khān (1954) vii, 447a
ʿAlī Riḍā-i ʿAbbāsī (XVII) i, **400b**; iv, 1124a
ʿAlī Riḍā Pasha (1919) ii, 813a; iv, 296b; vi, 984b
ʿAlī Riḍā Tabrīzī (XVI) viii, 788a, 789a
ʿAlī al-Ṣanhādjī (XVI) xi, 112b
ʿAlī Sārī → ʿAlī b. Kamāl al-Dīn
ʿAlī Shafīḳ Özdemir v, 145a
ʿAlī Shāh → Agha Khān II; ʿAlī ʿAdil-Shāh; ʿAlī Barīd Shāh; Wādjid ʿAlī Shāh
ʿAlī Shāh (vizier) (XIV) i, 627a; iii, 1122b
ʿĀlī Shāh Čak (1578) s, 131b, 167a
ʿAlī Shahīd Pīr (Bīdjāpūr) i, 1203b
ʿAlī Shanẓūra (Mūrītāniyā) (1727) vii, 614b
ʿAlī Shanẓūra b. Haddī, amīr (Mūrītāniyā) (1757) vii, 624b
ʿAlī Shaʿrāwī (XX) iii, 516a
ʿAlī Sharīʿatī (1977) vii, 762b
ʿAlī al-Sharīf, Mawlāy vii, 392b; s, 114a
ʿAlī Sharmarke (Zaylaʿ) (XIX) i, 1172b
ʿAlī Shēr Ḳāniʿ → Ḳāniʿ
ʿAlī Shīr Beg → Mīr ʿAlī Shīr Hawāʾī
ʿAlī Shīr Khān (Baltistān) (XVI) i, 1004b
ʿAlī Shīr Khurd Abū Malik Mughīth (XIV) vi, 272a
ʿAlī Shīr Nawāʾī → Mīr ʿAlī Shīr Nawāʾī
ʿAlī Shukr Beg (Bayram Khān) i, 1135a
ʿAlī Suʿāwī (XIX) ii, 473b, 474a; vi, 92b; vii, 599b
ʿAlī al-Ṣulayḥī (1081) vii, 861a, 996a
ʿAlī al-Ṭawīl (XII) i, 161b
ʿAlī Tegīn (ʿAlītigin) (Ilek-khān) i, 424b, 662a; ii, 4b; iii, 1114a; v, 76a; vi, 66a; s, 176b
ʿAlī Wāsiʿ → Wāsiʿ ʿAlīsī (ʿAlī b. Ṣāliḥ)
ʿAlī Werdī Khān (1756) i, **400b**; ii, 371a
ʿAlī Yakan (XX) vii, 713b
ʿAlī Yūsuf, Shaykh (1913) ii, 466b; iii, 516a; viii, 699a; s, 121b
ʿAlī al-Zaḳḳāḳ → al-Zaḳḳāk
ʿAlī-ābād iv, 1015a
ʿAlibek Aldamov ii, 18a
Alicante → Laḳant
Alidada → Asṭurlāb
ʿAlids i, 45b, 48b, 73b, 103a, b, 125b, 143a, 149a, 290b, **400b**, 550b, 688a, 713a, 1035b, 1352a; ii, 168b, 191a, 192b, 851b; iii, 22a, 242a, 616a, 753a, 984b; iv, 88b; v, 1238b; vi, 627b, 669b, 938b
Alif → Hidjāʾ
Aligarh i, 288a, **403a**, 1300a; ii, 97a, 132b, 426b; v, 283a; vi, 78a, 368b, 461b, 488b, 489a, 503b; viii, 241a; s, 4b, 106b, 247a
– movement iii, 433a; iv, 793a; vi, 612a; s, 74a, 107b, 247a
– university ii, 426b
ʿAliḳīn vi, 547b
ʿAlīkozāy, Banū ii, 629a
Alilat → al-Lāt
ʿĀlim → ʿUlamāʾ
ʿĀlim, Mīr (Bukhārā) (XX) i, 1296a; ii, 700b
ʿĀlima i, **403b**; ii, 1029b, 1048b
Alimtu i, 419a

ʿĀlim Allāh, Shaykh (XIX) s, 247a
ʿĀlim Khān (Khōḳand) (XIX) iv, 631b; v, 29b
ʿAlīnagar ii, 7a
Alindjaḳ i, **404a**; v. 491b
Aliou Faye, Cheikh (XX) vi, 705b
Alip-manash → Alpamïsh
ʿAlishāh b. Būka Awbahī (XV) vii, 685a
Alīsaʿ b. Ukhṭūb (Elisha) i, **404a**
ʿAlīshānzāde Ismāʿīl Ḥaḳḳi → Ismāʿīl Ḥaḳḳī Pasha
Alīṭ (Aledo) i, 7a, 43b; iii, 904b; iv, 672b; vii, 767b, 775b
ʿAlītigin → ʿAlī Tegīn
Aliwāl Khān i, 1209b
ʿAlīwiyya (Mostghanem) ii, 224b
ʿĀliya vi, 28a
ʿAlīzāy (Mahsūd), Banū ii, 629a; vi, 86a
Aljamía i, **207a**, **404b**, 502b; iv, 317a; vii, 243a; s, 81a, 397a
Aljamiado → Aljamía
Aljarafe → al-Sharaf
ʿAlḳa → ʿUḳūba
ʿAlḳama (VII) vii, 258b
ʿAlḳama b. ʿAbada al-Tamīmī (VI) i, **405b**; iii, 1177b; iv, 998b, 1087b
ʿAlḳama b. Dhī Djadan (al-Mathāmina) vi, 830b; viii, 979b, 980a
ʿAlḳama b. Ṣafwān b. Umayya ix, 440b
ʿAlḳama b. ʿUlātha (VII) i, 441b, 442a, 690a
al-ʿAlḳamī i, **405b**
Alkanna → al-Ḥinnāʾ
Alḳāṣ Mīrzā (Ṣafawid) (1549) i, **406a**; viii, 73a
Alkendi → al-Ḳindī, Abū Yūsuf Yaʿḳūb
All-India Muslim League v, 779b, 780a, 1080b; vii, 678b; viii, 241a; s, 4b
ʿAllāf b. Ḥassān (XI) ii, 484a, b
al-ʿAllāf, Isḥāḳ b. Wahb b. Ziyād (869) viii, 14a
Allāh i, 275a, 333a, 349b, **406a**, 773b, 776a; ii, 96a, 220b, 396a, 449a, 493b, 518a, 554a, 593b, 772b, 898b; iii, 28b, 82b, 497a, 870b, 917b, 1093b, 1196a; v, 3b, 411b
al-Allaḥ b. ʿAbd al-Wahhāb, Imām Aflaḥ (Rustamid) (872) ii, 441b; iii, 655a; vi, 841a; vii, 895a; viii, 639a; x, 100a
Allāh b. Sulaymān (ʿAzdī) (868) vi, 900a
Allāh Akbar → Takbīr
Allāh Ḳulī Beg (XI) iv, 808a
Allāh Ḳulī Khān (Gakkhar) (1705) ii, 973b; vii, 574b
Allāh Ḳulī Khān (Khīwa) (1842) iv, 1065a; vii, 574b; s, 46a, 228a
Allah Temple of Islam vii, 702b
Allāh Yār Kattaḳur Ghānī, Ṣūfī (1723) x, 65a
Allāh Yār Khān Āṣaf al-Dawla (XIX) vii, 454a
Allāh Yār Thānī → Murtaḍā Ḥusayn
Allāhābād i, **417b**; ii, 426a; v, 1218b; s, 325b
Allāhdād, Mawlānā (1582) s, 74a
Allāhumma i, **418a**
Allāhwardī (Allāh Wirdī) Khān (1613) i, 8a; ii, 1091b; iii, 585b; v, 672b, 825a; vii, 547b
ʿAllāḳa (X) ii, 483b; iii, 77a
al-ʿAllāḳī, wādī i, **418a**; ii, 214a; iv, 567b, 965b, 967a; viii, 90b, 863a
ʿAllāl al-Fāsī (1974) vii, 416a; s, **63b**
ʿAllaliyyīn s, 350b
ʿAllālū (XX) vi, 752a,b, 754b
ʿAllama Kamāl al-Dīn (Čishtiyya) (XIV) ii, 54a
ʿAllāma-i Ḥillī → al-Ḥillī, Djamāl al-Dīn Ḥasan
ʿAllāmī → Abu ʾl-Faḍl ʿAllāmī
ʿAllāmī, Shaykh → Abu ʾl-Faḍl ʿAllāmī
Allān → Alān
ʿAllān al-Warrāḳ al-Shuʿūbī (IX) vi, 829a
Allāt → al-Lāt
ʿAllawayh al-Aʿsar (850) i, 160a; s, 17b, **64a**
Allidina Visram (1916) x, 781a
ʿAllūya → ʿAllawayh
ʿAlma → ʿĀlima
Alma Ata i, **418b**; vi, 769b
Alma-dagh → Elma-dagh
Almada, almaden → al-Maʿdin
Almadia (raft) → Safīna
Almagest → Baṭlamiyūs
Almaḳah vi, 561a, 562a, b
Almalïgh i, **418b**; iii, 1120b; v, 858b; ix, 621b; s, 240a
Almanac → Anwāʾ; Taʾrīkh
Almani Omar (Fūta Djallon) (1872) ii, 960a
Almanon → al-Maʾmūn b. Hārūn al-Rashīd (ʿAbbāsid)
Almanzor → al-Manṣūr bi-ʾllāh

Almās i, **419a**; v, 353b, 550a, 965a
Almās Beg Ulugh Khān → Ulugh Khān
Almee → ʿĀlima
Almeria → al-Mariyya
Almicantarat → Muḳanṭarāt
Almodovar → al-Mudawwar
Almogávares i, **419b**
Almohads → al-Muwaḥḥidūn
Almoravids → al-Murābiṭūn
Almuñecar → al-Munakkab
Alodia → ʿAlwa
Alōr s, 163a
Alp i, **419b**
Alp Arghūn, Shams al-Dīn (Atabeg) (1271) iii, 1100a; v, 826b; vi, 494b
Alp Arslān, ʿAḍud al-Dawla Abū Shudjāʿ (Saldjūḳ) (1072) i, 329a, **420a**, 465b, 507b, 510a, 660b, 731a, 1041b, 1051b. 1336b; ii, 5a, 340a, 347b, 856a; iii, 86b, 196a, 197a, 471b, 1098b; iv, 27a, 291b, 347b, 348a, 458a, 807b, 840a; v, 388a, 489a; vi, 242b, 243a, 273b, 275a, 379b, 524a; vii, 120b, 693a; viii, 69b, 70a, 941a; s, 14b, 65a, 245b
Alp Arslān b. Rigwān (Saldjūḳ) (1113) viii, 947b
Alp Khān (1316) ii, 695a, 1124a; iv, 419a; s, 105b
Alp Khān b. Dilāwar → Hūshang Shāh Ghūrī
Alp Ḳush Kūn-i Khar (XII) i, 865b
Alp Takīn (Alp Tigin) (Fāṭimid vizier) (979) i, 823b, 824a; ii, 483a, 854a; iii, 246a, 841a; iv, 663b
Alp Takīn (Alp Tigin) (Ghaznawid) (963) i, 226b, **421b**, 984b; ii, 1049a; iii, 46b; iv, 24a; vi, 65a, 433a
Alp Tigin → Alp Takīn
Alp Yörük → Ḥusām al-Dīn Alp Yörük
Alpamïsh i, **421b**; iii, 116a
Alpetragius → al-Biṭrūdjī
Alphabet → al-Hidjaʾ, Ḥurūf-
Alpharas → Nudjūm
Alphonso → Alfūnsho
Alpī b. Timurtash (Artuḳid) (1176) i, 664b; iii, 1119a, b
Alptakīn Bakdjur, amīr (X) iii, 398a
Alpuente → al-Bunt
Alpujarras → al-Busharrāt
Alruccaba → Rukba
Alsh i, **422b**, 492a; s, 144b
Alṭāf Ḥusayn Ḥālī (1914) vi, 838a; vii, 662a, 668a; ix, 433b
Altai(ï) i, **422b**
Altaians i, **423a**; iii, 115a
Altair → Nudjūm
Altamġa, Āltamgha ii, 14b, 157b
Altamish → Iltutmish
ʿAlth i, **423a**
Altï Parmak (1623) i, **423b**
Altï Shahr (1623) i, **423b**
Altïlïk → Sikka
Altïn i, **423b**
Altïn Köprü i, **424a**
Altïn Ordu i, **424a**; iv, 280b
Altïntash, (Anatolia) i, **424a**
Altïntash (Salkhad) (XII) viii, 128a
Altïntash, Tādj al-Dīn b. Masʿūd II (Rūm Saldjūḳ) (XIV) i, 431b
Altïshahr s, 522b, 523a
Altun Djan (1063) vi, 482a
Alṭūniya → Malik Alṭūniya
Altūntāsh al-Ḥādjib, Abū Saʿīd (Khwārizm-Shāh) (1032) i, 278a, **424b**; iv, 1066b; vi, 780b; s, 176b
Aludel → al-ʿUthāl
Alughu Khān i, 1188a; ii, 3a, b; v, 38b
ʿAlūk → al-Djinn
Alula (Somalia) ix, 715b
Alus, Sermed Mukhtār (1952) s, **64b**
al-Ālūsī, Āl i, **425a**
al-Ālūsī, Abu ʾl-Thanāʾ (1853) i, **425a**; vi, 113a
al-Ālūsī, Maḥmūd Shukrī (1924) i, **425b**, 596b vi, 614a
Alvand Dīv (1596) vi, 515a, b
ʿAlwa i, **425b**; viii, 89a, b, 91a; ix, 698a
ʿAlwa bint Zurayḳa i, 1289b
Alwāḥ → Lawḥ
Alwand → Aḳ-Ḳoyunlu
Alwand b. Yūsuf b. Uzun Ḥasan (Aḳ-Ḳoyunlu) (1504) i, 311b, 312a; ii, 937a; iv, 186b, 1048b; viii, 767a
Alwand Kūh i, **426a**
Alwār i, **426b**
Ama → ʿAbd
al-Aʿmā al-Tuṭīlī (1130) i, **426b**, 595b, 602a; iii, 729b; vii, 811b
Amad, Banū i, 1078a
ʿAmādiya i, **426b**; v, 460a

Amādjūr, Banū iii, 1137a; vi, 600b
Amādjūr, ibn al-Athīr (Govenor of Palestine) (IX) i, 278b; iv, 89b;
Amadou Ḥamā Allāh Ḥaydara → Ḥamā Allāh
Amadu Bamba Mbacké → Ahmad(u) Bamba Mbacké
Amadu Sēku → Aḥmad al-Shaykh
Amagdūl (Mogador) vi, 741b
al-ʿAmāʾid vi, 562a
al-Aʿmāḳ → al-ʿAmḳ
ʿAmʿaḳ, Shihāb al-Dīn Bukhārī (1147) vi, 276b; viii, 971a; s, **64b**
ʿAmal i, 171a, **427a**; ii, 898a
ʿAmala iii, 1106a, b
ʿAmāla (tribe) v, 617a
ʿAmāla i, 439a;
Amālī → Tadrīs
ʿAmālīḳ i, **429a**; ii, 917a; iii, 1270a; v, 994b
Amalric I ii, 318a, b
Amān i, **429a**; ii, 227b, 248a, 303b, 341b, 565a; iii, 197b, 547a, 1179b, 1180a, 1181b, 1182a; v, 179a
Amān, Mīr (XIX) i, **430b**; iii, 376a; v, 201b
Amān Allāh → Afghānistān
Amān Allāh Khān (Kurdistān) (1825) vi, 484a; ix, 6b
Amān Allāh Khān, King (Afghānistān) (1960) i, 232b, 626b; ii, 531b, 657a, 658b; v, 37a, 1079a, b; vi, 86b, 169b, 262a, 768a; vii, 220b, 291a, 355a; s, **65b**, 237b
Amān Allāh b. Khusraw Khān Nā-kām (1867) ix, 6b
Amān al-Mulk (Chitral) (XIX) ii, 30b, 317a
Amānat (1858) i, **430b**
Amānat Khān (Tādj Maḥall) (XVII) vii, 333b
Amānī (Māzandarān) (1651) viii, 776a
Amanos ii, 982a; v, 810b; vi, 778a
Amantnāg iv, 177b
Amanus → Amanos
ʿAmar, Mawlāy (XVI) vi, 1009b
ʿAmāra i, **431a**; s, 179a
ʿAmāra Dūnḳas (Fundj) (1533) ii, 943b, 944a; iv, 892b
ʿAmārāt, Banū i, 483a
Amarkot i, **431a**
al-ʿAmarrada (Muʿāwiya, Banū) vi, 473a
al-Aʿmash, Sulaymān (765) i, 104b, **431b**; ii, 293a; iii, 843a; iv, 1112b; vi, 70b, 740a; vii, 607a; viii, 387a
Amasya i, 12b, **431b**; iii, 215a; iv, 576b, 1159a; vi, 70b, 740a
Amasyalı̊ Meḥmed Efendi → Memek Čelebi
Amasyawī, Maḥmūd b. Adham (XVI) viii, 544b
Amazigh → Berbers
Ambāla i, **432b**, 1348a; s, 203a
Ambēr vi, 601b
Ambassador → Elči, Rasūl
Ambon i, **433a**
Ambra → ʿAnbar
ʿAmda Ṣeyōn (Ṣion) (1344) i, 176b; ii, 175a; iii, 3b
ʿAmdjad ʿAlī Shāh (Nawwāb) (1847) vii, 301a
al-Amdjad Bahrāmshāh → Bahrām Shāh
Āmeddji i, **433a**; ii, 339a
Ameer ʿAlī → Amīr ʿAlī
Amengku Rat I (1677) (Mataram) s, 201a, 607b
Amengku Rat II (1703) Mataram) s, 607b
Amengku Rat III (1708) (Mataram) s, 607b
Amengku Rat IV (1726) (Mataram) s, 607b
Aménokal i, **433b**
Amēthī (Awadh) ii, 558a; vi, 272a
Amghar i, **433b**;
Amghār, Banū vi, 592b; vii, 587a; ix, 507b
Amhūrān vi, 81a
Āmid → Diyār Bakr
ʿAmīd (title) i, **434a**; vi, 275a
ʿAmīd al-Dawla Ibn Djahīr ii, 384a, b
ʿAmīd al-Dīn al-Abzārī al-Anṣārī (1227) i, **434a**
ʿAmīd al-Mulk al-Kundurī → al-Kundurī
Amīd Tūlakī Sūnāmī (XIII) s, **66b**
al-Āmidī (981) i, 154a, b; vi, 438a, 709b; vii, 978b
al-ʿAmīdī, Abū Saʿd Muḥammad b. Aḥmad (1042) vii, 772a; s, 362a
al-Āmidī, ʿAlī b. Abī ʿAlī al-Taghlabī (1233) i, **434b**; iii, 1025a, b; vii, 296b
al-ʿAmīdī, Rukn al-Dīn (1218) i, **434b**
ʿAmīḳ (lake) s, 239a
ʿĀmil (ʿawāmil) i, **436a**
ʿĀmil (ʿummāl) i, 19b, **435a**, 1255a; ii, 118b, 328a; iii, 284a, b; iv, 941a

ʿĀmila, Banū i, **436a**; ii, 573b; v, 632a; vi, 477a; vii, 780a
al-ʿĀmilī, ʿAlī b. Zayn al-Dīn (1557) vi, 550a
al-ʿĀmilī, al-Ḥurr → al-Ḥurr al-ʿĀmilī
al-ʿAmilī, Muḥammad b. Ḥusayn Bahāʾ al-Dīn, Shaykh (1621) i, **436b**; ii, 761a; iv, 725b; v, 872b, 873b; vii, 94a, 132a, 203b, 475b; viii, 778a, 893b; s, 308b
al-ʿĀmilī, Sayyid Aḥmad al-ʿAlawī (1633) vii, 94b
al-ʿĀmilī, Shahīd al-Awwal Muḥammad b. Makkī (1384) vii, 169b; s, 56b
al-ʿĀmilī, Shahīd al-Thānī Zayn al-Dīn → Shāhid al-Dīn
al-ʿĀmilī, Shaykh ʿAlī al-Karakī (1534) vi, 550a, b
Amīn (poet) (1620) vi, 837a
al-Amīn → Abū Ḳubays
Amīn (āmēn) i, **436b**
Amīn (umanā) i, **437a**, 633a, 975b, ii, 105a
Amīn, Ḳāsim → Ḳāsim Amīn
al-Amīn, Muḥammad b. Hārūn al-Rashīd (ʿAbbāsid) (813) i, 18a, 77b, 143b, 160a, **437a**, 897a, 899b, 1034b, 1036a; ii, 235a, 730b, 731a; iii, 231b, 274a, 360a, 618a; iv, 17a, 1091a; vi, 205b, 331a, 333a, b, 379a, 606a, 668b; s, 22b, 116b
Amīn Arslān, amīr (XIX) iii, 593a
al-Amīn Bey (Ḥusaynid), (Tunisia) (XX) i, 1110b; iii, 637a; s, 11a
Amīn b. ʿAḳīl (XX) vi, 177a
al-Amīn b. Ḥamad, Shaykh (XIX) vi, 628b
Amīn al-Dawla → Ibn al-Tilmīdh
Amīn al-Dawla b. Muḥammad Ḥusayn Khān (Iṣfahān) (1834) iv, 104b, 105a, 476a
Amīn al-Ḥusaynī, Muftī (1974) ii, 913b; iv, 961a; v, 336b, 337a; vi, 31b, 388b; vii, 765a; viii, 445b; s, **67a**
Amīn Khwādja Khānlïḳ (Lukchun, Turfan) (1760) x, 677a
Amīn Rāzī (XVI) vii, 530a
Amīn al-Sayyād (Demirdāshiyya) s, 209a
Amīn al-Sulṭān (1907) vi, 292a; vii, 432a
Amīn Taḳī al-Dīn (XIX) s, 159b
Amīna (Wife of Solomon) i, **438a**
Amīna Aḳdas (XIX) vi, 484b
Amīna bint Wahb b. ʿAbd Manāf umm Muḥammad (576) i, 42b, 169a, **438a**; iii, 362b; vi, 168b, 621b
Amindivi (Islands) v, 587a; vi, 206b
Amīndjī b. Djalāl b. Ḥasan (1602) s, **70b**
Amīnī, ʿAlī (XX) vii, 447b, 448a
Amīr (title) i, 19b, **438b**, ii, 507b; iii, 45b; iv, 941b, 942a; v, 686a, 1251b
ʿĀmir s, 81b
ʿĀmir, Banū (Beni Amer, Beni Amor) i, 1a, **440b**; ii, 252b, 709a; iii, 6a, 7b; v, 522a
ʿĀmir, Banū (Yamāma) vi, 625a
ʿĀmir I (Ṭāhirid) (1466) i, **440b**; iii, 746a
ʿĀmir II (Ṭāhirid) (1517) i, **441a**; ii, 730a; iii, 746a; v, 807b
ʿĀmir ʿAbd Allāh (ʿAlī) Abu ʾl-Fazārī (X) s, 306a
ʿĀmir (Djaʿda) → Djaʿda (ʿĀmir)
ʿĀmir b. ʿAbd al-Ḳays al-ʿAnbarī (VII) i, **441a**, 960a
ʿĀmir b. ʿAbd al-Wahhāb → ʿĀmir II
ʿĀmir b. Dāwud (Aden) (1538) iv, 901b
ʿĀmir b. Abī Djawshān (929) ix, 363a
ʿĀmir b. Ḍubāra (VII) i, 49a; iii, 802b; iv, 99b, 447a
ʿĀmir b. Fuhayra i, 110a; iii, 366b
ʿĀmir b. Kurayz s, 267b
ʿĀmir b. Luʾayy, Banū iii, 819b; vi, 139a, 145a, 334a, 477b, 543b
ʿĀmir b. Mismaʿ (VII) vi, 640b
ʿĀmir b. Rabīʿa b. ʿUḳayl (Djabrid) s, 234a
ʿĀmir b. Ṣaʿṣaʿa, Banū i, 382b, **441a**, 544b; ii, 72a, 353b, 895b, 1023a; iii, 168b; v, 101b, 526a, 583b, 640b, 954a; vi, 543b, 918a; vii, 373b; s, 178a
ʿĀmir b. Shahr (VII) iii, 123a
ʿĀmir b. Ṭāhir → ʿĀmir I
ʿĀmir b. al-Ṭufayl (630) i, 441b, **442a**, 690a, 1232b; iii, 136b; iv, 1106a
Amīr Aḥmad Khān (Maḥmudābād) (1973) vi, 78b
Amīr Ākhūr i, **442b**; iv, 217b
Āmir ʿAlam Khān (1753) s, 507a
Amīr ʿAlī, Sayyid (1928) i, 38b, **442b**; iii, 431b, 532b; iv, 170b; vi, 461b; s, 73b
Amīr ʿAlī Barīd b. Ḳāsim Barīd (Barīd Shāhīs) (1517) i, 1047a, 1200a; ii, 1135a; iii, 425b, 1159b, 1160a, b; vi, 63b
Amīr ʿAlī Ḥusaynī (1526) vi, 514b
Amīr-i Amīrān (XII) iii, 87a
Amīr Bashkurt (XIV) i, 1075b
al-Āmir bi-Aḥkām Allāh (Fāṭimid) (1130) i, 215b, **440a**, 814b, 1091b; ii, 170b, 857b,

858a, b; iii, 54b; iv, 944a; vi, 143b; vii, 163b
Amīr Bukhārī, Shaykh (XV) vii, 595a
Amīr Dād i, **443b**
Amīr Doladay (Awnik) (XV) iv, 586a, b
Amīr al-Ḥādjdj i, **443b**; iv, 679a
Amīr Ḥamza → Ḥamza b. ʿAbd al-Muṭṭalib
Amīr Ḥasan Khān b. Nawwāb ʿAlī Khān (1858) vi, 77b
ʿAmīr al-Hintātī (1370) iii, 462a
Amīr Hishmat al-Mulk ʿAlam Khān (III) (1891) s, 507b
Amīr Ḥusayn, a(d)miral (XVI) i, 441a; ii, 322a, 1127b; iv, 32b
al-Amīr al-Kabīr i, **444a**; v, 792b
al-Amīr al-Kabīr, Muḥammad (XVIII) s, 411a
Amīr Kabīr, Mīrzā Muḥammad Taḳī Khān (1852) i, 833b; ii, 649b; iii, 554b, 1105b, 1107a; iv, 70b, 394a, 395b, 396b, 398a, 787a, b, 1043a; v, 919a; vi, 20a; vii, 299a, 431b, 1003a; s, **70b**
Amīr Khān (1834) i, 282b, **444a**, 1195b; ii, 567a
Amīr Khān Turkmān (XVI) iii, 157b
Amīr Khusraw Dihlawī (1325) i, **444a**, 1212b, 1329a; ii, 56b, 504a, 794a; iii, 249a, 439a, 453a, 456b, 492a; iv, 66b, 759b, 1010a, 1136a; v, 937b, 1104b; vii, 337b, 340b, 754b; ix, 241b; x, 113b; s, 46b, 105a, 124a
Amīr Kiyāʾīs (Lāhīdjān) s, 363b
Amīr Kulāl (XIV) vii, 933b
Amīr Madjlis i, **445a**
Amīr Masʿūd → Masʿūd I b. Maḥmūd
Amīr Mīnāʾī (1900) v, 959a, 960b, 962a
Amīr Muḥammad Zamān (Kalāntar) iv, 475b
Amīr Muʿizzī, hidjāʾ iii, 356a
Amīr al-Mulk (Chitral) (XIX) ii, 30b
Amīr al-muʾminīn i, 21b, 79b, 83b, **445a**; ii, 676a
Amīr al-muslimīn i, 79b, **445b**
Amīr Niẓām, Ḥasan ʿAlī Khān (1899) s, **71a**
ʿĀmir Rabīʿa, Banū (ʿUḳayl) i, 942a, b; iv, 664a, b
Amīr Rūḥānī (XIII) iii, 1155b
al-Amīr al-Ṣaghīr, Muḥammad (XIX) s, 411a
Amīr Sayyid Bayan (1294) ix, 623a
Amīr Shāh Ḳāsim Bēglār (1547) iii, 1030a
Amīr Shāhī (Sarbadarid) vii, 442a; ix, 49a
Amīr Shāhī b. ʿAbd al-Karīm (Marʿashī) (1531) vi, 514b, 515a
Amīr silāḥ i, **445b**
Amīr Sulṭān (Bukhāra) (1429) viii, 136b
Amīr Sulṭān Muḥammad (Maklī) (XVII) vi, 190a
Amīr al-umarāʾ i, 19a, 20a, b, **446a**, 899b, 1040a; ii, 507b; v, 622a
Amīr Wālī (Astarābād) (1379) vi, 512a
Amīr Yashbak ii, 172b
Amīr Zayn al-Dīn (Marʿashī) (1562) vi, 516b
Amīra Ḳubād (XVI) i, 1066b
Amīrān, ṣūfī (XIV) i, 195b
Amīrānshāh b. Ḳāwurd (XI) i, 827a
Amīrghaniyya → Mīrghāniyya
ʿĀmirī i, **446a**
al-ʿAmīrī (Meknès) (XIX) vi, 249b
al-ʿĀmirī, Abu ʾl-Ḥasan Muḥammad b. Yūsuf (992) i, 235b; ii, 949a; vi, 351b; s, **72b**
al-ʿĀmirī, ʿĀlī b. ʿAbd al-Ḥadjdj al-Ghazzī (1777) vii, 470a
Amīrī, Muḥammad Ṣādiḳ Adīb al-Mamālik (1917) iv, 71a; vi, 114b; vii, 662a; s, **73a**
Amīr-i Aʿzam Sangsarī (XX) v, 664a
Amīr-i Niẓām → Taḳī Khān, Mīrzā
ʿĀmirids i, 76a, 84b, **446a**; iii, 495b, 743a; vi, 188b, 344b, 432a; vii, 590a
Āmiriyya iii, 54b; iv, 200b, 201a
Amirutzes, George (XV) vi, 69b, 71a
Amizmiz vi, 142a
al-ʿAmḳ i, **446b**; vi, 505b; s, 243a
ʿAmlūḳ, King i, 429a
ʿAmm, Banu ʾl- vi, 920b
al-ʿĀmma wa ʿl-Khāṣṣa → al-Khāṣṣa
ʿAmmān i, **447a**, 975b; vi, 31b, 32a, b, 546a; x, 887a
Amman, Mir → Amān, Mīr
ʿAmmār, Banū i, **448a**; ii, 353b, 568b; vii, 408a; x, 213b
ʿAmmār b. ʿAmr (VIII) iv, 1003b
ʿAmmār b. Yāsir, Abu ʾl-Yaḳẓān (657) i, **448b**, 704b; ii, 846a; iii, 29b, 241a, 874a; vi, 139b, 675b; ix, 554a; s, 354b
ʿAmmār b. Yazīd → Khidāsh
ʿAmmār b. Yāsir (VII) ix, 555a
ʿAmmār al-Baṣrī (IX) vi, 636b; vii, 517b

ʿAmmār al-Khāridjī (865) vii, 413b
ʿAmmār al-Mawṣilī (XI) i, **448b**, 785b
ʿAmmāra bint Ḥamza (VII) ii, 372a,
ʿAmmāriyya i, 371b, **449a**
Ammī → Mūsā b. ʿĪsā
ʿAmmūn, Iskandar s, 159b
ʿAmmūriya i, 154a, **449a**; ii, 237a; vi, 740a, 774b
Amorium → ʿAmmūriya
Amphila Bay vi, 642b
Amr i, 414b, **449b**, 1170a
ʿAmr b. ʿAbd al-Mālik al-Warrāḳ (IX) iv, 1005a
ʿAmr b. Abī Ṣayfī (VII) iv, 821a
ʿAmr b. Abī Sufyān (VII) i, 151a
ʿAmr b.ʿAdī (III) i, **450b**; v, 633a
ʿAmr b. al-Ahtam (676) i, **450b**
ʿAmr b. ʿĀmir al-ʿAzdī (VI) vi, 564b
ʿAmr b. al-ʿĀṣ al-Sahmī (663) i, 111a, 207a, 208b, 383b, 384a, **451a**, 531b, 659b, 812b, 932a, 966a, 1049a, 1098a, 1343b; ii, 306a, 327b, 372a, 625b, 910b, 957b, 1024b, 1056a; iii, 540b, 587a, 889b, 975b; iv, 132b, 424a, 514a, 841b, 1103b; v, 90b, 318a, 799b; vi, 362a, 411a, 452b, 648a, 649a, b, 656a, 666a, 669a, 671a, 672b, 674b, 677a, 740b; vii, 153b, 155b, 265a, 356b, 372b, 393b, 509b, 862b; ix, 554b; x, 816a; s, 157a, 267b
ʿAmr b. ʿAwf, Banū i, 771b; vi, 646b, 649a
ʿAmr b. Bakr al-Tamīmī (VII) iii, 887a, b
ʿAmr b. Bāna (Bānata) → Ibn Bāna
ʿAmr b. Dīnār (742) vii, 398a, 758a
ʿAmr b. Djamīl (VIII) s, 326b
ʿAmr b. al-Djamūḥ (VII) s, 230a
ʿAmr b. al-Djuʿayd iv, 421a
ʿAmr b. al-Ḥadjdjādj al-Zubaydī (VII) iii, 609b, 610b
ʿAmr b. al-Ḥārith (VI) vii, 841a
ʿAmr b. Ḥarmala, Rabīʿa b. Sufyān → Muraḳḳish al-Aṣghar
ʿAmr b. Ḥazm (Nadjrān) (VII) iv, 927b
ʿAmr b. Hind (Lakhmid) (568) i, **451b**, 772a; iii, 226b; v, 633b, 640a; vi, 477a; vii, 563a, 568b, 591b, 763b
ʿAmr b. Ḥurayth al-Makhzūmī (VIII) i, 1242b; vi, 140b; ix, 826a
ʿAmr b. Ḳamīʾa (530) i, **452a**, 963b; iii, 1177b, 1178a; vii, 580b, 581a
ʿAmr b. Ḳiʿās vii, 592a
ʿAmr b. Kirkira (VIII) s, 20b, **73b**
ʿAmr b. Kulthūm (VI) i, **452a**; iii, 222b; iv, 998a; v, 633b; vii, 254b
ʿAmr b. al-Layth (Ṣaffārid) (902) i, 278a, **452b**, 1001a, 1294a; ii, 191b, 553b, 812a, 1048b; iii, 344b, 1202a; iv, 21a, b, 22a, 100a, 188b, 266a, 975a; v, 158a; vi, 661a; vii, 418a, 760a, 777b; viii, 63a, 796a; s, 125b
ʿAmr b. Luḥayy i, **453a**; ii, 572a; iii, 537a; iv, 91b, 421b; v, 76b, 77a, b, 692a; vi, 373b
ʿAmr b. Maʿdīkarib (VII) i, **453a**; viii, 1051b
ʿAmr b. Masʿada (832) i, 279b, **453b**
ʿAmr b. Muḥammad b. al-Ḳāsim (VIII) vi, 439b
ʿAmr b. al-Mundhir III b. Māʾ al-Samāʾ (Lakhmid) vii, 591b
ʿAmr b. al-Nuʿmān (VII) i, 53a, 771b, 1283a; iv, 1187b; v, 995a
ʿAmr b. Saʿd b. Mālik b. Ḍubayʿa → Muraḳḳish al-Aṣghar
ʿAmr b. Saʿīd al-Ashdaḳ (684) i, 58a, 76b, **453b**; ii, 360b; iii, 226b, 271a, 608b; vi, 622a, b
ʿAmr b. Sālim al-Tudjībī (IX) i, 250b; v, 78a, b
ʿAmr b. Shimr s, 233a
ʿAmr b. Shuʿayb b. Muḥammad (736) vii, 576b
ʿAmr b. Sufyān → Abu ʾl-Aʿwar al-Sulamī
ʿAmr b. Tamīm → Tamīm
ʿAmr b. ʿUbayd (761) i, 274a, **454a**; iii, 985a, 1142b; iv, 370b; vi, 458a; vii, 398b, 783a
ʿAmr b. ʿUbayd Allāh al-Aḳṭaʿ (amīr) (863) i, 1103a, b; ii, 234b, 237a, b
ʿAmr b. ʿUmayr b. ʿAwf (VII) s, 355a
ʿAmr b. Umm Iyās i, 1241b
ʿAmr b. Usāma (Lakhmid) vii, 591b
ʿAmr b. al-Zubayr (681) i, 55a, 453b; iii, 970a
ʿAmr al-Ashaddīn x, 173b
ʿAmr al-Ḍāʾīʿ → ʿAmr b. Ḳamīʾa
ʿAmr al-Ḳays b. ʿAmr (IV) i, 526a
ʿAmr Makkī (IX) iii, 100a, 102a
ʿAmr Muzayḳiyāʾ i, 771a
Amram → ʿImrān
al-ʿAmrāwī, Idrīs b. Muḥammad (1878) vii, 391b
al-ʿAmrī → Muḥammad b. ʿUthmān; ʿUthmān b. Saʿīd

al-ʿAmrī, Abū ʿAmr ʿUthmān b. Saʿīd (880) viii, **812a**
al-ʿAmrī, Abū Djaʿfar Muḥammad b. ʿUthmān (917) viii, **812a**
Amrī Shirāzī, Abu 'l-Ḳāsim Muḥammad Ḳūhpāyaʾī (1591) viii, 115b
Amri Abedi (1964) vi, 612b, 613a
Amritsar i, **454a**, 1348a; s, 242a
Amrōhā s, **73b**
Amrōhāʾī, Maṣḥafī (XIX) s, 74a
ʿAmrūn al-Yaḥṣūbī (1007) iv, 289b
ʿAmrūs b. Fatḥ (IX) i, 120b
ʿAmrūs b. Yūsuf (IX) iii, 74a; s, 82a
ʿAms → Nuṣayrīs
Āmūū Daryā i, 222a, b, 313b, **454b**, 459b, 607a; 607a; ii, 1a, 2a; iv, 502b, 1060b; v, 24a, 388b, 581b, 868a; vi, 65a, 418a, 419a, 720a; s, 281a
ʿAmūd i, **457b**
ʿAmūdā the Great (town) ii, 235b
al-ʿAmūdayn, Ḳalʿat (fort) vi, 777b, 778b
al-ʿAmūdī, Āl ii, 173b
al-ʿAmūdī, Muḥammad Saʿīd (XX) vi, 175b, 176b, 177b
al-ʿAmūdī, Shaykh vii, 515b
ʿAmūdja-zāde → Ḥusayn Pasha, ʿAmūdja-zāde
Āmul i, 237a, **459a**; ii, 746a; iv, 644a, 646b; vi, 433a, 510b, 511a, b, 512a, b, 513a, b, 514b, 515b, 516a, 618b; s, 298a, 363b
Āmul (Čārdjūy) (Turkmen) i, **459a**, iii, 255a; iv, 583b; s, 228a, 281a, 335a, 356b, 357a
Amulets → Siḥr
Āmulī → Awliyā Allāh; Karīm al-Dīn
al-Āmulī → Ḥaydar-i Āmulī
Āmulī, ʿAbd al-Munʿim (XVI) viii, 542a
Āmulī, Ṭālib (1626) ix, 241b; x, **164b**
ʿAmūr, Banū i, 371b, 460b
ʿAmūr, Djabal → Djabal ʿAmūr
Amurath vii, 592b
Āmūya (Āmul, Turkmen) i, 459b
Āmūzagār, Djamshīd (XX) vii, 450b
ʿAmwās i, **460b**
Āna → Sikka
ʿĀna i, **461a**
Anadolu i, 292b, 322b, **461b**; ii, 8a, 83b, 966b; iii, 211a, 215b; v, 291b, 881a, 978a, 979a, 1144b; ix, 796b
Anadolu (eyālet) i, **480b**, 1160a; ii, 32b, 722a
Anadolu Ḥiṣārî i, **481a**, 1251b, 1318a; iii, 483a
Anadolu Kavaghî i, 481a, 1252a
Anāhīd → Zuhara
Anahilwada → Anhalwāra
ʿAnāḳ bint Ādam i, **481a**
Anakkaza, Banū (Borkou) i, 1258a
Anamur i, **481a**
ʿĀnān b. David (VIII) i, 481b; iv, 604a, b, 606a
Anand Ram Mukhliṣ (1750) iv, 1127b, 1128a
Ananda b. Mangalay b. Ḳūbīlay (1307) iv, 553b
Anandpāl (XI) vi, 65b
ʿAnāniyya i, **481b**; iv, 604a
Anapa i, 63a, **481b**; ii, 25b
Anas b. Abī Unās (VII) iii, 224b
Anas b. Ḳays b. al-Muntafiḳ (VII) vii, 582a
Anas b. Mālik (709) i, 52a, 431b, **482a**; iii, 40b, 586b, 947b; iv, 899a; vi, 266b, 651b
Anas b. Mudrik (Khathʿam) (VII) iv, 1106a
ʿĀnāt s, 130a
Anatolia → Anadolu
Anatomy → Tashrīḥ
Anavarza → ʿAyn Zarba
Anaw i, 701a
ʿAnaza (spear) i, **482a**, 1215a
ʿAnaza, Banū i, **482b**, 528b, 545a, 873b, 1093b; ii, 184b; iii, 293a, 1253b; vi, 733b; vii, 782b; viii, 643a, 668b
Anazarba → ʿAyn Zarba
ʿAnazeh, Banū i, 1277a
al-Anbābī, Muḥammad (1895) i, 819b, 1019b
Anbaduḳlīs i, 235b, **483b**; iii, 869a
ʿAnbar i, **484a**, 837b
al-Anbār i, 17a, **484b**, 1073b; ii, 195a, 946b; iv, 911b; vi, 333b, 633b; vii, 729b
ʿAnbar, Banū 'l- → Tamīm
ʿAnbar al-Sakhartī (XIV) viii, 986a
al-ʿAnbārī → ʿĀmir b. ʿAbd al-Ḳays
al-Anbārī, Abū Bakr Muḥammad b. al-Ḳāsim (940) i, 185a, **485b**; vi, 634a, 822b; vii, 307a; viii, 14b, 646a
al-Anbārī, Abu 'l-Barakāt Kamāl al-Dīn (1181) i, **485b**; iii, 550b, 706b, 934b; v, 242b; vi, 196a; vii, 914b
al-ʿAnbarī, Abu 'l-Ḥasan ʿUmar b. Wāsil (924) viii, 840b
al-ʿAnbārī, Abū Muḥammad (916) i, **486a**

al-ʿAnbarī, ʿUbayd Allāh b. al-Ḥasan (785) ix, 204a
ʿAnbasa b. Isḥāḳ (856) vi, 674b
ʿAnbasa b. Maʿdān (640) vi, 920b
ʿAnbasa al-Aʿwar (al-Ḳabḳ) (X) iv, 346b
al-Anbīḳ i, **486a**
Anbiya v, 651b, 652b
Ancyra → Anḳara
ʿAndalīb → Mīrzā Ḥusayn Khān b. Ṣabā
al-Andalus i, 58b, 75b, 76a, 79b, 82a, 85b, 86b, 121b, 134b, 162a, 165b, 242a, 390a, 427b, **486b**, 1046a, 1148a, 1319b; ii, 129b, 130a, 331a, 601b; iii, 220a, 1055a; v, 877a, 1118b, 1119a, 1149b; vi, 280a, 428a, 430b, 469b, 520a, 601a, 841b, 851b, 881a, 1043b; vii, 590a; ix, 505b; x, 105b; xi, 191b; s, 103a
- agriculture i, **491b**; ii, 901a; v, 878a
- governors i, **493a**, b; iii, 46a, 587b, 702a
- history i, 44a, 320b; ii, 72a; iii, 762b, 789b, 805b, 848a; iv, 494b, 1156b
- literature, culture i, 404b, **497a-503b**, 599a; ii, 729a, 988a; iii, 70a, b, 657b, 702a, 771b; iv, 1006b-1008a; v, 218b, 744b, 1128a
- in North Africa i, 92b, **496a**; ii, 161a; v, 1190b
Andaman isles iii, 407a
Andarāb i, **504a**
Andarāba s, 125b
Andarūn → Enderūn
Anḍawr vi, 80a
Anday, Melih Cevdet (XX) iv, 545a
Andelas (Sumatra) ix, 852a
Andi, Banū i, **504a**, 756a; ii, 86b, 88b
Andidjān i, **504b**, 847b; ii, 791b, 792a; v, 461a; vi, 557b, 769a
Andirīn vi, 508b, 509a
ʿAndjar → ʿAyn al-Djarr
Andjudān iv, 201b; viii, 115b; s, 528a
Andjuman i, **505a**, xvi; ii, 429b, 433a, 434a, b; iv, 39b, 789b
Andjuman-i Khuddām-i Kaʿba vii, 678b; s, 4b, **74a**, 293b
Andkh(w)ūy i, **506a**, 530b; vi, 494b; ix, 431a; s, 281a
Aneiza → ʿUnayza
al-Anf, Banū iv, 201a
Anfā i, **506a**; vi, 573a
Angād vi, 141b
Angeli → Amirutzes, George
Angels → Malāʾika
Anglovič, Michael (1485) vi, 70a
Angohrān s, 129a
Angora → Anḳara
Angres, Banū s, 246b
Anhalwāra i, **506b**; ii, 1123b, 1124a; vii, 911b, 957a
Ānī i, 421a, **507a**; 637b, 638a, 639a; iv, 347b, 670a; v, 452a; vi, 64b, 274a; ix, 169a
Animals → Ḥayawān
Ānis (Yemen) vi, 436b
Anīs, Mīr Babar ʿAlī (1874) i, **508b**; ii, 73b; iii, 119b; vi, 610b, 611b; s, **74b**, 358b
Anīs al-Dawla (XVIII) vi, 529b
ʿAnḳāʾ i, **509a**; iii, 169a; iv, 928a; ix, 615b
ʿAnḳā, Muḥammad (1962) x, 958b
ʿAnkabūt i, **509a**
Ankalāy (Zandj) (IX) vii, 526b
Anḳara i, **509b**, 974b; vii, 776a; s, 47b, 318a
- university ii, 425b
Anḳārawī → Ismāʿīl Anḳārawī
al-Ankubarda (ar) (Lombardy) → Īṭaliya
Anmār, Banū i, 73a, 865a
Anna → Sikka
al-ʿAnnāba (Bône) i, **511b**; iv, 359b; vi, 427a, 741a; s, 103a, 156a
Annam iii, 1210b, 1211a
ʿAnnāzids i, **512a**; iii, 258b; v, 453b
Anniyya i, **513b**
ʿAns, Banū vi, 566a; vii, 591b
Anṣāb → Nuṣub
ʿAnsabā (river) vi, 628a
Anṣār (Sudan) v, 1249a, b, 1251a, 1252b
al-Anṣār i, 45a, 55a, 110a, 305a, **514a**, 545a, 771a, 990b; ii, 728b; iii, 226b, 285b; iv, 1187a; v, 435a, 995a, 996b; s, 10a
ʿAnsāra i, **515a**
al-Anṣārī → ʿAbd al-Ḳuddūs; Abū Zayd; al-Awsī; Zakāriyyāʾ
al-Anṣārī (XV) s, 125a
al-Anṣārī, Abu 'l-Ḳāsim Sulaymān b. Nāṣir s, 346b
Anṣārī, Djābir b. ʿAbd Allāh → Djābir b. ʿAbd Allāh
Anṣārī, Muḥammad Amīn (XIX) s, 74a, 75a
Anṣārī, Shaykh b. ʿAbd Allāh Ibrāhīm (XX) x, 147a
Anṣārī, Shaykh Ḥusayn (XIX) s, 75a

Anṣārī, Shaykh Murtaḍā (1864) v, 1087b; vi, 552a, b; vii, 960b; s, **75a**
al-Anṣārī al-Harawī, ʿAbd Allāh (1089) i, 69b, 417a, **515b**, 936b; iii, 84a, 161a, 177b, 821b, 1148b; iv, 63b, 473a, 697a, 1057b; vi, 353a, 381a, 454b, 455b; viii, 539a, 574b; s, 292a
al-Anṣārī al-Ḥusayn b. Yaḥyā (VIII) s, 82a
Anṣāriyya vi, 582a
Anshary, Isa (XX) vi, 731b, 732a
al-ʿAnsī → Abu 'l-Mughīra; ʿUmar b. Hāniʾ
al-ʿAnsī, al-Aswad (Yemen) (VII) vii, 592a
ʿAnṣra → ʿAnṣāra
al-Anṭākī vi, 114a
al-Anṭākī, Dāwūd (1599) i, **516a**, 594a; ii, 238a; iv, 1134a; s, 40b
al-Anṭākī, Yaḥyā b. Saʿīd (1066) i, **516a**; iii, 81b
Anṭākiya i, 182b, 466a, **516b**, 761b, 1125b; iii, 12b; v, 437a, 921b; vi, 3a, 322a, 379a, b, 381b, 505b, 506a, 507a, 544a, 578a, b; viii, 128a
Antalya i, 476b, **517b**; iv, 816b; vi, 120b; x, 412a,b
ʿAntar, Sīrat i, **518a**, 521b; ii, 236b, 238b; iii, 111b; v, 951b; vi, 78b, 752b
ʿAntar b. Shaddād (VI) ii, 236b; vii, 254b; viii, 239a
ʿAntara b. Shaddād (VI) i, 25a, **521a**; vi, 490a; vii, 254b; viii, 239a; s, 38b, 178b
ʿAntarī i, **522a**
Anṭarṭūs → Ṭarṭūs
Antel → Djelāl, Ṣadreddīn
Antemuru, Banū i, **522a**
Antep → ʿAyntāb
Antioch → Antākiya
Anṭūn Faraḥ → Faraḥ Anṭūn
Anūdjūr → Unūdjūr
Anūsha b. Abi 'l-Ghāzī, Khān (Khīwa) (1687) iv, 754a; vi, 417a; s, 281a, 420a
Anūsharwān (Chosroës I) i, **522b**
Anūshirwān (Ilkhān) (1353) ii, 47a
Anūshirwān, Khusraw → Kisrā
Anūshirwān b. Ḳābūs (XI) iv, 100b
Anūshirwān b. Khālid (1138) i, **522b**; iii, 221a, 327b, 1158a; iv, 265a; vi, 64a, b, 782a; vii, 735a
Anūshirwān b. Khātūn (Saldjūḳ) (XI) v, 388a
Anūshirwān b. Ṭughrilbeg v, 388a
Anūshtekin → Anūshtigin
Anūshtigin al-Duzbarī (general) (XI) ii, 484a, 854b; vii, 117a, 1017b
Anūshtigin Gharčaʾī (Khwārazm-shāh) (1097) ii, 1011a, 1082a; iv, 1064a, 1067a; viii, 942b; ix, 16a; s, 279a
Anūshtigin Shīrgīr (Nūshtagīn), amīr (XII) i, 1359b
Anwāʾ i, **523a**; iv, 518b; s, 380b
Anwākshūṭ → Nouakchott
Anwar (XIX) ii, 222a
Anwār al-Ḥaḳḳ, shāh s, 293a
Anwār-i Suhaylī → Kalīla wa Dimna
Anwarī, Awḥad al-Dīn Khāwarānī (1189) i, **524a**, 1301a; ii, 1034a; iii, 1115a; vi, 608b; vii, 1019a; viii, 971a; s, 21b, 65a, 240a
Anwarī, al-Ḥādjdj Saʿdullah → Enwerī
ʿAnz b. Wāʾil, Banū i, 709a
Anzarūt s, **77b**
Aouguerout s, 328b
Apamea → Afāmiya
Apolaffar (Abū Djaʿfar) (amīr) (843) i, 1166a; iv, 275a
Apollonius of Tyana → Balīnūs
Aprīdī → Afrīdī
ʿĀr iii, 396a; s, 53a, **78a**, 191a
al-ʿĀra i, **524b**
al-ʿArab i, **524b**; iii, 1098a
ʿArab, Djazīrat al- i, 102b, **533b**; s, 213b
– administration i, **539a**, 976a
– demography s, 213b
– ethnography i, 39a, 436a, **543b**, 872a
– flora and fauna i, **540a**
– geography i, 156a, **534b**, 1230a, b; iii, 124a
– history i, **547a-555a**; 773a, 881a
ʿArab ʿIzzet Pasha s, **480a** (See also S.V.) ʿIzzet Hōlō
Arab League → al-Djāmiʿa al-ʿArabiyya
Arab Legion i, 46a; iii, 264b, 1258b
ʿArab Maḥmūd → Maḥmūd Shewḳat Pasha
ʿArab Muḥammad Khān (Shaybānid) (XVII) i, 120b; v, 24a
Arab Revolt i, 46a; ii, 289a, 872a; iii, 263b, 643b
Arab Socialist Union s, 8a, 9a
Araba i, 205b, **556b**; v, 659a
ʿAraba (Wādī ʿAraba) i, **558b**
Arababnī, Arabaynī i, 176b; iii, 3b
Arabesque i, 498b, 501a, **558b**; ii, 557a, 777b, 864a; iii, 219b; v, 232b, 991a

ʿArabfaḳīh, Shihāb al-Dīn (XVI) i, **561a**
ʿArabī Dafaʿ Allāh (XVII) i, 1157a; v, 1251a
ʿArābī Pasha → ʿUrābī Pasha
Arabia→ ʿArab, Djazīrat al-
Arabian Nights → Alf layla wa-layla
Arabic writing → Khaṭṭ
ʿArabistān i, **561b**; iii, 1102a; iv, 1171b; v, 80b, 81a; vi, 495a; vii, 673b, 675a
ʿArabiyya i, 157b, 501b, **561b**; ii, 167a, 280a, 306b; 468b, 472a, 490b; iii, 1216a, 1259a; v, 185b, 605b, 804a, 914a, 915b, 1091b, 1093a, 1203a, 1207a
al-ʿArabiyya (Ṭarīḳa) s, 411a
al-ʿArabiyya, Djazīrat i, 535b, **603a**
ʿArabkīr i, **603a**
Arabs → al-ʿArab; Mustaʿriba
ʿArabshāhids → Khwārazm
ʿArab-zāde vi, 971a
ʿAraḍ i, 128b, **603b**
ʿArād → al-Muḥarraḳ
al-Aʿrāf i, **603b**
ʿArafa, ʿArafāt i, 43b, **604a**; iii, 31b, 35b; vi, 45a, 105b, 148a, 154a, 155a, 162a, 169b, 659a; s, 33a
ʿArafa, Mawlāy → Muḥammad b. ʿArafa
ʿArafa, Sīdī (al-Ḳayrawān) (XVI) iii, 69a; iv, 828a
Arafale vi, 643b
Araghūn s, **80a**
Arai Hakuseki (1725) xi, 223a
al-ʿArāʾish i, 356a, **604b**; v, 1245b; s, 29a
Arāk → Sultānābād
Arāk (Iran) s, 342a
al-Arak (Alarcos) i, 165b, **605b**
Arakan i, **606a**, 1333a; ii, 32a
Arakʿel of Tabrīz s, 275a
Arāḳim, Banū x, 91a
Aral Sea i, 456a, **606b**; s, 169a, 244b
Ārām Shāh (Muʿizzī, Delhi) (1211) ii, 267a; iii, 416a, 1155a; s, 360a
Arar → Harar
Ararat → Aghrî Dagh
Aras, Araxes → al-Rass
Arat, Reshīd Raḥmetī (1964) s, **82a**
Arayabnī → Arababnī
Arbāʿ, Banū i, 371b
Arbaʿa (Mānd) vi, 384b
Arbaʿī x, 141a
Arbāb → Rabb
Arbad → Irbid
ʿArbān i, **608a**
Arbaʿūn Ḥadīthan s, **82b**
Arbela → Irbid
Arbeles → Irbil
al-ʿArbī (Larbi) Bakkūsh, Banū s, 387a
Arbil v, 440a, 445a, b, 455a, b, 456a, b, 457b, 460b
ʿArbīlī, Ibrāhīm (XIX) ii, 471a
Arbira → Irbil
Arbūna (Narbonne) i, **608b**; iii, 495a; v, 1121a
Archidona → Urdjudhūna
Architecture i, 457b, **608b**; ii, 288a, 340b, 557a; iii, 142, 143, 228b, 1123b, 1267a; iv, 236a, b; v, 12a, 1136a
– al-Andalus i, **497b**; ii, 1014b-1019a
– India, Indonesia ii, 598a, 1103b; iii, 148a, 440b, 1227b
Arči i, **624b**, 756a; ii, 88b
Arcos → Arkush
Arcot (Ārkāt) i, **624b**; iii, 320a; vi, 535b
Arctic → Baḥr al-Ẓulma (al-Ẓulumāt)
Arḍ i, **625a**; ii, 93a, 900b
ʿArḍ → Istiʿrāḍ
ʿArḍ ḥāl i, **625a**
Arḍ al-Sidra → Saḳḳāra
Arḍ al-Ṭibr, – al-Dhahab vii, 245b
Arḍ al-Waḳwaḳ vii, 245b
Ardabb → Kayl
Ardabīl i, **625a**, 837a; ii, 88a, 598b; iv, 7b, 49a, 1170a; v, 244a; vi, 120a, 498b, 499a, 500a, 633b; viii, 755a, b; s, 139a, 140a
al-Ardabīlī, Aḥmad b. Muḥammad (1585) viii, 778b
Ardabīlī, Mīrzā Naṣr Allāh Ṣadr al-Mamālik (XIX) vii, 453a
Ardabīlī, Ṣafī al-Dīn → Ṣafī al-Dīn
al-Ardabīlī, Uways al-Laṭīfī (XV) viii, 542b
Ardahān i, 468b, **626a**, 643b
Ardakān i, **626a**; s, 342a
Ardalān i, **626b**; v, 170a; vi, 495b
Ardashāt i, 645b
Ardashīr (Bāwandid) → Ḥusām al-Dawla
Ardashīr I (Sāsānid) (241) i, 2b, 305b, 528a, 548b, **626b**, 1341b; ii, 16b, 135b, 925b; iii, 112b, 113a, 394a; iv, 809b; vi, 633a
Ardashīr II (Sāsānid) (383) i, 626b; ix, 74b
Ardashīr III (Sāsānid) (629) i, 626b; ix, 80a
Ardashīr Khurra → Fīrūzābād
Ardibehisht → Taʾrīkh

Ardistān i, **626b**; iv, 99b; v, 1147b; vi, 365b; s, 23b
Ardjastānī, Muḥammad Ḥusayn b. ʿAbd Allāh Shahrābī (XIX) vi, 609b
al-ʿArdjī, ʿAbd Allāh b. ʿUmar (738) i, 10b, 305a, **626b**; ii, 428b, 1011b, 1029b, 1030b
Ardjīsh i, **627a**; iv, 587a
Ardjīsh-Dagh → Erdjiyās Daghi̊
Ardjumand Bānū Bēgam (XVII) vii, 332b
Ardjun Singh, Guru (Sikh) (1605) ii, 380b; iii, 424a; vii, 315a
Ardjūna (Arjona) vii, 1021a
Ardumusht s, 36a, 37a
Ardzruni i, 637a, b
Areg (Reg) → ʿIrḳ
Areshgūl → Arshgūl
ʿArfadja b. Harthama al-Bārikī (VII) ii, 811b
Argan i, **627b**
Arghana → Ergani, Arghani
Arghen → Hargha
Arghiyān s, **83a**
Arghūn (Mongols) i, 148a, 227b, 228a, **627b**; iii, 420a, 632b; vi, 189b
Arghūn → Il-Khāns
Arghūn b. Abaḳa (Īlkhān) (1291) i, 346b; ii, 606b, 607b; iii, 1122a; iv, 31a, 621a; v, 102b, 662b, 827a; vi, 16a, 494a, 502a; viii, 702b
Arghūn Āḳā (XIII) ii, 606a; iv, 30b
Arghūn al-ʿAlāʾī (Miṣr) (XIV) vii, 170b; viii, 986a; ix, 154b
Arghūn al-Dawādār (1312) vi, 323a
Arghūn al-Nāṣirī (1330) iii, 954b; vii, 992a
Arghūn Shāh (1331) viii, 894b
Arghūn Shāh (1349) iii, 818a
Arghūn Shāh b. Kilidj Arslan II (XIII) i, 431b
Argungu (Gwandu) ii, 1146b
Argyrocastro → Ergiri
al-Arḥabī, Mālik b. Kaʿb (VII) viii, 118b
al-Arḥabī, Yazīd b. Ḳays (VII) viii, 853b
ʿArīb (singer) (IX) iv, 821b; x, 810b
ʿArīb b. Saʿd al-Kātib al-Ḳurṭubī (980) i, 491b, 600a, **628a**; viii, 352a, 822b
al-ʿĀriḍ → Ibn Saʿdān
al-ʿĀriḍ (Nadjd) i, 72b, 126b, **628b**
ʿArīḍa, Nasīb (1946) v, 1254b, 1255a, b; vi, 91a
ʿArīf i, 438b, **629a**; iv, 532a
ʿĀrif → Djalāl al-Dīn; Muḥammad
ʿArīf, ʿAbd al-Bāḳī (1713) vi, 112b
ʿĀrif, ʿAbd al-Raḥmān (XX) v, 469a
ʿĀrif, ʿAbd al-Salām (1963) iii, 1259a; iv, 719a; v, 468b, 469a; vi, 29a
ʿĀrif, Abu ʾl-Ḳāsim (1934) iv, 789b
ʿĀrif, Amīr → ʿĀrif Čelebī
ʿĀrif, Mīrzā Abu ʾl-Ḳāsim (1934) s, **83b**
ʿĀrif al-ʿĀrif (XX) s, 67b
ʿĀrif Čelebī (1320) s, **83b**
ʿĀrif Hikmet (calligrapher) (1918) iv, 1126b
ʿArif Hikmet Bey (1859) i, 71a, **630a**; v, 263b, 1005a
ʿĀrif Ḥikmet Hersekli → Hersekli
ʿĀrif Pasha (XIX) iv, 876b
ʿĀrif al-Shihābī (XX) iii, 519a, b
ʿĀrif, Ulu → ʿĀrif Čelebī
ʿĀrif al-Zayn (1960) vii, 780b
ʿĀrifī, Mawlānā Maḥmūd (1449) iv, 67a; s, **84a**
Ari̊gh Böke b. Toluy b. Činghiz Khān (Mongol) (1266) i, 1188a; ii, 3a, 45b; iv, 811b; v, 38b, 300a; vii, 230a
Arīn → Ḳubbat al-Arḍ
al-ʿArīsh i, **630b**; vi, 195a
Aristotelian School → s, **605b** (See also S.V.) Mushattā
Aristotle → Arisṭūṭālīs
Aristotle, Theology of i, 349b, 416b, 449b, 514a, 631a; ii, 554b, 949a; iii, 644a, 942b; v, 701a, 842a
Arisṭūṭālīs i, 178b, 235b, 342a, 349b, 350a, 419b, 513b, **630b**, 736b, 795b, 1083b, 1155b, 1340a; ii, 101b, 249a, 358b, 493a, 550a, 740a, 765a, 770a, 779b, 948b; iii, 21b, 29b, 301b, 509a, 596b, 915b, 942b, 1130a; vi, 203b, 220a; xi, 245a
Ariyaruk (XI) ii, 336a
ʿĀriyya i, **633a**
Arḳa → ʿIrḳa
Arkalī Khān b. Fīrūz Shāh II Djalāl al-Dīn Khaldjī (XIV) i, 1036a; iv, 920b, 921a
al-Arḳam b. Abi ʾl-Arḳam Makhzūmī (624) i, **633b**; vi, 138a
Arkān → Rukn
Ārkāt → Arcot
Arkiko vi, 641b, 642a, b, 643a, b
Arkush i, 6a, **633b**; vii, 761a
Armāʾīl (VIII) vi, 744a
Armenia → Armīniya
Armenian (language) iv, 350b, 351b; v, 1a

Armenians i, 470b, 638b, 666a; ii, 65b; iii, 214b; iv, 8a, 99a, 240b, 241b, 476a, 485b; v, 1a, 136b, 462b; ix, 163a, 167a; s, 274b, 275a, b
Armīniya i, 10a, 18a, 64b, 77a, 465a, 470a, **634a**, 660a, 1052a; ii, 37a, 678b; iii, 12b; iv, 89b, 90a, 344b, 345b, 347b; v, 292a; vi, 230b, 274a, 334a, 335a, 337b, 338a, 427b, 499a, 670b; xi, 135a; s, 225b, 365a
Armiyā → Irmiyā
Arnab s, **84b**
Arnawutluḳ (Albania) i, **650a**, 1090b, 1118b, 1162a; ii, 184a, 721a; iv, 342b, 1173b; v, 265a, 276b, 284b; vi, 59b, 71b, 74a; s, 149b
Arnedo → Arnīṭ
Arnīṭ i, **658a**
ʿArnūn → Ḳalʿat al-Shaḳīf
Aror → Arūr
Arpa i, **658a**
Arpā Khān (Keʾün) (Čingizid) (1336) ii, 45b, 401a; iii, 1208a
Arpalïḳ i, **658a**
Arrabal iii, 74a; xi, 248a
ʿArrāda i, 556b, **658b**; iii, 469b, 470a, 482a
Arradjān i, **659a**; vi, 120a; s, 119a
al-Arradjānī, Abū Fāris Shudjāʿ (932) ii, 591a
al-Arradjānī, Nāṣiḥ al-Dīn Abū Bakr Aḥmad (1149) i, **659b**; iv, 863b; viii, 971a; s, 326b
al-Arradjānī, Yaḥyā b. Bishr (IX) i, 128b
ʿArrāf i, **659b**; iv, 421b
ʿArrām al-Sulāmī (IX) ix, 817b
Arrān i, 639a, 642a, **660a**, 1041a; ii, 975b; iii, 1110b; iv, 344b, 345b, 347b, 573a; vi, 274a, 275b, 337a, 500a
Arri(u)zafa → al-Ruṣāfa (al-Andalus)
ʿArṣat Nīl (Marrākush) vi, 596b
Arsenius (patriarch) (1010) iii, 79a
ʿArsh → Kursī
ʿArsh (Algeria) i, **661a**; iv, 362a
Arshad al-Dawla (1911) vii, 432b
Arshakawan vi, 201a
Arshashdib → Arči
Arshgūl i, **661b**; s, 376b
Arshīn → Dhirāʿ
Arslan i, **661b**
Arslan b. Āḳ Sunḳur → Arslān Abīhī
Arslan b. Saldjūḳ (1034) i, **661b**, 1292a; ii, 4a, b, 1108b; iii, 1114a
Arslan b. Toghrïl b. Muḥammad, Muʿizz al-Dīn (Saldjūḳ) (1176) iii, 1110b; vi, 482a, 500a; viii, 239b
Arslan Āba, Atabeg → Āḳ-Sunḳur II
Arslan Abīhī, Nuṣrat al-Dīn (Marāgha) (1175) i, 300b; ii, 764b
Arslan Agha (XVII) vii, 319a
Arslan Arghūn (Saldjūḳ) (1096) i, **662a**, 1051b, 1331b; iv, 1067a; vii, 489b
Arslan Beg (Abkhāz) (XIX) i, 101a
Arslan Beg b. Balangirī → Khāṣṣ Beg Arslān
Arslan Isrāʾīl → Arslān b. Saldjūḳ
Arslan Khān (Dihlī) (XIII) vi, 47b, 48a
Arslan Khān (Ḳarlūḳ) (XIII) iii, 1115a, 1120a; iv, 808b; ix, 67a
Arslan Khān b. Ḳïlïdj Arslan II (Saldjūḳ) (XII) viii, 15b
Arslan Khān Aḥmad → Aḥmad Khān b. Ḥasan
Arslan Khān Muḥammad b.ʿAlī (Ilek-Khān) (1024) v, 45b; viii, 942b; s, 245b
Arslan Khān Muḥammad II (Samarḳand) (XII) ix, 15b
Arslan Khātūn bint Čaghrï Beg Dāwūd (XI) iv, 26b, 466a
Arslan Shāh b. Ḳïlïdj Arslān II (Rūm Saldjūḳ) (XII) viii, 15b
Arslan Shāh I b. Kirmān Shāh, amīr (Saldjūḳ) (Kirmān) (1142) iv, 466a; v, 159b; vii, 535b; viii, 945b
Arslan Shāh b. Masʿūd III (Ghaznawid) (1118) i, 217b, 940a; ii, 893b, 1052a; vii, 535b; ix, 15b
Arslan Shāh b. Masʿūd (Zangid) → Zangids
Arslan Shāh b. Tughrïl Shāh II (Saldjūḳ) (1176) i, 940b; iii, 197b; v, 160a; viii, 944b
Arslan Tepe vi, 230a
Arslanlï → Sikka
Arsūf i, **662b**; vi, 322a
Artena → Eretna
Artsrunids (Armīniya) vii, 656a, b; xi, 135a
Artuḳ b. Ekseb (Artuḳid) (1091) i, 662b; ii, 384b; v, 328a; vi, 274b; viii, 947a
Artūḳ İnaḳ (1740) vi, 418a; s, 420a
Artuḳids i, 466b, 467a, 639a, **662b**; ii, 344a, 613b; iii, 507a, 1099a, 1118a, 1197b; iv, 464b; v, 454b; vi, 274b, 540b, 542b, 930b; vii, 273b; ix, 68b; s, 266b
Artvin i, **667b**; ii, 62a

ʿArūba → Taʾrīkh
ʿArūḍ i, **667b**; ii, 159b, 834b; iii, 672a; iv, 57a, 326b, 714b, 1187b
ʿArūḍ risālesi i, **849a**
Arūḍī → Niẓāmī ʿArūḍī
ʿArūdj (Barbarossa) (1518) i, 367b, 368a, **677b**; ii, 520a, 537b, 839b; iv, 361a, b, 1155b; v, 504a; vii, 64b; s, 80b
Arung Palakka (Sulawesi) (1696) ix, 813b
Arūr i, **679a**; v, 817a
ʿArūs, Banū i, 604b
ʿArūs resmi i, **679a**; ii, 147a
al-ʿArūsī al-Tilimsānī → Ibn ʿArūs
ʿArūsiyya i, **679b**; iii, 713b; vi, 355a; x, 248a; s, 93a
Arwā bint Aḥmad al-Sayyida (Sulayḥid) (1138) ix, 816a, b
Arwād/Ruwād i, 935b; iii, 475a; vi, 538a; s, 120b
Arwand-rūd → Shaṭṭ al-ʿArab
Arya Damar (Palembang) iii, 1219a
Arya Dilah (ʿAbd Allāh) (Palembang) (1486) viii, 245a
Arya Kusuma ʿAbd al-Raḥīm, Susuhunan (Palembang) (1706) viii, 245a
Aryāṭ al-Ḥabashī viii, 979b
Arzachel → al-Zarkālī
Arzan i, **679b**; ii, 712a
Arzan al-Rūm → Erzurum
Ārzāw i, **680a**
Arzila → Aṣīla
Ārzū, Khān (1756) i, **680a**; iv, 526b
Ās → Alān
Ās (myrt(l)e) s, **87a**
ʿAṣā i, **680b**; iv, 377b
al-Asʿāʾ (Mahra) vi, 81a
ʿAṣaba → Mīrāth
ʿAṣabiyya i, **681a**; ii, 962b; iii, 830b; iv, 46a
Asad → Minṭakat al-Burūdj; Nudjūm
al-Asad (lion) i, **681a**
Asad, Banū i, 99a, 528a, b, **683a**, 1241a, 1358b; iii, 1177a; vi, 145a, 146a, 965a; vii, 373b
Asad, Banū (ancient tribe) i, **684b**; ii, 71b; iv, 820a; v, 348a; s, 19b, 20a, 304b
Asad b. ʿAbd Allāh al-Kasrī (738) i, **684b**, 760a, 1001a, 1033a, 1293a; ii, 1010b; iii, 223b, 493b; iv, 54b, 926b; v, 2a, b, 47b, 76a, 856a; vii, 1016a; x, 590a, 925a
Asʿad b. Abī Yaʿfur (Yuʿfir) (Ḥiwālid) (943) iii, 124b; iv, 661a; vi, 439a; s, 335a
Asad b. al-Furāt (ḳāḍī) (828) i, 248b, 249b, 250a, **685a**; iii, 817a; iv, 733a, 829b; v, 1159b; vi, 279a, 280b, 751a; vii, 186b; viii, 843b; ix, 584a, 669b
al-Asʿad Ibn Mammātī → Ibn Mammātī
Asad b. Mūsā b. Ibrāhīm (827) s, **87b**
Asʿad b. Shihāb (Ṣanʿāʾ) (XI) iii, 125b
Asʿad b. Zurāra (VII) vii, 649b
Asʿad Abū Karib al-Ḥimyarī (Tubbaʿ) iv, 318b
Asad Allāh b. Ḥasan b. Riḍā al-Dīn (Marʿashī) (XV) vi, 513b, 514a
Asad Allāh b. Mīr Zayn al-Dīn Marʿashī, Amīr (1555) vi, 516b
Asad Allāh ʿAlam (1978) vii, 448a; s, 507b
Asad Allāh Ḥusaynī Marʿashī, Sayyid (1576) vi, 516b
Asad Allāh Iṣfahānī (XVII) i, **685b**
Asad Allāh Mīrzā (XIX) viii, 100b
Asʿad al-ʿAẓm (1757) iii, 120b; iv, 1016a; v, 925b, 926a; vi, 455a; xi, 334a
Asad al-Dawla → Ṣāliḥ b. Mīrdās
Asad al-Dīn → Shīrkūh
Asad al-Dīn Muḥammad b. al-Ḥasan (Ṣanʿāʾ) (XIII) v, 1241a
Asʿad Efendī → Esʿad Efendī
Asʿad Kāmil, Tubbaʿ i, 548b; ii, 865a; iii, 540b; iv, 318b; v, 895a
Asad al-Kasrī → Asad b. ʿAbd Allāh
Asad Khān Lārī (Berar) (XVI) iii, 1160b
Asad al-Lukaymī (1765) i, 60b; viii, 385a
Asʿad Pasha al-ʿAẓm, Khān (1752) ii, 287b, 288a; iii, 120b; v, 925b; vi, 455a
Asʿad al-Shidyāk (1830) ii, 801a
Asadābādh i, **685b**
Asadābādī, Sayyid Djamāl al-Dīn s, 53b, 290b
Asadī (dynasty), (Ḥims) iii, 399b
al-Asadī, Abu ʾl-Rūḥ ʿĪsā b. ʿAlī b. Ḥassān (XIII) s, 392b
Asadī, Abū Manṣūr ʿAlī b. Aḥmad al-Ṭūsī (XI) vii, 567b
Asadī, Abū Naṣr Aḥmad b. Manṣūr al-Ṭūsī (XI) i, **685b**; ii, 439b; iv, 61b, 62b, 525b, 1123b
Asadī, ʿAlī b. Aḥmad b. Manṣūr al-Ṭūsī (XI) i, **685b**
al-Asadī, al-Ḥasan b. Dubays (1018) vi, 921a

al-Asadī, Ḥusayn (ḳāḍī) (1300) vi, 15b
al-Asadī, ʿĪsā (XIII) iv, 745a; v, 9a; vii, 948a; s, 175b
al-Asadī, Ismāʿīl b. Sammār (VIII) ix, 827b
al-Asadī, Manṣūr b. al-Ḥusayn (amīr) (XI) vii, 271a
al-Asadī, Manẓūr b. Mart̲h̲ad viii, 377a
Asadiyya (S̲h̲īrkūh) vi, 320a
Āṣaf b. Barak̲h̲yā i, **686a**, 775a; ix, 823a
Āṣaf al-Dawla (Ḳād̲j̲ār) (XIX) iv, 393a, b
Āṣaf al-Dawla, (Nawwāb, Awad̲h̲) (XVIII) i, 153a, 757a, b, 813b, 1095a; ii, 265a, 499a, 870b; iii, 1163a; v, 635a, 636a; ix, 90a; s, 358b, 359a
Āṣaf D̲j̲āh I, Niẓām al-Mulk (Ḥaydarābād) → Niẓām al-Mulk Čin Ḳi̊li̊č K̲h̲ān
Āṣaf D̲j̲āh VII → ʿUt̲h̲mān ʿAlī K̲h̲ān
Āṣāf-D̲j̲āhs (Ḥaydarābād) i, 686a, 1015b, 1170a; ii, 99b; iii, 318b
Āṣaf K̲h̲ān (1554) ii, 1129a
Āṣaf K̲h̲ān, Abu ʾl-Ḥasan (1641) i, **686a**, 1347b; ii, 381a, 813b; iv, 1020a; v, 601a; vi, 190a; vii, 574a; viii, 125a
al-Āṣafī al-Ulug̲h̲k̲h̲ānī → Ḥād̲j̲d̲j̲ī al-Dabīr
ʿAsākir, Banū ii, 283a; iii, 713b
al-Aṣamm → Muḥammad b. ʿUmar
al-Aṣamm, Abu ʾl-ʿAbbās Muḥammad b. Yaʿḳūb al-Nīsābūrī (957) i, **686b**; viii, 53a
al-Aṣamm, Abū Bakr (Naṣr b. Abī Layt̲h̲) (Miṣr) (VIII) s, 90b
al-Aṣamm, Abū Bakr ʿAbd al-Raḥmān b. Kaysān (Baṣra) (817) iii, 1166a; vi, 737b; vii, 546b, 784b; s, **88b**, 226b
al-Aṣamm, Abu ʾl-ʿAbbās Muḥammad al-Nīsābūrī (957) i, 142b, 686b
al-Aṣamm, Muḥammad b. Abi ʾl-Layt̲h̲ (840) vii, 4a
al-Aṣamm, Sufyān b. al-Abrad al-Kalbī (VII) i, **686b**, 810b; ii, 809a; iii, 716b; iv, 753a
Asandamur Kurd̲j̲ī (Tripoli) (XIV) vii, 991b
Asar Kale → ʿAmmūriya
Asās → Ismāʿīliyya
ʿAsas i, **687a**; iv, 103b
Asas al-Sunna → Asad b. Mūsā b. Ibrāhīm
Asātigīn (Mosul) (870) vi, 900a
Asāṭīr al-Awwalīn iii, 369a; s, **90b**
Asāwira (Persians) vi, 875b
Aṣba → Iṣbaʿ
al-Aṣbag̲h̲ (838) vi, 279a
Aṣbag̲h̲ b. al-ʿAbbās (1196) s, 382a
Aṣbag̲h̲ b. ʿAbd Allāh b. Wānsūs (812) vi, 568a
Aṣbag̲h̲ b. K̲h̲alīl vii, 400a
Aṣbag̲h̲ b. Nabīl (XI) vii, 248b
Asbag̲h̲ b. Wakīl (IX) ix, 584b
al-Aṣbag̲h̲ (al-Asyaʿ) al-Kalbī (VII) i, 84b; ii, 625a; iv, 493b, 494a
al-Aṣbaḥī (XIII) vi, 182b; vii, 28b
Asben → Aïr
Ascalon → al-ʿĀsḳalān
Aṣfar (yellow) i, **687b**; v, 700b, 706b
al-Aṣfar al-Muntafiḳ (X) iv, 663b
Aṣfar, Banu ʾl- i, 688a
Asfār b. Kurdūya (Bag̲h̲dād) (X) s, 398a
Asfār b. S̲h̲īrawayhī (S̲h̲īrōya) (931) i, **688a**; ii, 192a; iii, 255a; iv, 23a, 661b, 859b; vi, 115b, 539a; s, 357a
Aṣfī (Safi) i, 85a, 141a, 687b, **688b**; vi, 573a, 589a, 594a, 741b; vii, 387a; s, 29a, 401b
Asfizār → Sabzawār
al-Asfizārī, Abū Ḥākim al-Muẓaffar b. Ismāʿīl (1121) vii, 196b
al-Aʿs̲h̲ā i, **689b**
al-Aʿs̲h̲ā, Maymūn b. Ḳays (625) i, 196a, 442b, **689b**; 963b, 1081b; iv, 1002a, 1008b; vii, 190b, 208b, 254b, 980b; viii, 883b; ix, 9b; s, 197b
Aʿs̲h̲ā Hamdān (702) i, **690b**; ii, 190b; iii, 123a, 354a, 716b; vi, 193a, 604a, 605a
Aṣḥāb → Ṣaḥāba
As̲h̲ʿab (771) i, **690b**
Aṣḥāb al-ḥadīt̲h̲ → Ahl al-ḥadīt̲h̲
Aṣḥāb al-kahf i, **691a**, 998a; iv, 724a
Aṣḥāb al-rass i, 509a, **692a**; iii, 169a
Aṣḥāb al-raʾy i, **692a**; ii, 889a
Aṣḥāb al-uk̲h̲dūd i, 692a, **692b**
al-As̲h̲ad̲j̲d̲j̲ al-Muʿammar → Abu ʾl-Dunyā
As̲h̲āḳa Bās̲h̲, Banū iv, 387b, 389a, 390b
Ashām i, **692b**; iv, 460b
Aʿs̲h̲ār → ʿUs̲h̲r
al-ʿAs̲h̲ara al-Mubas̲h̲s̲h̲ara i, **693a**
As̲h̲ʿarī, Banū vi, 221b, 493a
al-As̲h̲ʿarī (1444) i, 1154a; ii, 740b
al-As̲h̲ʿarī, Abū Burda (721) i, **693b**; vii, 635b
al-As̲h̲ʿarī, Abu ʾl-Ḥasan (935) i, 129a, 204b, 275a, 589b, **694a**, 958b, 1039a; ii, 412a, 449b, 554a, 569b, 570a, 931a; iii,

767a, 1037b, 1063a, 1144a, b, 1164b, 1170b, 1173b; iv, 271b, 470a; v, 526b; vi, 353a, 376a, 846b; vii, 187b, 546b, 1051a; s, 347a, 392a
al-As<u>h</u>ʿarī, Abū Mūsā (662) i, 304a, 383b, 384a, 693b, **695a**, 704a; ii, 414b, 415b, 811b, 1120a; iii, 1015b; iv, 13b, 99b, 220a; v, 406b, 451a, 499b; vi, 565b, 647b, 649a, 920a; vii, 207a; ix, 98a; s, 89b
al-As<u>h</u>ʿarī, Aḥmad b. Muḥammad (IX) viii, 387b
As<u>h</u>ʿarīyya i, 179a, 333a, b, 334a, 335a, 410b, 411a, b, 412a, b, 413a, 415b, **696a**, 714a, 958b; ii, 102b, 365a, 449b, 493b, 605a, 608a, 618a, 833b, iii, 171b, 330a, 465b, 767a, 1072b, 1144b, 1146a; iv, 107b, 108a, 172b, 183a, 365b, 366a, 469a, 616a, 692a, 693a; v, 527a; vi, 218b, 447b, 448a; s, 30a, 343b, 346b
al-As<u>h</u>ʿat<u>h</u> b. <u>D</u>jaʿfar al-<u>Kh</u>uzāʿī → al-<u>Kh</u>uzāʿī
al-As<u>h</u>ʿat<u>h</u> b. Ḳays (661) i, 42b, 625b, **696b**, 864a; ii, 198b; iii, 242b, 715a, 888b; v, 119b; viii, 97a; ix, 553b; s, 337b
al-As<u>h</u>daḳ → ʿAmr b. Saʿīd al-As<u>h</u>daḳ
As<u>h</u>d<u>j</u>aʿ, Banū vii, 561b
al-As<u>h</u>d<u>j</u>aʿ b. ʿAmr al-Sulamī (VIII) i, **697a**
As<u>h</u>hab (Mālikī) (819) vi, 279a; viii, 844a
ʿĀs<u>h</u>iḳ i, 193b, **697b**; ii, 990b; iii, 374a; iv, 706a; v, 275a
ʿĀs<u>h</u>iḳ, Muḥammad b. ʿU<u>th</u>mān b. Bāyezīd (XVI) i, **697b**; ii, 588a; v, 982a; s, 330b
ʿĀs<u>h</u>iḳ Čelebi (Pīr Meḥmed of Prizrin) (1571) i, **698a**; iv, 1137a; v, 116a, 693a; x, 55a; s, 83a
ʿAs<u>h</u>iḳ Pas<u>h</u>a (1333) i, 419b, **698b**; iii, 375a; v, 173a
ʿAs<u>h</u>iḳ Weysel (1973) s, **91a**
ʿĀs<u>h</u>iḳ-pas<u>h</u>a-zāde (1484) i, **699a**; ii, 1044b; iii, 23a
ʿAs<u>h</u>iklu, Banū iv, 577b
As<u>h</u>īr i, **699a**, 1319b; ii, 114b; iv, 459a; vi, 728a, b; ix, 18a
ʿĀs<u>h</u>ir Efendi (XIX) ii, 474a
ʿAs<u>h</u>īra i, **700a**; iv, 334a, b, 595a; v, 472a
As<u>h</u>k (XIX) iii, 376a
ʿAs<u>h</u>ḳābād i, 320b, **700b**; vi, 621b, 720a; x, 686a
As<u>h</u>ḳīlūla, Banū (Tu<u>d</u>jībids) iv, 729b; vi, 222b; vii, 1021a; xi, 15a
As<u>h</u>kū<u>d</u>ja → Dar<u>gh</u>in
As<u>h</u>lūn <u>Kh</u>ātūn umm al-Nāṣir Muḥammad b. Ḳalawūn (Mamlūk) (XIV) vii, 991a
al-As<u>h</u>mūnayn → U<u>sh</u>mūnayn
As<u>h</u>nās, vizier (IX) vii, 653a; s, 106a
As<u>h</u>ot → As<u>h</u>ūṭ
As<u>h</u>rāf → <u>Sh</u>arīf
As<u>h</u>raf (Čūbānid) → Malik As<u>h</u>raf
As<u>h</u>rāf (faction) iii, 88a; v, 349b
As<u>h</u>rāf (India) iii, 411a
As<u>h</u>raf (town, Māzandarān) i, 8b, 198a, 329a, 434b, **701a**, 780b, 799a, b. 940b, 971a; ii, 284a, 347b; iii, 504a; iv, 502b, 817b; vi, 516b, 528a; s, 140b
As<u>h</u>rāf (Sudan) i, 49b, 765a; ii, 124a; v, 1250a, b
al-As<u>h</u>raf I Muẓaffar al-Dīn, al-Malik (Ayyūbid) (1220) → al-Malik al-As<u>h</u>raf Mūsā I Muẓaffar al-Dīn (Ayyūbid)
al-As<u>h</u>raf (Rasūlid) (1296) vi, 81b; vii, 30a
As<u>h</u>raf b. ʿAbd al-ʿAzīz (Af<u>gh</u>anistān) (1729) i, 229b, 270a, 291a; iii, 604b; v, 461a
al-As<u>h</u>raf b. al-ʿĀdil, al-Malik (Ayyūbid) (1198) → al-Malik al-As<u>h</u>raf b. al-ʿĀdil
As<u>h</u>raf ʿAlī, Sayyid vii, 132b
As<u>h</u>raf ʿAlī b. ʿAbd al-Ḥaḳḳ al-Fārūḳī (1943) i, **701b**; iii, 433b, 1174a, b
As<u>h</u>raf ʿAlī <u>Kh</u>ān (1772) i, **702a**
As<u>h</u>raf bint Riḍā <u>Sh</u>āh Pahlawī (XX) vi, 486b
As<u>h</u>raf al-Dīn Gīlānī (1934) iv, 71a; vii, 754b; s, **91b**
As<u>h</u>raf <u>D</u>jahāngīr al-Simnānī (1405) i, **702b**, 859a; ii, 51b, 392a, 1115a
al-As<u>h</u>raf Ismāʿīl (Rasūlid) (1401) viii, 457a
al-As<u>h</u>raf <u>Kh</u>alīl b. Ḳalawūn (Mamlūk) (1293) vi, 322b; vii, 461b, 991b
As<u>h</u>raf <u>Kh</u>ān (<u>Kh</u>aṭṭ) (1572) iv, 1127b
al-As<u>h</u>raf Mūsā b. Ibrāhīm (Ayyūbid) (1262) iii, 399b, 989b; vi, 321b, 381a; vii, 273a, b
As<u>h</u>raf-og<u>h</u>lu Rūmī (XIV) iii, 43b
As<u>h</u>raf Og<u>h</u>ullarî i, **702b**, 1256b; iv, 621a
As<u>h</u>raf Rumī, ʿAbd Allāh (1493) i, 704a
al-As<u>h</u>raf <u>Sh</u>aʿbān II b. Ḥusayn (Mamlūk) (1376) vi, 195a, 424a, 548a
al-As<u>h</u>raf ʿUmar (Rasūlid) (1296) viii, 457a
As<u>h</u>rafī → Sikka
al-As<u>h</u>rafī, Sayf al-Dīn Ḳaratāy Ibn ʿAbd al-ʿAzīz (1376) vi, 580b

Ashrafiyya (Mamlūk) i, **704a**; v, 73a; vi, 316b, 320a
Ashras b. ʿAbd Allāh al-Sulamī → al-Sulamī
al-ʿAshshāb i, **704a**
al-Ashtar, Malik b. al-Ḥārith (VII) i, 382b, **704a**; ii, 89b, 416a; iii, 1265a; iv, 1035a; v, 499b, 954a
Ashtardjān vi, 366a
Ashtarkhānids → Djānids
Āshtiyānīs (Irān) vii, 653b
Ashturka (Astorga) s, **92a**
Ashur → Athūr
Ashur Ada vii, 455a
ʿĀshūrāʾ i, 265a, **705a**, 823b, 1352a; iii, 635a; s, 190a
Ashūṭ I (Armenia) (890) i, 507a, 637a; v, 488b
Ashūṭ II (Armenia) (929) i, 507a, 637b; ii, 679b
Ashūṭ III (Armenia) (977) i, 507a, 637b; ii, 680a; iv, 670a
Ashūṭ IV (Armenia) (1040) i, 638a
Ashūṭ Msaker (Bagratid) (IX) i, 507a
al-ʿĀṣī (Orontes) i, 239a, **706a**; ii, 555b, 556a; s, 243a
Āṣif al-Dawla (Iṣfahān) (XIX) iv, 105a
Aṣīla i, **706a**; v, 1118b; vi, 573a
ʿĀṣim → Čelebi-zāde Ismāʿīl ʿĀṣim
ʿĀṣim Aḥmad (1819) i, **707a**, 1327b; ii, 536b; v, 951b; vi, 340b
Asim, Dj. (XX) vi, 768b
ʿĀṣim b. ʿAbd Allāh al-Hilālī (VIII) ii, 601a; iii, 223b, 1202a
ʿĀṣim b. Abi ʾl-Nadjdjūd (745) i, **706b**; iii, 63a; v, 127b, 128a
ʿĀṣim b. Djamīl al-Yazdadjūmī (X) ii, 1095b
ʿĀṣim b. Thābit al-Anṣārī (VII) v, 40b, 41a
ʿĀṣim b. ʿUmar b. al-Khaṭṭāb (VII) vi, 344b
ʿĀṣim al-Aḥwal (VIII) i, 104b
Asỉm Bezirci (XX) vi, 95b
Asim Degel (Kano) (XIX) iv, 550b
ʿĀṣim Efendi Ismāʿīl → Čelebi-zāde
ʿĀṣim al-Sadrātī (VIII) iii, 654a, b; vi, 312a
ʿAsīr (Arabia) i, 98a, 106b, 539a, **707b**, 811b, 881b; v, 391b; vi, 151a, 156b, 192a; s, 3b, 30a, 278b
Asīr (Mānd) vi, 384b
Asīr, Djalāl al-Dīn (1639) i, **707b**; iv, 69a; viii, 776a
Asīrgarh i, **710a**; ii, 815b; iv, 1023a
Asīrī (XIX) s, 109b
Āsitāna → Istanbul
Asiuṭ → Asyūṭ
Āsiya (Pharaoh's wife) i, **710b**; ii, 848a, 917b; vi, 629a, 652b
Ask (Damāwand) ii, 106b; v, 660b, 661a, 664a
ʿĀskalān i, 9b, **710b**, 946b; ii, 911a, 912a, 1056a; iv, 958b; v, 331a; vi, 230a, 652a; s, 121a
al-ʿAskalānī → Ibn Ḥadjar
al-ʿAskalānī, ʿAlāʾ al-Dīn b. Ẓāfir (XII) vii, 1040a
al-ʿAskar → Djaysh
al-ʿAskar → Sāmarrāʾ
al-ʿAskar (al-Fusṭāṭ) ii, 958b, 959a
ʿAskar Khān Afshār Arūmī (XIX) s, 290a
ʿAskar Mukram i, **711b**; s, 12b, 37b
ʿAskarī i, **712a**; ii, 147a; iv, 231b, 242a, b, 563a, 564a
al-ʿAskarī, Abū Aḥmad al-Ḥasan (993) i, **712b**; viii, 14a; s, 38a
al-ʿAskarī, Abu ʾl-Ḥasan ʿAlī b. Muḥammad al-Naḳī / al-Hādī (X. Imām) (868) i, **713a**; iii, 246b; vii, 443a, 459b; viii, 1040b; s, 95a, 127b
al-ʿAskarī, Abū Hilāl (1010) i, 590b, **712b**, 759a, 857b; ii, 386a; iv, 249a; vi, 438a, 823a; vii, 527b
al-ʿAskarī, al-Ḥasan → al-Ḥasan al-ʿAskarī
ʿAskarī b. Bābur (Mughal) (XVI) i, 228b, 1135b; iii, 575b, 576a; iv, 523b
ʿAskerī → ʿAskarī
Askia al-Ḥādjdj Muḥammad → Muḥammad b. Abī Bakr (Songhay)
Aṣl → Uṣūl
al-Aslaʿ b. ʿAbd Allāh al-ʿAbsī s, 177b
al-Aṣlaḥ i, **713b**
Aslam, Banū v, 78b; vii, 356b, 561b
Aslam b. Zurʿa al-Kilābī (681) vii, 123b
Aslam, Ēm (XX) v, 204a, b
Asmāʾ bint ʿAbd al-ʿAzīz b. Marwān (746) vi, 664a
Asmāʾ bint Abī Bakr (693) i, 109b, 110a, **713b**; ix, 742a; s, 311a
Asmāʾ bint Mukharriba (VI) i, 115b; iii, 169a; vi, 145b
Asmāʾ bint al-Nuʿmān al-Djawniyya iii, 63b
Asmāʾ bint ʿUmays (659) i, 44a, 109b,

400b; ii, 372a, 844b, 846a; iv, 1106b; vii, 393a
al-Asmāʾ al-Ḥusnā i, 408a, **714a**; ii, 753a
al-Aṣmaʿī, Abū Saʿīd ʿAbd al-Malik (828) i, 105b, 108b, 115a, b, 125b, 158a, 167b, 338a, 520b, 521b, 588b, **717b**, 772a, 921a, 1241a; ii, 952b; iii, 136a; iv, 249a; vi, 625b; vii, 254b, 279b, 306b, 526b, 831b; s, 15b, 17b, 20a, 33a, 128b, 277a, 317b, 394b
al-Aṣmaʿiyyāt → al-Aṣmaʿī
Āsmāngird Mountains vi, 384a
al-Asmar, ʿAbd al-Salām al-Faytūrī (1574) vi, 355a; s, **93a**
al-Asnawī (1370) vi, 133a
Asparukh (Bulghar) (VII) x, 692a
Asper → Aḳče
ʿAṣr i, **719a**
Asrāfīl → Isrāfīl
Āṣṣ → Alān
Assab i, **719a**; ii, 113a; vi, 643b; ix, 715a
Aṣṣāda, Banū vi, 741b, 742a, 744a
Assadollah Alam (Asad Allāh ʿAlam) s, 507b
ʿAssāf al-Naṣrānī (XIII) iii, 951b
al-ʿAssāl, Awlād → Ibn al-ʿAssāl
al-ʿAssālī, Aḥmad b. ʿAlī al-Ḥarīrī (1638) iv, 992a
al-ʿAssāliyya iv, 992a
Assam i, **719a**; vi, 489a
ʿAṣṣār, Muḥammad (1377) i, **720a**; iv, 67a
ʿAssās i, 687b
Assenids i, 1302a
Assiout → Asyūṭ
Assuan → Uswān
Assyria → Athūr
Astarābādh i, **720a**; ii, 1141a; iii, 212b, 1102a; iv, 389a, b, 390a, b, 855b; vi, 14b, 494b, 495a, 512a, b, 513b, 514b, 515b; s, 139b, 356b, 357a, 363b, 380a
al-Astarābādhī i, **720b**
al-Astarābādī, Muḥammad Yūsuf (XVI) vi, 516b
al-Astarābādhī, Raḍī al-Dīn (1285) i, **721a**; iii, 781a, 861b; vii, 914b
al-Astarābādhī, Rukn al-Dīn (1317) i, **721a**
al-Astarābādī, Djalāl al-Dīn Muḥammad Yūsuf (Ṣadr) (XVI) vi, 18a, 516b
Astarābādī, Faḍl Allāh (1384) viii, 114b, 540a
Astarābādī, Ghiyāth al-Dīn Muḥammad b. Ḥusayn b. Muḥammad (amīr) (Ḥurūfī) ii, 733a, 735a
Astarābādī, Ibrāhīm b. Walī Allāh (XVI) viii, 540b
al-Astarābādī, Mīrzā Muḥammad b. ʿAlī (1619) vi, 550b; s, 56b
al-Astarābādī, Muḥammad Amīn (1640) viii, 779b
Astarābādī, Muḥammad Bāḳir → al-Dāmād
al-Astarābādī, Mullā Muḥammad Amīn b. Muḥammad Sharīf (1624) vi, 550b; vii, 298a; s, 56b, 57a
Asṭarlāb → Asṭurlāb
Astarte → al-Lāt
Astorga → Ashturḳa
Astrakhān i, **721b**, 1108a; ii, 44a, 179a; iv, 280b, 576a; v, 138a, b; vi, 416b; s, 318a
Astrakhānids → Djānids
Asṭurlāb i, **722b**; iii, 808b, 924a, 928b, 1136b; v, 46a; vi, 374b
al-Asṭurlābī, ʿAlī b. ʿĪsā (831) vi, 600a
al-Asṭurlābī → al-Badīʿ
al-Aʿsūm (Yemen) vi, 474a
al-Aswad b. Kaʿb al-ʿAnsī (632) i, 110b, **728a**, 738a; iii, 223b; iv, 1135b; viii, 94a; s, 116a
al-Aswad b. al-Mundhir III (VI) ii, 71b, 72a
al-Aswad b. Yaʿfur (VI) i, **728b**; iv, 998b; s, 256a, 394b
al-Aswad b. Yazīd vii, 258b
Aswan → Uswān
al-Aṣyaʿ al-Kalbī → al-Aṣbagh al-Kalbī
Asylum → Bast, Bīmāristān
Asyūṭ i, **728b**; ii, 424a; v, 515a; vi, 119a, 361a, 671b; s, 5a, 40b, 121b
al-Asyūṭī, Shams al-Dīn (1416) ix, 539a
Ata (father) i, **729a**
ʿAṭāʾ i, **729a**; ii, 360a; vi, 205b
ʿAṭāʾ b. Abī Rabāḥ (732) i, 123a, **730a**; ii, 538b, 886b, 888b; vii, 631b, 636a; s, 232b, 386b
ʿAṭāʾ b. Yasār al-Hilālī (722) iv, 369a
ʿAṭāʾ Allāh Efendi (XVI) i, 1235a; iv, 322b
ʿAṭāʾ Allāh Efendi, Shānī-zāde → Shānī-zāde
ʿAṭāʾ Allāh ʿOthmān-oghlu (1767) iv, 593a
ʿAṭāʾ Bey, Meḥmed (1919) i, **730b**
ʿAṭāʾ Bey, Ṭayyārzāde (1877) i, **730b**
ʿAṭāʾ Ilāhī, Banū iii, 1107b
ʿAṭāʾ al-Ḳasm, Shaykh (XX) vi, 538b

ʿAṭāʾ, Khwādja (XIV) s, 105b
ʿAṭāʾ Malik Djuwaynī → al-Djuwaynī, ʿAlāʾ al-Dīn
ʿAtāba i, **730b**
Atabak (Atabeg) i, 3b, 20b, 639a, **731a**, 1081a, 1276b; iii, 1016a; iv, 26a, 32a, 219a, b, 466b; v, 689b, 826a, 828a
Atābak al-ʿAsākir i, **732b**; v, 73a
ʿAtabāt s, **94a**, 104a
Atabeg → Atabak
Atabia (Mamprusi, Ghana) (1741) ii, 1003b
Atač, Nūr Allāh (1957) s, **96a**, 98b
ʿAṭāʾī, ʿAṭāʾ Allāh b. Yaḥyā (1635) i, **732b**
ʿAṭāʾī, Newʿi-zāde (1635) i, **732b**; viii, 8b, 164a
Atak i, **733a**; iv, 1102a, 1159b
Ātäk → Abīward
Ataliḳ i, **733b**; s, 96b
ʿAtama i, **733b**
At(a)man viii, 189b, 192a
Atar i, **733b**; v, 654a
Atargatis vi, 378b, 382a
al-Ātāsī, M. Hāshim (XX) iv, 138a
Atatürk (Muṣṭafā Kemāl Pasha) (1938) i, 75b, 470b, 511a, 641b, **734a**, 777a, 783a, 1255b;ii, 104b, 392a, 430b, 432a, 466b,475b, 497b, 531b,595b, 630a, 644b, 700a, 701b, 712b; iii, 526b, 622a; iv, 124a, 169a, 297b, 611b, 873a, 934a, b, 935b, 946b; v, 906a, 1099b; vi, 94b, 288a, 304b, 470a, 610a, 757b; vii, 188a, 284a, 677b, 764b; viii, 168b, 251a, 1053b; x, 694a; s, 41b, 63a, 98a, 282a, 329a
ʿAṭawiyya vii, 859a
Ātāy → Čay
Atay, Fāliḥ Rifḳī (1971) s, **98a**
Atazir / Athacir → al-Tasyīr
Atbara i, **735a**, 1172a, 1239b; iv, 686a; v, 1251b
Atbedj → Athbādj
Ātbēgī → Atabak
Atchin, Atcheh → Atjèh
ʿAteiba → ʿUtayba
Atek i, **735a**
Atesh v, 370a; vii, 531a; s, 98b
Ātesh → Mādjūs
Āteshizāde Memi Shāh (1531) ii, 1042b
ʿAṭf i, **735b**
Aṭfar → Djabala b. al-Ḥārith
Aṭfīḥ i, **735b**
Aṭfiyāsh (Aṭfayyish), Muḥammad b. Yūsuf (1914) i, **736a**; viii, 993b
Atga Khān (XVI) vii, 331b
Athāfit (Yemen) s, 22a, 335a
Athar i, **736a**, 1199a
al-Āthār al-ʿUlwiyya i, **736b**; iii, 30a
Athāth v, 1158a; s, **99a**
Athbādj, Banū i, 533a, 1246b; iii, 138a, 386a, 548a; iv, 479a; v, 1179a; vi, 728b; vii, 994a; s, 62b
Athbedj → Athbādj
Athens → Atīna
Athīr, Banū iii, 723b, 961a
Athīr-i Akhsikatī (1174) iv, 62a; viii, 971a
ʿAthlīth i, **737b**
ʿAthr/ʿAththar i, **737b**; vi, 436a
Athūr s, **100a**
ʿĀṭif Efendi (XVIII) iii, 590a
ʿAtīḳ b. ʿAbd al-Wāḥid b. Ziyād b. al-Muhallab (VIII) vii, 359b
ʿAtīḳ b. Aslam b. Yadhkur, Banū vi, 830b
ʿĀtīḳa bint ʿAbd al-Malik b. al-Ḥārith (VIII) vi, 140b
ʿĀtīḳa bint Aḥmed III (Ottoman) (1724) vi, 860b
ʿĀtīḳa bint Muʿāwiya i, 113b
ʿĀtīḳa bint Shudha (IX) vii, 518a
ʿĀtīḳa bint Zayd (VII) i, **738a**
Atil i, 721b, **738a**; iv, 280a, 1173a, 1176a, 1177b, 1178b; v, 1013b
Atīna i, **738b**
ʿAtīra i, **739b**; s, 221b
Ātish, Khwādja Ḥaydar ʿAlī (1847) ii, 84b; x, 878a; s, **102a**
Ātishī (Kandahar) (1565) ix, 241a
ʿAṭiyya (Mirdāsid) (1065) vi, 544a
ʿAṭiyya, Banū iii, 642b
ʿAṭiyya, Muḥammad (XX) viii, 727b
ʿAṭiyya b. al-Aswad al-Ḥanafī (688) iv, 534b; vii, 859a
Atjèh (Aceh) i, 88a, 92a, **739b**; iii, 1218b, 1220a, 1233a; v, 20b, 21b; vi, 43a, 234b, 235a, b, 236b, 239b, 240a, 732b; vii, 71b; ix, 154a; x, 222a; s, 199b
– war i, **743b**; iii, 1223a, 1228b
al-ʿAtk i, 538b, **747b**
Atlagic Meḥmed Pasha (XVII) v, 775a
Atlamish (Awnik) (XIV) iv, 586a
Atlas i, 364b, 460a, **748a**; v, 1184b, 1186b
Aṭrābulus → Ṭarābulus

al-Aṭrash → al-Mādharāʾī
Atrek (river) i, **749b**; vi, 495a, 716b
Atsïz b. Muḥammad b. Anūshtigin (Khwārazmshāh) (1156) i, **750a**; ii, 603a; iii, 196b; iv, 29a, 1067a; v, 311b; vi, 415b, 620b; viii, 63b; ix, 16a; s, 245b
Atsïz b. Uvak (1079) i, **750b**, 870a; ii, 282a, 856b, 911b; iii, 160a; v, 328a; vii, 121a, 731a; viii, 946b
ʿAttāb b. Asīd (634) i, **751a**
ʿAttāb b. Saʿd b. Zuhayr, Banū x, 91a
ʿAttāb b. Warḳāʾ (Iṣfahān) (VII) i, 810b
al-ʿAttābī, Kulthūm b. ʿAmr (835) i, **751a**, 857b; vi, 437b
al-ʿAṭṭār (1824) vi, 113a
al-ʿAṭṭār (druggist) i, **751b**; iv, 95b; s, 42b
ʿAṭṭār, Aḥmad ʿAbd al-Ghafūr (XX) vi, 175b
al-ʿAṭṭār → Dāwūd b. ʿAbd al-Raḥmān
al-ʿAṭṭār, Ḥasan b. Muḥammad (1835) i, **755a**, 819b; ii, 356b; viii, 523b
ʿAṭṭār, Hāshim (XIX) iv, 775b
ʿAṭṭār, Khwādja ʿAlāʾ al-Dīn (1393) vii, 934a
ʿAṭṭār, Shaykh Farīd al-Dīn (1220) i, 146a, **752b**; ii, 98b, 1041b, 1138a; iii, 373a; iv, 62a, 63a, 65a, 402a; vi, 73a, b, 85b, 762a; vii, 440a, 528b; viii, 83b, 580a; ix, 862b; x, 958a
ʿAṭṭār, Shaykh Khwādja Ḥasan (XV) s, 50b
ʿAttāra (Yemen) vi, 192a
ʿAṭṭārīn (Ḳurṭuba) vi, 188b
ʿAṭṭāsh, ʿAbd al-Malik → Ibn ʿAṭṭāsh
Attila (Hun) (453) x, 691b
Attock → Atak
Aurès → Awrās
Ausa (Dakhan) vi, 63b
Austria → Nemče
Avars i, 504a, 624b, **755a**, 998b; ii, 86a, b, 141b, 251a; iii, 157a; iv, 342b, 343a, 344b, 351a, 571b, 631b, 1172a; v, 55b, 81b, 579b; x, 691b
Avaristān ii, 86a
Avempace → Ibn Bādjdja
Avenetan, Avennathan → Ibn al-Haytham
Avennasar → al-Fārābī
Avenzoar → Ibn Zuhr, Abū Marwān
Averroes → Ibn Rushd
Avesta i, 236a; iii, 112b; iv, 11a; v, 1110a
Avetis Sulṭān-Zāda (XX) s, 365b
Avicenna → Ibn Sīnā
Avram Camondo → Camondo
Avroman → Hawrāmān
Avshar (Anatolia) vi, 420b
Āwa i, **756b**
ʿAwaḍ b. Ṣāliḥ (ʿAwlaḳī, Banū) (XX) i, 767a
Awadh (Oudh) i, 153a, **756b**, 809a, 1330a; ii, 808b, 870b; iv, 276b, 908a; v, 635a, 1033b, 1240a; vi, 48a, 49b, 77b, 244b, 272a, 535b, 537a; vii, 300b, 412a, 433a; viii, 793b; s, 76b, 95a, 102b, 247a, 292a, 312b, 358b, 360a
– Nawwābs i, 856a, 1330a; iii, 61a, 451a, 1163a
Awadhī (Eastern Hindī) iii, 456b; vi, 272a
ʿAwādhil → ʿAwdhalī
Āwadj → Āwa
Awadjïḳ vi, 200b, 201a
Awāʾil i, **758a**, 772b
Awāl (Baḥrayn) vi, 357b
ʿAwāliḳ → ʿAwlaḳī
ʿAwālim → ʿĀlima
Awami League viii, 243a
ʿAwāmil → ʿĀmil
al-ʿAwāmir, Banū i, **759b**
ʿAwāna b. al-Ḥakam al-Kalbī (764) i, **760a**; v, 947b; vii, 268b
Awar → Avars
al-Aʿwar → Abū Yaʿḳūb al-Khuraymī
ʿAwāriḍ i, **760a**; ii, 147a; iv, 234b
al-ʿAwāṣim i, 145a, 239a, 465b, 517a, **761a**, 909b, 996a, 1292b; ii, 36a; vi, 230b, 332b; s, 243a, b
al-Awāzim, Banū i, 546a, **762a**; iii, 642a, 1068a
ʿAwda b. Ḥarb Abū Tāyih (Ṭayyiʾ), Shaykh (XX) iii, 643a; x, 885a
Awdaghost i, **762a**; 1002a; iii, 288b, 657a; v, 653a; vi, 742b; vii, 585a
ʿAwdhalī i, **762b**; ii, 675b
ʿAwdhila → ʿAwdhalī
Awdj → Nudjūm
Awdjila i, **763a**, 1049a, b
ʿAwf b. ʿAṭiyya iv, 998a
ʿAwf b. Badr al-Fazārī s, 177b
Awfāt i, 176b, **763b**; iii, 3b, 5b
ʿAwfī, Muḥammad (1232) i, 94b, **764a**, 780a, 1131a; iii, 373a, 1155b; v, 385b; vii, 529b; s, 21a, 22a, 416a

Awghānī, Banū i, 218a
Awḥad al-Dīn ʿAbd al-Wāḥid (1385) ii, 330a
Awḥad al-Zamān → Abu 'l-Barakāt Hibat Allāh
Awḥadī (mystic) (XIV) iii, 635a
al-Awḥadī (1408) vi, 194a
Awḥadī Marāghaʾī (1338) x, 321b
Awḥadī, Rukn al-Dīn (1337) i, **764b**; iv, 67b
Awḥadī Taḳī al-Dīn Muḥammad al-Ḥusaynī → Taḳī Awḥadī
Awḳāf → Waḳf
Awḳāt → Waḳt
ʿAwl i, 320a, **764b**
Awlād → name of ancestor
Awlād al-Balad i, **765a**; v, 1250a, 1251b
Awlād Dulaym, Banū vi, 741b
Awlād Ḥassān vii, 613b, 614a, 616a
Awlād Khalīfa iv, 382b
Awlād Mṭāʿ vi, 594a
Awlād al-Nās i, 102a, **765a**, 1060a; iii, 99b; iv, 552b
Awlād Nāṣir vii, 613b
Awlād Saʿd Allāh vi, 743a
Awlād al-Shaykh i, **765b**, 802b
Awlād Sīdī Shaykh vi, 252a; viii, 794b
Awlād Sulaymān s, 164a, b
Awlād Yūnus vi, 743a
ʿAwlaḳī i, **766b**; ii, 675b
Āwlīl (island) ii, 1121b; vii, 57a
Awliyāʾ → Walī (Saint)
Awliyā Allāh Āmulī, Mawlānā (XIV) i, 871b; iii, 810b
Awliyā ata i, **767a**
Awliyar, Shaykh (XVI) iv, 723b
Awlonya i, 656a, **767b**
ʿAwn, Āl iii, 263a, 605b
ʿAwn Allāh Kāẓimī → al-Kāẓimī, Meḥmed
ʿAwn b. ʿAlī x, 41b
ʿAwn b. Djaʿfar b. Abī Ṭālib (VII) s, 92b
ʿAwn al-Dīn al-Tutunčī, imām (XIII) vii, 9b
ʿAwn al-Rafīḳ, Sharīf (1905) ii, 91a; vi, 151a
Awraba, Banū i, 1037a; iii, 1031b; v, 517b, 518a; vi, 889b; xi, 132b; s, **102b**
Awrangābād i, **768a**; ii, 55a, 99b, 262b; iii, 450b; vi, 53a, 369b
Awrangābād Sayyid i, **768a**
Awrangābādī, ʿAbd al-Razzāḳ → Shāh Nawāz Khān
Awrangzīb ʿĀlamgīr I (Mughal) (1707) i, 199b, 218a, 229a, 253a, 432b, 624b, **768a**, 954a, 1069a, 1161a, 1166a, 1193b, 1202b, 1210a, 1219a, 1300a, 1329b, 1331a; ii, 99b, 121a, 132a, 134b, 162a, 379a, 488b, 504a, 558a, 566b, 1049b; iii, 199a, 200b, 202a, 308b, 424b, 427a, 430a, 450b, 453b, 492b; iv, 93a, 286b, 514a, 914b, 1128a; v, 47b, 598b, 1135b, 1259a; vi, 126b, 310a, 369b, 407a, 456b, 534b, 535a, 536a, 610b, 612a, 696b; vii, 194a, 315a, b, 318a, 333b, 339b, 346a, 443b; viii, 253b; s, 55b, 57b, 126b, 142b, 246b, 258a, b, 292a, 410b, 420b
Awrangzīb Khān → Bādshāh Khān
Awrās (Aurès) i, 170a, 171b, 366a, 367a, 748b, **770a**, 1037a; iv, 383a, 459b; v, 696a; vi, 434b, 435a; s, 103a
Awrigha, Banū i, 1049a
al-Aws, Banū i, 514a, 544b, **771a**, 1283a; iii, 812a; iv, 835b, 1187a; v, 995a; vi, 373b, 374a, 472a; vii, 367a, 852b; s, 229b, 230a
Aws b. Ḥadjar (VI) i, **772a**; vi, 605b; x, 586a
Aws b. Ḥāritha b. Laʾm i, 1241a
Aws b. Maghrāʾ vii, 843a
Awsan iv, 746a
Awshār → Afshār
Awsī, Āl vi, 646a
al-Awsī al-Anṣarī, ʿUmar b. Ibrāhīm iii, 181a
Awtād i, 95a, **772a**
al-ʿAwwāʾ → Nudjūm
ʿAwwād, Tawfīḳ Yūsuf (XX) v, 189b, 190b
Awwal i, **772a**
al-ʿAwwām b. al-Zadjdjādj (Baḥrayn) (XI) iv, 764b
al-ʿAwwām b. ʿAbd al-ʿAzīz al-Badjalī (VIII) i, 134b
al-ʿAwwānī, Ibrāhīm (1320) vi, 353b
al-Awzāʿī, Abū ʿAmr ʿAbd al-Raḥmān (774) i, 164b, **772b**, 1137b; ii, 489a, 889b, 1026b; vi, 263b, 281a, 352b; vii, 398a; viii, 713a; ix, 7a; s, 384b
Awzal → al-Hawzālī, Muḥammad b. ʿAlī
Ay Khanum vi, 764b
Ay Aba, Djuyūsh Beg (1120) i, 300b; vi, 64a, 500a, 782a; vii, 235a, 408a
Ay Aba, al-Muʾayyid (Nīshāpūr) (1172) ix, 16b; x, 742b
Ay Tak, Ikhtiyār al-Dīn (Rayy) (XII) ii, 253a; ix, 16b

Āya, āyāt i, **773b**; iv, 616a; v, 422a
Aya Mavra → Levkas
Aya Sofya i, 75a, **774a**; iv, 225a, b, 226a
Aya Solūk i, **777b**
Aya Stefanos → Yeshilköy
Aʿyān i, 657a, **778a**, 1304a; ii, 33b, 640b, 724a; iii, 1187b
ʿAyān Kāzarūnī, Shaykh s, 51b,
Aʿyāṣ (Umayya) vi, 626a; s, **103b**
Āyās (town) i, **778b**, 946b; ii, 38a; iii, 475a
Ayās, Mawlānā (1451) vi, 70a
Ayās Pasha (1539) i, 293b, **779a**; ii, 203b
Ayash vi, 226b
Āyāt → Āya
Āyatullāh (Ayatollah) (title) s, **103b**
Āyatullāh Kāshānī → Kāshānī
Āyatullāh Ḳumī → Ṭabāṭabāʾī, Sayyid Āḳā Ḥusayn b. Muḥammad
Ayāz (1507) vi, 51a
Ayāz, Abu ʾl-Nadjm (1057) i, **780a**
Ayāz, Amīr (1105) i, **780a**
Ayāz b. Alp Arslān (Saldjūḳ) (1072) vi, 273b
Aybak, al-Muʿizz ʿIzz al-Dīn al-Muʿaẓẓamī (Mamlūk) (1248) i, 732a, **780b**, 804a, 944b; ii, 284a; iv, 210a, 484b; v, 571a, 627b, 821a; vi, 321b, 668b; vii, 148a, 166b, 274a, 989b; viii, 989a, 995a; s, 250a
Aybak Ḳuṭb al-Dīn → Ḳuṭb al-Dīn Aybak
Aybak al-Turkumānī, ʿIzz al-Dīn (1257) i, 732a, 804a, 944b; vi, 321b; ix, 176a
Aybar, Mehmet Ali (XX) iv, 124b
Aybeg → Aybak
ʿAydarūs, Āl i, **780b**
ʿAydarūs, ʿAbd Allāh (1461) i, **781a**
al-ʿAydarūs, ʿAbd al-Ḳādir i, 255b, 594b, **781a**; iv, 449b
al-ʿAydarūs, Abū Bakr (1508) i, 181b, **781a**; iv, 450a; vi, 132b, 354b
ʿAydarūs, ʿAlī Zayn al-ʿĀbidīn (1632) i, **781b**
ʿAydarūs b. ʿAlī (1948) i, 767a
ʿAydarūs b. ʿUmar al-Ḥabshī (1895) i, 782a
Aydemir, Colonel Talât (XX) iii, 204a
ʿAydhāb i, **782b**, 1158a; ii, 130b; v, 514b, 519a; vi, 195a, b; vii, 164b; viii, 863b;
Aydid, Muḥammad Faraḥ (general) ix, 721a
Aydimur → ʿIzz al-Dīn Aydimur
Aydi̊n i, 467b, **782b**, 1234b; v, 505b, 506a, 557b; vi, 372b, 716b, 975a
– Edict of vi, 496b
Aydi̊n-oghlu i, 346a, 778a, **783a**, 807a; ii, 599a; vi, 1018b; vii, 939b
Aydi̊n Reʾīs (Cacciadiavolo) (XVI) iv, 1156a, b
Ay-Doghmi̊sh (1205) vi, 500b
Aydoghu b. Kushdoghan → Shumla
Ayesha Bai (Kerala) vi, 460b
ʿAyhala b. Kaʿb → al-Aswad b. Kaʿb al-ʿAnsī
ʿĀyid, Banū i, 98b; vii, 921a
ʿĀyisha Kargīli Diz → Ṭāḳ
al-Ayka → Madyan
Aykaç, Fāḍil Aḥmed (XX) iii, 357b
Ayla i, 558b, **783b**; x, 883a
Aylūl → Taʾrīkh
Aymak i, **784a**; s, 367a
Aymal Khān, Afghān (XVII) i, 970b
Aymān → Ḳasam
Ayman b. Khuraym (VII) i, **784b**; s, 273a
ʿAyn → Hidjaʾ
ʿAyn (eye) i, **785a**; iv, 954a
ʿAyn (evil eye) i, **786a**; iv, 1009a
ʿAyn, aʿyān (sight) i, **784b**; ii, 486b
ʿAyn, ʿuyūn (spring water) i, 538b, 1232a
ʿAyn al-Baḳar vi, 652a
ʿAyn Dārā iv, 834b
ʿAyn al-Dawla (Ṣadr-i Aʿẓam) (XX) ii, 650b, 651a; viii, 140a
ʿAyn Dilfa i, **786b**
ʿAyn Djālūt (battle) (1260) i, 21b, **786b**, 1125a; ii, 284b; iii, 184a; v, 571b; vi, 314b, 321b, 543b; vii, 167a
ʿAyn al-Djarr i, **787b**; vi, 623b; s, 229b
ʿAyn Ḥunayn vi, 179b
ʿAyn al-Ḳuḍāt al-Hamadhānī → ʿAbd Allāh b. Abī Bakr al-Miyānadjī
ʿAyn al-Mulk Māhrū (XIII) s, 105b
ʿAyn al-Mulk Multānī (1322) i, 764a; ii, 12b, 218b; iii, 405b; iv, 759a, 922a; v, 635a; vi, 309b; s, **105a**
ʿAyn Mūsā i, **788a**
ʿAyn Shams i, **788a**; ii, 424a; vi, 75b, 411a, 412b, 413a
ʿAyn al-Tamr i, **788b**; x, 791a
ʿAyn Temushent i, **789a**
ʿAyn al-Warda i, **789a**; vii, 522a
ʿAyn Warḳa s, 159b
ʿAyn Yashīr i, 699b
ʿAyn Zarba i, **789a**; ii, 37b; vi, 505b, 775a
ʿAyn Zubayda vi, 164b, 177b, 179a

Ayna Čās̲h̲negīr, Sayf al-Dīn, amīr (XIII) i, 510a
Aynabak̲h̲tī i, **790a**; iv, 882a; v, 504a; s, 80b
Aynāl → Īnāl
Aynalu, Banū iv, 9b
ʿAynayn → al-D̲j̲ubayl
ʿAynayn, Āl Bū iv, 751b
al-ʿAynī (1487) vii, 537a
al-ʿAynī, Abū Muḥammad Badr al-Dīn (1451) i, 138a, 595a, **790b**, 1128a; iii, 488b; iv, 966b; v, 489b; vi, 194a; vii, 172b, 969b
ʿAynī ʿAlī (1617) vi, 508b
ʿAynī, Ḥasan Efendi (1837) i, **790b**
ʿAyniyya i, 51a; ii, 1094b; v, 889b, 892a
ʿAynṭāb i, 262a, **791a**; ii, 206; vi, 231a, 378a, 507a, 508b
al-ʿAynṭabī, Muḥammad S̲h̲ākir b. al-Ḥād̲j̲d̲j̲ Ibrāhīm Ḥilmī (1877) vi, 913b
ʿAynṭūra s, 33b
Ayodhyā → Awadh
Ayr → Aïr
al-ʿAyrayn Mnt. vi, 745a
Ayrumlu K̲h̲āns vi, 200b
ʿAys̲h̲e → ʿĀʾis̲h̲a
Ayt i, **792a**
Ayt Atta, Banū x, 82b
Ayt Idrasen s, 113b
Ayt Immūr, Banū vi, 590a
Ayt Isḥāḳ s, 223a
Ayt Mūsā s, 113b
Ayt Yūsī s, 113b
Aytāk̲h̲ al-Turkī (849) vii, 777b; s, **106a**
Ayt̲h̲ Zekrī (1914) s, 403b
Āytigīn, Ik̲h̲tiyār al-Dīn (XIII) vii, 915b
Aytimis̲h̲ al-Bad̲j̲asī, amīr (1400) ii, 781a, b
Ayudhya (XV) vi, 212b
Ayuka (1724) vi, 416b
Ayüke K̲h̲ān, Kalmuk (1678) i, 1076a
Aywalık i, **792a**
Aywān → Iwān
Aywaz (ʿAywāḍ) i, **792a**
Ayyām al-ʿAd̲j̲ūz i, **792b**
Ayyām al-ʿArab i, 566a, **793a**
ʿAyyān (Yemen) vi, 438b
Ayyār → Taʾrīk̲h̲
ʿAyyār (ʿayyārūn) i, 256b, **794a**, 900a, b, 902a, b, 955a, 1355b; ii, 961b, 962a, 1043b; iv, 445a
ʿAyyās̲h̲ b. Lahīʿa (IX) i, 153b
al-ʿAyyās̲h̲ī (marabout) (1641) v, 48b; viii, 899a
al-ʿAyyās̲h̲ī, Abu ʾl-Naṣr Muḥammad (IX) i, **794b**; iv, 711b; vi, 188a
al-ʿAyyās̲h̲ī, Abū Sālim ʿAbd Allāh (1679) i, **795a**; ii, 161a; iii, 736b
Ayyil i, **795a**
Ayyūb (Job) i, **795b**; 242a
Ayyūb, Ras̲h̲īd (1941) v, 1254b, 1255a, b
Ayyūb (of Edessa) (IX) i, 213a
Ayyūb b. Abi Yazīd al-Nukkārī (X) i, 163b; iii, 1042a; vi, 727b
Ayyūb b. Aḥmad al-Tag̲h̲libī (IX) vi, 900a
Ayyūb b. Ḥabīb al-Lak̲h̲mī (VIII) i, 58b; iv, 477b
Ayyūb b. al-Raḳḳī iv, 92a
Ayyūb b. Salama (VIII) vi, 139a
Ayyūb b. Shād̲h̲ī b. Marwān (XII) i, 796b
Ayyūb b. Tamīm b. al-Muʿizz (Zīrid) (XII) iii, 788a
Ayyūb Anṣārī (VII) s, 292a
Ayyūb K̲h̲ān (1914) i, 232a, **796b**; iv, 537b
Ayyūb K̲h̲ān (1974) iii, 533b, 565b, 566a; v, 1081b; vi, 78b; viii, 242b
Ayyūb Ṣabrī Pas̲h̲a (1890) i, **796b**
Ayyūb al-Sak̲h̲tiyānī iv, 370b
Ayyūbids i, 197b, 215a, 435b, 439b, 552b, 666b, **796b**, 814b, 816a, 1125a, 1206b, 1276b, 1316b; ii, 65a, 283b, 305b, 329b, 344b, 506a, 858a; iii, 120b, 228b, 473a, 507a; iv, 429b, 816b, 817b; v, 454b, 627b, 739a, 1245a; vi, 149a, 194a, 231a, 261b, 326b, 327a, 429a, b, 433b, 673b, 931a; vii, 164a, 998a; ix, 596b; xi, 190a; s, 154a, 338a, 387b, 396a
– literature iii, 753a, 967a
al-ʿAyyūḳ → Nud̲j̲ūm
ʿAyyūḳī (XI) iv, 57b, 62b; vi, 833
ʿAzab i, **807a**; iv, 230b, 723a
Āzād, Abu ʾl-Kalām (1958) iii, 431b; iv, 170b; v, 7a, b; vi, 461b; s, 4b, **106a**, 247b
Āzād, Muḥammad Ḥusayn (1910) i, **807b**; ii, 222a; iii, 93b; vii, 556a, 668a; s, 74b, **107a**
Āzād Bilgrāmī, G̲h̲ulām-ʿAlī (1786) i, **808a**, 1219b; vi, 271b; vii, 530b
Āzād K̲h̲ān (Afg̲h̲ān) (XVIII) i, 190a; iii, 1103a; iv, 390a, 639b
Āzādī s, **107b**
al-ʿAzafī, Abu ʾl-Ḳāsim (XIII) viii, 690b

ʿAzafī, Banu ʾl- iv, 355b; s, 45b, **111b**
Azahari, Shaykh A.M. (Brunei) (XX) s, 152a, b
Azaḳ (Azov) i, **808b**; vi, 56a, 1025b
Azal → Ḳidam
Azalay i, **808b**, 1222a; ii, 368a, b
Azalī i, **809a**; vi, 292a
Aʿẓam b. Awrangzīb (Mughal) (1707) vii, 341b
Aʿẓam Humāyūn → Malik Mughīth (Mālwā); Maḥmūd II Khaldjī
Aʿẓam-i Humāyūn b. Sayf al-Dīn Ghūrī, vizier (XIV) iv, 908a
Aʿẓam Khān I (Rādjpūt) (XVII) i, 809a; iv, 1018b; vii, 333b
Aʿẓam Khān II (Rādjpūt) (1771) i, 809a
Aʿẓam Khān (Mālwa) (XVI) v, 1a
Aʿẓam Khān Bārakzay → Muḥammad Aʿzam b. Dūst Muḥammad
Aʿẓam Shāh Ghiyāth al-Dīn (Bengal) (1419) ii, 216b; v, 638a
Aʿẓam Shāh (Mughal) → Muḥammad Aʿẓam b. Awrangzīb
Aʿẓamgarh i, **809a**; iii, 433a; ix. 433b
ʿAzamiyya (Ṭarīḳa) → Abu ʾl-ʿAzāʾim
Azammūr i, **809b**; vi, 573a, 594a, 740a, 741b
Āzar i, **810a**; iii, 980a
Azar Kaywan (1618) v, 1114a
Azarbāydjān → Adharbāydjān; Azerbaydjān
al-Azārīfī, Abū Muḥammad ʿAbd Allāh (1800) vi, 113a
Azāriḳa i, 77a, **810a**; iii, 40b, 657b; iv, 15a, 44b, 99b, 269a, 752b, 1075b; v, 157b; vii, 123b, 357a, 877b; x, 762a
Azarquîel → al-Zarḳālī
ʿAzāz (battle of (1030)) i, 239a; v, 106a; vii, 117b
ʿAzāzīl i, **811a**
Azd, Banū i, 304a, 529b, 544b, 548b, **811b**, 1140b; ii, 246b; iii, 223a, 782a; v, 77a; vi, 564b, 640b; x, 3a; s, 222b
al-Azd b. al-Ghawth vi, 565b
Azda bint al-Ḥārith b. Kalada (VII) s, 354b
Azdadja → al-Barānis
al-Azdamūrī, Sayf al-Dīn Manku Bāy (1415) vi, 580b
al-Azdī→ Abū Manṣūr; Abu ʾl-Muṭahhar; ʿĪsā b. Rayʿān; Yazīd b. Ḥātim
al-Azdī, ʿAbd al-ʿAzīz b. ʿAbd al-Raḥmān (IX) vi, 332a
al-Azdī, Abu ʾl-Khaṭṭāb vi, 774a
al-Azdī, Abū Muḥammad Yūsuf, ḳāḍī (X) s, 284a
al-Azdī, Abū Zakariyyāʾ (945) i, **813a**; viii, 518a
al-Azdī, ʿAlī b. Aḥmad (IX) viii, 53a
al-Azdī, Dhu Tādj Laḳīṭ b. Mālik s, 693b
al-Azdī, Djunada b. Abī Umayya (VII) viii, 569a
al-Azdī, Hārūn b. Mūsā viii, 818b
al-Azdī, Ismāʿīl b. Isḥāḳ b. Ḥammād al-Ḳāḍī (895) vi, 280b; s, **113a**, 384a
al-Azdī, Muḥammad b. al-Muʿallā s, 394b
Azemmūr → Azammūr
Azerbāydjān, Ādharbaydjān (republic) i, 188b, **191b**, ii, 595a; iii, 530a; v, 1213b;
Azerī → Ādharī
Aẓfarī (1818) i, **813b**
Azghār vi, 741b
al-Azhar i, **813b**; ii, 495a, 854a, 863a; iii, 841a, 986b; iv, 144a, 444a, 907b; v, 910b, 1124a; vi, 87b, 170a, 237b, 361a, 414a; ix, 260b; s, 18a, 40b, 121b, 132b, 262b, 408a, 411a
al-Azharī (XI) vi, 634b
al-Azharī, Abū Manṣūr Muḥammad (980) i, 719a, **822a**; iv, 524b; vi, 914a; vii, 209b; viii, 14a; s, 20a, 38a, 250b
al-Azharī, Aḥmad (1748) i, **821b**
al-Azharī, Ibrāhīm (1688) i, **821b**
al-Azharī, Ismāʿīl (XX) iii, 524a
al-Azharī, Khālīd (1499) i, **821b**, 1314b
ʿAẓīm Allāh Khān (1859) i, **822a**
ʿAẓīm al-Shān b. Bahādur Shāh I (XVIII) i, 914a, 1025b; ii, 7a, 379a, 810a
ʿAzīma i, **822b**; ii, 545a
ʿAẓīmābād → Bānkīpūr
Azimech → Nudjūm
al-ʿAẓīmī (1161) i, **823a**
Azimut → al-Samt
al-ʿĀzir → Lazarus
al-ʿAzīz (Ayyūbid) → al-Malik al-ʿAzīz ʿUthmān
al-ʿAzīz (Ḥammādid) (1121) iii, 138b
ʿAzīz b. Ḥātim (VII) vii, 922a
ʿAzīz ʿAlī al-Maṣrī (XX) s, 299b
al-ʿAzīz bi-ʾllāh Nizār (Fāṭimid) (996) i, 533a, 788a, 814b, 816a, **823a**, 1153b,

1218a; ii, 854a, 855a, 860a; iii, 76b, 128b, 130a, 246a, 385b; iv, 663b; vi, 199b, 435b, 545a, 670a, 673b; vii, 162a, 357b, 910b
ʿAzīz Ḍiyāʾ al-Dīn b. Zāhid (XX) v, 1005b
ʿAzīz Efendī → ʿAlī ʿAzīz Giridli
ʿAzīz Khammār (Amrohā) (XIV) s, 73b
ʿAzīz Miṣr i, **825b**
Aziz Nesin (XX) vi, 95b
ʿAzīz Saghrūshnī (XX) vi, 755b
al-ʿAzīz ʿUthmān b. al-Ādil b. Ayyūb (Ayyūbid) (XIII) ix, 739a
ʿAzīza bint al-Ghiṭrīf b. ʿAṭāʾ (VIII) s, 326b
ʿAzīza ʿUthmāna (XVIII) iii, 605a
ʿAzīzat al-Dīn Akhshāwrā Khātūn bint Mawdūd b. ʿImād al-Dīn Zangī (1213) vi, 871b
ʿAzīzī (1585) i, **825b**
ʿAzīzī → Ḳara-čelebi-zāde
ʿAzīziyya x, 250a; xi, 295a
Azkūtigīn b. Asātigīn (IX) vi, 900a
ʿAzl i, **826a**
al-ʿAzm, Āl v, 925a
ʿAzmī Gedizī (XVI) v, 952a
ʿAzmī-zade, Muṣṭafā (1631) i, **826a**; iii, 91b
Aẓnag → al-Sanhadjī, Ibrāhīm b. ʿAbd Allāh
Azophi → al-Ṣūfī, Abu ʾl-Ḥusayn
Azores → al-Djazāʾir al-Khālida
Azougui → Atar
Azov → Azaḳ
Azov, Sea of- → Baḥr Māyuṭis
Azra Erhat (XX) vi, 95b
ʿAzrāʾīl → ʿIzrāʾīl
al-Azraḳ ix, 673a
al-Azraḳī s, 271b, 272a
al-Azraḳī, Abu ʾl-Walīd (VII) i, 591a, 609a, **826b**; ii, 757b
Azraḳī Harawī, Zayn al-Dīn (1130) i, **827a**; iv, 61b; viii, 970b
Azraḳī Kurds → Zraḳī
Azraḳites → Azāriḳa
Azrū s, **113a**
Azuel → Abū Muḥammad al-Zubayr b. ʿUmar
Azūg(g)i (Azuḳḳī) vii, 587b, 613a
Azulejo → Khazaf
Āzurda, Ṣadr al-Dīn (1868) i, **827b**; ii, 736a
ʿAzza → Kuthayyir
ʿAzza al-Maylāʾ (VII) i, **828a**; ii, 1073b; iii, 812a; iv, 821b; viii, 853a
ʿAzzāba iii, 95a, 96a
ʿAzzān b. Ḳays (ʿUmān) (1871) i, 554b, 1283a; iv, 1085a; viii, 993a; s, 355b, 356a
ʿAzzān b. Tamīm (893) i, 813a

B

Bāʾ → Hidjāʾ; Mawāzīn
Bā i, **828a**
Bā ʿAbbād i, **828b**
Bā Aḥmad → Bā Ḥmād
Bā ʿAlawī, Āl i, 77b, 780b, **828b**; iv, 885b, 887b; x, 303a
Bā Faḍl → Faḍl, Bā
Bā Faḳīh → Faḳīh, Bā
Bā Ḥassān → Ḥassān, Bā
Bā Ḥmād, Aḥmad b. Mūsā, vizier (1900) i, 57b, 357a; ii, 820a; iii, 562b; v, 1193a; vi, 589b; s, **114a**, 336b
Bā Hurmuz → Hurmuz, Bā
Bā Kathīr → Kathīr, Āl
Bā Kāzim → Kāzim, Bā
Ba Lobbo i, 303b; ii, 914b; iii, 39b
Bā Madhidj → al-Suwaynī, Saʿd b. ʿĀlī
Bā Makhrama → Makhrama, Bā
Bā Ṣurra ii, 173b
Baalbek → Baʿlabakk
Bāb (gate) i, **830a**; v, 989b
Bāb (Shīʿa) i, **832b**; ii, 97b; iv, 39a, 51b, 70b, 854b
al-Bāb (Buṭnān) i, 1349a, 1357b, 1358a; vi, 378a
Bāb, ʿAlī Muḥammad Shīrāzī, Sayyid (1850) i, **833a**, 1030b; iv, 39a, 51b, 70b, 696a; vii, 422a; viii, 679a; ix, 404a
Bāb Abraz (Baghdād) s, 384a
Bāb al-Abwāb (Darband) i, 32a, **835b**; iv, 342a, 1173a; vi, 740a, b; vii, 71a
Bāb Adjyād (Makka) vi, 167a
Bāb Aghmāt (Marrākush) vi, 591a, 596a
Bāb Agnaw (Marrākush) vi, 596b
Bāb al-Aḥmar (Marrākush) vi, 596b
Bāb-i ʿĀlī (Istanbul) i, **836a**; iv, 568a, 1126a
Bāb Allāh (Damascus) s, 49a
Bāb Allāh (Ternate) (XVI) vi, 116b
Bāb Allān → Bāb al-Lān

Bāb Aylān (Marrāku<u>sh</u>) vi, 590b, 591a, 592a, 596a; s, 124b
Bāb al-Aza<u>dj</u> (Ba<u>gh</u>dād) s, 192b
Bāb Banī <u>Sh</u>ayba (Makka) vi, 708b
Bāb Banī Sulaym (Baṣra) vi, 709a
Bāb Berrīma (Marrāku<u>sh</u>) vi, 596b
Bāb Dabbā<u>gh</u> (Marrāku<u>sh</u>) vi, 592a, 596a
Bāb al-<u>Dh</u>ahab (Ba<u>gh</u>dād) i, 896a, 897a
Bāb al-<u>Dj</u>ābiya (Damascus) vi, 122b, 548a
Bāb <u>Dj</u>amā'iz (Makka) vi, 160a
Bāb al-<u>Dj</u>īsa (Fès) s, 126a
Bāb Dukkāla (Marrāku<u>sh</u>) vi, 590a, b, 596a, 597a
Bāb al-Durayba (Makka) vi, 175a, 177a
Bāb al-Farādīs (Damascus) vi, 122b
Bāb Fās → Bāb al-<u>Kh</u>amīs
Bāb Futūḥ (Fès) vi, 123b
Bāb al-Futūḥ (Miṣr) vii, 149a, 150a
Bāb al-<u>Gh</u>adr iv, 685a
Bāb al-Ḥadīd (Cairo) vi, 414a
Bāb al-Ḥamra (Fès) vi, 124a
Bāb al-Ḥarb (Ba<u>gh</u>dād) vi, 123b
Bāb Ḥiṭṭa (al-Ḳuds) vi, 626b
Bāb-i Humāyūn (Istanbul) i, **836b**; iv, 568a
Bāb Ibrāhīm (Makka) vi, 154b
Bāb I<u>gh</u>lī (Marrāku<u>sh</u>) vi, 596b
Bāb Kaysān (Damascus) vi, 122b
Bāb al-<u>Kh</u>amīs (Marrāku<u>sh</u>) vi, 590a, 596a
Bāb al-<u>Kh</u>awḳa (Málaga) vi, 220b
Bāb Ḳṣība (Marrāku<u>sh</u>) vi, 596b
Bāb Ḳubbat Zamzam (Makka) vi, 166a
Bāb al-Kuḥl (Marrāku<u>sh</u>) vi, 596b
Bāb al-Lān (Bāb Allān) i, **837a**; iv, 342b
Bāb al-Ma<u>kh</u>zen (Marrāku<u>sh</u>) vi, 596a
Bāb Maʿlā (Makka) vi, 122b
Bāb al-Malik (Suʿūd) (Makka) vi, 167b
Bāb al-Mandab i, **837b**, 932a
Bāb-i Ma<u>sh</u>ī<u>kh</u>at (Istanbul) i, **837b**
Bāb Messūfa (Marrāku<u>sh</u>) vi, 596a
Bāb Muḥriḳ (Marrāku<u>sh</u>) vi, 596a
Bāb Nfīs (Marrāku<u>sh</u>) vi, 596a
Bāb al-Rabb (Marrāku<u>sh</u>) vi, 591a
Bāb al-Raḥā (Marrāku<u>sh</u>) vi, 596a
Bāb al-Riyāḥ (Málaga) vi, 220b
Bāb al-Sāʿāt (Damascus) vi, 671a
Bāb al-Ṣafā (Makka) vi, 154b, 666b
Bāb al-Ṣa<u>gh</u>īr (Damascus) vi, 122b, 538a
Bāb al-Salām (Makka) vi, 153a, 160b, 167a, 177a, 709a
Bāb al-Saliḥa (Marrāku<u>sh</u>) vi, 596a
Bāb-i Serʿaskeri (Istanbul) i, **838a**; ii, 513a; iii, 552b
Bāb al-<u>Sh</u>ammāsiyya (Ba<u>gh</u>dād) vii, 485a
Bāb Ta<u>gh</u>zūt (Marrāku<u>sh</u>) vi, 596a
Bāb al-Ṭāḳ (Ba<u>gh</u>dād) i, 897a, 898b, 900a, b; s, 192b, 194a, 381a
Bāb al-Ṭubūl (Marrāku<u>sh</u>) vi, 596b
Bāb Tūmā (<u>Sh</u>ay<u>kh</u> Raslān, Damascus) vi, 122b, 545b
Bāb Umm Hāni' (Makka) vi, 167a
Bāb al-ʿUmra (Makka) vi, 160b
Bāb al-Wādī (Málaga) vi, 220b
Bāb Yīntān (Marrāku<u>sh</u>) vi, 596a
Bāb al-Zumurrud (Ba<u>gh</u>dād) vi, 519b
Bāb Zuwayla (Cairo) vi, 367b; s, 408a
Baba i, **838b**
Baba b. Ḥamā Allāh (Ḥamālī) (XX) iii, 108a
Bābā Ādam (1119) i, 1168a; ii, 216a
Baba Afḍal al-Dīn Muḥammad (1256) i, **838b**
Baba ʿAlī b. Ṣāliḥ b. Ḳuṭb al-Dīn (XIV) ii, 989b
Baba ʿAlī Mest-i ʿA<u>dj</u>emī (XVI) iv, 1137a
Baba ʿAlī Na<u>djdj</u>ār (XV) s, 423b
Baba Ardalān i, 626b
Baba Ayyūb (Chitral) ii, 29b
Baba Beg (1898) i, **839b**
Baba Dā<u>gh</u>i̊ → Babada<u>gh</u>i̊
Bābā Eskisi → Babaeski
Baba <u>Gh</u>or iii, 16a
Baba Girāy (1522) i, 838b
Baba Ḥasan → Ḥasan Baba
Bābā Ḥasan, Amīr (1460) vi, 513b
Baba Ḥātim → Sālār <u>Kh</u>alīl
Baba Ilyās vi, 354b
Baba Isḥāḳ (XIII) i, 698b, 843b, 1161b; ii, 989a
Baba Ismāʿīl Kubrawī (XV) s, 353b, 423b
Baba <u>Kh</u>ān, Bābā<u>kh</u>ān → Fatḥ ʿAlī <u>Sh</u>āh b. ʿAbd al-Ma<u>dj</u>īd
Baba <u>Kh</u>o<u>sh</u>īn (XI) i, 262b, 841b; v, 823a
Baba Nūr al-Dīn Ri<u>sh</u>ī (1438) s, **114a**
Baba Ratan → Ratan, Bābā Ḥā<u>djdj</u>ī
Baba Sāhib → Bhāskar Rāo
Bābā Sawindīk (XII) x, 33b
Baba Ṭāhir ʿUryān (1010) i, 262b, **839b**; iii, 106a; iv, 62a; x, 377b
Baba Toma (XIX) iv, 352a
Baba ʿU<u>th</u>mān (XV) s, 353b
Baba Walī Ṣaḥib i, 506a; iii, 245b

Babadaghĭ i, **842b**; ii, 612a, 613a
Babadjān b. Pinchas, Solomon (XIX) iv, 310b
Bäbädjik (canton) vi, 201a, b
Babaeski i, **843a**
Bābāʾī i, 698b, 838b, **843b**; iv, 817a; viii, 191b
Bābāʾī b. Farhād (XVII) iv, 310a
Bābāʾī b. Luṭf (XVII) iv, 310a
Bābak Yaḥyā b. Muʿādh al-Khurramī (838) i, 52b, 153b, 154a, 241a, 625b, 660b, **844a**, 1072b; ii, 228a, 623b, 893a; iii, 274b, 471a; iv, 17a, 344b, 646a; v, 64b, 856a; vi, 335a, 337a, b, 338a, b, 499a, 504b; vii, 497b, 776a, 777a; s, 116a
Bābalyūn (Babylon, Egypt) i, **844b**; vii, 147b
Bābān, Āl i, **845a**; v, 460b; ix, 830a
al-Bābānī, Aḥmad al-Faḳīh (XVII) i, 845a
Bābar → Bābur
Babari (Gobir) (1770) iv, 549a
al-Bābartī → Akmal al-Dīn
Bābā-Ṭāhir (XI) viii, 579b
Babatu (XIX) ii, 1003b
al-Babāwī → Shams al-Dīn Muḥammad
Babba Zakī iv, 549a
Babbaghāʾ i, **845b**
al-Babbaghāʾ, Abu ʾl-Faradj (1007) i, 120a, **845b**; ii, 198a; vii, 770b; s, 119b
Bābil (Babylon) i, **846a**; vi, 218a, 413a, 633b
Bābīs i, 304b, 833a, **846b**, 1099b; v, 102a, 502a; vi, 485a, 552a, b, 939b; vii, 422a, b, 440b, 1003b; viii, 114a; ix, 741a; s, 53b, 54b, 71a, 77a
Babrak Karmal (XX) vii, 291a
Baʿbūd al-ʿAlawī (XVIII) vi, 112b
Bābul → Bārfurūsh
Bābūlā vi, 507a
Bābulkānī, Sayyid Haybat Allāh (XV) vi, 514a
Bābulkānī Sayyids (XV) vi, 513b
Bābūnadj s, **114b**
Bābur b. ʿUmar Shaykh b. Abī Saʿīd, Ẓahīr al-Dīn (Mughal) (1530) i, 218a, 227b, 228a, 252b, 627b, **847b**, 864b, 970a, 1069a, 1139b, 1192b, 1212a, 1323b, 1347b, ii, 29a, 47b, 120b, 264b, 271a, 792a, 973a, 978a, 1049b, 1122b, 1144a; iii, 199b, 200b, 202a, 317a, 422b, 448b, 492b, 995b; iv, 186b, 357a, 410a, 536b, 914b, 1021b; v, 36b, 45b, 250b, 649a, 687a, 885a, 1135a; vi, 52a, 63b, 410a, 425a, 557b, 693a; vii, 105b, 135a, 138b, 218a, 313b, 316b, 329a; viii, 767b; x, 722b; s, 1b, 312a, 313a, 324b, 325a, 329b, 331b
Bābur Mīrzā → Abu ʾl-Ḳāsim Bābur
Bābur-nāma i, 80b, 607a, **848b**; ii, 909b
Babylon (Egypt) → Bābalyūn
Babylon (Mesopotamia) → Bābil
Bačča-yi Saḳāō (Saḳaw) (1928) i, 232b; ii, 658b; v, 1079a; vi, 86b; s, 66b
Bachtarzi (Bāsh Ṭarzī, Muhyī ʾl-Dīn) (XX) vi, 752a, 754b
Bäčkām → Badjkam
Backergunge → Bāḳargandj
Bactria i, 226a; v, 229a
Bād-i Hawā i, 656b, **850a**; ii, 147a
Badāʾ i, 265b, **850a**
Badajoz → Baṭalyaws
Badakhshān i, 46b, 87a, 223b, **851b**; ii, 43a; iii, 575a; iv, 202b, 205b; vi, 612b; vii, 129b, 134b; s, 50b, 125a, b, 258b, 367b
Badakhshānī, Shams al-Dīn (XIV) s, 73b
Badal (Bedel) i, 760b, **855a**; ii, 147a
Badal → Abdāl; Naḥw
Badan → Djism
Badan Singh (XVIII) i, 1193a
Bādarāya → Badra
Badasht vii, 422a
Badāʾūn (Budāʾūn) i, **855b**; ii, 274b; iii, 441b; iv, 749b; v, 1135a; vi, 47b, 48a, b, 62a; vii, 433a; viii, 571b; s, 73b, 74a
Badāʾūnī, ʿAbd al-Ḳādir (1615) i, **856a**, 1136a, b; ii, 871a; vii, 342a; s, 21a, 117b, 206b, 378a
Badāʾūnī, Sayyid Mīr Muḥammad (XVIII) vi, 953a
Badawī → Aḥmād al-Badawī
al-Badawiyya → Aḥmad al-Badawī
Badawlat → Yaʿḳūb Beg (Kāshghar)
Baddh Uwaysī → al-Dhawnpūrī, Sayyid Muḥammad
Baddāyā vi, 544a
Bādghīs / Bādhghīs i, **857a**; 253a; v, 47a; vi, 331a, 428a, 492b, 617b, 633b; x, 926b; s, 367b
Bādgīr v, 1148b; s, **115a**
Bādh (Marwānid) (Diyār Bakr) (983) i,

329a, 637b; ii, 344a; iii, 128b; v, 452b, 453a; vi, 540b, 626a, 930b
Bādhām (Khurāsān) vi, 618a
Bādhām, Bādhān (Yemen) (632) i, 102a, 728a; vi, 565b; s, **115b**
Bādhān Fayrūz → Ardabīl
Badhandūn → Bozanti
al-Badhdh i, 844a; vi, 335a, 504b; vii, 777a; s, **116a**
Badhl al-Kubrā (839) iv, 821b; s, **116b**
Badīʿ i, 587b, 592a, **857b**, 981b; iii, 663b, 665a, 799b; iv, 248b; v, 319a, 321b, 898a, 900a
al-Badīʿ (palace) (Marrākush) vi, 594b, 596b
Bādī I-IV (Fundj) ii, 944a, b
Bādī II (Sinnār) (1681) ix, 650b
Bādī III (Sinnār) (1716) ix, 650b
Badīʿ, Ḥasan iv, 72b, v, 198a
al-Badīʿ al-Asṭurlābī (1139) i, **858b**; iii, 780b
Badīʿ al-Dīn Shāh Madār (1440) i, 702b, **858b**; xi, 117a
Badīʿ al- Zamān → al-Hamadhānī
Badīʿ al-Zamān b. Ḥusayn Bayḳarā (XV) i, 627b; iii, 603a; iv, 1020b
Badīʿ al-Zamān b. Shāhrukh (XVII) i, 853a
Badīʿ al-Zamān Mīrzā (XV) i, 406a; vi, 514b
Badia y Leblich → ʿAlī Bey al-ʿAbbāsī
Badīha → Irtidjāl
Badīl → Abdāl
Bādīnān → Bahdīnān
al-Badīhī, Abu 'l-Ḥasan (X) viii, 615a
Bādis i, **859b**
Bādīs b. Ḥabbūs (Zīrid) (Gharnāṭa) (1073) i, 6a, 130b, 1310a; ii, 1012b, 1015a; iii, 147b; vi, 221a, 222a, b, 728b; vii, 761a, 766b
Bādīs b. al-Manṣūr (Zīrid) (Ifrīḳiyya) (1016) i, **860a**; iii, 137a; iv, 479a; v, 1179a, 1182a, b; vi, 841b; vii, 474a, 481b
al-Bādisī, ʿAbd al-Ḥaḳḳ (1322) i, 596a, **860a**; viii, 503b
al-Bādisī, Abū Ḥassūn ʿAlī → Abū Ḥassan ʿAlī
al-Bādisī, Abū Yaʿḳūb Yūsuf (XIV) i, **860a**
Bādiya s, **116b**
Bādj (tax) i, **860b**; ii, 147a; iii, 489b
Bādj (Firdawsī) i, **862a**
Bādja (al-Andalus) i, **862a**, 1092a; ii, 1009a
Bādjaddā i, **863b**
Bādjalān, Banū i, **863b**
al-Badjalī → Budayl b. Ṭahfa; Djarīr b. ʿAbd Allāh
al-Badjalī, Abū Bakr b. ʿAbd Allāh, Ibn Shādhān al-Rāzī (986) ix, 811b
al-Badjalī, Djibrīl b. Yaḥyā al-Khurāsānī (757) vi, 775a
al-Badjalī, al-Ḥasan b. ʿAlī b. Warsand i, **863b**; s, 402b
Badjaliyya i, 863b; s, 402b
Badjanāk → Pečeneg
al-Bādjarbaḳī (1312) ii, 377a
Bādjarmā (Bādjarmaḳ) i, **864a**
Bādjarwān i, **864a**
al-Badjasī → Aytimish
Bādjat al-Zayt (Tunisia) i, 862a, 863a
Badjāwa → Bedja
Bādjawr i, **864a**
Badjdjāna (Pechina) i, **864b**; vi, 575b
al-Bādjī, Abū Saʿīd Khalaf (1230) vi, 355a
al-Bādjī, Abu 'l-Walīd (1081) i, **864b**; iii, 542b; vi, 279a, 281b; vii, 293a; ix, 187b
Bādjī Rāo I (Marāthā) (1728) i, 710a, 1053a, 1195a; iii, 320a; vi, 535a; vii, 316a, 457a
Bādjī Rāo II (Marāthā) (1818) vi, 535b
Bādjī Rāo, Raghunnāth (1761) vi, 535a
Badjīla, Banū i, **865a**; iv, 925b, 1105b; v, 617a; vi, 441b, 447a; vii, 347b, 592a; x, 3a; s, 37b
Badjimzā (Bagimzā) i, **865b**
Bādjisrā i, **865b**
Badjkam, Abu 'l- Ḥusayn, amīr (941) i, **866a**, 1040a, 1046b; iii, 127a, 345a, 902b; vi, 206a; vii, 484a, 994b
al-Bādjurbaḳī (Ṣūfī) vi, 216b
Bādjūrī, Ibrāhīm b. Muḥammad (1860) i, 151a, 413a, 819b, **867b**; ii, 451a, 727b; iv, 173a, 693b, 1108a
Badlīs → Bidlīs
Badr, Āl i, 759b
Badr, battle of (624) i, **867b**; ii, 950b; v, 1162a; vi, 138a, 146b, 603b, 650a; vii, 369b; s, 44b, 230a, 351b
Badr (Slave of Abd ad-Raḥmān I) (VIII) x, 848a
Badr (pīr), Shaykh Badr al-Dīn (1440) i, **868b**

Badr b. Aḥmad (Zaydī) (XX) ix, 2a
Badr b. ʿAmmār al-Asadī → Badr al-K͟hars͟hanī
Badr b. Hasan(a)wayh (Hasanūya) (1000) i, 512b, 1030b; ii, 749a; iii, 244b, 258a, b; iv, 294a; v, 229b, 452b, 1124b; vi, 653a; s, 118b, 119a
Badr b. Hilāl (ʿAnnāzi) (XI) i, 513a
Badr b. Muhalhil (ʿAnnāzid) (XI) i, 513a
Badr b. Ṭuwayriḳ (Ḥaḍramī) (XVI) xi, 6a
Badr Bū Ṭuwayriḳ (1570) i, 553b; iii, 291b; vi, 82b; ix, 425a, 439a; s, 515a
Badr al-Dawla Sulaymān (Artuḳid), Aleppo (XIII) i, 663b, 983a
Badr al-Dīn b. D͟jamāʿa → Ibn D͟jamāʿa
Badr al-Dīn b. Ḳāḍī Samāwnā (1416) i, 312b, **869a**; ii, 599b; vi, 976a; vii, 594b
Badr al-Dīn Awliyā (Arakan) i, 606b
Badr al-Dīn al-Ḥasan b. ʿAlī (Rasūlid) (1214) vi, 433b
Badr al-Dīn al-Ḥasan b. Ḥūd (1300) x, 320b
Badr al-Dīn al-Ḥasanī, S͟hayk͟h (XX) vi, 538b
Badr al-Dīn al-Hās͟himī (1423) vi, 353a
Badr al-Dīn Ibrāhīm (Ḳarāmān-og͟hlu) (XIV) iv, 621b, 622a
Badr al-Dīn Ibrāhīm b. K͟huteni (Ermenak) (XIII) iv, 620a
Badr al-Dīn K͟hurāsānī, K͟hwād͟ja (XIII) ii, 81a; s, 157b
Badr al-Dīn Luʾluʾ → Luʾluʾ
Badr al-Dīn Muḥammad I, II, III → Faḍl Allāh, Āl
Badr al-Dīn Muḥammad al-Hamdānī (XIII) iv, 1188b
Badr al-D͟jamālī (vizier) (1094) i, 638b, 832a, **869b**, 926b, 1228a, 1316a; ii, 484b, 857b, 863b; iii, 253b; iv, 424b, 568a; v, 91b, 328a, 514b; vi, 367a, 453b, 673b; vii, 149b, 163a, 510b, 725a, 730b; viii, 464a, 864a; s, 390a
al-Badr al-Ḥabas͟hī (1221) x, 320b
Badr (Ḥād͟jib) (X) x, 851a
Badr al-Ḥammāmī (Iṣfahān) (X) iv, 100a
Badr al-Kabīr (IX) iv, 494a
Badr K͟hān D͟jazīri (XIX) v, 462a, b
Badr al-K͟hars͟hanī, amīr (942) i, **870b**; vii, 770a
Badr al-Muʿtaḍidī, Abu ʾl-Nad͟jm (902) i, 11a, 1223a; ii, 1080a; vii, 395a, 760a; s, **117b**
Badr al-Ṣaḳlabī (X) viii, 880a
Badra i, **870b**
Badrān b. Muḳallid (ʿUḳaylid) (XI) viii, 394a
Badrān b. Ṣadaḳa (Asadī) (XII) iv, 911b
Badras͟hayn (Umm ʿĪsā) vi, 411a
Badr-i Čāčī (1346) ix, 241b; s, **117b**
Badr-i D͟jahān K͟hānum (1797) vi, 484a
al-Badrī (XV) ii, 900b
al-Badrī (1800) vi, 112b
al-Badrī, Sayf al-Dīn Aynabak (1376) vi, 580b
Badrk͟hānī, D͟jalādat (1951) i, **871a**
Badrk͟hānī, T͟hurayyā (1938) i, **871a**
Bāds͟hāh K͟hān (1925) ii, 317a
Bādūrayā i, **871b**, 899b; v, 566b
Bādūsbānids i, **871b**; iii, 255a; iv, 808a; v, 663a, b; vi, 938b; s, 297b, 298a
Badw i, 14b, **872a**, 1049b, 1149b, 1230a, 1239b, 1288b; ii, 92b, 174b, 342b, 455a, 1005b, 1055a, 1059b; iii, 190b, 1261b; iv, 960b, 961a; v, 334a; vi, 32b, 33b, 478b, 490a
– language v, 1205b, 1206a, b
Baena → Bayyāna
Baeza → Bayyāsa
Baezay Mohmands vii, 220a
Bāfaḳī, S͟haraf al-Dīn (1570) viii, 542b
Bafilo → Kubafolo
Bafur (Adrār) i, 211a
Bagamoyo vi, 370a
Bagauda (Kano) (X) iii, 275b; iv, 548b, 551a
Bağdatlı Ismail Paşa → Ismāʿīl Pas͟ha Bag͟hdādli
Bāgerhāt ii, 486b; iii, 444a
Baggāra → Baḳḳāra
Bāg͟h (Garden) → Būstān
Bāg͟h (Town) → Nikāpur
Bāg͟hān vi, 384b
al-Bag͟hawī, ʿAbd Allāh b. Muḥammad (X) vi, 634a
al-Bag͟hawī, Abū Muḥammad al-Farrāʾ (Ibn al-Farrāʾ) (1122) i, **893a**; ii, 382a; iii, 24b
al-Bag͟hawī, ʿAlī b. ʿAbd al-ʿAzīz (870) vi, 822a
Bāg͟hāya iv, 422b
Bag͟hbūr → Fag͟hfūr
Bāg͟hčeköy vi, 57a

Bāghče Sarāy i, **893a**; ii, 1113a; v, 138a, 140b
Baghdād i, 8a, 17a, 18a, b, 19a, 21a, 291a, 438a, 576a, 616a, 866b, **894b**, 975a, b. 1038a; ii, 128b, 184b, 391a, 579b, 964a; iii, 702b, 1255a, 1256b, 1258a; iv, 20a, 215a, 652b; v, 33a, b, 458a, 928b; vi, 16a, 28b, 45a, 55b, 56b, 59b, 73b, 113b, 118a, 119b, 123b, 149b, 198a, 199a, 205a, 269b,270b, 273a, 275a, 332b, 333b, 335a, b, 338b, 405b, 428a, b, 450a, 494a, 499b, 501a, 517a, 532b, 539b, 541b, 600a, 606a, 613b, 635a, 656b, 668a, 669b, 671b; 13a, b, 15b, 33a, 95a, 102a, 113a, 182b, 191b, 192a, 199a, 225b, 267b
– commerce i, 905b, 907a; ii, 745b; iii, 218a, 1252b
– history i, 1309b; iii, 692b, 756a, 897a
– institutions i, 212b, 899a, 900a, 902a, 903a, 906b, 1223a; ii, 127a; iii, 140a, 159b, 160b; v, 1127a, 1148a
– monuments i, 11b, 52b, 616b, 831a, 832b, 896a-904b, 1354a; iii, 1268a; iv, 378a
– university ii, 424b
Baghdād Khātūn bint Amīr Čūbān (1335) i, **908b**; ii, 68a, 980b
Baghdād Yolu i, 475a
al-Baghdādī → ʿAbd al-Ḳādir; ʿAbd al-Latīf; Abu ʾl-Khayr al-Ḥusayn; Bahāʾ al-Dīn; al-Khaṭīb; Madjd al-Dīn
al-Baghdādī, ʿAbd al-Ḳāhir Abū Manṣūr (1037) i, **909a**; ii, 96a, 296a; iii, 1140a; iv, 183a-b, 667b; vi, 636b; vii, 54b, 296b, 1051b; viii, 497b
al-Baghdādī, ʿAbd al-Wahhāb (1031) ix, 19a
Baghdādī, Aḥmad Saʿīd (XIX) vii, 903a
Baghdādī, Mawlānā Khālid (1827) vii, 935b, 936b
al-Baghdādī, Muḥammad b. al-Mubārak b. Maymūn (XII) vii, 527a
al-Baghdādī, Muḥammad b. al-Sukrān (XIII) viii, 860a
al-Baghdādī, Sīdī Maḥmūd (XVI) viii, 18b
Bāgh-i Firdaws vi, 51b
Bāgh-i Nīlūfar (Dhōlpūr) vii, 329a
Bāgh-i Shaʿbān vi, 51b
Bāghistān s, 50b
Baghl i, **909a**; iv, 1146a
Baghlī → Dirham
Baghrās (Pagrae) i, 239a, **909b**, 1134a; vi, 623b
Baghyughu, Aḥmad (Mali) vi, 258b
Baghyughu, Muḥammad (Mali) vi, 258b
Bagirmi (Baghirmi) i, **910a**; v, 278b, 357b; s, 164a, b
Bagrat III v, 489a
Bagrat IV iv, 346b; v, 489a
Bagrat V v, 491a
Bagratids i, 100b, 101a, 466a, 507a, 637b, 638a; iv, 346b, 347b, 669b; v, 488b, 489a, 496a
Bagulal, Banū i, 504a; iv, 630b
Bagzāda, Āl iii, 292a
Bāh i, **910b**; ii, 552a
Bahāʾ Allāh, Mīrzā Ḥusayn ʿAlī Nūrī (1892) i, 833b, 834b, 846b, 847a, **911a**, 916a; iii, 325b; iv, 51b, 696a; v, 698b, 1172b; vii, 921b; s, 77a
Bahāʾ al-Dawla (1507) viii, 783b
Bahāʾ al-Dawla wa-Ḍiyāʾ al-Milla, Abū Naṣr Fīrūz (Būyid) (1012) i, 512a, 899b, 1354a; ii, 348b, 749a; iii, 219b, 244b, 258b, 388a, 671b; iv, 378a; v, 348a, 1028a; vi, 199a, 206a, 261b; vii, 270b, 497a; s, 4b, **118a**
Bahāʾ al-Dīn (vizier Gudjarāt) (1482) vi, 50b
Bahāʾ al-Dīn al-ʿĀmilī → al-ʿĀmilī
Bahāʾ al-Dīn Baghdādī (XII) iii, 1243a
Bahāʾ al-Dīn Ḳara ʿUthmān (Aḳ Ḳoyūnlū) (1400) vi, 901a,
Bahāʾ al-Dīn Muḥammad b. Djuwaynī (1279) ii, 607b; iv, 102a
Bahāʾ al-Dīn Sām (Bāmiyān) (1205) i, 1001b; ii, 1101b, 1103a
Bahāʾ al-Dīn Sām I (Ghūrid) (1149) ii, 382a, 928b, 1096b, 1100b
Bahāʾ al-Dīn Sām II (Ghūrid) (1213) ii, 1103a
Bahāʾ al-Dīn Shākir (XX) iv, 285a, 872b
Bahāʾ al-Dīn Sulṭān al-ʿUlamāʾ Walad b. Ḥusayn (XIV) ii, 393b; vi, 887b
Bahāʾ al-Dīn Zakariyyāʾ (Suhrawardī) (1262) i, **912a**; iii, 635a, 1269a; v, 26a; vii, 550a; ix, 298b; x, 255b; s, 10b, 353b
Bahāʾ al-Dīn Zuhayr (1258) i, 570b, 595b, **912b**; ii, 1032b; iii, 875b
Bahāʾ al-Ḥaḳḳ → Bahāʾ al-Dīn Zakariyyāʾ
Bāhā Lāl Dās Bayrāgī (XVII) ii, 134b
Bahāʾ Walad (1231) x, 320b

al-Bahāʾ Zuhayr → Bahāʾ al-Dīn Zuhayr
Bahādur i, **913a**
Bahādūr Gīlānī (1494) ii, 1127b; v, 1258a; vi, 63a,b
Bahādur Girāy I (Crimea) (1641) iv, 178b
Bahādur K̲h̲ān Gīlānī → Bahādur Gīlānī
Bahādur K̲h̲ān II (Dāwūdpōtra) (1617) ii, 185b
Bahādur K̲h̲ān b. Muẓaffar S̲h̲āh (Gud̲j̲arāt) (1526) vi, 52a, 270b, 310a
Bahādur K̲h̲ān Rohilla (1658) viii, 572b
Bahādur S̲h̲āh → Niẓām S̲h̲āh
Bahādur S̲h̲āh I (Mug̲h̲al) (1712) i, 781b, **913b**, 1012b, 1068b, 1195a, 1210a; ii, 30a, 558a; iii, 427a; iv, 507b, 598b; vii, 315b, 318b, 722b; viii, 48b
Bahādur S̲h̲āh II (Mug̲h̲al) (1862) i, **914a**, 953b, 1012b; ii, 221b; vii, 316b
Bahādur S̲h̲āh (Fārūḳid) ii, 815b
Bahādur S̲h̲āh Gud̲j̲arātī (1537) i, **914b**, 1193b; ii, 322b, 815a, 1128b; iii, 16a, 199b, 421b, 422a, 425b, 575b, 1160a; vi, 52a, 407a, 535a; vii, 314a; s, 335b
Bahāedin S̲h̲ākir → Bahāʾ al-Dīn S̲h̲ākir
Bahāʾī Meḥmed Efendi (1654) i, **915a**
Bahāʾīs i, 263b, 833a, 847a, **915b**; iii, 325b; iv, 39a, 51b; vi, 292a, 720a; vii, 921b
Baḥammou (Berber) s, 328a
Bahār, Muḥammad Taḳī (1951) i, **918b**; iv, 71a, b; vi, 276b, 609a; vii, 662a, 754b, 879b; s, 110a, 334a
Bahār, Rāy Tēkčand iv, 526b
Bahār K̲h̲ān b. Daryā K̲h̲ān Noḥānī (1530) s, 203a
Bahār-i Dānes̲h̲ → ʿInāyat Allāh Kanbū
Bahāristān → D̲j̲āmī
Bahārlū, Banū i, **919a**; iii, 1109b; iv, 9b; v, 668b
Bahasa Indonesia iii, 1215b, 216b, 1217a, b; s, 150b
Bahās̲h̲ima s, 25b
Bahasnā (Marʿas̲h̲) vi, 507a, b
Bahāwal K̲h̲ān I (Dāwūdpōtrā) (1749) i, 919b; ii, 186a
Bahāwal K̲h̲ān II-V → Dāwūdpōtrās
Bahāwalpūr i, **919b**; ii, 185b, 186a, 669a
Bahbūd̲h̲ b. ʿAbd al-Wahhāb (Zand̲j̲ī) (IX) vii, 526b
Baḥdal b. Unayf (657) i, **919b**; vi, 545a, 924b; vii, 267b
Bahdīnān i, 427a, **920a**; v, 460a
Bahd̲j̲at K̲h̲ān (Čandērī) (1514) ii, 12b; vi, 54b
Bahd̲j̲at Muṣṭafā Efendi (1834) i, 707a, **921a**; ii, 356b
Baḥḥāra i, 929a
Bāhila, Banū i, **920b**, 1096b; v, 541a; vi, 545a; s, 243a
al-Bāhilī, ʿAbd al-Raḥmān (VII) i, **921b**; iv, 343b, 1173b
al-Bāhilī, Abu ʾl-Ḥasan Sallām (vizier) vi, 111a
al-Bāhilī, Abū Naṣr Aḥmad (845) i, 717b, 718b, **921b**; vii, 831b
al-Bāhilī, Abū ʿUmar (X) vi, 846b
al-Bāhilī, al-Ḥusayn → al-Ḥusayn b. al-Daḥḥāk
al-Bāhilī, Salmān → Salmān b. Rabīʿa
Bahimiyya, Banū vi, 474a
Baḥīra → Buḥayra
Baḥīra (she-camel) i, **922a**
Baḥīrā (monk) i, **922a**, 1276b
al-Bāhirī, Bakr b. Ḥassād (Ḥammād) iii, 889b
Bahis̲h̲ī → D̲j̲anna
Bāḥit̲h̲at al-Bādiya → Malak Ḥifnī Nāṣif
Bāhiya (Marrākus̲h̲) vi, 589b; s, 114a
Bahlā (Oman) i, 140b; xi, 225a
al-Bahlawī → Abu ʾl-Muʾt̲h̲ir
Bahlōlzay, Banū vi, 86a
Bahlūl (Kurds) i, **923a**
Bahlūl (Morocco) vi, 773b, 815b
Bahlūl b. Marzūḳ s, 82a
Bahlūl Gwāliyārī, S̲h̲ayk̲h̲ (XVI) vii, 440a
Bahlūl Lōdī (Dihli) (1489) i, 218a, 1322a; ii, 47b, 48b, 270, 498b, 1131a, 1144a; iii, 418a, 419b, 420a, 485a, 632a, 633b; iv, 276b; v, 31b, 598a, 783a, b; vi, 62a; s, 1b, 10b, 203a
Bahlūl Pas̲h̲a (1825) i, 923b
Bahmaʾī, Banū iii, 1107a
Bahman → Taʾrīk̲h̲
Bahman b. Isfandiyār (Kayānid) iv, 809b; ix, 70b
Bahman b. Kayūmart̲h̲ (Kāwūs, Banū) iv, 808a; v, 663a
Bahman Lārīd̲j̲ānī, Malik (1596) vi, 515b
Bahman Mīrzā (Ḳād̲j̲ār) (XIX) iv, 393a, b, 398a; vii, 455b
Bahman S̲h̲āh → ʿAlāʾ al-Dīn Ḥasan Bahman

Bahmandīz iii, 501b; iv, 815b; v, 229a
Bahmanids i, 768a, **923b**, 1047a, 1170a, 1200a, b, 1203b; ii, 99b, 120b, 158b, 180a; iii, 15a, 114a, 420b, 446b; iv, 514a; v, 1a, 1258a; vi, 50b, 53b, 54a, 62b, 63b, 66b, 67a, 87a, 127b, 269b, 369a, 407a, 692a, 695a; vii, 943a; viii, 73b; x, 895a; xi, 1a, b; s, 280a
Bahmanyār, Abu 'l-Ḥasan (1067) i, **926a**
Bāḥmīn (Bohemians) viii, 4a, 874a; s, 170b
al-Bahnasā i, **926a**, 945a
Bahnūd b. Saḥwān iv, 503b
Baḥr → ʿArūḍ
Baḥr (river) i, **926b**; v, 949b
Baḥr al-Abyaḍ → Baḥr al-Rūm
Baḥr Adriyas i, **927a**, 935b
Baḥr al-Aḥmar → Baḥr al-Ḳulzum
Baḥr al-Aswad → Baḥr Bunṭus, Ḳarā Deniz
Baḥr Āzāk → Baḥr Māyuṭis
Baḥr al-Banāt i, **927a**
Baḥr Bunṭus i, **927a**, 935b; iv, 575a; v, 313a
Baḥr al-Dardūs iv, 514b
Baḥr al-Djabal i, 929a
Baḥr Fāris (Persian Gulf) i, **927b**, 930a; ii, 577b; iii, 1251b; iv, 500b; v, 66a, 507a, 572a; s, 222b
Baḥr al-Ghazāl i, **929a**, 1156b; v, 1248b, 1249b, 1250b; vi, 304a; viii, 39b
Baḥr al-Hidjdjāna vi, 546a
Baḥr al-Hind i, **930a**; ii, 584a; iii, 856b; v, 940b
Baḥr al-Khazar (Caspian) i, 3b, 191a, **931a**; iv, 1b; vi, 129b, 415a; vii, 71a; s, 245b
Baḥr al-Khazar, (Caspian) provinces iv, 6b-7a, 16a, 18b, 19a
Baḥr Khʷarizm → Aral Sea
Baḥr al-Ḳulzum i, **931b**; iii, 856b; iv, 686b; v, 367b
Baḥr Lūṭ i, **933a**
Baḥr al-Maghrib → Baḥr al-Rūm
Baḥr Māyuṭis i, **933b**; iv, 576b
Baḥr al-Muḥīṭ i, **934a**
Baḥr al-Muẓlim → al-Baḥr al-Muḥīṭ
Baḥr al-Nīl → al-Nīl
Baḥr Nīṭas → Baḥr Bunṭus
Baḥr al-Rūm i, **934b**, 936b; ii, 577b; v, 503a
Baḥr al-Shāmī → Baḥr al-Rūm
Baḥr Tīrān i, 935b
Baḥr Uḳiyānūs → al-Baḥr al-Muḥīṭ
Baḥr al-ʿUlūm, ʿAbd al-ʿAlī al-Lakhnawī (1810) i, **936b**; ii, 104a; viii, 69a; s, 292b, 293a, b
Baḥr al-ʿUlūm, Sayyid Mahdī (XIX) s, 135a
Baḥr Ushmūm vi, 440b
Baḥr al-Warank i, 934a, 935b
Baḥr al-Zandj i, 484a, **937b**
Baḥr al-Ẓulma (Ẓulumāt) → al-Baḥr al-Muḥīṭ
Baḥra (Makka) vi, 152b
Bahrāʾ, Banū i, **938a**
Bahrāʾič ii, 1047b; vi, 47b, 48a, 49b, 783b; s, 280a
Bahrāidj → Djawnpur
Baḥrain → al-Baḥrayn
Baḥrak, Djamāl al-Dīn (1524) i, **938a**
Bahrām i, **938b**
Bahrām (1140) i, 638b, **939a**; ii, 858a; iii, 55a
Bahrām I-IV (Sāsānids) i, 938b; v, 169a, 1113b; vi, 421a; ix, 72b, 75a
Bahrām V Gūr (Sāsānid) (438) i, 226a, 568b, 939a; iv, 53a; v, 816b; vi, 617b; ix, 75b
Bahrām b. Lashkarsitān iv, 807a
Bahrām Bayḍāʾī (XX) vi, 764a
Bahrām Čūbīn i, 939a; iii, 113a, 584b; vi, 502a, 608b, 745a; viii, 119b; ix, 78b
Bahrām al-Ismāʿīlī i, 1017a
Bahrām Khān Khʷādja (1873) vi, 484b
Bahrām Khān Māzandarānī (XIV) ii, 814a; vii, 458b
Bahrām Khān Turkbačča (1405) vi, 294b
Bahrām-Lam → Ibrāhīm Ināl
Bahrām Pasha (Yemen) (1575) viii, 521a
Bahrām Pasha (the Great) (Kurd) (1667) i, 920a
Bähram Rähmanaw (1961) vi, 770b
Bahrāmshāh, Fakhr al-Dīn (Mengüčekid) (1220) vi, 1016b; viii, 77a
Bahrām Shāh (Ṣafawid) (XVI) viii, 775b
Bahrām Shāh, Muʿizz al-Dīn (Muʿizzī, Delhi) (1242) ii, 267b, 609a, 973a; vii, 195a
Bahrām Shāh b. Masʿūd, Yamīn al-Dawla (Ghaznāwid) (1157) i, 94b, 217b, 227a, **940a**; ii, 382a, 1052a, 1100b; v, 159b, 501a; vi, 783a; vii, 535b, 1016b; ix, 15b, 116a

Bahrām Shāh b. Tughrıl Shāh (Saldjūḳid) (1174) i, **940b**; v, 160a; viii, 945b
Bahrām Shāh al-Malik al-Amdjad (Ayyūbid) (1229) i, 803b, **940b**, 971a
Bahrām Sīs (723) vi, 633b
al-Baḥrānī → Muḥammad b. ʿAlī
al-Baḥrānī, ʿAbd ʿAlī b. Aḥmad al-Dirāzī (1763) s, 57a
al-Baḥrānī, ʿAbd Allāh b. Ḥādjdj Ṣāliḥ al-Samāhīdjī (1723) x, 936a, b; s, 57a
Baḥrānī, Sayyid Mādjid (1619) vii, 475b
al-Baḥrānī, Yūsuf b. Aḥmad (1773) iii, 1152a; s, 57a
al-Baḥrayn ("the Two Seas") i, **940b**; iv, 664a, 751b, 764a, 953a, 1130b; v, 1057b; s, 234b, 318a, 417a
Baḥrayn (Baḥrain) i, 19a, 55a, 72b, 73a, b, 120a, 233b, 535b, 540a, 553b, **941a**, 976a; ii, 108b, 177a, 452b; vi, 37a, 148a, 333b, 357b, 439a, 551a, 621b, 625b; vii, 449b, 464a, 570b
Baḥri Mamlūks → Mamlūks
Baḥriyya (navy) i, **945b**; s, **119b**
Baḥriyya (Mamlūk regiment) i, 804a, **944b**; iv, 424b, 428a, 430a; v, 571a, b; vi, 320a; s, 392b
Baḥriyya (oasis) i, **945a**
Baḥriyye vekāleti i, 948b
Baḥrūn (Kamarān) ii, 235b
Bahrūr → Bhakkar
Baḥshal, Allām b. Sahl al-Wāsiṭī (901) i, **949a**; viii, 518a
Bahshamiyya ii, 570a; vii, 785b
Baḥth i, **949a**
Bahū Bēgum ii, 870b
Bahū (Bao) s, 242a
Bahurasīr → al-Madāʾin
Bahūṣiyya i, 375b
al-Bahūtī al-Miṣrī (1641) i, **949a**; iii, 162a
Bahw i, **949b**
Baḥya ibn Paḳūda iv, 487a
Baikal i, **950b**
Bāʾikbāk (IX) vii, 794a
Bailo → Bālyōs
Bairam Ali vi, 618a, 621b
al-Baʿīth (VIII) i, **950b**
Bajazet → Bāyazīd
Bajun Islands vi, 370a; ix, 715a
Baḳāʾ wa-Fanāʾ i, **951a**; iii, 546a; iv, 1083b, 1163a
Baḳʿa → Buḳʿa
al-Baḳʿa → al-Biḳāʿ
Baḳāʾī i, 1104a
Bākalamūn → Abū Ḳalamūn
Baḳar i, **951b**
Bāḳar, Āghā i, 952a
Baḳar, ʿīd → Bayram; ʿĪd
Bāḳargandj i, **951b**
Baḳāriṭṭa (Buḳraṭūn) → Buḳrāṭ
Bakāwalī iii, 376b
Baḳāyā i, 1145a
Bākbāk i, 278b; iii, 955b
Bakdjūr (991) i, 824b; ii, 483a; iii, 129b, 841a; v, 1211a; vii, 115b
Bakhʿa vi, 308a, b
Bākhamrā i, **952a**; vi, 428a
Bākharz i, **952a**; vi, 495b
al-Bākharzī, Abu 'l-Ḥasan ʿAlī b. al-Ḥasan (1075) i, **952b**, 1132a; vii, 527b; viii, 71b, 513b, 970b; s, 31a
al-Bākharzī, Sayf al-Dīn → Sayf al-Dīn al-Bākharzī
Bakhīt, Shaykh i, 821a
Bakhīt al-Muṭīʿī al-Ḥanafī (1935) s, **121b**
al-Bakhrāʾ i, 57b, **952b**; xi, 128a; s, 117a
Bakhshī i, **953a**; iv, 268b, 269a, 757b; v, 686b
Bakhshī Aḥmad Khān iii, 61b
Bakhshīsh i, **953a**
al-Bakhshiyya iv, 992a
Bakht Buland (XVII) vii, 899a
Bakht Girāy ii, 1114a
Bakht Khān (1859) i, **953b**; ii, 809a
Bakhtanaṣṣar → Bukht-naṣar
Bakhtariyya bint Khurshīd Maṣmughān → Buḥturiyya bint Khurshīd
Bakhtāwar Khān (1685) i, **954a**; vii, 322a
Bakhtī i, **954b**
Bakhtī, amīr v, 1179a
Bakhtigān i, **954b**
Bakhtīshūʿ → Bukhtīshūʿ
Bakhtiyār → Muḥammad b. Bakhtiyār Khaldjī
Bakhtiyār Abū Manṣūr (Būyid) (978) s, 449a
Bakhtiyār Sandjabī → Sindjābī
Bakhtiyār, ʿIzz al-Dawla (Buwayhid) (967) i, 11b, 211b, **954b**, 1350b; ii, 748b; iii, 46b, 128a, 246a, 258a, 704a, 730a, 1176a, 1201b; iv, 24a, 208b, 293b; vi, 540a; vii, 799a; s, 13a, 36a, 118b, 398a
Bakhtiyār-nāma i, **955a**; iii, 373a, 377a
Bakhtiyārī, Banū i, **955b**; iii, 1102a, b,

1103a, 1105a, 1110a; iv, 5b, 8a, 9a, 98b, 706a; v, 664a, 822a, 824a, 825a, 826a, 829b, 830a; vi, 495a; vii, 453b; viii, 1080b; s, 142b, 146a, 147b, 365b
Ba<u>kh</u>ṭūs (queen) ii, 234a
al-Baḳīʿ s, 311b
Bāḳī, Maḥmūd ʿAbd al- (1600) i, 292b, **956a**; ii, 221a; iv, 1137b; vi, 609b; viii, 8b; s, 324a
Baḳī b. Ma<u>kh</u>lad, Abū ʿAbd al-Raḥmān (889) i, 600a, **956b**; iii, 692b; vi, 132a; vii, 400a
Bāḳī bi-'llāh, <u>Kh</u>wā<u>dj</u>a (1603) i, **957a**; iii, 432b; vii, 937b, 938a; x, 256a; s, **121b**
Baḳīʿ al-<u>Gh</u>arḳad (cemetery, Madīna) i, **957b**; vi, 168b, 263b, 651b; vii, 276a
Baḳī <u>Kh</u>ān Čela Ḳalmāḳ ii, 1085a
Bāḳī Muḥammad (calligrapher) iv, 1127b
Bāḳī Muḥammad <u>Kh</u>ān (XVII) i, 8a; ii, 44b, 446a
Bāḳi̊<u>kh</u>anli̊, Bāki̊<u>kh</u>ānov (1847) i, 193b, **958a**
Bakīl → Ḥā<u>sh</u>id wa-Bakīl
al-Bāḳillānī, Abū Bakr Muḥammad (1013) i, 212a, 413a, 696b, 858a, **958b**; ii, 294a, 570b, 765a, 774b; iii, 544a, 1020a, 1063a, 1144b; iv, 108a, 183a, 272a, 378b, 470b, 616a, 949a; v, 426b; vi, 280b, 351b, 447b, 448a; vii, 312a; ix, 887a; s, 26b, 343b, 345a, 346b
Bāḳir b. Māhān iii, 988a
Bāḳir <u>Kh</u>ān <u>Kh</u>urāskānī iv, 104b, 391a
Baḳi<u>sh</u> iii, 1106b
al-Bāḳiyat us-Ṣāliḥat College (Vellore) vi, 462a
Baḳḳ → Ḳaml
Baḳḳ iv, 522a
Bakka → Makka
al-Baḳḳa (799) i, 100a
Bakkāʾ i, **959a**
al-Bakkāʾī, Aḥmad (1864) v, 394a; vi, 259b
al-Bakkāʾi, Ziyād iii, 801a
Baḳḳāl i, **961a**
Baḳḳam i, **961b**
Bakkār (island) i, **961b**
Bakkār b. ʿAbd Allāh b. Musʿab (809) xi, 243a
Bakkār b. Ḳutayba (883) ix, 547b
Baḳḳāra, Banū i, 49b, **962a**; ii, 122a, 124a; v, 266b, 1249a, 1250a, 1251b; viii, 171b
Bʿaḳlīn vi, 28a
Baḳliyya i, **962b**; iv, 661a
al-Bakr, Aḥmad Ḥasan v, 469a
Bakr, Banū i, 526b, 527a, 529b, 962b, 1339a; ii, 71b; iii, 222b; v, 116b, 346a, 362a; vi, 490a, 733b; vii, 266a, 373b
Bakr b. ʿAbd al-ʿAzīz b. Abī Dulaf iii, 126a, 619a; iv, 718b
Bakr b. ʿAbd Manāt (VII) v, 78a, b, 79a
Bakr b. Ḥassād (Ḥammād) al-Bāhirī iii, 889b
Bakr b. Ḥumrān al-Aḥmarī (VII) vii, 690a
Bakr b. <u>Kh</u>āri<u>dj</u>a iv, 1003b
Baka b. <u>Kh</u>unays al-Kūfī (VIII) vi, 613b
Bakr b. al-Muʿtamir (810) vi, 332a
Bakr b. al-Naṭṭāḥ, Abu 'l-Wāʾil (808) s, **122a**
Bakr b. Uk<u>h</u>t ʿAbd al-Wāḥid b. Zayd (VIII) vi, 457b
Bakr b. Wāʾil, Banū i, 545a, **962b**; ii, 241a, 343b; iii, 166b, 1254a; iv, 321b; vi, 640b; ix, 381b; x, 400b; s, 122a
Bakr b. Zadlafa, Banū ix, 306b
Bakr al-Aʿwar al-Ha<u>dj</u>arī al-Ḳattāt (VIII) vii, 348a
Bakr Beg (XVIII) i, 845a
Bakr Ṣidḳī (1939) ii, 1045a; iii, 1258b; viii, 141b, 445b; s, 672b
Bakr Ṣū Bā<u>sh</u>ī (XVII) i, 904a, **962b**; iii, 1257a
al-Bakra<u>dj</u>ī, Ḳāsim b. Muḥammad b. ʿAlī al-Ḥalabī (1756) vi, 913b
Bakrān, Muḥammad vi, 415b
al-Bakrī → ʿAbd al-ʿAzīz; Abū ʿUbayd
al-Bakrī → Bakriyya; Ṣiddīḳī
al-Bakrī b. Abi 'l-Surūr (1619) i, **965a**
al-Bakrī, Abu 'l-Ḥasan Aḥmad b. ʿAbd Allāh (XIII) i, **964b**; ii, 159a; vii, 100b
al-Bakrī Aḥmad Murād (XX) x, 324b
al-Bakrī, Muḥammad (poet) (1586) viii, 425a
al-Bakrī, Muḥammad b. ʿAbd al-Raḥmān al-Ṣiddīḳī (1545) i, **965b**; iv, 451b, 505b
al-Bakrī, Muḥammad b. Ayyūb (Walba) (XI) i, 6a; vii, 761a
al-Bakrī, Muḥammad b. Muḥammad b. Abi 'l-Surūr (1650) i, **965a**
al-Bakrī, Muḥammad b. Yūsuf, Ibn al-Warrāḳ vi, 946a
al-Bakrī, Muḥammad Ṭawfīḳ b. ʿAlī (1932) vi, 113b; s, **122b**, 132b

al-Bakrī, Muṣṭafā b. Kamāl al-Dīn (1749) i, 60a, b, **965b**; iv, 991b, 992a; vi, 112b, 627a; s, 44a
al-Bakrī, Shaykh → Shaykh al-Bakrī
al-Bakrī al-Khwārazmī, Ḍiyā' al-Dīn (1172) vi, 352b
Bakriyya i, **966a**
Bakriyya → Bakr b. Ukht ʿAbd al-Wāhid
al-Bakriyya i, **966a**; s, 122b
Baḳt i, 32a, **966a**
Baktamur Djilliḳ (1412) vii, 723a, b
Baktāsh al-Fakhrī, Badr al-Dīn (XIII) iv, 485a
Baktimur al-Silāḥdār, amīr (1300) vi, 545b
Bākū i, 191b, **966b**; iii, 530b; iv, 348a; vi, 129b, 769b; vii, 71a; s, 73a, 136a, 365a, b
Baʿḳūba i, **967b**
Bāḳūm (Bāḳūl) → ʿEnbāḳōm
Bakumpai s, 151a
Bākusāyā i, 870b, **968a**
al-Bākuwī, ʿAbd al-Rashīd Ṣāliḥ (1402) vii, 71a
Baʿl i, 491b, **968a**
Bal-Faḳīh → Faḳīh, Bal-
Bālā i, **969b**
Baʿla v, 692b
Balʿā' b. Ḳays vi, 349a
Bālā-ghāt i, **970a**
Bālā Ḥiṣār i, **970a**; ii, 978a, 1119a
Bālā Murghāb vi, 617b
Bālā Pīr → Ghāzī Miyān
Balābādh → Balāwāt
Baʿlabakk i, 940b, **970b**, 1051a, 1214b; vi, 193b, 303a; vii, 693a
Balaban (XV) iv, 140a
Balabān al-Tabbākhī, amīr (1279) vi, 579b
Balabān Zaynī, al-Dawādār, Sayf al-Dīn, amīr (1281) iv, 483b; vi, 579b
Balabanköy vi, 57a
Balad ʿAns s, 22b
al-Balādhurī, Aḥmad b. Yaḥyā (892) i, 591a, 635b, 760a, **971b**; ii, 131b; iii, 608a; iv, 275a, 342b; vi, 359a, 363a, 493a
Baladiyya i, **972b**
Bālādjī Rāo II (Pēshwā) (1761) vi, 535b; vii, 446a
Bālādjī Rāo Visvanāth (1719) vi, 535a
Balāgh iv, 203b
Balāgha i, 858a, **981b**, 1114a, b, 1116a; ii, 824a
Balaḳ (Mts) vi, 559a
Balak, Nūr al-Dawla Balak b. Bahrām (Artuḳid) (1124) i, 664b, 732a, **983a**, 1025a; ii, 110b; iii, 87a; iv, 1084a; v, 106a; vi, 380a
Bālaḳ b. Ṣāfūn → ʿŪdj b. ʿAnāḳ
Balakhsh i, 851b
Bālakī (tribe) i, 1031a
Balaklava i, **983b**
Balʿam i, **984a**
Balʿamī, Abū ʿAlī Muḥammad (974) i, 4216, **984b**; iv, 504a; vi, 433a; vii, 85b; x, 14a; s, 297b
Balʿamī, Abu 'l-Faḍl Muḥammad (940) i, **984b**; s, 265b
Bāl-ʿanbar → Tamīm
Balandjar i, 921b, **985a**; iv, 343b, 344a, 1173a
al-Balansī, ʿUbayd Allāh b. ʿAbd Allāh (IX) viii, 870b
Balansiya (Valencia) i, 446b, 495a, **985a**, 1288a; iii, 673a; iv, 468a; ix, 351a; s, 143a
Bālāpur s, 280a
Balʿarab (Yaʿfurid) (1692) xi, 292a
Balarm (Palermo) i, 250b, **986a**; ii, 115a, 864a; iv, 497a, 979b; vi,650a, 653a
Balāsāghūn i, **987a**; iii, 1114b; iv, 581a, 582a; v, 858a; s, 240a
Bālāsarīs (XX) ix, 404b
Balash (Sāsānid) (488) ix, 76b
Balāṭ (Miletus) i, 950a, **987b**; vi, 366a
Balāṭ i, **987b**
Balaṭ (Balad) s, 123b
Balāṭ (road) i, **988a**
Balāṭ al-Shuhadā' i, 86b, 493a, 988a, **988b**
al-Balāṭa → Shantarīn
al-Balaṭī, Abu 'l-Fatḥ ʿUthman (1202) s, **123b**
Balāṭunus i, **989b**
Balawī, Banū → Baliyy
al-Balawī, Abū Zamʿa vi, 712b
Balāwāt i, **989b**
Balawhar → Bilawhar wa-Yūdāsaf
al-Balawī (X) i, 96b, **990a**; iii, 745b
Bālāy Miyān → Ghāzī Miyān
Baʿlbak → Baʿlabakk
Balban, Ghiyāth al-Dīn Ulugh Khān (Muʿizzī, Dihlī) (1287) i, 217b, 1036a; ii, 12b, 120a, 260b, 268a, 272b, 973a, 1084a, 143b; iii, 168a, 416a, 441b, 492a; iv, 749b,

818a; v, 629b, 638a, 685a, 1135a; vi, 47b, 48a, b, 368b, 532b; vii, 193b; s, 66b, 73b, **124a**
Balban, Muḥammad b. Ghiyāth al-Dīn (1287) vi, 609a; s, 124b
Balbār (Ḥammādid) (XI) vi, 427a
Bālčand (painter) (XVII) vii, 339a
Baldj b. Bishr (742) i, 76a, 82a, 134b, 490a, **990b**; iii, 494a; iv, 494b; v, 367a
Baldj b. ʿUḳba al-Azdī (748) vii, 524b
Balearic Isles → Mayurḳa
Balewa, Abubakar Tafawa iii, 282b; iv, 774a
Balfour Declaration vi, 388a
Bālfurūsh → Bārfurūsh
Bal-Ḥāf → Ibn al-Ḥāf
Balharā i, **991a**; ii, 352a
Balḥārith → Ḥārith b. Kaʿb
Balhīb vi, 877b
Bāli (al-Ḥabash) i, 176b, **991b**; iii, 6a
Bali (Indonesia) iii, 1213b, 1214b, 1219b, 1223a; v, 785a
Balī → Baliyy
Balī, Banū vii, 921a; viii, 863a
al-Baʿlī, ʿAbd al-Raḥmān (1778) iii, 162a
Bali Bey b. Yaḥyā Pasha (Mohács) (1526) i, 1163b; ii, 201b; vii, 219a
Bālī Efendi (Vize) vi, 228a; ix. 705b
Baliabadra i, **992a**
Bāligh i, **993a**
Balîḳ i, 610b; ii, 971b
Bālik i, **993b**
Bālikesrī/Bālîkesīr i, **993b**; iv, 628b; vi, 588a
Balīkh (river) vi, 378b, 733a
Balîkhane i, 1279a
Bālîm Sulṭān i, 1162a; viii, 12a
Balīnūs (of Perge) → al-Nadjdjār
Balīnūs/Balīnās of Tyane (Apollonius) (VIII) i, 737a, **994a**; ii, 93b, 359a; iii, 464a; v,111b; vi, 637b; vii, 833b; s, 270a
Bālis i, **995b**; vi, 733a, b
Bālis-Maskana vi, 378a, 379b, 380a, 381b, 382a
Balisāna vi, 576a
al-Bālisī → Muḥammad b. Musallam
Bālish i, **997b**
Bālish (Vélez) i, **996a**; vi, 576a
Baliyy, Banū i, 990a; iii, 363b; v, 317b, 318a, b
Baliyya i, **997b**
al-Balḳāʾ, Banū i, **997b**, 1149a; vi, 371b; s, 117a
Balkā Khaldjī (XIII) iii, 1155b
Balkā-takīn i, 226b
Balkan i, 468a, **998a**; ii, 33b; iv, 297a
Balkar i, **1000a**; ii, 23a; iv, 325a, 596b
Balḳar vii, 352a
Balḳayn → Ḳayn
Balkh i, 8a, 17b, 46b, 147b, 223b, 296a, 662a, 684b, 768b, **1000b**, 1033a; ii, 4b, 43a, 201a; iii, 134b; iv, 809b; vi, 14b, 273b, 313b, 494b, 522a, 608b, 618b, 620b, 780b; s, 97a, 125b, 227b, 326a, 340b, 416b, 419b
Balkha(r) iv, 343a
Balkhān i, **1002a**; vi, 415b, 416a; s, 280b
Balkhash i, **1002a**
al-Balkhī → Abū Maʿshar
al-Balkhī, Abū ʿAlī Muḥammad ii, 918b
al-Balkhī, Abu 'l-Ḳāsim (931) i, **1002b**; iii, 979b; iv, 1162b; v, 702a; vii, 312a, b, 784b; s, 14b, 335b
Balkhī, Abu 'l-Muʾayyad (X) ii, 918b; xi, 360b
al-Balkhī, Abū Muṭīʿ (799) i, 124a; vii, 606b
al-Balkhī, Abū Zayd Aḥmad b. Sahl (934) i, **1003a**; ii, 579b, 581a; iii, 57b, 787b, 1077b; iv, 223a, 1079a; vi, 639b, 640a; vii, 493a, 538b; viii, 372b; s, 72b, 265a, 266a, 386b
al-Balkhī, Burhān al-Dīn al-Sikilkandī (1153) vi, 847b
al-Balkhī, Ḥamīd al-Dīn Abū Bakr (1164) vii, 567b
al-Balkhī, Ḳawām (Ḳiwām) al-Mulk Abū ʿAlī vi, 932a
Balkhī, Muẓaffar Shams (1401) vi, 131b
al-Balkhī, Nuṣayr b. Yaḥyā (881) vi, 846a
al-Balkhī, Shaḳīḳ b. Ibrāhīm (809) vii, 647a; viii, 254b
al-Balkhī al-Warrāḳ, Abu 'l-Djaysh al-Muẓaffar b. Muḥammad (977) vii, 312a, b
Balkis → Bilḳīs
Balkuwārā → Sāmarrāʾ
Ballā, Sīdī, Abū Muḥammad Ibn ʿAzzūz (1789) s, **124b**
Ballabh Rāy', Rādja i, 952a

Ballahara → Balharā
al-Ballūtī → Abū Ḥafṣ ʿUmar; Mundhir b. Saʿīd
Balōč → Baluč
Balshas, Balshiči i, 653b
Bālṭa Līmānī (treaty) (1838) i, **1003b**; vii, 429a, 467b
Balṭadjî i, **1003b**
Balṭadjî Muḥammad Pasha → Muḥammad Pasha
Bālṭa-oghlū Sulaymān Beg i, 1003b
Baltic Sea → Baḥr al-Warank
Baltistān i, **1004b**; vi, 696b; viii, 136a; s, 242a, 423b
Balūč, Baluchis i, 211b, 225a, 546a, **1005a**, 1354b; iii, 633b, 1098a, 1107b; iv, 10b; v, 153a, 673b, 674b; vi, 50b, 193b, 342b; s, 143b, 147a, 270b, 331a, b, 332a, b
Balūčistān i, **1005a**; ii, 669a, 1083b; iv, 3b, 8a, 364a; v, 101b, 520b, 580b; vi, 65b, 192b; viii, 240b; s, 71b, 222a, 270b, 329b
Balwant Singh i, 1166a
Balyā b. Malkān iv, 904b
Balyānī, Awḥād al-Dīn (1288) x, 320b
Balyemez i, **1007b**, 1062b
Bālyōs, Bālyōsi **1008a**; ii, 60b
Balyūnash s, **124b**
Bam i, **1008a**; iii, 502a; iv, 1052a; v, 148b, 149b, 151a; s, 127a, 327a
Bamako i, **1008b**; vi, 260a
Bambāra i, 297a, **1009a**; ii, 252a; iii, 39b; iv, 314a; vi, 258b, 259a, b, 260a, 402b; s, 295b
Bāmiyān i, **1009a**; ii, 1101a; s, 367a, b, 787a
Bampūr i, **1010a**; vi, 192b
Bān i, **1010b**
Banādir iv, 885b, 886a
Banākat i, **1010b**
Banākath x, 349a
Banākitī i, **1011a**
Banāras → Benares
Banarsidas vii, 323a
Bānās, Nahr i, 1029b
Banat → Temesvar
Banāt Ḳayn iv, 493b
Banāt Naʿsh → Nudjūm
Bānat Suʿād i, **1011b**; iv, 316a, b
Banbalūna i, 83b, **1011b**, 1079b; v, 1119a; vii, 1039b
Band i, **1012a**; v, 862b, 867-9
Band, military → Naḳḳāra-Khāna
Band-i Amīr i, 212b, 1012a; v, 867b
Band-i Bahman vi, 384a
Band-i Ḳīr iv, 675b; v, 867b
Band-i Mīzān v, 867a, b
Bāndā i, **1012b**
Banda Bayrāgī i, 432b, 914a, 1022b; ii, 28b, 380b
Banda islands i, **1012b**
Banda Nawāz → Sayyid Muḥammad
Bandanīdjīn i, 968a
Bandar i, **1013a**
Bandar b. Fayṣal b. ʿAbd al-ʿAzīz Āl Suʿūd (XX) s, 305b
Bandar ʿAbbās i, 928a, **1013a**, 1172b, 1282a, 1283a; iii, 585a; iv, 1170b; v, 148a, 151b, 152a, 183b, 673a, 674a; viii, 773a
Bandar Kung → Kung
Bandar(-i) Linga → Linga
Bandar Nādiriyya → Būshahr
Bandar Pahlawī i, **1013b**; iv, 7a
Bandar Seri Begawan (Bandar Brunei) s, 151b
Bandar Shāpūr i, 1342a
Bandar Tawayih (Tawwāhī) i, 180b
Bandayr ii, 620b, 621a
Bandirma i, **1014a**; vi, 587b
Bandj, bang i, **1014b**; ii, 1068b; iii, 266b
Bandjarmasin i, **1014b**; s, 150a, b, 151a, 199b
Bandjī b. Nahārān Shansabānī ii, 1099b
Bandjūtakīn (992) vi, 506b
Bānegā ix, 727b
Bangakh i, 219a
Bangāla i, 400b, 606a, **1015a**; ii, 183b, 751b, 1092a; iii, 14b, 419a, 422a, 427b, 444a, 533a, 631b; iv, 210b; vi, 49b, 61b, 273a, 343a, 535b, 693a; vii, 79a; viii, 68a; s, 247a
Bangalore v, 1259b, 1260a, b
Banganapalle i, **1015b**
Bangash, Banū i, 218b, 219a; v, 250b; vii, 220a
Bangka i, **1015b**; vi, 239a
Bangla → Fayḍābād
Bangladesh v, 1082a; viii, 241b, 243a
Banhā i, **1015b**
Bani (Annam) iii, 1210b, 1212a
Banī Suwayf i, **1016a**
Banians vi, 734b, 735b

al-Bānīdjūrī → Dāwūd b. ʿAbbās
Bānīdjūrids (Abū Dāwūdids) i, 504a; v, 76a; vii, 477b; x, 602a; s, **125a**
Banīka i, **1016a**
Bāniyās (Buluniyās, Balanea) i, **1016b**; vii, 198b; viii, 129a, 131a
Baniyās (Paneas) i, **1017a**; iv, 200a; vi, 577b, 578a, b, 579b, 580b, 582a, b, 789b; vii, 198b, 274a, b; s, 204b
Bāniyās, Nahr → Bānās
Banjaluka i, **1017b**, 1263b, 1265b, 1266b, 1270b
Banking → Djahbadh and Ṣayrafī
Bānkīpūr i, **1018a**; vi, 198b
Banmana → Bambāra
Bannāʾ → Bināʾ
al-Bannāʾ, Aḥmad b. Muḥammad → al-Dimyāṭī
al-Bannāʾ, Ḥasan (1949) i, **1018b**; ii, 429b; iii, 518a, 1068b, 1070a
Bannāʾī, ʿAlī b. Muḥammad (XV) vii, 685a
Bannāʾī, Kamāl al-Dīn (1513) i, **1019a**; ii, 208a
al-Bannānī, Abū ʿAbdallāh Muḥammad b. ʿAbd al-Salām b. Ḥamdūn (1750) i, **1019b**
al-Bannānī, Abū ʿAbdallāh Muḥammad b. Ḥasan (1780) i, **1019b**; vi, 279a
al-Bannānī, Āl i, **1019b**; s, 405a
Bannū i, **1020a**; v, 251a, 501a; vi, 86a; s, 329b
Bannʿučīs i, 1020a
Bantam (Banten) iii, 1219b, 1223b; vi, 235a; s, 199b, 201a, 202a, 374b
Banū, followed by the name of the eponymous ancestor of a tribe, see in general under the name of that ancestor
Banu 'l-Afṭas → Afṭasids
Banu 'l-ʿAnbar b. ʿAmr. Ḥārith b. ʿAmr → Tamīm
Banu 'l-Djulandā i, 812b
Banū Isrāʾīl i, 264b, **1020a**; vi, 737a, b
Banū Maslama → Afṭasids
Bañuelo ii, 1015a
Banūr i, **1022a**; ii, 28b; s, 1b
al-Banūrī, Ādam (1643) i, **1022b**
Banwālī Dās Walī vii, 343b
Banya i, 700a
Banyan v, 807b
Banyar i, **1023a**
Bānyās → Baniyās
Banzart (Bizerta, Tunesia) i, **1023b**; vii, 269b; s, 145a
Bāʾolī i, **1024a**; v, 884b, 888b
Bāonī i, **1024b**
Bar Bahlūl → Abu 'l-Ḥasan b. Bahlūl
Bar Dīṣān → Ibn Dayṣan
Bar Hebraeus → Ibn al-ʿIbrī
al-Bāra i, 145b, **1024b**
al-Barāʾ b. ʿĀzib (691) i, 98b, **1025a**; iv, 858b
al-Barāʾ b. Maʿrūr (622) i, **1025a**, 1241b; v, 82b
Bāra Sayyids i, **1025b**
Bārā Wafāt i, **1026a**
Barāʾa i, 207a, 811a, **1026b**; ii, 78b, 79b, 308a
Baraba i, **1028a**
Barābīsh, Banū vi, 741b
Barābra i, **1028b**; viii, 92a
Baradā (river) i, **1029a**; ii, 1105a; viii, 118b
Baradā (Djayhūn) i, **1030a**
Baradān i, **1030a**
Barādhiʿī, Abū Saʿīd (X) vii, 538a
Barādūst i, **1030b**
Barāghīth i, 1049b
Baraghwāṭa → Barghawāṭa
Barāhima i, 173a, **1031a**, 1092b; ii, 166b; iii, 905a; v, 550a; s, 93a
Barahūt → Barhūt
Barak i, 1233b
Barak Baba (1307) i, **1031b**; ii, 1085b
Barak Ḥādjib → Burāk Ḥādjib
Barak Khāns → Būrak Khān
Baraka i, **1032a**; iii, 305b; v, 745a
Baraka (ṣūfī) s, 3a
Baraka Khān (Mamlūk) → al-Saʿīd Nāṣir al-Dīn Baraka (Berke) b. Baybars
Baraka Khān (Mongol) → Berke Khān
Baraka Umm Ayman (VII) x, 913a
Barakai i, 1190a
Barakāt I b. Ḥasan b. ʿAdjlān, Sharīf (1455) i, **1032a**; vi, 149b
Barakāt II b. Muḥammad b. Barakāt I, Sharīf (1525) i, **1032b**; ii, 527b; iv, 552b; vi, 150a
Barakāt III b. Muḥammad b. Ibrāhīm (1682) i, **1032b**
Barakāt IV b. Yaḥyā (1723) i, **1032b**
Barakāt b. Mūsā, Zayn al-Dīn (al-Zaynī) (XVI) iv, 514a, 552a, 553a
Barākish (Yathill) vi, 88b

Bārakzay i, 87a, 95b, 231a; ii, 628b, 629a; s, 65b
Baramendana Keita ii, 1132a
al-Barāmika i, 2b, 10a, 14a, 17b, 107b, 143b, 160a, 271b, 364a, 751b, 897a, **1033a**; ii, 40b, 78a, 305a, 576b; iii, 231a; iv, 221b, 447a, 756a; vi, 276a, 334b, 335b, 336a; vii, 518a; xi, 186b; s, 130a, 225b
Bārāmūla s, 167a
Baran → Bulandshahr
Barʾān (temple) vi, 562a
al-Barandjār i, 1305b
Barānī, Bārānlu → Ḳarā Ḳoyunlu
Baranī, Ḍiyāʾ al-Dīn (1357) i, **1036a**; iv, 210b; vi, 121b; vii, 988a; s, 105a, b, 409a, b
al-Barānis i, **1037a**, 1349b; vi, 741a; s, 102b
Baranta i, **1037b**
Barār → Berār
Baraṭ vi, 436b
Barāthā i, **1038a**, 1040a; s, 400b
Barawa (Brava) i, **1038a**; vi, 128b, 129a, 704a
al-Barāwī, Masʿūd b. Sulṭān Shafīʿ ʿAlī b. Sulṭān Muḥammad (1888) vi, 967a
al-Barāwī, Shaykh Muḥyī al-Dīn b. al-Shaykh al-Ḳaḥṭānī (Zanzibar) (XIX) vi, 964a
al-Barāwī, Uways b. Muḥammad (1909) x, 249b
Barāz (Barāzbanda) (VIII) iv, 16a; v, 64a
Barbā i, **1038b**
Bārbad (Bārbadh) iv, 53b; vi, 102b, 276a; viii, 278a
al-Barbahārī, al-Ḥasan b. ʿAlī (941) i, 277a, **1039a**; iii, 159a, 734b; iv, 172b, 470a; vi, 446b, 627b; viii, 14b
Bārbak Shāh b. Bahlūl Lōdī ii, 47b, 270b, 498b; iii, 420a, 632a, 633b
Bārbak Shāh Ilyās (XV) iii, 14b; s, 203a
Barbarī, Barābira → Barābra
Barbarīs → Hazāras
Barbarossa → ʿArūdj; Khayr al-Dīn
Barbary → al-Maghrib
Barbashturu i, 83b, **1040b**; v, 1119b; x, 824a; s, 152b
Barberousse → ʿArūdj; Khayr al-Dīn
al-Barbīr (1811) vi, 113a
Barcelona → Barshalūna
Barčlīgh-kent s, 246a
Barčuk (Uychur Ḳaghan) (1209) x, 676b
Bardalla, Abū ʿAbd Allāh Muḥammad (1721) s, **125b**
Bardas Sclerus (X) i, 212a
Bardasīr/Guwāshīr ix, 667a
Bardesanes → Ibn Dayṣān
Bardhaʿa (Barda) i, 660a, b, **1040b**; iv, 346b; v, 397a; vi, 499a
al-Bardhaʿī, Abū Saʿīd (1009) vi, 278b, 279a
al-Bardīdjī, Abū Bakr (914) vii, 576a; viii, 516a
Bardistān vi, 384b
Bardja (Berja) vi, 576a
Bardjalūna → Barshalūna
Bardjawān, Abu ʾl-Futūḥ (1000) i, **1041b**; ii, 858a; iii, 77a; iv, 1091b
Bārdjīk iv, 1173b
Bardo → Tūnis
Bardsīr v, 147b, 148b, 150a, b, 152a, b
Bardsīrī → Āḳā Khān Kirmānī
Bareilly, Barēlī i, **1042b**; iii, 60b, 61b; viii, 571b; s, 73b, 420b
Bārfurūsh (Bābul) i, **1043a**; vi, 511a
Bārfurūshī, Nadīm (1825) iv, 1035a
Barghash b. Saʿīd b. Aḥmad, Bū Saʿīd (1888) i, 37b, **1043b**, 1282b; v, 1030b, 1031a; vi, 129a; vii, 35a; s, 355b
Barghawāṭa, Banū i, 157a, **1043b**; ii, 275b, 1008b; v, 654b, 1160a, 1189a, 1199b; vi, 134a, 741a, 743b; vii, 585a
al-Barghawāṭī, Saḳḳūt (1083) viii, 690a
Bārgīn-farākh → Ḳarā-köl
Bārgīr iv, 219b; v, 686b
Barghūth → Ḳaml
Bārha Sayyids viii, 73a; s, **126a**
Barhebraeus → Ibn al-ʿIbrī
Barhūt i, **1045a**
Bari iv, 275a
al-Barʿī (XI) vi, 898a
Barī Bēgam (XIX) iii, 336a
Bārī Ṣāḥiba (Bīdjāpūr) (XVII) vii, 514b
Bariba ii, 94a; iv, 538b; v, 281a
Barīd i, **1045a**, 1039b; ii, 487a, 969b; iii, 109b, 182a; iv, 215b; v, 1142b
Barīd Shāhīs (Bīdar) i, **1047a**, 1200a, b, 1201a; iii, 421b, 425a, b, 447a; vi, 68a, 126a, 368a, 695b; vii, 289a
al-Barīdī, Abū ʿAbd Allāh (941) i, 866a, b, 867a, 1046b; ii, 454a; iii, 127b; vi, 921a; vii, 484a, b, 994b

al-Barīdī, Abu ’l-Ḥusayn i, 1046b, 1047a
al-Barīdī, Abu ’l-Ḳāsim i, 1047a; iii, 1175b
al-Barīdī, Abū Yūsuf i, 1046b, 1047a
Bāri̱dj̱ān → Bāriz
Bāridīs (al-Ahwāz) xi, 168a
Bāriḥ i, **1048a**
al-Bāriḥ iv, 290b
Bārimmā → Ḥamrīn, D̲jabal
Bārīn vi, 378b, 381a, 429a
Barīra (680) i, **1048a**
Barisan Hizbullah (XX) vi, 730b
Bari̱sẖk (Brechk) vi, 404a, b
Barito (river) s, 150b
Bariyya iv, 980b
Bāriz, D̲jabal s, **127a**
al-Bārizī, Kamāl al-Dīn (XV) iii, 799b; iv, 642a
Barḳa i, **1048b**, 1169a; ii, 160b, 161b; iii, 296b; v, 694b, 695b, 758a, 760a; vi, 455b, 945b; s, 1a
Barḳa (Ḳumm) s, 127a
Barḳaʿīd i, **1050a**
al-Barkat ii, 1022b
al-Barḳī, Abū D̲jaʿfar Aḥmad b. Muḥammad (IX) s, **127a**, 266a
Barḳiyya ii, 318a, b, 858b
Barḳūḳ b. Anas, al-Malik al-Ẓāhir Sayf al-Dīn (Mamlūk) (1399) i, 14b, 138a, 816b, 869a, **1050a**, 1109a, 1138a; ii, 24a, 105b, 239b, 285b, 330a, 337b; iii, 48b, 185a, 187a, 188a, 190a, 299b, 756b, 799b, 1198a; iv, 432b, 642a; v, 628a, 1141a; vi, 195a, 231b, 323b, 324a, 326b, 327a, 541a, 547b, 548a, 674a; vii, 171b, 407b; viii, 987a
Barḳūt i, 950b
Barkyārūḳ b. Malik-S̲h̲āh (Sald̲j̲ūḳ) (1105) i, 314a, 353a, 466a, 513a, 664a, 731a, 780a, **1051b**, 1070b, 1336b; ii, 282a, 384b; iii, 196a; iv, 28b, 101b, 102a; v, 437a; vi, 64a, 275a, 499b, 540b; vii, 408a, 489b, 541a, 755a; viii, 72a, 81b, 716a, 942a; s, 279a, 382b, 384a
Barlaam and Josaphat → Bilawhar wa Yūdāsaf
Barlās, Banū v, 182a
Barmak i, 1001a, 1033a, b
al-Barmakī → D̲jaʿfar b. Yaḥyā
Barmakids → Barāmika
al-Barnāwī, ʿAbd Allāh (1677) xi, 123a
Barniḳ → Beng̲h̲āzī
Barōda i, **1053a**; vi, 535b
Bārōg̲h̲il ii, 29a
Barr al-D̲jazāʾir → Algeria
al-Barrāḍ b. Ḳays al-Kinānī ii, 883b; iii, 285b; v, 116b
al-Barrādī, Abu ’l-Faḍl (XIV) i, 120b, 167a, **1053a**; ii, 140b; iii, 235b
al-Barrādī, Abu ’l-Ḳāsim (XV) vi, 311a, 948b
Barrāḥ ii, 103a
Barrāk b. G̲h̲urayr Āl Ḥumayd → Barrāk b. ʿUrayʿir
Barrāk b. ʿUrayʿir Āl Ḥamīd (XVII) iv, 765a, 925a
Barre, Muḥammad Siyad (XX) ix, 720a
Bārs Ṭūg̲h̲ān iv, 911b
Barṣawmā al-Zāmir, Isḥāḳ (804) s, **128a**
Barsbāy, al-Malik al-As̲h̲raf Abu ’l-Naṣr (Mamlūk) (1438) i, 138a, 354b, 945b, 1032b, **1053b**; ii, 6a, 286a; iii, 20a, 99b, 186a, 190a, 923a, 1198a; iv, 133b, 267b, 433b, 642a, 643a; v, 304a; vi, 324a, b; vii, 173a; s, 39a, 43b, 273b
Bārsbīk → Bārd̲j̲īk
Bars̲h̲alūna i, 75b, **1054b**; ii, 485b
Bars̲h̲ambū, Sayf al-Dīn ʿAbd Allāh (XIV) viii, 90b
Bars̲h̲āna vi, 576a
Bars̲h̲awīs̲h̲ → Nud̲j̲ūm
Barṣīṣā i, **1055a**
Barsk̲h̲ān iv, 213a; xi, 335b
Barsṭog̲h̲an (XI) ii, 391a
Barṭāʾīl ii, 486b
Bartang i, 853b, 854a
Bārūd i, **1055b**; iii, 191a; v, 687a, 979a
al-Bārūdī, Maḥmūd Sāmī Pas̲h̲a (1904) i, 597b, **1069b**; vii, 184a, b, 528b, 903a; s, 132b
Barūd̲j̲ird (Burud̲j̲ird) i, **1070b**; v, 828b, 829a, b; s, 75a, 157b, 384a
al-Bārūk (S̲h̲ūf) vi, 343b
al-Bārūnī, ʿAbd Allāh i, 1070b
al-Bārūnī, Sulaymān (1940) i, **1070b**; ii, 595a
al-Bārūsī, Abu ’l-Ḥasan Sālim vi, 224b
Barwānī → Ibrā
Barzak̲h̲ i, 940b, **1071b**, 1093a; ii, 581b; iv, 120b
Barzamān vi, 507a
Bārzān i, **1072a**; v, 467b; vii, 714a
Barzand i, **1072a**

al-Barzandjī (1691) xi, 232a
al-Barzandjī, Djaʿfar b. Ḥasan (1765) vi, 350b, 354b; vii, 100b, 103a
Barzandjī, Muṣṭafā (XX) ix, 831a
Barzandjī, Shaykh Maḥmūd (1956) v, 466b, 467b; viii, 463b; ix, 831a
Bārzānī → Muṣṭafā Bārzānī
Barzbān, Prince ii, 85b
Barzikanī iii, 258a
Barzū-nāma i, **1072b**
Barzūya i, **1073a**
Basadar s, 145a
Basaraba (Voyvoda, Wallachia) (XIV) x, 693a
al-Basāsīrī, Abu 'l-Ḥārith Arslān al-Muẓaffar (1060) i, 20b, 513a, 900b, **1073a**, 1355a; ii, 348b, 856a; iii, 159b, 891b, 1255b; iv, 26b, 457b, 458a, 911b; v, 73b; vi, 272b, 966a; vii, 270b, 730b, 731a; s, 29b
Basbās s, **128b**
Bāshā → Pasha
Bashan → ʿŪdj
Bashariyya vii, 647b
Bashdefterdār → Daftardār
Bashdjirt (Bashkir, Bashkort, Bashkurt) i, **1075a**, 1305a; ii, 995b; v, 1011b, 1012a, 1019a, b, 1020b
Bashdjirt (Bashkir) literature x, **731b**
Bashi̊-bozuḳ i, **1077b**; v, 35b
Bashīr (general) (838) vi, 775b
al-Bashīr b. al-Mundhir (IX) iii, 652a
Bashīr b. Saʿd (633) i, **1077b**; viii, 118b
Bashīr Čelebi (XV) i, **1078a**
Bāshīr Ibrāhīmī → Ibrāhīmī
Bashīr Ḳāsim Malḥam ii, 636a
Bashīr Kizlar-aghasi̊ (XVIII) iii, 253a
Bashīr Shihāb I b. Ḥusayn (1706) ii, 635a; vi, 344a, 346a
Bashīr Shihāb II, Amīr (Lebanon) (1840) i, **1078a**, 1138a, 1281a; ii, 444a, 635b; iii, 999b; v, 792b; vi, 303b; vii, 670b; s, 159b, 162b
al-Bashīr al-Wansharīsī, Shaykh (1130) iii, 959b; vi, 592a
Bashīrā (XIV) iv, 1019b
Bashkard, Bashākard, Bashkardia v, 352b; s, **129a**
Bashkent (battle of) (1473) vi, 72a, 979b
Bashkirs → Bashdjirt
al-Bashkunish i, 82a, 1011b, **1079b**; v, 1121a
Bashkort → Bashdjirt
Bashkurt → Bashdjirt
Bashḳut, Djewād Fehmī (1971) s, **129b**
Bashli̊k, Bashluk iv, 706a
Bashmaḳ → al-Naʿl al-Sharīf
Bashmaḳli̊k i, **1079b**
Bashmuḥāsaba → Māliyya
Bashshār b. Burd, Abū Muʿādh (VIII) i, 10a, 143b, 331b, 587b, 857b, **1080a**; ii, 551b, 1031b; iii, 135b, 1019b, 1262b; iv, 54b, 1003b; vi, 267a, 625b, 635b; vii, 694b, 982a; viii, 377b, 984b; s, 58b
Bashshār b. Muslim iii, 41b
Bashshār al-Shaʿīrī (VIII) i, **1082a**; vii, 517a
al-Bashshārī → al-Muḳaddasī
Bashtak (1341) vi, 323a, b
Bāshūra i, 831a
Bashyāčī, Elijah (1490) iv, 605b, 606a, 607b
Bashwakīl → Başvekil
Bāṣiʿ (Bāḍiʿ) → Maṣawwaʿ
Basil I (IX) i, 182b
Basil II (1026) i, 638a; ii, 855a; iii, 77a, 130b; v, 820b
Baṣinnā iv, 654a
al-Baṣīr, Abū ʿAlī (IX) i, **1082a**; v, 118a
Baṣīrī, Aladja (1535) i, **1082b**
Baṣīrī (tribe) iv, 9b; v, 668b
Bāsirī iii, 1106a, b
al-Basīt i, **1083a**
Basīṭ → ʿArūḍ
Basīṭ wa murakkab i, **1083b**
Basiyeh, el- vi, 582b
Basmačis i, 1077a, **1084a**; ii, 366b, 700b; iv, 792b; vi, 557b
Basmala i, **1084a**; ii, 303a; iii, 122b; v, 411b
Basmil i, 1240a; x, 689b
Basques → al-Bashkunish
al-Baṣra i, 40b, 62b, 76b, 86a, 131b, 236b, 389a, 529b, 549b, 695a, 810b, 907a, **1085a**; ii, 385a, 391a, 414b; iii, 1254b, 1257a; iv, 640a; v, 57a, 646a, 950b; vi, 112a, 119b, 139b, 140a, 196a, 198a, 199a, 262b, 266b, 267a, 270b, 272b, 279b, 280b, 333b, 334b, 335b, 336b, 344b, 345b, 359a, 362a, 363a, b, 428a, 477a, 509a, 606a, 620a, 640b, 647b, 653a, 656b, 658a, 660a, b, 664a, 668a, 670b, 671a, 677a, 679a, b, 709a, 710b, 735a; vii, 67a; s, 12b, 15b,

17b, 18b, 20a, 24a, 26a, 27b, 31a, 32a, 35a, 41a, 88b, 113a, 119a, 122a, 179a, 198b, 225b, 243a, 284b, 352a, 354b, 384b, 385a, 389b
– commerce i, 1086a, 1087a, b; ii, 130b; iii, 1252b
– monuments i, 610a; iii, 1268a
– school of i, 4b, 569b, 587b, 717b
al-Baṣra (Morocco) i, **1087b**; iii, 149a
al-Baṣrī → ʿAlī b. Abi ’l-Faradj
al-Baṣrī, Abu ’l-Ḥasan Aḥmad b. Muḥammad b. Sālim (967) viii, 840b, 993b
al-Baṣrī, ʿAbd al-Djalīl (1854) s, 162b
Bassein, treaty of vi, 535b
Bassora → al-Baṣra
Bast i, **1088a**; iii, 1170a; iv, 51a
Basṭ i, **1088b**; iii, 361a; iv, 326a
Basta (Baza, Spain) i, **1089a**; s, 144b
Bastām vi, 201b
Bastū vi, 574b
al-Basūs bint Munḳidh i, 565a, **1089a**; v, 362a; vi, 490a, 640b; s, 234b
Başvekalet Arşivi i, 626a, **1089b**; ii, 82b, 128a
Başvekil i, **1091a**
al-Baṭāḥira, Banū i, **1091a**; vi, 80a, 84b
al-Baṭāʾiḥ → al-Baṭīḥa
al-Baṭāʾiḥī (1192) vii, 164a
al-Baṭāʾiḥī, Abū ʿAbd Allāh (al-Maʾmūn) (vizier) (XII) i, 440a, **1091b**; ii, 127a, 130a, 858a, 859b; iv, 429a
al-Baṭāʾiḥī, Muḥammad → Muḥammad al-Baṭāʾihī
al-Baṭāʾinī, ʿAlī b. Abī Ḥamza (IX) vii, 647b
Batak iii, 1214b, 1220a, 1225b
Baṭalyaws i, 6a, 161a, **1092a**; iii, 498b
al-Baṭalyawsī, Abū Muḥammad ʿAbd Allāh Ibn al-Sīd (1127) i, 602a, **1092b**; ii, 838a; iv, 1007b; v, 929b; vi, 111a; vii, 280b
Batavia i, 980b; ii, 390b; iii, 1221b
Baʿth (resurrection) i, **1092b**
Baʿth → Nabīʾ
Baʿth party iv, 125a, b, 126a; v, 486a, b, 1048b; vi, 470b; viii, 247a; s, 7b
Batha s, 166a
al-Bathaniyya i, **1093a**; iii, 293a
al-Baṭḥāʾ (Algeria) vii, 186b
al-Baṭḥāʾ (Makka) vi, 144b, 147a
Baṭḥarī → al-Baṭāḥira
Báthory ii, 704a
al-Baṭīḥa i, **1093b**; iii, 1175b; v, 865a; vii, 484b, 650a; s, 118b, 119a, 243a
Bāṭil → Fāsid wa bāṭil
Bāṭin i, 1039a, 1099a, b; ii, 97b, 169a; iii, 662a; iv, 203a, b
al-Bāṭin i, **1097b**
al-Bāṭina (plain) i, 536b, 541a, **1098a**; vi, 734b
Bāṭina Yāl Saʿd s, 355b
Bāṭiniyya i, 256b, 839a, **1098b**, 1332b; ii, 169a, 282a, 733b, 734a, 1040b, 1094b; iv, 25b, 28b-29a, 47a, 101b-102a; vi, 547a; vii, 408a
al-Bātiya → Nudjūm
Batjan i, **1100a**
Baṭlamiyūs (Ptolemy) i, **1100a**; ii, 357b, 577b, 578a, 763a; iii, 788b, 906b, 1135b, 1136b; iv, 517b, 1182b; v, 762a; vi, 377b, 639b
Baṭn i, **1102a**
Baṭn al-Agharr s, 198b
Baṭrīḳ → Biṭrīḳ
Batriyya, Butriyya iii, 244a, 1166a; s, 48b, **129b**
Batrūn i, **1102b**
al-Batt s, 23a
Baṭṭāl v, 332b
al-Baṭṭāl, ʿAbd Allāh (740) i, 243b, **1102b**; iii, 493b
al-Baṭṭāl, Sayyid (840) i, **1103b**; ii, 110a, 234b, 237b; iii, 115a; iv, 845b; v, 951b
Baṭṭāl b. ʿAbd Allāh s, 223a
Baṭṭāl Ḥuseyin Pasha (1801) ii, 25b, 207b
al-Battānī, Abū ʿAbd Allāh (Albatenius) (929) i, 589b, 727a, **1104b**; iii, 228a, 1137a; v, 84b; vi, 374b, 377b, 600b; vii, 680a; viii, 101b; s, 412b, 413b
al-Battī → Abu ’l-Ḥasan al-Battī
Bātū b. Djūčī b. Čingiz Khān (Mongol) (1255) i, 135a, 467a, **1105a**, 1106b, 1187b, 1308a; ii, 3a, 44a, 571b; iv, 849a; v, 491a; vi, 419b, 420a; vii, 230a; viii, 162b; s, 203b
Bātūʾids i, 1105a, b, **1106b**, 1308a; ii, 315b, 1112a; iii, 1121b; iv, 349b, 1064a; v, 136b, 137a; vi, 457a, 492b; s, 203b
Batumi i, 468b, **1108a**
Baʿūḍ iv, 522a
al-Bāʿūnī i, **1109a**

Bāvī (tribe) iii, 1107a
Bawānātī, Muḥammad Bāḳir (1891) iv, 70b
Bāwand(ids) i, 237a, 872a, **1110a**; iii, 254b, 810a; iv, 207b, 645b; vi, 511b, 632a, 745a, 938a; s, 298a, 309a, 356b, 416a
al-Bawandī, Shaykh → ʿAbd al-ʿAzīz al-Bawandī
Bāward → Abīward
Bawāzīdj i, **1110b**
Bāwiyān v, 896a
Bāwiyya, Banū vii, 675a
Bawraḳ (Būraḳ) s, **130b**
Baxar s, 325a
Bay (Bey) i, **1110b**; ii, 146b, 638b
Bayʿ i, **1111a**
al-Bayʿa i, 1111a, **1113a**; ii, 302b, 308a; iv, 943b, 944a; vi, 205b
al-Bayāḍ vi, 439a
al-Bayāḍī, Kamāl al-Dīn (1687) vi, 848a
al-Bayālika vi, 230b
Bayān i, **1114a**; v, 898a, 899b
Bayān b. Samʿān al-Tamīmī (737) i, **1116b**; ii, 1094b; iv, 837a; vii, 348a, 388b
Bayān al-adyān ii, 74a
Bayānā iii, 441b; vi, 53b, 368b
Bayāndur, Abu 'l-Fatḥ Beg → Abu 'l-Fatḥ Beg Bayāndur
Bayāniyya iii, 1265b; iv, 837a
Bayar, Celâl (XX) ii, 204a, 432b, 596a; iii, 527a; vi, 1011b
Bayarku (Banū) x, 687b
Bayās → Payas
al-Bayāsī, Yūsuf b. Muḥammad (1255) iii, 111a
Bayāt (Türkmen) i, **1117a**; iii, 1101b, 1102b, 1108a; iv, 387a; v, 828a, b; vi, 201a, 202b
Bayʿat al-ḥarb i, 314b; v, 995b
Bayʿat al-nisāʾ i, 314b; v, 995b
Bayʿat al-riḍwān s, **131a**
Bāyazīd I Yîldîrîm (Ottoman) (1403) i, 21b, 313a, 346a, 394a, 432a, 468a, 481a, 510b, 517b, 640a, 783b, 842b, 947b, 988a, 999a, **1117b**, 1251b, 1263a, 1303a, 1334a; ii, 11b, 239b, 292a, 611a, 684a, 697a, 722a, 984a, 989b, 990a, 1086a; iii, 1183a, 1248a; iv, 586a, 600b, 623a; v, 539a, 677a; vi, 3b, 231b; vii, 348b; viii, 193a; s, 314b
Bāyazīd II (Ottoman) (1512) i, 293a, 310b, 432a, 510b, 842b, 1061a, **1119a**, 1207b, 1225b, 1253a; ii, 26a, 62a, 118b, 291b, 420b, 529a, 530a, 612a, 685a, 715a, 879a, 1087b; iii, 213a, 341a; iv, 92a, 230b, 291b, 463a, 565a, 1159a; v, 269a, 589b, 677b; vi, 324b, 525b, 530a, b, 606b, 795a; vii, 272a; viii, 8a, 767b
Bāyazīd (town) i, **1117b**; vi, 55b, 200b, 201a, b
Bāyazīd b. Uways al-Djalāyir i, 1117b; ii, 4016
Bāyazīd b. ʿAbd Allāh Anṣārī (Kānīgurām) (1572) i, 220a, 225b, 238a, **1121b**; iii, 430a, 575b; vii, 327b; viii, 468a
Bāyazīd Bayāt (XVI) vii, 342b
Bāyazīd al-Bisṭāmī → Abū Yazīd al-Bisṭāmī
Bāyazīd Khān Kararānī ii, 183b
Bāyazīd Khān Maḥmūdābād vi, 77b
Bāyazīd Kötürüm (XIV) iv, 108b
Bāyazīd Pasha (XV) vii, 594b
Bāyazīd Sarwānī → ʿAbbās Sarwānī
Baybars I, al-Malik al-Ẓāhir Rukn al-Dīn al-Bunduḳdārī (Mamlūk) (1277) i, 21a, 280b, 354a, 517a, 553a, 662b, 711a, 786b, 804b, 945b, 946a, 966b, 989b, 1017a, 1046a, **1124b**, 1126b, 1127b, 1188a; ii, 38a, 170b, 285a, 568b, 693b, 966a; iii, 20a, 48a, 109b, 184b, 189a, 399b, 402b, 473a, 504b, 506a, 679a, 832b, 1121a; iv, 87b, 216b, 402b, 431a, 432b, 483b, 484b, 609a, 655a, 842b, 843a, 944b; v, 571b, 801b; vi, 45a, 46a, 143b, 149b, 195a, 258a, 315b, 321b, 322a, 324a, 325b, 326a, 352a, 359b, 419b, 440b, 507b, 543b, 579b, 654a, b, 659b, 663a, 666a, 667b, 669a, 672b, 673b, 777b, 790b; vii, 148a, 166b, 167a, b, 168b, 479b, 729a, 990b; viii, 90b, 147a, 464a, 995b, 999b; s, 391a
Baybars II al-Malik al-Muẓaffar Djāshnikīr (Mamlūk) (1310) i, **1126b**, 1325a; iii, 952a; iv, 429a, 433b; vi, 359b; vii, 169b, 176a, 635b, 991b
Baybars (usurper) (1312) vi, 323a
Baybars, Sīrat i, **1126b**
Baybars al-Djāshenkīr (Čāshnegīr) → Baybars II
Baybars al-Manṣūrī (Mamlūk general) (1325) i, **1127b**; vi, 317b; s, 388b

Baybughā (u) Rūs (amīr) (XIV) vi, 316b; vii, 993a
Bāybūrd i, **1128a**; ii, 223b
al-Bayḍā᾽ (el-Beizā᾽) (Fārs; Yemen) i, **1128b**; vii, 779a
Baydaḳ → Shaṭrandj
Baydamūr (XIV) iii, 818a
Baydarā (amīr) (Miṣr) (XIII) iv, 964b, 965b; v, 595a; vii, 169a
al-Bayḍāwī, ʿAbd Allāh (1286) i, **1129a**; ii, 95b; iv, 912b; vi, 218a, 219a
al-Baydhaḳ, Abū Bakr (XII) i, 78a, 122a, 389a, **1129b**; iii, 958b; v, 1209a; vi, 592a; x, 346a
Baydju Noyon (Mongol) (XIII) i, 467a; ii, 38a, 712a; iv, 814a, 843a; v, 271b; vii, 479a; viii, 949a
Baydu (1295) i, **1129b**; ii, 982a; iii, 1122b; v, 162b, 553b
Bayero (1903) ii, 1146b
Bāyezīd → Bāyazīd
Bāyezīd Kötürüm → Bāyazīd Kötürüm
Bāyezīdli (XIX) vi, 508b
Bayhaḳ i, **1130a**, 1131b; s, 343a
al-Bayhaḳī → al-Ḥākim al-Djushamī
Bayhaḳī Sayyids s, **131b**, 329a
al-Bayhaḳī, Abū Bakr Aḥmad (1066) i, **1130a**; iii, 24b; v, 1126b
al-Bayhaḳī, Abū Djaʿfar (1167) vi, 914a
al-Bayhaḳī, Abū Djaʿfar Aḥmad (1110) s, 289b
al-Bayhaḳī, Abu ᾽l-Faḍl Muḥammad (Dabīr) (1077) i, **1130b**; ii, 336a, 1053a; v, 1224b; vi, 108a, 115a, 193a, 353a, 410a, 433a, 780b, 987a; s, 245b
al-Bayhaḳī, Abū Saʿīd → al-Ḥākim al-Djushamī
al-Bayhaḳī, Aḥmad s, 354a
Bayhaḳī, Djaʿfarak (1150) iv, 525b
al-Bayhaḳī, Ibrāhīm b. Muḥammad (X) i, 759a, **1132a**
Bayhaḳī, Sayyid Muḥammad (1505) s, 423b
al-Bayhaḳī, Ẓahīr al-Dīn Abu ᾽l-Ḥasan ʿAlī (1169) i, 594b, **1131b**; vi, 824a, 913b; s, 245b
al-Bayhaḳī, Zayd b. al-Ḥasan s, 236a
Bayḥān (wadi) i, **1132b**; iii, 208a; iv, 746a, b; s, 337a
Bayḥān al-Kaṣāb i, **1133a**; ii, 675b; iv, 681a
Bayhasiyya i, 113a; iii, 661a
Bayıldım Ḳaṣrı vi, 57a
Bayındır (tribe) i, 311a, **1133b**; ii, 200b; iii, 1100b; iv, 463a
Bāyirāt iv, 1036a
al-Baykandī, Abū ʿAmr ʿUthmān b. ʿAlī (1157) vi, 558a
Bāyḳarā (Tīmūrid) (1416) i, **1133b**; iv, 33a
Bāyḳarā, Sultan Ḥusayn Mīrzā b. Manṣūr (Tīmūrid) (1506) vii, 129b, 133b, 929a, 935a; viii, 750a, 1012a; x, 514a; s, 423a
Bāykbāk → Bākbāk
Baylaḳān i, **1134a**; vi, 337a; vii, 498a
al-Baylamān → Madjlis
Baylān i, **1134a**
Baynūn i, **1134b**; viii, 979b
Bayra vi, 576a
Bayraḳ → ʿAlam
Bayraḳdār i, **1134b**; iv, 679a
Bayraḳdār Muṣṭafā Pasha → Muṣṭafā Pasha Bayraḳdār
Bayram → ʿĪd
Bayram, Muḥammad (1889) i, 597a
Bayram ʿAlī (town) i, **1135a**
Bayram ʿAlī Khān (Ḳādjār Türkmen) (1785) i, **1135a**; vi, 621a
Bayrām Beg i, 1067a
Bayram Khān, Khān-i Khānān Muḥammad (1560) i, 80b, 316a, **1135a**, 1194b; ii, 156a; iii, 423b; iv, 1020a; v, 629b; vi, 131a; vii, 314a, 320a; s, 312a
Bayrām Khʷadja (1380) iii, 1100b; iv, 584a
Bayram Pasha (1657) iii, 357a; iv, 573b
Bayram al-Tūnusī (1889) v, 1160b
Bayrām-i Walī → Ḥādjdji Bayrām
Bayrāmiyya i, 312b, 313a, 423b, 511a, **1137a**, 1235a; iii, 43a; vi, 226a; x, 252a; s, 283a
Bayrānwand (tribe) v, 617a
Bayrūt i, **1137a**; ii, 129b, 635b; vi, 28a, 343b, 469b; viii, 131a
– institutions ii, 424a
Baysān i, **1138b**; vi, 543b, 547a, b
Bayṣar b. Ḥām vi, 411b
Bāysonḳor → Bāysonghor
Bāysonghor b. Shāh Rūkh, Ghiyāth al-Dīn (Tīmūrid) (1433) i, **1139a**; ii, 919b, 1076a; iv, 1123a, 1124a; vii, 602b
Bāysonghor b. Maḥmūd (1493) i, **1139b**

Bāysonghor b. Yaʿḳūb (Samarḳand) (XV) i, 312a, **1139b**
Bāysonghor, Muḥammad b. s, 43b, 84a
Bāysunkur → Bāysonghor
Bayt i, **1139b**; ii, 113b; iv, 1146b, 1148a
Bayt, abyāt i, 668a
Bayt Asgedē vi, 628b
Bayt Balḥāf vi, 80b
Bayt Bāraʿfīt vi, 80b
Bayt Djibrīn (Bethgibelin) i, **1140a**; ii, 911b; s, 204b
Bayt Fāʿis vi, 438b
Bayt al-Faḳīh i, **1140b**; s, 30b
Bayt Grayza vi, 735b
Bayt Ḥarāwīz vi, 80b
Bayt al-Ḥikma i, 589a, 899a, **1141a**; iii, 872a; v, 1125a; vi, 336b
al-Bayt al-ḥarām i, 1139b
Bayt Kalshāt vi, 80b
Bayt Ḳamṣīt vi, 80b
Bayt Ḳayʿāl i, 759b
Bayt Laḥm i, **1141a**
Bayt al-Maḳdis → al-Ḳuds
Bayt al-māl i, 729b, **1141b**; ii, 144b, 325a; v, 1251b, 1252a; s, 200a
al-Bayt al-Muḳaddas → al-Ḳuds
Bayt Rās i, **1149a**; s, 117a
Bayt Rayb vi, 438b
Bayt Ṣamūdat vi, 80b
Bayt Thuwār vi, 80b
Bayt al-ṭirāz iii, 344b; iv, 216b
Bayt Ziyād vi, 80b
Bayt Zaʿbanāt vi, 80b
Bayṭār i, **1149b**
al-Bayṭār, Ṣalāḥ al-Dīn iv, 161b
Bāytūz (X) i, 1348b; v, 691a
Bayulî, Banū vi, 416b
Bayundur, Banū i, 311a, b; x, 689b
Bayyāna (Baena) i, **1150a**
Bayyāsa (Baeza) i, **1150a**
al-Bayyāsī, Abū Muḥammad (1127) iv, 116a; vi, 339b
Bayyina i, **1150b**
Bayyūmiyya i, 281a, **1151b**
Bayzara i, **1152a**; iv, 745a
Bāz (Mānd) vi, 384b
Bāz, Āl vi, 177a
Bāz Bahādur b. Shudjāʿ Khān, Malik Bāyazīd (Mālwa) (1570) i, **1155a**; ii, 815a; iii, 421b, 453b; vi, 310a, 407a
Bāz Bahādur (palace) vi, 407a, b
Baza → Basta
Bāzabdā iv, **639a**
Bāzahr (Bezoar) i, **1155b**; v, 672a, 1229a
Bāzār → Sūḳ
Bāzargān → Tidjāra
Bāzargān, Mahdī (XX) iv, 166a; vii, 450a, 762b, 763a
al-Bazdawī, b. Aḥmad al-Nasafī vii, **968b**; s, 132a, 225b
al-Bazdawī, ʿAbd al-Karīm b. Mūsā (X) vi, 846a
al-Bazdawī, Abu 'l-Yusr (1099) iii, 1165a; vi, 847b; x, 931a; s, 690a
al-Bazdawī (al-Pazdawī), ʿAlī b. Muḥammad (1089) iii, 1024a, 163b; x, 932b
Bazh → Bādj
Bāziʿ (Baʾziʿ) b. ʿUrayʿir (XIX) iv, 925b
Bazīgh b. Mūsā (VIII) i, **1156a**; iv, 1132b
Bāzinḳir i, **1156b**
Bazirgan i, **1157a**
Bazmān, Kūh-i iv, 3b
Bazm-i Ṣūfiyya-yi Hind s, 4b, 293b
Bāzūkiyyūn i, **1157a**; iii, 1108b; iv, 1029b; v, 459a
Bāzyār i, 1152b, 1153a
al-Bazzār (1349) i, 273b; vi, 353b
al-Bazzāz (town) vi, 921b
al-Bazzāz, ʿAbd al-Raḥmān (1971) iv, 782b, 783a
al-Bazzāz, Abū Bakr Muḥammad b. ʿAbd Allāh (965) vii, 648a
Bazzāzistān → Ḳayṣariyya
Beaufort, Castle → Ḳalʿat al-Shaḳīf
Beč i, **1157b**
Bécharré → Bsharrā
Bečkem → Badjkam
Bedel-i ʿAskerī → Badal
Bedel-i Naḳdī → Badal
Bēdel → Bīdil
Bedestān → Bezzāzistān
Bedj → Beč
Bedja (Budja) i, 1a, 782b, **1157b**, 1172a, 1239b; iii, 5b; iv, 686a, b, 687a; v, 99a, 368b; vi, 628a; viii, 90b, 863a; s, 243b
– language v, 521b, 523a
Bedjkem (X) vii, 800a
Bēdjwān i, 863b
Bedouins → Badw
Bedr al-Dīn, Shaykh (XVI) vii, 349a
Bedr al-Dīn b. Shaykh Ḳāsim (1479) vii, 56b

Bedri Rahmi Eyuboğlu → Eyyūbog̲h̲lu, Bedrī Raḥmī
Beersheba → Bīr al-Sabʿ
Beg, Bey i, **1159a**; ii, 507b; v, 629b
Beg b. Yaḥyā Pas̲h̲a (XVI) vii, 239b
Begam Anis Kidwai (XX) vi, 489a
Begam Anwara Taimur (XX) vi, 489a
Begam Ḥabībullāh (XX) vi, 489a
Begam Liyāḳat ʿAlī K̲h̲ān (XX) vi, 489b
Begam Mohammad Ali (XX) vi, 489a
Begam Nasim Wali Khan (XX) vi, 489b
Begam Nusrat Bhutto (XX) vi, 489b
Bēgam Ṣāḥib(a) → D̲j̲ahānārā Begam bint S̲h̲āh D̲j̲ahān
Bēgam Sulṭān (VII) ii, 922a
Begarhā, Maḥmūd I, Sayf al-Dīn (1511) ii, 500a, 922a, 1127b; v, 26b, 1216b; vi, **50a**, 54a; ix, 64a, 869a; x, 435b
Begdili i, **1159b**; iii, 1100a
Bēglār iii, 1030a
Beglerbegi i, 368a, 468b, 978a, **1159b**, 1191a; ii, 146a, 201b, 722a, 723b
Begrā → Begarhā
Begteginids i, **1160b**; ii, 347b; v, 144b
Begtimur → S̲h̲āh-i Arman
Begtūzūn (998) vi, 65a, 433a
Begum i, **1159a**, 1161a
Bēḥān → Bayḥān
Behāristān → D̲j̲āmī
Behdīn v, 1113a, b, 1114a
Beḥera → Buḥayra
Behesnī → Besni
Behis̲h̲t → D̲j̲anna
Behistūn → Bīsutūn
Behman → Bahman
Behnesā → Bahnasā
Behrām → Bahrām
Behrasīr v, 945a, 946a
Behzād → Bihzād
Beirut → Bayrūt
el-Beizāʾ → al-Bayḍāʾ
Beja → Bād̲j̲a
Bekaa → al-Biḳāʿ
Bekār odalari iv, 236a
Bekbulatovič, Simeon → Sāyin Bulāt
Bekči iv, 234b
Bekeč/G̲h̲āzī Arslan Tegin (Ḳarak̲h̲ānid) x, 689b
Bekrī Bābā vi, 1015b
Bekrī Muṣṭafā Ag̲h̲a (XVII) i, **1161b**; iii, 375a; viii, 185b
Bektās̲h̲ al-Fāk̲h̲irī (IVX) i, 571a
Bektās̲h̲ Walī → Ḥād̲j̲d̲j̲ī Bektās̲h̲
Bektās̲h̲iyya i, 309b, 653a, 768a, 844a, **1161b**; ii, 202b, 292a, 968a; iii, 600b, 662b; iv, 168a, 811b, 951b; v, 283b, 285a; vi, 89a, 510a, 810a; viii, 2b, 8b, 161b, 210b, 244a, 343b, 744b; x, 251b, 412b, 418b; s, 95b
Bēla → Las Bēla
Belalcázar → G̲h̲āfiḳ
Belediye → Baladiyya
Beled̲j̲ik → Bīred̲j̲ik
Belen → Baylān
Beles̲h̲ → Bālis̲h̲
Beleyn i, **1163a**
Belgrade i, 268a, 269b, 293a, 656a, **1163a**; iv, 239a, 969b; v, 262a, 263a; vi, 70a
Belhūba, Belhīt → Abu ʾl-Hawl
Belīg̲h̲, Ismāʿīl (1729) i, **1165b**
Belīg̲h̲, Meḥmed Emīn (1760) i, **1165b**
Belitung → Billiton
Belkasem Krim → Ibn al-Ḳāsim Karīm
Bello, Alhaji Aḥmadu iii, 282b; iv, 549b, 550a, 774a
Belomancy → Istiḳsām
Béloutchistan → Balūčistān
Ben-ʿamma iii, 389a
Ben Ayed ii, 460a
Ben Badīs → Ibn Bādīs
Ben Bella, Aḥmad (XX) iii, 564a; v, 1070b
Ben Cheneb (S̲h̲neb) → Ibn Abī S̲h̲anab
Ben Ganah i, 1247a
Ben Ghedahem → Ibn G̲h̲id̲h̲āhum
Ben Sedira iii, 689b, 690b
Benares, Banāras, Kās̲h̲ī i, **1165b**; vi, 369b, 602a; s, 47a
Benavent i, **1166a**
Benavert (1068) i, **1166b**
Bender → Bandar
Bender (Bessarabia) i, **1166b**; vi, 56a
Beng → Band̲j̲
Bengal → Bangāla
Bengali i, **1167a**
Beng̲h̲āzī i, 1049a, 1050a, **1169a**; v, 759b, 760a; s, 164b
Beni Amer → Āmīr, Banū
Benī Mellāl s, **132a**
Benī Menāser → Manāṣir, Banū
Beni-Saf s, 376b
Beni Suef → Bani Suwayf
Benia → Banya

Benjamin → Binyāmīn
Benjamin b. Mishal iv, 310a
Benlāk → Bennāk
Bennāk i, **1169b**; ii, 32b
Benue (river) i, 179a
Benyāmīn → Ibn Yāmīn
Beograd → Belgrade
Berār i, 924b, **1170a**; ii, 815b, 981b; iii, 425a, 1159a; v, 1a; vi, 63a, 68a, 87a, 536b; s, 279b, 280a
Berāt i, **1170a**; ii, 32b, 119a; iii, 1180b, 1187a
Berātlı̊ i, **1171b**
Berber (language) i, 171a, 374b, 379a, 568b, 573b, 578b, 763a, 770a, 792a, 889a, 1044b, 1177a, 1180-5; ii, 109b, 460a, 591b, 873b, 992b; iv, 307b, 1149a; v, 754b, 760a, 1206a; x, 118b; s, 397a
– territory i, **1171b**; v, 1249b
Berberā i, **1172b**; ix, 715a
Berberi i, **1173a**
Berbers i, 32a, 47b, 79b, 86b, 92a, 125a, 163b, 167b, 171a, 207b, 244b, 245a, 254b, 355b, 367a, 374b, 379a, 532b, 699a, 770a, 990b, 1043b, 1049a, b, 1071b, **1173a**, 1238a, 1246b, 1321a; ii, 57b, 992b; iii, 494a, 982b; iv, 75a, b, 307b, 339a, 359a, 415a, b, 562a; v, 517b, 744a, 1156b, 1160a, 1187a; vi, 39b, 310b, 741a, 773b, 815a, 840a, 899a, 923a, 943b, 948a, 1038a, 1042a; vii, 611a; viii, 616a; ix, 844b; s, 145a, 153a, 376b
– in al-Andalus i, 5b, 6a, b, 76a, 82a, b, 490b, 494a, b, 1176a, 1249a; ii, 505a, 541b; iii, 12a, 147a, 495b, 1043b; v, 1239b
– ethnography i, 370b, 1037a, **1173a**, 1349b; iii, 295b, 1039a; iv, 360b, 511b; v, 1196b
– religion i, **1178a**; ii, 1079a; iii, 134b
Berdī Beg Khān (Golden Horde) (1360) i, 325a, 1107b; ii, 401a; x, 560b
Berdi Khodja iv, 584a, b
Bergama i, **1187a**; iv, 628a; vi, 740a; s, 137b
Bergi → Birge
Berke b. Djočī, Khān (Batu'id) (1266) i, 1106a, b, **1187b**; ii, 44a; iii, 185a, 679a; iv, 30b, 349b; v, 301a; vi, 322a, b, 419b, 420a, b; vii, 168a, 974a
Berkečār b. Djūčī (Mongol) (1269) vi, 420a
Berk-yaruk → Barkyārūk
Béroia, Bérrhoia → Karaferye
Bertam (Malacca) vi, 207b
Besermyans i, **1188b**
Beshike i, **1189a**
Beshiktash ii, 1042b; iv, 233a; v, 905a, 949a; vi, 57a
Beshiktash Sāḥil Sarāyı̊ vi, 57a
Beshīr Agha (Ḳı̊zlar aghası̊) (1730) vi, 55b, 56b
Beshīr Agha (Malāmī) (1662) vi, 228a
Beshlik ii, 28b
Beshparmak i, **1189a**
Besika Bay → Beshike
Beskesek-Abaza i, **1189a**
Besleney ii, 21b, 22a
Besni (Bahasnā) i, **1190b**; vi, 505b
Bessarabia → Budjāk
Bet (island; fortress) vi, 50b
Bēt → Bayt
Betelgeuze → Nudjūm
Bēth Aramāyē (IV) vi, 633a
Bethlehem → Bayt Laḥm
Bēwarāsp vi, 744a, b
Bey → Bay
Beyānī (Muṣṭafā of Rusčuḳ) (1597) x, 55a
Beyatlı̊ → Yaḥyā Kemāl Beyatlı̊
Beyhan, Princess ii, 999a
Beylerbeyi → Beglerbegi
Beylik i, 368a, **1191a**; ii, 338b
Beyoghlu i, 973a, b; iii, 1181a; s, 314a, 315b
Beyrouth → Beirut
Beyshehir i, 703a, 703b, **1191b**; iv, 620b, 622a, 623a; s, 137a
Bežeta (Bezzeta, Bezhiti) ii, 251a; iv, 571b
Bezistān → Ḳayṣariyya
Bezm-i ʿĀlem → Walide Sultān
Bezoar → Bāzahr
Bezzāzistān iii, 212b, 213a; iv, 226b, 227a, b; v, 559b
Bhagwān Dās (XVI) iv, 709a
Bhagwanis i, 173a
Bhagwant Rāy (XVIII) i, 1330a
Bhakkar i, **1192a**; iii, 633a
Bhakti ii, 51b; iii, 435b, 456b
Bharatpūr i, **1192b** 1193a; ii, 488b; iii, 1158b; s, 358b
Bharoč i, **1193a**; ii, 1129a; iii, 444b; s, 358b
Bhāskar Rāo (XIX) ii, 220a

Bhāskara i, 133a
Bhattā-Shāh s, 327b
Bhaṭṭi i, **1193b**; iii, 225b
Bhattinda i, **1193b**; vi, 47b, 48b; vii, 279a
Bhawāni Rām (XVIII) ii, 219a
Bhīkam Khān b. Maḥmūd Khān Sharḳī (Djawnpūr) (1458) vi, 62b
Bhīls iv, 1023b
Bhīls(a) vi, 55a, 309a
Bhīm-Dēv (Radjpūt) (1423) vi, 50b; s, 242a
Bhimpāl (Rādjā) (1026) vi, 65b
Bḥīra (Rabat) vi, 293b
Bhitāʾī, Shāh ʿAbd al-Laṭīf (1752) i, **1194b**; vii, 328a, 376b; ix, 637a; x, 322a
Bhittanni vi, 86a
Bhōdja, Rādja i, 1197a; ii, 218b, 219b
Bhōdjpur iii, 638b
Bhōnslē, Raghudjī (1803) vi, 535b
Bhōnslē, Shāhdjī (1664) vi, 534b
Bhōnslēs vi, 534a, 535b, 536a
Bhōpāl (town) i, **1196b**; vi, 535b
Bhōpāl (state) i, **1195a**; vii, 421a
Bhūčar Mōrī (Sōrath) vii, 131b
Bhutto, Benazir (2007) vi, 489b; viii, 243b
Bhutto, Zulfiqar Ali (1979) v, 1081b; vi, 489b; viii, 243a; xi, 518a
Bī Ammāñ → Ābādī Begum
Biʿa → Kanīsa
Bībān i, **1197a**
Bībī i, **1197b**
Bībī Aḳā Malik → al-Djawnpūrī
Bībī Djamāl (XIII) ii, 49b
Bībī Khānım (Khānum) → Masdjid-i Djāmiʿ (Samarḳand)
Bībī Khātūn (Khwārazm) (1257) vi, 482b
Bībī Khwunza iii, 632a
Bībī Rādjī Sharḳī (Djawnpur) (1452) vi, 62a, b
Bibgha Arūs (amīr) (XIV) vii, 462a
al-Biblāwī, ʿAlī b. Muḥammad (1905) s, 123a, **132b**
Bible i, 118a, 564b; iii, 1205a; iv, 303a, 308b, 312a
Bibliography i, **1197b**
Bičaḳdji-zāde Muṣṭafā Čelebī i, 775b
Bičitr (painter) (XVII) vii, 339a
Bīd vi, 494a
Bidʿ → al-Dawḥa (Ḳaṭar)
Bidʿa i, 277a, 1039a, **1199a**; iv, 141b
Bīdar i, 924a, 925a, b, 1047a, b, **1199b**, 1323a; iii, 425b, 447a; v, 295b, 888b, 1135a, 1215a, b; vi, 53b, 63a, b, 66b, 67b, 68a, 269a, 368b, 369a, 407a, b, 537a, 695b
Bidʿat ii, 147a
Bīdil, Mīrzā ʿAbd al-Ḳādir (1721) i, **1201a**; ii, 865b; vii, 341b, 529a
Bīdjān, Aḥmed (XV) i, **1202a**; ii, 587b; iii, 43b
Bidjanagar → Vidjayanagara
Bīdjāpūr i, 199a, 768b, 769a, 913b, 924b, 1015b, **1202b**, 1323b; iii, 15a, 287b, 288a, 425a, b; v, 884b, 888b, 1259a, b; vi, 62b, 63b, 68a, 122a, 126a, b, 127a, 271b, 369a, b, 456b, 534b, 535a, b, 537b; vii, 404b; s, 246b
– monuments i, 1203b, 1204b; iii, 446b, 447b; v, 295a, 1216a
Bidjār s, 142a, b
Bidjanagar → Vidjayanagara
Bidjay Rāy i, 1194a
Bidjāya (Bougie) i, 155a, 165a, 678a, **1204b**; ii, 130a, 747b, 863b; iii, 67a, b, 138a, b, 500a; iv, 359b, 360b, 361b, 479b; v, 531a; vi, 320a, 404b, 426b, 573a; s, 113b
Bīdjbehāra s, 114a
Bidjnawr i, 288a, **1206a**; s, 73b, 74a
Bidlīs (Bitlis) i, **1206a**; v, 457a, 458b, 459a; vi, 242b
Bidlīsī, Abu ʾl-Faḍl (1574) i, 1208a; iv, 704b
al-Bidlīsī, ʿAmmār (1194) ix, 778a
Bidlīsī, Idrīs (1520) i, **1207b**; ii, 1136b; v, 457a, b, 481b
Bidlīsī, Sharaf al-Din Khān (XVII) i, 1207a, **1208b**; v, 458a, b, 481b; vi, 931b; ix, 6b
Bīdrī i, 1201a
Biga s, 330a
Bīgha i, **1209a**
Bīgha → Misāḥa
Bighāʾ ii, 551a, b; v, 778a; s, **133a**
Bihādhīn → Iʿtimāzāda, Muḥammad
Bihāfarīd x, 926b
Bihʾāfrīd b. Farwardīn (749) i, **1209a**; iv, 44b, 910a; v, 1111b
Bihār i, **1209b**; iii, 423b; v, 783b; vi, 47a, b, 49a, 131a, 273a, 343a, 409b, 410a, 535b; vii, 314a; s, 167a, 203a, 325b
Bihār Sharīf vi, 131b, 410a
Bihār-i Dānish → ʿInāyat Allāh Kańbū
al-Bihārī, Muḥibb Allāh (1707) i, 937a, b, **1210a**; iii, 435a

Bihāristān → Djāmī
Bihbihān i, 659a; iii, 1107a; v, 876a; s, 134b
Bihbihānī, Āḳā ʿAbd al-Ḥusayn (XVIII) s, 135a
Bihbihānī, Āḳā Muḥammad ʿAlī (XVIII) s, 135a
Bihbihānī, Āḳā Sayyid Muḥammad Bāḳir Waḥīd (1793) vi, 551a, 552a; viii, 46b, 541a; s, 57a, **134b**
Bihbihānī, Muḥammad ʿAlī s, 135a
Bihbahānī, Sayyid ʿAbd Allāh (XX) viii, 140a; s, 104a, 365b
Bihbahānī, Sayyid Muḥammad (XX) vii, 300a
Bihbūd Khān, sardār (XVIII) iv, 390a
Bihisht → Djanna
Bihishtī, Aḥmed (1511) i, **1210b**; iv, 129a; v, 1105b; vi, 1023a
Bihḳubādh i, 789a, **1210b**
Bihrangī, Ṣamad (1968) v, 200b; s, **135a**
Bihrūz al-Khādim (amīr) (XII) i, 797a; vii, 734b, 913b
Bihrūz (Amīr) (1577) i, **1211a**
Bihrūz Khān (1631) i, **1211a**
Bihzād, Kamāl al-Dīn (1533) i, 205b, **1211a**; vii, 602b; viii, 787b; s, 138b, 139a, b
al-Biḳāʿ i, 787b, **1214a**; ii, 750a; v, 790a, 739b; s, 154a, 250a
al-Biḳāʿī, Burhān al-Dīn (1480) x, 394b
Bikbāshī → Biñbashi
Bikrami era i, 1239a
Biḳratīs → Buḳrāt
Bilād al-Barbarā (Barābara) vii, 245b
Bilād al-Djarīd → Djarīd
Bilād al-Islām ii, 131b, 581b; iv, 173a
Bilād Shām x, 191a
Bilād Shāwir (Yemen) vi, 438b
Bilād al-Sūdān i, 156b; ii, 121b, 137a; vi, 281b, 401a
Bilād al-Sufāla vii, 245b
Bilād-i thalātha **i, 1214b**
Bilād Yāfiʿ (Yemen) vi, 439a
Bilād al-Zandj iii, 653a; vii, 245b
Bilāl b. Abī Burda al-Ashʿarī (739) i, 694a; ii, 232a, 245a; iii, 155a, 650a; iv, 919a, 926b
Bilāl b. Djarīr al-Muḥammadī (1151) i, **1214b**
Bilāl b. al-Ḥārith (VII) i, 336b
Bilāl b. Rabāḥ (638) i, 24b, 110a, 188a, 482a, 1141b, **1215a**; ii, 846b; vi, 361b, 675a, 677a, 738b
Bilāl b. Tawʿa (VII) vii, 689b
Bilāliyyūn → Muslimūn: Black Muslims
Bilʿam → Balʿam
Bīlāwar v, 460b
Bilawhar wa-Yūdāsaf i, 2b, **1215b**; iv, 63a
Bīlbak al-Khāzindār, amīr (XIII) i, 816b
al-Bilbālī, Makhlūf b. ʿAlī (Kano) (XVI) iv, 550a
Bilban Tabakhī (amīr) (1297) vi, 507b
Bilbās (confederation) i, **1217b**; vi, 502b
Bilbāy (Yalbāy/Yilbāy), al-Ẓāhir Sayf al-Dīn (Mamlūk) (1467) vii, 727a
Bilbays i, **1218a**; s, 159a
Bilbīsī, Madjd al-Dīn (1399) viii, 635b
Bile → Bīredjik
Bileam → Balʿam
Biledjik i, **1218b**; iii, 215a; viii, 181a; s, 282a
Bilen vi, 643a
Bilgä Ḳaghan (734) x, 687b
Bilgā Takīn (Bilge Tegīn), amīr (974) i, 421b; ii, 978a; vi, 522b; s, 284b
Bilgrām i, **1218b**; vii, 445a
Bilgrāmī → Ghulām Nabī
Bilgrāmī, ʿAbd al-Djalīl (1725) i, 808a, **1219a**
Bilgrāmī, ʿAbd al-Wāḥid vii, 956b
Bilgrāmī, Sayyid ʿAlī (1911) i, **1219b**
Bilḳīs i, 262a, **1219b**; ii, 218a; iii, 541b; vi, 468a, 562a, 565b, 615a; viii, 665a, 979a, b; ix, 823a
Billawr (Ballūr) i, **1220b**; v, 965a
Billiton i, **1221a**; vi, 293a
Billūr Köshk i, **1221a**; iii, 375a
Bilma i, **1221b**
Bilmedje i, **1222a**
Bilmen, Ömer Nasuhī (XX) iii, 163b
Bīmāristān i, 899a, **1222b**; ii, 283b, 1015b, 1120a; iii, 195b; iv, 485b; v, 1006a; s, 273b, 274a, 381a
Bīmund (Bohemund) ii, 237b
Bin ʿAbd al-Krīm (Rīf) (XX) → Muḥammad b. ʿAbd al-Karīm
Bin ʿAlī (Mirbāṭ) vi, 83b
Bin ʿArībat (Raysūt) vi, 83b
Bināʾ i, **1226a**
Biñbashi i, **1229a**

Bingöl i, **1229a**
Bingöl Dagh i, **1229a**
Binkath x, 348b
Binn (Druze) s, **135b**
Bint al-Khuss → Hind bint al-Khuss
al-Binya vi, 572a
Binyāmīn i, 261a, 262a, **1229b**
Bīr (district) vi, 269a
Biʾr i, 538b, **1230a**; s, 318b
Biʾr Aḥmad (Yemen) i, 345a
Biʾr ʿAlālī (Čad) s, 165a
Biʾr ʿAlī (Mahra) vi, 81b
Biʾr al-Hudhā (Arabia) vi, 455b
Biʾr Maʿūna (Arabia) i, 442b, **1232b**; v, 41a; vi, 604a
Biʾr Maymūn (Arabia) i, **1232b**
Biʾr Rūma (Medina) viii, 892a
Bīr al-Sabʿ (Beersheba) i, **1233a**
Bīr Singh Dēva, Rādjā (1394) i, 117b; ii, 380a; vi, 49a, 534a
al-Bīra i, **1233a**, b; viii, 128b
Biraima iv, 352a
Bīrbal → Radja Bīrbal
Bīrbal Kāčrū s, 332a, 333a
Bīrdjand i, **1233a**; iv, 4a-b; s, 507b
Bīrdjandī, Niẓām al-Dīn b. Muḥammad Ḥusayn (1527) viii, 541b
Bīredjik i, **1233b**; vi, 378a, 509a, 539b
Birge i, **1234b**
Birgewī (Birgili), Meḥmed (1573) i, 332b, **1235a**; iv, 560a
Bi̊rghos → Lüleburgaz
Birkat al-Ḥabash (Cairo) vi, 671b; vii, 509b
Birmali Sala Pate (Fulbe) (XIX) ii, 942a
Birnin-Katsina iv, 773b
Birr i, **1235b**
Birs (Nimrūd) i, **1235b**
Bīrūn i, **1236a**; ii, 15a, 1089a
al-Bīrūnī (1030) xi, 499a
al-Bīrūnī, Abu ʾl-Rayḥān Muḥammad (al-Khwārazmī) (1050) i, 87a, 119a, 213a, 419a, 455b, 591b, 725a, 726b, 1014b, 1031a, b, 1131a, 1220b, **1236a**; ii, 584a; iii, 9a, 30b, 113b, 405a, 406a, 459a, 858a, 1206b; iv, 358b, 707a, 754a, 1061a, 1063a; v, 86a, b, 1025b; vi, 66a, 185a, 374b, 450b, 600b, 638a, 726b; vii, 199a, 977a; s, 56a, 59b, 249b, 251b, 253a, 327b, 363a, 413b
Birzāl, Banū i, **1238a**; iv, 254b, 665b; vi, 434b, 727a
al-Birzālī, ʿAlam al-Dīn al-Ḳāsim (1339) i, **1238a**; ii, 522b; iv, 863b; viii, 458b
al-Birzāli, Muḥammad b. ʿAbd Allāh (Ḳarmūna) (XI) i, 6a; vii, 761a
Bisāṭ v, 1158b; vi, 664b; vii, 336a; s, **136a**
al-Bisāṭī, Muḥammad b. Aḥmad (ḳāḍī) (1438) vi, 280a
Bisbarāy b. Harigarbhdās (Karkarni) (XVII) i, **1239a**
Bīsha (Yemen) i, 538a, b, **1239a**; vi, 435b; x, 10b
Bīsharʿ i, **1239b**
Bishāra al-Khūrī s, 159b
Bishārīn, Banū i, 1b, 1172a, **1239b**
Bishbali̊ḳ i, **1240a**; ix, 621b; x, 676b
Bishkek → Pishkek
Bishndās (painter) (XVII) vi, 425b, 426a; vii, 339a
al-Bishr (battle) i, **1240b**
Bishr b. Abī Khāzim (VI) i, **1241a**; vi, 349a
Bishr b. al-Barāʾ (628) i, **1241b**
Bishr b. Dāwūd b. Yazīd b. Ḥātim b. Ḳabīsa b. al-Muhallab (IX) vii, 360a
Bishr b. Ghiyāth al-Marīsī (833) i, **1241b**; ii, 373a, 388a; iv, 1163b; vii, 5b; s, 89a, 90a
Bishr b. al-Ḥārith → Bishr al-Ḥāfī
Bishr b. Marwān (Umayyad) (693) i, **1242b**; ii, 788a; iii, 40b, 73a, 715a; vii, 145b, 357a
Bishr b. al-Muʿtamir (825) i, 454a, 587a, **1243a**; iii, 1143b, 1266a; vi, 336b, 458a, 636b; vii, 259a, b, 546b, 604a; viii, 388a; ix, 454b; s, 89b, 225b, 226a, b
Bishr b. Ṣafwān (VIII) i, 50a; ii, 327b; iii, 169b
Bishr b. al-Walīd (VIII) i, **1244a**; iii, 990b
Bishr al-Ḥāfī, Abūnaṣr (840) i, **1244a**; vi, 350b; vii, 647a; ix, 57a, 866b; s, 384b
Bishr-i Yāsīn → Abu ʾl-Ḳāsim
Bishtāsb b. Luhrāsb (Kayānid) iv, 809b
Biskra i, **1246b**; v, 1181a
Bismillāh → Basmala
Bisṭām (Basṭam) i, **1247a**; s, 149a, 235a
Bisṭām b. Ḳays (615) i, 343a, 963b, **1247b**, ii, 72a
Bisṭām b. ʿUmar al-Ḍabbī → al-Ḍabbī, Bisṭām

al-Bisṭāmī, ʿAbd al-Raḥmān (1454) i, **1248a**; ii, 376a
al-Bisṭāmī, Abū Yazīd → Abū Yazīd
al-Bisṭāmī, ʿAlāʾ al-Din → Muṣannifak
al-Bisṭāmī, ʿAlī b. Ṭayfūr (XVII) vii, 988b
Bīstī → Sikka
Bīsutūn (Bihistūn) i, **1248b**; v, 169a; vi, 494a
Bīsutūn, Malik (1500) vi, 514b
Bīsutūn b. Djihāngīr b. Kāwūs (1507) iv, 808a
al-Bīṭār, Ṣalāḥ al-Dīn (XX) iv, 125a
Bitik, bitikči i, **1248b**; iv, 757a
Bitlis → Bidlīs
Bitolja → Manastir
Biṭrawsh i, **1249a**; ii, 744a; v, 510a
Biṭrīḳ (Patricius) i, 642b, **1249b**; v, 620a
al-Biṭrīḳ b. al-Nakā (VIII) viii, 423b
al-Biṭrūdjī, Nūr al-Dīn (Alpetragius) (XIII) i, **1250a**; iii, 957a; iv, 518a; viii, 102a
Biyābānak i, **1250a**
Biya-pīsh → Gīlān-i Biyā Pas
Biyār, al-Biyār s, **149a**
Biyārdjumand → Biyār
Bïyïḳlï ʿAlī Āghā (XVIII) i, 396a
Bïyïḳlï Meḥmed Pasha → Meḥmed Pasha Bïyïḳlï
Bizāʿā → Buzāʿā
Bīzabān → Dilsiz
Bizerta → Banzart
Bizye/Vize vi, 290b
Black Sea → Baḥr Bunṭus; Ḳarā Deniz
Blida → Bulayda
Boabdil → Muḥammad XII (Naṣrid)
Bobastro → Barbashturu
Bodrum i, 476b, **1250b**
Bodufenvalugē Sīdī (Maldives) (1969) vi, 247a
Boghā al-Kabīr → Bughā al-Kabīr
Boghā al-Sharābī → Bughā al-Sharābī
Boghā Ṭarkhān (VIII) iii, 493b
Boghaz → Boghaz-iči
Boghaz-iči i, **1251a**; v, 243a
Boghaz Kesen → Rūmeli Ḥiṣār
Boghdān (Moldavia) i, 4b, 310b, 1120a, **1252b**; v, 39b; s, 510b
Bōgrā i, **1253b**
Bohemia → Čeh
Bohorās (Bohras) i, 172a, **1254a**; ii, 170b; iii, 381a, 434a, b, 544b; iv, 199b, 888a; v, 942b; vi, 246a; vii, 222b, 725a; x, 403a; s, 70b
Bohorās, Dāwūdī x, 103b
Bohtān → Kurds
Bokar Biro (Fūta Djallon) (XIX) ii, 960b, 1132b
Bokar Salif Tall iii, 108a
Bokhārā → Bukhārā
Bolān Pass ix, 531a
Böke Budhrač (Yabāku) x, 689b
Bolēday Balūč s, 222a
Bolor Dagh → Pamir
Bolu i, **1255b**; s, 98b
Bölük i, 657a, 999b, **1256a**, 1278a; ii, 1098a, 1121a
Bölük-Bashï i, **1256b**
Bölük-bashï, Aḥmed Durmush (XIX) s, 149b
Bölük-bashï, Rïḍā Tewfīḳ (1949) iv, 933a; s, **149b**
Bolwadin i, **1256b**; s, 238b
Bombay City i, 979a, **1257a**; ii, 426a; vi, 536b; s, 47a, 247a
Bombay state i, **1257a**
Bondū, Bundū → Senegal
Bône → al-ʿAnnāba
Bonneval, Comte de → Aḥmad Pasha Bonneval
Borāḳ (1428) x, 812b
Bordj → Burdj
Bori cult (Hausa) iii, 278a
Böri Bars b. Alp Arslan (Saldjūḳ) (1095) i, **1331b**; viii, 81b
Böri b. Tughtigin (1132) x, 216b
Böri Tigin → Ibrāhīm Tamghač Khān
Boris (Bulghar Ḳaghan (888) x, 692a
Börklüdje Muṣṭafā (Bürklüdje Muṣṭafā) (XV) i, 869b; ii, 599b
Borkou i, **1257b**
Borku s, 165a, 166a
Borneo i, **1258b**; iii, 1213a, b, 1215b, 1225b; v, 309b, 539b; s, **150a**
Bornū i, 35a, **1259a**; iii, 276a; iv, 541a, b, 548b, 567a; v, 278b; x, 122b; s, 164a, b, 165a
Borsippa → Birs
Börte Fudjin (XIII) ii, 41b, 42a, 571a
Borusu i, 1290b, 1291a, b
Bosna i, 4a, 97a, 285a, 310a, 656b, 1018a,

1261a; ii, 211b, 681b; v, 32a, 263b, 774a; vi, 59b, 69a, 89b, 227b, 327b; vii, 244a; viii, 171b; ix, 28b; x, 697b; s, 281b
Bosna-sarāy → Sarajevo
al-Bosnawī, ʿAlī Dede (1598) i, 759a
Bosnia → Bosna
Bosphorus → Bog͟haz-iči
Boṣrā (Bostra) i, **1275b**, 1316a, b; v, 1138a, b, 1139a; vi, 123b, 364a, 546b; s, 117a
Bostān Čelebī (1630) iv, 190a
Bostānd͟jì i, **1277b**; iv, 1100b
Bostānd͟jì-bas͟hì i, **1278b**
Bostānzāde, Muṣṭafā Efendi (1570) i, **1279a**
Bostānzāde, Meḥmed Efendi (1598) i, **1279b**; iv, 884a
Botlik͟h, Banū i, 504a; iv, 630b
Boṭṭīwa, Banū i, 680a
Bou Maza xi, 138b
Bou Regreg vi, 142b
Bou Saada (Algeria) s, 134a
Bouddha → Budd
Bouira → Sūḳ Ḥamza
Boumedienne, Houari → Abū Madyan, Hawwārī
Bourguiba, Ḥabīb (XX) ii, 470b, 639a; iii, 524a, 563b, 636b; v, 915a, 1068b, 1161a; vii, 416a
Bourguiba, Muḥammad (XX) vi, 750a
Bourzey → Barzūya
Boyer Aḥmad, Banū iv, 5b
Boynu-Yaralì Meḥmed Pas͟ha (1649) v, 257a
Boz Aba (Atabeg) (1146) vi, 482a, 782a; vii, 406b; viii, 944a, 978b
Bozan (al-Ruhā) (XI) viii, 947a
Bozanti i, **1280a**; v, 257a, b
Bozd͟ja-ada (Tenedos) i, **1280b**; v, 257a, b
Bozo (Sudan) ii, 251b
Bozoḳ → Yozgat
Bozoḳlu Muṣṭafā Pas͟ha (XVII) i, 268a
Boztepe, K͟halīl Nihād (1949) iii, 357b; s, 324b
Brādost, Banū v, 460a; x, 898a
Brāhīm Lakudī (XX) vi, 750a
Brahima bi Saidu (Fulbe) (1817) ii, 942a
Brahmans → Barāhima
Brahōīs, Brahūīs i, 1005a, b; ii, 388a; iv, 10b, 364b; v, 102a, 684b; s, 222a
Brahūʾī → Brahōīs
Braẓila → Ibrail
Brava → Barawa
Brechk → Baris͟hk
Brēlwī → Aḥmad Brēlwī
Brid͟j Baratpūr (XVIII) i, 1193a
Broach → Bharūč
Brousse → Bursa
Brunei vi, 241a; s, 150a, **151b**
Brusa → Bursa
Bryson → Tadbīr al-Manzil
Bs͟harrā i, **1280b**
Bteddīn i, **1281a**
Bū → Kunya
Bū ʿAlī, Banū ii, 440b
Bū ʿAlī Čag͟hānī → Abū ʿAlī Čag͟hānī
Bū ʿAlī Ḳalandar → Abū ʿAlī Ḳalandar
Bū ʿAmāma (XIX) i, 369b, 1281b; ii, 885b
Bū ʿAzza → Abū Yaʿazza
Bū Bakr b. Sālim, S͟hayk͟h (Ḥaḍramawt) s, 420b
Bū Dali (D͟jid͟jelli) ii, 538a
Bū D͟hanayn, Āl (ʿAd͟jmān) s, 42a
Bū D͟jaʿd (Morocco) vi, 890b
Bū Falāḥ, Āl (Abū Ẓabī) i, 1313b
Bū Falāsā, Āl i, 1313b; ii, 618b
Bū Ḥamīr, Āl i, 1313b
Bū Ḥanak (Ḥasan b. Ḥusayn) (Ḳusṭanṭīna) (1754) v, 531b, 532a
Bū Ḥasan, Āl → ʿArab, D͟jazīrat al-
Bū Ḥmāra (1909) i, 57b, 357a, **1281a**; ii, 620a, 820a, 1116a; iii, 62b; v, 1193a
Bū Ḳabrīn (1798) iv, 361a
Bū Kamya (Kalyān Ḥasan Bey) (1736) (Ḳusṭanṭīna) v, 531b
Bū K͟hraybān, Āl (al-Būraymī) i, 1313b; s, 42a
Bū Muḥammad, Āl (ʿAmāra) i, 431a, 1096a, b; vii, 582a; s, 243a
Bū Naṣr (1032) vi, 522a, b
Bū Ngāb (1850) vi, 252a
Bū Saʿāda (Algeria) s, 224a
Bū Saʿīd, Banū (Algeria) vi, 404b, 405a
Bū Saʿīd, Āl (ʿUmān/Zanzibar) i, 539b, 554a, 1038b, **1281b**; iv, 887a, b; v, 507b, 655b; vi, 358a, 735a, b; s, 332b, 355b
Bū ʾl-Sbaʿ (Marrākus͟h) vi, 595b
Bū S͟hāmis, Āl (al-Buraymī) i, 1313b; s, 42a
Bū S͟henṭūf → Muḥammad b. Nāṣir
Buʿāt͟h i, **1283a**; iv, 1187b; v, 436a, 995a; vii, 366b
Bubakar Sori (Fulbe) (XIX) ii, 942b

Bubashtru (Bobastro), Barbashturu vii, 569a; s, **152b**
Bučaķ → Budjāķ
Bučāķčī, Banū v, 154b
Bucharest → Bükresh
Buda → Budīn
Budapest → Budīn
Budayl b. Ṭahfa al-Badjalī (VIII) ii, 188a, 488a
Budayl b. Warķā᾽ al-Khuzā῾ī (630) i, **1283b**; vii, 372b
Budd i, **1283b**
Budha iii, 405b; iv, 534b, 535a; vi, 967b; x, 673a
Buddha → Budd
Buddhists → Sumaniyya
Buddūma (Buduma) (lake, Čād) iv, 540b; s, 165a
Būdh-Ardashīr → al-Mawṣil
Budhiya → Budha
Budhan, Shaykh (XVI) i, **1284a**
Būdhāsaf → Bilawhar wa-Yūdāsaf
Budīn (Buda) i, 1164a, **1284b**; ii, 1133b, 1134a; iii, 998a; v, 1022a, b; s, 171a
Budja → Bedja
Budjāķ i, 1253b, **1286b**; vi, 58b
Budjatli̊ → Bushatli̊s
Budjayr b. Aws al-Ṭā᾽ī (VII) s, 37b
Budjnūrd i, **1287a**; vi, 495a; vii, 454a; s, 235a
Budūḥ ii, 370a; s, **153a**
Budukh → Shāh Dagh
Buganda x, 778b
Bughā al-Kabīr al-Turkī (862) i, 551a, 637a, 844a, **1287a**; ii, 1024a; iv, 345a, 1175a; v, 997a; vii, 778a, 794a; viii, 120b; xi, 178a
Bughā al-Sharābī al-Ṣaghīr al-Turkī (868) i, **1287b**; ii, 679a, 1080a; iv, 88b, 89a; v, 488b; vi, 504b; vii, 390a, 593a, 722b, 777b, 793b
Bughdān → Boghdān
Bughrā Khān → Muḥammad II b. Sulaymān (Ķarakhānid)
Bughrā Khān b. Balbān b. Mūsā (Ķarakhānid) (XIII) i, 444a, 997a; ii, 268a; iv, 818a, 920b; v, 685b; s, 124b
Bughra Khān Hārūn (Ilek-Khān) (1102) i, 987a; ii, 254a; iii, 1113b, 1114a; viii, 110a
Bughra Khān Hārūn/Ḥasan (Ķarakhānid) (X) viii, 110a; s, 549b
Bughrā Khān b. Mūsā (Ķarakhānid) (992) i, 987a; ii, 254a
Bughra Khān (Yaghma) x, 689a
Bughračuķ (Harāt) (X) iv, 189b
al-Bughṭūri, Makrīn b. Muḥammad (XIII) i, **1287b**
Buginese vi, 116a, b; s, 151a
Bugtīs (Kilāt) s, 332a
Buḥayra (lake) i, **1288a**
Buḥayra (Beḥera, Egypt) i, **1288a**; iii, 299b; iv, 134a; s, 244a, 268a
al-Buḥayra (Battle of) (1130) i, 1288a; vi, 592a, 945a
al-Buḥayra al-Mayyita al-Muntina → Baḥr Lūṭ
al-Buhriy, Hemedi b. Abdallah (1922) s, 351b
Buḥayrat Anṭākiyya i, 446b
Buḥayrat Khʷarizm → Aral
Buḥayrat Lōdi → Bahlūl Lōdī
Buḥayrat Māyuṭis → Baḥr Māyuṭis
Buḥayrat Nastarāwa → Burullus
Buḥayrat Tinnīs viii, 38b
Buḥayrat Yaghrā → Buḥayrat Anṭākiyya
Buhlūl, al-Madjnūn al-Kūfī (X) i, **1288b**
Buhlūl, Shaykh (XVI) iii, 455b
Buhlūl b. Rāshid (799) i, 1289a; viii, 843b
al-Buḥturī, Abū ῾Ubāda (897) i, 118b, 153b, 154a, 386b, 592a, **1289a**; iii, 111a, 573a, 693a; v, 935a; vi, 625b; vii, 527a, 982a; xi, 156b; s, 16b, 25a, 26a, 277b
Buḥturids ii, 634b; iv, 834b
al-Buḥturiyya bint Khurshīd (Dābūyid) (IX) v, 69b; vi, 335a, 745a
Būķ i, **1290b**
Buķ῾a i, **1292b**; s, **154a**
Buķa (Oghuz) (XI) i, **1292a**
Buķa Temür → Ṭughā Tīmūr
Būķalā i, **1292b**; iii, 290a
Būķalamūn → Abū Ķalamūn
Bukar (Bāru) Dā῾ū (Songhay) (XV) vii, 393b
Bukar Garbai (Kanemi, Bornū) (XX) i, 1260b; v, 359a
Bukarest → Bükresh
al-Buķay῾a i, **1292b**; vi, 579b; s, 154a
Buķayķ → Abķayķ
Bukayr b. Māhān (744) i, **1292b**; ii, 601a; iv, 446b, 837b; v, 2a, 3a; vii, 396a
Bukayr b. Wishāḥ (696) i, 47b, **1293a**
Bukhār Khudāt (VII) i, 1293b, 1294a; s, 327a

Bukhārā i, 320, 36a, 46b, 71a, 103a, 121a, 141b, 147b, 750a, 853a, **1293b**; ii, 2b, 43a, 446a, 932b, 1096a; iv, 188b, 189b, 310a; v, 28b, 541b, 853b, 856b, 858a, 859b, 966b, 1149a; vi, 77a, b, 115b, 130b, 333a, 340a, 365b, 418a, b, 419a, 433a, 621a, 764b, 766a, 769b; vii, 477b, 1015a; viii, 749a; ix, 427a; s, 49a, 50b, 65a, 66a, 97a, 107a, 145a, 227b, 228a, 261a, 265a, 281a, 326b, 340a, 419b, 420a; s, 467a
al-Bukhārī → Ṣalāḥ al-Dīn b. Mubārak
al-Bukhārī, Aḥmad al-Faḍl (XI) vii, 199b
Bukhārī, Amīr Aḥmad (1516) vii, 936a
al-Bukhārī, Muḥammad b.ʿAbd al-Bāḳī (XVI) i, **1296b**
al-Bukhārī, Muḥammad b. Ismāʿīl (870) i, 791a, 808a, 892b, **1296b**; ii, 125b; iii, 24a, 27b, 512b, 778a, 803a, 862a, 909b, 948b; iv, 736b; vi, 112a, 353a; vii, 361b, 537b; s, 87b, 232b, 404b
al-Bukhārī, Muḥammad ʿAlī Khān (XIX) ii, 618a
Bukhārī, Mullā Sayfī (1503) viii, 543a
al-Bukhārī, Nūr al-Dīn al-Ṣābūnī (1184) vi, 848a
Bukhārī, Shaykh Muḥammad Murād (1729) vii, 936b
al-Bukhārī al-Ghundjār, Muḥammad b. Aḥmad (1021) viii, 748b
Bukhārlïk (Bukharidīs) i, **1297a**
Bukhl i, **1297b**
Bukht-Naṣ(ṣ)ar (Nebuchadnezzar) i, 846a, **1297b**; ii, 112b; iv, 809b; vi, 412b
Bukhtīshūʿ i, 212b, **1298a**; iii, 872b; iv, 649a; s, 379b
Būḳīr → Abūḳīr
Bukovina → Khotin
Buḳrāṭ (Hippocrates) ii, 402b; iii, 897b; iv, 406b; s, **154b**
Bükresh i, **1298b**
Buḳūm, Banū i, **1299a**
Būlāḳ i, **1299b**; ii, 167a; iv, 425a, 442a, b; vi, 797b, 801b; vii, 69a
Būlala (Kanem) iv, 541a; s, 164a
Bulandshahr i, **1299b**; vi, 49b, 50a, 294b
Būlātmūriyān, Banū iv, 860a
Bulāy (Poley/Aguilar de la Frontera) i, **1300b**
Bulāy, battle of (891) x, 850b
Bulayda (Blida) i, **1300b**
al-Bulayṭī → al-Balaṭī, Abu 'l-Fatḥ
Bulbul i, **1301a**; ii, 1133a
Bulbul Shāh (1327) iv, 708a; s, **156a**
al-Buldadjī (1284) iii, 163b
Buldur → Burdur
Bulgaria i, 394a, **1302a**; ii, 610b, 611a; v, 534a, 1014b; x, 698a
Bulghār i, 998b, 1000a, 1075b, 1105a, **1304b**; ii, 21a, 69b, 202b, 853b, 1107b; iii, 759a; iv, 280a, 648b, 1173a; v, 1011a; vi, 420a; vii, 352a; x, 691b
Bulghār-dagh → Toros
al-Bulghārī → Sharaf al-Dīn Husām al-Dīn; Yaʿḳūb b. Nuʿmān.
Bulghār-maʿden → Toros
Bulgur s, 775b
Bulgur Tekke Mescid (Konya) v, 255b
Bulkiah I (Brunei) (XVI) s, 152a
Bulkiah, Sultan Sir Hassanal (XX) s, 152b
al-Bulḳīnī, ʿAbd al-Raḥmān b. ʿUmar (1421) i, 138a, **1308b**; iii, 777b
al-Bulḳīnī, Muḥammad b. Muḥammad (1485) i, **1309a**
al-Bulḳīnī, Muḥammad b. ʿUmar (1389) i, **1308b**
al-Bulḳīnī, Ṣāliḥ b. ʿUmar (1464) i, **1308b**
al-Bulḳīnī, Sirādj al-Dīn ʿUmar (1403) i, **1308b**; iii, 699a
al-Bulḳīnī, ʿUmar b. Raslān (1403) i, **1308b**; vii, 692a
Bullhē Shāh, ʿAbd Allāh (1767) vii, 328a; viii, 256a; x, 322a
Bullū, Banū s, 148a
Buluggīn b. Bādīs b. Ḥabūs b. Zīrī (Zīrid) (1057) i, 491b; vi, 222b
Buluggīn b. Muḥammad (Ḥammādid) (1062) iii, 137b
Buluggīn b. Zīrī b. Manād (Zīrid) (984) i, 699b, 824a, 1044b, 1088a, **1309a**; ii, 520a, 821b, 854a; iii, 1036b, 1043a; v, 1010b, 1176a, b, 1177a; vi, 431b, 728a, 947a; vii, 64b, 486a; viii, 688b
Bulūgh → Bāligh
Būlūghān, amīr (Mongol) iv, 1047a
Bulukkīn → Banya
Buluniyās → Bāniyās
Buluwādīn → Bolwadin
Bumin (553) x, 687a
Būna (Bône) → al-ʿAnnāba
Bunān b. ʿAmr al-Ḍārib (IX) s, 284b
Bundār al-Iṣbahānī → Ibn Lizza
Bundār → Muḥammad b. Bashshār

al-Bundārī, al-Fatḥ b. ʿAlī (XIII) i, 523a, **1309b**; iii, 918b; iii, 1158a; vi, 430a
Bundēlas, Banū vii, 443b
Bundū → Senegal
al-Bunduḳdārī → Baybars I
Bunduḳī → Sikka
Bunduḳiya → Wenedik
al-Būnī, Abu 'l-Abbās (1225) ii, 376a; iii, 596a; iv, 1134a; v, 222b; s, 153a, **156a**
Bunkan, Muḥammad (1537) x, 36b
Bunn → Ḳahwa
Buñsuz (Ḳarāmān-og̲h̲lu) (XIII) iv, 619b, 620a
al-Bunt (Alpuente) i, **1309b**
Bunyāt (Buk̲h̲āra) (VIII) i, 1294a
Būr s, 515a
al-Burādiʿī ʿAlī (1737) iii, 162a
al-Burāḳ i, **1310a**; ii, 71a, 108a, 785b; vii, 376b
al-Burāḳ b. ʿAbd Allāh (VII) iii, 887a, b
Burāḳ (Baraḳ), ḥād̲j̲ib (Ḳutlug̲h̲ K̲h̲ān) (1235) i, **1311a**; ii, 393a; iv, 32a, 583b; v, 161b, 553a
al-Burāḳ (Baraḳ) K̲h̲ān (Čag̲h̲atay) (1271) i, **1311b**; ii, 1b, 3b, 45a, 791b; iv, 811b; v, 39a; vi, 420a
al-Burāḳ Reʾīs (1499) iv, 882a
al-Burak al-Ṣarīmī (Ṣuraymī) (660) s, **157a**
Būrān bint al-Ḥasan b. Sahl (884) i, 897b, **1312a**; ii, 731b; iii, 243b, 345b; vi, 335b
Būrāniyya → Baḳliyya
Burayda i, 873a, **1312b**; iv, 717a
Burayda b. al-Ḥuṣayb (680) i, **1313a**; v, 78b; vii, 983a
Burayka ii, 454b
Burayka (Banū Rabīʿa) (755) vi, 540a
al-Buraymī i, 539b, **1313b**; s, 42a, 417b
Burd, Banū → Ibn Burd
Burda i, **1314b**; iii, 1232a; iv, 316a, 940a; v, 6b, 734a; s, 159a
Burd̲j̲ i, 248b, **1315a**; iii, 475a
Burd̲j̲ → Nud̲j̲ūm
Burd̲j̲ al-Ṣabī vi, 578b, 582b
Burd̲j̲ān (Bylg̲h̲ār) i, 1305a
Burd̲j̲īs → Mamlūks
Burd̲j̲iyya (regiment) i, 1050b, **1324b**; iv, 486a; vi, 316b, 322b
al-Burd̲j̲umī (al-Burd̲j̲amī) (1033) i, 900b; ii, 962a
al-Burd̲j̲umī, Abu 'l-S̲h̲ibl (IX) iv, 1005a; xi, 151a
al-Burd̲j̲umī, ʿImrān b. Fuḍayl (Tamīm) (VII) ix, 865b
Burdur i, **1325a**
Bure (Amphila Bay) vi, 642b
Burgas i, **1325b**
Burg̲h̲az, Būrg̲h̲ūs → Lüleburgaz
al-Burg̲h̲āzī, Yaḥyā b. K̲h̲alīl i, 323b, 324b; ii, 968a
Burg̲h̲ul v, 42a
Burg̲h̲us̲h̲ (Burgos) i, **1326a**
Burg̲h̲ūt̲h̲ → Ḳaml; Muḥammad b. ʿĪsā (Burg̲h̲ūt̲h̲)
Burg̲h̲ūt̲h̲iyya i, **1326a**; vii, 868b
Burgos → Burg̲h̲ūs̲h̲
Burhām(n)iyya i, 281a; ii, 166a
al-Burhān i, **1326b**; iii, 543b
Burhān I (Niẓām-S̲h̲ahī) (1553) i, 914b, 1069a; iii, 425b, 426a, 1160 a, b; viii, 73a, b
Burhān II (Niẓām-S̲h̲ahī) (1595) ii, 815a, 921b; iii, 426b; vi, 271b; vii, 300a; viii, 73b
Burhān III (Niẓām S̲h̲āhī) (1632) viii, 74a
Burhān, Āl-i (Buk̲h̲ārā) i, 1295a, **1327b**; iii, 1115a; v, 858a; viii, 749a
Burhān Muḥammad Ḥusayn b. K̲h̲alaf al-Tabrīzī (XVII) i, 1056b, **1327b**; iv, 526a
al-Burhān b. Abī S̲h̲arīf vi, 87b
Burhān Asaf (XX) vi, 95a
Burhān al-Dīn, Ḳāḍī Aḥmad (1398) i, 311b, 432a, 1117b, 1118a, **1327b**; ii, 706a; iv, 623a, 843a, 871a; viii, 581b; s, 324a
Burhān al-Dīn G̲h̲arīb, Mawlānā (1337) i, **1328b**, 1331a; ii, 48a, 51b, 55a, b, 816a; s, 352b
Burhān al-Dīn Ḳuṭb-i ʿĀlam (1453) i, **1329b**; ii, 1125b
Burhān al-Din al-Marg̲h̲īnānī → al-Marg̲h̲īnānī
Burhān al-Dīn Muḥaḳḳiḳ, Sayyid (XIII) ii, 393b
Burhān al-Dīn Naṣr b. Aḥmad-i D̲j̲ām (XII) i, 283a
Burhān ʿImād S̲h̲āh (ʿImād S̲h̲āhī) (1574) iii, 425a, 1161a
Burhān al-Mulk (Nawwāb, Awad̲h̲) (1739) i, 757a, **1330a**; ii, 870a; iv, 666a; v, 635a; vii, 316a; viii, 793b; s, 325b
Burhānī, ʿAbd al-Malik (1073) vii, 489a
Burhānī Abū Muʿizzī (1116) vi, 276b

Burhānpūr i, **1330b**; ii, 816a; iii, 446b; vi, 52a, 67b, 369a, 535b, 690a
al-Burhānpūrī, Muḥammad b. Faḍl Allāh (1590) ix, 296b
al-Būrī s, 390b
Būrī → Tādj al-Mulūk
Būrī Takīn → Ibrāhīm Tamghač Khān
Buri-Bars (1095) i, 662a, **1331b**
Būrids i, 216a, **1332a**; ii, 282a
al-Būrīnī, al-Ḥasan (1615) i, **1333a**; vii, 469b
Burḳat al-Amhār vi, 81a
al-Burḳān (Kuwayt) i, 536b; s, 50a
Burke Sulṭān (XV) i, 135a
Bürklüdje Muṣṭafā → Dede Sulṭān
Burḳuʿ, Ḳaṣr s, **157a**
Burma i, 606a, **1333a**; xi, 492b
Burne (Mali) vi, 258a
Būrrūdh (river) s, 356b
Bursa i, 4a, 298a, 1225b, **1333b**; ii, 746b; iii, 210b, 211b, 212b, 214a, 215a, 216a; iv, 574a, 1159b; v, 32b, 651a; vi, 3a, 120b, 228a, 366a, 530b; viii, 175b; s, 170a, 282b
Bursa Edict vi, 496b
Bursalï → Aḥmad Pasha
Bursalï, Djelīlī Ḥamīd-zāde (1569) v, 1105b
Bursalï Ṭāhir (XX) ii, 980b; iv, 284b
al-Bursawī, Muḥammad b. ʿAbd al-Ḥalīm (XVIII) vii, 469b
Bursuḳ (1089) i, 1052b, **1336a**
Bursuḳ b. Bursuḳ (XII) i, 1336b, 1337a; iii, 1118b; v, 924b
al-Bursukī → Aḳ Sunḳur
al-Burt i, **1337a**
Burṭās/Burdās i, 1305b, **1337b**; ii, 69b, 817a
Burtuḳāl i, 58b, **1338b**
Burūdj → Minṭakat al-
Burūdjird → Barūdjird
Burūdjirdī, Muḥammad Ḥusayn Ṭabāṭabāʾī, Āyatullāh al-ʿUẓmā (1961) iv, 165b; vi, 548b, 552a, b, 553a; vii, 300a, 448a, 762b; s, 104a, **157b**
Burūdjirdī, Shaykh Asad Allāh (1854) s, 75a
Buruḳlus (Proclus) i, 234b, **1339b**; ii, 765a, 929b; iii, 1129b; iv, 129b
Burullus i, **1340b**
Burushaski s, **158b**
Burūsho s, 158b
Burzō(ē) (VI) i, 1359a; iv, 503a, b
al-Burzulī, Abu 'l-Ḳāsim (1438) i, **1341a**; vii, 1052b
Busayra → Ḳarḳīsiyā
Būshahr (Būshīr) i, 928a, 1013b, **1341a**; iii, 1191a; iv, 851a; vi, 358a
Busḥāḳ, Fakhr al-Dīn Aḥmad b. Ḥallādj (1424) i, **1342a**; iii, 355b; iv, 66a; vii, 567b; viii, 45b; s, 415b
Busḥāḳ-i Aṭʿima → Busḥāḳ, Fakhr al-Dīn
Būshandj i, **1342b**; iv, 1073a
al-Būshandjī, Abu 'l-Ḥasan b. Sahl (X) vi, 224a
al-Bushārrāt i, **1343a**
Bushatlïs i, 653a, 657a; iv, 588a; v, 276b, 775a
Būshīkrī, Muḥammad b. ʿAbd Allāh (1865) x, 346b
Būshīr → Būshahr
Bushra (X) iv, 459b
al-Bushrawī, ʿAbd Allāh b. al-Ḥādjdj Muḥammad al-Tūnī (1666) s, 57a
Būṣīr, Abūṣīr i, **1343a**; iii, 961b; iv, 774a; vi, 411a, 624b; s, 159a
al-Būṣīrī, Sharaf al-Dīn (1294) i, 595b, 821b, 1011b, 1070b, 1314b; iii, 720b; iv, 316a, 1134a; v, 958b; s, **158b**, 404b
Busr b. Abī Arṭāt (VII) i, 109a, 695b, **1343b**; ii, 481a; iii, 782a; v, 532b, 533a; ix, 555a; s, 230b
Busr al-Ḥarīrī v, 593b
Buṣrā → Boṣrā
Bust i, **1344a**; ii, 1054a, 1100b; v, 230a, 690b, 691a; vi, 345a, 523a; viii, 795b
Būstān i, **1345b**; ii, 908b, 1019a; v, 888b
Būstān Efendi (1570) ii, 880b
al-Bustānī, Āl s, **159a**
al-Bustānī, ʿAbd Allāh (1930) s, **159b**
al-Bustānī, Buṭrus b. Būlus (1883) i, 596b; ii, 428b, 467a; iv, 525a; v, 794b; vi, 712a; vii, 902b; s, **159b**
al-Bustānī, Buṭrus b. Sulaymān (1969) s, **160a**
al-Bustanī, Karam (1966) s, **160b**
al-Bustānī, Saʿīd b. Salīm (1977) v, 188a; vii, 903a; s, **160b**
al-Bustānī, Salīm b. Buṭrus (1884) v, 188a; vii, 902a; s, 160a, **161a**
al-Bustānī, Sulaymān b. Khaṭṭār (1925) i, 597b; iii, 112a; s, **161b**
al-Bustānī, Wadīʿ (1954) vi, 615b; s, **162a**

al-Bustī, Abu 'l-Fatḥ (1010) i, **1348b**; iv, 61a
al-Bustī, Abū Ḥātim Muḥammad b. Ḥibbān (965) v, 1126b; vii, 692a
al-Buṭāḥ (Baʿūḍa) vi, 267b
Buṭāna (Kasala) iv, 686a, b
Buṭayn → Nudjūm
Buṭnān, wādī i, **1348b**, 1357b; vi, 378a
Butr, Banū i, **1349b**; vi, 310b, 741a, 815a, 840a; ix, 894b
Butriyya → Abtariyya
Buṭrus Ghālī (XX) vii, 715b
Buṭrus Karāma (1851) s, **162b**
Buṭrus al-Tūlawī (1745) ii, 795a
al-Buwayb (battle) (636) iv, 386a
Buwayhids/Būyids i, 19a, 20a, 131b, 211b, 434a, 439b, 512b, 551b, 696a, 866b, 899b, 1045b, 1073b, **1350a**; ii, 144a, 178b, 192b, 214b, 326a, 487a, 506a, 748b, 1050b; iii, 46b, 159a, 1201b, 1255b; iv, 18a, 19a, 23a, b, 46b, 100b, 208b, 221b, 266a, 293b; v, 621b, 622a, 824a; vi, 66a, 148a, 261b, 272b, 275a, 433a, 440a, 549a, 600b, 669b, 941b; vii, 477b, 723b; viii, 472a; ix, 595b; xi, 186b; s, 12b, 23a, 56b, 118a, b, 119a, b, 192a, 267b, 363a
Buwayr Aḥmadī (tribe) iii, 1107a
al-Buwayṭī, Yūsuf b. Yaḥyā (840) vii, 4a
Buxar i, **1357b**
Būyids → Buwayhids
Büyük Ada vi, 588b
Büyük Sulaymān Pasha → Sulaymān Pasha Büyük
Buyuruldu i, **1357b**
Buzāʿā i, 1349a, **1357b**; viii, 131a
Būz-Abeh (1137) i, **1358a**; iv, 498a
Būzači (Boz Ḥādjī) (peninsula) vi, 415a, 416b; s, 168b, 169a
Buzākha i, **1358b**
Būzān (XI) i, 1336b
Buzan (1334) ii, 4a
Būzār → Ong Khān
al-Būzdjānī → Abu 'l-Wafāʾ
Buzghāla Khāna ii, 116a
al-Būzīdī, Muḥammad (1814) iii, 696b, 697a, 700b
Buzurdjmihr → Buzurgmihr
Buzurg b. Shahriyār (956) i, 203b, 204a, 570b, **1358b**; ii, 583b; vi, 704a; vii, 245b; viii, 292b, 595a; ix, 698b
Buzurgmihr (Buzurdjmihr) (VI) i, **1358b**; iv, 53b, 503a, b; viii, 106b
Buzurg-ummīd, Kiya (1138) i, 353b, **1359b**; v, 656b
Byblos → Djubayl
Byzantins → Rūm
Byzantion → Istanbul
Byzantium → Rūm
Bžedukh → Čerkes

C

Cabra → Ḳabra
Čāč → Tashkent
Cacciadiavolo, Aydin Reʾīs (XVI) iv, 1156a, b
Čāčī, Badr al-Dīn Muḥammad → Badr-i Čāčī
Čač-nāma iii, 459a; vii, 405b; s, **162a**
Čad, Chad iv, 540a, b, 566b; xi, 10b, 11b; s, **163b**, 218a
Cádiz/Cadix → Ḳādis
Čādur (chador) v, 749b, 750a
Caesar → Ḳayṣar
Caesarea → Ḳaysariyya; Kayseri; Sharshal
Caffa → Kefe
Čaghal-oghlu → Čighālazāde Sinān Pasha
Čaghaloghlu (quarter of Istanbul) iv, 722a; ix, 937a
Čaghānī, Abū ʿAlī Aḥmad b. Muḥtādj (955) iv, 100b; vi, 115b; v, 76a; vii, 477b; viii, 110a, 597b, 996b, 997a, 1027b; s, 125b
Čaghāniyān ii, **1a**; vii, 477b; s, 50b, 386b
Čaghān-rūd ii, **2a**
Čaghatay Khān b. Čingiz-Khān (1241) i, 418b, 1105b; ii, **2a**, 3a, 43a, 44a, 269a, 571b; iii, 198a, 1120a; iv, 584a; vi, 77b, 494b, 518a
Čaghatay Khānate i, 120b, 1295b, 1311b; ii, **3a**, 45b; iii, 1100a; iv, 274a, 587a; v, 858a, b; s, 96b, 98a, 227b, 240a, 246a
– literature i, 813b; ii, 792a; iii, 317a; iv, 527a; v, 836a, 859b; s, 46a, b; x, 708a, **721a**
Čaghatayids xi, 288a

Čaghatays (Ulus Čaghatay) x, 511b
Čaghmīnī → al-Djaghmīnī
Čaghrï-Beg Dāwūd (Saldjūḳ) (1060) i, 662a, 1159a; ii, **4a**, 1108b; iii, 1114a; iv, 25a, 26b, 347b; v, 58a; vi, 620b; viii, 69b; s, 195a
Chalos → Ḳuwayḳ
Čahār Aymāḳ, Banū i, 224b; ii, **5b**
Čahār Bāgh (Iṣfahān) s, 275a
Čahār-Lang i, 955b; iii, 1105a, b; v, 822b
Čahār Maḥall iv, 98a, b; s, 147b
Čāhbār i, 1282a, 1283a
Caïd → Ḳāʾid
Čāʾildā, Shaykh (XV) s, 73b
Caïn → Ḥābīl wa Ḳābīl
Cairo → al-Ḳāhira; Miṣr
Čaḳa (Tzachas) (XI) i, 466a; ii, 686b; v, 505a; s, 168b
Čaḳa b. Noghay (XIV) i, 1302b; ii, 610b
Čaḳa Bey (Saldjūḳ) (1090) vii, 47a; viii, 890a; ix, 679b
Čakarsaz i, 424b
Čakïrdjï-bashï ii, **6a**, 614b
Čak, Tādjī (XVI) s, 423b
Čaḳmaḳ, al-Malik al-Ẓāhir Sayf al-Dīn (Mamlūk) (1453) i, 138b, 281a, 1032b; ii, **6a**, 239b, 598b; iii, 187a, 1198a; vi, 195a; vii, 173b
Čakmak Mustafa Fevzi (Kavaklï) (1950) ii, **6b**; iii, 527a
Čaks, Banū iii, 420a; iv, 709a; vii, 300b; s, 131b, **167a**, 324b, 354a, 423b
Čākur, Mīr (Balūcistān) i, 1005b
Čala → Bukhārā
Čalabī → ʿUnwān, Muḥammad Riḍā
Calabria → Ḳillawriya
Calatayud → Ḳalʿat Ayyūb
Calatrava → Ḳalʿat Rabāḥ
Calcutta (Kalikātā) i, 979a; ii, **7a**, 426a; v, 201b; vi, 198b; s, 106a, 247a
Čāldïrān (battle) (1514) i, 1030b, 1066b; ii, **7b**; iv, 35a, 186b; v, 35a, 457a; vi, 200b, 201a, b, 541a; viii, 768a; ix, 128b
Calendar x, 258b
Čalï Bey (1416) i, 947b
Calicut → Kalikat
Caliz → Khalisioi
Čam ii, **8b**; iii, 1209a
Čamalal, Banū i, 504a; iv, 630b
Čambāl (river) vi, 536a
Cambay → Khambāyat
Cambodia → Ḳimār
Cameroons ii, **9a**; s, 218a
Camieniec → Kaminča
Čamishgezek v, 459a; vi, 71a
Čamlïbel, Fārūḳ Nāfidh (1973) s, **167b**, 324b
Camondo, Avram (1873) s, **168a**
Čampā (Champa) → Ṣanf
Čāmpānēr ii, **10b**, 1127a; iii, 445b, 482a, 575b; v, 1216b; vi, 50a, b, 51a, b, 52a, 53b, 270a, 310a; vii, 314a
Campiña → Kanbāniya
Čʿan (Laz) v, 713b, 714a
Čanaḳ-ḳalʿe Boghazï i, 4b, 1252a; ii, **11a**, 209a; iv, 628b, 884b, 1169b; v, 259a
Canary Islands → al-Djazāʾir al-Khālida
Čand Bībī bint Ḥusayn I (Niẓām Shāhī) (1604) viii, 74a
Čānd Mīnār vi, 368b, 369a
Čandā Ṣāḥib → Ḥusayn Dūst Khān
Čandarlï → Djandarlï
Čandar-oghlu → Isfendiyār-oghlu
Čānd Bībī bint Ḥusayn I (Niẓām Shāhī) (1604) i, 81a, 303a, 1202b; iii, 15b, 426b, 626a; viii, 74a
Čandērī ii, **12b**; iii, 446a; v, 644b; vi, 52b, 53a, 54b, 55a, 62a, 126a; s, 331b
Candia → Ḳandiya
Čandra Bhān Brahman (1663) vii, 343a
Čandrā Sēn (Bulandshahr) (1193) i, 1300a
Čandragiri iii, 148b
Canea → Ḥānya
Čanēsar, Malik Sinān al-Dīn (XIII) iii, 1155b
Canestrine → Ḳinnasrīn
Čangshi (Čaghatay Khānat) (1338) ii, 4a; xi, 336a
Canik → Djānīk
Čankïrï ii, **13a**; v, 248a, 257a
Cannanore → Kannanur
Čannēy Khān (Dāwūdpōtr) ii, 185a
Cantemir → Ḳantimūr
Canton → Khānfū
Čao i, 903a; ii, **14a**, 982a; iv, 31a
Čapakčur → Bingöl
Čapan-oghlu → Derebey
Čapanoghlu Aḥmad → Aḥmad Pasha
Čapanoghlu Djalāl al-Dīn Pasha (XIX) iii, 88b

Čapan-oghullarî (Čobān-oghullarî) i, 469a; ii, 206b, 207a; iv, 843b; s, **171b**
Čapan-zāde Agāh Efendi (1885) ii, 207b, 466a
Čapar b. Ḳaydu (Mongol) (XIV) ii, 3b, **14b**, 45b; vi, 783a; s, 240a
Capsa → Ḳafsa
Caracul → Karakay
Carcastillo → Ḳarḳastal
Čārdjūy → Āmul
Čārī (river) s, 327a
Čarkhī, Mawlānā Yaʿḳūb (1447) vii, 934a
Čarlowicz → Ḳarlofča
Carmathians → Ḳarmaṭī
Carmona → Ḳarmūna
Carnatic → Karnatak
Carpenitze → Kerbenesh
Carthage → Ḳarṭādjanna
Casablanca → Dār al-Bayḍāʾ
Casbah → Ḳaṣaba (town)
Casena → Katsina
Čāshna-gīr ii, **15a**
Čashnagīr-bashî ii, **15a**
Caspian Sea → Baḥr al-Khazar
Castamina, Castemol → Ḳasṭamūnī
Castilla → Ḳasṭīliya
Castille → Ḳashtāla
Castillo del Hierro → Firrīsh
Castriota, Georges → Iskender Beg
Castro giovanni → Ḳaṣryānnih
Cata → Ḳaṭā
Čatāldja ii, **15b**
Catania → Ṣiḳilliya
Čātgām → Chittagong
Caucasus → Ḳabḳ
Čāʾūsh (çavuş) ii, **16a**
Cavalle → Ḳawāla
Čawdharī Khāliḳ al-Zamān (XX) vi, 78a
Čawdor(s) (Čawdîr), Banū ii, **16a**; vi, 416a, b; s, 143b, **168b**
Čawgān ii, **16b**, 954a, 1035b; v, 688a
Čawhān ii, 1122b; iii, 167b, 168a, 225a; v, 1023a
Čawli → Fakhr al-Dawla; Mubāriz al-Dīn
Čawlî Saḳāwu (amīr) (XII) vii, 408a
Cawnpore → Kānpur
Čawundur → Čawdor
Čay ii, **17b**, 904b; v, 1145b
Čāy-khāna s, **169a**
Čaylaḳ Tewfīḳ (1892) ii, 474a; s, **170a**
Čečens ii, **18a**; iii, 1235b, 1236a; iv, 351a; vii, 351b; x, 920b
Čeh s, **170b**
Celal Nuri Ileri → Ileri, Djelāl Nūrī
Celebes → Sulawesi
Čelebī ii, **19a**, 394b
Čelebi Efendi → Djalāl al-Din Rūmī; Muḥammad b. Aḥmad Ṭāhā-zāde
Čelebi-zāde Ismāʿīl ʿĀṣim (1760) ii, **19b**, 1076a
Čeltükdji → Kürekčis
Cemalettin Mahir → Kemal Tahir
Cenap Şehabettin → Djanāb Shihāb al-Dīn
Čendereli → Djandarlî
Čepni, Banū ii, **20b**
Cercina, Cercinitis → Ḳarḳana
Čeremiss ii, **20b**
Cerigo → Čoka Adasî
Čerkes i, 32b, 64b, 470b, 732b, 1000a, 1050b, 1189b; ii, **21a**, 172b, 458a, 781b; iii, 316a; iv, 345b, 350a, 351a, 569a, 597a; v, 139a, 288a; vi, 315b, 325b, 382b; vii, 351a; x, 921a
Čerkes Edhem (1949) ii, **25b**
Čerkes Ḥāfiẓ Meḥmed Pasha (XIX) vi, 232a; viii, 84b
Čerkes Ismāʿīl Pasha (1861) ii, 878b
Čerkes Meḥmed Tewfīḳ (1949) ii, 25b, 26a
Čerkes Reshīd (1951) ii, 25b, 26a
Čerkeshī, Muṣṭafā (1814) ix, 155b
Čerkeshiyya iv, 991b
Česhme (source) ii, **26a**
Česhme (town) vi, 69a
Česhmīzāde, Muṣṭafā Rashīd (1770) ii, **26b**
Çetin Altan (XX) vi, 95b
Ceuta → Sabta
Cevat Rifat Atilhan s, 296b
Cevat Şakîr Kabaağackhlî → Haliḳarnas Balîḳčîsî
Ceylon i, 177b; ii, **26b**, 577a; v, 297a
Čeyrek ii, **28b**
Chaanba, Banū s, 328b
Chad → Čad
al-Chādirchī, Kāmil (XX) iv, 125a
Chah → Shāh
Cham → Čam; Ḥām
Chamba → Djāba
Chamito-Sematic → Ḥām; Sām
Chandax → al-Khandaḳ

Čhat ii, **28b**, 29a
Čhatr, Čhattar → Miẓalla
Chaudhri Raḥmat ʿAlī (XX) viii, 241a
Chaul (naval battle) (1508) vi, 51a
Chechaouen → Shafshāwan
Cheikh → Shaykh
Cheikho → Shaykhū, Luwīs
Chélif v, 1173b, 1175a, 1179a, b, 1180a; vi, 404a, b
Chella → Shāla
Cheng Ho (XV) v, 849b, 850a; vi, 283a, viii, 279b; ix, 715b; s, 746b
Cherchell → Sharshāl
Chérif → Sharīf
China → Kansu; Panthay al-Ṣīn, Tu Wen-Hsiu
Chin-chi-pʾu v, 847a, b, 848a, b
Chinguetti → Shinḳīt
Chionites i, 225b, 226a; iii, 303b
Chios → Saḳi̊z Ada
Chitral ii, **29a**, 317a; vi, 780a; s, 158b
Chittagong i, 606a, 1333a; ii, **31b**; iv, 177b
Chleuh → Sh(u)lūḥ (Marrākush); Tashelḥīt
Chocim → Khotin
Chole (island) → Mafia
Chonae → Khōnās
Chorfa → Sharīf
Chosroës → Kisrā
Čhotā Panduʾā vi, 368b
Čhotī Begam (XIX) ii, 83b
Chum, Hajji (Zanzibar) (XX) s, 351b
el-Cid → al-Sīd
Čift-resmi i, 999a, 1169b; ii, **32a**, 146b, 907a; iv, 211a
Čiftlik i, 1264b, 1266a, b, 1268b, 1269a; ii, **32b**, 907a
Čighālazāde Sinān Pasha (1605) i, 8a, 267b, 904a; ii, **33b**; iii, 1001a; s, 238b
Čihil Sutūn palace (Iṣfahān) vi, 526b, 527b; s, 257a, 259b, 325b
Čiḥrāzād → Humāy
Cilicia i, 184a; ii, **34b**, 65b
Čilla → Khalwa
Čimkent ii, **39a**
Čīn → al-Ṣīn
Cin → Djinn
Čīnārūd vi, 495a
Čīn-Kālān → Khānfū
Či̊n Ḳilic Khān, Nizām al-Mulk, Āṣaf Djāh (1748) viii, **73a**
Či̊n-Temür (XIII) ii, 606a; s, 246a
Cinema (sīnimā) ii, **39b**
Čingāne ii, **40b**
Čingiz Khān (Mongol Great Khān) (1227) i, 121a, 227a, 418b, 879b, 1295a; ii, 2a, 38a, **41a**, 393a, 571a, 607a, 894a; iii, 198a, 472a; iv, 30a; v, 391b, 858a; vi, 16a, 77a, 417b, 537a, 809b; vii, 232a, b, 997b; s, 176b
Čingiz Khān (Gudjarāt) (1567) vii, 133b
Čingizids ii, **44a**; iv, 723b; s, 97a
Čīnī Darwāza (Māhūr) vi, 87a
Čīnīōt (Cīnyōt) ii, **47a**
Cintra → Shintara
Čirāgh ʿAlī (1895) iii, 431b; iv, 170b
Čirāgh-i Dihlī (1356) ii, **47b**, 51a, 54a, 55a, b, 392a, 1114b; iii, 429b
Čirāghān (palace, Istanbul) ii, **49a**; vi, 531b
Circars → Sarkārs
Circassians → Čerkes
Circesium → Ḳarḳīsiyā
Čirkīn, Bāḳir ʿAlī vii, 534a
Čirmen ii, **49a**
Cirta → Ḳusṭanṭīna
Čishtī, Khwādja Ḳuṭb al-Dīn Mawdūd (1181) vi, 872a
Čishtī, Muʿīn al-Dīn Ḥasan Sidjzī (1236) i, 72b, 208a, 912a, 1024a; ii, 48b, **49b**, 50b, 378b, 796b; iii, 429a; v, 546b; vi, 697b, 867a; vii, 932a; x, 255b; s, 5a, 293b, 353b
Čishtī, Shaykh Ibban (XVI) s, 74a
Čishtī-Niẓāmī s, 293a, 360b
Čishtī-Ṣābirī → Ṣābiriyya
Čishtiyya i, 95a; ii, **50b**, 137b, 296b, 421a, 796b, 1115b; iii, 167b, 429a, 433a, 1174b; iv, 48a, 507a, 1026b; vii, 898a; s, 5a, 312b, 313a, 353a; x, 322b
Čishumī, Khwādja Tādj al-Dīn ʿAlī b. Shams al-Dīn (Sarbadārid) (1351) ix, 48a
Čitawr, Čitōr iii, 457a, 482b; vi, 53a, b, 55a, 270a, 272a, 309b, 310a, 407a, 1027a; s, 105a
Čitr → Ghāshiya
Čitrāl → Chitral
Čittagong → Chittagong
Čiwi Ilyāsii (XV) ii, 56b
Čiwi-zāde, ʿAbdī Čelebi (1552) ii, 56b
Čiwi-zāde, Muḥammad (1587) ii, **56b**; vii, 469a

Čiwi-zāde, Muḥyi al-Dīn Shaykh Muḥammad (1547) ii, **56b**
Cizrî, Melayê (XVII) v, 482a
Claudias → Ḳalāwdhiya
Čōbān → Čūbān
Čoban Girāylar ii, 1113b
Čobān-oghullarî → Čapan-oghullarî
Čoghondur i, 99b
Coilom → Kūlam
Coïmbra → Ḳulumriyya
Čoka → Ḳumāsh
Čoka Adasî ii, **57a**
Čökermish, amīr (XII) vii, 408a
Cölemerik ii, **57a**; v, 456b
Collyridians vi, 629b
Colomb-Béchar ii, **57b**
Colonia → Shābīn Ḳarā Ḥiṣār
Čomaḳ Baba (Marʿash) vi, 510a,
Comania → Dasht-i Ḳîpčaḳ
Comans → Ḳipčaḳ
Comnenus, Alexis (1118) v, 103b, 505a, 712b
Comnenus, Isaac Ducas (XII) v, 302b
Comnenus, John (1143) ii, 37a, 110b; v, 712b; vi, 380a
Comnenus, Manuel (1180) i, 466b, 289b, 791b; ii, 37a, b, 111a, 715a; v, 104a
Comores → Ḳumr
Conakry → Konakry
Congo (river-country) ii, **58a**; iv, 749b, 750b
Constantine III (al-Ḳurdj)(1414) v, 492a, b
Constantine → Ḳusṭanṭīna
Constantinus Africanus i, 381a; ii, **59b**; s, 271b
Constantin of Lampron (XIII) ii, 37b, 38a
Constantinople → Istanbul; Ḳusṭanṭīniyya
Constanza → Köstendje
Consul ii, **60b**
Čōpān → Čūbān
Čopan-ata ii, **61a**, 69b
Coptos → Ḳifṭ
Copts → Ḳibṭ
Coran → al-Ḳurʾān
Čorbadjî ii, **61b**
Córdoba → Ḳurṭuba
Corea → al-Sīlā
Corfu → Körfüz
Coria → Ḳūriya
Corinth → Kordos
Čorlu ii, **62a**; s, 282a
Čorlulu ʿAlī Pasha → ʿAlī Pasha Čorlulu
Cormaghun (XIII) iv, 349b, 670a
Coromandel → Maʿbar
Coron → Ḳoron
Corsica s, 120b
Čoruh (Corukh) ii, **62a**
Čorum ii, **62a**; s, 394b
Cos → Istanköy
Cossacks → Kazakh; Kazaḳ
Côte d'Ivoire (Ivory Coast) ii, **62b**
Cotonou → Kotonou
Čowdors → Čawdor, Banū
Crac → Karak
Crac des Chevaliers → Ḥiṣn al-Akrād
Črār (Srīnagar) s, 114b
Crimea → Ḳîrîm
Croia → Krujë
Crusades i, 197b, 198a, 215b, 341a, 466a, 517a, 519a, 552b, 662b, 710b, 737b, 778a, 783a, 784a, 798b, 799b, 910a, 1014a, 1017a, 1025a, 1045b, 1073a, 1102b, 1118b, 1125b, 1137b, 1139a, 1190b, 1218a, 1358a; ii, 37a, **63b**, 130a, 163a, 856a, 911b, 983b, 1056a; iii, 86b, 292b, 324b, 472b, 474b, 503b,504a, 1045a; iv, 291b, 483a, 485a, 842a, 958b; v, 103b, 303a, 330a, b, 800b, 924a; ix, 167a, b: s, 204b, 205a
Ctesiphon iii, 1254b; v, 945a, 946a; s, 298a
Ču ii, **66b**; iv, 212b
Čūbak, Ṣādiḳ (XX) iv, 73a; v, 200a; s, 60a
Čūbān, amīr (1327) i, 347a, 468a, 703a, 908b; ii, **68a**, 69a; iii, 1122b; iv, 621b, 672a, 738a, 817b; v, 554b; vi, 482b; viii, 753a; ix, 821b
Čūbānids ii, **67b**, 401a; vi, 482b; x, 44a
Čūčak Bēgam (XVI) iii, 633b
Cuenca → Ḳūnka
Čufut Ḳalʿe i, 893a, b
Čūha Sulṭān Tekkelu (1525) vi, 514b
Čuka → Ḳumāsh
Čukurova → Cilicia
Čulābīs → Afrāsiyāb
Čulāḳ-Sūrkhay-Khān (XVIII) ii, 87b; v, 296b
Čulawī, Amīr Ḥusayn Kiyā (XVI) vi, 515b
Čulîm ii, **68b**
Cumania x, 693a
Cümhuriyet → Djümhūriyyet
Čunār vi, 47a, 62a
Čūpān (herdsman) ii, **69a**; s, 319b, 321a
Čūpān-ata → Čopan-ata
Čūpān, Amīr → Čūbān

Čūpānbegī → Ḳūbčūr
Čūrāman Djāt (XVIII) i, 1193a; ii, 810b
Cuttack x, 894b
Čuvash i, 557a; ii, **69b**; iv, 528a, 849b, 853b, 1177a; viii, 618b; x, 417b, 691b
Čuwash i, 246a, 1307b, 1338a; ii, **69b**; iv, 280a, 281a, 608b
Čuwash literature x, **732a**
Cyprus → Ḳubrus
Cyrenaïca → Barḳa
Cyrillus b. Laḳlaḳ (1243) s, 396a
Cyrrhus → Ḳūrus
Cyrus → al-Muḳawḳis
Czechoslovakia → Čeh

D

Daʿʿān, Treaty of (1911) vi, 35b
al-Daʿʿār, Banū s, 338a
Daʾb → Adab
al-Dabarān → Nudjūm
Ḍabb ii, **70a**; s, 286b
Dābba ii, **71a**
Ḍabba, Banū ii, 71b; vi, 33a
Ḍabba b. Muḥammad al-Asadī (X) iv, 637b
Ḍabba b. Udd b. Ṭābīkha ii, **71b**
Dabbāgh (tanner) s, **172a**
al-Dabbāgh, Abū Zayd ʿAbd al-Raḥmān (1300) vi, 353b; s, **172b**, 395a
al-Dabbāgh al-Fāsī (1719) vi, 356b
al-Dabbāgh, Ḥusayn Ṭāhir (1927) vi, 157b
Dabbāgh-zāde Meḥmed Efendi, Shaykh al-Islām (1687) vi, 983a
al-Dabbās → Abu ʾl-Khayr Ḥammād
al-Ḍabbī, Abu ʾl-ʿAbbās (1008) viii, 389b
al-Ḍabbī, Abū Djaʿfar (1203) i, 602b; ii, **72a**
al-Ḍabbī, Abū ʿIkrima ʿĀmir b. ʿImrān (864) vi, 822b; vii, 306b
al-Ḍabbī, Abu ʾl-Ṣaydāʾ x, 844b
al-Ḍabbī, Bisṭām b. ʿUmar (VII) iii, 649b, 658b
al-Ḍabbī, al-Mufaḍḍal b. Muḥammad (780) iii, 136b, 706b, 985a, 1178a; vii, 306b, 841a; s, 15b, 38b
al-Ḍabbī, al-Mufaḍḍal (II) b. Salāma b. ʿĀsim (903) ii, 135b, 807b; vi, 215a, b, 822b; s, 177a, **631a**
al-Ḍabbī, al-Musayyab b. Zuhayr (791) vii, 645b; s, 327a
Dābiḳ ii, **72b**, 360b, 912a; vi, 544a
Dabiḳ ii, **72b**
Dabīl → Dwīn
Al-Dabīlī, Abū Mūsā (IX) i, 162b
Dabīr (scribe) iv, 758b, 759a; s, **173a**
Dabīr, Mīrzā Salāmat ʿAlī (1875) i, 508b; ii, **73a**; iii, 119b; vi, 610b, 611b; s, 74b
Dabistān al-Madhāhib ii, **74a**
Ḍābiṭ i, 975a; ii, **74a**
Ḍābiṭa Khān (Rohilla) (1785) i, 1206a; ii, 1092b; iii, 61a; vii, 869b; viii, 572b
Dābō(ē) → Dābūya
Ḍabōt vi, 82a
Ḍabṭ ii, **74b**, 155b, 156a
Ḍabṭiyya ii, **74b**; iv, 611b
Ḍabuʿ, Ḍabʿ s, **173b**
Dābū vi, 510b, 511a
Dābul vi, 63a, 66b
Dabūsiyya s, **176b**
Dābūya/Dābūyids i, 871b; ii, **74b**; iv, 207b, 644a; v, 69a; vi, 335a, 941a; s, 297b, 298a, b
Dacca → Dhākā
Ḍād ii, **75a**
Dada → Dede
Dadaloghlu (1870) ii, **75b**
Dadan al-ʿUlā (oasis) → Dedan (al-ʿUlā)
Dadanitic s, 505b
Dādhawayh (VII) i, 728a
Dād-Beg Ḥabashī (XI) s, 279a
Dādhburzmihr b. Farrukhān (734) ii, 74b, 809a; s, 299a
Dadjādja ii, **76a**
al-Dadjdjāl i, 932a; ii, **76a**, 486b; iv, 408b; v, 800a
Dādū, Pīr (1593) v, 26b
Daff → Duff
Ḍafīr, Banū ii, **77a**
Dafn → Dhunūb, Dafn al-
Daftar i, 1090a, b; ii, **77b**, 82a, b, 147b, 563a; iv, 1047b; viii, 149b
Daftar-i Khāḳānī i, 999a; ii, **81b**, 147b
Daftardār i, 480b; ii, **83a**, 723b; iv, 560b
Dāgh, Nawwāb Mīrzā Khān (1905) ii, **83b**; iii, 119a; v, 961b
Dagh-Čufut ii, 86b, 88b, 89a
Dāgh u Taṣḥīḥa v, 685b, 686b; s, **176b**

Daghfal vi, 828b
Dāghistān i, 504a, 755a, 756a, 958a; ii, **85a**, 206a, 746b; iii, 157a; iv, 343a, b, 350a, 846b; v, 55b, 246a, 382a, 617b, 618a, 729b; vi, 55b, 56b; vii, 352a; viii, 642b; ix, 283b x, 921b; s, 143a, 484a
Daghūgh, Banū vi, 742a
Dagno iv, 139b
Dahak (Ghazna) vi, 783a
Dāhār (VIII) iv, 534b
Daḥdaḥ (Damascus) vi, 122b
Dahdam → Lamlam
al-Ḍaḥḥāk → Zuhāk
Ḍaḥḥāḳ, Azhd ii, 106b, 1099a; v, 449a
al-Ḍaḥḥāk b. Ḳays al-Fihrī (684) i, 53b, 704b; ii, **89a**, 360a; iii, 270b, 687b; vi, 545a, 546b, 622a; vii, 268a, b, 464a; viii, 119a
al-Ḍaḥḥāk b. Ḳays al-Shaybānī (746) ii, **90a**; iv, 1076a; vi, 624a; vii, 546a, 693b; ix, 767a
Daḥḥāk b. Muzāḥim (724) v, 1123a
al-Daḥḥāk b. ʿUthmān (770) ix, 566b
Dahhām b. Dawwās (XVIII) vii, 410a
Dahhānī, Khwādja (XIII) viii, 972a, b
Daḥḥūn, Banū iii, 12a
Ḍāḥik, Mīr (XVIII) s, 358b
Dahinda (river) vi, 294b
Ḍāhir (Yemen) i, 762b
Dāhir (Sind) (VIII) vii, 405b; s, 163a
Ḍāhir al-ʿUmar → Ẓāhir al-ʿUmar
Dāḥis ii, 873a, 1023a; s, **177a**
Dahistan → Dihistān
Dahlak islands ii, **90b**, 709b; vi, 642a; vii, 861a
Daḥlān, Aḥmad b. Zaynī (1886) i, 66a; ii, **91a**; vi, 176a, b
al-Dahmānī, Sīdī Abū Yūsūf vi, 353b
al-Dahnāʾ i, 537a; ii, **91b**; viii, 1048a
al-Dahnadj ii, **93a**
Dahomey ii, **93b**; v, 279b
Dahr ii, **94b**
Dahriyya ii, **95a**, 770b; vi, 737b; s, 89a
Daḥshūr ii, **97b**
Dāʿī i, 832b; ii, **97b**
Dāʿī, Aḥmad b. Ibrāhīm (1472) ii, **98a**; iii, 1243a
Dāʾira → Dawāʾir
Dāʾira Saniyya s, **179a**
Daḳahliyya ii, **99a**; vi, 440b
Dakar s, **179a**
Dakhadayev, Muḥammad ʿAlī (1918) vi, 129b
Dakhalieh → Daḳahliyya
Dakhan (Deccan) i, 81a, 117b, 923b; ii, **99a**; iii, 15a, 420b; v, 937a, 1214b, 1215a, b; vi, 50b, 53b, 54a, 62b, 126b, 271a, 309a, b, 406b, 488b, 534a, 536b; vii, 79b, 632a; viii, 67b; s, 74b, 335b
Dakhanī (Dakhni) → Urdū
Dakhaw → ʿAlī Akbar Dihkhudā
Dakhīl ii, **100a**; iii, 1018a; iv, 412a
al-Dākhil → ʿAbd al-Raḥmān I; al-Ḥasan
al-Dākhila and al-Khāridja → al-Wāḥāt
Dakhtanūs vi, 603a
Dakibyza → Gebze
Daḳīḳī, Abū Manṣūr Muḥammad (X) ii, **100a**, 918b, 1035b; iii, 113a; iv, 60b, 62b
al-Daḳḳāḳ, Abū ʿAbd Allāh (XII) i, 137b; ii, **100b**
al-Daḳḳāḳ, Abū ʿAli (1015) v, 526b
Dakkanī, Walī (1707) v, 959b, 961a, 1106a
Daḳūḳāʾ i, 184a, 512b; ii, **101a**; vi, 500b
Dāl ii, **101a**
al-Dalāl, Abū Zayd Nāḳid (762) iv, 1087b; s, **183a**
Dalāṣī (al-Dalāṣīrī) → al-Buṣīrī
Dalhama → Dhu ’l-Himma
Ḍāliʿ i, 446a; ii, 675b
Dālī b. Aḥmad al-Maʿḳūr ii, 122b
Dalīl (sign) ii, **101b**; iii, 543b
Dalīl Baḥr → Dālī b. Aḥmad al-Maʿḳūr
Dalīpgarh i, 1020a
Dallāl ii, **102b**; iii, 213a; v, 1004a, 1005a
Dalmā ix, 658b
Dalmatia s, **183b**
Dalmāw vi, 49b
Daltāwa ii, **103a**
Dalūka, queen iii, 71b; vi, 412b, 413a
al-Dalw → Minṭaḳat al-Burūdj; Nudjūm
Dām → Sikka
Dam (blood) s, **188b**, 221b
Damā (ʿUmān) vi, 735b
Dāma al-ʿUlyā (Ḥawrān) vi, 303a
Dāmād ii, **103b**
Dāmād ʿAlī Shehīd (1725) i, 268b; iv, 1039b; vii, 217a; ix, 14b
al-Dāmād al-Astarābādī, Mīr (1630) ii, **103b**; vi, 550a; vii, 94a, 547b; viii, 541b; s, 308b

Dāmād Ferīd Pasha (1923) ii, **104b**, 431b, 533b, 630b; iii, 595a; iv, 873a, b; vi, 984a
Dāmād Pasha → ʿAlī Pasha; Ḥasan Pasha; Ibrāhīm Pasha; Sinān Pasha
Dāmād-zāde Fayḍ Allāh Efendi, Shaykh al-Islām (XVI) vi, 1004b
Dāmādjī (XVIII) i, 1053a
al-Dāmaghānī, Abū ʿAbd Allāh al-Ḥusayn b. ʿAlī (1166) s, **192b**
al-Dāmaghānī, Abū ʿAbd Allāh Muḥammad b. ʿAlī (1085) s, **191b**, 192a, b
al-Dāmaghānī, Abū ʿAbd Allāh Muḥammad b. ʿAlī, Tādjal-Ḳuḍāt (1122) s, **192b**
al-Dāmaghānī, Abū ʿAbd Allāh Muḥammad b. al-Ḥusayn (1218) s, **194a**
al-Dāmaghānī, Abū Djaʿfar ʿAbd Allāh b. Muḥammad Muhadhdhib al-Dawla (1124) s, **192b**
al-Dāmaghānī, Abū Djaʿfar Yaḥyā b. Djaʿfar (1232) s, **194a**
al-Dāmaghānī, Abu 'l-Faḍl Muḥammad b. al-Ḥasan (1196) s, **193b**
al-Dāmaghānī, Abu 'l-Fatḥ Muḥammad b. ʿAlī (1180) s, **193b**
al-Dāmaghānī, Abu 'l-Hasan ʿAlī (1119) s, **194a**
al-Dāmaghānī, Abu 'l-Ḥasan ʿAlī b. Aḥmad (1188) s, **193a**
al-Dāmaghānī, Abu 'l-Ḥusayn Aḥmad b. ʿAlī (1145) s, **192b**
al-Dāmaghānī, Abu 'l-Ḳāsim ʿAbd Allāh b. al-Ḥusayn (1219) s, **193b**
al-Dāmaghānī, Abū Manṣūr Djaʿfar b. ʿAbd Allāh (1172) s, **193a**
al-Dāmaghānī, Abū Muḥammad al-Ḥasan b. Aḥmad (1186) s, **193a**
al-Dāmaghānī, Abū Muẓaffar al-Ḥusayn b. Aḥmad (1183) s, **193a**
al-Dāmaghānī, Abū Naṣr al-Ḥasan b. ʿAlī (1160) s, **192b**
al-Dāmaghānī, Abū Saʿīd al-Ḥasan b. ʿAbd Allāh (1179) s, **193a**
al-Dāmaghānī, ʿAbd Allāh b. al-Ḥusayn b. ʿAbd Allāh (fl. 1102) s, 194a
al-Damāmīnī, Badr al-Dīn Muhammad b. ʿUmar (1423) iv, 135a
al-Damāmīnī, Tādj al-Dīn (1331) iv, 641a
Ḍamān i, 1144a; ii, **105a**; iv, 323b, 324a, 326a, 404b, 1046a
Damanhūr (Buḥayra) i, 1288a, b; ii, **105b**; vii, 421a
Damanhūr al-Shahīd ii, **105b**
Damascus → Dimashḳ
Damāwand i, 358b; ii, **106a**; iv, 402; v, 89a, 657b, 659b, 660a; vi, 335a, 337b, 744a, b; s, 298a
Damawiyya iv, 334b
Dambat vi, 201a, b
Damdam → Lamlam
Damēlī ii, 31a, 138b
Dāmghān ii, **107a**; iv, 701b; v, 377b, 378a; vi, 115b, 365a, 453a, 513a; s, 149a, 192a, 357a
Dāmghānī, Ḥasan-i (Sardabārid) (1361) ix, 48b
Dāmghānī, Shams al-Dīn (XIV) ii, 1124b; iii, 14b; iv, 218b
Damietta → Dimyāṭ
Ḍamīr → Naḥw
al-Dāmir iv, 686b
Damir Ḳapu → Dar-i Āhanīn
al-Damīrī, Muḥammad b. Mūsā (1405) i, 509a, 594b; ii, **107b**; iii, 306b, 307b, 313a; vi, 218b, 904a; s, 392b
Ḍamīrī al-Iṣfahānī (1578) vi, 271a; viii, 775b
al-Damlūdjī, ʿAbd Allāh (XX) vi, 153a, b
Damḳōt vi, 81a
Ḍamma → Ḥaraka
al-Dammām ii, **108a**, 175b, 569a; iii, 238b
Dammār, Banū i, 6a; vi, 899a, 946b; vii, 761a
Damnāt (Demnate) ii, **109a**; vi, 741a
al-Damnātī → ʿAlī b. Sulaymān
al-Ḍamrī, ʿAmr b. Umayya (VII) vii, 517b, 863a
al-Damurdāshī, Aḥmad (XVIII) ii, **109b**
Dānā Shahīd, Shāh (1270) vii, 550a
Danāgla viii, 92a, b
Dānaḳ → Sikka
Danāḳil/Danāḳla → Danḳalī
Danānīr al-Barmakī (IX) i, 1036a; s, 116b
Dandānḳān, Dandānaḳān vi, 66a, 453a; vii, 407a; s, **195a**, 245b
al-Dandarāwī, Abu 'l-ʿAbbās (1950) s, 279a
al-Dandarāwiyya x, 249a; s, 279a
Dāndēsh → Khāndēsh
al-Dānī, Abū ʿAmr (1053) ii, **109b**, 112a; iii, 753b; iv, 731b; v, 128a; vi, 188b, 189a; vii, 553a
al-Danī, Abū Bakr Muḥammad → lbn al-Labbāna

Daniel → Dāniyāl
Dānis, Banū s, 513b
Dānish, Aḥmad Makhdūm (1897) s, 109b, 290a, 467a
Dānishgāh → Djāmiʿa
Dānishmand Khān (XVII) vii, 321b
Dānishmend, Malik Aḥmad Ghāzī (XI) i, 465b, 466a, b, 1103b, 1104a; ii, 37a, 110a, 1044a; iii, 115a; viii, 36a
Dānishmend Tigin (XIII) i, 418b
Dānishmendids i, 431b, 466b, 510a, 639a, 665a, 666a; ii, 13b, **110a**; iv, 627b, 737b; v, 103b, 106a; vi, 231a; s, 154b
Dāniya ii, **111b**; v, 631b
Dāniyāl ii, **112b**, 377a; iv, 654a
Dāniyāl b. Akbar (Mughal) (1604) i, 80b, 1331a; ii, **113a**, 851b, 871a; iv, 1017b; vi, 814b; viii, 74a
Dāniyāl b. Shaʿya i, 388b
Dāniyāl Biy Atalîḳ (Mangît) (1785) i, 1295b; iv, 310a; vi, 418b, 419a, 621a; s, 97a
Dāniyār b. Ḳāsim Khān (1486) iv, 723b
Danḳalī i, 176b, 765a, 1028b; ii, **113a**, 351a, 615a; iii, 4a, 5b; v, 1248b
Dār ii, **113b**; iv, 236a, b, 1015a, 1016b; v, 23a
Dār-i Āhanīn ii, **115b**
Dār al-ʿahd i, 1253a; ii, **116a**
Dār-i Alān → Bāb al-Lān
Dār al-Baḥr s, 62b
Dār al-Bayḍāʾ (Casablanca) i, 506a, 977b; ii, **116b**, 727a; vii, 387a; s, 63b, 134a, 145a, 223b
Dār al-Bayḍāʾ (Marrākush) vi, 596b
Dār al-Ḍarb i, 24a, 1335b; ii, **117b**, 205b, 874b; iii, 41b; iv, 134b, 230b; v, 264b, 488b
Dār al-Djihād i, 1163b
Dār Fartīt i, 929a, b
Dār Firʿawn (Manf) vi, 413b
Dār al-Funūn → Djāmiʿa
Dār al-Funūn (Tehran) vi, 291a
Dār Fūr i, 35a, 49b, 929a, b, 962a; ii, **121b**, 351a; v, 267a, 1248b, 1249b; vi, 281b; xi, 11a; s, 164a
Dār al-Ḥadīth ii, **125b**, 283a; v, 1129a; s, **195a**
Dār al-Ḥadīth (Makka) vi, 173b
Dār al-Hamara iii, 149a
Dār al-Ḥarb i, 429b; ii, **116a**, 126a, 131b
Dār al-Ḥikma i, 816a, 1141a; ii, **126b**, 169b, 859b; iii, 78b; v, 1033a, 1125b
Dār al-ʿIlm i, 899a; ii, **127a**, 169b; iii, 78b; v, 1125a, b, 1126a, 1129a; s, 95b
Dār al-Imāra (Baghdād) i, 899b, 900a, 901a; ii, 128b
Dār al-Islām i, 116a, **127b**, 131b; iii, 546b; iv, 173a, b
Dār al-Ḳurʾān wa ʾl-Ḥadīth ii, 126a
Dār al-Maḥfūzāt al-ʿUmūmiyya ii, **128a**
Dār al-Mamlaka (Baghdād) i, 901a, 1352b, 1354a
Dār al-Mizān vi, 384b
Dār al-Muṣannifīn (Lakhnaw) ii, 132b
Dār al-Nadwa (Makka) ii, **128b**
Dār Runga (Čad) s, 164b
Dār al-Saʿāda → Saray
Dār al-Saʿāde Aghasî → Saray-Aghasî
Dār al-Ṣabbāghīn viii, 985a
Dār al-Salām ii, **128b**
Dār al-Sawdāʾ vi, 563b
Dār es-Salaam ii, **128b**; v, 1031a; vi, 370a
Dār al-Shifāʾ (Turkey) i, 1225b
Dār al-Shifāʾ (Srīnagar) s, 353b
Dār al-Shifāʾ (Tehran) s, 23b
Dār al-Ṣināʿa ii, **129b**; iii, 271b; s, 120a
Dār Ṣīnī s, **197a**
Dār al-Ṣulḥ ii, **131a**
Dār al-Tablīgh al-Islāmī (Ḳum) iv, 166b
Dār al-Takiyya al-Miṣriyya (Makka) vi, 178a
Dār al-Taḳrīb bayna ʾl-Madhāhib al-Islāmīyya (Cairo) iv, 165b
Dār al-Taḳrīb → Ikhtilāf
Dār Tāma ii, 123b
Dār al-Ṭibāʿa → Maṭbaʿa
Dār Ṭirāz → Ṭirāz
Dār al-ʿUlūm i, 817b, 818a, 819a, 820a; ii, **131b**, 205a; v, 909a, 910b; vi, 602a; vii, 418b; s, 18a, 262b
Dār al-ʿUmma (Marrākush) vi, 596a
Dār al-Wikāla iv, 136a
Dāra (Abyssinia) i, 176b
Darʿa → Adhriʿāt
Darʿa (Draʿ) (town; province) ii, **133b**; v, 1185a; vi, 540a, 589b, 590b; s, 29a, 402b
Dārā, Dārāb (Dareios) ii, **132b**; iv, 809b
Dārā Shukōh b. Shāh Djahān I (Mughal) (1659) i, 229a, 768b, 769a, 781b, 1136a, 1166a; ii, 54b, **134a**, 378b; iii, 202a, b,

436a, 459a; iv, 69a; vi, 368b; vii, 189a, 327a, b, 343a, 452b; viii, 540b; s, 308b
Dārāb → Dārābdjird
Dārāb Khān (1625) i, 81b
Dārābdjird i, 43b, 896b; ii, **135b**; vi, 384a, 494a, 640b
Dārābī, Ḥakīm ʿAbbās s, 308b
Darabukka ii, **135b**
Därädiz vi, 504a
Daragaz vii, 454a
Darak s, **198a**
Darāk → Dawraḳ
Daraḳhsh i, 1233b
al-Dāraḳuṭnī, Abu ʾl-Ḥasan ʿAlī b. ʿUmar (995) ii, **136a**; iii, 24b, 758a, 768b; viii, 517a; s, 400b
Darandollä Nomads (Maḳdishū) vi, 129a
al-Darazī, Muḥammad (1019) ii, **136b**, 631b; iii, 80b, 154b
Ḍarb → Dār al-Ḍarb; Sikka
Ḍarb → Madīna
Ḍarb Āl ʿAlī iii, 208a
Ḍarb al-Arbaʿīn ii, 122a, **137a**
Ḍarb al-Fīl i, 707b
Ḍarb al-Ḥadjdj vi, 546a
Ḍarb al-Kunhurī i, 748a; ii, 568b
Ḍarb al-Saʿāda (Cairo) vi, 75b
Ḍarb Zubayda ii, 92a; s, **198b**, 304b
Darband → Derbend
Ḍarbkhāne → Dār al-Ḍarb
Darbukka → Darabukka
Darčīn s, 327a
Dard, Khʷādja Mīr b. Khʷādja Muḥammad Nāṣir (1785) ii, **137b**; vii, 555b, 939a; x, 878a; s, 358b
Dardanelles → Čanaḳ-kalʿe Boghazi̊
Dardic and Kāfir Languages ii, **138a**; iv, 711b; v, 649a; s, 158b
Dardīr (1786) vi, 279a
al-Dardīr i, 867b
Dardīriyya ii, **139b**
Dardistān ii, **140a**; s, 167a
Dārdjān vi, 384b
al-Dardjīnī, Abu ʾl-ʿAbbās Aḥmad b. Saʿīd (XIII) i, 167a, 1053b; ii, **140b**; iii, 96b, 656b; vi, 311a, 945a
Dareios → Dārā
Dargāh ii, **141b**; iv, 26a
Darghin i, 756a; ii, 86b, 89a, **141b**; iv, 846a, b; v, 285b
Darghūth viii, 763b
Darī (court language) ii, **142a**; iv, 55a; vi, 768a
al-Darʿī (XVIII) vi, 350a
Darʿī, Moses (XII) iv, 605b
Darial, Dariel → Bāb al-Lān
Ḍarība ii, **142b**; s, **199b**
Dārim → Tamīm
al-Dārimī, ʿAbd Allāh b. ʿAbd al-Raḥmān (869) ii, **159a**; iii, 24b; vii, 663a
al-Dārimī, Sufyān b. Mudjāshiʿ (VII) iv, 832b
Dārin → Tārūt
al-Ḍarīr, Ḥāmid al-Dīn (1267) vii, 969a
Ḍarīr, Muṣṭafā (XIV) ii, **159a**
Ḍarīsa, Āl vi, 310b, 311a, 312a
Darius, King → Dārā, Dārāb
Ḍariyya ii, **159b**
al-Darʿiyya → al-Dirʿiyya
Darḳāwa i, 368b, 371a; ii, **160a**, 224a; iii, 261b, 696a, 701a, 968a; s, 371a
Darḳāwī, Abū Ḥāmid al-ʿArabī (1823) x, 247b
Darḳāwī Muḥammad al-Ḥarrāḳ (1845) vi, 250b
Darna i, 1049a; ii, **160b**
Dārōd, Banū vii, 390a
Darōhar s, 163a
Daron → al-Dārūm
Darra Gaz vi, 495b
Darrās al-Fāsī (X) iv, 341a; v, 1208b
Darshan ii, **162a**
Darsim ii, 193a; v, 465a
Dart → Djerīd
Dārūgha ii, **162a**; iii, 491a; iv, 103b, 268b; s, 97a
Darul-Islam (Indonesia) vi, 117a, 732a, b
Darūliyya → Eskishehir
al-Dārūm i, 1140a; ii, **163a**
Ḍarūra ii, **163b**; iii, 306b; iv, 692b
Darvīsh khusraw (1593) iv, 860b
Darwāz vi, 618b
Darwīsh ii, **164a**; iv, 49b; s, 154a
Darwīsh ʿAbdī (1647) iv, 1126a
Darwīsh ʿAlī (Aleppo) (XX) viii, 449a
Darwīsh ʿAlī, Cangī-yi Khāḳānī (XVII) viii, 543a
Darwīsh ʿAlī Khān (1556) i, 722a
Darwīsh Khēl Wazīrī, Banū vi, 86a; vii, 220a
Darwīsh Khusraw (1593) viii, 115b

Darwīsh Muḥammad Naḳḳāsh (XVI) i, 1211b
Darwīsh Muḥammad Tarkhān (1467) vii, 90b
Darwīsh Riḍā (1631) viii, 116b
Darwīsh Waḥdatī (1909) vi, 614b
Darwīza, Akhund (XVI) i, 1121b, 1123a
Daryā ʿImād Shāh (ʿImād Shahī) (1561) iii, 425a, 1160b, 1161a
Daryā Khān → Ẓafar Khān Lodī II
Daryā Khān Noḥānī (1524) ii, 1129a; v, 72a; s, **203a**
Daryā-begi ii, **165b**
Daryā-yi Shāhī / Riḍāʾiyya → Urmiya (lake)
Dās, Rādjā Bhagwān (XVI) s, 167a
Dāsenī → Ṭasinī
al-Dashtakī, Ghiyāth al-Dīn Manṣūr b. Muḥammad (1541) iv, 610a; viii, 778a, 781b, 783a, 785b
Dashtakī, Ṣadr al-Dīn Muḥammad (1498) viii, 781b
Dashtī → Muḥammad Khān (1881)
Dashtī (Mānd) vi, 384b
Dasht-i Arzhan vi, 493b
Dashtī, ʿAlī (XX) iv, 73a; v, 199a
Dasht-i Kavīr iv, 2a; s, 149a
Dasht-i Ḳipčaḳ vi, 314a, b, 315a, 322a, 417b; x, 562b; s, **203b**
Dasht-i Lūṭ iv, 2a, b, 4b; v, 147b, 352b
Dasht-i Rūn vi, 496a
Dashtistān vi, 384b
Daskara ii, **165b**
Dastadjird ii, **166a**
Dāstān-i Ḳahramān → Ḳahramān-nāma
al-Dāstānī, Shaykh Abū ʿAbd Allāh (X) i, 162b; iv, 1058a
Dast-i Mayṣan vi, 633b
Dastūr → Dustūr
Dastūr Dīnār (Ḥabshī) (1504) iii, 15a; vi, 63a, b
Dasūḳ i, 817b; viii, 698b; s, 18a
al-Dasūḳī, Ibrāhīm b. ʿAbd al-ʿAzīz (1287) ii, **166a**
al-Dasūḳī, Ibrāhīm b. Ibrāhīm (1883) ii, **167a**; vi, 279a; x, 190a
al-Dasūḳī, Ibrāhīm b. Muḥammad (1513) ii, **167b**
Dātā Gandj → Hudjwīrī
Datbūrdjmatūn (Dābūyid) (737) vi, 941a
Dathīna ii, **167b**, 675b; iv, 746a, 747b
Datoʾ Patimang vi, 116b
Datoʾri Bandang vi, 116b
Datoʾri Tiro vi, 116b
Dattū Sarwanī (XVI) s, 313a
Dāʾūd → Dāwūd
Dāʾū-Potra → Bahāwalpūr
David → Dāwūd
David II the Restorer → Dawid II Aghmashenebeli
David b. al-Hītī (XV) iv, 605b
Davudpaşa (Istanbul) vi, 529b
Dawāʾ → Adwiya
Daʿwā ii, **170b**
Daʿwa, daʿawāt i, 832b; ii, 97b, **168a**; iv, 203b; 815a
Dawā Khān → Duwā Khān
Dawādār ii, **172b**; iv, 759a
al-Dawādār, Sayf al-Dīn Aḥmad Aḳbughā b. ʿAbd Allāh (1383) vi, 580b
al-Dawādārī, Ibn Aybak (1336) vii, 167a
Dawāʾir ii, **172b**
Dawʿan, wādī ii, **173b**
al-Dawʿanī, Muḥammad b. ʿAlī Djirfīl (1497) vi, 132b
al-Daw(w)ānī, Muḥammad b. Asʿad Djalāl al-Dīn (1502) i, 326b, 329a; ii, **174a**; iv, 267b, 471b, 850b; v, 53b; vii, 143b, 272a, 478b; viii, 781a, 1047b
Dawār ii, **174b**; s, 318b
Dāwar → Zamīn-i Dāwar
Dāwar Bakhsh b. Khusraw b. Djahāngīr (XVII) i, 686b; v, 74a; vii, 315a
Dawārō i, 176b; ii, **175a**; iii, 3b; vi, 128b
al-Dawāsir, Banū i, 233b, 545b, 873b; ii, 108b, **175b**; v, 40a; vi, 191b
Dawāt v, 988b; s, **203b**
Dawāwida, Banū i, 1247a
al-Dawḥa (Ḳaṭar) ii, **177a**; iv, 751a, b
Dawḥat Bilbūl (Arabia) iv, 681a
Dawid b. Georgi Lasha (Kurdj) (1273) v, 491a
Dawid b. Luarsab → Dāwūd Khān (Georgia)
Dawid II Aghmashenebeli (1125) iv, 348b; v, 489b; vi, 64b; viii, 943b; ix, 170a
Dawit I (Ḥabash) (1411) iii, 4a
Dāwiyya and Isbitāriyya i, 293b, 1119b, 1250b; ii, 6a, 529b; iii, 325b, 504a, 1006b; iv, 483b; v, 342b; vi, 578b, 579a, b, 580a; viii, 569a; s, **204b**

Dawla ii, **177b**; iv, 293b; v, 621b, 623a
Dawlat-Begs s, 367b
Dawlat Čak (XVI) s, 324b
Dawlat Girāy I (1577) ii, **178b**; v, 137a, 138a, b
Dawlat Girāy II (1713) ii, 1047a; iv, 569a; v, 140b
Dawlat Girāy III (1717) i, 270b, 1287a
Dawlat Ḳāḍī (Bengali) (XVII) i, 606b
Dawlat Khān (Rādjpūt) (XVII) i, 809a
Dawlat Khān b. Shudjāʿ (1555) i, 1155a
Dawlat Khān Lōdī (1414) i, 218a; iii, 417b, 485a; vi, 49a, b, 50a; s, **206a**
Dawlat Khān Lōdī (1525) i, 848a; ii, 271a; iii, 420b, 995b; v, 598a
Dawlat Muḥammad Āzādī (XVIII) vi, 130b
Dawlat-Shāh (amīr) b. ʿAlāʾ al-Dawla (XV) ii, **179a**; vi, 276a; vii, 530a; x, 516a; s, 65a, 84a, 415a
Dawlatābād i, 1322b, 1329a; ii, 99b, **179b**; iv, 922b; v, 884a; vi, 54a, 126a, 131b, 269a, 271a, 368b, 369a, 535b; vii, 412a; s, 57b, 105a, b, 279b, 352b
– monuments i, 1323b; ii, **180a**, 442a
al-Dawlatābādī, Shihāb al-Dīn (1445) i, 702b, 859a; ii, **180b**
Dawlatyār s, 367a
Dawr s, **206b**
Dawraḳ ii, **181a**; v, 89a
Daws → Azd
Dawsa ii, **181b**
Dāwūd (King David) i, 261a; ii, **182a**; iv, 947b
Dāwūd (Gudjarāt) (1459) vi, 50a
Dāwūd b. ʿAbbās al-Bānīdjūrī (873) i, 1001a; s, 125a, b
Dāwūd b. ʿAbd Allāh b. Idrīs al-Faṭānī (XIX) ii, **183a**; vi, 235b
Dāwūd b. ʿAbd al-Raḥmān al-ʿAṭṭār (IX) i, 827a
Dāwūd b. Abī Dāwūd (khuttalan) (IX) xi, 255a; s, 125b
Dāwūd b. al-ʿĀḍid (Fāṭimid) (1207) iv, 200b
Dāwūd b. Abū Hind (VIII) i, 104b
Dāwūd b. ʿAdjab Shāh (Bohorā) (1588) i, 1254b; iv, 201a; ix, 824b, 829a
Dāwūd b. ʿAlī b. ʿAbbās (VIII) i, 43a; iv, 973b
Dāwūd b. Idrīs II (Idrīsid) (VIII) iii, 1035b; iv, 632b
Dāwūd b. Khalaf al-Ẓāhirī (884) i, 337a; ii, **182b**, 889b, 890a; v, 239b; vii, 570a
Dāwūd b. Ḳuṭb Shāh (Bohorā) (XVI) i, 1254b, 1255a; iv, 201a; ix, 824b
Dāwūd b. Maḥmūd b. Muḥammad b. Malik-Shāh (Saldjūḳ) (1131) i, 300b, vi, 64a, 500a, 782a
Dāwūd b. Marwān al-Raḳḳī → al-Muḳammiṣ
Dāwūd b. Rawḥ b. Ḥātim b. Ḳabīṣa b. al-Muhallab (VIII) vii, 360a
Dāwūd b. Suḳmān (Artuḳid) (XII) i, 664b 983b; iii, 507a
Dāwūd b. Sulaymān (Mikhlāf) (X) ii, 517a
Dāwūd b. Sulaymān (Kilwa) (1170) v, 106b, 1157b
Dāwūd b. Yazīd b. Ḥātim b. Ḳabīṣa b. al-Muhallab (820) vii, 360a, 694a
Dāwūd al-Anṭāḳī → al-Anṭāḳī
Dāwūd Atba, Ḥādjdj (XX) vi, 165b
Dāwūd Barakāt (XX) s, 159b
Dāwūd Burhān al-Dīn → Dāwūd b. Ḳuṭb Shāh
Dāwūd al-Faṭānī → Dāwūd b. ʿAbd Allāh
Dāwūd Khākī, Bābā (Čak) (XVI) s, 167b
Dāwūd Khān (Pasha) (1549) vii, 721a
Dāwūd Khān, Dāwūd Pasha (1851) i, 330b, 905b; ii, **184b**, 813a; iii, 1257b; s, 75a
Dāwūd Khān, Dāwūd Pasha (1875) ii, **184b**, 637a
Dāwūd Khān (Carnatic) (XVIII) i, 624b
Dāwūd Khān (Fārūḳī) (1508) ii, 814b
Dāwūd Khān (Rohilla) (1725) iii, 59b; viii, 426a, 572a, b
Dāwūd Khān b. Luarsab (al-Kurdjī) (XVI) v, 493a
Dāwūd Khān Ḳara, Dāwūd Pasha Ḳara (1623) ii, **183b**; vii, 707b
Dāwūd Khān Kararānī (1576) ii, **183a**; ii, 202b, 423b; vi, 342b
Dāwūd Khān Ḳodja, Dāwūd Pasha Ḳodja (1498) ii, **184a**; iv, 231a; vi, 3a, 72a
Dāwūd Khān Ḳurayshī (XVII) i, 1210a
Dāwūd Pasha al-Kurdjī (1816) vi, 797a
Dāwūd Khān, Nawwāb (Maḥmūdābād) vi, 77b
Dāwūd Pasha (mutaṣarrif) (1851) ii, **184b**
Dāwūd Pasha (1875) ii, **184b**
Dāwūd Pasha (1470) vi, 72a, 1025b
Dāwūd-Shāh Mengüček (XIII) iv, 817b, 871a

Dāwūd al-Ṭāʾī (781) i, 124a
Dāwūdis i, 552b, 1255a; ii, 98a; iv, 201b
Dāwūdiyya → Ẓāhiriyya
Dāwūdiyya, Banū (Masīla) vi, 728b
Dāwūdpōtrās i, 230a; ii, **185a**
al-Dawwānī (1501) i, 326b, 329a
Dāya → Rāzī, Nadjm al-Dīn
Ḍayʿa i, 1145b; ii, **187b**
Dayak s, 150b, 151a
Dayā Bahādur (1728) ii, 219a
Dayānat Khān (XVII) ii, 336b, 868b
al-Daybaʿ (1537) vii, 911b
Daybul (Sind) ii, **188a**; iii, 441a; iv, 597b; vi, 405b, 691a; vii, 71a, 405b; ix, 75b; s, 243a
Daydabān ii, **189a**
Ḍayf ii, **189a**; iii, 1018a
Ḍayfa Khātūn (Ayyūbid) (1242) iii, 87b; vii, 990a
Dayi̊ i, 368a; ii, **189a**
Dayi̊ Ḳarača Pasha (1456) viii, 10a
Dayla-rustāḳ vi, 511b, 513a
Daylam i, 20a; ii, **189b**, 732a, 1111a; iv, 19a, 345b, 346a, 1078a; vi, 120a, 433b, 744a; vii, 655b; viii, 586a, 807b; xi, 242, 539b; s, 297b, 298a, 299a, 363a
Daylamān s, 335a
al-Daylamī, Abu ʾl-Ḥasan (XI) iii, 823a
al-Daylamī, Abū Ṭāhir Ilyās (1069) s, 192b
al-Daylamī, Muhadhdhab al-Dīn ʿAlī (1244) vii, 479a
al-Daylamī, Muḥammad b. al-Ḥasan (1307) vi, 917b
Daylamī, Banū (Yemen) s, 22b
Daylamīs x, 897b
Daylamis i, 190a, 688a, 839b, 1350a, 1354a, 1355b; ii, **190a**, 506a, 1082b, 1111b; iii, 197a, 671b, 1201b; iv, 208a, 465a, 859a; vi, 115b, 499a; vii, 655b; s, 118b, 309a, 356b
al-Daymartī vi, 829a
Dayn s, **207a**
Dayr ii, **194b**
Dayr ʿAbd al-Raḥmān ii, **195b**
Dayr al-ʿĀḳūl ii, **196a**; vi, 728b; vii, 410b, 771a, 801b
Dayr al-Aʿwar ii, **196b**
Dayr al-Balaḥ vi, 31a
Dayr al-Djamādjim i, 42b; ii, **196b**, 304b; iv, 289a, 495a, b; v, 639b; vii, 408b
Dayr al-Djāthalīḳ ii, **197a**; vii, 408b, 650a
Dayr Kaʿb ii, **197b**
Dayr al-Ḳamar s, 159a, 160b
Dayr Ḳunnā ii, **197b**
Dayr Ḳurra ii, **197b**
Dayr Murrān ii, **198a**,b; vi, 599b
Dayr Mūsa ii, **198b**
Dayr al-Rummān ii, 198b
Dayr Samʿān ii, **198b**; iii, 130a
Dayr al-Suryānī (wādī al-Naṭrūn) i, 201a, 624a; ii, 195b
Dayr al-Zaʿfarān vi, 542a, b
Dayr al-Zōr ii, **198b**; iv, 655a
Dayrī, Banū v, 333a
Daysam b. Ibrāhīm al-Kurdī (X) i, 190a; ii, 680a; v, 451a; vii, 656a; x, 42b, 897b
Daysam b. Isḥāḳ (X) vii, 633a
Dayṣāniyya ii, **199a**; v, 384b
Dayyir vi, 384b
Dayzan → al-Ḥaḍr
al-Ḍayzan b. Djabhala iii, 51a
Dazā, Banū i, 1258a; s, 165a
Dead Sea → Baḥr Lūṭ
Dēbal → Daybul
Debaroa → Debārwā
Debārwā vi, 642a; viii, 235b
Debbeb, Fitawrāri (XIX) vi, 643a
Debdou → Dubdū
Deccan xi, 1a, 144a
Dedan (al-ʿUlā) i, 547b; v, 761b, 762a; vi, 88b
Dede ii, **199b**
Dede Aghač ii, **200a**
Dede Ḳorḳut i, 311a, 419b; ii, 75b, **200a**, 1109a; iii, 374a; viii, 163b
Dede Sulṭān i, 869b; ii, **200b**
Dede ʿUmar Sikkīnī (XV) iii, 43b
Defter → Daftar
Defter Emini ii, **201a**
Defterdār → Daftardār
Defterdār ʿAlī Pasha (1695) vii, 708a
Dehās ii, **201a**
Dehhānī, Khodja (XIII) ii, **201a**
Dehkān → Dihḳan
Dehkhudā, ʿAlī Akbar (1955) s, **207b**
Deir ez-Zor → Dayr al-Zōr
Deldoul s, 328b
Delhemma → Dhu ʾl-Himma
Delhi → Dihlī
Deli ii, **201a**
Deli Birader → Ghazālī, Meḥmed

Deli Ḥasan Pasha (XVII) ii, 208b; iv, 499a, 595a
Deli Muṣṭafā (Bostandjî) (XIX) i, 1278b
Deli-Orman ii, **202a**
Delvina ii, **203a**
Demak (1546) s, 150b, 199b, 201a, 202a
Demavend → Damāwand
Demesne → Ḍayʿa
Demetrius b. Sefer-beg (Abkhāz) (1822) i, 101a, 1132a
Demetrius Cantemir (Hospodar) → Ḳantimūr, Ḳantimīr
Demir → Kemal Tahir
Demir Baba (Bektāshī) ii, 202b
Demir Khān b. Ḳarāmān (1333) iv, 622a
Demir Khān b. Karasî (XIV) iv, 628a
Demir Kapî → Dar-i Āhanīn
Demirbash ii, **203b**
Demirdāsh Bāshā, ʿAbd al-Raḥmān Muṣṭafā (1929) s, 208b
Demirdāshiyya i, 1152a; iv, 991b; vi, 88a; s, **208a**
Demirel, Süleymān (XX) x, 695a
Demirtash → Timurtash
Demnat → Damnāt
Demokrat Parti ii, **204a**, 569a, 645a; iv, 124b; v, 264a, 1038b
Demokritos → Dīmuḳrāt
Demotika → Dimetoḳa
Denau (Āmū Dāryā) s, 281a
Dendi (Songhai) ii, 94a
Deneb → Nudjūm
Denia → Dāniya
Deñizli ii, **204a** v, 557a, 588b; vi, 420b; s, 44b, 138a
Denktaş, Rauf (XX) v, 308a, b, 1078a
Deoband ii, 55a, 132a, b, **205a**, 437a; v, 1135b; vi, 462a; x, 38bs, 66b, 74a, 292b, 293b
Deōgīri → Dawlatābād
Derʿa → Adhriʿāt
Dēra Fatḥ Khān ii, 205b; iii, 633b
Dēra Ghāzī Khān → Dēradjāt
Dēra Ismāʿīl Khān → Dēradjāt
Dēradjāt i, 1005b; ii, 185b, 186a, b, **205b**, 206a; iii, 633b; vi, 86a, b; viii, 253b; ix, 819b; s, 329b, 331b, 332a, 507b
Derbend (Bāb al-Abwāb) i, 32a, 835b, 921b, 1066b; ii, 85b, 87b, 88a, 115b, **206a**; iv, 342b, 344a, b, 346a, 348a, b; vi, 129b, 740a; vii, 572b
Derbouka → Darabukka
Derde Shay (Čad) (1939) s, 165a, b, 166b
Derdli, Ibrahim (1845) ii, **206b**
Derdli Kātib (Bektāshī) ii, 202b
Derebey i, 469a; ii, **206b**, 446b
Deren (Atlas) i, 748a
Dergāh → Dargāh
Derna → Darna
Dersim ii, **208a**
Derwīsh Ḥasan Pasha → Derwīsh Pasha (1603)
Derwīsh Meḥmed (1512) vi, 125a
Derwīsh Meḥmed Pasha (1655) ii, **209a**, 339a; iii, 1248a
Derwīsh Meḥmed Pasha (1777) ii, **209a**
Derwīsh Meḥmed Pasha (1837) i, 241a, 1078b; ii, **209b**
Derwīsh Meḥmed Ẓillī (1648) ii, 717b; v, 18a
Derwīsh Pasha (1603) i, 1271a; ii, **208a**
Derwīsh Pasha (1606) ii, **208b**, 287b; iv, 572b; v, 641a
Derwīsh Pasha (Kozan) (XIX) vii, 525a
Derwīsh Waḥdetī, ḥāfiẓ (XX) ii, 475a; iv, 283b
Destour ii, 639a; iii, 524a
Devagiri → Dawlatābād
Deval Devi (XIX) ii, 269a, 695a, 1124a; iv, 922a
Deve Boynu ii, **210a**
Devedji ii, **210b**
Develi Ḳara Ḥiṣār → Ḳara Ḥiṣār
Develū, Banū (Ḳādjār) iv, 389a; vi, 483b
Devkoṭ ii, 297a
Devshirme i, 36a, 206b, 268b, 269b, 656b, 712a, 807a, 999b; ii, **210b**, 1086a, 1087a; s, 269b
Dēwal → Daybul
Dewal Dewi → Deval Devi
Dewlet → Dawlat
Dewlet-berdi (Girāy) (XV) iii, 44a
Dey → Dayî
Deymer → Hüsnü, Shefīḳ
Dghughī → Sīdī Abu ’l-Ḥasan ʿAlī b. Ḥamdūsh
Dghughiyyīn s, 350b
al-Dhabḥānī, Muḥammad b. Saʿīd (1470) iv, 449b
Dhabīḥ Bihrūz (1971) vi, 764a
Dhabīḥa ii, **213a**; s, 221b
Dhafār → Ẓafār, Ẓufār

Dhahab ii, **214a**, 1002a, 1003a; v, 964a, 965b, 967a, 970a, 977a
al-Dhahabī → Aḥmad al-Dhahabī; Aḥmad al- Manṣūr
al-Dhahabī, Shams al-Dīn Abū ʿAbd Allāh (1348) i, 70a, 74b, 594b, 595a, 965a, 1238b; ii, 125b, **214b**, 522b, 523a; iii, 756a, 954b; vi, 349b, 350a, 352b, 353a; vii, 212b, 537b, 576b; viii, 458b, 517a; s, 225b, 311b, 386b, 400a
al-Dhahabī, Shaykh (1977) vii, 291b
Dhahabiyya → Kubrāwiyya
Dhahirah → al-Ẓāhira (Oman)
al-Dhahr → al-Ẓahr
Dhahran → Ẓahrān
Dhākā (Dacca) ii, 7a, **216a**, 426a; vi, 369b, 806a
Dhākir, Kāṣim Bey (1857) i, 193b; ii, **217a**
Dhakwān b. ʿAmr al-Fuḳaymī → al-Fuḳaymī, Dhakwān b. ʿAmr
Dhāl ii, **217b**
Dhala → Ḍāliʿ
Dhalūl i, 541a
Dhamār ii, **218a**; vi, 433b, 436a; s, 335a
Dhamarʿalī Yuhabirr (IV) vi, 563b
al-Dhammiyya ii, **218a**, 570a
Dhanab → Nudjūm
Dhāndā (river) vi, 49b
Dhār ii, **218b**, 276b, 1124a; iii, 446a; vi, 309b; s, 105a
Dharr b. ʿAbd Allāh (VII) vii, 605b
Dharra ii, **219b**
Dhārūr (district) vi, 269a
Dharwān b. Thaʿlaba, Banū ix, 817a
Dhārwār ii, **220a**
Dhāt ii, **220a**; v, 1261a, 1262a
Dhāt al-Himma → Dhu 'l-Himma
Dhāt al-Ṣawārī (naval battle) (655) i, 51b, 936a; vii, 155a; ix, 444b; s, 120b, **221b**
Dhātī (1564) i, 956a; ii, **220b**, 737b; iv, 1137b
Dhawḳ ii, **221a**, 1041a
Dhawḳ, Muḥammad (1854) i, 807b, 914b, 1116a; ii, 83b, 84a, **221b**; iii, 1095a; iv, 716b; v, 960a, b, 961b; s, 107a
Dhawū ʿAbd Allāh iii, 263a
Dhawū Barakāt (Makka) iii, 263a; vi, 150a, b
Dhawū Ḥassān, Banū vi, 141b, 741a
Dhawū Manṣūr, Banū vi, 141b, 142b, 143a
Dhawū Masʿūd (Makka) vi, 150b
Dhawū ʿUbayd Allāh, Banū vi, 141b
Dhawū Zayd (Makka) iii, 263a; vi, 150a, b, 151a
Dhawwāḳ → Čāshna-gīr
al-Dhiʾāb ii, **222b**; iv, 79a
Dhiʾb ii, **223a**
Dhiʾb, Banū ix, 84a
Dhihnī, Bayburtlu (1859) ii, **223b**
Dhikr i, 346b; ii, 55b, 160a, 164b, **223b**, 891b; iii, 1051a; iv, 94b, 487b, 992b; s, 313a
Dhikrīs (Zikrīs) v, 1230b; s, **222a**
Dhimār → Dhamār
Dhimma i, 429b, 811a; ii, **227a**; iv, 1146b
Dhimma (capacity) ii, **231a**
Dhimmī → Ahl al-Dhimma
Dhira i, 98b
Dhirāʿ ii, **231b**
Dhiyāb b. Bādi (Ḳerrī) (XVIII) iv, 893a
Dhofar → Ẓafār (Oman)
Dhū Bīn s, 22a
Dhū, dhī, dhā i, 194b, 195a; ii, **232b**
Dhu 'l-Aktāf → Shāpūr II
Dhū-Amīr vi, 563b
Dhū Awān vi, 647a
Dhū Djadan (Ḥimyar) vi, 829b; viii, 980a
Dhū Djibla ix, 1b
Dhu 'l-Faḳār (sword) i, 742a; ii, **233a**; vi, 528a, 537a
Dhu 'l-Faḳār al-Kurdī (XVI) i, 903b; iii, 1257a
Dhu 'l-Faḳār Alī Khān b. Raḥmat Khān (XVIII) iii, 61b
Dhu 'l-Faḳār Bahādur (XIX) i, 1012b
Dhu 'l-Faḳār Bey (XVIII) ii, 233b
Dhu 'l-Faḳāriyya ii, **233a**; iv, 723a, 852a; vi, 325a, b
Dhu 'l-Fiḳār ʿAlī Bhutto → Bhutto, Zulfiqar Ali
Dhu 'l-Fiḳār Khān (Abdālī) (XVIII) i, 295b, 1025b; ii, 379a, 810a
Dhū Ḥazfar, Banū (Mārib) vi, 561b
Dhu 'l-Ḥidjdja → Taʾrīkh
Dhu 'l-Himma i, 1102b, 1103b, 1104a; ii, **233b**
Dhū Ḥiwāl, Banū xi, 342a
Dhū Ḥusā, Day of s, 178a
Dhū Ḥusayn vi, 566a
Dhu 'l-Ḳaʿda → Taʾrīkh
Dhu 'l-Ḳadr (Turkmen) i, 468a, b, 1190b; ii, 8a, **239a**, 724b; iii, 1105a; iv, 553a,

562b, 843a; vi, 231b, 324b, 507b, 508b; vii, 271b, 645a; ix, 129a
Dhū Ḳār i, 690a, 964a; ii, **241a**; iv, 289a; v, 634a; viii, 120a
Dhū Ḳarad vii, 371a
Dhu 'l-Ḳarnayn → Iskandar
Dhu 'l-Ḳarnayn b. ʿAyn al-Dawla (1162) ii, 111a
Dhu 'l-Ḳaṣṣa (battle) x, 162a
Dhu 'l-Khalaṣa i, 865b; ii, **241b**; iv, 1106a
Dhu 'l-Khimār → al-Aswad b. Kaʿb al-ʿAnsī
Dhu 'l-Kifl (Ayyūb) (Prophet) i, 404b; ii, **242a**; vi, 652b; x, 542b
Dhū l-Madjāz (Makka) x, 90a, 789a
Dhū Marmar iv, 201a
Dhu 'l-Marwa v, 316b
Dhū Matāra vi, 473a
Dhū Muḥammad (Mārib) vi, 566a
Dhu 'l-Nūn (Dānishmendid) (1173) ii, 111a; vi, 507a; viii, 132a
Dhu 'l-Nūn, Abu 'l-Fayḍ al-Miṣrī (861) i, 274a, 718a; ii, **242a**; iii, 83b; iv, 990a; vi, 354a, 570a; viii, 892a
Dhu 'l-Nūn Ayyūb al-ʿIrāḳī vi, 91a
Dhu 'l-Nūn Beg Arghūn (1507) i, 627b; iv, 536b; v, 579b
Dhu 'l-Nūnids i, 7a, 202b; ii, **242b**; v, 392a; vii, 778b
Dhū Nuwās, Yūsuf Ashʿar (VI) i, 549a, 692b; ii, **243b**; v, 120b, 776b; vi, 829b; vii, 872a; s, 229b
Dhū Raydān i, 548a, b; vi, 561a
Dhu 'l-Riyāsatayn iv, 51b
Dhu 'l-Ruḳayba v, 526a
Dhu 'l-Rumma (735) i, 586b; ii, 92b, **245a**; vii, 403b, 536b, 981b; viii, 377b; s, 42b
Dhu 'l-Shanātir (ʿUmān) vii, 551a
Dhu 'l-Sharā ii, **246a**; iv, 321b; v, 1156b
Dhu 'l-Tādj Laḳīṭ b. Mālik al-Azdī s, 693b
Dhū ʿUthkulān vi, 830b
Dhū Yazan → Sayf
Dhuʾayb b. Mūsā (1151) iii, 134a; iv, 200b
Dhubāb ii, **247b**
Dhūbān, Shaykh s, 263a
Dhubyān, Banū ii, 71b, 873b, 1023a; vii, 841a; s, 177a, 178a
Dhūdhū Miyān b. Ḥādjdjī Sharīʿat Allāh (1860) vii, 291a
Dhufār → Ẓufār
Dhuhl, Banū vi, 333a, 649a
Dhuhl b. Thaʿlaba i, 963a
al-Dhulayḥ viii, 377a
Dhunnūnids → Dhu 'l-Nūnids
al-Dhunūb, Dafn ii, **248a**, 303b ; iv, 407a
Dhurr → Ḳamḥ
Diāgha (Mali) vi, 258b
Ḍībāb → ʿĀmir b. Ṣaʿṣaʿa
Dībādj → Ḳumāsh
Dībādj b. Filshāh (Gīlān) (1300) vi, 907b
al-Dībadjāt → Maldives
Dibbiyya s, 159a, b, 161b, 162a
al-Dibdiba ii, **248b**
Diʿbil (860) i, 154a, 1290a; ii, **248b**; iv, 929a; v, 375a; vi, 604a, b, 625b; vii, 694b; viii, 83a; s, 32b, 35b
Dibir, ḳāḍī (1827) i, 756a
al-Dibsī → Yaʿḳūb
Ḍīdān b. Fahhād → Ibn Ḥithlayn
Ḍidd i, 184b; ii, **249a**
Dīdebān → Daydabān
Didja al-ʿAwrāʾ → Shaṭṭ al-ʿArab
Didjla i, 184a, 191a, 634b, 1094b, 1095a, b; ii, **249a**; iii, 1251a; iv, 654a, 675a; v, 442a, 645b, 646b, 864b, 945a; s, 37a
Dido i, 756a; ii, 86b, 88b, **251a**; iv, 344b, 571b; v, 55b
Dienné (Sudān) i, 303a; ii, **251b**; vi, 258b, 259a
Difrīgī → Diwrīgī
Diglal ii, **252b**
Digurata → Ossetes
Dihātī → Muḥammad Masʿūd
Dihgāns i, 224a, b
Dih-i Khwāraḳān vi, 502 a, b
Dih-i Naw → Djand
Dihistān ii, **253a**; vi, 415b, 493b, 717a; s, 299a
al-Dihistānī, ʿAbd al-Djalīl, vizier (XI) i, 1052b
Dihḳan ii, **253b**; v, 853a, 854a
Dihkhudā, ʿAlī Akbar (XX) iv, 71a, 527a
al-Dihlawī, ʿAbd al-Ḥaḳḳ → ʿAbd al-Ḥaḳḳ b. Sayf al-Dīn
al-Dihlawī, Aḥmad Ḥasan (XIV) s, 409a
al-Dihlawī, Nūr al-Ḥaḳḳ → Nūr al-Ḥaḳḳ al- Dihlawī
al-Dihlawī, Ghulām ʿAlī (1824) vii, 936b
al-Dihlawī, Shāh ʿAbd al-ʿAzīz (1824) → ʿAbd al-ʿAzīz al-Dihlawī
al-Dihlawī, Shāh Walī Allāh (1762) i, 297b, 593a, 937a; ii, 138a, 205b, **254a**,

437a; iii, 324a, 358b, 430b, 432b, 435a, b; v, 833a; vii, 290b, 316a, 328a, 938b; s, 126b, 292b
al-Dihlawī, Shaykh ʿAbd Allāh (XX) vi, 164b
al-Dihlawī, Shaykh ʿAbd al-Ḥaḳḳ → ʿAbd al-Ḥaḳḳ Sayf al-Dīn
Dihlī ii, 205a, **255b**; iii, 420a; v, 883b, 1135a; vi, 48b, 49a, 50a, 53a, 61b, 65b, 126a, 270b, 273a, 294b, 309a, b, 369b, 406b, 535b, 537a, 602a, 650a, 658b, 664b; vii, 314a, 854b; x, 593b; s, 57b, 66b, 74a, 102a, 247a, 353a, b, 385b
– history i, 230a, 914a, 953b; ii, **255-9**; v, 6a
– monuments i, 1321b, 1324a, 1348a; ii, 254a, **259-66**; iii, 287b, 441a, 442a, b, 443a, 449a; iv, 268b; v, 1214b, 1219b
Dihlī Sultanate i, 34a, 1036a, 1321b; ii, 153b, **266b**, 336a, 1124a; iii, 198b, 201a, 416a, 417a, 420a; iv, 218a, 759a; v, 598a, 685a, 1214b; vi, 368a, 488a; vii, 193b; viii, 67b; ix, 785b; s, 117b, 124a, 203a, 206a, b, 258a, 284b, 359b, 409a
– art ii, **274a**
Dihm, Banū vi, 474b
Dihram vi, 384b
Dihwārs i, 224a
Diḥya b. Khalīfa al-Kalbī (670) ii, **274b**, 363b, 846a; iv, 492b, 839a; vii, 212a
Diḥya b. Musʿab (Miṣr) (VIII) vii, 160b
Dīk ii, **275a**
Dīk al-Djinn al-Ḥimṣī (849) ii, **275b**; ix, 453b
al-Dīkdān s, **222b**
al-Dikdikidjī (1775) vi, 215a
Dikka ii, **276a**
Dikwa (Bornū) i, 1259b, 1260a, b; ii, 10b
Dil Hersek iii, 341b
al-Dilāʾ v, 1191b; vi, 356b, 607a; s, 29a, **223a**
al-Dilāʾī, Muḥammad b. Abī Bakr (1636) vi, 112b; s, 223a
al-Dilāʾī, Muḥammad al-Masnāwī (1724) vi, 112b, 350a
al-Dilāʾī, Muḥammad b. Maḥammad b. Abī Bakr al-Murābiṭ (1678) s, 223b
Dilāʾiyyūn s, 223a
Ḍilāl bint Lamak vii, 190a
al-Dilam iv, 1072b, 1073a
Dilāwar Khān (Ḥabshī) (1492) iii, 15a
Dilāwar Khān (Ḥabshī) (1588) ii, 921b, 922a; iii, 15b, 426b
Dilāwar Khān Ghūrī (Mālwā) (1405) ii, 218b, 219a, 270b, **276a**, 1125a; iii, 417a, 638a; vi, 52b, 309b, 406b, 407b
Dilāwar Khān Lōdī (XVI) iii, 995b; iv, 1020a
Dilāwar Pasha (1622) ii, **276b**
Dilāzāk, Banū i, 218b
Dildār ʿAlī (1819) iii, 434a
Dilpasand Khān (1486) vi, 63a
Dilras Bān, Begum (1657) vi, 131b
Dilshād Khātūn (1352) i, 908b; ii, 68a; viii, 997b
Dilsiz ii, **277a**
Dimashḳ i, 153b, 256a, 551b, 824a, 870a, 975a, b, 1029a, b, 1332a; ii, **277b**, 360a, 541a, 1105a, 1106a; iii, 714a, 931b, 958a; iv, 174b, 214b; v, 993a; vi, 44b, 68b, 118b, 122b, 198a, 266b, 362b, 363b, 455a, 471a, 545a, 648a, 649b, 652a, 653a, 656b, 657a, 666b, 668a, 680b, 681a, 871b; viii, 128a,b, 728b; ix, 792b; s, 20b, 37a, 49a, 195a, b, 199a, 239a, 268a
– the Great Mosque i, 610b, 622a; ii, 280b, 281a, 282a, b, 286a, 956a, b; iii, 286b, 921a
– institutions i, 1224a; ii, 283a, b, 286a, 288a, b, 289a, 290a, 424a; iii, 139b; v, 1127a
– monuments i, 831a, 1316a; ii, 280b, 283a, 284b, 285a, 286a, 287b, 1106a; iii, 142a; v, 217b, 1139a, 1140a
Dimashḳ Khodja b. Sālim (1404) ii, 614a
Dimashḳ Khʷādja (Čūbānid) (1327) ii, **68a**
al-Dimashḳī → Abū ʿUthmān; Ibn Isrāʿīl; Saʿīd b. Yaʿḳūb; Shams al-Dīn Muḥammad
al-Dimashḳī, Shams al-Dīn (1327) i, 594b; ii, **291a**; iv, 1081b; v, 1012b; vi, 111b; s, 45a, 130b
al-Dimashḳī Sharīf ʿIzz al-Dīn (1315) viii, 156b
Dimdim vi, 502b
Dimetoḳa (Dimotiḳa) ii, **291b**; vi, 290b
Dimlī → Zāzā
Dīmuḳrāt s, 154b
Dimurdāsh b. Djūbān → Tīmūrtāsh b. Čūbān
Dimyāṭ i, 946b; ii, 63b, 72b, **292a**; iv, 520b; v, 92a; vi, 440a, b, 547b; vii, 69b; s, 120b

al-Dimyāṭī ʿAbd al-Muʾmin al-Shāfiʿī (1306) ii, **292b**; vi, 183b
al-Dimyāṭī, al-Bannāʾ (1705) ii, **293a**
al-Dimyāṭī, Nūr al-Dīn (XIII) ii, **293a**
Dīn ii, **293b**; iv, 171b, 174a; v, 621b, 622b, 623a, b, 629a
Dīnādjpur ii, **297a**
Dīnār ii, 120b, **297a**, 768b; v, 964a, 965b
Dīnār, Malik (Oghuz) (1195) ii, **299a**, 1109a; iii, 1099b; v, 160b; viii, 946b; ix, 34b
Dīnawar ii, **299a**; iv, 13b; v, 169b; vi, 493a, 502a, 539a; s, 17b
al-Dīnawarī, Abū Bakr (1014) vi, 671b
al-Dīnawarī, Abū Ḥanīfa Aḥmad (895) i, 135b, 213a, b, 718b; ii, **300a**; v, 1025a; vii, 83b, 831b; s, 42b, 128b, 249b, 277a, 314a
al-Dīnawarī, Abū Saʿīd Naṣr b. Yaʿḳūb (1009) ii, **300b**; iii, 772a; viii, 646a, b; s, 259a
al-Dīnawarī al-Miṣrī (922) vi, 353a
Dīnāwariyya xi, 511b
Dindān ii, **301a**
Dinet, Alphonse s, **224a**
Dīn-i Ilāhī (1581) i, 317a; ii, **296a**; iii, 423b, 459a; vi, 131a
Dionysos → Dhu ʾl-Sharā
Dioula ii, 63a; v, 252b
Dioscorides → Diyusḳuridīs
Diplomatic ii, **301b**
Dīpalpūr vi, 49a, b, 50a, 62a, 294a
Diponegara, Pangeran (Yogyakarta) (1855) s, 608a
Dīr (Morocco) s, 132a
Dīr (Pakistan) i, 864a; ii, 30b, **316b**
Dir → Somali
Dirač → Drac
Ḍirār b. ʿAmr al-Ghaṭafānī al-Kūfī (815) i, 333b; iii, 1037a, 1143a, 1166a; iv, 692b; vi, 458a; vii, 54b, 259a, 260a, 546b, 566a, 784b; s, 88b, 89a, **225b**
Ḍirār b. Ḥusayn (VIII) ii, 72a
Ḍirār b. al-Azwar al-Asadī (833) vi, 268a
Ḍirār b. al-khaṭṭāb (633) ii, **317b**; iii, 975b; iv, 775a; vi, 603b; ix, 864b
Dire Dawa ii, **317b**
Ḍirghām b. ʿĀmir, Abu ʾl-Ashbāl (1164) i, 197a; ii, **317b**, 856b; viii, 130b, 831b
Dirham ii, 119a, 121a, **319a**, 991b; iii, 1116a; iv, 248b; v, 855a, 964a, 965b
Dirham b. Naṣr b. Ṣāliḥ (VII) iv, 20b; viii, 795b
al-Dirʿiyya i, 628b; ii, 159b, **320b**; iii, 678b; iv, 925a, b, 1072b; v, 508a; vi, 150b; vii, 410a; ix, 903b; s, 30b
Dirlik ii, **322a**
Diū ii, **322a**; vi, 51a, 52a, 233b, 270a
Divehi Rājjē → Maldives
Divine Scripture → Zabūr
Divittār → Dawādār
Dīw ii, **322b**, 1125a, 1128a, b; iv, 332a; vi, 938b
Dīw Sulṭān Rūmlū (XVI) v, 492b; x, 108b, 137a
Dīwān (administration) i, 19b, 279b, 316b, 382a, 729a, b, 801b, 905b, 1003b, 1141b, 1143a, 1145b; ii, 304b, 305b, **323a**, 360a, 505b;iv, 26a, 937b; v, 500b; s, 210a
Dīwān (collection) i, 143b, 1070a; ii, **323a**, 999b
Dīwān-Begi s, 97a, **227b**
Dīwān-i Humāyūn ii, **337b**
Dīwān Sāwan Mal (XIX) s, 332a
Dīwān al-Shūrā → Madjlis al-Shūrā
Dīwān Shurfā Khān (1638) vi, 190b
Dīwāna → Muẓaffar Shāh Shams al-Dīn Ḥabshī
Dīwāna Maḥmūd Čelebi (XVI) vi, 887b
Dīwānī i, 1145b; ii, 128a, 332b; iv, 1125b, 1127b
Dīwāniyya ii, **339b**
Dīwdād → Abu ʾl-Sādj
Diwrīgī ii, **340a**
Diwrīghī, Fakhr al-Dīn Muḥammad al-Salghūr (1236) viii, 1005b
Diwrigli-zāde Shams al-Dīn Muʾayyad Čelebi (1447) vii, 272a
Ḍiyāʿ → Ḍayʿa
Diya i, 29a, 31b, 171b, 338a, 892a; ii, 228a, **340b**; iv, 766b; v, 180a
Ḍiyā al-Dīn (Marand) vi, 504a
Ḍiyā al-Dīn, Sayyid (XX) iv, 398b
Ḍiyā al-Dīn b. al-Athīr → Ibn al-Athīr
Ḍiyāʾ al-Dīn Abū Muḥammad Saʿīd b. Asʿad (XII) vi, 558a
Ḍiyāʾ al-Dīn Muḥammad → ʿAlāʾ al-Dīn Muḥammad
Ḍiyāʾ al-Dīn Yūsuf (1513) vii, 935a
Ḍiyāʾ al-Dīn Yūsuf b. Muʿīn al-Dīn Djāmī (1394) viii, 749b

Ḍiyā Gökalp → Gökalp, Ziya
Ḍiyā al-Ḥaḳḳ → Zia ul-Haqq
Ḍiyā' al-Mulk b. Niẓām al-Mulk (XI) viii, 72b
Ḍiyā Pasha → Ẓiyā Pasha
Ḍiyā' al-Salṭana (XIX) vi, 484a
Diyālā (river) i, 184a; ii, **343a**; v, 442a; vi, 335b, 614a, 616a; vii, 912b
Diyānat → Dayānat
Diyār Bakr i, 4b, 8a, 639a, 662b, 664a, 665b, 666a, 1054a; ii, 8a, **343b**, 384b, 523b, 707a; iii, 1197b; iv, 90b, 816b; v, 453a, 457b; vi, 3a, 242b, 270b, 341b, 366a, 420b, 539b, 541a, b, 626a, b, 627a, 633a, 667a; vii, 1017a; viii, 53b, 133a; s, 36b, 37a, 63a, 250a, 266b
Diyār Muḍar i, 11a, 119b, 804a; ii, **347a**, 523b; vi, 379b, 380b
Diyār Rabī'a ii, 344a, **348a**, 523b; vi, 379b, 539b, 540b, 781a; s, 37a
al-Diyārbakrī, Ḥusayn (1582) ii, **349a**
Diyusḳuridīs i, 3a, 213a, b; ii, **349a**; iii, 147b, 259a, 737b, 928a; iv, 254b; s, 43a, 59b, 78a, 114b
Diz (river) v, 81a, 887a
Diza (castle) vi, 505a, 618a
Dizai (Kurds) ii, 571a; v, 471b, 473b
Dizfūl ii, **350a**; iv, 7b, 675a; v, 830a; 867b; vi, 494b; vii, 673a; s, 75a, b
Diz-gāh vi, 384b
Dizi-i Pisar-i 'Umāra → al-Dīkdān
Diz-i Siyāh v, 63a, 828a, 831b
Dizmār iv, 1044a, b
Dja'āfira, Banū viii, 863b
al-Dja'alī, Muḥammad (XVI) v, 267a
Dja'aliyyūn ii, **351a**, 944b; v, 1248b; s, 164a
Djabā → Bennāk
Djaba → Djebe
Djāba (Chamba) ii, **352a**
Djabaev → Djambul Djabaev
al-Djabal → al-Djibāl
Djabal Abān al-Aḥmar (Arabia) viii, 613a
Djabal Abān al-Asmar viii, 613a
al-Djabal al-Aḥmar (Cairo) iv, 425b; vii, 509a
Djabal al-Akhḍar i, 207b, 1048b, 1049a; v, 759b, 760a; viii, 566a, b; ix, 774b
Djabal 'Āmil vi, 550a; vii, 301b, 407b
Djabal 'Āmila i, 436a; iv, 484a
Djabal 'Ammāriyya vii, 865a
Djabal 'Amūr i, **460a**; iv, 481b; s, 144b
Djabal Anṣāriyya vi, 577b, 578b, 789a
Djabal Aswad vi, 546a, 547a
Djabal 'Awf i, 208a
Djabal 'Aybān ix, 1a
Djabal Babor i, 749b; iv, 359a, 360b
Djabal Baḥrā vi, 578b, 579a; vii, 117b
Djabal Balaḳ al-Awsaṭ vi, 562b, 563a
Djabal Balaḳ al-Ḳiblī vi, 562b
Djabal-i Barakāt → Yarpūz
Djabal Bāriz v, 148a, 153b; s, **127a**
Djabal Bishrī vi, 378a
Djabal Dana Tagh vi, 382a
Djabal Daran → Atlas
Djabal Dhukhār vi, 439a
Djabal Djawshīn vii, 119a
Djabal Djūdī → Djūdī, Djabal
Djabal al-Dukhkhān vi, 358a
Djabal Ḍulā' iv, 779b
Djabal Durūd vi, 170a
Djabal al-Durūz vi, 31a, 1034b
Djabal Fāruh vi, 220b
Djabal Gillīz vi, 589a, 591a, 592a, b, 593a, 594b, 596b
Djabal al-Ḥadīd vi, 591a
Djabal Ḥadjar viii, 436a,b
Djabal Ḥamrīn i, 184a; iii, **149a**; s, 100a
Djabal al-Ḥārith → Aghridāgh; Djudī
Djabal Hindi vi, 155a
Djabal Kabkāb vi, 179b
Djabal Ḳalamūn vi, 308a
Djabal al-Ḳarāni' x, 392a
Djabal Ḳāsiyūn → Ḳāsiyūn, Djabal
Djabal al-Ḳilāl i, 935b
Djabal al-Lukkām vi, 774b, 778b, 791a
Djabal Ma'ādid vi, 435a
Djabal Madhrūb vi, 729a
Djabal Masār s, 22a
Djabal Maswar vi, 436a, 438b, 439a
Djabal Mūsā s, 124b
Djabal Nafūsa i, 139a, 1186a; ii, 369a, 441b; iii, 657b, 927b; iv, 78a, 919b; vi, 311a, 312a, 452b, 453a; vii, **894b**; ix, 289b
Djabal Nuḳum ix, 1a
Djabal al-Nūr vi, 154b, 168b
Djabal al-Raḥma i, 604a; iii, 35b; vi, 168b, 169b
Djabal Ramm i, 169b
Djabal Rayyo i, 489a
Djabal Ṣabir vi, 474b; x, 118a
Djabal Sablān vi, 494a

Djabal Saʿd (Makka) vi, 179b
Djabal Ṣāfir vi, 566a
Djabal Salmā vii, 865a
Djabal Samaʿān vi, 382b
Djabal Sarāt x, 3a
Djabal Says s, 117a, b, **228b**
Djabal Shammar i, 536b; iii, 326b; ix, 290a; s, 3b, 304b, 407b
Djabal al-Sikkīn → Djabal al-Lukkām
Djabal Sindjār viii, 147a
Djabal al-Sirādj ii, 817b
Djabal al-Summāḳ iv, 200a; vii, 117b
Djabal Taḳarbūst iv, 478b, 479a, b
Djabal Ṭāriḳ i, 79b, 124b, 439a; ii, **352b**
Djabal al-Ṭayr i, 535b
Djabal Tays vi, 436a, 438b
Djabal Thabīr → Thabīr, Djabal
Djabal Thawr iii, 760a; vi, 168b, 579b
Djabal Timatrīn vii, 611a
Djabal Titteri ix, 18a
Djabal Tukhlā vi, 438b
Djabal Ṭūr → Ṭūr ʿAbdīn
Djabal Ṭuwayḳ → Ṭuwayḳ
Djabal Yashkur (Cairo) vii, 147b, 510a
Djabal al-Zallādj vi, 355a
Djabal Zarhūn vi, 889a; s, 53a, 350b
Djabala (Nadjd) ii, **353b**; iii, 49a; v, 526a, 640a, b
Djabala (Syria) ii, **353a**; vi, 577b, 578a, 579b, 582a
Djabala b. al-Ayham (VII) i, 1339a; ii, 24b, **354a**; iv, 820b
Djabala b. al-Ḥārith (VI) iv, 556b; s, **229b**
al-Djabanyānī (979) vi, 354a
Djaʿbar, Ḳalʿat ii, **354a**; vi, 378a, 381b; vii, 118b
Djaʿbar b. Sābiḳ (XI) ii, 354b
Djabarites → Djabrids
Djābarkā xi, 223b
Djabart (Djabara) i, 763b; ii, **355a**, 709a, 710a; iii, 5a, b; v, 522a
al-Djabartī, ʿAbd al-Raḥmān (1825) i, 707a, 819b; ii, 109b, **355a**; vi, 87b, 316b, 327a, 543a; s, 38b, 302a
Djabarūt → ʿĀlam
Djabbāna v, 23a, 347a
Djabbānat al-Sabīʿ vii, 523a
al-Djabbār → Nudjūm
Djabbār b. Djazʾ viii, 377a
Djabbāra i, 942b; iv, 9b
Djabbāriyya, Banū vi, 614a
Djabbārlu vi, 201b
Djabbul ii, **357a**; viii, 131a
al-Djabbūl i, 1349a; ii, **357a**; iii, 85a; viii, 131a
Djabbūya → Yabghu
Djābir III (Āl Ṣabāḥ) (XX) viii, 669a
Djābir, Banū vi, 741b; s, 356a
Djābir b. ʿAbd Allāh al-Anṣārī (697) vii, 398a, 757b; s, 75a, 94a, **230a**
Djābir b. Aṭaḥ (Geber) (XII) i, 1250a; ii, **357a**; viii, 102a; x, 940b; s, 413b
Djābir b. Ḥayyān (VIII) i, 131b, 235b, 247a, 995a, 1100b, 1156a; ii, 357a, **357b**, 370b, 375a, 949b; iii, 267a, 378a; v, 112a, 113a; vi, 204a; vii, 558a, 833b; viii, 52b; s, 270a
Djābir b. Ḥunayy vii, 307b
Djābir b. Malik b. Labīd (IX) vii, 633a
Djābir b. Zayd (711) ii, **359b**; iii, 648b, 649a, b, 652a
Djābir al-Djuʿfī (745) vii, 348a, 399a; ix, 492a; s, **232b**
al-Djābiya ii, 280a, **360a**; vi, 544a, 545a, 546b, 622a, b; s, 117a, 229b
Djabr i, 371b; ii, 365a, 388b; s, **233a**
al-Djabr wa ʾl-Muḳābala ii, **360b**; iv, 1070a
Djabr b. ʿAtīḳ (VII) vii, 32b
Djabr b. al-Ḳāsim (X) ii, **362b**
Djabrāʾīl/Djibrīl ii, **362b**, 846a, 847a; v, 210a; vi, 217a, 219b, 629a, 675a; s, 231a
Djabrāʾīl b. Bukhtīshūʿ (827) i, 1223a, 1298a
Djabrāʾīl b. Yaḥyā → Djibrāʾīl b. Yaḥyā
Djabrān Khālīl Djabrān (1931) i, 597a; ii, **364a**, 404a, 471b; v, 188b, 1254b, 1255a, b, 1256b; vi, 75b, 91a; vii, 902a; viii, 88a
Djabrī Saʿdallāh → Saʿd Allāh Djabrī
Djabrids i, 942b; ii, 176a; iv, 764b; x, 913b; s, **234a**
Djabriyya i, 249b, 257b; ii, **365a**; iii, 1142b; iv, 271b
Djabuk (Türkmen) (1113) i, 983a
al-Djābiya xi, 291a
Djaʿd b. Dirham → Ibn Dirham
Djaʿda (ʿĀmir), Banū i, 233b, 446a; ii, **365a**; iv, 745b
Djaʿda b. Kaʿb → ʿĀmir b. Ṣaʿṣaʿa
Djadd, Banū ʾl- iii, 748a

al-Djadd b. Ḳays s, 131a
Djaddāla (Gudāla), Banū vii, 584a
Djadhīma b. ʿĀmir, Banū ii, **365b**; vi, 268b, 649a; s, 189b
Djadhīma b. ʿAwf, Banū iv, 764a
Djadhīma al-Abrash (al-Waḍḍāḥ) (III) i, 14a, 196b, 450b; ii, **365b**; iv, 820a; vii, 850a; x, 191a; s, 272a
al-Djaʿdī → Marwān II (Umayyad)
al-Djaʿdī (1190) ix, 187b
Djadīd ii, **366a**, 932b; iv, 792a, 848a; viii, 753a
Djadīda → Manzil Bashshū
al-Djadīda (Morocco) i, 56a, 85a, 291a, 356b, 809b; ii, **366b**; vi, 755b
Djadīdism s, 467a
Djadīs → Ṭasm
Djādisiyya → al-Ḳādisiyya
Djādjarm s, 83a, **235a**
al-Djādjarmī, Badr al-Dīn b. ʿUmar (1287) s, **235b**
al-Djādjarmī, Muḥammad b. Badr (XIV) vii, 529b; s, **235b**
Djadjnagar (Orissa) vi, 48a, 67a
Djādū ii, **368a**; s, 15b
Djādū (Tripolitania) ii, **368b**
Djadwal ii, **370a**
al-Djady → Nudjūm
Djāf, Banū i, 512b; ii, **370b**, 481a
Djaʿfar (Ḳarmaṭī) (X) iv, 663b
Djaʿfar, Banū i, 441b, 442a; v, 489b; vii, 186a
Djaʿfar b. ʿAbd Allāh (X) i, 1306b, 1307b
Djaʿfar b. ʿAbd al-Raḥmān (X) v, 1009b
Djaʿfar b. Abī Ṭālib (629) i, 109b, 118b, 152b; ii, **372a**; iii, 1266a; v, 398b; vi, 141b, 350b; vii, 372b, 374b, 393a, 756b, 862b; s, 92b
Djaʿfar b. Abī Yaḥyā, Shams al-Dīn Abu ’l-Faḍl (1177) s, **236a**
Djaʿfar b. ʿAlī b. Ḥamdūn al-Andalusī (982) i, 1044b, 1238a, 1309a; ii, **372b**; iii, 1042b; v, 1176a, b, 1177a; vi, 727b, 728a, 1038a; vii, 487a
Djaʿfar b. ʿAlī (Tiṭīs) (XI) iv, 346b, 347b; v, 489a, b
Djaʿfar b. al-Faḍl (IX) vi, 106a
Djaʿfar b. al-Faḍl b. al-Furāt → Ibn al-Furāt, Djaʿfar
Djaʿfar b. Fahardjis (IX) v, 451b
Djaʿfar b. Falāḥ al-Kutāmī (X) vii, 488a
Djaʿfar b. al-Hādī (IX) s, 116b
Djaʿfar b. Ḥarb (X) vii, 312a
Djaʿfar b. Ḥarb al-Hamadhānī (850) ii, **373a**; iii, 1037a, 1266a; iv, 126b, 629b; vi, 636b; vii, 790a
Djaʿfar b. Hārūn (803) iv, 645a
Djaʿfar b. al-Ḥasan b. al-Uṭrūsh (X) vi, 115b; s, 356b, 357a
Djaʿfar b. Ḥinzāba (1001) iv, 419b
Djaʿfar b. Ismāʿīl (1899) vii, 100b
Djaʿfar b. Khiḍr → Kāshif al-Ghiṭāʾ al-Nadjafī
Djaʿfar b. Ḳudāma al-Kātib v, 319a, b
Djaʿfar b. al-Manṣūr bi-’llāh (Zaydī) (1001) vi, 436a, 439a
Djaʿfar b. Manṣūr al-Yaman (X) ii, 861b; s, **236b**
Djaʿfar b. Mubashshir (848) ii, **373a**; iii, 1266a; vii, 605a; ix, 824b; s, 89a
Djaʿfar b. Muḥammad → Abū Maʿshar al-Balkhī
Djaʿfar b. Muḥammad (Kalbid) (X) iv, 497a; ix, 670a
Djaʿfar b. Muḥammad, Sharīf (Mūsāwid) (X) iii, 262b; vi, 148a
Djaʿfar b. Muḥammad b. Aḥmad b. Hudhār (IX) s, 1a
Djaʿfar b. Muḥammad b. al-Ashʿath (VIII) vii, 646a
Djaʿfar b. Muḥammad b. Ḥamdān al-Mawṣilī (934) ii, 127a; v, 1125a; vi, 784b
Djaʿfar b. Muḥammad b. Ḳūlūya al-Ḳummī (979) vii, 312a
Djaʿfar b. al-Muktafī bi’llāh viii, 103a
Djaʿfar b. al-Sammāk al-ʿAbdī (VIII) iii, 649b, 650a
Djaʿfar b. Sulaymān (ʿAbbāsid) (792) iii, 876a, 878a; vi, 263b; vii, 114a; viii, 536b, 996b
Djaʿfar b. Sulaymān al-Makramī (dāʿī)(XVII) vi, 190b, 191a
Djaʿfar b. Yaḥyā al-Barmakī (803) i, 14a, 718a, 1034a, b, 1035b, 1045a, 1114b, 1298a; ii, 78a, 195a, 281b, 305a, 731a; iii, 233a; vi, 331a; xi, 243a, b
Djaʿfar b. Yūsuf (1019) iv, 497a
Djaʿfar al-ʿAskarī (XX) x, 885b; s, 672b
Djaʿfar Beg (1520) ii, **373b**
Djaʿfar Čelebi (1515) ii, **374a**, 839b
Djaʿfar al-Falāḥ (971) ii, 854a; iii, 246a

Djaʿfar Kāshif al-Ghiṭāʾ, Shaykh (XIX) vi, 13b, 551a, b
Djaʿfar Khān Gakkhaŕ (1801) iii, 336a
Djaʿfar Khān Zand (1789) iii, 1191a; iv, 104b, 391a; v, 825b, 835a; s, 336a, 405b
Djaʿfar al-Khuldī (960) ix, 65b
Djaʿfar Ḳulī Khān (Ḳādjār) (XVIII) iv, 104b, 391a
Djaʿfar Mīr (1765) ii, **371a**, 1091b
Djaʿfar Mullā (XIX) s, 53a
Djaʿfar Pasha (Yemen) (1617) vi, 437a
Djaʿfar al-Ṣādiḳ b. ʿAlī Zayn al-ʿĀbidīn i, **781b**
Djaʿfar al-Ṣādiḳ b. Muḥammad al-Bāḳir (Imām) (765) i, 48a, 134a, 402a, 402b, 1082a, 1116b, 1156a, 1245a; ii, 168b, 357b, 359a, **374a**, 377b, 761a, 857a; iii, 496b, 616b, 682b, 1061a, 1166b; iv, 114b, 1132a, b, 1134a; v, 1236b; vi, 12a, 219a, 334b; vii, 348a, 388b, 645b, 932a; ix, 423a, 770a; s, 231b, 232b, 233a, 401a
Djaʿfar al-Sarrādj → al-Sarrādj, Abū Muḥammad
Djaʿfar Sharīf b. ʿAlī al-Ḳurayshī al-Nāgōrī (XIX) ii, **375a**; vi, 126b, 127a, 228b
Djaʿfar al-Ṭayyār → Djaʿfar b. Abī Ṭālib
Djaʿfar b. Yaḥyā b. Khālid b. Barmak (803) i, 1034a; iii, 233a; vi, 438a
Djaʿfar Zattallī (1713) iii, 358b; ix, 213b
Djafāra (Libya) v, 759b; vi, 452b
Djaʿfarābād s, 246b
al-Djaʿfarī (1744) vi, 354b
Djaʿfarī, Abū ʿAlī Muḥammad (Ḳazwīn) (1033) iv, 859b
Djaʿfarids (Ḥimyar) vi, 831b
Djaʿfariyya ii, 375a; iv, 50b, 764a; vi, 27a, 28a, 37a, 56b; vii, 778a
Djaff, Banū v, 471b
Djafna, Banū vii, 841a
Djafr → Ghanam
Djafr ii, **375b**; iii, 595b; iv, 1129a; vi, 216a
al-Djafūl → Mālik b. Nuwayra
al-Djāfūra i, 537a
Djagat → Dwārkā
Djagat Singh (XVII) iv, 543b
Djaghatay → Čaghatay
Djaghatu vi, 502a, b
al-Djaghbūb ii, **378a**; v, 759b, 760a; s, 165a
al-Djaghmīnī, Maḥmūd (XIV) ii, **378a**
Djāghurī iii, 304a
Djāgīr ii, 155b, 156b, 158a, 272b, 378b; s, 126b, 131b
Djaḥādila, Banū iii, 363b, 541a
Djahān Ārā bint Shāh Djahān (XVI) ix, 195b, 196a
Djahan Khān Pōpalzaʾi (XVIII) ii, 186a
Djahan Khānum bint Kāmrān Mīrzā (XX) vii, 432a
Djahān-Pahlawān Muḥammad → Djihān-Pahlawān Muḥammad
Djahan Shāh b. Bahādur Shāh (Mughal) (XVIII) i, 914a; ii, 379a
Djahānābād v, 264b
Djahānārā Begam bint Shāh Djahān (1681) i, 253b, 1161a; ii, 50a, **378b**, 627b; vi, 126b, 488b; vii, 333a
Djahāndād Khān (1906) ii, 974a
Djahāndār Shāh (1713) i, 241b, 914a, 1025b; ii, **379a**, 810a
Djahāndār Shāh (1878) i, 853a
Djahāngīr b. Akbar (Mughal) (1627) i, 8b, 81a, 117b, 118a, 238a, 252b, 253a, 297b, 686a, 1331b, 1347b; ii, 54b, 121a, 157a, 162a, **379b**, 503b, 840a; iii, 424a, 434a, 450a, 492b; iv, 279a, 282a, 543a, 709a, 1017b; v, 598a, 600b, 1135b, 1214a; vi, 127a, 269b, 368b, 369b, 407a, 424b, 425b, 426a, 488a, 516b, 534a; vii, 139a, 189a, 194a, 204a, b, 221a, 315a, 317b, 331a, 338b, 343a, 345b; viii, 125a; s, 1b, 142b, 167b, 258a, 259b, 313b, 366b
Djahāngīr b. Kāwūs Pādūspānī, Malik (XV) vi, 514a
Djahāngīr Djalīlī (1938) iv, 72b
Djahāngīr Khān (Kazakh) (1652) x, 681b
Djahāngīr Muḥammad Khān (XIX) i, 1195b, 1197a
Djahāniyān-i Djahān Gasht, Makhdūm-i → Djalāl al-Dīn Ḥusayn al-Bukhārī
Djahannam i, 334b; ii, **381b**
Djahānpanāh i, 1322b; ii, 258a, 259a; v, 888b, 1214b; vi, 49b, 294a, 532b, 692a
Djahānshāh (Ḳara Ḳoyunlu) → Djihānshāh
Djahānshāh (Mughal) → Shāh Djahān
Djahān-Sūz, ʿAlāʾ al-Dīn Ḥusayn (Ghūrid) (1161) i, 940a; ii, **382a**, 1049b, 1052b, 1100b, 1101a, 1103b; iii, 196a; v, 691a; vi, 198b
Djahān u Arghiyān s, 83b
Djahāz Maḥall vi, 407b

Djahbadh i, 898b, 1144b; ii, 78b, 79b, 324b, 325a, **382b**; iv, 1032b
Djahḍam b. ʿAbd Allāh (VIII) iii, 986a
Djaḥdar b. Ḍubayʿa vi, 640b
al-Djaḥḥāf b. Ḥakīm (Ḥukaym) al-Sulamī (VII) i, 1241a; viii, 630b
Djāhidiyya → Khalwatiyya
Djāhiliyya i, 890a; ii, **383b**, 998b, 1073a; iii, 305b; iv, 998a; vi, 430a; s, 33a, 189a
Djaḥīm → Nār
Djahīr, Banū ii, 344a, **384a**; vi, 274b, 275a; vii, 540b, 693a, b, 755b; viii, 70b
al-Djāḥiẓ, Abū ʿUthmān al-Baṣrī (868) i, 10b, 105b, 127a, 176a, 214b, 266a, 271b, 316a, 585a, 588b, 717b, 857b, 1115a, 1243b, 1297b; ii, 95b, 300a, **385a**, 536b, 552a, 590b, 824a, 951b, 1097a; iii, 312a, 354b, 367b, 389b, 990a, 1143a, 1263a; iv, 490b, 822b, 949a; v, 113b, 778b, 1224a, 1225a, b; vi, 109a, 115a, 313b, 346b, 351a, 539a, 605a, 607b, 634b, 636b, 640a, 903b; vii, 279b, 401a, 494a, 567a, 580b, 985b; viii, 95a, 535a, 839a; ix, 454b; s,13b, 24a, 25a, 35b, 45a, 73b, 85b, 88b, 124a, 263a, 273a, 286a, 294b, 316b, 318a, 392b, 402a
Djahlāwān ii, **387b**
Djahm b. ʿAtiyya (VIII) iv, 447a
Djahm b. Ṣafwān al-Samarḳandī (746) i, 274a, 1242a; ii, **388a**; iii, 224a, 747b; vii, 784b; x, 343b; s, 225b
Djahmiyya i, 124a, 275a, 976b, 333b, 334a, 335a, 410b; ii, 365a, **388a**; iii, 161b, 822a, 1143a, 1171a; iv, 469a, 1087a; vii, 604a; viii, 87b
al-Djahrāʾ (battle, 1920) iv, 680b, 681a
Djahriyya (Kansu) iv, 554b
Djahrum v, 671b
al-Djahshiyārī, Abū ʿAbd Allāh (942) i, 361a; ii, **388b**; iii, 371a; s, 48b
Djahwarids i, 5b, 6a; ii, **389a**; vi, 189a; vii, 766b
Djaḥẓa, Aḥmad b. Djaʿfar (936) i, 1036a; ii, **389b**
Djai Singh (XVII) i, 768b, 769a
Djaʾilda, Shaykh al-Islam (XV) vi, 53b, 62a
Djāisī, Malik Muḥammad (XVI) iv, 922a
Djāʾiz i, 2a; ii, **389b**
Djāʾiza → Ṣila
Djakam, amīr (1407) ii, 781b
Djakarta i, 980b; ii, **390a**, 426b; iii, 1214a
Djakat → Zakāt
Djakīm (Djakūn) (Aleppo) vi, 541a
Djaḳmaḳ → Čaḳmaḳ
Djaksu b. Tumbine Khān (Mangi̊t) vi, 417b
Djaʿl → Tazyīf
Djalāhima, Banū iv, 751a
Djalāʾirids → Djalāyir
Djalāl, Muḥammad ʿUthmān → Muḥammad ʿUthmān Djalāl
Djalāl b. Abi ʾl-Khayr Djazāʾirī, Shaykh (XV) vii, 672a
Djalāl b. Shīr Shāh Sūrī (Bengal) (XVI) vi, 47b
Djalāl Āl-i Aḥmad (1969) viii, 116a
Djalāl al-Dawla (title) ii, **390b**
Djalāl al-Dawla Shīrzīl, Abū Ṭāhir (Būyid) (1044) i, 131b, 512b, 1073a; ii, **391a**, 856a; iii, 860a; iv, 379a, 457a, b, 653a; vi, 261b, 270b, 272b, 965b; vii, 271a; s, 119a
Djalāl al-Dīn b. Bayazīd Anṣārī (Rawshānī) (XVI) i, 238a, 1123a
Djalāl al-Dīn b. Maḥmūd Khān (Kālpī) (1437) vi, 61b, 66b
Djalāl al-Dīn b. Shīr Shāh Sūrī (Bihār) (1545) ii, 271a; vi, 47a
Djalāl al-Dīn, Djalāl Khān (Bihār) (1534) vi, 47a
Djalāl al-Dīn Lōdī (XVI) ii, 271a; iii, 420b, 995a
Djalāl al-Dīn Aḥsan (1339) ii, **391b**; vii, 412a
Djalāl al-Dīn ʿĀrif (1930) ii, **391b**
Djalāl al-Dīn Bāyazīd (Isfendiyār-oghlu) (1385) iv, 108b; viii, 189b
Djalāl al-Dīn al-Dawānī → al-Dawānī
Djalāl al-Dīn Ḥasan → Ḥasan III Rukn al-Dīn (Nizārī)
Djalāl al-Dīn Ḥasan b. ʿAlī b. Ṣadaḳa (vizier) (1128) vii, 735a
Djalāl al-Dīn Ḥusayn al-Bukhārī (1384) i, 702b, 868b; ii, 186b, **392a**; iii, 434a; vi, 228b; vii, 1048b; x, 255b; s, 10b
Djalāl al-Dīn Iskandar b. ʿUmar Shaykh (Tīmūrid) (XV) vii, 529a
Djalāl al-Dīn Ḳaratāy i, 732a; iv, 813b; v, 1145a
Djalāl al-Dīn Khaldjī → Fīrūz Shāh II
Djalāl al-Dīn Khwārazm-shāh Mangubirtī (1231) i, 190a, 227a, 301a, 329a, 353b,

508a, 665a, 799a, 919b, 1010a, 1206b, 1311a; ii, 2a, 43b, 188b, 267b, 284a, **392b**, 606a, 680b, 711b, 975b, 1049b, 1083a; iii, 196b, 197a, 1112a; iv, 30a, 102a, 349a, 817b, 1068a; v, 31b, 455a, 490b; vi, 48b, 381a, 500b; vii, 231a, 273b, 498a, 549a, 666a, 727b, 871a, 973b, 990b, 998a; x, 43a; 898a
Djalāl al-Dīn Khᵂārazmī, Sayyid (XIV) viii, 45a
Djalāl al-Dīn Mangubirtī → Djalāl al-Dīn Khwārazm Shāh
Djalāl al-Dīn Mīrān Shāh b. Tīmūr (XV) vii, 133a
Djalāl al-Dīn Mīrzā (Ḳādjār) (XIX) vii, 438b; s, 23b
Djalāl al-Dīn Muḥammad → Muḥammad Shāh Gaṇeśa
Djalāl al-Dīn Pasha (Bosna) (XIX) i, 1268a
Djalāl al-Dīn Rūmī, Mawlānā (1273) i, 109b, 234a, 347a, 698b, 752b, 753b, 780a, 843b, 916b, 1194b; ii, 221a, **393b**; iii, 429b, 602a, 711a; iv, 65a, 67a, 190a, 570a; v, 255a, 676b; vi, 87a, 354b; vii, 480a, 754b, 1019a; s, 49b, 83b, 108a
Djalāl al-Dīn Surkh Bukhārī, Sayyid (XIV) x, 767a
Djalāl al-Dīn Tabrīzī → Tabrīzī, Djalāl al-Dīn
Djalāl al-Dīn Ṭayyibshāh (Faḍlawayh) (1282) ii, 737a
Djalāl al-Dīn Thanesarī → Thanesarī, Djalāl al-Dīn
Djalāl Ḥusayn Čelebi (XVII) ii, **397b**
Djalāl Khān (Bahmānid) (XV) iii, 577a
Djalāl Khān (Bihār) → Djalāl al-Dīn (Bihār)
Djalāl Nūrī → Ileri, Djelāl Nūrī
Djalāl Redjāʾīzāde → Redjāʾīzāde
Djalālābād ii, **397b**; iv, 409b; vii, 407a; s, 66b, **237a**
Djalālakmār-parčīn vi, 511a
Djalālī (brigands) i, 1334b; ii, 183b, 209a, 1046b; iii, 237b, 1002a, 1248b; iv, 499a, 594a, 843b; v, 258b, 270a, 677b; vi, 525b; s, **238a**
Djalālī (calendar) ii, **397b**; iv, 52a; vi, 275b; viii, 71b
Djalālī (islet) vi, 734b, 735a
Djalālī, Banū (Kurds) vi, 201b
Djalāliyya (Suhrawardiyya) vi, 225b
Djalāl-zāde Muṣṭafā Čelebi (1567) ii, **400a**; iii, 998b; iv, 565b, 566a
Djalāl-zāde Ṣāliḥ Čelebi (1565) ii, **400b**
Djalāl-zāde Ṭāhir Čelebi (XV) viii, 213b
Djaʿlān viii, 566a
Djālandhar/Čālandhar vi, 783a
Djalaw Khān (Kart) (1327) iv, 672a
Djalāyīn s, 357a
Djalāyir/Djalāyirid i, 66b, 190a, 311b, 508a, 861a, 903b, 1128b; ii, 348b, **401a**; iii, 1123a, 1256b; iv, 32a; v, 45b; vi, 482b, 494b, 502b, 901a; viii, 998a; x, 44a; s, 364a
Djalī (calligraphy) iv, 1123a, b, 1125b, 1126a; v, 224a
Djālī → Djawālī
Djalīlī, Āl (Mosul) ii, **402a**
Djālīnūs (Galen) (199) i, 213a, 234a, 327a, b, 344b, 388a, 1198a; ii, 60a, 249a, **402b**, 765a, 771a, 780b, 929b; iii, 266b, 579a, 906b; iv, 129a, 329b, 330a, b, 406b; vi, 449a; s, 154b, 271a, 379b
Djālīsh → Shālīsh
Djāliya ii, **403b**, 470b; v, 1253a
Djaʿliyyīn, Banū i, 1a, 765a
Djallāb, Djallābiyya i, 1349b; ii, **404b**
Djallāba Hawwāra (tribe) iii, 300a
Djāllandharī → Ḥafīz
Djalliḳiyya → Djillīḳiyya
Djālo i, 763a
Djālor ii, **405a**; iii, 441b; viii, 244b
Djalūlāʾ (ʿIrāḳ) ii, **406a**; iv, 13b, 386a
Djalūlāʾ (al-Ḳayrawān) vii, 269b
Djālūt (Goliath) ii, **406a**
Djālwand (tribe) v, 617a
Djalwatiyya i, 1137a
Djalwī b. Turkī Āl Saʿūd (1853) i, 1313a
Djām (Ghūr) ii, **406b**; v, 1148a; vi, 365b, 368b
Djām (valley) vi, 495a
Djām ʿAlī Khān III (1896) v, 684b, 685a
Djamʿ, djamāʿa ii, **406b**
Djām Firūz (XVI) i, 627b; iii, 632b
Djām Mīr Khān I (1818) v, 684b
Djām Mīr Khān II (1869) v, 684b, 685a
Djām Nanda (XVI) i, 627b; iii, 420a, 634a
Djām Niẓām al-Dīn (Gudjārāt) (1473) vi, 50b,
Djāmaʿ al-Fnā (Marrākush) vi, 589b

Djāmaʿ Ibn Ṣāliḥ (Marrākush) vi, 590b
Djām Niẓām al-Dīn Nindō (Rādjpūt) (1509) vi, 189b
Djamāʿa i, 171a, 276b, 373b, 770b, 1179b; ii, **411a**, 885b; iii, 98a; iv, 154b, 362a; v, 1198b
Djamāʿa, Banū iii, 749a
Djamāʿat-i Islāmī iii, 433a; vi, 461b, 462a; viii, 242b
Djamādjim → Ḥumāḥim
Djāmakiyya ii, **413b**; vi, 276b
Djamal → Ibil
al-Djamal (battle) (656) i, 43b, 55a, 308a, 383b, 448b, 704b; ii, **414a**
Djamāl → ʿIlm al-djamāl
al-Djamal al-Akbar (842) vii, 4a
Djamāl al-Dīn b. Nubāta → Ibn Nubāta al-Miṣrī
Djamāl al-Dīn b. Yaghmūr (1264) s, 463a
Djamāl al-Dīn ʿAbd al-Ghānī (XIII) vii, 274a
Djamāl al-Dīn Abū Bakr b. Mughulṭay (1389) vii, 350a
Djamāl al-Dīn al-Afghānī (1897) i, 64b, 327a, 332a; ii, 97a, **416b**, 429a, 417a, 650a, 932b, 933b; iii, 250b, 514a, b, 1145b, 1149b, 1170a; iv, 112a, 159a, 162b, 164a, b, 397b, 720b, 946a; vi, 292a, 360a, 414a, 462a; vii, 184a, 418b, 716a, 813a; viii, 248a; s, 76a, 106b, 244b, 248a, 296a
Djamāl al-Dīn Aḳḳūsh al-Afram al-Shāmī (1303) vi, 545b, 547b; viii, 156b, 157a
Djamāl al-Dīn Aḳsarayī (1389) ii, **419b**
Djamāl al-Dīn al-Ardistānī (1474) v, 53b; xi, 360b
Djamāl al-Dīn Efendi (1919) ii, **420a**
Djamāl al-Dīn Gīlī (1253) s, 633a
Djamāl al-Dīn Hānsawī → Hānsawī
Djamāl al-Dīn al-Ḥillī → al-Ḥillī, Djamāl al-Dīn
Djamāl al-Dīn Ibrāhīm, Shaykh al-Islām (1306) iv, 1040b, 1046b
Djamāl al-Dīn Iṣfahānī, Muḥammad b. ʿAbd al-Razzāḳ (1192) iv, 62a, 515b; vi, 608b; s, **239b**
Djamāl al-Dīn al-Iṣfahānī → al-Djawād al-Iṣfahānī
Djamāl al-Dīn Ismāʿīl (Munḳidh, Banū) (1229) vii, 579b
Djamāl al-Dīn al-Ḳāsimī → al-Ḳāsimī
Djamāl al-Dīn al-Khiḍr, Ḥākim (XIV) vi, 231a
Djamāl al-Dīn Maḥmūd b. ʿAlī, Ustādār (1397) iii, 773b; vi, 199b
Djamāl al-Dīn Muḥammad (Būrid) (1140) i, 1332a
Djamāl al-Dīn Muḥammad b. Aḥmad b. ʿAbd Allāh (1498) ii, 730a
Djamāl al-Dīn Muḥammad Sām (XIV) ix, 112a
Djamāl al-Dīn al-Ustādār (Miṣr) (XV) vii, 172a
Djamāl al-Dīn Yāḳūt (Ḥabshī) (1239) i, 1194a; ii, 1084a; iii, 14a
Djamāl al-Ḥusaynī (1520) ii, **420a**
Djamāl Karshī (XIV) ii, 3b; v, 39a; s, **240a**
Djamāl Khān, Ḥadjdjī (1770) i, 231a, 295b
Djamāl al-Mulk (vizier) (1104) i, 440a
Djamāl al-Mulk Muḥammad b. Niẓām al-Mulk (1082) viii, 72a, 81b
Djamāl Pasha → Djemāl Pasha
Djamālī, ʿAlāʾ al-Dīn ʿAlī b. Aḥmad (1526) vii, 478b; ix, 401b
Djamālī, ʿAlī (1526) ii, **420a**
Djamālī, Ḥāmid b. Faḍl Allāh (1536) ii, **420b**
Djamālī Kambo, Shaykh (1535) s, 312a
al-Djamāliyya (Ṭarīḳa) iv, 991b, 992a
Djamālzāda, Muḥammad ʿAlī (XX) iv, 73a, 789b; v, 199a
Djamar (Ḳum) vi, 493a
Djambul → Awliyā ata
Djambul Djabaev (1945) i, 767a; ii, **421a**
Djamdār ii, **421b**
Djāmiʿ → Masdjid
Djāmiʿ, Banū iv, 337a
Djāmī, Khʷādja Muḥammad Yūsuf (XIX) vii, 935b
Djāmī, Mawlānā Nūr al-Dīn ʿAbd al-Raḥmān (1492) i, 88b, 146a, 347b, 753a, 1082b, 1211b; ii, **421b**; iii, 131b, 373a, 710b, 711a; iv, 64b, 66b, 650a, 1010a, 1073b; v, 482a, 650b, 1104b; vi, 225a; vii, 478b, 530a, 662a, 935a; viii, 540b, 704a, 800b; x, 322a; s, 46b, 83a, 415a
al-Djāmiʿ al-Azhar → al-Azhar
Djāmiʿ al-Zaytūna → Zaytūna
Djāmiʿa i, 56b; ii, **422b**; iii, 250b; iv, 70b; v, 365a, 904b, 919a

al-Djāmiʿa al-ʿArabiyya i, 46a, 279b; iii, 264a; iv, 783a, 947a; viii, 246b; s, **240a**
Djāmiʿat Umm al-Ḳurā (Makka) vi, 174a
al-Djāmiʿayn vi, 965b; vii, 497a
Djāmid → Naḥw and Ṭabīʿa
Djamīl, Ṭanburī → Ṭanburī Djamīl
Djamīl b. ʿAbd Allāh al-ʿUdhrī (701) i, 10b; ii, **427b**, 1031a; vi, 468a; vii, 978a; s, 42b
Djamīl Nakhla al-Mudawwar (1907) ii, **428a**
Djamīl Ṣadīḳī al-Dhahāwī vi, 609a
Djamīl Ṣalībā (XX) vi, 538b
Djamīla (singer) (VII) ii, **428b**, 1011b; iii, 931b; iv, 821b
Djamīla bint al-Ḥasan Nāṣir al-Dawla (Ḥamdānid) (X) s, 36b, 37a
Djamʿiyya ii, **428b**, 650b; iii, 514b; iv, 924a
Djamʿiyyat al-ʿahd iii, 520b
Djamʿiyyat al-djāmiʿa al-ʿarabiyya iii, 520b
Djamʿiyya al-Ḥiṣāfiyya al-khayriyya s, 371a
Djamʿiyyat al-iṣlāḥ al-shaʿbī iii, 521b, 522a
Djamʿiyyat al-Ḳaḥṭāniyya iii, 519b
Djamʿiyyat al-nahḍa iii, 519a
al-Djamʿiyya al-tashrīʿiyya v, 1060b, 1064a
Djamʿiyyat ittiḥād Miṣr al-fatāt ii, 429a; iii, 514b; vii, 852a
Djamʿiyyat-i ʿUlamāʾ-i Hind s, 4b, 106b
al-Djammāʿīlī, Taḳī al-Dīn (XIV) iii, 867b
Djammāl s, **241b**
al-Djammāz, Abū ʿAbd Allāh (861) ii, **437b**; iii, 879a; vii, 847a
Djammū s, **241b**
Djamnā ii, 255b, 265b, **437b**; s, 313a
al-Djamra ii, **438a**; iii, 36a
Djāms (Sammā) ix, 634b
Djamshīd ii, **438b**; iv, 12a, 220b, 221a, 1104b
Djamshīd b. Sulṭān Aḥmad (Gilān-i Biyāpīsh) (XVI) vi, 483a
Djamshīd Ḳarīn Ghawrī (1400) vi, 512b
Djamshīdī, Banū i, 224b, 857a; ii, 5b; iii, 1107b
Djamuḳa (Mongol) (XII) ii, 42a, 571a
Djamunā (river) v, 885b
Djāmūs s, **242b**
Djān b. Yār Muḥammad (Činglizid) (XVI) ii, 44b
Djān ʿAlī Khān (Ḳāsimov) (1535) iv, 723b, 849b
Djān Bābā (Maklī) (1608) vi, 190a
Djān Begam bint ʿAbd al-Raḥīm Khān, Khān-i Khānān (XVI) ii, 44b; vi, 488b
Djān-i Djanān → Maẓhar
Djanāb Shihāb al-Dīn (Cenap Şehabettin) (1934) ii, **439b**, 474b; iii, 261b; vi, 93a, b
Djanāb-i Ṭāhira → Ḳurrat al-ʿAyn
al-Djanaba, Banū (ʿUmān) i, 1091b; ii, **440b**; iii, 270a; vi, 729a
Djanāba ii, **440b**
al-Djanad (Ḥaḍramawt) vi, 138b, 140b, 438b; s, 337b
al-Djanad (Taʿizz) x, 118a
al-Djanad (Taʿizz) ix, 816a
al-Djanadī, Abū ʿAbd Allāh (1332) i, 255b; ii, **441a**; viii, 458b
Djanāḥ al-Dawla Ḥusayn (amīr) (1103) iii, 398b; viii, 519a
al-Djanāḥiyya i, 49a; ii, **441a**; iii, 1266a; iv, 44b, 838a
al-Djanāwanī, Abū ʿUbayda (IX) ii, 369a, **441b**; iii, 657b; iv, 919b
al-Djanāwunī → Abū Zakariyyāʾ
al-Djanāwunī, Abū Yaḥyā Tawfīḳ (XIII) i, 1287b
Djanāza ii, **441b**
Djanb, Banū v, 954b
Djanbās Ḳalʿa i, 831a; iii, 502b
Djānbāz ii, **442b**
Djānbāzān ii, **443a**
Djānbeg Girāy Khān (1635) i, 310b; iii, 252a
Djanbī i, 125a; vi, 312a
al-Djanbīhī, Muḥammad b. ʿAbd al-Nabī (1927) s, **244a**
Djānbirdi al-Ghazālī → al-Ghazālī
Djānbulāṭ i, 1078a; ii, **443b**; v, 106a, 793a
Djānbulāṭ, Shaykh Ḳāsim (XVIII) i, 1078a; ii, 444a, 636a
Djānbulāṭ-oghlu ʿAlī Pasha (1607) i, 4a, 182b, 267b; ii, 443b, 635a, 750a; iii, 88a; iv, 499a; vii, 600b; s, 239a
Djand ii, 571b; iii, 472a; iv, 542b; v, 247a; ix, 557b; s, **244b**
Djandaba b. al-Ḥārith al-Kilābī ii, 234a
Djandaḳ xi, 238a, b, 303a
Djandal b. al-Rāʿī (VIII) viii, 120b

Djāndār ii, **444a**; v, 685a
Djāndār (Anadolu) i, 467b
Djandārids (1400) vi, 975a
Djandarli̊ i, 348a; ii, **444b**, 722a; iv, 292a; v, 1023b
Djandarli̊ ʿAlī Pasha b. Khayr al-Dīn Khalīl Pasha → ʿAlī Pasha Čāndārli̊-zāde
Djandarli̊, Ibrāhīm Pasha (1429) ii, **444b**, 721a
Djandarli̊, Ibrāhīm Pasha b. Khalīl (1500) ii, **445a**; iv, 231a; vi, 1025b; vii, 594b, 595a, 644b
Djandarli̊, Khalīl Pasha b. Ibrāhīm (1453) → Khalīl Pasha Djandarli̊
Djandarli̊ Khayr al-Dīn Khalīl Pasha (1387) ii, **444b**; vii, 594a; viii, 192b, 193a
Djandī, Bābā Kamāl (1273) x, 251a
al-Djandī, Yaʿḳūb b. Shīrīn, ḳāḍī (XII) s, 246a
Djandjīra iii, 15b; s, **246a**
Djandjis → Gangā
Djandjū ix, 440b
Djandōl ii, 317a
Djandrāwar (river) vii, 20b
Djandūba → Djanbī
Djangalī ii, **445b**; v, 310b
Djangī Yūsuf Dede (1669) iv, 190a
Djānī Beg (Shaybānid) (1528) i, 46b; iv, 391b
Djānī Beg Abū Iskandar Khān (Tarkhān) (1601) i, 80b; vi, 190a
Djānī Beg al-ʿAzīzī (amīr) (1485) i, 841a; vii, 173a
Djānī Beg Batuʾid (1357) x, 88b
Djānī Beg Maḥmūd Khān (Batuʾid) (1357) i, 325a, 808b, 1107b; ii, 401a; viii, 753a, 755b; ix, 42a
Djānī Beg Mīrzā (Arghūn) (1599) i, 628a; vii, 129b
Djāni Bēgum bint ʿAbd al-Raḥīm Khān (XVII) i, 81a
Djānī Khān Ḳāshḳāy (1823) iv, 706a
al-Djandī, Muʾayyid al-Dīn (1300) viii, 753b; x, 320b; xi, 39a; s, 753a
Djānib ʿAlī Efendi (XVIII) vi, 56a
Djānībak al-Ṣūfī, amīr (XV) i, 1054b; iii, 923a
Djānībak al-Ẓāhirī (1463) v, 73a
Djānibeg Girāy → Djānbeg Girāy
Djānībeg Khān i, 325a, 808b, 1107b; ii, 401a
Djānids i, 1295b; ii, 44b, **446a**; v, 273b; viii, 232a; x, 681b; s, 97a, 227b, 419b
Djānīk ii, **446b**
Djānīkli ii, 207a, 446b
Djānīkli Ḥādjdjī ʿAlī Pasha (1785) ii, 207b, **446b**
Djānim al-Ashrafī, ḳāshif (Miṣr) (1522) vi, 325a
Djānim al-Ashrafī (Syria) (1462) v, 73a; vii, 727a
Djāni̊m-Khodja Meḥmed Pasha (admiral) (1730) vi, 55b; vii, 1036b; viii, 266a, 288a
Djān-Ḳalʿa s, 244b
Djānḳī ii, 334b; vi, 724b; s, 163a
Djankirmān → Özi
Djanna i, 334b; ii, **447a**
Djannāba ii, **452a**
al-Djannābī, Abū Muḥammad Muṣṭafā (1590) ii, **452b**; iv, 406a
al-Djannābī, Abū Saʿīd Ḥasan (913) i, 11a, 73b, 551b; ii, **452b**; iv, 198a, 661a, 664a, 764a; vii, 760b
al-Djannābī, Abū Ṭāhir (943) i, 485a, 551b; ii, **452b**; iii, 236a, 238a; iv, 198b, 661b, 662a, b, 664a; vii, 541b; s, 305a
al-Djannābī, Aḥmad b. Abī Ṭāhir (951) vi, 435b
al-Djannābī, Aḥmad b. Saʿīd (X) vii, 488a
al-Djannābī, al-Ḥasan al-Aʿṣam b. Aḥmad b. Saʿīd (X) vii, 488a
al-Djannābī, Saʿīd b. Abī Saʿīd (X) ii, 452b; iv, 664a
Djanpulāt → Djanbulāt
Djānū → ʿUthmān Ādam
Djanza → Gandja
Djār → Djiwār
al-Djār ii, **454b**; vii, 42b, 69b
Djara iv, 335b, 338b, 340a
Djarāblus vi, 378a, b
Djarād ii, **455a**
Djarāda → al-Djarādatān[i]
al-Djarādatān[i] iv, 820b; s, **246b**
Djarādjima (Mardaïtes) i, 761a; ii, **456a**; vi, 505b
Djaralī and Datolī, Banū vi, 48a
Djarār (peninsula) vi, 641b
Djarash i, 208a; ii, **458a**

Djarāwa, Banū iii, 1039b, 1041b; iv, 422b, 479a, b; v, 1174b
al-Djarāwī, ʿAbd al-ʿAzīz (Miṣr) (IX) vii, 160b
Djarba (Djerba) (island) ii, **458a**, 461a; iv, 1156a; v, 503b; x, 213b; s, 15b, 80b
Djarba (battle) (1560) ii, **461a**
al-Djarbāʾ ii, **461b**; x, 883a
Djarbādhakān → Gulpāyagān
Djardamur (XIV) vi, 580b
al-Djardjarāʾī, al-ʿAbbās b. al-Ḥasan (908) ii, **461b**; iii, 619b, 767b, 892b; vii, 541b, 543a
al-Djardjarāʾī, Abu ʾl-Ḳāsim ʿAlī b. Aḥmad (1045) ii, **462a**; iii, 79a; vi, 198a; vii, 483a, 729b
al-Djardjarāʾī, Aḥmad b. al-Khaṣīb (879) i, 1289b; ii, **461b**; iii, 835a, 1085a; vii, 583a, 653a
al-Djardjarāʾī, Muḥammad b. al-Faḍl (864) ii, **461b**
al-Djarḥ wa ʾl-taʿdīl i, 1199b; ii, **462a**
Djarhud (Ustūnāwand) vi, 744b
Djārī → Khaṭaʾ
Djarīb → Kayl
Djarīd, Bilād al- ii, **462b**; iv, 739b, 740a; vii, 186b
Djarīda i, 279b, 287a, b, 288a, 289b, 871a, b; ii, 288b, 289b, 364a, 403b, 404a, 417b, 418a, 428a, 429a, **464b**, 596b; iv, 73; iv, 70b, 71a, b, 112a, 124a, 681b, 857a, 876a; v, 438a, 484b, 838b, 1254b, s, 247a
Djarīda (military) ii, 78b, 79a, 80a
Djarīma ii, **479b**
Djarīr, Awlād ii, 509b
Djarīr b. ʿAbd Allāh al-Badjalī (640) i, 865b; ii, 241b; vi, 710a; vii, 797b; viii, 82b; ix, 553b
Djarīr b. ʿAbd al-Ḥamīd (804) vii, 662b
Djarīr b. ʿAbd al-Masīḥ → al-Mutalammis
Djarīr b. ʿAṭiyya (728) i, 158b, 196a, 331a, 436b, 586a, 950b, 1080a; ii, 245b, **479b**, 788b; iii, 42a, 354a, 853b; vi, 267a, 475a, 604b, 606a, 625a; vii, 114a, 145b, 261a, 402a, 546a, 920b; viii, 120b, 377b; s, 15a, 273a
Djarīr b. Ḥammād b. Zayd (IX) s, 384b
Djarīr b. Yazīd (780) vi, 937b
Djarīriyya x, 11a, 12b
Djāriya → ʿAbd
Djāriya b. Ḳudāma (VII) ii, **480b**; iii, 782a
Djarkent (Panfilov) vi, 768b
Djarkh → Ḳaws
Djarm, Banū vi, 477b
al-Djarmī, Abū ʿUmar (839) vii, 279b; ix, 317b
al-Djarmī, Muslim b. Abī Muslim (IX) viii, 874b
al-Djarmūzī, al-Ḥasan b. al-Muṭahhar (XVIII) vii, 514b
Djarr → Naḥw
Djarrāḥ ii, **481b**
al-Djarrāḥ, Banū xi, 186a
al-Djarrāḥ b. ʿAbd Allāh al-Ḥakamī (730) i, 837a, 985a; ii, **482a**; iii, 493b; iv, 344a, 1173b; vi, 623a; ix, 254a; x, 844b
al-Djarrāh b. ʿAmr ii, 236a
Djarrāḥids i, 386b, 784a; ii, 197b, **482b**, 854a; iii, 767b; v, 327b; vii, 461a, 760a
Djarrūn (Djahrum) vi, 384a
Djarshīḳ → Djirra
Djārsīf → Garsīf
al-Djārūd b. Abī Sabra ʿAbd al-Ḳays (630) i, 73a, 942a; vii, 114b
al-Djārūdiyya ii, **485a**; iii, 1166a; vii, 459b; s, 129b, 130a, 400b
Djarūmiyya, Banū vi, 371b
Djarūn → Bandar ʿAbbās
Djarunda i, 82a; ii, **485a**
Djarwal (Makka) vi, 156b, 161a, 178b
Djarwānids s, 234a
Djāsak ii, **486a**; v, 675a
Djasīm al-Dīn (XX) i, 1169a
Djasīm b. Djābir (XIX) iv, 751b
Djasīm b. Muḥammad (Āl Thānī) (1913) iv, 751b, 752a, 953b
Djasrat b. Shaykhā (1442) v, 31b, 598a; 783a; vii, 279a; ix, 118b
al-Djaṣṣāṣ, Aḥmad (981) ii, **486a**; vii, 562a; ix, 36a
al-Djassāsa i, 932a; ii, **486b**
Djassawr (Jessore) ii, **486b**; vi, 46b
Djastanids → Djustānids
Djāsūs ii, **486b**; iii, 181b
Djaswant Rāo Holkar (XIX) i, 444a
Djaswant Singh (1678) i, 768b, 769a; ii, 567a; iii, 202a
Djāt, Banū (Zuṭṭ) i, 224b, 253a, 1005a, 1193a; ii, **488a**, 504a, 797b, 928b, 1122a, 1131b; iii, 197b; iv, 364b; vi, 50b; s, 163a
Djätä (Mogholistān) xi, 336a

Djāta b. Sumar Rādja Pāl (Druze) vii, 544b
Djāvuldur, Banū → Čāwdor
Djāwa → Djāwī
al-Djawād al-Iṣfahānī, Abū Djaʿfar (Djamāl al-Dīn) (1164) i, 604a, 1160b; ii, **489a**; vi, 870a
Djawād Karbalāʾī, Sayyid (XIX) s, 53a
Djawād Pasha (1900) ii, **489b**
Djawāhir → Djawhar
al-Djawāhirī, Muḥammad Mahdī (XX) ix, 230a
Djawālī ii, 327a, 329a, **490a**, 561a
al-Djawālī, Abū Manṣūr (al-Mawṣil) (XII) vi, 380a; vii, 983b
al-Djawālīḳī, Abū Manṣūr Mawhūb (1114) i, 485b, 593a; ii, **490a**; iii, 733a; iv, 913a; vii, 262a
al-Djawālīḳī, Hishām b. Ṣāliḥ (VIII) viii, 387b; ix, 109a
Djāwān (al-Baḥrayn) i, 941b
Djāwān, Mīrzā Kāẓim ʿAlī (815) ii, **490b**; v, 644b
Djāwān Mardi → Futuwwa
Djāwānī Kurds → Djāf
Djawānrūd ii, **491a**
Djāwars s, **249b**
al-Djawāsim → Ḳawāsim
al-Djawāzir, Banū i, 1096b
al-Djawbarī, ʿAbd al-Raḥīm (XIII) iii, 487b, 511a; vii, 495a; ix, 70a; s, 43a, **250a**
Djawdhar (X) ii, **491a**, 1080b
Djawdhar, Pasha (XVI) i, 289a; ii, 977b
Djawf i, 1313b; ii, **491b**; vi, 88b, 433a, 474b, 559b, 566a; ix, 90n
al-Djawf ii, **492a**, 624b
Djawf Kufra ii, **492b**; s, 164b, 165a
Djawhar (substance) i, 128b, 784b; ii, 220a, **493a**
Djawhar (jewel) i, 1157b; ii, 1119b; iii, 30b; v, 965a; s, **250b**
Djawhar Āftābačī (XVI) ii, **494a**; vii, 342b
Djawhar b. ʿAbd Allāh al-Ṣiḳillī (992) i, 814a, 824a; ii, **494b**, 853a, b, 860a, 1080b; iii, 246a, 768b, 785b, 1036b, 1042b; iv, 275b, 663b, 1091b; v, 1160a, 1176a; vi, 650a, 673b; vii, 148b, 162a, 482b; viii, 40b, 90b, 879a, 880a, 1068b
al-Djawhar b. Sakkum al-Gudālī (XI) vii, 584a, 621b
Djawhar al-ʿAdanī, Ṣūfī (XII) vi, 133a
Djawhar al-Ḳanḳabāʾī (1440) i, 814b
Djawhar-Shādh (XV) vi, 714b
al-Djawāhirī (1002) x, 33a
Djawharī, Banū vi, 657b
al-Djawharī, al-ʿAbbās b. Saʿīd (828) vi, 600a; s, 411b, 412b, 414a
al-Djawharī, Abū Naṣr Ismāʿīl (1009) ii, **495b**, 926b; iii, 733a, 738b; iv, 524b, 527b; vii, 190a; viii, 378b, 661a; s, 38b, 240a, 289a, b
al-Djawharī, Muḥammad s, 395b
al-Djawharī, Muḥammad Ibrāhīm Harawī Ḳazwīnī (1837) vi, 609b
al-Djawharī, Ṭanṭāwī (1940) vi, 360b; vii, 439b; s, **262b**
Djāwī ii, **497a**; vi, 151b
Djāwīd, Meḥmed (1926) ii, **497b**, 616a; iv, 285a, 297b
Djāwīdhān b. Sahl (**1926**) i, 844a; v, 64b **??**
Djāwīdhān Khirad iv, 504b; s, **263a**
Djawkān → Čawgān
al-Djawl i, 536a
Djawlakiyya iv, 473a, b
al-Djawlān ii, **498a**; vi, 455a, 546b; s, 229b
Djawn, Banu 'l- v, 119a
Djawn al-Khaḍārim (Yamāma) vii, 858b
Djawnā Khān → Muḥammad b. Tughluḳ
Djawnā Khān (Shamsābād) (1456) vi, 62b
Djawnpūr ii, 270b, **498b**, 925a; iii, 419a, b, 420a, 442b, 444a, 632a, 1003a; iv, 276b; v, 783b, 889a, 1135a, 1216b; vi, 49a, b, 50a, 52a, 53b, 61b, 62a, b, 273a, 294b, 309b, 368a, 406b, 407b, 693b; vii, 79b, 314a, 573b; ix, 356a; s, 206b, 325a
al-Djawnpūrī, Maḥmūd (1652) i, 593a
al-Djawnpūrī, Sayyid Muḥammad (1505) ii, **499b**; v, 1230b; vii, 458a
Djawsaḳ (Djawsat) vi, 541a
Djawsaḳ al-Khāḳānī (Sāmarrāʾ) i, 1346a; vii, 9a, 766a; viii, 1039b; ix, 44b, 49b
Djawshakānī, Niʿmat Allāh (XVII) s, 139a
Dhawū Ḥassān, Banū vi, 741a
al-Djāwulī, Abū Saʿīd ʿAlam al-Dīn Sandjar (amīr) (1344) iv, 960a; v, 628a
Djāwuliyya iv, 960a
Djaww → Djawf
al-Djawwād Yūnus b. Mawdūd b. al-ʿĀdil (1243) i, 766b
al-Djawwānī (1192) ii, **501a**
Djawz s, **264a**
al-Djawzāʾ → Minṭaḳat al-Burūdj; Nudjūm
al-Djawzahar ii, **501b**

Djay iv, 98b, 99b, 100a, 106a
Djāyasī → Malik Muḥammad Djāyasī
Djayb-i Humāyūn ii, **502b**
Djayfar b. Djulanda i, 451a
Djayḥān (river) ii, 35a, b, **502b**; vi, 505b, 507a, b
al-Djayhānī, Abū ʿAbd Allāh Aḥmad b. Muḥammad (978) s, 265b
al-Djayhānī, Abū ʿAbd Allāh Muḥammad b. Aḥmad b. Naṣr (922) i, 434a; ii, 581a; iv, 1079b; vi, 628a, 640a; viii, 1027a; s, **265a**, 376b
al-Djayhānī, Abū ʿAlī Muḥammad b. Muḥammad (942) i, 984b, 1003a; iv, 847a; viii, 1027a; s, **265a**, b
Djayḥūn → Baradā
Djayḥūn → Āmū Daryā
al-Djayla s, 356a
Djayn ii, **503a**, 1123b
Djaypāl, Rādjā (Hindū Shāhī) (986) ii, 1050b, 1123a; iii, 460b; vi, 65b; viii, 299b
Djaypūr (Jaipur) ii, **503b**; vi, 127b, 602a; s, 260a
Djayrūt vi, 82a
Djaysalmer s, 312b
Djaysh ii, **504a**; v, 685a; vi, 142a
Djayshān s, 335a
Djaysh b. Ṣamṣāma (X) i, 1042a; ii, 483b; iii, 77a
Djaysinha s, 163a
al-Djayṭālī (1329) ii, **515a**; iii, 95a, 97b
Djayyān i, 1343a; ii, **515b**; iii, 498b
Djayyāsh b. Nadjāḥ → Nadjāḥids
Djayzān (Djāzān) i, 109a; ii, **516a**
Djāz-Muryān s, 129a
Djazʾ b. Muʿāwiya (641) vi, 920b
Djazāʾ ii, **518a**
al-Djazāʾir (Algiers) i, 34b, 67b, 367b, 368b; ii, 115b, 425b, **519b**; iii, 251b, 606b; iv, 359b; vi, 58b, 59b, 134b, 573a; s, 325b
al-Djazāʾir Banū → al-Djawāzir
al-Djazāʾir dey → Dayi̊
Djazāʾir-i Baḥr-i Safīd ii, **521b**; vi, 588b
Djazāʾir Ibn Khalfān → Khūriyān Mūriyān
al-Djazāʾir al-Khālida ii, **522a**; v, 755b
Djazāʾir al-Saʿādāt → al-Djazāʾir al-Khālida
al-Djazāʾirī → Ḳaddūra al-Djazāʾirī
al-Djazāʾirī → Aḥmad b. ʿAbd al-Raḥmān
al-Djazāʾirī, ʿAlī b. Hilāl (XV) s, 380a
al-Djazāʾirī, Muḥammad b. Muḥammad (XIX) vi, 113b
al-Djazāʾirī, Niʿmat b. Muḥammad (1718) vi, 112b
al-Djazāʾirī, Sayyid Niʿmat Allāh (1700) vii, 476a
al-Djazāʾirī, Shaykh Ṭāhir (1920) iii, 519a; iv, 159a; vii, 901a; viii, 906b, 908a
Djazāʾirli Ghāzī Ḥasan → Djezāʾirli Ghāzī Ḥasan Pasha
al-Djazarī (1429) vii, 1039b
al-Djazarī, Badīʿ al-Zamān Abu ʾl-ʿIzz (XII) v, 861b; vi, 111a; s, **266b**
al-Djazarī, Shams al-Dīn Muḥammad b. Ibrāhīm (1338) ii, **522b**; iv, 965a; vii, 141a; viii, 458b
al-Djazarī, Shams al-Milla wa ʾl-Dīn (1301) s, **267a**, 371b, 372b, 373a, b, 400a
Djazarī Ḳāsi̊m Pasha (1485) iv, **722a**; vi, 1025b
al-Djazīra (Algiers) xi, 138b
Djazīra (island) ii, **523a**
al-Djazīra (Djazīrat Aḳūr) i, 11b, 12b, 198a; ii, 64b, 249b, 344b, 347a, 348a, **523a**; iii, 933b, 1250b, 1252a; v, 453b, 457a, 458a; vi, 139a, 273b, 331a, 337a, 378a, 427b, 428b, 429b, 539b; s, 101a, 266b
al-Djazīra al-khaḍrāʾ (Algeciras) i, 6a, 12b, 58a, 1057b; ii, **524b**; v, 1119a; vi, 430b
Djazīrat al-ʿArab → ʿArab, Djazīrat al-
Djazīrat Banī Naṣr vi, 453b
Djazīrat Firʿawn i, 784a
Djazīrat Ibn Kāwān → Kishm
Djazīrat Ibn ʿUmar → Ibn ʿUmar, Djazīrat
Djazīrat Ḳays → Ḳays, Djazīrat
Djazīrat al-Khiḍr → ʿAbbādān
Djazīrat Sharīḳ ii, **525b**; vi, 457a
Djazīrat Shuḳr ii, **526a**
Djazīrat Ṭarīf i, 7a, 492a
Djazm → Naḥw
al-Djazr (Syria) v, 921a, b, 922a
al-Djazr wa ʾl-madd → Madd
Djazūla, Banū ii, **526b**; vi, 741a, 742a, 744a
al-Djazūlī (al-Gazūlī), ʿAbd Allāh b. Yāsīn → ʿAbd Allāh b. Yāsīn
al-Djazūlī, Abū ʿAbd Allāh al-Samlālī (1465) i, **527a**; iii, 70a, 721b; vi, 743a, 773b; viii, 723a
al-Djazūlī, Abū Mūsā ʿIsā (1209) ii, **528a**; iii, 733a

al-Djazūlī, Ibn Makhlūf al-Nuwayrī (1318) viii, 156a
al-Djazūlī, Muḥammad b. ʿAbd Allāh al-Ḥaḍīkī (1775) vi, 356b
al-Djazūlī, Sīdī Muḥammad b. Slīmān (1465) vi, 591a, b
al-Djazūliyya i, 245a; ii, 528a; iii, 339b; iv, 93b, 380a; vi, 356a; x, 247b; s, 223a
al-Djazzār → Ibrāhīm b. Mūsā al-Kāẓim
Djazzār s, **267a**
al-Djazzār Pasha, Aḥmad (1804) i, 341b, 1078a; ii, 444a, 635b, 912a; iii, 325b; iv, 842b; vi, 327b; viii, 75b; s, **268a**
Djebe (Mongol) (XIII) i, 836a, 987a; ii, 43a
Djebedji i, 807b, 1061b; s, **269b**
Djebel → Djabal
Djebeli, djebelü ii, **528b**, 1090a
Djeblé → Djabala
Djedda → Djudda
Djedīd → Djadīd
Djek → Shahdāgh
Djekermish al-Mawṣilī (XII) i, 1052a
Djelal ed-Din Roumi → Djalāl al-Dīn Rūmī
Djelāl Meḥmed Ḳulī-zāde (XX) viii, 683b
Djelāl Sāhir (XX) vi, 94a; s, 98a
Djelali → Djalālī
Djelālzāde → Djalālzāde
Djellāb, Banū x, 589b
Djem b. Meḥemmed II (Ottoman Prince) (1495) i, 293a, 510b, 1119a, b, 1334b; ii, **529a**; iii, 341a; iv, 463a, 738a; vi, 324b, 1025a; viii, 569b
Djemāʿa → Djamāʿa
Djemāl al-Dīn Bey (Derebey) (XIX) viii, 167a
Djemāl Pasha (Young Turk) (1922) ii, 289b, 431a, **531a**, 637b, 699b; iv, 284b, 872b, 906b; vi, 304a, b, 615a; s, 98a
Djemāl Pasha (Makka) (XIX) vi, 151b
Djemalī Efendi → Djamālī, ʿAlī
Djemʿiyyet → Djamʿiyya
Djemʿiyyet-i ʿIlmiyye-i ʿOthmāniyye ii, **532a**
Djemshīd → Djamshīd
Djenānī → ʿĀṣim, Aḥmad
Djenāze Ḥasan Pasha → Kaḥyā Ḥasan Pasha
Djendereli → Djandarli̊
Djenné → Dienné
Djerba → Djarba
Djerīd ii, **532a**, 954a
Djerīd → Djarīd, Bilād al-
Djerime → Djarīma
Djevrī vi, 836a
Djewād Shākir → Haliḳarnas Bali̊ḳči̊si̊
Djewān Bakht b. Bahādur Shāh II i, 914a
Djewānshīr line (Mughal) iv, 573a
Djewdet, ʿAbd Allāh (1932) ii, 430b, 474b, 475a, **533a**, 1117a; iii, 393a; iv, 168b, 169a; vi, 93a, 94a
Djewdet Pasha → Aḥmad Djewdet Pasha
Djewher Sulṭān bint Selīm II (XVI) viii, 316b
Djezāʾirli Ghāzī Ḥasan Pasha (1790) i, 63a; ii, 26b, **533b**; iii, 992b; iv, 455b, 588b, 853a; v, 764a, 1248a; vi, 325b; vii, 179a
Djezzar → Djazzār
Djibāl ii, **534b**
al-Djibāl i, 49a, 437b; ii, **534b**; vi, 64a, b, 66a, 117b, 120a, 332b, 333a, b, 337b, 338a, b, 539a, 574b, 653a, 781b
Djibāl Ḳarīn i, 1350a; ii, 534b; iv, 97b, 465a; v, 169a; vi, 937b; s. 43b
Djibāl Pādūspān vi, 938a
Djibāliyya, Banū iii, 642a
Djibāliyyūn (Tunisia) vi, 251a
al-Djibāwī, Ḥasan (1504) viii, 729b; 730b
al-Djibāwī, Saʿd al-Dīn → Saʿd al-Dīn al-Djibāwī
Djibāya i, 533b; iv, 244b
Djibbālī (language) vi, 84a; s, 339b
Djibouti → Djibūtī
Djibrāʾīl b. Yaḥyā (Samarḳand) (VIII) viii, 1032b
Djibrān → Djabrān
Djibrīl → Djabrāʾīl
Djibrīl b. ʿUmar (1785) viii, 18b
Djibūtī ii, **535b**; vi, 643b; ix, 717a; x, 71a
Djidʿatī, Banū vi, 128b
al-Djidd wa ʾl-hazl ii, **536a**
Djidda → Djudda
Djidjelli ii, **537a**; iv, 361a, 362a
Djīdjī Ānaga (Umm Mīrzā ʿAzīz Kōka) (XVI) vii, 131a
al-Djifār viii, 385a; x, 480b, 481a
Djigdjiga (Ogādēn) vii, 389b; viii, 161b
Djihād i, 7a, 31b, 179b, 250b, 276b, 314a, 445b, 664a; ii, 64a, 65a, 126a, 504b, **538a**; iii, 180a, 181b; iv, 772a, 796b; v, 1243b, 1250a

Djihādiyya i, 1157a; v, 267b, 1252a
Djihān-Pahlawān Muḥammad b. Eldigüz (Ildeñizid) (1186) i, 300b; iii, 47b, 1110b, 1111a, b; s, 416a
Djihān Shāh (Ḳara Ḳoyunlu) (1467) x, 964b
Djihāngīr (Mughal) → Djahāngīr
Djihāngīr b. ʿAlī (Aḳ-ḳoyunlu) (1453) i, 311b, 312a; vi, 541a
Djihāngīr b. ʿAzīz (Banū Kāwūsh) (1596) iv, 808a
Djihāngīr b. Süleymān II Ḳānūnī (Ottoman) (1553) iv, 232a; v, 727a
Djihānshāh (Ḳara Ḳoyunlu) (1467) i, 147b, 311b; iv, 34a, 102b, 587b, 588a; vi, 513b; viii, 766b; x, 514a
Djihār (idol) vii, 463b
Djihinnām (VII) i, 690a
Djīl Djawbara b. Farrukhān Djīlānshāh (696) s, 298a
Djīl Djīlān → Djīl Djawbara
Djilāla, Djilālism iv, 381b, 382b, 383a; s, 351a
Djilālī b. Idrīs → Bū Ḥmāra
Djilālī Mthīr əd (XIX) vi, 250a
al-Djīlālī al-Rūgī (1908) vi, 1009b
Djīlān s, 297b, 298a
Djilaw Khān (Čūbānid) (1327) ii, 68a
Djild ii, **540a**
al-Djildakī, ʿIzz al-Dīn Aydamir (1342) iv, 1134a; v, 112a, 971a, b, 973a; s, **270a**
al-Djīlī → ʿAbd al-Ḳādir al-Djīlanī
al-Djīlī, Ḳuṭb al-Dīn → ʿAbd al-Karīm al-Djīlī
Djīlīs, Banū vi, 539a
al-Djillī, Muḥammad b. ʿAlī (994) viii, 146b
Djilliḳ ii, **541a**, 1021a; s, 117a
Djillīḳī → Ibn Marwān al-Djillīḳī
Djillīḳiyya (Galicia) ii, **541b**; v, 781b; vi, 221b; s, 92a
Djilwa ii, **542b**
Djīlwa, Mīrzā Abu 'l-Ḥasan (1896) vii, 132a
Djilwatiyya ii, **542b**; iii, 538b; iv, 191b
Djīm ii, **543b**
Djimār vi, 105b
Djimat ii, **545a**
Djimmā ii, **545a**
Djimrī (XIII) i, 467a; ii, 204b, 989a
Djimrī (rebel) (XIII) iv, 620a; viii, 831b
Djināḥ, Muḥammad ʿAlī (1948) i, 1196b; ii, **545b**; iii, 532b, 1204b; iv, 299a; v, 780a; vi, 78a, b; viii, 241b, 254b
Djinās → Tadjnīs
Djināza → Djanāza
Djinbāwāy s, 244a
al-Djinbayhī/al-Djunbayhī → al-Djanbīhī
Djindjī vi, 535a
Djindji Khwādja → Ḥusayn Djindji
Djinīn vi, 543b
Djinn i, 187a; ii, 323a, 518b, **546b**; iii, 273b, 669a, 1050a; iv, 264b; v, 1101a, 1202a; s, 52b, 371a
Djinn ʿAlī Pasha (XVIII) viii, 197a
Djins (genus) ii, **550a**
Djins (sex) ii, **550b**
Djirān, al-ʿAwd (VIII) viii, 120b
Djirāb al-Dawla ii, 178b
Djiʿrāna vi, 266a; vii, 373a
Djirdjā → Girgā
al-Djirdjāwī, ʿUthmān (XVIII) iv, 852b
Djirdjent ii, **553a**; iv, 496b
Djirdjī Zaydān → Zaydān, Djirdjī
Djirdjīs ii, **553a**
Djirga v, 1079a; s, **270a**
Djirm → Djism
Djirm (Badakhshān) i, 851b
Djirra (river) ix, 310a
Djīruft i, 810b; ii, **553b**; iv, 4a; v, 148b, 149a, 150b; vi, 493b; vii, 357a; s, 129a
Djīsh → Gīsh
Djism ii, **553b**
Djisr ii, **555a**, 716a; iv, 555a
al-Djisr, Shaykh Ḥusayn (1909) vi, 355a; viii, 446b
Djisr Banāt Yaʿḳūb ii, **555a**; viii, 757b
Djisr al-Ḥadīd ii, **555b**
Djisr al-Khashab vi, 547a
Djisr Manbidj → Ḳalʿat al-Nadjm
Djisr al-Shughr ii, **556a**; iv, 1015a
Djisr al-Walīd vi, 774b
Djisr-i Muṣṭafā Pasha s, 149b
Djiṣṣ ii, **556b**
Djītal → Sikka; Wazn
al-Djiṭālī → al-Djayṭālī
Djiti Shahr → Altı̊ Shahr
al-Djiwāʾ i, 539b; ii, **557b**
Djīwan (1717) ii, **558a**
Djiwār i, 429b, 890b; ii, **558b**; iii, 1017b
Djīza (Gizeh) i, 125b; iii, 173b; vi, 195b, 411a, 652a; vii, 147a, 148a, b; s, 407b
Djīzān → Djayzān
al-Djīzī, Abū Muḥammad (870) ii, **559a**

Djizya i, 656a, b, 1090b, 1144a, 1146a; ii, 121a, 131a, 142b, 146b, 151b, 154a, 227a, 272a, 490a, **559a**; iii, 1181a; iv, 500a, 939a, 1033a, 1095a; v, 92b, 262b, 500b
Djoči Khān → Djuči b. Čingiz Khān
Djōdhpur ii, **567a**
Djogdjakarta ii, 426b, 427a
Djolof (language) ii, **567a**; ix, 119a; x, 602a
Djowān Mīr (XIX) iv, 730b
Djuʿayl, Banū v, 318a
al-Djuba → al-Djawf
Djubar, Banū iv, 361a, b
Djubārāt, Banū vii, 921a
Djubayl (Lebanon) ii, **568a**; v, 789a, 793a; ix, 268a
al-Djubayl (Saʿūdi Arabia) ii, **568b**
al-Djubayla i, 628b; ii, **569a**
Djubayla (island) vi, 729b
Djubba → Libās
Djubbaʿdīn vi, 308a, b
al-Djubbāʾī (Zandjī) (IX) vii, 526b
al-Djubbāʾī, Abū ʿAlī Muḥammad (915) i, 4b, 128b, 412a, 694a; ii, 449b, **569b**, 802b; iii, 465b, 1143a, 1165b; iv, 183a, 693a, 1162b, 1163a; vi, 846b; vii, 312a, 784a, 975b; ix, 551b; s, 13b, 88b, 90b, 344a, b, 345b, 347a
al-Djubbāʾī, Abū Hāshim ʿAbd al-Salām (933) i, 4b, 411a; ii, 218b, **570a**; iii, 171b, 832a, 1143a, 1165b; v, 702a; vii, 784a; viii, 534a; s, 12b, 13b, 25b, 32a, 226b, 343b, 346b, 348a
Djubūr ii, **570b**; s, 101b
Djuči b. Čingiz Khān (Mongol) (1227) i, 1105a, 1106b, 1187b, 1188a; ii, 2a, 43a, 44a, **571a**; vi, 417b; s, 96b, 246a, 459a
Djučids s, 340a
Djudāla → Gudāla
Djudayʿ b. ʿAlī al-Kirmānī (VIII) iii, 224a; vii, 1016a
Djudda i, 380b, 546b, 1032b, 1054b; ii, 91b, **571b**; iii, 11b, 362b, 760b, 1067a; v, 808a; vi, 33b, 34b, 35a, 144b, 148a, 150b, 151a, 157a, 163a, 195b, 324a, 641b; vii, 173a
Djudhām, Banū i, 436a, 528b, 532a, 630b, 1140a; ii, **573b**; v, 594a, 632a, b, 897b; vi, 221b, 622a, 727b; vii, 372a, 921a; viii, 466a, 865a
Djudhām (leprosy) s, **270b**
al-Djudhāmī, Abū ʿAbd Allāh (XIII) s, 381b
al-Djudhāmī, al-ʿAlāʾ b. Mughīth (763) i, 82a, 862a; iv, 665b
al-Djudhāmī, Ibn al-Ṣabbāgh (XIII) vii, 811b
al-Djudhāmī, ʿUthmān b. ʿAbd al-Ḥakam (779) vi, 280b
Djudhayma al-Abrash i, 788b
Djūdī, Djabal i, 251b; ii, **573b**; s, 36a
Djūdī al-Mawrūrī (813) ii, **574b**
Djudjayn b. Thābit ii, 590b
Djufayna iii, 586b
al-Djufayna vi, 563b
Djuʿfī, Banū ii, 1059b, 1061b
al-Djuʿfī, al-Mufaḍḍal b. ʿUmar (Khaṭṭābī) (VIII) vii, 647b
al-Djuʿfī, Muḥammad b. Mūsā b. al-Ḥasan b. al-Furāt (ḳāḍī) (IX) viii, 146a
al-Djufra ii, **575a**
Djufriyya vi, 640b
Djughrāfiyā i, 1102a; ii, **575b**; iv, 1078a-1083a
Djuḥā ii, **590b**; vii, 1018a
al-Djuhanī → ʿAbd Allāh b. Unays; Maʿbad
al-Djuhanī, ʿAbd al-Sharīḳ vii, 581a
al-Djuhanī, ʿAmr b. Murra (VII) viii, 82b
Djuhaymān → al-ʿUtaybī, Djuhaymān b. Muḥammad
Djuhayna → Ḳudāʿa
al-Djuhaynī, Muḥammad b. Dīnār (798) vi, 280b
Djuke-Tau → Zhukotin
Djūlāmerg → Čölemerik
al-Djulandā, Āl i, 812b, 813a, 1098a; iv, 500b; 1098a; viii, 85a; ix, 77a, 775a; x, 816a; s, 222b, 223a
al-Djulandā b. Kanʿān s, 222b
al-Djulandā b. Masʿūd b. Djaʿafar (VIII) i, 550b; **ii, 592b**; iii, 652a; ix, 775a, s 693b
al-Djulandā Imām (752) x, 816a
Djulbān (Aleppo) (XIV) vi, 381b
Djulfā i, 8a, 643a; iv, 476a; vi, 291a; viii, 773b; s, **274b**
Djulfār → Raʾs al-Khayma
Djullanār s, **277a**
al-Djulūdī, ʿAbd al-ʿAzīz b. Yaḥyā iv, 927a
al-Djulundā b. Masʿūd b. Djaʿafar (VIII) → al-Djulandā b. Masʿūd b. Djaʿafar
Djumʿa (Yawm al-) ii, **592b**
Djumʿa, Imām (Iṣfahān) (XIX) s, 169b

Djumādā → Taʿrīkh
Djumaḥ Banū vi, 137b, 145a; s, 284a
al-Djumaḥī → Abū Dahbal; Ibn Sallām
al-Djumaḥī, Saʿīd b. ʿAbd al-Raḥmān (790) s, 225b
Djumayla, Banū i, 233b
Djumblāṭ → Djānbulāṭ
Djumhūr b. al-ʿIdjlī (VIII) iv, 99b
Djumhūriyya ii, **594a**, 644b
al-Djumhūriyya al-ʿarabiyya al-muttaḥida ii, 649a, 674a; iii, 264b, 1259a; v, 1061a; vi, 36b, 280b; s, 2b, 7b
Djümhūriyyet Khalḳ Fîrkasî i, 734b; ii, 432b, **595b**; iii, 526b; iv, 124b, 791b, 988a; v, 1038a
Djumla → Naḥw
Djūnā Khān → Muḥammad b. Tughluḳ
Djūnāgarh (Ḳāthiawār) ii, **597a**, 1127a; iii, 451a; vi, 50b, 190a, 270a, 419b; s, 246b
Djunayd, Shaykh (Ṣafawid) (1460) ii, **598b**; iii, 315b, 1006b; vi, 613b; viii, 766b, 777a
Djunayd (Aydînoghlu) (1425) i, 309a, 346a, 783b; ii, **599a**; vi, 975b; vii, 594b, 645a, 711a
al-Djunayd, Abu ʾl-Ḳāsim al-Baghdādī al-Nihāwandī (911) i, 162a, 415b; ii, **600a**; iii, 823b; iv, 114b; vi, 225a, 569b, 570a; vii, 871a; ix, 57a; x, 116b; s, 350a
al-Djunayd b. ʿAbd Allāh al-Murrī (734) i, 1292b; ii, **600b**; iv, 708a
al-Djunayd b. ʿAbd al-Raḥmān (VIII) vii, 629b; s, 252a
al-Djunayd b. Ibrāhīm → Ṣafawids
Djunayd Khān (Turcoman) (XX) v, 24a, b
Djunaydib akhū Banī Rawāḥa s, 177b
Djunaydiyya i, 868b
Djunayr vi, 63a
al-Djunbulānī al-Djannān, Abū Muḥammad ʿAbd Allāh (900) viii, 146a
Djunbulāṭ → Djānbulāṭ
Djund i, 76a, 82a, 134b, 248a, 490a, b, 729b, 991a; ii, 505a, **601a**; v, 685a
Djund (province) v, 125a
Djundab b. Khāridja al-Ṭāʾī i, 1241b; viii, 377a
Djundaysābūr → Gondēshāpūr
Djundī → Ḥalḳa (soldiers)
Djundīsāpūr → Gondēshāpur
Djundub b. Djunāda → Abū Dharr al-Ghifārī
Djūngars x, 677a
Djūnī vi, 303a
Djunnar ii, **602a**; vi, 269a
Djūr → Fīrūzābād
Djuradh s, **285b**
Djurash (Yemen) s, 326b
Djurʾat (1810) ii, **602a**
Djuraydj (Gregorius) i, 1021b; ii, **602b**; vi, 630b
al-Djurayrī, Abū Muḥammad (924) viii, 840b
Djurbadhāḳān → Gulpāyagān
Djurd (Durūz) vi, 343b, 344a
Djurdjān → Gurgān
Djurdjānī, Fakhr al-Dīn → Gurgānī
al-Djurdjānī, ʿAbd al Ḳāhir (1078) x, 129a
al-Djurdjānī, Abu ʾl-ʿAbbās (1089) viii, 428a
al-Djurdjānī, Abū Bakr ʿAbd al-Ḳāhir (1078) i, 590b, 858a, 982a, 1115b; ii, 824b; iii, 834b, 1020a; iv, 250b, 251a, b, 864a; v, 899a, 900b, 1026a; vi, 218a, b, 340a, 348b; vii, 261a, 528a, 771b, 773b, 914b; ix, 455a; s, **277a**
al-Djurdjānī, Abu ʾl-Ḳāsim (XI) s, 14b
al-Djurdjānī, ʿAlī b. ʿAbd al-ʿAzīz Abu ʾl-Ḥasan (1001) iv, 249b; vii, 772a; ix, 57a; s, 652a
al-Djurdjānī, ʿAlī b. Muḥammad al-Sayyid al-Sharīf (1413) i, 342b, 343a, 351a, 714b, 715b, 1327a; ii, 294a, **602b**, 608a, 774a; iii, 330a, 664b, 1147b; iv, 123a, 272a; vi, 354b; vii, 821b; x, 89a
al-Djurdjānī, Ismāʿīl b. al-Ḥusayn (1136) i, 213b; ii, **603a**; s, 271b
al-Djurdjānī, Mīr Sayyid Sharīf (1413) viii, 45b, 541b
al-Djurdjāniyya → Gurgandj
Djurdjīs b. Djibrīl b. Bukhtīshūʿ (VIII) i, 212b, 1298a
Djurdjūma ii, 456a, 457b
Djurdjura i, 369b; ii, **603a**; iv, 359a, 360a, 361a, 362b
Djurhum (Djurham), Banū i, 563a; ii, **603b**; iii, 389b, 739a; iv, 185a, 448b; v, 77a, b, 763a; vi, 145a, 738a
al-Djurhumī, ʿIṣām b. Shahbar (VI) vii, 841a
Djurm ii, 479b, **604a**
Djurmāghūn (XIII) iv, 102a
Djurmāʾīs v, 163a

al-Djurr, Shukr Allāh (XX) v, 1256a, b
al-Djurūmiyya v, 65a, 183a
Djurzān → al-Kurdj
Djusham (Djishum) s, 343a
Djusham b. Muʿāwiya, Banū ii, 626b; v, 48b; vi, 134a, b, 741b
Djusnas Abū FarruKhān (VIII) s, 298b
Djustān I b. Marzubān (Djustānid) (960) ii, 191a; v, 452; vi, 499b; vii, 656b
Djustān II (Djustānid) ii, 191a, b; iii, 245a
Djustān III (Djustānid) (IX) vii, 655b
Djustān b. Sharmazan (X) x, 897b
Djustān b. Wahsūdān ii, 192a
Djustān (King, Daylam) (VIII) xi, 242b
Djustānids ii, 191a, 193b; iii, 254b; v, 602b, 603a; vii, 655b; s, 356b
Djūtid Shurafāʾ ix, 507b
Djuwayn ii, **604b**; iv, 5a; s, 235a
al-Djuwaynī, ʿAbd Allāh b. Yūsuf (1047) i, 952b; ii, **605a**; iv, 149b; v, 526b
al-Djuwaynī, ʿAbu ʾl-Maʿālī (Imām al-Ḥaramayn) (1085) i, 410b, 411a, 485a, 593a, 1130b; ii, 570b, **605a**, 1038b, 1040a; iii, 330a, 914a, 1019b, 1024b, 1145a; iv, 149b, 257b, 272a; vi, 376a, 448a, 456a, 739a; vii, 296b, 781a; viii, 63a; s, 343b, 346b, 347a, b, 348a, 403a
al-Djuwaynī, Abū Muḥammad viii, 63a
al-Djuwaynī, ʿAlāʾ al-Dīn ʿAṭā-Malik (1283) i, 902b; ii, **606a**; iii, 738a; iv, 865a; v, 311b; vii, 234b; viii, 342b; s, 94b
al-Djuwaynī, Bahāʾ al-Dīn Muḥammad (1279) ii, 607b; viii, 342b; xi, 193b; s, 235b
Djuwaynī, Muntadjab al-Dīn Badīʿ (XII) ix, 16b
al-Djuwaynī, Shams al-Dīn (Ṣāḥib dīwān) (1284) ii, 334a, **607a**; iii, 572b, 1269a; iv, 620b; v, 868b; vii, 234b; viii, 342b 702b, 806a; xi, 193b; s, 235b
Djuwaynī Sharaf al-Din Harūn (1286) ii, 607b; viii, 806a
Djuwayra → Abū Duʾād al-Iyādī
Djuwayriyya bint Abī Djahl (VII) i, 751a
Djuwayriyya bint al-Ḥārith (VII) v, 78b
Djūybārī Khʷādja Muḥammad Islām (1563) x, 250b
Djūybārīs s, 228a
Djuyum → Djuwayn
Djuyūsh Beg, Ay Aba (1120) i, 300b; vi, 64a, 500a, 782a; vii, 235a, 408a
Djuzʾ (atom) ii, 220a, **607b**
Djuzʾ (Ḳurʾān) → Ḳurʾān
Djuzʾ (in poetry) → ʿArūḍ
Djūzdjān (Gūzgān) ii, 1b, **608b**, 798b; vi, 65b, 618a; s, 125b, 367b, 376a, b, 386b
al-Djūzdjānī, Abū ʿAmr Minhādj al-Dīn (1270) i, 1131a; ii, **609a**, 1099a; iii, 1155b
al-Djūzdjānī, Abū Sulaymān (890) vi, 846a
al-Djūzdjānī, Abū ʿUbayd (XI) iii, 331a, 941a, b; vi, 638a; viii, 542a
al-Djūzdjānī, Ibrāhīm b. Yaʿḳūb (873) viii, 515b
Dnieper → Özı
Dōʾāb ii, **609b**, 868a; vi, 48a, 49a, 50a, 63b, 65b, 294b; x, 891b; s, 57b, 124a, 126a, 206b
Dōʿān → Dawʿān
Dobʿa iii, 6a
Dobrotič (XIV) ii, 611a, 971b
Dobrudja i, 1302a; ii, **610a**, 909a, 971b; v, 277b; x, 699b
Dōdāīs i, 1005b; s, 332a
Dodecanese → On iki Ada
Ḍofār → Ẓafār
Dogali vi, 643b
Doğan Avcioğlu (XX) vi, 95b
Döger (Ghuzz) i, 666b; ii, **613b**, 1107b
Döger Sālim Beg (XIV) iv, 584b, 586a
Doghandjî ii, **614a**
Dōgrās iv, 709b; s, 241b
Doğu-Bayazitğ → Bāyazīd
Doha → al-Dawḥa
Doḳūz Khātūn (1265) iii, 569b, 1122a; vii, 973a
Dolma Baghče → Istanbul
Dōmbkī → Balūčistān
Dome of the Rock → Ḳubbat al-Ṣakhra; Masdjid al-Aḳṣā
Donanma ii, **615a**
Donbolī → Dumbulī, Banū
Dongola i, 50a; ii, **615a**; vi, 574b; vii, 425b; viii, 89b, 90b; ix, 155a; s, 278b
Dönme ii, **615b**
Dönüm → Miṣāḥa
Dorylaion → Eskishehir
Dōsa → Dawsa
Dōst Muḥammad → Dūst Muḥammad
Douar → Dawār
Draʿ/Draa → Darʿa
Drač ii, **616b**

Dragman → Tardjumān
Dragut → Ṭurghud ʿAlī Pasha
Drīshak tribe → Balūčistān
Druzes → Durūz
Duʿāʾ ii, 302a, 314b, **617a**; iv, 715b; v, 74a, b, 621b, 956b, 960a
Duʾa Khān → Duwā Khān
Dūʿan → Dawʿan
Dubai → Dubayy
Dubays I b. ʿAlī (Mazyadid) (1081) i, 684a, 1073b, 1074a, 1075a; iii, 390a; iv, 911a; vi, 965b; vii, 118a
Dubays II b. Ṣadaḳa I (Mazyadid) (1135) i, 300b, 314a, 684a; iv, 493b, 911b; vi, 64a, b, 544a; vii, 733a, b
Dubayy i, 166b, 928b, 1313b; ii, **618b**; iv, 778a; vi, 37b; s, 416b
al-Dubb → Nudjūm
Dubdū ii, **619b**
Dubrovnik → Raghūsa
Duče Meḥmed Pasha (XVII) i, 656b
Dūdāniyya → Dido
Dudekulas v, 648b
Dūdhū Miyān i, 952a; ii, 784a
Dudjayl → Kārūn
Dudlebs (Dūlāba), Banū s, 170b
Duero → Wādī Duwayro
Duff ii, **620a**
Dughāgha → Daghūgh, Banū
Dūghlāt (Dūḳlāt) ii, 45b, **621b**; ix, 649a
Dūghlāt, Mīrzā Muḥammad (1534) viii, 136a
Ḍuḥā ii, **622b**
al-Duhaym b. Khalīl, Aḥmad (949) s, 113a
Duhmān, Banū vi, 649a
Duhn → Khazaf
Dukaginzade Yaḥyā Beg (1582) vi, 836a
Duḳāḳ b. Tutush (Saldjūḳ) (1104) i, 664a, 731b, 1052a, 1332a; ii, 282a; iii, 398b; vi, 930b; viii, 947a; x, 600a
al-Dūkālī, ʿAbd al-Wāḥid s, 93a
Dukayn al-Rādjiz b. Radjāʾ al-Fukaymī (723) ii, **622b**
Dukayn al-Rādjiz b. Saʿīd al-Dārimī (727) ii, **622b**
Dukchi Ishān (XIX) iv, 113a
Dukhān → Tütün
Dukhtar Khāṣṣa vi, 488a
Dukkāla, Banū ii, **623a**; vi, 595a, 741a, b, 743a
al-Dukkālī, Abū Shuʿayb b. ʿAbd al-Raḥmān (1937) iv, 159b; viii, 905b
Dūlāb → Nāʿūra
Dūlāb (Daylam) iv, 725a
al-Dūlābī, Muḥammad b. Aḥmad (923) viii, 516a
Dulafids ii, **623a**; iv, 100a
Dūlandī bint Arghun b. Abaka (İlkhān) (XIV) ii, 68a
Dulaym, Banū i, 461a; ii, **623b**
Duldul ii, **624a**
al-Dulfīn → Nudjūm
Dulghadir → Dhu ʾl-Ḳadr
Dulūk i, 791b; ii, **624a**; vi, 506b, 507a
Dūmānlū vi, 384b
Dūmat al-Djandal (al-Djawf) i, 55a, 384a, 525a, 882b, 969a; ii, **624b**; iv, 492b, 928a, b; vi, 544b; vii, 371a, 373b, 693b; x, 784a
Dumayr ii, 1021b
Dumbulī, Banū ii, 193a; v, 460a
Dumbulī Khāns → Kurds
al-Dumistiḳ Ḳurḳāsh (X) vi, 230b
Dūna, Banū vi, 310b
Dunama b. Aḥmad (Bornu) (XIX) i, 1260a
Dunama Dibbalemi (Kanem) (XIII) iv, 567a
Dūnash b. Labrāṭ vii, 661a
Dunaysir ii, **626a**; v, 248a; vi, 540a
Dunbāwand → Damāwand
Dunbulī → Dumbulī
Dündar Beg → Falak al-Dīn Dündar
Dungan (Dōngan, Tungan) → al-Ṣīn
Dungans (Tungans, Tʾung-kan) i, 418b; v, 363b, 364a; x, **629a**; xi, 256a
Dungar Sen (XV) vi, 53a
Dunghuzlum → Deñizli
Dungina → Ḳayalîḳ
Dunhuang x, 707a
Dunḳulā → Dongola
Dunūh/Dumūya/Dumuwayh vi, 412b
Dunyā i, 2a, 325a; ii, 295a, **626b**
Dunyā Khātūn (Artuḳid) (1367) vi, 540b
Durač, Durrës → Drač
Dūrāh Pass ii, 29a
Durand Agreement (1893) i, 87b
Durand Line vi, 86b; s, 66a, 270b
al-Duraybī, Āl i, 1312b
Durayd b. al-Ṣimma (630) ii, **626b**; iii, 578a; iv, 1027a; vi, 605a
Durazzo → Drač
Dūrbāsh ii, **627b**
Durčaʾi, Sayyid Mahdī (1944) vii, 95b

Durčaʾi, Sayyid Muḥammad Bāḳir (1923) vii, 95b; s, 157b
Durgaras → Dōgrās
Durkānī → Balūčistān
Ḍurmā vi, 191b
al-Durr i, 95b; ii, 557b, **628a**; iv, 764b; v, 572b, 675a, 819a
Durrānī i, 72b, 95a, 217b, 219b, 230a, b, 295a; ii, **628b**, 1001b; iii, 202a, 428a; iv, 357a, 537b; s, 66b, 270a, 332b
Dürrī Meḥmed Efendi (1736) ii, **629a**
Dürrīzāde ʿAbd Allāh Bey (1923) ii, 105a, **630a**
Dürrīzāde Meḥmed ʿĀrif Efendi (1800) ii, **629b**; iii, 604a, 1002b
Dürrīzāde Muṣṭafā Efendi (1775) ii, **629b**
Dürrīzāde Seyyid ʿAbd Allāh (1828) ii, **630a**
Dürrīzāde Seyyid Meḥmed ʿAtāʾ Allāh (1785) ii, **629b**
Dursun b. ʿAdjlān Ḳarasi̊ (XIV) iv, 628a
Dursun Beg (1461) vi, 70b, 71a
Dursun Meḥmed Pasha (1691) i, 174b
al-Durūʿ, Banū ii, **630b**; iii, 1004b
Durūn (Darūn) i, 320b
Durūz i, 68a, 483a, 552a, 571a, 1042a, 1078b, 1093b; ii, 98a, 136b, **631b**, 749b, 1026b; iii, 21a, 76b, 293a; iv, 199a, 332a, 484a, 834b; v, 791b, 793b; vi, 26a, b, 27b, 30b, 31a, 41b, 42a, 343a, 387b; vii, 117b; x, 192a, b; s, 49a, b, 135b, 206b, 268b, 269a, 371a
Dusares → Dhu ʾl-Sharā
Dushanbe vi, 769a; x, 66a
Dushmanziyār → Kākawayhids
Dushmanziyārī, Banū iii, 1106b
Dūst Bū Saʿd Dada (XI) i, 147b
Dūst Muḥammad (painter) (XVI) vii, 602b; viii, 787b, 788a
Dūst Muḥammad Khān (1740) i, 1195a, 1197a
Dūst Muḥammad Khān (1863) i, 231a; ii, 417a, **637b**; iv, 537b; v, 48a; s, 237b, 367b
Dustūr i, 170a; ii, 79a, 151a, **638a**; iii, 186b
Duwā Khān (Čaghatay) (1306) i, 504b; ii, 3b, 14b, 45a, 268b; iv, 31b, 32a
Duwaydār → Dawādār
Duwayḥ (Dongola) s, 278b
al-Duwayhī → Iṣṭifān al-Duwayhī
al-Duwayḥī, Ibrāhīm al-Rashīd (1874) vi, 354b; s, **278b**
Duwayḥis (XVIII) iv, 925a
Duyūn-i ʿUmūmiyye ii, **677a**
Dūzakh → Djahannam
Duzdāb → Zāhidān
Düzmedje Muṣṭafā → Muṣṭafā Čelebi, Düzme
Dwārkā ii, **678a**, 1127a; vi, 50b
Dwīn (Dabīl) i, 636a, 638a, 645a, b; ii, **678a**; vi, 504b, 648a; vii, 395a; ix, 169a
Dyābāt vi, 293b
Dyallo i, 303a
Dyula (Mali) vi, 258b
Dzabic, A.F. (1918) i, 1271b, 1274a; ii, **681b**
Dzambul Dzabaev → Djambul Djabaev
Dzhek iv, 1029a; v, 284b
Dzungharia ix, 648b, 649b
Dzunghars → Zunghars

E

ʿEbedyeshuʾ/ʿAbdīshūʾ vi, 115a
Ebionites viii, 676a
Eblis → Iblīs
Ebu ʾl-Suʿūd Efendi → Abū ʾl-Suʿūd
Ebüzziya Tevfik (Abu ʾl-Ḍiyāʾ Tewfīḳ) (1913) i, 289b; ii, 474b, **682a**; vi, 92b, 93a, 372b; vii, 532a
Ecevit (XX) x, 696a
Ecija → Istidja
Edebiyyāt-i Djedīde ii, **683a**
Edessa → al-Ruhā
Edfū → Adfū
Edhem, Čerkes → Čerkes Edhem
Edhem, Khalīl → Eldem, Khalīl
Edhem Pasha → Ibrāhīm
Edigü (Noghay) (1419) i, 1108a; ii, 44a, 1112a; iii, 117a; vi, 417b; viii, 86a; x, 563a
Edindjik vi, 587b
Ediou (Noghay) (XV) vi, 417b; viii, 86a
Edirne i, 269a, 398b, 999a, 1078a, 1279a, 1334a; ii, **683a**; iii, 352a; iv, 590a; vi, 55a, 59b, 70a, 74a, 290b; s, 149b, 274a, 330b

– institutions i, 1225b; ii, 686a, 1133b
– monuments ii, 684a, b, 685a, b; iv, 592a, 722b, 1159a; v, 225a
Edirneli Naẓmī → Naẓmī
Ed̲j̲e K̲h̲alīl ii, 983b
Edrei → Ad̲h̲riʿāt
Edremit ii, **686b**
ʿEdrūs → ʿAydarūs
Efe → Zeybek
Efendi i, 75a; ii, 19a, **687a**
Eflāḳ (Wallachia) i, 340b, 1118b, 1298b; ii, 611b, **687b**, 688b, 703a, 915; iii, 1004a; vi, 58b, 59b; viii, 609a
Egerdir → Eğridir
Eğil vi, 541a
Eğin ii, **689a**
Eğri ii, **689b**
Eğri Dag̲h̲ → Ag̲h̲rï Dag̲h̲
Eğriboz (Euboea) ii, **691a**; v, 722b; vi, 71b
Eğridir ii, **691b**
Egypt → Miṣr
Ekbez s, 171b, 172a
Ekdālā iii, 634b
Ekinči b. Ḳočḳar (1097) iv, 1067a; v, 385b; s, **279a**
Ekrem Bey (1914) i, 287b, 558a; ii, 440a, **692a**; iii, 357b; iv, 930b; v, 195b; vi, 373a
Ekrem ʿÖmer Pas̲h̲a (1854) vi, 68b
El Ḳaghan (eastern Türk) x, 687a
Elam, Elamite v, 830b
Elath → Ayla
Elaziğ → Maʿmūrat al-ʿAzīz
Elbasan i, 652b, 655b; ii, **693a**; iv, 140a
Elbaz, Raphael Moise vi, 293a
Elbistān ii, 239a, b, 240a, **693a**; iv, 463a; v, 73b; vi, 231b, 322a, 366a, 505b, 507a, b, 508a, b, 509a
Elburz → Alburz
Elchasaites → Ṣābiʾ; Ṣābiʾa
Elche → Als̲h̲
Elči ii, **694a**; iv, 31b
Eldem, K̲h̲alīl Edhem (1938) ii, **694b**; iii, 993b
Eldigüz, Eldigüzids → Ildeñiz, Ildeñizids
El-Erg → D̲j̲ālo
Elesbaas i, 103a
El-Gāʿda i, 460b
El-Hajj Malik El-S̲h̲abazz → Malcolm X
Elias Andrawus s, 301a
Eličpur vi, 54a; s, **279b**
Elijah → Ilyās
Elijah Muhammad (1975) vii, 703a
Elisha → Alīsaʿ
Elkass mirza → Alkāṣ mīrzā
Ellora → Elurā
Elma Dag̲h̲ï ii, **694b**, 982a; v, 810a, b
Elmalï ii, **695a**
Eloche → Als̲h̲
Eltüzer İnaḳ K̲h̲ān (K̲h̲īwa) (1806) vii, 574b; s, 420a
Elurā ii, **695a**
Elvira → Ilbīra
Elwān Čelebi i, 698b; ii, 62b; vi, 354b
Elwend → Alwand
Emānet → Emīn
Emanet-i Muḳaddese ii, **695b**
Emba (river) vi, 417b, 418a
Ememik → al-Yamāmī
Emesa → Ḥims
Emil iv, 581a
Emil K̲h̲wād̲j̲a (Ḳoca) (XIV) x, 590b
Emīn i, 1090b; ii, 147b, **695b**
Emin, Mehmed → Yurdakul, Mehmed Emin
Emīn Pas̲h̲a ii, 636b
Emīn Pas̲h̲a (E.C. Schnitzer) (1892) ii, **696a**; v, 1250b
Emīne Sulṭān (XVIII) i, 394b; s, 282b
Eminek (1475) ii, 1112b; vi, 1016b
Emir → Amīr
Emīr Buk̲h̲ārī, S̲h̲eyk̲h̲ (1421) vi, 530b
Emir Efendi of Ḳāsim Pas̲h̲a (XVI) vi, 228a
Emīr Süleymān → Sulaymān Čelebi
Emīr Sulṭān (1429) ii, 103b, **697a**; s, 282b
Emīrōf Murād, Ebu ʾl-Fārūḳ → Mīzānd̲j̲ï Meḥmed Murād
Emniyyet-i ʿUmūmiyye ii, 74b
Empedocles → Anbāduḳlīs
Emr → Amr
Emrāh s, 91b
Emreli ii, **697b**; vi, 588b
ʿEnbāḳōm i, 609a; vii, 74a; s, 396b
Enderūn ii, **697b**, 1089a, 1091a; iv, 1097a
Enderūn-i Hümāyūn Kütübk̲h̲ānesi vi, 198b
End̲j̲ümen → And̲j̲uman
ʿEnes̲h̲ vi, 506a
Enez → Enos
Engürü → Ankara
Engürüs → Mad̲j̲āristān; Ungurus
Enif → Nud̲j̲ūm
Enīs ʿAwnī → Akagündüz

Enīs Behīdj s, 168a
Enīs Redjeb Dede, Shaykh (1734) vii, 575a
Enna → Ḳaṣryānnih
Ennaya vi, 582b
Ennayer → Yinnāyir
Ennedi s, 165a, 166a
Enoch → Idrīs
Enos ii, **698a**
Enwer Pasha (1922) i, 63b; ii, 431b, 531a, b, **698a**; iii, 1199b; iv, 284b, 285b, 297a, b; v, 537b; vi, 983b; viii, 251a
Enwerī, Ḥādjdjī Saʿd Allāh (1794) ii, **702b**
Enzel → Inzāl
Enzeli → Bandar Pahlawī
Ephesus → Aya Solūḳ
Ephthalites → Hayāṭila
Erač vi, 62a
Erbakan, Necmettin (XX) iv, 791b; x, 696b
Erbīl → Irbīl
Erciyas → Erdjiyas
Erdebīl → Ardabil
Erdek (Gulf of) vi, 587b, 588a
Erdel ii, **703a**
Erden ʿAlī → ʿAlāʾ al-Dīn Beg
Erdjīsh → Ardjīsh
Erdjiyas Daghi̊ ii, **705a**; iv, 845b
Ereğli ii, **705a**; iv, 575b, 621a
Erekle → Irakli̊ II
Eretna i, 432a, 510b; ii, 401a, **705b**; iv, 622b, 843a
Erg → Ṣaḥrāʾ
Erganí ii, **707a**
Ergen, Özbeg Khān s, 246a
Ergene Khātūn → Orki̊na Khātūn
Ergenekon ii, **707b**
Ergin, Osman (1961) ii, **708a**
Ergiri ii, **708b**
Ergun, Saʿd al-Dīn Nüzhet s, **280a**
Eritrea ii, **709a**; iii, 6a; vi, 628a
Eriwan → Rewān
Ermenak, Ermenek ii, **710a**; iii, 1006b; iv, 619a, 622a, b
Ermine → Farw
Erota vi, 628b
Ersari̊, Banū i, 224a; v, 582a; vi, 416a, b; s, 143b, 147a, **280b**
Ersoy → Mehmet Akif Ersoy
Ertoghrul i, 329b, 340a; ii, **710b**, 715b; viii, 180b, 192a; ix, 706a
Ertoghrul, Bursa i, 1218b; ii, 711a
Ertoghrul b. Bāyazīd (1392) ii, **711a**
Erzen → Arzan
Erzerum → Erzurūm
Erzindjān i, 639a, 1328a; ii, 33a, **711a**; iv, 817b
Erzurūm (Ḳālīḳalā) i, 4a, 465a, 636a, 639a; ii, 210a, 425b, 711b, **712a**, 945b; iii, 212b, 214b; iv, 394b, 817b; v, 33b; s, 136a, 308a
Esad, Mehmed (Shaykh Muḥammad Asʿad) (1931) vii, 937a
Esʿad Efendi, Aḥmed (1814) ii, **712b**
Esʿad Efendi, Meḥmed (1625) ii, **713a**; iv, 900b
Esʿad Efendi, Meḥmed (1753) ii, **713b**, 931b; iv, 527b
Esʿad Efendi, Meḥmed (1778) ii, **713b**
Esʿad Efendi, Meḥmed (1848) i, 630a; ii, 465b, **714a**; vi, 59a
Esʿad Mukhliṣ Pasha, Saki̊zli̊ Aḥmed (1875) ii, 636b; vi, 69a; vii, 205b; s, **281b**
Esʿad Pasha (1932) iv, 873b
Esāme → Yeni Čeri
Esdras → Idrīs; ʿUzayr
Esen Bugha I ii, 3b
Esen Bugha II (XV) i, 148a; ii, 45b; v, 859a
Esen Buḳa, Khān (1318) x, 590b
Esen Tayshi (XV) iv, 512a
Esendal, Memdūḥ Shewket (1952) v, 194b, 197a; s, **282a**
Eshām → Ashām
Eshkindji ii, 528b, **714b**
Eshḳiyāʾ iii, 317b
Eshref → Ashraf
Eshref, Meḥmed (1912) s, **282b**
Eshref Edib (1910) vi, 986a
Eshref, Rüshen (Ünaydin) (XX) iv, 874b
Eshref-i Rūmī → Eshrefoghlu
Eshrefiyye s, 282b
Eshrefoghlu ʿAbd Allāh (1469) s, **282b**
Eski Baba → Babaeski
Eski Ḳapli̊dja iv, 570a
Eski Ḳarā Ḥiṣār → Īsdje Ḳarā Ḥiṣār; Ḳarā Ḥiṣār
Eski Malaṭya vi, 232a
Eski Sarāy → Sarāy
Eski Üdjüm s, 82a
Eskishehir ii, **715a**
Eṣnāf → Ṣinf
Esne → Isnā
Esrār Dede (1796) ii, 999a; vi, 610a; s, **283a**

Estrangelo iii, 963b
Eszék ii, **715b**
Esztergom ii, **716a**; v, 641a, 1022a; vi, 75a; s, 171a
Etājā, Etaya → Itāwā
Etawah → Itāwā
Ethiopia → al-Ḥabash
Ethiopians → Ḥabasha
Etil → Itil (river)
Et-Meydani → Istanbul
Euboea → Eğriboz
Euclid → Uḳlīdish
Eugène of Savoy i, 269b, 292a, 395a; iv, 969b
Eunuchs (Makka) vi, 168a
Euphrates → al-Furāt
Eutychius → Saʿīd b. Biṭrīḳ
Eve → Ḥawwāʾ
Ev-göčü iv, 239b
Evora → Yābura
Evran → Akhī Ewrān
Evren, Kenan (XX) x, 696a
Evrenos → Ewrenos
Ewliyā Čelebi (1684) i, 310b, 843a, 993a, 1076a; ii, 589b, **717b**; iii, 7a; iv, 185b; v, 726b, 816a; vi, 411b; vii, 599a; s, 171b, 187a, 208b, 315b, 330b
Ewrāḳ i, 1090a
Ewrenos Beg, Ghāzī (1417) ii, **720a**, 722a; iv, 628b; v, 772a; vi, 71a; vii, 237a, 645a; s, 330a, b, 331a
Ewrenos-oghullarî i, 340b, 1118b; ii, **720b**
Eyālet i, 468b, 469a, 640b, 906b, 974a, 1263b; ii, **721b**
Eylūl → Taʾrīkh
Eymir (Eymür) ii, **724a**
Eyvān → Īwān
Eyüp → Eyyüb
Eyyüb iv, 214a, 226a, 231a, 233a, b, 235a, 238b, 244b; vi, 3a, 55b, 125a, 530b; s, 315a
Eyyūb Agha Ḳarā ʿOthmān-oghlu iv, 593b
Eyyüb Ṣabrī iv, 284b
Eyyūbī Aḥmad Pasha (1731) vi, 55b
Eyyūboghlu, Bedrī Raḥmī (1975) s, **283a**
Eyyūboghlu, Ṣabāḥ al-Dīn Raḥmī (1973) s, **283b**
Ezafe → Iḍāfa
Ezan adî iv, 181a
Ēzānā (IV) iii, 10a
Ezbek (XV) iv, 462b, 463a
Ezbekiyya iv, 442a, b
Ezekiel → Ḥizḳīl
Ezelī → Azalī
Ezra → Idrīs; ʿUzayr

F

Fāʾ ii, **725a**
Faḍāʾil → Faḍīla
Fadak ii, **725a**, 844b; vi, 621b, 875a; vii, 398a; xi, 178a
Faḍāla ii, **727a**; vii, 387a
al-Faḍāli, Muḥammad (1821) i, 334a, 867b; ii, **727b**
Fadʿān i, 483a
Faddāʿ, Āl (Mecca) vi, 177a
Faddān → Misāḥa
al-Faddaynī (IX) x, 883a
Fadhlaka ii, **727b**
al-Fāḍil → al-Ḳāḍī al-Fāḍil
Fāḍil Bey, Ḥüseyn (1810) ii, **727b**
Fāḍil Ḥüsnī Dağlarca s, 150a
Fāḍil Khān → al-Bihārī
Fāḍil Pasha, Muṣṭafā, Mîṣîrlî (1875) ii, 474a, 642a, 682a, **728a**, 935b; iii, 357a, 593a; iv, 875b, 876a; xi, 332a
Fāḍil al-Warṯilānī (XX) xi, 248a
al-Fāḍil b. Yaḥyā b. Khālid al-Barmakī (808) → al-Faḍl b. Yaḥyā b. Khālid al-Barmakī
Fāḍil Yuldash i, 422a
Faḍīla i, 327b, 960b; ii, **728b**; v, 331b; vi, 350a, 351a
Fāḍiliyya v, 889b, 892a
Fadjīdj → Figuig
al-Fadjīdjī i, 1154a
Fadjr → Ṣalāt
Fadjr-i Ātī → Fedjr-i Ātī
Faḍl III b. Faḍl II (Shaddādid) (1130) ii, 680b; vi, 274a; ix, 170a (see also *s.v.* Faḍlūn b. Shaddād)
Faḍl (poet) iii, 1202b
Faḍl, Āl iv, 87b; viii, 986b
Faḍl, Bā ii, **729b**
al-Faḍl b. al-ʿAbbās i, 137a

al-Faḍl b. ʿAbd al-Ṣamad al-Raḳā<u>sh</u>ī (IX) vii, 414b
Faḍl b. Abī Yazīd (948) i, 164a; vi, 435a
al-Faḍl b. Aḥmad al-Isfarāʾinī (1013) ii, **730a**, 919a; iv, 107b
Faḍl b. ʿAlī al-ʿAbdalī i, 95b; v, 602a, b
Faḍl-i ʿAlī <u>Kh</u>ān i, 809a
al-Faḍl b. <u>D</u>jaʿfar b. al-Furāt → Ibn al-Furāt, Abu ʾl-Fatḥ
al-Faḍl b. al-Ḥubāb al-<u>D</u>jumaḥī (917) s, **284a**
al-Faḍl b. Ḳārin iv, 493b
al-Faḍl b. Marwān (vizier) (X) (864) ii, **730b**; iv, 929a; vii, 679a, 776b
Faḍl b. Muḥammad (<u>Sh</u>addādid) iv, 1176b
Faḍl b. Nuʿayr, Āl iii, 400a
al-Faḍl b. al-Rabīʿ b. Yūnus (822) i, 107b, 143b, 437b, 438a, 1035a, 1298a; ii, **730b**; iii, 45b; iv, 17a; vi, 331b, 333b, 335a, 336a, 438a; vii, 646a; viii, 351a. 838b; s, 48a, 304b
al-Faḍl (al-Mufaḍḍal) b. Rawḥ al-Muhallab (794) vii, 360a; viii, 465b
al-Faḍl b. Sahl b. Za<u>dh</u>ānfarū<u>kh</u> <u>Dh</u>u ʾl-Riyāsatayn (818) i, 271b, 400a, 437b, 1035b; ii, **731a**; iii, 231b, 243b; v, 621a; vi, 331b, 332b, 333b, 334a, b, 335b, 941a; vii, 215a, 558b, 694b; viii, 100b; s, 15a
al-Faḍl b. Ṣāliḥ (vizier) (X) i, 823b, 824a; ii, 483a; iii, 79b, 128b; vii, 910b; xi, 129a
al-Faḍl b. <u>Sh</u>ā<u>dh</u>ān iv, 660b, 661b; s, 89b
al-Faḍl b. Yaḥyā b. <u>Kh</u>ālid al-Barmakī (808) i, 241a, 1033b, 1034a, b; ii, 191a, 540b, **732a**; iii, 233a, b; iv, 356b, 419b, 631b, 1164a, 1174b; v, 855b; vi, 331a, b, 437b, 438a; vii, 646a, b; viii, 145a; ix, 496a; xi, 242b
Faḍl al-Ḳaṣabānī (1052) x, 461b
Faḍl al-<u>Sh</u>āʿira, al-Yamāmiyya (871) s, **284b**
Faḍl Allāh, Aḥmad → Ibn Faḍl Allāh al-ʿUmarī
Faḍl Allāh Āl i, 1046a; ii, 305b, **732a**; iii, 758b; iv, 509b
Faḍl Allāh → Ra<u>sh</u>īd al-Dīn
Faḍl Allāh b. ʿĪsā Ta<u>sh</u>kandī iv, 505a
Faḍl Allāh b. Muḥibb Allāh i, 1333a
Faḍl Allāh b. Rabeh i, 1260a
Faḍl Allāh b. Rūzbihān <u>Kh</u>un<u>dj</u>ī (1521) → <u>Kh</u>un<u>dj</u>ī, Faḍl Allāh b. Ruzbihān
Faḍl Allāh b. Saʿīd (947) vii, 569b
Faḍl Allāh Bal<u>kh</u>ī → Iḳbāl <u>Kh</u>ān
Faḍl Allāh Dabbās iv, 966b
Faḍl Allāh <u>D</u>jamālī → <u>D</u>jamālī
Faḍl Allāh Efendi iv, 194a
Faḍl Allāh Ḥurūfī (1394) i, 1162a; ii, 685a, **733a**, 924a; iii, 600a, 601a; vi, 226b; vii, 105b, 226b; viii, 8a
Faḍl Allāh <u>Sh</u>īrāzī xi, 174a
Faḍl Allāh Zāhidī (XX) vii, 655a
al-Faḍl al-Hada<u>th</u>ī vii, 785a
Faḍl-i Ḥaḳḳ (1862) i, 827b, 953b; ii, 104a, **735b**, 736a; iv, 196a, 197a
Faḍl al-Ḥaḳḳ (Bengal) (XX) iii, 533a
Faḍl al-Mawlā Muḥammad v, 1250b, 1251a
Faḍl al-<u>Sh</u>āʿira al-Yamāniyya (871) viii, 856a
Faḍlawayh, Banū ii, **736b**; ix, 157a; s, 326a
Faḍlawayh b. ʿAlī <u>Sh</u>abānkāraʾī (Kurd) (1071) i, 420a; ii, 736b; iii, 1097b; iv, 222a, 807b; viii, 946a; ix, 157a
Faḍlawī iii, 337a; v, 824b, 826b
Faḍlī (Fadhlī) ii, 675b, **737a**
Faḍl-i Imām (1829) i, **736a**
Faḍlī, Meḥmed (Ḳara Faḍlī) (1563) i, 1301b; ii, **737b**, 1133a; v, 957b
Faḍlūn b. Abi ʾl-Suvār iv, 773a
Faḍlūn b. Minučihr iv, 670a
Faḍlūn b. <u>Sh</u>addād iv, 346b; v, 489a
Faḍlūya → Faḍlawayh b. ʿAlī <u>Sh</u>abānkāraʾī
Fadu, Fadwa → Fidya
Fa<u>gh</u>fūr ii, **738a**
Fa<u>gh</u>fūr (porcelain) iii, 345b (see also *s.v.* Ṣīnī)
Fahd ii, **738b**
Fahd Banū iii, 759b
Fahd b. ʿAbd al-ʿAzīz (Āl Suʿūd) (XX) v, 1004a; vi, 158a; ix, 905a
Fahd b. Ibrāhīm iii, 77a, 78a
al-Fāhikī i, 1154a; ii, 740b
Fahīm, Aḥmad → al-Fār
Faḥl (Fiḥl) ii, **743a**; x, 883a
Faḥm v, 965a, 967b
Faḥm, Banū iii, 363b; s, 183a
Fahmī al-Mudarris (XX) vi, 615a
Fahra<u>dj</u> vi, 192b; s, 127a
Fahrasa i, 70b, 96b, 1019b, 1092b; ii, **743b**; iii, 837b; vi, 406a; s, 303a
Faḥṣ al-Ballūṭ ii, **744a**

Fā'ik, amīr (Harāt) (X) ii, 799a,
Fā'ik Khāṣṣa (994) vi, 65a, 340a, 433a; viii, 110a, 1028a
Fā'ik al-Niẓāmī al-Ṣaḳlabī (X) viii, 880a
Fā'ik Sa'īd v, 195a
Fā'il → 'Illa
Fā'il → Naḥw
Fā'iz (1683) vi, 837b
al-Fā'iẓ bi-Naṣr Allāh i, 9b; ii, 857a; iv, 944a
Faizullah Khodja → Khodjaev
Faḳāriyya → Dhu 'l-Faḳāriyya
Faḳ'as, Banū iv, 490b
al-Faḳ'asī, al-Naẓẓār b. Hāshim viii, 376a
Fakhdh, Fakhidh i, 700a → 'Ashīra, Ḳabīla
Fākhita bint Abī Hāshim b. 'Utba (VII) iv, 929b; vi, 139a, 622a; vii, 268a
Fakhkh ii, **744b**; iii, 22a; vi, 147b
Fakhr Ārā'ī (1949) vii, 446b
Fakhr al-Dawla Abū 'Alī (X) iv, 859a
Fakhr al-Dawla Abu 'l-Ḥasan 'Alī (Buwayhid) (997) i, 59b, 211b, 212a; ii, **748b**; iii, 258a, 671b; iv, 100b, 358a; vi, 66a, 600b; vii, 272b; s, 118b, 323a
Fakhr al-Dawla Abū Manṣūr Kūfī (IX) iv, 859a
Fakhr al-Dawla Čawlī i, 1012a; ii, 823b; iii, 1097b; iv, 29a, 850b; v, 868a; s, 382b
Fakhr al-Dawla Ḥasan b. Shāh (Bāwandid) (1349) i, 237a, 1110a; vi, 511a; s, 363b, 364a
Fakhr al-Dawla Ibn Djahīr → Djahīr, Banū
Fakhr al-Dawla Muḥammad b. Djahīr i, 1206b; ii, 384a, b; v, 453a
Fakhr al-Dīn I b. Ma'n (1544) ii, 634b, **749b**; iv, 483b
Fakhr al-Dīn II b. Ḳurḳumāz b. Ma'n (1635) i, 267b, 1138a; ii, 443b, 634b, 749b, 912a; iii, 205b, 325a; iv, 834b; v, 792b; vi, 343b, 345a, 580b; vii, 600b, 911a; viii, 182b, 758b; ix, 99a; s, 49a, 159a
Fakhr al-Dīn (Maḳdishū) (XIII) vi, 128b
Fakhr al-Dīn b. Abi 'l-Faradj (Ustādār) (XV) vii, 271b
Fakhr al-Dīn b. Luḳmān (XIII) vii, 729b
Fakhr al-Dīn b. Mīr-i Buzurg al-Mar'ashī (1405) vi, 512a, b
Fakhr al-Dīn b. al-Sā'ātī (XII) vi, 663a
Fakhr al-Dīn 'Abd Allāh b. al-Hādī iii, 685a
Fakhr al-Dīn 'Adjemī (al-'Adjamī) (1468) ii, 685a, 879a; ix, 400b
Fakhr al-Dīn Aḥmad Ḳarāmān-oghlu iv, 622a, b
Fakhr al-Dīn 'Alī (1288) viii, 831a
Fakhr al-Dīn 'Alī Ṣafī (1532) iv, 704a
Fakhr al-Dīn 'Alī Tabrīzī → Ṣāhib Atā
Fakhr al-Dīn Čishtī → Shāh Fakhr al-Dīn
Fakhr al-Dīn Gurgānī (XI) → Gurgānī, Fakhr al-Dīn As'ad
Fakhr al-Dīn Harātī (ḳāḍī al-ḳuḍāt) (1300) vi, 16a
Fakhr al-Dīn Ibn Shaykh al-Shuyūkh (1250) vi, 321a
Fakhr al-Dīn Ibrāhīm b. Luḳmān iii, 679b
Fakhr al-Dīn 'Īsā b. Ibrāhīm al-Mawṣilī (XIII) iii, 956a; vi, 628a
Fakhr al-Dīn 'Iṣāmī → 'Iṣāmī
Fakhr al-Dīn Ḳara Arslan, amīr (Ḥiṣn Kayfā) (1149) vi, 870b
Fakhr al-Dīn Kart iv, 672a
Fakhr al-Dīn Mādjid iii, 774a
Fakhr al-Dīn Muḥammad b. Manṣūr Mubārak Shāh → Fakhr-i Mudabbir Mubārak Shāh
Fakhr al-Dīn al-Marāghī (1258) vi, 501a
Fakhr al-Dīn Mar'ashī, Sayyid v, 663a; vi, 511a, b, 512a, b
Fakhr al-Dīn Mas'ūd ii, 1100b, 1101a
Fakhr al-Dīn Mubārakshāh (XIV) ii, **751b**, 1099a; viii, 622a
Fakhr al-Dīn Muḥammad b. Ḥasan b. 'Allāma al-Ḥillī s, 364a
Fakhr al-Dīn Muḥammad (Kart) (1307) ix, 112a
Fakhr al-Dīn Muḥammad b. 'Umar al-Rāzī (1210) i, 113a, 342b, 411a, 594a, 1115b; ii, 393b, 449b, **751b**, 756b, 771a, 773b, 825b, 971a, 1025b; iii, 172a, 302a, b, 330a, 1020a, 1237b; iv, 120a, 183b, 251b, 367a, 406a, 669a; vi, 132a, 353a, 450a, 636b, 637b, 627b, 908a; vii, 55a, 199b; viii, 95a, 134a, 541a; ix, 887a; s, 25b, 90b, 343b, 396b
Fakhr al-Dīn Muḳrī, amīr (1285) vi, 580a
Fakhr al-Dīn Pīrīoghlu iv, 671a
Fakhr al-Dīn 'Uthmān b. al-Ḥādjdj Yūnis (Ma'n) (1506) vi, 343a

Fakhr al-Dīn Yūsuf b. al-Shaykh i, 711a, 766a
Fakhr al-Dīn Zāhid i, 868b
Fakhr-i Ḳawwās v, 1027a
Fakhr-i Mudabbir Mubārak Shāh (1236) iii, 181a, 196a, 197a, 344a, 481b, 1155b, 1202a; iv, 267a; v, 546b, 688a; vii, 193a, 679a, 988a; s, **284b**
Fakhr-i Mudabbir viii, 814b
Fakhr al-Muḥaḳḳiḳīn (1369) vi, 549b
Fakhr al-Mulk (b.) ʿAmmār i, 448a; vii, 408a; ix, 410b (see also *s.v.* ʿAmmār, Banū)
Fakhr al-Mulk Muḥammad b. ʿAlī → Ibn Khalaf, Abū Ghālib
Fakhr al-Mulk al-Muẓaffar b. Niẓām al-Mulk (1096) i, 1052b; ii, 1039b; vi, 14a, 489b; viii, 81b
Fakhrā → Fakhr al-Dīn Mubārakshāh
Fakhrī (XIV) vi, 835b
Fakhrī (1618) ii, **755b**
Fakhrī, Bā ii, **756a**
Fakhrī, Shams al-Dīn Muḥammad (XIV) ii, **755b**; iv, 526a, b
Fakhrī Pasha v, 998a
Faḳīh i, 7a, 250a, 279b, 289a; ii, **756a**; v, 1124b, 1208a, 1248a
Faḳīh, Bal (Bā ʿAlawī) ii, **756b**
al-Faḳīh, Ibrāhīm v, 190a
al-Fākihī, Abū ʿAbd Allāh Muḥammad b. Isḥāḳ (IX) i, 591a, 827a; ii, **757a**; vi, 106a
Faḳīr ii, **757b**; v, 1124b, 1208a, 1248
Faḳīr of Ipi (1960) vi, 86b; viii, 282b; xi, 198a; s, **285a**
Faḳīr Muḥammad Khān ii, **758a**
Faḳīr Muḥammad Lahorī i, 827b
Faḳīrī, Kalkandelenli (XVI) ii, **758a**; ix, 410a
Faḳḳara → Foggāra
Faḳr-i ʿadjam iv, 52a
Fāḳūdh vi, 630a
Fāl v, 670b, 671b, 672a
Faʿl ii, **758b**
Fāl-nāma ii, **760b**
(al-) Faladj i, 233a, 539a, 1313b; vii, 843b (see also *s.v.* al-Aflādj)
Falādj al-Muʿallā x, 854a
Falak ii, 761b
Falak ʿAlā-i Tabrīzī ii, 81a
Falak al-Dīn b. Aḳ-Sunḳur II (XII) i, 300b; vi, 500b
Falak al-Dīn Dündar ii, 692a; iii, 132b; iv, 622a
Falak al-Maʿālī Manūčihr (Ziyārid) (1029) vi, 453a
Falaḳa ii, **763b**
al-Falakī, Maḥmūd Pasha (1885) ii, **764a**
Falakī Shirwānī (1155) ii, **764a**; iii, 1162a; iv, 62a, 348b; s, 333b
Falāsifa i, 351a, 414b, 415a; ii, **764b**; iii, 169b, 303a, 1146b, 1147b; iv, 366b, 469a, 794b; v, 237a, 238a, 702b; vi, 448b
Fālidj iii, 665b
Fāliḥ Rîfḳî Atay (XX) ii, 432a; vi, 94b; s, **98a**
Falilu Mbacké (1968) vii, 609b; x, 575b
Fallāḥiya → Dawraḳ
Fallāḳ ii, **767b**; iv, 954b
Fallāta ii, 767b
al-Fallātī, al-Ṭāhir b. Ibrāhīm iv, 773b
(al-) Fallūdja (ʿIrāḳ) ii, **768a**; vi, 616a
Fallūdja (Miṣr) s, 6a
Fallūs b. Tutush (Saldjūḳ) (XII) viii, 995a
(al-) Fals i, 203a; iii, 393a; vi, 374a
Falsafa i, 414b, 415a, 427b; ii, 450a, 618a, 752b, 764b, **769b**, 898a; iii, 75a, 329b; iv, 615b, 794b, 986b; v, 1129b
Fālūghus ii, 236a
Famagusta → Maghōsha
Fāmiya i, **215a**, 706a; vi, 378b, 381a; vii, 725a
Fanāʾ → Baḳāʾ
Fanak ii, **775a**; iii, 809a
Fanākatī, Aḥmad (1282) iv, 1020a
Fanār → Fener; Manār
al-Fanārī, Aḥmad i, 99a
al-Fanārī, Muḥammad ii, 602b
Fanar(a)ki (Istanbul) vi, 359b
Fanduruskī → Abū Ṭālib
Fānī → Navāʾī
Fannā Khusraw → ʿAḍud al-Dawla Fannā-Khusraw
Fānnū bint ʿUmar b. Yīntān (Almoravid) (1147) ii, 1013b; vii, 626b
Fāo → al-Fāʿū
Faʾr s, **285b**
Farʿ → Furūʿ (tax)
al-Fār, Aḥmad Fahīm iii, 368a
al-Faraʿ s, 335a
Fārāb ii, **778a**; viii, 478b; s, 244b, 245a, 289a, b; ix, 557b

al-Fārābī, Abū Ibrāhīm Isḥāḳ b. Ibrāhīm (961) ii, 496a; s, **289a**
al-Fārābī, Abū Naṣr (950) i, 179a, 234b, 236a, 327b, 328a, 342a, b, 350b, 427a, 589a, 630b, 631b, 1102a; ii, 96a, 765b, 770b, **778b**, 949a; iii, 329b, 509b, 729a, 876b, 911b, 942b, 1148a; v, 113b, 702b; vi, 97b, 204b, 220a, 347a, 348b, 442b, 446b, 447b, 449a, b, 450a, 637a, 674a, 905a; vii, 682b, 683a, 1051a; viii, 123b, 421b; s, 289b, 408b
Faradj, al-Malik al-Nāṣir b. Barḳūḳ (Mamlūk) (1412) i, 138a; ii, 24a, 285b, **781a**; iii, 187a, 189b, 190a, 774a, 827b; iv, 428a; vi, 324a, 326b, 327a; vii, 168a, 172a
Faradj, Muḥammad ʿAbd al-Salām (1982) vii, 291b
Faradj b. Sālim iii, 753a
al-Faradj baʿd al-Shidda → Nādira
Farāfra, Farāfira i, 945a; ii, **782a**; xi, 33a
Farāh ii, **782b**; s, 222a
Faraḥ Anṭūn (1922) i, 597a; ii, **782b**; iii, 514b; vi, 414a, 598b; vii, 902a
Faraḥ Dībā (XX) vii, 447a
Faraḥābād i, 8b; ii, **783a**; vi, 526b, 939a
Farāhānī → Ḳāʾim-maḳām-i Farāhānī
Farāhānī, Mīrzā Ḥusayn Khān s, 109a
Farāʾiḍiyya i, 719b; ii, **783b**, 797b; iii, 433a; vii, 291a
Farāmarz, ʿImād al-Dawla → ʿImād al-Dawla
Farāmarz b. ʿAlī → ʿAlāʾ al-Dawla
Farāmarz b. Muḥammad (Marʿashī) vi, 515a
Farāmurz (Kākūyid) → Abū Manṣūr Farāmurz
Farāmūsh-Khāna ii, 433b; vi, 291b; s, **290a**
Farangī Maḥall → Lakhnaw (monuments)
Farangī Maḥall, Āl vii, 300b; viii, 68b; s, 4b, 5a, 74a, b, **292a**, 360b
Faras ii, **784b**; iii, 314b, 890b; iv, 214a-219b; v, 689a, b
Faras (al-Marīs) vi, 574b
Faras al-Māʾ s, **294a**
Farasān i, 535a, 738a; ii, 787b; x, 90b
Farasnāma iv, 218b
Farāwa i, 320b; vi, 780b; vii, 26a
al-Farawī, Muḥammad b. Muḥ. b. ʿAlī s, 83a
al-Farazdaḳ (728) i, 43a, 105a, 158b, 331a, 586a, 772a, 950b, 1248a; ii, 479b, **788a**, 998b; iii, 248a, 354a, 608b; iv, 819a; vi, 344b, 476a, 477b, 539a, 545a, 604b, 709b; vii, 114a, 144a, 261a, 402a, 920b, 981a, b; s, 647b
al-Fard → Nudjūm
Fard, Wallace D. (1934) vii, 702b
Fardoonji, Kavasji Mulla (XIX) vii, 222b
al-Farfarūn → Farāfra
Farghalūs → Asbagh n. Wakīl
Farghānā i, 46b, 148a, 330b; ii, **790a**; iii, 1060b; iv, 632a; v, 29a, 31a, 45a, 966b; vi, 337a, 557a, b, 769b; vii, 313b, 477b; viii, 236b; s, 51b, 97b, 327b, 406b
al-Farghānī, Abū Manṣūr Aḥmad (1007) ii, **793a**; viii, 14b
al-Farghānī, Abū Muḥammad ʿAbd Allāh (972) ii, **793a**
al-Farghānī, Aḥmad b. Kathīr (Alfraganus) (861) i, 589b; ii, 763a, **793a**; iii, 1137a; vi, 374b; vii, 39b, 539b, 680a
Farhād Khān Ḳaramanlï (1596) iv, 808a; v, 663a; vi, 515b
Farhād Mīrzā (Ḳādjār) ii, 827a; s, 95a
Farhād Mīrzā Muʿtamad al-Dawla s, 302a
Farhād Pasha → Ferhād Pasha
Farhād wa-Shīrīn ii, **793b**; iv, 601b, 730b; v, 650b; viii, 278a; s, 831a
Farhang iv, 525b
Farhangistān-i Irān i, 505a; ii, 952b; v, 1095b, 1096a, b; xi, 222b
Farḥāt, Djarmānūs (1732) i, 571b, 596b; ii, **795a**
Farḥāt, Ilyās v, 1256b; vi, 308a; viii, 584b
Farḥāt b. Saʿīd i, 1247a
Farḥāt ʿAbbās iii, 525a; iv, 784b
Farḥāt al-Mulk ii, 1124b
Farīburz b. Garshāsp iv, 349a
Farīburz b. Sāllār iv, 348a, b; s, 326a
Farīd (pearl) s, 253a
Farīd Bukhārī, Shaykh (XVII) vi, 1031a; vii, 938a; s, 122a
Farīd al-Dīn → ʿAṭṭār
Farīd al-Dīn Masʿūd Gandj-i Shakar, Shaykh (1265) ii, 51a, **796b**; iii, 167b, 429a, 435b, 456b; v, 546b, 611a; viii, 68a, 240a; xi, 119a; s, 73b, 353a
Farīd Murtaḍā Khān Bukhārī, Shaykh iv, 543b
Farīd Pasha → Dāmād Ferīd Pasha
Farīd Wadjdī (1907) vi, 955b

Farīḍa → Farāʾiḍ, Farḍ
Farīḍa (queen) → Ṣafīnāz
Farīdkōṭ ii, **797b**
Farīdpur ii, **797b**
Farīdūn → Ferīdūn Aḥmed Beg
Farīdūn b. Abtiyān (or Abtīn) (Afridūn) ii, 106b, **798a**; iii, 105a, 112b; iv, 12a; v, 661a; vi, 744a; viii, 312b; x, 672a
Farīdūn, Djalāl al-Dīn → ʿĀrif Čelebī
Fārigh (1591) iv, 68a; viii, 776a
Farīghūnids ii, 608b, **798b**, 1099b; vi, 65b, 340a; vii, 407a; s, 125b, 376a, 386b
Farīḳ → Abū Sinbil
al-Fāriḳī, Abu ʾl-Ḳāsim (1001) vii, 281b; s, 824a
al-Fāriḳī , Shihāb al-Dīn iv, 642a
Farīmān vi, 495b; vii, 762b
Fāris ii, **800a**
Fāris (Marīnid) (1415) vi, 594a
Fāris b. ʿĪsā (X) iii, 103a
Fāris b. Muḥammad → Ḥusām al-Dīn Abu ʾl-Shawḳ
Fāris al-Dīn Aḳṭāy al-Mustaʿrib al-Djamadār (1254) i, 944b; v, 571a; vi, 321b; vii, 166b
Fāris al-Dīn Ilbeki al-Sāḳī al-Ẓāhiri (Ṣafad) (1298) vi, 777b
Fāris al-Dīn al-Shidyāḳ, Aḥmad (1887) i, 596b; ii, 464b, 466a, **800b**, 927a; iii, 665a; v, 1090a; vi, 598b; vii, 902a, b; ix, 229b; s, 40a
Fāris Nimr → Nimr, Fāris
al-Fārisī → Abū Ḥulmān; Kamāl al-Dīn; Salmān
al-Fārisī, ʿAbd al-Ghāfir (1048) vii, 26b; xi, 48a; s, 343a
al-Fārisī, Abū ʿAlī al-Ḥasan (987) i, 87a; ii, **802b**; iii, 754b, 880b; iv, 182a; vi, 188b, 635b; vii, 914a; viii, 615a; s, 13a, 19a, 277a, 361b
al-Fārisī, Abu ʾl-Ṭāhir Muḥammad b. al-Ḥusayn (1058) vi, 354a; vii, 474a
al-Fārisī, ʿAlāʾ al-Dīn ʿAlī b. Balbān (1339) viii, 836a
al-Fārisī, Kamāl al-Dīn (1319) viii, 558a
al-Fārisī , Muḥammad b. Abī Bakr (XIII) xi, 497a
al-Fārisī, Muḥammad b. al-Ḥasan s, 277a
al-Fārisī, ʿUmāra b. Wathīma b. Mūsā b. al-Furāt (902) vii, 284a
al-Fārisī, Wathīma b. Mūsā b. al-Furāt (851) vii, 284a
al-Fārisī al-Dimashḳī, Abū Ḥulmān (951) viii, 840b
Fārisiyya → Īrān
al-Fārisiyya Djazīrat i, 535b; ii, **803a**
Farja i, 705b
Farḳ → Faṣl
Farḳad al-Sabakhī (VIII) vi, 613b
al-Farḳadānī → Nudjūm
Fārkat (parkent) s, 51a
al-Farma (port) i, 32a, 216a; vii, 43a
Fārmad s, 14b
al-Fārmadhī → Abū ʿAlī al-Fārmadī
Farmān ii, 303b, 309a, **803a**; iii, 1189b; iv, 1131b
Farmān-Farmā, Ḥusayn ʿAlī Mīrzā (XIX) iv, 105a, 392b; vii, 453b; ix, 477a
Fārmāsūn → Māsūniyya
Farmāsūniyya xi, 359a; s, 290a, **296a**
Farmūl ii, **806b**
Faro → Shantamariyyat al-Gharb
Farouk → Fārūḳ
al-Farrāʾ, Abū Zakariyyāʾ Yaḥyā b. Ziyād al-Kūfī (822) ii, **806b**; iii, 846b; v, 174a, 351a; vii, 280a, 914a; viii, 573a; s, 22b, 631a, b
al-Farrāʾ, Muḥammad b. Aḥmad (X) vi, 224a
Farrakhan, Minister Louis (XX) vii, 703b
Farrān v, 41b, 42b
Farrukh-Hormizd i, 188b
Farrukh-Shāh → ʿIzz al-Dīn Farrukh-Shāh
Farrukh-Siyar, Abu ʾl-Muẓaffar Muḥammad Muʿīn al-Dīn (Mughal) (1719) i, 1025b, 1026a; ii, 7a, 121a, 379b, 567a, 808a, **810a**; iii, 427a; iv, 279b; vi, 321b, 339b, 346a; vii, 443b; viii, 73a; s, 126b
Farrukh Beg (painter) (XVII) vi, 426a
Farrukh Khān Amīn al-Dawla (1856) vi, 291b; vii, 1004a; s, 108b, 290b
Farrukhābād ii, **808a**; iii, 61a; vii, 443b; s, 106b
Farrukhān b. al-Zaynabī (VII) vi, 745a, b; viii, 471a
Farrukhān Gīlān-shāh (Djīlānshāh) (680) iv, 207b; s, **297b**
Farrukhān the Great (Dābūyid) (728) ii, 74b, **809a**; v, 69a; s, **297b**
Farrukhī, Muḥammad Ibrāhīm → Farrukhī Yazdī

Farrukhī Sīstānī, Abu 'l-Ḥasan (1037) i, 1301a; ii, **809b**; iv, 61a; vi, 66a, 453a, 608a, b, 609a; s, 108a
Farrukhī Yazdī, Muḥammad iv, 71a, 789b; xi, 238b, **309a**; s, 110a
Farrukhrū Parsay iv, 1152a
Farrukhyasār iii, 316a; iv, 350a
Farrukhzād b. Masʿūd i, 1131a; ii, 5a, 1052a
Fārs i, 2b, 8a, 43b, 49a, 131b, 132a, 211b, 212a, 659a, 695b, 731b, 954b, 1350a, 1356a, 1358a; ii, **811a**; iii, 1097a; iv, 19b, 774a, 1046b; v, 450b, 665b; vi, 17b, 120a, 272b, 273a, 275b, 332a, 337b, 365a, 383b, 384a, b, 416a, 482a, 484b, 493b, 494a, 524a, 621b, 633b, 677a; s, 91a, 118b, 147b, 222b, 302a, 326a, 379b, 383b
Fārs al-Liwāldjān vi, 384b
Farsh → Ḳālī
Farsh → Mafrūshāt
Farshūṭ viii, 866a
Fārsī → Īrān
Fārsī, Abu 'l-khayr (XVI) viii, 542a
Fārsistān → Īrān
al-Farsy, Sheikh Abdulla Salem (1982) ix, 917b; s, 576b
Fartanā iv, 821a
Farthiyya iii, 660a
Fārūḳ → Anṣārī, Shaykh Murtaḍā
Fārūḳ, Day of s, 178a
Fārūḳ, King (1965) ii, 648b; iii, 517a, 572a; v, 1062a; vii, 904b, 905a; s, 5b, 6b, 299a
al-Fārūḳ → ʿUmar b. al-Khaṭṭāb
al-Fārūḳī, ʿAbd al-Bāḳī (1862) i, 330b; ii, **813a**
al-Fārūḳī, Kamāl iii, 1023b
al-Fārūḳī, Mullā Maḥmūd (1652) ii, **813a**
al-Fārūḳī, Rādjā → Malik Rādjā Fārūkī
al-Fārūḳī, Shaykh Djalāl al-Dīn (XVII) ii, 54b
al-Fārūḳī, Shaykh Muḥammad Maʿṣūm (XVII) vii, 602a
al-Fārūḳī, Shaykh Niẓām al-Dīn (XVII) ii, 54b
Fārūḳids ii, **814a**, 1084b
Farwa(h) b. Musayk (VII) i, 728a; ii, 177b, 1096a; iv, 927b; v, 954a; vii, 592a; s, 692b
Farwa b. Namfal iii, 1265b
Farwān ii, **817b**
Farwardīn → Ta'rīkh
Faryāb (Gūzgān) ii, **817b**; iii, 223b; vi, 915a; ix, 431a
Fāryāk → Fāris al-Shidyāḳ
Faryūmadī, Ghiyāth Dīn b. ʿAlī vii, 821b; ix, 158b; x, 552b
Faryūmadī, ʿIzz al-Dīn Ṭāhir (1270) viii, 342b
Fās i, 35a, 47a, 70b, 86a, 92b, 355b, 687b, 977b, 1225a; ii, **818a**, 835a; iii, 62b, 149a, 694b, 814a; iv, 774b; v, 877a, 1178a, 1189a; vi, 38a, 40a, 123b, 124a, 141b, 142b, 199b, 248a, 251a, 281a, 293a, 356a, 404a, b, 422a, 431b, 571b, 572a, b, 573a, b, 589a, 591a, 592a, 594a, b, 595a, b, 664a, 675a, 741b, 742b; vii, 641a; viii, 440b; s, 10a, 23a, 26b, 28b, 40a, 47b, 63b, 113b, 126a, 133b, 223b, 350b, 387b, 389a, 390b
– institutions i, 1224b; ii, 819a, 1822b; iii, 140a; v, 1190a, 1208a
– monuments i, 85a, 499b, 1346b; ii, 818b, 821-823; iv, 632a; v, 1150a, b, 1151b, 1152a, 1153a
Fās al-Bālī ii, 819a, 822a, b, 823a; iii, 448b; vi, 293a
Fās al-Djadīd ii, 819a, 820b, 822a, b, 823a; iii, 448b, 499a
Fasā ii, **823b**; vi, 120a, 384a, 640b; s, 302a
Fasād → Fāsid, Kawn
Fasā'ī, Ḥādjdjī Mīrzā Ḥasan (XIX) vi, 384a; s, **302a**
Fasāna → Afsāna
Fasandjus, Banū ii, **827a**
al-Fasāsīrī → al-Basāsīrī
al-Fasawī, Yaʿḳūb b. Sufyān (890) viii, 516a
al-Fāshir (el-Fasher) ii, 122a, **827b**
Fāshōda i, 929b; ii, **828a**; ix, 746b
al-Fāsī → Ibn Abī Zarʿ
al-Fāsī, ʿAbd al-Kabīr (1879) s, **303a**
al-Fāsī, ʿAbd al-Ḳādir b. ʿAlī (1680) i, **70b**, 86a, 139a, 795a; s, **302b**, 325b
al-Fāsī, ʿAbd al-Raḥmān b. ʿAbd al-Ḳādir (1685) vi, 255b, 350a, 356b; s, **302b**
al-Fāsī, ʿAbd al-Raḥmān b. Muḥammad (1626) i, **86a**, 139a, 428a; s, **302b**
al-Fāsī, ʿAbd al-Salām b. Muḥammad (1895) s, **10a**
al-Fāsī, Abu ʿAbd Allāh Maḥammad → Mayyāra, Abū ʿAbd Allāh Maḥammad

al-Fāsī, Abū ʿAbd Allāh Muḥammad (1722) s, **303a**, 403b, 404b
al-Fāsī, Abū ʿAbd Allāh Muḥammad (1765) s, **303a**
al-Fāsī, Abū ʿAbd Allāh Muḥammad (1799) s, **303a**
al-Fāsī, Abū Ḥafṣ ʿUmar (1774) s, **303a**
al-Fāsī, Abū Ḥāmid Muḥammad s, 404b
al-Fāsī, Abū ʿImrān al-Ghafdjūmī (XI) vii, 584a
al-Fāsī, Abū Madyan Muḥammad (1768) s, **303a**
al-Fāsī, Abu ʾl-Maḥāsin (1604) i, **138b**, v, 1029a; s, **302b**
al-Fāsī, Abū Mālik ʿAbd al-Wāḥid (1799) s, **303a**
al-Fāsī, Aḥmad al-Ḥāfiẓ b. Abi ʾl-Maḥāsin (1612) s, **302b**
al-Fāsī, Āl s, **302a**
al-Fāsī, ʿAllāl (1974) iv, 159b; vii, 416a; s, **63b**
al-Fāsī, al-ʿArabī (1642) i, 428a
al-Fāsī, David b. Abraham (X) iv, 305b, 605a; vii, 539b
al-Fāsī, Ḥamdūn b. al-Ḥādjdj (1817) → Ibn al-Ḥādjdj, Ḥamdūn b. ʿAbd al-Raḥmān al-Fāsī
al-Fāsī, Isaac (b.) (1103) iv, 306b; vii, 540a
al-Fāsī, Muḥammad b. ʿAbd al-Salām (1799) vi, 130b
al-Fāsī, Muḥammad b. Muḥammad s, 371a
al-Fāsī, Muḥammad b. Sulaymān (1823) vi, 247b, 250b
al-Fāsī, Muḥammad al-ʿArbī b. Abi ʾl-Maḥāsin (1642) i, 139a; s, **302b**
al-Fāsī, Muḥammad al-Mahdī (1698) iii, 971b; vi, 350a, 351a, 356a; s, **302b**
al-Fāsī, Muḥammad al-Ṭāhir (1868) s, **303a**
al-Fāsī, Muḥammad al-Ṭayyib (1701) ii, 1022a; s, **303a**
al-Fāsī, Sayyid Aḥmad b. Idrīs (1837) vi, 628b
al-Fāsī, Sīdī ʿAbd al-Ḳādir s, 302b, 325b
al-Fāsī, Taḳī al-Dīn (1429) ii, **828b**; iii, 760a
Faṣīḥ Dede (1699) ii, **833a**
Faṣīḥī (1670) viii, 776a
Fāṣila ii, **834b**
Faṣīla ii, **835a**
al-Fāsiyya (ṭarīḳa) v, 949a; vi, 454b
al-Fāsiyyūn i, 70b, 138b, 139a; ii, **835a**; iv, 379b; s, 223b, 302a
Faskāt ū-Mzāl → Abū Ḥafṣ ʿUmar
Faṣl ii, **836b**
Faṣl → Filāḥa, Mafṣūl
Fatā i, 256b; ii, **837a**, 961a, 1043b; iv, 705a
al-Fatāwā al-ʿĀlamgīriyya i, 1331a, 954a; ii, 157b, 736a, **837a**; iii, 163b, 435a
Fatḥ → Ḥaraka
al-Fatḥ b. Khāḳān (861) i, 1082b, 1289b; ii, 385b, **837b**; vi, 110b, 111a; vii, 528a, 559a, 777b, 985b
al-Fatḥ b. Khāḳān al-Ishbīlī (1134) i, 602a; ii, **838a**; iii, 354b, 734a, 807b
Fatḥ ʿAlī Khān (1746) vi, 56b, 939b
Fatḥ ʿAlī Khān (Ḳādjār) (1750) vii, 853a
Fatḥ ʿAlī Khān (Ḳuba) (1765) ii, 206a; v, 296b
Fatḥ ʿAlī Khān Dāghistānī (1720) iii, 604a; iv, 389b; v, 663b
Fatḥ ʿAli Khān Devel iv, 391b, 392a, 597b; vi, 483b
Fatḥ ʿAlī Khān Tālpūr iii, 323b; iv, 597b, 1160a; ix, 635a
Fatḥ ʿAlī khund-zāda → Akhund-zāda, Mīrzā Fatḥ ʿAlī
Fatḥ ʿAlī Shāh (Ḳādjār) (1834) i, 13b, 246a, 304b, 682b, 1030b; ii, 335b, **838b**, 1083b; iii, 114a, 348b, 554a, 1103b, 1104a, 1191a; iv, 38b, 51a, 391a, b, 392a, b, 393a, 703b, 1040b; v, 371b, 750a, 1222a; vi, 276b, 483b, 484a, b, 516b, 524a, 525a, 528a, b, 529b, 551a, b, 715a, 803b; vii, 298b, 603a, 960b; viii, 58a, 665b; s, 57a, 94b, 108b, 336a, 405b
Fatḥ ʿAlī Shāh b. ʿAbd al-Madjīd Khān (XX) x, 961a
Fatḥ Allāh ʿImād al-Mulk, vizier (1482) ii, 981a; iii, 1159a; vi, 62b, 63a; vii, 459a
Fatḥ Allāh al-Shīrāzī, Mullā ii, 132a, 156b; s, 353b, 410b
Fatḥ Djang i, 231b
Fatḥ al-Dunyā wa ʾl-Dīn Djalāl Shāh Sulṭānī → Maḥmud Khān, Nāṣir al-Dīn (Kālpī)
Fatḥ Girāy I ii, 1046b, 1113b
Fatḥ Girāy II iv, 569a
Fatḥ al-Ḳalʿī (Aleppo) (1016) vii, 116b;
Fatḥ Khān (Barakzay) i, 230b, 231a; ii, 637b

Fatḥ Khān (Dawūdpōtrā) ii, 187a
Fatḥ Khān (Gudjaratī) → Maḥmud I Begrā
Fatḥ Khān b. Malik ʿAmbar (XVII) i, 781b; iii, 15b, 626a; viii, 74b
Fatḥ Khān Harāwī (1452) vi, 62a
Fatḥ Shāh Djalāl al-Dīn ii, 797b; iii, 14b; vi, 46b; s, 131b
Fatḥa iii, 172b
Fatḥābād ii, 32a, 180a, 797b; iii, 442b; v, 1216b
Fatḥiyya → ʿAbd Allāh b. Djaʿfar al-Ṣādiḳ
Fatḥnāme ii, **839b**; v, 1028b; vii, 535b
Fatḥpūr Sīkrī i, 252b, 1024a, 1324a; ii, **840a**; iii, 287b, 449b; v, 1135b, 1218a; vi, 127a, b, 190b, 294b, 368b; viii, 267b; ix, 46b; s, 378a
Fātiḥ-Camii iv, 229a
Fātiḥa ii, **841a**; v, 425a
al-Fātik → Nadjāḥ, Banū
Fāṭima bint Abī Muslim v, 65a, b
Fāṭima bint ʿAmr b. Makhzūm i, 42b, 80a
Fāṭima bint Asad b. Hāshim i, 152b; ii, 850a
Fāṭima bint Barrī i, 280b
Fāṭima bint Djāsim (XIX) vi, 614a
Fāṭima bint al-Ḥasan b. ʿAlī (VII) vii, 398a
Fāṭima bint al-Ḥusayn s, 95a
Fāṭima bint Ḳays al-Fihriyya (VII) x, 913b
Fāṭima bint Maẓlūm ii, 234a
Fāṭima bint Muḥammad (633) i, 15a, 187a, 381b, 382a, 400b; ii, 725a, **841b**; iii, 1232a; vi, 468a, 469a, 629a, 646a, 652a; s, 92b, 231a
Fāṭima bint Muḥammad IX (Naṣrid) s, 399a
Fāṭima bint Muḥammad al-Fihrī iv, 632a
Fāṭima bint al-Mundhir III b. al-Nuʿmān (Lakhmid) (VI) vii, 604a
Fāṭima bint ʿUmar b. Ḥafṣ iii, 694a
Fāṭima Khānîm s, 331a
Fāṭima Khātūn vi, 367a
Fāṭima Khātūn umm ʿĀrif Čelebi (XIII) ix, 858b; s, 83b
Fāṭima Lärä i, 841b
Fāṭima al-Maʿṣūma v, 369b, 370b, 371b
Fāṭima Sulṭān bint ʿAbd al-Medjīd (Ottoman) (1854) vi, 860b
Fāṭima Sulṭān bint Aḥmad III (Ottoman) (1731) i, 269b, 395a; ii, 49a; iii, 1002a; iv, 969b; vi, 55b
Fāṭima Sulṭan bint Ibrāhīm (Ottoman) (1646) vi, 865a
Fāṭima Sulṭān bint Selīm i, 291b
Fāṭima Zahrāʾ Khānîm iv, 875a
Fāṭimids i, 20a, 48b, 83b, 163a, 196b, 215b, 367a, 403a, 435b, 440a, 551b, 710b, 797b, 798a, 832b, 869b, 986a, 1074a, 1175b, 1354b; ii, 281b, 453b, 494b, 506a, **850a**, 911a; iii, 656a, 785a, 932a; iv, 198b, 200b, 204a, 378b, 458b; v, 327b, 620b, 623b, 738a, 1175b, 1243b; vi, 1b, 65b, 117b, 120b, 140b, 148a, 194a, 195a, 199b, 261b, 274b, 275a, 280b, 379b, 385b, 423b, 518a, b, 519a, b, 520a, 668b, 669b, 670a, 671a, 673b, 674b, 676a, 712b, 713a, 849a; vii, 160a, 162a; ix, 266a, 507a, 596b; xi, 188a; s, 120b, 236b, 254b, 256b, 326a, 338a, 389a
- administration i, 1148b; ii, 80a, 126b, 145b, 326a, 328a, **860a**; iii, 47b, 360a; iv, 943b, 1092a
- art, architecture i, 200b, 830a, 1319b; ii, 747a, 821b, **862b**; iv, 428b; v, 217a
Fāṭin b. Tamzīt b. Ḍarī, Banū i, 1349b; vi, 310b, 815a, 840a, 1042a
Fāṭin (Dāwūd) (1867) ii, **864b**
Faṭma ʿAliyye Khanîm i, 286a
Fatra ii, **865a**
Fattāḥ Wālī vi, 751a
Fattāḥī (1448) i, 256b; ii, **865a**; v, 650b; iv, 67a; viii, 48b
al-Fattāl, al-Ḥasan b. ʿAbd al-Karīm s, 380a
Fatwā i, 40a, 176a, 399b; ii, 304a, 306a, **866a**, 890a; ix, 400a
Faṭwāka, Banū vi, 742a; x, 77a
al-Fāʾū v, 66a
Fāʾw/Fāw, Ḳaryat al-/Wādī al- ii, **867b**; viii, 576a; s, 506a, 831b
Fawātiḥ al-suwar (al-Ḳurʾān) v, 412a
Fawdj → Ḥarb, Lashkar
Fawdjdār ii, **868a**; s, 57b
Fawrī, Aḥmad (1571) ii, **869a**; iv, 716a; v, 649b
Fawzī, Ḥusayn i, 598a
Fawzī al-Maʿlūf → Maʿlūf
Fawziyya bint Fuʾād al-Awwal (XX) ii, 654b; vii, 446b
Fayʾ i, 704a, 1142a, 1144a; ii, **869a**; iv, 973a, 1031a, 1141b; vii, 636a, b; xi, 299 a, b

Fayḍ → Muḥsin-i Fayḍ-i Kāshānī
Fayd, Ḥiṣn s, 198b, 199b, **304b**
al-Fayḍ b. Abī Ṣāliḥ (789) i, 106b; ii, **870a**; viii, 93b; s, 17b
Fayd b. Ḥām b. ʿAmalīḳ → Zayd al-Khayl al-Ṭāʾī
Fayḍ Aḥmad Fayḍ (1984) x, 879b
Fayḍ Allāh, Ḥādjdj (XVIII) vii, 444a
Fayḍ Allāh, Shaykh (1575) i, 1168a; ix, 85a
Fayḍ Allāh al-ʿAlamī i, 352b
Fayd Allāh Bey i, 1030b
Fayḍ Allāh Efendi, Shaykh al-Islām (1702) ii, 19b; iii, 627a; vi, 55a; vii, 708a; viii, 752b; s, 63a
Fayḍ Allāh Khān iii, 60a, b, 61b; viii, 426b
Fayḍ Athār iv, 103b; vi, 18b
Fayḍ al-Kashī i, 596a
Fayḍ Muḥammad Khān i, 1195a, 1197a
Fayḍābād ii, 1a, **870a**; s, 74b, 102a, 358b
Fayḍī (Fayyāḍī) → Muḥsin-i Fayḍ-i
Fayḍī Abu ʾl-Fayḍ b. Shaykh (1595) ii, **870b**; vii, 592b; xi, 566b
Fayḍ-i Kāshānī (1680) vi, 550b; vii, **475b**. 548a; viii, 136a, 779b; s, 57a, 305a
al-Fayḍiyya iv, 992a; vi, 454b
Faydj → Fuyūdj
Fayḍullāh → Fayḍ Allāh
Fāyiz, Awlād iv, 637b
Faylaka (island) v, 572a, 573b, 574a
Faylasūf ii, **872a**
Faylī iii, 1102b, 1106a; v, 823b, 829b
Fayoum → al-Fayyūm
Fayrūz → Fīrūz
Fayṣal I b. al-Sharīf al-Ḥusayn (Hāshimite) (1933) i, 46a, 684a; ii, 289b, 429b, 661a, **872a**; iii, 263b, 293a, 605b, 1258b; iv, 782b; v, 1044a, 1046b, 1091b; vi, 262a, 304a, 387a, 538a, 615a, b, 616a; vii, 442b; viii, 141a, 246a; x, 885a; s, 67b
Fayṣal II b. Ghāzī (Hāshimite) (1958) ii, 674b, **872b**; iii, 264a; viii, 141b, 142b
Fayṣal b. ʿAbd al-ʿAzīz (Āl Suʿūd) (1975) i, 98b; iii, 1066a; iv, 261a; vi, 34b, 155a, 156a, 166a, b, 169b; vii, 765a; ix, 904b; s, **305b**
Fayṣal b. Ḥusayn → Fayṣal I
Fayṣal b. Suʿūd (Āl Suʿūd) (1840) ii, 320b; vi, 151a, viii, 438b; x, 943b
Fayṣal b. Sulṭān al-Dawīsh (Mutayr chief) iii, 1065b, 1066a, 1067a, b; iv, 681a; v, 575a, 998a, b; vii, 782b
Fayṣal b. Turkī (Āl Bū Saʿīd, Oman) (1913) i, 1282; vi, 729b; ix, 904a; s, 356a
Fayṣal b. Turkī (Āl Suʿūd) (1865) i, 98b, 554b; ii, 108b, 176b; iv, 751b, 765a, 1073a; viii, 548a; ix, 904a; xi, 43b
Fayshān iii, 166b; vi, 80b; s, 694b
Faytūriyya s, 93a
al-Fayyāḍ b. ʿAlī b. Muḥammad b. al-Fayyāḍ (IX) vii, 460a, 905b
Fayyāḍ Beg iii, 1198b
Fayyāḍī → Fayḍī
al-Fayyūm i, 1145a; ii, **872b**; iv, 774a; vi, 88b, 119a, 219b, 671b, 674a; s, 379a
al-Fayyūmī → Saʿadya al-Fayyūmī
al-Fayyūmī (1333) x, 32b, 124b, 125a
al-Fayyūmī (1614) vi, 112a
Fayyūmi, Nathanael (b.) iv, 304b
Fayzabad → Fayḍābād
Fayẓī → Fayḍī
Faza vi, 129a; xi, 449a
Fazāra, Banū ii, 122a, b, **873a**, 1023b; iv, 493b; v, 267a; vii, 488a, 629b; x, 959b; s, 177a, b
al-Fazārī → Ibrāhīm b. Muḥammad
al-Fazārī, Abū Isḥāḳ (805) viii, 498b; ix, 771a, b
al-Fazārī, Abu ʾl-Ḳāsim Muḥammad (956) s, **306a**
al-Fazārī, Muḥammad b. Ibrāhīm (790) iii, 1136a,b; iv, 517b; vii, 401b; viii, 874a; xi, 498a
al-Fazārī al-Ibāḍī, ʿAbd Allāh b. Yazīd viii, 112b; s, 225b
Fāzāz ii, **873b**; vi, 591b, 741a; ix, 820a; s, 113b
Fāzil Ḥusayn Bey → Fāḍil Bey
Fazl, Fazlī → Faḍl, Faḍlī
Fazlullāh → Faḍl Allāh
Fāzūghlī ii, **874b**
Fazyl → Fāḍil
Fazzān i, 35a, 39a; ii, **875a**; iii, 296b; iv, 542a; v, 759b; s, 163b, 164b
Fedākārān-i Millet Djemʿiyyeti iv, 857a
Fedala → Faḍāla
Fedjr-i Ātī ii, **877b**; iii, 261a; v, 271b; viii, 838a, b
Fedū → Fidya

Fehīm-i Ķādim → Fehīm, Undjuzāde Muṣṭafā
Fehīm, Süleymān (1846) i, 284b; ii, **878a**; viii, 167a
Fehīm, Undjuzāde Muṣṭafā (1648) ii, **878a**
Fehīm Pasha (1908) ii, **878a**
Fehmī, Sheykh Ḥasan → Ḥasan Fehmī Efendi
Fehmī, Sheykh Muṣṭafā (1881) ii, **878b**
Feisal → Fayṣal
Fellāgha → Fallāķ
Fellani → Fulbe
Fellata → Fallāta
Fenārī, ʿAlāʾ al-Dīn ʿAlī b. Yūsuf Bālī (1497) ii, **879b**
Fenārī, Muḥyi ʾl-Dīn Meḥmed (1548) ii, **879b**; vii, 225a; ix, 896a
Fenārī, Shems al-Dīn Meḥmed (1431) i, 299b; ii, 602b, **879a**; v, 681a
Fenārī-zāde ii, **879a**
Fener ii, **879b**; iv, 241a; x, 237b
Fenerbāghčesi vi, 55b, 57a
Fennec → Fanak
Feodosia → Kefe
Feraḥ ʿAlī Pasha ii, 25a
Ferdī ii, **880a**
Ferdosi → Firdawsī
Ferghānā → Farghānā
Ferhād Pasha (1595) ii, 240a, **880b**; iii, 1001a; v, 493a; vi, 228a, 510a; vii, 596b; viii, 291a; ix, 127a; s, 238b
Ferhād u-Shīrīn → Farhād wa-Shīrīn
Ferhād Sokolovic (Sokollu) i, 1017b, 1018a, 1263b; v, 775a
Ferhat → Farhat
Ferhat Hashed (Tunisia) (XX) vii, 416b
Ferīd Čelebi (engraver) (XVII) vii, 472b
Ferīd Pasha → Dāmād
Ferīdūn Aḥmed Beg (1583) i, 312b; ii, 56b, 128a, 589a, 839b, **881a**; iii, 1045b, 1243a; vi, 1006b; vii, 7a, 596a; viii, 544b; s, 330a
Ferishte-oghlu i, 1162a
Ferkhwān (Dābūyid) (728) vi, 941a
Fermān → Farmān
Fērōz → Fīrūz
Fērōz Mīnār (1490) vi, 368b
Fērōzkōh → Fīrūzkūh
Fērōzshāh → Fīrūzshāh
Ferret → Ibn miķraḍ
Fès → Fās
Fethi Naci vi, 95b
Fethiye i, 476b; x, 126a
Fetoua → Fatwā
Fetwa → Fatwā
Fetwākhāne i, **837b**; ii, 867a; iii, 552b
Fevrī → Fawrī
al-Fewet ii, 1022b
Fewzī (1747) i, 1271a
Feyḍ Allāh → Abū Saʿīd-zāde Feyḍ Allāh
Feyzioğlu, Turhan ii, 646a
Fez (town) → Fās
Fezzān → Fazzān
Fidāʾ iii, 183a; v, 647a, b; s, **306b**
Fidāʾī (fidāwī) ii, **882a**; iii, 254a; viii, 442a; s, 306b
Fidāʾī Khān Kōka vii, 333b
Fidāʾiyyān-i Islām ii, **882a**; iii, 529b; iv, 40b, 52a, 165a, 790a; s, 158a
Fiḍḍa ii, **883a**, 1139a; v, 964a, 965b, 966a, 967a, 970a, 977a
Fidjār, ḥarb al- (VI) i, 53a; ii, 627a, **883b**; iii, 203b, 285b, 389a; v, 3b, 101b, 434b; vi, 145b, 146a, 266a, 477b; xi, 142b
Fidya ii, **884a**; s, 306b
Fighānī, Shīrāzī (Bābā) (1519) i, 860b; ii, **884a**; iv, 69a; vii, 342a, 667b; viii, 776a; x, 892a
Fighānī, Ramaḍān (1532) ii, **884b**; iii, 998a; iv, 715b
Figuig (Fadjīdj) ii, **885a**; vi, 571b
Fiḥl → Faḥl
Fihr, Banū iv, 828b; vi, 145a; s, 302a
al-Fihrī → ʿAbd al-Raḥmān; al-Daḥḥāk b. Ķays
al-Fihrī, ʿAbd Allāh b. Ḥabīb (VIII) x, 848a
al-Fihrī, Abū Isḥāķ (XIII) ii, **885b**
al-Fihrī, Ḥabīb b. ʿUbayd → Ḥabīb b. ʿUbayd al-Fihrī
al-Fihrī, Nāfiʿ b. ʿAbd al-Ķays (VII) vii, 154a; viii, 89b
al-Fihrī, Yūsuf b. ʿAbd al-Raḥmān (756) x, 848a, b
Fihrist → Fahrasa; Ibn al-Nadīm; Ṭūsī
Fiķāriyya (Mamlūk) vi, 319a
Fiķh i, 26a, 86a, 106a, 142b, 169b, 170a, 272b, 274a, 338a, 428a, 436b, 910b; ii, 605b, **886a**, 1069a; iii, 103b, 435a, 647a, 901a; iv, 204a; v, 1129b
Fiķh Akbar I i, 187b, 332b, 335a; iv, 172a, 693b; vii, 577a
Fiķh Akbar II i, 187b, 411a; ii, 294a; iii, 286b; iv, 172a, 470b, 693b; vii, 577a

Fiḳh Akbar III iii, 466a; iv, 693b
al-Fiḳī, Muḥammad Ḥāmid (XX) vi, 897a
Fikr ii, **891b**
Fikret, Tevfik → Tewfīḳ Fikret
Fikrī, ʿAbd Allāh Pasha (1890) ii, **892a**; vi, 113b, 602b
Fikrī, Amīn Pasha ii, 892a
Fīl ii, **892b**, 1049b; iii, 201a, 345b; iv, 215a, 217b, 218b, 219b, 647b; v, 687a, 690a
al-Fīl ii, **895a**
Fiʿl ii, **895b**; v, 578a, b, 579a
Fīʿl, afʿāl ii, **898a**
Filāḥa ii, 32b, **899a**; iii, 964a
Filʾakovo s, 171a, b
Fīlālīs → ʿAlawīs
Fīlān iv, 343a
Fīlān-Shāh iv, 343a; s, 700a
Filardūs al-Rūmī vi, 506b
Filasṭīn i, 111a, 197b, 216a, 451a, 975b; ii, 854a, **910b**; iii, 523b; iv, 834b; v, 912a; vi, 29a, 388a, 796b; vii, 9b; s, 67b
– literature ii, 468a
Filibe i, 1302b; ii, **914a**; vi, 1029b; x, 920a; s, 328b, 330a
Filīmūn ii, 916b
Filkhāna → Pīlkhāna
Filori ii, **914b**
Fils → Fals
Fīn iv, 694b, 695b
Find al-Zimmānī vi, 477a
Fi̊ndi̊ḳli̊ ii, 62a; iv, 231b, 233a
Fi̊ndi̊ḳli̊li̊ Süleymān Efendi ix, **414a**
Fi̊ndi̊ḳoghlu, Ḍiyāʾ al-Dīn Fakhrī (1974) s, **308a**
Findiriskī, Mīrzā Abu ʾl-Ḳāsim (1640) vii, 452b, 547b; s, **308a**
Finike ii, 695a; s, 221b
Finkenstein (treaty) ii, 839a; iv, 38b, 395b; v, 495b; s, 620b
Finyāna, Fiñana ii, **915b**
Firabr ii, **915b**
Firandj → al-Ifrandj
Firārīs vi, 981b
Firāsa i, 146b; ii, **916a**; v, 100a, 235a
Firʿawn ii, **917a**; iii, 1175a; vi, 412a
Firaydan ii, 905b; iv, 97b, 98a, b
Firda → Furḍa
Firdaws ii, 448b, 451a
Firdawsī (Ferdosi) (1020) i, 205b, 358b, 505a, 686a, 1072b, 1139b, 1309b, 1354a; ii, 132b, 740a, 794a, 798a, 894b, **918a**, 1050b; iii, 112b, 113a, 122a, 371a, 637b; iv, 62b; vi, 66a, 608b; viii, 76a, 77b, 80a; s, 108a
Firdawsī silsila vi, 131b
Firdewsī rūmī (XV) ii, **921a**
Firdousi → Firdawsī
Firīdun → Farīdūn
Firind v, 971b, 972a, b; s, 740a
Firishta → Malāʾika
Firishta, Muḥammad Ḳāsim Hindū Shāh Astarābādī (1623) i, 199a; ii, **921b**; vi, 121b, 294a; vii, 342b; s, 206b
Firisdhte-oghlu, ʿAbd al-Laṭīf (Ibn Malak) (XV) ii, **923b**; x, 539a
Firishte-oghlu, ʿAbd al-Madjīd (1469) ii, **924a**
Firḳa → Ḥizb, al-Milal wa ʾl-niḥal, Ṭarīḳa
Firḳān (al-Akhbār) i, 260b, 261a, b, 263a
Firkovič, Abraham iv, 606a, 1175a
Firmān → Farmān
Firouz → Fīrūz
Firrīm (Pirrīm) ii, 928b; iv, 644a, b; vi, 632b, 936a; s, **309a**
Firrīsh (Castillo del Hierro) ii, **924a**
Fīrūhā s, 154b
Fīrūz (ḍāʿī) vi, 438b
Fīrūz (Gūr) i, 43b; ii, **925b**; vi, 365a, 384a,b
Fīrūz (Sāsānid) (484) ix, 76a
Fīrūz (vizier) (1400) vii, 56a
Fīrūz b. Daryā ʿImād al-Mulk (1574) iii, 1161b
Fīrūz b. Kabk s, 125b
Fīrūz b. Radjab → Fīrūz Shāh III (Ṭughluḳ)
Fīrūz b. Yazdigird III (Sāsānid) (VII) v, 181a; ix, 621b
Fīrūz Bey i, 340b, 1118b; ii, 611b, 688a; x, 413b, 457b
Fīrūz al-Daylamī i, 728a; iv, 1134b; x, 785a; s, 116a
Fīrūz Djang I, Ghāzī ʾl-Dīn Khān (XVII) vii, 446a
Fīrūz Djang II → Muḥammad Panāh, Mīr
Fīrūz Djang III → ʿImād al-Mulk, Ghāzī al-Dīn
Fīrūz Ḥusayn iv, 571a
Fīrūz Shāh Khaldjī → Khaldjīs
Fīrūz Shāh I Rukn al-Dīn (Muʿizzī, Dihlī) (1236) ii, 267b; vi, 488a

Fīrūz Shāh II Djalāl al-Dīn (Khaldjī, Dihlī) (1296) i, 444b, 855b, 1036a, 1202b; ii, 179b, 256b, 268a; vi, 406b, 488a; vii, 457b
Fīrūz Shāh III Rukn al-Dīn (Tughluḳid, Dihlī) (1388) i, 432b, 855b, 1036a, b, 1156b; ii, 48a, 120b, 270a, 392a, 814a, **924b**, 1047b, 1124b; iii, 202b, 416b, 434a; iv, 218b, 276a, 368a, 543a, 749b, 1019a; vi, 273a, 294a, 368a, 532b, 533a, 537a, 692a, 693b, 866b; vii, 194a, 195a, 412a, 679b; viii, 1047b; s, 73b, 105b, 238a, 325a, 409b
– administration ii, 154a, 336a, 566b, 924b, 1084b; iii, 492a
– constructions i, 1322b; ii, 258a, 262a, b, 274b, 438a, 498b, 909b, 925a, 928b; iii, 225a, 442a, 485a; v, 549a, 884a, 885b, 1135a
Fīrūz Shāh (Mughal) ii, 809a
Fīrūz Shāh, ʿAlāʾ al-Dīn (Bengal) (1533) i, 1168a; v, 639a; vi, 47a
Fīrūz Shāh b. Radjab (Tughluḳid) (1388) x, 591b
Fīrūz Shāh, Sayf al-Dīn (Bengal) (1490) iii, 14b, 422a; v, 639a; vi, 46b
Fīrūz Shāh Tādj al-Dīn (Bahmānid) (1422) i, 1200a; ii, 1114b; ii, 15a, 417b; vi, 67b; vii, 289a
Fīrūz Shāpūr (Anbār) i, 484b; vi, 633a
Fīrūzābād (Djūr) (Adhharbāydjān) ii, **925b**; iv, 989b; vi, 384b; ix, 70a
al-Fīrūzābādī, Abu ʾl-Ṭāhir al-Shīrāzī (1415) ii, 801b, **926a**; iii, 765a; iv, 524a, b; vi, 796a; vii, 445a
Fīrūz, Madjd al-Dīn (XIV) viii, 458b
Fīrūzadj ii, **927b**
al-Fīrūzādjiyya i, 866a
Fīrūzānids ii, **928a**; iii, 255a
Fīrūzkūh (Harāt) ii, **928a**, 1096b, 1101a; ix, 110a
Fīrūzkūh (Ṭabaristān) ii, **928b**; vi, 511b, 512b, 514b; s, 309b
Fīrūzkūhī i, 224b; ii, 5b; iii, 1107b
Fīrūzpūr ii, **928b**
Fishārakī, Sayyid Muḥammad vii, 918b; s, 342a
Fishek → Shenlik
al-Fishtālī → ʿAbd al-ʿAzīz b. Muḥammad
Fisḳ → Fāsiḳ
Fiṭahl vi, 820a
Fīthāghūras i, 235b; ii, 765b, **929a**
Fitna ii, **930b**; iii, 494b, 495b; v, 1109b; xi, 310a, 311b
Fiṭnat ii, **931b**; iii, 269a
Fiṭr → ʿĪd al-fiṭr
Fiṭra ii, **931b**
Fiṭrat, ʿAbd al-Raʾūf (XX) ii, **932a**; x, 63b, 961a
al-Fītūrī Tlīsh (1943) vi, 252b
Fityān → Fatā
Flores iii, 1219b; vi, 116b; ix, 977a; s, 761a
Flori → Filori
Foča i, 476a, 1270b; iii, 214b; vii, 244a, b; vii, 391b
Fodié Sylla iii, 108a
Foggāra ii, 875b; iv, 529a, 532b
Fomalhaut → Nudjūm
Fondouk → Funduḳ
Fort Jesus → Mazrūʾī; Mombasa
Fortūn b. Mūsa iv, 713a
Fortunate Islands → Djazāʾir al-Saʿādāt
Fostat → al-Fusṭāṭ
Fouad → Fuʾād
Fouta Djallon → Fūta Djallon
Fraga → Ifragha
Frāmarz Shāh ii, 30a
Franc-Maçonnerie → Farāmush-Khāna; Farmāsūniyya; Māsūniyya
Frankincense → Lubān; Mibkhara
Frasa → Ifrāgha
Frasheri i, 650b (see also *s.v.* Sāmi, Shems ül-Dīn)
Frāsiyāb → Afrāsiyāb
Fraxinetum i, 935b; ii, **933b**, v, 503a
Frederick II (Hohenstaufen) i, 461a, 1141b; iii, 157b; vi, 413a, 579b, 637b, 638a; vii, 273b, 274a; ix, 582b
Freetown ix, 550b, 551a
Frīsa iv, 94a, 95a
Frolinat s, 166a, b
Frunze → Pishpek
Fuʾād al-Awwal (Egypt) (1936) i, 13b; ii, **934a**; iii, 516a, 517a; v, 1061a; vi, 45a, 155b, 262a; vii, 765a; viii, 60a; s, 18b, 299a
Fuʾād al-Khaṭīb (XX) vi, 153b, 176a
Fuʾād Pasha iv, 857a; v, 631a
Fuʾād Pasha Kečedjizāde (1869) i, 284b, 286b, 397a, 397b; ii, 185a, 429a, 637a, **934b**; iii, 553a; iv, 295b, 460b; vi, 68b; s, 281b
Fuat Köprülü → Köprülü

al-Fuḍayl b. ʿIyād (803) i, 274a, 284a, 1246a; ii, **936a**; iii, 752a; viii, 496a, 547a
Fuḍayl b. al-Zubayr al-Rassān ii, 485a
Fū<u>dh</u>an<u>dj</u> s, **309b**
al-Fu<u>dj</u>āʾa (VII) iv, 752b
al-Fu<u>dj</u>ayra ii, **936b**; vi, 38a; ix, 349a, b; s, 416b
al-Fūdūdī i, 129b
al-Fuḍūl iii, 389b
Fuḍūlī, Muḥammad b. Sulaymān (1556) i, 956b; ii, 206b, **937a**; iv, 704b, 1137b; v, 1105b; vii, 576b; viii, 581b, 775b; s, 83a, 324a
Fu<u>gh</u>ān → A<u>sh</u>raf ʿAlī <u>Kh</u>ān
Fujairah → al-Fu<u>dj</u>ayra
Fuḳahāʾ al-Madīna al-Sabʿa v, 997b; s, **310b**, 380b
Fuḳarāʾ i, 1b, 483a
al-Fuḳaymī, <u>Dh</u>akwān b. ʿAmr ii, 998b
al-Fuḳaymī, Muḥammad b. <u>Dh</u>uʾayb viii, 377a
Fula ii, 939a, 940b, 942b
Fūlād b. <u>Sh</u>ansab ii, 1099a
Fūlād <u>Kh</u>ān s, 335b
Fūlād-Sutūn i, 132a; iii, 1201a; v, 73b; vi, 272b, 273a; ix, 157b
Fūlād Turkbačča (XV) vii, 279a
Fūlā<u>dh</u> v, 971b, 978b
Fulani → Fulbe
Fulayḥ b. al-ʿAwrāʾ i, 118a; iii, 996a; s, 116b
Fulaymūn → Aflīmūn
Fulayta, Banū ix, 807a
Fulbe i, 179a, 303a, 910b, 1259a, 1260a; ii, 9b, 10a, 94a, 251b, 767b, **939a**, 959b, 960b, 1132a, 1144b; iii, 276b, 646a; iv, 549a; vi, 281b; vii, 435b; viii, 19b; x, 142a, 602a; s, 164a
Fulful b. Saʿīd i, 860a; v, 1176b, 1180b, 1182a
Fulfulde → Fula
Fulk (of Anjou) (XII) iv, 779a; s, 204b
Fulūs → Fals
Fūman ii, 74b, **943b**; s, 298a
Fūmanī → ʿAbd al-Fattāḥ Fūmanī
Fūmin → Fūman
Fūmoluṭī, Aḥmad iv, 889a; vi, 385a
Fun<u>dj</u> i, 425b, 1158a; ii, 252b, 615a, **943b**; iv, 686b, 891b; v, 267a; viii, 91a
Funduḳ ii, **945a**; iv, 135b, 136a, 1015a
Fünfkirchen → Pécs
Fung → Fun<u>dj</u>
Fūr, Fūrāwī ii, 122a, 123a; v, 1250b
al-Fūrakī, Abū Bakr iii, 1165a
al-Furāt i, 405b, 467b, 468a, 634b, 994a, 1094b, 1095a; ii, 250a, 686b, **945a**; iii, 1251a; iv, 482a; v, 441b, 864b; s, 37a
al-Furāt, Banū iii, 750a, b, 767b; iv, 189a; v, 953a; xi, 186a
Furḍa ii, **948a**
al-Furḍa (river) vii, 114a
al-Furḍa (town) → Raḥba (Raḥbat Mālik b. Ṭawḳ)
Furḍat Nuʿm → Raḥba (Raḥbat Mālik b. Ṭawḳ)
Furdat al-ruʾūs ii, 149a, 948a
Furfūriyūs (Porphyry) i, 234b; ii, 550a, 780a, **948b**, 955a; iv, 92a; ix, 403a
Furgač → ʿIzzet Pa<u>sh</u>a, Aḥmed
Furḳān ii, **949b**; x, 317b, 318a, 319a, b
Furḳān (<u>Sh</u>īʿī group) vii, 763a
Furḳān b. Asad → Jeshuah b. Judah
Furḳān, Banū ii, 463a
Furn v, 41b, 42b
al-Furs ii, **950b**
Fürstenspiegel → Siyāsa
Furūʿ (law, doctrine) i, 257b, 277a; ii, 182b, 889b; iii, 162a, 182a
Furūʿ (poetic) i, 671a, b
Furūʿ (tax) i, 1144a; iv, 1041a
Furū<u>gh</u>, Abu ʾl-Ḳāsim <u>Kh</u>ān (XIX) ii, **951b**
Furū<u>gh</u>, Muḥammad Mahdī b. Muḥammad Bā<u>gh</u>ir Iṣfahānī (XIX) ii, **952a**
Furū<u>gh</u> al-Dīn → Furū<u>gh</u>, Muḥammad Mahdī b. Muḥammad Bā<u>gh</u>ir Iṣfahānī
Furū<u>gh</u> Farru<u>kh</u>zād vi, 609a
Furū<u>gh</u>ī, Mīrzā ʿAbbās (1858) ii, **952a**; iv, 69b
Furū<u>gh</u>ī, Mīrzā Muḥammad Iṣfahānī (XVIII) ii, **952a**; iv, 69b
Furū<u>gh</u>ī, Muḥammad ʿAli → Muḥammad ʿAli Furū<u>gh</u>ī
Furū<u>gh</u>ī, Muḥammad Ḥusayn (1943) ii, **952a**
Furūḳ ii, 605a
Furūsiyya i, 520a; ii, 786b, **952b**; v, 688a, 689a, b; vi, 913a
Fusayfisāʾ i, 610b, 611b, 612a; ii, 955a; iv, 1167b; v, 13b, 16b, 17a, 298b
Fū<u>sh</u>han<u>dj</u> → Bū<u>sh</u>an<u>dj</u>
Fusṭāṭ (tent) iv, 1147a

al-Fusṭāṭ i, 126a, 197a, 451b, 531b, 532a, 844b, 950b, 1346a; ii, 114b, 130a, 746a, **957b**, 1064b; iii, 79b, 675a; iv, 323b, 424a, b; vi, 186a, 195a, 362a, 363a, b, 410b, 647b, 648a, 649a, 660a, 666a, 668a, 670b, 671a; vii, 158b; s, 1a, 136b
– Djāmiʿ ʿAmr i, 610a, 619a, 624a, 814a; ii, 958a, 959a
Fuṣūṣ fi ʾl-Ḥikma i, 414b; ii, 780a
Fūṭa v, 737b
Fūta Djallon ii, 941b, **959a**, 1131b, 1132a; vi, 281b; viii, 16b; ix, 550b
Fūta Tōro x, 602a, b
Fūthāghūras → Fīthāghūras
Futūḥ b. Muḥammad b. Marwān al-Aṣghar vi, 625b
Futūḥa (musician) vi, 488a
Futūḥāt → Ṭarābulus (al-Shaʾm)
al-Futūḥī, Tādj al-Dīn i, 949b
al-Futūḥī, Takī al-Dīn (1572) i, 949b; vii, 311b
Futuwwa i, 21a, 256b, 277a, 321b, 322a, 520a, 794b, 900b; ii, 433a, **961a**, 1044a; iii, 671b, 1256a; iv, 705a; vi, 225a; vii, 998b
Fütüwwetnāme i, 323a, b; ii, 967b, 968a, b
Futyā → Fatwā
al-Fuwaṭī, Hishām → Hishām b. ʿAmr al-Fuwaṭī
al-Fuwaṭī, Kamāl al-Dīn → Ibn al-Fuwaṭī
Fuwwa vi, 119a; viii, 438a
Fuyūdj i, 1045b; ii, **969b**
Fuzūlī → Fuḍūlī
Fyzabad → Fayḍābād

G

Ğa Ssuling → Ma Chung-ying
Gaban ii, **970a**
Gabès → Ḳābis
Gabon ii, **970a**
Gabr ii, **970b**
Gabrī (Mānd) vi, 384b
Gabriel → Djabrāʾīl
Gadāʾī (poet) v, 836a; vii, 91a
Gadāʾī Kambō, Shaykh ʿAbd al-Raḥmān (1568) i, 1136a; ii, 421a; v, 836a; s, **312a**
Gaddafi, Muʿammar → al-Ḳadhdhāfī
Gaddāla → Djaddāla, Banū; Gudāla
Gadjapatis vi, 67a
Gadmīwa, Banū vi, 742a, b, 743a; x, 530b
Gaeda i, 1258a
Gāēkwār i, 1053a; ii, 1129b; vi, 535b; viii, 244b
Gafinā (Marʿash) vi, 506b
Gafsa → Ḳafṣa
Gafuri → Ghafūrī, Madjīd
Gagauz, Banū i, 1287a, 1302b; ii, 610a, b, **971a**; iv, 600b, 814a; vi, 420b; x, 698b; xi, 149a
Gagik I i, 507b, 638a; ii, 680a
Gagik II i, 638a; ii, 680b; iv, 670a
Gagik-Abas i, 638b
Gagik Ardzrunī i, 637a
Gagrawn → Muṣṭafābād
Gāhāmbārs ii, 398a; vii, 15b
Gāhānbārs → Gāhāmbārs
Gāikwāŕ → Gāēkwar
Gakkhaŕ ii, **972a**, 1131b, 1155b; v, 31b
Galata → Ghalaṭa
Galata-Saray → Ghalaṭa-Sarāyi̊
Gälbāghī v, 460b
Galdan (Zunghar Khān) (XVII) s, 523b
Galen → Djālīnūs
Galena → al-Kuḥl
Galicia → Djillīḳiya
Galla → Oromo
Gallabāt → Ḳallabāt
Galla-dār (Mānd) vi, 384b
Gallipoli → Gelibolu
Gamasāb, Gamasiyāb → Karkha
Gambia ii, **974b**
Gambīrī ii, 138b
Gambra → Bandar ʿAbbās
Gamron (Gomron) → Bandar ʿAbbās
Gana, Banū i, 1247a; viii, 794b; ix, 764a; x, 589b; xi, 366a
Ganāfa, Ganaveh → Djannāba
Gandamak s, 237b
Gandamak, Treaty of v, 501b, 580b; ix, 531b
Gandāpur i, 219a; ii, **975a**
Gandāwa → Ḳandābīl
Gandhāra → Ḳandahār
Gandhi, M.K. i, 317b; v, 7b; s, 4b, 480b, 481a, 526a
Gandj ʿAlī Khān iv, 476a; v, 164a

Gandja (Djanza, Elizavetpol) i, 8a, 191b, 660b, 1041b; ii, **975a**, iv, 1176b; v, 490a, 495b; vi, 55b, 56a, 64b, 85b, 274a; vii, 453a; ix, 169a; s, 143a
– (treaty) (1735) viii, 771b
Gandjābā → Ḳandābil
al-Gandjī, Muḥammad b. Yūsuf v, 1236b, 1237a
Gandj-i-Shakar → Farīd al-Dīn Masʿūd
Gandjvar b. Isfandiyar s, 263b
Gando ii, 94a (see also *s.v.* Fulbe)
Gandu iii, 277b
Ganfīsa, Banū vi, 742a
Gangā ii, **976a**
Gangāwatī vi, 63a
Ganges → Gangā
Gangōh s, 313a
Gangōhī, Shaykh ʿAbd al-Ḳuddūs (1537) ii, 54b, 55a, 56a; xi, 118b; s, **312b**, 572a
Gangōhī, Rashīd Aḥmad (1905) x, 442b
Gangōhī, Rukn al-Dīn Muḥammad b. ʿAbd al-Ḳuddūs (1537) s, 313a
Ganja iii, 266b
Ganza → Gandja
Gao (Mali) ii, **976b**; v, 222a; vi, 259a; vii, 393b; viii, 16b, 848a; ix, 753b, 756b; s, 295b
Gāon sabhā i, 758a
Gaourang i, 910b
Gardīz ii, **978a**
Gardīzī, Abū Saʿīd (XI) ii, **978b**; v, 1001a; vii, 21a; s, 136a, 245a, 266a, 326b
Gardīzī, Shāh Yūsuf vii, 550a
Garĕbĕg → ʿĪd, Indonesia (Islam)
Gargar vi, 507a; x, 966b
Gaṙhī vi, 47a
Gaṙhī Saʿādat iii, 335b
Gaṙhī Ḥabībullāh iii, 335b
Garmādūz s, 116a
Garmrūdī, ʿAbd Allāh s, 290b
Garmsīr → Ḳishlaḳ
Garnāna, Banū vi, 742a
Garrūs iii, 1102b, 1108b; s, 71a
Garrūsī, Amīr-i Niẓām s, 73a
Garshāsp (heroe) viii, 636b, 1011a, b
Garshāsp II, ʿAlāʾ al-Dawla Abū Kālīdjār (Kākūyid) (1119) iv, 466a, b; vi, 908a; x, 553b
Garshāsp, ʿIzz al-Dīn v, 828a
Garshāsp b. Muḥammad iv, 466a
Garsīf ii, **978b**; vi, 142b; vii, 642a
Gasprali̊ (Gasprinski), Ismāʿīl (1914) i, 894a; ii, 366a, 474b, **979a**; iv, 630b; vii, 764b; viii, 250b; s, 47a, 123a
Gasprinski → Gasprali̊
Gāthā (prem-) iii, 456b; iv, 53a
Gaṭṭāya iv, 95a
Gāṭū, gaṭṭū, gaṭwa iv, 743b
Gaur → Gabr
Gāvír → Gabr
Gavras i, 664b, 983a; vi, 1016b
Gāvur → Kāfir, Gabr
Gavur-Ḳalʿa (Marw) vi, 619a, b
Gawakuke vii, 435b
Gawālior → Gwāliyar
Gāwān, Maḥmūd → Maḥmūd Gāwān
Gāwar-Bātī i, 225a; ii, 31a, 138b
Gāwbāra → Gīl Gawbarā
Gāwdūk vi, 502a
Gawhar Amān ii, 30a; s, 327b
Gawhar Khātūn (XI) vii, 679b
Gawhar Shād i, 147b, 148b; vi, 366a; x, 520a
Gawhar-i Murād → Sāʿidī, Ghulām Ḥusayn
Gawhar-i Tādj ʿĀbida Sulṭān i, 1196b
Gāwilgaṙh ii, **981a**; iv, 921a; vii, 314b; s, 280a
Gawr → Gabr
Gawr (Bengal) ii, 976a, b; iii, 444a, 634b; v, 638a; vi, 46b, 47a, b, 368b; vii, 314a
Gawur → Kāfir
Gāwur Daghlari̊ ii, **982a**; s, 171b
Gaykhātū b. Abaḳa (Il-Khānid) (1295) i, 703a, 1129b; ii, 14a, **982a**, 1043a; iii, 284a, 1122a; iv, 31a, 621a; v, 162b, 553b, 827a; vi, 16a, 502a, 1017b; vii, 232a
al-Gaylānī, Rashīd ʿĀlī → Rashīd ʿAlī
Gayō → Atjeh
Gayōmard, Shams al-dīn (malik) (Rustamdār) ii, 268a; iii, 1270a; iv, 818b, 920b; vi, 513a, b; x, 110b
Gaz (measure) s, **313b** (see also *s.v.* Misāḥa)
Gaza → Ghazza
Gaziantep → ʿAyntāb
Gaz-i-ilāhī ii, 982b; iv, 1055b; vii, 139a, b; s, 313b
Gazūla, Gazūlī → Djazūla, Djazūlī
Gāzurgāh viii, 267a; x, 515a
Gāzurgāhī vi, 73b
Geben → Gaban
Geber → Gabr, Madjūs

Geber → Djābir b. Aflaḥ
Gebīr → Gabr
Gebze (Dakibyza) ii, **982b**; vi, 366a
Gečid resmi ii, 147a
Gedaref → al-Ḳaḍārif
Gedi, Gede ii, **983a**; iv, 888b; vi, 283b, 704a
Gedik → Ṣinf
Gedik Aḥmed → Aḥmad Pasha Gedik
Gediz Čayi̊ ii, **983a**
Geg i, 650a, 651a (see also *s.v.* Arnawutluḳ)
Gehenna → Djahannam
Geladjo i, 303a
Gelenbe ii, 715a; s, 282b
Gelibolu i, 947b; ii, 11b, **983a**; iv, 571b; vi, 71b, 587b; viii, 193a; s, 41b, 149b
Gemlik (Kios) ii, **987a**; vi, 588b
Genāwah → Gnāwa
Genč ʿAlī Pasha (1736) vi, 56a
Genč ʿOthmān ii, 75b
Genç Spor Klübü iv, 138a
Genghis Khan → Činghiz Khān
Genil → Shanīl
Geniza ii, **987b**; v, 738b
George, Saint → Djirdjīs
Georgia → Abkhāz; al-Kurdj
Gerard of Cremona (1187) vii, 738b
Gerasa → Djarash
Gerdek resmi → ʿArūs resmi
Geredelī Ḥadjdjī Khalīl (1831) ix, 156a
Germany-V Nemče
Germiyān i, 243b, 467b; ii, 204b; vi, 975a
Germiyān-oghullari̊ i, 346a, 510b, 1256b; ii, **989a**; v, 359b, 539a; vii, 593b
Gerona → Djarunda
Gerri → Ḳerrī
Gessi Pasha s, 164b
Gēsū Darāz ii, 1135a; vi, 369a; xi, 119a
Geṭna i, 733b
Gevele iv, 620a; vi, 71b
Gevherī, Meḥmed (1737) ii, **990a**
Geygellis ii, 40b
Geyvān Ketkhudā (XVI) vii, 244b
al-Ghāb (river) i, 1073a; ii, **990b**; vi, 578b
Ghāba ii, **991a**
Ghabāghib vi, 546a, b, 548a
Ghaban iv, 1165b
al-Ghabrāʾ i, 521b; s, 177b, 178a
Ghaḍāʾirī iv, 61a; x, 745a, 869b
Ghadāmès ii, 875a, 876b, **991b**
al-Ghaḍanfar → Abū Taghlib, Ḥamdanids
al-Ghaḍanfarī, Abū ʿAbd Allāh (1020) ix, 819a
Ghaḍanfer Dede (1566) ii, 1088a; vi, 226b, 227a, 228a
Ghadār → Khazaf
Ghadīr Khumm i, 1025a, 1325b; ii, **993a**; vii, 276b; ix, 420b, 429b; xi, 161b
al-Ghāḍirī ii, **994b**
Ghadjar ii, 40b
Ghaffārī, Aḥmad b. Muḥammad (1567) i, 423b; ii, **994b**; vii, 199b
Ghāfiḳ i, 1249a; ii, 744a, b; s, 313a
Ghāfiḳī → ʿAbd al-Raḥmān al-Ghāfiḳī
al-Ghāfiḳī, Abū Djaʿfar Aḥmad (1146) i, 156a, 214a, 345a, 594b, 1156a; ii, 995a; iii, 737a; vi, 263a, 264b, 350b; s, **313b**, 383a, 397a
al-Ghāfiḳī, Abu ʾl-Ḳāsim → al-Kabtawrī
al-Ghāfiḳī, Muḥammad b. Ḳassūm b. Aslam (XII) i, 449a; ii, **995a**
Ghāfir, Banū i, 545b; ii, 630b; iii, 403b; viii, 993a; x, 816b; s, 355b, 356a
Ghāfirī → Ghāfir, Banū
Ghafūrī, Medjīd (1934) ii, **995a**
Ghaghauz → Gagauz
Ghāʾib ii, **995b**
Ghāʾiṭa → Ghayṭa
Ghalāfiḳa ii, **996a**
Ghalaṭa i, 973a, b; ii, 833a, 999a; iv, 225b, 228b, 231b, 239a, 240b, 244a, 1158b; v, 313a, 533b; vi, 3a; s, 168a, **314a**
Ghalaṭa-Sarāyi̊ ii, **996b**; v, 904b; vi, 57a
Ghalaṭāt-i Meshhūre ii, **997a**
Ghalča i, 225a, 853b; ii, **997b**
Ghaldan Khān iii, 1120b
Ghaldjī → Ghalzay
Ghālī → Ghulāt
Ghālī, Rashīd v, 190a
Ghālib (ʿAlīgarh) vi, 612a
Ghālib, Ismāʿīl → Ismāʿīl Ghālib
Ghālib, Mīrzā Asad Allāh (1869) ii, 735b, **1000a**, 1036b; iii, 93b, 1095b; iv, 716b; v, 961b; vii, 341b, 376b; s, 334a, 360b
Ghālib, Sharīf (1813) i, 1299a; ii, 176b; iii, 363b; v, 62b; vi, 150b (see also *s.v.* Wahhābiyya)
Ghālib b. ʿAbd al-Raḥmān al-Ṣiḳlabī (981) ii, **997b**; iii, 31a, 74b, 1036b; v, 626a, 1008a; vi, 431a
Ghālib b. ʿAlī b. Hilāl iii, 403b
Ghālib b. Ṣaʿṣaʿa (VII) ii, 788a, **998a**

Ghālib Dede, Meḥmed Esʿad Shaykh (1799) ii, **999a**; iii, 90b; iv, 190b; vi, 610a; s, 283a
Ghālib Pasha → Meḥmed Saʿīd Ghālib Pasha
Ghaliev, Mīr Saʿīd Sulṭān (XX) vi, 585b, 586b
Ghāliya i, 1299a
Ghallābakhshī ii, 155b, 156a, 157b
Ghalzay (Afghān) i, 88a, 95a, 217b, 219b, 229a, b, 1013b; ii, 812a, **1001a**; iii, 604b; iv, 537a, 917b; vii, 853b; s, 66b, 237b, 329b, 367a, 763b
Ghamātiyyūn iii, 339a
Ghāmid, Banū ii, **1001b**; iii, 363b; ix, 302a
al-Ghammād, Muḥammad b. ʿAlī al-Wadjdī (1624) vi, 350a
al-Ghamr b. Yazīd (750) vii, 798a
Ghamr dhī Kinda i, 526b; v, 119a; viii, 353a
Ghāna i, 211a, 762a; ii, 94a, **1003a**; iii, 288b; v, 386b, 387a, 653b; vi, 258a, 259b, 281b; vii, 612b; viii, 16b; ix, 754a; s, 217b
Ghāna (Sudān) ii, **1001b**; iii, 657a
Ghanam i, 876a; s, **316b**
Ghanānand iii, 457b
Ghanī, Muḥammad Ṭāhir Ashaʾī (1688) ii, **1004a**
Ghanī b. Aʿṣur b. Saʿd b. Ḳays ʿAylān, Banū i, 920b; ii, **1004b**; vi, 545a
Ghānim, Khalīl → Khalīl Ghānim
Ghanīma i, 1142a, 1144a; ii, 146b, 154b, 504b, 869a, **1005a**; iii, 183a;iv, 1141b; v, 689b
Ghanīmat Kundjāhī, Muḥammad Akram (1690) ii, **1006b**; s, 322a
Ghānimids ii, 517a; v, 333a
Ghāniya, Banū i, 92b, 161b, 165a, 367a, 533a, 798a, 1176a, 1205b; ii, 112a, 526a, **1007a**; iii, 1055b; iv, 337b, 416a, 479b; vi, 404a, 728b; vii, 897a, 989a; viii, 563a; s, 80b
Ghanm b. ʿAwf, Banū i, 683b; vi, 649a
Ghār s, 327a
Ghār Ḥirāʾ vi, 168b
al-Ghār al-Muḳaddas iii, 207a, 959a
Ghār al-Shuyūkh ii, 1024b
Ghār Thawr vi, 168b
Gharb (Durūz) vi, 343b, 344a
Gharb (Morocco) ii, **1008b**; iii, 300b; v, 1185b; s, 350b, 387b
Gharb al-Andalus ii, **1009a**; x, 795a
al-Gharbiyya ii, **1009b**; vi, 453b, 580b; s, 18a, 40a
Ghardaḳa vii, 53b
Ghardāya ii, **1010a**; iii, 97b; viii, 794b
Ghardjistān, Gharshistān ii, **1010b**; vi, 65b, 617b, 618a; s, 376b
Gharīb i, 157b, 275b; ii, **1011a**; iii, 25b
Gharībān ii, 443a, 921b, 1097b
Ghāribī (Persian poet) s, 528a
al-Ghāribī, Muḥammad b. Sulayyim s, 355b
Gharībīs → Āfāḳīs
al-Gharīḍ (VIII) ii, **1011b**; iii, 950a
Ghārim ii, **1011b**; s, 207b
Gharīm iv, 811a
Ghariyyān iii, 1064a
Gharnāṭa (Granada) i, 6a, 43b, 84a, 491b, 495b, 1057b; ii, **1012a**; iii, 135a, 220a, 836b, 1110a; vi, 606b; vii, 1020a, 1028a
– Alhambra → al-Ḥamra
– monuments i, 1225a, 1320b; ii, **1014b**; iii, 144a, 498b
al-Gharnāṭī → Abū Ḥāmid; Abu Ḥayyān; al-Ḥādjdj
Ghars → Kars
Ghars al-Dawla b. Shumla i, 240a
Ghars al-Dīn Khalīl (Ramaḍān-oghlu) (1510) viii, 418b
Ghars al-Dīn-zāde iii, 340a
Ghars al-Niʿma iv, 127a (see also *s.v.* Abu 'l-Ḥasan Muḥammad b. Hilāl (Ṣābiʾ)
Gharsiya b. Shandjuh s, 80b
Gharsiya b. Wanḳu i, 1079b; s, 129b
Ghārūḳa s, **322b**
Gharyān, ʿAbd al-Madjīd iv, 720b
Ghaṣb ii, **1020a**; vii, 285a; ix, 62b, 63a
Ghāshiya ii, **1020a**
Ghaṣība i, 233a; ii, 320b, 321a
Ghasīl al-Malāʾika (623) ii, **1020b**; ix, 204b
Ghassāl s, **322b**
Ghassān b. ʿAbbād (Samarkand) i, 271b; vi, 335b; viii, 1026a, 1032a
Ghassān b. Ḥāmid (VIII) viii, 536b
Ghassān al-Kūfī ii, 1022a
al-Ghassānī, Abū ʿAbd Allāh (XVII) ii, **1021b**; s, 130b
al-Ghassānī, Abū ʿAlī (1104) iii, 976b; viii, 635a
al-Ghassānī, Abu 'l-Ḥasan Muḥammad b. Aḥmad b. Djumayʿ ix, 8b

Ghassānids i, 405b, 526a, 548b, 890a, 1140b, 1249b; ii, **1020b**; iii, 272b, 292b; iv, 492b, 839a, 1145a; v, 633b; vi, 303a, 544b, 564b; vii, 840b; viii, 119b; s, 117a, 229b
Ghassāniyya ii, **1022a**
Ghassāsa, Banū vi, 1009a
Ghāt ii, 875a, 876b, **1022a**
Ghaṭafān, Banū ii, 627a, **1023a**; iii, 285b; iv, 1139a, 1144a; vii, 370b, 463b, 629b; s, 177a, 178a
al-Ghaṭafānī, Ḳaʿnab b. Damra viii, 376a
Ghaṭān (Ḳaḥṭān), Banū vii, 782b
Ghaṭaṭ i, 541b; iv, 743b
al-Ghaṭghaṭ i, 628b; iii, 361b; vi, 152b; x, 943b, 944a
Ghāts vi, 67a, 421b
Ghātwāls ii, 868b
al-Ghawār ii, **1024a**
Ghawāzī → Ghāziya
al-Ghawr i, 998a, 1138b; ii, **1024b**; viii, 527a
al-Ghawrī, Sultan → Ḳānsūh al-Ghawrī
al-Ghawth x, 402b; s, 37b
Ghawth Muḥammad Khān i, 1195b
Ghawthī Dede ii, 833a
Ghawwāṣī (poet) (1650) iii, 376a; vi, 837b
Ghayba ii, **1026a**; iii, 907a, 1167a; iv, 277b; v, 1236a; vii, 443a, b; xi, 103a
al-Ghayḍa (Mahra) vi, 81a
Ghayghāya, Banū vi, 742a
Ghayl al-Khārid → al-Khārid, Wadī
Ghaylān b. Muslim ii, **1026b**; iii, 1142b; iv, 271b, 370a, 371b
Ghaylān b. ʿUḳba → Dhu 'l-Rumma
Ghayn ii, **1026b**
Ghayr, ghayra iv, 272b, 273a
Ghayr Mahdī → Muḥammad al-Djawnpūrī
Ghayṭa ii, **1027b**; vii, 207b; xi, 574a
Ghayth (Mahra) vi, 82b
al-Ghayṭī, Muḥammad b. Aḥmad b. ʿAlī (1576) vii, 100b
al-Ghayṭī, Nadjm al-Dīn (XVI) ix, 915a
al-Ghazāfī (1589) vi, 112a
Ghazal i, 10b, 107b, 586a, 592a, 677b; ii, **1028a**; iv, 57b, 62a, 65a, 714b; v, 836a; vii, 96a; s, 323b
Ghazāl ii, **1036b**; iv, 649a
al-Ghazāl, Yaḥyā b. Ḥakam al-Bakrī (IX) i, 83a, 601a, 934b; ii, 516a, **1038a**; iii, 702a; v, 1119b; vii, 275a
al-Ghazālī, Abu 'l-Futūḥ s, 384a
al-Ghazālī, Abū Ḥāmid Muḥammad al-Ṭūsī (1111) i, 25b, 92a, 274a, 326b, 327b, 333a, 347a, 350a, 351a, 390b, 411a, 412b, 414a, 416a, 427b, 513b, 593a, 595b, 696b, 714a, 715a, 826a, 839a, 1099b; ii, 96a, 144b, 225b, 451a, 605b, 765b, 767a, 773a, 834a, **1038b**, 1069b; iii, 254a, 512a, 544a, 683b, 712b, 915a, 958b, 1024b, 1029a, 1063b, 1148a, 1149a, 1168a, 1205b; iv, 25b, 149b, 257b, 279b, 487a, 697b, 895a; v, 54b, 329b; vi, 11b, 14a, 73b, 110b, 204b, 211a, 219a, 279b, 280a, 281a, 347a, 447a, 448b, 452a, 739a, 905b; vii, 143b, 296b, 445a, 465a, 585b, 591a, 755a, 986a; viii, 71b, 95b, 125a, 547b; x, 468; s, 2b, 15a, 153a, 293a, 305b
al-Ghazālī, Aḥmad b. Muḥammad (1126) ii, 1038b, **1041b**; iv, 64a, b; viii, 539b; s, 2b
al-Ghazālī, Badr al-Dīn (1577) x, 5a
al-Ghazālī, Djānbirdī (1521) i, 779a; ii, 287a, **1042a**; iii, 88a, 400a; vi, 325a; x, 211b; s, 524b
Ghazālī, Meḥmed (1535) ii, **1042a**; vi, 610a
Ghazālī Mashhadī (1572) vii, 340b; viii, 775b
Ghazan Khān (Hunza) iii, 581a
Ghazan Khān Maḥmūd (Il-Khānid) (1304) i, 205b, 861a, 903a, 1011a, 1031b, 1126b, 1129b; ii, 47a, 285b, 311b, 1043a, 1045b; iii, 189b, 198a, 284a, 399b, 490b, 951b, 1089b, 1099b, 1122b, 1124a, b; iv, 31a, b, 48b, 621a, 637b, 818a, 945a, 975b, 976a, 1038b, 1045b; v, 162b, 312a, 554b, 662b, 872b; vi, 15a, b, 16a, 19b, 117b, 120a, b, 483a, 494a, b, 501b, 502a, 524a, b, 545b, 547b, 601b, 714b; vii, 169a, 232a, 507a, 991b; viii, 156b; xi, 18b; s, 59a, 94b
Ghāzāniyye iii, 1124b, 1125a
Ghazāt → Ghazw
Ghāzī (ghuzāt) i, 322b; ii, 505b, **1043b**; iii, 196a
Ghāzī I, II (Zangids) → Sayf al-Dīn Ghāzī I, II
Ghāzī, Amīr → Gümüshtegin
Ghāzī b. Fayṣal (Hāshimite) (1939) ii, 872b, **1045a**; iii, 264a, 1258b; v, 1044b; vii, 919a; viii, 141b

Ghāzī b. Ḥassān (1168) vi, 380b
Ghāzī b. Ṣalāh al-Dīn → al-Ẓāhir Ghāzī
Ghāzī Beg b. Djānī Beg, Mīrzā (Arghūn) iii, 1030a; vii, 129b
Ghāzī Čelebī ii, **1045a**; v, 505b; ix, 654a
Ghāzī ʾl-Dīn Ḥaydar i, 757b; ii, **1045b**; v, 635a, 637a, 1238a
Ghāzī ʾl-Dīn ʿImād al-Mulk (Ḥaydarābād) vi, 535b
Ghāzī ʾl-Dīn Khān → ʿImād al-Mulk; Muḥammad Panāh, Mīr; Shihāb al-Dīn, Mīr
Ghāzī ʾl-Dīn Khān iii, 320b
Ghāzī Evrenos Beg → Ewrenos
Ghāzī Girāy I (1524) ii, **1046a**, 1113b
Ghāzī Girāy II (1607) ii, **1046a**; v, 138b
Ghāzī Girāy III (1708) ii, **1047a**; iv, 569a; v, 140b
Ghāzī Ḥasan Pasha (XVIII) → Djezāʾirli Ghāzī Ḥasan Pasha
Ghāzī Khān Čak (1566) iv, 709a; s, 167a, **324b**, 335b, 353b
Ghāzī Khunkʸār → Murād I (Ottoman)
Ghāzī Khusrew-bey → khosrew beg
Ghāzī Ḳirān b. Sulṭān Aḥmad i, 1030b; ix, 727a, b
Ghāzī-Ḳumuḳ → Ḳumiḳ
Ghāzī Malik → Ghiyāth al-Dīn Tughluḳ I
Ghāzī Meḥmed Pasha → Muḥammad Pasha Bushatlı̊
Ghāzī Miyān, Sālār Masʿūd (1033) i, 756b, 855b; ii, **1047b**; iv, 210b; vi, 783b; viii, 252a; xi, 119a; s, 280a
Ghāzī Muḥammad → Ḳāḍī Muḥammad
Ghāzī Shāh Čak → Ghāzī Khān Čak
Ghāzīpūr vii, 314a; s, 203a, **325a**
Ghāziya i, 404a, 1036a; ii, **1048a**
Ghāziyan i, 1014a
Ghaziyya i, 483a, 528b
Ghazna i, 222b, 223a, 226b, 940a; ii, 382a, **1048b**, 1054a, 1103b; vi, 65a, b, 198b, 276b, 368b, 433a, 453a; s, 66b, 329b
Ghaznawī, Shaykh Raḍiyy al-Dīn ʿAlī-yi Lālā (1244) viii, 458a
Ghaznawids i, 226b, 420a, 421b, 434a, 439b, 1130b, 1342b, 1344b; ii, 4b, 266b, 336a, 893b, **1050a**, 1083a, 1109a; iii, 47a, 197a, 415b, 438b, 471a; iv, 18b, 24a-25a, 61a, 189b, 208b, 217b, 266b, 357a, 696b, 758b; v, 58a, 597b, 691a, 956b; vi, 64a, 193a, 198b, 261b, 273b, 521b, 522a, 523a, b, 524a, 532b, 620b; vii, 193a, 477b, 653a, 679a; ix, 158b; s, 21a, b, 119a, 242a, 284b, 333a, 386b
– art, architecture ii, 1053b, 1103b
Ghaznī iii, 336b; s, 41a, 367a
Ghaznī Khān b. ʿĀdil Khān II (Khāndesh) (1508) vi, 51a
Ghaznī Khān Muḥammad b. Alp Khān Hūshang (Ghūrī, Mālwa) (1436) iii, 638b; iv, 219a, 1067b; vi, 52b, 309b
Ghazw, Ghazwa i, 885b, 892a; ii, 64a, b, 509b, 1043b, **1055a**; v, 768a, 1161b
al-Ghazwānī, Sīdī ʿAbd Allāh (1528) vi, 591a, 597a
Ghazza ii, **1056a**; iii, 187b; v, 801b; vi, 31a, 118b; ix, 210a, b; s, 20b, 326a
al-Ghazza (Mecca) vi, 161b
al-Ghazzāl, al-Malakī (1777) vii, 387b; s, **325b**
al-Ghazzālī → al-Ghazālī
Ghazzan Khān b. Ḳāsim Khān ii, 316b
Ghazzāwī, Āl vi, 345b
al-Ghazzāwī, ʿAlī Bey (al-Kabīr) i, **391b**; iv, 852b; vii, 420b; x, 189a (see also *s.v.* ʿAlī Bey (Bulūṭ Ḳāpān))
al-Ghazzī, Abū Isḥāḳ (1129) viii, 971a; s, **326a**
al-Ghazzī, Nadjm al-Dīn (1651) i, 100a, 594b; vi, 352a; vii, 469b
Ghdāms → Ghadāmès
Gheghāya iii, 207a
Gheraba i, 371b
Ghība → Pandjāb
Ghidhāʾ ii, **1057a**; iii, 79a; s, 318b
Ghidjuwānī, Khʷādja ʿAbd al-Khāliḳ (1220) vii, 933b, 934a; viii, 933b, 934a
Ghifār, Banū ii, **1072b**; v, 58b, 116b; vii, 561b
al-Ghifārī, al-Ḥakam b. ʿAmr (VII) vii, 357a
Ghighāya vi, 590b (see also *s.v.* Gheghāya)
Ghīlān, Ḳāʾid iv, 729b
Ghilmān → Ghulām
Ghilzay → Ghalzay
Ghināʾ ii, **1072b**; iv, 821a; v, 480b
Ghirbāl ii, 620b, 621a, 1074a
Ghirbīb b. ʿAbd Allāh (797) ii, **1075b**; vii, 808a
Ghirsh (Ghūrsh) → Sikka
Ghīṭa → Ghayṭa
al-Ghiṭāʾ, Shaykh ʿAlī Kāshif (1838) s, 75b

al-Ghīṭānī, Djamāl vi, 469a; x, 799a
Ghiṭrīf, Āl i, 812a
al-Ghiṭrīf b. ʿAṭāʾ al-Djurashī (VIII) v, 855a, b; s, **326b**
Ghiṭrīf b. Ḳudāma (VIII) vii, 949a
al-Ghiṭrīfī, Muḥammad b. Aḥmad s, 326b
Ghiyār ii, **1075b**; v, 736b, 744b; xi, 571b, 572a
Ghiyāth (dāʿī) iv, 661b
Ghiyāth b. Muḥammad s, 271b
Ghiyāth Beg → Iʿtimād al-Dawla (Mīrzā Ghiyāth Beg)
Ghiyāth al-Dīn (Ḳaraʾuna Turk) vi, 692b
Ghiyāth al-Dīn b. Kamāl al-Dīn (Marʿashī) (1400) vi, 512a, b, 513a
Ghiyāth al-Dīn b. Maḥmūd Khaldjī I (Mālwā) (1451) vi, 53b, 54a, 407a
Ghiyāth al-Dīn b. Rashīd al-Dīn Faḍl Allāh (XIV) vii, 404b
Ghiyāth al-Dīn Aʿẓam Shāh → Aʿẓam Shāh
Ghiyāth al-Dīn Balban → Balban
Ghiyāth al-Dīn Djāmī (1522) s, 139a
Ghiyāth al-Dīn Girāy ii, 1112b; iii, 44a
Ghiyāth al-Dīn al-Ḥādjdjī (Muẓaffarid) vii, 820a
Ghiyāth al-Dīn Iṣfahānī vi, 907b
Ghiyāth al-Dīn Kaykhusraw → Kaykhusraw II
Ghiyāth al-Dīn Maḥmūd → Maḥmūd III (Bengal)
Ghiyāth al-Dīn Maḥmūd (Ghūrid) (1212) ii, 267a, 752a, 1103a; iv, 917b; v, 546a
Ghiyāth al-Dīn Maḥmūd b. Meḥmed Beg (Menteshe) (1385) vi, 1018b
Ghiyāth al-Dīn Masʿūd b. ʿIzz al-Dīn Kay Kāʾwūs → Masʿūd II (Rūm Saldjūḳ)
Ghiyāth al-Dīn Muḥammad (1328) ix, 1a
Ghiyāth al-Dīn Muḥammad I (Saldjūḳ) (1118) vii, 983b
Ghiyāth al-Dīn Muḥammad b. Ḥusayn → Astarābādī
Ghiyāth al-Dīn Muḥammad b. Rashīd al-Dīn (1336) viii, 541b; s, 415b
Ghiyāth al-Dīn Muḥammad b. Sām I (Ghūrid) (1202) → Muḥammad b. Sām I, Ghiyāth al-Dīn
Ghiyāth al-Dīn Muḥammad Eretna i, 1327b; ii, 239a, 706a, 712b
Ghiyāth al-Dīn Muḥammad al-Kurtī i, 361b, 764b, 908b; ii, 68a, 238a; iii, 1022a; iv, 672a
Ghiyāth al-Dīn Naḳḳāsh (XV) ii, **1076a**
Ghiyāth al-Dīn Pīr ʿAlī iv, 672a
Ghiyāth al-Dīn Pīrshāh (Khwarazm) (1230) i, 1311a; ii, 393a; vi, 277
Ghiyāth al-Dīn Shīrāzī iv, 1073b
Ghiyāth al-Dīn Tughluḳ I (Tughluḳid) (Dihlī) (1325) i, 104b, 444b, 1322a; ii, 120a, 154b, 257a, 262a, 269b, 274b, 922b, **1076a**; iii, 201a, 416b, 441b, 492a; iv, 759b, 921b, 924a; v, 885a; vi, 126a, 127b; vii, 550a; s, 105b, 409a
Ghiyāth al-Dīn Tughluḳ Shāh II (Tughluḳid) (Dihlī) (1389) ii, **1077a**; vi, 61b
Ghiyāth Mutaṭabbir → Sabzawārī, Muḥammad ʿAlāʾ al-Dīn
Ghiyāth al-Umma → Bahāʾ al-Dawla Fīrūz
Ghom → Ḳumm
Ghōr (Afghānistān) s, 367a
Ghōrāt (Afghānistān) v, 353a; vii, 218b; s, 367a
Ghōrband iv, 356a; s, 367b
Ghōriya Khēl(s) i, 218b; vii, 220a
Ghourides → Ghūrides
Ghouristan → Ghūr
Ghubār iii, 468b, 469a, 1140a; iv, 1124a, 1125b
Ghubayrā s, **327a**
Ghubrīn, Banū, ii, 1077b (see also *s.v.* Ghubrīnī)
Ghubrīnī ii, **1077b** ; ix, 358a, b
al-Ghubrīnī, Abū Mahdī ʿĪsā (1412) iii, 712a, 843b, 844a; xi, 15b
al-Ghubrīnī, Ḥadjdj b. ʿAwda ix, 358b
Ghudāna, Banū vi, 268a
Ghudiyyāt v, 267a
Ghudjdāma, Banū vi, 742a
Ghudjduwān ii, **1077b**; x, 88b
Ghudjdu(a)wānī, ʿAbd al-Khāliḳ (1220) ii, **1077b**; viii, 539b; xi, 116a; s, 521a
Ghufrān ii, **1078a**
Ghufrān Maʿāb → Naṣīrābādī
Ghūl ii, **1078b**; s, 52b
Ghulām i, 7b, 8a, 1278a; ii, 507a, 551b, 837a, **1079b**, 1103a; iii, 195a; iv, 36a, 242a; v, 245a, 691b, 820a
Ghulām-Ḥusayn Ṣādighī (1985) vi, 764a
Ghulām Aḥmad i, 301a, 302b; iii, 433b
Ghulām ʿAlī Āzād → Āzād Bilgrāmī
Ghulām ʿAlī, Shāh (1824) iii, 433b; vii, 938b
Ghulām Farīd iv, 507b; v, 611a
Ghulām Ḥalīm → ʿAbd al-ʿAzīz al-Dihlawī

Ghulām Ḥaydar Khān ii, 638a; ix, 446b
Ghulām Ḥusayn, Rādja (XX) vi, 78a
Ghulām Ḥusayn Khān Tabāṭabāʾī (1815) ii, **1091b**; viii, 573a
Ghulām Ḥusayn "Salīm" (1817) ii, **1092a**
Ghulām Isḥāḳ Khān viii, 243b
Ghulām (Ḳādir) Khān (Rohilla) (1789) i, 813b; ii, **1092b**; iii, 428a; vii, 316
Ghulām Khalīl, Aḥmad (IX) i, 1039a; iv, 1083b; viii, 139b; ix, 873b
Ghulām al-Khallāl (974) i, 274a, 274b; ii, **1093a**; iii, 158b, 735a; iv, 990a, 1083b; v, 10a
Ghulām Muḥammad iii, 565a, b; iv, 710b
Ghulām Muḥammad b. Tīpū Sulṭān ii, 7b
Ghulām Nabī Bilgrāmī i, 1168b; iii, 457b
Ghulām Naḳshband Lakhnawī i, 1219a
Ghulām Shāh Kalhōrā ii, 186a; iii, 323b; iv, 544b
Ghulām Shāhīs i, 295b
Ghulām Thaʿlab (957) ii, **1093a**; v, 608a; vi, 916b; s, 361a
Ghulām Yaḥyā iii, 430b
Ghulām Zafariy vi, 768b
Ghulāmī (XVIII) vi, 611a
Ghulāt i, 51a, 1098b; ii, **1093b**; iii, 662a
Ghulayfiḳa → Ghalāfiḳa
Ghuldja → Ḳuldja
Ghumāra, Banū i, 161a; ii, **1095a**; v, 1204a, b; vi, 741a, b, 743b
Ghumdān ii, **1096a**; viii, 664b, 979b
Ghumīk ii, 85b; iv, 348a
Ghundjār (802) ii, **1096a**
Ghunm → Ghanīma
Ghūr ii, **1096b**; vi, 66a, 365b; s, 376b
Ghurāb ii, **1096b**, 1098b; ix, 388a
al-Ghurāb (1771) vi, 113a
Ghurāb → Safīna
al-Ghurāb → Nudjūm
Ghurabāʾ, Ghurebā ii, **1097b**, 1120b
Ghurābiyya ii, **1098b**
al-Ghuraf s, 515a
Ghūrak (Ṣughd) (737) i, 241a; viii, 1032b
al-Ghuraynī, ʿAbd al-Raḥmān b. Sulaymān s, 44a
Ghurbat → Ḳurbat
al-Ghurfa s, 515a
Ghūrī → Dilāwar Khān, Mālwā
al-Ghūrī (Mamlūk) → Ḳānsūh al-Ghawrī
Ghūrids i, 217b, 218a, 223b, 227a, 420a, 852a, 1010a, 1344b; ii, 266b, 382a, 894a, 1049b, 1052b, 1096b, **1099a**; iii, 197b, 415b, 471b; iv, 210a; v, 597b; vi, 193a, 198b, 309b, 618a; vii, 433a, 997a, b; viii, 253a; s, 242a, 284b
Ghurūsh → Sikka
Ghusl ii, **1104a**; iii, 315b, 1053a; iv, 264b
Ghūṭa i, 1029b; ii, 278a, 290b, 541a, **1104b**; vi, 378a, 544b, 545b, 546a, 566a; vii, 212a
Ghuwaynim, Banū vi, 371b
Ghuzāt → Ghāzī
Ghuzāt al-baḥr i, 1205b; ii, 521a, 526a, 678a; iii, 627b
al-Ghuzūlī, ʿAlāʾ al-Dīn (1412) i, 361b; ii, **1106b**; vii, 1040a; s, 115b
Ghuzz (Oghuz) i, 147b, 181b, 190a, 227a, 239b, 311a, 512b, 524a, 607b, 660b, 661b, 662a, 729a, 1001b, 1029a, 1073b, 1133b, 1292a; ii, 20b, 200a, 613b, 724a, 971a, 1101b, **1106b**; 1110a; iii, 1098b, 1115a; iv, 18b, 26a-b, 29b, 101a, 347a, 614a, 1176a; v, 58b, 59a, 126a, 160a, b, 453b, 855b; vi, 243b, 272b, 415b, 416a, 493b, 499b, 620b, 714b; vii, 543b; viii, 943a, 1005a; x, 688b, 689b; s, 168b, 195a, 244b, 280b, 333b
Giafar → Djaʿfar
Giālpō i, 1004b
Giaour → Gabr, Kāfir
Gibel → Djabala
Gibralfaro → Djabal Fāruh
Gibraltar → Djabal Ṭāriḳ
Gibran → Djabrān
Gičkīs s, 222a, 332a
Gīl ii, 1111a; s, 356b, 363a
Gīl Gawbarā ii, 74b; iv, 644b; viii, 651a; s, 298a, 299a
Gīlakī, Amīr i, 1250a
Gīlakī, Abu 'l-Ḥasan b. Muḥammad x, 22b
Gīlakī, Shams (al-)Dīn viii, 599a
Gīlān i, 8a, 46b, 60a, 91a, 389a, 1014a; ii, 189b, 190a, 445b, 903b, **1111a**; iii, 211a, 212a, 214b; v, 602b, 604a; vi, 66b, 433b, 483a, 499a, 512a, b, 513a, b, 514a, 515b, 516a; viii, 449b; s, 13a, 23b, 139b, 299a, 356b, 357a, 363a, 365b
Gīlān Shāh iv, 815a; xi, 540b
Gīlānī, Masīḥ al-Dīn Abu 'l-Fatḥ (1589) viii, 542b
Gīlānī, Mullā Shamsa (1686) viii, 782a
Gīlānī, Muḥammad Makhdūm (1517) x, 255b

Gīlān-i Biyāpīsh iv, 475b; v, 602b, 603a; vi, 18a, 483a, 515b, 516a
al-Gildakī → al-Djildakī
Gilgamesh iv, 902b, 903a; ix, 830a
Gilgit (Pakistan) ii, 30a, b, 1112a; iii, 581a; vi, 127a; viii, 240b; s, **327b**
Gilit iii, 1259b
Gīlīz iii, 207a
Gimbri → Ḳonbur
Gindibu i, 524b
Ginukh → Dido
Giorgi II v, 489b
Giorgi III iii, 1110a; v, 490a
Giorgi III Lasha v, 490a, b; x, 555a
Giorgi V v, 491a
Giorgi VI v, 491b
Giorgi XI → Gurgīn Khān
Giorgi XII v, 495a
Girāy i, 893a; ii, 44b, 1046a, **1112a**; iv, 499b; v, 137a
Girdhār Bahādur ii, 219a
Girdkūh i, 353a; iii, 501b; viii, 599a
Giresün ii, **1114a**
Girgā ii, **1114a**
Girgenti → Djirdjent
Girishk ii, **1114b**
Girit → Iḳrītish
Girīz, girīzgāh iv, 715b
Girnār (Gudjarāt) ii, 1130b; vi, 50a, b; ix, 869a
Gīsh i, 47a, 356a; ii, 146b, 509b, 510b; vi, 134a (see also *s.v.* Djaysh)
Gīsū Darāz, Muḥammad (1422) ii, 54a, 55a, 56a, **1114b**; iii, 418a, 429b, 434a, 436a; iv, 962a; s, 353a
Giwa i, 956a
Gizduvan → Ghudjduwān
Gīza, Gizeh → al-Ḳāhira
Gjinokastër → Ergiri
Glāwa, Banū ii, **1116a**; vi, 742a, 743a
Glāwī Madanī ii, 1116a; iii, 62a
Glāwī Tihāmī ii, 1116b; vi, 890b; s, 634a
Gnāns iii, 1163b; iv, 206a
Goa i, 924a, 978b; ii, 1128a; iii, 422a; vi, 63a, b, 67a
Gobān → Ḳobān
Göbek adî iv, 181a
Godāvarī vi, 67b, 87a, 269a
Göde, Aḥmad → Göwde, Aḥmad
Godoberi, Banū i, 504a; v, 597b
Gogo → Gao
Gōgul Prashād Rasā (XIX) vii, 475b
Goḥa → Djuḥā
Gök Tepe ii, **1116b**
Gokalā Djāt iv, 177b
Gökalp, Ziyā (Ḍiyāʾ) (1924) i, 327a; ii, 345b, 475b, **1117a**; iv, 123b, 169a, 791a; v, 264a, 271b; vi, 6b, 94a; viii, 251a; s, 47b, 150a, 167b
Gökbürī, Muẓaffar al-Dīn → Muẓaffar al-Dīn Gökbürī
Gökčay → Gökče
Gökče Mūsā ii, 614a
Gökče-göl ii, **1118a**
Gökče-deniz ii, **1118a**
Gökče-Tengiz ii, **1118a**
Göklän ii, **1118a**; iii, 1108a; vii, 935b; s, 571a
Göksu ii, 946a, **1118b**; vi, 539b; ix, 112a
Göksün ii, **1118b**; vi, 505b, 509a; s, 239a
Golan → al-Djawlān
Golconda → Golkondā
Gold Coast → Ghana
Golden Horde → Bātūids; Ḳipčaḳ; Sarāy
Golden Horn → Ghalaṭa; Istanbul; Takhtaḳalʿe
al-Golea → al-Ḳulayʿa
Goletta → Ḥalḳ al-wādi
Golfe Persique → Baḥr Fāris
Goliath → Djālūt
Golkondā i, 768b, 769b, 924a, 1323b; ii, 158b, **1118b**; iii, 318b, 426b, 448a; v, 549b; vi, 126b, 369b, 535a; vii, 458b
Golubac vi, 70b
Gōmal Pass iv, 1143a; vi, 86a; xi, 494b; s, 329b
Gōmal (river) → Gūmāl
Gombroon → Bandar ʿAbbās
Gomut vi, 128b
Gondar i, 49b; iii, 5a, 7a; iv, 687a
Gondēshāpūr i, 212b, 516b, 1223a; ii, 577a, **1119b**; iii, 872b; v, 919a; vi, 599b; x, 452b; s, 354a
Gonduruḥmaan, shaykh (XIX) x, 71b
Gondwāna i, 316a; vi, 50b, 54a; vii, 898b
Gongo vi, 422a (see also *s.v.* Kankan)
Gönüllü ii, **1120b**
Gora, Abdallāh Suleymān v, 483a
Gora-Mokra viii, 166b
Gōrgān → Gūrgān
Gördes ii, **1121a**; s, 136b, 138a, 282b
Gorein, Djabal iv, 478b, 479b

Görele s, 283a
Gorgan → Gurgān
Göridje → Korča; Manastir
Göridjeli Ḳoči Beg → Ḳoči Beg
Gorno-Badakhshān i, 853a; viii, 245a; x, 66b
Gorwekht s, 285a, b
Gōsiōs, 52a
Gourara (Gurāra) v, 1165a; vi, 141a; x, 757b; s, **328a**
Govind Singh, Guru (Sikh) (1708) i, 913b; ii, 928b; vii, 315b
Govindapur ii, 7a
Gövsa, Ibrāhīm ʿAlāʾ al-Dīn (1949) iii, 1199b; s, **328b**
Gowardhan (painter) (XVII) vii, 339a
Göwde, Aḥmad (Aḳ-Ḳoyunlu) (1397) i, 312a, 1082b; ii, 184a
Goyum → Djuwayn
Gōzgān → Djuzdjān
Grabadin i, 345a
Grain(e) (Grane Kuwayt) v, 572a; x, 956a
Gran → Esztergom
Grañ → Aḥmad Grañ
Granada → Gharnāṭa
Grane → Grain(e)
Great Horde i, 1108a; ii, 44a; v, 137a, b; vi, 1016b; x, 622b, 623a
Greece, Turks in x, 699a
Greeks → Yūnān
Grenade → Gharnāṭa
Gresik i, 980b; xi, 120b; s, 201b
Greyhound → Salūḳī
Guadalajara → Wādī 'l-Ḥidjāra
Guadalquivir → al-Wādi 'l-Kabīr
al-Gūdālī, Yaḥyā b. Ibrāhīm → al-Djawhar b. Sakkum
Guadarrama → al-Sharrāt
Guadelmedina → Wādi 'l-Madīna
Guadiana → Wādī Yāna
Guadix → Wādī Āsh
Guanche i, 1180b
Guardafui (Ra's ʿAsīr) ii, **1121b**
Gudāla ii, **1121b**; v, 653b; vii, 612b; x, 548a
Gūdarz iv, 815b, 816a
Gūdjar i, 224b; ii, **1122a**, 1123a; iii, 335b
Gudjarāt i, 506b, 561b, 924a, 1053a, 1254b; ii, 11a, 814b, 816a, **1123a**; iii, 16a, 421b, 444b, 857a, 1010a; iv, 199b, 202b, 901b; v, 26b, 1117a, 1216b; vi, 47a, 49b, 50b, 51a, b, 53a, 126b, 127a, b, 233b, 271a, 294b, 309b, 342b, 368b, 369a, b, 406b, 407b, 410b, 535a, b, 536a, 642a, 694a; vii, 79b, 133a, b; viii, 68a; ix, 785b; s, 105a, 200a, 312a, 335b
Gudjarātī i, 1255a; ii, **1130b**; viii, 126a
Gudjarī, Gudjurī ii, 31a, 1122b
Gudjrāṅwāla ii, **1130b**; iii, 63a
Gudjrāt i, 80b; ii, **1131a**
Gudmanā → ʿAfīfī
Guellala → Ḳallala
Guerara → Ḳarāra
Guergour s, 144b,
Guersif → Garsīf
Guezebida i, 1221b
Guinea ii, **1131b**; v, 252a
Gujarat, Gujerat → Gudjarāt
Gujarati → Gudjarātī
Guklān → Göklän
Gul ii, **1133a**
Gul Čandra iii, 570a
Gul Gumbād (Gumbādh) v, 295a
Gul Khātūn s, **329a**
Gulāb Sīngh ii, 30a, 140a; iii, 336a; iv, 709b; s, 242a
Gulʿanbar → Shahrizūr
Gülbaba i, 1286a; ii, **1133b**
Gulbadan Bēgam (1603) ii, **1134b**; vii, 342b
Gülbāng ii, **1135a**; x, 418a
Gulbargā i, 924b, 925a, 1323a; ii, 54a, **1135a**; iii, 15a, 442a, 446b; v, 295b; vi, 127b, 369a
Gülek Boghaz ii, 35a, **1135b**
Gulia, Dimitri i, 101b
Gulia, Wallace vi, 302a
Gulistān i, 241b, 680a, 1212b; ii, 839a, **1135b**; iv, 392b, 394b
Gulistān (treaty) i, 958a; v, 495b, 657a; x, 88b
Gülkhāne i, 74b; ii, 147b, **1135b**; vi, 285b
Gulkunda → Golkondā
Güllü (Agop Vartovian) vi, 758a, 759a
Gülnüsh (Emetü 'llāh) Sulṭān (1715) iv, 233b, 1100a; xi, 131b
Gulpāyagān ii, **1135b**; vi, 14a
Gulpāyagānī, Muḥammad Riḍāʾ (Āyatullāh) (XX) vi, 553b; vii, 762b
Gulrukh Bēgum bint Mīrzā Kāmrān (XVI) iv, 523b; vii, 133a, 134a
Gulshanī, Ibrāhīm b. Muḥammad (1534) ii, 345b, **1136a**; iii, 393a; iv, 991b
Gulshanī Ṣarūkhānī (XV) ii, **1137b**

Gülshaniyya ii, 1137b; vi, 886a; ix, 149b
Gülshehrī (1317) ii, **1138a**; v, 173a; viii, 972a
Gulshīrī, Hūshang v, 201a
Gūm ii, **1138b**; iv, 784b
Gūmāl (Gomal) (river) s, **329b**
Gumi, Abū Bakr b. Maḥmūd (1992) x, 122b
Gümrük → Maks
Gumukh → Kemākh
Gümüldjīne s, **329b**
Gümüshāne, Gümüshkhāne i, 645b, 1128b; ii, **1139a**; v, 966a, 977a
Gümüshkhānewī, Shaykh Ḍiyāʾ al-Dīn (1894) vii, 937a
Gümüshtegin b. Dānishmend, Amīr Ghāzī (1134) i, 466a, b, 664b, 983a, 1276b; ii, 110b, 1139b; vi, 231a, 506b
Gunābādī, Sulṭān ʿAlī Shāh (Niʿmat Allāhī) (1909) i, 841a; viii, 47a
Gunābādīs x, 327b
Gunābādiyya iv, 51b
Gunbad-i ʿAlawiyān (Hamadān) (1220) vii, 12b
Gunbad-i Ghaffāriyya vi, 501b
Gunbadh → Ḳubba
Gunbadh-i Ḳābūs ii, **1139b**, 1141b; iv, 6b, 358a
Gunḍāfa, Banū vi, 743a
Güneri Bey i, 703a; iv, 620b, 621a, b; v, 677a
Güntekin, Reşat Nuri → Reshād Nūrī
Gunzalị̊ → Khunzal
Gūr → Fīrūzābād
Gura ii, 709b; vi, 643a
Gūrān ii, **1139b**; iii, 292a, 1109a; v, 168b
Gūran, Shaykh Abu 'l-Fatḥ (1536) s, **331b**
Gūrānī, Shams al-Dīn → Gūrānī, Sharaf al-Dīn
Gūrānī, Sharaf al-Dīn (1488) ii, **1140b**
Gūrānī, Shihāb al-Dīn → Gūrānī, Sharaf al-Dīn
Gūrānī (language) i, 262b, 840a, 863b; ii, 1140a; iii, 1261a
Gurāra → Gourara
Gurčānī s, **331b**
Gurdjistān → Kurdj
Gürdjü ʿAbd al-Nabī iv, 766a
Gürdjü Meḥmed Nedjib Pasha (1850) vi, 68a; vii, 937a
Gürdjü Meḥmed Pasha → Meḥmed Pasha, Gürdjü
Gürdjü Muṣṭafā Pasha iv, 723a
Gurgān i, 3b, 40a; ii, 253a, 746a, 1139b, **1141a**; iii, 501b; iv, 6b, 10a, 19a; vi, 66a, 115b, 130b, 334b, 336a, 415b, 493a, b, 494a, 495a, 539a, 726b, 780a; s, 13a, 86b, 235a, 277a, 298a, 326b, 356b
Gurgandj i, 120b, 456a, b; ii, 2a, 43b, 571b, **1141b**; iv, 1061b, 1063b, 1064a, b, 1066a; v, 858a; vi, 65b, 340a; x, 88b, 892b; s, 246a, 280b
Gurgānī → Djurdjānī
Gurgānī, Abu 'l-Haytham iv, 60b
Gurgānī, Fakhr al-Dīn Asʿad (XI) ii, **1142b**; iv, 62b; vi, 632b, 833a; viii, 100a, 885b; xi, 210a; s, 108a
Gurgīn, King → Giorgi
Gurgīn Beg x, 898a
Gurgīn Khān i, 229a; iii, 603b, 604a; v, 493b; vii, 573a
Gurgīn Milād v, 661a, 670a
Gurieli i, 1108b
Gūrjara-Pratīhāras → al-Djurz
Gūrkhān (Ḳara-Khitāy) (XII) i, 987a, 1131a; ii, 791b, **1143a**; iii, 1114b; iv, 581b, 582a; vii, 410a; xi, 335b
Gürpinar → Ḥusayn Raḥmī
Gürsel, General ii, 646a; s, 677a
Gurush ii, 119a, b; viii, 564b
Gurz v, 691b; s, 740b
Güwāhī (XVI) vi, 826b, 836a
Guwākharz → Bākharz
Guwayn → Djuwayn
Gūyān → Djuwayn
Güyük b. Ögedey b. Činghiz Khān (Mongol Great Khān) (1248) i, 1105b; ii, 3a, 45b; vi, 77b, 524a; vii, 230a; x, 569a, b
Guyum iv, 9b
Guzarati → Gudjarātī
Güzel Ḥiṣār → Aydın
Güzeldje Ḥiṣār → Anadolu Ḥiṣārı̊
Gūzgān → Djūzdjān
Gwādar i, 1282a; v, 684b; vi, 192b; s, **332a**
Gwāliyār ii, **1143b**; iii, 995b; v, 1216a; vi, 49a, 53a, 65b, 127b, 535b; s, 331b
Gwāliyārī, Muḥammad Ghawth (1562) → Muḥammad Ghawth Gwāliyārī
Gwandu ii, **1144b**; vii, 435b
Gwaris (Nigeria) viii, 20a, 21a
Gwāṭar Bay s, 332b
Gyromancy → Raml

H

Hāʾ iii, **1a**
Ḥāʾ iii, **2a**
al-Habāʾa, Day of s, 177a, 178a, b
al-Habāʾa, Well of s, 177a, 178a
Ḥabāb, Banū ii, 709a, 710a
al-Ḥabāb (1232) vi, 592b
Ḥabāba (723) i, 1149a; ii, 428b, 1011b; iii, **2b**; iv, 821b; xi, 311b
Ḥabābiḍ (Mārib) vi, 563a, b
Habar Awal i, 1172b, 1173a; iii, 206b
Ḥabash, (864) xi, 499a
Ḥabash, Ḥabasha i, 39a, 44a, b, 80a, 84b, 102b, 111a, 286b, 547b, 561a, 763b, 991b; ii, 91a, 535b, 545a; iii, **2b**, 950b, 1137a; iv, 1088a; v, 116b, 950b, 1137a, 1250a; vi, 137b, 144b, 146b, 152a, b, 161a, 194a, 269b, 560a, 564a, b, 646b, 677b, 829b, 1002a; viii, 808b; ix, 535b
Ḥabash (musician) s, 64a, 183a
Ḥabash ʿAmīd, Ḳuṭb al-Dīn (XIII) ii, 2b, 3b; viii, 893b; ix, 110a
Ḥabash al-Ḥāsib al-Marwazī (IX) i, 159b; ii, 577a; iii, **8a**, 1137a; v, 85a; vi, 543a, 600a; vii, 29a; ix, 179b; x, 267a; s, 413b
Ḥabash, Ikhtiyār al-Mulk Rashīd al-Dīn Abū Bakr (XIII) viii, 814b
Ḥabash Khān (XV) iii, 14b; vi, 47a
Ḥabash Khān Sīdī Miftāḥ iii, 16b
Ḥabasha i, 24b, 102a; ii, 244b, 940a; iii, **2b**; xi, 242a
Ḥabashat iii, **9a**
Ḥabashī, Abū Shudjāʿ Yaḥyā (XI) vii, 489b
Ḥabashī, Ḳaṣr vi, 295a
al-Ḥabashī b. Muʿizz al-Dawla (X) vii, 485a
Ḥabashī b. ʿUmar → Aḥmad b. ʿUmar
Ḥabaṭ iii, **10b** (see also *s.v.* Ḥawṭa)
Ḥabawnā, Wādī i, 538a; viii, 575b
Ḥabba iii, **10b**
Ḥabba Khātūn (XVI) s, **332a**
al-Ḥabbāl, Abū Isḥāḳ (XI) viii, 707b
al-Ḥabbāl al-Miṣrī s, 390b
Ḥabbān iii, **11a**
Habbāniyya, Banū ix, 760b; x, 4b
Habbāniyya, lake ii, 947b; iii, 1250b
Ḥabbūs → Ḥabūs
Ḥabesh iii, **11a**, 157b; viii, 183b, 184a, 235a, b
Ḥabeshī ʿAlī Agha (1678) vi, 991a
Ḥabeshī Meḥmed Agha ii, 1088a; iii, 175b
Ḥabīb b. ʿAbd al-Malik (VIII) iii, **11b**
Ḥabīb b. Abī Thābit al-Kūfī (738) iii, 874a; ix, 553a
Ḥabīb b. Abī ʿUbayda al-Fihrī (VII) i, 86a, b, 990b; v, 367a; vi, 923a; ix, 584a, 753b; x, 848a
Ḥabīb b. Aws → Abū Tammām
Ḥabīb b. Gannūn (Benguennoun) (1864) vi, 250b
Ḥabīb b. Ḥabīb b. Yazīd b. al-Muhallab (VIII) vi, 311b
Ḥabīb b. Maslama al-Fihrī (662) i, 325a, 635b, 636a, 660a, 1349a; ii, 276a, 456a, 678b; iii, **12b**, 20a; iv, 343b, 654b, 870b; v, 487b; vi, 230b; vii, 922a
Ḥabīb b. al-Muhallab (VIII) vii, 359a
Ḥabīb b. Murra (VIII) vii, 629b; x, 883a
Ḥabīb b. Muẓāhir iii, 610a
Ḥabīb b. ʿUmar Tal i, 297a
Ḥabīb b. Yazīd b. al-Muhallab s, 41a
Ḥabīb Allāh b. Khalīl Allāh iv, 961b, 962a
Ḥabīb Allāh II → Bačča-i Saḳaw
Ḥabīb Allāh Khān, Amīr (Afghanistān) (1919) i, 88a, 232a; iii, **13a**; v, 1079a; vi, 807a; s, 65b, 237b
Ḥabīb Boulares (Bu ʾl-ʿArīs) vi, 751b
Habīb Hassan Touma vi, 103a
Ḥabīb Iṣfahānī iv, 72a; x, 234a
Ḥabīb Khān Huwayda vi, 154b
Ḥabīb al-Nadjdjār i, 517a; iii, **12b**
Ḥabīb al-Raḥmān v, 803a
Ḥabīb Ṣāliḥ b. Ḥabīb ʿAlawī v, 655b, 656a
Ḥabīb Shāh s, 167a, 324b
Ḥabība bint Khāridja i, 109b
Ḥabība Saldjūḳ-Khātūn i, 1328a
Ḥabība Sulṭān Begum viii, 1037b
Ḥabībī i, 193a
Ḥabībīs iii, 12a
Hābīl wa-Ḳābīl i, 178a, 181a; iii, **13b**; iv, 724a
Hābil-oghlu i, 431b
Ḥābiṭiyya → Aḥmad b. Ḥābiṭ
Ḥabla Rud iv, 1029b, 1030a
Habous → Waḳf
Ḥabsān → Djadjīra
Ḥabshī ii, 816a, 1084b, 1129a; iii, **14a**, 419a, 422a, 631b; v, 687b; vi, 63a, 269a
al-Ḥabshī, Aḥmad b. Zayn (1732) i, 829b

Ḥabsiyya s, **333a**
Habṭ vi, 741b
Ḥabūḍa xi, 380b
Ḥabūḍīs s, 338b
Ḥabūs b. Ḥumayd iii, 688a
Ḥabūs b. Māksan ii, 516a, 1012b, 1015a; iv, 355a
Ḥāč Ovasi̊ → Mezö-Keresztes
Haci̊lar s, 172a
al-Hada (plain) vi, 160b
Ḥaḍāna iii, **16b**
Hadanduwa i, 1158a, b; iv, 686b
Ḥadārib i, 1157b, 1158a, 1239b; ix, 88a
Ḥādārim iii, 11a; vi, 734b
Ḥadath iii, **19b**
al-Ḥadath i, 1190b; iii, **19b**; v, 1239a; vi, 505b, 506a
Ḥadd i, 382a, 383a; ii, 632a; iii, **20a**, 204b; iv, 770b, 771b; v, 730b, 731b
Ḥaddā', Treaty of iii, 1067a; viii, 644a; ix, 673b; s, 237a
Ḥaddād, ʿAbd al-Masīḥ v, 1254b, 1255a, b; s, 788a
al-Ḥaddād, Abū Ḥafṣ vi, 225a
Ḥaddād Banū iv, 540b
Ḥaddād, Marie Anṭūn (XX) vii, 903a
Ḥaddād, Nadjīb i, 597a
Ḥaddād, Niḳūlā (XX) vii, 903a; s, 788a
Ḥaddād, Nudra v, 1254b, 1255a, b
Ḥaddād, al-Ṭāhir (1935) iv, 161a; s, **334a**
Haddūḳa, A.H. ben v, 191a
Hadendoa → Bedja
Ḥādha s, 198b
Hadhbānīs (Kurds) v, 451b, 453b; vi, 499b; x, 897b
Ḥadhf → Naḥw
Ḥadhw iv, 412a
al-Hādī, Ibrāhīm b. ʿAlī b. Aḥmad vi, 113b
al-Hādī ilā 'l-Ḥaḳḳ (ʿAbbāsid) (786) i, 14a, 17b, 402b, 1034a, 1045b, 1298a; iii, 20a, **22a**, 29a, 231a, 232b, 617a, 742a, 996a; iv, 645a, 858b, 1164a; vi, 140b, 331a, b, 332a; s, 22a, 326b
al-Hādī ilā 'l-Ḥaḳḳ Yaḥyā al-Rassī (Zaydī) (911) i, 551b; iii, 617b; v, 1241a; vi, 433a, 435b, 436b, 439a; vii, 773a, 786a; s, **334b**, 358a
al-Hādī ʿIzz al-Dīn b. al-Ḥasan (Yemen) (XV) vii, 996a
Hādī Sabzawārī → Sabzawārī
al-Ḥadīd iii, **22b**; iv, 819b; v, 964b, 966a, 967b, 971a, 978a, 1166b
Ḥadīd → Nudjūm
Ḥadīd, Shaykh vi, 733b
Ḥadīd (Djadīd) al-Ḳāra (Ḥudjūr) vi, 436b
Ḥadīdī (XVI) iii, **22b**
Ḥadīdīn, Banū vi, 733b
al-Ḥāḍina iii, **23a**
Ḥādir (IX) s, 48b
Ḥāḍir Ṭayyi' x, 402b
al-Ḥādira (VII) iii, **23a**
Ḥadīth i, 25b, 258b, 326a, 410a, 566a, 589b, 1021a, b; ii, 71a, 125b, 448a, 729a, 889a; iii, **23b**, 369b, 435a; iv, 148a, b, 172a, 767b, 983b, 995a, 1107a, 1112a, 1135b; v, 1123b, 1132b, 1232a, b
– literature i, 59a, 60b, 106b, 158b, 273b; ii, 159a; iii, 927a
– scholars i, 104b, 129a, 143a, 272b, 275b, 485b, 791a, 1130a, 1296b; ii, 136a, 292b, 301a; iii, 82a, 821a, 848b, 860b, 874a
Ḥadīth Ḳudsī i, 88b; iii, **28b**, 101b; s, 83a
Ḥadītha ii, 623b; iv, 855b
Ḥadītha b. al-Faḍl b. Rabīʿa (XIII) vii, 461b
Ḥadīthat al-Furāt iii, **29b**
Ḥadīthat al-Mawṣil iii, **29a**
Ḥadīthat al-Nūra → Hadīthat al-Furāt
Hadiyya iii, 343a, 346b, 347b, 350a
Hadj → Ḥadjdj
Hadjar → al-Ḥasā
Ḥadjar (Baḥrayn) i, 73a, b; ii, 452b
Hadjar (district) vi, 633b, 875a; vii, 374a, 570b
Ḥadjar (town) iii, **29b**
Ḥadjar (stone) iii, **29b**; iv, 1128b; v, 117b
Ḥadjar (Yemen) s, 135b, 136a
al-Ḥadjar, Djabal i, 536b; ii, 936b
al-Ḥadjar al-Aswad i, 178a, 551b, 867a; ii, 453a; iv, 317a, b, 319a, b, 321b, 662a, b; v, 10a, 77b, 78a
Ḥadjar Bādis i, 859b
Hadjar Ḥarīb iii, 208b
Hadjar b. Ḥumayd i, 1132b, 1133a; iv, 747a
Hadjar Ḥinū 'l-Zarīr iii, 208a; iv, 747a
Ḥadjar Ismāʿīl vi, 165b
Hadjar Kuḥlān i, 1132b; iv, 746b, 747a
Ḥadjar al-Nasr iii, **30b**; vii, 641b
Ḥadjar Shughlān vi, 507b

Ḥadjar al-Shurafāʾ → Ḥadjar al-Nasr
Ḥadjar Tarbiyat vi, 486b
Hadjarayn ii, 173a; iii, **31a**; vi, 132b
al-Ḥadjarī ʾl-Andalūsī, Aḥmad b. Ḳāsim (XVII) vii, 243b
Hadjbūn al-Randāḥī, Abu ʾl-ʿAbbās s, 112a
Ḥadjdj i, 178a, 443b; iii, **31b**, 927a, 1052b; iv, 320b, 322a; v, 424b, 897a, b, 1003a, 1004a; vi, 169a, 195a; vii, 65b
Ḥādjdj(ī) iii, 38b
al-Ḥādjdj ʿAmmār (XIX) viii, 399b
al-Ḥādjdj, Baʿl ii, 730a
al-Ḥādjdj al-ʿArbī v, 596b
al-Ḥādjdj Bashīr (1843) viii, 399b
al-Ḥādjdj al-Gharnāṭī x, 480a
al-Ḥādjdj Ḥammūda (1787) iii, **38b**
al-Ḥādjdj Masʿūd vi, 593b
Ḥādjdj Muḥammad Ṭrīḳī iii, 247a
al-Ḥādjdj Sālim Suwarī (XV) ix, 757a; xi, 137b, 138a
al-Ḥādjdj ʿUmar b. Saʿīd Tāl (Tukulor) (1864) i, 297a, 303b; ii, 63a, 252b, 941b, 1132b; iii, **38b**, 107b, 289a; ix, 122a, 141b; x, 602b
Ḥādjdja vi, 436b; viii, 456b
Ḥadjdjādj → Ḳutlugh Khāns
Ḥadjdjādj, Banū iv, 115b
al-Ḥadjdjādj, Abū Djaʿfar (X) iv, 911a; vii, 497a
al-Ḥadjdjādj b. ʿAbd al-Malik b. Marwān ii, 280b, 304b, 480a; iii, 73a, 573b
Ḥadjdjādj b. Arṭāt i, 896b
Ḥadjdjādj b. Hurmuz i, 512b
Ḥadjdjādj b. Yūsuf b. Maṭar al-Ḥāsib (IX) iii, **43a**, 1136b, 1138b; vii, 83a, 1050a; viii, 550b, 559a; s, 411b
al-Ḥadjdjādj b. Yūsuf al-Thaḳafī (714) i, 42b, 54a, 55b, 76b, 77b, 105a, 142a, 482a, 485, 550a, 690b, 714a, 810b, 1005b, 1094b; ii, 27a, 195b, 197a, b, 561b, 788b; iii, **39b**, 247b, 649a, 715a, b, 716a, 717a, 841b, 970a, 1255a, 1267a; iv, 15a, 99b, 319b, 531b, 724b, 753a, 1075b, 1076a; v, 541a, 735b, 947b; vi, 44b, 139a, 147a, 336b, 656a, 660b, 669a, b, 691a, 967b; vii, 114b, 357b, 359a, 405b, 652b, 1030b; x, 816a, 843b; s, 230b, 243a, 354b
Ḥadjdjādj Sulṭān b. Terken Khātūn (Kirmān) (XIII) vi, 482b
Ḥadjdjām → Faṣṣād
al-Ḥadjdjām → al-Ḥsan b. Muḥammad b. al-Ḳāsim (Idrīsid)
Ḥādjdjī I, al-Muẓaffar ii, 24a; iii, 48a, 239b; vii, 992b
Ḥādjdjī II, al-Malik al-Ṣāliḥ Ṣalāḥ al-Dīn (Mamlūk) (1412) i, 1050b, 1051a; ii, 159a; vii, 171b; viii, 987a, b
Ḥādjdjī ʿAbd Allāh vi, 354a
Ḥādjdjī Aḥmad iv, 1082b
Ḥādjdjī ʿAlī-ḳulī Khān Bakhtīyarī (Sardār Asʿad) v, 826a; viii, 450a; s, 291a
Ḥādjdjī ʿAlī Pasha i, 268a, 394a
Ḥādjdjī ʿĀrif Beg (Haci Ârif Bey) (1885) ix, 418a
Ḥādjdjī Bayrām Walī (1429) i, 312b, 509b, 511a, 869a, 1137a, 1202a; ii, 542b; iii, **43a**; vi, 226a; s, 282b
Ḥādjdjī Beg → Riḍwān Begovič
Ḥādjdjī Bektāsh Walī (XIII) i, 299a, 1161b, 1162a; ii, 20b; iii, 315a; iv, 811b; viii, 12a
Ḥādjdjī al-Dabīr (XVII) s, **335b**
Ḥādjdjī Dāwūd ii, 87b; v, 296b
Ḥādjdjī Djābir Khān (Kaʿb) (1881) iv, 1171a; vii, 675a
Ḥadjdjī Gerey → Ḥadjdjī Girāy
Ḥādjdjī Ghulām Ḥusayn (1840) vii, 454b
Ḥādjdjī Girāy (1466) i, 1252b; ii, 44b, 1112b, 1113a; iii, **43b**; iv, 868b; v, 137a
Ḥādjdjī Hāshim s, 336a, 405b
Ḥādjdjī Hüseyn Agha iv, 593a
Ḥādjdjī Ibrāhīm Khān Kalāntar (XIX) iii, 1106a; iv, 391b, 392a, 394a, 476a, 706a; v, 835a; s, **336a**
Ḥādjdjī Ilbegi (XIV) ii, 291b; vi, 290b; vii, 593a
Ḥādjdjī Ismāʿīl Agha i, 284b
Ḥādjdjī Kamāl (Čanderī) (XV) vi, 52b; vii, 531b
Ḥādjdjī Ḳawām al-Dīn Shīrāzī s, 336a
Ḥādjdjī Khalīfa → Kātib Čelebi
Ḥādjdjī Khān (Mālwā) (XVI) vi, 310a (see also *s.v.* Shadjāʿat Khān)
Ḥādjdjī Khān (Dāwūdpōtrās) → Fatḥ Khān (Dāwūdpōtrās)
Ḥādjdjī Khān (XVIII) v, 674a; ix, 743b
Ḥādjdjī Maḥmūd ʿAlī s, 336a
Ḥādjdjī Mawlā iv, 922a
Ḥādjdjī Mīrzā Āghāsī i, 833b; iii, 554b; iv, 393a, b, 394a, 395b, 978b; v, 876a, 1222a

Ḥādjdjī Mīrzā ʿAlī Khān → Faḳīr of Ipi
Ḥādjdjī Muḥammad i, 1124a
Ḥādjdjī Mullā Aḥmad Narāḳī → Narāḳī, Mullā Aḥmad
Ḥādjdjī Mullā Sulṭān Gunābādī (1909) x, 397a
Ḥādjdjī Mullā Taḳi Barakānī i, 304b
Ḥādjdjī Muṣliḥ al-Dīn (XVII) vii, 349a
Ḥādjdjī Nasīm Oghlu → Nasīm Oghlu
Ḥādjdjī Niʿmat Allāh → Niʿmat Allāh
Ḥādjdjī Pasha (XIV) i, 299b; iii, **45a**
Ḥādjdjī Raʾīs Djamāl, Āl (Mānd) (1725) vi, 384b
Ḥādjdjī Ṣāḥib Turangzay vii, 220b
Ḥādjdjī Shādgeldī i, 432a; ii, 419b
Ḥādjdjī Shāh b. Yūsuf Shāh (Yazd) (XIV) vii, 820a; xi, 306b
Ḥādjdjī Shaykh ʿAbbās ʿAlī Kaymān (XX) x, 397b
Ḥādjdjilu iv, 577b
Ḥādjdjiyān vi, 384b
Hadji → Ḥādjdjī
Hadji Abdul Malik Karim Amrullah → Hamka
Ḥādjib i, 5b, 94a; ii, 507b; iii, **45a**, 360a; iv, 421b; s, **336b**
Ḥādjib b. Zurāra (VII) ii, 354a; iii, **49a**; v, 640b
Ḥādjib b. Begtoghdï (1035) vi, 780b
Ḥādjib al-Tāʾī iii, 650b
Ḥādjib Tatar, Amīr (XI) x, 897b
Ḥadjiewad → Karagöz
Ḥādjīpūr vi, 47a
al-Ḥādjir s, 198b
Hādjir, Banū iii, **49b**
Ḥādjiz i, 940b, 1071b
Ḥādjiz b. ʿAwf i, 812a
Ḥādjō Agha i, 871b
Ḥadjr i, 993b; iii, **50a**
al-Ḥadjr (Banū) i, 811b
al-Ḥadjr b. al-Hinw (Banū) i, 811b, 812a
al-Ḥadjr b. ʿImrān (Banū) i, 812a
Ḥadjr, Wādī s, 337a
al-Ḥadjūn (Mecca) vi, 122b, 123a
Hadjw iii, 358b
Ḥaḍn i, 536a; iii, 363a; v, 62b
al-Ḥaḍr (Hatra) i, 196b; iii, **50b**; vi, 921b
Ḥaḍra iii, **51a**; iv, 942a; s, 93a
al-Ḥadrabī i, 782b
Ḥaḍramawt i, 39b, 55a, 110b, 257a, 538a, 546b, 547b, 549b, 551b, 554a, 780b, 828b; iii, **51b**; vi, 132b, 191b, 194a, 473a, b; s, **336b**, 420b, 515b
Ḥaḍramawt, Banū vi, 472a
Ḥaḍramawt b. Ḥimyar s, 337a
al-Ḥaḍramī, Abū ʿAbd Allāh (XIV) vi, 356a
al-Ḥaḍramī, Ḳāḍī Muḥammad b. al-Ḥasan al-Mūrādī (1095) vii, 587b, 613a
Ḥaḍrat Bēgam i, 296a
Ḥaḍrat Maḥall, Bēgam i, 953b
Ḥaḍrat al-mallūk iv, 382b
Ḥaḍrat Mīrzā Bashīr al-Dīn Maḥmūd Aḥmad i, 302a
Ḥaḍrat Tādj Faḳīh (1180) vi, 410a
Ḥaḍrat-i Rāz iv, 51b
Ḥaḍūr b. ʿAdī b. Malik iii, 53a
Ḥaḍūr (Nabī) Shuʿayb i, 536a; iii, **53a**
Hady iii, **53b**
Hadyā i, 176a; iii, 3b
al-Ḥāf b. Ḳuḍāʿa b. Mālik b. Ḥimyar b. Ḳaḥṭān (Mahra) vi, 81b
Ḥafar al-Bāṭin → Bāṭin
Ḥaffār (Hafar) iv, 675a; v, 65b, 66a
al-Ḥāfī → Bishr
Hafik v, 248a
Ḥāfiẓ → Ḳurʾān
al-Ḥāfiẓ (Fāṭimid) (1146) i, 814b, 939b, 1215a; ii, 170b, 855a, 857b; iii, **54b**; iv, 200a, b; vii, 163a
Ḥāfiẓ, ʿAbd al- (ʿAlawī) (1937) i, 58a, 357b, 1281b; ii, 820a, 1116a; iii, **62a**, 562b; v, 890b, 1193b; vi, 249a, 595b, 596b; vii, 39a; s, 47b
al-Ḥāfiẓ, Mawlāy → Ḥāfiẓ, ʿAbd al-Ḥāfiẓ, Mullā s, 292a
Ḥāfiẓ, Shams al-Dīn Muḥammad Shīrāzī (1389) i, 153a, 1301a; ii, 439b, 760b, 1034a; iii, **55a**; iv, 56b, 65b, 909b; v, 671a; vi, 956b; vii, 458b, 480b, 821b; s, 35a, 415a
Ḥāfiẓ ʿAbd Allāh i, 1023a
Ḥāfiẓ-i Abrū (1430) i, 607a, 1131a; iii, **57b**, 574b; iv, 1082a
Ḥāfiẓ ʿAfīfī Pasha iii, 515b; s, 301a
Ḥāfiẓ Agha i, 289b
Ḥāfiẓ Aḥmad, Mawlawī iv, 626a
Ḥāfiẓ Aḥmed Agha (XVIII) viii, 570b
Ḥāfiẓ Aḥmed Pasha (1632) i, 4a, 962b; ii, 635a, 750b; iii, **58a**; iv, 483b; v, 33a, 34a, b, 458a; vii, 598a
Ḥāfiẓ al-Asad v, 1049a; s, 672a

Ḥāfiẓ al-Dimashḳi → Ibn ʿAsākir
Ḥāfiẓ al-Dīn → al-Nasafī
Ḥāfiẓ Djāllandharī (1982) iii, 119b; vi, 838b
Ḥāfiẓ Djawnpūrī i, 1284a
Ḥāfiẓ Ghulām Rasūl Shawḳ ii, 221b
Ḥāfiẓ Ibrāhīm, Muḥammad (1932) i, 597b; iii, **59a**; iv, 159b, 967b; vi, 113b, 414a, 538b, 955b; s, 57b
Ḥāfiẓ Ismāʿīl Haḳḳī ii, 637b, 698b, 699b
Ḥāfiẓ Muṣṭafā s, 282b
Ḥāfiẓ ʿOthmān (1699) iv, 1125a; vii, 905a
Ḥāfiẓ Raḥmat Khān (Rohilla) (1774) i, 1042b, 1043a; iii, **59b**; vii, 707a; viii, 426b, 572b
Ḥāfiẓ Ramaḍān iii, 515b
Ḥāfiẓ al-Samarḳandī, Abu ʾl-Layth Naṣr (X) i, 137a
Ḥäfiẓ Sh. Äbdusämätaw vi, 770a
Ḥāfiẓ Tanı̊sh (XVI) s, **340a**
Ḥāfiẓ Wahba, Shaykh (XX) vi, 153a, b, 155b, 159b, 161a
Ḥāfiẓa Maryam umm ʿInāyat Allāh Khān (XVIII) vi, 131b
Ḥāfiẓābād iii, **62b**
Ḥāfiẓī, Mawlūd b. Mawhūb (XX) viii, 902a, b
Ḥāfiẓiyya (guard) iii, 54b
Ḥāfiẓiyya (Ismaʿīlīs) iv, 200b
Ḥāfiẓiyya (school) iii, 156a
Ḥafīẓ-uddīn iv, 505a
al-Ḥafnāwī, Abu ʾl-Ḳāsim viii, 126a
al-Ḥafnāwī. Muḥammad b. Sālim (1767) viii, 399a
Ḥafrak iii, **63a**
Ḥafṣ b. Abi ʾl-Miḳdām iii, 660a; ix, 470b
Ḥafṣ b. Sulaymān al-Khallāl → Abū Salama
Ḥafṣ b. Sulaymān (796) i, 707a; iii, **63a**
Ḥafṣ al-Fard, Abū ʿAmr (IX) iii, **63b**; s, 88b, 225b
Ḥafṣa bint al-Ḥādjdj (1190) iii, **66a**
Ḥafṣa bint ʿUmar b. al-Khaṭṭāb (665) i, 308a; ii, 414b; iii, **63b**; vi, 575b, 652a
Ḥafṣids i, 92b, 121b, 122b, 124b, 155a, 445b, 533a, 770b, 863a, 1027b, 1046a, 1148b, 1176b, 1205b, 1246b, 1341a; ii, 145a, 146a, 307b, 459b, 463b, 537a, 1077b; iii, 38b, **66a**; iv, 338a; v, 530b, 626a, b, 1190a, 1247a; vi, 216b, 281a, 355a, 404a, 572b, 593b, 728b, 742b; vii, 1023b; s, 93a, b, 111b, 307b
Ḥafṣiyya iii, 660a; ix, 470b
Haft Gunbad i, 925b; vi, 127b
Haft-Lang i, 955b; iii, 1105a,b; v, 825b
Haft Paykar viii, 662b
Haft Sīn vi, 528b
Hagar iv, 184b, 185a; ix, 28a
Haggada iv, 307b, 308a; vii, 639a
Ḥāḥā, Banū iii, **69b**; vi, 741a, b, 742a, b, 743a, b
al-Ḥāḥī, ʿAbd Allāh b. Saʿīd (1602) x, 346a
al-Ḥāḥī, Yaḥyā b. ʿAbd Allāh b. Saʿīd → Yaḥyā b. ʿAbd Allāh b. Saʿīd al-Ḥāḥī
Ḥāḥiyyūn iii, 339a
Haifa → Ḥayfā
Ḥāʾik → Libās
Ḥāʾik s, **340b**
al-Ḥāʾik, Muḥammad (XVIII) iii, **70a**
Ḥāʾil → Ḥāyil
Ḥāʾir (Ḥayr) i, 535b, 613b; iii, **71a**
al-Ḥāʾir (Nadjd) vi, 191b; ix, 738b, 739a
Ḥāʾir al-Aʿizza → al-Ḥāʾir
Ḥāʾir Subayʿ → al-Ḥāʾir
Ḥāʾirī, ʿAbd al-Karīm Yazdī (1937) iv, 1028b; vi, 553a, b; vii, 919a; s, 157b, 158a, **342a**
Ḥāʾirī, Mīrzā Muḥammad Taḳī (XX) vi, 553a; ix, 480b
Ḥāʾiṭ al-ʿAdjūz iii, **71a**
Haji, M.K. (Mappila) vi, 462b
Haji, V.K. Kunyahamad vi, 459b
Haji Misbach ix, 52b
Haji Miskin (Padri) (XIX) viii, 238a
Hajira Begam (XX) vi, 489a
Hajira Masroor (XX) vi, 489b
Ḥaḳāʾiḳ iii, **71b**, 134a
Ḥaḳāḳiyya iv, 668a
Ḥakam iii, **72a**
al-Ḥakam I b. Hishām (Umayyad, Cordova) (822) i, 11a, 12b; ii, 1038a; iii, **73b**; iv, 216b; vi, 139b, 568a; vii, 160b; x, 849b; s, 82a
al-Ḥakam II al-Mustanṣir bi-ʾllāh (Umayyad, Cordova) (976) i, 156b, 494a, 498b, 601b, 628a, 864b, 950a, 1088a, 1291a; ii, 956a, 957a; iii, 30b, 46a, **74b**, 762b; v, 71b, 511a, 1119a; vi, 198a, 199a, 431a, b, 432a, 728a; vii, 208a, 487a, 569b; viii, 632a; ix, 740b; x, 852a
al-Ḥakam b. ʿAbdal (VII) i, 1243a; iii, **72b**; s, 52a

al-Ḥakam b. Abi ʾl-ʿĀṣ ii, 811b; vi, 621b, 622b
Ḥakam b. ʿAmr al-Ghifārī ii, 1072b; x, 601b
al-Ḥakam b. Ḳanbar (VIII) iii, **73a**; vii, 694b
al-Ḥakam b. al-Muṭṭalib b. ʿAbd Allāh b. al-Muṭṭalib (VIII) vi, 381a
Ḥakam b. Saʿd, Banū ii, 516b; iii, **73b**; s, 697a
Ḥakam b. Saʿīd al-Ḳazzāz iii, 496a
al-Ḥakam b. al-Ṣalt (VII) vii, 394b; xi, 474a
al-Ḥakam b. ʿUtayba s, 129b
al-Ḥakam b. al-Walīd II iii, 990b
al-Ḥakam Abū Marwān I s, 103b
Ḥakam al-Wādī (singer) (VIII) v, 936b; vii, 798a
al-Ḥakamī → Abū Nuwās; al-Djarrāḥ b. ʿAbd Allāh; ʿUmāra b. ʿAlī
Hakari → Ḥakkārī
Ḥakhām, Simon iv, 310b
Ḥaḳīḳa iii, **75a**, 1240b; v, 1261a, 1262a
Ḥaḳīḳat, Shāh Ḥusayn (XIX) vii, 475a
Ḥakīm → Ṭabīb
Ḥakīm Ātā (1186) iii, **76b**; x, 250a
Ḥakīm, Banu ʾl- vii, 1022a; viii, 616a
Ḥakīm, Mīrzā → Muḥammad Ḥakīm
Ḥakīm, Rukna Kāshī (XVI) x, 164b
al-Ḥākim, Tawfīḳ → Tawfīḳ al-Ḥakīm
al-Ḥākim I bi-Amr Allāh (ʿAbbāsid, Cairo) (1302) ii, 966a, iii, 679a; iv, 944b; vi, 322a; vii, 167b, 729b
al-Ḥākim bi-Amr Allāh (Fāṭimid) (1021) i,620a, 814b, 816a, 1029a, 1042a, 1141a, 1218a; ii, 125b, 126b, 127a, 136b, 169b, 229a, 232b, 483b, 495b, 631b, 854a, 855a, 857a, 859b, 911b; iii, **76b**, 130b, 154a; iv, 199a, 944a; v, 91b, 327b, 1125b; vi, 148b, 198a, 199b, 366b, 367a, 600b, 626a, 650a, 653a, 663b, 665b, 671b, 672b, 673b; vii, 162a, 295a, 482b, 510a; xi, 129a; s, 136a, 267b, 323a
Ḥakīm b. Djabala al-ʿAbdī vi, 193a
Ḥakīm b. Ḥizām i, 151b; i, 151b; iv, 898b; xi, 475a
Ḥakīm Abu ʾl-Fatḥ Gīlānī (1588) iii, 245b; vii, 341a; viii, 123b; x, 892a
Ḥakīm Adjmal Khān (Dihlī) (1886) vi, 488b
Ḥakīm Ata (1186) i, 299a; iii, **76b**
Ḥakīm ʿAyn al-Mulk i, 856b,
Ḥakīm-Bashi̊ → Ḥekīm-Bashi̊
al-Ḥākim al-Djushāmī (1101) xi, 479a; s, 14b, 90b, **343a**
Ḥākim Ghulām Nabī (XIX) vii, 555a
Ḥakīm Idrīs → Bidlīsī, Idrīs
Ḥakīm Maysarī iv, 63a; vi, 833b
al-Ḥākim al-Naysābūrī Ibn al-Bayyiʿ (1014) ii, 136a; iii, 25a, 27a, 28a, **82a**; viii, 63a; x, 29b
al-Ḥākim al-Shahīd iii, 163a
al-Ḥakīm al-Tirmidhī (930) vi, 821a; viii, 746b, 747a; xi, 110a, b, 111a s, 753a
Ḥakīmoff, Karīm Khān (XX) vi, 153b
al-Ḥaḳīr → Maysara
Ḥaḳīrī al-Ādharbāydjānī v, 1105b
Ḥaḳḳ → Ibrāhīm Ḥaḳḳī Pasha (1918)
Ḥaḳḳ i, 60b, 275a; ii, 294b; iii, **82b**
Ḥaḳḳ al-Dīn i, 763b
Hakkārī (Hakkâri) iii, **83a**, 1109a; v, 452b, 454b, 456b, 459b, 462b
al-Hakkārī, ʿAdī → ʿAdī b. Musāfir
al-Hakkārī, ʿAlāʾ al-Dīn ii, 966a; iii, 680a
al-Hakkārī, Ibn ʿAbd Allāh iv, 137a
al-Ḥakkārī, ʿIsā iv, 613a
Ḥaḳḳī → ʿAbd al-Ḥaḳḳ b. Sayf al-Dīn; Ibrāhīm Ḥaḳḳī; Ismāʿīl Ḥaḳḳī
Ḥaḳḳī, Maḥmūd Ṭāhir (XX) vii, 903a
Ḥaḳḳī, Yaḥyā v, 190b, 191a, 192a; xi, **250b**
Ḥāl (attribute) s, **343b**
Ḥāl (grammar) → Naḥw
Ḥāl, aḥwāl (Ṣūfī) i, 411a, 603b, 1088b; ii, 570a; iii, **83b**
Ḥalab i, 256a, 824b, 983b; ii, 795a; iii, **85a**, 120a, 129a, b, 130b, 212b, 1118b; v, 561a, 923b, 925b, 1211a; vi, 117b, 118b, 198a, 231a, b, 323a, 345b, 372b, 377b, 378b, 379a, b, 381b, 429a, 505b, 507b, 508b, 544a, 547b, 578a, 598a, 667a; viii, 127b, 729b; ix, 795a; xi, 453a; s, 19a, 36a, 37b, 49a, 197a, 239a
– history i, 823a; iii, 695b
– institutions i, 1224a; ii, 83b, 424a; iii, 89a, 139b
– monuments i, 830a, 1317b; iii, 87a, b, 88a, b; v, 1139a
Ḥalabdja ii, 370b, 371a; ix, 219a
al-Ḥalabī, Abu ʾl-Ṣalāḥ (XI) vii, 313a
al-Ḥalabī, Abu ʾl-Ṭayyib ʿAbd al-Munʿim b. Ghalbūn vi, 188b
al-Ḥalabī, Aḥmad (1708) vi, 356b

al-Ḥalabī, Burhān al-Dīn (1549) iii, **90a**, 163b, 711a
al-Ḥalabī, Nūr al-Dīn (1635) iii, **90b**
Ḥalaḳat Dimashḳ al-saghīra iii, 519a
Ḥalāl wa-Ḥarām → Sharīʿa
Ḥalam b. Shaybān (X) vii, 549a
Halāward s, 125a
Ḥalbas al-Rabīʿī (Marand) (VII) vi, 504a
Ḥālet Efendi (1822) i, 399a, 399b; ii, 209b; iii, **90b**, 628b; iv, 295a
Ḥaletī, ʿAzmi-zāde Muṣṭafā (1631) i, 826a; iii, **91b**; viii, 581b, 582a
Ḥaletī ʿAlī Aʿlā, Ḥasan iv, 991b
Halevi, Judah iv, 304b; vii, 812a
Halevi, Moses ben Joseph iv, 305a
al-Ḥalf iv, 687b, 689a
Ḥalfāʾ iii, **92a**
Ḥalfā, Wādī xi, **15b**
Ḥalfā al-Djadīd(a) viii, 92b; xi, 15b
al-Ḥalfawī, Ḳāsim (1591) vi, 350a
Ḥālī → Bannāʾī
Ḥālī → Ḥaly
Ḥālī (ʿAlīgaṙh) vi, 612a
Ḥālī, Alṭāf Ḥusayn (1914) i, 807b; iii, **93b**, 119b, 433a; iv, 170b; v, 202a, 962a; vi, 838a; vii, 662a, 668a; s, 74b, 106a, 107a, b
Halide Edīb → Khālide Edīb
al-Ḥalīfān → Ṭayyiʾ, Banū
Haliḳarnas Balïḳcïsï (1973) v, 195a, 197a; s, **348b**
Halil Kut → Khalīl Pasha
Halīladj iv, 357a; s, **349a**
Ḥalīm b. Muḥammad ʿAlī i, 142a; s, 296a
Ḥalīma iii, **94a**
Ḥalīma bint Abī Dhuʾayb (VI) i, 957b; iii, **94a**; viii, 362b, 697b
Ḥalīma Begī Āghā → ʿĀlamshāh Begum
Ḥalīmī, Luṭf Allāh, Ḳāḍī (XV) iv, 526a; vii, 272a
Ḥalḳ Fïrkasï → Khalḳ Fïrkasï
Ḥalḳ al-Wādī i, 281b; iii, **94b**; ix, 631b; x, 811a; s, 80b
Ḥalḳa (councils) i, 817a; ii, 141a; iii, **95a**; v, 1129a, 1134a, 1158b
Ḥalḳa (soldiers) i, 765b, 947a; iii, **99a**, 185b
Ḥalḳa (sūfism) → Taṣawwuf
Ḥalḳa (tactic) iii, 187b
Halkevi → Khalḳevi
Halkevleri i, 734b; ii, 596b
Halkodalarï ii, 596b; iv, 988a
al-Ḥallādj, al-Ḥusayn b. Manṣūr b. Maḥammā (922) i, 46a, 324b, 387b, 416a, 753a, 754a, 951a, 1128b; ii, 197b, 223b, 734a, 891b; iii, 83a, **99b**, 165b, 620a, 669b, 700a, 1207a; iv, 114b, 615b, 616b; v, 543b; vi, 279b; vii, 94b; s, 385b
Ḥallādjīn v, 559a
Ḥallādjiyya ii, 224b; iii, 103a, b, 823b
Ḥallāḳ s, **350a**
al-Ḥallāniyya i, 535b; iii, 270a; v, 70a
Ḥālūmat al-ṭibāʿ al-tāmm iv, 260a
Halvetiyye → Khalwatiyya
Ḥalwa → Ghidhāʾ
Ḥaly (Yaʿḳūb, Farʿūn) iii, **104b**; vi, 150a
Ḥaly Abbas → ʿAli b. al-ʿAbbās
Haly Imrani → al-ʿImrānī, ʿAlī b. Aḥmad
Halys (river) → Kïzïl-Irmāk
Ḥām b. Nūḥ iii, **104b**; v, 521a, b; vi, 411b
Ḥamā(h) → Ḥamāt
Ḥamā Allāh Ḥaydara iii, 107a, b, 108a, 289a
al-Ḥamād (plain) i, 536b; iii, 1253a
Ḥamad b. ʿĪsā iv, 954a
Ḥamad, Āl i, 1098b
Ḥamad b. Aḥmad Āl-Bū Saʿīdī (1792) vi, 963b; x, 817a
Ḥamad ʿImrān i, 1239b
Ḥamad Wad al-Madjdhūb, Fakī (1776) s, **555b**
Ḥamāda, Banū ii, 568b; vii, 780a
Ḥamāda of Murzuḳ ii, 875a
al-Hamadānī → ʿAlī al-Hamadānī
Hamadānī, ʿAbd al-Samad (XIX) vii, 453a
Hamadānī, Abū Yaʿḳūb Yūsuf (1140) 1, 299a, 515b; ii, 1078a; vii, 933b; viii, 539b; x, 250a; s, 521a
Hamadānī, Mīr Sayyid ʿAlī (1385) i, 1004b; viii, 539b; ix, 857a
Hamadhān (Hamadān) i, 426a, 840a; iii, **105a**, 761b; iv, 3a, 7b, 13b, 465a; v, 171a; vi, 332a, b, 333a, 482a, 484a, b, 493a, 500a, 539a, 600b, 653b; s, 2b, 84a, 118b, 142b
al-Hamadhānī, Abū Saʿd ʿAlī s, 119b
al-Hamadhānī, Aḥmad Badīʿ al-Zamān (1008) i, 116a, 331b, 590b; ii, 246a; iii, **106a**, 368a, 373a, 764a, 1264a; iv, 1069b; v, 132b, 768b, 1010a; vi, 107b, 108b, 379a, 756a; vii, 495a; viii, 735b; s, 17a, 31a

al-Hamadhānī, ʿAyn al-Ķuḍāt → ʿAbd Allāh b. Abī Bakr al-Miyānadjī
al-Hamadhānī → Ibn al-Faķīh; Yūsuf
al-Hamadhānī, Muḥammad ʿAbd al-Malik x, 14a
Ḥamādisha (ṭarīķa) vi, 250b; s, 53a, **350b**
Ḥamadu → Aḥmadu
Hamāhullāh (1943) vi, 260a; xi, 123a
Ḥamāʾil → Siḥr; Tamāʾim; Ṭilasm
al-Ḥamal → Minṭaķat al-Burūdj; Nudjūm
Ḥamal b. Badr al-Fazārī s, 177b, 178a
Ḥamāliyya i, 1009a; ii, 63a, 94b; iii, **107a**; vi, 260a, 705a
Ḥamāllāh, Shaykh → Ḥamā Allāh Ḥaydara
Ḥamām iii, **108b**; v, 924b
Ḥamāma, Banū ii, 464a; s, 144b
Ḥamāma b. al-Muʿizz b. ʿAṭiyya v, 1177b
Hāmān ii, 917b; iii, **110a**; iv, 673a
Ḥamar-wēn (Maķdishu) vi, 129a
Hāmarz iii, **110b**, 586a
Ḥamāsa i, 154b, 584b, 586a, 892a; iii, **110b**; s, 32b, **351a**
Hamasāla iv, 1045a
Ḥamāt i, 118b, 609b; iii, **119b**; v, 923a, 925a; vi, 118b, 230b, 321b, 323a, 378b, 379b, 380b, 429a, b, 545b, 547b, 577b, 578a, 681a; viii, 127b
Hamawand iii, **121b**; ix, 830b
Ḥamawī → Saʿd al-Dīn Ḥamawī
Ḥamawī, Ķāḍī b. Kāshif al-Dīn (XVI) viii, 783b
al-Ḥamawī → Ibn Ḥidjdja; Yāķūt
Ḥamawiya, Banū → Awlād al-Shaykh
Ḥamawiyya (province) vi, 79a
Ḥamawiyya (ṭarīķa) vii, 620a
al-Hamaysaʿ b. Ḥimyar iii, 124a
Ḥamḍ, Wādī al- i, 538a; iii, **121b**; xi, 14a
Ḥamd Allāh, Shaykh (1520) iv, 1125a; x, 409a
Ḥamd Allāh Mustawfī al-Ķazwīnī (1339) i, 358b, 903a; iii, 114a, **122a**; iv, 859a, b, 863a, 1051b, 1052a, 1081b, 1082a; vi, 202a, 505a, 901a, 907b; vii, 754a; s, 235a, 382b
Ḥamdala iii, **122b**; v, 74a
Ḥamdallāhi (Mali) i, 303a; ii, 941b; iii, 39b; vi, 259b
Hamdān, Banū i, 544b, 548a; iii, **123a**; v, 346a; vi, 191a; vii, 591b, 592a, 777a; ix, 1b
Ḥamdān b. Ḥamdūn (Ḥamdānid) (IX) iii, 126a, 619a; iv, 89b; vi, 540a, 900a; vii, 760a
Ḥamdān b. al-Ḥasan Nāṣir al-Dawla (X) iii, 127b, 128a; vi, 540a
Ḥamdān Abū ʿAndja iv, 687a
Ḥamdān Ķarmaṭ b. al-Ashʿath (IX) i, 95b; iii, **123b**; iv, 198a, b, 660b; vi, 157b; viii, 922a
al-Hamdānī → (ʿĪsā) b. ʿUmar
al-Ḥamdānī, Abū Muḥammad al-Ḥasan (Ibn al-Ḥāʾik) (971) i, 534a; iii, 123b, **124a**, 1077a; iv, 335a; v, 110b, 113b; vi, 81a, 829b; s, 341b
Ḥamdānids (Syria) i, 19a, 119b, 215a, 439b, 637b, 679b, 824b, 1046b, 1354b; ii, 281b, 348b, 524a; iii, **126a**, 398a; iv, 23b, 24a; vi, 379a, 626a, 900b, 930a; vii, 484b, 656b, 723b
Hamdānids (Yemen) iii, **125a**, 259b; v, 820a, b; vii, 411a; s, 62a
Ḥamdawayh b. ʿAlī b. ʿIsā b. Māhān vi, 334b
al-Ḥamdawī, Abū ʿAlī Ismāʿīl s, **352a**
Ḥamdī (1911) iv, 806b
Ḥamdī, Ḥamd Allāh (1503) iii, **131a**; v, 1105b
Ḥamdī, Ibrāhīm (Yemen) xi, 274b
Ḥamdī Bey → ʿOthmān Ḥamdī Bey
Ḥamīd al-Dīn, Āl (Yemen) xi, 274a
Ḥamdīs b. ʿAbd al-Raḥmān al-Kindī i, 248a
Ḥamdūn, Abū ʿĀlī → Abū ʿAbd Allāh al-Andalusī
Ḥamdūn, Banū → Ibn Ḥamdūn
Ḥamdūn b. al-Ḥādjdj (1817) → Ibn al-Ḥādjdj, Ḥamdūn b. ʿAbd al-Raḥmān al-Fāsī
Ḥamdūn b. Ismāʿīl b. Dāwūd al-Kātib (IX) iii, 784a; vii, 518b
Ḥamdūn al-Ķaṣṣār, Abū Ṣāliḥ (884) iii, **132a**; vi, 223b, 224b
Ḥamdūn Shalbī (XIX) vi, 251a
Ḥamdūn al-Ṭāhirī (1777) vi, 356b
al-Ḥamdūnī → al-Ḥamdawī, Abū ʿAlī Ismāʿīl
al-Ḥamdūniyya vi, 224b
Ḥamdūshiyya ix, 173b; x, 248a
Hamengku Buwono I (1792) s, 607b, 838a
Hamengku Buwono III s, 838a

Hamengku Buwono IX ix, 852b, 892b; s, 608a, 838a
Hamengku Buwono X s, 838a
Hami → Ḳomul
Ḥāmī (Ḥaḍramaut) iii, **132a**
Ḥāmī-i Āmidī (1747) iii, **132b**
Ḥāmī 'l-Ḥaramayn → Khādim al-Ḥaramayn
Hamian i, 372a
Ḥamīd, Ḥamīd-oghullari̊ i, 467b, 468a; ii, 692a; iii, **132b**; iv, 210b; vii, 593a
Ḥamīd, Sayyid s, 1b
Ḥāmid, Shaykh (1412) vi, 226a
Ḥamīd, Shaykh Ḥādjdjī (Khalīfa) (XVI) vii, 440a
Ḥāmid b. al-ʿAbbās (923) i, 387a; iii, 100b, 101a, **133a**, 739a, 767b; iv, 100a; v, 737a
Hāmid b. Djamālī Dihlawī → Djamālī, Hāmid b. Faḍl Allāh
Ḥāmid b. Muḥammad al-Murdjibī → al-Murdjibī
Ḥāmid b. Mūsā 'l-Ḳayṣarī i, 869a; iii, 43b
Ḥāmid b. Saʿīd i, 1281b
Ḥāmid ʿAbd al-Mannān, Shaykh (XX) vi, 171b
Ḥamīd Allāh Khān i, 1195b, 1196a, b
Ḥamīd al-Anṣārī s, 247b
Ḥamīd al-Dawla iii, 1158b
Ḥamīd al-Dawla Ḥātim (XII) iii, 125b; vi, 433a
Ḥamīd al-Dīn, Āl (Zaydī) ix, 2a
Ḥamīd al-Dīn b. ʿAmʿaḳ → Ḥamīdī b. ʿAmʿaḳ
Ḥamīd al-Dīn Balkhī (1156) vi, 114b
Ḥamīd al-Dīn Ḳāḍī Nāgawrī (1244) vii, 925a; s, **353a**, 571b
Ḥamīd al-Dīn al-Kirmānī → al-Kirmānī, Ḥamīd al-Dīn
Ḥamīd al-Dīn, Shaykh → Ḥamīd al-Dīn Ḳāḍī Nāgawrī
Ḥamīd al-Dīn Ṣūfī Nāgawrī Siwālī (1276) ii, 51a, 55b; vii, 898a; s, **353b**
Ḥamīd Efendi iv, 682a; vii, 599b (see also *s.v.* ʿAbd al-Ḥamīd II)
Ḥāmid Efendi (ḳāḍī-ʿasker) ii, 56b
Ḥamīd Efendi (XVI) (mufti) ix, 710b
Ḥāmid Efendi (shaykh al-Islām) ii, 718a
Ḥamīd Ḳalandar i, 1329a; ii, 48b, 55b; s, 352b
Ḥamīd Kashmīrī i, 72a
Ḥamīd Khān (vizier) (Dihlī, Djawnpūr) (XV) iii, 485a; iv, 1018b; v, 783b; vi, 62a
Ḥamīd Khān (Ḥabshī) iii, 15b; iv, 1018b
Ḥamīd al-Maḥallī (1254) vi, 351b, 352a
Ḥamīd Pasha → Khalīl Ḥamīd
Ḥamīda Bānū Begam i, 316a, 1135b; iii, 455b
Ḥamīda (Ḥumayda) bint Ṣāʿid al-Barbariyya (VIII) vii, 645b
Ḥamīdābād → Isparta
Ḥāmidī (1485) iii, **133b**
al-Ḥāmidī, ʿAlī b. Ḥātim (Ḥamdānid, Yemen)(1209) iii, 125b, **134a**; v, 954b; vii, 411a; s, 62a
al-Ḥāmidī, ʿAlī b. Ḥātim (Ḥamdānid, Yemen) (1174) vi, 433a
al-Ḥāmidī, Ḥamīd al-Dīn (1164) iii, **134b**; vi, 632b
al-Ḥāmidī, Ḥātim b. Ibrāhīm (1199) iii, **134a**; vii, 411a; s, 62a
al-Ḥāmidī, Ibrāhīm b. al-Ḥusayn (1162) iii, 72a, **134a**; iv, 200b, 204b; v, 894a; vi, 439b; vii, 411a
Ḥāmidī b. ʿAmʿaḳ s, 65a
Ḥamīdiyya iii, 961a; v, 462b; vi, 155a, 156b, 778b
al-Ḥamīdiyya shādhiliyya (ṭarīḳa) viii, 744a
Ḥamīdīzāde Muṣṭafā Efendi → Muṣṭafā Efendi
Ḥamīd-oghullari̊ → Ḥamīd
Ḥamīdū i, 368b; ii, 538a
Ḥā-Mīm b. Mann al-Muftarī (927) i, 1178b, 1186a; ii, 1095b; iii, **134b**; vi, 741b, 743b
Hamīrat s, 42a
Hamka vi, 240b
Ḥamladji̊ i, 1278a
al-Ḥamma (Alhama) i, 492b; ii, 463a, 464a; iii, **135a**; vi, 221b, 431a; xi, 212a, b
Ḥammād, Banū → Ḥammādids
Ḥammād b. Abī Ḥanīfa al-Nuʿmān i, 124a; iii, 512a
Ḥammād b. Abī Sulaymān (738) i, 123a; ii, 888b; v, 239b; x, 29a
Ḥammād b. Buluggīn (Zīrid) (1028) i, 860a; iii, 137a; iv, 479a; vi, 841b; vii, 474a; ix, 18a
Ḥammād b. Djarīr al-Djabarī (IX) xi, 178a
Ḥammād b. Isḥāḳ iii, 820a; iv, 111a

Ḥammād b. Isḥāḳ b. Ismāʿīl (881) s, **384b**
Ḥammād b. Salama (783) vii, 662b; xi, 244a
Ḥammād b. ʿUdayy s, 305a
Ḥammād b. Zayd b. Dirham (Mālikī) (795) vi, 263b; s, **384b**
Ḥammād b. al-Zibriḳān (VIII) iii, 135b, 136a; iv, 1003b; vii, 798b
Ḥammād ʿAd͟jrad (777) i, 160a, 1080b; iii, **135a**, 136a; iv, 1003b; vii, 798b; viii, 884a, 996b
Ḥammād al-Barbarī iii, 233a
Ḥammād al-Dabbās (1131) i, 69a; ix, 778a
Ḥammād al-Rāwiya (772) i, 718b; iii, 135b, **136a**, 641b, 1177b; iv, 316b, 919a, 1003b; vi, 442a; vii, 254a, 305b, 661a, 798b; viii, 545b
Ḥammāda iii, **136b**
al-Ḥammādī, Yaḥyā b. Lamak b. Mālik (dāʿī) (X) vii, 725b
Ḥammādids i, 79a, 165a, 533a, 699b, 860a, 1176a, 1204b, 1246b, 1319b; ii, 115a, 145b, 537a, 747b; iii, 137a, 386a; iv, 478b; v, 59b, 60a, 1179a; vi, 426b, 427a, 728b; vii, 481b
Ḥammāl iii, **139a**
Ḥammām iii, **139b**, 148b; v, 13b, 14a, b, 16a
Ḥammām b. Munabbih (749) viii, 657a; ix, 7b
Hammam Ali s, 101b
Ḥammām Bourguiba v, 52a
Ḥammām Ḳarā Ḥiṣār iv, 580b
Ḥammām Mask͟hūṭīn vi, 738b
Ḥammām al-Ṣarak͟h iii, 141b, **146a**; s, 229a; 514a
Ḥammām Sittī Maryam vi, 631b
Ḥammāma b. Zīrī iii, 1043a
Ḥammār, lake i, 1095b
Ḥammū b. Malīl (XI) viii, 763b
Ḥammu Ḳiyu s, 53a
Ḥammūda Bey (1659) ii, 459b; iv, 825b, 828a
Ḥammūda Bey (Pas͟ha) (1814) iii, 94b, 636a; iv, 403a; viii, 763a
Ḥammūdids i, 403a, 495a; ii, 525a; iii, **147a**, 938b, 1037a; vi, 222a, 842a; s, 398b
Hammūya, Muḥammad b. (1135) s, 3a
Hāmōn, Moses (1554) iii, **147b**; iv, 308b
Hampī iii, **147b**, 451a
Ḥamrāʾ al-Asad s, 230a
Ḥamrāʾ (Persians) vi, 875b
al-Ḥamrāʾ iii, **148b**
al-Ḥamrāʾ, G͟harnāṭa i, 459a, 495b, 497b, 500a, 682a, 1321a, 1347a; ii, 115a, 556b, 1012b, **1016b**, 1019a, b; iii, 973a; v, 219b
Ḥamrīn, D͟jabal → D͟jabal Ḥamrīn
Hams͟hin v, 713a
Ḥamūd b. ʿAbd Allāh, S͟harīf (XVII) vii, 782b
Ḥamūd b. Muḥammad Abū Mismār i, 709a; ii, 517b; v, 808a
Ḥamūda b. Murād ii, 189b; x, 634a, b
Ḥamūda Pas͟ha → Ḥammūda Bey (1814)
Ḥamūla iii, **149b**
Hāmūn i, 222a; iii, **150a**; xi, 516b
Ḥamūs vi, 507b
Ḥamūya, Muḥammad b. (1135) viii, 703b
Ḥamūya, Saʿd al-Dīn v, 300b, 301a (see also Saʿd al-Dīn Ḥammūʾī)
Hamza iii, **150a**
Ḥamza, Amīr → Ḥamza b. ʿAbd al-Muṭṭalib
Ḥamza (Malāmī) (1561) vi, 227b, 228a
Ḥamza b. ʿAbd Allāh → Ḥamza b. ʿAbd al-Muṭṭalib
Ḥamza b. ʿAbd Allāh (K͟hārid͟jī) → Ḥamza b. Ādarak
Ḥamza b. ʿAbd Allāh b. al-Zubayr (VIII) vi, 262b
Ḥamza b. ʿAbd al-Muṭṭalib (VII) i, 80a, 115b; iii, 114b, **152b**, 455a, 1234b; iv, 896b, 994b, 1106b; v, 197b, 1161b; vi, 240a, 604a, 650b; x, 782b; s, 92b, 103b
Ḥamza b. Ādarak (K͟hārid͟jī) (828) i, 207a; ii, 978a; iii, 153a, 233b; v, 158a; vi, 331b, 337b; viii, 795b; ix, 683a; xi, 458b
Ḥamza b. Aḥmad b. ʿUmar b. Ṣāliḥ → Ibn Asbāṭ al-G͟harbī
Ḥamza b. ʿAlī b. Aḥmad (1018) ii, 136b, 632a; iii, 80b, **154a**; iv, 199a; vii, 544a
Ḥamza b. ʿAlī b. Rās͟hid (Mandīl) (XIV) vi, 404b, 405a
Ḥamza b. ʿAmmāra → Ḥamza b. ʿUmāra
Ḥamza b. Asad → Ibn al-Ḳalānisī
Ḥamza b. Bīḍ (734) iii, **154b**
Ḥamza b. Ḥabīb (772) iii, **155a**
Ḥamza b. Muḥammad al-Ḥanafī iii, 155b
Ḥamza b. Turg͟hūd (1554) vii, 537a

Ḥamza b. ʿUmāra i, 1116b; iv, 837a; v, 433b
Ḥamza b. ʿUthmān i, 311b, 312a; iii, 156b
Ḥamza Beg (Aḳ-ḳoyunlu) i, 767b; iii, **156b**; iv, 292a; vi, 541a; ix, 124a; x, 737b
Ḥamza Beg (Imām) (1834) i, 755b; ii, 88b; iii, **157a**
Ḥamza Fanṣūrī (XVI) i, 742a; iii, **155b**, 1220a, 1233a; vi, 235b; s, 728a
Ḥamza Fatḥ Allāh (XIX) vii, 434a
Ḥämzä Häkimzadā Niyaziy (Ḳoḳan) (1929) vi, 767b, 769b
Ḥamza Ḥāmid Pasha (1770) iii, **157a**
Ḥamza al-Ḥarrānī iii, **155b**
Ḥamza al-Iṣfahānī, al-Muʾaddib (961) i, 144b; iii, **156a**, 371a; vi, 823a; ix, 100b; x, 226a; s, 382b
Ḥamza Makhdūm (1578) s, **353b**
Ḥamza Mīrzā (Ṣafawid) (1586) iii, **157b**; iv, 861a; vii, 600b
Ḥamza Mīrzā Hishmat al-Dawla (XIX) vii, 675a
Ḥamza Pasha (1768) iii, **157b**
Ḥamza Pasha Nishandjî iv, 566a
Ḥamzat Thadasa i, 756a
Ḥamzawī ii, 98a; iii, 153b; iv, 128b
Ḥamzāwī, Rashād v, 190b
Ḥamzāwīs vi, 227b; x, 252a
Ḥamzawiyya vi, 224a, 227b; x, 252a
Ḥamzevī → Ḥamzawī
Ḥamziyya i, 207a; iii, 153a, 653b, 658b
Ḥanābila i, 272b, 696a, 900a, 949a, 1040a; ii, 388a; iii, **158a**, 677b, 699b, 731a, 752a, 766a, 784b; iv, 173a; v, 9b; vi, 446b; xi, 40a; s, 29b
– doctrine i, 333b, 338b, 339a, 414a; ii, 411b; iii, 17a, 1144b, 1148a, 1149a, 1164b, 1171b; iv, 172b, 183b, 691a, 990a
al-Ḥanafī, Abu 'l-ʿAlāʾ Aḥmad b. Abī Bakr al-Rāzī (XII) vi, 111a
al-Ḥanafī, Abu 'l-Ḳāsim b. ʿAbd al-ʿAlīm vi, 352b
al-Ḥanafī, Aḥmad b. Muḥammad Rūmī s, 49b
Ḥanafī Aḥmad (XX) vii, 439b
Ḥanafī-Māturīdī iii, 1149b, 1171a, 1172b, 1173a; iv, 172a, 470a, b, 693b
Hanafites → Ḥanafiyya
Ḥanafiyya i, 70b, 123a, 164a, 332b, 338a, b, 340a, 803a; ii, 829b; iii, 6b, 17a, 90a, **162b**, 350b, 756b, 848b, 1024b; iv, 404a, b, 690a; vi, 2a, 3a, 557b; s, 23a
Ḥanbal b. Hilāl i, 272b
al-Ḥanbalī (1503) vi, 353a
Ḥanbalīs, Ḥanbalites → Ḥanābila
Ḥanbalī-zāde vi, 971a
Ḥanbīl i, 689a
Handasa → ʿIlm al-handasa
Handjām vi, 358a
Ḥandūs → Sikka
Handžič (al-Khāndjī) (1944) s, **354a**
al-Ḥanfāʾ s, 177b
Hāniʾ b. Hāniʾ s, 298b
Hāniʾ b. ʿUrwa al-Murādī (680) iii, **164b**, 609b; vii, 400b, 592a, 689b, 690a
Ḥanīf iii, **165a**; vi, 146a
Ḥanīfa b. Ludjaym, Banū i, 545a,b, 963a; ii, 569a; iii, **166b**; vi, 648b; s, 122a, 178a
Ḥanīfa, Wādī → Wādī Ḥanīfa
Ḥanīna vi, 750a
Ḥannā (Aleppo) (XVIII) i, 359a
Ḥanna bint Djaḥsh (VII) vii, 649b
Ḥanna umm Maryam vi, 630a; xi, 249a
Hansaliyya iii, **167a**; ix, 173b; x, 247b
Hānsawī, Djamāl al-Dīn (1260) iii, **167b**, 168b; s, 67a
al-Ḥansh (Idrīs b. ʿAlī) (1901) vi, 250b
Hanshīr i, 661a
Hanshīr Dwīmīs iv, 826b
Hānsī iii, **167b**, 225b; vi, 780b
Hānswī → Hānsawī
Ḥantama bint Hāshim b. al-Mughīra vi, 139a
Hantīfa, Banū vi, 742a
Ḥanūt iii, 403b, 404a
Ḥānya iii, 983b, 1086a, b; iv, 539b; vi, 1001a; ix, 697b
Ḥanẓala b. Abī ʿĀmir → Ghasīl al-Malāʾika
Ḥanẓala b. Abī Sufyān i, 151a; ii, 1020b
Ḥanẓala b. Ḳatāda (Mecca) (XIII) vi, 149a
Ḥanẓala b. Mālik, Banū iii, **168b**; v, 640a; vi, 267a, b, 268a
Ḥanẓala b. Ṣafwān i, 509a; iii, **169a**
Ḥanẓala b. Ṣafwān al-Kalbī (VIII) i, 86b, 509a; iii, **169a**, 494a; iv, 826a
Ḥanẓala b. al-Sharḳī i, 115b
Ḥanẓala b. Thaʿlaba iii, 1022b
Ḥanẓala Bādghīsī iv, 55a
Haoussa → Hausa
Haouz → Ḥawz

Ḥāra ii, 230a; iii, **169b**
al-Ḥāra (Marrākus̲h̲) vi, 590a
Harābī i, 1049b
Ḥaraḍ vi, 191b; vii, 861b
Ḥarāfīs̲h̲ → Ḥarfūsh
Ḥaraka wa-Sukūn iii, **169b**; iv, 731b
Ḥarakta, Banū s, 144b
Haram (pyramid) iii, **173a**
Ḥarām (Mamlūks) vi, 327b
Ḥarām, Banū vi, 649a
Ḥaram (enclose) i, 892b; iii, 294a,b, 1018a; iv, 37a, 322a; v, 810a, 1003a, 1201a
Ḥaram Bilḳīs vi, 562a (see also *s.v.* Maḥram Bilḳīs)
al-Ḥaram al-S̲h̲arīf iii, **173b**; v, 341b, 343b, 344a, 1143b, 1144a; vi, 153a, 707a
al-Ḥaramayn iii, **175a**; iv, 956b; vi, 153a, 155b; vii, 466a; s, 304b
Hārand s, 116a, 332a
Harar i, 976a; iii, 3b, 4b, **176a**; viii, 161b
Ḥarari ii, 154b; iii, 7b, 176a
Ḥaras → Ḳaṣr
al-Ḥarāsīs, Banū iii, **176a**; vi, 84b; s, 819a
Harāt (Herāt) i, 7b, 8a, 47b, 91a, 147b, 222b, 223a, 227b, 228b, 1067b; ii, 1101b; iii, **177a**, 471b, 603a; iv, 39a, 394b, 523b, 672a; v, 58b, 59a, b, 873a, 993a; vi, 54a, 408a, 512a, b, 513a, b, 514b, 627b, 633b, 715a, 765a, 780a; vii, 92a, 453a, 455a, 481b, 1052b; viii, 704a, 1012b; s, 38a, 41a, 50b, 71a, 138b, 139b, 140a, 142a, 340a, 380a, 423b, 460a
Ḥarāṭīn → Ḥarṭānī
al-Harawī → al-Anṣārī al-Harawī
al-Harawī, Abu 'l-Faḍl (X) iv, 1183a; vi, 600b
al-Harawī, Abū ʿUbayd al-Ḳāsim b. Sallām (837) v, 607b; vi, 924a
al-Ḥarawī, ʿAlī b. Abī Bakr (1215) ix, 262b, 582a
Harawī, Ibn Ḥusām (1355) vii, 754b
al-Harawī, Maḥmūd b. Muḥammad s, 406b
al-Harawī, Mīr ʿAlī (calligrapher) (XVI) viii, 787b
Harawī, Mīrzā → ʿAbd al-Raḥmān Harawī
al-Harawī, Mollā Miskīn (XV) vii, 969b
al-Harawī, Muḥammad iv, 801a
al-Harawī al-Mawṣilī, ʿAlī (1215) i, 89a; iii, 71b, **178a**, 181a, b, 511a; iv, 958b; v, 214b
Ḥarāz (Yaman) iii, **178b**; iii, 134a; iv, 201a; vi, 191b, 192a; ix, 816a; s, 407a
Harāz (river) v, 659b, 660a
Ḥarāzem, Sīdī → Ibn Ḥirzihim
Ḥarāzim (1815) vi, 356b (see also *s.v.* ʿAlī Ḥarāzim b. al-ʿArabī Barāda)
Ḥarb, Banū iii, **179b**, 363b, 1065b; v, 998a
Ḥarb (war) iii, **180a**; v, 687a
Ḥarb b. Umayya i, 1241b; ii, 883b; iii, **203a**; s, 103b
Ḥarb Akademisi iii, 204a
Ḥarba → ʿAnaza; ʿAsā; Ḳaḍīb; Silāḥ
Ḥarbāʾ iii, **203b**
Harbaḳa iv, 726a
Ḥarbī i, 429b
al-Ḥarbī → Ibrāhīm al-Ḥarbī
Harbin s, 82a, b
al-Ḥarbiyya (quarter) i, 895a; vi, 335a; viii, 588b; s, 785a
al-Ḥarbiyya (sect) iii, 1265b; iv, 837b; vi, 335a, b (see also *s.v.* al-Ḥāris̲h̲iyya)
Ḥarbiyya (La Forbie), Battle of iii, 989b; viii, 989a
Ḥarbiye ii, 425b, 513b; iii, **203b**; v, 903b
Ḥareket Ordusu iii, **204a**
Ḥarf i, 345b; iii, 172a, **204b**, 597b, 598a, b; iv, 867b
Ḥarfūs̲h̲ (amīrs) i, 971a; iii, **205b**
Ḥarfūs̲h̲, Muḥammad (amīr) (1850) vi, 308a
Ḥarfūs̲h̲, ḥarāfīs̲h̲ ii, 963a; iii, **206a**
Hargeisa iii, **206b**
Harg̲h̲a, Banū iii, **207a**; vi, 742a, b, 744a
Hari Čand iii, 225a
Hari Čand, Diwān ii, 140a
Harī Rūd iii, **207b**; v, 872b, 873b; vi, 713b; s, 367a
Harī Singh (Mahārād̲j̲ā) ii, 140a; iv, 710a; s, 327b
Harī Singh Nalwa (governor, general) i, 970b; ii, 1131a; iii, 336a
Ḥarīb (district/wādī) iii, **207b**; iv, 747a
Ḥārik → Ḥurrāk
Ḥārim i, 239a; iii, **208b**
Ḥarīm i, 35b; ii, 114b; iii, **209a**; v, 871b, 1149a
Harim b. Ḥayyān i, 73b
Harim b. Sinān ii, 1023a; vii, 629a; xi, 557a

Ḥarīmī ii, 794b; v, 269b (see also *s.v.* Ḳorḳud b. Bāyazid (1513))
Harīpur iii, 336a
Ḥarīr ii, 904b; iii, **209b**, 400b; iv, 135a, 339b, 676b; v, 39a, 604b; s, 340b
al-Ḥarīrī, Abū Muḥammad ʿAlī (1247) iii, 222a, 811b; viii, 525b
al-Ḥarīrī, Abū Muḥammad al-Ḳāsim al-Baṣrī (1122) i, 523a, 570b, 591a, 669b; iii, **221a**, 733a, 834b, 1264a; iv, 913a; v, 207b, 608b; vi, 109a, b, 110a, 132b, 199a; vii, 388a; viii, 736a; s, 31a, 123b
Ḥarīriyya iii, **222a**; vi, 88a; viii, 525b
Ḥarīsh → Karkaddan
al-Ḥārith Banū vi, 436a; ix, 817a; s, 335a
al-Ḥārith, Djabal i, 251b; ii, 574a
al-Ḥārith b. ʿAbd al-ʿAzīz b. Abī Dulaf ii, 623b
al-Ḥārith b. ʿAbd al-Muṭṭalib i, 80a; vi, 350b; ix, 420a
al-Ḥārith b. Abi ʾl-ʿAlāʾ Saʿīd al-Taghlibī → Abū Firās
al-Ḥārith b. Abī Ḍirār (VII) v, 78b; viii, 1003b
al-Ḥarīth b. Abī Rabīʿa ii, 196a; v, 1232a
al-Ḥārith b. Abī Shām (Ghassānid) (634) vi, 546b;
al-Ḥārith b. ʿAmr (Kinda) (1528) i, 526b; iii, 1177a; v, 118b; vi, 951a; ix, 77a
al-Ḥārith b. Asad → al-Muḥāsibī
al-Ḥarīth b. ʿAwf → al-Ḥārith b. Ẓālim
al-Ḥārih b. Badr al-Fazārī s, 177b
Ḥarīth b. Bazīʿ iv, 713a
Ḥārith b. Djabala (Ghassānid) (569) i, 102b, 405b, 548b, 1249b; ii, 1020b; iii, 94a, **222a**; iv, 726a, 1138a; v, 633a, b; s, 229b
al-Ḥārith b. Fihr, Banū vi, 145a
al-Ḥārith b. Ḥammām i, 115b; iii, 221a
al-Ḥārith b. Ḥilliza al-Yashkurī iii, **222b**; vii, 254b; s, 272b
al-Ḥārith b. Hishām b. al-Mughīra Makhzūmī (VII) i, 115b; vi, 138b, 139a; s, 32b
Ḥārith b. Kaʿb, Banū ʾl- iii, **223a**; vii, 276a, 872a
al-Ḥārith b. Kalada b. ʿAmr al-Thaḳafī (634) ii, 1120a; iv, 820b; vi, 637b; x, **452a**; s, 133b, **354a**
al-Ḥārith b. Khālid al-Makhzūmī (VII) i, 308b; vi, 140a
al-Ḥārith b. Miskīn (ḳāḍī) (864) vi, 279a, 663b, 673a; s, 726b
al-Ḥārith b. Ṣabīra s, 172a
al-Ḥārith b. Sharīd ix, 864a
al-Ḥārith b. Suraydj (746) i, 530a, 684b; ii, 388a, 1026b; iii, **223b**, 471a, 1202a; iv, 44b, 370a; v, 57a, 76a, 854a; vii, 606a, 664a, 1016a
al-Ḥārith b. Talid al-Ḥaḍramī iii, 653b, 654a
al-Ḥārith b. Thaʿlaba s, 229b
al-Ḥārith b. Tirmāḥ s, 136a
al-Ḥārith b. Waʿla i, 690a
al-Ḥārith b. Ẓālim al-Kilābī ii, 234b
al-Ḥārith b. Ẓālim al-Murrī (VII) ii, 1023a, b; iii, 812a; vii, 629a; s, 178a
al-Ḥārith al-Ḥaffār (VIII) viii, 350b
al-Ḥārith al-Ḳubāʿ b. ʿAbd Allāh b. Abī Rabīʿa b. al-Mughīra vi, 140a
Ḥārith al-Muḥāsibī → al-Muḥāsibī
Ḥāritha b. Badr al-Ghudānī (684) iii, **224b**, 1261b; iv, 1002b
Ḥāritha b. Djanāb, Banū i, 771b; vi, 649a; vii, 267b
Ḥāritha b. al-Ḥadjdjādj → Abū Duʾād al-Iyādī
Ḥāritha b. Ḳaṭan i, 969a
al-Ḥāritha b. al-Nuʿmān ii, 843a
Ḥāritha, Banū iii, 227a; x, 211a, 783a
al-Ḥārithī, Abushiri b. Salim (XIX) iv, 889a; x, 195a
al-Ḥārithī, Muḥammad b. Ṭāhir s, 62a
al-Ḥārithī, Ṣāliḥ b. ʿAlī (ʿUmān) (1896) viii, 993a; s, **355a**
al-Ḥārithī, Ziyād b. ʿAbd Allāh (VIII) viii, 531a
al-Ḥārithiyya iii, 659a, 1266a; iv, 837b, 838a; v, 63b, 945b
Hariyānā iii, 168a, **225a**
Ḥarka ii, 509b; v, 1221a
Harkand (Bangladesh) ix, 877b
Harkarn b. Mathurādās (XVII) iii, **225b**
Ḥarmala b. Yaḥyā (858) vii, 691b
Harmas, Harmīs → Hirmis
Ḥarra i, 535a; iii, **226a**, 362a
al-Ḥarra i, 50b, 55a; iii, **226a**; v, 997a
Ḥarrān i, 16b, 106b, 119b, 136b; ii, 347b, 348a; iii, **227b**, 287a; v, 593b; vi, 338a,

380b, 539b, 623b, 624a, 667a, 670b, 781b; viii, 672b; x, 845a; s, 36b
al-Ḥarrānī → Abu 'l-Fatḥ; Ḥamza; Ibrahīm b. Dhakwān; ʿĪsā b. ʿAlī; Nadjm al-Dīn
al-Ḥarrānī, Muḥammad b. Salama (867) ix, 661a
Ḥarrānians, Ḥarrāniens → Ṣābiʾa
Harrar → Harar
Ḥarrat al-Buḳūm i, 1299a
Ḥarrat Ḥaḍn i, 1299a
Ḥarrat Khaybar i, 452b; iii, 121b; viii, 613a, b
Ḥarrat al-Raḥāh iii, 121b
Ḥarrat Rahaṭ iii, 121b; s, 198b
Ḥarrat ʿUwayriḍ iii, 121b
Ḥarrat Wāḳim → al-Ḥarra
Harsusī (language) i, 575a; iii, 176b; vi, 84b
Ḥarsūsī → al-Ḥarāsīs
Ḥarṭānī i, 371a; ii, 133b, 877a; iii, **230b**; v, 1197a; s, 328b
Harthama b. ʿArfadja al-Bāriḳī (650) iii, 29a; vi, 899b
Harthama b. Aʿyan (816) i, 149b, 437b; ii, 196b, 886a; iii, **231a**, 233a, 243b, 982a; iv, 16b; vi, 333a, b, 334a, b; vii, 227b
Harthama b. Naṣr s, 106a
Harūd → Harī Rūd
Hārūn b. ʿAbd Allāh (890) vi, 900a
Hārūn b. ʿAbd Allāh al-Badjalī (896) ix, 767a
Hārūn b. Altūntāsh i, 424b; iv, 1067a
Hārūn b. al-Faradj (XI) iv, 605a; vii, 539b
Hārūn b. Gharīb (934) i, 688b, 962b; iii, 126b; vii, 414a
Hārūn b. ʿImrān iii, **231b**; vi, 630a
Hārūn b. Khumarawayh (Ṭulūnid) (905) iii, 745b; s, 812a
Hārūn b. al-Mahdī → Hārūn al-Rashīd
Hārūn b. Mūsā (Multān) ii, 892b; viii, 818b
Hārūn b. Mūsā b. Sharīk (885) i, 321a
Hārūn b. Sayf al-Dīn b. Muḥammad Faḍl ii, 123b
Hārūn b. Sulaymān (892) vi, 900a
Hārūn b. Yaḥyā i, 775a, 1033b; iii, **232**a, 1044b; vi, 89a
Hārūn b. al-Yamanī al-Mukhālif iii, 659b
Hārūn Bughra Khān → Bughra Khān Hārūn
Hārūn (Ḥasan) Khān b. Sulaymān (Ḳarakhānid) vi, 274a
Hārūn al-Rashīd (ʿAbbāsid) (809) i, 14a, 18a, 107b, 118a, 144b, 164b, 247b, 364a, 437a, 485a, 510a, 550b, 697a, 1034a, 1035, 1298a; ii, 191a; iii, 22b, 231a, **232b**, 344b, 345b, 996a, 1044b; iv, 16b, 97b, 858b, 940b, 1164a; v, 174b, 533b, 1239a; vi, 2a, 140b, 147b, 205b, 263b, 264b, 331a, 379a, 437b, 468b, 499a, 506a, 544a, 578a, 660b, 665a, 714a, 744b, 752b; vii, 518a, 646a; viii, 411a, 412a; xi, 242b, 243a; s, 22b, 26a, 48a, 64a, 122a, 128a, 198b, 199a, 225b, 251b, 252a, 263a, 304a, 326b, 372a
– constructions i, 182b, 199b, 616b, 761a, 789b; ii, 36a, 1120a; iii, 228a, 235a
Hārūn al-Sharī ii, 524a; iii, 126a, 619a
al-Hārūniyya iii, **234b**; vi, 506a; x, 744b
Ḥarūnum vi, 562b
Ḥarūrāʾ i, 40b; iii, **235a**; vii, 523b
Ḥarūrites i, 40b, 384a, 385b; iii, 235a; iv, 1074b (see also *s.v.* Ḥarūrāʾ)
Harūsindān b. Tīrdādh s, 357a
Hārūt wa-Mārūt i, 811b; iii, **236b**; vi, 216b, 218a, 737a, 738a
Ḥarz iv, 1038a
Harzam vi, 540b
al-Ḥasā i, 72b, 100a, 538b, 539a; iii, **237b**; iv, 663b, 664a, b, 764b, 925a, b; v, 684a; vi, 157b, 274b, 435b, 734b; vii, 301b, 782b; s, 135b, 234a, 380a
Ḥasab wa-nasab i, 892b; iii, **238b**
Ḥasab Allāh b. Muḥammad Faḍl ii, 122b
Hasākira → Haskūra
Ḥasan (in ḥadīth literature) iii, 25a
al-Ḥasan I, Mawlāy (ʿAlawī) (1895) i, 290b, 356b, 357a, 1281a; ii, 109a, 820a, 823a, 885b, 1116a; iii, **240a**, 256a, 536a, 562a; v, 890a, 1192b, 1193a; vi, 134b, 135a, b, 589b, 595b, 743a; s, 114a
al-Ḥasan II (ʿAlawid) ii, 673b; iii, 564a; v, 1072b, 1073a, 1195a
Ḥasan I (Nizārī) → Ḥasan-i Ṣabbāḥ
Ḥasan II (Nīzārī) (1193) i, 353b; iv, 28a, 200a, 205a; viii, 442a
Ḥasan III Rukn al-Dīn (Ismāʿīlī) (1221) i, 353b; iv, 205b, 860a; vii, 1000b
al-Ḥasan, Abū ʿAbdallāh Muḥammad iii, 69a; iv, 1157a
Ḥasan, Bayhaḳī Sayyid s, 131b

Ḥasan, al-Malik al-Nāṣir Nāṣir al-Dīn (Mamlūk) (1361) i, 765b, 1050b; iii, **239b**, 900b; iv, 431b, 940a; v, 1141a; vii, 171a, 992b
al-Ḥasan, Mawlāy → al-Ḥasan (ʿAlawid); al-Ḥasan, Abū Abdullāh
Ḥasan, Mīr Ghulām (1786) vi, 838a; s, **358b**
Ḥasan, Mullā (Farangī Maḥall) s, 292a
Ḥasan, Pīr v, 27a
Ḥasan, Shaykh (Čūbānid) vi, 482b
Ḥasan b. ʿAbd Allāh → Nāṣir al-Dawla Ḥasan
al-Ḥasan b. ʿAbd al-Raḥmān (XI) vii, 413a
Ḥasan b. Abi ʾl-Ḥasan → Japheth al-Barḳamānī
al-Ḥasan b. Abī ʾl-Haydjāʾ → Nāṣir al-Dawla Ḥasan
al-Ḥasan b. Abī Numayy II, Sharīf ii, 517b; s, 234b
Ḥasan b. Aḥmad al-Karmaṭī v, 368b
Ḥasan b. ʿAdī i, 195b
Ḥasan b. ʿAdjlān, Sharīf (1426) ii, 828b; vi, 149b
al-Ḥasan b. Aḥmad (Mombasa) (XVII) v, 104b; vii, 226b
Ḥasan b. Aḥmad Bahmanī iii, 577a
Ḥasan b. ʿAlī → al-Ḥasan al-Utrūsh; Ibn Makūlā; Niẓām al-Mulk
Ḥasan b. ʿAlī (Ḥamdānid) (896) vi, 900a
al-Ḥasan b. ʿAlī (Zanzibar) vii, 250a
al-Ḥasan b. ʿAlī (Zīrid) iii, 138b, 933a
al-Ḥasan b. ʿAlī b. Abi ʾl-Ḥusayn (Kalbid) i, 986b; ii, 853a; iv, 496b; v, 105b; ix, 585a
al-Ḥasan b. ʿAlī b. Abī Ṭālib (Imām) (669) i, 40b, 43b, 86a, 163b, 194b, 385a, 550a, 697a; ii, 843a, 848b; iii, **240b**, 607b, 889b; v, 945b; vi, 334a, 652a, 668b; vii, 265b, 688b; s, 401a
Ḥasan b. ʿAlī al-Baṣrī → Japheth b. Eli
al-Ḥasan b. ʿAlī al-Maʾmūnī i, 149b
Ḥasan b. ʿAlī Shāmma ii, 167a
al-Ḥasan b. ʿAlī ʿUmar al-Marrākushī i, 727a; ii, 586b; v, 1209b; s, 413b
al-Ḥasan b. ʿAmmār i, 1042a; ii, 858b; iii, 76b, 77a; iv, 497a; v, 1160a
Ḥasan b. Asad Allāh (Marʿashī) (1476) vi, 514a
al-Ḥasan b. Ayyūb (X) vi, 636b; x, 18a
Ḥasan b. al-Bākir iv, 859a
Ḥasan b. Bālī Efendi (Malāmī) (XVI) vi, 228a
Ḥasan b. Buwayh (Būya) → Rukn al-Dawla Ḥasan
Ḥasan b. al-Faḍl iv, 637b
Ḥasan b. Faraḥ b. Ḥawshab b. Zādān al-Kūfī → Manṣūr al-Yaman
Ḥasan b. Farīghūn ii, 799b
al-Ḥasan b. Fīrūzān (Daylamī) (X) ii, 928a; vi, 115b
Ḥasan b. Gannūn (Djannūn) (Idrīsid) (985) i, 1088a; iii, 30b, 74b, 1036b; vi, 431a, b; vii, 942b
Ḥasan b. Ḥabīb vi, 196b
Ḥasan b. al-Ḥāfiẓ i, 939b; iii, 55a
al-Ḥasan b. Hāniʾ → Abū Nuwās
Ḥasan b. Ḥārūn i, 866a
Ḥasan b. Ḥassūna iv, 686b
al-Ḥasan b. Ḥayy → al-Ḥasan b. Ṣāliḥ b. Ḥayy
al-Ḥasan b. Hibat Allāh Ibn ʿAsākir iii, 713b;
Ḥasan b. Hibat Allāh Makramī (1775) iv, 201a; vi, 191b,
al-Ḥasan b. al-Ḥusayn iv, 646b, 647a
Ḥasan b. Idrīs (dāʿī muṭlaḳ) s, 358b
al-Ḥasan b. al-Imām al-Manṣūr bi-ʾllāh al-Ḳāsim (Zaydid) (1639) vii, 270a
al-Ḥasan b. Ismāʿīl, Mawlāy (ʿAlawid) vii, 387a
al-Ḥasan b. Ismāʿīl Āl Shibām al-Makramī iv, 201a; vi, 192a
Ḥasan b. Ḳaḥṭaba (754) i, 16a, 103a, 449b; ii, 196b, 679a, 715a; iii, 802b; iv, 447a, b; vi, 417b; ix. 612b
Ḥasan b. Ḳāsim (Idrīsid) → Ḥasan b. Gannūn
Ḥasan b. al-Ḳāsim al-Dāʿī ilā ʾl-Ḥaḳḳ (Ḥasanid) (928) i, 688a; ii, 191b, 192a, b; iii, 254b; vi, 115b, 941b; s, **356a**
Ḥasan b. Ḳatāda b. Idrīs, Sharīf (XIII) iv, 749a; vi, 149b
al-Ḥasan b. Khālid al-Ḥāzimī, Sharīf s, 30b
al-Ḥasan b. al-Khaṣīb → Ibn al-Khaṣīb
Ḥasan b. Khayr al-Dīn → Ḥasan Pasha (Algiers)
al-Ḥasan b. Maḥbūb (XI) i, 758b; vii, 732a
al-Ḥasan b. Makhlad → Ibn Makhlad
al-Ḥasan b. al-Manṣūr bi-ʾllāh al-Ḳāsim b. Muḥammad (Zaydī) (1613) vi, 437a
al-Ḥasan b. Marwān v, 453a

al-Ḥasan b. Muḥammad (ʿAlawid) → al-Ḥasan I, II
al-Ḥasan b. Muḥammad (Buwayhid) → al-Muhallabī
al-Ḥasan b. Muḥammad (Khayrātid) i, 709b; ii, 518a
al-Ḥasan b. Muḥammad (Nizārī) → al-Ḥasan II, III
al-Ḥasan b. Muḥammad Āl ʿĀʾiḍ i, 709b
Ḥasan b. Muḥammad al-ʿAṭṭār → al-ʿAṭṭār, Ḥasan b. Muḥammad
al-Ḥasan b. Muḥammad b. al-Ḥanafiyya (705) v, 1026b; vi, 636b; s, **357b**
Ḥasan b. Muḥammad b. Ḳalāwūn (Mamlūk) (1350) vi, 413b
al-Ḥasan b. Muḥammad b. al-Ḳāsim (Idrīsid) iii, 1036a; vii, 641b
al-Ḥasan b. Muḥammad b. Samāʿa al-Ṣayrafī al-Kūfī (Wāḳifī) (876) vii, 647b
Ḥasan b. Muḥammad Abū Numayy, Sharīf (1601) vi, 150a; s, 234b
Ḥasan b. Muḥammad Naẓẓām al-Nīsābūrī s, 413a
al-Ḥasan b. Mūsā (923) vii, 786a
Ḥasan b. Nāmāwar ii, 194a
Ḥasan b. Nūḥ al-Hindī (1533) s, **358b**
Ḥasan b. al-Nuʿmān (VII) vi, 751a
al-Ḥasan b. Rabāḥ s, 352a
Ḥasan b. al-Ṣabbāḥ → Ḥasan-i Ṣabbāḥ
al-Ḥasan b. Ṣafī (1173) vi, 110b
al-Ḥasan b. Sahl (850) i, 149b, 271b, 316a, 897b, 1298a, 1312a; ii, 731a, b; iii, **243b**, 345b, 951a, 987b; iv, 17a; vi, 334a, b, 335a, b, 336a; vii, 404a; s, 15a, 263b
al-Ḥasan b. Ṣāliḥ b. Ḥayy (784) iii, **244a**; xi, 224b; s, 48a, 130a
al-Ḥasan b. Sanbar (or Shanbar) iv, 664a
Ḥasan b. Sulaymān (Ilek-Khān) (1102) iii, 1114a; xi, 359b
al-Ḥasan b. Sulaymān II (Kilwa) (1333) v, 1157b; ix, 699a, 700b
al-Ḥasan b. Sulaymān al-Anṭākī iii, 824b
al-Ḥasan b. Suwār (1017) i, 631b, 632a; vi, 204a, 347a, 845b
Ḥasan b. Tīmūrtāsh (Čūbānid) → Ḥasan Küčük
al-Ḥasan b. ʿUbayd Allāh b. Tughdj iii, 956a; iv, 660b, 663a
Ḥasan b. Ustādh-Hurmuz, ʿAmīd al-Djuyūsh (1011) iii, **244b**; vi, 965b; viii, 1050b; s, 118b, 119a
Ḥasan b. Wahb i, 153b, 154a
al-Ḥasan b. Yūsuf → al-Ḥillī, Djamāl al-Dīn
al-Ḥasan b. Zayd b. al-Ḥasan (783) i, 45b; iii, **244b**, 786b; vii, 879a
al-Ḥasan b. Zayd b. Muḥammad (al-ḍāʿī al-kabīr) (884) i, 352b; ii, 191a; iii, 245a; iv, 46b; v, 662a; vi, 745b, 941a; vii, 390a, 410b, 418a, 723a, 786a, 794a; viii, 625b; x, 105a
al-Ḥasan b. Zayn al-Dīn (1602) iii, 588b; vii, 298a; viii, 777b
Ḥasan b. Ziyād al-Luʾluʾī i, 124a; iii, 163a
Ḥasan ʿAbd al-Shukūr, Shaykh (XX) vi, 175b
Ḥasan Abdāl iii, **245a**
Ḥasan Agha (1545) i, 1247a; iii, **245b**
Ḥasan Agha (author) v, 261a
Ḥasan Agha (Aydi̊noghlu) ii, 599a
Ḥasan Akhmīnī i, 330a
Ḥasan al-Akhram iii, 80b, 154a
al-Ḥasan ʿalā dhikrihi ʾl-salām → Ḥasan II (Ismāʿīlī)
Ḥasan ʿAlī b. Djahānshāh i, 148a; iv, 588a
Ḥasan ʿAlī b. Fatḥ ʿAlī Shāh (Ḳādjār) (XIX) vi, 484b
Ḥasan ʿAlī Bārha i, 1025b, 1026a; ii, 379a, 810a; iv, 279b; s, 126b
Ḥasan ʿAlī Manṣūr (1965) iv, 42a; vii, 448b; s, 530a
Ḥasan ʿAlī Mīrzā Shudjāʿ al-Salṭana (Shīrāz) (XIX) iv, 313a, 393a; vii, 453b, 454a
Ḥasan ʿAlī Munshī (XVI) vii, 988a
Ḥasan ʿAlī Shāh → Agha Khān
al-Ḥasan Amīrkā b. Abi ʾl-Faḍl al-Thāʾir s, 363a
al-Ḥasan al-Aʿṣam (977) i, 551b; ii, 854a; iii, **246a**; iv, 663a, b; s, 36b
Ḥasan al-ʿAskarī, Abū Muḥammad (XI, Imām) (874) iii, **246b**; vii, 443a; viii, 146a, 1040b; s, 95a
Ḥasan Baba, dey (1683) iii, **247a**, 629a
Ḥasan Baba Ḳāʾimī (1691) s, **506b**
Ḥasan Balfiyya ii, 233b; iv, 852a
al-Ḥasan al-Bannāʾ → al-Bannāʾ
al-Ḥasan al-Bashīr (Sūdān) (XX) ix, 750b
al-Ḥasan al-Baṣrī (728) i, 105a, b, 454a, 718a, 1080b; ii, 293a, 729a, 891b; iii,

247b, 682b, 947b, 948a; iv, 142a, 212a, 369a, 486a, 734a, b; v, 209b, 936a, 1231b; vi, 266b, 351a, 457b, 709b; vii, 783a, b; s, 230b, 323b, 350a, 358a
Ḥasan Bāwand → Fakhr al-Dawla Ḥasan
Ḥasan al-Bawwāb i, 195b
Ḥasan Bāyḳarā → Bāyḳarā
Ḥasan Bedr al-Dīn, Pasha (1912) vi, 372b, 373a; s, **359b**
Ḥasan Bey al-Djuddāwī iii, 992a, b
Ḥasan Bey-zāde (1636) iii, **248b**
Ḥasan Bey Melikor Zerdabi → Zerdabi
Ḥasan Buzurg, Shaykh (Djalāyirid), (1337) i, 903b, 908b; ii, 68a, b, 401a, 706a; iii, 1122b, 1208b; vi, 502b
Ḥasan Čelebi → Ḳinalizāde
al-Ḥasan al-Dākhil, sharīf iii, 256b
Ḥasan Dihlawī (1336) iii, **249a**; vi, 609a
Ḥasan Djalāyir → Ḥasan Buzurg
Ḥasan Djūrī, Shaykh (Marʿashī) (XIV) vi, 511a
Ḥasan Esīrī (XVII) viii, 5a
Ḥasan, Fakhr al-Dawla (Bāwandid) (1349) → Fakhr al-Dawla Ḥasan b. Shāh
Ḥasan al-Faḳī (XX) vi, 176b
Ḥasan al-Fārūḳī ii, 814b; iii, 638a
Ḥasan Fasāʾī → Fasāʾī, Ḥādjdjī Mīrzā Ḥasan
Ḥasan Fehmī (1909) iii, **251a**; iv, 284a
Ḥasan Fehmī Efendi (1881) iii, **250a**; iv, 168b
Ḥasan Fehmī Pasha (1910) ii, 473b; iii, **249b**
Ḥasan Gangū → Muḥammad I (Bahmānid)
Ḥasan Ghaznawī Ashraf s, 416b
Ḥasan al-Ikhnāʿī i, 280b
Ḥasan-ili s, 168b
Ḥasan ʿIzzet Pasha ii, 104b, 699b
Ḥasan Kabīr al-Dīn, Pīr iv, 202b; v, 26a; ix, 85a
Ḥasan Kāfī i, 310a, 1271b
Ḥasan Karlugh, Sayf al-Dīn (Multān) (1249) i, 227a; vi, 48a, b
al-Ḥasan al-Kātib (XI) vii, 683b, 976a, 1024a
Ḥasan Khān (Ḳarakhāni) → Ḥasan b. Sulaymān
Ḥasan Khān Bāyburdī iv, 1044b
Ḥasan Khān Ḳāshḳāy iv, 706a
Ḥasan Khān Sālār (Mashhad) (1849) vi, 715a
Ḥasan el-Kheyūn i, 684a
Ḥasan Küčük (Čūbānid) (1343) ii, **68a**, 401a, b, 706a; iii, 1122b, 1208b
Ḥasan Malik of Čadura s, 366a
Ḥasan Mīrzā b. Muḥammad Khudābanda (1576) vi, 515a
Ḥasan Muḳaddam (1925) vi, 764a
al-Ḥasan al-Mustanṣir (Ḥammūdid) vi, 222a
al-Ḥasan Nāṣir al-Dawla, Amīr s, 36a
Ḥasan Nithārī s, 340a
Ḥasan Niẓāmī (XIII) v, 546b; s, **359b**
Ḥasan Pasha → Djezāʾirli Ghāzī; Kāhya; Khādim; Küčük; Ṣokollī; Tiryākī; Yemenli; Yemishdji
Ḥasan Pasha (Algiers) (1572) iii, **251a**; iv, 1158a; v, 362a
Ḥasan Pasha (Baghdād) (1723) i, 905a; iii, **252a**, 1257b
Ḥasan Pasha (Mora) (XVII) vii, 239b
Ḥasan Pasha (Yemen) (1604) vi, 436b
Ḥasan Pasha, Dāmād (1713) iii, **252b**
Ḥasan Pasha, Sayyid (1748) iii, **253a**; iv, 233b
Ḥasan Pasha, Sherīf (1791) ii, 534a; iii, **253a**; s, 331a
Ḥasan Pasha Čataldjali (1631) iii, **252a**; iv, 92a
Ḥasan Pasha Predojevič i, 1266a; ix, 681a
Ḥasan al-Rammāḥ (1294) i, 1056a; vii, 885b
Ḥasan al-Rayyī s, 252b
Ḥasan-i Djūrī, Shaykh (1842) ix, 48a
Ḥasan-i Bēg Rūmlū (XVI) iii, **253b**
Ḥasan-i Ṣabbāḥ (1124) i, 215b, 352b, 353a,b, 1359b; ii, 98a, 194a, 858b; iii, **253b**, 544b, 725a; iv, 199b, 200a, 205a; vi, 918a; vii, 541a; viii, 72a, b, 84a
Ḥasan Ṣabrī iii, 515b; s, 300b
Ḥasan Sezāʾī (1738) iv, 991b; viii, 167a
Ḥasan Shāh b. Gul Khātūn (Kashmīr) s, 131b, 242a, 329a, 423b
Ḥasan Shāh Bahmanī → ʿAlāʾ al-Dīn Ḥasan Bahman Shāh
Ḥasan Shāh (1484) s, 353b
Ḥasan Shīrāzī, Mīrzā viii, 140a; x, 41a; s, 54a
Ḥasan Sidjzī (XIV) s, 577a
Ḥasan the Tailor vi, 228a, b
Ḥasan al-Turābī (Sūdān) (XX) ix, 750b; s, 673a

Ḥasan al-Uṭrūsh Abū Muḥammad b. ʿAlī Zayn al-ʿĀbidīn, Imām (917) i, 688a, 1350b; ii, 191b; iii, **254a**; iv, 19a; v, 603a; vi, 516a, 941b; vii, 542b, 645b, 995b; s, 356b, 363a
Hasanābād ix, 6b, 681a
Ḥasanak, Abū ʿAlī Ḥasan (1032) iii, **255b**; vi, 916a; vii, 26b; viii, 63a
Ḥasanayn al-Ḥiṣāfī → al-Ḥiṣāfī
Ḥasanī iii, **256a**
Ḥasan-ī Buzurg (1356) viii, 997b
Ḥasanī, Ḥasaniyyūn (Ḥasanids) i, 403a; ii, 572b; iii, **256b**; v, 1191b; vi, 140b, 148a; ix, 507a
Ḥasanī, Ibrāhīm al- v, 133a
al-Ḥasaniyya iii, 660a
Hasankeyf → Ḥiṣn Kayfā
Ḥasanmat (Sawādkūh) (1545) vi, 515a
Ḥasanwayh al-Barzikānī i, 211b; ii, 299b, 748b; iii, **258a**, 703b; v, 452b; s, 118b
Ḥasanwayhids i, 1030b; iii, **258a**; v, 824a; ix, 727a
Ḥasanzāde Meḥmed Efendi iv, 737a
Ḥāṣbayyā vi, 28a, 31a; s, 606a, b
Ḥasdāy b. Shaprūṭ (975) ii, 349b; iii, **259a**; viii, 626a, 813b
Ḥashā iv, 272b, 273a
Ḥasharāt al-arḍ iii, 307b; v, 390a; s, 288a
Ḥāshid wa-Bakīl, Banū iii, **259a**; v, 807b; vi, 436a
Hāshim, Abū Ibrāhīm Shīrāzī s, 405b
Hāshim, Aḥmed (1933) iii, **260a**
Hāshim, Banū → Hāshimids; Hāshimiyya; Ḥidjāz; Makka; Muḥammad
Hāshim, Labība (XX) vii, 903a; x, 797b
Hāshim, Shehu i, 1260a; v, 358b
Hāshim b. ʿAbd al-ʿAzīz (IX) i, 85b; vii, 569a
Hāshim b. ʿAbd Manāf i, 15a, 80a, 115b; ii, 1056a; iii, **260a**, 262b, 265a, 1093a; v, 41b
Hāshim b. Sulaymān (Mecca) (XX) vi, 165b
Hāshim b. ʿUrwa vi, 263a
Hāshim b. ʿUtba iii, **260a**; viii, 696b; x, 774b
Hāshim ʿAlī (1756) vi, 611a
Hāshim al-Ātāsī (XX) iv, 138a; v, 1047a; vi, 538a
Hāshim (Sayyid) b. Ḥasan (Bayhaḳī) s, 131b
Hāshim Baba ii, 543b
Hāshim Bey (XIX) vii, 685b
Hāshim Khān (1933) vi, 86b
Hāshim Khodjandī iv, 505a
Hāshim Musabbaʿāwī ii, 123a; v, 267a
Hāshim al-Ṭaʿʿān vii, 145b
Hāshim Ushkūrī s, 23b
Hāshim al-Zawāwī (1947) vi, 176b
al-Hāshimī, ʿAlī b. Sulaymān viii, 101b
al-Hāshimī, Shaykh (1961) iii, **261b**
Hāshimids (Bāb al-Abwāb) i, 835b; iv, 345a; ix, 488b
Hāshimids (Ḥidjāz, ʿIrāḳ, Jordan) i, 41a; iii, **263a**, 1065b, 1066b; vi, 31b; s, 3b
Hāshimids (al-Hawāshim, Mecca) i, 552a; iii, **262b**; vi, 137b, 138a, 145a, 146a, 148b, 149a, 441b; ix, 507a
Hāshimiyya (ʿAbbāsids) i, 15a, 17a, 258a; iii, **265a**; iv, 446a, 837a; v, 1b-2b; vi, 624b; x, 841a, 845a
al-Hāshimiyya (capital) i, 17a, 895b; iii, **265b**; iv, 729a; vi, 345a
Hāshimiyya (Djilwatiyya) ii, 543b
al-Ḥashīr i, 233b
Ḥashīsh i, 1014b; iii, **266a**; ix, 202b
Ḥashīshiyya (Nizārīs) i, 353a; ii, 170b, 882a; iii, **267b**; v, 922a; vi, 577b
Ḥāshiya i, 816b; iii, **268b**
Ḥāshiya (entourage) → Ḳaṣr
Ḥashm-i ḳalb iii, 199a; v, 685a
Ḥashm-i aṭrāf v, 685a
Ḥashm-i bilād-i mamālik v, 685a
Ḥashmet (1768) iii, **269a**, 357a; viii, 9a
Ḥashr → Ḳiyāma
Hashtād-Sar s, 116a
Hashtarūd vi, 498b, 502a, b
al-Ḥashw i, 671b; ii, 825a, b; iii, 269b; vii, 914a
Ḥashwiyya i, 410b; iii, **269b**, 905b; iv, 470a
Ḥāsib → ʿIlm al-ḥisāb
Ḥāsik iii, **269b**; vi, 80a
Ḥāsikī → al-Ḥāsikiyya
al-Ḥāsikiyya i, 535b; iii, 270a; v, 70a, b
Ḥaśirān vi, 80b
al-Ḥaṣkafī iii, 163b
Haskūra (Hasākira), Banū v, 652a; vi, 741a, 742a, 743a, b; ix, 18b
Ḥasrat Mohānī (1951) v, 7a; s, **360a**
Ḥāssa → Ḥiss
Ḥassān, Bā iii, **270a**
al-Ḥassān b. al-Djarrāḥ al-Ṭaʾī (1024) ii, 482b; iii, 246a; vii, 117a

Ḥassān b. Gümüshtigin, amīr (1123) vi, 380a
Ḥassān b. Mālik b. Baḥdal al-Kalbī (688) ii, 89b, 360a; iii, **270b**; iv, 493a, 929b; vi, 622a; vii, 267b
Ḥassān b. Mufarridj (XI) ii, 483b, 484a, 855b; iii, 80a; iv, 842a; v, 1211b; x, 482a, b
Ḥassān b. al-Nuʿmān (699) i, 77b, 862b, 1023b; ii, 130a; iii, **271a**; iv, 336b, 415b, 422a, b, 423a, 739b, 829b; vii, 643a
Ḥassān b. Thābit b. al-Mundhir (659) i, 50b, 145a, 828b, 1149a; ii, 541a, 993b, 1020b; iii, 271b, 354a, 975b; iv, 835b, 1002a; vi, 475a, 575a, 605a; vii, 361b; s, 9b
Hassani → Ḥasanī
Hassū Taylī (1603) s, **361a**
Ḥassūn, Rizḳ Allāh ii, 471a
Ḥassūna, Banū v, 352a
Ḥassūna b. ʿAmmār viii, 449a
Ḥassūna al-Laylī vi, 251a
Ḥassūna al-Nawawī i, 819b, 820a; v, 838b
Hastādān vi, 495b
Ḥātam Khān, Malik ʿAlī Sardjāndār i, 444b
Hatay (Alexandretta) i, 468b, 517a; iii, **273a**; iv, 138b; vi, 387b, 538a
Hataylā Pir → Ghāzī Miyān
Hātī Khān ii, 973a
Ḥāṭib b. Abī Baltaʿa iv, 821a; vii, 511b
Hātif iii, **273a**, 668b
Hātif Iṣfahānī, Aḥmad (1783) iii, **273b**; viii, 448b; x, 235b
Hātifī, ʿAbd Allāh (1521) iii, 114a, **274a**; iv, 1010a, 1073b; v, 1105a; viii, 775a
Ḥaṭīm → Kaʿba
Ḥātim, Banū xi, 269a; s, 61b, 387b, 388a
Ḥātim b. Aḥmad al-Ḥātimī v, 954b; s, 263a
Ḥātim b. ʿAlī al-Zurayʿid v, 954b, 1244b
Ḥātim b. al-Ghashīm al-Mughallasī iii, 125b
Ḥātim b. Harthama b. Aʿyan (IX) i, 844a; iii, 231b, **274a**; v, 297b; vi, 333a, 335a
Ḥātim b. al-Ḥumās iii, 125b
Ḥātim al-Ahdal i, 255b, 781a
Ḥātim al-Ṭāʾī b. ʿAbd Allāh (VI) i, 195a, 364a, 1241b; ii, 961a; iii, **274b**, 343a; iv, 705a; vi, 474b; s, 234b
al-Ḥātimī, Abū ʿAlī Muḥammad (998) iv, 249b; vii, 772a; s, **361a**; 708a
Ḥātimids s, 236a
Hatra → al-Ḥaḍr
Hatta ii, 663a, 664a, 665b
Ḥaṭṭin → Ḥiṭṭīn
Hausa i, 179b, 1259a; ii, 10a, 479a; iii, **275a**; iv, 773b; viii, 20a; ix, 761a
– language, literature i, 179b; ii, 479a; iii, 278b; iv, 567b; v, 222b
Havāyī i, 1063a
Ḥawāla ii, 147b; iii, **283a**; iv, 405b
al-Ḥawānīt vi, 728b, 775b
Ḥawār i, 535b; xi, 547a
Ḥawārī iii, **285a**
Ḥawārī Rasūl Allāh → al-Zubayr b. al-ʿAwwām
Ḥawāshī → Ḥāshiya
Ḥawāshib → Ḥawshabī
al-Hawāshim → Hāshimids
Hawāwīr iii, 300a; ix, 760b
Hawāzin, Banū i, 12a, 544b; ii, 627a, 883b; iii, **285b**, 578a; vi, 266a, b; vii, 373a; viii, 697b; x, 788a, 79a; s, 177b
Hawbas vi, 561a
Ḥawḍ (basin) ii, 461b; iii, **286a**
Ḥawḍ (cistern) iii, **286b**; v, 884a, 888a
Ḥawḍ (Mauritania) iii, **288b**; v, 890a, 892a
al-Ḥawḍ (Almería) vi, 576a
Hawdha b. ʿAlī (VII) i, 689b, 690a, 964a; iii, 166b; vii, 664b; x, 57a
Ḥawdhān vi, 191b
al-Ḥawf viii, 39a; x, 617b
(al-) Ḥawf al-Gharbī viii, 39a; ix, 357a
(al-) Ḥawf al-Sharḳī viii, 39a; ix, 357a
Ḥawfī iii, **289b**; vi, 248a
Ḥāwī iii, **291a**, 335a
Ḥāwī iii, **291a**
Ḥawīza (Ḥuwayza) i, 1096a; iii, **291b**; v, 80b; vii, 672a; ix, 856a
Ḥawr al-Ḥammār viii, 613b; ix, 368b
Ḥawra iii, **291b**
Ḥawra → al-Dhiʾāb
Hawrāmān iii, **292a**
Ḥawrān i, 1079a, 1093b, 1277a; ii, 1021a; iii, **292a**; vi, 303a, 349a, 545b, 547a
Hawsam (Rūdisar, Gilān) vi, 513a; vii, 995b; x, 430b; s, **363a**
al-Hawsamī, Abū Djaʿfar s, 363a
Ḥawshabī iii, **293b**
Hawshanī vi, 216b
Ḥawṭa iii, **294a**; s, 420b
al-Ḥawṭa iii, **294b**
Ḥawwāʾ iii, **295a**, 330b

Ḥawwāʾ → Ḥāwī; Ruḳya
al-Ḥawwāʾ → Nudjūm
Hawwāra, Banū i, 250a, 254b, 1049a; ii, 979a, 1114b; iii, 66b, **295b**, 653b; iv, 481b, 568a; v, 515b; vi, 311a, 312a, 324a, 434b, 727a; vii, 186a, 420b; viii, 865a
al-Ḥawwārī, Abu 'l-Ḥasan (XIII) vi, 355a
Hawwārī, Abū Madyan → Abū Madyan, Hawwārī
al-Hawwārī, Abū Yaḥyā Zakariyyāʾ b. Ibrahīm ix, 289b
al-Hawwārī, ʿĪsā b. Ḥamdūn al-Midyūnī vi, 1043b
al-Hawwārī, Muḥammad b. Aḥmad vi, 196b; xi, 15a
Ḥawwārīn → Ḥuwwārīn
Ḥawz iii, **300b**; vi, 589a, b; s, 48a, 144b
al-Hawzālī, Muḥammad b. ʿAlī (1749) x, 326a
Hayākil i, 835a
Hayʾa (astronomy) → ʿIlm al-hayʾa
Hayʾa iii, **301a**
Ḥayāt iii, **302a**
Ḥayāt, Shaykh iii, 228b, 229a, 230a, b
Ḥayāt b. Mulāmis → Ḥaywa b. Mulāmis
Ḥayāt Allāh Khān ii, 973b
Ḥayāt Muḥammad Khān i, 1195a
Ḥayātī → ʿAbd al-Ḥayy, Shaykh
Ḥayātī, Shaykh Meḥmed (XVIII) viii, 166b, 167a
Ḥayātī-zāde iii, **303a**
Hayāṭila (Huns) i, 226a, b, 852a, 857a; ii, 1a; iii, 177a, **303b**, 584b; iv, 356a, 536a, 1172a, 1173b; v, 56b, 57a, 76a, 354b; vi, 633b, 720a; x, 303a, 691a; s, 327a
Ḥayawān iii, **304b**, 311b; v, 991b
Haybat Khān Niyāzī s, 324b
Ḥayḍ iii, **315b**
Ḥaydar iii, **315b**; viii, 766b
Ḥaydar (clan) s, 105b
Ḥaydar (general) s, 301a
Ḥaydar, Āl iv, 857a
Ḥaydar, Amīr (Bukhārā) i, 1295b
Ḥaydar, Ghāzi 'l-Dīn → Ghāzi 'l-Dīn
Ḥaydar, Malik al-ʿUlamāʾ Mullā s, 4b, 292b
Ḥaydar, Mīr i, 530b
Ḥaydar, Naṣīr al-Dīn (Nawwāb) (1837) i, 757b; v, 1240a; vii, 301a
Ḥaydar b. ʿAlī Ḥusaynī Rāzī (XVII) iii, **316a**
Ḥaydar b. Djunayd, Shaykh (Ṣafawid) (1488) i, 923a; iii, **315b**; iv, 34a,b, 573a; v, 243b; viii, 237b, 766b, 777a
Ḥaydar b. Kāʾus → al-Afshīn
Ḥaydar al-Afshīn → al-Afshīn
Ḥaydar ʿAlī Khān Bahādur (Mappila) (1782) i, 296b, 625a, 1015b; iii, **316b**, 428a; iv, 547a; v, 1259a, b, 1260a; vi, 459b, 535b; vii, 897b
Ḥaydar Bāmātōf (1872) vii, 205b
Ḥaydar Beg i, 153a
Ḥaydar Mīrzā Dūghlāt Muḥammad (1551) i, 1002a; ii, 621b; iii, **317a**; iv, 213b, 410a, 612a, 708b; vii, 218a; s, 131b, 167a, 324b, 366a
Ḥaydar Ḥaydar (Syria) vi, 469a; x, 799a
Ḥaydar Khān ʿAmū Ughlī (1921) s, **365a**
Ḥaydar Ḳulī Sulṭān (Afshār) (XVI) i, 240a; vii, 673a
Ḥaydar Malik (VII) s, 332b, **366a**
Ḥaydar Pasha (Yemen) (XVII) iv, 828a; vii, 270a
Ḥaydar Shāh b. Zayn al-ʿĀbidīn (Kashmīr) s, 131b, 329a
Ḥaydar Shāh Lakhkhī i, 432b
Ḥaydar Shihāb (Maʿn, XVIII) ii, 443b, 444a; v, 792b; vi, 344a
Ḥaydar al-Shihābī (1835) ii, 594b; vi, 345b, 346a; viii, 986a
Ḥaydar al-Zāwaʾī, Ḳuṭb al-Dīn (1221) xi, 295a
Ḥaydar-i Āmulī, Bahāʾ al-Dīn (1385) iv, 49b, 698a; xi, 161a; s, **363b**
Ḥaydar-oghlu Meḥmed (XVII) i, 4a; iii, **317b**; iv, 766a
Ḥaydara b. Mahdī i, 345a
Ḥaydarābād (Deccan) i, 924a, 1170a; ii, 99b, 426b, 1119a; iii, **318a**; iv, 219b; v, 550b; vi, 87a, 369b, 489b, 535b, 536a, b, 696a; viii, 67a, 73a; s, 4b, 47a, 280a
– institutions ii, 426b; iii, 318b, 322b
– monuments iii, 319a, 448a
– Niẓām of i, 1170a, 1202b; iii, 318b, 322a
Ḥaydarābād (Sind) iii, **323b**
Ḥaydarān iii, 137b, **324b**, 386a; vi, 712b
Ḥaydarānlū (Mākū) i, 1031a; vi, 201b
Ḥaydarī, Ḥaydar Bakhsh iii, 376b
Ḥaydarīkhāna s, 336a
Ḥaydarīs iv, 99a, 860b; ix, 513a
Ḥaydariyya iv, 474a; x, 250a; xi, 295a, 463a

Haydj (Baḥrayn) x, 90a
Haydut i, 1267a
Ḥayfā i, 946b; iii, **324b**, 365a; vi, 45b, 322a
al-Ḥayfī, ʿAbd al-Djalīl b. Muḥammad b. al-Musallam vii, 491a
Ḥāyil, Ḥāʾil iii, **326b**; s, 3b, 305a
al-Ḥayḳ i, 181a
Haykal, Muḥammad Ḥusayn i, 597b, 598a; ii, 467a; iv, 173a; v, 188b, 189b; vi, 956a; s, 6b, 58a
Haykal al-Zahra i, 488b
al-Ḥayḳār (Aḥiḳar) v, 811b, 812a, 813a
al-Ḥayḳutān ix, 777a
Haylāna, Banū i, 250b; vi, 592a, 742a
al-Ḥaymā iii, **327a**; vi, 84b, 192a, 436b
Haymana i, 511a; vi, 226b
Ḥayr → Ḥāʾir
Ḥayra iv, 95a
Hayrabolu vi, 227b; ix, 875b; x, 414b
Ḥayratī (1553) iv, 68a; viii, 775b
Ḥayrīdj s, 337a
Ḥays x, 901a; s, **366b**
al-Ḥays s, 30b
Hays (tiller) vii, 22b
Ḥayṣa Bayṣa (1179) iii, **327b**, 819b; vi, 64b
al-Hayṣam al-Hamdānī iii, 233a
Hayṣamiyya (city) i, 233b
Hayṣamiyya (sect) iv, 668a
Hayṭal → Hayāṭila
al-Haytham (dāʿī) vi, 439a
Haytham b. ʿAbd Allāh (870) vi, 900a
al-Haytham b. ʿAdī (821) i, 759b; iii, 136a, **328a**; vi, 828b; vii, 258a; s, 38b
al-Haytham b. al-Haytham (Ibāḍī) (IX) vii, 546b
al-Haytham b. Muḥammad (IX) ix, 488a
al-Haytham b. al-Rabīʿ b. Zurāra → Abū Ḥayyā al-Numayrī
al-Haythamī (1563) vii, 191b
Haythūm → Hethum
Hayūlā ii, 554a; iii, **328a**; x, 530a
Haywa b. Mulāmis al-Ḥaḍramī iv, 115a
Ḥayy i, 306a; iii, **330a**
Ḥayy b. Yaḳẓān iii, **330b**, 944a, 957a, 974b
Ḥayya iii, **334b**; iv, 95a
Ḥayya b. Turkī b. Djalwī s, 305b
Ḥayyān b. Djabala iv, 646b
Ḥayyān b. Khalaf → Ibn Ḥayyān
Ḥayyān al-Sarrādj iv, 837a; v, 433b; viii, 372a
Hazadj → ʿArūḍ
Hazār Afsāna i, 361a, b; iii, 313b
Hazār Ustūn (palace) v, 1214b; vi, 532b; x, 594a
Hazāras (Afghānistān) i, 88a, 224a, b, 229a, 857a, 1010a, 1173a; ii, 5b; iii, 335a, 1100b, 1107b; s, **367a**
Hazāras (Pakistān) iii, **335b**
Hazāradjāt s, **367a**
Hazārasp i, 421a, 750a, b, 872a; ii, 194a; iii, **336b**; s, 228b, 420a
Hazārasp, Malik iii, 337a, b; v, 826b
Hazārasp Muḥammad (XV) vi, 512b
Hazāraspids iii, **336b**; iv, 32a; v, 824b, 826b
Hazārāt i, 139b
Hazārdjarīb vi, 512a, b, 515a; s, 140b, 309b
Hazārfann → Ḥusayn Hezārfenn
Hazāristān i, 223b
Hazārmard → ʿUmar b. Ḥafṣ b. ʿUthmān b. Ḳabīṣa
Hazārnao i, 238b
Hazhīr → ʿAbd al-Ḥusayn
Ḥāzī i, 659b; iv, 421a, b
Ḥāzim b. ʿAlī ii, 484b
Ḥāzim b. Muḥammad al-Ḳarṭādjannī (1285) iii, **337b**; iv, 672b; vi, 196b, 348b; xi, 27b
Ḥāzim b. Zayd al-Djahḍamī s, 384b
Ḥazīn, Muḥammad b. Abī Ṭālib (Shaykh ʿAlī) (1766) i, 680b, 1166a, 1301a; iii, 313b, **338b**; iv, 69b; vii, 300b, 530a; s, 108a
Hazīrān → Taʾrīkh
Hazmīra, Banū ii, 623a; iii, 339a; vi, 592a, 741b
al-Hazmīrī → Abū ʿAbd Allāh Muḥammad; Abū Zayd ʿAbd al-Raḥmān; Abū Yaʿazzā; Abū Zayd
al-Hazmīrī ʾl-Marrākushī (1280) vi, 356a
Hazmīriyyūn iii, **338b**
Hazradja, Banū vi, 742a, 743b
Hazrat, Āl s, 66b
Ḥazza v, 555a
Hazzāʿ b. Muḥammad i, 1032b
Hebron → al-Khalīl
Hedjaz → al-Ḥidjāz
Ḥefeṣ ben Yaṣlīaḥ iv, 306a
Hegira → Hidjra
Heis (Somalia) ix, 715a
Hejar, ʿAbd al-Raḥmān v, 483a
Ḥekīm-Bashi̊ iii, **339b**, 1152b

Ḥekīm-og͟hlu ʿAlī Pas͟ha → ʿAlī Pas͟ha Ḥakīm-og͟hlu
Heliopolis i, 788a; iv, 442b; vii, 140b (see also *s.v.* ʿAyn S͟hams)
Helmand, Helmend → Hilmand
Helphand, Alexander Israël (XX) iv, 123b; vi, 94a; 584a
Ḥelvā v, 642a, b; vi, 810a
Hemedi al-Buhriy (XX) vi, 612b; s, 351b
Hēmū i, 316a, 1136a; iii, 423a; ix, 894b
Henoch → Idrīs
Hephthalites → Hayāṭila
Heraclea → Ereğli
Herat → Harāt
Herātī (pattern) s, 142a
Herātī (tribe) iv, 10b
Hercules, Pillars of → Ḳādis
Hereke → Ḳālī
Hergan Kale → ʿAmmūriya
Herī Rūd → Harī Rūd
Herīz s, 142b
Hermes → Hirmis
Hersek → Bosna
Hersekli ʿĀrif Ḥikmat i, 1302a; iii, 1200b
Hersek-og͟hlu → Hersek-zāde
Hersek-zāde, Aḥmed Pas͟ha (1517) i, 244a, 1264b; iii, **340b**; iv, 565a; v, 774b; vi, 1025b
Herzegovina → Bosna
Ḥesene i, 483a
Hes͟hdek i, 1075b
Hethum I i, 639b; ii, 37b, 38a; iv, 817a; x, 43b
Hethum II ix, 679a
Heybeli Ada → Marmara
Hezārfenn → Ḥusayn Hezārfenn
Hezārg͟hrad iii, **342a**, 998b
Hezārpāre Aḥmed Pas͟ha (1648) iii, 318a, 983b; v, 272b
Hiba (gift) iii, **342b**; iv, 217b
Hiba (gift *inter vivos*) iii, **350a**
al-Hība → Aḥmad al-Hība
Hibat Allāh b. ʿAbd al-Wāḥid vi, 349b
Hibat Allāh b. ʿAlī → Ibn Mākūlā
Hibat Allāh b. D̲jamīʿ → Ibn D̲jamīʿ
Hibat Allāh b. al-Ḥusayn s, 267a, 372a (see also *s.v.* al-Badīʿ al-Asṭurlābī)
Hibat Allāh b. Ibrāhīm (1747) vi, 191b
Hibat Allāh b. Maḥfūẓ iii, 931a
Hibat Allāh b. Mākūlā → Ibn Mākūlā, Hibat Allāh
Hibat Allāh b. Malkā → Abu ʾl-Barakāt
Hibat Allāh b. Muḥammad (XII) iii, **351b**; v, 815a
Hibat Allāh b. Nāṣir al-Dawla ix, 108a, b
Hibat Allāh b. al-S͟had̲jarī (1148) vii, 527a; s, 840b
Ḥibr → Kitāba
Ḥibrī (1676) iii, **351b**
Ḥidāʾ → Ḥudāʾ
Ḥidād → ʿIdda, Libās
al-Hidāya al-Islāmiyya iv, 907a
Hidayat → Riḍā Ḳulī K͟hān
Hidāyat (Borneo) s, 150b
Hidāyat, Ṣādiḳ (1951) iii, **352a**; iv, 73a, b; v, 199b; s, 780a
Ḥidhāʾ → Libās
Hid̲jāʾ i, 442b, 584b, 586a; iii, **352b**; iv, 56a; s, 394a
al-Hid̲jāʾ, Ḥurūf → Ḥurūf al-hid̲jāʾ
Ḥid̲jāb i, 306b; iii, **359a**; v, 740a
Ḥid̲jāba → Ḥād̲jib
al-Hid̲jar iii, **361b**, 1064b; ix, 291a, 904b
al-Ḥid̲jārī, Abū Muḥammad ʿAbd Allāh b. Ibrāhīm (1188) i, 602b; iii, 926a; vii, 492a, 811a
al-Ḥid̲jāz i, 25a, 37a, 46a, 77a, 103a, 268b, 272b, 315a, 443b, 539a, 554b; ii, 572b, 660a, 1030a; iii, 34b, 263b, **362a**, 606a, 1066b; iv, 1002a; v, 519a, b, 1127b; vi, 9a, 33a, b, 34a, 45b, 87b, 139b, 144b, 150b, 156a, 264a, 266a, 280a, b, 332a, 334a, b, 336a, 360b, 433b, 435b; s, 3a, b, 4b, 10a, 20a, 198b, 305b
– dialect i, 573b, 574a
– Ḥid̲jāz railway i, 64b, 315a; ii, 289a; iii, 34b, 293a, 326a, 363a, **364a**, 605b; v, 998a; vi, 361a; x, 885a
Ḥid̲jāzī, Muḥammad iv, 73a; v, 199a, 1096a
Hid̲jd̲jāna vi, 544b
Ḥid̲jr iv, 317a, 319b; vi, 147a
al-Ḥid̲jr (Saudi Arabia) iii, **365b**; vi, 455a; x, 436a (see also *s.v.* al-ʿUlā)
Hid̲jra (emigration) iii, **366a**
Hid̲jra (fiḳh) s, **368a**
Hid̲jra, hud̲jra → Hid̲jar
Hid̲jris v, 131b; x, 432b
Hid̲jwiyya iv, 715b
Hidrellez → K͟hiḍr-ilyās
al-Ḥifnī, Yūsuf b. Sālim (1764) vi, 112b
Ḥifnī Nāṣif (XIX) vi, 219b, 602b, 1090b

Hīfūḳraṭīs (Īfūḳraṭīs) → Buḳrāṭ
Ḥifẓ → Ḳirāʾa, Ḳurʾān
Ḥifẓī (XVIII) vi, 826b
Ḥikāya iii, **367a**; iv, 895b; v, 187a, 812a, 951b
Ḥikma iii, **377b**; iv, 120a; s, 324a
Ḥikmān, Banū ii, 631a; iii, 1038a; vi, 729a
Ḥikmat Abū Zayd iv, 1152a
Ḥikmat Sulaymān iii, 521b, 1258b
Ḥikmet, Aḥmad → Aḥmad Ḥikmet
Ḥikr s, **368b**; iii, 1017b
Ḥīla → Ḥiyal
al-Hilāl ii, 403b, 466b, 472b; s, 106a
Hilāl iii, **379a**
Hilāl, Banū i, 93b, 167b, 367a, 374a, b, 441a, 532b, 533a, 770b, 863a, 1049a, 1176a, 1204b; ii, 526a; iii, 138a, 324b, **385b**; iv, 337a, 739b, 827b, 830b; v, 60a, 760a, 1182b, 1196b; vi, 134a, b, 141a, 606a, 712b, 741a, b; vii, 482b, 483a, 731b; viii, 863b; ix, 16a, 895a; s, 62b, 328a
Hilāl b. Abī Hilāl al-Ḥimṣī (883) ix, 481a; s, 412a
Hilāl b. al-Aḥwāz al-Tamīmī (720) iv, 535a; vi, 954b
Hilāl b. Asʿar (700) vi, 954b
Hilāl b. Badr i, 512b; iii, 258b; ix, 295b, 727a
Hilāl b. Mardanīsh i, 161a; iii, 865a
Hilāl b. al-Muḥassin b. Ibrāhīm al-Ṣābiʾ (1056) i, 1354a, 1356b; ii, 80a; iii, 46a, 344a, **387b**, 741b; v, 624b; vi, 520b, 522a; viii, 674b
Hilāl b. Umayya v, 730b
al-Hilālī, Abu ʾl-Abbās al-Sidjilmāssī (1761) v, 647b; s, **370a**
Hilālī, Badr al-Dīn (1529) i, 1301b; iii, **388a**; s, 46b
Ḥilf iii, **388b**; v, 581a, b, 596b
Ḥilf al-Fuḍūl i, 44b, 110a; iii, **389a**; v, 435a; vi, 137b, 145a, b, 146a
Ḥilla, Banū iii, 578a
al-Ḥilla i, 684a; iii, **389b**; v, 34a; vi, 64b, 270b, 966a; vii, 297b; viii, 716a; s, 179a, 326a
al-Ḥillī, Djamāl al-Dīn Ḥasan b. Yūsuf (ʿAllāma-i Ḥillī) (1325) ii, 774a; iii, **390a**, 1152a; iv, 277b, 762b; vi, 13a, 549a, b; vii, 132a, 297b, 417b, 1043b; viii, 777b; s, 56b, 380a
al-Ḥillī, Muʿizz al-Dīn Muḥammad (1891) x, 135b
al-Ḥillī, Nadjm al-Dīn Djaʿfār b. al-Ḥasan (Muḥaḳḳiḳ-i awwal) (1277) iii, **390b**; vi, 549a; vii, 297b; viii, 777b
al-Ḥillī, Naṣīr al-Dīn al-Kāshānī s, 364a
al-Ḥillī, Niʿmat Allāh (1533) viii, 778a
al-Ḥillī, Ṣafī al-Dīn → Ṣafī al-Dīn al-Ḥillī
al-Ḥillī, Shumaym (1204) iii, 111a, 221b; vi, 352a; ix, **501a**; xi, 265b
al-Ḥillī, Taḳī al-Dīn Ḥasan iii, 1152a
al-Ḥillī al-Wāsiṭī vi, 434a
Ḥilm ii, 536a; iii, **390b**; v, 435a
Hilmand i, 222a; iii, **392a**; v, 690b, 868a; s, 367a
Ḥilmī, Aḥmed Shehbenderzāde (1913) iii, **392b**
Ḥilmī, Ḥüseyn → Ḥusayn Ḥilmī Pasha
Ḥilmī, Refīq v, 483b
Ḥilmī, Tunalī (1928) iii, **393a**
Ḥilmī Bey (XIX) vii, 191b
Ḥilmī Efendi, Aḥmed (1878) iii, **392b**
Ḥilmī Pasha → Ḥusayn Ḥilmī Pasha; Kečiboynuzu Ibrāhīm
al-Ḥilmiyya (Cairo) vi, 75b
Ḥimā i, 442a; iii, 294b, **393a**; iv, 488a, 1143b; s, 304b
Ḥimā Ḍariyya i, 441a; ii, 159b; iv, 1144a; viii, 120a; s, 234b
Ḥimā Kulayb ii, 159b
Ḥimār iii, **393b**
Ḥimār al-Djazīra -> Marwān II (Umayyad)
Himatnagar ii, 1125a; iii, 1010a (see also Aḥmadnagar (Gudjarāt))
Ḥimāya i, 1144a; ii, 143b; iii, **394a**, **b**, 1113a
Ḥimṣ i, 57b, 85a, 119b, 609b, 1125a; ii, 590b; iii, **397a**, 1118b; vi, 139a, 221a, 321b, 322a, b, 406a, 506a, 545a, b, 578a, 580a, 623b, 648a; s, 154a, 162b
– buildings iii, 401a, b, 402a
Ḥimṣ, battle of (1280) iii, **402b**
Ḥimṣ (Morocco) vi, 293a
al-Ḥimsī, ʿAbd al-Masīḥ b. ʿAbd Allāh b. Nāʿima (IX) x, 954b; xi, 261b
Hīmū → Hēmū
Ḥimyar xi, 379a (see also *s.v.* Yaman)
Ḥimyar (language) i, 564a; iii, 124b
Ḥimyar, Banū i, 195a, 544b, 1259b; ii, 223a, 244a; iii, 52a; iv, 448a; v, 119a, 120b, 315a; ix, 7a; s, 337b

Ḥimyar b. Sabaʾ vi, 565b
al-Ḥimyarī → Ibn ʿAbd al-Munʿim; al-Sayyid al-Ḥimyarī; Nashwān b. Saʿīd
al-Ḥimyarī, Abu 'l-Walīd Ismāʿīl b. Āmir (1048) vii, 528a, 964a, 1046a, b
al-Ḥimyarī, ʿAlī b. Nashwān b. Saʿīd vi, 433b
al-Ḥimyarī, Ṣāliḥ b. Manṣūr (VIII) vii, 941a; viii, 522a
Hinā, Banū iii, **403b**, 537b; vi, 735a; s, 355a, b; viii, 85b
Ḥināṭa iii, **403b**
Hināwī → Hinā, Banū
Hind (India) i, 91a, 172a, 177b, 287b, 295b, 435b, 978b, 1068b; ii, 119b, 336a, 566a, 1084a; iii, 198b, **404b**, 481a; iv, 170a-b; v, 562a, 888a; vi, 49b, 131a, 368a, 439a, 532b, 688b, 804b; vii, 13b, 79a; s, 21a, 219b
– agriculture ii, 909a; iii, 407b, 410a; iv, 1055b; v, 883b
– architecture i, 830b, 1321b; v, 294b
– ethnography iii, 409b; vi, 489a
– geography ii, 576b; iii, 404b; v, 938b
– institutions ii, 426a, 437a; iii, 491b, 532a, 1204a; iv, 268a, b; v, 1080b, 1101a, 1134b
– languages, literature i, 808a; ii, 1092a; iii, 164a, 412a; v, 232a
– music iii, 452b
Hind bint Abī ʿUbayda iii, 984a
Hind bint ʿAwf b. Zubayr s, 92b
Hind bint al-Khuss iii, **454b**; iv, 472a; viii, 377a
Hind bint al-Nuʿmān b. al-Mundhir v, 777b; ix, 565b
Hind bint ʿUtba b. Rabīʿa (VII) iii, 152b, **455a**; iv, 332a; vi, 145b, 477a; vii, 145a; 264a; x, 944b
Hinda Gilan vi, 489b
Hindāl b. Bābur (Mughal) (1551) i, 228b; iii, **455b**, 575a, b; vii, 130b, 131a
Hindī iii, 1b, 413b, **456a**, 460b
al-Hindī → al-Shiblī, Abū Ḥafs
Hindī, Sabk-i → Sabk-i Hindī
Hindibāʾ ii, 1058a; s, **370b**
Hindiyya i, 405b, 406a; ii, 339b
Hindū i, 756b; iii, **458b**; iv, 794a
Hindūka al-Astarābādī (amīr) (XV) vi, 513b
Hindū-Kush i, 221b, 223a, 1009b; ii, 29a; iii, **459b**; iv, 409b, 410b; vi, 621a
Hindū-shāh b. Sandjar Gīrānī i, 522b; iii, 956a; vii, 404b
Hindūshāhīs iii, **460b**; v, 649a; vi, 65b; viii, 253a; s, 662a
Hindūstān → Hind
Hindustānī i, 1167a; iii, **460b**; v, 644b
Hindustānī Beg → Gūran, Shaykh
Hinglādj → Las-Bēla
Hinn iv, 489b; s, **371a**
Ḥinnāʾ iii, **461a**; v, 1b; s, 776a
Ḥinṭa → Ḳamḥ
Hintāta, Banū iii, 207a, **461b**; vi, 593b, 594a, 742a, 743a
al-Hintātī → ʿAmīr al-Hintātī
al-Hintātī, ʿAbd al-Wāḥid b. Abī Ḥafs (XIII) vii, 989a
Hippocrates → Buḳrāṭ
Ḥirāʾ, Ḥarāʾ iii, **462a**, x, 98b
al-Ḥīra i. 450b, 451b, 452a, 526a, 564b, 610a, 890a; iii, **462b**, 1254a; iv, 13b, 14a, 998b; v, 119a, 632a, b, 634a, b; vi, 145b, 633b, 660a; vii, 840b, 841a; viii, 121b; x, 90a, 191a; s, 91a, 272b
Hiraḳla → Eregli
Hiran Mīnār vi, 368b
Ḥirār → Ḥarra
Ḥirbāʾ iii, **463a**; s, 191a
Ḥirfa → Ṣinf
al-Ḥīrī, Abū ʿUthmān vi, 225a; ix, 811b
Hirḳil iv, 383b
Hirmis i, 247a; iii, **463b**; iv, 120b; v, 111b; ix, 667a; x, 500b; xi, 495b; s, 270a, 407b
Ḥirth iii, 537b; s, 355a, b
Ḥirz → Tamāʾim
Ḥisāb → ʿIlm al-ḥisāb; Muḥāsaba
Ḥisāb (theological) iii, **465a**; v, 224b
Ḥisāb al-ʿaḳd iii, **466a**
Ḥisāb al-djummal iii, **468a**; v, 224b
Ḥisāb al-ghubār iii, **468b**
al-Ḥiṣāfī, Ḥasanayn (1910) vi, 355a, 454b; s, 18a, **371a**
al-Ḥiṣāfiyya al-Shādhiliyya s, 371a
Ḥiṣār (fortress) iii, **483a**
Ḥiṣār (Mā warāʾ al-Nahr) iii, **483a**
Ḥiṣār (siege) iii, **469a**; iv, 798b
Ḥiṣār, Abdülhak Şinasi (1963) iii, 260a, **484a**; v, 197a
Ḥiṣār Fīrūza ii, 134a; iii, 168a, 225b, 442b, **484b**; v, 884a, 855b; vi, 50a; s, 206b
Ḥiṣār-i Muḥammad → Narwar

Ḥisba i, 26b, 344b, 477a, 629b, 752a, 898b, 972b, 977b, 1335a; ii, 228b, 519b, 1064a; iii, 140a, **485b**, 681a, 960b; iv, 245a, 1161b; v, 280a, 876a; vi, 136a
Ḥisbān viii, 1000a; x, 884a
Hi<u>sh</u>ām I, Abu 'l-Walīd, al-Riḍā (Umayyad, Cordoba) (796) i, 493b, 494a, 497b; iii, **495a**; x, 849a; s, 92a
Hi<u>sh</u>ām II, al-Muʾayyad bi-'llāh (Umayyad, Cordoba) (1013) i, 6a, 75b, 84b, 494a,b; ii, 389a; iii, 46a, 74b, 147a, 220a, **495b**, 746b, 755b; v, 1239a, b; vi, 222a, 431a, 852a; vii, 292b; ix, 740b; x, 848b; s,183a
Hi<u>sh</u>ām III al-Muʿtadd bi-'llāh (1036) i, 1309b; iii, **496a**, 542a, 938b; x, 584a
Hi<u>sh</u>ām, Mawlāy (Fīlālī) (1793) ii, 510b; vi, 595a, b; ix, 819b
Hi<u>sh</u>ām, Sayyidī (Sīdī, marabout) (XIX) vi, 743a
Hi<u>sh</u>ām b. ʿAbd al-<u>Dj</u>abbār iii, 819a
Hi<u>sh</u>ām b. ʿAbd al-Malik (Umayyad) (743) i, 142a, 613a,b, 1102b, 1292b; ii, 85b, 117b, 327b, 600b, 1026b; iii, **493a**, 747b; iv, 726a, 727a; v, 16b; vi, 139b, 230b, 428a, 623b, 676a, 740a, 829a; vii, 269a, 398a; s, 10a, 31b, 251b, 252a
Hi<u>sh</u>ām b. ʿAbd al-Malik al-Aṣ<u>gh</u>ar (800) vi, 140b
Hi<u>sh</u>ām b. ʿAbd Manāf iv, 838a
Hi<u>sh</u>ām b. ʿAmr al-Fuwaṭī (842) i, 4b; iii, **496b**, 1266a; vii, 259a, 784b; x, 83b; s, 89a, 226b
Hi<u>sh</u>ām b. ʿAmr al-Ta<u>gh</u>libī iv, 535a, 536a, 708a
Hi<u>sh</u>ām b. al-Ḥakam, Abū Muḥammad (kalām) (795) i, 128a, 850a; ii, 374b, 554a; iii, **496b**, 1037a, 1063a; iv, 182b, 271b, 692b, 1132a; v, 384b; vi, 737b; vii,259a, b, 312b, 645b, 646a; viii, 387b; s, 89a, 225b, 392a, 393b
Hi<u>sh</u>ām b. Ismāʿīl (Medina) (VII) i, 2b; vi, 139b, 140a; xi, 482b
Hi<u>sh</u>ām b. Ḳubayb b. Rusaḥ iii, 125b
Hi<u>sh</u>ām b. al-Mu<u>gh</u>īra, Banū vi, 140b
Hi<u>sh</u>ām b. al-Mu<u>gh</u>īra al-Ma<u>kh</u>zūmī (VI) vi, 137b
Hi<u>sh</u>ām b. Muḥammad al-Kalbī → al-Kalbī
Hi<u>sh</u>ām b. ʿUrwa b. al-Zubayr (763) ii, 887b; iii, 810b, 811a; vi, 107a; x, 29b; s, 661a
Hi<u>sh</u>ām b. al-Walīd b. al-Mu<u>gh</u>īra vi, 139a, b
al-Hi<u>sh</u>āmī (musician) v, 936b; xi, 351a; s, 64a, 183a
Ḥi<u>sh</u>na, Banū v, 317b
Hismaic x, 436b; s, 506a
Ḥiṣn iii, **498a**; iv, 1139b
Ḥiṣn b. ʿUmāra → al-Dīkdān
Ḥiṣn al-Akrād i, 1292b; iii, **503a**; vi, 322a, 579a, b, 581b, 582a; s, 204b
Ḥiṣn Arkanāʾ vi, 231a
Ḥiṣn Banī Ba<u>sh</u>īr vi, 221b
Ḥiṣn Daī s, 132a
Ḥiṣn Dikbāya → al-Dīkdān
Ḥiṣn al-Fara<u>dj</u> i, 165b; s, 724a
Ḥiṣn al-<u>Gh</u>urāb iii, **506a** (see also *s.v.* Ḥusn <u>Gh</u>urāb)
Ḥiṣn al-Ḳaṣr iii, 791a; s, 724a
Ḥiṣn al-Kawkab ii, 234b
Ḥiṣn Kayfā i, 664b, 665a, 666b, 804b, 1067a, 1068a; ii, 344b; iii, **506b**; v, 459a; vi, 626a; vii, 579a; viii, 133a, b; s, 250a
Ḥiṣn Liyyīṭ → Alīṭ
Ḥiṣn al-Mahdī iii, 501b; iv, 674b
Ḥiṣn Manṣūr → Adiyaman
Ḥiṣn al-Ṭāḳ iii, 501b; 502a
Ḥiṣn al-ʿUḳāb vi, 742b
Ḥiṣn al-Wād vi, 221b
Ḥiṣn Ziyād → <u>Kh</u>arpūt
Ḥiṣnī (ṣūfī) (1426) vi, 350a
Ḥiss iii, **509a**
Ḥiṣṣa, Ḥiṣṣe → Tīmār, Waḳf
Hissar → Ḥiṣār
Hīt ii, 947a; iii, **510a**; x, 82b
Ḥiṭṭān b. Kāmil b. ʿAlī (Munki<u>dh</u>, Banū) (1183) vii, 578b, 579b
Ḥiṭṭīn, Ḥaṭṭīn (1187) i, 798a, 946b; iii, **510b**; vi, 578b; s, 205b; xi, 234b
Ḥiwālids vi, 438b, 439a
Ḥiyāḍ → Ḥawḍ
Ḥiyal iii, 159b, **510b**; iv, 253b, 863a; s, **371b**, 632a
Ḥizām b. <u>Gh</u>ālib iv, 215a
Ḥizb, Aḥzāb ii, 224a; iii, **513a**
Ḥizb (political) ii, 429b; iii, **514a**
Hızır → <u>Kh</u>aḍir; <u>Kh</u>iḍr
Ḥizḳīl ii, 242a; iii, **535a** (see also *s.v.* <u>Dh</u>ū 'l-Kiṭ)
Hizzān, Banū i, 482b
Hlivne → Livno

Ḥmād u-Mūsā, Sīdī (1563) i, 35a; ii, 527a; iii, **535b**; v, 132b; vi, 350a
Ḥmādsha → Ḥamādisha
Ḥnayshiyya iv, 95a
Hobyo Sultanate (Somalia) ix, 717b
Hōbyōt (Mahrī) vi, 84b; ix, 439b; s, 339b
Hoca → Khwādja
Hochow v, 847b, 848a, 851a, 851b
Hodh → Ḥawḍ
Hodja Aḥmed Sulṭān i, 1076b
Hodna → Ḥuḍna
Hoesein Djajadiningrat (1960) s, **374b**
Hofuf → al-Hufūf
Ḥogariyya → Ḥudjriyya
Hoggar Ahaggar
Holkar, Djaswant Rāo (Marāṭhā) vi, 535b, 536a
Holkar, Malhar Rāo (Marāṭhā) vi, 535b
Holkar, Tukodjī Rāo (Marāṭhā) vi, 535b
Homs → Ḥimṣ
Honaz → Khōnās
Hor → Khawr
Horde iii, **536a**; viii, 174b
Hormizd I → Hurmuz I
Hormizd II (Sāsānid) (309) ix, 73b, 309b (see also *s.v.* Hurmuz II)
Hormizd III (Sāsānid) (459) iii, 303b; ix, 76a (see also *s.v.* Hurmuz III)
Hormizd IV (Sāsānid) (590) i, 939a; v, 378a; ix, 78b (see also *s.v.* Hurmuz IV)
Hormuz → Hurmuz
Hormuzd Ardashīr → al-Ahwāz
Hoshangshāh Ghōrī → Ghūrids
Hōt → Balūčistān
Hotin → khotin
Houri → Ḥūr
Hubal iii, **536b**; iv, 263b, 264a, 320a, 321a; v, 77b; vi, 373b; viii, 728a
Hubayra b. ʿAbd Yaghuth (al-Makshūḥ) vii, 591b
Hubayra b. Abī Wahb iii, 975b
Ḥubaysh b. Duldja (684) vi, 622b
Ḥubaysh b. al-Ḥasan al-Dimashkī (IX) s, **375b**
Ḥubaysh b. Mubashshir ii, 373b
Ḥubaysh, Muḥammad s, 411a
Ḥubb → ʿIshk
Ḥubbā ii, 551b; v, 77b, 78a, 519b
Ḥubus → Wakf
al-Ḥubūs, Banū iii, **537a**
Hūd (prophet) i, 169a, 828b, 1045a; iii, **537b**; iv, 448b; v, 421a; vi, 81a, b, 83b, 106a, 652b
Hūd, Banū → Hūdids
Hūd b. Muḥkim (IX) x, 86b
Hudā ii, 294a; xi, 26a
Hudā Shaʿrāwī Pasha, Madame (XX) iii, 360a; v, 740a; vi, 470a, 927b; xi, 26a
Hüdāʾī, ʿAziz Maḥmūd (1628) ii, 542b, 543a; iii, **538a**; iv, 191b, 972a; vii, 597b
al-Huḍaybī, Ḥasan iii, 518a, 1069a, b; iv, 160a
al-Ḥudaybiyya (628) iii, **539a**; iv, 320a; vi, 146b; vii, 371b; s, 131a
al-Ḥudayda (628) i, 709b, 1140b; iii, 327a, b, **539b**; vi, 192a; s, 30b
al-Hudaylī Ṣāḥib al-Kāra (1627) vi, 132b
al-Ḥuḍayn of Ūk s, 326b
al-Ḥuḍayn b. al-Mundhir (718) iii, **540a**
Ḥudayr b. ʿAmr b. ʿAbd b. Kaʿb (VII) vii, 123a
Ḥudayr b. Simāk (VII) i, 771b, 1283a; iv, 1187b; viii, 697b
Ḥudayr, Banū ix, 511b
al-Ḥudayrī, Shaykh ʿUthmān b. al-Shaykh ʿAlī viii, 18b
Hudhalī i, 115a; iii, 540b
al-Hudhalī → Abū Dhuʾayb; Abū Kabīr; Abū Ṣakhr; Saʿīd b. Masʿūd
Ḥudhayfa → ʿUyayna b. Ḥiṣn
Ḥudhayfa b. ʿAbd b. Fukaym b. ʿAdī → al-Kalammas
Ḥudhayfa b. Badr al-Fazārī ii, 873a, b, 1023a; s, 177a, b, 178a
Ḥudhayfa b. al-Yamān al-ʿAbsī (VII) i, 190a, 448b; iii, 512a, 1059b; v, 945b; vii, 189b
Hudhayl, Banū i, 149a, 545a; iii, 363b, **540a**; v, 763a; vi, 349a, 373b, 374a; ix, 908b; x, 3a
Hudhayl b. ʿAbd al-Malik, Abū Muḥammad (1044) ix, 307b
al-Hudhayl b. Hubayra x, 91b
al-Hudhayl b. ʿImrān al-Taghlibī (656) vi, 954a, x, 91b
Hudhayl b. Khalaf b. Lubb viii, 478b
Hudhud iii, **541b**, x, 91b, 777b, 778a
Hūdids (Banū Hūd) i, 1040b; iii, **542a**, 849b; v, 683a; vi, 222b, 339b, 577a; vii, 1020b; viii, 690a; s, 80b, 81a, 381b

Ḥudjarīyya i, 866a; ii, 507a, 1080a,b; iii, 545b, 902b; iv, 1091b, 1092a
al-Ḥudjāwī, Mūsā i, 949b; iii, 162a
Ḥudjaylān b. Ḥamad iv, 717b
Ḥudjdja i, 832b; ii, 97b, 98a; iii, 254a, **543b**; iv, 203b
Ḥudjdjādj (Morocco) iii, 339a
Ḥudjr, Banū vi, 649a
Ḥudjr b. ʿAdī al-Kindī (VII) i, 693b; ii, 89b; iii, 242a, **545a**, 1265b; v, 349a, 499b; vii, 266b, 400b, 521b
Ḥudjr b. al-Ḥārith i, 99a, 527a, 683b; ii, 785a; iii, 1177a; v, 118b
Ḥudjr Ākil al-Murār i, 526b, 548b, 1241b; v, 118b, 119a
Ḥudjra iii, **545b**
Ḥudjrat al-Aghawāt (Mecca) vi, 166a
Ḥudjriyya, Banū iii, **545b**; v, 895a
Ḥudjūr (Yemen) vi, 436b, 437a
al-Ḥudjwīrī, Abu 'l-Ḥasan ʿAlī (1072) i, 794b; ii, 55a; iii, 84a,b, 435b, **546a**, 570b; iv, 616b, 697a; vi, 225a, b
Hudna ii, 127b, 131a, 303a; iii, **546b**; vi, 727a, 728a, b
Ḥudna (Hodna) i, 749a; iii, **547b**; iv, 478b; s, 144b
Ḥudūd iii, **548a**
Ḥudūd al-ʿĀlam i, 5a, 967a; ii, 581a, 799b; iii, 406a; iv, 223b, 342a, 1079b; v, 107b, 1011a; s, **376a**
Ḥudūth iii, 1050b, iv, 509a; v, 96a, b
Ḥudūth al-ʿālam iii, **548a**
Huelva → Walba
Huesca → Washka
Huete → Wabdha
Ḥufāsh iii, **548b**
al-Hufhūf → al-Hufūf
al-Hufūf iii, 237b, **548b**; iv, 925b; vii, 282b; s, 234b
Hūglī ii, 976a, b; vii, 444a
Hui ix, 303b; x, 629a; xi, 346b
al-Ḥukamāʾ i, 95a
Ḥukaym b. Djabala ii, 415a; iii, 583a
Ḥukm i, 257a, 1170b; ii, 273a, 294a; iii, 306b, **549a**; v, 241b
Hukōm i, 742b, 746b
Ḥukūk iii, **551b**
Ḥüküm → Ḥukm
Ḥukūma i, 384a; iii, **551b**
Ḥükūmet i, 469a; iii, 552a
Ḥulā (ornaments) → Libās
al-Ḥūla (lake) iii, **568b**
Ḥūla (town) iii, **568b**
Hūlāgū b. Toluy b. Čingiz Khān (Mongol Īl-Khānid) (1265) i, 21a, 190a, 329b, 353b, 665a, 787a, 902b, 1086b, 1188a, 1314b; ii, 47a, 194a, 204b, 284b, 376b, 606a, 966a, 1056b; iii, 208b, **569a**, 1121a; iv, 30b, 349b, 482a, 521a; v, 455b, 491a, 598a, 826b; vi, 16a, 48b, 149b, 198a, 381b, 482a, b, 501a, b, 504b, 505a, 540b, 601a; vii, 230a, 753b, 984a, 990b
Hūlāgū (Lahore) iii, **569b**
al-Ḥulal al-Mawshiyya iii, **570a**
Hülegü, fief of ix, 860a; x, 44b
Ḥulm → Taʿbīr al-Ruʾyā
Ḥulmāniyya iii, **570b**
Hultāna, Banū vi, 742a
Hulu Sungai s, 150b
Ḥulūl iii, 102b, **570b**; iv, 283a
Ḥulwān (donative) → Inʿām; Māl al-bayʿa; Pīshkash
Ḥulwān (Egypt) iii, **572a**
Ḥulwān (ʿIrāḳ) iii, **571b**; v, 89b, 460b; vi, 336a, 410b, 539a; ix, 64b; s, 122b, 273a
Ḥulwān (tax) ii, 148b
al-Ḥulwānī, Shīʿī (X) vi, 727b
al-Ḥulwānī, Abu 'l-Fatḥ → Abu 'l-Fatḥ al-Ḥulwānī
Huma (Marāgha) vi, 502b
Humā (bearded vulture) iii, **572a**
Humā (poet) (1873) iv, 70a
Ḥumāḥim i, 181a
Humai iv, 567a
Humām, Nāṣir al-Dīn ii, 318a
Humām b. Yūsuf, Hawwāra Shaykh (XVIII) i, 1029a; iii, 300a; iv, 723a; vii, 179a, 420b, 445a
Humām al-Dīn b. ʿAlāʾ Tabrīzī (1314) iii, **572b**; vi, 609a
al-Ḥumās b. Ḳubayb iii, 125b
Humāy (Čihrāzād) iv, 809b
Humāy, Humāya → Humā
Ḥumayd, Banū i, 862b, 1289b; iv, 765a; s, 355b
Ḥumayd b. ʿAbd al-Hamīd al-Tūsī (825) i, 316a; iii, **573a**
Ḥumayd b. Ḥurayth al-Kalbī ii, 1023b; iv, 493a

Ḥumayd b. Ķaḥṭaba (Marw al-Rūdh) (777) vi, 618a
Ḥumayd b. Maḥmūd ii, 484b
Ḥumayd b. al-Ṭawīl (759) x, 29b
Ḥumayd b. Thawr al-Hilālī (VII) iii, **573a**; iv, 744b; vii, 864b
Ḥumayd (Ḥamīd) b. Yaṣāl (X) iii, 1036b; v, 1175b; vii, 641b
Ḥumayd b. Ziyād (922) vii, 906a
Ḥumayd al-Arķaṭ (VIII) i, 1297b; iii, **573b**
Ḥumayḍa, Amīr iii, 952b
Ḥumayḍa b. Muḥammad i, 1032b
Ḥumayḍa bint Saʿīd al-Barbariyya → Ḥamīda bint Saʿīd al-Barbariyya
al-Ḥumaydī, ʿAbd Allāh b. al-Zubayr (834) vii, 706a
al-Ḥumaydī, Abū ʿAbd Allāh (1095) i, 94b; ii, 72a; iii, **573b**, 790b
al-Ḥumayma iii, **574a**; vi, 427b; vii, 396a, 399b
Ḥumaynī i, 782a
Ḥumayr, Banū vi, 263a
Humāyūn (epithet) iii, 572b, **574a**
Humāyūn, Nāṣir al-Dīn (Mughal) (1556) i, 80b, 228b, 252b, 316a, 413a, 628a, 852b, 914b, 962a, 970a, 1135b, 1192a, 1218b, 1323b; ii, 120b, 155a, 259a, 264b, 271a, b, 494a, 498b, 973a; iii, 199b, 348a, 422b, 423a, 449a, 455b, 485a, 492b, **575a**, 633a; iv, 475a, 523b, 533b, 537a, 1022a; v, 598a, 1217a; vi, 47a, b, 52a, 126b, 128a, 131a, 310a, 407a, 410a, 456b, 525b, 693a; vii, 130b, 138b, 314a, 316b, 319a, 329a, 337b, 340b, 345a, 573b, 928b; s, 3a, 312a, 313a, b, 325a
Humāyūn Shāh Bahmanī (1461) iii, 421a, b, **577a**; iv, 908a; vi, 66b; vii, 458b
Humāyūn-nāma ii, 1134b; iv, 505a; vii, 481a
Ḥumlān (Yemen) vi, 438b
Hummām, Banū viii, 866a
Ḥumrān b. Abān (Baṣra) (780) i, 441a; vi, 878b, 920b; s, 661b
Ḥumrīn → Ḥamrīn, Djabal
Ḥums iii, **577b**; x, 160b; xi, 558b
Ḥumūd b. ʿAzzān s, 355b
Ḥumūm, Banū vi, 473b, 474a, b, 475a
Hūn i, 120a
Ḥunayn (Mecca) i, 9a, 12a; iii, 500a, **578a**; vi, 147a, 266a; vii, 373a, 389a
Hunayn (seaport) s, **376b**
Ḥunayn b. Isḥāķ al-ʿIbādī (873) i, 213a, 234a, 235a, 236a, 327a, 570a, 589a, 631b, 785b, 1014b, 1149b; ii, 60a, 300b, 349b, 358b, 402b; iii, **578b**, 977a; iv, 110a, 254b; v, 133b, 701b; vi, 204a, 376a, 637a, b; vii, 403b, 538b, 539b, 559a; x, 453a; s, 52b, 375b
Hungary (Madjār, Madjāristān) i, 267b, 291b, 398a, 698a, 1075b, 1163b; ii, 562b, 716a; iii, 1001a; iv, 591b; v, 373a, **1010b**
Huns (Khʷiyon/Hsiung-nu) → Hayāṭila
Hunza and Nagir iii, **581a**; s, 158b, 367b
Ḥūr ii, 447b, 449a, 1037b; iii, **581b**; viii, 271b
Ḥūrānī, Akram iv, 125a
Ḥurayḍa iii, 52a; s, 337b
Ḥurayfish al-Makkī iv, 1006b
Ḥuraymilā iii, **582b**
Hurayriyya iv, 838a; viii, 461b
al-Hūrīnī, Naṣr i, 596b
Ḥurķūṣ b. Zuhayr al-Saʿdī (VII) ii, 415a; iii, **582b**
Ḥurķūs, Banū i, 43b; vi, 954a
Ḥurma Wuld ʿAbd al-Djalīl (1828) vii, 624a
Hurmuz iii, **583b**
Hurmuz I (Sāsānid) (273) iii, 584a, b
Hurmuz II (Sāsānid) (309) iii, 584a (see also *s.v.* Hormizd II)
Hurmuz III (Sāsānid) (579) iii, 584a (see also *s.v.* Hormizd III)
Hurmuz IV (Sāsānid) (590) iii, 584a; vi, 633a (see also *s.v.* Hormizd IV)
Hurmuz (Hormuz) i, 8a, 535b, 553a, 928a, 942b, 1013a; iii, **584b**, 1121b; iv, 500b, 764b; v, 149a, 150b, 183a, 671b, 673a, 675b; vi, 50b, 735a; s, 115a, 129a, 234b
Hurmuz, Bā iii, **586a**
Hurmuz, Bā, ʿAbd al-Raḥmān b. ʿUmar (1508) iii, 586a; vi, 132b
al-Hurmuzān (644) iii, 582b, **586a**; iv, 97a; vi, 633b, 920a
Ḥurr iii, **587b**
al-Ḥurr b. ʿAbd al-Raḥmān al-Thaķafī (VIII) iii, **587b**; v, 510a; s, 81b
al-Ḥurr b. Yazīd (680) iii, **588a**, 609a; x, 407b
al-Ḥurr b. Yūsuf ii, 328a; x, 762b
al-Ḥurr al-ʿĀmilī, Shaykh al-Islām (1708) vi, 550b

al-Ḥurr al-ʿĀmilī, Shaykh Muḥammad b. al-Ḥasan (1693) iii, **588a**, 1152a; iv, 165b; vii, 132a; s, 57a
Ḥurr Riyā b. Yazīd iv, 638a
Ḥurrāk iv, 456b
Ḥurra-yi Khuttalī s, 125b
Ḥurriyya iii, **589a**, 1062b, 1063b
Ḥürriyet we Iʿtilāf Fịrkasị ii, 104b; iii, 520a, **594b**
Ḥurūf, ʿIlm al- ii, 376b, 734b; iii, **595b**
Ḥurūf al-hidjāʾ iii, 204b, 205a, **596b**
Ḥurūfī → Faḍl Allāh
Ḥurūfiyya i, 193a, 260a, 720b, 1099b, 1162a, 1248a; ii, 733a, 924a, 1095a; iii, **600a**; iv, 48b, 721b; v, 823a; vi, 226b, 228a, 549b
Ḥusām, Fakhr al-Dīn ii, 318a, b
al-Ḥusām b. Ḍirār → Abu ʾl-Khaṭṭār
Ḥusām al-Dawla → Malik b. ʿAlī al-Barānī
Ḥusām al-Dawla Ardashīr b. Ḥasan iii, 810a; iv, 516a; v, 662b; ix, 191b
Ḥusām al-Dawla Ardashīr b. Kīnakhʷār i, 1110a
Ḥusām al-Dawla al-Muḳallad (ʿUḳaylid) → al-Muḳallad b. al-Musayyib. Ḥusām al-Dawla
Ḥusām al-Dawla Shahriyār (Bāwandid) s, 363b
Ḥusām al-Dawla Tāsh ii, 748b, 749a; iv, 358a
Ḥusām al-Dīn → Timurtash
Ḥusām al-Dīn (Ḳapūdān) ii, 26b
Ḥusām al-Dīn, Malāmī Shaykh (1553) vi, 226b, 227a, b, 228a
Ḥusām al-Dīn b. Abī ʿAlī iii, 967a
Ḥusām al-Dīn b. ʿAlī Shīr ii, 989a
Ḥusām al-Dīn Abu ʾl-Shawḳ → Abu ʾl-Shawḳ Fāris
Ḥusām al-Dīn Alp Yörük iv, 738a
Ḥusām al-Dīn Čelebi (1284) ii, 19a, 394b, 395a; iii, **602a**; vi, 338b; ix, 298b, 858b
Ḥusām al-Dīn Ghulām Ḥusayn (1938) vi, 191a
Ḥusām al-Dīn Ḥasan (Marʿash) (1208) vi, 507b
Ḥusām al-Dīn Khān ii, 1124a
Ḥusām al-Dīn Luʾluʾ → Luʾluʾ, Ḥusām al-Dīn
Ḥusām al-Dīn ʿUmar (XII) viii, 671a, 749a; xi, 286b
Ḥusām Girāy i, 310b
Ḥusām Khān v, 783a, b
Ḥusām Khān (Gudjarāt) s, 335b
Ḥusām al-Salṭana (1848) vi, 715a
Ḥusām-zāde Muṣṭafā Efendi (XV) iii, 1243a; vii, 478b
al-Ḥusart, Maḥmūd Khalīl Shaykh x, 74a
al-Ḥuṣayb → Zabīd
al-Ḥusayma v, 80a; viii, 440b; s, **377a**
Ḥusayn, admiral → Amīr Ḥusayn
Ḥusayn I b. Uways (Djalāyirid) (1382) i, 66b; ii, 401b; iv, 584b; viii, 998a
Ḥusayn II (Djalāyirid) ii, 401b
Ḥusayn I, Shāh (Ṣafawid) (1722) vii, 222b, 318b; viii, 771a
Ḥusayn (Hidjāz) → al-Ḥusayn b. ʿAlī, Sharīf
Ḥusayn (Jordan) → Ḥusayn b. Ṭalāl
Ḥusayn, Mawlāy (Fīlālī) (1794) vi, 595b
Ḥusayn, Mullā i, 833a, b, 846b, 847a; v, 502a, 664a
Ḥusayn, Sharīf (1880) i, 106b; vi, 151a
Ḥusayn b. ʿAbd Allāh → Ibn Sīnā
Ḥusayn b. ʿAbd al-Raḥmān al-Ahdal → Ibn al-Ahdal
Ḥusayn b. ʿAbd Allāh Rawāḥī (1189) viii, 459b
Ḥusayn b. ʿAbd al-Wahhāb ii, 845b, 849a
Ḥusayn b. Abī Bakr al-ʿAydarūs i, 782a
Ḥusayn b. Abī Manṣūr al-ʿIdjlī (VIII) vi, 441b
Ḥusayn b. Aḥmad → Abū ʿAbd Allāh al-Shīʿī; Ibn Khālawayh
Ḥusayn b. Aḥmad al-Makramī (XX) vi, 190b
Ḥusayn b. Aḥmad al-Shahīd ii, 730a
Ḥusayn b. ʿAlī → Ibn Mākūlā; al-Maghribī; al-Ṭughrāʾī
Ḥusayn b. ʿAlī (Abū ʿArīsh) (XIX) vii, 515a
Ḥusayn b. ʿAlī (Ḥusaynid) (1740) i, 1110b; iii, **604b**, 635b; iv, 828b
Ḥusayn b. ʿAlī (Khayratīd) ii, 518a
Ḥusayn b. ʿAlī, Ṣāḥib Fakhkh (786) i, 402b, 551a; ii, 745a; iii, **615b**; vii, 646a
Ḥusayn b. ʿAlī, Sharīf/King (1931) i, 39a, 98b, 555a, 709b; ii, 289b, 429b, 531b, 572b; iii, 263a, b, 363b, **605a**, 1065b, 1066b; iv, 782b, 947a; v, 62b, 63a, 998a, 1055a, b; vi, 45b, 151b, 152a, 154a, 160b, 161b, 166a, 262a, 304a, 615a, b; vii, 764b; s, 3b, 4b, 293b

Ḥusayn b. ʿAlī b. Abī Ṭālib (680) i, 44b, 55a, 113b, 385a, 430b, 508b, 550a, 711a; ii, 843a, 848b, 912a; iii, 119b, 164b, 242a, 588a, **607a**; iv, 637a; vi, 77b, 147b, 537a, 604a, 605b, 608a, 609a, 610b, 675b, 737a, 958b; vii, 267b, 470a, 478a, 688b, 689a; s, 94a, 128a, 352a, 401a
Ḥusayn b. ʿAlī b. ʿAlī b. Muḥammad b. Djaʿfar al-Ḳurashī (1268) s, **62a**
Ḥusayn b. ʿAlī b. Ḥanzala → ʿAlī b. Ḥanzala
Ḥusayn b. ʿAlī b. ʿĪsā b. Mahān (IX) i, 437b; iii, 859a; vi, 333b
Ḥusayn b. ʿAlī b. Luhrasp i, 237b
Ḥusayn b. ʿAlī al-Marwazī (amīr) i, 278a, 1003a; iv, 661b; vii, 968b
Ḥusayn b. ʿAlī Pasha i, 236b, 554a, 1087a
Ḥusayn b. ʿĀlim b. Abi ʾl-Ḥasan Ḥusaynī → Ḥusaynī Sādāt Amīr
Ḥusayn b. Amīn al-Ṣayyād vi, 88a; s, 209a
Ḥusayn b. Asad Allāh (Marʿashī) (XV) vi, 514a
Ḥusayn b. Dadjn s, 81b
Ḥusayn b. al-Ḍaḥḥāk (864) iii, **617b**; iv, 1003a, 1004a, b; v, 778b; vii, 694b; ix, 453b; s, 25a
Ḥusayn b. Djaʿfar v, 292a; s, 352a
Ḥusayn b. Djaʿfar al-Nāṣir xi, 479a
Ḥusayn b. Djanbulāṭ ii, 443b
Ḥusayn b. Djawhar ii, 495b; iii, 79a, b; v, 623b
Ḥusayn b. al-Faḍl al-Badjalī s, 392a
Ḥusayn b. Fakhr al-Dīn ii, 635a, 751a
Ḥusayn b. Ḥamdān (918) iii, 126a, **619a**; iv, 493b, 494a
Ḥusayn b. Ḥamza iii, 156a
Ḥusayn b. al-Ḥusayn (1838) iii, **606b**
Ḥusayn b. Ibrāhīm al-Natīlī ii, 349b
Ḥusayn b. al-Imām al-Manṣūr bi-ʾllāh al-Ḳāsim (Zaydid) (1640) vii, 270a
Ḥusayn b. ʿImrān b. Shāhīn i, 212a; iii, 1176a
Ḥusayn b. Iskandar-i Shaykhī (Marʿashī) (1402) vi, 512b
Ḥusayn b. Ismāʿīl (IX) vii, 390a
Ḥusayn b. Ismāʿīl (XIX) vi, 901a
Ḥusayn b. al-Ḳāsim b. ʿUbayd Allāh (vizier) (932) i, 387b; ii, 178a; iii, 768a; iv, 1094a; ix, 594b
Ḥusayn b. Maḥmūd (XIX, Mozambique) s, 628b
Ḥusayn b. Maḥmūd, Khwādja (1339) vi, 505a
Ḥusayn b. Manṣūr → al-Ḥallādj
Ḥusayn b. Manṣūr b. Bāyḳarā, Mīrzā (Tīmūrid) (1506) i, 148a, 227b, 228a, 627b, 847b, 920a, 1082b; ii, 334a; iii, 177b, **603a**; iv, 34a, 48b, 536b; v, 59a, 389a; vi, 514b, 715b; vii, 90a; s, 423a
Ḥusayn b. Muḥammad → al-Rāghib al-Iṣfahānī
Ḥusayn b. Muḥammad b. Nāṣir, Sharīf (1640) vi, 566a
Ḥusayn b. Muḥammad Marʿashī, Abū Manṣūr (1030) vi, 517a
Ḥusayn b. Muḥammad al-Marw al-Rūdhī i, 893a
al-Ḥuṣayn b. al-Mundhir → al-Ḥuḍayn b. al-Mundhir
Ḥusayn b. Numayr al-Sakūnī (686) i, 55a, 810a; iii, **620b**; v, 119b; vii, 521b; ix, 826b; xi, 310a
Ḥusayn b. al-Ruḳād iii, 153a
Ḥusayn b. Saʿīd (Djabrid) s, 234b
Ḥusayn b. Saʿīd b. Ḥamdān iii, 127b, 129a; v, 923b
Ḥusayn b. Salāma (Ziyadid) (1012) i, 181b; ii, 517a; xi, 370a
Ḥusayn b. al-Ṣiddīḳ al-Ahdal i, 255b, 781a
Ḥusayn b. Sulaymān (Ṣafawid) (1726) i, 1068a; ii, 87b; iii, 348b, **603b**, 1102b, 1190b; iv, 37a, 104a, 1043b, 1092b; v, 493b, 494a, 1087a
Ḥusayn b. Ṭāhir al-Ṭāʾī iv, 188b
Ḥusayn b. Ṭalāl b. Amīr ʿAbd. Allah (Kāshimit) (1999) (Jordan) ii, 674b; iii, 264b; x, 886b; s, 7b, 9a
Ḥusayn b. ʿUmar (Ibn Dirham) (X) s, **386a**
Ḥusayn b. Uways → Ḥusayn I (Djalāyirid)
Ḥusayn b. Ẓāhir al-Wazzān iii, 79a
Ḥusayn b. Zikrawayh (Ḳarmaṭī) (X) iii, 619a; iv, 494a, 660b; viii, 831a
Ḥusayn Abū Muḥammad → Nāṣir al-Dawla Ḥusayn
Ḥusayn al-Afṭas (IX) vi, 148a
Ḥusayn Aḥmad Madanī ii, 55a, 205b; iii, 432a
Ḥusayn al-Ahwāzī iii, 123b
Ḥusayn Akhlāṭī i, 869a
Ḥusayn ʿAlā ii, 882b; viii, 512b
Ḥusayn ʿAlī (Dakhan) (1718) vi, 535a

Ḥusayn ʿAlī b. Fatḥ ʿAlī Shāh (Ḳādjār) (XVIII) vi, 484b
Ḥusayn ʿAlī Khān Bārha i, 1015b, 1025b, 1026a, 1219b, 1330a, b; ii, 379b, 804a, 810a; iv, 279b, 392b, 393a, 507b; s, 126b
Ḥusayn ʿAlī Mīrzā Farmān-Farmā b. Fatḥ ʿAlī Shah (Ḳādjār) (1834) ii, 812b; iii, 1106b, 1107a; vii, 675a
Ḥusayn ʿAlī Nūrī, Mīrzā → Bahāʾ Allāh
Ḥusayn al-Aṣghar i, 137a, 552a
Ḥusayn ʿAwnī → Akagündüz
Ḥusayn ʿAwni Pasha (1876) i, 285b; iii, **621a**; vi, 68b, 372b; vii, 599b
Ḥusayn Bādkūbaʾi, Sayyid s, 23b
Ḥusayn Beg b. Tay Bugha iv, 584a, b
Ḥusayn Beg Djald ix, 856b
Ḥusayn Bey (Egypt) ii, 321b
Ḥusayn Bey (Tunis) (1835) iii, 636a; iv, 828b; vii, 717b
Ḥusayn Djahānsūz → Djahānsūz
Ḥusayn Djāhid (Yalçin) (1957) i, 287b; ii, 474b, 475a, b, 497b; iii, **621b**; iv, 872b; s, 98a
Ḥusayn Djajadiningrat → Hoesein Djajadiningrat
Ḥusayn Djalīlī (1743) vi, 901a
Ḥusayn Djindji Khodja (1648) iii, **623a**, 983a, b; iv, 178b, 720a; vi, 1001a
Ḥusayn Dūst Khān i, 625a
Ḥusayn Efendi (Djindji Khodja) → Ḥusayn Djindji Khodja
Ḥusayn Efendi (Hezārfenn) → Ḥusayn Hezārfenn
Ḥusayn Fahmī Ṣādiḳ s, 299b
Ḥusayn Hezārfenn (1678) ii, 110a; iii, **623b**; viii, 564b
Ḥusayn Ḥilmī Pasha (1922) iii, **624a**; iv, 123b; vi, 74a
Ḥusayn Ḳāʾinī iv, 199b
Ḥusayn Kāmil b. Ismāʿīl Pasha (1917) i, 13b; iii, **624b**; vi, 166a; ix, 379a; s, 40b
Ḥusayn Ḳaraʾunas, Amīr (1369) x, 510b
Ḥusayn al-Khalīʿ → al-Ḥusayn b. al-Ḍaḥḥāk
Ḥusayn Khalīfa Pasha i, 2a, 1172a
Ḥusayn Khān (Patiyāla) i, 856b
Ḥusayn Khān (Ḳaytāḳī) ii, 87a; v, 296b
Ḥusayn Khān, Mīrzā (XIX) vi, 291b; vii, 455b; viii, 665b
Ḥusayn Khān b. Aḥmad Sulṭān Bayat (1835) vi, 202b
Ḥusayn Khān b. Manṣūr Beg v, 829b
Ḥusayn Khān b. Nādir Shāh vi, 202b, 203a
Ḥusayn Khān b. Riḍa Ḳulī Khān (XIX) v, 312a
Ḥusayn Khān Ādjūdān-bāshī i, 833b
Ḥusayn Khān Farmulī viii, 430b
Ḥusayn Khān Mushīr al-Dawla, Mīrzā (XIX) ii, 649b; iii, 555a; iv, 397b, 398a, 787a; v, 1086a; vi, 20b; vii, 1004a
Ḥusayn Kharmīl (Harā) iii, 471b
Ḥusayn Khaznadār (XX) vi, 177b
Ḥusayn Kiyā, Sayyid (Marʿashī) (XV) i, 237b; ii, 734b; vi, 512b, 513a
Ḥusayn Ḳulī Āḳā iv, 389b
Ḥusayn Ḳulī Khān (1655) i, 1068a
Ḥusayn Ḳulī Khān (Ḳādjār) (XVIII) iv, 104b, 391a, 392a; vi, 484a
Ḥusayn Ḳulī Mīrzā ii, 838b; ix, 476b
Ḥusayn al-Kurdī i, 1032b; ii, 572a; iv, 552b; ix, 135b
Ḥusayn Lawāsānī, Malik Sulṭān v, 663a, b
Ḥusayn al-Mahdī, Imām s, 22a
Ḥusayn al-Muṣaylihī vi, 627a
Ḥusayn al-Nadjdjār vii, 392b, 868a, b; viii, 122b
Ḥusayn al-Nāṣir s, 363a, b
Ḥusayn Niẓām Shāh I (1565) iii, 426a, **625b**, 1160b; viii, 75a
Ḥusayn Niẓām Shāh II (1589) ii, 921b; iii, **626a**; viii, 75b
Ḥusayn Niẓām Shāh III (1633) iii, **626a**; viii, 76a
Ḥusayn Nūrī Ṭabarsī iii, 588b
Ḥusayn Pasha → Silāḥdār
Ḥusayn Pasha, Agha (1849) iii, **628a**, 999b; v, 36a
Ḥusayn Pasha, ʿAmūdja-zāde (1702) i, 481a; iii, **626b**; iv, 233b, 657b; vii, 708a, 917b; xi, 267a
Ḥusayn Pasha, Deli (1659) i, 904b; iii, **626a**; v, 258b
Ḥusayn Pasha, Ḥādjdj ii, 402a
Ḥusayn Pasha, Küčük (1803) i, 948a; ii, 534b; iii, **627a**; v, 35b
Ḥusayn Pasha, Sharīf v, 808b
Ḥusayn Pasha b. Afrāsiyāb (1668) i, 236b, 1087a; vi, 112a
Ḥusayn Pasha Mezzomorto (1701) iii, **629a**; viii, 891a; x, 571a
Ḥusayn Raḥmī (1944) iii, 357b, 375a, 593a, **630a**; s, 64b

Ḥusayn al-Rayyī s, 252b
Ḥusayn Rushdī Pasha iii, 625a
Ḥusayn Ṣāḥib al-Shāma iii, 398a; iv, 660b; xi, 405a
Ḥusayn Sarḥān (XX) vi, 177b
Ḥusayn Sarrādj (XX) vi, 177b
Ḥusayn Shāh, ʿAlāʾ al-Dīn (Ḥusayn-Shāhī) (1519) i, 719b, 1015a; ii, 32a; iii, 14b, 422a, **631b**, 632a, 634b; vi, 47a; ix, 85b
Ḥusayn Shāh Arghūn (1555) i, 627b, 962a; iii, 575b, **632b**, 634a
Ḥusayn Shān Čak s, 167a, 325a, 366b
Ḥusayn Shāh Langāh I (1502) i, 1005b; ii, 47a; iii, 419a, **633b**
Ḥusayn Shāh Langāh II (XVI) iii, 633a, **634a**
Ḥusayn Shāh Sharḳī (Djawnpūr) (1495) ii, 270b, 271a, 498b; iii, 419b, 420b, 453b, 631b, **632a**; iv, 1136a; v, 783b; vi, 694a; ix, 355a
Ḥusayn Shāhīs (Bengal) i, 606a; ix, 728a
Ḥusayn Sirrī iii, 515b; s, 300b
Ḥusayn Sirrī ʿĀmir (general) s, 301a
Ḥusayn Ṣūfī (Khwarazm) (XIV) iv, 1064a; x, 89a
Ḥusayn-i Tabrīzī i, 777a
Ḥusayn Wafā ii, 433b
Ḥusayn Wāʿiẓ → Kāshifī
Ḥusaynābād iii, **634b**, 1163a
Ḥusaynābād (Lakhnawtī) v, 638a
al-Ḥusaynī, Mīr Ḥusayn (1499) vi, 114a; viii, 543a
al-Ḥusaynī, Muḥammad ʿAbd al-Ḥasīb (1654) vii, 94b
al-Ḥusaynī Dālān iii, **634b**
al-Ḥusaynī al-Ḥaḍramī, Abū Bakr (XVI) vi, 112a
Ḥusaynī Sādāt Amīr (1328) iii, **635a**, iv, 474a; vi, 73a, 834a
al-Ḥusaynī, Ṣadr al-Dīn (XIII) s, **378a**
Ḥusaynids (Medina) i, 402a, 403a, 552a; vi, 148a, 627b
Ḥusaynids (Tunisia) i, 281b, 863a, 1111a; ii, 463b; iii, 605a, **635b**
Ḥusaynīs iii, 523b; s, 67a
Ḥusayniyya-yi Irshād iv, 167a; vii, 762b; ix, 328b
al-Ḥusayniyya → al-Ḥasaniyya
al-Ḥusayniyya (oasis) vi, 160b, 163a
al-Ḥusayniyya (Mawālī) → Khashabiyya
al-Ḥusayniyya (Zaydī) v, 1237b; vi, 441b; ix, 507a
Ḥusayn-zāde ʿAlī s, 47a
Hüseyin Aywansarayī (XVIII) vii, 532a
Hüseyin Cahid → Ḥusayn Djāhid Yalčin
Hüseyin Raʾūf Bey (XX) vii, 229a
Hüseyin Pasha (beglerbeg) iv, 594b
Ḥüseyn Agha Ḳarā ʿOthmān-oghlu iv, 593b
Ḥüseyn Beg, Ḥamīd-oghlu ii, 692a; iii, 133b; iv, 210b
Ḥüseyn Beg Gradaščević viii, 520a
Ḥusayn Djāhid Yalčin (XX) i, 287b; iv, 930b, 933a; vi, 93a, 94b
Ḥüseyn Ḥilmī Pasha (1910) vi, 983b; vii, 206b
Ḥüseyn-i Lāmekānī (Malāmī) (1625) vi, 228a
Ḥūsh iii, **637b**; xi, 52b; s, 381b
Ḥūsh Rīḥāniyya ii, 1105b
Hūsh-Rübā ii, 999b
Hūshang (mythological king) iii, **637b**; iv, 445a; v, 377b; x, 110b; s, 263a, b
Hūshang b. Dilāwar Khān → Hushang Shāh Ghūrī
Hūshang Shāh Ghūrī (Mālwā) (1432) i, 924a; ii, 218b, 270b, 276b, 814b, 1125a; iii, 418a, **638a**, 1003a; iv, 219a, 513a; v, 1a; vi, 52b, 53a, 54a, 272a, 309b, 406b, 407a, b; vii, 278b, 279a, 957a
Hūshangābād vi, 309b
Hushaym b. Bashīr al-Sulamī (799) i, 272b; iv, 110b, 149a; vii, 662b
Ḥūshī → Waḥshī
al-Ḥusnī, Muḥammad b. Abi 'l-Khayr (XVI) ix, 180a
Ḥusn Djahān Khānum (Ḳādjār) (XVIII) vi, 484a
Ḥusn Ghurāb iii, 52a, b (see also *s.v.* Ḥiṣn al-Ghurāb)
Ḥusn al-Khātima iii, 1246a
Ḥusnī al-ʿArabī, Maḥmūd iv, 125a
Ḥusnī al-Zaʿīm → al-Zaʿīm, Ḥusnī
Ḥüsnü, Shefīḳ iv, 124a; vi, 94b; ix, 523b
Ḥüsnü Pasha iii, 357a
Hüsnümansur → Adiyaman
Husrev → Khusrev
al-Ḥuṣrī → Abū ʿAbd Allāh al-Ḥuṣrī
al-Ḥusrī, Abu 'l-Ḥasan (982) ix, 432b
al-Ḥuṣrī, Abu 'l-Ḥasan ʿAlī (1095) iii, **640a**; vii, 483b

al-Ḥuṣrī, Abū Isḥāḳ al-Ḳayrawānī (1022) i, 591a; iii, **639a**; vi, 108b, 109a, 438a, 606b; vii, 483b; s, 62b
al-Ḥuṣrī, Abū Saʿīd (IX) vii, 785a
al-Ḥuṣrī, Sāṭiʿ iv, 783a; x, 908a; s, 792a
Ḥussāb i, 1145b
Hussein Onn vi, 241b, 242a
al-Ḥūt → Nudjūm; Yūnus; Zīdj
al-Ḥuṭam b. Ḍubayʿa iv, 764a, 832b; vii, 797a; s, 694a
al-Ḥuṭayʾa (Djarwal b. Aws) (VII) i, 1297b; iii, 136b, 272a, 354a, **641a**, 941a; vi, 625b
Hutaym, Banū i, 528b, 546a; iii, **641b**; ix, 814b
al-Ḥuṭaym (Ḥadjar Ismāʿīl, Mecca) vi, 165b
Huwa Huwa iii, **642b**, 644a; v, 543b
Huwala i, 941b, 942b; ii, 181a; iv, 777b
al-Huwaydira → al-Ḥādira
al-Ḥuwayrith b. Nuḳayẓ b. Wahb ii, 842b
al-Ḥuwayṭāt, Banū i, 315a; ii, 626a; iii, **642b**; iv, 335a; ix, 316b, 374a; x, 885a
al-Ḥuwayyiṭ → Fadak
Ḥuwayza → Ḥawīza
al-Ḥuwayzī, ʿAbd ʿAlī b. Djumʿa al-ʿArūsī s, 57a
Huwiyya iii, **644a**
Ḥuwwārīn, Ḥawwārīn (Syria) iii, **645b**; vii, 268a
Ḥuyyay b. Akhṭab (VII) v, 436a; vii, 852b; viii, 817a
Hvar, island of s, 185a
Hyderabad → Ḥaydarābād

I

Ibād → Naṣārā
ʿIbād Allāh Beg ii, 83b
Ibadan iii, **646a**; xi,338a
ʿIbādāt i, 277a; iii, **647a**; iv, 154b
ʿIbādat Khāna s, **378a**
al-Ibāḍīyya i, 57a, 120b, 121a, 125a, 134a, 139a, 140b, 141b, 166b, 167a, 171b, 188b, 249b, 250b, 371a, 736a, 759b, 770b, 810a, 813a, 1028a, 1043b, 1053b, 1175a; ii, 129a, 140b, 170a, 359b, 368b, 592b, 1010a; iii, 95a, **648a**, 924b, 927b, 1168a; iv, 78a, 1076a, 1077a; v, 697b, 997a, 1230a; vi, 38a, 84a, 311a, b, 637a, 945a, 948a; viii, 112b; ix, 425a, 766a, 775a; x, 99b, 816a; xi, 212a; s, 15a, 88b, 90a, 225b, 337b, 338a, 355a, b
Ibʿādiyya (Abʿādiyya) ii, 148b, 149a; s, **379a**
Ibāḥa (I) iii, **660b**
Ibāḥa (II) ii, 136b; iii, **662a**; iv, 997a
Ibāḥatiya iii, 434a, **663a**
Ibāḥiyya → Ibāḥa (II)
Ibāḥiyyūn ii, 1031a
ʿIbāra iv, 114a, b; s, 753a
Ibb iii, **663b**; v, 1244b; s, 236a
Ibdāʿ i, 450a; iii, **663b**, 1051b; iv, 986b, 987a
Ibdāl iii, **665a**
Ibil i, 541a, 880b, 882a; ii, 1055a; iii, 32b, **665b**; iv, 676b, 677a
Ibiza → Yābisa
Ibkishtīn s, 159a, 161b
Iblīs i, 45b, 71b, 177a, b, 181a, 262a, 796a, 811b, 1093a; ii, 547a; iii, **668a**; vi, 217b, 218a; x, 1b; s, 136a
Ibn iii, **669b**
Ibn ʿAbbād → ʿAbbādids; al-Muʿtamid; Muḥammad b. Ismāʿīl; Ibn ʿIyād
Ibn ʿAbbād (Ṣiḳilliyya) → Benavert
Ibn ʿAbbād al-Rundī (1390) iii, **670b**, 720a, 722b; viii, 616a; xi, 532a; s, 404b
Ibn ʿAbbād al-Ṣāḥib Ismāʿīl (995) i, 59b, 119b, 126b, 590b, 712b, 1352b, 1354a; ii, 570a, 749a, b; iii, 487a, **671a**, 677a, 704a, 764b; iv, 61a, 524b, 862b, 1069b; v, 1028b; vii, 273a, 312a, 495a, 560a, 771b; viii, 71a; s, 4a, 13a, b, 24a, 38a, 118b, 124a, 393a
Ibn ʿAbbāda (1310) viii, 157a
Ibn ʿAbbādī s, 416b
Ibn al-Abbār, Abū ʿAbd Allāh (1260) i, 594b, 602b; ii, 308a; iii, 66b, **673a**, 704b, 762b, 803b, 904a; iv, 468a; vi, 216b; vii, 569a; ix, 339b, 350b; x, 585a; s, 382a, 388a
Ibn al-Abbār, Abū Djaʿfar Aḥmad (1041) iii, **673b**
Ibn ʿAbbās → ʿAbd Allāh b. al-ʿAbbās
Ibn al-ʿAbbās (Belabbès) (XIX) vi, 250b
Ibn al-ʿAbbās al-Ṣaghīr (XVI) ix, 20b

Ibn al-ʿAbbās al-ʿUbbādī xi, 140a
Ibn ʿAbbūd al-Fāsī (XVI) vi, 248b
Ibn ʿAbd Allāh → Ism
Ibn ʿAbd al-Barr al-Namarī, Āl (1070) i, 108a, 600a; iii, **674a**; vi, 264b, 281b; vii, 293a, 553a; s, 26b
Ibn ʿAbd al-Hādī → Yūsuf b. ʿAbd al-Hādī
Ibn ʿAbd al-Ḥakam, Abū ʿAbd Allāh (882) iii, **674b**; ix, 183a; x, 11b
Ibn ʿAbd al-Ḥakam, Abu ʾl-Ḳāsim (871) iii, **674b**, 775a, 1047b; vi, 411a, b, 412a, b, 413b, 944b; vii, 153b; viii, 829a; xi, 106a; s, 88a, 800a
Ibn ʿAbd al-Ḥakam, Abū Muḥammad (829) iii, **674b**; vi, 279a
Ibn ʿAbd al-Haḳḳ i, 903a
Ibn ʿAbd Kān, Abū Djaʿfar ii, 305a, 328a
Ibn ʿAbd al-Karīm al-Ragrāgī ii, 1007b
Ibn ʿAbd al-Malik al-Marrākushī (1301) iii, **675a**; s, 397a
Ibn ʿAbd al-Munʿim al-Ḥimyarī i, 156b, 280a, 488a, 1054b; iii, **675b**, 1033a; vi, 220b, 411b, 412b; viii, 612b, 613a; s, 171a
Ibn ʿAbd Rabbih (940) i, 590a, 600b, 601a, 667b; ii, 246a; iii, **676b**; iv, 1188a; vi, 603b, 904a; vii, 254b, 528b, 811b, 985b; viii, 376b, 499a, 873b; ix, 515a; s, 16b
Ibn ʿAbd al-Raḥīm (1285) vi, 580a
Ibn ʿAbd al-Raʾūf i, 157a; iii, 486b; iv, 735a; ix, 790a, b, 791a
Ibn ʿAbd al-Salām al-Marrākushī iv, 1134a
Ibn ʿAbd al-Ṣamad (XI) iii, **677a**
Ibn ʿAbd al-Wahhāb (1792) i, 554a, 593a, 942b; ii, 176b, 320b, 321a, 569a; iii, 162a, 295a, 582b, **677b**; iv, 717b, 925a; vi, 462a; ix, 903b; xi, 39b
Ibn ʿAbd al-Ẓāhir, Fatḥ al-Dīn iii, 679b, 680a
Ibn ʿAbd al-Ẓāhir, Muḥyi ʾl-Dīn (1292) iii, **679a**; iv, 464b, 965a; v, 22b; vi, 326a; ix, 180b
Ibn ʿAbdal → al-Ḥakam b. ʿAbdal
Ibn ʿAbdūn, Abū Muḥammad al-Fihrī (1134) i, 591a, 602a; iii, **680b**, 813b; vi, 606b; vii, 778b
Ibn ʿAbdūn Muḥammad b. Aḥmad al-Ishbīlī (XII) i, 156a, 157a, 390b, 1148b; iii, 486b, **681a**; vi, 124a; vii, 587a, 778b; s, 134a
Ibn ʿAbdūn al-Yāburī (1134) xi, 226a
Ibn ʿAbdūs al-Djahshiyārī → al-Djahshiyārī, Abū ʿAbd Allāh
Ibn ʿAbdūs, Aḥmad (1079) iii, **681b**, 973b, 974a; xi, 133b
Ibn ʿAbdūs, Muḥammad (XII) iii, **681a**
Ibn Abī ʿAbda (917) vii, 633a; x, 851a
Ibn Abi ʾl-ʿAḳb vi, 216b
Ibn Abī ʿAḳīl (Tyre) (XI) vii, 731a
Ibn Abī ʿĀmir → al-Manṣūr bi-ʾllāh (Almanzor)
Ibn Abi ʾl-Ashʿath (X) s, 271b, **379b**
Ibn Abi ʾl-ʿAshshār (X) ix, 846b
Ibn Abī ʿAṣrūn, Sharaf al-Dīn al-Mawṣilī (1189) i, 766a; iii, 87a, 120b, **681b**; vi, 380b
Ibn Abī ʿAtīḳ iii, **682a**; vii, 857b
Ibn Abi ʾl-ʿAwdjāʾ (772) i, 1081a; iii, **682b**
Ibn Abī ʿAwn (933) iii, **683**a; vii, 528a; xi, 153b
Ibn Abī ʿAzafa → ʿAzafī
Ibn Abi ʾl-ʿAzāḳir → Muḥammad b. ʿAlī al-Shalmaghānī
Ibn Abi ʾl-Baghl → Muḥammad b. Yaḥyā
Ibn Abi ʾl-Bayān (1236) i, 1224b; iii, **683a**, 749b; v, 251b
Ibn Abī Dabbūs iii, 67a; iv, 338a
Ibn Abī Dalīm (962) vi, 280a
Ibn Abi ʾl-Dam iii, **683b**, 967a
Ibn Abī Dāʾūd v, 406a, 804a
Ibn Abī Dīnār al-Ḳayrawānī (XVII) iii, **683b**; vi, 840b
Ibn Abi ʾl-Ḍiyāf (1874) iii, **684a**
Ibn Abi ʾl-Djawād (ḳāḍī) (849) viii, 844b
Ibn Abī Djumʿa → Kuthayyir
Ibn Abī Djumhūr al-Aḥsāʾī (XV) iv, 278a; s, **380a**
Ibn Abī Duʾād → Aḥmad b. Abī Duʾād
Ibn Abi ʾl-Dumayna → al-Hamdānī
Ibn Abi ʾl-Dunyā, Abū Bakr al-Baghdādī (894) i, 326a, 590a; iii, **684a**, 922b; iv, 212a; vi, 214b; x, 33a; s, 670a
Ibn Abi ʾl-Fawāris vi, 438b
Ibn Abī Ghudda iv, 509b, 510b
Ibn Abī Ḥadīd (1926) vi, 957a
Ibn Abi ʾl-Ḥadīd (1257) iii, **684b**; vii, 784a, 904a, 1043b; ix, 114a, 819a; s, 25b
Ibn Abī Ḥadjala, Aḥmad b. Yaḥyā al-Tilimsānī (1375) iii, **686a**, 1135a; vi, 111b; ix, 367b

Ibn Abī Ḥaṣīna (1065) iii, **686b**; v, 935a
Ibn Abī Ḥātim al-Rāzī → Abū Muḥammad al-Rāzī
Ibn Abi 'l-Ḥawwārī (IX) vi, 569b
Ibn Abī Ḥudhayfa → Muḥammad b. Abī Ḥudhayfa
Ibn Abī Hurayra (956) ix, 187b
Ibn Abī Ḥuṣayna → Ibn Abī Ḥaṣīna
Ibn Abi 'l-Iṣbaʿ (1256) v, 840a; vii, 491a; viii, 427a; x, 450b
Ibn Abī Khālid s, 112a
Ibn Abi 'l-Khayr → Abū Saʿīd b. Abi 'l-Khayr
Ibn Abī Khaythama (892) iii, **687a**, 803b; vii, 649a
Ibn Abī Khāzim → Bishr b. Abī Khāzim
Ibn Abi 'l-Khinzīr ix, 585a
Ibn Abī Khinzīr, Āl (X) viii, 52b
Ibn Abi 'l-Khiṣāl (XI) vii, 587a
Ibn Abī Ḳuḥāfa → Abū Ḳuḥafa b. ʿĀmir
Ibn Abī Laylā, Muḥammad (ḳāḍī) (765) i, 123b; ii, 232a; iii, **687a**, 938a; v, 711b; viii, 388a
Ibn Abī Laylā al-Akbar (VII) iii, 155a, **687a**
Ibn Abi 'l-Layth iv, 289b; vii, 4a, 5a
Ibn Abī Madyan (XVI) ix, 20b
Ibn Abī Muslim → Yazīd b. Abī Muslim
Ibn Abi 'l-Rabīʿ ii, 743b, 744a; iii, 741a; iv, 355b; x, 584b, 607b
Ibn Abī Rabīʿa → ʿUmar b. Abī Rabīʿa
Ibn Abī Randaḳa al-Ṭurṭūshī → al-Ṭurṭūshī
Ibn Abi 'l-Ridjāl, Abu 'l-Ḥasan ʿAlī al-Ḳayrawānī (XI) iii, **688a**, 902b, 936a; iv, 830b; vii, 483b; viii, 108b
Ibn Abi 'l-Ridjāl, Aḥmad (1092) iii, **688b**
Ibn Abi 'l-Sādj → Muḥammad b. Abi 'l-Sādj
Ibn Abī Saʿīd al-Mawṣilī vi, 902b
Ibn Abī Saʿīd ʿUthmān b. Saʿīd al-Mawṣilī (X) vi, 637b
Ibn Abi 'l-Ṣaḳr → Muḥammad b. ʿAlī b. ʿUmar
Ibn Abi 'l-Ṣalt → Umayya b. Abi 'l-Ṣalt
Ibn Abi 'l-Samḥ → Mālik b. Abi 'l-Samḥ
Ibn Abī Sarḥ → ʿAbd Allāh b. Saʿd
Ibn Abī Shanab (1929) iii, **689a**
Ibn Abī Sharīf, Kamāl al-Din v, 333a
Ibn Abi 'l-Shawārib iii, **691a**
Ibn Abī Shayba (849) i, 758b; iii, **692a**; vii, 663a, 691b; ix, 555b; x, 399a; s, 698a
Ibn Abi 'l-Surūr → al-Bakrī
Ibn Abī Ṭāhir Ṭayfūr (893) i, 108b, 591b, 751b, 1081a, 1082b; iii, **692b**, 757a, 820a; vii, 985b; viii, 537b; x, 14a; s, 122b
Ibn Abī Ṭalḥa (737) x, 86a
Ibn Abī Ṭayyiʾ (1228) i, 150a, 823a; iii, **693b**
Ibn Abī ʿUmāra, Aḥmad (1283) iii, 67a, 825b; iv, 338a, 416a, 828a; viii, 763b
Ibn Abī Usāma iii, 922b
Ibn Abī Uṣaybiʿa, Muwaffaḳ al-Dīn (1270) i, 213a, 214a, 235b, 247a, 571a, 594b, 803b; iii, 683a, **693b**, 737a; vi, 198a, 215a, 637b, 726b; viii, 103a; s, 25a, 45a, 154b, 290a, 313b, 379b, 391a, 397b
Ibn Abī ʿUyayna the Elder (819) iii, **694b**; vi, 333b
Ibn Abī ʿUyayna the Younger (VIII) iii, **694a**
Ibn Abī ʿUyayna → Muḥammad b. Abī ʿUyayna
Ibn Abī Yaʿlā → Abu 'l-Ḥusayn; Abū Khāzim
Ibn Abī Zamanayn (1009) iii, **694b**; vii, 538a
Ibn Abī Zarʿ (XIV) i, 290b; ii, 145b; iii, **694b**; v, 652b, 653a, 1209a; xi, 427a; s, 27a, 376b
Ibn Abi 'l-Zawāʾid → Sulaymān b. Yaḥyā
Ibn Abī Zayd al-Ḳayrawānī (996) i, 106a; iii, **695a**; iv, 341a, 830b; vi, 188b, 278b, 710a, 942b; vii, 387b, 473b, 538a; viii, 497b; s, 395a
Ibn Abi 'l-Zinād (790) s, 310b, **380a**
Ibn ʿĀbidīn, Muḥammad Amīn (1842) iii, 163b, **695b**; s, 172a
Ibn ʿĀbidīn, ʿAlāʾ al-Dīn (1888) iii, **695b**
Ibn al-Ādamī (920) iii, 1137a; vii, 210a; ix, 641a
Ibn Aḍḥā (ḳāḍī) (XI) ii, 1013b; vii, 563b
Ibn Adham → Ibrāhīm b. Adham
Ibn ʿAdhārī → Ibn ʿIdhārī
Ibn ʿAdī s, 400b
Ibn al-ʿAdīm, Kamāl al-Dīn (1262) i, 594b, 823a; iii, 693b, **695b**; v, 927b; vii, 115b; viii, 498b
Ibn ʿAdjarrad, ʿAbd al-Karīm i, 207a

Ibn al-Adjdābī, Abū Isḥāḳ al-Ṭarābulusī (1251) iii, **696a**; vi, 183b, 374b; s, **380b**
Ibn ʿAdjība (1809) iii, 262a, **696a**; s, 390b
Ibn ʿAdjlān ii, 1031b; ix, 226a
Ibn Ādjurrūm (1323) iii, **697a**; vii, 392a
Ibn al-ʿAdjūz → Alīsaʿ
Ibn al-ʿAfīf al-Tilimsānī (1289) i, 596a; iii, **697b**
Ibn al-Afṭas i, 242a; ii, 389a, b; x, 915a; iii, 680b
Ibn al-Ahdal i, 255b; iii, 711a
Ibn al-Aḥmar iii, **697b**; v, 1209a; vi, 310b, 311a, 604a; s, 112a
Ibn al-Aḥnaf → ʿAbbās b. al-Aḥnaf
Ibn al-Ahtam → ʿAmr b. al-Ahtam; Khālid b. Ṣafwān
Ibn ʿĀʾidh (847) iii, **698a**
Ibn ʿĀʾisha (Almoravid) i, 389b, 1337b; ii, 526b; iv, 672b; vii, 633b
Ibn ʿĀʾisha, Ibrāhīm b. Muḥammad (824) iii, **698b**; vi, 335a, 336a
Ibn ʿĀʾisha, Muḥammad (VIII) ii, 428b; iii, **698b**
Ibn ʿĀʾisha, Muḥammad b. Ḥafṣ iii, **698b**
Ibn ʿĀʾisha, ʿUbayd Allāh iii, **698b**
Ibn al-Akfānī al-Asadī, al-Ḳaḍī (1014) s, **381a**
Ibn al-Akfānī, Hibat Allāh b. Aḥmad (1129) iii, 930b; s, **381a**
Ibn al-Akfānī, Muḥammad b. Ibrāhīm (1348) vii, 30a; x, 456b; s, 45a, **381a**
Ibn Akhī Ḥizām i, 1149b
Ibn ʿAḳīl (1071) iv, 215b
Ibn ʿAḳīl, ʿAbd Allāh (1367) i, 126b, 1308b; iii, **698b**, 861b
Ibn ʿAḳīl, Abu ʾl-Wafāʾ ʿAlī (1119) i, 69b, 273b, 276b; iii, 103a, 160a, **699a**, 751a, 843a; iv, 172b, 513b; v, 234b; vi, 637a; vii, 296b, 566a, 755a; s, 194b
Ibn ʿAḳnīn, Yosēf iii, 542b; iv, 304b, 306a
Ibn Aktham → Yaḥyā b. Aktham
Ibn al-Aʿlam i, 87a; vi, 600b; x, 368a
Ibn ʿAlī → Muḥammad b. ʿAlī wuld Rzīn (Tāfīlālt)
Ibn ʿAlīwa (1934) iii, **700b**, 968a; iv, 95b, 326b; ix, 174a
Ibn ʿAlḳama, Abū Ghālib Tammām (IX) iii, **701b**
Ibn ʿAlḳama, Tammām b. ʿĀmir (896) i, 601a; iii, **702a**
Ibn ʿAlḳama, Muḥammad b. Khalaf ix, 533a
Ibn al-Alḳamī, Muʾayyad al-Dīn (1258) i, 406a; iii, 684b, 685a, **702a**; vi, 549b; vii, 727b; x, 746b
Ibn al-ʿAllāf (930) iii, **702b**
Ibn al-Aʿmā (1293) vi, 111a
Ibn Amādjūr iii, **702b**; vii, 28b
Ibn/Wuld al-Aʿmash (1695) vii, 1052b
Ibn al-ʿAmīd → Ibn al-Kalānisī; al-Makīn
Ibn al-ʿAmīd, Abu ʾl-Faḍl (970) i, 212a, 434a, 590b, 1352b, 1354a; ii, 305a; iii, 258a, 671a, b, **703a**, 1242b; iv, 1182a; vi, 539a, 600b; vii, 144a, 196b, 656b, 771a; viii, 598a; s, 72b, 124a, 263b
Ibn al-ʿAmīd, Abu ʾl-Fatḥ ʿAlī (976) i, 126b; iii, 258a, 671a, **704a**, 730a, 780b; v, 621a; s, 72b
Ibn al-Amīn Maḥmūd Kemāl → Inal
Ibn ʿĀmir, Abū ʿUmar (736) iii, **704b**
Ibn Amīr Ḥādjib (Mali) (XIV) vi, 421b
Ibn Amīra (1258) ii, 526b; iii, **704b**; viii, 573b; x, 131b
Ibn ʿAmmār → ʿAmmār, Banū; al-Ḥasan b. ʿAmmār; Ṭarābulus
Ibn ʿAmmār, Abu ʾl-Abbās Aḥmad (XVIII) iii, **705a**
Ibn ʿAmmār, Abū Bakr Muḥammad (1086) i, 6b, 7a, 602a; iii, 542b, **705b**, 904b, 963a; vi, 852b; vii, 633b, 766b, 768a
Ibn ʿAmmār (ḳāḍī, ʿAmmār, Banū) (1072) vii, 120b, 731a
Ibn ʿAmmār al-Kutāmī → al-Ḥasan b. ʿAmmār
Ibn ʿAmr al-Ribāṭī (1822) s, **381b**
Ibn Amsāyib (1768) ix, 20b
Ibn al-Anbārī → al-Anbārī, Abū Bakr Muḥammad
Ibn al-ʿArabī, Abū Bakr Muḥammad (ḳāḍī, 1148) iii, **707a**, 748b, 798b, 807b; iv, 290a; vi, 738a; x, 739b; xi, 521a
Ibn al-Aʿrābī, Muḥammad b. Ziyād (845) ii, 248a; iii, 686a, **706b**; iv, 111a; vi, 821b; vii, 305b, 306b, 402a, 831b; x, 433b; s, 38b, 122a
Ibn al-ʿArabī, Muḥyī ʾl-Dīn (al-Shaykh al-Akbar) (1240) i, 60a, 71a, b, 88b, 90a, 347a, 388b, 594a, 596a, 869a, 937a, 1092b, 1103a; ii, 296b, 376a, 377a, 450b; iii, 29a, 51b, 90a, 262a, 429b, **707b**, 798b,

871a, 910b, 952a, 1240a; iv, 49b, 114b, 813b; v, 166a, 433a, 544a, 614a, 1160b; vi, 73a, 216b, 247b, 280a, 351a, b, 354a, 570a, b; vii, 95b, 480b; viii, 715b, 753a; x, 317a; s, 93b, 208b, 293a, 313a, 363b, 364a, b, 380a
Ibn ʿArabshāh, Aḥmad b. Muḥammad (1450) i, 137a, 595a; iii, 309a, **711b**; iv, 506b; vi, 316a, 632b, 971a; vii, 710b
Ibn ʿArafa, Abū ʿAbd ʿAllāh al-Warghammī (1401) i, 1341a; iii, 68b, **712a**, 827b; vi, 281a, 728b
Ibn Arfaʿ Raʾs v, 112a; s, 270a
Ibn Arfaʿ Rāsuh s, 23a
Ibn al-ʿArīf, Abu 'l-Abbās Aḥmad (1141) ii, 100b; iii, **712a**, 732a, 816b
Ibn al-ʿArīf, al-Ḥusayn iii, **713a**; viii, 868b
Ibn ʿArrām (Miṣr) (XIV) vii, 171a
Ibn Arṭāṭ → Ibn Sayḥān
Ibn ʿArūs, Sīdī b. ʿArūs (1463) i, 679b; iii, 69a, **713b**; vi, 250a; s, 93a
Ibn ʿAsākir, Abu 'l-Ḳāsim ʿAlī (1176) i, 150a, 594b; ii, 126a, 283b, 993b; iii, **713b**, 767a; vi, 122b, 353a; viii, 518a
Ibn ʿAsākir, Amīn al-Dawla (1288) vi, 350b
Ibn Asbāṭ al-Gharrī (1520) viii, 986a
Ibn al-Ashʿath → Ḥamdān Ḳarmaṭ
Ibn al-Ashʿath ʿAbd al-Raḥmān (704) i, 77a, 690b, 1086a, 1344b; ii, 197a; iii, 40b, 247b, **715a**, 841b; iv, 15a, 356b; v, 119b, 349a, 1231b; vi, 311b, 946a; vii, 114b, 359b, 408b, 606a; viii, 799b; x, 843b; s, 26a, 358a
Ibn al-Ashʿath Muḥammad → Muḥammad b. al-Ashʿath al-Khuzāʿī
Ibn ʿĀshir, Abu 'l-Abbās (1362) iii, 670b, 701b, **719b**, 843b; s, 390b
Ibn ʿĀshir (1631) vi, 933a
Ibn al-Ashtar → Ibrāhīm b. al-Ashtar
Ibn al-Ashtarkūwī (1143) vi, 110b
Ibn ʿĀshūr (1698) iii, **720a**
Ibn Āshūr, Muḥammad al-Fāḍil iii, 720b; iv, 159b, 924b
Ibn ʿĀshūr, Muḥammad al-Ṭāhir (1868) i, 1314b; iii, **720b**; iv, 159b; vi, 635b
Ibn ʿĀṣim, Abū Bakr (1426) i, 427b, 602a; iii, **720b**, 948b; vi, 824b; vii, 392a
Ibn ʿAsḳalādja (985) vi, 431b
Ibn ʿAskar, Abū ʿAbd Allāh (1578) iii, **721a**; vi, 356a, b; ix, 190a
Ibn ʿAskar, Muḥammad b. ʿAlī al-Ghassānī (1239) vi, 220b, 221b, 222b; s, **381b**
Ibn al-ʿAssāl, Abu 'l-Faḍl iii, **721b**
Ibn al-ʿAssāl, al-Ṣafī Abu 'l-Faḍāʾil iii, **721b**; x, 18a
Ibn al-ʿAssāl, al-Asʿad iii, **721b**, 1205b
Ibn al-ʿAssāl, al-Muʾtaman iii, **721b**, v, 92b; ix, 848b; s, 396a, b
Ibn al-ʿAssāl, al-Amdjad iii, **721b**
Ibn al-Aswad iii, 712b
Ibn ʿAṭāʾ (al-Ḥallādj) vi, 569b
Ibn ʿAṭāʾ Allāh (1104) vii, 538a
Ibn ʿAṭāʾ Allāh (1215) vi, 279a
Ibn ʿAṭāʾ Allāh al-Iskandarī (1309) i, 351b; ii, 225a, b; iii, 670b, **722b**, 952a; ix, 172a, b; s, 387a, 404a, b
Ibn Aʿtham al-Kūfī (IX) i, 984b; iii, **723a**; vii, 400b; viii, 873b
Ibn al-Athīr, ʿAlāʾ al-Dīn (1329) viii, 802a
Ibn al-Athīr, Ḍiyāʾ al-Dīn (1239) ii, 826a; iii, 221b, 487a, **724a**; iv, 252a, 755b; vii, 978b; s, 177b
Ibn al-Athīr, ʿIzz al-Dīn (1233) i, 594b, 595a, 683a, 794a, 1115b; iii, **724a**; v, 821a
Ibn al-Athīr, Madjd al-Dīn (1210) iii, **723b**; vi, 350b; viii, 753b
Ibn ʿAṭiyya al-Muḥāribī ii, 744a; viii, 524b, 708a
Ibn ʿAṭiyya al-Numayrī xi, 181b
Ibn al-ʿAṭṭār al-Isrāʾīlī i, 344b; vii, 807b, 1041b
Ibn ʿAṭṭāsh, ʿAbd al-Malik (XI) i, 353a; iii, 253b, 254a, **725a**; iv, 101b
Ibn ʿAṭṭāsh, Aḥmad → Aḥmad b. ʿAṭṭāsh
Ibn Āwā iii, 309b, **725b**, 809a
Ibn al-ʿAwdjā → Ibn Abi 'l-ʿAwdjāʾ
Ibn ʿAwn Allāh (988) x, 159a
Ibn ʿAwn al-Asadī vii, 312b
Ibn al-ʿAwsadjī i, 762b
Ibn al-ʿAwwām (ḳāḍī) (1010) vi, 671a
Ibn al-ʿAwwām (XIII) x, 147a
Ibn al-ʿAwwām al-Ishbilī, Abū Zakariyyāʾ (1130) ii, 902a; iv, 1145b; vii, 202b, 203b, 906b; viii, 632b; s, 128b, 370b
Ibn Ayās → Ibn Iyās
Ibn al-ʿAydarūs → ʿAbd al-Ḳādir al-ʿAydarūs; Abū Bakr al-ʿAydarūs
Ibn ʿAyshūn (XII) viii, 819a
Ibn ʿAyshūn al-Sharrāṭ (1697) vi, 356b

Ibn ʿAyyād → Ibn ʿIyād
Ibn al-Azraḳ al-Fāriḳī (1154) iv, 348b; vi, 626b, 930a
Ibn ʿAzzūz, Sīdī Ballā (1789) vi, 354b; s, **382a**
Ibn ʿAzzūz al-Ḳusanṭīnī xi, 501a, b, 502a
Ibn ʿAzzūz, Abu ʾl-Ḳamr vii, 591a
Ibn Bābā al-Kās̲h̲ānī → al-Ḳās̲h̲ānī, Abu ʾl-ʿAbbās
Ibn Bābas̲h̲ād̲h̲ (XI) → Ṭāhir b. Aḥmad b. Bābas̲h̲ād̲h̲
Ibn Bābawayh (1179) → Muntad̲j̲ab al-Dīn
Ibn Bābawayh (I) (Bābūya), Abū D̲j̲aʿfar al-Ḳummī (991) i, 120a, 162b, 1216a, 1352a; ii, 848a; iii, 24b, **726b**, 1266a; iv, 182b; v, 363b, 370b; vi, 107a; vii, 312a, 758b, 786a; viii, 778a; s, 23b
Ibn Bābs̲h̲ād̲h̲ i, 131b
Ibn Bābūyā → Ibn Bābawayh
Ibn Bādīs, ʿAbd al-Ḥamīd (1940) iii, **727a**, 1003b; iv, 146b, 147b, 151a, 159a, 784b; v, 597a; viii, 765a, 902a
Ibn Bādīs → Muʿizz b. Bādīs
Ibn Bād̲j̲d̲j̲a (Avempace) (1139) i, 234b, 594a, 631b, 1250a; ii, 771a, 773b, 838a; iii, 302b, 542b, **728a**, 849b; v, 704a; vi, 87a, 204b; vii, 58a, 683b, 811b; viii, 534b
Ibn Badrūn (XII) iii, 680b; vi, 606b
Ibn al-Bag̲h̲dādī ii, 362a
Ibn al-Bāg̲h̲andī (925) vii, 706b
Ibn Baḥdal → Ḥassān b. Mālik al-Kalbī
Ibn Bahlūl → Abu ʾl-Ḥasan b. Bahlūl
Ibn Bahmāniyār (XI) viii, 72a
Ibn Bahrīz vi, 204b
Ibn al-Baʿīt̲h̲ (IX) iv, 88b; vi, 504a, b; vii, 778a
Ibn Baḳī (1150) i, 595b, 602a; iii, **729b**, 851b; vii, 811b
Ibn al-Bāḳillānī → al-Bāḳillānī
Ibn Baḳiyya (X) i, 11b; iii, 704a, **730a**, 780b; x, 435a; s, 398a
Ibn Bākūya i, 147a
Ibn al-Baladī iii, **730b**, 950b; vii, 726b
Ibn Balʿām, Judah iv, 306a
Ibn al-Balk̲h̲ī (1116) ii, 823b; iii, 1097a, b; vi, 493b; ix, 310a; s, **382b**
Ibn Bāna (Bānata) (891) ii, 1074a; iii, **730b**; s, 64a
Ibn al-Bannāʾ al-Bag̲h̲dādī (1079) iii, **730b**; s, 30a
Ibn al-Bannāʾ al-Marrākus̲h̲ī (1321) iii, 339a, **731a**; iv, 477a, 725a; v, 1209b; vi, 375a; vii, 137a; xi, 501b
Ibn Baraka → Abū Muḥammad b. Baraka
Ibn Barhān (1126) x, 461b
Ibn Barniyya al-Kātib (X) viii, 811b
Ibn Barrad̲j̲ān (1141) ii, 100b; iii, 712b, **732a**, 800b, 816b
Ibn Barrī, Abu ʾl-Ḥasan ʿAlī (1331) iii, **732b**
Ibn Barrī, Abū Muḥammad (1187) ii, 490b; 528a; iii, 818b, **733a**
Ibn Bas̲h̲kuwāl (1183) i, 156a, 594b, 602b, 1092b; iii, 673a, **733b**, 762b, 803b, 976a
Ibn Bas̲h̲rūh (1166) ix, 587a
Ibn Baṣṣāl, Muḥammad b. Ibrāhīm (1105) ii, 901a, b, 902a; vii, 906b; x, 147a
Ibn Bassām (IX) iii, **734b**
Ibn Bassām al-S̲h̲antarīnī (1147) i, 602a; ii, 838a; iii, 354b, 677a, **734a**, 789b, 807b, 934b; vii, 528a, 811a; ix, 308b
Ibn Baṭṭa al-ʿUkbarī (997) i, 1040a; iii, 159b, **734b**; iv, 172b, 183b, 469b; v, 10a; vi, 122b, 123a, 447a; viii, 497b; s, 17a, 362a
Ibn Baṭṭūṭa, S̲h̲ams al-Dīn al-Ṭand̲j̲ī (1368) i, 96b, 186b, 323a, 593b, 775a, 903a; ii, 391b, 586a; iii, **735b**; iv, 649a; v, 671a, 827a, 1126a; vi, 121b, 258a, b; s, 73b, 203b, 210b, 295b
Ibn al-Bawwāb, Abu ʾl-Ḥasan ʿAlī Ibn al-Sitrī (1022) i, 1354a; iii, **736b**, 887a; iv, 1122b; vii, 281b, 728a; viii, 151a; x, 408b, 409a; xi, 264a
Ibn Bayhas (IX) vii, 279b
Ibn al-Bayṭār (1248) i, 156a, 214b, 516a, 594b, 704a; ii, 349b, 1068a; iii, 267a, 693b, **737a**; iv, 627a; vii, 58a; s, 43a, 78a, 313b, 370b, 397a
Ibn al-Bazzāz al-Ardabīlī (1391) vi, 354b; viii, 801b; s, **382b**
Ibn Bībī al-Munad̲j̲d̲j̲ima (XIII) i, 1197b; iii, **737b**; viii, 705a, 972a; 59a
Ibn Biklāris̲h̲ (1100) iii, 754a; x, 346a; s, **383a**
Ibn al-Birr (XI) iii, **738b**, 818b, 859b; ix, 582a, 587a
Ibn al-Birzālī → al-Birzālī
Ibn Bis̲h̲r → ʿUt̲h̲mān b. ʿAbd Allāh
Ibn Bis̲h̲r i, 1312b; iii, 773a

Ibn Bishr al-Ashʿarī (874) vi, 829a
Ibn Bishrūn iii, 929a; v, 1109b
Ibn al-Biṭrīḳ → Saʿīd b. al-Biṭrīḳ; Yaḥya b. al-Biṭrīḳ
Ibn al-Buʿayth → Ibn al-Baʿīth
Ibn Buhlūl (930) iii, **739a**
Ibn Buḳayla i, 927b; iii, **739a**; ix, 84b
Ibn Bukhtīshūʿ ii, 894b; vii, 1040a
Ibn Bulbul → Ismāʿīl b. Bulbul
Ibn Burd → Bashshār b. Burd
Ibn Burd al-Akbar (1027) iii, **739b**
Ibn Burd al-Aṣghar (1054) iii, **740a**
Ibn Burghūth → Muḥammad b. ʿUmar ibn Burghūth
Ibn Buṭlān, al-Mukhtār (1068) i, 32b; iii, **740b**, 906b; v, 930b; vi, 110a, 638a
Ibn Crispīn, Moses iv, 305a
Ibn Daʾb (787) iii, **742a**; v, 1103a; ix, 827a
Ibn al-Dabaythī → Ibn al-Dubaythī
Ibn Dabba → Yazīd b. Miḳsam
Ibn al-Ḍaḥḥāk → Ḥusayn b. al-Ḍaḥḥāk
Ibn Dāhir → Djaysinh b. Dāhir
Ibn Daḳīḳ al-ʿĪd (1302) i, 96a; ii, 214b; iii, 900b; v, 515a; ix, 813a; s, **383b**
Ibn al-Daḳḳāḳ → Ibn al-Zaḳḳāḳ
Ibn al-Dāmād → al-Dāmād al-Astarābādī
Ibn Danān, Saʿdyā iv, 305b
Ibn Dāniyāl, Shams al-Dīn al-Mawṣilī (1310) i, 570b, 595b; iii, **742a**; iv, 602b, 1136b; vi, 114b; vii, 495a
Ibn Dāra → Ibn Sabʿīn
Ibn Darrādj, ʿAbd Allāh i, 1094a; viii, 799b
Ibn Darrādj al-Ḳaṣṭallī (1030) i, 592b, 601b; iii, **742b**, 936b; viii, 420a; xi, 401a
Ibn Darrādj al-Ṭufaylī → Ṭufaylī, Abū Saʿīd ʿUthmān
Ibn Dārust (1093) s, 29b, **383b**
Ibn al-Dawādārī (XIV) iii, **744a**
Ibn Dāwud, Abraham iv, 304b
Ibn Dāwūd, Muḥammad (909) ii, 183a, 1032b; iii, 100b, 102a, **744b**, 762b, 792b, 949a, b; vii, 527b; viii, 14b
Ibn al-Dāya (941) i, 990a, b, 1101b, 1156a; ii, 305a; iii, **745b**; x, 617a
Ibn al-Dāya, Madjd al-Dīn Abū Bakr ix, 411a (see also *s.v.* Madjd al-Dīn Abū Bakr)
Ibn al-Daybaʿ, Abū ʿAbd Allāh al-Zabīdī (1537) iii, **746a**; vi, 474b, 897b
Ibn Dayṣān i, 48a; ii, 199a, b
Ibn Dhakwān, ʿAbd Allāh (1000) iii, **746b**
Ibn Dhakwān, Abu ʾl-ʿAbbās Aḥmad (1022) iii, 739b, **746b**
Ibn Dhakwān, Abū Bakr Muḥammad (1043) iii, **747a**
Ibn Dhakwān, Abū Ḥātim Muḥammad (1023) iii, **747a**
Ibn Dhi → al-Hamdānī, Abū Muḥammad al-Ḥasan (al-Ḥāʾik)
Ibn Diḥya, ʿUmar b. al-Ḥasan (1235) ii, 1038b; iii, 702a, **747a**; v, 1119b; vi, 896a
Ibn Dīnār → ʿIsā b. Dīnār; Mālik b. Dīnār; Muḥammad b. al-Ḥasan b. Dīnār; Yazīd b. Dīnār
Ibn Dirham, al-Azdī s, **384a**
Ibn Dirham, Djaʿd (742) iii, **747b**, 1019a; iv, 926b; vi, 623a; x, 342a, 343b
Ibn Dirham ʿUmar b. Muḥammad (940) s, **386a**
Ibn Dirham Yaʿḳūb b. Ismāʿīl b. Ḥammād (845) s, **384b**
Ibn Dirham Yūsuf b. ʿUmar (967) s, **386a**
Ibn Dirham Yūsuf b. Yaʿḳūb b. Ismāʿīl b. Ḥammād (910) s, **385a**
Ibn al-Djadd, Abū ʿĀmir Aḥmad (1155) iii, **748a**
Ibn al-Djadd, Abū Bakr Muḥammad (1190) iii, **748b**
Ibn al-Djadd, Abu ʾl-Ḥasan Yūsuf (XI) iii, **748a**
Ibn al-Djadd, Abu ʾl-Ḳāsim Muḥammad (1121) iii, **748a**; ix, 506a
Ibn Djaʿfar (894) i, 141a; iii, **748b**
Ibn Djaḥdam → ʿAbd al-Raḥmān al-Fihrī
Ibn Djahīr → Djahīr, Banū
Ibn Djahīr, Abū Naṣr → Fakhr al-Dawla Muḥammad b. Djahīr
Ibn Djahīr, ʿAmīd al-Dawla (1100) ii, 384a, b; iii, 774b; vii, 693b, 755b; viii, 586b, 587a
Ibn Djahīr, Fakhr al-Dawla → Fakhr al-Dawla Muḥammad b. Djahīr
Ibn Djahīr, Zaʿīm al-Ruʾasāʾ (1113) ii, 384b; vii, 755b
Ibn al-Djahm → ʿAlī b. al-Djahm; Muḥammad b. al-Djahm
Ibn Djahwar, Abī Ḥazm → Abu ʾl-Ḥazm Djahwar

Ibn Djahwar, Abu 'l-Walīd i, 155b, 242a; ii, 389a; iii, 789a, 973b, 974a; v, 586b
Ibn Djalaf viii, 655a
Ibn al-Djallāl (XI) vii, 413a
Ibn Djamāʿa (1416) vii, 537a
Ibn Djamāʿa, Āl (XIV) iii, **748b**; v, 333a
Ibn Djamāʿa, Badr al-Dīn (1333) i, 439b; iii, 711a, 748b, 952a; iv, 949b; v, 333a; vii, 168a
Ibn Djamāʿa, Burhān al-Dīn Ibrāhīm (1388) iii, 748b, 749a; viii, 458B
Ibn Djamāʿa, ʿIzz al-Dīn (1366) iii, 699a, 748b
Ibn Djāmiʿ, ʿAbd al-Karīm s, 164a
Ibn Djāmiʿ, Abu 'l-Ḳāsim Ismāʿīl (IX) i, 118a; iii, **749b**, 996a; s, 26a, 116b
Ibn Djāmiʿ, Hibat Allāh → Ibn Djumayʿ, Hibat Allāh al-Isrāʾīlī
Ibn Djāmiʿ, ʿĪd → ʿĪd b. Djāmiʿ
Ibn Djanāḥ (XI) iii, **750a**; viii, 538b
Ibn Djarāda → Abū ʿAbd Allāh b. Djarāda
Ibn Djarrāḥ → Djarrāḥids
Ibn al-Djarrāḥ (1024) vii, 117a
Ibn al-Djarrāḥ, Muḥammad b. Dāwūd (908) i, 386b; ii, 197b; iii, 619b, **750a**; xi, 127a; s, 24b, 284b
Ibn al-Djaṣṣāṣ, Ḥusayn (Ḥasan) (927) iii, **750b**; v, 49b
Ibn al-Djaṣṣāṣ, Isḥāḳ iii, **750b**
Ibn al-Djawālīḳī → al-Djawālīḳī, Abū Manṣūr Mawhūb
Ibn al-Djawzī, Abu 'l-Faradj (1200) i, 69b, 70a, 274b, 275b, 594a, 595a, 802b; ii, 590b, 964a; iii, 160b, 700a, 735a, **751a**, 752b, 803a; vi, 105a, 266b, 350b, 351a, 352b, 353a, 354a, 634b; viii, 517a; s, 16b, 408a
Ibn al-Djawzī, Muḥyi al-Dīn iii, 161a, 752a
Ibn al-Djawzī, Sibṭ (1256) i, 150a, 595a; iii, 700b, **752b**; iv, 173a, 1099b; v, 1236b; vi, 243a, 354a; vii, 986a
Ibn al-Djazarī, Abu 'l-Khayr (1429) i, 594b; iii, **753a**; vii, 622a
Ibn al-Djazarī, Shams al-Dīn iii, 705b, **753a**
Ibn Djazla (1100) i, 1057a; iii, **754a**; iv, 331a; x, 454b
Ibn al-Djazzār al-Ḳayrawānī (1004) i, 803b; ii, 60a; iii, **754a**; iv, 830b, 906b, 1097b; viii, 822a
Ibn al-Djiʿābī, Abū Bakr Muḥammad b. ʿUmar (966) vii, 312a
Ibn al-Djīʿān (1480) vii, 174b; viii, 468a, 844b, 894b
Ibn al-Djillīḳī, ʿAbd al-Raḥmān b. Marwān (889) i, **85b**, 494a, 1092a, 1339a; ii, 1009a; vi, 568a; vii, 808a
Ibn Djinnī (1002) i, 143b; ii, 774b, 802b; iii, **754b**, 934b, 1128b; iv, 122b, 123a, 182a; v, 242b, 804b, 840b; vii, 772a, 914b; s, 19a
Ibn al-Djiyāb (1150) vii, 137a
Ibn al-Djuʿayd iv, 421a; vii, 591b
Ibn Djubayr, Abu 'l-Ḥusayn al-Kinānī (1217) i, 330a, 593b, 602b, 901a; ii, 143a, 228b; iii, 736a, **755a**; v, 1160b; vi, 106b, 148b, 195b, 380b; s, 205a
Ibn Djudʿān → ʿAbd Allāh b. Djudʿān
Ibn Djuhayr → Ibn Djahīr
Ibn Djuldjul, Abū Dāwūd al-Andalusī (994) i, 214a, 600b; iii, **755b**; iv, 254b; vi, 641a; s, 52b, 59b, 309b, 397a
Ibn Djumayʿ, Hibat Allāh al-Isrāʾīlī (1198) iii, 683a, **749b**; v, 251b; x, 455a; s, 386a
Ibn al-Djumayyil → Ibn Diḥya
Ibn Djuraydj , ʿAbd al-Malik b. ʿAbd al-ʿAzīz al-Makkī (767) vi, 263b; vii, 398a, 662b, 758a; ix, 7a; x, 29a; s, 18a, **386a**
Ibn Djuzayy (1355) iii, 721a, 736a, 755a, **756a**
Ibn Ḍubāra → ʿĀmir b. Ḍubāra
Ibn al-Dubaythī (1239) iii, **756a**; x, 791a; xi, 264b
Ibn Duḳmāk, Sārim al-Dīn al-Miṣrī (1406) iii, **756b**; vi, 411b, 653a; vii, 174b
Ibn al-Dumayna (VIII) iii, **756b**; iv, 1106b; vi, 477a
Ibn Durayd, Abū Bakr al-Azdī (933) i, 125b, 564a, 590a; ii, 1093b; iii, 512a, **757a**; iv, 123a, 524b; v, 608a; vi, 108b, 195b, 196a, b, 199a, 347b, 604b, 634a; vii, 26a, 262a; viii, 14b, 376a; s, 361a, 388a
Ibn Durustawayh (957) i, 185a; ii, 807b; iii, **758a**; iv, 501b; vii, 279b; x, 399a
Ibn Ezra, Mūsā iii, 770b; iv, 307a; vii, **642a**
Ibn Faḍl Allāh al-ʿUmarī (1349) i, 214a, 595a, 607a, 1139a, 1149a; ii, 303a, 305b, 732b; iii, 7a, 71b, **758a**, 1242b; iv, 431b,

510a, 742b; vi, 118b, 424a, 572a, 667b, 670a; ix, 869a; s, 395b
Ibn Faḍlān (X) i, 1305a, 1306b, 1307a; ii, 1107b; iii, **759a**; iv, 753b, 1063b, 1066a; vi, 724b; s, 265a, b
Ibn Fahd iii, **759b**
Ibn Fahd, ʿIzz al-Dīn ʿAbd al-ʿAzīz (1515) iii, **760b**
Ibn Fahd, Muḥibb al-Dīn Djār Allāh (1547) iii, **760b**
Ibn Fahd, Nadjm al-Dīn ʿUmar (1480) iii, **760a**
Ibn Fahd, Taḳi 'l-Dīn Muḥammad (1466) iii, **760a**; ix, 605b
Ibn Fahd, Taḳi 'l-Dīn Abū Bakr iii, 760
Ibn Fahd al-Ḥillī viii, 135a
Ibn al-Faḥḥām (1122) iii, **760b**; ix, 587a
Ibn al-Faḳīh (IX) i, 203b, 645b; ii, 580a, b; iii, 106a, **761b**, 1077b; iv, 131b, 1099a; vi, 640a; s, 56a, 265a
Ibn Falīta, Aḥmad b, Muḥammad b. ʿAlī (1363) ix, 565b
Ibn al-Fallāḥī ii, 858a
Ibn Fallūs → al-Mārdīnī, Abu 'l-Ṭāhir
Ibn al-Faraḍī (1012) i, 600b; iii, 733b, **762a**, 789b, 848a; vii, 400a; x, 585a
Ibn Faradj al-Djayyānī (X) i, 601a; iii, 734a, **762b**
Ibn Faraḥ al-Ishbīlī (1300) iii, **763a**
Ibn Faraḥ al-Kurṭubī (1273) iii, **763a**
Ibn Farḥūn, Burhān al-Dīn al-Yaʿmarī (1397) i, 280a, 594b; iii, **763b**; vi, 280a
Ibn al-Fāriḍ (1235) i, 60a, 89a, 596a, 816a, 1333a; ii, 363b; iii, **763b**; iv, 1006b
Ibn Farīghūn → Farīghūnids
Ibn Farīghūn, Shaʿyā (X) s, 376a, **386b**
Ibn Fāris, Abu 'l-Ḥusayn al-Lughawī (1004) i, 345b, 568a; iii, 111a, 672a, **764a**; iv, 524b; vi, 351a; vii, 914b; s, 346a
Ibn al-Farrāʾ → al-Baghawī
Ibn al-Farrāʾ, Abū Yaʿlā (1066) i, 273b, 435b, 1040a; iii, 159a, b, 512b, 699b, 730b, 735a, **765b**, 784b, 1165a; iv, 458b; vii, 927a; s, 195a
Ibn Farrūkh v, 1159b
Ibn Farrūkh, Rabīʿ s, 688b
Ibn Fasandjus, Abu 'l-Faḍl al-ʿAbbās ii, 827a
Ibn Fasandjus, Abu 'l-Faradj i, 11b; ii, 827a
Ibn Fasandjus, Abū Muḥammad ʿAlī ii, 827a
Ibn Fatḥūn, Abu 'l-Ḳāsim (1114) viii, 635a
Ibn Fāṭima ii, 586a; ix, 307b
Ibn Fattūḥ vi, 110a
Ibn Fendīn → al-Ifrānī, Abū Ḳudāma Yazīd
Ibn Firishte → Firishte-oghlu
Ibn Firnās → ʿAbbās b. Firnās
Ibn al-Funduḳ (XII) vii, 26b; viii, 81b, 82a, 996b; ix, 617a (see also *s.v.* al-Bayhaḳī, Ẓāhir al-Dīn Abu 'l-Ḥasan ʿAlī)
Ibn Fūrak (1015) ii, 125b; iii, **766b**; iv, 107b, 108a, 183a
Ibn al-Furāt (828) vi, 278b
Ibn al-Furāt, Abu 'l-ʿAbbās Aḥmad (904) i, 386b; iii, **767b**
Ibn al-Furāt, Abu 'l-Faḍl Djaʿfar (1001) ii, 136a, 495a; iii, **768b**, 840b; v, 953b
Ibn al-Furāt, Abu 'l-Fatḥ al-Faḍl (938) iii, 79a, **768a**; v, 953b; vi, 845b; xi, 584b
Ibn al-Furāt, Abu 'l-Ḥasan ʿAlī b. Muḥammad (vizier, 924) i, 386b, 835b; ii, 461b; iii, 100b, 133a, 619b, 739a, 750b, **767b**, 824a, 886b; iv, 265a, 1063b; v, 857a, 953a; vi, 352a, 498a, 518a; vii, 397a, 542a, b, 543a, 575b, 653a
Ibn al-Furāt, Abu 'l-Khaṭṭāb Djaʿfar (909) iii, **768a**
Ibn al-Furāt, Muḥammad (1405) iii, 693b, **768b**
Ibn al-Furāt, ʿUmar (818) iii, **767a**
Ibn Fūrradja (1141) vii, 772a; s, 652a
Ibn al-Fuwaṭī (1323) iii, **769a**
Ibn Gabirol (1058) iii, **770a**; iv, 304a; vii, 642b; viii, 475b
Ibn Ghalbūn iii, **770b**
Ibn Ghalbūn → Muḥammad b. Khalīl
Ibn Ghālib al-Gharnāṭī (1175) ii, 100b; iii, **771b**
Ibn Ghānim (1279) i, 1186a; iii, **772a**; vii, 909a; s, 830a
Ibn Ghānim (1596) iii, **772a**
Ibn Ghāniya → ʿAlī b. Ghāniya; Yaḥyā b. Ghāniya
Ibn Ghannām (1294) iii, **772a**
Ibn Ghannām, Shaykh (1810) iii, **772b**
Ibn al-Gharābīlī → Ibn Ḳāsim al-Ghazzī
Ibn Gharsiya, Abū ʿAmir Aḥmad (XI) iii, **773a**; vii, 292b; ix, 515a
Ibn al-Ghasīl → ʿAbd Allāh b. Ḥanẓala

Ibn al-Ghassāl vi, 606b
Ibn Ghaybī (1435) vii, 190b, 191a, 207b, 208a, 209a, b; viii, 347a; x, 769a, 839b; ix, 11b
Ibn Ghāzī, Abū ʿAbd Allāh (1513) iii, **773b**; vi, 890a
Ibn Ghāzī al-Ḳayrawānī vi, 712b
Ibn Ghidhāhum (1867) vii, 452a, 718a, b; s, **387a**; 482a
Ibn Ghiyāth (Ghayyāth), Isaac iv, 306a
Ibn Ghurāb (1406) iii, **773b**, 923a
Ibn Giḳaṭilia, Moses iv, 306a
Ibn Gīṭūn Wulā al-Ṣaghīr vi, 251b, 607a
Ibn al-Habbāriyya (1115) iii, 309a, 354b, **774a**, 799b, 1264b; iv, 504a, 506a; viii, 971b; s, 26b
Ibn al-Ḥabḥāb → ʿUbayd Allāh b. al-Ḥabḥāb
Ibn Ḥabīb, Muḥammad → Muḥammad b. Ḥabīb
Ibn al-Ḥabīb al-Andalusī (853) i, 600a, 718b; iii, 272b, **775a**; vi, 278b, 279a; x, 453b
Ibn Ḥabīb al-Dimashḳī (1377) i, 119a, 595a; iii, **775a**; vi, 351a
Ibn Ḥābiṭ → Aḥmad b. Ḥābiṭ
Ibn al-Ḥaddād (poet, 1088) iii, **775b**; x, 172a
Ibn al-Ḥaddād (ḳāḍī) iii, 898b
Ibn al-Ḥaddād, Muḥammad Amezẓiyān viii, 399b
Ibn al-Ḥaddādiyya vi, 477a
Ibn al-Hadhbānī, Naṣr al-Dīn (amīr, 1389) vi, 580b
Ibn Ḥadjar al-ʿAsḳalānī (1449) i, 275b, 594b, 595a, 791a, 1297a; ii, 159a, 215a, 743b; iii, 25b, 730b, **776a**, 818b; iv, 142b, 642b; vi, 36a, 194a, 280b, 353a, 785a; vii, 212b, 576b, 581b; viii, 458b, 517a; x, 934b; s, 88a, 388b
Ibn Ḥadjar al-Haytamī, Abu ʾl-ʿAbbās (1567) i, 965a; iii, **778b**, 856a; iv, 451a, 741b; v, 1235a; vi, 88a, 133a, 352b; vii, 458a
Ibn al-Ḥādjdj, Abū ʿAbd Allāh (1336) iii, **779b**; iv, 957b; vi, 214b, 654b, 896b
Ibn al-Ḥādjdj, Abu ʾl-ʿAbbās al-Ishbīlī (1249) iii, **779b**
Ibn al-Ḥādjdj, Abu ʾl-ʿAbbās al-Sulamī (1856) iii, **780a**
Ibn al-Ḥādjdj, Abū ʿAbd Allāh al-Sulamī (1857) iii, **780a**
Ibn al-Ḥādjdj, Abu ʾl-Barakāt al-Balāfiḳī (1370) iii, **780a**
Ibn al-Ḥādjdj, Abū Isḥāḳ Ibrāhīm iii, **780a**
Ibn al-Ḥādjdj, Ḥamdūn b. ʿAbd al-Raḥmān al-Fāsī (1817) vi, 249b, 356b; s, **387b**, 390b
Ibn al-Ḥādjdj, Muḥammad al-Ṭālib iv, 774b; s, 387b
Ibn al-Ḥādjdj, Shīth b. Ibrāhīm al-Ḳifṭī (1002) iii, **780a**
Ibn al-Hadjdjādj, Abū ʿAbd ʿAllāh (1001) i, 133b, 858b; ii, 552a, 1032b; iii, 354b, **780a**, 1264a; vi, 468b; vii, 771a; s, 26a, 398b, 723b
Ibn Ḥadjdjādj al-Ishbīlī i, 135b; ii, 901b
Ibn al-Ḥādjib, Djamāl al-Dīn al-Mālikī (1248) i, 721a; iii, **781a**, 861a; iv, 414b; vi, 278b, 279a; vii, 132a, 296b, 914b
Ibn Ḥādjib al-Nuʿmān (XI) iii, **781b**
Ibn al-Ḥaḍramī, ʿAbd Allāh b. ʿAmr (658) ii, 480b, 481a; iii, **782a**; vii, 265b
Ibn al-Ḥāf (Bal-Ḥāf) iii, 295a, 506b; vi, 81b
Ibn Ḥafsh iv, 722b
Ibn Ḥafṣūn → ʿUmar b. Ḥafṣūn
Ibn al-Ḥāʾik → al-Hamdānī
Ibn al-Hāʾim (1021) v, 333a; vi, 132b
Ibn al-Hāʾim (XII) xi, 462b, 501a, b
Ibn al-Hāʾim (Miṣr) (1412) iii, 1140a; vi, 543a
Ibn al-Ḥakīm al-Rundī (1309) iii, 833b, 834a, 909a; vii, 1022b
Ibn Ḥamādu (1231) iii, **782b**; s, 803a
Ibn Ḥamāma → Bilāl b. Rabāḥ
Ibn Ḥamdīn, Abu ʾl-Ḳāsim Aḥmad iii, 850a, 851b
Ibn Ḥamdīn, Muḥammad iii, 712b, 849a, b, 958b; iv, 290a
Ibn Ḥamdīs (1132) i, 592b, 602a, 1205a; ii, 1033a; iii, 138a, **782b**; iv, 1007a; v, 60b
Ibn Ḥamdūn (Ismāʿīli) vi, 439b
Ibn Ḥamdūn, Abu ʾl-Maʿālī (1166) iii, **784a**; vi, 108b; vii, 726b
Ibn Ḥamdūn Aḥmad b. Ibrāhīm (IX) iii, **783b**; vi, 728a; s, 17b
Ibn Ḥāmid (1012) iii, 159a, b, 765b, **784b**; v, 10a
Ibn Ḥammād → Ibn Ḥamādu
Ibn Ḥammādī (Relizane) (XIX) vi, 249b
Ibn Ḥammūd iv, 733b

Ibn Hamushk i, 161a; ii, 516a, 1014a; iii, 850b, 865a; iv, 116a, 665b
Ibn al-Ḥanafiyya → Muḥammad b. al-Ḥanafiyya
Ibn Ḥanbal → Aḥmad b. Ḥanbal
Ibn al-Ḥanbalī (1563) iii, 90b; vii, 136a
Ibn al-Ḥanbalī (1141) x, 951b
Ibn Hāniʾ al-Andalusī (973) i, 60b, 592a; ii, 855b, 861b; iii, **785a**; iv, 496b; vi, 728a; s, 62b
Ibn Ḥānish (ḳāḍī, 1328) viii, 157b
Ibn al-Ḥannāṭ (1045) iii, **786a**, 939b
Ibn al-Ḥanẓaliyya → Abū Djahl
Ibn Ḥarb → ʿAbd Allāh b. ʿAmr; ʿAbd Allāh b. Sabaʾ
Ibn Ḥarb → Muḥammad b. al-Mughīra b. Ḥarb
Ibn al-Ḥārith (971) x, 585a
Ibn al-Ḥārith al-Khushanī → al-Khushanī, Abū ʿAbd Allāh
Ibn Harma (VIII) iii, **786b**; iv, 1004b; v, 1156a; ix, 848a; s, 638a
Ibn al-Ḥasan al-Nubāhī → al-Nubāhī
Ibn Ḥashīsh (ḳāḍī, 1328) viii, 157b
Ibn Ḥassūn (ḳāḍī, Mālaḳa, 1182) vi, 222b
Ibn Ḥātim, Badr al-Dīn (1295) s, **387b**
Ibn Ḥawḳal (980) i, 96a, 488a, 1003a, 1041a; ii, 577b, 581a, 582a, 1002a; iii, 131a, 405b, **786b**; iv, 223a, b, 1079a, 1081a; v, 555a; vi, 120b, 313b, 639b, 640a; vii, 493a; s, 94b, 244b, 376b
Ibn Ḥawshab → Manṣūr al-Yaman
Ibn al-Ḥawwās (XI) ii, 553a; iii, **788a**, 956a; iv,733b; ix, 585b
Ibn al-Haytham (1039) i, 785b, 816a, 1102a; ii, 362a; iii, **788a**, 1135b; iv, 515b, 518a, 1059b; v, 397b, 536a, 703b, 1025b; vi, 376b, 377a, 450b, 637b; vii, 106b, 282b; viii, 102a, 560b; s, 412a, 413a, 414a
Ibn al-Haythamī i, 593a; iii, 856a
Ibn al-Ḥayy (1064) vii, 413a
Ibn al-Hayyabān iv, 270a
Ibn Ḥayyān, Abū Marwān (1076) i, 82b, 155b, 600b, 1040b; iii, **789a**; v, 1119b; vi, 221b, 431b; vii, 492b, 553a, 1042b
Ibn Ḥayyawayh iii, 922b; xi, 102b
Ibn Ḥayyūs, Abu ʾl-Fityān (1081) i, 1070a; iii, 686b, **790a**; vi, 539a
Ibn Ḥāzim → Muḥammad b. Ḥāzim
Ibn Ḥazm, Āl iii, **790a**
Ibn Ḥazm, Abū Bakr (1011) iii, **790a**, 939a
Ibn Ḥazm, Abu ʾl-Mughīra (1046) iii, **790b**, 901b, 938b
Ibn Ḥazm, Abū Muḥammad ʿAlī (1064) i, 84a, 147a, 265b, 414a, 427b, 497a, 590a, 600a, 601b, 865a; ii, 96b, 765a; iii, 308a, 744b, **790b**, 870b, 901b, 1019b, 1024a; iv, 113b, 142a, 272a; v, 703b, 704a; vi, 221b, 281b, 346b, 444b, 445a, b, 446a, b, 943b; vii, 55a, 293a, 553a; viii, 981a; s, 45a, 362b, 396b
Ibn Ḥazm, Abū Rāfiʿ al-Faḍl b. ʿAlī (1068) iii, **790b**
Ibn Ḥazm, Abū ʿUmar Aḥmad b. Saʿīd (1012) iii, **790a**
Ibn Ḥibbān (965) i, 1348b; iii, **799a**; viii, 516b, 836a
Ibn Hibintā iv, 810a; vi, 711a; viii, 103b
Ibn Ḥidjdja al-Ḥamawī (1434) i, 595b, 982b, 1109b; iii, **799b**, 1006a; vii, 1039b; x, 125a
Ibn Hilāl al-Ṣābiʾ → Ghars al-Niʿma Muḥammad
Ibn Hindū (1019) i, 236a; iii, 703b, **800a**; s, 72b
Ibn Ḥinzāba → Ibn al-Furāt, al-Faḍl
Ibn Ḥirzihim, ʿAlī (1163) i, 137b; iii, 732a, **800a**; vii, 587b; xi, 112a
Ibn Hishām, ʿAbd al-Malik (828) i, 158b; iii, 272b, **800b**; v, 41a, 1161b
Ibn Hishām, Abū Muḥammad ʿAbd al-Malik (833) vii, 361a; ix, 161a
Ibn Hishām, Djamāl al-Dīn (1360) i, 126b, 593a, 821b; iii, **801a**; iv, 414b; vii, 914b; s, 404b
Ibn Hishām al-Lakhmī (1182) v, 608b, 609b; vi, 196a; xi, 548b; s, **388a**
Ibn Ḥithlayn (XX) iii, 1067b, 1068a
Ibn Hubal (1213) iii, **802a**
Ibn Hubayra, ʿAwn al-Dīn al-Shaybānī (1165) vii, 406b, 679b, 726a; viii, 943b
Ibn Hubayra, ʿUmar (VIII) ii, 1023b; iii, **802a**, 1157b
Ibn Hubayra, Yaḥyā al-Shaybānī (1165) i, 122b; iii, 160b, 751a, **802b**, 1157b; iv, 912a, 942b; v, 623a, 1016a
Ibn Hubayra, Yazīd b. ʿUmar (Ḳaysī) (VIII) i, 16a, 103a, 107b, 123a; ii, 1023b; iii, 266a, **802a**, 1255a; iv, 447b,

728b, 1132b; vi, 345a, 427b, 624a, b; vii, 388b; x, 844a, 845a
Ibn Hubayra, Yūsuf b. ʿUmar iii, **802a**
Ibn Ḥubaysh (1188) iii, **803b**; iv, 468a; viii, 819a
Ibn Hūd → Hūdids
Ibn Hūd al-Māssī ii, 1009b; iii, 771b
Ibn Ḥudaydj → Muʿāwiya b. Ḥudaydj
Ibn Hudhayl, Abu 'l-Ḥasan ʿAlī (XIV) i, 594a; ii, 786b; iii, **804a**
Ibn Hudhayl, Abū Bakr Yaḥyā viii, 347b
Ibn Ḥudayr (al-Andalus) (X) vi, 431a
Ibn al-Humām, Kamāl al-Dīn (1457) iii, 164a; iv, 256b; vi, 848a
Ibn Ḥumayd → Sulṭān b. Bidjād
Ibn Ḥumayd al-Makkī iii, 162b
Ibn Ḥumayd al-Rāzī, ʿAbd Allāh x, 11a, b
Ibn Hurmuz (VIII) vi, 263b
Ibn Ḥusām (1470) iii, 114b; vi, 836b
Ibn Ḥusām Harawī vii, 754b
Ibn al-ʿIbrī (Bar Hebraeus) (1286) i, 214a; iii, **804b**; iv, 482a; vi, 231a, 502a; s, 314a
Ibn ʿIdhārī al-Marrākushī (1312) i, 157a; iii, 789b, **805b**; iv, 830a; v, 1209a; vi, 311b; vii, 584a; s, 389b
Ibn Idrīs (1201) vii, 297b; s, 534a
Ibn Idrīs, Abu 'l-ʿAlāʾ (1879) iii, **806b**
Ibn Idrīs, Abū ʿAbd Allāh Muḥammad (1847) iii, **806a**
Ibn Idrīs, Aḥmad → Aḥmad b. Idrīs, Sharīf
Ibn al-Iflīlī (1050) iii, **806b**
Ibn Igit (XII) i, 1249a; ii, 744b
Ibn al-Ikhshīd, Abū Bakr Aḥmad (938) iii, **807a**; vii, 312a; x, 14b; s, 12b, 13a
Ibn Ilyās s, 327a
Ibn al-ʿImād al-Ḥanbalī (1679) i, 594b; iii, 162a, **807b**; s, 267b, 381a
Ibn al-Imām (1155) viii, 819a
Ibn al-Imām al-Shilbī (XII) iii, **807b**
Ibn ʿInaba (1424) iii, **807b**
Ibn ʿIrāḳ, Abū Naṣr Manṣūr b. ʿAlī (1036) i, 1236a, b, 1237a; iii, **808b**; iv, 1182a, b; vi, 543a
Ibn al-ʿIrāḳī → Abū Zurʿa
Ibn ʿĪrs iii, **808b**
Ibn ʿĪsā → ʿAlī b. ʿĪsā b. al-Djarrāḥ
Ibn ʿĪsā → Muḥammad b. ʿĪsā al-Ṣufyānī
Ibn ʿĪsā, Maḥammad (1607) iii, **809b**
Ibn ʿĪsā b. Madjd al-Dīn i, 309b
Ibn-i Isfandiyār (XIII) iii, **810a**; vi, 745a; s, 357a
Ibn Isḥāḳ, Muḥammad b. Yasār (767) i, 158b, 588a; iii, 23b, 272b, 800b, **810b**, 1205b; iv, 370a; v, 1161b, 1162b, 1163a; vii, 283b, 361a; s, 87b, 358a
Ibn Isrāʾīl al-Dimashḳī (1278) iii, **811b**
Ibn al-Īṭnāba al-Khazradjī (VII) iii, **812a**
Ibn Īṭūwafat, Abū Ḥātim Yaʿḳūb b. Ḥabīb b. Midyan (XIV) vi, 311b
Ibn ʿIyād ix, 170b
Ibn ʿIyād (ḳāʾid) (XII) v, 631b; ix, 865a; x, 106a
Ibn Iyās (1524) i, 571a, 595a; iii, 206a, **812a**; x, 622a
Ibn Kabar, Abu 'l-Barakāt (1320) s, **388b**, 396a
Ibn al-Ḳābisī → al-Ḳābisī, Abu 'l-Ḥasan ʿAlī
Ibn Ḳabṭūrnu (Kabṭūrna), Abu 'l-Ḥasan iii, **813b**
Ibn Ḳabṭūrnu, Abū Bakr ʿAbd al-ʿAziz (1126) iii, **813b**
Ibn Ḳabṭūrnu, Abū Muḥammad Ṭalḥa (XII) iii, **813b**
Ibn al-Ḳaddāḥ iii, 922b
Ibn al-Ḳāḍī, Shihāb al-Dīn al-Miknāsī (1616) i, 96b; iii, **814a**; vi, 351a; x, 548b; xi, 15b; s, 223a
Ibn al-Ḳāḍī (Kabyle) → Aḥmad b. al-Ḳāḍī
Ibn Ḳāḍī Samāwnā → Badr al-Dīn b. Ḳāḍī Samāwnā
Ibn Ḳāḍī Shuhba, Badr al-Dīn (1470) iii, **814b**, 818a; iv, 641b; vi, 352a, 353a, 580b; ix, 493b, 494a
Ibn Kaḍīb al-Bārī iii, 1241a
Ibn Ḳādūs i, 440a
Ibn al-Ḳaʿḳāʿ al-Makhzūmī v, 997b
Ibn al-Kaʿkī, Shams al-Dīn (XIII) vii, 274a; viii, 987b
Ibn Kākūya → ʿAlāʾ al-Dawla Muḥammad b. Dushmanziyār
Ibn Ḳalāḳis (1172) iii, **814b**; iv, 967b; viii, 42b; ix, 587b
Ibn al-Ḳalānisī (1160) iii, **815a**; iv, 181a; vi, 243a; vii, 564a; s, 204b
Ibn al-Ḳalānisī (vizier) s, 197a
Ibn al-Kalbī → al-Kalbī
Ibn al-Kalbī (819) → al-Kalbī, Hishām b. Muḥammad

Ibn Kamāl → Kemalpasha-zāde
Ibn Ḳamīʾa → ʿAmr b. Ḳamīʾa
Ibn Kammūna (1284) iii, **815b**; ix, 220a
Ibn Ḳanbar → al-Ḥakam b. Ḳanbar
Ibn Karategin iii, 703a
Ibn al-Kardabūs vii, 286b
Ibn Karib → Abū (Ibn) Karib
Ibn al-Ḳāriḥ v, 933b, 1212a, b, 934a; s, 37b
Ibn al-Karkhī, ʿImād al-Dīn (ḳāḍī) (XII) viii, 439b
Ibn Ḳarnas (1273) vi, 111a
Ibn Karrām → Muḥammad b. Karrām
Ibn Ḳaṣī (Banū) iii, **815b** (see also *s.v.* Ḳāsī, Banū)
Ibn Ḳasī, Aḥmad (1151) i, 1339a; ii, 1009a, b; iii, 712b, 732a, **816a**; v, 586b
Ibn Ḳāsim → Muḥammad b. Ḥāzim
Ibn Ḳāsim al-Ghazzī (1512) i, 151a; iii, **817a**
Ibn al-Ḳāsim Karīm iv, 362b, 363a
Ibn al-Ḳāsim al-ʿUtāḳī (806) ii, 889b; iii, **817a**; vi, 264b, 278b, 279a, 280b; viii, 843b
Ibn al-Ḳasīra (XI) vii, 587a
Ibn al-Ḳāṣṣ (X) vi, 183a; x, 15b
Ibn Kathīr, Abū Maʿbad (VIII) iii, **817b**
Ibn Kathīr, ʿImād al-Dīn (1373) i, 273b, 595a; iii, 700a, **817b**, 927a, 954b; v, 571a; vi, 106b, 353a; vii, 212b, 284a
Ibn al-Ḳaṭṭāʿ, ʿAlī (1121) iii, 738b, **818b**, 859b; iv, 497b; vii, 528a, 772a; ix, 587a
Ibn al-Ḳaṭṭāʿ, ʿĪsā (1006) iii, **819a**
Ibn al-Ḳaṭṭān, Abu ʾl-Ḳāsim (1163) iii, 327b, **819b**; s, 396b
Ibn al-Ḳaṭṭān the Elder (1231) s, **389a**
Ibn al-Ḳaṭṭān the Younger i, 78a, 389a; s, **389b**
Ibn al-Kattānī (1029) iv, 823b; vii, 528a; xi, 401a
Ibn al-Kawwāʾ i, 382b
Ibn Ḳays al-Ruḳayyāt (VII) i, 1243a; iii, 572a, **819b**; vii, 402a; viii, 42b; x, 162b
Ibn Kaysān, Abu ʾl-Ḥasan Muḥammad al-Naḥwī (911) iii, **820a**; v, 1131a; vii, 279b; viii, 14b; s, 389b
Ibn al-Ḳaysarānī (1174) viii, 910b
Ibn al-Ḳaysarānī, Abu ʾl-Faḍl (1113) i, 100a; iii, **821a**; v, 330a; vi, 214b
Ibn al-Ḳaysarānī, Sharaf al-Dīn (1154) iii, **821b**
Ibn al-Kayyāl → al-Kayyāl, Aḥmad b. Zakariyyāʾ
Ibn al-Kayyāl (1532) vi, 214b
Ibn Ḳayyim al-Djawziyya (1350) i, 273b, 274b, 276a, 276b, 593a, 982b, 1114b, 1116b; ii, 449a; iii, 161b, 513a, 745a, **821b**, 952b, 953a, 1020a; iv, 151b, 1134a; v, 114a; vi, 217b; vii, 419b
Ibn al-Ḳazzāz vii, 400a
Ibn Kemāl (XV) ii, 220b; vi, 1025b
Ibn Kerboghāʾ (Tatar, XIV) vi, 231a
Ibn Khafādja, Abū Isḥāḳ (1139) i, 602a; ii, 526b; iii, **822b**, 849b, 971a; iv, 1007a; vi, 606b; vii, 261b, 1046b
Ibn Khafīf, al- Shaykh al-Shīrāzī (al-Shaykh al-Kabīr, 982) iii, 103a, **823a**; iv, 46a, 851b; viii, 840b, 994a; ix, 432b, 778a, b; xi, 111b
Ibn Khaḳān (1134) viii, 819a
Ibn Khāḳān (1063) → Ibn Khān
Ibn Khāḳān, ʿAbd Allāh (926) iii, **824b**
Ibn Khāḳān, al-Fatḥ → al-Fatḥ b. Khāḳān
Ibn Khaḳān, Muḥammad (924) iii, **824a**; vii, 397a, 653a
Ibn Khāḳān, ʿUbayd Allāh b. Yaḥyā (vizier, 877) i, 1082b; iii, **824a**, 844b, 879b, 880a; vii, 583a, 766a, 777b, 778a; x, 11b; s, 25a
Ibn Khāḳān, Yaḥyā (IX) iii, **824a**
Ibn al-Khāl (1705) ix, 101a
Ibn Khalaf (Ibāḍī) iv, 920a; v, 623b; viii, 688a
Ibn Khalaf, Abū Ghālib Muḥammad b. ʿAlī (1016) s, 119a, b, **390a**
Ibn Khalaf, Abū Shudjāʿ Muḥammad (1073) s, **390a**
Ibn Khalaf, ʿAlī b. ʿAbd al-Wahhāb al-Kātib (XI) s, 390a, **390b**
Ibn Khalaf Murādī viii, 655a
Ibn Khalaf al-Warrāḳ (XI) vi, 198a
Ibn Khalāṣ iii, 921b, 925a; viii, 690b; s, 111b
Ibn Khālawayh (980) i, 120a, 258b; iii, 124b, **824b**, 874b, 880b; v, 927b; vi, 188b, 196a; viii, 14a; s, 37b, 361b
Ibn Khaldūn, ʿAbd al-Raḥmān (1382) i, 15a, 286b, 376b, 579b, 593b, 595a, 659b, 681a, 816b, 858a, 959a, 1116b; ii, 285b, 308a, 586b, 767a, 774b; iii, 68b, 711a, **825a**, 1147a; iv, 260a; v, 782a, 1160b; vi, 188a, 194a, 199b, 216b, 220a, 248a,

255b, 258a, 280a, 310b, 311a, b, 348b, 728b; vii, 254b; s, 87b, 102b, 308a, 377a, 396a
Ibn Khaldūn, Abū Zakariyāʾ Yaḥyā (1379) i, 123a; iii, 826b, **831b**; vi, 728b
Ibn al-Khalīlī (vizier) viii, 759a
Ibn al-Khallād → al-Rāmahurmuzī
Ibn Khallād iii, **832a**; vii, 785a; s, 12b, 32a
Ibn Khallikān (1282) i, 72a, 594b, 669b, 1161a; ii, 285a; iii, 814a, **832b**, 934a; v, 481b; vi, 262b, 263a, b, 673b; s, 25b, 400a
Ibn Khamīs (1308) iii, **833a**
Ibn Khamīs (Āl Badr) i, 759b
Ibn Khamīs al-Mawṣilī al-Shāfiʿī (1157) vi, 354a
Ibn al-Khammār iii, 895a
Ibn Khān vii, 120a
Ibn al-Kharrāṭ al-Ishbīlī (1180) viii, 635b
Ibn Kharūf al-Rundī al-Ishbīlī (1212) iii, 861b, 927a; viii, 574a; ix, 371a, 524b
Ibn al-Khashshāb, ʿAbd Allāh (1172) iii, 803a, **834a**
Ibn al-Khashshāb, Abu ʾl-Ḥasan i, 983b; iii, 87a
Ibn al-Khaṣīb, Abū ʿAlī Aḥmad (IX) iii, **835a**; iv, 742b; vii, 722b; viii, 856a
Ibn al-Khaṣīb, Abū Bakr (IX) iii, **835a**
Ibn al-Khaṣīb, Aḥmad → al-Djardjarāʾī
Ibn al-Khaṣīb, Aḥmad b. ʿUbayd Allāh → al-Khaṣībī
Ibn al-Khaṭīb, Abū ʿAbd Allāh Lisān al-Dīn (1375) i, 594a, b, 602a; ii, 306a; iii, 756a, 826b, 827a, **835b**, 972b; v, 626a, 707b, 782a; vi, 111b, 187a, b, 220b, 221a; vii, 811b, 1024a; viii, 376b; s, 23a, 52b, 382a
Ibn Khaṭīb Dārayyā i, 759a
Ibn Khātima (1369) iii, **837a**, 855a; v, 609a; viii, 407a; s, 388b
Ibn al-Khaṭīr Masʿūd (XIII) viii, 15b
Ibn Khaṭṭāb → al-Khaṭṭābī
Ibn Khaṭṭāb al-Hawwārī ii, 875b
Ibn Khayr al-Ishbīlī (1179) i, 156a, 1198a; ii, 743b; iii, 221a, **837b**; vi, 111a; s, 88a
Ibn al-Khayyār al-Djayyānī (Fès, XII) vii, 679a
Ibn al-Khayyāṭ, Abū Bakr Muḥammad (932) iii, **837b**; vi, 539a
Ibn al-Khayyāṭ, Abū al-Ḥasan ʿAlī (X) iii, **838a**
Ibn Khayyāṭ al-ʿUṣfurī (854) iii, **838b**; v, 947b; vii, 265a, 268b; viii, 515a
Ibn Khazar b. Ṣūlāt iii, 1041b; v, 1175a, b, 1180b
Ibn Khāzim → ʿAbd Allāh b. Khāzim
Ibn Khims al-Taghlibī s, 178a
Ibn Khurradādhbih (911) i, 32a, 589b, 761b; ii, 579a, 580a; iii, **839a**, 1077b; v, 319b; vi, 183a, 215b, 313b, 379b, 639b, 640a; s, 266a, 327a, 376b
Ibn Khuwayzmindād vi, 279a
Ibn Khuzayma, Abū Bakr i, 1039b; iii, 799a; x, 389a
Ibn al-Ķifṭī, Djamāl al-Dīn (1248) i, 213a, 235b, 247a, 631a, 803b; ii, 770a, 771b; iii, **840a**; vi, 215a; viii, 103a; s, 17a, 25b, 32b, 45a, 289a, 362a
Ibn Killis, Abu ʾl-Faradj Yaʿķūb (991) i, 816a, 823b; ii, 127a, 169b, 483a, 857b, 859b, 860a; iii, 130a, 404b, **840b**; v, 623a, 1124a, 1125b; vi, 667b, 670a, 673b
Ibn Kīrān, Abū ʿAbd Allāh (1812) v, 353b; s, **390b**
Ibn Kīrān, Muḥammad b. ʿAbd al-Madjīd s, 390b
Ibn al-Ķirriyya (703) i, 1115a; iii, **841b**; viii, 830a
Ibn al-Ķiṭṭ (901) iii, **842a**
Ibn Ķiwām (XIII) vi, 354b
Ibn Ķubṭūrna → Ibn Ķabṭūrnu
Ibn Ķudāma al-Maķdisī (1223) i, 273b, 277a, 949b; iii, 159a, 161a, 677b, 700a, 735a, 752a, 766b, **842b**; iv, 212a; v, 10a; vi, 122b, 123a, 353b, 636b; vii, 311b; viii, 497b; s, 322b
Ibn Ķudwa iv, 669a
Ibn al-Ķuff, Amīn al-Dawla (1286) ii, 481b; ix, 804b; s, 130b, 271b, **391a**
Ibn Kullāb al-Baṣrī (855) v, 97a; vii, 312b, 787b, 843b; viii, 649a; ix, 552a; s, 391b
Ibn Kunāsa (823) i, 523a; iii, 136a, **843a**; v, 374b
Ibn Kundādjīk → Isḥāk b. Kundādj(īķ); Muḥammad b. Isḥāķ
Ibn Ķunfudh al-Ķusanṭīnī (1407) iii, 339a, 719b, 731b, **843b**; vi, 356a
Ibn Ķuraysh, Judah iv, 305a, b
Ibn al-Kurdī ii, 633a
Ibn Ķurhub i, 139a; ii, 853a; iv, 275b; viii, 879a

Ibn Kurr (XIV) vii, 685a
Ibn al-Kus̲h̲ayrī iii, 160a, 1266a
Ibn Ḳutayba, Abū Muḥammad ʿAbd Allāh al-Dīnāwarī (889) i, 10b, 131a, 307a, 326b, 589a, 758b, 1092b; ii, 249a, 300a, 865a; iii, 28a, 512a, **844b**, 1263b; iv, 212a, 718a; v, 1026b; vi, 107b, 110b, 111b, 263a, 344b, 348a, 636a; vii, 254b, 978a, 985a; viii, 496a; s, 42b, 227a, 273a, 380b, 392b
Ibn Ḳutayba al-Marzūḳī vi, 374b
Ibn Kut̲h̲ayyir al-Ahwāzī vi, 351b
Ibn al-Ḳūṭiyya, Abū Bakr (977) i, 600a; iii, 702a, 789b, 845b, **847b**; vi, 430b
Ibn Ḳutlūbug̲h̲ā (1474) i, 594b; iii, 164a, **848b**; vi, 194a
Ibn Ḳuzmān, Abu 'l- Aṣbag̲h̲ ʿĪsā (X) iii, **849a**
Ibn Ḳuzmān, Abū Bakr Muḥammad b. ʿAbd al-Malik (al-Akbar) (1114) iii, **849a**
Ibn Ḳuzmān, Abū Bakr Muḥammad b. ʿĪsā (al-Aṣg̲h̲ar) (1160) i, 501b, 595b, 602a; iii, **849b**; iv, 1007b; v, 744a, 1207a
Ibn Ḳuzmān, Abu 'l-Ḥusayn (1196) iii, **849b**
Ibn Ḳuzmān, Abū Marwān ʿAbd al-Raḥmān (1169) iii, **849b**
Ibn al-Labbād → ʿAbd al-Laṭīf al-Bag̲h̲dādī
Ibn al-Labbān (Mālikiyya, 1054) iii, 766b; iv, 863a; vi, 279a
Ibn al-Labbāna, Abū Bakr (1113) i, 602a; iii, 677b, **853a**; iv, 1007a; vi, 606b; vii, 811b
Ibn Lad̲j̲aʾ (VII) iii, **853b**
Ibn Lahīʿa, ʿAbd Allāh (790) iii, **853b**; v, 1162a; vi, 412a; x, 946b; xi, 179b; s, 87b, 755b
Ibn Lankak (970) iii, **854a**; v, 43b; s, 32a, b
Ibn Layt̲h̲ (XI) vii, 413a; x, 394a
Ibn Lazza → Ibn Lizza
Ibn al-Liḥyānī (Ḥafṣid, 1317) iii, 67b, 825b; v, 1247a; x, 462b
Ibn Lirra → Ibn Lizza
Ibn Lisān al-Ḥummara iii, **854a**
Ibn Lizza iii, 820a, **854b**
Ibn Luʾayy, K̲h̲ālid iii, 1065b, 1066b, 1068a; v, 63a
Ibn Lubb vi, 281b
Ibn Luʾluʾ s, 119b
Ibn al-Lunḳuh ii, 901b
Ibn Luyūn, Abū ʿUt̲h̲mān al-Tud̲j̲ībī (1349) ii, 902a; iii, **855a**; vii, 200b
Ibn Māʾ al-Samāʾ, ʿUbāda (1030) iii, **855a**; vii, 492b, 811b
Ibn Maḍāʾ (1195) iii, 747a, **855b**; iv, 468a; viii, 635b
Ibn Maḍā(ʾ) Abū ʿAbd Allāh Muḥammad x, 178a
Ibn Maʿdīkarib → ʿAmr b. Maʿdīkarib
Ibn al-Madīnī, ʿAlī b. ʿAbd Allāh (853) vii, 260b; viii, 515b
Ibn Mād̲j̲a (887) ii, 108a; iii, 24a, 692b, **856a**; s, 232b
Ibn al-Mad̲j̲dī (1506) vi, 543a
Ibn Mād̲j̲id, S̲h̲ihāb al-Dīn Aḥmad (1500) i, 553b, 932a; ii, 517b, 583a, 586a; iii, **856a**; iv, 1082b, 1083a; v, 941a, 1025a; vi, 82b, 283a, 359a, 374b; vii, 51a, 245a; viii, 100a, 102b
Ibn al-Mād̲j̲is̲h̲ūn (829) iii, 876a, 879a; iv, 87a; v, 711b; vi, 279a
Ibn Mād̲j̲ūr → Ibn Amād̲j̲ūr
Ibn al-Mag̲h̲āzilī iii, 367b; xi, 169a
Ibn al-Mag̲h̲ribī → ʿAlī b. al-Ḥusayn al-Mag̲h̲ribī
Ibn Māhān, ʿAlī b. ʿĪsā (808) i, 437b; iii, 233b, 234a, 345b, **859a**, 1202a; iv, 16b, 645a, 718b; vi, 331b, 332a, b, 334a, 335a; viii, 385b
Ibn Maḥfūf → ʿAbd Allāh b. Maḥfūf
Ibn al-Maḥrūḳ (vizier, 1329) vii, 1023a
Ibn al-Māḥūz → ʿUbayd Allāh b. al-Māḥūz; Zubayr b. al-Māḥūz
Ibn Mak̲h̲lad, al-Ḥasan (882) ii, 197b, 389b; iii, **859b**; vii, 410b, 477a, 766a
Ibn Mak̲h̲lad, Ṣāʿid (889) iii, **859b**; iv, 126b, 189a; vii, 410b, 766a; ix, 594b; x, 826b
Ibn Mak̲h̲lad, Sulaymān b. al-Ḥasan (X) i, 387b; iii, **859b**
Ibn Mak̲h̲lūf → al-D̲j̲azūlī, Ibn Mak̲h̲lūf al-Nuwayrī
Ibn Makkī (Ḳābis) i, 950a; ii, 515a
Ibn al-Makkī (musician) s, 64a
Ibn Makkī, Abū Ḥafṣ ʿUmar (XI) iii, 738b, **859b**; v, 608a, b; s, 388a
Ibn Makkī 'l-ʿĀmilī, Muḥammad → Muḥammad b. Makkī 'l-ʿĀmilī
Ibn al-Maklātī iii, 788a, 956a

Ibn Makram b. Sabāʾ b. Ḥimyar al-Aṣghar vi, 190b, 191a
Ibn Mākūlā, Abū ʿAbd Allāh iii, 766a
Ibn Mākūlā, ʿAlī (XI) iii, **860b**; iv, 718b; viii, 56a, b, 518b
Ibn Mākūlā, al-Ḥasan b. ʿAlī (1030) iii, **860a**; iv, 718b
Ibn Mākūlā, Hibat Allāh (XI) iii, **860a**; iv, 718b
Ibn Malak → Firishte-oghlu, ʿAbd al-Laṭīf
Ibn Mālik, Abū ʿAbd Allāh al-Djayyānī (1274) i, 126a, 602b; iii, 699a, **861a**, 966b; vi, 132b; vii, 388a, 914b; s, 404b
Ibn Mālik, Badr al-Dīn (1287) v, 898a, 900b; viii, 894a
Ibn Mālik al-Yamanī (XI) iii, **862b**
Ibn Malka → Abu ʾl-Barakāt
Ibn Malka, Judah iv, 305a
Ibn Mammātī, Abu ʾl-Malīḥ (XI) iii, **862b**
Ibn Mammātī, al-Asʿad b. Muhadhdhab (1209) i, 800b, 801b; ii, 900a; iii, 734a, 747b, **862b**, 894b; iv, 135b, 613b, 1181b; v, 92a; vi, 118b, 141a; vii, 164a; viii, 913a; s, 408a
Ibn Mammātī, al-Muhadhdhab (1182) iii, **862b**; v, 92a
Ibn al-Maʾmūn → al-Baṭāʾiḥī
Ibn Maʿn al-Andalusī (XVII) vi, 350a
Ibn Manda (XI) iii, **863a**; x, 10b
Ibn Manda, ʿAbd al-Raḥmān (1078) iii, 161a, **863b**
Ibn Manda(h), Abū ʿAbd Allāh (1005) i, 142b; iii, 161a, **863b**
Ibn Manda, Yaḥyā (1118) iii, **864a**; s, 193a
Ibn Manglī, Muḥammad al-Nāṣirī (XIV) v, 1229b; vii, 43b, 885b, 948a; s, 175b, **392b**
Ibn Mangudjak i, 664b; ii, 110b
Ibn Manẓūr, Muḥammad b. Mukarram (1311) i, 822a; iii, **864b**; iv, 524b; vi, 349b, 351a, 374b, 906a; vii, 445a, 561b; x, 33a
Ibn Mardanīsh (1172) i, 79b, 160b, 986a, 1288a, 1347a; ii, 115a, 516a, 526b, 1013b; iii, 850b, **864b**; iv, 116a; v, 392b; ix, 351b
Ibn al-Māristāniyya (1202) iii, 161a, 803a; vi, 430a
Ibn Maʿrūf, Abū Muḥammad (ḳāḍī al-ḳuḍāt) vii, 358b; viii, 614b
Ibn Marwān → Abū ʿAlī b. Marwān
Ibn Marwān, al-Djillīḳī, ʿAbd Allāh (X) v, 498b; vii, 569a; x, 850a, b; xi, 225b
Ibn Maryam (1605) iii, **865b**; ix, 345a
Ibn al-Marzubān → Muḥammad b. Khalaf
Ibn Marzūḳ, Aḥmad b. Muḥammad s, 403a
Ibn Marzūḳ, Muḥammad VI al-Ḥafīd (1438) i, 1314b; iii, 720b, **866a**
Ibn Marzūḳ, Shams al-Dīn Abū ʿAbd Allāh al-Tilimsānī iii, **865b**; xi, 15b
Ibn Marzūḳ, Shams al-Dīn Muḥammad IV (1379) iii, **866b**; v, 1160b, 1209a; vi, 359a, 441a, 572a; ix, 345a; s, 403a
Ibn Marzūḳ → ʿUthmān b. Marzūḳ
Ibn Masʿada → ʿAmr b. Masʿada
Ibn Maṣāl (1150) i, 9a, b, 198b; ii, 858b; iii, **868a**; x, 149b; xi, 382b
Ibn Masarra, Muḥammad b. ʿAbd Allāh (931) i, 484a, 497a, 600a; ii, 774b; iii, 712b, **868b**; vi, 280a; vii, 570a; x, 159a; xi, 548b
Ibn Māsawayh (857) i, 589b, 785b, 1223a; iii, 578b, **872a**; x, 453a; s, 271b, 303b, 314a
Ibn Mashīsh → ʿAbd al-Salām b. Mashīsh
Ibn al-Māshiṭa (X) iii, **873a**
Ibn al-Mashṭūb (XIII) vi, 381a; viii, 434a
Ibn Māssa s, 249b, 314a
Ibn Maṣṣāla al-Ibāḍī iii, 655b, 659b
Ibn Masʿūd, ʿAbd Allāh b. Ghāfil (VII) i, 114b, 687a; ii, 888b; iii, 41b, 540b, **873b**; iv, 378a; v, 127a, 350b, 406a, 407a, 409b; vi, 671a; vii, 187a, 258b; s, 227a, 311b
Ibn Masʿūd al-Khushanī ii, 743b; s, 306a
Ibn Masʿūd al-Shīrāzī s, 271b
Ibn Maʿṣūm (1705) viii, 427a; x, 305b, 451a, b; s, 695b
Ibn Maṭrūḥ (1251) iii, 833a, **875b**
Ibn Mattawayh (XI) i, 59b, 343a; iv, 615b; s, **393a**
Ibn Maʿtūḳ (XVII) vii, 673b
Ibn al-Mawlā, Muḥammad b. ʿAbd Allāh (VIII) iii, **876a**
Ibn al-Mawṣilī ii, 962a
Ibn Maymūn, Abū ʿImrān Mūsā (Maimonides) (1204) i, 214b; iii, 267a, **876a**; iv, 304b, 306b; vii, 804b; viii, 96a, 538b; s, 52b
Ibn Mayyāda, Abū Sharāḥīl (754) iii, **878a**; iv, 1003a; vi, 951a, 954a; vii, 516b, 629b

Ibn Māza, Burhān al-Dīn iii, 163b
Ibn Mengüček → Ibn Mangudjak
Ibn Mibrad → Yūsuf b. ʿAbd al-Hādī
Ibn Mīkāl iii, 757a, b
Ibn Miḳsam al-Naḥwī (965) v, 127b; s, **393a**
Ibn al-Miʿmār (1244) ii, 964a, 965a, 966a; vii, 999b
Ibn Misdjaḥ (VII) iii, **878b**, 883a, 950a
Ibn Miskawayh → Miskawayh
Ibn Miskīn iv, 134b
Ibn Mītham al-Tammār (VIII) s, **393b**
Ibn Muʿādh s, 372a, 373b
Ibn al-Muʿadhdhal, ʿAbd al-Ṣamad (854) iii, **878b**; viii, 378a; s, 352a
Ibn al-Muʿadhdhal, Aḥmad (IX) i, 1114b; iii, 879a
Ibn al-Muʿallim → al-Mufīd
Ibn Muʿammar → Muḥammad b. Mushārī
Ibn Muʿayyā iii, 808a
Ibn Mubārak (Maṣyad) vi, 790b
Ibn al-Mubārak, ʿAbd Allāh (797) i, 124a, 1244a; iii, 512b, **879b**; vi, 263b; vii, 758a; viii, 498a; s, 87b, 386b
Ibn al-Mubārak al-Lamaṭī → al-Lamaṭī
Ibn al-Mudabbir, Abu ʾl-Ḥasan Aḥmad (884) i, 278b; ii, 144a, 328a; iii, **879b**; v, 91a; vi, 195a; vii, 161a
Ibn al-Mudabbir, Ibrāhīm (892) iii, 745b, **879b**, 880a, 1242b; ix, 396a, b; s, 35a, b
Ibn Mudjāhid, Aḥmad b. Mūsā (936) i, 105b; iii, 101a, 817b, **880b**, 936a; v, 127b, 128a, 408b, 409a; vi, 188b; vii, 292b
Ibn al-Mudjāwir, Yūsuf b. al-Ḥusayn al-Shīrāzī (1204) iii, **881b**
Ibn al-Mudjāwir, Yūsuf b. Yaʿḳūb al-Dimashḳī (1291) i, 571a; iii, **880b**; vi, 81a, 474a
Ibn Mufaḍḍal (VIII) viii, 387b
Ibn Mufarrigh (689) iii, 354a, 620b, **881b**, 1261b; iv, 536a; vi, 920b; ix, 116b
Ibn Muṭiḥ, Akmal al-Dīn (1602) iii, **882b**
Ibn Muṭiḥ, Burhān al-Dīn (1400) iii, 162a, **882b**
Ibn Muṭiḥ, Shams al-Dīn (1362) iii, **882b**
Ibn Mughīth → ʿAbd al-Malik b. Mughīth
Ibn al-Muhallab → Muhallabids; Yazīd b. Muhallab b. Abī Ṣufra
Ibn Muḥammad (XIV) ix, 67a
Ibn Muḥayṣin ii, 293a; iv, 91a
Ibn Muḥriz (VIII) i, 828a; iii, 2b, 878b, **883a**; ix, 9b; xi, 350b; s, 273a
Ibn Muḥriz (al-Marḳab) (XII) vi, 578a, b
Ibn Muḥriz al-Wahrānī (1179) vi, 111a, 262a, 279a
Ibn al-Muḳaddam, Amīr Shams al-Dawla (XII) ii, 283b; v, 924b; viii, 910b
Ibn al-Muḳaffaʿ, ʿAbd Allāh (756) i, 65b, 66a, 176a, 306b, 326b, 569b, 588a, 784b, 1216b; ii, 951a; iii, 113a, 313b, 372b, **883a**, 1019b, 1263a; iv, 92a, 503b, 504a, b, 755b, 948b, 1098a; vi, 109a, 204a, 539a; vii, 359b, 566a, 985a; viii, 107b, 996b; xi, 512bs, 85b, 88b, 263b
Ibn al-Muḳaffaʿ, Sāwīrūs/Severus (X) iii, **885b**; vi, 144a; vii, 164a
Ibn Mukarram → Ibn Manẓūr
Ibn Muḳashshir iii, 81a
Ibn Muḳbil, Abū Kaʿb al-ʿĀmirī (VII) vi, 403b; s, 10a, **394a**
Ibn al-Mukhtār (Timbuktu) (XVII) vi, 258b
Ibn Muḳla (940) i, 387b, 866a, b, 1040a, 1046b; ii, 305a, 388b; iii, 127a, 345a, 736b, **886b**, 902b, 936a, 1157a; iv, 423b, 1094a, 1122b; vii, 397a, 414a, 728a; viii, 151a
Ibn Mukram i, 132a; iii, 101b
Ibn Muldjam, ʿAbd al-Raḥmān al-Murādī (661) i, 385a; iii, **887a**; iv, 1075a; vii, 265b, 592a; s, 157a
Ibn Munādhir ii, 1011a; iii, 354b, **890a**
Ibn al-Munadjdjim → ʿAlī b. Yaḥyā; Yaḥyā b. ʿAlī
Ibn al-Mundhir (X) s, 726b
Ibn al-Mundhir (XII) ix, 441a
Ibn al-Mundhir (XIV) iii, **890b**; iv, 216a, 1145b
Ibn Munīr → al-Ṭarābulusī al-Raffāʾ
Ibn al-Munḳidh → Usāma b. Munḳidh; Munḳidh, Banū
Ibn Munḳidh, Abu ʾl-Ḥasan (1079) vii, 122a
Ibn Munḳidh, ʿAlī b. Muḳallad (XI) vii, 121a
Ibn al-Murābiʿ (1350) iii, **891a**; vi, 111b
Ibn Murrāna vi, 216b
Ibn al-Murtaḍā → Muḥammad b. Yaḥyā al-Murtaḍā
Ibn al-Murtaḍā s, 25b, 225b

Ibn Musāfir → Muḥammad b. Musāfir
Ibn al-Musayyab (VII) viii, 645b; s, 770b
Ibn al-Muslima, Abu 'l-Ḳāsim ʿAlī (1058) i, 1073b, 1074b, 1356a; iii, 766a, 860b, **891a**; iv, 457b; v, 73b; vi, 272b
Ibn al-Mutawwadj (1330) vi, 653a
Ibn Muṭayr (VIII) iii, **892a**
Ibn al-Muʿtazz, Abu 'l-ʿAbbās ʿAbd Allāh (ʿAbbāsid) (908) i, 144a, 386b, 446a, 590a, 592a, 857b, 971b, 981b, 1132a; ii, 197b, 1032b; iii, 100b, 619b, 702b, 750b, **892a**, 955b, 1020a; iv, 90a, b, 491a, 1004a, 1005a; v, 319a, b, 321b; vi, 206a, 348a, 437b, 438a, 605a, 635b; vii, 277a, 541b, 963a, 1040a; viii, 376a, 378a; s, 25a, 31b, 35a, 122b, 385a, b
Ibn al-Muthannā iii, 1137a; iv, 1071a; ix, 641a
Ibn Muṭīʿ → ʿAbd Allāh b. Muṭīʿ
Ibn Muʿṭī, Abu 'l-Ḥusayn Yaḥyā (1231) ii, 528b; iii, **893b**, 966b; vii, 914b
Ibn al-Muṭrān (1191) vi, 845a; x, 455a
Ibn al-Muwaḳḳit (1949) iii, 570a, **893b**; iv, 159b; viii, 692a
Ibn Muyassar, Tādj al-Dīn (1278) iii, **894a**; vi, 144a; xi, 320b
Ibn Muzāḥim → Naṣr b. Muzāḥim
Ibn al-Muzawwiḳ → Ibn al-Sadīd
Ibn Muzayn (XI) vii, 766b; ix, 308b
Ibn al-Nabīh (1222) iii, 48a, **894b**; iv, 1006a
Ibn al-Nadīm (995) i, 105a, 151b, 213a, 235a, 247b, 1081a, 1197b, 1354a; ii, 771b, 1093b; iii, 370b, **895a**, 1045a, 1151a; iv, 53b, 1119a; v, 207b; vi, 198b, 634b, 906a; s, 45a, 88b, 127b, 225b, 371b, 372b
Ibn al-Nadīm (1046) ix, 114a
Ibn al-Nadjdjār, Muḥibb Allāh (1245) iii, 756a, **896b**; vi, 353a; vii, 728a, 773b
Ibn al-Nadjdjār (1572) i, 949b
Ibn Nādjī, Abu 'l-Ḳāsim (1435) vi, 353b, 355b; s, 173a, **394b**
Ibn al-Nafīs, ʿAlāʾ al-Dīn (1288) i, 713b; iii, 694a, **897a**, 944b; vi, 354a; x, 355b
Ibn al-Naḥḥās (950) iii, **898b**; v, 121b; vii, 254b
Ibn al-Naḥwī (1119) iii, 800a, b; iv, 481a; x, 124b
Ibn al-Nāḳid iii, 683a
Ibn Nāḳiyā, ʿAbd Allāh (1092) iii, **899a**; vi, 110a
Ibn al-Naḳūr s, 195a
Ibn Nāṣir (al-Nāṣirī) s, **395a**
Ibn Nāṣir, Aḥmad b. Maḥammad (1717) s, **395a**
Ibn Nāṣir, al-Ḥusayn b. Muḥammad (1680) iv, 325b; s, **395a**
Ibn Nāṣir, Maḥammad b. Muḥammad (1674) iv, 325b; xi, 352a; s, **395a**
Ibn al-Nāṣir, Muḥammad b. ʿAbd al-Salām (al-Kabīr) (1823) s, **395b**
Ibn Nāṣir, Muḥammad (al-Makkī) b. Mūsā (1729) s, **395a**
Ibn Nāṣir al-Darʿī ii, 161a
Ibn Nāṣir al-Salāmī x, 461b
Ibn Nasṭūrus → ʿIsā b. Nasṭūrus
Ibn al-Naṭṭāḥ (866) iii, **899a** (see also *s.v.* Bakr b. al-Naṭṭāḥ)
Ibn al-Naẓar (XII) iii, **900a**
Ibn Nāẓir al-Djaysh iv, 510a; s, 395b
Ibn Nubāta al Fāriḳī (984) iii, **900a**; v, 75b; vi, 930a
Ibn Nubāta al-Miṣrī (1366) i, 1154a; iii, 781a, 799b, **900a**; iv, 471b, 864a
Ibn Nubāta al-Saʿdī (1014) vi, 110a
Ibn Nudjaym, Zayn al-Dīn al-Miṣrī (1562) i, 27a, 593a; ii, 163b; iii, 163b, **901a**; vi, 971b; vii, 969b
Ibn Nūḥ → Muḥammad b. Nūḥ
Ibn Nuʿmān (al-mufīd) (1022) viii, 615a
Ibn Nuṣayr → al-Namīrī, Muḥammad b. Nuṣayr
Ibn Pakūdā, Baḥya iv, 303b, 304b, 487a
Ibn Rabban → al-Ṭabarī
Ibn al-Rabīb (1038) iii, 790b, **901b**
Ibn Radjab, ʿAbd al-Raḥmān (1392) iii, 161b, 700a, 803b, **901b**, 954b; iv, 990a; viii, 516a
Ibn al-Rāhib (1290) vi, 143b; s, **396a**
Ibn Raḥīḳ (XI) vi, 183a
Ibn Raḥmūn vii, 282b
Ibn Rāhwayh, Isḥāḳ b. Ibrāhīm (853) iii, 844b, 846a, **902a**; vii, 691b, 706b
Ibn Rāʾiḳ (amīr) (942) i, 19a, 20a, 446a, 866a, b, 870b, 1040a, 1046b; ii, 144a, 453b, 1080b; iii, 46a, 86a, 127b, 768b, 887a, **902b**, 1255b; iv, 215a; vii, 411b, 484a, 800a, 912b, 994b; xi, 186b
Ibn al-Raḳā ii, 389a

Ibn al-Raḳīḳ, Abū Isḥāḳ Ibrāhīm al-Ḳayrawānī (1027) iii, **902b**; iv, 830b, 1007a; vii, 483b, 528b, 1040a
Ibn al-Rakkāḍ i, 759b
Ibn al-Raḳḳāḳ → Ibn al-Zaḳḳāḳ
Ibn Rāmīn (VIII) viii, 996b
Ibn al-Ras͟hīḳ (Mālikiyya) (1234) vi, 279a
Ibn Ras͟hīḳ, Abū ʿAlī Ḥasan al-Ḳayrawānī (1063) i, 858a; iii, 354b, 640a, 688a, **903a**, 936a; iv, 250a, 867a; vi, 605a, 606b; vii, 254b, 277a, b, 309b, 483a, 661a, 978b; viii, 427a; s, 27a, 62b, 394b
Ibn Ras͟hīḳ, Abū Muḥammad (Murcia) (XI) i, 6b; iii, 706a, **904b**; vii, 633b, 767a
Ibn Rawāḥa → ʿAbd Allāh b. Rawāḥa
Ibn al-Rāwandī (al-Rēwendī) (X) i, 129a, 130a; 373b, 780b; iii, **905a**, 1019b; iv, 1162b; v, 120b; vi, 458a; vii, 566a; s, 12b, 14a, 225b
Ibn al-Rawwād (Tabrīz) vi, 504b
Ibn Raysūn al-ʿAlamī (1645) vi, 356b
Ibn Rayyān vi, 113b
Ibn Razīḳ i, 1283a
Ibn Rāzga → al-S͟hinḳīṭī, Sīdī ʿAbd Allāh b. Muḥammad b. al-Ḳāḍī
Ibn Razīn i, 1092b (see also *s.v.* Razīn, Banū)
Ibn al-Razzāz al-D̲j̲azarī iii, 511a; x, 33b (see also *s.v.* al-D̲j̲azarī, Badīʿ al-Zamān Abu ʾl-ʿIzz)
Ibn al-Riḍā → Ḥasan al-ʿAskarī
Ibn Riḍwān, Abu ʾl-Ḥasan (1061) iii, 740b, 741b, **906a**, 977a; vi, 638a; vii, 282b, 510b; viii, 42a; ix, 249a; x, 454b; s, 30a
Ibn Rizām (951) i, 48a, b, 95b, 96a; iv, 662b; vi, 917b
Ibn Rubayʿān, ʿUmar ii, 354a; iii, 1068a
Ibn Rūḥ, Abu ʾl-Ḳāsim al-Nawbak͟htī (938) iii, 133a, **907a**; vii, 379b, 443b, 1043b
Ibn Ruhayb → Ḳiṭfīr
Ibn al-Rūmī (896) i, 592a; iii, 354b, **907b**, 955b; iv, 1005a; vi, 253a, 603a, 605a, 625b, 955b; vii, 566b, 963b, 982a; viii, 376a, 377b; ix, 387a; xi, 156b, 157b; s, 58b, 352b
Ibn al-Rūmiyya, Abu ʾl-ʿAbbās (1240) iii, 798b; vi, 779a; ix, 258a; s, 313b, **396b**
Ibn Rus͟hayd (1321) iii, 834a, **909a**; iv, 355b
Ibn Rus͟hd xi, 216b
Ibn Rus͟hd (1141, ḳāḍī) vii, 400a
Ibn Rus͟hd, Abu ʾl-Walīd al-Ḥafīd (Averroes) (1198) i, 162a, 179a, 209b, 214a, 234b, 327b, 342b, 350b, 415a, b, 594a, 630b, 982b, 1154b; ii, 96b, 765b, 766a, 771a, 773b; iii, 170a, 509b, 644b, 729a, 748b, **909b**, 978a, b, 1132a, 1149a; v, 704a, 843a; vi, 205a, 220a, 279a, 281b, 348b, 449a, b, 450a, 590b; vii, 288a, 387b, 539a, 805b; viii, 96a; s, 397b
Ibn Rus͟hd, Abu ʾl-Walīd Muḥammad al-D̲j̲add (1126) vii, 247b; s, **397b**
Ibn Rusta, Abū ʿAlī Aḥmad (912) i, 100b, 775a; ii, 579b, 580a, b; iii, 232a, **920a**; vi, 640a, 656b; viii, 612b
Ibn Rustam → ʿAbd al-Raḥmān b. Rustam
Ibn Saʿāda (1170) iii, **921a**
Ibn al-Sāʿātī, Aḥmad b. ʿAlī x, 932b
Ibn al-Sāʿātī, Bahāʾ al-Dīn iii, **921a**
Ibn al-Sāʿātī, Fak͟hr al-Dīn Riḍwān (1230) iii, **921a**
Ibn al-Sāʿātī, Muẓaffar al-Dīn Aḥmad (1295) iii, **921a**; vii, 969a
Ibn Sabaʾ, Bahāʾ al-Dīn (1207) → ʿAbd Allāh b. Sabaʾ
Ibn al-Ṣabbāg͟h (XI) iii, 950a; ix, 170b; s, 29b
Ibn Sabʿīn ʿAbd al-Ḥaḳḳ (1269) i, 594a, 772b; iii, **921b**; vi, 451b, 637b
Ibn Saʿd, Abū ʿAbd Allāh Muḥammad (845) i, 140a, 591a, 694a; iii, 838b, **922a**; vi, 262b, 263a; vii, 361b
Ibn al-Ṣābūnī (1320) viii, 156b
Ibn Ṣadaḳa iii, 221a; ix, 103b (see also *s.v* Ṣadaḳa, Banū)
Ibn Saʿdān, Abū ʿAbd Allāh al-Ḥusayn b. Aḥmad (984, vizier) i, 127a, 159a; vii, 304b; s, 361b, **398a**
Ibn Ṣaddīḳ, Joseph iv, 304b
Ibn al-Sadīd (1430) iii, **923a**
Ibn al-Sadīd (1324) iii, **923a**
Ibn Ṣadr al-Dīn al-S͟hirwānī i, 327a
Ibn Saʿdūn → Yaḥyā b. Saʿdūn
Ibn al-Ṣaffār, Abu ʾl-Ḳāsim Aḥmad al-Andalusī (1035) iii, **924a**, 1137a; vii, 210b, 413a; ix, 641a; xi, 500a

Ibn al-Ṣaghīr (902) iii, **924b**; vi, 841a, 947b
Ibn Ṣaghīr al-Barbarī al-Maṣmūdī iv, 920a
Ibn Ṣāḥib al-Ṣalāt (XII) iii, **924b**
Ibn Sahl al-Isrāʾīlī (1251) i, 602a; iii, **925a**, 1047a; iv, 1007b; vii, 811b; viii, 833b
Ibn Saḥnūn, Muḥammad iii, 681a; v, 503b
Ibn al-Sāʿī (1276) iii, 896b, 897a, **925b**; vii, 727b, 728a; s, 284b
Ibn Saʿīd → al-Mundhir b. Saʿīd
Ibn Sāʿid (Ḥawrān) iv, 552b
Ibn Saʿīd, Abū Djaʿfar → Abū Djaʿfar Ibn Saʿīd
Ibn Saʿīd al-Maghribī (1286) i, 119a, 602a, 602b; iii, 807b, **926a**; iv, 1081a; v, 1012a, 1020b; vi, 111a; vii, 186a, 528a, 824b; s, 86a, 266a
Ibn al-Ṣāʾigh (1375) vi, 193b
Ibn al-Ṣāʾigh (Ifrīḳiya) (XI) vi, 942b
Ibn al-Ṣāʾigh al-ʿArūḍī (1322) iii, **926b**
Ibn al-Saḳḳāʾ (XI) iii, 73b
Ibn al-Saḳḳāʾ (1176) viii, 892a
Ibn al-Ṣalāḥ (1154) viii, 99b; x, 934b
Ibn al-Ṣalāḥ, Taḳī 'l-Dīn (1245) ii, 462a; iii, 25b, 27a, 818b, **927a**, 1108a; vi, 353a; vii, 631a; viii, 459b
Ibn Salām b. ʿUmar (ʿAmr) (XI) iii, **927a**; vi, 311a
Ibn Salāma (Mālikiyya) iii, 712a, 827a, 828b; vi, 263b
Ibn al-Sal(l)ār → al-ʿĀdil b. al-Salār
Ibn Sālim iii, 570b
Ibn Sālim al-Kalāʿī → al-Kalāʿī, Abu 'l-Rabīʿ b. Sālim
Ibn Sallām → Abū ʿUbayd al-Ḳāsim b. Sallām
Ibn Sallām al-Djumaḥī (846) iii, 272b, 353b, 698a, **927b**, 1177b; vii, 580b, 978a; ix, 662b; s, 284a
Ibn Sallāmī al-Maghribī, Abū ʿUthmān (983) vi, 280a
Ibn al-Ṣalt, Aḥmad b. Muḥammad s, 400b
Ibn al-Salʿūs iv, 964b, 965a
Ibn Samadjūn (XI) i, 214a; iii, **928a**; s, 313b, 314a; x, 768a
Ibn al-Samāʿī (1275) vi, 352a
Ibn Samʿān (Zandjī) (IX) vii, 526b
Ibn al-Samḥ (1035) i, 600b; iii, **928b**, 1137a; v, 1109b; s, 25a
Ibn Sammāk iii, 570a
Ibn Samʿūn → Abu 'l-Ḥusayn b. Samʿūn
Ibn Samura → ʿUbayd Allāh Ibn Samura
Ibn Sanāʾ al-Mulk, Abu 'l-Ḳāsim (1211) i, 595b; ii, 1033a; iii, **929a**; vi, 255b; vii, 528a, 812a
Ibn al-Ṣāniʿ → Ibn Yaʿīsh, Muwaffaḳ al-Dīn
Ibn Sarābiyūn, Suhrāb (X) iii, **929b**
Ibn Sarābiyūn, Yuḥannā (IX) → Yuḥannā b. Sarābiyyūn
Ibn Ṣāra (1124) vii, 261b; ix, 308a
Ibn Ṣārah s, 352b
Ibn al-Sarāya → Ṣafī al-Dīn al-Hillī
Ibn al-Sarrādj → Ibn al-Ḳiṭṭ
Ibn al-Sarrādj (al-Ḥalabī) (1325) vii, 30a, 210b; viii, 575a
Ibn al-Sarrādj, Abū ʿAlī iii, 842a
Ibn al-Sarrādj (family name) s, **398b**
Ibn al-Sarrādj, Muḥammad b. ʿAlī (XIV) iii, **930a**
Ibn al-Sarrādj, Abū Bakr Muḥammad al-Naḥwī al-Baghdādī (928) iii, **930a**, 1128a; vii, 279b, 914a; x, 4a
Ibn al-Ṣarṣarī iii, 952a (see also *s.v.* Ibn Ṣaṣra)
Ibn Ṣaṣra/Ṣaṣarrā iii, 475b, **930b**; viii, 156b
Ibn Saʿūd → ʿAbd al-ʿAzīz Āl Suʿūd
Ibn al-Sawdāʾ → ʿAbd Allāh b. Sabaʾ
Ibn Sawda → Ibn Sūda
Ibn Sawwār i, 1086b; ii, 127a; viii, 417a
Ibn Sayāba → Ibrāhim b. Sayāba
Ibn Sayf II iii, 604a
Ibn Sayḥān (VII) iii, **931b**; iv, 1002a
Ibn al-Ṣayḳal (1302) viii, 805b
Ibn al-Ṣayrafī, Abū Bakr Yaḥyā (1162) i, 389b; iii, **932b**; vii, 584a
Ibn al-Ṣayrafī, Tādj al-Riʾāsa (1147) ii, 80a, 304b, 305a; iii, 932a, 1242b; vi, 423b
Ibn Sayyār al-Warrāḳ (X) ix, 93b, 576a
Ibn al-Sayyid (995) i, 600a
Ibn Sayyid al-Nās, Fatḥ al-Dīn (1334) iii, **932b**; vi, 111b; vii, 388a; ix, 661a
Ibn Shābāsh, Abu 'l-Ḥasan ʿAlī b. Faḍl (1052) ix, 159a
Ibn al-Shabbāṭ iii, 1048a; iv, 402b, 403a
Ibn Shaddād, ʿAbd al-ʿAzīz iii, **933a**
Ibn Shaddād, Bahāʾ al-Dīn (1235) iii, **933b**; vi, 430a

Ibn Shaddād, ʿIzz al-Dīn al-Ḥalabī (1285) i, 946a; iii, **933b**, 938a; vi, 381a, 930a
Ibn Shaddād Yūsuf s, 197a
Ibn Shādhān (993) viii, 14a
Ibn Shādhān (1034) ix, 65a
Ibn Shādhān al-Rāzī → al-Badjalī, Abū Bakr Muḥammad b. ʿAbd Allāh
Ibn al-Shadjarī al-Baghdādī (1148) i, 485b, 1241a; iii, 110b, 111a, 834a, **934b**; vii, 527a
Ibn Shahīd (Ḥafṣid) s, 111b, 112a
Ibn al-Shahīd, Abū Ḥafs ʿUmar (XI) iii, **934b**; vi, 114b
Ibn Shāhīn → Nissīm ben Yaʿḳob Ibn Shāhīn
Ibn Shāhīn, ʿUmar b. Aḥmad (995) viii, 517a
Ibn Shāhīn al-Ẓāhirī (XV) iii, **935a**
Ibn Shahrāshūb, Abū Djaʿfar (1192) i, 120a; ii, 848a; iii, **935a**, 1151b; vi, 351b
Ibn Shākir → al-Kutubī
Ibn Shaḳīshaḳa s, 197a
Ibn Shaḳrūn al-Miknāsī (XVIII) s, 40a, b, **399b**
Ibn Shālib al-Yahūdī (XI) i, 7a; viii, 813b
Ibn al-Shalmaghānī → Muḥammad b. ʿAlī al-Shalmaghānī
Ibn Shanabūdh (939) i, 1039b; iii, **935b**; v, 127b, 409a; s, 386a, 393b
Ibn Shanbūdh → Ibn Shanabūdh
Ibn Shankā (1173) vii, 707a
Ibn Shannabūdh → Ibn Shanabūdh
Ibn Sharaf, Abu 'l-Faḍl (1139) i, 602a; iii, **936b**
Ibn Sharaf al-Ḳayrawānī (1067) iii, 903b, **936a**; iv, 830b; v, 43b; vi, 108b, 109a, 110a, 606b; vii, 483a; s, 27a, 62b, 394b
Ibn Sharāfī, Ṣafī al-Dīn v, 92a
Ibn al-Shārī (XIII) s, 388b
Ibn al-Sharīf al-Darḳāwī (XIX) ii, 160a; vii, 263a
Ibn Sharya, ʿAbīd/ʿUbayd al-Djurhumī iii, 370a, **937a**; iv, 211b; vi, 197b; viii, 408a; ix, 967a; xi, 35b
Ibn al-Shāṭir (1375) iii, 1137b; iv, 518a, 810a; vi, 543a, 602a; vii, 30a, 210b; viii, 102a
Ibn Shaykh (Masraḥ) (XX) vi, 755a
Ibn al-Shaykh al-Balawī i, 602a; iii, 773b
Ibn Shaykh Ḥiṭṭīn → al-Dimashḳī, Shams al-Dīn
Ibn Shaykh al-Salāmiya → Ibn al-Ṣāʾigh al-ʿArūḍī
Ibn Shibl (1080) iii, **937b**; iv, 1005b; xi, 180b
Ibn Shihāb i, 830a, 1002b; ix, 671a, b
Ibn Shihāb al-Zuhrī → al-Zuhrī, Ibn Shihāb
Ibn al-Shiḥna al-Ḥalabī, Muḥibb al-Dīn (1485) i, 119a; iii, **938a**; vi, 230a, 381b, 382a
Ibn Shīrzād (X) vii, 723b
Ibn Shīt al-Kurshī i, 801b; ii, 329b
Ibn Shubruma (761) iii, 687b, **938a**; x, 541b
Ibn Shudjāʿ Farrukhshāh v, 76b
Ibn Shuhayd, Abū ʿĀmir (1035) i, 591a, 601b; iii, 346b, 355a, 370b, 740a, 786a, 790a, b, **938b**; iv, 1007a; v, 114b, 778b; vi, 109b, 110a; vii, 495a; viii, 533b; ix, 455b; s, 250a
Ibn Shukr i, 800b, 801b; xi, 190a, b
Ibn al-Sīd al-Baṭalyawsī → al-Baṭalyawsī
Ibn Sīda (Sīduh), Abu 'l-Ḥasan (1066) i, 600a, 601a; ii, 300b; iii, **940a**; iv, 524b; vi, 374b; vii, 772a
Ibn al-Sikkīt (858) i, 772a, 1241a; ii, 300a; iii, 803a, **940b**; iv, 1027b; vii, 831b, 841b; s, 15b, 394b
Ibn al-Simāṭ v, 1247b
Ibn Sīmdjūr ii, 749a; vi, 340a
Ibn Sīnā xi, 216b
Ibn Sīnā, Abū ʿAlī al-Ḥusayn (Avicenna) (1037) i, 74b, 112a, b, 147a, 179a, 213b, 234b, 327b, 342a,b, 350b, 415a, 427a, 434b, 589a, 630b, 772b, 784b, 785b, 839a, 926a, 1084a, 1236a, 1327a, 1354a; ii, 96a, 221a, 378b, 450a, 481b, 550a, 764b, 765a; iii, 30a, 170a, 329b, 330b, 333b, 509b, 543b, 897b, 916a, **941a**, 974b, 1028a, 1130b; iv, 120a, 331a, 358b, 366b, 466b, 615b; v, 842b, 1261b, 1262b; vi, 73b, 97b, 204b, 220a, 347a, 348b, 446b, 449b, 450a, b, 467a, 600b, 616b, 637a, 638a, 907a; vii, 200b, 682b, 683a; viii, 95a, b, 123b, 541a; x, 453b; s, 24a, 40b, 59b, 72b, 270a, 271b, 305b, 308a, 314a, 380a
Ibn Sinān al-Khafādjī (1060) i, 1070a; vii, 120a; x, 450b; xi, 53a
Ibn Sīrīn, Abū Bakr Muḥammad (728) ii, 300b; iii, **947b**; v, 1232a; vi, 266b; viii, 374b, 645b

Ibn al-Sitrī → Ibn al-Bawwāb
Ibn Sūda (Tāwdī, Fès) iii, **948a**
Ibn Sūda, Abū ʿAbd Allāh Muḥammad al-Tāw(u)dī (1795) iii, **948b**; vi, 356b
Ibn Sūdūn i, 571a; s, 721a
Ibn al-Ṣūfī (IX) iii, 808a; viii, 863b
Ibn al-Ṣuḳāʿī al-Naṣrānī (1325) s, **400a**
Ibn Sukkara (995) ii, 1032b; iii, 852a; ix, 342a, 453b; xi, 51b; s, 352b
Ibn Sukkara (1120) viii, **707b**
Ibn Ṣulayḥa (ḳāḍī) (XII) ii, 353b; vi, 578a
Ibn Sulaym al-Aswānī (X) iii, **949a**; viii, 40b
Ibn Ṣumādiḥ → al-Muʿtaṣim Ibn Ṣumādiḥ
Ibn Sumayya → Ziyād b. Abīhi
Ibn Surāḳa (Damascus) i, 773a
Ibn Surāḳa al-ʿĀmirī, Muḥammad (1019) vi, 106b, 183a, b
Ibn Surāḳa al-Shābiṭī ix, 513a
Ibn Suraydj, Abu ’l-Abbās Aḥmad (918) iii, 100b, **949a**; ix, 36a, 893b
Ibn Suraydj, ʿUbayd Allāh (714) i, 118a, 828a; ii, 428b, 1011b; iii, **950a**; iv, 315b; vi, 262a, b; vii, 681b
Ibn al-Sūrī ii, 350a
Ibn Surūr al-Maḳdisī (XIII) vi, 637a
Ibn Suʿūd → ʿAbd al-ʿAzīz Āl Suʿūd
Ibn Suwār, ʿAbd al-Ḳādir b. Muḥammad (1605) vi, 88a
Ibn Suwār (1017) i, 737a; vi, 204b, 347a; x, 360b
Ibn Suwār, Āl vi, 88a
Ibn Suwayṭ ii, 77a
Ibn Swīkāt (Bessouiket) (XVIII) vi, 249b
Ibn al-Taʿāwīdhī (1188) i, 212b; iii, 891b, **950a**
Ibn Ṭabāṭabā (934) vii, 277a; s, 649b
Ibn Ṭabāṭabā, Muḥammad b. Ibrāhīm (815) i, 149b, 402b; iii, 243b, **950b**; vi, 334a
Ibn Tafrāgīn iii, 49a, 68a, 826a, 867a; v, 1151a, 1247a
Ibn Taghrībirdī → Abu ’l-Maḥāsin
Ibn al-Ṭaḥḥān (XI) iv, 821a; vii, 684a, 1042a
Ibn Ṭāhir → ʿAbd Allāh b. Ṭāhir
Ibn Ṭāhir, Abū Bakr Aḥmad b. Isḥāḳ (Murcia) (1119) vii, 633b
Ibn Talḥa al-ʿAdawī al-Rādjī ii, 376a; v, 1236b
Ibn Ṭālib (888) viii, 844a
Ibn Talīd (al-Mawṣil) (700) vi, 900a
Ibn Ṭalūt iv, 459a
Ibn al-Tammār → Ibn Mītham
Ibn Ṭarf → Sulaymān b. Ṭarf
Ibn al-Ṭathriyya iii, 757a; v, 526a; vi, 477a; ix, 867a
Ibn Ṭayfūr (Mertola) i, 6a; vii, 761a
Ibn Taymiyya, Madjd al-Dīn iii, 161a, 951a, 953b
Ibn Taymiyya, Taḳī al-Dīn Aḥmad (1328) i, 69b, 195a, 266b, 272b, 273b, 274b, 275b, 276a,b, 277a, 333a, 411b, 425a, 553a, 593a, 696a, 827b, 959a, 1238b; ii, 51a, 230a, 285b, 294a, 295a, 411b, 752b, 931a, 966a; iii, 161b, 162a, 429b, 512b, 700a, 711a, 722b, 752a, 821b, **951a**, 1148b, 1171b, 1207a; iv, 142a, 149b, 257b, 258b, 366a, 381b, 469b; v, 426a; vi, 34a, 122b, 176b, 353b, 360b, 447a, 452a, 651b; vii, 169b, 212a, 291b, 296b, 419b, 462a; viii, 125a, 147a, 156b, 534a, 759a; s, 354a
Ibn al-Tayyān → Tammām b. Ghālib
Ibn al-Tayyān(ī) x, **178a**; i, 600a
Ibn al-Ṭayyib al-Baṣrī → Abu ’l-Ḥusayn
Ibn al-Ṭayyib al-ʿIrāḳī, Abu ’l-Faradj (1043) i, 328a, 388a; ii, 780a, 929b, 948b; iii, 740b, **955a**, 1205b; vi, 204b, 637b, 638a; vii, 1031a; s, 25a, 396b
IbnThawāba, Abu ’l-ʿAbbās Aḥmad (890) iii, **955a**
IbnThawāba, Abu ’l-Ḥusayn Djaʿfar (897) iii, **955b**; vii, 653a
Ibn al-Thumna (1062) iii, 782b, 788a, 838a, **956a**; ix, 585b, 670a
Ibn Tīfalwīt iii, 542b, 728a, 849b
Ibn al-Ṭiḳṭaḳā, Ṣafī al-Dīn (XII) i, 157b, 595b; iii, 702a, **956a**; vi, 627b; vii, 404b
Ibn al-Tilmīdh, Abu ’l-Ḥasan, Amīn al-Dawla (1165) i, 111b, 344b, 858b, 1224a,b; iii, **956b**; vi, 727a
Ibn Ṭūbī, Mūsā iv, 307a
Ibn Ṭufayl, Abū Bakr Muḥammad (1185) i, 162a, 594a, 1250a; ii, 773b, 1039b; iii, 330b, 333a, 729a, 910a, 911b, **957a**; vi, 590b; vii, 805b
Ibn Ṭūlūn → Aḥmad b. Ṭūlūn

Ibn Ṭūlūn, Shams al-Dīn al-Ṣāliḥī (1546) i, 571a; iii, **957b**; iv, 1161b; vi, 352b, 354b, 359b, 685a; s, 195b
Ibn Tūmart al-Mahdī, Muḥammad (1130) i, 78a, 121b, 122a, 251a, 389b, 390a, 592b, 1129b, 1176a, 1186a, 1205a; ii, 307b; iii, 207a, **958b**; iv, 290a, 558a; v, 626a, 744b, 1160b, 1199b; vi, 281a, 339b, 592a, b, 597a, 742b, 743b; vii, 591a, 801b
Ibn Ṭumlūs (Alhagiag bin Thalmus) (1223) iii, **960a**; vi, 450b
Ibn Ṭumlūs (Umayyad) iii, 31a
Ibn Turayk, Abu 'l-ʿAlāʾ iii, 782a
Ibn al-Ṭuwayr, Abū Muḥammad (1220) i, 801b; iii, **960b**; iv, 1145b; vi, 850a; vii, 150b; viii, 831b, 832a
Ibn ʿUbayya v, 333b
Ibn ʿUdjayl i, 1140b
Ibn Udhayna → ʿUrwa b. Udhayna
Ibn ʿUkāsha (1078) i, 6b; vii, 766b
Ibn ʿUḳba → Mūsā b. ʿUḳba
Ibn ʿUḳda, al-Hamdānī (944) s, **400b**
Ibn al-Ukhuwwa, Ḍiyāʾ al-Dīn (1329) iii, **960b**; vii, 29a; ix, 288a; s, 273b
Ibn ʿUlayya, Abū Isḥāḳ Ibrāhīm b. Ismāʿīl (832) vi, 263b; viii, 711b; s, 90a
Ibn ʿUmar → ʿAbd Allāh b. ʿUmar b. al-Khaṭṭāb; Yaʿḳūb b. ʿUmar al-Maghribī
Ibn ʿUmar, Djazīrat (Cizre) iii, **960b**; v, 447b, 458b; vi, 539b, 627a, 781a; s, 267a
Ibn ʿUmāra → al-Dīkdān
Ibn Umayl (X) ii, 358a, b; iii, 464b, **961b**; v, 112a; s, 270a
Ibn ʿUmayr vi, 248a
Ibn Umayya i, 1343a
Ibn Umm Maktūm vi, 677a
Ibn ʿUnayn (1233) i, 1070a; iii, **962a**; vi, 539a
Ibn Unays vi, 646a
Ibn ʿUrayba v, 1247b
Ibn ʿUṣfūr (1271) iii, 338a, **962b**; vii, 914b; ix, 347a; x, 361a
Ibn al-ʿUshārī (1049) ii, 729a; vi, 350b
Ibn Ustādh-Hurmuz, Abū ʿAlī al-Ḥasan → Ḥasan b. Ustādh-Hurmuz
Ibn Uthāl (666) i, 85a; vi, 139b, 140a, 654b; x, 452b
Ibn ʿUthmān al-Miknāsī (1799) vii, 387b; s, 308a, **401a**
Ibn ʿUyayna → Sufyān b. ʿUyayna
Ibn Wadʿān s, 83a
Ibn Wāfid (1074) i, 345a, 600b; ii, 901a; iii, **962b**; s, 314a
Ibn Wahb → ʿAbd Allāh b. Sabaʾ
Ibn Wahb, ʿAbd Allāh al-Ḳurashī (813) iii, **963a**; iv, 87a; vi, 264b, 265a; vii, 691b
Ibn Wahb, Abu 'l-Ḥusayn (X) s, **402a**
Ibn Wahb al-Kātib (X) viii, 427a, 737b
Ibn Wahbūn (1092) iii, 734a, **963a**; ix, 233a
Ibn Wahhās → al-Khazradjī, Muwaffaḳ al-Dīn
Ibn al-Waḥīd (1312) vii, 840a; s, 589a
Ibn Waḥshiyya (IX) i, 247a; ii, 358a, 455b, 900a; iii, **963b**; iv, 120b, 659a; v, 112a, 222b, 997a; vii, 200a, 203b, 257b, 837a; viii, 677b; s, 59b, 310a, 392b
Ibn Waḳār, Joseph iv, 305a
Ibn Walmiya iv, 337a, b, 339a
Ibn al-Wannān (1773) i, 290b; iii, **965b**; vii, 388a, 1007b; s, 381b
Ibn al-Wardī, Sirādj al-Dīn (1457) i, 594b; ii, 587b; iii, **966a**; iv, 1081b
Ibn al-Wardī, Zayn al-Dīn (1349) i, 119a; iii, 772b, **966b**; iv, 471b; v, 548a; vi, 111b, 185b; vii, 537a
Ibn Warḳāʾ v, 647b; vi, 195b
Ibn Warsand (IX) s, **402b**
Ibn Waṣīf al-Ṣābiʾ iii, 464a; vi, 411b; vii, 141b; xi, 106b **163a**
Ibn Waṣīf Shāh → Ibn Waṣīf al-Ṣābiʾ
Ibn Wāṣil, Abū ʿAbd Allāh (1298) iii, 934a, **967a**; vi, 144a, 429b, 580a; s, 204b, 205a
Ibn Wāsūl (Midrārid) (X) vi, 1038a, 1041a; vii, 486b
Ibn Waththāb ii, 484b; viii, 590b
Ibn Waṭwāṭ (1318) vii, 1040a
Ibn Wazīr → Sidrāy b. Wazīr
Ibn Wazīr, Ibrāhīm b. Muḥammad al-Ḥādawī (Zaydī) (1508) vi, 112a
Ibn al-Wazzān s, 398a
Ibn Yaʿīsh, Muwaffaḳ al-Dīn (1245) i, 571a; ii, 896a; iii, 551a, **968a**; vi, 448b, 637b; vii, 914b
Ibn Yaʿīsh, Solomo(n) (1603) iii, **967b**
Ibn Yaʿīsh, Solomon (1345) iii, **967b**
Ibn Yaʿīsh, Yaḥyā (XII) iii, **967b**
Ibn Yāḳūt → Muḥammad b. Yāḳūt
Ibn Yalbaḳ iii, 46a; iv, 423b, 424a

Ibn Yallas, Muḥammad (1927) iii, 261b, **968a**
Ibn Yāmīn (Benyāmīn) (1520) vi, 226b, 228a
Ibn-i Yamīn, Amīr Fakhr al-Dīn Faryūmadī (1368) iii, **968a**; iv, 66a; viii, 448b; ix, 49a; s, 540a
Ibn-i Yamīn Shiburghānī (1596) iii, **968b**
Ibn Yāsīn → ʿAbd Allāh b. Yāsīn
Ibn al-Yasmīn (1204) vi, 543a
Ibn Yūnus → Abu ʾl-Muẓaffar b. Yūnus
Ibn Yūnus (1059) vi, 279a
Ibn Yūnus (vizier) (1188) x, 554b
Ibn Yūnus (Yūnis), Abu ʾl-Ḥasan ʿAlī al-Ṣadafī (1009) ii, 584a; iii, 9a, **969b**, 1137a; iv, 810a, 1079a; v, 85a, b; vi, 598a, 599b, 600b; vii, 202b; s, 115b, 413b
Ibn Yūnus, Abū Saʿīd (958) iii, **969b**; x, 11a
Ibn Zabāla vi, 666b; viii, 1043b
Ibn al-Zabīr (698) i, 1243a; iii, 165a, **970a**
Ibn al-Zadjdjādj i, 942a
Ibn Ẓafar, Abū ʿAbd Allāh Ḥudjdjat al-Dīn (1170) iii, 309a, **970a**; iv, 506a; vii, 986a; ix, 587b
Ibn al-Zaʿfarānī, Abū ʿAbd Allāh vii, 868b
Ibn Ẓāfir, Djamāl al-Dīn al-Azdī (1216) iii, 894b, **970b**; vii, 528a
Ibn Zāghū, Abu ʾl-ʿAbbās Aḥmad (1441) ix, 247a
Ibn Zāghū, Aḥmad b. Muḥammad x, 499b; s, 403a
Ibn Zāghū, Muḥammad b. Aḥmad iv, 477a
Ibn Zakī iii, 708a
Ibn al-Zaḳḳāk (1133) i, 602a; iii, 823a, **971a**; iv, 1007a; vii, 1046b
Ibn Zakrawayh → Ḥusayn b. Zakrawayh; Yaḥyā b. Zakrawayh
Ibn Zakrī s, **402b**
Ibn Zakrī al-Fāsī (1731) s, **403b**
Ibn Zakrī, Muḥammad Saʿīd v, 1029b; viii, 126a
Ibn Zakrī al-Tilimsānī (1494) xi, 140a; s, **402b**
Ibn Zākūr (1708) ii, 838a; iii, **971b**
Ibn Zamraḳ (1393) i, 602a; iii, 836a, **972b**; vii, 811b, 1025a
Ibn al-Zarḳala → al-Zarḳalī
Ibn Zarḳūn iii, 680b, 798b; iv, 468a; viii, 574a
Ibn Zawlāk → Ibn Zūlāk
Ibn Zayd (1465) vi, 352b
Ibn Zayd, Rabīʿ viii, **351a**
Ibn Zaydān, ʿAbd al-Raḥmān (1946) iii, **973a**; vi, 250a; s, 401b
Ibn Zaydūn, Abu ʾl-Walīd (1070) i, 591a, 592b, 601b; ii, 1033a; iii, 681b, 706a, **973b**; v, 377a; vi, 751a; vii, 661a, 766b, 768a; viii, 533b
Ibn Zaylā, Abū Manṣūr al-Ḥusayn (1048) iii, **974b**; vi, 638a; vii, 207b, 683b; ix, 10a
Ibn al-Zayyāt, Abū Yaʿḳūb al-Tādilī (1230) iii, **975a**; vi, 355b
Ibn al-Zayyāt, Muḥammad b. ʿAbd al-Malik (vizier) (847) iii, **974b**; vii, 191b, 652b, 776b, 777b; xi, 178b; s, 106a
Ibn Zekri → al-Zawāwī, Muḥammad Saʿīd b. Aḥmad
Ibn al-Zibaʿrā, ʿAbd Allāh iii, **975a**; vi, 605a
Ibn Ziyād → ʿUbayd Allāh b. Ziyād
Ibn Ziyād (Zabīd) (1568) iii, 779a; x, 481b; s, 338a
Ibn al-Zubayr → ʿAbd Allāh b. al-Zubayr; ʿAmr b. al-Zubayr; Muṣʿab b. al-Zubayr
Ibn al-Zubayr, Abū ʿAbd Allāh (870) iii, **976b**
Ibn al-Zubayr, Abū Djaʿfar (1308) iii, 762b, **976a**
Ibn Zuhr iii, **976b**; iv, 289b; ix, 258a; s, 392b
Ibn Zuhr, Abu ʾl-ʿAlāʾ (1130) iii, 850a, **976b**
Ibn Zuhr, Abū Bakr Muḥammad (1198) iii, **978b**; vii, 811b; ix, 258a
Ibn Zuhr, Abū Marwān (1161) i, 162a; ii, 481b; iii, 910b, **977b**; vi, 590b; viii, 652b
Ibn Zuknūn i, 273b
Ibn Zūlāḳ (Zawlāḳ), Abū Muḥammad (996) iii, **979a**; vii, 164a, 487b; viii, 42b
Ibn Zumruḳ → Ibn Zamraḳ
Ibn Zurʿa (1008) i, 235a; iii, **979b**; xi, 261a; s, 398b
Ibnou-Zekri → Ibn Zakrī
Ibo → Nigeria
ʿIbra iv, 557a, b, 1031b, 1038a
Ibrā (ʿUmān) s, 355b, 356a
Ibrā (al-Sharḳiyya) ix, 356b; x, 817a; s, 355b
Ibrāḍism iv, 739b

Ibrāhīm (Abraham) i, 177a, 315b; ii, 280a, 1106a; iii, 37a, 165a, **980a**; iv, 184a, b, 318a, b, 956a, b, 959a-b; v, 20a, 421a, 423b, 550b; vi, 105b, 144b, 218b, 566a, 645a, 738a; ix, 383a, b; s, 317a
Ibrāhīm I (Aghlabid) (812) i, 24a, 247b, 248a, 250a; iii, 233a, **981b**, 1032a; iv, 827a; vi, 133b, 295a; ix, 684a
Ibrāhīm II, Aḥmad b. Muḥammad (Aghlabid) (902) i, 24a, 248b, 249a, 250b, 619b; iii, 297b, **982b**; iv, 275b, 337a; v, 105a, 777b; vii, 11a; s, 1a
Ibrāhīm (Ghaznavid) → Ibrāhīm b. Masʿūd II
Ibrāhīm (Ḳaramānid) (1451) vi, 978a
Ibrāhīm (Ottoman) (1648) iii, 623a, **983a**; iv, 884b; v, 272b; vi, 202b, 345b
Ibrāhīm (Ṣafawid) (1447) viii, 766a
Ibrāhīm (Umayyad) i, 57b, 1244a
Ibrāhīm, al-Malik al-Manṣūr → Ibrāhīm b. Shīrkūh
Ibrāhīm, Sultan, Dār Fūr → Ibrāhīm b. Muḥammad Ḥusayn
Ibrāhīm b. ʿAbd Allāh b. al-Ḥasan b. al-Ḥasan (ʿAlid) (762) i, 45b, 103b, 123a, 402b, 952a, 1080a; iii, 616a, **983b**; vi, 263b, 334a, 428a; vii, 114b, 305b, 306a, 358b, 359b, 388b, 784a, 1043b; s, 48b, 130a
Ibrāhīm b. ʿAbd Allāh b. Yazīd b. al-Muhallab (IX) vii, 360a
Ibrāhīm b. ʿAbd al-Djalīl (vizier) (XIV) vi, 441a
Ibrāhīm b. ʿAbd al-Wāḥid iii, 843a
Ibrāhīm b. Abī Ḥātim Aḥmad al-ʿAzafī s, 112b
Ibrāhīm b. Abi 'l-Haytham (XI) vii, 773a
Ibrāhīm b. Abī Salama s, 62a
Ibrāhīm b. Abi 'l-khayr iv, 310a
Ibrāhīm b. Adham (777) i, 162b, 274a; ii, 36b, 353b; iii, 843a, **985b**; viii, 892a
Ibrāhīm b. Aḥmad (Aghlabid amīr) (962) vi, 453a; vii, 76a; ix, 396a
Ibrāhīm b. Aḥmad (Ṣamānid) (X) viii, 110a
Ibrāhīm b. ʿAlāʾ al-Dawla b. Bāysonghor i, 147b
Ibrāhīm b. ʿAlī → al-Shīrāzī
Ibrāhīm b. ʿAlī b. Ḥasan al-Saḳḳāʾ (1881) iii, 250a, **986b**
Ibrāhīm b. ʿAlī b. ʿĪsā i, 387b
Ibrāhīm b. al-Ashʿar s, 399a
Ibrāhīm b. al-Ashtar al-Nakhaʿī (691) i, 50b, 76b; iii, 620b, **987a**; iv, 836a, 1186b; vi, 623a; vii, 650b; viii, 589b; x, 763b
Ibrāhīm b. Ayyūb ii, 79b, 383a
Ibrāhīm b. Benyāmīn, Shaykh (Malāmī) (XVI) vi, 228a
Ibrāhīm b. Bughāmardī iv, 494a
Ibrāhīm b. Dhakwān al-Ḥarrānī (VIII) iii, **987b**
Ibrāhīm b. Djalāl al-Dīn Aḥsan iii, 225a
Ibrāhīm b. Djibrīl iv, 356b
Ibrāhīm b. al-Fakhkhār al-Yahūdī viii, 813b
Ibrāhīm b. Ghurāb (Miṣr) (XV) vii, 172a, 176b
Ibrāhīm b. al-Ḥadjdjādj (911) iv, 822a; vi, 899a
Ibrāhīm b. Ḥammād (935) viii, 363a; s, **385a**
Ibrāhīm b. Ḥaydar b. Djunayd (Ṣafawid) (XV) viii, 766b
Ibrāhīm b. Hilāl → al-Ṣābiʾ, Abū Isḥāḳ Ibrāhīm b. Hilāl
Ibrāhīm b. Hishām b. Ismāʿīl al-Makhzūmī iv, 370a; vi, 139b; xi, 473b
Ibrāhīm b. Ḥusām al-Dīn Ḥasan (Marʿash) (XIII) vi, 507b
Ibrāhīm b. al-Ḥuḍayn al-Ḳūṣī xi, 459a
Ibrāhīm b. Ilyās viii, 1026a
Ibrāhīm b. ʿĪsā Khān Tarkhān I (1558) vi, 189b, 190a
Ibrāhīm b. Ismāʿīl al-Aṭrash ii, 637a
Ibrāhīm b. Ismāʿīl b. Yasār iv, 190a
Ibrāhīm b. Ḳarātakīn ii, 1109b; iv, 614a
Ibrāhīm b. Ḳays i, 1283a
Ibrāhīm b. Khālid → Abū Thawr
Ibrāhīm b. al-Mahdī (ʿAbbāsid) (839) i, 272a, 1312b; ii, 731a, 1072a; iii, 745b, 767b, 872b, **987b**, 996b; iv, 17a, 940a; v, 69b; vi, 205b, 335a, b, 336a; vii, 404a, 518b; xi, 53a; s, 64a
Ibrāhīm b. Mālik → Ibrāhīm b. al-Ashtar
Ibrāhīm b. Marzubān (X) ii, 680a; vi, 499b; vii, 636b, 655b, 656b, 657a; x, 897b
Ibrāhīm b. Masʿūd II (Ghaznawid) (1099) ii, 5a, 1052a, 1100a; iv, 942b; v, 622b; vi, 273b, 274a; vii, 193a; s, 21a
Ibrāhīm b. al-Mudabbir → Ibn al-Mudabbir, Ibrāhīm
Ibrāhīm b. Muhādjir iv, 667b

Ibrāhīm b. Muḥammad (632) vi, 575a, 650b; vii, 374b
Ibrāhīm b. Muḥammad b. Abī ʿAwn (934) vii, 397b
Ibrāhīm b. Muḥammad b. ʿAlī, al-Imām (749) i, 15b, 16a, 141a; iii, **988a**; iv, 446b; vi, 332b, 333a, 334b, 620b; vii, 396a
Ibrāhīm b. Muḥammad b. Fahd al-Makramī iv, 201a
Ibrāhīm b. Muḥammad b. Ṭalḥa (VII) vii, 522a
Ibrāhīm b. Muḥammad ʿAlī Pas̲h̲a (1848) vi, 541b; ix, 903b
Ibrāhīm b. Muḥammad al-Fazārī (804) ii, 36b
Ibrāhīm b. Muḥammad Ḥusayn i, 929b; ii, 123b
Ibrāhīm b. Muḥammad Ẓāfir al-Madanī v, 949a; xi, 298b
Ibrāhīm b. Mūsā I iii, 262b
Ibrāhīm b. Mūsā al-Kāẓim (IX) iv, 855b; vi, 148a, 334b; s, 95a
Ibrāhīm b. Muzayn i, 600a
Ibrāhīm b. Naṣr (X) vii, 477b
Ibrāhīm b. Sahl → Ibn Sahl al-Isrāʾīlī
Ibrāhīm b. Sayāba (809) iii, **989a**
Ibrāhīm (Sayyid) b. Sayyid Muḥammad (Bayhaḳī) s, 131b
Ibrāhīm b. S̲h̲āhruk̲h̲ (1435) iii, 337a, b, **989a**; iv, 221b; v, 827b; ix, 475a
Ibrāhīm b. S̲h̲īrkūh (1246) iii, 399b, **989b**
Ibrāhīm b. Sīmd̲j̲ūr (X) viii, 110a, 1027b
Ibrāhīm b. Sinān (X) iv, 1182b; vii, 405a; viii, 560b; x, 428b
Ibrāhīm b. al-Sindī b. S̲h̲ahāk (IX) iii, **990a**; vii, 259a
Ibrāhīm b. Sulaymān al-S̲h̲āmī → al-S̲h̲āmī, Ibrāhīm b. Sulaymān
Ibrāhīm b. ʿUmar al-Biḳāʿī al-S̲h̲āfiʿī iv, 92a
Ibrāhīm b. al-Walīd I (Umayyad) (750) iii, 704b, **990b**; vi, 623b, 624a
Ibrāhīm b. Waṣīf S̲h̲āh → al-Waṣīfī, Ibrāhīm b. Waṣīf S̲h̲āh
Ibrāhīm b. Yaḥyā (800) ix, 182a
Ibrāhīm b. Yaḥyā al-Suḥūlī iii, 688b
Ibrāhīm b. Yaʿḳūb al-Isrāʾīlī al-Ṭurṭūs̲h̲ī (X) i, 157a; iii, **991a**, 1045a; v, 719a, 1012b, 1013a, 1014a; viii, 875a; s, 170b
Ibrāhīm b. Yūsuf b. Tās̲h̲ufīn ii, 838a; iii, 728a, 822b, 977b; ix, 363a
Ibrāhīm ʿĀdil S̲h̲āh I i, 199a; iii, 15b, 426a, 626a, 1160b, 1161a; v, 1216a
Ibrāhīm ʿĀdil S̲h̲āh II (1627) i, 199b, 781b, 1200a, 1202b, 1203a,b, 1204a; ii, 921b, 922a; iii, 15b, 426b, 453b; v, 1216a; vi, 271b; vii, 341a
Ibrāhīm Ag̲h̲a → Kečiboynuzu Ibrāhīm Pas̲h̲a
Ibrāhīm Āg̲h̲ā Mustaḥfiẓān iv, 426a, 431a, 437b
Ibrāhīm Āg̲h̲ā, Zurnazen-bas̲h̲ı̊ (XVII) vi, 1007b
Ibrāhīm al-Aḥdab (1891) iii, **991b**; v, 1103b; vi, 113b, 913b; s, 40a, 161a
Ibrāhīm Aḥmad Barzānī (XX) vii, 714a
Ibrāhīm al-ʿAwwānī (1320) s, 172b
Ibrāhīm al-Bād̲j̲ūrī → Bād̲j̲ūrī, Ibrāhīm b. Muḥammad
Ibrāhīm Bahādur b. Meḥmed i, 783b; ii, 599a
Ibrāhīm Bayyūd (XX) viii, 902b
Ibrāhīm Beg (Tād̲j̲īk) (XX) iii, 483b
Ibrāhīm Beg b. Ork̲h̲ān Beg (Ментес̲h̲e) (1360) vi, 1018a, b
Ibrāhīm Beg Ḳarāmān-og̲h̲lu iv, 623b, 624a; v, 677a
Ibrāhīm Bey (Faḳārī, Miṣr) (XVII) vii, 178b
Ibrāhīm Bey (Tunis) iii, 605a; iv, 828b
Ibrāhīm Bey Isfendiyār Og̲h̲lu iv, 108b
Ibrāhīm Bey al-Kabīr (1816) iii, **992a**; iv, 853a; vi, 325b; vii, 179a, 420b
Ibrāhīm al-Dasūḳī → al-Dasūḳī, Ibrāhīm b. Ibrāhīm; al-Dasūḳī, Ibrāhīm b. Muḥammad
Ibrāhīm Derwis̲h̲ Pas̲h̲a (1896) ii, 878b; iii, **992b**
Ibrāhīm al-D̲j̲azzār i, 551a
Ibrāhīm Edhem Pas̲h̲a (1893) i, 285b; ii, 694b; iii, **993a**; iv, 190b, 191a
Ibrāhīm al-Fazārī iii, 976a
Ibrāhīm Fūda (XX) vi, 175b
Ibrāhīm Guls̲h̲enī → Guls̲h̲anī, Ibrāhīm b. Muḥammad
Ibrāhīm Ḥaḳḳī (1780) i, 1072a; ii, 450b; vii, 839a; s, 614b
Ibrāhīm Ḥaḳḳī Pas̲h̲a (1918) ii, 533b; iii, **993b**, 1188b; vi, 74a; vii, 547b

Ibrāhīm al-Ḥalabī → al-Ḥalabī, Burhān al-Dīn
Ibrāhīm al-Ḥāmidī → al-Ḥāmidī
Ibrāhīm al-Ḥarbī (898) i, 718a; iii, 706b, **994b**; s, 304b
Ibrāhīm al-Hāshīmī, Sharīf iv, 919b
Ibrāhīm Ḥilmī Pasha → Kečiboynuzu Ibrāhīm Ḥilmī
Ibrāhīm Ḥusayn Mīrzā (Mīrzās, Gudj arāt) iv, 666a; vii, 133a, 134a
Ibrāhīm al-Imām → Ibrāhīm b. Muḥammad b. ʿAlī
Ibrāhīm Ināl i, 420a, 512b, 1074a; ii, 5a; iii, 258b; iv, 26b, 466a, 807a; v, 388a, 454a, 489a; vii, 1017b; x, 553a, b
Ibrāhīm Kāhya → al-Ḳāzdughlī, Ibrāhīm
Ibrāhīm Karāma s, 162b
Ibrāhīm Ḳaṭarāghāsī iii, 88b
Ibrāhīm Katkhudā (1754) i, 391b
Ibrāhīm al-Khalīl → Ibrāhīm (Abraham)
Ibrāhīm Khalīl Khān ii, 490b; iv, 573a
Ibrāhīm Khān (1622) iii, **995a**
Ibrāhīm Khān (Ḳazān) iv, 849a
Ibrāhīm Khān (Lār) v, 672b
Ibrāhīm Khān, Ẓahīr al-Dawla v, 155b, 164b
Ibrāhīm Khān b. Aḥmad iv, 581b
Ibrāhīm Khān Avar i, 755b
Ibrāhīm Khān Fatḥ Djang (Bihār) (1617) vi, 410a
Ibrāhīm Khān Kākar (XVII) vi, 410a
Ibrāhīm Khān Sarwānī ix, 448a
Ibrāhīm Khān Sūr (Bengal) (1534) ii, 271b; vi, 47a; vii, 965b; ix, 894a, b
Ibrāhīm khan Zangana v, 169b
Ibrāhīm Khān-zāde ii, 999a; iii, 995a
Ibrāhīm khāṣṣ Oda-Bashi̊ → Ibrāhīm Pasha (Maḳbūl)
Ibrāhīm al-Khawwāṣ (903) x, 377b; s, 823a
Ibrāhīm Ḳuṭb Shāh i, 1047b, 1048a; ii, 1119a; iii, 319b; v, 550a; vii, 943b; viii, 73a
Ibrāhīm Lōdī (Delhi) (1526) i, 252b, 848a, 1068b; ii, 271a; iii, 168a, 420b, **995a**; v, 784a; viii, 253b; s, 203a, 331b
Ibrāhīm al-Mawṣilī (804) i, 10b, 107b, 108a, 118a; iii, 749b, 989a, **996a**; iv, 822a; vii, 518a, 563a; s, 17b, 64a, 116b, 128a, 183a
Ibrāhīm al-Māzinī s, 57b
Ibrāhīm Mīrzā b. Sulaymān Mīrzā (1560) vii, 135a
Ibrāhīm Mīrzā (Ṣafawid) (1517) viii, 1212a
Ibrāhīm Mīrzā b. Bahrām Shāh (Ṣafawid) (1568) viii, 775b
Ibrāhīm, Muḥammad al-Bashīr (1965) iii, **1003b**; iv, 158b
Ibrāhīm al-Mūsawī s, 423a
Ibrāhīm Mussu → Karamoko Alfa
Ibrāhīm Müteferriḳa (1745) i, 63b, 270a, 1271b; ii, 589b, 704b; iii, **996b**; v, 641b; vi, 800a; vii, 794b; viii, 859b; xi, 138a
Ibrāhīm Naʿīm al-Dīn ii, 990b
Ibrāhīm al-Nakhaʿī (714) ii, 888a, b; iii, 512a; v, 350b, 731a, b; vi, 925b; vii, 258b
Ibrāhīm Nasir (Maldives) vi, 246a
Ibrāhīm Pasha → khodja Ibrāhīm Pasha; Shāḳshāḳī Ibrāhīm Pasha; Shayṭān Ibrāhīm Pasha
Ibrāhīm Pasha (Maḳbūl) (1536) i, 293b; ii, 400a, 722b, 884b, 1042b, 1136a; iii, **998a**, 1183b; iv, 333b, 1137b; v, 650a; vi, 759a; vii, 177b, 225a, 713a; viii, 202b; ix, 833b; s, 315b
Ibrāhīm Pasha (al-Mawṣil) (XIX) vi, 542a
Ibrāhīm Pasha, Ḥādjdjī iii, 91b; iv, 594b, 595a
Ibrāhīm Pasha, Ḳarā (1687) iii, **1001b**
Ibrāhīm Pasha b. khalīl Djandarli̊ → Djandarli̊, Ibrāhīm Pasha b. Khalīl
Ibrāhīm Pasha b. Muḥammad ʿAlī Pasha (1848) i, 182b, 244a, 341b, 399a, 975a, 1079a, 1134a, 1138a, 1234a; ii, 38b, 108b, 288a,b, 321a,b, 514a, 636a, 912a; iii, 89a, 300a, 326b, 400a, 628b, **999a**; iv, 130b, 609b, 717b, 765a, 925b; v, 36a, 322b, 335a, 539b, 1253b; vi, 75a, 232a, 508b, 778a; vii, 182b, 217b, 241a, 515a; viii, 84b, 484b
Ibrāhīm Pasha al-ʿAẓm (XVI) v, 591b, 925b
Ibrāhīm Pasha Dāmād (1601) i, 270b, 826b; ii, 20a, 34a, 49a, 103b, 634b; iii, 342b, **1000b**; iv, 233b; vi, 800b
Ibrāhīm Pasha Katkhudā i, 68b
Ibrāhīm Pasha Millī v, 463a
Ibrāhīm Pasha Nevshehirli (1730) i, 269b, 270a, 836b, 1004b; ii, 20a; iii, 997b, **1002a**; iv, 969b; v, 641a, b, 642a, b, 643a, b; vi, 55b, 1005a; viii, 11a

Ibrāhīm Pasha Ṭawīl i, 236b; vi, 112b
Ibrāhīm Pečewī → Pečewī
Ibrāhīm Pūr-i Dāwūd iv, 71a (see also Pūr-i Dāwūd, Ibrāhīm)
Ibrāhīm al-Rashīd al-Duwayḥī (1874) vii, 124a; viii, 990a; s, 279a
Ibrāhīm Rawḍa (Bīdjāpūr) i, 1204a; v, 295a; vi, 126a
Ibrāhīm al-Riyāḥī (1849) x, 465a
Ibrāhīm al-Ṣābiʾ → al-Ṣābiʾ, Abū Isḥāḳ Ibrāhīm b. Hilāl
Ibrāhīm al-Sadjīnī s, 44b
Ibrāhīm Sālār iii, 703b
Ibrāhīm Ṣāliḥ b. Yūnis al-Ḥusaynī (XX) x, 464b
Ibrāhīm Shāh Sharḳī (Djawnpūr) (1440) i, 702b, 859a, 1300a; ii, 51b, 180b, 499a; iii, 14b, 419a, **1003a**; iv, 513a; vi, 61b, 294b; vii, 278b, 279a; s, 206b
Ibrāhīm al-Sharīf → Ibrāhīm Bey (Tunis)
Ibrāhīm Shāshī s, 50b
Ibrāhīm al-Shāṭibī iv, 381b
Ibrāhīm Shināsī → Shināsī
Ibrāhīm Shīrāzī, Ḥādjdjī (1801) s, **405b**
Ibrāhīm Sori Maudo ii, 942a, 960a, 1132a
Ibrāhīm al-Ṣūlī (857) i, 10a; x, 129a; s, 720a
Ibrāhīm Tamghač Khān iii, 1114a,b, 1115b; iv, 200a
Ibrāhīm Temo ii, 430b
Ibrāhīm al-Yashrūṭī → Ibrāhīm b. Muḥammad Ẓāfir al-Madanī
Ibrāhīm al-Yāzidjī → al-Yāzidjī, Ibrāhīm
Ibrāhīm Yināl → Ibrāhīm Ināl
Ibrāhīma Mussu → Karamoko Alfa
Ibrahimu Dabo iv, 549a
Ibrail i, 269a; ii, 612a; iii, **1004a**
ʿIbrī → Yahūd
ʿIbrī iii, **1004b**
Ibrīḳ v, 989a; x, 769b; s, **406a**, 778a
Ibrīm → Ḳaṣr Ibrīm
Ibrīm (Piromi) i, 1029a; 11, 1110b; viii, 90a; s, 35b (see also *s.v.* Abū Sinbil)
Ibrishīm, Ibrisīm → Ḥarīr
ʿIbriyyūn iii, 1004b
Ibruh i, 348a, 487b, 489a; iii, 74a, **1005a**
al-Ibshīhī, Aḥmad iii, 1006a
al-Ibshīhī, Bahāʾ al-Dīn (1446) ii, 536b; iii, 392a, **1005a**; vi, 115a, 823b, 904b; xi, 564a; s, 350a
al-Ibshīhī, Shihāb al-Dīn iii, 1006a
Ibshīr Muṣṭafā Pasha → Ipshir Muṣṭafā Pasha
Ibtidāʾ iii, **1006a**; iv, 152a, 264a
Ibuḳrāṭ(īs) → Buḳrāṭ
Ibyār (Djazīrat Banī Naṣr) vi, 453b
Ič-oghlanı̊ i, 394a, 395a; ii, 1087b, 1088b; iii, **1006b**
Ičil ii, 34b; iii, **1006b**; iv, 617a
Içoglan → Ič-oghlanı̊
ʿĪd iii, **1007a**; v, 477a
ʿĪd b. Djāmiʿ i, 752a
ʿĪd al-aḍḥā i, 1b; iii, **1007b**
ʿĪd al-fiṭr iii, **1008a**; v, 714b
ʿĪd al-ghadīr iv, 1110b; vi, 851b
ʿĪd al-kabīr → ʿĪd al-aḍḥā
ʿĪd-i Ḳurbān iv, 103b
ʿĪd al-naḥr vi, 850a, 851a, b (see also *s.v.* ʿĪd al-aḍḥā)
al-ʿĪd, Muḥammad iv, 159b
al-ʿIdāda → al-Asturlāb
Iʿdādiyye i, 285b; x, 206b
al-Īdadjfaghī, Awfā b. Abū Bakr (1883) vii, 622b
Iḍāfa → Nisba
Iḍāfa iii, **1008a**
Iḍam → Ḥamḍ, Wādī al-
Iʿdām → Ḳatl
Īdar ii, 1124b, 1125a, b, 1128a; iii, **1010a**; vi, 51a, 1028a
Iddī, Āl s, 269a
Iddighām → Idghām
Idfū → Adfū
Idghām iii, **1013a**
Idgish v, 254a
Idgü Bahādur Barlās v, 163b
Idhāʿa iii, **1014a**; x, 134b
Īdhadj (Māl-Amīr) iii, **1015b**; iv, 675b; v, 826b, 827a, 830b; vi, 494b; viii, 417a; ix, 500a
Idhkhir iv, 322a; 819b; x, 900a
Idil → Itil (river)
Idhn i, 429b; iii, 1016a, 1181b
Idhnnāme i, 679a
Idī Amīn x, 780b
ʿIdī (Mahra) vi, 83b
Idibaʾil i, 525a
Īdj → Īg
Īdjāb i, 1111b; iii, **1017a**
Idjār, idjāra iii, **1017a**; v, 126b
Idjāra iii, **1017b**

Idjāza i, 66a, 90b, 96a, 142b, 319b, 817a; ii, 304a; iii, 27a, 491a, **1020b**; iv, 412b, 634a, 950b, 1125b; v, 1125a, 1132b
Idjāza → Ḥadjdj
Idjdhāb iv, 95a
al-Īdjī, ʿAḍud al-Dīn (1355) i, 342b, 593a, 715a, 715b; ii, 608a, 774a; iii, **1022a**, 1176a; iv, 737a; vi, 218a, 848a; vii, 480b; viii, 45a
Idjil i, 809a
ʿIdjl Banū i, 963a, b, 964a, b; iii, **1022b**; iv, 718a, b; vi, 441b; x, 400b
ʿIdjl b. Ludjaym iii, 1022b; s, 122a
al-ʿIdjlī → Abu ʾl-Nadjm al-ʿIdjlī; al-Aghlab; al-Ḳāsim b. ʿĪsā
al-ʿIdjlī, Abu ʾl-Aḥwaṣ ʿUmar b. al-Aḥwaṣ (759) i, 134b; vi, 946a
al-ʿIdjlī, Abū Dulaf → al-Ḳāsim b. ʿĪsā
al-ʿIdjlī, Abū Manṣūr (738) i, 1099a; ii, 1094a; vi, **441b**; vii, 347b, 398b, 459b; s, 510a
al-ʿIdjlī, Aḥmad b. ʿAbd Allāh (875) viii, 516a
al-ʿIdjlī, Asʿad b. Masʿūd b. khalaf (1203) vi, 914a
al-ʿIdjlī, Harūn b. Saʿīd ii, 377b; s, 130a
al-ʿIdjlī, al-Madhʿūr b. ʿAdī (VII) vii, 796b
al-ʿIdjlī, al-Mughīra b. Saʿīd Ghālī (737) i, 141a, 1099a, 1116b; ii, 1094a; iv, 926b; vi, 441b; vii, 388b, 399a; s, 103b, 232b
al-ʿIdjlī, Muḥammad b. Nūḥ vii, 3a
al-ʿIdjlī, Murra al-Rudaynī ix, 680b
ʿIdjliyya s, 130a
Idjmāʿ i, 259b, 1199b; ii, 182b, 411b, 888b; iii, **1023a**, 1061b; iv, 154a; v, 239a
Idjnāwn ii, 369a
Idjtihād i, 259b, 276a; iii, 954a, 1025b, **1026a**; iv, 152b-154a, 1101a; v, 241a
Idjtimāʿ iv, 259a; v, 577b; vii, 1050b (see also *s.v.* Istiḳbāl)
al-Idkawī, ʿAbd Allāh (1770) vi, 112b
Iḍmār ii, 786b; iii, **1027b**; xi, 508b
Idrāk ii, 891b; iii, **1028a**; viii, 649a
Idrākī Bēglārī (XVII) iii, **1029b**
Idrīs (the hidden) vi, 227b, 228a
Idrīs (prophet) iii, **1030b**; vi, 412b, 651a; viii, 387a
Idrīs, ʿImād al-Dīn (1468) x, 403b
Idrīs, Mawlāy → Idris II b. Idrīs
Idrīs al-Mutaʿayyid (Malaga) (1039) x, 144b
Idrīs (nāʾib) (Maṣawwaʿ) vi, 642b
Idrīs, Suhayl iv, 525b; v, 191b
Idrīs, Yūsuf v, 191a, b; x, 797b, 798a
Idrīs I (al-Akbar) b. ʿAbd Allāh (Idrīsid) (793) i, 402b, 1037a, 1175b; ii, 745a, 818a, 874a; iii, 616b, 617a, **1031a**; v, 1175a, 1189a; vi, 140b, 742b, 815b; vii, 389b; xi, 132b; s, 103a
Idrīs II (al-Aṣghar) b. Idrīs I (Idrīsid) (828) i, 1088a; ii, 818a, 874a; iii, **1031b**; v, 1189a, 1200a, 1201a; vi, 742b; s, 103a
Idrīs II al-ʿAlī (Ḥammūdid) (1055) vi, 222a
Idrīs I al-Sanūsī (1982) (Lybia) i, 1049b, 1071b; ii, 667b; iv, 262a; v, 697a, 758a, b, 1066a; vi, 262a; ix, 24a
Idrīs b. Abī Ḥafṣa vi, 625b
Idrīs b. Aḥmad al-Ḥabūḍī s, 338b
Idrīs b. ʿAlī → al-Ḥansh
Idrīs b. ʿAlī b. Ḥammūd (Ḥammūdid) (1039) vi, 222a
Idrīs b. Bā Ḥmād s, 114a
Idrīs b. al-Ḥasan, ʿImād al-Dīn (1468) s, **407a**
Idrīs b. al-Ḥusayn, Sharīf (1625) s, **407b**
Idrīs b. Muḥammad al-Arbāb ii, 944a
Idris Abdul Wakil (XX) xi, 450b
Idrīs Alooma (Alawōma) iv, 567b; s, 164a
Idrīs Atuma i, 1259b
Idrīs Bidlīsī → Bidlīsī, Idrīs
Idrīs al-Maʾmūn, Abu ʾl-ʿUlāʾ (Almohad) (1232) i, 1176b; iii, 207b; iv, 116a, 117b; vi, 592b, 593a, 595b
al-Idrīsī, Abū ʿAbd Allāh (1166) i, 157a, 168a, 214a, 488a, 594a, 602b, 1337b; ii, 578a, 582a, 585a; iii, 7a, 405a, **1032b**, 1077a; iv, 274b, 1080b; vi, 283a, 350b, 639b, 640a; vii, 245b; ix, 589b; s, 92a, 171a, 376b
al-Idrīsī, Abū Djaʿfar → al-Idrīsī, Djamāl al-Dīn
al-Idrīsī, Abū Djaʿfar, Sharīf vi, 411a, 412b; viii, 428a, 895a; s, 123b
al-Idrīsī, Djamāl al-Dīn s, **407b**
al-Idrīsī, Muḥammad b. ʿAlī i, 98b, 277b, 709b; ii, 518a; v, 758a, 808b, 809a
Idrīsids i, 156b, 403a, 1044a; ii, 145b, 818a, 821a, 853a, 1095b; iii, 30b, **1035b**; iv, 632a, b; vi, 134a, 712b
Idrīsiyya i, 87b, 277b, 555a, 709b; ix, 24b, 173a; s, 278b; 697a

Iḍṭirār iii, **1037a**; vi, 448a
Iduḳ Ḳut i, 1240a, b; x, 676b
ʿIdwa s, 408a
al-ʿIdwī al-Ḥamzāwī, Ḥasan (1885) v, 1237a; s, **408a**
Ifāḍa iii, 32a, b, 36a
al-ʿIfār ii, 631b; iii, **1037b**
Ifāt → Awfāt
ʿIffat b. Aḥmad Āl Thunayyān s, 305b
ʿIffat Ārāʾ Bēgum i, 813b
ʿIffat al-Salṭana iv, 392a
ʿIffatiyya vi, 485b
Ifgan vii, 263a
Iflāḳ → Eflāḳ
al-Iflīlī → Ibn al-Iflīlī
Iflīmūn → Aflīmūn
Ifnī iii, **1038a**; vii, 391b; viii, 671b; x, 551b
Ifoghas i, 210b; iii, **1038b**
Ifrād iii, 35a, 53b; x, 865b, 866a
Ifrāgha iii, **1038b**
Īfran, Banū (Īfrānids) i, 6a, 367a; iii, **1039a**; v, 1164b, 1175a, 1179a, 1245b; vi, 311b; vii, 761a
al-Ifrandj i, 9b, 82b, 197a, 198b, 216a, 639b, 664a, 784a, 798a, 804a, 932b, 946a, 983a, 1017a, 1025a, 1054b, 1125b, 1332a; ii, 63b, 282b, 292b, 318b, 912a; iii, 325a, 398b, 503b, **1044a**, 1118b; iv, 520b, 642a, 779a; v, 921b, 924b; x, 81b; s, 205a
al-Ifrānī (Īfranī), Abū ʿAbd Allāh (1743) i, 315b; iii, **1046b**; vi, 188a, 350b, 351a, 356b, 594b; s, 28b
al-Ifrānī, Abū Ḳudāma Yazīd b. Fendīn (803) iii, 1041b; viii, 112b
al-Ifrānī, Ayyūb b. Abī Yazīd (X) viii, 632a
al-Ifrānī, Yaʿlā b. Muḥammad b. Ṣāliḥ (X) vii, 263a
Ifrāṭ, Ifrāṭ fi ʾl-Ṣifa → Mubālagha
al-Ifrīḳī, ʿAbd al-Aʿlā b. Ḥudaydj (or Djuraydj) (VIII) vi, 923a; ix, 767b
Ifrīḳiya i, 50a, 79a, 86a, 92b, 104a, 124b, 134b, 156b, 166a, 247b, 248a, 532b, 1321a; ii, 331b, 852b, 998a; iii, 1032a, 1040b, **1047a**; iv, 175a, b, 176b, 177a; v, 503a, 723b, 877a; vi, 280a, 434a, 457a, 606a; vii, 70a; s, 1a, 62b, 306a
– language, literature i, 568b
ʿIfrīt ii, 323a; iii, **1050a**; s, 52b
Ifruḳlus → Buruḳlus
Iftāʾ ii, 866a, b
Iftikhār al-Dīn Muḥammad al-Bukhārī iv, 860a
Iftikhār Khān (XVII) vii, 331b, 432b
Īg ix, 156b, 158a
Igal, Muḥammad Ḥādjdjī Ibrāhīm (XX) ix, 718b, 719a
Igdir, Banū (Oghuz) vi, 416a, b; x, 412b, 413a; s, 168b, 169a
Igerwān s, 113b
Ighār i, 1144b; iii, **1051a**, 1088b; iv, 1032a
Igharghar iii, **1051a**
Ighlān s, 395a
Ighrāḳ, Ighrāḳ fi ʾl-Ṣifa → Mubālagha
Ighraḳ, Sayf al-Dīn iv, 918a
Igīlīz → Gīlīz
Igli v, 964b; vi, 742a, b, 743b, 744a; ix, 900b
Igliwa → Glāwa
Īhām → Tawriya
Iḥdāth iii, 664b, **1051a**
Ihlīladj → Halīladj
Iḥrām iii, 35a, 36b, **1052b**; v, 329a; vi, 918a; viii, 356b; x, 864b
Iḥṣān → Muḥṣan
Iḥsān, Aḥmad → Aḥmad Iḥsān
Iḥsān ʿAbd al-Ḳuddūs (XX) v, 190a; vi, 468b; ix, 558b; x, 797b
Iḥsān Allāh (Djudda) (XX) vi, 157b
Iḥsān Allāh Khān ii, 445b; v, 310b
Iḥsās → Ḥiss
Iḥtisāb → Ḥisba
Iḥtishām al-Dawla v, 674b; s, 302a
Iḥyāʾ iii, **1053b**
Īḳāʿ viii, 421b; s, **408b**
ʿIḳāb (punishment) → ʿAdhāb; ʿAdhāb al-Ḳabr; Djazāʾ; Ḥadd; Taʿzīr; ʿUḳūba
al-ʿIḳāb (battle 1212) i, 495b; iii, **1055a**; vii, 989a; x, 606a
ʿIkabb (VI) i, 826b; vii, 563a
Iḳāla i, 319b; iii, **1056b**
Iḳāma i, 188b; iii, **1057a**
Iḳbāl, Āl s, 338a
Iḳbāl, Sir Muḥammad (1938) i, 327a; ii, 546b, 1036b; iii, 119b, 432a, **1057a**; iv, 170b; v, 601a; vi, 461b, 838b; vii, 297a, 422a
Iḳbāl b. Sābiḳ-i Sīstānī i, 347b
Iḳbāl al-Dawla → ʿAlī b. Mudjāhid al-Āmirī
Iḳbāl Khān → Mallū Iḳbāl Khān

Iḳbāl Khān (Mālwā) (XVI) vi, 54b
Iḳbāl-nāma iv, 127b, 128b
Iḳbāl al-Sharābī (XIII) vii, 727b
Iḳbāl-i Sistānī → Iḳbāl b. Sābiḳ-i Sistānī
Īkdjān v, 540a, b; vi, 727b
Iḳfāʾ → Ḳāfiya
Ikhlāṣ iii, **1059b**
Ikhlāṣī, Shaykh Meḥmed iv, 761a
Ikhlāṣī, Walīd x, 799a
Ikhmīm → Akhmīm
al-Ikhnāʾī, Taḳī al-Dīn iii, 953a
Ikhshīd (title) iii, **1060b**
al-Ikhshīd → Kāfūr, Abu 'l-Misk; Muḥammad b. Tughdj
Ikhshīdids i, 435b, 439b, 551b, 1042a; ii, 130a, 281b; iii, 129a, 768b, 979a, **1060b**; iv, 418a; s, 120b
Ikhshīdiyya viii, 614b
Ikhshīn (river) ix, 310a
Ikhtilādj iii, **1061a**; v, 100a; s, 235b
Ikhtilāf i, 155a; iii, 160b, **1061b**
Ikhtisān, Muḥammad Ṣadr ʿAlāʾ (XIV) s, **409a**
Ikhtiyār i, 413a; iii, 1037a, **1062b**
Ikhtiyār al-Dīn Abu 'l-Mudjāhid Ḳādir Khān (Kālpī) (1432) vi, 61b
Ikhtiyār al-Dīn Alṭūniya → Malik Alṭūniya
Ikhtiyār al-Dīn Aytaḳ ii, 253a; ix, 16b
Ikhtiyār al-Dīn Āytigīn → Āytigīn, Ikhtiyār al-Dīn
Ikhtiyār al-Dīn Ghāzī Shāh ii, 751b
Ikhtiyār al-Dīn Ḥusayn vii, 988a
Ikhtiyār al-Dīn Muḥammad khāldjī → Muḥammad Bakhtiyār Khaldjī
Ikhtiyār al-Dīn Munshī iv, 1124a
Ikhtiyār al-Dīn Zangī (XIII) vii, 973b
Ikhtiyār Heyʾeti i, 972b
Ikhtiyār Khān (Dihlī) (XV) vi, 49b, 50a
Ikhtiyār Khān Ṣiddīḳī (Gudjarāt) (XVI) vi, 52a
Ikhtiyārāt (anthologies) → Mukhtārāt
Ikhtiyārāt (hemerology) iii, **1063b**; iv, 518b
Ikhtiyāriyya s, **409b**
al-Ikhwān (Wahhābīs) ii, 469a; iii, 361b, **1064a**; iv, 680b, 681a, 1133b; v, 574b, 998a, b; vi, 46a, 152b, 157b; ix, 904b; s, 3b
al-Ikhwān al-Djumhūriyyūn x, 96b, 97a
al-Ikhwān al-Muslimūn i, 416b, 1018b; ii, 429b, 882b; iii, 162b, 518a, 557b, **1068b**; iv, 161b, 206b; vi, 360b; viii, 717a; s, 6a, b, 7a, 300b
Ikhwān al-Ṣafāʾ i, 247a, 350b, 589b, 659b, 737a, 772a, 1156a; ii, 93a, 358b, 361b, 554b, 579a, 765b, 766a, 774b; iii, 21b, 134a, 171a, 301a, 313a, 329a, 1059b, **1071a**, 1130a, 1139a, 1171b, 1207a; iv, 367a, 548a, 663a; v, 703a; vi, 99a, 450b, 905b; vii, 954b; s, 321a, 414a
Ikhwāniyyāt ii, 302a; iv, 1005b; viii, 536b, 537a
Ikhwat Yūsuf vii, 10b
al-Iklīl → Nudjūm
Iklīl al-Malik s, **410a**
Iḳlīme khātūn (Marʿash) vi, 509b
Iklān → Akli
Iḳlīm i, 489b, 988a; iii, **1076b**; iv, 223a, 273b; v, 398a
Iḳna → Ḳunā
Ikrāh i, 319a; s, **410b**
Iḳrār iii, 511b, **1078a**; ix, 845b
Iḳrār Khān ix, 83b
ʿIkrima b. Abī Djahl (VII) i, 115b, 151a, 690b, 812b; ii, 895b; iii, 653b, **1081b**; vi, 84a, 138a, b, 546b, 1038a; viii, 155a; ix, 6a; s, 232b, 386b
Iḳrītish (Crete) i, 83a, 121b, 397b, 935b, 1249a; ii, 130a, 489b; iii, 621a, **1082a**; iv, 539a, 766a, 1054a, 1157b; v, 503a; vi, 58b; s, 120b, 186a
al-Iḳrītishī iii, 1085b
al-Iksīr iii, 961b, **1087b**; v, 113b; xi, 495b
Iḳṭāʿ i, 533b, 802a, 1144a, b, 1146b, 1353a; ii, 187b, 508a; iii, **1088a**; iv, 18a, 26a, 32a, 323b, 975a, 1043b; v, 688a, 862b
Iḳtibās iii, **1091b**
Iḳtiḍāb → Tadjnīs; Takhalluṣ
Iktisāb → Kasb
Iḳwāʾ → Ḳāfiya
Īl iii, **1092a**
Īl-Arslān iii, 1110b; iv, 29b, 658b, 1067b; viii, 444b; x, 419b; s, 245b
Īlāʾ → Ṭalāḳ
Īlāf iii, **1093a**; vi, 145b
Ilāh iii, **1093b**
Ilāhābād → Allāhābād
Ilāhī iii, **1094a**; v, 275a
Ilāhī, Mollā ʿAbd Allāh (1491) vii, 754a, 936a; xi, 612a; x, 322a; s, 51b
Ilāhī Bakhsh "Maʿrūf" (1826) iii, **1095a**

Ilāhī Era s, **410b**
Ilāhiyyāt i, 343a, 415a; iii, 1147b; v, 842a
Īlāḳ s, **411a**
Ilak Khān → Ilek-Khāns
Īlāt iii, **1095b**
Ilbīra (Elvira) i, 49a; ii, 1012a, 1014b; iii, **1110a**; iv, 739a; vi, 221b
al-Ilbīrī → Abū Isḥāḳ al-Ilbīrī
Ilče i, 469b; iii, 1092b
Ilči → Elči
İlčī, Mīrzā Abu 'l-Ḥasan Khān s, 108b, 290a, b
Ildeñiz (Ildegiz, Eldigüz), Shams al-Dīn (atabeg) (1175) i, 190a, 300b; iii, **1110b**, 1112a; vi, 275b, 482a, 500a; vii, 406b, 730b, 922b; viii, 239a, 944a; ix, 270a, 195a
Ildeñizids (Eldigüzids, Ildigizids) ii, 975b; iii, **1110b**; iv, 348b, 349a; vii, 922a
Ilek-Khāns (Ḳarakhānids) i, 236b, 421a, 987a, 1295a; ii, 1b, 4b, 791b, 893b, 1143b; iii, 345b, **1113a**; iv, 572b, 581a, 658b, 699a; v, 857b; vi, 340a, 809b; vii, 193a; x, 222b, 689a, 707b; xi, 287b; s, 176b, 240a, 245b, 326a
Ileri, Djelāl Nūrī (1938) iii, **1117a**
Ileri, Sedād Nūrī iii, 1117a
Ileri, Ṣubḥī Nūrī iii, 1117a
Ileri, Tevfik v, 282b
Iletmish → Iltutmish
Īlgaz → Čankiri̊
Ilghāz → Muʿammā
İlghāzī I Nadjm al-Dīn (Artuḳid) (1184) i, 664a, 665b, 983a, 1337a; iii, 87a, **1118a**; v, 124b; vi, 64b, 380a, 540b, 544a, 966a; vii, 578b, 725b, 733b, 983b
Ilghāzī II b. Nadjm al-Dīn Alpī (Artuḳid) (1122) iii, **1119a**
Ilḥād → Mulḥid
Ilhām iii, 28b, **1119b**
İlhami Soysal (XX) vi, 95b
Ili (river and town) iii, **1120a**; iv, 512b; v, 363b (see also *s.v.* Ḳuldja)
Iličpur → Eličpur
Īli̊dja iii, **1120b**; iv, 569b, 570a
Ilig Naṣr (Karakhānid) (X) iii, 1113b; iv, 189b; viii, 110a, 236b, 1028a; s, 459b
Ilīgh (Morocco) ii, 527a; vi, 743a; viii, 440a; x, 405b
Īliyā → al-Ḳuds
Īlīyā (metropolitan) vi, 620a
Īlīyyā Abū Māḍī (XX) viii, 88a; s, **27b**
Ilḳās Mīrzā iv, 103a
Īlkhānī → Taʾrīkh
Īlkhāns i, 227a, 329b, 346a, 467a, 468a, 470a, 510b, 666a, 703a, 861a, 872a, 902b, 1106b, 1128a; ii, 45a, 47a, 401a; iii, 122a, 473a, 569b, **1120b**, 1256a; iv, 31a, 48a, b, 349b; v, 58b, 455b, 677a; vi, 15a, b, 65a, 66a, 120a, 273b, 274a, 315b, 321b, 322a, 366a, 482b, 492b, 493a, 494a, 501b, 521b, 524a, b, 549b, 714a, 724b, 854b, 931b; viii, 168b, 175a, 443a,b; ix, 268b, 474b, 597a; x, 43a; s, 59a, 64b, 126b, 235b, 383a, 409b
– administration i, 1159a; ii, 81a, 83a, 311a, 313a, 334a, 903a; iii, 47b, 284a, 348a, 1089a; iv, 559b, 757a, 1045a, 1046a, b
– art/architecture iii, 1123b, 1127b; v, 1148a
ʿIlla i, 1327a; iii, **1127b**
Illā iv, 272b; v, 241b
ʿIllaysh, Muḥammad b. Aḥmad (1882) ix, 23a; s, **411a**
Illig agreement vii, 389b
ʿIlliyyūn iii, **1132b**; iv, 987b
ʿIlm iii, **1133a**; v, 1123b
ʿIlm al-aktāf → Katif, ʿIlm al-
ʿIlm al-Dīn al-Anṣārī → Wazīr Khān
ʿIlm al-djamāl iii, **1134a**
ʿIlm al-handasa s, **411b**
ʿIlm al-hayʾa i, 1100b; ii, 586b; iii, 302a, 703a, 789a, **1135a**; iv, 491b, 1059a, 1182b; v, 46a, b, 83a-87b, 397a, 542b, 547a; xi, 496b
ʿIlm al-ḥisāb iii, **1138a**; iv, 1070a; v, 527b
ʿIlm al-ḥurūf → Ḥurūf
ʿIlm al-ikhtilādj → Ikhtilādj
ʿIlm al-kaff → al-Kaff
ʿIlm al-kalām ii, 605b, 608a, 618a, 898b, 931a; iii, 543b, 664b, 1132a, **1141b**; iv, 366b
ʿIlm al-manāẓir → Manāẓir
ʿIlm al-mīḳāt → Mīḳāt
ʿIlm al-ridjāl iii, **1150b**; vi, 312b; vii, 581b
ʿIlm al-tarādjim iii, 1151a
ʿIlmiyye iii, **1152a**; vii, 545a
Ilsh → Alsh

Īls͟haraḥ Yaḥḍib (Yaḥṣib) ii, 1096a; iii, 10a; vi, 561b
Iltizām ii, 147b, 148a; iii, **1154a**; iv, 324a, 1096a; v, 93b; vii, 550b, 551a; s, 238b (see also *s.v.* Mültezim)
Iltizām (rhetoric) → Luzūm mā lā yalzam
Iltutmis͟h b. Ēlam K͟hān, S͟hams al-Dīn (Muʿizzī, Dihlī) (1236) i, 208b, 432b, 764a, 856a, 912b, 1192a, 1209b, 1218b; ii, 50a, 120a, 153b, 260a, 266b, 267a, b, 274b, 609a, 1084a, 1143b; iii, 416a, 441a, 492a, **1155a**; iv, 533b; v, 549a, 597b, 629b, 883b, 1134b; vi, 48a, 189b, 309a, 368a, 406b, 488a, 532b, 691b; vii, 193b, 549a; viii, 81a; s, 124a, 284b, 353a, 360a
Iltüzer K͟hān iv, 1068a; v, 24a
ʿIlwa, Banū → Muṭayr, Banū
Ilyās (Elijah) i, 404b, 1214b; iii, **1156a**; iv, 903a; v, 5a
Ilyās, Amīr (Ḳūm) (1428) vi, 513a
Ilyās b. Aḥmad iv, 859a
Ilyās b. Ḥabīb i, 86b
Ilyās b. Ḥamīd iii, 132b
Ilyās b. Ilyasaʿ s, 356b
Ilyās b. Isḥāḳ iv, 698b
Ilyās b. Manṣūr al-Nafūsī (Ibāḍī) → Abū Manṣūr Ilyās al-Nafūsī
Ilyās b. Yuḥannā i, 593b
Ilyās Beg (Mirāk͟hor) v, 265a, b
Ilyās Beg b. Meḥmed Beg (Mentes͟he) (1421) ii, 599a; v, 506a; vi, 1018b
Ilyās Farḥāt v, 1256b; vi, 308a; viii, 584b
Ilyās K͟hān s, 331b
Ilyās (Iliyyā) al-Naṣībī (Elias of Nisibin) (1046) ii, 199a; vi, 118b, 119b, 120b; vii, 1031b
Ilyās Pas͟ha (XV) vii, 594b , 713a
Ilyās Pas͟ha (Anatolia) (XVII) s, 49a
Ilyās Pas͟ha Umm Birayr (Kordofān) (XIX) v, 267b
Ilyās S͟hāh, S͟hams al-Dīn (Bengal) (1358) i, 1015a, 1168a; ii, 751b; iii, 202b, 416b; v, 638a; vi, 46b, 244b; viii, 5b, 258b
Ilyās S͟hāhīds (Bengal) vi, 46b, 244b; viii, 258b, 373b; ix, 728a
Ilyas-og͟hlu ii, 207b
Ilyasaʿ (X) iii, 1156b; v, 158b
Ilyasaʿ (al-Yasaʿ) (VIII) v, 593b; viii, 985b
Ilyasaʿ b. ʿĪsā al-G͟hāfiḳī s, 802b
Ilyāsids iii, **1156b**; v, 158b
Īmāʿ → Is͟hāra
ʿImād, Mīr (XVI) vii, 442a
ʿImād Abu ʾl-Ḳāsim (XII) vi, 608b
ʿImād al-Dawla, ʿAlī b. Būya (Buwayhid) (949) i, 211b, 866b, 1046b, 1350a; ii, 178b; iii, 197a, **1157a**; iv, 23a, b, 100a, b, 222a; v, 1213a; vi, 115b, 261b, 539a; vii, 484a, b; viii, 597b, 598a
ʿImād al-Dawla b. Hūd iii, 542b, 543a, 728a
ʿImād al-Dawla Farāmarz iii, 1162a
ʿImād al-Dawla Sāwtigin → Sāwtegin
ʿImād al-Dīn, Amīr (Astarābād) (XV) s, 380a
ʿImād al-Dīn, Mīr (Murtaḍāʾī) (XIV) vi, 512a
ʿImād al-Dīn b. Arslān S͟hāh v, 454b
ʿImād al-Dīn b. Ibrāhīm b. Ḥusām al-Dīn Ḥasan (Marʿas͟h) (XIII) vi, 507b
ʿImād al-Dīn b. Mawdūd Zangī II (1180) vi, 781a, b, 871a; viii, 131b
ʿImād al-Dīn b. Ṣalāḥ al-Dīn → al-Malik al-ʿAzīz ʿImād al-Dīn
ʿImād al-Dīn b. Sayf al-Dīn ʿAlī Aḥmad b. al-Mas͟hṭūb (Manbid͟j) (1202) vi, 381a
ʿImād al-Dīn Abu ʾl-Fatḥ ʿUmar b. ʿAlī i, 765b
ʿImād al-Dīn ʿAlī, Faḳīh-i Kirmānī (773) iv, 1010a; vi, 834a; s, **414b**
ʿImād al-Dīn al-Bag͟hdādī (1335) vii, 135b, 136a, b
ʿImād al-Dīn Darguzīnī (1150) vi, 782a
ʿImād al-Dīn Ḥasan b. ʿAlī s, 83a
ʿImād al-Dīn Ismāʿīl → al-Ṣāliḥ ʿImād al-Dīn
ʿImād al-Dīn al-Kātib al-Iṣfahānī (1201) i, 150a, 523a, 594a, 595a, 801b, 1309b; iii, 222a, 834b, **1157b**; iv, 613b; v, 528b; vi, 430a, 606a; vii, 527b, 726b; s, 123b, 205a, 326a, 378b
ʿImād al-Dīn Kumal (Balk͟h) (XII) ix, 16b
ʿImād al-Dīn Muḥammad b. Aḥmad b. Ṣāʿid (ḳāḍī) vi, 14a
ʿImād al-Dīn Muḥammad b. Ḳāsim ii, 27a
ʿImād al-Dīn Muḥammad Suhrawardī ix, 784b
ʿImād al-Dīn Rayḥān → Rayḥān, ʿImād al-Dīn
ʿImād al-Dīn ʿUmar al-S͟hayk͟h i, 766b
ʿImād al-Dīn Zangī I b. Aḳ Sunḳur (Zangid) (1146) i, 426b, 1332a; v, 332a, 454a,

b, 922a; vi, 64a, 380a, 545b, 606a, 782a, 870a, 900b; vii, 543b; viii, 127a; ix, 68b
ʿImād al-Dīn Zangī II vi, 781a
ʿImād al-Mulk (Multān) iii, 634a; s, 335b
ʿImād al-Mulk Fatḥ Allāh → Fatḥ Allāh ʿImād al-Mulk
ʿImād al-Mulk Abu 'l-Ḳāsim (XI) viii, 81b
ʿImād al-Mulk, Ghāzī al-Dīn (1746) i, 295a, 1024b; iii, 61a, **1158a**; v, 598b
ʿImād Shāh (Berār) (XVI) i, 1160a; vi, 51a
ʿImād Shāhīs (Berār) i, 1170a; ii, 981b; iii, 425a, 447a, **1159a**; vi, 68a, 368a, 536b, 695b; s, 280a
ʿImādī (Shahriyārī) (XII) iii, **1161b**; s, **416a**
ʿImād-i Ḥasanī-i Sayfī iv, 1124b
ʿImādiyya → ʿAmādiya
Imāla iii, **1162a**
Imām → Imāma, Masdjid
Imām al-Ḥaramayn → al-Djuwaynī, ʿAbd al-Malik
Imām al-Hudā → Abu 'l-Layth al-Samarḳandī
Imām-bārā iii, **1163a**; v, 1033a
Imām Ḳulī Khān (Fārs) (1632) i, 8b, 120b; ii, 446a, 812a, 975b; iv, 387b, 399a; v, 493a, 673a; vii, 673b; s, 340b
Imām Ḳulī Mīrzā b. ʿAbbās I (Ṣafawid) (XVII) viii, 770b
Imām Ḳulī Mīrzā ʿImād al-Dawla v, 170b
Imām Ma (Yunnan) (XIX) viii, 260b
Imām Shāh (1513) iii, **1163a**; iv, 202b; v, 26b; ix, 85a
Imām Shāh Nizār (1722) iv, 201b
Imām-Shāhīs → Sat-panthīs
Imām al-Suhaylī → al-Suhaylī, Sīdī ʿAbd al-Raḥmān
Imām Yaḥyā iv, 296b
Imāma i, 27a, 276b, 832b; ii, 660b, 931a, 1094a; iii, 547a, 954a, **1163b**; iv, 50a, 182b, 184a, 234b, 277b, 278b, 456b, 943b, 944a, 948a, 987b; v, 166b, 1236a; s, 327b
Imāmīyya i, 393a, 445b, 850a; iii, 497a, 1166b; iv, 610a; v, 1236a, b; s, 25b
Imāmzāda iii, 1124a, **1169b**; iv, 702a
Imāmzāda Abu 'l-Faḍl wa-Yaḥyā (Maḥallat Bālā) (1300) vii, 12b
Imāmzāda Karrār (Buzān) (1143) vii, 12b
Imāmzāda Shāh Ḥusayn (Warāmīn) (1330) vii, 13a
Imāmzāde (Shāh) ʿAbd al-ʿAẓīm → Shāh ʿAbd al-ʿAẓīm al-Ḥasanī
Īmān i, 276b, 335a, 1242a; ii, 294a; iii, **1170b**; iv, 171b, 172a, 173a, b
al-Imārāt al-ʿArabīyya al-Muttaḥida iv, 778b; v, 1058a; vii, 301b; ix, 658b, 659a; x, 853b; s, 2b, 42a, **416b** (see also *s.v.* Abū Ẓabī; ʿAdjmān; Dubayy; al-Fudjayra; Raʾs al-Khayma; al-Shāriḳa; Umm al-Ḳaywayn)
Imārat al-nubuwwa → Nubuwwa
ʿImāret → khayr; Waḳf
Imazighen i, 433b, 1143a; x, 118b
al-Imbābī, Muḥammad s, 411b
Imbros → Imroz
Imdād Allāh al-Hindī al-Makkī (1899) i, 701b; ii, 54b; iii, **1174a**
Imdād Ḥusayn Khān Nāṣir Djang ii, 808b
Imeretie → al-Kurdj
Imeum i, 741b
ʿImm i, 239a; vi, 871a
Imraʾ al-Ḳays → Imruʾ al-Ḳays
Imrālī → Emreli
ʿImrān (ʿAmrām) i, 177a; iii, **1175a**; vi, 218b, 628b, 630a
ʿImrān (Sind) iv, 535a
ʿImrān b. Faḍl iii, 125b
ʿImrān b. Ḥiṭṭān (703) iii, 889b, **1175a**; vii, 123b; ix, 766b; s, 284a
ʿImrān b. Muḥammad b. Sabaʾ i, 181b; xi, 572a
ʿImrān b. Mukhallad i, 248a
ʿImrān b. Mūsā (840) vi, 967b
ʿImrān b. Mūsā al-Barmakī i, 1036a
ʿImrān b. Shāhīn (979) i, 211b, 955a, 1096a; iii, 730a, **1175b**; vii, 358a, 484b, 818a
al-ʿImrānī, ʿAlī b. Aḥmad (955) i, 132b; iv, 340b; viii, 108a
al-ʿImrānī, Ibrāhīm al-Shalḳānī iv, 992a
al-ʿImrānī, Muʿīn al-Dīn (XIV) i, 133a; iii, **1176a**
al-ʿImrānī al-Shīrāzī (XVI) iv, 309b
ʿImrānid/ʿImrāniyya ix, 507b
Imroz i, 947b, 1280b; ii, 522a; iii, **1176a**; v, 763b, 764b
Imruʾ al-Ḳays iii, **1176b**
Imruʾ al-Ḳays (Lakhmid) (328) i, 548b, 564b; v, 633a; vii, 871b, 945b
Imruʾ al-Ḳays, Banū (Sulaym) ix, 817a
Imruʾ al-Ḳays b. ʿĀbis al-Kindī (VII) iii, 1176b
Imruʾ al-Ḳays b. ʿAwf v, 120a

Imruʾ al-Ḳays b. Ḥudj̲r (550) i, 99a, 405b, 452a, 527a, 583b, 1152a; ii, 241b, 550b, 785a, 1028b; iii, **1177a**; iv, 263b, 839a; v, 119a, 633a; vi, 261a, 477b; vii, 254b, 261a; x, 90a; s, 38a, 58b, 259a
Imruʾ al-Ḳays ʿAdī b. Rabīʿa al-Tag̲h̲libī (al-Muhalhil) (VI) i, 144b; iii, 1176b, 1178a; vii, 580b, 581a, 979a; x, 782a; xi, 280b, 281a
Imtiyāzāt ii, 912b; iii, **1178b**; iv, 38b, 808b
Imẓad iii, **1195b**
In s̲h̲āʾ Allāh iii, **1196a**
ʿInab → K̲h̲amr
İnaḳ iv, 1065a; v, 392a; s, 97b, **419a**
ʿInāk i, 780b; viii, 995b
Inaḳids s, 420a
Īnāl (kās̲h̲if) (Miṣr) (XVI) vi, 325a; vii, 177b
Īnal, Ibnülemin (1957) iii, **1199a**
Īnāl, İnālids ii, 344a; iii, **1197b**
İnal, İnalčuḳ (1220) iii, **1198a**
İnāl al-Adj̲rūd, al-Malik al-As̲h̲raf Sayf al-Dīn (Mamlūk) (1461) i, 352a; iii, **1198a**; vii, 173b, 727a
Inālū → Abū ʿUmar Inālū
Inʿām iii, 347b, **1200b**; viii, 750a; ix, 894a
Inʿām al-Ḥasan (1995) x, 38b
ʿInān (841) iii, **1202b**
İnānč K̲h̲ān vii, 974a
Inanč K̲h̲ātūn → Inānd̲j̲ (Inanč) K̲h̲ātūn
Inānd̲j̲, Ḳiwām al-Dīn (Rayy) (1161) i, 300b; ii, 333b; iii, 1110b; vi, 500a, b; viii, 472a
Inand̲j̲ Bīg̲h̲ū, Amīr (Māzandarān) (1065) vi, 935b
Inānd̲j̲ (Inanč) K̲h̲ātūn (S̲h̲āh-i Arman) (XII) iii, 1111b; ix, 193a
Īnānlū iv, 858b
Inari Konte (Mali) (XIV) vi, 421b
Iʿnāt → Luzūm mā lā yalzam
ʿĪnāt s, 337b, **420b**
ʿInāya i, 89b, 90a, 415a; iii, **1203a**; iv, 366b
ʿInāyat (India) s, 292b, 293b
ʿInāyat Allāh (Afg̲h̲ānistān) s, 65b, 66b
ʿInāyat Allāh ʿAlī (1858) vii, 291a
ʿInāyat Allāh Kan̊bū (1671) iii, **1203b**
ʿInāyat Allāh K̲h̲ān → al-Mas̲h̲riḳī, ʿInāyat Allāh
ʿInāyat Allāh K̲h̲an (1726) vi, 131b; vii, 322a, 722b
ʿInāyat Allāh K̲h̲ān (1681) s, **420b**
ʿInāyat Allāh K̲h̲an (1682) s, **420b**
ʿInāyat Allāh K̲h̲ān b. Ḥāfiẓ Raḥmat iii, 61a
ʿInāyat Allāh K̲h̲ān b. Ẓafar Aḥsan ii, 1004b
India → Hind
India, Muslim ix, 800b
Indian Congress Party iv, 277a; s, 106b
Indian National Congress iii, **1204a**; iii, 461a; vi, 78a; viii, 241a, 273a; ix, 378b; s, 4b, 480b, 526a
Indian Ocean → Baḥr al-Hind; Baḥr al-Zand̲j̲
Ind̲j̲īl i, 264a; iii, **1205a**
Ind̲j̲ili Čavus̲h̲ iii, 375a
Īnd̲j̲ū iii, 55b, **1208a**; iv, 31b, 32a, 975b, 1094a; v, 163a; s, 235b
Īnd̲j̲ū S̲h̲īrāzī, D̲j̲amāl al-Dīn Ḥusayn iv, 526a
Ind̲j̲ūids → Ind̲j̲ū
Indochina iii, **1208b**
Indonesia iii, 502b, **1213a**; iv, 175b; v, 940b; s, 220a
– administration i, 980b; iii, 566a; vi, 42b
– ethnography iii, 1214b
– geography iii, 1213a
– history ii, 19a, 595a, 662b; iii, 534a, 1218-1230
– institutions ii, 426b
– languages, literature i, 88a, 92a; iii, 1215a, 1230b; iv, 1128a; v, 205a, 226b, 227a, 228b; vi, 239a; viii, 153a
Indus → Mihrān
Inebak̲h̲tı̊ → ʿAynabak̲h̲tı̊
Infiʿāl → Fiʿl
Infiṣāl → Waṣl
Infūsen → al-Nafūsa
Ingalaga, Panembahan Senopati (Mataram) (1601) s, 607a
Ingiliz Muṣṭafā ii, 511b
Ingus̲h̲ ii, 18a, b; iii, **1235b**; vii, 351b, 352a; s, 491b, 492a
Inḥiṣār s, **421a**
Inkār iii, 1078b, **1236b**
Inḳilāb → T̲h̲awra
Innāyir → Yinnāyir
Innib (Marʿas̲h̲) vi, 507a
Inniya v, 1262a, b, 1263b
Inönü, Erdal x, 696a
Inos(z) → Enos
Inṣāf iii, **1236b**

Insān iii, **1237a**
al-Insān al-Kāmil i, 117b; iii, **1239a**; v, 543b; viii, 125b
Inshā' i, 594a, 595a; ii, 306b; iii, **1241b**; iv, 705a, 760a
Inshā' Allāh Khān (1818) ii, 602a; iii, 358b, 376b, 458a, **1244a**; v, 959a, 960b, 961b; vii, 668a, 669b
Inshāṣ (Palace) s, 301a
Institut d'Egypte iii, **1245a**
Institut des Hautes Études Marocaines s, **421b**
Institut des Hautes Études de Tunis s, **422a**
Intī → Hintāta
al-Īntī (Hintāta), Abū Ḥafṣ ʿUmar (XII) i, 79b, **121b**, 161a; vi, 222b
Intidāb → Mandate
Intihā' iii, **1246a**
Intiḥār iii, **1246b**
Intiḳālī iv, 978a
Inzāl → Waḳf
Inzāl s, **423a**
Ipsala (Kypsela) ii, 720a; vi, 290b
Ipshīr Muṣṭafā Pasha (1665) i, 4b; iii, 318a, 983b, **1248a**; v, 257a; ix, 844b; xi, 152b
Iʿrāb i, 566a, 569b, 570a, 576b; iii, 697a, **1248b**; v, 567b (see also *s.v.* Ḥaraka wa-Sukūn; Kasra)
Irāde i, 414b, 1170a, b; iii, **1250a**; iv, 1131b
Īradj Khān i, 702a
Īradj Mīrzā (1925) iv, 71b; vi, 609a, 834b; s, 84a
ʿIrāfa i, 629a; iv, 421b, 422a
ʿIrāḳ iii, **1250a**; iv, 719a; v, 912a; vi, 16a, 28a, 45b, 82b, 119b, 225a, 337a, 345a, 387a, 467b, 469b, 470a, 517a, 624a, 797a; vii, 9a; ix, 87a; s, 179a, 198b, 259a
- art, architecture i, 609b, 1226a; iii, **1266b**; v, 292b, 293a, 1148a
- ethnography i, 39a, 872b; iii, **1253a**; v, 440a, 466b
- geography i, 431a, 461a; iii, **1250a**; iv, 1b; v, 146a, 864b, 886b
- history i, 16a, 18b, 21a, 33a, 46a, 53b, 76b, 77a, 111a, 140b, 211b, 383a,b, 388b, 400a, 549b, 1087a, 1350b; ii, 579b, 872b; iii, 263b, 521a, 558a, 560b, 1066a,b, **1254a**; iv, 15a, 16b-17b, 261b
- institutions ii, 424b; v, 1044a, 1093b
- languages, literature i, 568b, 576a; ii, 468b; iii, **1259a**
- sects i, 15a; iii, **1265a**
ʿIrāḳ(-i) ʿAdjamī → al-Djibāl
al-ʿIrāḳī, ʿAbd al-Raḥīm, Shaykh (XVI) iii, 817b, 927a; vii, 565a
al-ʿIrāḳī, Fakhr al-Dīn (1289) iii, 635a, 710b, **1269a**; iv, 65b, 67b, 474a; v, 166a; vii, 480a; viii, 540a
al-ʿIrāḳī, Sayyid Shams al-Dīn (1526) s, **423a**, 353b, 366b
al-ʿIrāḳī, Zayd al-Dīn (1404) vii, 290a; x, 934b
Irakli II v, 296b, 494b, 495a; vii, 854a; ix, 254b
Īraḳlīdis Abū Buḳrāṭ s, 154b
Iram i, 169a, b; iii, **1270a**; ix, 169b
Iram Dhāt al-ʿImād i, 169a, b, 181a; ii, 364b; iii, **1270b**; ix, 407a
Īrān i, 38a, 62b, 270a, 291a, 406a; ii, 966b, 1135b; iv, **1a**, 163b, 785a; vi, 11a, 119b, 291a, 471a, 491b, 517a, 521a, 761b, 803a, 825b, 853a; vii, 1a, 12a, 76a; s, 129a, 214b, 332b
- administration i, 978a; ii, 150a, 308b, 332b, 514b, 649b, 1081b; iii, 194b, 213b, 347b, 554a; iv, 1034a; v, 1042a
- art, architecture iii, 501b; iv, 288a, b; v, 292b; s, **448a**, **453a**
- demography s, **214b**
- ethnography i, 36a; iv, 7a-11a; v, 439b, 466a
- geography ii, 902b; iv, 1a-8a; v, 865a
- institutions ii, 426a, 433a; iii, 527b; v, 919a, 1094b
- languages, literature i, 1132a; ii, 308b; iii, 355a, 372b; iv, 52b-75a, 308a, 714a; v, 228b; s, **425a**
- mythology iv, 12a-13a
- sects iv, 43a-52b
Īrānī → Mughals
Īrānshahr → Nīshāpūr
al-Īrānshahrī → Abu 'l-ʿAbbās al-Īrānshahrī
Iraten iv, **75a**
Irbid i, 998a; iv, **75b**; vi, 603a
Irbil i, 1160b; iii, 1268a; iv, **76a**; v, 144b, 145b; vi, 781b
al-Irbilī, ʿIzz al-Dīn (1326) viii, 806a
al-Irbilī, al-Ḳāsim ii, 214b
al-Irbilī, Ṣalāḥ al-Dīn (1234) viii, 583b

al-Irbilī, Sharaf al-Dīn iii, 832b
ʿIrḍ iv, **77a**; vi, 146a, 475a; vii, 581a; x, 888b
al-ʿIrḍ (valley) i, 628b; iii, 166b
Irdānā Bī v, 29a
al-Irdjānī, Abū Yaḥyā Zakariyyāʾ (X) ii, 369a; iii, 656a; iv, **78a**
ʿIrfān Pasha iv, 879a
Irian Barat iii, 1213a, b, 1215a
Irič (erachli) ii, 274b; vii, 79a, b; s, **458b**
Īridj Shāhnawāz Khān i, 80b, 81b, 769a, 1331a
ʿIrgha → ʿIrḳa
al-ʿIrʿīr ii, 176a
ʿIrḳ, ʿurūḳ i, 537a; ii, 92a; iv, **78b**
ʿIrḳ → Ṣaḥrāʾ
ʿIrḳ al-Luʾluʾ → Ṣadaf
ʿIrḳa (Arḳa) ii, 321b; iv, **79a**; vi, 579a; xi, 47b
Irmiyā iv, **79a**; v, 442b
Irōn → Ossetes
Iron Gate → Bāb al-Abwāb; Dar-i āhanīn
Irsāliyye iv, **79b**, 435b; v, 35a; vi, 811b; viii, 994b
Irtidjāʿ → Radjʿiyya
Irtidjāl iv, **80b**; viii, 376b
Irtifāʿ → Falak; ʿIlm al-Hayʾa
Irtish (Irtysh) s, 245a, **458b**
Īrwānī, Muḥammad s, 76a
al-Iryānī ʿAbd al-Raḥmān (Yemen) xi, 274b
al-ʿĪṣ iii, 152b
al-ʿĪṣ, Umayya b. ʿAbd Shams s, 103b
ʿĪsā, Āl iv, 87b, 88a
ʿĪsā, Nahr i, 897a; ii, 250a; iv, **86b**, 88b
ʿĪsā, al-Ẓāhir i, 666b
ʿĪsā b. Abī Hishām (XII) viii, 653b
ʿĪsā b. Abī khālid (819) vi, 336a, 337a
ʿĪsā b. Aḥmad al-Dawsarī v, 40a, b
ʿĪsā b. Aḥmad al-Rāzī i, 321a, 600b
ʿĪsā b. ʿAlī (ʿAbbāsid) iii, 883a
ʿĪsā b. ʿAlī (Marʿash) (778) vi, 506a
ʿĪsā b. ʿAlī (physician) i, 388a
ʿĪsā b. ʿAlī b. ʿĪsā i, 387b; iii, 895a
ʿĪsā b. ʿAlī Āl Khalīfa iv, 953b
ʿĪsā b. ʿAlī al-Ḥarrānī iv, 340b
ʿĪsā b. Abān (836) viii, 839b; ix, 392b
ʿĪsā b. Bāyazīd I (Ottoman) vi, 974a
ʿĪsā b. Dīnār al-Ghāfiḳī (827) i, 600a; iv, **87a**; vi, 281a
ʿĪsā b. Djābir, faḳīh (XV) vii, 243a; ix, 255b
ʿĪsā b. Djaʿfar (IX) iii, 907b
ʿĪsā b. Djaʿfar b. (Abi) al-Manṣūr (Baṣra) (VIII) vii, 646a; ix, 775a; xi, 427b
ʿĪsā b. Djaʿfar al-Ḥasanī (Mecca) (994) vi, 435b
ʿĪsā b. Gümüshtigin (XII) vi, 380a
ʿĪsā b. al-Haytham al-Ṣūfī (860) iv, 1162a, b; vii, 785a
ʿĪsā b. Hishām (mukaddī) iii, 221a; v, 1010a; vi, 108a, 109a; vii, 495a
ʿĪsā b. Idrīs II ii, 874a; iii, 1035b
ʿĪsā b. Idrīs (Dulafid) ii, 623a
ʿĪsā b. Ismāʿīl al-Aḳsarāʾī → al-Aḳsarāʾī
ʿĪsā b. Khalāt (ʿUkaylid) (XI) viii, 394a
ʿĪsā b. Khalīd b. al-Walīd → Abū Saʿd al-Makhzūmī
ʿĪsā b. Maʿdān (Makrān) (1030) vi, 193a
ʿĪsā b. Maʿḳil i, 1293a
ʿĪsā b. Maryam i, 177a, 265a, 272a, 1020b, 1141a; ii, 280a; iii, 1206a; iv, **81a**; v, 41a, 421a, 423b, 1231a; vi, 218b, 628b, 629b, 726a
ʿĪsā b. Māsardjīs vi, 641a
ʿĪsā b. Māssa vi, 637b
ʿĪsā b. Mayzad al-Aswad (757) vi, 1038a; ix, 768b
ʿĪsā b. Miskīn i, 249b
ʿĪsā b. Muḥammad (ḳāḍī) ix, 441a
ʿĪsā b. Muḥammad b. Abī Khālid (826) vi, 335b
ʿĪsā b. Muḥammad b. Aydi̊n iii, 45a
ʿĪsā b. Muḥammad b. Sulaymān i, 661b
ʿĪsā b. Muhannā (1284) iii, 403a; iv, **87b**; vii, 461b
ʿĪsā b. Muhīn (Marʿash) (1271) vi, 507b
ʿĪsā b. Mūsā (ʿAbbāsid) (783) i, 96a, 134a, 618b, 952a, 1033b; iii, 984a; iv, **88a**; v, 1238a; vi, 332a, 333a, 427b, 428a, b; vii, 389a; x, 791b; s, 31b
ʿĪsā b. Mūsā (Ḳarmaṭī) i, 96a, 962b; iv, 198b, 662a, b, 838a
ʿĪsā b. Mūsā al-Nūsharī v, 327a
ʿĪsā b. Nasṭūrus i, 823b, 824b; ii, 858a; iii, 77a
ʿĪsā b. Rayʿān al-Azdī iii, 655b; v, 696a, b
ʿĪsā b. Ṣāliḥ (Sharḳiyya Hināwī, ʿUmān) (1896) s, 355b, 356a
ʿĪsā b. Ṣāliḥ (ʿUmān) (1946) i, 1283a; viii, 993a
ʿĪsā b. Salmān iv, 954a

ʿĪsā b. al-Shaykh al-Shaybānī (882) ii, 344a; iv, **88b**; vi, 930a; viii, 149a; x, 617a
ʿĪsā b. ʿUmar al-Hamdānī iv, 91a
ʿĪsā b. ʿUmar al-Thaḳafī (766) i, 42b; iv, **91a**, 919a; v, 567a; vii, 815a; viii, 573a, 661a
ʿĪsā b. ʿUthmān b. Fūdī iii, 281b, 282a
ʿĪsā b. Yaḥyā i, 213a, 1236b; iii, 579b
ʿĪsā b. Yūsuf al-ʿIrāḳī iii, 1246b
ʿĪsā b. Zakariyyāʾ ii, 140b
ʿĪsā b. Zayd b. ʿAlī iii, 244a; v, 1238b; s, 48a, 130a
ʿĪsā b. Zurʿa → Ibn Zurʿa
ʿĪsā Aydinoghlu i, 778a, 783b
ʿĪsā al-Asadī → al-Asadī, ʿIsā
ʿĪsā Beg b. Evenros ii, 721a; iv, 139b
ʿĪsā Beg b. Isḥāḳ (Bosnia) (XV) iv, 140a; vii, 244a
ʿĪsā Bey i, 1263a, 1264b
ʿĪsā Čelebi i, 510b; ii, 599a; vi, 1018b
ʿĪsā al-ʿĪsā ii, 468a
ʿĪsā Ḳāʾimmaḳām (Irān) s, 70b
ʿĪsā Khān Iʿtimād al-Dawla iii, 554a
*ʿĪsā Khān Tarkhān I (1565) i, 1192a; ii, 216b; iii, 1030a; vi, 189b, 190a; ix, 728a
ʿĪsā Khān Tarkhān II (1644) vi, 190a
ʿĪsā al-Khaṭṭī (VII) vii, 546a
ʿĪsā al-Kinānī al-Ḳayrawānī (1875) vi, 355b
ʿĪsā al-Laghwāṭī, al-Ḥādjdj (1737) vi, 249a
ʿĪsā al-Nūsharī (908) vi, 674a; vii, 543a
ʿĪsā Sawādjī (XV) viii, 750b
ʿĪsā al-Suktānī i, 428a
ʿĪsā ʿUbayd (1922) vi, 957a
ʿĪsā al-Ẓāhir (Artuḳid) (1406) vi, 540b, 541a
Isaac → Isḥāḳ
Isaac b. Abraham (1594) iv, 605b
Isāf wa-Nāʾila iv, **91a**; vi, 349a, 737a, 738b; viii, 756b; ix, 97b; s, 133a
Īsāghūdjī iv, **92a**
Isaiah → Shaʿyā
Isakča iv, **92a**
ʿIsām, Banū viii, 690a
ʿIsām al-khawlānī (902) vi, 926b
ʿIṣāmī, Fakhr al-Dīn (XIV) ii, 153b; iii, 1155b; iv, **92b**; vi, 48b, 532b; ix, 241b; s 105b
ʿIsāmī, ʿIzz al-Dīn iv, 92b, 210b
Īsānpur vi, 369a
Īsar-dās (XVIII) ii, 566b; iv, **93a**
ʿIsāwā, ʿĪsāwiyya i, 371a; iv, **93b**; vii, 36b; s, 325b, 350b, 351a
ʿIsāwī → Naṣārā
al-ʿIsāwiyya (al-Iṣfahāniyya) i, 130a; iv, **96a**; ix, 73b
Iṣbaʿ iv, **96b**
Iṣbahān → Iṣfahān
Isçehisar, Ischtschi Ḥiṣār → Īsdje Ḳarā Ḥiṣār
Īsdje Ḳarā Ḥiṣār iv, 578a
Iṣfabadh b. Sāwtigīn al-Turkumānī iv, 208a
Iṣfahān i, 142b, 643a; ii, 335a; iv, **97a**, 131b, 977b, 979a; v, 874a; vi, 17a, b, 18b, 20a, 198b, 274b, 275a, b, 332b, 365b, 366a, 486a, 494b, 515a, 516a, b, 523a, 525b, 526b, 527a, 539a, b, 552b, 633b; viii, 70a; ix, 46a; s, 23b, 43b, 54a, 75a, 95b, 140b, 141b, 142a, 157b, 169b, 257a, 274b, 275a, 308a, 326a, 336a, 363b, 365b, 380a, 384a
– history iii, 156a, 863b, 864a; iv, 7b, 37a, 97a-105b, 465a, b; v, 1157a
– institutions ii, 426a; iii, 1124a; iv, 101b, 103a; s, 139a
– monuments i, 400b; iii, 1124b, 1125a; iv, 36b, 105b-107a, 1137a; v, 1148b, 1149a
Iṣfahān b. Ḳarā Yūsuf iv, 587a, b, 588a
al-Iṣfahānī → Abu ʾl-Faradj; Abū Nuʿaym; ʿAlī b. Ḥamza; Djamāl al-Din Muḥammad; al-Djawād; Ḥamza; Ibn Dāwūd; ʿImād al-Dīn al-Kātib; al-Rāghib Rūkn al-Dīn
al-Iṣfahānī, Abu Mūsā Muḥammad iii, 821a
al-Iṣfahānī, Ḥādjdjī Āḳu Nūr Allāh s, 342b
al-Iṣfahānī, Ḥādjdjī Sayyid Abu ʾl-Ḥasan Mūsawī (1946) vi, 552b, 553a; vii, 301a; s, 158a, 342a
al-Iṣfahānī, Mīrzā Abū Ṭālib s, 108a, 290a
al-Iṣfahānī, Niẓām al-Dīn (1281) viii, 583b
al-Iṣfahānī, Shams al-Dīn Abū ʿAbd Allāh Muḥammad b. Maḥmūd (ḳāḍī) (1289) vi, 381b
al-Iṣfahānī, Shaykh Faḍl Allāh, Shaykh al-Sharīa (1920) vi, 552b; s, 342a
Iṣfahāniyya → ʿĪsāwiyya
Isfahsālār → Ispahsālār
Isfandiyār Khān i, 120b; s, 91a
Isfandiyār b. Adharbād iv, 662a
Isfandiyār b. Bishtāsb iv, 809b; viii, 637a
Isfandiyār Khān v, 24a; s, 281a

Isfarāʾinī → al-Isfarāyīnī
Isfarāyīn iv, 107a; vii, 19b
al-Isfarāyīnī → Ṭāhir b. Muḥammad al-Isfarāʾinī
al-Isfarāyīnī, Abu ʾl-ʿAbbās al-Faḍl b. Aḥmad (vizier) (1013) ii, 919a; iv, 107a; vi, 915b
al-Isfarāyīnī, Abū Ḥāmid (1015) ii, 136a; v, 345a; ix, 187b, 188a
al-Isfarāyīnī, Abū Isḥāḳ Ibrāhīm (1027) iv, 107b, 183a; ix, 187b
al-Isfarāyīnī, Saʿd al-Dīn i, 827a
Isfendiyār Og̲h̲lu i, 1256a; iv, 108b, 737b, 738a
Isfendiyār Og̲h̲lu, Mubāriz al-Dīn (Ḳasṭamuni) (1440) iv, 108b; vi, 974b; vii, 644a
Isfendiyār Og̲h̲lu Ismāʿīl Beg (Sinop) (1460) iv, 108b; vi, 71a; vii, 594b; ix, 654b
Isfendiyār Og̲h̲lu S̲h̲emsī Aḥmed Pas̲h̲a (Ḳi̊zi̊l Aḥmedli̊) (1580) iv, 108b; vii, 596a
Isfīd Diz → Ḳalʿe-i Sefīd
Isfīd̲h̲ (Safīd̲j̲/Sipih) → Nuṣratābād
Isfīd̲j̲āb ii, 778b; v, 856a; ix, 557b, 659b; x, 222b; s, **459a** (see also *s.v.* Sayrām)
al-Isfīd̲j̲ābī, Abū Manṣūr Muḥammad b. Ḥasan (997) s, 459b
Isfinṭ → Afsantīn
Isfizārī, Abū Ḥātim Muẓaffar (1100) viii, 542a
Isfizārī, Muʿīn al-Dīn Muḥammad Zamčī (XIV) i, 67a; vii, 928a; s, **460a**
ʿIs̲h̲āʾ → Ṣalāt
Isḥāḳ (Isaac) iii, 980a; iv, **109a**, 184a, b
Isḥāḳ (Ḳarmaṭī) iv, 663b
Isḥāḳ, Adīb (1885) ii, 417b, 429a, 466b, 467b; iv, **111b**; vii, 902b; viii, 992b, 993a; x, 444b
Isḥāḳ, Banū vii, 390a
Isḥāḳ b. Abraham b. Ezra i, 111b
Isḥāḳ b. ʿAlī b. Yūsuf (Almoravid) (1146) i, 79a; vi, 592a; vii, 585b; xi, 20a
Isḥāḳ b. ʿAlī al-Ruhāwī viii, 588b
Isḥāḳ b. Alp Takīn (G̲h̲aznawid) i, 226b, 421b; vi, 433a
Isḥāḳ b. Ayāz ii, 322a
Isḥāḳ b. Ayyūb, Tag̲h̲libī (870) iv, 89b; vi, 900a; x, 93a
Isḥāḳ b. Aʿẓam K̲h̲ān i, 88a
Isḥāḳ b. G̲h̲āniya ii, 112a
Isḥāḳ b. Ḥunayn (910) i, 234b, 589a, 631b, 784b, 1340a; ii, 362a; iii, 579a, 1045a, 1136b; iv, **110a**; vi, 204a, 347a; vii, 83a; s, 411b, 412a
Isḥāḳ b. al-Ḥusayn (geographer) iii, 1077a
Isḥāḳ b. Ibrāhīm b. Muṣʿab (Ṭahirid) (849) i, 153b; x, 105a, s, 106a
Isḥāḳ b. Ibrāhīm b. Ḥusayn b. Muṣʿab (Ṭāhirid) (833) vi, 336b, 337b; vii, 2b, 776b
Isḥāḳ b. Ibrāhīm b. Wahb al-Kātib (X) i, 982a, 1115a; vii, 661a
Isḥāḳ b. Ibrāhīm Ḳarāmān-og̲h̲lu iv, 624a
Isḥāḳ b. Ibrāhīm al-Mawṣilī (850) i, 118a, 718a; ii, 246a, 1011b; iii, 698b, 730b, 989a, 996b; iv, **110b**, 822a; v, 319b; vi, 97b, 103a, 262a; vii, 518b, 559a, 681b, 682a, 976a, 1042b; s, 64a, 128b, 183a
Isḥāḳ b. Ibrāhīm al-Muṣʿabī → Isḥāḳ b. Ibrāhīm b. Muṣʿab
Isḥāḳ b. ʿImrān ii, 60a; iv, 627a, 829b; s, 303b, 314a
Isḥāḳ b. Ismāʿīl, amīr iv, 345a, 669b; v, 488a, b
Isḥāḳ b. Ismāʿīl b. Ḥammād (860) s, **384b**
Isḥāḳ b. Kundād̲j̲(īḳ) (Mosul) (891) i, 279a; ii, 524a; iv, 89b, 90a; v, 49a; vi, 900a; vii, 766a
Isḥāḳ b. Maḥmas̲h̲ād̲h̲ iv, 668a, 669a
Isḥāḳ b. Muḥammad b. G̲h̲āniya ii, 1007a
Isḥāḳ b. Muḥammad al-Aḥmar (IX) vii, 517a
Isḥāḳ b. Murād iv, **111a**
Isḥāḳ b. Mūsā al-Hādī (IX) vi, 335a
Isḥāḳ b. Mūsā b. S̲h̲uʿayb (XIV) iv, 964a
Isḥāḳ b. Rāhwayh → Ibn Rāhwayh
Isḥāḳ b. Sulaymān al-Isrāʾīlī (955) i, 785b; ii, 60a; iii, 754a; iv, **111b**, 304a, 627a, 829b; viii, 661b; xi, 486a; s, 197b, 314a
Isḥāḳ b. Zayd b. al-Ḥārit̲h̲ al-Anṣārī i, 49a; ii, 441a; iv, 838a
Isḥāḳ Bāb → Isḥāḳ al-Turk
Isḥāḳ Barbarossa i, 678a, b
Isḥāḳ Efendi (1835) iv, **112b**
Isḥāḳ Efendi (1734, S̲h̲ayk̲h̲ al-Islām) ii, 629b, 713b
Isḥāḳ K̲h̲ān Karaʾī iii, 1107b
Isḥāḳ k̲h̲uttalānī i, 392b; v, 301a; viii, 134b
Isḥāḳ al-Mawṣilī → Isḥāḳ b. Ibrāhīm al-Mawṣilī

Isḥāḳ Pas̲h̲a (1453) vi, 70a, 1025b
Isḥāḳ Pas̲h̲a (Georgia) (1728) v, 494a, b
Isḥāḳ al-Raffāʾ iv, 797a, 800b
Isḥāḳ Sükūtī (1903) ii, 474b; iii, 393a; iv, **113a**
Isḥāḳ al-Turk iv, 16b; v, 64a; xi, 294b
Isḥāḳābād vi, 115b
Isḥāḳids (Fūmin) viii, 450a
Isḥāḳiyya (Black Mountain) s, 522b, 523a
Isḥāḳiyya (Karrāmiyya) iv, 668a; v, 945b
Isḥāḳiyya (sect) → Kazarūniyya
Ishakovič → Üsküb
Isḥāḳzāy ii, 629a, 1001b
Is̲h̲ān iv, **113a**; v, 823b
Īs̲h̲āns vi, 768a
Is̲h̲āra iv, **113b**
Is̲h̲bāʿ (Elisabeth) vi, 630a,
al-Is̲h̲bīlī → Abu 'l-k̲h̲ayr; al-Fatḥ b. k̲h̲āḳān; Ibn al-k̲h̲arrāṭ; Ibn k̲h̲ayr; al-Ruʿaynī
Is̲h̲bīliya (Sevilla) i, 5b, 6b, 7a,b, 83a, 162a, 491a, 493a; iii, 681a; iv, **114b**; vi, 361b, 364a, 431a, 597a; s, 388a
– constructions i, 499b, 501b, 1226b; iii, 498b; iv, 117a-118b
Īs̲h̲īk-āḳāsī iii, 47b; iv, **118b**
Is̲h̲im K̲h̲ān ii, 45a
ʿIs̲h̲ḳ i, 416a; ii, 552a; iii, 103a; iv, **118b**
Is̲h̲kās̲h̲im (Badak̲h̲s̲h̲ān) i, 853b; s, **460a**
Is̲h̲kās̲h̲imī i, 225a, 854a
Isḳāṭ s, **466a**
ʿIs̲h̲k̲h̲an ii, 1118a
ʿIs̲h̲ḳī, Muḥammad Riḍā Mīrzāda (1924) iv, 789b; vi, 609a, 764a; vii, 662a, 754b; viii, 513a; s, 110a, **460b**
ʿIs̲h̲ḳiyya x, 250b
Ishḳodra (Shkodër, Albania) i, 285a, 654a, 657a; iv, 588b; s, **161b**, 281b, 359b
Is̲h̲mael → Ismāʿīl
Ishmaelite v, 1014b, 1015b, 1019a
Īs̲h̲ōʿdᵉnaḥ vi, 648b
Is̲h̲rāḳ → al-Dāmād
Is̲h̲rāḳ ii, 774a; iv, 50b, **119b**
Is̲h̲rāḳīyyūn i, 234b, 351a, 416b, 596a; iv, **120b**; v, 1262b; viii, 593b
Is̲h̲tar → Manāt
Is̲h̲tib (Štip) iv, **121b**; vi, 89a, 888b
Is̲h̲tiḳāḳ (etymology) iv, **122a**
Is̲h̲tiḳāḳ (rhetoric) → Tad̲j̲nīs
Is̲h̲tik̲h̲ān (Transoxania) iii, 1060b; s, **462b**
Is̲h̲tirāk → Tawriya
Is̲h̲tirākiyya iv, **123b**
Īs̲h̲ūrūni iv, 301b
Īs̲h̲war-dās → Īsar-dās
Īs̲h̲war Singh (Ud̲j̲d̲j̲ayn) (1455) vi, 62a
Isʿird → Siʿird
al-Isʿirdī, Nūr al-Dīn ibn Rustum (1258) iv, 1006a; ix, 574a; s, **462b**
Iskāf (Iskāfī) s, **463a**
al-Iskāfī, Abū ʿAlī Muḥammad b. Aḥmad b. al-D̲j̲unayd (X) vii, 312b
al-Iskāfī, Abū D̲j̲aʿfar Muḥammad (854) iv, **126b**; vi, 636b; s, 13b
al-Iskāfī, Abu 'l-Faḍl D̲j̲aʿfar (IX) iv, **126b**
al-Iskāfī, Abū Isḥāḳ Muḥammad (968) iv, **127a**
al-Iskāfī, Abu 'l-Ḳāsim D̲j̲aʿfar iv, 127a
Iskān iii, 1002b; s, **463b**
Iskandar, Banū vi, 938b
Iskandar (Ḳarā-ḳoyunlu) iv, 587a, b, 702b; ix, 197b
Iskandar II (Atjèh) i, 743a, b; iii, 1220a; viii, 279b; ix, 296a
Iskandar b. Kayūmart̲h̲ iv, 808a; v, 663a; vi, 938b; viii, 651a
Iskandar b. ʿUmar S̲h̲ayk̲h̲ (XV) i, 1342a; ix, 197a, 667b
Iskandar, D̲h̲u 'l-Ḳarnayn i, 935a, 1101a, 1206b; ii, 112b, 133a, 278b; iii, 181a; iv, **127b**, 131a, 498a; vi, 207b; viii, 79b
Iskandar al-Afrūdīsī i, 342a; ii, 550a, 771a; iii, 728b; iv, **129a**
Iskandar Ag̲h̲a b. Yaʿḳūb (Abkaryus) (1885) iv, **130b**; vi, 352a
Iskandar Beg → Iskender Beg
Iskandar Beg al-S̲h̲ahīr bi-Muns̲h̲ī (1632) iv, 130b; vi, 202a, 483a, 495a; viii, 787b
Iskandar al-Dimas̲h̲ḳī iv, 129a
Iskandar K̲h̲ān b. D̲h̲ānī Beg (Shībānid) (1583) i, 46b, 970a; ii, 44b; s, 340a, **466a**
Iskandar Muda (1636) i, 743a, b; iii, 1220a; ix, 296a; s, 199b, 200b
Iskandar-nāma i, 299b, 325a; iii, 113a; iv, 62b, **127b**, 902b, 904a
Iskandar Pās̲h̲a iv, 435b
Iskandar-i S̲h̲ayk̲h̲ī b. Afrāsiyāb (1403) i, 237a; vi, 511a, 512a, b
Iskandar S̲h̲āh (Malacca) (XVI) vi, 207b
Iskandar T̲h̲ānī → Iskandar II

al-Iskandariyya (Egypt) i, 13a, 32a, 121b, 396b, 531b, 947a, 976a, 1288a; ii, 65a; iii, 1082b, 1193b; iv, **132a**; vi, 45b, 140b, 324a, b, 358b, 359a, b, 378b; vii, 68a; s, 1a, 5a, 120b, 121b
– institutions ii, 424a; v, 92a
al-Iskandariyya (towns) iv, **131a**
Iskandarūn (Alexandretta) i, 468b, 476b; ii, 35b; iv, **138a**; vi, 509b; x, 310b
Iskandarūna (Skandelion) iv, 131a, 138a
Iskeče ix, 156a; s, 330a
Iskender Beg (1468) i, 309b, 651b, 654b; ii, 721a; iv, **138b**, 574b; v, 724a, 725a; vii, 595a
Iskender Čelebi i, 1083a; ii, 1042b; iii, 998b; iv, 1137b; vi, 610a
Iskender Pas̲h̲a i, 268a; ii, 704b; iii, 998a; v, 682b; viii, 182a
Iṣlāḥ i, 383a; iv, **141a**; s, **466b**
Islām ii, 294a; iv, 44a-52a, 171b
İslâm Ansiklopedisi s, 42a, 615b
Islām, encyclopaedias → Mawsūʿa
Islām Girāy I (Crimea) (1532) iv, **178a**; viii, 832a, b
Islām Girāy II (Crimea) (1588) ii, 1113b; iv, **178b**; v, 137a; x, 811a
Islām Girāy III (Crimea) (1654) iv, **178b**; v, 139b, 719b; vi, 986b; vii, 62a
Islām K̲h̲ān i, 719b; ii, 216b, 797b; ix, 894a
Islām K̲h̲ān Sarwānī s, 203a
Islām S̲h̲āh Niʿmat Allāh Yazdī (XVI) vi, 483a
Islām S̲h̲āh b. S̲h̲īr S̲h̲āh Sūr (Delhi) (1554) i, 432b; ii, 259a, 271a, b; iii, 199b, 423a, 492b; ix, 894a; s, 1b, 3a
Islāmābād (India) ii, 32a; iv, **177b** (see also *s.v.* Chittagong)
Islāmābād (Pakistan) iv, **177b**
Islāmī D̲j̲amāʿat vi, 78b
Islāmī D̲j̲umhūrī Ittiḥād viii, 244a
Īṣlitan iii, 1039a, 1040a; vi, 948a
Islambol → Istanbul
Isly (river) iv, **179a**; vii, 391a
Isly, Battle of i, 67b, 85a; vii, 391a
Ism (name) ii, 302a; iv, **179a**; v, 396a
Ism (in grammar) iv, **181b**
ʿIṣma iii, 1024a; iv, **182b**
ʿIṣma K̲h̲ātūn (XII) vii, 755b
Ismaël → Ismāʿīl
Ismāʿīl (Ishmael) iii, 980a; iv, **184a**, 318a; v, 1014b; vi, 105b, 106a, 144b
Ismāʿīl (engineer) (1272) vi, 406a
Ismāʿīl (Izmail, town) iv, **185a**
Ismāʿīl , Imām → Ismāʿīl b. D̲j̲aʿfar al-Ṣādiḳ
Ismāʿīl I, Abu ’l-Walīd (Naṣrid) (1325) i, 1057b; vii, 1020a, **1023a**
Ismāʿīl II, Abu ’l-Walīd (Naṣrid) (1360) vii, 1020b, **1024a**
Ismāʿīl (Nog̲h̲ay) (1563) viii, 86b
Ismāʿīl I (Rasūlid) ii, 926a; iv, 1188b
Ismāʿīl I S̲h̲āh (Ṣafawid) (1524) i, 193b, 228a, 237b, 262b, 311b, 625b, 627b, 903b, 920a, 1019a, 1030b, 1087a, 1120a,b, 1211b; ii, 8a, 44b, 254b, 310b, 344b, 374a, 812a, 937a, 967a; iii, 114a, 177b, 274a, 316a, 585a, 1101a; iv, 34b, 49b, 102b, **186a**, 389a, 610a, 855a; v, 457a, 492b, 603b; vi, 714b; vii, 176b, 300a, 316b, 672b; viii, 115b, 750b, 765b, 767a; ix, 128b; s, 94b, 95a, 138b, 147b, 382b
Ismāʿīl II S̲h̲āh (Ṣafawid) (1577) i, 7b, 1208b; ii, 310b; iii, 157b; v, 825a; iv, **188a**; vii, 442a
Ismāʿīl III S̲h̲āh (Ṣafawid) ii, 311a; iv, 104b, 390a, b, 639b; v, 825b; ix, 597b; xi, 443b
Ismāʿīl I b. Aḥmad I (Sāmānid) (907) i, 278a, 452b, 984b, 1001a, 1294a; iv, 21b, 22a, **188b**, 658b; v, 58a, 853a, 856a; vi, 365b; vii, 418a, 760a; viii, 63a, 500a, 796b, 1026b
Ismāʿīl II b. Nūḥ II (Sāmānid) (1004) iv, **189b**; v, 622b; viii, 1028a; s, 176b, 245a
Ismāʿīl, Abu ’l-Faḍl i, 1332a, b; ii, 282a; iii, 120a
Ismāʿīl, Mawlāy (ʿAlawid) → Mawlāy Ismāʿīl
Ismāʿīl b. ʿAbbād → Ibn ʿAbbād al-Ṣāḥib
Ismāʿīl b. ʿAbbād al-Muʿtaḍid i, 5b, 6a
Ismāʿīl b. ʿAbbās → Ismāʿīl I (Rasūlid)
Ismāʿīl b. ʿAbd al-Ḥaḳḳ v, 60a, b
Ismāʿīl b. ʿAbd al-Raḥmān b. D̲h̲i ’l-Nūn ii, 243a; v, 392a; x, 584a, 605b
Ismāʿīl b. Abī K̲h̲ālid (763) vii, 576a
Ismāʿīl b. Abi ’l-Ḳāsim D̲j̲aʿfar b. al-Uṭrus̲h̲ i, 688a; iii, 255a
Ismāʿīl b. Abī Sahl al-Nawbak̲h̲tī i, 143b
Ismāʿīl b. Abī Uways (841) vii, 691b

Ismāʿīl b. Aḥmad Ankarāwī (1631) iii, 711a; iv, **190a**; viii, 306a; ix, 59b
Ismāʿīl b. ʿAlī b. ʿUt̲h̲mān al-T̲h̲aḳafī s, 163a
Ismāʿīl b. ʿAmmār (VIII) viii, 996b; ix, 452a, 827b
Ismāʿīl b. Bulbul, vizier (892) iii, 739a, 767b, 955a; iv, **189a**; vii, 766a, 975a
Ismāʿīl b. D̲j̲aʿfar b. Sulaymān b. ʿAlī (Baṣra) vi, 335a
Ismāʿīl b. D̲j̲aʿfar al-Ṣādiḳ (VIII) i, 402b, 550b; ii, 851a; iv, 198a, 1133a; v, 1242b; vi, 333b; vii, 645b
Ismāʿīl b. D̲j̲āmiʿ → Ibn D̲j̲āmiʿ, Ismāʿīl
Ismāʿīl b. Gīlākī (Ismāʿīlī, Ṭabas) (XII) vii, 489b, 535b
Ismāʿīl b. Haydar b. D̲j̲unayd (Ṣafawid) (XV) viii, 766b
Ismāʿīl b. Isḥāḳ b. Ismāʿīl b. Ḥammād → al-Azdī
Ismaʿīl b. Ismāʿīl b. Ḥammād (910) s, **385a**
Ismāʿīl b. al-Ḳāsim → Abu ʾl-ʿAtāhiya
Ismāʿīl b. K̲h̲alaf (1065) ix, 587a
Ismāʿīl b. Māzin iii, 299b
Ismāʿīl b. Muḥammad (amīr) (Ḳadmūs) (XIX) viii, 923a
Ismāʿīl b. Muḥammad b. ʿAlī Kurd Taymūr (XIX) vi, 75a
Ismāʿīl b. Muḥammad al-Nīsābūrī ii, 496b; iii, 738b
Ismāʿīl b. Mūsā b. Mūsā iv, 713a; v, 683a
Ismāʿīl b. Mūsā al-Kāẓim i, 402b; vii, 645b; s, 95a
Ismāʿīl b. Nūḥ (1004) → Ismāʿīl II b. Nūḥ II
Ismāʿīl b. Sebüktigin (X) ii, 799a, 1050b; iv, **189b**; vi, 65a
Ismāʿīl b. Ṣubayḥ al-Ḥarrānī, kātib al-sirr (VIII) vi, 333b
Ismāʿīl b. ʿUbayd Allāh (Sūs) (VIII) vi, 923b
Ismāʿīl b. Yāḳūtī i, 1051b, 1052a; iv, 28b; vi, 274b; viii, 941b
Ismāʿīl b. Yasār al-Nisāʾī (VIII) i, 206b; iv, 54a, **189b**; vii, 310a, 648b
Ismāʿīl b. Yūsuf b. Ibrāhīm al-Saffāk (IX) vi, 106a, 148a; vii, 390b, 794a
Ismāʿīl b. Yūsuf al-Baṣrī iv, 1004a
Ismāʿīl b. Yūsuf al-Uk̲h̲ayḍir i, 551a; x, 792a
Ismāʿīl b. Ziyād al-Nafūsī iii, 654a; iv, 336b
Ismāʿīl ʿĀdil S̲h̲āh iii, 425b, 1160a, b; vii, 943b
Ismāʿīl Ag̲h̲a Čengič (1840) viii, 520a, b
Ismāʿīl Ag̲h̲a Ṣīmḳo ʿAbdoy i, 1030b; iv, 622b; v, 466a; ix, 245b
Ismāʿīl ʿĀṣim Efendi → Čelebi-zade
Ismāʿīl al-Aṭras̲h̲ ii, 636b, 637a
Ismāʿīl al-Azharī (Sudan) ix, 748b
Ismāʿīl Bey (Miṣr) (1791) iii, 992a; iv, 853a; vii, 179b
Ismāʿīl Bey (Serez) i, 778b, 1304a; ii, 640a
Ismāʿīl Bey b. Īwāẓ Bey iv, 723a
Ismāʿīl Bey Isfendiyār-og̲h̲lu iv, 108b
Ismāʿīl Bey Ḳutḳashînlî ii, 217a
Ismāʿīl al-D̲h̲abīḥ (engineer) (XX) vi, 165b
Ismāʿīl D̲j̲ānbulāt iv, 284b, 285b
Ismāʿīl Gasprinski → Gasprali̊
Ismāʿīl G̲h̲ālib (1895) iii, 993b; iv, **190b**; viii, 183a
Ismāʿīl Ḥaḳḳi b. Ibrāhīm Manāstîrlî (1912) s, **468b**
Ismāʿīl Ḥaḳḳi ʿĀlīs̲h̲ān (1944) ii, 637b; iv, **191a**
Ismāʿīl Ḥaḳḳī Balṭad̲j̲îog̲h̲lu (1978) iv, 1126b; vi, 988a; s, **468b**
Ismāʿīl Ḥaḳḳī al-Brūsawī (1725) ii, 475a, 542b; iv, **191a**
Ismāʿīl Haḳḳī Pas̲h̲a, Ḥāfiẓ (1911) ii, 698b, 699b; vi, 983b
Ismāʿīl Husrev (XX) vi, 95a
Ismāʿīl Kāmil Pas̲h̲a ii, 351b, 615b, 874b, 1110b
Ismāʿīl Kemāl i, 657b; iv, 195b
Ismāʿīl K̲h̲ān ii, 45b
Ismāʿīl K̲h̲ān Ḳashḳāy iv, 706a
Ismāʿīl K̲h̲andān i, 424b; iv, 1067a
Ismāʿīl al-k̲h̲as̲h̲s̲h̲āb ii, 356b
Ismāʿīl al-Manṣūr → al-Manṣūr (Fāṭimid)
Ismāʿīl Mīrzā b. Ṭahmāsp (Ṣafawid) vi, 483a
Ismāʿīl Muk̲h̲ i, 923b; ii, 99b, 180a, 1124b; iv, 907b
Ismāʿīl al-Muntaṣir → Ismāʿīl II b. Nūḥ II
Ismāʿīl Og̲h̲lan S̲h̲ayk̲h̲ (Malāmī) (1529) vi, 226b, 227a, b, 228a
Ismāʿīl Pas̲h̲a → Čerkes Ismāʿīl Pas̲h̲a
Ismāʿīl Pas̲h̲a b. al-ʿAẓm v, 925b
Ismāʿīl Pas̲h̲a b. Bahrām i, 920a
Ismāʿīl Pas̲h̲a b. Ibrāhīm Pas̲h̲a, Khedive (1879) i, 37b, 142a, 825b, 929a, 1069b; ii, 149b, 167a, 423b, 514a, 642a, 647a,

728a, 892a, 934a; iii, 4b, 360a, 593a, 1000a, 1193b; iv, **192a**, 441b, 442a; v, 4a, 909a, 1060a, 1248a; vi, 23a, b, 25a, 68b, 75a, 192a, 197a, 342a, 643a, 794b; vii, 182b, 183b; viii, 40b, 58b; s, 40a, 179a, 296b, 299b, 379a, 408b
Ismāʿīl Pas̲h̲a b. Muḥammad ʿAlī Pas̲h̲a (1822) vii, 425b; viii, 40b; ix, 229b, 301a
Ismāʿīl Pas̲h̲a Ayyūb ii, 123b
Ismāʿīl Pas̲h̲a Bag̲h̲dādl̊ (1920) i, 905a; s, **429a**
Ismāʿīl Pasha Nis̲h̲ānd̲j̲l̊ (1690) iv, **193b**; v, 258b; vii, 239b
Ismāʿīl Rūmī (1953) iv, 382a, b; xi, 114b
Ismāʿīl Ṣabrī (1953) iv, **194b**
Ismāʿīl Ṣabrī Pas̲h̲a (1923) iv, **194b**
Ismāʿīl Ṣafā (1901) iv, **195a**
Ismāʿīl S̲h̲āh → Ismāʿīl I, II, III
Ismāʿīl S̲h̲ahīd, Muḥammad (1831) ii, 735b; iii, 431a, 436a; iv, **196a**; vii, 442a
Ismāʿīl Ṣidḳī (1948) ii, 934b; iii, 515b, 516a, 517a; iv, **197b**; ix, 151b; xi, 253a; s, 58a
Ismāʿīl al-Tamīmī ii, 633a; vi, 113a
Ismāʿīlawayh (X) ix, 698b
Ismāʿīlī, Banū (Maḳdis̲h̲ū) vi, 128b
Ismāʿīlī (S̲h̲abānkāra) iii, 1097b
Ismāʿīlīyya i, 20a, 48a, 95b, 103b, 125a, 134a, 160a, 216b, 225b, 353a, 402b, 550b, 551a, 832b, 872a, 1052b, 1254b, 1332b, 1350b, 1358a; ii, 168b, 194a, 301a, 375a, 453b, 631b, 859a; iii, 80a, 123b, 253b, 254a, 411b, 433b, 862b, 1155b; iv, 28a, 29b, 30b, 46b-47a, **198a**, 660b, 859b, 887b, 910a; v, 25b, 1033a; vi, 65a, 190b, 191a, 219b, 274a, 322a, 438b, 499b, 500a, 791b; viii, 83a, 586b, 942a; s, 95b, 206b, 248b, 358b, 407a, 411a
– doctrine i, 160b, 414b, 450a, 834b, 1098b, 1099b; ii, 97b, 136b, 848b, 1066a, 1070a; iii, 71b, 232a, 1071a, 1130a; iv, 183a, 203a; v, 167a, b, 1242b
Ismāʿīliyya (town) iv, 193a, **206b**; s, 6a
ʿIsmān, Adan Abdulla (Somalia) (IX) ix, 718b
ʿIsmat Allāh Buk̲h̲ārāʾī (XV) x, 813b
Ismat Chughtai (XX) vi, 489a
ʿIṣmatiyya i, 903a
Iṣmet Inönü (1973) i, 734b, 1255b; ii, 6b, 26a, 432b, 595b, 596a; iii, 1199b; iv, 873b, 934a; s, 98b, **469b**
Isna iv, **206b**; v, 386a; vi, 366b
Isnād i, 259a; ii, 302a; iii, 25a, 26a; iv, **207a**; v, 947a
Ispahbad̲h̲ i, 73a, 1110a; iv, **207a**, 208b, 465a; v, 662a; vi, 633b; vii, 570a; s, 309a
al-Ispad̲h̲iyyūn vii, 570a
Ispahdūst al-Daylamī (X) vii, 485a
Ispahsālār ii, 507b; iii, 47a; iv, **208a**; vi, 519a; xi, 197b
Ispand b. Ḳara Yūsuf (Ḳara Ḳoyunlu) (1444) vii, 672a
Isparta iv, **210b**
Ispend̲j̲e ii, 32a, 146b, 915a; iv, **211a**, 563a; viii, 487a, b
Isperuk̲h̲ K̲h̲ān i, 1305a
Ispirīzāde Aḥmed Efendi v, 643b
Isrāʾ → Miʿrād̲j̲
Israel, Israël → Filasṭīn; Yaʿḳūb
Israel ha-Maʿārābī iv, 605b, 606a
Isrāfīl i, 1093a; iv, **211a**, 292b; v, 770a; vi, 217a; vii, 557a; s, 256a
Isrāʾīl, Banū i, 264b, **1020a**; vi, 737a, b
al-Isrāʾīlī → Ibrāhīm b. Yaʿḳūb; Isḥāḳ b. Sulaymān
al-Isrāʾīlī, Abu ʾl-Faḍl b. Abi ʾl-Bayān (XI) i, 344b; viii, 108a
al-Isrāʾīlī, Ibn al-ʿAṭṭār → al-Kōhēn al-ʿAṭṭār
Isrāʾīliyyāt iv, **211b**
İssi̊k-kul iv, **212b**
Istabba (Estapa) vi, 221b
Iṣṭabl ii, 696a; iv, **213b**, 266a; vi, 537b; vii, 88a
Iṣṭak̲h̲r (town) i, 43b, 1355b; ii, 925b; iv, **219b**; vi, 120a, 650a, 651a, 656a, 661a
Istak̲h̲r (cistern) v, 869b
al-Iṣṭak̲h̲rī → Abū ʿAmr al-Iṣṭak̲h̲rī
al-Iṣṭak̲h̲rī, Abū Isḥāḳ Ibrāhīm (950) i, 133a, 488a, 835b, 1003a, 1354a; ii, 581a,b, 582a; iii, 405b, 787a; iv, 220a, **222b**, 1079a; v, 1012a; vi, 313b, 639b, 640a; vii, 493a; s, 327a
al-Iṣṭak̲h̲rī, Abū Saʿīd (940) ii, 1099a; iii, 486a
Istami (Is̲h̲temi) b. Bumin, Yabgu (575) x, 687a
Istān → Ustān

Istanba → Abū Isḥāḳ Ibrāhīm al-Harawī
Istanbul i, 13b, 37a, 109a, 293b, 294a, 394a, 466b, 467a, 973a, 974b, 1334b; ii, 63b, 83b, 708b, 907b; iii, 216b; iv, **224a**; v, 694a, 882a; vi, 45b, 57a, 372b, 531b; s, 53b, 67b
– fires iv, 237a-238b
– institutions i, 1225b; ii, 425b; iii, 140a, 1137b; v, 366a
– monuments (VIII) i, 774a, 830b, 1318a; iii, 143b; iv, 225b, 232a, 720a, 1159a; v, 67a, 243a, 261a, 533b; s, **470b**
– population iv, 238a-244b
– streets iv, 235a-237a
Istanköy → On Iki Ada
Istār iv, **248b**
Istiʿāra iv, **248b**; s, 278a
Istibdād → Ẓulm
Istibrāʾ i, 28a, b, 1027a; iii, 1012a; iv, **252b**
Istibṣār, Kitāb al- ii, 874b; iii, 675b; iv, **254a**
Istidja iv, **254a**, 355a; x, 243a, b
Iṣṭifan b. Basīl iv, **254b**
Iṣṭifan al-Duwayḥī (1704) iv, **255a**; vi, 345b; s, 602a, 603a, 798b
Istifhām iv, **255a**
Istiḥḍār iv, 264b
Istiḥsān ii, 164a; iii, 1237a; iv, **255b**, 269b
Istiḳbāl iv, **259a**; vii, 490a
Istiḳbāl (paper) iv, 681b
Istikhāra iv, **259b**; viii, 646b
Istikhdām → Tawriyya
Istiḳlāl iv, **260b**; v, 1194b, 1195a
Istiḳsām iv, **263a**
Iṣṭilāḥat ii, 765b; v, 805b
Istilḥāḳ s, **475a**
Istimṭār iii, 305b; iv, 270a
Istiʾnāf iv, **264a**
Istinbāt → Māʾ; Rifāya
Istindjāʾ iv, **264b**
Istinshāḳ iv, **264b**
Istinzāl iv, **264b**
Istiʿrāḍ i, 810a; ii, 507b; iv, **269a**, 1076b; v, 19b
Istiʿrāḍ, ʿarḍ iv, **265a**
Istiṣḥāb i, 276a; iv, **269b**
Istishrāḳ → Mustashriḳūn
Istisḳāʾ i, 109a; ii, 617b; iv, **269b**; v, 736a, 1202a; ix, 94b
Istiṣlāḥ → Istiḥsān
Istiṭāʿa i, 413b; iv, **271a**
Istithnāʾ i, 276b; ii, 302a; iii, 1079b, 1196a; iv, **272b**
Istiwāʾ, Khaṭṭ al- iv, **273a**
Istōnī (Istolnī) Belghrād ii, 208b; iv, **273b**
Istravshan → Ura-Tepe
Īṭāʾ iv, 413a
Iṭāʿa → Ṭāʿa
ʿItāb b. Warḳa iv, 99b
Iʿtāḳ → ʿAbd
Italy → Īṭaliya
Īṭaliya i, 293a; iv, **274b**, 413b; v, 758a;
Iʿtaraḍa iv, 269a
Itāwa iv, **276a**
Itāwā (Etājā) iv, **276a**; vi, 62a
Itāy al-Bārūd i, 1069b; s, 244a
Itbāʿ → Muzāwadja
ʿItbān b. Malik (VII) vi, 649a, 650a
Iṭfīr → Ḳiṭfīr
Ithbāt iv, **277a**
Ithm iv, 1106b, 1107a; s, **475a**
Ithnā-ʿashariyya i, 134a, 765a, 1130a, 1142a, 1350b, 1352a; ii, 375a, 1093b; iii, 380a, 433b, 544b, 726b, 1021a, 1150b, 1166b; iv, 46b, 47b, 49b-50a, 186a, **277a**, 888a; vi, 16a, 312b; vii, 780a; ix, 507a; s, 56b, 134b, 248b
Iʿtibār Khān (1623) ii, 1085a; iii, 225b; iv, **279a**
Iʿtiḳād iv, **279a**
Iʿtiḳād Khān (XVIII) iv, **279b**; s, 167b
Iʿtikāf iv, **280a**; vii, 846b; viii, 417b
Itil → Atil
Itil (river) iv, **280a**, 1175b
Iʿtimād (al-Rumaykiyya) (XI) iii, 706a; vii, 766b; viii, 617b
Iʿtimād al-Dawla → Shafīʿ Mazandarānī
Iʿtimād al-Dawla (Ibrāhīm Shīrāzī) s, 405b
Iʿtimād al-Dawla (Mīrzā Ghiyāth Beg) (1622) i, 253b; ii, 380b; iv, **282a**, 543b; vi, 369b; vii, 195a, 331b; viii, 268a
Iʿtimād al-Dawla (title) iv, **281b**; v, 630a
Iʿtimād al-Dawla Ḳamar al-Dīn Khān (XVIII) vii, 446a
Iʿtimād al-Ḥaram vi, 529a
Iʿtimād Khān (Gudjārāt) (XVI) ii, 1129a; vii, 134a; s, 335b
Iʿtimād al-Salṭana → Muḥammad Ḥasan Khān Ṣāniʿ al-Dawla
Iʿtimādpur vi, 128a

Iʿtimāzāda, Muḥammad iv, 73b
Iʿtiṣām al-Dīn (XVIII) iii, 1046a; s, 108a, **475b**
ʿItḳ → ʿAbd
ʿİtḳnāme iv, **282b**
al-Iṭlāḳiyya iii, 284a
ʿIṭr → ʿAnbar; Misk
Ittibāʿ iv, 152a; x, 809a
Ittiḥād iii, 571a; iv, **282b**
al-Ittiḥād al-ʿarabī ii, 674b
al-Ittiḥād al-ʿarabī ʾl-ishtirākī s, 671b
Ittiḥād-i Islām (committee) ii, 445b
Ittiḥād-i Islām (periodical) iii, 393a
Ittiḥād-i Muḥammedī Djemʿiyyeti iv, **283b**
al-Ittiḥād al-Lubnānī ii, 467b; iii, 519b
al-Ittiḥād al-Sūrī iii, 520b
Ittiḥād we Teraḳḳī Djemʿiyyeti i, 734a; ii, 430b, 643b, 698b; iii, 204a, 251a, 526a, 994a; iv, 283b, **284a**, 611b, 872a, b, 873a; v, 905b, 1036a; vi, 74a; viii, 446b; s, 41b, 47b, 149b
Ittiḥādiyya iii, 161b, 821b, 822a, 952a
Ittiṣāl → Ittiḥād
Ivanko → Yanko
Ivory Coast → Côte d'Ivoire
Iwā i, 919a
ʿIwaḍ iv, **286a**
ʿIwaḍ Beg (Kurd) vi, 202a
ʿIwaḍ Pasha, Ḥādjdjī, vizier (XV) i, 1334a; vii, 594b
ʿIwad Wadjīh (XVII) iv, **286b**
Īwān i, 950a, 1228b; ii, 114a, b, 115b; iv, **287a**, 1073b, 1137a, 1138b, 1141b, 1146b
ʿIwāẓ (ʿIwāḍ) Bey ii, 233b
ʿIwāẓ (Iwāḍ) Khaldjī, Ghiyāth al-Dīn ii, 267b; iii, 1155a
ʿIwāẓ Khaldjī, Ḥusayn al-Dīn i, 393b
ʿIyāḍ, Banū ii, 196b, 197b; iv, **289a**, iv, 1133b; v, 77a, b, 639b, 640a; x, 140b
ʿIyāḍ b. Ghānm (VII) i, 329a, 635b, 679b, 695a, 1206b; ii, 344b, 523b, 624a, 625b; iii, 20a, 228a; iv, 841b; vi, 379a, 540a, 930a; vii, 983a; viii, 410a, 433b, 589b; ix, 68b
ʿIyāḍ b. Mūsā al-Sabtī al-Ḳāḍī (1149) i, 602b; ii, 743b; iii, 680b, 707b, 867b; iv, 183b, **289b**, 912b; v, 71b, 1208b; vi, 263a, 280a, b, 349b, 351a, 353b, 591a, 712a; vii, 584a, 625a, 691b; viii, 690b; x, 122a; s, 27a
Iyāḍ b. Sūd, Banū iv, 289b
al-ʿIyāḍī → Muḥammad al-Tūnisī
al-ʿIyāḍī, Abū Naṣr Aḥmad b. al-ʿAbbās (890) vi, 846a
ʿIyāfa ii, 760a, 916a; iv, **290b**
ʿIyāl Manṣūr iii, 49b
ʿIyāl Zāyid ii, 175b, 176a
Iyāla → Eyālet
ʿIyān vi, 436a
al-ʿIyānī, Djaʿfar b. al-Ḳāsim (XI) s, 22a
al-ʿIyānī, al-Ḥusayn b. al-Ḳāsim (Zaydī Imām) (1013) v, 1237b; vii, 773a; s, 22a
al-ʿIyānī, al-Manṣūr Bi ʾllāh al-Ḳāsim (Zaydī Imām) vi, **435b**; vii, 773a; xi, 479b; s, 557a
ʿIyār → Sikka
ʿIyār-i Dānish → Kalīla wa-Dimna
Iyās b. Ḳabīsa al-Ṭāʾī (611) i, 689b, 690a; ii, 241a; x, 62a, 402b; s, **475b**
Iyās b. Muʿāwiya (793) iii, 650a; iv, **291a**; s, 757b
Iyās b. Muḍārib (VII) vii, 522b
Īzadyār b. Masʿūd i, 217b
Izâfet → Iḍāfa
Iʿzāz al-Dawla Marzubān b. ʿIzz al-Dawla Bakhtiyār (Būyid) (X) iv, 293b; vii, 358a
Iẓhār al-Ḥasan b. Inʿām al-Ḥasan (1996) x, 38b
Izmail → Ismāʿīl (Izmail)
Izmīd/Izmit v, 250a; vi, 587b, 588b; s, **476a**
Izmīr (Smyrna) i, 464a, 476a, 783b, 1335b; ii, 599a, b; iii, 210b, 214b; v, 505a, 1170a; vi, 68b; vii, 70b; s, 44b, 67b, **477b**
– institutions ii, 425b
Izmir-oghlu → Djunayd (Aydın-oghlu)
Iznīḳ i, 477a; ii, 746b; iv, **291b**, 702a, 1169a, b; v, 103b; vi, 366a; viii, 175b; s, 204a, 330b
– monuments iv, 291b, 292a
al-Iznīḳī, Abu ʾl-Faḍl Mūsā i, 137a
al-Iznīḳī, Ḳuṭb al-Dīn iii, 711a; v, 547a
Izraʿ v, 593b
ʿIzrāʾīl iv, **292b**; v, 210a; vi, 217a
ʿIzz al-Dawla iv, **293b**
ʿIzz al-Dawla Bakhtiyār → Bakhtiyār, ʿIzz al-Dawla
ʿIzz al-Dawla al-Bakrī → ʿAbd al-ʿAzīz al-Bakrī
ʿIzz al-Dīn b. ʿAbd b. al-Salām → ʿAbd al-Azīz b. ʿAbd al-Salām
ʿIzz al-Dīn b. al-Athīr → Ibn al-Athīr

ʿIzz al-Dīn b. ʿAwn al-Dīn b. Hubayra (XII) vii, 726b; viii, 943b
ʿIzz al-Dīn b. Djahāndār ii, 379b; iii, 200a
ʿIzz al-Dīn b. Shudjāʿ al-Dīn v, 828a, b, 829a
ʿIzz al-Dīn Abu ʾl-ʿAsākir Sulṭān (Shayzar) (1154) vi, 791a; ix, 410b (see also *s.v.* Abu ʾl-ʿAsākir Sulṭān b. Sadīd al-Mulk ʿAlī)
ʿIzz al-Dīn Abū Bakr al-Dubaysī (amīr) (al-Mawṣil) (1160) iii, 961a; vi, 870b
ʿIzz al-Dīn Ala-Tagh (XIV) xi, 135b
ʿIzz al-Dīn Aybak (Mamlūk) → Aybak, al-Muʿizz ʿIzz al-Dīn al-Muʿaẓẓamī
ʿIzz al-Dīn Aybak al-Turkumānī (1257) i, 732a, 804a, 944b; vi, 321b; ix, 176a, b
ʿIzz al-Dīn Aybak al-Turkī al-Ẓāhirī (Ḥimṣ) (1363) vi, 547b
ʿIzz al-Dīn Aydamur al-ʿIzzī al-Naḳīb (1303) vi, 547b
ʿIzz al-Dīn Aydimur al-Ḥillī i, 814b
ʿIzz al-Dīn Farrukh-Shāh v, 1139b
ʿIzz al-Dīn Ḥasanī Rikābī, Sayyid (Marʿashī) (1393) vi, 512b
ʿIzz al-Dīn Ḥusayn ii, 1100a; v, 828b; ix, 110a
ʿIzz al-Dīn Ibrāhīm b. al-Muḳaddam (1181) vi, 380b, 381a
ʿIzz al-Dīn Kaykāwus → Kaykāʾūs I, II
ʿIzz al-Dīn Khān-i Ayāz s, 66b
ʿIzz al-Dīn khaṭṭāb b. Maḥmūd b. Murtaʿish (1325) vi, 548a
ʿIzz al-Dīn al-Maṣrī (XX) vi, 755a
ʿIzz al-Dīn Masʿūd I (Zangid) (1193) iii, 1119a; vi, **780b**, 900b; viii, 79b; xi, 454a
ʿIzz al-Dīn Masʿūd II (Zangid) (1218) viii, 79b, 127a, b; ix, 411a
ʿIzz al-Dīn Shīr iv, 586a
ʿIzz al-Dīn Sūghandī, Sayyid vi, 511a
ʿIzz al-Dīn al-Sulamī → al-Sulamī, ʿIzz al-Dīn ʿAbd al-ʿAzīz b. ʿAbd al-Salām
ʿIzz al-Dīn Usāma (XII) i, 208a; iv, 779a; x, 883b
ʿIzz al-Dīn al-Wafāʾī (XV) x, 313a
ʿIzz al-Mulk i, 1052b; viii, 81a
ʿIzzat al-Dawla (Ḳādjār) (XIX) vii, 431b, 818b; s, 70b
Izzat Sultan (XX) vi, 770b
al-ʿIzzatī, Muḥammad b. Luṭf Allāh b. Bayrām (XVII) vii, 469b
ʿIzzet ʿAbed Pasha i, 64a; iii, 364a
ʿIzzet Bey ii, 641a
ʿIzzet Efendi iv, 1126a
ʿIzzet Hōlō ʿArab ʿIzzet Pasha (1924) s, **480a**
ʿIzzet Molla i, 558a; ii, 934b; iv, **295a**; v, 710b, 1083b; viii, 171b
ʿIzzet Muḥammad Pasha iii, 627b
ʿIzzet Pasha → Aḥmad ʿIzzet; Ḥasan ʿIzzet
ʿIzzet Pasha, Aḥmed Furgaç (1937) iv, **296a**; vi, 984a; vii, 229a; s, 300a
ʿIzzī Süleymān Efendi (1755) iv, 298b

J

Jacob → Isrāʾīl; Yaʿḳūb
Jacob ben Eleazar (Toledo) vi, 114b
Jacob b. Reuben iv, 605b
Jacob b. Simeon iv, 605b
Jacobites → Yaʿkūbiyya
Jaén → Djayyān
Jaffa → Yāfā
Jagellons ii, 179a; v, 719b; vii, 219a
Jain → Djayn
Jaipur s, 140b, 142b (see also *s.v.* Djaypur)
Jajce i, 1018a, 1263b; vi, 71b, 979a
Jakarta → Djakarta
Jaleel, K.A. vi, 461a
Jamia Millia Islamia (al-Djāmiʿa al-Milliyya al-Islāmiyya) ii, 426b; s, **480a**
Jamna (river) → Djamnā
Janina → Yanya
Janissiries → Yeñi Čeri; Yerliyya
Japan → al-Yābānī
Japara iii, 1219a; s, 201a, b
Japheth → Yāfith
Japheth b. Eli iv, 305b, 605a
Japheth al-Barḳamānī iv, 605b
Jassy → Yash
Jata (Mogholistān) x, 590b
Játiva → Shāṭiba
Jatts → Zuṭṭ
Java i, 170b, 174a, 981a; ii, 352a, 497a; iii, 566b, 1213a, b, 1214b, 1218b, 1219b, 1222a, b, 1226a; iv, 1128a; v, 225b, 226b, 227b, 1154b; vi, 42b, 43b, 239a, 517a
Jawnpur → Djawnpur

Jaxartes → Sīr Daryā
Jbala v, 1185b, 1200b, 1203b; vii, 36b
Jehlam (river) s, 156a
Jellābas → Djallāb
Jenghiz Khan → Činghiz Khān
Jeremiah → Irmiyya
Jerez → Sharīsh
Jericho → Rīḥā
Jerusalem → al-Ḳuds
Jeshuah b. Judah (Abu ʾl-Faradj Furḳān) (XI) iv, 305a, 605a, 607a; vii, 539b
Jessore → Djassawr
Jesus → ʿĪsā b. Maryam
Jethro → Shuʿayb
Jews → Yahūd
Jimeno, Count i, 161a; iii, 771b
Jinnah → Djināḥ
Jnān b. Ḥalīma vii, 39a
Jnān al-ʿAfīya (Marrākush) vi, 596b
Jnān Riḍwān (Marrākush) vi, 596b
Job → Ayyūb
Jōʾēl, Rabbi iv, 505b
Joel of Dotawo vii, 545a
Johannes Grammaticus → Yaḥyā al-Naḥwī
John the Baptist → Yaḥyā b. Zakariyyāʾ
Johor vi, 116b, 208a, 232b, 235a, b, 236a, b, 239a; viii, 303a, 1042a; s, 150b, 151b
Jolo (island) iii, 1218b; viii, 303a, b
Jonah → Yūnus
Jordan (river and country) → al-Urdunn
Joseph → Yūsuf
Joseph b. Noah → Yūsuf b. Nūḥ
Joseph ha-Rōʾeh → Yūsuf al-Baṣīr
Joshua → Yūshaʿ
Joshua ben Judah → Jeshuah b. Judah
Jomblatt → Djānbulāṭ
Jou-Jan (Zhouan-Zhouan/Zhuan-Zhuan) ix, 531b; x, 303a, 335a, 687a, 691a
Jubba (river) ix, 412a, 714b
Judaeo-Arabic i, 574b; iv, **299a**; v, 206b; s, 669b
Judaeo-Berber iv, **307b**
Judaeo-Persian iv, **308a**
Jumbe, Aboud (XX) xi, 450b

K

Ḳāʿa ii, 114b; iv, 428b; viii, 545b; ix, 175b, 176a
Ḳaʿādi → al-Djarādatān[i]
Ḳaʾan → Khāḳān
Ḳāʿān (China) vi, 501b
Ḳāʾānčīs iv, 30b
Ḳaʾānī, Ḥabīb Allāh (1854) ii, 433b; iii, 373a; iv, 69b, **313a**; vi, 609b; vii, 661b
Kaarta (Mali) ii, 1002a; iii, 39a; iv, **313b**; vi, 259a
Kaʿb, Banū i, 441a; iii, 1102b, 1107a; iv, **314b**, 740a, 765a; v, 81a; vii, 674b, 675a; ix, 898b
Kaʿb b. ʿAmr, Banū v, 78b, 79a; viii, 1002b
Kaʿb b. Asad v, 436a
Kaʿb Asad xi, 240b
Kaʿb al-Ashraf (625) iv, **315a**; vi, 145a, 603b
Kaʿb b. Djuʿayl al-Taghlabī (VII) iv, **315a**; x, 92b
Kaʿb b. Mālik, Abū ʿAbd Allāh (670) i, 50b; iii, 272b, 354a, 975b; iv, **315b**; vi, 604a
Kaʿb b. Māma i, 115b
Kaʿb b. Saʿd al-Ghanawī ii, 1005a; vi, 817b
Kaʿb b. Zuhayr (VII) i, 1011b, 1314b; ii, 528b; iv, **316a**, 510a; v, 6b, 734a, 958b; vi, 467b, 896a; vii, 981a; xi, 155a
Kaʿb al-Aḥbār, Abū Isḥāḳ (652) i, 926b; ii, 363; iii, 370a; iv, 212a, **316b**, 1135b; v, 324a, 1231b; vi, 247b
Kaʿba i, 55b, 136a, 178a, 268a, 453a, 551b, 608b, 867a, 892b, 1054a; ii, 247a, 453a, 603b, 695b; iii, 33a, 40a, 101a, 980b; iv, 184a, b, 260a, **317a**; 926a; v, 77b, 78a, 434a, b, 435b, 520a, 990b; vi, 46a, 105b, 148a, 157b, **166b**, **180b**, 645a, b, 646b, 651a, 658b, 659a, 664a, 665a, 669b, 677b, 708b
Ḳabā, ḳabāʾ v, 739b, 743b, 748a, b, 749a, b
al-Kaʿba al-Yamāniya ii, 241b
Ḳabača, Nāṣir al-Dīn → Nāṣir al-Dīn Ḳabača
Kabadian → Ḳubādhiyān
Ḳabādiyān → Ḳubādhiyān
Ḳabadj Khātūn i, 1293b
Ḳābādū, Maḥmūd b. Muḥammad (1871) viii, 401b; s, **481**
Kabāʾir i, 1242a; ii, 833a; iii, 797a; iv, 995a, 1107b, 1108b; s, 483b

Kabak → Kebek
Ḳabaḳbāzī → Laʿb
Ḳabaḳdjî-oghlu Muṣṭafā (Yamak) (1808) ii, 713a; iv, **322b**; vii, 710a
Ḳabakulaḳ Ibrāhīm Agha (1730) vi, 55b; viii, 288a
Ḳabāla (Ādharbāydjān) i, 659b; ii, 817a; ix, 254a
Ḳabāla(t) i, 1144a; ii, 145b; iv, **323a**, 1032a, 1040a; ix, 253a
Ḳaban vi, 201a
Kabard, Banū i, 1000a, 1189b; ii, 21b, 22a, b; iii, 1235b; iv, 324b, 596b; v, 288b; x, 920b
Kabards → Kabard, Banū
Kabarega (Bunyoro) (1899) x, 779a
al-Kābarī, Muḥammad (XV) xi, 122b
Ḳabartay i, 62b; ii, 25a, 1113a; vi, 56a (see also *s.v.* Kabard, Banū)
Ḳabāṭiyya vi, 543b
al-Ḳabbāb, Abū Muḥammad al-Tamgrūtī (1635) iv, **325b**; vi, 350a
Ḳabbān → Mīzān
al-Ḳabbānī, Aḥmad Abū Khalīl x, 233a
al-Ḳabbānī, Djamāl al-Dīn Abū ʿAlī al-Kaʿbī (1697) vi, 112a
al-Ḳabbānī, Muḥammad vi, 798b
Ḳabbānī, Nizār Tawfīḳ (1998) s, **482b**
Ḳabḍ (contraction) i, 1088b; iii, 361a; iv, 326a
Ḳabḍ (possession) iii, 350a; iv, **325b**
Kabdān, Ahl vi, 1009a
Ḳabdjaḳ al-Manṣūrī, Sayf al-Dīn (Ḥamāt) (1310) vii, 991b (see also *s.v.* Sayf al-Dīn Ḳîpčaḳ al-Manṣūrī)
al-Kaʿbī, Abu 'l-Ḳāsim al-Balkhī (932) i, 204b; ii, 518b; vi, 846b; s, 32a, 225b
Kabid iv, **327a**
Ḳābiḍ, Mollā (1527) iv, **333b**; v, 41b; vi 227a; vii, **225a**
Ḳabīḥa umm al-Muʿtazz (IX) s, 252b
Ḳābīl → Hābīl wa-Ḳābīl
al-Ḳābil (al-Sharḳiyya) ix, 256v; s, 355b
Ḳābil Khān iv, 760a
Ḳabīla i, 700a; iv, **334a**, 362a
Ḳabīlīs (Yemen) vi, 491a
Kabīr (poet) (ca. 1448) i, 1166a; iii, 456b, 459b; v, 630b; s, **483a**
Kabīr Khān (Multān) (XIII) v, 597b; vi, 48a, b
Kabīra (grave sin) s, **483b** (see also *s.v.* Kabāʾir)
Ḳābis (Gabès) i, 950a; iv, **335b**; vi, 134a, 141a, 452b; s, 11a, 334a
Ḳabīṣa b. Abī Ṣufra (VIII) vii, 359a
al-Ḳabīṣī, ʿAbd al-ʿAzīz Abu 'l-Ṣaḳr (X) iv, **340b**
al-Ḳābiṣī (Ibn-), Abu 'l-Ḥasan al-Maʿāfirī (1012) iv, **341a**; vi, 188b, 353b; s, 26b
Kābiya b. Ḥurḳūs (Māzin) vi, 954b
al-Ḳabḳ i, 18a, 270b, 380a; iv, 324b, **341b**; v, 287b, 288b, 495b; vii, 351a; s, 136a, 143a, 169a, 218b; s, **483b**
Ḳablān al-Ḳāḍī al-Tanūkhī ii, 443b
Ḳabludja → Ḳaplîdja
Kābora vi, 258b
Kabou iv, **351b**
Ḳabr iv, **352a**; v, 214b
Ḳabr Hūd i, 1045a; iii, 538a; s, 337b, 515a
Ḳabra iv, **355a**
Kabsh → Badw (IIa); Silāḥ; Yürük; Zakāt
al-Kabsh (Miṣr) i, 1325a; vii, 147b
Kabsha/Kubaysha s, 394a
Kabsha bt. Wāḳid b. ʿAmr iii, 812a
al-Ḳabtawrī, Abu 'l-Ḳāsim (1304) iv, **355b**
Ḳabṭūrnuh, Banū 'l- s, **501b**
Kabūd Djāma vi, 494a
Kabudhān s, 130b; x, 896b
Kābul i, 72a, 86a, 87b, 222a, b, 223a, 226b, 238a, b, 970a, 1347b; iii, 576a; iv, 175a, **356a**; v, 649a; vi, 86b, 122a, 342b, 419a; vii, 313b; xi, 198a; s, 41a, 63a, 66a, b, 122a, 237a, b, 270a, 285a
– university ii, 426a
Ḳabūl → Bayʿ
Ḳabūl Aḥmad ii, 1046a
Kābul-Shāhs iv, 208a, 356b
Ḳabūla al-Hindī iii, 104b
Kābulistān iv, **357b**
Ḳabūn vi, 547b
Kābūn b. Taṣūla (Sūs) (946) vi, 434b
Ḳābūs (Lakhmid) (574) v, 633b; vii, 568b
Ḳābūs b. Muṣʿab ii, 917b
Ḳābūs b. Saʿīd b. Taymūr (Āl Bū Saʿīd) (XX) vi, 735b; x, 814b; xi, 231a
Ḳābūs b. Wushm(a)gīr b. Ziyār (Ziyārid) (1012) i, 211b, 591a, 1110a, 1236a; ii, 748b, 1139b; iv, **357b**; v, 1028a; vi, 632a; vii, 987b; viii, 383a; s, 13a, 361b
Ḳābūs-nāma i, 794b; iv, 815a

Kabyle, language i, 1184a, b; iv, 361a
Kabyles i, 371a, 371b, 372a, 374a, 1177b; ii, 537b, 603; iii, 607a; iv, 360b-363a
Kabylia i, 171a, 365a, 369b, 433b; ii, 603; iv, 75b, **358b**; vi, 427a, 475a, 586b; x, 118bs, 190a
Kačawča s, 74a
Kačč̣h(ī) Gandāwa iv, **364a**, 534b; v, 689b; vi, 50b
Ḳaḍāʾ (divine decree) i, 89b, 90a, 413a, 413b; ii, 618a; iv, **364b**, 365a
Ḳaḍāʾ (religious duty) i, 169b
Ḳaḍā (region) i, 469a
al-Ḳaḍāʾ wa ʾl-Ḳadar iv, **365a**
Ḳadāḥ v, 989b
Ḳadam v, 95b
Ḳadam Rasūl Allāh → Ḳadam Sharīf
Ḳadam Sharīf ii, 258b; iv, **367b**; vi, 126a; s, 661b
Ḳadamgāh s, **501b**
Ḳāḍan, Ḳāḍī (Mahdawī) vii, 327b; ix, 637a
Ḳaʿdān al-Fāyiz, shaykh (XVIII) viii, 882b
Ḳadar i, 89b, 90a, 407a, 408b, 413a, 413b, 958b; ii, 365a, 374b, 618a; iii, 659a, 870b; iv, **365a**; v, 3b
Kadarbirt vi, 231a
al-Ḳaḍārif (Gedaref) iv, 686a, 687a; ix, 601b; s, 555b
Ḳadariyya i, 124a, 276b, 412b; iii, 248a, 494b, 990b, 1142b; iv, 366a, **368a**, 734b, 938a; v, 936a; vi, 279b; s, 358a
Ḳadāsa iv, **372a**
Ḳaddāḥids i, 48b; ii, 851b
Ḳaḍḍām, Muḥammad b. ʿUmar Bā (1544) vi, 132b
Ḳaddūr al-ʿAlamī (Meknès) (1741) iv, **372b**; vi, 249b, 253a, 255a, b
Ḳaddūr wuld Muḥammad al-Burdjī → Bū Ngāb
Ḳaddūra al-Djazāʾirī (1687) iv, **373a**
Ḳadhf i, 29b; iii, 20b; iv, **373a**; v, 730b; xi, 510a
al-Ḳadhdhāfī, Muʿammar v, 759a, 1067a; viii, 22b, 247a, 328a; ix, 689a
Ḳāḍī i, 491a, 741b; ii, 119a, 519b, 867a, 888a, 890b; iii, 487b, 492a, 1152b, 1153a; iv, 365a, **373b**, 941a; v, 631a, 1133a, b
Ḳāḍī b. Muḥammad b. Walmiya iv, 337a
Ḳāḍī Aḥmad viii, 787b
Ḳāḍī ʿAskar i, 480b, 712a; iii, 1152b; iv, **375b**, 735b; vi, 1a; ix, 209a
Ḳāḍī ʾl-djamāʿa iv, 374b
Ḳāḍī Djihān Ḳazwīnī (XVI) viii, 775b; x, 109b
al-Ḳāḍī ʾl-Fāḍil, Abū ʿAlī ʿAbd al-Raḥmān (1200) i, 150a, 594a, 801b; ii, 127a, 305b, 329b; iii, 679b, 863a, 901a; iv, **376a**, 613b, 614b; vi, 198a, 423b, 430a, 664a; vii, 164b; viii, 653b; s, 124a
Ḳāḍī al-Harawī → al-ʿAbbādī, Abu ʿĀsim
Ḳāḍī Ismāʿīl (860) vi, 279a
Ḳāḍī ʿIyāḍ → ʿIyāḍ b. Mūsā al-Sabtī
Ḳāḍī Khān, Fakhr al-Dīn (1196) iii, 163b; iv, **377**; vi, 558b
Ḳāḍi ʾl-Ḳuḍāt i, 164b; iv, 374a
Ḳāḍī Meḥmed → Lālezārī, Shaykh Meḥmed
Ḳāḍī Muḥammad (1947) ii, 88b; iii, 157a; iv, **377a**; v, 466a, b, 1213a, b
Ḳāḍī Nuʿmān → Nuʿmān
Ḳāḍī Nūr Allāh → Nūr Allāh al-Sayyid
Ḳāḍī al-Rashīd b. al-Zubayr s, 251b
Ḳāḍī al-Saʿīd → Ibn Sanāʾ al-Mulk
al-Ḳāḍī Ṣāʿid → Ṣāʿid al-Andalūsī
Ḳāḍī al-Tahartī → Ibn al-Rabīb
Ḳaḍīb i, 482a; iv, **377b**, 940a; viii, 852b; ix, 10b
Ḳadīm v, 96a, b
Ḳādimīs ii, 366b; v, 1115a; s, 466b
Ḳadi̊n → Marʾa; Sarāy
al-Ḳādir → al-Asmāʾ al-ḥusnā
al-Ḳādir b. Dhi ʾl-Nūn (XI) ii, 243a; v, 392a; vii, 288b, 633b; x, 605b, 606a (see also *s.v.* Yaḥyā al-Ḳādir)
al-Ḳādir bi-ʾllāh (ʿAbbāsid) (1031) i, 1352b, 1353a, 1355a; iii, 159a, 255b, 256a, 735a, 860a; iv, **378a**, 940b, 942a; vi, 65a, 206a, 522a, b; vii, 312b; s, 14b, 118a, b, 119a, 253b, 361b
al-Ḳāḍir Khān → Ikhtiyār al-Dīn Abu ʾl-Mudjāhid Ḳādir Khān
al-Ḳādir Khān, Yūsuf (Ilek-khān) (1034) → Yūsuf Ḳādi̊r Khān
Ḳādir Shāh (Mallū Khān) (Mālwā) (XVI) iii, 421b, 422b, 426a; iv, 276b; vi, 310a, 407a; ix, 448a
Ḳāḍir Walī → Shāh al-Ḥamīd ʿAbd al-Ḳādir
Ḳadirgha Limani̊ ii, 985a; vi, 588a
Ḳādirī, ʿAbd al-Madjīd s, 74a
al-Ḳādirī, ʿAbd al-Salām → al-Ḳādirī al-Ḥasanī, Abū Muḥammad

al-Ḳādirī, Abū ʿAbd Allāh (1773) iv, **379a**; s, 404b
Ḳādirī Čelebī iv, 333b; vii, 225a
al-Ḳādirī al-Ḥasanī, Abu 'l-ʿAbbās (1721) iv, **379b**
al-Ḳādirī al-Ḥasanī, Abū ʿAbd Allāh (1695) iv, **380a**
al-Ḳādirī al-Ḥasanī, Abu 'l-Faḍāʾil → al-Ḳādirī al-Ḥasanī, Abu 'l-ʿAbbās
al-Ḳādirī al-Ḥasanī, Abū Muḥammad (1698) iv, **380a**, 382a, 1085a; vi, 350a
Ḳādiriyya i, 69a, 257b, 281a, 303a, 371a, 782a, 1009a, 1173a, 1260b; ii, 10a, 58b, 63b, 94b, 134b, 164a, 535b, 710a, 975a, 1003b, 1004a; iii, 103b, 160b, 176a, 646b; iv, **380b**, 549b, 951a; v, 287b, 393b, 475a; vi, 203b, 259b, 260a, 354b, 356b, 643b, 705a; vii, 246a, 620a; viii, 18b; x, 247b; s, 5a, 182b, 282b, 283a, 293a, 303a, 322a
Ḳādiriyya Bakkāya ii, 1132a
Ḳādis iv, **383a**
al-Ḳādisiyya (al-Kūfa) (635) ii, 893b; iii, 194b, 1254b; iv, 384b, **385b**, 775a; v, 634a; vi, 266b; viii, 112b
al-Ḳādisiyya (Sāmarrāʾ) iv, **384a**; vii, 795a; ix, 882a
Kadiwala sayyids v, 26b
Ḳādiyānī → Aḥmadiyya
Ḳāḍī-zāde Aḥmed Shams al-Dīn v, 27b
Ḳāḍī-zāde ʿAlī i, 1284b
Ḳāḍī-zāde ʿAlī Pasha vii, 601a
Ḳāḍī-zāde Meḥmed Beg (XVI) i, 293b
Ḳāḍī-zāde Meḥmed Efendi (1635) vii, 598a; x, 755a
Ḳāḍī-zāde Rūmī (1432) iv, 702b; viii, 1036a; s, **502a**
Ḳāḍī-zāde-i Rūmī (1436) i, 393a, 869a; iv, 702b; vi, 601b; viii, 542a
Ḳādjārs i, 13b, 36a, 190b, 246b, 296a, 720b, 1250b; ii, 150a, b, 151a, 309a, 334b, 433b, 654b, 656a; iii, 554a, 1100a, 1101b, 1103b; iv, 38a, 51a, 294a, **387b**, 577b, 1052b; v, 371b, 461b, 630a; vi, 13b, 18b, 202b, 276b, 366a, 483b, 521b, 523a, b, 526a, 528a, b, 529a, b, 548b, 551b, 552b, 554b, 856b; vii, 440b, 678a; x, 47b; s, 70b, 71a, 104a, 257a, b, 260b, 302a, 336a, 405b
Ḳādjār, Banū iii, 1100a, 1101b, 1103b; iv, **387a**
al-Kadjgharī → ʿAbd al-Ghāfir
Kadkhudā i, 978a; iv, 103b, **893b**; ix, 645b, 732a (see also *s.v.* Ketkhudā)
Ḳadm-i Rasūl → Ḳadam Sharīf
Ḳadmūs iv, 200a; vi, 578a, b, 582a, 789b; viii, 147a
Ḳadr → Ḳaḍā; Ramaḍān
Ḳadr Khān → Ḳādir Khān
Ḳadrī (XVII) iii, 114a; iv, **399a**
Ḳadrī Bey ii, 657b; iv, 853a
Ḳadrī Shīrāzī iv, 399a
Ḳāf (Mts) i, 926b; iii, 332a; iv, 342a, **400b**; ix, 101b
al-Kāf (El-Kef) iii, 167a; iv, **402b**; ix, 902a
Kāf (k) iv, **399a**
Ḳāf (ḳ) iv, **400a**
Kafa → Kefe
Kafāʾa iv, **404a**, 1161b; viii, 871b
al-Kafādjī i, 1056b
Kafāla ii, 105a; iii, 1179a; iv, **404b**
Kafan xi, 150a; s, **502b**
Kafar Ṭāb vi, 378b, 381a; vii, 577b, 578a, 817a
Kafarbayya vi, 774b, 775a, b
Ḳafes ii, 338b; s, **503a**
al-Kaff s, **505a**
al-Kaff (ʿIlm-) iv, **405b**
Kaff → ʿArūḍ; Ḳuʿūd
Kaffa → Kefe
al-Ḳaffāl al-Shāshī (947) ix, 187b; x, 349a
Kaffāra iv, **406b**, 688a, 768a
Kāfī → Ḥasan Kāfī
al-Kāfī Zaʿīm al-Ruʾasāʾ ii, 384b
Kafīl → Kafāla
Ḳāfila → Karwān; Tidjāra
Ḳāfilat al-Sūdān ii, 137b
Kāfir i, 224b, 225a; iv, **407b**, 410b; v, 649a
Kāfir (language) ii, 138a, b; iv, 409b
Kāfiristān i, 223b; ii, 140a; iv, **409a**; vi, 66a; s, 237a, b
Kāfirkūb(āt) iv, 44b, **411a**
Kāfirnihān i, 455a; ii, 2a
Ḳāfiya ii, 834b; iv, **411b**; v, 320b
al-Kāfiyadjī (1447) iv, **414b**; vii, 491a
Kāfiyya v, 740a
Ḳafīz → Makāyīl
Kafr ʿAwaḍ Allāh Ḥidjāzī s, 262b
Kafr al-Ḥiṣāfa s, 371a
Kafr Mandūr vi, 408a
Ḳafsa (Gafsa) i, 161b, 165a; iv, **414b**, 739b; v, 1181b; vi, 355b
Ḳafṭān v, 737b, 739b, 752a; x, 88a

Kaftar s, 127a
Kāfūr (camphor) iv, **417b**
Kāfūr, Abu 'l-Misk (Ikhshīdid) (968) i, 34a, 1042a; ii, 793b, 1080b; iii, 768b, 840b; iv, **418a**, 673b, 1091b; v, 327a, b, 619a; vi, 545a; vii, 147b, 161b, 411b, 488a, 770b
Kāfūr, Malik, Hazār-Dīnārī (1316) i, 444b; ii, 12b, 179b, 269a, 272a, 1084b, 1085a, 1124a; iv, **419a**, 921b, 922a, 923b, 1023a; v, 938a, 1258b; vi, 270b; vii, 289a, 457b; s, 105a
Ḳāf-zāde Fāʾiḍī (XVII) i, 1165b; viii, 6b
Kāf-zāde Fayḍ Allāh Efendi (1611) viii, 6b
Kāghad (Kāghid) ii, 311a; iv, **419b**, 742a, 1114b; v, 854b; viii, 149b; xi, 150a
Kaghalgha → Ḳalghay
Kāghān iii, 335b; xi, 244a
Ḳaghan → Khāḳān
Kāghitkhāne i, 1279a; vi, 55b, 57a
Kahar Muzakkar (XX) vi, 117a; ix, 814b
al-Kahf → Aṣḥāb al-Kahf
Kahf al-Dawla wa 'l-Islām → Maḥmūd b. Sebüktigin
al-Ḳaḥḥāl → ʿAlī b. ʿĪsā al-Kaḥḥāl
Kāhī (1580) s, **505a**
Kāhin i, 585b, 659b; iv, **420b**; v, 235a, 420a, 422a, 1101a; vii, 564b; viii, 728b, 732b, 733a
al-Kāhina i, 367a, 770b, 1175a; iii, 271a, b, 296a, 1039b; iv, **422a**; vi, 751a, 753b; x, 20a
al-Ḳāhir bi-'llāh (ʿAbbāsid) (950) i, 19a, 1039b; ii, 1080b; iii, 46a, 126b, 345a, 886b; iv, **423b**, 940a; vi, 206a, 539a; vii, 414a, 541b, 575b
Ḳāhir b. ʿAlī b. Ḳānit v, 926a
al-Ḳāhir al-Falak (Miṣr) vii, 148b
al-Ḳāhira i, 9a, 396b, 451b, 551b, 832a, 976a; ii, 128a, 495a, 854a, 958b; iii, 81a, 756b, 813a; iv, 215b, **424a**; v, 993a; vi, 44b, 45a, 122b, 123a, 186a, 445a, 649b, 656b, 657a; ix, 791b
– cemeteries iv, 425a
– fortifications iv, 428b, 429b, 430b, 436a; v, 92a
– madrasas iv, 430a, 432a, 437a; v, 1125b, 1127b, 1140b, 1141a
– modern city iv, 441b-444b
– monuments i, 620a, 621a-624, 813-821, 863a, b; iii, 81a, 190a; iv, 424a-428b, 438a, b, 439a, 440a
– mosques i, 620a, 814b; iv, 428b, 430a, 431a, 436b, 437b, 444b; v, 93a, 500b
– population iv, 443a, b
– tombs iv, 425a-428b, 429b, 430b, 434a
– university i, 818a; ii, 132a, 424a; iv, 441b, 444a
Kāhiya iv, 894b
Kahka → Ḳahḳaha
Ḳahḳaha i, 99b; iv, 188a; viii, 1012b
al-Kaḥlaba Hubayra b. ʿAbd Hanāf ix, 864a
Kahlān b. Sabaʾ i, 544b; ii, 573b
Kahlān b. Abī Lawā (Maṭmāṭī) (XI) vi, 842a
Kahlān, Banū i, 436a; ii, 516b; iv, 448a
Kahlās, Banū vi, 50b
Kāhrabāʾ → Kahrubā
Kahramanmaraş vi, 509a, b; x, 571b
Ḳahramān Mīrzā (1842) iv, 393a; vii, 453a, 454a, b
Ḳahramān-nāma i, 152b; iv, **444b**
Kahrubā iv, **445b**; vi, 556b
Ḳahrūn b. Ghannūsh v, 59b
Ḳaḥṭaba b. Shabīb al-Ṭāʾī (749) i, 16a, 16b, 108b, 141a, 1033b; iii, 988b; iv, 99b, **445b**; vi, 332b, 333a, b, 345a; vii, 360a
Ḳaḥṭān i, 544b, 545b, 873b; ii, 176a; iii, 363b, 1065b; iv, **447b**; vi, 75a, 371b; s, 338a, 506a
Ḳaḥṭānī (leader) viii, 657b
al-Ḳaḥṭānī (Maḳdishū) vi, 128b, 472b
al-Ḳaḥṭānī, Muḥammad b. ʿAbd Allāh (Mecca) (1979) vi, 157b, 158b
Ḳaḥṭānī tribes vii, 838b; viii, 466a, 882b; s, 817b, 818a
Ḳaḥṭānite/Qahtanite s, **505b**
Ḳahwa i, 540a, 1140b; ii, 1063a; iii, 179a; iv, **449a**, 741b; v, 109b; x, 754b
Kaḥyā → Ketkhudā
Kaḥyā (Djenāze) Ḥasan Pasha (1810) iv, **455b**
Ḳāʾid i, 977a; ii, 507b; iv, **456a**; v, 1198b
al-Ḳāʾid b. Ḥammād (Ḥammādid) (1054) iii, 137a; v, 623b, 1177b; vii, 482b

al-Ḳāʿida (al-Qaeda) s, 786b, 787a
Ḳaïdes iv, 384b
Ḳāʾif → Ḳiyāfa
al-Ḳāʾim, Ḳiyām al-Dīn (1793) ix, 214a
al-Ḳāʾim bi-Amr Allāh (ʿAbbāsid) (1075) i, 132b, 420a, 461b, 1073b, 1074b, 1075a; ii, 384a; iii, 86b, 159b, 196a, 345b, 860b, 891a; iv, 26b, **457a**, 942a, b; v, 388b; vi, 243b, 272b, 275a, 674a; viii, 70a,b; s, 192a, b, 194a
al-Ḳāʾim bi-Amr Allāh (ʿAbbāsid) (1455) iii, 1198b
al-Ḳāʾim bi-Amr Allāh (Fāṭimid) (946) i, 699b, 1355b; ii, 491a, 851a, 853a; iv, **458b**; v, 1243b, 1246b; vi, 434b, 727b; vii, 642a; s, 62b, 236b
al-Ḳāʾim bi-Amr Allāh Āl Muḥammad (Mahdī) iv, 203b, 204a, **456b**; v, 1235b
al-Ḳāʾim bi-Amr Allāh Khān iii, 60a
Ḳāʾim-maḳām ii, 444a; iv, **461b**; vii, 906a
Ḳāʾimī, Ḥasan Baba (1691) s, **506b**
Ḳāʾim-maḳām-i Farāhānī, Abu ʾl-Ḳāsim (1835) iv, 70b, 394a, **462a**; s, 73a
Ḳāʾim-maḳām-i Farāhānī, ʿĪsā (1822) iv, **462a**; v, 919a
Ḳāïmāz i, 1160b
Ḳāʾime i, 693a; ii, 935b; iv, **460a**; x, 203a
Ḳāʾin (Qayen) v, 354b, 355a, b; s, **507b**; xi, 1233a, b
Kairowan → Ḳayrawān
Kaisos → Ḳays b. Salama
Ḳāʾit Bāy, al-Malik al-Ashraf ʿAbd al-Naṣr (Mamlūk) (1496) i, 281a, 349a, 553a, 815a, 1060a, 1119b, 1190b, 1234a, 1281a, 1317b; ii, 166b, 286a, 529b, 530a; iii, 48b, 186b, 346a; iv, 133a, 429a, 432a, **462b**, 563a, 642b, 960a; v, 304a, 1143b; vi, 150a, 315a, 323b, 324a, b, 359b, 367b, 580a, 709a; vii, 61b, 173b, 175b, 295a, 727a; s, 208a, b
Ḳāʾit Bāy b. Muḥammad i, 1032b
al-Ḳaʿḳāʿ iv, **463b**
Ḳaʿḳāʿ b. ʿAbd Allāh b. Abī Ḥadrad iv, 463b
al-Ḳaʿḳāʿ b. ʿAmr (VII) iv, **464a**
Ḳaʿḳāʿ b. ʿAṭiyya al-Bāhilī iv, 463b
Ḳaʿḳāʿ b. Ḍirār al-Tamīmī iv, 463b
Ḳaʿḳāʿ b. Ḥakīm al-Azdī iv, 463b
Ḳaʿḳāʿ b. Khulayd al-ʿAbsī iv, 463b
al-Ḳaʿḳāʿ b. Maʿbad al-Tamīmī iv, 463b
Ḳaʿḳāʿ b. Nafr → al-Ṭirimmāḥ b. ʿAdī b. ʿAbd Allāh al-Djubayr
Ḳaʿḳāʿ b. Shawr b. ʿIḳāl al-Dhuhlī iv, 463b
Kākāʾī, Banū i, 262b; ii, 101a; ix, 153a
Kākaṛ, Banū xi, 494b; s, **507b**
Kʾakh ii, 22a
Kakheti v, 486b, 493a; s, 484b
Kakhtā (Kʸākhta) iv, **464a**; vi, 507a
Kākī (Mānd) vi, 384b
Kākī (Masraḥ) vi, 754a
Kākī, Āl vi, 115b
Kākī, Ḳutb al-Dīn Bakhtiyār (1235) xi, 118b
Kāḳshāls iii, 423b
Kākudam (desert) vii, 584a, 612b
Ḳāḳūn ii, 911a; iv, 842b; x, 616a
Kākūyids/Kākwayhids i, 1356a; iv, **465a**; v, 824a; vi, 66a; x, 553a
Kalā (island) → Kalah
Ḳalʿa → Agadir; Burdj; Ḥiṣār; Ḥiṣn; Ḳaṣaba
Ḳalʿa i, 904a, b
al-Ḳalʿa (castle) iv, **467a**
al-Ḳalʿa (Ḥammād) → Ḳalʿat Banī Ḥammād
al-Ḳalʿa al-Bayḍāʾ → Ḳalʿe-i Sefīd
al-Ḳalʿa Kuhrūd v, 661a, 662a; vi, 511b
Kalā-rustāḳ vi, 511b
al-Kalābādhī (990) ii, 891b; iii, 84a, 102b, 986a, 1060a; iv, **467a**, 616b, 696b, 697a
Kalaband (Ottoman) → Nafy
Ḳalafat ii, 61b
Kalah (Kalāh) ii, 105a; iv, **467b**, 502a, b; vi, 234a, 1020b; vii, 71b; xi, 367a
Kalāh-bār i, 930a; iv, 468a
Ḳalaʿī (tin) → Ḳalʿī
al-Kalāʿī → Khālid b. Maʿdān
al-Kalāʿī, Abu ʾl-Rabīʿ b. Sālim (1237) i, 1019b; iii, 804a; iv, **468a**; vii, 388a; viii, 819b
al-Kalāʿī, Ibn al-Ghafūr vii, 261a
al-Kalāʿī, Muḥammad b. Ibrāhīm b. al-Maḥābī vi, 830b
Ḳalʿa-i Dukhtār iv, 288a; v, 657b
Ḳalʿa-i Iṣṭakhr iv, 221b, 222a
Ḳalʿa-i Sefīd → Ḳalʿe-i Sefīd
Ḳalʿa-i Sulṭāniyya → Ḳalʿe-i Sulṭaniyye
Ḳalʿa-yi Dabūs s, 176b
Ḳalāla i, 1221b; iv, 777a; vi, 435a

Kalām i, 60b, 113a, 266a, 333a, 342b, 409b, 410a, 414a, 415b, 694b; ii, 95b, 449a, 608a, 618a, 824b; iii, 103b, 171b; iv, 46a, **468b**, 508b, 985a; v, 238a,b
Ḳalam (pen) iv, **471a**, 472a
Ḳalam (secretariat) iv, **471b**
Kalām (theology) → ʿIlm al-Kalām
Ḳalam al-Ṣāliḥiyya iv, 822b
Ḳalama i, 1231a; iii, 176b
Kalaman i, 98a
Ḳalamdan → Ḳalam; Kitāba
Ḳalamdār iv, 471b; v, 988b
Ḳalamkārī iv, **471b**
al-Ḳalammas iv, **472a**
Ḳalamūn vi, 544b; viii, 446a, b
Kalan (town) iv, 467b; x, 628a
Ḳalān (Mongol tax) iv, 31a, 1050a, b
Kalān, Mīrzā i, 853a
Ḳalandar iv, 58b, **472b**, 473a; vi, 225b, 228b; ix, 298a; s, 352b
Ḳalandar Bakhsh → Djurʾat
Ḳalandariyya i, 104b; ii, 165a, 395a; iv, **473a**; vi, 224a, 228b; viii, 3a; x, 250b
Ḳalandariyyāt → Ḳalandar
al-Ḳalānisī, Aḥmad b. ʿAbd al-Raḥmān s, 392a
al-Ḳalānisī, Badr al-Dīn Muḥammad i, 344b
Ḳalānisiyya (Damascus) vi, 193b; s, 197a
Ḳalansuwa iv, 940a; v, 734b, 735a; s, **508a**
Kalāntar iv, 103b, 472b; **474a**, 705b; v, 155b; s, 275b, 405b
Kalāntar, Mīrzā Muḥammad s, 405b
Kalār ii, 190b; s, 335a
Kalārud vi, 745b
Kalasʾa s, 242a
Kalaṣa ii, 31a, 138b
al-Ḳalaṣādī, Abu ʾl-Ḥasan ʿAlī (1486) iv, **476b**, 725b; ix, 20a
Kalāt, Kilāt, Kelāt → Balūčistān
Ḳalāt (Kalʿat) Abī Sufyān i, 145b a
Ḳalʿat Abī Ṭawīl → Ḳalʿat Banī Ḥammād
Ḳalʿat ʿAdjādj vi, 357b
Ḳalʿat Aḳdja vi, 231a
Ḳalʿat al-Akrād vi, 231a
Ḳalʿat Ayyūb (Calatayud) iv, **477b**
Ḳalʿat al-Azraḳ i, 780b
Ḳalʿat Banī ʿAbbās iv, **478a**
Ḳalʿat Banī Ḥammād i, 367a, 1319b, ii, 863b; iii, 137a; iv, **478b**, 1166a; ix, 18a
Ḳalʿat Bayḍāʾ vi, 378a
Ḳalʿat Dawsar, Ḳalʿat Djaʿbar → Djaʿbar, Ḳalʿat
Ḳalʿat al-Djisr vii, 578a
Ḳalʿat Ḥammād → Ḳalʿat Banī Ḥammād
Ḳalʿat Huwwāra iv, **481b**
Ḳalʿat Khayrān vi, 576a
Ḳalʿat al-Muḍīḳ i, 215a; vi, 789a
Ḳalʿat al-Muhaylba → Balāṭunus
Ḳalʿat al-Nadjm iv, **482a**; vi, 378a, 379a, 381a, 429a, 733a, b
Ḳalʿat Namrūd → al-Subayra
Ḳalʿat Nawḥamām vi, 231a
Ḳalʿat al-Rabaḍ (ʿAdjlūn) vi, 547b
Ḳalʿat Rabāh (Calatrava) iii, 1055a, b; iv, **482b**
Ḳalʿat al-Rūm → Rūm Ḳalʿesī
Ḳalʿat al-Shaḳīf iv, **482b**
Ḳalʿat Sharḳāt → Athūr
Kalʿat Yaḥmūr vi, 579a, 789b
Ḳalaṭa → Ghalaṭa
Ḳalʿat-i Nādirī iv, 38a; v, 59a, **102b**
Ḳalāʾun → Ḳalāwūn
Ḳalāwdhiya iv, **484a**
Ḳalawriya → Ḳillawriya
Ḳalāwūn, al-Malik al-Manṣūr (Mamlūk) (1290) i, 200b, 944b, 971a, 1016b, 1102b, 1127b, 1138a, 1224a, 1324b; ii, 38a, 285a, 305b, 353b; iii, 99a, 186b, 189a, 399b, 402b, 403a, 474b, 679b, 775b, 832b; iv, 464b, **484a**; v, 591a, 628a, 1140b; vi, 45a, 195a, 315b, 322b, 326b, 381b, 545b, 577b, 579b, 580a, 581b, 673b, 719a, 777b; viii, 90b, 147a; s, 205b, 389a
Kalaybar s, 116a
Ḳalʿa-yi Bākhta vi, 502a
Ḳalʿa-yi Shahriyār vi, 384b
Ḳalʿa-yi Zohāk vi, 501a
Ḳalaylîḳoz Aḥmed Pasha (1704) iv, 969a; vi, 991a; vii, 917b
Ḳalb (heart) iv, **486a**
Kalb (dog) i, 1031b; ii, 223a; iv, **489b**
Kalb, Banū i, 550a, 920a, 986b; ii, 90a, 553a; iii, 619a, 838a; iv, 370b, 492b, 496a, 820a; v, 105b, 1232a; vi, 221b, 333b, 379a, 435b, 544b, 545a, 546b, 622a, 623b, 624a, 717b; vii, 267b; s, 178a
Kalb ʿAlī Khān ii, 84a; v, 959a
Kalb b. Wabara iv, **492b**, 496a, 834a
Kalbāsī, Ḥādjdj Muḥammad Ibrāhīm s, 76a, 135a
Kalb-i ʿAlī Khān (Afshār) i, 240b

al-Kalbī, ʿAbbās b. Hishām (1609) iv, **496a**
al-Kalbī, Aḥmad b. Ḥasan (969) iv, 496b; ix, 585a
al-Kalbī, Aḥmad b. Yūsuf al-Akḥal (1030) iii, 788a; iv, 497a
al-Kalbī, ʿAlī b. al-Ḥasan iv, 496b; ix, 585a
al-Kalbī, ʿAlī b. Abi ʾl-Ḥusayn (938) iv, 496b
al-Kalbī, Ḥasan b. ʿAlī ix, 585a
al-Kalbī , Hishām b. Muḥammad (819) i, 210a, 758b; iii, 608a, 1047b; iv, 91b, **495a**; v, 350b; vi, 215b, 828b; vii, 402a, 967b; viii, 149b, 546a; s, 31b, 177a
al-Kalbī, Khālid b. Arṭāṭ viii, 82b
al-Kalbī, Muḥammad b. al-Sāʾib (763) iv, **495a**; viii, 983b; s, 90b
al-Kalbī, al-Sāʾib b. Bishr iv, 494b
al-Kalbī, Sulaymān b. Yaḳẓān s, 82a
Kalbids (Syria) ii, 484a; iii, 619a; iv, 370b
Kalbids (Sicily) i, 920a, 986b; ii, 553a; iv, **496a**; v, 105b; vii, 486b; ix, 585a
Ḳalʿe → Ḳalʿa
Ḳalʿe-i Isfīd → Ḳalʿe-i Sefīd
Ḳalʿe-i Sefīd iv, **497b**
Ḳalʿe-i Sulṭāniyye ii, 11b
Kalembaina vii, 435b
Ḳalender Shāh → Ḳalandar Oghlhi̊ Meḥmed
Ḳalenderi → Ḳalandarīyya
Ḳalender-oghli̊ Meḥmed Pasha (1609) i, 267b, 510b, 826b, 1162b, 1334b; iii, 91b; iv, **499a**; viii, 197a; s, 239a
Ḳalghay ii, 1113b; iv, **499b**; vi, 734b, 735a, 989a
Ḳalhāt iii, 653a; iv, **500b**; vi, 734b, 735a
al-Ḳalhātī iii, 235b
Kalhōṙā i, 229b, 230b; ii, 185a, b, 186a; iii, 323b; iv, 364b; ix, 440a, 634b
Kalhūr v, 168b, 460b, 617a; 659a
Kali → Ḳāḍī
Ḳalʿī (Ḳalaʿī) (tin) iv, 467b, **502a**; v, 964b, 967b
Ḳālī → Erzurūm
Ḳālī (carpet) → Bisāṭ
Ḳālī (pasture) vi, 493b
al-Ḳālī, Abū ʿAlī al-Baghdādī (967) i, 156a, 590a, 600a; iii, 845a; iv, **501a**; vi, 344b, 430b, 713a, 822b, 916b; vii, 404a, 569b; viii, 14b
Kāl-i Shūr iv, 107a; s, 235a
Ḳalīb i, 538b, 1230a
Kalīdar s, 83b
Kālif i, 455a; iv, **502b**; s, 281a
Kalikat iv, 547a, 642b; v, 360b; vi, 459a; s, **508b**
Ḳālīḳalā → Erzurūm
Kalikātā → Calcutta
Ḳāliḳūt vii, 71b (see also *s.v.* Kalikat)
Kalīla wa-Dimna i, 2b, 326b, 524b, 756a; ii, 758a, 951b; iii, 309a, 313b, 372b, 377a, 863a, 883b; iv, **503a**, 704a; s, 85b
Ḳalīm, Abū Ṭālib (1651) iv, **506b**; vi, 271b; vii, 341a; viii, 991b
Kalīm Allāh → Mūsā
Kalīm Allāh b. Maḥmūd Shihāb al-Dīn (Bahmānīd) (1538) i, 923b, 1047a, 1200a; vi, 63b
Kalīm Allāh Djahānābādī (1729) ii, 55a; iv, **507a**
Kalima i, 450a; iv, 83a, **508a**
Kalimantan i, 1258b; iii, 1213a, b, 1215b, 1225b; vi, 43a, b, 116b, 239a; s, 150a, b, **509b** (see also *s.v.* Borneo)
Kalīmī → Yahūd
Kālindjār v, 546a; vi, 48a, 65b, 916a; ix, 448a
Kalinin → Porsi̊
Káliz → Khalisioi
Ḳalḳaliyyūn s, 302b
al-Ḳalḳashandī (nisba) iv, 511a
al-Ḳalkashandī, Shihāb al-Dīn Aḥmad (1418) i, 119a, 239b, 430a, 595a, 761b; ii, 301b, 305b, 328a, 487a; iii, 344b, 487a, 1242b; iv, **509a**, 742b, 1119a; v, 627a; vi, 108b, 112a, 118b, 185b, 198a, 352a, 381b, 906b; vii, 257b; viii, 537a; s, 1a, 203b
Kalkhur iii, 1102b, 1109a
al-Kallāʾ i, 1086a; vii, 67b
Ḳallabāt i, 49b; ii, 768a; iv, 686a, 687a; v, 1250a; vi, 643b; x, 143a
Ḳallala iv, **511a**
Ḳalmuk i, 121a, 135a, 422a, 722a, 1002b, 1028a; ii, 21b, 25a, 39a, 47a; iii, 117a, 1120b; iv, 213b, **512a**, 584a; v, 134b; vi, 371a, 416b, 418a; x, 677a; s, 169a, 281a, 419b
Ḳalpaḳ ii, 1113b; v, 751b
Kalpī iii, 443b, 638b; iv, **513a**; vi, 53b, 61b, 62a; vii, 278b, 279a; ix, 785b; s, 206b
al-Ḳalshanī i, 863a
Ḳalūdiya → Ḳalawdhiya
Ḳālūn (835) vii, 878a; xi, 152b

Ḳalūniya iv, 578b
al-Ḳalūṣ (Zandjī) (IX) vii, 526b
Ḳālūs̲h̲ s, 269a
Kalwād̲h̲ā iv, **513a**; v, 566b; vi, 656b
al-Kalwad̲h̲ānī, Abu 'l-K̲h̲aṭṭāb (1117) iii, 160a, 735a, 766b; iv, **513b**; x, 114a; s, 193a
al-Kalwad̲h̲ānī, ʿUbayd Allāh b. Muḥammad xi, 33b
Ḳalyān, Ḳalyūn → Baḥriyya; Safīna
Kalyāni i, 768a, 1047a, 1323b; iii, 426a, 626a, 1160a, 1161a; iv, **513b**
Kalyar ii, 54b; s, 313a
Ḳalyūb iv, **514a**; vi, 119a; s, 371a
al-Ḳalyūbī, S̲h̲ihāb al-Dīn (1596) iv, **515a**; ix, 483a; s, 726b
al-Ḳalyūbī, ʿAlī b. Muḥammad iv, 643a
al-Ḳalyūbiyya ix, 357a; s, 121b
Kām Bak̲h̲s̲h̲ i, 913b, 1202b
Ḳamaʿa b. K̲h̲indif v, 76b, 77a
Kamadjas i, 1258a
Ḳamaḥ → Kemāk̲h̲
Kamāl → Kemāl
Kamāl, S̲h̲ayk̲h̲ s, 361a
Kamāl al-Dawla S̲h̲īrzād (G̲h̲aznawid) (1115) vi, 783a
Kamāl al-Dīn b. Ḳawām al-Dīn (Marʿas̲h̲ī) (1358) vi, 511a, b, 512a, b, 513b
Kamāl b. Arslan K̲h̲ān Maḥmūd (Ḳarā-K̲h̲ānid) s, 245b
Kamāl b. Mir-i Buzūrg (Marʿas̲h̲ī) vi, 516a
Kamāl b. Muḥammad (Marʿas̲h̲ī) vi, 513b
Kamāl b. S̲h̲ams al-Dīn, Mīr (Marʿas̲h̲ī) (1502) vi, 514b
Kamāl b. Yūnus (XIII) vi, 638a
Kamāl Abu 'l-Faḍl Muḥammad al-S̲h̲ahrazūrī (1160) vi, 870b
Kamāl Abu 'l-Maʿālī Muḥammad b. al-Amīr Nāṣir al-Dīn Muḥammad (XV) vii, 295a
Kamāl Aḥmad b. Ṣadr al-Dīn i, 766b
Kamāl al-Dīn Gurg ii, 405b, 1124a; s, 685a
Kamāl al-Dīn Ismāʿīl (Ismāʿīl-i Iṣfahānī) (1237) iv, 62a, **515b**; vi, 609a; s, 235b, 239b
Kamāl al-Fārisī (XIV) iii, 1137a, 1139a; iv, **515b**, 804b; v, 397b, 547a; vi, 183b, 377a
Kamāl Ḥusayn Beg i, 1191b
Kamāl Ibn al-ʿAdīm → Ibn al-ʿAdīm
Kamāl Ḳazwīnī ii, 54a
Kamāl Marʿas̲h̲ī, Sayyid v, 663a
Kamāl Muḥammad, vizier (1150) vi, 782a
Kamāl S̲h̲īr ʿAlī → Bannāʾī, Kamāl al-Dīn
Kamāl al-Dunyā wa 'l-Dīn al-Ḥasan b. Masʿūd (Maṣyād) (XIII) vi, 790b
Kamāl Ismāʿīl-i Iṣfahānī → Kamāl al-Dīn Ismāʿīl
Kamāl K̲h̲ān Rustamī (1649) ii, 973b; vi, 837a
Kamāl K̲h̲udjandī (1400) i, 1301a; iv, **516b**; viii, 510a
Kamāl al-Mulk b. ʿAbd al-Raḥīm iii, 1201a
Kamāl al-Mulk al-Simīrumī (1118) vi, 64a; vii, 679b; 754a, b
Kamāl al-Mulk Pas̲h̲a-zāde → Kemāl Pas̲h̲a-zāde
Kamāl al-Wizāra → Aḥmad Maḥmūdī
Kamālī (1611) viii, 776a
al-Kamāliyya (Ṭarīḳa) iv, 991; ix, 155b
Kamāliyya bt. Abī Bakr iii, 760a, b
Kaman i, 606b
Kamanča → Malāhī
Ḳamāniča iv, **516b**; v, 260b; ix, 135a
al-Ḳamar iv, **517a**
Ḳamar (singer) iv, 822a
Ḳamar, Banū (Mahra) vi, 82b
Ḳamar al-Dīn Čīn Ḳilič K̲h̲ān → Āṣaf Djāh I, Niẓām al-Mulk
Ḳamar al-Dīn Dūg̲h̲lāt ii, 622a; x, 561a, 590b; xi, 336a
Ḳamar al-Dīn K̲h̲ān i, 295b; iii, 59b, 1158a
Ḳamarān i, 535b, 539a; iv, **519a**; vii, 514; ix, 135b
Ḳambar Dīwāna iii, 482b
Kambayāt/Kanbāya vi, 271a
Kamenetz Podolski → Ḳamāniča
Kāmfīrūz i, 1128b; iv, 705b; vi, 493b
Kāmgār iv, 1018b
Ḳamḥ ii, 904a, 1062b; iv, **519b**
Kamieniec → Ḳamāniča
Kāmil → ʿArūḍ
Kāmil → Shaʿbān I
Kāmil, al-Malik al-, b. al-ʿĀdil (Ayyūbid) (1238) → al-Malik al-Kāmil I b. al-ʿĀdil
Kāmil, al-Malik al-, b. al-Muẓaffar (Ayyūbid) (1260) → al-Malik al-Kāmil II
Kāmil, Muṣṭafā → Muṣṭafā Kāmil
Kāmil ʿAyyād (XX) vi, 538b
Kāmil Dāg̲h̲istān (XX) vi, 538b

Kāmil Ḥusayn iii, 1207b; iv, 85b
Kāmil al-Ḥusaynī s, 67a, b, 68a
Kāmil Nuʿmanaw Yās͟hin (XX) vi, 768b
Kāmil Pas͟ha (1912) i, 286a; ii, 643b, 698b; iii, 520a, 595a, 605b, 624a; iv, 284a; vi, 983b
Kāmiliyya (Cairo) iii, 932b; vi, 320a; s, 197a
Kāmiliyya (S͟hiʿī sect) i, 1080b; viii, 818b; s, **510a**
Kamīn iii, 202b
Ḳamīs i, 1016b; v, 733b, 748b, 749b; s, 323a
Kamk͟h → Kemāk͟h
Ḳaml iv, **521b**
Kamlān, Banū iii, 297b, 298a; vi, 434b, 435a, 727a, b
al-Kammad (1704) iii, 971b; iv, **522a**
al-Ḳammāṭ, Muḥammad (1479) vi, 132b
Kammūn iv, **522a**; vii, 951b
al-Kammūnī, Muḥammad (XI) iv, **523a**
Ḳammūniya → Ḳamūniya
Kāmrān, Mīrzā b. Bābur (Mug͟hal) (1557) i, 228b; ii, 973a; iii, 422b, 423a, 455b, 485a, 575a, b, 576a, 633b, 634a; iv, **523b**, 537a; vii, 130b, 131a, 135a, 220a, 314a, 337b
Kāmrān Mīrzā (1860) iv, 393b; vi, 484b; vii, 818b
Kāmrān S͟hāh Durrānī (1828) i, 230b; ii, 637b; iv, **523b**
Kāmrūp i, 719b; iv, **524a**; vi, 48a
Ḳamṣar iv, 694b; v, 869a
Ḳāmuhul vi, 967b
Ḳamūniya iv, 825b, 826b
Ḳāmūs ii, 585b, 801b, 926b; iii, 760a,b; iv, **524a**; v, 837a, 1093a
Ḳān → K͟hān
Kān wa-kān iv, **528a**; v, 372b
Ḳanā → Ḳunā
Ḳanāʿat S͟hāh Atalïḳ s, 98a
al-Ḳaʿnabī, ʿAbd Allāh b. Maslama vii, 691a
al-Kaʿnabī, ʿAbd al-Raḥmān vi, 280b
Kanaka (IX) viii, 106b
Kanākir vi, 546a
Kānamī → Kānemī
Kanʿān iv, **528b**; v, 521b
Ḳanān b. Mattā (VII) viii, 535b
Kanʿān Pas͟ha → Kenʿān Pas͟ha
Kanarese → Kannada
Ḳanāt ii, 875b; iv, 8b, **528b**, 600b; v, 866a, b, 875b, 878b, 968b, 1108b
Kanāta → Kunta
al-Ḳanāṭir iv, 555a, b; s, 230a
Ḳanāṭir Firʿawn iv, 556b
Ḳanāṭir al-Tisʿa xi, 422a
Ḳanawāt iv, **533a**; vi, 546b
Kan(n)awd͟j ii, 808b; iv, 276a, **533b**; vi, 48a, 49b, 65b, 273a, 294b, 309a, 410a; vii, 407a; s, 21a, 312a
Ḳanbalū (island) i, 930a; v, 940a; vi, 784b; viii, 292b; ix, 715b
Ḳanbāniya iv, **534a**; v, 509b
Ḳanbar ʿAlī Beg v, 665b, 673a
Ḳanbar Beg iv, 749b
Kanbāya i, 930a; iii, 444b (see also *s.v.* K͟hambāyat)
Kanbō, S͟hayk͟h D͟jamālī (1534) s, **510b**
Kanbō(h), Muḥammad Ṣāliḥ → Muḥammad Ṣāliḥ Kańbū
Kanchandas i, 173a
Kānčī vi, 67b
Ḳand → Sukkar
Kand b. K͟hars͟hbūn (Mohmand) vii, 220a
Ḳandābīl iv, 364a, **534a**; x, 673a
Ḳandahār i, 5a, 8b, 72a, 80b, 95b, 222b, 223a, 768b, 1323b; ii, 134b, 628b; iv, 37b, **535a**; vi, 768a; vii, 130b, 131a, 313b, 318b, 438a, 854b; s, 63a, 66b, 367b, 423b
Ḳandahār, Ḳand͟hār (Deccan) iv, **538a**; v, 579b
Kānd͟halawīs x, 39a
Kandi ii, 94a; iv, **538b**
Kandia Koulibali iii, 39a
Ḳandīl → Ḳindīl
Kandilli (Istanbul) vi, 57a; vii, 599a
Ḳandiya iv, **539a**, 590b; v, 260a, 261a
Kand͟j Pas͟hā i, 1078b
Kandūrī iv, **540a**; ix, 154a
Kanem (Kānim) i, 1259b, 1260a; ii, 369a, 876a; iv, **540a**, 566b; vi, 281b; s, 163b, 164a, 165a
Kanembū i, 1260a; iv, 540b, 566b; s, 163b
Kānemī (language) ii, 441b; iii, 657b; iv, 566b
al-Kāne(i)mī, ʿAbd Allāh (XIX) vii, 435b
al-Kāne(i)mī, S͟hayk͟h Muḥammad al-Amīn (1837) i, 1260a; ii, 942a; iii, 38b; iv, **541b**, 541b, 567a; v, 357b; vii, 435b; ix, 516a; x, 122b; s, 164b

Kanesh → Kültepe
Kangarids → Musāfirids
Kangāwar → Kinkiwar
Kanglî s, 97b, 420a
Ķanghli, Ķanķlî i, 987a; iv, **542a**, 613a; s, 97b
Kāńgŕā iv, **542b**; vii, 989a; viii, 869a
Kānī, Abū Bakr (1791) iv, **544a**; vi, 826b
Ķāniʿ, Mīr ʿAlī Sher (1788) iv, **544b**
Kānī, Muṣṭafā iv, 795b, 796a
Kāniguram i, 225a; vi, 86a, b
Ķāniʿī, Aḥmad b. Maḥmūd al-Ṭūsī (XIII) iv, 504b; vii, 1017a; viii, 971b
Kanik, Orhan Veli (1950) iv, **545a**
Kanīsa iv, **545a**; vi, 649b
Kanīsat al-Ghurāb i, 488b
Kanīsat al-Ķiyāma iv, 545b
Kanīsat al-Ķumāma iv, 545b
Kanīsat al-Sawdāʾ vi, 775a
Kān-i Zand vi, 384a
Kanizsa, Kanizhe iii, 1001a; iv, **546b**, 637a, 878a; xi, 546a
Kankan ii, 1132a, b; viii, 1049a
Kankarides → Kurds
Kankdiz v, 297a; xi, 223b
Kankiwar → Kinkiwar
Ķanķlî → Ķanghli
Kankūt ii, 155b, 156a
Kannada (language) ii, 218a; iii, 147b; v, 1258b
Kannanūr (Cannanore) iv, **546b**; v, 587a; vi, 206b
Kannās iv, **547b**; s, 323b
Ķannāṣ ix, 99a
Kannudj → Kanawdj
al-Kannī, Abu ʾl-ʿAbbās s, 236a
Kano iii, 275b, 276a; iv, **548a**; v, 1165b; vi, 258b; xi, 123a
Kapudan-i Deryā → Kapudān Pasha
Kānpur (Cawnpore) iv, **551b**; vi, 78a; s, 360b
Ķanṣ → Ṣayd
Ķānṣawh Bey iv, 723a
Ķānṣawh al-Ghawrī (Ķānṣūh al-Ghūrī) (Mamlūk) (1516) i, 315a, 815a, 1032b, 1057b, 1059a, 1060a; ii, 72b, 286a, 955a, 1127b, 1136b; iii, 346b, 760b, 813a; iv, 435a, b, 451a, **552a**; vi, 45a, 315a, 324b, 325a, 367b; vii, 175b, 176b; ix, 129a, b; s, 43b
Ķansāwuķ Beg ii, 25a
Kansu iv, **553a**; v, 844b, 845a, b, 846a, 848a, b, 850b; vii, 230b; x, 707a
Ķānṣūh al-Ghūrī → Ķānṣawh al-Ghawrī
Ķānṣūh Pasha (Yemen) (XVII) vii, 270a
Ķanṭara (bridge) ii, 555a, 716a; iv, **555a**
al-Ķanṭara (Algeria, Spain, Egypt, Syria) i, 424a; iv, 555b; vi, 727a
Ķanṭarat al-ʿĀshir (Wāsiṭ) vii, 348a
Ķanṭarat Umm Ḥakīm vi, 546b
Ķanṭarat Zaynab iv, 556a
Kantemiroğlu → Ķantimīr, Demetrius
Ķantimīr, Demetrius (1723) i, 269a, 271a; viii, 65b; ix, 832b; s, **510b**, 548b
Ķantimīr Pasha (Silistria) (XVII) i, 310b, 1287a
Ķāntū ix, 440b
Ķānūn i, 152a, 170a, 171a, 975b; ii, 79a, 81b, 147a, 519a; iv, **556b**, 946b
Ķānūn (music) → Malāhī
Ķānūnnāme i, 268a, 656b, 861b, 862a, 1147b, 1169b; ii, 83a; iv, 557a, **562a**
Ķānūn Ṣanʿāʾ iv, 741b; ix, 2b
Ķānūn al-Siyāsatnāma iii, 556b
Ķānūngo ii, 156b; viii, 271a
Ķanūnī Süleymān viii, 641a; ix, 131b, 199b, 200a (see also *s.v.* Süleymān (Sulayman the Magnificent))
Kanuri i, 179b, 809a, 1221b, 1259a, b; ii, 10b, 368b; iv, **566b**
Kānwa s, 331b
Kanz, Banu ʾl- (Awlād al-Kanz) iv, **567b**; vi, 574b; viii, 90a, b, 863b
Kaole vi, 370a
Ķapan ii, 147a; iii, 489b; iv, 226b, 228b; vi, 980b
Kāparbandj vi, 53b
Kapgan Ķaghan x, 687b
Ķapî iv, **568a**
Ķapî-aghasî → Ķapu Aghasî
Kapî daghî vi, 587b, 588a
Kapî Kahyasî → Sarāy
Kapî ķullarî i, 35b, 102a, 206b, 1256b; ii, 1090b, 1097b, 1120b; iv, 242b, 243a, 568a; v, 249b; s, 269b
Kapî Ķulu → Ordu
Ķapîdjî iv, **568a**
Kapilendra (ca. 1467) i, 924a; x, 895a
Kapilēshwar vi, 67a
Ķaplan Girāy I (Crimea) (1738) iv, **568b**; vi, 55b; vii, 854a; viii, 288a
Ķaplan Girāy II (Crimea) (1771) iv, **569b**

Ḳaplan Muṣṭafā Pasha (1680) s, **511a** (see also *s.v.* Muṣṭafā Pasha Ḳaplan)
Ḳaplidja iii, 1120b; iv, **569b**
Ḳapu Aghasi ii, 1047a; 1088a; iv, **570b**, 1093a
Ḳapuča iv, **571b**
Ḳapudan Pasha (Ḳaptan Pasha) i, 269b, 948b, 1209a, 1266a, b, 1267b, 1268b; ii, 165b, 521b; iv, **571b**, 970b, 1158a; vi, 588b
Kār Kiyā, Mirzā ʿAlī (XV) vi, 515b; viii, 767a; x, 312a
Kār Kiyā Muḥammad II (Marʿashī) (1474) vi, 514a; xi, 394a
Ḳarā iv, **572b**
Karā (province) s, 203a
al-Ḳarā, Banū i, 98a, 536a; v, 116b; vi, 80a, 83b, 84a, b
al-Ḳarā (Damascus) vi, 734a
Ḳara Aghač (Mand) vi, 384a
Ḳara Aghač (Manisa) s, 282b
Ḳara Aḥmad → Aḥmad Pasha, Ḳara
Ḳara Aḥmed Shātiroghlu s, 91b
Ḳara Āmid → Diyār Bakr
Ḳara Arslān, Fakhr al-Dīn (Artuḳid) (1167) i, 664b, 665a; iii, 507a; vi, 507a, 870b; vii, 579a
Ḳara Arslān Beg → Ḳāwurd b. Čaghri Dāwūd
Ḳara ʿaynī → Čāldirān
Ḳarāba iv, **595a**; vi, 875b
Ḳarābādhīn → Aḳrābādhīn
Ḳarābāgh ii, 1135b; iv, 389a, **573a**; v, 397a; vi, 291a, 366a, 494a, b; vii, 498a; xi, 301b; s, 47a, 139b, 143a
Ḳarā Bahādur s, 324b
Ḳarabāsh Welī, ʿAlī ʿAlāʾ al-Dīn (1686) i, 965b; iv, 991b; ix, 155b, 156a
al-Ḳarābāshiyya iv, 991b, 993a
Ḳarā Bayat i, 1117a; iii, 1101a, b
al-Karābīsī, Abū ʿAlī al-Ḥusayn b. ʿAlī (859) iv, **596a**; vii, 260b, 312b
al-Karābīsī, Aḥmad b. ʿUmar iv, **596a**
al-Karābīsī, Asʿad b. Muḥammad (1174) iv, **596b**
al-Karābīsī, Ḥusayn b. ʿAlī ix, 186b; x, 78a; s, 546b
Ḳarā Biyik-oghlū i, 396a
Ḳarā Boghaz vi, 417a; s, 281a
Ḳarā Boghdān → Boghdān
Ḳaračay i, 1000b; ii, 23a; iv, **596b**; v, 288a; vii, 352a; x, 691a; s, 489a, 494a, 498a
Ḳaračay-Balḳar i, 1000b; iv, 596b, 1177a; viii, 618b; x, 691a
Ḳaračay-Čerkes Autonomous Oblast/ Region iv, 325a, 597a; s, 498b
Karačelebi-zāde, Āl i, 915b; iv, 298b, **573a**
Karačī (Adharbāydjān) ii, 41a; v, 818a
Karāčī i, 1006a; ii, 426b; iv, **597a**; v, 356a, 1222b; s, 332b
Karāčī trial vii, 421b
Ḳarāčīl vii, 412a
Ḳara-Ḍagh (Montenegro) iii, 992b; iv, **574a**, 589a, 1054a; v, 263a; vi, 69a
Ḳarā Dāwūd Pasha → Dāwūd Pasha (1623)
Ḳarā Deniz iv, **575a**; vii, 70b
Karadeniz Ereğlisi ii, 705a
Ḳara Dewletshāh (1400) vi, 974a
Ḳara Dhu ʾl-Ḳādir (XIV) vii, 462a
(al)-Karadj (Karadj Abī Dulaf) ii, 623b; vi, 493a, 495b; s, 17b, 122b
Ḳaradja (amīr) iii, 398b, 503b; iv, 210a
Ḳara Beg → Zayn al-Dīn Ḳaradja b. Dul-ḳādir (Dhu ʾl-Ḳadr)
Ḳara Beg (1445) i, 511a
Ḳara Beg (1456) vi, 70a
Ḳara Beg b. ʿAbd Allāh, Ghāzī (1411) ii, 985b
Ḳara Dagh (Adharbāydjān) i, 348b; v, 810b; vi, 504a, 539b; s, 116a
Ḳara Dagh (al-Djazīra) vi, 539b
Ḳaradja Beg → Zayn al-Dīn Ḳaradja b. Dulḳādir (Dhu ʾl-Ḳadr)
Ḳaradja Ḥiṣār ii, 710b, 715b; iv, 580b, **598b**
Ḳaradja Shehir → Ḳaradja Ḥiṣār
al-Karādjakī (XI) vii, 313a
Ḳaradja-oghlan i, 677b; ii, 75b; iv, **599a**; s, 91b, 324a
al-Karadjī, Abū Bakr Muḥammad (XI) i, 133b; iv, **600a**, 703a; viii, 551b; s, 119b, 390a
Karadj-i Abū Dulaf vi, 494a
Ḳarā Evlī iii, 1100a
Ḳarā Faḍlī → Faḍlī, Meḥmed
al-Ḳarāfa (al-Kubrā and Ṣughrā) → al-Ḳāhira, cemetries
Karaferye iv, **600b**
al-Ḳarāfī (1285) vi, 279a, 280a, 638a; ix, **436a**; x, 112a

Ḳaragan Bay vi, 416b
Ḳaraghūl, Banū vi, 614a
Ḳaragöz i, 152a, 792b, 1161b; iv, **601a**, 1136b; vi, 373a; vii, 657b
Ḳaragöz Meḥmed Beg (XVI) vii, 244b
Ḳarā Gözlü iii, 1102b, 1109a; iv, **577b**
Ḳaragozlu, Muḥammad Ḥusayn Khān (1825) vii, 453a
Ḳarā Ḥasan iv, 1156a, b
Ḳarā Haydar-oghlu → Haydar-oghlu Meḥmed
Ḳarā Ḥiṣār iv, **578a**
Ḳarā Ḥiṣār Adalia → Ḳarā Ḥiṣār-i Teke
Ḳarā Ḥiṣar Develi iv, 624a, 843a, b
Ḳarā Ḥiṣar-i̊ Behrāmshāh (Bayrāmshāh) iv, 579b
Ḳarā Ḥiṣar-i̊ Demirdji iv, 579b
Ḳarā Ḥiṣar-i̊ Ṣāḥib → Afyūn Ḳarā Ḥiṣār
Ḳarā Ḥiṣar-i̊ Sharḳī, Shabkhāne → Shābīn Ḳarā Ḥiṣār
Ḳarā Ḥiṣar-i Teke iv, 579b
Ḳarā-Hülegü i, 1311b; ii, 3a, b
Ḳarāʾī iii, 1102b, 1107b; v, 154b
Ḳarā Ibrāhīm Pasha → Ibrāhīm Pasha, Ḳarā
Ḳarāʾīm → Karaites
Karaites, Ḳarāʾiyyūn iv, 305a, b, **603b**; v, 136b, 326b; x, 697b
al-Karak i, 804b; iv, **609a**; vi, 321b, 322a, b, 323a, 547b; vii, 989b, 991b, 992b; viii, 989a; s, 391a
Ḳaraḳalpaḳ i, 422a, 1076b; ii, 971a; iii, 116b; iv, **610b**; vi, 418a, b; s, 97b, 839a
Ḳaraḳalpaḳ literature x, **731a**
Ḳarā Kemāl iv, 285b; ix, 499a
Ḳarā Khalīl Djandarli̊ → Djandarli̊, Khayr al-Dīn Khalīl Pasha
Ḳarā Khalīlzade iv, 506a
Ḳarā Khān Ustādjalū (1516) vi, 541b, 992b
Ḳarā Khān (Awliyā Ata) i, 767a
Karakh iv, 347a
Ḳarākhān → Khayr Khān
Ḳarakhānid (language) iv, 700a
Ḳarakhānids → Ilek-khāns
Ḳarā Khiṭāy i, 750a, 987a, 1001b, 1240a, 1295a, 1311a; ii, 43a, 67a, 607a, 1101b, 1109a; iii, 1114b; iv, 29a, b, 30a, 32a, 542b, **580b**, 1067b; v, 38b, 134b; vi, 481b, 557b; vii, 997b; viii, 943a; x, 543a
al-Karakī, Nūr al-Dīn ʿAlī (1534) ii, 104a; iv, **610a**; vi, 550a, b; vii, 298a; viii, 777b; x, 40b; s, 516b
Ḳarā Kirgiz → Kirgiz
Karak Nūḥ iv, **609b**; s, 380a
Ḳarakol iv, **611a**
Ḳarā-köl i, 1135a; iv, 213b, **583b**; s, 97a, 227b, 318a
Karakol Djemʿīyyetī iv, **611b**
Ḳaraḳorum (town) ii, 45b, 606b; iv, **612b**, 915a; vi, 482b; viii, 162b, 599a
Ḳaraḳorum Mountains iv, **611b**; x, 854b; s, 158b
Karaköy v, 557b; viii, 602b; s, 314b
Ḳarā Ḳoyunlu i, 190a, 311b, 508a, 666b, 903b, 919a; ii, 334a, 344b, 401b, 598b, 711b; iii, 1100b, 1256b; iv, 33b, 34a, **584a**; v, 456b; vi, 201a, 483a, 493a, 495a, 515b, 541a; vii, 271b; x, 45a, 963b
Ḳarākul → Ḳarā-köl
Ḳaraḳum (desert) iv, **613a**; vi, 416a, 621a
Ḳarākum (town) iv, 542b, 613a
Ḳaraḳūna (island) ii, 235a
Ḳarāḳūsh, Bahāʾ al-Dīn al-Asadī (1201) iii, 173b; iv, 424b, **613a**; vi, 430a; vii, 151a, 816b, viii, 467b, 913b
Ḳarāḳūsh, Sharaf al-Dīn al-Armanī (1212) i, 161b, 165a, 533a, 797b, 798a; ii, 575a, 875b, 1007b, 1008a, 1110a; iii, 173b; iv, 210a, 337b, 424b, **614a**, 739b
Ḳarā Maḥmūd → Medhi, Maḥmūd Efendi (Gelibolu)
Ḳarā Maḥmūd Pasha, Ishḳodrali̊ Bushatli̊ (1796) i, 657a; iv, **588a**; v, 276b; vii, 719b; s, 461b
Ḳarā Mambuche vi, 382a
Ḳara Timurtash Pasha ii, 722a; x, 698a
Ḳara Yoluḳ ʿUthmān (1435) x, 963b
Karam i, 311b; s, **511a**
al-Karam, Banū → Zurayʿids
Karam, Yūsuf → Yūsuf Karam
al-Karam b. Yām i, 181b
Karam Allāh Kurḳusāwī i, 929b; ii, 696b; v, 1250b
Karāma iv, **615a**
Ḳaramān i, 354b, 468a; iv, **616b**, 621a; v, 881b
Ḳaramān (town) iv, 616b
Ḳaramān b. Nūre Ṣūfī i, 467a, 468a; iv, 619b, 620a; x, 569b

Ḳaramānī Akhaweyn Meḥmed Čelebi (XVI) vi, 970b
Ḳaramānī Meḥmed Pasha → Meḥmed Pasha Ḳaramānī
Ḳarāmānids → Ḳaramān-oghullari̊
Ḳaramānlī ii, 161a, b, 876a, 876b, 971b; iv, **617a**
Ḳaramānlī Aḥmad Bey iv, 617a
Karamanlidika xi, 149a
Ḳaramān-oghlu, ʿAlāʾ al-Dīn ʿAlī (1379) i, 394a, 1118a; iv, 622b, 623a; v, 680a
Ḳaramān-oghlu Ibrāhīm Beg (1468) ii, 239b, 705b; vi, 71b; vii, 594b
Ḳaramān-oghlu Meḥmed (XV) vii, 644a
Ḳaramān-oghullari̊ (Ḳaramānids) i, 240b, 244a, 292b, 1117b, 1118a; ii, 103b, 239b, 529b, 607b, 692a, 705b, 710b; iii, 1006b; iv, **619a**, 843a; v, 254a, 677a, b, 1144b; vi, 975a; vii, 271b, 479b; viii, 16a
Karāmat ʿAlī Djawnpūrī (1873) i, 952a; iv, 170a, **625b**
Karamba ii, 1132b
Ḳarāmīd → Khazaf
Ḳarāmiṭa → Ḳarmaṭī
Karāmiyya → Karrāmiyya
Karamoko Alfa ii, 960a, 1132a, b
Karamoko Oule Wattara v, 253a
Ḳarā Muḥammad i, 311b, 1051a; iv, 584b
Karamuk → Bolwadin
Ḳarā Murād Pasha iv, 766a
Ḳaramürsel v, 250a; vi, 587b
Ḳarā Mūsā i, 293b
Ḳarā Muṣṭafā Pasha → Kemānkesh Ḳarā Muṣṭafā Pasha
Ḳarā Muṣṭafā Pasha Firārī i, 236b; iii, 1001b
Ḳarā Muṣṭafā Pasha Merzifonlu (1683) i, 948a, 1284b; ii, 522a, 572b; iv, **589b**; v, 261b, 272b, 720b; vi, 202b, 982b; viii, 4b; ix, 697b
Ḳarāmiṭa → Ḳarmaṭī
Karandal → Ḳalandar
Ḳaranful iv, **626b**
Ḳaranfūl b. Malik Sarwar (Djawnpūr) (XIV) iii, 14b; vi, 273a
Ḳaranghu vi, 498b, 501a
Karaosmanoğlu/Ḳarā ʿOthmān-Oghli̊ → Ḳarā ʿUthmān-oghullari̊
Ḳarapapakh iv, **627a**; vii, 353a
Ḳarā Pīrī Beg Ḳādjār iv, 387b, 389a
Ḳarār → Mūsīḳī
al-Ḳarār i, 897a
Ḳarāra iii, 97b
Ḳarasaḳal i, 1076b
Ḳarashahr ix, 621b
Ḳarāshams al-Dīn ix, 617b; s, 540b
Ḳarasi̊ i, 467b, 468a, 994a, 1187a; ii, 686b; iv, **627b**; vi, 587b; viii, 176a
Ḳarasi̊-chi → Ḳarasi̊
Ḳarasi̊-eli i, 468b
Ḳarā Sonḳor (atabeg) (1140) i, 1358a; ii, 975b
Karasta i, 1205b
al-Ḳarasṭūn iv, **629a**; vii, 195b
Ḳarā-ṣū → al-Furāt
Ḳarā-ṣū → Khāsa
Ḳara-ṣu (Mākū) vi, 200b; vii, 498b
Ḳaraṣū-Bāzār iv, **629b**
Ḳarāsunḳur, Shams al-Dīn al-Manṣūrī (Aleppo) (1328) iv, 432b; v, 1142b; vi, 501b; vii, 991b; viii, 157a
Ḳārat al-Kibrīt ii, 631a; iii, 1038a
Ḳarata, Banū i, 504a; iv, **630b**
Karataï, Banū i, 1338a
Ḳarā Takīn → Ḳaratigin
Karatau vi, 415a
Ḳaratāy → Djalāl al-Dīn Ḳaratāy
Ḳaraṭāy (Ḳirtay) al-ʿIzzī al-Khāzindārī s, **511b**
Ḳaratekin (Čanki̊ri̊) (XI) ii, 14a
Ḳaratigin iv, **631a**; s, 228a
Ḳaratigin al-Isfīdjābī (X) i, 852a; ii, 1082a; s, 356b, 459b
Ḳarātisa s, 42a
Ḳaraṭughan vi, 512a, 515b, 745b
Ḳarā Ulus (nomads) iv, 584a; vi, 242b
Ḳarā ʿOthmān-oghi̊ i, 469a, 783a; ii, 206b, 207a; iv, **592b**; v, 1170b; vi, 541a, 931b
Ḳaravul → Karakol
Ḳarāvulān iv, 860a
Ḳara Üweys Čelebi (XVI) vii, 596a; ix, 710b
Ḳarawī (language) i, 575a
al-Ḳarawī, al-Shāʿir v, 1256b; ii, 471b
al-Ḳarawiyyīn → Masdjid al-Ḳarawiyyīn
Karawnas → Nīkūdārīs
Ḳarāwul vi, 20b (see also *s.v.* Karakol)
Ḳaray, ḳaraylar iv, 608a
Karay, Refīḳ Khālid (1965) iii, 357b; iv, **635b**, 812a; v, 194b, 196b; vi, 94b; ix, 655b; s, 96a, 98b
al-Ḳarayāt iv, 680b

Ḳarā Yazîdjî (Djalālī) (1602) iv, 499a, **594a**, 843b; vi, 981b; viii, 197a; ix, 874a; s, 238b
Ḳarā Yülüḳ ʿUthmān i, 311b, 1054a, 1328a; ii, 614a; iii, 186a, 190a; iv, 586b, 587a, b, 871a; ix, 843a
Ḳarā Yūsuf Ḳaraḳoyunlu (1410) i, 311b, 666b, 791b, 1119a; ii, 401b, 614a; iv, 33b, 586a, b, 587a; vi, 202a, 541a, 976b; vii, 105b, 271b
Karbalāʾ i, 1168b; ii, 938a; iii, 115a, 119b, 610a; iv, **637a**; v, 1033a; vi, 113a, 123b, 516b, 537a, 604a, 609b, 611a; vii, 456b, 690b, 778a; s, 74b, 75a, 94a, b, 134b, 231b
Karbalāʾī Ḳurbān s, 70b
Kārbān → Kārwān
Karbughā al-Mawṣilī (1098) i, 517a, 1052a; vi, 544a
Ḳardā and Bāzabdā iii, 126b; iv, **639a**
Kardan (steppe) vi, 56b
Ḳardagh iv, 76a
al-Kardarī, al-Bazzāzī iii, 163b
al-Kardarī, Muḥammad b. Muḥammad (1424) vi, 352b
al-Kardarī, Shams al-Aʾimma (1244) vii, 969a
Kardj → Kerč
Ḳardū, Karduchoi v, 447b, 448a, b
Ḳardū (Mountain) ii, 574a
al-Kardūdī, Abū ʿAbd Allāh (1849) iv, **639a**
Karghandede vi, 541b
Karghawayh, Karghūyah i, 119b; iii, 129b; v, 923b
Kārgudhār iii, 1193a
Ḳāriʾ → Ḳirāʾa; Ḳurʾān; Ḳurrāʾ
Ḳārī, Niẓām al-Dīn Maḥmūd (XV) iii, 355b; iv, 66a
al-Ḳārī → ʿAlī al-Ḳārī al-Harawī
Ḳarība (singer) → Ḳurayba
Ḳarība (tax) v, 259a
Karibʾīl Bayān ix, 91b
Karibʾil b. Dhamarʿalī vi, 561b, 562b
Karibʾil Watar vi, 560b; ix, 91a, 166a
Karibʾil Yuhanʿim vi, 562a
Karibīya → Kuraybiyya
Kārim iv, 640b
Karīm al-Dīn al-Āmulī (1310) iii, 952a
Karīm al-Dīn al-Kabīr → Ibn al-Sadīd (1324)
Karīm Khān (Nagar) s, 327b
Karīm Khān Zand (Zands) (1779) i, 190a, 230a, 246b, 393b, 1341b; ii, 311a, 812a; iii, 1102b, 1103a, 1191a, 1257b; iv, 104b, 390a, b, **639b**, 695a, 1056b; v, 617a, 674a, 825b; vi, 495a, 551a, 715a; vii, 582b, 674b; s, 405b
Karīm Shāh → Agha Khān IV
Karīm Thābit s, 301a
Karīma vi, 434b
Kārimī i, 800a; ii, 144b; iii, 776b; iv, 136a, b, 137a, **640a**; v, 514b; vi, 324a; s, 43a
Ḳārin i, 47b; iv, 644a
Ḳarīn iv, **643b**
Ḳarīn (Mts.) s, 298a
Ḳārin b. Shahriyār Bāwand i, 1110a; iv, 645b, 646b; s, 363b
Ḳārin b. Wandād-Hurmuzd iv, 645a
Karin-ābād (Karnobat) i, 1302b, 1303a; ii, 1047a
Ḳārinids iv, 207b, **644a**; v, 661a; vi, 337b, 745a, 938b; s, 298a, 309a
Karīnov, Islom x, 962a
Karîshdîran Süleymān Beg iv, 225a
Kāriyān v, 1110a, 1112a; v, 668b; vi, 384b
Kārīz → Ḳanāt
Karkaddan iv, **647a**; v, 1228a; s, 295a
Ḳarḳana iv, **650b**
Karkand → Karkaddan
Karkarn → Bisbarāy
Ḳarkashandī, Banū v, 333a
Ḳarḳastal s, 80a
al-Karkh (Baghdād; Sāmarrāʾ) i, 896a; iv, **652a**; vi, 428b, 613b; s, 13a, 172a, 192b, 193a
Karkh Bādjaddā vi, 613b
Karkha (river) iii, 1251a; iv, **653b**, 675a; v, 830a, 867b; vii, 674b, 675a; ix, 113b
Karkha (town) ix, 898a
Karkhāyā i, 1223a; iv, 652b
al-Karkhī → al-Karadjī
al-Karkhī, Abū ʿAlī Muḥammad s, 25b
al-Karkhī, Abu ʾl-Ḥasan (952) ix, 36a; s, 12b, 13a, 14a, 36a
al-Karkhī, ʿAlī b. Ḥasan ii, 486a
al-Karkhī, Badr al-Dīn Muḥammad (1597) viii, 562a
al-Karkhī, Ḥasan Fatḥ (Malāmatī) (XIX) vi, 224a
al-Karkhī, Maʿrūf b. al-Fayzurān → Maʿrūf al-Karkhī

Karkhina → Kirkūk
Karkī s, 281a
Ķarķīsiyā iv, **654b**, 897b, 898a; s, 117a
Kārkiyā ii, 194a; v, 603a, b, 604a
Karkūr iv, **655b**
Karlî-Īli; Karlo-Īli iv, **656a**; v, 725b, 726a; s, 836a
Ķarlofča iv, **657a**; v, 721a, 727b; vii, 708a; ix, 135a; xi, 492a, 517b; s, 187a
Karlowitz → Ķarlofča
Ķarluķ ii, 67a, 1107b; iii, 335b, 1113a, 1116b; iv, 188b, 213a, **658a**, 917a; v, 854b, 855b, 856a, 857a; x, 689a; s, 326b
Karm iv, **659a**
Ķarmāsīn → Kirmānshāh
Ķarmaṭī (Ķarāmiṭa) i, 11a, 19a, 73b, 95b, 194b, 387a, 551a, 822a, 824a, 867a, 942a, 1086a, 1276b, 1354b; ii, 98a, 168b, 281b, 385a, 452b, 482b, 495b, 854a, 1070a; iii, 123b, 126b, 238a, 246a, 255b, 380b, 619a, 799a; iv, 22b, 198a, 494a, **660b**, 764a; v, 327a, 348a, 923a; vi, 128a, 148a, 274b, 435b, 585a; vii, 484b, 543a, 652a, 760b, 769a, 770a; viii, 72a, 862b; s, 12b, 36b, 117b, 199a
Karmīniyya s, 176b
Karmisīn → Kirmānshāh
Ķarmūna i, 6a, 1238a; iii, 498b; iv, **665a**
Ķarn i, 1290b; iv, 825b; vii, 269b
al-Karnabāʾī (Zandjī) (IX) vii, 526
Karnāl ii, 973b; iv, **665b**; vi, 456b
Karnātak i, 624b; iii, 316b; iv, **666b**; vi, 535a; vii, 459a
Ķarnaw vi, 88b
Karnobat → Karin-ābād
Karōṙī ii, 156b
Karpenésion, Karpenisi → Kerbenesh
Karra vi, 48a
al-Ķarra iii, 582b
Ķarrād v, 132a, b
Karrāmiyya i, 187b, 411a, 714a; ii, 218b, 752a, 791a, 931b, 1103a; iii, 177b, 767a, 1145a, 1165a, 1173a; iv, 46a, 183b, 469a, **667a**, 1025b; v, 328b; vii, 577a; viii, 63a; s, 149a
Karranāy i, 1291b
Ķarrī → Ķerrī
Ķarrīṭa i, 206a
Kārrūn vi, 384a
Karrūṣa i, 206a
Ķars i, 468b, 637b, 638a, 640a, 641b; iv, 627a, b, **669b**, 854a; vi, 55b, 56a, 274a, 508a, b, 1002b, 1003a
Ķarṣana → Ķurṣān
Karsh → Kerč
Ķarshī i, 1019a; ii, 4a; iii, 1236b; iv, **671b**, 694a, b; v, 858b; vi, 418a; vii, 925a
Karshūnī iv, **671b**
Kart i, 227a, 1343a; iii, 177b, 1121b; iv, 32a, **672a**; v, 58b; vii, 218b; viii, 83a; x, 88b, 89a, 552b
Ķarṭādjanna i, 51b, 77b; iii, 271a; iv, **672b**; v, 1188a
al-Ķarṭādjannī → Ḥāzim al-Ķarṭādjannī
Ķarṭas → Ķirṭās
Ķarṭasa ii, 105b
Kartasura ix, 892a
Kartli iv, 1174b; v, 486b, 487a, 494a; s, 484b
Kartosoewirjo, S.H. vi, 731b
Karūbiyya vi, 219b
Kārūd → Ķalʿa Kuhrūd
Karūkh iv, **673a**
Karume, Abeid (1972) xi, 450b
Ķārūn i, 909a; iv, **673a**
Kārūn (river) i, 8b; iii, 1251a; iv, 6a, 9a, 654a, **673b**; v, 65b, 66a, 80b, 867a, 869a; xi, 472b, 473a
Kārwa iii, 197b; s, 471a
Kārwān iv, **676a**
Ķarwāsh b. al-Muķallad (ʿUkaylid) (1050) i, 1073b; iii, 80b, 860a; iv, 378b, 911a; v, 896b; vi, 965b; vii, 118a; x, 787a; s, 119a
Ķarwasha iv, **679b**
Ķarya iv, **680a**
al-Ķarya al-Ḥadītha → Djand
Ķarya al-Suṭā iv, **680b**
Ķarya al-ʿUlyā iii, 1066a; iv, **680b**; v, 574b
Ķaryat Djilyāna vi, 221b
Ķaryat al-Fāʾw/Fāw → Fāʾw/Fāw, Ķaryat al-/Wādī al-
Ķaryat al-Ḥaddādīn vi, 744b
al-Karyatayn i, 43b; iv, 532a; viii, 423b; s, 117a
Kārzai, Ḥamīd s, 787a
Karzīn → Abū ʿUbayda Muslim b. Abī Karīma al-Tamīmī
Kārzīn vi, 384a
Karzūbī iii, 1097b
al-Ķaṣāb iv, **681a**

Ḳaṣab iv, **682a**
Ḳaṣāb, Teodor (1897) iv, **681b**; vi, 373a
Ḳaṣab al-dharīra s, 42b
Ḳaṣab al-sukkar iv, **682b**
Ḳaṣaba (town) i, 1320a; iii, 498b; iv, **684b**, 685b
Ḳaṣaba (citadel) i, 974b; iv, **685a**; v, 654b
Ḳaṣaba Benī Mellāl → Benī Mellāl
Ḳaṣaba B. Kush s, 132a
Kasādī, Āl vii, 496a
Käsäg → Kabards
Kāsagarān Madrasa s, 23b
Ḳasak → Čerkes
Kasala i, 1158b; iv, **686a**; v, 1251a; vii, 124b
Ḳasam iv, **687b**; v, 178b, 179b
Ḳasāma i, 1151a; ii, 342b; iv, 687b, **689b**
Ḳāsān → Kāshān
al-Kāsānī, ʿAlāʾ al-Dīn (1189) iii, 163b; iv, **690a**; vii, 758b; viii, 532b; ix, 548a
Kasap → Ḳaṣāb
Ḳaṣaṣ → Ḳiṣṣa
Kasb i, 413b, 414a, 696b; ii, 365a; iii, 1037a, b; iv, 272a, **690b**
Kasbah → Ḳaṣaba (town)
Kasf → Kusūf
Ḳāsh i, 1158a, b
Kash (Shahr-i Sabz) iv, **694a**, 711b; v, 181a, 858b; ix, 46a; s, 97b
Kashad al-Djuhanī v, 316a, b
Kashaf-Rūd vi, 495a, 713b; x, 741a; s, 83a
Kashak (Kasak) → Čerkes
Kāshān i, 11a; ii, 746a; iii, 144b, 1125b; iv, **694b**, 1040a, 1047b, 1167a; v, 171a, 370a; vii, 72b, 960b; s, 71a, 75b, 139a, b, 141a, 142a, 450a
Kashāna (Kashāta) (Berber) vi, 310b
al-Ḳāshānī, ʿAbd al-Razzāk → ʿAbd al-Razzāk al-Ḳāshānī
al-Ḳashānī, Abu ʾl-ʿAbbās Aḥmad (1116) iv, **696a**
al-Kashānī, Abū Ṭālib → Ḳalīm Abū Ṭālib
Kāshānī, Afḍal al-Dīn (1256 or 1265) x, 320b (see also *s.v.* Bābā Afḍal al-Dīn Muḥammad)
Kāshānī, Āḳā Muẓaffar s, 308b
Kāshānī, Āyātullāh Abu ʾl-Ḳāsim (1962) ii, 882b; iii, 529b; iv, 165a, **695b**, 790a; vii, 300a, 446b, 654b
al-Kāshānī, Ghiyāth al-Dīn → al-Kāshī, Djamshīd
Kāshānī, Ḥādjdjī Mīrzā Djānī (1852) iv, **696a**; viii, 114a
Kāshānī, ʿImād al-Dīn Yaḥyā (XIV) viii, 806b
Kāshānī, ʿIzz al-Dīn Maḥmūd (1334) ix, 780b; s, 415b, 784a
Kāshānī, Maḳṣūd s, 139a
Kāshānī, Mullā Muḥsin Fayḍ → Muḥsin-i Fayḍ-i Kāshānī
al-Kashānī, Taḳī al-Dīn Muḥammad (XVI) vii, 478a
Kashf iv, **696b**
Kashfahān ii, 556a
Kashfī, Sayyid Djāʿfar (1850) vi, 551b; vii, 298b
Kashgān (river) iv, 654a; v, 830a
Kashghāī → Ḳashḳaʾī
Kāshghar i, 46b; iii, 1114a; iv, **698b**; v, 38a, b, 846a; vi, 273b, 274a, 512b, 618b, 765b, 767a, 768b; x, 812a; xi, 256a; s, 240a
Kāshgharī, Khwādja Yūsuf (XIX) vii, 935b
Kāshgharī, Maḥmūd (XI) iii, 115b, 1114a, 1116a; iv, 525a, 527a, **699b**, 1080b; vi, 415b; vii, 567b; viii, 160b, 161a; xi, 359b; s, 168b, 280b, 289b
Kāshgharī, Saʿd al-Dīn (1456) → Saʿd al-Dīn Kāshgharī
Kāshī → Benares
Kāshī iv, **701a**; v, 600a
al-Ḳāshī, Abu ʾl-ʿAbbās Aḥmad → al-Ḳāshānī, Abu ʾl-ʿAbbās Aḥmad
al-Kāshī (al-Kāshānī), Ghiyāth al-Dīn Djamshīd b. Masʿūd (1429) iii, 1137b, 1139b, 1140a; iv, **702b**, 725b, 726a; vi, 112b, 601a; vii, 136a; viii, 542a; x, 267b; s, 502a
Kāshī, Ḥasan b. Maḥmūd (1310) viii, 423a
Kāshī, ʿImād al-Dīn b. Masʿūd (XVI) viii, 783b
Kāshī, Kāmāl al-Dīn Ḥusayn b. Masʿūd (1546) viii, 783b
Kāshī, Masʿūd b. Maḥmūd (1539) viii, 783b
Kāshī, Muḥammad Bāḳir b. ʿImād al-Dīn (XVI) viii, 783b
Kāshī, Nūr al-Dīn b. Kamāl al-Dīn (1561) viii, 783b
al-Ḳashīb (Mārib) vi, 561b
Kāshif, Muḥammad Sharīf (1653) iv, **703a**

Kāshif al-Ghiṭāʾ, Āyatullāh (XX) vi, 553b; x, 140a
Kāshif al-Ghiṭāʾ, Shaykh ʿAlī (1838) s, 75b
Kāshif al-Ghiṭāʾ, Shaykh Djaʿfar al-Nadjafī (1812) iv, **703b**; vi, 551a, b; vii, 298b, 302b; s, 57a
Kāshif al-Ghiṭāʾ, Shaykh Mūsā s, 75a
Kāshifī, Kamāl al-Dīn Ḥusayn b. ʿAlī al-Wāʿiẓ (1504) i, 430b; iii, 274b, 351b, 372b, 490a; iv, 68a, 504b, **704a**, 1035a; vi, 609b, 761b, 762a; vii, 1017a; viii, 465a, 540b; s, 46b
Kashīnā, Kashnā → Katsina
al-Kashināwī, Muḥammad (1655) iv, 773b
Kashīsh-Daghi → Ulu Dagh
Ḳashḳāʾī, Ḳāshḳāy ii, 925b; iii, 1105a, 1106a, 1110a; iv, 8a, 9a, b, **705b**; vii, 1050a; ix, 477b; x, 369a; xi, 385b; s, 142b, 146a, 147b
Ḳashka-Daryā i, 530b; vi, 418a, 619a
Ḳāshḳār → Chitral
Kashkasha i, 709a; iv, 399b; ix, 278b
Kashkūl iv, **706b**
Kashlī Khān → Sayf al-Dīn Aybak b. Iltutmish
Kashmīr i, 71a, 231a, 392b, 856b; ii, 140a; iii, 317a, 420a; iv, **706b**; v, 588b; vi, 125b, 128a, 368a, 426a, 696b, 780a; viii, 68a; ix, 785b; s, 63a, 114b, 131b, 156a, 167a, 241a, 242a, 324b, 327b, 332a, 333a, 366a, b, 423a, b
– monuments i, 1347b, 1348a; iii, 448a
Kashmīrī (language) ii, 138a; iii, 413b; iv, 707a, **711b**; xi, 472a
Kashmūla, Banū vi, 902a
al-Kashnāwī, Muḥammad (1732) iv, 773b; x, 809b
Kashshāfa iii, 185a; x, 164a
al-Kashshī, Abū ʿAmr Muḥammad b. ʿUmar (951) i, 134a, 794b; iii, 1151a; iv, **711b**; vi, 312b; viii, 517b
Ḳashtāla (Castile) iv, **712a**, 739a; v, 781b; s, 80b
al-Ḳashtālī, Aḥmad (XIV) vi, 356a
Ḳasī, Banū i, 494a, 658a; iii, 815b; iv, 477b, **712b**; v, 683a; s, 80b, 82a
Ḳāṣid → Safīr
Ḳaṣid Oghlu → Ḳāzdughliyya
Ḳaṣīda i, 583b, 586a, 592a, 601b, 668a, 671b, 676b, 677a, 1290a; ii, 293a, 1028b; iii, 1178a; iv, 57a-b, 59a-b, 65a, **713b**; v, 930b, 956a, 957a, 958b, 963a
Ḳaṣīdat al-burda i, 1011b; v, 958b, 963a; x, 346b
al-Ḳāsim (al-Muʾtamin, ʿAbbāsid) (IX) vi, 331a
al-Ḳaṣīm (Nadjd) i, 1312b, 1313a; iv, **717a**; vi, 153a; viii, 613a; s, 3b, 304b, 305a
Ḳāsim (Qassem), ʿAbd al-Karīm (1963) iii, 1259a; iv, **719a**; v, 468a, 1213b; vi, 29a; vii, 714a; viii, 446a
Ḳāsim, S.M. iv, 711a
al-Ḳāsim b. ʿAbbād (ḳāḍī) (XI) vi, 222a
al-Ḳāsim b. Aḥmad I (1638) iv, **717a**
al-Ḳāsim b. Aḥmad b. Bāyazīd (1518) iv, **716b**
al-Ḳāsim b. ʿAlī b. ʿUmar s, 48b
al-Ḳāsim b. Aṣbagh (951) i, 600a, 1150a; iii, 845a, 848a; iv, **717b**; v, 71a; vii, 400a
al-Ḳāsim b. Djihāngīr (Aḳ-ḳoyunlu) (1445) i, 311b; vi, 542b
al-Ḳāsim b. Djiryāl al-Dimashḳī s, 267a
al-Ḳāsim b. Ḥammūd (Ḥammūdid) (1021) i, 6a, 985b; iii, 147a, 786a; vi, 222a; vii, 761a
al-Ḳāsim b. Ḥasan iii, 610b; vi, 783b
al-Ḳāsim b. Ibrāhīm al-Rassī (Zaydī Imām, Yemen) (860) vi, 435b, 436b; vii, 546b, 773a, 786a; viii, 388a, 980b; x, 111b
al-Ḳāsim b. Idrīs II i, 1088a; iii, 1035b
al-Ḳāsim b. ʿĪsā al-Idjlī (840) i, 153b, 315b; ii, 623a; iv, **718a**; vii, 777a; s, 17b, 122a
al-Ḳāsim b. Ḳuṭlubugha (1474) ix, 36a
al-Ḳāsim b. Maḥfūẓ al-Baghdādī (XIII) vii, 29a
al-Ḳāsim b. Muḥammad (Ḳatar) → Djāsim b. Muḥammad
al-Ḳāsim b. Muḥammad (faḳīh) (VII) vii, 393a
al-Ḳāsim b. Muḥammad b. Abī Bakr s, **311b**
al-Ḳāsim b. Muḥammad, al-Kabīr → al-Manṣūr bi-llāh al-Kāsim b. Muḥammad
al-Ḳāsim b. Muḥammad al-Muʾayyad v, 1242a
al-Ḳāsim b. al-Rashīd iv, 859a; v, 647a
al-Ḳāsim b. ʿUbayd Allāh b. Sulaymān (vizier) (904) ii, 178a; iii, 767b, 892b, 908a; iv, 110a, 293b; v, 621b; vii, 543a, 679a; ix, 594b; s, 118a

al-Ḳāsim b. ʿUmar iii, 651b
al-Ḳāsim b. ʿUmar (amīr) ii, 635b
al-Ḳāsim b. Yūsuf b. al-Ḳāsim iii, 309a
al-Ḳāsim Agha (XVII) iv, **719b**; v, 257a
Ḳāsim ʿAlī (painter) i, 1211b, 1213a
Ḳāsim ʿAlī, Mīr (1777) i, 1357b; ii, 1091b; iii, 61a; vii, **573a**; viii, 573a
Ḳāsim Amīn (1908) i, 597a; ii, 423a; iii, 59a, 360a, 593a; iv, **720a**; vi, 220a, 470a, 957b; vii, 901a; s, 244b
Ḳāsim-i Anwar (1433) ii, 19a; iv, 66a, **721a**, 1073b; viii, 540a
Ḳāsim Arslān (1587) s, **511b**
Ḳāsim Barīd (Barīd Shāhī) (1504) i, 1047a, b, 1200a; iii, 15a, 421a; vi, 63a, b
Ḳāsim Beg ii, 529b; iv, 594a, 624a, b
Ḳāsim Čelebi b. Bāyazīd (1417) iv, **716b**
Ḳāsim al-Dawla al-Bursuḳī → Āḳ Sunḳur al-Bursuḳī
Ḳāsim Djān, Munshī i, 72a
Ḳāsim Djānbulāt (Jumblat) → Djānbulāt, Shaykh Ḳāsim
Ḳāsim Gannūn (Djannūn) iii, 1036b
Ḳāsim Ghanī iii, 55a, 56b
Ḳāsim al-Ḳaysī (XX) vi, 614a
Ḳāsim Khān (XVI) vii, 330a; s, 167b
Ḳāsim Khān Mīr Baḥr (Afshar) i, 240a; iv, 709a; s, 132a, 167b
Ḳāsim Khān (Tatar) i, 721b; iv, 723a, 849a
Ḳāsim al-Khaṣāṣī → al-Khaṣāṣī
Ḳāsim Pasha ii, 813a
Ḳāsim Pasha, Djazarī (1485) iv, **722a**; vi, 1025b
Ḳāsim Pasha, Ewliyā (1485) iv, **722a**
Ḳāsim Pasha, Güzeldje (1552) iv, 233a, **722b**; vii, 239b; ix, 896a
Ḳāsim al-Rassī b. Ṭabāṭabā vi, 433a; ix, 507a
Ḳāsim-Shāh iv, 201b; v, 26a
Ḳāsim Shaykh (XVI) xi, 115b
al-Ḳāsim al-Wāthiḳ iii, 147b
Ḳāsim Yughayta ii, 330b
Ḳāsim Yūsuf → Ḳāsim Čelebi
Ḳāsim al-Zarhūnī (1550) vi, 894a
Ḳāsimī, Āl → al-Ḳawāsim, Āl
Ḳāsimī, Djamāl al-Dīn (1914) iv, 159a; vi, 360a, b; viii, 906b
Ḳāsimī, Shaykh Ṣaḳr b. Muḥammad s, 418a 418a, b
Ḳāsimī, Shaykh Ṣaḳr b. Sulṭān s, 418a
Ḳāsimī Gunabādī (1574) iii, 114a; viii, 775a
Ḳāsimiyya (Egypt) ii, 233a; iii 300a; iv, **722b**; vi, 319a, 325a, b, 327b
Ḳāsimiyya (Yemen) iii, 255a; vi, 436b
Ḳāsimov ii, 44b; iv, **723a**, 849a, b; v, 721b
Kāsi̊mpasha (Istanbul) vi, 57a, 587b, 588a, b; viii, 317a; s, 314b, 315b
al-Ḳaṣīr (monastery) iii, 78a
al-Ḳaṣīr, ʿAbd al-Raḥmān b. Aḥmad b. (1180) vi, 111a
al-Kasirḳī → Nūr al-Dīn ʿAbd al-Raḥmān al-Kasirḳī
Ḳāsiyūn, Djabal iv, **724a**; vi, 599b; vii, 558b; s, 197a
Kaskar iv, **724b**; xi, 166a
al-Kaskarī, Isrāʾīl (872) vii, 1031b
Ḳaṣr s, **512a**
Kasr (fraction) iv, **725a**, 731b
Ḳaṣr (palace) iv, 236b
Ḳaṣr ʿAbd al-Karīm → al-Ḳaṣr al-Kabīr
Ḳaṣr Abī Dānis ii, 1009b; s, **513b**
Ḳaṣr al-Abyaḍ → Khirbat al-Bayḍāʾ
Ḳaṣr Adjwad b. Zamīl s, 234b
Ḳaṣr al-Aghāliba → al-ʿAbbāsiyya (Ifrīḳiya)
Ḳaṣr al-Amīr vi, 455b
Ḳaṣr al-ʿAynī v, 907b; x, 416a; s, 38a
Ḳaṣr Banī Muḳātil x, 791b
Ḳaṣr Baḥr → Ḳaṣr al-Mulk
Ḳaṣr Burḳuʿ vii, 944b; s, 117a
Ḳaṣr Firʿawn → Walīla/Walīlī
Ḳaṣr al-Ḥallābāt s, 117a
Ḳaṣr al-Ḥasanī i, 897b, 898a, 1312b; iii, 243b
Ḳaṣr al-Ḥayr al-Gharbī i, 613a; ii, 557a, 1021a; iii, 71a, 141b, 310a, 494b; iv, **726a**; vi, 680a; viii, 452a; s, 117a
Ḳaṣr al-Ḥayr al-Sharḳi i, 613a, 613b, 831a; iii, 71a, 494b; iv, **727b**, 1011b; s, 117a
Ḳaṣr Hishām → Khirbat al-Mafdjar
Ḳaṣr Ibn Abī Aḥmad vi, 457a
Ḳaṣr Ibn Hubayra iii, 265b, 266a; iv, **728b**; vii, 836a; xi, 249b
Ḳaṣr Ibrīm vi, 574b; vii, 545a; viii, 90a
al-Ḳaṣr al-Kabīr (Alcazarquivir) i, 706b; iii, 62b; iv, **729a**; v, 1191a; vi, 741b, 743a
Ḳaṣr al-Ḳadīm → al-ʿAbbāsiyya (Ifrīḳiya)
Ḳaṣr al-Kawkab iv, 479b
Ḳaṣr Kharāna → Kharāna
Ḳaṣr Kutāma → al-Ḳaṣr al-Kabīr

Ḳaṣr al-Luṣūṣ → Kinkiwar
Ḳaṣr al-Madjāz → al-Ḳaṣr al-Ṣaghīr
Ḳaṣr al-Mannār iv, 479b; vi, 427a
Ḳaṣr Maṣmūda → al-Ḳaṣr al-Ṣaghīr
Ḳaṣr al-Mulk iv, 479b
Ḳaṣr al-Mushāsh s, **514a**
al-Ḳaṣr al-Ṣaghīr i, 56a, 706b; iv, **729b**; v, 1190b; vi, 741b; viii, 723b
Ḳaṣr al-Salām (al-Raḳḳa) iv, 479b; viii, 411a
Ḳaṣr al-Shawḳ s, 44a
Ḳaṣr Ṭūbā s, **514b**
Ḳaṣr Yānī → Kaṣryānnih
Kasra iii, 172b; iv, **731a**
Ḳaṣrān v, 661b
Kasrānī i, 1007b
Kasrawī Tabrīzī, Aḥmad (1946) ii, 882b; iii, 114a; iv, 166b, **732a**, 789b; v, 1097b, 1098a
al-Ḳasrī, Asad b. ʿAbd Allāh (VIII) i, **684b**; ii, 608b; 1010b; iii, 223b, 224a; vii, 1016a; viii, 1026a (see also *s.v.* Asad b. ʿAbd Allāh al-Kasrī)
al-Ḳaṣrī, Khālid b. ʿAbd Allāh (vizier) (738) vii, 75b
al-Ḳaṣrī, Muḥammad b. Khālid b. ʿAbd Allāh (VIII) vii, 798b
Ḳaṣr-i Aḥnaf → Marw al-Rūdh
Ḳaṣr-i Shīrīn i, 624a, 1345b; ii, 793b, 794a; iv, **730b**; vi, 56b
Ḳaṣryānnih iv, **733a**; ix, 584b
Ḳāṣṣ iv, **733b**; v, 186a, b, 187a, 951a; vi, 468a; ix, 552b
Ḳaṣṣāb, Ḥaydar-i (Sarbadārid) (XIV) ix, 48b
Kassāḥ → Kannās
Kassala → Kasala
Ḳassām ii, 483a; iii, 128b; iv, **735b**; vi, 4b
Ḳassām (rebel) i, 824a, b; iii, 841a; s, 37a
Ḳaṣṣār → Ghassāl
al-Ḳaṣṣār, Abū ʿAbd Allāh (1531) iv, **736a**
Ḳaṣṣāra, Abu 'l-Ḥusayn ʿAlī (1843) iv, **736b**
al-Ḳaṣṣāriyya vi, 224b
al-Ḳaṣṣāṣīn s, 300b
Ḳaṣṣārī iii, 132a
(al-)Ḳasṭal s, 230a, **514b**
al-Ḳasṭallānī, Abu 'l-ʿAbbās Aḥmad b. Muḥammad (1517) i, 1297a; iv, **736b**; v, 398b; vi, 87b, 112a
Ḳasṭallānī (Kestelī), Muṣliḥ al-Dīn Muṣṭafā (1495) iv, **737a**; vii, 272b
al-Ḳasṭallī, Abū ʿAmr vi, 350a
Kastamonu → Ḳasṭamūnī
Ḳasṭamūnī iv, 108b, **737a**; v, 693b, 966b, 977b, 1145b; vi, 69a, 120b; s, 274a
Ḳasṭīlya (Castille) → Ḳashtāla
Ḳasṭīliya (Ilbīra) iii, 1110a; iv, **739a**
Ḳasṭīliya (Tunisia) ii, 462b, 463a; iv, **739b**; vi, 435a; x, 789b, 790a (see also *s.v.* Djarīd, Bilād al-)
Kastoria → Kesriye
Kastriota, George → Iskender Beg
Ḳasṭūn ii, 484a; vi, 507a
Ḳaṣūr ii, 929a; viii, 256a
Ḳāt iv, **741a**
Ḳaṭʿ iv, **741b**
Ḳaṭʿ al-Ṭarīḳ → Ḳatl; Sariḳa; Ṣuʿlūk
Ḳaṭā iii, 573a; iv, **743a**
Ḳaṭā Sarāy iv, 579b
Ḳaʿṭaba iv, **745b**
Ḳatabān i, 548a, 1132b; iii, 208a; iv, **746a**; vi, 560b, 561a; viii, 350a
Katāda, Banū iii, 261b, 881a; ix, 507a
Ḳatāda b. Diʿāma (735) i, 104b; iv, 370b, **748b**; v, 1232a; viii, 853a; s, 755a
Ḳatāda b. Idrīs, Sharīf (Abū ʿUzaiyyiz) (1221) i, 552b, 1032a; iii, 262b; iv, **748b**; vi, 433b; vii, 998b
Ḳatāda b. Mūsā II b. ʿAbd Allāh (Sharīf) vi, 149a
Ḳatāda b. Salāma al-Ḥanafī iv, 832a
Katahr iv, **749a**; viii, 571b, 572b; s, 73b, 206b
Ḳaṭāʾiʿ ii, 187b; iv, 323a, b, **754b**, 973a, 1031a; v, 23a, 347a
al-Ḳaṭāʾiʿ i, 279a; ii, 958b, 959a
Katak → Orissa
Kataman v, 21b
Ḳaṭāmi bint al-Shidjna iii, 887a, 888a
Ḳaṭʿān b. Salma al-Zawāghī (811) vi, 840b
Katanga ii, 58b; iv, **749b**
Ḳataniya → Ṣiḳiliyya
Ḳaṭar i, 536a, 539b, 941a, 944a; ii, 177a; iv, **750b**, 953b; v, 1058a; vi, 37a, b, 358a; vii, 301b, 449b; xi, 547a; s, 417a, b
Ḳaṭarī b. al-Fudjāʾa (Azraḳī) (697) i, 686b, 810b; iii, 40b; iv, 207b, 269a, **752b**, 938a, 1075b; v, 157b; vii, 357b; x, 124b
Katavolenos, Thomas vi, 70b
Katbughā → Kitbughā

Kateb Yacine (XX) vi, 754a
al-Katf al-Buṣrī vi, 548a
Kā<u>th</u> ii, 1142a; iv, **753b**, 1063b, 1064b, 1066b; vi, 340a; ix, 220b
Kathāwat s, 325a
Ka<u>th</u>īr, Banū vi, 82b, 83b
Ka<u>th</u>īr al-Nawwā' s, 129b
Ka<u>th</u>īr b. Saʿd v, 2a, b
Ka<u>th</u>īrī, Āl iii, 291b; iv, 10a; v, 184a; vi, 132b; vii, 496a; ix, 115a; xi, 235b; s, 337b, 338b; s, **515a**, 542b
Ḳāṫhiyāwār → <u>D</u>junagaṙh
Ka<u>th</u>rā x, 788b
Katī ii, 31a, 138b; iv, 409b, 410b
Ḳāṭiʿ, ʿAlī Afḍal (XVI) viii, 784b
Kaʿti, Maḥmūd (Souinke) (1593) iv, **754a**
Ḳaṭīʿa → Ḳaṭāʾiʿ
Kātib i, 981b; ii, 324b; iii, 740a, 1242b; iv, **754b**; v, 1238b
Kātib Čelebi (1657) i, 478b, 594b, 698a, 758a, 1198a; ii, 110a, 589a, 590a; iv, 168a, **760b**, 1082b; vi, 352b, 906a; vii, 48b, 917b; s, 171b, 289b
Kātib Ferdī (1537) ii, 879b; vi, 542b
Kātib al-Iṣfahānī → ʿImād al-Dīn al-Kātib al-Iṣfahānī
al-Katība iv, 1139b, 1141a, b
al-Kātiba, Munya xi, 160b
al-Kātibī, Na<u>dj</u>m al-Dīn Dabīrān (1276) iv, **762a**
Kātibī, <u>Sh</u>ams al-Dīn (1435) iv, **762b**
Kātib-i Rūmī → Sīdī (ʿAlī) Reʾīs
Kātibzāde Meḥmed Refīʿ iv, 1126a
al-Ḳaṭīf i, 73a, 942b; ii, 452b; iv, **763b**; vi, 735a; vii, 301b, 859a; x, 960a; s, 234a
Katif, ʿIlm al- iv, **763a**
Ḳaṭīfe iii, 216b, 217b
al-Ḳaṭīfī, Ibrāhīm b. Sulaymān (XVI) iv, 610a; s, **516b**
al-Ḳaṭīʿī → Abū Bakr al-Ḳaṭīʿī
al-Ḳaṭīʿī al-Ba<u>gh</u>dādī iii, 756a
Ḳatīl, Mīrzā iii, 1244b
Katīn → <u>Kh</u>ātūn (title)
Ḳaṭirān → Ḳaṭrān
Ḳātir iii, 1105b, 1106a
Ḳāṭi̊r<u>dj</u>ī-ogh<u>l</u>i̊ Meḥmed Pa<u>sh</u>a (1668) i, 4b; iii, 317b; iv, **765b**
Ḳaṭʿiyya iv, 743a
Kat<u>kh</u>udā → Ket<u>kh</u>udā
Kat<u>kh</u>udā Marzubān i, 955b
Kat<u>kh</u>udā Pa<u>sh</u>a → Ibrāhīm Pa<u>sh</u>a Kat<u>kh</u>udā
Ḳatl iv, **766b**; x, 406b
Ḳaṭlān, ʿAbd al-Fattāḥ (1931) viii, 907a
Kator → Kāfiristān
Kaṫra Mīrānpūr iii, 61b
Katrabbul → Ḳuṭrabbul
Ḳaṭrān iv, **772b**; s, 320b
Ḳaṭrān, Ḥakīm (XI) iv, 61b, 525b, **773a**; vii, 498a; viii, 585b; ix, 169b
Ḳaṭrāna iii, 364b; x, 885a
Katsina iii, 275a, 276a; iv, 549b, **773b**; x, 142b
Ḳatta-Kur<u>gh</u>an i, 1296a; vi, 418a
Kattān iv, **774a**
al-Ḳaṭṭān, Yaḥyā b. Saʿīd (813) viii, 515a, 983b; ix, 771a
al-Kattānī, Āl iv, **774b**
al-Kattānī, Abū ʿAbd Allāh <u>Dj</u>aʿfar b. Idrīs (1905) iv, 774b; v, 1029b
al-Kattānī, Muḥammad b. <u>Dj</u>aʿfar (1927) iii, 468b; iv, 774b; v, 1209b; ix, 508a; x, 381b; s, 350b, 404a, b
al-Kattānī, <u>Sh</u>arīf Muḥammad al-Kabīr b. ʿAbd al-Wahhāb (XX) viii, 905b
al-Kattānī, <u>Sh</u>ay<u>kh</u> Abu 'l-Asʿad Muḥammad ʿAbd al-Ḥayy (1912) iv, 774b; viii, 905b
al-Kattānī, ʿUmar b. Ṭāhir (1891) iv, 774b
Kattāniyya viii, 905b
al-Ḳāṭūl Abi l-<u>D</u>jund viii, 1039a
al-Ḳāṭūl al-Kisrawī vii, 912b; viii, 1039a
al-Ḳāṭūl iv, 384a
Ḳaṭwān Steppe (battle) (1141) iii, 1114b; iv, 581b; ix, 16b; x, 543a
Katwar → Kāfiristān
Ḳavād<u>h</u> I ii, 439a; iii, 571b (see also *s.v.* Ḳawā<u>dh</u> I)
Kavafoğlu → Atač, Nūr Allāh
Kavakli̊ → Čakmak, Mustafa Fevzi
Kavala → Ḳawāla
Kavala <u>Sh</u>ahīn → <u>Sh</u>ahīn Pa<u>sh</u>a
Kavas → Ḳawwās
Kāveh → Kāwah
Kavol ii, 41a
Ḳavuḳ iv, 806a, b; v, 751a
Kāwa (journal) iv, 775a, 789b; x, 136a
Kāwa (Kābī) → Kāwah
Ḳawad → Ḳiṣāṣ
Ḳawā<u>dh</u> I (Sasānid) (531) i, 3a, 1041a, 1094a, 1134a; ii, 78a, 253a; iii, 571b; vi, 378b, 949a; ix, 214a, 76b; s, 127a, 297b

Ḳawādh II → Ḳubādh II
al-Ḳawādhiyān → Ḳubādhiyān
Kāwah (Kāveh) iv, **775a**; vi, 745b; xi, 554b
Ḳawāʿid Fiḳhiyya s, **517a**
al-Kawākibī, ʿAbd al-Raḥmān (1902) i, 597b; iii, 593b; iv, 143b, 144a, 145b, 151a, 159a, 162b, **775b**, 782b; vi, 360a; vii, 764b; viii, 360a, 447a, 907a; ix, 517b
al-Kawākibī, Nadjm al-Dīn (XVI) viii, 543a
Ḳawāla (Kavala) iv, **776a**; vii, 423a; xi, 66b
Ḳawām, Aḥmad Adharbāydjān (XX) i, 190b; ii, 653b; iii, 529a; v, 630b
Ḳawām al-Dīn b. Shāh Shams al-Dīn, Shāh viii, 135b
Ḳawām al-Dīn Abu l-Ḳāsim iii, 1162b
Ḳawām al-Dīn I al-Marʿashī, Sayyid (Mīr-i Buzurg) i, 237a; vi, 510b, 511a, 512a, b, 515a, b
Ḳawām al-Dīn II b. Riḍā al-Dīn (Marʿashī) (1407) vi, 512b, 513a, b
Ḳawām al Dīn al-Mulk iii, 1106a; v, 674b
Ḳawām al-Dīn Zawzanī iv, 1034b
Ḳawām al-Salṭana (XX) viii, 512a; xi, 221b
Kawār i, 1221b; iv, 567a, **777a**; vi, 384a; x, 789b
al-Ḳawārīrī, ʿUbayd Allāh b. ʿAmr (849) vii, 691a
al-Ḳawāsim, Āl i, 928a, 1282a; ii, 619a; iv, 751a, **777b**; v,70b, 183b, 507b, 508a, 765a; vi, 735a, b; viii, 435a, 436a; s, 42a
Ḳawāsma, Banū viii, 91a
al-Kawfanī → al-Abīwardī
Kāwī → Kāwah
Kawīr s, 61a
Kawīr, Dasht-i iv, 2a, b, 9b; viii, 694b; xi, 238a
Kawkab → Nudjūm
Kawkab al-Hawāʾ iv, **778b**; v, 120b
Kawkabān iii, 134a; iv, **779a**; vi, 433b, 434a, 436b
Kawkaw → Gao
Ḳawlīs i, 323a; v, 818b
Ḳawm iii, 411a; iv, **780b**, 785b
Ḳawm (military) → Gūm
al-Ḳawmā → al-Ḳūmā
Ḳawmiyya iv, **781a**; vi, 586a; x, 908a; xi, 175b; s, 240a (see also *s.vv.* Pan-arabism; Waṭaniyya)
Kawn wa-fasād iv, **794b**
Kawōm → Ḳawm
al-Kawr i, 536a, b
Kawr al-ʿAwd i, 766b
Kawr ʿAwdhilla i, 766b, 1023b, 1132b (see also *s.v.* ʿAwdhalī)
Kawr al-ʿAwāliḳ i, 536a
Ḳawriya → Ḳūriya
Ḳaws ii, 506b; iii, 469b, 470a, 476a; iv, **795b**
Ḳaws Ḳuzaḥ iv, **803a**; v, 700a; vii, 825a
Ḳawṣara ii, 526a; iv, **805a**; v, 503a
Ḳawṣūn al-Nāṣirī (Miṣr) (1342) vi, 323a, b; vii, 170b, 992a; viii, 432a
al-Kawthar ii, 448b; iii, 286a; iv, **805b**; x, 788b
Kawtharī (Hamadān) (1606) viii, 776a
Kawthariyya viii, 46b
Ḳawuḳlu iv, **806a**; viii, 179a
Ḳāwurd b. Čaghrï Beg Dāwūd (amīr) (Kirmān) (1074) i, 420a, 552a, 664b, 665a; iii, 195a, 507a, 1097b, 1098a; iv, 26b, 27b, 101a, **807a**; v, 158b, 353a; vi, 273b; vii, 193a; viii, 70a, 945b, 946a; s, 127a
*Kāwūs (Sāsānid) i, 241a; vi, 632a, 745a; x, 925a
Kāwūs, Banū iv, **808a**; vi, 938b
Kāwūs b. K(G)ayūmarth (1467) iv, 808a; v, 663a; vi, 513a
al-Ḳawwāmī, Badr al-Dīn (XII) viii, 582a
Ḳawwās iv, **808b**
al-Ḳawwās (1591) vi, 112a
al-Ḳawwās Bagdādī iii, 109a
Kaya → Ketkhudā
Kayalars v, 582a
Ḳayalïḳ iv, **808b**; viii, 317b
Kayānīds i, 236b; iii, 113a; iv, 12b, 128a, **809a**; ix, 75a, 76a (see also *s.vv.* Kay Kāʾūs; Kay Khusraw; Kay Ḳubād)
Kaybar (battle) (1029) vii, 117a
al-Kayd iv, **809b**, 1186a
al-Ḳayd iii, 208a
Kaydaḳ → Ḳaytaḳ
Ḳaydū (Tīmūrid) i, 1133b
Ḳaydu Khān b. Ḳashi (Mongol) (1303) i, 504b, 1311b, 1312a; ii, 3a, b, 45a, b; iv, 808b, **811b**; v, 39a, 300a; vi, 420a, 782b, 783a; s, 240a
Ḳayghusuz Abdāl (1415) iv, **811b**; viii, 2b

Kaygili, ʿOthmān Djemāl (1945) iv, **812a**; s, 64b
Ḳāyi, Banū ii, 1128a; iv, **812b**; viii, 181b; x, 689b
Ḳayib Khān i, 1076b
Ḳāyināt iv, 4a, b
Kayir Buḳu Khān s, 246a
Ḳayir Tigin → Ḳaratigin
Ḳayir Toḳu Khān (XII) ix, 558a
Ḳayitbāy → Ḳāʾitbāy (Mamlūk)
Kaykāʾūs I b. Kaykhusraw I (Rūm Saldjūḳ) (1220) i, 313a, 336b, 467a, 510a; ii, 37b, 966b; iii, 708a; iv, 575b, **813b**; vi, 381a, 632a; viii, 15b, 949a
Kaykāʾūs II ʿIzz al-Dīn (Rūm Saldjūḳ) (1279) i, 1188b, 1302b; ii, 204b, 610b, 971a, 1006b; iv, 600b, **813b**; v, 104b, 254a, 286a; vi, 420b, 507b; vii, 479b; viii, 949b, 975a
Kaykaʾūs (Kayānid) iv, 809a, **813a**
Kaykāʾūs b. Iskandar (Ziyārid) (XI) iv, **815a**; vi, 761b; vii, 987b; s, 96b, 429a, b
Kaykāʾūs Shāh (Bengal) (1301) ix, 83b
Kay Khusraw (Kayānid) i, 236b; iv, 809a, **815b**; ix, 696b
Kay Khusraw I b. Ḳilidj Arslān II (Rūm Saldjūḳ) (1211) i, 346a, 466b, 517b; ii, 111a; iii, 708a; iv, **816a**, 1061b; vi, 507a
Kay Khusraw II b. Kayḳubād I, Ghiyāth al-Dīn (Rūm Saldjūḳ) (1245) i, 432a, 467a, 838b; ii, 38a; iv, **816b**; v, 271b, 286a, b; vi, 528a; vii, 193a, 479a, 990b; viii, 949a, 975a
Kay Khusraw III b. Rukn al-Dīn Ḳilidj Arslān (Rūm Saldjūḳ) (1284) i, 703a; iv, 620b, **817a**; viii, 15b
Kay-Khusraw b. Maḥmūd Shāh (Īndjūʾid) (1338) iii, 1208a, b; vii, 820a
Kay Ḳubād (Kayānid) iv, 809a; viii, 637a
Kayḳubād I ʿAlāʾ al-Dīn (Rūm Saldjūḳ) (1237) i, 329a, 354b, 355a, 424b, 467a, 510a, 665a, 799b, 1191b; ii, 38a, 444b, 692a, 710b, 711b; iii, 215b, 738a; iv, 521a, **817b**, 818b, 1006b, 1084b; v, 255a, 285b; vi, 381a; vii, 273b, 871a; viii, 949a, 975a
Kayḳubād II b. Kaykhusraw I (Rūm Saldjūḳ) (1257) iv, **818a**; ix, 12b
Kayḳubād III (Rūm Saldjūḳ) (1303) i, 467b; ii, 201a; iv, **818a**; viii, 949b
Kayḳubād, Muʿizz al-Dīn (Dihlī) (1290) i, 444b; ii, 256b, 268a; iv, **818a**, 920b; s, 73b
Kayḳubādiyya iv, **818b**
Ḳayl iv, **818b**; ix, 675b
Kayl → Makāyīl
Ḳayla i, 697a
Ḳayla bt. Kāhil b. ʿUdhra x, 774a
Ḳayla, Banū i, 514a, 771a, 772a; v, 995a; vi, 477a
Kaylif → Kālif
Kay-Luhrāsb → Kayānids
Kaylūkarī s, 243b
Kaymak → Kīmāk
Ḳaymāz, Ḳutb al-Dīn (amīr) (1175) iii, 891b; vii, 707a, 726b
Ḳaymaz Kāfūrī → Ṣārim al-Dīn Ḳaymaz Kāfūrī al-Manbidjī
Ḳaymaz al-Zaynī, Mudjāhid al-Dīn (1198) viii, 127a
Ḳayn iv, **819a**
Ḳayn, Banu ʾl- i, 684b; iv, **819b**; ix, 673a
Ḳayna i, 32b; ii, 551b, 1073b; iv, **820b**; vi, 468a; s, 247a
Ḳaynuḳāʿ, Banū i, 53a; ii, 363b; iv, **824a**; v, 996a; vii, 367a, 370a, 561b; viii, 871a
Kayor, Kingdom of s, 179b
Kayra ii, 122a, b, 124b
al-Ḳayrawān i, 77b, 86b, 125a, 134b, 163b, 248a, 249a, 532b, 1175a; iii, 386a, 655a, 903b; iv, 479a, 532b, **824b**; v, 518a, 877b, 1159a; vi, 120b, 188b, 297b, 280b, 311b, 312a, 364a, 404b, 426b, 434b, 441a, 606a, 648b, 712b, 727a; viii, 843b; x, 790a; s, 26b, 62b, 103a, 144a, b, 145a, 172b, 274a, 303b, 306a, b, 394b
– constructions i, 457b, 624a, 1346a; ii, 863a, iii, 287b; iv, 825b, 828b-831b
– great mosque i, 248b, 619b, 621a, 950a; ii, 746a; iii, 271b; iv, 829b, 1165b; v, 220b
al-Ḳayrawānī → Ibn Abī Zayd
al-Ḳayrawānī, Abū Bakr Muḥammad b. al-Labbād (944) ix, 182a
al-Ḳays → Ḳaws Ḳuzaḥ
al-Ḳays (island) → Kīsh (Ḳays, Djabal)
al-Ḳays (ḳāḍī) (Fusṭāṭ) (643) vi, 671a
al-Ḳays b. Abī Ḥazim (703) vii, 576a
al-Ḳays b. Abī Muslim al-Māṣir (VII) vii, 605b
al-Ḳays b. ʿAmr al-Nadjāshī s, 10a
al-Ḳays b. ʿĀṣim iii, 1022b; iv, **832a**; xi, 496a; s, 693a

al-Ḳays b. al-Haytham al-Sulamī i, 47b, 1001a; iv, 14b
al-Ḳays b. Hubayra b. ʿAbd Yaghūth (VII) i, 110b; vii, 592a
Ḳays b. al-Ḥudādiyya ix, 864b
al-Ḳays b. al-Ḥusayn iii, 223b
al-Ḳays b. al-Imām Aḥmad i, 1282a; s, 355b
al-Ḳays b. al-Khaṭīm (620) iii, 272a, 941a; iv, **835b**; vi, 708a; vii, 65b; viii, 1041b
al-Ḳays b. Maʿdīkarib i, 689b, 696b; v, 119a
al-Ḳays b. al-Makshūḥ al-Murādī i, 110b, 728a; iv, 1134b; vii, 592a; s, 693b
al-Ḳays b. Masʿūd al-Shaybānī i, 690a
al-Ḳays b. Muḥammad al-Ḥirāmī ii, 517b
al-Ḳays b. al-Mulawwaḥ (VII) v, 1102b; viii, 78a; x, 775a
al-Ḳays b. al-Muntafiḳ vii, 582a
al-Ḳays b. Saʿd i, 44a; iii, 241a, b, 242a
al-Ḳays b. Salāma b. al-Ḥārith i, 527a; iii, 1177b; v, 118b
al-Ḳays b. Thaʿlaba, Banū i, 73a, 963b, 964a; x, 219a, 400b
al-Ḳays b. Yarwātiḳ (961) vii, 613a
al-Ḳays b. Zuhayr b. Djadhīma al-ʿAbsī i, 115b; ii, 873a, 1023a; s, 177a, b, 178a
al-Ḳays ʿAbd al-Rashīd (Pashtūn) i, 218b; xi, 494b
Ḳays Aylān, Banū i, 76b, 329a, 529b 532a, 544b, 643a, 1241b; ii, 89a, 327b; iii, 1255a; iv, 314b, 493a, 494b, **833b**; vi, 221b, 265b, 266a, b, 303a, 333a, b, 334a, 345b, 544b, 545a, 546b, 620b, 622a; ix, 817a; x, 116a
Ḳaysaba b. Kulthūm xi, 63b; s, 37b
Kaysān b. al-Muʿarraf al-Hudjaymī, Abū Sulaymān (VII) iii, 820b
Kaysān Abū ʿAmra (VII) iv, 836a, b; vii, 523a; ix, 422a
Kaysāniyya i, 850b; ii, 1094b; iii, 1265b; iv, **836b**, 1086b; v, 350a, 433b, 552a, 1235b; xi, 294b; s, 357b
Ḳayṣar iv, **839a**
Ḳayṣar, Banū i, 928a
Ḳayṣar Shāh b. Zamān i, 230b
al-Ḳaysarānī, Abu ’l-Faḍl b. Ṭāhir → Ibn al-Ḳaysarānī, Abu ’l-Faḍl
al-Ḳaysarī, Dāwūd b. Maḥmūd (1350) iii, 709a; v, 545a; x, 322a; s, 364a, b
Ḳaysāriyya iv, **840a**
Ḳayṣariyya (Caesarea) iii, 475b; iv, **841a**; vi, 322a
Ḳayṣariyya (Kayseri) iv, 623b, **842b**; v, 1145a, b; vi, 230b, 322a, 505b; s, 146a, 274a
Ḳaysar-nāma s, 41a
Kayseri → Ḳayṣariyya
Ḳaysī, Abū ʿAbd Allāh Muḥammad b. Djaʿfar (1172) x, 346a
Ḳaysīs s, 82a
Kaysūm (Keysun) i, 761b; vi, 334a, 336b, 506b, 507a; vii, 1016b; xi, 464a; s, **518a**
Ḳaysūn i, 1190b; viii, 130a
Ḳayt al-Radjabī iv, 552a
Ḳaytaḳ (Kaytagh) ii, 86b, 89a, 141b; iv, 345b, 350b, **846a**, 1176b
Ḳaytās Bey i, 56a, 395a
Ḳayṭās Pasha ix, 254b
Ḳāytbāy → Ḳāʾitbāy
Kayūmarth b. Bīstutūn iv, 808a
Kayūmarth, Shams al-Dīn → Gayōmard, Shams al-Dīn
Kayūs b. Ḳubād i, 1110a
Kayūsiyya (Bāwand) i, 1110a; viii, 383a
al-Kayyāl, Aḥmad b. Zakariyyāʾ iv, **847a**
Ḳayyān iv, 822b
Kayyarā s, 101b
al-Ḳayyāra iii, 1022b
Ḳayyim iv, **847b**
Ḳayyūm Nāṣirī (1902) iv, **848a**
Ḳāz → Ḳabḳ
Kaza → Ḳaḍāʾ
Kaza → Khāsa
Ḳazaghān iv, 32a
Ḳazaḳ i, 120b, 135b, 268a, 418b, 481a, 722a, 1076b, 1077a, 1252a, 1287a; ii, 25a, 44b, 446a, 613a, 995b, 1066b; iii, 116b, 531b; iv, 40a, 178b-179a, 512b, 611a, **848a**; v, 134b, 135a; vi, 415a, 416b, 457a, 768b; vii, 353a; s, 169a
– literature x, **729a**
Kazākhstān ii, 44b; v, 135b; vi, 417a, 768b; x, 677b, 680b; s, **518b**
Kazalinsk iv, 1065a; ix, 660a; s, 244b
Ḳāzān i, 1075b, 1108a, 1308a; ii, 44b, 179a, 1113a; iv, 280b, 723b, **849a**; s, 82a, b, 96b
Ḳazan Khān (Čaghatay) (1347) ii, 4a; vii, 925a, 933b
Kāzarān s, 73a

Kāzarūn (Kāzirūn) i, 240a; iv, **850b**; vi, 494a
al-Kāzarūnī, ʿAbd Allāh (Diyār Bakr) (XI) vi, 626b, 930b
Kāzarūnī, Shaykh Abū Isḥāḳ (1033) i, 147a, 162b, 1129a, 1245b; iv, **851a**; v, 1112a
Ḳāzbēgī → Sikka
Kazbek → Ḳabḳ
al-Ḳāzdughlī, Ibrāhīm Kahyā (Miṣr) (1754) iv, 852a, b; vii, 179a
al-Ḳāzdughlī, Muṣṭafā ii, 233b; iv, 852a
Ḳāzdughliyya ii, 233b; iv, **852a**; vi, 325b; vii, 420a
Kāzh → Kāth
Kazi-asker → Ḳāḍī ʿAskar
Ḳāzī-Ḳūmuḳ → Lak
Kazi Mulla → Ghāzī Muḥammad
al-Kāẓim → Mūsā al-Kāẓim
Kāzim, Bā i, 767a
Kāẓim Bey, Mīrzā s, 76a
Ḳāẓim Ḳadrī, Ḥusayn (934) iv, **853a**
Kāẓim Karabekir Pasha (1948) i, 641b; ii, 6b; iv, 671a, **853b**; x, 418a
Kāẓim Rashtī, Sayyid (1843) iv, 51a, **854a**; v, 502a; vii, 422a, 440b, 454b; ix, 404a
Kāẓimayn (Kāẓimiyya) i, 903b; iv, **854b**; vi, 551a, 797a; vii, 397a, 485a; s, 57a, 77a, 94a, 95a
Kāẓimī → Sikka
al-Kāẓimī, ʿAbd al-Muḥsin (1935) iv, **856a**; ix, 230a
al-Kāẓimī, ʿAbd al-Nabī b. ʿAlī (1840) iv, **856b**
al-Kāẓimī, Ḥaydar b. Ibrāhīm (1849) iv, **856b**
al-Kāẓimī, Meḥmed Sālim (1914) iv, **857a**
al-Kāẓimī, Murtaḍā Mushfiḳ iv, 72b; v, 198b
Kāẓimiyya → Kāẓimayn
Kazimov → Ḳāsimov
Kazirūn → Kāzarūn
Ḳazwīn i, 8b, 688b; iv, 7b, 857b; v, **875b**; vi, 56b, 64a, 271a, b, 333a, 365a, 366a, 494a, 511b, 512b, 515a, b, 516a, 525b, 715a; viii, 115b, 389a; s, 43b, 83b, 84a, 139a, 336a, 423a
– monuments iv, 862b
al-Ḳazwīnī, ʿAbd al-Djalīl s, 56b
al-Ḳazwīnī, Abū Ḥātim Maḥmūd (XI) iv, **863a**; vii, 200a
al-Ḳazwīnī, Djalāl al-Dīn Abū ʿAbd Allāh (Khaṭīb Dimashḳ) (1338) i, 858a, 982b, 1116a; ii, 824a; iv, **863b**; v, 898a, b, 900b; vii, 277b, 388a, 537a; viii, 894a
al-Ḳazwīnī, Djalāl al-Dīn Zakariyyāʾ (XV) vii, 988a
al-Ḳazwīnī, Ḥamd Allāh → Ḥamd Allāh Mustawfī
al-Ḳazwīnī, Khalīl (1677) viii, 779a
al-Ḳazwīnī, Nadjm al-Dīn ʿAbd al-Ghaffār (1266) iv, 509b, **864b**
al-Ḳazwīnī, Sayyid Mahdī s, 135a
al-Ḳazwīnī, Shāh Ṭāhir b. Shāh Raḍī al-Dīn (1549) vii, 300a; viii, 389a
al-Ḳazwīnī, Zakariyyāʾ b. Muḥammad (1283) i, 157a, 204a, 419b, 571a, 594b, 836a; ii, 587b; iii, 30a, 313a, 991b; iv, **865a**, 1081b; vi, 185b, 218b, 374b, 501b, 904a; s, 128b
Kazzāz (Iran) i, 1117a; iii, 1102b; ix, 859b
al-Ḳazzāz, Abū ʿAbd Allāh Muḥammad b. ʿUbāda (1021) iv, **867a**; vii, 483b, 811b
al-Ḳazzāz → Ḥakam b. Saʿīd al-Ḳazzāz
al-Ḳazzāz, Muḥammad b. Djaʿfar iii, 936a
al-Ḳazzāz, Muḥammad b. ʿUbāda iii, 855b; vii, 811b
al-Ḳbāb (Fès) vi, 123b
Kebbawa ii, 1144b, 1146a; viii, 20b
Kebbi (Nigeria) ii, 942a, 1144b; iv, 549a; viii, 20a, b
Kebek Khān (Čaghatay) (1326) ii, 4a, 14b, 45a; iv, 419a, 671b, 921b; v, 858b; vii, 925a
Kebra Nagast i, 1220a
Kēč → Kīdj/Kīz
Kēč Makrān → Makrān
Keče → Libās
Kečedjīzāde → Fuʾād Pasha Kečedjīzāde; ʿIzzet Mollā
Kechla i, 689a
Kēčī i, 1007a
Kečiboynuzu Ibrāhīm Ḥilmī Pasha (1825) iv, 569b, **867b**
Kĕdah iii, 1218a, 1219b; iv, 467b; vi, 232b, 234a, 236b; viii, 275b, 276a, 286a (see also *s.v.* Kalah (Kalāh))
Kediri v, 1155a, b; s, 202a
Kĕdjuruns i, 740a
Kef, le- → al-Kāf
Kefalia Shahīn → Shahīn Pasha

Kefe iii, 44a, b; iv, 576a, **868a**, 892a; v, 141a; viii, 480a
Kel Ḥasan iv, 806b
Kelantan iii, 385a; vi, 212b, 232b, 236a, b, 241a; viii, 275b, 276a, 286a
Kelāt → Kalāt
Keldibek iii, 117a
Kelek i, 424a, 476a; iv, **870a**; viii, 810b
Kelesh-beg (Prince) i, 101a
Kēlvē-Māhīm → Māhīm
Kemākh iv, **870b**
Kemāl, ʿAlī (1922) iv, **871b**
Kemāl, Meḥmed Nāmiḳ (1888) i, 61b, 62a, 74b, 630b; ii, 430b, 473b, 474a, 682a, 692b, 878a, 1047a; iii, 592a; iv, **875a**; v, 1172b; vi, 68b, 69a, 92b, 372b, 373a, 610a; vii, 599b; ix, 240b, 443b; s, 98a, 324b
Kemāl al-Dīn → Kamāl al-Dīn
Kemāl Pasha-zāde (1534) i, 89a, 698a, 1208a; ii, 552b, 997b, 1137a; iii, 164a, 596b, 708b; iv, 333b, **879b**; vi, 227a, 609b, 724b; vii, 225a; viii, 44a; ix, 401b
Kemāl Reʾīs (1511) ii, 588a; iv, **881b**; v, 506b; vii, 1038a; viii, 308a, b
Kemāl Tahir (Demir) (1973) iv, **882a**; v, 197a, 282b
Kemāl of Eğridir, Ḥādjdjī s, 50b
Kemāliye → Eğin
Kemānkesh ʿAlī Pasha (1624) ii, 713a; iv, **884a**; vii, 597b, 707b
Kemānkesh Ḳara Muṣṭafā Pasha (1643) ii, 804b; iii, 623a, 626b, 983a, 1001b; iv, 455b; v, 249a, vi, 1001a
Kemkhā iii, 216b
Ḳenā → Ḳunā
Kenʿān Pasha (1659) i, 843a; iv, **884b**; v, 258a; ix, 62a
Keneges, Banū vi, 419a
Kenèh → Ḳunā
Kenesari Khān v, 135b
Kenya i, 38a; ii, 974b; iv, **885a**; vi, 283a; ix, 714a; s, 248a, b
Kenz → Kanz, Banu ʾl-
Kerala → Malabar
Kerala Muslim League vi, 460b
al-Kerak → Karak
Kerasūn → Giresün
Kerbānsarāyi iv, 228a
Kerbela → Karbalāʾ
Kerbenesh iv, **891b**
Kerboka i, 485a
Kerbughā → Karbughā al-Mawṣilī
Kerč iii, 44a; iv, **891b**; v, 141a, 312b, 313a; viii, 877a
Keren i, 1163a; ii, 709a; iii, 4b; vi, 643a
Kerey → Giray
Kereyt, Kereit ii, 42a, b, 1112b
Kerimba (islands) iv, **892a**; xi, 448b
Kerkenna → Ḳarḳana
Kerkha → Karkha
Kerkuk → Kirkūk
Kerkur → Karkūr
Kermān → Kirmān
Kermān Shāh → Kirmān Shāh
Kermiyān → Germiyān
Ḳerrī iv, **892b**
Kertch → Kerč
Kesh → Kash
Keshan i, 558a; ii, 720a, 986b, 987a; vi, 290b; x, 920a
Keskes → Kuskusu
Kesr-i mīzān ii, 83a
Kesriye (Kastoriá) iv, **893a**; viii, 611a
Kesriyeli Aḥmed Pasha (1746) vi, 56b
Kestelī, Kestellī → Ḳasṭallanī, Muṣṭafa
Ketāma → Kutāma
Ketapang s, 150b
Kētehr → Katahr
Ketendji ʿÖmer Pasha-zade Meḥmed iii, 318a
Ketkhudā ii, 1121a; iii, 1180a; iv, 8b, 476a, **893b** (see also *s.v.* Kadkhudā)
Ketkhudā Ḥasan Pasha → Kaḥyā Ḥasan Pasha
Ketkhudā-zāde Süleymān (XIX) vi, 73b
Kfar ʿAḳāb vi, 303a, 305a
Khāʾ ii, 1026b; iv, 671b, **894b**
Khabar (information) iii, 369a; iv, **895a**; v, 1103a
Khabar (grammar) iv, **895b**
Khabar al-wāḥid iv, **896a**; vii, 781b, 1057b; xi, 395b
Khabbāb b. al-Aratt (VII) iv, **896b**
Khabbāz v, 41b, 42a; vi, 808b; x, 102a
Khabīr al-Mulk, Ḥasan Khān s, 53b
Khabīr al-Mulk, Rūḥī Khān s, 53b
al-Khabīth ʿAlī Muḥammad v, 451b
Khabn → ʿArūḍ
Khabrāʾ iv, **897b**; v, 40a
Khābūr (rivers) i, 608a; iv, 655a, **897b**; vi, 378a, 379a, 539b, 733a

Khābūr al-Ḥasaniyya ii, 249b; iv, 898a; s, 37a
Khabūshān → Ḳūčān
al-Khabūshānī i, 197a; viii, 913b
Khadāʿī (singer) (IX) vii, 413a
al-Khaddām, ʿAbd Allāh b. Muḥammad iv, 515b
Khaḍḍār i, 961a
Khaddāsh → Khidāsh
Khader, U.A. vi, 464b
Khadīdja (Ibn Khaldūn) vi, 422a
Khadīdja bint Khuwaylid (619) ii, 363b, 845b; iii, 152b; iv, **898b**; vi, 145b, 146a, 152b, 168b, 469a, 476b, 629a, 650b
Khadīdja bint Ṭahmāsp vi, 483a
Khadīdja bint al-Ḥasan s, 95a
Khadīdja Begum ii, 598b; iii, 315b; iv, 391a
Khadīdje bint Aḥmed III (Ottoman) (1724) vi, 860b
Khadīdje Sulṭān (1524) iii, 998b; vi, 864b
Khadīdje Sulṭān bint ʿAbd al-Ḥamīd I (Ottoman) (1775) vi, 859b
Khadīdje Sulṭān bint Meḥemmed IV i, 96b; ii, 684b; iii, 216a, 252b; viii, 318b
Khadīdje, Ṭurkhān Ṣulṭān iii, 998a, b; iv, 1100a; x, **679a** (see also *s.v.* Ṭurkhān Ṣulṭān)
Khadija Masroor (XX) vi, 489b
Khādim i, 33a; iv, **899a**, 1087a
Khādim al-Ḥaramayn iv, **899b**, 946a; ix, 905a
Khādim Ḥasan Pasha Ṣoḳollï (1598) i, 956b; iv, **900b**, 1093a
Khādim Pasha → ʿAlī Pasha; Sinān Pasha; Sulaymān Pasha
Khādim Süleymān Pasha (1547) iv, 435b, **901a**, 1093a; v, 35a, 534b, 1022b; vii, 779b; viii, 235a
al-Khaḍir (al-Khiḍr) i, 117a, 347a, 1284a; ii, 1026a; iii, 1156a; iv, 674b, 810b, **902b**; v, 17b, 800b; vi, 123b
al-Khaḍīr, Banū i, 546a; iv, 717a, **905b**
al-Khaḍir, Djazīrat iv, **906a** (see also *s.v.* ʿAbbādān)
al-Khaḍir Ghaylān (Tandja) (XVII) vi, 891b; viii, 440b, 899a; x, 184a
al-Khaḍir, Muḥammad b. al-Ḥusayn (1958) iv, **906a**
al-Khaḍir (Khiḍr) b. ʿAlī s, 263b
al-Khaḍir al-Mihrānī, Shaykh (Miṣr) (XIII) vii, 169b
Khaḍiriyya i, 277b
Khwādja (title) iv, **907a**; v, 26a
Khwādja ʿAbd al-Ṣamad (XVI) vii, 317a, 337b, 338a
Khwādja Āfak (Hidāyat Allāh b. Muḥammad Yūsuf (XVII) s, 523a
Khwādja Aḥrār → Aḥrār, Khwādja ʿUbayd Allāh
Khwādja ʿAlī (Sarbandārid) (1386) ix, 48b
Khwādja ʿAlī b. Ṣadr al-Dīn (1429) ii, 350b; viii, 753a, 756a, 766a
Khwādja ʿAlī ʿAzīzān-i Ramītanī s, 522a
Khwādja Bāḳī bi-'llāh → Bāḳī bi-'llāh
Khwādja Bāyazīd b. Bahlūl Lōdī (XV) vi, 62a
Khwādja Djahān Sarwār (Sharḳī) iii, 570a; iv, **907b**; x, 593a (see also *s.v.* Malik Sarwar)
Khwādja(-i) Djahān Turk iv, 908a; vi, 66b, 67a
Khwādja Faḍl Allāh Abu 'l-Laythī (1460) vii, 90a
Khwādjā Ghulām Farīd iv, 302b, 507b, 611a
Khwādja Ghulām Turk (1463) iv, **908a**; vi, 66b, 67a
Khwādja Ḥusayn → Thanāʾī
Khwādja Muḥammad b. Maḥmūd al-Ḥāfuẓī (1419) viii, 272b; xi, 115b
Khwādja Muḥammad Akbar b. Saʿd-Dīn Kāshgharī viii, 800b
Khwādjagān (order) iv, 47b; vi, 72b; x, 250b; s, **520b**
Khwādjagānlïk i, 433a; iv, 908b
Khwādjagī Kāʾānī Dakhbidī, Mawlānā (1542) x, 250b; s, 122a
Khwādja-i Djahān Aḥmad Ayāz (1351) i, 1036b, 1166a; ii, 814a; iii, 570a; iv, **907b**
Khwādja-i Djahān Astarābādī (XV) iv, **908a**
Khwādja-i Djahān Aʿẓam-i Humāyūn iv, **908a**
Khwādja-i Djahān Dakhnī (XV) iv, **908a**
Khwādja-i Djahān Nūr al-Dīn iv, **907b**
Khwādja-i Djahān Surūr (XIV) iv, **907b**
Khwādja Isḥāḳ b. Aḥmad Khwādjagi (1599) s, 522b, 523a
Khwādja Isḥāḳ Khuttalānī ix, 857a

Khʷādja Kamāl al-Dīn (1932) i, 302b
Khʷādja Khiḍr iv, 905a, **908a**
Khʷādja Mīr Dard → Dard
Khʷādja Muʿīn al-Dīn Ḥasan Sidjzī → Čishtī, Muʿīn al-Dīn Ḥasan
Khʷādja Muḥammad Islām Djūybarī x, 250b
Khʷādja Niyāz Ḥadjdjī ix, 649b
Khʷādjas s, **522b** (see also *s.v.* Khōdjas)
Khʷādja Shams al-Dīn v, 827a; ix, 861b
Khwādjagi Kāʿāhī Kakhbidī, Aḥmad Mawlānā ii, 48b; s, 122a, 522b
Khʷādjayn, Fayḍ Allāḥ (1937) x, 961a
Khʷādja-zāde → Khōdja-zāde
Khʷādjās, Khodjas s, **522b**
Khʷādjegān-i Dīwān-i Hümāyūn iv, **908b**; vi, 340b
Khadjkhadj (943) vi, 921a
Khʷādjū Kamāl al-Dīn Kirmānī (1361) i, 1301a; iv, 66a, b, 909b, 1010a; vi, 608b; vii, 662a, 754b, 821b; viii, 885a
Khadjuri Kač vi, 86a
al-Khaḍrāʾ (palace) vii, 268b
Kh(ʷ)āf iv, **910a**, 1073a; s, 57b, 420b
Khafādja, Banū i, 528b; iv, **910b**; v, 348b; vii, 118a; s, 119a
Khafādja b. Sufyān b. Sawādan (IX) ix, 584b, 670a
al-Khafādjī (1073) ii, 824b; iv, 250a
al-Khafādjī, Abū ʿAlī b. Thimāl (1008) viii, 394a
al-Khafādjī, Shihāb al-Dīn al-Miṣrī (1659) i, 68a, 594a, 1056a; iii, 222a; iv, **912a**; vii, 262a, 470a, 527b; viii, 736a
Khafāra ii, 143b; iii, 394a, b, 396b; iv, **913a**
Khafḍ (Khifāḍ) iv, **913a**; vi, 469b, 475b (see also *s.v.* Khitān)
al-Khʷāfī, Abū Manṣūr ʿAbd Allāh iv, 910a
al-Khʷāfī, Faṣīḥ al-Dīn Aḥmad iv, 910b, 1068a
al-Khʷāfī, Niẓām al-Dīn ʿAbd al-Raḥīm v, 872b, 873b
al-Khʷāfī Khān (1732) i, 769b; iv, **914a**
Khwārazmian Language s, **425a**
Khafīf → ʿArūḍ
Khafiyye i, 64a
Khafr vi, 384a
Khaibar → Khaybar
Khʷāharzāde, Badr al-Dīn (1253) vii, 969a
Khāʾin Aḥmad → Aḥmad Pasha Khāʾin
Khāʾir Bey (1522) ii, 1042a; iv, 451a, 553a; vi, 325a, 327a; vii, 176b, 177a; s, **524a**
Khāḳān iii, 335b; iv, 343b, **915a**, 1010b, 1174a, 1176b, 1177a; vi, 809b; viii, 621b; x, 688a
Khāḳān → Fatḥ ʿAlī Shāh
Khāḳānī, Afḍal al-Dīn Ibrāhīm Shīrwānī (1199) i, 677a, 680a; iv, 62a, 63b, 348b, **915a**; v, 619b; vi, 608b, 1016b; s, 108a, 239b, 333b
Khāḳān, Ibn, Muḥammad b. ʿUbayd Allāh → Ibn Khāḳān, Muḥammad
Khāḳān, Ibn, Mūsā b. ʿUbayd Allāh vi, 230a
Khāḳān Meḥmed Bey (1606) iv, **916a**; s, 83a
Khāḳānī, Ḳāḍī Nūr Allāh (XVII) vii, 988a
Khāḳānids → Shirwān Shāhs
Khāḳānīyān → Ilek-Khāns
Khakhay, Banū i, 219a; vii, 220a; viii, 299b
Khākhīṭ (Kakhetʾi, Georgia) iv, 1174a; viii, 873b
Khāksār (India) iv, **916b**
Khaksār (Dervishes, Iran) iv, 52a, ix, 168a; ix, 785a; s, 753b
Khalʿ s, **524b**
Khāl, Akhwāl iv, **916b**
Khāl, Khayalān → Firāsa
Khalʿa → Khilʿa
Khalā iv, 272b, 273a
Khaladj, Banū i, 99b, 217b; ii 1001a; iii, 1106b, 1108b; iv, 705b, 706a, **917a**; v, 369b; ix, 86a
Khaladjistān iv, 918a; v, 369b; ix, 86a
Khalaf, Banū ʾl- ii, 463b
Khalaf b. ʿAbd al-Malik → Ibn Bashkuwāl
Khalaf b. Aḥmad (Sidjistān) (1008) i, 160a; ii, 1082a; iii, 471a, 502a; iv, 208b; vi, 109a; ix, 683b; s, 601b
Khalaf b. Ḥayyān al-Aḥmar, Abū Muḥriz (796) i, 105b, 115b, 143b, 718b, 1081a; ii, 248b; iii, 136a; iv, **919a**
Khalaf b. Hishām iii, 155b
Khalaf b. Mubārak al-Ḳuṣayyir iii, 403b
Khalaf b. Mulāʿib al-Ashhabī (1106) i, 215a; iii, 398b; iv, **919a**; vii, 578a; viii, 922a, b

Khalaf b. al-Samḥ (IX) i, 139a; ii, 441b; iii, 659b, 1040a; iv, 919b; v, 1230a; viii, 639a
Khalaf al-Aḥmar (821) i, 115b; iii, 136a, 742a; vi, 625b; viii, 545b; x, 3a
Khalaf Allāh, Muḥammad Aḥmad i, 821a; ii, 452a; iv, 161b
Khalafids viii, 797b
al-Khalafiyya iii, 659b, 1168a; iv, 47a, **919b**; viii, 639a; xi, 466a
Khalandj iv, 1085b; v, 107b
al-Khalandjī, ʿAbd Allāh b. Muḥammad b. Abī Yazīd (851) vii, 5a
al-Khalaṣa iv, 263b
Khaldī v, 448a
Khaldjī Samarkandī, ʿAbd al-Salām s, 121b
Khaldjīs (Mālwā) i, 393b; ii, 268a, 1084a; iii, 441b; iv, 268b, 818b, 918a, **920b**; v, 688b; vi, 52b-55a, 198b, 271a; vii, 193b; s, 124b, 280a, 352b, 353a, 409a
Khaldūn, Banū iv, 115b; s, 111b, 723b
al-Khaldūniyya (al-Djamʿiyya) ii, 436b; iv, **924a**; viii, 449a, 765a, b; s, 11a
Khalfūn (Amīr) iv, 275a
Khāliʿ Ḳasam i, 829a
Khālid, Banū i, 873b; ii, 77a, 108b; iii, 238a; iv, 765a, **925a**; v, 333a; vi, 334a, 336a; vii, 410a, 782b
Khālid b. ʿAbd Allāh b. Khālid b. Asīd (VII) i, 1242b; iii, 715a; vii, 650a; viii, 400b
Khālid b. ʿAbd Allāh al-Ḳasrī (743) i, 207a, 684b, 865b, 1094b, 1116b, 1242b; ii, 36a; iii, 42a, 493b, 650a, 715a, 747b, 802b, 1255a; iv, 913b, **925b**; v, 347a, 374a; vi, 441b, 665a, 666b, 667a, 669b; vii, 347b, 348a, 357a; xi, 116b; s, 232b
Khālid b. ʿAbd al-ʿAzīz (Āl-Suʿūd) (1982) vi, 158a; ix, 915a
Khālid b. ʿAbd al-Malik al-Marwarrūdhī (831) iv, 1182b; vi, 600a; xi, 498b
Khālid b. ʿAbd al-Raḥmān al-Muhādjir (666) vi, 140a
Khālid b. Abī Djaʿfar al-Barḳī s, 127b
Khālid b. Aḥmad al-Dhuhlī i, 1296b
Khālid b. al-ʿĀṣī b. Hishām (680) vi, 140a
Khālid b. Asīd s, 267b, 386a
Khālid b. Barghash i, 1282b
Khālid b. Barmak (767) i, **1033b**; ii, 305a; vi, 745a, 941a
Khālid b. Djaʿfar b. ʿĀmir ii, 1023a; iii, 812a
Khālid b. Fayṣal b. ʿAbd al-ʿAzīz (Āl Suʿūd) s, 305b, 306a
Khālid b. Ḥamīd al-Zanātī v, 367a; vi, 923b; ix, 767b
Khālid b. Ibrāhīm, Abū Dāwūd v, 76a, 181b; vi, 332b; ix, 391b
Khālid b. Luʿayy (XX) vi, 152a, b, 153a, b
Khālid b. Maʿdān al-Ṭāʾī iv, 446a; v, 19b
Khālid b. Maʿdān b. Abī Kurayb al-Kalāʿī iv, 369a
Khālid b. Manṣūr → Ibn Luʿayy
Khālid b. Muḥammad, Shaykh s, 418a
Khālid b. Nazzār vi, 264b
Khālid b. Ṣafwān b. al-Ahtam i, 1297b; iv, **927a**; v, 132a
Khālid b. Saʿīd b. al-ʿĀṣ (635) iv, **927a**; vi, 546b; viii, 1051b
Khālid b. Shāhsuwār Bek i, 1157a
Khālid b. Sinān al-ʿAbsī i, 509a; ii, 1024a; iii, 169a; iv, **928a**; vi, 381a
Khālid b. Suʿūd (Āl Suʿūd) (1841) ix, 904a
Khālid b. al-Walīd b. al-Mughīra Makhzūmī (642) i, 110b, 111a, 145b, 208b, 484b, 549b, 788b, 964a, 1139a, 1215b, 1240b, 1343b, 1358b; ii, 279b, 366a, 625a, b, 1023b; iii, 85b, 223b, 397b, 578a, 739b, 1254b; iv, 13b, 289b, 407a, **928a**, 1106b; v, 458a; vi, 138a, b, 139a, 267b, 268a, 505b, 544b, 546b; vii, 356b, 370a, 372b, 549b, 756b; ix, 80a; x, 782b; s, 230b
Khālid b. Yazīd (Mukaddī) vii, 494a, 858a
Khālid b. Yazīd b. Ḥātim iii, 694a, b
Khālid b. Yazīd b. Muʿāwiya (Umayyad) (704) ii, 360b; iii, 271a, 398a; iv, **929a**; vi, 197b, 198a, 622a, b; vii, 268a; s, 270a
Khālid b. Yazīd b. Mazyad al-Shaybānī (IX) i, 154a; ii, 679a
Khālid b. Yazīd al-Kātib al-Tamīmī (883) iv, **929a**; ix, 848a
Khālid al-ʿAbd (VIII) vii, 662b
Khālid Baghdādī al-Kurdī, Mawlanā (1827) v, 475a, 486a; vii, 935b; x, 250b
Khālid al-Barmakī → al-Barāmika
Khālid Beklū i, 1157a
Khālid Ḍiyāʾ (Ziyā) (1945) i, 287b; iii, 260b; iv, 636b, **930a**; v, 194b, 195b; vi, 1003a
Khālid Fakhrī v, 271b; s, 168a

Khālid al-Ḳasrī → Khālid b. ʿAbd Allāh al-Ḳasrī
Khālid Kurdī (XIX) vii, 939a
Khālid al-Marwarrūdhī → Khālid b. ʿAbd al-Malik al-Mawarrudhī
Khālid Muḥammad Khālid (XX) vi, 467a
Khālid Muḥyī al-Dīn s, 6a
Khālid Pasha Ḳara ʿOthmān-oghlu iv, 593b
Khālida (Djarīr) vi, 604b
Khālid bint Arkam, Banū iii, 975b
al-Khālidāt → al-Djazāʾir al-Khālida
Khālide Edīb (1964) iii, 622b; iv, 931b, **933a**; v, 194b, 196a; vi, 94a, 386a; ix, 499a; s, 41b, 480b
al-Khālidī (Muʿtazilī) vii, 312a
al-Khālidī, Rūḥī (1913) iv, **936a**
al-Khālidiyyān[i] (X) ii, 195a; iv, **936b**; vii, 935b, 936b; viii, 989b; s, 639a
al-Khalīdj vi, 587b, 667b
Khalīdj Amīr al-Muʾminīn i, 932a; v, 368a; vii, 149a; ix, 357a
al-Khalīdj al-Banādiḳī i, 935b
Khālidj al-Ḥākimī → Khālidj Amīr al-Muʾminīn
Khalīdj al-Ḳusṭanṭīniyya i, 927a, 935a, b; vi, 587b
Khalīdj Miṣr → Khalīdj Amīr alMuʾminīn
Khalīdj al-Nāṣirī i, 1299b
Khalīfa (caliph) iii, 344a; iv, **937a**, 1076b; v, 435a, b, 621a, 624a
Khalīfa, Āl i, 233b, 540a, 554a, 942b; ii, 108b, 176b; iii, 23a; iv, 751a, **953a**; v, 508a, b, 573b; vi, 358a; vii, 464a; x, 956a
Khalīfa, Shaykh (Māzandarān) (XIV) ix, 48a
Khalīfa b. Abi ʾl-Maḥāsin (XIII) i, 388b; iv, **954a**; x, 355a
Khalīfa b. ʿAskar (XX) ii, 767b; iv, **954b**
Khalīfa b. Bahrām s, 309a
Khalīfa b. Khayyāṭ → Ibn Khayyāṭ al-ʿUṣfurī
Khalīfa b. Muḥammad iv, 953a
Khalīfa b. Shakhbūṭ i, 166b
Khalīfa b. Warrū v, 1182b
Khalīfa ʿAbd Allāh (1899) → ʿAbd Allāh b. Muḥammad al-Taʿāʾishī
Khalīfa al-Safṭī (1879) vi, 354b
Khalīfa Shāh Muḥammad (XVIII) iv, **954b**
Khalīfa Sulṭān Ḥusayn b. Muḥammad b. Maḥmūd (Marʿashī) (1653) vi, 516b; viii, 780a
Khalīfat al-Masīḥ i, 301b
Khalīfat al-Masīḥ (Armenian Catholicos) viii, 607a
Khalīfe → Khalīfa
Khāliḳ, Abū Anīs vi, 611a; s, 74b
al-Khalīl → Ibrāhīm
al-Khalīl (Hebron) ii, 911b; iv, **954b**; vi, 654b, 662b, 675a; x, 176a; s, 823b
Khalīl, Banū (Mārib) vi, 561b
Khalīl, al-Malik al-Ashraf Ṣalāḥ al-Dīn (Mamlūk) (1293) i, 341b, 737b, 1127b, 1324b; ii, 912a, 966a; iii, 325a, 679b; iv, 485b, **964b**; v, 595a
Khalīl b. Aḥmad (791) i, 11a, 106a, 587a, 588b, 668b, 669b, 670b, 674a, 675b; iii, 948b; iv, 412a, 524b, **962a**, 1187b; v, 711a, 806b; vi, 129b, 130a, 199a; vii, 262a, 560b, 569b; ix, 11a, 525b; s, 73b, 289b, 408b
Khalīl b. Alī Čandarli̊ → Djandarli̊, Khayr al-Dīn Khalīl Pasha
Khalīl b. Badr b. Shudjāʿ v, 826b, 828a
Khalīl b. Isḥāḳ b. Ward (941) i, 163b; ii, 553a; iv, 459b, 979b; ix, 586a
Khalīl b. Isḥāḳ, Ibn al-Djundī (1374) i, 1019b; iii, 781b; iv, **964a**; vi, 278b, 279a, 281b, 313b, 710a; vii, 387b, 538a, 1052b
Khalīl b. Ismāʿīl v, 801b
Khalīl b. Ḳalāwūn, al Malik al-Ashraf Ṣalāḥ al-Dīn (Mamlūk) (1293) iv, **964b**; vi, 195a, 322b, 507b; vii, 167b, 168b; ix, 884a; x, 612b
Khalīl b. Zayn al-Dīn Ḳaradja (Dhu ʾl-Ḳadr) ii, 239a, b; vi, 507b
Khalīl b. Uzun Ḥasan ii, 1136b; iv, 1048b; x, 964a
Khalīl Allāh (1884) → Shihāb al-Dīn al-Ḥusaynī
Khalīl Allāh, Shāh imām (1817) iv, 201b
Khalīl Allāh b. Niʿmat Allāh Nūr al-Dīn (1456) viii, 45b, 46a, 48a
Khalīl Allāh b. Shāh Niʿmat Allāh Kirmānī → Khalīl Allāh But-Shikan
Khalīl Allāh But-Shikan b. Khalīl Allāh b. Shāh Niʿmat Allāh Kirmānī (1460) i, 1200b; iv, **965b**; vi, 63a
Khalīl Allāh (Shīrvān-Shāh) iv, 587b
Khalīl Atā → Ḳazan Khān (Čaghatay)
Khalīl Bahādur iv, 621a
Khalīl Beg (Ḳarāmān-oghlu) iv, 621b, 622a, b

Khalīl Bey iv, 828a, b
Khalīl Bey (XX) viii, 463b
Khalīl Dede, Shaykh (XVIII) vii, 572b
Khalīl Edhem → Eldem
Khalīl Efendi-zāde (1754) iv, **966a**
Khalīl Ghaffa i, 600a
Khalīl Ghānim (1903) ii, 471a; iii, 593a; iv, **966b**
Khalīl Gibran → Djabrān Khalīl Djabrān
Khalīl Ḥamīd Pasha i, 63a, 1064b; ii, 534a, b, 629b; iv, 211a
Khalīl Ḥilmī s, 98a
Khalīl al-Khūrī ii, 466a; x, 81b
Khalīl Mīrzā i, 1211b
Khalīl Mīrzā (Tīmūrid) → Khalīl Sulṭān
Khalīl Muṭrān (1949) iii, 59a, b; iv, **966b**; vi, 414a; s, 34a
Khalīl Naṣr (XX) vi, 797a
Khalīl Nūrī Efendi iv, 544a
Khalīl Pasha Djandarli̊ (1453) ii, 445a, 721a; iv, **968b**; vi, 70a, 978a; viii, 194b; xi, 384a
Khalīl Pasha Ḥādjdjī Arnawud (1733) iii, 1002a; iv, **969a**
Khalīl Pasha Ḳayṣari̊yyeli (1629) i, 4a, 268a; iv, **970a**; vi, 994a, 998b; viii, 182a; ix, 59a
Khalīl Pasha Kut → Enwer Pasha
Khalīl Sarkīs ii, 467b
Khalīl Ṣūfī → Niʿmat Allāh b. Aḥmad
Khalīl Sulṭān b. Mīrānshāh b. Tīmūr (Tīmūrid) (1409) vii, 105b; viii, 892b; ix, 315b; x, 543b, 812a
Khalīl Ṭūṭaḥ (XX) vi, 615b
Khalīl Yakhshī Beg i, 309a; ii, 599b
Khalīl al-Ẓāhirī (XV) vi, 382a, 791a; vii, 286a; ix, 850b
Khalīlī (1485) iv, **972b**
al-Khalīlī, Imām Muḥammad b. ʿAbd Allāh (ʿUmān) (1954) viii, 993b; s, 356a
Khalīlī, Shams al-Dīn (1365) v, 83b, 85a, 87a, b; vi, 543a
Khāliṣ ii, 103a
Khāliṣa ii, 272b, 906b; iv, **972b**, 1035b; v, 688b; vi, 496a
Khāliṣa (lady-in-waiting) s, 198b
al-Khāliṣa (citadel) iv, **979b**
Khāliṣī, Shaykh Mahdī s, 342a
Khalisioi v, 1015a, 1018b
Khalḳ iii, 663b, 664b; iv, **980a**
Khalḳ Fi̊rḳasi̊ i, 734b; ii, 432a, 595b
Khalḳevi iv, **988a**; v, 906b; vi, 95a
Khalkha Banū (Mongolia) iv, 988b; xi, 226b
Khalkha (river) iv, **988b**
Khalkhāl (Ādharbāydjān) iv, **989a**; vi, 494a
Khalkhālī, Muḥammad Ṣāliḥ s, 308b
Khallād b. ʿAmr b. al-Djamūḥ s, 230a
Khallād b. Khālid iii, 155b
Khallād b. al-Minḳarī (VIII) viii, 573a
al-Khallāl, Aḥmad b. Muḥammad Abū Bakr (923) i, 274a, b; ii, 1093a; iii, 158b, 735a; iv, **989b**; vi, 636a
Khallukh → Ḳarluḳ
Khalwa iii, 1011a; iv, 381b, 383a, **990a**, 992b; v, 23a, 1201a, b
Khalwatiyya i, 95a, 965b, 1137a; ii, 164b, 203b, 224a, 542b, 1137b; iv, 721b, **991a**; vi, 627a; viii, 19a; ix, 299a; x, 247b, 252a; s, 40b, 44a, 208a
Khamāsa → Muzāraʿa
Khambāyat (Cambay) iii, 444b; iv, **993b**; vi, 233b, 283a, 369a, 694a; vii, 49a; s, 358b
Khambhāt → Khambāyat
Khameneʿī vii, 300a
Khamīs (military) iii, 182a, b
Khamīs b. ʿAbd Allah (Uganda) x, 779a
Khamīs (Thursday) iv, 994a, 1009a
Khamīs Mushayṭ iv, **994a**; vi, 158a; ix, 908a
Khamlīdj viii, 364b, 621a; ix, 620a
Khamlīkh → Khamlīdj
Khamr ii, 1058b, 1059b, 1062a, 1069a; iii, 78b, 400b; iv, 135b, **994b**
Khamriyya i, 584b; iv, **998a**; viii, 803a
Khamsa (No. 5) i, 786a; iv, **1009a**
Khamsa (poem) iv, **1009b**; v, 1104a
Khamsa/Khamseh, Banū iii, 1106a, 1110a; iv, 9b; s, 146a, 147b
Khamse → Wilāyāt-i Khamse
Khāmūsh Ḳi̊zi̊l Arslan b. Özbek (Ildeñizid) (1191) i, 301a; iii, 1112a; vi, 501a; x, 554b
Khān (title) iii, 1113b; iv, **1010b**; v, 629b
Khān (staging-post) iv, 228a, b, 236a, 435a, 677b, **1010b**; v, 1124b
Khan Abdul Wali Khan (XX) vi, 489b
Khān Aḥmad (Ardalān) v, 33b, 34a
Khān Aḥmad Khān i, 1208b

Khān(-i) Ārzū (1739) iv, 526b; vii, 96a; ix, 90a
Khān Asad vi, 384a
Khān Ātash i, 262b
Khān ʿAyyāsh vi, 544b
Khān Baba → Bayram Khān, Khān-i Khānān Muḥammad
Khān Bahādur Khān i, 953b, 1043a; viii, 572b
Khān Balïḳ/Bālïḳ → Khānbalïḳ
Khān Begī Khānum i, 406a
Khān Danūn vi, 546b, 548a b
Khān Dawrān (XVIII) vii, 457a, 899a
Khān Djahān ʿAlī (1459) → Khāndjā ʿAlī
Khān Djahān Lōdī ii, 381a; iii, 424a; iv, **1017b**
Khān Djahān Maḳbūl → Khān-i Djahān Maḳbūl Tilangānī
Khān al-Khalīlī (al-Ḳāhira) s, 5a
Khān, ʿAbd al-Ghaffār (1988) v, 251a; vii, 220b; viii, 282a; s, **525b**
Khān Khānān iv, 210b, **1019b**; v, 629b
Khān Khānān Maḥmūd b. Fīrūz iv, 920b, 1019b
Khān al-Ḳuṣayr vi, 544b
Khān Lādjīn vi, 544b
Khān Shaykhūn iv, 1011a; vi, 455a
Khān Sulṭānī, ʿAbd al-Rashīd (XIV) vi, 49a
Khān Yakdas i, 1030b
Khān Yūnis vi, 31a; ix, 630b
Khān Zamān ʿAlī Ḳulī Khān (1566) vii, 340b; ix, 196a; s, 505a
Khān al-Zayyāt vi, 548a
Khāna Pasha i, 845a
Khanagāh, Khānaḳah → Khānḳāh
Khanāṣir → Khunāṣira
Khanāzir → Khinzīr
Khānbalïḳ iv, 420a, **1020a**; xi, 487b
Khʷand Mir (1524) ii, 500a
Khandaḳ i, 121b; ii, 130a; iii, 1083a, 1084a, b, 1086b; iv, **1020b**; vi, 604a; s, 351b
Khandaḳ → Ḳandiya
al-Khandaḳ (al-Andalus) (939) vi, 431b
Khandaḳ al-ʿAbīd (Miṣr) vii, 149b
Khandaḳ Sābūr v, 80b, 634a; ix, 309b
Khandaḳ Ṭāhir i, 897b
Khʷāndamīr (1535) i, 456a, 1211b, 1213a; iv, **1020b**; vii, 127a, 602b
Khande Rāo iii, 316b
Khāndēsh ii, 113a, 270b, 814a, 816a, 1125a; iii, 418b, 422a, 446b; iv, **1022a**; vi, 50b, 52a, 53a, 54a, b, 67b, 310a, 695a; s, 335b
Khāndjā ʿAlī (1459) ii, 486b; iii, 444a; ix, 877b
Khandjara → Čankïrï
al-Khāndjī → Handzič
Khandwa vi, 53a
Khāne iv, 243a, b
Khānfū iv, **1024a**; vii, 67b, 72a; ix, 619a, b, 626b
Khān-i Ārzū → Khān(-i) Ārzū
Khān-i Djahān → Rāo Mandalik Čudāsama
Khān-i Djahān Maḳbūl Tilangānī, Ḳiwām al-Mulk (1368) ii, 925a, 1084b; iv, 907b, **1019a**; vii, 795b
Khān-i Shahīd → Muḥammad b. Balban
Khan-i Zinyān vi, 384a
Khāniḳīn i, 845a; iv, 447b, **1024b**
al-Khanīnī vi, 113b
Khānḳāh iv, 433a, **1025a**; v, 1129b; vi, 501b; s, 49b
Khānlar Khān Iʿtiṣām al-Mulk iv, 787a
Khānlarī, Parwīz Nātil iii, 56b; iv, 71b, 72a, 714b; x, 234b
Khannāb s, 327a
Khannās i, 262a
al-Khansāʾ (Tumāḍir bint ʿAmr) (644) i, 12a; ii, 627a; iii, 941a; iv, **1027a**; v, 710a; vi, 603a; x, 305a
Khansā (Khinsā) iv, 1024a, **1026b**
Khʷānsalār ii, 15a
Khʷānsārī, Aḳa Ḥusayn s, 308a
Khʷānsārī, Āyatullāh Aḥmad (1985) vi, 553b,
Khʷānsārī, Muḥammad Bāḳir (1895) iv, **1027b**; v, 1089a
al-Khʷānsarī, Muḥammad Riḍā al-Raḍawī s, 75a
Khʷānsārī, Muḥammad Taḳī Mūsawī (1952) iv, **1028b**; s, 157b
Khanuwā iii, 202a; vii, 314a
Khān-zāda Bēgum iv, **1029a**
Khanzīt i, 983a; iv, **1029a**
Khaputs iv, **1029a**; v, 284b, 729b
Khʷār iv, **1029b**; vi, 744b
Kharābshahr iii, 501b
Kharādj i, 861b, 969a, 990b, 1143b; ii, 116a, 131a, 142b, 146b, 154a, 187b, 559b, 561b, 562b, 566a, 869b; iii, 1088a; iv, 14a,

b, 15b, 323a, b, 755a, 939a, 974a, **1030b**; v, 872a; vi, 496a
al-Kharadjī, Abū Bakr Muḥammad iv, 529b, 530a
Khārag ii, 452a, 812b; iv, **1056a**; v, 81a, 507b; vi, 619a
al-Kharāʾiṭ i, 1045b
al-Kharāʾiṭī (939) i, 326a; iii, 745a; iv, **1057a**
Kharaḳānī, Abu ʾl-Ḥasan (1033) i, 147a, 515b, 780a; ii, 1078a; iv, **1057a**; x, 958a; s, 14b, 521a
Khara-Khula iv, 512a
al-Kharaḳī, Abū Bakr Muḥammad (1138) iv, **1059a**
al-Kharaḳī, Aḥmad b. Isḥāḳ iv, 1004a
al-Kharaḳī, Bahāʾ al-Dīn → al-Kharaḳī, Abū Bakr Muḥammad
al-Kharaḳī, Shams al-Dīn → al-Kharaḳī, Abū Bakr Muḥammad
Khārān iv, **1059b**; v, 102b, 684b; vi, 192b
Kharāna iv, **1060a**
Kharāsūya bint Djustān III vii, 655b
Kh^{w}ārazm i, 46b, 47a, 135a, 424b, 455b, 662b, 1131a; ii, 3a, 16a, 1141b; iii, 196a, 502a; iv, 753b, **1060b**; v, 24b, 542a, 857b; vi, 65b, 277b, 337a, 415b, 495a, 512a, 620a, 676a, 726b, 765a; ix, 428a; x, 708a; s, 168b, 169a, 245b, 279a, 289b, 420a
Kh^{w}ārazm-Shāhs i, 20b, 21a, 227a, 424b, 732a, 750a, 804a, 1132a; ii, 606b, 1053a, 1101a, b; iii, 471b, 1115a, 1155a; iv, 29a-30a, 349a, b, 542b, 583a, 817b, 1063b, **1065b**; v, 38b, 331a, 1014a, 1015b, 1018b; vi, 65b, 261b, 381b, 505a, 618a; viii, 63b; x, 743a; s, 245b, 279a
al-Kh^{w}ārazmī, Abū ʿAbd Allāh Muḥammad (XI) iv, **1063a**, 1068b; vii, 913a; s, 130b, 371b, 387a
al-Kh^{w}ārazmī, Abū Bakr, Shaykh al-Ḥanafiyya (1012) vi, 634b
al-Kh^{w}ārazmī, Abū Bakr Muḥammad b. al-ʿAbbās (993) i, 590b; ii, 78b; iii, 6b, 106b; iv, 1063a, **1069b**; vi, 108b, 905a; vii, 26a; ix, 56b; x, 426a
al-Kh^{w}ārazmī, Abū Djaʿfar Muḥammad b. Mūsā (847) i, 132b, 379b, 589b, 722b; ii, 360b, 577b, iii, 405a, 469a, 929b, 1137a, 1139a; iv, 1063a, **1070a**, 1078a, 1175b; vii, 210a; viii, 101b, 549b, 550a; s, 43a, 412b, 413b; xi, 498a
Kh^{w}ārazmī, Kamāl al-Dīn Ḥusayn (1551) x, 251a
al-Kh^{w}ārazmī, Abu ʾl-Ḳāsim vi, 108b
al-Kh^{w}ārazmī, Abu ʾl-Muʾayyad al-Muwaffaḳ b. Aḥmad (1172) vi, 351b, 415b
al-Kh^{w}arazmī, Aḥmad b. Muḥammad b. Isḥāḳ s, 343a
al-Kh^{w}ārazmī, Tādj al-Dīn (1436) ix, 863a
Kh^{w}arazmian (language) iv,1062b; x, 690
Kharbga iv, **1071b**; v, 109a
Khārčīnī → Khārṣīnī
Kharda vi, 535b
al-Khardj i, 538b; iv, **1072b**
al-Khārdj → Khārag
Khardja → Muwashshaḥ
Khārdje, Khārga → al-Wāḥāt
Khardjird → Khargird
Khardjlïḳ ii, 714b
Kharera vi, 294b; vii, 947a
Kharfūsh → Ḥarfūsh, ḥarāfīsh
Kharg → Khārag
Khargird iv, 910b, **1073a**; v, 1137b, 1148b; x, 520a; xi, 424a
al-Khargūshī, al-Wāʿiẓ (1015) iv, **1074a**
al-Kharība al-Sawdāʾ → al-Sawdāʾ (al-Kharība)
Kharibtā vii, 394b
al-Khārid, Wādī i, 538a; iv, **1074a**; ix, 90b
Kharid i, 829b
al-Khāridja → al-Wāḥāt
Khāridja b. Ḥiṣn al-Fazārī i, 690a; ii, 1023b; iii, 23b
Khāridja b. Ḥudhāfa i, 451b
Khāridja b. Zayd b. Thābit al-Anṣārī s, **311a**
Khāridjites i, 16a, 40b, 49a, 54b, 55a, 77a,113a, 120a, 158a, 163a, 207a, 248a, 332b, 367a, 384a, b, 445b, 451b, 550b, 686b, 810a, 942a, 972a, 1044a, 1110b, 1178b, 1242b; ii, 90a, 166a, 416a, 523b, 524a, 978a, 1095b; iii, 153a, 233b, 583b, 648a, 651a, b, 652a, 715b, 1164a, 1265a; iv, 15a, 20b, 415b, 673a, 753a, 827a, **1074b**; v, 499a, 855a, 945b, 1189a; vi, 84a, 279b, 311b, 331a, 345a, 623b, 740a; vii, 265b, 266b, 562a; ix, 754a, 766a; x, 816a; s, 122b, 157a, 284a
– doctrine i, 124a, 128b, 187b, 257b, 335a, 1027b; ii, 833b; iii, 19b, 235b, 658b, 661a, 1167b; iv, 938a, **1076a**

Kharīṭa, Khāriṭa iv, **1077b**
Khʷārizm/ī → Khʷārazm
Khark v, 878b, 879b, 880b
Khark (island) → Khārag
Kharkūshī → Khargūshī
al-Khwārizmī → Muḥammad b. Maḥmūd
Kharlukh → Ḳarluḳ
Kharm → ʿArūḍ
Kharpūt → Khart(a)pert
Kharrāna s, 229a
al-Kharrāz, Abū Saʿīd (890) i, 959b; iv, **1083a**; ix, 548b; x, 314b; xi, 23a; s, 748b
Kharrūba → Makāyīl
al-Kharrūbī, Muḥammad b. ʿUmar b. ʿAbd al-ʿAzīz iii, 776b
al-Kharrūbī, Zakī al-Dīn iii, 776b; iv, 641b, 642a
Kharshbūn i, 218b; vii, 220a
Khʷarshi ii, 251a
Khārṣīnī iv, **1084a**; v, 970b
Khart(a)pert (al-Khartabirtī) i, 665a, 983a; iii, 128a; iv, 1029a, **1084a**; vi, 231a, 341b, 507a, b; vii, 999b; viii, 133a; s, 37a
Kharṭūm i, 49b, 168b; v, **70a**, 1249b
– institutions i, 976a; ii, 424a
Kharūṣ, Banū iii, 653a; iv, **1084b**; viii, 993b
al-Kharūṣī, Saʿīd b. Khalfān al-Khalīlī → Saʿīd b. Khalfān al-Khalīlī
al-Kharūṣī, Salīm b. Rashīd i, 1283a; iv, 1085a; viii, 85b
al-Kharūṣī, Wārith b. Kaʿb → Wārith b. Kaʿb al-Kharūṣī
Khāṣ Pūlād-Khān ii, 88a
Khaṣab viii, 436b, 437a
Khāsa-Čay (river) i, 184a; v, 145a, 441b
al-Khaṣāsī, Abu ʾl-Faḍl Ḳāsim (1673) iv, 379a, 380a, **1085a**
Khashab iv, **1085a**; v, 108b, 655b
al-Khashabāt iv, **1086a**; vi, 359a
Khashabiyya iii, 987a; iv, 411b, 836b, **1086a**; vii, 357a
Khashkhāsh i, 934b; ii, 522b
Khashm Djazra/Khaṭma i, 536b
Khashm al-Girba viii, 92b
Khasht → Khōst
Khāṣī iv, **1087a**; vi, 317b
al-Khaṣīb → Ibn al-Khaṣīb
al-Khaṣīb b. ʿAbd al-Ḥamīd i, 143b; iii, 835a
al-Khaṣībī, Abū ʿAbd Allāh al-Ḥusayn b. Ḥamdān (957) viii, 146b
al-Khaṣībī, Abū ʿAlī Aḥmad → Ibn al-Khaṣīb
al-Khaṣībī, Aḥmad b. ʿUbayd Allāh (940) iii, 835a; iv, **1094a**
al-Khāsir → Salm b. ʿAmr al-Khāsir
Khāṣṣ i, 850a, 1080a, ii, 83a, 103b; iv, 238b, 972b, **1094a**
Khāṣṣ, Khāṣṣa (Iran) → Khāliṣa
Khāṣṣ Aḥmed Beg ii, 985b
Khāṣṣbek, al-Amīr al-Kabīr Niṣrat al-Dīn → Āḳ-Sunḳur al-Aḥmadīlī
Khāṣṣ Beg Arslān b. Balangirī (Palang-eri), amīr (1153) i, 300b; iv, **1097a**; vi, 275b, 782b; vii, 406b
Khāṣṣ Murād Pasha (1473) vi, 72a; x, 965b; s, 471a
Khāṣṣ Oda ii, 277b, 1088b, 1089b; iv, **1097a**; v, 18a, b, 938b, 939a
Khāṣṣa i, 491a, 1099a; ii, 188a; iv, 36a, 972b, 976a, b, 977a, 1044a, 1094a
Khāṣṣa (occult) iv, **1097b**
Khāṣṣa ʿaskeri i, 1278b
Khāṣṣa niwīs iv, 759a
Khāṣṣa wa ʾl-ʿĀmma iv, **1098a**; v, 605b
Khāṣṣadārs i, 238b; iv, 1143a; xi, 198a
al-Khaṣṣāf, Abū Bakr Aḥmad (874) i, 1113a; iii, 163a, 512b s, 141b, **526a**
al-Khāṣṣakī, Sayf al-Dīn Shaykh Ibn ʿAbd Allāh al-Ṣafawī (1398) vi, 580b
Khāṣṣakī Muḥammad Pasha i, 904b
Khāṣṣakiyya iv, **1100a**
Khāṣṣekī i, 1225b, 1279a; iv, **1100a**; v, 66b; xi, 130b
Khāṣṣköy iii, 629a; iv, 242a, 1096b; vi, 72a
Khaṭaʾ iv, 768b, 769b, **1100b**
al-Khatādjī, Shihāb al-Dīn s, 362a
Khaṭāʾī → Ismāʿīl (Ṣafawid)
Khaṭak i, 218b; iv, **1102a**; v, 72a, 250b, 251a
Khātam, Khātim ii, 306a, 307a, 311b, 315a; iv, **1102b**; s, 256b
Khathʿam, Banū (1071) i, 442a, 811b, 812a; iv, **1105b**; vi, 435b, 436a; viii, 82b; x, 3a
Khāthira, Day of s, 177b
Khaṭīʾa iv, **1106b**
Khaṭīb i, 981b; iv, **1109b**; v, 74a
Khaṭīb, Abū Bakr s, 195a

Khaṭīb al-Baghdādī (1071) i, 123b, 142b, 321b, 333a, 591b, 616b, 898a, 1309b; ii, 462a; iii, 27b, 512b, 735a, 754a, 860b; iv, **1111a**; v, 1129b; vi, 263a, 634b, 674a; viii, 518a; ix, 65a; s, 32b, 323a, 326a, 361a
Khaṭīb Dimashḳ → al-Ḳazwīnī, Khaṭīb Dimashḳī
Khaṭīb al-Iskāfī (1030) viii, 390a; s, 669a
Khatib Muhammad Maulavi (1964) vi, 462a
Khātim → Khātam
Khātima v, 960a
Khātimī → Muʾayyad-zāde (Müʾeyyed-zāde)
al-Khārimī, ʿAbd Allāh b. Yazīd (VII) vii, 522a
Khatlān → Khuttalān
Khatma, Khitma ii, 78b, 79b; iv, **1112b**; x, 74b
Khaṭma, Banū i, 514b, 771a
al-Khaṭmī, ʿAbd Allāh b. Yazīd (VII) vii, 522a; ix, 826b
Khatmiyya i, 277b, 1029a, 1158b; ii, 710a; iii, 6a, 523b; iv, 686b; x, 249a (see also *s.v.* Mīrghaniyya)
Khaṭṭ i, 1354a; ii, 311a, 777b; iv, **1113a**, 1123b, 1125a; v, 210b-233b *passim*, 379b, 992a;
Khaṭṭ (Chinese Islam) s, **526b**
Khaṭṭ (geomancy) iv, **1128b**
al-Khaṭṭ (Persian Golf) iv, **1130b**
Khaṭṭ al-Istiwāʾ → Istiwāʾ, Khaṭṭ al-
Khaṭṭāb, Banū (Almeria) ii, 875b; vi, 743a; x, 105b, 586a; xi, 466a, b
al-Khaṭṭābī, ʿAbd al-Karīm (XX) iii, 701a
al-Khaṭṭābī, Abū Sulaymān ix, 887a
al-Khaṭṭābī, Ḥamd b. Muḥammad (996) iii, 1020a; iv, **1131b**; viii, 374b; ix, 887a
Khaṭṭābiyya i, 486a, 1082a; iv, 203a, **1132a**; vii, 517a; viii, 1047a
al-Khaṭṭār (Ḳurzul) s, 177b
Khaṭṭāra iv, 532b; vi, 589a
Khaṭṭ-i Humāyūn/Khaṭṭ-i̊ Sherīf i, 74b, 282a, 397a, 855a, 1090a; ii, 314a; iii, 553b; iv, **1131a**; v, 904b; x, 201a
Khatuḳāy ii, 25a
Khātūn (title) iv, **1133a**
Khātūn (Bukhārā) (vii) ix, 249b
Khātūn al-ʿIṣma bint Malik-Shāh (Saldjūḳ) (XII) vii, 408a
Khātūnābādī, Mollā Muḥammad Bāḳir (XVIII) vii, 222b
Khātūnī, Muwaffaḳ al-Dawla Abū Ṭāhir (XII) vi, 351b; vii, 529b; s, 65a
Khāwa iii, 643a; iv, **1133a**; viii, 882b; s, **535a**
Khāwa (Luristān) v, 617a, 830a
Khāwa bt. Ḥakīm b. Umayya (VII) s, **527b**
Khāwābī (Fortress) viii, 147a; x, 310a
Khawand → Ākhūnd
Khāwandagār i, 260b, 261b, 262a
Khāwarān/Khābarān vi, 914b
Khawāridj → Khāridjites
Khawārizm(ī) → Khʷarazm(ī)
al-Khawarnaḳ i, 196b; iv, **1133b**; v, 633a
Khawāṣṣ → Khāṣṣ, Khāṣṣa
Khawāṣṣ Khān (XVI) vi, 54b; s, 685b
Khawāṣṣ al-Ḳurʾān iv, **1133b**
Khawātūnābādi, Muḥammad Ṣāliḥ (1704) vii, 476a
Khawbar → Khōbar
Khawla i, 400b
Khawla bint Ḥakīm i, 307b; ix, 89b
Khawla bt. al-Hudhayl b. Hubayra x, 91b
Khawla umm Muḥammad b. al-Ḥanafiyya i, 400b; vii, 402b
Khawlān, Banū i, 881b; iv, **1134a**; vi, 436a; s, 22a
al-Khawlānī, ʿAbd al-Raḥmān b. Ismāʿīl b. Kulāl → Waḍḍāḥ al-Yaman
al-Khawlānī, Abū Idrīs (699) iv, **1135a**, 1136a
al-Khawlānī, Abū Muslim (682) iv, 1135a, **b**
Khawr i, 536a, 538b, 1094b, 1095a, b; ii, 618b
Khawr Dawraḳ ii, 181b
Khawr Fakkān ii, 936b; ix, 349a
Khawr Ghanāḍa ii, 618b
Khawr Ghubb ʿAlī viii, 436b
Khawr Ḥabalayn viii, 436b
Khawr al-Ḥammār ix, 801b, 802a
Khawr Ḥasan v, 508a, b
Khawr Ḥassān iv, 751a
Khawr Mūsā ii, 181b
Khawr al-Shamm viii, 436b
Khawr Rawrī xi, 380a
Khawr al-ʿUdayd iv, 751b; x, 773b
Khayāl iii, 453b, 632b; iv, **1136a**
Khayāl, Mīr Muḥammad Taḳī (1759) iv, **1136a**

Khayāl al-ẓill iv, 602b, **1136b**; viii, 409a; 418a; ix, 70a
Khayālī ii, 937a; v, 5a; x, 352b
Khayālī (Meḥmed) Bey (1556) iv, **1137a**
Khaybar (629) i, 9a, 435a; ii, 725a, 844b; iv, **1137b**; v, 250b; vi, 150a, 738a; vii, 371b; viii, 299a, b; s, 351b
Khaybar (Khyber) Pass i, 238a, b; iv, **1143a**; vii, 220a, 548b; ix, 440a; s, 329b
Khaydāḳ → Ḳaytaḳ
Khaydhār → al-Afshīn Ḥaydar
Khāyir Bey al-ʿAlāʾī i, 315a
Khāyir Bey al-Djarkasī s, 38a
al-Khayl iv, 495b, **1143a**; v, 75b
Khayma iv, **1146b**; v, 444a
Khayr iv, **1151a**
Khayr b. Muḥammad b. al-Khayr v, 1176a, b, 1179a
Khayr b. Muḥammad b. Khazar iii, 1042a, b; v, 1175a, b
Khayr b. Nuʿaym (ḳāḍī) (740) vi, 671a
Khayr Allāh Efendi (1865) i, 61a; iv, **1153a**; vi, 758b, 759a
Khayr Bak (amīr) (1499) vi, 580b
Khayr al-Bayān i, 220b, 1122a, 1123a, b
Khayr al-Dīn, Ustād iv, **1158b**
Khayr al-Dīn Čandarli̊ → Djandarli̊
Khayr al-Dīn Pasha Barbarossa (1546) i, 367b, 368a, 512a, 678a, 947b, 1023b, 1300b; ii, 189b, 353a, 520a, 522a, 537b, 722b, 839b; iii, 69a, 94b, 245b, 1086a; iv, 361a, b, 572a, 656b, 828a, **1155a**; v, 268b, 270b, 504a, 1010b; vi, 141a, 529b; vii, 48a, 940a; viii, 569b; s, 80b
Khayr al-Dīn Pasha al-Tūnusī (1890) i, 285b; ii, 436a; iii, 562a, 591b, 636b; iv, 924a, **1153b**; v, 949a; vi, 69a; vii, 433b, 434b, 451b, 452a, 901a
Khayr al-Dīn Rāghib Pasha ii, 207b
Khayr al-Manāzil → M. Māham Anaga
Khayr Khān iii, 398b, 399a
Khayr al-Nassādj (914) vii, 1029b; ix, 432a
Khayr Shāh, Sayyid iv, 1160b
Khayrābād ii, 205a; iv, **1159b**; s, 420b
Khayrān (ʿĀmirid) (1038) i, 84a; ii, 1012b; iii, 147a; vi, 576a, b; vii, 633a; xi, 465b, 559a
Khayrāt, Āl i, 709a, 709b; ii, 517b, 518a; vi, 191b; s, 30a
Khayrat, Maḥmūd (XX) vii, 903a
al-Khayrī, Rāshid v, 204a
Khayriyye Sulṭān bint Maḥmūd II (Ottoman) (1830) vi, 860a
Khayrpūr ii, 258b, 263b, 264a, 669a; iii, 443a; iv, **1159b**
Khayrullāh Efendi i, 61a
Khayrullāh Efendi (Grand Vezir) i, 921a
al-Khayrūn iii, 155b
Khaysh iv, **1160b**; vii, 128a
Khayshan iv, 553b
al-Khaytānī, Shaykh Muḥyī al-Dīn b. Shaykh b. ʿAbd Allāh xi, 450a
Khaywān xi, 271a; s, 335a, 834a
al-Khayyāmī, Abū Ḥafṣ ʿUmar → ʿUmar Khayyām
Khayyāṭ iv, **1161a**
al-Khayyāṭ, Abu ʾl-Ḥusayn (913) i, 129a, 1002b; ii, 386b, 1026b; iii, 905b, 1144a; iv, **1162a**; vii, 785a; s, 12b, 225b
al-Khayyāṭ, Abū ʿAlī Yaḥyā (835) iv, **1162a**; viii, 107a
al-Khayyāṭ, ʿUthmān v, 769a; vii, 963b
al-Khayyāṭī, Sadīd b. Muḥammad (XII) viii, 893b
al-Khayzurān bint ʿAṭāʾ al-Djurashiyya (789) i, 633b, 1034a, 1035a, 1298a; iii, 22b, 231a, 232b; iv, **1164a**; v, 737b, 1239a; vi, 650b; s, 326b
Khazaf ii, 745a; iv, **1164b**
Khazʿal Khan (1936) iv, **1171a**; viii, 512b
Khazāʿil i, 1096b; ii, 339b
Khazaʾil (King) i, 525b
Khazar i, 18a, 100b, 625b, 660a, 835b, 837a, 864a, 921b, 931a, 985a, 1000a, 1305a, b, 1307a, b; ii, 85b, 86a, 482b, 1107b; iii, 234a, 759a; iv, 280a, 343a, b, 344a, b, 346b, 608b, 891b, **1172a**; v, 382a, 488a, 1013b; vi, 415b, 428a, 623a, b, 740a; s, 106a, 297b; x, 690a, 692a
– language iv, 1178b
Khazar, Banū v, 1174b, 1175a, 1176b, 1179b; x, 498b; s, 843b
Khazar b. Ḥafṣ b. Maghrāw v, 1174b
Khazarān i, 738a, b; iv, 346b, 1176a, 1178a; viii, 623a
Khazaria i, 837a; iv, 1174b, 1176b, 1177b
Khāzim b. Khuzayma i, 550b; ii, 592b; iii, 652a; viii, 462a; x, 816a, 927a
Khāzim b. Muḥammad iii, 501b
Khāzin ii, 304b; iv, **1181b**

al-Khāzin, Abū Djaʿfar (961) i, 1003a, 1100b; ii, 362a; iv, 629b, 1080a, **1182a**; vi, 600b; s, 412a
Khazīne ii, 1088b; iv, **1183b**
Khazīne-i Enderūn i, 1147a; iv, 1183b, 1184a
Khazīne-i Ewrāḳ i, 75a, 1089b; iii, 484a
al-Khāzinī, Abu ʾl-Fatḥ (XI) iii, 1137a; iv, **1186a**; vi, 601a; vii, 196b, 199b, 203b; viii, 655a; ix, 3a
al-Khāzir (river) iv, 493a, **1186b**; vii, 523b
Khazīr, Battle of iii, 620b
Khaznadār, Khāzindār iv, **1186b**
Khaznadār, Muṣṭafā → Muṣṭafā Khaznadār
al-Khazradj, Banū i, 50b, 53b, 514a, 544b, 771a, 1283a; iii, 812a; iv, **1187a**; v, 995a; vi, 373b, 374a, 472a; vii, 367a, 852b; s, 229b, 230a
al-Khazradjī, Abū Dulaf (X) → Abū Dulaf al-Khazradjī
al-Khazradjī, Ḍiyāʾ al-Dīn iv, **1187b**
al-Khazradjī, Muwaffaḳ al-Dīn (1410) ii, 441a; iv, **1188b**
al-Khazradjiyya → al-Khazradjī, Ḍiyāʾ al-Dīn
Khazrūn, Banū v, 1182a, b, 1183a; vi, 404a, 946b; ix, 545b, 894b; x, 213a
Khazrūn b. Fulfūl b. Khazar (976) v, 1178a; vi, 404a, 1041a
Khazrūn b. Saʿīd v, 1182b
Khazz → Ḥarīr
Khedive → Khidiw
Khedive Ismāʿīl → Ismāʿīl Pasha
Khēma → Khayma
Khemshili, Khemshin v, **1a**
Khenafsa s, 328a
Khērla v, **1a**, 924a; vi, 53a; s, 280a
Khettara iv, 529a
Kheyūn b. Djenāh i, 684a
Khibāʾ iv, 1147a
Khiḍāb v, **1b**; ix, 312a, 383b
Khidāsh (Khaddāsh) (736) i, 15b, 1293a; iv, 15b, 45a, 446a, 837b; v, **1b**, 63b; vii, 396a
Khidāsh b. Zuhayr al-Aṣghar (VII) v, **3b**; vii, 581a; s, 394b
Khidhlān i, 413b; v, **3b**, 833b
Khi̊ḍi̊r → Khayr al-Dīn Pasha Barbarossa
Khi̊di̊r b. ʿAbd Allāh (XV) vii, 685b
Khidīw (Khedive) v, **4a**
al-Khiḍr → al-Khaḍir
al-Khiḍr b. Aḥmad, Taghlibī vi, 900a
Khiḍr Beg Aydi̊noghlu i, 778a, 783b; iii, 1183a; v, 506a
Khiḍr Beg b. Ḳāḍī Djalāl al-Dīn (1459) iv, 225a, 737a; v, **4b**; vi, 1023a; ix, 400b, 630b; s, 528a
Khiḍr Beg b. Köse Mīkhāl vii, 34b
Khiḍr Ghaylān → al-Khaḍir Ghaylān
Khiḍr Ḥusayn → al-Khaḍir, Muḥammad b. al-Ḥusayn
Khiḍr-Ilyās ii, 915b; v, **5a**; vi, 421a, 810a
Khiḍr Ilyās Agha xi, 336b
Khiḍr Khān (Multān) (1395) iv, 1148a; vi, 49b, 50a, 294b; x, 593a; s, 206b
Khiḍr Khān (Sayyids, Delhi) (1421) i, 444b; ii, 120b, 258b, 269a, 270b, 695a; iii, 417b, 418a, 485a; iv, 276b, 419a, 922b, 923b; v, **5b**, 598a, 782b, 783a; vii, 193b, 313a, 549a; ix, 118b; s, 73b
Khiḍr Khān b. Ibrāhīm (Ḳarakhānid) (1081) iii, 1115b; vi, 274a; s, 65a
Khiḍr Khʷādja (Mongolistān) (1399) x, 590b, 677a
Khiḍr Khʷādja Čaghatāy ii, 1134b
Khiḍrawayh, Aḥmad vi, 225a
Khiḍrellez → Khiḍr-Ilyās
al-Khiḍrima i, 963a; iii, 166b; x, 792a
Khifāḍ → Khafḍ
Khifāra → Khafara
Khilʿa i, 24a; iii, 215b, 344b, 346b; v, **6a**, 620a, 737a, 752a; vii, 664a
Khilāfa → Khalīfa
Khilāfat movement i, 443a; ii, 255a; iii, 1204b; iv, 793b; v, **7a**; vi, 459b; vii, 421b, 678b; viii, 241b, 249a; s, 4b, 293b, 360a
Khilāt → Akhlāt
Khildjī → Khaldjī
Khillaut, Khilut v, 7a
Khimar, Banū iv, 10b
Khinalug ii, 89a; v, **8a**, 729b
Khindif, Banū i, 545a; vi, 477a
Khinsā → Khansā
Khinzīr v, **8a**; vi, 382b
al-Khiraḳī, Abu ʾl-Ḳāsim (946) i, 277a; iii, 159a, b, 734b, 784b; v, **9b**
Khirāsh b. Umayya viii, 1003a; s, 350a
Khirbat al-Bayḍāʾ v, **10a**
Khirbat al-Mafdjar i, 613b; ii, 955b; iii, 71a, 142b, 310a, 494b; iv, 701b, 1164b; v, **10b**, 338a; s, 117a, 251a

Khirbat al-Minya ii, 955b; v, **17a**; s, 117a, 229a
Khirḳa iv, 474a; v, **17b**, 737a; vii, 608b; viii, 306a
Khirḳa-yi̊ Saʿādet → Khirka-yi̊ Sherīf
Khirḳa-yi̊ Sherīf ii, 695b, 1088b; v, **18a**, 761b; x, 567a
Khīrkhān b. Ḳarādja iii, 120a, 1118b
Khirkī → Awrangābād
al-Khirniḳ vi, 603a; x, 219a
al-Khirrīt al-Nādjī (VII) v, **19b**, 451a
al-Khirshī vi, 279a
Khiṣāʾ iv, 1087b, 1090b
Khiṣālī (Budin) (1651) vii, 531b
Khīsh ii, 905a, b; iv, 1038b
Khiṭa → Ḳarā Khiṭāy
Khiṭāʿī → ʿAlī Akbar
Khitān iv, 913a; v, **20a**, 471a (see also *s.v.* Khafḍ)
Khitans v, 375b; vii, 234b
Khiṭaṭ v, **22b**
Khiṭāy → Ḳarā Khiṭāy; al-Ṣīn
Khiṭba v, **22b**; ix, 94a
Khitma → Khatma
Khiṭṭa v, **23a**
Khīwa i, 36a, 71a, 99b, 120b, 456a, 456b, 1296a; ii, 16a, 446a; iv, 611a, 1060b, 1064b, 1065a; v, **23b**, 859b; vi, 130b, 417a, 418a, 419a; s, 46a, 66a, 73a, 419b, 420a
Khīwa Khānate iv, 1065a; v, 24a, 392a; s, 97b, 169a, 228a, 281a
Khiyābān (Mashhad) vi, 715b
Khiyābān, Shaykh Muḥammad (1920) iv, 789b; v, **24b**; s, 110a, 365b, 366a
Khiyāla → Khayl
Khiyām → Khayma
al-Khiyāmī, Muḥammad iii, 812a
Khiyār v, **25a**
Khiyār (theology) → Ikhtiyār
Khiyār b. Sālim al-Ṭaʾī iii, 652a
Khiyār al-Madjlis iii, 1017a; viii, 818b
al-Khiyarī (1672) vi, 455a
Khizāna i, 68a, 212b, 270a, 280a, 391a, 396b, 601a, 626a, 736a, 776a, 816b, 819a, 826b, 893b, 899a, 1018a, 1053a, 1139b, 1211b, 1272a, 1354a; ii, 7b, 126b, 127a, 132b, 290a, 714a, 837b, 871a, 885a; iii, 627a, 708b, 769a, 777b, 896a, 973a, 1200a, 1234b (see also *s.v.* Maḳtaba)
Khizānadār → Khāzindār
Khizāne-i ʿāmire → Khazīne
Khizr, Khizir → Khiḍr
Khizrūn, Banū vii, 761a
Khloṭ → Khulṭ
Khmelnitsky, Boghdan iv, 178b, 179a
Khmer → Ḳimār
Khnīfra s, 223a
Khō, Banū ii, 31a, b
Khōbar → al-Khūbar
Khōdja i, 36a, 172a, b, 246b, 552b, 1254a, 1333b; ii, 45b, 47b, 58b, 129a, 170b; iii, 381a, 434b, 545a; iv, 202b, 206a; v, **25b**, 942b; viii, 84a, 307a; s, 332a
Khodja Čelebi → Abu ʾl-Suʿūd Muḥammad b. Muḥyi ʾl-Dīn al-ʿImādī
Khodja Čiwizāde → Muḥyi ʾl-Dīn Shaykh Muḥammad
Khodja Dāwūd Pasha → Dāwūd Pasha
Khodja Debhānī (XIII) viii, 210b
Khodja Efendi Saʿd al-Dīn (1599) i, 826a, 956a; ii, 713a; iii, 91b, 248b; iv, 900b; v, **27a**, 682b; vii, 596a, b
Khodja Eli → Ḳodja Eli
Khodja Ibrāhīm Pasha i, 395a
Khodja Kenʿān Pasha i, 843a; iv, 885a
Khodja Muṣṭafā Pasha (1512) viii, 10a
Khodja Muṣṭafā Pasha (1529) iii, 341b; iv, 231a, 882a; vi, 1023a
Khodja Muṣṭafā Pasha (Istanbul) vii, 1055b; ix, 875a, b
Khodja Rāghib Pasha → Rāghib Pasha
Khodja Sinān Pāshā (1486) → Sinān Pasha, Khodja (1486)
Khodja Sinān Pasha (1596) → Sinān Pasha, Khodja (1596)
Khodja Ṭāhir Efendi (Prizren) (XIX) viii, 340b
Khodja Yūsuf Pasha i, 63a, 174b; ix, 133a
Khodjaev (1938) ii, 932b; v, **28a**
Khodjand → Khudjand
Khōdjas (Kāshgharia) xi, 288a (see also *s.v.* Kh^{w}ādjas)
Khōdjazāde iii, 1149a
Khōī (Khūy) v, **28b**; vi, 120a, 200b, 201a, b, 202a, b, 243b, 494b, 502a, 504a; s, 365b
Khoḳand i, 71a, 504b, 1296a; ii, 45a, 67b, 440a, 792a; v, **29a**, 46a, 274a, 364a, 399b; vi, 371a, 419a, 557b; s, 97b, 98a, 228b, 420a
Khōkars, Banū ii, 972b, 1053a; v, **31a**, 598a; vii, 410a; ix, 119a, 693a

Khomayr → Khumayr
Khomeinī → Khumaynī
Khōnās i, 243b; ii, 204b; viii, 831b
Khorā iv, 231a; vi, 53a; ix, 680a
Khorāsān → Khurāsān
Khorkhut s, 245a
Khorsābād → Khursābād
Khō shāb ix, 417a
Khosham s, 363a (see also *s.v.* Hawsam)
Khoshḳadam → Khushḳadam, al-Malik al-Ẓāhir
Khosraw → Anūshirwān; Amīr Khusraw; Khosrew; Khusraw; Kisrā; Parwīz
Khosraw Agha → Khusraw Pasha Bosniak
Khosrew, Mollā (1480) ii, 126b; iii, 163b, 164a; v, **32b**; vi, 980a; vii, 595a; ix, 401a
Khosrew Beg Ghāzī (Bosnia) (1541) i, 1139b, 1263b, 1270b, 1272a; ii, 201b; v, **31b**; ix, 29b; s, 185a
Khosrew Pasha Bosniak → Khusraw Pasha Bosniak
Khosrew Pasha Deli (Dīvāne) (1544) iv, 902a; v, **35a**; vii, 911b; 706b
Khosrew Pasha, Meḥmed (1855) v, **35b**
Khōst v, **36b**, 501a, b; 1079b; vii, 438a, 573b; xi, 198a; s, 66a
Khotan i, 423b; iii, 1115b; v, **37a**; vi, 274a; ix, 617b; x, 628b; xi, 297a; s, 98a
Khotin v, **39b**, 260b, 720a, 766a
Khowár ii, 31a, 138b; s, 158b
Khoybūn i, 871a, b
al-Khubar i, 874a; ii, 175b; v, **40a**
Khubayb b. ʿAdī al-Anṣārī (VII) v, **40b**
Khubayb b. Yasāf (VII) x, 839b
Khūbmesīḥīs iv, 333b; v, **41a**
al-Khubūb i, 1312b, 1313a
Khubz ii, 1058a; v, **41b**; vii, 262b; viii, 652b
al-Khubzaʾaruzzī, Abu ʾl-Ḳāsim (938) v, 42a, **43a**; vii, 114b; ix, 55b
Khudā Bakhsh (1908) i, 1018a; v, **43b**
Khudā-Yār Khān → Yār Muḥammad Khān
Khudābanda → Muḥammad Khudābanda; Uldjaytū Khudābanda
Khudādād i, 359a
Khudādād b. Miḥrāb Khān v, 521a
Khudāwand v, **44a**
Khudāwand Khān (Gudjarāt) (1526) iii, 1160a; vi, 51b; ix, 893a
Khudāwand Khātūn (Saldjūḳ) (1332) viii, 15b
Khudāwand Muḥammad iv, 201b
Khudāwendigār i, 468b; iv, 564a; v, **44b**; vii, 592b; ix, 691b; xi, 332b, 333a
Khudāyār Biy (Mangit) (XVIII) vi, 418b
Khudāyār Khān (Kalhōrā) ii, 186a
Khudāyār Khān (Khoḳand) (1875) v, 30a, b; vi, 769a
Khudaybakhsh iv, 202b
Khudāydād ii, 622a
Khudāydād (Yasawī) xi, 116b
Khudāynāma iii, 884a; iv, 11a, 809a
Khudayr, Banū vi, 902a
Kūdjān → Ḳūčān
Khudjand v, 30b, **45a**, 400a; vi, 77a
Khudjand, Āl-ī s, 239b
Khudjandī, Abu ʾl-Ḳāsim iv, 101b
Khudjandī, Abū Maḥmūd Ḥāmid (1000) v, **46a**; vi, 600b, viii, 574a
Khudjandī, Ḍiyāʾ al-Dīn ʿAlī Turka (1431) vi, 73a
Khudjandī, Muʾayyad al-Dīn s, 364b
Khūdjī → Khūzī
Khudjistān v, **47a**
al-Khudjistānī → Aḥmad b. ʿAbd Allāh al-Khudjistānī; Muḥammad b. ʿAbd Allāh al-Khudjistānī
Khufāf b. Nadba/Nudba i, 12a; ix, 864a
Khugiyani s, 237b
Khūʾī (Khōī), Ayatullāh Ḥādjdjī Sayyid Abu ʾl-Ḳāsim (1992) vi, 553b; vii, 301b, 919a; s, 641b
Khūʾī Naṣīr (Nāṣir) al-Dīn x, 320b
Khuḳand → Khoḳand
Khulʿ → Ṭalāḳ
Khulafāʾ Sayyids (Iṣfahān) vi, 516b
Khulayd b. ʿAbd Allāh al-Ḥanafī (VII) viii, 62b
Khulayd b. Kaʾs (VII) viii, 62b
Khulayd ʿAynayn ii, 569a
Khuld vi, 564b
al-Khuld (Palace) i, 897a, b
Khuldābād i, 768a; v, **47a**; vi, 126a, b, 127a; vii, 315b
Khulḳ → Akhlāḳ
Khulm (town) ii, 638a; v, **47b**, 389a
Khulm (river) v, 47b
Khulnā vi, 46b; ix, 872b
Khulṭ, Banū v, **48b**; vi, 592b, 741b, 743a; viii, 899a; x, 169a

Khumār Beg i, 852a; viii, 245b
Khumārawayh b. Aḥmad b. Ṭūlūn (Ṭūlūnid) (896) i, 314b, 1290a; ii, 281b; iii, 745b, 750b; iv, 1090b; v, **49a**; vi, 657a, 676b; vii, 161a, 395a, 510a, 760a, 801b, 910b; x, 616b; s, 1a
Khumartāsh b. ʿAbd Allāh al-ʿImādī iv, 213b, 862b
Khumartāsh al-Sulaymānī i, 732a
Khumaynī, Āyatollāh Ruḥollāh Mūsawī (1989) v, 372a; vi, 487a, 549a, 553b, 554a, b; vii, 298b, 300a, 301b, 448a, b, 449a, 450a, b, 762b, 860b; x, 61b; s, 95b, 104a, 342b; s, **530a**
Khumayr v, **50b**; x, 641b
Khumays b. Ḥudhāfa iii, 63b
Khumayyis, Āl/ʿIyāl ii, 631b
Khumayyis al-ʿĀtī viii, 449a
Khumayyis Tarnān (1964) viii, 449a
Khumbara i, 1063a; iii, 478b
Khumbaradjï i, 1062a; v, **52b**
Khumbaradjī Aḥmed Pasha → Aḥmad Pasha Bonneval
Khumm → Ghadīr al-Khumm
Khums i, 1085b, 1142a; ii, 146b, 156b, 869b; s, **531a**
Khumurtāsh al-Ḥāfiẓī, Abu ʾl-Muẓaffar (amīr) (1141) iii, 399a; viii, 832a
Khumurtāsh al-Sulaymānī i, 732a
Khūnadj (Khūna) iv, 420a; vii, 508a
al-Khūnadjī ix, 20a, 344b
Khunāṣira v, **53a**
Khunātha bint Bakkār (1746) v, **53b**
Khunayfghān vi, 384b
Khunayḳ al-Ghirbān vi, 142a
Khundj v, 666b, 670b, 671a; vi, 384b
Khundjbāl → Khundj-ū-Fāl
Khundj-ū-Fāl v, 671b; vi, 384b; ix, 668a
Khundjī, Faḍl Allah b. Rūzbihān (1521) iv, 1036b; v, **53b**, 873a; vi, 14a; vii, 928a, 988a; ix, 428b, 733a
al-Khunūs (Aljonós) vi, 221b
Khunzal ii, 251a; v, **55b**
Khūr iv, 6a; xi, 238a, b
Khurāfa iii, 369b, 370a; vi, 819b; v, 187b
Khurāsān i, 3b, 16a, 18a, 19b, 43a, b, 52b, 59a, 77a, 99b, 108b, 141a, 147b, 149a, 228a, b, 230a, 246b, 278a, 296b, 437b, 529a, 684b, 964a, 1052a, 1293a, 1294a; ii, 4b, 43b, 1109a; iii, 163a; iv, 1051b; v, 2a, **55b**, 541a; 852b, 869a, 1238b; vi, 16a, 64b, 65a, 66a, 73a, 115b, 224b, 225a, 273b, 280b, 331a, b, 337a, 365b, 416a, 427b, 428a, 432b, 433a, 450a, 493a, 494b, 495a, 511a, 512a, 513b, 514b, 516b, 523a, 526b, 617b, 618a, 624b, 633b, 634a, 663b, 677a, 713b, 715b; vii, 266a, 396a, 409b, 410b, 440b, 453a, b, 477b; viii, 62b; s, 14b, 15a, 24a, 31b, 38a, 57b, 66b, 72b, 83a, 84a, 139b, 140a, 142a, 149a, 195a, 204a, 235a, 259a, 263a, 265a, 266a, 281a, 299a, 326a, b, 363b, 420b
– administration ii, 505a, 561a; v, 56b
– ethnology iii, 1107b; iv, 20a; v, 56a, b
– history ii, 978b; iv, 15a-b; v, 56b-59b
Khurāsān, Banū v, **59b**
Khurāsānī → Badr al-Dīn Khurāsānī
al-Khurāsānī, Ākhūnd Mullā Muḥammad Kāẓim (1911) v, **61a**; vi, 552b, 553a; vii, 299b; ix, 216b, 217a, 479b; x, 497b; s, 76a, 95b
al-Khurayba v, 761b, 762a; viii, 356b (see also *s.v.* Dedan)
Khuraym vi, 606a
Khuraym al-Nāʿim i, 784b
al-Khuraymī → Abū Yaʿḳūb al-Khuraymī
Khuraz Bek (Mangït) (XVIII) vi, 418a
Khūrī i, 1006b
al-Khūrī, Fāris (1962) iii, 519a; v, **62a**
al-Khūrī, Rashīd Salīm → al-Ḳarawī, al-Shāʿir
al-Khūrī, Shukrī ii, 471b
Khūriyā-Mūriyā → Khūryān-Mūryān
al-Khurma v, **62b**; ix, 739a
Khurma-rūd ii, 1141a
Khurram (Prince) → Shāh Djahān I (Mughal) (1666)
Khurramābād i, 840a; v, **63a**, 830a, 831b
Khurramdīnī → Khurramiyya
Khurramiyya (Khurramdīniyya) i, 149b, 241a, 844a; iii, 234a; iv, 17a, 45a, 100a, 838b; v, **63b**, 243b, 823a; vi, 338b, 951b; vii, 664a
Khurramshahr i, 1342a; ii, 181a; iv, 6a; v, **65b**; ix, 369a; s, 57a (see also *s.v.* Muḥammara)
Khurrem Sulṭān (1558) i, 1225b; iii, 147b, 998b; iv, 232a, 1100a; v, **66a**, 333b, 720a, 802a; vii, 713a
Khursābād v, **67b**; vi, 365a
Khurshāh → Rukn al-Dīn Khurshāh

Khurshān b. Ḳubād al-Ḥusaynī → Niẓām-Shāhī
Khurshīd (Dābūyid, Ṭabaristān) (761) ii, 74b; iii, 501b; v, **68b**; vi, 744b, 941a; s, 298b
Khurshīd, K.H. iv, 711a
Khurshīd Aḥmed Pasha (Morea) (XIX) i, 399a, b; ii, 637a; iii, 88b; vii, 249b; x, 834b
Khurshīd (Silūrzī) i, 513b
Khurshīdī v, 828a
al-Khurṭūm → Kharṭūm
Khurūdj (grammar) iv, 412a
Khurūdj (literature) x, 123a
Khūryān-Mūryān i, 535b, 540a, 1282b; v, **70a**; vi, 729b
Khusdār → Kalāt; Ḳuṣdār
al-Khushanī, Abū ʿAbd Allāh (981) i, 600b; iii, 789b; v, **71a**; vi, 353b; vii, 400a; viii, 117b, 518a
al-Khushanī → Ibn Masʿūd al-Khushanī
al-Khushanī, Ibn ʿAbd al-Salām ix, 38a
Khushḥāl Khān Khaṭak (1689) i, 218b, 221a; iv, 1102a; v, **72a**
Khushaysh b. Aṣram (867) iv, 368b; viii, 388a
Khushḳadam, ʿImād al-Mulk (Gudjarāt) (1526) vi, 51b, 52a
Khushḳadam, al-Malik al-Ẓāhir (Mamlūk) (1467) ii, 239b; iii, 1198b; iv, 960a; v, **73a**; vi, 318b, 727a, 791a; s, 38a
Khusraushāhī, Hādī iv, 167a
Khusraw → Amīr Khusraw; Khosrew Beg; Kisrā I, II
Khusraw b. Djahāngīr → Khusraw Sulṭān
Khusraw Beg → Khosrew Beg
Khusraw Fīrūz, al-Malik al-Raḥīm (1057) i, 132a, 513a, 1073b, 1352b, 1356a; ii, 192b; iv, 457b; v, **73b**
Khusraw Fīrūz (Djustānid) s, 357a
Khusraw Fīrūzān ii, 192a
Khusraw Khān Barwārī ii, 269a, 272a, 1076a, 1084a; iii, 416b; iv, 923b; s, 105b
Khusraw Malik, Tādj al-Dawla (Ghaznawid) (1186) vii, 1016b
Khusraw Mīrzā iii, 554b; iv, 787a; vii 454a; x, 737b; s, 70b, 108b
Khusraw Parvīz → Kisrā II
Khusraw Pasha Bosniak (1632) i, 4a, 1159b, 1208b; ii, 1091a; iv, 971b; v, **32b**, 256b, 458a
Khusraw Pasha Dīvāne (Deli) → Khosrew Pasha Deli
Khusraw Shāh → Ghaznawids
Khusraw Shāh, Nāṣir al-Dīn → Khusraw Khān Barwārī
Khusraw Shāh b. Bahrām ii, 1052b; v, 691a
Khusraw Sulṭān (Mughal) (1622) i, 686a; ii, 380a; iv, 282a; v, **74a**; vii, 131b, 315a, 331b
Khusrawānī v, 185a
Khusrawgird vi, 365b
Khusrawī, Muḥammad Bāḳir Mīrzā (1950) iv, 72b; v, 198a; viii, 448a; ix, 402b
Khusraw-zāde v, 609b
Khusrew → Khosrew; Khusraw
Khusūf → Kusūf
al-Khuṣūṣ vi, 775a; viii, 874a
al-Khutaʾītī (ḳāḍī) (Aleppo) (XI) vii, 693a
Khuṭarniyya vi, 633b; vii, 521b
Khutarniyya (garments) i, 1236a
Khuṭba i, 20b, 132a, 261b; ii, 593a; iii, 35b; iv, 945a, 1110a; v, **74a**; vi, 657b, 668b
Khuttal → Khuttalān
Khuttalān ii, 1052a; v, **75b**; vii, 477b; s, 125a, b
Khuttalānī, Isḥāḳ (1423) v, 301a; viii, 134b; ix, 857a
Khuttalī iv, 216a; s, 125b
Khuwāra → Djand
al-Khuwārizmī → al-Khʷārazmī
Khuwayr → Khawr Ḥassān
Khuwwa → Khafāra
Khūy → Khōī
al-Khūyī, ʿAbd al-Muʾmin (painter) viii, 961a
al-Khūyī, Ḥasan b. ʿAbd al-Muʾmin (XIV) viii, 544a
Khuzāʿa, Banū i, 453a, 1283b; v, **76b**, 434b; vi, 145a, 333a, 374a; vii, 356b
al-Khuzāʿī, ʿAbd Allāh b. al-Haytham (IX) vi, 333a
al-Khuzāʿī, Abū ʿAlī Muḥammad b. ʿAlī b. Razīn → Diʿbil
al-Khuzāʿī, Abū Muḥammad i, 827a; x, 162b
al-Khuzāʿī, Aḥmad b. Naṣr b. Malik (845) vii, 4b; viii, 1051b; xi, 178a, b
al-Khuzāʿī, Ḥamza b. Mālik s, 326b
al-Khuzāʿī, Malik b. al-Haytham (IX) vi, 332a, b, 335a

al-Khuzāʿī, Muḥammad b. al-Ashʿath (IX) vi, 333a
al-Khuzāʿī, al-Muṭṭalib b. ʿAbd Allāh vi, 335a, b
al-Khuzāmā v, **80a**; s, 377a
Khuzayma, Amīr Ismāʿīl Khān (XVIII) s, 507a
Khuzayma b. Khāzim b. Khuzayma al-Tamīmī (IX) v, 488a; vi, 332b, 335b, 499a
Khuzayma b. Thābit al-Anṣārī (VII) v, 621a; vi, 710a; ix, 555a
Khuzdar → Ḳuṣdār
Khūzistān i, 3a, 131b, 239b, 240a, 305b, 437b, 528b, 561b, 659a, 695a, 866b, 1350a; ii, 903a; iii, 291b; iv, 6a, 42b; v, 65b, **80a**, 824a, 831a, 866b, 867a; vi, 117b, 120a, 272b, 333b; vii, 672a, 675a; ix, 855b; s, 12b, 37b, 61a
Khvarshi̊ v, **81b**
Khʷadāy-nāmak → Khudāynāma
Khʷaja Nizamuddin viii, 242a
Khʷāsh (village) v, 147b; ix, 54a
Khʷāsh b. Yūsuf (1009) vii, 43b
Khyber Pass → Khaybar
Kianghrī → Čanki̊ri̊
Kiari, Modibbo i, 179b
Kiari, Muḥammad al-Amīn i, 1260a
Kiaya → Ketkhudā
Kibar v, 868b
Ḳibla i, 609b; ii, 213b; iv, 318a; v, **82a**, 323b, 1140b, 1141a, 1169a
Ḳi̊bri̊sli̊ Meḥmed Emīn Pasha (1860) i, 397a; vi, 1032a
al-Kibrīt v, **88b**, 706b
Ḳibṭ i, 435b, 471a, 532a, 803a, 1146b; ii, 229b, 330a, 560b, 958a; iii, 4a, 721b, 886a; v, **90a**
al-Ḳibṭī → Čingāne
Ḳidāḥ iv, 488a
Ḳidam i, 333b; v, **95a**
Kidara i, 226a; iii, 303b
Kīdj (Kīz) vi, 193a
Ḳidjmās (amīr) (Damascus) (1382) ii, 286a; vi, 580b
Ḳidwāʾī → Mushīr Ḥusayn Ḳidwāʾī
Kifāyat Khān iv, 1128a
Ḳifṭ v, **90a**, 92a, 99a, 514a
al-Ḳifṭī → Shīth b. Ibrāhīm
al-Ḳifṭī, ʿAlī b. Yūsuf → Ibn al-Ḳifṭī
al-Ḳifṭī, Yūsuf b. Ibrāhīm s, 289a
Kihāna ii, 322b, 760a; iv, 263b, 420b, 763a, 1128b; v, **99b**; vi, 247a; viii, 94a
Kihsan v, 1148b
Kijumwa, Muhammad bin Abu Bakari (XX) vi, 612b
Ḳīḳān, Kīkān → Kalāt
Kilā → Kalah
al-Ḳilā → al-Ḳily
al-Ḳilāʿ → al-Ḳalʿa (castle)
Ḳilʿa Rāy Pithorā i, 1321b; ii, 256a, b, 259a; v, 1214b
Kilāb b. Rabīʿa, Banū i, 441a, b, 442a; ii, 71b, 159b, 234a, 235a, 238a; v, **101b**, 459a, 923a; vi, 379a; vii, 115a, 693a; viii, 863b
Ḳilāba bt. al-Ḥārith b. Kalada s, 355a
al-Kilābī (820) vii, 831b
al-Kilābī, Abu ʾl-ʿAbbās Aḥmad b. Saʿīd (939) v, 923b; vii, 115a
al-Kilābī, Abu ʾl-Fatḥ ʿUthmān b. Saʿīd (944) vii, 115a; ix, 105a
al-Kilābī, Safr b. ʿUbayd viii, 632a
al-Kilāʿī, ʿAyyād (ʿAbbād; ʿImād) b. Naṣr iv, 403a
al-Kīlānī, Rashīd ʿAlī → Rashīd ʿAlī al-Gaylānī
Kilār ii, 1088b
Kilāt (Kalāt, Kelāt) (Balūčistān) i, 39a, 99b, 230a, 1006a; iii, 564b; iv, 364b, 395a, 535a, 1059b; v, **101b**, 580a, 684b; vi, 192b, 193a, 502b; s, 22a, 332a
Kilāt-i Nādirī v, **102b**
Ḳi̊lburun v, **103a**
Kili i, 1253a, 1287a; iii, 253b
Kilī, Banū v, 459b
Kilia i, 1119b; iv, 92a
Ki̊li̊çzāde Ḥaḳḳī iv, 169a
Kilīd al-Baḥr → Čanaḳ-ḳalʿe Boghazi̊
Ḳi̊li̊dj Alayi vi, 529b-531b
Ḳi̊li̊dj ʿAlī Beg v, 48a
Ḳi̊li̊dj ʿAlī Pasha → ʿUlūdj ʿAlī
Ḳi̊li̊dj Arslan I b. Sulaymān b. Ḳutlumush (Rūm Saldjūḳ) (1107) i, 466a, b, 664a, 732a; ii, 110a, b; v, **103b**; vii, 408a; viii, 948a
Ḳi̊li̊dj Arslan II b. Masʿūd I (Rūm Saldjūḳ) (1192) i, 431b, 466b; ii, 111a; iv, 575b; v, **104a**, 254b; vi, 507a, 777a; vii, 816b; viii, 129b, 130a, 133a, 948b, 975a
Ḳi̊li̊dj Arslan III b. Rukn al-Dīn (Rūm Saldjūḳ) (XIII) ii, 691b; v, **104b**

Ḳïlïdj Arslan IV Rukn al-Dīn b. Khusraw II (Rūm Saldjūḳ) (1265) iv, 619b, 620a, 813b, 814a; v, **104b**, 254a; vii, 479a, b
Ḳïlïdj Arslān b. al-Malik al-Manṣūr (Ayyūbid) (1220) vi, 429b
Ḳïlïdj Bek i, 1157a
Ḳilidjūrī v, 9a
Kilifi v, **105a**
Ḳīlīḳiya → Cilicia
Killah → Kalah
Ḳillawriya iv, 496b; v, **105a**
Killigil ii, 701b, 702a
Killiz v, **105b**
Kilmek Abiz i, 1076b
Kilōgharī s, 352b
Kilwa iv, 886a, 892b; v, **106a**, 223b, 1157b; vi, 128a, b, 283a, b, 370a, 704a, 774a; ix, 700b
al-Ḳily v, **107a**
Kimäk v, **107b**, 126a; iv, 542a; x, 690; s, 245a
Ḳimār i, 343a; v, **108b**, 616b, 768b
Ḳimār (Khmer) ii, 9a; iii, 1208b; v, **108a**; 227a
al-Kīmāriyyūn (al-Ṣābiʾa) vi, 921a
al-Kīmiyāʾ iii, 965a; iv, 673b; v, 110a; xi, 495b
Ḳinā iv, 207a; v, 515b, 519b (see also *s.v.* Ḳunā)
Kinabalu, Mount s, 150a
al-Ḳināʾī, ʿAbd al-Raḥīm (1195) viii, 864b
Kīnakhʷāriyya i, 1110a; s, 363b
Kınalı vi, 588b
Ḳïnalïzāde ʿAlāʾ al-Dīn (1572) iv, 471b; v, **115a**
Ḳïnalïzāde Ḥasan Čelebī (Bursa) (1603) v, **116a**; x, 55a; xi, 132a
Kināna b. Bishr (VII) vii, 269a
Kināna b. Khuzayma, Banū i, 545a; ii, 625a, 627a, 883b; iv, 334a; v, **116a**; vi, 145a
Kināya v, **116b**; s, 278a
Kinda, Banū i, 526b, 548b, 583b, 683b, 697a; ii, 354a; iii, 52b; v, 23a, **118a**; vi, 311a, 441b, 472a, 477b; ix, 77a; x, 90a; s, 326b, 337b, 506a
al-Kindī, ʿAbd al-Masīḥ iii, 165b; v, **120b**
al-Kindī, Abū ʿUmar (961) i, 153b; v, **121b**; vi, 412a; ix, 114a, b
al-Kindī, Abū Yūsuf Yaʿḳūb b. Isḥāḳ (866) i, 154a, 234b, 235a, 327b, 328a, 344b, 589a, 631a, 1003b, 1100b; ii, 376b, 578b, 765b, 771b, 872a; iii, 169b, 303a, 664a; iv, 332b, 418a, 763b, 795a; v, 113b, **122a**, 237b, 398b, 702b, 950a; vi, 99a, 204b, 338b, 376b, 449a, 637a; vii, 681a, b, 682a, 1031b; viii, 108a, 302a; ix, 35a; s, 72b, 78a, 251b, 271b, 412a
al-Kindī, ʿAlī b. Muḥammad (VIII) viii, 573a
Ḳindīl → Miṣbāḥ
Ḳiniḳ, Banū viii, 938a; x, 689b
Kinkiwar v, **123b**, 169a
Ḳinnasrīn i, 135a, 761a, b; ii, 624a; v, **124a**, 921a; vi, 338b, 379a, 380b, 506a, 544a, 623b
Ḳinṭār → Makāyīl
Ḳïpčaḳ i, 135a, 927a, 1075b, 1105a, 1188b, 1302a; ii, 24a, 43a, 44b, 610a, 1108a, 1109a; iii, 1115a; iv, 32b, 349a, 350a, 527a, 542a, 892a; v, 30a, 108a, **125b**; vi, 321a, 325b; vii, 166a; x, 690b; s, 97b, 203b, 245b, 392b, 420a
Ḳïpčak, Sayf al-Dīn ii, 285b; vi, 545b, 777b
Ḳïr Shehir → Ḳïrshehir
Kirāʾ v, **126b**
Ḳirāʾa → Tadrīs
Ḳirāʾa(t) i, 114a, 565b, 567b; ii, 293a; iii, 434b, 704b, 761a, 817b; iv, 822a; v, **127a**; s, 393b
Ḳirāḍ iv, 691b; v, **129b**
Ḳirān iii, 35a, 53b; iv, 259a; v, **130b**
Ḳīrāṭ ii, 769a; iii, 10b (see also *s.v.* Makāyīl)
Ḳiraynūn, Āl vi, 81b
Ḳird v, 5b, **131a**; ix, 440b; s, 174b, 191b
Kirdi ii, 9b, 10a; xi, 11b; s, 569a
Kirdï-Kalal → Ḳarata, Banū
Ḳïrdjalï i, 1304a; ii, 971b
Kiresun → Giresün
Ḳirghiz → Ḳïrgïz
Ḳïrgïz i, 224a, 853b, 1076b, 1077a; ii, 66b, 67b, 571a; iii, 116a, 117a; iv, 10a, 213b, 631b; v, **134a**, 247a; vi, 370b, 371a, 770b; vii, 353b; viii, 178a; x, 688b
– literature x, **728a**
Kirid → Iḳrītish
Ḳïrïm i, 4b, 62b, 270b, 293a, 893a, 1108a, 1119b; ii, 24b, 25a, 1112a; iii, 44b; iv, 499b, 568b, 608a, 891b; v, **136a**, 719b; s, 96b

Ḳi̊ri̊m Khānat v, 141b, 142a, 312b
Ḳi̊ri̊mčaḳ x, 697b
al-Kirimī, Diyā' al-Dīn ʿAbd Allāh al-Ḳazwīnī x, 88b
Ḳirḳ-Khān vi, 538a
Ḳi̊rḳ Kilise v, **143b**, 815a
Ḳi̊rghi̊z x, 688b
Ki̊rgi̊zstān s, **536a**
Ḳi̊rḳgöz (bridge) vi, 230a, 231b
al-Ḳirḳisānī, Abū Yaʿḳūb Yūsuf (Karaite) (X) iv, 96a, 306b, 605a; vii, 539b, 566a
Ḳirḳīsiyā vi, 622b (see also *s.v.* Ḳarḳīsiyā)
Ḳi̊rḳlareli → Ḳi̊rḳ Kilise
Kirkūk v, 144a; vi, 55b, 56b, 614a; vii, 714b
Ḳi̊rk-yir iii, 44b
Kirmān i, 8a, 86a, 131b, 132a, 211b, 420a, 731b, 830b, 1005a, 1311a, 1350a; ii, 299a, 746b, 1051a; iii, 1156b; iv, 14b, 19b, 391b, 807a, 1046b, 1170a; v, **147a**, 294a, 835a, 1114a, 1116a; vi, 66a, b, 72b, 115b, 272b, 273b, 331b, 368b, 481b, 493b, 494a, 633b; s, 53a, 71b, 118b, 122b, 127a, 129a, 139b, 140b, 142a, 147b, 326a, 327a
Kirmān (Karmān) b. Menteshe Beg (1300) vi, 1018a
Kirmānī, Awḥad al-Dīn (1238) v, **166a**; vi, 381b; viii, 753b; ix, 298a
Kirmānī, ʿAlā' al-Dīn (1870) viii, 542a
Kirmānī, Ḥādjdjī Mīrzā Muḥammad Karīm Khān (XIX) → Shaykhiyya
Kirmānī, Ḥamīd al-Dīn Aḥmad (1020) i, 450a; iii, 72a, 134a; iv, 204a; v, **166a**; vii, 968b, 1006b
Kirmānī, Kamāl al-Dīn → Khʷādjū Kamāl al-Dīn Kirmānī
Kirmānī, Mīrzā Āḳā Khān s, 109b
Kirmānshāh iv, 7b; v, **167b**; vi, 491b, 493a, 495b, 498b; s, 73a, 84a, 135a, 142b
Kirmāsin → Kirmānshāh
Kirmāstī v, **171b**
Ḳirmid v, 585b, 1215a
Kirmīsīn → Kirmānshāh
Ḳirmiz i, 645b; ii, 681a; v, 586a
Kirovabad → Gandja
Ḳirsh → Sikka
Ḳi̊rshehir i, 323b, 324a; v, **172a**
Ḳirṭās i, 531b; ii, 307a; iv, 742a; v, **173b**
Ḳīr-wa-Kārzīn vi, 384a
Ḳirwāsh b. Muḳallad (Mawṣil) (XI) ii, 391a; iv, 378b; v, 896b; x, 787a; xi, 180b
Kisā' → Libās
al-Kisā'ī, Abu 'l-Ḥasan ʿAlī b. Ḥamza (805) ii, 806b, 807b; iii, 155a; v, **174a**, 351a; vi, 331a; vii, 280a; viii, 573a; s, 22b, 128b
al-Kisā'ī, Madjd al-Dīn (X) iv, 60b; v, **175b**
al-Kisā'ī, Ṣāḥib Ḳiṣaṣ al-Anbiyā' (Abū Bakr Muḥammad) iii, 306a; v, **176a**, 180b, 233b; vii, 284a
Kisakürek, Necip Fazil (1983) ii, 432b; s, **538a**
Kisangani v, **176b**
Ḳiṣāṣ ii, 341a; iv, 770a; v, **177a**
Ḳiṣaṣ → Ḳiṣṣa
Ḳiṣaṣ al-anbiyā' i, 169a; iv, 673b; v, 176a, **180a**, 186b, 193b, 197b, 205a
Kīsh (Ḳays, Djabal) i, 552a, 942b, 1355a; iii, 881a; iv, 500b, **832a**; v, 670b, 671a; s, 222b
Kīsh (Shahr-i Sabz) i, 1066b; iv, 694a, 711b; v, **181a**, 858b; vii, 925a
Ḳi̊shlaḳ v, **182b**
Ḳi̊shlāḳ (Khʷār) iv, 1029b
Kishlū Khān (Delhi) (XIII) iii, 202b; iv, 920b; vi, 48b
Kishm, Badakhshān i, 851b
Ḳishm (island) iii, 653a; iv, 399a, 777b; v, **183a**, 675a, b, 765a
Ḳishn v, **184a**; vi, 80a, 82a, b; ix, 808b
Kishōr Singh, Maharao (1821) vi, 419b
Ḳishr iv, 451a, 452a, 741a
Kishsh → Kash; Kish
al-Kishshī, Abū Shakūr al-Sālimī (XI) vi, 847b
Kishtwār s, 242a
Kishwar ii, 577a, 579b, 951b
Ḳisma, ḳismet v, **184a**
Kisrā v, **184b**
Kisrā (Ḳarmaṭī) iv, 663a, b
Kisrā I Anūshirwān (Sāsānid) (579) i, 102a, 516b, 522b, 549a, 835b, 1094a; ii, 114a, 190b, 740a; iii, 304a; iv, 14a, 265a, 839a; v, 184b; vi, 230b, 378b, 632a, 633a, 637b, 648a, 653b, 660b, 664b, 745a; vii, 912b; ix, 77b; s, 115b, 127a, 255b, 299a, 354b
Kisra II Parwīz b. Hormuzd II (Sasānid) (628) i, 510a, 996a, 1094a; ii, 793b; iii, 219a; iv, 730b, 1133b; v, 184b, 633b; vi, 201b, 276a, 537a, 633a; vii, 841a; viii, 77b, 119b; ix, 79a; s, 298b
Kisrawān vi, 343b, 344a; ix, 494a, b; s, 33b

al-Kisrawī, Abu ʾl-Ḥasan ʿAlī (IX) v, **185b**
Kissa → Khāsa
Ḳiṣṣa, Ḳiṣaṣ ii, 306a; iii, 369a, 374a; v, **185b**, 951a
Ḳiṣṣa Čahār Darwīsh i, 430b; iii, 373a
Ḳisṭ → Makāyīl
al-Kīsumī, Abū Riḍā s, 363a
Kiswa (town) ii, 541a; iv, 317b, 319b; vi, 546b, 547a, 548a
Kiswa iv, 317b; vi, **166a**
Ki-swahili → Swahili
Ḳiṭʿa (poetry) vii, 509a; s, **538b**
Kitāb i, 30a, 274a; ii, 214a, 302b; iii, 1127a; iv, 353b; v, **207a**
Kitāb al-Djilwa v, **208b**
Kitāb al-Istibṣār → Istibṣār, Kitāb al-
Kitāba i, 30a; ii, 302b, 328b; iii, 27a; ix, 549b
Kitābāt v, **210b**, 754b, 761b, 992b
Kitābi̊ Dede Ḳorḳud → Dede Ḳorḳut
Kitābkhāna → Maktaba
Kitai → Ḳarā Khiṭāy
Kitāmiyya → Shādhiliyya
Kʾi-tan vi, 456a; ix, 16a (see also *s.v.* Ḳarā Khiṭāy)
Ḳitarā → Ḳithāra
Kitau vi, 385a
Kitbugha al-Manṣūrī, al-Malik al-ʿĀdil (Mamlūk) (1297) i, 1126b, 1324b; ii, 285a; iii, 954b; iv, 965b; v, 595a; vi, 322b; vii, 168b, 169b, 991b; viii, 156b, 995b
Kitbugha Noyon (XIII) i, 786b; vii, 167a
Kitchener, Lord i, 13b, 46a; ii, 828a
Ḳiṭfīr i, 825b; v, **233b** (see also *s.v.* ʿAzīz Miṣr)
Ḳithāra v, **234a**
al-Kitmān → al-Ibāḍiyya; Khāridjites; Taḳiyya
Ḳiṭmīr → Aṣḥāb al-Kahf; Kalb
Ḳiṭrān → Ḳaṭrān
Kivar → Kibar
Ḳiwām al-Dawla → Bahāʾ al-Dawla Fīrūz
Ḳiwām al-Dīn Darguzīnī (Ansabādhī) (XII) vi, 64b
Ḳiwām al-Dīn Niẓām al-Mulk (vizier) (1497) s, 460a
Ḳiwām al-Din Shīrāzī iv, 910b, 1073b
Ḳiwāmī (Gandja) (XII) iv, 59b; vi, 609b; s, 416b
Kiyā Abu ʾl-Faḍl (Thāʾirid) s, 363a
Kiyā Buzurg-Ummīd (XII) vi, 918a
al-Kiyā al-Harrāsī, Shams al-Islām (1010) v, **234b**; vii, 562a, 755b; s, 347a
Ḳiyāfa ii, 211a, 916a, b; v, **234b**
Kiyā-i Djalāl vi, 515b
al-Ḳiyāma i, 186b; iv, 47a, 205a, b; v, **235b**
Ḳiyāmatābād vi, 501b
Ḳiyān → Ḳayna
Kiyāna (Zāb) iv, 479a; vi, 435a
Kiyār iv, 97b
Ḳiyās i, 276a, 1199b, 1327a; ii, 102a, 182b; iii, 795a, 1025b, 1026a; iv, 153b, 256a; v, **238b**
Ḳiyāt s, 46a, 97b
Kiybad Çiftliği → Kayḳubādiyya
Ḳi̊z v, **242b**
Ḳi̊z Kulesi v, 243a; vi, 359b
Kiẓāma iv, 532b
Ḳizduwān s, 246a
Ḳızıl Adalar vi, 588a, b
Ḳi̊zi̊l Aghač vii, 497b
Ḳi̊zi̊l Aḥmedli̊ → Isfendiyār Oghlu Shemsī Aḥmed Pasha
Ḳi̊zi̊l Arslan, Khāmūsh → Khāmūsh Ḳi̊zi̊l Arslan
Ḳi̊zi̊l Arslan ʿUthmān iii, 1111a, b, 1112a; xi, 393a
Ḳi̊zi̊l-bāsh i, 1b, 224a, 262a, 1162a, 1229b; ii, 20b, 202b; iii, 253b, 316a, 1101a; iv, 34b, 35a, b, 36b, 186b, 188b; v, **243a**, 437b, 749a; vi, 483a; x, 108b
Ḳi̊zi̊l-elma (Ḳi̊zi̊l-alma) v, **245b**; vi, 979a
Ḳi̊zi̊l-irmāḳ v, 172a, **246b**; x, 759b
Ḳi̊zi̊l-ḳum iv, 613a; v, **246b**
Ḳi̊zi̊l-üzen v, **247a**; vi, 502a; vii, 189b; viii, 808a; ix, 196b (see also *s.v.* Safīd Rūd)
Kizimkazi(-Dimbani) v, **247b**; vi, 1023a
Kīzkānān → Kilāt
Ḳi̊zlar Aghasi̊ i, 295a; iii, 175b; iv, 568b; v, 243a, 247b
Klementi i, 651b, 652a, 656b; ii, 563b
Klis i, 1263b; v, 774b, 775a
Ḳnīṭra iv, 556b
Kōbad → Ḳubādh
Ḳobān iv, 674b, 675a
Köbeči → Ḳubači
Ḳocaeli → Kodja-eli
Kocha i, 719b
Ḳoč Ḥiṣār v, **247b**; vi, 231b, 541b
Ḳoči̊ Beg (XVII) i, 712a; iii, 983a; iv, 168a; v, **248b**, 266a; vii, 598a; viii, 184b
Ḳočḳar (river) iv, 212b

Ḳočo x, 676a; s, **540a**
Ḳodja → Khodja
Ḳodja-eli i, 468b; v, **250a**
Kogh-Vasil (Kaysūm) (XII) i, 1190b; vi, 776b
Kōhāt i, 238b; v, **250b**
al-Kōhēn al-ʿAṭṭār v, **251a**
al-Kōhīn → al-Kūhin
Kohinoor → Kūh-i Nūr
Kōhistān → Ḳūhistān
Kōh-rūd → Ḳuhrūd
Kōʾil → Aligarh; Koyl
Ḳoḳan → Khoḳand
Kökbürī → Gökbürī, Muẓaffar al-Dīn
Kokča (river) i, 851b, 852a
Kökildäsh vi, 130b
Kök-Türk (inscriptions) vi, 809b; viii, 178a
Kökülü-oghlu ii, 207a
Kōlatirri Rādjās iv, 547a; v, 587a
Kölbay Toghis uli vi, 767a
Koléa i, 67b; v, 362a
Kolhāpur vi, 535a
Ḳolonborna i, 1062b
Köl Tegin → Kültigin
Ḳomač iii, 47b
Ḳōmis → Ḳūmis (Comes)
Komo vi, 422a
Komoten → Gümüldjīne
Ḳomul v, 846a; vi, 768a; xi, 343a, b; s, **541a**
Konakry v, **252a**
al-Konawi → al-Ḳūnawī
Konbur → Dāghistān
Kong ii, 63a; v, **252b**
Ḳongrat → Ḳungrāt
Konkan iii, 426a; vi, 50b, 269a, b; vii, 919b; viii, 300b; s, 246a, **541b**
Ḳonḳirat → Ḳungrāt
Ḳonya (Ḳūniya) i, 466b, 468a, 477b, 703a, 807a; ii, 202a, 746b; iv, 575b, 621a, b, 622a, 1167b; v, **253b**, 589a, 676b, 677b, 881a; vi, 59b, 71b, 120b, 275b, 366a, 710b; s, 83b, 137a, 146a, 280b
– monuments v, 254b, 1145a, 1146a
Ḳonya (Ḳaramān) Ereğlisi ii, 705b
Kopak → Sikka
Köpek Khān → Kebek Khān
Köpek, Saʿd al-Dīn → Saʿd al-Dīn Köpek
Köprü → Vezīr Köprü
Köprü ḥaḳḳi ii, 147a
Köprü Ḥiṣārī v, **256a**
Köprülü (viziers) i, 1064a; v, **256a**
Köprülü ʿAbd Allāh Pasha (1724) vi, 505a; vii, 854b
Köprülü Aḥmed Pasha vi, 982b; s, 171a
Köprülü Fāḍil Aḥmed Pāsha (1676) i, 68b, 1032b; ii, 635a, 833a; iii, 477a, 1086b; iv, 516b, 539a, 590a, 591a; v, 258b, **259a**, 720b, 766a; vi, 982b; s, 171a
Köprülü Fāḍil Muṣṭafā Pasha (1691) i, 268a; iv, 193b, 194a, 233b; v, **261a**; vi, 983a
Köprülü Meḥmed Fuʾād (1966) ii, 596a; vi, 93b, 94a; v, **263b**; s, 82b
Köprülü Meḥmed Pasha (1661) i, 4b; ii, 1090b; iii, 626b; iv, 233b, 589b, 720a; v, **256b**; vi, 345b, 982b; vii, 900a; ix, 697b
Köprülü Nuʿmān Pasha (1719) i, 268b, 269a, 395a; v, **262b**
Köprülüzāde Meḥmed Fuʾād → Köprülü Meḥmed Fuʾād
Ḳopuz → ʿŪd
Kōrā Djahānābād iii, 61a; v, **264b**
Korah → Ḳārūn
Koraltan, Refik ii, 596a; vi, 1011b
Korča v, **264b**
Kordjāna ii, 235b
Kordofān i, 35a, 962a; ii, 123a; v, **266b**, 1249a, b; vii, 425b; s, 164a
Ḳordos v, **268b**
Korea → al-Shīla
Körfüz i, 395a; iv, 1157b; v, **268b**, 838a; s, 835b
Körgüz ii, 606a; xi, 285b
Koridjan (battle of) vi, 55b
Koritza → Korča
Ḳorḳmaz Maʿn ii, 634b, 749b; iii, 205b; iv, 834b
Ḳorḳud b. Bāyazīd (1513) i, 1120b; ii, 1042b; v, **269a**; xi, 162a
Ḳorḳud Dede → Dede Ḳorḳut
Köroghlu (XVI) i, 792b, 1255b; ii, 75b; iii, 117a, 374b; v, **270a**; s, 239a
Ḳoron v, **270b**
Ḳoryürek, Enīs Behīdj (1949) v, **271a**; viii, 177b
Kôs → Ḳūṣ
Kōs Mīnārs vi, 368b
Köse ʿAlī Pasha (XVII) v, 258b; vii, 899b
Köse Dagh v, **271b**; vi, 231a; vii, 990b
Köse Mikhāl ʿAbd Allāh (XIV) vii, 34a; viii, 192a

Köse Mūsā Pasha iv, 322b
Kösem Wālide/Kösem Sulṭān (Māhpaykar) (1651) iii, 623a, 983a; iv, 233b, 717a, 884b, 971b; v, **272a**; vii, 597b
Ķosh-begi v, **273a**; s, 97a, 228a, 419b
Köshk v, **274a**
Ķoshma v, **274b**; x, 736b
Ķoshuķ → Ķoshma
Kosi (river) vi, 47a
Ķoṣowa, Kosovo v, **275b**; vi, 74a, 89a; vii, 593b, 595a; viii, 335b
Kossaian v, 830b
Köstendil → Küstendil
Köstendje v, **277a**; vii, 696a
Köszeb (Güns) s, **542a**
Kōt Kāńgŕā → Kāńgŕā
Kota Kota v, **278a**
Kota Tengah vi, 116b
Kota Waringin s, 150b
Kotah vi, 419b, 536a
Köten (Ķipčaķ) (XIII) x, 693a
Koti iv, 1029b
Kotlā vi, 49b
Koťlā Mubārakpur (Delhi) vi, 126b
Kotoko iii, 98a; v, **278a**
Kotonou v, **279a**
Kotumble → Kudummul
Ķotur-čay vi, 200b, 201a, b, 202b, 504a
Kötürüm → Djalāl al-Dīn Bāyazīd (Isfendiyar Oghlu)
Ķotuz → Ķuṭuz, al-Malik al-Muẓaffar
Kōtwāl ii, 868a; iii, 199a, 493a; v, **279b**
Kōtwālī Darwāza vi, 46b
Kouandé v, **280b**
Koulougli → Ķul-oghlu
Koumiss → Kumis (Ķimiz)
Kounta → Kunta, Banū
Koweit → Kuwayt
Köy v, **281b**
Köy enstitüleri v, **281b**; s, 283b, 811b
Koyama vi, 370a
Koyl v, **283a**; s, 331b
Ķoylu Ḥiṣār v, **283a**
Ķoyul Ḥiṣār v, 283a, **b**
Ķoyun Baba v, **283b**; viii, 189b
Ķoyunlū iv, 389a
Kozak → Kazakh
Ķōzān i, 285a, b; v, **283b**; ix, 678a (see also *s.v.* Sīs)
Ķozan-oghullari ii, 207a; v, **284a**; ix, 679a
Kozhikode vi, 206b
Ķožoñ v, 275b
Ķrān → Sikka
Krawang s, 202a
Ķrim → Ķirim
Ķriz iv, 1029a; v, **284b**
Kroumir → Khumayr
Kroyo → Krujē
Krujë i, 309b, 654a; iv, 139a, b, 140a; v, **284b**
Krum (Bulghar) ix, 702b; x, 692a
Krushevats → Aladja Ḥisār
Ksar, Ksour → Ķaṣr; Ķaṣaba
Ķsentīnī → al-Ķusanṭīnī, Rashīd
Ķṣība → Ķaṣaba (town)
Kuala Lumpur i, 980a; ii, 426b; vi, 232b, 241a; ix, 647a; s, 642a
Ķuʿaytī, Āl i, 554b; iii, 291b; vi, 81b; vii, 496a; s, 337b, 338b, 515b, 516a, **542a**
al-Ķuʿaytī, ʿUmar b. ʿAwaḍ (XIX) vii, 496a; s, 542b
Ķuba → Ķubba
Ķubā (Farghānā) ii, 791a
Ķubāʾ (al-Madīna) vi, 646b, 647a, 649a, 654a, 659b, 677a
Ķubači ii, 86b, 89a; iv, 1169a, 1170a; v, **285b**
Ķubād b. Sulṭān Ḥusayn i, 920a
Ķubādābād iv, 702a, 818a; v, **285b**
Ķubādh I b. Fīrūz (Sasānid) → Ķawādh I
Ķubādh II (Sasānid) (628) ix, 80a; xi, 3a
Ķubādh b. Yazīd iv, 347a
Ķubādhiyān i, 455a; ii, 1a, 2a, 577b; v, **286b**
Ķubādja → Nāṣir al-Dīn Ķabāča
Ķubād-oghlu (1400) vi, 974a
Kubafolo/Bafilo v, **287a**
Kuban i, 1305a
Ķuban (river) ii, 21a; v, **287b**
Kūbarā vi, 507b
Ķubāṭī iv, 774a
Ķubāwī, Abū Naṣr Aḥmad (XII) vii, 966a
Kubayh ii, 137b
Kubaysha vi, 476b (see also *s.v.* Kabsha)
Ķubba (Ķuba) v, **296a**; s, 143a
Kubba (palace) s, 301a
Kubba (tent) iv, 1147a; vi, 651b
Kubba (tomb) iv, 352b, 434a; v, 214b, **289a**, 1139b
al-Ķubba (Ķubbat al-ʿĀlam/al-Arḍ) v, **297a**
Ķubbat al-ʿĀlam → al-Ķubba

Ḳubbat al-Arḍ → al-Ḳubba
Ḳubbat al-Bārūdiyyīn (Marrākush) vii, 587a
Ḳubbat al-hawāʾ iii, 274a; v, **297b**
Ḳubbat al-Ṣakhra i, 77b; ii, 911a, 978a; iii, 174b, 381a; v, **298a**; vi, 665b, 666a, 707a; vii, 8b
Ḳubbe wezīri v, **299b**
Ḳūbčūr iii, 1099b; iv, 31a, 1042a, 1050a, 1051b; v, **299b**; vii, 233b
Ḳubilāy b. Toluy b. Čingiz Khān (Mongol Great Khān) (1294) i, 1188a, 1311b; ii, 3a, 45b, 47a; iii, 472a; iv, 811b; v, 38b, 39a, **300a**; vi, 406a, 420a, 524a; vii, 230a
Ḳubilāy Noyon iv, 583b, xi, 335b
Kubrā, Shaykh Aḥmad b. ʿUmar Nadjm al-Dīn (1220) i, 754b; iv, 1064a; v, **300a**; vii, 870b; viii, 539b, 703a; ix, 110a, 784b; x, 251a; s, 423a
Ḳubrat (Bulghar) (VII) x, 692a
Kubrāwiyya iv, 48a, 49a, 51b; v, 300a, 301a-b; vi, 549b; x, 251a, 328a; s, 353b
Ḳubrus i, 109a, 152a, 798b, 935b, 945b, 1054a; ii, 522a; iii, 186b, 189a, 1182b, 1198b; v, **301b**, 1077a, 1171a; vi, 324b; vii, 720b; s, 53a, 120b, 221b
Ḳubruslu → Ḳibrisli̊
Kubu v, **309b**
Kūč → Ḳufṣ
Kuča ix, 617b; x, 248b; s, 136b, 540b
Kūča-i Arg vi, 20b
Kučak → Wiṣāl, Kučak
Kūčak Khān Djangalī, Mīrzā (1921) ii, 445b; iv, 398b, 789b; v, **310a**; viii, 450a; s, 110a, 366a
Ḳūčān v, **311a**; vi, 495a; s, 83a
Kucha → Kuča
Küčlük (Nayman Mongol) (XIII) i, 418b, 987b; ii, 42b, 43a, 791b; iii, 1114b; iv, 583a; v, 38b; xi, 335b
Küčük, Aḥmad Pasha (1636) ii, 635a, 751a; vi, 345b; s, **49a**
Küčük ʿAlī Oghullari̊ ii, 207b; s, 172b, **543a**
Küčük Bālī Beg → Yaḥyā Pasha-zāde Küčük Bālī Beg
Küčük Bostān i, 1279b
Küčük Čelebi-zāde → Čelebi-zāde
Küčük Ḥasan Pasha i, 904b
Küčük Ḥusayn Pasha → Ḥusayn Pasha, Küčük
Küčük Ḳaynarča (treaty, 1774) i, 56b, 62b, 311a, 470b, 893b; ii, 26b, 60b, 688b; iii, 589b, 1186a; v, 141a, **312b**, 495a; vii, 63a, 275b; ix, 133b
Küčük Köy s, 330a
Küčük Meḥmed (Janissary, Miṣr) (1694) iv, 852a; vii, 178b
Küčük Meḥmed Čelebi viii, 422b
Küčük Meḥmed Khān i, 721b; ii, 44a
Küčük Muṣṭafā → Muṣṭafā Čelebi
Küčük Saʿīd Pasha (1914) i, 285b; iii, 993b; v, **313b**
Küčük Suleymān Pasha i, 905b; iii, 91a
Küčük Sulṭān i, 1076a; iv, 591a
Kučum Khān (Sibir) (XVI) ii, 45a; v, 314b; viii, 161a
Küčümids i, 1076a
Ḳuḍāʿa, Banū i, 1a, 545a, 563b, 962a; ii, 122a, 572a; iii, 363b; v, **315a**; vi, 145a, 649a; vii, 267b; viii, 91a; x, 788a, 842b
Ḳuḍāʿa b. Mālik b. Ḥimyar vi, 82a
al-Ḳuḍāʿī, Muḥammad b. Salāma (ḳāḍī) (1062) vii, 164a; viii, 895a; ix, 472a
al-Ḳuḍāʿī, Yūsuf b. ʿAlī (XII) iii, 221a
Kūdakiyya v, 65a
Ḳudam b. Ḳādim (480) ii, 540b; viii, 407b
Ḳudāma b. Djaʿfar al-Kātib al Baghdādī (932) i, 590b, 730a, 857b, 982a, b; ii, 579a, b, 580b; iii, 354b; iv, 249a; v, **318b**; vi, 313b, 348a, 605b, 640a; vii, 277a, 978b; viii, 496b; s, 266a, 402a, 649b
Ḳudār al-Aḥmar (Uḥaymir) i, 169b; iii, 1270a
Ḳudayd vi, 373b, 374a; s, 312a
Ḳuddūs → Muḥammad ʿAlī Bārfurūshī Ḳuddūs
Kudjuk (Küčük) b. al-Nāṣir Muḥammad (Mamlūk) (1341) vi, 323b; vii, 992b
Kudjūr iv, 808a; vi, 511b
Ḳudra iv, 271b, 272b; iv, 692b, 693a; v, 576a, b
Kudrī iv, 743b
al-Ḳuds (Jerusalem) i, 215b, 352a, 549b, 797b, 799b, 975b, 1310a; ii, 63b, 911b; iii, 1158a; v, 82b, 92a, **322a**, 1127b; vi, 118b, 378b, 648a, 665a; vii, 274b; s, 154a (see also *s.v.* al-Masdjid al-Aḳṣā)
- monuments ii, 911a; iii, 174a,b; v, 327b, **339a-344a**, 1143a, b
- population v, 328b, 329a, 334a, 336a, b

Ḳudsī → Bakîkhānlî
al-Ḳudsī, Abū Ḥāmid Muḥammad (1483) iii, 772b; vi, 412b, 413b; vii, 140b, 141a, 165a, 175b, 176b; viii, 464b
Ḳudsī, Muḥammad Djān (1646) v, **344b**; vii, 341a, b; viii, 776a; ix, 241b
al-Ḳudsī, Nāẓim ii, 662a
Ḳudsiyya Bēgam i, 1195b, 1196a, 1197a
Küdüdjin bint Tash Möngke (XIV) ix, 474b
Kudummul v, **345a**
al-Ḳudūrī, Abu 'l-Ḥusayn/al-Ḥasan Aḥmad (1037) i, 310a, 791a; ii, 390a, 486a; iii, 163a; v, **345a**; vii, 310b; s, 192a
Kudyat al-ʿAbīd vi, 589a
al-Kūfa i, 16a, 76b, 77a, 103a, 704a; ii, 196b, 415b, 453a; iii, 843a, 1252b, 1254b, 1255a; iv, 911a; v, 174a, **345b**, 945b; vi, 119b, 140b, 266b, 333b, 334b, 335b, 336b, 345a, 364b, 427b, 428a, b, 441b, 620a, 624a, 647b, 651a, 656b, 659b, 660a, b, 667a, 668a, 670b, 675b, 679a, b, 691a; vii, 396a, 769a, b; viii, 696b; ix, 826a; s, 15b, 16a, 19a, 48a, 198b, 225b, 230b, 304b, 357b, 358a, 389b, 393b, 400b, 401a
– ethnography i, 529b, 568a; v, 346a, b
– literature ii, 729a, 806b; iv, 1003a; v, 350b
– monuments i, 610a; v, 347a, b, 348b
Kuffār → Kāfir (infidel)
al-Kūfī, Abū Djaʿfar (931) vi, 351b
al-Kūfī, Furāt b. Furāt (922) x, 86b
al-Kūfī, Abu 'l-Ḳāsim ʿAlī b. Aḥmad (963) vii, 517b
al-Kūfī, ʿAlī b. Ḥāmid b. Abī Bakr s, 163a
al-Kūfī, Muḥammad b. Sulaymān s, 335a
al-Kūfī, Shams al-Dīn Maḥmūd vi, 606a
Kūfic ii, 67a, 91a, 260b, 372b, 709b; iv, 1121a, 1122a, 1123a, 1125a; v, 217a-221b, 229b-230b, 350b
Ḳūfičīs → Ḳufṣ
Kufr → Kāfir
Kufra ii, 492b, 493a; v, **351b**, 759b, 887a
Ḳufṣ i, 1005a, b, 1354b; iii, 1098a; iv, 807a; v, 152b, **352b**; s, 129a
Kūghūn s, 327a
Ḳuḥāfa x, 189a
Kūhak → Čopan Ata
Kūhandil Khān i, 231a, b; v, 102a
Kuḥaylat al-ʿAdjūz ii, 785b
Kūh-Gīlū (Kūh-Gälū) i, 240a; iii, 1107a; iv, 5b, 9a; v, 822a, 824b, 826b, 827a, 829b, 830b; vi, 496a
Kūh-Gīlūya → Kūh-Gīlū
al-Kūhī, Abū Sahl Waydjān vi, 600b; s, 119b, **543b**
Kūh-i Bābā i, 221b; iii, 460a; v, **353a**; s, 367a
Kūh-i Bāričī → Bāriz, Djabal
Kūh-i Bazmān iv, 3b; ix, 54a
Kūh-i Binālūd s, 83a
Kūh-i Darang vi, 384a
Kūh-i Hazār Masdjid s, 127a
Kūh-i Iṣṭakhr iv, 221b
Kūh-i Kalāt iv, 4a
Kūh-i Ḳārin iv, 644a; s, 309a
Kūh-i Lālazār s, 127a
Kūh-i Mānd vi, 384a
Kūh-i Marra-yi Shikaft vi, 384a
Kūh-i Mōrpīsh ix, 54a
Kūh-i Nār vi, 384a
Kūh-i Nūḥ → Aghrî Dagh
Kūh-i Nūr iii, 348a; v, **353b**; vii, 854b
Kūh-i Raḥmat iv, 221a
Kūh-i Rang v, 830a
Kūh-i Shāh Djahān s, 83a
Kūh-i Surkh iv, 4a
Kūh-i Taftān iv, 3b
al-Kūhin v, **353b**; s, 390b
al-Kūhīn al-ʿAṭṭār → al-Kōhēn al-ʿAṭṭār
Ḳūhistān i, 1233a; v, 56a, **354a**; vi, 274a, 696b; s, 66b, 149a
Ḳūhistānī (language) ii, 138b; v, 356a
al-Ḳuhistānī (d. 1543) iii, 163b
Kūh-kamarāʾī, Ḥādjdj Sayyid Ḥusayn (1881) vii, 299b; s, 76a
Kūhkamarī, Ḥudjdjat (Āyatullāh) (XX) vii, 762b
al-Kuḥl i, 785a; 1089a; iii, 22b; v, **356a**
Kuḥlan vi, 436a
Kuḥlān al-Sharaf s, 723b
Kuhna-Abīward i, 99b
Kuhna-Ḳahḳaha i, 99b
Ḳuhrūd (Kōh-rūd) v, **357a**, 869a; vi, 511b; vii, 13a
Kūhyār Bāwand iv, 645b, 646b, 647a
Kūka → Kūkawa
Kūkaltāsh, Khān Aʿẓam ʿAzīz Muḥammad (XVI) vii, 458a
Kūkaltāsh, Khān-i Djahān (XVII) ii, 488b

Kūkawa (Kūka) i, 1260a, b; v, **357b**; s, 164b
Ḳuḳli Meḥmed Beg v, 724b; viii, 388a
Kūko iii, 246a; iv, 361a, b
Ḳul ii, 25b, 147b; v, **359a**, 630a
Ḳul Muṣṭafā Ḳayi̊kdji̊ (XVII) v, **359b**
Ḳul-Bābā Kökältāsh s, 340a
Ḳūla (town) v, **359b**
Kulāb → Khuttalān
Kulāčī ii, 975a; iv, 597a
Külāh v, 751b
Kulāl (amīr) (1379) vii, 933b; viii, 45a
Kūlam (-Malāy) v, **360a**, 937b
Ḳulansiya → Ḳalansuwa
al-Ḳulayʿa v, **361a**
Ḳulayʿat (Syria) vi, 579a
Kulayb vi, 490a
Kulayb b. Rabīʿa al-Taghlibī i, 1089a; ii, 159b; iii, 393a; v, **362a**; s, 234b
Kulayb Wāʾil i, 526b, 793b; ii, 738b
al-Kulaynī (al-Kulīnī), Abū Djaʿfar Muḥammad (939) i, 1352a; iii, 726b, 1266a; v, **362b**; vi, 12a, 549a, 552a; vii, 132a, 548a; s, 56b, 103b
Kulbarga → Gulbarga
Ḳuldja (Ghuldja) iii, 1120b; v, **363b**; vi, 768b; x, 221a
Külek Boghaz → Cilicia
Ḳulī Khān Maḥram i, 80b, 117b
Ḳulī Khān, Padshān (1682) s, 420b
Ḳulī Ḳuṭb al-Mulk, Sulṭān (Ḳuṭb Shāhī) (1518) ii, 922b, 1084b, 1118b, 1119a; iii, 15a, 421a; v, 549b, 1258a; vi, 63a, b, 696a
Ḳūlī Shāh i, 1120b; v, 677b
al-Kulīnī, Abū Djaʿfar Muḥammad → Kulaynī
Kullābiyya iii, 1164b; iv, 469a; s, 392a
Ḳullar-āḳāsī iv, 36b; v, 359b; viii, 770a
Kulliyya ii, 423a, b; iv, 435b; v, **364b**
Ḳulliyya i, 767a
Kulliyyat al-Ādāb i, 176a
Külliyye v, **366a**
Ḳulluḳ-aḳčasi̊ → Čift-resmi
Ḳul-oghlu i, 369a, 371a, 1119a; ii, 173a, 520b; iii, 340a; iv, 481b; v, **366b**, 1010b, 1247b
Ḳuloghlu (poet) (XVII) v, **367a**; viii, 722a
Kūlsara vi, 498b, 501a
Kulsāriʿ → Ḳuṭb al-Dīn
Kültepe s, 100b
Kulthūm (Ḳubāʾ) vi, 647a
Kulthūm b. ʿAmr al-ʿAttābī → al-Attabī
Kulthūm b. ʿIyāḍ al-Ḳushayrī (741) i, 86b, 990b, 1175a; iii, 169b, 494a; v, **367a**; ix, 870b
Kültigin (prince) iv, 583b; v, 854a; viii, 231a; x, 687b, 688a
Ḳulughlī → Kuloghlu
Ḳulumriya (Coimbra) i, 390a, 1338b; v, **367a**; ix, 308b
Ḳuluz (Vólos) s, **544a**
al-Ḳulzum i, 931a, 932a; ii, 129b; v, **367b**; ix, 912a
Ḳum(m) (Ghom) i, 16b; iii, 1124b, 1169b; iv, 7b; v, 292b, 350a, **369a**; vi, 21a, 271a, 332b, 337b, 366a, 493a, 513a, 514a, 516b, 548b, 553a, b, 554a, b, 627b, 634b, 714b; viii, 387a; s, 56b, 104a, 127a, b, 139a, 157b, 158a, 305a, 342a
Kuma (river) s, 169a
al-Ḳūmā/al-Ḳawmā v, **372b**
Ḳumān ii, 202b; v, 126a, **373a**; x, 690b
Ḳumān Ḳipčaḳ confederation x, 692b
Kumārī → Ḥasan, al-Malik al-Nāṣir Nāṣir al-Dīn (Mamlūk) (1362)
Ḳumāsh iii, 344b, 1126b; v, 151a, 216b, **373b**, 748a
Kumasi ii, 1003b; vii, 103b
Kumatgī iii, 287b
Kumayl b. Ziyād i, 89a; viii, 306b
Ḳumayr, Banū viii, 1002b
al-Kumayrī b. Zayd al-Asadī (743) viii, 83a, 122b
al-Kumayt b. Maʿrūf v, 374a
al-Kumayt b. Thaʿlaba v, 374a
al-Kumayt b. Zayd al-Asadī (743) i, 402a; ii, 1011a; v, **374a**; viii, 83a, 122b
Ḳumbara → Khumbara
Kumbaradjī → Khumbaradji̊
Kumbhalgaṛh vi, 53a
Ḳumbi Ṣāliḥ → Ḳunbi Ṣāliḥ
Ḳumī → Malik Ḳumī
Kumīdjīs ii, 1a; iv, 631b; v, 75b, **375b**
Ḳumi̊ḳ → Ḳumuḳ
Kumi̊s (Ḳi̊mi̊z) iv, 998a; v, **375b**
Ḳūmis (Comes) i, 491a; v, **376a**
Ḳūmis (Manf) vi, 411b
Ḳūmis (province) v, **377a**; vi, 120a, 332b, 333a; s, 149a, 192a, 298a, 309b
Ḳūmis b. Antunyān v, 376b
al-Ḳūmisī, Daniel iv, 604a, b
Kūmiya (berber) v, **378b**; vi, 310b, 815a

Ḳumḳum v, 988a
al-Ḳummī, Aḥmad b. Muḥammad b. al-Ḥasan b. al-Walīd (X) vii, 312a
al-Ḳummī, ʿAlī b. Ibrāhīm b. Hāshim (X) vi, 351b; vii, 399a
al-Ḳummī, Ḥādjdjī Āḳā Ḥusayn vi, 552b; s, 158a, 342b
al-Ḳummī, Ḥasan b. Muḥammad (X) iii, 1096b, 1169b; s, **544b**
al-Ḳummī, Ḳāḍī Aḥmad Ibrāhīm Ḥusaynī (XVI) v, **379a**
al-Ḳummī, Ḳāḍī Saʿīd (1692) v, 371a; vii, 476a
al-Ḳummī, Madjd al-Dīn Barāwistānī ix, 191b
al-Ḳummī, Mīrzā Abu 'l-Ḳāsim (1817) vi, 551b; vii, 298b
al-Ḳummī, Muḥammad (vizier) (XIII) vii, 727b
al-Ḳummī, Muḥammad b. ʿAbd Allāh (IX) viii, 89b
al-Ḳummī, Muḥammad b. Aḥmad b. Dāwūd b. ʿAlī (978) vii, 312a b
al-Ḳummī, Mullā Muḥammad Ṭāhir (1686) viii, 136a
al-Ḳummī, Saʿd b. ʿAbd Allāh (911) iv, 661b; vii, 459b, 517a
al-Ḳummī, Sayyid Muḥsin b. Muḥammad al-Riḍawī s, 380a
al-Ḳummī, Sayyid Ṣadr al-Dīn s, 134b
Ḳumr (Comoro Is.) i, 170a, 522a; v, **379b**, 939a, b, 940b; vi, 82b, 203b
al-Ḳūm-Rīshī, Shihāb al-Dīn iv, 810a; x, 691a, 920b
Ḳumuḳ ii, 89a, 141b; v, **381b**, 617b
Ḳumuḳ (language, literature) v, 382b, 383a, 617b
Ḳumul → Ḳomul
Kumūn v, **384a**; s, 89a, 226a
Ḳumūsh i, 767a
Kumzārī i, 575a
Kun iv, 982b
Ḳun, Banū v, 373a, b, **385a**; x, 689b
Ḳūn (Kunān) Ḳipčaḳ x, 690b
Kun Laszlo (Lászo the Cuman) (1290) x, 693a
Ḳunā v, **385b**, 1161a
Kunaŕ iv, 409b, 411a; vii, 957b
Kunāsa v, 347a, b
al-Ḳūnawī, ʿAlāʾ al-Dīn i, 596a; iii, 953a
al-Ḳūnawī, Ṣadr al-Dīn → Ṣadr al-Dīn
Ḳunayṭira → Ḳanṭara
Ḳunayṭra (Lubnān) vi, 31a, 455a
Kunāz, Banū iv, 568a
Kunbāṣ v, 1168b-1169b
Ḳunbi Ṣāliḥ ii, 1002a; v, **386b**; vii, 612b
Kund-Sūlḳān s, 423a
Kundar (river) s, 329b
Kundjāh/Kandjāh ii, 1006b; s, 322a
Kundjpura i, 296b; iv, 666b
Kundur → Lubān
al-Kundurī, ʿAmīd al-Mulk (1064) i, 420a, 421a, 434a, 952b; ii, 192a, 605a; iii, 1148b, 1201a; iv, 458a; v, **387b**; vi, 523b; viii, 69b, 70a; s, 192a
Ḳunduz i, 853a, 1009a; v, 388b; xi, 134a
Ḳunfudh, Banū ix, 817a
Ḳunfudh, Ḳunfadh v, **389b**
Ḳunfudh b. ʿUmayr (VII) vii, 468b
al-Ḳunfudha i, 98b; v, **391a**; vi, 154a
Kung v, 673a, b, 765a; s, 716b, 717b
Kung-ming x, 574b
Ḳungrāt i, 422a, 607b; ii, 41b, 45a; iv, 610b, 1065a; v, 24a, 273b, **391b**; vi, 418a; vii, 574b; s, 97b, 169a, 420a
Kūnī ḳadar iv, 203a
Ḳūniya (Ḳamūniya) iv, 826b
Ḳuniya → Ḳonya
Ḳūnka v, **392a**; s, 143a
Ḳunṣul → Consul
Ḳunṣul, Ilyās v, 1257a
Ḳunsul, Zakī v, 1257a
Kunta, Banū i, 809a; iv, 382a; v, **393a**, 889b, 1166a; vi, 259b, 357a; vii, 613b; ix, 756a
al-Kuntī, Aḥmad al-Bakkāʾī x, 826a
al-Kuntī, Shaykh Sīdī al-Mukhtār (1811) v, 393a; vi, 259b; vii, 623a; x, 509a
Küntoghdi̊ (Atabeg) (1121) vi, 64a, 500a; x, 42b
Ḳunūt v, **395a**; x, 359a
Kunūz i, 1028b, 1029a
Kunya ii, 302a; iv, 179a; v, 116b, **395b**
Kunyipakki Sahib, C.O.T. (XX) vi, 461a
Kuominchün horde v, 845a, b
Kur (river) i, 634b; v, **396b**, 866a, 867b
Ḳurʾ, Ḳurūʾ iii, 1011a; iv, 253b
Kūr Galdwan ii, 828a
Kūra i, 489b; v, **397b**
Ḳurʿa iv, 259b; v, **398a**
al-Kura (sphere) v, **397a**
Ḳurakh v, 729b, 730a

Kuram (river) → Kurram
Ḳurama v, **399b**
Ḳurʿān i, 1258a
Ḳurād b. Ḥanīfa iii, 49a
Kuraibiya → Kuraybiyya
Ḳurʾān i, 55a, 77b, 107a, 383b, 549a, 565b, 567b, 585b, 922b, 1084b, 1199b, 1242a, 1345b; ii, 126a, 388b, 728b, 834b, 841a, 949b; iii, 24a, 41b, 65a, 152a, 369a, 513b, 874b, 1127a; iv, 81a-84b, 146a, b, 469b, 902b, 980b-986b, 1133b; v, 127a, **400a**; x, 72b; s, 642a
– chronology v, **414b**
– commentaries i, 89a, 104b, 117a, 120a, 126a, 143a, 152a, 302a, 310a, 352b, 425a, 701b, 958b, 1129a; iii, 696b, 753b, 845b, 880b; iv, 495a, 508a, 704b, 705a, 734b; v, 512b, 513b
– history v, **404a**, 426a
– interpretations i, 24b, 38b, 90a, 128b, 158b, 204a, 257a, 264a, 267a, 272a, 275a, 325a, 338a, 561b, 603b, 691a, 788a, 935b, 968b, 1021a, 1026b, 1055a, 1071b, 1326b; ii, 71a, 95a, 128b, 219b,383b, 447a, 549b, 617a, 626b, 869b, 917a, 949b, 950a, 1025a; iii, 172a, 359a, 465a, 543b, 661a, 795a, 797a, 912a, 1091b, 1172a, 1205a; iv, 1106b
– language v, **419a**
– Muḥammad and v, **402b**, 415a, 1101a
– readings, readers v, **406a**
– references i, 169a, 177a, 187a, 209a, 384a, 406-417, 448b, 453a, 514a, 680b, 714a, 773b, 795b, 850b, 922a, 940b, 1020a,b, 1032a, 1092b, 1150b, 1297b; ii, 168a, 182a, 214a, 223b, 293b, 363a, 447a, 536a, 551a, 576a, 848a, 1061a; iii, 13b, 53b, 165a, 209b, 235b, 295a, 302a, 377b, 379a, 537b, 668b, 980a, 1237a,b, 1239b; iv, 141a, 171b, 184a, b, 353b, 365b, 407a, b, 486b, 508b, 595a, 692a, 766b, 805b, 994b; v, 186a, 236a, b, 400b, 698a
– scholars i, 40a, 68b, 105a, 114a, 120a, 152a, 696a, 706b, 1129a; ii, 254a; iii, 155a, 753b, 880b, 936a, 1081b; iv, 1112b; v, 128a, 174a
– translations i, 68b, 88b, 404b; ii, 255a; iv, 891a, 1123a; v, **429a**
al-Kūrānī, Ibrāhīm (1690) v, **432b**, 525b; s, 28a
al-Kurānī, S͟hams/S͟haraf/S͟hihāb al-Dīn → Gurānī, S͟haraf al-Dīn
Kūrānkid͟j iii, 902b; iv, 215a
al-Ḳuras͟hī → ʿAbd al-Ḳādir al-Ḳuras͟hī
al-Ḳuras͟hī (Transoxania) (XIII) viii, 582a
al-Ḳuras͟hī, Abū Bakr b. Muʿāwiya (al-Andalus) (X) vi, 430b
al-Ḳuras͟hī, Abu ’l-Ḥasan → al-Kurs͟hī, Abu ’l-Ḥasan
al-Ḳuras͟hī, Abu Zayd Muḥammad → Abū Zayd Muḥammad b. Abī ’l-K͟haṭṭāb
al-Ḳuras͟hī, ʿAlī b. Ḥazm (1288) vii, 1040a
al-Ḳuras͟hī, ʿAlī b. Muḥammad (1215) → ʿAlī b. Muḥammad b. D͟jaʿfar al-Kuras͟hī
al-Ḳuras͟hī, ʿAlī b. Muḥammad (1405) vi, 280a
al-Ḳuras͟hī, D͟jamāl iv, 525b
Kurayb ii, 77b
Kurayb b. K͟haldūn vii, 808a
Ḳurayba iv, 821a
Ḳurayba bint Abī Ḳuḥāfa → Umm Farwa
Kuraybiyya iii, 1265b; iv, 639a, 836b, 837a; v, **433b**; viii, 383a
al-Ḳurayniyya i, 628b
Ḳuray s͟h i, 80a, 382b, 545a, 549a, 565a, 890b, 891b, 1073b, 1074a, b, 1241b; ii, 128b, 348b, 627a, 883b; iii, 7b, 285b, 363b, 389a, 577b, 975b, 1093a; v, 116b, 316a, b, **434a**, 520a, b, 581a; vi, 137b, 145a, b, 267b, 349a, 422a, 439b; x, 841a; s, 284a
Ḳuray s͟h b. Badrān (ʿUkaylid) (1061) vi, 966a; vii, 693a
Ḳuray s͟h al-Biṭāḥ v, 581b; vi, 145a
Ḳuray s͟h al-Ẓawāhir vi, 145a
Ḳurayya (Bag͟hdād) i, 901a, b
Ḳurayyāt (ʿUmān) vi, 734b
Ḳurayyāt al-Milḥ v, **435b**
Ḳurayẓa, Banū i, 381b; iv, 270a; v, **436a**, 996a; vi, 649a, 738b; vii, 367a, 370b, 561b, 852b
Kurāz b. Mālik al-Sulamī (695) vi, 920a
al-Ḳuraẓī → Muḥammad b. Kaʿb al-Kuraẓī
Ḳurba → Ḳarāba
Kurbāl v, 668a, b, 867b, 868a
Kurbālī, S͟hud͟jāʿ al-Dīn (1462) vi, 73a
Ḳurbān v, **436b**
Ḳurbat ii, 40b; v, 818a, b
Kurbuḳa, Kür-Bug͟ha (1102) v, **437a**

Ķürčī v, **437a**
Ķürčībā<u>sh</u>ī iii, 1102a; iv, 36b, 209b; v, 437b, 630a; viii, 769b; x, 109b
Kurd ʿAlī, Muḥammad Farīd (1953) i, 598a, 990a, b; ii, 290a; iv, 159a; v, **437b**, 1090b; vii, 813b
Kurd Hamza ii, 750a
Kürd <u>Sh</u>ey<u>kh</u> Ḥasan (Čemi<u>sh</u>gezek) (XV) vi, 71a
Kurdī (dog) iv, 491a
al-Kurdī, Muḥammad Amīn (1914) ii, 225a; v, 475b, **486a**
Kurdī, <u>Sh</u>ay<u>kh</u> ʿAlī (1519) vii, 935a
Kurdish (language) i, 840a, 871b, 1006b; ii, 1139b; iii, 1b, 1260b; iv, 351a, b; v, 208b, 209a, b, **479a**, 1105a
Kurdistān i, 8a, 62b, 845a; ii, 8a; iv, 3a-b, 19b; v, **438b**; vi, 491b, 492b, 494a, 495a, 502a; ix, 829a, 831a; s, 72a, b
– economy v, **472b**
– history v, **447b**
– inhabitants v, **444a**, 456a, b
– folklore/literature v, **480b**
– religion v, **474b**
– society v, **470a**
– workers party (PKK) x, 696a
al-Kur<u>dj</u> (Gur<u>dj</u>, Gur<u>dj</u>istān) (Georgia) i, 8a, 100b, 420b, 636a, 642a, 644b; ii, 162b; iii, 1112b; iv, 342b, 347b, 348b, 349a, b, 351a, b, 391b, 476a, 670a, 1174b; v, **486b**; vi, 500a, b, 505a; vii, 352a; x, 966a
– languages iv, 350b; v, 486b
Kur<u>dj</u>ī Muķaddam al-Bur<u>dj</u>iyya i, 1325a
Kurdo<u>gh</u>lu <u>Kh</u>izir Reis i, 743b
Kurds i, 190a, 195b, 251a, 470b, 471b, 474a, 512a, 513a, 575a,644a, 750a, 796b, 871a, 920a, 1030b, 1072a, 1207a, 1208b, 1287a, 1354b, 1356a; ii, 57a, 184b, 208a, 1110b, 1139b; iii, 83a, 258a, 961a, 1096b, 1102b, 1109a, 1254a; iv, 5b, 8a, 9a, 10a, 377b; v, 145a, 146b, 312a, **438b**, 617a, 822a, 1213a, b; vi, 201a, 382b, 384b; viii, 173bs, 71b, 119a; x, 48b
Kürdü<u>dj</u>in bint Abi<u>sh</u> <u>Kh</u>ātūn (1319) vi, 482a
Kurdufān → Kordofān
Kürekčis i, 760b; v, 880a, b
Ķurḥ v, **497b**; xi, 19a
Ķurhub b. <u>Dj</u>ābir al-<u>Kh</u>uzāʿī v, **498a**
Kūri iv, 540b
Kuria Muria (islands) → <u>Kh</u>ūryān-Mūryān
Ķūriltāy iv, 499b; v, **498a**; vi, 482b
Kürin v, **498a**, 729b, 730a
Kürin (<u>Kh</u>ānat) → Lez<u>gh</u>in
Ķūriya i, 242b; v, **498b**
Kurkī s, 421a
Ķurķūb v, **498b**
Ķurķumāz b. Yūnis Maʿn (1516) vi, 343a, b
Ķurķūra i, 325b; v, 492b
Kurr → Kur (river)
Ķurra iv, 521b
Ķurrāʾ v, 349b, 409a, **499a**
Ķurrāʾ, Banū ii, 741a; iii, 79b; vii, 117a, 730a
Kurra, Muḥammad ii, 123a; v, 267a
Ķurra b. <u>Sh</u>arīk (714) ii, 305a, 323b, 327b; iv, 742a, 1103b; v, **500a**; vi, 648a, 662a; vii, 75a, 158b; viii, 537b
Kurram (river) v, 37a, **501a**; s, 329b
Ķurrat al-ʿAyn Ṭāhira, Fāṭima umm Salmā (1852) i, 834a, 846b, 847a; iv, 70b; v, **502a**; vi, 485a
Ķurṣān iv, 1056b; v, **502b**; vii, 387b
al-Ķurṣāwī, ʿAbd al-Naṣīr (1822) s, 467a
al-Kur<u>sh</u>ī, Abu ʾl-Ḥasan iv, 729a
Kursī ii, 276a; v, **509a**; vi, 663b; s, 99a
Ķūrṣūl → Bo<u>gh</u>ā Tar<u>kh</u>ān
Kurt → Kart
Kürt Ḥāfiẓ (1474) vi, 72a
Ķurt Ḥasan b. <u>Dj</u>unayd ii, 599b
al-Kurtī (vizier) → <u>Gh</u>iyā<u>th</u> al-Dīn Muḥammad al-Kurtī
Kūrtigīn (Daylamī) (X) vii, 800a
Ķurṭuba (Córdoba) i, 5b, 6b, 82a, 83a, 85b, 390b, 491b, 493a, 494b; iii, 74a, 140a, 496a, 762a; v, 318b, **509b**, 1008b, 1239b; vi, 186a, 279b, 364a, 431a, 521a; vii, 766b; s, 152b, 397b
– great mosque i, 459a, 498b, 500b, 618b, 950a, 1228a, 1319b; ii, 956a, b; iii, 495a; v, 510b
Ķurṭuba, <u>Dj</u>ibāl i, 488b
al-Ķurṭubī → ʿArīb b. Saʿd; Ibn Faraḥ
al-Ķurṭubī, Abu ʾl-ʿAbbās v, 512b
al-Ķurṭubī, Abū ʿAbd Allāh (1272) v, **512b**
al-Ķurṭubī, Abū Muḥammad (1092) vi, 110a, 629a
al-Ķurṭubī, Maslama b. al-Ķāsim (964) x, 12a
al-Ķurṭubī, Yaḥyā b. ʿUmar (1172) v, **513b**
Ķurūʾ → Ķurʾ

Ḳūrū s, 165a
Kuruca vi, 70b
Kurukshetra x, 442a
Ḳurūn Ḥamāt (battle) (1175) vi, 781a
Kurūr i, 272a
Ḳūrus i, 761a; vi, 506a, 507a; s, **544b**
Ḳūrūsh (Cyrrhus) vi, 378a
Ḳūṣ v, 99a, b, **514a**, 519a; vi, 119a; viii, 864a; s, 383b
Kūs owasi̊ → Ḳoṣowaʾ
Kuşadasi̊ vi, 1011b
Kūsān vi, 745a, b
Ḳusanṭīna → Ḳusṭanṭīna
al-Ḳusanṭīnī, Rashīd (1944) v, **515b**; vi, 752a, 754b
al-Kūsawī al-Djāmī, Shams al-Dīn Muḥammad i, 283a, b
Kusayla b. Lamzam i, 367a, 1175a; iii, 296a; iv, 336b, 422b, 827a; v, **517b**; x, 790a; s, 103a
al-Ḳusayr → Abū Zaʿbal
al-Ḳusayr (al-Ḥīra) i, 450b
al-Ḳusayr (port) v, 386a, **518b**; vi, 195a, 545b
al-Ḳusayr ʿAmrā i, **612a**; iii, 141b, 146b, 310a; vii, 82a; s, 117b, 251a
Ḳuṣayy ii, 128b; iii, 260a, 975b; iv, 320a, 421b; v, 77b, 78a, 116b, 434b, **519b**, 581a, 692b; vi, 145a, 349a
Ḳuṣdār v, 102a, **520b**; vi, 65b, 193a; ix, 121b
Kūsh iv, 528b; v, **521a**; viii, 89a
Ḳushadali̊, Ibrāhīm (1845) ix, 156a
Kushadasī i, 777b, 778a
Kushādjim, Maḥmūd b. al-Ḥusayn al-Sindī (961) i, 1153b; ii, 740b; iii, 809a; iv, 1005b; v, **525a**, 1229b; vi, 403b; vii, 646b, 851a, 949a; viii, 377b, 1022a; s, 175b, 203b
Kushan Empire i, 225b; s, 237a, 426b
Kushāna vi, 839a
Kushānūsh al-Burdjān (Bulgar) ii, 235a
al-Ḳushashī, Ṣafī al-Dīn (1661) v, 433a, **525b**; viii, 728b
Ḳushayr b. Kaʿb i, 233b, 442a; v, 526a
Ḳushayr, Banū i, 107a; v, **526a**; vii, 115a; ix, 104b
al-Ḳushayrī, Abu ʾl-Ḳāsim (1074) i, 146b; ii, 125b, 605a; iii, 589a; iv, 697a; v, **526a**, vi, 225a, 569b, 614a; vii, 100a; x, 314b; s, 14b, 15a
al-Ḳushayrī, Abu ʾl-Naṣr (1120) v, **527a**
al-Ḳushayrī, Abu ʾl-Ḳāsim v, **526a**
al-Ḳushayrī, Muḥammad b. Saʿīd (945) viii, 412b
al-Ḳushayrī, Sawwār b. Awfā (VII) v, 710a; vii, 843a
Ḳush-begi → Ḳosh-begi
Ḳushči v, 273a
Ḳūshdji (1348) ii, 774a
al-Ḳūshdjī → ʿAlī al-Ḳūshdjī
Kushitic → Kūsh
Kūshiyār b. Labān iii, 1137a, 1139b; iv, 1071a; v, **527a**; viii, 554b; x, 267a
Kushka i, 1173a; vi, 621b
Ḳushtemür iii, 197a
Kushterī, Shaykh iv, 601b
al-Ḳushūrī → Naṣr al-Ḳushūrī
Ḳush-yalwa, Banū vi, 501a
al-Ḳūṣī, ʿAbd al-Ghaffār b. Nūḥ (1307) viii, 458b
al-Ḳūṣī, Ibrāhīm b. al-Ḥuḍayn → Ibrāhīm b. al-Ḥuḍayn al-Ḳūṣī
Ḳūsira → Ḳawṣara
Kuskusū v, **527b**
Ḳuṣmān iv, 717a, b
Ḳuss b. Sāʿida (912) i, 585b; v, **528b**; vii, 73b; x, 789a
Ḳuṣṣās → Ḳāṣṣ, Ḳaṣṣa
Ḳusta (Maṣyad) vi, 790b
Ḳusṭā b. Lūḳā al-Baʿlabakkī (912) i, 328a, 589a, 727a; ii, 771b, 900a; iii, 378a; iv, 329b, 600a; v, 397b, **529b**; vi, 637b; vii, 559a, b; s, 412a
Kustāndīl → Constantine III
Ḳusṭanṭīna i, 155a; v, **530a**; vi, 427a
Ḳusṭanṭīniyya iv, 224a; v, **532b**; x, 821b
Küstendil iv, 121b; v, **534a**
Ḳusṭūs al-Rūmī ii, 900a
Kusūf v, **535b**
al-Ḳūṣūnī, Badr al-Dīn iv, 451b
Ḳuṣūr i, 1321b (see also *s.v.* Ḳaṣr)
Kūt al-ʿAmāra v, **537a**; vii, 582b
Kūtab vi, 499b, 501a
Ḳutadghu Bilig i, 299a, 677b, 987a; iv, 700a; v, 275a, **538a**; x, 62b
Kütāhiya (Kütahya) i, 182b; ii, 747a; iv, 1169b; v, **539a**; vi, 59b, 525b; viii, 84b; s, 49a, 359b
Kütahya Edict vi, 496b
Kutai v, **539b**; vi, 240a; s, 151a
Ḳutalmish → Ḳutlumush b. Arslān Isrāʾīl

Kutāma (Ketama) Banū i, 104a, 249a, 367a, 1037a, 1042a, 1175b, 1177b, 1178b, 1309b; ii, 852b; iii, 77a; iv, 199a, 827b, 830a; v, **540a**; 1160a, 1243a; vi, 435a, 727a, b, 728a; ix, 18a
al-Kutamī, ʿAbd al-Karīm iv, 729a
al-Ḳutāmī, Djaʿfar b. Kulayd (1038) vii, 120b
al-Ḳuṭāmī, ʿUmayr b. Shuyaym (719) iv, 315b; v, **540b**
al-Kutāmī al-Fāsī, Abu 'l-Ḥasan ʿAlī → Ibn al-Ḳaṭṭān the Elder
Kutawaringin vi, 240a
Ḳutayba, Banū i, 920b
Ḳutayba b. Muslim (715) i, 529b, 684b, 921a, 1001a, 1293b; ii, 1a, 601a, 790b; iii, 41a, 304a, 471a, 493b; iv, 1062a; v, 47b, 181a, 378a, **541a**, 853b, 854a, 1111a; vii, 359a, 1016a; viii, 67a; s, 299a
Ḳutayba b. Saʿīd (854) vii, 691a
Ḳutayba b. Tughshāda i, 1294a, b
Ḳutaybids vi, 640b
Ḳuṭayfa s, 117a
Kutayfāt → al-Afḍal Kutayfāt
Ḳutayla (VII) vii, 873a
Ḳutayla (musician) (1330) viii, 806a
Ḳutayla bint ʿAbd al-ʿUzzā i, 109b, 713b
al-Ḳuṭb i, 95a, 280a; iv, 950a; v, **542b**; s, 323b
al-Ḳuṭb, Sayyid ii, 452a; iii, 1069b, 1070a; iv, 160a, 166a; ix, **117a**; x, 373a
al-Ḳuṭb ʿAlī, Shaykh iii, 456b, 457a
al-Ḳuṭb al-Awliyāʾ → ʿAbd al-Salām Khundjī
Ḳuṭb al-Dīn → al-Nahrawālī, Ḳuṭb al-Dīn
Ḳuṭb al-Dīn I (Ḳutlugh-Khān) vii, 796a
Ḳuṭb al-Dīn II (Ḳutlugh-Khān) → Shāh Djahān b. Suyurghatmïsh
Ḳuṭb al-Dīn (Bengal) s, 366b
Ḳuṭb al-Dīn, Malik iv, 672a
Ḳuṭb al-Dīn, Mullā i, 936b; ii, 132a; s, 292a, 293a; viii, 68b
Ḳuṭb al-Dīn, Nayrīzī (1759) x, 328a
Ḳuṭb al-Dīn b. Tekish (Khʷārazm-shāh) → ʿAlāʾ al-Dīn Muḥammad b. Tekish
Ḳuṭb al-Dīn Abu 'l-Fatḥ Muḥammad Khān (Ḳutlugh-Khān) (1257) v, 161b, 162a, 553a, b; vi, 482b
Ḳuṭb al-Dīn Aḥmad (Ḥekīm-bashï) iii, 340a
Ḳuṭb al-Dīn Aḥmad Abu 'l-Fayyāḍ → al-Dihlawī, Shāh Walī Allāh
Ḳuṭb al-Dīn Aḥmad Shāh (Gudjarāt) (1451) vi, 53b, 1027b
Ḳuṭb al-Dīn Aḥmad Shāh II (1458) ii, 1125b
Ḳuṭb al-Dīn Aybak (Muʿizzī, Delhi) (1210) i, 208b, 393b, 403b, 506b, 756b, 855b, 1209b, 1300a, 1321b; ii, 256a, 260a, 266b, 267a, 1084a, 1103a, 1123b; iii, 168a, 415b, 1155a; iv, 210a, 1127a; v, 283a, **546a**, 549a; vi, 368a, 691a, b; vii, 409b, 410a, 433a; viii, 81a; s, 284b, 359b, 360a
Ḳuṭb al-Dīn Bakhtiyār Kākī (1235) i, 104b, 1024a; ii, 796b; v, **546b**, 549a; s, 353a
Ḳuṭb al-Dīn Ḥabash ʿAmīd → Ḥabash ʿAmīd, Ḳuṭb al-Dīn
Ḳuṭb al-Dīn Ḥasan al-Ghūrī ii, 1100a
Ḳuṭb al-Dīn Il-Ghāzī (Mārdīn) (1183) vi, 781b
Ḳuṭb al-Dīn Ināl b. Ḥassān (Manbidj) (1168) vi, 380b
Ḳuṭb al-Dīn Ismāʿīl b. Yāḳūtī (XI) vi, 274b
Ḳuṭb al-Dīn al-Iznīḳī (1418) iii, 711a; v, **547a**
Ḳuṭb al-Dīn Kulsāriʿ i, 731a
Ḳuṭb al-Dīn Mawdūd b. Zankī → Mawdūd b. ʿImād al-Dīn Zankī
Ḳuṭb al-Dīn Mubārak → Mubārak Shāh I
Ḳuṭb al-Dīn Mubāriz (Shanānkāra) ix, 158a, 667b
Ḳuṭb al-Dīn Muḥammad (Ghūrid) i, 940a; ii, 382a, 928a, 1096b, 1100b
Ḳuṭb al-Dīn Muḥammad b. Anūshtigin (Khwārazmshāh) (1127) iv, 1067a; vi, 415b; viii, 943a; ix, 16a s, 279a
Ḳuṭb al-Dīn Muḥammad b. ʿImād al-Dīn Zangī (XII) viii, 127a
Ḳuṭb al-Dīn al-Rāzī ii, 774a; viii, 386b
Ḳuṭb al-Dīn Shīrāzī (1311) ii, 399a, b; iii, 1137b; iv, 1059b; v, **547a**; vi, 99a, 601a, 907b; vii, 204a, 684b; viii, 860b; ix, 481a
Ḳuṭb al-Dīn Yūsuf b. Yaʿḳūb (vizier) (XII) vii, 535b
Ḳuṭb al-Dīn-zāde Muḥammad (1480) v, 547a, **548b**
Ḳuṭb Khān (Monghyr) (1533) vi, 47a
Ḳuṭb Khān Lōdī (XV) iii, 632a; iv, 513a; v, 783a; vi, 62a, b

Ḳuṭb Mīnār v, 546b, **548b**; vi, 361b, 368a, b, 369a, 691b
Ḳuṭb al-Mulk → Ḳulī Ḳuṭb al-Mulk
Ḳuṭb Shāhīs (Golkondā) i, 1048a; ii, 1119a; iii, 318b, 426a, 427a, 448a; v, **549b**; vi, 68a, 126b, 369a, 610b, 696a, 837b; vii, 80a, 300a; s, 302a
Ḳuṭb al-Yaman al-Ahdal i, 255b
Ḳuṭba b. Aws → al-Ḥādira
Ḳuṭb-i ʿĀlam → Burhān al-Dīn
Ḳuṭbids ii, 517b
Kūthā v, 550b
Ḳutham b. al-ʿAbbās (676) iii, 876a; v, **551a**; viii, 1032a
Kuthayyir b. ʿAbd al-Raḥmān (Kuthayyir ʿAzza) (723) i, 402a; ii, 1029b; iv, 836b, 1086b; v, 433b, **551b**; vi, 604a; vii, 978a
Kuthayyir b. Waslās b. Shamlāl (VIII) vi, 744a
Ḳuṭlu Beg i, 311b
Ḳuṭlūdumūr (Amīr) vi, 15a
Ḳutlugh al-Aḥmadīlī i, 300b
Ḳuṭlugh Inanč b. Pahlawān (1195) iii, 1111b; vi, 921a; viii, 945a
Ḳutlugh Khān (XIII) vi, 48a, b; viii, 979a; s, 246a
Ḳutlugh Khānids i, 1311a; v, 161b, **553a**
Ḳutlugh Murād Khān s, 46a, 420a
Ḳutlugh Shāh Manḳut ix, 831b
Ḳutlugh Shāh Noyan (1307) v, **554a**
Ḳutlugh Terken xi, 286a, b
Ḳutlugh Tīmūr iv, 1064a
Kutlughtakin i, 731b
Ḳutlumush b. Arslān Isrāʾīl (Saldjūḳ) (XI) i, 420a, 1074a; iii, 195b; iv, 120a; v, 388a, b; vi, 274b; viii, 948a
Ḳuṭlūshāh vi, 545b; xi, 18b
Ḳuṭn ii, 904b; v, **554b**
Ḳuṭr v, **566b**; vii, 794b
Ḳuṭrabbul v, **566b**
Ḳuṭrub ii, 1078b; v, **566b**
Ḳuṭrub, Abū ʿAlī Muḥammad b. al-Mustanīr (821) v, **567a**; vii, 82b, 312b, 402a, 546b
Kuttāb → Kātib
Kuttāb (school) iv, 436a; v, **567b**, 909a, b, 911b, 1123a
al-Kutubī, Abū ʿAbd Allāh al-Dimashḳī (1363) v, **570b**
al-Kutubī, Muḥammad b. Ibrāhīm (1318) vi, 945b
al-Kutubiyya → Marrākush
Ḳutulmish → Ḳutlumush b. Arslān Isrāʾīl
Kütüphane → Maktaba
Ḳuṭuz, al-Malik al-Muẓaffar (al-Muʿizzī Mamlūk) (1260) i, 786b, 1125a; ii, 284b; iii, 184b, 1121a; iv, 484b, 641a; v, **571a**; vi, 321b, 322a, 543b, 790b; vii, 166b, 167a, 729a
al-Kuʿūb → Kaʿb, Banū
Ḳuʿūd v, **572a**; vii, 859b
Ḳuwā iii, 648b; iv, 330b
Ḳuwādhiyān → Ḳubādhiyān
Kuwait → al-Kuwayt
Kuwayk, Banū iv, 137a
Ḳuwayḳ, Nahr s, **545a**
al-Kuwayt i, 39b, 233b, 534a, 540a, 762a, 976a; ii, 176b, 469a, 673a; iii, 1066a, b; iv, 680b, 925a; v, **572a**, 1057a; vi, 36b; vii, 449b; viii, 668b; s, 3b, 50a
– university ii, 425a
Ḳuwwa iv, 271b; v, **576a**
Ḳuwwat al-Islām (Mosque, Delhi) ii, 256a, 274b; iv, 420a; vi, 368a
al-Ḳuwwatlī → Shukrī al-Ḳuwwatlī
Kuybishev iv, 281a
Ḳuyudju Murād Pasha → Murād Pasha Ḳuyudju
Ḳūz (Agoz) vi, 741b
Ḳuz-Balïgh i, 987a (see also *s.v.* Balāsāghūn)
Ḳuzaḥ iv, 803a
Ḳuzaḥ (Deity) iii, 32b; ix, 409a; xi, 221a
Kūzakunānī, Ṣunʿ Allāh (1523) vii, 935a
Ḳuzdār → Ḳuṣdār
Ḳuzmān, Banū vii, 778b; s, **545b**
Ḳuz-Ordu → Balāsāghūn
Ḳuz-Ulush i, 987a (see also *s.v.* Balāsāghūn)
Kwanadi v, **579b**
Kwararafas (Nigeria) viii, 20a, b
Kwaťta v, 101b, **579b**; ix, 447a; s, 507b
Kypsela → Ipsala
Kythera → Čoka Adasï

L

Laʿaḳat al-dam, Banū v, 581a; vi, 137b, 145a; vii, 783a; s, 189b
Laârba → Arbāʿ
Laʿb → Laʿib
Labāb v, 581b
Labakī, Naʿʿūm ii, 471b
Labbai v, 582a; vi, 206b, 503a, b
Labbayka → Talbiya
Labbès iv, 361a
Labībī (XII) v, 583a; vi, 609a
Labīd b. Rabīʿa (660) v, 583b; vi, 603a; vii, 254b; viii, 377a; s, 178b
al-Labīdī (1048) vi, 354a
Labin v, 584b
Labla (Niebla) i, 6a; ii, 1009a; iii, 748b; v, 586a; vi, 431a
Laccadives i, 170b; iv, 547a, b; v, 587a; vi, 206b
Ladā<u>kh</u> v, 588a; s, 156a, 242a
Lā<u>dh</u>iḳ (Amasya) v, 589a
Lā<u>dh</u>iḳ (Denizli) i, 204a; v, 589b
Lā<u>dh</u>iḳ (Konya) v, 589a
al-Lā<u>dh</u>iḳī vii, 685a
al-Lā<u>dh</u>iḳiyya v, 589b; vi, 322b, 379b, 577b, 578a, 579b, 582a; vii, 578a; viii, 128b; s, 133b
Lā<u>dh</u>ū <u>Sh</u>āh, Mawlānā s, 353a
Ladik vii, 272a
Lādīḳ → Deñizli
La<u>dj</u>āʾ v, 593a; vi, 544b, 546a
La<u>dj</u>āya s, 103a
La<u>dj</u><u>dj</u>ūn (town) v, 593b; vii, 756b;, x, 211b
Lā<u>dj</u>īn, al-Malik al-Manṣūr Ḥusām al-Dīn (Mamlūk) (1299) i, 622b, 1126b, 1128a, 1325a; ii, 38a, 285a, 958b; iii, 286b, 951b; iv, 437b, 964b, 965b; v, 594b; vi, 322b, 323a, 507b, 667a, 669b; vii, 169b
La<u>dj</u>nat al-fatwā i, 819b
Lafiyar Toga ii, 1146a
Lafẓ iii, 846a; v, 320b, 321b; s, **545a**
La-Garde-Freinet → Fraxinetum
La<u>gh</u>ïm, la<u>gh</u>ïmlar i, 1063a, 1064a; iii, 479b
La<u>gh</u>ïm<u>dj</u>ïlar i, 1062a
La<u>gh</u>mān → Lam<u>gh</u>ān
La<u>gh</u>wāt, Banū v, 1181a
Lagūṭ b. ʿAlī (Ma<u>gh</u>rāwī) (1057) vi, 742b
Laḥad → Ḳabr
Laḥam (Mt.) vi, 576a
Laḥn s, **546b**
Lahāna, Banū vii, 186a
Lāharī, Bandar vi, 537a
Lāhawr i, 1323a, 1324a, 1347b, 1348a; ii, 134b, 267b, 380a; iii, 450a; v, 31b, 597a; vi, 47b, 48a, b, 49b, 65b, 190a, 369b, 488b, 516b, 535b, 691a; vii, 279a, 854b; s, 21a, 47a, 63a, 142b, 247a, 284b, 333a, 360a
– monuments v, 599b, 1217b, 1219b
– university ii, 426a; iv, 1127a, b
Lāhawri → ʿAbd al-Ḥamīd
Laḥ<u>dj</u> → Laḥi<u>dj</u>
Lah<u>dj</u>at-i Sikandar <u>Sh</u>āhī iii, 453b
al-Laḥ<u>dj</u>ī, Muslim s, 236a
Laḥi<u>dj</u> i, 39b, 95b, 181a; ii, 192a, 193a, 675b; iii, 294a; v, 601b, 604a; vi, 36a, b; vii, 779a; ix, 738b; x, 106b; s, 338a
Lāhī<u>dj</u>ān ii, 192a, 193a; v, 602b, 604b; vi, 502a, 513a, 514a, 515b; s, 363a, b
Lāhī<u>dj</u>ī, ʿAbd al-Razzāḳ (1616) v, 605a; vii, 548a
Lāhī<u>dj</u>ī, <u>Sh</u>ams al-Dīn Muḥammad (1506) v, 604b, 605b
al-Lāḥiḳī → Abān b. ʿAbd al-Ḥamīd
Lahistān → Leh
Laḥn al-ʿāmma v, 605b, 803b; vi, 248; s, 388b
Lahndā v, 610a
Lahore → Lāhawr
Lāhōrī, <u>Gh</u>ulām Sarwar vi, 131b
Lāhūt wa-Nāsūt i, 351a; v, 611b
Lāhūtī, Abu 'l-Ḳāsim (1957) iv, 71a; v, 614b; vi, 608b; vii, 754b; s, 110a
Laʿib v, 478b, 615a
al-Lāʾiḥa al-Asāsiyya ii, 647b
Lāʾiṭ → Liwāṭ
Lak (Kurds) i, 755b, 756a; ii, 86b, 87a, 141b; iii, 1102b, 1109a; iv, 344a, 351a; v, 154b, 616b, 822b, 825b
Laḳ (Caucasus) v, 617b
Laḳab ii, 302a; iv, 180a, 293b, 294a; v, 618b
al-Laḳānī, ʿAbd al-Salām iv, 613b
Laḳant v, 631b
Lakay, Ibrāhīm ii, 701a

Lakha, Banū vi, 741a
Lakhanawatī (Gawr) x, 894b
Lakhdar Ben Khlouf (XVI) vi, 254b
Lakhm, Banū ii, 573b; v, 632a; x, 788a
al-Lakhmī (1085) vi, 279a, 942b
al-Lakhmī, Abu 'l-ʿAbbās → ʿAzafī, Banu 'l-
al-Lakhmī, Abū Ḥasan (1085) vii, 538a
al-Lakhmī, Abu 'l-Ḳāsim → ʿAzafī, Banu 'l-
al-Lakhmī, ʿAlī b. Rabāḥ s, 81b
al-Lakhmī, Muḥammad → ʿAzafī, Banu 'l-
al-Lakhmī al-Sabtī, Muḥammad b. ʿAlī s, 388b
Lakhmids i, 73a, 405b, 450b, 451b, 526a, 532a, 548b, 684b, 890a; ii, 1021a; iii, 462b, 1254a; iv, 1144b; v, 632a, 632b; vi, 97a, 221b; viii, 119b; s, 229b
Lakhnaw ii, 132a, b, 205a; iii, 451a; v, 634b, 1033b; vi, 78a, 537a, 611a; s, 74a, b, 102a, 106a, 247a, 292b
– monuments i, 66a; ii, 132a; v, 7a, 636a, 1135b
Lakhnawtī i, 393b, 1015a; ii, 270a; v, 637b; vi, 48a, 244b; s, 124a
Laḳīṭ al-Iyādī v, 639b
Laḳīṭ b. ʿĀmir b. al-Muntafiḳ (VII) vii, 582a
Laḳīṭ b. Bukayr b. al-Nadr (806) vii, 463b
Laḳīṭ b. Mālik al-ʿĀtikī i, 812b
Laḳīṭ b. Yaʿmur al-Iyādī (VI) iv, 289a; v, 639b
Laḳīṭ b. Zurāra (VI) ii, 353b; iii, 168b; v, 640a; vi, 603a; ix, 424b; s, 37b
Laḳḳūt b. Yūsuf i, 251a
Lakshadweep → Laccadives
Lakshmap Singh iii, 458a
Lakz → Lezgh
Lāl Kunwar ii, 379a
Lala iii, 340a; iv, 37a; s, **547a**
Lālā ʿAbla (Morocco) vii, 415b
Lālā ʿĀʾisha bint Muḥammad V b. Yūsuf (ʿAlawid) (XX) vii, 415b
Lālā Fāṭima Zahrāʾ bint Muḥammad V b. Yūsuf (ʿAlawid) (XX) vii, 415b
Lālā Mālika bint Muḥammad V b. Yūsuf (ʿAlawid) (XX) vii, 415b
Lālā Meḥmed Pasha (1606) → Meḥmed Pasha, Lālā, Shāhīnoghlu
Lālā Muṣṭafā Pasha → Muṣṭafā Pasha Lālā
Lāla Ratan Čand s, 126b
Lala Shāhīn Pasha → Shāhīn Lala Pasha
Lālā Yāḳūt umm Muḥammad V b. Yūsuf (ʿAlawid) (XX) vii, 415a
Lāle v, 172b, 642a, 644a
Lāle dewrī i, 270a, 558a; iii, 1002b; v, 641a
Lālezarī, Shaykh Meḥmed (XVIII) v, 644a
Lālezarī, Shaykh Meḥmed Ṭāhir (1789) v, 644a
Lālī → Shāh Sulṭān Muḥammad
Lālish v, 644a
Lalitpur v, 644b
Laʿlīzāde ʿAbd al-Bāḳī vi, 226a, 228a
Lālkōt ii, 256a, b, 259a
Lālla Khadīdja i, 371b
Lālla Masʿūda (1557) vi, 597a
Lallā ʿŪda vi, 591a
Lallūdjī Lāl (1835) ii, 491a; iii, 458a; v, 644b
Lām v, 644b
Lām, Banū i, 431a, 528b, 1096a, b; iii, 1107b; iv, 10a, 552b; v, 81a, 645b; vii, 582a, 673b
Lamak (Lamech) v, 646b; vi, 215b; vii, 681a
Lamak b. Mālik, al-ḳāḍī (dāʿī) (XI) iv, 199b; vii, 271a, 732a
Lamās, Banū vi, 744a
Lamasar → Lanbasar
Lamas-ṣūū v, 647a; s, 306b
al-Lamaṭī, Abu 'l-ʿAbbās b. al-Mubārak (1743) v, 647b; vi, 356b
al-Lamaṭī, Aḥmad al-Ḥabīb (1751) v, 647b
Lamāya, Banū vi, 221b, 310b
Lambadis v, 648a
Lamdiyya, Banū v, 1010b
Lamech → Lamak
Lamghān iv, 409b, 411a; v, 649a, b
Lamghānāt v, 648b, 782a; s, 237a
Lamghānī, Abū Yaʿḳūb Yūsuf (1209) vii, 785b
Lāmiʿī, Abu 'l-Ḥasan (1067) v, 649b
Lāmiʿī Čelebi, Shaykh Maḥmūd b. ʿOthmān (1531) ii, 869a; v, 649b; vi, 354a, 609b; vii, 567b, 936a, 1018a
Lāmiʿī Gurgānī, Abū 'l-Ḥasan (1067) viii, 970b
Lamīn → al-Amīn b. Ḥamad, Shaykh
Lamine Bey → al-Amin Bey
Lamlam v, 651a

Lamṭ iii, 347a; v, 651b, 1227b
Lamṭa, Banū v, 651b, 652a; vii, 587a
Lamṭī, Wadjdjādj b. Zalwī (XI) vii, 583b, 584a, b
Lamtūna, Banū i, 211a, 251a, 389b, 1176a, 1178b; ii, 1122a; v, 652b; vi, 741a, 742a, b, 744a; vii, 584a, 613a, b; ix, 18a
al-Lamtūnī, Abū Bakr b. ʿUmar (1075) i, 211a, 251a, 1176a; ii, 1002b, 1122a; iii, 288b; v, 653b, 654a; vii, 584b, 585a, 613a
al-Lamtūnī, Awbik b. Ačfagha (1674) vii, 614a
al-Lamtūnī, Limtād (Limtān) b. Nafīr (XI) vii, 585a
al-Lamtūnī, Yaḥyā b. ʿUmar (1055) vii, 584b
Lamu v, 655a, 963a; vi, 283a, 385a, 612b, 613a, 704a
al-Lān → Alān
Lanbasar iii, 501b; v, 656a
Langāh, Ḥusayn Shāh → Ḥusayn Shāh Langāh
Langar iv, 1073b
Langar Khān Langāh iii, 634a
Lankabālūs → Nicobar Islands
Lankar Čak → Čaks
Lankoran v, 656b
Lankuran → Kankoran
Laodicaea → Lādhiḳ, Lādhiḳiyya
Laos iii, 1208b
Lār (island) v, 674b
Lār, Lārīdjān v, 657a, 670b
Lār, Lāristān v, 604b, 665a
Larache → al-ʿArāʾish
Lārak → Djāsak
Lāranda i, 468a; iv, 621a, b, 624a; v, 676b, 1145b; vi, 71b
al-Lārī → Muṣliḥ al-Dīn
Lārī (coin) → Lārīn
Lārī, ʿAbd al-Ghafūr (1507) vii, 935a
al-Lārī, Muḥammad b. Ṣalāḥ (1572) v, 682a
al-Lārī, Muṣliḥ al-Dīn ii, 345b; v, 682a
Lārī, Yahuda iv, 309b
Lārī Čelebi iii, 340a
Laribunder iv, 597b
Laribus → al-Urbus
Lārida v, 682b
Lāridjān s, 357b
Lārīdjānī, Amīr-i Mukarram → Mīrzā Muḥammad Khān b. ʿAbbās
Larin ii, 120b; v, 672a, 683b
Larissa → Yenishehir
Lāriz v, 661a, 664b
Las Bēla v, 684a; vi, 192b; s, 222b
Lascaris, Theodore iv, 816a, b
Lāsh ii, 605a
Lāshārīs s, 332a
Lashgarniwīs iv, 757b
Lāshīn, Maḥmud Ṭāhir (1954) v, 189a; s, 547b
Lashkar → ʿAskar Mukram
Lashkar (army) v, 685a
Lashkarī (Daylamī) iv, 100a
Lashkarī, ʿAlī b. Mūsa iv, 347b, 773a
Lashkarī b. Mardī Ziyārid (X) vii, 498a, 656a; x, 42b
Lashkar-i Bāzār i, 1345a; ii, 1054a, 1082b, 1083a; v, 690b; vi, 65b; ix, 45a
al-Lāt Banū i, 151b; iv, 321b; v, 692a; vi, 373b, 374a, 645b; vii, 347a; x, 116a
Latakia → al-Lādhiḳiyya
Laṭīf b. Muẓaffar Shāh (Gudjarāt) vi, 51b, 52a
Laṭīfī, ʿAbd al-Laṭīf Čelebi (1582) v, 116a, 693a
Lawandar vi, 511b
Lawāsān vi, 511b
Lawāta, Banū i, 207b, 440a, 1049a, 1174b, 1349b; iii, 1040a; v, 694b; vi, 435a, 591b, 943b
al-Lawātī, Abū Muḥammad (1133) v, 697b
Lawei s, 150b
Lawḥ i, 90a, 851a; 911b; iv, 354a; v, 698a; s, 93a, 231a
al-Lawḥ al-maḥfūẓ → Lawḥ
Lawn v, 698b
Lawsha v, 707b
Lâye s, 182b
Layl and Nahār v, 707b
Laylā bint al-Djūdī ii, 625b
Laylā bint Masʿūd i, 400b
Laylā bint Nuʿmān iii, 255a; iv, 23a, 1066a
Layla al-Akhyaliyya (VII) iv, 912a; v, 710a; vi, 477b, 603a; vii, 843a
Laylā Khānïm (1847) v, 710a
Laylā Khānïm (1936) iii, 1117a; v, 710b
Laylā-u Madjnūn → Madjnūn wa-Laylā
Laylān vi, 498b, 502a
Laylat al-barāʾa i, 1027b → Ramaḍān
Laylat al-Ḳadr iv, 280a → Ramaḍān
Laylī ii, 191a

Laylī b. Nuʿmān → Laylā b. Nuʿmān
Layth Banū vii, 392b
al-Layth b. Faḍl (802) vi, 119a
al-Layth b. Mahaṭṭa (Tanūkh) x, 190b
al-Layth b. al-Muẓaffar (784) iv, 963a; v, 711a; vii, 190a
al-Layth b. Saʿd (791) v, 711b; vi, 263b; s, 87b
Layth b. ʿAlī iii, 619b
Layth b. Kahlān iii, 856b, 857b
al-Laythī, Naṣr b. Shabath vi, 334a
al-Laythī, Yaḥyā b. Yaḥyā (848) i, 83a; vi, 279a, 281a; 165a
Lāyzān iv, 343a
Laz i, 100b, 469b, 471b, 474b; iv, 350a, 351a, 576b; v, 712a
Lazarus v, 714b
Lazistān v, 712a, 713a, b
Lazz, Āl i, 759b
League of Arab States → Arab League
Lebanon → Lubnān
Lebaran v, 714b
Lebna Dengel vi, 642a
Lebou v, 694b, 753b
Leff i, 1179b; v, 715a
Lefḳosha v, 716a
Leh (Poland) i, 4a, 1119b; iv, 178b, 179a, 516b, 590b; v, 139b, 140a, b, 260b,719a, 766a, b
Lēk → Lakz
Lekë Dukagjin i, 170b, 652a
Lemdiya → al-Madiyya
Lemnos → Limni
Lenkoran → Lankoran
Leninabad → Khudjand
Leo Africanus (XVI) iv, 339b; v, 723a
Leo I (Armenia) i, 182b; ii, 37a
Leo II (Armenia) ii, 37b
Leo III (Armenia) iv, 1174a; vi, 381b, 580a
Leo IV (Armenia) iv, 1174a
Leo V (Armenia) i, 790a; ii, 38b
Leon → Liyūn
Lepanto → Aynabakhtï
Lerida → Lārida
Lesbos → Midilli
Lesh v, 724a
Leskofdjalï Ghālib ii, 878a; iii, 1200b; s, 324b
Letur s, 143a
Leucas → Levkas
Levante → Sharḳ al-Andalus
Levend → Lewend
Levi b. Japheth iv, 605a
Levice s, 171a
Levkas (island) iv, 656a; v, 725b
Lewend iii, 317b; v, 506b, 728a; vi, 56b; vciii, 185a
Lewnī (painter) (1732) vii, 603a; s, **548a**
Leylā Saz → Laylā Khānïm (1936)
Lezgh ii, 86a, 89a; iii, 604a; iv, 343a; v, 494a, 498a, 617b, 713a, 729b
Lezgi → Lezgh
Li Xun (Persian) (X) x, 460a
Liʿān i, 1150b; iv, 689a; v, 730a
Liʿb → Laʿib
Libān → Lubnān
Libās ii, 206b; v, 6a, 476a, 732a
Liberia v, 753a
Lībiyā i, 39b, 1071a, 1177a; ii, 94a, 667a, 676a; iii, 385a, 1049a; iv, 262a; v, 696a, 753b, 1066a; vi, 467b, 1043b; s, 216a
– demography s, 216a
– inscriptions v, 221b, 754b
– literature ii, 470b
– university ii, 425a; v, 912a
Libn → Labin
Libya → Lībiyā
Libyan i, 1180b, 1185a; v, 694b
Lifardjān vi, 384a
Liḥya → Liḥya-Yï Sherīf
Liḥyān, Banū i, 562b; v, 761b; vi, 349a; vii, 371a
al-Liḥyānī, ʿAlī b. Ḥāzim v, 763a
Liḥyānite → Liḥyān
Liḥya-yi Sherīf v, 761a
Likaylik, Muḥammad Abū ix, 651a
Likaylik, Nāṣ
Līlī b. al-Nuʿmān s, 356b, 357a
Līm, Līmūn → Muḥammadāt
Limassol → Ḳubruṣ
Limbang Valley s, 152b
Limni v, 257b, 763b
Linga v, 507b, 674b, 765a
Liongo s, 351a, b
Liparit (Georgian) vi, 626b
Lipḳa v, 765b
Liptako ii, 942a
Lisān v, 803a, 805a
Lisān al-ʿArab → Ibn Manẓūr
Lisān al-Dīn Ibn al-Khaṭīb → Ibn al-Khaṭīb
Lisān al-Ḥummara → Ibn Lisān al-Ḥummara

Lisānī (1533) iv, 68b
Lisbon → al-Us͟hbūna
Lis͟hbūna i, 1338b
Liṣṣ v, 767b
Līṭānī, Nahr al- iv, 483a
al-Līt͟h vi, 153b, 154a
Lit͟hām v, 744a, b, 745a, 769a
Lithuania v, 137b, 140a, 765b
Little, Malcolm → Malcolm X
Liu (T)Chiai-lien → Liu (T)Chih
Liu (T)Chih (XVIII) v, 770a
Livadya v, 772a
Livno v, 774a
Liwāʾ i, 349a; ii, 507b; iii, 383b, 384b; v, 776a
Līwā → al-D̲jiwāʾ
Liwāʾ-i S͟herīf → Sand̲jaḳ-i S͟herīf
Līwān → Īwān
Liwāṭ v, 776b; vi, 317b; xi, 509b
Liyāḳat ʿAlī K͟hān (1951) iii, 532b; v, 779b; vi, 489b; viii, 242a
Liyāḳat al-Lāh iii, 119b
Liyūn (Léon) v, 781a
Liyya (Ṭāʾif) vi, 266a
Lob nor (lake) x, 302a
Lobbo → Aḥmadu Lobbo; Ba Lobbo
Lōdī, ʿAlam K͟hān (XVI) i, 848a; ii, 271a, 1129a; iii, 420b
Lōdīs (Delhi) i, 756b; ii, 258b, 263b, 264a, 270b, 274b; iii, 442b; iv, 513a; v, 782a; vi, 46b, 49a, 126a, 127b, 369a, 488a; vii, 795b; s, 1b, 313a
Loe D̲jirga s, 66a
Logone v, 278b
Loja → Laws͟ha
Loḳmān, Seyyid → Luḳmān b. Sayyid Ḥusayn
Lombardy → Īṭaliya
Lombok i, 1219b, 1226a; v, 785a
Lope b. Musa → Lubb b. Mūsā
Lor, Lorī → Lur, Lurī
Loralai district (Balūčistān) s, 331b
Los Pedroches → Faḥṣ al-Ballūṭ
Lot → Lūṭ
Lōtōn → K͟hotan
Louxor → al-Uḳṣur
Lowarāʾī ii, 29a
Lōya D̲jirga i, 232b; ii, 657b
Luarsab I (al-Kurd̲jī) (XVI) v, 492b, 493a
Luʿba v, 616a
Lubān (incense) v, 786a; vi, 83b, 666a; x, 117a
Lubb b. Muḥammad iv, 713a
Lubb b. Mūsā b. Ḳāsī (863) vii, 288b
Lubb b. Mūsā b. Mūsā iv, 713a
Lubka → Lipḳa
Lubnān (Lebanon) i, 975b, 1078a, b; ii, 185a, 403b, 443b, 444a, 595a, 661a; iii, 559a; iv, 834b; v, 787a, 1253a; vi, 26b, 387b, 467b, 470a, 796b; s, 641b
– history iv, 261b
– industries iii, 211a; v, 791b, 795b
– institutions ii, 424a; iii, 523a; v, 912a, b, 1051a
– language, literature i, 575a; ii, 467a
Lubūd v, 798a
al-Lubūdī s, 267b, 341b
Lucena → al-Yussāna
Lucera → Lūs͟hīra
Lucknow → Lak͟hnaw
Ludd v, 798b
Lūdhiāna v, 803a
Lūd̲jāra → Lūs͟hīra
al-Lud̲jd̲j i, 1083b
Lug͟ha iv, 122a, b, 524a; v, 803a
Lug͟ha, ʿIlm al- → Lug͟ha
Lug͟hat-nāma → Dehk͟hudā
al-Lug͟hawī → Abu ʾl-Ṭayyib
Lug͟hz v, 806b
Luhayfa bint Abū Safyān i, 145b
al-Luḥayya v, 807a; vi, 192a; s, 30b
Luhrāsb iv, 809a
al-Lukām → al-Lukkām, D̲jabal
Luḳaṭa v, 809b
al-Lukkām, D̲jabal ii, 982a; v, 810a, b; vi, 778a
al-Luḳaymī → Asʿad
Lukayz i, 73a
Luḳmān b. ʿĀd i, 146a, 984a; ii, 112b; iii, 309a; v, 811a; vi, 235a, 565b
Luḳmān b. Sayyid Ḥusayn (1601) v, 813b
Luḳmānd̲ji b. Ḥabīb Allāh (1760) v, 814b
Lüleburgaz v, 815a
Lūlī ii, 40b, 41a; v, 816b; ix, 64b
Lulon → Luʿluʿa
Luʾluʾ (pearl) v, 819a, 969b
Luʾluʾ (eunuch, Aleppo) (1116) i, 1337a; iii, 86b, 1118b; vi, 578a
Luʾluʾ (amīr) iii, 398a

Luʾluʾ, Badr al-Dīn (Zangid) (1259) i, 195b, 1161a; ii, 348b; iii, 961a; iv, 76b; v, 821a; vi, 321b, 352a, 900b; vii,727b, 728b, 990b; ix, 45b
Luʾluʾ, Ḥusām al-Dīn i, 784a, 932b; v, 368b
Luʾluʾ al-Kabīr al-D̲j̲arrāḥī (1009) iii, 130b; v, 820a, 923b; vii, 116a
Luʾluʾa (fortress) ii, 36a, b, 37b; vi, 338a
al-Luʾluʾī, al-Ḥasan b. Ziyād (819) vi, 331a; vii, 758a
Lummān b. Yūsuf (930) ix, 586b
Lummasar i, 1359b
Lūnī (river) s, 329b
Lur(s) i, 513a, 955b; iii, 1096b, 1097b, 1102b; iv, 5b, 8a, 9a; v, 616b, 817a, 821a; s, 147b
Lūrā v, 234a
Lūrī v, 816b, 817a
Lūrī → Lūlī
Lurī (langue) iii, 1261a; v, 818a, 823a, b
Lur-i Buzurg iii, 1097b; v, 826a
Lur-i Kūčik iii, 1106a; v, 821b, 824b, 826a, 828a, 829b
Luristān i, 8a, 732a, 840a; iii, 337a, 1102a; v, 63a, 617a, 817b, 824a, 828a, 829b; vi, 491b, 494b, 495a, b
Lūrḳa v, 832b
Lūs̲h̲īra iv, 274b
Lusignan v, 303a
Lustre painting iv, 1167a
Lūṭ (Lot) v, 421a, 776b, 832b; vi, 495b
Lūṭ b. Yaḥyā → Abū Mik̲h̲naf
Lūt Das̲h̲ī-i → Ḍas̲h̲ī-ī Lūṭ
Luṭf (grace) v, 833b
Luṭf → Amān; Mīr
Luṭf ʿAlī Beg Ād̲h̲ar (1781) iv, 69b; v, 834a; vii, 530a
Luṭf ʿAlī K̲h̲ān iii, 604a
Luṭf ʿAlī K̲h̲ān Zand (1794) i, 246b, 1008b; ii, 812a; iv, 391a, b, 476a; v, 164b, 835a; viii, 665b; s, 336a, 405b
Luṭf Allāh, Mullā s, 353b
Luṭf Allāh b. Wad̲j̲īh al-Dīn Masʿūd (Sarbadārid (XIV) ix, 48b → IX. 49b
Luṭf Allāh K̲h̲ān s, 76a, b
Luṭfī (1463) ii, 1133a; v, 835b
Luṭfī, ʿAbd al-Mad̲j̲īd v, 189b
Luṭfī, Mollā iv, 880a
Luṭfī, Muṣṭafā → al-Manfalūṭī
Luṭfī Beg → Luṭfī Pas̲h̲a
Luṭfī Efendi (1907) i, 286a, 972b, 974a; ii, 714a; iii, 515a, 593b; v, 836b
Luṭfī Pas̲h̲a (1562) v, 268b, 837b
Luṭfī al-Sayyid, Aḥmad (1963) v, 838b, 1092a; vi, 955b; vii, 441b, 901a
Luṭfiyya → S̲h̲ād̲h̲iliyya
Lūṭī iv, 99b; v, 776b, 839a
Lutpulla Mutällip (1945) vi, 768a
Luwāta → Lawāta
Luxor → al-Uḳṣur
Luzon s, 152a
Luzūm mā lā yalzam v, 839b, 931a, 932a
Lydda → Ludd

M

Māʾ i, 1029b, 1094-7; ii, 343b; v, 859b, 1007a, 1108b; s, **548a**
Ma, Banū (N.W. China) → Wu Ma
Māʾ al-Ward s, **550a**
Maʿabiyat → al-Mabyāt
Māʾ al-ʿAynayn al-Ḳalḳamī, S̲h̲ayk̲h̲ (1910) i, 734a; v, 889b; ix, 446a; s, 47b
Maʿād v, 892b
Maʿadd i, 102b, 544b, 549a; iv, 448a, b; v, 894b
Maʿadd (amīr) → al-Muʿizz li-Dīn Allāh (Fāṭimid)
Maʿadd b. ʿAdnān v, 315a, 894b
Maʿādī, Banū i, 1097a; vii, 672a
Maadid s, 144b
Maʿāfir v, 895a
al-Maʿāfirī, Abu ʾl-Ḥasan ʿAlī (1208) v, 895b
al-Maʿāfirī, Abu ʾl-K̲h̲aṭṭāb ʿAbd al-Aʿlā (Imām) (761) vi, 311b, 312a, 946a
al-Maʿāfirī, ʿAmr (Miṣr) (VIII) vii, 160b
al-Maʿāfirī, Muḥammad b. K̲h̲ayrūn iv, 825b
al-Maʿāfirī, Saʿīd b. ʿAbd Allāh (VIII) vi, 280b
Maʿalt̲h̲āyā v, 896a
al-Maʿāmirī, Suʿūd b. Baʿīd (1878) vii, 227a

Maʿān v, 897a
al-Maʿānī i, 784b, 858a; ii, 550a
Maʿānī ʾl-shiʿr iii, 110b
al-Maʿānī wa ʾl-bayān v, 898a
Maʿārif v, 902b
Maʿarrat Maṣrīn (Miṣrīn) v, 921a
Maʿarrat al-Nuʿmān i, 1289a; v, 922a; vi, 429a; viii, 119a
al-Maʿarrī, Abu ʾl-ʿAlāʾ (1058) i, 108a, 131a, 591a, 592b, 1092b, 1290b; ii, 127b; iii, 640b, 686b, 1019b; v, 840a, 922b, 926b, 927a, 1211a, 1212b; vi, 616b; vii, 261a; viii, 470b; s, 32b, 37b, 119b, 289a
al-Maʿarrī, Abū Ghālib Ḥumām b. al-Faḍl al-Muhadhdhib vi, 578a
Maʾāṣir ii, 143a
Maʾāthir al-Umarāʾ i, 241b, 808a; iii, 340b; iv, 814b; v, 935b
Maʿazza, Banū viii, 866a
Maba s, 164a
Maba language (Wadāī) xi, 11b
Maʿbad b. Wahb (singer) (743) i, 118a; ii, 428b; iii, 698b; iv, 821b; v, 936b; vi, 262a, b
Maʿbad b. al-ʿAbbās b. ʿAbd al-Muṭṭalib i, 862b
Maʿbad al-Djuhanī (703) ii, 1026b; iii, 1142a; iv, 370a, 371a, b; v, 935b; vii, 567a
Maʿbad Mūsā vi, 651a
Mā baʿd al-ṭabīʿa v, 841a
Ma Chʾao-ching → Ma Hua-lung
Ma Chung-ying (XX) v, 844b
Ma Fu-chʾu (XIX) x, 575a
Ma Hu-shan v, 846b
Ma Hua-lung (1871) iv, 554b; v, 847a, 850b; viii, 240a
Ma Huan (XV) v, 849a; vi, 212a
Ma Ming-hsin (XVIII) iv, 554b; v, 847b, 850b
Mā warāʾ al-Nahr i, 8a, 103b, 147b, 454b, 1188a, 1294a, 1312a; ii, 3b, 45a, 587a, 1108a; iv, 175a, 188b; v, 852b; vi, 77a, b, 274a, 331b, 418a, 432b, 512a, b, 656a; s, 50b, 97a, b, 122a, 176b, 192b, 228a, 244b, 326b, 340a, 411a
Ma Yüan-chʾang iv, 554b
Maʿbar (Coromandel) iii, 407a; v, 937a, 1122a; vi, 271a
al-Maʿbarī, Shaykh Zayn al-Dīn (XVI) v, 938a
Mābeyn i, 64a; v, 938b
Mābeyndji I → Mābeyn
Mabkhara → Mibkhara
Mablaḳa iv, 747a, b
Mabnā al-Ḥashradj vi, 563b,
Mabramān (IX) vii, 279b
al-Mabyāt v, 498a
Māčar iv, 350a
Macassar → Makassar
Macedonia → Māḳadūnyā
Macina → Masīna
Macoraba → Makka
Ma-chu (Mazhu) (1710) ix, 623b
Mad Mullah → Muḥammad b. ʿAbd Allāh Ḥassān al-Mahdī
Madaba x, 884b
Madagascar v, 939a; vi, 774a
– language v, 942b, 943b
al-Madāʾin i, 77a, 810b; iii, 241b; iv, 386a; v, 945a; vi, 333b, 335b, 427b, 648a, 653b, 664b; s, 118a, 263b
Madāʾin Ṣāliḥ → al-Ḥidjr
al-Madāʾinī, Abu ʾl-Ḥasan (830) i, 758b, 760a; ii, 1097a; iii, 682a, 723a, 1263a; iv, 291a, 927a, v, 946b; vi, 350b; vii, 281a
Madali Khān → Muḥammad ʿAlī Khān (Khōkand)
Maʿdān vi, 193a; s, 243a
Maʿdān al-Shumaytī s, 510a
al-Madanī, Aḥmad Tawfīḳ iv, 159b
al-Madanī, Ibn Maʿṣūm (1692) vii, 527b
al-Madanī, Muḥammad Ẓāfir (1854) s, 481a
al-Madanī, Shaykh Muḥammad i, 808a; iii, 28b; v, 948b, 949a
Madaniyya v, 948b; vi, 454b; s, 371a
Madār, Shāh → Badīʿ al-Dīn
Madārī i, 859a
Mādar-i Shāh iv, 1015a, 1016b
al-Madd wa ʾl-djazr v, 949b
Mādda iii, 328b, 329b
Maddāḥ iii, 368a; iv, 735a; v, 951a; vi, 373a
Maḍḍar, Shaykh iii, 206b
Māddiyya ii, 97b
Maʿden ii, 707a
Madghalīs iii, 852a
Mādghīs i, 1349b
Madḥ → Madīḥ
al-Madhār/Maysān vi, 633b, 920a
al-Madhār vi, 921b

al-Māḏharāʾī, Āl (884) iii, 979a; v, 50a, 953a; vi, 670a, 671b; vii, 161b
al-Māḏharāʾī, Abū Bakr Muḥammad (956) v, 953b
al-Māḏharāʾī, Abū Zunbur al-Ḥusayn (929) v, 953a
al-Māḏharāʾī, ʿAlī b. Aḥmad (897) v, 953a
al-Maḏhārī, Abu ʾl-Ḥasan (1189) vi, 921a
Madhav Rāo iii, 316b; vi, 535b
Maḏhhab iii, 52a; v, 1129a, 1141b, 1150b; vi, 436a; s, **551a**
Maḏhḥiḏj, Banū i, 544b, 728a; v, 120b, 953b; vi, 141b, 472a; vii, 777a ; viii, 94a
Madḥiyya → Madīḥ
Mādhō Lāl Ḥusayn (XVI) vii, 327b
Maʾḏhūn 1, 29a; ii, 97b; iii, 50b
Māḍī v, 954b
Madīḥ/Madḥ iv, 714b; v, 931a, 955a; vi, 351a
Maʿdī-Karib Yaʿfir (Tubbaʿ) (ca. 520) ii, 244a; v, 118b; x, 576a
Maʿdin ii, 29b, 924a; v, 963b
al-Maʿdin v, 993b
Maʿdin Banī Sulaym s, 198b
Maʿdin al-Naḳira s, 198b
Madīna (urbanism) s, **551a**
al-Madīna i, 45a, 50b, 53a, 110b, 609a; ii, 592b, 854a; iii, 362a, 1067a; v, 994a; vi, 1a, 33a, b, 34a, b, 45b, 118a, 139b, 140b, 147a, 148a, 157a, 263b, 264a, 280b, 344a, 621b, 645b, 666b, 668a; s, 198b, 267b, 335a, 337b
– city v, 1000-1007
– constitution of v, 995b
– history iii, 896b; iv, 335b; v, 994a
– population v, 999a, b, 1003a
– university v, 1005b
al-Madīna al-Zāhira v, 1007b, 1239b; vi, 431a, 455b
Madīnat Fās ii, 818a; iii, 1031b, 1032a
Madīnat Ibn Hubayra iii, 266a
Madīnat ʿIzz al-Islam-V Ṣabra (al-Manṣūtiyya)
Madīnat al-Manṣūr → Baghdād
Madīnat al-Nuḥās s, **554b**
Madīnat al-Salām i, 894b; viii, 974b
Madīnat Sālim (Medinaceli) ii, 998a; v, 1008a
Madīnat al-Zahrāʾ i, 84a, b, 202a, 459a, 498a, 950a; ii, 745b, 747b, 957a; iii, 498b; iv, 1165b; v, 510b, 1008b; vi, 431a
Madīnat Zāwī i, 511b
al-Madīnī → Abū Ayyūb; Muḥammad b. ʿUmar
Maḍīra v, 1010a
al-Madiyya (Médéa) v, 1010a; vi, 404a, b
Madjabra i, 763b
Madjāḏhīb ii, 944b; iv, 686b
al-Madjāḏhīb, Banū s, **555b**
Madjālis → Madjlis
Madjalla → Medjelle
Madjallat al-Azhar i, 819a, 820b
Mādjān (canal) vi, 619b
Madjānīḳ i, 1057a, 1059a
Madjanna x, 789a
Madjapahit iii, 1219a, 1221b; s, 201a, 202a
Madjar, Madjaristān v, 1010b
al-Madjarra v, 1024b
al-Mādjashūn (781) vi, 264a
Madjāz i, 158b; iii, 898b; v, 1025b
Madjbūb iv, 1087a
Madjd al-Dawla, Abū Ṭālib Rustam b. Fakhr al-Dawla (Būyid) (1029) iii, 764b; iv, 100b, 465a; v, 1028a; vi, 66a; s, 118b
Madjd al-Dīn → Hibat Allāh b. Muḥammad
Madjd al-Dīn b. Abī Ṭālib b. Niʿma (Balkh) vi, 608b
Madjd al-Dīn b. al-Athīr → Ibn al-Athīr
Madjd al-Dīn b. al-Dāya (Munḳiḏh, Banū) (XII) vii, 578b
Madjd al-Dīn Abū Bakr (1168) vi, 380b
Madjd al-Dīn Baghdādī (1209) i, 347a, 764a; vii, 870b; viii, 703a
Madjd al-Dīn Barāwistanī al-Ḳummī (vizier) ix, 181b
Madjd al-Dīn Isḥāḳ iii, 708a
Madjd al-Dīn Muḥammad, ḳāḍī (Gulpāyagān) vi, 14a
Madjd al-Dīn Muḥammad al-Ḥusaynī al-Madjdī (XVII) viii, 893b
Madjd al-Mulk al-Balāsānī (1099) i, 1052b, 1336b; ii, 333b; v, 1028b; vii, 754a; viii, 81b
Madjd al-Mulk Sīnakī iv, 787b
Madjd al-Mulk Yazdī ii, 334a, 607b
al-Madjdal i, 846a
Madjdalyābā (fortress) vii, 910b
Madjdhūb, Abū Zayd ʿAbd al-Raḥmān (1569) v, 1029a; vi, 248b, 356b, 756a
Madjdhūb, Muḥammad (1831) s, 555b
Madjdhūbī → Madjāḏhīb
al-Madjdhūbiya → al-Madjāḏhīb

Madjdī b. ʿAmr v, 316b
Madjd-i Hamgar s, 235b
Madjīd b. Saʿīd b. Sulṭān (ĀlBū Saʿīd) x, 817a
al-Madjdjāsī, Muḥammad b. al-Ḥasan s, 126a
al-Madjdjāwī, ʿAbd al-Ḳādir (1913) v, 1029b
Madjdūd b. Masʿūd b. Maḥmūd (Ghaznawid) (1041) iii, 168a; vi, 780b
Madjghariyya → Madjar
al-Madjhidjī, Muḥammad b. al-Ḥasan i, 600b; iii, 791b
Madjhūl ii, 897a; iii, 26b
Madjīd, Banū ix, 739b
Mādjid b. Saʿīd (1870) i, 1282b; ii, 129a; v, 1030a; s, 355b, 356a
Mādjid b. ʿUrayʿir iv, 925b
Mādjid al-Kurdī (XX) vi, 157a
Madjīd Ṭūbiyā vi, 469a
Madjīdiyya → Ḥāfiẓiyya
Madjīdiyya library (Mecca) vi, 175b
Mādjir (tribe) s, 387a
al-Mādjishūn, ʿAbd al-Malik (828) vi, 280b
al-Madjisṭī → Baṭlamiyūs
Madjkasa Berbers s, 111b
Madjlis i, 891b, 974a, b, 975a, 976a, 979b, 1035b; ii, 87a; iii, 528a, 529a; v, 920a, 1031a
Madjlis al-Aʿyān ii, 658b, 659b; iii, 528a; v, 262b, 1035b, 1044a, 1054a
Madjlis Ḳiyādat al-Thawra s, 6b
Madjlis-niwīs iv, 758a
Madjlis al-nuwwāb v, 1044a, 1051b, 1054a, 1060b, 1061a, 1064a, 1066b
Madjlis al-shaʿb v, 1049a, 1059b, 1061b, 1065a
al-Madjlis al-Sharʿī al-Islāmī al-Aʿlā s, 68a
Madjlis ul-Islam il-Aʿlā Indonesia iii, 1229b
Madjlis-i Khāṣṣ iii, 553a
Madjlis Ḳuṭub ii, 797b
Madjlis al-Nuẓẓār ii, 647a; iii, 557a
Madjlis-i shūrā ii, 658b, 660a; v, 1042a, 1058a, 1059a, 1082b
Madjlis Shūrā al-Nuwwāb ii, 647a, 659b
Madjlis al-umma v, 1044a, 1054a, 1057a, 1061a, 1066b, 1068b
Madjlis-i ʿumūmī ii, 643a; v, 1035a, b, 1085b
Madjlis-i wālā v, 1084b, 1085a
Madjlis-i wükelā ii, 643a
al-Madjlisī, Muḥammad Bāḳir → Madjlisī-yi Thānī
al-Madjlisī, Muḥammad Taḳī → Madjlisī-yi Awwal
Madjlisī-yi Awwal, Muḥammad Taḳī (1659) v, 1087a, 1088b; vi, 550b; vii, 94a
Madjlisī-yi Thānī, Muḥammad Bāḳir (1698) i, 593a; iii, 588b, 1169b; iv, 278a; v, 1086b, 1087a, 1089b; vi, 550b, 551a; vii, 94a, 132a, 298a, 935b; viii, 136a, 779a; ix, 854a; s, 134b
Madjmaʿ al-baḥrayn i, 935b, 940b; iv, 903a, b
al-Madjmaʿ al-ʿIlmī i, 572b; v, 438a, 1090a; s, 11b
al-Madjmaʿ al-ʿIlmī al-ʿArabī i, 572a; ii, 290a
al-Madjmaʿ al-ʿIlmī al-Miṣrī → Institut d'Égypte
Madjmaʿ al-Lugha al-ʿArabiyya i, 572b; s, 11b
Madjmaʿ-i Ukhuwwat ii, 434a
Madjnūn ii, 1031a; iii, 273a, 841b; v, 1101a; vi, 468b
Madjnūn Banī ʿĀmir → Madjnūn Laylā
Madjnūn Laylā v, 1102b
Madjrā iv, 412a, b
Madjrīṭ iv, 533a; v, 1107a
al-Madjrīṭī, Abu al-Ḳāsim Maslama (1007) i, 600b, 1101a; iii, 924a, 1072b; v, 1109a; vi, 412a, 413b, 601a, 711b; viii, 52b, 677b; ix, 568b
Māʿdjūdj → Yāʿdjūdj wa-Māʿdjūdj
Madjūs (Norsemen) i, 83a, 494a, 864b; ii, 525a; iii, 74b; iv, 115b; v, 503b, 586a, 1013a, 1118a
Madjūs (Zoroastrians) i, 15b, 83a, 264a, 626a, 1354b; ii, 638a, 970b, 1035b, 1124a; iv, 43a, 54a, 910a, 1063a; v, 157a, 370b, 1110a, 1121b; vi, 337a, 633b, 675a; x, 439b
al-Madjūsī → ʿAlī b. al-ʿAbbās al-Madjūsī
Madjūsiyān ii, 162b
Madjzūʾ i, 671a
Madmūn v, 1121b
Madras i, 979a; ii, 426a; v, 1122a; s, 47a, 247a
Madrasa i, 20b, 593a, 899a, 1272a; iii, 1124a, 1227b, 1255b, 1264a; iv, 28a,

167b, 288b, 1025b; v, 255b, 907b, 1123a, 1200a
Madrasa Abū ʿInāniyya (Fès) s, 223b
Madrasa ʿĀdiliyya (Damascus) vi, 671b; vii, 274a
Madrasa As̲h̲rafiyya (Damascus) v, 1143a, b, 1144a; vi, 193b, 664a
Madrasa As̲h̲rafiyya (Aleppo) (1210) vii, 10a
Madrasa Čaḳmaḳiyya (Damascus) vi, 187a
Madrasa Dammāg̲h̲iyya (Damascus) vi, 664a
Madrasa Dār al-siyādat (Kirmān) vii, 480b
Madrasa D̲j̲amāl al-Dīn vi, 674b
Madrasa D̲j̲amāliyya (Cairo) vi, 672b, 673a
Madrasa Fāḍiliyya (Cairo) vi, 198a, 664a
Madrasa al-Falāḥ (Mecca) vi, 173b
Madrasa al-Firdaws (Aleppo) (1235) vii, 10a
Madrasa al-Ḥākim (Cairo) vi, 193b
Madrasa Halawiyya (Aleppo) (1245) vii, 14a
Madrasa al-Ḥasan (Cairo) vi, 193b
Madrasa Ḥaydariyya (Ḳazwīn) (1220) vii, 12b
Madrasa Iḳbāliyya (Damascus) vi, 193b
Madrasa Ḳalawūn (1285) vii, 11a
Madrasa Ḳalender-K̲h̲āne (Istanbul) vii, 272a
Madrasa K̲h̲āniyya (Buk̲h̲ārā) vi, 782b
Madrasa K̲h̲ātūniyya (Mārdīn) vi, 542b
Madrasa K̲h̲ōd̲j̲a Bedr al-Dīn (Mīlās) vii, 56a
Madrasa al-Ḳuḍāʿiyya (Damascus) vii, 469a
Madrasa al-Ḳumḥiyya (Cairo) viii, 913b
Madrasa al-Mad̲j̲diyya vi, 677b
Madrasa Maḥmūd Gawan (Bīdar) vi, 695b
Madrasa al-Maḥmūdiyya (Cairo) vi, 199b
Madrasa Masʿūdiyya (Diyār Bakr) vii, 13a
Madrasa Mustanṣiriyya (Bag̲h̲dād) (1234) i, 902a, b, 903a; v, 1127a; vi, 198a; vii, 727b, 728a, b
Madrasa Niẓāmiyya (Bag̲h̲dād) (1067) i, 901b, 902a; iv, 458a; v, 1126a, 1127a; vi, 198a, 635a, 657b; vii, 728a; viii, 71b, 82a; s, 4b, 29b, 192a, b, 326a
Madrasa Niẓāmiyya (Čis̲h̲tiyya) ii, 55a
Madrasa Niẓāmiyya (Damascus) s, 197a
Madrasa Niẓāmiyya (Marw) s, 326a
Madrasa Niẓāmiyya (Farangī Maḥall) s, 4b, 292a, 293a
Madrasa Patnā (1630) vi, 697b
Madrasa al-Rāḳiya (Mecca) vi, 173b
Madrasa Ṣāḥibiyya vi, 672b, 673a
Madrasa al-Ṣāliḥiyya (Cairo) vi, 671b; vii, 565a
Madrasa S̲h̲ādbak̲h̲tiyya (Aleppo) vii, 10a
Madrasa S̲h̲īrghāzī (K̲h̲īwa) vi, 130b
Madrasa Sitt Riḍwiyya (Mārdīn) vi, 542b
Madrasa Sulṭāniyya (Aleppo) (1223) vii, 10a
Madrasa Tād̲j̲iyya (Bag̲h̲dād) s, 384a
Madrasa al-Ẓāhiriyya (Damascus) ii, 286a, 290a; vi, 671b
Madrasa Zindjīriyya (Mārdīn) vi, 542b
Maḍraṭān s, 352a
Madrid → Mad̲j̲rīṭ
Madura ii, 391b; iii, 1213b, 1219a, 1226a; v, 1154b; vi, 43b; s, 202b, **556a**
al-Madya → al-Madiyya
Madyan S̲h̲uʿayb v, 1155b
Māf, Manāfa → Manf
Mafāk̲h̲ir i, 892a
Mafāk̲h̲ir al-Barbar iii, 782b; v, 1156b
al-Māfarrūk̲h̲ī, Mufaḍḍal b. Saʿd (XI) v, 1157a
Mafia (island) v, 1157b; vi, 370a
Mafḥaḳ iii, 327a
Mafḳūd ii, 995b
Mafraḳ s, 157a, **556a**
Mafrūs̲h̲āt v, 1158a
Mafṣūl v, 1159a
Magal s, 182a
Magan (Makkan) vi, 192b; ix, 774b
Magas iv, 345b, 349b
Maggan b. Kāmil b. D̲j̲āmiʿ iii, 386b
Magh i, 952a
Mag̲h̲ā (Muḥammad) b. Mansa Mūsā (Mali) (XIV) vi, 421b
Mag̲h̲āfir iii, 64b
Mag̲h̲āg̲h̲ā (Egypt) s, 408a
Mag̲h̲āg̲h̲a (tribe) v, 695a, b, 697a
Mag̲h̲āʾir S̲h̲uʿayb v, 1156a
al-Mag̲h̲āmī (900) vi, 352b
Mag̲h̲āra ii, 14a
Mag̲h̲āriba v, 1159a
Mag̲h̲azberd vi, 202b
al-Mag̲h̲āzī iii, 698a; v, 996a, 1161b
Mag̲h̲īla, Banū iii, 1040b, 1041a; v, 1164a; vi, 221b, 310b, 311b, 815a

al-Maghīlī, Muḥammad b. ʿAbd al-Karīm (1503) ii, 977b; iii, 276a; iv, 548b, 549b, 550a; v, 1165a; vii, 394a; viii, 18a; x, 122a
Maghlova ix, 630a
Maghmadās i, 125a; iii, 654a
Maghnāṭīs v, 1166b
Maghnisa i, 1225b; iv, 593b; v, 1169b
Maghōsha (Famagusta) v, 1171a; vi, 372b
Maghrāwa, Banū i, 122b, 1246b; ii, 821b; iii, 1041b, 1042a; v, 596a, 1173b; vi, 404a, b, 435a, 728b, 742b; vii, 722a
al-Maghrāwī, Abū Fāris ʿAbd al-ʿAzīz (1605) vi, 248b, 249a, 254b, 607a
al-Maghrāwī, Sīdī ʿAbd Allāh i, 1127a
al-Maghrāwī, ʿUbayd Allāh Aḥmad b. Bū Djumʿa (XVI) vii, 243a
al-Maghrib (North Africa) v, 1183b; ix, 789bb
al-Maghrib (al-Mamlaka al-Maghribiyya Morocco) i, 18a, 47a, 50a, 57b, 78b, 84b, 92a, 162a, 288b, 355a-357b, 366b, 1058a, 1231b, 1321a; ii, 130b, 619b, 748a; iii, 38a, 66a, 163a, 204a, 251b, 256b, 1038a, 1041a, 1049b; iv, 262b; v, 742b, 1149b, 1150a, 1159a, 1175a, b, 1184a; vi, 38a, 123b, 248a, 439a, 606a, 750a, 798b, 841b, 1036b; vii, 11a, 70a, 587a; viii, 61b, 794a, 905a; ix, 820a; s, 103a, 190b, 215a, 223a
– administration i, 171a, 428a, 917b, 1148b; ii, 145a, 307b, 413a, 673b, 676a; iii, 395b, 561b, 562a, 563b, 564a; iv, 784b; v, 1072a, 1198b
– demography s, 215a
– ethnography i, 34b, 39a, b, 533b, 1177b; ii, 160a; iii, 298b; iv, 329b, 331b, 332b; v, 696b, 1164b, 1196a, 1207b
– geography v, 1184a
– history v, 1188a
– institutions ii, 425b; iii, 525a; v, 917b, 1094a, 1150b
– languages, literature i, 96a, b, 156b, 315b, 571b, 578b; ii, 469b; iii, 806b, 814a, 902b; v, 757a, 1203a, 1159a; vi, 248a, 606a, 798b, 1036b
– monuments v, 289b, 1152a, 1153b, 1201a
– religion v, 1199a
al-Maghrib al-Aḳṣā vi, 141a
al-Maghribī → ʿAbd al-Ḳādir; Abu 'l-ʿAbbās; Muḥammad Shīrīn
al-Maghribī, Abu 'l-Ḥasan ʿAlī b. al-Ḥusayn (1009) i, 824b; iii, 79a; v, 928a, 1210b
al-Maghribī, Abu 'l-Ḳāsim al-Ḥusayn b. ʿAlī (1027) ii, 483b; iii, 80a, 896b; v, 929b, 1211b; vii, 1017a, 1031b
Maghribī, Aḥmad Khattū (1446) i, 1329b; ii, 1125b; v, 1209b; s, 10b
al-Maghribī, ʿAlī b. ʿĪsā (1835) viii, 399b
al-Maghribī, Banū v, 1210a
al-Maghribī, al-Ḥusayn b. ʿAlī (965) v, 1210b
al-Maghribī, Muḥyi 'l-Dīn (1281) vi, 601a, b
al-Maghribī, Saʿīd vii, 613a
Maghribī al-Shanḳīṭī (XX) vi, 75b
Maghumi i, 1259b; iv, 566b
Māghūs, Banū vi, 742a, 743b
Māgir, Banū vi, 741b
Māgiriyyūn iii, 339a
Māgres s, 167a
Māh Baṣra iv, 13b; v, 1212b
Māh Kūfa → Dīnawar
Māh-Peyker ii, 183b
Maḥa i, 1028b
Mahābād v, 466a, 1213a; vi, 502a; vii, 714a
Mahābat Khān (Mughal) (1634) i, 81a, 686a; ii, 180a, 381a; iv, 1018a, b, 1020a; v, 250b, 1214a; vi, 488a; viii, 125a
Mahābat Khān II (Mughal) v, 1214b
Mahābat Khān (Shīr) → Muḥammad Mahābat Khān
Maḥabba ii, 55b; iii, 103a; iv, 94b, 119b
Maḥabbat Khān (Bareilly) ii, 602a; iii, 61b
Mahābhārata i, 856b
al-Maʿhad al-ʿIlmī al-Suʿūdī vi, 173b
Maʿhad al-Nūr (Mecca) vi, 174a
Maʿhad al-Ṭibbī al-ʿArabī (Damascus) vi, 304a
Mahadba s, 144b
Mahādila → al-Ahdal
al-Mahādjir i, 766b
Mahāʾimī, ʿAlāʾ al-Dīn b. Aḥmad (1431) vii, 920a
Maḥall i, 317a; v, 1214b
al-Maḥalla v, 1220b; vi, 119a
Maḥallat Daḳalā v, 1221b
al-Maḥalla al-Kubrā ii, 1009b; v, 1221a
Maḥallat Sharḳiyūn v, 1221b
Maḥallat Abū ʿAlī s, 18a

Maḥallātī, Āghā Khān I, Sayyid Ḥasan ʿAlī Shāh (1881) i, 246a, b, 1008b; iv, 201b; v, 27a, 164b, 1221b; vii, 454b
Maḥalle iv, 229b-231b, 234a, 238a, 239b; v, 1222b
al-Maḥallī, Djalāl al-Dīn (1459) v, 1223a; viii, 42b
Maham → Mahīm
Māham iii, 455b
Māham Anga (XVI) i, 1136b; vii, 330b
Maḥāmīd, Banū i, 1299a; vi, 251a
Maḥammad b. Abī Bakr (1636) vi, 187a, 188a; s, 223a
Maḥammad b. Aḥmad b. ʿAbd Allāh Huḍīgī (1775) s, **556b**
Maḥammad b. Muḥammad al-Ḥafīd (al-Aṣghar) (1731) vi, 933a
Maḥammad b. al-Sharīf, Mawlāy (ʿAlawid) (1664) i, 355b; vi, 250a
Maḥammad ʿAbdille → Muḥammad b. ʿAbd Allāh Ḥassān al-Mahdī
Maḥammad al-Ḥādjdj → al-Dilāʾ
Maḥammad al-Shaykh (Saʿdid) (1557) vi, 594a, b, 597b
Maḥammad al-Shaykh al-Aṣghar (Saʿdid) (1655) vi, 595a
Māhānasar vi, 512a
Mahanḍ Bāba b. ʿUbayd (1860) vii, 622b
al-Māhānī → Muḥammad b. ʿĪsā b. Aḥmad
Māhānī, Ustādh Muʾmin b. Ḳuṭb al-Dīn s, 139a
Mahārashtrā vi, 63a, 536b; s, 246b
Mahari → Kotoko
Maḥārim → Ḥarīm
Maḥasī i, 1029a
Maḥāsin i, 981b
al-Maḥāsin wa-ʾl-masāwī v, 1223b
Mahāt v, 651b, 1227a
Mahathir Mohamad, Datuk Seri (XX) vi, 241b, 242a
Maḥbūb b. al-Raḥīl al-ʿAbdī, Abū Sufyān (VIII) iii, 651a; v, 1230a
Maḥbūb ʿAlī Khān ii, 84a; iii, 322b
Maḥbūba (singer) iv, 821b, 822b
Maḥbūbī, Āl-i v, 858a; viii, 749a
al-Maḥbūbī, Aḥmad b. ʿUbayd Allāh (1232) viii, 749a
al-Maḥbūbī, Maḥmūd iii, 163b
al-Maḥbūbī, Shams al-Dīn Muḥammad b. Aḥmad (XII) viii, 749a
al-Maḥbūbī, ʿUbayd Allāh b. Masʿūd (1346) vi, 848a; viii, 749a
al-Maḥbūbiyyūn iii, 659b
Mahd Awliyāʾ Khayr al-Nisāʾ Begum (XIX) vi, 483a, 515a; s, 71a
Mahdawīs ii, 500a; iii, 492b; v, 1230b; s, 222a
Mahdī → al-Djawnpūrī; Ibn Tūmart al-Mahdī; Muḥammad b. ʿAbd Allāh Ḥassān
al-Mahdī (restorer) ii, 851a; iii, 1167a; iv, 203b, 204a, 278b, 456b, 662a; v, 1230b; vi, 216a, 247b
al-Mahdī (Fāṭimid) → al-Mahdī ʿUbayd Allāh
al-Mahdī, Abū ʿAbd Allāh Muḥammad (ʿAbbāsid) (785) i, 59b, 103b, 107b, 402b, 550b, 710b, 897a; ii, 143b, 159b, 234b, 281b, 305a; iii, 20a, 22a, 232b, 265b, 616a, 749b, 876a, 996a, 1015b; iv, 88b, 645a, 838a, 939b, 940b, 1164a; v, 69b, 1233a, 1238a; vi, 106a, 139b, 140a, 147b, 205b, 263b, 334b, 428a, b, 493a, 506a, 625a, 636b, 673a, 707b, 708b, 744b, 745a, 821b; vii, 306b, 507a, 645b; x, 227a; s, 17b, 35a, 48b, 89a, 94a, 199a, 225b, 304b, 326b, 352a
al-Mahdī, Muḥammad b. Hishām b. ʿAbd al-Djabbār (Umayyad) (1010) i, 84b; ii, 485b; iii, 495b; v, 1107b, 1239a; s, 153a
al-Mahdī (Sudanese) → Muḥammad Aḥmad b. ʿAbd Allāh
al-Mahdī b. Abī ʾl-Faḍl Djaʿfar, al-Thāʾir fī ʾllāh vi, 941b
Mahdī b. ʿAlwān al-Shārī (al-Ḥarūrī) (IX) vi, 335b
Mahdī b. Sayyid Riḍā Ḥusaynī, Sayyid (XVII) vii, 132a
Mahdī b. Tawālā ii, 874a
al-Mahdī Aḥmad (Zaydid) (1681) vii, 270a
Mahdī ʿAlī Khān (XIX) iv, 170b; v, 1240a
Mahdī Baḥr al-ʿUlūm, Sayyid s, 157b
Mahdī Khān Astarābādī (XVIII) iv, 69b; v, 1240a; s, 46b
Mahdī Ḳulī Hidāyat v, 24b
Mahdī Ḳulī Khān iv, 573a
Mahdī Ḳuli Sulṭān i, 240a
al-Mahdī li-Dīn Allāh Aḥmad b. al-Ḥasan b. al-Ḳāsim (Zaydī Imām) (1681) i, 554a; v, 1241b; vii, 779a

al-Mahdī li-Dīn Allāh Aḥmad b. al-Ḥusayn (Zaydī Imām) (1258) v, 1241a
al-Mahdī li-Dīn Allāh Aḥmad b. al-Ḥusayn (Zaydī) (1013) s, **556b**
al-Mahdī li-Dīn Allāh Aḥmad b. Yaḥyā b. al-Murtaḍā (Zaydī Imām) (1437) v, 1241a; vii, 55a
Mahdī al-Mniaï (XX) vi, 755a
al-Mahdī ʿUbayd Allāh (Fāṭimid) (934) i, 48a, 104a, 249a, 1175b, 1178b, 1238a; ii, 168b, 453a, b, 850b, 852a, b, 860b, 861b; iii, 123b, 785a; iv, 198a, b, 204a, 458b, 660b; v, 1175a, 1237b, 1242a, 1246a; vi, 434b, 439a, 712b, 727a, 1039b; vii, 575b, 641a, 941b; viii, 922a; s, 236b
Mahdī ʿUlyā bint ʿAbd Allāh → Mahd Awliyāʾ Khayr al-Nisāʾ Begum
Mahd-i ʿUlyā umm ʿAbbās I (1600) vi, 939a
Mahdids i, 552b; iii, 125b; v, 1244a; vii, 861b
al-Mahdiyya (Sudan) ii, 63b, 124a; iii, 5a; iv, 952b; v, 267b, 1247b; vii, 124b
al-Mahdiyya (town Morocco) i, 356a; iii, 500a; v, 1245a; s, 144b
al-Mahdiyya (Tunisia) i, 163b, 700a, 830a, 1319b; ii, 853a, 862b, 956a; iii, 138b, 470b; iv, 460a; v, 1243a, 1246a; vi, 427a, 434b, 455b, 712b, 727b; s, 11a
al-Mahdjar v, 1253a
Maḥdjūr iii, 50a
Maheskar vi, 53b
Maḥfūr iv, 897b
Maḥfūẓ iii, 26b
Maḥfūẓ, ʿAlī al-Bārūnī s, 15b
Maḥfūẓ, Nadjib v, 190b, 191a, b
Māh-i Mulk Khātūn s, 65a
Māhī Sawār ii, 32a
Mahīm (Maham) v, 1257b; vii, 919b
Māhīm v, 1258a
Māhir, ʿAlī (1960) s, **557b**
Mahisūr iii, 428a; v, 1216a, 1258b; vi, 459b, 535b
– monuments v, 1259b
Mahisūr (Mysore) in Tīpū Sultān x, 532b
Māhiyya i, 513b, 514a, 785a; v, 1261a
Maḥkama vi, 1a
Maḥkama (Algeria) s, **557b**
Maḥkama (Brunei) s, **568b**
Maḥkama (Malaysia) s, **567b**
Maḥkama (Indo-Pakistan sub-continent) s, **560b**
Maḥkama (Singapore) s, **566b**
Maḥkama (Tunisia) s, **559a**
Maḥlūl vi, 44b
Maḥmadīl vi, 499b
Maḥmal iii, 34a; vi, 44b
Mahmand → Mohmand
Maḥmashādh iv, 669a
Maḥmūd (Samarḳand) s, 65a
al-Maḥmūd, Āl (Yemen) vii, 779b
Maḥmūd, Sayyid (Nīshāpūr) s, 360a
Mahmud, Sultan (Malacca) vi, 209a, 212b, 213a
Maḥmūd I Nāṣir al-Dīn b. Ilyās Shāh (Bengal) (1459) vi, 46b
Maḥmūd II Nāṣir al-Dīn (Bengal) (XV) ii, 486b; vi, 46b
Maḥmūd III Ghiyāth al-Dīn (Bengal) (1538) iii, 422b; vi, 47a
Maḥmūd I, Nāṣir al-Dīn b. Iltutmish (Delhi) (1266) i, 1194b, 1300a, 1322b; ii, 260a, 267b, 268a, 274b, 609b, 973a, 1047b; iv, 749b; v, 546a; vi, 47b, 127b, 273a, 368b; s, 124a
Maḥmud II Nāsir al-Dīn b. Sulṭān Muḥammad Shāh Tughluḳ (Delhi) (1412) i, 1068b; ii, 218b, 270a, 276b, 498b, 1125a; iii, 417b; iv, 533b, 543a; vi, 49a, 294a, b, 406b; vii, 313b; s, 206b
Maḥmud I Sayf al-Dīn, Begarhā (Begrā, Gudjarāt) (1511) i, 924a, 1068b, 1200a; ii, 10b, 54a, 597b, 678a, 814b, 1127a; iii, 421b; v, 26b, 1216b; vi, 50a, 53b, 54a, 269b, 270a
Maḥmūd II b. Muẓaffar Shāh I (Gudjarāt) (1526) vi, 51b
Maḥmūd III Abu ʾl-Futūḥāt Saʿd al-Dīn (Gudjarāt) (1554) i, 1135b; ii, 1128b; iv, 901b; vi, 52a
Maḥmūd II b. Muḥammad Khān (Ḳarakhānid) (1164) ix, 16b
Maḥmūd I Ghāzī (Ottoman) (1754) i, 56a, 776a; iv, 900b; v, 643b; vi, 55a; vii, 319a
Maḥmūd II (Ottoman) (1839) i, 61a, 399a, 790b, 836b, 948a; ii, 209b, 684a, 714a; iii, 91a, 628b; iv, 295b; v, 19a, 36a, 816a, 903b, 1084b; vi, 58a, 196b, 284b, 341a, 508b, 531a, 541b; vii, 425b, 547a, 677b; viii, 59a, 84b; s, 168a, 211b

– reforms i, 469a, 657a, 778b, 783a, 837b, 838a, 905b, 972b, 1226a, 1304a; ii, 202a, 207a, 339a, 512b, 513b, 519b, 563a, 615a, 641b, 724a, 907b, 1091a; iii, 203b, 384b, 552b, 1153b, 1257b
Maḥmūd I b. Turkān Khātūn (Saldjūḳ) (1094) i, 1051b, 1070b; vi, 275a; vii, 541a; viii, 81b, 942a; s, 384a
Maḥmūd II b. Muḥammad b. Malik-Shāh (Saldjūḳ) (1131) i, 300a, 353b, 858b; ii, 894a; iii, 195a, 345a, 1118b, 1255b; iv, 29a, 466a; vi, 63b, 500a, 782a; vii, 733b; viii, 81b, 943b; s, 3a
Maḥmūd (Mirdāsid) (1074) vi, 544a
Maḥmūd b. ʿAbd al-Djabbār i, 82b
Maḥmūd b. Abī Saʿīd i, 148a, 852b; iii, 483b; iv, 410a; v, 389a
Mahmūd b. Aḥmad of Ḳalhāt (XIII) iv, 500b
Maḥmūd b. ʿAlī (XIV) s, 83a
Maḥmūd b. Amīr Walī vii, 849a
Maḥmūd b. Bābur (Tīmūrid) (XV) vi, 513b, 514b
Maḥmūd b. Būrī → Shihāb al-Dīn Maḥmūd
Maḥmūd b. Ghiyāth al-Dīn (Ghūrid) (XIII) vii, 410a
Maḥmūd b. Ghulām Muḥammad Ṭarzī iii, 13b
Maḥmūd b. Ḥamza al-Ḥamzāwī ii, 182b
Maḥmūd b. Iltutmish (Muʿizzī, Delhi) vii, 193b
Maḥmūd b. Ismāʿīl → Luʾluʾ, Badr al-Dīn
Maḥmūd b. Maḥmūd b. Bābur (Tīmūrid) vi, 513b
Maḥmūd b. al-Malāḥimī s, 393a
Maḥmūd b. Malikshāh → Maḥmud I (Saldjūḳ)
Maḥmūd b. Mīr Ways (Ghalzay) (XVIII) i, 229a, b, 1008b; ii, 1001a; iii, 604a, b; iv, 37a, 537a; viii, 771a
Maḥmūd b. Muḥammad-V Mīrem Čelebi
Maḥmūd b. Nāṣir Raʾīsiyya ii, 29b
Maḥmūd b. Naṣr → Rashīd al-Dawla Maḥmūd
Maḥmūd b. Sebüktigin (Ghaznawid) (1030) i, 217b, 226b, 424b, 506b, 662a, 780a, 1020a, 1036b, 1068b, 1130b, 1194a, 1218b, 1300a, 1356a; ii, 119b, 308b, 488b, 597a, 730a, 799a, 809b, 919a, 972b, 1043b, 1049a, 1050b, 1099b, 1123b; iii, 195a, 196b, 197b, 255b, 347b, 415b, 1113b; iv, 24b, 189b, 294b, 410a, 543a, 1066b, 1150b; v, 956b, 1028b; vi, 65a, 193a, 276a, 406b, 410a, 440a, 517a, 600b, 606a, 691a, 715b; vii, 407a, 549a; viii, 110a, 253a, 1028a; ix, 45a; x, 869b; s, 125b, 252b, 253b, 280a, 284b, 305a
Maḥmūd b. Turghut Oghlu iv, 624b
Maḥmūd b. ʿUmar b. Muḥammad Aḳīt (Timbuktu) (XV) vii, 394a
Maḥmūd b. Walī s, 227b, 419b
Maḥmūd b. Zangī b. Aḳ Sunḳūr (Zangid) (XII) vii, 10a
Maḥmūd b. Zangī, Nūr al-Dīn → Nūr al-Dīn Maḥmūd b. ʿImād al-Dīn Zangī
Maḥmūd Aḥmad i, 735a, 765a, 929b; ii, 124a; v, 267b, 268a, 1250b, 1251a, b
Maḥmūd Ālūsī-zāde → Maḥmūd Shukrī
Maḥmūd ʿAyyād iv, 1153b
Maḥmūd ʿAẓmī Pasha, amir al-Ḥadjdj (XX) vi, 155a
Maḥmūd Beg (Ḳarāmān-oghlu) iv, 621b
Maḥmūd of Betl-Kakhab rosso i, 765a
Maḥmūd Bey iii, 636a
Maḥmūd Čelebi (XVII) vii, 472b
Maḥmūd Djalāl al-Dīn iv, 1125b
Maḥmūd Ekrem Bey → Ekrem Bey
Maḥmūd Esʿad vi, 94b
Maḥmūd Gāwān, Khwādjā ʿImād al-Dīn (1482) i, 199a, 924a, b, 925a, 1200a, 1323a; iii, 15a, 421a, 577a, 1159b; v, 1135a; vi, 53b, 62b, 66b, 269a, 369a; vii, 459a b, 353b;
Maḥmūd Ghalzai → Maḥmūd b. Mīrways
Maḥmūd Ghazān → Ghazān Khān
Maḥmūd of Ghazna Maḥmūd b. Sebüktigin
Maḥmūd Ghilzay b. Mīr Ways (XVIII) ix, 854b
Maḥmūd Ghizhduwānī s, 46b
Maḥmūd Ghūrī → Ghiyāth al-Dīn Muḥammad b. Sām
Maḥmūd Gokaldāsh i, 628a, 1192a
Maḥmūd Ḥamdī Ḥamūda, dr. vi, 178a
Maḥmūd al-Hamzāwī iii, 156a
Maḥmūd Ḥasan ii, 437a; v, 7a
Maḥmūd Ḳābādū iv, 1153b
Maḥmūd Karantao ii, 1003b
Maḥmūd Kārī i, 1342b; iii, 355b
Maḥmūd Kemāl → Īnal

Maḥmūd Khaldji I b. Malik Mughīth (Mālwā) (1469) i, 924a, 1200a; ii, 12b, 219a, b, 1125b; iii, 418b, 638b; v, 1a; vi, 50b, 51a, 52b, 62a, 67a, 87a, 272a, 309b, 406b, 407b; s, 280a
Maḥmūd Khaldjī II b. Nāṣir al-Dīn Shāh (Mālwā) (1531) i, 914b; ii, 12b, 1128a; iii, 421b; vi, 54b, 309b, 310a, 407a, 970a
Maḥmud II Khān (Ḳarākhānid) (1141) iii, 1114b, 1116b; iv, 581b; v, 45b
Maḥmūd Khān, Naṣīr al-Dīn (Kālpī) (XV) vi, 61b
Maḥmūd Khān, Nawwāb (Mughals) vi, 77b
Maḥmūd Khān b. Laṭīf b. Muẓaffar Shāh (Gudjarāt) vi, 52a
Maḥmūd Khān b. Nāṣir i, 1006a
Maḥmūd Khān b. Yūnus (XVI) x, 349a
Maḥmūd Khān Lōdī, Masnad-i ʿAlī s, 73b
Maḥmūd Khān Māzandarānī, Mushīr al-Wizāra s, 23b
Maḥmūd Khān Rohillā i, 1206a
Maḥmūd al-Khwārazmī → Maḥmūd Yalawač
Maḥmūd Khayrām (Aḳshehir) (1269) ix, 61a
Maḥmūd Khōdja Behbudiy (1919) vi, 767a, 769a, b
Maḥmūd Kokaltāsh → Maḥmūd Gokaldāsh
Maḥmūd Lāmiʿī Čelebī → Lāmiʿī Čelebī Shaykh Maḥmūd b. ʿOthmān
Maḥmūd Langāh iii, 633a, 634a
Maḥmūd al-Malāḥimī s, 25b
Maḥmūd al-Masʿadī (XX) vi, 750b
Maḥmūd Mukhtār Pasha (XX) iv, 284a; vii, 525b
Maḥmūd Nedīm Pasha (1883) i, 56b, 285b; iii, 250b, 621a; iv, 681b; vi, 68a
Maḥmūd Pasha → al-Falakī; Ḳara Maḥmūd; Ṭayyār
Maḥmūd Pasha (Yemen) (1567) vi, 72a; vii, 600a
Maḥmūd Pasha Welī (1474) ii, 691a, 722b; iv, 230a, 1017a; vi, 69b; s, 282b
Maḥmūd Pasīkhānī iii, 600b; viii, 114b
Maḥmūd Raʾīf (XIX) vi, 725a
Maḥmūd Rashīd Efendi vi, 113b
Maḥmūd Riyāḍ s, 240b
Maḥmūd Samarḳandī, Mawlānā (XV) ii, 678a; vi, 50b
Maḥmūd Shabistarī (Shabustarī) (1318) iv, 67b; vi, 72b; viii, 540a
Maḥmūd Shāh (Bahmanī) i, 923b, 1047a; iii, 15a, 421a, 1159b
Maḥmūd Shāh (Özbeg) i, 853a; ii, 30b
Maḥmūd Shāh, Khwādjā vii, 271a
Maḥmūd Shāh Durrāni i, 230b; ii, 637b, 839a
Maḥmūd Shāh Īndjū iii, 1208a
Maḥmūd Shāh Khaldjī → Maḥmūd I Khaldjī
Maḥmūd Shāh Nāṣir al-Dīn (1412) (Tughluḳid) x, 593a
Maḥmūd Shāh Sharḳī (Djawnpūr) (1458) ii, 270b, 499a; iii, 419b; vi, 61b; ix, 355a
Maḥmūd Shewḳat Pasha (1913) i, 64a; ii, 15b, 431a, 531a, 682b, 698b; iii, 204a, 595a, 994a; iv, 296b, 297a; vi, 73b, 614b, 983b
Maḥmūd Shihāb al-Dīn (Bahmanī) (1518) vi, 62b
Maḥmūd Shukrī al-Ālūsī → al-Ālūsī, Maḥmūd Shukrī
Maḥmūd Ṭarābī (1238) i, 1295a; v, 858a; vi, 77a
Maḥmūd Tardjumān (1575) vi, 74b
Maḥmūd Ṭarzī s, 65b, 109b
Maḥmūd Taymūr (1973) i, 597b, 598a, b; v, 187b, 189a, b, 192a; vi, 75a, 414b
Maḥmūd Ṭayyār → Ṭayyār Maḥmūd Pasha
Maḥmūd Ṭoghrïl Ḳara Khān b. Yūsuf Ḳadïr Khān (Marghīnān) (1075) vi, 557b
Maḥmūd Tughluḳ → Maḥmūd II (Dihlī)
Maḥmūd Urmewī ii, 345b; v, 5a
Maḥmūd Yalawač (XIII) ii, 2b, 791b; iv, 1020a; v, 38b, 858a; vi, 77a
Maḥmūd Zarkūn i, 280a, 289a
Maḥmūdābād (Mughān) ii, 1127a, 1129a; iii, 445b; vi, 494a
Maḥmūdābād, Āl vi, 77b
Maḥmūdek Khān iv, 723a, 849a
Maḥmūdī, Banū v, 460a
Maḥmūdī Beg (Mākū) (1639) vi, 202b
Maḥmūd-i Kutubī (1402) vii, 481a
Maḥmūd-i Zāwilī → Maḥmūd b. Sebüktigin
al-Maḥmūdiyya viii, 114b; s, 371a
Maḥmūdpūr vi, 691a
Mahmut Makal (XX) vi, 96a
Māhpaykar → Kösem

Mahr i, 172b, 174a, 209a; vi, 78b, 476a
Mahra i, 110b, 543b; iii, 9a, 652a; v, 184a; s, 339b
Mahra, Banū vi, 80a, 83b, 84a, b
Mahra b. Ḥaydān b. ʿAmr b. al-Ḥāf vi, 81b; ix, 403a
Maḥram Bilḳīs vi, 84a, 561b, 562a
Mahrattās → Marāthās
Mahrī i, 575a; iii, 176b; vi, 84a; s, 339b
Mahriyya iii, 666a, 667b
Māhrū iv, 758b
Mahsatī iv, 62a; vi, 85b
Mahsūd, Banū vi, 86a; s, 285a
Maḥsūsāt vi, 87a
Māhūʾī Sūrī, Marzbān vi, 620a
Māhūr vi, 87a, 269a
Maḥw iv, 277a
Maḥyā i, 1040a; vi, 87b
Mai s, 569a
Māʿi Daya Kawr i, 432b
Maimonides, Abraham iv, 305a, 306a, b
Maimonides, Moses → Ibn Maymūn
Mai Tatsine (1980) s, **569a**
Ma-in (town) vi, 283a
Maʿīn, Banū i, 525a, 548a; v, 183b; vi, 88b, 561a; ix, 91a
Maʿīn al-Din i, 803a
Maʿīn al-Djawf vi, 433a; ix, 91a
Mainu Kano, Malam iv, 549b
Majorca → Mayurḳa
Maḳābir Ḳuraysh → Kāẓimayn
Maḳʿad ii, 114b
Māḳadūnyā vi, 88b
Maḳāla ii, 802a; vi, 90a
Makalla → al-Mukallā
Maḳām (music) iii, 83b; vi, 96b
Maḳām ʿAbd al-ʿAzīz (al-Gharrā) vii, 10a
Makām al-Ḥanafī vi, 165b
Maḳām Ibrāhīm iv, 317b, 318a, b; vi, 104b, 165b, 708b
Maḳām-i Aʿlā i, 918a
Maḳāma iii, 106b, 221b, 373a; iv, 64a; vi, 107a; s, 267a
Maḳāmāt ii, 246a; iii, 899a
Mākān b. Kākī, Abū Manṣūr (940) i, 688a, 866a, 867a, 1350a; ii, 928a; iii, 255a, 1157a; iv, 23a; v, 158a; vi, 115b, 539a; s, 357a
Makanpur s, 358b
Makanta Jigi (Fajigi) vi, 422a
Makarfi, Malam Shuʿaibu iii, 283a
Makāri → Kotoko
Maḳāsid al-Sharīʿa s, **569b**
Makassar iii, 1219b; v, 1155a; vi, 116a; ix, 877a; s, 151a, 199b, 201b
Makāyīl vi, 117a
Maḳbara (Iran) vi, 122a; s, **570b**
Maḳbūl Ibrāhīm Pasha → Ibrāhīm Pasha (Maḳbūl)
Maḳdishū iii, 3a; iv, 885b; v, 131b; vi, 128a, 370a, 704a
al-Maḳdisī (966) vii, 284a
al-Maḳdisī, ʿAbd al-Ghanī (1203) iii, 161a, 735a, 752a, 842b; vi, 350b
al-Maḳdisī, ʿAbd al-Karīm b. ʿAbd al-Raḥmān iv, 511a
al-Maḳdisī, Abū ʿAbd Allāh (1000) → al-Muḳaddasī
al-Maḳdisī, Abū ʿAbd Allāh (1343) iii, 763a
al-Maḳdisī, Abū Bakr b. Muḥammad iv, 511a
al-Maḳdisī, Abu ʾl-Ḥasan al-Rabʿī (1137) vi, 713a
al-Maḳdisī, Abū Sulayman Muḥammad iii, 1071b; v, 330a
al-Maḳdisī, Ḍiyāʾ al-Dīn (1245) vi, 350b; s, 195b
al-Maḳdisī, Ibrāhim b. ʿAlī iv, 511a
al-Maḳdisī, Muḥammad b. ʿAlī i, 949b
al-Maḳdisī, Shihāb al-Dīn vii, 295a
al-Maḳdisī, Naṣr b. Ibrāhīm s, 326a
Makhač-ḳalʿe
al-Makhaḍīb → al-Mukhaḍḍaba
al-Makhāʿī → al-Shādhilī ʿAlī b. ʿUmar
Makhāridj al-Ḥurūf iii, 598a; vi, 129b
Makhāziniyya iv, 456b
al-Makhdūm → Sharīf Awliyā Karīm
Makhdūm, Shaykh (Mappila) vi, 461b
Makhdūm Djahāniyān s, 10b
Makhdūm Ḥāmid Gandj Bakhsh ii, 186b
Makhdūm Ḳulī (Firāḳī) (1782) iv, 853b; v, 859b; vi, 130b
Makhdūm al-Mulk, Sharaf al-Dīn (ʿAbd Allāh Sulṭānpūrī) (1582) vi, 131a
Makhdūm al-Mulk Manīrī (Manērī) (1381) vi, 131a, 410a
Makhdūm Shāh Dawlat (Abū Yazīd) (1608) vi, 410a, b; vii, 331b
Makhdūma-yi Djahān Nargis Bēgam vi, 66b, 488b
Makhdūm-i ʿĀlam (Bihār) vi, 47a

Makhdūm-i Djahāniyān → Djalāl al-Dīn Ḥusayn al-Bukhārī
Makhfī (Zīb al-Nisāʾ Begum) (1702) vi, 131b, 488b; vii, 341b
Makhiwal s, 361a
Makhkhan Singh iii, 336a
Makhlad, Banū vi, 132a
Makhlad b. Kaydād al-Nukkārī → Abū Yazīd al-Nukkārī
Makhlad b. Yazīd, ḳaḍī vi, 132a
Makhlaṣ → Takhalluṣ
Makhlūf, Muḥammad (XX) vi, 280a
Makhrama, Abū Muḥammad al-Ṭayyib (1540) vi, 132b
Makhrama, ʿAfīf al-Dīn ʿAbd Allāh (1565) vi, 132b
Makhrama, ʿAfīf al-Dīn Abu ʾl-Ṭayyib (1497) vi, 132b
Makhrama, Bā (Abū) i, 255b; iii, 881a; vi, 132b
Makhrama, ʿUmar b. ʿAbd Allāh (1545) vi, 132b
Makhredj vi, 133a
Makhṭūṭa → Naskha
Mākhūkh (Banū Wamānū, XI) iii, 138a; vi, 427a
Makḥūl b. Abī Muslim al-Dimashḳī (730) iv, 356b, 369a; vii, 631b; viii, 713a
Makhzan i, 79b, 288b, 355b, 368b, 369a, 1145b, 1191a; ii, 146a, 326b, 510a, b; v, 48b, 1191a, 1192b, 1193a, 1198b; vi, 133b; s, 336b
Makhzen → Makhzan
Makhzen, Banū vi, 589b, 590b
Makhzūm, Banū i, 9a, 115b; iii, 3b, 975b; vi, 137b, 145a, 262b, 649a; vii, 362a; s, 32b
al-Makhzūmī, ʿAbd al-Raḥmān b. Zayd b. Muḥammad b. Ḥanzala (852) vii, 5a
al-Makhzūmī, Abū ʾl-Ḥasan al-Ḳurashī (1189) v, 863a; vi, 140b; vii, 164a
al-Makhzūmī, Hāniʾ ix, 84b
al-Maʿḳil, Banū i, 93b, 211a, 355b, 356a, 374b, 533a; ii, 134a; iii, 256b, 288b, 300b; v, 1196b; vi, 134a, b, 141a, 741a, b; vii, 613b
Maʿḳil b. Ḍirār → al-Shammākh b. Ḍirār
Maʿḳil b. ʿĪsā iv, 718b; s, 122b
Maʿḳil b. Ḳays al-Riyāḥī v, 19b
Maʿḳil b. Sinān al-Ashdjaʿī iii, 226b, 227a
Makīn vi, 86a
al-Makīn b. al-ʿAmīd, Djirdjis (1273) vi, 143b, 629b; s, 396a, 400a
Makīna (Fès) vi, 136a
Mākisīn iv, 898a
Makk i, 1171b; ii, 615a
Makka (Mecca) i, 12a, 35a, 55a, 77a, 80a, 136a, 151b, 549a, 551b, 552b, 890b, 976a, 1032b, 1232b; ii, 453a, 854a; iii, 33b, 260a, 362a; iv, 318b, 321b, 335b; v, 77a; vi, 33a, b, 34b, 44b, 45a, 118a, 137b, 139b, 140b, 144b, 320a; s, 3b, 106a, 198b, 267b, 278b
– geographical description vi, 144b, 720a
1. The pre-Islamic and early Islamic periods
i. Pre-Islamic Mecca vi, 144b
ii. Mecca and the beginnings of Islam vi, 146a, 644b
iii. Mecca from 632 to 750 vi, 147a
2. From the ʿAbbāsid to the modern period vi, 147b
i. Mecca under the ʿAbbāsids down to the foundation of the Sharīfate (750-961) vi, 147b, 663a
ii. From the foundation of the Sharīfate to Ḳatāda (ca. 960-1200) vi, 148a, 617a, 672b, 674b, 676a, 677b
iii. The rule of Ḳatāda and his descendants down to the Wahhābī period (ca. 1200-1788) vi, 149a
iv. The Sharīfate from the Wahhābī period to its end. The Kingdom vi, 150b
3. The Modern City vi, 152a
i. communications vi, 178b
ii. economy vi, 162b
iii. education and cultural life vi, 173a
iv. floods vi, 179b
v. health care vi, 178a
vi. libraries vi, 175a
vii. literature i, 826b, 965b; ii, 91b, 590a, 757a, 829a; iii, 760a; v, 850a; vi, 177a
viii. al-Masdjid al-Ḥarām and other religious buildings vi, 164b
ix. the physical city vi, 161b

x. pilgrimage vi, 169a
xi. politics and administration vi, 152a
xii. population and society vi, 159a
xiii. press vi, 176a
xiv. seizure of the Ḥarām vi, 157b
xv. water supply vi, 179a
4. Mecca as the centre of the world vi, 180b
i. the determination of the sacred direction vi, 181b
ii. Islamic sacred geography vi, 183a
iii. the orientation of Islamic religious architecture vi, 185b
iv. the orientation of the Kaʿba vi, 181a
Maḳḳara vi, 187a
al-Maḳḳarī, Muḥammad b. Muḥammad vi, 187a
al-Maḳḳarī, Shihāb al-Dīn Abu 'l-ʿAbbās al-Tilimsānī (1632) i, 157a, 595a; iii, 814a; v, 1159b, 1160b; vi, 112a, 187a, 247b; 1042b; s, 223a, 381a
al-Maḳḳarī, al-Djadd (1357) ix, 364a
Makkhourēbi → Maghrāwa
al-Makkī → ʿAbd al-Wahhāb; Abū Ṭālib; Ibn Ḥumayd
Makkī, Abū Muḥammad al-Ḳurṭubī (1045) vi, 188b
Makkī, Banū v, 696a; viii, 763b
al-Makkī, al-Muwaffaḳ b. Aḥmad vi, 352b
Makkī b. Kāmil b. Djāmiʿ iv, 337b
al-Makkiyya al-Fāsiyya → Madaniyya
al-Maklātī, Muḥammad b. Aḥmad (1631) iii, 468b; vi, 112b
Maklī vi, 189b
Maḳlūb iii, 26a
Makna (port) vii, 373b
Makramat Khān i, 254a
al-Makramī, ʿAbd Allāh b. Aḥmad b. Ismāʿīl (dāʿī) vi, 191a
al-Makramī, ʿAbd Allāh b. ʿAlī (dāʿī) vi, 191b
al-Makramī, Aḥmad b. Ḥasan b. Ismāʿīl vi, 192a
al-Makramī, ʿAlī b. Muḥsin Āl Shibām (1936) vi, 192a
al-Makramī, Ḍiyāʾ al-Dīn Ismāʿīl (1770) vi, 191b
al-Makramī, Djābir b. al-Fahd (XVII) vi, 191a
al-Makramī, Ḥasan b. Ismāʿīl b. Muḥsin āl Shibām (1872) vi, 192a
al-Makramī, Ibrāhīm b. Ṣafī al-Dīn (1683) vi, 191a
al-Makramī, Ṣafī al-Dīn Muḥammad (1633) vi, 190b, 191a; ix, 829a
Makramids i, 552b; ii, 517b; iii, 179b; iv, 201a; vi, 191a; ix, 829a
Makrān i, 211b, 1005a; iii, 1121b; iv, 3b; v, 684a; vi, 65b, 192b, 780a; vii, 405b; s, 129a, 222a, 332a, b
Makrand Ray i, 1042b
Makrānī i, 1005a, 1007a
Maḳrīn b. Muḥammad al-Bughṭūrī → al-Bughṭūrī
al-Maḳrīzi, Tāḳī al-Dīn Abu 'l-ʿAbbās (1442) i, 138b, 594b, 595a, 791a, 965b; ii, 107b, 327a, 328a; iii, 268b, 488b, 676a, 679b, 756b; v, 29b, 863a; vi, 119a, 122b, 143b, 193b, 317b, 353a, 363a; s, 210b, 273b, 295a, 388b, 396a
Makrūh vi, 194b
Maks (Mukūs) i, 170a, 1144a; ii, 142b, 146a; iii, 1182b; iv, 134b, 323a, b, 324a; vi, 194b, 323a, 573b
al-Maḳs (Miṣr) vii, 150a; s, 120b
al-Maḳsī (vizier) (XIII) vi, 672b
al-Maḳsī, Shihāb al-Dīn (XIII) vii, 29b
Maḳṣūra → Masdjid
Maḳṣūra i, 240a; ii, 115b; vi, 195b
Maktab vi, 196b
Maktaba iv, 635a; v, 38a, 43b, 159a, 261a, 338a, 371b, 641b, 890b, 1005a, 1125a, 1212b; vi, 197b
al-Maktaba al-Ahliyya vi, 614b
Maktabdār, ʿAlāʿ al-Dīn (1486) vii, 935a
Maktabī al-Shīrāzī (XV) iv, 1010a; v, 1105a; vi, 833a
Maḳtal iii, 374a
Maḳṭūʿ ii, 563b; iii, 25b
Maktūbāt ii, 55b, 56a; s, **571b**
al-Maktūbiyya (Marʿash) vi, 509b
al-Maḳtūl → al-Suhrawardī
Makua, Banū s, 574a
Maktūm b. Baṭī b. Suhayl ii, 619a
Mākū vi, 200b, 504a
Makua vi, 203b

al-Maḳūlāt vi, 203b
Maḳurra 1029a
al-Maḳwa s, 50a
Māl ii, 148a, 150b; iv, 1034a; vi, 205a
Māl al-bayʿa iii, 1201b; vi, 205b
Māl Khātūn (1325) i, 348a; xi, 131a
Māla ii, 905b
Malaʾ s, **573a**
al-Maʿlā (Maḳbara, Mecca) vi, 160a, 168b, 179b
Malabar iv, 547; v, 360a, 937a; vi, 206a, 234a, 245a, 458a, b, 459a, b, 463a
Malacca i, 979a, b; iii, 1218b, 1219b, 1225b; iv, 467b; vi, 116b, 207a, 232b, 233b, 234a, 235a, b, 237a, 240b; s, 199b
Malāfita ii, 235b
Málaga → Mālaḳa
Malāhī vi, 214a
Malāḥim ii, 377a; vi, 216a
Malāʾika vi, 216b
Malak, Malʾak → Malāʾika
Malak Ḥifnī Nāṣif (1918) vi, 219b, 470a
Malak Ṭāʾūs i, 263a
Malaka vi, 220a
Mālaḳa (Málaga) i, 6a, 43b, 1321a; ii, 747b; iii, 498b, 500a, 681a; vi, 220b, 339b; vii, 1028b; s, 381b
Malal → Mali
Malam vi, 223a
Malāmatiyya i, 313a, 794b, 1137a, 1239b, 1245a; ii, 395a, 963b; iii, 132a, 662b, 899a; iv, 46a, 472b, 473a, 1109b; vi, 223b; s, 361a
Mālamīr → Īdhadj
Mālān → Mālīn
Malang vi, 228b
Malāryā (Malaria) v, 867a; vi, 229a
al-Malaṭī, Abu 'l-Ḥusayn (987) vi, 230a
Malaṭya ii, 234b; vi, 230a, 507a, b, 508b, 541a, 544a, 740a
al-Malaṭyawī (Malaṭī), Muḥammad b. Ghāzī (1202) vi, 632a
Mālawās vi, 309a
Malawi, Muslims in- s, **574a**
Malay language i, 41b, 88a, 92a; ii, 27b, 549b; iii, 377a, 1215b, 1216a, 1220a, 1231a, 1234a; iv, 1128a; v, 205a; vi, 239a
Malay peninsula vi, 207a, 232b
Malays (people) vi, 239a; s, 150b
Malaysia i, 41b, 979a; iii, 377a, 385a, 502b, 1214b, 1219b; v, 226a, b, 227a, 228a, b; vi, 239a, 240b; s, 220b
Malāzgird (1071) i, 420b, 465b, 510a; v, 539a; vi, 242b, 379b; viii, 70a
Malcolm X (1965) vii, 703a
Mālda (Māldah, Māldaha) vi, 244b, 368b
Maldives iii, 385a, 407a; iv, 547a, 1085b; v, 587a; vi, 245a
Male (Maldives) vi, 245a, b
Malfūẓāt ii, 55b; iii, 435b; s, **577a**
Malḥam b. Ḥaydar ii, 635b
Malḥam b. Maʿn ii, 635a
Malḥama vi, 247a
Malḥūn i, 571b; v, 1207a; vi, 247b
Mali ii, 63a, 94a; iii, 276a, 657a; iv, 313b; vi, 257b, 281b, 401a, 421b, 572b; viii, 1049a; ix, 121b, 756a; s, 218a, 295b
Māli-Amīr → Īdhadj
Māl-i Irsāliyye → Irsāliyye
Malībār → Malabar
al-Malīdjī, Muḥammad Muḥyi 'l-Dīn (XVII) ix, 316a
Malifattan vi, 503a
Malīḥ (Mleh) vi, 230b
Malik (title) ii, 858a; iv, 818b; v, 627b; vi, 261a
Mālik b. Abi 'l-Samḥ al-Ṭāʾī (754) iii, 698b; vi, 262a
Malik b. Adham al-Bāhilī iv, 447a
Mālik b. al-ʿAdjlān i, 771a; iv, 1187b; v, 995a
Malik b. ʿAli al-Barānī, Shāh (Djand) s, 245b
Mālik b. ʿAlī al-Ḳaṭanī i, 600a
Mālik b. ʿAlī al-Khuzāʿī s, 122b
Mālik b. ʿAmr al-Ḥimyarī v, 315a
Mālik b. Anas (796) i, 164a, 280a, 338b, 412a, 550b, 588b, 685a, 773b,957b, 966b, 1244b; ii, 889b; iii, 23b, 24a, 763b,811a, 817a, 963a; iv, 146a, 257a, 718a; v, 711b, 712a, 731b, 997b; vi, 262b, 278a, 337a, 352b, 366a, 658a, 739a; vii, 649a; s, 384b
Mālik b. Asmāʾ b. Khāridja iv, 1002b
Mālik b. ʿAwf b. Saʿd b. Rabīʿa al-Naṣrī (VII) ii, 627a; iii, 286a, 578a; vi, 265b
Mālik b. Badr al-Fazārī s, 177b
Mālik b. Baḥdal vii, 267b
Mālik b. Dīnār al-Sāmī (748) i, 1080b; vi, 266b, 459a; viii, 354b; x, 394b

Mālik b. Fahm, Banū iv, 500b; x, 191a, 816a
Mālik b. Ḥimyar vi, 82a
Mālik b. al-Ḥāri<u>th</u> al-Na<u>kh</u>aʿī → al-A<u>sh</u>tar
Mālik b. Ḥu<u>dh</u>ayfa b. Badr al-Fazārī s, 178b
Mālik b. Mismaʿ (691) i, 964b; iii, 540a; vi, 640b
Mālik b. Nuwayra b. <u>Dj</u>amra, Abu 'l-Mi<u>gh</u>wār (634) vi, 267a; vii, 768b; xi, 179a
Mālik b. Rabīʿa b. Riyāḥ al-Hilālī s, 92b
Mālik b. al-Rayb (714) vi, 954b
Mālik b. Ṭawḳ i, 751b, 1289b; s, 122b
Mālik b. Zuhayr s, 177b
al-Malik al-ʿĀdil I, Abū Bakr Muḥammad b. Ayyūb, Sayf al-Dīn (Ayyūbid) (Aleppo, Damascus Egypt, Diyār Bakr) (1218) i, 197b, 665a, 798b, 799b, 800a, b, 803b, 996a, 1316b; ii, 283b, 284a, 347b; iii, 87b, 228b, 504a; iv, 430a, 483b, 520a, 568a, 609a, 613b; vi, 261b, 380b, 381a, 429a, b, 434a, 540b, 547b, 781b; vii, 164b, 273a, 461b, 989b; viii, 127a
al-Malik al-ʿĀdil II, Abū Bakr Sayf al-Dīn b. al-Malik al-Kāmil (Ayyūbid) (1248) i, 198b, 766a, b
al-Malik al-Afḍal b. Ṣalāḥ al-Dīn (Ayyūbid) (1225) i, 197b, 198a, 215a, 732a, 798b, 1017a; ii, 283b; iii, 724a, 876b; iv, 376b; vi, 380b, 381a, 547b; vii, 998b; viii, 995a
Malik Aḥmad b. Malik Ḥasan Niẓām al-Mulk (1496) vi, 63a
Malik Aḥmad Baḥrī (Niẓām <u>Sh</u>āhī) (1510) i, 295a, 303a; ii, 814b, 1048b; iii, 15b, 1159b; vi, 51a, 63a, 269a; viii, 73b; s, 246a
Malik Aḥmad <u>Gh</u>āzī → Dāni<u>sh</u>mend
Malik Aḥmad Pa<u>sh</u>a v, 461a
Malik Altūniya i, 1194a; ii, 973a
Malik ʿAmbar (ʿAnbar) (1626) i, 81a, 768a, 781b, 1204a; ii, 158b; iii, 15b, 202b, 424a, 426b; iv, 1018a, 1023a; vi, 269a, 534b; vii, 204b, 957a; viii, 74a
al-Malik al-Am<u>dj</u>ad → Bahrām <u>Sh</u>āh (Ayyūbid)
Malik Andīl → Fīrūz <u>Sh</u>āh, Sayf al-Dīn
Malik ʿArab (Anḳara) (XII) ii, 110b
Malik Arslān (<u>Dh</u>u 'l-Ḳadr) (1465) vi, 507b
Malik Arslān b. Masʿūd → Arslān <u>Sh</u>āh b. Masʿūd (<u>Gh</u>aznawid)
Malik Arslan b. Sulaymān ii, 239b
al-Malik al-A<u>sh</u>raf I Muẓaffar al-Dīn (Ayyūbid) (Damascus), (Diyār Bakr) (1220) vii, 989b, 990b
al-Malik al-A<u>sh</u>raf I Muẓaffar al-Dīn b. al-Malik al-ʿĀdil (Ayyūbid) (Damascus), (Diyār Bakr) (1237) vi, 540b, 665b, 931a; vii, 989b, 990b, 998b
Malik A<u>sh</u>raf b. Amīr Čūbān (Čūbānid) (1357) i, 325a; ii, 401a; iii, 1208b; vi, 501a; viii, 753a, 766a
al-Malik al-A<u>sh</u>raf b. al-ʿĀdil (Ayyūbid) (1198) vii, 998b
al-Malik al-A<u>sh</u>raf ʿUmar (Rasūlid) (1296) x, 147a
al-Malik al-A<u>sh</u>raf <u>Sh</u>aʿbān → <u>Sh</u>aʿban II
al-Malik al-Awḥad Na<u>dj</u>m al-Dīn b. al-Malik al-ʿĀdil (Ayyūbid, Diyār Bakr) (1210) i, 198a, 329a, 799a; vi, 931a
Malik Ayāz (1522) ii, 322a, 1127b, 1128a; vi, 269b
al-Malik al-ʿAzīz b. <u>Dj</u>alāl al-Dawla <u>Sh</u>īrzīl, Abū Manṣūr (Būyid) (1049) i, 132a; ii, 391a; iii, 1201b; vi, 270b; vii, 1018a
al-Malik al-ʿAzīz <u>Gh</u>iyā<u>th</u> al-Dīn Muḥammad (Ayyūbid), (Aleppo) (1237) iii, 934a; vi, 381a, b
al-Malik al-ʿAzīz Muḥammad (Ayyūbid) (1237) vi, 381a
al-Malik al-ʿAzīz Ṭu<u>gh</u>tioīn b. Ayyūb (Ayyūbid, Yemen) (1197) x, 303a
al-Malik al-ʿAzīz ʿU<u>th</u>mān b. al-Malik al-ʿĀdil (Ayyūbid) (1237) vii, 274a
al-Malik al-ʿAzīz ʿU<u>th</u>mān ʿImād al-Dīn b. Ṣalāḥ al-Dīn (Ayyūbid), (Egypt) (1198) i, 197b, 198a, 798b, 1214b; ii, 283b; iv, 376b, 613b; vi, 381a, b; vii, 165a
al-Malik al-ʿAzīz Yūsuf → Yūsuf b. Barsbāy
al-Malik al-ʿAzīz Ẓahīr al-Dīn Tu<u>gh</u>takin (Tu<u>gh</u>tigin) (Ayyūbid), (Yemen) (1197) i, 664a, 731b, 1332a, 1337a; ii, 282a, 353b, 458a; iii, 120a, 398b, 503b, 1118b; iv, 200a; vi, 433b
Malik Bahrām v, 782b
Malik Dīnār (1195) → Dīnār, Malik
Malik Dīnār (1319) → Ẓafar <u>Kh</u>ān (Gu<u>dj</u>arāt)

Malik Djahān Khānum bint Muḥammad Ḳāsim Ḳādjār (XIX) vii, 453a
al-Malik al-Djawād Yūnus (Ayyūbid) vii, 989b
Malik Djīwan → Malik Djuwān
Malik Djuwān i, 769a; ii, 134b
Malik Fīrūz v, 782b, 783a
Malik Ghāzī (Ḳïrshehir) v, 172b
Malik Ghāzī Shaḥna (architect) vi, 692a
Malik Gopī vi, 51b, 270a
Malik Ḥasan Niẓām al-Mulk Baḥrī (1481) vi, 62b, 63a, 67a, b, 269a; vii, 459a
Malik Ḥifnī Nāṣif → Nāṣif, Malik Ḥifnī
Malik Kāfūr → Kāfūr Hazār-Dīnārī
Malik Kālā v, 782b, 783a
Malik al-Kalām → Malik Ḳummi
al-Malik al-Kāmil I Nāṣir al-Dīn b. al-ʿĀdil (Ayyūbid), (Egypt) (1238) i, 14b, 198a, 665a, 765b, 766a, 798b, 799a, b, 800b, 803a, 804a, 940b; ii, 65b, 126a, 292b, 347b, 911b; iii, 504a, 747a; iv, 200b, 520a, 818a; v, 331a; vi, 359b, 381a, 413a, 429b, 440a, 547b; vii, 147b, 273a, b, 727b, 989b, 998b; viii, 127a; ix, 167b; s, 197a, 392b, 407b
al-Malik al-Kāmil II b. al-Muẓaffar (Ayyūbid, Mayyāfāriḳīn) (1260) iv, 521a; vi, 931b
Malik Kardī (Marāgha) vi, 502b
Malik Karib Yuʿmin vi, 563b
Malik Khātūn bint Malikshāh I (XI) vii, 540b
Malik Khurram ii, 405b
Malik Khushnūd (1646) vi, 837b
Malik Ḳummi (1616) i, 1203a; vi, 271a; vii, 340b, 341a
Malik Maḥmūd (Mengüček) (XII) iv, 871a
Malik Maḥmūd (Sīstān) (XVIII) vii, 853a
al-Malik al-Manṣūr → Nadjm al-Dīn Ghāzī Ḳalawūn (Mamlūk)
al-Malik al-Manṣūr Muḥammad b. ʿUmar (Ayyūbid), (Ḥamāt) (1220) iii, 697b; vi, 380b, 381b, 429a, 777b, 816b, 999a; s, 205b
al-Malik al-Manṣūr ʿUmar (Rasūlid) s, 338b
Malik Masʿūd (amīr al-Mawṣil) (1120) vi, 500a
al-Malik al-Masʿūd (Artuḳid) s, 250a
al-Malik al-Masʿūd Yūsuf (Ayyūbid), (Yemen) (1229) i, 552b
al-Malik al-Muʾayyad → Abu 'l-Fidā (Ayyūbid)
al-Malik al-Muʾayyad Shaykh (Mamlūk) (1421) ii, 24a, 781b; iii, 48a, 99b, 186a, 187a; iv, 431b, 586a, 623b; vi, 580b; vii, 168a, 169a, 172b, 271a
al-Malik al-Muʿaẓẓam Tūrān-Shāh-V Tūrān-Shāh
al-Malik al-Muʿaẓẓam Sharaf al-Dīn ʿĪsā b. al-Malik al-ʿĀdil I (Ayyūbid, Damascus) (1227) i, 198a, 434b, 780b, 799a, b, 804a, 1124b; ii, 284a; iii, 399b, 747a, 962a, 967a; iv, 520b, 779a, 842a; v, 331a, 925a; vii, 273a, 989b; viii, 987b
al-Malik al-Muʿaẓẓam Sharaf al-Dīn Tūrān-Shah (Ayyūbid), Damascus, Diyār Bakr, Egypt/ Damascus/Ḥiṣn Kayfa, Āmid) (1249) i, 198a, 434b, 780b, 799a, b, 804a, 1124b; ii, 284a; iii, 399b, 747a, 962a, 967a; iv, 520b, 779a, 842a; v, 331a, 925a; vi, 321a, 326a, 381a, b, 440b; vii, 166a; viii, 988b
Malik Mubārak Shāh Ḳaranfal (Sharḳī) (1461) iii, 14b, 419b; ix, 355a
al-Malik al-Mughīth (Karak) (XIII) vii, 167b
Malik Mughīth (Mālwā) (1443) vi, 52b, 271b, 406b, 407b, 695a
Malik Muḥammad b. Ghāzī (Malaṭya) (1141) iv, 506b, vi, 507a
Malik Muḥammad Djāyasī (Djāysī) (1542) iii, 457a, vi, 272a
Malik Muḥammad Nādjī s, 366a
al-Malik al-Muʿizz ʿIzz al-Dīn Aybak (Mamlūk) (1257) i, 732a, 804a, 944b; vi, 668b
Malik al-Mutakallimīn iv, 789a
Malik Muẓaffar b. Bahrāmshāh → Malik Ghāzī Shaḥna
al-Malik al-Muẓaffar Shihāb al-Dīn Ghāzī b. al-Malik al-ʿĀdil (Ayyūbid), Diyār Bakr) (1244) i, 197b, 798b, 1160b; ii, 347b; iii, 120a, 683b; iv, 614a, 640b; vi, 931a; vii, 273b, 974a
al-Malik al-Muẓaffar Taḳī al-Dīn ʿUmar b. Nūr al-Dawla (Ayyūbid), (Ḥamāt) (1191) vi, 380b, 381a, b, 429a, 430a; vii, 816a
Malik Nāʾib → Kāfūr Hazār-Dīnārī
al-Malik al-Nāṣir I Ṣalāḥ al-Dīn Yūsuf b. Ayyūb (Saladin) (Ayyūbid), (Egypt) (1193) i, 96b, 150a, 197b, 353b, 517a,

552b, 662b, 665a, 711a, 797a, 814b, 832a, 932b, 971a, 989b, 1016b, 1138a, 1140a, 1358a; ii, 64b, 127a, 144a, 163a, 283b, 292b, 344b, 353b, 461b, 501b, 556a, 856b, 959a, 1056a; iii, 87a, 99a, 120a, 208b, 228b, 399b, 474a, 510b, 693b, 751b, 933b, 120a, 208b, 228b, 399b, 474a, 510b, 693b, 751b, 933b, 934a, 1157b, 1158a, 1201a; iv, 137a, 376b, 429b, 613a, 640b, 877b, 899b, 944a; v, 92a, 330b, 455a, 800b, 924b, 1127b; vi, 143b, 149a, 195a, b, 261b, 320a, 380b, 429a, 430a, 540b, 543b, 547a, 578b, 579a, 606a, 656a, 657a, 667b, 668a, 671b, 673b, 676a, b, 708a, 733b, 780b; viii, 131b, 910a; ix, 267b; s, 121a, 123b, 154a, 205a, 941a

al-Malik al-Nāṣir II Ṣalāḥ al-Dīn Dāwūd b. al-Malik al-Muʿaẓẓam (Ayyūbid, Aleppo, Damascus) (1259) i, 804b; ii, 284a, b, 348a; iii, 87b, 186b, 187b, 399b, 933b, 989b; iv, 521a; vi, 321b; vii, 166b, 274a, 727b, 728b, 989b; s, 197a, 391a, 463a

al-Malik al-Nāṣir, Ṣalāḥ al-Dīn Yūsuf (al-Nāṣir Yūsuf) (Ayyūbid), (Aleppo), (Damascus) (1260) vii, 321b, 989b, 990a

Maliks of Nimrūz ix, 683b

Malik al-Nuḥāt → al-Ḥasan b. Ṣafī

Malik Rādjā Fārūḳī ii, 814a; iii, 417a; iv, 1023a

al-Malik al-Raḥīm, Abū Naṣr (Būyid) (1058) vi, 272b

Malik al-Sādāt Ghāzī → Sayyid Masʿūd

al-Malik al-Saʿīd (Artuḳid) → Ghāzī I (Artuḳid)

al-Malik al-Saʿīd (Mamlūk) → al-Saʿīd Baraka Khān

al-Malik al-Ṣāliḥ (Samudra-Pasè) (1297) i, 742b; iii, 1218b, 1225b; viii, 279a

al-Malik al-Ṣāliḥ ʿImād al-Dīn Ismāʿīl (Ayyūbid), (Damascus), (Egypt) (1245) i, 711a, 766b, 799a, 804a; ii, 284a; iii, 989b; iv, 483b; vii, 990b; viii, 464a, 987b; s, 255b

al-Malik al-Ṣāliḥ Nadjm al-Dīn Ayyūb → al-Ṣāliḥ Nadjm al-Dīn Ayyūb

al-Malik al-Ṣāliḥ Nūr al-Dīn → Nūr al-Dīn Maḥmūd b. ʿImād Zangī

al-Malik al-Ṣāliḥ Shams al-Dīn → al-Malik al-Muʿaẓẓam Shams al-Dīn

Malik Sandjas → Alp Khān

Malik Sārang vi, 270a

Malik Sarwar (Sharḳī) (1399) ii, 270b, 498b, 1084b; iii, 14b, 417a, 419b; iv, 276b, 533b, 907b; vi, 49a, 273a

Malik Shaʿbān vi, 50a

Malik Shāh → Kh(w)ādja-i Djahān Turk

Malik-Shāh I b. Alp Arslan (Saldjūḳ) (1092) i, 243b, 353a, 421a, 465b, 517a, 552a, 639b, 662b, 664a, 731a, 750b, 780b, 870a, 901a, 1051b, 1336b; ii, 282a, 344a, 347b, 384b, 397b, 406a; iii, 86b, 195a, 208b, 471b, 1114b, 1202a; iv, 27a, b, 28a, 101a, 458a, 807b; v, 159b; vi, 13b, 16a, 63b, 273a, 379b, 482a, 523b, 524a, 540b, 600a, 618a, b, 620b, 627a, 628a; vii, 15b, 489a, 540b, 679b, 693a, b; viii, 69b, 941a; x, 267b; s, 14b, 73b, 94b, 383b

Malik-Shāh II b. Berk-Yaruḳ (Saldjūḳ) (1105) vi, 275b

Malik-Shāh III b. Maḥmūd b. Muḥammad (Saldjūḳ) (1152) iv, 1097a; vi, 64a, 275b; viii, 944a

Malik-Shāh b. Ḳilidj Arslan I (Saldjūḳ) (1107) vi, 275b, 578a

Malik-Shāh b. Ḳilidj Arslan II (Saldjūḳ) (1192) vi, 275b

Malik-Shāh b. Tekish (Khwārazm-Shāh) (1197) viii, 63b; s, 246a

al-Malik Shahānshāh b. al-Muẓaffar, Taḳī al-Dīn (Ayyūbid) (XII) vii, 816b

Malik al-Sharḳ → Malik Sarwar

Malik Shīr Khān i, 1194b

Malik al-Shuʿarāʾ iv, 56a; vi, 276a

Malik Sy, Cheikh El-Hadji vi, 705b

Mālik al-Ṭāʾī → Mālik b. Abi ’l-Samḥ al-Ṭāʾī

Malik Tādj al-Dīn s, 105b

Malik al-Tudjdjār ii, 602a, 814b; v, 1258a; vi, 276b

Malik Ṭuḥfa vi, 50a

Malik Yak Lakhī s, 105b

Malik Yāḳūt Sulṭānī iii, 16a

Malik Yüz Beg vii, 193b

al-Malik al-Ẓāhir Ghāzī b. Ṣalāḥ al-Dīn (Ayyūbid, Aleppo) (1216) i, 197b, 798b, 803a, 989b, 996a, 1316b; ii, 37b, 353b, 556b; iii, 87b, 178a, 208b, 399b, 693b, 863a; iv, 482a; v, 924b; vi, 380b, 381a, 429a, b, 507a, 540b, 544a, 547b, 579a

al-Malika al-Sayyida al-Ḥurra (Sulaymid) (1138) x, 403a; vii, 725b

Mālikāne i, 728a; iv, 1096a; vi, 277b

al-Mālikī s, 306b
al-Mālikī, Abū ʿAbd Allāh Muḥammad (1046) vi, 353b
Malikī, Khalīl iii, 529a, b; s, 60b
Malikī b. Muḥammad ii, 1146b
Mālikiyya i, 249b, 338b, 339a, 494a; ii, 618b, 828b, 859b, 1010a; iii, 6b, 17a, 308b, 350b, 695a; iv, 87a-b, 290a, 341a, 404b; v, 895b; vi, 2a, 278a; xi, 248b; s, 113a
Malikī → Djalālī
Malik-nāma i, 421a
Malikpur i, 1322b; ii, 260a
Malik-yi Djahān vi, 488a
Malikzāda Fīrūz b. Tādj al-Dīn Turk (1389) vi, 61b
Malīla i, 356b; iii, 298b; s, 325b
Mālīn i, 952b
Malindi iv, 887a, b, 888b; vi, 283a, 385a; vii, 226a
Malinké ii, 63a; v, 252b; vi, 257b; xi, 137b, s, 295b
Māliyyāt → Māl
Māliyye i, 1090b; ii, 83b; vi, 283b
Malḳara vi, **290b**; ix, 631b
Malkoč-oghulları̊ (XIV) i, 340b; vii, 34a; s, **578a**
Malkom Khān, Mīrzā Nāẓim al-Dawla (1908) ii, 650a; iii, 554b; iv, 72a, 73b, 164a, 397b, 788a; v, 919b, 1086a; vi, 291a, 763b; vii, 438b, 1003b; s, 23b, 53b, 71b, 108b, 109a, 290b
Malla Khān iv, 631b; v, 30a
Mallāḥ i, 181a; i, 230a; vi, 292b, 591b
Mallal vi, 401a, b
Mallālī (XVI) ix, 29b
Mallel → Mālī
Malloum, General s, 166b
Mallū Iḳbāl Khān (1405) i, 1300a; iii, 417b; iv, 533b; vi, 49a, b, 294a; s, 206a
Mallū Khān → Ḳādir Shāh
Malta/Mālṭa i, 250b, 936a; ii, 801b; iii, 251b; vi, 295a; s, 47b, 55a, 120b
Maltese language vi, 295b
Maltese literature vi, 298b
Malthai → Maʿalthāyā
al-Maʿlūf, Āl vi, 303a
al-Maʿlūf, Amīn Fahd (1943) vi, 304a
al-Maʿlūf, Djamīl (1950) vi, 304b
al-Maʿlūf, Djurdj Ḥassūn (1965) vi, 307b
al-Maʿlūf, Fawzī (1930) iii, 112a; v, 1257a; vi, 306b
al-Maʿlūf, Ibrāhīm (Abū Nātiḥ) (XV) vi, 303a
al-Maʿlūf, ʿĪsā Iskandar (1956) vi, 303a, 305a
al-Maʿlūf, Kayṣar Ibrāhīm (1961) vi, 304b
Maʿlūf, Lūwīs (Louis) (1947) iv, 525a; vi, 303b
al-Maʿlūf, Mīshāl (Michel) (1942) v, 1256a; vi, 305a
al-Maʿlūf, Nāṣīf (1865) vi, 303b
al-Maʿlūf, Shafīḳ (1976) v, 1256b, 1257a; vi, 306a
al-Maʿlūf, Shaykh Aḥmad vi, 303a
al-Maʿlūf, Yūsuf Nuʿmān (1956) vi, 304a
Maʿlūlā vi, 308a
Mālwā i, 208a, 923b, 924a, 1026a, 1155a; ii, 219a, 276a, 1125a; iii, 421a, b, 446a, 481b, 638a; v, 1216a; vi, 50b, 51a, 52a, 53a, 54a, 55a, 61b, 270a, 272a, 309a, 342b, 368a, 406b, 407b, 533b, 536a, 694b, 953a, 970a, 1027b; vii, 79b, 314a; viii, 68a; s, 105a, 280a, 331b
Malwiyya (Moulouya) v, 1185a, 1187a; vi, 141a, b
Malzūza, Banū vi, 310b
al-Malzūzī → Abū Ḥātim al-Malzūzī
Mama Bonfoh iv, 352a
Mamadjān (Ḳumm) vi, 493a
Mamadu Djoue ii, 960a, 1132b
Mamadu Mustafa Mbacké (1945) vii, 609b
al-Māmaḳānī, ʿAbd Allāh b. Muḥammad al-Nadjafī (1933) vi, 312b
Mamaḳānī, Shaykh Muḥammad Ḥasan b. ʿAbd Allāh (1905) vi, 553a
Mamālīk iv, 36a, 976b, 977b, 1044a
al-Mamālik, Mīrzā Yūsuf Mustawfī (XIX) vii, 1004a, b
Mamand, Banū vii, 220a
Maʿmar b. al-Muthannā → Abū ʿUbayda
Maʿmar b. Rashīd (770) vii, 662b; ix, 7a, b, 661a
Maʿmar Abu 'l-Ashʿath s, 88b
Māmash i, 1217b
Mamassanī, Banū iii, 1102b, 1106b; iv, 9a, 498b; v, 822a, 825a, 829b; vii, 453b; s, 147b
Mamay (Tatar) i, 1107b
Māmāy Bey iv, 723a

al-Mambassī, Muḥammad b. Aḥmad b. Shaykh (1890) vii, 227a
Mamdūḥ v, 956a, 959b
al-Māmī, al-Shaykh Muḥammad (1865) vi, 313a; vii, 619a, 624b, 626a
Mamikonians i, 636b; ii, 679a; vi, 623b
Māmiya al-Rūmī iv, 451b
Mamlaka vi, 313b
Mamlān i, 638a
Mamlūk i, 34a; ii, 506b; vi, 314a
Mamlūks (Burdjī) i, 33a, 34a, 63a, 182b, 468a, 666b, 786b, 804a, 905b, 910a, 971a, 1119b, 1138a, 1190b, 1288b; ii, 38a, 65b, 284b, 292b, 340a, 348a, 572a, 1043b, 1056b; iii, 120b, 402b; iv, 31b; v, 373b, 739b; vi, 194a, 195a, 261b, 321a, 530a, 545b, 580b, 668b, 669b, 671b, 673b, 674a, 724b, 979b; vii, 165a; ix, 129a, 168a, 596b; x, 966b; xi, 26b, 293b; s, 205b, 395b
– administration i, 34a, 102a, 435b, 444a, 765a, 816b, 1046a, 1349a; ii, 23b, 102b, 172b, 230a, 301b, 330a, 414a, 421b, 508b; iii, 48a, 346a, 758b, 773b; iv, 210a, 267b; v, 332a, b, 627b, 628a; s, 138a, 393a
– art, architecture i, 1316b; iv, 430b; v, 218a, 1140b; s, **578b**
– history i, 1128a; iii, 775b, 813a; iv, 462b
– military i, 445b, 944b, 945b, 1058b, 1324b; ii, 130a, 444b; iii, 99a, 184a, 472b
– Numismatics (IV) s, **591b**
al-Mammasī (944) vi, 353b; s, 306b
Mammeri, faḳīh (XX) vii, 415b
Mams vi, 434b
Mamūḳ b. Ibāḳ iv, 849a
al-Maʾmūn → al-Baṭāʾiḥī
al-Maʾmūn b. Hārūn al-Rashīd (ʿAbbāsid) (833) i, 18a, 78a, 271a, b, 272b, 279a, 316a, 399b, 400a, 402b, 437a, 844a, 1280a; ii, 235a, 281b, 505b, 726b, 730b, 731a, 911a; iii, 173a, 228a, 231b, 234a, 243b, 618a, 987b, 1148a; iv, 17a, 45b, 645a, b, 939b, 940b; vi, 148a, 198a, 205b, 331a, 340a, 411a, 438a, 499a, 599b, 606a, 619b, 620b, 635b, 649b, 662a, 665a, 668b, 710b, 714a; vii, 147b, 358b; s, 15a, 22b, 26a, 32b, 35a, 88b, 144a, 252b, 263a, 338a, 384b, 408a
– reforms i, 589a, 114a; ii, 198a, 232a, 578a
al-Maʾmūn, Abu ʾl-ʿAlāʾ (Almohad) (1232) i, 1176a; iii, 207b; iv, 116a, 117b; vi, 339b
Maʾmūn I Khʷarazmshāh ii, 1142a; iv, 1066b
Maʾmūn II Khʷarazmshāh i, 1236b; iv, 1066b
al-Maʾmūn b. al-Baṭāʾiḥī → al-Baṭāʾiḥī
al-Maʾmūn b. Dhu ʾl-Nūn (Toledo) (1075) i, 6b, 986a; ii, 243a, 901a; iv, 665b; vii, 766b; viii, 867b
Maʾmūn b. Muḥammad, Abu ʾl-ʿAbbās (Maʿmūnid Khʷārazm-Shāh) (997) vi, 340a
al-Maʾmūn b. Muḥammad al-Shaykh al-Mahdī i, 55b, 56a
al-Maʾmūn (ʿAbbāsid) (833) x, 227a
al-Maʾmūnī, Abū Ṭālib ʿAbd al-Salām (993) vi, 340a
Maʾmūnids → Khʷarazm-Shāhs
Maʾmūniyya (Marrākush) vi, 596b
Maʾmūr vi, 340b
Maʿmūr Khān, ʿAbd al-Karīm v, 600a
al-Maʿmūra → al-Mahdiyya (town, Morocco)
al-Maʿmūra (al-Maṣṣīṣa) vi, 778b
Maʿmūrat al-ʿAzīz (Elaziğ) iv, 1084b; vi, 341b, 539b
Maʿmūriyye Ḳalʿesi i, 481a
Maʿn, Banū i, 181b, 552a, 767a; ii, 634b, 635a, 749b; iv, 834b; v, 259a, 602a, 792b; vi, 343a; ix, 439a; s, 49b, 338a
Maʿn b. Aws al-Muzanī (VII) vi, 344a, 477a
Maʿn b. Ḥātim iii, 125b
Maʿn b. Muḥammad b. Ṣumādiḥ al-Tudjībī (1052) iii, 740a; vi, 344b, 576b
Maʿn b. Zāʾida, Abu ʾl-Walīd al-Shaybānī (769) i, 364a, 964b; iii, 892a; vi, 344b, 576b; vi, 345a, 625a; viii, 462a, 996b; ix, 391b; s, 338a, 386b
Mān Singh (1614) ii, 1144a; iii, 632a; vi, 342b; vii, 129b, 131b
Maʿnā v, 320b, 321b; vi, 346a
Manād b. Manḳūs (X) ix, 18a
Manāf vi, 349a
Manāhil, Banū vi, 83b
al-Manākha iii, 179a, 327a; vi, 192a

al-Manākhī, Dja'far b. Ismā'īl (905) vi, 439a
Manāḳib v, 1209a; vi, 263a, 349a
al-Manāma i, 540a, 941a, b, 942b; vi, 357b; vii, 464a; s, 42a
Manāniyya (Mānawiyya) vi, 421b
Manār, Manāra (lighthouse) iv, 132b, 383b; vi, 358b
al-Manār vi, 360a
Manāra, Manār (Minaret) vi, 361b
Manāra (Marrākush) vi, 596b
Manārat al-'Abd iv, 638a, b
Manārat al-'Arūs (Damascus) vi, 362b
Manārat al-Mudjīda vi, 364b
Manas iii, 116a; vi, 370b
Manashshā i, 823b
al-Manāṣīr, Banū i, 371a, 372a; vi, 371b
Manāstir → Monastir
Manāstir (Bitola) vi, 371b
Manāstirli Meḥmed Rif'at (1907) vi, 372b; s, 359b
Manāt iii, 540b; iv, 322a; v, 692a, b, 995b; vi, 373b, 645b
Manāwa, Banū vi, 435a
Manāzdjird/Manāzgerd → Malāzgird
al-Manāzī → Malāzgird
al-Manāzī, Shaykh Abū Naṣr (1050) vi, 930b
al-Manāzil (lunar mansions) i, 1225a; iii, 83b; iv, 517a; vi, 374a
Manāẓir i, 98a; vi, 376a
Manbasa → Mombasa
Manbidj i, 119b; vi, 377b, 429a, 505b, 506b
al-Manbidjī, Naṣr al-Dīn iii, 952a
Manbik → Manbidj
Mancus ii, 298b
Mānd (Fārs) vi, 383b
Manda iv, 885b; v, 655a; vi, 385a
Mandaeans → Ṣābi'a; Ṣubba
Mandakhā vi, 385a
Mandalgarh vi, 53a, b
Mandalī vi, 614a
Mandān vi, 744b
Mandara ii, 114b
Mandasor vi, 53a, 55a, 270a, 272a, 310a
Mandats vi, 385b
Mande vi, 400b
Mandesh ii, 1099b
Mandīl (cloth) v, 735a, 749b; vi, 402b
Mandīl, Awlād/Banū v, 1180a; vi, 404a
Mandil b. 'Abd al-Raḥmān b. Abī Nās (XIII) v, 1180a; vi, 404a
Mandīl al-amān iii, 188a – iii, 192b
Mandīlsar vi, 498b
Mandingos, Mande ii, 1132a; iii, 275b; vi, 400b, 401a, 422a; viii, 20b; s, 295b
Mandīsh (Ghūr) vii, 407a
Māndistān vi, 383b, 384b, 385a
Mandjak al-Nāṣirī iii, 775b, 818a
Mandjaḳ Pasha (1669) vii, 469b
Mandjak al-Yūsufī iv, 425b
Mandjanīḳ i, 658b; ii, 188a; iii, 201b, 469b, 472b, 482a; vi, 405a
Mandjar (river) vi, 53b
Māndjhan, Mīr Sayyid iii, 457a
al-Mandjūr, Abu 'l-'Abbās Aḥmad al-Fāsī (1587) vi, 406a
Mandsore s, 331b
Māndū ii, 219a, 276b, 1128a; iii, 421b, 446a, 638a, b; v, 1216a; vi, 52b, 53a, 54a, b, 272a, 309b, 310a, 406b; vii, 314a, b
Mandūb vi, 408a
Mandūr, Muḥammad b. 'Abd al-Ḥamīd Mūsā (1965) v, 1257b; vi, 408a; viii, 88a; s, 58b
Manēr (Manīr) vi, 131a, 409b
Manērī, Sharaf al-Dīn Aḥmad → Makhdūm al-Mulk
Manērī, Sharaf al-Dīn Yaḥyā (1391) xi, 11b
Manf (Minf, Munf, Munayf) vi, 410b
al-Manfalūṭ vi, 119a, 414a; viii, 865a; s, 40b, 383b
al-Manfalūṭī, Muṣṭafā Luṭfī (1924) i, 597a; iv, 159b; v, 188a; vi, 75b, 414a, 956a; vii, 901b
Manfā'ūs b. 'Adīm (king) vi, 412a
Manfish → Manf
Manfiyya → Mafia
Manfūḥa i, 628b
Mangat Rai i, 606b
Manghir/Māngir → Sikka
Mangishlak vi, 415a; s, 168b, 169a, 245b, 280b, 281a
Mangistau Mts vi, 415a
Mangit (tribes Özbek) i, 1295b; ii, 44b, 446a; v, 182a, 273b; vi, 416b, 417b; s, 97a, b, 228a, 281a, 419b, 420a
Mangits (dynasty, Bukhārā) vi, 418b, 621a
Mangḳūt → Mangit

al-Manglī, Muhammad → Muḥammad al-Manglī
Mangrol vi, 419b
Mangū → Möngke
Mangū-Tīmūr, Khān (Mongol) (1280) vi, 419b
Mangubars → Mengubars
Mangudjak → Mengüček
Mangūr i, 1217b
Mangūtakīn (991) i, 824b, 1042a; ii, 483b, 855a; iii, 77a, 130a; v, 820a, b, 928a; vi, 545b
Manhūk i, 671a
Manīʿ iii, 228a
Māni vi, 420b; x, 227a
Mānī (Manichaeism) (274) xi, 511a
al-Maʿnī, Aḥmad (amīr) (XVII) vi, 346a
Mānī b. Fāttik (Fātik) (274) vi, 421a; viii, 675b
Manīʿ b. Ḥassān, Abu 'l-Fityān (1026) iv, 911a
Mānīʿ b. Rabīʿa al-Muraydī (XV) i, 553a; ii, 320b, 321a
Mānīʿ b. Shabīb b. Waththāb (XI) xi, 181a
Manîc (river) s, 169a
Manichaeism i, 130a; iii, 885a; iv, 43b, 1025a; v, 853a; vi, 421a; viii, 672a, 676a
Maʿnids (peace) s, 159a
Maʿnids → Maʿn, Banū
al-Manīʿī, Abū ʿAlī Ḥassān (1089) viii, 403a
Manīḳa vi, 578b
Mānikpūr vi, 48a; s, 203a
Manila s, 152a
Manisa → Maghnisa
Mankalī-Bughā iii, 818a
Manḳashlāgh vi, 415b
Mānkdīm Shashdiw (1034) vii, 786a, 787a
Mankit → Mangit
Mankubirnī → Djalāl al-Dīn Khwārazm-Shāh
Mankurūs b. Khumātigin (XII) viii, 851a
Manna (Soninke) x, 142a
Männan Uyghur (1955) vi, 768b, 769b
al-Mannāwī, Aḥmad b. Muḥammad s, 403a
al-Mannūbiyya i, 309a
Manōhar (painter) (XVII) vi, 425b; vii, 339a
Manōhar, Manōhargarh (fortress) vi, 421b
Mān-rūd v, 821b, 831b
Mansā Mūsā (Mali) (1337) iii, 275b; iv, 641a; vi, 258a, b, 402a, 421b; vii, 588a; viii, 847b
Mansā Sulaymān (Mali) vi, 258a
Mansā Ulī (Walī) (Mali) vi, 258a
Manṣab, Manṣabdār v, 685b, 688b; vi, 422b
Mansārām i, 1166a
Manshiya (palace, Marrākush) vii, 387a
Manshūr ii, 303a, 309a; vi, 423a
Manshūrāt s, 594a
Mansūkh → Nāsikh
Manṣūr (painter) (1624) vi, 424b; vii, 339a
al-Manṣūr Abū Djaʿfar ʿAbd Allāh (ʿAbbāsid) (775) i, 12b, 17a, 23b, 43a, 45b, 59b, 86b, 103b, 123a, 141b, 212b, 402b, 454a, 485a, 952a, 1030a, 1033b, 1080b, 1232b, ii, 178a, 576b; iii, 135b, 266a, 984a; iv, 939a, b, 940b; v, 69b, 326a, 620b, 1160a, 1233a, 1238a; vi, 140a, 147b, 230b, 263b, 278a, 311b, 331a, 333a, 345a, 427a, 439b, 506a, 540a, 625a, 659b, 691a, 707b, 710b, 744b, 821b; vii, 113b, 388b, 396a, 628a, 645b; viii, 462a; s, 17b, 31b, 267b, 304b, 306b, 384b, 385b, 386b
– foundation of Baghdād i, 616a, 895a, 896a, 897a
al-Manṣūr (Afṭasid) → Ibn al-Afṭas; ʿAbd Allāh b. Muḥammad b. Maslama
al-Manṣūr (Almohad) → Abū Yūsuf Yaʿḳūb
al-Manṣūr (Ḥammādid) → al-Manṣūr b. al-Nāṣir
al-Manṣūr (Marīnid) → Yaʿḳūb al-Manṣūr
al-Manṣūr (Marwānid, Diyār Bakr) (1096) vi, 627a
Manṣūr (Moghol Khān) (1545) x, 677a
al-Manṣūr (Zīrid) s, 62b
al-Manṣūr, Madīnat → Baghdād
al-Manṣūr, Muḥammad b. Abī Djaʿfar (777) vii, 76a
Mansur, Sultan (Malacca) (XV) vi, 209a, 212b
al-Manṣūr b. Abī ʿĀmir al-Maʿāfirī → al-Manṣūr bi-'llāh (Almanzor, al-Andalus)
Manṣur b. Abī Mālik (al-Maʿkil) (1287) vi, 142a
al-Manṣūr, Aḥmad (Saʿdid) → Aḥmad al-Manṣūr
Manṣur b. ʿAbdūn ii, 858a; iii, 79a; v, 1211a

al-Manṣūr b. Aʿlā al-Nās → al-Manṣūr b. al-Nāṣir
Manṣūr b. ʿAlī b. ʿIrāḳ Djīlānī → Ibn ʿIrāḳ
Manṣūr b. Bādja (IX) vi, 437b
al-Manṣūr b. Buluggīn (Zīrid) (996) i, 824a, 1309a; iii, 137a; s, 62b
Manṣūr b. Djumhūr (744) vi, 439b; s, 232b
Manṣūr b. Dubays I (Mazyadid) (1086) i, 684a; vi, 966a
Manṣūr b. Fakhr al-Dīn b. Ḳurḳumāz Maʿn (1635) vi, 343b
Manṣūr b. Ḳarātegīn iv, 100b; viii, 110a
Manṣūr b. Ḳutlumush b. Arslān Isrāʾīl (Saldjūḳ) (1078) i, 1336b; vi, 274b; viii, 948a
Manṣūr b. Luʾluʾ iii, 80b, 130b; v, 623b, 820b
al-Manṣūr b. al-Mahdī (ʿAbbāsid) (817) vi, 335a, b, 650a
Manṣūr b. Maymūn iv, 346b, 347a
Manṣūr b. Muḥammad b. Aḥmad b. Yūsuf b. Ilyās (XV) viii, 542b; x, 355a
Manṣūr b. Muḥammad al-Azdī al-Harawī (ḳāḍī) (1048) vi, 913b
al-Manṣūr b. al-Mutawakkil i, 242b
al-Manṣūr b. al-Nāṣir (Ḥammādid) (1105) i, 1205a; iii, 138a, 753a; iv, 479a; vi, 140a, 426b
Manṣūr b. Naṣr al-Tunbudhī i, 248a; iv, 827b
Manṣūr b. Nūḥ I, Abū Ṣāliḥ (Sāmānid) (976) i, 421b, 984b, 1294b; ii, 100a; v, 430a; vi, 432b; s, 149a, 259a, 265b
Manṣūr b. Nūḥ II, Abu ʾl-Ḥārith (Samānid) (999) i, 1236a; vi, 65a, 433a; s, 259a
Manṣūr b. Saʿīd (Marwānid) (1085) v, 453a; vii, 693b
Manṣūr b. Yazīd al-Ḥimyarī vii, 694b
Manṣūr b. Yūnus Buzurg (IX) vii, 647b
al-Manṣūr ʿAbd Allāh b. Ḥamza (Zaydī Imām) (XIII) vii, 773a
al-Manṣūr ʿAlāʾ al-Dīn ʿAlī (Mamlūk) (1382) ii, 159a
al-Manṣūr ʿAlī b. al-Mahdī ʿAbd Allāh (Zaydī Imām) (XIX) vii, 515a
Manṣūr Ata i, 299a
Manṣūr al-Bahūtī → al-Bahūtī al-Miṣrī
al-Manṣūr bi-ʾllāh (Almanzor) (al-Andalus) (1002) i, 75b, 446a, 489b, 494a, 499a, 601b, 628a, 1055a, 1238a, 1338b; ii, 373a, 485b, 542a, 998a; iii, 46a, 74b, 495b, 713a, 743a, 746b; iv, 216b, 712b; v, 133a, 511a, 626a, 781a, b, 1007b, 1008a, 1107b, 1177b; vi, 430b, 520b, 842a, 852a; vii, 570a, 942b; viii, 632a; ix, 740b; x, 852b; s, 92b, 125a
al-Manṣūr bi-ʾllāh (Zaydī Imām) (XVIII) vii, 515a
al-Manṣūr bi-ʾllāh, Ismāʿīl (Fāṭimid) (953) i, 163b, 1238a; ii, 491b, 861b; iv, 460a; v, 1246b; vi, 434a, 728a; vii, 485b; s, 144b, 236b
al-Manṣūr bi-ʾllāh ʿAbd Allāh b. Ḥamza (Zaydī Imām) (1217) v, 1240b; vi, 433b; s, 236b, 363b
al-Manṣūr bi-ʾllāh ʿAlī (Imām) (1809) s, 30b
al-Manṣūr bi-ʾllāh al-Ḳāsim b. ʿAlī al-ʿIyānī (Zaydī Imām) (1003) vi, 435b
al-Manṣūr bi-ʾllāh al-Ḳāsim b. Muḥammad (Zaydī Imām) (1620) v, 1241b; vi, 436a, b; vii, 996a; ix, 2a; s, 30b
al-Manṣūr al-Dhahabī (Saʿdid) (1603) vi, 406a, 607a, 933a
al-Manṣūr Ḥādjdjī (Mamlūk) (1390) vi, 548a
al-Manṣūr al-Ḥusayn b. al-Mutawakkil (Zaydī Imām) (1747) vi, 191a
Manṣūr al-Namarī (805) vi, 437b, 625a
al-Manṣūr Ṣalāh al-Dīn Muḥammad s, 395b
Manṣūr al-Shihābī ii, 444a, 635b
al-Manṣūr ʿUmar (Rasūlid) (1249) viii, 436a
al-Manṣūr ʿUthmān b. Djaḳmaḳ (Mamlūk) (1453) vii, 727a
Manṣūr Ushurma, Shaykh ii, 18a, 88a
Manṣūr al-Yaman al-Nadjdjār al-Kūfī (Ibn Ḥawshab) (914) i, 103b, 551b; ii, 852a; iv, 198a, b, 661a; vi, 438b; s, 236b
Manṣūr Zalzal vi, 97b, 103a; s, 128b
al-Manṣūra (Miṣr) vi, 314b, 440a; vii, 166a
al-Manṣūra (Sind) vi, 439b, 691a
al-Manṣūra (Tilimsān) iii, 470b; vi, 440b, 572a
al-Manṣūrī → al-Manāṣīr, Banū
al-Manṣūriyya → Ṣabra
al-Manṣūriyya (Ifrīḳiyya) iv, 479a; s, 62b, 236b
Manṣūriyya (Mamlūk) vi, 316a, 322b
al-Manṣūriyya (Miṣr) vii, 162a; s, 62b, 236b

Manṣūriyya (Shīʿī) i, 258a; vi, 441b
Manṭiḳ, ʿIlm al- vi, 442a
al-Manṭiḳī → Abū Sulaymān al-Manṭiḳī
Mantzikert → Malāzgird
Mānū, Ḳaṣr vi, 452b
Mānū Djān Khānum bint Āghā Muṭahhar (XVIII) vii, 444a
Manūčihr I b. Yazīd iv, 347a
Manūčihr II b. Faridūn ii, 764a, 798a; iv, 348b, 915a
Manūčihr b. Ḳābūs (Ziyārid) (1029) iv, 100b, 358a, 465a; v, 662a; vi, 66a; s, 235a
Manūčihr Iḳbāl (1977) vii, 450b
Manūčihr Khān (Luristān) (XVII) vii, 674a
Manūčihr Khān Muʿtamid al-Dawla (1847) i, 833b; iv, 1091b; v, 825b; vi, 803b; vii, 557a, 675a
Manūčihrī, Abu ʾl-Nadjm Dāmghānī (1041) i, 1301a; iv, 61a; v, 1104a; vi, 453a; vii, 661b; s, 35a
Manūf al-Suṭā vi, 453b
Manūf al-ʿUlyā vi, 453b
al-Manūfī, ʿAbd Allāh – al-Mālikī (1347) vi, 454a
al-Manūfī, ʿAbd al-Djawwād b. Muḥammad (1658) vi, 454a
al-Manūfī, Abu ʾl-ʿAbbās Aḥmad b. Muḥammad (1521) vi, 454a
al-Manūfī, Abu ʾl-Ḥasan ʿAlī (1532) vi, 454a
al-Manūfī, Maḥmūd Abu ʾl-Fayḍ (1972) vi, 454b
al-Manūfī Manṣūr b. ʿAlī (1722) vi, 454b
al-Manūfī, Muḥammad b. Ismāʿīl (1452) vi, 454a
al-Manūfī, Ramaḍān al-Ashʿath vi, 454a
al-Manūfiyya al-Aḥmadiyya vi, 454a
Maʿn-zāda, Ḥusayn b. Fakhr al-Dīn II al-Maʿnī (1690) vi, 343b, 345a
Manzah Bint al-Sulṭān i, 699b, 700a
Mantzikert → Malāzgird
Manzil (lunar mansion) → Manāzil
Manzil (stage) vi, 454b
Manzil Bashshū (Ifrīḳiya) vi, 455b, 457a
al-Manzila Bayn al-Manzilatayn vi, 457b
Manẓūr ʿAlī Khān ii, 1092b
Mao (Kānim) s, 165a, b, 166a
Mappila i, 172a; iii, 411b; iv, 547a; v, 587a; vi, 206b, 245a, 458a; vii, 49a
Mār ghat (Margat) → al-Marḳab
Mār Ghātūm (Margathum) → al-Marḳab
Mār Kābān (Marckapan) → al-Marḳab
Mār Kābūs (Markappos) → al-Marḳab
Mār Sābā v, 330a
al-Marʿa (1214) xi, 112b
al-Marʾa (woman) iv, 720a, b; v, 587b, 895b; vi, 466a
– education v, 905a, b, 907a, 909a
– in South East Asia s, **594b**
Marʿā (pasture) vi, 490a
Marādjiʿ al-taḳlīd iii, 491a, b
Marādjil umm al-Maʾmūn (ʿAbbāsid) vi, 331a
Marāfiḳ ii, 325a; vi, 498a
Marāgha i, 300a, 301a; vi, 494a, 498a, 504b, 601a, b; vii, 395a
– observatory iii, 1125a, 1135b, 1137b
Marāghaʾī, Zayn al-ʿĀbidīn (1910) iv, 72a, 164b, 789a; s, 109b
al-Marāghī, ʿAbd al-Ḳādir (1435) vii, 684b, 1042b; s, 409a
al-Marāghī, Muṣṭafā iv, 159b; v, 429b
al-Marāghī, Ṣadr al-Dīn iv, 862b
Marah Rusli (XX) vi, 240b
Mārahrawī → Aḥsan Mārahrawī
Marāʿī iv, 1042a, b
Maraḳiyya iii, 474b
Marakkayar v, 582a; vi, 503a
Marand iii, 1125a; vi, 504a; s, 365b
Marandj vi, 783a
Marandjīṣa iii, 1040b, 1041a
Marʿash i, 4a, b, 1190b; vi, 380a, 505b
al-Marʿashī → al-Shushtarī, Sayyid Nūr Allāh b. Sharīf Marʿashī
Marʿashī, Ḳawām al-Dīn (Mīr-i Buzurg) i, 237a
Marʿashī-Nadjafī, Āyatallāh Shihāb al-Dīn vi, 516b, 517a, 553b
Marʿashīs vi, 510b, 549b; vii, 672b
Marāṣid ii, 143a
Marāsim vi, 518a
Marāt (Wādī Rahyū) vi, 404a
Marāthās i, 208b, 230a, 253a, 296a, 400b, 403b, 418a, 625a, 757a, 796b, 808a, 952a, 1170a, 1202b, 1300a, 1330a, 1331a; ii, 99a, 219a, 808b, 1092b, 1130a; iii, 15b, 60b, 202b, 316b, 320a, 424b, 427b; iv, 1023b; v, 1259a; vi, 269a, b, 310a, 407a, 534a; vii, 315b, 443b, 457a, 899a; viii, 74a, 253b, 300b, 382b; s, 55b, 246b
Marāthī vi, 536b
Marātib vi, 536b

Marāzīg vii, 897a, b
Marāziḳa → Ibn Marzūḳ, Muḥammad VI
Marbaṭ (Marbiṭ) vi, 537b
Marbaṭ al-Dimm vi, 563b
Marcionites-V Marḳiyūniyya
Marcuella → Marḳwīz
Mardam, ʿAdnān b. Khalīl (XX) vi, 538b
Mardam, Djamīl (1961) vi, 538a
Mardam, Khalīl (1959) vi, 538b
Mardān-shāh (Maṣmughān) (VII) vi, 744b
Mardanīsh → Ibn Mardanīsh
Mardanīsh, Banū s, 80b
al-Mardāwī, ʿAlāʾ al-Dīn (1480) iii, 162a, 766b
Mardāwidj b. Ziyār (Ziyārid), 935) i, 125b, 688a, b, 866a, 1350a, b, 1354a; ii, 192b, 299b, 454a, 1082a, 1141b; iii, 105b, 195b, 255a, 1157a; iv, 19a, 23a, 100a, 661b; vi, 115b, 521b, 523a, 539a; viii, 597b; s, 357a
Marḍī (Murḍā) Ibn al-Ṭarsūsī (XIII) vii, 885b
Mārdīn (Māridīn) i, 311b, 664a, 665b, 666b; ii, 344b; iii, 1118a; iv, 898a; v, 248a, 457b, 1145a; vi, 111b, 539b; x, 527a; s, 36a
al-Mārdīnī (1591) vi, 112a
al-Mārdīnī, ʿAbd Allāh b. Khalīl (1406) vi, 542b
al-Mārdīnī, Abu ʾl-Ṭāhir Ibn Fallūs (1252) vi, 542b
al-Mārdīnī, Muḥammad b. Muḥammad, Sibṭ al-Mārdīnī (1506) vi, 543a
Mardj (Shūf) s, 159a, 160b
al-Mardj → Barḳa
Mardj ʿAdhrāʾ vi, 544b, 545b
Mardj al-Aṭrākhūn vi, 778b
Mardj Banī ʿĀmir vi, 543b
Mardj Dābiḳ iv, 553a; vi, 231b, 325a, 544a
Mardj al-Dībādj vi, 776b
Mardj al-Ḳassāb vi, 545b
Mardj Rāhiṭ i, 5a, 920a, b; ii, 90a, 1106a; iv, 493a; vi, 544a, 622a; vii, 268b; viii, 756b
Mardj al-Shaḥm vi, 774b
Mardj al-Ṣuffar vi, 544b, 545a, 546a; vii, 462a; viii, 756b
Mardj ʿUyūn ii, 234b; vi, 430a
Mardjaʿ-i Taḳlīd v, 371b; vi, 548b; s, 75b, 76a, 103b, 158a
Mardjān (amīr) (1521) i, 938a
Mardjān (amīr) (Zabīd) (1022) vii, 861a
Mardjān (Baghdād) i, 903b
Mardjān (coral) vi, 556a
Mardjanī i, 1307a
al-Mardjanī, Shihāb al-Dīn (1889) s, 467a
Mardjumak Aḥmad → Merdjümek, Aḥmed b. Ilyās
Mardūd iii, 26b
Marea → Māryā
Mār Ghāt (Margat) → al-Marḳab
Mār Kābān (Marckapan) → al-Marḳab
Mār Kābūs (Markappos) → al-Marḳab
Marghelān → Marghīnān
Marghīnān (Marghelān) ii, 792a; v, 29a, b; vi, 557a
al-Marghīnānī, ʿAbd al-ʿAzīz b. ʿAbd al-Razzāḳ (1084) vi, 558b
al-Marghīnānī, Abu ʾl-Fatḥ Zayn al-Dīn vi, 558b
al-Marghinānī, Abu ʾl-Ḥasan Naṣr b. al-Ḥasan viii, 383b
al-Marghīnānī, Abu ʾl-Ḥasan Ẓahīr al-Dīn (1112) vi, 558b
al-Marghīnānī, Bahāʾ al-Dīn ii, 3b
al-Marghīnānī, Burhān al-Dīn Abu ʾl-Ḥasan (1197) iii, 163b; vi, 557b, 558b; ix, 36a
al-Marghīnānī, al-Ḥasan b. ʿAlī vi, 558a
al-Marghīnānī, ʿImād al-Dīn al-Farghānī vi, 558b
al-Marghīnānī, Muḥammad Abu ʾl-Fatḥ Djalāl al-Dīn al-Farghānī → al-Marghīnānī, ʿImād al-Dīn al-Farghānī
al-Marghīnānī, ʿUmar Niẓām al-Dīn al-Farghānī vi, 558b
al-Marghīnānī, Ẓahīr al-Dīn al-Ḥasan (XII) vi, 558b
Marḥala vi, 558b
Mari → Čeremiss
Mari → Ḳayyim
al-Marʿī iii, 954b
Mārī Hills s, 331b
Mārī Ilyās Ziyāda → Mayy Ziyāda
Mārī Jāta (Sunjata, Mali) vi, 421b
Mariamites vi, 629b
Mārib (Maʾrib) i, 102b, 549a, 890b; ii, 785a, 1060b; iii, 223a; v, 811a; vi, 474b, 559a; viii, 663a; s, 336b, 337a
Mārid s, **598a**; iii, 1050a; ix, 406b
Mārida (Merida) i, 493a, 1319b; ii, 1009a; iii, 74a, 288a, 498b, 499b; vi, 567b

al-Māridānī, ʿAlī iii, 818a
Māridīn → Mārdīn
al-Māridīnī, Sibṭ iii, 1141a
Maʿrifa ii, 358a; iii, 262a, 1133a; iv, 847a; vi, 568b
al-Mārighnī, Abū ʿAmr ʿUthmān b. Khalīfa (XII) viii, 113a
Mārīkala vi, 780b
Marīnā, Banū x, 79b
Marindja → Bahčekent
Marīnids (Banū Marīn) i, 92b, 93a, 122b, 124b, 129b, 155a, 167b, 290b, 367b, 445b, 495b, 1148b, 1176b, 1346b; ii, 146a, 353a, 819a, 822a, 979a, 1095b; iii, 49a, 68a, 386b, 462a, 825b; iv, 116b, 338a, 633b; v, 531a, 626b, 1128a, 1150a, 1190a, 1208a; vi, 134a, b, 142a, 222b, 281a, 293a, 310b, 404a, 440b, 441a, 571a, 593a, 741b, 742b, 743a; vii, 37a, 613b, 803a, 1021b, 1022a, b; ix, 545b; xi, 182a; s, 45b, 103a, 112a, 113b, 318a, 336b
al-Marīs (Nobatia) vi, 574b; viii, 88b, 89b
al-Marīsī → Bishr b. Ghiyāth
al-Marīsiyya i, 1242a
Māristān → Bīmāristān
Maritsa → Merič
Māriya (the Copt) (637) iii, 64a; vi, 575a, 650b; vii, 372a, 396b
Mariya Ulfa (XX) x, 77a
al-Mariyya (Almería) i, 32a, 489a, 864b; iii, 135a, 498b, 712b; v, 219a; vi, 344b, 575b; vii, 70a; s, 383a
Māriya bint al-Ḥārith b. Djulhum umm al-Aswad (Lakhmid) (VI) vii, 568b
Mariyyat Badjdjāna → al-Mariyya (Almería)
Māriz s, 129a
Marka vi, 258b
al-Markab (Margat) i, 118b, 1016b; iv, 485a; vi, 345b, 577a
Markab (observatory) → Marṣad
Markha, Wādī iv, 747a
Markhassa i, 640b
Mārk(i)siyya (Marxism) vi, 583a
Markiyūniyya (Marcionites) s, **599b**
Markwīz s, 80a
Marmara Deñīzī i, 463a; vi, 587a
al-Marmarāwī, Aḥmad Shams al-Dīn b. ʿĪsā (1504) iv, 992a, b
Marmoucha s, 145a
Marnīsa, Banū vi, 1009a
Maronites i, 1280b, 1281a; ii, 65b, 467b, 637a, 750a, 795a; iii, 523a; iv, 255a; v, 791a, b, 792a; s, 268b, 269a
Marrakesh → Marrākush
Marrākūsh i, 79a, 251a, 289a; ii, 818b, 819a, b, 1116b; iii, 148b, 462a, 501a, 675a, 975a; iv, 533a; v, 654a, b, 1186b, 1208a; vi, 38b, 124a, 142b, 187a, 250a, 293b, 339b, 340a, 350a, 351a, 364a, 406a, 521a, 571b, 573a, 572b, 588b, 742b; vii, 391a; ix, 47a; s, 29a, 48a, 103a, 114a, 124b, 389a, 397b, 401b
– Djāmiʿ al-Kutubiyyīn → Masdjid al-Kutubiyya-literature i, 1224b; iii, 806b
– monuments i, 56a, 58b, 85a, 161b, 289a, 459a, 499b, 1320b, 1346b, 1347a; v, 1153b; vii, 391a
al-Marrākushī → ʿAbd al-Wāḥid; al-Ḥasan b. ʿAlī ʿUmar; Ibn ʿAbd al-Malik; Ibn al-Bannāʾ
al-Marrrākushī, Abū ʿAlī al-Ḥasan b, ʿAlī (1280) i, 727a; ii, 586b; v, 1209b; vi, 598a; vii, 201b, 210b; viii, 575a; s, 413b
Marrāsh, ʿAbd Allāh (XIX) vi, 598b
Marrāsh, Faṭh Allāh (XIX) vi, 598b
Marrāsh, Fransīs b. Faṭh Allāh (1874) iii, 591b; vi, 598b
Marrāsh, Maryāna vi, 598b, 599a
Marrīs s, 332a
Mars (planet) → al-Mirrīkh
Marsā → Mīnāʾ
Marsā ʿAlī → Ṣikilliyya
Marsā ʾl-Kharaz vi, 556b
Marsā Mūsā s, 125a
Marsā Zafran → Maghmadās
Marṣad (observatory) i, 1141a; iv, 702b; vi, 599b
Marṣafā vi, 602a
al-Marṣafī, al-Ḥusayn (1890) iii, 593b; iv, 1098a; vi, 602a
Marsūm ii, 303a, b,
Martaba s, **600b**
Martapura s, 151a
Martel, Charles i, 86b, 493a, 988b
Marthiya i, 508b, 584b; ii, 73a; iv, 1027a; v, 611b, 635b, 1033b; vi, 602b
Martolos i, 1164a; vi, 613a; viii, 609a
Marūčak → Marw-i Kūčik

Maʿrūf → Ilāhī Bakhsh
Maʿrūf Balkhī, Abū ʿAbd allāh (X) s, **601b**
Maʿrūf, Banū i, 1096a
Maʿrūf al-Karkhī, Abū Maḥfūẓ b. Fīrūz (815) iv, 653a; vi, 354a, 613b, 614a; vii, 647a, 871a
Maʿrūf al-Ruṣāfī (1945) i, 597b; iii, 1264b; vi, 614a; ix, 230a
al-Maʿrūf wa ʾl-Munkar → al-Nahy ʿan al-Munkar
Mārūn s, 269a
Mārūn, Yūḥannā v, 791a
Mārūn al-Naḳḳāsh → al-Naḳḳāsh
Mārūniyya (Maronites) i, 1280b, 1281a; ii, 656b, 467b, 637a, 750a, 795a; iii, 523a; iv, 255a; v, 791a, b, 792a; s, 268b, 269a, **602a**
Mārūt → Hārūt wa-Mārūt
Marw al-Rūdh vi, 334a, 617b, 627b
al-Marw al-Rūdhī → Ḥusayn b. ʿAlī; Ḥusayn b. Muḥammad
Marw al-Shāhidjān (Marw) i, 16a, 18a, 47b, 750a, 1007a, 1067a, 1293b, 1294a; ii, 4b, 43b; iv, 131b; v, 56b, 58b, 293a, 554b, 868b; vi, 199b, 205b, 331b, 332b, 333b, 334b, 335b, 337b, 419a, 427b, 493b, 600a, 617b, 618a, 627b, 628a, 633b, 656a; s, 89a, 195a, 240a, 281a, 326a, 357a
al-Marwa → al-Ṣafā
Marwān I b. al-Ḥakam b. Abi ʾl-ʿĀṣ (Umayyad) (684) i, 453b, 1242b; ii, 89b, 360b, 415b, 416a, 726a; iii, 65a, 227a, 242b, 270b, 607b, 620b, 932a; iv, 493a, 929b, 938b; v, 74b, 451a; vi, 544b, 545a, 546b, 621b, 623a, 625a, 626a, 641a, 653b, 659a, 661b, 671b; vii, 269a; s, 10a, 52b, 230b
Marwān II b. Muḥammad b. Marwān b. al-Ḥakam (Umayyad) (750) i, 43a, 53b, 57b, 65b, 100b, 103a, 108b, 354a, 660b, 787b, 835b, 837a, 1244a, 1343b; ii, 130a, 505a, 523b, 958a; iii, 29a, 228a, 229b, 398a, 493b, 651b, 802b, 990b; iv, 344a, b, 370b, 447b, 1174a; vi, 147b, 506a, 623a, 626a, 641b, 656a; vii, 497b, 910b; x, 844b
Marwān (miller) (X) vi, 626a
Marwān, ḳāḍī vi, 670b
Marwān b. ʿĀbī Djanūb → Marwān al-Aṣghar b. Abī Djanūb
Marwān b. ʿĀbid al-Mutaʿāl (1911) vi, 627a
Marwān b. Ḥafṣa (VIII) ix, 665b
Marwān b. al-Ḥakam → Marwān I
Marwān b. al-Haytham al-Sulaymī ii, 234a
Marwān b. Muḥammad → Marwān II
Marwān b. Yazīd b. al-Muhallab (VIII) vii, 359b; s, 41a
Marwān al-Akbar b. Abī Ḥafṣa (797) ii, 248b; iii, 1202b; vi, 345a, 437b, 625a
Marwān al-Aṣghar b. Abi ʾl-Djanūb vi, 625a
Marwān al-Ḥimār → Marwān II b. Muḥammad (Umayyad)
Marwān al-Khalfāwī (1329) vi, 627a
Marwānids (Diyār Bakr) i, 13a, 81b, 82b, 95b, 118a, 493b, 1206b; ii, 344a; iii, 676b; iv, 27b; v, 453a; vi, 270b, 274b, 540b, 626a, 930a; viii, 70b; s, 103b
Marwānids (Umayyads) i, 13a, 118a; vi, 626a; s, 103b
Marwānids (Umayyads, al-Andalus) i, 81b, 493b; iii, 676b
Marwāniyya vi, 627a
Mārwār → Djōdhpur
Marwārīdī (XVI) vii, 473a
al-Marwarrūdhī, al-Ḥusayn (1070) vii, 781a
al-Marwarrūdhī,Khālid b. ʿAbd al-Malik (831) iv, 1182b; vi, 600a
al-Marwazī → Abū Saʿīd; Abū Yaḥyā; Ḥabash al-Ḥāsib
al-Marwazī, Abu ʾl-Abbās iv, 55a
al-Marwazī, Abū Bakr (888) i, 274a, b, 1039a; iii, 159a; vi, 627b
al-Marwazī, Abu ʾl-Faḍl (XI) vi, 627b
al-Marwazī, Abū Isḥāḳ (951) ix, 187b
al-Marwazī, Abu ʾl-Ḳāsim al-Fūrānī (1079) vii, 781a
al-Marwazī, Abū Ṭālib ʿAzīz al-Dīn (XIII) vi, 627b
al-Marwazī, Aḥmad b. ʿAlī (905) vii, 706b
al-Marwazī, Aḥmad b. Bishr (973) vii, 538a
al-Marwazī, Ghassān b. Muḥammad (849) vii, 5a
al-Marwazī, Ibrāhīm b. Aḥmad (951) vii, 538a
al-Marwazī, Sharaf al-Dīn Masʿūdī (XIII) viii, 542a
al-Marwazī, Sharaf al-Zamān Ṭāhir (1120) v, 385b, 1011a, b; vi, 628a
Marw-i Kūčik vi, 617b; s, 281a
Mary → Maryam

Mārya (Marea) vi, 628a
Maryab vi, 565a
Maryam (Mary) ii, 848a; iii, 1175a, 1206a; iv, 81b, 82a; v, 90a; vi, 628b
Maryam Begum (XVIII) vi, 483b
Maryam Khānum (XIX) vi, 484a
Maryam Umīd Muzayyin al-Sulṭān (XX) vi, 486a
Marzbān (Ṭamīsha) v, 661b; s, 298a
Marzbān b. Sharwīn (X) vi, 632a, b
Marzbān (Marzubān)-nāma iv, 63b, 506b; v, 1028a; vi, 632a
Marzpān (Marzubān) vi, 633a
Marzubān (Daylamī) (X) vi, 499b
Marzubān b. Bakhtiyār → Ṣamṣam al-Dawla (Būyid)
Marzubān b. Djustān ii, 191a
Marzubān I b. Muḥammad (Musāfirid) (957) i, 190a, 660b, 1041b; ii, 680a; iii, 703a; iv, 345b, 346a, 662b; v, 452a; vii, 655b; viii, 998b
Marzubān b. Rustam b. Shahriyār iii, 372b; iv, 506a; v, 1028a
al-Marzubān b. Rustam b. Sharwīn → Marzbān b. Sharwīn
Marzubān b. Wahrīz (Yemen) (VI) vi, 633b
al-Marzubānī, Abū ʿUbayd Allāh al-Baghdādī (994) i, 154b, 758b; iii, 879a; vi, 634a, 709b; vii, 312a; viii, 14a; s, 24b, 33a, 400b
Marzūḳ b. Maẓlūm ii, 234b
al-Marzūḳī, Abū ʿAlī Aḥmad b. Muḥammad (1030) i, 154a; vi, 635b; vii, 307a
al-Masʿā vi, 165b, 167a
Maṣāff iii, 156b
Maṣāffiyya ii, 1080b; iii, 45b
Masāḥa iv, 1037b, 1038a
Masāʾil wa-adjwiba i, 274a, 320a; vi, 636a
Masākira s, 356a
al-Masʾala al-minbariyya i, 765a
al-Masʾala al-Suraydjiyya iii, 949b
Masāliḥ i, 761a
al-Masālik wa ʾl-Mamālik i, 488a; vi, 639b
Masāmiʿa, Āl vi, 640b
Maṣāmida → Maṣmūda, Banū
Masardjasān vi, 620a
Māsardjawayh (Māsardjīs) vi, 640b; s, 52b
Māṣarm vi, 384a
al-Masāwī → al Maḥāsin wa ʾl-Masāwī
Maṣawwaʿ i, 932a, 976a; ii, 91a; iv, 687a; vi, 641b; viii, 184a, 235b
Mascara (Algeria) → al-Muʿaskar
Mascate → Masḳaṭ
Masculin (in grammar) → Mudhakkar
Masdjid (mosque) i, 497-500, 608-624, 830a, 1200b; ii, 777b; iii, 1124a; iv, 229b; v, 366a, 1123b, 1124a, b; vi, 644b
Masdjid/Masdjid-i

Abarḳūh (1415) vi, 685a
al-ʿAbbās (Yemen) (XIII) vi, 683b
ʿAbdallāhābād (Khurāsān) (XII) vi, 684b
Abī Bakr (Mecca) vi, 651a
Abī Dulaf (Sāmarrāʾ) vi, 364b, 365a; vii, 9a
Abī Hurayra (al-Madīna, Djīza, al-Ramla, Yubnā) vi, 652a, b
ʿAdī b. Ḥātim vi, 653a
Ādīna (Ḥaḍrat Pānduā) (1374) vi, 693b; vii, 79a; ix, 575b
Ādīna (Sabzawār) (879) vii, 76b
Afḍal Khān (Bīdjāpur) (1653) vi, 689b, 696a
Afḍal Khān (Gulbargā) vi, 698b
Afyon (1273) vi, 682b
Aghmāt (704) vi, 743b
Aḥmad Shāh (Aḥmadābād) (1414) vii, 79b
Aḥmad Yasawī (Turkestan) (1394) vi, 685a
Aḥmed Ghāzī (Mīlās) (1378) vii, 56a
Aḥmed Pasha (Istanbul) (1562) vi, 687a
ʿĀʾisha (Mecca) vi, 650b
Akbar (Adjmēr) (1570) viii, 315b
Āḳbughawiyya (Cairo) vi, 672b
Akhī Elvān (Ankara) (1382) vi, 683a; vii, 78b
ʿAkk (ʿAkkā) vi, 652b
al-Aḳmar (Cairo) (1125) vi, 657a, 667b, 683a; vii, 150b, 504a; viii, 314b
al-Aḳṣā (Jerusalem) (VII) i, 3a, 201a, 610a, 618b; ii, 263a, 911a; iv, 367b, 1169b; v, 298a, 299a, 323b, 325a, 340b, 342b, 343a; vi, 31b, 362a, 655a, 657a, 659b, 662a, 677b, 680a, 707a; s, 205a
al-Aḳṣā (Ḳudus, Java) vi, 708a
Āḳsarāy (Shahr-i Sabz) (1396) viii, 315b
Āḳsunḳur (Miṣr) (1412) vi, 654a, 667b; vii, 78b
ʿAlāʾ al-Dīn (Bursa) (1335) vi, 686a
ʿAlāʾ al-Dīn (Ḳonya) (1135) vi, 366a, 682b, 683a; vii, 78a

ʿAlāʾ al-Dīn (Niğde) (1223) vi, 682b, 686a; vii, 13a, 79a; viii, 15b
Aladja ʿImāret (Selānīk) (1486) ix, 124a
Alaeddin (Ankara) (1197) vii, 78b
ʿAlī → al-Nadjaf
ʿAlī (Iṣfahān) (1522) vi, 685b; viii, 787b
ʿAlī (Ḳuhrūd) vii, 13a
ʿAlī b. Yūsuf (Marrākush) vi, 590b, 597a
ʿAlī Barīd (Bīdar) (1576) vi, 695b
ʿAlī Ḳulī Agha (Iṣfahān) vi, 686a
ʿAlī Shāh (Tabrīz) (1310) vi, 685a; viii, 315b
ʿAlī Shahīd Pīr (Bīdjāpūr) vi, 696a
Alif Khān (Dhōlkā) iii, 445a
ʿAmādiyya (1153) vii, 77b
al-ʿAmr (al-Fusṭāṭ) (641) vi, 193b, 362a, 363a, 653b, 654a, 656b, 657a, b, 658b, 659a, 660b, 661b, 662a, 663a, b, 664a, b, 665b, 666a, 667b, 668a, 670a, b, 671a, 672b, 673a, b, 674a, 675a, 679a, 740b; vii, 8b, 159a
ʿAmr (Ḳūs) (1155) vii, 77b
Andā (Bīdjāpur) vi, 689b, 696a
Arbaʿa Rukūn (Maḳdishū) (1268) vi, 128b, 370a
Ardabīl vi, 684b
Ardahāl vii, 19a
Aŕhāʾī-dinkā Djhōńpŕā (Adjmēr) (1236) vi, 691b; vii, 13b; viii, 267a, 315b
Aŕhāʾī Kangūra (Kāshī, Banāras) vi, 689b, 694a; vii, 79b
al-Arḳam b. al-Arḳam (Mecca) vi, 168a
Arslanhane Cami (Ankara) (1290) vii, 13b
al-Ashʿath vi, 653a
Ashrafiyya (Taʿizz) (XIII) vi, 683b; x, 118a
Ashtardjān (1315) vi, 684b, 685a
al-ʿAskar (Cairo) (785) vi, 662a, 668a
al-ʿAssālī (Damascus) (XVII) s, 49b
Atabegī (Naw) (Shīrāz) (XIII) viii, 701b
Atalā (Djawnpur) (1376) vi, 689a, 693b, 697a; viii, 315b
ʿAtīḳ Djāmiʿ (Tarabzun) (1461) x, 217a
ʿAtīḳ (Prizren) viii, 338a
Ayazma Djāmiʿi (Üsküdār) (Scutari) (1758) vii, 709b; x, 924a
al-ʿĀyin (1240) i, 780b
Ayodhya (1528) vii, 329a
al-Azhar (Cairo) (1085) vi, 654a, 662a, b, 663b, 665a, b, 667b, 668a, 671b, 672b, 673a, b, 677b, 679b, 680a, b; vii, 10b, 150a
Azirān (1325) vi, 685a

Bāb Aylān (Marrākush) vi, 590b
Bāb Dukkāla (Marrākush) vi, 590b, 597a; viii, 725a
Bādal Maḥall Darwāza (Čandērī) vi, 695b
Badjistān (XV) vi, 685a
al-Badriyya (Jerusalem) vi, 672b
Bādshāhī (Lāhawr) (1673) vi, 369b, 698a; vii, 333b
al-Baghla (Medina) vi, 650b
Baʿlabakk (XII) vi, 679b, 680a
Balkh (X) vi, 680a
Banābashi̊ (Sofya) ix, 705b
Barā Gumbad (Delhi) vii, 79a
Barā Sōnā (Gawr) (1526) vi, 693b
al-Barātha (Kalwādhā) (940) vi, 656b
Baŕī (Čhōtā Panduʾā) (XIV) vi, 368b; vii, 79a
Barḳūḳ (Cairo) (1410) vii, 78b
Barūdjird (Burūdjird) vi, 365a
Bashan (X) vi, 684b
Basṭām vi, 684b
al-Bayʿa (Medina) vi, 650b
Bayraḳli̊ (Prizren) (1573) viii, 339a
Bāyazīd II (Amasya) (1486) vii, 79a; ix, 629b
Bāyazīd II (Istanbul) (1506) vi, 687a
Baybars (Cairo) (1269) vi, 683a; viii, 315a
Bēgam Shāhī → Masdjid Maryam Zamānī
Begampur (Delhi) (1325) vi, 692a, 693b; viii, 315b
Berrīma (Marrākush) vi, 590b
Beyşehir (1296) vi, 682b
Bhadreshwar (Gudjarāt) (X) vi, 689a, 691a
Bharoč (XIV) vi, 692a
Bībī Khānum (Samarḳand) (1399) vi, 685a, b
Bībī Kī (Burhānpur) vi, 695a
Bilāl (Mecca) vi, 651a
Birrābād vi, 684b
Bīshāpūr vi, 683b
Blād al-Ḥaḍar (Tozeur) vii, 12a
Bū Fatātā (Susa) (838) vii, 11a
Bū ʿInāniyya (Maghrib) vi, 663a

Bukhārā vi, 684a
Büyük (Sofya) (XV) ix, 704b

Čamkatta (Gawr) (1475) vi, 693b
Čār Sutūn (Tirmidh) (XI) vi, 684b
Careva Dzamiya (Sarajevo) (1566) ix, 30a
Čashum vi, 686a
Čelebi Sulṭān Meḥemmed (Dimetoka) vi, 686b
Čhōta Panduā vi, 693a
Čhōta Sōnā (Gawr) (1493) vi, 693b
Čihil Sutūn (Ziyāratgāh) (1485) vi, 685a
Čīnili Djāmiʿ (Üsküdār) (1640) x, 924a; xi, 131b

Dābgīr (Thattā) (1588) vi, 698b; ix, 638b
Dāʿī Angā (Lāhawr) (1635) vi, 697b, 698b
Dakar vi, 705a
Damrī (Aḥmadnagar) vi, 695b
Dandānḳān (XI) vi, 684b
Dār al-ʿIlm (Cairo) vi, 671b
Dashtī (1325) vi, 685a
Dawlatābād (XIV) vi, 692a
Dāwūd vi, 645a
Defterdār Kapi̊si̊ (Istanbul) vi, 57a
Dhamār (Yemen) (XIII) vi, 683b
Dhibin (1250) vi, 683b
Dhū Ashraḳ (1019) vi, 683b
Dhu 'l-Kiṭ b. Ayyūb vi, 652b
Dialmath (Senegal) vi, 705a
al-Dibs s, 234b
Diggaron (Hazāra) vi, 684b
Dilāwar Khān (Khed) vi, 695b
Dilāwar Khān (Māndū) (1405) vi, 695a
Divri i (1180) vi, 682b, 683a
Diyārbakir (1091) vi, 682b
Dizdār Naṣūḥ (Mostar) (XVI) vii, 244b
Djālōr (XIV) vi, 692a
Djamāʿat Khāna (Delhi) (1325) vi, 691b; vii, 79a
Djamāl ʿAbd al-Nāṣir Mosque (Tripoli) (1970) x, 214b
Djamālī (Delhi) (1536) vi, 693a, 697a
Djāmiʿ (Abyāna) (1077) vii, 77a
Djāmiʿ (Āgrā) (1648) vi, 697b; vii, 80a, 333a; viii, 268b, 316a
Djāmiʿ (Aḥmadābād) (1423) vi, 694b; viii, 267b
al-Djāmiʿ Aḥmadī (Ṭanṭā) x, 189a
Djāmiʿ (Ardistān) (1158) vii, 12b; viii, 314b
Djāmīʿ (Ashtardjān (1315) viii, 315a
Djāmiʿ (Badāʾūn) (1223) vi, 691b
Djāmiʿ (al-Baṣra) → Masdjidī
Djāmiʿ (Benares) vii, 334a
Djāmiʿ (Bīdar, – Solah Khamba) (1423) vi, 695b
Djāmiʿ (Bīdjāpūr, – Ibrāhīm) (1550) vi, 696a
Djāmiʿ (Burhānpur) (1589) vi, 695a
Djāmiʿ (Čāmpānēr) (1518) vi, 694b
Djāmiʿ (Čandērī) vi, 695a; vii, 79b
Djāmiʿ (Delhi) vii, 80a, 452b; viii, 268a, 316a
Djāmiʿ (Djawnpur) (1438) vi, 694a
Djāmiʿ (Fahradj) (IX) vii, 12a
Djāmiʿ (Fatḥpur Sikrī) (1574) vi, 690a, 697a; vii, 14a, 80a, 330b, 331a, 333b
Djāmiʿ (Fīrūzshāh Kōtlā) (1354) vi, 692b
Djāmiʿ (Gāwilgarh) (1488) vi, 695b
Djāmiʿ (Golkondā) (1518) vi, 696a
Djāmiʿ (Gulbargā) (1367) vi, 690a, 695a; vii, 80a
Djāmiʿ (Harāt) vii, 78b; viii, 314b
Djāmiʿ (Ḥaydarābād) (1597) vi, 696b
Djāmiʿ (Irič) (1412) vi, 692b; vii, 79a
Djāmiʿ (Iṣfahān) (1314) vii, 12b; viii, 314b
Djāmiʿ (Itāwā) vi, 694a; vii, 79b
Djāmiʿ (Khambāyat) (1325) vi, 692a
Djāmiʿ (Khudābād) vi, 698b
Djāmiʿ (Kirmān) (1550) vi, 698b; vii, 13a
Djāmiʿ (Lahore) (1673) viii, 316a
Djāmiʿ (Lamu) (1511) vii, 80a
Djāmiʿ (Lāt-, Dhār) (1404) vii, 79b
Djāmiʿ (Mahdiyya) (920) viii, 314b
Djāmiʿ (Māndū) (1454) vi, 406b, 407a, b, 695a; vii, 79b
Djāmiʿ (Manṣūra, Sind) vi, 691a
Djāmiʿ (Mathurā) (1660) vi, 839a; vii, 334a
Djāmiʿ al-Miḥyās s, 38a
Djāmiʿ (Mīrath) (1556) vii, 113a
Djāmiʿ (Monastir, Tunisia) (1000) vii, 228b
Djāmiʿ (Muḥammadiyya) vii, 77a
Djāmiʿ (Murādābād) (1632) vii, 601b

Djāmiʿ (Nāyin/Nāʾīn) (1311) vii, 12a, 78a; viii, 314a
Djāmiʿ (Plewna) (XVI) viii, 318b
Djāmiʿ (al-Rāfiḳa/al-Raḳḳa) (VIII) viii, 411a
Djāmiʿ (Rezaʾiye/Riḍāʾiyya) (1277) vii, 12b
Djāmiʿ (Rhohankhed) (1582) vi, 695b
Djāmiʿ (Samarḳand) (1403) viii, 315b, 1036b
Djāmiʿ (Sāmarrāʾ) (852) viii, 314a, 1039b
Djāmiʿ (Shāhdjahānābād) (1656) vi, 689a; vii, 333a
Djāmiʿ (Shīrāz) (IX) vii, 12a
Djāmiʿ (Shushtar) vii, 76b
Djāmiʿ (Solah Khamba, Bīdar) (1423) vi, 695b
Djāmiʿ (Srīrangapattana) vi, 369b
Djāmiʿ (Sūsa) (851) ix, 901b
Djāmiʿ (Suryān) vii, 78a
Djāmiʿ (Ṫhaṫṫá) (1657) vii, 333a
Djāmiʿ (Tunis) i, 950a, 1228a
Djāmiʿ (Ungwana, Kenya) (1500) vii, 80a
Djāmiʿ (Warāmīn) (1326) viii, 314b
Djāmiʿ (Yazd) (1375) vii, 13a
Djāmiʿ (Zawāra) (1156) vii, 12b; viii, 314b
Djāmiʿ al-abyaḍ (al-Ramla) viii, 424a
Djāmiʿ Ibrāhīm (Bīdjāpūr) (1550) vi, 696a
Djāmiʿ al-kabīr (al-Ramla) viii, 424a
Djāmiʿ al-Muẓaffar (Taʿizz) viii, 456b
Djāmiʿ al-Sulṭān (Rawḍa) (1481) viii, 464b
Djāmiʿ Yūsuf (Bīdjāpur) (1512) vi, 696a
al-Djanad (Yemen) vi, 683b
Djenne (Mali) vi, 705a
Djibla (Yemen) (1087) vi, 683b
al-Djilāʾ (Ṣanʿāʾ) vi, 683b
al-Djinn (m. al-Bayʿa, m. al-Ḥaras) (Mecca) vi, 168b, 650b
Djirdjis (Mosul) vi, 652a
Djumʿa (Iṣfahān, ca 771) vi, 719b; s, 453b
Djuyūshī (Cairo) (1085) vii, 150b
al-Dulāmiyya (Damascus) vi, 672b
Dunaysir (1204) vi, 682b, 683a

Ek Mīnār kī (Rāyčūr) (1513) vi, 695b
Emīn Pasha (Prizren) (1831) viii, 339b
Erzurum (1135) vi, 682b
Eşrefoğlu (Beyşehir) (1297) vii, 78a
al-Faḍīkh (al-Madina) (625) vi, 650b

Fahradj (IX) vi, 679b
Fakhr al-Dīn (Maḳdishū) vi, 704b
Faryumad (XIII) vi, 684b
al-Fatḥ (Medina) vi, 650b
Fatḥpurī (Āgra) vi, 697b
Fātiḥ (Istanbul) (1463) vi, 57a, 687a, b; viii, 842b
Firdaws (1201) vi, 684b
Fīrūzshāh (Turbat-i Djām) (1442) vi, 684b; viii, 315a

Gawhar Shād (Harāt) (1418) vi, 685a
Gawhar Shād (Mashhad) (1418) vi, 685a
Gaz (1315) vi, 685a
al-Ghamurī (Cairo) vi, 88a
Ghāzī al-Dīn Khān (Delhi) vii, 334a
Girgā viii, 865b
Gök (Amasya) (1266) vi, 686a
Guédé (Senegal) vi, 705a
Gulbarga vii, 458b
Gulpāyagān (1116) vi, 684a
Gunbād (Ziyāratgāh) (1483) vi, 685b
Gunmant (Gawr) (1484) vi, 693b

al-Ḥadjdjādj b. Yūsuf al-Thaḳafī (Wāsiṭ) vii, 8b
Ḥadjdjī Khātūn (Samsun) (1694) viii, 1053a
Ḥafṣa Khaṭun (Selānīk) (1467) ix, 124a
Hafshūya (XIV) vi, 684b
Ḥakim (Iṣfahān) (1656) vi, 686a; viii, 789a
al-Ḥākim (Cairo) (991) vi, 656b, 663b, 667b, 670a, 671b, 679b, 680a, b; viii, 314b; x, 103b
Halwar (Senegal) vi, 705a
al-Ḥarām (Mecca) vi, 164b, 659b, 675a, 708a
Ḥarrān vi, 679b, 680a
Ḥasan (Rabat) (1195) vi, 682a
Hilāl Khān Ḳāḍī (Dhōlkā) (1333) vi, 369a, 694a
Hūd (ʿAkkā, Damascus, Ḥaḍramawt) vi, 652b
Hüdavendigār Cami (Bursa) vi, 366a
al-Ḥuddān vi, 670b
al-Ḥusayn → Karbalāʾ

Ḥusayniyya (Farīzhand) vii, 77a
Hūshang (Māndū) vii, 79b

Ibb (Yemen) vi, 683b
Ibn Ṣāliḥ (Marrākush) (1331) vi, 597a
Ibn Ṭūlūn (Cairo) (878) vi, 651a, 656b, 662a, b, 663a, b, 664b, 665a, 667a, 668a, 670a, 671b, 672b, 673a, 674b, 679b, 680a; vii, 10a, 510a
Ibn Yūsuf (Marrākush) vi, 38b, 590a, 591a, 594b, 597b
Ibrāhīm (m. Bilāl, Mecca) vi, 168b, 651a
Ibrāhīm (Munyat Ibn al-Khaṣīb) vi, 651a
Ibrāhīm Rawḍa (Bīdjāpūr) (1626) vi, 696a
al-Idjāba (Medina) vi, 650b
Ikhlāṣ Khān (Bīdjāpūr) (1560) vi, 696a
Ilyās Bey (Miletus) (1404) vi, 366a
Imām (Iṣfahān) (1637) viii, 789a
Imām ʿAlī al-Riḍā (Mashhad) (1215) vii, 13a, 78a
Imām al-Hādī Yaḥyā (Ṣaʿda) (X) vi, 683b
Imām Ḥasan (Ardistān) (1158) vi, 684b; viii, 314b
Imāmzāda Ismāʿīl (Barz) vii, 77a
ʿImāret (Ankara) (1427) i, 511a
ʿĪsā Bey (Selcuk) (1374) vi, 366a, 683a
Iṣfahān vi, 685a
Ishbīliya (1175) vi, 682a
Iṣṭakhr vi, 679b
Istiḳlāl (Jakarta) vi, 700b

Kābulī Bāgh (1526) vi, 693a
Kačpura (1530) vii, 329a
Kadj (1325) vi, 685a
Kafarbayya vi, 774b
al-Kāfūrī vi, 661b
Ḳāyit Bāy vi, 454a; s, 44a
al-Ḳalʿa (Cairo) vi, 662a
Kalān (1387) vi, 692b
Kālī (Bīdar) (1694) vi, 695b
al-Kallāsa (Damascus) vi, 666b
Kamāl Mawlā (Dhār) (1392) viii, 267b
al-Ḳamḥiyya (Cairo) vi, 671b
Kānpūr vii, 421b
al-Ḳarāfa vi, 657b
al-Ḳarakhāniyya (Samarḳand) (XI) vi, 679b
al-Ḳarāsunḳuriyya (Cairo) vi, 672b
al-Ḳarawiyyīn (Fès) (859) ii, 821-3; iv, 632a; v, 1152a, 1190a, 1208a; vi, 38b, 136a, 187a, 199b, 406a, 591a, 681b; vii, 504b, 587a; s, 126a, 303a
Karīm al-Dīn (Bīdjāpur) (1320) vi, 695b
al-Ḳaṣaba (Tunis) (1232) vi, 457a
al-Ḳaṣba (Marrākush) (1185) vi, 682a
Kāshān (1462) vi, 685a
Ḳāṣimiyye (Sekānīkī) (1492) ix, 124a
Ḳayrawān (836) iv, 828b; vi, 679a, b, 680a, b; vii, 11a, 76a
Kayseri (1140) vi, 682b
Kemayoran (Surabaya) vi, 700b
Khadīdja (Mecca) vi, 650b
al-Khāḍir (Damascus) vi, 652b
Khwādja Siyāh Pūsh (Sistān) vi, 691b
Khān Muḥammad Mirdha (Dhākā) (1706) vi, 698a
Khāṭirī (Cairo) vii, 78b
Khaybar (628) vi, 650b
al-Khayf (Minā) (1467) vi, 168b, 650b, 654a; vii, 65a
Khayr al-Manāzil (Delhi) vi, 690a; vii, 330b, 331a
Khayr al-Manāzil (Māham Anaga) (1561) vi, 696b
Khirkī (Delhi) vi, 690a, 692b; vii, 195a
Khishtī (Maḥmūdpūr) (1021) vi, 691a
Khudāwendigār (Čekirge) (XIV) vii, 594a
Khünkär (Üsküb) (1436) x, 922b
Ḳila-yi Kuhna (Delhi) (1542) vii, 13b
Kilwa vi, 704b
Ḳïrḳ Ḳïz (Termez) vi, 691b
Kisimkazi (Zanzibar) (1107) vi, 704a; vii, 80a
Kubbeli Djāmiʿ (Afyūn Ḳaraḥiṣār) (1341) viii, 831b
Kūča Mīr (Nātanz) (XII) vi, 684b
Ku-chʾie Lou Djāmiʿ (Chʾeng-tʾu) ix, 919b
Kuhna (Purāna Ḳilʿa. Delhi) (1535) vi, 693a; viii, 267b, 315b
Kukli Meḥmed Bey (Prizren) (1538) viii, 338b
Ḳum(m) vi, 684b
Ḳurtuba (787) vi, 679a, b, 680a, 682a
Ḳurwa (Irān) vi, 684a
Kuṭa Deḍé (Java) vi, 701a
Ḳuṭb Shāhī (1585) vii, 79b
al-Kutubiyya (Marrākush) (XII) i, 79a, 166a, 1226b; vi, 589b, 590b, 596a, 597a, 682a; vii, 11b, 504b

Ḳuwwat al-Islām (Dihlī) (1199) ii, 256a; vi, 689a, b, 691a; viii, 315b

Lāl Darwāza (Djawnpur) (1447) vi, 62b, 694a
Lālbāgh (Dhākā) (1678) vi, 698a
Lāleli vii, 709b
Langar kī (Gulbargā) (1435) vi, 695b
Lāt (- Djāmiʿ) (Dhār) (1404) viii, 267b
Lattan (Gawr) (1475) vi, 693b
Lindjān (XIV) vi, 684b
Liyya (Ṭāʾif) (629) vi, 650b
Lōdī (Khayrpur) (1494) vi, 692b, 693a; viii, 315b

Madrasa (Patnā) (1630) vi, 697b
Magogoni (Dār es-Salaam) vii, 80b
Magribija (Sarajevo) (XVI) ix, 31a
Mahābat Khān (Peshāwar) viii, 300a
al-Mahdiyya (Tunisia) (X) vi, 367a
Maḥmūd Pasha (Prizren) (1821) viii, 339b
Makkā (Bīdjāpur) vi, 689b
Makka (Ḥaydarābād) (1617) vi, 696b
al-Maḳs (Cairo) vi, 656b, 671b, 672b
Malatya (1237) vi, 682b
Malik ʿĀlam (Aḥmadābād) (1422) vi, 694b
Malik Mughīth (Māndū) (1432) vi, 272a; vii, 79b
Malika Djahān Bēgam (Harāt) (1586) vi, 696a
Manisa (1376) vi, 683a
al-Manṣūr (Baghdād) vi, 671b, 674a
Mardjān (Baghdād) i, 903b
Maribud (1462) vi, 685a
al-Māridānī (Cairo) (1340) vi, 719a
Maryam Zamānī (Lahore) (1614) vi, 697a; vii, 331b
Mashhad vi, 684b
Masīla (Mʾsila) (Zāb) vi, 187a, 435a, 727a
Maydān (Abyāna) (1103) vii, 14a
Maydān (Kāshān) (XV) vii, 78b
Mayyāfāriḳīn (1155) vi, 682b, 683a
Medina (al-Rawḍa) vi, 677a
Meḥmed Pasha (Amasya) (1486) vii, 79a
Merām (Ḳonya) (1402) vi, 682b
Mihrimah (Istanbul) (1568) vi, 687a; ix, 630a
Mihtar-i Maḥall (Bīdjāpūr) vi, 696a
Miḳyās (al-Djazīra) vi, 656b
Mīnā (Āgra) vi, 697b
Minyā (1154) viii, 864a
Mīr Čaḳinaḳ (Yazd) (1436) vi, 685a
Miṣriyān (XI) vi, 684b; vii, 12b
Mopti (Mali) vi, 705a
Mostar (1474) vii, 244b
Mōth kī (Khayrpur) (1505) vi, 693a
Mōtī (Āgra) (1653) vi, 698a; viii, 269a
Mōtī (Lahore) (1645) vi, 697b
al-Muʾayyad (Cairo) vi, 657a, 665b, 671b, 672b, 674b; vii, 272a
Mudjarrad Kamāl (Gulbargā) (1400) vi, 695b
Muḥāfiẓ Khān (Aḥmadābād) (1492) vi, 694b
Muḥammad b. Tīpū Sulṭān (1842) vii, 79b
Muḥammad ʿAlī (Cairo) (1857) vii, 151b, 427b
Mungēr (Bihar) vii, 129b
Murādiyye (Manisa) (1583) vii, 597a; ix, 69b
al-Mustanṣiriyya (Baghdād) vi, 663a
Mutʿa (Córdoba) x, 159a
al-Muṭahhar (Cairo) s, 244a
al-Muẓaffar (Taʿizz) (XIII) vi, 683b; x, 118a
al-Mwāsīn (Marrākūsh) vi, 590a, b, 591b, 594b, 597a

al-Nabī (Medina) vi, 659b, 660b, 666a, 677b, 680b
Nagīna (Āgra) (1630) vi, 697b; viii, 316a
Nāʾīn/Nāyin (Irān) (X) vi, 365a, 679b, 684a
Nakhčivān (1186) vi, 684b
Namāzgāh (Ḳarshī) vii, 329a
Namira (Ibrāhīm al-Khalīl) (Arafa) vi, 154a, 168b
al-Nāṣir Muḥammad b. Ḳalawūn (Cairo) (1318) vi, 683a
al-Nāṣiriyya (Cairo) vi, 671b, 672b
Nawwāb Sardār Khān (Aḥmadābād) (1660) vi, 698b
Ndioum (Senegal) vi, 705a
Niksar (1145) vi, 682b
Nīlūfer ʿImāreti (Iznīḳ) (XIV) vii, 594a
Nīrīz (Irān) (973) vi, 684a
Nīshāpūr (XV) vi, 685a

Niẓāmiyya (Abarḳūh) (1325) viii, 315a
al-Nukhayla (Cordova) vi, 188b
Nūr-i ʿOthmāniyye (Istanbul) vi, 56b, 57a

Orhan Gazi (Bilecik) vi, 686a

Pādshāhī (Lāhawr) (1673) viii, 269a
Pāʾīn (Farīzhand) vii, 77a
Pānipat (1528) vi, 693a; vii, 329a
Pātan (XIV) vi, 692a
Patthar (Srīnagar) (1620) vii, 331b
Pīrī Meḥmed Pasha (Istanbul) viii, 307b

Rabba (Ṭāʾif) vi, 655b
Rada (Yemen) (XIII) vi, 683b
Raḳḳa (IX) vi, 680a
Ramazan Efendi (Khodjamustafapasha) (1585) vi, 687a
Rānī Rūpawātī (Aḥmadābād) (1510) vi, 694b, 695a
Rānī Siprī (Sabarī) (Aḥmadābād) (1514) vi, 369a, 694b
Ras Mkumbuu (Pemba) vi, 370a
Rāshida (Cairo) vi, 649a, 650a, 656b, 671b
Rasūlids (Taʿizz) vi, 683b
al-Rawḍa (Yemen) (XIII) vi, 683b
al-Raʾya (Mecca) vi, 650b
al-Rifāʿī (Cairo) (XIX) viii, 526a
Rīgistān (Samarḳand) (1417) vi, 685a
Rūm Meḥmed Pasha (Üsküdār) (1471) x, 924a
Rushkhar (1454) vi, 685b
Rüstem Pasha (Istanbul) (1561) ix, 630a

Sadrettin Konevi (Konya) (1274) vii, 13b
Sahib Ata (Konya) (1358) viii, 315a
al-Ṣāḥibiyya (Cairo) vi, 672b
Sāla (1232) i, 780b
Ṣalāḥ al-Dīn (Mīlās) (1330) vii, 56a
Ṣāliḥ (ʿAkkā) vi, 652b
al-Ṣāliḥ Nadjm al-Dīn (Cairo) (1250) vii, 504a
al-Ṣāliḥ Ṭalāʾiʿ (Cairo) (1160) vi, 674a, 719a
Salik (Basīrhāt) (1305) vi, 693a
Ṣalkhad (1232) i, 780b; viii, 995b
Sāmarrāʾ (852) vi, 679b, 681a; vii, 9a
Sambhal (1526) vi, 693a; vii, 329a
Ṣanʿāʾ (VII) vi, 681a
Sandjar (Kālī) (Delhi) vi, 690a
Sandjar (Niẓām al-Dīn) (1370) vi, 692b
Sangān-i Pāʾīn (1140) vi, 684b
al-Ṣarghitmishiyya vi, 674b
Sar-i Rīg (1424) vi, 685a
Sarkhēdj (1451) vi, 694b
Sarm vi, 686a
Sātgunbadh (Dhākā) vi, 698a
al-Ṣawmaʿa (Hūt, Yemen) (XIII) vi, 683b
Sayyid ʿĀlam (Aḥmadābād) (1412) vi, 694b
Sayyida Ruḳayya (Cairo) (1133) vii, 504a
Şehzade (Istanbul) (1548) vi, 687a
Selimiye (Edirne) (1576) vi, 687b; vii, 79a; ix, 619b
Sfax (849) vi, 680a; vii, 76b
Shāh (Iṣfahān) (1612) vi, 685b
Shāh (Mashhad) (1451) vi, 190b, 366a, 685b
Shāh ʿĀlam vi, 692b
Shāh Bāzār (Gulbargā) (1360) vi, 695a
Shāhdjahān (Thattā) (1647) vi, 698b
Shāh Djahānī (Adjmēr) (1638) vi, 697b
Shāh Hamadān (Shrinagar) vi, 696b
Shāh Muḥyī ʾl-Dīn (Čarkh) (XII) vii, 14a
Shāh-i (Ghardjistān) (1175) vi, 691b
Shāh-i Djāmiʿ (Bari Khatu) (XIII) vi, 691b
al-Shams (Karbalāʾ) vi, 650a, b
Shaykh ʿAbd al-Nabī (Delhi) (1575) vii, 330b
Shaykh Bārha (Ẓafarābād) (1311) vi, 694a
Shaykh Ḥasan Muḥammad Čishtī (Aḥmadābād) (1565) vi, 694b
Shaykh Luṭf Allāh (Iṣfahān) (1602) vi, 685b, 719b; viii, 789a
Shaykh Muʿīn al-Dīn Čishtī (Adjmēr) (1570) vii, 330b
Shaykhū (Cairo) vii, 78b
Shehzāde (Istanbul) ix, 629b
Shem b. Nūḥ (Ṣanʿāʾ) vi, 651a
Shibām (X) vi, 683b
Shīrāz (XVI) vi, 684b, 685a
Shuʿayb vi, 652b
al-Shuhadāʾ (Yogyakarta) vi, 700b
Shūnīziyya (Baghdād) ix, 65b
Sīdī ʿAbd Allāh al-Ḥadjdjām vi, 891a
Sīdī Bel ʿAbbās (Marrākush) vi, 590b

Sīdī Bū Marwān (ʿAnnāba) (1033) s, 156a
Sīdī Saʿīd al-Ḥabshī (Aḥmadābād) (1572) vi, 694b
Sīdī ʿUḳba (al-Ḳayrawān) vi, 364a
Simāk (al-Kūfa) vi, 653a
Simnān (XI) vi, 684b
Sīn (1136) vi, 684b
Sīrāf (Irān) (VIII) vi, 683b; vii, 12a
Sirha (Yemen) vi, 683b
Siu (Kenya) (1523) vii, 80b
Sivas vi, 682b
Ṣofu Sinān Pasha (Prizren) (1613) viii, 339a, 340a
Sokollu (Istanbul) (1572) vii, 79a
Sonahrī (Delhi) (1751) vi, 698a
Srīnagar ix, 734b, 735a
Sulaymān (Iṣṭakhr) vi, 650a
Sülaymāniyye (Istanbul) (1557) vi, 687a, b; ix, 629b
al-Sulṭān (Baghdād) (XI) vi, 275a
Sultan Ahmed (Istanbul) (1616) iv, 233a; vi, 687b
Sulṭān Ḥasan (Cairo) (1356) vi, 683a; vii, 78b, 151b; viii, 315a
Sultan Meḥemmed (Prizren) viii, 338b
Sulṭān Muḥammad (Merzifon) vii, 480a
Sūsa (850) vi, 679b, 680a, 683b

Tabrīz (1465) vi, 685b
Tādj Maḥall vi, 697b
Takhlatan Baba (Khurāsān) (XII) vi, 684b
Tamur (Yemen) (XI) vi, 683b
Ṭarābulus al-Gharb (XIV) vi, 683b
Tārīkhāna (Dāmghān) (X) vi, 679b, 684a; vii, 12a, 78b; viii, 314a; s, 453b
al-Ṭaybarsiyya (Cairo) vi, 672b
Tekkeci Ibrāhīm Agha (Istanbul) (1590) vi, 687a
Thāntipāra (Gawr) (1480) vi, 693b
Tīla (Lakhnaw) s, 292a
Tilimsān vii, 11b, 587a
Timbuktu vi, 705a
Tinmāl (1153) vii, 12a, 504b
Tithid (Yemen) (XIII) vi, 683b
Tivaouane (Senegal) vi, 706b
Tolī (Golkondā) (1633) vi, 369b, 696b
Tulaytula (Toledo) (X) vi, 680a
Tunis (864) vi, 679a, 680a, b

Uç Şerefeli (Edirne) (1447) vi, 686b; ix, 629a
Ūkha (Bayāna) (1316) vi, 692a
Ulu Cami (Birgi) (1312) vi, 683a
Ulu Cami (Bitlis) (1160) vi, 686a
Ulu Cami (Bursa) (1394) vi, 686b; vii, 594a
Ulu Cami (Divriği) (1228) vi, 366a; vii, 79b; viii, 315a
Ulu Cami (Edirne) (1403) vi, 686b
Ulu Cami (Erzurum) (1179) vii, 13a
Ulu Cami (Kiziltepe) (1204) vii, 13a
Ulu Cami (Malaṭya) vi, 231a
Ulu Cami (Siirt) vii, 78a
Ulu Cami (Sivrihisar) (1272) vii, 78a
Ulu Djāmiʿ (Afyūn Ḳaraḥiṣār) viii, 831b
Ulu Djāmʿ (Sīwās) (XII) ix, 689b
ʿUmar → al-Ḳuds
ʿUmar (Boṣrā) vii, 9a
ʿUmariyya (Mosul) vii, 9b
Umayyads (Damascus) (710) vi, 662b, 663a, 664a, 666b, 670b, 671a, 674a, 677a; vii, 9a, 10a
Umm Kulthūm (1122) vii, 10b
al-ʿUmra (Mecca) vi, 168b
Urfa (XII) vi, 682b
Urmiya/Riḍāʾiyya (XIII) vi, 684b

Wālādjāhī (Madras) s, 292b, 293a
Wālide Djāmiʿ (Üsküdār) (1708) x, 924a
Wālide-yi ʿAtīḳ (Üsküdar) (XVII) xi, 131a
Warāmīn (1322) vi, 685a
al-Wazīr (Baghdād) vi, 614b
Wazīr (Kāshān) vi, 686a
Wazīr Khān (Lahore) (1634) vi, 697a; vii, 333a

Yaḥyā al-Shabīh (Cairo) (1150) vii, 504a
Yaʿḳūb Bey (Prizren) viii, 338b
Yaʿḳūb al-Manṣūr (Marrākush) (1195) vii, 12a
Yaʿḳūb wa-Yūsuf (Cairo) vi, 651a
Yazd (1330) vi, 683b, 684b, 685a; viii, 315a
Yazd-i Khāst vi, 684a
Yeñi Djāmiʿ (Istanbul) (XVII) xi, 131a
Yeñi Djāmiʿ (Yeñi Djumʿa Djāmiʿi (Tarādzun) (1500) x, 217a
Yeşil Cami (Bursa) (1413) vi, 686b; vii, 13b

Yeşil Cami (Iznīḳ) (1378) vi, 686a
Yi̊ldi̊ri̊m Bāyazīd (Bursa) (1390) vi, 686b
Yi̊ldi̊z-Dede (Istanbul) vi, 57a
Yivli Minare (Antalya) (1373) vi, 683a
Yūnis (Niniveh) vi, 662b
Yūsuf Agha al-Ḥīn (Cairo) (1625) vi, 719a

Ẓafār Dhibin (Yemen) vi, 683b
al-Ẓāhir (Cairo) vii, 151b
al-Ẓāhiriyya (Cairo) vi, 674b
Zawāra (1133) vi, 684b
Ziyāratgāh (Harāt) (1482) vi, 685a

Masdjidī (Baṣra) vi, 709a
Masdjid-i Sulaymān (Iran) s, 291a
Masdjumi, Mashumi iii, 534a, b, 1230a
Maṣfīwa, Banū vi, 742a
Masfūt s, 42a
al-Masḥ ʿAlā ʾl-Khuffayn vi, 709b
Māshāʾ Allāh i, 722b, 1101b; iii, 8b; v, 130b; vi, 710b
Māshaʾ Allāh b. Atharī (IX) vi, 710b;viii, 106b
Maṣḥaf → Muṣḥaf
Maṣḥaf-räsh v, 208b, 209a, b, 210a
Mashaʾiyya (Mashshāʾiyya) iv, 120b
Mashāḳa, Mīkhāʾil (1888) vi, 712a
Mashāriḳa v, 1159a; vi, 712a
Mashawasha vi, 943b
Mashāwiriyya iv, 456a
Mashāyikh iv, 167b
Mashāyikh, Pīr v, 27a
Mashdūf iii, 289a
Mashhad (town) i, 8a, 400b, 1067a; ii, 173b; iv, 7b, 38a; v, 59a, b, 289a, 1149a; vi, 190b, 336a, 418b, 484a, 495b, 510b, 516a, 526b, 550b, 553b, 713b; s, 53a, 71a, 73a, 75a, b, 139b, 365a, b, 380a, 423b
– history and development since 1914 s, **603b**
– university ii, 426a
Mashhad (shrine) s, **604b**
Mashhad Abī Hurayra vi, 652a
Mashhad ʿAkk (ʿAkkā) vi, 652b
Mashhad ʿAlī → al-Nadjaf
Mashhad Dhu ʾl-Kiṭ b. Ayyūb vi, 652b
Mashhad Djirdjis (Mosul) vi, 652a
Mashhad al-Ḥāʾir s, 94a
Mashhad Hūd (ʿAkkā, Damascus), (Ḥaḍramawt) vi, 652b
Mashhad al-Ḥusayn → Karbalāʾ
Mashhad al-Kāẓimī → Kāẓimayn
Mashhad al-Khaḍir (Damascus) vi, 652b
Mashhad Rabba (Ṭāʾif) vi, 655b
Mashhad Ṣāliḥ (ʿAkkā) vi, 652b
Mashhad Shāh-i (Ghardjistān) (1175) vi, 691b
Mashhad Shuʿayb vi, 652b
al-Mashhadān → Karbalāʾ
Mashhadī, Mīr Sayyid Aḥmad (XVI) vii, 442a
Mashhad-i Miṣriyān (XI) ii, 253b; vi, 716b
Mashad-i Murghāb vi, 383b
Mashhūr vi, 717a
Mashīʾa i, 414b
Mashkēl (valley, Balūčistān) vi, 192b
Mashrabiyya (turned wood) v, 1153a; vi, 717b
Mashriḳ v, 1159a; vi, 720a
Mashriḳ al-Adhkār i, 918a; vi, 720a
al-Mashriḳī, ʿInāyat Allāh iv, 916b
Mashrūʿ ii, 390a
Mashrūbāt vi, 720b
Mashrūṭiyya → Dustūr
Mashshāʾiyya (Peripatetic School) s, **605b**
Mashṭūr i, 671a
al-Maʿshūḳ (Takrīt) vii, 414a
Mashʾūm ii, 759a
Mashwara (Mashūra) ii, 641b; vi, 724a
Mashyakha (Mashīkha) vi, 725b
al-Masīḥ (Messiah) iv, 82b; vi, 726a
Masīḥ b. Ḥakam iv, 329a
Masīḥ al-Dimashḳī s, 314a
al-Masīḥī al-Djurdjānī, ʿIsā b. Yaḥyā (1010) vi, 726b
Masik → al-Ḥārith Djabal
Māsikha iv, 796b
al-Masīla, wādī i, 538b; s, 337a
Masīla (Mʿsila) (Zāb) iv, 479a, b; vi, 187a, 435a, 727a; s, 62b
Masīna (Fulbe) i, 303a, b; ii, 941b; iii, 39b; vi, 259b, 281b
Maʾṣir vi, 728b
Maṣīra i, 535b; vi, 729a
Masjumi vi, 730a
Maṣḳala b. Hubayra v, 19b
Maskana vi, 733a
Masḳaṭ i, 536a, 539a, 554b, 942b, 1071b, 1098b, 1282b, 1283a, 1314a; iv, 500b; v,

183b; vi, 38a, 729b, 734a; s, 332b, 355b, 356a
Maskh ii, 95b; iii, 305b, 306a; v, 131a; vi, 736b
Maskin ii, 197a; vii, 359b
Maṣlaḥa i, 276a, 276b; ii, 254b; iii, 954a; iv, 257a, b, 258a; vi, 738b
Maslama, Banū → Afṭasids
Maslama b. ʿAbd al-Malik b. Marwān (Umayyad) (738) i, 12b, 449b, 835b, 837a, 996a, 1033b, 1094b, 1102b, 1187a; ii, 85b, 234a, 236b, 237a; iii, 493b, 1255a; iv, 343b, 344a, 843a, 870b, 938b, 973b, 1173b; v, 533a; vi, 363a, 623a, b, 740a; vii, 359a, 408b; viii, 6b; s, 31b
Maslama b. Makhlad al-Anṣārī (VII) x, 790a
Maslama b. Mukhallad (Mukhlid) b. al-Ṣāmit (682) ii, 327b; vi, 660b, 661b, 663a, 664b, 676b, 677a, 740b; vii, 266b
Maslama al-Madjrīṭī → al-Masjrīṭī
Maṣmūda, Banū i, 1176a, 1177b, 1178b, 1350a; ii, 623a; iii, 69b, 207a, 959a; iv, 730a; vi, 590b, 592a, 593b, 741a, 802a
al-Maṣmūdī (Shāʿir) (XVII) vi, 249a
al-Maṣmūdī, Yaḥyā b. Yaḥyā (848) vi, 264a, b
Maṣmughān (Damāwand) v, 661b; vi, 335a, 744a
Maṣmughān b. Wandā-Ummīd (864) vi, 745b
Masnad-i ʿAlī → Daryā Khān Noḥānī
al-Masnāwī, Abū ʿAbd Allāh (1724) s, 223b, 403b, 404a
Mason Bey (XIX) vi, 643a
Maṣr al-ʿAtīḳa ii, 958a
Maṣraf Defteri vi, 745b
Masraḥ (theatre) iv, 73b; vi, 746a
Masraḥī v, 516b
Masraḥiyya iv, 73b
Masrūḳ vii, 258b
Masrūḳ b. Abraha s, 115b
Masruḳān i, 711b; iv, 674a
Masrūr (eunuch) (IX) ii, 1079b; vi, 752b
Masrūr b. al-Walīd i, 1244a; iii, 990b
Māssa, Banū vi, 773b
Massāḥ iv, 1041b
al-Massāḥ, Aḥmad al-Faḍl vii, 196b
Massalajem (Madagascar) vi, 774a
Maṣṣālī Ḥādjdj iv, 362b
Massar i, 1166b; iv, 275a
Massassi → Bambara
Massenya i, 910a, b
al-Māssī → Ibn Hūd
al-Maṣṣīṣa (Mopsuestia) i, 42b; ii, 35b; vi, 338a, 505b, 506a, 650a, 774a; vii, 777a; viii, 874a
Massūfa i, 389b
Massūfa, Banū vii, 584b
al-Massūfī → Barrāz
al-Massūfī, Muḥammad b. ʿAbd b. Yanūmar (XIV) vii, 625a
al-Massūfī, Yaḥyā b. Ghāniya (1148) vii, 586a
Mast ʿAlī Shāh (Niʿmat-Allāhī) (XIX) viii, 46b
Masṭawa, Banū vi, 743a
Mastūdj vi, 779b
Masʿūd, Badr al-Dīn Khurshīdī v, 828b
Masʿūd, Sayyid Salār Ghāzī → Ghāzī Mīyān, Sālār Masʿūd
Masʿūd, Sīdī (Marrākush) vi, 501b
Masʿūd I b. Maḥmūd b. Sebüktigin (Ghaznawid) (1040) i, 147a, 217b, 278a, 424b, 459a, 1005b, 1130b, 1236b, 1344b, 1356a; ii, 4b, 1049a, 1051a, 1053a, 1083a, 1100a; iii, 167b, 195b, 255b, 345a, 482b, 1201b; iv, 25a, 100b, 1067a; v, 624a; vi, 65b, 66a, 193a, 453a, 521b, 522a, b, 523a, 524a, 714b, 780a; vii, 19a, 257a, 477b; viii, 69b; s, 195a, 235a, 245b
Masʿūd II (Ghaznawid) (1049) ii, 1051b
Masʿūd III ʿAlāʾ al-Dawla (Ghaznawid) (1115) ii, 1052a, 1100a; vi, 783a; vii, 535a, 783a; s, 21a, b
Masʿūd I b. Muḥammad b. Malik-Shāh (Rūm Saldjūḳ) (1152) i, 181b, 182b, 300a, 466b, 522b, 684a, 731b; ii, 37b, 110b, 1083a; iii, 20a, 196b, 345a, 1110b, 1255b; v, 253b; vi, 64a, 275b, 500a, 506b, 507a, 782a, 870b; vii, 406b, 543b, 733b, 734b; viii, 439a, 943b, 974b
Masʿūd II (Rūm Saldjūḳ) (1305) i, 703a; iv, 620b, 621a, 817b; vi, 231a
Masʿūd I (Zangid) iii, 1119a
Masʿūd II b. Arslān Shāh ʿIzz al-Dīn (Zangid) (1218) viii, 127b
Masʿūd b. ʿAmr al-Atakī (683) i, 304a, 810a; vii, 114b, 877b
Masʿūd b. Ibrāhīm → Masʿūd III (Ghaznawid)

Masʿūd b. ʿIzz al-Dīn Kay-Kāwūs II (Rum Saldjūḳ) (XIII) vi, 420b
Masʿūd b. al-Kāmil (Ayyūbid) (XIII) vi, 149b, 433b
Masʿūd b. Mawdūd → Masʿūd II (Ghaznawid)
Masʿūd b. Mawdūd b. Zangi (Zangid), al-Mawṣil) (1193) vi, 780b
Masʿūd b. Menteshe Beg (1319) vi, 1018b
Masʿūd b. Saʿd b. Salmān → Masʿūd-i Saʿd-i Salmān
Masʿūd Bak ii, 55a, 1115a; iii, 429b
Masʿūd Beg b. Maḥmūd Yalawač (1289) i, 1240b, 1312a; ii, 2b, 3a, 791b; iv, 808b; v, 38b, 858a; vi, 77a, b, 782b
Masʿūd Bilālī iii, 197a
Masʿūd Khān b. Muḥammad Shāh Ghūrī (XV) vi, 52b, 309b
Masʿūd al-Khurāsānī vi, 524a
Masʿūd Mīrzā Ẓill al-Sulṭān (XIX) vi, 291b
Masʿūd Rukn al-Dīn Mawdūd (Artuḳid) (1232) iv, 521a
Masʿūd Shāh, ʿAlāʾ al-Dīn ii, 267b
Masʿūd-Shāh Īndjū iii, 1208a, b; iv, 498b
Masʿūd al-Surunbākī (Muwallad) (X) xi, 225b
Masʿūd al-Ṭāhirī al-Djūṭī s, 404a
Masʿūd Yalavač → Masʿud Beg b. Maḥmūd Yalavač
Masʿūd I (Zangid) → ʿIzz al-Dīn
Masʿūd b. Muṣṭafā Barzānī (XX) vii, 715a
Masʿūd b. al-Nāṣir (XVI) vii, 37b
al-Masʿūdī, Abu ʾl-Ḥasan ʿAlī b. al-Ḥusayn (956) ii, 361a, 591b, 837a, 851b; ii, 579b, 580b, 583b, 865a; iii,166a, 405b, 739b, 1206b; iv, 345b; v, 950a, 1012a; vi, 107b, 195b, 640a, 784a, 905a; vii, 187b, 245b; s, 42b, 56a, 295a
Masʿūd-i Rāzī (1039) vii, 19a
Masʿūd-i Saʿd-i Salmān (1121) i, 252b; iii, 456b; iv, 61b; vi, 608a, b, 762a, 783a; vii, 535a, 754b; s, 333a, b, 334a
Masʿūdiyya Madrasa vi, 782b
Maʿṣūm (title) ii, 86b, 88a
Maʿṣūm, Khwādja Muḥammad Murād (XVIII) vii, 936b, 938a
Maʿṣūm Khān (Mangit) → Murād b. Dāniyāl Biy Ataliḳ
Maʿṣūm ʿAlī Shāh Dakkanī (Niʿmat Allāhī) (1797) i, 283b; iv, 51a; viii, 46a,b; s, 23b
Maʿṣūm Beg Ṣafawī iv, 188a
Maʿṣūm Nāmī → Mīr Muḥammad Maʿṣūm, Nāmī
al-Maʿṣūmī, Abū Saʿīd (XI) vi, 638a
Maʿṣūm-i pāk i, 1162a
Māsūniyya → Farāmūsh-Khāna; Farmāsūniyya
Masūsa (tribe) v, 695b
Maṣyād iv, 200a; vi, 577b, 789a; vii, 578b
Maṣyāf → Maṣyād
Maṭābikh Kisrā i, 685b
Maṭāf iv, 318a
al-Maṭāliʿ (ascensions) vi, 792b
al-Maṭāmīr → Maṭmūra
al-Matamma v, 1251a; vi, 794b
Matan s, 150b
Maṭar, Ilyās Dīb (1910) s, **606a**
Maṭar (Mawālī) s, 17b
Mataram (Java) iii, 1219b, 1221b; v, 1155a, b; ix, 852b, 892a; s, 150b, 199b, 201a, 202a, **606b**
Maṭariyya vi, 631b
Maṭbaʿa (printing) i, 282a, 289b, 640b, 641a, 906b, 907b, 1071a, 1299b; ii, 464b, 472b, 533a, 589b, 682b; iii, 136, 993b, 997b; iv, 70a-b, 143a, 310a, 311a, 607b; v, 190a, 641b, 1254b; vi, 794b; s, **608a**
al-Maṭbaʿa al-Kāstiliyya s, 408a
Maṭbaʿa al-Madīna al-Munawwara s, 18a
Maṭbaʿa-i ʿĀmire v, 313b
Maṭbakh vi, 807a; s **608b**
Matdjar al-Sulṭānī iv, 136a, b
Mātem gedjeleri i, 1162a
Maṭghara, Banū vi, 310b, 815a, 923a
Mathal ii, 102a; iii, 369b; iv, 248b; v, 424b; vi, 815b
Mathālib i, 892a; vi, 349b, 828a
al-Mathāmina i, 195a; vi, 829b
Mathānī → al-Ḳurʾān
Mathnawī (in Arabic) → Muzdawidj
Mathnawī (in Persian, Turkish, Urdu) i, 677a; ii, 395a, 396a; iv, 58a, b, 62a-63a, 66b-67a; v, 201b, 650b, 1106a; vi, 832a; s, 324a
Mathurā iv, 177b; vi, 343a, 369b, 602a, 839a
al-Maṭlaʿ vi, 839a
Maṭmāṭa, Banū vi, 251a, 310b, 840a, 1009a
Maṭmūra vi, 338a, 842a

Matn vi, 843a
Matn (Durūz district) vi, 343b, 344a
Maṭraḥ vi, 734b, 735b, 843a
Maṭraḳčï, Naṣūḥ al-Silāḥī (1564) vi, 843b
Maṭrān, Khalīl → Muṭrān
Matruh iv, 529a
Matrūk → Marʾa (Turkey)
Mattā b. Yūnus (Yūnān) al Ḳunnāʾī Abū Bishr (940) i, 151b, 631b, 737a, 982b; ii, 779a; iii, 112a, 368a; iv, 252b; vi, 204a, 443b, 444a, 844b; vii, 1031a; viii, 614b
Matthias Corvinus (1490) vii, 219a
Matun (Khōst) vi, 86b
al-Māturīdī, Abū Manṣūr (944) i, 124a, 589b; iii, 1145a; iv, 272a; vi, 846a; s, 90b
Māturīdiyya i, 334a, b, 343a, 410b, 411a, b, 413b, 696a; ii, 834a; iii, 330a, 465b; iv, 183b, 365b; vi, 847a
Maulavi, E.K. (XX) vi, 462b
Maulavi, Khatib Muhammad (1964) vi, 462a
Maulavi Abussabah Ahmedali (Mappila) (1971) vi, 461a
Maumoon Abdul Gayoom (Maldives) (XX) vi, 246a
Maʿūna vi, 848b
Mauritania → Mūrītāniya (al-Yadālī)
Mauritius vi, 848b
Mawākib vi, 849b; s, **612b**
Mawāl, mawāliya i, 404a; iii, 289b
Mawālī → Mawlā
Mawāliyā vi, 867b
al-Māwardī, Abu 'l-Ḥasan ʿAlī (1058) i, 119a, 328b, 435b, 439b, 982b, 1356a; ii, 116a, 131a; iii, 159b, 486a, 766a, 1165a, 1237a; iv, 173a, 457b, 458b, 949b; vi, 11a, 496a, 820a, 869a; vii, 296b, 506b; viii, 95a; x, 918a; s, 192a, 525a
Mawāt iii, 1053b; iv, 1036a; vi, 869b
Mawāzīn vi, 117a
Mawḍūʿ iii, 26b
Mawdūd b. Altuntakin (amīr, Mosul) (1113) i, 1332b; ii, 282a; vii, 983b
Mawdūd b. ʿImād al-Dīn Zankī, Ḳuṭb al-Dīn (Zangid, Mosul) (1170) i, 1160b; ii, 489b; iii, 961a; vi, 870a; vii, 406b; viii, 127b
Mawdūd b. Masʿūd b. Maḥmūd (Ghaznawid) (1048) i, 278a; ii, 5a, 1051b; iv, 815a; vi, 780b, 871b; vii, 407a
Mawdūdī → Abu 'l-ʿAlāʾ Mawdūdī
Mawdūdī (Mawdoodi), Sayyid Abu 'l-ʿAlāʾ (1979) vi, 872a; viii, 242b; xi, 518a
Māwiya vi, 474b
Mawḳif vi, 874a; s, **613a**
Mawlā i, 30b, 569a, b, 890b; ii, 324a, 951a; iii, 388b, 412a, 719a, 1152b; iv, 44a-b, v, 925b, vi, 874a
Mawlā ʿAlī b. Muḥammad b. Falāḥ (XV) vii, 672a
Mawlā (Mūl) 'l-Ḳṣūr → al-Ghazwānī, Sīdī ʿAbd Allāh
Mawkā Ṣandalī → Muḥammad bū Ḥurmuz
Mawlāʾīs iv, 202b
Mawlānā v, 627a
Mawlānā ʿAbd Allāh → Makhdūm al-Mulk
Mawlānā ʿAlī Aḥmad (Delhi) vii, 473b
Mawlānā Darwīsh Muḥammad (XVI) vii, 337b
Mawlānā Dūst (Kābul) (XVI) vii, 337b, 473b
Mawlānā Ḥasan Kawkabī (XVI) vii, 676b
Mawlānā Ibrāhīm (Delhi) vii, 473b
Mawlānā Khālid Baghdādī al-Kurdī (1867) v, 475a, 486a; x, 250b
Mawlānā Khūnkār vi, 882b
Mawlānā Maḳṣūd (Herat) vii, 473b
Mawlānā Muḥammad ʿAlī (1951) i, 302b; v, 7a, b
Mawlānā Rūmī → Djalal al-Dīn Rūmī
Mawlānā Yūsuf (painter) (XVI) vii, 337b
Mawlawī → Djalāl al-Dīn Rūmī
Mawlawī, Mullā ʿAbd al-Raḥīm Taydjawzī (1883) vi, 883a
Mawlawiyya i, 234a, 1161b; ii, 164b, 224a, 226b, 393b; iv, 48a, 65b, 190b; vi, 354b, 530b, 883a; ix, 858a; x, 251b s, 83b, 283a
Mawlāy (ʿAlawī/Saʿdī title) v, 627a; vi, 888b
Mawlāy → ʿAlawids: al-Rashīd b. al-Sharīf; ʿAbd Allāh b. Ismāʿīl; Muḥammad III b. ʿAbd Allāh; Sulaymān, Abū 'l-Rabīʿ b. Muḥammad; ʿAbd al-Raḥmān b. Hishām; Muḥammad IV b. ʿAbd al-Raḥmān; ʿAbd al-ʿAzīz b. al-Ḥasan; ʿAbd al-Ḥāfiẓ (al-Ḥāfiẓ); Yūsuf b. al-Ḥasan; Muḥammad V b. Yūsuf; Saʿdids: ʿAbd Allāh al-Ghālib bi-'llāh; Aḥmad al-Manṣūr al-Dhahabī
Mawlāy ʿAbd Allāh b. Ibrāhīm (Idrīsid Sharīf) (1678) xi, 201b

Mawlāy ʿAbd Allāh b. Muḥammad b. Yūsuf (ʿAlawid) (XX) vii, 415b
Mawlāy Bū ʿAlī (Marrākush) (XV) vi, 594a
Mawlāy al-Ḥarrānī (Tāfilālt) (1672) vi, 891b
Mawlāy al-Ḥasan → al-Ḥasan I, Mawlāy
Mawlāy Ḥasan b. Muḥammad V b. Yūsuf (ʿAlawid) (XX) vii, 415b
Mawlāy Ḥasan b. Yūsuf (ʿAlawid) (XX) vii, 415a
Mawlāy Idrīs (Fès) vi, 124b
Mawlāy Idrīs b. Yūsuf (ʿAlawid) (XX) vii, 415a
Mawlāy Idrīs, Zāwiyat (town) v, 1188b; vi, 889a
Mawlāy Ismāʿīl b. al-Sharīf (ʿAlawid) (1727) i, 34b, 47a, 159b, 289a, 365a; ii, 17b, 173a, 367b, 510a, 819b, 823a, 1022a; iii, 231a, 499b, 1047a; iv, 214a; v, 49a, 53b, 1191b, 1245b; vi, 135a, 142b, 250a, 293b, 591a, 595a, 596b, 891b; vii, 37b; s, 40a, 113b, 114a, 125b, 126a, 132a, 223b, 399b
Mawlāy Maḥammad al-Shaykh I, Abū ʿAbd Allāh al-Mahdī (al-Imām) (Saʿdid) (1557) vi, 893
Mawlāy Maḥammad al-Shaykh II, al-Maʾmūn (Saʿdid) (1613) vi, 894b
Mawlāy Maḥammad al-Shaykh III b. Mawlāy Zaydān al-Ṣaghīr (Saʿdid) (1655) vi, 894b
Mawlāy al-Saḳlī (XVI) ix, 758a
Mawlāy Yūsuf b. al-Ḥasan (ʿAlawid) (1926) i, 357b; ii, 160a; iv, 634b; vii, 415a; s, 48a
Mawlāy Zīdān (Saʿdī) (1628) ix, 545b
Mawlid 3. in the Maghrib s, **613a**
Mawlid/Mawlūd i, 281a, 1004a, 1161a; v, 1200b; vi, 895a
Mawlid al-Nabī (Mecca) vi, 168a
Mawlid Sayyidatnā Fāṭima (Mecca) vi, 168a, 650b
Mawlidiyya (Mawli(ū)diyyāt i, 58b; vi, 248a, 897b
Mawrūr (Morón) i, 6a; vi, 898b
al-Mawrūrī → Djūdī
Mawsidsh (Mawshid) vii, 513b
al-Mawṣil i, 731b, 732a, 866b, 907a, 975b, 1074a; ii, 90b, 348a, 385a; iii, 127a, 218a, 1256b, 1258a, 1267b; iv, 584b; v, 145b, 437a, 451a, b, 454a, 463b, 821a; vi, 55b, 56b, 69a, 75a, 198a, 243b, 270b, 378b, 379b, 380a, b, 387a, 471a, 500a, 502b, 539b, 541a, 624a, 626a, 648a, 652a, 667a, 733b, 780b, 870a, 899a; viii, 131b; xi, 451a, 454a; s, 36a, b, 37a, 49b, 100a, 192b, 379b
al-Mawṣilī, ʿAbd Allāh b. Muṣṭafā al-Fayḍī (XIX) vi, 113b
al-Mawṣilī, Bakr b. al-Ḳāsim b. Abī Thawr (X) vi, 902b
al-Mawṣilī, Ibn Abī Saʿīd vi, 902b
al-Mawṣilī, al-Muʿāfā b. ʿImrān (800) x, 8b
al-Mawṣilī, Muḥammad b. Yaḥyā b. Abī Manṣūr (IX) vi, 215a
al-Mawṣilī, Murr b. ʿAlī viii, 53a
al-Mawṣilī, Tādj al-Dīn b. Muḥammad (1361) vii, 257b
al-Mawṣilī, Ubayy b. Kaʿb vii, 494a
al-Mawṣilī, ʿUthmān b. ʿAlī al-ʿUmarī (1770) vi, 112b, 114a
Mawsim vi, 233a, 903a; s, 53a
Mawsūʿa vi, 903b
Mawsūʿa 3. in Turkish s, **614a**
Mawsūʿa 5. in Urdu s, **616a**
Mawt vi, 910b
al-Mawwāḳ vi, 279a
Mawwāl → Mawāliyā
al-Mawzaʿī, Shams al-Dīn ʿAbd al-Ṣamad (1621) vi, 911b
Mawzūna → Sikka
Maybūʿ ix, 673a → IX, 700b
Maybud vi, 912a
al-Maybudī, Khaṭīr al-Mulk (vizier) (1119) i, 1052b; vi, 912a
al-Maybudī, Mīr Ḥusayn al-Manṭiḳī (XVI) vi, 912a
al-Maybudī, Rashīd al-Dīn (XII) vi, 912a
Maydān ii, 954b; vi, **912b**
Maydān-i Mashḳ vi, 529a
al-Maydānī, Abū ʾl-Faḍl Aḥmad al-Naysābūrī (1124) i, 794a; ii, 590b; iii, 992a; iv, 525b; vi, 478a, 823b, 913a
al-Maydānī, Shaykh ʿAbd al-Ghānī (1881) viii, 908a
al-Maydī v, 808b
Mayfaʿ i, 538a; s, 337a
Mayhana, Mīhana i, 147a; vi, 914b
al-Mayhanī (XII) iii, 1243a
Mayhanī, Muḥammad b. ʿAbd al-Khāliḳ (XI) vii, 679b
al-Mayhanī, Shaykh Abū Saʿīd s, 154a

al-Mayl vi, 914b
Maylāʾ vi, 442a
Maylī (Harāt) (1576) viii, 775b
Maymad s, 116a
Maymana ii, 608b, 609a; vi, 915a; ix, 431a
Maymandī, Abu 'l-Ḳāsim Aḥmad b. Ḥasan (Shams al-Kufāt) (1032) i, 278a; iii, 255b, 345a; vi, 453a, 522a, 915b; vii, 653a, 679a
Maymandī, Manṣūr b. Saʿīd s, 21a
al-Maymandī i, 278a; iii, 255b, 345a
al-Maymanī al-Rādj(a)kūtī, ʿAbd al-ʿAzīz (1978) vi, 916a
Maymūn iii, 574b; v, 132b
Maymūn b. Aḥmad ii, 1082b; iv, 347a
Maymūn b. ʿAmr (928) ix, 586b
Maymūn b. al-Aswad al-Ḳaddāḥ (765) i, 48a; ii, 851b; v, 1242b; vi, 917b
Maymūn b. Djaddār (Yiddar) (1155) ii, 1013b; vii, 591a
Maymūn b. Mihrān, Abū Ayyūb (735) vi, 878a, 916b
Maymūn b. Yiddar → Maymūn b. Djaddār
Maymūna (Malta) iii, 362b; vi, 295b; s, 311a
Maymūna bint al-Ḥārith (681) vi, 918a; vii, 372b
Maymūn-Diz i, 1359b; iii, 501b; vi, 917b
al-Maymūnī, Abu 'l-Malīḥ (VIII) vi, 917a
al-Maymūnī, ʿAmr b. Maymūn b. Mihrān (VIII) vi, 917a
al-Maymūnī, Djaʿfar b. Burḳān (VIII) vi, 917a
Maymūniyya i, 48a
Mayo ii, 464a
Maysalūn (battle, 1920) vi, 918a; viii, 141a
Maysān vi, 918b
Maysara al-ʿAbdī i, 1292b
Maysara al-Maṭgharī (740) i, 1175a; v, 1189a; vi, 815a, 923a; viii, 638a; ix, 767b
al-Maysī, Luṭf Allāh (1622) viii, 779a
al-Maysir i, 1111b; iv, 263b; v, 108b; vi, 923b; s, 394b
Maysūn bint Baḥdal b. Unayf al-Kalbiyya (680) i, 920a; vi, 924b; vii, 267b; x, 867b
Maysūr (936) i, 163b; iii, 1036b; iv, 459a, b
Maysūr (Mysore) → Mahisur
Mayta ii, 1069a; vi, 924b
al-Maʿyūf, Banū vi, 303a
Mayūrḳa i, 490a, 1055a; ii, 111b, 1007a; iii, 704b; iv, 1157a; vi, 457a, 926a, 989a; s, 120b, 307a
al-Mayūrḳī → al-Ḥumaydī, Abū ʿAbd Allāh
al-Mayūrḳī, Abū Bakr Muḥammad (1142) iii, 712b, 732a
al-Mayūrḳī, Abu 'l-Ḥasan ʿAlī (1082) vi, 927a
Maywātīs iii, 433b
Mayy Ziyāda (Mārī Ilyās Ziyāda) (1941) vi, 927a
Mayyāfāriḳīn i, 665a, 679b; ii, 344b; iii, 129b, 900a; iv, 521a; vi, 119b, 270b, 540a, 626a, b, 928a, 1017a; s, 36b, 37a
Mayyāra, Abū ʿAbd Allāh Maḥammad al-Akbar (1662) vi, 406b, 932b; s, 404a
Mayyūn i, 535b, 539a, 837b; vi, 933a
Maʿz → Ghanam
Māza, Banū iii, 163a
Mazagan → al-Djadīda
Mazagran vi, 248b
Mazāḳī v, 261a
Maẓālim i, 209a, 387b; ii, 145b, 519b; vi, 933b
Māzandarān i, 8a, b, 147b, 148a, 237a; ii, 903b; iv, 808a; v, 663a, b, 664a; vi, 202b, 415b, 510b, 511b, 512a, b, 513a, b, 514a, b, 515a, b, 516a, 632b, 726b, 935b; viii, 650b; s, 239b
al-Māzandarānī, ʿAbd Allāh b. Muḥammad b. Kiyā (1363) ii, 81a
Māzandarānī, Mullā Muḥammad Ṣūfī (XI) i, 840b
Māzandarānī, Saʿīd al-ʿUlamāʾ (XIX) vi, 552a; s, 95b
Mazandjān v, 456b
Mazang ii, 41a
Māzar → Ṣiḳiliyya
Mazār → Maḳbara; Ziyāra
Mazār-čub vi, 936a
al-Māzarī, Abū ʿAbd Allāh (al-Imām) (1141) vi, 942b; vii, 228a
al-Māzarī, Abū ʿAbd Allāh Muḥammad al-Iskandarānī (1135) vi, 943a
al-Māzarī, Abū ʿAbd Allāh (al-Zakī) (1118) vi, 943a; ix, 587a
Mazarʾi, Āl v, 223b; s, 355b
Mazār-i Sharīf i, 530b, 1001b; vi, 765a, 942a; s, 94a, 281a

Mazāta, Banū vi, 310b, 311a, 943b
al-Mazātī, Abu 'l-Rabīʿ Sulaymān b. Yakhlaf (1078) vi, 946b, 948a
al-Mazātī, Dūnās b. al-Khayr (XII) vi, 946b
Mazdaeans iv, 11a-12b, 43a; vi, 337a, 949a
Mazdak (Mazdaḳ) (531) i, 2b; v, 63b; vi, 949a
Mazdakites i, 844a; ii, 228a; v, 63b, 64a, 853a; x, 440a
Mazdalī b. Sulankān i, 986a; ii, 1013a
Maẓhar (theophany) vi, 952a
Maẓhar, Ismāʿīl iv, 125a
Maẓhar, Maryam (XX) vii, 903a
Maẓhar, Mīrzā Djāndjānān (1781) iii, 430b; iv, 507a; vi, 953a; vii, 327b, 533a, 938b
Maẓhar al-Dīn Ibn Nishāṭī (XVII) vi, 837b
al-Mazimma s, 377b
Māzin, Banū vi, 953b
al-Māzīnī, Abū ʿUthmān Bakr b. Muḥammad (863) iv, 122b, 822a; vi, 954a, 954b; vii, 279b, 281a
al-Māzinī, Ibrāhīm ʿAbd al-Ḳādir (1949) i, 597b; v, 189a, b; vi, 91a, 414b, 415a, 955b; vii, 441a
al-Māzinī, Muḥammad b. ʿAbd Allāh vii, 538a
al-Māziyār → Ḳārinds
Maẓlūm vi, 958b
Mazouna → Māzūna
Mazraa → Mezere
Mazraʿa vi, 959a
Mazrūʿī, Banū iv, 887a, b, 889b; vi, 961b; vii, 227a
al-Mazrūʿī, Shaykh al-Amīn b. ʿAlī (1947) iv, 890b; vi, 962b; x, 195b; s, 248a
Māzūn ix, 775a
Māzūna (Dahra) vi, 404a, b; vii, 263a
Mazyad, Banū (Mazyadids) i, 300b, 512a, 684a, 1052b, 1086a, 1096a; iv, 27b; vi, 64a, 270b, 380a, 500a, 965a; vii, 726b; viii, 71b, 716a; s, 119a, 326a
Māzyār b. Ḳārin b. Wandā(d)hurmuz (Ḳārinid) (841) i, 52b, 241a; iv, 20b, 207b, 645b, 646a, b; v, 64b; vi, 337b, 338b, 745a, b; vii, 776a; x, 17b; s, 309a
Mazyata s, 103a
Mbacké, Āl → Amadu Bamba; Falilu; Mamadu Mustafa
Mbārak b. Gharīb (1696) vi, 962a
Mbārak al-Mazrūʿī iv, 889b
Mboamaji (Tanzania) vi, 370a
Mbweni vi, 966b
Meʾālī (1535) vi, 610a, 967a
Mecca xi, 42a
Mecelle → Medjelle
Mech(h)ed → Mashhad
Mechitar i, 640b
Meclis → Madjlis
Mecque, La → Makka
Mēd vi, 385a, 967a
Medan vi, 239a
Meddāḥ → Maddāḥ
Medea → al-Madiyya
Medeniyyet vi, 968a
Medḥī, Dervīsh Ḥasan (XVII) vi, 969b
Medḥī, Maḥmūd Efendi, Ḳara Maḥmūd (Gelibolu) (1597) vi, 969a
Medḥī, Nūḥ-zāde Seyyid Muṣṭafā Čelebi (1680) vi, 969a
Medīḥī, Meḥmed (Istanbul) (1672) vi, 969b
Medīḥī, Muṣṭafā Čelebi (Sīrōz) (XVI) vi, 696b
Medina (Saudi Arabia) → al-Madīna
Medina (Maghrib) v, 347b, 348a, 1108a; vi, 969b
Medina Sidonia → Shadūna
Medinaceli → Madīnat Sālim
Mēdinī Rāʾī (Rādjpūt) (1527) ii, 13a, 1128a; iii, 421b; vi, 970a
Mediouna s, 144b, 145a
Mediterranean Sea → Baḥr al-Rūm
Medjdī, Meḥmed Čelebi (1591) vi, 970b
Medjelle i, 285a; iii, 164a, 250a, 661a; iv, 168b; vi, 971a
Medjerda (river) vi, 727b
Medjīdiyye → Sikka
Medjīdiyye (Medgidia) ii, 28b, 119b; vi, 972b
Medjlis → Madjlis
Medjlis-i Wālā vi, 972b
Medrese → Madrasa
Meerut → Mīrath
Mefkhari → ʿAṭāʾ Bey, Meḥmed
Meguiden s, 328a
Méhari vi, 83b

Meharza s, 328a
Mehedak → al-Mahdiyya
Meḥemmed (turkish form of "Muḥammad") vi, 973b
Meḥemmed I Čelebī b. Bāyazīd I (Ottoman) (1421) i, 299b, 394a, 432a, 468a, 510b, 869b, 988a; ii, 98a, b, 239b, 599a, 611b, 684a, 984b, 990a; iii, 356b, 711b; iv, 623b; vi, 531a, 973b; viii, 193b
Meḥemmed II Fātiḥ (Ottoman) (1481)) i, 312b, 468a, 739a, 767b, 777a, 992b, 999a, 1007b, 1061a, 1062a, 1119a, 1163b, 1253a, 1334b; ii, 239b, 291b, 374a, 529a, 612a, 684a, 691a, 839b, 982b, 1140b; iii, 190b, 213a; iv, 140a, 224b, 225a, 576a, 624a, 969a; vi, 70a, 71a, 291a, 507b, 530a, b, 588a, 724b, 800a, 913b, 978a; vii, 465b, 550b, 739b; viii, 194a; x, 965b; s, 257a, 283a, 315b
– administration i, 310b, 470a, 640b, 655b, 1256a, 1265b; ii, 82b, 118b, 211b, 337b, 338a, 687a, 715a, 907a, 1086b; iii, 1181a, 1183a; iv, 225a, 238a, 376a, 560a, 563a, 564b, 900a; v, 850a, 882a
– constructions i, 481a, 775b, 836b, 1078a, 1225b, 1251b; ii, 11b, 684b; iv, 225a, b, 226a, 228a-230b
Meḥemmed III (Ottoman) (1603) i, 310a, 380b, 956a; ii, 34a, 690a, 880b; iii, 1185a; iv, 900b; v, 19a, 27b; vi, 202a, 981a
Meḥemmed IV Awdjî (Ottoman) (1687) i, 1278b; ii, 345b, 684a, b; iii, 983b, 1185a; iv, 590a, b; v, 260a, b, 261b, 272b, 720b; vi, 56b, 295b, 345b, 982a; vii, 89a; x, 679a; s, 257b
Meḥemmed V Reshād (Ottoman) (1918) i, 64a; vi, 166a, 983a; vii, 525b; viii, 59b
Meḥemmed VI Waḥīd al-Dīn (Ottoman) (1926) i, 734a; ii, 104b; iv, 873a, b, 946b; vi, 530b, 531b, 984a
Mehkeme → Maḥkama
Meḥmed, Mehmet → Meḥemmed
Meḥmed II (Ḳaramānid) (1413) vi, 975b
Meḥmed b. ʿAlāʾ al-Dawla Bozḳurd (Dhu 'l-Ḳadr) (1515) vi, 509b
Meḥmed b. ʿAlī al-Fenārī iv, 244b
Meḥmed Agha (XV) vi, 69b, 70a
Meḥmed Agha (Ḳule Aghasî) (XIX) s, 281b
Meḥmed ʿĀkif (1936) vi, 985a
Meḥmed ʿAlī Pasha → Muḥammad ʿAlī Pasha
Meḥmed ʿĀshîḳ → ʿĀshîḳ
Meḥmed ʿAṭāʾ (1919) s, 96a
Meḥmed Baghčesarāyī (1651) vi, 986b
Meḥmed Balṭadjî → Meḥmed Pasha Balṭadjî
Meḥmed Beg b. Ibrāhīm Beg (Menteshe) (1370) vi, 1018b
Meḥmed Beg b. Yaʿḳūb I (Germiyān-Oghullarî) (XIV) ii, 989b; ix, 418b
Meḥmed Behdjet iv, 195a
Meḥmed Bîyîklî Pasha → Meḥmed Pasha, Bîyîklî
Meḥmed Čelebi → Ghazālī, Meḥmed; Meḥemmed I
Meḥmed Čelebi Üsküdarī ii, 442b
Meḥmed Djelāl (XIX) vii, 532a
Meḥmed Edīb (XVII) vi, 778a
Meḥmed Emīn ʿAlī Pasha → ʿAlī Pasha Muḥammad Amīn
Meḥmed Emīn b. Muṣṭafā Feydī Ḥayātī-zāde (XII) iii, 30
Meḥmed Emīn Pasha (XVIII) vii, 709a
Meḥmed Emīn al-Toḳadī (1745) vii, 724b
Meḥmed Emīn Yurdakul (1944) vi, 986b; viii, 251a; s, 47b, 149b
Meḥmed Emnī Beyefendi (XVIII) vi, 56a
Meḥmed Esʿad → Esʿad Efendi; Ghālib Dede
Meḥmed Farrūkh Pasha (XVI) s, 234b
Meḥmed Girāy I (Crimea) (1523) vi, 989a
Meḥmed Girāy II (Crimea) (1584) viii, 184b
Meḥmed Girāy, Derwīsh (XVIII) vi, 989a
Meḥmed Ḥafīd (XIX) vii, 257b
Meḥmed Ḥākim Efendi (1770) ii, 26b; vi, 989b
Meḥmed Khalīfe b. Ḥüseyn (1687) vi, 990b
Meḥmed Khusrew, Defterdār (Miṣr) (XIX) vii, 425b
Meḥmed Lālā Pasha → Meḥmed Pasha, Lālā
Meḥmed Lālezārī → Lālezārī
Meḥmed Nedjātī (XVII) s, 171b
Meḥmed Pasha (wālī Erzerūm) (1647) vi, 202b
Meḥmed Pasha (Yemen) (XVII) vi, 437a; vii, 270a
Meḥmed Pasha, Aydînlî (XVI) vii, 514a

Meḥmed Pasha, Balṭadjî (1712) i, 269a, 395a, 1004b; vi, 991a; vii, 839a
Meḥmed Pasha, Bîyîḳlî (1521) ii, 345a, b; v, 248b, 457b; vi, 541b, 992b
Meḥmed Pasha, Bushatlî i, 675a; iv, 588b
Meḥmed Pasha, Čerkes (1625) i, 174b; v, 33a; vi, 993a
Meḥmed Pasha, Dalṭaban (XVIII) vii, 708a
Meḥmed Pasha, Djalīlī ii, 402a
Meḥmed Pasha, Djerrāḥ (XVI) vi, 981a
Meḥmed Pasha, Elmās (1697) vi, 993a; vii, 708a
Meḥmed Pasha, Gürdjü (I) (Khādim) (1626) vi, 994a; vii, 707b
Meḥmed Pasha, Gürdjü (II) (1666) vi, 994b
Meḥmed Pasha, ʿIwaḍ (1743) vi, 995a
Meḥmed Pasha, Ḳaramānī (1481) vi, 995b
Meḥmed Pasha, Kōra i, 920a
Meḥmed Pasha, Lālā, Melek-Nihād (II) (1595) vi, **996b**
Meḥmed Pasha, Lālā, Shāhīnoghlu (1606) i, 267b, 1284b; ii, 716b; iv, 499a; v, **640b**; vi, 996b
Meḥmed Pasha, Melek, Dāmād (1802) vi, 997b
Meḥmed Pasha, Muḥsin-zāde (1774) i, 56b, 62b; iii, 158a, 253a; vi, 998a; vii, 708b
Meḥmed Pasha, Öküz (1620) ii, 635a; iv, 970b; vi, 998b; viii, 182a
Meḥmed Pasha Rāmī (1707) i, 349b; iv, 657b; vi, 999b; ix, 60a
Meḥmed Pasha, Rūm(ī) (1478) vi, 71b, 72a, 1000a
Meḥmed Pasha Saḳîzlî (XVII) x, 214a
Meḥmed Pasha Ṣarî → Ṣarî Meḥmed Pasha
Meḥmed Pasha, Silāḥdār iv, 437b
Meḥmed Pasha Ṣoḳollī → Ṣoḳollī, Ṣoḳollu
Meḥmed Pasha, Sulṭān-zāde (1646) iii, 623a, 983a; vi, 1000b
Meḥmed Pasha, Tabanîyassî (1639) vi, 1001a
Meḥmed Pasha, Tiryāḳī (1751) i, 267b; iv, 546b, 878a; vi, 1001b; ix, 557b
Meḥmed Pasha Yegen (Gümrükčü) (1745) i, 56b, 292a; ii, 534a; iv, 544a; v, 729a; vi, 995a, 1002b
Meḥmed Pasha Yegen, Ḥādjdjī Seyyid (1787) i, 56b; ii, 534a; iv, 544a; vi, 1003a
Meḥmed Radīf Pasha i, 709b
Meḥmed Rāshid → Rāshid, Meḥmed
Meḥmed Rashīd (wālī Syria) (XIX) s, 296a
Meḥmed Raʾūf (1931) vi, 1003a
Meḥmed Reʾīs, Ibn Menemenli (XVII) vi, 1003b
Meḥmed Rüshdī Pasha (XIX) vii, 599b
Memed Ṣādîḳ iv, 284b
Meḥmed Saʿīd Ghālib Pasha (1829) iv, 295b; vi, 1003b
Meḥmed Saʿīd Pasha (XIX) vi, 69a
Meḥmed Ṣāliḥ Efendi (Ḥekimbashî) (XIX) i, 973a
Meḥmed Ṣāliḥ Efendi, Shaykh al-Islām (1762) vi, 1004a
Meḥmed Shākir Pasha (1914) s, 348b
Meḥmed Sherīf (XIX) s, 63a
Meḥmed Ṭāhir, Bursalî (1925) ii, 980b; vi, 284b; s, **616b**
Meḥmed Tewfīḳ Efendi, Khodja (XIX) s, 149b
Meḥmed Yîrmîsekiz Çelebi Efendi (1732) iii, 997b, 1002a; v, 641b, 642a; vi, 1004b; viii, 859b
Meḥmed Zaʿīm (XVI) vi, 1006b
Meḥmet ʿĀkif Ersoy iv, 169a
Mehri → Mahrī
Mehtar ii, 30b
Mehter vi, 1007a
Mehterkhāne → Mehter
Meknes → Miknās
Melāmīlik x, 252a
Melazo vi, 560a
Melek Aḥmed Pasha ii, 718a
Melek Meḥmed Pasha iv, 455b
Melek Ṭāwūs → ʿIzrāʾīl
Melilla (Malīla) i, 356b; iii, 298b; vi, 120b, 1008b; vii, 387a, 391b, 641b; s, 325b
Melilot → Iklīl al-Malik
Melitene i, 1103a, b, 1104a; ii, 110a, b, 238a; iv, 484a
Melkites → Rūm
Mellāḥ → Mallāḥ
Mellita iv, 650b, 651b
Melukhkha vi, 192b
Memdūḥ Pasha (XIX) i, 825b
Memdūḥ/Shewket Esendal → Esendal
Memek Čelebi (1600) iii, 175b
Memi Shāh → Āteshīzāde Memi
Memish Beg (XVI) ii, 1046a
Memon → al-Maymanī al-Rādj(a)kūtī

Memon (Gudjarāt) i, 172a; vi, 1009b
Memphis → Manf
Menangkabau → Minangkabau
Menderes, Adnan (1961) ii, 204a, 432b, 596a; iii, 527a; vi, 1011b
Menderes, Büyük- vi, 1010a
Menderes, Eski- vi, 1011b
Menderes, Küçük- vi, 1011a
Menekshe (Monemvasia) vi, 1013b
Menelik II (Ethiopia) (1913) viii, 161b
Menemen vi, 1015b
Menemendji-oghlu ii, 207a
Menemenli-zāde Meḥmed Ṭāhir (1902) vi, 1016a
Mêng-Kuan iv, 554b
Mengli Girāy I (Crimea) (1515) i, 293a, 843a, 893a, 1166b; ii, 1112b, 1113a; v, 137a, 138a, 719b; vi, 1016a; viii, 236a
Mengü-Bars b. Böri-Bars (Saldjūḳ) (XII) i, 1336b, 1358a; vii, 408a
Mengüček (Mangūdjak) (Mengüčekids) (Erzindjān) (XII) i, 466a, b, 467a, 639a, 983a; ii, 340a, 711b; iv, 578b, 871a; vi, 231a, 1016b
Mensūkhāt vi, 1017a
Menteshe-eli i, 467b, 988a, 1250b; ii, 204b, 599a; v, 505b, 506a; vi, 1017a
Menteshe Beg (1296) vi, 1018a
Menteshe-Oghullarî vi, 1018a; vii, 56a, 348b
Menūtum → Manāt
Mēʾō vi, 48a, 1019a; s, 124a
Merca (Somalia) vi, 129a, 170a
Mercimek Ahmet → Merdjümek
Merdjān, beglerbegi (XVI) iv, 571a
Merdjümek, Aḥmed b. Ilyās (XV) vi, 1019a
Mere Ḥuseyn Pasha (XVII) vii, 707b
Merguez → Mirkās
Mergui (Burma) vi, 1020a
Merič (river) vi, 1022a
Merida → Mārida
Merinids → Marīnids
Merka vi, 127a, 354a, 1022b
Merkez, Shaykh Muṣliḥ al-Dīn (1552) vi, 1023a
Merkez Ḳalʿesi vi, 778a
Merkit ii, 42a, 43a, 571a
Mersin i, 476b; vi, 1023b
Mersiye → Marthiya
Mertola → Mīrtula
Mertvîy Kultuk (bay) vi, 417a
Merv → Marw al-Shāhidjān
Merv-Rūd → Marw al-Rūdh
Merwārā → Rādjāsthān
Merzifūn (Mārsiwān, Merzifon) iv, 589b; v, 1147a; vi, 1023b
Mesdjid → Masdjid
Mesfīwa vi, 590b
Meshʿale vi, 1024a
Mesh(h)ed → Mashhad
Mesh(h)ed ʿAlī → al-Nadjaf
Mesh(h)ed Ḥusayn → Karbalāʾ
Meshrūṭa, Meshrūṭiyyet → Dustūr
Mesīḥ Meḥmed Pasha, Khādim (1589) vi, 1024b
Mesīḥ Pasha (1501) vi, 1025a
Mesīḥī (1512) vi, 1026a
Mesopotamia → al-Djazīra; Irāḳ
Messahallah → Māshāʾ Allāh
Meṣṣālī al-Hādjdj (Messali Hadjdj) iii, 524b; iv, 785a
Messiah → al-Masīḥ
Mesta (river) vi, 89a
Mesue → Ibn Masāwayh
Mevlānā Yūsuf Sinān Germiāni → Sheykhī Čelebi
Mēwār vi, 53a, b, 54a, 1027a
Mēwāt vi, 48a, 49b, 1028b; vii, 278b
Mēwātī → Mēʾō
Mewḳūfātčî, Mewḳūfātī vi, 1029a
Mewlānā ʿĪsā vi, 836a
Mewlānā Khūnkār → Mawlānā Khūnkār
Mewlānā Saʿd al-Dīn (ḳāḍī) (XVI) vii, 225a
Mewlewiyyet, Mollalîḳ iv, 375a; vi, 133b, 1029b
Mewlūd → Mawlid
Meydān Česhmesi vi, 57a
Mezere → Maʿmūrat al-ʿAzīz
Mezīd Beg (1400) vi, 974a
Mezistre (Mystras) s, **616b**
Mezö-Keresztes (Battle of) (1596) iv, 499a; v, 27b; vi, 1030a; s, 238b
Mezzomorto → Ḥusayn Pasha Mezzomorto
Mgīld, Bānū s, 113b, 145a
Mḥammad b. al-Khayr (Belkheīr) (XIX) vi, 252a
M'ḥammad Bey (Tunis) (1859) vii, 717b
Miʾān Bhuʾā, Masnad-i ʿAlī (XVI) vi, 1030b
Mibkhara v, 987b

Michael → Mīkāl
Michael b. Sefer Beg (Abkhāz) (1864) i, 101a
Michael of Tinnīs (XI) vii, 164a
Midād ii, 307a, 311a; vi, 1031b
Miʿdān → Maʿādī, Banū
Miʿdhana → Manār, Manāra
Midḥat, Aḥmed → Aḥmad Midḥat
Midḥat Djemāl Kuntay (1951) v, 197a
Midḥat Pasha (1884) i, 63b, 285b, 286a, 289b, 906b, 907b, 1096a, 1097a, 1304a; ii, 288b, 289a, 468b, 642a, 909a, 935b; iii, 621b, 1257b; iv, 638a, 765b, 876b; v, 904b; vi, 69a, 372b, 797a, 1031b; vii, 599b
Midianite → Madyan Shuʿayb
Midilli (Mytilene) vi, 69a, 71a, b, 1035b
Midjmar s, 23b
Miḍrab iv, 1147a
Midrār, Banū (Midrārids) i, 83a, 1175b; ii, 495a; vi, 1038a
Midyān Ḥaḍrat (Shaykh ʿAbd Allāh) (XVII) vii, 432b
Midyāt vi, 539b, 542a
Midyūna (Madyūna), Banū vi, 310b, 1042a
al-Midyūnī, ʿIsā b. Ḥamdūn (XI) vi, 1043b
Mifrash (Mafrash; Mifresh) vii, 1a
Miftāḥ v, 990a
Miftāḥ al-Ḥikma i, 995b
Miftāḥ al-Mulk → Mīrzā Maḥmūd b. Yūsuf
Miftāḥ al-ʿUlūm i, 594a, 858a, 982a
Mihdī Bāzargān vi, 549a
Mihir Bhodja Pratīhāra ii, 1122b, 1123a
Mihmān s, **618a**
Mihmindār iv, 1043a; vii, 2a
Miḥna i, 811a; ii, 931a; iii, 1148a; v, 426a, 1124a; vi, 338a; vii, 2b
Mihnī, Banū (Kirmān) v, 153b
Mihr → Taʾrīkh
Mihr Āfrūz vi, 488a
Mihr ʿAlī (painter) vii, 603a
Mihr al-Nisāʾ → Nūrdjahān
Miḥrāb vii, 7a
Miḥrāb Khān i, 1006a; v, 102a
Mihrabānids ix, 183b
Mihragān (Mihradjān) ii, 798b; vi, 523a; vii, 15a
Mihragān (Mihradjān) b. Rūzbih vii, 19b
Mihrān (Indus) i, 222a; iii, 408a; iv, 597b; v, 872b; vii, 20b
Mihrān Efendi (XIX) ii, 474b, 475a; iv, 872b
Miḥrāth vii, 21b
Mihrawlī ii, 259a, 266a
Mihrgān → Mihragān
Mihribān (river) vi, 745b
Mihrī Khātūn (1512) vii, 23b
Mihrī Māh Sulṭān bint Sulaymān II (Ottoman) (1578) iii, 147b; v, 66b; vi, 862a; vii, 6b
Mihrishāh Sulṭān iv, 233b
Mihrumāh Sulṭān iv, 231b
Mihtar → Mehter
Mihyār b. Marzawayh (Marzōye) al-Daylamī (1037) i, 592b; vi, 603a, 605b; vii, 24b, 982b; s, 119b
Mihzam, Banū s, 24b
Mīkāl (Mīkaʾīl) (archangel) ii, 363b, 846b; vi, 217a, 219b; vii, 25a
Mīkāʾīl b. Djaʿfar i, 1306b, 1307b
Miʿkāl (al-Riyāḍ) s, 234b
al-Mīkālī, Abu ʾl-Faḍl (amīr, XI) vii, 527b; s, 343a
Mīkālīs (Khurāsān) vi, 196a; vii, 25b; x, 426a
Mīḳāt iii, 362b, 1052b; vii, 26b
Miḳdād b. ʿAmr (653) ii, 846b; iii, 873b; vii, 32a, 517b
Miḳdād Aḥmed Pasha (1791) ii, 207b
al-Miḳdādī, Muṭahhar b. Muḥammad (1650) vii, 94b
al-Miḳdām → Yaḥyā III (Idrīsid)
Mīkhāʾīl Mushāka (XIX) vi, 99a
Mīkhāʾīl Nuʿayma ix, **229a**
Mīkhāʾīl al-Ṣabbāgh (1816) vii, 33a
Mīkhāl-oghlu vii, 34a
Mikhāl-oghlu Ghāzī ʿAlī Bewy (1507) viii, 318a
Mīkhāl-oghlu Meḥemmed (XV) vii, 644b
Mīkhāl-oghlu Mīkhāl Beg (XV) vii, 712b
Mīkhāl-oghullarī i, 340b
Mikhdham (sword) vi, 374a
Mikhlāf/Makhālīf ii, 517a, b; vii, 35a
Mikhlāf al-Sulaymānī ii, 517a; vi, 191b; s, 30a
Mikindani (port) vii, 35a
Miḳlama iv, 471b
Miḳlāṣiyya xi, 511b
Miknās (al-Zaytūn) (Meknès) i, 85a, 356a, 134b; ii, 819b; iii, 973a; v, 1192a; vi, 141b, 293a, 356a, 406a, 571b, 572a, 595a; vii, 35b, 387a; ix, 47a; s, 53a, 103a, 350b, 397b, 399b

Miknāsa, Banū i, 1349b; vi, 741a, 923a; vii, 36b
al-Miknāsī, Abū Allāh Muḥammad b. Ḥamza (XIX) vi, 356b
al-Miknāsī, Maṣāla b. Ḥabūs (924) ii, 853a; iii, 1036a; vii, 641a, b, 941b
Miḳyās (Nilometer) iii, 572a; v, 91b, 862b; vi, 413a, 618b; vii, 39b; viii, 41b
Mīlād vii, 40b
Milāḥa (Navigation) ii, 583a, 586a; iii, 856b, 627b; vii, 40b
al-Milal wa 'l-Niḥal vii, 54a
Milān, Banū vi, 201b
Mīlānī, Āyatullāh Muḥammad (1975) iv, 165b; vi, 553b
Mīlās (Milas) vii, 55a; s, 138a
Miletus → Balāṭ
Milḥ v, 250b, 435b, 965a, 967b, 976a, 981b; vii, 57a
al-Mīlī, Mubārak iv, 157a, 159b
Mīl-i Nādirī vi, 365b
Mīl-i Rādkān (Gurgān) vi, 713b
Miliana → Milyāna
Milk (ownership) i, 28b, 661a; iv, 1035b; vii, 60b
Milkān vi, 562b
Milla (religion, sect) ii, 294b; iv, 174a; vii, 54b, 61a
Millat → Millet
Millet (religion, religious community) i, 470a; ii, 6b; iii, 1180b; iv, 785b, 790b; vii, 61b
Millī, Banū vi, 541b
Millī Kongre ii, 431b
Milliyyat iv, 785b
Milyāna, Miliana vi, 404a, b; vii, 64a
Mīm vii, 64b
Miʿmār-bas̲h̲ī iv, 235a, b
Mīmiyya → Muḥammadiyya
Minā (Mecca) iii, 32b, 36a; vi, 140b, 169b; vii, 65a; viii, 379a,bs, 33a, 317a, 350a, 357b
Mīnāʾ (port) vii, 66a
Mīna, Ḥannā v, 190b, 191a
Mīnāʾ al-Aḥmadī s, 50a
Mīnāʾ al-Fahl vi, 735b
Mīnāʾ Ḳābūs vi, 736a
al-Mīna (Mīnās) ii, 1056a
Mīnāb s, 129a
Minaeans → Maʿīn
Mināʾī i, 201b; iv, 1167a; vii, 72b
Minangkabau i, 170b, 173b, 174a; iii, 1214b, 1222b, 1225b, 1228a; vii, 73b; viii, 237b; s, 151a
Mīnār, Minaret → Manāra
Minbar i, 202b, 776a; vii, 73b
Miñbas̲h̲ī i, 1229a
Mindanao → Phillippines
Mindū, S̲h̲ayk̲h̲ (XIV) vi, 231a
Minglī Girāy K̲h̲ān → Menglī Girāy I
Minhād̲j̲-i Sirād̲j̲ → al-D̲j̲ūzd̲j̲ānī
Minicoy vi, 206b; vii, 80b
Minḳād, Wādī s, 157a
al-Minkarī → Naṣr b. Muzāḥim
Minnet Beg-Og̲h̲lu Meḥmed Beg (XV) vi, 70b
Minorca → Minūrḳa
Minṭaḳat al-Burūd̲j̲ vii, 81b
Minṭās̲h̲ (Mamlūk) (1390) i, 1050b, 1051a; ii, 239b; iii, 187a; vi, 231b; vii, 170b, 462a
Minṭās̲h̲ (Türkmen; amīr) (1321) vi, 381b
Minūčihrī → Manūčihrī
Minūf, Minūfī → Manūf, Manūfī
Minūfiyya s, 44a
Minūrḳa iv, 1157a; iv, 1157a; vii, 87a
al-Minyā (province) s, 18a, 408a
Minyā al-Ḳamḥ vi, 408a
Minyat ʿAfīf s, 44a
Mīnyo, Nahr i, 489a
Mīr (title) vii, 87b
Mīr ʿAbd Allāh K̲h̲ān Marʿas̲h̲ī (XVI) iv, 364b; vi, 515b
Mīr Aḥmad b. Ramaḍān (Ramaḍān-og̲h̲lu) (1416) viii, 418b
Mīr Āk̲h̲ūr vii, 88a
Mīr ʿAlāʾ al-Mulk Marʿas̲h̲ (XVI) vi, 516b
Mīr ʿAlī K̲h̲ān (Mīr Taymūr) (Marʿas̲h̲ī) (XVI) vi, 515a
Mīr ʿAlī S̲h̲īr Nawāʾī, Niẓām al-Dīn (1501) i, 292b, 504b, 813b, 1019a, 1082b, 1211b, 1212b; ii, 179a, 421b, 422a, 792a; iii, 177b, 358a, 603a; iv, 66a–b, 1010a, 1020b; v, 835b; vi, 768a; vii, 90a, 473a, 530a, 567b, 935a; s, 83a, 324a; viii, 581b
Mīr ʿAlī Tabrīzī iv, 1124b
Mīr Amān → Amān, Mīr
Mīr At̲h̲ar (1794) vi, 837b
Mīr ʿAzīz K̲h̲ān b. ʿAbd Allāh (Marʿas̲h̲ī) (XVI) vi, 515a
Mīr Babar ʿAlī → Anīs
Mīr-i Buzurg → Marʿas̲h̲ī, Ḳawām al-Dīn
Mīr-i Dāmād Astarābādī → al-Dāmād

Mīr Damīr (XIX) vi, 611a, b
Mīr Dard (XVIII) vii, 328a
Mīr Dja'far → Dja'far, Mīr Muḥammad
Mīr Dja'far 'Alī (1713) vi, 612a
Mīr Djumla, Muḥammad Sa'īd (1663) i, 719b, 769a; ii, 216b, 1135a; iii, 318b, 427a; iv, 1020a; vi, 63a; vii, 93b
Mīr Ghulām Ḥasan → Ḥasan, Mīr Ghulām
Mīr Ḥusayn Khān (Mar'ashī) (XVII) vi, 515a,
Mīr Ḳāsim 'Alī (1777) vii, 93b
Mīr Ḳawām al-Dīn (Mar'ashī) (XV) vi, 514a
Mīr Khalīḳ Abū Babar 'Alī Anīs (XIX) vi, 611a
Mīr Khudādād v, 102b
Mīr Lawḥī, Sayyid Muḥammad (XVII) v, 1088a; vii, 94a
Mīr Ma'sūm → Mīr Muḥammad Ma'sūm, Nāmī
Mīr Mīrān Ghiyāth al-Dīn (Yazd) (XVI) viii, 775b
Mīr Mithar 'Alī (1831) vii, 291a
Mīr Muḥammad b. Ḳāḍī Ḳalandar (Ṣūfī) → Miyān Mīr
Mīr Muḥammad Ḥusayn Shahristānī (XIX) vi, 516b
Mīr Muḥammad Ma'ṣūm, Nāmī (1606) i, 962a, 1192b; iii, 245b; vii, 96a, 317b
Mīr Muḥammad Taḳī Mīr (1810) ii, 1036b; iii, 119a, 358b, 376a; v, 961b; vi, 611a, 837b; vii, 96a, 533a; x, 878a
Mīr Muhannā (Khār(a)g) iv, 1056b
Mīr Munnū → Mu'īn al-Mulk b. Ḳamar al-Dīn
Mīr Muṣawwir Abū Mīr Sayyid 'Alī (XVI) vii, 337b
Mīr Nadjm al-Dīn b. Aḥmad (Mar'ashī) vi, 516a
Mīr Nūr Allāh (naḳīb, Ṣafawid) (XVI) vi, 516a
Mīr Sāmān i, 316b
Mīr Sayyid 'Alī b. Amīr Asad Allāh Mar'ashī (XVI) vi, 516b; vii, 317a, 337b, 338a
Mīr Shams al-Dīn iv, 709a
Mīr Shīr 'Alī → Afsūs
Mīr Taḳī Mīr → Mīr Muḥammad Taḳī
Mīr Taymūr → 'Abd al-Karīm b. 'Abd Allāh (Mar'ashī)
Mīr Turāb → Sālār Djang
Mīr Ways (Ghalzay) (XVIII) i, 218b, 226b, 229a; ii, 1011a; iii, 603b; iv, 537a; vii, 318b; viii, 771a; ix, 854b
Mīrāb → Mā', Irān
Mi'rādj i, 1310b; ii, 448b; vii, 97b
Mi'rādj 6. in persian literature s, **618a**
Mīrafāb i, 1171b, 1172a
Mīrak Ḥusayn Yazdī s, 204a
Mīrak Naḳḳāsh i, 1211a, b
Mīrān Ṣāḥib → Shāh al-Ḥāmid 'Abd al-Ḳāḍir
Mīrān Muḥammad Shāh I (Fārūḳī; Khāndesh) (1537) ii, 815a, 1128b; iii, 422a, 1160a; vi, 52a; vii, 105a
Mīrān Muḥammad Shāh II (Fārūḳī; Khāndesh) (1576) ii, 815a; iii, 1161a, b; vii, 134a
Mīrān Ṣāḥib → Shāh al-Ḥamīd 'Abd al-Ḳādir
Mīrān Shāh b. Tīmūr (Tīmūrid) (XVI) s, 604b
Mīrān Shāh 'Alī (Aḥmadnagar, XVI) iii, 626a
Mīrān Shāh Ḥaydar (XVI) iii, 625b
Mīrāndjī → Miyān Mīr, Miyāndjī
Mīrānī ('Umān) vi, 735a
Mīrānīs (Balūčī) ii, 185b
Mīrānshāh b. Tīmūr Lang (Tīmūrid) (1408) i, 66b; ii, 733a, b; iii, 600b; iv, 914b, 1029a; vi, 714b; vii, 105b
Mir'āt (mirror) v, 988a; vii, 105b
Mir'āt al-Aḥwāl ii, 466a, 471a
Mīrāth i, 1142b; vii, 106b
Mīrath (Meerut) vii, 113a
Mīrāthī, 'Imād al-Dīn iv, 1041a
al-Mirbad (al-Baṣra) i, 1080a, 1086a; vi, 709b; vii, 113b, 843a, 873a; s, 172a
al-Mirbāṭ iii, 270a; vi, 83b; vii, 53a, 114b
Mirčea ii, 611a
Mirdās, Banū (Mirdāsids) i, 442a, 1349a; iii, 86a, 686b; v, 459a; vi, 626b; vii, 115a
Mīrdās b. Udayya, Abū Bilāl (680) iii, 169a, 648a, 1175b; iv, 1075b; vii, 123a; ix, 766a
Mīrem Čelebi (1525) iv, 810a; viii, 541b
al-Mīrghanī, Ḥasan b. Muḥammad iv, 686b
al-Mīrghanī, Muḥammad 'Uthmān (1851) i, 1029a; vii, 124a; s, 278b
Mīrghaniyya/Khatmiyya i, 277b, 1029a, 1158b; ii, 710a; iii, 6a, 523b; iv, 686b; vii, 124a; viii, 92b

Mīrī (Amīrī) i, 1147b; ii, 148a; vii, 125a
Mīrī, Shaykh ii, 768a
Mīr-i Buzurg → Ḳawām al-Dīn I al-Marʿashī, Sayyid
Mīr-i Khātūn bint Arghu Āḳā (XIV) viii, 999a
Mīr-i Mīrān vii, 95b
Miriamiyya vi, 631b
Mīrim Čelebī (1525) s, 502b
Mīrim Kösesi (1550) ix, 209a
Mirkās (Mirḳās) vii, 126b
Mīrkhwānd, Muḥammad b. Khwāndshāh (1498) iv, 1020b; vii, 128b; s, 46b
Mīrmīran i, 1160a
al-Mirrīkh (Mars) vii, 127a
Mirsaid Mirshakar (1993) x, 65b
Mīrtula (Mārtula) i, 6a; ii, 1009b; vii, 127b
Mirwaḥa vii, 127b
Mirwāt → Čeh
Miryam → Maryam
Mīrzā (Mirzā) (title) vii, 129a
Mīrzā ʿAbd Allāh → Burton, Sir Richard
Mīrzā ʿAbd Allāh Khān → Shihāb Turghīzī
Mīrzā Abū Ṭālib (Ṣadr) vi, 18a
Mīrzā Abu ʾl-Ḥasan Raḥīm → Yaghmā Djandaḳī
Mīrzā Aḥmad Khān (XVIII) vii, 129b
Mīrzā Āḳā Tabrīzī (XIX) vi, 763b
Mīrzā ʿAskarī b. Bābūr (Mughal) (1558) vii, 130b
Mīrzā ʿAzīz Kūka (Kōka) b. Shams al-Dīn Aḥmad Ghaznawī (1624) i, 80b, 507a; ii, 815a; vii, 129b, 131a, 134a, 331b, 938a, 1055a
Mīrzā Buzurg → Ḳāʾim-maḳām-i Farāhānī, ʿIsā
Mīrzā Buzurg → Wafā, Mīrzā Ḥasan
Mīrzā Djaʿfar Ḳarādjadāghī (XIX) vi, 763a
Mīrzā Ghālib → Ghālib, Mīrzā Asad Allāh
Mīrzā Ghulām Aḥmad Ḳādiyānī → Aḥmadiyya
Mīrzā Ḥasan Khān → Wuthūḳ al-Dawla
Mīrzā Ḥaydar Dūghlāt → Ḥaydar, Mīrzā
Mīrzā Hindāl → Hindāl, Mīrzā, Abū Nāṣir Muḥammad
Mīrzā Ḥusayn Khān Sipahsālār (XIX) vi, 763a; s, 109a
Mīrzā Ḥusayn Khān b. Ṣabā (1848) viii, 665b
Mīrzā Ibrāhīm Adham (XVII) vii, 132b
Mīrzā ʿĪsā Ḳāʿimmaḳām (XIX) vi, 551b
Mīrzā Iskandar (1415) v, 163b
Mīrzā Kalīč Beg (1929) ix, 627a
Mīrzā Kāmrān → Kāmrān, Mīrzā b. Bābur
Mīrzā Khān (Aḥmadnagar, 1600) ii, 921b; iii, 626a; s, 327b
Mīrzā Khān (Badakhshān, 1520) i, 852b
Mīrzā Khān Sulṭān Maḥmūd (Marʿashī) (XVI) vi, 515a
Mīrzā Kūčik → Wiṣal, Mīrzā Muḥammad Shafīʿ
Mīrzā Maḥmūd b. Yūsuf (XX) vii, 257b
Mīrzā Malkum → Malkom Khān Mīrzā
Mīrzā Meḥemmed Isfendiyār-oghlu iv, 108b
Mīrzā Muḥammad Ḥakīm → Muḥammad Ḥakīm, Mīrzā
Mīrzā Muḥammad Khalīl Marʿashī Ṣafawī (1805) vi, 516b
Mīrzā Muḥammad Khān b. ʿAbbās Ḳulī Khān (XX) v, 664a, b
Mīrzā Muḥammad Muḳīmī (1665) vi, 837a
Mīrzā Muḥammad Taḳī Kashānī → Sipihr
Mīrzā Muḥammad Zamān → Muḥammad Zamān, Mīrzā
Mīrzā Muḳīm Abu ʾl-Manṣūr Khān → Ṣafdar Djang
Mīrzā Naṣr → Shihāb Iṣfahānī
Mīrzā Rafīʿ al-Dīn, ṣadr → Nāʾīnī, Mīrzā
Mīrzā Rafīʿā (XVIII) vi, 17a, 18a, b
Mīrzā Rafīʿā, Muḥammad b. Ḥaydar, Ḥusaynī Ṭabāṭabāʾī Nāʾīnī (1673) vii, 132a
Mīrzā Ṣādiḳ Khān → Amīrī
Mīrzā Ṣafī → Ṣafī Mīrzā b. Shāh Sulṭān
Mīrzā Ṣāliḥ (XIX) ii, 649b
Mīrzā Sayyid Djaʿfar Khān Tabrīzī, Muhandis Bashī (1862) vii, 678a
Mīrzā Sayyid Muḥammad Mutawallī (Marʿashī) → Shāh Sulaymān II (Ṣafawid)
Mīrzā Shādmān b. Mīrzā ʿAzīz Kōka (XVII) vii, 131b
Mīrzā Shafīʿ Māzandarānī (1819) s, 336a, 406b, **620b**
Mīrzā Shafīʿ Wādiḥ Tabrīzī (1852) s, **621b**
Mīrzā Shams al-Dīn b. Mīrzā ʿAzīz Kōka (XVII) vii, 131b
Mīrzā Taḳī Khān → Amīr Kabīr
Mīrzā Yaḥyā Dawlatābādī (XX) ix, 741b
Mīrzā Yaḥyā Nūrī → Subḥ-i Azal

Mīrzā Yaʿḳūb Abū Malkom Khān (XIX) vi, 291a
Mīrzā Zakī (XVIII) vi, 527b
Mīrzāʾī → Aḥmadiyya
Mīrzāpur vii, 132b
Mīrzās (Gudjarāt, Badakhshān ii, 1129a, b; iii, 422a, 423b; vi, 342b; vii, 131a, b, 133a, 314b
Mīrzā-yi Shīrāzī-yi Buzurg → Shīrāzī, Mīrzā Muḥammad Ḥasan
Mīrzā-yi Shīrāzī-yu Kūčik → Shīrāzī, Muḥammad Taḳī b. Muḥibb ʿAlī Ḥāʾirī
Mīrzā-zāde Meḥmed Emīn-V Sālim
Mirz Tursunoda (1977) x, 65b
Misāḥa (survey) vii, 137b
Misāḥa, ʿIlm al- vii, 135a
Misalla (obelisk) vii, 140b
Misʿar b. Fadakī iv, 269a
Misʿar b. Muhalhil → Abū Dulaf
Miṣbāḥ → Sirādj
Misbaḥa → Subḥa
Misher vi, 420b
Mishkān vi, 494a
Mīshmast iii, 1103a
Mishmish vii, 141b
Mishowdagh vi, 504a
Misis → al-Maṣṣīṣa
Misiṭṭāsa i, 1037a
Misk vii, 142a
Miskawayh (Ibn), Abū ʿAlī Aḥmad (1030) i, 127a, 234b, 326b, 327b, 328a, 328b, 590a, 1353b, 1354a; ii, 80a, 174a; iii, 703b, 955a, 1237a; vi, 199a, b, 571a, 638a; vii, 143a; s, 72b, 119b, 263b, 398b
Miskīn ii, 757b; vii, 144b
Miskīn al-Dārimī (708) vii, 145a
al-Mislaḥ s, 198b
Mismaʿ b. Shihāb vi, 640b
al-Mismaʿī, ʿAbd Allāh b. Ibrāhīm (X) iii, 1015b; iv, 100a
Miṣr C.2 the city from 1798 till the present day s, **621b**
Miṣr D.8 the British occupation and the Egyptian parliamentary monarchy 1882–1952 s, **623a**
Miṣr D9 Republican Egypt 1952 to the present s, **625a**
Miṣr (Egypt) i, 13b, 21a, 215b, 396a, 451a, 531b, 638b, 750b, 797b, 800a, 801a, 870a, 1054a, 1107a; ii, 495a, 668a, 853b, 854a, 914a; iii, 4b, 264a, 384b, 395a, 653b, 1259a; v, 556b, 558b, 1060a; vi, 22b, 82b, 118b, 288b, 337b, 366b, 467b, 469b, 471a; vii, 10a, 146a; viii, 906b; s, 120b, 216a
– administration i, 976a; ii, 148a, 327a, 595a, 647a; iii, 556a, 1154a, 1185b, 1193b; iv, 192b, 193a, 323b, 1033b
– agriculture iii, 625a, 1154a
– demography s, 216a
– education v, 907b, 1091b
– ethnography i, 35a, 37b, 39a; iii, 299b; v, 317b
– history i, 138b, 965a; ii, 355b; iii, 675a, 756b, 813a, 894b; v, 121b
– institutions ii, 126b, 128a, 129b, 132a, 423b; iii, 1068b; iv, 192b
– language, literature i, 74b, 142a, 568b, 575a; ii, 465a, 466a, 764a; iii, 935a
– monuments v, 290a
– statesment i, 51b, 58a, 293b, 391b, 1069b; ii, 764a
Miṣr Bay iv, 552a
Miṣr(īm/āyim) b. Bayṣar b. Ḥām vi, 411b
Miṣr al-fatāt (Young Egypt) ii, 429a; iii, 518a; s, 5b
Misrāḳlî → Sulaymān Pasha
Misrāta (Miṣrāta), Banū iii, 1040a; v, 948b; vii, 186a
al-Miṣrī, ʿAzīz ʿAlī (XX) viii, 140b, 141a
al-Miṣrī, ʿAbd Allāh b. ʿAbd al-Ḥakam vi, 264b
Miṣrī Efendi → Niyāzī
Miṣṣīs (Mopsuestia) → Maṣṣīṣa
Missolonghi vi, 59a
Mistra vi, 70b
Mistāwa → al-Nukkār
Misurata → Misrāta
Miswāk vii, 187a
al-Miswar b. Hāniʾ (XII) vi, 312a
Mīthāḳ vii, 187b
Mīthāḳ-i Millī vii, 188a
Mithāliyya iv, 507a
Mithḳāl → Dīnār; Ḥabba; Istār
Mithḳāl, Amīr v, 1141b, 1142a
Mitīdja → Bulayda
Mitwālī s, 268b, 269a
Miʿwadh → Ḥamāʾil
al-Miyādīn → al-Raḥba
Miyān-duʾāb vi, 502b
Miyān-du-rūd iv, 645a; vi, 745b; s, 298a
Miyān Gul Djān (XX) ii, 317a
Miyān Gul Gul Shāhzāda (XX) ii, 317a

Miyān Ḥasan Khān Sūrī (XV) ii, 271a
Miyān Mīr, Miyādjī, Bālā Pīr (1635) ii, 134b; vii, 189a, 327b
Miyān Muṣṭafā Gudjarātī (1575) ii, 500a
Miyān Rādjū (1607) vi, 269b
Miyāna (Miyānidj) vii, 189b
Miyānābād iv, 107b
Mizāb iv, 318a
Mizādj s, **627b**
Miʿzaf(a) vii, 189b
Mizʿal Khān iv, 1171a
Miẓalla iv, 214a, 1147a; vi, 521a; vii, 191b
al-Mīzān → Minṭaḳat al-Burūdj
al-Mīzān (balance) ii, 358b; iii, 212b, 465b; iv, 600a, 1186a; vii, 195b
Mīzān (Ottoman weekly) vii, 204b
Mīzāndjî Meḥmed Murād Bey (1917) ii, 474b; iv, 871b; vii, 204b, 205a
Miẓhar → Maẓhar
Mizmār vii, 206b
Mizwala (sundial) vii, 210a
Mizwār i, 687b; vii, 211b
al-Mizza (Mezzé) vi, 624a; vii, 212a
al-Mizzī, Djamāl al-Dīn Abu 'l-Ḥadjdjādj al-Kalbī (1341) iii, 817b, 818a, 952a, 954b; vii, 30a, 212a, 576b, 692a; viii, 517a
al-Mizzī, Muḥammad b. Aḥmad (XIV) viii, 575a
Mkwaja vi, 370a; vii, 213a
Mleh (Mlech) i, 182b, 639a; ii, 37b
Moa (Tanzania) vi, 370a
Moab s, 190b, 191a
Mobadh vii, 213b
Mocha/Mokhā → al-Mukhā
Modibbo Adama (1848) i, 179b, 180a; ii, 9b, 942b
Modibo Muḥammad (XV) vi, 258b
Modon v, 270b, 271a; vii, 216b
Möʾetüken b. Čaghatay i, 1010a; ii, 2a
Mogadishu → Maḳdishū
Mogador → al-Suwayra
Mogholistān ii, 45a, b, 622a; v, 858a; vi, 77a, b; vii, 218a; s, 96b
Moghols vii, 218b
Mogul → Mughal
Moḥā u Aḥmad al-Ahansalī iii, 167a
Mohács (Mihāč) vi, 74b; vii, 218b; viii, 185a; s, 171a
Mohamed bin Nasor Shaksi (XX) vi, 612b
Mohamman ii, 1145b
Mohammed Racim (Rāsim) (XX) s, 224b
Mohān s, 360a
Moḥand u l-Hādj iv, 363a
Mohmand vii, 220a, 548b; s, 237b
Mohur vii, 221a
Moidu Moulavi, E. (Mappila) (XX) vi, 460a
Moidu Padiyath (Mappila) (XX) vi, 464b
Mois Dibra iv, 139b, 140a
Moïse → Mūsā
Mokhā → al-Mukhā
Moḳrānī i, 369b, 1197a; iv, 478b
Moktar Ould Daddah (al-Mukhtār Wuld Dāddāh) vii, 615b
Moldavia → Boghdān
Molesalam Grasias i, 172a
Mollā (title) vii, 221a
Mollā Arab (Muftī) (1483) ix, 400b
Mollā Bādjī (Bāshī, Bāshigarī) → Mollā
Molla Bīlāl (XIX) x, 221a
Mollā Čelebi → Muḥyi 'l-Dīn Meḥmed al-Djamālī
Mollā Ḳābid (1527) vii, 225a b
Mollā Khusraw → Khusraw, Mollā
Mollā Kūrānī → Gurānī, Sharaf al-Dīn
Mollā Naṣr al-Dīn → Naṣr al-Dīn Khodja
Mollā Ṣadrā → Mullā Ṣadrā
Moluccas iii, 1219a, 1226a
Mombasa i, 1282a; iv, 886a; v, 655b; vi, 129a, 283b, 370a; vii, 225a; s, 248a, 355b
Mōmnas → Satpanthīs
Monastir (Tunisia) i, 1319a; vii, 227b
Monastir (Yugoslavia) → Manāstir
Moncef Bey → Munṣif Bey
Mondros (Mudros) vii, 229a
Monemvasia → Menekshe
Monghyr → Mungīr
Möngke b. Toluy b. Čingiz Khān (Mongol Great Khān) (1260) i, 1105b, 1106a, 1187b, 1240b, 1311b; ii, 3a, 45b; iii, 1121a; iv, 814a; v, 299b, 300a; vi, 77b; vii, 230a
Möngke-Temür (Batuʾid), (1280) i, 1188b; ii, 812a, 1112a
Mongolia iv, 988b; vii, 230b; x, 687a
Mongols i, 21a, 121a, 190a, 227a, 329b, 353b, 354b, 508a, 639b, 660b, 786b, 791b, 804b, 872a, 879b, 902b, 1105a, 1240b, 1295a, 1308a; ii, 3b, 38a, 41b, 67b, 194a, 229b, 285b, 344b, 393a, 707b, 746a, 928b, 1142a; iii, 87b, 105b, 177b, 402b, 702b, 1121a; iv, 30a-32a, 48a-b, 349a, 485a,

512a, 562b, 612b, 817a, 921b, 1049b-1051b; v, 58b, 456a, 748b; vi, 48a, b, 77a, 198b, 314b, 482b, 492b, 493b, 494a, 500b, 501a, 540b, 545b, 547b, 606a; vii, 230b; viii, 472b; ix, 474a, 811b; x, 690b; xi, 26b, 293a; s, 184a, 246a, 256a, b
– art iii, 1125b, 1126a,
– histories ii, 606b; iii, 114a
– warfare ii, 1083b; iii, 183b, 188a, 197b, 472a, 1099b
Montenegro → Ḳaradag͟h
Moors i, 31b; ii, 27a; vii, 235b
Mopla(stan) → Māpilla
Mora (game) iv, 114a
Mora (Morea) ii, 534a, 691a, 985a; iii, 91a, 212a; iv, 241a; v, 268b, 270b, 717b; vi, 58b, 59a, b, 71b; vii, 236b; s, 149b
Morādābād → Murādābād
Moravia → Čeh
Mordve i, 1338a
Mordves → Burṭās
Morea → Mora
Morikubala Dore ii, 1132a
Moriscos i, 55b, 404b, 496a, 496b, 502a, 1343a; iv, 239a, 673a; v, 504b; vii, 241b; s, 81a
Moro National Liberation Front (MNLF) viii, 304b, 305a
Morocco → al-Mag͟hrib, al-Mamlaka al-Mag͟hribiyya
Moron → Mawrūr
Mora → Muk͟hārad͟ja
Moros (Philippines) viii, 303b, 304a
Moses → Mūsā
Moses of K͟horen s, 274b
Moses b. Eleazar → Mūsā b. al-ʿĀzār
Moses Hāmōn → Hāmōn, Moses
Mossadegh → Muṣaddiḳ, Muḥammad
Mossi vi, 402b
Mostaganem → Mustag͟hānim
Mostar vii, 244a
Mosul → al-Mawṣil
Moudros → Mondros
Moulay → Mawlāy
Moulay Hafid → Ḥāfiz, ʿAbd
al-Moulouya → Malwiyya
Moulay Ḥasan, Sulṭān → al-Ḥasan I, Mawlāy
Mourre → Mora
Moyinkutty Vaidyar (1891) vi, 464a
Mozambique vi, 203b, 283a; vii, 245a; ix, 698b; xi, 283a; s, **628a**
Mozarab i, 82b, 491a, 494a, 1339a; v, 367b, 376a; vii, 246b; s, 92a, 397b
Mrābṭīn i, 1049b
Ms͟hatta → al-Mus͟hattā
Msīd → Kuttāb
Msīla → Masīla
Mt. D'eli vi, 207a
Mtambwe Mkuu vii, 249b
M'tir, Banū s, 145a
Mtugga, Banū vi, 743a
al-Muʿābada (Mecca) vi, 154a, b, 161b, 170a
Mu'addib v, 568a
Muʿād͟h b. ʿAfrāʾ vi, 645b
Muʿād͟h b. D͟jabal (VII) i, 460b, 694a, 695a; ii, 372a; iv, 771a; v, 241a; vii, 635b
Muʿād͟h b. al-Nuʿmān i, 771b; iii, 812a
Muʿād͟h al-Harrā' (802) viii, 573a; x, 361a
Muʿād͟ha al-ʿAdawiyya (VII) viii, 354b
Mu'ad͟hd͟hin → Ad͟hān; Masd͟jid
Mu'ad͟hd͟hinzāde ʿAlī Pas͟ha iii, 251b; iv, 571b
Muʿad͟jd͟jal i, 172b
al-Muʿāfa b. Ṭāwūs vi, 900a
al-Muʿāfā b. Zakariyyāʾ (1000) i, 154a; iii, 42a, 824b; viii, 546a
Muʿāfī iv, 1045a
Muʿāhada (earlier times) → ʿAhd; Baḳṭ; Imtiyāzāt
Muʿāhada (modern times) vii, 250a
Muʿāhid s, **630b**
Muʿāhidūn v, 376a
Muʾāk͟hāt vii, 253b
al-Muʿallafa Ḳulūbuhum i, 12a, 266b; vii, 254a
Muʿallaḳ iii, 26a
al-Muʿallaḳāt iii, 136a, 222b, 1178a; vii, 254a
Muʿallal iii, 26a
Muʿallim v, 568a
Muʿallim Nād͟jī (1893) ii, 474b; iv, 195b, 874b, 930b; vii, 255a
al-Muʿallim al-T͟hālit͟h → al-Dāmād
Muʿāmalāt i, 277a; iv, 560b; vii, 255b
Muʿammā v, 806b; vii, 257a
Muʿammāʾī → al-Ḥusaynī, Mīr Ḥusayn
Muʿammar i, 117a, 519b; vii, 258a
Muʿammar, Āl (Tamīm) ii, 321a; iii, 678a

Muʿammar b. ʿAbbād al-Sulamī, Abū ʿAmr (830) i, 1243a; iii, 1143a; vii, 259a; s, 88b, 226a
Muʿammar b. al-Aḥmar iv, 1132b; v, 702a
al-Muʿammarī → Abū Manṣūr al-Maʿmarī
al-Muʿammar al-Maghribī → Abu 'l-Dunyā
Muʿammir → Muʿammar
al-Muʿammariyya → al-Khaṭṭābiyya
Muʿanʿan iii, 26a; vii, 260a
Muʾannath → Mudhakkar
Muʿanṣar b. Ḥammād v, 1179b
Muar (Malacca) vi, 207b
Muʿāraḍa (collation) → Muḳābala
Muʿāraḍa (opposition) vii, 261a
Muʿarrab vii, 261b
Muʾarridj, Abū Fayd al-Sadūsī (819) vi, 138b, 821b, 822a; vii, 967b; s, 73b
Muʾarrikh → Kh(w)āndamīr
al-Muʿaskar (Mascara) vii, 262b
Muʿattib, Banū vii, 347a
Muʿaṭṭib ibn Ḳushayr iv, 839b
Muʿaṭṭila → Taʿṭīl
Muʿāwada vii, 263b
Muʿāwiya, Banū v, 118b; vi, 473a
Muʿāwiya I b. Abī Sufyān b. Ḥarb (Umayyad) (680) i, 40b, 43b, 85b, 194b, 275b, 710b, 760a, 1137b; ii, 35b, 89b, 116a, 128b, 129b, 280b, 323b, 343b, 456b, 911a, 931a, 1093b; iii, 20a, 241a, b, 391b, 397b, 455a, 545a, 607b, 1163b; iv, 315a, 493a, 734a, 841b, 938a, 973a, 1074b; v, 302a, 324b, 1123a; vi, 139a, b, 140a, 147a, 193a, 197b, 230b, 247b, 336b, 334b, 362a, 363a, 505b, 547b, 621b, 622a, 626a, 650b, 654b, 657b, 660b, 661b, 662a, 665a, 666a, 668b, 669b, 670a, 774a; vii, 254a, 263b, 269a, 347a, b, 358b, 393b, 689a; ix, 584a; x, 841b; s, 10a, 88a, 89b, 103b, 133b, 157a, 221b, 230b, 243a, 394a
– conflict with ʿAlī i, 383a, b, 384a, 451b, 549b, 636b, 704b, 1343b; ii, 480b, 625b; iii, 12b, 889b
Muʿāwiya II b. Yazīd b. Muʿāwiya I (Umayyad) (684) ii, 89b; iii, 270b; iv, 369b; vi, 544b, 545a, 546b, 622a, 626a; vii, 268a
Muʿāwiya b. al-ʿĀṣ s, 103b
Muʿāwiya b. Bakr al-ʿImlāḳī iv, 820b; s, 246b
Muʿāwiya b. al-Ḥārith al-Ṣimma ii, 627a
Muʿāwiya b. Hishām (Umayyad, al-Andalus) (735) i, 1103a; iii, 494b; vii, 269a
Muʿāwiya b. Ḥudaydj b. Djafna al-Sakūnī al-Tudjībī (672) iv, 825b, 826a; vi, 740b; vii, 269a, 393b; x, 212b
Muʿāwiya b. al-Mughīra s, 103b
Muʿāwiya b. Ṣāliḥ vi, 221a
Muʿāwiya b. ʿUbayd Allāh → Abū ʿUbayd Allāh
Muʿāwiya b. ʿUḳayl vii, 582a
Muʿawwidhatāni vii, 269b
Muʿayn, Banū → Maʿīn, Banū
al-Muʿayṭī, al-Muntaṣir bi-'llāh (Denia) (XI) ii, 111b; vii, 292b
al-Muʾayyad (Rasūlid) (1322) vii, 30a
al-Muʾayyad (Ṣāliḥid) (X) vii, 641b
al-Muʾayyad, Āl (Yemen) vii, 779b
al-Muʾayyad, Shafīḳ iii, 519b
al-Muʾayyad b. al-Mutawakkil ʿalā 'llāh (ʿAbbāsid) (IX) vii, 777b
al-Muʾayyad Aḥmad b. Īnāl (Mamlūk) (1461) v, 73a; vii, 727a
al-Muʾayyad bi-'llāh → Hishām II (Umayyad), (al-Andalus)
al-Muʾayyad bi-'llāh (Zaydī Imām) → Yaḥyā b. Ḥamza al-ʿAlawī
al-Muʾayyad bi-'llāh, Aḥmad b. al-Ḥusayn (Imām) (1020) vii, 786a; s, 13a, 335b, 363a
al-Muʾayyad bi-'llāh Muḥammad, Ibn al-Imām al-Mutawakkil ʿalā 'llāh Ismāʿīl (1668) vii, 270a
al-Muʾayyad bi-'llāh Muḥammad (Zaydid) (1644) i, 553b; vi, 436b, 437a; vii, 270a, 514b, 779a
Muʾayyad al-Dawla (Būyid) vi, 659a
Muʾayyad Dāwūd (Rasūlid) (XIV) ix, 338a
al-Muʾayyad fi 'l-Dīn Allāh Abū Naṣr al-Shīrāzī (dāʿī) (1077) i, 132b, 832b, 1074a; ii, 98a, 169a, 855b, 856a; iii, 905b; iv, 47a; v, 930a; vii, 270b, 732a; ix, 221a
Muʾayyad al-Mulk b. Niẓām al-Mulk (XII) i, 1052a, b; vii, 408a, 489b
al-Muʾayyadiyya (Mamlūk) vi, 303b
Muʾayyadzāde (Ḳāḍī ʿasker) (1507) i, 1082b
Muʾayyad-zāde (Müʿeyyed-zāde), ʿAbd al-Raḥmān b. ʿAlī Čelebi (1516) vii, 23b, 272a; viii, 1b
Muʿayyid al-Dawla, Abū Manṣūr Būya (Būyid) (984) i, 211b, 1350b; ii, 748b;

iii, 258a, 671a, 704a; iv, 100b. 358a; vii, 272b; s, 13a
Muʾayyid al-Dīn, wazīr (1195) iv, 974b
Muʾayyid al-Dīn al-ʿArḍī (al-ʿUrḍī) (1266) vi, 501b, 601a
Muʾayyid al-Dīn Djandī (1300) viii, 753b
Muʾayyid al-Mulk ʿUbayd Allāh b. Niẓām al-Mulk (XI) i, 1036a; viii, 70b, 81b
Muʿayyir al-Mamālik, Dūst ʿAlī (XIX) vi, 481b, 484a, b
Muʿaẓẓam, Prince → Bahādur Shāh I
al-Muʿaẓẓam Sharaf al-Dīn, ʿĪsā, al-Malik → al-Malik al-Muʿaẓẓam Sharaf al-Dīn
al-Muʿaẓẓam Sulaymān (Ayyūbid, Sanʿāʾ) (XIII) vi, 433b
Muʿazzaz Khān (Nawwāb) (XVIII) vii, 129b
Mūbad Shāh ii, 74a
Mübādele (exchange) vii, 275a
Mubāḥ → Aḥkām; Sharīʿa
Mubāhala (Mulāʿana) i, 265a; ii, 848b, 849b; vii, 276a
Mubālagha vii, 277a
Muballigh → Dikka; Masdjid
Mubāraʾa i, 1027a
Mubārak, Āl iii, 582b
Mubārak (Āl Ṣabāḥ) (1915) viii, 668b
Mubārak (Āmirid) i, 446b, 985b
al-Mubārak b. Kāmil b. ʿAlī (Munḳidh, Banū) (1193) vii, 579b
Mubārak Abu ʾl-Aṭbāḳ (Mbārk Bū Leṭbāḳ) vi, 250a
Mubārak Āl Ṣabbāh ii, 673a; v, 574a, b
Mubārak Ghāzī (Bengal) vii, 278b
Mubārak, Ḥusnī (XXV) s, 626b
Mubārak Khān (Khāndēsh) (XVI) vi, 310a
Mubārak Khān ʿAbbāsī ii, 186b
Mubārak Khān I Dāwūdpōtrā ii, 185b, 186a
Mubārak Khān II Dāwūdpōtrā ii, 186a
Mubārak Khān Fārūḳī ii, 814b
Mubārak Khān Lūḥānī i, 1136b
Mubārak Khān Noḥānī s, 203a
Mubārak al-Maghribī al-Bukhārī i, 449a
Mubārak Nāgawri (al-Mahdawī) i, 117a; ii, 870b,
Mubārak Shāh (Badakhshān) i, 852b
Mubārak Shāh II (Fārūḳī) (1566) ii, 815a, 816a; iii, 422a; vi, 52a
Mubārak Shāh I Ḳuṭb al-Dīn (Khaldjī) (1320) i, 444b; ii, 120a, 179b, 258b, 269a, 1084b, 1085b; iii, 416b; iv, 419b, 923b; vi, 62a, 126b, 692a; vii, 457b; s, 105b
Mubārak Shāh II b. Khiḍr Khān, Muʿizz al-Dīn (Sayyid, Delhi) (1434) i, 1323a; ii, 270b; iii, 638b; iv, 513a; vii, 195a, 278b; ix, 118b, 119a
Mubārak Shāh b. Ḳara Hölegü i, 1311b; ii, 3a, b
Mubārak Shāh al-Marwarrūdhī (XIII) viii, 581b; s, 285a
Mubārak (Sayyid) b. Sayyid Ibrāhīm (Bayhaḳī) s, 131b
Mubārakābād i, 1323a; ii, 258b; vii, 279a
Mubārakpur ii, 258b, 263b
Mubārakshāh (1375) viii, 806b
al-Mubāriz Aḳdjā (amīr) (XIII) vi, 381a
Mubāriz al-Dīn Čawlı̊ ii, 693b
Mubāriz al-Dīn Muḥammad (Muẓaffarid) (1364) ii, 737a, 812a; iii, 56a, 1022a; iv, 498b, 672a; v, 163a, 554a; vii, 480b, 820a, b; ix, 198b; s, 415a
Mubāriz al-Dīn Muḥammad Bey i, 703a
Mubāriz Khān (Deccan) ii, 99b; iii, 318b, 320a
Mubāriz Khān (Delhi) → Muḥammad Shāh V
Mubāriz al-Mulk (XVI) vi, 270a
al-Mubarḳaʿ (Sufyānid) (841) vi, 338b; vii, 279a; xi, 178a
al-Mubarrad, Abū ʾl-ʿAbbās Muḥammad b. Yazīd al-Azdī (898) i, 97b, 125b, 321b, 590a, 1223b; ii, 300a; iii, 930a, 1263b; iv, 122b; v, 948a; vi, 348a; vii, 279b, 390b, 914a; ix, 317b, 387b; x, 4a, 433a; s, 25a, 27b, 352a, 389b
al-Mubarraz vii, 282b
Mubashshir b. Fātik, Abu ʾl-Wafāʾ (XI) i, 235b, 236a, 247a; iii, 463b, 906b; vii, 282b
Mubashshir b. Sulaymān iii, 853a
Mubashshir wa-Bashīr vi, 219b
Mubayyaḍiyya xi, 294b
al-Mubayyiḍa → al-Muḳannaʿ
Mubham iii, 26a
Mūbiḳāt iv, 1107b, 1109a
Mubīn, Mullā (Farangī Maḥall) s, 292b
Mubtadaʿ vii, 283a
Mudabbadj iii, 26a
Mudallas iii, 26a
Mudanya vi, 587b; vii, 284a
Muḍar → Rabīʿa

Muḍar, Banū iv, 832b, 833b; v, 76b, 77a; vi, 727b; vii, 266a, viii, 352b
Muḍāraba vii, 284b
Muḍāriʿ i, 108a; v, 954b; vii, 285b
Muḍarites i, 529b, 544b, 684b; iii, 233a
Mudarris, Sayyid Ḥasan (1936) vii, 300a
Mudarrisī, Taḳī iv, 73b; v, 200b
Muḍarriṭ al-Ḥidjāra → ʿAmr b. Hind
al-Mudawwana (Ibāḍī) → Abū Ghānim
al-Mudawwana (Mālikī) → Saḥnūn
al-Mudawwar (Almodovar) vii, 286a a
Mudawwar, Djamīl v, 188a
Mudawwara vii, 286a; x, 885a
al-Mudayna → Surt
al-Muddaththir/al-Muzzammil vii, 286a
al-Muḍayrib s, 355b
Mudejar iv, 118a; vii, 242a, 249a, 286a; s, 81a
Mudgal vii, 289a, 458b
Mudhakkar vii, 289b
al-Mudhaykhira vi, 439a
Mudghalīs (1181) viii, 804a
Mudīr vii, 290a
Mudīriyya ii, 828a
Mudjaddid vii, 290a, 296b
Mudjaddidīs i, 297b; vii, 936b
Mudjāhid → Rasūl, Banū
Mudjāhid al-ʿĀmirī → Mudjāhid al-Muwaffaḳ b. ʿAbd Allāh
Mudjāhid, al-Muwaffaḳ b. ʿAbd Allāh al-ʿĀmirī (Denia) (1044) i, 446b; ii, 111b, 112a, 837a; iii, 743b, 773a; vii, 292a; viii, 880a,b
Mudjāhid, Sayyid Muḥammad s, 75a
Mudjāhid b. Djabr al-Makkī, Abu ’l-Ḥadjdjādj (718) vii, 293a, 758a; viii, 1014b s, 386b
Mudjāhid al-Dīn Ḳāymāz, amīr (1199) i, 798b; vi, 781a
Mudjāhids (Denia) vi, 926b
Mudjāhidin-i islām iv, 52a
Mudjāhidūn i, 1333b; ii, 140b, 316b; iii, 335b, 1068a; iv, 196b, 729b; xi, 237a
Muʿdjam → Ḳāmūs
Mudjannada i, 490a
Mudjāshiʿ b. Masʿūd al-Sulamī v, 157b
Mudjassima → Tashbīh
Mudjāwir v, 1134a; vii, 293b
Mudjawwaza → Tülbend
Mudjbira → Djabriyya
Mudjdjāʿa b. Siʿr iii, 41a; iv, 534b
Mudjdjān iv, 1002b, 1003a, 1004a
Mudjīb al-Raḥmān v, 1082a
Mudjīr al-Dīn al-ʿUlaymī, Abu ’l-Yumn (1522) iii, 161b, 954b; iv, 958a; v, 322b; vi, 658b; vii, 294b
Mudjīr al-Dīn Abak → Abu Saʿīd Abak
Mudjīr al-Dīn Amīrshāh iv, 738a; s, 59a
Mudjīr al-Dīn Aybak viii, 128a
Mudjīr-i Baylaḳānī (1197) iv, 62a; s, 239b, **630b**
Muʿdjiza iv, 615a, b, 616a, b; vii, 295b
Mudjrā → Madjrā
Mudjtabā Mīrlawḥī → Nawwāb-i Safawī
Mudjtahid iii, 1025b, 1026b; iv, 278a, 1101a; vii, 295b; ix, 914a; s, 103b
Mudjtathth vii, 304a
Mudjūn vii, 304a
Mudlidj b. Muhannā (XV) vii, 462b
al-Mudlidjī, Abū ’l-Ḳāsim (X) i, 127a
al-Mudlidjī, ʿAlḳama b. Mudjazzaz (VII) vii, 863a
Muḍmar vii, 304b
Mudradj iii, 26a
Mudros → Mondros
Muḍṭarib iii, 26a
Muezzin → Muʾadhdhin
Mufādana iv, 324a
Mufaḍḍal s, 38b
al-Mufaḍḍal b. Abī Faḍāʾil (XIV) vii, 305a; s, 388b
al-Mufaḍḍal b. Maʿshar vii, 581a
al-Mufaḍḍal b. Muḥammad b. Yaʿlā al-Ḍabbī → al-Ḍabbī
al-Mufaḍḍal b. Salama (903) s, **631a**
al-Mufaḍḍal (II) b. Salama b. ʿĀsim al-Ḍabbī → al-Ḍabbī
Mufaḍḍal b. Ṣāliḥ s, 233a
al-Mufaḍḍal b. ʿUmar al-Djuʿfī iv, 1132b, 1133a
al-Mufaḍḍal b. Yazīd b. al-Muhallab vii, 359a; s, 41a
Mufaḍḍaliyya → al-Khaṭṭābiyya
al-Mufaḍḍaliyyāt vii, 306b
Mufākhara i, 584b, 586b; iv, 77b, 448b; v, 1223b; vii, 308b
al-Mufarradj b. Sallām iv, 275a
Mufarridj b. Daghfal al-Ṭāʾī (Djarrāḥid) i, 824a, b; ii, 482b, 483a, 854b; iii, 77a, 79b, 128b, 841a; iv, 841b; s, 37a
Mufarridj b. al-Djarrāḥ v, 327b
Mufaṣṣal s, **632a**

Mufāwaḍa vii, 310a
al-Mufawwaḍ, Dja'far b. al-Mu'tamid ('Abbāsid) (IX) i, 278b; vii, 766a
Müfettish s, **632a**
al-Mufīd, Shaykh Abū 'Abd Allāh al-'Ukbarī (1022) iii, 1266a; iv, 182b; vi, 219a, 549a; vii, 312a, 758b; viii, 372b; s, 56b, 89b
Mufliḥ → Abū Ṣāliḥ Mufliḥ
Mufrad i, 95a, 1083b; vii, 313a
al-Muftarī → Ḥā-mīm
Muftī → Fatwa; Shaykh al-Islām
Müftī-zāde (Müftüoghlu) Aḥmed → Aḥmad Ḥikmet
Mugan Ḳaghan (572) x, 687a
Mughalmārī → Tukarō'ī
Mughals i, 81a, 117b, 199a, 228b, 229a, b, 238a, 252b, 316a, 768a, 769a, 1069a, 1159a, 1161a, 1168b, 1347b; ii, 120b, 155a, 157a, 265a, 336b, 806a, 815a, 868a, 1084b, 1129b; iii, 199a, 201a, b, 411a, 422b, 424b, 448b; iv, 268b, 563a, 709a, 759b, 1056a; v, 72a, 629b; vi, 77b, 198b, 310a, 422b, 424b, 488a, 533b, 534a, b, 696b, 813b; vii, 80a, 129b, 194a, 313b, 795b, 943b; ix, 598a; s, 131b, 167b, 246b, 252b, 253a, 257b, 258b, 280a, 335b
– constructions v, 888b, 889a, 1215a, 1216b
Mughalānī Bēgam i, 296a; iii, 1158b
al-Mughallis, Abū 'Abd Allāh al-Ḥusayn s, 119b
Mughals xi, 118b
al-Mughammas (Mecca) vii, 346b
Mūghān s, 143a
Mūghān steppe vi, 56a, 492b, 494a, 495b, 527b
Mughannī ii, 1073a, b
Mughārasa vii, 346b
al-Mughāwir → Almogávares
al-Mughayyabāt al-Khams vii, 346b
Mughīra, Banū i, 98a; vi, 138a, 139a
al-Mughīra b. 'Abd Allāh → al-Uḳayshir al-Asadī
al-Mughīra b. 'Abd Allāh b. 'Umar b. Makhzūm vi, 137b
al-Mughīra b. 'Abd al-Raḥmān b. Makhzūm vi, 139a, 140b
al-Mughīra b. 'Abd al-Raḥmān III (al-Andalus) (X) vi, 431a
al-Mughīra b. Abī Burda al-Ḳurashī (VIII) v, 1160a
al-Mughīra b. Abī Ṣufra (VIII) vii, 359a
al-Mughīra b. Khālid b. Makhzūm vi, 140a
al-Mughīra b. Sa'īd al-Badjalī → al-Mughīriyya
al-Mughīra b. Sa'īd al-'Idjlī, Ghālī (737) i, 141a, 1099a, 1116b; ii, 1094a; iv, 926b; vi, 441b; vii, 388b, 459b; s, 103b, 232b
al-Mughīra b. Shu'ba, Abū 'Abd Allāh al-Thaḳafī (668) i, 111a, 382b, 695a, 714a; iii, 40a, 545a, 1265b; iv, 385a; v, 346b; vi, 710a, 920a; vii, 27a, 347a; ix, 421a
Mughīra b. Sunyer (X) x, 303b
al-Mughīriyya i, 1116b; vii, 347b, 459b
al-Mughīth, al-Malik (Ḥims) (XIII) vi, 381a
Mughīth, Malik (Hind) (XV) iii, 418b, 638b
Mughīth al-Rūmī i, 493a; v, 510a
al-Mughīth 'Umar b. Ayyūb (1244) iv, 609a; viii, 989a
Mughla (Muğla) vii, 348b
Mughniyya, Muḥammad Djawād (1979) vii, 780b
Mughrāna, Banū vi, 742a
Mughulistān → Mogholistān
Mughuliyya iv, 420a
Mughultāy (1290) ix, 661a
Mughulṭāy b. Ḳilīdj b. 'Abd Allāh (1361) vii, 350a; viii, 156b
Mughulṭāy 'Alā' al-Dīn (1307) viii, 158a
Muḥāḍara iv, 697a, b
Muḥaddith → Ḥadīth
al-Muhadhdhab, al-Ḳāḍī iv, 214b
Muhadhdhab al-Dīn v, 272a
al-Muhadhdhab b. Mammātī → Ibn Mammātī
Muhadhdhib al-Dawla 'Alī b. Naṣr s, 118b, 119a
Muhādjarat movement v, 171a
Muhādjir vii, 350b
Muhādjir, Banu 'l- i, 65b; ii, 305a; iv, 478a; s, 82a
al-Muhādjir b. 'Abd Allāh al-Kilābī s, 31b
al-Muhādjir b. Abī Umayya b. al-Mughīra Makhzūmī (VII) i, 110b; vi, 138b, 139b; viii, 97a
al-Muhādjirūn i, 54b, 515a; iii, 226b, 366b, 874a; v, 995b; vii, 356a

Muḥāfiẓ Khān (XVI) ii, 1127a; vi, 52a, 54b
Muḥakkak iv, 1123a, 1125a
al-Muḥakkik (1277) vii, 297b
Muḥakkik-i Awwal → al-Ḥilmī, Nadjm al-Dīn
Muḥakkima → Khawāridj; Taḥkīm
al-Muḥakkima al-ūlā → Harūrites
Muḥāl → Manṭiḳ
Muhalhil ii, 1028b
al-Muhalhil b. Muḥammad i, 512b, 513a
al-Muhalhil b. Rabīʿa → Imruʾ al-Ḳays ʿAdī b. Rabīʿa al-Taghlibī
al-Muhallab b. Abī Ṣufra, Abū Saʿīd al-Azdī (702) i, 55a, 76b, 77a, 304a, 810b, 1242b; iii, 40b; iv, 15a, 752b, 1075b, 1145b; v, 57a; vii, 357a, 523b; s, 357b
al-Muhallabī → Yazīd b. Ḥātim
al-Muhallabī (1246) vii, 772a
al-Muhallabī, Abu 'l-Ghanāʾim al-Mufaḍḍal (X) vii, 358a
al-Muhallabī, Abu 'l-Ḥusayn al-Ḥasan b. Aḥmad (990) vii, 357b; viii, 16b
al-Muhallabī, Abū Muḥammad al-Ḥasan b. Muḥammad (vizier) (963) i, 118a, 126b, 1352b; iii, 780a, 854a; vi, 965b; vii, 358a, 771a; s, 13a, 32b, 362a, b
Muhallabids i, 158a, 305a; iii, 649b, 981b; vi, 428a, 640b; vii, 358b, 1016a; viii, 465b; s, 352a; x, 541b
al-Muḥallī, Ḥamīd b. Aḥmad vi, 433b, 434a
Muḥallil v, 109b; s, 632a
Muḥammad, the Prophet (632) i, 453a, 514a, 728a, 959a, 1020b, 1021a, 1092b, 1283b; ii, 168a, 227a, 363a, 538b, 593a, 758b, 932a, 1061a; iii, 32a, 33a, 90b, 435a, 800b, 933a, 1231b, 1240b; iv, 316a, 356a, 994b, 996b; v, 75a, 402b, 734a; vi, 146a, 652a; vii, 360b, 570b
– beliefs concerning the Prophet i, 178a, 187b, 264a, 266a, 267a, 306b, 314b, 333a, 336b, 337a, 349a, 443a, 1310a, b, 1314b; ii, 363b, 376a, 847a, 883b, 950a, 993a, 1005b, 1058b, 1098b; iii, 94b, 256a, 462a, 607a, 1018b; iv, 270a, 319a, 367b, 821a, 1074a; v, 82a
– companions i, 114b, 129a, 343b, 881b, 405a, 448b, 514a, 695a, 1077b, 1313a; ii, 728b; iii, 582b, 873b, 1024a; iv, 896b, 927a; v, 406a
– history iv, 736b; v, 415a, 771a
– life events i, 12a, 53a, 109b, 110a, 115b, 136b, 151a, 152b, 307b, 381b, 442b, 451a, 509b, 549a, 609a, 633b, 771b, 868a, 922a, 1011b; ii, 113b, 372a, 461b, 625a, 725a, 842b, 846b, 873b, 953a, 993b, 1023b; iii, 33a, 64a, 94a, 223a, 240b, 286a, 366b, 539a, 578a, 975b; iv, 320a, b, 771a, 824a, 832b, 898b, 927b, 928b, 1020b, 1103a, 1138b; v, 78b, 79a, 316a, b, 317a, 436b, 995b, 1161b
– relics i, 109a, 736a, 1314b; ii, 695b; iv, 367b, 368a; v, 761a
Muhammad, K.T. (Mappila) vi, 464b
Muhammad, N.P. (Mappila) vi, 464b
Muḥammad II b. Muḥammad I al-Sharīf, Mawlāy (ʿAlawid, 1664) vi, 142b
Muḥammad, Sultan of Brunei s, 151b
Muḥammad (Bayhaḳī Sayyid) s, 131b
Muḥammad I (ʿAbbādid) i, 5b, 242a; iv, 115b
Muḥammad II (ʿAbbādid) → al-Muʿtamid
Muḥammad I (Aghlabid) i, 248b, 250b
Muḥammad II (Aghlabid) i, 249a, 250b, 1152a
Muḥammad I (ʿAlawid) i, 355b; s, 113b
Muḥammad II b. Muḥammad I al-Sharīf, Mawlāy (ʿAlawid) (1664) i, 355b; v, 1191b; vi, 142b
Muḥammad III b. ʿAbd Allāh, Sīdī (ʿAlawid) (1790) i, 47b, 356a, 506b; ii, 116b, 146a, 308a, 367b, 510b, 727a, 820a; iii, 339b, 395b, 966a; iv, 634a, 635b; v, 1192a; vi, 249a, 250a, 293b, 589a, 597a, 842b; vii, 39a, 387a, 391a; viii, 507b; s, 40b, 325b, 401a, b
Muḥammad IV b. Abd al-Raḥmān, Sīdī (ʿAlawid) (1873) i, 315b, 356b, 357a; ii, 332a, 510b; iii, 562a, 806b; vi, 249a, 250b, 595b, 798b; vii, 391a; s, 114a, 303a
Muḥammad V b. Yūsuf (ʿAlawid) (1961) i, 357b, 358a; ii, 673b, 1116b; iii, 564a; iv, 634b, 635b, 775a; v, 1072a, 1194b; vi, 262a; vii, 415a
Muḥammad I (Bahmanid) (1375) vi, 67a; vii, 458a; xi, 1a
Muḥammad II (Bahmanid) (1397) vii, 458b
Muḥammad III, Shams al-Dīn Lashkarī (Bahmanid) (1482) vi, 67a, b; vii, 458b
Muḥammad I (Ḥafṣid) → al-Mustanṣir
Muḥammad II (Ḥafṣid) → Abū ʿAṣīda

Muḥammad III (Ḥafṣid) → Abū Darba
Muḥammad IV (Ḥafṣid) → al-Muntaṣir
Muḥammad V (Ḥafṣid) → Abu ʿAbd Allāh Muḥammad V
Muḥammad I b. al-Ḳāsim b. Ḥammūd al-Mahdī (Ḥammūdid) (1048) iii, 147b
Muḥammad III (Ḥammūdid) iii, 147b
Muḥammad I (Ismāʿīlī) i, 353b, 1359b; iv, 859b
Muḥammad II (Ismāʿīlī) i, 353b; iv, 205a
Muḥammad III, ʿAlāʾ al-Dīn (Ismāʿīlī, Alamūt) (1255) i, 353b; iv, 205b; vi, 790b; s, **632b**
Muḥammad I (Ḳarak͟hānid) iii, 1114a
Muḥammad II b. Sulaymān Bug͟hrā K͟hān (Ḳarak͟hānid) (1130) iii, 1114b; vii, 535b; x, 689a
Muḥammad I (Ḳarāmānid) → Muḥammad b. Ḳarāmān
Muḥammad II (Ḳarāmānid) iv, 623b
Muḥammad IV (Marīnid) iii, 832a, 836a
Muḥammad I b. Naṣr al-G͟hālib (Naṣrid) (1273) i, 495b, 1089a; ii, 307b, 1014a, 1015b, 1016b; iii, 826b; vi, 222b, 577a; vii, 1020a, 1021b; s, 381b
Muḥammad II al-Faḳīh (Naṣrid) (1302) ii, 1016b; vi, 222b, 521a; vii, 1020a, 1021b
Muḥammad III al-Mag͟hlūʿ (Naṣrid) (1309) iii, 833b; vii, 563b, 1020a, 1022a
Muḥammad IV, Abū ʿAbd Allāh (Naṣrid) (1333) iv, 355b; vii, 1020b, 1023a
Muḥammad V al-G͟hānī bi-'llāh, Abū ʿAbd Allāh (Naṣrid) (1359) i, 1225a; ii, 115a, 1017a; iii, 804a, 835b, 972b; vii, 1020b, 1024a
Muḥammad VI al-G͟hālib bi-'llāh, Abū ʿAbd Allāh (El Bermejo) (Naṣrid) (1362) vii, 1020b, 1024a
Muḥammad VII, Abū ʿAbd Allāh (Naṣrid) (1408) iii, 804a, 972b; vii, 1020b, 1025a
Muḥammad VIII al-Mutamassik (El Pequeño) (Naṣrid) (1429) vii, 1020b, 1025b, 1026a; s, 399a
Muḥammad IX al-G͟hālib bi-'llāh (El Zurdo) (Naṣrid) (1453) vii, 1020b, 1025b, 1026a; s, 399a
Muḥammad X, Abū ʿAbd Allāh (al-Aḥnaf/ El Cojo) (Naṣrid) (1447) vii, 1020b, 1026a; s, 399a
Muḥammad XI (El Chiquito) (Naṣrid) (1455) vii, 1020b, 1026a
Muḥammad XII, Abū ʿAbd Allāh (Boabdil) (Naṣrid) (1492) i, 501b; vi, 222b; vii, 1020b, 1026b; s, 399a
Muḥammad XIII b. Saʿd (al-Zag͟hal) (Naṣrid) (1489) vii, 1020b, 1026b, 1027b
Muḥammad I-VI (Ottoman) → Meḥemmed I-VI
Muḥammad I (Āl Ṣabāḥ) (1896) viii, 669a
Muḥammad I G͟hiyāt͟h al-Dīn b. Malik S͟hāh (Sald͟jūḳ) (1118) i, 522b, 664a, 684a, 780a, 1052a, 1336b; ii, 975b; iii, 47a, 196a, 197b, 254a, 1097b; iv, 28b, 29a, 101b, 102a; v, 159a, b, 662a; vi, 64a, 275a, b, 493b, 499b; vii, 408a, 529b; viii, 81b, 716a, 942b; s, 382b
Muḥammad I Mug͟hīt͟h al-Dīn b. Arslan S͟hāh (Sald͟jūḳ) (1156) vi, 853a
Muḥammad II b. Maḥmūd b. Muḥammad b. Malik-S͟hāh (Sald͟jūḳ) (1159) i, 684a, 865b; iv, 1097a; v, 160b; vi, 64a, 500a, 871a; vii, 406a; viii, 944a
Muḥammad I b. ʿAbd al-Raḥmān II (Umayyad), (al-Andalus) (886) i, 11a, 83a, 85b, 494a, 498a, 957a; iii, 816a; iv, 713a; v, 510b, 1107b; vi, 926b; vii, 248a; x, 850b
Muḥammad II b. His͟hām al-Mahdī (Umayyad) (1010) → al-Mahdī (Umayyad)
Muḥammad III b. ʿAbd al-Raḥmān al-Mustakfī (Umayyad) → al-Andalus, Umayyads of Spain
Muḥammad II al-Burtuḳālī (Waṭṭāsid) (1525) i, 706b; vii, 37b
Muḥammad, al-ʿĀlim b. Ismāʿīl (ʿAlawid) (XVIII) iii, 49b; vi, 595a
Muḥammad, Awlād ii, 876a
Muḥammad b. ʿAbbād → Muḥammad I (ʿAbbādid)
Muḥammad b. ʿAbbād i, 1166b
Muḥammad b. ʿAbbās (Ḳād͟jār) → Ḳād͟jār
Muḥammad b. al-ʿAbbās b. al-Baṣrī → Ṣāḥib al-Rākūba
Muḥammad b. al-ʿAbbās b. Mandīl vi, 404a
Muḥammad b. al-ʿAbbās al-Yazīdī iii, 23b
Muḥammad b. ʿAbd Allāh → Ibn al-Abbār, Abū ʿAbd Allāh (1260); Ibn al-K͟haṭīb Abū ʿAbdallāh, Lisān al-Dīn (1375); Ibn Mālik, Abū ʿAbdallāh al-D͟jayyānī (1274)

Muḥammad b. ʿAbd Allāh → Muḥammad III (ʿAlawid)
Muḥammad b. ʿAbd Allāh (Ḥamāliyya) → al-Sharīf al-Akhḍar
Muḥammad b. ʿAbd Allāh (Ḥasanid) s, 232b
Muḥammad b. ʿAbd Allāh b. ʿAbd al-Ḥakam (882) → Ibn ʿAbd al-Ḥakam, Abū ʿAbd Allāh
Muḥammad b. ʿAbd Allāh b. ʿAbd al-Ḥakam (Mālikī) (845) vii, 4b
Muḥammad b. ʿAbd Allāh b. al-Ḥasan b. al-Ḥasan, al-Nafs al-Zakiyya (ʿAlid) (762) i, 45b, 103b, 123a, 402a, b, 550b; ii, 485a, 745a; iii, 256b, 616a; v, 1233a, b; vi, 263a, b, 332a, 334a, 427b; vii, 348a, 358b, 359b, 388a, 459b, 645b; ix, 423b, 761b
Muḥammad b. ʿAbd Allāh b. Khāzim i, 1293a
Muḥammad b. ʿAbd Allāh b. al-Muḳaffaʿ i, 631a; iii, 883b
Muḥammad b. ʿAbd Allāh b. Saʿīd al-Yaharī iii, 124a
Muḥammad b. ʿAbd Allāh b. Shabīb (IX) s, **633b**
Muḥammad b. ʿAbd Allāh b. Ṭāhir Dhī ʾl-Yamīnayn (867) vii, 390a, 722b; viii, 856a
Muḥammad b. ʿAbd Alllāh b. Yūnus (1059) ix, 586b
Muḥammad b. ʿAbd Allāh b. Ẓafar al-Ṣaḳalī → Ibn Ẓafar
Muḥammad b. ʿAbd Allāh b. Ziyād → Muḥammad al-Ziyādī
Muḥammad b. ʿAbd Allāh Āl Khalīfa iv, 953b
Muḥammad b. ʿAbd Allāh al-Ghālib → Muḥammad al-Maslūkh
Muḥammad b. ʿAbd Allāh Ḥassān al-Mahdī (1920) i, 1172b; vii, 389b; viii, 162a, 990a
Muḥammad b. ʿAbd Allāh al-Kharūṣī iv, 1085a
Muḥammad b. ʿAbd Allāh al-Khudjistānī iii, 254b
Muḥammad b. ʿAbd Allāh al-Sāmarrī iii, 161a
Muḥammad b. ʿAbd Allāh al-Shintināwī vi, 627a
Muḥammad b. ʿAbd Allāh Yumn al-Dawla i, 1310a
Muḥammad b. ʿAbd Allāh b. Ziyād (Ziyādid) (859) xi, 370a
Muḥammad b. ʿAbd al-ʿAzīz b. Suʿūd v, 998b
Muḥammad b. ʿAbd al-Bāḳī (1583) ix, 101b
Muḥammad b. ʿAbd al-Djabbār (XI) x, 853a
Muḥammad b. ʿAbd al-Ḥalīm (1681) vii, 469b
Muḥammad b. ʿAbd al-Ḳādir al-Kardūdī → al-Kardūdī
Muḥammad b. ʿAbd al-Karīm (Rīf) (1963) vii, 416b; viii, 523a, 905b; s, **633b**
Muḥammad b. ʿAbd al-Malik → Ibn Ṭufayl; Ibn al-Zayyāt; Ibn Zuhr
Muḥammad b. ʿAbd al-Malik (Umayyad) (700) vi, 900a
Muḥammad b. ʿAbd al-Malik b. Ayman i, 600a
Muḥammad b. ʿAbd al-Malik al-Ṭawīl s, 80a
Muḥammad b. ʿAbd al-Malik al-Zayyāt ii, 385b
Muḥammad b. ʿAbd al-Muʿīn b. ʿAwn, Sharīf iii, 263a, 605b; vi, 150b, 151a
Muḥammad b. ʿAbd al-Muʾmin i, 79b, 160b; iii, 386b
Muḥammad b. ʿAbd al-Raḥīm → Ibn al-Furāt
Muḥammad b. ʿAbd al-Raḥmān (886) x, 824a
Muḥammad b. ʿAbd al-Raḥmān b. Abi ʾl-Baḳāʾ (XIII) vi, 824b
Muḥammad b. ʿAbd al-Raḥmān b. Abī Ziyān (1733) → Ziyāniyya
Muḥammad b. ʿAbd al-Raḥmān al-ʿAṭawī (864) vii, 392b
Muḥammad b. ʿAbd al-Raḥmān al-Gashtulī (1793) viii, 399a
Muḥammad b. ʿAbd al-Raḥmān al-Ḳāʾim bi-amr Allāh (Saʿdid) (1517) vi, 893a
Muḥammad b. ʿAbd al-Razzāḳ (X) vi, 499b; vii, 656a; viii, 1028b; x, 232a
Muḥammad b. ʿAbd al-Ṣamad iv, 381a
Muḥammad b. ʿAbd al-Wahhāb → Ibn ʿAbd al-Wahhāb
Muḥammad b. ʿAbdūn vi, 450a

Muḥammad b. Abi 'l-ʿAbbās iii, 135b
Muḥammad b. Abī ʿAffān, Imām (IX) x, 816b
Muḥammad b. Abī ʿĀmir → al-Manṣūr b. Abī ʿĀmir
Muḥammad b. Abī Bakr → Ibn Ḳayyim al-Dj̲awziyya; Ibn Sayyid al-Nās
Muḥammad b. Abī Bakr (al-Ṣiddīḳ) (VII) i, 44a, 109b, 451b; iii, 241a; vi, 740b; vii, 269a, 393a; s, 92b
Muḥammad b. Abī Bakr (Songhay) (1538) ii, 977b; vii, 393b; ix, 756b
Muḥammad b. Abi 'l-Dj̲awarī (IX) ix, 670a
Muḥammad b. Abī Ḥud̲h̲ayfa (657) vii, 393a, 394b
Muḥammad b. Abi 'l-Ḳāsim → Ibn Abī Dīnār
Muḥammad b. Abī Muḥammad → Ibn Ẓafar
Muḥammad b. Abī Muḥammad Ibn Abi 'l-Zinād (VIII) s, 380b
Muḥammad b. Abī Rawḥ Luṭf Allāh b. Abī Saʿīd i, 145b
Muḥammad b. Abi 'l-Sād̲j̲ al-Afs̲h̲īn (Sād̲j̲id)(901) i, 145b; ii, 524a, 679b; v, 49a; vii, 395a; viii, 745a
Muḥammad b. Abī Tawād̲j̲īn al-Kutāmī i, 91b
Muḥammad b. Abī ʿUyayna b. al-Muhallab (VIII) vii, 359b, 395a
Muḥammad b. Abī Yūsuf Yaʿḳūb (al-Nāṣir) → al-Nāṣir, Muḥammad b. Abī Yūsuf
Muḥammad b. Abī Zaynab → Abu 'l-K̲h̲aṭṭāb
Muḥammad b. ʿAffān iii, 652b
Muḥammad b. Afrāsiyāb vi, 511a
Muḥammad b. al-Ag̲h̲lab → Muḥammad I (Ag̲h̲labid)
Muḥammad b. Aḥmad → Muḥammad II (Ag̲h̲labid); Abu 'l-Muṭahhar al-Azdī; Ibn al-ʿAlḳamī; Ibn Iyās; Ibn Rus̲h̲d
Muḥammad b. Aḥmad (Āl-i Burhān) (1219) viii, 749a
Muḥammad b. Aḥmad, Abu 'l-S̲h̲alaʿlaʿ ii, 851a
Muḥammad b. Aḥmad b. ʿAlī b. Dj̲ābir al-Hawwārī (XIV) xi, 15a
Muḥammad b. Aḥmad b. Karīm al-Dīn (1578) ix, 316a
Muḥammad b. Aḥmad b. K̲h̲ayrāt vi, 191b
Muḥammad b. Aḥmad b. Rus̲h̲d vii, 538a
Muḥammad b. Aḥmad b. Sālim (909) viii, 993b
Muḥammad b. Aḥmad Abī ʿAwn iii, 683a
Muḥammad b. Aḥmad al-Andalusī (XI) vii, 413a
Muḥammad b. Aḥmad al-Ḥabūḍī s, 338b
Muḥammad b. Aḥmad al-Ḥuḍīgī ii, 527a
Muḥammad b. Aḥmad Ibn Ṭāhir (Mursiya) (XI) vii, 767a
Muḥammad b. Aḥmad al-Iskandarānī (XIX) vii, 395b
Muḥammad b. Aḥmad al-Manṣūrī vi, 665a
Muḥammad b. Aḥmad Mayyāra i, 428a; iii, 721a
Muḥammad b. Aḥmad (S̲h̲arwān-S̲h̲āh) iv, 346b
Muḥammad b. Aḥmad al-S̲h̲aybānī iv, 90b
Muḥammad b. Aḥmad Ṭāhāzāde iii, 88a
Muḥammad b. al-Aḥmar → Muḥammad I (Naṣrid)
Muḥammad b. ʿĀʾid i, 98b, 106b, 709b; v, 808b
Muḥammad b. Āḳā Rustam Rūzafzūn vi, 514b
Muḥammad b. ʿAḳīl (1806) vii, 115a
Muḥammad b. ʿAlī → Ibn ʿArabī; Ibn ʿAskar (1239); Ibn Bābawayh; Ibn Dj̲awād al-Iṣfahānī; Ibn Muḳla; Ibn al-Ṭiḳṭaḳā; Ibn Waḥs̲h̲iyya
Muḥammad b. ʿAlī, Sayyid (1600) viii, 778b
Muḥammad b. ʿAlī b. ʿAbd Allāh al-ʿAbbās (743) i, 15a, 48b, 124b, 381a; ii, 168b; iii, 1265b; iv, 15b, 837a; v, 2a, 3a; vii, 396a, 399a
Muḥammad b. ʿAlī al-Layt̲h̲ (Ṣaffarid) (911) viii, 796a
Muḥammad b. ʿAlī b. Muḥallī (Marrākus̲h̲) vi, 593a
Muḥammad b. ʿAlī b. Yūsuf ii, 1007a
Muḥammad b. ʿAlī b. ʿUmar (1105) vii, 397a
Muḥammad b. ʿAlī al-Baḥrānī iii, 588b
Muḥammad b. ʿAlī al-Barḳī s, 127a
Muḥammad b. ʿAlī al-Fenārī → Meḥmed b. ʿAlī al-Fenārī
Muḥammad b. ʿAlī al-Hamadānī i, 392b
Muḥammad b. ʿAlī al-Idrīsī → al-Idrīsī, Muḥammad b. ʿAlī

Muḥammad b. ʿAlī al-Idrīsī (ʿAsīr) vi, 192a
Muḥammad b. ʿAlī al-Riḍā (835) i, 713a; iii, 1167a; vii, 313a, 396b; s, 95a, 127b
Muḥammad b. ʿAlī al-Shalmaghānī (934) ii, 218a, 1094b; iii, 101a, 683a; vii, 397a, 812a
Muḥammad b. ʿAlī Sipāhīzāde i, 119a; ii, 587b
Muḥammad b. ʿAlī wuld/u Rzīn (Tāfīlālt) vi, 249b
Muḥammad b. ʿAlī Zayn al-ʿĀbidīn al-Bāḳir (V. Imām) (735) vi, 441b, 917b; vii, 95a, 348a, 388b, 397b, 459b; ix, 168a, 422b; s, 129b, 231a, 232b, 233a
Muḥammad b. ʿĀmir Abū Nuḳṭa al-Rufaydī i, 709a
Muḥammad b. Amīr Ghāzī (Dānish mendid) vi, 506b
Muḥammad b. ʿAmmār b. Yāsir i, 448b
Muḥammad b. Āmsāyb (Ben Msayeb) vi, 249a, 253b
Muḥammad b. ʿAnnāz i, 512a; iii, 258b, 571b
Muḥammad b. al-ʿArabi → Ibn al-ʿArabī
Muḥammad b. al-ʿArabiyya i, 47b
Muḥammad b. ʿArafa (1976) (ʿAlawī) i, 357b, 358a; v, 1194b; s, **634a**
Muḥammad b. ʿĀrif b. Aḥmad ʿAbd al-Ḥaḳḳ s, 313a
Muḥammad b. Aṣbagh (Bayyāna) (915) vii, 400a
Muḥammad b. Aṣbagh b. Labīb (938) vii, 400a
Muḥammad b. Aṣbagh b. Muḥammad (918) vii, 400a
Muḥammad b. Aṣbagh al-Azdī vii, 400a
Muḥammad b. al-Ashʿath b. Kays al-Kindī (686) iii, 715a; vii, 400b, 523a, 689b
Muḥammad b. al-Ashʿath al-Khuzāʿī (761) i, 134b; iii, 654b, 981b, 1040b, 1041b; iv, 827a; vi, 841a
Muḥammad b. Arslan → Muḥammad I (Saldjūḳ)
Muḥammad b. ʿĀshūr al-Kindī → Ibn ʿĀshūr
Muḥammad b. ʿĀṣim i, 600a
Muḥammad b. ʿAttāb v, 488a
Muḥammad b. ʿAṭṭū al-Djānātī (Marrākush) vi, 593a
Muḥammad b. ʿAwaḍ b. Lādin al-Ḥaḍramī vi, 166b, 167b
Muḥammad b. ʿĀyid → Muḥammad b. ʿĀʾid
Muḥammad b. ʿAyshūn al-Sharrāṭ iv, 380a
Muḥammad b. ʿAyyāsh ii, 1014b
Muḥammad b. Aẓhar i, 1212b
Muḥammad b. Badr al-Dīn al-Munshiʿ (1592) i, 310a
Muḥammad b. al-Baʿīth (Buʿayth) (IX) iv, 88b; vi, 504b; x, 42a
Muḥammad b. Bakhtiyār → Muḥammad Bakhtiyār Khaldjī
Muḥammad b. Baḳiyya b. ʿAlī → Ibn Baḳiyya
Muḥammad b. Balban ii, 268a; s, 67a, 124b
Muḥammad b. Bānī iii, 326b
Muḥammad b. Barakāt i, 553a, 1032b; ii, 517b
Muḥammad b. Barakāt I b. Ḥasan b. ʿAdjlān, Sharīf (1497) i, 553a, 1032b; ii, 517b; vi, 150a
Muḥammad b. Bashīr → Muḥammad b. Yasīr
Muḥammad b. Bashīr (Bushayr) (IX) vii, 460a, 517a, 647b
Muḥammad b. Bashshār Bundār (866) vii, 691b; x, 11b
Muḥammad b. Bilāl, Kurd (906) vi, 900b
Muḥammad b. Bughā (IX) vii, 477a
Muḥammad b. Buzurg-Ummīd → Muḥammad I (Ismāʿīlī)
Muḥammad b. Dāwūd → Ibn Ādjurrūmī; Ibn Dāwūd, Muḥammad
Muḥammad b. Dāwūd b. al-Djarrāḥ → Ibn al-Djarrāḥ
Muḥammad b. al-Djabbār ii, 1009a
Muḥammad b. Djābir b. ʿAbd Allāh s, 231a
Muḥammad b. Djaʿfar → Djaʿfar b. Abī Ṭālib; al-Kattānī; al-Ḳazzāz; al-Kharāʾiṭī; al-Muntaṣir bi-'llāh; al-Rāḍī
Muḥammad b. Djaʿfar al-Azkawī → Ibn Djaʿfar
Muḥammad b. Djaʿfar al-Ṣādiḳ al-Dībādj (IX) i, 145a, 402b, 551a; vi, 334b
Muḥammad b. al-Djahm al-Barmakī i, 153b, 1036a; iii, 355a; vii, 401a
Muḥammad b. Djarīr ii, 790b
Muḥammad b. al-Djazarī → Ibn al-Djazarī, Abu 'l-Khayr

Muḥammad b. Dumlādj (1075) vii, 121b
Muḥammad b. Dushmanziyār → ʿAlāʾ al-Dawla
Muḥammad b. Eretna → Ghiyāth al-Dīn Muḥammad
Muḥammad b. al-Faḍl b. Māhān (Sind) (IX) vi, 967b
Muḥammad b. Faḍl Allāh iii, 155b
Muḥammad b. al-Faḍl al-Djardjaraʿī → al-Djardjarāʾī
Muḥammad b. Fakhr al-Dīn Muḥammad iii, 457b
Muḥammad b. Falāḥ iv, 49a
Muḥammad b. Farāmarz → Khosrew Mollā
Muḥammad b. Farīd (Dihlī Sayyid) (1443) ix, 118b, 119a
Muḥammad b. Farīghūn → Abu'l-Ḥārith
Muḥammad b. Fayṣal b. ʿAbd al-ʿAzīz Āl Suʿūd s, 305b
Muḥammad b. Fuḍayl viii, 486a
Muḥammad b. al-Furāt → Ibn al-Furāt, Muḥammad
Muḥammad b. Ghāzī (Dānishmend) ii, 110b; iv, 843a
Muḥammad b. Ghāzī → Malik Muḥammad b. Ghāzī (Malaṭya)
Muḥammad b. Gümüshtigin (Dānishmendid) (1142) viii, 948b
Muḥammad b. Habbāriyya (1115) viii, 376ab
Muḥammad b. Ḥabīb Abū Djaʿfar (859) i, 158b; ii, 480a; iii, 820a, 907b; vi, 822b; vii, 401b; x, 2b; s, 177a
Muḥammad b. al-Ḥādjdj ii, 1013a; iii, 542b
Muḥammad b. Hādjdjādj iv, 665b
Muḥammad b. al-Ḥadjdjām ii, 1009b
Muḥammad b. Ḥamad al-Sharḳī ii, 936b
Muḥammad b. Ḥammād b. Isḥāḳ Ibn Dirham s, 385a
Muḥammad b. al-Ḥanafiyya b. ʿAlī b. Abī Ṭālib (700) i, 15a, 41a, 48b, 55b, 124b, 381a, 402a, 959a, 1116b; ii, 168b, 1026a, 1094b; iii, 608b, 1232b, 1265b; iv, 836b, 1086b; v, 433b, 552a, 1231a, 1235b; vi, 240a, 350b; vii, 402b, 521a; ix, 421b; s, 48b, 343a, 357b, 401a
Muḥammad b. al-Ḥanash iv, 552b
Muḥammad b. Ḥanbal i, 272b
Muḥammad b. Hāniʾ → Ibn Hāniʾ
Muḥammad b. al-Ḥārith b. Bashkīr (IX) vii, 190a
Muḥammad b. al-Ḥarsh → Bū Dalī
Muḥammad b. Hārūn (IX) iii, 254b; vii, 418a
Muḥammad b. Hārūn (Rasūl) (XII) viii, 455a
Muḥammad b. Ḥasan → Muḥammad II, III (Ismāʿīlī)
Muḥammad b. al-Ḥasan → Ibn Durayd; Ibn Ḥamdūn; al-Shaybānī, Abū ʿAbd Allāh
Muḥammad b. Ḥasan (Sayyid Bayhaḳī) s, 131b
Muḥammad b. al-Ḥasan b. ʿAlī → al-Ḥurr al-ʿĀmilī
Muḥammad b. al-Ḥasan b. Dīnār (864) vii, 403b
Muḥmmad b. Ḥasan al-Ḥurr → al-Ḥurr al-ʿĀmilī
Muḥmmad b. Ḥasan b. Idrīs (Dāʿī Muṭlaḳ) s, 358b
Muḥammad b. Ḥasan al-Sarakhsī i, 146a
Muḥammad b. al-Hayṣam iv, 668a
Muḥammad b. al-Haytham i, 154a
Muḥammad b. Ḥāzim b. ʿAmr al-Bāhilī (IX) vii, 404a
Muḥammad b. Hazzāʾ b. Zaʿal ii, 619a
Muḥammad b. Hilāl b. al-Muḥassin al-Ṣābiʾ viii, 103a
Muḥammad b. Hindū-shāh Nakhčiwānī (XIV) vii, 404b
Muḥammad b. Hishām b. Ismāʿīl (VIII) i, 627a; vi, 139b
Muḥammad b. Hishām b. ʿAbd al-Djabbār → al-Mahdī (Umayyad)
Muḥammad b. al-Hudhayl → Abu 'l-Hudhayl al-ʿAllāf
Muḥammad b. Ḥumayd al-Ṭūsī iii, 573a
Muḥammad b. Hurmuz (X) viii, 797a
Muḥammad b. Ḥusām iv, 68a
Muḥammad b. Ḥusayn → Meḥmed Khalīfe; al-Sharīf al-Rāḍī
Muḥammad b. Ḥusayn (Ḥusaynid) iii, 635b; iv, 828b
Muḥammad b. Ḥusayn b. al-Astarābādī → Ghiyāth al-Dīn Muḥammad
Muḥammad b. Ibrāhīm → Simdjūr, Banū
Muḥammad b. Ibrāhīm II b. Ṭahmāsp (ʿĀdil-Shāhi) (1656) vii, 404b
Muḥammad b. Ibrāhīm b. Ḥadjdjādj iv, 115b
Muḥammad b. Ibrāhīm b. Ṭabāṭabā → Ibn Ṭabāṭabā

Muḥammad b. Idrīs → Ibn Idrīs
Muḥammad b. Idrīs II (Idrīsid, 836) i, 1088a; ii, 874a; iii, 1035b
Muḥammad b. Idrīs b. ʿAlī b. Ḥammūd (Mālaḳa) (1048) vi, 222b
Muḥammad b. Ilyās → Abū ʿAlī
Muḥammad b. ʿĪsā (1582) vi, 112b; viii, 526a
Muḥammad b. ʿĪsā (Burghūth) (IX) i, 1326b; iii, 1037a; iv, 692b; vii, 867a, 868b
Muḥammad b. ʿĪsā b. Aḥmad al-Māhānī (866) ii, 362a; iv, 1182b; vi, 600b; vii, 405a; s, 412a, 413b
Muḥammad b. ʿĪsa al-Mukhtār (1524) xi, 113a
Muḥammad b. ʿĪsa al-Ṣufyānī al-Mukhtārī iv, 93b
Muḥammad b. Isḥāḳ → Abu 'l-ʿAnbas al-Ṣaymarī; Ibn Isḥāḳ, Muḥammad; Ibn al-Nadīm
Muḥammad b. Isḥāḳ b. Ghāniya ii, 112a, 1007a
Muḥammad b. Isḥāḳ b. Kundādj(īk) iv, 90a, 494a; vi, 540a, 900a
Muḥammad b. Isḥāḳ b. Manda → Ibn Manda, Abū ʿAbd Allāh
Muḥammad b. Isḥāḳ b. Maḥmashādh i, 146b; iv, 668b
Muḥammad b. Ismāʿīl b. Djaʿfar i, 48a; ii, 375a; iii, 123b, 1072a, 1167b; iv, 198a, 203b, 204a, 1133a
Muḥammad b. Ismāʿīl Ibn ʿAbbād iii, 740a
Muḥammad b. Ismāʿīl al-Maymūn (7th ismāʿīlī Imām 795) s, **634b**
Muḥammad b. Kaʿb al-Ḳurazī i, 140a; v, 436a, b
Muḥammad b. Ḳāʾitbāy (Mamlūk) (1499) vii, 175b
Muḥammad b. Ḳalawūn → al-Nāṣir Muḥammad
Muḥammad b. al-Ḳalḳashandī → Ibn Abī Ghudda
Muḥammad b. Ḳara Arslan i, 665a; iii, 507a
Muḥammad b. Ḳaramān i, 467a; ii, 204b, 989a; iv, 620a, b
Muḥammad b. Ḳārin → al-Māziyār
Muḥammad b. Karrām ii, 1011a; iv, 183b, 667a
Muḥammad b. al-Ḳāsim → al-Anbārī
Muḥammad b. al-Ḳāsim (ʿAlid) (IX) i, 52b; ii, 485a; iii, 74a; vii, 776a
Muḥammad b. al-Ḳāsim (al-Djazīra al-Khaḍrāʾ) (XI) vi, 222b
Muḥammad b. Ḳāsim (Sind) (710) vi, 206b, 439b, 691a, 967b
Muḥammad b. al-Ḳāsim b. Ḥammūd iii, 786a; iv, 115b
Muḥammad b. al-Ḳāsim al-Thaḳafī (715) i, 679a, 1005b, 1068b, 1192a; ii, 27a, 154a, 188a, 488a, 1123a; iii, 41a, 323b, 482a; iv, 533b; vi, 206b, 439b, 691a, 967b; vii, 405b, 548b; viii, 253a; s, 163a, 243a
Muḥammad b. al-Ḳāsim b. ʿUbayd Allāh iv, 424a
Muḥammad b. Khalaf b. al-Marzubān (921) iii, 111a, 820a; vii, 406a
Muḥammad b. Khālid i, 1034b, 1035a, 1036a
Muḥammad b. Khalīfa b. Salmān (XIX) ii, 108b; iv, 953a, b
Muḥammad b. Khalīl iv, 535a
Muḥammad b. Khalīl Ibn Ghalbūn iv, 617b
Muḥammad b. Khaṭīb (Ḳuṣdār) (XII) vii, 535a, 536a
Muḥammad b. al-Khayr Ibn Khazar iii, 1042b; v, 1176a
Muḥammad b. al-Khayr b. Muḥammad v, 1176b, 1177a
Muḥammad b. Khazar b. Ḥafṣ v, 1174a
Muḥammad b. Khazar al-Maghrāwī (X) vii, 486a
Muḥammad Ibn Khazar al-Zanātī → Ibn Khazar b. Ṣūlāt
Muḥammad b. Khunays i, 1293a
Muḥammad b. Khuzāʿī (VI) ix, 817b
Muḥammad b. Lope (Lubb) Ibn Ḳasī iii, 816a; iv, 713a
Muḥammad b. Maḥammad b. Abī Bakr al-Murābiṭ s, 223b
Muḥammad (al-Mahdī) b. al-Manṣūr s, 31b
Muḥammad b. Maḥmūd (Saldjūḳ) → Muḥammad II (Saldjūk)
Muḥammad b. Maḥmūd b. Sebüktigin (Ghaznawīd) (1041) ii, 1051a; iii, 1201b; vii, 407a
Muḥammad b. Maḥmūd al-Khwārazmī i, 124a
Muḥammad b. Maḥmūd al-Ḳabrī → Muḳaddam b. Muʿāfa al-Ḳabrī
Muḥammad b. al-Makkī vi, 354b

Muḥammad b. Makkī al-ʿAmilī (1384) vi, 13a; vii, 407a
Muḥammad b. Malikshāh → Muḥammad I (Saldjūḳ)
Muḥammad b. Maʿn b. Ṣumādiḥ al-Tudjībī (Abū Yaḥyā) (Almeria) (1097) iii, 775b, 934b; vi, 576b
Muḥammad b. Mānī (XI) xi, 124a
Muḥammad b. Manṣūr → Sayf al-Ḥaḳḳ Abu ʾl-Mafākhir
Muḥammad b. Manṣūr (Sarakhs) (XII) ix, 5a
Muḥammad b. al-Manṣūr bi-ʾllāh al-Ḳāsim b. Muḥammad (Ḳāsimī Zaydī) (XVII) vi, 436b
Muḥammad b. Marwān I b. al-Ḥakam (Umayyad) (719) i, 42a, 77a, 100b, 1041a; ii, 523b; iii, 29a; vi, 505b, 740a, 917a; vii, 408b
Muḥammad b. Marwān al-Aṣghar b. Abi ʾl-Djanūb vi, 625b
Muḥammad b. Marzūḳ → Ibn Marzūḳ
Muḥammad b. Maslama al-Awsī al-Anṣārī (VII) i, 382b; iv, 315a; vii, 852b
Muḥammad b. Masʿūd i, 1132a
Muḥammad b. Mawlāy ʿArafa (ʿAlawid) (XX) vii, 416b
Muḥammad b. Mawlāy Ismāʿīl (ʿAlawid) (1706) vii, 38b
Muḥammad b. al-Miʿmār → Ibn al-Miʿmār
Muḥammad b. Mīrānshāh b. Tīmūr (Tīmūrid) vii, 104b, 105b
Muḥammad b. Muʿayḳil ii, 492b
Muḥammad b. al-Mubārak b. Maymūn (1201) viii, 401a
Muḥammad b. al-Mubāriz ii, 736b
Muḥammad b. al-Mughīra b. Ḥarb s, 352a
Muḥammad b. al-Mukhtār Igdhaburgha b. Yadhrinan (Mauritania) → al-Yadālī
Muḥammad b. Muḥammad → Abu ʾl-Wafāʾ; al-Ghazālī; Ibn ʿĀṣim; Ibn Djahīr; Ibn al-Habbāriyya; Ibn Nubāta al-Miṣrī; ʿImād al-Dīn al-Kātib al-Iṣfahānī; Simdjūr, Banū
Muḥammad b. Muḥammad b. Abi ʾl-Luṭf i, 759a
Muḥammad b. Muḥammad b. Zayd i, 149b; iii, 951a
Muḥammad b. Muḥammad Čiwizāde ii, 56b
Muḥammad b. Muḥammad al-Djayhānī → al-Djayhānī
Muḥammad b. Muḥammad b. al-Shiḥna (1485) vii, 537a
Muḥammad b. Muḥammad al-Shīrāzī → Ibn Khafīf
Muḥammad b. Muhannā → Nuʿayr
Muḥammad b. Mukarram → Ibn Manẓūr
Muḥammad b. Mukaththir iv, 748b
Muḥammad b. al-Munkadir vi, 263a
Muḥammad b. Murād (XV) vii, 207b
Muḥammad b. Murtaḍā → Fayḍ-i Kāshānī
Muḥammad b. Mūsā (ʿAbd al-Wādid) → Abū Zayyān II
Muḥammad b. Mūsā b. Shākir → Mūsā, Banū
Muḥammad b. Mūsā b. Shākir (IX) vi, 600a
Muḥammad b. Mūsā al-Khʷārazmī → al-Khʷārazmī
Muḥammad b. Mūsā (Kudatli) i, 756a
Muḥammad b. Musāfir (Musāfirid) (941) vi, 539a
Muḥammad b. Musāfir Kangarī (Ṭārum) (X) ii, 192a; vi, 539a
Muḥammad b. Musallam al-Bālisī iv, 641a
Muḥammad b. Mushārī ii, 321b
Muḥammad b. al-Mustanīr → Ḳuṭrub
Muḥammad b. Muṭarrif vi, 264b
Muḥammad b. al-Muthannā (866) vii, 691a
Muḥammad b. al-Muwallad iv, 89a
Muḥammad b. al-Muwayliḥt → al-Muwayliḥt, Muḥammad
Muḥammad b. al-Muẓaffar (Muẓaffarid) (XIV) ii, 401b; iv, 221b
Muḥammad b. Nāṣir (1674) x, 170b
Muḥammad b. Nāṣir (Bū Shenṭūf) (Marrākush) (1525) vi, 594a
Muḥammad b. Nūḥ (890) viii, 85a
Muḥammad b. Nūḥ al-ʿIdjlī (833) i, 272b; vii, 3a
Muḥammad b. al-Nuʿmān → Shayṭān al-Ṭāḳ
Muḥammad b. al-Nuʿmān, ḳāḍī (X) i, 823b; ii, 169b; iii, 76b
Muḥammad b. Nūr (Baḥrayn) (IX) i, 813a, 942a; iii, 652b; ix, 775a; x, 816b
Muḥammad b. Nuṣayr al-Namīrī i, 713a
Muḥammad b. Rāfiʿ (859) vii, 691a
Muḥammad b. Rāʿiḳ → Ibn Rāʿiḳ

Muḥammad b. Ramiya, Shaykh (XX) x, 196a
Muḥammad b. Rashīd → Rashīd, Āl
Muḥammad b. Razīn → Abu 'l-Shīṣ al-Khuzāʿī
Muḥammad b. Rushayd iv, 337a, b
Muḥammad b. Sabaʾ i, 181b, 1214b, 1215a; iv, 200b; v, 1244b
Muḥammad b. Saʿd → Ibn Mardanīsh
Muḥammad b. Saʿd b. Abī Waḳḳās iii, 717a
Muḥammad b. Saʿd al-Awfī iii, 922b
Muḥammad b. Saʿdān s, 177a
Muḥammad b. Sahla (XVIII) vi, 250b
Muḥammad b. Saḥnūn al-Tanūkhī (870) iii, 681a; v, 503b; vii, 409a, 1052b
Muḥammad b. Saʿīd b. Hārūn (Ukhshūnūba) (XI) i, 6a; ii, 1009a; vii, 761a, 766b
Muḥammad b. Ṣāliḥ (1909) vii, 389b; s, 279a
Muḥammad b. Ṣāliḥ (Suʿūd, Āl) (al-Dirʿiyya) (1765) i, 554a; ii, 321a; iii, 162a, 678b
Muḥammad b. Ṣāliḥ al-Īfranī (1767) iii, 1042a
Muḥammad b. Sālim → Ibn Wāṣil
Muḥammad b. al-Salīm, Ḳādī al-Ḳurṭuba (X) vi, 430b
Muḥammad b. Sālim al-Ḥifnī (1767) iv, 992a
Muḥammad b. Ṣaʿlūḳ iii, 254b, 255a
Muḥammad b. Sām I, Ghiyāth al-Dīn (Ghūrid) (1203) i, 208b, 217b, 1165b, 1192b, 1194a, 1300a; ii, 119b, 266b, 752a, 922b, 972b, 1049b, 1052b, 1101a, b, 1122b, 1123b; iii, 414b, 433b; iv, 666b, 669a; v, 501a, 782b; vi, 65b, 365b, 618a; vii, 409b; viii, 63b, 81a, 253a; s, 242a, 284b, 360a
Muḥammad b. Sām I, Muʿizz al-Dīn Muḥammad (Ghūrid) (1206) vii, 409b, 433a, 549a; viii, 63b
Muḥammad b. Sayf al-Dīn, ibn Aydamir (1310) s, **635a**
Muḥammad b. Shabīb vii, 606b, 784b
Muḥammad b. Shādān iii, 856b, 857b
Muḥammad b. Shaddād (Shaddādids) (VIII) ii, 680a; ix, 169a; x, 927a
Muḥammad b. Shahriyār, Ispahbad s, 356b
Muḥammad b. Shihāb → al-Zuhrī, Muḥammad b. Shihāb
Muḥammad b. al-Shiḥna (1412) vii, 469a
Muḥammad b. Shīrkūh iii, 399b
Muḥammad b. Sīrīn → Ibn Sīrīn
Muḥammad b. Slīmān al-Djazūlī, Sīdī vi, 597b
Muḥammad b. Subayyil, Shaykh (XX) vi, 157b
Muḥammad b. Sulaymān (Ḥasanid) i, 551a; iii, 135b, 617a, 682b
Muḥammad b. Sulaymān (Ḳarakhānid) i, 1294b; iii, 1114b, 1115a
Muḥammad b. Sulaymān b. ʿAbd Allāh b. al-Ḥasan (Idrīsid) (IX) iii, 1032a, 1035b; vi, 841b
Muḥammad b. Sulaymān Kāshgharī Yïghan Beg (vizier) (1124) ix, 16b
Muḥammad b. Sulaymān al-Kātib (X) ii, 281b; iii, 126a, 345a, 759a; vii, 543a
Muḥammad b. Sulaymān al-Rūdānī (XVII) i, 1032b
Muḥammad b. Sulaymān al-Tanakabunī (XIX) i, 113a; v, 197b
Muḥammad b. Sūrī ii, 1096b, 1099b
Muḥammad b. Surūr al-Ṣabbān b. al-Ḳunfudha (1899) vi, 177b
Muḥammad b. Suʿūd (Āl Suʿūd) (1765) vii, 410a
Muḥammad b. Tādjīt al-Maṣmūdī v, 498b
Muḥammad b. Ṭāhir → Ibn al-Ḳaysarānī, Abū 'l-Faḍl
Muḥammad b. Ṭāhir b. ʿAbd Allāh (Khurasān) (908) ii, 1082b; iv, 20b, 21a, 667b; vii, 390b, 410b
Muḥammad b. Ṭāhir II (Ṭāhirid) (Khurasān) (884) x, 105a
Muḥammad b. Ṭāhir al-Ahdal i, 255b
Muḥammad b. Ṭāhir al-Ḥārithī (1188) vii, 410b
Muḥammad b. al-Ṭayyār (VIII) vii, 398b
Muḥammad b. al-Ṭayyib, Sīdī i, 303a, 367b; iv, 383a
Muḥammad b. al-Ṭayyib al-ʿAlamī → al-ʿAlamī
Muḥammad b. Tekish → ʿAlāʾ al-Dīn Muḥammad
Muḥammad b. Thābit b. al-ʿAbbās b. Mandīl (XIV) vi, 404b
Muḥammad b. Thābit b. al-ʿAmmār (XIV) x, 213b
Muḥammad b. Thānī ii, 177a; iv, 751b
Muḥammad b. Tughdj al-Ikhshīd (Ikhshīdid) (946) i, 870b; ii, 36b, 281b, 305a, 1080b;

iii, 86a, 129a, 768b; iv, 418a, 459a; v, 91b, 327a, 953b; vi, 379a; vii, 115a, 148a, 161a, b, 411a, 800a; viii, 464a; s, 120b
Muḥammad b. Tughluḳ (Tughluḳid) (1351) i, 756b, 855b, 868b, 923b, 1036a, b, 1165b, 1192a, 1199b, 1300a, 1322a, 1329a; ii, 48a, 50a, 51a, 99b, 120a, 154b, 179b, 218b, 220a, 258a, 269b, 276b, 597a, 924b, 1076b, 1084b, 1124b, 1135a; iii, 202b, 416b, 428b, 442a, 453a, 492a; iv, 218b, 514a, 538a, 907b, 923b, 1019a; v, 598a; vi, 131b, 532b, 692a, 837b, 867a, 1027b; vii, 194a, 221a, 345b, 411b, 473a; x, 591a; s, 73b, 105b, 117b, 352b, 409a, b
Muḥammad b. Tūmart → Ibn Tūmart
Muḥammad b. ʿUbayd Allāh → Abu 'l-Maʿālī
Muḥammad b. ʿUmar b. ʿAbd al-Raḥmān b. al-Ḥārith (VIII) vi, 140b
Muḥammad b. ʿUmar b. Lubāba i, 600a
Muḥammad b. ʿUmar al-Aṣamm ii, 100b
Muḥammad b. ʿUmar Ibn Burghūth (1056) vii, 412b
Muḥammad b. ʿUmar al-Kashshī → al-Kashshī, Abū ʿAmr
Muḥammad b. ʿUmar al-Madīnī iv, 742a
Muḥammad b. ʿUmar al-Tūnusī → al-Tūnusī
Muḥammad b. Umayya b. Abī Umayya (IX) vii, 413a
Muḥammad b. ʿUrayʿir (XVIII) iv, 925a
Muḥammad b. ʿUthmān (ʿAbd al-Wādid) → Abū Zayyān I
Muḥammad b. ʿUthmān al-ʿAmrī (916) i, 713a; vii, 443b
Muḥammad b. Waḍḍāḥ (IX) vii, 400a
Muḥammad b. al-Walīd → al-Ṭurṭushī
Muḥammad b. Wandarīn, Abū Djaʿfar (Bāwandid) (XI) v, 230a; vi, 713b; viii, 383a
Muḥammad b. Wānūdīn ii, 744b
Muḥammad Ibn Warsand b. al-Ḥasan s, 402b
Muḥammad b. Wāsiʿ i, 959b
Muḥammad b. Waṣīf (X) vii, 413b; viii, 797b
Muḥammad b. Wāṣil al-Tamīmī v, 158a
Muḥammad b. Yaḥyā → Ibn Bādjdja
Muḥammad b. Yaḥyā b. Abī Ṭālib → ʿAzafī
Muḥammad b. Yaḥya al-Barmākī ii, 1036a
Muḥammad b. Yaḥyā al-Dhuhlī i, 1296b
Muḥammad b. Yaḥyā al-Yaḥṣubī i, 6a; ii, 1009a; v, 586b
Muḥammad b. Yaʿkūb al-Nīsābūrī → al-Aṣamm, Muḥammad
Muḥammad b. Yāḳūt, Abū Bakr (935) ii, 453b; iii, 46a; iv, 100a, 127a; vii, 413b, 542a
Muḥammad b. Yallas → Ibn Yallas, Muḥammad
Muḥammad b. Yasār iv, 190a
Muḥammad b. Yasīr al-Riyāshī, Abū Djaʿfar (IX) iii, 309a; vii, 414a
Muḥammad b. Yazīd → Ibn Mādja; al-Mubarrad
Muḥammad b. Yazīd (wālī, Ḳayrawān) (VIII) i, 50a; iii, 587b
Muḥammad b. Yazīd (Sharwān-Shāh) iv, 345b
Muḥammad b. Yazīd b. Ḥātim (Muhallabid) (IX) vi, 333b
Muḥammad b. Yināl al-Tardjumān (X) x, 236a
Muḥammad b. Yūsuf → Abū Ḥayyān; Muḥammad V (ʿAlawid)
Muḥammad b. Yūsuf b. Aḥmad → Muḥammad I (Naṣrid)
Muḥammad b. Yūsuf b. Hūd (XII) ii, 1014a; iii, 543a; iv, 116a, 254b; vi, 339b
Muḥammad b. Yūsuf b. Ibrāhīm (Ḥasanid) (IX) vi, 148a
Muḥammad b. Yūsuf b. al-Sarrādj → Ibn al-Sarrādj
Muḥammad b. Yūsuf b. Yaʿḳūb → Ibn Dirham, Muḥammad b. Yūsuf b. Yaʿḳūb
Muḥammad b. Yūsuf al-ʿĀmirī → al-ʿĀmirī, Abū 'l-Ḥasan Muḥammad b. Yūsuf
Muḥammad b. Yūsuf al-Sanūsī → al-Sanūsī
Muḥammad b. Zakariyya (XVII) vii, 469b
Muḥammad b. Zakariyyāʾ al-Rāzī → al-Rāzī → al-Rāzī Abūbakr Muḥammad b. Zakariyyāʾ
Muḥammad b. Zayd b. Muḥammad (Zaydī) (900) ii, 191b; iii, 245a, 254b; iv, 189a; v, 662a; vii, 417b, 1015b; s, 335a
Muḥammad b. Ziyād s, 338a
Muḥammad b. Ẓufar (XII) viii, 749a
Muḥammad ʿAbābsa (1953) vi, 251a

Muḥammad ʿAbbās Shāh (Ḳādjār) (1848) vi, 276b, 484a, 715a
Muḥammad ʿAbd Allāh al-ʿĀdil s, 389a
Muḥammad ʿAbd Allāh, Shaykh (1965) s, **635b**
Muḥammad ʿAbd al-Ḥayy al-Kattānī iv, 774b
Muḥammad ʿAbd al-Karīm ʿAlawī → ʿAbd al-Karīm Munshī
Muḥammad ʿAbd al-Karīm Ṣābūn ii, 123b
Muḥammad ʿAbd al-Munʿim i, 13b
Muḥammad ʿAbdīlle Ḥassān → Muḥammad b. ʿAbd Allāh Ḥassān
Muḥammad ʿAbduh (1905) i, 38b, 327a, 414a, 416a, 597a, 817b; ii, 97a, 417b, 429a, 451b, 465b, 471a, 1065b; iii, 59a, 1020a, 1145b, 1149b; iv, 112a, 143b, 144a, 146b, 149b, 151a, 159a, 162b, 321b, 471a, 720b, 856a; v, 187a; vi, 23a, 24b, 25a, 41b, 75b, 219b, 237b, 238a, 360a, 361a, 414a, 462a, 607a, 739b; vii, 418a, 421a, 434b, 713b, 716a, 813a, 900b, 901a; viii, 446b, 698b, 900b, 902b, 906b; s, 64a, 121b, 123a, 244b, 248a, 296a
Muḥammad Abdurrahiman Sahib (Mappila) (XX) vi, 460a
Muḥammad ʿĀbid Khān (XVIII) (Bitlīs) vi, 505a
Muḥammad ʿĀbid Ḥusayn, Ḥādjdjī (XIX) ii, 205a
Muḥammad Abu ʾl-Dhahab (1775) vii, 420a
Muḥammad Abū Ḥatīm i, 940a
Muḥammad Abū Likaylik (XIX) ii, 944b
Muḥammad Abū Madyan b. ʿAbd al-Raḥmān (Dār Fūr) (XIX) ii, 123b
Muḥammad Abū Numayy, Sharīf (1566) vi, 150a
Muḥammad Abū Raʿs al-Nāṣirī (1822) vi, 250a
Muḥammad Abū Samḥ ʿAbd al-Ẓāhir, Shaykh (XX) vi, 173b
Muḥammad Abū Zayd (XX) vii, 420b
Muḥammad ʿĀdil-Shāh (1656) i, 199b, 1202b, 1204a, b
Muḥammad V ʿĀdil-Shāh → Muḥammad Shāh V
Muḥammad Afḍal Khān → Afḍal Khān Barakzay
Muḥammad al-Afshīn → Muḥammad b. Abi ʾl-Sādj
Muḥammad Afshīn b. Dīwdād (Sādjid) (IX) vi, 499a
Muḥammad Aghā (Turkče Bilmez) (XIX) vii, 515a
Muḥammad Aḥmad b. ʿAbd Allāh al-Mahdī (1885) i, 49b, 50a, 168b, 735a, 765a, 929b, 962a, 1172a; ii, 123b, 828a; iv, 687a, 952b; v, 70a, 267b, 1247b, 1248b; vi, 281a; viii, 170b
Muḥammad Akbar Ḥusaynī ii, 56a
Muḥammad Akbar Khān i, 231b; ii, 638a; s, 237b
Muḥammad ʿAkī vii, 220b
Muḥammad ʿĀkif Pasha (1845) vi, 610a
Muḥammad Akmal, Mullā s, 134b
Muḥammad Āl Khalīfa → Muḥammad b. Khalīfa b. Salmān
Muḥammad al-ʿAlamī i, 352a
Muḥammad ʿAlī (Andjumān) v, 7a; s, 5a, 74a, 247b, 293b, 360a
Muḥammad ʿAlī (Lahore) vii, 422a
Muḥammad ʿAlī (Mustaʿlī) i, 1254b
Muḥammad ʿAlī, Prince iii, 1199b; s, 300a
Muḥammad ʿAlī (Rāmpūr) (1931) vii, 421a; viii, 249a
Muḥammad ʿAlī b. Muẓaffar al-Dīn → Muḥammad ʿAlī Shāh Ḳādjār
Muḥammad ʿAlī b. Tawfīḳ i, 13b
Muḥammad ʿAlī Bahāʾī i, 915b
Muḥammad ʿAlī Bārfurūshī Ḳuddūs, Mullā (1849) i, 833b, 847a; vii, 422a
Muḥammad ʿAlī Furūghī (XX) ii, 952a; v, 1095b, 1096a, b, 1097a; vii, 446b
Muḥammad ʿAlī Ḥazīn (1766) viii, 542a
Muḥammad ʿAlī Ḥudjdjat-i Zandjānī, Mullā (1851) vii, 422b
Muḥammad ʿAlī Kānpūrī ii, 132b
Muḥammad ʿAlī Khān, Nawwāb i, 625a; iv, 666b
Muḥammad ʿAlī Khān Ḳashḳāy iii, 1106b; iv, 706a
Muḥammad ʿAli Khān (Khoḳand) iv, 631b; v, 30a
Muḥammad ʿAlī Khān al-Bukhārī → al-Bukhārī
Muḥammad ʿAlī Maghribī (XX) vi, 176b
Muḥammad ʿAlī Māhir ii, 1004b
Muḥammad ʿAlī Mīrzā b. Fatḥ ʿAlī Shāh (Ḳādjār) (1823) iv, 394b, 861b; v, 170a
Muḥammad ʿAlī Muḥammad Khān (XX) vi, 78a

Muḥammad ʿAlī Nāṣiḥ iv, 71b
Muḥammad ʿAlī Pasha (1849) i, 13a, 35a, 182b, 404a, 554b, 571b, 755a, 1078b, 1172a, 1288b, 1299a, b; ii, 123b, 128a, 148b, 149a, 288b, 356a, 423b, 465a, 514a, 647a; iii, 218b, 238a, 556a, 999a, 1086b, 1154a, 1193b; iv, 442a, 490a; v, 267a, b, 907b, 1085b, 1248a; vi, 22b, 24b, 58b, 59b, 60b, 75a, 150b, 151a, 197a, 232a, 325b, 327a, 330a, 341a, 453b, 469b, 602b, 643a, 718a, 719a; vii, 151b, 241a, 423a, 720a; viii, 484b, 485a; ix, 903b; s, 30a, b, 38a, 179a, 301b, 379a
Muḥammad ʿAlī Riḍā (XX) vi, 176b
Muḥammad ʿAlī Shāh b. Muẓaffar al-Dīn (Ḳādjār) (1925) ii, 650b, 651b, 652a; iv, 39b, 392a, 398b, 789b; vi, 502b, 553a, 715a; vii, 431b, 918b; viii, 140a; ix, 191b; s, 53b, 72a, 91b, 291a, 365b
Muḥammad ʿAlī Zaynal Riḍā (XX) vi, 173b, 176b, 178a
Muḥammad ʿAlī-i Zandjānī i, 847a
Muḥammad al-ʿĀlim b. Mawlāy Ismāʿīl (ʿAlawid) (XVIII) vi, 595a; s, 126a
Muḥammad Amīn (Amīnā Ḳazwīnī) (XVII) vii, 443b
Muḥammad Amīn (China) → Ma Ming-hsin
Muḥammad Amīn (Shāmil) (XIX) i, 1190a
Muḥammad Amīn, Inaḳ (XVIII) iv, 1065a; v, 24a; s, 420a
Muḥammad Amīn, Shaykh (Tokat) (1745) vii, 936b
Muḥammad Amīn Badakhshī i, 1023a
Muḥammad al-Amīn Bey iv, 262b
Muḥammad Amīn Bukhārī s, 419b
Muḥammad Amīn Dīdī (Maldives) (XX) vi, 246a, b
Muḥammad al-Amīn al-Kānemī → al-Kānemī, Muḥammad al-Amīn
Muḥammad Amīn Khān (1518) iv, 849a
Muḥammad Amīn Khān (1855) s, 46a
Muḥammad Amīn al-Kurdī → al-Kurdī
Muḥammad Amīr Aḥmad Khān, Rādjā (1973) vi, 78a
Muḥammad Amīr Pandja Kash ii, 83b
Muḥammad Anūsha iv, 1064b, 1068a
Muḥammad Anwar Shāh al-Kashmīrī al-Hindī iv, 84b
Muḥammad ʿĀrif i, 287b; ii, 391b
Muḥammad al-Aṣghar b. al-Maʾmūn (ʿAbbāsid) (IX) vi, 331b
Muḥammad ʿĀshiḳ → ʿĀshiḳ, Muḥammad
Muḥammad al-ʿAṭṭār, Shaykh (XIX) vii, 670b
Muḥammad al-Awḳaṣ b. ʿAbd al-Raḥmān, Ḳāḍī (VIII) vi, 140b
Muḥammad ʿAyn al-Dawla iii, 1114a
Muḥammad Aytīmur (Sarbadārid) (1346) ix, 48a
Muḥammad Aʿẓam b. Awrangzīb i, 913b, 1201b; ii, 216b; iii, 457b
Muḥammad Aʿẓam b. Dūst Muḥammad i, 232a; ii, 417a, 638a
Muḥammad Aʿẓam b. Pāyinda Khān i, 231a; ii, 637b; v, 501b
Muḥammad Bā Faḍl (1497) vi, 132b
Muḥammad Badāʿūnī → Shaykh Niẓām al-Dīn Awliyāʾ
Muḥammad al-Badr, Imām (yemen) (1962) iv, 745b; xi, 274a
Muḥammad Bahāwal Khān → Bahāwal Khān
Muḥammad Baḥrī Pasha ii, 990b
Muḥammad Baḳāʾ b. Ghulām Muḥammad Sahāranpūrī (1685) vii, 432b
Muḥammad Bakhtiyār Khaldjī (1206) i, 393b, 1209b; ii, 267b, 297a, 1103a; v, 638a; vi, 244b; vii, 433a, 573a
Muḥammad Bāḳī b. ʿĪsā Khān Tarkhān, Mīrzā (1585) i, 628a; vi, 190a
Muḥammad Bāḳī Naḳshbandī → Bāḳī bi-ʼllāh
Muḥammad Bāḳir, Abū Djaʿfar → Muḥammad b. ʿAlī Zayn al-ʿĀbidīn Bāḳir
Muḥammad Bāḳir b. Muḥammad Taḳī al-Madjlisī → Madjlisi-yi Thānī
Muḥammad Bāḳir, Abū Djaʿfar → Muḥammad b. ʿAlī Zayn al-ʿĀbidīn
Muḥammad al-Bāḳir, Amīr (Imām Muḥammad-Shāhī) (1796) iv, 202a
Muḥammad Bāḳir Iṣfahānī, Hājjī Shaykh (1883) vii, 918b
Muḥammad Bāḳir al-Madjlisī → al-Madjlisī
Muḥammad Bāḳir Mīrzā b. ʿAbbās I (Ṣafawid) (1614) viii, 770b
Muḥammad Bāḳir Mīrzā Khusrawī (XX) ix, 402b
Muḥammad Bāḳir Nadjm-i Thānī (1637) i, 848a, 1019a; vii, 433a, 988a

Muḥammad Bāḳir Shaftī s, 75a
Muḥammad Bāḳir-i Bihbihānī iv, 51a
Muḥammad al-Balʿamī → al-Balʿamī
Muḥammad al-Baṭāʾiḥī (Ḳādiriyya) iv, 381a
Muḥammad al-Baṭāʾihī (Rifāʿiyya) iv, 350a
Muḥammad Bayram I (1800) vii, 433b
Muḥammad Bayram II (1831) vii, 433b
Muḥammad Bayram III (1843) vii, 433b
Muḥammad Bayram IV (1861) vii, 433b
Muḥammad Bayram al-Khāmis iv, 1154a; vii, 433b, 901a
Muḥammad Beg (Turcoman) ii, 204b
Muḥammad Beg Aydinoghlu i, 783a; ii, 989a, 1044b
Muḥammad Beg Ḳarāmānid → Muḥammad b. Ḳarāmān; Muḥammad II (Ḳarāmānid)
Muḥammad Beg Ustādjlū i, 1067a
Muḥammad Behdjet → Meḥmed Behdjet
Muḥammad Bello b. Shaykh ʿUthmān b. Fūdī (1837) vii, 435b; viii, 356b; x, 122b
Muḥammad Bey (Ḥusaynid) (1859) i, 977a; ii, 638b; iii, 561b, 636a; vi, 798b; vii, 436b
Muḥammad Bey b. Aḥmad Bey Mirzā (XVII) i, 1208b
Muḥammad Bey b. Maḥmūd (Tunisia) (1663) i, 1049a; ii, 161a; vi, 840b
Muḥammad Bey b. Yaḥyā i, 1164a, b
Muḥammad Bey Abu ʾl-Dhahab → Abu ʾl-Dhahab, Muḥammad Bey
Muḥammad Bey Abu ʾl-Dhahab → Muḥammad Abu ʾl-Dhahab
Muḥammad Bey al-Alfī (1807) i, 1288b; iv, 853a; vii, 423b
Muḥammad Bey Khālid → Muḥammad Khālid Zuḳal
Muḥammad Bey Khusraw ii, 123b, 351b; iv, 686b; v, 267a
Muḥammad Bey Minnet-oghlu i, 1263b
Muḥammad Bey ʿUthmān Djalāl (1898) vii, 437a
Muḥammad Boḍu Takurufānu (Maldives) (XVI) vi, 245b
Muḥammad Burhān al-Dīn b. Ṭāhir Sayf al-Dīn x, 103b
Muḥammad al-Bukhārī → al-Bukhārī
Muḥammad al-Bulālī i, 929a
Muḥammad al-Burtuḳālī → Muḥammad II (Waṭṭāsid)
Muḥammad Čavush iv, 592b
Muḥammad Čelebī (Ottoman) → Meḥemmed I
Muḥammad Čelebi b. Burhān al-Dīn i, 1328a
Muḥammad Čelebi Efendi → Yirmisekiz Čelebi Meḥmed
Muḥammad Čelebi Üsküdarī → Meḥmed Čelebi Üsküdarī
Muḥammad Čurbak vii, 410a
Muḥammad Dāʾim ii, 28b
Muḥammad Dāwūd Khān (1978) v, 1079b; vii, 438a
Muḥammad Dāwūd Shāh (Atjèh) (1903) i, 744a
Muḥammad Demirdāsh al-Muḥammadī s, 208a
Muḥammad al-Dībādj → Muḥammad b. Djaʿfar
Muḥammad Djaʿfar Ḳaradja-Dāghī Munshī (XIX) i, 332a; vii, 438b
Muḥammad Djaʿfar Khān → Djaʿfar Mīr
Muḥammad Djamāl al-Dīn Huvadu (Maldives) (XVI) vi, 245b
Muḥammad Djamālī ii, 420a
Muḥammad Djān i, 232a
Muḥammad al-Djawād ʿAlī al-Riḍā al-Taḳī (835 Imām) → Muḥammad b. ʿAlī al-Riḍā
Muḥammad Djawād al-Djazāʾirī s, 28a
Muḥammad al-Djawnpūrī → al-Djawnpūrī, Sayyid Muḥammad
Muḥammad Djayāsī → Malik Muḥammad Djayāsī
Muḥammad Djūkī i, 135a, 148a; s, 51a
Muḥammad al-Durrī (XX) vi, 755a
Muḥammad Edīb ii, 590a
Muḥammad Efendī Aḳ Kirmānī i, 310b
Muḥammad Efendī Čiwizāde ii, 57a
Muḥammad Emīn (Crimea) (1519) viii, 832a
Muḥammad Emīn b. Hadjdjī Meḥmed i, 295a
Muḥammad Emīn b. Muṣṭafā → Meḥmed Emīn b. Muṣṭafā Feyḍī Ḥayātī-zāde (XII)
Muḥammad Emīn Pasha iii, 1199a
Muḥammad-Enweri Kadić i, 1271b
Muḥammad Eretna → Ghiyāth al-Dīn Muḥammad
Muḥammad Eshref iii, 357b

Muḥammad Faḍl b. ʿAbd al-Raḥmān (Dār Fūr) (1838) ii, 123b
Muḥammad al-Fāḍil b. Ā<u>sh</u>ūr → Ibn Ā<u>sh</u>ūr, Muḥammad al-Fāḍil
Muḥammad Fāḍil al-Ḳalḳamī v, 889b, 890a
Muḥammad al-Faḥḥām iv, 165b
Muḥammad al-Faḳīh → Muḥammad II (Naṣrid)
Muḥammad Farīd → Abū Ḥadīd
Muḥammad Farīd Bey b. Aḥmad Farīd Pa<u>sh</u>a (1919) iii, 515a; vii, 439a, 716a
Muḥammad Farīd Wa<u>dj</u>dī (1954) vii, 439b
Muḥammad Fasan<u>dj</u>us → Abu 'l-Fara<u>dj</u> Muḥammad Fasan<u>dj</u>us
Muḥammad Fatḥ Allāh Barakāt iii, 516a
Muḥammad Ferīd → Dāmād Ferīd Pa<u>sh</u>a
Muḥammad al-<u>Gh</u>ālib bi-'llāh → Muḥammad I (Naṣrid)
Muḥammad al-<u>Gh</u>ānī → Muḥammad V (Naṣrid)
Muḥammad <u>Gh</u>ar<u>dj</u>istānī i, 227a
Muḥammad <u>Gh</u>aw<u>th</u> (Gwāl(i)yār) (1562) ii, 1144a; iii, 430a, 436a; vi, 127b; vii, 439b
Muḥammad <u>Gh</u>ūri → Muḥammad b. Sām, <u>Gh</u>iyā<u>th</u> al-Dīn; – Muʿizz al-Dīn; Muḥammad <u>Sh</u>āh <u>Gh</u>ūrī
Muḥammad Girāy I ii, 1046a, 1113a; iv, 849b
Muḥammad Girāy II iv, 178b; v, 138b
Muḥammad Girāy III i, 310b; v, 719b
Muḥammad Girāy IV ii, 25a; v, 139b, 719b
Muḥammad Gīsū Darāz → Gīsū Darāz
Muḥammad Gulandām iii, 56a
Muḥammad Gūlēd, <u>Sh</u>ay<u>kh</u> (1918) ix, 722b
Muḥammad al-Ḥabīb Bey (Ḥusaynid) (1929) iii, 636b
Muḥammad al-Ḥabīb (Mauritania) (1860) vii, 614b
Muḥammad Hādī b. al-Lawḥī (XVII) vii, 95b
Muḥammad al-Hādī Bey (Ḥusaynid) (1906) iii, 636b
Muḥammad al-Ḥā<u>dj</u><u>dj</u> b. Maḥammad b. Abī Bakr (XVII) vi, 187a
Muḥammad Ḥāfiẓ Ibrāhīm → Ḥāfiẓ Ibrāhīm
Muḥammad Ḥākim, Mīrzā (1585) i, 316a, 733a, 1122b; iii, 423b; iv, 410b; v, 649b; vi, 342b; vii, 573b; s, 122a, **636b**
Muḥammad Ḥakīm Biy (Mangi̊t) (XVIII) vi, 418b
Muḥammad Ḥāmid al-Faḳī (XX) vi, 176b
Muḥammad Ḥāmid <u>Kh</u>ān ii, 597b
Muḥammad Harsānī, <u>Sh</u>ay<u>kh</u> (XX) vi, 171b
Muḥammad Ḥasab Allāh ii, 91b
Muḥammad Ḥasan (Zarrīn ḳalam) s, 167b
Muḥammad Ḥasan ʿAwwād (XX) vi, 176b
Muḥammad Ḥasan Faḳī (XX) vi, 177b
Muḥammad Ḥasan Gīlānī s, 23b
Muḥammad Ḥasan <u>Kh</u>ān Ḳā<u>dj</u>ār i, 701b; iii, 1103a; iv, 389b, 390a, b, 639b
Muḥammad Ḥasan <u>Kh</u>ān Ṣanīʿ al-Dawla (1896) ii, 433b, 952a; iv, 70b; vii, 440a; x, 233b; s, 71b, 75b
Muḥammad Ḥasan Kutubī (XX) vi, 178a
Muḥammad Ḥasan Mīrzā i, 262b
Muḥammad Ḥasan Wazzānī (Morocco) (XX) vii, 416a
Muḥammad Hā<u>sh</u>im Āṣaf Rustam al-Ḥukamāʾ vi, 483b
Muḥammad al-Hā<u>sh</u>imī → al-Hā<u>sh</u>imī
Muḥammad Ḥasan Nūrī, Mīrzā s, 23b
Muḥammad al-Ḥāsib (861) vii, 39b
Muḥammad Ḥaydar Dug<u>h</u>lāt → Ḥaydar Mīrzā
Muḥammad al-Ḥifnī (XVIII) ii, 167a; vi, 627a
Muḥammad al-Hilālī → Muḥammad al-Bulālī
Muḥammad Ḥusayn b. Bahrām b. <u>Sh</u>āh Ismāʿīl I, Mīrzā (Ṣafawid) (XVI) vii, 129b
Muḥammad Ḥusayn b. Muḥammad Faḍl ii, 123b, 124b
Muḥammad Ḥusayn ʿAṭā <u>Kh</u>ān iii, 376a
Muḥammad Ḥusayn Āzād (1910) vii, 668a
Muḥammad Ḥusayn Bu<u>sh</u>rūʾī, Mullā (1849) vii, 422a, 440b
Muḥammad Ḥusayn Dū<u>gh</u>lāt ii, 622b; iii, 317a
Muḥammad Ḥusayn Haykal (1956) vi, 176b; vii, 441a, 713b
Muḥammad Ḥusayn <u>Kh</u>ān Develū iv, 390a, b
Muḥammad Ḥusayn <u>Kh</u>ān Nāẓim al-Dawla iv, 104b, 578a
Muḥammad Ḥusayn <u>Sh</u>ahriyār iv, 71b
Muḥammad Ḥusayn Tabrīzī (XVI) vii, 442a

Muḥammad al-Ḥusaynī al-Bukhārī s, 10b
Muḥammad Ibn Gīṭūn vi, 607a
Muḥammad Ibn al-Zayn viii, 886b
Muḥammad Ibrāhīm Dhawḳ → Dhawḳ
Muḥammad Ibrāhīm al-Ghazzāwī (XX) vi, 175b
Muḥammad Ibrāhīm al-Zarben x, 71b
Muḥammad al-Idrīsī → al-Idrīsī
Muḥammad Iḳbāl → Iḳbāl, Muḥammad
Muḥammad al-Ilkhān ii, 401a
Muḥammad al-Ikhshīd → Muḥammad b. Ṭughdj al-Ikhshīd
Muḥammad ʿIllīsh ii, 167a
Muḥammad Ilyās (1944) iii, 433b; x, 38a; xi, 358a
Muḥammad Īndjū iii, 1208b
Muḥammad ʿĪsā Tarkhān i, 628a, 1192a; iii, 1030a
Muḥammad Isfandiyārī → Nīmā Yūshīdj
Muḥammad Ismāʿīl b. ʿAbd al-Ghānī al-Shahīd → Ismāʿīl Shahīd, Muḥammad
Muḥammad Ismāʿīl Khān Nūrī v, 155b, 165a
Muḥammad Ismāʿīl Mērathī (1917) vi, 838b
Muḥammad ʿIṣmatī (XVII) vii, 469b
Muḥammad ʿIzzat Darwaza (Darwazeh) (1984) vii, 442b
Muḥammad Ḳāḍī s, 51b
Muḥammad Ḳādirī (XVII) vii, 925b
Muḥammad Ḳadrī Pasha (XIX) iii, 164a; vi, 23b, 27a, 29b
Muḥammad al-Ḳāʾim al-Mahdī (XII. Imām) (940) i, 402b; iii, 247a; vii, 443a; s, 95a
Muḥammad Kāshānī, ḳaḍī (ṣadr) (XVI) vi, 18a
Muḥammad al-Ḳāʾim bi-Amr Allāh i, 245a
Muḥammad Kāmil Pasha v, 314a
Muḥammad Ḳaramānlı̊ iv, 617b
Muḥammad Ḳāsim (painter) (XVII) vii, 603a
Muḥammad Ḳāsim, Mawlawī (XIX) ii, 205a; iii, 431a
Muḥammad Ḳāsim Khān b. Sulaymān Ḳādjār (XIX) vi, 484b
Muḥammad Ḳāsim Khān Mīr-i Baḥr (XVI) i, 253a
Muḥammad Kāẓim, Munshī (1681) vii, 342b, 443b
Muḥammad Kāẓim Khurāsānī (XX) s, 54a
Muḥammad al-Khāḍir b. al-Ḥusayn → al-Khāḍir, Muḥammad b. al-Ḥusayn
Muḥammad Khwādja i, 808b
Muḥammad Khālid Zuḳal ii, 123b,124a, 827b; v, 1250a
Muḥammad Khān (1609) s, 523a
Muḥammad Khān, Dashtī (1881) vi, 384b
Muḥammad Khān, Sayyid (1864) s, 46a
Muḥammad Khān (Ḳarakhānid) → Muḥammad I, II, III; Muḥammad b. Sulaymān
Muḥammad Khān (Turcoman) iv, 389b
Muḥammad Khān b. Aḥmad Shāh (Gudjarāt) (XV) vi, 52b
Muḥammad Khān b. Balban s, 124a
Muḥammad Khān b. Ḥadjdjī Muḥammad Kirmānī (1906) ix, 409b
Muḥammad Khān Awḥadī (Bayāna) (XV) vi, 53b; vii, 278b, 279a
Muḥammad Khān Bangash Karlānī, Nawwāb (1743) ii, 808a, 1085a; vii, 443b
Muḥammad Khān Ḳoyunlū iv, 390b
Muḥammad Khān Madjd al-Mulk Sinakī iv, 397b
Muḥammad Khwārizmshāh → ʿAlāʾ al-Dīn Muḥammad Khwārizm Shāh
Muḥammad al-Khayrātī, amīr (XVIII) vi, 191b
Muḥammad al-Khiḍr Ḥusayn (XX) vii, 439b
Muḥammad Khodja iii, 605a
Muḥammad Khor (XIX) viii, 463b
Muḥammad Khudābanda (XVI) vii, 478a
Muḥammad Khusraw Pasha (XIX) ii, 292b; vi, 285a
Muhammad Koya, C.H. (Mappila) (XX) vi, 460a
Muḥammad Ḳulī Khān Ḳāshḳāy iv, 706a
Muḥammad Ḳulī Ḳuṭb Shāh, Sultan (1611) iii, 318b, 319a, 426b; v, 550a, 630a, 961a; vi, 610b, 837b
Muḥammad Ḳuṭb Shah iii, 427a
Muḥammad Lashkarī → Muḥammad Shāh III (Bahmanī)
Muḥammad Lārī → Lārī, Muḥammad b. Ṣalāḥ
Muḥammad al-Liḥyānī → Muḥammad III (Ḥafṣid)
Muḥammad Māḍī → Abu ʾl-ʿAzāʾim

Muḥammad Mādjid al-Kurdī, Shaykh (XX) vi, 175b, 176a
Muḥammad Mahābat Khān I (1770) ii, 597b
Muḥammad Mahābat Khān (1960) ii, 598a
Muḥammad Mahdī (Djawnpūr) v, 1230b; s, 222a
Muḥammad al-Mahdī (Ḥammūdid) → Muḥammad I (Ḥammūdid)
Muḥammad al-Mahdī (Saʿdid) v, 1191a
Muḥammad al-Mahdī (Sanūsī) ii, 493a; s, 165a
Muḥammad al-Mahdī (Umayyad) → Muḥammad II (Umayyad)
Muḥammad al-Mahdī b. Muḥammad ʿAlī al-Sanūsī (1902) ix, 25b
Muḥammad Mahdī Khān → Mahdī Khān Astarābādī
Muḥammad Maḥmūd ii, 934b; iii, 516a, 517a, 518b; s, 18a
Muḥammad al-Makhlūʿ → Muḥammad II (Naṣrid)
Muḥammad al-Makkī (IX) vii, 401a
Muḥammad al-Māmī, Shaykh v, 891b, 892a
Muḥammad al-Manglī i, 1154a; ii, 740b
Muḥammad al-Mānṣālī (XX) vi, 752a
Muḥammad al-Maslūkh i, 56a, 706b; ii, 367b; iii, 721a
Muḥammad Masʿūd (Miṣr) (XX) vi, 602b
Muḥammad Masʿūd, Dihātī (1947) iv, 72b; v, 199a
Muḥammad Mīrāb, Shīr → Muʾnis (Khīwa)
Muḥammad Mīrzā → Muḥammad Shāh (Ḳādjār)
Muḥammad Muʿaẓẓam Bahādur Shāh b. Awrangzīb → Bahādur Shāh I (Mughal) (1712)
Muḥammad Mubārak Khān → Mubārak Khān
Muḥammad Mufīd (XVII) iii, 490b
Muḥammad Muḥsin (XX) iv, 626a
Muḥammad Muḥsin al-Ḥādjdj (1812) vii, 444a
Muḥammad Muḳīm Khān → Muḳīm Khān
Muḥammad Muʾmin Khān Muʾmin (1851) vi, 838a
Muḥammad al-Mundhir ii, 1009a
Muḥammad al-Muntaṣir → Muḥammad b. Idrīs II
Muḥammad Murād Beg → Murād Beg
Muḥammad al-Murtaḍā li-Dīn Allāh b. al-Hādī, Abu ʾl-Ḳāsim (Rassī Zaydī) (922) vii, 444b, 773a; s, 335b
Muḥammad Murtaḍā al-Zabīdī (1791) i, 596b, 782a; ii, 355b, 927a, 948b; iv, 524b; vii, 445a; viii, 728b
Muḥammad Mūsā (Kudatli) ii, 87b
Muḥammad al-Mustaʿīn → Muḥammad VII (Naṣrid)
Muḥammad al-Mustakfī → Muḥammad III (Umayyad)
Muḥammad al-Mustaʿlī → Muḥammad III (Ḥammūdid)
Muḥammad al-Muʿtamid → al-Muʿtamid
Muḥammad al-Mutawakkil al-Maslūkh → Muḥammad al-Maslūkh
Muḥammad al-Muẓaffar → al-Muẓaffar (Afṭasid)
Muḥammad Muzammil Allāh Khān, Sir (1938) vi, 165b
Muḥammad al-Nadjdjār, al-Ḥādjdj (Marrākush) (XIX) vi, 249b, 250b
Muḥammad Nadjīb (Neguib) (1984) ii, 648b; vii, 445b; s, 6a, 7a, 301a
Muḥammad al-Nafs al-Zakiyya → Muḥammad b. ʿAbd Allāh b. al-Ḥasan b. al-Ḥasan, (ʿAlid)
Muḥammad al-Nasawī ii, 962a
Muḥammad al-Nāṣir (Almohad) → al-Nāṣir, Muḥammad b. Abī Yūsuf Yaʿḳūb
Muḥammad al-Nāṣir (Naceur Bey, Ḥusaynid) (1922) iii, 636b; vi, 750a
Muḥammad Nāẓim iii, 581a
Muḥammad Nergisi i, 1271a
Muḥammad Nuṣrat Nuṣratī (1684) vi, 837a
Muḥammad Pāʾīzī iii, 114a
Muḥammad Panāh, Mīr (Ghāzī al-Dīn Khān, Fīrūz Djang II) (1752) iii, 1158a; vii, 446a
Muḥammad Pasha → Meḥmed Pasha; Derwīsh Meḥmed Pasha; Duče Meḥmed Pasha; Kalender-oghlū Meḥmed Pasha; Khāṣṣakī Meḥmed Pasha; Köprülü Meḥmed Pasha; Ṣofu Meḥmed Pasha; Soḳollu Meḥmed Pasha
Muḥammad Rabaḍān i, 404b
Muḥammad Rabbānī (2001) s, 787a
Muḥammad Rafīʿ Bādhil iii, 114b

Muḥammad Raḥīm Biy (Mangit) (XVIII) vi, 418b
Muḥammad Raḥīm Khān (Atalīḳ, Khīwa) (1825) i, 1295b; ii, 116a; iv, 610b, 1065a; v, 24a, 29a; vii, 574b; s, 46a, 97a, 420a
Muḥammad Raḥīm Khān II, Sayyid (1872) s, 46a, 228b
Muḥammad Rashād → Meḥemmed V
Muḥammad al-Rashīd → Muḥammad b. Ḥusayn (Ḥusaynid)
Muḥammad al-Rashīd, Bey (1759) viii, 448a
Muḥammad Rashīd Pasha (XIX) i, 906b; iii, 628b, 999b; v, 36a, 462a
Muḥammad Rashīd Riḍā → Rashīd Riḍā
Muḥammad Rasūl Khān ii, 598a
Muḥammad Raʾūf iii, 622b
Muḥammad Rezā Shāh → Muḥammad Riḍā Shāh Pahlawī
Muḥammad Riḍā b. Sangīn ʿAlī ii, 29b
Muḥammad Riḍā Aḥsan Allāh → Ẓafar Khān
Muḥammad Riḍā ʿIshkī → ʿIshḳī, Muḥammad Riḍā
Muḥammad Riḍā Khān iii, 1106b
Muḥammad Riḍā Mīrāb b. Er Niyāz Bek → Āgahī
Muḥammad Riḍā al-Shabībī v, 1093b
Muḥammad Riḍā Shāh Pahlawī (1980) ii, 653a; iii, 454a; iv, 40b-42b, 165a; v, 721b, 920b, 1042b, 1098a; vi, 21b, 22a; vii, 300a, 446a, 715a
Muḥammad Rinānī iv, 104b; v, 834a
Muḥammad al-Ṣādiḳ Bey (Tunis) (1882) i, 37a; ii, 638b; iii, 562a, 636b; iv, 1154a; vii, 434b, 437a, 451b, 717b, 718a; viii, 61a
Muḥammad Ṣafī al-Dīn (Sukadana, Borneo) viii, 1042a
Muḥammad al-Ṣaghīr s, 208b
Muḥammad al-Ṣaghīr b. Yūsuf i, 863a
Muḥammad Saʿīd → Khalīl Efendi-zāde; Marīnids
Muḥammad Saʿīd → Saʿīd Pasha b. Muḥammad Pasha (Khedive)
Muḥammad Saʿīd (Mīr Djumla) → Mīr Djumla, Muḥammad Saʿīd
Muḥammad Saʿīd b. Muḥammad ʿAlī Pasha (1863) vii, 182b
Muḥammad Saʿīd Abu 'l-Khayr (XX) vi, 157a
Muḥammad Saʿīd ʿAbd al-Maḳsūd (XX) vi, 176b, 177b
Muḥammad Saʿīd Ashraf (1708) vi, 131b
Muḥammad Saʿīd Bābaṣēl ii, 91b
Muḥammad Saʿīd Sarmad (1659) ii, 134b; iii, 492b; vii, 452b
Muḥammad Sāḳī Mustaʿidd Khān → Mustaʿidd Khān
Muḥammad Ṣāliḥ Beg (Kalāntar) (1621) iv, 476a
Muḥammad Ṣāliḥ Kanbō (XVII) iii, 1203b; v, 600b; vi, 418a; vii, 342b; s, **636b**
Muḥammad Ṣāliḥ Naṣīf, Shaykh (XX) vi, 176a, b
Muḥammad Ṣāliḥ Shīrāzī iv, 787a
Muḥammad Sālim, ḳāḍī iv, 410b
Muḥammad Sambo b. ʿUthmān b. Fūdī (XIX) xi, 123b
Muḥammad al-Sammān i, 92a
Muḥammad Shāh I (Bahmanid) i, 924b, 925b, 1068b; ii, 1119a
Muḥammad Shāh II (Bahmanid) i, 925b, 1200a; iii, 417b
Muḥammad Shāh III Lashkarī (Bahmanid) 1, 923b, 1047a, 1200a, 1323a; iii, 1159a; s, 280a
Muḥammad Shāh (Ḳādjār) (1848) i, 246b; ii, 812b, 839a; iii, 554a; iv, 38b, 105a, 392a, 393a; vi, 804a; vii, 299a, 422b, 452b; viii, 58a; s, 71a, 94b, 108b
Muḥammad Shāh I ʿAlāʾ al-Dīn (Khaldjī, Delhi) (1316) i, 444b, 506b, 710a, 1036a, b, 1068b, 1202b, 1322a; ii, 99b, 120a, 154b, 179b, 256b, 260b, 268b, 272b, 405a, 1084b, 1124a; iii, 201a, 416a, 434a, 492a; iv, 218b, 419a, 921a-923b; v, 883b; vi, 121b, 406b; vii, 457b; s, 73b, 105a, 176a, 279b, 325a
Muḥammad Shāh I b. Djahān-Shāh Nāṣir al-Dīn (Mughal) (1748) i, 229b, 295b, 834a, 1026a, 1042b, 1166a, 1330a; iii, 59b, 520a, 454a; iv, 666a; vi, 310a, 456b, 535a, 602a; vii, 316a, 319a, 339b, 443b, 446a, 457a, 854b
Muḥammad Shāh IV (Sayyid), (Delhi) (1443) ii, 270b; v, 598a, 783a, b; vi, 53a
Muḥammad Shāh V (Delhi) ii, 271b, 1144a; iii, 423a
Muḥammad Shāh (Sharḳī) (1458) ix, 355a

Muḥammad Shāh II b. Tughluḳ Shāh I (Tughluḳid), (Delhi) (1351) → Muḥammad b. Tughluḳ
Muḥammad Shāh III b. Fīrūz Shāh (Tughluḳid), (Delhi) (1393) iv, 276a; vi, 273a
Muḥammad Shāh (Djawnpūr) → Muḥammad b. Fīrūz Shāh III (Tughluḳ)
Muḥammad Shāh, Sultan (Malacca) (XV) vi, 210b
Muḥammad Shāh b. Ḥadjdjādj v, 162b, 163a, 554a
Muḥammad Shāh b. Ḥasan Shāh (Kashmīr) s, 131b
Muḥammad Shāh b. Malik Shāh (Kirmān) (Saldjūḳ) (1156) viii, 945b
Muḥammad Shāh Djahān Khān ii, 317a
Muḥammad Shāh Fārūḳī → Mīrān Muḥammad I, II
Muḥammad Shāh Gaṇeśa ii, 797b; iii, 419a; viii, 259b
Muḥammad Shāh Ghūrī → Ghaznī Khān b. Hushang Shāh Ghūrī (Mālwā)
Muḥammad Shāh Karīm (Gudjarāt) (1451) ii, 1125b; iii, 1010a; vi, 50a, 53b
Muḥammad Shāh (Kashmīr) s, 324b, 423b
Muḥammad Shāh Khudābanda b. Ṭahmāsp I (Ṣafawid) (1588) i, 7b, 8b; iii, 157b; vi, 17b, 483a, 515a, 526a
Muḥammad Shāh Khusraw ii, 316b, 317a
Muḥammad Shāh Özbeg i, 853a
Muḥammad Shāh Sayyid → Muḥammad Shāh IV (Dihlī)
Muḥammad Shāh Tangal (Mappila) (XVIII) vi, 463a
Muḥammad Shāhī imāms iv, 201b, 202a
Muḥammad Shāhī Nizāriyya → Ismāʿīliyya
Muḥammad Shākir Efendi iv, 618a
Muḥammad Shams al-Dīn Shāhīn (1894) x, 65a
Muḥammad al-Sharīf → Muḥammad I (ʿAlawid)
Muḥammad Sharīf, Khalīfa i, 765a; v, 1249a, 1250a, b, 1251b
Muḥammad Sharīf b. Dūst Muḥammad → Muʿtamad Khān
Muḥammad Sharīf b. Iʿtimād al-Dawla iv, 282a
Muḥammad Sharīf al-Adhamī (XI) vi, 379b
Muḥammad Sharīf Ḳābil → Ḳābil Khān
Muḥammad Sharīf Khān ii, 316b, 317a
Muḥammad Sharīf al-Nadjafī (XVII) vii, 457b
Muḥammad Sharīf Pasha → Sharīf Pasha
Muḥammad Sharīf al-ʿUlamāʾ, Mullā s, 75a
Muḥammad al-Sharīf , Sultan (Wadāī) (1858) xi, 11b; s, 164b
Muḥammad Sharḳī iii, 419b
Muḥammad al-Shaṭṭī → al-Shaṭṭī, Muḥammad
Muḥammad Shaybānī → Shaybānī Khān
Muḥammad al-Shaybānī → al-Shaybānī
Muḥammad al-Shaykh (Saʿdid) (1557) vii, 37b
Muḥammad al-Shaykh al-Mahdī i, 245a; iii, 251a
Muḥammad al-Shaykh II al-Maʾmūn i, 605a, 1058a; iii, 810a; s, 29a
Muḥammad Shībānī → Shībānī Khān Muḥammad
Muḥammad Shirān i, 393b
Muḥammad Shīrīn Maghribī (1406) i, 1301a; iv, 66a
Muḥammad al-Ṣūfī, Shaykh s, 353b
Muḥammad Ṣūfī Māzandarānī → Māzandarānī, Mullā Muḥammad Ṣūfī
Muḥammad Ṣughrā i, 1218b
Muḥammad Sulṭān Bayātī iii, 1101a
Muḥammad Sulṭān Pasha (Miṣr) (XIX) vii, 184b
Muḥammad Sulṭān Rūmī i, 1168a
Muḥammad Surūr al-Ṣabbān (XX) vi, 166a, 175b
Muḥammad Ṭāhir → Pīr ʿAlī
Muḥammad al-Ṭāhir → Ibn ʿĀshūr
Muḥammad Ṭāhir (1672) iv, 286b; vii, 139b
Muḥammad Ṭāhir b. ʿĀlī Patani Gudjarātī (1578) vii, 458a
Muḥammad Ṭāhir Ashaʿī → Ghanī
Muḥammad Ṭāhir al-Kurdī (XX) vi, 176b, 177a, 178a
Muḥammad Ṭāhir al-Ṣiḳillī al-Ḥusaynī iv, 736a
Muḥammad al-Taḳī → Muḥammad al-Djawād
Muḥammad Taḳī, Mīrzā v, 169b
Muḥammad Taḳī ʿAlī Ābādī ii, 433b

Muḥammad Taḳī Bahār → Bahār
Muḥammad Taḳī Iṣfahānī, Shaykh → Āḳā Nadjafī
Muḥammad Taḳī Khān (Fārs) (XVIII) vi, 735a
Muḥammad Taḳī Khān, Mīrzā → Taḳī Khān, Mīrzā Muḥammad (Amīr Kabīr)
Muḥammad Taḳī Khān Pisyān (XX) s, 110a, 366a
Muḥammad Taḳī Ḳummī (1990) x, 139b
Muḥammad Taḳī Madjlisī → Madjlisī-yi Awwal
Muḥammad Taḳī Mīr → Mīr Taḳī Mīr
Muḥammad Taḳī Siphir (1880) iv, 70a; ix, 658a
Muḥammad Ṭalʿat → Ṭalʿat, Meḥmed
Muḥammad Tapar → Muḥammad I Ghiyāth al-Dīn b. Malik Shah (Saldjūḳ)
Muḥammad al-Tawdī → Ibn Sūda, Abī ʿAbd Allāh
Muḥammad Tawfīḳ → Tawfīḳ Pasha
Muḥammad Tawfīḳ Makkī (XX) vi, 176a
Muḥammad al-Ṭawīl (XX) vi, 153a
Muḥammad Taymūr (1921) vi, 75a, b
Muḥammad Tayrāb ii, 123a; v, 267a
Muḥammad Ṭayyib ii, 205b
Muḥammad al-Ṭayyib al-Anṣārī v, 998b
Muḥammad Tewfīḳ → Tewfīḳ Meḥmed; Čerkes Meḥmed Tewfīḳ
Muḥammad Tīmūr i, 1019a
Muḥammad Tughluḳ → Muḥammad Shāh II, III (Dihlī)
Muḥammad Ture → Muḥammad b. Abī Bakr (Songhay)
Muḥammad al-Tūnisī s, 306a
Muḥammad ʿUbayd Allāh b. Hazārmard v, 451b
Muḥammad Ulugh Khān s, 335b
Muḥammad ʿUmar b. ʿAbd al-Raḥmān iii, 13a
Muḥammad ʿUmar al-Tūnisī ii, 137a
Muḥammad ʿUthmān Djalāl (1898) i, 597a; vi, 746a; vii, 901b, 902b; s, **637a**
Muḥammad ʿUthmān al-Mīrghānī → al-Mīrghānī
Muḥammad Wāʿiẓ-i Kāshifī → Kāshifī, Kamāl al-Dīn Ḥusayn b. ʿAlī al-Wāʿiẓ
Muḥammad Walī Khān ii, 435b, 652b
Muḥammad Wārith s, 46b
Muḥammad wuld Ahmad Yūra (1921) vii, 622b
Muḥammad wuld Tulba al-Yaʿḳūbī (1856) vii, 625b
Muḥammad Yādgār (Tīmūrid) (1470) vii, 90b
Muḥammad al-Yaḥṣubī → Muḥammad b. Yaḥyā
Muḥammad Yaḥyā, Khwādja s, 51b
Muḥammad al-Yālūshī (XIX) vii, 407b
Muḥammad Yūsuf al-Kāzarūnī i, 1218b
Muḥammad Ẓāhir Shāh i, 232b
Muḥammad al-Zākī ʿUthmān i, 1172a
Muḥammad Zamān Khan → Abū Ridjāʿ
Muḥammad Zamān Khān b. Asʿad Khān (Djalālābād) (XIX) s, 237b
Muḥammad Zamān Mīrzā (XVI) vii, 314a; s, **637b**
Muḥammad Zanjina ii, 1003b
Muḥammad al-Ẓāfir iv, 1154b
Muḥammad Zayd al-Ibyānī (XIX) vi, 23b
Muḥammad al-Ziyādī i, 551a; v, 602a
Muḥammada vii, 361b
Muḥammadābād → Bīdar; Čāmpānēr; Ghāzīpūr; Gudjarāt; Kalpī
Muḥammadan Union → Ittiḥād-i Muḥammedī Djemʿiyyeti
al-Muḥammadī, Ḳānī-Bay b. ʿAbd Allāh (amīr) (XV) vi, 580b
Muḥammadī Harawī (XVI) vii, 603a; viii, 514a
Muḥammad-i Khaṭībī s, 333b
Muḥammad-i Waṣīf iv, 55a
Muḥammad-i Zamān, Mīrzā (XVI) i, 914b; ii, 322b, 1128b; iii, 422b; iv, 1021a; vi, 52a
Muḥammadī b. Djahāngīr v, 829a
al-Muḥammadiyya → Faḍāla
Muḥammadiyya (ʿĀlids) vii, 459a
Muḥammadiyya (al-Ḳāhira) iii, 992a
Muḥammadiyya (Manṣūriyya) ii, 1094b; vi, 441b; vii, 459b
Muḥammadiyyah (Indonesia) i, 745b, 746a; iii, 534a, 1229a; vi, 730a; s, 151a
Muḥammadnagar → Golkondā
Muhammadu Bello ii, 942a, 1145a; iii, 38b, 276b
Muhammadu dan Amu iv, 550b, 551a
Muhammadu Marwa → Maitatsine
Muḥammadzays → ʿAbd al-Raḥmān Khān (Bārakzay); Afghānistān; Amān Allāh Khān; Ḥabīb Allāh Khān
Muhamman Alwali iv, 549a

Muhamman Rumfa (1499) iv, 549a, 550a
Muḥammara iv, 675a, b; v, 66a; vii, 461a
Muḥammira v, 64a, 65a
Muhandis-khāne → Muhendiskhāne
Muhannā, Banū i, 403a, 1313a; iv, 88a; vii, 461a; viii, 986b; ix, 507a
Muhannā b. ʿĪsā b. Muhannā (1334) iii, 952a; iv, 88a; vii, 461b
Muḥannā b. Naṣīr, Mīr v, 507a, b
Muḥārib, Banū vi, 145a; vii, 463a
Muḥārib b. Mūsā vi, 878b
al-Muḥāribī → Ibn ʿAṭiyya
Muhārish i, 1074b; 1075a
Muḥarraf iii, 26a
al-Muḥarrak (island) i, 941a; vi, 357b, 358a; vii, 464a
al-Muḥarram vii, 464a
Muḥarram, Aḥmad iii, 112a
Muḥarrik → ʿAmr b. Hind
Muḥarrirān iv, 757b
Muḥāsaba ii, 81a; vii, 465a
Muḥasayn, Āl iv, 1171a
al-Muḥāsibī, Abū ʿAbd Allāh al-Ḥārith b. Asad (857) i, 277a, 326b, 694b, 1245b; ii, 242b, 450b; iii, 83b, 466a, 720a; iv, 212a; vii, 101a, 465a, 466b; viii, 547a; x, 314b; s, 125b, 392a
Muḥaṣṣil vii, 467b
al-Muḥassin (Muḥsin) b. ʿAlī b. Abī Ṭālib (VII) vii, 468b
al-Muḥassin Ibn al-Furāt (X) i, 387a; iii, 702b, 767b; vii, 397a, 653a
al-Muḥassin al-Tanūkhī → al-Tanūkhī
Muḥaṣṣiṣ-i mamlakat iv, 475a
Muḥāwere iv, 602a
al-Muḥaydatha (al-Muḥayditha) vi, 303a; s, 27b
Muḥaysīn iv, 10a
Muḥdath ii, 96b; iii, 1051b; v, 96b
Muḥdathūn s, **637b**
Muhendiskhāne i, 63a, ii, 425b; v, 903a, 908a
Muḥibb Aḥmed "Diranas" (1980) vii, 469a
Muḥibb Allāh Allāhābādī ii, 54b, 55a, 134b; s, 293a
Muḥibb Allāh Bihārī → al-Bihārī
Muḥibb al-Dīn → al-Ṭabarī
Muḥibb al-Dīn al-Khaṭīb (1969) iii, 519a; iv, 160a; s, **640a**
Muḥibbī → Sulaymān I
al-Muḥibbī, Faḍl Allāh (1671) vii, 469b
al-Muḥibbī, Muḥammad al-Amīn (1699) i, 68b, 594b; vii, 469b, 527b, 772a
al-Muḥibbī, Muḥibb al-Dīn Abu 'l-Faḍl (1608) vii, 469a
al-Muḥillūn vii, 470a
Mühimme Defterleri i, 1090b; vii, 470a
al-Muḥīṭ → al-Baḥr al-Muḥīṭ
Muḥkam (XIX) vi, 611a
Muḥkam Čand s, 332a
Muhr ii, 121a, 311b, 806a; vii, 472a; s, 256b
Muhrdār iv, 1104a
Muḥrim iii, 1052b, 1053a
Muḥriz, Banū vi, 578a
Muḥriz b. Khalaf, (Sīdī Maḥrez) (1022) iii, 695a; iv, 341a; vi, 354a; vii, 473b
Muḥriz b. Ziyād iii, 386a, b; iv, 827b; v, 59b, 60b
al-Muḥriza iv, 674b
Muḥṣan vii, 474b; xi, 509b
Muḥsin, Ḥādjdjī Āḳā s, 342a
Muḥsin, Mawlā → Fayḍ-i Kāshānī
Muḥsin b. Farīd i, 181b, 767a
Muḥsin b. al-Ḳāʾid iii, 137b
Muḥsin b. Sālim iii, 294a
Muḥsin ʿAlī Muḥsin (XIX) vii, 475a
Muḥsin al-Amīn (1952) vii, 780b
Muḥsin Fānī ii, 74a
Muḥsin al-Ḥakīm, Āyatullāh Shaykh (1970) vi, 553a, b; vii, 301b
Muḥsin Khān Ghāzī i, 1123a
Muḥsine iii, 998b
Muḥsin-i Fayḍ-i Kāshānī, Muḥammad b. Murtaḍā → Fayḍ-i Kāshānī
Muḥsin-zāde → ʿAbd Allāh Pasha Muḥsin-zāde; Meḥmed Pasha Muḥsin-zāde
al-Muhtadī bi-'llāh (ʿAbbāsid) (870) iv, 89a; vi, 670a; vii, 476b; s, 402a
Muḥtādj, Abū ʿAlī Aḥmad Čaghānī (Muḥtādjid) (955) ii, 1b; iv, 60b
Muḥtādj, Abū Bakr Muḥammad b. Muẓaffar b. (Muḥtādjid) (941) vii, 477b
Muḥtādjids vii, 477b
Muḥtaram Shāh I ii, 29b
Muḥtaram Shāh II ii, 30a
Muḥtaram Shāh III ii, 30a
Muḥtasham-i Kāshānī (1587) iv, 68a; vi, 271a, 608b, 609a, b, 610b; vii, 477b; viii, 775a,b

Muḥtasib i, 26b, 344b, 477a, 629b, 752a, 898b, 977b; ii, 228b, 519b; iii, 485b, 487a, 490a, 492a; v, 280a, 876a
al-Muḥtasib → Abū ʿAbd Allāh al-Shīʿī
Muḥyī 'l-Dīn, Shaykh (Čishtī) (XVI) vi, 272a
Muḥyī 'l-Dīn b. ʿAbd al-Ẓāhir (XIII) vi, 424a
Muḥyī 'l-Dīn b. al-ʿArabī → Ibn al-ʿArabī
Muḥyī 'l-Dīn Khaṭīb (XX) vi, 176a
Muḥyī 'l-Dīn Khayyāṭ (XX) vi, 614b
Muḥyī 'l-Dīn Lārī (1526) vii, 478b
Muḥyī 'l-Dīn Masʿūd b. Ḳilidj Arslan II i, 510a
Muḥyī 'l-Dīn Meḥmed al-Djamālī (XVI) vii, 478b
Muḥyī 'l-Dīn Muḥammad b. Aḥmad al-Walīd (Yemen) vi, 433b
Muḥyī 'l-Dīn Muḥammad Čiwi-zāde ii, 56b
Muḥyi 'l-Dīn Shāh Meḥmed Fenārī-zāde ii, 879b; iv, 333b
Muḥyī 'l-Dīn Yaḥyā b. Faḍl Allāh ii, 732a; iii, 758b
Muḥyī-i Gülshenī ii, 1136a
Muʿīd → Mustamlī
al-Muʿīd li-dīn Allāh (XI) vi, 566a
Muʿīn (painter) (XVII) vii, 603a
Muʿīn al-Dīn b. Sharaf al-Dīn Farāhī → Mullā Miskīn
Muʿīn al-Dīn ʿAlī → Ḳāsim-i Anwār
Muʿīn al-Dīn Djāmī, Shaykh (XIV) viii, 749b
Muʿīn al-Dīn Ḥasan b. Ṣadr al-Dīn i, 766a, b
Muʿīn al-Dīn Ḥasan Čishtī → Čishtī
Muʿīn al-Dīn Ḳattāl (XV) vii, 440a
Muʿīn al-Dīn Mukhtaṣṣ al-Mulk (vizier) (1127) ix, 15b
Muʿīn al-Dīn Natanzī (XV) vi, 483a, 494b
Muʿīn al-Dīn Sulaymān Parwāna (1277) iii, 1269a; iv, 619b, 814a, 817a; vii, 479a; viii, 15b, 949b
Muʿīn al-Dīn Unur (Anar) (XII) i, 1332a; ii, 282a; iii, 399a; vii, 579a; viii, 128a
Muʿīn al-Dīn Yazdī (1387) vii, 480b
Muʿīn al-Fuḳarāʾ → Aḥmad b. Muḥammad (Maḥmūd)
Muʿīn al-Miskīn (1501) vii, 481b
Muʿīn al-Mulk b. Ḳamar al-Dīn i, 295b, 296a; iii, 1158b
Muʿīn al-Mulk Abu 'l-Maḥāsin, Sayyid al-Ruʿasāʾ (XI) vii, 489b
Muʿīnsiz s, **640b**
al-Muʿizz (Mamlūk) → ʿIzz al-Dīn Aybak (Mamlūk)
al-Muʿizz b. Bādīs (Zīrid) (1062) i, 533a, 860a, 1023b; iii, 137a, 324b, 385b, 386a, 688a, 695a, 903a, 936a; iv, 199a, 497a, 805a, 827b; v, 59b, 530b, 1182b, 1246b; vii, 474a, 481b, 731a, 994a; s, 26b, 62b
al-Muʿizz b. Muḥammad b. Walmiya iv, 337a
al-Muʿizz b. Zīrī b. ʿAṭiyya v, 1177b, 1178b, 1179a
Muʿizz al-Dawla, Aḥmad b. Būya (Būyid) (967) i, 11b, 19b, 20a, 419a, 711b, 866b, 899b, 1047a, 1352a; ii, 178b, 994a, 1082b; iii, 127b, 195b, 1156b, 1157a, 1175b, 1202a; iv, 23a, b, 266a, 855a; vi, 539a; vii, 358a, 484a, 723b, 799a, 995a; s, 13a, b, 36b, 127a, 259a, 362a
Muʿizz al-Dīn al-Kurtī iv, 672a
al-Muʿizz li-Dīn Allāh, Maʿadd (Fāṭimid) (975) i, 592a, 814a, 823a, 1175b; ii, 195a, 329a, 491b, 494b, 495a, 853a, b, 855a, 860a, b, 861b, 963a, 994a, 1099a; iii, 246a, 298b, 785b, 840b, 886a, 1084a; iv, 198b, 662b, 663b; v, 862b; vi, 673b, 727b, 728a, 1040b; vii, 162a, 485a; viii, 117a; ix, 45a; s, 62b, 236b, 252b
Muʿizz al-Dīn Ḥusayn ii, 1049b
Muʿizz al-Dīn (Shihāb al-Dīn) Muḥammad b. Sām (Ghūrid) → Muḥammad b. Sām I, Ghiyāth al-Dīn
Muʿizz al-Dīn Sandjar (Marw) iii, 603a
Muʿizz al-Dīn Sandjar Shāh b. Sayf al-Dīn Ghāzī II (Zangid) (XII) vi, 781a
al-Muʿizz Ismāʿīl b. Ṭughtakīn (Ayyūbid) (XIII) vi, 433b, 434a
Muʿizzī, Amīr Abū ʿAbd Allāh (1147) iii, 356a; vi, 275b, 276a, b, 609a
Muʿizzī b. Burhānī iv, 61b, 466b; s, 384a
Muʿizzī Naysābūrī, Muḥammad b. ʿAbd al-Malik (1125) vii, 489a; viii, 71b, 76a, 970b
Muʿizziyya ii, 1083a; vi, 321b
Muʿizziyya (Sicily) → Taormina
Mujibur Rahman (XX) viii, 243a
Muḳābal iii, 84a; iv, 259a
Muḳābala (law) iv, 193a
Muḳābala (opposition) vii, 490a

al-Mukaʿbar (Baḥrayn) (VI) vii, 763b
Muḳaddam vii, 492a
Muḳaddam, Aḥmad Khān (XIX) vi, 502b
al-Muḳaddam, Banū vi, 381a, 502b
Muḳaddam, Dr. Muḥammad (XX) v, 1098a
Muḳaddam b. Muʿāfā al-Ḳabrī (911) i, 601a; iv, 355a; vii, 492a, 811a
Muḳaddas Khurāsānī, Bābī vii, 303a
al-Muḳaddasī, Shams al-Dīn Abū ʿAbd Allāh Muḥammad (X) i, 488a, 570b; ii, 127a, 581a, 582a; iii, 761b, 1078a, 1252b; iv, 45b, 220a, 223a, 1079a, 1088a; v, 328b, 330a; vi, 119a, b, 120b, 144b, 199a, 313b, 359a, 378a; vii, 492b; s, 266a, 363a, 392a
Mukaddī iv, 735a; vii, 493b
Muḳaddima vii, 495b
al-Mukaḥḥal → ʿAmr b. al-Ahtam
Muḳāʿis, Banū iv, 832a
Muḳali ii, 43a
al-Mukallā i, 182a, 554b; ii, 173b; vi, 81b, 84a, 177a; vii, 496a; s, 338b
al-Muḳallad b. al-Musayyib, Ḥusām al-Dawla (ʿUḳaylid) (1000) vi, 900b; vii, 497a
Muḳallad b. Naṣr b. al-Munḳidh (1059) vii, 577b
Mukallafa ii, 79b
Muḳallid → Ḳaṣṣ; Maddāḥ; Taḳlīd
al-Muḳammiṣ iv, 304a
Mūḳān (Mūghān) vi, 499a; vii, 497b; ix, 221a
Mūḳān b. Dalūla (X) vii, 498a
al-Muḳannaʿ (VIII) i, 141b, 1294a; ii, 1107a; iii, 617a; iv, 16b, 45b; v, 64a, 181b, 855a, 1238b; vii, 500a, 664a; s, 411a
Muḳannī iv, 529b
Muḳanṭarāt vii, 500b
Muḳāraʿa → Mukhāradja
Muḳāraḍa → Ḳirāḍ
Muḳarbaṣ(s) vii, 500b
Mukārī vii, 501b
Muḳarnas i, 1229a; ii, 777b, 864a; iv, 481a; vi, 366b; vii, 501b
Muḳarrab Khān (Delhi) (XIV) vi, 49a, b, 294a, b
Muḳarrab Khān (Gakkhaŕ) (XVIII) ii, 973b, 1131b
Mukarram b. Yām → al-Karam b. Yām
al-Mukarram Aḥmad b. ʿAlī al-Ṣulayḥī i, 181b, 552a; iii, 125b
al-Muḳarrariyya iii, 284a
Mukarrib i, 547b; vi, 562b, 563a
Mukarzal, Naʿʿūm ii, 471a
Mukarzal, Sallūm ii, 471b
Muḳāsama ii, 158a; iv, 1032a, 1037b, 1038a, 1055b; vii, 506b
Mukāshafa iv, 696b, 697a, b
Mukāsir ii, 97b
Muḳāṭaʿa i, 642b, 651b, 1080a, 1144b; ii, 33b, 118b, 147b, 188a, 907b; iii, 284a; iv, 225b, 323b, 1038a, 1046a; v, 792a, b; vii, 508a
Mukātaba i, 30a; ii, 302b, 328b; iii, 27a
Muḳātil b. ʿAṭiyya al-Maghrāwī (X) v, 1176b, 1177a, 1178b; vi, 605b
Muḳātil b. Mismaʿ (VIII) vi, 640b
Muḳātil b. Sulaymān b. Bashīr al-Azdī (767) vii, 508b, 571a, 607a; x, 160b, 391a; s, 90b
Muḳaṭṭaʿāt iv, 58a; vii, 509a
al-Muḳaṭṭam ii, 288b, 403b, 466b; vi, 122b, 123a, 413a; vii, 509a
al-Muḳawḳis (VII) i, 1016a; v, 90b; vi, 413a, 575a; vii, 154b, 372a, 509b, 511a
Muḳawwiyāt s, **640b**
Muḳayyin iv, 822b
al-Mukhā i, 932b, 1140b; iv, 449b, 450a; vii, 513b; s, 30b
al-Mukhabbal b. Rabīʿa s, 394b
al-Mukhaḍḍaba iii, 49b
Mukhaddirāt → Afyūn; Bandj
Mukhaḍram i, 12a, 140a; vii, 516a
Mukhallafāt i, 1147b, 1148a; vii, 517a
al-Mukhammas → al-Musammaṭ
Mukhammisa iv, 1132b, 1133a; vii, 459b, 468b, 517a
Mukhāradja vii, 518a
Mukhāriḳ, Abu 'l-Muhannāʾ b. Yaḥyā (844) vii, 518a; xi, 178a; s, 64a
Mukhāriḳ b. Shihāb (620) vi, 954a
Mukharrim i, 897b, 900a, 901a
al-Mukharrimī → Abū Saʿd al-Mubārak
Mukhāṭara vii, 518b
Mukhattam vii, 519a
Mukhayriḳ (VII) ii, 844b
Mukhbir al-Salṭana → Mahdī Ḳulī Hidāyat
Mukhliṣī → Muṣṭafā b. Süleymān I
Mukhtār vii, 519a
Mukhtār (al-Maʿḳil) vi, 141b
al-Mukhtār b. Abī ʿUbayd al-Thakafī (687) i, 5a, 15a, 41a, 45a, 50b, 55a, 76b, 304a,

850b; ii, 198b, 523b; iii, 236a, 715a, 718a, 987a, 1255a, 1265b; iv, 44b, 836a, b; v, 349b, 350a; vi, 640b; vii, 357a, 400b, 403a, 470a, 521a, 605b, 650a, 689a; ix, 421b; x, 843a; s, 357b
al-Mu_kh_tār b. ʿAwf al-Azdī, Abū Ḥamza (748) i, 550b; ii, 141a; iii, 651b, 658a; iv, 1076a; vi, 147b; vii, 524b; x, 845a; s, 337b, 338a
Mu_kh_tār b. Maḥmūd al-Zāhidī iv, 1062b
Mu_kh_tār b. ʿUmar Tal i, 297a
Mu_kh_tar Auez Ulï (1961) vi, 768b
Mu_kh_tār al-Baḳḳālī, al-Ḥā_dj_dj (1839) vi, 249a, b, 250b, 255b
Mu_kh_tār Bey (Maṣawwaʿ) (XIX) vi, 643a
al-Mu_kh_tār al-Kabīr, Sīdī v, 393b, 394a
al-Mu_kh_tār Muḥammad b.ʿĪsā (1524) x, 248a
Mu_kh_tār Pa_sh_a, _Gh_āzī Aḥmed (1919) vi, 372b; vii, 525a
Mu_kh_tār Pa_sh_a Tepedelenli (XIX) i, 398b, 399a
al-Mu_kh_tār al-Ṣa_gh_īr, Sīdī v, 394a
al-Mu_kh_tāra i, 133b, 389a; ii, 4441; vii, 526a
Mu_kh_tārāt vii, 526b
Mu_kh_tārī, Sirā_dj_ al-Dīn (1159) s, 416a
Mu_kh_tārī _Gh_aznawī, Abū ʿUmar ʿU_th_mān b. ʿUmar (1118) vii, 535a
Mu_kh_tāriyya v, 393b, 394a
al-Mu_kh_tārūn v, 50a
Mu_kh_taṣar vii, 536a
Mu_kh_taṣṣ _Kh_ān (XVI) iv, 276b; vi, 546
Muḳīm b. Ar_gh_ūn _Kh_ān i, 227b, 627b; ii, 1049b; iv, 357a, 536b
Muḳīm Abu ʾl-Manṣūr _Kh_ān, Mīrzā (Ṣafdar _Dj_ang) vii, 195a
Muḳīm _Kh_ān Sārawī v, 663b
Muḳḳrān, Ūlād iv, 478b
Muḳrā vii, 540a
Mukram i, 711b
Mukrān → Makrān
Muḳrānī → Moḳrānī
Mukrī, Banū iii, 1102b, 1109a; v, 460b; vi, 128b; viii, 895b
al-Mukrī (Morocco) vii, 415a
al-Muḳriʾ, Muḥammad vi, 374b
al-Muḳriʾ al-Rāzī, ʿAbd al-_Dj_abbār b. ʿAbd Allāh (XII) x, 40a
Mukrī Kurds (amīrs) vi, 502b; ix. 92b
Mukrianī, Husayn Huznī v, 483b
Muḳrim i, 942b
Muḳrin iv, 764b
Muḳrin, Banū i, 553b
Mukrin b. A_dj_wad s, 234b
Muḳtaʿ ii, 272b, 273a, 508a; v, 862b
al-Muḳtabis i, 82b, 600b
Muḳtaḍab vii, 540a
al-Muḳtadī bi-Amr Allāh (ʿAbbāsid) (1094) i, 901a; iv, 458a, 942b; vi, 274b, 275a, 379b, 523b; vii, 540a; viii, 70b; ix, 481b; s, 192b, 194a
al-Muḳtadir bi-ʾllāh (ʿAbbāsid) (932) i, 19a, 387a, 446a, 688b, 867a, 898a, 899a, 936a; ii, 344b, 383b, 388b, 462a, 1080b; iii, 100b, 126b, 344b, 388a, 619b, 691b, 692a, 739a, 750b, 757b, 767b, 768a, 886b, 892b, 1201b; iv, 214b; v, 132a, 737b; vi, 206a, 498a, 518a, 539a; vii, 414a, 541b, 575b; s, 118a, 192a, 199a, 372a, 385b
al-Muḳtadir b. Hūd → Aḥmad I (Hūdid)
al-Muktafī bi-ʾllāh(ʿAbbāsid) (908) i, 11a, 19a, 898a; ii, 461b; iii, 345a, 892b, 1044b; iv, 494a, 940a; vi, 275a; vii, 542b; s, 118a, 304b
al-Muktafī li-Amr Allāh (ʿAbbāsid) (1160) i, 865b; iii, 160b, 197a, 1255b; vi, 275b, 870b; vii, 543b; s, 193b
Muktagīrī s, 280a
al-Muḳtanā, Bahāʾ al-Dīn (XI) i, 552a; ii, 632b; iii, 154b; vii, 544a
al-Muḳtaṭaf ii, 288b, 403b, 428a, 466b
al-Muḳurra (al-Maḳurra) iv, 568a; vi, 574b; vii, 544b; viii, 89b
Mukūs → Maks
al-Mulāʾī → Abū Nuʿaym
Muladī → Muwallad
Mulāṭafa, mulaṭṭifāt ii, 304a
Mula_thth_amūn v, 652b, 744a, 769b
Mūlāy → Mawlāy
Mūlāy ʿAlī Bū _Gh_ālem iv, 729a
Mūlāy Būʿazzā i, 159b
Mulāy Bushʿīb → Abū _Sh_uʿayb
al-Mulayda (battle) (1891) viii,439a; s, 3b
Mulayḥ b. al-Ḥakam viii, 377a
Mülāzemet vii, 545a
Mulāzim vii, 545b
Mulāzimiyya v, 1252a, b
Mulham, Dir_gh_ām Nāṣir al-Muslimīn (XII) ii, 318a, b
Mulḥid vii, 546a
Mulḥim (Maʿn) (XVII) vi, 343b

Mūlid → Mawlid
Mulk v, 623a; vii, 546b
Mulk Amān (Chitral) (XIX) ii, 30a
Mulk-Ārā (Ḳādjār) (XIX) vi, 484a
Mulkiyya ii, 425b, 692a; iv, 909a; v, 904a; vii, 547a
Mullā → Molla
Mullā ʿAbd al-Razzāḳ Lāhidjī → Lāhidjī ʿAbd al-Razzāḳ
Mullā Apāḳ s, 331b
Mullā-bāshī iv, 104a
Mullā Hādī Sabzawārī → Sabzawārī, Ḥādjdj Mullā Hādī
Mullā Ilāhī, ʿAbd Allāh (1490) vii, 754a, 936a; s, 51b
Mullā Miskīn (1501) i, 423b
Mullā Muḥsin → Muḥsin-i Fayḍ-i Kāshānī
Mullā Muḥyī al-Dīn (Wazīristān) (1913) xi, 198a
Mullā Nūr Muḥammad (Wāna) (XX) xi, 198a
Mullā Pōwindā → Mullā Muḥyī al-Dīn
Mullā Ṣadrā Shīrāzī, Ṣadr al-Dīn (1640) i, 596a; ii, 104a, 774a; iii, 103b, 664a, 1130b; iv, 50b, 121a, 509a; v, 605a; vii, 132a, 452b, 475b, 547b; viii, 541b, 782a; xi, 216b; s, 24a, 305a, 308a, b
Mullā Shāh Badakhshī (1661) ii, 134b; vii, 189a; ix, **196a**
Mullā Shaydā → Shaydā, Mullā
Mullā ʿUmar (Ṭālibān) s, 787a
Mullā Wadjhī (1609) vi, 837b
Mullagorī, Banū vii, 548b
Mullāʾī i, 225b; iii, 1102b
Multān i, 218a, 230b, 628a, 912a; iii, 419b, 433b, 441b, 443b, 633a, b, 634a, 1155b; iv, 199a; v, 26a, 782b, 783a, 885a; vi, 48a, b, 49b, 50a, 65a, b, 112a, 127b, 131a, 294b, 691a, 695b; vii, 405b, 409b, 412a, 548b; viii, 68a, 253a; s, 10b, 66b, 105a, 284b, 329b, 332a, 423b
Multān Mall i, 218a
al-Multazam iv, 318a
Mültezim (Multazim) ii, 147b, 148a, b; iii, 1154a; vii, 550b
Mulūk al-Ṭawāʾif (Persia) vii, 551a
Mulūk al-Ṭawāʾif (Reyes de Taifas) i, 6a, b, 94b, 130b, 155b, 242a, 495a, 865a, 1320a; ii, 331b; iii, 496a, 640a, 791b; vii, 552a
Mumahhid al-Dawla Saʿīd Abū Manṣūr (Marwānid) (Diyār Bakr) (1011) i, 1298b; iii, 130b; v, 453a; vi, 626a, 930b; vii, 116a
Mumayyiz → Bāligh
al-Mumazzaḳ i, 74a
Muʾmin vii, 554b
Muʾmin (Mōmin), Ḥakīm Muḥammad Khān (1851) vii, 555a
Muʾmin b. Aḥmad i, 1306b, 1307b
Muʾmin b. al-Ḥasan i, 1306b, 1307b
Muʾmin ʿĀrif (Yamanī) vi, 410a
Muʾmin Khān (Gudjarāt) i, 1053a; ii, 1130a;
Muʾmin Khān (poet) (1851) iii, 119b; v, 961b
Muʾmina Khatun iii, 1110b
Muʾminids → al-Muwaḥḥidūn
Mūmiyāʾ vii, 556a
Mumtaḥin al-Ḍawla s, 109a
Mumtāz, Barkhwurdār b. Maḥmūd Turkmān (XVIII) vii, 557a
Mumtāz Efendi (1871) iv, 1126a
Mumtāz Khan → Iʿtibar Khān
Mumtāz Maḥall (1631) i, 253b, 686a, 1161a, 1331a; vii, 557a; x, 58b
Munā vi, 154a, 155a, 162a
Munabbāt, Banū vi, 142a, b
Munādī vii, 557a
Munādjāt vii, 557b
Munadjdjim vii, 557b
al-Munadjdjim (IX) vi, 99a
Munadjdjim, Abu 'l-ʿAbbās Hibat Allāh (X) vii, 561a
Munadjdjim, Abū ʿAbd Allāh Hārūn (901) vii, 561a, 559b
Munadjdjim, Abū Aḥmad Yaḥyā (912) vii, 559a
Munadjdjim, Abū ʿAlī Yaḥyā (830) vii, 558b
Munadjdjim, Abu 'l-Ḥasan Aḥmad (939) vii, 559b
Munadjdjim, Abu 'l-Ḥasan ʿAlī (888) vii, 559a
Munadjdjim, Abu 'l-Ḥasan ʿAlī (963) vii, 560a
Munadjdjim, Abū ʿĪsā Aḥmad (X) vii, 559b
Munadjdjim, Abu 'l-Ḳāsim Yūsuf (X) vii, 560a
Munadjdjim, Abū Manṣūr Abān (VIII) vii, 558b

al-Munadjdjim, ʿAlī b. Hārūn (X) s, 362b
Munadjdjim, Banu ʾl- i, 1141a; vii, 358b, 558b; s, 375b
al-Munadjdjim, Kanka al-Hindī vi, 412a
al-Munadjdjim, Yaḥyā b. ʿAlī (913) iv, 111a; v, 516b; vii, 681b
Munadjdjim Bāshī → Münedjdjim-bashi̊
Munāfara iv, 77b
Munaffidh i, 1148b; ii, 146a
al-Munāfiḳūn i, 53b; v, 996a, b; vii, 561a, 852b
Munāhada → Mukhāradja
Munakhkhal b. Djamīl s, 233a
al-Munakhkhal al-Yashkurī vii, 562b, 841a
al-Munakkab vii, 563b
Munāṣafa vii, 564a
Munāshada vii, 564b
al-Munāwī, ʿAbd al-Raʾūf (1621) iii, 29a; vii, 565a
al-Munāwī, Yaḥyā (Shaykh al-Islām) (XVI) vii, 565a
al-Munawwar, Muḥammad b. s, 154a
al-Munawwar ʿAlī Shāh (1884) iv, 51a
al-Munayyir vi, 114a
al-Munayzila s, 234b
Munāẓara iii, 431b; v, 1130b, 1223b; vii, 565b
al-Munāzī, Abū Naṣr Aḥmad v, 929b
Munāzil, ʿAbd Allāh (Malāmatiyya) vi, 225a
Mundā iii, 412a
al-Mundhir I (Lakhmid) i, 939a; v, 633a
al-Mundhir III Ibn al-Nuʿmān (Lakhmid) (554) i, 99a, 115b, 451b, 526b, 527a, 548b; ii, 1021a; iii, 94a, 222a, 462b; v, 633a, 640a; vi, 951a; ix, 77a
al-Mundhir IV (Lakhmid) (580) v, 633b; vii, 568b
al-Mundhir b. al-Ḥārith b. Djabala (Ghassānid) (582) i, 1249b; ii, 244b, 1021a, b; v, 633b; vii, 568b; viii, 630a
al-Mundhir b. Ḥassān al-ʿAbdī vi, 677a
al-Mundhir b. Māʾ al-Samāʾ → al-Mundhir III
al-Mundhir b. Muḥammad (Umayyad), (al-Andalus) (888) i, 49a, 85b; vi, 222a; vii, 568b; s, 92a, 153a
al-Mundhir b. al-Muḳtadir ii, 112a
al-Mundhir b. al-Nuʿmān (VII) vii, 671a
al-Mundhir b. Saʿīd al-Ballūṭī (966) i, 497a, 600a; ii, 744b; vii, 569a
al-Mundhir b. Sāwā (Sāwī) (VII) vii, 570a
al-Mundhir b. Yaḥyā al-Tudjībī iii, 147a, 743a
al-Mundhirī, Abū Muḥammad al-Ḳawī s, 194a
al-Mundhirī, Muḥammad b. Djaʿfar i, 114b, 822a
Mundjī i, 225a
Münedjdjim Bashi̊ (1702) i, 836a; ii, 110a; iii, 392b; iv, 1175a; vii, 572b; viii, 1a; s, 59a
Munghyr → Mungīr
Mungi Śivgaon (treaty) vi, 535a
Mungīr i, 1209b, 1210a; vi, 47a; vii, 573a
Municipality → Baladiyya
Münīf (1733) s, 83a
Münīf Muṣṭafā Efendi (XVIII) vi, 56b
Münīf Pasha (1910) ii, 473b, 532a, 682b; vi, 92b; vii, 573a, 813b
Munʿim Khān (Munʿim Beg) (1575) i, 1136b; ii, 183b, 498b, 499b; iv, 1020a; v, 638b; vii, 133b, 330b, 573b; ix, 196a
Munīr al-Dawla (XIX) vi, 484b
Munīr al-Khādim (X) vi, 545b
Munīr Lāhawrī (1644) vii, 574a
Munīra al-Mahdiyya (1965) x, 144a
Münīrī Belghrādī i, 324b; ii, 968b
Muʾnis (Khīwa) (1829) vii, 574b
Muʾnis (Lakhnaw) (XIX) vi, 611b
Muʾnis ʿAlī Shāh, Ḥādjdj Mīrzā ʿAbd al-Ḥusayn (Niʿmat Allāhī) (1953) viii, 47b
Muʾnis Dede Derwīsh (1732) vii, 575a
Muʾnis al-Faḥl (-al-Khāzin) (914) vii, 575a
Muʾnis al-Khādim → Muʾnis al-Muẓaffar
Muʾnis al-Muẓaffar, Abu ʾl-Ḥasan, al-Khādim (933) i, 11a, 19a, 34a, 386b, 387a, 446a; ii, 191b, 325b; iii, 46a, 126b, 619b, 620a; iv, 22b, 423b; v, 1243b; vii, 192a, 414a, 541b, 575a, 994b
Muʾnis b. Yaḥyā al-Mirdāsī iii, 386a; iv, 337a
Muʾnisa (Kayna) s, 252b
Munkar (Ḥadīth) vii, 575b
Munkar wa-Nakīr i, 187a, 334b; iii, 1231b; iv, 667b; vi, 217b, 219b; vii, 576b
Munḳidh, Banū vi, 789b; vii, 577b; ix, 410a
Munsariḥ → ʿArūḍ
Munshī vii, 580b
Munshi Abdullah (1854) vi, 240b

Mun<u>sh</u>ī ʿAṭāʾ Muḥammad (1855) ix, 440a
Mun<u>sh</u>ī Harkaran (XVII) vii, 343a
Mun<u>sh</u>ī Mawlawī → ʿAbd al-Karīm Mun<u>sh</u>ī
Mun<u>sh</u>ī Nawal Ki<u>sh</u>ōr (1895) x, 879a
Mun<u>sh</u>ī Nawbat Rāʾe Naẓar (XIX) vi, 612a
Munṣif vii, 580b
Munṣif Bey iii, 636b
Munṣifa (Munṣifāt) vii, 580b
Munta<u>dj</u>ab al-Dīn (1179) vii, 581a
Munta<u>dj</u>ab al-Dīn Abu ʾl-Ḥasan ʿAlī al-Ḳum(m)ī) (XII) iii, 1151b
Munta<u>dj</u>ib al-Dīn, "Zar Ba<u>kh</u>sh" (<u>Kh</u>uldābād) vi, 127a
al-Muntafiḳ, Banū i, 270b, 684a, 873a, 942a, 1086a, 1087a, 1096a, b; ii, 77a; iii, 1107b, 1257b; v, 81a; vii, 582a, 674a; ix, 801b; s, 119a, 234b
al-Muntafiḳ b. ʿĀmir b. ʿUkayl, Banū vii, 582a
Muntafiḳ district (ʿIrāḳ) vi, 615a; vii, 582a
Munṭaḳa i, 297a
al-Munta<u>kh</u>ab → Abū Zakariyyāʾ Yaḥyā III
Munta<u>kh</u>ab al-Dawla iv, 842a
al-Muntaṣir (Ḥafṣid) iii, 69a; iv, 416a
al-Muntaṣir bi-ʾllāh (ʿAbbāsid) (862) i, 402b; ii, 461b, 837b; vi, 625b; vii, 583a, 777b
al-Muntaṣir b. Abi ʾl-ʿAbbās (Marīnid) (XIV) vi, 594a
al-Muntaṣir b. Abī Liḥya (Gafsa) (XI) vi, 355b
al-Muntaṣir b. <u>Kh</u>azrūn v, 1181a, 1182b
Muntazah (palace) s, 301a
Muntaẓirī, Āyatullāh (XX) vi, 554a; vii, 300a
Munūf → Manūf
Munyat al-Aṣba<u>gh</u> (Miṣr) vii, 149a
Munyat Ibn al-<u>Kh</u>aṣīb vi, 651a
Murabbaʿ → Musammaṭ
Murabbīh Rabbuh b. Māʾ al-ʿAynayn, <u>Sh</u>ay<u>kh</u> (1942) vii, 621a
al-Murābī, Abu ʾl-ʿAbbās iv, 736a
Murābiṭ → Ribāṭ
al-Murābiṭūn (Almoravids) i, 7a, 78b, 165a, 242b, 251a, 367a, 389a, 495a, 602a, 986a, 1092a, 1176a; ii, 134a, 1007a; iii, 207a, 800a, 959a, 1043a; v, 744a, 1178b, 1189b; vi, 134a, 216b, 259a, 279b, 281a, 427a, 520b, 571b, 576b, 590b, 592a; vii, 583b, 613a; viii, 616b; ix, 754b, 899b; s, 27a, 80b
– administration i, 445b, 1148b; ii, 145b, 230a; v, 626a
– constructions i, 499a, 1320b; ii, 818b, 821b, 1015a; iii, 300b; iv, 633a; v, 1150a
– history i, 44a, 156b; iii, 932b; v, 653b
Murād I (Ottoman) (1389) i, 322b, 394a, 468a, b, 481a, 510b, 1117b, 1191b, 1263a, 1302b, 1325b; ii, 15b, 210b, 291b, 444b, 684b, 983b; iv, 376a, 623a, 945a; v, 44b, 276a; vi, 89a, 290b, 530b; vii, 592b; viii, 193a; s, 314b, 331a
Murād II (Ottoman) (1451) i, 199a, 468a, 654b, 655b, 992a, 1061a, 1225b, 1248a, 1252b, 1334a; ii, 82b, 98a, 210b, 443a, 599b, 684a,b, 685a, 697a, 703a, 721a, 984b, 990a, 1086a; iv, 139b, 624a, 656a, 968b, 1093a; v, 1170a; vi, 70a, 73a, 530a, b; vii, 594b; viii, 193b; s, 274a, 315a
Murād III (Ottoman) (1595) i, 775b, 1017b, 1208b; ii, 82b, 208a, 442b, 615a, 881a; iv, 638a; v, 27b, 766a, 814b, 1170a; vi, 377a, 505a, 601b, 799a; vii, 595b, 601a; s, 138a
Murād IV (Ottoman) (1640) i, 4a, 310b, 424a, 468b, 475a, 481a, 775b, 826a, 904a; ii, 49a, 119b, 345b, 718a; iii, 91b, 352a, 357a, 626a, 1257a; iv, 451b, 574a, 717a, 728b; v, 18b, 34b, 272b, 493b; vi, 150a, 202b, 232a, 345b; vii, 319a, 597b; s, 49a, b, 94b, 171b, 315b
Murād V (Ottoman) (1904) i, 63b; ii, 49a, 642a; iv, 876a, b; vii, 599a; s, 63a
Murād b. Amīr <u>Sh</u>āhī, Sulṭān (Marʿa<u>sh</u>ī) (XVI) vi, 514b, 515a
Murād II b. Mīrza <u>Kh</u>ān, Mīr Sulṭān (Marʿa<u>sh</u>ī) (XVI) vi, 515a
Murād A<u>gh</u>a (1556) x, 213b
Murād, Banū iii, 223a; v, 954a; vi, 472a; vii, 591b
Murād Beg (Tar<u>dj</u>umān) (XVI) x, 237a
Murād, Ḥā<u>dj</u><u>dj</u>ī → <u>Sh</u>āmil
Murād, Muḥammad (Mat-Murad, Dīwān-begi) (XIX) s, 228b
Murād b. Aḥmad b. Bāyazīd iv, 716b
Murād (<u>Sh</u>āh-) b. Akbar (Pahari) (Mu<u>gh</u>al) (1599) i, 81a; ii, 981b; vi, 814b; vii, 592a; viii, 74a
Murād b. Dāniyāl Biy Atalīḳ, <u>Sh</u>āh (Mangīt) (1785) vi, 418b, 419a, 621a; s, 97a

Murād b. Djem (1523) ii, 530b; viii, 570a
Murād b. Mālik b. Udad vii, 591b
Murād b. Yaʿḳūb i, 311b, 312a
Murād Bakhsh b. Shāh Djahān (1661) i, 768b; ii, 134b; iv, 914b; vi, 345b; vii, 599b, 601b
Murād Beg (Ḳunduz) (1838) i, 853a; ii, 638a
Murād Beg Tardic v, 774b
Murād Bey, Muḥammad (neo-Mamlūk) (1801) iii, 992a; iv, 853a; vi, 325b; vii, 179a, 180b, 420b; ix, 229a; s, 38b
Murād Bey Abū Bālā (1702) iv, 828a
Murād Bey Sulaymān (XX) vi, 93a, 614b
Murād Girāy (Crimea) (1683) iv, 178b; v, 140a; vi, 989a
Murād Ḥādjdjī → Shāmil
Murād Khān b. Ismāʿīl Pasha i, 920a
Murād Khān (Kashmīr) → Iʿtiḳād Khān
Murād Pasha (1473) iv, 230a
Murād Pasha Ḳuyudju (1611) i, 267b, 511a, 904a; ii, 635a, 750a; iv, 499a, 970a; vii, 275b, 600a; viii, 237a; s, 239a
Murād Raʾīs v, 504a
Murād Sulṭān i, 1076b
Murād-suyu (Murat Su) → al-Furāt
Murādābād iv, 749b; vi, 48a, 49a, 50a vii, 601b; s, 73b, 74a, 321b
Murādī → Murād III; Murād IV
al-Murādī, ʿAbd al-Raḥmān (1803) vii, 602a
al-Murādī, Abū Bakr Muḥammad b. al-Ḥasan al-Ḥaḍramī, Imām (1096) vii, 613a
al-Murādī, ʿAlī (1771) vii, 602a
al-Murādī, Ḥusayn (1774) vii, 602a
al-Murādī, Muḥammad (1755) vii, 602a
al-Murādī, Muḥammad Khalīl al-Ḥusaynī (1791) i, 594b; ii, 355b, 839b; vi, 345b; vii, 602a
al-Murādī, Muḥammad b. Manṣūr (IX) s, 48b
al-Murādī, Murād b. ʿAlī al-Ḥusaynī al-Bukhārī (1720) vii, 602a
al-Murdī, al-Rabīʿ (884) ix, 182a, 187a
al-Murādī, ʿUmar b. ʿAbd Allāh (VIII) vi, 923a
Murāḳaba → Muḥāsaba
Muraḳḳaʿ vii, 602b
Murakkab i, 1083b
Muraḳḳish al-Akbar (VI) vii, 306a, 603a
Muraḳḳish al-Aṣghar i, 963b; iv, 998a, b; vii, 604a
al-Muraysīʿ vii, 356b; viii, 820a
Murcia → Mursiya
Murḍā b. ʿAlī i, 798a; vi, 406a
Murdādh → Taʾrīkh
al-Murdār, Abū Mūsā (840) iii, 1019b, 1266a; vi, 636b; vii, 546b, 604a
Murdi-čay (river) vi, 498b
Murdjān i, 781a
Murdjiʿa i, 123b, 124a, 249b, 276b, 1241b; ii, 833b, 931a, 1022a; iii, 807b, 1142b, 1164a, 1171a; iv, 408a; vi, 457b; vii, 508b, 605b; s, 358a
Murdjiʿābād (Balkh) vii, 606b
al-Murdjibī, Ḥāmid b. Muḥammad (Tippu Tip) (1905) iv, 750a, b; v, 176b; vii, 607b
al-Murdjibī, Muḥammad b. Djuma (1881) x, 194b
Murghāb (river) i, 222b, 313b, 853b; v, 868b, 873b; vi, 617b, 618a, b, 621a; vii, 608b
Murīd vii, 608b
Murīdiyya (Murīdism) (Senegal) ii, 63b; iii, 157a; vii, 609a; ix, 146a; s, 182a
Mūristus (Mūrṭus/Mīrisṭus) (868) vii, 610a
Mūrītāniyā i, 211a, 1177b; ii, 672a, 676a, 1122a; iii, 231a, 288b, 385a; v, 697a, 1074a; vi, 142a; vii, 611a; ix, 445b; s, 182b, 218a
al-Mūriyānī, Abū Ayyūb Sulaymān b. Makhlad (771) vii, 628a
Murra, Banū (Āl-) i, 545b, 873b; ii, 176b, 725b, 1023b; vi, 371b; vii, 461b, 488a, 628b, 630a, 840b; s, 5a
al-Murrī, al-Djunayd iii, 223b
al-Murrī, Ṣāliḥ iv, 734b
Mursal iii, 26a; vii, 631a
Murshid vii, 631b
Murshid Ḳulī Khān (1658) i, 7b, 786b; ii, 157b, 488b, 810a; iv, 976b; vii, 632a
Murshidābād (Bengal) vi, 369b; vii, 444a, 632b
Murshidī → ʿAbd al-Raḥmān b. ʿĪsā
Murshidiyya → Kāzarūniyya
al-Mursī → Yāḳūt
al-Mursī, Abu 'l-ʿAbbās (1287) v, 17b; ix, 172a, b; x, 247a; s, 159a
Mursiya (Murcia) i, 6b, 58b, 82b, 489a, 1320a, 1347a; ii, 115a; iii, 706a, 904b; iv,

672b; vi, 339b, 521a; vii, 633a; x, 105b; s, 144b
al-Murtaḍā → ʿAbd al-Raḥmān IV (Umayyad), (al-Andalus)
Murtaḍā I Niẓām Shāh (Niẓām Shāhī) (1588) ii, 815a, 921b; iii, 426b, 1161a; vi, 271b; viii, 73b
Murtaḍā II Niẓām Shāh (Niẓām Shāhī) (1610) iii, 15b; iv, 1018b; vi, 269b; viii, 74a
al-Murtaḍā (Almohad) (1266) s, 112a, 389a, b
Murtaḍā (Hind) s, 329b
al-Murtaḍā, al-Sharīf Abu 'l-Ḳāsim, ʿAlam al-Hudā (1044) i, 130a, 154b, 1352a; ii, 127b; iii, 1266a; iv, 182b; v, 363a; vi, 458a, 549a, b, 634b; vii, 313a, 634a, 786a, 903b; viii, 462b; s, 23a, 25b, 56b, 95a
(al-)Murtaḍā b. al-ʿAfīf (XIII) vii, 634b
Murtaḍā b. ʿAlī Sārī b. Kamāl al-Dīn (Marʿashī) (XV) v, 663a; vi, 513a
Murtaḍā b. Kamāl al-Dīn (Marʿashī) (XV) vi, 512b, 513a
Murtaḍā b. Riḍā al-Dīn (Marʿashī) (XV) vi, 513b
Murtaḍa ʿAlī ii, 88a
Murtaḍā Anṣārī, Shaykh (1864) vii, 299a
Murtaḍā Baktāshī ii, 735a,b
Murtaḍā al-Dawla Manṣūr b. Luʾluʾ al-Kabīr (1010) vii, 116a
Murtaḍā Ḥusayn i, 1219a
Murtaḍā Ḳulī Khān (XVIII) iv, 390b, 391a
Murtaḍā Ḳulī Khān Iḳbāl al-Salṭana (Mākū) (1923) vi, 203a
Murtaḍā Ḳulī Khān Shāmlū (XVII) iv, 1124b; viii, 784a
Murtaḍā Ḳulī Khān Wakīl al-Mulk (XIX) v, 165a
Murtaḍā Pasha (XVII) i, 4b, 236b; v, 34b, 258a, b, 1023a; viii, 7a
Murtaḍāʾids vi, 512a
Murtadd iv, 408a, 771a, 1076b; v, 179a; vii, 635a
Murtadi → (al-)Murtaḍā b. al-ʿAfīf
Murtahin iv, 488b
Murūʾa (Muruwwa) ii, 961a; vii, 636b
Murud s, 246b
Murwan-Ḳru i, 100b; v, 487b, 488a
Murzuḳ (Libya) i, 38a; ii, 876a; vii, 638a
Muş vi, 242b
Mūsā (Moses) ii, 280a, 917b; iii, 231b, 1175a; iv, 293a, 903a, b, 904a; v, 421a, 423b; vii, 638b
Mūsā, Aḥmad (IX) vii, 640a, b
Mūsā, Banū i, 84b, 403a; vi, 600a; vii, 640a; viii, 559b; x, 428b; s, 267a, 371b, 372b, 373a, 412b
Mūsā, Muḥammad (873) vii, 640a
Mūsā Mzuri (1861) x, 194b
Mūsā, Salāma iv, 125a
Mūsā I al-Djawn iii, 262b, 984b
Mūsā II b. ʿAbd Allāh (Mūsāwid) iii, 262b; vi, 148b
Mūsā b. ʿAbd Allāh b. Ḥasan → Mūsā I al-Djawn
Mūsā b. ʿAbd Allāh b. Khāzim (Tirmidh) (705) i, 48a, 529b; iii, 304a; x, 542a, 576b
Mūsā b. Abi 'l-ʿĀfiya (938) ii, 853a, 979a; iii, 1036a; iv, 459a; vi, 1008b; vii, 641a, 942a
Mūsā b. Abī Djābir al-Azkānī iii, 652a
Mūsā b. al-Amīn (ʿAbbāsid) (IX) vi, 332b
Mūsā b. al-ʿĀzār (Moses b. Eleazar) (X) i, 344b
Mūsā b. ʿAzra (1135) vii, 642a
Mūsā b. Bughā (877) i, 278b, 1287b; ii, 191a; iii, 29a, 245a; iv, 493b, 859a; vii, 477a, 801a
Mūsā b. Djaʿfar → Mūsā al-Kāẓim
Mūsā b. Fortūn iv, 712b
Mūsā b. Ḥafṣ iv, 645b
Mūsā b. al-Ḥārith (Kinda) vii, 671a
Mūsā b. Ḥudayr i, 600a
Mūsā b. Ibrāhīm b. Shīrkūh → al-Ashraf Mūsā
Mūsā b. ʿImrān (prophet) vi, 412b
Mūsā b. ʿĪsā (799) (ʿAbbāsid) i, 162b; x, 810b
Mūsā b. Kaʿb al-Tamīmī (VIII) vi, 332b, 744b
Mūsā b. Maḥmūd Ḳādīzāda Rūmī Ṣalāḥ al-Dīn (XV) x, 813b
Mūsā b. Maymūn → Ibn Maymūn
Mūsā b. Muḥammad b. Abī Bakr (Songhay) (XVI) vii, 394a
Mūsā b. Mūsā Ibn Ḳasī i, 1012a; iii, 815b; iv, 712b; s, 82a
Mūsā b. Nuṣayr (716) i, 58b, 492b, 1079b, 1242b, 1338b; ii, 1009a, 1095b; iii, 271b;

iv, 115a, 494b, 665a; v, 1189a; vi, 134a, 568a, 742a; vii, 643a; s, 81b, 125a
Mūsā b. Rabīʿa b. Mānīʿ al-Muraydī ii, 569a
Mūsā b. Shākir (IX) vii, 640a
Mūsā b. Shākir, Banū vii, 559a, s, 413b, 414a
Mūsā b. Ṭalḥa v, 1231a
Mūsā b. ʿUḳba al-Asadī (758) v, 1162a, 1163a; vii, 644a
Mūsā b. ʿUmar b. ʿĀmir b. Kunnu (XVII) vi, 642b
Mūsā b. Yaḥyā (Barmakid) (835) i, 1036a; vi, 332a
Mūsā ag Amāstan i, 255a
Mūsā Aydinoghlu i, 783b; ii, 599a
Mūsā Beg (Ḳarāmān-oghlu) iv, 621b, 622a
Mūsā Beg b. Ibrāhīm Beg (Menteshe) (1375) vi, 1018b
Mūsā Čelebi b. Bāyazīd I (Ottoman) (1413) ii, 291b, 599a, 611b, 684a; vi, 973b; vii, 644a
Mūsā al-Hādī → al-Hādī ilā 'l-Ḥaḳḳ (ʿAbbāsid)
Mūsā Ḥarfūsh ii, 750a; iii, 205b
Mūsā al-Kāẓim (VII. Imām) (799) i, 108a, 402b, 550b, 850b; ii, 374b, 375a; iii, 233b, 497a, 616b; iv, 855a, b, 1132b; v, 1236a; vi, 921b; vii, 396b, 645b, 672a; s, 95a, 383a, 402b
Mūsā Khān Pūlādī i, 1136b
Mūsā Pasha, Ḳāʾim-Maḳām (XVIII) vii, 709b
Mūsā Rayna s, 423b
Mūsā al-Ṣadr, Imām (1978) vii, 301b; viii, 388a; ix, 315a, 884a; s, **641b**
Mūsā Shahawāt^{in}, Abū Muḥammad (VIII) iv, 190a; vii, 648b
Mūsā Sulaymān iii, 370b
Muṣʿab (Miṣr) (785) vii, 160b
Muṣʿab b. ʿAbd Allāh al-Zubayrī (851) vii, 649a
Muṣʿab b. ʿUmayr (625) vii, 649b
Muṣʿab b. al-Zubayr, Abū ʿAbd Allāh (691) i, 55a, 76b, 304a, 453b, 810b, 1242b, 1243a, 1349a; ii, 197a; iii, 40a, 715a, 970a, 1255a, 1265b; iv, 494b; v, 731a; vi, 139a, b, 622a, 623a, 640b; vii, 357a, 400b, 408b, 523b, 649b; ix, 421b; s, 357b, 380b
Musābaḳa s, **642a**
al-Muṣʿabayn i, 1133a
Musabbaʿāt ii, 122a,b; v, 267a
al-Musabbiḥāt vii, 650b
al-Muṣabbiḥī (1030) iii, 81a, 894b; vii, 115b, 163b, 650b
al-Muṣʿabī, Abā Yazmū (XIII) iii, 96b, 97a
al-Muṣʿabī, Abu 'l-Ṭayyib (X) vii, 652a
Muṣādara i, 1144a; ii, 152b; iv, 463b; vii, 652b
Musaddas → Musammaṭ
Muṣaddiḳ, Muḥammad (1967) i, 978b; ii, 653a, 882b; iii, 529b; iv, 41b, 695b, 790a, 1028b; v, 630b, 1042b; vii, 447a, 653b; s, 60b, 110b, 158a
al-Muṣaffāt → Ḥamīda bint Ṣaʿīd al-Barbariyya
Musāfir s, **642b**
Musāfirids i, 98b, 637b, 638a, 1041b; ii, 192a, 680a; iv, 345a, 346a; vi, 66a, 499a, b; vii, 655b; ix, 169b
Musāhama → Mukhāradja
Muṣaḥḥaf iii, 26a
Muṣāḥib vii, 657b
Muṣāḥib Muṣṭafā Pasha (1686) i, 96b; ii, 684b; vii, 839a
Muṣāḥib-Zāde Djelāl (Musahip-zade Celal) (1959) vii, 657b
Musāʿid (al-Matamma) (1820) vi, 794b
Musāḳāt v, 871b; vii, 658b
Musālima i, 491a
al-Muṣallā i, 482a; v, 1141a, 1147a; vi, 653b; vii, 658b
al-Muṣallā al-ʿAtīḳ (Baghdād) vi, 653b
al-Muṣallā al-Ḳadīm (Cairo) vi, 654a
Muṣallā Khawlān (Cairo) vi, 653b
Musallamī iv, 1045a
Musallim al-Tardjāwī v, 267a, b
Musalmānī i, 952a
Musalmānī Bānglā i, 1167a
Musalsal iii, 26a; iv, 1124a, 1125b
Musāmaḥāt ii, 303a
Musammaṭ i, 677b; iv, 715a; vii, 660b
Musandam i, 536a; v, 508a
Muṣannaf vii, 662b
al-Musannāt vii, 393b
Muṣannifak, ʿAlā al-Dīn ʿAlī al-Bisṭāmī al-Ṣiddīḳī (1470) i, 867b; vi, 995b, 663a
Muṣarrif-zāde → Shefīḳ Meḥmed Effendi
Musāwāt iii, 530b; vii, 663a
al-Mūsawī i, 256a
al-Mūsawī, Sayyid Sharaf al-Dīn → Bulbul Shāh

Mūsawī Shīʿa s, 402b
Mūsāwids i, 552a; iii, 262b
Musāwir b. Sawwār al-Warrāḳ (VIII) vii, 663b
Mūsāwīs (Ḥasanids) (Mecca) vi, 148a, b; ix, 507a
Mūsāwīs (Persia) → Mūsā al-Kāẓim
Muṣawwaʿ → Maṣawwaʿ
Musawwida iii, 617a; vii, 664a
Musaylima b. Ḥabīb, Abū Thumāna al-Kadhdhāb (633) i, 110b, 964a; ii, 1060a; vi, 138b, 675b; vii, 664b; viii, 52a, 739a
al-Musayyab b. ʿAlas (VI) vii, 306b, 764a
al-Musayyab b. Nadjaba (685) ix, 826b
al-Musayyab b. Zuhayr al-Ḍabbī → al-Ḍabbī
Muscat → Masḳaṭ
Müsellem (müsellim) i, 1268b; ii, 33a; vii, 665a
Museveni x, 781a
Mūsh (Muş) i, 644a; vi, 242b; vii, 665b
Mushāʿ i, 661a; vii, 666b
Mushāʿara vii, 667b; ix, 434a
Mushabbiha → Tashbīh
Muṣḥaf v, 207a; vii, 668b
al-Muṣḥafī, Djaʿfar b. ʿUthmān (982) i, 601b, 628a; iii, 346b; vi, 431a, 926b; viii, 833b
Muṣḥafī, Shaykh Ghulām Hamadānī (1824) iii, 358b, 1244a; vii, 475b, 669b; s, 102a
Mushāhada iv, 697a
Mushāḳa, Mīkhāʾīl b. Djirdjīs (1888) vii, 670b, 686a
al-Mushaḳḳar (port) vii, 570b, 671a, 859b
al-Mushallal (Ḳudayd) vi, 373b; vii, 694a
Mūshār/Minshār vi, 231a
Mushāraka vii, 671b
Mushārī b. Saʿūd (1821) ii, 321b
Mushārī b. Saʿūd b. Djalwī (XX) vi, 155b
al-Musharraf b. Muradjdjaʾ v, 330a, 332a
Musharrif al-Dawla (1025) i, 131b; ii, 391a; iv, 378b; viii, 595b
Mushaʿshaʿ i, 1096a; iii, 1256b; iv, 49a; v, 80b; vi, 549b; vii, 672a; viii, 777b; ix, 856a
Mushāt iii, 187a
al-Mushattā (al-Mshattā) i, 613b, 615a, 616a; iii, 310a; v, 183a; vii, 675b; s, 117a
Mushfiḳī, ʿAbd al-Raḥmān (1588) vii, 676b
Mushidd i, 802a
Mushīr vii, 677a
Mushīr al-Dawla, Mīrzā Sayyid Djaʿfar Khān (1862) iv, 787a, 788a; vii, 678a; s, 108b
Mushīr Ḥusayn Ḳidwāʾī vii, 678b; s, 4b, 74a
Müshīr, müshīriyyet i, 1111a; ii, 724a
Mushk-i ʿĀlam i, 232a
Mushkān → Abū Naṣr Mushkān
Mushrif ii, 146a; iv, 759a; vii, 678b
Mushrif al-Kurdī, Ḥusayn (amīr) (XVI) vii, 514a
Mushrik → Shirk
Mushtāḳ ii, 433b; iv, 69b
Mushtāḳī s, 1b
Mushtarī (planet) vii, 680a
al-Mushtarik (Mushtarak) i, 184b; vii, 680b
Mūsī i, 261a
Mūsīḳī/Mūsīḳā i, 1124a; iii, 974b; v, 477b; vii, 681a; viii, 448b
Muṣlī Čawush i, 267b
Muṣliḥ iv, 141a
Muṣliḥ al-Dīn Lārī → al-Lārī, Muṣliḥ al-Dīn
Muṣliḥ al-Dīn Muṣṭafā b. Shaʿbān (1561) vi, 991a
Muṣliḥ al-Dīn Muṣṭafā al-Ḳaraḥiṣārī → Akhtarī
Muṣliḥ al-Zandjī (IX) vii, 526b
Muslim iv, 171b, 173a, b, 176a, b, 177a; v, 1015a, 1019a; vii, 688b
Muslim, league → al-Rābiṭa al-Islāmiyya
Muslim, non-arab → Mawlā
Muslim b. ʿAḳīl b. Abī Ṭālib (680) i, 337b; iii, 164b, 608a, 609a, 620b, 715a; vi, 438b; vii, 400b, 521b, 592a, 688b; viii, 119a; ix, 421b
Muslim b. ʿAwsadja al-Asadī (VII) vii, 689a
Muslim b. al-Ḥadjdjādj (875) i, 114b, 1297a; ii, 159a; iii, 24a, 708b, 803a, 909b; vii, 260a, 361b, 631a, 691a, 706a; viii, 516a; s, 232b
Muslim b. Ḳuraysh, Sharaf al-Dawla (ʿUḳaylid) (1085) i, 517a, 664a; ii, 282a, 347b, 348b, 384b; iii, 86b, 686b, 790a; vi, 274b, 546b; vii, 120b, 577b, 692b; viii, 947a; x, 787a
Muslim b. Ḳutayba vi, 604a

Muslim b. Saʿīd al-Kilābī (VIII) vi, 633b; vii, 1016a
Muslim b. ʿUbays (VII) i, 810a; vii, 858b, 877b
Muslim b. ʿUḳba al-Murrī (VII) i, 45a, 55a, 76b; ii, 89b, 1023b; iii, 226b, 227a, 620b; v, 997a; vi, 622a; vii, 629b, 693b
Muslim b. al-Walīd al-Anṣārī (823) i, 10a, 587b, 857b; ii, 248b; iii, 73a, 1264a; iv, 1004b; vi, 437b, 604b; vii, 413a, 694a, 982a
Muslim Educational Society vi, 461a
Muslimiyya vi, 544a
Muslimūn vii, 695a
Muslin → al-Mawṣil
Muslu Čawush (1608) vii, 600b; s, 239a
Musnad i, 273b, 275b; iii, 25b; vii, 704b
Mussoorie s, 66a
Mustacaplioğlu, Esat Adil iv, 124b
al-Mustaḍīʾ, Mawlāy (ʿAlawid) (1740) i, 47b; vi, 595a
al-Mustaḍīʾ bi-Amr Allāh (ʿAbbāsid) (1180) i, 212b, 273a; iii, 751a; vii, 707a; s, 193b
Mustadjāb Khān Bahādur, Nawwāb (1774) vii, 707a
Mustadrika vii, 868b
Muṣṭafā I (Ottoman) (1638) ii, 183b, 713a; iv, 884a; v, 272a; vii, 707b
Muṣṭafā II (Ottoman) (1703) i, 96b, 398a; ii, 684a; iv, 1104b; v, 18b, 262b; vi, 5a, 55a; vii, 707b
Muṣṭafā III (Ottoman) (1773) i, 1004a; ii, 49a; iii, 158a, 269a; iv, 892a; vii, 708b
Muṣṭafā IV (Ottoman) (1808) iv, 322b; vi, 58a; vii, 709b; viii, 75b
Muṣṭafā (walī, Ḳonya) (XV) i, 244a; ii, 184a
Muṣṭafā b. Ḥādjdjī Ākā Muḥsin, Sayyid s, 342a
Muṣṭafā b. Ibrāhīm (Mēṣṭfa bēn Bqāhīm) (XIX) vi, 250b, 253b, 255b
Muṣṭafā b. Idrīs (amīr) (1788) vi, 791b
Muṣṭafā b. Ismāʿīl (1843) ii, 173a; vii, 434a, b, 452a b
Muṣṭafā b. al-Ḳādī Ṭāhā (XIX) vii, 205a
Muṣṭafā b. Kamāl al-Dīn al-Bakrī → al-Bakrī, Muṣṭafā b. Kamāl al-Dīn
Muṣṭafā b. Meḥemmed I (Ottoman) (1425) vii, 594a
Muṣṭafā b. Sülaymān Ḳānūnī (Ottoman) (1553) i, 1301b; ii, 737b, 738a; iii, 147b; vii, 713a; viii, 641a
Muṣṭafā b. Umūr II ii, 599b
Muṣṭafā ʿAbd al-Rāziḳ (1947) vii, 713a
Muṣṭafā Abū Muḥammad Bayram al-Khāmis vii, 433b
Muṣṭafā Abū Ṭāhir al-Ḥusaynī s, 67a
Muṣṭafā Agha (Dār al-Saʿāda Aghasi̊ (XVII) iv, 194a, 590b
Muṣṭafā Agha, Dede (XIX) vii, 519a
Muṣṭafā Agha ʿOthmān-oghlu iv, 593a
Muṣṭafā ʿAlī → ʿAlī, Muṣṭafā b. Aḥmad Čelebi
Muṣṭafā ʿĀṣim s, 328b
Muṣṭafā al-Baghdādī (1148) vii, 9b
Muṣṭafā Barzānī, Mullā (1979) i, 1072a; v, 467a, b, 468a, b, 469a, b, 1213b, 1214a; vii, 714a
Muṣṭafā Beg (Shūshīk) (XVII) vi, 202b
Muṣṭafā Beg b. ʿIwaḍ Beg al-Maḥmūdī (Mākū) (XVI) vi, 202a
Muṣṭafā Behdjet Efendi → Bahdjat Muṣṭafā
Muṣṭafā Bey Čapan-oghlu ii, 207b
Muṣṭafā Čalabi Ṣābūndjī (Mosul) (XX) vi, 901b
Muṣṭafā Čelebi → Bičaḳdji-zāde; Djalālzāde
Muṣṭafā Čelebī (Küčük Muṣṭafā) b. Meḥemmed I (1423) ii, 990a; vii, 712b
Muṣṭafā Čelebi, Düzme, b. Bāyazīd I (1422) i, 783b, 899b; ii, 599b, 684a, 697a, 721a; v, 763b; vii, 237a, 594b, 710a
Muṣṭafā Dāʿī, Shaykh v, 952a
Muṣṭafā Davidovič ii, 979b, 980a
Muṣṭafā li-Dīn Allāh → Nizār b. al-Mustanṣir
Muṣṭafā Djinānī (1585) viii, 213b, 215a
Muṣṭafā Efendi (Masraḥ) (XIX) vi, 759a
Muṣṭafā Efendi b. Sahrab (XVII) vi, 247b
Muṣṭafā Fāḍil Pasha → Fāḍil Pasha
Muṣṭafā Feyḍī iii, 303a
Muṣṭafā ʿIzzet Efendi i, 776a
Muṣṭafā Kabakči̊ → Kabakči̊
Muṣṭafā Kāmil Pasha (1908) i, 597a; iii, 59a, 515a; iv, 967a; vii, 439a, 715a; viii, 49a; ix, 151b
Muṣṭafā Kʸahyā al-Ḳādughlī (Miṣr) (XVII) vii, 178b

Mustafā Kemāl Pāsha → Atatürk
Muṣṭafā Kemāl Pasha (town) → Kirmāstī
Muṣṭafā Khān i, 1155a
Muṣṭafā Khayrī Efendi, Ürgüplü (1921) vii, 716b
Muṣṭafā Khaznadār (1878) i, 282a; iii, 636a, b; iv, 1153b, 1154a; vii, 436b, 451b, 452a, 717b; s, 387a
Muṣṭafā Khodja iii, 636a
Muṣṭafā al-Manṣūrī ix, 517a
Muṣṭafā al-Marāghī, Shaykh s, 300a
Muṣṭafā Nadjīb Pasha iv, 618a
Muṣṭafā al-Naḥḥās Pasha ii, 934b; iii, 515b, 516a, 517a; s, 5b, 300a, b
Muṣṭafā Nāʾilī Pasha (XIX) i, 397a; vi, 68b
Muṣṭafā Naʿīm → Naʿīmā
Muṣṭafā Naẓīf Efendi (XVIII) vi, 56b
Muṣṭafā Nihat Özön (1980) vii, 658a
Muṣṭafā Nūrī Pasha ii, 636b
Mustafa Oğulcuk → Esendal
Muṣṭafā Pasha → Ḳara; Khodja; Köprülüzāde; Muṣāḥib; Soḳollu
Muṣṭafā Pasha (XIII) vii, 11a
Muṣṭafā Pasha (1623) ii, 751a
Muṣṭafā Pasha (1760) i, 1152a
Muṣṭafā Pasha (Sūria) (1850) vi, 308a
Muṣṭafā Pasha, Bayraḳdār (ʿAlemdār) (1808) i, 778b, 1304a; ii, 207a, 512b, 640a, 641b, 713a; iv, 322b; vi, 58a; vii, 710a, 719a
Muṣṭafā Pasha, Bushatlï (1860) i, 657a; v, 276b; vii, 719b
Muṣṭafā Pasha, Čelebi (XIX) vii, 710a, 719a
Muṣṭafā Pasha, Ipshīr → Ipshīr
Muṣṭafā Pasha, Isfendiyār-oghlu iv, 108b
Muṣṭafā Pasha, Ḳara Shāhīn (1564) vii, 720a; viii, 521a
Muṣṭafā Pasha, Köprülü → Köprülü
Muṣṭafā Pasha, Lala (1580) i, 380a, 468b; iv, 670b; v, 305a, 493a; vi, 455a; vii, 720b; viii, 184a
Muṣṭafā Pasha Kaplan i, 905a
Muṣṭafā Pasha al-Nashshār (1555) vii, 721a
Muṣṭafā Pasha Ṭūḳān al-Nābulusī s, 20b
Muṣṭafā Rāḳim iv, 1125b
Muṣṭafā Reshīd Pasha → Reshīd Pasha, Muṣṭafā
Muṣṭafā Riyāḍ Pasha (Miṣr) (XIX) iii, 514b, 515a; vii, 184a
Muṣṭafā Ṣafī Efendi v, 18a
Mustafa Yalïnkat → Esendal
Muṣṭafā Zühdi s, 171b
Muṣṭafābād ii, 597b, 1127a; vi, 50b, 53a, 55a
Muṣṭafānagar vi, 67b
Mustafīd iii, 25b
Mustaghānim (Mostaganem) vi, 754a; vii, 721b
Mustaḥabb vii, 722b
Mustaʿidd Khān, Muḥammad Sāḳī (1723) i, 954a; vii, 342b, 722b
al-Mustaʿīn bi-ʾllāh, Abū ʾl-ʿAbbās Aḥmad b. Muḥammad (ʿAbbāsid) (866) i, 21b, 145a, 278b, 897b, 1287b; v, 1160a; vii, 390b, 722b
al-Mustaʿīn bi-ʾllāh, Abu ʾl-Faḍl (ʿAbbāsid) (1430) ii, 781b; vii, 168a, 723a
al-Mustaʿīn (Hūdid) → Aḥmad II; Sulāyman b. Hūd
al-Mustaʿīn (Umayyad) → Sulaymān al-Mustaʿīn
al-Mustakfī bi-ʾllāh (ʿAbbāsid) (949) i, 20a, 1352b; vii, 484b, 723b
Mustakhīrūn iv, 259b
Mustakhridj v, 376a; vii, 724a
Müstaḳīm-zāde, Saʿd al-Dīn Sulaymān (1788) vii, 724a, 936b
Muṣṭalaḥāt i, 572a
Mustaʿlī bi-ʾllāh, Abu ʾl-Ḳāsim Aḥmad (Fāṭimid) (1101) i, 215b, 353a, 1254a; ii, 170b, 857a; iv, 200a; vii, 725a; viii, 83a Mustaʿlī-Ṭayyibī Ismāʿīlis vii, 411a, 725a; ix, 824b, 829a; s, 61b, 62a, 70b, 358b, 407a
Muṣṭaliḳ, Banu ʾl- v, 78b; vi, 648b; vii, 371a; viii, 820a
Mustaʾmin → Amān
Mustamlī v, 1133b; vii, 725b
al-Mustamsik (ʿAbbāsid) (1517) vii, 394a
al-Mustandjid (I) bi-ʾllāh (ʿAbbāssid) (1170) i, 212b, 684a; iii, 160b, 730b, 751a; vi, 54a; vii, 707a, 726a; s, 193b
al-Mustandjid (II) bi-ʾllāh (ʿAbbāsid) (1479) iii, 1198b; vii, 727a
al-Mustanīr → al-ʿIdjlī, Abū Manṣūr
al-Mustanṣir (I) bi-ʾllāh, Abū Djaʿfar (ʿAbbāsid) (1242) i, 21b; iii, 203b, 219b; vi, 322a; vii, 727a
al-Mustanṣir (II) bi-ʾllāh, Abu ʾl-Ḳāsim (ʿAbbāsid, Cairo) (1261) i, 21b; ii, 966a; iv, 944b; vii, 167b, 729a

al-Mustanṣir, Abū Yaʿḳūb Yūsuf (Almohad) s, 389a
al-Mustanṣir bi-ʾllāh, Abū Tamīm (Fāṭimid) (1094) i, 200b, 215a, 814b, 832b, 869b, 901b, 1073b, 1074b; ii, 169a, 855b, 856a, 857b, 859a, 861b, 958b; iii, 686b; vi, 453b, 626b, 707b; vii, 162b, 271a, 282b, 483a, 729b; s, 260b, 390a
al-Mustanṣir, Abū Muḥammad (Ḥafṣid) (1277) i, 21a, 1152a, 1346b; iii, 66b, 338a, 673a, 705a; iv, 179a; vi, 196b, 404a
al-Mustanṣir (Hūdid) → Aḥmad III
al-Mustanṣir II (Nizarī Imām) iv, 206a; v, 26b
Mustapha Kateb (Masraḥ) (XX) vi, 754a
Mustaʿrib → Mozarab
Mustaʿriba vii, 732b
al-Mustarshid bi-ʾllāh, Abū Manṣūr al-Faḍl (ʿAbbāsid) (1135) i, 353b, 522b, 858b, 901a; iii, 345a, 1255b; iv, 29b, 942b; vi, 64a, b; vii, 733a; s, 194a
Mustashār vii, 732b
Mustashār al-Dawla Tabrīzī iv, 787b; s, 53b
Mustashriḳūn vii, 735b
al-Mustaʿṣim bi-ʾllāh, Abū Aḥmad ʿAbd Allāh (ʿAbbāsid) (1258) i, 21a, 902b, 919a; iv, 30b; vi, 606a; vii, 166b, 753b; s, 199a, 252b
Mustawdaʿ ii, 851b
Mustawfī ii, 83a, 333b; iv, 977b; vii, 753b
Mustawfī, Abū Naṣr Muḥammad (XI) vii, 535a
Mustawfī, Ḥamd Allāh → Ḥamd Allāh Mustawfī al-Ḳazwīnī
Mustawfī al-mamālik ii, 335a, b
al-Mustawrid b. ʿUllafa (663) iii, 1265b; vi, 920a; vii, 347b
Mustazād i, 677b; vii, 754b
al-Mustaẓhir bi-ʾllāh (ʿAbbāsid) (1118) i, 659b, 901a; ii, 385a; iii, 351b; vi, 275a; vii, 408a, 755a; s, 194a, b, 326a
al-Mustaẓhir bi-ʾllāh → ʿAbd al-Raḥmān V
Müstethna Eyāletler vii, 756a
Muʾta (town) ii, 372b; vi, 604a; vii, 372b, 756a
Mutʿa i, 209a; ii, 551b; vii, 757a; s, 133a
Mūtā ii, 190b
al-Muṭāʿ v, 544a
Mutaʿarriba vii, 759b
Mutadārik iv, 412b; vii, 759b
al-Muʿtadd → Hishām III
al-Muʿtaḍid bi-ʾllāh, Abu ʾl-ʿAbbās b. al
Mutesa (Uganda) (1884) x, 779A
al-Muʿtaḍid bi-ʾllāh, Abū ʿAmr b. ʿAbbād (ʿAbbādid) (1069) i, 5b, 155b, 242a, 1040b, 1339a; ii, 389a, 1009a; iii, 496a, 640a, 705b; iv, 115b; v, 586b; vii, 249a, 760b
al-Mutadjarrida vii, 563a, 841a
Mutafarriḳa, Ibrāhīm → Ibrāhīm Müteferriḳa
al-Muṭahhar b. al-Mutawakkil ʿalā ʾllāh (Yemen) (1572) vii, 721b, 761b, 779b; viii, 235b
al-Muṭahhar b. Sharaf al-Dīn iv, 201a
al-Muṭahhar b. Ṭāhir al-Maḳdisī, Abū Naṣr (X) v, 65a, 330a; vii, 762a
al-Muṭahhar al-Hillī 1, 593a
Muṭahhar of Kara (XIV) x, 593a
Muṭahharī, Āyatullāh Murtaḍā (1979) iv, 166a; vii, 762b
Muṭahharten Bey i, 1119a; iv, 871a
Muʿtaḳ i, 30b
Mutaḳārib vii, 763a
Mutakāwis → Ḳāfiya
al-Mutalammis (580) i, 451b; vii, 763a
Muʿtamad Khān, Muḥammad Sharīf (1639) vii, 342b, 343a, 764a
Muʾtaman al-Dawla Isḥāḳ Khān i, 680a
Muʾtaman al-Khilāfa iv, 613a
al-Muʾtaman al-Sādjī i, 515b; iii, 730b
Muʾtamar vii, 764b
al-Muʿtamid Ibn ʿAbbād (Muḥammad b. ʿAbbād al-Muʿtaḍid) (ʿAbbādid) (1095) i, 6a, b, 251a, 592b, 601b; ii, 389b, 874a; iii, 677a, 706a, 783a, 853a, 905a, 963a, 973b; iv, 115b, 1007a; vi, 215b, 216a, 606b, 669b; vii, 553a, 633b, 761a, 766a, 775b; s, 1a
al-Muʿtamid ʿalā ʾllāh (ʿAbbāsid) (892) i, 18b, 279a, 637a, 897b; ii, 389b; iii, 247a, 839b; vi, 215b, 216a, 606b, 669b; vii, 390b, 765b; s, 16a, 402a
al-Muʿtamīd (Zīrid) iv, 117a
al-Muʿtamid b. Abī ʿInān (Marrākush) (XIV) vi, 593b
Muʿtamid al-Dawla → Ḳarwāsh b. al-Muḳallad
Muʿtamid al-Dawla iii, 1105b; v, 646a
al-Muʾtamin b. Hārūn al-Rashīd (IX) vi, 332a

al-Muʾtamin Ibn Hūd, Yūsuf b. Aḥmad (Hūdid) (1083) vii, 768a
Mutammim b. Nuwayra (VII) vi, 267a, 603a; vii, 308a; **768b**
al-Mutanabbī, Abū ʾl-Ṭayyib Aḥmad (955) i, 119b, 212b, 592a, 601a, 827b, 845b, 1249b; ii, 802b; iii, 338a, 672a, 738b, 743b, 754b, 780a, 807a, 1264a; iv, 418b, 867b, 1069b; v, 927b, 934b; vi, 253a, 605b, 616b, 956b; vii, 261a, 769a, 982b; s, 24a, 27b, 32b, 58b, 277b, 361b, 651b
Mutanabbī al-G͟harb viii, 420a
Mutarādif → Ḳāfiya
al-Muṭarrif (835) vi, 279a
Muṭarrif b. ʿAbd Allāh al-Marwānī (894) vi, 899a; s, 153a
al-Muṭarrif b. al-Mug͟hīra b. S͟huʿba (Mandāʾin) (VII) iii, 40b
Muṭarrif b. S͟hihāb b. ʿAmr al-S͟hihābī (1067) vii, 772b
Muṭarrifiyya vii, 772b; s, 22b, 236a
al-Muṭarrizī, Burhān al-Dīn Abu ʾl-Fatḥ Nāṣir (1213) v, 319a, b, 320b; vii, 190a, 773b, 914b
Mutaṣarrif vii, 774a
Mutaṣarrifiyya iv, 794a; v, 1253a, b
Mutas͟hābih i, 275a, 409a, 412a
al-Muʿtaṣim biʿllāh → Yaḥyā b. al-Nāṣir b. al-Manṣūr
al-Muʿtaṣim bi-ʾllāh b. Hārūn al-Ras͟hīd (ʿAbbāsid) (842) i, 11b, 16b, 18b, 52b, 153b, 241a, 271a, 273a, 279b, 437b, 449b, 510a, 844a, b, 897b, 1096a, 1287b, 1346a; ii, 235b, 328a, 505b, 730b, 1079b; iii, 618a; iv, 97b, 215a, 646b; vi, 198a, 206a, 319b, 335a, b, 337b, 338a, b, 379a, 504b, 625b, 666a; vii, 279a, b, 776a; s, 106a, 127b, 243a, 252b, 384b
al-Muʿtaṣim, Muḥammad b. Maʿn b. Ṣumādiḥ al-Tud͟jībī (Tud͟jībid) (1091) iii, 775b, 934b; vii, 501a, 775b
al-Muʿtaṣim bi-ʾllāh → Yaḥyā b. al-Nāṣir b. al-Manṣūr
al-Mustaʿṣimī → Yāḳūt
Mutaṭawwiʿa (Muṭṭawiʿa) vii, 776b
al-Mutawakkil ʿalā ʾllāh, Abu ʾl-Faḍl (ʿAbbāsid) (861) i, 18b, 271b, 273a, 386a, 620b, 637a, 713a, 1287b, 1289b; ii, 130a, 281b, 292b, 324b, 385b, 437b, 837b, 1080a; iii, 579a, 618a, 691a, 824a, 940b; iv, 637b, 940b; v, 1111a; vi, 106a, 206a, 504b, 625b, 656b, 660a, 663a, 667a; vii, 279b, 280b, 777b; s, 16b, 26a, 35a, 48a, 64a, 94b, 106a, 117b, 199a, 252a, b, 384b, 392a
al-Mutawakkil I (ʿAbbāsid, Cairo) (1406) vi, 548a
al-Mutawakkil III, Muḥammad (ʿAbbāsid, Cairo) (1517, d. 1543) i, 21b; iv, 945b; vii, 911b
al-Mutawakkil ʿalā ʾllāh (Afṭasid) (1095) vii, 778a
al-Mutawakkil (Hūdid) → Muḥammad b. Yūsuf b. Hūd
al-Mutawakkil Aḥmad b. Sulaymān iii, 125b; v, 1240b; s, 236a
al-Mutawakkil ʿalā ʾllāh Aḥmad b. Sulaymān (Zaydī) (XII) vi, 433a
al-Mutawakkil ʿalā ʾllāh Ismāʿīl b. al-Ḳāsim, Imām (Zaydī) (1676) ii, 517b; iii, 688b; v, 1241b; vi, 437a; vii, 514b, 778b
al-Mutawakkil ʿalā ʾllāh S͟haraf al-Dīn Yaḥyā, Imām (Zaydī) (1555) vi, 436b; vii, 779b
al-Mutawakkil Muḥammad b. Yaḥyā b. Muḥammad, Imām (Zaydī) (XIX) i, 555a; vii, 515a
Mutawakkilī Kingdom (Yemen) → Yaḥyā b. Muḥammad
Mutawālī (Métoualis) vii, 780a
al-Mutawallī, Abū Saʿd (1086) vii, 781a
al-Mutawassiṭ → ʿAbd al-Raḥmān II
Mutawātir iii, 25b; iv, 412b; vii, 781b
Muṭawwif vii, 782a
Muṭayr, Banū i, 545b; ii, 77a; iii, 1065b, 1068a; iv, 680b; vii, 782b
Muṭayyabūn → Laʿaḳat al-Dam
Muṭayyabūn, Banū i, 151a;v, 581a, b; vi, 137b, 145a
Mutayyam al-Hās͟himiyya iv, 821b; s, 116b, 252b
Muṭayyan, Muḥammad b. ʿAbd Allāh b. Sulaymān al-Ḥaḍramī (909) viii, 517b
Mutazawwid͟jāt i, 308b
Muʿtazila i, 4b, 59b, 127b, 266a, 271a, 272a, 326a, 454a, 694a, 1002b, 1243a; ii, 365a, 373a, 388a, 449a, 569b; iii, 496b, 658b, 699a, 1142b, 1143a, 1148a, 1150a, 1165b, 1266a; iv, 46a, 366a, 379a, 1162a; vi, 218b, 331b, 336a, b, 337a, b, 338a, 376a, 448a, 457b, 458a, 467a; vii, 783a; xi, 6b; s, 12b, 16b, 17a, 23a, 25a, b, 30a,

31b, 56b, 88b, 103a, 225b, 306a, 335b, 343a, b, 344a, 391b, 392a, 393a
– doctrine i, 17b, 128a, 178b, 187b, 204b, 209a, 334a, 410a-415b, 713b, 714a, 1092b; ii, 518a, 618a, 772a, 833b; iii, 171b, 465b, 661a, 672a, 1063a, 1146a; iv, 126b, 172a, 183a, 271b, 408a, 469a; v, 576b, 702a
al-Muʿtazila (Shīʿites) vii, 793b
al-Muʿtazz bi-'llāh b. Djaʿfar (ʿAbbāsid) (869) i, 273a, 278b, 897b, 1287b; ii, 36b, 1079b; iv, 89a, 126b; v, 1160a; vii, 390b, 477b, 777b, 793b
Müteferriḳa vii, 794a
Müteferriḳa, Ibrāhīm → Ibrāhīm Müteferriḳa
Müterdjim ʿĀṣim → ʿĀṣim, Aḥmad
Müterdjim Meḥmed Rüshdī (XIX) vi, 69a
al-Muthaḳḳib al-ʿAbdī (590) i, 74a; viii, 421b
Muthallath (triangle) vii, 794b
Muthamman vi, 127b; vii, 795a
al-Muthannā, Muḥammad b. ʿAbd Allāh (IX) vii, 649a
al-Muthannā b. Ḥāritha (635) i, 111a, 964a; ii, 241a; iii, 194b, 1254b; iv, 13b, 385a; vi, 920a; vii, 796b
Muthbita → Ahl al-ithbāt
Muṭīʿ b. Iyās al-Kinānī (785) i, 160a; ii, 1031b; iii, 135b; iv, 1003b; vii, 797b; viii, 884a, 996b; ix, 387a; xi, 155b
al-Muṭīʿ li 'llāh (ʿAbbāsid) (974) i, 211b, 1352b; iii, 128a; vi, 786a; vii, 358a, 724a, 799a; s, 36a
al-Muṭīʿa s, 121b
Muṭʿim b. ʿAdī (VII) vii, 366a, 1045a
Muṭʿim al-Ṭayr iv, 91b
Muṭlaḳ vii, 799b
Muṭrān, Khalīl → Khalīl Muṭrān
al-Muttaḳī li 'llāh b. al-Muḳtadir (Abbāsid) (968) i, 867a; iii, 127b; vi, 206a; vii, 723b, 800a; s, 386a
al-Muttaḳī, ʿAlī b. Ḥusām al-Dīn (1567) vi, 247b; vii, 458a
al-Muttaḳī al-Hindī, ʿAlī (1567) i, 593a; ii, 500b; iii, 435a; vii, 800b
Muṭṭalib, Banū i, 258a; vi, 145a; vii, 361b
al-Muṭṭalib b. ʿAbd Manāf i, 80a, 115b; iii, 1093a
Muttaṣil iii, 25b
al-Muṭṭawwiʿ, Tamīm b. Baḥr (IX) viii, 178a
Muṭṭawwiʿa → Mutaṭawwiʿa
Mütügen → Mö'etüken
Muwāḍaʿa iv, 253b; vii, 801a
al-Muwāfaḳa wa 'l-djamāʿa ii, 78b
Muwaffaḳ (ʿAbbāsid) (902) i, 11a, 14b, 19a, 249a, 592a, 637a, 896a, 897b, 898a, 964b, 1141a; ii, 128b, 325b, 344b, 524a, 1080a; iii, 344b, 761b, 767b, 818a, 892b, 908a; iv, 21b, 22a, 42b, 90a, b, 189a, 265b, 940b, 49b; vi, 540a, 658a, 669b, 671a, 673a, 729a, 807b; vii, 395a, 759b, 910b; s, 117b, 284a
al-Muwaffaḳ b. al-Mutawakkil (ʿAbbāsid) (880) i, 18b, 145a, 278b, 279a, 389a, 898a; ii, 196a, 1080a; iii, 859b, 908a, 976b; iv, 189a, 655a, 940b; v, 49a, b; vi, 673a, 921a; vii, 766a, 801a; viii, 796as, 117b, 384b, 385a, 402a
al-Muwaffaḳ, Abū ʿAlī b. Ismāʿīl (X) s, 118b
Muwaffaḳ b. ʿAlī al-Harawī, Abū Manṣūr i, 213b, 686a, 1014b; iii, 267a; iv, 1123b
Muwaffaḳ al-Dīn b. Ḳudāma → Ibn Ḳudāma
Muwaffaḳ al-Dīn Abu 'l-Maʿālī Aḥmad iii, 684b, 685a
Muwaffaḳ al-Dīn Yaʿḳūb s, 391a
al-Muwaffaḳiyya vi, 921a
Muwaffiḳ al-Mulk → Ibn al-Tilmīdh
al-Muwaḥḥidūn (Almohads) i, 78a, 92b, 94b, 122a, 160b, 165a, 367a, 495b, 602a, 1176a, 1205b, 1339b; ii, 112a, 527a, 818b, 1007b, 1009b, 1110b; iii, 207a, 300b, 461b, 771b, 864b, 959b; v, 744b, 1189b, 1199b; vi, 134a, b, 141b, 216b, 404a, 520b, 521a, 571b, 572b, 573b, 577a, 589a, 596b, 597a, 741a, 742b, 852b; vii, 585b, 801b; viii, 616b; s, 103a, 111b, 113b, 153a, 336b; x, 213a
– administration i, 1148b; ii, 145b, 230a, 307b; iv, 943b; v, 626a
– constructions i, 1320b; ii, 822a; iii, 499b; iv, 633b
– history i, 94b; iii, 570a, 924b; iv, 337b; v, 530b
al-Muwaḳḳar vii, 807a
Muwaḳḳit → Mīḳāt
Muwallad vii, 807a

Muwalladūn i, 49a, 491a, 494a; iii, 770b
Muwāraba vii, 808b
al-Muwāṣafa ii, 79a
Muwāṣala → Wiṣāl
Muwas̲h̲s̲h̲aḥ i, 426b, 595b, 601a, 602a; ii, 1033a, 1074a; iii, 729b, 851b, 855b, 929a; vii, 809a
Muwāṭin vii, 812b
al-Muwayliḥī, Ibrāhīm (1906) vii, 813a, 902b
al-Muwayliḥī, Muḥammad (1930) i, 597a; iii, 59b; vi, 113b, 114b; vii, 814a, 902a; viii, 736b
Muways b. ʿImrān b. D̲j̲umayʿ (VIII) vii, 414b, 784b, 815a
Muwaẓẓaf ii, 158a
Muwīs, Baḥr xi, 422a
Muyaka b. Mwinyi Haji al-G̲h̲assaniy (1837) iv, 887a; vi, 612b; vii, 227a
Muzabbid al-Madanī vii, 857a
Muzafar, sultan (Malacca) (XV) vi, 209a, 212a, b
al-Muẓaffar (1008) → ʿAbd al-Malik b. Abī al-Maʿāfirī
al-Muẓaffar (Afṭasid) → ʿAbd al-Malik al-Muẓaffar
al-Muẓaffar (Artuḳid) i, 665a
al-Muẓaffar (Ayyūbid) → al-Malik al-Muẓaffar ʿUmar
Muẓaffar (Balansīya) i, 446b, 985b
Muẓaffar (Maḳdis̲h̲ū) (XVI) vi, 128b
al-Muẓaffar, Abu ʾl-Fatḥ ii, 1142b
al-Muẓaffar b. ʿAlī (986) iii, 1176a; vii, 818a
Muẓaffar b. Kaydur (834) vii, 3b
Muẓaffar II b. Maḥmūd S̲h̲āh (Gud̲j̲arāt) (1526) vii, 478b; viii, 64b
al-Muẓaffar b. al-Malik al-Manṣūr (XIII) vi, 429b
al-Muẓaffar b. al-Manṣūr → ʿAbd al-Malik b. Abī ʿĀmir al-Maʿāfirī
al-Muẓaffar b. Muḥammad Ḳāsim-i Muẓaffar D̲j̲unābādī (1596) x, 146a
Muẓaffar b. Nad̲j̲m al-Dīn G̲h̲āzī I, Saʿīd (Artuḳid, Mārdīn) (XIII) vi, 540b
Muẓaffar Aḥmad (XX) vii, 848a
al-Muẓaffar Aḥmad b. al-Muʾayyad S̲h̲ayk̲h̲ (Mamlūk) (1421) iii, 1198a; vii, 272a
Muẓaffar ʿAlī (painter) (XVI) viii, 787b
Muẓaffar Barlās vii, 90b
Muẓaffar Beg Turkamān (XVI) vi, 514b
Muẓaffar al-Dīn b. ʿAlī S̲h̲īr ii, 989a
Muẓaffar al-Dīn b. Naṣr Allāh Mangi̊t (Buk̲h̲ārā) (1885) v, 30b; vi, 419a
Muẓaffar al-Dīn b. Nuṣrat al-Dīn (Marʿas̲h̲) (XIII) vi, 507b
Muẓaffar al-Dīn Gök-büri (Irbil) (1207) i, 300b, 1160b, 1161a; iii, 228b; iv, 76a-b; v, 477a; vi, 500b, 895b; vii, 273b, 727b, 817b; viii, 127b
Muẓaffar al-Dīn Muḥammad S̲h̲āh → Muḥammad S̲h̲āh b. Ḥad̲j̲d̲j̲ād̲j̲
Muẓaffar al-Dīn S̲h̲āh (Ḳād̲j̲ār) (1907) i, 1088b, 1296a; ii, 310b, 650a, b; iii, 555b; iv, 392a, 393b; vi, 276b, 291b, 529b; vii, 431b, 818a; viii, 58b; s, 72a, 84a
Muẓaffar al-Dīn Yuluḳ (Yavlaḳ) Arslan (1292) iv, 738a; viii, 544a
Muẓaffar D̲j̲ang i, 153a; iii, 320b
Muẓaffar Ḥusayn → Fidāʾī K̲h̲ān Kōka
Muẓaffar K̲h̲ān (S̲h̲āh) iv, 631b
Muẓaffar Muḥammad (S̲h̲abānkāra) (1260) ix, 158a
Muẓaffar al-Mulk ii, 31a
Muẓaffar Murtaḍāʾī, Sayyid (Hazārd̲j̲arīb) (1596) vi, 515a, b
Muẓaffar Sayf al-Dīn Ḥād̲j̲d̲j̲ī I (Mamlūk) (1347) ii, 24a; iii, 48a, 239b
Muẓaffar S̲h̲āh I Gud̲j̲arātī (1411) i, 506b, 1193a, 1300a, 1329b; ii, 218b, 270b, 276b, 322a, 405b, 597b, 1124b, 1125a; iii, 417a, 638a; vi, 50a
Muẓaffar S̲h̲āh II (Gud̲j̲arātī) (1526) ii, 322a, 405b, 1128a; iii, 422a, 1010a; vi, 54b, 55a, 269b, 270a
Muẓaffar S̲h̲āh III (Gud̲j̲arātī) (1593) i, 80b, 156a, 938b; ii, 678a, 815a, 1129a; vi, 52b; vii, 131b
Muẓaffar S̲h̲āh (Malacca) (1459) ix, 852a
Muẓaffar S̲h̲āh S̲h̲ams al-Dīn Ḥabs̲h̲ī, Dīwāna (1493) ii, 1084b; iii, 14b, 631b; vi, 47a
Muẓaffar S̲h̲ams Balk̲h̲ī (1400) vii, 819b
al-Muẓaffar Yūsuf (Rasūlid) (1295) viii, 456a, 457a; s, 338b, 387b, 388a
Muẓaffarids i, 3b; ii, 401b; iii, 56a, 57b, 1208b; iv, 32a, 102b, 498b; v, 163b; vi, 493a; vii, 480b, 820a; s, 327a, 335b, 415a
Muẓaffarnagar s, 126b
Muẓaffarpur vii, 822a

al-Muzanī, Abū Ibrāhīm (878) i, 686b; vii, 409a, 822a, 824b; viii, 497b
Muzāraʿa ii, 187b, 905b; iv, 1154a; v, 871b; vii, 822b
al-Muzarrid (VI) ix, 11a
Muzāta, Banū vi, 727a
Muzāwadja vii, 823a
Muzawwir v, 1004a
al-Muzayḳiyāʿ → ʿAmr b. ʿĀmir
Muzayna (Muzayyin), Banū (Shilb) i, 6a; ii, 1009a; vi, 344a; vii, 356b, 761a, 824a
Muzdalifa iii, 32b, 36a; vi, 105b, 162a, 169b; vii, 825a; s, 33a
Muzdawidj i, 2b, 587a; iv, 58a; vii, 825b
Muẓhir al-Shāwī (1958) vi, 616b
Muzn (Māzandarān) vi, 937b
Muznī, Banū i, 1247a
Mwana Mkisi (Mombasa) vii, 226a
Mwanga (Uganda) (1888) x, 779b
Mwengo b. Athumani, Bwana s, 351b
Mwinyi, Ali Hasan (XXI) xi, 450b
Mysia iv, 627b, 628a
Mysore → Mahisūr
Mystras → Mezistre
Mytilene → Midilli
Mzāb i, 171b, 687a; ii, 1010a; iii, 96a, 97b, 98b, 656b; vi, 364b; vii, 826a; s, 15b
Mzābites i, 371a; ii, 1010a; iii, 95a, 97a, b, 145a

N

Naʿām vii, 828a
al-Naʿāʾim s, 320b
Nabʿ iv, 797b
Nabaʿ iii, 369a
Nābal i, 936a
al-Nabarāwī, ʿAbd Allāh (1859) vii, 831a
Nabāt i, 213a; ii, 908b, 1038a, 1058b; vii, 831a
Nabaṭ (Nabīṭ) (Nabataeans) i, 528a, 548a, 563a, 564b, 1096a; ii, 246b, 278b, 1060a; iii, 366a; iv, 995a; v, 762a, 1156a; vi, 230b, 373b; vii, 834a
Nabaṭī (poetry) vi, 230b, 373b; vii, 838a
al-Nabātī → Abu 'l-ʿAbbās
Nabaṭiyya (Djabal ʿĀmil) vii, 407b
Nabawiyya ii, 964a
Nabaz iv, 180a
Nabeul s, 11a, 145a
Nabhān (Ṭayyiʾ) s, 305a
Nabhān, Banū i, 553b; iv, 885b, 886b; vii, 838b; viii, 85a, 287a
al-Nabhānī, Ḥimyar b. Nāṣir (ʿUmān) (1920) viii, 993b
Nabī v, 423b
Nabī Dhu 'l-Kifl → Dhu 'l-Kifl (b. Ayyūb)
Nabī Djirdjīs → Djirdjīs
Nabī Yūnus → Nīnawā
Nābī Yūsuf (poet) (1712) vi, 826b, 886b, 991b, 999b; vii, 839a; s, 83a, 324a
Nabīdh iv, 996a; vii, **840a**
Nābigha al-Dhubyānī (VI) i, 196a, 1149a, 1241b; ii, 1020b; iii, 1261a; vii, 254b, 563a, 840b; viii, 119b; s, 178b
al-Nābigha al-Djaʿdī, Ḳays b. ʿAbd Allāh (698) i, 115b; iv, 315b; v, 710a; vi, 625a; vii, 842b
al-Nabīt i, 771b
Nābita ii, 386b; vii, 843b
Nabl iv, 799a
Nabob → Nawwāb
Nabtāb i, 440b; ii, 252b
Nabuchodonosor → Bukht-naṣar
Nābulus iv, 834b, 835a; vi, 543b; vii, 844a
al-Nābulūsī → ʿAbd al-Ghānī b. Ismāʿīl
al-Nābulusī, Shams al-Dīn (1394) v, 9b
al-Nābulusī, ʿUthmān b. Ibrāhīm i, 800b, 801b; ii, 329b; v, 862b
Naceur Bey → Muḥammad al-Nāṣir
Nacir Ed Dine → Dinet, Alphonse
Nadhīr vii, 845a
Nadhīr Aḥmad Dihlawī (1912) iii, 359a; v, 203a; vii, 845b; x, 879b
Nadhīr Ḥusayn → Sayyid Nadhīr Ḥusayn
Nadhr iv, 688a; vii, 846a; s, 221b
Nadhr al-Islām, Ḳāḍī (1976) i, 1169a; vii, 847b
Nadhr Muḥammad b. Dīn, Khān (Djānid) (1651) i, 1195b, 1197a; vii, 849b; ix, 411b
Nadīm vii, 849b
al-Nadīm → Ibn al-Nadīm
Nadīm, ʿAbd Allāh (1896) i, 597a; ii, 429a; v, 909b
Nadīm, Aḥmad → Nedīm, Aḥmed
al-Nadīm, al-Sayyid ʿAbd Allāh (1896) vii, 716a, 852a

Nadir → Naẓīr al-Samt
Naḍīr, Banu 'l- i, 53a; ii, 869b; iv, 1139a, 1140b; v, 436a, 996a; vi, 647a, 650b; vii, 367a, 370a, 852b
Nādir Khān (Gakkhar) (1853) ii, 973b
Nādir Khān (Mahsūd) (XX) vi, 86b
Nādir Mīrzā b. Shāh Rukh (Afshārid) (XVIII) vi, 715a
Nādir Shāh Afshār (Afshārid) (1747) i, 71b, 95a, 190a, 229a, b, 240b, 270a, 291a, 295a, 395b, 431b, 460a, 625b, 701b, 905a, 928a, 970b, 1001b, 1005b, 1008b, 1020a, 1087a, 1217b, 1281b, 1295b, 1330a, 1341b; ii, 88a, 186a, 206a, 265b, 310b, 350b, 1049b, 1114b, 1131b; iii, 106a, 177b, 427b, 485a, 1103a, 1257b; iv, 37b-38a, 50b, 104a, 357a, 389b, 390a, 537a, 638a, 666a, 978a, 1048b; v, 103a, 164a, 312a, 461a, 494a, 643a, 1240a; vi, 55b, 56a, b, 202b, 310a, 418b, 495a, 502b, 527b, 528b, 529a, 535b, 551a, b, 715a, 939b; vii, 222b, 299a, 316a, 457a, 674b, 853a; viii, 9a, 253b, 771b; x, 47a; s, 94b, 97b, 237b, 251b, 259a, 260b, 276a, 281a, 336a, 358b, 420a
Nādir Shāh Bārakzay (1933) ii, 232b, 658b; v, 1079a; vii, 438a
Nādira ii, 536b; iii, 369b; vii, 856b
Nādira 2. in Swahili literature s, **643a**
al-Naḍīra bint al-Ḍayzan iii, 51a
Nādira Begam (XVII) ii, 135a
Nādira Khānim (1842) vi, 768a
Nadīr-i Nādirpūr iv, 72a
Nādiya (Nabadwip) vii, 433a
Nadjadāt iii, 1167b; vii, 562a, 858b
al-Nadjaf i, 385a; iv, 703b; vi, 88a, 351b, 516a, b, 552b; vii, 859b; s, 54b, 75b, 76a, 91b, 94a, b, 104a, 119a, 157b, 342a, 380a
Nadjaf Khān i, 253a, 403a; iv, 666a; v, 283a
Nadjaf-Ḳulī (Ḳādjār) s, 290b
al-Nadjafī, Fakhr al-Dīn al-Ṭurayḥī (1674) vii, 528a
Nadjafī, Hādjdjī Shaykh Muḥammad Ḥasan Iṣfahānī (1849) vi, 552a, b; s, 75b
Nadjafī, Shaykh Dja'far (1812) s, 134b, 135a
Nadjāḥ (Tihāma) (XI) s, 22b
Nadjāḥ b. Salama (IX) vii, 653a
Nadjāḥids i, 552a, 552b; v, 1244a, b; vii, 861b
Nadjāsa, Banū vi, 311a
al-Nadjāshī (negus) i, 482a; iii, 10a; vi, 145b, 653b; vii, 372a, 862a
al-Nadjāshī, Aḥmad b. 'Alī (1063) iii, 1151b; vi, 785a; vii, 313a; ix, 114a; s, 233a
al-Nadjāshī (poet) → Ḳays b. 'Amr
Nadjāt, Mīr 'Abd al-'Āl (1714) vii, 864a
Nadjātī → Nedjātī
Nadjd i, 233a, 539a, 554a; ii, 159b, 320b, 660a; iii, 362b, 1066b, 1067b; iv, 717a, 1143b; vi, 9a, 33a, b, 34a, 56b, 81a, 84a, 150a, 156b, 191b, 266a, 267b; vii, 864a; s, 3b, 234b, 304b, 318a
– dialect i, 573b
Nadjd b. Muslim iv, 1103b
Nadjd al-Djāḥ s, 22b
Nadjda b. 'Āmir al-Ḥanafī al-Ḥarūrī (691) i, 55a, 120a, 550a, 810a, 942a; iii, 661a; iv, 764a, 1076a; vii, 858b; s, 338a
Nadjdashī Ḳays b. 'Amr (669) s, **643b**
al-Nadjdī → 'Abd Allāh b. Ibrāhīm
al-Nadjdjād, Abū Bakr iii, 159a, 734b
al-Nadjdjār → Balīnūs (of Perge)
Nadjdjār, Banū vi, 474b, 645b
al-Nadjdjār, 'Abd al-Wahhāb v, 180b
al-Nadjdjār, Abū Ḥāmid Aḥmad b. Muḥammad s, 343a
al-Nadjdjār, al-Ḥusayn b. Muḥammad Abū 'Abdallāh (IX) i, 204b, 1242a; iv, 271b, 692b, 1187b; vii, 392b, 546b, 604a, 866b
al-Nadjdjāriyya i, 1326a; vii, 868a
Nadjdjārzāda, 'Abd al-Raḥīm → Ṭālibov
Nadjdiyya i, 77a; s, 338a
Nādjī, Ibrāhīm (1953) vii, 868b
Nadjīb (Neguib) → Muḥammad Nadjīb
al-Nadjīb b. Muḥammad (1600) viii, 18b
Nadjīb b. Sulaymān al-Ḥaddād (1899) vi, 746a, 751b, 755a; vii, 869a
Nadjīb Allāh Khān iii, 336a
Nadjīb 'Azūrī (XX) iii, 519a
Nadjīb al-Dawla (Rohilla) (1770) i, 296a, 1042b, 1206a; iii, 61a, 1158b; vii, 869b; viii, 572a,b
Nadjīb al-Dīn 'Alī b. Buzghush (1279) viii, 860a
Nadjīb al-Dīn Firdawsī (1291) vi, 131a, 410a
Nadjīb Diyāb s, 28a
Nadjīb Khān → Nadjīb al-Dawla
Nadjīb Muḥammad Surūr (1978) vii, 869b

Nadjīb Pasha iv, 638a
Nadjīb al-Rīḥānī (1949) ii, 39b; vi, 746b, 750b
Nadjīb Ziyāb (XX) ii, 471a
Nadjībābād vii, 870a
Nadjīram vi, 384b
Nadjis vii, 870a
Nādjiya, Banū v, 19b
Nadjm al-Dawla Khumārtigin s, 382b
Nadjm al-Dīn, Adda Mulla (Pathān) vii, 220b
Nadjm al-Dīn Ayyūb Abū Ṣalāḥ al-Dīn (1173) viii, 132b
Nadjm al-Dīn Ibn Abī Asrūn iii, 681b, 682a
Nadjm al-Dīn Alpï (Artuḳid), (Mārdīn) (1176) vi, 930b
Nadjm al-Dīn-i Dāya (1256) s, 364a, b
Nadjm al-Dīn Il Ghāzī I (Artuḳid) (1122) ix, 11b
Nadjm al-Dīn Ghāzī II, al-Malik al-Manṣūr (Artuḳid) (1312) viii, 802a
Nadjm al-Dīn al-Ḥarrānī (XIV) viii, 624a
Nadjm al-Dīn Ismāʿīl vi, 790b
Nadjm al-Dīn Ḳārin → Ḳārin b. Shahriyār Bāwand
Nadjm al-Dīn Abu 'l-Ḳāsim Muḥammad → Kānī
Nadjm al-Dīn al-Bādarāʾī (1257) s, 463a
Nadjm al-Dīn Kubrā (1221) xi, 116a
Nadjm al-Dīn al-Miṣrī (XIII) vii, 29b
Nadjm al-Dīn Muḥammad (vizier) (1335) ix, 191b
Nadjm al-Dīn Rāzī Dāya (1256) vi, 15a; vii, 870b; viii, 539b; 972a; ix, 862a
Nadjm-i Thānī → Muḥammad Bāḳir Nadj m-i Thānī (1637)
Nadjrān i, 151b, 538a, 555a; ii, 127b, 131a, 244b; iii, 223a; vi, 190b, 191a, 192a, 371b, 433a, 436a, 559b; vii, 373b, 871b; ix, 729a; s, 335a
al-Nadjrānī, ʿAlī b. ʿAbd Allāh b. ʿUtba s, 393a
Nadjwā iii, 81a
al-Naḍr b. al-Ḥārith b. ʿAlḳama (VII) i, 358b; iii, 370a; vii, 369b, 872b; s, 91a
Naḍr b. Kināna i, 1021b
al-Naḍr b. Saʿīd al-Ḥarashī, Ḳaysī (VIII) i, 53b; ii, 90a; vi, 624a
al-Naḍr b. Shumayl al-Māzinī (820) iii, 155a; vi, 954b; vii, 873a; s, 317b
Nadrūma (Nedroma) v, 397a; vii, 873b; s, 144b
Nadvat ul-Mujahideen (Mappila) vi, 462b
Nadwa → Dār al-Nadwa
Nadwat al-ʿUlamāʾ (Lakhnaw) ii, 132b; iii, 433a; vii, 874b
Nadwī, Sayyid Sulaymān (1953) ii, 132b; iii, 435a, 1174a; vii, 875b
Nafādh iv, 412a
Nafaḳa iii, 1011b; s, **643b**
Nafaḳat al-safar iii, 184a, 186a
Nafal → Ghanīma
Nafar iv, 9b
Nafas → Nafs; Nefes
al-Nafāthiyya iii, 659b
Naffātī → Nafāthiyya
Naffis (river) vi, 742a, b, 743b
Nāfiʿ (ḥadīth) (735) i, 140a; vi, 278b; vii, 876a
Nāfiʿ b. ʿAlḳama ii, 1011b
Nāfiʿ b. ʿAbd al-Ḳays al-Fihrī (VII) vii, 154a
Nāfiʿ b. Abd al-Raḥmān al-Laythī (785) i, 718a; iii, 155b, 732b; v, 127b, 997b; vi, 263a; vii, 878a
Nāfiʿ b. al-Azraḳ al-Ḥanafī al-Ḥanẓalī (683) i, 120a, 810a; iii, 367a, 648b; vi, 457b, 636a; vii, 858b, 877a
Nāfiʿ b. al-Ḥārith b. Kalada s, 354b
Nāfiʿ b. Kalada s, 354b
Nāfiʿ b. ʿUmar (735) x, 29a
Nāfidh, Aḥmed iv, 877b, 878a
Nāfidh, Fārūḳ (XX) viii, 221a
Nāfila vii, 878a
Nafīr → Nefīr
Nafīs b. ʿIwaḍ s, 271b
Nafīsa, al-Sayyida (mausoleum) vii, 879a
Nafīsa bint al-Ḥasan b. Zayd b. al-Ḥasan (824) vii, 879a
Nafīsī, Saʿīd (1966) vii, 879b
Nafs iv, 487a; vii, 880a
al-Nafs al-Zakiyya → Muḥammad b. ʿAbd Allāh b. al-Ḥasan b. al-Ḥasan (ʿAlid) (762)
Nafṭ i, 967a, 1055b, 1056a, 1059a, 1068b; ii, 507a; iii, 470a, 475b; vii, 884a
Nafṭa (Nefṭa) (Tunisia) vii, 890b
Nafṭa (Ḳasṭīliya) s, 402b
Nafūd i, 537a, 1312b; ii, 92a; vii, 891a
al-Nafūsa, Banū (Infūsen) i, 1349b; iii, 654a, 655b; vi, 452b, 453a; vii, 892a
Nafūsa, Djabal → Djabal

al-Nafūsī, Abū Sahl al-Fārisī (Rustamid) (VIII) vii, 895a
Nafy vii, 895b
Nafza, Banū vii, 896b
Nafzāwa, Banū i, 1349b; vii, 896b
al-Nafzāwī, Muḥammad ii, 552b
Nagar vii, 897b; s, 327b
Nagarkōt → Kāngrā
Nāgawr iii, 441b; v, 884a; vi, 48b; vii, 134b, 898a; s, 353a, b
Nāgawrī, Shaykh Ḥamīd al-Dīn Suwali (1274) vii, 898a
Nāgawrī, Shaykh Mubārak (1593) vii, 898a
Naghmī, Naghamī v, 951b
Naghrallā, Banu ʾl- i, 491b
Nagir → Hunza and Nagir
Nagīsa vi, 742a
Nāgōshias i, 1255a
Nagpur vi, 535b; vii, 898b
Nagyvárad vii, 899b
Nahār → Layl and Nahār
Nahāwandī → ʿAbd al-Bāḳī
al-Nahāwandī, Benjamin iv, 604a, b, 606b
Nahḍa iv, 142b, 143b; v, 794b; vii, 900a
al-Nahḍa (al-Ḳāhira) s, 5b
Nahdat al-ʿUlamāʿ iii, 534a, b, 1229b, 1230b
Nahdatul Ulama (Nahdat al-ʿUlamāʾ) iii, 534a, b, 1229b, 1230b; vi, 730a; s, 151a
al-Nahdayn ix, 1a
Nahdī, Banū vi, 221b
Nahdj al-Balāgha vii, 903b
al-Naḥḥās, Abū Djaʿfar (950) vii, 569b; viii, 14a
al-Naḥḥās, Muṣṭafā (1965) vii, 904b; xi, 26a
al-Naḥḥāsīn (al-Ḳāhira) s, 5a
Naḥīfī, Süleymān (1739) vii, 905a
Nahīk Mudjāwid al-Rīḥ iv, 91b
al-Nahīkī, ʿAbd Allāh b. Muḥammad (X) vii, 460a, 905b
al-Nahīkī, Abu ʾl-ʿAbbās ʿUbayd Allāh (IX) vii, 906a
Nāḥiye iv, 229b, 230a, b; vii, 906a
Naḥiyy Tūnb iv, 778a, b; s, 417b
Naḥl vii, 906a
Nahr i, 52b, 1029b, 1094b; ii, 438a; iv, 133b, 193a; v, 368a, 885a, 886a; vii, 909b
Nahr Abī Fuṭrus i, 103a; vii, 910a
Nahr al-ʿĀṣī → al-ʿĀṣī
Nahr al-Aʿwadj vi, 546a, 547b
Nahr al-ʿAwdjāʾ → Nahr Abī Fuṭrus
Nahr Bāniyās vi, 577b
Nahr Ḥūrīth → Aḳ-Ṣū
Nahr ʿĪsā ibn ʿAlī → ʿĪsā, Nahr
Nahr al-Isḥāḳī x, 141a
Nahr Ḳadīsha (Tripoli in Syria) x, 214b
Nahr al-Kalb vi, 343b
Nahr al-Khawṣar vi, 900b
Nahr al-Ḳubāḳib vi, 230a
Nahr al-Ḳuwayḳ vi, 544a
Nahr al-Maʿḳil vii, 67a; s, 16a
Nahr al-Malik → Didjla
Nahr Markiya vi, 577b
Nahr al-Ratīn → Shāpūr (river)
Nahr Ṣughd → Zarafshān
Nahr Tīrā s, 352a
Nahr al-Ubulla vii, 67a
Nahr Yazīd s, 197a
Nahr Zubayda vi, 900b
Nahr al-Zuṭṭ s, 243a
al-Nahradjūrī, Abū Aḥmad iii, 1071b
al-Nahradjūrī, Abū Yaʿḳūb (X) vi, 224a
al-Nahrawālī, Ḳuṭb al-Dīn Muḥammad (1582) vii, 911b
al-Nahrawān i, 40b, 384b; ii, 250a, 343b; iii, 236b; iv, 1075a; vii, 912b
al-Nahrawānī, Abū Ḥakīm (1161) iii, 751a
Nahray ben Nissim ii, 988b
Nahrwāla → Anhalwāra; Pātan
Naḥw iv, 122a; v, 804a; vii, 913a
Naḥwī v, 1133b
al-Nahy ʿan al-Munkar s, **644b**
Nāʾib vii, 915a
Naʾib ʿĀlim Khān (1866) vi, 942a
Naʾib al-Salṭana → Nāʾib
Nāʾif b. ʿAbd al-ʿAzīz (Āl Suʿūd) (XX) vi, 158a
Naïl, Awlād i, 371b
Nāʾila → Isāf
Nāʾilī (1634) i, 1302a
Nāʾilī (Pīrī-zāde) (Nāʾilī-yi Ḳādim) (1666) ii, 1000a; vii, 916a; s, 324a
Nāʾilī, Ṣāliḥ (1876) vii, 916a
Naʿīm, Aḥmed s, 83a
Naʿīm, Āl iv, 752a; s, 42a
Naʿīm, Muṣṭafā → Naʿīmā
Naʿīm al-Dīn (Naʿimī) (XVIII) vii, 917a
Naʿīmā (Muṣṭafā Naʿīm) (1716) vi, 343b, 345b, 725a, 990b; vii, 917a
Nāʾīn (Nāyin) vii, 918a

Nāʾīnī, Mīrzā Muḥammad Ḥusayn Gharawī (1936) iv, 164b; vi, 553a; vii, 301a, 918b; s, 109b, 342a
Nāʿinī, Mīrzā Rāfīʿ al-Dīn (1688) vi, 516b; viii, 779a
Nāʿiṭ vi, 566a
Naitias (Naʾitas) vii, 919b
Najāra, Israel iv, 310a
Naḳā vii, 920a
Naḳab al-Ḥadjar xi, 47b
Nakad i, 1078a
Naḳāʾiḍ vii, 920a
al-Naḳb vii, 920b
Naḳd vii, 921a; s **646b**
Naḳḍ al-Mīthāḳ vii, 921a
Nakhaʿ, Banū xi, 219a
al-Nakhaʿī al-Aḥmar al-Kūfī, Isḥāḳ b. Muḥammad (899) vii, 460a
al-Nakhaʿī, Ḥafṣ b. Ghiyāth (809) viii, 388a
al-Nakhaʿī, Ibrāhīm b. Yazīd (717) vii, 921b
Nakhāwila v, 998b, 999b
Nakhčiwān i, 8a, 191b; vi, 200b, 202b, 365b; vii, 922a; viii, 175a
Nakhdjawānī, Muḥammad b. Hindūshāh (XIV) iii, 284a, 1243a; iv, 526a; v, 872b; vi, 15a, 456a; ix, 5a
Nakhidjevan s, 275a
Nakhkhās i, 32b
Nakhl vii, 923a; ix, 763b
Nakhla i, 540a; ii, 1058a; iii, 237b; iv, 995b; v, 595b; vi, 146b; vii, 356b, 369b, 924b
Nakhla al-Mudawwar s, 161a
Nakhlī → Ḥāfiẓ Tanîsh
Nakhshab vii, 925a
Nakhshabī, Shaykh Ḍiyāʾ al-Dīn (1350) iv, 69a; vii, 925a
al-Naḳīʿ iv, 1144a
Naḳīb iii, 184a; iv, 267a; v, 1131b; vii, 926a; s, 208b
al-Naḳīb, ʿAbd al-Raḥmān iii, 521a
Naḳīb al-Ashrāf iii, 1152b; iv, 103b, 474b; vii, 926b; s, 122b, 132b
Naḳībī → Mīr Lawḥī
Naḳīḍa → Naḳāʾiḍ
Nakīr → Munkar wa-Nakīr
Naḳīr (drink) iv, 995b
Nāḳiṣ → Yazid (III) b. al-Walīd (I)
Nakiye, Elgün (Khanîm) iv, 933b
Naḳḳāra-khāna vii, 927b
Nakkārī → Yazīdīs
Naḳḳāsh → Ghiyāth al-Dīn
al-Naḳḳāsh, Mārūn b. Ilyās (1855) i, 597a; vi, 746a; vii, 930a
Naḳḳāsh, Muḥammad → Darwīsh Muḥammad
al-Naḳḳāsh, Salīm → Salīm b. Khalīl
Naḳḳāsh ʿAlī Pasha v, 649b
Naḳḳāsh Ḥasan Pasha (1622) vii, 931a
Naḳḳāsh-khāna iv, 1169a; vii, 931a
Naḳl vii, 932a; s, **658b**
Naḳsh → Kitābāt
al-Naḳshabandī, ʿAbd al-Ḥaḳḳ (XX) v, 1005b
Naḳshband, Bahāʾ al-Dīn (1389) x, 250b
Naḳshband, Muḥammad b. Muḥammad Bahāʾ al-Dīn al-Bukhārī (1389) vi, 354b; vii, 933a; viii, 539b, 704a; s, 50b, 364b
Naḳshbandiyya i, 755b, 782a, 1072a, 1137a, 1295b; ii, 18a, 88a, 91b, 137b, 293a, 296b, 711b, 879a, 1078a; iii, 38a, 432b, 662b; iv, 48b; v, 53b, 475a, 486a, 851a, 859a; vi, 224a, 225b, 354b, 408a, 953a; vii, 934b; viii, 237b; s, 50b, 51b, 71a
Naḳshdjam vii, 124a
Naḳshe (Naxos) vii, 939b; ix, 483b
Naḳsh-i Djahān (palace, Iṣfahān) vi, 525b, 526b
Naḳsh-i Radjab iv, 220b
Naḳsh-i Rustam (Shāpūr) ii, 135b; iv, 220b, 221a, b
Nakūk → Abu ʾl-ʿAlāʾ b. Yaʿḳūb
Nakūr (Nukūr) v, 1119a; vi, 120b; vii, 641b, 941a; s, 377a
Nāḳūs i, 188a; vii, 943a
Naʿl v, 733a, 735b, 736a, 752b
al-Naʿl al-Sharīf s, **660a**
Naldrug iii, 448a; vii, 943a
Nalgunda vi, 66b
Nāma vii, 943b
al-Namalī, Muḥammad b. Ḥassān ii, 552a
Namāra vi, 261a; vii, 944a
Namā-rustāḳ vi, 513a
Namāz → Ṣalāt
Namāzgāh vii, 947a
Nāmdār Khān b. Salābat Djang s, 280a
Nāmdjīn → Bāḥmīn
Nāme → Nāma
Nāmī → Mīr Muḥammad Maʿṣūm
Nāmiḳ Kemāl → Kemāl, Meḥmed Nāmiḳ

Nāmiḳ Pas͟ha i, 906b
Namir/Nimr vii, 947b
Namir b. Ḳāsiṭ, Banū i, 545a; vi, 437b; s, **661b**
al-Namir (Namr) b. Tawlab al-ʿUklī (644) vii, 563a, 950b
Nāmir al-Hawāʾ → Namāra
al-Namīrī, Muḥammad b. Nuṣayr (IX) viii, 146a
Naml vii, 951a
Namrūd vii, 952b;viii, 49a; s, 101a
Nāmūs ii, 486b; vii, 953b
Nānā Ṣāḥib i, 822b; iv, 551b
Nānak (Gurū –, Sikh)) (1538) iii, 456b; vii, 956b; viii, 253b; ix, 576b
Nanda → D̲j̲ām Nanda
Nandana s, **662a**
Nāndeŕ vii, 957a
Nand̲j̲arād̲j̲ iii, 316b
Nandurbār vii, 957a
Nangrahār (Ningrahār) vii, 957b; s, 237a, b
Naples → Nābal
Nār iii, 78a; iv, 237a; vii, 957b
Nār al-ḥarratayn iv, 928a; v, 1110a, 1111a, 1112a, 1113a, 1115b
Narāḳ (Nirāḳ) vii, 960b
Narāḳī, Muḥammad Mahdī b. Abī D̲h̲arr (1794) vii, 960b
Narāḳī, Mullā Aḥmad (1829) vi, 552a; vii, 960b; s, 75b
Narameikhla, King i, 606a, 1333a
Nārand̲j̲ vii, 961b
Narāyan Singh ii, 47b
Narbadā/Narmadā (river) vi, 310a, 535a, 536a
Narbonne → Arbūna
Nārbūta Beg (K̲h̲ān) v, 29a
Nard v, 109a, 110a; vii, 963a
Nard̲j̲is vii, 963b
Naré-Famaghan vi, 401b
Narela vi, 62a
Narg̲h̲īla → Tütün
Nargūnd ii, 220a
Nariman Narimanov s, 365a
Nārimān Ṣādiḳ s, 299b
Narin (river) ix, 659a
Nark̲h̲ iii, 489a; vii, 964a
Narmās̲h̲īr (Narmāsīr) vii, 965a
Narnāla iii, 1161b; vii, 314b, 965a
Nārnawl vi, 128a; vii, 965b
Nars (Kūfa) vi, 438b
Narseh (Sāsānid) iv, 753b; ix, 73a
Nars̲h̲ak̲h̲ī, Abū Bakr Muḥammad (X) i, 1294a, b; v, 856b; vii, 966a; viii, 749a, 1027a; s, 125b, 326b, 327a
Narsingh Ray s, 206b
Narwar s, 10b
Nasā (Nisā) i, 320b, 701a; vii, 966b
Nasā (K̲h̲urāsān) x, 88b
Nasab iii, 238b; iv, 179b, 495b; vii, 967a
Nasaf → Nak̲h̲s̲h̲ab
al-Nasafī, Abū ʿAbd Allāh i, 125b, 160b, 414b; iv, 198a, 203b, 661b, 662b; v, 167a
al-Nasafī, Abū Ḥafṣ ʿUmar Nad̲j̲m al-Dīn (1142) i, 333a; 593a; iii, 901b; iv, 737a; vi, 47b, 218b, 558a, 848a; vii, 781b, 969a
al-Nasafī, Abu ʾl-Ḥasan Muḥammad b. Aḥmad al-Bazdawī (943) i, 125b, 160b, 414b; iv, 198a, 203b, 661b, 662b; v, 167a; vi, 846b; vii, 968b
al-Nasafī, Abu ʾl-Muʿīn al-Makḥūlī (1114) vi, 846a, 847b; vii, 546b, 968b
Nasafī, ʿAzīz-i al-Dīn (1300) viii, 703b; x, 321a
al-Nasafī, Ḥāfiẓ al-Dīn Abu ʾl-Barakāt (1310) iii, 163b; vi, 848a; vii, 969a
al-Nasāʾī Abū ʿAbd al-Raḥmān (915) iii, 24a; vi, 132b; vii, 969b; s, 87b
al-Nasāʾī al-Madlid̲j̲ī, Aḥmad iv, 509b
Nasaḳ ii, 156a, 157a, 158a
Naṣārā i, 31b, 264b, 265a, b, 470a, 1020a, 1040b; ii, 229a, b, 230a, 459a, 637a, 859b; iii, 77b, 1206a, b; iv, 43b, 76b, 241a, 243b; v, 141b, 265a, 326b, 330b, 334a, 335b, 793b, 795b, 799a, 1020a; vii, 970a; x, 248a
al-Nasawī, Abū Naṣr Muḥammad b. ʿAbd al-Raḥīm (XI) vi, 638a
al-Nasawī, Muḥammad b. Aḥmad (XIII) i, 1354a
al-Nasawī, Muḥammad b. Manṣūr i, 434a
al-Nasawī, S̲h̲ihāb al-Dīn Muḥammad (1249) vii, 973b; s, 632b
Naṣb vii, 974b
Nasd̲j̲ → Bisāṭ; Ḥarīr; Ḳuṭn; Libās; Ṣūf
Nas̲h̲aʾkarib ix, 675b
Nas̲h̲ās̲h̲ībī, Isʿāf (XX) vi, 615b
Nas̲h̲ās̲h̲ībī, Rāg̲h̲ib (XX) vi, 615b
Nas̲h̲ās̲h̲ībīs iii, 523b
Nas̲h̲āṭ, Mīrzā ʿAbd al-Wahhāb (1828) vii, 975a
Nas̲h̲awā → Nak̲h̲čiwān

al-Nāshiʾ al-Akbar, Abu ʾl-ʿAbbās (906) vii, 605a, 975a; viii, 886a; ix, 454a; s, 89b, 225b, 265a
Nashīd vii, 975b
Nāshira al-Yarbūʿī s, 26a
Nashīṭ i, 828a; iii, 878b; vii, 976a
Nashḳ, Banū iv, 335b
Nashshān → al-Sawdāʾ
Nashtakīn → al-Darazī
Nashwān b. Saʿīd al-Ḥimyarī (1177) i, 564a; iii, 124a; vi, 565a, b, 829b; vii, 976b; x, 147a; s, 225b, 289b, 339b
Nasī (intercalation) vii, 977a
Nasī (title) iv, 472a; vii, 977b
Nasīb i, 583b, 584a; ii, 1028a, b; iv, 488a, 714a, 715a; v, 930b, 956a; vii, 978a
Nasīb ʿArīḍa (XX) viii, 88a
Nasīb Djanbulāṭ ii, 444a
al-Naṣīb(īn)ī, Abū Isḥāḳ Ibrāhīm b. ʿAlī vii, 312a; s, 13b
Naṣībīn iv, 898a; vi, 427b, 539b, 542a, 626a, b, 633a, 667a; vii, 983a; s, 36a, 37a
Nāṣif, Malik Ḥifnī i, 597b; iii, 360a; iv, 720b
Nāṣīf al-Yāzidjī → al-Yāzidjī
Naṣīḥat al-Mulūk vii, 984b
al-Nāṣiḥī, Abū Muḥammad s, 343a
Nāsikh → Naskh
Nāsikh, Shaykh Imām Bakhsh (1838) ii, 84b; vii, 988b; s, 102a
al-Nāsikh wa ʾl-Mansūkh → Naskh
Nasīm, Dayā Shankar Kawl (1832) vii, 989a
Nasīm Oghlu Aḥmad b. Ḥasan (XVIII) i, 310a
al-Nāṣir (ʿAbbāsid) → al-Nāṣir li-Dīn Allāh
al-Nāṣir al-Dīn Muḥammad Shāh (Tughluḳid) x, 593a
al-Nāṣir (Fīlālī) (1745) vi, 595a
al-Nāṣir (Mamlūk) → Ḥasan, al-Malik al-Nāṣir Nāṣir al-Dīn; al-Nāṣir Muḥammad
al-Nāṣir (Marrākush) (1514) vi, 594a
al-Nāṣir (Umayyad) → ʿAbd al-Raḥmān III
al-Nāṣir, Abu ʾl-Saʿādāt Muḥammad i, 1060a
Nāṣir, Banū vii, 675a; s, 395a
al-Nāṣir, Ibrāhīm al-Malīḥ b. Muḥammad (Yemen) (XI) vi, 436a
Nāṣir, Khwādja Mīr (1758) vii, 939a
al-Nāṣir, al-Malik al-Nāṣir Nāṣir al-Dīn → Ḥasan, al-Malik al-Nāṣir (Mamlūk)
al-Nāṣir, Mawlāy i, 605a
al-Nāṣir, Muḥammad b. Abī Yūsūf Yaʿḳūb al-Manṣūr (Almohad) (1213) i, 166a; ii, 819a, 1007b; iii, 1055a; iv, 337b; vii, 989a
al-Nāṣir, Yūsuf b. Yaḥyā b. Aḥmad (Yemen) (XI) vi, 436a
al-Nāṣir b. ʿAlennās (ʿAlnās) (Ḥammādid)) (1089) i, 1205a; iii, 137b, 386a; iv, 479a; v, 59b; vi, 427a; vii, 993b
al-Nāṣir b. Barḳūḳ (Mamlūk) (XV) vi, 193b
Nāṣir b. Faradj Allāh, amīr (XV) vii, 672b
al-Nāsir b. al-Ghālib bi-ʾllāh (Saʿdī) (1595) vi, 1009b
Nāṣir b. Khalīfat al-Bāʿūnī i, 1109a
Nāṣir b. Mubārak iv, 752a
Nāṣir b. Muhannā (XVII) vii, 462b
Nāṣir b. Murshid (Yaʿrubid) (XVII) i, 554a; viii, 435b; x, 816b; xi, 292a
al-Nāṣir ʿAbd Allāh b. Ḥasan, Imām (Yemen) (1840) vii, 996a
al-Nāṣir Aḥmad (Rasūlid) → Aḥmad b. Ismāʿīl
al-Nāṣir Aḥmad b. al-Nāṣir Muḥammad (Mamlūk) (1344) vii, 992b
Nāṣir ʿAlī Shāh Malik-niyā (Niʿmat-Allāhī) (XX) viii, 46b
Nāṣir ʿAlī Sirhindī (1697) vii, 1005b
Nāṣir al-Dawla → Ibn Baḳiyya
Nāṣir al-Dawla (Kirmān) s, 53a
Nāṣir al-Dawla (Labla) v, 586b
Nāṣir al-Dawla, Abū Muḥammad al-Ḥasan (Ḥamdānid) (968) i, 119b, 866b, 870b, 1352b; ii, 178b, 524b; iii, 126b, 127a, 346a, 902b; vi, 930a; vii, 397a, 983b, 994b; s, 36b, 379b
Nāṣir al-Dawla b. Sikandar iii, 322a
Nāṣir al-Dawla Badr → Badr b. Ḥasan(a)wayh
Nāṣir al-Dawla Ḥusayn ii, 856a, 857b, 858b; iii, 129a
Nāṣir al-Dawla Ibn Ḥamdān, Sulṭān al-Dawla (Miṣr) (1073) vii, 730a, b
Nāṣir al-Dawla Manṣūr b. Niẓām al-Dīn (Marwānid, Diyār Bakr) (1085) vi, 626b
Nāṣir al-Dīn → Čirāgh-i Dihlī; Humayūn; Maḥmūd I, II (Bengal)

Naṣīr al-Dīn, Shaykh (XIV) s, 352b
Nāṣir al-Dīn b. Ḥasan Karlugh i, 227a
Nāṣir al-Dīn b. Kamāl al-Dīn (Marʿashī) (XV) vi, 513a
Nāṣir al-Dīn b. Ḳawām al-Dīn (Marʿashī) (XV) vi, 512b
Naṣīr al-Dīn b. Muḥammad b. al-Naḳīd (XIII) vii, 727b
Nāṣir al-Dīn b. Musallam (1373) iv, 643
Nāṣir al-Dīn b. al-Muẓaffar Taḳī 'l-Dīn ʿUmar (Ayyūbid) (Manbidj) (XII) vi, 380b
Nāṣir al-Dīn b. Sayyid-i Adjall (1292) ix, 623a
al-Nāṣir li-Dīn Allāh (Zaydī Imāms) vii, 995b
al-Nāṣir li-Dīn Allāh, Abu 'l-ʿAbbās Aḥmad (ʿAbbāsid) (1225) i, 20a, b, 322b, 1150a; ii, 327a, 964a, 1044a; iii, 109b, 160b, 488b, 1256a; iv, 29b, 749a, 942b; vi, 429b, 430a, 433b, 434a; vii, 728b, 996b; viii, 111a; s, 193b, 378b s
al-Nāṣir li-Dīn Allāh, Aḥmad Abu 'l-Ḥasan b. Yaḥyā al-Hādī ila 'l-Ḥaḳḳ, Imām (Yemen) (937) vii, 995b, 996b
Nāṣir al-Dīn al-Asad iv, 820b, 821a
Nāṣir al-Dīn Awbik b. Ačfagha → al-Lamtūnī, Awbik b. Ačfagha
Naṣīr al-Dīn Djaḳar (XII) vii, 734a
al-Nāṣir al-Dīn Faradj (Mamlūk) (1412) vii, 271b, 723a
Nāṣir al-Dīn Ḳabāča (Kubādja) (XIII) i, 764a, 1192a, 1194a; ii, 267b, 393a, 609a, 1103a; iii, 416a, 1155a; v, 597b; vii, 410a, 549a; s, 360a
Nāṣir al-Dīn al-Kaymarī iv, 842b
Nāṣir al-Din Khaldjī ii, 381a
Nāṣir al-Dīn Maḥmūd (Artuḳid, Diyār Bakr) (1222) s, 266b
Nāṣir al-Dīn Maḥmūd b. Iltutmish → Maḥmūd I (Delhi)
Nāṣir al-Dīn Maḥmūd b. Yaḥyā → Čirāgh-i Dihlī
Nāṣir al-Dīn Meḥmed Beg (Ḳaramānid) (XV) vii, 271b
Nāṣir al-Dīn Muḥammad b. Dhu 'l-Karnayn ii, 111a
Nāṣir al-Dīn Muḥammad b. Khalīl ii, 239b
Nāṣir al-Dīn Muḥammad b. Muḥammad (1462) vi, 193b
Nāṣir al-Dīn Muḥammad Shāh (Dōʾāb) s, 126b
Nāṣir al-Dīn Muḥammad al-Zurayḳ iii, 155b
Nāṣir al-Dīn Mukram b. ʿAlāʾ s, 326a
Nāṣir al-Dīn Munshī (XIV) vi, 481b
Nāṣir al-Dīn Shāh (Ḳādjār) (1896) i, 626b, 833b, 846b, 847a, 916a, 1088b; ii, 152b, 418a, 433b, 649b, 650a; iii, 554a, 1103b; iv, 39a, 72a, 392a, 393a, 696a, 788a, 855b; v, 659a, 919b, 1085b; vi, 19a, 20a, b, 21a, 277a, 291b, 481b, 484a, b, 485b, 528b, 529b, 551b, 715a, 763a, 804a; vii, 440a, b, 573b, 918b, 1003a; viii, 58a; s, 23b, 41a, 70b, 71a, 94b, 108b, 260b, 290b, 302a
Nāṣir al-Dīn Shāh b. Ghiyāth al-Dīn (Mālwā) (1510) vi, 54b, 309b, 407a
Nāṣir al-Dīn al-Ṣūrī (amīr) (XII) vi, 870a
Nāṣir al-Dīn Ṭāhir b. Fakhr al-Mulk al-Muẓaffar (1153) viii, 81b
Naṣīr al-Dīn al-Ṭūsī (1274) i, 113a, 326b, 328b, 353b, 393a, 450a, 594a, 721a, 839a, 1198a; ii, 362a, 399b, 607b, 765b, 774a; iii, 24b, 103b, 390a, 726b, 1122a, 1137b, 1151b, 1266a; iv, 48b, 121a, 205b, 976a, 1028a, 1036a; v, 547a; vi, 450a, 501a, b, 549b, 601a, b; vii, 143b; viii, 135a; s, 412a, 413a, 414a
Nāṣir Djang (Farrukhābād) → Imdād Ḥusayn Khān
Nāṣir Djang (Ḥaydarābād) iii, 320a, b
al-Nāṣir Faradj b. Barḳūḳ → Faradj, al-Malik al-Nāṣir Zayn al-Dīn (Mamlūk, 1412)
al-Nāṣir (al-Fattāḥ) vi, 112b
Nāṣir al-Ḥaḳḳ Abū Muḥammad iv, 19a
al-Nāṣir li-'l-Ḥaḳḳ → Ḥasan al-Uṭrūsh
al-Nāṣir al-Ḥasan b. ʿAlī b. Dāwūd, Imām (Yemen) (1596) vii, 996a
al-Nāṣir al-Ḥasan b. ʿIzz al-Dīn, Imām (Yemen) (1523) vii, 996a
al-Nāṣir Ḥasan b. al-Nāṣir Muḥammad (Mamlūk) (1361) viii, 992b
al-Nāṣir al-Kabīr → Ḥasan al-Uṭrūsh
Nāṣir Khān (Bengal) (1442) vi, 46b
Nāṣir Khān (Kālpī) (XV) vi, 53b, 61b
Naṣīr Khān II b. Miḥrāb Khān (Balūčistān) (1857) i, 1006a
Naṣīr Khān b. Muẓaffar Shāh → Maḥmūd II b. Muẓaffar Shāh (Gudjarāt)

Nāṣir Khān (Brahūī, 1795) i, 230a, 296a, 1006a, 1010b; iv, 1059b; v, 102a, 580a; s, 222a, 332b
Nāṣir Kh̲ān Fārūḳī (Kh̲āndesh̲, 1437) i, 710a, 1329a, 1331a; ii, 814b, 1125a; iii, 419a, 638a
Nāṣir Kh̲ān Ḳāshḳāy iv, 706b
Naṣīr Kh̲ān Lārī (XVIII) v, 673b, 674a
Naṣīr Kh̲ān Lārī (XIX) v, 674a
Nāṣir Kh̲ān Noḥānī s, 203a
Nāṣir-i Kh̲usraw (1060) i, 137a, 233b, 450a, 552a, 852a, 1220b; ii, 584b, 861a, 997b; iii, 328b, 1130b; iv, 61b, 63a, 199b; v, 175b, 930a, 956b; vi, 119b, 626b, 652b, 672b; s, 108a, 203b, 208a
Nāṣir Mīrzā i, 228a, 852b
al-Nāṣir Muḥammad (Ṣāḥib al-Mawākib), Imām (Yemen) (XVII) vii, 515a
al-Nāṣir Muḥammad b. Isḥāḳ b. al-Mahdī Aḥmad, Imām (Yemen) (1753) vii, 996a
al-Nāṣir Muḥammad b. Ḳāʾit Bāy (Mamlūk) (1498) vi, 324b, 501b; vii, 172b, 993a
al-Nāṣir Muḥammad b. Ḳalāwūn (Mamlūk) (1341) i, 118b, 610b, 779a, 1126b, 1127b, 1128a, 1299b, 1324b; ii, 38a, 68a, 285a, b, 330a; iii, 99a, 189b, 220a, 346b, 744b, 890b, 923b, 952b; iv, 136b, 424b, 430b, 464b, 609a, 834b, 864a, 965b; v, 373b, 595a, 1140b; vi, 195a, 231a, 258a, 314b, 315b, 318a, 322a, b, 323a, 324a, 326a, b, 367a, b, 381a, 424a, 455a, 545b, 547b, 662a; vii, 168b, 169b, 170a, 176a, 991a; viii, 90b, 156b, 157a, 864b; s, 395b
Nāṣir al-Mulk (Čitrāl) ii, 31a
Nāṣir al-Mulk (Irān) (XX) ii, 652a, b; vii, 432a
al-Nāṣir al-Ṣagh̲īr al-Ḥusayn b. al-Ḥasan (Caspian Zaydī) (1083) vii, 995b
al-Nāṣir Salāḥ al-Dīn, Imām (Yemen) (1391) vii, 996a
al-Nāṣir Ṣalāḥ al-Dīn Yūsuf (Ayyūbid) (1259) → al-Malik al-Nāṣir II
al-Nāṣir(ī) al-Salāwī, Sh̲ihāb al-Dīn (1897) → Aḥmad al-Nāṣirī
al-Nāṣir b. Yūsuf → al-Malik al-Nāṣir Ṣalāḥ al-Dīn Yūsuf (Ayyūbid)
Nāṣira (Damascus) vi, 545a
Nāṣira (Nazareth) vi, 631a; vii, 1008a
Nāṣirābād → Sīstān
Nāṣirābādī, Mawlānā Sayyid Dildār ʿAlī (Gh̲ufrān Maʿāb) (1820) vii, 300b
Nāṣirābādī, Sayyid ʿAlī Akbar (1909) vii, 301a
Nāṣirābādī, Sayyid Ḥusayn b. Dildār ʿAlī (1856) vii, 300b
Nāṣirābādī, Sayyid Muḥammad b. Dildār ʿAlī (1867) vii, 300b
Nāṣirābādī, Sayyid Muḥammad Taḳī (1872) vii, 301a
al-Nāṣirī → Ibn Nāṣir; Aḥmad al-Nāṣirī al-Salāwī
Nāṣir-i Kh̲usraw, Abū Muʿīn al-Ḳubādh̲iyānī (1060) iv, 61b, 63a, 199b; v, 175b, 930a, 956b; vi, 119b, 626b, 652b, 672b; vii, 141a, 163a, 535b, 730a, 732a, 1006a; s, 108a, 203b, 208a
al-Nāṣirī, Muḥammad Makkī (XX) viii, 906a
al-Nāṣiriyya → Bid̲j̲āya
Nāṣiriyya (Caspian region) s, 363a
Nāṣiriyya (Damascus) s, 197a
Nāṣiriyya (Farad̲j̲) vi, 316b
Nāṣiriyya (Morocco) i, 290a, b; ii, 134a; vi, 713a; s, 395a
Nāṣiriyya (Yemen) iii, 255a
al-Nāṣiriyya (order) vii, 1009a
al-Nāṣiriyya (town) vii, 1009a
Nāṣirwand v, 603a
Nask̲h̲/al-Nāsik̲h̲ wa ʾl-Mansūk̲h̲ i, 265b, 850b; iii, 28a, 898b; iv, 170a; v, 415b; vii, 1009b
Nask̲h̲ī → K̲h̲aṭṭ; Kitābāt
Nasnās/Nisnās → Ḳird
Nasr (deity) vii, 1012a
Nasr (vulture) vii, 1012b
Naṣr I b. Tamgh̲ač Kh̲ān (Ḳarakh̲ānid) (1080) i, 1295a; iii, 1114b, 1115a; iv, 217b; vi, 273b, 275b; viii, 748b
Naṣr I b. Aḥmad b. Sāmān-kh̲udā (Sāmānid) (892) i, 1294a; iv, 21b, 188b; viii, 1026b; s, 265b
Naṣr II b. Aḥmad b. Ismāʿīl, amīr (Sāmānid) (943) i, 278a, 1294b; ii, 1082b; iii, 254b, 759a, 1156b; iv, 22b; v, 856b; vi, 115b, 539a, 608b, 853a; vii, 397b, 652a, 1015a; viii, 110a, 1027a; s, 265a, 411a
Naṣr (Mosul) (IX) vi, 900a
Naṣr b. ʿAbbās b. Abi ʾl-Futūḥ i, 9b, 198b; ii, 318a; iv, 514a
Naṣr b. Abī Layth̲ → al-Aṣamm, Abū Bakr (Miṣr)
Naṣr b. Aḥmad → al-Kh̲ubzaʾaruzzī

Naṣr b. ʿAlī, Ilig Khān (Özkend) (XI) iii, 1113b; vi, 65a; viii, 242b
Naṣr b. ʿĀṣim iv, 731b
Naṣr b. Ibrāhīm (Ilek-Khān) s, 65a
Naṣr b. Khalaf (Sīstān) (XII) vii, 535b
Naṣr b. Maḥmūd (Mirdāsid) iii, 790a
Naṣr b. Marzūḳ s, 88a
Naṣr b. Muʿāwiya, Banū vi, 265b, 266a
Naṣr b. Muḥammad, Abu 'l-Djuyūsh (Naṣrid) (1314) iii, 833b; vii, 1020a, 1022b
Naṣr b. Muḥammad al-Samarḳandī → Abu 'l-Layth
Naṣr b. Murshid, Imām (Yaʿrubid) (XVII) vi, 735a
Naṣr b. Muzāḥim, Abu 'l-Faḍl al-Minkarī (827) i, 383b; vii, 1015b; x, 107b; s, 233a
Naṣr b. Nuṣayr al-Ḥulwānī (X) vi, 195b; vii, 418a, 1015a
Naṣr b. Sadīd al-Mulk ʿAlī (Munkidh, Banū) (1098) vii, 578a
Naṣr b. Ṣāliḥ b. Mirdās (Mirdāsid) (1029) vii, 117a
Naṣr b. Sayyār al-Laythī (748) i, 16a, 206b, 529b, 1293b; ii, 561a; iii, 224a, 471a, 493b, 802b, 988a; iv, 15b, 446b; v, 57a, b, 711a, 854a; vi, 331b, 620b; vii, 1015b; x, 845a
Naṣr b. Sebüktigin iv, 189b; v, 1126b
Naṣr b. Shabath al-ʿUḳaylī (IX) i, 52b; ii, 524a; iii, 950b; vi, 336b, 337a; vii, 1016b
Naṣr Āl Madhkūr i, 942b
Naṣr Allāh (Afghānistān) s, 65b, 237b
Naṣr Allāh, ḳāḍī (Baghdād) (XIII) vi, 77b
Naṣr Allāh (Mangit) (1860) vi, 419a
Naṣr Allāh (amīr) (Bukhārā) i, 1296a; iv, 694b; v, 30a, 46a
Naṣr Allāh b. ʿAbd al-Ḥamīd iii, 372b; iv, 504b
Naṣr Allāh b. ʿAbd al-Raḥmān i, 232b; iii, 13a
Naṣr Allāh b. al-Djazarī s, 267a
Naṣr Allāh b. Muḥammad b. ʿAbd al-Ḥamīd (Naṣr Allāh Munshī) (XII) iv, 64a; vii, 1016b; s, 21b
Naṣr Allāh Iṣfahānī, Mīrzā (XIX) iv, 164a
Naṣr Allāh Mīrzā b. Nādir Shāh (Afsharid) vii, 457a
Naṣr al-Dawla, Abū Naṣr Aḥmad b. Marwān (Marwānid) (Diyār Bakr) (1061) ii, 384a, 484b; iii, 344b; v, 453a; vi, 626a, b, 930b; vii, 1017a
Naṣr al-Dīn (Berber) (XIX) i, 1172a
Naṣr al-Dīn Ibrāhīm (XII) vii, 816b
Naṣr al-Dīn Khodja (Nasreddin Hoca) i, 313a; ii, 591a; iii, 375a; vii, 1018a; s, 170b
Naṣr Khān → Naṣr I (Ḳarakhānid)
Naṣr al-Ḳushūrī iii, 45b, 101a, 886b
Naṣr al-Mulk (Ḳarā Gözlü) iv, 578a
Naṣrābādī, Muḥammad Ṭāhir (XVII) vii, 530a; s, 340b
Naṣrat Shāh ii, 218b
Naṣrawī → Naṣārā
Naṣrid Maliks (Sīstān) ix, 683b
Naṣrids (Banū Naṣr/Banu 'l-Aḥmar) i, 495b, 500a; ii, 307b, 1015b, 1016b; iii, 499a; v, 625b; vii, 1020a; s, 112b, 256b, 307a, 398b; vi, 221a, 222b, 521b, 572a
Nāṣriyya (Yūsuf) (Ayyūbid) vi, 320a
Naṣṣ vii, 1029a
al-Nassādj vii, 1029b
Nassādjī iv, 1042b
Nassads vii, 1029b
Naṣṣār, Nadjīb ii, 468a
Nasser, Colonel → ʿAbd al-Nāṣir, Djamāl
Nastaʿlīḳ → Khaṭṭ
Nasṭūr vii, 362a
Nasṭūriyyūn (Naṣāṭira) ii, 67a, b, 1120a; iii, 886a, 1122a, 1206a; v, 121a, 896b; vi, 542a; vii, 1030a; viii, 173b
Naṣūḥ Pasha (1614) i, 268a; ii, 443b, 750a, b; vi, 999a; vii, 1033a; s, 238b
Naṣūḥ Pasha ʿOthmān-oghlu i, 395a
Naṣūḥ al-Silāḥī i, 904b
Naṣūḥī, Muḥammad (1718) ix, 155b
al-Naṣūḥiyya iv, 991b
Nāsūt v, 611b, 612a
Naʿt ii, 302a; iv, 715b; vii, 1034a
Naṭanz iii, 1124b; vii, 1034a
Naṭanzī, Ḥusayn (XV) iv, 525b; ix, 42a
Nathr s, **662b**
Nathrī, Shaykh Mūsā iv, 72b; v, 198a
Natīdja vii, 1034b
Nāṭiḳ bi-'l-Ḥaḳḳ (Mūsā b. al-Amīn) (ʿAbbāsid) (IX) iv, 203a, b; vii, 1034b
al-Nāṭiḳ bi-'l-Ḥaḳḳ, Abū Ṭālib iii, 832a; s, 13a, 343a
Nātil-Rustāḳ (Rustamdār) vi, 511b, 513a
al-Natīlī → al-Ḥusayn b. Ibrāhīm
National Front (Iran) iv, 41a, b, 42a
Nationalism → Waṭaniyya

Naṭrūn i, 1068b; v, 965a, 979b; vii, 1035a; s, 130b
Natsir, Mohammed (XX) vi, 731b, 732a
Naṭṭāḥa → Ibn al-Khāṣīb, Abū ʿAlī
Nauplion vii, 1035a
Nāʿūra i, 492a, 1232a; iii, 29b; v, 860b, 861a, 863b, 864a, 969a; vii, 1037a
Navarino vii, 426a, 1037b
Navarra vii, 1039b
Navas de Tolosa, Las → al-ʿIḳāb
Nawʿ → Anwāʿ
Naw Bahār i, 1033a; vii, 1039a
al-Nawādjī, Shams al-Dīn Muḥammad (1455) vii, 1039b
Nawāʾī, ʿAlī Shīr → Mīr ʿAlī Shīr Nawāʾī
Nawālī → Naṣūḥ aḳ Hiṣārī
Nawār (bint ʿamm al-Farazdaḳ) vi, 476a
Nawār → Čingāne; Lūlī; Zuṭṭ
al-Nawāwī, Muḥammad b. ʿUmar al-Djāwī (XIX) vii, 1040b
al-Nawawī, Muḥyi al-Dīn Abū Zakariyyaʾ (1277) iii, 25b, 763a, 779a, 860b, 927a; iv, 1108a; v, 20a; vi, 133a, 263a, 353a, 651b; vii, 691b, 1041a; viii, 425a; s, 83a, 390b
Nawba iii, 453b; vi, 521a; vii, 927b, 1042a
Nawbakht vi, 710b, 834b; vii, 1043b
al-Nawbakhtī, Abu ʾl-Ḳāsim al-Ḥusayn (938) vii, 542b; viii, 812a
al-Nawbakhtī, Abū Sahl Tīmādh (924) vii, 312a, b, 786a, 1043b, 1044a
al-Nawbakhtī, al-Faḍl b. Abī Sahl (IX) vii, 1044a
al-Nawbakhtī, Ḥasan (786) vii, 1043b
al-Nawbakhtī, al-Ḥasan b. Mūsā (922) iii, 497b; vii, 786a, 1044a; s, 225b, 393b
al-Nawbakhtī, Ḥusayn b. Rūḥ → Ibn Rūḥ
al-Nawbakhtī, Ibrāhīm b. Isḥāḳ b. Abī Sahl (X) vii, 1043b
al-Nawbakhtī, Isḥāḳ b. Ismāʿīl (X) vii, 542a
Nawbandadjān vii, 1044b
Nawf, Banū ix, 90b
Nawfal b. Asad b. ʿAbd al-ʿUzzā x, 2b
Nawfal, Banū v, 435a; vi, 145a; vii, 1045a
Nawfal, Hind (XX) vii, 903a
al-Nawfalī, Āl vii, 1045a
Nawʿī, Muḥammad Riḍā (1610) vii, 1046b
Nawr al-Ward v, 827b
Nawriyya vii, 1046a
Nawrōdjī, Dādābhāʾī ii, 545b
Nawrūz iv, 8b, 477a; vi, 521b, 523a, 526b, 527a, 528b, 529a, 857a; vii, 15b, 1047a
Nawrūz, Amīr (Marāgha) (XIII) i, 1130a; ii, 1043a; iv, 878a; v, 554a; vi, 502a
Nawrūz Aḥmed Khān i, 46b; iv, 512a
Nawrūz al-Ḥāfiẓī al-Ẓāhirī (1414) ii, 781b; iii, 186a; vii, 271b, 723a
Nawrūznāma iv, 64a
Nawshahr s, 131b
Nāwūsiyya ii, 375a; vii, 645b, 1048a
Nawwāb/Nawāb (title) vii, 1048a
Nawwāb Islām Khān vi, 690a
Nawwāb Mīrzā Dāgh → Dāgh, Nawwāb Mīrzā Khān
Nawwāb Mīrzā Shawḳ (1871) vi, 838a
Nawwāb Sayyid Ṣiddīḳ Ḥasan Khān (1890) i, 259b, 827b, 1196a; vii, 1048b; s. 293a
Nawwāb Shāh Djahān Begum (XX) vii, 1048b
Nawwāb Wazīr Khān vii, 189b
Nawwāb Wazīrs (Awadh, Oudh) s, 74b, 325b
Nawwāb-i Ṣafawī ii, 882b; iii, 529b; iv, 165a
Nawwāf b. Nūrī Shaʿlān (1921) viii, 644a
Naxos → Naḳshe
Nāy (Ghazna) vi, 783a; s, **667a**
Naybčari ii, 97a
Nayman ii, 42a; s, 97b, 420a
Nayrab iv, 724a
Nayrīz (Nīrīz) vii, 1049b
al-Nayrīzī, Abu ʾl-ʿAbbās al-Faḍl (X) i, 727a; vii, 1050a
al-Nayrīzī, Abū Manṣūr (900) iii, 1137a; v, 85b; vii, 199b
Naysābūr → Nīshāpūr
al-Naysābūrī → al-Nīsābūrī
al-Naysābūrī, al-Ḥasan b. al-Muẓaffar s, 289b
Nayzak iv, 811a
Naẓar i, 949a; vii, 1050a
Nazar Beg b. Ghāzī Beg (Somāy) (1669) ix, 727b
Naẓar Muḥammad Khān i, 768b
Nazareth → al-Nāṣira
Nazhūn iii, 850a
Nāzila vii, 1052a
Nāẓim, Dr iv, 284b, 285a
Nāẓim, Muṣṭafā (1696) vii, 1054a
Nāẓim, Nabī-zāde i, 287b; ii, 699b, 700b

Nāẓim, Yaḥyā (1726) vii, 1054a
Nāẓim Farrūkh Ḥusayn (1670) vii, 1052b
Nāẓim Ḥikmet (Ran) (Nāẓim Hikmet Borzecki) (1963) iv, 882b; vii, 1053a
Nāẓim Pasha (Baghdād) (XX) i, 906b; ii, 624a, 698b; iii, 402a; iv, 296b, 297a; vi, 614b
Naẓīr (-al-Samt) vii, 1054b
Nāẓir al-maẓālim → Maẓālim
Naẓīrī, Muḥammad Ḥusayn (1612) vii, 340b, 341a, 1054b; ix, 241a
Nāẓir-zāde iii, 538a
Nazlī (queen) s, 299a
Nazli Ilicak (XX) vi, 95b
Naẓm s, **668a**
Naẓmī, Meḥmed Edirneli (1555) vii, 531b, 1055b
Naẓmī, Sheykh Meḥmed b. Ramaḍān (1701) vii, 1055b
Naẓmī-zāde Murtaḍā (1705) vi, 1019b
Nāzūk (X) iii, 768a; vii, 542a
al-Nāẓūr vii, 1056a
Nazwā → Nizwā
al-Nazwī, Abū Bakr Aḥmad b. ʿAbd Allāh al-Kindī al-Samdī (1161) viii, 800a
al-Naẓẓām, Abū Isḥāḳ Ibrāhīm b. Sayyār (835) i, 128b, 272a, 713b, 737a; ii, 386a, 518b, 569b; iii, 302b, 1143a, 1266a; iv, 183a, 615a; v, 240b, 384a, b, 893b; vi, 335a, 336b, 636b, 737b; vii, 259a, b, 401a, 546b, 567a, 604a, 784b, 1057a; x, 83bs, 90b, 226a, 393b
Ndiassâne s, 182b
Ndjamena s, 166b
Nebuchadnezzar → Bukht-Naṣar
Nečari → Nayčari
Necdet Sancar (1975) viii, 251b
Necip Fazil Kısakürek (XX) vi, 95b
Nedīm → Nadīm
Nedīm, Aḥmed (1730) i, 270a, 1302a; ii, 1000a; iii, 1002b; iv, 574a, 715b; v, 641a, b, 642a; vi, 198b; viii, 1a; s, 324a
Nedjātī, Muṣṭafā v 282a
Nedjātī Bey, ʿĪsā (1509) i, 292b; ii, 221a; vi, 609b, 610a; vii, 24a; viii, 1b; s, 324a
Nedjīb ʿAsim (1935) iv, 791a
Nefes v, 275a; viii, 2b
Nefʿī, ʿOmar Efendi (1635) iii, 357a; iv, 715b; vi, 886b; viii, 3a; s, 282b, 324a
Nefīr (trumpet) i, 1291a, b; viii, 3b
Nefīrī Behrān (XVI) vi, 1007b
Nefṭa ii, 463a, 464a
Negara Dār ul-Islām iii, 1228b; vi, 731b
Negev → al-Naḳb
Negri Sembilan vi, 232b
Negroponte → Eğriboz
Neguib, Muḥammad → Muḥammad Nadjīb
Negübey → Nīkpāy
Negus → al-Nadjāshī
Nellur vi, 67b
Nemče viii, 4a
Nememcha i, 371b; ii, 464a; s, 144b
Nepal viii, 5a
Nergisī (Nergisī-zāde), Meḥmed Efendi (1635) viii, 6b
Neshʾet Khōdja Süleymān (1807) viii, 7a
Neshrī (1520) viii, 7b
Nesīmī, Sayyid ʿImād al-Dīn (1417) iii, 600b; vi, 226b; viii, 8a; s, 324a
Nesin, Aziz iii, 357b; iv, 882b; v, 195a
Nestorians- → Nasṭūriyyūn
Nevruz, Emīr → Nawruz, Amīr
Nevzāt, Refiḳ iv, 123b
New Persian Language s, **426b**
New Saray i, 1188b
Newābād vi, 57a
Newāʿī → Navāʿī
Newʿī, Yaḥyā b. Pīr ʿAlī (1599) vii, 597a; viii, **8b**, 581b; s, 83a
Newʿī-zāde ʿAṭāʾī → ʿAṭāʾī
Newres, ʿAbd al-Razzāḳ (Newres-i Ḳadīm) (1762) viii, 9a
Newres-i Djedīd (1876) viii, 9a
Newrokop viii, 9b
Newshehir viii, 11a
Newshehirli Ibrāhīm Pasha → Ibrāhīm Pasha Newshehirli
Newzād, Tewfik iv, 930b
Nēzak Ṭarkhān → Nīzak Ṭarkhān
Nʾgaous → Niḳaws
Niani (Mali) vi, 258b
Niassenes s, 182b
Nibrāwī → al-Nabarāwī
Nībūlī (Nicopolis) viii, 35a
Nicaea → Iznīḳ
Nicander s, 59b
Niccolò II Gattilusio (Lesbos) (XV) vi, 71a
Niccolò da Canale (Euboea) (XV) vi, 72a
Nicephorus Phocas (X) i, 789b; iii, 86a, 120a, 398a, 1084a, b; v, 921b, 923b; vii, 487a, b
Nicobar Islands iii, 407a; viii, 12a

Nic(k)opolis → Niḳbūlī
Nicosia → Lefḳosha
Nidjābat Khān iv, 666b
Niebla → Labla
Niffar (Nuffar) viii, 12b
al-Niffarī, Muḥammad b. ʿAbd al-Djabbār (976) viii, 13b
Nifṭawayh, Abū ʿAbd Allāh (934) i, 822a; vi, 634a; vii, 279b, 403b; viii, 14a; x, 386a
Nīgde (Niğde) vi, 366a, 508b; viii, 15b
Nigde, Ḳāḍī Aḥmad of s, 59a
Niger (river) viii, 16b
Niger (state) vi, 281b, 401a; viii,17b; s, 218a
Nigeria i, 39a, 179a; ii, 10a, 942a; iii, 275a; vi, 281b; viii, 19b; xi, 337b; s, 217a
Nigīsa iv, 53b
Nihāl Čand Lāhawrī (XIX) viii, 23a
Nihāwand i, 16a; iv, 13b, 447a, 653b; v, 1212b, 1213a; vi, 332b, 493a; vii, 853b; viii. 23a; s, 297b
al-Nihāwandī, ʿAbd al-Bāḳī (1632) vii, 343a; viii, 24a
al-Nihāwandī, Aḥmad b. Muḥammad (790) vi, 599b; xi, 498b
Nihāya viii, 24a
Nihḍat-i Āzādī iv, 166a
Nīk ʿĀlam Khān i, 1193a
Nikāba viii, 25b
Nikāḥ viii, 26b
Nikāpur vi, 269a
Niḳaws s, 103a
Nīkpāy ii, 3a
Niksar (Neo-Caesarea, Bythynia) viii, 36a; s, 154a
Nīkūdārīs (Negüderis) vii, 218b, 233a
Nīḳūlāʾūs (Nicolas of Damascus) viii, 36b
Nīl (Dye) i, 540b, viii
Nīl (indigo) viii,
al-Nīl (river) i, 735a, 929a; iii, 71b; iv, 133b, 424b, 442b; v, 862a, 863a, 1249b; vi, 401a; viii, 37b; s, 413a
Nīl Kanth (Māndū) vi, 407a
Nīlambar i, 719b
Nile xi, 15b
Nīlūfer Khātūn (XIV) viii, 43a
Nīm-dih vi, 384b
Nīmā Yūshīdj iv, 71b; viii, 43a
Niʿmat Allāh, Hādjdjī i, 261b
Niʿmat Allāh b. Aḥmad b. Mubārak al-Rūmī (1561) i, 776b; iv, 526a; viii, 44a
Niʿmat Allāh b. Ḥabīb Allāh Harawī (XVII) vii, 220a; viii, 44b
Niʿmat Allāh Harawī s, 1b
Niʿmat Allāh Nūr al-Dīn Walī al-Kirmānī (1431) → Niʿmat-Allāhiyya
Niʿmat Allāh Walī → Niʿmat-Allāhiyya
Niʿmat Khān, ʿAlī (1710) viii, 48a
Niʿmat-Allāhiyya i, 925b, 1342a; iv, 49b, 51b, 66a, 951b, 961b; v, 157a, 1222a; vi, 66b, 549b, 551a; viii, 44b; s, 134b, 156a
Niʿmatīs iv, 99a, 860b
Niʿmatullāhī x, 326a, 327b
Nimr (Shandī) (XIX) vi, 794b
Nimr, Banū iv, 834b
Nimr, Fāris (1951) ii, 467a; v, 1090b; vii, 902b; viii, 48b
al-Nimr b. Ḳāsiṭ iv, 493b
Nimr Muḥammad ii, 351b
Nimrān i, 1239b
Nimrūd → Namrūd
Nimrūz → Sīstān
Nims (mongoose) viii, 49b
Nimzat s, 182b
Nīnawā viii, 50b
Nindru s, 74a
Ninive(h) → Nīnawā
Ning-Hsia viii, 51a
Nioro iii, 289a
Nippur → Niffar
Nīrandj viii, 51b
Nīrīz i, 954b; viii, 52b
Nirīz (Fārs) → Nayrīz
Nirun (Mongols) vi, 417b
Nisā → Nasā
Niṣāb (Yemen) vi, 81a
Nīsābūr → Nīshāpūr
al-Nisābūrī → Ismāʿīl b. Muḥammed; al-Ḥākim
al-Nīsābūrī (1327) ix, 887a
al-Nīsābūrī, Aḥmad b. Ibrāhīm (dāʿī) (XI) vii, 732a
al-Nīsābūrī, al-Faḍl b. Shādhān (873) vii, 460b
al-Nīsābūrī, al-Ḥasan b. Muḥammad, Abu 'l-Ḳāsim (1052) viii, 53a
al-Nīsābūrī, al-Ḥasan b. al-Muẓaffar (1050) s, 289b
al-Nīsābūrī, Muḥammad b. al-Mundhir vii, 569b
al-Nīsābūrī, Sahl b. ʿUthmān (XII) vi, 713a

al-Nīsābūrī, Salama b. Shabīb (IX) vii, 409a
al-Nīsābūrī, Yaḥyā b. Yaḥyā (839) vii, 691a
Nīsān (month) viii, 53b
Nīsān, Banū i, 256a; iii, 1197b; viii, 53b
Nīsānids → Nīsān, Banū
Nisba iv, 180a; viii, 53b
Niṣf al-Nahār viii, 56b
Nish vi, 56a, b, 70b; viii, 56b
Nishān i, 1170b; ii, 309a; vi, 537a; viii, 57b;
Nishāndjï iv, 560b, 561a; viii, 62a
Nishāndjï, Khodja → Djalālzāde Muṣṭafā Čelebi
Nīshāpūr i, 3b, 452b, 750a; ii, 4b, 43b, 746b; iii, 472a; iv, 669a; v, 58a, 354a, 526b, 1126b; vi, 14a, 115b, 120a, 128b, 223b, 224b, 273b, 340a, 523a, 600a, 620b, 627b, 633b, 657a, 661a, 670b, 671a, 715a, b, 780b; viii, 62b; s, 14b, 21a, 32a, 72b, 149a, 204a, 235a, 251a, 253a, 254b, 259b, 263b, 299a, 343a, 357a, 359b, 392a
Nīshāpūrī, Ẓāhīr al-Dīn (1184) viii, 64a
Nishāt ii, 433b
Nishdān iv, 488a
Nishtār, Sardār ʿAbd al-Rabb iii, 532b
Niṣībīn/Nisibis → Naṣībīn
Nisnās → Nasnās
Nissīm b. Yaʿḳūb, Ibn Shāhīn (1062) iv, 306b; s, **669b**
Nīṭas → Baḥr Bunṭus
Nithār viii, 64a
Nitra s, 171a
Niyāḥa viii, 64b
Niyāzi, Banū iii, 423a
Niyāzī, Shams al-Dīn Meḥmed (Miṣrī Efendi) (1694) viii, 65a
Niyāzī Bey (XX) i, 63b; ii, 698b; viii, 65b
Niyya viii, 661
Nīzak, Ṭarkhān (Hephtalite) (710) i, 857a, 1001a; iii, 304a; iv, 208a; v, 57a, 541b; viii, 67a; ix, 80b
Niẓām (title) viii, 67a
Niẓām ʿAlī Khān (Ḥaydarābād) (1802) iii, 320b; viii, 67b
Niẓām Badakhshī (1584) viii, 67b
Niẓām Burhānpūrī i, 1331a; ii, 837b
Niẓām al-Dawla b. Marwān v, 453a
Niẓām al-Dīn (amīr-i dād) iv, 818a
Niẓām al-Dīn, Mullā Muḥammad (1748) i, 936b; ii, 132a; v, 1135b; vi, 354b; viii, 68b; s, 292a, b, 293a
Niẓām al-Dīn b. al-Ḥakīm (1358) viii, 806a
Niẓām al-Dīn Aḥmad b. Muḥammad Muḳīm al-Harawī (1594) i, 60b, 856b, 857a; ii, 922a; vii, 342a; viii, 67b; s, 302a
Niẓām al-Dīn Awliyāʾ, Shaykh (Čishtī) (1325) i, 444b, 856a, 1024a, b, 1036b, 1328b; ii, 48a, 50a, 51a, 55a, b, 1076b; iii, 249a; iv, 921b; v, 884b; vi, 126b, 131a, 198b, 691b; viii, 68a; x, 255b; xi, 119a; s, 352b, 353a
Niẓām al-Dīn Awrangābādī ii, 55a; iv, 507b
Niẓām al-Dīn Maḥmūd (Shabānkāra) (XII-XIII) ix, 158a
Niẓām al-Dīn Maḥmūd, Shaykh (XIII) s, 414b
Niẓām al-Dīn Naṣr b. Naṣr al-Dawla (Marwānid) (Diyār bakr) (1079) vi, 626b
Niẓām al-Dīn Shāmī → Shāmī, Niẓām al-Dīn (Ḥaydarābād)
Niẓām al-Dīn Thānesarī → Thānesarī
Niẓām al-Dīn ʿUmar s, 197a
Niẓām al-Islām, Ḥādjdjī (XIX) vi, 529a
Niẓam Khān (prince) → Sikandar Shāh Lōdī
Niẓām al-Milla → Malik b. ʿAlī al-Barānī
Niẓām al-Mulk → Ibn Rāwal Djay Singh
Niẓām al-Mulk (Dōʿāb) s, 126b
Niẓām al-Mulk b. Abī Saʿd al-Djunaydī i, 764a
Niẓām al-Mulk Āṣaf Djāh → Niẓām al-Mulk Čin Ḳïlïč Khān (Ḥaydarābād)
Niẓām al-Mulk Čīn Ḳïlïc Khān, Ḳamar al-Dīn (1748) i, 710a, 1026a, 1170a, 1193a, 1200a, 1201b, 1330b. 1331a; ii, 99b, 981b; iii, 318b, 320a, 427b; iv, 1023b; vi, 535a, b; vii, 446a; viii, 67a, 73a; ix, 246b; s, 280a
Niẓām al-Mulk Dakhnī iii, 1159b
Niẓām al-Mulk Ḍiyāʾ al-Mulk Aḥmad (XII) vii, 408b
Niẓām al-Mulk Ḥasan (vizier) (XII) ix, 16b
Niẓām al-Mulk al-Ṭūsī (1092) i, 353a, 421a, 552a, 593a, 696a, 731a, 1051b, 1130a; ii, 5a, 344a, 384b, 605a, 963b, 1083a; iii, 253b, 347b, 774b, 1088b, 1099a; iv, 25b, 26a, 27b, 807b, 942b,

1073b; v, 387b, 388b, 625a, 1126b, 1127a, 1128b, 1137b; vi, 13b, 14a, 16a, 20b, 66a, 273b, 274b, 275a, 521b, 523b, 605b, 608b, 627a, 949a; vii, 408a, b, 540b, 679a, 987a, b; viii, 69b, 971b; xi, 193a; s, 14b, 29b, 30a, 384a
Niẓām ʿAskarī s, **670a**
Niẓām Shāh (Bahmanid) (1463) ii, 1127a; vi, 50b, 53b, 488b
Niẓām-Shāhī (1565) viii, 73a
Niẓām-Shāhīs i, 303a, 768a, 1170a; ii, 180a; iii, 425a, 426a, 447a, 1161a; vi, 63a, 67a, 368a, 536b, 695b; vii, 943a; viii, 73b; s, 246a, 259a
Niẓāmī, Ḥasan (XIII) viii, 81a
Niẓāmī, Niẓām al-Dīn Abū Muḥammad (1202) i, 680a, 1213a; ii, 794a, 966b, 1143a; iii, 114a, 1112a; iv, 62b, 63a, 66b, 92b, 127b, 128a, 1009b; v, 1104a; vi, 1016b; s, 46b, 415a
Niẓāmī, Shāh Ḳudrat Allāh s, 293a
Niẓāmī ʿArūḍī Samarḳandī, Aḥmad b. ʿUmar b. ʿAlī (1156) vi, 91b, 276a, 726b, 833a; viii, 76b; s, 333a, 359b
Niẓām-i Djedīd ii, 207a, 511b, 512a, b, 713a; iv, 322b; v, 35b, 907b; viii, **75a**
Niẓāmī Gandjawī, Djamāl al-Dīn (XIII) viii, 76b
Niẓām-i Shāmī → Shāmī, Niẓām al-Dīn
Niẓām-i Wafā iv, 71b
Niẓāmiyya (Āl Niẓām al-Mulk) i, 1051b, 1052b; ii, 1083a; vi, 275a; viii, 81b
Niẓāmiyya → Madrasa
Niẓāms (Ḥaydarābād) vii, 316a
Nizamuddin ii, 262b, 263a; iii, 442b
Nizār b. Maʿadd i, 544b; v, 894b; viii, 82a; ix, 554a
Nizār b. al-Mustanṣir (Fāṭimid) (1095) i, 215b, 353a, 552b; ii, 170b, 857a, 858b; iv, 28a, 200a; vii, 725a; viii, 83a, 84a
Nizārī Ḳuhistānī, Ḥakīm Saʿd al-Dīn (1320) i, 1233a; iv, 67b; viii, 83b
Nizārīs i, 20b, 215b, 246a, b, 352b, 353a, 440a, 552b, 659a, 853b, 1052b, 1099b, 1126a, 1233a, 1254a, 1359b; ii, 64b, 98a, 170b, 859b, 882a, 1039a, 1040b; iii, 72a, 254a, 267b, 268a, 544b, 1169a; iv, 47a, 200a, 201b, 202a, b, 944a; v, 25b; vii, 578a, b, 755a; viii, 84a, 126a, 133b, 442a, 598b; s, 95b, 527b, 632b
– doctrine iv, 205a
Nizhād iv, 785b
Nizīb vi, 60b, 541b; viii, 84b
Nizwā (Oman) i, 1071b; iii, 652b; vii, 838b; viii, 85a; ix, 775a
Noah → Nūḥ
Nobatia → al-Marīs
Noghay (Tatars) i, 721b, 1000a, 1075b, 1189b, 1287a; ii, 25a, 44b, 89a; iv, 569b; v, 140b, 141a, 314b; vi, 371a, 415a, 416b, 417b, 418a, 457a; vii, 351a; viii, 85b
Noghait, Noḳāy (amīr) (1299) i, 1107a, 1188b; ii, 44b, 610a; iii, 117a; vi, 420a
Noghay (1299) x, 690b
Nógrad s, 171a
Nokra ii, 91a
Nomadism i, 872-892; iii, 1096a; iv, 263b, 1177b; v, 472b, 648a, 658a, 659a, 1197b
Nonhera s, 325a
Noradin (prince, Mākū) vi, 202a
North-West Frontier Provice → Wazīrīs Yāghistān
Noria → Nāʿūra
Nouakchott vii, 615b; viii, 86b
Nové Zámky v, 259b, 260a, 261a; s, 171a
Noyan (title) viii, 87a
Nuʿaym → Naʿīm, Āl
Nuʿaym b. Ḥammād (840) ii, 388a; vii, 4a; viii, 87b
Nuʿaym b. Khāzim b. Khuzayma al-Tamīmī (IX) vi, 335a
Nuʿaym b. Muḳarrin (VII) vi, 744a, b
Nuʿayma, Mikhāʾīl i, 598a; v, 188b, 189b, 1254b, 1255a, b, 1256b; vi, 91a, 409a; viii, 88a
al-Nuʿaymī, ʿAbd al-Ḳādir (1521) ii, 585b; viii, 504b; s, 195b
Nuʿayr b. Ḥiyār b. Muhannā, amīr (1400) ii, 614a; iv, 88a; vii, 462a
Nūba, Banū i, 966a; ii, 127b, 131a, 940a; iv, 485b; v, 266b; 268a, 521b; vi, 281b; s, 19b
Nūba (Nubia) viii, 88b
Nūba languages viii, 91b
al-Nubāhī (Mālaḳa) (XIV) vi, 112a, 221b, 222b; s, **679b**
Nūbār Pasha (1899) ii, 696b; iii, 1194b; viii, 93a
Nubāta, Banū i, 665a
Nubāta b. ʿAbd Allāh al-Ḥimnānī (IX) viii, 93b
Nubāta b. Ḥanẓala al-Kilābī iv, 447a

Nubia → Nūba
Nubuwwa viii, 93b
al-Nudjabā᾽ i, 95a; v, 995b
al-Nudjayr viii, 97a
Nudjūm iv, 492a; v, 100b, 1024b; viii, 97b
Nudjūm, Aḥkām al- i, 1101a; iii, 1063b; viii, 105b
Nufayʿ b. Masrūḥ → Abū Bakra
Nufayla → Ibn Buḳayla
Nuffār i, 382b, 383a
Nūḥ → Djuḥā
Nūḥ (prophet) i, 177a; iv, 528b; 609b; v, 421a; vi, 106a, 218b; viii, 108b
Nūḥ, Banū vi, 899a
Nūḥ I b. Naṣr b. Aḥmad (Sāmānid) (954) iv, 22b, 23a, 24b; vi, 261b, 608b; vii, 477b; viii, 109b, 1027b; s, 35a
Nūḥ II b. Manṣūr b. Nūḥ I (Sāmānid) (997) i, 985a; ii, 100a, 799a; vi, 65a, 340a, 915b; viii, 110a, 1028a; s, 265b
Nūḥ b. Asad ii, 791a; iii, 1113b; viii, 1026a
Nūḥ b. Muṣṭafā (1659) viii, 110b
Nūḥ b. Shaybān b. Mālik b. Mismaʿ (VIII) vi, 640b
Nuḥām viii, 110b
Nūhānīs (Bihār) vi, 47a
Nuḥās v, 964b, 966a, 967b, 970b, 977b; viii, 111b
Nuhu Mbogo (1921) x, 780a
al-Nukabā᾽ → al-Nudjabā᾽
Nūḳān vi, 714a
al-Nukayr vi, 507b
al-Nukhayla viii, 112b
Nukhayridjan ii, 197b
al-Nukkār (al-Nakkāra) viii, 112b, 639a
al-Nukkārī → Abū Yazīd
Nukkāriyya (Ibāḍī) vi, 840b
Nuḳḳawī iv, 860b
al-Nuḳra viii, 114a
al-Nuḳrāshī iii, 1069a; s, 58a
Nuḳṭat al-Kāf viii, 114a
Nuḳṭawiyya iii, 600b; iv, 50a; vi, 433b; viii, 114b
Nukūr s, 103a
Nukuz, Banū vi, 418a; s, 97b, 420a
Nūl al-Aḳṣā v, 652a, b, 654a
Nūl Lamṭa xi, 20a
al-Nuʿmān I (Lakhmid) i, 196b; iv, 1133b; v, 633a
al-Nuʿmān II (Lakhmid) v, 633a
al-Nuʿmān III b. al-Mundhir IV (Lakhmid) (601) i, 73a, 196a, 452a, 728b, 1241a; ii, 241a, 354a; iii, 812a; iv, 1024b; v, 583b, 633b; vii, 563a, 568b, 840b, 841a; viii, 119b, 278a, 918b; ix, 79b
al-Nuʿmān b. Abī ʿAbd Allāh Muḥammad al-Maghribī, ḳāḍī (974) ii, 859a, 861b; iii, 308a, 1084b; vi, 438b; viii, 117a; s, 70b, 402b
al-Nuʿmān b. ʿAbd al-ʿAzīz iii, 1085a, b
al-Nuʿman b. ʿAdi (al-Nuʿmān b. ʿAdī) (VII) vi, 920a
al-Nuʿmān b. Bashīr al-Anṣārī (684) i, 952b, 1078a; iii, 226b, 272b, 398a, 608b; iv, 1187b; v, 922b; vii, 689a; viii, 118b
al-Nuʿmān b. Djasr iv, 820a
al-Nuʿmān b. al-Ḥārith b. al-Ayham (Ghassānid) (VI) viii, 630a
al-Nuʿmān b. Muḥammad (957) viii, 715b
al-Nuʿmān b. al-Muḳarrin (VII) viii, 23b
al-Nuʿmān b. al-Mundhir → al-Nuʿmān III (Lakhmid)
al-Nuʿmān b. Mundhir (Ghassānid) ii, 1021a, b
al-Nuʿmān b. ābit → Abū Ḥanīfa
al-Nuʿman al-Gharūr v, 634a
Nuʿmān Pasha → Köprülüzāde
al-Nuʿmānī, Muḥammad b. Ibrāhīm (956) viii, 811b
Numāyish → Masraḥiyya
Numayr (IX) i, 551a
Numayr, Banū ii, 347b; iii, 228a; vi, 379a, 546b; vii, 117b
Numayr b. ʿĀmir b. Ṣaʿṣaʿa, Banū viii, 120a
al-Numayrī, Abū Ḥayya → Abū Ḥayya
al-Numayrī, Djaʿfar Muḥammad (1985) v, 1065a; viii, 92b; ix, 748b
Numidian v, 754b, 755a
Nūn viii, 120b
Nūniyya iv, 668a
Nupe (Nigeria) viii, 20b
Nūr viii, 121b
Nūr Afzā (garden) s, 366b
Nūr ʿAlī Shāh b. Ḥadjdjī Niʿmat Allāh (1895) i, 261b
Nūr Allāh b. Aḥmad al-Miʿmār, ustādh (XVII) iv, 507a
Nūr Allāh Beg v, 462a

Nūr Allāh al-Sayyid Sharīf al-Marʿashī al-Shushtarī (1610) i, 721a; ii, 380b; iii, 434a, 1152a; vi, 54b, 516a; vii, 132a, 300a, 672a,b; viii, 123b
Nūr Bānū Wālide Sulṭān (Murād III) (1583) vii, 595b; viii, 124a, 818a
al-Nūr Bey Muḥammad ʿAnḳara i, 1156b; ii, 123b
Nūr al-Dawla Balak b. Bahrām b. Artuḳ (Artuḳid) → Balak Nūr al-Dawla
Nūr Dawlat Girāy Khān iv, 723b
Nūr al-Dīn (Crimean title) → Girāy
Nūr al-Dīn (deputy) iv, 500a
Nūr al-Dīn (Khōdja) (dāʿī) → Satgur Nūr
Nūr al-Dīn, ʿAbd al-Ḳādir (1987) viii, 126a
Nūr al-Dīn b. Edigü (Noghay) (1440) viii, 86a
Nūr al-Dīn Arslān Shāh I b. Masʿūd b. Mawdūd b. Zangī (Zangid), Mosul (1211) vi, 781b; vii, 9b, ,728b; viii, 127a
Nūr al-Dīn Djibrāʾīl b. Bahāʾ al-Dīn Djadja (XIII) v, 172a, b
Nūr al-Dīn Maḥmūd b. Zangī (Zangid) (1174) i, 150a, 197a, 198b, 215a, 446b, 639a, 664b, 791b, 797a, 971a, 1017a, 1025a, 1224a, 1332a, b, 1349a; ii, 64b, 111a, 126a, 283a, 318a, b, 347b, 354b, 856b; iii, 87a, 109b, 208b, 228b, 399a, 504a, 681b, 714a; iv, 482a, 1088a; v, 104a, 924b, 1129a; vi, 380a, b, 507a, 545b, 547a, 606a, 663a, 708a, 733b, 780b, 870a, b; vii, 163b, 578b, 579a, 726b, 816a; viii, 127b; ix, 486a; xi, 453a; s, 195a
Nūr al-Dīn Muḥammad II (Nizārī) (1210) viii, 133b, 442b
Nūr al-Dīn Munshī (XIII) vii, 974a
Nūr al-Dīn Pasha iv, 873b
Nūr-Djahān (Mihr al-Nisāʾ) (1645) i, 253b, 686a, 1161a; ii, 380b; iv, 282a, 709a, 914b; v, 600b, 601a; vi, 488b; vii, 327b; viii, 124b; s, 366a
Nūr al-Ḥaḳḳ b. ʿAbd al-Ḥaḳḳ Dihlawī (XVII) vii, 432b; viii, 134a
Nūr Ḳuṭb al-ʿĀlam, Sayyid (1416) i, 1168a; ii, 51b; iii, 1003a; viii, 125a
Nūr Muḥammad Alīzay i, 295b
Nūr Muḥammad (Kalhorā) (1754) i, 431b, 1192a; ix, 440a
Nūr Muḥammad Shāh iv, 202b; v, 26b
Nūr Muḥammadī iii, 1240a; viii, 125a; s, 411b
Nūr Satgur (1094) viii, 125b
Nur Sutan Iskandar (XX) vi, 240b
Nūr Turk iii, 433b
Nūr Waḥī (Vahitov) Mullā (1918) s, 784a
Nūrbakhsh, Sayyid Muḥammad b, Muḥammad b. ʿAbd Allāh (1464) i, 392b; iv, 48b; v, 301a; vi, 73a; viii, 134a; s, 423a
Nūrbakhshī, Shams al-Dīn Muḥammad b. Yaḥyā al-Lāhiğī (1515) viii, 135b
Nūrbakhshiyya i, 392b; v, 301a, 604b; vi, 549b; vii, 300b; viii, 134a; s, 366b, 423a, b
Nurculuk viii, 136b
Nūrī (gypsies) viii, 138a
al-Nūrī (932) vi, 569b
al-Nūrī, Abu ʾl-Ḥusayn Aḥmad al-Baghawī (907) iii, 1247a; iv, 990b; viii, 139b; x, 314b
Nūrī, Mīrzā → Bahāʾ Allāh; Ṣubḥ-i Azal
Nūrī, Mīrzā Āḳā Khān, Iʿtimād al-Dawla (XIX) vii, 1003b
Nūrī, Shaykh Faḍl Allāh (1909) vii, 918b; viii, 140a; ix, 192b; s, 110a
al-Nūrī b. Shaʿlān (XX) i, 483a; ii, 492b, 626a
Nūrī Bīmāristān (Damascus) vi, 193b
Nuri Killigil → Enwer Pasha
Nūrī (Nuri) Pasha (Killigil) i, 191b, 1071a; ii, 701b
Nūrī al-Saʿīd (1958) ii, 872b; iii, 521b, 522a; v, 1045a; vi, 615a, 616a; viii, 140b, 246a, 445b; s, 7a
Nūrī Shaʿlān (XX) viii, 644a
Nūrīn vi, 504b
Nūristān → Kāfiristān
Nūriyya (Cairo) s, 197a
Nursī, Sheykh Badīʿ al-Zamān (Bediuzzaman Said Riza-Nursi) (1960) viii, 143a
Nurullah Ataç (1957) vi, 95b
Nūrzāy ii, 629a
Nuṣayb ii, 1029b
Nuṣayb al-Akbar b. Rabāḥ, Abū Miḥdjān (730) viii, 145a
Nuṣayb al-Aṣghar, Abu ʾl-Ḥadjnāʾ (IX) viii, 144b
Nuṣaybin → Naṣībīn
Nuṣayr b. Ṣāliḥ al-Ibāḍī iii, 655a
Nuṣayrīyya (Nuṣayris) i, 134a, 470b, 471b,

688a, 832b, 1082a, 1098b, 1099b; ii, 358b, 994a, 1070b, 1094b; iv, 202a, 1133a; vi, 582a, 791b; viii, 145b; s, 207a, 364b
al-Nūshādir viii, 148a
al-Nūshadjān b. Wahrīz s, 354b
al-Nūsharī (al-Nawsharī), Abū Mūsa (IX) viii, 149a
al-Nūsharī, wālī (X) iv, 89a; vi, 670b
Nūshirwān → Anūshi(a)rwān
Nushshāb iv, 799a
Nūshtagin → Anūshtigin
al-Nushū' Abū Shākir s, 396a
Nushūr → Ḳiyāma
Nuskha viii, 149a
Nuṣrat Allāh, ḳāḍī (XIV) vi, 77b
Nuṣrat Bībī vi, 488a
Nuṣrat al-Dīn b. Ibrāhim b. Ḥusām al-Dīn Ḥasan (Marʿash) (XIII) vi, 507b
Nuṣrat al-Dīn b. Khāmūsh (Atabeg) (1210) i, 301a; vi, 501a
Nuṣrat al-Dīn b. Sāḥib ʿAṭā' i, 243b
Nuṣrat al-Dīn Abū Bakr → Abū Bakr b. Pahlawān Muḥammad
Nuṣrat al-Dīn Aḥmad Ibn Hazārasp iii, 337a, b, 1016a; v, 827a
Nuṣrat al-Dīn Amīr-Amīran b. ʿImād al-Dīn Zangī (XII) vi, 870a, b; viii, 127b
Nuṣrat al-Dīn Arslān Āba → Aḳ-Sunḳūr II
Nuṣrat al-Dīn Khāṣṣ-bek → Arslan Abīhī
Nuṣrat al-Dīn Muḥammad b. ʿAlā' al-Dīn (Marāgha) (XIII) vi, 500b
Nuṣrat al-Dīn Yaḥyā (Muẓaffarid) (1393) vii, 480b
Nuṣrat Khān (Delhi) (XIV) i, 506b, 1192a; ii, 1124a; iv, 922a; vi, 49a, b
Nuṣrat Khātūn vi, 488a
Nuṣrat Shāh (Bengal) (1532) iii, 422b, 632a; v, 638b; vi, 47a
Nuṣrat Shāh (Delhi) ii, 270a
Nuṣrat Shāh II (Tughluḳid) (1399) vi, 294a, b
Nuṣratābād viii, 154a
Nuṣratī, Muḥammad Nuṣrat (XVII) iii, 119a; viii, 154b
Nuṣub viii, 154b
al-Nuwayrī, ʿImād al-Dīn (1317) viii, 157b
al-Nuwayrī, Muḥammad b. al-Ḳāsim al-Iskandarānī (1374) vii, 171b; viii, 155b
al-Nuwayrī, Shihāb al-Dīn Aḥmad (1332) i, 595a, 794a, 1116b; iv, 334a, b, 485b; vi, 144a, 311b, 340b, 906b; viii, 156a; s, 43a, 128b
Nuzha → Miʿzaf
Nyasaland → Malawi
Nyitas i, 173a

O

Ob (river) viii, 160a
Oba v, 472a
Obat iv, 648b
ʿObhadya, ʿObhedel → ʿĪsāwiyya
Oblučica → Isakča
Ochialy → ʿUlūdj ʿAlī
Ochrida → Okhri
Ocsónoba → Ukshūnuba
Oczakov → Özi
Odjaḳ i, 947b, 1256a, b, 1267a, 1277b; ii, 1091a; iv, 167b; viii, 161a; s, 409b
Odjaḳlîḳ → Odjaḳ
Odon → Khotan
Ofen viii, 161b
Ogādēn vii, 389b; viii, 161b
Ögedey (Mongol) (1241) i, 227a, 1105a, b; ii, 2a, b, 3a, 43a, 44a, 45b, 606a, 928b; iv, 584a, 612b; v, 38b, 858a; vi, 77a, b, 482b; vii, 230a, 234a; viii, 162a
Oghlan → Ghulām(iv)
Oghul viii, 163a
Oghul Ḳaymish ii, 45b
Oghur iv, 1172a, b; x, 691b
Oghurdjik Alp s, 280b
Oghuz → Ghuzz
Oghuz-Khān (Kaghan) ii, 1109a; iii, 115b, 314b; v, 125b
Oghuznāma iii, 115a; viii, 163a
Ohrid → Okhrl
Oirats ii, 44b; v, 595a
Oḳču-zāde, Meḥmed Shāh Beg (1630) viii, 164a
Okello, John (XX) xi, 450b
Okhrī (Ohrid) viii, 164b
Oktay → Ögedey
Oktay Rifat (Horozcu) (1988) viii, 168a
Öküz Meḥmed Pasha ii, 635a; iv, 970b; viii, 182a

Okyar, ʿAlī Fethi ii, 432a; iv, 297b, 872b; viii, 168b
ʿÖlah → ʿUlah
Oläng-i Ḳurūḳ vi, 541b
Old Man, the → Muḥammad III b. Ḥasan
Old Man of the Mountain, The → Rās̲h̲id al-Dīn Sinān
Öldjeytü, G̲h̲iyāt̲h̲ al-Dīn Muḥammad K̲h̲ār-(K̲h̲udā)banda (Mongol Īlk̲h̲ān) (1316) i, 162a, 347a, 903a, 1031b; ii, 14b, 194a, 1111b; iii, 57b, 390a, 952b, 1122b, 1124b, 1127a; iv, 32a, 48b; v, 554b, 630a; vi, 13a, 323a, 494b, 501b, 502b, 540b, 549b; vii, 13a, 462a, 992a; viii, 168b; s, 83b
Olendirek viii, 169b
Olg̲h̲un, Meḥmed Ṭāhir (Tahir Olgun) (1951) viii, 170a
Oman → ʿUmān
Omar Ali Saifuddin, Sultan Sir s, 152a
Omar, Ömer → ʿUmar
Omar Khayyām → ʿUmar al-K̲h̲ayyām
Omar, Sultan (1876) Terengganu) x, 419a
Omdurman (Umm Durmān) i, 50a, 976a; v, 70a, 1249b, 1250b, 1251b; viii, 170b
ʿÖmer b. Mezīd (XV) vii, 531b
ʿÖmer ʿĀs̲h̲iḳ (1707) viii, 171a
ʿÖmer Beg (Mora) (XV) vii, 237a
ʿÖmer Beg (Naḳs̲h̲e) (XIV) vii, 940a
ʿÖmer Ḍiyāʾ al-Dīn s, 83a
ʿÖmer Efendi (XVIII) viii, 171b
ʿÖmer Fuʾādī (1636) ix, 155b
ʿÖmer Seyf ül-Dīn (Ömer Seufeddin) (1920) ii, 440a; iii, 357b; iv, 636b; vi, 93b; viii, 172a, 251a; s, 55a, 98b, 282a
Omo v, 522a, 523b
On Iki Ada (Dodecanese) viii, 172b
On Oḳ Union (XVII) x, 691b
Oner, amīr (XI) vii, 541a
Ong K̲h̲ān i, 418b; ii, 42a, 571a, 1112b
Oporto → Burtuḳāl
Orakzay Pathāns vi, 127a
Orāmār (Oramar) viii, 173a
Oran → Wahrān
Orbay, Ḥüseyin Raʾūf (1964) iv, 297b; vii, 229a; viii, 174a
Orda i, 1105a, 1106b; ii, 44a, 571b
Orda b. D̲j̲oči x, 560b
Ordu viii, 174a
Ordūbād vii, 922a; viii, 174b
Ören, Ḳalʿe (Orenkale, Orenburg) s, 245a, **679a**
Öreng Timur → Urang Temür
Örenkale → Ören, Ḳalʿe
Oreto → Urīt
Orfa → al-Ruhā
Orgiba D̲j̲adīda vi, 590a
Orik, Nahīd Ṣırrī (Nahit Sirri Örik) (1960) viii, 175a
Orissa → Urisā
Ork̲h̲ān (pretender) (XV) vi, 978a
Ork̲h̲ān b. ʿOt̲h̲mān I G̲h̲āzī (Ottoman) (1362) i, 175a, 318a, 348a, 468a, 468b, 994a, 1187a, 1229a, 1334a; ii, 337b, 443a, 686b, 722a, 982b, 1045a; iii, 212a; iv, 291b, 628a, 969a; v, 248b, 283b; viii, 175a, 192b
Ork̲h̲ān b. Sulaymān Čelebi (XV) vii, 644b, 645a
Ork̲h̲ān Beg b. Masʿūd b. Mentes̲h̲e Beg, S̲h̲ud̲j̲āʿ al-Dīn (1344) vi, 1017b
Ork̲h̲ān Kemāl, Mezmed Rās̲h̲id (Orhan Kemâl Ögütçü) (1970) viii, 177a
Ork̲h̲an Seyfī (Orhan Seyfi Orhon) (1972) viii, 177b; s, 168a
Ork̲h̲an Welī Kanik s, 150a
Ork̲h̲on (river) i, 1240a; viii, 177b
Orki̊na K̲h̲ātūn i, 418b; ii, 3a, b
Ōmuqī i, 225a, 1006b
Ōrmuqs i, 217a, 224a
Oromo (Galla) i, 176b; ii, 545a, b, 974a; iii, 5b, 6a; iv, 88b; v, 522a, 524a; viii, 178a
Orontes → al-ʿĀṣī
Orta viii, 178b
Orta oyunu iv, 806b; vi, 373a; viii, 178b
Ortač, Yūsuf Ḍiyā (Yusuf Ziyā Ortaç) (1968) viii, 179a
Ortaḳči̊-ḳul ii, 1090b
Oruč Owasi̊ s, 239a
Orud̲j̲ b. Timurtas̲h̲ ii, 599b
Örüg-Temür b. Ananda iv, 553b
Osama bin Laden → Usāma b. Lādin
Ösek → Eszék
Ös̲h̲ → Uččh
Osman → ʿUt̲h̲mān
Osman dan Fodio → ʿUt̲h̲mān Ibn Fūdī
Osman Digna → ʿUt̲h̲mān Digna
Osman Nūrī → Ergin, Osman Nūrī
Osmanov Muḥammad v, 383a
Osrus̲h̲ana → Usrus̲h̲ana
Ossetia iv, 349b
Ossetians i, 354a, 837a, 1000a; viii, 179b
Ossetic (language) iv, 351a, b

Ostāḏh → Ustāḏh
Ostādsīs → Ustāḏhsīs
Ostrovica vi, 70b
ʿOtba (ʿOtūb), Banū → ʿUtba, Banū
Otčigin ii, 2b
Ötemish iv, 849b
ʿOth̲mān, Āl-i → V ʿOth̲mānli̊
ʿOth̲mān I, G̲h̲āzī (Ottoman) (1326) i, 467b, 1191a; ii, 710b, 715b; iv, 375a; vi, 724b; viii, 180b; ix, 12b
ʿOth̲mān II b. Aḥmad I (Ottoman) (1622) i, 395b, 1253b; ii, 183b, 277a, 713a; iv, 971a; vii, 707b; viii, 182a
ʿOth̲mān III b. Muṣṭafā II (Ottoman) (1757) i, 395b; vi, 56b, 57a; viii, 182b
ʿOth̲mān b. Ertog̲h̲rul (XIII) v, 256a
ʿOth̲mān Ag̲h̲a (Tard̲j̲umān (XVII) x, 237a
ʿOth̲mān Efendi (XVIII) vii, 709a; viii, 709a
ʿOth̲mān Faḍlī, S̲h̲ayk̲h̲ (XVII) iv, 191a
ʿOth̲mān Ḥamdi Bey (1910) ii, 210a, 694b; iii, 993b; viii, 183a
ʿOth̲mān K̲h̲od̲j̲a (Buk̲h̲ārā) (XX) ii, 700b
ʿOth̲mān Nūrī → Ergin, Osman
ʿOth̲mān Pas̲h̲a (G̲h̲āzī) (Plewna) (1877) viii, 319a
ʿOth̲mān Nūrī Pas̲h̲a (Ḥid̲j̲āz) (XIX) vi, 151a, 176a
ʿOth̲mān Pas̲h̲a (Rumeli) (XVIII) vi, 613b
ʿOth̲mān Pas̲h̲a al-Kurd̲j̲ī (XVIII) iii, 325a; v, 925b
ʿOth̲mān Pas̲h̲a Özdemir-og̲h̲lu (1585) i, 697b; ii, 880b, 1046b; v, 249a, 270a; vii, 600b; viii, 183b, 235b
ʿOth̲mān Pas̲h̲a al-Ṣādiḳ (Damascus) (XVIII) vii, 420b; s, 20b
ʿOth̲mān Pas̲h̲a, Yegen (1689) iv, 194a; viii, 185a
ʿOth̲mān Pazar (Osman Pazar) viii, 185a
ʿOth̲māniyya → Ergani
ʿOth̲mānli̊ i, 8a, 21b, 190a, 467a-468b, 640a, 767b, 791b, 808b, 942b, 998b, 1060b-1064b, 1119b, 1128b, 1218b, 1250b, 1252a, 1321a; ii, 286b, 345a, 634b, 710b, 989b, 1056b; iii, 88a, 1086b, 1183a; iv, 35a, b, 36b, 37b, 1156a; v, 493a, 494a, 716a, 726a, 739b, 974a; vi, 134b, 529b, 541b, 566a; ix, 269b
– administration i, 435b, 1159a, 1225b; ii, 118a, 146b, 230b, 313b-316a, 429b-433a, 562b-565b, 1085b-1091a; iii, 164a, 190b-193b, 211b-215b, 349a, 476a-480b, 489a, 552b, 997a; iv, 268a, 560a, 562b, 678b, 893b, 945b-947a, 1053b, 1094b; v, 249a, 334a, b, 878b, 1035a, 1082b; vi, 1b, 3a, 529b, 858a
– architecture iv, 236a, 570a; v, 292a, b
– education v, 902b
– history v, 814a
– literature ii, 587b; iii, 352a; iv, 527a, 877b, 878a, 1153a; v, 28a
– in Egypt vii, 177a
ʿOth̲mānli̊ Ḥürriyet D̲j̲emʿiyyeti iv, 284a
ʿOth̲mānli̊ Ik̲h̲tilāl Fi̊rḳasi̊ iii, 393a
ʿOth̲mānli̊ Ittiḥād we Teraḳḳī D̲j̲emʿiyyeti → Ittiḥād we Teraḳḳī D̲j̲emʿiyyeti
ʿOth̲mānli̊ Sosyalist Fi̊rḳasi̊ iv, 123b
ʿOth̲mān-zāde Aḥmad Tāʾib (1724) vi, 69b; viii, 188a; s, 83a
ʿOth̲mānd̲j̲i̊k (Osmancik) viii, 189a
ʿOth̲mānli̊ viii, 190a
Otranto i, 293a
Otrār-V Utrār
Ottomans (viziers) xi, 194b
Ötüken viii, 231a; x, 688a
Ouadai → Wadāī
Oualata → Walāta
Ouargla → Wargla
Ouarou Ouari v, 281a
Ouarsenis → Wans̲h̲arīs
Oubangui-Chari s, 165b
Oudh → Awadh
Oued Nīnī iv, 422b
Oued Saoura s, 328a
El-Oudiane ii, 464a
Oued → Wādī
Oud̲j̲da → Wad̲j̲da
Ould Dādda, Muk̲h̲tār v, 1074b, 1075a
Ouled → Awlād
Ouolof → D̲j̲olof
Ourdou → Urdu
Oxus → Āmū Daryā y iv, 1150b
Oymāḳ v, 243b, 245a
Oyo (Nigeria) viii, 20b, 231b; xi, 337b
Oyrats → Kalmuk; Wāfidiyya

Özal, Turgut (1993) x, 695a; s, 681a
Ozan i, 697b; viii, 232a
Özbeg b. Muḥammad Pahlawān (Ildeñizid) (1225) vi, 501a, 632a; viii, 234b
Özbeg b. Pahlawān i, 353b; ii, 393a, 975b; iii, 1112a; s, 378b
Özbeg Khān (Batuʿid) (1341) i, 908b, 1107a; v, 136b; ix, 42a; s, 203b
Özbegistan → Uzbekistan
Özbeg(s) i, 8a, 46b, 47a, 135a, 148a, 224a, 227b, 228b, 406a, 530b, 839b, 847b, 852b, 1001b, 1066b, 1067b, 1107b, 1295b; ii, 44b, 792a; iii, 116b, 177b; iv, 35a, b, 36b, 186b, 1064b; v, 55a, 389a, 859a; vi, 416b, 418b, 419a, 557b, 621a, 714b, 715a, 942a; vii, 91b, 316b; viii, 232as, 46a, 51a, 66a, 97a, b, 168b, 169a, 340a, 419b; x, 109a, 690b
Özbeg – literature x, **721a**
Özbeg-Tatars vii, 353a
Özbek (Mongol) (1341) x, 690b
Özdemir-oghlï ʿOthmān Pasha → ʿOthmān Pasha
Özdemir Pasha (1560) iii, 4b, 11b; iv, 450a; v, 628a; vi, 642a; vii, 721b, 761b; viii, 235a; ix, 2a
Özdemir-Zāde ʿOthmān Pasha (1585) x, 46a
Özï (Özü) i, 1287a; iii, 252a; v, 103a; vi, 56a; viii, 236a
Özkend (Uzkend) ii, 791b; viii, 236b
Özü → Özï

P

Pāʾ (Bāʾ-i farsī) viii, 237a
Pādhūspān → Ruyān
Pādhūspānids → Bādūsbānids
Pādishāh viii, 237a
Pādishāh Khātūn bint Terken Khātūn (XIII) v, 162a, b, 553b; vi, 482b
Padri iii, 1222b; viii, 237b
Pādshāh Bēgam i, 1161a; ii, 378b
Paghmān (Kābul) vi, 768a; s, 65b
Pahang vi, 232b
Pahārpūr vi, 62a
Pahlawān viii, 238b
Pahlawān Bahādur (XIX) ii, 30b
Pahlawān Maḥmūd Pūryār Khwārazmī vi, 73b
Pahlawān Muḥammad b. Ildeñiz, Nuṣrat al-Dīn (Ildeñizid) (1186) vi, 500a, b, 781b; vii, 922b; viii, 239b, 944b
Pahlawi (Pahlavi) ii, 1142b; iii, 113a, 1136b; iv, 40a; viii, 38b, 239b
Pahlawi (language) v, 229a, 660b, 1112a; s, 429a
Pāʾī viii, 239b
Pai Yen-hu (Muḥammad Ayyūb) (1882) v, 848a; viii, 240a
Paisā → Paysā
Pajang (Java) s, 607a
Pāk Pātan (Pākistān) viii, 240a
Pakhtūn → Pashto
Pakistan ii, 29b, 132a, 437a, 545b, 595a, 598a, 668b, 676a, b; iii, 385a, 409b, 440a, 532a, 564b; iv, 1b, 171a, 711a; v, 501a, 599a, 780b, 1081a; vi, 489a, 772a; vii, 355a-356a; viii, 240b; s, 220a, 327b, 331b, 332a
Pākistān, N.-W. → Wazīrīs; Yūsufzāy
Paku Buwono → Surakarta
Pakubuwana I (1709) (Mataram) s, 607b
Pakubuwana II (1749) (Mataram) s, 607b
Pakubuwana III (1788) (Mataram) s, 607b
Pālāhang viii, 244a
Palam (Delhi) s, 206b
Palamāw (Palamū) i, 1210a; viii, 244b
Palangka Raya s, 150a
Pālānpur viii, 244b
Palembang vi, 207b, 236b, 239a; viii, 245a; s, 150b, 200a, 201a
Palermo → Balarm
Palestine → Filasṭīn
Palghat/Palkheo vi, 206b, 535a
al-Palimbānī → ʿAbd al-Ṣamad
Palmyra → Tadmur
Palmyrena → al-Bakhrāʾ
Pambak → Panbuk
Pamir Agreement s (1919) i, 87b
Pamir language → Ghalča
Pamirs i, 454b, 853a, b; ii, 997b; vi, 419a; viii, 245a
Pamplona → Banbalūna
Pāmpūr s, 332a

Pamuk-ova → Aḳ Ḥiṣār
Pan-Arabism viii, 245b, 447a
Pan-Islamism viii, 143b, 248a, 359b, 360a, b
Pan-Turkism viii, 250a
Panāh ʿAlī Khān iv, 573a
Panāhī i, 955b
Panbuk v, 557a
Pāñč Pīr → Pandj Pīr
Panča Sila ii, 663a; iii, 534b, 1230a; vi, 731a
Pančatantra i, 42a, 1359b; iii, 313b; iv, 503a, 506a
Pančāyat i, 758a, 978b; v, 1114b, 1115a
Pandačuk s, 333a
Pandārī ii, 156a
Pandit Dayā Shankar Nasīm (1843) vi, 838a
Pandj (river) i, 454b
Pandj Pīr (Pačpiriyā) i, 868b, 969b; viii, 252a
Pandja ʿAlī (al-Mawṣil) vii, 9b
Pandjāb i, 72a, b, 230a; ii, 426a, 1050b; iii, 443b; v, 886a; vi, 48a, b, 368a, 532b, 535b; viii, 240b, 252b; s, 21a, 63a, 66b, 203a, 241a, 367a
Pandjābī iii, 1b; v, 610a; viii, 255a
Pandjdih i, 87b; vi, 618a; viii, 257a
Pandjhīr, Pandjshīr i, 504a; v, 968b; viii, 258a; s, 125b
Pāndū (Čak) s, 167a
Pāndu'ā (Pāndvā) iii, 4441; viii, 258b
Pandjwāy → Ḳandahār
Pangulu → Penghulu
Pānīpat i, 296b, 1053a; iii, 61a; vi, 535b; vii, 313b, 314a, 316a; viii, 253b, 258b, 430b
Pānīpāt (battle) (1526) i, 848a, 1068b; iii, 199b, 200a, 995b; v, 784a; s, 312a, 313a, 325a, 331b
Pānīpatī, Ḳāḍī Thanāʾ Allāh (1810) vii, 938b
Pānipātī, Niẓām al-Dīn s, 308b
Panjgūrī i, 1007a
Pānka iv, 1160b
Pantelleria → Ḳawṣara (Ḳūsira)
Panthay viii, 259b
Papyrus i, 531b; ii, 307a; iv, 742a; v, 173b; viii, 149b, 261b
Para ii, 119b; s, 325a
Para (Paros) (island) viii, 265b
Pāra (coin) ii, 119b; viii, 266b
Parāčī i, 224a, 225a; v, 649a
Parakou ii, 94b
Paramāra ii, 218b
Paramēśvara (Malacca) (XV) ix, 852a
Parasang → Farsakh
Parasramdēv s, 242a
Parčīn-Kārī viii, 267a
Parda-dār iii, 46b; viii, 270b
Parendā i, 1323b; vi, 67b; viii, 270b
Pargana i, 317a; ii, 156b; viii, 270b
Parī (Peri) viii, 271a
Parī Khān Khānum bint Ṭahmāsp vi, 483a
Parias (al-Andalus) viii, 272a
Pariyān (river) v, 868a
Parkent → Fārkat
Parmaḳ ḥisābi̊ i, 677b
Paropamisus (Mountains) i, 221b; s, 367b
Pārs → Fārs
Pārsā, Khwādja Muḥammad (1420) vi, 225b; vii, 934a, b; viii, 458b, 539b
Pārsāʾiyya viii, 272b
Pārsī Language s, 429b, 431a
Pārsīs ii, 1124a; v, 1114a, b, 1115a, 1116a, 1117a; vii, 222b; viii, 273a
Parsiyā → Bīr Sāl
Partai Islam Se Malaysia viii, 275b
Partai Nasional Indonesia vi, 731a
Partai Sarekat (Serikat) Islam Indonesia iii, 1229b, 1230a; vi, 731a
Pathāns s, 525b
Parwān → Farwān
Parwāna → Muʿīn al-Dīn Sulaymān Parwāna
Parwāna-Oghullari̊ vii, 480a
Parwānačī viii, 276b
Parwīn Iʿtiṣāmī (1941) iv, 71b; vi, 486a, 609a; viii, 285a; s, 110a
Parwīs (Mughal) (1626) viii, 74a
Parwīz → Kisrā II
Parwīz (Parwez), Ghulām Aḥmad (XX) iv, 171a
Parwīz, Khusraw (II) (Sāsānid) (628) viii, 277b, 918b
Parwiz b. Djahāngīr i, 81a, 1331a; v, 1214a
Parwīz al-Rūmī (1579) vii, 537a
Paryāb → Faryāb
Pasai, Pasè i, 742b; iii, 1218b; vi, 234b, 240a; s, 199b
Pasak vi, 202a
Pasantren → Pesantren

Pasargadae s, 129a
Pasarofča (Passarowitz) i, 269b; iii, 1002a; v, 641b; vi, 56a; viii, 278a
Pasè viii, 279a
Pas̲h̲a (title) i, 368a; viii, 279b
Pas̲h̲a D̲j̲ūdar (XVI) (Tinbuḳtu) ix, 756b
Pas̲h̲a Ḳapusu (Wezīr Ḳapusu) viii, 281b
Pas̲h̲aī (language) i, 225a; ii, 138b
Pas̲h̲aīs i, 224b; iv, 410a; v, 356a, 649a
Pas̲h̲alîḳ viii, 282a
Pas̲h̲alimanî vi, 588a
Pas̲h̲a-Yigit i, 654a, 1118a, b,
Pas̲h̲ang b. Yūsuf S̲h̲āh II v, 827b
Pas̲h̲maḳlîk iv, 1095a
Pas̲h̲to i, 217a, **220a**, b, 1124a; ii, 31b, 101b, 1103b; iii, 1b; iv, 538a, 1102a; v, 72a, 356a; xi, 237a; s, 41b, 367a, 367a
Pas̲h̲tūn xi, 494b; s, 237b, 786b
Pas̲h̲tūnistan vii, 220b; viii, 282a
Pas̲h̲tūnistān Movement s, 285b
Pasir s, 151a
Pasir (Kalimantan Timur) viii, 283a
Pasisir (Java) viii, 284a
Passarowitz → Pasarofča
Paswan-og̲h̲lu ʿOt̲h̲mān (1807) i, 398b, 778b, 1304a; ii, 971b; iii, 628a; viii, 284b
Paswē vi, 502a
Patan i, 80b, 506b; ii, 1124a; iii, 444b
Pātan viii, 285a
Patani (Thailand) viii, 285b
Pate (island) iv, 885b, 886a, b; v, 655a, b; vi, 385a, 612b, 963a; vii, 838b; viii, 286b; ix, 686a; s, 351b, 355b
Pathāns i, 216b, 218a, 769a, 864a; iii, 411a; vi, 86a; viii, 244b; ix, 440a; s, 270a, 285a, 329b
Patiālā i, 1194b; ii, 488b; s, 66b
Patih Yūnus iii, 1219a
Patnā i, 1018a; vi, 198b, 409b; viii, 287a
Pátrai, Patras → Baliabadra
Paṭrīk (patriarch) viii, 287b
Patrona K̲h̲alīl (1731) i, 97a, 270b; iii, 1002b; v, 643a; vi, 55b, 995a; viii, 287b
Patta → Pate
Paulus of Aigina s, 52a
Pavagarh vi, 51a, 270a
Pawan (river) s, 150b
Pawlā viii, 288a
Payag (painter) (XVII) vi, 426b
Payās vii, 69b; viii, 288a
Pāygāh iv, 218a, b
Payg̲h̲ū viii, 288b
Pā-yi Bābān vi, 620a
Payinda K̲h̲ān i, 12b, 230b, 231a; ii, 637b
Paykand v, 853b; viii, 500a
Paylāwag̲h̲ s, 331b
Paysā (Pice) viii, 288b
Pʿaytarakan s, 116a
Pazārd̲j̲îḳ vi, 508b, 509a
Pāzavārīs vi, 514a, 515b
al-Pazdawī, Abu 'l-Yusr → al-Bazdawī
Pāzūkī → Bāzūkiyyūn
Pāzvandog̲h̲lu → Paswan-og̲h̲lu
Pazyryk s, 136b, 145a, 146a, 148a
Peacock Throne → Tak̲h̲t-i Ṭāwūs
Pečenegs i, 607b, 1305b, 1307b; ii, 237a; iv, 1175b, 1176b; v, 1011a, 1013b, 1014a, 1015b, 1016b, 1017a, b, 1018a; viii, 289a, 875a; x, 689b, 690b, 692b
Pečewī, Ibrāhīm (1649) i, 1286a; viii, 291a; s, 171a
Pechina → Bad̲j̲d̲j̲āna
Pécs viii, 291b
Ped̲j̲īn vi, 1017b
Pedro de Alfonso (Moses Sefardi) (1110) vii, 737a
Pedroche → Biṭraws̲h̲
Pégon iii, 1234b
Pehlewān → Pahlawān
Pekin → K̲h̲ānbalîḳ
Peloponnesus → Mora
Pemba Island vi, 370a, 784b; viii, 292a; ix, 715b
Pembela Tanah Air vi, 730b
Pemuda Pusa i, 745b
Pen name → Tak̲h̲alluṣ
Penang i, 979b; vi, 232b, 237a, 240b; viii, 292b
Penbe v, 558b, 559a
Penče i, 1357b; ii, 314b; viii, 293b
Pend̲j̲ik ii, 210b, 1087a; viii, 293b
Pengangā (river) vi, 87a
Penghulu viii, 294a
Peninsula, Arabic → ʿArab, D̲j̲azīrat al-
Peñon iv, 1156b
Penyengat (island) vi, 237a
Pera → Beyog̲h̲lu
Perak vi, 232b, 235a, 236a, b; viii, 295a
Pérez, Ivan → Ibrahim Taybilī
Pergamon → Bergama
Peripatetic School → Mas̲h̲āʾiyya
Perim → Mayyūn

Perlak vi, 210b, 234b
Perlis vi, 232b, 236b
Perovsk → Ak Masdjid
Persatuan Islam vi, 731b
Persatuan Ulama-ulama Seluruh Atjèh i, 745b, 746b, 747b
Persepolis iv, 221a, b, 535b
Persia (viziers) xi, 192b
Persian Gulf → Baḥr Fāris
Persian Tobacco Concession s, 53b, 54b
Pertew Edhem Pasha (1873) iv, 112b; viii, 296a
Pertew Meḥmed Pasha (XVI) viii, 295b
Pertew Meḥmed Saʿīd Pasha (1837) viii, 295b
Pērūz Shāpūr → al-Anbār
Perwāne b. ʿAbd Allāh (XVI) vii, 531b
Perzerin → Prizren
Pesantren viii, 296a
Peshāwar i, 223a, 238b, 282b, 970a; ii, 426b; iv, 196b; v, 251a; viii, 299a; s, 41a, 237a
Pēshdādī iv, 12b
Pēshwā viii, 300b, 342a; s, 246b
Pest viii, 301b
Petančic, Feliks (Petancius) s, 185b
Peter the Venerable (1156) vii, 737b
Petro Varadin → Waradīn
Petroleum
– Gulf iv, 752a, 778b, 1057a, 1171b; v, 40b, 573a
– Irāḳ v, 146a
– Iran iv, 41b, 42b; v, 81a, 831b
– Lībiyā v, 758b, 760b
Petrol industry → Nadjd; Nafṭ
Petrus Alfonsi (1130) viii, 302a
Peul → Fulbe
Peyāmī Ṣafā v, 196b; vi, 95b
Phanariot → Fener
Pharos iv, 132b, 133a
Philadelphia (Anatolia) → Alashehir
Philby, Harry St. John Bridger (1960) viii, 302a
Philippines iii, 1219b; vii, 236b; viii, 303a; s, 152a
Philopon, John → Yaḥyā al-Naḥwī
Philoponus → Yaḥyā al-Naḥwī
Phonetics → Sawṭiyya
Pickthall, Mohammed Marmaduke William (1936) viii, 305b
Pie → Pāʾī
Pihānī, Mīr Ṣadr-i Djahān (XVI) viii, 749b
Pīl → Fīl
Pīlakhna s, 331b
Pīlībhīt iii, 60b
Pīlkhāna(e) → Fīl
Pindārī i, 1195b; vi, 536a
Pīr iii, 411b; iv, 202b, 206a; viii, 306a
Pīr Aḥmad b. Ibrāhīm Beg (Ḳarāmān-oghlu) (1475) iv, 624a, b; vi, 71b
Pīr Aḥmad b. Pashang (Hazāraspid) (1408) iii, 337a, b; v, 827b
Pīr ʿAlī (Kart) → Ghiyāth al-Dīn Pīr ʿAlī
Pīr Budak iv, 586b
Pīr Dede Sulṭān (XIII) vi, 1023b
Pīr Ḥasan Beg iv, 584b, 586a
Pīr Ḥusayn iii, 1208b
Pīr Ḥusayn b. Sahat iv, 670a
Pīr Ilyās vii, 23b
Pīr Meḥmed Wehbī Khayyāṭ (1848) ii, 878b
Pīr Muḥammad b. Djihāngīr b. Khalīl b. Tīmūr (1406) i, 227a; ii, 1049b; iii, 417a; iv, 536b; vi, 49b, 524a, 525a; vii, 313b; ix, 197a
Pīr Muḥammad Khān (Mālwa) (1561) i, 1155a; ii, 815a; iii, 576a; vi, 310a
Pīr Pandjāl Pass vii, 332a
Pīr Ṣadr al-Dīn (XV) viii, 307a; ix, 637a
Pīr-Shāh → Ghiyāth al-Dīn
Pīr Shams (al-Dīn) viii, 307a
Pīr Tārīk → Bāyazid Anṣārī
Pīr ʿUmar iv, 871a
Pīrāk vi, 512a, b
Pīrān i, 1217b
Pirate Coast → al-Sāḥil
Pîremêrd → Tewfîq, Hacî
Pīrī Beg b. Kalb ʿAlī Beg iv, 1045a
Pīr-i Kāmil i, 1121b, 1122a
Pīrī Meḥmed Pasha (1532) i, 293b; ii, 400a; iii, 341b; iv, 232a, 566a; viii, 307b
Pīrī Pasha (Istanbul) s, 168b
Pīrī Reʾīs b. Hādjdjī Meḥmed Muḥyi ʾl-Dīn (1553) i, 936b; ii, 588a, 590a; iv, 882a, 1082b; vi, 588a, 735a; vii, 47b; viii, 308a
Pīrī-zāde Meḥmed Ṣāḥib i, 286b; viii, 309b
Pirlepe (Prilep) vi, 89a; viii, 310a
Pīrpanthī s, **681a**
Pīrpanthis i, 173a
Pīrūzābād → Fīrūzābād

Pisar-i Kākū → ʿAlāʾ al-Dawla Muḥammad b. Dushmanziyār
Pīshāwarī, Adīb iv, 789b
Pīshdādids iv, 809a; viii, 312a; ix, 54b
Pīshīn v, 579b, 580b
Pishkān (cap) s, 332a
Pīshkash ii, 150b, 152b; iii, 347b; viii, 312b
Pīshkūh iii, 1106a; v, 826a, 829b, 830a, b
Pīshpek ii, 67b; viii, 313a a
Pīshtāḳ v, 599b, 600a; viii, 313b
Pīshyān ii, 106b
Pisḳopiye v, 265b
Pist viii, 316b
Pithorā Rāy → Prithvī Rādj
Piyāle Pasha (1578) ii, 461a; iv, 233a, 571b; v, 304b; vii, 940a; viii, 316b
Piyārē, Shaykh s, 313a
Plato → Aflāṭūn
Pleven → Plewna
Plewna viii, 317a
Plotinus → al-Shaykh al-Yūnānī
Plovdiv → Filibe
Poitiers → Balāṭ al-Shuhadāʾ
Poland → Leh
Polemon al-Kāhin (Manf) vi, 411b
Polemon of Laodicea → Aflīmūn
Poley → Bulāy
Polnyi Wakuf → Aḳ Ḥiṣār
Pomaks i, 1000a, 1304a; viii, 320a
Pondok → Pesantren
Ponnani vi, 206b, 461b, 462a, 463a
Pontianak viii, 324a; s, 150a, b, 151a, 199b
Poole, E. → Elijah Muhammad
Poona → Pūna
Popalzāy i, 95b; ii, 629a
Pornäk (Türkmen) vi, 201a
Port Said viii, 324b; s, 7b
Port Sudan iv, 687b
Portal → Pīshṭāḳ
Porto-Novo ii, 93b, 94a, b; v, 279b
Portugal → Burtuḳāl
Posta (Postage stamps) viii, 325b
Posta (Postal services) viii, **325**b
Pōthōhārī v, 611a
Potiphar → Ḳiṭfīr
Powinda, Mullā (1913) vi, 86a, b
Pozanti → Bozanti
Prang Sabil i, 747a; viii, 333a
Pratap Singh i, 426b; iv, 709b
Pratīhāra ii, 1122b
Prawiranegara, Sjafruddin vi, 731b, 732b
Prayāg → Allāhābād
Prēm Čand (1936) iii, 458b; v, 204a; viii, 333b
Presbyter Johannes → Prester John
Prester John s, **681b**
Preveze (Prevesa) viii, 334b
Prilep → Pirlepe
Prishtina viii, 335b
Prithvī Rādj i, 217b, 1194a; ii, 50a, 256a, 1122b; iii, 168a
Prizren viii, 349a
Proclus → Buruḳlus
Proto-Ismāʿīliyya → Ismāʿīl b. Djaʿfar al-Ṣādiḳ
Prūmīyon iii, 963b
Pseudo-al-Wāḥidī vi, 823b
Ptolemy → Baṭlamiyūs
Pʾu Shou-keng (XIII) viii, 341a
Puasa (Ramaḍān) s, **682a**
Pukkoya Tangal P.M.S.A. (1975) vi, 460a, b
Pul → Fulbe
Pular → Fula
Pulūr v, 657b, 659b
Pulwar iv, 220b, 221b
Pūna vi, 534b, 535b; viii, 341b
Punč-Bārāmūla s, 423b
Pundja ii, 1125a
Puniāl vi, 127a; s, 327b
Punjab → Pandjāb
Pūr Dāʾūd iv, 789b
Purānā Ḳilʿa vi, 126a
Pūr-i Bahāʾ-i Djāmī (XIII) viii, 342a
Pūr-i Dāwūd, Ibrāhīm (1968) viii, 343a
Purnā (river) s, 279b
P.U.S.A. → Persatuan Ulama
Pusht-i Kūh iii, 1106a; v, 646b, 829b, 830a; vi, 491b
Pushto → Pashto
Pushtūn s, 237b
Pushtūnistān → Pashtūnistān
Pushtūnwālī s, 787b
Pūst viii, 343b
Pūst-neshīn viii, 343b
Putiphar → Ḳiṭfīr
Pythagoras → Fīthāghūras

Q

Qasr → Ḳaṣr
Qassem → Ḳāsim, ʿAbd al-Karīm
Qatar → Ḳaṭar
Qayen → Ḳāʾin
Qena → Ḳunā
Qìltu iii, 1259b
Qom → Ḳumm
Quedah → Kedah
Queen of Sheba → Bilḳīs
Quetta → Kwatta
Quiloa → Kilwa
Quilon → Kūlam
Quinsai → Khansā
Qurat ul-Ain Hyder (XX) vi, 489b
Qwl → Ḳayl

R

Rāʾ (letter) viii, **343a**
Raʿamsās (Raʿamsīs) vii, 140b
Raʿāya → Raʿiyya
Rabʿ viii, **344a**
Rabāb i, 1124a; viii, **346a**
al-Rabadha iv, 1144a; vi, 622b; viii, **349a**; s, 198b
al-Rabaḍiyyūn iii, 1082b
Rabāḥ b. ʿAdjala i, 659b
Rabāḥ b. Djanbulāt ii, 443b
Rabāḥ b. ʿAmr al-Ḳaysī (796) viii, 354b; x, 60b
al-Rabaḥī, Yūsuf b. Sulaymān (1056) ii, 575a; viii, **349b; ix, 528b**
al-Rabaʿī, Abu ʾl-Ḥasan (1029) viii, 349b
Raʿbān vi, 506b, 507a; vii, 816b; viii, 129b, 911a; ix, 107b; i, 761a
Rabat → Ribāṭ al-Fatḥ
Rabb viii, **350a**
Rabbath, Edmund iv, 783a
Rabeh (Rabah/Rābiḥ) i, 180a, 910b, 1260a; v, 358b
Rabghūzī, Nāṣir al-Dīn (1310) vii, 193a; viii, **350a**
Rabīʿ (month) viii, 350b
al-Rabīʿ b. Dāʾūd (VIII) i, 157b
al-Rabīʿ b. Ḥabīb al-Baṣrī (791) iii, 651a; v, 1230b; vii, 663a; viii, 836a
al-Rabīʿ b. al-Ḳaṭṭān (946) vi, 353b
al-Rabīʿ b. Ṣabīḥ (777) vii, 662b
al-Rabīʿ b. Sulaymān ii, 559b; iii 1036a
al-Rabīʿ b. Yūnus, Ḥādjib (785) ii, 730b; iii, 45b, 135b; iv, 1164a; vi, 331b, 438a; viii, 350b
Rabīʿ b. Zayd (Recemundus) (X) i, 628b; vii, 248b; viii, **351a**
al-Rabīʿ b. Ziyād al-ʿAbsī s, 177b, 178a, b
al-Rabīʿ b. Ziyād al-Ḥārithī (VII) i, 1313a; iv, 14b, 356b; v, 57a, 157b; vi, 620a; x, 601b; xi, 458b; xi, 521a
Rabīʿa, Banū i, 1a, 72b, 526b, 529b, 544b, 545b, 964b, 1029a, 1096b, 1158a; v, 537a; vi, 333b, 504a, b, 540a; vii, 266a, 461a, 675a; viii, 90b, 91a, 352b, 863a; s, 122a
Rabīʿa b. Abī ʿAbd al-Raḥmān ii, 888b, 1067b
Rabīʿa b. ʿAmr al-Djarashī (VII) vi, 545a
Rabīʿa b. Farrukh (Rabīʿat al-Raʾy) (749) vi, 263a, 278b; 688b
Rabīʿa b. Ḥāritha b. ʿAmr b. ʿĀmir I 453a; v, 77a
Rabīʿa b. Kaʿb (al-Aratt) b. Rabīʿa vi, 141b
Rabīʿa b. Kaʿb al-Aslamī i, 266b
Rabīʿa b. Muḳaddam i, 518b, 520a
Rabīʿa b. Mukhāshin vii, 74a
Rabīʿa b. Naṣr ix, 84b
Rabīʿa b. Nizār vi, 437b; x, 89b, 400b; s, 661b
Rabīʿa b. Riyāḥ al-Hilālī s, 92b
Rabīʿa b. Rufayʿ ii, 627a
Rābiʿa al-ʿAdawiyya al-Ḳaysiyya (801) vi, 266b; viii, **354b**
Rābiʿa Dawrānī (Awrangābād) vi, 369b; vii, 333b
Rābiʿa Ḳuzdārī iv, 61a
Rabīʿat al-Raʾy → Rabīʿa b. Farrukh
Rabīb al-Dawla Abū Manṣūr (1119) viii, 235a, **356a**
Rābigh (Bandar) iii, 362b; vi, 153b, 154a, 166a; viii, **356b**
Rābiḥ (Bornu) → Rabeh

Rābiḥ b. Faḍl Allāh (1900) i, 1157a; v, 278b; viii, **356b**; s, 164b
Rabīʿiyyāt viii, 357a
Rabīn b. al-Rāḍī → al-Sharīf al-Rāḍī
al-Rābiṭa (al-Mariyya) vi, 576a; viii, 359a
al-Rābiṭa al-Adabiyya vi, 538b
al-Rābiṭa al-Islāmiyya ii, 132a, 546a; iii, 532b, 534a, 1204b; iv, 793a; vi, 461a; viii, **359b**; ix, 905a
al-Rābiṭa al-Ḳalamiyya ii, 364a; v, 1255a; vi 307b; viii, 88a; ix, 230a, b; s, 28a
al-Rābiṭa al-Sharḳiyya s, 121b
Rabwah i, 302a; iii, 411b
Rachel → Rāḥīl
Raḍāʿ (Riḍāʿ) viii, **361a**, 824a
Radawlī → Rudawlī
Radd viii, 362b
Raḍḍiya Sulṭāna i, 1194a; ii, 120a, 267b, 973a, 1143b; iii, 14a, 433b, 1156a
Raden Patah iii, 1219a; v, 1155a
Raden Raḥmat → Sunan Ampel
Raden Trenggana iii, 1219b
Rādhān, Nahr i, 184a
al-Rādhāniyya i, 32a; ii, 817a; iii, 1044b; iv, 1088b; v, 368a; vii, 43a, 69b; viii, **363b**, 620b
Rādhanpūr viii, 367b
al-Rāḍī → al-Rundī, Abū Khālid Yazīd
al-Rāḍī, al-Sharīf → al-Sharīf al-Rāḍī
al-Rāḍī bi-'llāh, Abu 'l-ʿAbbās Aḥmad b. al-Muḳtadir (ʿAbbāsid) (940) i, 19a, 866 b, 1038a, 1298b; ii, 453b; iii, 46a, 127a, 159a, 345a, 346a, 902b; iv, 424a, 940b; vii, 994b; viii, **368a**; s, 386a, 719a
Raḍī al-Dīn Abū Saʿīd al-ʿIrāḳī (1166) vi, 824a
Raḍī al-Dīn al-Hanbalī (1563) v, 609b
Rāḍī al-Dīn Ḥasan al-Ṣaghānī → al-Ṣaghānī
Rāḍī al-Dīn, shaykh (Bhāgalpūr) i, 954a
Rādī Kiyā, Sayyid ii, 194a; v, 603b; s, 363b
Radīf iv, 57a; v, 836a; viii, **368b**
Rāḍiye Kalfa (XVI) vii, 596a
Raḍiyya Begum → Raḍiyya Sulṭāna
Raḍiyya Sulṭān Bēgum (1722) iv, 638a
Raḍiyyat al-Dunyā wa-'l-Dīn bint Iltutmish (Dihlī, 1240) vi, 261b, 488a; viii, **371a**
Radjʿā i, 51a; i, 79a; iv, 457a, 837a; v, 236a, 433b; viii, **371b**
Radjāʾ b. Ayyūb al-Ḥiḍārī (IX) ii, 198a; vii, 279a, b; xi, 178a
Radjāʾ b. Ḥaywa (730) s, **682a**
Rādjā Aḥmad (Farukī) → Malik Rādjā
Rādjā ʿAlī Khān → ʿĀdil Shāh IV
Rādjā Bhādj → Bhōdja
Rādjā Bīrbal i, 229a; ii, 296b; iii, 457b
Rādjā Chait Singh (Rāja) i, 757a
Rādjā Dāhir i, 1068b; ii, 188a, 1123a
Rādjā Djay Singh I, II → Djay Singh Sawāʾī
Rādjā Ganesh (Bengal) (1418) iii, 417b, 1003a; vi, 46b ; viii, **373b; ix, 355b**
Rādjā Mān Singh i, 229a, 1210a, 1254a; ii, 296b, 1144a; v, 638b; x, 895a; s, 333a
Rādjā Prithiwīrādj s, 325a
Rādjā Rām I, 913b; ii, 488b, 1091b; iii, 424b
Rādjā Shitāb Rāyʿ i, 702a
Rādjā Srī i, 1218b
Rādjā Suhādeva s, 156a, 167a, 366a
Rādjā Todar Mall (XVII) vi, 67a, 269b; viii, 74a
Radjaʿa v, 892b, 894b b
Radjab (month) viii, **373b**
Radjab ʿAlī Beg Surūr, Mīrzā v, 202a; ix, 895a
Radjab Dīwān-Begi s, 228b
Radjab Pasha v, 34b
Radjabiyya iii, 35a
al-Radjabiyyūn i, 95a
Rādjāma(u)nd(a)rī I, 924b; vi, 67a, 269a
Rādjarām b. Śivādjī (XVII) vi, 535a
Rādjāsthān vi, 49b, 1027a; s, **683b**
Radjaurī s, 324b
Radjaz i, 142a, 673b; ii, 246a, 1073a; iv, 80b, 714a; viii, **375b**, 733a
al-Radjdjāf I, 1157a; v, 1250b, 1251a
Radjdjāla iii, 187a
Rādjgīr vi, 131a
Rādjī iii, 114b
Radjʿiyya (Irtidjāʿ) viii, **379a**
Radjm viii, 379a
Rādjmahal v, 638b; vi, 343a; viii, **381a**
Rādjpūts i, 208b, 252b, 413a, 913b; ii, 271b, 272a, 567a, 597b, 1122a; iii, 202a, 423b; v, 264b; vi, 50b, 52a, 54b, 127b, 309a, 342b, 1019a, 1027a; vii, 315b; viii, **381b**; s, 55b, 73b, 126b, 332a, 353b
Radjrādja (Regraga) viii, 671b
Rādjshāhī ii, 426b; v, 638b
Rādkān vi, 495b; viii, 383a
Radloff iii, 116b

Radmān i, 1132b; s, 22b
al-Rādūyānī, Muḥammad b. ʿUmar (1114) ii, 809b; iv, 59b; v, 841a; viii, **383a**
Raḍwā i, 536a; v, 433b; vii, 388b; viii, **383b**
Rafʿ → Ṭalāḳ
Rafʿ (grammar; tradition) viii, **383b**
Rafaḥ vi, 31b; viii, **385a**
Rafanea vi, 578a
al-Raffāʿ, Muḥammad b. ʿAlī (XII) ix, 4b
al-Raffāʿ, al-Sarī al-Mawṣilī (X) iv, 936b; viii, 633a; ix, 55b
Rāfiʿ b. Har<u>th</u>ama (896) i, 452b; ii, 191b; iv, 21a, b; vii, 418a; viii, 63a, **385b**
Rāfiʿ b. al-Lay<u>th</u> b. Naṣr b. Sayyār (IX) ii, 1b; iii, 233b, 234a, 859b; iv, 16b, 17a, 658b; v, 45a, 711a, 855b; vi, 331b, 333a; viii, **385b**
Rāfiʿ b. Makkī b. <u>Dj</u>āmiʿ iv, 337a, b
Rafīʿ al-Dara<u>dj</u>āt (Pād<u>sh</u>āh) (XVIII) i, 1026a; ii, 810b; vi, 535a; vii, 457a; s, **686b**
Rafīʿ al-Dawla <u>Sh</u>āh <u>Dj</u>ahān II (Mu<u>gh</u>al) → <u>Sh</u>āh <u>Dj</u>ahān, Rafīʿ al-Dawla
Rafīʿ al-Dīn, Mawlānā <u>Sh</u>āh Muḥammad b. <u>Sh</u>āh Walī Allāh (1818) viii, **386a**
Rafīʿ al-Dīn Nāʾinī s, 23b
Rafīʿ al-<u>Sh</u>ān i, 914a, 1210a; ii, 379a
Rāfiʿ al-Ṭahṭāwī → al-Ṭahṭāwī
al-Rāfiḍa (al-Rawāfiḍ) iii, 308a; iv, 46b; v, 236a; vi, 744a, 916b; viii, **386b**; s, 86a
al-Rāfiʿī, ʿAbd al-Karīm (1226) viii, 389a
al-Rāfiʿī, Muṣṭafā Ṣādiḳ i, 598a; iii, 1018b
Rafīḳ, Aḥmad → Aḥmad Rafīḳ
Rafīḳ <u>Kh</u>ān i, 87b
al-Rāfiḳa vi, 331b; viii, 410b; s, 48b
Rafsan<u>dj</u>ān viii, **389b**
Rafsan<u>dj</u>ānī, ʿAlī Akbar Hā<u>sh</u>imī, Ḥu<u>dj</u>djat al-Islām (XX) vi, 554a; vii, 300a; viii, 389b
al-Ra<u>gh</u>āma vi, 153b
al-Rā<u>gh</u>ib al-Iṣfahānī, Abu 'l-Ḳāsim (XI) ii, 125b; vii, 561b; viii, **389b**; s, 172a, 463b
Rā<u>gh</u>ib Pa<u>sh</u>a, <u>Kh</u>o<u>dj</u>a Meḥmed (1763) i, 965b; iii, 157a, 269a; vi, 826b; vii, 708b, 839a; viii, 183a, **390b**
Ra<u>gh</u>īwa I, 1037a; s, 103a
Raghunnāth Bā<u>dj</u>ī, Rād (Marātha) (XVIII) vi, 535b
Ragrāga, Banū ii, 623a; vi, 591a, 741b, 742b, 743a, 744a
Ra<u>gh</u>ūsa (Ragusa) i, 999a, 1266a; iv, 1055a; viii, **391a**; s, 183b, 184a, b
Raḥā → Ṭāʿūn
Raḥābum vi, 562b, 563a, b
Raḥāmina, Banū iii, 300b; vi, 741b; vii, 391a
al-Raḥba (Raḥbat Mālik b. Ṭawḳ) vii, 271a; viii, 168b, **393b**; s, 36a
Rahbāniyya viii, **396b**
al-Raḥbī iii, 693b
Raḥbiyyān s, 356a
Rah<u>dj</u> al-<u>gh</u>ār iv, 482b
Raḥḥāl (Nahār al-Ra<u>djdj</u>āl) b. ʿUnfuwa (VIII) vii, 664b
Raḥḥāṣiyya ii, 964a
Rāhib viii, **397a**
al-Rāhib Anbā Buṭrus → al-Sanā al-Rāhib
Rāhib Ḳuray<u>sh</u> → Abū Bakr b. al-Mu<u>gh</u>īra al-Ma<u>kh</u>zūmī
Rāḥil viii, **397a**
Raḥīl viii, **397b**
Raḥīm → Allāh; Basmala; al-Ḳurʾān; Raḥma
Raḥīm Ba<u>kh</u><u>sh</u> ii, 187a
Raḥīm Ḳulī <u>Kh</u>ān s, 46a
Raḥīm Yār <u>Kh</u>ān → Bahāwal <u>Kh</u>ān
Raḥma iv, 488a; viii, **398a**
Raḥma b. <u>Dj</u>ābir (1826) i, 928a; ii, 108b; iv, 751a, 765a; v, 508a, b
Raḥmān → Allāh; Basmala; al-Ḳurʾān; Raḥma
Raḥmān Bābā (XVIII) vii, 328a
Raḥmāniyya i, 371a; ii, 224a; iv, 362b, 993b ; viii, 399a; x, 247b
Raḥmat Allāh, <u>Sh</u>ay<u>kh</u> ii, 54a
Raḥmat Allāh <u>Kh</u>ān ii, 316b
Raḥmat al-Nisāʾ Nawāb Bāʾī i, 913b
Raḥmat ʿAlī <u>Sh</u>āh, Zayn al-ʿĀbidīn (Niʿmat-Allāhī) (1861) viii, 47a, b
Rähmätullä Atäḳoziyew Uy<u>gh</u>un (XX) vi, 770b
Raḥmī, Hüseyin (Ḥusayn) iii, 630a; iv, 284b, 285a, b, 932a; v, 195b
Ramiya of Bagamoyo, <u>Sh</u>ay<u>kh</u> (XX) x, 196a
Rahn viii, 400a
Rahnamā, Zayn al-ʿĀbidīn iv, 166b
Raḥraḥān v, 640a, b; vi, 268a
Rāhu ii, 502a

al-Rāʿī i, 196a; ii, 245a; s, 24b
Rāʿī Čand Pūrbīya → Mēdinī Rāʿī
al-Rāʿī al-Numayrī (714) viii, 120b, 400b
al-Rāʾid al-Tūnusī viii, **401a**
Rāʾiḳ (VII) viii, 402a
Rainder (port) vi, 53b
Raïs (XX) vi, 754a
Raʾīs (chief) iv, 474b; v, 1131b; viii, **402a**
Raʾīs Ahl Naghd → Adjwad b. Zāmil
Raʾīs Ḥāmid i, 928a
Raʾīs al-Kuttāb → Reʾīs ül-Küttāb
Raʾīsiyya ii, 29b; v, 154a
Raʿiyya (Reʿāyā) i, 712a, 999b, 1169b, 1266b; iv, 563a, 564a, 565a, 1096a; v, 262a, 880b; viii, **403b**
Rajāʾ b. Ḥaywa v, 325b
Raja Muda (Penyengat) vi, 237a
Rajputana iv, 922a
Rakʿa viii, 406b
Rakāsh, Banū i, 2b
al-Raḳāshī → Abān b. ʿAbd al-Ḥamīd
Raḳāshīs iv, 734b
Rakhīk, Awlād iv, 637b
Rakhshān (valley) vi, 192b
Raḳīb viii, **406b**
Rāḳid viii, **407a**
al-Raḳīḳ al-Ḳayrawānī → Ibn al-Raḳiḳ
al-Raḳīm → Aṣḥāb al-Kahf
Raḳḳ (Riḳḳ) viii, **407b**
Raḳḳa (ceramic) iv, 1167b, 1168a
al-Raḳḳa i, 11a, 457b, 831b; iii, 1268a; vi, 336a, 378b, 379b, 381b, 428a, b, 599b, 600b, 622b, 733b; viii, 131b, **410a**; s, 36a, 413b
Raḳḳāda i, 24a, 250b, 1346a; ii, 955b; iv, 829a, 830b; vi, 434b, 727b; viii, **414b**; s, 144a
Raḳḳāṣ viii, 415a
al-Raḳḳī → Aḥmad al-Raḳḳī; al-Muḳammiṣ
al-Raḳḳī, Sulaymān b. Djarīr ix, 824a; s, 130a
Rákoczy, George (II) v, 257b, 258a, b
Raḳṣ viii, **415b**
Rām-Hurmuz vi, 198a, b; viii, **416b**; s, 90a
Rām Narāyan ii, 1091b
Rām Rāy i, 1047a; iii, 626a
Rama Čandra iv, 922a, b
Ramad viii, **417a**
Ramaḍān (month) viii, **417b**
Ramaḍān, Saʿīd (XX) iv, 160a
Ramadān Efendi → Bihishtī
Ramaḍān-oghullari̊ i, 182b, 183a, 468b, 790a; ii, 38b; iv, 623a; vii, 271b; viii, **418a**
Ramaḍān-zāde Meḥmed Čelebi Pasha Yeshildje (1571) vi, 70a; viii, **419a**
Rāmadeva, Rādja iv, 419a, b
al-Ramādī (1013) i, 601b; v, 744a, 779a; viii, **419b**
al-Rāmahurmuzī, Abū Muḥammad al-Ḥasan (971) iii, 27a; vi, 821a; vii, 491a; viii, **420b**; x, 934a
Ramal iii, 883a; viii, **421a**
Rāmčandra ii, 179b; s, 366a
Ramdan Aban iv, 362b
Rāmdjird v, 868a
Rāmī Meḥmed Pasha (1707) → Meḥmed Ramī Pasha
Rāmī Tabrīzī, Sharaf al-Dīn (XIV) viii, **422a**
al-Ramīmī (al-Rumaymī), Muḥammad b. Yaḥyā (XI) vi, 577a
Ramiro III (Léon) (X) vi, 431b
Rāmisht → Abu ʾl-Ḳāsim Rāmisht
Raml ii, 220b, 761b; iv, 1128b; v, 943a; viii, 423b
al-Ramla i, 618b, 1030a; ii, 483b, 911a; iii, 287b; v, 326a, 328a, 329a, 799b, 800b; vi, 506a, 652b, 661b, 668a; viii, **423b**; s, 20b, 37a
al-Ramlī, ibn al-Nābulusī (973) s, **686b**
al-Ramlī, Malik (Karaite) iv, 604a
al-Ramlī, Muḥammad b. Aḥmad (1595) iii, 779a; viii, **424b**
al-Rammāl → Aḥmad b. ʿAlī b. Zunbul
Rāmpūr i, 218a; vi, 198b, 611b; vii, 421a; viii, **425b**; s, 73b, 292a, b
Ramy al-Djimār s, **687b**
Ramz viii, **426b**
Ran → Nāẓim Ḥikmet
Rānā Kumbha iii, 418b; iv, 53a; vi, 309b, 1027b
Raʿna Muṣṭafā Efendi (1832) viii, 11a
Rānā Sāngā (Mēwār) (1528) vi, 270a; vii, 314a; viii, 382b, **430b**
Ranbīr Singh iv, 709b; ix 734b
Rančī s, 106b
Rand, Banu ʾl- iv, 415b, 416b, 739b; v, 1181b; x, 646b
Randjit-dēv s, 242a
Randjīt Singh (1839) i, 230b, 432b, 454b, 1020a, 1347b; ii, 47b, 186b, 929a, 1131a;

iii, 336a; iv, 196b, 709b; v, 353b, 599a; viii, 253b: ix, 693b; s, 242a, 332a
Rangīn, Saʿādat Yār Khān (1835) viii, 431a
Rangoon viii, **431a**
Rānikūh vi, 115b
al-Rānīrī, Nūr al-Dīn (Nuruddin) (1666) i, 88a, 742a; iii, 1220a, 1233a, 1234a; vi, 235b, 240a; viii, 294a
al-Ranisūl vi, 221b
Rank viii, **431b**
Rann (river) vi, 50b
Ranthambor vi, 48a, 53a
Rāo Mandalik Čudāsama (Djūnāgarh) (XV) vi, 50b
Rāo Pahār Singh iii, 61b
Rapak viii, **433a**
Raprī vi, 62a
Raʾs viii, **433b**
Raʾs al-ʿĀm viii, **433b**
Raʾs Asīr → Guardafui
Raʾs al-ʿAyn (ʿAyn Warda) i, 789a; iv, 898a; vi, 437b, 539b ; viii, **433b**
Raʾs Burūm vii, 496b
Rāʾs ḍarbat ʿAlī i, 539a; vi, 81a
Raʾs al-Djibāl → Musandam
Raʾs al-Djufayr vi, 358a
Raʾs al-Ḥadd vi, 729a
Raʾs Ḥāfūn vi, 128a
Raʾs Kalbuh vi, 735b
Raʾs al-Khayma i, 928a; iv, 777b; v, 508a, 765a; vi, 38a; viii, **435a**; s, 416b
Raʾs al-Khums → Raʿs al-Rubʿ
Raʾs al-Māʾ vi, 547b
Ras Mkumbuu (Pemba) vi, 370a
Raʾs Musandam viii, **436b**
Raʾs (al-)Tannūra viii, **437b**
Raʾs al-tīn (palace) s, 301a
Raʾs al-Wādī i, 1171b
Rasāʾil → Risāla
Rasāʾil al- Ḥikma ii, 633a
al-Rasʿanī vi, 114a
Raṣāṣ v, 964b, 967a
Rashāʾida, Banū (Rashāyida) iii, 642a; viii, **437b**
Rāshayyā vi, 28a
Rasheed Jahan (XX) vi, 489a
Rashīd (1734) vii, 839a
Rashīd (Rosetta) vii, 69b; viii, **438a**; s, 18a, 120b
al-Rashīd (ʿAbbāsid) (809) → Hārūn al-Rashīd
Rāshid (freedman) (VIII) iii, 1031a
Rashīd, Āl i, 554b, 1313a; ii, 176b, 492b; iii, 1066a; iv, 481b; 717b, 1073a, 1142b; v, 574b; vi, 83b, 985b; viii, **438b**; ix, 904a; s, 3b, 145a, 350a, b
Rāshid, Meḥmed (1735) viii, **441a**
Rāshid, N.M. (1975) viii, **441b**
Rāshid b. ʿAmr al-Djudaydī (675) vi, 967b
Rashīd b. Ḥumayd (ʿAdjmān) (XX) s, 42a
Rāshid b. Iyās b. Muḍārib (685) vii, 522b
al-Rashīd b. Maʾmūn (Almohad) → ʿAbd al-Wāḥid II al-Rashīd
Rāshid b. Maṭar al-Ḳāsimī Raʾs al-Khayma (XVIII) iv, 777b
Rāshid b. Mughāmis (Baṣra) (XVI) iii, 1257a; iv, 764b; s, 234b
Rāshid b. Muḥammad (Mandīl) (XIV) vi, 404b
Rashīd b. al-Naḍr (ʿUmān) (890) iii, 757a
Rāshid b. Saʿīd (ʿUmān) (XI) iii, 653b
Rāshid b. Saʿīd al-Maktum, Shaykh (Dubayy) (XX) s, 418b
al-Rashīd (Mawlāy) b. al-Sharīf (Filālī) (1672) i, 355b; ii, 510a, 819b, 823a; iv, 729b; v, 1191b; vi, 142b, 250a, 595a, 743a; viii, **440a**; s, 223b, 377b
Rashīd ʿAlī al-Gaylānī (al-Djīlānī) 1965) iii, 264a, 521b, 522a, b, 1258b; vi, 616a; viii, 141b, **445a**; ix, 831a; s, 69a
Rashīd Ayyūb (XX) viii, 88a
al-Rāshid bi'llāh, Abū Djaʿfar al-Manṣūr (ʿAbbāsid) (1138) i, 353b; iii, 1255b; viii, **439a**
Rashīd al-Dawla Maḥmūd b. Naṣr (Mirdāsid) (1074) iii, 86a, 790a; v, 924a; vi, 379b, 578a
Rashīd al-Dīn b. Faḍl Allāh → Rashīd al-Dīn Ṭabīb
Rashīd al-Dīn b. Khāḳānī Shirwānī (1175) vi, 608b
Rāshid al-Dīn Sinān b. Salmān b. Muḥammad al-Baṣrī (1193) i, 353b; iv, 206a; vi, 578a, 790a; viii, 134a, **442a**
Rashīd al-Dīn Ṭabīb, Faḍl Allāh (1318) i, 595a, 1011a; ii, 334a, 1043b, 1109b; iii, 57b, 122a, 215b, 1045a, 1089b, 1122b; iv, 31b, 975b, 1035b, 1037a; vi, 15b, 16a, 457a, 481b; viii, 163b, 169a, **443a**; ix, 870a; s, 280b

Rashīd al-Dīn Waṭwāṭ (1177) iv, 62a, 267b; v, 902b; viii, 383b, **444b**, 543a, 971a; ix, 297b; s, 240a
Rāshid Efendi iv, 845a, 874a
Rashīd Khān i, 1124a
Rashīd Karāma b. ʿAbd al-Ḥamīd (Tripoli) x, 216a
Rashīd Muḥammad Pasha → Meḥmed Rashīd Pasha
Rashīd Pasha (Kurdistān) (1837) vi, 541b
Rashīd Pasha, Muṣṭafā → Reshīd Pasha, Muṣṭafā
Rashīd Riḍā, Sayyid Muḥammad (1935) i, 46a, 598a; ii, 170b, 294b, 295b, 451b, 466b; iii, 162b, 520b, 1168b; iv, 142a, b, 143b-149a, 159a, 162b, 775b, 782b, 947a; vi, 360a, b, 361a, 462a, 739b, 897a; vii, 419a, 764b; viii, **446a**, 901a; s, 151a, 248a
Rāshid Rustum s, 224b
Rashīd Yāsimī (1951) viii, 448a
Rashīdī (XI) vi, 276b; s, 65a
al-Rashīdī, Muḥammad Gūlēd s, 279a
al-Rashīdiyya (order) s, 279a
al-Rashīdiyya (al-Djamʿiyya) viii, **448b**; x, 249a
Rāshidūn iii, 1164a, 1168b; iv, 937b; vi, 875b; s, 528b
Rashmaya vi, 712a
Rasht ii, 1111a; iv, 7b, 631a; viii, **449b**; s, 91b
Rasht, treaty of (1732) viii, 771b
Rashtī, Ḥabīb Allāh s, 76a
Rashtī, Sayyid Kāẓim (1844) viii, **450b**; ix, 404a
Rāshṭrakūṭa → Balharā
Rashwa iii, 343b; viii, **451a**
Rāsim, Aḥmad → Aḥmad Rāsim
Raslān, Banū vi, 791b
Rasm viii, **451b**
Rasmī → Aḥmad Rasmī
al-Rass (Araxes) i, 252a, 634b; v, 397a, 441b; vi, 200b, 201a, b, 504a; viii, **453a**; s, 116a, 274b
al-Rass → Aṣḥāb al-Rass
al-Rassī, al-Ḳāsim b. Ibrāhīm (Zaydī) (860) viii, **453b**
Rassids i, 403a; vi, 436b; viii, **454b**; ix, 507a
Rasūb (sword) vi, 374a
Rasūl v, 423b; viii, **454b**
Rasūlids i, 552b, 553a, 803b; iv, 1188b; v, 895b, 1241a; vi, 81b, 433b, 434a; vii, 996a; viii, **455a**; x, 118a; s, 338a, 387b
Ratan, Bābā Ḥādjdjī i, 1194b; vii, 258b; viii, **457b**
Ratan Nāth Sarshār (1903) x, 879a
Ratanpūr vi, 53a
Raṭhors i, 769a; ii, 567a; iv, 93a; vi, 53a; s, 55b, 420b; viii, 381b
Rātib viii, **459a**
Raṭl → Makāyil
Raʾūf, Muḥammad → Muḥammad Raʾūf
Rauf Bey i, 836b; ii, 6b
Raʾūf Pasha iii, 4b; v, 36b
Ravi s, 63a, 242a
Ravza → Khuldābād
Rawāfiḍ (see also, *s.v.* al-Rāfiḍa) i, 257b, 864a; ii, 605a; viii, 386b
Rawāḥa, Banū viii, **459a**
Rāwal Djay Singh (Čāmpāner) (XV) vi, 51a
Rāwal Rāy Singh (Djaysalmēr) (XVIII) ii, 186a
Rāwalpindi viii, 460a
Rāwalpindi (treaty) (1919) s, 66a
Rawān iv, 732b
Rāwandān i, 239a; viii, **460a**
al-Rawandī, ʿAbd Allāh (VIII) iv, 837b; viii, 461a
al-Rawandī, Abu 'l-Ḥusayn (864) viii, 95a
al-Rāwandī, Abū Hurayra (VIII) iv, 838a; viii, 461b
al-Rāwandī, Ḥarb b. ʿAbd Allāh (764) viii, 461a
al-Rāwandī, Maḥmūd b. Muḥammad iv, 1074a
Rāwandī, Muḥammad b. ʿAlī (XIII) vi, 275b; viii, **460b**
Rāwandiyya i, 15b, 17b; iv, 45b, 837b; vi, 345a, 428a, b, 744b, 853a; viii, **461a**
Rawāndiz viii, **463a**
Rāwar vi, 493b
Rawḍa (Khuldābād) vi, 126a
al-Rawḍa (Roda, island) i, 944b; iv, 424b, 430a; vii, 147a, 148a; viii, **463b**; s, 120b
Rawḍa-Khʷānī viii, 465a
Rawḍakhʷān iv, 50b
Rawḥ b. Ḥātim b. Ḳabīṣa b. al-Muhallab (791) iii, 655a; v, 69b; vii, 360a; viii, **465b**, 996b

Rawḥ b. Zinbāʿ al-Djudhāmī (703) i, 436a, 1242b; ii, 360b, 573b; iii, 270b, 1175b; vi, 622a; vii, 694a; viii, **466a**
Rāwī (reciter) i, 566b, 584b; iv, 735a; viii, **466b**
Rawī (rhyme letter) iv, 412a, 413a
Rāwīnī s, 83a
Rawḳ iii, 99a, 863a, 1090a; iv, 557b; viii, **467b**
Rāwnīr s, 83a
al-Rawshan i, 1239b
Rawshaniyya i, 1123b; vi, 342b; vii, 220a; viii, **468a**
Rawther v, 582a; viii, **469a**
al-Rawwād b. al-Muthannā (VIII) viii, 469b
al-Rawwād al-Azdī (Ādharbāydjān) (IX) vi, 499b; x, 42a
al-Rawwād, Abū Manṣūr b. Muḥammad al-Amīr (Tabrīz) (XI) x, 42b
Rawwādids (Banū Rawwād) (XI) i, 190a, 300a, 638a; iv, 346a; vi, 499b; vii, 656b; viii, **469b**; x, 42b
Raʾy s, **687b**
Ray → Rayy
Ray Čand Pūrbiya (Raʾī Cand Pūrbīya) vi, 54b, 407a
Rāya → Liwāʿ
Rāyčūr iii, 425a, b; vi, 368b, 369a; vii, 289a; viii, **470a**
Rayda (Rīda) viii, **470a**
Raydan (Ḥimyar) viii, 664a
Raydān al-Saḳlabī i, 1042a; iv, 1091b
al-Raydāniyya iii, 184b; vi, 325a; ix, 630b; x, 622a
Raydūn iii, 31a
Rayḥān, ʿImād al-Dīn (XIII) ii, 609b, 1084a; vi, 47b, 48a, b
Rayḥān, Muʾayyid al-Dīn (atabeg) (XII) v, 159a, 160a; viii, 946a
Rayḥāna v, 436b
al-Rayḥānī, Amīn (1940) i, 597a; v, 1254b, 1255b, 1256b; vi, 113b, 614b; viii, **470b**
Rāyin s, 327a
Raymānites vi, 80b
Raymond II of Tripoli s, 204b
Raymond Lull (1315) vii, 737b
Raymond Martin (1286) vii, 737b
Rayna vi, 511b, 744b
Raypūr vi, 53a
Raysūt vi, 83b; vii, 53a; viii, 914b
Rayṭa (ʿAbbāsid) (VIII) i, 107b; iv, 1164a
Rayṭa bint Abi 'l-ʿAbbās al-Saffāḥ (VIII) vi, 139b
al-Rayy i, 125b, 1356a; ii, 127a, 190a, 191a, 192b, 746a; iii, 219b, 287a; iv, 465b, 1167a; v, 661b, 662a, 1028b, 1137b, 1238a; vi, 14b, 64a, b, 66a, 115b, 117b, 120a, 198b, 199a, 273a, 332a, b, 333a, 340a, 428a, 500a, b, 522b, 524a, 539a, 600b, 627b, 633b, 744b, 745a; viii, **471a**; s, 13a, 15a, 23b, 32a, 33a, 56b, 72b, 118b, 236a, 297b, 309a, 356b, 357a, 416a, 423b
Rayya (Reyyo) vi, 221b, 222a; viii, **473b**
Rayyān b. al-Aslaʿ s, 178b
al-Rayyān b. al-Walīd ii, 917b
Razgrad → Hezārghrad
al-Rāzī → Fakhr al-Dīn al-Rāzī
al-Rāzī, ʿAbd al-Raḥmān Ibn Abī Ḥātim (938) ii, 462a; viii, 516b
al-Rāzī, Abū Bakr Aḥmad b. Muḥammad (955) xi, 151a
al-Rāzī, Abū Bakr Muḥammad b. Zakariyyāʿ (935) i, 112a, 125b, 213b, 235a, 327b, 328a, 344b, 381a, 387b, 486a, 589b, 1223b, 1224a, 1340b; ii, 359a, 780b, 1068a; iii, 328b, 944b; iv, 329b, 847a; v, 112a, 167b; vi, 204b, 247a, 347a, 449a, 616b, 629a; vii, 196b; viii, 123a, **474a**; x, 453a; s, 14a, 52b, 271b, 314a, 392b
al-Rāzī, Abū Ḥātim Muḥammad b. Idrīs (890) viii, 516b, 998a
al-Rāzī, Abu 'l-Ḥusayn (958) vi, 353a
al-Rāzī, Abū Zurʿa ʿUbayd Allāh b. ʿAbd al-Karīm (878) viii, 516a
al-Rāzī, Aḥmad b. ʿAbd Allāh (1068) viii, **477b**, 518a
al-Rāzī, Aḥmad b. ʿAbd Allāh b. Ḥumayd (862) x, 11a
al-Rāzī, Aḥmad b. Muḥammad b. Mūsā (955) i, 156b, 488a, b, 489b, 600b; iii, 771b; iv, 718a; x, 585b
Rāzī, Amīn Aḥmad (XVII) viii, **478a**
Rāzī, Djamāl al-Dīn Abu 'l-Futūḥ Khuzāʿī (XII) viii, 541a
al-Rāzī, Ibn al-Muʿaẓẓam (XIII) vi, 111b
Rāzī, Ḳuṭb al-Dīn (1364) ii, 774a; viii, 514a, b
Rāzī, Mīr ʿAskar ʿĀdil Khān (1696) vii, 1006a

al-Rāzī, Muḥammad b. Muḳātil (841) vi, 846a
Rāzī, Nadjm al-Dīn "Dāya" (1256) → Nadjm al-Dīn Rāzī
Razīḳ (canal) vi, 619a, b
Razīn, Banū viii, **478b**; ix, 307a; s, 80b
Razīn b. Muʿāwiya al-Saraḳusṭī, Abu 'l-Ḥasan (1129/1140) viii, **479a**
Razmak (town) xi, 198b; s, 285a
Razmārā, General Ḥādjdjī ʿAlī (1951) ii, 882b; iv, 41a; vii, 447a
Rbīʿā → Rabīʿ
Reʿāyā → Raʿiyya
Reconquista i, 494a, 495a, 496a; v, 367b
Red Sea → Baḥr al-Ḳulzum
Redīf → Radīf
Redīf Pasha (Yemen) (XIX) vii, 525a
Redjāʾī-zāde Aḥmed Djewdet (XIX) vii, 532a
Redjāʾī-zāde Maḥmūd Ekrem → Ekrem Bey
Redjāʾī-zāde Meḥmed Djelāl Bey (1882) viii, **480a**
Redjeb Pasha, Topal (1632) iii, 252a; vii, 598a; viii, **480a**
Refet Pasha i, 836b; iv, 636a
Refīʿ Djewād iv, 873b
Refiʿī (XV) viii, 8a, **480b**
Refīḳ Khālid Ḳaray → Karay, Refiḳ Khālid
Reg viii, **481a**
Rehanina → Raḥāmina
Reʾīs Efendi Rāmī (XVIII) vii, 708a
Reʾīs ül-Küttāb (Reʾīs Efendi) viii, **481b**
Reji iv, 930b
Relizane (region) iii, 298a; vi, 249b; vii, 186b
Rembau (Rumbow) viii, **483b**
Remmāl Khʷādja (XVI) viii, 833a
Republic, Arabic, Union → al-Djumhūriyya al-ʿarabiyya al-muttaḥida
Rēr Faḳīh → Muḳrī
Rēr Shēkh → ʿAḳabī
Resava vi, 70b
Reshād Nūrī (Reşad Nuri Güntekin) (1956) v, 196b; viii, **483b**; s, 96a
Reshīd → Rashīd
Reshīd Efendi (XIX) vi, 372b
Reshīd Pasha, Muṣṭafā (1858) i, 284b, 309b, 396b, 397b, 505b, 1089b; ii, 693a, 934b; iii, 592a, 993a; v, 36a, b; vi, 68a, b, 285a, b; vii, 468b, 532a, 720a; viii, 59a, 484b, 726b; ix, 443a; s, 168a
Resht → Rasht
Resm viii, **486a**
Resmī Efendī Aḥmad → Aḥmad Rasmī
Rewān (Eriwān) i, 8a, 640a, 643a, 644a, 645a, b; vi, 202b; viii, **487a**; s, 365a
Rewān Ḳaṣr vi, 55b, 56b
Rēwand b. Bēwarāsp Adjdahāk (al-Mawṣil) vi, 899b
Rewānī (1524) viii, 489b
Rey Lobo → Ibn Mardanīsh
Reyes de Taifas → Mulūk al-Ṭawāʾif
Rezā Shāh → Muḥammad Riḍā Shāh Pahlawī
Rezzou → Ghazw
Rḥama b. Djābir b. ʿAdhbī (Djalāhima) x, 956b
Rḥāmma, Banū vi, 590b, 595b
Rhodes → Rodos
Rhodope vi, 89a; vi, 1022a
Riau Archipelago vi, 208a, 236b, 237a, 239a; viii, **490b**
Riʿāyat Shāh → ʿAlāʾ al-Dīn
Ribā i, 693b, 1111b, 1112b; iv, 691b
Ribā b. in modern commercial usage s, **690b**
al-Ribāb (Ḳayna) s, 247a
Ribāṭ i, 5a, 248b, 901b, 1023b; ii, 36a, 71b, 539b; iii, 499a; iv, 380b, 434a, 677a, 1026a; v, 856a, 1129b, 1150a, 1200b; vi, 359a; viii, **493b**
Ribāṭ al-Fatḥ (Rabat) i, 34b, 35a, 79b, 832b, 1225a, 1226b, 1228a, 1320b; iii, 143b, 499a; v, 504b, 1245b; vi, 39a, 40a, 142b, 293b, 294a, 364a, 521a, 597a; viii, **506b**; s, 144b, 223b
– university ii, 425b
Ribāṭ Sayyidī Shikar (Tansift) vi, 743b
Ribāṭ-i Sharaf vi, 691b; viii, **508b**
Riḍāʿ → Raḍāʿ
Riḍā (mysticism) viii, **509a**
Riḍā, Meḥmed b. Meḥmed (1671) viii, **509b**
Riḍā ʿAbbāsī (artist) (XVII) i, 1213b, viii, **509b**, 788a
Riḍā Čelebi (XVII) vii, 472b
Riḍā al-Dīn b. Ḳawām al-Dīn al-Marʿashī (XIV) vi, 511b, 512a, b, 513a, 515b, 516b

Riḍā al-Dīn Abu 'l-Maʿālī (XIII) vi, 790b
Riḍā Khān → Riḍā Shāh Pahlawī
Riḍā Kirmānī, Mīrzā (XIX) s, 53b
Riḍā Kiyā, Sayyid (Gīlān) (XV) vi, 513a
Riḍā Ḳulī b. Nādir Shāh (Afshārid) (1747) v, 103a
Riḍā Ḳulī Khān b. Muḥammad Hādī (1871) iv, 70a, 526b, 1065a; vii, 530a; viii, **510a**; ix, 658a; s, 46b
Riḍā Ḳulī Khān Ḳādjār (XVIII) iv, 391a; v, 663b
Riḍā Ḳulī Mīrzā b. Ḥusayn ʿAlī Mīrzā Farmān-Farma (XIX) iv, 393a; s, 290b
Riḍā (Rizā) Nūr (1942) iii, 595a; iv, 113a, 791b, 872b; viii, **511a**
Riḍā Shāh (Pahlawī) (1941) i, 5b, 190b, 720b, 978a, b, 1014a; ii, 445b, 514b, 654a, 903a, 1112a; iii, 528b, 1110a, 1193a; iv, 40a, b, 52a, 398b, 789b, 1172a; v, 826a, 920a, 1042b, 1095a, b; vi, 203a, 486a, b; vii, 223a, 299b, 447a, 654a; viii, 511a; s, 84a, 91b, 110a, 207b, 342b
Rḯḍā Tewfīḳ → Bölük-bashi̊, Rḯḍā Tewfīḳ
Riḍāʾī, Āḳā (XVII) viii, **514a**
Riḍāʾiyya (Rezaiyyeh) → Urumiyya
al-Ridda s, **692b**
Riḍiyya → Raḍiyyat al-Dunyā bint Iltutmish
Ridjāl iv, 711b; viii, **514b**
Ridjāl al-ghayb i, 94b, 772a; ii, 1025b
Riḍwān (angel) ii, 846a, b
Riḍwān (ḥādjib) (1359) iii, 836a; vii, 1023b, 1024a
Riḍwān (Paradis) viii, 519a
Riḍwān b. Muḥammad al-Sāʿātī (XIII) viii, 654b; s, 371b, 372b
Riḍwān (Ruḍwān) b. Tutush (Saldjūḳ, Aleppo) (1113) i, 664a, 1052a; ii, 169b, 282a; iii, 86b, 398b; v, 921b, 924a, b; vi, 380a, 546b; vii, 725b; viii, **519a**, 947a; x, 167b, 600a
Riḍwān b. Walakhashī (vizier) (XII) i, 939b; ii, 858a, b; iii, 55a; iv, 137a; v, 627b; viii, 831b; ix, 372b
Riḍwān Bannigash (Banegas) vii, 1026a; s, 399a
Riḍwān (Rizvān) Begovič, ʿAlī Pasha (1851) i, 1268b; vii, 244b; viii, **519b**
Riḍwān Bey (amīr al-ḥadjdj) (Miṣr) (1656) ii, 233a; iv, 723a; vi, 325a; vii, 178b
Riḍwān Kāhya al-Djulfī iv, 852b
Riḍwān Pasha (1585) viii, **521a**
Rīf i, 749b, 859b; ii, 820b; iii, 499b; v, 1184b, 1185b, 1194a; vi, 356a, 361a; viii, 440b, **521b**; s, 191a, 377b
Rifāʿa, Banū vi, 649a
Rifāʿa Bey al-Ṭahṭāwī (1873) i, 571b, 596b, 755a; ii, 641b, 801a; iii, 590b; iv, 1155a; v, 907b, 908a, b, 909a; vi, 725a, b; vii, 427a, 901b, 902a, b, 915b; viii, **523b**
Rifāda i, 9a, 80a
al-Rifāʿī, Abu 'l-ʿAbbās Aḥmad b. ʿAlī (1183) vi, 354b, 463a; viii, **524b**
al-Rifāʿī, Aḥmad b. Sulaymān (1291) vii, 11a
Rifāʿiyya i, 281a; ii, 16a, 164b, 1134a; iii, 122b, 291a, 952a; vi, 88a; viii, 340b, **525b**; x, 252a
Rifat, Oktay iv, 545a
Rifʿat, Ṣādiḳ → Ṣādiḳ Rifʿat Pasha
al-Rīfī → Aḥmad al-Rīfī
Rīgha, Banū v, 1181a, b
Rīgistān i, 1294b
Rīḥ (wind) viii, **526b**
Rīḥā (Aleppo) viii, **527b**
Rīḥā (Jericho) viii, **527a**
al-Rīḥānī, Amīn → al-Rayḥānī
Riḥla viii, **528a**
al-Rijeby, Mādjid b. Djābir (1808) vii, 227a
Rikʿa → Khaṭṭ
Rikāb (stirrup) viii, **528b**
Rikābdār (Rikībdār) viii, **529b**
Riḳḳ → Raḳḳ
Rimāya → Ḳaws
Rimm (Druze) s, 135b
Rinčana s, 156a
Rind viii, **531a**
Rinds, Banū i, 1005b; s, 332a
Risāla viii, **532a**
Rīshahr (battle, 637) i, 1341a; ix, 311a
Rishīs i, 1031a; s, 114b
Rissani x, 82b
Riwāḳ (Ruwāḳ) viii, **544b**
Riwāya viii, **545b**
Riyāʾ (Riʾāʾ) viii, **547a**
al-Riyāḍ i, 628b, 1231a; ii, 425a, 569b; iv, 1073a; vi, 33a, 34b, 151a, 152b; viii, **547b**; ix, 904a; s, 3b
Riyāḍ al-ʿArūs (Marrākush) ii, 527b; vi, 597b

Riyāḍ Pasha (Miṣr) (XIX) vii, 184b
Riyāḍ al-Ṣulḥ (Lubnān) (XX) v, 787b, 794b
Riyāḍī (Mollā Meḥmed) (1644) viii, **548b**
al-Riyāḍiyyāt (al-Riyāḍa) viii, **549b**
Riyāfa viii, **562a**
Riyāḥ, Banū i, 161b, 533a; ii, 463b; iii, 66b, 137b, 386a; iv, 337a; v, 48b; vi, 728b, 741b; viii, **562b**
Riyāḥ b. ʿUthmān b. Ḥayyān al-Murrī (VIII) vii, 388b, 629b
al-Riyāḥī → Abu ʾl-Hindī; Maʿḳil b. Ḳays
al-Riyāḥī, Muḥammad b. Yaḥyā i, 600a
Riyāḥiyya iv, 837a
Riyāl viii, **563b**
Riyāla (Bey) viii, **564a**
Riyām, Banū vi, 82b; viii, **566a**
al-Riyāshī, Abu ʾl-Faradj (871) vii, 279b, 281a; ix, 652b
Rizā → Riḍā
al-Rizaḳ al-aḥbāsiyya ii, 148b
Rizām b. Sābiḳ iv, 838a
Rizāmiyya v, 63b
Rizayḳāt Baḳḳāra i, 929a, 962a; ii, 122a, 123b
Rize ii, 62a; viii, **566b**
Rizḳ i, 204b; viii, **567b**
Rizḳ Allāh Ḥassūn → Ḥassūn
Rizwan → Riḍwān
Rōb (Ar. Ruʿb; Hindūkush) s, 426b
Rodos i, 293a, 935b, 945b, 1250b; ii, 6a; iv, 1169b; v, 506b; viii, **568b**; s, 222a
Rodosto → Tekirdagh
Roem, Mohammed (XX) vi, 731b, 732b
Roger II (Sicily) i, 79a; ii, 585a, 855a; iii, 1032b; iv, 337b, 651a; v, 1246b; ix, 585b
Rōh viii, **571a**; s, 1b
Rohilkhand i, 218a; iv, 749b; viii, **571a**
Rohillas (Rohilas) i, 253a, 856a, 953b, 1042b, 1206a; iii, 59b, 61b, 427b; viii, 426a, **572b**
Rohtak v, 1258a; vi, 49a, 50a; s, **695a**
Rōhtās ii, 1091b; iii, 449a; vi, 343a; viii, **573a**
Rōhtāsgarh viii, **573a**
Romanus IV Diogenes (XI) vi, 242b, 243a
Rome → Rūmiya
Ronda → Runda
Rosetta → Rashīd
Rōshān, Pīr Bāyezīd i, 853b, 854a; vii, 220a
Roshānārā (1671) vii, 333b
Rōshānī i, 225a
Rōshāniyya → Rawshaniyya
Rostom (Kay Khusraw, Georgia) (1658) v, 493b; x, 479b
Rotulla dynasty (Prizren) viii, 339b
Rouiched vi, 754a
Rouzathul-Uloom (Feroke, Mappila) vi, 462a
Roxelana → Khurrem Sulṭān
Rozagī → Rūzagī
al-Ruʾāsī i, 105b; ii, 806b; vii, 280a
al-Ruʾāsī, Muḥammad b. Abī Sāra al-Nahwī (VIII) viii, **573a**
al-Ruʾāsī, ʿUthmān b. ʿĪsā al-ʿĀmirī (IX) vii, 647b
al-Ruʿaynī, Abu Djaʿfar (1377) s, **695a**
al-Ruʿaynī, Abu ʾl-Ḥasan al-Ishbīlī (1267) ii, 743b; iv, 468a; viii, **573b**
Rubʿ viii, **574a**
al-Rubʿ al-Khālī i, 537a, b, 539a, 759b, 1231a; vi, 371b; viii, **575b**
Ruʿba b. ʿAdjdjādj al-Tamīmī (762) i, 142a, 207b, 1154b; iii, 73a, 573b, 1262a; vii, 208b, 546a; viii, 377a, 577a; s, 31b, 286b
Rubāʿī (pl. Rubāʿiyyāt) i, 677a; iv, 58a, 62a; v, 166a; viii, **578b**
Rūbandj vi, 937b
Rubāṭ I (Sinnār) (1644) ix, 650b
Rubayyiʿ b. Zayd ii, 176b; v, 62b
Rubenids i, 182a, 466a, 639a, 790a
Rubghūzī → Rabghūzī
al-Ruburtayr (Reverter) (1145) i, 78b, 390a
Rūdakī, Abū ʿAbd Allāh Djaʿfar (940) i, 1216a; iv, 53a, 60b, 63a, 504b, 773b; v, 956a; vi, 276a, 609a, b; viii, 76a, **585a**; s, 35a
al-Rudānī (1693) vi, 264a
Rudawlawī, Aḥmad ʿAbd al-Ḥaḳḳ s, 312b, 313a
Rudawlī ii, 54b; s, 293a, 312b
Rudaynī, Banū x, 42a
Rūdhbār (Rūdbār) iii, 254a; iv, 859b; v, 149a, b, 247a; vi, 493b; viii, **586a**
al-Rūdh(a)bārī (X) vii, 164a
Rūdhrāwar viii, **586b**
Rūdhrawārī, Abū Shudjāʿ Muḥammad b. al-Ḥusayn (1095) ii, 384b; iii, 258b; vii, 294a; viii, 70b, **586b**; s, 398a
Rūd-i Shahr s, 97a

Rūdisar → Hawsam
Rūdj vi, 578b
Rūdjū' viii, **587a**
Ruḍwān → Riḍwān
Rufā'a x, 96b
Rūfus al-Afsīsī viii, **588a**
Rufus of Ephesus → Rūfus al-Afsīsī
Rūḥ → Nafs
Rūḥ Allāh → Khumaynī, Āyatollāh / Nafs I.B.
Rūḥ al-Amīn Khān al-'Uthmānī i, 1219a
al-Ruhā (al-Ruhā') i, 466a, 639b, 1054a; ii, 63b, 347b; vi, 243b, 378b, 379b, 381b, 507b, 626b; viii, 127b, **589a**
al-Ruhā Edessa xi, 180b, 452a
Rūhānī → Amīr Rūḥānī
Rūḥānī (XX) iv, 71b
Rūḥāniyya viii, **593b**
Rūḥī (1511) iii, 91b; viii, **594a**
Rūḥī, Shaykh Aḥmad (XIX) s, 53a
Rūhī Fāḍil Efendi (1528) viii, 594a
Rūhiyyè Khānum (Mary Maxwell, XX) i, 916a
Ruhmī viii, **594b**
al-Ruhūnī, Muḥammad (1815) vi, 356b
al-Ruḳabā' → Abdāl
Ruḳayya bint Hāshim b. 'Abd Manāf i, 80a
Ruḳayya bint Muḥammad (624) i, 136b; ii, 845a; viii, **594b**
Ruḳayya Bēgam bint Mīrzā Hindāl (1626) iii, 456a
Rukhām s, **695b**
al-Rukhkh viii, **595a**
al-Rukhkhadj i, 86a; viii, **595a**
al-Rukhkhadjī, Abu 'l-Faradj (IX) viii, 595b
al-Rukhkhadjī, Mu'ayyid al-Mulk (XI) viii, 595b
Rukhṣa viii, **595b**
Rukhṣatī s, 91b
al-Ruḳ'ī, al-Ḥādjdj al-Khayyāṭ (1703) s, 403b, 404a
Rukn (pl. arkān) viii, **596b**
Rukn al-Dawla, Atabeg (Fārs) s, 382b
Rukn al-Dawla, Abū 'Alī al-Ḥasan b. Būya (Buwayhid) (976) i, 211b, 419a, 955a; ii, 178b, 680a, 928a; iii, 258a, 703a, 704a, 1157a; iv, 23a, b, 100b, 859b; v, 452b; vi, 499b, 539a, 600b; vii, 656b, 777a; viii, **597b**; s, 36b, 259a
Rukn al-Dawla Khān → I'tiḳād Khān
Rukn al-Dīn → Ḳïlïdj Arslan IV
Rukn al-Dīn b. 'Abd al-Ḳādir al-Djīlī iii, 751b
Rukn al-Dīn b. Burāḳ (Kutlugh- Khānid) i, 1311b; v, 161b, 162a, 553b
Rukn al-Dīn b. Ēlam Khān (Dihli) (XIII) vii, 193b
Rukn al-Dīn Aḥmadīlī i, 300b
Rukn al-Dīn 'Alā' al-Dawla → 'Alā' al-Dawla al-Simnānī
Rukn al-Dīn Bārbak b. Maḥmūd I (Bengal) (1474) vi, 46b; viii, **598b**
Rukn al-Dīn Čanda ii, 1077a
Rukn al-Dīn al-Iṣfahānī ii, 125b
Rukn al-Dīn Kart (1283) iv, 536b, 672a
Rukn al-Dīn Khur-Shāh (Nizārī) (1257) i, 354a; ii, 606a; iv, 201b; vi, 918a; viii, **598b**
Rukn al-Dīn Kilidj Arslān → Kilidj Arslān IV
Rukn al-Dīn Mas'ūd I b. Ḳïlïč Arslan I (Rūm Saldjūḳ) (1156) viii, 128a
Rukn al-Dīn Mawdūd, shaykh ii, 54a
Rukn al-Dīn Sām b. Lankar iv, 466b
Rukn al-Dīn al-Samarḳandī → al-'Amīdī
Rukn al-Dīn Sulaymān II Shāh (Rūm Saldjūḳ) (1204) i, 431b, 510a; iv, 575b, 816a; vi, 632a
Rukn al-Dīn Ṭughrïl II → Ṭughrïl II, Rukn al-Dīn
Rukn al-Dīn Ṭughrïl III → Ṭughrïl III b. Arslān Rukn al-Dīn
Rukn al-Dīn Yūsuf → Yūsuf Shāh II
Ruknā Masīḥ al-Kāshānī (1655) iv, 1128a; viii, 776a, 851a
Ruknābād (Āb-i Ruknī) viii, **599b**
al-Ruknī, 'Alā' al-Dīn Aydughdī, Amīr (XIII) iv, 960a
Ruḳya viii, **600a**
Rūm i, 18a, 54b, 76b, 77a, 83a, 121b, 182b, 346a, 420b, 465b, 468a, 470a, 517a, 637b, 638b, 639a, 679b, 789b, 1128a, 1319a; ii, 14a, 81a, 345a, 347b, 456a, 712a, 853a; iii, 77a, 128b, 129b, 233b, 271a, 344b, 1046a, 1083b, 1089a; iv, 175a, 839a; v, 104a, b, 124b; vi, 97a, 316b, 379b; viii, **601a**
Rūm Ḳal'esī (Ḳal'at al-Rūm) vi, 322b; viii, **606b**
Rūm Meḥmed Pasha (XV) → Meḥmed Rūm(ī) Pasha
Rūm Saldjūks → Saldjūks

Rūma → Rūmiya
Rumania ii, 688a, b
Rūmeli i, 97a, 396a, 398a, b, 469a, 697b, 998b, 1160a, 1304b; ii, 83a, 443a, 722a; iv, 232b; v, 261a, 881a; vi, 89a, 372a; viii, 606a, **607b**; s, 268b
Rumeli Ḥiṣārī i, 1251b, 1318a; iii, 483a; viii, 611b
Rumeli Kavaghī i, 481a, 1252a
Rūmeli Pāyeli Ibrāhīm Efendi (XVIIII) vi, 55a
Rumelia → Rūmeli
Rūmī viii, **612a**
al-Rūmī → Ashraf; Djalāl al-Dīn; Ḳusṭūs
Rūmī Khān i, 1062a, 1068b; iii,482a
Rūmiya (Rome) iv, 274b, 275a; v, 945a, b; viii, 612b
Rūmlū, Banū iii, 1101b
Rūmlū, Nūr ʿAlī Khalīfa (XVI) viii, 768a
Rumman, Banū i, 1246b
al-Rummānī, Abu 'l-Ḥasan ʿAlī b. ʿĪsā (994) i, 126b, 858a, 1115b; iii, 1020a; iv, 249a; v, 242b, 426b; vii, 312a, 914a; viii, **614a**; ix, 317b; s, 13a, 27b, 362b
Rūna s, 21a
Runda i, 6a, 11b; vii, 1022a, b; viii, **615b**
al-Rundī → Ibn al-Ḥakīm
al-Rundī, Abū Khālid Yazīd (1091) viii, 617b
Rūnī, Abu 'l-Faradj → Abu 'l-Faradj b. Masʿūd Rūnī
Rūpiyya (rupee) ii, 121a; viii, **618a**
Rūpmātī i, 1155a; vi, 407a, b
Rūs i, 4a, 625b, 738b, 836a; iii, 759a; iv, 346b, 347a, 348b, 1175b, 1176a; v, 1120a, b, 1121b; viii, **618b**; ix, 169a
al-Ruṣāfa viii, **629b**
al-Ruṣāfa (al-ʿAbbāsiyya) i, 24a, 1320a
al-Ruṣāfa (al-Andalus) vi, 431a; viii, 631b
al-Ruṣāfa (Baghdād) i, 897a, b, 898b, 901a, 902b; viii, 629b; s, 193b, 386a, 400b
Ruṣāfa (al-Nuʿmān) vi, 378a, 624a; s, 117a
al-Ruṣāfa (Syria) vi, 378a, 624a; viii, **630a**; s, 117a
al-Ruṣāfī, Abū ʿAbd Allāh Muḥammad b. Ghālib (1177) i, 602a; vi, 111a; viii, 632b, 633a
al-Ruṣāfī, Maʿrūf → Maʿrūf al-Ruṣāfī
Rusčuk (Ruse) viii, **633b**
Rūshanī, Dede ʿUmar (1487) s, **696b**
al-Rushāṭī, Abū Muḥammad (1147) viii, **635a**
Rushayd b. Kāmil b. Djāmiʿ iv, 337a, b
Rushayd al-Daḥdāḥ ii, 795b
Rushdī, Fāṭima (XX) vi, 750b
Rushdī Malḥaṣ (XX) vi, 176b
Rushdī Pāshā → ʿAbd al-Raḥmān; Ḥusayn Rushdī Pasha; Shirwānī-zāde
Rüshdiyye i, 285b, 1272a; v, 904a, b, 905a
Russians → Rūs
Russo-Persian Wars x, 48a
Russo-Turkish wars (1769-1774) i, 4b, 294b, 948a; iii, 193a, 253a
– (1877-1878) ii, 88b, 613b; iii, 993a
Rustāḳ viii, **636a**
al-Rustāḳ (ʿUmān) iv, 1085a; viii, **636a**; s, 355b
Rustaḳubādh i, 711b
Rustam (Shāh-nāma) iii, 113a, 114a, 153b; iv, 809a,b, 813a; viii, **636b**
Rustam I, Shāh Ghāzī (Bāwandid), (Ispahbadiyya) (1163) v, 662a; vi, 938b
Rustam II (Bāwandid), Kāʾūsiyya b. Sharwīn II (980) s, 309a
Rustam II, Shams al-Mulūk Shāh Ghāzī (Bāwandid), (Ispahbadiyya) (1209) i, 1110a; iii, 810a; vi, 938b
Rustam b. Bahram b. Shāh Ismāʿīl I, Mīrzā (Ṣafawid) (1641) vii, 129b
Rustam b. Farrukh Hurmuzd (637) viii, **638a**
Rustam b. Maḳṣūd (Aḳ Ḳoyunlu) (1497) i, 312a; iv, 186b, 387a, b; viii, 766b
Rustam b. Nūr al-Dīn Khurshīdī (Luristān) (XIII) v, 828a
Rustam Khān (Ḳaytaḳ) → Rustum Khān
Rustam Khān, Mīr (Khayrpūr) (XVIII) i, 1192b
Rustam Khān b. Karagözlu (XIX) vii, 453a
Rustamdār iv, 808a; v, 663a, b; vi, 511a, b, 512a, b, 513a, b, 514a, b, 515a; viii, 650b
Rustamdārī, Banū vi, 515b
Rustamdārī, Ḥusayn ʿAḳīlī (1571) vi, 908b
al-Rustamī, Ḥusayn b. ʿAmr (IX) vii, 215a
Rustamids (Rustumids) i, 83a, 167a, 445b; ii, 141a, 145b, 852b; iii, 655a, 658b, 924b; vi, 452b; viii, **638a**; x, 99b
Rüstem Pasha (1561) i, 291b, 1279b; ii, 685a; iii, 147b; iv, 232a; v, 35b, 67a; vi, 228b; vii, 6b, 713a, 720b; viii, 202b, **640b**
al-Rustughfanī, Abu 'l-Ḥasan (X) vi, 846a

Rustum and Isfandiyār s, 91a
Rustum (Ḳādisiyya) ii, 893b; iii, 195a, 1254b; iv, 385b
Rustum-Khān (Ḳaytaḳ) (XVII) ii, 87b; iv, 846b; vii, 601b
Rusudan (Queen, Georgia) (1247) v, 490b; x, 555a
Rusūkhī, Ismāʿīl s, 83a
Ruswā, Mirzā Muḥammad Hādī (1931) v, 203b, 1106b; viii, **641b**; ix, 161a; x, 879b
Ruṭaynā iv, 679b
Rutbīl → Zunbīl
Rutul (Dāghistān) viii, **642b**
Ruwād → Arwād
Ruwāla, Banū i, 483a, 873b, 1093b; ii, 492b; iii, 1018a; vi, 46a, 490b; viii, **643a**
Ruwāndiz → Rawāndiz
Ruwaydjān vi, 384a
Ruwaym (910) iii, 823b; vi, 570a; x, 377a
Ruʾyā iii, 600a; iv, 259b, 260a; viii, **645a**
Ruʾyā-i ṣādiḳa iv, 72b
Rūyān ii, 74b; iv, 808a; v, 661b; vi, 337b, 539a; viii, **650b**; s, 297b
Rūyānī, Abu 'l-Maḥāsin iv, 859b
Ruʾyat Allāh i, 411b; viii, **649a**
Ruʾyat al-Hilāl viii, **649b**
Rūyīn-diz i, 300b, 301a; vi, 500a-501b
Rūzafzūn (Sawādkūh) (1517) vi, 515b, 938b
Rūzafzūn, Aḳā Rustam (sipahsālār) (XVI) vi, 514b
Rūzafzūn, ʿAlī b. Iskandar (sipahsālār) (XV) vi, 513b, 514a
Rūzafzūn, Bahrām (sipahsālār) (XV) vi, 513b
Rūzafzūn, Iskandar (sipahsālār) (XV) vi, 513a
Rūzafzūn, Muḥammad (XVI) vi, 514b, 515a
Rūzakī (Rozagī), Banū v, 458b, 459a
Rūzakī, Sayyid Aḥmad Beg (XVI) vi, 931b
Rūzbahān b. Windād-Khūrshīd iii, 703a, 1202a
Rūzbahān Baḳlī → Rūzbihān al-Baḳlī
Rūzbih b. Buzurdjmihr vi, 660a
Rūzbihān al-Baḳlī al-Shīrāzī (1209) iii, 823a; iv, 851b; v, 53b; viii, 429a, **651b**; x, 320b
Rūzbihān al-Wazzān al-Miṣrī v, 300b
Ruzhekī → Ruzāgī
Rūznāma viii, **652a**
al-Rūznāmadj ii, 78b, 79b, 81a
Rūznāmedji viii, **652a**
al-Ruzz ii, 904a, 907a, 1062b; iv, 519b; v, 879b; viii, **652b**
Ruzzīk b. Ṭalāʾiʿ, Abū Shudjāʿ (vizier) (1163) i, 197a; ii, 318a; iv, 376a; viii, **653b**
Rzewuski, Wenceslas Severin (1831) viii, **654a**

S

Ṣaʿ viii, **654a**
Sāʿa iii, 921a; v, 708b; viii, **654b**
Saʿāda viii, **657b**
Saʿāda, Anṭūn iii, 523a, b; iv, 125a
Saʿāda, Banū viii, 708a
Saʿādat b. Muḥammad Girāy II iv, 178b
Saʿādat ʿAlī Khān, Nawāb (Awadh) (1814) i, 757b, 809a; iii, 1244a; v, 637a; viii, **660b**
Saʿādat Allāh Khān i, 624b
Saʿādat Girāy Khān I ii, 179a, 1046a, 1113b; iv, 178a
Saʿādat Ḥasan Mantō (1955) x, 880a
Saʿādat Khān → Burhān al-Mulk, Nawwāb
Saʿādat Khān Bahādur → Burhān al-Mulk, Mīr Muḥammad Amīn, Nawwāb
Saʿādat Khān Swātī iii, 335b
Saʿādat Yār Khān → Ṣādiḳ Muḥammad Khān III
Saʿādatābād Square (Iṣfahān) vi, 526b
Saadia Gaon → Saʿadyā al-Fayyūmī
Saʿadyā ben Yōsēf, Saʿīd Yaʿḳūb Yūsuf al-Fayyūmī (942) i, 343a; ii, 95b; iv, 304a, 305b, 306a, 604a; vii, 786a; viii, **661a**; ix, 10a
Saʿālīk → Suʿlūk
al-Sāʿātī, Muḥammad s, 371b, 373a, b
Sabʿ, Sabʿa viii, **662b**
Ṣaʿb Dhu 'l-Ḳarnayn al-Ḥimyarī vi, 565b
Ṣabā, Fatḥ ʿAlī Khān (1822) iii, 114a; iv, 69b; vi, 276b

Saba (Queen) → Bilḳīs
Sabaʾ (Sabeans) i, 548a, b; iii, 9a; vi, 88b, 560a, 561a, 562a, 831b; viii, **663a**; ix, 91a; s, 337a
Ṣabā (zephyr) ii, 1035a
Sabāʾ b. Abī ’l-Suʿūd i, 1214b; iii, 134a; v, 954a
Sabaʾ b. Aḥmad (Ṣulayḥid) (1098) vii, 773a; ix, 1b
Sabaʾ b. Managhfād ii, 1095b
Sabaʾ b. Yashdjub b. Yaʿrub b. Ḳaḥṭān vi, 560a
Sabaʾ al-Aṣghar s, 337b
Sabab i, 671b, 672a; iii, 1129b; viii, **666b**
Sabaea → al-Ṣābiʾa
Sabah (Borneo) vi, 232b, 241a, 242a; viii, **668a**; s, 150a
Ṣabāḥ (jeweller) s, 251b
Ṣabāḥ, Āl i, 233b, 540a; ii, 176b; v, 573b, 574a; viii, **668b**
Ṣabāḥ I (Ṣabāḥ, Āl) (1756) viii, 668b
Ṣabāḥ al-Dīn (“Prens” Sabahattin) (1948) ii, 430b, 474b, 475a; iii, 593a; viii, **669a**
Ṣabāḥ al-Dīn ʿAlī v, 195a, 197a
Sabahattin Ali (1948) vi, 95b; viii, **669b**
Sabahattin (Raḥmī) Eyuboğlu → Eyyūboghlu, Ṣabāḥ al-Dīn Raḥmī
al-Sabāʿī (966) vi, 353b
Sabaeans → Sabaʾ; Ṣābiʾ
Sabaʿiyya i, 382b; iii, 1265a; s, 357b
Ṣabandja viii, 670b
Sabarta → Isparta
Sabasṭiyya viii, **670b**
Sabʿat Khawātim v, 222b
Sabʿatayn s, 337a
Sabʿatu Ridjāl (Marrākush) vi, 591a; viii, **671b**
Ṣabbāgh viii, **671b**
al-Ṣabbāgh, Aḥmad b. Muṣṭafā al-Sikandarānī s, 44a
Ṣābiʾ (Sabians: Ḳurʾān, ʿIrāḳ, Ḥarrān) viii, **672a**
al-Ṣābiʾ, Abū Isḥāḳ Ibrāhīm b. Hilāl (994) i, 591b, 955a, 1354a; ii, 305a; iii, 258a, 387b, 671b, 703b, 780a; iv, 756b; viii, 674a; s, 4a, 19a, 398a
al-Ṣābiʾ, Ghars al-Niʿma b. Hilāl (X) x, 14a
Ṣābiʾa (Mandaeans) i, 264a, 527b; iii, 9b, 52a, 166a, 228a, 1075b; v, 120a, 895a; vi, 247a, 337a, 338a, 413b, 559a, 613b, 950b; viii, **675a**; ix, 801b; s, 336b
Sabians → Ṣābiʾ
Ṣābiʾat al-Baṭāʾiḥ → Ṣābiʾa
Ṣābiʾat Ḥarrān → Ṣābiʾa
Ṣabīḥ s, 251b
al-Sabīʿī, Abū Isḥāḳ (745) vii, 398b
al-Sabīʿī al-Hamdānī s, 400b
Sābiḳ b. Maḥmūd b. Ṣāliḥ (Mirdāsid) (1079) iii, 790a; vii, 577b
Sābiḳ b. Sulaymān b. Harāth b. Mūlāt, Ibn Dūnās vi, 842a; vii, 186a
Sābiḳ al-Barbarī (IX) xi, 151a
Sabīka umm Muḥammad b. ʿAlī al-Riḍā vii, 396b
al-Sābiḳūn viii, **678b**
Sabīl iv, 435b; viii, **679a**
Ṣābir (Lombardia) iv, 275b; v, 1244a
Ṣābir b. Ismāʿīl al-Tirmidhī (Adīb Ṣābir) (1142) viii, **683a**, 971a
al-Ṣābir, ʿAlāʾ al-Dīn ʿAlī b. Aḥmad s, 313a
Ṣābir, Mīrzā ʿAlī Akbar (1911) viii, **683b**
Ṣābiriyya ii, 54a; s, 313a
Sabirs (Central Asia) iv, 1172a, b, 1178b
Sabʿiyya i, 178b; iv, 203a, b; viii, **683b**
Sabk (Shibl) al-Daylamī (902) viii, 631a
Sabkatī → Maḥmūd I Ghāzī (Ottoman)
Sabkha ii, 877b; viii, **685a**
Sabk-i Hindī ii, 999b, 1034a; iv, 60a, 68b-69a; viii, **683b**
Sabk-i ʿIrāḳī iv, 60a; viii, 683b
Sabk-i Khurāsānī iv, 60a; viii, 683b
Sabk-i Turkistānī iv, 60a; viii, 683b
Sābla iv, 674a, 675a
Ṣabr (patience) viii, **685b**
Ṣabr (aloe) viii, **687b**
Ṣabra (al-Manṣūriyya) ii, 114b, 861b, 863a; iv, 830a, b; vi, 435a; viii, **688b**
Ṣabra (Sabratha) vi, 452b; viii, **687b**
Sabra b. Maʿbad vii, 757b
Sabra b. Nakhf b. Abī Ṣufra (VIII) vii, 359b
Sabt (Sabbath) viii, **689a**
Sabta (Ceuta) i, 83b, 356b; iv, 355b; v, 1192a; vi, 216b, 431b, 572a, 573a, 574a, 592a, 594a, 595a, 596a; vii, 387a, 391b, 641b; viii, **689b**; s, 111b, 124b, 125a
al-Sabtī b. Hārūn al-Rashīd i, 1289a
al-Sabtī, Aḥmad b. Djaʿfar al-Khazradjī, Abu ’l-ʿAbbās (1205) iii, 893b, 975a; viii, 690b, **691a**, 715b

al-Sabtī, Abu 'l-Ķāsim (1358) vi, 196b
al-Sabtī, Ķāḍī Abu 'l-Faḍl ʿIyāḍ b. Mūsā (1149) vii, 625a
al-Sabtī, Muḥammad b. ʿIyāḍ vi, 111a, 355a
Sabuktakīn/Sabuktigīn → Sebüktegin
Ṣābūn viii, **693a**
al-Ṣābūnd̲j̲ī, Ḥusayn iv, 852b
Ṣābund̲j̲ī, Louis (1931) viii, **693b**
Sābūr (1022) x, 915a
Sābūr, D̲h̲u 'l-Aktāf → S̲h̲āpūr II
Sābūr b. Abī Ṭāhir iv, 664a
Sābūr b. Ardas̲h̲īr, Abū Naṣr (1025) i, 242a, 899a, 1352b; ii, 127a; vi, 199a; viii, **694a**; s, 119b, 361b
Sābūr b. Sahl b. Sābūr (869) i, 344b, 1224a; viii, **694a**
Sābūr al-D̲j̲unūd → S̲h̲āpūr I
Ṣābūrī, Abū Muḥammad Taķī Bahār (XIX) vi, 276b
Ṣabyā s, 278b, **696a**
Sabz ʿAlī (Ramaḍān ʿAlī) (1938) viii, **694b**
Sabzawār (Harāt; K̲h̲urāsān) iii, 968b; vi, 13a; vii, 76b, 90a; viii, 694b; ix, 47b; s, 41a
al-Sabzawārī, Abū Saʿīd al-Ḥasan b. al-Ḥusayn (1450) iv, 704b
Sabzawārī, Ḥad̲j̲d̲j̲ Mullā Hādī (1878) iv, 50b; viii, **695a**; s, 41a
Sabzawārī, Muḥammad ʿAlāʾ al-Dīn (XV) viii, 542b
Sabzawārī, Muḥammad Bāķir (1679) viii, 779a; s, 308a
Sabzawārī, S̲h̲āh Riḍā (XVII) vii, 1052b
Sabzawārī, S̲h̲ams al-Dīn (1300) ii, 394a; v, 26a; vii, 550a
Saččal Sarmast (1827) v, 611a; ix, 637a
Ṣād viii, **695b**
Saʿd (atabeg Fārs) (XIII) vi, 482a; viii, 978b
Saʿd (Mamlūks) vi, 327b
Saʿd b. Zangī (Salg̲h̲urid) (1260) vi, 608b; viii, **720a**
Saʿd b. Abī Waķķāṣ (671) i, 140a, 336b, 382b, 445a, 485a, 697a; iii, 260a, 587a, 739b, 874a, 1254b; iv, 385a, b, 775b, 796a; v, 345b, 451a, 945a; vi, 647b, 648a, 649a, 653b, 659a, 660a, 664b, 702a; vii, 75a, 364a, 394b, 783b; viii, **696a**; ix, 44b, 618a, 661b
Saʿd b. ʿĀʾid̲h̲ al-Ķaraẓ s, 172a
Saʿd b. al-ʿĀṣ iv, 858b
Saʿd b. Bakr, Banū iii, 94a, 363b; vi, 648b; viii, **697b**
Saʿd b. Fahm, Banū x, 2b
Saʿd b. Fayṣal b. ʿAbd al-ʿAzīz Āl Suʿūd s, 305b
Saʿd b. Mardanīs̲h̲ → Ibn Mardanīs̲h̲
Saʿd b. Masʿūd (VII) vii, 521a; ix, 421b; x, 431a
Saʿd b. Muʿād̲h̲ b. al-Nuʿmān al-As̲h̲halī (627) i, 514b, 771b; v, 436b; vi, 374a, 645a, 646b; vii, 370b, 371a; viii, **697b**
Saʿd b. Muḥammad → Ḥayṣa Bayṣa
Saʿd b. Rabīʿ (VII) vii, 254a
Saʿd b. ʿUbāda (634) i, 514b; v, 996b; vii, 356b, 1020a; viii, **698a**
Saʿd (I) b. Zangī Abū S̲h̲ud̲j̲āʿ ʿIzz al-Dīn (Salg̲h̲urid) (1226) i, 434a; iv, 1037a, 1041a; v, 161a; viii, **701a**, 978b
Saʿd b. Zayd Manāt al-Fizr, Banū i, 102a; ii, 71b; viii, **701b**; s, 31a, 178a
Saʿd Allāh K̲h̲ān (XVII) vii, 321b
Saʿd Allāh K̲h̲ān, Mullā (Sartōr Faķīr, Bunēr) (XIX) ii, 317a
Saʿd Allāh K̲h̲ān ʿAllāmī al-Tamīmī ii, 47b; iv, 759b
Saʿd Allāh K̲h̲ān Rohilla iii, 60a, b
Saʿd Allāh Lāhorī iii, 634a
Saʿd Allāh Pas̲h̲a (Diyār Bakr) (XIX) vi, 542a
Saʿd al-ʿAs̲h̲īra, Banū vii, 591b
Saʿd, Atabeg of Fārs → Salg̲h̲urids
Saʿd al-Aysar v, 49a, 50a
Saʿd Buh s, 182b
Saʿd al-Dawla, (Jew, Bag̲h̲dād) (1291) i, 903a; iii, 1122a; iv, 48a; vii, 234b
Saʿd al-Dawla b. al-Ṣafī al-Abharī (1291) viii, **702a**
Saʿd al-Dawla S̲h̲arīf I, Abu 'l-Maʿālī (Ḥamdānid) (991) i, 119b; iii, 86a, 128a, b, 129b; v, 820a, 923b; s, 37a
Saʿd al-Dawla al-Ṭawās̲h̲ī → al-Ṭawās̲h̲ī
Saʿd al-Dīn (1599) → K̲h̲od̲j̲a Efendi
Saʿd al-Dīn (Rūyīn-diz) vi, 501a
Saʿd al-Dīn (Ethiopia) i, 176b, 763b
Saʿd al-Dīn Hammūʾī (1252) viii, 135a, **703a**; s, 235b, 364b
Saʿd al-Dīn Ibn al-ʿArabī viii, 753b
Saʿd al-Dīn K̲h̲iḍr i, 766b
Saʿd al-Dīn Köpek b. Muḥammad (1240) viii, **704b**

Saʿd al-Dīn Muḥammad al-Kāshgharī (1456) ii, 421b, vii, 935a; viii, **704a**
Saʿd al-Dīn al-Shaybānī al-Djibāwī (XIII) viii, 728b
Saʿd al-Dīn Taftāzānī → al-Taftāzānī
Saʿd al-Dīn al-Warāwīnī (1246) iv, 506b; vi, 632a, b, 658b
Saʿd al-Ḳaraẓ vi, 677a
Saʿd (Saʿīd) al-Khayr b. ʿAbd al-Malik (Umayyad) (VIII) vii, 398a
Saʿd al-Mulk Abu ʾl-Maḥāsin, wazīr (XII) vi, 275b; vii, 754a; x, 42b
Saʿd wa-Naḥs viii, **705a**
Saʿd Zaghlūl Pasha (1927) ii, 417b, 423a, 467a, 934a; iii, 59a, 516a; iv, 197b, 856a; v, 910a; vi, 607a; vii, 439a, 904b; viii, **698a**; xi, 25b; s, 58a
Sada (festival) vi, 523a
Ṣaʿda (Yemen) vi, 433a, b, 435b, 436a, 437a, 566a; viii, **705b**; s, 22a, 236a, 335a, 407a
Ṣadā viii, 706b
Saʿdābād i, 232b; v, 642a
Ṣadaf v, 819b; viii, **707a**
al-Ṣadafī, Abū ʿAlī Ḥusayn b. Muḥammad (1120) iv, 290a; viii, 635a, **707b**
Ṣadāḳ viii, **708b**
Ṣadaḳa i, 1142a, 1144a; iii, 350a; iv, 1151b; v, 424b; viii, 708b
Ṣadaḳa, Banū viii, 716a
Ṣadaḳa I b. Manṣūr (Mazyadid) (1108) i, 684a; iii, 197b, 389b, 774b; iv, 27b, 29a, 911b; vi, 380a, 966a; vii, 408a, 755b; viii, 716a, 942b
Ṣadaḳa II b. Dubays II (Mazyadid) (1138) vi, 966a
Ṣadaḳa b. Abi ʾl-Ḳāsim Shirāzī iii, 373a; iv, 63b
Ṣadaḳa b. ʿAlī (VII) x, 897a
Ṣadaḳa b. ʿAlī al-Azdī (IX) vi, 337a
Ṣadaḳa b. Yūsuf al-Falāḥī (1048) vii, 118b
al-Saʿdān[i] viii, **716b**
Saʿdaniyya iii, 291a
al-Sadārā → Sudayrī
Sadaśiv Rāo (Marāthās) (XVIII) vi, 535b
al-Sādāt, Anwar (1981) v, 1062a; vii, 291b, 451a; viii, **716b**; s, 5b, 6a, 306a
Sādāt-i Marʿashī iv, 48b
Sadd al-Dharāʾiʿ viii, **718a**
Ṣaddām Ḥusayn (XX) vii, 715a; viii, 247a
Saddūm (XVIII) vii, 616a
Sadekov s, 365b
al-Saʿdī, ʿAbd al-Malik b. Muḥammad b. ʿAṭiyya (VIII) vii, 524b
al-Saʿdī, ʿAbd al-Raḥmān b. ʿAbd Allāh (Timbuktu) (1656) i, 595a; vi, 258b; viii, **718b**
Saʿdī, Abū ʿAbd Allāh Musharrif al-Dīn b. Muṣliḥ (1292) i, 241b, 680a, 780a, 1301a, 1345b; ii, 1034a, 1035a, b; iii, 93b, 373a, 573a; iv, 65b, 67b; vi, 608b, 609a, 825b, 833a; vii, 480b; s, 46b, 415a; viii, 540a, **719a**, 892a
al-Saʿdī, Abū Shudjāʿ Shāwar b. Mudjīr (XII) viii, 653b
Saʿdī b. Abi ʾl-Shawk i, 513a
Saʿdī Čelebi iii, 90a; iv, 333b
Sadīd al-Mulk ʿAlī (Munḳidh, Banū) (1082) vii, 577b
Saʿdids (Saʿdians) i, 55b, 56a, 58b, 93a, 245a, 288b, 355a, 403a, 496b, 689a, 1058a, 1149a; ii, 134a, 146a, 164b, 181b, 510a, 819b, 823a; iii, 70a, 251b, 257a, 426a, 1047a; v, 627a, 1191a, b; vi, 134b, 142b, 187b, 248b, 594a, 596a, 741b, 743a, 888b; vii, 37b; viii, **723a**; ix, 545b; s, 28b, 29a, 223b, 336b
Ṣādiḳ, Colonel iii, 595a
Ṣādik, G.M. iv, 711a
Ṣādiḳ Beg iv, 593b
Ṣādiḳ Ḥalwāʾī, Mawlānā s, 122a
Ṣādiḳ Hidāyat → Hidāyat, Ṣādiḳ
Ṣādiḳ Khān Shakākī i, 1030b; ii, 838b; iii, 1109a
Ṣādiḳ Khān Zand i, 1087a; iv, 104b; v, 674a
Ṣādiḳ al-Mahdī (Sūdān) (XX) ix, 749b
Ṣādiḳ Muḥammad Khān I (Dāwūdpōtrā) (1746) ii, 185b, 186a
Ṣādiḳ Muḥammad Khān II (1825) ii, 186b
Ṣādiḳ Muḥammad Khān III ii, 186b
Ṣādiḳ Muḥammad Khān IV (1899) ii, 187a
Ṣādiḳ Muḥammad Khān V (1956) ii, 187a
Ṣādiḳ Muṭṭalibī i, 432b
Ṣādiḳ Rifʿat Pasha, Meḥmed (1857) iii, 552a, 591a; viii, **726a**
Ṣādiḳī (coin) viii, **726b**
Ṣādiḳī Bēg (painter) vii, 603a; viii, 776b, 787b
al-Ṣādiḳiyya, al-Madrasa v, 915a; viii, **726b**
Sādin iv, 421b; viii, **728a**

Ṣadīna, Banū vi, 310b
Sadir, A. (XX) vi, 768b
Ṣādirāt ii, 152a; iv, 1041a, 1042a
Sadīrī, Muḥammad Mu'min (XVII) vii, 475b
Sa'diyya viii, **728b**
Sādj viii, **732b**
Sadj' i, 591a, 594a, 673b; ii, 307a; iii, 1242b; v, 420a, 839b; viii, **732b**
Sadjāḥ, Umm Ṣādir bint Aws b. Ḥikk (VII) i, 110b, 247b, 451a; iii, 169a, 224b; iv, 463b; vi, 267b, 268a, 675b; vii, 665a; viii, **738b**
Sadjāḥī → Sadjāḥ
al-Sadjāwandī, Abū 'Abd Allāh (1165) viii, **739a**
al-Sadjāwandī, Sirādj al-Dīn (XIII) iii, 163b; viii, **739b**
Sadjda viii, **740a**
Sadjdjād Ḥusayn iii, 359a
Sadjdjāda iv, 950a; viii, **740b**
al-Sādjī, Abū Yaḥyā Zakariyyā' (909) viii, 840b
Sādjids i, 145a, 190a, 637a, 660b; ii, 679b; iv, 22a, b; v, 489a; vi, 539a; vii, 922a; viii, **745a**
Sādjiyya i, 866a; ii, 1080b
Sadjsin v, 1016a, b
Sādjūr (river) vi, 377b, 378a, 379a, b, 82a
Sadok Bey (1860) vi, 798b
Sadōzays i, 229a, 230a, 295a
Ṣadr (chest) viii, **746a**
Ṣadr (eminent person) viii, **748a**
Ṣadr (Ḳumm) s, 157b
al-Ṣadr, Muḥammad Bāḳir (Āyatullāh) (1980) vii, 301b
Ṣadr al-Dīn → Rinčana
Ṣadr al-Dīn (Kashmīr) iv, 708a
Ṣadr al-Dīn (vizier) (Gaykhātū, b. Abaḳa) (XIII) vii, 232a
Ṣadr al-Dīn, Pīr iv, 202b
Ṣadr al-Dīn Ardabīlī b. Ṣafī al-Dīn Ardabīlī (1391) viii, **752b**; s, 382b
Ṣadr al-Dīn 'Aynī (1954) viii, **753a**; x, 65b
Ṣadr al-Dīn Azurda → Āzurda, Ṣadr al-Dīn
Ṣadr al-Dīn al-Baṣrī (XIII) vi, 352a
Ṣadr al-Dīn Khālidī (vizier) (XIII) xi, 192b
Ṣadr al-Dīn Ḳūnawī (1274) iii, 708a, b, 710b, 1269a; vi, 247b; viii, 210b, 703b, **753a**, 860a
Ṣadr al-Dīn Muḥammad b. Ghiyāth al-Dīn Manṣūr (1498) viii, 543a
Ṣadr al-Dīn Muḥammad Shīrāzī → Mulla Ṣadrā Shīrāzī
Ṣadr al-Dīn Mūsā, Shaykh iv, 721a
Ṣadr al-Dīn Mūsā b. Ṣafī al-Dīn Ardabīlī (1391) iv, 721a; viii, **755a**, 766a
Ṣadr al-Dīn ibn Sanī al-Dawla, Ḳāḍī (1260) s, 463a
Ṣadr al-Dīn Ṣadr (Āyatullāh) (XX) vii, 762b
Ṣadr al-Dīn Sheykhoghlu (XIV) vi, 632b
Ṣadr al-Dīn Shīrāzī → al-Shīrāzī, Ṣadr al-Dīn
al-Ṣadr al-Shahīd Ḥusām al-Dīn 'Umar (1141) vi, 558a
Ṣadr al-Sharī'a al-Thānī iii, 163b
Ṣadr al-Ṣudūr i, 316b, 1327b
Ṣadrā Shīrāzī → al-Shīrāzī, Ṣadr al-Dīn
Sadrātā i, 1246b; v, 697b; viii, **756a**
al-Sadrātī → 'Āṣim; Abū Ya'ḳūb
Sadrettin Celal (Ṣadr al-Dīn Djelāl) (XX) iv, 124a; vi, 94b, 95b
Ṣadr-i A'ẓam i, 1091a; ii, 333a, 335b; iii, 554a, 555a; iv, 393b; v, 631a; viii, **751b**
Ṣadūḳ, Shaykh-i → Ibn Bābawayh
Sa'dullāh Pasha iii, 592b
al-Sa'dūn, 'Abd al-Muḥsin (XX) vii, 582b
Sa'dūn, Āl → al-Muntafiḳ
Sa'dūn, Banū → al-Muntafiḳ, Banū
Sa'dūn, Nāṣir Pasha (XIX) vii, 582b
Sa'dūn, Shaykh Manī' (XVIII) iii, 1191a; vii, 582a
al-Sa'dūn, Shaykh Manṣūr (XIX) vii, 582b
Sa'dūn b. Manṣūr (Muntafiḳ, Banū) (1911) vii, 582b
Sa'dūn b. Muḥammad Āl Ghurayr ii, 321a; iv, 925a
Sa'dūn al-Surunbāḳī i, 85b
al-Ṣafā vi, 544b, 546a; viii, **756b**
al-Ṣafā (Mecca) ii, 71a; vi, 162a, 165b, 167a, 178a; viii, **756a**; s, 175a
Ṣafā, Bābā, Ḥādjdjī (1740) x, 251a
Ṣafā Girāy (Ḳazan) (1531) viii, 832a
Ṣafā' Khān iv, 849b
Ṣafad vi, 343b; viii, **757a**
al-Ṣafadī, al-Ḥasan b. Abī Muḥammad (XIV) viii, 759a
Ṣafadī, Muṭā' v, 191a
al-Ṣafadī, Ṣalāḥ al-Dīn Khalīl b. Aybak (1363) i, 594b; ii, 285b; iv, 863b; v,

609a; vi, 112a, 143b, 196a, 198b, 247b; vii, 170b, 306b, 390b; viii, 458b, 672a, **759a**; x, 68b, 395a; s, 48b, 381a, 388a, b, 400a
Ṣafāʾī (1725) viii, 991a
Ṣafaitic vi, 349a; viii, **760b**
Safāḳus (Sfax) v, 220b; viii, **762b**
al-Ṣafāḳusī, ʿAlī al-Sharafī (XVI) vi, 185b; vii, 47b
al-Safāḳusī, Maḥmūd b. Saʿīd Maḳdīsh (1813) viii, **763a**
Ṣaʿfān vi, 191b
Ṣafar (month) viii, **764b**
Ṣafar (Sfar), Muḥammad al-Bashīr (1917) viii, **765a**
Safar (journey) viii, **764b**
Ṣafarov, ʿAlī Ḳulī s, 71b
Ṣafātene i, 562b
Ṣafawids, Ṣafawiyya i, 190a, 311b, 1066a-1068b, 1120a; ii, 7b, 598b; iii, 177b, 220a, 315b, 1100a; iv, 34a-37b, 49a, 68b, 103a-104a, 118b, 130b, 186a, b, 187a, 387b, 537a, 670b; v, 33b, 34a, 59a, 379a, 603b, 749a; vi, 11a, 18b, 226a, 271a, 483a, b, 493a, 495a, 510b, 515b, 521b, 522b, 523a, 525a, 548b, 549b, 550a, b, 724b, 855a, 931b; viii, 755a, **765b**; ix, 475b; x, 45b; s, 51b, 71a, 139a, 227b, 257a, 308a, 327a
– administration i, 36a, 240a, 1088a, 1159a, 1346a; ii, 150a, b, 162b, 311b, 334a, 967a, 1083b; iii, 47b, 198b, 490b, 1257a; iv, 474b, 757b, 860b, 951b, 976b, 1048b, 1052b, 1092b; v, 244a, 630a, 869a
Ṣafawiyya (order) s, 382b, 383a
Ṣafdar ʿAlī b. Ghazan Khān iii, 581a
Safdar ʿAlī b. Saʿādat Allāh i, 625a
Ṣafdār Djang (Awadh (Oudh), 1754) i, 757a; ii, 808b, 870a; iii, 60a, b, 1158b, 1163a; vi, 128a, 369b, 353b, 537a; vii, 316a, 334a; viii, **793b**
Ṣaff iv, 334b; viii, **793b**
al-Saffāḥ → Abu ʾl-ʿAbbās al-Saffāḥ
al-Ṣaffār, Ismāʿīl b. Abī Naṣr (1069) viii, 748b
al-Ṣaffārī, Abū Isḥāḳ Ibrāhīm (XII) viii, 749a
Ṣaffārids i, 18b, 23b, 226b, 439b, 452b, 1354b; ii, 191b, 962b, 1082b; iii, 346a; iv, 20b-21b, 188b, 208b; vi, 65b, 193a, 274a, 620b, 872a; vii, 766a; viii, **795a**; s, 113a
al-Ṣāffāt viii, **798a**
Saffet Bey (XIX) vi, 758b
Ṣafī (Fakhr al-Dīn ʿAlī Kāshifī) (1532) iv, 69a, 704a; vii, 1019a; viii, **800b**
Safi (port) → Aṣfī
Ṣafī/Ṣawāfī i, 1144a; iv, 972b, 973a; viii, **798b**
Ṣafī I, Shāh (Ṣafawid) (1642) i, 228b; ii, 104a, 335a; iii, 220b, 348b, 1190a; iv, 977a; v, 1089b; vi, 516b, 550b; vii, 318a, 476a; viii, 770b; s, 63a, 83b, 276a
Ṣāfī II, Shāh (Ṣafawid) (1694) → Sulaymān Shāh
Safi, Banū s, 237b
Ṣafī ʿAlī-Shāhīs x, 327b
Ṣafī ʿAlī-Shāhiyya ii, 434a; iv, 52a; viii, 47a
Ṣafī Amīr al-Muʾminīn → Bahāʾ al-Dawla Fīrūz
Ṣafī (Sofi)-Čay vi, 498b, 501a, b
Ṣafī al-Dīn ʿAbd Allāh b. Shukr iii, 863a
Ṣafī al-Dīn ʿAbd al-Muʾmin (1294) ii, 1074a; vii, 191a, 209a
Ṣafī al-Dīn al-Ardabīlī (Ṣafawid) (1334) i, 625b, 1197b; ii, 967a; vi, 131b, 354b; viii, 766a, 801a; s, 139a, 382b
Ṣafī al-Dīn al-Ḥillī (1351) i, 595b, 666b, 858a, 982b; ii, 1033a; iii, 852a, 1264b; iv, 1006a; vi, 248a; vii, 495a, 661a, 812a; viii, 111a, 376a, 378a, **801b**; ix, 70b
Ṣafī al-Dīn al-Urmawī, ʿAbd al-Muʾmin (1294) vi, 99a, 102b; vii, 683b, 684a, 1042b; viii, **805b**; s, 408b, 409a
Ṣafī Ḳuli Khān i, 229b, 904a
Ṣafī Mīrzā b. Shāh Ṣulṭān Ḥusayn (Ṣafawid) (XVIII) vi, 56b; viii, 771b
Ṣafiābād i, 701b
Ṣafī Sayf Khān, Mīrzā (XVII) vii, 574a
Safīd Kūh i, 222a; viii, **807b**; s, 237b
Safīd Rūd ii, 189b; iv, 6b; v, 602b, 866a; vi, 498b, 500a; viii, **807b**; s, 356b, 363a
Safīdpūsh iv, 409b
Safīna vii, 53a; viii, **808a**
Ṣafīnāz Dhu ʾl-Fiḳār s, 299b
Ṣafīpur s, 293a
Safīr ii, 590a; iii, 590a; viii, **811b**
Safīrī (XX) vi, 754a
Sāfīthā (chastel blanc) vi, 579a; viii, **815b**
Ṣafiyat al-Nisāʾ bint Muḥammad Akbar b. Awranzīb (XVII) iv, 93a

Ṣafiyya bint Amīr Abū ʿAbd Allāh b. Mardanīsh (Martinez) (XII) vi, 339b
Ṣafiyya bint Ḥuyayy b. Akhṭab (670) i, 55b, 1022a; ii, 275a; iv, 1140a; v, 619b; vi, 658b; vii, 852b; viii, **817a**
Ṣafiyye Wālide Sulṭān (Cecilia Baffo) (1605) i, 267b; iv, 233b, 900b; vii, 595b; viii, 124a, **817b**
Ṣafḳa viii, **818a**
Safvet-bey Başagič i, 1271b
Ṣafwān b. Idrīs (1201) viii, **819a**
Ṣafwān b. al-Muʿaṭṭal al-Sulamī (638) i, 307b; iii, 272a; iv, 870b; viii, **819b**
Ṣafwān b. Ṣafwān al-Anṣarī i, 1080b; viii, **818b**
Ṣafwān b. Umayya i, 115b, 151a
Ṣafwat Pasha (XIX) vi, 151b
Ṣafwat al-Mulk iii, 399a
Sagartians v, 448b
Sagbāns ii, 512b
Sagh Gharībler → Ghurabāʾ
al-Ṣaghānī, Aḥmad b. Muḥammad (X) vi, 600b
al-Ṣaghānī, Raḍiyy al-Dīn Ḥasan (1252) i, 856a; iii, 435a, 1155b; iv, 504a; vi, 113b; vii, 190a, 637b; viii, **820a**
Ṣaghāniyān → Čaghāniyān
Ṣaghīr (child) viii, **821b**
Saghîr Aḥmed-zāde Meḥmed Bey (XIX) vi, 68b
Saghrouchen, Aït s, 145a
Sagrajas → al-Zallāḳa
Saguiet-el-Hamra s, 294a
Ṣaḥāba viii, **827b**
Saḥabī al Astarābādhī, Kamāl al-Dīn (1601) iv, 68b; viii, **829a**
Sahand vi, 494a, 498a, b, 499b, 500b
Sāhādjī (Marātha) s, 246b
Sahara, Algerian → Wargla
Sahāranpūr district viii, **829b**; s, 312b
al-Sahbāʾ i, 538b; iv, 1072b; viii, **830a**
al-Ṣaḥbāʾ → Umm Ḥabīb
Saḥbān Wāʾil viii, **830a**
Ṣaḥḥāflar-Sheykhī-zāde Esʿad Meḥmed Efendi (1848) viii, 564b
Ṣāḥib viii, **830b**
Ṣāḥib b. ʿAbbād → Ibn ʿAbbād
Ṣāḥib ʿĀdil ii, 736b
Ṣāḥib ʿAṭāʾ Fakhr al-Dīn ʿAlī (XIII) i, 243b, 313a; ii, 81a; iv, 620a, b, 817a; vii, 479b
Ṣāḥib Atā Oghullarî viii, **831a**
Ṣāḥib al-Bāb viii, **831b**
Ṣāḥib al-Djawāhir → Nadjafī, Ḥadjdjī Shaykh Muḥammad Ḥasan Iṣfahānī
Ṣāḥib Fakhkh → al-Ḥusayn b. ʿAlī
Ṣāḥib al-Fuṣūl, Shaykh Muḥammad Ḥusayn s, 75b
Ṣāḥib Girāy Khān I (Crimea, 1551) i, 1075b; ii, 25a, 1113a; iv, 178a, 849b; v, 138a; viii, **832a**
Ṣāḥib al-Ḥamrāʾ i, 829a
Ṣāḥib al-ḥimār → Abū Yazīd al-Nukkārī
Ṣāḥib al-Khabar iv, 895b
Ṣāḥib Khān b. Nāṣir al-Dīn Shāh (Khaldjī, Mālwā) (XVI) ii, 12b, 1128a; vi, 54b
Ṣāḥib Ḳirān viii, **833a**
Ṣāḥib-Ḳirān-nāma (1062) iii, 114b, 153b
Ṣāḥib al-Madīna viii, **833b**
Ṣāḥib al-Nāḳa → Yaḥyā b. Zikrawayh
Ṣāḥib al-Rākūba iv, 1005b
Ṣāḥib al-Shāma Abū ʿAlī al-Muḥassin (Ṣābiʾ); Ḥusayn b. Zikrawayh
Ṣāḥib al-Zandj → ʿAlī b. Muḥammad al-Zandjī
Ṣaḥīfa viii, **834b**
Ṣaḥīḥ i, 791a, 1297a; ii, 389b; iii, 25a; viii, **835b**
al-Sāḥil (Sahel) i, 539b; ii, 619a, 936b; iv, 778a; viii, **836b**
al-Sāḥilī, Abū Isḥāḳ al-Gharnāṭī (1346) ix, 757b
Sāhir, Djelāl (Celal Sahir Erozan) (1935) viii, **838a**
Sahl b. Abān iii, 856b, 857b
Sahl b. Bishr i, 1100b, 1102a; viii, 107a, 108a
Sahl b. Hārūn b. Rāhawayh (830) i, 1141a; iii, 309a, 1263a; vi, 108b, 920b; viii, **838b**
Sahl b. Maṣlīaḥ, Abu ʾl-Surrī (Karaite) iv, 605a
Sahl b. Muḥammad al-Ṣuʿlukī i, 686b
Sahl b. Saʿd vi, 79a, 645b
Sahl b. Salāma al-Anṣārī (IX) vi, 335a, b, 336a
Sahl b. Sunbāṭ (IX) i, 660b, 844b; iv, 344b; ix, 254a
Sahl al-Dīn al-Kūhī ii, 362a
Sahl al-Tustarī, Abū Muḥammad (896) i, 1039a; iii, 100a, 159a; vi, 225a, 570a, 672b; viii, 123a, **840a**; ix, 548b; x, 60b, 86b

Sahl al-Warrāḳ s, 306b
Sahla bint Suhayl b. ʿAmr (VII) vii, 394b
Sahlān b. Musāfir iii, 258a
al-Sahlī, Abu 'l-Ḥusayn (XI) vi, 638a
Sahl-i Sumbatian → Sahl b. Sunbāṭ
Sahlids vi, 334b
Sahm → Ashām
al-Sahm viii, **841b**
Sahm, Banū vi, 137b, 145a
al-Sahmī, Ḥamza b. Yūsuf (1038) viii, 518a, **842b**
Ṣaḥna viii, **843a**
Ṣaḥn-i Thamān (Medāris-i Thamāniyye) viii, **842b**
Saḥnūn, ʿAbd al-Salām b. Saʿīd al-Tanūkhī (854) i, 249b, 250b, 685a; iii, 681a, 817a; v, 503b; vi, 265a, 278b, 279a, 352b, 353b, 739a; vii, 387b, 409a, 1052b; viii, 638a, **843a**
Saho iii, 6a; v, 522a; vi, 628a
al-Saḥrā' i, 307a, 748b, 770a, 1177b, 1231b; iii, 288b; v, 653a, 755b, 757b, 890a, 1187b; vi, 83b; viii, **845b**; s, 328
Ṣaḥrāwīs (Morocco) vii, 584a
al-Ṣaḥṣāḥ b. Djandaba ii, 234a, 237b
Sahsārām iii, 449a; vi, 127b; viii, **850a**
al-Saḥūl viii, **850b**
Saḥūr v, 372b
Ṣahyūn vi, 322b; viii, **850b**
Ṣāʾib, Mīrzā Muḥammad ʿAlī (1676) iv, 69a; vii, 341a, b; viii, 776a, **851a**
al-Sāʾib b. Abi 'l-Sāʾib al-Makhzūmī (VIII) iv, 898b; vii, 293a
al-Sāʾib b. Bishr → al-Kalbī, al-Sāʾib
Sāʾib Khāthir (683) i, 828a; ii, 428b, 878b; viii, **852b**
Ṣaʿid (Mawālī) s, 17a
al-Ṣaʿīd/ Ṣaʿīd Miṣr vii, 156b; viii, **861b**
Ṣāʿid, Āl-i s, 239b
Saʿīd, Banū (Alcalá) s, 382a
Saʿīd, Banū (Mānbidj) vi, 382a
Saʿīd b. ʿAbd Allāh (VIII) viii, 985a
Saʿīd b. ʿAbd Allāh (Ḳishn) (XVI) vi, 82b
Saʿīd b. ʿAbd al-Malik (Umayyad) (VIII) vi, 900a
Saʿīd b. ʿAbd al-Raḥmān b. al-Ḥakam s, 10a
Saʿīd b. Abī ʿArūba (773) vii, 662b; viii, **853a**; s, 386b
Saʿīd b. Abīb (XIX) vii, 608a
Saʿīd b. Aḥmad, Imām (Bū Saʿīd) (1783) i, 1281b
Saʿīd b. ʿAmr al-Ḥarashī (VIII) i, 864a, 1134a; iii, 493b, 802b; v, 45a, 854a; vi, 623b, 820a
Saʿīd b. al-ʿĀṣ b. Saʿīd b. al-ʿĀṣ b. Umayya (678) i, 695b, 704a; ii, 1141b; v, 56b, 499b; vi, 344b, 621b; viii, **853a**; ix, 826a; s, 103b, 298a
Saʿīd b. Asad b. Mūsā b. Ibrāhīm s, 88a
Saʿīd b. al-ʿĀṣī (VII) vii, 497b
Saʿīd b. Bā Ḥmād s, 114a
Saʿīd b. Bahdal al-Shaybānī ii, 90a; ix, 766b
Saʿīd b. Barakāt i, 1032b
Saʿīd b. Bashīr iv, 748b
Saʿīd b. al-Biṭrīḳ (Eutychius) (940) vi, 143b; viii, **853b**
Saʿīd b. al-Djubayr (713) iv, 926a; vi, 107a; vii, 758a; ix, 555a; s, **697b**
Saʿīd b. al-Ḥakam (1282) vii, 87a
Saʿīd b. Ḥamdān vii, 414a
Saʿīd b. Hibat Allāh i, 111b; iii, 754a
Saʿīd b. Ḥumayd (871) viii, **856a**; s, 25a, 284b, 352a
Saʿīd b. al-Ḥusayn al-Anṣārī iv, 712b
Saʿīd b. Idrīs b. Ṣāliḥ (VIII) vii, 941a
Saʿīd b. ʿĪsā, Shaykh ii, 173b
Saʿīd b. Ḳays al-Hamdānī iii, 123b, 241b
Saʿīd b. Khafīf al-Samarḳandī vii, 210a
Saʿīd b. Khalfān al-Khalīlī iv, 1085a; s, 355b, 356a
Saʿīd b. Khālid b. ʿAbd Allāh al-ʿUthmānī (VIII) vii, 648b
Saʿīd b. Khazrūn b. Fulful v, 1180b
Ṣāʿid b. Makhlad → Ibn Makhlad, Ṣāʿid
Saʿīd b. Manṣūr (842) vii, 663a, 691b; ix, 874a
Saʿīd b. Masʿūd I i, 424b
Saʿīd b. Masʿūd al-Hudhalī iii, 950a
Ṣāʿid b. Muḥammad al-Ustuwāʾī i, 146b
Saʿīd b. Mukhallad v, 621a
Saʿīd b. al-Musayyab al-Makhzūmī (713) ii, 888a; iii, 948a; v, 1124a, 1231b; vi, 140a; vii, 631b; ix, 204a; x, 29a, 821a, b; s, 311b
Saʿīd b. Naṣr al-Dawla (Marwānid, Diyār Bakr) (1079) vi, 626b
Saʿīd b. Muslaṭ i, 709b
Saʿīd b. Sabandād s, 352a

Saʿīd b. Saʿīd b. al-ʿĀṣ (VII) ix, 787a
Saʿīd b. Salm b. Kutayba (IX) ix, 487a
Saʿīd b. Sulṭān, Sayyid (Āl Bū Saʿīd) (1856) i, 37b, 554b; iv, 887b; v, 183b; vi, 129a, 735b, 962a; vii, 227a; viii, **856b**; x, 194b, 818b; xi, 449b; s, 355b
Saʿīd b. Taymūr b. Fayṣal (Āl Bū Saʿīd, ʿUmān) (1970) i, 1071b; iii, 1005a; vi, 735b; viii, 85b; x, 817a
Saʿīd b. ʿUthmān b. ʿAffān (VII) v, 181a, 551a; vii, 357a
Saʿīd b. Yaʿḳūb al-Dimashḳī, Abū ʿUthmān (950) i, 1223b, 1340a; ii, 948b; vi 902b; viii, **858b**
Saʿīd b. Yarbūʿ Makhzūmī (VII) vi, 138b
Saʿīd b. Yūsuf al-Ahansalī iii, 167a
Saʿīd b. Zayd (670) viii, **857a**
Saʿīd Abū Bakr (1948) viii, **857b**
Saʿīd Abu ʾl-Faḍāʾil Saʿīd al-Dawla al-Mawṣilī (Ḥamdānid, Aleppo) (1002) iii, 130a; v, 928a; vi, 230b
Saʿīd al-Aḥwal (Nadjāḥid) (1089) ix, 816a
Saʿīd ʿĀlimkhān (amīr) (Bukhārā) vi, 771a
Ṣāʿid al-Andalusī (1070) i, 235b; ii, 951b; vii, 55a, 413a, 551b, 553a; viii, **867b**
Saʿīd Atā (1218) i, 299a; x, 250a
Said Atba i, 371b
Ṣāʿid al-Baghdādī, Abu ʾl-ʿAlāʾ (1026) i, 601b; iii, 713a; vi, 713a; viii, **868a**
Saʿīd al-Bānī, Shaykh (XX) vi, 538b
al-Saʿīd Baraka Khān i, 1234a; ii, 285a; iii, 679a; iv, 484b
Saʿīd al-Dīn Farghānī (Saʿīd-i Farghānī) (1292) viii, **860a**; x, 320b
Saʿīd Djanbulāṭ ii, 444a; iii, 991b
Saʿīd al-Djīlānī (Shāmī Pīr) (XX) vi, 86b; xi, 198a
Saʿīd Efendi/Pasha, Meḥmed Čelebi-zāde (1761) iii, 997b; vi, 1005a; viii, **859a**
Saʿīd al-Fayyūmī iv, 111b
Saʿīd al-Ḥabshī iii, 16a
Saʿīd Ḥalīm Pasha (1917) ii, 698b, 699a; vi, 983b; vii, 717a
Saʿīd Imām-zāde iii, 269a
Saʿīd Khān i, 852b; iii, 317a
al-Saʿīd al-Muʿtaḍid Abu ʾl-Ḥasan ʿAlī (Almohad) (1248) v, 48b; vi, 593a
al-Saʿīd Nāṣir al-Dīn Baraka (Berke) b. Baybars (Mamlūk) (1280) vi, 322b, 326b
Saʿīd Nursī → Nursī, Sheykh Badīʿ al-Zamān
Saʿīd of Palu, Shaykh (XX) vi, 888a
Saʿīd Pasha, Muḥammad b. Muḥammad ʿAlī Pasha (Khedive) (1863) ii, 149b, 423b; iii, 1193b, 1194a; iv, 192a, 442a; v, 908b; vi, 23b, 25a, 75a; vii, 182b, 290a, 428b; viii, **859b**; s, 379a
Saʿīd Pasha, vizier (1912) ii, 643b; iii, 595a; vi, 983b; vii, 525b
Saʿīd Pasha Küčük → Küčük Saʿīd Pasha
Saʿīd al-Suʿadāʾ (Khānḳāh) iv, 433a; vi, 454a; viii, **861a**
Saʿīd al-Yaḥṣubī al-Maṭarī iv, 115a
Saïda → Saʿīda
Saʿīda (town) viii, **868b**
Sāʿida b. Djuʾayya i, 115a; vii, 980b
Saʿīdā Gīlānī (XVII) viii, **869a**
Saʿīdābād → al-Sīradjān
Ṣaʿīdī s, 9b
Saʿīdī, Āl ii, 167b
Sāʿidī, Ghulām Ḥusayn v, 200b
Saʿīdov, Hārūn v, 618b
Saʿīdpūr s, 325a
Ṣāʾifa viii, **869b**
Saifa Arʿad iii, 3b
Saifawa i, 1259b; s, 164a
Ṣāʿ viii, **871a**
Ṣāʿin al-Dīn Turka (1432) viii, 540a
Ṣāʿīn Ḳalʿa viii, **871b**
Ṣāʿin Khānī, Banū (Türkmen) vi, 495a
Saʿīr viii, **872a**
Saʿīr → Suʿayr
Saʾis iv, 215b
Sāʾis s, 113b
al-Sāḳ viii, **872a**
Saḳa v, 882b
Saka (language) v, 37a, b
Saka, Banū v, 375b
al-Sakākīnī, Ḥasan b. Muḥammad (1342) vi, 279b
Sakākīnī, Khalīl (XX) vi, 615b
Saḳal v, 761a, 768a
Saḳal-i̊ Sherīf → Liḥya-yi Sherīf
Ṣaḳāliba i, 32a, 76a, 490b, 909b; iv, 344a, 1088b; v, 1120b; vii, 941b; viii, 623a, **872b**; s, 297b
Sakan b. Saʿīd i, 600b
Saḳar viii, **881a**
Saḳar, Banū v, 582a
Saḳarya (river) v, 880b; viii, 191a, 192a, **881a**; ix, 653b
Sakata → Sokoto

al-Saḳaṭī i, 32b, 157a; iii, 486b, 681a
al-Sak͟hāwī → ʿAlam al-Dīn al-Sak͟hāwī
al-Sak͟hāwī (1378) vi, 280a
al-Sak͟hāwī, S͟hams al-Dīn (1497) i, 594b, 595a, 1109b, 1110a, 1309a; iii, 746a, 777b, 814b; iv, 509a; v, 54a; vi, 194a; vii, 296b; viii, **881b**; ix, 913b
Ṣak͟hr → Abū Sufyān
Ṣak͟hr (demon) ii, 106b
Ṣak͟hr, Banū i, 528b; iv, 335a; viii, **882b**
al-Sak͟htiyānī, Ayyūb (VIII) vii, 607a
Sāḳī viii, **883b**
al-Saḳīfa, Saḳīfat Banī Sāʿida viii, **887b**
Sakīna viii, **888b**
Sāḳī-nāma iv, 59a
Sakīna bint Ḥusayn → Sukayna bint al-Ḥusayn
Sākiya → Māʾ
Sāḳiya al-Ḥamrāʾ i, 1176b; v, 890a, 892a; vi, 142a; vii, 584a; s, **698b**
Saḳi̊z (Chios) i, 268b; iii, 210b, 252b, 629b; v, 557a; vi, 69a; viii, **889b**; s, 281b
Saḳi̊zli̊ Aḥmad Asʿad iv, 966b
Saḳi̊zli̊ Edhem Pas͟ha → Ibrāhīm Edhem Pas͟ha
Saḳi̊zli̊ Ohannes Pas͟ha (XIX) ii, 473b
al-Ṣakk ii, 79a, 382b; s, **699a**
Saḳḳā → Saḳa
Saḳḳāʾ viii, **892a**
al-Saḳḳāʾ → Ibrāhīm b. ʿAlī b. Ḥasan
Sakkākī (1400) viii, **892b**
al-Sakkākī, Abū Yaʿḳūb Yūsuf (1229) i, 594a, 858a, 982a, 1116a; iv, 251b, 864a; v, 898a, 899b, 900b, 902b, 1026a; vii, 537a; viii, 427a, **893b**
Sakkākiyya iii, 660a
Sakkān, Ṣayḥkān → Mānd
Saḳḳāra viii, **894b**
Saḳḳīz viii, **895b**
al-Saḳlāwiyya, Nahr i, 485b
Ṣaḳr b. Muḥammad b. Sālim al-Ḳāsimī iv, 778b
Ṣaḳr b. Rās͟hid al-Ḳāsimī iv, 778a
Saḳr b. Sulṭān i, 1314a
Sakrūd͟j s, 269a
Saksāwa/Saksīwa, Banū vi, 742a, 743a
Saḳsīn vi, 415b; viii, **895b**
Saktāna, Banū vi, 742a
Sakūn v, 119b
Sakūra vi, 258a
Salā (town) i, 85a, 780b, 1224b; iii, 500a, 1043a; v, 290a, 504a, b; vi, 124a, 293a, b, 294a, 356a, 572a, 573a, 592a, b, 741a, 742b; viii, **898b**; s, 63b, 145a, 397b
Ṣalābat D͟jang (XVIII) ii, 180a; iii, 320b; iv, 1023b; s, 280a
Ṣalābat K͟hān II (XVII) vi, 456b; viii, 74b
Saladin → al-Malik al-Nāṣir I Ṣalāḥ al-Dīn (Ayyūbid)
Salād͟jiḳa v, 154a
Salaf i, 1112b; viii, **899b**
al-Salaf wa ʾl-K͟halaf viii, **910a**
Salafiyya i, 272b, 416b, 425b; ii, 295a, 412a; iii, 701a, 727b, 1145b; iv, 142b, 145b-160b; v, 595b, 597a; vii, 387b, 415b; viii, 447b, **900b**; s, 63b
Ṣalāḥ (S͟hād͟hilī) (1645) i, 352b
Ṣalāḥ ʿAbd al-Ṣabūr (1981) viii, **909a**
Salāḥ Bey (Constantine) (XVIII) i, 1247a
Salah Birsel (XX) vi, 96a
Ṣalāḥ al-Dīn, al-Malik al-Nāṣir Abu ʾl-Muẓaffar Yūsuf b. Ayyūb (Saladin) → al-Malik al-Nāṣir I Ṣalāḥ al-Dīn
Ṣalāḥ al-Dīn b. Mubārak al-Buk͟hārī iv, 298b
Ṣalāḥ al-Dīn Abū Fāṭima K͟hātun s, 83b
Ṣalāḥ al-Dīn K͟hudā Bak͟hs͟h v, 44a
Ṣalāḥ al-Dīn, S͟haykh (Maldives) (1950) vi, 247a
Ṣalāḥ al-Dīn Mūsā → Ḳāḍī-zāde-i Rūmī
Ṣalāh al-Dīn al-Ṣafadī → al-Safadī
Ṣalāḥ al-Dīn, al-Malik al-Nāṣir Abu ʾl-Muẓaffar Yūsuf b. Ayyūb (Saladin) → al-Malik al-Nāṣir I Ṣalāḥ al-Dīn (Ayyūbid)
Ṣalāḥ al-Dīn Zarkūb ii, 394b, 397a
Ṣalāḥ Raʾīs i, 1247a
Ṣāliḥ Reʾīs Beylerbeyi (XVI) v, 506b; x, 589b
Salakta vi, 364a
Ṣalāla vi, 735b, 736a; viii, **914b**; s, 337a
Salam iv, 326a; v, 559a; viii, **914b**
Salām viii, **915b**
Salama, Banū → Tud͟jībid
Salāma, Būlus iii, 112a
Salama b. al-Akwaʿ vii, 757b
Salama b. ʿĀṣim (854) i, 10b; ii, 807a; vi, 822a; x, 433b
Salama b. Bud͟jayr ix, 422b
Salama b. Dīnār (757) viii, **918a**
Salāma b. D͟jandal (VI) viii, **918a**
Salama b. al-Faḍl (805) x, 11b

Salama b. al-Ḥārith i, 527a; v, 118b
Salama b. Kuhayl s, 129b
Salāma b. Saʿīd iii, 653b
Salāma b. Ẓarib iv, 832b
Salāma al-Ḥidjāzī (XX) vi, 75b, 750a; vii, 438a
Salama al-Khayr v, 526a
Salāma Mūsā (1958) vi, 584a; viii, **919a**; ix, 517a
Salamān and Absāl viii, **920a**
Salamanca → Shalamanka
Salāmat ʿAlī → Dabīr
Salāmat Allāh s, 293b
al-Salāmī, Muḥammad iii, 821a
Salāmish (Süleymish) b. Baybars, Badr al-Dīn (Mamlūk) (1279) iv, 484b; vi, 322b
al-Salāmiyya iv, 202a; vi, 429a, 546b; viii, **921a**; s, 93b, 101a
Sālār (military chief) viii, **924a**
Salar (N-W. China) viii, **923b**
Salār (XIV) i, 1126b, 1139a, 1325a; iii, 952a; vi, 323a
Salar (tribe) iv, 553b, 554b; v, 850b, 851a
Sālār al-Dawla b. Muḥammad ʿAlī Shāh (Ḳādjār) (XX) ii, 652b; iv, 393b; v, 171a, 466a, 826a; vii, 432a, b
Sālār al-Dawla (Ḳādjār) iv, 393b a
Sālār al-Daylamī (XI) vii, 313a
Sālār al-Dīn, Shaykh (XV) s, 114a
Sālār Djang (1883) ii, 158b; iii, 322b; viii, **924b**
Sālār Khalīl (Andkhoy) v, 230a
Sālār al-Manṣūrī (XIV) vii, 991b
Sālār Masʿūd Ghāzī → Ghāzī Miyān
Ṣalāt i, 188a; ii, 593b, 617a; iii, 1057a; iv, 321a, 771b; v, 74a, b, 75a, 82a, b, 395a, 424b, 709a; viii, **925a**
Sālāt (Zāb) vi, 435a
Ṣalāt al-Khawf viii, **934a**
al-Ṣalatān i, 74a
Ṣalāt-i Maʿkūsa s, 313a, **699a**
Ṣalawāt → Ṣalāt
al-Salawī, ʿAbd al-Ḳādir b. ʿAbd al-Raḥmān vi, 351b
Ṣalb viii, **935a**
Saldjūḳ b. Duḳāḳ s, 245a
Saldjūḳids i, 20b, 98b, 236b, 465b, 510a, 639a, 661b, 799b, 900b, 1001a, 1336b, 1356a; ii, 4a, 344a, 855b, 1051a, 1108a; iii, 471b, 891b, 1255b; iv, 18b, 20a, 25a-29b, 208b, 294b, 347a, 1067a; v, 58a, 159b, 623a, 739a, 748a; vi, 64a, 148b, 198a, 231a, 261b, 274a, 327a, 366a, 379b, 453a, 482a, 493b, 499b, 523a, b, 524a, 530a, 540b, 549b, 550b, 620b, 809b, 854a, 872a, 900b; vii, 163b; viii, 163a, 472a, **936a**; ix, 266b; s, 29b, 59a, 119a, 146a, 149a, 154a, b, 168b, 192a, 195a, 205a, 245b, 279a, 326a, 378a; x, 42b, 690a
– administration i, 256a, 318a, 340a, 420a, 434a, 439b, 731a, 1045b, 1159a; ii, 80b, 229b, 506a, 1083a; iii, 47a, 1088b, 1098b; iv, 267a, b, 807a, 975a; v, 159a; vii, 679b
– art, architecture v, 217b, 1144b
– literature i, 570b; iii, 1158a
Saldjūḳids Rūm i, 215a, 346a, 466b, 467b, 477a, 510a, 702b, 843b, 1107a, 1159b, 1190b; ii, 13b, 344b, 444b, 712a, 989a; iii, 215b, 737b; iv, 294b, 464b, 813b; v, 103b, 104a, 271b; viii, 948a
Saldjūḳ-Shāh b. Muḥammad b. Malik-Shāh (Saldjūḳ) (1131) vi, 64a, 782a; viii, 943b
Saldjūḳ-Shāh b. Salghur-Shāh b. Saʿd (Salghūrid) (1263) i, 1358a; iv, 498a; vi, 482a
Salé → Salā
Saleha Abid Husain (XX) vi, 489a
Salghir → Salur, Banū
Salghūrids ii, 812a; iii, 337a, 1099b; iv, 29b; viii, **978b**; ix, 474a
Salḥīn (Salḥum/Silḥīn) vi, 561b, 562a; viii, **979b**
Sali Bahādur (Mongol, XIII) vi, 48b
al-Ṣalīb viii, **980a**
Salifu bi Hama ii, 942a
Ṣāliḥ (prophet) v, 124b, 421a; vi, 106a, 652b; viii, **984a**
Ṣāliḥ (rāwī) (IX) i, 154a, 274b
al-Ṣāliḥ (Artuḳid, Mārdīn) (1408) vi, 540b, 541a
Salīḥ, Banū i, 14b, 403a, 526a; viii, 981b; ix, 507a
Ṣāliḥ b. ʿAbd al-Ḳuddūs (783) i, 128a; ii, 1072a; iv, 1004a; vi, 820b; viii, **984b**
Ṣāliḥ b. ʿAbd al-Raḥmān (VIII) vii, 359a
Ṣāliḥ b. Aḥmad b. Ḥanbal i, 273b; iii, 158b
Salīḥ b. ʿAlī (Sharḳiyya Hināwī) → al-Ḥārithī, Ṣāliḥ b. ʿAlī

Ṣāliḥ b. ʿAlī b. ʿAbd Allāh b. al-ʿAbbās (769) i, 108b; iii, 398a; iv, 375b; vi, 428a, 506a, 775a; viii, 921b, **985a**
Ṣāliḥ b. Djanāḥ vii, 637b
Ṣāliḥ b. Ḥusayn Djibil i, 762b
Ṣāliḥ b. Kuthayr iii, 659a
Ṣāliḥ b. Manṣūr (Artuḳid, Mārdīn, 1367) vi, 540b
Ṣāliḥ b. Mirdās, Asad al-Dawla (Mirdāsid) (1029) ii, 484a; iii, 86a, 130b, 398b; v, 921b, 929a, 933a; vi, 379b; vii, 116a, 577b
Ṣāliḥ b. Muḥammad Sharīf al-Adhamī (XI) vi, 379b
Ṣāliḥ b. Musarriḥ (VII) ix, 766b
Ṣāliḥ b. al-Naḍr (ʿayyār) (IX) viii, 795b
Ṣāliḥ b. Rashīd iii, 234a, 618a
Ṣāliḥ b. Saʿīd al-Ḥimyarī (864) vii, 941b
Ṣāliḥ b. Ṭarīf (al-Bar(a)ghwāṭī) (795) i, 1044a, b, 1178b, 1186a; v, 1199b; vi, 743b; viii, **985a**
Ṣāliḥ b. Waṣīf (870) vii, 477a, 794a
Ṣāliḥ b. Yaḥyā b. Ṣāliḥ b. Ḥusayn (1436) i, 946b; v, 791b; viii, **985b**
Ṣāliḥ, ʿAlī ʿAbd Allāh (Yemen) (1990) xi, 275a
al-Ṣāliḥ ʿAlī b. Ḳalāwūn (Mamlūk) (1290) vi, 322b, 367b
al-Ṣāliḥ Ayyūb → al-Ṣāliḥ Nadjm al-Dīn
Ṣāliḥ Bey (Ḳāsimī) iv, 723a
Ṣāliḥ Bey (Algeria) iii, 300a; v, 531b, 532a
Ṣāliḥ Čelebi → Djalālzāde
Ṣāliḥ Efendī (XVIII) vii, 30b
Ṣāliḥ al-Fallāḥ (1748) vi, 327b
al-Ṣāliḥ ʿImād al-Dīn Ismāʿīl, al-Malik (Mamlūk) (1345) vii, 992b; viii, **986a**; s, 255b
al-Ṣāliḥ Ismāʿīl b. Badr al-Dīn Luʾluʾ, al-Malik (1261) vi, 900b; viii, **988a**
al-Ṣāliḥ Ismāʿīl b. al-Malik al-ʿĀdil (Ayyūbid) (XIII) vii, 274a
al-Ṣāliḥ Ismāʿīl b. Nūr al-Dīn Maḥmūd (Zangid) (1180) i, 1358a; ii, 283b; iii, 87a; vi, 781a; viii, 910b
Ṣāliḥ ʿIṭirdjī, Shaykh (XIX) vi, 175b
Sāliḥ Muḥammad Djamāl (XX) vi, 176a
al-Ṣāliḥ Nadjm al-Dīn Ayyūb, al-Malik (Ayyūbid) (1249) i, 198b, 711a, 766a, b, 801a, 802b, 804a, 912b, 944b, 1124b; ii, 284a, 347b; iii, 184b, 875b, 967a, 989b; iv, 430a, b, 521a; v, 628a, 922a; vi, 143b, 314a, b, 320a, 321a, 325b, 326a, 507b; vii, 147b, 148a, 164b, 666a, 990a; viii, **988b**
al-Ṣāliḥ Nāṣir al-Dīn Muḥammad, al-Malik (Mamlūk) (1421) viii, **987b**
al-Ṣāliḥ Nūr al-Dīn, al-Malik → Nūr al-Dīn Maḥmūd b. ʿImād al-Dīn Zangī
Ṣāliḥ Pasha (1919) vi, 984b; vii, 188b
Ṣāliḥ Reʾīs v, 506b
al-Ṣāliḥ, al-Malik b. al-Malik al-Ashraf Shaʿbān II (Mamlūk) (1389) i, 1050b, 1051a; ii, 159a
al-Ṣāliḥ Ṣalāḥ al-Dīn Ḥādjdjī, al-Malik (Mamlūk) (1412) viii, 987a
al-Ṣāliḥ Ṣalāḥ al-Dīn Ṣāliḥ, al-Malik (Mamlūk) (1360) iii, 239b; viii, 986b
Ṣāliḥ Ṣidḳī Ef. Hadžihusejnović i, 1271b
al-Ṣāliḥ Ṭalāʾiʿ → Ṭalāʾiʿ b. Ruzzīk
Ṣāliḥ al-Yamanī, Shaykh (1696) ii, 87b
Ṣāliḥa Sulṭān bint Aḥmed III (Ottoman) (XVIII) vi, 862a
Ṣāliḥa Sulṭān bint Maḥmūd II (Ottoman) (XIX) vi, 860a
al-Ṣāliḥī, Abu ʾl-Ḥusayn iv, 986a; vii, 606b
Ṣāliḥī, Muḥammad b. Muslim iv, 1163a; v, 806a
Ṣāliḥī, Muḥammad b. Yūsuf (1536) ix, 661a
al-Ṣāliḥī al-Ḥadjdjār (1329) viii, 156a
Ṣāliḥids vii, 941a, b, 942a, b
Ṣāliḥiyya (cemetery, Damascus) vi, 123a
al-Ṣāliḥiyya (al-Djazīra) viii, **989b**
al-Ṣāliḥiyya (Miṣr) iii, 184b; vi, 325b
al-Ṣāliḥiyya (Syria) iv, 532b; viii, **989b**; s, 20b
Ṣāliḥiyya (regiment) i, 1325a
Ṣāliḥiyya (ṭarīḳa) viii, **990a**; s, 279a
Ṣāliḥiyya (Zaydī) iii, 244a
al-Ṣāliḥūn viii, **990a**
Ṣāliḥ-zāde Meḥmed Emīn (XVIII) vii, 724b
Sālik v, 1029a
Sālim viii, **990b**
Sālim (Mirzā-zāde Meḥmed Emīn) (1743) viii, **990b**
Sālim, Abu ʾl-ʿAlāʾ (mawlā) (VIII) iv, 755b; vii, 985a; viii, 532b, 533a; x, 226a
Sālim, Banū vi, 647a, 650a
Sālim, Muḥammad Ḳulī (1647) viii, **991b**
Salīm b. ʿAbd Allāh, Jumbe v, 278a
Sālim b. ʿAbd al-Raḥmān (XIII) viii, 631a

Sālim b. ʿAbdallāh i, 277b
Sālim b. Abī Ḥafṣa s, 129b
Sālim b. Aḥmad al-Nafrawī s, 44a
Salīm b. Akbar → Djahāngīr
Sālim b. Dhakwān vii, 562a
Sālim b. Ghalbūn i, 250b
Sālim b. Idrīs al-Ḥabūḍī s, 338b
Sālim b. Ḳāsim iv, 749a
Salīm b. Khalīl al-Naḳḳāsh (1884) iv, 112a; vii, 902b; viii, **992b**
Sālim b. Mālik ii, 354b
Sālim b. Mubārak Āl Ṣabāh iii, 1066a; iv, 680b; v, 574b
Sālim b. Muḥammad, ʿIzz al-Dīn (1606) viii, **991b**
Sālim b. Mustafād (1024) vii, 116b
Sālim b. Rāshid (ʿUmān) (1920) viii, **993b**
Sālim b. Rashīd (937) ix, 585a
Sālim b. Sulṭān i, 1282a; viii, 856b
Sālim b. Thuwaynī s, 355b
Sālim al-ʿAydūdī vi, 251a
Salīm Bābān i, 291a, 1217b
Salīm al-Bishrī s, 132b
Sālim of Burullus (VIII) vi, 775a
Salīm Čishtī, Shaykh (XVI) ii, 379b, 840a, b; vi, 127a, b, 690a; viii, 514a
Salīm Fāris ii, 801a; iii, 593a
Sālim Isḥāḳ (1948) ix, 370a
Salīm Ḳabūdān i, 929a
Sālim al-Kharūsī i, 1283a
Sālim Maghribī i, 280b
Salīm al-Naḳḳāsh iv, 112a
Salīm Rubayy ʿAlī (Yemen) (1978) xi, 276b
Salīm Shāh → Islām Shāh Sūrī
Sālim al-Tūmī i, 678a; ii, 520a
Salīma, Banū iv, 500b; vi, 645a, 647b, 649a, 653b; s, 131a
Salīma Sulṭāna Bēgum (XVI) i, 1136a, b; ii, 380a; vi, 488b
Salīmgarh vi, 132a
al-Sālimī (XIV) iii, 935a
al-Sālimī → ʿAbd Allāh b. Ḥumayyid
al-Sālimī, Abū Muḥammad ʿAbd Allāh b. Ḥumayd (1914) i, 736a; viii, **993a**; s, 356a
Sālimiyya (Baṣra) i, 153a; iii, 269b; viii, 840b, **993b**; x, 60b
Salimu, al-Ḥādjdj → Karamba
Salmin Amour (XX) xi, 450b
Sāliyāne (Salyāne) viii, **994a**
Ṣalkhad (Ṣarkhad) (town) i, 780b; iii, 293a; vii, 274a; viii, **994b**; s, 391a
al-Sallāl, ʿAbd Allāh (Yemen) (1967) ix, 2a; xi, 248a, 274b
Sallām, Āl i, 95b
Sallām al-Tardjumān (IX) x, 236a; xi, 178b; s, **699b**
Sallāma Umm al-Manṣūr (Abbāsid) (VIII) vi, 427b
Sallāma al-Zarḳāʾ ii, 428b; iii, 2b, 682a; iv, 821b; viii, **996b**
Sallāmat al-Ḳass viii, **996b**
al-Sallāmī s, 326b
al-Sallāmī, Abū ʿAlī al-Ḥusayn b. Aḥmad al-Bayhaḳī (X) viii, **996b**
al-Sallāmī, Madjd al-Dīn Ismāʿīl (XIV) vi, 315b; vii, 170a, 176a
Sallārids → Musāfirids
Salm b. ʿAmr al-Khāsir (802) i, 1081b; vi, 437b; viii, **997a**
Salm b. Ḳutayba (776) iv, 493b; vii, 798b
Salm b. Ziyād b. Abīhī, Abū Ḥarb (692) i, 5a, 47b; v, 853b; vii, 357a; viii, **997b**; s, 26a
Salmā → Adjaʾ wa-Salmā
Salmāʾ bint ʿAmr Umm ʿAbd al-Muṭṭalib b. Hāshim (VI) i, 80a; iii, 260a; vi, 474b; vii, 757a
Salma b. Saʿd → Salāma b. Saʿīd
Salma bint al-Ṣāʾigh umm al-Nuʿmān III (Lakhmid) (VI) vii, 568b
Salmān, Banū vi, 436a
Salmān, Masʿūd-i Saʿd-i (1121) vi, 783a; viii, 448b; s, 21a
Salmān, Shaykh ii, 181a; iv, 314b, 675a
Salmān b. Ḥamad i, 944a; iv, 954a
Salmān b. Rabīʿa al-Bāhilī (VII) i, 635b, 636a, 660a, 921b, 1041a; iv, 343b; ix, 254a, 488a
Salmān al-Fārisī (VII) i, 114a, 258a, 922b; ii, 846a, b, 847a, 850a, 1094b; iii, 470b; v, 430a, 945b, 946a; vi, 225b; vii, 370b, 460a, 517a, b; viii, 711b, 998a; ix, 819b; s, **701b**
Salmān Pāk → Salmān al-Fārisī
Salmān Sāwadjī (1376) i, 300a, 764b; ii, 439b; iv, 66a, 67a; viii, 448b, **997b**
Salmāniyya viii, **998a**
Salmās (Irān) viii, **998a**
Salmās (Mākū) vi, 203a

Salmōn ben Yerūḥim → Sulaymān b. Ruhaym
Sāl-nāme i, 75a, 975a; viii, **898a**
Salomon → Sulaymān
Salonica → Selānīk
Salor, Banū → Salur, Banū
Salsabīl viii, **999a**
Ṣalṣāl (giant) viii, 972b
al-Salṭ (al-Salt) (town) viii, **999b**
al-Ṣalt b. Mālik (IX) i, 140b, 141b; iii, 748b, 757a
Salṭana viii, **1000b**
Saltes → Shalṭīsh
Saltuḳ-oghullarî (Erzurum) i, 639a; ii, 712a; iv, 578b, 670a; viii, **1001b**
Saltūḳids → Saltuḳ-oghullarî
Salūḳī iv, 491a; viii, **1001b**
Salūḳiyyīn ii, 352a, 1122b
Salūl, Banū viii, **1002a**
Salur, Banū v, 582a; vi, 416a, b; viii, **1005a**; s, 146b, 280b, 281a
Salur Ḳazan s, 280b
Salvatierra → Shalbatarra
Salwā viii, **1006a**
Salwān (Morocco) vi, 892a
Sālyāne ii, 83a, 723a
Sām (Shem) viii, **1007a**
Sām (Sīstān) viii, **1011a**
Sām Mīrzā b. Shāh Ismāʿīl I (1566) i, 228b; iv, 68b; vii, 530a; viii, 775b, **1012a**
Samāʾ (heaven) viii, **1014a**
Samāʿ viii, **1018a**
Sāma b. Luʾayy, Banū vi, 266b
Samāʾ al-Dawla (Ayyūbid) (1028) iii, 331a
al-Ṣamad, al-Ḥusayn b. ʿAbd (1576) viii, 777b
Ṣamad Khān (Marāgha) (XX) vi, 502b
Samāḥa, Masʿūd v, 1255b
Samak viii, **1020b**
Samakatān → al-Nudjūm
Samālū (al-Maṣṣīṣa) vi, 778b
Samana vi, 47b, 48b, 50a, 294b, 664b
Samandağ → al-Suwaydiyya
Samandal viii, **1023b**
Samandar ii, 86a; iv, 1173a
al-Samʿānī, ʿAbd al-Karīm b. Muḥammad Tādj al-Dīn (1166) i, 146b, 594b; iii, 327b, 756a; vi, 263a, 846a; vii, 776b; viii, **1024b**; ix, 847b; s, 195a, 246a, 304a, 326a, b
al-Samʿānī, Abu ʾl-Ḳāsim (1140) viii, **1024a**
Sāmānids i, 33a, 125b, 278a, 421b, 434a, 439b, 570b, 662a, 688a, 1001a, 1294a, 1344b, 1354b; ii, 192b, 253b, 748b, 791a, 1050b, 1082b; iii, 46b, 1113b, 1116a; iv, 18b, 21b-22b, 60b, 188b, 189a, 266b, 1066a; v, 622b, 856a, b; vi, 65a, b, 66a, 115b, 261b, 276a, 340a, 432b, 433a, 522a, 557b, 620b, 720a, 832b, 941b; vii, 193a, 477b, 1015a; viii, 472a, **1025b**; x, 741b; s, 21b, 35a, 72b, 149a, 204a, 245a, 356b, 411a
Sāmānkhudāt i, 685a
Samannūd vi, 119a; viii, **1031a**
Ṣamanto vi, 508a
Samar iii, 369b
Samara → Kuybishev
Samarinda s, 150a, 151a
Samaritans → al-Sāmira
Samarḳand i, 32a, 46b, 135a, 147b, 148a, 848a; ii, 43a, 61b, 746a; iii, 711b, 799a, 1137b; iv, 33a; v, 541b, 551a, 853b, 1149a; vi, 16a, 186a, 273b, 418a, 419a, 494b, 513a, 524b, 525a, 601b, 618b, 633b, 720a, 765a, 767a, 769a; vii, 313b; viii, **1031b**; ix, 427a; s, 50b, 97a, 125b, 340a
al-Samarḳandī → ʿAbd al-Razzāḳ; Abu ʾl-Layth; Abū Muḳātil; al-Hāfiẓ; Djahm b. Ṣafwān; al-Hāfiẓ; Nīẓāmī ʿArūdī
al-Samarḳandī, ʿAlāʾ al-Dīn Abū Bakr Muḥammad (1145) iv, 690a; vi, 846a
Samarḳandī, Bābā Ḥaydar (1550) vii, 936a
Samarḳandī, Badr al-Dīn v, 301a
al-Samarḳandī, Nāṣir al-Dīn (1258) vii, 969b
al-Samarḳandī, Shams al-Dīn Muḥammad Ashraf (1303) vii, 566a; viii, **1038a**
Samarḳandī, Sharaf al-Dīn Ḥusayn b. Ḥasan (XIII) viii, 542a
Sāmarrāʾ i, 18b, 211b, 897b; ii, 745b; iii, 1255a; iv, 215a, 384a, 653b, 1166a; v, 293a; vi, 198a, 338b, 364a, b, 504b, 552b, 600a, 656b, 660a, 667a; vii, 776b; viii, **1039a**; ix, 44b; s, 94a, 95a, 106a, 251a, 256a, b, 342a
– dams ii, 948a; iii, 1251a
– great mosque i, 620a, b, 622b, 830a, 1228a, 1315b; iii, 287a
– monuments i, 457b, 1346a; ii, 114a; iii, 1267b

al-Samarrī → ʿAlī b. Muḥammad; Muḥammad b. ʿAbd Allāh
al-Samarrī → al-Simmārī
Samastha Kerala Jamiat-ul-Ulema (Mappila) vi, 460b
al-Samaṭrānī → Shams al-Dīn
Samāwa (ʿIrāḳ) vii, 582b, 769a; viii, **1041a**
al-Samawʾal b. ʿĀdiyāʾ i, 565a; iii, 1177a; iv, 303a; viii, **1041a**
Samawʾal b. Yaḥyā al-Maghribī (1175) i, 520b, 690a; ii, 238a, 552b; iv, 600a; s, **702b**
al-Samawʾal Maghribī (1175) x, 112a, 960b
Sambas viii, **1042a**; s, 150a, b, 151a
Sambāṭ I i, 507a, 637a; ii, 679b
Sambāṭ II i, 507b, 637b, 638a
– Śambhadjī (Marātha) (1689) i, 769b; iv, 1023b; vi, 535a; s, 246b
– Śambhadjī II b. Rādjarām (Marātha) (1760) vi, 535a, b
Sambhal → Murādābād
Ṣamgh viii, **1042b**
al-Samḥ b. Mālik al-Khawlānī i, 608b; iii, 587b; v, 510a; s, 81b
Samhar vi, 641b, 642b
al-Samhūdī, Nūr al-Dīn Abu ʾl-Ḥasan ʿAlī (1506) vi, 653a, 658b; viii, **1043a**; s, 234b, 304b, 350a
Sāmī (1733) vii, 839a
al-Samt (Azimuth) viii, **1054a**
al-Sāmī, ʿAbd al-Aʿlā b. ʿAbd al-Aʿlā (805) viii, 853a
Sāmī, Shems ül-Dīn (1904) viii, **1043b**
Sāmī al-Bārūdī iii, 59a
Sāmī Bey → Shams al-Dīn Sāmī
Sāmī Pasha (XX) ii, 637b
al-Sāmira viii, **1044a**
al-Sāmirī viii, **1046a**
Sāmiriyya → al-Sāmira
Samīṣād vi, 508b
al-Samlālī, Aḥmad b. Mūsā (1564) vi, 350a
al-Samlālī, al-Sayyida Maryam bint Masʿūd al-Sūsī (1751) vi, 357a
al-Samlālī, Yibūrk vi, 350a
Samlis ii, 770b
Sammā (dynasty, Sind) i, 627b; iii, 419b; vi, 189b; viii, **1047a**
Sammād → Kannās
al-Sammāk, Abū Djaʿfar (IX) ix, 57a
al-Ṣammān i, 536b; ii, 92a; viii, **1048a**
al-Ṣammān, Muḥammad b. ʿAbd al-Karīm (1775) iv, 991b; x, 248b
al-Sammāniyya iv, 991b, 993a; x, 4b, 248b
Sammāsī, Khwādja Muḥammad (XIV) vii, 933b
Sammūr → Fanak; Farw
Sammūra (Zamora) iii, 842a
al-Samn i, 541a; ii, 1057b; viii, **1048b**
Sāmogarh iii, 202a, b
Samori Turé (1900) i, 297a; ii, 63a, 1003b, 1132b; v, 253a; viii, **1048b**
Samos → Sīsām
Sampit s, 150b
Samrū (Sumrū), Bēgam (1836) viii, **1049b**
al-Ṣamṣām, Ḥasan i, 986b; iii, 788a; iv, 497a
Ṣamṣām al-Dawla (Iran) (XX) iii, 1193a
Ṣamṣām al-Dawla, Abū Kālīdjār (Būyid) (998) viii, **1050a**
Ṣamṣām al-Dawla, Shāh Nawāz Khān (1758) → Maʾāthir al-Umarāʾ
Ṣamṣām al-Dawla Marzubān (Būyid) (998) i, 1351a; ii, 749a; iii, 128b, 244b; iv, 220a; v, 452b; s, 4a, 118a, 119b, 398a
Ṣamṣām al-Salṭana, Nadjaf Ḳulī Khān (1930) viii, **1050b**
al-Ṣamṣāma i, 453a; viii, **1051b**
Samsat → Sumaysāṭ
Ṣāmsūn (Samsun) i, 476b; ii, 20b, 446b; iv, 575b; viii, **1052a**
Samudra, Pangeran s, 150b
Samudra-pasai (Sumatra) vi, 210b, 702a
Samuel → Ushmūʾīl
Samuel ben Ḥofni (1034) iv, 305b; vii, 539b
Samuel b. Moses al-Maghribī iv, 306b, 605b
Samuel b. Nagrella i, 130b; ii, 1012b, 1016b
Samūʾīl b. Yaḥyā b. ʿAbbās al-Maghribī al-Andalusī (1174) vii, 199b
Samūm viii, **1056a**
Ṣanʿāʾ i, 102b, 440b, 551a, 554b; ii, 1096a; iii, 125a; v, 808b; vi, 36a, 138b, 433b, 436a, b, 437a, 438b, 439a, 559a, 566a, 651a, 667a, 677a; vii, 270a; viii, 184a, 235b; ix, **1a**; s, 22a, b, 61b, 62a, 115b, 236a, 335a, 337b, 338a, 387b
Ṣanāʿ (near Ṣanʿāʾ) s, 236a
Sanāʿ al-Mulk al-Ḥusayn i, 440a
al-Sanā al-Rāhib s, 396a
Sānabād(h) vi, 335b, 714a

Sanābira iv, 664b
Sanad (Sind) b. ʿAlī (864) vi, 600a; vii, 196b, 199b; s, **703a**
Sanadjāt ix, **3a**
al-Sanādjiḳ iii, 186b
al-Ṣanāfīrī iii, 776a
Sanāʾī, Abu 'l-Madjd Madjdūd b. Ādam (1180) i, 764b, 1019a; iv, 57b, 61b, 63a; vi, 609a; vii, 535b; ix, **3b**; s, 240a, 334a, 416b
Ṣanam ix, **5b**
al-Ṣanam iv, 384a
Ṣanam kādis ix, **6a**
Ṣanamayn vi, 548a
Sanandadj ix, **6b**; s, 136b, 145b
al-Ṣanʿānī, ʿAbd al-Razzāḳ b. Ḥammām (827) v, 1162a; vii, 571b, 663a; viii, 374a; ix, **7a**; x, 86a
al-Ṣanʿānī, Abū Firās Daghtham (Duʿaym) (XII) vi, 433b
al-Ṣanʿānī, Ḍiyāʿ al-Dīn Shaʿbān (1736) ix, **8a**
al-Ṣanʿānī, Ḥanash b. ʿAbd Allāh (VIII) s, 81b
al-Ṣanʿānī, Muḥammad b. ʿAbd al-Aʿlā (869) x, 11b
Ṣanāriyya iv, 345a; v, 487b, 488a
Ṣanʿatī (1644) vi, 837a
Ṣanʿatīzāda, ʿAbd al-Ḥusayn iv, 72b; v, 198a
Ṣanāw vi, 80a
Sanāwa-Shumba vi, 384b
al-Ṣanawbarī, Abū Bakr Muḥammad b. Aḥmad (945) iv, 55b; vi, 604b; vii, 566b; ix, **8a**, 652b
Sanbar b. al-Ḥasan iv, 664a
Sanbāt → Sambāṭ
Sancho Garcès Abarca (Navarra) (X) vi, 431b
Sancho Garcia (Castille) (XI) i, 75b, 76a
Sancho Gimeno → Jimeno
Sanchuelo → ʿAbd al-Raḥmān b. Muḥammad b. ʿAbī ʿĀmir
Sand Seas, Arabian → Nafūd
Sandābil i, 116a; ix, **9a**
Ṣandal (X) iv, 459a
Ṣandal (sandal) ix, **9a**
Ṣandal al-Ḥalabī (X) vi, 1040a
Ṣandj (sindj) ix, **9b**
Sandjābī, Karīm (XX) vii, 451a, ix, 642b
Sandjaḳ i, 468b, 469a, 652a, 655b, 1263b, 1264a; ii, 722b, 723b; iv, 563b, 1094b; v, 776a; ix, **11b**
Sandjaḳ Beyi → Sandjaḳ
Sandjaḳdār i, 1135a
Sandjaḳ-i Sherif v, 19a; ix, **13b**
Sandjan v, 1113a, b
Sandjar b. Malik-Shāh Nāṣir al-Dīn (Saldjūḳ) (1157) i, 94b, 283a, 353b, 504a, 524a, 662a, 687a, 750a, 940a, 1001b, 1052a, 1132a; ii, 81a, 333b, 382a, 893b, 1052a, 1100a, 1101a, 1109a, 1143b; iii, 196a, b, 336b, 345a, 1099a, b, 1114b; iv, 18b, 29a, b, 217b, 466a, 581b, 1067a, 1186a; v, 58b, 439a, 454a; vi, 14a, b, 64a, b, 85b, 493b, 524a, 600a, 620a, b, 628a, 782a, 966a; vii, 408a, 489b, 543b, 733b, 755a, b; viii, 76a, 81b, 942b; ix, **15a**; s, 65a, 245b, 279a, 326a, 333b, 682a
Sandjar Abū Shudjāʿī i, 1138a, 1324b
Sandjar al-Ḥalabī (XIII) vi, 322a, b
Sandjar Shāh b. Sayf al-Dīn Ghāzī II (Zangid) (XII) vi, 781a, b
Sandjar Shāh b. Ṭughān Shāh (Saldjūḳ, Harāt) (1187) viii, 63b
Sandjar Sihwastānī (XIII) vi, 48a
Sandjīl (Mons Peregrinus) x, 215a
Ṣandūḳ iv, 227b Ṣanf (Champa) ii, 8b; iii, 1209a; v, 227a; vi, 234a; ix, **17a**
Sangamēshwar vi, 67a
Sangat Singh i, 432b
Sang-i Maghribī i, 1068b
Sangīn ʿAlī I ii, 29b
Sangīn ʿAlī II ii, 30a
Sāngrām, Mahārānā ii, 1128a; iii, 1010a
Ṣanhādja, Banū Ḥammād i, 699a, 700a, 762a, 1174b, 1175b, 1309a, 1319b, 1350a; ii, 115a, 873b, 1121b; iv, 199a, 479b; v, 652b, 653a, 769b, 1177b, 1204a, b; vi, 221b, 259b, 404b, 427a, 728a, 741a, 742a, b, 744a, 1009a; vii, 486a, 583b, 585b, 612b, 994a; viii, 18b; ix, **18a**; xi, 514a; s, 113b
al-Ṣanhādjī, Abu 'l-Gharīb → Ibn Shaddād, ʿAbd al-ʿAzīz
al-Ṣanhādjī, Ibrāhīm b. ʿAbd Allāh (1597) x, 346a
al-Ṣanhādjī, Sīdī Yūsuf b. ʿAlī (1196) vi, 591a
Ṣanhādjiyyūn iii, 339a

Sanḥān (Yemen) vi, 436b
al-Sanhūrī, ʿAbd al-Razzāḳ (1971) vi, 739b; ix, **18b**
al-Sanhūrī, Abu ʾl-Ḥasan (1484) ix, **19a**
al-Sanhūrī, Abu ʾl-Nadja → Sālim b. Muḥammad
al-Sanhūrī, ʿAlī (XVI) vi, 454a
Ṣāniʿ i, 898b; iv, 819a
Ṣāniʿ al-Dawla → Muḥammad Ḥasan Khān
al-Sāniḥ iv, 290b
Sanīn Ḥusayn ii, 124a
Sāniya → Nāʿūra
Saniyya Lands s, 179a
Sankarani vi, 258b
Sankhodhar → Bet
Ṣannādj al-ʿArab → Ibn Muḥriz
Saʿnōnī i, 531a
Sansār Čand iv, 543b
Sanskrit iii, 412b, 1136a, 1215b, 1216a; v, 540a
Santa Cruz i, 245a
Santa Maria de Alarcos → al-Arak
Santa Maria de Algarve → Shantamariyat al-gharb
Santa Maura → Levkas
Santarem → Shantarīn
Santaver → Shantabariyya
Sante Bennūr v, 1259b; vi, 696a
Santiago de Compostela → Shant Yāḳub
Santūr ix, **19b**
Santurin Adasi ix, **20a**
Ṣanūʿ, Yaʿḳūb (XIX) vii, 902b
Sanua, James → Abū Naḍḍāra
Sanūb → Sinob
al-Sanūsī, Abū ʿAbd Allāh Maḥammad b. Yūsuf (1490) i, 333a, 334a, 593a, 696a, 867b, 1019b; iii, 780a; ix, **20a**; s, 403a, b
al-Sanūsī, al-Mahdī b. Muḥammad v, 352b
Sanūsī, Sheykh Sayyid Aḥmad (1933) vi, 530b; ix, **23b**
al-Sanūsī, Sīdī Muḥammad b. ʿAlī (1859) ii, 224a, 378a, 492b; iv, 952b; v, 760a; vi, 355b; vii, 434a; ix, **22b**; s, 164b, 278b
Sanusi, Sir Muhammadu, amīr (Kano) (XX) iv, 550a
Sanūsiyya i, 136a, 277b, 763a, 1049b, 1071a, 1258b, 1260b; ii, 161b, 165a, 224a, 378a; iv, 541b, 777a, 952a, 954b; v, 352a, 760a; viii, 19a; ix, **24b**; x, 249a; s, 164b
Saphadin → al-Malik al-ʿĀdil I Abū Bakr Muḥammad b. Ayyūb, Sayf al-Dīn
Sār, Banū (Ḥaḍramawt) vi, 82a
Šar Planina vi, 89a
Sāra (Bible) ix, **26b**
Sarā → Sarāy
Sāra (singer) iv, 821a
Sara, Banū s, 163b, 165b, 166a, b
Sāra b. Aḥmad al-Sudayrī s, 3b
Sarāb ix, **27a**
Saracens v, 1014b, 1019a; ix, **27b**
Sarāfīl, Sarāfīn → Isrāfīl
Saragossa → Saraḳusṭa
Sarajevo i, 1263a, b, 1265b, 1266b, 1267a, b, 1268a, b, 1270b, 1273a; v, 32a; ix, **28b**
Sarakata i, 741a, b
Sarakhs i, 47b; v, 293b; vi, 335b, 495a, 620b, 633b; ix, 5a, **34a** x, 89a; s, 195a
al-Sarakhsī, ʿAbd al-Raḥmān b. ʿAbd al-Karīm (XII) ii, 752a
al-Sarakhsī, Abu ʾl-ʿAbbās Aḥmad b. al-Ṭayyib (899) i, 339a, 590a, 1003b; ii, 578b; vi, 204b; vii, 683b, 1031b; ix, **35a**
al-Sarakhsī, Muḥammad b. Aḥmad Shams al-Aʾimma (1096) iii, 163a, b, 1024a; v, 130a; vi, 215a, 452a, 558a, 640a; ix, **35b**
al-Sarakhsī, Luḳmān (shaykh) ix, 34b
Sarāḳūdj iii, 186a
Saraḳusṭa (Saragossa) i, 82a, 390a, 493a, 495b; iii, 542a, b, 728a, 1093a; v, 219a; vi, 520b; vii, 768a; ix, **36a**; s, 81b, 82a, 383a
– monuments i, 497b, 499a
al-Saraḳusṭī, Abu ʾl-Ḳāsim Thābit (925) ix, **38a**
al-Saraḳusṭī, Abū Muḥammad Ḳāsim b. Thābit (914) ix, **38a**
al-Sarāḳusṭī, Muḥammad (XV) vi, 281b
Sarāna iv, 1042b
Sarandīb (Sri Lanka/Ceylon) ix, **39a**
Sarandjām i, 260b, 262a
Sārang Khān v, 31b
Sārang Khān Lōdī (Tughlukid) (XV) vi, 49a, b, 294a
Sārangpūr vi, 53a; ix, **39a**
Sarāparda ix, **39b**
al-Sarāt i, 536a, 707b, 811b ; iii, 362a; vi, 144b, 266a; ix, **39b**
Saraṭān ix, **40a**
Sarawak vi, 232b, 241a; ix, **40b**; s, 150a, 151a, 152a

Sarāy ix, **44a**
Saray (Astrakhān) i, 1106a, b, 1108a; iv, 349b, 350a; vi, 420a; ix, **41b**; s, 203b
Sarāy (Baghdād) i, 904b, 906a
Sarāy-aghası ii, 1088a, 1089a; iv, 571a
Saray Bosna s, 354a
Sarāy-Mulk Khātūn (XV) vii, 193b
Saray Ovası → Sarajevo
Sarāy-i Hümāyūn → Sarāy
Sarbadārids iii, 968b, 1123a; iv, 32a, 48b; v, 59a; vi, 13a, 511a, 515b, 549b; ix, **47b**, 158b; x, 552b
Sarbadars → Sarbadārids
Sarbandīs iv, 10b
Sarbuland Khān i, 1053a, 1330a
Sarčam iii, 1125a
Sardāb ii, 114a; ix, **49b**
Sardāniya i, 86b; ix, **49b**; s, 86b. 120b
Sardār (Sirdār) ix, **50b**
Sardār, Amīr Khān (1826) vii, 453a
Sardār Muḥammad ʿAzīz (XX) vii, 438a
Sardār Muḥammad Hāshim Khān i, 232b
Sardār Muḥammad Ibrāhīm iv, 711a
Sardhanā ix, **50b**
Sardinia → Sardāniya
Sardj ix, **51a**
Sardjūn b. Manṣūr (VII) iv, 755a; vii, 268a
Sardjūn b. Manṣūr al-Rūmī (VIII) x, 226a
Sardsir → Kıshlaḳ
Sarekat Islam iii, 534a, 1223b, 1229a; ix, **51b**
Ṣarf iv, 326a; ix, **53a**; s, **703a**
Ṣarfrāz Khān i, 400b; ii, 371a
Ṣarghatmush (Sarghitmish) al-Nāṣirī (1358) iii, 239b, 699a; iv, 424a; vi, 323b, 367b; vii, 170b
Sargūdjā vi, 53a
Ṣarghūn II v, 68a, b
Sarḥadd ix, **54a**
Sarhang ix, **54a**
Sārī (Ḳumān) v, 373a
Sārī/Sāriya (town, Māzandarān) vi, 511a, b, 512a, b, 513a, b, 514a, b, 515b, 517a, 745b; ix, **54b**; s, 298a, 309a, 356b, 357a
al-Sarī b. al-Ḥakam b. Yūsuf al-Balkhī (820) vii, 160b; ix, **55a**
al-Sarī b. Manṣūr → Abu ʾl-Sarāyā
Ṣarı ʿAbd Allāh Effendī (1661) iii, 711a; ix, **59a**
al-Sarī al-Aḳṣam iv, 1132b
Ṣarı Beyoghlı Muṣṭafā iv, 593a
Ṣarı-čay vi, 201a
Sarı Demir Tash Pashā iv, 623a
Sarı Kenʿān Pasha → Kenʿān Pasha
Sarı Kürz (Görez) (1521) ix, **59b**
Sarı Meḥmed Pasha (1717) ix, **60a**
Sarı Muṣṭafa Pasha iv, 969b
Sar-i Pul ix, **26b**, 431a
al-Sarī al-Raffāʾ ix, **55b**
al-Sarī al-Saḳaṭī, Abu ʾl-Ḥasan (867) i, 1245b; ii, 600a; vi, 613b; vii, 467b; ix, **56b**
Ṣarı Ṣalṭuḳ Dede (VII) i, 299a, 838b, 842b, 843a, 993a, 998b, 1031b; ii, 610b, 612a; iii, 115a; iv, 628a, 885a; ix, **61a**
Ṣarīfa i, 1097a
al-Ṣarīfīnī s, 195a
al-Ṣarīfīnī, Shuʿayb b. Ayyūb (875) viii, 14a
Sarighshin iv, 1178a
Sāriḳ → Sariḳa
Sarıḳ (tribe) s, 143b, 146b, 281a; s, 706b
Sariḳa ix, **62b**; s, **707a**
Sarikat → Shirka
Ṣārim b. Sayf al-Dīn (Mukrī) (XVI) ix, 92b
Ṣārim al-Dīn (al-Ṣārimī) Ibrāhīm b. al-Muʾayyad Shaykh (Mamlūk) (1420) vii, 271b
Ṣārim al-Dīn Ḳaymaz Kāfūrī al-Manbidjī (XIII) iv, 483b; vi, 381a
Ṣārim al-Dīn Mubārak (Alamūt) vi, 790b
Sar-i-mūsh iv, 811a
Ṣarı-ṣu vi, 200b, 201a
Sarīr (Avaristān) ii, 86a; iv, 343a, 346a
Sarı-Tash (mountain) vi, 416b
Sāriya → Sārī
Sarkan Bashkurt i, 1075b
Sarkār s, **710a**
Sarkār Āḳā ix, **63b**; 404b
Sarkārs i, 316b; iii, 320b
Sarkash iv, 53b; vi, 276a
Sarkel → Sharkil
Ṣarkhad → Ṣalkhad
Sarkhāstān iv, 646b, 647a
Sarkhēdj (Aḥmadābād) iii, 445a, b; vi, 51a; ix, **64a**
Sarkīs, Khalīl ii, 467b
Sārliyya ix, **64a**
Sarmad → Muḥammad Saʿīd Sarmad
Sarmada vi, 578b
Sarmast, Saččal v, 611a
Ṣarmis → Čeremiss
Sāroēē → Sārūya

Sarpul-i Dhuhāb ix, **64b**
Sarrādj → Sardj
Sarrādj, ʿAbd al-Ḥamīd s, 8a
al-Sarrādj, Abū ʿAlī → Ibn al-Sarrādj, Abū ʿAlī
al-Sarrādj, Abū Muḥammad Djaʿfar b. Aḥmad (1106) i, 69a, 516al vi, 263b; ix, **65a**
al-Sarrādj, Abū Naṣr (988) iii, 546b, 589a; viii, 429a, 579b, 583b, 994a; ix, **65b**
al-Sarrādj, Banū → Ibn al-Sarrādj
al-Sarrādj, Yaḥyā iii, 670b
al-Sarrādj al-Baghdādī → al-Sarrādj, Abū Muḥammad
Ṣarrāf s, **710a**
al-Ṣarrāf, Aḥmad (XIX) vii, 903a
Sarrasins → Saracens
Ṣarrūf, Yaʿḳūb (1912) i, 597a; vii, 902b, 903a; ix, **66b**
Ṣarṣar x, 588a
al-Ṣarṣarī (1160) vi, 898a
Sarshār, Ratan Nāth iii, 359a, 376a; v, 202b
Sar-shumārī ii, 151b; iv, 1042b
Sārt (Tādjīks) v, 30a, 273b; vi, 557b; ix, **66b**
Ṣart (Sardes) ix, **68a** x, 63a, b, 66b
Sartaḳ i, 1106a, 1187b
Saru, Banū vi, 474a
Ṣaru Ṣaltuḳ → Ṣarı̊ Ṣaltı̊ḳ
Sarūdj ix, **68b**
Sarudja (Sarı̊dja) iii, 317b
Ṣarudja Pasha ii, 985b
al-Sarūdjī, Abū Zayd vi, 115a; ix, 68b
Saruḳ (town) s, 142b
Sārūḳ (river) vi, 502b
Ṣarūkhān (dynasty) i, 467b, 654a; v, 505b, 506a, 1169b; vi, 975a, 1015b, 1018b; ix, **69a**
Ṣarūkhān-oghulları̊ → Ṣarūkhān
Sarūkhānī → Gulshanī
Saru-ḳurghan vi, 502b
Sarūr iii, 376a
Sārūya ii, 74b
Sarvantikʿar vi, 776b
Sarwār Khān (Tank) (XIX) s, 329b
Sarwar al-Mulk (XV) vii, 279a
al-Sāwī, Djamāl al-Dīn (1232) x, 251a
Sarwistān ix, **69b**; s, 327a
Sasa Beg (1308) i, 783a
Ṣaʿṣaʿa i, 382b
Sasaks (Lombok) v, 785a, b
Sāsān (Kayānid) iv, 809b
Sāsān, Banū vii, 495a; ix, **70a**; s, 250a
Sāsānids i, 66a, 226a, 938b, 1041a, 1094a; ii, 77b, 190a, 951a; iii, 50b, 113a, 177a, 304a, 470b, 884a; iv, 13a-b, 219b, 850b; v, 56b, 184b, 634a, 831a, 1110a; vi, 11a, 97a, 261a; ix, **70b**; s, 116a, 251a, 297b
– art, architecture ii, 742b, 743a
Sasarām → Sahsarām
Sāsī b. Muḥammad (XX) vi, 251a
Sası̊ Buḳa (Özbeg) s, 246a
Sastroamidjojo, Ali (XX) vi, 732a
Ṣāṣūn v, 459a
Satalia → Antalya
Sātgāʿon (Bengal) ix, **83b**
Satgur Nūr iv, 202b; v, 26a; viii, 125b
Sati-Beg (Il-Khānid) (1319) ii, 68a, b, 401a; vi, 482b
Sāṭiʿ al-Ḥuṣrī (1968) ii, 1117b; v, 905b; s, **711b**
Saṭīḥ b. Rabīʿa iii, 739b; ix, **84a**, 440b
Satpanth iv, 206a
Satpanthīs i, 173a; iii, 1163a; iv, 202b; ix, **85a**
Satr s, **712a**
Sattār Khān s, 365b
Satuḳ Bughra Khān → ʿAbd al-Karīm Khān
Saturdjı̊ Meḥmed Pasha v, 27b
Saturiḳ iii, 1125a
Satya Pīr (Bengal) iii, 422b; ix, **85a**
Saʿūd → Suʿūd
Saʿūd b. ʿAzzān b. Ḳays s, 356a
Saudi Arabia → al-Suʿūdiyya
Saʿūdiyya → al-Suʿūdiyya
Saʿudj-Bulāḳ → Sāwdj-Bulāḳ
Saul → Ṭālūt
Sava (river, Bosnia) vi, 56a
Sava (town, Afghānistān) ii, 746a
Savak iv, 41b
Savak (Savaz) ii, 70a
Sāwa (Sāva) (Persia) ii, 746a; v, 868b; vi, 64a; ix, **85b**
al-Sawād (Malaṭya) i, 382b; ii, 577a; iv, 1140b; v, 345b, 347b; vi, 230b, 633b, 738b; ix, **87a**; s, 59a
Sawād b. Ghanm b. Kaʿb b. Salima, Banū vi, 649a
Sāwadjī, Saʿd al-Dīn (1312) viii, 169a; ix, 86b

al-Sāwadjī, ʿUmar b. Sahlān (1145) ix, 782a
Sawādkūh vi, 511b, 513a, 514a, b, 515a; vii, 440b
Sawādkūhīs vi, 512a
Ṣawāfī → Ṣāfī
Sawāʿī → Djay Singh
Sawākin i, 782b, 1158a, 1172a; iv, 643a, 687a; v, 1249b, 1251a; vi, 642b, 643a; viii, 235b; ix, **87b**
Sawalān vi, 501a, 504a
Sawār (amīr) (Aleppo) (XII) v, 124b, 125b, 922a; vi, 380a
Ṣawda (Zawda), Banū vi, 742a
al-Sawdāʾ (al-Khariba) ix, **90b**
al-Sawdāʾ (Khūriyā Mūriyā) i, 535b
Sawdā, Mīrzā Muḥammad Rafīʿ (poet) (1781) i, 241b; iii, 119a, 358b; iv, 716b; v, 959a, b, 961a; vi, 611a; vii, 669b, 998b; ix, **90a**; x, 878a; xi, 2a; s, 109b, 358b
Sawda bint Zamʿa b. Ḳayyis (674) i, 307b; vi, 646a; ix, **89b**; s, 172a
Sawdān i, 1166b; iv, 275b
Sāwdj-Bulāḳ v, 1213a; vi, 498b, 502a, b; ix, 92a
Sawdjî, Sawdjī ix, **93a**
Sawdjī Beg b. Ertoghrul ix, 93a
Sawdūb, amīr (nāẓir al-Azhar) (XV) vi, 672b
al-Sāwī, Djamāl al-Dīn iv, 473a, b
Sāwī (Sāwadjī), Zayn al-Dīn ʿUmar b. Sahlān (XII) viii, 542a
Sawīḳ ix, **93b**
al-Ṣawīra (Mogador) vi, 589a; vii, 391b, a
Ṣawlat al-Dawla Khān iv, 706b
Ṣawlat Djang ii, 1091b
Sawm ix, **93b**
Ṣawm v, 424b; ix, **94a**
al-Ṣawmaʿī → Aḥmad b. Abi ʾl-Ḳāsim
Sāwra (valley) s, 28b
Sawra b. Ḥurr al-Tamīmī ii, 600b
Sawrān s, 245a, b
Sawrāshtra ii, 1123b, 1130b
Sawsanī, Abū Sahl iii, 256a
Sawte(i)gin, ʿImād al-Dīn (Ghulām) (XI) i, 660b; ii, 1082b; iii, 471b; iv, 348a; vi, 274a; x, 480b; s, 383b
Ṣawtiyya ix, **95b**
Sāwudjbulāgh s, 73a
Sawuran Ḳalʿe → Sarvantikʿar
Sawwār b. ʿAbd Allāh s, 113a
Sawwār b. Ḥamdūn ii, 1012b
Saʿy iii, 35a, 36b; iv, 185a; ix, **97b**
Sayābidja i, 761b; ix, **97b**
Sayābiga → Sayābidja
Ṣayd ix, **98b**
Ṣaydā (Sidon) iii, 474b; iv, 483a, 484a; ix, **99a**; s, 49a, 120b, 268a
al-Ṣaydana/al-Ṣaydala ix, **100a**
al-Ṣaydāwī, Shams al-Dīn Muḥammad (1506) ix, **101a**
Saydnāyā (Maʿlūlā) vi, 308a
Sayf (sword) ii, 1122a; iv, 502b; v, 972b, 973a
Sayf b. Dhī Yazan (Sīrat) i, 102a; ii, 1096a; iv, 566b; vi, 830a; ix, **101b**; xi, 302a; ix, 52a; s, 115b, 164a
Sayf b. Sulṭān I (Yaʿrubid) (1711) v, 507a; vi, 735a; viii, 85a; xi, 292a
Sayf b. Sulṭān II (Yaʿrubid) (1743) i, 1281b; vi, 735a; x, 816b; xi, 292b
Sayf b. ʿUmar al-Tamīmī (809) i, 51a, 629a; iv, 385a; v, 324a; vi, 267b; viii, 638a; ix, **102a**; s, 701b
Sayf b. Zāmil b. Djabr s, 234a
Sayf ʿAlī Beg i, 1135a
Sayf ʿAyn al-Mulk iii, 1161a
Sayf al-Dawla Abu ʾl-Ḥasan ʿAlī (Ḥamdānid) (967) i, 118a, 119b, 329a, 517a, 679b, 789b, 791b, 845b; ii, 36b, 178b, 344a, 693b; iii, 20a, 86a, 127a, b, 129a, b, 398a, 404b, 507a, 824b, 900a; v, 124b, 525a, 923b; vi, 242b, 379a, 506b, 545a, 775b, 930a; vii, 115b, 411b, 770a, b, 983b, 995a, b; ix, **103a**, s, 12b, 36a, 37b, 361b, 362a
Sayf al-Dawla Aḥmad b. Hūd → Aḥmad III (Hūdid)
Sayf al-Dawla Maḥmūd b. Ẓahīr al-Dawla (Ghaznawid) (1076) ii, 1052a; vi, 783a; s, 21a, 24a
Sayf al-Dawla Ṣadaḳa s, 326a
Sayf al-Dīn → al-ʿĀdil I
Sayf al-Dīn (Aleppo) (XII) vi, 380b
Sayf al-Dīn (Shansabānid/Ghūrid) ix, **110a**
Sayf al-Dīn b. Afrāsiyāb (Marʿashī) (XIV) vi, 511a
Sayf al-Dīn Aybak b. Iltutmish (XIII) vi, 47b
Sayf al-Dīn ʿAzāz al-Ṣāliḥī, amīr (1298) vi, 777b
Sayf al-Dīn Bākharzī, Abu ʾl-Maʿālī (1261)

i, 347b; v, 301a; viii, 539a; ix, **110a**, 862b; x, 251a
Sayf al-Dīn Balabān al-Djukāndār (1306) viii, 158a
Sayf al-Dīn Bizlār al-Manṣūrī, amīr (1298) vi, 777b
Sayf al-Dīn Dengiz (XIV) vi, 231a
Sayf al-Dīn Fīrūz → Fīrūz Shāh (Bengal)
Sayf al-Dīn Ghāzī I b. ʿImād al-Dīn (Zangid) (1149) i, 1160b; ii, 489b, 1045a; iii, 327b; vi, 870b; viii, 127b; ix, 12b
Sayf al-Dīn Ghāzī II (Zangid) (1160) ii, 1045a; vi, 781a, 871b
Sayf al-Dīn ʿImād al-Dīn Farāmurz s, 416a
Sayf al-Dīn Ḳipčaḳ al-Manṣūrī (1310) vi, 545b, 777b
Sayf al-Dīn al-Malik al-Nāṣirī ii, 126a
Sayf al-Dīn Muḥammad ii, 1101a, 1103a
Sayf al-Dīn-oghlu (Tripoli) (XVII) vii, 707b
Sayf al-Dīn Sunḳur, atābeg (XIII) vi, 434a
Sayf al-Dīn Sūrī i, 940a; ii, 382a, 1100a
Sayf al-Dīn Tungur (XIV) vi, 544a
Sayf al-Ḥaḳḳ Abu 'l-Mafākhir Muḥammad b. Manṣūr (XII) ix, 4a
Sayf al-Islām Badr ii, 674b
Sayf al-Mulk Ibn ʿAmrūn (al-Kahf) (XII) vi, 789b
Sayf al-Mulūk (Khāndesh) s, 335b
Sayf al-Raḥmān ii, 31a
Sayfī (XVI) i, 323a; v, 314b
Sayfī ʿArūḍī Bukhārī (XV) ix, **111b**
Sayfī Harawī (XIV) ix, **112a**
Saygun, Adnan iii, 1094b
al-Sayḥ i, 233a
Ṣayhad (desert) vi, 566a; s, 337a
Sayḥān (Saros) i, 184a; ii, 35a, 502b; ix, **112a**
Sayḥūn → Sir Daryā
Sayhūt s, 337a
Sāyigh, Fatḥ Allāh (XIX) ix, **113a**
Sāyigh, Tawfīḳ (1971) ix, **113b**
Sāyin Bulāt iv, 723b
Ṣaymara (town) ix, **113b**
al-Ṣaymarī, Abu 'l-ʿAbbas Yaʿḳūbī ii, 552a; ix, **114a**
al-Ṣaymarī, Abū ʿAbd Allāh Muḥammad (XI) ix, 668b; s, 25a
al-Ṣaymarī, Abu 'l-ʿAnbas → Abu 'l-ʿAnbas al-Ṣaymarī
al-Ṣaymarī, Muḥammad b. ʿUmar (927) vii, 785b
Saymūr vii, 919b
Sayr b. ʿAbd Allāh (Usrūshana) (893) x, 925a
al-Ṣayrafī, Muḥammad b. Badr (942) ix, **114a**
al-Ṣayrafī, Shihāb al-Dīn ʿAbd Allāh (XIV) viii, 806b
Sayram (Isfīdjāb) s, 459b
Sayrām (town) ii, 39a, 45b; ix, **114b**, 621b
Say'ūn, Saywūn (Ḥaḍramawt) vi, 132b; vii, 496b; ix, **115a**; s, 337b, 338b
Sayūna ix, 699a, b
Ṣayyād, Banū iv, 10b
al-Ṣayyād, ʿIzz al-Dīn Aḥmad (1271) viii, 525b
al-Ṣayyādī, Muḥammad Abu 'l-Hudā (1909) vi, 88a; viii, 526a
Sayyāḥ, Ḥādjdj s, 109b
Sayyi'a iv, 1106b
Sayyid (Saʿīd) (title) i, 1022b; ii, 687b; iii, 411a; v, 627a; ix, **115a**
Sayyid ʿAbd al-ʿAẓīm Mīrzā → Aghā-bakhsh
Sayyid Abū Bakr iii, 1218b
Sayyid Abū Bakr (Sharīf al-Hāshim) (Sulu) (XV) viii, 303b
Sayyid Āghā Ḥasan → Amānat
Sayyid Aḥmad b. ʿAbd al-Raḥmān iv, 780a
Sayyid Aḥmad b. ʿAlawī Marʿashī (1144) vi, 517a
Sayyid Aḥmad b. Muḥammad b. ʿAlī Mūsāwī Marʿashī (XIX) vi, 516b
Sayyid Aḥmad Brēlwī → Aḥmad Brēlwī
Sayyid Aḥmad Khān → Aḥmad Khān, Sir Sayyid
Sayyid Aḥmad Shāh, Mīrzā v, 164a
Sayyid Akbar i, 238b; iv, 1143a
Sayyid ʿAlī Dūghlāt ii, 622a
Sayyid ʿAlī Hamadānī (1384) viii, 134b
Sayyid ʿAlī Khān ii, 47b
Sayyid ʿAlī Muḥammad → Bāb
Sayyid ʿAlī Muḥammad Shād ʿAẓīmābādī (1927) vi, 838b
Sayyid ʿAlī Naṣr (1961) vi, 764a
Sayyid ʿĀlim Khān, amīr (Mangit) (1920) vi, 419a
Sayyid Awlād ʿAlī Khān (1803) vii, 1048b
Sayyid al-Awwal i, 606b

Sayyid ʿAẓīm i, 193b
Sayyid Badrān b. Falāḥ (Mus͟haʿs͟haʿ) (XVI) vii, 673a
Sayyid Baṭṭāl → al-Baṭṭāl
Sayyid Burhān K͟hān iv, 724a
Sayyid Darwīs͟h (1923) x, 144a
Sayyid Ḍiyāʾ al-Dīn (XX) vii, 654a; s, 84a
Sayyid D͟jaʿfar b. Nūrbak͟hs͟h (XVI) viii, 135b
Sayyid D͟jalāl al-Dīn Buk͟hārī (XIV) ix, 673
Sayyid Dūst Muḥammad b. Sayyid Ḳuṭb al-Dīn s, 325a
Sayyid Falāh b. Muḥsin (Mus͟haʿs͟haʿ) (1514) vii, 673a
Sayyid Fatḥī (XVIII) vi, 56b
Sayyid Fayyāḍ (Mus͟haʿs͟haʿ) (XVI) vii, 673a
Sayyid Ḥasan b. Ḥamza b. ʿAlī Marʿas͟h (968) vi, 517a
Sayyid Ḥasan Beg (XVIII) iv, 201b
Sayyid Ḥasan G͟haznawī (1161) ix, **116a**
Sayyid Ḥasan Mudarris (1938) vii, 223b
al-Sayyid al-Ḥimyarī, Abū Hās͟him (789) i, 431b; ii, 136a; iii, 882a; iv, 836b; v, 552b; vi, 604a, 635b; ix, **116b**, 454a
Sayyid Ḥasan Taḳīzāda → Taḳīzāda, Sayyid Ḥasan
Sayyid Ḥusayn ʿAli K͟hān Bārha → Bārha Sayyids
Sayyid Isḥāḳ ii, 733a
Sayyid Kāẓim Ras͟htī → Ḳāẓim Ras͟htī
Sayyid K͟hān ii, 973b
Sayyid Ḳuṭb (1966) viii, 907b; ix, **117a**
Sayyid Ḳuṭb al-Dīn b. Sayyid Masʿūd (XIV) s, 325a
Sayyid Maḥmūd D͟jawnpūrī ii, 500a
Sayyid Mansab (1922) iv, 887a
Sayyid Manṣūr (XVI) xi, 115b
Sayyid Masʿūd s, 325a
Sayyid Mīrān Hās͟himī (1697) vi, 837b
Sayyid Mubārak b. Muṭṭalib b. Badrān (Mus͟haʿs͟haʿ) (1616) vii, 672a, b
Sayyid Muḥammad, Mīr s, 340a
Sayyid Muḥammad, Mīrzā (XIX) s, 23b, 74a
Sayyid Muḥammad b. ʿAlī → al-Idrīsī
Sayyid Muḥammad b. Falāḥ (Mus͟haʿs͟haʿ) (1465) vii, 672a
Sayyid Muḥammad b. Sayyid ʿAlāʾ al-Dīn ii, 967b
Sayyid Muḥammad b. Sayyid ʿAlī al-Hamdānī iv, 708b
Sayyid Muḥammad Buzurg-Sawār i, 262a; ii, 194a
Sayyid Muḥammad Dāmād (Āyatullāh) (XX) vii, 762b
Sayyid Muḥammad D͟jawnpūrī → al-D͟jawnpūrī
Sayyid Muḥammad K͟hān (Awadh) (XIX) ii, 1046a
Sayyid Muḥammad K͟hān (Delhi) s, 247a
Sayyid Muḥammad Mīrzā Dug͟hlāt ii, 622b
Sayyid Muḥsin (Mus͟haʿs͟haʿ) (1499) vii, 672b
Sayyid Murād iv, 1158a
al-Sayyid Murtaḍā i, 266a, b
Sayyid Murtaḍā Efendi, S͟hayk͟h al-Islām (1750) vi, 1004b
Sayyid Nad͟hīr Ḥusayn i, 259b
Sayyid Nūḥ ii, 588b
Sayyid al-Ruʾasāʾ Ibn Kamāl al-Mulk (1083) viii, 72a
Sayyid Sad͟jd͟jād b. Badrān (Mus͟haʿs͟haʿ) (XVI) vii, 673a
Sayyid S͟hams al-Dīn (XV) vi, 62a
Sayyid Ṣiddīḳ Ḥasan → Nawwāb Sayyid Ṣiddīḳ
Sayyid al-Tābiʿīn → Saʿīd b. al-Musayyab
Sayyid Ṭālib al-Rifāʿī al-Naḳīb iii, 520a
Sayyid Yaḥyā b. Sayyid Ḳuṭb al-Dīn s, 325a
al-Sayyida → ʿĀʾis͟ha al-Mannūbiyya
al-Sayyida al-ʿAlawiyya bint Wat͟ht͟hāb Sābiḳ al-Numayrī (XI) xi, 181a
Sayyida ʿĀtiḳa vii, 10b
Sayyida Ḥurra bint Aḥmad i, 181b, 552a; ii, 856a; iii, 134a; iv, 200b
al-Sayyida al-Kubrā → Ṣubḥ
Sayyida Ruḳayya vii, 10b
Sayyida umm Fak͟hr al-Dawla iv, 465a; v, 1028a, b
Sayyida Zaynab bint Muḥammad al-S͟hahāriyya (1702) vii, 879a; ix, 201b
Sayyids (Delhi) vi, 50a, 692b; vii, 795b; ix, **118b**
Sayyidī Abū Saʿīd i, 863b
Sayyid-i Ad͟jall S͟hams al-Dīn ʿUmar (1279) xi, 346b
Sāz ix, **120a**; s, 91b
Sbīṭla → Subayṭila

Sbuk → Subuk
Scanderbeg → Iskender Beg
Scenites i, 527b
Schnitzer, Carl → Emīn Pasha
Scutari → Üsküdār
Sea → Baḥr
Sea of Aral → Aral
Sea of Azov → Baḥr Māyuṭis
Sea of Marmara → Marmara Deñizi
Seʿādet Girāy Khān I (Crimea) (1532) viii, 832a
Seʿadya → Saʿīd
Sebastiyya → Sabastiyya
Sebeos (bishop) i, 635b, 636b
Sebḥa → Sabkha
Sebou (river) → Sabū, Wādī
Sebük-eri (X) viii, 796b
Sebüktegin, Abū Manṣūr Nāṣir al-Dawla (Ghaznawid) (977) i, 11b, 142b, 226b, 421b, 424b, 899b, 1348b; ii, 799a, 978a, 1049a, 1050b; iii, 46b, 197a, 415b; iv, 24b, 208b, 917b; v, 622b, 649a; vi, 65a, 193a; vii, 193a, 987a; viii, 67b, 110a, 797b, 1028a; ix, **121a**; s, 284b
Secuna (Cordova) → Shaḳunda
Secunderabad → Sikandarābād
Sedrata ii, 115a
Seethi Sahib, K.M. (1960) vi, 460a, 462a
Sefāretnāme → Safīr
Sefawa iv, 566b
Sefer-beg i, 101a
Sefer Ghāzī (Agha) iv, 178b, 630a
Sefrou → Sufrūy
Segbān s, **713a**
Segestan → Sīstān
Segovia → Shaḳūbiyya
Segu, Segou i, 297a; iii, 39a; vi, 259a, b, 402b; ix, **121b**
Seguiat el Hamra → al-Sāḳiya al-Ḥamrāʾ
Segura → Shaḳūra
Sèh Nurullah (Shaykh Nūr Allāh) (XVI) ix, 852b
Sehī Bey (1548) ix, **122a**
Sehī of Edirne (1548) x, 55a
Sekou Ouattara v, 252b
Sekou Touré ii, 1133a
Seku Hamadu → Aḥmadu
Selāmlïḳ ii, 114b; ix, **123a**
Selangor vi, 232b, 236b, 242a
Selānīk vi, 69a, 74a, 89a, 150b; ix, **123a**; s, 63a, 269b
Selānīkī, Muṣṭafā Efendi (1600) ix, **126b**
Selayar vi, 116a
Selčuk → Aya Solūk
Selčuk b. Toḳaḳ Temir Yalïgh x, 690a
Seldjen-oghlu iii, 1199a
Seldjuḳs/Seldjuḳides → Saldjūḳids
Selīm I (Yavuz) (Ottoman) (1520) i, 21b, 182b, 310b, 329b, 362a, 396a, 441a, 468a, 475a, 477a, 553b, 1032b, 1120b, 1207b, 1208a, 1234a; ii, 7b, 38b, 72b, 240a, 286a, b, 291b, 340a, 373b, 374a, 400a, 420b, 634b, 684a, 722b, 968a, 1042a; iii, 213b, 216a, 341b, 708b, 1183b; iv, 376a, 553a, 716b, 868b, 880a, 899b, 900a, 945b, 1156a; v, 269b; vi, 150a, 231b, 315a, 325a, 530a, b, 531a, 544a, 588a, 795a; vii, 176b, 272b, 319a; viii, 195b; ix, **127a**; s, 274a
Selīm II (Ottoman) (1574) i, 152a, 329b, 380a, 775b; ii, 25a, 82b, 737b; iii, 1183b; v, 67a, 138b, 814a; vi, 708b; viii, 124a, 195b, 770b; ix, **131b**
Selīm III (Ottoman) (1807) i, 63a, 790b, 948a, 1064b, 1165a, 1171b, 1252a, 1268a, 1278a; ii, 12a, 83b, 206b, 339a, 511b, 512a, 684a, 694a, 697a, 712b, 999a; iii, 384b, 627b; iv, 168a, 322b, 589a, 900b; v, 725a; vi, 6a, 58a, 284b, 725a, 757b, 801b, 912b; vii, 275a, 424a, 709b; viii, 59a, 75a; ix, **132b**
Selīm Girāy I (Crimea) (1704) i, 893b; ii, 990b, 1047a; iv, 569a; v, 140a; ix, **134b**
Selīm Girāy II (Crimea) (1748) vi, 1002b
Selīm Girāy III (Crimea) (1771) i, 4b; v, 141a
Selīm Meḥmed Pasha v, 36a
Selīm Pasha ii, 636a
Selmān Reʾīs (1527) iv, 552b; ix, **135a**
Selwī (Sevlievo) ix, **136a**
Semāʿ Khāne → Samāʿ
Semarang s, 201a
Semaun s, 151b
Sembat Bagratuni (Armenia, 914) iv, 90a; vii, 395a
Semedirek (Samothrace) ix, **137a**
Semendire (Smederovo) s, **714a**
Semendria → Smederovo
Semetey b. Manas (Kïrghïz) vi, 371a
Semey (Semipalatinsk) vi, 768b
Semīr Aḥmed Pasha (XVI) vii, 7a
Semireč(i)ye → Yeti Su vi, 274a, 618b; vii, 218a

Şemo, Ereb v, 484a
Sencer Divitçioğlu (XX) vi, 96a
Sened-i Ittifāḳ ii, 640a,b
Senegal ii, 94a, 567a; vi, 259b, 281b; vii, 609a; ix, **137b**; x, 465a, 575a; xi, 123a; s, 179a, 182a, 218a → Dakar
Senekʿerim i, 638a
Senghor Léopold Sédar ix, 144b
Senkere (Sankara) ix, **148b**
Senna → Sanandadj
Sennār → Sinnār
Senneh s, 136b, 142b, 145a
Senoufo ii, 63a; v, 252b
Şenyurt vi, 542a
Sepoy → Sipāhī
Sepoy Mutiny (1857) s, 325b
"Septimains" → Sabʿiyya
Serajévo → Sarajevo
Serʿasker → Bāb-i Serʿasker
Serbest Fırka s, 47b
Serbest(iyyet) iii, 589b
Serbia → Ṣirb
Serçe Liman vii, 45b
Seringapatam → Shrīrangapattanam
Serḳīn, Awlād v, 596a, b
Serres (Serrai) → Siroz
Servet → Ṭāhir Bey
Seth → Shīth
Sétif vi, 435a; s, 145a
Sevan → Gökče-Tengiz
Sevdalinka i, 1271a
"Seveners" → Sabʿiyya
Severus → Ibn al-Muḳaffaʿ
Sèves, Colonel → Sulaymān Pasha al-Faransawī
Sevilla → Ishbīliya
Sevin Beg → Khān-zāda Bēgum
Sevindj b. Būrī iii, 120a
Şevket Süreyya Aydemir (XX) vi, 95a
Sewindj (amīr, Türkmen) (XIII) vi, 501a
Seychelles ix, **149a**
Seydī Aḥmed Pasha v, 258b
Seydī ʿAlī Pasha v, 764a
Seyf ül-Dīn, ʿÖmer → ʿÖmer Seyf ül-Dīn
Seyfī (1590) ix, **149b**
Seyhan → Sayḥān
Seyit Vehbi, Hüseyin / Wehbi-yi Ḳadīm (Ewwel) → Wehbī, Sayyidī Ḥusayn
Seyrānī (XIX) vi, 826b
Seyrek-zāde vi, 971a
Seytek (Ḳirghiz) vi, 371a
Seyyid → Sayyid
Sezāʾī Ḥasan Dede (1738) ii, 686a; ix, **150a**
Sezāʾī, Sāmī Pasha-zāde (1936) v, 194a, 195a; ix, **150a**
Ṣfar, Bashīr iv, 159b
Sfax → Safāḳus
Sgrafiatto iv, 1166b
Shaaban Robert (1962) vi, 612b, 613a; ix, **150b**
Shaʿanba v, 361b, 362a
Shaʿb i, 535a; iv, 334a, 746a, 819a; ix, **150b**
Shaba → Katanga
Shaʿbadha (Shaʿwadha) ix, **152b**
Shabak, Banū i, 990a; iv, 187b; ix, **152b**
Shabakhtān ix, **153b**
Shaʿbān (month) ix, **154a**
Shaʿbān I, al-Malik al-Kāmil (Mamlūk) (1345) iii, 48a; v, 1141a; ix, **154b**
Shaʿbān II, al-Malik al-Ashraf Nāṣir al-Dīn (Mamlūk) (1377) i, 790a, 1050b; ii, 970a; iii, 346b; vii, 171a; ix, **154b**; s, 395b
Shaʿbān Welī (1568) ix, 155b
al-Shābandar, ʿAbd al-Raḥmān iii, 522b
al-Shaʿbāniyya i, 426b; iv, 991b, 992a; ix, **155a**
Shabānkāra, Banū iii, 1097a; v, 161a, 450b, 454a, 671a; vii, 408a; viii, 701b; ix, **156b**; s, 326a, 382b
Shabānkāraʾī, Muḥammad b. ʿAlī (1358) i, 1131a; vii, 987a; ix, **158b**
Shābarān ix, 488b
Shābāshiyya ix, **159a**
Shabath b. Ribʿī (VII) vii, 522b
al-Shābb al-Ẓarīf → Ibn al-ʿAfīf al-Tilimsānī
Shabbānāt, Banū vi, 141b, 142a, b, 294a, 595a
al-Shabbās (1052) iv, 663b
Shabbatay Ṣebī (1676) ii, 615b, 987a; ix, **159a**
Shabbaz → Kāth
al-Shābbī, Abu 'l-Ḳāsim (1934) i, 598b; ix, **160a**
al-Shābbī, Muḥammad al-Masʿūdī (XVII) vi, 355b
Shabelle → Shebelle
Shābbī Sīdī ʿArfa viii, 763a

Shabbīr Ḥasan Khān Djosh (1982) ix, **161a**
Shābbiyya iii, 69b; iv, 828a
al-Shaʿbī, ʿĀmir b. Sharāḥīl (722) ix, **162b**
al-Shaʿbī, al-ḳāḍī al-Kūfī (721) vi, 670b; vii, 631b; viii, 387a; s, 232b
Shabīb b. Badjara iii, 887a, 889a
Shabīb b. al-Barṣāʿ vii, 629b
Shabīb b. Shayba, Abū Maʿmar (VIII) ix, **163b**
Shabīb b. Waththāb b. Sābiḥ al-Numayrī (1068) vii, 118a; xi, 180b
Shabīb b. Yazīd b. Nuʿaym al-Shaybānī (697) i, 77a, 693b; iii, 40b, 203b, 649b, 715b, 1168a; iv, 369b, 1075b; ix, **164a**, 766b
Shabīb al-Nadjrānī iv, 369b
Shabībiyya iv, 369b
Shābīn Ḳarā Ḥiṣār iv, 578b
Shabistar vi, 72b, 73a
Shabistarī, Maḥmūd-i → Maḥmūd Shabistarī
Shabistarī, Mudjtahid (XX) iv, 166b
Shaʿbiyya → al-Nukkār
Shābkhāne iv, 579a
Shabrīṭ b. al-Ṭawīl, Banū s, 82a
Shabṭūn (819) ix, **165a**
al-Shābush(t)ī, Abu 'l-Ḥasan ʿAlī (988) ii, 127a, 195a; vi, 199b; vii, 390b; ix, **165b**
Shabwa iii, 52a,b; vi, 80b, 559a, 560b; ix, **165b**; s, 336b, 337a, b
Shādagān ii, 181a
Shadd ix, **166b**
Shaddād, Banū → Shaddādid
Shaddād b. ʿĀd i, 181a; iii, 173b, 1270b; ix, **169a**
Shaddād Abū ʿAntara s, 178a
Shaddād b. ʿAmr (VII) i, 44b; ix, **169a**
Shaddādids i, 420b, 421a, 507b, 639a, 660b, 796b; iv, 345a, 347a, b, 670a; v, 452a, 489a; vi, 64b, 274a; ix, **169a**
Shādgeldī → Ḥādjdjī Shādgeldī
Shādh (title) xi, 224a
Shādhdh iii, 25b, 26b
Shadhfarī vi, 384a
Shādhī iii, 115a
Shādhī Ayyūb → Ayyūb b. Shādhī
al-Shādhilī, Abu 'l-Ḥasan ʿAlī b. ʿAbd Allāh al-Djabbār al-Zarwīlī (1258) i, 1b, 91b, 309a, 1019b; iii, 513b, 722b; iv, 449b; vi, 280a, 355a, b, 356a; ix, **170b**; x, 247a; s, 350b
al-Shādhilī, ʿAlī b. ʿUmar (1418) i, 781a; iv, 449b, 450a, b, 741a; vii, 513b
al-Shādhilī, Shams al-Dīn Abu 'l-Fatḥ b. Wafāʿ al-Iskandarī (1358) vi, 112a
al-Shādhiliyya i, 70b, 371a, 596b, 679b, 966a, 1260b; ii, 160a, 224a,b; iii, 339b, 535b, 670b; iv, 992b; v, 948b; vi, 88a, 203b, 454b; vii, 246a; viii, 18b; ix, **172b**, 507b; x, 247a; s, 18a, 44a, 93a, 208b, 223a, 244a, 278b, 408a, 411a
Shadhkān → Shāpūr
Shadhūna → Shadhūna
Shādī Khān (Bengal) (1442) vi, 46b
Shādīābād → Māndū
Shadirwān iv, 481a; v, 1146a; ix, **175a**
Shadjāʿat Khān (Gudjarāt) (1701) iv, 93a
Shadjāʿat Khān (Mālwā) (1554) vi, 310a, 407a
Shadjar(at) al-Durr, umm Khalīl (1257) i, 732a, 766a; vi, 45a, 261b, 321a, b, 327a; vii, 166b, 990a; viii, 989a; ix, **176a**
al-Shadjdjār i, 704a
Shadūna (Media Sidonia) ix, **176b**
Shādyākh vi, 854a
Shafāʿa i, 334b, 958b; ii, 306b; ix, **177b**
al-Shafaḳ ix, **179b**
Shāfiʿ b. ʿAlī al-ʿAsḳalānī (1330) vi, 144a, 352a; vii, 167a; ix, **180b**
Shafīʿ Māzandarānī, Mīrzā s, 336a, 406b, **620b**
Shafīʿa Yazdī (1670) iv, 1124b; ix, **186a**
al-Shāfiʿī, al-Imām Abū ʿAbd Allāh Muḥammad b. Idrīs (820) i, 123b, 155a, 259a, 272b, 551a, 588b, 773a, 1130b, 1199a, 1242a; ii, 102b, 889b; iii, 24a, 63b, 162b, 674b, 1024a; iv, 256a, 425a, 430a, 896a; v, 240a, 731b, 1131a, 1142a; vi, 113b, 263b, 265b, 352b, 353a, 451b, 452a, 605a, 652b, 739a; vii, 691b; viii, 497b; ix, **181a**
al-Shāfiʿī, Muḥammad b. al-Ḥasan (1277) vi, 354a
Shāfiʿiyya i, 150b, 338a, 339a; ii, 559a; iii, 6b, 17a, 512b, 687b; iv, 46a, 47b, 172b, 269b; v, 109b; vi, 2a, 3a; ix, **185a**
Shafīḳ Manṣūr (1925) viii, 360a
Shāfil (Yemen) i, 446a
Shafshawa(ān)/Shīshāwa i, 55b; vi, 742b, 743b; ix, **189b**
Shaftī, Sayyid Muḥammad Bāḳir (1844) vii, 302b, 453b; s, 75b, 135a

Shafūniyya vi, 544b
Shāgirds iii, 217b
Shāh/Shāhanshāh (titles) v, 630a, b; ix, **190b**
Shāh b. Mīkāl (Mīkālī) (914) vii, 26a
Shāh ʿAbbās I, II, III (Ṣafawid) → ʿAbbās
Shāh ʿAbd Allāh (1485) ix, 369b; x, 256a
Shāh ʿAbd al-ʿAẓīm al-Ḥasanī (864) ii, 650b; vi, 21a; ix, **191a**
Shāh ʿAbd al-ʿAzīz al-Dihlawī → ʿAbd al-ʿAzīz al-Dihlawī
Shāh ʿAbd al-Ḳādir Dihlawī → ʿAbd al-Ḳādir Dihlawī
Shāh ʿAbd al-Laṭīf → Bhitāʾī
Shāh ʿAbd al-Raḥīm al-ʿUmarī i, 1023a; ii, 254a; v, 1135b
Shāh Abu ʾl-Ḳāsim Sulṭān → Bēglār
Shāh Afḍal (Chitral) (1795) ii, 30a
Shāh Afḍal II b. Muḥtaram Shāh II (Chitral) (1853) ii, 30a
Shāh ʿĀlam I Bahādur Shāh (Mughal) → Bahādur Shāh
Shāh ʿĀlam II, Djalāl al-Dīn ʿAlī Dhawhar (Mughal) (1806) i, 813b; ii, 121b, 186a, 808b, 1092b; iii, 428a; vi, 535b, 536a, 537a; vii, 94a, 316a, 346a; viii, 5b; ix, **192b**
Shāh ʿĀlam b. Burhān al-Dīn Ḳuṭb-i ʿĀlam (XV) i, 1329b
Shāh ʿĀlam Khān iii, 59b
Shāh ʿAlī Khān iv, 723b, 849b
Shāh-i Arman (Turcomans, Akhlāṭ) i, 329a; vi, 781b; ix, **193a**
Shāh Bandar ix, **193b**
Shāh Beg Arghūn i, 227b, 228a, 627b, 961b, 1192a; iii, 420a, 632b; iv, 535a, 536b
Shāh Bēgam (1605) vii, 331b
Shāh Budāgh Khān, amīr (XVII) vi, 407a
Shāh Dagh s, **716a**
Shāh Dāʿī Shīrāzī (poet) (XV) viii, 45b
Shāh Dawla, pīr (1713) ii, 1131b
Shāh Djahān I (Mughal) (1666) i, 60b, 66a, 81a, 199b, 208a, 228b, 252b, 253a, 686b, 710a, 856a, 1161a, 1200a, 1324a, 1329b, 1331a, 1347b; ii, 99b, 121a, 157b, 162a, 180a, 446a, 598b; iii, 424a, 450a, 492b, 1204a; iv, 507a, 543a, 914b, 1018a, b; v, 74a, 598a, 600a, 688a, 1135b, 1214a; vi, 126b, 131b, 345b, 407a, 426a, 456b, 533b; vii, 139b, 189a, 194a, 204a, b, 315a, 318a, 332a, 339a, 346a, 404b, 443b; viii, 74a, b; ix, **195a**; x, 58b, s, 63a, 142b, 167b, 258a, b, 313b, 366b, 420b
Shāh Djahān II, Rafīʿ al-Dawla (Mughal) (1719) i, 914a, 1026a; vii, 457a
Shāh Djahān III (Mughal) (1760) vii, 316a
Shāh Djahān b. Suyurghatmïsh (1306) v, 163a, 554a
Shāh Djahāngīr Hāshimī (1539) s, 505a
Shāh Djalāl Mudjarrad Ḳunyāʾī (XIV) ix, 611a
Shāh Dūst → Fatḥ Khān
Shāh Fāḍil ii, 30a
Shāh Faḳīr ʿAlwī (1780) ix, 440a
Shāh Fakhr al-Dīn ii, 55a, 56a; iii, 436a, 1158b
Shāh Fulādī (peak) i, 221b
Shāh Ghāzī Rustam I iv, 266a
Shāh al-Ḥamīd ʿAbd al-Ḳādir (Marakkayar) (1600) vi, 503b
Shāh Ḥātim Dihlawī iii, 119a
Shāh Ḥusayn Abbāsī v, 829a
Shāh Ḥusayn Khān i, 1219a
Shāh-i Djangal Bash ii, 205a
Shāh Ismāʿīl I, II, III (Ṣafawids) → Ismāʿīl I, II, III
Shāh Ismāʿīl Ghāzī ʿArabī (XV) ii, 297a; viii, 598b
Shāh Kābulī i, 1201a
Shāh Ḳāḍān (Khalīfa) (XVI) vii, 440a
Shāh Ḳādirī, Mullā ii, 134b, 378b
Shāh Kalīm Allāh Djahānābādī ii, 55a; iii, 432b
Shāh Ḳāsim b. Muḥammad Nūrbakhsh s, 423b
Shāh Ḳāsim Fayḍbakhsh b. Nūrbakhsh (1511) viii, 135b
Shāh Ḳāsim Huwaʾllāhī i, 1201a
Shāh Ḳāsim Sulaymānī (1606) vii, 132b
Shāh Katōr → Muḥtaram Shāh II
Shāh Khāmūsh iv, 202b
Shāh Ḳulī Ḳādjār iv, 389a
Shāh Ḳulī Sulṭān iv, 476a
Shāh Madār → Badīʿ al-Dīn
Shāh Maḥmūd (Muẓaffarid) (1375) ii, 401b
Shāh Mālang iv, 202b
Shāh Malik b. ʿAlī Yabghu (Ghuzz) (XI) ii, 4b, 1108a; iv, 1067a; vi, 416a; ix, **195b**
Shāh Manṣūr Shīrāzī (1581) ix, **195b**
Shāh-i Mashhad v, 1147b, 1148a

Shāh Meḥmed b. Ḳarā Yūsuf iv, 586b, 587b
Shāh Mīnā v, 634b, 636a
Shāh Mīr (Mīrzā) → Shams al-Dīn Shāh Mīrzā
Shāh Mīr b. Mīr Ḳawām al-Dīn (Marʿashī) (XVII) vi, 516a
Shāh Mīrs s, 167b
Shāh Mīrzā Zarkash vii, 95b
Shāh Muḥammad b. ʿAbd Aḥmad (1661) ix, **196a**
Shāh Muḥammad ʿAlī (Ḳādjār) (1909) v, 24b; vi, 21b
Shāh Muḥibb Allāh b. Khalīl Allāh (XV) vi, 63a
Shāh Muḥibb Allāh b. Shāh Niʿmat Allāh (Kirmān) (XV) vi, 66b
Shāh Muḥibb Allāh Ilāhābādī (XVII) viii, 69a
Shāh Murād (Bukhārā) (1800) vi, 418b, 766a
Shāh Muẓaffar (Muẓaffarid) (1353) i, 1211b; vii, 820b
Shāh Muẓaffar al-Dīn (Ḳādjār) (1907) vi, 21a; vii, **818a**
Shāh Naṣīr (XVIII) ii, 221b
Shāh Nawāz I (Vakhtang, Georgia) (XVII) v, 493b
Shāh Nawāz II (Giorgi XI, Georgia) (1688) v, 493b
Shāh Nawāz Khān Awrangābādī (1759) i, 229a; iii, 603b; v, 493b, 935b; vi, 131b, vii, 343a,
Shāh Nawāz Khān (Chitral) ii, 30a
Shāh Nawāz Khān (Iridj) → Iridj Shāhnawāz Khān
Shāh Niʿmat Allāh → Niʿmat Allāhiyya
Shāh Niyaz Aḥmad ii, 55a
Shāh Nizām al-Dīn i, 853a
Shāh Nizār iv, 201b
Shāh Nūr Muḥammad ii, 55a
Shāh Raḍī al-Dīn i, 852b; iv, 202b; vii, 300a
Shāh Rafīʿ al-Dīn i, 69a; iii, 430b, 431a; iv, 196a; viii **386a**
Shāh Rūd v, 656b; ix, **196b**; s, 149a
Shāh Rukh (Afshārid) (1795) vi, 715a
Shāh Rukh (Čaghatayid) → Shāh Rūkh Mīrzā b. Tīmūr
Shāh Rukh I (Miñ, Khoḳand) (XVIII) ii, 45a; v, 29a
Shāh Rukh Mīrzā b. Ibrāhīm Mīrzā (Badakhshān Mīrzās) (1607) vii, 135a; s, 43b
Shāh Rukh Mīrzā b. Tīmūr Lang (Tīmūrid) (1447) i, 66b, 90b, 227a, 1001b, 1054a, 1133b; ii, 6a, 270b, 792a; iii, 57b, 58a, 114a, 346b, 778a; iv, 33a, b, 34a, 102b, 586b, 587a, b, 642b, 721b, 945a, 1020a, 1040b; v, 858b; vi, 16a, 61b, 324b, 505a, 512b, 513a, b, 619a, 621a, 714b, 976b; vii, 173a, 313b, 928a; viii, 750a; ix, **197a**; x, 513b, 812a; s, 49a, 84a
Shāh Rustam v, 829a
Shāh Saʿd Allāh Gulshān (1728) xi, 125b
Shāh Ṣafī I → Ṣafī I Shāh
Shāh Shudjāʿ (Afghānistān) → Shudjāʿ al-Mulk Durrānī
Shāh Shudjāʿ (Bengal) i, 229a, 606a, 768b, 769a, 1333a; ii, 216b, 813b
Shāh Shudjāʿ b. Mubāriz al-Dīn (Muẓaffarid) (1384) ii, 401b; iii, 56a; iv, 498b; v, 827b, 828b; vii, 480b, 481a, 820b; ix, **198b**; s, 415a
Shāh Sulaymān I (Ṣafawid) (1694) → Sulaymān Shāh
Shāh Sulaymān II (Ṣafawid) (1763) vi, 18a, 483b, 516b
Shāh Sulaymān (Taunsa, Čishtiyya) ii, 56a
Shāh Sulṭān bint Selīm I (1575) ix, **199b**
Shāh Sulṭān bint Selīm II (1580) ix, **200b**
Shāh Sulṭān Ḥusayn I (Ṣafawid) (1722) vi, 16b, 18a, 483b, 525a, 551a, 856a; vii, 62a; viii, 771b
Shāh Sulṭān Muḥammad Badakhshī i, 852b
Shāh Ṭāhir al-Ḥusaynī (Muḥammad Shāhī) (1545) ix, **200b**
Shāh Ṭahmāsp I, II (Ṣafāwids) → Ṭahmāsp I, II
Shāh-Temir (fortress) vi, 418a
Shāh Turkān umm Fīrūz Shāh I Rukn al-Dīn (Delhi) (XIII) vi, 488a; viii, 371b
Shāh Walī Allāh al-Dihlawī → al-Dihlawī
Shāh Walī Khān i, 232b
Shāh Wilāyat (XII) vii, 965b
Shāhābād ii, 1120a; s, 313a
Shahāda i, 332b, 407b; iii, 269b; ix, **201a**
Shāhanshāh (title) → Shāh
Shaḥāra, Banū vi, 80a
Shaḥāra (Yemen) vi, 436b; ix, **201b**
Shahāridja ix, **202a**

Shāh-bandar i, 1013a; vi, 209b; s, 199b, 200a, **716a**
Shahbanderzāde → Ḥilmī, Aḥmed
Shahbāz Girāy ii, 25b, 1114a
Shāhbāz Ḳalandar iv, 474a
Shahdānadj ix, **202a**
Shāhdiz iii, 725b; iv, 200a
Shāhdjahān Bēgam i, 1196a, 1197a
Shāhdjahānābād i, 253a; ii, 258a, 259a; iii, 450b; v, 889a; vii, 332b, 333b
Shāhdjahānpūr s, 292b
Shāhdjī Bhōnsla (XVII) i, 769a, 1202b; vi, 534b; viii, 74b
Shāhgarh → Kanawdj
al-Shaḥḥām, Abū Yaʿḳūb Yūsuf (IX) i, 128b; ii, 569b; iv, 1163a; vii, 604a; ix, **202b**; s, 226b
Shāhī (coinage) ix, **203a**
Shāhī (island) vi, 501b, 504b
Shāh-i Zinda (Timūrid) s, 154b 54b
Shāhid iv, 354a; ix, **207a**
Shahīd ix, **203b**
Shahīd (Shuhayd) b. al-Ḥusayn al-Balkhī (927) vi, 609a; ix, **208b**; s, 35a
al-Shahīd al-Awwal → Muḥammad b. Makkī
Shahīd Balkhī → Shahīd (Shuhayd) b. al-Ḥusayn
Shahīd Muḥammad Pasha iv, 970a
al-Shahīd al-Thānī, Zayn al-Dīn b. ʿAlī (1557) vi, 13a; viii, 777b; ix, **209a**; s, 56b
Shāhidbāzī v, 166a
Shāhidī (1550) vii, 349a
Shāhīn (XX) s, 109b
Shahīn (Spāhbed) (VII) ix, 79b
Shahīn, Āl ix, **210a**
Shāhīn, Banū → ʿImrān b. Shāhīn
Shāhīn, Dizh → Sāʿīn Ḳalʿa
Shāhīn, Lala (1388) i, 653b, 1159b, 1302b; ii, 683b, 722a, 914a, 1086a; iv, 1093a; vi, 290b; vii, 593a; ix, **211a**
Shāhīn, Mawlānā (XVI) iv, 309a, b; vii, 510b
Shāhīn b. ʿAbd Allāh (XIV) ix, 211a
Shāhīn Girāy i, 310b
Shāhīn Girāy Khān i, 63a; ii, 447a; v, 141a, b
Shāhīn Lālā Pasha (1388) i, 1159b, 1302b; ii, 683b, 722a, 914a; vi, 290b; vii, 593a
Shāhīn-i Shīrāzī (XIV) ix, **211a**
Shahmār vi, 937b
Shahmardān b. Abi ʾl-Khayr al-Rāzī (1120) vi, 908a; x, 146a
Shahms al-Dīn ʿItāḳī (XVII) x, 356a
Shāhnāmedjī ix, **211b**
Shāhnawāz Khān (1659) vi, 131b
Shahnāz Āzād (XX) vi, 486a
Shahnāz bint Muḥammad Riḍā Shāh Pahlawī (XX) vii, 447a
Shāhpūr vi, 62a
Shahr ("town") ix, **212a**
Shahr b. Bādhām i, 728a; s, 116a
Shahr b. Ḥawshab (718) vii, 576a
al-Shahrāfī vi, 247b
Shahrān iv, 994a
Shahrangīz (Shahrashūb) ix, **212a**
Shahrashūb → Shahrangīz
Shahrastān vi, 663b, 664b; viii, 439b
al-Shahrastānī, Abu ʾl-Fatḥ Muḥammad b. ʿAbd al-Karīm (1153) i, 129a, 130a, 151b, 234b, 247a, 450a, 483b, 1340b; ii, 96b, 764b, 767a, 930a; iii, 328b, 496b; iv, 847a; vi, 347a, 476a; vii, 55a; ix, **214b**; s, 25b, 43b, 343b, 345a
al-Shahrastānī, Muʿīn al-Dīn iii, 600a
al-Shahrastānī, Sayyid Muḥammad ʿAlī (1967) ix, **216b**
Shahrazād i, 361a, 362a, b; ix, **217b**
Shahrazūr (Shahrizūr) ix, **218a**
al-Shahrazūrī, Kamāl al-Dīn Abu ʾl-Faḍl Muḥammad (XII) viii, 132a
al-Shahrazūrī, Muḥyī ʾl-Dīn (ḳāḍī) (1190) vi, 111a; ix, **219b**
al-Shahrazūrī, Shams al-Dīn (XIII) i, 236a; iv, 121a; ix, **219b**
al-Shahrazūrī, Ṭaḳī ʾl-Dīn Ibn al-Ṣalāḥ → Ibn al-Ṣalāḥ
al-Shahrazūrī (vizier) (XII) iii, 1157b
Shahrbarāz (630) iv, 342b; ix, 79b, 80a; xi, 290b
Shahrdārī i, 978b
Shahr-i Bābak v, 152a, b
Shahr-i Bilḳīs iv, 107b
Shahr-i Khān v, 30a
Shahr-i Kurd vi, 719b
Shahr-i Naw i, 952b; vi, 53a
Shahr-i Sabz → Kash; Kish
Shahr-i Sīstān → Zarang
Shāhrekīs iv, 10b

Shahrīr → Taʾrīkh
Shahristān i, 320b; iv, 98b; ix, **220a**; s, 406b
Shahriyār I (Kayūsiyya, Bāwandid) (825) i, 871b; iv, 645b
Shahriyār II (Kayūsiyya, Bāwandid) (930) s, 356b
Shahriyār III b. Dārā (Kāʿūsiyya, Bāwandid) (1006) i, 1110a; ii, 919b; s, 309a
Shahriyār, Sayyid Muḥammad (1988) ix, **220b**
Shahriyār b. Djahāngīr i, 686b; ii, 381a; iv, 1018a
Shahriyār b. al-Ḥasan (XI) ix, **221a**
Shahriyār b. Khusraw b. Djahāngīr (XVII) vii, 315a
Shāriyār b. al-Maṣmughān → al-Māzyār b. Ḳārin
Shahrizūr i, 16a, 261a; v, 33b, 34a, 144b, 145b, 455b; viii, 463a; ix **218a**
Shahr-kent → Djand
Shāhrūkh → Shāh Rūkh
Shāhrukh, Mīrzā i, 230a, b, 246b, 295b; v, 59a; s, 43b
Shāhrukh Bī v, 29a; s, 97b
Shāhrukhī ii, 120b
Shāhrukhiyya i, 148a, 1011a; s, 51a
Shahrwīn b. Rustam Bāwand i, 871b; s, 356b
al-Shāshī, Abū Bakr Muḥammad al-Ḳaffāl (975) x, 349a
Shāhsivan (Shāhsewan), Banū iii, 1102a, 1108b, 1109a, 1110a; iv, 9b, 858b; vii, 498a; ix, **221a**
Shāhsuwār (Dhu ʾl-Ḳadr) (1472) i, 182b; ii, 38b, 239b; iii, 186b; iv, 462b; vi, 778a
Shāh-Takhtī (Araxes) vi, 203a
Shāhū b. Śambhadjī (Marāthā) (1749) i, 913b; ii, 219a; iv, 1023b; vi, 535a, b, 536a
Shahu Misham (Mombasa) vii, 226a
Shāhwardī b. Muḥammadī v, 829a, b
Shāh-zāda → Miyān Gul Gul Shāhzada
Shāh-zāda (Bīdjāpūr) ii, 1084b
Shāh-zāda Aḥmad v, 823a
Shāh-zāda Shāhrukh b. Muḥammad Bāḳī Tarkhān (Tarkhānid), Maklī) (1584) vi, 190a
Shāʾiḳiyya, Banū vi, 794b; s, 278b
Shāʿir 1. a. Pre-islamic and Umayyad period ix, **225a**
Shāʿir b. From the ʿAbbāsid period to the Nahda s, **717b**
Shāʿir c. From 1850 to the present day xi, **228b**
Shāʿir d. in Muslim Spain ix, **230b**
Shāʿir e. The folk poet in Arab society ix, **233b**
Shāʿir 2. in Persia xi, **236b**
Shāʿir 3. in Turkey ix, **239a**
Shāʿir 4. in Muslim India ix, **240a**
Shāʿir 5. in the Western and central Sudan ix, **242b**
Shāʿir 6. in Haussaland ix, **244a**
Shāʿir 7. in Malaysia and Indonesia ix, **244a**
Shāʾista Khān iv, 177b
Shakāk, Banū ix, **245a**
Shaḳāḳī (Shiḳaghī), Banū iii, 1102b, 1109a; ix, **246b**
Shakānī iii, 1097b
Shakar Gandj → Farīd al-Dīn Masʿūd
Shakarkheldā ix, **246b**
Shaḳāwa ix, **246a**
Shaker Beklū i, 1157a
Shaḳḥab, Battle of → Mardj al-Ṣuffar
Shakhab, Tell al- iii, 189a; vi, 545b, 546b, 547a, b, 548a
Shakhbūṭ b. Dhiyāb i, 166b
Shakhbūṭ b. Sulṭān i, 166b; iv, 778b
Shakhṣ i, 409b, 785a; ix, **247a**
Shakīb Arslān, Shaykh (1946) iii, 524b, 525a; iv, 159a; v, 794b; vii, 415b, 765a; ix, **248a**; s, 159b
Shaḳīf ʿArnūn → Ḳalʿat al-Shaḳīf
Shaḳīḳat al-Nuʿmān ix, **248b**
Shākir (ʿUḳba b. Nāfiʿ) (VII) vi, 743b
Shākir (Zāb) vi, 435a
Shākir, Aḥmad Muḥammad (1958) ix, **249a**
Shākir, Banū → Mūsā b. Shakīr, Banū
Shākir Pasha v, 462b
al-Shākiriyya ix, **249b**
Shaḳīshaḳiyya s, 197a
Shakk ix, **250a**
Shakkāf s, 111b, 112a
Shakkāziyya ix, **251b**
Shakkī iv, 350a; ix, **253b**
Shakla bint al-Maṣmughān (Damāwand) (IX) vi, 335a
Shakshāk ii, 621a
Shāḳshāḳī Ibrāhīm Pasha i, 268a
Shakūbiyya ix, **255a**

Shakunda ix, **255b**
al-Shaḳundī, Abu 'l-Walīd (1231) vi, 221a; vii, 191a, 207a, 209a; ix, **256a**
Shaḳūra i, 7a; ix, **256a**
Shaḳyā b. ʿAbd al-Wāḥid al-Miknāsī i, 82a, 634a
Shāl, Shālkot → Kwatta
Shāl(l)a → Salā
Shalla (Chella) ix, **258b**
al-Shalāḥī (XIV) vi, 215b; vii, 190a, b
Shalamanḳa (Shalamantiḳa) ix, **256b**
Shaʿlān (Ruwala, Banū) viii, 644a
Shalanba (Dunbāwand) vi, 744b
al-Shalawbīn, Abū ʿAlī ʿUmar (1247) iii, 338a; ix, **257b**
Shalbaṭarra ix, **258b**
Shālīmār i, 1347b, 1348a; vii, 332a, 333a; s, 63a
Shālīsh (Djālīsh) s, **722a**
Shallāl, Banū vi, 902a
al-Shalmaghānī, Abū Muḥammad → Muḥammad b. ʿAlī al-Shalmaghānī
Shalṭīsh (Saltés) i, 6a, 155b; ix, **259a**
Shaltūt, Maḥmūd (1963) iv, 159b; ix, **260b**; s, 158a
al-Shalūbīnī ii, 528b
Shālūs iii, 254b; s, 356b
Sham (Balučistān) s, 331b
Sham (Tabrīz) vi, 601b
al-Shām/al-Shaʿm (Syria) i, 4b, 17a, 19a, 46a, 103a, 111a, 145a, 279a, 383b; ii, 595a, 661a, b, 676a, 854a; iii, 85a, 184a, 233a, 263b, 521a, 522b, 559a, 560b, 1254b; iv, 206a; vi, 25b, 59b, 60b, 64b, 273b, 364a, 378b, 387b, 467b, 469b, 470a, 796b; vii, 9b, 69b; viii, 906b; ix, **261b**
– art, architecture i, 609b, 1226a; v, 291a, b
– demography s, 212a
– ethnography v, 440a, 469b, 1253b
– history iv, 261b; v, 438a
– institutions ii, 125b, 424a; iii, 99b, 521a; v, 912a, b, 1046b, 1090b
– language, literature i, 568b, 575a; ii, 468a
– products iii, 211a, 218b; ix, **261b**
Shāma ix, **281a**
Shamʿa ix, **281b**
Shamākha → Shīrwān
Shamākhī ii, 87b; iii, 604a; iv, 350a; vi, 320a
Shamāmūn (Nubia) iv, 485b
Shaman ix, **282a**
Shaman Khēl, Banū (Pathān) vi, 86a
al-Shamardal b. Sharīk al-Yarbūʿī (VIII) viii, 377b; ix, **282b**
Shamash (ʿIrāḳ) vi, 650a
Shāmāt s, 327a
Shamb(h)adjī i, 913b; s, 55b
Shamʿdānī-zāde ii, 211b; iv, 761a
Shamdīnān i, 427a; ix, **262b**
Shamʿī (XVII) i, 1208b, 1345b
al-Shāmī (1585) vi, 214b, 352b
al-Shāmī, Abū Bakr (1095) s, 194a
al-Shāmī, Ibrāhīm b. Sulaymān (IX) i, 83a
Shāmī, Nizām al-Dīn (XV) iii, 57b, 58a; ix, **283b**
Shāmī Pīr → Saʿīd al-Gīlānī
Shāmil (Dāghistān) (1871) i, 755b, 756a; ii, 18a, 87b, 88b; iii, 157a; iv, 631a; v, 618a; ix, **283b**
Shāmil-ḳalʿe → Makhač-ḳalʿe
Shamir b. Dhi 'l-Djawshan (686) iii, 609b, 610b; iv, 836a; s, **722a**
al-Shamir/Shimr → Shamir b. Dhi 'l-Djawshan
Shamīrān → Tārom
Shamkh, Banū s, 37b
Shāmkhāl ii, 87a; v, 382a, b, 618a
Shāmlū i, 1159b; iii, 1100a, 1109b; iv, 577b; v, 243b
Shāmlū-Ustadjlū iii, 157b
Shammāʿ ix, **288a**
al-Shammākh b. Ḍirār al-Ghaṭafānī (643) i, 1154b; vii, 843b; viii, 377a; ix, **288b**; s, 304b
al-Shammākh b. Shudjāʿ (Shirwān) (IX) ix, 487a
Shammākha (town) ix, **289b**, 487a
al-Shammākhī al-Ifrānī, Abu 'l-ʿAbbās Aḥmad (1522) i, 121a, 125a, 167a, 1186a, 1287b; iii, 656b, 927b; vi, 311a, 840b; ix, **289b**
al-Shammākhī, Abū Sākin ʿĀmir i, 1053b
Shammār, Banū i, 528b, 873b; ii, 77a, 492b; iii, 180a, 326b, 1065b, 1253b; v, 348a; vi, 371b, 614a, 733b, 902a; vii, 582a; ix, **290a**; s, 101b
Shammar Yuharʿish (300) i, 548b; iii, 10a; x, 575b
Shammās (monk) ii, 234a

Shammās b. ʿUthmān, Makhzūmī (VII) vi, 138a
al-Shammāsiyya (Baghdād) i, 897b, 899b; vi, 599b
Shampa → Ṣanf
Shamrīn vi, 230b
Shams (sun) ix, **291a**
Shams bint Riḍa Shāh Pahlawī (XX) vi, 486b
Shams al-ʿAmāra (palace, Tehran) vi, 529b
Shams Badrān s, 8b, 9a
Shams al-Dawla Abū Ṭāhir (Būyid) (1021) i, 512b, 1354a; iii, 671b; v, 1028a; ix, **295b**; s, 118b
Shams al-Dawla Sulaymān i, 664b
Shams al-Dīn → al-Dimashķī; Djuwaynī; Ildeñiz; al-Ṣaydāwī; Shams-i Tabrīzī
Shams al-Dīn (Bahmanid) i, 1200a
Shams al-Dīn (Bengal) (1442) → Ilyās Shāh
Shams al-Dīn (Malaysia) vi, 235b
Shams al-Dīn (Miʿmār, Khwārazm) (XII) vi, 14b
Shams al-Dīn, Pīr iv, 202b; v, 26a
Shams al-Dīn Kurt I (Kart, Ḥarāt) (1285) iii, 177b; iv, 672a
Shams al-Dīn II b. Rukn al-Dīn Kurt (Kart, Harāt) (1329) iv, 536b, 672a
Shams al-Dīn b. ʿAbd al-Malik, amīr (Sindjār) (1149) vi, 870b
Shams al-Dīn b. Djamshīd Ķārīn (Marʿashī) (XV) vi, 512b
Shams al-Dīn b. Nadjm al-Dīn Ismāʿīl (Maṣyād) (XIII) vi, 790b
Shams al-Dīn b. Kamāl al-Dīn (Marʿashī) (XV) vi, 514a, b, 516a
Shams al-Dīn b. Murtaḍā (Marʿashī) (XV) vi, 513b
Shams al-Dīn b. Taman Djāndār iv, 108b
Shams al-Dīn (Ķarāmān-oghlu) iv, 622b
Shams al-Dīn ʿAbd al-Malik (1200) vi, 381a
Shams al-Dīn Abū Rādjāʿ ii, 597b
Shams al-Dīn ʿAlī Shāh Kart (Kurt) (Harāt) (1308) viii, 83b
Shams al-Dīn Āmulī (1307) vi, 908a
Shams al-Dīn al-Ānī (XIV) vi, 13a
Shams al-Dīn Dandānī (1457) vi, 1027b
Shams al-Dīn al-Dimashķī (1327) vi, 111b
Shams al-Dīn Dīv (XVI) vi, 515a
Shams al-Dīn Ibrāhīm Shāh (Sharķī) (1440) ix, 355a
Shams al-Dīn Īletmish → Īltutmish
Shams al-Dīn ʿIrāķī, Mīr s, 353b, 366b
Shams al-Dīn Ķara-Sunķur (amīr) Ārdharbāydjān) vi, 501b
Shams al-Dīn Ķārin Ghawrī (Marʿashī) (XV) vi, 512b
Shams al-Dīn Khān (1835) ii, 83b
Shams al-Dīn Lāhidjī (Gīlānī) (XVI) vi, 18a
Shams al-Dīn Māhūnī iii, 633a, 634a
Shams al-Dīn Muḥammad III Lashkarī (Bahmanid) (1482) vi, 62b, 407a; vii, 458b
Shams al-Dīn Muḥammad b. Ķays al-Rāzī → Shams-i Ķays
Shams al-Dīn Muḥammad b. Rukn al-Dīn Khur-Shāh (Nizārī) (1310) ix, **285b**
Shams al-Dīn Muḥammad b. Murtaḍā (Marʿashī) (1452) vi, 513a
Shams al-Dīn Muḥammad al-Babāwī ii, 330b
Shams al-Dīn Muḥammad al-Dimashķī i, 775a, 1327b
Shams al-Dīn Muḥammad Ghūrī (1203) ii, 1101a
Shams al-Dīn Muḥammad Tabrīzī → Shams-i Tabrīzī
Shams al-Dīn Ṣāliḥ, al-Malik al-Ṣāliḥ (Artuķid, Mārdīn) (1364) vi, 111b; viii, 802a
Shams al-Dīn al-Samarķandī s, 413a
Shams al-Dīn al-Samaṭrānī (1630) i, 742a; iii, 1220a, 1233a; viii, 294a; ix, **296a**
Shams al-Dīn Sāmī Bey Frasherī (XIX) i, 298b; ii, 474a; v, 195a; vi, 92b, 373a
Shams al-Dīn Shāh Mīrzā Swātī iv, 708a; s, 167a
Shams al-Dīn Sulṭānpūrī, Shaykh (XVI) vi, 131a; s, 3a
Shams al-Dīn-i Sīrādj ʿAfīf (XIV) ix, **296b**
Shams al-Maʿālī → Ķābūs b. Wushmagīr b. Ziyār
Shams-Māh Khātūn (Dhu 'l-Ķadr) (X) vi, 509b
Shams al-Mulk ʿUthmān b. Niẓām al-Mulk (XII) i, 522b, 902a; vi, 64b; viii, 81b
Shams al-Mulk Naṣr → Naṣr I (Ķarakhānid)
Shams al-Mulūk → Duķaķ; Rustam

Shams al-ʿUrafāʾ, Sayyid Ḥusayn Ḥusaynī (1935) viii, 46b
Shamsa ix, **298b**
Shamsābād vi, 62a, b
Shamsān i, 98b
Shamshān i, 180b
Shams-i Fakhrī → Fakhrī Shams al-Dīn Muḥammad
Shams-i Ḳays (XIII) i, 982b; iv, 59b, 64b, 714a; v, 1027a; viii, 578b; ix, **297a**; s, 21b, 431a
Shamsī Khān v, 33b
Shams-i Munshī → Nakhdjawānī, Muḥammad
Shams-i Tabrīz(ī) (1247) ii, 394a; v, 26a; ix, **298a**
Shamsī Pasha iv, 108b
Shamsī-yi Aʿradj Bukhārī (XIII) viii, 749a
Shamshīr b. Azar s, 327b
Shamshīr Bahādur i, 1012b
Shämsiddin Shäräfiddinaw Khurshid (1960) vi, 768b
Shamsīyān iv, 473b
Shamsiyya ii, 1070b; iv, 203a, 473b, 991b; v, 26a; vi, 542a; ix, **299a**
Shamsūn (Samson) ix, **300a**
Shamʿūn vi, 575a
Shamwīl (Samuel) ix, **301b**
al-Shanāwī, Aḥmad i, 829b
Shanbal i, 829a
Shandī ii, 351b; ix, **301b**
Shandjwilo, Shandjūl → ʿAbd al-Raḥmān b. Abī ʿAmīr
Shandūr ii, 29a
al-Shanfarā iv, 744b, 919a; vii, 308a, 309a; ix, **301a**; s, 176a
Shangānī (Maḳdīshū) vi, 129a
Shānī (XVII) viii, 776a ; xi, 444a
Shanish vi, 576a
Shānī-zāde Meḥmed ʿAṭāʾ Allāh Efendi (1826) ii, 713a; iii, 590a; v, 1083b; vi, 725a; ix, **303a**
Shanḳīr s, 295a
Shann, Banū i, 73a, 74a
Shans adāsi → Ada Ḳalʿe
Shansabanī ii, 1099a, 1100a, 1101a
Shanshiya → Djidʿatī
Shansi (Shan-hsi) ix, **303b**
Shant Mānkash (Simancas) ix, **304a**
Shant Yāḳub (Santiago de Compostela) i, 494b; ix, **304b**
Shantabariyya (Santaver) ii, 243a; iii, 299a; ix, **305b**
al-Shantamarī, Abu 'l-Ḥadjdjādj (1083) i, 521b, 601a; iii, 111a, 807a, 963a; ix, **306a**
Shantamariyyat al-Gharb (Faro) i, 6a; ix, **306a**
Shantamariyyat al-Sharḳ (Albarracin) ix, **307a**
Shantarīn (Santarem) i, 161b, 1338b; ix, **308a**
Shanūʿa i, 812a; ix, 775a
Shāpūr (river) vi, 383b; ix, **309b**
Shāpūr (town) iv, 850b; ix, **310b**
Shāpūr (Sābūr) I b. Ardashīr (Sāsānid) (270) i, 484b, 516b, 788b; ii, 1119b; iii, 50b; iv, 675b; v, 573b; ix, **309b**
Shāpūr II b. Hormizd II (Sāsānid) (379) i, 225b, 484b, 548b; iii, 303b; v, 640a; vi, 633a; ix, 73b, **309b**
Shāpūr III (Sāsānid)) ix, 75a, 309b
Shāpūr b. Shahriyār Bāwand iv, 645b
Shāpūr al-Djunūd → Shāpūr I
Shāpūr-Kh(w)āst v, 831b
Shāpūr Mīrzā Iʿtiḳād Khān (1650) vii, 574a
Shār ix, **311a**
Shaʿr ix, **311b**
Sharāb → Mashrūbāt
Sharabyānī, Mullā Muḥammad Ḳāẓim Fāḍil (1904) vi, 553a
Sharaf ix, **313b**
al-Sharaf (Aljarafe) i, 7a, 135b; iv, 115a; s, **723b**
al-Sharaf (Sharaf Ḥadjūr) s, **723a**
al-Sharaf (Yemen) vi, 436b
Sharaf al-Dawla Muslim b. Ḳuraysh (ʿUḳaylid) (1085) iii, 228a; vi, 379b; vii, **693**
Sharaf al-Dawla, Abu 'l-Fawāris Shīrdhīl (Būyid) (989) i, 1354a; iii, 244b; vi, 600b; ix, **314a**; s, 118a, 398a
Sharaf al-Dīn, ʿAbd al-Ḥusayn b. al-Sayyid Yūsuf al-Mūsāwī al-ʿĀmilī (1957) vii, 301b; ix, **314b**
Sharaf al-Dīn, Ḥasan Rāmī → Rāmī Tabrīzī
Sharaf al-Dīn, Mawlānā s, 353a
Sharaf al-Dīn b. Ḳawām al-Dīn al-Marʿashī (XIV) vi, 512a, b
Sharaf al-Dīn Abū Tawwāma ii, 216a
Sharaf al-Dīn ʿAlī Yazdī (1454) vii, 343b; ix, **315b**

Sharaf al-Dīn Husām al-Dīn al-Bulghārī i, 1307b
Sharaf al-Dīn ʿĪsā → al-Muʿaẓẓam ʿĪsā
Sharaf al-Dīn Khān → Bidlīsī
Sharf al-Dīn Mawdūd al-Mawṣilī, amīr (XII) vi, 547a
Sharaf al-Dīn Saʿd Allāh i, 322b, 346b, 510b
Sharaf al-Dīn Shāh Wilāyāt vii, 601b
Sharaf al-Dīn Yaḥyā Manerī (1371) i, 868b; x, 255b
Sharaf Djihān (1560) viii, 775b
Sharaf Khwādja, Shaykh s, 280b
Sharaf al-Maʿālī i, 440a
Sharaf al-Mulk (vizier) (1227) i, 301a; vi, 500b, 501a, 505a; s, 359b
Sharaf al-Mulk b. Ḳuraysh (ʿUḳaylid) (1080) vii, 122a
Sharaf-nāma iv, 127b, 128a, b
Sharaf Rashīdov (1983) x, 961b
al-Sharafa s, 335a
al-Sharafī, ʿAlī b. Aḥmad iv, 1082a
al-Sharafī, Muḥammad b. ʿAlī iv, 1082b
Sharafshāh b. Djaʿfarī iv, 859b
Sharāḥīl Dhū Yazan ii, 244b
Sharahim Shaumar (XX) vi, 768b
al-Shaʿrānī, ʿAbd al-Wahhāb b. Aḥmad (1565) i, 596a; iii, 901a; v, 1237a; vi, 87b, 88a, 821a; vii, 565a; viii, 425a; ix, **316a**, 914a
al-Shaʿrānī, Sulaymān b. Mūsā (IX) vii, 526a
al-Shaʿrāniyya vi, 88a; s, **724a**
Sharar, ʿAbd al-Ḥalīm v, 203b, 635b
Sharāra, ʿAbd al-Laṭīf iv, 783a
al-Sharārāt i, 546a, 873a; iii, 642a; ix, **316b**
al-Sharāt ii, 535a; ix, **317a**
Sharāwiḥ, Banū vi, 82a
Sharbithāt vi, 84b
Shardja s, 42a
al-Shardja → al-Shāriḳa
Shārekī → Shāhrikī
Sharḥ ix, **317a**
Shari (river) i, 910a; s, 164b
Shāriʿ ix, **320b**
Sharīʿa i, 152a, 170a, 173b, 260b, 353b, 1099b, 1142b, 1143a; ii, 146b, 660a, b, 668a; iii, 76a, 164a, 662b; iv, 156b, 556b, 559a; v, 860a, 870b; ix, **321a**
Shariat Act (1937) i, 172a, b
Sharīʿat Allāh, Ḥādjdjī (1839) i, 952a; ii, 783b; iv, 625b; vii, 291a
Sharīʿatī, ʿAlī (1977) vii, 451a; ix, **328a**
Sharīʿatī, Muḥammad Taḳī iv, 166a; ix, 328a
Sharīʿatmādarī (Āyatullāh, Ḳum) (1986) vi, 553b; vii, 300a; ix, **329a**
Sharīf (pen-name) ix, **337b**
Sharīf (title) ix, **329b**
al-Sharīf, Mawlāy → Muḥammad I (ʿAlawid)
Sharīf ʿAbd al-Raḥmān (Pontianak) (1808) viii, 324a
al-Sharīf Abū Muḥammad Idrīs (1314) ix, **338a**
Sharīf Aḥmad (Abū ʿArīsh) s, 30b
al-Sharīf al-Akhḍar iii, 107a, 289a
al-Sharīf al-ʿAḳīlī (XI) ix, **338b**
Sharīf Āmulī (XVI) ix, **339a**
Sharīf Awliyā Karīm al-Makhdūm (Jolo) (XIV) iii, 1218b; viii, 303a
al-Sharīf al-Djurdjānī → al-Djurdjānī
al-Sharīf al-Gharnāṭī (1359) ix, **339b**
al-Sharīf al-Ḥusaynī (1374) vi, 353a
al-Sharīf al-Idrīsī → al-Idrīsī
Sharīf Muḥammad Kabungsuwan (XVI) viii, 303b
al-Sharīf al-Murtaḍā → al-Murtaḍā al-Shārīf Abu 'l-Ḳāṣim
Sharīf Pasha, Muḥammad (Miṣr) (1887) i, 1070a; iii, 515a; vii, 184b; ix, **340a**
Sharīf Pasha Ṣabrī s, 300a
al-Sharīf al-Rāḍī (1016) i, 592b, 1352a; iii, 244b, 463a, 780b, 1266a; iv, 277b; vi, 603a, 604b, 605b; vii, 24b, 313a, 634a, 903b; ix, **340b**; s, 23a, 95a
al-Sharīf al-Rundī (1285) vi, 606b
al-Sharīf al-Talīḳ (1005) ix, **343a**
al-Sharīf al-Tilimsānī (Ahl) iii, 670b, 866b; ix, **343b**
Sharīfī, Mīrzā Makhdūm iv, 860b
Sharīfīs (Irān) iv, 51b
Sharīfī-zāde (1630) vi, 354a
Sharīfs (Mecca) i, 552a; vi, 148a; vii, 319b
Sharīfs (Morocco) → Shurafāʾ
Sharifu Badruddini (Lamu) vi, 613a
Shāriḥ ül-Menār-zāde Aḥmed (1641) ii, 751a; vii, 917b; ix, **348a**
Sharīk b. al-Aʿwar al-Ḥārithī (VII) vii, 689b

Sharīk b. Shaykh al-Mahrī (750) i, 1294a; iv, 16a; xi, 522a
Sharīk al-ʿAbsī ii, 525b
Sharika ix, **348a**
al-Shāriḳa (Shardjah) i, 166b, 928b; ii, 619a, 936b; iv, 777b; vi, 37b; ix, **349a**; s, 42a, 416b, 418a
Sharīsh (Jerez) ix, **349b**
al-Sharīshī, Abu 'l-ʿAbbās (1222) i, 602a; iii, 221b; vi, 110b; ix, **350a**
Shāriya (singer) ix, **350b**
Sharḳ al-Andalus i, 82b; ix, **351a**
Sharḳāt s, 101b
Sharḳawa (Sherkāwa) ix, **352b**
al-Sharḳāwī, ʿAbd al-Raḥmān (1987) i, 819b; ix, **353a**
Sharḳāwiyya s, 40b
Sharkhā i, 176b; iii, 3b
Sharkhub vi, 547a
Sharḳī ix, **353b**
al-Sharḳī b. al-Kutāmī (767) ix, **354a**
Sharḳī, Ibrāhīm (XV) vi, 49b, 50a
Sharkids → Sharkīs
Sharkil iv, 1175a, 1176a, 1178a; vi, 384a
Sharḳīs (Djawnpūr) i, 756b; iii, 632a; iv, 533b, 534a; vi, 46b, 53b, 61b, 294b, 693b; viii, 68a, 125a; ix, **355a**; s, 203a, 325a
Sharḳishla s, 91b
al-Sharḳiyya (Baghdād) i, 901b, 1011a; s, 385b
al-Sharḳiyya (Miṣr) vi, 408a, 411b; ix, **356b**
al-Sharḳiyya (ʿUmān) vi, 84b; ix, **356b**
Sharm al-Shaykh s, 8b
al-Shārrāṭ i, 487a, 489a; ix, **357b**
Sharshal (Cherchell) iv, 1156a; vi, 371b, 404a, b; ix, **357b**; s, 145a
Sharṭ ix, **358b**
al-Shartūnī, Saʿīd b. ʿAbd Allāh (1912) s, **724b**
Sharūr iv, 186b, 389a; viii, 767a
Sharvashidze i, 101a; v, 496a
Sharwān → Shirwān
Sharwīn I b. Surkhāb (Kāyūsiyya, Bāwandid) (797) vi, 745b; xi, 242b
Sharwīn Mts iv, 645b, 646b; s, 298a
Shāsh (Tashkent) → Čāč
al-Shāshī → ʿAbd Allāh b. Maḥmūd; Abū Bakr
Shashmaḳom vi, 768b; ix, **360b**
al-Shāshī, Aḥmad b. Muḥammad (955) ix, 36a
Shaṭā ix, **361a**
Shaṭḥ (Shaṭḥiyya) ix, **361b**
Shāṭiba ix, **362b**
al-Shāṭibī, Abū Isḥāḳ (1388) iv, 149b; vi, 739b; ix, **364a**
al-Shāṭibī, Abu 'l-Ḳāsim (1194) iv, 736b; vi, 130b; vii, 622a; ix, **365a**
al-Shāṭibī, Muḥammad b. Sulaymān iv, 137a
Shāṭir Djalāl (XVI) vii, 478a
Shāṭir Beg Muḥammad i, 840b
Shatm s, **725b**
Shaṭnīl s, 135b, 136a
Shatrandj i, 1359a, b; ii, 955a, 1038b; iii, 775a; v, 110a, 478b; ix, **366b**
Shaṭṭ ix, **368a**
Shaṭṭ al-Amaya (Aʿmā) iv, 674a, b
Shaṭṭ al-ʿArab i, 5a, 133b, 1086b, 1087b; ii, 175b; iii, 1251b; iv, 6a, 674b, 675a; v, 65b, 66a; vii, 449b, 582b, 675a; ix, **368a**
Shaṭṭ Bamishīr (Behemshīr) iv, 674b, 675a
Shaṭṭ al-Ḳadīmī iv, 674a
Shaṭṭ Ḳobān (Goban) → Shaṭṭ al-Amaya
Shaṭṭ al-Nīl viii, 13b
al-Shaṭṭanawfī, Nūr al-Dīn (1314) i, 70a, 596a; iii, 160b; viii, 525a
Shaṭṭārī, Shaykh ʿAbd Allāh (XVI) vii, 440a
Shaṭṭāriyya i, 88a, 1284a; iii, 1233b; vii, 440a; viii, 237b; ix, **369b**
al-Shaṭṭī, Muḥammad Djamīl ii, 182b; iii, 161b
Shāʾul, Anwar v, 189b; ix, **370a**
Shawādhdh v, 128a
Shawāhid ix, **370b**
Shawānkāra → Faḍlawayh, Banū; Shabānkāra
Shāwar, Abū Shudjāʿ (vizier) (1169) i, 197a, 797a; ii, 318a, b, 856b, 858b, 959a; iv, 376a; viii, 130b; ix, **372b**
al-Shawāribī iv, 514b
al-Shawbak vii, 989b; ix, **373a**
Shawdhab (or Bistam) al-Yashkurī (VIII) iii, 650a; x, 821b
Shāwī dialects ix, 376a
al-Shāwī, Abu 'l-ʿAbbās (1605) ix, **374a**
al-Shāwirī, ʿAbd Allāh b. al-ʿAbbās (dāʿī) (IX) vi, 439a

Shāwīsh → Čāʾūsh
al-Shawīsh (al-Djawīsh), ʿAbd al-ʿAzīz (XX) vii, 716a
Shāwiya, Banū i, 371a, 372a, 770a; ii, 117a; viii, 794b; ix, **374b**
Shāwiya (Chaouïa) x, 169b
Shawḳ ix, **376b**
Shawḳ, Taṣadduḳ Ḥusayn (1871) ix, **377b**
Shawḳa vii, 672a
Shawḳal ii, 86b, 87a
al-Shawkānī, Muḥammad b. ʿAlī (1839) iv, 142b; vii, 297a; ix, **378a**
Shawkat ʿAlī (1938) vi, 78a, 459b; viii, 249a; ix, **378a**; s, 5a, 74a, b, 293b, 360a
Shawkat Bukhārī (1695) i, 1301b; ix, **378b**
Shawkat Djang ii, 371b, 1091b
Shawḳī, Aḥmad (1932) i, 597b, 598a; iv, 856a; vi, 307a, 409a, 414a, 607a, 956a; vii, 422a, 903a; ix, 229b, **379a**; s, 34a, 57b
Shawḳī Efendī Rabbānī (1957) i, 916a, 917b; vii, 921b; ix, **380a**
al-Shawshāwī vii, 622a
al-Shawwāf, ʿAbd al-Wahhāb iv, 719a
Shawwāl ix, **380b**
Shāy → Čay
Shayʾ ix, **380b**
Shayʿ al-Ḳawm ix, **382b**
Shaʿyā ix, **382b**
Shayāḍima vi, 744a
al-Shayb wa'l- shabāb ix, **383a**
Shayba, Banū iv, 317a, b, 318a, 320b; vi, 148b, 168a; vii, 362a; ix, **389b**
Shayba b. ʿUthmān → Shayba, Banū
Shaybak Khān Uzbek (XVI) vi, 514b
Shaybān, Banū iii, 1103a; iv, 88b-90b; v, 362b; vi, 345a, 546b, 624a, 640b, 900a, 930a; ix, **391a**; s, 15b
Shaybān b. Djoči (Batuʾid) ii, 44b, 67b x, 560b
Shaybān al-Ṣaghīr iii, 988b; iv, 447a
al-Shaybānī → al-Daḥḥāk b. Ḳays; ʿĪsā b. al-Shaykh; Yazīd b. Mazyad
al-Shaybānī, Abū ʿAbd Allāh Muḥammad b. al-Ḥasan (805) i, 123a, 124a, 164b, 588b; iii, 162b, 512b; iv, 377a, 691a; vi, 24a, 264b; vii, 310b, 537b, 662b; ix, 35b, **392b**
al-Shaybānī, Abū ʿAmr Isḥāḳ b. Mirār (820) iv, 524b; vi, 197b; vii, 831b, 841a, 843a; ix, **394b**; s, **15b**, 394b
al-Shaybānī, Abū Dāwūd Khālid b. Ibrāhīm al-Dhuhlī (XI) vi, 332b
al-Shaybānī, Abu 'l-Ḳāsim Hibat Allāh s, 193a
al-Shaybānī, Abū Naṣr Fatḥ Allāh (1890) iv, 70a; ix, **395b**
al-Shaybānī, Abu 'l-Sarāyā al-Sirrī b. Manṣūr (IX) i, **150a**; vi, 334a
al-Shaybānī, Aḥmad b. ʿĪsā b. Shaykh (IX) i, 145a; iv, 903a, b; vi, 88b, 540a; vii, 760a
al-Shaybānī, Aḥmad b. Mazyad (Ḳaysī) (IX) vi, 333b
al-Shaybānī, Ibrāhīm b. Muḥammad (911) ix, **396a**
Shaybānī Khān (Shaybānid) (1510) → Shībānī Khān
Shaybānids s> Shībānids al-Shaybī, ʿAbd Allāh b. ʿAbd al-Ḳādir (XX) vi, 160b, 165b
Shaydā, Mullā ix, **396b**
Shayfta, Muṣṭafā Khān iii, 93b
Shāyista Khān i, 606a, 769a; ii, 32a, 216b
Shaykh (title) iii, 411a, 721a; iv, 335a, 678a; v, 1131a, 1133a; ix, **397a**
Shaykh (Mamlūk) → al-Muʾayyad Shaykh
Shaykh b. ʿAbd Allāh b. Shaykh (1) i, 781a
Shaykh b. ʿAbd Allāh b. Shaykh (2) i, 781b
Shaykh b. Muḥammad b. Ṣāliḥ (1919) viii, 990a
Shaykh ʿAbd Allāh (Kashmīr) iv, 710a, b
Shaykh ʿAbduh i, 1070a; v, 188a
Shaykh Abū Isḥāḳ (Īndjūid) (1356) vii, 820a
Shaykh Ādam, Ṣafī al-Dīn (1621) ix, **398a**
Shaykh ʿAdī → ʿAdī b. Musāfir
Shaykh Aḥmad (Durban) (1886) ix, 730b
Shaykh al-Aḳl i, 1078b
Shaykh ʿAlī b. Uways ii, 401b; iv, 584b
Shaykh ʿAlī Āghā b. Fatḥ ʿAlī Khān (Ḳādjār) v, 296b
Shaykh ʿAlī Khān Zand iv, 390b
Shaykh Badr al-Dīn (XV) vii, 645a
Shaykh al-Bakrī i, 966a; ii, 165a, 181b
Shaykh al-balad ix, **398b**
Shaykh Dāwūd Kirmānī (1574) x, 255b
Shaykh Djunayd → Djunayd Shaykh
Shaykh Ghālib → Ghālib Dede, Shaykh
Shaykh al-Ḥara → Ismāʿīl Pāshā
Shaykh Ḥasan-i Buzurg (Djalāyirid) x, 552b

Shaykh Ḥusayn (Ethiopia) (1200) ix, **398b**
Shaykh Ibrāhīm (Sharwan-Shāh) iv, 350a, 586b
Shaykh al-Islām i, 837b; ii, 420b, 867a, b; iii, 250a, 552b, 1152a; iv, 168a, 573b; v, 1083b; vi, 6b; ix, **399b**
Shaykh al-Islām Yaḥyā iii, 1200b; s, 324a
al-Shaykh al-Kabīr → Ibn Khafīf
al-Shaykh al-Kāmil iv, 93b
Shaykh Khiḍr (1586) vii, 189a
Shaykh Maḥmūd i, 262b
Shaykh al-Maḥmūdī (Aleppo) (XV) vii, 723a, b
Shaykh Manṣūr ii, 25b
Shaykh Mīrzā ʿAlī Shahristānī, Ḥādjdj (Marʿashī) vi, 516b
Shaykh Muʾayyad i, 1328a
Shaykh Muḥammad (painter) vii, 603a
Shaykh Mūsā Barāhima ii, 166b
Shaykh Mūsā Nathrī (1968) ix, **402a**
Shaykh al-Raʾīs Abu 'l-Ḥasan Mīrzā (Ḳādjār) vi, 292a
Shaykh Rifāʿa → al-Taḥṭāwī
Shaykh Rukn al-Dīn Abu 'l-Fatḥ (1334) x, 255b
Shaykh Saʿd vi, 650a
Shaykh Saʿdī → Saʿdī, Abū ʿAbd Allāh
Shaykh Ṣafī → Ṣafī al-Dīn Ardabīlī
al-Shaykh Saʿīd (Bāb al-Mandab) vi, 933a; ix, **402b**
Shaykh Saʿīd → Ṣafī al-Dīn Ardabīlī
Shaykh Saʿīd Naḳshbandī v, 463b, 464b
Shaykh Saʿīd Shaʿbān (Tripoli) (XX) x, 216a
Shaykh Ṣāliḥ (XX) vi, 791b
al-Shaykh al-Ṣāliḥ → ʿAbd Allāh al-Shaykh
Shaykh Saʿūd iv, 638a
al-Shaykh al-Shīrāzī → Ibn Khafīf
Shaykh al-Ṭāʾifa → al-Ṭūsī, Muḥammad b. al-Ḥasan
Shaykh al-Ṭayyib al-Madjdhūb ii, 122b; iv, 687a
al-Shaykh al-Yūnānī i, 234b; ii, 765a; iii, 942b; ix, **403a**
Shaykh Yūnus → Küčik Khān Djangalī
Shaykh Yūsuf → Abidin Tadia Tjoessoep
Shaykh Zāde → Sheykh Zāde
Shaykh Ẓāhir i, 341b
Shaykh Zayn i, 849a, b
Shaykha → Shīkha
Shaykhā Khokar (XIV) v, 31b; vi, 49b
Shaykhān (river) vi, 539b
Shaykhī → Shaykhiyya
Shaykhiyya (theology) i, 304b, 850b; iv, 51a, 854a, b; vi, 551b; vii, 422a, 440b; ix, **403b**; s, 305a
Shaykhī (poets) ii, 990a; iii, 43b
Shaykhiyān vi, 384b
Shaykhiyya-Djūriyya (ṭarīḳa) iv, 48b; vi, 511a
Shaykhū, amīr (XIV) vi, 413b
Shaykhū, Luwīs (L. Cheikho) (1927) ix, **405b**
Shaykhū al-ʿUmarī → Ibn Faḍl Allāh al-ʿUmarī
Shaykhūn al-ʿUmarī (1357) i, 444a; iii, 239b; vi, 327a, 367b; vii, 993a
al-Shaykhūniyya vi, 454a
Shaykhūpūra vi, 368b
Shāyḳiyya ii, 351a, 615b, 944b; ix, **406a**
Shaymāʾ bint Ḥalīma (VII) viii, 697b
al-Shayṭān i, 177a; iii, 668b, 1050a; iv, 643b; ix, **406b**
Shayṭān Ibrāhīm Pasha i, 1284b
Sheyṭan al-Ṭāḳ (Muḥammad b. al-Nuʿmān) (VIII) ii, 374b; ix, **409a**
Shayyād ix, **409b**
Shayzar (town) vi, 118b, 606a; vii, 577b, 578a; ix, **410a**
al-Shayzarī, ʿAbd al-Raḥmān b. Naṣr (1193) i, 800b; ii, 482a; iii, 486b
al-Shayzārī, Abu 'l-Ḥasan ʿAlī iii, 761a
al-Shayzarī, Amīn al-Dīn (XIII) ix, **411a**
Shawrī → Shiḥrī
Sheba, Queen of → Bilḳīs
Shebek → Shabak
Shebelle (river) ix, **412a**, 714b
Shebīn Ḳarā Ḥiṣār → Ḳarā Ḥiṣār
Shebsefa Kadi̊n (1805) ix, **412b**
Shefīḳ Ḥüsnü (XX) iv, 124a; vi, 94b
Shefīḳ Meḥmed Efendi (1715) ix, **412b**
Shefḳatī, ʿAlī iv, 681b
Shehe Mvita (Mombasa) vii, 226a
Shehīd ʿAlī Pasha → Dāmād ʿAlī Pasha
Shehir Emāneti ix, **413a**
Shehir Emīni → Shehir Emāneti
Shehir Ketkhüdasi̊ i, 974a; ix, **414a**
Shehr → Shahr
Shehremānet i, 972b, 974b, 975a
Shehremīni i, 972b, 974a
Shehr-i Sebz → Kash
Shehzāde (title) ix, **414a**

Shehrīzāde Aḥmed b. Müdhehhib ii, 589b
Shehu (Bornū) i, 1260a, b; v, 359a
Sheikh → Shaykh
Sheker Bayramî → ʿĪd al-Fiṭr
Shekhu Aḥmadu (Shaykh Aḥmad, Mali) (XIX) vi, 259b
Shekib Efendi ii, 636b
Shela (Lamu) vi, 385a, 963b
Shemʿdānī-zāde Süleymān Efendi (1779) ix, **414a**
Shemʿī (XVI) ix, **414b**
Shems al-Dīn Günaltay (1961) ix, **415b**
Shemsī vi, 886a
Shenlik ix, **416b**
Shen-si (Shaanxi) v, 848a; ix, **415b**
Shepherd, the (astronomy) s, 321a
Shēr Aḥmad Khān iv, 711a
Shēr Shāh Sūr → Shīr Shāh Sūrī
Shēr Singh → Shīr Singh
Sherāga ii, 510a, b
Sherārda ii, 510a
Sherbet ix, **417a**
Sheref, ʿAbd al-Raḥmān (1925) ix, **417a**
Sherefli Ḳočhisar v, 247b
Śḥerí → Djibbālī
Shērs (Shārs) (Ghardjistān) ii, 1010b; vi, 65b
Shērzād b. Masʿūd ii, 1052a; s, 21a
Shesh Bolūḳī Reshkūlī s, 148a
Shetiyya iv, 401b
Shewkī Beg (Şevki Bey) (1896) ix, **417b**
Sheykh Badr al-Dīn (Samāwnā) x, 253b
Sheykh Ghālib → Ghālib Dede, Shaykh
Sheykh Ḥasan Efendi → Sezāʾī
Sheykhī Čelebi (Germiāni) (1429) iii, 356b; vi, 835b; viii, 211a; ix, 240a
Sheykh-oghlu, Ṣadr al-Dīn (1401) viii, 211a; ix, **418a**
Sheykh-zāde → Sheykh-oghlu
Sheykh-zāde Aḥmed (Aḥmed-i Miṣrī) (XV) ix, **419a**
Sheytānlîḳ (island) ix, **419a**
Sheyyād Ḥamza (XIII) viii, 972b; ix, **419b**
Shīʿa i, 15a, 16b, 20a, 51a, 124b, 130a, 149b, 224a, 347a, 382a, 399b, 402a, 589b, 713a, 794b, 832b, 941b, 1040a, 1120a, 1162a, 1198a, 1254a; iii, 411b, 434a, 1265a; iv, 34b, 46b, 277b, 855a; v, 1033a; vi, 11a, 272b, 476a, 548b; vii, 854a, 921b; viii, 777a; 342a, 367b, 402a, b, 423b
– doctrine i, 188a, 258a, 334a, 339b, 402a, 1026b, 1098b, 1113b, 1352a; ii, 374b, 539a, 834a; iii, 78b, 242b, 544b, 664a, 1130a; iv, 19a, 278b, 698a; v, 1235b; ix, **420a**, 819a; x, 49b; s, 305a
Shiʿār ix, **424a**
Shiʿb ʿAlī (Mecca) vi, 168a
Shiʿb Djabala vi, 603a; vii, 582a; ix, **424b**; s, 177a, 178a
Shibām vi, 132b, 439a; vii, 496a; ix, **425a**; s, 337b, 338a, 407a
Shibām Aḳyān vi, 436a
Shibām al-Ghirās → Shibām
Shibām Ḥaḍramawt → Shibām
Shibām Ḥarāz → Shibām
Shibām Kawkabān → Shibām
Shiban (Aḳ Orda) s, 96b
Shibān → Shaybān
Shībānī Khān Muḥammad (Özbeg) (1510) i, 627b, 847b, 849a, 1001b, 1019a, 1211b, 1295b; iii, 198a, 1101a; iv, 1036b; v, 54b, 55a, 59a, 859a; vi, 418a, 714b; vii, 928a; viii, 768a; ix, **426a**, 684a; x, 722a; s, 51b
Shībānids i, 8a, 46b, 120b, 121a, 228b, 637a, 690a, 963b, 964b, 1110b; ii, 44b, 72a, 792a; iv, 9b, 1064b; v, 859a, b; viii, 232a; ix, **428a**; s, 96b, 227b, 340a, b
Shibarghān (town) ix, **431a**
Shibīn al-Kūm vi, 453b
Shibithth ix, **431b**
Shibl al-Dawla → Mirdās, Banū
Shiblī (Sārī) (XV) vi, 514a
al-Shiblī → Ibn Shibl
al-Shiblī → al-Hindī, Sirādj al-Dīn al-Ḥanafī
al-Shiblī, Abū Ḥafṣ (1372) ix, **433a**
al-Shiblī, Abu ʾl-Ḳāsim (Abū Bakr) Dulaf b. Djaḥdar (945) i, 387b; iv, 990a; vi, 280a, 569a; ix, **432a**
al-Shiblī, Badr al-Dīn al-Dimashḳī (1367) i, 758b, 759a
Shiblī, Shaykh (945) viii, 8a
Shiblī academy → Dār al-Muṣannifīn
Shiblī al-Aṭrash ii, 637a
Shiblī al-Mallāṭ s, 159b
Shiblī Nuʿmānī, Muḥammad (1914) ii, 132b, 489a; iii, 433a; v, 960a, 1136a; vi, 612a; vii, 875b; ix, **433b**; x, 879b; s, 106a, b, 293a

Shifāʿī Iṣfahānī, Ḥakīm Sharaf al-Dīn (1628) iv, 69a; ix, **434a**
Shīdān vi, 494a
al-Shidyāḳ → Asʿad al-Shidyāḳ; Fāris al-Shidyāḳ
al-Shidyāḳ, Āl vi, 712a
Shifāʾī, Muẓaffar b. Muḥammad al-Ḥusaynī (1556) viii, 783b; x, 458a
Shifāʾī, Sharaf al-Dīn (1627) iv, 69a, viii, 776a, 851a
Shigaley → Shāh ʿAlī
Shighnān → Shughnān
Shigi-Ḳutuku (Mongol) (XIII) xi, 284b
Shīḥ ix, **434b**
Shihāb, Banū ix, **435a**
Shihāb al-Dawla → Mawdūd b. Masʿūd
Shihāb al-Dīn → Muḥammad b. Sām I, Muʿizz al-Dīn
Shihāb al-Dīn, Pīr v, 26a
Shihāb al-Dīn b. ʿAlāʾ al-Dīn, Sayyid iii, 155b
Shihāb al-Dīn b. Nāṣir al-Dīn Shāh (Mālwā) (XVI) vi, 54b
Shihāb al-Dīn Abū ʿAbd Allāh Yaʿḳūb → Yāḳūt al-Rūmī
Shihāb al-Dīn Aḥmad b. Mādjid → Ibn Mādjid
Shihāb al-Dīn Aḥmad b. ʿAbd al-Ḳādir (XVII) vii, 290b
Shihāb al-Dīn Aḥmad b. Abū Bakr Marʿashī (1467) vi, 517b
Shihāb-al-Dīn Aḥmad b. Faḍl Allāh → Ibn Faḍl Allāh al-ʿUmarī
Shihāb al-Dīn Dawlatābādī → al-Dawlatābādī
Shihāb al-Dīn al-Ḥusaynī, Shāh (1884) ix, **435b**
Shihāb al-Dīn al-Ḳarāfī (1285) vi, 185a; ix, **436a**
Shihāb al-Dīn al-Ḳūṣī (1255) vi, 429b
Shihāb al-Dīn Maḥmūd (Bahmanid) (1518) vi, 62b; vii, 289a
Shihāb al-Dīn Maḥmūd b. Būrī i, 1332a; ii, 282a; iii, 399a
Shihāb al-Dīn Maḥmūd b. Ḳarādja iii, 120a
Shihāb al-Dīn Maḥmūd b. Takash al-Ḥārimī (Ḥamāt) (1176) vi, 790a
Shihāb al-Dīn Mālik ii, 354b
Shihāb al-Dīn al-Maḳsī (XIII) vii, 210b
Shihāb al-Dīn al-Miṣrī al-Ḥanafī → al-Khafādjī
Shihāb al-Dīn Muḥammad Ghūrī → Muʿizz al-Dīn Muḥammad b. Sām
Shihāb al-Dīn Shāhīn Pasha → Shāhīn Pasha
Shihāb al-Dīn Shīrāshāmak iii, 420a; iv, 708a
Shihāb al-Dīn ʿUmar → ʿUmar Shāh
Shihāb al-Dīn ʿUmar b. Muʿīn al-Dīn Djāmī (XIV) viii, 749b
Shihāb Iṣfahānī (1874) ix, **436a**
Shihāb Mahmrā s, 66b
Shihāb Turshīzī (1800) ix, **436b**
al-Shihābī (1800) iv, 69b
al-Shihābī → ʿAbd al-Khāliḳ; Aḥmad; Ḥaydar; Manṣūr
Shihābids i, 1078a; ii, 634b, 635a; iv, 834b; v, 259a; s, 268a, b, 269a
Shiḥna ix, **437a**
al-Shiḥr i, 554b; iv, 901b; v, 656a, 786a, b; vi, 81b, 133a, 385b; vii, 51a, 496a; ix, **438b**; s, 337b, 338a, b
Shiḥrī (Shaḥrī) ix, **439a**
Shiḳāḳ, Banū i, 1031a
Shikār aghalarî ii, 6a
Shikārī ix, **439a**
Shikārpūr ii, 185b, 186a; ix, **440a**
Shikasta → Khaṭṭ
Shīkha iv, 823b
Shiḳḳ ix, **440b**
Shiḳḳa Banāriya → al-Kāf
Shiḳḳdār ii, 273a, 868a
al-Shīla (al-Sīla) (Korea) ix, **440b**
Shilb (Silves) i, 6a, 165b, 862a, 1339a; ii, 1009a; iii, 816b; ix, **441a**
al-Shilbī → Ibn al-Imām
al-Shilbī, Maryam bint Abī Yaʿḳūb (XI) ix, 441b
al-Shilbiyya (XII) ix, 441b
al-Shillī, Abū ʿAlawī Muḥammad b. Abū Bakr (1682) i, 828b; vi, 352a; ix, **441b**
Shilluk ii, 828a, 944a
Shīmā bint Ḥalīma (VI) viii, 362b
Shimr (Ḥusayn b. ʿAlī) vi, 737a
Shimrān vi, 20b
Shimshāṭ ix, **442a**
al-Shimshāṭī, Abu 'l-Ḥasan (X) ix, **442a**
Shimʿūn vi, 631b
Shīn → Sīn

Shīnā, Salmān (1978) ix, **442b**
Shinās vii, 53a
Shināsī, Ibrāhīm Efendi (1871) i, 61b, 294a, 298a, 973a; ii, 466a, 473b, 682a; iii, 591b; iv, 875b; vi,92a, 373a, 758a, b; ix, **443a**
Shīnī (Shīniyya, Shānī) ix, **444a**
Shinḳīṭ/Shindjīṭ i, 211a, 733b; vii, 611a, 623b, 624a; ix, **445a**
al-Shinḳīṭī, Aḥmad b. al-Amīn (1913) v, 892a; vii, 624a; ix, **445b**; s, 123a
al-Shinḳīṭī, Muḥammad b. al-Mukhtār (1882) x, 249a
al-Shinḳīṭī, Sīdī ʿAbd Allāh b. al-Ḥādjdj Ibrāhīm (1878) vii, 624a
al-Shinḳīṭī, Sīdī ʿAbd Allāh b. Muḥammad b. al-Ḳāḍī (Ibn Rāzga) (1730) vii, 624a
al-Shinḳīṭī, al-Ṭālib Abū ʿAbd Allāh (Bilaʿmash) (1695) vii, 624a
Shintara (Cintra) ix, **446b**
Shinwārīs i, 238a; s, 66b, 237b
al-Shinshawrī, ʿAbd Allāh (1590) vii, 135a
Shiʿr 1. in Arabic a. the Pre-Modern Period ix, **448b**
Shiʿr b. the modern period ix, **462a**
Shiʿr 2. in Persian ix, **465b**
Shiʿr 3. in Turkish ix, **467b**
Shiʿr 4. in Urdu ix, **469b**
Shiʿr 5. in Malay and Indonesian s, **727a**
Shiʿr 6. in Swahili → Swahili. 2. Literature
Shiʿr 7. in Hausa ix, **470b**
Shīr → Asad
Shīr Afḍal ii, 30b, 317a
Shīr Afkan → ʿAlī Ḳulī Khān Istadjlū
Shīr ʿAlī (vizier, Mashhad) (XV) vi, 715b
Shīr ʿAlī Khān b. Dōst Muḥammad (Afghānistān) (1879) i, 87a, 231b, 232a, 796b; ii, 417a, 638a; iv, 537b; vi, 807a; ix, **446b**
Shīr ʿAlī Khān (Khōkand) (1845) v, 30a
Shīr Khān → Shīr Shāh Sūrī (Delhi)
Shīr Khān (Bengal) (1272) i, 1254a
Shīr Khān Bābī ii, 597b
Shīr Khān Lōdī (XVII) vii, 530b
Shīr Muḥammad Mīrāb, ʿAwaḍ, al-Khīwaḳī → Muʾnis (Khīwa) (1829)
Shīr Shāh Sūr (Afghān, Delhi) (1545) i, 218a, 228b, 252b, 316a, 1015a, 1135b, 1155a, 1209b, 1218b, 1323b; ii, 13a, 121a, 154b, 155b, 259a, 271a, 272b, 498b, 973a, 1122b, 1144a; iii, 199b, 201b, 422b, 423a, 449a, 575b; iv, 276b, 1127b; v, 598a, 687b; vi, 47a, b, 48b, 127b, 131a, 272a, 310a, 407a; vii, 131a, 138b, 195a, 314a, 317a, 325a, 344b, 680a, 965b; ix, **448a**, 894a; s, 1b, 3a, 176b, 203a, 312a, 325a
Shīr Singh ii, 140b; iii, 336a; iv, 196b
Shīr wa-Khurshīd → Nishān
Shiraʾ ix, **470b**
al-Shiʿrā (Sirius) ix, **471b**; s, 320b
Shīrangapattanam → Srīrangapattanam
Shīrāshāmak → Shihāb al-Dīn Shīrāshāmak
Shīrawayh (Shīrūy Kawādh II) (Sāsānid) (628) xi, 3a
Shīrawayh, Abū Shudjāʿ (1115) iii, 105b; ix, **472a**
Shīrāz i, 36a, 132a, 1341b; ii, 812a; iii, 55b, 1208b; iv, 7b, 220a; v, 835a; vi, 120a, 128b, 198b, 199a, 272b, 283a, 383b, 384a, 408a, 484b, 516a, 517a, 551a, 627b, 671b, 764a; vii, 820a, b; ix, **472b**; s, 38a, 118b, 119b, 142b, 147b, 291a, 302a, 305a, 336a
– institutions i, 212b; ii, 426a
– monuments i, 127a; iii, 1124b
Shīrāzī (Kilwa) ix, **489a**
al-Shīrāzī → al-ʿAbbās b. al-Ḥusayn; Ḳuṭb al-Dīn
Shīrāzī, ʿAbd al-Hādī (Āyatullāh) (1962) vi, 553b; ix, **480a**
al-Shīrāzī, Abū ʿAbd Allāh iv, 1074a
al-Shīrāzī, Abu ʾl-Faradj iii, 161a, 766b
al-Shīrāzī, Abu ʾl-Ḥasan ii, 649b; iv, 787a; v, 61a
al-Shīrāzī, Abu ʾl-Ḥusayn (XII) ix, **481a**
al-Shīrāzī, Abū Isḥāḳ (1083) iii, 899a; vi, 655a; vii, 397a, 540b; viii, 71b; ix, 65a, **481a**; s, 29b, 192a
Shīrāzī, Elwān (XV) vi, 73a
Shīrāzī, Ḥasan al-Mahdī al-Ḥusaynī (Āyatullāh) (1980) ix, **481a**
Shīrāzī, Mahdī b. al-Sayyid Ḥabīb Allāh al-Ḥusaynī (1960) ix, **480a**
Shīrāzī, Mīrzā ʿAlī Agha (1936) ix, **480a**
Shīrāzī, Mīrzā Muḥammad Ḥasan (1895) vi, 552b; vii, 299a, 918b; ix, **479b**; s, 76a, 77a
Shīrāzī, Mīrzā Muḥammad Taḳī b. Muḥibb ʿAlī Ḥāʿirī (1920) vi, 552b; ix, **480b**
Shīrāzī, Mīrzā Ṣāliḥ (XIX) s, 108a, 290b
Shīrāzī, Mīrzā al-Sayyid Ismāʿīl (1888) ix, **480a**

al-Shīrāzī, Muḥammad b. Iyās i, 344b
al-Shīrāzī, Nūr al-Dīn Muḥammad b. Abi ʾl-Ṭayyib (XIV) vi, 847b
Shīrāzī, Rafīʿ al-Dīn (1620) ix, **483a**
al-Shīrāzī, Ṣadr al-Dīn → Mullā Ṣadrā Shīrāzī
Shīrāzī, Shaykh Hāshimī (XIX) vii, 440b
Shīrbaz vi, 506b
al-Shirbīnī, Yūsuf b. Muḥammad (XIII) i, 571b, 595b; ix, **483a**
Shire (Syros) ix, **483b**
Shīrgīr → Anūshtigin Shīrgīr
Shīrī → ʿAlī Beg Hersek-zāde
Shīrīn → Farhād wa-Shīrīn
Shirin Begī ii, 1113b; iv, 630a
Shīrīn Bika Āḳā bint Ṭaraghay (Tīmūrid) (1385) viii, 1036a
Shīrīn Maghribī, Muḥammad ix, **484a**
Shirk ix, **484b**
Shīrkūh, al-Mudjāhid (Ḥims) (XIII) viii, 988b
Shīrkūh, Abu ʾl-Ḥārith b. Shādī (1169) i, 197a, 197b, 797a; ii, 318b, 856b, 858a; iii, 399a, 862b; iv, 210a; vi, 320a, 322a, 380b, 547b, 871a; vii, 163b, 726b; viii, 127b, 130a, b, 131a; ix, **486a**
Shīrkūh I, Asad al-Dīn iii, 399b
Shīrkūh II b. Nāsīr al-Dīn Muḥammad al-Mundhirī (1258) (Ḥims) viii 988b
Shirmake, ʿAbd al-Rashīd (Somalia) (1969) ix, 718b, 719b
Shīrpūr i, 1254a
Shirriz vi, 744a, b
Shīr-rūd-dūhazār vi, 512b
Shīrwān (Sharwān, Shirwān) i, 8a, 191b, 406a, 958a; ii, 86a, 193a; iii, 211a; iv, 343a, 344b, 346a-350a; v, 296a, 458b; vi, 55b, 56b, 64b, 320a, 416b, 500a, 516b; ix, **487a**; s, 139b, 143a, 326a, 333b
Shirwān (river) → Diyālā
Shīrwān-Shāh iv, 348a; vi, 274b; ix, **488a**
Shīrwān Shāhs i, 835b, 967b; ii, 1082b; iv, 345a, b, 348a, 350a
al-Shirwānī, Fatḥ Allāh al-Muʾmin (1453) vii, 685a, 976a
al-Shirwānī(-zāde), Meḥmed/Muḥammad Rushdī(/Rüshdü) Pasha (1875) i, 285a; iii, 621a; vi, 175b; vii, 205b
Shīrwānī, Yaḥyā (1463) x, 252a
Shīrwānī, Zayn al-ʿĀbidīn (1837) viii, 117a; xi, 484a
Shīrzādiyān iv, 860a
Shisar xi, 5b
Shishaklī, Adīb al- ii, 662a; v, 1048a
Shishāwa vi, 142a, 743b
Shishman i, 1118b, 1302b, 1303a; ii, 611a
Shishmanids i, 1302b
Shīth b. Ādam (Seth) i, 178a, 247a; vi, 901a; ix, **489b**
Shīth b. Bahrām ii, 1099b
Shīth b. Ibrāhīm al-Ḳifṭī iii, 780a
Shīthānī ii, 1100a, 1101a
Shiṭrandj → Shaṭrandj
Shīv(w)ādjī b. Shādjī Bhōnsle (Marāthā) (1680) i, 199b, 769a, 1202b; ii, 99b, 602a, 1129b; iii, 15b, 202b, 424b, 427a; iv, 1023a; vi, 269b, 534b, 535a, 536a; vii, 315b, 404b; viii, 74b; s, 246b
Shivādjī II b. Rādjarām (Marāthā) (XVIII) vi, 535a
Shiw Prasād iii, 458a
Shīz v, 1110a, 1112a; ix, **490b**
Shkarawa i, 1189b, 1190a
Shkodra → Ishkodra
Shlūḥ → Tashelhīt
Shoa i, 763b; ii, 10a, b; iii, 3b; iv, 540b
Shodhi Efendi → Shawkī Efendi Rabbānī
Shoghi → Shawḳī
Shoghi Efendi → Shawḳī Efendi
Shōlāpūr iii, 426a, 626a, 1160a, 1161a; ix, **490b**
Shor Bazaar s, 66b
Shorfā → Sharīf; Shurafāʾ
Shrārda (rebel) (XIX) i, 84b; vi, 595b
Shrīnagar → Srīnagar
Shrīrangapattanam iii, 451a; v, 1259a, 1260a, b
Shriwardhan s, 246b
Shu → Ču
Shuʿāʿ al-Salṭana (Ḳādjār) (XX) ii, 652b; iv, 393b; vii, 432a, b
Shuʿayb (prophet) ix, **491a**
Shuʿayb I b. ʿUmar (880) i, 680b; v, 421a, 1156a, b; vi, 1035b
Shuʿayb b. Djalāl al-Dīn Manīrī (XV) vi, 354a
Shuʿayb b. al-Ḥabḥāb al-Azdī i, 104b
Shuʿayb b. Mahdam iii, 53a
Shuʿayb b. al-Muʿarrif viii, 112b
Shuʿayb b. Muḥammad b. ʿAbd Allāh (VIII) vii, 576b
Shuʿayb b. Sahl (842) vii, 4a

Shuʿayb b. Ṣāliḥ viii, 657b
al-Shuʿayba vi, 144b; s, 50a
Shuʿaybiyyūn iii, 339a
Shuʿba b. ʿAyyāsh (808) i, 105b; iii, 63a; vi, 263b; s, 18a, 232b
Shuʿba b. al-Hadjdjādj (777) i, 445b; vii, 260a; viii, 515a; ix, **491b**
Shubāṭ → Taʾrīkh
Shubayl b. ʿAzra al-Ḍubaʿī (757) ix, 766b
Shubha ii, 831b; iii, 21b; ix, **492b**
Shubrā al-Khayma (Damanhūr) ii, 105b; vi, 303a
Shubrāwī, Shaykh ʿAbd Allāh i, 819b, 1152a
Shubruma b. al-Ṭufayl iii, 938a
Shūdhī xi, 112b
Shudjāʿ, Shaykh (Khalwatī) (1588) vii, 596a; ix, 155b
Shudjāʿ b. al-Ḳāsim (IX) vii, 723a
Shudjāʿ b. Shāh Djahān iii, 634b; ix, 195b; s, 258b
Shudjāʿ al-Dawla, Mīrzā Djalāl al-Dīn Nawwāb, Awadh (1775) i, 680a, 702a, 757a, 1042b, 1357b; ii, 870b; iii, 61a, b, 1158b, 1244a; v, 637a; viii, 426a; ix, 90a, **493a**
Shudjāʿ al-Dīn Khurshīd v, 828a
Shudjāʿ al-Dīn Orkhan b. Menteshe vii, 56a
Shudjāʿ al-Dīn Sulaymān Pasha iv, 108b
Shudjāʿ Khān (Mālwā) (1554) i, 1155a; vi, 407a
Shudjāʿ al-Mulk, Nawwāb (Awadh) (XVIII) vii, 707a
Shudjāʿ al-Mulk b. ʾAmān al-Mulk ii, 30b
Shudjāʿ al-Mulk Bukhārī iii, 634a
Shudjāʿ al-Mulk Durrānī (Afghanistān) (1839) i, 72b, 230b, 231a, b; ii, 186b, 638a, 1001a; iv, 537b; v, 102a; vi, 806b; s, 270a
Shudjāʿ al-Salṭana → Ḥasan ʿAlī Mīrzā
Shudjāʿī, Shams al-Dīn (XIV) ix, **493b**
al-Shūf ii, 749b; vi, 343a, 344a; ix, **494a**; s, 159a
Shufʿa i, 172b; v, 878b; ix, **494b**
Shufurwa, Sharaf al-Dīn (XII) iv, 62a; viii, 971b; ix, **495a**
Shughnān (Shighnān) i, 851b, 853b, 854a; iv, 202b; ix, **495b**
Shughnī (language) i, 225a
Shughr ii, 556a
al-Shuhadāʾ (Mecca) ii, 744b; vi, 147b, 153a
Shuhāra → Shahāra
Shuhaym, Banū s, 356a
Shuhūd → Shāhid
Shuḥūra (pass) vi, 546a
Shukāʿa (Shukāʿ) ix, **496b**
Shukr ix, **496b**
Shukr b. Abi ʾl-Futūḥ (Musāwī) (1061) vi, 148b
Shukr Allāh, Mīrzā (XVI) vii, 442a
Shükr Allāh Efendī (XVII) v, 19a
Shukrān, Banū vii, 263a
Shukrī, ʿAbd al-Raḥmān (1958) vi, 955b; ix, **998a**; s, 58a
Shukrī al-Khūrī → al-Khūrī
Shukrī al-Ḳuwwatlī ii, 290a; ix, 561a
Shukrī Muṣṭafā (1978) vii, 291b; x, 61b, 122b
Shukriyya iv, 686a, b, 687a
Shükrü, Midḥat iv, 284b
Shükrü (Shükrī) Bey, Aḥmed (1926) iii, 1199a; ix, **499a**
Shükūfe ii, 908b
Shūl (China) ix, **499a**
Shūl (amīrs) (XIII) v, 826b; vi, 482a
Shuʿla iv, 69b
Shulayr, Djabal i, 489a
Shūlistān iv, 498a; v, 824a, 829b; ix, **499b**
Sh(u)lūḥ (Marrākush) i, 1181b, 1182a, b, 1183a, b, 1350a; vi, 590b, 591b, 743b
Shūmān ix, **500b**
Shumaym, Abu ʾl-Ḥasan ʿAlī (1204) ix, **501a**
al-Shumaym al-Ḥillī iii, 111a, 221b
Shumayṭiyya (Sumayṭiyya) i, 509a; ix, **501b**
al-Shumaysī (Mecca) vi, 154b
Shumayyil, Shiblī b. Ibrāhīm (1917) iv, 125a; **501b**, 517a
Shumen → Shumnu
Shumla (Khūzistān) (XII) i, 239b, 513b; vi, 58b, 59b; vii, 707a, 726b
Shumnu ix, **502a**, 702b
Shungwaya (Somalia) ix, **504a**
al-Shūnī, Nūr al-Dīn (1537) vi, 87b, 88a
al-Shūnīzī → Kāẓimayn
Shunḳub ix, **504b**
Shūrā i, 84b; ii, 866a; v, 1084a; ix, **504b**
Shurafāʾ (Shorfāʾ) i, 355a, b, 368b, 371b, 403a; iii, 1037a; v, 1187b, 1191a, b,

1200a, 1201b; vii, 36a; viii, 440a; ix, **507a**, 899b
Shuraḥbīl b. ʿĀmir (684) vi, 677a
Shuraḥbīl b. al-Ḥārith (al-Mathāmina) i, 527a; v, 118b; vi, 829b
Shuraḥbīl b. Ḥasana (639) i, 111a, 341a, 1139a, 1149a; ii, 498a; iii, 397b, 569a; iv, 927b; v, 119b; vi, 546b; ix, 262b, **508b**
Shuraḥbīl b. al-Simṭ al-Kindī (VII) i, 1343b; iii, 168b; ix, 553b
Shuraḥbīl b. Yaḥṣib (Mārib) vi, 561b
Shuraḥbiʾil Yaʿfur (Mārib) vi, 561b, 563b
Shurāt → Khāridjites
Shurayḥ b. al-Ḥārith b. Ḳays (ḳāḍī) (695) vi, 670b; ix, **508b**
Shurā-yi Dewlet → Madjlis al-Shurā
Shurbubba vii, 614a
Shurīda, Muḥammad Taḳī (1826) ix, **509b**
Shurṭa ii, 505a, 507a, 510a; iii, 487b; iv, 373b; ix, **510a**
Shurūṭ → Sharṭ
Shūsh → al-Sūs
Shūsha iv, 573a; s, 47a
Shushānī → Shwāshna
Shūshtar (Shūshtar, Tustar) i, 695a, 711b; ii, 350b; iv, 674a, 675b; v, 451b, 867a; vi, 494b, 516a, 627b, 672b; vii, 673a, b; ix, **512a**
al-Shūshtarī, ʿAbd al-Laṭīf Mūsawī Djazāʾirī s, 108a, 290a
al-Shushtarī, Abu ʾl-Ḥasan ʿAlī (1269) i, 501b; iii, 921b; iv, 1006b; vii, 56b, 812a; ix, **513a**; x, 320b; s, 264a
al-Shushtarī, Sayyid ʿAbd al-Ḥusayn Marʿashī (XIX) vi, 517a
al-Shushtarī, Sayyid Niʿmat Allāh al-Djazāʾirī s, 57a
al-Shushtarī, Sayyid Nūr Allāh → Nūr Allāh al-Sayyid Sharīf al-Marʿashī
Shustar → Shushtar
Shuʿūb iv, 334a
Shuʿūbiyya i, 16b, 158a, 206b, 276a, 1080b; ii, 729a, 951b; iii, 353b, 773b, 846a, 885a; iv, 16a, 54b, 190a, 786a; vi, 215a, 313b, 880b; viii, 880b; ix, **513b**; s, 17b, 404b
Shuʿurī Ḥasan Efendī iv, 526b
Shuwa i, 1259b; ix, **516a**; s, 164a
Shuwaymiyya vi, 84b
al-Shuwayr vi, 305a, 307b
Shuwḥālīshoʿ (VIII) s, 599b
al-Shwayfāt vi, 304a
Shuyūʿiyya iii, 594a; ix, **517a**
Shyāḍma, Banū vi, 591a
Sī ʿAbd al-Ḥayy al-Kettānī (XX) vii, 416b, 417a
Sī Aḥmad al-Bakkāy iii, 39a
Sī Faṭmī ben Slīmān (XX) vii, 417a
Si Mohand (Mhand) x, 119a
Siak Sri Infrapura → Sumatra
Sialkōt → Siyālkūt
Al-Sīb (Damā) vi, 735b
Ṣibā iv, 488b
Sība, Bilād al- s, **729a**
Sibāʿ b. ʿAbd al-ʿUzzā al-Khuzāʿī iv, 896b
Sibāʿ b. Nuʿmān iv, 16a
al-Sibāʿī, Muṣṭafā iii, 1069b, 1070a; iv, 160a; viii, 906b
Sibāʿī, Yūsuf v, 190a
Sibāḳ → Faras
Sībawayh(ī), Abū Bishr ʿAmr b. ʿUthmān (796) i, 321b, 588b; ii, 896a; iii, 204b, 205a, 1162a; iv, 122b, 255a, 399b; v, 174b, 803b; vi, 130a, 346b, 443b, 635b; vii, 262a, 277a, 281b, 914a; ix, **524a**; s, 22b
Sībāy iii, 400a; iv, 552a, b, 553a
Siberia → Sibir
Siberia-Tukic Languages x, **732b**
Sībī (Sīwī) ix, **531a**; s, 270b
Sibir ix, **531b**
Sibir, Khān of (XV) ii, 45a
Sibṭ → Ibn al-Djawzī; Ibn al-Taʿāwīdhī; al-Mārdīnī, Muḥammad b. Muḥammad
Sicily → Ṣiḳilliyya
al-Sīd i, 986a; ii, 526b; iii, 542b, 770b; ix, **533a**; s, 81a
Sidama iii, 2b
Sidamo v, 524b
Siddi Lebbe ii, 28a
al-Ṣiddīḳ ix, **534b**
Ṣiddīḳ Ḥasan Khān al-Kannawdjī → Nawwāb Sayyid Ṣiddīḳ Ḥasan Khān
Ṣiddīḳa Dawlatābādī (XX) vi, 486a, b
al-Ṣiddīḳī → al-Firūzābādī
al-Ṣiddīḳī (Bakriyya) ix, **535a**
Ṣiddīḳī, Shāh Ghulām Muḥammad Ṣūfī (XX) ix, 730b
Ṣiddīḳī Shaykhs (Maḥmūdābād) vi, 77b
Sidḥ vi, 84a
Sidhpūr ix, **535a**
Sidi ix, **535b**

Sīdī ʿAbd Allāh al-Khayyāṭ (Talaghza) vi, 891a
Sīdī Abu ʾl-Ḥasan ʿAlī b. Ḥamdūsh (1718) vi, 891a; s, 350b
Sīdī Aḥmad (Banū ʿAbbās) iv, 478a, b
Sīdī Aḥmad b. ʿAlī iv, 350a
Sīdī Aḥmad u-Mūsā → Ḥmad u-Mūsā
Sīdī Aḥmad b. Yūsuf → Aḥmad b. Yūsuf
Sīdī Aḥmad al-Bakkāʾī (1514) v, 393a; ix, 758a
Sīdī Aḥmad Dghughī → Sīdī Abu ʾl-Ḥasan ʿAlī b. Ḥamdūsh
Sīdī ʿAlī → Sīdī Abu ʾl-Ḥasan ʿAlī b. Ḥamdūsh
Sīdī ʿAlī b. Khlef b. Ghālib → Mūlāy ʿAlī Bū Ghālem
Sīdī ʿAlī Arulatī iv, 349b
Sīdī ʿAlī Čelebi (1554) vii, 51a
Sīdī ʿAlī Ḥarzūz (1549) vi, 894a
Sīdī ʿAlī al-Mzālī (Fès) vi, 124a
Sīdī ʿAlī Reʾīs (1562) i, 386b; vii, 319a; ix, **535b**
Sīdī Badr → Muẓaffar Shāh Ḥabshī
Sīdī Bel-ʿAbbās al-Sabtī iv, 729a; vi, 589b, 590b, 591a, 596a
Sīdī Bel-Abbès → Sīdī Bu ʾl- ʿAbbās
Sīdī Ben Aḥmed iv, 729a
Sīdī Ben ʿAmmār → Ibn ʿAmmār, Abu ʾl-ʿAbbās
Sīdī Ben ʿArūs → Ibn ʿArūs
Sīdī Ben Slīmān → al-Djazūlī
Sīdī Berridjāl → Ibn Barradjān
Sīdī Bou Said → Sayyidī Abū Saʿīd
Sīdī Bū ʿAzzā → Abū Yaʿzā
Sīdī Bu ʾl-ʿAbbās ix, **536b**
Sīdī Bū Madyan → Abū Madyan
Sīdī Bū ʿUthmān vi, 595b; s, 48a
Sīdī Bū Yaʿḳūb → Abū Yaʿḳūb Yūsuf al-Bādisī
Sīdī Būshta (Abu ʾl-Shitāʾ) s, 405b
Sīdī ʾl-Ḥādjdj v, 596a
Sīdī Ḥammū i, 1186a
Sīdī Ḥarāzam (Fès) vi, 123b
Sīdī Lakhḍar Bakhkhlūf (al-Akhḍar) (XVI) vi, 248b, 249a, 253b
Sīdī Khalīl → Khalīl b. Isḥāḳ al-Djundī
Sīdī Lahsen Lyūsī (1691) ix, 769b
Sīdī Maḥmūd al-Baghdādī (XVI) ix, 758b
Sīdī Maḥrez → Muḥriz b. Khalaf
Sīdī Muḥammad → Muḥammad I-V (ʿAlawid)
Sīdī Muḥammad b. ʿAbd Allāh (ʿAlawid) → Muḥammad III b. ʿAbd Allāh, Sīdī
Sīdī Muḥammad b. ʿĪsā (XV) vii, 36b
Sīdī Muḥammad b. al-Mukhtār v, 394a
Sīdī Muḥammad b. al-Ṭayyib → Muḥammad b. al-Ṭayyib
Sīdī Muḥammad ʿAbd Allāh (Ḥamāliyya) → al-Sharīf al-Akhḍar
Sīdī Muḥammad al-ʿAyyāshī ii, 367b
Sīdī al-Mukhtār (1811) ix, 758a
Sīdī al-Muntaṣir al-Muḥammad (XIV) vii, 638a
Sīdī Muwallih iv, 921a
Sīdī (ʿAlī) Reʾīs ii, 588b, 589b; iii, 856b; ix, 535b
Sīdī al-Ṣāḥib → al-Balawī, Abū Zamʿa
Sīdī ʿUḳba → ʿUḳba b. Nāfiʿ
Sīdī Yāḳūt (Ḥabshī) s, 246a
Ṣādiḳ Zalīlī (Sidiḳ Zälili) (XVIII) vi, 768a; ix, 295b
Sīdiyya Bābā, Shaykh (XIX) vii, 609a
Sīdiyya al-Kabīr (1868) vii, 623a
Sidjādī, ʿAlāʾ al-Dīn v, 481b
Sidjdjīn iii, 1132b; ix, **538a**
Sidjill i, 9b, 1090a; ii, 79a, 302b, 308b; ix, **538a**
Sidjilmāsa ii, 885a; iii, 149a, 256b; v, 1175a, 1177a, 1178a; vi, 142a, b, 571b, 573a, 593a, 727b, 743b, 815a, 1038a; vii, 585a; viii, 440a; ix, **545a**; s, 28b, 29a, 295b, 370a, 389b
al-Sidjilmāsī, Abū Muḥammad al-Ḳāsim (XIV) vii, 277a; viii, 427a; ix, **546a**
al-Sidjilmāsī, ʿAlī (1647) vii, 626b
Sidjistān → Sīstān
al-Sidjistānī → Abū Bakr; Abū Dāwūd; Abū Ḥātim; Abū Sulaymān
al-Sidjistānī, ʿAbd Allāh (1929) ix, **546b**
Sidjn ix, **547a**
al-Sidjzī → Abū Yaʿḳūb; Aḥmad; Amīr Ḥasan
al-Sidjzī, ʿAbd Allāh (IX) vii, 410b
al-Sidjzī, Abū Saʿīd viii, 108a
Ṣidḳ iv, 487b; ix, **548b**
Ṣidḳa Kaʿkī (XX) vi, 163b
Ṣidḳī → Bakr Ṣidḳī; al-Zahāwī
Ṣidḳī, Muḥammad iv, 148b; v, 191a
Sidon → Ṣaydā
Sidona → Shadūna
Sidr ix, **549a**

Sidrat al-Muntahā ix, **550a**
Sidrāy b. Wazīr i, 1339a; ii, 1009a; iii, 816b
al-Sidrī s, 35b
Sīduh → Ibn Sīda
Sierra Leone ix, **550b**; s, 217b
Sīf al-Naṣr ii, 876a
Sīf ʿUmāra s, 222b, 223a
Ṣifa/Ṣifāt i, 333b, 410b; ii, 550b; iv, 182a; ix, **551a**
Ṣifātiyya i, 334a
Sīfawayh al-Ḳāṣṣ (VIII) ix, **552b**
Ṣiffīn, battle of i, 40b, 51b, 304a, 383b, 448b, 451b, 697a; iii, 12b; v, 936a; vi, 139a, 378b; vii, 693b; ix, **552b**; x, 107a; s, 89b, 230b
al-Ṣifr ix, **556b**
Sigetwār (Szigetvar) ii, 881b; ix, **557b**
Sïghnāḳ (Sughnāḳ) (town) ix, **557b**; x, 561as, 245a, 246a
al-Sïghnāḳī, Ḥusām al-Dīn (1314) vii, 969a
Ṣiḥāfa / Ṣaḥāfa 1. in the Arab Middle East ix, **558a**
Ṣiḥāfa / Ṣaḥāfa 2. North Africa ix, **563b**
Ṣiḥāfa / Ṣaḥāfa 3. the Arab Diaspora ix, **565a**
Ṣiḥāfa / Ṣaḥāfa 4. Persia s, **730a**
Ṣiḥāfa / Ṣaḥāfa 5. Turkey s, **731b**
Siḥāḳ v, 777b; ix, **565b**
Sihālī s, 292a
Sihām al-Mulk s, 365a
Siḥr i, 1084b; iv, 770a; v, 100b; ix, **567b**
Ṣihrīdj → Ḳanāt
Ṣihyawn (Sion) ix, **571b**
Siʿird (Siʿirt) ix, **573b**
Sīkān vi, 493b
Sikandar → Iskandar
Sikandar (Gudjarāt) ii, 1128b
Sikandar b. ʿAlī ʿĀdil-Shāh (ʿĀdil-Shāhs) (1700) i, 199b, 769b, 12102b; vi, 837a
Sikandar b. Muẓaffar Shāh I (Gudjarāt) (1526) vi, 51b
Sikandar b. Sulṭān Fatḥ Shāh (Kashmīr) (XVI) s, 324b
Sikandar Bēgam i, 1195b, 1197a
Sikandar b. Ḳuṭb al-Dīn, But-Shikān (Kashmīr) (1410) iii, 420a; iv, 708a, b; ix, **575b**; s, 131b
Sikandar Djāh (Ḥaydarābād) (XIX) iii, 322a; vi, 806a
Sikandar Khān (Satwas) (XVI) vi, 54b, 55a
Sikandar Shāh I, ʿAlāʾ al-Dīn (Tughluḳid, Delhi) (1393) vi, 49a
Sikandar Shāh I (Bengal) (1390) i, 719b; viii, 258b; ix, **575b**
Sikandar Shāh II Lōdī (Lōdīs, Delhi) (1517) i, 252b, 914b, 1323a; ii, 12b, 155a, 205a, 271a, 421a, 498b, 1048a, 1114a; iii, 420b, 439a, 453b, 492a, 631b, 632a; v, 784a, b, 1135a; vi, 51b, 126a, 410a, 970a, 1030b; vii, 139a; s, 10b, 73b, 203a, 312a, 313a, b
Sikandar Shāh III Aḥmad Khān Sūr (Sūrīs, Delhi) (1555) i, 316a, 1135b; ii, 271b; iii, 423b, 576a
Sikand(a)ra iv, 131b; vi, 369b
Sikandarābād/Secundarabad → Ḥaydarābād
Siḳāya i, 9a, 80a
Sikbādj ix, **576a**
Sikhs i, 72a, 230a, b, 231a, 282b, 296a, b, 454a, 913b, 970b, 1020a; ii, 28b, 637b, 929a, 973b; iii, 63a, 225b, 245b, 335b, 336a, 435b; iv, 666a, 709b; v, 597b, 598b; viii, 253b, 254b; ix, **576b**; s, 242a, 332a
Ṣiḳilliyya i, 86a, b, 248b, 250a, 935b; ii, 130b, 853a; iii, 220a, 299a, 657b, 788a; iv, 274b, 275b, 459b, 496a, b, 805a; v, 697a, 1243b; vi, 337b, 435b, 455b, 1043b; ix, 507b, **582a**; s, 120b, 303a
Sikka ii, 117b; iii, 256a, 384a; iv, 190b, 220a, 467a, 945a, 1177b; v, 965b, 966a; ix, **591b**
Sikkat al-Ḥadīd ix, **600b**
al-Sikkīn (XI) ii, 858b; vii, 732a
al-Sikkīt ii, 300a; iii, 940b
al-Ṣiḳlabī, ʿAbd al-Raḥmān iv, 672b
Sīkūl iv, 213a
Ṣila ix, **603a**; x, 11a
al-Silafī, al-Ḥāfiẓ Abū Ṭāhir Ḥāfiẓ (1180) iv, 137a; vi, 429a; ix, 65a, **607**b
Silāḥ i, 1055b; ii, 506b; v, 973a; s, **734**b
Silāḥdār ix, **609**b
Silāḥdār ʿAlī Pasha → ʿAlī Pasha Silāḥdār
Silāḥdār Findïḳlï Meḥmed Agha (1726) v, 18b; ix, **610**b
Silāḥdār Dāmād ʿAlī Pasha → ʿAlī Pasha Dāmād
Ṣilāḥdār Ḥusayn Pasha i, 905a
Silāḥdār Muṣṭafā Pasha (XVII) vi, 232a
Sile s, 136a
Silhādī i, 914b

Silhet (Sylhet) ix, **610**b
Silifke (Seleucia) iii, 1007a; ix, **611**a
Silistre i, 4b; ii, 611b; iii, 253a; iv, 878a; viii, 236a
Silivri Kapîsî iv, 232b
Siliwan → Mayyāfāriḳīn
Silm, Āl i, 759b
Silsila ix, **611**a
Silsilat al-Dhahab s, 173a
Silves → Shilb
al-Sīm, lughat ix, **611**b
Silwān vi, 629a
Simāk b. Makhrama (VII) ix, 553b
Simancas → Shant Mānkash
Simāṭ iv, 957a, b
Sīmāvī, Sedād ii, 475a, b
Simaw (Simav) ix, **612**a; s, 359b
Simawna-Oghlu Badr al-Dīn → Badr al-Dīn b. Ḳāḍī (Simawne)
al-Sīmāwī → Abu 'l-Ḳāsim Muḥammad al-ʿIrāḳī
Simdjūr, Banū i, 1354b
Sīmdjūr al-Dawātī s, 357a
Sīmdjūrī, Abū ʿAlī b. Abī 'l-Ḥasan (994) v, 624b; vi, 65a, 340a; viii, 110a, 1027b
Sīmdjūrī, Abu 'l-Ḥasan Muḥammad b. Ibrāhīm (X) viii, 110a, 1028a; x, 945a
Sīmdjūrids i, 1354b; ix, **612**a
Simferopol i, 312a
Simḥah Isaac b. Moses iv, 606a
Sīmīn Dānishwar (XX) vi, 486a
Sīmiyāʾ iv, 264b; ix, **612**a
Ṣimkān vi, 384a
Ṣīmḳo → Ismāʿīl Agha Ṣīmḳo
al-Simmarī, Abu 'l-Ḥasan ʿAlī b. Muḥammad (941) viii, **812**a
Simnān (town) vi, 366a, 492a; ix, **613**b; s, 73a, 309b
al-Simnānī → ʿAlāʾ al-Dawla; Ṭāʿūs
al-Simnānī, Abū Djaʿfar Muḥammad (1052) ix, **614**b
al-Simnānī, Abu 'l-Ḥasan Aḥmad s, 194a
Simoom → Samūm
Simplicius → Samlis
Simsār → Dallāl
Simsim ix, **614**b
al-Simṭ b. al-Aswad v, 119b
Sīmurgh i, 509a, 753a; ii, 106b, 1099b, 1138a; iii, 112b; iv, 402a; ix, **615**a
Sīn/Shīn (letters) ix, **615**b
al-Ṣīn (China) i, 91a, 390b, 927b; ii, 42b, 45b, 477b, 583a, 1076a; iii, 653b, 1115b; iv, 553a; v, 364a, 770a, 854b; ix, **616b, 617a, 617b, 622**b; x, 460b, 475b; s, **746**b
Ṣīn/ʿĪn Kalān (Khānfū/Canton) ix, **626**b
Ṣ)nā (language) ii, 139a
Sīnāʾ (Sinai) ix, **625**a
Ṣināʿa ix, **625**b
Sinād iv, 412b
Sinai → Sīnāʾ; al-Tīh; al-Ṭūr
Sinān (architect) (1588) i, 511a, 768a, 843b, 1256b; ii, 685b, 686a, 705b; iii, 144b; iv, 232a, b, 233a, 1017a, 1158a; v, 67a, 815b, 837b, 882a; vi, 868b, 687a; ix, **629**a
Sinān (685) iv, 534b; s, 131a
Sinān (ketkhudā) (XVI) vi, 436b
Sinān, Rāshid al-Dīn → Rāshid al-Din Sinān
Sinān b. Salama b. al-Muḥabbiḳ al-Hudhalī (VII) vi, 193a
Sinān b. Sulaymān ii, 484a
Sinān b. Thābit i, 387b, 867a, 899a
Sinān b. ʿUlayyān al-Kalbī (1024) vii, 117a
Sinān Pasha → Čīālazāde; Khodja
Sinān Pasha (grand vizier) (1596) vii, 912a
Sinān Pasha (Tunis) (XVI) vii, 433b
Sinān Pasha, Khādim (1517) ii, 1042a; iii, 341b; iv, 1093a; ix, 14b, **630**b b
Sinān Pasha, Khodja (1486) ix, **630**b
Sinān Pasha, Khodja (1596) i, 340b, 697b, 1298b, 1303b; ii, 34a, 287b, 688a, 880b; iii, 94b; v, 1023a; vi, 996b; vii, 433b, 762a; viii, 184a; ix, **631**a
Sinān Pasha Dāmād i, 292b; ii, 985b; iv, 230b
Sinān Pasha al-Kaykhiyā (Yemen) (1608) vi, 436b; vii, 514a; viii, 339a
Sinān Pasha-zāde Meḥmed Pasha iv, 594b
Sinandadj → Sanandadj
Sindbād-nāme iii, 313b, 373a
Sind (Sindh) i, 43b, 228a, 229b, 230b, 246b, 627b, 962a, 1194b; ii, 74a, 153b, 185a; iii, 323b, 404b, 415a, 419b, 448b; iv, 199b, 202b, 597b, 793a, 1160a; vi, 48a, 50b, 193a, 368a, 439a, 489a, 640b, 689a, 691a; vii, 314a, 388b; viii, 68a, 240b; ix, **632**a; s, 252a
Sindābūr (Sandābūr) ii, 1127b; ix, **638**b
Sindān (Sandān) ix, **638**b
Sindbād ix, **638**b
Sindbād al-Ḥakīm (Syntipas) ix, **640**a

Sindhī (language) i, 1007b; ii, 101b; ix, 636a
Sindhia ii, 1144a
Sindhind i, 11a; iii, 1137a; ix, **640**b
Śīndhīyā, Djayappa (Marāthā) (XVIII) vi, 535b
Śīndhīyā, Mahādadjī Rāo (Marāthā) (1794) ii, 1092b; vi, 535b, 536a
Sindhu (Indus Riyer) s, **748**a
al-Sindī → Abū ʿAṭāʾ; Abū ʿAlī; Abū Maʿshar
Sindī, Banū i, 1246b
al-Sindī, Abū ʿAlī (XI) s, **748**a
al-Sindī, Raḥmat Allāh b. ʿAbd Allāh (1585) vii, 294a
al-Sindī b. Shāhik (IX) iii, 990a; vi, 332a, 335a; vii, 259a, 646b
Sindjābī (Sendjāwī), Banū ix, **641**b
Sindjār (town) iii, 1268a; vi, 539b, 599b, 781a, 870b; vii, 9a; s, 381a, 413b
Sindjār, Djabal viii, 147a; ix, **643**a
al-Sindjārī, Ḥasan al-Makzūn (amīr) (XIII) viii, 147a
Sindjas, Banū v, 1179a, b, 1181a, b, 1182a
Sind-Rūdh vii, 20b; s, 366b
Sinet → Khitān
Ṣinf i, 477a; ii, 967a; iii, 217b; iv, 894a; ix, **644**a
Singapore i, 979a; ii, 426b; vi, 207b, 236b, 237a, 241a; ix, **646**b; s, 220b
Singkawang s, 151a
Ṣinhādja i, 79a, 84a, 355b, 356a, b, 367a; ii, 623a
Ṣīnī (porcelain) iv, 1168b, 1169a, 1170a; v, 857a; ix, **647**a
Sīnimā → Cinema
Sinkāt iv, 686b, 687a
Sinkiang ii, 43a; v, 846a, b; ix, **648**b; xi, 228b
Sinna (senna) → Sanandadj
al-Sinnabra vi, 547a, 622b; viii, 423b; s, 117a
Sinnār i, 35a; ii, 943b; v, 267a; vii, 425b; ix, **650**b
Sinnawr ix, **651**b
Siounik (Arrān) vi, 337a
Sinūb (Sinop) i, 476b; iv, 575b, 577a, 813b; v, 505b; vi, 70b, 71a; ix, **653**b
Sipāhī i, 1264b, 1265a, 1268b; iii, 191a, b, 192b; iv, 565a, 1095b; ix, **656**a
Sipāhī Meḥmed v, 775a
Sipāhī oghlanlarï i, 102a, 1004a
Sipahsālār → Ispahsālār
Sipihr Shukōh ii, 134b
Sipihr, Suhrāb (1880) iv, 70a; ix, **658**a
Sīr b. Abī Bakr i, 7a, 242b; ii, 1013a; iv, 116a
Ṣīr Banī Yās, Djazīrat i, 535b; ix, **658**b
Sïr Daryā (Jaxartes) i, 135a, 607a; ii, 778a, 790a, 791a; v, 30b, 45a, 46a; vi, 557a; ix, **659**a; s, 244b, 245a, b
Sir Sayyid → Aḥmad Khān
Sīra iii, 369b, 374a; v, 1161b, 1163b; ix, **660**b
Sīra Shaʿbiyya ix, **664**a
Sirādj v, 986b; ix, **665**a
Sirādj ʿAfīf, Shams al-Dīn ix, **296**b; s, 105b
Sirādj al-Dawla Mīrzā Maḥmūd (Nawwāb) (1757) i, 400b; ii, 7a, 371a, 1091b; ix, **666**b
Sirādj al-Dīn al-Awrangābādī (1763) vi, 837b
Sirādj al-Dīn Djunaydī, Shaykh vi, 369a
Sirādj al-Dīn al-Ḥanafī → al-Hindī
Sirādj al-Dīn Muẓaffar b. al-Ḥusayn (1237) vi, 790b
Sirādj al-Dīn ʿUthmān → Akhī Sirādj al-Dīn ʿUthmān, Shaykh
Sirādj al-Ḳuṭrub ix, **667**a
al-Sīradjān (town) ix, **667**a
Sīrāf (port) i, 550b, 552a, 927b, 1355a; ii, 130b; iv, 500b, 1085b; v, 670b; vi, 365a, 385b; vii, 52a, 66b; ix, **667**b; s, 118a
al-Sīrāfī, Abū Muḥammad Yūsuf (995) ix, **689**b
al-Sīrāfī, Abū Saʿīd (979) i, 97b, 126b; ii, 896b; vi, 443b, 444a, b, 845b; vii, 281a, 490b, 914a; viii, 614b; ix, 327b, **668**b; s, 362b
al-Sīrāfī, Aḥmad b. ʿAlī b. al-ʿAbbās b. Nūḥ (1022) viii, 811b
Sirāikī → Lahnda; Sind, Language
Siraḳūsa (Syracuse) ix, **669**b
Ṣirāṭ ix, **670**b
Sīrat al-Amīr Ḥamza iii, 153b, 376a, 1207a
Sīrat ʿAntar → ʿAntar
Sīrat Banī Hilā → Hilāl Banū
Sīrat al-Baṭṭāl → Dhu ʾl-Himma
Sīrat al-Dalhama → Dhu ʾl-Himma
Sīrat al-Mudjāhidīn → Dhu ʾl-Himma
Sīrat Sayf b. Dhī Yazān → Sayf Ibn Dhī Yazān

Sīrat ʿUmar b. al-Nuʿmān → ʿUmar b. al-Nuʿmān
Ṣirb (Serbia) i, 1163b, 1165a; v, 276a; vi, 70a; ix, **671**a; s, **748**b
Sardāb v, 12b; ix, **49**b
Sirdār → Sardār
Sīrdjān v, 150a, 151a, 152a, b; s, 327a
Sirfandakār vi, 507b
Sirḥān b. Saʿīd b. Sirḥān (XVIII) vii, 838b
Sirhind i, 1194a; vi, 50a, 62a; ix, **673**b; s, 126b, 313a
Sirhindī, Mawlānā ʿAbd al-Ḳādir (XVI) vi, 131a; s, 3a
Sirhindī, Shaykh Aḥmad al-Farūḳī (1624) → Aḥmad Sirhindī
Sirhīndī, Yaḥyā (XV) s, 105a
Sirī s, 206b
Sīrī i, 1322a; ii, 256b, 269a; iii, 481b; iv, 921b; vi, 49a, 50a, 294a
Sīrīn bint Shamʿūn (VII) vi, 575a
Sirʿīn (Lebanon) vi, 303a
Sirius → al-Shiʿra
Sirkap s, 259b
Siroz (Serres) ix, **673**b; s, 330a
Sirr s, **752**b
Sirrī Pasha (XIX) i, 907b, 1018b
Sīrwā(n) vi, 742a
Ṣirwāḥ vi, 80b, 560b, 562b, 831a; ix, **675**b
Sirwāl ix, **676**a
Siryākūs (Cairo) vi, 454a
Sīs i, 8a; ii, 36a, 38a; v, 283b; vi, 507b, 508b, 724b; ix, **678**a
Sisak → Sisḳa
Sīsām (Samos) ix, **679**b
Sīsar ix, **680**a
Sisḳa (Sisak) ix, **681**a
Sisodiās vi, 53a
Sīstān i, 5a, 43b, 86a, 147b, 211b, 222b, 223a, 452b, 1344a; ii, 5a, 49b, 903b; iv, 4b, 19a-b, 54a, b, 55a; v, 57a, 390a, 868a; vi, 65b, 331b, 333a, 337b, 345a, 368b, 640b; viii, 795a; ix, **681**b; xi, 254b, 458b; s, 21a, 26a, 326b
Sīstānī → Farrukhī-i Sīstānī
Sistova → Zistova
Sitāra iii, 360a; iv, 823b
Siti binti Saad (1950) ix, **685**a
Sitr ix, **685**a
Sitt al-Mulk bint al-ʿAzīz (Fāṭimid) (1023) ii, 484a, 855b, 857a; iii, 80b; iv, 944a; vii, 116b, 482b; ix, **685**b
Sitt al-Nisāʾ vi, 488b
Sitt al-Tudjdjār iv, 136a
Sittī Khātūn (Dhu ʾl-Ḳadr) (XV) ii, 895a; vi, 507b, 978a
Siu (Siyu) ix, **686**a; s, 355b
Sivas → Sīwās
Sīvāsiyya iv, 991b
Sīwa ix, **686**b
Sīwādjī (Marātha) → Shiv(w)ādjī
Siwāk → Miswāk
Siwāl s, 353b
Sīwās i, 511a; iv, 1167b; v, 248a; vi, 72a, 120b, 231a, 232a, 275b, 315b; ix, **689**b; s, 146a, 274a
Sīwāsī, ʿAbd al-Aḥad Nūrī (1651) vi, 227b; ix, 299b
Sīwāsī, ʿAbd al-Madjīd (1639) ix, 299b
Sīwāsī, Ḳara Aḥmad Shams a-Dīn (1597) ix, 299a
Sīwistān (Sind) vii, 189a, 412a
Siwri Ḥiṣār ix, **681**b
Siyāgha → Sāʾigh
Siyāhčashm iv, 661b
Siyāh-Ḳalem (XV) ix, **692**a
Siyāh-Kūh vi, 415a, b
Siyāh-pūsh iv, 409b, 410b
Siyāḳat ii, 128a, 332b, 952a; iv, 1124a, 1125b; ix, **692**b
Siyākh vi, 384a, b
Siyālkūt (Sialkot) ix, **693**a; s, 241b
al-Siyālkūtī, ʿAbd al-Ḥākim (1657) i, 297b, 1022b; ix, **693**b
Siyārwardiyya iv, 342b
Siyāsa ix, **693**b
Siyāsat-nāma → Naṣīḥat al-Mulūk
Siyāṭ (785) xi, 350b
Siyāwakhsh b. Mihrān b. Bahrām-Čubīn (VIII) vi, 744b
Siyāwush (b. Kay Ḳāʾūs II) i, 703a; iv, 620a, b, 813b, 815b, 1061b; v, 274b; ix, **696**b
Siyāwush Pasha, Abāza (1688) i, 380b, 1284b; iv, 193b; vi, 983a; vii, 275b; viii, 185a; ix, **697**b
Siyāwush Pasha Kanizheli (1602) ix, **697**a
Siyer → Sīra
Sjahrir ii, 664a, b
Skandelion → Iskandaruna
Skanderbeg → Iskender Beg
Skārdū i, 1004b
Sḳīfa ii, 115b

Skiros vi, 71b
Sklēros s, 37a
Skopje → Üsküb
Skutari → Ishkodra
Slavs → Saḳāliba
al-Slāwī → al-Nāṣir al-Salāwī
Slēmān, Awlād ii, 876a
Slīmān → Sulaymān
Sliman ben Ibrahim s, 224a, b
Slīmān Benaissa (XX) vi, 754a
Slovakia → Čeh
Smacids i, 733b, 734a
Smala → Zmāla
Ṣmara v, 890a, b
Smbat → Sambāṭ
Smederovo vi, 70a, b, 71a
Ṣmyr (Shakla) bint Khurshīd (Ṭabaristān) (VIII) vi, 745a
Smyrna → Izmīr
Soaïtou Mamadou v, 279b
Sōba (town) i, 425b; iv, 892b; ix, **698**a
Socotra → Suḳuṭrā
Socrates → Suḳrāṭ
Sodom v, 833a
Soekarno → Sukarno
Soekiman, Dr. → Sukiman, Dr.
Sofāla vi, 128a; ix, **698**b
So-fei-er, Sayyid ix, 622b, 623a
Sofia → Ṣofya
Ṣofta (Sukayn) ix, **702**a
Ṣofu Meḥmed Pasha (XVII) iii, 983b
Ṣofu Sinān Pāsha (1615) viii, 339a
Ṣofya (Sofia) vi, 70b; ix, **702**b
Sogguen ii, 1095b
Soghdia → Ṣughd
Soghdian Language ix, 772b; s, **425**b
Sögman-āwā vi, 201a
Sögüd (Sögüt) ix, **706**a
Sögüdjuk i, 63a
Sōhāg ii, 1114b
Sohar → Ṣuḥār
Sohrān, amīr (Barādūst) i, 1031a
Sohrān, Banū v, 460b
Soḳḳar vi, 200b, 201a, b, 202b
Sökmen → Alp; Artuḳids; Shāh-i Arman
Sokna ii, 575b
Ṣoḳollï-zade Ḥasan Pasha iv, 594b, 901a
Ṣoḳollu Meḥmed Pasha (1579) i, 291b, 1018a, 1264b; ii, 56b, 103b, 704a, 881a; iii, 995a; v, 815b; vi, 72b; vii, 595b, 596a, 720b; ix, **706**b; x, 959a
Ṣoḳollu Muṣṭafā Pasha i, 1285b, 1286a; ii, 880b; v, 775a
Sokolovic → Ṣoḳollu
Sokoto ii, 1145a; iii, 277a; iv, 549b; vi, 281b; vii, 435b, 436a; viii, 20b; ix, **711**a
Soḳoṭra, Soḳoṭrī → Suḳuṭra
Sol Gharībler → Ghurabāʾ
Ṣolaḳ ix, **712**a
Ṣolaḳ-zāde. Meḥmed Hemdemī (1658) iii, 249a; ix, **712**b
Soldaïa → Sudak
Solomon → Sulaymān
Soltangaliev → Sulṭān ʿAlīūghlī
Somalia Somaliland i, 176b, 553a, 1038a, 1172b; ii, 113b, 535b; iii, 4a, 5b; v, 522a, 524a; vi, 128a, 283a; viii, 162a; ix, **713**a
Ṣōmāy ix, **727**a
Sōmnāth → Sūmanāt
Somniani bay vi, 192b
Sonārgāʾon i, 868b; ii, 216a, 751b; vi, 131a; ix, **728**a
Songarh vi, 407a
Songhay i, 1259b; ii, 94a, 252a, 977a; iii, 1038b; iv, 549a, 754b; vi, 258b, 259a, b, 281b, 402b; vii, 393b; viii, 724a; ix, **728**a, 756b; x, 89b, 122a; xi, 337b
Songo Mnara Island vi, 370b; vii, 838b
Soninké iii, 288b; iv, 314a; vi, 258a, 401a
Sonḳor (Sunḳur) ix, **730**a
Sonnī ʿAlī (1492) ii, 252a, 977a; ix, 756b; x, 122a
Soofie Saheb → Ṣiddīḳī, Shāh Ghulām Muḥammad Ṣūfī
Sōpūr iv, 707b
Soraya → Thurayya
Sorgatmix → Suyurghatmīsh b. Noradin
Sorguč → Tulband
Sori, Ibrāhima Mwado ii, 942b, 960a, 1132a
Sorḳoḳtani umm Möngke (XIII) vi, 782b; vii, 230a; ix, 110b
Sosso vi, 401b
Soudan → Sūdān
Sūf (Souf) ix, **763**b; s, 145a
Soumangourou (Sosso, Mande) vi, 402a
Soundiata vi, 402a
Sousse → Sūsa
South Africa, Islam in ix, **730**a; s, **754**a
Soy iii, 374a
Soyinadji (Soyin Ḥādjī), Banū vi, 416b; s, 168b, 169a

Soyūrghāl ix, **731**b
Soyurghatmïsh → Suyūrghatmïsh
Spahi → Sipāhī
Spahpat → Ispahbadh
Spain → al-Andalus
Spartel (Morocco) ix, **734**a
Sphinx → Abu 'l-Hawl
Split i, 1267a; v, 774b; s, 186a
Spring in Arabic Literature → Zahriyyāt
Spring in Ottoman Literature → Rabīʿiyyāt
Sri Lanka → Ceylon; Sarandīb
Srīnagar iii, 448a; iv, 707b; ix, **734**a; s, 114a, 131b, 156a, 332a, 333a, 353b, 366a, b, 423b
Śrīrangapattanam ix, **736**b
Śrīvijaya vi, 207b, 234a
Stenka Razin (1671) viii, 450a
Stephanos → Iṣṭifan b. Basīl
4Štip → Ishtib
Stuhlweissenburg → Székesfehérvár
Su (water) ix, **736**b
Sū (Ghazna) vi, 783a
Su-Lu i, 684b; iii, 493b
Su-ssu-shi-san iv, 454b; v, 851b
Suakin → Sawākin
al-Suʾālātī, Muḥammad b. Muḥammad (XVII) vii, 470a
Suʿāwī, ʿAlī (1878) ix, **737**b
Suʿayr ix, **738**a
Ṣūba i, 316b; ix, **738a**
Ṣūbadār ii, 337a; ix, **738**b
Ṣubāḥ, Āl x, 956a
Ṣu Bashï ix, **736**b
Ṣubashï Tigin (ḥādjib) (XI) iii, 47a; vi, 523a; vii, 928a
Subayʿ (Sabayʿ), Banū i, 628b; iii, 363b; v, 62b; ix, **738**b
Subayʿa bint ʿAbd Shams (VI) vi, 477b
al-Subayba ix, **739**a
Subayḥī, Banū ix, **739**b
Subayta (Isbayta) ix, **739**b
Subayṭila (Sufetula) ix, **740**a
Ṣubba (Mandaeans) i, 1096a; iii, 1254a; vi, 247a; viii, 672a, 675a
Sübetey i, 836a; ii, 43a; iv, 107b; v, 311b
Ṣubḥ → Ṣalāt
Ṣubḥ (sultana) (X) vi, 430b, 431a
Ṣubḥ al-Bashkunsiyya ix, **740**b
Ṣubḥa ix, **741**b
Subḥān ix, **742**b
Subḥān-Ḳulī Khān s, 419b
Subḥān Werdī Khān (XIX) ix, 6b
Ṣubḥī, Muṣṭafā iv, 124a
Ṣubḥ-i Azal Mīrzā Yaḥyā Nūrī (Bābī) (1912) i, 809a, 833b, 847a, 911b; iv, 51b, 696a; viii, 114a; ix, **741**a; s, 53b
Ṣubḥī Meḥmed Efendi (1769) ix, **743**a
al-Subkī (town) ix, **743**b
al-Subkī, Bahā al-Dīn Abū Ḥāmid Aḥmad (1371) ii, 107b; iv, 863b
al-Subkī, Shāfiʿī ʿulamā ix, **744**a
al-Subkī, Shaykh Maḥmūd b. Muḥammad (1933) vi, 897a; ix, 745b; s, 244b
al-Subkī, Tādj al-Dīn Abū Naṣr ʿAbd al-Wahhāb (1370) i, 593a, 594b, 1308b; ii, 215a; iii, 818a, 954b; vi, 353a, 847b, 869a; vii, 212b, 296b; ix, **744**b
al-Subkī, Taḳī al-Dīn Abu 'l-Ḥasan, Shaykh al-Islām ʿAlī (1355) ii, 215a, 926a; iii, 822a, 954b; viii, 125b
al-Subkī Taḳī al-Dīn Abu 'l-Fatḥ Muḥammad (1344) iii, 711a; ix, **744**a
al-Subkiyyūn ix, **745**b; s, 244b
al-Subūʿī, al-Subūʿī b. Muḥammad iv, 828b
Subuk i, 637b; ii, 679b
Subuktigîn → Sebuktegin
Subutāi → Sübetey
Suchow iv, 553b, 554a; v, 848a
Suʿdā, Sūdābeh iv, 813a
Ṣūdāḳ (Crimea) → Sughdāḳ
Sūdān i, 49a, 279b, 289a, 297a, 1058a; ii, 121b; iii, 657b; iv, 262a; v, 70a, 1248a, b; vi, 467b, 594b, 646b; viii, 724a; ix, 698a, **746**a; x, 96b; s, 217b
– administration i, 976a, 1156b; ii, 595a, 668a; iii, 385a; v, 1063b
– ethnography i, 1a, 37b, 39a, 1058a; ii, 767b, 1110b; iii, 300a; v, 317b, 318b
– institutions ii, 425a; iii, 523b
– language, literature i, 575b; ii, 467a; iii, 949a
Sūdān, Banū vii, 672a
Sudān, Bilād al- ix, **752**b
Sudayf b. Maymūn (764) vi, 724a; ix, **761a**-b
Sudayrī (al-Sadārā) i, 748a; ii, 175b; ix, **762**a
al-Suddī, Ismāʿīl b. ʿAbd al-Raḥmān (745) vii, 758a; viii, 387a; ix, **762**a
al-Sūdī, Aḥmad b. ʿAbd Allāh b. Sālim (1634) ii, 730a
Sūdī, Aḥmed (1596) ix, **762**a

Sudjān Rāy Bhandārī (XVIII) i, 241b; ix, **762**b
Sudjdjā ix, **763**a
al-Suds al-fakhrī v, 46b
Suez → al-Suways
Sūf → Wādī Sūf
Ṣūf (wool) ix, **764**b
Sufāla (ʿUmān) viii, 85a
Ṣufayna s, 198b
Sufetula → Subayṭila
Ṣuffa → Ahl al-Ṣuffa
Ṣūfī → Taṣawwuf
al-Ṣūfī → ʿAbd al-Raḥmān al-Ṣūfī
al-Ṣūfī, Abu ʾl-Ḥusayn viii, 102b
Ṣūfī Islām (1807) vii, 935b
Ṣūfids iv, 1064a
Ṣūfīgarī v, 244a
al-Ṣūfisṭāʾiyyūn (Sophists) ix, **765**a
Ṣūfiyāna ix, **765**b
al-Ṣūfiyya (Damascus) vi, 122b
Ṣufriyya iii, 648a, 654b, 657b, 1040b, 1175a; vi, 311b; vii, 123b, 815a; viii, 638a, b; ix, **766**a
Ṣufrūy (Sefrou) (town) vi, 142b; ix, **769**a; s, 191a
Suftadja ii, 382b; iii, 283b; ix, **769**b
Sufyān, Banū v, 48b; vi, 741b, 743a
Sufyān b. ʿAwf al-Ghāmidī (VII) vi, 505b
Sufyān b. Khālid al-Liḥyānī v, 763a
Sufyān b. Muʿāwiya al-Muhallabī (VIII) iii, 883b; vii, 360a
Sufyān b. Mudjīb al-Azdī (VII) x, 215a
Sufyān b. ʿUyayna (811) i, 272b, 827a, 960b; vi, 263b; vii, 662b; ix, 7a, 182a, **772**a; s, 386b
Sufyān b. Yazīd b. al-Muhallab (VIII) vii, 359b
Sufyān al-ʿAbdī, Abū ʿAbd Allāh (739/794) ix, **776**a
Sufyān al-Hudhalī (VII) vi, 646a
Sufyān al-Thawrī (778) ii, 538b, 889b; iii, 155a, 687b, 843a; vi, 263b, 353a, 671b; vii, 607a, 662b, 758a; viii, 354b, 983b; ix, 7a, **770**b; s, 232b, 384b
Sufyān al-Yamanī i, 829a
al-Sufyānī s, **754**b
Sufyānids i, 17a; ii, 281b; iv, 457a, 494a; v, 1232a; vi, 139b, 333b; vii, 693b; ix, **772**b; s, 103b
al-Ṣughd (Soghdia) ii, 67a, 790b; iii, 1060b; v, 181a, 541b, 542a, 852b, 854a; viii, 1031b; ix, **772**b; s, 64a, 65a, 176b
Sughdāḳ iv, 575b, 576a, 817b; vi, 575, 576a; ix, **773**b
al-Sughdī → Abū Ḥafṣ Sughdī
Sughnāk → Suḳnāḳ
Sughundjak Noyan iv, 1046b
Sūhādj → Sōhāg
Ṣuḥār (ʿUmān) i, 563b, 1098a, 1281b; iv, 500b; vi, 385b, 734b, 735a; vii, 66b, 67a, 838b; viii, 85a; ix, **774**b; s, 234b
Ṣuḥār al-ʿAbdī iii, 650a
Ṣuhayb (VII) iii, 587a
Ṣuhayb, Banū vi, 878b
Suhayl vi, 645b
Suhayl b. ʿAmr (ʿĀmir, VII) i, 115b, 151a
Suhayl b. Bayḍāʾ (VII) vi, 659a
Suhayl, Saʿd b. ʿAbd Allāh (XIX) vi, 352a
al-Suhaylī, Sīdī ʿAbd al-Raḥmān (Imām al-Suhaylī) (1185) vi, 591a; vii, 538a; ix, 661a; s, 382a, s, **756**a
Suḥaym ʿAbd Banī ʾl-Ḥasḥās (657) ix, **776**b
Suḥaym b. Wathīl al-Riyāḥī (VII) ii, 998b; ix, 227a, 776b
Ṣuḥbatiyya i, 195b
Suhrāb (al-Ḥīra) (574) v, 633b; vii, 568b
Suhrāb b. Āḳā Rustam Rūzafzūn (Marʿashī) (XVI) vi, 514b
Suhrāb Khān, Mir (Khayrpūr) (1830) iv, 1160a
Suhraward (town) ix, **777**b
Suhrawardī, Abu ʾl-Nadjīb ʿAbd al-Ḳāhir b. ʿAbd Allāh (1168) vi, 131b; vii, 608b; ix, **778**a
Suhrawardī, Ḥusayn Shahīd iii, 533a, b
al-Suhrawardī, Shams al-Dīn (1340) viii, 805b
Suhrawardī, Shaykh ʿAbd Allah (XV) s, 10b, 11a
Suhrawardī, Shaykh Bahāʾ al-Dīn → Bahāʾ al-Dīn Zakariyyāʾ Suhrawardī
al-Suhrawardī, Shihāb al-Dīn Abū Ḥafṣ ʿUmar (1234) i, 347a, 596a; ii, 55a, 964b, 966b; iv, 516a, 990b; vi, 111a, 224a, 225a, b, 468b, 571a; vii, 480b, 608b, 728b, 871a, 997b, 998b, 999b; viii, 506a; ix, **778**b; s, 313a, 353a, 380a, 414b, 415b; x, 255b; xi, 216b

al-Suhrawardī, Shihāb al-Dīn Yaḥyā b. Ḥabash al-Maḳtūl (1191) i, 234b, 351b, 416b, 595b, 803a; ii, 774a; iii, 1131b; iv, 64a, 119b, 120b, 943a; vi, 111a; vii, 548a; ix, **782**a; s, 41a, 67a
Suhrawardiyya i, 912a; ii, 421a; iii, 823a; iv, 48a, 1026b; vi, 225b; ix, 780b, **784**b; s, 10b, 156a, 312a, 353a
al-Suhūl i, 628b
Sūḳ i, 898b; ii, 959a, 962a; iii, 486b; iv, 136a; v, 665b; ix, **786b, 789b, 791b, 792, 796a,b, 800**b; s, **756**a
al-Sūḳ (Sahara) → Tādemekket
Sūḳ al-Ahwāz → al-Ahwāz
Sūḳ al-ʿAṭṭārīn s, 422b
Sūḳ al-Gharb (Bairūt) s, 162a
Sūḳ Ḥamza iv, 479a, b
Sūk al-Khamīs vi, 595b
Sūḳ Kutāma iv, 729b
Sūḳ al-Shuyūkh (town) ix, **801**b
Sūḳ al-Thulathāʾ i, 899b, 900a; s, 381a
Sukadana s, 150b, 201a
al-Suḳāʿī vi, 143b
Sukarno (Soekarno) (1970) ii, 663a, 664a, 665a, 666a; iii, 534a; vi, 731a, 732a, b, 733a; s, **759**b
Sukayn → Sofya
Sukayna bint al-Ḥusayn b. ʿAlī (VII) i, 305a; ii, 1011b; vii, 650b; ix, **802**a
Sukhf ii, 552a; iii, 354b, 780b; ix, **804**a
Sūkhrā (Kārinid) iv, 644a; vi, 745b
Sūkhrāniyyān → Ḳārinids
Sukhum (Iskhum) i, 100b, 101a, b
Soekiman, Dr. vi, 731b, 732a, b
Sukkar i, 305b; ii, 904a, 1062b, 1064b; iv, 682b; ix, **804**b
al-Sukkarī, Abū Saʿīd al-Ḥasan b. al-Ḥusayn (888) i, 107a, 154b, 158b, 331a, 718b; ii, 245b; iii, 820a; v, 768a; vii, 402b; ix, **805**a; s, 37b, 394b
al-Sukkarī, Aḥmad (XX) s, 371a
Suḳmān b. Artuḳ al-Ḳuṭbī (amīr) (Akhlāṭ) (1104) i, 300a, 329a, 639a, 664a, 666a, 983a, 1052a; iii, 507a, 1118a; v, 454a; vi, 499b, 500a, 540b, 546b, 930b; vii, 726a; ix, 68b
Suḳmān II (Shāh-i Arman) (1185) iii, 1119a; ix, 193a
Suḳmān al-Ḳuṭbī (Shāh-i Arman) (1112) ix, 193a; x, 42b
Sukmāniyya iv, 483b
Suknā ix, **805**b
Suḳnāk Tigin i, 418b
Suḳrāṭ i, 235b; ix, **805**a; s, 154b
al-Suktānī → ʿĪsā al-Suktānī
Sukūn → al-Ḥaraka wa ʾl-sukūn
Sukūt ix, **806**b
Sükūtī, Isḥāḳ → Isḥāḳ Sükūtī
Suḳuṭrā i, 535b; iii, 270a, 652a; v, 184a; vi, 82a, b; ix, **806**b
al-Ṣulaba i, 546a, 873a, b
Sulaḥfā ix, **811**a
Sulāma, Banū vii, 266a, 672a
al-Sulamī → Abu ʾl-Aʿwar; Yazīd b. Usayd
al-Sulamī, ʿAbd Allāh b. Khāzim (VII) i, **47**b; vii, 357a
al-Sulamī, Abū ʿAbd al-Raḥmān Muḥammad b. al-Ḥusayn (1021) i, 146a, 266a; vi, 223b, 821a; viii, 579b, 583b; ix, **811**b; x, 86b; s, 343a
Sulamī, Abu ʾl-Faḍl Muḥammad (X) viii, 110a
al-Sulamī, al-Ashras b. ʿAbd Allāh (VIII) ii, 600b; iii, 493b; x, 844b
al-Sulamī, ʿĀsim b. Ḳays (640) vi, 920b
al-Sulamī, ʿIzz al-Dīn ʿAbd al-ʿAzīz b. ʿAbd al-Salām (1262) vi, 351a; ix, **812**b
al-Sulāmī, Djamāl al-Islām iii, 714a
al-Sulamī, Ḳays b. al-Haytham (VII) viii, 62b
al-Sulamī, Muʿammar b. ʿAbbād vi, 347a; vii, **259**a
al-Sulamī, Yazīd b. Usayd (VIII) ix, 488a
Sulawesi ii, 19a; iii, 1213a, 1214b, 1219b, 1220, 1226a; vii, 71b; ix, **813**b; s, 151a
Sulawesi Selatan vi, 116a
Ṣulayb, Banū iii, 642a; ix, **814**b
al-Ṣulayḥī, ʿAlī b. Muḥammad (Ṣulayḥid) (1066) iv, 199b, 664a; vi, 148b; vii, 730b; ix, 816a; s, 22a, 62a
Ṣulayḥids i, 552a; ii, 170b, 856a; iii, 125a, 259b; iv, 199b; vii, 163a, 731a; viii, 706a; ix, **815**b; s, 62a, 236a, 338a, 407a
Sulayk b. al-Sulaka iv, 1106b; vi, 477a, b; ix, 864a
Sulaym, Banū i, 12a, 108a, 374b, 532b, 533a, 544b, 1049a, 1232b, 1240b; ii, 234a, 235a, 741a; iii, 66b; iv, 1144a; v, 760a; vi, 145b, 712b; vii, 372b; viii, 863b; ix, **817**a; s, 199a

Sulaym b. Ayyūb al-Rāzī (1055) x, 461b
Sulaym b. Ḳays al-Hilālī (714) ix, **818**b
Sulaymā bint ʿAṣar al-ʿUḳaylī s, 394a
Sulaymān Mountains ii, 205b; ix, **819**b; s, 329b, 331b
Sulaymān I (Ottoman) (1421) vi, 531a
Sulaymān the Magnificent (1566) → Süleymān
Sulaymān Shāh I (Ṣafī II) (Ṣafawid) (1694) iv, 1092b; v, 1087a; vi, 256a, 257a, b, 855b; viii, 771a; ix, **820**b
Sulaymān Shāh II (Ṣafawid) (1750) iv, 390a; s, 276a
Sulaymān, Awlād i, 1258b
Sulaymān, Banū v, 927a
Sulaymān, Mawlāy, Abu ʾl-Rabīʿ b. Muḥammad (ʿAlawid) (1822) i, 315a, 356b; ii, 117a, 160b, 308a, 510b, 820a, 885b; iv, 634a; v, 1192a; vi, 113a, 250b, 293a, b, 595b, 596b, 597a; vii, 39a; ix, **819**b; s, 113b, 114a, 132a, 390b, 401b
Sulaymān al-Mustaʿīn (Umayyad, Cordoba, 1016) ii, 243a, 516a, 1012a; iii, 147a, 495b, 1043b; v, 1239b; x, 853a; s, **762**b
Sulaymān, Shaykh (Kaʿb) → Salmān, Shaykh
Sulaymān (traveller) ii, 583b, 1123b
Sulaymān b. ʿAbd Allāh b. Ṭāhir (I) (Ṭāhirid) (IX) vii, 390b; x, 105a
Sulaymān b. ʿAbd al-Malik (Umayyad) (717) i, 50a, 58a, b, 77b, 124b, 305a, 1030a; ii, 72b, 327b, 911a; iii, 42a, 85b, 155a; v, 533a, 799b, 1231a; vi, 544a, 666b, 668a, 669b; vii, 148a, 359a; ix, **821**a; s, 311b
Sulaymān b. ʿAbd al-Raḥmān I al-Dākhil (Umayyad, al-Andalus) (1016) ii, 1009a; iii, 74a, 495a; iv, 254b, 672b; s, **762**b
Sulaymān b. ʿAbd al-Raḥmān al-Ṣanīʿ (1969) vi, 175b
Sulaymān b. ʿAbd al-Wahhāb iii, 678b
Sulaymān b. ʿAddū (Murābiṭ) (1060) vii, 585a
Sulaymān b. Aḥmad vi, 637b
Sulaymān b. Aḥmad (Brunei) s, 152a
Sulaymān b. ʿAlī b. ʿAbd Allāh (ʿAbbāsid) (789) i, 43a, 105a, 1080b; iii, 883a; iv, 495a; vii, 414b; ix, **822**b; s, 352a
Sulaymān b. ʿAlī al-ʿAbbāsī (al-ʿAbsī) → Sulaymān b. ʿAlī b. ʿAbd Allāh
Sulaymān b. ʿAlī al-Hāshimī (786) vi, 262b, 428a; vii, 114a
Sulaymān b. al-Ashʿath → Abū Dāʾūd al-Sidjistānī
Sulaymān b. Bāyazīd I (Ottoman) (1411) vi, 973b
Sulaymān b. Čaghrï Beg Dāʾūd i, 420a; ii, 5a; iii, 1201a; iv, 27a
Sulaymān b. Dāʾūd b. al-ʿĀḍid iv, 200b
Sulaymān b. Dāwud (King Solomon) i, 686a; iii, 236b, 541b, 836; iv, 221a, 1104b; v, 423b; ix, **832**b
Sulaymān b. Djaʿfar b. Fallāḥ i, 1042a; ii, 483b; iii, 77a
Sulaymān b. Djāmiʿ (Zandjī) (IX) vii, 526a, b
Sulaymān b. Djarīr al-Raḳḳī (Zaydī) (VIII) i, 851a; vii, 787b; viii, 387a; ix, **824**a; s, 225b, 392a
Sulaymān b. Ghālib (IX) ix, 55a
Sulaymān b. Ghāzī iii, 507b
Sulaymān b. Ḥabīb b. al-Muhallab (VIII) vii, 359b
Sulaymān b. al-Ḥakam → Sulaymān al-Mustaʿīn
Sulaymān b. Ḥasan al-Hindī (1597) iv, 201a; vi, 190b, 191a; ix, **824**b, 829a
Sulaymān b. al-Ḥasan b. Makhlad → Ibn Makhlad, Sulaymān b. al-Ḥasan
Sulaymān b. Ḥassān → Ibn Djuldjul
Sulaymān b. Hishām b. ʿAbd al-Malik (Umayyad) (VIII) i, 787b, 1103a; ii, 90b; iii, 398a, 990b; vi, 623b, 624a; s, 183a
Sulaymān b. Hūd al-Mustaʿīn ii, 243a; iii, 496a, 542a; iv, 478a
Sulaymān b. Kathīr al-Khuzāʿī (750) i, 15b, 16a, 103b, 141a, 1293a; iii, 988a; v, 3a; vi, 620b; vii, 396a; ix, **825**a
Sulaymān b. Ḳatta vi, 604a
Sulaymān b. Ḳïlïdj Arslan II → Rukn al-Dīn Sulaymān II
Sulaymān b. Ḳuṭulmïsh b. Arslan Isrāʾīl (Saldjūḳ) (1086) i, 182b, 346a, 465b, 517a, 909b, 1336b; ii, 354b; iii, 86b, 195b, 208b; iv, 291b; v, 103b; vi, 274b; vii, 693b; viii, 947a; ix, **825**b
Sulaymān b. Mihrān → al-Aʿmash
Sulaymān b. al-Mundhir ii, 112a
Sulaymān b. Mūsā II (Mūsāwīd) (737) iii, 262b; vi, 148b, 917a

Sulaymān b. Ruḥaym iv, 305b, 605a
Sulaymān b. Shihāb s, 81b
Sulaymān b. Ṣurad al-Khuzāʿī (685) ii, 196b, 523b; iii, 608a, 620b; iv, 637b; vii, 521b; ix, 431b, **826**a; x, 398a
Sulaymān b. Ṭarf i, 709a, 737b; ii, 517a
Sulaymān b. Ṭawḳ (XI) vii, 116b
Sulaymān b. ʿUfayṣān iv, 1072b
Sulaymān b. Wahb al-Kātib (vizier) (905) vii, 477a, 766a; viii, 427a; s, 402a
Sulaymān b. al-Walīd (Umayyad) (717) vi, 740a; vii, 643b; s, 183a
Sulaymān b. Yaḥyā (VIII) ix, **827**a
Sulaymān b. Yaʿḳūb b. Aflaḥ iii, 660a
Sulaymān b. Yasar → Fuḳahāʾ al-Madīna
Sulaymān b. al-Zubayr Raḥma i, 929b, 1157a; ii, 123b
Sulaymān Abū Ghaliyya (XX) vi, 171b
Süleymān ʿAskerī ii, 699b
Sulaymān Azhar (XX) vi, 165b
Sulaymān al-Balansī → Sulaymān b. ʿAbd al-Raḥmān I
Sulaymān Beg b. Nāṣir al-Dīn Muḥammad (Dhu ʼl-Ḳadr) (1454) vi, 509b
Sulaymān Beg Bābān (XVII) i, 845a
Sulaymān Beg Bālṭa-oghlū → Bālṭa-oghlū
Sulaymān Beg b. Khalīl Beg Ḳarāmān-oghlu (1361) iv, 622b
Sulaymān Bek b. Muhammad Bek iv, 506b
Sulaymān Bey Ashraf-oghlu i, 703a; iv, 620b, 621a
Sulaymān Bey Čapen-oghlu ii, 207b
Sulaymān Bey Isfendiyār-oghlu iv, 108b
Sulaymān Čelebi (Ḳadiʿasker) (XV) i, 312b; ii, 98a; iii, 132a
Sulaymān Čelebi b. Bāyazīd (Ottoman) (1411) i, 394a, 654a; ii, 98a, 159a, 599a, 611b, 684a, 984b; iii, 1183a; vii, 644a, b
Sulaymān Djāndārid i, 1117b, 1118a
Sulaymān al-Ḥarīrī al-Tūnisī s, 40a
Sulaymān Kāhya v, 532a
Sulaymān Kararanī i, 316a; ii, 183a
Sulaymān al-Ḳardāhī (XX) vi, 750a
Sulaymān Khān (XVI) vi, 541b
Sulaymān Khān (wālī) (XIX) vii, 440a; ix, 6b
Sulaymān Khān al-Thānī → Bihrūz Khān
Sulaymān Khēl, Banū s, **763**b
Sulaymān al-Mahrī (1553) ii, 586a; iii, 856b; iv, 97a, 1082b, 1083a; v, 941a, b; vi, 82b, 359a; vii, 51a; viii, 100a, 102b; ix, **827**b
Sulaymān Mīrzā b. Khān Mirzā (Badakhshān Mīrzās) (1589) i, 228b, 852b, 1123b; iii, 528a, b; vii, 135a
Sulaymān al-Mustaʿīn (Umayyad, Andalus) (1016) → Sulaymān b. ʿAbd al-Raḥmān I al-Dākhil
Sulaymān al-Naḥwī al-Ḥalabī ii, 795a
Sulaymān Pasha → Kücük Suleymān Pasha
Sulaymān Pasha (1819) i, 1078b; ii, 635b
Sulaymān Pasha (1932) iv, 791a
Sulaymān Pasha b. Orkhan (Ottoman) (1359) i, 510b; ii, 683b, 983b; vi, 290b, 291a, 887b; vii, 592b; viii, 175b, 176a; ix, **843**b
Sulaymān Pāsha Babān (1754) i, 845a
Sulaymān Pasha Büyük (1802) i, 62b, 905b, 1087a; ii, 184b; iii, 1257b
Sulaymān Pasha al-Faransāwī (Colonel Joseph Sève) (1860) ii, 514a; iii, 999b, 1000a; iv, 428a; v, 907b, 908a; vii, 425b; ix, **828**b
Sulaymān Pasha Isfendiyār-oghlu (XIV) iv, 738a
Sulaymān Pasha Khādim → Khādim Süleymān Pasha
Sulaymān Pasha Mis(z)rāḳlî, Abu Laylā (1749) i, 199a, 905a, 1087a; iii, 1110b
Sulaymān Shafīḳ Kamālī Pasha (XX) i, 98b, 709b
Sulaymān Shāh b. Muḥammad b. Malik-Shāh (Saldjuḳ) (1161) vi, 64a, 871a; vii, 406b, 543b; viii, 943b, 944b, 975a
Sulaymān Shukōh b. Dārā i, 768b; ii, 134b
Sulaymān Shukōh b. Shāh ʿĀlam (XVIII) ii, 602a; iii, 1095a; vii, 669b
Sulaymān Solong ii, 122b
Sulaymān al-Tādjir s, 56a
Sulaymānān iv, 674b
al-Sulaymānī iii, 799a
Sulaymānī Kurds v, 459b
Sulaymānī Payraw (1933) x, 65b
Sulaymānīs (Mecca) i, 403a, 709a; ii, 517a; v, 1244b; vi, 148b; ix, 507a, **829**a
Sulaymānis (Hind) i, 552b, 1255a; ii, 98a; iv, 201a

Sulaymāniyya (town/district, ʿIrāḳ) v, 467b; vi, 614a; viii, 199a; ix, **829**b
Sulaymān-nāme i, 826b; ii, 921a
Sulaymān-shāh b. Parčam Īwāʿī i, 919a
Sulaymanu iv, 549a
Sulduz (Süldüz), Banū (Mongol) ix, **831b**
Suldūz (Ādharbāydjān) ix, **832**a
Süleman Dhatī (1738) s, **763**b
Sülemish iv, 621a
Süleymān (Sulayman the Magnificent) (Ottoman) (1566) i, 152a, 293a, 398a, 406a, 432a, 468b, 553b, 557b, 842b, 956a, 1117b, 1128b, 1163b, 1250b, 1253b; ii, 612a, 715b; iii, 147b; iv, 638a, 1157a; v, 630b; vi, 3a, b, 4b, 5a, 228b, 496b, 508a, b, 510a, 609b, 893b; vii, 225a, 239a, 319a; viii, 4a, 195b; ix, **832**b; s, 94b, 95a, 154a, 238a, 274a, 315b; x, 109a
– administration i, 712a, 469a, 1266a; ii, 103b, 118b, 287a, 907a; iii, 213b, 1183a; iv, 565a, b, 900a; v, 882a
– constructions i, 768a, 1134a, 1166b, 1225b; ii, 12a, 345b; iv, 232a; v, 333b
– literature ii, 400a, 588b, 869a; iv, 574a
Süleymān II (Ottoman) (1691) v, 262a; vii, 319a; ix, **842**a
Süleymān Čelebi b. Bāyazīd (Ottoman) (1411) i, 394a, 654a; ii, 98a, 159a, 599a, 611b, 684a, 984b; iii, 1183a; vii, 644a, b; ix, **843**a
Süleymān Čelebi, Dede (1422) ix, **843**a
Süleymān Efendi → ʿIzzī Süleymān Efendi
Süleymān Pasha Berkīn-Zade Bargjini (1616) x, 533a
Süleymān Pasha, Malaṭyalï (1687) ix, **844**b
Süleymān Pasha (Mohács) vii, 219b
Süleymān Shāh Germiyān-oghlu (1387) i, 299b; ii, 98a, 989b; v, 359b, 539a; ix, 418b
Süleymaniyye (Istanbul) iv, 232a; vi, 366b
Süleymanlï (Zeytūn) vi, 508b, 509a
Ṣulḥ i, 1143b; ii, 131a; iv, 14b; ix, **845a**
Ṣulḥ-i-ḳull i, 117b, 317a; ix, **846**a
al-Ṣūlī, Abū Bakr Muḥammad b. Yaḥyā (946) i, 10a, 144b, 154a, 590a, 867a; iii, 466b, 893a, 908b; vi, 198b, 352a, 634a; vii, 279b, 559a; ix, 8b, **846**b; s, 24b, 35b, 37b, 118a, 386a
Sūlī b. Ḳaradja ii, 239b
Sullam ix, **848**b; s, 396b
Sulṭān (title) iv, 942a, b; v, 628a; ix, **849**a
Sulṭān I b. Sayf (Yaʿrubid) (1680) v, 507a; vi, 735a, 843a; xi, 292a
Sulṭān II b. Sayf (Yaʿrūbid) (1719) v, 507a; vi, 735a; ix, 775b; xi, 292a
Sulṭān b. ʿAbd al-ʿAzīz (Āl-Suʿūd) (XX) vi, 158a, b
Sulṭān b. Aḥmad (Bū Saʿīd) (1804) i, 1282a; v, 183b; vi, 735b; s, 332b
Sulṭān b. Bidjād (Āl Ḥumayd) (XX) ii, 354a; iii, 1065b, 1066b, 1067b; vi, 152a, b
Sulṭān b. Ḥāmid al-Ḳaysī iv, 925a
Sulṭān b. Muḥammad b. Ṣaḳr iv, 778b
Sulṭān b. Ṣaḳr i, 928a; ii, 619a; iv, 778a
Sulṭān b. Salāmah iv, 752a
Sulṭān b. Sayf Imām (Yaʿrūbid) (XVII) vi, 735a; x, 816b
Sulṭān b. Thumāl iv, 911a
Sulṭān Ādam Gakkhar ii, 973a; iii, 576a
Sultan Agung ii, 390b; iii, 1221b; s, 201a, b
Sultan Aḥmad (Djalāyirid) → Aḥmad b. Uways
Sulṭān Aḥmad Khān Avar i, 755b
Sulṭān Aḥmad Mīrzā i, 847b
Sulṭān ʿAlī (calligraphe(r)) (XVI) viii, 787b
Sulṭān ʿAlī Kātib i, 1212a, b
Sulṭān ʿAlī Oghlu → Sulṭān Galiev
Sulṭān ʿAlī Sadōzay i, 231a
Sulṭān ʿAlī Ūghlī (Soltangaliev) (1940) iii, 532a; iv, 792b; s, **783**b
Sulṭān al-Aṭrash ii, 290a, 637b
Sulṭān Bāhū (Jhang) (1691) vii, 328a; viii, 256a
Sulṭān-Band (Marw) vi, 621a, b
Sulṭān Bāyazid Dūrī iv, 1127b
Sulṭān Begādā → Maḥmūd I Begrā (Gudjarāt)
Sulṭān al-Dawla Abū Shudjāʿ (Būyid) (1024) i, 131b; ii, 391a; iv, 378b; vi, 626a; ix, **854**a; s, 119a, b
Sulṭān al-Dawla Arslān Shāh (Ghaznawid) (1115) vi, 783a
Sulṭān Djahān Bēgum (XX) i, 1195b, 1196a, 1197a; vii, 1049a
Sulṭān Ghārī (Delhi) vii, 195a
Sulṭān Ghāzī Shāh Čak → Ghāzī Khān Čak
al-Sulṭān al-Ḥanafī s, 18b
Sulṭān Ḥasan Mīrzā Nayyir al-Dawla (XIX) s, 23b
Sulṭān Ḥusayn, Shāh (Ṣafawid) (1726) vi, 16b, 18a, 483b, 525a, 551a, 856a; vii, 62a; viii, 771b; ix, **854**a

Sulṭān Ḥusayn Bayḳara → Ḥusayn Bayḳara
Sulṭān Ḥusayn Lingāh → Ḥusayn Shāh Langāh I
Sulṭān Ḥusayn Mīrzā → Ḥusayn I (Ṣafawid)
Sulṭān Ibrāhīm (Fārs) (XVI) vi, 17b
Sultan Ibrāhīm Nūr al-Dīn (Maldives) (XIX) vi, 246a
Sulṭān Isḥāḳ → Sulṭān Ṣoḥāk
Sulṭān Ismāʿīl Shāh (Čak) s, 324b
Sulṭān-Ḳalʿa vi, 619a, b, 620a, 621a
Sulṭān Khalīl b. Uzun Ḥasan iv, 267b
Sulṭān Khātūn i, 1117b; v, 679b
Sultān Ḳulī → Ḳulī Ḳuṭb al-Mulk
Sulṭān Maḥmūd Māhīsawār i, 1168a
Sulṭān Muḥammad (painter) viii, 788a
Sulṭān Muḥammad b. Awrangzīb vii, 315b
Sulṭān Muḥammad b. Muḥammad b. Falāḥ (Mushaʿshaʿ) (XV) vii, 672b
Sulṭān Muḥammad al-ʿĀdil (Maldives) (XII) vi, 245b
Sulṭān Muḥammad Khān (Bārakzay) i, 231a; ii, 637b
Sulṭān Muḥammad Khān Ḳāshḳāy iv, 706a
Sulṭān Muḥammad Mīrzā b. ʿAbbās I (Ṣafawid) (XVII) viii, 770b
Sulṭān Muḥammad Shāh → Maḥallatī, Agha Khān
Sulṭān Naṣīr al-Dīn Ghāzī Čak → Ghāzī Khān Čak
Sulṭān Nithār Bēgam (1624) vii, 331b
Sulṭān Öñü (Eskishehir) ix, **855**a
Sulṭān Saʿīd (Shaybānid) (1572) vii, 677a
Sulṭān Sandjar (Tīmūrīd) (XV) i, 147b
Sulṭān Sārang ii, 973a
Sulṭān Sayyid Saʿīd (Bū Saʿīd) → Saʿīd b. Sulṭān, Sayyid
Sulṭān Sehāk (XV) ix, **855**a
Sulṭān Shāh (Ghūrīd) (XII) vi, 618a
Sulṭān Shāh b. Il Arslan (Khwārazmī) (XII) ii, 253a, 1101b; iv, 583a, 1067b; ix, 34b
Sulṭān-Shāh b. Ḳāwurd (Saldjūḳ, Kirmān) (1085) iii, 86b, 87a; v, 159b; vi, 273b
Sulṭān Shāh b. Riḍwān (Saldjūḳ) (1123) viii, 947b
Sulṭān Shāh Lōdī b. Malik Bahrām (1431) v, 782b, 783a
Sulṭān Shāhzāda → Bārbak Shāh Ḥabshi
Sulṭān Ṣoḥāk i, 260b, 261b, 262a, b
Sulṭan Sulaymān (Tu Wen-Hsiu) (XIX) viii, 260b; x, **574**b
Sulṭān Taḳī Sulṭān (Sõmāy) (XVII) ix, 727b
Sulṭān al-Ṭalaba (festival) ix, **857**b
Sulṭān Uways b. Idgü v, 163b, 584b
Sulṭān Walad b. Djalāl al-Dīn Rūmī (1312) i, 147a; ii, 394a; iv, 67a; vi, 833a, 835b, 883a, 886b; viii, 972b; ix, 298a, **858**a; s, 49b, 83b
Sulṭān Ways Mīrzā i, 852b
Sulṭān Yaʿḳūb (Aḳ-Ḳoyunlu) → Yaʿḳūb b. Uzun Ḥasan
Sulṭāna bint Aḥmad al-Sudayrī s, 305b
Sulṭāna Čand Bībī (Aḥmadnagar) vi, 488b
Sulṭānābād (towns) ix, **859**a; s, 73a
Sulṭānābād-i Čamčamāl vi, 494a
Sulṭāniyya (Djibāl)) i, 261a; iii, 1124b; iv, 1167b; v, 294a; vi, 494a, 495b, 528b, 540b; viii, 169a; ix, **859**b; s, 83b
Sulṭāniyya (Maklī) vi, 189b
Sulṭānpūr vi, 131a
Sulṭānpūrī, ʿAbd Allāh (Makhdūm al-Mulk) (1584) v, 1235b; s, **3**a
Sultansky, Mordecai iv, 606a
Sulṭān-zāde Isḥāḳ Bey iv, 112b
Sulṭānzāde Muḥammad Pasha → Muḥammad Pasha Sulṭānzāde
Sulu archipelago → Philippines
Su-lu (Türgesh Kaghan) (738) x, 560a
Sulūk ix, **861**b
Ṣulūḳ → Wādī ʾl-ʿArab
Ṣuʿlūk v, 768a; ix, **863**b; s, 37a
al-Ṣuʿlūkī, Abū Sahl Muḥammad (980) ix, **868a**
al-Ṣuʿlūkī, Abu ʾl-Ṭayyib (1611) ix, **868b**
Ṣumādiḥ, Banū vi, 576b; s, **766**a
Sumak s, 136a
Sumāmī, Muḥammad ʿĀbid (XVIII) vi, 953a
Sūmanāt (Somnāth) ii, 597a, 598a, 1123b, 1125a; vi, 63b; viii, 1047a; ix, **868**b
Sumaniyya (Buddhists) i, 15b, 17b, 953a, 1031a, 1092b, 1284a, 1333b; ii, 972b; iii, 335b, 1122a; iv, 43b, 356a, 512b; v, 37b, 853a; ix, **869**a
Sumatra iii, 1213a, b, 1214b, 1215b, 1218a, 1219a, 1225b; v, 226a, b; 227b, 228a, b; vi, 43a; vii, 73b; ix, **870**b
al-Ṣumayl (Cordoba) (VIII) x, 848b

al-Ṣumayl b. Ḥātim Abū Djawshān al-Kilābī (759) i, 135a; iii, 602a; iv, 494b; ix, **870**b; s, 81b, 82a
Sumayr iii, 41b
Sumaysāṭ vi, 230b, 505b; ix, **871**b
al-Sumaysāṭī → al-Shimshāṭī
Sumayṭiyya vii, 645b
Sumayya umm ʿAmmār b. Yāsir (VII) ix, 205b; s, 354b
Sumbar (river) vi, 716b
Sumbawa (Sunda) i, 1219b, 1226a; ix, 877a
Sumerā/Sumrā (Sind) viii, 1047a; ix, **872**a
Sumhuʿalī Yanūf b. Dhamarʿalī vi, 562b
Sumhuʿalī Yanūf b. Yadaʿʾil Dharīḥ vi, 559b, 562a, b, 562b
Summ (samm) ix, **872**a
al-Ṣummān → al-Ṣammān
Sumayya bint Khubāṭ s, 354b
al-Simnānī, Abū Djaʿfar iii, 544a, 1146b; ix, **614**b
Sumnūn (Samnūn) b. Ḥamza (910) ix, **873**a
Ṣunʿ Allāh b. Djaʿfar al-ʿImādī (1612) ix, **873**b
Suna II Kabaka (1856) x, 778b
Sūnām s, 66b
al-Sunāmī, ʿUmar b. Muḥammad (1333) s, **766**b
Sunan ix, **874**a
Sunan Ampel (1467) iii, 1219a
Sunan Bonang iii, 1218b, 1219a
Sunan Giri iii, 1218b, 1219a; v, 1155a
Sunaq-qurghan (Sïghnāḳ) s, 245a
Sunbādh (Khurāsān) vi, 427b, 744b; ix, **874**b
al-Sunbāṭī, Aḥmad b. ʿAbd al-Haḳḳ iv, 451a
Sunbūḳ → Milāḥa; Safīna
Sunbul Khānum (XVIII) vi, 484a
Sünbül Sinān Efendi (1500) vi, 1023a
al-Sunbula → Minṭaḳat al-Burūdj
Sunbuliyya/Sünbüliyye iv, 991b, 992a; vi, 1023a; ix, **875**a
Sünbül-zāde Wehbī (1809) ix, **876**a
Sunda islands iii, 1213a, 1226a; v, 785a; ix, **877**a
Sundarban ix, **872**b
Sundjata Keita (XIII) vi, 258a; ix, 756a
Sungur Bey Shamsī Pasha → Shams al-Dīn b. Taman
Sunḳur/Sonḳor (town) ix, **877**b
Sunḳur b. Mawdūd Muẓaffar al-Dīn (Salghurid) (1161) ii, 812a; iii, 1097b; v, 826b; viii, 978b
Sunḳur Agha (Niğde) (XIV) viii, 15b
Sunḳur al-Ashḳar (Damascus) (XIII) ii, 285a; iii, 403a, 832b; iv, 88a, 485a; v, 594b; vi, 322b; vii, 461b; viii, 851a
Sunna i, 175b, 258b, 275b, 325b, 773a, 1039b, 1199a; ii, 859a, 888b; iii, 953b, 994b; iv, 142a-b, 147b, 148a; ix, **878**a
Sünnet Odasï vi, 55b
Sunnī i, 1254a; ii, 64b, 283a, 290a, 859b, 931b; iii, 87a, 411b, 1168b
Sunni ʿAlī → Songhay
Sunʿullāh Efendi (XVII) vii, 600b
Suphi Ezgi (1962) ix, 418a
Sūr ix, **881**b
Ṣūr (Tyr) i, 215b; iv, 129b; v, 789a; ix, **883**a; s, 120b
Ṣūr (ʿUmān) vi, 729b; vii, 53a; ix, 356b
Sūr, Afghān i, 228b; iii, 423a; s, 1b
Sūr Dās iii, 457a
Sur (Ḳaṣr) al-Ḥadjar (Marrākush) vi, 596b
Sura (Ḳurʾān) v, 409b; ix, **885**b
Ṣūra (image) i, 1084a; ix, **889**a
Sūra Maʾmūniyya i, 1003b; ii, 578b
Surabaya s, 150b, 202b
Surādik iv, 1147a
Sūradj Kund ii, 255b
Sūradj Mal Djāt → Bharatpūr
Suradjgarh vi, 47a
Surāḳā b. ʿAmr i, 921b; iv, 342b
Surāḳa b. Bukayr (VII) vii, 497b
Surāḳa b. Mirdās al-Aṣghar (699) ix, **892**a
Surakarta (Mataram) vi, 43a; ix, **892**a; s, 607b
Surapati (1766) (Mataram) s, 607b
Sūrat (India) v, 1114a, b; vi, 53b, 233b, 534b; vii, 71b; ix, **893**a
Ṣurat al-arḍ ix, **893**b
Sūrat Singh s, 361a
al-Suraydjiyya, al-Masʾala ix, **893**b
Ṣuraym ii, 71b
Sūrghān Shīra ii, 67b
Sürgün iv, 225a, 238a, 239a; v, 305b; s, **767**a
Surhāb-mat vi, 515a
Surḥūbiyya → al-Djārūdiyya
Sūrī → Sūrs
Sūrīd (king) vi, 411b

Sūriyā (Syria) → al-S͟hām
Surk͟hāb i, 512b, 513a
Surk͟hāb b. ʿAnnāz i, 513b; v, 824b, 828a
Surk͟hāb b. Badr i, 513a; v, 454a
Surk͟hāb b. Bāw iv, 644b
Surk͟hāb Beg i, 406a
Ṣurk͟hābiyya iv, 1086b
Sūrk͟hay K͟hān → Čulāḳ-Sūrk͟hay
Sūrk͟hāy-Mīrzā ii, 87a
Surk͟h-rag vi, 384a
Sürmeli ʿAlī Pas͟ha → ʿAlī Pas͟ha Sürmeli
Ṣurna s, 136a
Ṣurra i, 483b; iv, 1133b; ix, **894**a
Ṣurrat al-Ḥaramayn iv, 1133b
Sūrs (Afg͟hans, Delhi) vii, 795b; ix, **894**a
Sursuḳ iii, 514b; vi, 543b
Surt (town) vi, 946a; ix, **894**b
Surūmī, bā, ʿAbd Allāh b. Aḥmad al-S͟hiḥrī (1536) vi, 133a
Surūr, Mīrzā Rad͟jab ʿAlī Beg (1867) ix, **895**a
Surūr al-Fātikī (XII) v, 1244b
Surūr, Nad͟jīb → Nad͟jīb Muḥammad Surūr
Surūrī, Kashānī Muḥammad Ḳāsim (XVI-XVII) i, 380a; iv, 526a; ix **896**b
Surūrī, Muṣliḥ al-Dīn (1562) ix, **895**b
Surūrī, Seyyid ʿOt͟hmān (1814) ix, **896**b
Surūs͟h, Muḥammad ʿAlī K͟hān (1868) iv, 70a; ix, **897**a
Sūryānūs ii, 770b
Sūs (licorice) ix, **897**b
al-Sūs (Sūsa, S͟hūs͟h) (K͟hūzistān) i, 86a, 245a; ii, 527a; v, 1178b, 1187b; vi, 494b, 589a, b; 590b, 591b, 594a, b, 595a, 633b, 741a, 742b, 743b; vii, 643b; ix, **898**a; s, 29a, 40a, 47b, 133b, 336b, 402b
al-Sūs al-Aḳṣā (Morocco) ix, **899**a
Sūsa (Sousse, Tunisia) i, 248b, 620a, 1319a; ii, 130a; iii, 499b; iv, 654a; v, 830a; vi, 113b, 141b, 142a, b, 143a, 295a, 434b; ix, **901**a
Sūsan (Sawsan) ix, **902**b
Sūsand͟jird iv, 654a; v, 498b
Sūsū, Banū i, 762b; vi, 258a
Susuhunan → Agung
Sūsūn iv, 1042b
Sutan Takdir Alisjahbana vi, 240b
Sūtānuti ii, 7a
Sutaylı̊ iv, 584a
Sutled͟j i, 919b; v, 885b
Sütlüd͟je iv, 233a; s, 168b
Sutra ix, **902**b
Sutūda, Manūčihr s, 376a
Suṭūḥiyya i, 280b; x, 189a
Suʿūd, Āl (dynasty) i, 98b, 554b, 942b, 1313a; ii, 176b, 320b, 573a; iii, 363b; iv, 717b, 765a, 778a, 953a, 1072b; v, 574b, 575a; ix. **903**a; s, 30a
Suʿūd b. ʿAbd al-ʿAzīz Āl Suʿūd) (1814) ii, 321a; iv, 765a, 925b; vi, 150b, 191b; ix, 903b; xi, 41b
Suʿūd b. ʿAbd al-ʿAzīz (Āl Suʿūd) (1964) i, 555a, 958a; ii, 660b; vi, 156a, 169b; ix, 904b
Suʿūd b. Fayṣal b.ʿAbd al-ʿAzīz (Āl Suʿūd) (1860) ii, 176b; iv, 1073a; s, 305b
Suʿūd b. Fayṣal b. Turkī (Āl Suʿūd) (1874) ix, 904a
Suʿūd b. Muḥammad b. Muḳrin (1724) vii, 410a
Suʿūd al-Kabīr iv, 1073a
Suʿūdī, Abu ’l-Faḍl al-Mālikī (XVI) ix, **905**a
Suʿūdī (Abu ’l-Suʿūdī) b. Yaḥyā al-Dimas͟hḳī (1715) ix, **905**b
Suʿūdī, Sayf al-Dīn (1335) ix, **905**b
al-Suʿūdiyya, al-Mamlaka al-ʿArabiyya (Saudi Arabia) i, 39a, b, 534a, 539a, 1314a; ii, 425a, 557b, 660a; iii, 363a; v, 1056b; vi, 33a, 144b; ix, **905**b; s, 417b
Suut Kemal Yetkin (XX) vi, 95b
Suwāʿ iii, 540b; **908**b
Suwār (Sawar) i, 1305b, 1306b; v, 686a; ix, **909**a
al-Suwārī → al-Ḥād͟jd͟j Sālim
Suwayd b. al-K͟hadhdhāk i, 74a
Suwayd b. Muḳarrin i, 1247a; iv, 207b, 644a; v, 378a; s, 297b
Suwayd al-Haramī s, 366b
Suwaydān iv, 751b
Suwaydī, Banū v, 459a
al-Suwaydī, ʿAbd Allāh b. al-Ḥusayn al-Bag͟hdādī (1760) vi, 112b
al-Suwaydī, ʿAbd al-Raḥmān b. ʿAbd Allāh (1786) vi, 113a
al-Suwaydī (Ibn al-), ʿIzz al-Dīn (1292) ix, **909**b
Suwaydiyya vi, 579a; ix, **916**a
Suwayf, Banū → Banī Suwayf
Suwayḳa (Medina) xi, 242b
Suwayḳat Ibn Mat͟hkūd vii, 186b
al-Suwaynī, Saʿd b. ʿAlī (1453) s, **767**b

al-Suwayra (Morocco) ix, **910a**
al-Suways (Suez) i, 13a, 315a, 554b; iv, 206b; v, 368b; vi, 195a; ix, **912a**; s, 6b
Sūyāb ii, 67a; ix, **913a**; x, 560a, 689a; xi, 335b
Sūyūmbigi, Princess iv, 850a
Suyūrg͟hāls ii, 150b, 152a; iv, 1043b
Suyūrg͟hatmis͟h b. Ḳuṭb al-Dīn, D̲jalāl al-Dīn Abū Muẓaffar (1294) v, 162a, b, 553b, 554a; vi, 482a
Suyūrg͟hatmīs͟h b. Noradin (XV) vi, 202a
Suyūrg͟hatmīs͟h b. Terken K͟hātūn (Kirmān) (XIII) vi, 482b
Suyūrsāt ii, 152a; iv, 1043a
Suyūṭ → Asyūṭ
al-Suyūṭī, D̲jalāl al-Dīn (1505) i, 27a, 72a, 429a, 594b, 595a, 721a, 729a, 759a, 1110a, 1198a, 1309a; ii, 826b; iii, 90a, 435a, 697a, 711a, 957b; iv, 550a, 863b; v, 419b, 1223a, 1235a; vi, 112a, 181a, 194b, 262b, 263a, b, 264b, 351b, 352b, 353a, 354a, 454a, 907a; vii, 175a, 254b, 261b, 262a, 290b, 296b, 394a; ix, 757b, **913a**; s, 352b, 388a
Sūz, Sayyid Muḥammad Mīr (1798) ix, **916a**
Sūzanī (Sozanī). Muḥammad b. ʿAlī al-Ṣamarḳandī (1166) iii, 355b; iv, 62a; viii, 749a, 971a; ix, **916b**; s, 65a
Sūzī Čelebi (1524) vii, 34b; viii, 338a; ix, **916b**
Sūzmanī, Banū → Lūlī
Svatopluk → Čeh
Svištov → Zis͟htowa
Swahili ii, 59a, 129a; iv, 886b, 888b; v, 177a, 205b, 223a, 655b, 962b; vi, 612b, 827b; ix, **917a**
Swāt (Pakistan) i, 864a; v, 356a; vi, 127a; ix, **918b**
Swimon I b. Luarsab (al-Kurd̲jī) (1600) v, 493a
Sy, el-Had̲ji Abdoul Aziz s, 182a
Sy, el-Had̲ji Malick s, 182a
Sylla → Fodié; Yaʿḳūba
Sylhet → Silhet
Syntipas → Sinbād al-Ḥakīm
Syr Darya → Sı̊r Daryā
Syros (Syra) → S͟hire
Syriae → S͟hām
Syrianus → Sūryānūs
Szechuan (Ssŭ-ch'uan, Si-chuan) ix, **919a**
Szécsény s, 171a
Szeged ix, **920a**
Székesfehérvár ix, **920b**
Szigetrar → Sigetwār

T

Tāʾ x, **1a**
Ṭāʾ x, **1a**
Ṭāʿa x, **1b**
Taʾabbaṭa S͟harran i, 130b; ii, 1079a; iii, 540b; vii, 308a, 309b; x, **2b**
Taʿaddī x, **3b**
Taʿad̲jd̲jub x, **4a**
Taʿāʾīs͟ha i, 49b; ii, 122a, 124a; v, 1250a, b; x, **4b**
Taʿalluḳ (a) s, **767a**
Ṭaʿām x, **4b**
Taʿarrub x, **5a**
Taʿāsīf → ʿAlam al-Dīn Ḳayṣar
Taʿaṣṣub → ʿAṣabiyya
Taʿāwīd͟hī → Ibn al-Taʿāwīd͟hī
Taʿāwun x, **5b**
Taʿawwud͟h x, **7a**
Ṭābaʿ iv, 456b, 1105b
Tabaddul iii, 170b
Ṭabaḳa x, **7a**
al-Ṭabaḳa al-K͟hāmisa i, 1060a
Ṭabaḳ al-manāṭiḳ iv, 703a
Ṭabaḳāt i, 106a, b, 274b; ii, 922a; x, **7b**
Tabannin s, **768a**
Tabārakallāh i, 1032a; v, 425b
Ṭābarān vi, 714a
al-Ṭabarānī, Abu 'l-Ḳāsim (971) i, 273b; iii, 159a, 864a; x, **10b**; s, 400b
al-Ṭabarānī, Abū Kat͟hīr Yaḥyā al-Kātib (932) viii, 661b
al-Ṭabarānī, Surūr al-Ḳāsim (1034) viii, 146b
Ṭabarī (dialect) i, 872a
al-Ṭabarī, Abū D̲jaʿfar Muḥammad b. D̲jarīr (923) i, 51a, 140a, 459a, 567b, 591a, 628a, 760a, 984b; ii, 133a, 215a, 793a,

1111b; iii, 57b, 608a, 1062a, 1206b; v, 1130b; vi, 199a, 262b, 265a, 403b, 605a, 905a; ix, 547a; x, **11a**
al-Ṭabarī, Aḥmad b. ʿAbd Allāh (1295) iv, 797a; x, **16a**
al-Ṭabarī, ʿAlī b. Rabban i, 213b, 265b; iii, 378a; v, 701b; viii, 148b; x, 12a, **17a**, 453a; s, 314a
al-Ṭabarī, al-Ḳāḍī al-Imām Abu 'l-Ṭayyib (1058) i, 459a, 773a, 1039b; ii, 412a; iii, 302a; x, **15b**; s, 192a
al-Ṭabarī, Muḥibb al-Dīn (1251) vi, 106b, 350a, b, 351b
al-Ṭabarī, ʿUmar b. Farrukhān (VIII) vi, 710b; viii, 107a, 108a
Ṭabarīs s, 335a
Ṭabaristān i, 40a, 52b, 688a, 760a, 871b, 1110a, 1350a; iii, 233b, 245a, 810a; iv, 644a, b; v, 68b, 69b, 661a; vi, 66a, 115b, 120a, 148a, 335a, 337a, b, 511a, 517a, 527a, 539a, 744b, 780a, 935b; x, **18b**; s, 13a, 235a, 297b, 298a, 299a, 356b, 357a, 363a, b
Ṭabariyya (Tiberias) vi, 652b; x, **18b**
Tabarka v, 50b, 51b; x, **19b**
Tabarruʾ x, **20b**
Ṭabarsarān ii, 85b, 87b, 89a; iv, 343a, 345b; x, **22b**
Ṭabarsī → Ḥusayn Nūrī
al-Ṭabarsī, Raḍī al-Dīn (1153) i, 326a
Ṭabarsī, Shaykh Abū ʿAlī al-Faḍl vii, 422b, 441a
Ṭabas i, 1052b; v, 354b; 868b; x, **22b**
Ṭabāshīr x, **23a**
Ṭabāṭabāʾī, ʿAlīm Allāh (1743) ii, 1092a
Ṭabāṭabāʾī, Āyatullāh Muḥsin Ḥakīm (1970) s, 104a
Ṭabāṭabāʾī, Ḥudjdjat al-Islām Sayyid Muḥammad Ḳāẓim Yazdī (1919) vi, 552b
Ṭabāṭabāʾī, Sayyid Ḍiyāʾ al-Dīn (1969) i, 978a; iii, 529a; v, 310b; viii, 511b; x, **23b**
Ṭabāṭabāʾī, Sayyid Muḥammad Ḥusayn b. Muḥammad (Āyatullāh) (1947) iv, 166a, b; vi, 553a; vii, 762b
Ṭabāṭabāʾī, Sayyid Muḥammad Mahdī (baḥr al-ʿulūm) (1797) vi, 552a
Ṭabāṭabāʾī, Sayyid Ṣādiḳ Abū Sayyid Muḥammad Ṭabāṭabāʾī (XX) iv, 164a
Ṭabbākh x, **23b**
Ṭabbāl x, **24a**
Ṭabʿī (1670) vi, 837b
Ṭabīʿa x, **25a**
Ṭabīb → Ṭibb
al-Ṭabīb, ʿImād al-Dīn Maḥmūd b. Masʿūd (XVI) viii, 542b
Ṭabīʿiyyāt s, **769a**
Ṭabīʿiyyūn ii, 96a
Ṭābīnān v, 686a, b, 689a
Taʿbīr al-Ruʾyā s, **770a**
Tabissa i, 163a
Ṭābiʿūn i, 276a; iv, 149a; x, **28b**
Tabḳa vi, 382b
Ṭabkh x, **30a**
Ṭabl ii, 621a;, x, **32b**
Ṭabl-Khāna x, **34b**
Tablīgh iv, 166b
Tablīghī Djamāʿat x, **38a**; xi, 358a, 406b
Tabriʾa i, 1026b
al-Ṭabrisī (al-Ṭabarsī), Abū Manṣūr (XII) vii, 312b; x, **39b**, 85a
al-Ṭabrisī (al-Ṭabarsī), Amīn al-Dīn (1154) Abū ʿAlī al Faḍl vii, 422a, 441a; x, **40a**, 85a
al-Ṭabrisī (al-Ṭabarsī), Ḥādjdj Mīrzā Ḥusayn b. Muḥammad (1902) x, **41a**
Tabrīz i, 190b, 325a; ii, 8a, 435b; iii, 157b, 212b; iv, 7b, 33a, 392a; vi, 18b, 55b, 72b, 120a, 315b, 484b, 494a, 498a, b, 499a, b, 501b, 502a, b, 504a, b, 505a, 514a, 523b, 526b, 584a; viii, 184b; x, **41b**; s, 73a, 110a, 135a, 138b, 139a, b, 140a, 142a, 208a, 275a, 289a, 365b
– institutions ii, 426a, 1043a
– monuments i, 1124a, 1125a; iv, 702a
Tabrīzī x, **50a**
al-Tabrīzī, Abū Zakariyyāʾ Yaḥyā (1109) → al-Tibrīzī, Abū Zakariyyāʾ Yaḥyā (1109)
Tabrīzī, Aḥmad iii, 114a
Tabrīzī, Aḥmad Kasrawī → Kasrawī Tabrīzī
Tabrīzī, Bahāʾ al-Dīn Yaʿḳūb (XIII) vi, 73a
Tabrīzī Djalāl al-Dīn Suhrawardī (Bengal) (1244) xi, 119a; s, **771b**
Tabrīzī, Fakhr al-Dīn ʿAlī → Ṣāḥib ʿAtāʾ
Tabrīzī, Ḳāsim-i Anwār → Ḳāsim-i Anwār
Tabrīzī, Ibn Khalaf → Burhān
Tabrīzī, Muḥammad ʿAṣṣār → ʿAṣṣār
Tabrīzī, Muḥammad Ḥusayn → Muḥammad Ḥusayn Tabrīzī

al-Tabrīzī, Muḥammad Ḥusayn b. Khalaf → Burhān
Tabrīzī, Radjab ʿAlī s, 308a
Tabrīzī Shams-i → Shams-i Tabrīzī
Tabshīr s, **772a**
Tabūk i, 9a; vi, 158a, 455a, 647a, b, 650a; vii, 373b; x, **50b**;s, 351b
Tabula Smaragdina i, 995a
Ṭabūr x, **51a**
Tabūshkān iii, 224a
Tābūt v, 864a
Tacapas → Ḳābis
Tadallīs (Dellys) x, **51b**
al-Tadallisī, Sīdī Yaḥyā v, 1165a
Tadbīr x, **52b**
Taddart i, 372a
Tādemeket, Tādmekka iii, 657a; xi, 212b
Tadhkira ii, 80a, 179a, 304a; v, 193a; x, **53b**
Taʿdīl x, **55a**
Taʿdīl Bayn al Saṭrayn x, **55b**
Taʿdīl al-Zamān x, **55b**
al-Tādilī (XIII) vi, 741b
al-Tādilī Ibrāhīm b. Muḥammad (1894) x, **55b**
al-Tādilī, Yūsuf b. Yaḥyā, ibn al-Zayyād → Ibn al-Zayyād
Tādj v, 634a, 748a, 749a; x, **57a**
Tādj al-ʿAdjam (XII) i, 440a
Tādj al-Dawla → Tutush
Tādj al-Dawla (Labla) (1041) ii, 1009a; v, 586b
Tādj al-Dawla Muḥammad (Munḳidh, Banū) (1157) vii, 578b
Tādj al-Dawla Ṭāwūs Khānum Iṣfahānī (XVIII) vi, 484a
Tādj al-Dīn → al-Subkī
Tādj al-Dīn Firūz Shāh (Bahmānīd) (1422) xi, 1a
Tādj al-Dīn, Ḳāḍī ʾl-Ḳuḍāt (1262) vi, 667b
Tādj al-Dīn, Mawlānā s, 352b
Tādj al-Dīn, Pīr v, 26b
Tādj al-Dīn ʿAbd al-Madjīd (1343) ix, 666a
Tādj al-Dīn Abū Bakr s, 66b
Tādj al-Dīn (I) Abu ʾl-Faḍl Naṣr (Sīstān) (1073) ix, 683b
Tādj al-Dīn (II) Abu ʾl-Faḍl Naṣr (Sīstān) (1164) ix, 683b
Tādj al-Dīn Abu ʾl-Futūḥ (Alamūt, Maṣyād) (1239) vi, 790b
Tādj al-Dīn ʿAlī-Shāh (1318) viii, 169a, 443b
Tādj al-Dīn Ḥarb b. Muḥammad (Nīmrūz) (1213) ix, 682b
Tādj al-Dīn Ḥusayn b. Fakhr al-Dīn ʿAlī i, 243b
Tādj al-Dīn Inaltigin (1235) ix, 683b
Tādj al-Dīn Khandgāh (Ghaznawid) (XI) vi, 410a
Tādj al-Dīn Mukhtaṣ (1289) iv, 76b; vi, 653b
Tādj al-Dīn Muʿtazz iv, 738a
Tādj al-Dīn Yildiz Muʿizzī (1215) x, **60a**
Tādj Khān Narpalī (XVI) vi, 52a
Tādj Khātūn bint Muḥammad Bayhaḳī s, 131b
Tādj Maḥall i, 253b; ii, 47b, 287a; iii, 450b; vi, 126a, 127a, 1289a, 369b; vii, 332b; viii, 268b; x, **58b**
Tādj al-Mulk (Delhi) v, 6a
Tādj al-Mulk Abu ʾl-Ghanāʾim (1093) i, 1051b; iii, 774b; vi, 275a; vii, 541a; viii, 72a, 81b; s, **383b**
Tādj al-Mulūk bint Tīmūr Khān (XX) vii, 446a
Tādj al-Mulūk Būrī (Būrid) (1132) i, 1017a, 1332a, b; ii, 282a; iii, 120a; vi, 547a
Tādj al-Salṭana bint Nāṣir al-Dīn Shāh (Ḳādjār) (XX) vi, 481b
Tadjallī x, **60b**
Tadjammul Ḥusayn Khān ii, 809a
Tadjdīd x, **61b**
Tādjīk i, 224a, 530b, 853b, 854a, 857a, 1010a; iv, 310a, b, 313b; v, 244b, 614b, 857b, 858a; vi, 371a, 557b; ix, 682b; s, 98a, 237b, 367b; x, **62a**
Tādjīkī x, **64b**
Tādjīkistān i, 531a; x, **66a**; s, 819b
Tādjī-zāde Djaʿfer Čelebi (1516) vi, 967a; viii, 212a
Tādjir x, **67a**
Tadjmīr x, **67a**
Tadjnīs x, **67b**
al-Tadjrīshī, al-Amīr Muṣṭafā iv, 856b
Tādjuh (Tagus) x, **70b**
Tadjurra (Tadjura) x, **71a**
Tadjwīd x, **72b**
Tādlā vi, 141b, 592a, 741a, 742a, b; x, **75a**; s, 132a, 223a

Tadlīs x, **77a**
Tadmait s, 328a
Tādmakkat x, **78a**
Taḍmīn x, **78b**
Tadmur i, 563a; vi, 373b, 544b, 622a; x, **79a**; s, 117a
Tadrīs x, **80a**
Tādrus b. al-Ḥasan (1029) vii, 117a
Tadūra vi, 412b
Tadwān vi, 384a
Tadwīn x, **81a**
Tafaḍḍul Ḥusayn Khān i, 1043a; ii, 809a
Tafarnudj x, **81b**
Tafḍīl x, **82a**
al-Ṭaff (steppe) iv, 384b; x, **82a**
Tafīla x, 884b
Tāfīlālt i, 355b; iii, 256b; v, 1187b; vi, 135a, 141b, 142b, 143a, 248b, 249a, 590b, 742a; viii, 440a; ix, 545b; x, **82b**; s, 223b, 370a
Tafīsh vi, 562b
Tafkhīm x, **83a**
Tafna i, 67b
Ṭafra x, **83a**
Tafsīr i, 40a, 60b, 274b, 410a; ii, 363a; iii, 172a, 434b; iv, 147a, 984b; x, **83b**
Tāfta iii, 216b; x, **88a**
Taftāzān (Khurāsān) x, 88b
al-Taftāzānī, Saʿd al-Dīn Masʿūd (1390) i, 342b, 858a, 982b, 1019b, 1116a, 1345b; ii, 174a, 602b, 774b; iii, 163b, 711a, 1168a; iv, 414b; vi, 218b, 848a; vii, 388a; x, **88b**
Tagawst xi, 20b
Tagdaust → Awdaghust
Tagh Boyu → Akhāl Tekke
Taghā → Tughā
Taghāliba ii, 175b, 176a
Taghāza x, **89a**
Ṭaghī ii, 1124b
Ṭāghiya v, 692b; vi, 374a; x, 94a
Taghlib, Banū i, 526b, 527a, 528a, 545a, 963a, 1240b, 1241a; iii, 222b, 1254a; iv, 1143b; v, 362a; vi, 378a, 379a, 490a; vii, 373b; s, 86b, 178a
Taghlib b. Wāʾil, Banū ii, 176a; x, **89b**
al-Taghlibī, al-Ḥakam b. ʿAmr vi, 193a
Taghlibiyya viii, 730b
Taghrī Birdī al-Bashbughāwī ii, 781a, b, 782a
Taghrībirdī al-Ẓāhirī ii, 286a
Taghrīr x, **93a**
Ṭāghūt x, **93b**
Tagmut vi, 590b
Tagore, Rabindranath s, 162a
Tagus → Wādī Tadj
Ṭah, Shaykh Abū ʿUbayd Allāh (XIX) vii, 454b
Ṭā-hā x, **1b**
Ṭāhā, ʿAlī Maḥmūd (1949) x, **95a**
Ṭāhā Ḥusayn (1973) i, 565b, 598a, 890a; iv, 906b; v, 189a, b, 1092a; vi, 91a, 408a, 409a, 461a, 956a; vii, 441a, 713b; x, **95a**; s, 58a
Ṭāhā, Maḥmūd Muḥammad (1985) x, **96b**
Tahadjdjud x, **97b**
Tahamtan, Ḳuṭb al-Dīn i, 942b; iii, 585a; iv, 764b
al-Tahānāwī, Muḥammad Aʿlā (XVIII) i, 595a; iii, 170b, 1238b, 1241b; vi, 219a, 442a, b, 443a, b, 451a; x, **98a**
Taḥannuf iii, 165b, 166a
Taḥannuth x, **98b**
Ṭahār, Ṭahāra iv, 372b; v, 20b; x, **99a**
Tāhart i, 1175b; iii, 654b, 655a, 657a; v, 696b, 1164b; vi, 312a, b, 435a, 452b, 727b, 840b; vii, 263a; x, **99b**
al-Ṭaḥāwī, Aḥmad b. Muḥammad Abū Djaʿfar (933) i, 123b, 310a; iii, 163a; vi, 352b; vii, 822a; x, **101a**; s, 156a, 310b
Tahawwur Khān s, 420b
Taḥayyur iv, 95a
Taḥdjīr iii, 1054a
Ṭaḥḥān x, **102a**
Ṭāhir I b. al-Ḥusayn (Ṭāhirid) (822) x, **103a**
Ṭāhir II b. ʿAbd Allāh (Ṭāhirid) (859) iv, 20b; x, **105a**
al-Ṭāhir, ʿAlī Nāṣūḥ v, 412b
Ṭāhir b. Abū Ṭayyib iii, 107a
Ṭāhir b. Aḥmad b. Bābashādh (Wazīr) (1077) i, 131b; iii, 733a, 761a; x, **102b**
Ṭāhir b. Ghalbūn b. Abi ʾl-Ṭayyib al-Ḥalabī (1008) vi, 188b
Ṭāhir b. Hilāl b. Badr (XI) i, 512b; iii, 258b; ix, 295b
Ṭāhir b. al-Ḥusayn al-Būshandjī (Ṭāhirid) (822) i, 18a, 52b, 271b, 437b, 751b, 897b; ii, 524a; iii, 231b, 694b; iv, 17a, 20a, b, 645a; v, 57b, 621a; vi, 333a, b, 334a, 336a, b, 337b, 438a; vii, 985b, 1016b; s, 15a
Ṭāhir b. Ḥusayn al-Ahdal, Sayyid i, 255b

Ṭāhir b. Khalaf iii, 502a; s, 118b
Ṭāhir b. Muḥammad b. ʿAbd Allāh (999) x, **103b**
Ṭāhir b. Muḥammad b. ʿAmr (Ṣaffārid) (X) viii, 796b
Ṭāhir b. Muḥammad al-Isfarāyīnī iv, 107b
Ṭāhir b. Zayn al-ʿAbidīn s, 95a
Tahir Alangu (XX) vi, 95b; s, **61b**
Ṭāhir ʿAlī Sharīf (XX) vi, 751b
Ṭāhir al-Balkhī iv, 797a, 800b
Ṭāhir, Banū (Murcia) x, **105b**
Ṭāhir Beg, Meḥmed (1912) s, **773b**
Ṭāhir Dhu ʾl-Yamīnayn (VIII) viii, 590a; x, 14a
Ṭāhir Efendi iv, 882b
al-Ṭāhir al-Ḥaddād iv, 720b; viii, 858a
Ṭāhir al-Ḥawwa (XIX) vi, 252a
Ṭāhir al-Ḥusaynī s, 67a
Ṭāhir Ḥusaynī Dakkanī, Shāh iv, 202a; ix, **200b**
Ṭāhir Pasha (Miṣr) (1803) i, 1269a; v, 35b; vii, 423b
al-Ṭāhir Raḥāb (XX) vi, 251b
Ṭāhir Sayf al-Dīn, Abū Muḥammad (1965) x, **103b**
Ṭāhir Selām i, 630a
Ṭāhir Waḥīd, Mīrzā Muḥammad (1698) x, **104a**
Ṭāhira → Ḳurrat al-ʿAyn
Ṭāhirids i, 52b, 439b, 440b, 441a, 553a, 1008b, 1342b; ii, 253b, 505b, 1081b; iii, 245a, 746a; iv, 18b, 20a, b, 646a; v, 57b; vi, 336b, 338b, 620b; vii, 777b, 867a, 996a; s, 338b
Ṭāhirids, (al-Andalus) x, **105b**
Ṭāhirids, (Khurāsān) x, **104b**
Ṭāhirids, (Souh Arabia) x, **106b**
Taḥkīm x, **107a**
Tahlīl x, **108a**
Ṭahmān b. ʿAmr al-Kilābī x, **108b**
Ṭahmāsibī, Khalīl ii, 882b; s, 158a
Ṭahmāsp I, Shāh Abu l-Fatḥ (Ṣafawid) (1576) i, 228b, 291a, 329b, 406a, 967b, 1066b, 1068a, 1135b, 1208b, 1211a, b; ii, 310b, 334b; iii, 214a, 253b, 575b, 1101a, 1189b, 1191a, 1257a; iv, 35a, b, 102b, 103a, 188a, 537a, 610a; v, 244b, 492b; vi, 16b, 17b, 18b, 456b, 483a, b, 495a, 514b, 515a, 516b, 525b, 550a, b, 608b, 714b, 715a; vii, 314a, 316b, 317a, 440b, 478a, 928b; viii, 73a, 115b, 766a, 768b, 775b; ix, 834b; x, **108b**; s, 43b, 140a, 383a
Ṭahmāsp II, Shāh (Ṣafawid) (1740) i, 395b; iii, 604b, 1002b; iv, 37a, 389b, 390a; v, 663b; vi, 55b, 715a; vii, 853a; x, **110b**
Ṭahmāsp b. ʿAbbās I (Ṣafawid) (XVII) ii, 1083b
Ṭahmāsp b. Muḥammad Khudābanda (Ṣafawid) (XVI) i, 8b; iii, 157b; iv, 860b, 861a
Ṭahmāsp Ḳulī Khān → Nādir Shāh
Ṭahmāsp Mīrzā b. Shāh Sulṭān Ḥusayn (Ṣafawid) (XVIII) viii, 771b
Ṭahmūrath (Pīshdādid) i, 459a; v, 494b; ix, 54b; x, **110b**
Taḥnīt x, **111a**
Taḥrīf x, **111a**
Taḥrīr x, **112b**
Taḥṣīl x, **113a**
Taḥsīn Efendī (Pasha) i, 61b, 64a; iii, 1199a
Taḥsīn, Mīr Muḥammad Ḥusayn (XVIII) x, **113b**
Taḥsīn Wa-Taḳbīḥ x, **114a**
Taḥt al-Ḳalʿa (Damascus) vi, 455a
Taḥt al-Ḳalʿa (Istanbul) iv, 228a; s, 472a
al-Ṭahṭāwī, Rifāʿa Bey (1873) → Rifāʿa Bey
Tahūda iv, 827a
Ṭāḥūn x, **114b**
al-Ṭāʾī → Abū Tammām; Dāwūd; Djundab b. Khāridja; Ḥātim
al-Ṭāʾī (1778) vii, 969b
al-Ṭāʾī (al-Ṭūsī), Muḥammad b. Ḥumayd (IX) vi, 337a, b
Ṭāʾī, Banū viii, 53a
al-Ṭāʾiʿ li-Amr Allāh al-ʿAzīz (ʿAbbāsid) (1003) i, 212a, 955a, 1352b; ii, 195a; iii, 345a; vi, 522a, 667a, 669b; x, **115a**s, 23a, 118b
Taičiʿut ii, 41b
Ṭāʾif i, 9a, 55a, 609a; iii, 363a; v, 434b, 692b; vi, 145b, 147b, 151b, 152a, 157a, 160b, 162b, 224a, 266a, b, 405a, 650a, b; vii, 366a, 373a; x, **115a**; s, 3b, 133b, 134a, 152a, 318a, 354a, b
Ṭāʾifa x, **116a**
Ṭāʾifiyya x, **117a**
al-Ṭāʾir → Nudjūm
al-Ṭāʾir/al-Ṭayr v, 184b; x, **117b**

Taʿizz vi, 474b, 911b; vii, 270a, 761b; viii, 184a, 235b, 456a; x, **118a**; s, 338b
Ṭāḳ iii, 501b, 502a; v, 69b
al-Tāka (Ṭāḳā) → Kasala
Ṭāḳa (Ḥaḍramawt) vi, 83b
Taḳālīd s, **774b**
Taḳdīr x, **119b**
Takfīr x, **122a**
al-Takfīr wa 'l-Hidjra x, **122b**
Takafūr (Nicephorus Phocas) ii, 236a
Taḳalī v, 267a
al-Taʿkar (Ibb) ix, 816a
Takash → Tekish
Taḳbaylit x, **118b**
Takbīr x, **199b**
Takhalluṣ x, **123a**
Takhmīs x, **123b**
Takht-i Djamshīd (Iṣṭakhr) iv, 220b
Takht-i Fūlād (Iṣfahān) vii, 132a; s, 308a
Takht-i Rustam (Iṣṭakhr) iv, 221b
Takht-i Sulaymān (Saturiḳ) iii, 1125a; iv, 1166a, 1167b; vi, 499a
Takht-i Sulaymān Shīz x, 896b
Takht-i Ṭāwūs (Peacock Throne) vi, 528a; viii, 869a; x, 125a
Takhtadjı̊ x, **125b**
Takhṭīṭ al-Ḥudūd x, **126b**
Takhyīl x, **129a**
Taḳī Arānī (1939) s, 110a
Taḳī Awḥadī (ca. 1632) vii, 530a; x, **132a**
Ṭāḳ-i Bustān (Kirmānishāh) v, 169a
Taḳī Bāfḳī, Shaykh Muḥammad s, 342b
Taḳī al-Dīn → al-Muẓaffar
Taḳī al-Dīn, Ḳāḍī al-Ḳuḍāt (1280) vi, 673b
Taḳī al-Dīn b. Maʿrūf b. Aḥmad (1585) v, 27b; vi, 377a, 601b; vii, 30b; viii, 555b; x, **132b**; s, 372a
Taḳī al-Dīn Muḥammad b. Sharaf al-Dīn (XVII) x, **133a**
Taḳī al-Dīn al-Nabhānī (1977) x, **133b**
Taḳī al-Dīn al-Futūḥī → Ibn al-Nadjdjār
Taḳī al-Dīn ʿIrāḳī, Kh(w)ādja s, 415b
Taḳī al-Dīn ʿUmar → al-Malik al-Muẓaffar ʿUmar
Taḳī al-Dīn ʿUmar b. Turān Shāh (Ayyūbid) (XII) vi, 380b
Taḳī Kāshī vii, 530a; s, 415a, 415b
Taḳī Khān, Amīr Kabīr, Mīrzā (1852) → Amīr Kabīr
Taḳī Shīrāzī, Mīrzā Muḥammad s, 342a
Takidda (Takedda) x, **133b**
Taḳī Mīr, Mīr (XVIII) vii, 669b
Takin → Tegin
Takīn b. Tutush (Saldjūḳ) (XII) viii, 995a
Takirwan iv, 826a
Taḳiyya i, 402a, 811a, 1099a; v, 375a; x, **134b**; s, 230b
Taḳī-zāda, Sayyid Ḥasan (1970) v, 1097b; x, **136a**; s, 365b
Takkalū, Banū x, **136b**, v, 245a
Taḳlā, Bishāra and Salīm ii, 466b; iv, 967a; vii, 902b
Takla b. Hazārasp iii, 337a, b
Taklamakan → Tarim Basin
Taḳlīd i, 1039a; ii, 182b, 303a, 890a; iii, 1026b, 1173b; iv, 152a; x, **137a**
Taḳlīd-i Sayf → Marāsim 4
Taklīf x, **138b**
Taḳrīb x, **139b**
Takrīt (Tikrīt) iii, 1252b, 1268a; iv, 289a; vi, 143b, 966a; vii, 396b, 400b, 543b; viii, 716a; x, **140b**; s, 36b
al-Takrītī, ʿAbd al-Laṭīf b. Rushayd iv, 137a
Taḳrīẓ ii, 304a; s, **781a**
Takrūna x, **141b**
Takrūr i, 297a; ii, 941b, 970a; iii, 657a; vi, 87b, 258a, 259b, 281b, 320a; vii, 612b; ix, 138b, 139a, 752b; x, **142a**
Takrūrī → Takrūr
al-Takrūrī, Abū Muḥammad b. ʿAbd Allāh (X) vii, 612b
Takshīf iv, 678a
Taḳsīm vi, 57a; x, **143a**
Taḳsīṭ x, **144a**
Ṭaḳṭūḳa x, **144a**
Takūdār → Aḥmad Takūdār
Tākurunnā viii, 615b, 616a; x, **144b**
Taḳwā s, **781b**
Takwa Milinga (Manda) vi, 385a, b
Taḳwīm i, 285a; ii, 465b; v, 313b; x, **145a**
Takwīn x, **147b**
Ṭalab al-ʿIlm → ʿIlm
Ṭalaba (Ṭullāb) iii, 97b, 98a, b; v, 1134a; x, **148b**
Ṭalabānī, Djalāl (XX) vii, 714b, 715a
Ṭalabānī, Shaykh Riḍā v, 147a
Ṭalabīra (Talavera) x, **149a**
Ṭalāʾiʿ b. Ruzzīk (vizier) (1161) i, 9b, 196b; ii, 318a, 855b, 856b, 858a; iv, 429a, 944a; v, 514b; vii, 61b; viii, 130a, 864a; x, **149a**; s, 115b

Ṭalāḳ i, 27b, 28b, 172b, 173b, 174a, 177a, 178a, 179a; ii, 836b; iii, 19a, 949b, 952b; iv, 286a, 689a; x, **151a**
Ṭālaḳān ii, 43b; vi, 618a; x, **157a**
al-Ṭāl(a)ḳānī, Abu 'l-Ḥasan (995) vi, 820b, 823a
Ṭālaḳānī, Āyatullāh Sayyud Maḥmūd (1979) → Ṭāliḳānī, Āyatullāh Sayyud Maḥmūd (1979)
Ṭalāl b. ʿAbd Allāh b. al-Ḥusayn, King (1972) iii, 264b; x, 886b
Ṭalāl b. ʿAbd Allāh b. Ras͟hīd → Ras͟hīd, Āl
Ṭalāl b. ʿAbd al-ʿAzīz ii, 660b; iv, 1142b
al-Ṭalamanḳī, Abū ʿUmar Aḥmad (1037) x, **159a**
Talas (Transoxania) iv, 188b; vi, 420a; ix, 621b, 622a; x, 222a
Ṭalʿat Bey (Pas͟ha), Meḥmed (1921) x, **159b**
Ṭalʿat, Meḥmed → Ṭalʿat Pas͟ha Ḥarb
Ṭalʿat Pas͟ha Ḥarb ii, 431a, b, 497b, 698b, 699a, b; iii, 360a, 622b; iv, 284b, 285a, b, 636a, 720b; v, 1003b; vi, 615a, 983b; vii, 229a; s, 98a, 296b
Talbiya iii, 37a; v, 582a; x, **160a**
Ṭald͟jiʾa iii, 394a, 1113a
Talfīḳ x, **161a**
Ṭalḥa b. Ṭāhir (I) b. al-Ḥusayn (Ṭāhirid) (828) i, 52b, 272a; iv, 20b; vi, 337b; x, 104b
Ṭalḥa b. ʿUbayd Allāh al-Taymī (656) i, 43b, 110a, 308a, 381b, 382a, 383a; ii, 414b, 415b; iii, 1165b; iv, 316a; v, 316a; vi, 139b, 621b; vii, 364a; x, **161b**; s, 89b
Ṭalḥa b. Yaḥyā s, 113b
Ṭalḥa al-Naḍrī al-Layt͟hī i, 266b
Ṭalḥa(t) al-Ṭalaḥāt (684) x, **162b**; s, 26a
al-Ṭāliʿ x, **163a**
Ṭāliʿa x, **164a**
Ṭāliʿ Īmānī vii, 91b
Ṭālib → Ṭalaba
Ṭālib b. Abī Ṭālib i, 152b
Ṭālib b. Aḥmad i, 1306b, 1307b
Ṭālib Āmulī (1626) vii, 341a; ix, 241a; x, **164b**
Ṭālib al-Ḥaḳḳ (ʿAbd Allāh b. Yaḥyā) (748) s, **785a** i, 550b; ii, 592b; iii, 651b, 658a; iv, 1076a; v, 1230a; vii, 524b; s, 337b, 338a
Ṭālib Pas͟ha al-Naḳīb (XX) vi, 615b
Ṭālibān s, **786a**
Ṭalibids → ʿAlids
Ṭālibiyya s, 401a
Ṭālibūf (Ṭālibov), ʿAbd al-Raḥīm, Nad͟jd͟jārzāda (1911) iv, 72a, 164b, 789a; x, **164b**; s, 109b
Ṭālibzada → Ṭālibov
Ṭalīḳ → Tulaḳāʾ
Taʿlīḳ → Ṭalāḳ
Taʿlīḳ (Taʿlīḳa) x, **165a**
Ṭāliḳān vi, 511b, 512a
Ṭāliḳānī, Āyatullāh Sayyid Maḥmūd (1979) iv, 166a; vi, 549a, 553b; vii, 762b; x, **158a**
Taʿlīḳī-zāde, Meḥmed b. Meḥmed el-Fenārt (1603) x, **165b**
Tālikotā viii, 252a; x, **166a**
Talʿīk-zāde (XVII) vii, 931a
Ṭālis͟h vii, 497b, 498b, 935b; x, **166a**; s, 143a
Talkāta, Banū ix, 18a
Talk͟hīṣ → Muk͟htaṣar
Tall (Tell) x, **167a**
Tall Bās͟hir vi, 380a, 381b, 499b, 506b, 507a, 544a; x, **167a**
Tall, el-Had͟ji Omar s, 182a
Tall, el-Had͟ji Seydou Nourou s, 182a
Tall Ibn Maʿs͟har vii, 578b
al-Tall al-Kabīr x, **167b**
Tall al-Sulṭān vi, 781a
al-Tallaʿfarī S͟hihāb al-Dīn (1277) v, 110a; x, **168a**
al-Tallaʿukbarī, Hārūn b. Mūsā s, 400b
Talman (XVIII) vi, 56a
Talmīḥ iii, 1091b
Tālpūrs i, 230b; ii, 168a; iii, 323b; iv, 1160a; ix, 440a, 635a
Talsindah vi, 48a
Ṭālūt (Saul) i, 404b; x, **168b**
Ṭālūṭ b. al-Ḥusayn (Kilwa) (XIV) vi, 370a
al-Talutī ʿAlī ix, 20a
Tam, Banū i, 1190a
Ṭamaʿ ii, 79a
Tāmag͟hilt → Mag͟hīla
Tamahak → Ṭawārik.2
Tamahaḳḳ iii, 1038b
al-Ṭamāmī (al-Ẓamāmī), Abū Zakariyyāʾ (dāʿī) (IX) vi, 439a
Taman Siswa i, 746a
Tamanrasset i, 255a
Tamar (Georgian queen) v, 490a
Tamarurt vi, 743b

Tamashek → Ṭawārik.2
Tāmasna ii, 623a; vi, 741b, 742b; x, **169a**
Tamattuʿ iii, 35a, 36b, 53b
Tamazight (dialect) x, 118b, **169b**; s, 113b
Tāmdalt vi, 742b
Tamerlane → Tīmūr Lang
Tamgha i, 861b; ii, 147a, 310a; iii, 489b; iv, 31a, 1050a; x, **170a**
Tamghāč Khān → Muḥammad II b. Sulaymān Bughrā Khān (Ḳarakhānid)
Tamgrūt i, 290b; vi, 350a; x, **170b**; s, 395a
al-Tamgrūtī, Abu 'l-Ḥasan (1594) x, **171a**
Ṭāmī b. Shuʿayb al-Rufaydī ii, 518a
Tamil ii, 28a; v, 582a
Tamils → Rawther
Tamīm x, **176b**
Tamīm, Banū i, 47b, 304a, 343b, 528b, 529b, 545a, 963b, 1247b, 1293a; ii, 70a, 181a, 353b, 480b; iii, 49a, 295a, 1254a; iv, 717a, 832b; v, 346a; vi, 267a, b, 349a, 640b, 646a; vii, 123a, 266a, 373b; s, 177a, 243a
Tamīm b. Baḥr al-Muṭṭawwiʿ x, **171a**
Tamīm b. Buluggīn b. Bādīs (Mālaḳa) (1090) i, 43b; vi, 222b
Tamīm b. al-Muʿizz Li-Dīn Allāh Abū ʿAlī (Fāṭimid) (prince and poet) (985) ii, 852b, 857a, 861b; iii, 903b; vii, 661a; viii, 42b; x, **171b**
Tamīm b. al-Muʿizz, Abū Yaḥyā (Zīrid) (1108) vii, 731b, 994a; x, **172a**
Tamīm b. al-Muʿizz b. Bādīs iii, 137b, 138a, 386a, b; v, 60a
Tamīm b. Murr, Banū x, **172b**
Tamīm b. Naṣr b. Sayyār iv, 447a
Tamīm b. Yūsuf b. Tāsh(u)fīn (amīr) (Almoravid) (XII) i, 389b, 390a; ii, 516a, 901b, 1013a; vi, 110b, 742b; s, 397b
Tamīm b. Zīrī → Abu 'l-Kamāl
Tamīm al-Dārī (VII) i, 405a; ii, 306b, 486b; iv, 734a, 956a; vi, 657b ; viii, 1043a; x, **176a**
Tamīma x, **177b**
al-Tamīmī, Abu 'l-Ḥasan v, 10a
al-Tamīmī, Abū Khuzayma s, 309a
al-Tamīmī, Abū ʿUbayda Muslim b. Abī Karīma (Ibāḍī Imām) (VIII) viii, 113a
al-Tamīmī, al-Aswad b. Sarīʿ (635) vi, 671a
al-Tamīmī, Ismāʿīl (1832) vi, 113a
Tamīmīs iv, 463b; x, 175a, b; s, 305a
Tamir-Bugha al-Ashrafī → Minṭāsh (Mamlūk)
Tamir Khān Shūra (Buynaksk) x, 164b
Ṭamīsha s, 298a, 356b, 357a
al-Ṭamiyya (mountain) vii, 348a
Tamkīn (Kābul) iii, 84b; vii, 473b
Tammām, Abū Ghālib → Ibn ʿAlḳama
Tammām b. ʿĀmir → Ibn ʿAlḳama
Tammām b. Ghālib (1044) x, **178a**
Tammān al Tamīmī iii, 982a
Tammār x, **179a**
Tammūz x, **179b**
Tamthīl x, **179b**
Tamr → Nakhl
Tānā Shāh → Abu 'l-Ḥasan Ḳuṭb Shāh
al-Tanakabunī → Muḥammad b. Sulaymān
Tanas i, 678b; vi, 120b, 371b, 404a, b, 576a; x, **180a**
al-Tanasī Muḥammad (1494) x, **181b**; s, 403b
Tanāsukh ii, 136b; iv, 45a; x, **181b**
Tanawlīs iii, 336a
al-Tanāwutī (Ibāḍīs) (XI) x, **183a**
Tanbūr → Tunbur
al-Tandaghī, Muḥammad Fāl b. Muttāliyya (XIX) vii, 623a
Ṭandja i, 85a, 356a, 706b; vi, 39a, b, 40a, 135a, 136b; x, **183b**; s, 112a
Tandja Bāliya iii, 500a
Tandjūr vi, 535a, b
Tanfīdha ii, 308a
T'ang v, 38a
Tanga/Tanka ii, 119b, 120a; v, 785a; vi, 612b; x, **185a**
Tanganyika → Tanzania
Tanghiz → Tankiz
Tang-i Ḳashḳay vi, 384a
Tangier → Ṭandja
Tangistān s, 336a
Tangri Ḳaghan (741) x, 687b
Tangut ii, 2a, 42b, 43b; iii, 115b; iv, 553b
Tanḥūm ben Yōsēf ha-Yerushalmī iv, 306a
Tanibak, Sayf al-Dīn ii, 285b
al-Tanʿīm vi, 168b
Tank vi, 86a; s, 329b
Tanka → Tanga
Tankalūshā al-Bābilī (I) viii, 103b, 106b
Tankiz b. ʿAbd Allāh al-Nāṣirī al-Ḥusāmī (vizier) (1340) i, 119a, 1138a, 1214a; ii, 285b, 354b; iii, 952b; iv, 960a; vi, 323a, 455a, 548a; vii, 170b, 992a; x, **185b**

Tankizbughā (amīr) iv, 432b
Tannūr → Maṭbakh
Ṭannūs al-Shidyāḳ vi, 346a
Tanpinar, Aḥmed Ḥamdī (1962) x, **186a**; v, 195a
Tañrï x, **186b**, 688a
Tansar, Kitāb x, **188a**
Tānsen ii, 1144a; iii, 453b
Tansift vi, 741b, 742a
Tānsin (Mīrzā Tānsen) (1589) x, **188b**
Ṭanṭā i, 281a, 404a; ii, 1009b; iv, 367b; vi, 87b, 408a, 453b, 499a, 652b; x, **188b**; s, 40b
al-Ṭanṭarānī, Aḥmad b. ʿAbd al-Razzāḳ (XI) viii, 970b
Ṭanṭāwī Djawharī (1940) vii, 439b; s, **262b**
al-Ṭanṭāwī Muḥammad Ayyād (1861) x, **190a**
Tanūkh, Āl i, 528a; ii, 634b, 751a; iii, 85b; iv, 289a; x, **190b** s, 284a
al-Tanūkhī, ʿAbd Allāh (1480) ii, 633a; vii, 544a
al-Tanūkhī, Abū ʿAlī al-Muḥassin (994) i, 176a, 764a, 1249b; iii, 373a, 1263b; iv, 703a; v, 768b; vi, 108a; vii, 358b; viii, 579b, 583b; x, **192b**; s, 32b, 361a, 398a
al-Tanūkhī, Abu 'l-Ḳāsim ʿAlī b. Muḥammad (ḳāḍī) (1271) vi, 169a; vii, 358b; ix, 433a; s, 361a
al-Tanūkhī, Djamāl al-Dīn (1479) x, **192b**
al-Tanūkhī Muḥammad b. Saḥnūn → Muḥammad b. Saḥnūn al-Tanūkhī
al-Tanūkhī, Naṣr Allāh b. ʿAbd al-Munʿim (1274) viii, 87b
al-Tanwādjīwī, Sayyid ʿAbd Allāh (1732) vii, 622a
Tanwīn iv, 413a, b; x, **193b**
Ṭanyūs Shāhīn (1895) ii, 595a; iii, 591b; x, **193b**
Tanzania, Muslims in i, 39a; iv, 890a; x, 104a, **194a**; s, 248b
Tanzīl → Waḥy
Tanẓīm al-Nasl, Tanẓīm al-Usra x, **197a**
Tanẓīmāt i, 13a, 37a, 56b, 286a, 318a, 397a, 469a, 652a, 657a, 693a, 972b, 1090b, 1304a; ii, 33b, 682b, 936a; iii, 285a, 592b, 1188a; iv, 168a, 560b; v, 36b, 631a, 904a, 1084b; vi, 285b, 469b; viii, 198b, 200a, 206b; x, **201a**
Taormina iv, 496b
Taoudeni i, 809a; x, 89b
Taourirt vi, 141b
Tapanta, Banū i, 1189b, 1190a
Tapar, Muḥammad (Saldjūḳ) (XII) i, 353a, 1359b; vii, 755a
Tappa Ḥiṣār ii, 107a
Tāptī (river) iv, 1022b; s, 279b
Ṭapu i, 1090b; ii, 147a; x, **209b**
Taraʿōri s, **788a**
Ṭarab (emotion) iv, 823a; x, **210b**
Ṭārāb/Tārāb (Bukhārā) x, 211b
Taraba i, 1299a; v, 62b
Tarabai umm Shivādjī II (Marātha) (1700) vi, 535a
Ṭarabāy, Banū (Palestine) iii, 325a; v, 594a; x, **211b**
Ṭarābī, Maḥmūd (1238) vii, 749a; x, **211b**
Tarābīn, Banū vii, 921a
al-Ṭarābulsī, Abū Saʿīd Khalīfa b. Farḥūn iv, 1130a
Ṭarābulus al-gharb (Tripoli, Lybia) i, 1317a; v, 759b, 760b, 1183a; vi, 3a, 58b, 60b, 68b, 404a, 452b; x, **212a**; s, 1a, 163b
Ṭarābulus al-shām (Tripolis) i, 125a, 448a, 946b; iii, 474b; iv, 485a; v, 591a; vi, 118b, 322b, 323a, 345a, 360a, 580a; vii, 62b; x, **214b**
al-Ṭarābulusī, Muḥammad b. Shaʿbān (1611) vi, 355b
al-Ṭarābulusī al-Raffāʾ (1153) iii, 821b; x, **216b**
Tarabzun (Tredizond) i, 468b, 476b, 645a; v, 712b; vi, 69a, 70b, 71a; x, **216b**; s, 328b
Ṭaradiyyāt i, 587a, 1154b; iii, 309a
Ṭarafa b. al-ʿAbd al-Bakrī (VI) i, 451b; ii, 1028b; iii, 666b; iv, 998b; vi, 603a; vii, 254b, 604a, 763b; x, **219a**
al-Ṭarāʾifī, Aḥmad b. ʿAbdūs iv, 668a
Ṭarāʾifiyya iv, 668a
Tārā Khān s, 327b
Tarakzay Mohmands vii, 220a
Tarāna i, 677a
Tarančis (Kāshghar) x, **220b**
Tarannum iv, 413b
Taranto iv, 275b
Tārāpūr (Māndū) vi, 407a
Tārashni (1023) vii, 613a
Ṭarāwīḥ x, **222a**
Ṭarāz (Talas) x, **222a**
Tarbiya x, **223a**
Tarbiyat Khān (XVII) vii, 318b

Ṭard → Ṣayd
Tardī Beg i, 1135b, 1136a
Ṭardiyya x, **223a**
Tardj (Khathʿam) vi, 435b, 436a
Tardjama
– in literature x, **224a**
– translations from Greek and Syriac x, **225b**
– translations from middle Persian (Pahlavi) x, **231a**
– modern translations into Arabic (IX) x, **232b**
– modern translations into Arabic (XX) s, **788a**
– in modern Persian x, **233b**
– in Turkish x, **234b**
Tardjīʿ-band / Tarkīb-band i, 677b; iii, 273b; iv, 715a; x, **235b**
al-Tardjumān (Turdjumān) al-Mayūrḳī, ʿAbd Allāh (Fray Anselmo Turmeda) vi, 927a; x, **236a**
Tardu b. Isṭami (603) x, 687a, 691b
Ṭarfids i, 709a
Ṭarghī ii, 268b; iv, 921b
Ṭarī (gold coin) x, **238b**
Tari Taghāʾī iii, 968b
Taʿrīb
– in the sense of the rendering of foreign notions or words in Arabic x, **240a**
– arabicisation as a weapon of modern political policy s, **790b**
Ṭarīf (VIII) i, 493a, 1044a; x, **241a**
Ṭarīf, Āl (Yemen) vi, 30b; s, 335a
Ṭarīf, Djazīrat → Ṭarīfa
Ṭarīfa (Djazīrat Ṭarīf) i, 7a, 493a; vi, 573a; x, **241b**
Tarifiyt x, **242a**
Ṭarīfiyya (Ibāḍī) iii, 659a
Ṭarīḳ s, 794b
Ṭāriḳ b. Suwayd al-Ḥaḍramī iv, 995b
Ṭāriḳ b. Ziyād b. ʿAbd Allāh (VIII) i, 50a, 493a, 985b, 1175a; ii, 352b, 524b, 786a; iii, 298b; iv, 665a; vi, 221b, 744a; vii, 643b; x, **242a**; s, 92a, 822a
al-Ṭarīḳ al-Sharḳi iii, 362b
al-Ṭarīḳ al-Sulṭānī iii, 362b
Ṭarīḳa ii, 164a, 224a; iv, 47b, 167b, 168a; v, 1200a; vi, 87b; x, **243b**
Taʾrīkh ii, 307a, 315a; iii, 468a, 838b; x, **257b**
Taʾrīkh (dates and eras in the islamic world)
– in the sense of date, dating etc., etymology x, **258a**
– definitions x, **258a**
– the muslim calendar x, **258b**
– pre-islamic and agricultural calendars of the arabian pensula x, **259b**
– the Julian calendar in the islamic world x, **261a**
– the coptic calendar x, **261b**
– in Persia x, **261b**
– the tax year x, **262b**
– the turco-mongolian calendar x, **263a**
– muslim India x, **263b**
– era chronology in astronomical handbooks x, **264b**
– calendars and eras x, **264b**
– days since the dpoch x, **268b**
– conversions x, **269a**
– madakhil x, **270a**
– tables x, **270a**
– historical writing in the arab world **271a**
– origins to ca. 950 x, **271a**
– the central and eastern lands 950-1500 x, **276a**
– the period 1500-1800 s, **795a**
– the 19th and 20th centureis x, **280a**
– North Africa s, **799b**
– in muslim Spain x, **283a**
– Christian Arabic historiography x, **807a**
– in Persian x, **286a**
Taʾrīkh al-Bāb i, 836a; iv, 346a
Taʾrīkh al-Hind al-Gharbī iii, 1045b
Taʾrīkh al-Islām ii, 215a, b
Taʾrīkh al-Mustabṣir iii, 881a
Taʾrīkh al-Sūdān ii, 251b, 252a
Tāʾrīkh-i Djalālī → Djalālī
Taʾrīkh-i Ilāhī → Ilāhī Era
Taʾrīkh-i ʿOthmānī Endjümeni i, 505b, 1089b; ii, 475a
Tarīm b. Ḥaḍramawt b. Sabaʾ al Aṣghar x, 303a
Tarim Basin (Sinkiang) ix, 648a, 649b; x, **302a, 707a**
Tarīm (Ḥaḍramawt, Yemen) vi, 82b, 132b, 490a; s, 337b, 338a, 339a, 420b; x, **302b**
Tarīm al-Sukūn b. al-Ashras b. Kinda x, 303a

Tarīn iii, 335b, 336a
al-Ṭarḳ bi 'l-ḥaṣā → K̲h̲aṭṭ
Ṭark̲h̲ān (title) x, **303a**
Tarkīb band → Tard̲j̲īʿ Band
Tarisapally vi, 458b
Tariverdiov → Ḥaydar K̲h̲ān ʿAmū Ug̲h̲lī
Ṭarḳala (Sūs) vi, 741a
Tarkan K̲h̲ātūn bint ʿIzz al-Dīn Masʿūd b. Ḳuṭb al-Dīn Mawdūd (1242) vi, 871b
Tarkanrī i, 864a
Tark̲h̲ān, al-K̲h̲(ʷ)arizmī Ras (VIII) iv, 1174a
Ṭark̲h̲ān Nīzak → Nīzak Ṭark̲h̲ān
Tark̲h̲āns vi, 189b; ix, 634b
Ṭarkī (Ṭārk̲h̲ū) ii, 86a, 87a
Tarkīb-band → Tardjīʿ-band
Tarma ii, 114a
Tarmas̲h̲īrīn (Mongol) (1326) i, 418b; ii, 4a, 45a, 922b; v, 598a; vii, 113a, 412a
Ṭārom/Ṭārum (Daylam) ii, 192a; vi, 515b, 539a; vii, 497b, 655b, 657a; x, **311a**
Ṭarrakūna (Tarragona) x, **303b**
Ṭarrār x, **304a**
Ṭars̲h̲ x, **304b**
Tarṣīʿ x, **304b**
Ṭarsūs i, 183a; ii, 35b, 36b, 129b; vi, 338a, 506a, 775a; x, **306a**; s, 120b
al-Ṭarsūsī, Abū ʿAmr ʿUt̲h̲mān x, 307a
Ṭarsūsī → Abū Ṭāhir Ṭarsūṣī
al-Tarsūsī, Marḍī (Murḍā) b. ʿAlī b. Marḍī (XII) x, **307a**
al-Ṭarsūsī, Nad̲j̲m al-Dīn (1348) ix, 539a
al-Ṭarsūsī, ʿUt̲h̲mān b. ʿAbd Allāh (X) viii, 498b
Tartar → Tatar
Tārtāra vii, 548b
Tartīb x, **307b**
Tartiya-rustāḳ vi, 513a
Tarṭūs (Tortosa) i, 825a; vi, 538a, 577b, 578b, 579a, b, 581b; ix, 268a; x, **309b**
Tārūdānt (Taroudant) vi, 742a, 743b, 893a; ix, 900b; x, **310b**; s, 48a, 402b
Ṭārum (Daylam) → Ṭārom x, **311a**
Tārūt iv, 763b; vii, 142b
Tarwiya x, **312b**
al-Ṭāsa x, **312b**
Taṣadduḳ Ḥusayn → Nawwāb Mīrzā S̲h̲awḳ
Taṣawwuf i, 60a, 69a, 70b, 89a, 92a, 96a, 138b, 142b, 146a, 195a, 234b, 266b, 280a, 283a, 297b, 298b, 326a, 346b, 352a, 392b, 416a, 441a, 515b, 592b, 701b, 717a, 765b, 794b, 829a, 951a, 957a, 960b, 1088b, 1239b, 1244a; ii, 165a, 166b, 220b, 223b, 242b, 422b, 450a, 1025b, 1041a; iii, 75b, 83b, 103b, 262a, 363a, 662a, 697a, 707b, 752a, 763b; iv, 35a, 46a-b, 47b, 49a, 51b, 64b-65a, 114a, 183b, 467a, 508a, 554b, 616a, 950a, 1074a; v, 333a, 698b, 1235b; x, **313b**
Tasbīḥ → Subḥa
Taṣdīḳ i, 1242a; iv, 279a
Tās̲h̲ Farrās̲h̲ (XI) iii, 1097b; vi, 523a; ix, 157a
Tās̲h̲ Möngke (Mangū) b. Hūlāgū (Mongol) (1252) iv, 1047a; vi, 482a
Tas̲h̲ahhud x, **340b**
Tas̲h̲an vi, 974a
Tas̲h̲bīb ii, 1028b; iii, 1006a; iv, 714b; v, 958b
Tas̲h̲bīh i, 275a, 333b, 410b, 414b; iii, 160a; iv, 249b; x, **341a**
Tas̲h̲bīh Wa-Tanzīh i, 257b, 334a; ii, 388b; x, **341b**
Tas̲h̲elḥīt i, 433b, 1181b, 1182a, b, 1183b, 1186a; ii, 116b; ix, 900b; x, **344a**
Tās̲h̲fīn b. Tināmer (XII) i, 699b; vi, 427a
Taṣḥīf x, **347a**
Tās̲h̲kent i, 46b, 47a; ii, 45b; iii, 224a; v, 30a, b, 399b; vi, 767a, b; x, **348a**; s, 50b, 51a, 98a, 228b, 245a, b, 411a
Tās̲h̲k̲h̲ūd̲j̲a Asīrī (K̲h̲od̲j̲and) (1916) x, 65a
Tās̲h̲köprüzāde ʿIṣām al-Dīn (1561) i, 89a, 594b, 698a, 732b; iii, 164a, 467b; iv, 704b; vi, 907a, 971a; x, **351b**; s, 381b, 383b
Tās̲h̲köprüzāde Kemāl al-Dīn (1621) x, **351a**
Tās̲h̲köprüzāde, Muṣliḥ al-Dīn Muṣṭafā (1529) x, **351a**
Tas̲h̲kun Og̲h̲ullarî i, 1159b
Tas̲h̲lîd̲j̲alî Yaḥyā Taşlicalî (1582) ii, 937a; iv, 1137b; vi, 610a; vii, 531a; viii, 213a; x, **352a**
Tas̲h̲mūṭ b. Hūlāgū iv, 521a
Ṭas̲h̲öz (Thasos) v, 763b; x, **352b**
Tas̲h̲rīʿ x, **353a**
Tas̲h̲rīfāt → marāsim I; Nīs̲h̲ān
Tas̲h̲rīḥ x, **354b**
Tas̲h̲rīḳ vii, 65b; x, **356b**
Ṭas̲h̲tamur al-ʿAlāʾī ii, 24a, 1112a; vi, 718b
Ṭas̲h̲tikīn (amīr al-ḥad̲j̲d̲j̲) vi, 434a

Tāshufīn b. ʿAlī b. Yūsuf (Almoravid) (1145) i, 78b, 390b; ii, 100b, 744b, 1013b; iii, 850b; iv, 290a; x, **357a**
Tasili (Tassili) x, **357b**
Ṭasinī (Banū Yazīdī) v, 460a
Tasʿīr x, **358b**
Taṣliya vi, 87b; x, **358b**
Ṭasm, Banū x, **359a**
Tasmiya → Basmala
Taṣnīf x, **360a**
Tasnīm x, **360a**
Taṣrīf x, **360b**
Ṭassūdj x, **361a**
Ṭassūdj vi, 504a
Tasūdj-i Dashtī vi, 384b
Ṭasūdjī, ʿAbd al-Laṭīf iv, 72a; ix, 897b
Taṣwīr x, **361b**
al-Tasyīr x, **366a**
Tāt ii, 89a; iv, 313b; v, 604b; x, **368a**
Tatar x, **370a**, 699b
Tatar (literature) x, **730a**
Ṭāṭār, al-Ẓāhir Sayf al-Dīn b. al-Muẓaffar Aḥmad (Mamlūk) (1421) i, 1053b; iii, 186a; vii, 172b; s, 39a
Tātār Khān b. Muẓaffar Khān (Gudjarāt) (1403) ii, 1125a; vi, 49b
Tatār Khān (Lāhawr) (XIV) ii, 973a; iii, 570a
Tatar Khān Lūdī (XV) s, 242a
Tātār Khān Sarang Khānī (XVI) ii, 1144a; iii, 455b; s, 331b
Tatar Pazarcik x, **371b**
Taṭarruf x, **371a**
Tatars i, 32b, 269a, 721b, 722a, 808b, 893b, 1028a, 1106b, 1107a, 1108a, 1188b, 1287a, 1297a, 1302b; ii, 41b, 42b, 68b, 70a, 610b, 995b; iii, 403a; iv, 179a, 280b, 848a, 850a; vi, 378a, 381b, 420a, b, 544a, 547b; vii, 350b; viii, 250b; s, 171b
Tatars (Ḳazan) i, 1188b, 1307b; ii, 366a, 980a
Tatars (Crimea) i, 722a, 893b, 894a, 983b, 1000a, 1252a, 1286b; ii, 24b, 88a, 612b; iii, 531b; iv, 500a, 630a, b, 849b; v, 136a, 137b, 139a, b, 720a, 765b
Tatawlalī Maḥremī (1535) viii, 213a
Taṭbīḳ ii, 254b
Tathlīth x, **373b**
Tathr, Banū vii, 582a
Tātī iv, 858b; x, **369b**
Taʿṭīl → Tashbīh Wa-Tanzīh Taʿṭīl
Tatmīn → Taḍmīn
Tattaʿ vi, 590b
al-Tattawī → ʿAbd al-Rashīd al-Tattawī
Ṭāʾūḳ → Daḳūḳāʾ
Ṭāʿūn iii, 240a
Taurus → Toros
Tavī (Djamnū) s, 241b
Ṭavīla iv, 219a
Tavium ii, 62b
Tawābil → Afāwīh
Tawaddud x, **375b**
Ṭawāf x, **376a**
Ṭawāʾif → Mulūk al-Ṭawāʾif
Tawakkul x, **376b**
Tawakkul b. Bazzār → ibn al-Bazzār al-Ardabīlī
Tawakkul b. Tūlak-Beg (XVII) vii, 529b
Tawakkul Khān, (Kazakh) (XVI) iv, 512a; v, 135a
Tawallud x, **377a**
Tawallulī, Farīdūn iv, 72a
al-Tawʾamān → Minṭaḳat al-Burūdj
Tawargha vi, 311b
Ṭawāriḳ (Touareg) i, 36b, 39b, 170b, 210b, 254b, 307a, 371a, b, 433b, 809a, 1179b, 1221b, 1259b; ii, 368b, 509b, 740a, 977b, 1022b; iii, 726a, 1038b, 1195b; iv, 777a, 1150a; v, 221b, 754b, 759b, 769b; vi, 258b, 259b, 402b; x, **379a**; s, 164b
Ṭawāriḳ (language) x, **380b**
Tawārīkh-i Ḳosṭanṭiniyya i, 776b
Ṭawāsh^{in} i, 33a; iv, 1088a (see also, *s.v.* Khaṣī I)
al-Ṭawāshī, Bahādur al-Shihābī (amīr) (XIV) vi, 580b
al-Ṭawāshī, Saʿd al-Dawla i, 440a
Ṭawāshī Shudjāʿ al-Dīn ʿAnbar al-Lālā (1324) viii, 156b, 157b
Tawāt → Tuwāt
al-Ṭawāḥīn (Palestine) ix, 35a
Tawātur x, **381b**
Tawāyiha, Banū iii, 643a
Tawāzun al-Sulutāt, Faṣl al-Sulutāt x, **382a**
Tawba iv, 1108a, b; x, **385a**
Tawba b. al-Ḥumayyir Abū Ḥarb (674) iv, 912a; v, 710a; vi, 477b, 603a; x, **386a**
Tawba b. Namir al-Ḥaḍramī (ḳāḍī) vi, 673a
al-Ṭawfī, Nadjm al-Dīn (1316) iii, 700a; iv, 258a, b; vi, 739b
Tawfīḳ x, **386b**
Tawfīḳ, Sulaymān iv, 857a

Tawfīḳ Aḥmad s, 224b
Tawfīḳ al-Ḥakīm (1987) vi, 76b, 409a, 746b; x, **386b**
Tawfīḳ al-Madanī (XX) vi, 753b
Tawfīḳ Pas̲h̲a, Aḥmad (K̲h̲edive) (1892) i, 13b, 142a, 815a, 1069b; ii, 181b, 514a, 647b; iii, 557a; v, 94a; vi, 531b, 984a; vii, 184a, 434b, 437b; x, **388a**; s, 40a, 408b
Tawfīḳ Rifʿat Pas̲h̲a v, 1092a
Tawfīḳ Ṣidḳī, dr. (XX) vi, 360a
Tawḥīd x, **389a**; xi, 40a
al-Tawḥīdī → Abū Ḥayyān al-Tawḥīdī
Ṭawīl x, **389b**
Taʾwīl x, **390b**
Ṭawīl, Banū 'l- x, **390a**; s, 82a
al-Ṭawīl, Muḥammad Amīn G̲h̲ālib (XX) viii, 147b
al-Ṭawīl, Tād̲j̲ al-Dīn (1311) viii, 157a
Ṭawīl K̲h̲ālīl (D̲j̲alālī) s, 238b
Tawīl-og̲h̲lu Muṣṭafā (1608) vii, 601a
al-Ṭawīla x, **392a**
Tawke (Kazak̲h̲ K̲h̲ān) (XVIII) x, 681b
Tawḳīʿ x, **392b**
Tawḳīt → Miḳāt
Tawlūd (island) vi, 641b
Tawliyat, Abu 'l-Faḍl s, 158a
Tawrāt x, **393b**
Tawrīḳ x, **395a**
Tawriya x, **395a**
al-Tawrīzī, Nūr al-Dīn ʿAlī (1429) iv, 642b
Ṭāwūs (Ṭāʾūs) (Peacock) x, **396a**
Ṭāwūs b. Kaysān (724) i, 1245a; v, 1131b; s, 232b
Ṭāwūs al-ʿUrafāʾ, Saʿādat ʿAlī S̲h̲āh (1876) viii, 47a
Ṭāwūs (Ṭāʾūs) Sīmnānī, Ḳuṭb al-Dīn (XV) i, 91a, 148a
Ṭāwūsiyya x, **397b**
Tawwāb → Tawwābūn
Tawwābūn ix, 826a; x, **398a**
Tawwad̲j̲ vi, 383b; vii, 357a; x, **398b**
al-Tawwātī, Aḥmad al-Tihāmī (1715) s, 44a
al-Tawwazī (847) vii, 279b, 281a
Tawzar (Tozeur) → Tūzar
Tawzīʿ ii, 145b
Taxila s, 259b
al-Ṭayālisī, Abū Dāwūd (819) iii, 24a; vii, 706a; x, **398b**
al-Ṭayālisī, D̲j̲aʿfar b. Muḥammad (X) x, **399a**
Ṭayba vi, 190b, 191a
Ṭaybād viii, 267a
Ṭaybarṣ al-Wazīrī, ʿAlāʾ al-Dīn (XIII) i, 814b; iii, 228b; vi, 507b
Ṭaybug̲h̲ā al-As̲h̲rafī al-Bi(a)klimis̲h̲ī al-Yūnānī iv, 797a; vi, 543a
Ṭaybug̲h̲ā al-ṭawīl (1366) ix, 154b, 532a
Tayčiʾut, Banū vi, 417b
Ṭayf al-K̲h̲ayāl x, **400a**
Ṭayfūr iv, 811a
Ṭayfūr b. ʿĪsā → Abū Yazīd al-Bisṭāmī
Ṭayfūr al-Dīn i, 859a
Ṭayfūrids i, 862a
al-Taylasān → Tālis̲h̲
Taym b. Murra, Banū (Taym Ḳuray̲s̲h̲) vi, 145a, 263a; vii, 393a; x, **401a**
Taymāʾ i, 547b, 1231a; x, **401b**; s, 117a
Taym Allāh b. T̲h̲aʿlaba, Banū i, 963b; x, **400b**
Tayammum x, **399b**
Taymannīs i, 224b; ii, 5b; s, 367b
al-Taymī → Abū Ḥanīfat al-Nuʿmān
al-Taymī, Hilāl b. ʿUllafa (VII) viii, 638a
Taymūr, Maḥmūd → Maḥmūd Taymūr
Taymūr, Muḥammad (1921) i, 597b, 598a; v, 189a
Taymūr Muḥammad b. ʿAlī Kurd (XIX) vi, 75a
Taymūr b. Fayṣal (Bū Saʿīd) (1932) i, 1283a; vi, 735b
Taymūr Bak̲h̲tiyār (1970) vii, 448b
Taymūr Mīrzā iv, 393a; s, 290b
Taymūrī i, 224b; ii, 5b; iii, 1107b
al-Taymūriyya, ʿĀʾis̲h̲a (1902) i, 597b; vii, 903a
al-Ṭayr → al-Ṭāʾir
Tayrāb → Muḥammad Tayrāb
Ṭayy, Banū → Ṭayyiʾ
Ṭayyār al-Furāt → al-Ḳaʿḳāʿ b. Maʿbad
Ṭayyār Maḥmūd Pas̲h̲a (1807) ii, 207b; iv, 322b; vii, 719a
Ṭayyār Pas̲h̲a-zāde Aḥmed Pas̲h̲a v, 258a
al-Ṭayyāriyya → al-D̲j̲anāḥiyya
Ṭayyiʾ/Tayy, Banū i, 528a, b, 544b, 563b, 683a, 1241a; ii, 234b, 482b; v, 348a; vi, 262a, 472a, 474b; vii, 116b, 461a, b, 672a; viii, 865a; x, 62a, **402b**; s, 37b, 304b
Ṭayyiʾ, D̲j̲abala i, 203a; ii, 482b
al-Ṭayyib, Mawlāy (1679) s, 404a

al-Ṭayyib b. al-Āmir (Faṭimid) (XII) i, 440a; ii, 170b, 858b; iii, 1168b; iv, 200a; vi, 191a
al-Ṭayyib al-Sāsī (XX) vi, 176b
al-Ṭayyib al-Ṣiddīḳī (XX) vi, 114b, 755b, 756a
Ṭayyibdjī, Badr al-Dīn iii, 1204a
Ṭayyibī, Banū iii, 1107a
Ṭayyibī Ismāʿīliyya → Ismāʿīliyya
Ṭayyibiyya i, 371a; ii, 98a; iii, 71b, 134a, 1168b; iv, 200b, 201a, 204a, b; v, 166b; x, 247b, **403a**; s, 44a, 61b, **810a**
Ṭayyibshāh → Djalāl al-Dīn Ṭayyibshāh
Tavghač Bughra Khān (Kāshghar) (XI) xi, 222b, 359b
Ṭāz (amīr) → al-Ẓāhirī, Sūdūn min ʿAlī Bak
Tāzā i, 355b; iii, 499a; vi, 141b, 572a, 592a, 681b, 741a; x, **404a**; s, 63b, 377b
Tazerwalt/Tāzarwālt iii, 535b; vi, 589b, 743a, 744a, 774a; x, **405a**
al-Tāzī (1831) vi, 356b
al-Tāzī, Ibrāhīm b. Muḥammad (XV)) ix, 20b
Taʿzīr ii, 519a; ix, 547b, 548b; x, **406a**
Taʿziya ii, 848b; iv, 50b, 73b, 857a; v, 636b; x, **406b**
Tazwīr x, **408b**
Tazyīf x, **409b**
Tchad → Čad
Teba s, 152b
Tebessa x, **410b**; s, 144b, 145a, 387a
Tebou ii, 875a, 876a, 877a; v, 760a
Teda i, 1221b, 1258a; ii, 368b; iv, 541a; v, 352a; s, 163b, 164b, 165a, 166a
Tedjeddüd Fîrḳasî iv, 285b
Tedjen (river) vi, 494b
Tegüder, Aḥmad Īl-Khān (1284) i, 903a; ii, 606b; iii1122a; iv, 31a, 620b, 817b, 975b; v, 827a; x, **411b**
Tehran → Tihrān
T'eimuraz → Ṭahmūrath
Tekālīf x, **412a**
Teke-eli x, **412a**
Tekele b. Muẓaffar al-Dīn (Salghurid) (1198) viii, 978b
Teke-oghllarî (Turkmen) x, **412b**
Teke-oghlu i, 517b
Tekfur (Bursa) i, 1333b;, x, **413b**
Tekīn (933) v, 329b
Tekin Alp (Moïse Cohen) (XX) vi, 94a; viii, 251a
Tekine Mirza (XV) iii, 44a
Tekridagh (Tekirdağ) vi, 290b, 588b; x, **414a**
Tekish, ʿAlāʾ al-Dīn (Khwārazmshāh) (1200) ii, 253a, 606a, 1101b; iii, 1111b; iv, 29b, 102a, 583a, 1067b; vi, 482a, 908a, 997a, b; viii, 63b, 749a; ix, 111b; s, 245b
Tekish b. Il Arslān (Saldjūḳ) (XI) iv, 27b; vi, 273b; x, **414b**
Tekke i, 467b; ii, 695a; v, 269b; x, **415a**
Tekke (Türkmen) s, 143b, 145a, 146b, 147a, 281a
Tekkelū iii, 1105a
Teknedji-zāde Ibrāhīm Efendi i, 776a
Teleorman → Deli-Orman
Telingānā vi, 269a; vii, 412a, 459a; x, **416b**
Teliyāgarhī Pass vi, 47a
Telkhīṣ x, **416b**
Telkhīṣdji x, **416b**
Tell → Tall
Tell Abū Sēfe iv, 556a; vi, 378a
Tell ʿAdjāba → ʿArbān
Tell al-Aḥmar → Tell Abū Sēfe
Tell ʿArān vi, 380a
Tell Bāshir vi, 380a, 381b, 499b, 506b, 507a, 544a
Tell Espīd iv, 498b
Tell Ḥamdūn vi, 507b
Tell Kawkab vi, 539b
Tell el-Kebīr → al-Tall al-Kabīr
Tell Khālid vi, 544a
Tell el-Kheleyife i, 558b
Tell Muraybat vi, 733a
Telugu v, 648a
Temeshwār (Temesvár) i, 291b; v, 1023a; vii, 708a; x, **417a**
Temirboghā → Timurbugha
Temīr-Khān-Shūrā → Makhač-ḳalʿe
Templiers → Dāwiyya et Isbitāriyya
Temučin/temüdjin → Činghiz-Khān
Temüdjin → Činghiz Khān
Temürtash → Timurtash
Tenedos → Bozdja-ada
Ténès → Tanas
Tenggarong s, 151a
Tengku Abdul Rahman s, 152a
Tenouadjib iii, 289a
Tepebashî vi, 57a

Tepedelen → ʿAlī Pas̲h̲a Tepedelenli̊
Tepedelenli ʿAlī Pas̲h̲a → ʿAlī Pas̲h̲a Tepedelenli
Teptyar x, **417b**
Terak̲k̲īperver D̲j̲umhūriyyet Fi̊rkasi̊ ii, 432a, 596a; iv, 854a, 934b; x, **417b**s, 41b
Terd̲j̲ān x, **418a**
Terd̲j̲ümān ii, 476b, 980a; x, **418b**
Terd̲j̲ümān-i Aḥwāl ii, 466a, 473b, 908a
Terd̲j̲ümān (in mysticism) x, **418b**
Terd̲j̲üme Odasi̊ iii, 553b
Terek x, **418b**
Terengganu (Trengganu) vi, 232b, 236b, 239b; x, **419a**
Terengganu (Trengganu) (Demak) (1546) iii, 1219b; ix, 852b
Terengganu (Trengganu) (stone) vi, 210b, 234a
Terken K̲h̲ātūn (Turkān K̲h̲ātūn) (Ḳutlug̲h̲-K̲h̲ānide) (1281) v, 162a, 553b, 554a; vi, 482b; ix, 110b; **x, 419a**
(wife of Malik-S̲h̲āh, Sald̲j̲ūḳ) (1094) i, 1051b, 1070b; iv, 28b, 101b; vi, 274a, 275a, 482a; vii, 541a; viii, 72a; s, 384a; x **419b**
(wife of Tekis̲h̲, Sald̲j̲ūḳ) (1232) iv, 30a; vi, 482a, b; x **419b**
Ternate x, **419b**; s, 199b
Tesalya (Thessaly) x, **420b**
Tersāne x, **420a**
Terter I i, 1302b
Terter II i, 1302b
Tes̲h̲rīfātd̲j̲i ii, 338b
Tétouan → Tiṭṭāwīn
Teuku Muḥammad Ḥasan i, 745a, 746a, 746b
Teuku Nja' Arif i, 745a, 746a, 746b
Teuku Panglima Pòlém Muḥammad Dāwūd i, 744a, 746a
Teungku And̲j̲ōng i, 742a
Teungku di-Kuala → ʿAbd al-Raʾūf al-Sinkilī
Teungku Muḥammad Dāwūd Bevereuʾéh i, 746a, 747a
Tewfik Bey → Ebüzziya Tevfik
Tewfik Fikret (1915) i, 287b; ii, 440a, 474b, 475a; iii, 357b; iv, 169a, 195b, 931a; vi, 93a, 614b; vii, 469a; ix, 240b; x, **422b**; s, 98a, 149b
Tewfiḳ Meḥmed ii, 474a
Tewfīḳ Pas̲h̲a → Tawfīḳ Pas̲h̲a
Tewfîq, Hacî v, 482b
Tewḳiʿī ʿAbd ul-Raḥmān Pas̲h̲a (1676) viii, 752b
Teyran, Feqiyê v, 482a
T̲h̲āʾ x, **423b**
T̲h̲aʿāliba, Banū vi, 141a
al-T̲h̲aʿālibī, ʿAbd al-ʿAzīz (1944) viii, 901a; x, **424b**
al-T̲h̲aʿālibī, ʿAbd al-Raḥmān b. Muḥammad b. Mak̲h̲lūf (1468) vi, 143a; ix, 20b; x, **425a**, 427b
al-T̲h̲aʿālibī, Abū Manṣūr ʿAbd al-Malik b. Muḥammad (1038) i, 321b, 590a, 591a, 845b, 952b, 1348b; ii, 918b; iii, 1157b; iv, 54b, 1066b; v, 619a, 1226b; vi, 109a, 340a; vii, 262a, 470a, 527b, 986a; viii, 1028b; x, 68a, **426a**; s, 119b
al-T̲h̲aʿālibī, Abū Manṣūr al-Ḥusayn al-Marg̲h̲anī (XI) ii, 133b; iii, 114a; x, **425b**
al-T̲h̲aʿālibī, al-Shayk̲h̲ (XX) v, 1161a
al-T̲h̲aʿālibī, Sīdī ʿAbd al-Raḥmān ii, 520a
T̲h̲abāba b. Salama al-D̲j̲ud̲h̲āmī iv, 494b
T̲h̲abīr (D̲j̲abal) vi, 666b; vii, 65a; viii, 383b; x, **428a**
T̲h̲ābit, ʿAlāʾ al-Dīn (1712) vi, 826b; x, **428a**
T̲h̲ābit, Banū x, 213b (see also, *s.v.* ʿAmmār, Banū)
T̲h̲ābit b. al-ʿAbbās b. Mandīl (XIII) vi, 404a, b
T̲h̲ābit b. Arḳān (VII) vii, 756b
T̲h̲ābit b. Ḳays iii, 403b
T̲h̲ābit b. Ḳurra (Ṣābiʾ) (901) i, 235b, 589b, 1100b, 1101a; iii, 166a, 228a, 1135a, 1136b, 1138b; iv, 110b, 629a, 804b, 1078b; vi, 204a, 215a, 600b; vii, 83a, 210a, 559a; viii, 558a, 560a, 672b, 677b; x, **428b**; s, 59b, 271b, 411b, 412a, 414a
T̲h̲ābit b. Ḳuṭba (Buk̲h̲ārā) (VII) ix, 250a
T̲h̲ābit b. Naṣr al-K̲h̲uzāʿī (VIII) vi, 332a, 775a
T̲h̲ābit b. Nuʿaym (VIII) vi, 623b, 624a
T̲h̲ābit b. Sinān i, 1223b, 1353b; iii, 387b, 388a
T̲h̲ābit al-Ḥaddād, Abu 'l-Miḳdād s, 129b
T̲h̲ābit Ḳuṭna, Abu l-ʿAlāʾ T̲h̲ābit b. Kaʿb D̲j̲ābir (728) vii, 606a; x, **429b**
Thabraca → Tabarka

Thaddarth iv, 359a, 361b
Thadj x, **429b**
Thaghr al-Aʿlā (Araghūn) s, 80b
al-Thaghrī, Abū ʿAbd Allāh Muḥammad b. Yūsuf (XIV) ix, 347a
al-Thaghrī, Abū Saʿīd Yūsuf b. Muḥammad al-Ṭāʾī (IX) i, 1289a; x, **430a**
al-Thaghrī, Aḥmad (XV) vi, 222b
Thailand, islam in- v, 227a; x, **430a**
al-Thāʾir fi ʾllāh, Abu l-Faḍl (961) iii, 255a; vi, 941b; x, **430b**; s, 363a
Thāʾirids s, 363a
al-Thaḳafī → Abū ʿUbayd; ʿĪsā b. ʿUmar; Ismāʿīl b. ʿAlī b. ʿUthmān
al-Thaḳafī, Ahmad b. ʿUbayd Allāh (926) vi, 829a
al-Thaḳafī, al-ʿAlāʾ b. Djāriya vii, 570b
al-Thaḳafī, Ibrāhīm b. Muḥammad (896) x, **431a**
al-Thaḳafī, al-Mughīra b. Shuʿba (VII) vi, 499a
al-Thaḳafī, Muḥammad b. Ḳāsim → Muḥammad b. Ḳāsim al-Thaḳafī
al-Thaḳafī, Tammām b. ʿĀmir (vizier) (IX) vii, 569a
al-Thaḳafī, Yūsuf b. ʿUmar b. Muḥammad (744) iii, 493b; iv, 926a, 927a; v, 374b; vi, 139b, 140a, 441b; vii, 629b; x, **431b**; s, 127a, 232b, 251b
al-Thaḳafī, Yūsuf al-Barm (VIII) vi, 618a
Thaḳafīs vi, 266a, b, 646a, 657a
Thaḳīf, Banū i, 145a, 544b; iii, 286a, 363b; v, 520b; vi, 266a, 677a; vii, 347a; x, **432a**; s, 693a
Thala s, 387a
Thaʿlab (fox) x, **432b**
Thaʿlab, Abu ʾl-ʿAbbās Aḥmad b. Yaḥyā (904) i, 321b, 485b, 590a, 718b, 971b; ii, 245b, 806b, 1093b; iii, 758a, 820b; iv, 249a; v, 320a, 351a, 607b, 1033a; vi, 348a; vii, 277a, 280a, 282a, 312b, 390b, 914a; viii, 546a; ix, 318a; s, 15b, 25a, 388a, 389b; x, 69a, **433a**
Thaʿlab, Sharīf Ḥisn al-Dīn (XIII) viii, 864b
Thaʿlaba, Banū (Sulaym) ix, 817a; x, **433b**
Thaʿlaba b. ʿUḳāba, Banū i, 962b; ii, 71b
Thaʿlaba b. Salāma al-ʿĀmilī i, 134b; ii, 1009a; iii, 602a
Thaʿlaba b. Yarbūʿ, Banū vi, 267a, b, 268a
al-Thaʿlabī, Abū Isḥāḳ Aḥmad v, 180b
al-Thaʿlabī (al-Taghlibī), Muḥammad b. al-Ḥārith (IX) x, **434a**
al-Thaʿlabī Aḥmad b. Muḥammad al-Nīshābūrī (1035) vii, 283b; s, 90b
al-Thaʿlabiyya x, **434b**; s, 198b
Thaldj, Banū x, **435a**
Thallādj x, **435a**
Thālnēr iii, 446b; vi, 51a, 127b; x, **435b**
Thamādi → al-DjarādatānI
Thamal, amīr i, 449b
al-Thamara iii, 746a
Thāmir iv, 314b
Thamisṭiyus (themistius) (388) x, **435b**
Thamūd i, 145a, 169b, 548a; iii, 366a, 1270a; v, 763a; x, **436a**
Thamudic / Thamoudeen i, 562b, 564b; vi, 349a, 373b; x, **436b**, s 506a
Thānā (town) iii, 418b; x, **438b**
Thanāʾ Allāh, Mawlānā (XIX) iii, 431b
Thanāʾī (1587) viii, 775b; x, **439a**
Thanawiyya (dualists) x, **439b**
Thānesar (Thāneswar) x, **441b**
Thānesarī, Djalāl al-Dīn Muḥammad b. Maḥmūd (1582) x, **442a**; s, 313a
Thānesarī, Mawlānā Aḥmad (1412) x, **442a**
Thānesarī, Niẓām al-Dīn (1626) ii, 55a; x, **442b**
Thānī, Āl i, 539b; ii, 177b; iv, 751b
Thaniyyat al-Aḥisa x, 959b
Thaniyyat al-ʿUḳāb vi, 544b, 545a, 778b
Thānkawālā vi, 131a
Thannuris s, 229b
Thar (desert) vi, 65b
Thaʾr x, **442b**
Thaʾrān b. Dhamarʿalī Yuhabirr vi, 563b
Thaʾrān Yuhanʿim vi, 563b
al-Tharwānī, Muḥammad b. ʿAbd al-Raḥmān iv, 1003a
Tharwat ʿUkāsha s, 6a
Thasos → Ṭashöz
Thathul (Armenian) vi, 506b
Ťhaťťhā (Sind) i, 80b; iii, 448b, 633a; vi, 189b; viii, 1047b; x, **443b**
– history x, **443b**
– monuments s, **810a**
Thawāba b. Salāma i, 135a; iii, 602a
Thawbān b. Ibrāhīm → Dhu ʾl-Nūn, Abu ʾl-Fayḍ
al-Thawr → Minṭakat al-Burūdj
Thawr b. Yazīd v, 329b

Thawra x, **444a**
al-Thawrī → Sufyān al-Thawrī
Thawriyya iv, 46a
Theodosia → Kefe
Theophrastus i, 736b, 737b; s, 59b
Therwet-i Fünūn i, 287a; ii, 439b,440a, 474b, 692b, 877b; iii, 261a; iv, 931a; v, 194b, 195b; x, **445b**
Thessaly v, 772a; vi, 58b, 290a
Thiḳa x, **446a**
Thiḳat al-Mulk Ṭāhir b. ʿAlī ix, 4a
Thimāl b. Ṣāliḥ b. Mirdās (Mirdāsid) (1062) iii, 686b, 740b; v, 924a; vii, 117a
Thomas the Slav (IX) vi, 336a
Thughūr i, 465b, 761a, b, 789b; ii, 36a, 503a; vi, 230b, 775b; x, **446b**; s, 120a
Thulā x, **449a**
Thuluth iv, 1123b, 1125a, 1127b; v, 218a; s, 586a
Thumāl (amīr) iv, 911a
Thumāma b. Ashras, Abū Maʿn al-Numayrī (828) i, 271b; ii, 386a; iii, 1266a; vii, 604a, 784b; x, **449b**; s, 48b, 89a
Thumāma b. Uthāl i, 964a; iii, 167a; vii, 664b
Thurayya (ʿAbalāt, Mecca) (VIII) ii, 1011b
al-Thurayyā (Baghdād) i, 898a
Thurayyā bint Maḥmūd Ṭarzī (1968) s, 65b
Thurayyā (Sorayya) Isfandiyārī (XX) vii, 447a
Thureyyā, Meḥmed (1909) x, **450a**
Thuwaynī b. Saʿīd b. Sulṭān (Āl Bū Saʿīd) i, 1282b; v, 1030b; x, 817a
Ṭibāḳ x, **450b**
Ṭibb ii, 1120a; x, **452a**
Ṭibbiyye-i ʿadliyye-i Shāhāne ii, 996b; s, **810b**
Tibbu → Tubu
Tibesti x, **461a**; s, 163b, 165a, 166a
Tibet → Tubbat
Ṭībīs i, 942b
Tibrīz → Tabrīz
al-Tibrīzī, Abū Zakariyyāʾ Yaḥyā (1109) i, 69a, 154b, 593a, 794a; iii, 111a; v, 930a; vi, 824a; vii, 307b, 978b; x, **461a**
Tibrīzī, Shams al-Dīn → Sabzawārī, Shams al-Dīn
al-Tidjānī (Māsina) (1887) i, 297a; ii, 941b; ix, 853a
al-Tidjānī, Abū Muḥammad ʿAbd Allāh b. Muḥammad (1311) i, 207a; ii, 552b; iv, 339b; vi, 574a, 840b; ix, 853a; x, **462a**
al-Tidjānī, Sī Aḥmad b. Maḥmūd (1815) i, 297a; ii, 941b; iii, 107b; iv, 550b; vi, 706b; vii, 263a; ix, 22b; x, **463a**
Tidjāniyya i, 297a, 315b, 371a, 1009a, 1260b; ii, 10a, 63a, 94b, 432b, 975a, 1004a; iii, 38b, 107a, 289a, 646b; iv, 549b; v, 287b; vi, 259b, 260a, 356b, 705a, 706b; vii, 620a; x, **464a**; s, 165a, 182a, 371a, 387a
Tidjāra x, **466b**
Tidjīn-Rūd s, 309b
Tidore x, **475a**; s, 199b
Tʾieh-le (Ting-Ling) x, 691b
Tʾien Wu (1784) v, 851b; x, **475b**
al-Tifāshī, Sharaf al-Dīn Aḥmad b. Yūsuf (1253) i, 419b, 1220b; ii, 93b; iv, 881b; vi, 374b; vii, 82b, 1042b; x, **476a**
Tifinagh i, 1185a; v, 221b, 222a, 754b-757b; x, **476b**
Ṭiflī Aḥmed Čelebi (1660) v, 952a; x, **478a**
Tiflīs (Tiflis/Tbilisi) i, 644a; iv, 346b, 349a, 391b; v, 487a-489b, 493a, 495a, 497a; vi, 55b, 64b, 203a; vii, 453a; x, **478b**; s, 47a, 275a
Tiflīsī, Abu ʾl-Faḍl Ḥubaysh iv, 525b
al-Tiflīsī, Abū ʿImrān iv, 604a
al-Ṭighnārī, Abū ʿAbd Allāh (XII) ii, 901b; vii, 201a, 203b; x, **479b**
Tīghnīt vi, 201a
Tighremt i, 1321b
Tigin (Takīn) x, **480b**
Tigīnābād iv, 536b
Tigre (Tigrinya) ii, 709b; iii, 6a, 7b
Tigris (river) → Didjla
al-Tih (Faḥṣ al-Tīḥ) x, **480b**
Tihāma i, 536b, 539a; ii, 1025a; v, 808a, 809a, 1244a, b; vi, 35b, 191b; ix, 815b; s, 22b, 236a, 335a; x, **481a**
al-Tihāmī, Abu ʾl-Ḥasan (1025) vi, 626b; x, **482b**
Tihbat-i khurd → Baltistān
Tihran (Iṣfahān) x, **496a**
Tihrān (Teheran) i, 978a, 1088b; ii, 426a; iv, 7b, 391a; v, 876a; vi, 19b, 20b, 277a, 366a, 484b, 493a, 495b, 528b; x, **482b**; s, 23b, 41a, 73a, 142a, 291a, 423a
Ṭihrānī, Āghā Buzurg (1970) x, **496a**

Ṭihrānī, Ḥadjdjī Mīrzā Ḥusayn Khalīlī (1908) vi, 553a;x, **497b**; s, 95b
Tik Wa-Tum x, **498a**
Tikiya-yi Dawlat vi, 485a
Tikla b. Hazārasp v, 826b
Tikrīt → Takrīt
Tilangāna vi, 68a
Tilangānī, Khān-i Djahān Maḳbūl (1368) iv, 907b; vii, 795b
Tilimsān (Tlemcen) i, 92a, 93a, 122b, 124b, 155a, 168a, 367a, 678b; ii, 173a, 1008a; iii, 251a, 339b, 470a, 1041a, 1042b; v, 518a, 1175a, 1179a; vi, 141a, b, 142a, 187a, 249a, 281a, 311b, 404a, b, 405b, 427a, 440b, 441a, 572a, 573a, 592a, 593a, b, 681b; ix, 20b; s, 29a, 145a, 376b, 403a; x, **498b**
– literature iii, 832a, 865b
– monuments i, 499b; iii, 144a; v, 290a, 1151b
al-Tilimsānī → al-Sharīf
al-Tilimsānī, ʿAbd Allāh b. Muḥammad, Sharīf (1390) ix, **346b**
al-Tilimsānī, Abu ʾl-ʿAbbās Aḥmad (1490) ix, **347a**
al-Tilimsānī, Abū ʿAbd Allāh al-Sharīf (1369) ix, 364b (see also, *s.v.* al-Tilimsānī, Muḥammad b. Aḥmad, Sharīf)
al-Tilimsānī, Abu ʾl-Faradj (1463) ix, **347a**
al-Tilimsānī, Abū Yaḥyā , Sharīf (1423) ix, **346b**
al-Tilimsānī, ʿAfīf al-Dīn (XIII) i, 569a; viii, 13b, 753a; x, 500a
al-Tilimsānī, Ibn Saʿd (XVI) ix, 20b
al-Tilimsānī, Ibn Zāghū Aḥmad b. Muḥammad (1441) x, **491b**
al-Tilimsānī, Ibrāhīm b. abī Bakr (1291) x, **500a**
al-Tilimsānī, Muḥammad b. Aḥmad, Sharīf (1369) ix, **343b** (see also, *s.v.* al-Tilimsānī, Abū ʿAbd Allāh al-Sharīf)
al-Tilimsānī, Muḥammad b. Sulaymān (1289) x, **500a**
al-Tilimsānī, Sulaymān b. ʿAlī (1291) x, **500a**
Tilsam x, **500a**
Tīlūtān (Tayalūthān) (837) vii, 613a
Tīmār i, 652b, 654a, 655b, 656b, 999b, 1147b, 1264a, 1266b; ii, 32b, 33b, 82a, 147a, b; iii, 284b, 1089a; iv, 1094b; v, 249a, 880b, 881a; x, **502a**; s, 238b
Timāwī b. Ayyūb al-Millī (1838) vi, 541b
Timbuktu → Tinbuktū
Timimoun s, 328a, b
Tīmi̊shwār → Temeshwār
Ṭimm s, 135b
Timnaʿ i, 1132b; iv, 746b, 747a; vi, 88b, 559a, 560b
Timothy I (patriarch) (XIII) x, 17b, 227a, 374a
Timsāḥ (lake) x, **510b**
Timthāl → Ṣanam
Tīmūr Lang (Tīmūrid) (1405) i, 66b, 227a, 237a, 244a, 311b, 468a, 470a, 530b, 721b, 852b, 903b, 999a, 1046a, 1051a, 1107b, 1119a; ii, 45a, 86b, 120b, 204b, 239b, 270a, 285b, 697a, 781b, 990a; iii, 187b, 189b, 198a, 199b,417a, 827b, 1100b; iv, 32b-33a, 102b, 349b, 410a, 586a, 670a, 871a, 1104b; v, 182a, 457a, 491b, 858b; vi, 16a, 49b, 50a, 61b, 202a, 231b, 273b, 294b, 309b, 324a, 381b, 406b, 417b, 483a, 493a, 494b, 502b, 512a, b, 515b, 524b, 525a, 537a, 540b, 541a, 692b, 974a; vii, 171b, 172a, 498a, 644a, 666a, 710b, 821a; viii, 193a; ix, 46a. 597a; x, 44b, 510b, 560b, 593a, 898a; s, 49a, 94b, 242a, 327a
– literature ii, 591b; iii, 58a, 274a, 711b
Tīmūr Malik b. Urus Khān (XIV) x, 561a
Tīmūr Pasha Khān b. ʿAlī Khān Bayat (1895) vi, 203a
Tīmūr Shāh Durrānī (1793) i, 230a, b, 296a, 970b; ii, 186a, 628b, 952a; iii, 1158b; vi, 715a
Tīmūrbughā (Timurbughā), al-Ẓāhir (Mamlūk) (1468) iv, 462b; vi, 329a
Tīmūrbughā al-Afḍalī Minṭāsh (XIV) vi, 548a, 580b; vii, 170b, 462a; viii, 987b
Tīmūrids i, 135a, 147b, 227a, b, 1001b; ii, 45b, 309a, 334a, 792a; iii, 483b, 1256b; iv, 33a, 66a, 350a; v, 59a, 824b; vi, 17b, 366a, 483a, 515b, 521b, 522b, 524b, 557b; vii, 90a, 170b, 193b; 462a; viii, 987b; s, 71a, 138b, 227b, 256a, b, 313a; x, **513a**
– history iv, 914b; s, 96b
Tīmūrtāsh b. Amīr Čūbān (1328) i, 468a, 703a; ii, 68a, 706a; iv, 622a; vi, 315b, 372a
Tīmūrtāsh b. Ḳara ʿAlī Beg (1404) i, 738b, 1159b, 1302b; ii, 722a; x, 528a
Timurtāsh b. Nadjm al-Dīn Il-Ghāzī I

(Artuḳid) (1154) i, 664b; vi, 380a, 544a, 871b, 930b; x, **527a**
Tīmūrtāsh Oghullarî x, **528a**
Timzought → Tīmzūghat
Tīmzūghat vi, 405a
Tīn x, **529a**
Ṭīn x, **529b**
Ṭīna x, **530a**
al-Tinbuktī → Aḥmad Bābā
Tinbuktū (Timbuktu) i, 35a, 280a; ii, 252a; v, 394a; vi, 258b, 259a, b, 281b, 364b, 421b, 589b; viii, 718b; ix, 756b, 757a; x, **508a**; xi, 122b; s, 29a, 295b
Tindarma vii, 394a
Tindi, Banū i, 504a; iv, 630b
Tindūf (Tindouf) x, **530b**
Tinerkouk s, 328b
Tingitana v, 1188b; vi, 591b
Tingiz s, 195b
Tīnkalūs → Tankalūshā al-Bābilī
Tinmal, Tinmallal i, 459a; iii, 207b, 959a; vi, 592b, 682a, 742a, 743b; x, **530b**
Tinnīn (Draco) x, **531a**; s, 191a
Tinnīs ii, 72b; vii, 69b; x, **531b**
Tippu Tip → al-Murdjibī
Tipū Mastān Awliyā i, 625a
Tīpū Sulṭān (1799) i, 625a, 1015b; ii, 220a; iii, 119b, 316b, 322a; iv, 547b; v, 648a, 884b, 886a, 1259a, 1260a, b; vi, 459b, 735a; x, **532b**
Ṭīra ii, 758b, 759b, 760a, 1097a; iv, 290b
Tirāh i, 238a, b
Tirāhi i, 237b
Tīrān → Tihrān II
Tirana → Tiran
Tirān/a, Straits of x, **533a**; s, 8b
Ṭirāz i, 501a; ii, 301b, 302a; iii, 218a, 219a; v, 498b, 736b, 857a; x, **534b**; s, 144a, 341a
al-Ṭirāz iii, 863a
Tīre (Tire) x, **538b**
Tirebolu x, **539a**
Tirḥāla (Trik(k)ala) x, **539b**
al-Tīrhānī, Abu 'l-Ḥasan b. Bahlūl i, 737b
Tirhut (Bihar) x, **540b**; s, 409a
al-Ṭirimmāḥ b. ʿAdī b. ʿAbd Allāh al-Djubayrī (al-Ṭirimmāḥ al-Akbar) (VII) i, 1011a; vii, 402a; x, **541a**
al-Ṭirimmāḥ b. Djahm al-Ṭāʾī al-Sinbist x, **541a**
al-Ṭirimmāḥ al-Akbar (Kaʿkaʿ b. Nafr / Ibn Ḳays al-Ṭāʾī) (VII) x, **541a**
Tīris al-Gharbiyya vii, 625b
Tirmidh (Termez) ii, 1a, 4b, 43a; vi, 273b, 764b; x, **542b**
al-Tirmidhī, Abū ʿAbd Allāh Muḥammad b. ʿAlī al-Ḥakīm (936) x, 314b, **544a**
al-Tirmidhī, Abu 'l-Ḥasan ʿAlī al-Muzayyin (939) viii, 840b
al-Tirmidhī, Abū ʿĪsā Muḥammad b. ʿĪsā b. Sawra (892) i, 114b; iii, 24a, 25a, 27b, 707a; vi, 351a; viii, 123a, 516a; x, **546b**; s, 232b
al-Tirmidhī, Muḥammad b. ʿAlī al-Ḥakīm (X) viii, 404a
al-Tirmidhī,Sayyid Burhān al-Dīn Ḥusayn Muḥaḳḳikī (1240) x, **546b**
Tîrnowa (Tarnovo) x, **547a**
Ṭirs → raḳḳ I
Tīryākī Ḥasan Pasha (XVI) i, 267b; iv, 546b, 878a; ix, 557b
Tirza vi, 384b
Tishrīn x, **548a**
Tīshīt (Mauritania) vii, 624b
al-Tīshītī, Abū ʿAbd Allāh Muḥammad (1711) vii, 625a
Tīṭ (Tīṭt an Fiṭr/ʿAyn al-Fiṭr) vi, 741b; x, **548a**
Tiṭarī, Ṭiṭerī i, 368a, 699b; vi, 141a, 405a, 728a
Tiṭṭāwīn (Tetouan) vi, 39a, 40a, 293a, b, 294a, 574a; vii, 391b; x, **549a**
Tītū Mīr/Miyān, Sayyid Mīr Nithār ʿAlī (1831) vii, 291a; x, **580a**
Tivaouane s, 182a
Tiyāhā, Banū vii, 921a
Tiyek s, 171b, 172a
Tiyūl (Tuyūl) ii, 150b, 152a, 153a; v, 244b; x, **550b**
Tiyūywīn s, 402b
Tīz vi, 193a
Tīzī n'Maʿshū s, 48a
Tizi n-Test vi, 743b
Tizi Ouzou iv, 359b
Tizi-Telwet vi, 742a
Tīznīt vii, 583b; ix, 900b; s, 47b, 48a; x, **551a**
Tlemcen → Tilimsān
Tobacco Régie Concession vi, 20b, 485a, b; viii, 140a; ix, 479b; s, 71b, 77a, 104a
Tobiah b. Moses iv, 605b

Tobīrčiḳoghlū Ḳayib Khān → Ḳayib Khān
Tobna → Ṭubna
Tobol (river) x, **511b**
Tobol Tatar x, 551b
Toči vi, 86a
Tōdar Mal, Rādjā (Gudjarāt) (1589) ii, 156a, 183b; iii, 457b; vii, 131a, 134b; x, **552a**
Ṭodgha vi, 590b
Togan, Zekī Welīdī i, 1077a; ii, 700b
Togha, Temür Cīl-Khān (1353) x, **552a**
Ṭoghan Khān (Balāsāghūn) (XI) i, 987a
Toghdî beg (1033) vi, 853b
Toghluk → Tughluk
Toghril x, **552b**
Ṭoghrîl I (Ṭughril Beg) (Saldjūḳ) (1063) (Great Saldjūn) i, 20b, 132a, 420a, 512b, 513a, 627a, 839b, 900b, 1073b, 1074b, 1075a, 1336b, 1356a; ii, 4b, 5a, 192b, 348b, 680b, 855b, 856a, 1051a, 1108b; iii, 159b, 344b, 345b,471b, 891b, 1098b; iv, 25a, 26b-27a, 101a, 347b, 457b, 458a, 465b, 942a; v, 388a, b, 623a; vi, 64a, 242b, 272b, 274b, 482a, 500a, 521b, 523a, b, 626b, 847b, 966a; vii, 193a, 271a, 983a, 1017a, b; viii, 63b, 69b, 938b; x, **553a**; s, 14b, 29b, 192a, 195a
Ṭoghrîl II, Rukn al-Dīn b. Muḥammad b. Malik-Shāh (Saldjūḳ) (1134) i, 300b; iii, 196b; iv, 860a, vi, 64a, b, 782a, 809b; vii, 733b, 734a; viii, 943b; x, **554a**; s, 416a
Ṭoghrîl III b. Arslān, Rukn al-Dīn (Saldjūḳ) (1194) ii, 894a; iii, 1111a, b; iv, 948b, 1067b; vii, 997a; viii, 64a, 78a, 239b, 944a, b; x, **554b**; s, 378b, 416a
Ṭoghrîl b. Sonḳur Ḳuṭb al-Dīn (Salghurid) (1181) viii, 978b
Ṭoghrîl Shāh b. Ḳîlîdj Arslan II (Rūm Saldjūḳ) (1225) x, **555a**
Ṭoghrîl-tigin b. Ekinči b. Ḳočḳar (XII) vi, 415b; s, 279a
Toghuzghuz i, 1240a; x, **555b**, 687b, 691b
Togo-Islam in iv, 351b; vi, 281b; x, **557b**
Tohāna x, 98a
Tok Kenali (1933) viii, 286a
Tokar → Tūkar
Toḳat (Tokat) iii, 212b; v, 557b; x, **558b**
Tokat Köshkü vi, 57a
Toḳay Tīmūr b. Djoči b. Čingīa Khhān x, 560b
Toker, Samuel (XVII) x, 214a
Tokhma Ṣuyu vi, 232a
Tokhtu Khān ii, 610b
Toḳmaḳ ii, 67b; x, **560a**
Tokolors → Tukulors
Toḳtamîsh Girāy (Cremea) (1608) ii, 1047a, 1113b; iv, 1064a; v, 765b
Toḳtamîsh Khān, Ghiyāth al-Dīn (Batuʾid) (1395) i, 1107b; ii, 44a, b, 86b, 1112a; vi, 417b
Toḳtamîsh (Tokhtamîsh) Khān (Golden horde) (1406) x, 511a, **560b**
Toḳtoʾa ii, 42b
Toḳūḳān (Toghon) Abū Mangū-Tīmūr (Batuʾid) (XIII) vi, 419b
Töküsh i, 664a
Tōlā x, **563b**
Tolba → Sulṭān al-Ṭalaba
Toledo → Ṭulayṭula
Tolobey i, 808b
Toluy b. Čingiz Khān (1332) i, 227a, 1105a; ii, 43b, 45b; iv, 542b; vi, 621a; x, **564a**
Tomārā vi, 49a
Tomaševič, Stjepan (XV) vi, 71a
Tombalabaye, François s, 166a, b
Tombouctou → Tinbuktū
Tong Yabgu (western Türk) (630) x, 687b
Tonguç, Ismail Hakki (1960) v, 281b, 282a, b; s, **811b**
Tonk i, 444a, 1195b; x, **564b**
Ṭoñuzlu → Deñizli
Tonyukuk (691) x, 687b
Ṭop x, **564b**
Ṭop ʿArabadjîlarî i, 1061b
Ṭopal Meḥmed Pasha v, 257b, 764a
Ṭopal ʿOthmān Pasha (1733) i, 292a; v, 144b, 461b, 494a; vii, 853b; x, **564b**
Ṭopal ʿOthmān Pasha (1874) i, 1268b, 1272a; x, **565b**
Topal Redjeb Pasha (1632) vii, 598a
Topčîbashî, ʿAlī Merdān s, 47a
Ṭopdju → Ṭop
Ṭopdjular i, 1061b
Ṭopḳapî Sarāyî i, 836b, 1091a; ii, 694b, 996b; iv, 231b, 232b, 233a, 368a; v, 67a, b, 274a; vi, 198b; ix, 46b; x, **566a**
Ṭopkhāne i, 1061b; ii, 129b, 513a; iv, 233a; vi, 57a; s, 314b, 315b
Ṭopraḳ Ḳalʿe → Athūr
Ṭōr → al-Ṭūr
Torah → al-Tawrāt

Ṭorānī (dialect) vi, 542a
Töregene ii, 45b; vi, 482b; x, **569a**
Torghud ʿAlī (1565) x, 213
Torghud Banū x, **569b**
Torghud (commander) (XIV) x, **570a**
Torghud Eli x, **570b**
Torghud Reʾīs (1565) x, **570b**
Torī Khēl s, 285a
Torlaḳ Hū Kemāl i, 869b
Toros (Taurus mts.) i, 463a; ii, 35a; x, **571a**
Tortum s, 308a
Tosḳ i, 650a, 651a
Touareg → Ṭawāriḳ
Touareg (language) i, 792a, 1180b, 1182a, b, 1183a, b, 1185a
Touat → Tuwāt
Touba → Ṭūbā
Touggourt → Tuggurt
Tourkopo(u)loi (turcoples) x, **571b**
Tozeur → Tūzar
Trabzon → Tarabzun
Trabzonlu Hüseyn Rüshdī Pasha ii, 200a
Trahgām s, 167a
Tralleis → Aydi̊n
Transcaspia vi, 716b
Transcaucasia iv, 349a, b; v, 440a, 495b, 496b
Transjordan → al-Urdunn
Transoxania s, 816a (see also, *s.v.* Mā Warāʾ al-Nahr)
Transylvania → Erdel
Trāra i, 372a; v, 379a
Travnik (Bosnia) i, 1270b; x, **572b**
Trebizond → Tarabzun
Trengganu → Terengganu
Trengganu (Demak) (1546) → Terengganu (Demak) (1546)
Trengganu Stone → Terengganu Stone
Trestenik-oghlu Ismāʿīl → Ismāʿīl Bey (Serez)
Tribeni (Fīrūzābād) vi, 693a; x, **574a**
Tritočanpāl vi, 65b
Tripoli (Lībiya) → Ṭarābulus al-gharb
Tripolis → Ṭarābulus al-shām
Tripolitania i, 134b, 139a, 1071a; ii, 595a; iii, 296b, 654b, 655a, 1040a; iv, 617a, 919b; v, 758a, b, 759b, 760a, 1182a; vi, 248a, 310b, 312a, 361a, 945b
Troc → Muʿāwada
Troki iv, 608a, b
Trucial Coast → Sāḥil al-Imārāt al-ʿArabiyya al-Muttaḥida; ʿUmān
Trucial States → al-Imārāt al-ʿArabiyya al-Muttaḥida
Ṭrūd, Banū ix, 763b
Truna Jaya v, 1155a, b
Tskhum → Sukhum
Tsakhur x, **574b**
Tu Wen-Hsiu (1873) x, **574b**
Tualtae i, 354a
Tuʿām → al-Buraymī
Tuan Guru → Abdullah Kadi Abdus Salaam
Tuanku Imam Bonjol (Padri) (XIX) viii, 238b
Tuanku Maḥmūd i, 745b
Tuanku Radja Keumala i, 745a
Tuāreg → Ṭawāriḳ
Ṭūb v, 585b
Ṭūbā (Touba) x, **575a**; s, 182a
Ṭūbā Azimūda, Mrs. (XX) vi, 485b
Tubal b. Lamak ii, 620a; x, 32b
Tuban s, 201b
Tubbaʿ (Tabābiʿa) iii, 882a; viii, 979a; x, **575b**
Tubbat (Tibbat, Tibat) (Tibet) i, 71a, 1004b; x, **576a**
Tuberon, Ludovik Crijevic s, 185b
Ṭubna (Tobna) i, 125a, 1246b; iii, 1041b; vi, 311b, 312a, 727b; ix, 768b; x, **580a**
Tubu (Tūbū, Tibesti) i, 1258a; x, **580b**
Tūda iii, 529a, b, 530a
Tudeh party iv, 40b-41a, 41b, 790a; vii, 446b; s, 60b
Tudela → Tuṭīla
Tūdjī vi, 511a, b
Tudjīb, Banū (Tudjībīds) iii, 816a; iv, 478a, 713a; v, 119b, 120a, 683a; vi, 344b; x, **582b;** s, 80b, 82a
al-Tudjībī, ʿAbd Allāh b. Masʿūd (VIII) iii, 653b
al-Tudjībī, ʿAlam al-Dīn (1329) x, **584b**
al-Tudjībī, ʿAtīḳ (1030) vi, 353b
al-Tudjībī, al-Ḥasan b. Muḥammad b. al-Ḥusayn (XI) vii, 413a
al-Tudjībī, Muḥammad b. Hāshim (938) vi, 852a; vii, 248b
al-Tudjībī, Sulaym b. ʿItr (ḳāṣṣ, ḳāḍī) (VII) vi, 657b
al-Tudjībī, Sulaymān b. Khalaf (1081) vii, 537b

Tudjībīds → Tudjīb, Banū
Tūdjīn, Banū (Dynasty) i, 122b, 167b; vi, 404a; xi, 146a
Tudmīr (Murcia) vi, 576b; vii, 633a; x, **585a**
Tudmīr b. ʿAbdūs i, 58b; iii, 706a; iv, 672b; s, 81b
Tufāl Khān Dakhnī ii, 815a; iii, 425a, 1161a
Tufang i, 1066a, 1068a, b
Tufangčī i, 8a, 1068a, 1256b
Tufangčī-āķāsī iv, 36b; vi, 525b
Ṭufayl b. ʿAwf al-Ghanawī (ca. 608) i, 115b, 772a; ii, 1005a; x, **586a**
Ṭufaylī x, **586b**
Ṭufaylī, Abū Saʿīd ʿUthmān (IX) x, **587a**
Tuffāḥ x, **587a**
al-Ṭūfī, Nadjm al-Dīn (1316) x, **588a**
Tūfīķ iv, 359a
Tuggurt (Touggourt) x, **589a**
Tugh iii, 191b; v, 766b; x, **590a**
Ṭughā Tīmūr (Čaghatayid) (1291) ii, 3b, 44a, 401a; v, 663a; vi, 502b
Tughalčin iii, 417b
Ṭughān (amīr) (XV) vi, 667b
Tūghān b. Malik Ayāz (Diū) (XVI) ii, 322a
Tughān Arslān (Bidlīs) (1138) ii, 680b, 764b
Ṭughān Shāh Abū Bakr b. Alp Arslan II (Saldjūķ, Harāt) (1185) i, 827a; ii, 552a; viii, 63b, 970b
Tughāy (XIV) vii, 412b
Tughay Tīmūr (Čaghatayid) (1291) vi, 502b; ix, 48a
Ṭughdj b. Djuff b. Balakīn (922) ii, 281b; iv, 493b; s, **812a**
Tughluķ, Fīrūz v, 685b
Tughluķ, Malik → Ghīyath al-Dīn Tughluķ I
Tughluķ Shah → Ghiyāth al-Dīn Tughluķ I
Tughluķ Temür (Čaghatayid) (1363) ii, 45a, 622a; iv, 32b; ix, 649a; x, **590b**
Tughluķābād i, 1322a; ii, 257b, 262a; iii, 441b, 481b; v, 888a, 1215a; vi, 126a
Tughluķids (Delhi) v, 884a; vi, 198b, 369a, 488a, 692a; vii, 193b; x, **591a**; s, 206b
Ṭughrā ii, 310a, 311b, 314b, 804a, b; iv, 796b, 1104b; v, 232b; x, **595a**
Ṭughrā, Mullā (1667) x, **598b**
al-Ṭughrāʾī, Abū Ismāʿīl al-Ḥusayn s, 326b
al-Ṭughrāʾī, Muʾayyid al-Dīn al-Ḥasan (al-Ḥusayn) b. ʿAlī al-Iṣfahānī (1121) i, 206b; iii, 1264b; v, 112a, 114a; vi, 64a, 275b, 606a; viii, 971a; x, **599a**
Ṭughrïl-Arslan (Malaṭya) (XII) i, 983a; ii, 110b
Ṭughrïl Birār i, 1130b; ii, 1052a
Ṭughrïl Khān (Bengal governor) s, 124a
Ṭughrïl Khān (Ķarakhānid) i, 987a
Ṭughrïl Khān (Kereyt) → Ong Khān
Ṭughshāda i, 1293b
Ṭughtakīn → Ṭughtigīn
Ṭughtigīn (Ṭughtakīn), Ẓahīr al-Dīn Atabeg (Būrid) (1128) iii, 398b; vi, 547a, 578a, 789b; vii, 461b, 578b; viii, 947a, 999b; x, **600a**
Ṭughtigīn (Ṭughtakīn), Sayf al-Dīn (Ayyūbid) (XII) vii, 579b
Tuhāmī Glawi, al-Ḥādjdj (Marrakesh) (XX) vii, 416b, 417a
Tuhāmī Ḥabābū vii, 415a
Tuhāmī al-Madgharī (1856) vi, 249a, 250b, 253a
Tukal Bogha ii, 610b
Ṭūķān iv, 834b
Tūkar iv, 680b, 687a
Tukarōʾī iii, 202b; x, **600b**
al-Tuķatī (1495) vii, 537a
Ṭukhāristān i, 852a; vi, 273b; vii, 477b; x, **600b**; s, 125a
al-Tukhāwī, Muḥammad Aḥmad s, 371a
al-Tukhāwiyya s, 371a
Ṭūkhī, ʿAbd Allāh v, 190a
Tukhorghan → Dih-i Khwāraķān
Tukos the Babylonian → Tankalūshā al-Bābilī
Tuktamīr (892) vi, 900a
Tukulor x, **602a**
Tūlak (Khurasān) s, 66b
Ṭulaķāʾ (Sing. Ṭalīķ) x, **603a**
Tūlakī, Malik Ḍiyā al-Dīn i, 1194a
al-Tūlawī → Buṭrus
Ṭulayḥa b. Khuwaylid al-Asadī (642) i, 110b, 683b, 1358b; iv, 385b, 858b; x, **603a**
Ṭulayṭula (Toledo) i, 6b, 7a, 82b, 83a, 242b, 493a; iii, 12a, 74a, 702a; vii, 778b; x, **604a** 849a, b; s, 23a
al-Ṭulayṭulī, Abu ʾl-Ḥasan (X) x, **607b**
Ṭulb iii, 185b; x, **608a**
Tulband x, **608a**

Ṭulkarm x, **615b**
Tulsī Dās iii, 457a
Ṭulumbadjî i, 270a; iv, 234b, 237b; vi, 57a; x, **616a**
Ṭūlūnids i, 14b, 18b, 278a, 435b, 439b, 1346a; ii, 36b, 281b; vi, 373a; x, **616b**; s, 120b
Tulūy → Toluy
Ṭuʿma, Ilyās, Abū Faḍl (XX) x, **618b**
Tūmān x, **619a**
Tūmān, Amīr iv, 578a
Ṭūmān Bay, al-ʿĀdil Sayf al-Dīn (Mamlūk) (1501) iv, 552a
Ṭūmān Bay, al-Ashraf (Mamlūk) (1517) i, 779a; ii, 172b, 1042a; iii, 188a, 813a; iv, 552a, 553a; vi, 325a; vii, 174a, 176b; x, **621b**
Ṭūmār iv, 742a; v, 873b
Tūmārī i, 260b
Tumbāk → Tutun
Tumbatu x, **622a**
Tumbine Khān (Mongol) vi, 417b
Tümen x, **622b**
Tūn (Ḳūhistān) v, 355a; x, **623a**
Tun Abdul Razak (XX) vi, 241b
Ṭuna x, **623b**
Tunakābun vi, 936a
Tunb, Greater and Lesser iv, 778a, b; vii, 449b; viii, 435a; s, 417b; x, **624b**
al-Tunbudhī → Manṣūr b. Naṣr al-Tunbudhī
Tunbūr x, **624b**
Tunceli → Tundjeli
Tundjeli (Tunceli) ii, 208a; v, 465a; x, **628a**
Tundjur, Banū i, 1258a; ii, 122a; iv, 541a; xi, 11a; s, 164a
Tunganistan v, 846b; x, **628b**
Tungans x, **629a**
Tunggang Parangan, Tuan s, 151a
al-Tūnī, ʿAbd al-Muʾmin b. Khalaf al-Dimyāṭī (1306) ii, **292b**
Tūnī, Ḳuṭb al-Dīn, Ḥaydar (1426) x, 251a
Tūnis i, 86b, 163b, 248b, 281b, 1225a; ii, 130a, 189b, 1008b; iii, 94b, 145a, 605a; v, 1127b, 1151a; vi, 404b, 573a, 676b; s, 133b, 145a; x, **629b**
al-Tūnisī (1051) vi, 279a
al-Tūnisī, Maḥmūd Bayram (1961) x, **639b**
al-Tūnisī, Muḥammad b. ʿUmar (1857) ii, 122b, 827b; x, **640a**
al-Tūnisī, Shaykh Zayn al-ʿĀbidīn (XIX) x, **644b**
Tunisia i, 18a, 19a, 34b, 35a, 37a, 79a, 171a, 977a, 1177a, 1321a; ii, 413a, 526a, 595a, 638b, 676a, 748a; iii, 297a, 384b, 395b, 561b, 563a, b, 605a, 635b, 683b, 684a, 927b; iv, 175a, 262b, 403a, 824b, 954b, 1157a; v, 59b, 696a, 915a, 1067b; vi, 58b, 60b, 248a, 251b, 467b, 840a, 946b, 1043b; viii, 60b, 794b, 900b; x, **641a**; s, 11a, 215b, 254b
– demography s, 215b
– institutions ii, 425a, 436a; iii, 524a
– language, literature ii, 470a
– population v, 1181b
Tūnk iv, 213a
Tūnkath vi, 557b; s, 411a
Tunku Abdul Rahman (XX) vi, 241a, b, 242a
Tunocain s, 507a
Tunukābun vi, 513a, b, 514b
al-Tūnusī → Khayr al-Dīn
al-Tūnusī, Muḥammad b. ʿUmar (XIX) → al-Tūnisī, Muḥammad b. ʿUmar (XIX)
Tūpčiyān i, 1066a, 1068a, b, 1069a
Tüp-Karagan, cape vi, 417a
al-Ṭūr (Ṭōr) vi, 195a; viii, 865a; x, **663a**
Tur, ʿAbd al-Raḥmān Aḥmad (Somalia) ix, 722b
Ṭūr ʿAbdīn vi, 539b, 540a, 542a; x, **655a**
Tura Khāns i, 135a, 1075b
Turaba → Taraba
Ṭurābāy, Banū ii, 912a; vi, 543b
Turakhān Beg (1456) vii, 237a; x, **670b**
Ṭūrān (Tūrān) i, 236a; v, 314b; vi, 193a, 492a; x, **672a**
Tūrān-čar (Turīsha) s, 299a
Turanism viii, 250a
Ṭūrān (Ḳuṣdār) x, **679b**
Tūrān-Shāh I b. Ḳāwurd (Saldjūḳ, Kirmān) (1097) vi, 273b
Tūrān Shāh II b. Toghrïl (Saldjūḳ) (Kirmān) (1183) v, 160a, b
Tūrānshāh of Hurmuz (XIV) i, 942b
Tūrānshāh b. Ayyūb, al-Malik al-Muʿaẓẓam (Ayyūbid) (1180) Shams al-Dīn Tūrān-Shāh x, **673a**
al-Ṭurayf ii, 320b, 321a

Turayḥīb b. Bandar b. Shuḳayr iv, 680b, 681a
Turba x, **673b**
Turban → Tulband
Turbatī, Khwādjā Abu 'l-Ḥasan (1633) viii, 851b
Turbat-i Ḥaydarī vi, 495b; xi, 463a
Turbat-i Shaykh-i Djām i, 283a; iii, 1125a; x, **675b**; s, 41a, 367b
Türbe → Turba
Turcoman → Türkmen
Turcopoloi ix, 268a
Ṭurfa Āl al-Shaykh s, 305b
Turfān (Turpan) ii, 45b; iv, 529a; vi, 768a; x, **675b**; s, 136b
Turgay x, **677b**
Türgesh, Banū i, 684b; iii, 224a; iv, 583b; v, 854a, b, 855b; ix, 413a; x, 687b, 689a
Ṭūrghūd ʿAlī Pasha ii, 459b, 461a; iii, 69b; iv, 416a, 656b, 828a; v, 504a, 1247a
Turghut Oghlu Ḥasan Beg iv, 624a
Tūrī, Banū v, 501b
al-Ṭūrī, Muḥammad b. ʿAlī iii, 901b
Turīsha → Tūrān-čar
Turk, Atrāk vi, 316a
al-Turk, Niḳūlā b. Yūsuf b. Nāṣīf (ca. 1828) x, **678b**
Türk Odjaghi̊ (Odjaklari̊) ii, 431a, 432a; iv, 791a, 933b; x, **678a**; s, 47b
Türk Yurdu → Maḳāla.3
Turk b. Yāfit iv, 914b
Turkān Āḳā (Tīmūrid) (1383) viii, 1035a
Turkān Khātūn → Terken
Turkče Bilmez i, 709b; v, 391a, 808a
Türkčülük v, 264a
Türkeli → Avsha
Türkeş, Alparslan (XX) iv, 791b; viii, 251b
Turkey i, 13b, 37b, 39a, 62b, 74b, 238b, 281b, 462a, 734a, 871a, 972b; ii, 594b, 595a, 640a, 966b; iii, 213b; iv, 1b, 790b; v, 464b, 505a; vi, 366a, 470a, 496b, 757a, 799a, 809a, 826a; vii, 13a, 70b, 76a; x, **693b**; s, 214a
– demography s, 214a
– education v, 906a, 1099b
– ethnography v, 439b, 750b
– institutions i, 972b, 1225b; ii, 425b, 429b, 708b; iii, 526a; iv, 167b; v, 1037b
– languages ii, 473b; iii, 373b, 1115b; iv, 699b, 715a, 853b; v, 193a, 223b, 538a, 1100a, 1101a
Ṭurkhān Sulṭān (Tarkhān) (1683) iv, 233b; v, 273a; x, **679a**; xi, 131a; s, 257b
Ṭurkhān-oghlu ʿÖmer Beg (XV) v, 772a; vi, 71b
Turkhān-oghullari̊ i, 340b
Turkī b. ʿAbd Allāh b. Suʿūd (Āl Suʿūd) (1834) i, 554b; ii, 176b, 321b; iv, 765a, 953a, 1073a; vii, 782b; ix, 904a
Turkī b. Fayṣal b. ʿAbd al-ʿAzīz (Āl Suʿūd) (XX) vi, 158a; s, 305b
Turkī b. Saʿīd (Bū Saʿīd) (1888) i, 1283a; v, 183b, 1030b; s, 356a
Turkistān i, 36a, 72b, 147b, 223b; ii, 477a; iv, 175a; 792a; v, 858a, 859a; vi, 483b; x, **679a**; s, 51b, 66a, 125a, 143b, 240a
Turkistanis vii, 353a
Türkiye Büyük Millet Meclisi v, 1037b, 1040a
Türkiye Işçi Partisi iv, 124b
Türkiye Ishči ve Čiftči Sosyalist Fi̊rkasi̊ iv, 123b, 124a
Türkiye Komünist Partisi iv, 124a
Türkiye Sosyalist Fi̊rḳasi̊ iv, 123b, 124b
Türkmen i, 4a, 120b, 224a, 311a, 340a, 420b, 460a, 467a, 470b, 639a, 665b, 666b, 700b, 750b, 843b, 1133b; ii, 1108b, 1117a; iii, 1098b, 1108a, 1110a, 1256b; iv, 10a, 25b, 28b, 1065a; v, 24a, 104a, 145b; vi, 148b, 230b, 231a, 317a, 416a, b, 482a, 492b, 493b, 502b, 541a, 580b, 620b, 715a, 780b; ix, 826a; x 126b, **682a**, 698a; s, 49a, 75b, 143b, 146b, 147a, 168b, 280b
– literature x, **727b**
Türkmen Čay I (Turkomanchai) x, **685b**
Türkmen (Turghudlu) (Turcomans) vi, 71b
Turkmenistan x, **688a**; s, 838a
Türkoğlu vi, 509a
Turkomānčāy ii, 152a; iii, 1191b; iv, 38b, 394b; v, 495b; vi, 19b, 21a
Turkomānī, Shaykh Süleymān v, 173a
Turks i, 18b, 19b, 20b, 31b, 33a, 55b, 93a, 168a, 174b, 183b, 367b, 893b, 505b; ii, 601a, 980b, 1107a; iv, 671a; x, **686b**
Turks in the Dobrudja x, **699b**
Turks – folklore x, **734b**
Turks in Greece x, **699a**
Turks – history x, **687a**
Turks – language x, **701a**; s, 812b
Turks – literature x, **715a**; s, 814a
Turks – music x, **733a**
Turks outside Turkey x, **697a**

Turks – tribal history in Central Asia x, **689a**
Turks – Western Eurasia and Central Europe x, 691a
Turks in former Yugoslavia x, **697b**
Türkü x, **736a**
al-Turkumānī (amīr) (XIV) viii, 156b
al-Turkumānī, al-Madanī (1886) vi, 250b
Turla (Dnestr) vi, 56a
Turpan → Turfan
Turs → Rank; Silāḥ
Ṭurshīz (Ḳūhistān) x, **737a**; s, 149a
Ṭūrsūn Beg (XV) x, **737b**
Ṭursun Faḳīh x, **738a**
Tursun Yunus vi, 768a
al-Ṭurṭūshī, Ibn Abī Randaḳa Abū Bakr (1126) i, 594a, 602a; iv, 136b; v, 1160b; vi, 279a; vii, 986a; x, **739b**
Ṭuruf, Banū iii, 1107b; iv, 1170b; vii, 675a
Ṭuruḳ (Tanzania) x, 195b
Ṭūs v, 293b; vi, 331b, 335b, 633b, 714a, b; x, **740b**; s, 14b, 357a
Ṭūs, Malik (XIV) vi, 512a
Tushtarī, Shams al-Dīn Muḥammad i, 703b
al-Ṭūsī → ʿAlī b. ʿAbd Allāh; Asʿadī; Naṣīr al-Dīn; al-Sarrādj
al-Ṭūsī, Abu ʾl-ʿAbbās Aḥmad b. Masrūḳ (911) viii, 583b
al-Ṭūsī, Abū Djaʿfar (Shaykh al-Ṭāʾifa) (1066) iv, 711b; vi, 12a, 312b, 549a, 906a; vii, 297b, 313a, 459b, 581b, 634a; viii, 372b, 517b, 713b, 811b; x, 40a, 85a, **745a**, 935b; s, 56b, 233a
al-Ṭūsī, Abu ʾl-Ḥasan (786) vi, 821b, 822a
al-Ṭūsī ʿAlāʾ al-Dīn (1472) s, **815a**
al-Ṭūsī Ḳāniʿī, Aḥmad b. Maḥmūd iv, 504b, 1081a
Ṭūsī, Muḥammad (XI) vi, 907b
Ṭūsī, Muḥammad b. Ḥamīd (IX) viii, 53a
al-Ṭūsī, al-Muẓaffar i, 727a
al-Ṭūsī, Naṣīr al-Dīn Abū Djaʿfar Muḥammad (1274) vii, 132a; viii, 540b, 541a, 542a, 754a; x, **746a**; s, 633a
al-Ṭūsī, Sharaf al-Dīn viii, 553a
Tustar → Shushtar
al-Tustarī, Ḥasan b. Ibrāhīm b. Sahl (XI) ii, 858a
al-Tustarī, Sahl b. ʿAbd Allāh Abū Muḥammad (896) i, 1039a; ii, 858a; iii, 100a, 159a; vi, 225a, 570a, 672b; viii, 840a
Ṭūsūn (Tusun) b. Muḥammad ʿAlī Pasha (1816) iii, 362b, 999a; v, 997b; vi, 150b; vii, 424a, 425b
Tūt x, **752a**
Tutak x, **752b**
Tuṭīla iii, 816a; s, 80a, 81a, 82a; x, **752b**
al-Tuṭīlī, al-Aʿmā → al-Aʿmā al-Tuṭīlī
Tūtiyā v, 965a, 967b, 970b
Tutun x, **753a**
Tütünsüz Aḥmed Beg → Aḥmad Riḍwān
Tutush (I) b. Alp Arslān, Tādj al-Dawla (Saldjūḳ) (1095) i, 314a, 466a, 517a, 664a, 731a, 751a, 971a, 1051b, 1332a, 1349a; ii, 282a, 347b, 1039a; iii, 86b, 1118a; iv, 27b, 28b; v, 328a, 437a, 924a; vi, 274b, 379b, 540b, 546b, 930b; vii, 121b, 693a, 731a, 755a; viii, 81b, 519a, 947a; x, **756b**
Tutush b. Duḳāḳ (XII) viii, 519a
Ṭuwāna (Tyana) i, 11b, 12b; vi, 338a, 740a
Tuwāt / Twāt (Touat) i, 210b; v, 1165a, b; vi, 141a; viii, 794b; x, **757a**; s, 328a
al-Ṭuwayḳ (Tuēk) Djabal i, 536b, 628b, 747b; vii 865a; viii 575b; x, **758b**
Ṭuways, Abū ʿAbd al-Munʿim (711) ii, 620b, 1073b; iii, 878b; x, **759a**; s, 183a
Tuyūl iv, 1044a, 1045b; x, **550b**
Tuz Gölü x, **759b**
Tūzar (Touzeur) ii, 463a, 464a; iv, 740a; vii, 897a; x, **759b**
Ṭuzdju-oghullari̊ viii, 567a
Tūzīn, Banū s, 113b
Tūzūk x, **760b**
Tūzūn al-Turkī (945) iii, 127b; vii, 723b, 800a, 995a
Twelvers → Ithnā-ʿAshariyya
Tyana → Ṭuwāna
Tyawka Khān v, 135a
Tyre → Ṣūr
Tzachas → Čaka

U

U Nu i, 1333b; v, 431a
ʿUbād, Banū (Ṭayyiʾ) iv, 911b; vi, 649a
ʿUbāda b. Māʾ al-Samāʾ vii, 492b; iii, **855a**
ʿUbāda b. Ṣāmit v, 324b, 590a
Ubāgh (ʿAyn Ubāgh) x, **761a**
ʿUbar → Wabār
ʿUbayd, Banū vii, 582a
ʿUbayd b. Ayyūb al-ʿAnbarī (VIII) x, 2b
ʿUbayd b. Maʿālī iv, 430a
ʿUbayd b. Sharya → Ibn Sharya
ʿUbayd Abū Ziyād s, 355a
ʿUbayd Allāh Sulṭān Khān (Uzbek) (1539) s, **816a**
ʿUbayd Allāh, Shaykh (Kurd) (XIX) v, 462b; vi, 203a, 502b; vii, 935b; s, 71a
ʿUbayd Allāh b. al-ʿAbbās b. ʿAbd al-Muṭṭalib (704) i, 41a; iii, 241a, 242a, 617a; vi, 344b; x, **761a**
ʿUbayd Allāh b. ʿAbd Allāh (Ṭāhirid) (850) vii, 18b, 410b; x, 105a, 435a
ʿUbayd Allāh b. ʿAbd Allāh al-Hudhalī s, 311b
ʿUbayd Allāh b. Abī Bakra, Abū Ḥātim (698) iv, 356b; vii, 777a; x, **761b**
ʿUbayd Allāh b. Aḥmad b. Abī Ṭāhir (925) iii, 693a; iv, 21a; x, **761b**
ʿUbayd Allāh b. Aḥmad b. Ghālib (848) vii, 5a
ʿUbayd Allāh b. Arṭāh i, 399b
ʿUbayd Allāh b. Bashīr x, **762b**
ʿUbayd Allāh b. Djaḥsh (VII) vii, 862b
ʿUbayd Allāh b. Djibrīl (1058) vi, 351b
ʿUbayd Allāh b. Ḥabḥāb (741) i, 439a, 1157b; ii, 328a; iii, 494a; vi, 742b; vii, 159b, 613a; ix, 584a; x, **762b**
ʿUbayd Allāh b. al-Ḥurr (VII) vii, 650a; ix, 866b
ʿUbayd Allāh b. Idrīs II (Idrīsid) → ʿAbd Allāh b. Idrīs II (Idrīsid)
ʿUbayd Allāh b. Maḥmūd Shaybānid (1539) i, 1295b
ʿUbayd Allāh b. al-Māḥūz i, 810b
ʿUbayd Allāh b. Nabhān ii, 188a
ʿUbayd Allāh b. Samura iii, 717a, b
ʿUbayd Allāh b. al-Sarī b. al-Ḥakam (IX) vii, 160b
ʿUbayd Allāh b. Sulaymān b. Wahb (901) iii, 750a, 892b, 955b; iv, 90b; vii, 760a
ʿUbayd Allāh b. ʿUmar b. al-Khaṭṭāb (657) iii, 65a, 587a; ix, 554a; x, **763a**
ʿUbayd Allāh b. ʿUthmān x, 848b
ʿUbayd Allāh b. Yaḥyā → Ibn Khākān, ʿUbayd Allāh
ʿUbayd Allāh b. Ẓabyān (VII) vii, 650b
ʿUbayd Allāh b. Ziyād b. Abīhi (686) i, 3b, 76b, 304a, 337b, 1086a, 1293b; ii, 89b, 759b, 788a; iii, 164b, 226b, 270b, 588a, 608b, 609a, 715a, 882a, 987a, 1254b; iv, 1186b; v, 853b; vi, 622a, b, 665a, 675b, 677a; vii, 114b, 123b, 400b, 523a, b, 689b, 690a, b, 1045a; viii, 119a; ix, 411b, 826a; x, **763a**, 842b
ʿUbayd Allāh Aḥrār, Kh(w)ādja → Aḥrār, Khwādja ʿUbayd Allāh
ʿUbayd Allāh al-Djarrāz (1051) xi, 226a
ʿUbayd Allāh Khān Özbeg (1540) i, 228b, 1067b; iii, 388a; v, 55a; x, 109a; s, 51b, 340a
ʿUbayd Allāh Khān Özbeg (1711) v, 273b; s, 97a, 419b
ʿUbayd Allāh Khān Shībānī ix, 34b
ʿUbayd Allāh al-Mahdī → al-Mahdī ʿUbayd Allāh
ʿUbayd Allāh Sindhī s, 360a
ʿUbayd al-Ḥarfūsh (Ḥurayfīsh) iii, 206a
ʿUbayda (VIII) vi, 544a
ʿUbayda b. al-Djarrāḥ → Abū ʿUbayda ʿĀmir b. ʿAbd Allāh b. al-Djarrāḥ
ʿUbayda b. al-Ḥārith (623) vii, 32b
ʿUbayda b. Hilāl (680) vii, 123b
al-ʿUbaydalī, Sharīf Tādj al-Sharaf Muḥammad al-Ḥusaynī al-Ḥalabī (1267) viii, 895b
al-ʿUbaydī, Muḥammad b. ʿAbd al-Raḥmān (VIII) vi, 440a; vii, 527b
ʿUbayd-i Zākāni al-Ḳazwīnī (1369) iii, 355b, 373a, 1208b; iv, 66a, 67b; vii, 572b, 1019a; x, **764a**
ʿUbaydids ii, 852a; iii, 782b; ix, 507a; s, 306b
Ubayy b. Kaʿb (ca. 650) i, 104b; iv, 1112b; v, 127b, 406a, 407b; x, **764b**; s, 227a
al-Ubayyiḍ (El Obeid) v, 267b, 1249b; x, **765a**
al-ʿUbbād i, 137b; iii, 866a; vi, 572a; ix, 20b; s, 403a
Ubbadha (Ubeda) x, **765a**

al-ʿUbbādī, Abū ʿAbd Allāh Muḥammad s, 403a
ʿUbey s, 160a, 161a
Ubna (Khān al-Zayt) x, 913a
al-Ubrūḳ ii, 340b
al-Ubulla i, 43b, 1085a; ii, 143a; iii, 1252b; vi, 773b, 920a; vii, 66b; x, **765b**
Ubykh x, **766b**
Uččh ii, 791b; iii, 443b, 633a; v, 26a, b; vi, 48a, b, 49b, 127b; vii, 409b; ix, 785b; x, **766b**; s, 10b, 66b
Ucciali → Wuchali
Uclés → Uklīsh
ʿŪd x, **767b**
ʿŪda, ʿAbd al-Ḳādir iii, 1069b
ʿUdār ii, 1078b
Ūdāya, Banū i, 47a; ii, 510b, 820a; vi, 142b, 590a, b, 741b
al-ʿUdayd x, **773b**
Udaypur (Nēwar) vi, 127b, 342b; x, **773b**
Udfu → Adfū
al-Udfuwī, Abū Bakr (998) vi, 188b
Udgīr x, **773b**
Udhayna b. Hayrān b. Wahb Allāt (Odenatus II) (267) x, 79b
ʿUdhra, Banū ii, 427b, 1031b; v, 317b, 497b; vi, 415a, 472a, 477b; x, **773b**
ʿUdhrī x, **774b**
al-ʿUdhrī, Abu 'l-ʿAbbās Aḥmad b. ʿUmar Ibn al-Dalāʾī (1085) i, 157a; iii, 991b; vi, 431b, 576a; vii, 501a; x, **776a;** s, 80a, 92a
Udhruḥ → Adhruḥ
Udj ii, 611a, 613a, 1044b; x, **777a**
ʿŪdj (ʿĀdj b. ʿAnaḳ / ʿOg) x, **777b**
Udj-Bey → Udj
Udj-beyi i, 1118a; ii, 1044b; viii, 609a
Udjak i, 1217b
Ūdjān vi, 494a, b, 524a
ʿUdjayf b. ʿAnbasa (838) i, 11b; x, **778a**
ʿUdjayr b. ʿAbd Allāh al-Salūlī iv, 1002b
Udjda → Wadjda
Udjdjayn ii, 577a; iii, 1155b; v, 297a; vi, 54b, 62a, 65b, 309a, 602a; x, **778b**; s, 105a
al-Udjhūrī (1656) viii, 479b
ʿUdjma → ʿAdjam
al-ʿUdjmān i, 545b, 873b; iii, 238b, 1065b
ʿUdūl → ʿAdl
ʿUdwat al-Andalus iii, 1032a
al-Ufrānī → al-Ifrānī
Uftāde, Muḥyī al-Dīn ii, 542b, 543a; iii, 538b
Uganda, Muslims in x, **778b**
Uggwag → Wadjdjādj
Ughānān v, 163a
Ughurlu Muḥammad b. Uzun Ḥasan (Aḳ Ḳoyunlu) (XV) iv, 588a; vi, 72a
Uguday → Ögedey
Uḥayḥa b. al-Djulāḥ, al-Awsī x, **782a**
al-Uḥaymir al-Saʿdī ix, 866a
ʿUhda → Ḍarība .4
Uḥdjiyya v, 807a
Uḥud (625) vii, 370a; x, **782a**
Ujiji ii, 58b
ʿUḳāb x, **783b**
ʿUḳalāʾ al-Madjānīn s, **816b**
ʿUḳār (Mahra) vi, 82b
ʿUkāsha → ʿUkkāsha
Ukawafī s, 351a
Ukaydir b. ʿAbd al-Malik al-Sakūnī (VII) ii, 625a; v, 119b; x, **784a**
ʿUḳayl, Banū i, 421a, 442a, 512a, 942a, 1073a, 1356a; ii, 348b; iii, 129a; iv, 27b, 764a, b, 911a; vi, 379a, 546b; vii, 488a, 582a; x, **784b**; s, 37a, 119a
ʿUḳayl al-ʿUkbarī i, 116a
al-ʿUḳaylī, ʿAsar (VII) s, 394a
al-ʿUḳaylī, Isḥāḳ b. Muslim (VIII) vi, 427b; viii, 589b
al-ʿUḳaylī, Muḥammad b. ʿAmr (934) vii, 576b; viii, 516a
ʿUḳaylids (990-1169) vi, 270b, 274b, 379b, 626a, b, 900b; vii, 1017a; viii, 71b; x, **786b**
al-Uḳayshir al-Asadī (699) iv, 1002b; x, **787a**
al-Uḳayṣir ii, 1024a; x, **788a**
ʿUkāẓ i, 343a; iii, 760b; vi, 251b, 477b; vii, 309b; ix, 817b; x, **789a**
ʿUḳba b. Abī Muʿayṭ (624) i, 115b, 136b; ii, 842b; vii, 369b
ʿUḳba b. ʿĀmir al-Djuhanī (VII) vi, 740b; vii, 394b
ʿUḳba b. al-Ashʿath i, 150b
ʿUḳba b. al-Azraḳ (VII) vi, 665a
ʿUḳba b. al-Ḥadjdjādj al-Salūlī (VIII) i, 76a, 1011b, 1079b; vi, 923a
ʿUḳba b. Nāfiʿ b. ʿAbd al-Ḳays (683) i, 248b, 367a, 532b, 770a, 1175a, 1221b, 1259b; ii, 575a, 875b, 992a; iii, 667b; iv, 415b, 567a, 739b, 777a, 826a, b, 827a; v,

393a, 518a, 1189a; vi, 134a, 740b, 742a, 743b, 773b, 944b; viii, 18a; x, **789a**, 848a; s, 81b
ʿUḳba b. Ruʾba i, 1080b
ʿUḳba b. Salm (VIII) i, 45b, 1080b; vi, 820a
ʿUḳba al-Sulaymī (faḳīh, ḳāḍī) ii, 234b, 235a, 236a
ʿUkbānī, Āl s, 403a
al-ʿUḳbānī, al-Ḳāsim b. Saʿīd iv, 477a; s, 403a
ʿUḳbār (Zāb) vi, 435a
ʿUkbarā s, **817b**
al-ʿUkbarī → Ibn Baṭṭa
al-ʿUkbarī, ʿAbd Allāh b. al-Ḥusayn (1219) x, **790b**
al-ʿUkbarī, Abu ʾl-Baḳāʾ (1219) vi, 438a, 824b; vii, 772a
al-ʿUkbarī, al-Aḥnaf (X) vii, 495a
al-ʿUkbarī, Ismāʿīl iv, 604a
al-ʿUkbarī, Mīs̲h̲awayh iv, 604a
al-ʿUkbarī, Muḥammad b. ʿAbd al-Raḥmān (1267) viii, 428a
al-ʿUḳbī, Ṭayyib (XX) iv, 159b; viii, 903a
al-Uk̲h̲ayḍir, Banū (867-ca.1050) i, 403a, 551a, 618a, 831b, 1226b, 1315b; ii, 114a; iii, 262b, 1267b; iv, 88b, 384b; vi, 364b; ix, 507a; x, **792a**; s, 115b
Uk̲h̲ayḍir (castle) x, **791a**
al-Uḳḥuwāna vii, 117a
Ukiyānūs → al-Baḥr al-Muḥīṭ
ʿUḳḳāl → ʿĀḳil
ʿUkkās̲h̲a b. ʿAbd al-Ṣamad iv, 1004a
ʿUkkās̲h̲a b. Ayyūb al-Fazārī (742) iii, 169b; iv, 336b, 826a
ʿUkkāẓ, Bu i, 1247a
al-ʿUḳla (S̲h̲abwa) vi, 80b
al-ʿUklī, Abu ʾl-Wad̲j̲īh s, 85b
Uḳlīdis (Euclid) x, **792b**
al-Uḳlidīsī, Aḥmad b. Ibrāhīm iii, 1139b
Uklīd̲j̲ → Uḳlīs̲h̲
Uḳlīs̲h̲ (Ucles) i, 390a; iv, 596a, 600a, 1182a; v, 123a; x, **794a**
Ukraine v, 260b, 719a, b
Uks̲h̲ūnūba (Oesonoba) i, 1339a; ii, 1009a; x, **794b**
al-Uḳṣur (Luxor) vi, 366b; x, **795a**
Uḳṣūsa x, **796b**
ʿUḳūba x, **799a**
al-ʿUlā (oasis) i, 547b; v, 497b, 761b, 762a; vi88b; x, **800a**; s, 505b
Ūlād Slīmān iv, 540b, 541a
Ulag̲h̲ → Ulug̲h̲
Ulag̲h̲ Noyon i, 1010b
Ulag̲h̲či K̲h̲ān i, 1187b
al-ʿUlah, Banū ii, 167b
Ulaḳ x, **800a**
ʿUlamāʾ x, **801b**
al-ʿUlaymī, Mud̲j̲īr al-Dīn iii, 161b, 954b; v, 322b; vii, **294b**
Ulays, Banū ʾl- iv, 494a, 660b
ʿUlayya bt. al-Mahdī (825) x, **810b**
ʿUlayyān, Āl i, 1312b
Uld̲j̲aytū K̲h̲udābanda → Öld̲j̲eytü
Ulèëbalangs i, 741a, 742a, 744a, 744b, 745b, 747a
Ulema → ʿUlamāʾ
ʿUl(l)ayka vi, 578b, 791a
al-ʿUlt̲h̲ī, Isḥāḳ b. Aḥmad iii, 161a
ʿUlūd̲j̲ ʿAlī (1587) iii, 94b; v, 726b; x, 213b, **810b**
ʿUlūfe x, **811b**
ʿUlūfed̲j̲i̊ → ʿUlūfe
Ulug̲h̲ Beg b. Abī Saʿīd iv, 357a
Ulug̲h̲ Beg, Muḥammad Ṭarag̲h̲āy b. S̲h̲āh Ruk̲h̲ (Tīmūrid) (1449) i, 227b, 393a, 1295b; ii, 399a, 586b; iii, 1137b; iv, 584a, 702b; v, 858b; vi, 540b, 601b, 602a, 768a; x, **812a**
Ulug̲h̲ Bilge Iḳbāl K̲h̲ān i, 767a
Ulug̲h̲ K̲h̲ān (title) x, **814a**
Ulug̲h̲ K̲h̲ān, Almās Beg (K̲h̲ald̲j̲ī, Delhi) (XIV) i, 506b, 1193a; ii, 597a, 1124a; iv, 922a
Ulug̲h̲-K̲h̲ānī al-Āṣafī → Ḥād̲j̲d̲j̲ī al-Dabīr
Ulug̲h̲ K̲h̲ān-i Aʿẓam (XIII) i, 217b; ii, 609b
Ulug̲h̲ Muḥammad (Crimea) (1438) viii, 832a
Ulug̲h̲ Muḥammad (Meḥmed) K̲h̲ān (Golden Horde) (1446) i, 1252b, 1308a; ii, 44b; iii, 44a; iv, 849a
Ulus x, 513a, **814a**
ʿUlyā Ḥaḍrat (1965) s, 65b
ʿUlyāʾiyya i, 1082a, 1096a; x, **814b**
Umāma bint Abi ʾl-ʿĀs (VII) i, 400b
ʿUmān (Oman) i, 73a, 110b, 132a, 140b, 141b, 211b, 535a, 539b, 545a, 551b, 552a, 555a, 811b, 928a, 1013b, 1281b, 1283a,

1354b; ii, 592b; iii, 652a; iv, 500b, 777b, 807b, 1130b; v, 507a, 1059a; vi, 38a, 80b, 82b, 84b, 118a, 272b, 333b, 358a, 371b, 385b, 843a; vii, 301b, 449b, 514b, 838b; x, **814b**; xi, 292a; s, 42a, 118b, 178a, 222b, 234b, 332a, b, 338a, 355a, 417a, **817b**
al-ʿUmānī → al-Fuḳaymī, Muḥammad b. Dhuʿayb
ʿUmānīs v, 1185a; vi, 129a, 735a, b; vii, 226b, 227a; x, 816a; s, 574a, 818b
ʿUmar (I) b. al-Khaṭṭāb (644) i, 9a, 12a, 52a, 104b, 110a, 129a, 145b, 158b, 188a, 337b, 343b, 381b, 382a, 445a, 545b, 549b, 687a, 718a, 729a, 738a, 932a, 1085a, 1141a, b, 1143b, 1215b, 1343b; ii, 77b, 159b, 190b, 232a, 304b, 323b, 360a, 454b, 725b, 842b, 888b, 1006a, 1056a; iii, 64a, 65a, 586b; iv, 14a, 270b, 316b, 320b, 365a, 386a, 927b, 928b, 937b, 995b, 1140b, 1142a; v, 324a; vi, 1a, 105a, 138b, 139a, 140b, 147a, 168a, 193a, 350b, 351a, 362a, 379a, 467a, 476a, b, 575a, 604a, 636a, 645a, b, 647a, 648a, b, 650b, 651b, 652a, 654b, 658a, b, 659a, 660a, 661a, 665a, 666a, 668b, 671a, 675a, b, 724a, 737a, 738b; vii, 295a, 509b, 1030b; viii, 93b, 835a, b; ix, 504b; x, **818b**; s, 48b, 89b, 129b, 130a, 198b, 343a
ʿUmar II b. ʿAbd al-ʿAzīz b. Marwān (Umayyad) (720) i, 53b, 117a, 181b, 257b, 305a, 435a, 729b, 966b; ii, 36a, 72b, 198a, 227b, 304b, 327b, 480a, 561a, 622b, 726a; iii, 228a, 428b, 650a, 674b; iv, 369b, 742a, 939a, 997a; v, 53a, 590b, 923a, 1124a, 1231b; vi, 107b, 197b, 350b, 351a, 457b, 626a, 641a, 652a, 659a, 662a, 665a, 712b, 740a, 774b, 917a; vii, 8b, 27a, 157b, 398a; x, **821a**, 842a; s, 41a, 52b, 311b, 358a
ʿUmar, Banū iii, 299b, 1035b, 1097a
ʿUmar, al-Ḥādjdj (Toucouleur) (XIX) iii, **38b**; vi, 281b, 295b
ʿUmar (marabout, Marrākush) (1766) vi, 595a
ʿUmar b. al-ʿAbbās b. Mandīl (1277) vi, 404a
ʿUmar b. ʿAbd Allāh b. Abī Rabīʿa (712) i, 10b, 305a, 566a; ii, 427b, 428b, 1011b, 1029b, 1030b; iii, 682a; iv, 488b, 1008b; vi, 140b, 468a, 477b; vii, 694b, 981b; x, **822b**; s, 10a
ʿUmar b. ʿAbd Allāh al-Aḳṭaʿ (amīr) (Malaṭya) vi, 230b
ʿUmar b. ʿAbd al-ʿAzīz → ʿUmar II (Umayyad)
ʿUmar b. ʿAbd al-ʿAzīz (Dulafid) (IX) ii, 623b; vii, 395a
ʿUmar b. ʿAbd al-Muʾmin, vizier (XII) i, 160b; s, 61a
ʿUmar b. Abī Bakr (Songhay) (XV) vii, 394a
ʿUmar b. Abī Bakr, al-Ḥādjdj (Ghana) (1934) ii, 1004a
ʿUmar b. Abi ʾl-Ṣalt (Rayy) (VII) iv, 207b; v, 541a
ʿUmar b. Aḥmad b. ʿAbd al-ʿAzīz (Dulafid) (896) vii, 760a
ʿUmar b. ʿAlāʾ (VIII) vi, 744b, 941a; viii, 650b
ʿUmar b. ʿAlī → Ibn al-Fāriḍ
ʿUmar b. ʿAlī, al-Malik al-Manṣūr Nūr al-dīn (Rasūlid) (1250) i, 553a; v, 1241a, viii, 455b
ʿUmar b. ʿAlī b. al-Ḥasan vi, 334b
ʿUmar b. Arghūn Shāh (XIV) viii, 894b
ʿUmar b. Ayyūb → al-Muẓaffar, al-Malik
ʿUmar b. Bāyazīd Anṣārī i, 1123a, b
ʿUmar b. al-Fāriḍ → Ibn al-Fāriḍ
ʿUmar b. Ḥaddū (XIII) vi, 743a
ʿUmar b. Ḥafṣ → Muhallabids.iv
ʿUmar b. Ḥafṣ b. ʿUthmān b. Ḳabīṣa b. Abī Ṣufra (Hazārmard) (768) i, 125a; vi, 311b, 312a, 1042b; vii, 359b
ʿUmar b. Ḥafṣ al-Ballūṭī → Abū Ḥafṣ ʿUmar al-Ballūṭī
ʿUmar b. Ḥafṣūn (muwallad) (918) i, 83b, 494a, 997a, 1150a, 1300b, 1343a; ii, 516a, 915b, 1012b; iii, 785a, 842a; iv, 254b, 534a; v, 376b, 1243b; vi, 222a; vii, 248b, 563b, 569a, 808a, 941b; x, **823b**, 850b; s, 152b
ʿUmar b. Hāniʾ al-ʿAnsī iv, 370a
ʿUmar b. Ḥanẓala vi, 12a, b
ʿUmar b. Hubayra → Ibn Hubayra
ʿUmar b. Hubayra al-Fazārī (VIII) ii, 1023b; iii, **802a**
ʿUmar b. Ibrāhīm al-Khayyāmī → ʿUmar Khayyām
ʿUmar b. Idrīs II (Idrīsid) (IX) ii, 874a, 1095b; iii, 1035b; viii, 522a
ʿUmar b. Īmkaten (Ibāḍī) (VIII) iii, 654a; v, 696a

ʿUmar b. Ismāʿīl al-Hawwārī (1396) iii, 299b
ʿUmar b. al-Ḳāsim al-Nashshār i, 105b
ʿUmar b. al-Khaṭṭāb → ʿUmar I (Umayyad)
ʿUmar b. Khuraym al-Murrī (VIII) vii, 629b
ʿUmar b. al-Malik al-ʿĀdil Abū Bakr (Ayyūbid) (XIII) x, 884a
ʿUmar b. Mihrān (Miṣr) (VIII) vii, 160b
ʿUmar b. Mīrānshāh b. Tīmūr (Tīmūrid) (XV) vii, 105b
ʿUmar b. Muḥammad al-Kanemī i, 1260a; v, 357b, 358a
ʿUmar b. al-Nuʿmān i, 361b, 363a; ii, 238a
ʿUmar b. Ramaḍān al-Thalātī i, 121b
ʿUmar b. Rasūl (XIII) vi, 433b
ʿUmar b. Riyāḥ s, 129b
ʿUmar b. Rubayʿān → Ibn Rubayʿān
ʿUmar b. Saʿd b. Abī Waḳḳās (VII) iii, 588a, 609b, 611a; iv, 836a; vii, 523a, 690a
ʿUmar b. Saʿīd, al-Fūtī (1864) x, 122b, 464a, **825b**
ʿUmar b. Saʿīd, al-Ḥādjdj (Malī) (XIX) iii, 38b; vi, 259b; vii, 436a
ʿUmar b. Shabba b. ʿAbīda (878) i, 158b; v, 607b; x, **826b;** s, 38b
ʿUmar b. Sulaymān al-Shayẓamī → ʿUmar al-Sayyāf
ʿUmar b. ʿUbayd Allāh b. Maʿmar (VII) i, 120a, 810a, 1242b; vii, 671a
ʿUmar b. Wīghran b. Mandīl (XIV) vi, 404b
ʿUmar b. Yūsuf b. Rasūl, al-Malik al-Ashraf (Rasūlid) (1297) iii, 267a; vi, 829b
ʿUmar Agha Ḳara ʿOthmān-oghlu iv, 593a, b
ʿUmar ʿArab (XX) vi, 177b
ʿUmar Bamakhrama → Makhrama.3
ʿUmar the Cutler (1475) vi, 226a, b, 228b
ʿUmar Djaghāraʾī, Bahā al-Dīn (XV) vii, 126b
ʿUmar Djibrīl, Shaykh (Niger) viii, 18a
ʿUmar Efendi (XVIII) i, 1271b; ii, 20a; vi, 227b
ʿUmar Fākhūrī s, 224b
ʿUmar Fatḥī s, 301a
ʿUmar al-Ḥusaynī (faḳīh) (1530) vi, 143a
ʿUmar Khān b. Aḥmad Shāh (Gudjarāt) (1438) vi, 52b, 53a
ʿUmar Khān b. Nārbūta (Khokand) (1822) v, 29b; vi, 765b, 768a
ʿUmar Khān Avar i, 755b
ʿUmar Khān Kāsī ii, 54b; s, 313a
ʿUmar Khān Sarwānī → ʿAbbās Sarwānī
ʿUmar Khayyām (1123) i, 113a, 839a, 841a, 1132a; ii, 362a, 397b, 533b; iii, 1139a; iv, 54a, 62a, 64a; vi, 275b, 600a, 638a; viii, 76a, 552b, 580a, 971b; x, **827b**; s, 35a, 235b, 412a, 413a, b, 414a
ʿUmar Luṭfī (XX) x, 5b
ʿUmar Makram (1809) vii, 424a, 429b
ʿUmar Makram, al-Sayyid (1822) x, **834a**
ʿUmar al-Mālaḳī al-Zadjdjal (XV) vi, 112a
ʿUmar Mīrzā (Timūrid) (XV) iv, 586a; vi, 202a
ʿUmar al-Mukhtār v, 758a
ʿUmar al-Murtaḍā, Abū Ḥafṣ (Almohad) (1266) vi, 593a
ʿUmar al-Mutawakkil i, 242b; iii, 680b, 813b ʿUmar Nasuhī Bilmen → Bilmen
ʿUmar al-Nuʿmān ii, 234a; x, **834b**
ʿUmar Pasha (Baghdād) (XVIII) i, 199a, 905a; vi, 551a, 811b
ʿUmar Pasha Latas i, 1268b
ʿUmar al-Rūshanī ii, 1136b, 1137a, b; iv, 991b; s, 208a
Umar Said Tall, al-Hajj ix, 853b
ʿUmar al-Saḳḳāf (XX) vi, 154a
ʿUmar Ṣayrafī (XX) vi, 177b
ʿUmar al-Sayyāf ii, 527b
ʿUmar Seyf al-Dīn (Omer Seyfettin) → ʿÖmer Seyf ül-Dīn
ʿUmar Shaykh Mīrzā b. Tīmūr (Tīmūrid) (1394) vii, 133a; ix, 667b; x, **835a**
ʿUmar Shaykh Mīrzā II Küräcän b. Abī Saʿīd Mīrzā (Tīmūrid) (1494) i, 148a, 847b; ii, 792a; x, **835b**
ʿUmar Tal → al-Ḥādjdj ʿUmar
ʿUmar Ṭoghrïl Tigin b. Maḥmūd Ṭughrïl Ḳara Khān (Ḳarakhānid) (1074) vi, 557b
ʿUmar al-Ẓāhir → Ẓāhir al-ʿUmar
ʿUmāra, Banū iii, 757a; s, 222b
ʿUmāra b.ʿAḳīl viii, 120b; x, 69a
ʿUmāra b.ʿAlī al-Ḥakamī i, 197a, 552b, 593b
ʿUmāra b. ʿAmr i, 113b
ʿUmāra b. Khuraym al-Murrī (VIII) vii, 629b
ʿUmāra b. Wathīma (902) x, **835b**
ʿUmāra al-Yamanī (1174) ii, 861b; iii, 814b; v, 1244a; x, **836a**

al-ʿUmarī → ibn Faḍl Allāh al-ʿUmarī
al-ʿUmarī (Medina) (VIII) iii, 616a, 617a
al-ʿUmarī, ʿAbd al-Raḥmān (IX) i, 1158a; viii, 863a
al-ʿUmarī, Aḥmad → Ibn Faḍl Allāh
al-ʿUmarī, Amīn b. Khayr Allāh (1789) vii, 1040a
al-ʿUmarī, ʿIṣām al-Dīn ʿUthmān b. ʿAlī (XVIII) vii, 528a
al-ʿUmariyya i, 1009a; iii, 659b
Umaru Bakatara ii, 1146b
Umaru Salaga iv, 550b
al-Umawī, Yaʿīsh b. Ibrāhīm (1490) vii, 136a
Umay (wife of Tañri) x, 187a, 688a
ʿUmayr b. Bayān al-ʿIdjlī iv, 1132b
ʿUmayr b. Ḥubāb al-Sulamī ii, 800b, 1023b; iii, 819b; iv, 493a, 870b, 1186b; viii, 433b
ʿUmayr b. Saʿd al-Anṣārī (VII) vii, 264b; viii, 433b
ʿUmayr b. Shuyaym → al-Ḳuṭāmī
ʿUmayr b. Sinān al-Māzinī vi, 954b
Umayya, Banū vii, 362a, 552a; x, 840b
Umayya b. ʿAbd Allāh b. Khālid i, 148b, 1293a
Umayya b. ʿAbd al-Azīz, Abu ʾl-Ṣalt (1134) i, **149a**; x, **836b**
Umayya b. ʿAbd Shams (VII) x, **837b**
Umayya b. Abī ʾl-Ṣalt (VII) i, 44b, 418a, 565a, 584b; iii, 165b, 541b, 975b, 1206a; v, 180b; vi, 603b; vii, 363a; x, **839a**; s, 247a
Umayya b. Khalaf i, 1215a (VII) x, **839b**
Umayyads i, 16a, 43a, 45a, 49a, 51b, 55b, 76a, 103a, 439b, 550a, 920a; ii, 360a; iv, 15b-16a; v, 736a; vi, 1b, 118b, 194a, 379a, 518a, 519a, 669b, 676a, 875b; vii, 42b; ix, 263b, 264a, b, 491a; x, **840b**; s, 103b, 116b, 396b
– administration ii, 304b, 323b; iv, 755b, 938a
– constructions i, 609b, 612b; ii, 280b, 821b; v, 10b-16b, 17a, 216b, 325b
– literature i, 118a, 760a
Umayyads of Spain vi, 2a, 221a, 331a, 712b; x, **847b**
Umbay İnaḳ s, 420a
ʿUmdat al-mulk iv, 758b
Umīdī iv, 68b ; viii, 135b
Umm ʿĀṣim i, 58b
Umm al-Banīn bint al-Mughīra b. ʿAbd al-Raḥmān (VII) i, 400b; ii, 1023b; vi, 139a
Umm Djaʿfar viii, 884a
Umm Djundad vii, 261a
Umm Dubaykarāt (Sudān) i, 50a
Umm Dunayn (Maks) vi, 195a
Umm Faḍl bint al-Maʾmūn (IX) i, 713a; vii, 396b
Umm Farwa bint Abī Ḳuḥāfa (VII) vii, 400b
Umm Gharayāt i, 418a
Umm Ḥabīb bint al-Maʾmūn (IX) i, 400b; vii, 396b
Umm Ḥabība bint Abī Sufyān (VII) i, 151a; iv, 927b; vii, 264a, 862b
Umm Ḥakīm bint al-Ḥārith b. Hishām b. al-Mughīra (VII) vi, 139a, 546b, 547b
Umm al-Ḥasan Sitt al-Mashāyikh Fāṭima (XIV) vii, 407b
Umm Hāshim Fākhita bint Abī Hāshim b. ʿUtba (VII) vi, 622a; vii, 268a
Umm al-Ḥasan Fāṭima bint al-Ḥasan (IX) s, 334b
Umm Hishām (VIII) vi, 139b
Umm ʿĪsā bint Mūsā al-Hādī (VIII) vi, 331b
Umm al-Ḳaywayn vi, 38a; x, **853b**; s, 416b
Umm al-Khaḳān bint Amīr Kabīr Mīrzā Muḥammad Taḳī Khān vii, 431b
Umm Khalīl Shadjar al-Durr (XIII) vi, 321a, b; ix, 176a
Umm Khāridja vi, 478a
Umm al-Kitāb i, 89b; ii, 849a; iv, 203a; x, **854a**
Umm Kulthūm (1975) x, **855b**
Ümm Külthūm bint Aḥmed III (Ottoman) (1724) vi, 860b
Umm Kulthūm bint ʿAlī i, 109b, 136b, 308b; ii, 843a; iii, 889a; s, 13b
Umm Kulthūm bint Muḥammad (VII) x, **855a**
Umm al-Ḳurā x, **850a**
Umm al-Ḳuṣūr vi, 546a
Umm al-Ḳuwayn i, 928b; viii, 435a (see also, *s.v.* Umm al-Ḳaywayn)
Umm Mūsā iv, 637b; s, 94a
Umm al-Rabīʿ (Marrākush) v, 1185a; vi, 593a, b; x, 169a
Umm al-Raṣāṣ x, **856a**
Umm Rūmān bint ʿĀmir i, 109b, 110a, 307b

Umm Salama Hind bint Abī Umayya (679) i, 258a, 308a; ii, 846a; iii, 64a, 612b; iv, 927a; vi, 650b; x, **856b**; s, 230b
Umm Salama bint Mūsā al-Kāẓim (IX) vii, 647a
Umm Salama bint Yaʿḳūb b. Salama (VIII) vi, 139b
Umm Sharīḳ bint ʿAṣar al-ʿUḳaylī s, 394a
Umm ʿUthmān → Sallāma al-Zarḳāʾ
Umm al-Walad x, **857a**
Umm al-Walīd x, **859b**
Umm Zaynab iii, 954b
Umma x, **859b**
Umma Khān Avar i, 755b; ii, 87b
ʿUmmāl → ʿĀmil
Ummarār i, 1158b, 1239b
Ummī vii, 364b; x, **863b**
Umm-i Sinān, Shaykh (1658) viii, 65a
Ummīdī (1519) viii, 775a
ʿUmra x, **864b**
ʿUmrā Khān ii, 30b, 317a
ʿUmūm wa-Khuṣūṣ x, **866b**
Umur I Pasha, Bahāʾ Dīn ʿUmar (Aydïnoghlu) (1348) i, 346a, 653b, 783a, 1302b; ii, 683b, 983b; iii, 115a, 1086a; v, 505b, 506a; vi, 1036a; vii, 47b; viii, 890a; x, **867a**; s, 330a
Umūr II (Aydïnoghlu) i, 783b; ii, 599a
Umūr Beg/Pasha → Ümür I (Aydïnoghlu)
Umur Beg Timūrtāshoghlu v, 250a
Una (Gudjarāt) vi, 270b
Unayf Abū Maysūn → Unayf b. Daldja
Unayf b. Daldja (VII) x, **867b**
ʿUnayza i, 534a, 1312b; iv, 717a; vi, 153a; vii, 782b; x, **867b**
ʿUnāza → ʿUnayza
al-Ungudja → Zandjibār
United Arab Emirates → al-Imārāt al-ʿArabiyya al-Muttaḥida
United Arab Republic → al-Djumhūriyya al-ʿArabiyya al-Muttaḥida
al-Unḳalī, Unḳūriyya → Madjar
Unḳaliyyīn, Unḳūriyya → Madjar
ʿUnnāb x, **868a**
Ūnsā II (Sinnār) (1692) ii, 944a, b; ix, 650b
al-ʿUnṣulayn vi, 820b
ʿUnṣur x, **868b**
ʿUnṣur al-Maʿālī Kay Kāʾūs → Kāʾūs b. Iskandar
ʿUnṣurī, Abu ʾl-Ḳāsim Ḥasan (1039) iv, 61a, 62b; vi, 66a, 276a, 453a, 609a; vii, 19a; x, **869a**; s, 21b
Unūdjūr b. Muḥammad b. Ṭughdj (Ikhshīdid) (961) iii, 129a; iv, 418a, b; vii, 161b, 411b; ix, 99b
ʿUnwān x, **870b**
ʿUnwān Muḥammad Riḍā (1667) x, **872a**
Upanishads ii, 135a; iii, 436b
Ūparkōt ii, 597b, 598a; vi, 50b
Ura-Tepe (Ura Tübe/Uroteppa, Tādjīkistān) v, 29b, 30a; vi, 419a; s, 228a, **819b**
Ura Tübe → Ura-Tepe
ʿUrābī Pasha, Aḥmad (Miṣr) (1911) i, 141b, 142a, 815a, 1070a; ii, 28a, 417b, 514b; iii, 514a, 515a; vi, 586b, 602b, 643a; vii, 184a, b, 418b, 852a; x, 388b, **872a**; s, 132b, 408b, 411b
ʿUrābī Sidjīnī (XX) vi, 157a
ʿUrāʿir, Day of s, 178a
Ural river → Yayïḳ
Urang Temür ii, 1112a; iv, 868a
ʿUrayʿir, Banū iv, 925a, b
ʿUrayʿir (al-Aḥsāʾ) (XVIII) vi, 191b
ʿUrayma vi, 579a
Uraz Muḥammad Khān iv, 724a
al-Urbus i, 104a, 163a, 250b; iv, 403a
al-ʿUrḍī vii, 201a
Urdjudhūna (Archidona) vii, 569a; x, **873a**
Urdjūza → Radjaz
Urdū i, 430b, 505b, 807b, 827b; ii, 101a, 490b, 797a, 1036a; iii, 1b, 93b, 119a, 358b, 375b, 413a, 460b, 536b, 1057a, 1244b; iv, 716b; v, 201a, 635b, 958a, 1106a; vi, 62b; x, **873b**; s, 247a, 358b
– literature vi, 610b, 827a, 837a; vii, 667b
Urdumāniyyūn i, 83a, 494a; v, 1119b
al-Urdunn (Jordan; Jordan) i, 39a, 46a, 534a, 975b, 1017a; ii, 555a, 662b; iii, 264a, 560a, b; iv, 262a; v, 337b, 912a, 1053b; vi, 31b, 32a, 388a, 797a; x, **881a**; s, 251b
– West Bank v, 1054b, 1055a
ʿUrf x, **887b**
Urfa → al-Ruhā
Urfalï Nüzhet ʿÜmer Efendi (1778) vi, 632b
ʿUrfī Shīrāzī, Djamāl al-Dīn (1591) i, 680a; ii, 794b, 878a; iv, 69a; v, 958a; vi, 608b;

vii, 340b, 341a; viii, 775b; ix, 241b; x, **892a**
Urganč, Urgandj → Gurgandj
Urgenč x, **892b**
Urghan (Urghanūn) x, **893a**
Uriśā (Orissa) vi, 67a, b, 343a, 406b, 535b; vii, 459a; x, **894b**
Urīṭ iv, 482b
ʿUrḳūb iii, 396a; vi, 817a
Urm x, **896a**
Urmar → Orāmār
al-Urmawī, Ṣafī al-Dīn → Ṣafī al-Dīn
Urmiyā (Jeremiah) → Irmiyā
Urmiya v, 442b; vi, 120a, 500b, 502a; x, **897a**
Urmiya, Lake i, 191a; iii, 569b; vi, 72b, 498b, 502b, 504a, b; x, **896a**
ʿUrr ʿAdan → ʿAdan
ʿUrs (ʿUrus) x, **899b**
Urtuḳids → Artuḳids
ʿUrūba x, **907b**
ʿUrudj b. ʿĀdil (XVI) x, **908a**
Uruk/Erech → al-Warkāʾ
ʿUrūḳ al-Rumayla ii, 92a; viii, 1048a
Urumči v, 846a, b; vi, 767a, 768a
Urumiyya (Riḍāʾiyya) vi, 203a
Urus Khān (Tokay Tīmūrid) (XIV) ii, 44a; x, 560b
Urus Mīrzā i, 1075b
Uruzgān v, 353b; s, 367a
ʿUrwa b. Ḥizām b. Muhāṣir al-ʿUdhrī (650) x, **908b**
ʿUrwa b. Masʿūd b. Muʿattib al-Thaḳafī (630) iv, 839a; vii, 347a; x, **909a**
ʿUrwa b. Udayya (658) iii, 169a; vii, 123a
ʿUrwa b. Udhayna (VIII) x, **909b**
ʿUrwa b. al-Ward al-ʿAbsī (VII) i, 518b; ii, 1072b; iii, 941a; vii, 309b; ix, 864a; x, 2b, **910a**
ʿUrwa b. al-Zubayr b. al-ʿAwwām (711) i, 867b; iii, 24a; iv, 189b; v, 997b, 1161b; vii, 27a, 361a; viii, 533a; x, **910b**; s, 311a
ʿUrwa al-Raḥḥāl ii, 883b; iii, 285b; v, 101b
al-ʿUrwa al-Wuthḳā ii, 418a, 419a, 429a; vii, 419a
ʿUryān, Muḥammad (XVII) xi, 123a
Uryūla x, **913a**
Uşak → ʿUshāḳ
al-Usāma i, 682b
Usāma b. Lādin s, 787a
Usāma b. Munḳidh (b. Murshid) b. ʿAlī (1188) i, 9b, 570b, 593b, 665b, 680b, 1153b; ii, 64b, 318a, 739a, 740b, 1037a, 1065b; iii, 809a; iv, 514a; v, 9a, 330b; vi, 469b, 606a, 790a; vii, 577b, **578b**, 733b; viii, 133b, 913b; ix, 410b; s, 205a, 362a
Usāma b. Zayd b. Ḥāritha al-Kalbī (674) i, 110b, 382b; ii, 327b; v, 1161b; vi, 877a; vii, 374b; x, **913a**; s, 693a
Usāma b. Zayd al-Tanūkhī (720) ii, 327b; vi, 423b, 670b; viii, 41b
Usayd b. Ḥuḍayr i, 514b; iii, 285b; viii, 697b
Usays viii, 423b; s, 117a, 229a
al-Usayyidī, ʿUmar b. Yazīd (727) ix, 282b
al-ʿUṣba al-andalussiyya → al-Mahdjar
ʿUṣfūr al-Azdī iv, 796b
ʿUṣfūrids i, 553a, 942b; iv, 764b; x, **913b**
ʿUshāḳ (Uşak) x, **913b**; s, 137b
ʿUshāḳī-zāde iv, 930a; x, **919a**
ʿUshāḳī-zāde, Ibrāhīm b. al-Seyyid ʿAbd ül-Bāḳī (1724) x, **919b**
al-Ushbūna (Lisbon) i, 1338b; x, **914b**
al-Ūshī, ʿAlī b. ʿUthmān (1173) vi, 848a; x, **916a**
Ushmūm (idol) i, 126a
Ushmūm Ṭannāḥ (Miṣr) vi, 440a, b
Ushmūnayn vi, 624b; x, **916a**
al-Ushnandānī, Abū ʿUthmān Saʿīd (900) iii, 757a; vi, 347b
Ushnū (Ushnuh) vi, 494a, b, 500b; x, **916b**
ʿUshr x, **917a**
Ushrūsana i, 241a; vi, 337b, 338b; vii, 395a; s, 406b
ʿUshshāḳī, Ḥasan Ḥusām al-Dīn (1592) x, 919a, 920a
ʿUshshāḳī-Zāde x, **919a**
ʿUshshāḳī-Zāde, Ibrāhīm b. al-Seyyid (1724) x, **919b**
ʿUshshāḳiyya vi, 1004a; x, **920a**
ʿUshshāḳiyye Ṭarīḳa → ʿUshshāḳiyya
Ushurma, Manṣūr (1794) x, **920b**
Uskāf Banī Djunayd iii, 1267a
Üsküb i, 698a, 1263a; vi, 70b, 89a; x, **922a**
Üsküdār iii, 216b, 220a, 623a; iv, 233a, 244a, 720a, 1017a; v, 273a; vi, 3a, 57a, 227b, 529b; x, **923b**; s, 315a
Uslūdj b. al-Ḥasan ii, 860a; iii, 840b
Usman, Faqih (XX) vi, 732a
Usman dan Fodio → ʿUthmān b. Fūdī

Ūsmī (Utsmi) ii, 87a, 88a, 141b; iv, 846b
Usrū<u>sh</u>ana x, **924b**
Ustādār (Ustāddār) x, **925a**, 926a
Ustā<u>dh</u> x, **925b**
al-Ustā<u>dh</u> al-Aʿẓam → Bā ʿAlawī, Muḥammad b. ʿAlī (1255)
Ustā<u>dh</u> <u>D</u>jawwhar → <u>D</u>jawwhar b. ʿAbd. Allāh al-Ṣiḳillī
Ustā<u>dh</u>-Hurmuz iii, 244b
Ustā<u>dh</u>dār i, 33a, 801b; ii, 384b; iv, 294a
Ustā<u>dh</u>sīs iii, 177b; iv, 16b; v, 1111b; vi, 428a; x, **926b**
Usta<u>d</u>jlū, Aḥmad Beg (1576) vi, 16b
Ustā<u>d</u>jlū, Banū iii, 1101a, b, 1105a; viii, 769a
Ustā<u>d</u>jlū (Usta<u>d</u>jlu), Muḥammad (1507) vi, 541a, 931b
Ustān x, **927a**
Ustāndār x, **927b**
Usṭā<u>th</u> (Asṭā<u>th</u>) (IX) x, **927b**
Ustolnī Bel<u>gh</u>rād → Istōnī (Istolnī) Bel<u>gh</u>rād
Usṭūl x, **928a**
Ustūnāwand (<u>D</u>jarhud) i, 1034a; vi, 744b
Usṭūra iii, 369a
Ustuwā vi, 869a; x, **928b**
Üst-Yurt Plateau i, 607a; vi, 415a, 416b
Uṣūl x, **928b**
Uṣūl al-Dīn x, **930b**
Uṣūl al-Fiḳh x, **931b**
Uṣūl al-Ḥadī<u>th</u> x, **934a**
Uṣūlī (1568) viii, 212b; s, 83a
Uṣūlīs iv, 50a; s, 103b
Uṣūliyya vi, 549a, 550b, 551a; vii, 297b; viii, 779b; x, **935a**; s, 56b, 95b
Usuman iv, 549a, 550a
Usuman Dan Fodio → ʿU<u>th</u>mān b. Fūdī
Usuo<u>gh</u>ullarï s, 282b
Uswān (Aswan) v, 514b, 887a; vi, 366b; viii, 863b; x, **938a**; s, 7a, 8b, 35b, 36a, 57b
al-Uswārī, Abū ʿAlī (IX) iv, 734b; vii, 401a
al-Uswārī, Mūsā b. Sayyār iv, 734b
Ūsya iii, 1154b
Usyūṭ → Asyūṭ
al-ʿUtāb, Banū x, 91a
Uṭāmi<u>sh</u> (vizier) (863) vii, 390a, 722b, 723a
ʿUṭārid (Mercury) x, **940b**
ʿUṭārid b. Ḥā<u>d</u>jib iii, 49a
ʿUṭārid b. Muḥammad al-Ḥāsib (IX) i, 87a; x, **942b**
ʿUṭayba (Damascus) vi, 544b
ʿUtayba, Baḥr x, **944a**
ʿUtayba, Banū i, 545b; ii, 354a; iii, 1065b; vi, 159a, 177b; vii, 782b; x, **942b**
ʿUtayba b. Abū Lahab i, 136b
ʿUtayba b. al-Ḥāri<u>th</u> i, 1247b
al-ʿUtaybī, <u>D</u>juhaymān b. Muḥammad (XX) vi, 157b, 158a, b; x, 944a
ʿUṭayf b. Niʿma iv, 493b
ʿUtba (slave girl) (VIII) i, 107b; iv, 1164b
ʿUtba (ʿUtūb), Banū i, 482b, 942b
ʿUtba b. Abī Sufyān (VII) vi, 740b
ʿUtba b. Abū Lahab i, 136b
ʿUtba b. Farḳad al-Sulamī (VII) v, 896b; vi, 899b; viii, 1004a; ix, 818a; x, **897a**
ʿUtba b. <u>Gh</u>azwān (635) i, 1085a; iii, 583a; v, 80b; vi, 647b, 920a; x, **944b**; s, 354b
ʿUtba b. Ḳays b. Zuhayr al-ʿAbsī s, 177b
ʿUtba b. Rabī ʿa b. ʿAbd <u>Sh</u>ams (624) x, **944b**
al-ʿUtbī (869) i, 600a; vi, 278b
al-ʿUtbī, Abu ʿAbd Allāh Muḥammad (868) x, **945b**
al-ʿUtbī, Abu ʿAbd al-Raḥmān Muḥammad (842) x, **945b**
al-ʿUtbī, Abū <u>D</u>jaʿfar (vizier) (958) vii, 26a; x, **945a**
al-ʿUtbī, Abu ʾl-Ḥusayn (vizier) (982) vi, 340a; viii, 110a, 1027b, 1028a; x, **945a**; s, 72b, 265b
al-ʿUtbī, Abū Naṣr (vizier) vi, 340a
al-ʿUtbī, Abu Naṣr al-<u>D</u>jabbār (1036) i, 591b; vi, 278b; vii, 21a; x, **945a**
al-ʿUtbī, Āl x, **945a**
al-U<u>th</u>āl (al-A<u>th</u>al) x, **946a**
ʿU<u>th</u>mān I, II, III (Ottoman) → ʿOthmān I, II, III
ʿU<u>th</u>mān II Abū Saʿīd (Marīnid) (1331) iii, 909a; vi, 124a, 572b, 593b, 594a; s, 112b
ʿU<u>th</u>mān, Abū ʿUmar i, 1152b; ii,540a; iii, 69a
ʿU<u>th</u>mān, Banū (Maʿḳil) vi, 141b
ʿU<u>th</u>mān, Sayyid iii, 457a
ʿU<u>th</u>mān b. ʿAbd Allāh b. Bi<u>sh</u>r iii, 103a
ʿU<u>th</u>mān b. Abi ʾl-ʿĀṣ i, 695b; ii, 811b, 823b; iv, 14b
ʿU<u>th</u>mān b. Abī Bakr → ʿU<u>th</u>mān Digna
ʿU<u>th</u>mān b. Abī Bakr (Gidadd dan Laima) (XIX) vii, 435b
ʿU<u>th</u>mān b. Abī <u>Sh</u>ayba (853) vii, 691a
ʿU<u>th</u>mān b. Abi ʾl-ʿUlā, vizier (XIV) vii, 1023a, b

ʿUthmān b. Abī Yūsuf → ʿUthmān II (Marīnid)
ʿUthmān b. ʿAffān (655) i, 43b, 51b, 52a, 92b, 93a, 114b, 195a, 308a, 336b, 381b, 382a, 451b, 549b, 704a, 957b; ii, 414a, 1023b; iii, 240b, 272a, 539a, 583a, 587a, 1163b; iv, 937b; v, 405a, 996b; vi, 138b, 139a, 147a, 279b, 379a, 603a, 604a, 621b, 660a, 661b, 663b, 664a, 665b, 668b, 670a, 671a, 676a, 677a; vii, 263b, 394b; ix. 505a; x, **946a**; s, 10a, 89b, 129b, 130a, 131a, 198b, 221b, 230b, 304b, 343a
ʿUthmān b. Aḥmad → ʿUthmān b. Muʿammar
ʿUthmān b. ʿAnbasa b. Abī Sufyān (VII) vii, 268b
ʿUthmān b. al-ʿĀṣ (VII) iv, 220a; viii, 435b
ʿUthmān b. Čaghri̊ Beg Dāwūd (Saldjūḳ) (XI) vi, 273b
ʿUthmān b. Čaḳmaḳ ii, 6b; iii, 1198a
ʿUthmān b. Fūdī (Usman dan Fodio, Tukulor, Sokoto) (1817) i, 179b, 303a; ii, 941b, 942a, 1003b, 1144b; iii, 276b; iv, 549b; v, 394b, 1166a; vi, 281b; vii, 435b; viii, 18a, b; x, 122a, **949b**
ʿUthmān b. Ḥayyān al-Murrī (VIII) i, 113a; vii, 629b; ix, 821b
ʿUthmān b. Ḥunayf ii, 415a; iii, 583a
ʿUthmān b. al-Ḥuwayrith (VI) vi, 146a; xi, 142b
ʿUthmān b. Ḳaṭan iii, 715b; ix, 164b
ʿUthmān b. Khalīfa ʿAbd Allāh (Shaykh al-Dīn) (1900) v, 1250b, 1251b, 1252a
ʿUthmān b. Marzūḳ (1169) x, **951b**
ʿUthmān b. Maẓʿūn b. Ḥabīb (625) i, 957b; ii, 1060a; iii, 1017b; iv, 1089a; viii, 396b; x, **951b**
ʿUthmān b. Muʿammar ii, 321a; iii, 678a; iv, 925a; x, 959b
ʿUthmān b. Muḥammad Fodiye (Fūdī) → ʿUthmān b. Fūdī
ʿUthmān b. Niẓām al-Mulk, vizier (XII) vi, 64a; vii, 735a
ʿUthmān b. Saʿīd al-ʿAmrī (IX) i, 713a; iii, 247a; vii, 443b
ʿUthmān b. Ṣāliḥ (832) vi, 413b; viii, 854a
ʿUthmān b. Ṭalḥa i, 451a; iii, 975b; iv, 320b; x, 390a
ʿUthmān b. ʿUmāra b. Khuraym al-Murrī (VIII) vii, 629b
ʿUthmān b. al-Walīd II iii, 990b
ʿUthmān b. Yaghmurāsan (Mandīl) (XIII) i, 92b; vi, 404a, b
ʿUthmān Ādam (Djānū) (XIX) ii, 124a; v, 267b, 1250b
ʿUthmān Āghā Mustaḥfiẓān iv, 438a
ʿUthmān ʿAlī Khān ii, 99b; iii, 323a
ʿUthmān al-Battī v, 731a; s, 44b
ʿUthmān Batūr (1943) ix, 649b
ʿUthmān Bey al-Bardīsī (1807) ii, 292b; iv, 853a; vii, 423b
ʿUthmān Bey Dhu ʾl-Faḳār iv, 852a, b
ʿUthmān Dāy (Dayi̊/Dey, Tunis) (1610) i, 496a, b; ii, 161a; iv, 338b; vii, 243a
ʿUthmān Diḳna (Digna) b. Abī Bakr i, 49b, 1158b, 1239b; iv, 687a; v, 1249b, 1250a, 1251a; x, **952a**
ʿUthmān al-Djāzānī ii, 517b
ʿUthmān dan Fodio → ʿUthmān b. Fūdī
ʿUthmān al-Ḥaddād v, 51a
ʿUthmān Katkhudā al-Kazdughlī i, 815a
ʿUthmān Khān (Djālor) ii, 1127a
ʿUthmān Khān b. Ibrāhīm (Ḳarakhānid) (1212) iii, 1115a; iv, 583a, 1067b, 1068a; viii, 1033b
ʿUthmān al-Muḍāʾifī iii, 363b
ʿUthmān al-Nābulusī → al-Nābulusī
ʿUthmān Pasha → ʿOthmān Pasha
ʿUthmān Sirādj al-Dīn (XIX) vii, 935b
ʿUthmān Ulīdī (Bizerta) (XIX) vi, 251a
ʿUthmān al-Zandjīlī i, 181b; s, 338a
ʿUthmān al-Zindjārī x, 303a
ʿUthmān-i Marandī → Shāhbāz Ḳalandar
ʿUthmānids iv, 89b; x, 135a
ʿUthmāniyya x, **952a**
ʿUthmānzāde iv, 505a
ʿUthmānzay xi, 197b; s, 285a, 525b
Utrari → Utrār
al-ʿUṭrūsh → Ḥasan al-Uṭrūsh
Utsmi → Ḳaytaḳ
Uttar Pradesh vi, 489a; s, 74a, 325a, 360a
al-ʿUtūb, Banū iv, 751a; vi, 358a, 735a, b; viii, 668b; x, 955b
Uthūlūdjiyā (theology) x, **954b**
Utrār (Otrār) ii, 43a, 778b; x, **955a**
ʿUtūb x, **955b**
Uwaym b. Lāwudh (Lud) iii, 1270a
ʿUwaymir b. al-Ḥārith i, 113b, 114a; v, 730b
ʿUwayṣ → Aʿyāṣ

Uways I b. Ḥasan-i Buzurg (Djalāyirid) (1374) i, 325a, 720a, 1096a; ii, 401a, 733b; iv, 584b; vii, 189a; x, **957a**
Uways II b. Shāh Walad (Djalāyirid) (1421) x, **957b**
Uways b. Muḥammad b. Baykarā (Tīmūrid) (XV) i, 148a
Uways al-Ḳaranī (657) vi, 354a; vii, 472b, 592a; x, **958a**
Uways Muḥammad al-Bawārī, Shaykh (1909) ix, 722b
Uways Pasha (Yemen) (XVI) viii, 235b
Uwaysiyya x, **958a**
Uweys b. Meḥmed → Weysī
Üweys, Ḳara (1591) x, **958b**
al-ʿUyayna i, 628b; ii, 321a; iii, 677b, 678a; x, **959a**
ʿUyayna b. Ḥiṣn al-Fazārī (Uigur) (VII) i, 690a, 1077b, 1358b; ii, 873b, 1023a; v, 79b; ix, 115b; x, **959b**
Uyghur i, 1240a; ii, 2b, 311a, 315b, 840a, 1106b; iii, 115b, 116a, 217a, 1116a; iv, 699b; v, 846a, b; vi, 421b, 768a; vii, 353a; viii, 178a; s, 97b, 419a, 420a
– literature x, **725b**
Uyghur Khān (XVII) vii, 220a; x, 622b
Uyghur, On x, 687b, 688a
Uyrat → Kalmuks
ʿUyūn Dāwūdiyya vi, 230a
ʿUyūn Mūsā i, 788a
ʿUyūn Sīdī Mallūk vi, 892a
ʿUyūnids i, 73b, 552a, 553a, 942a; iii, 238a; iv, 764b; vii, 628b; x, **960a**
Uyvar s, 171a
Ūzār → Ong Khān
ʿUzayr (Ezra) x, **960a**
ʿUzayr (ʿIrāḳ) i, 265a; vii, 582b; s, 33b
al-ʿUẓayyim → al-ʿAḍaym
ʿUzayyiz b. Fayṣal iii, 1067b, 1068a
Uzbek/Üzbak/Ūzbīk → Özbeg
Uzbek (Özbeg) literature x, **721a**
Uzbekistān i, 531a; vi, 770a; x, **960b**
Uze → Ghuzz
Uzganī, Aḥmad b. Saʿd al-Dīn (X) x, 958a
Uzgend/Uzkend → Özkend
Uzuk (Ūzuk) ii, 806a; iv, 1104b; vii, 473b
Uzun Ḥasan (Ḥasan al-Ṭawīl) (Aḳ-Ḳoyunlu) (1478) i, 148b, 244a, 293a, 311b, 340a, 393a, 468b, 861b, 1067a, 1234a, 1252b; ii, 150a, 151a, 174a, 598b, 839b, 1136a; iii, 212b, 315b, 1101a; iv, 34a, 463a, 474a, 562b, 588a, 871a, 945a, 1048a; v, 492a; vi, 71a, 72a, 117b, 120a, 495a, 514a, 541a, 979a; vii, 173b, 666b, 727a; viii, 766b; x, 45b, **963b**; s, 208a
Uzun Khalīl i, 1257a
al-ʿUzzā iv, 321b; v, 692a, b; vi, 373b, 374a, 645b; x, **967b**

V

Vahrām → Bahrām
Vaikom Muhammad Basheer (XX) vi, 464b
Vakf-Mearif i, 1274b
Vakhtang (1676) → Shāh Nawāz I
Vakhtang (1724) v, 493b, 494a
Valachie → Eflāḳ
Valencia → Balansiya
Valenia → Bāniyās
Vālide Djāmiʿi → Yeni Djāmiʿ
Valona → Awlonya
Vambéry, Arminius (XIX) i, 64b; viii, 248a, 250b
Van (lake) → Wān
Van Ḳaraḥiṣārï iv, 579b
Van Kulu ii, 497a
Varna → Warna
Varvar ʿAlī Pasha iii, 318a, 983b, 1248a; v, 257a
Varvara (Bosnia) → Warwar
Vasak i, 939b; x, 76a
Vaspurakan i, 637b, 638a; xi, 135a, b
Vasvár, treaty of v, 259b; vi, 982b, 990b
Vāvār (Mappila) vi, 463b
Veda iii, 112b; iv, 206a
Vedat Nedim Tör (XX) vi, 95a
Velez → Bālish
Venice/Venise x, 966a
Vermudo II (Léon) (X) vi, 431b
Vērnāg iv, 709a; s, 366b
Verne s, 136a
Vérria → Karaferye
Vezīr Köprü v, 256a
Vidin → Widin

Vīdjāyanagara i, 199b; ii, 981a; iii, 147b, 417a, b, 421a, 425a, 426a, 1160b; v, 549b, 938a, 1258b; xi, **1a**
Vidyāpati (Vidyapati) i, 1168a; ix, 85b
Vienna → Viyana
Vietnam ii, 9a; iii, 1208b
Vikram → Bikrami
Vilayet → Wilāyāt
Vilches → Bildj
Vishtāsp → Bishtāsb
Viyana i, 294b, 1157b, 1285b; iv, 591b
Vize → Wize
Vizier → Wazīr
Vlad Drakul (XV) vi, 71a
Vlora → Awlonya
Vodin → Wodina
Voivode → Woywoda
Volga river → Itil
Volga Tatars → Ḳazan; Turks I
Volodimir I (Rūs) (1015) viii, 624a; x, 692b
Volos → Ḳuluz
Volubilis → Walīlī
Voynuḳ → Woynuk
Voyvoda → Woywoda
Vrančic, Antun (Verantius) s, 185b

W

Wā-Sōkht xi, **2a**
Wabāʾ iii, 240a; xi, **2a**
Wabar, Banū viii, 576a; xi, **4b**
Wabdha (Huete) i, 161a
Wād ʿAllāla x, 180a
Waʿd al-Banāt xi, **6a**
Wād Bū Regreg v, 1545b; vi, 135a
Waḍʿ al-Lugha v, 805b; xi, **7a**
Wad Madanī xi, **6a**
al-Waʿd Wa ʾl-Waʿīd xi, **6b**
Wadaʿ (Wadʿ) xi, **7b**
Wādaʿa (Yemen) vi, 436a; xi, 270b
Wadai → Wadāī
Wadāī (Ouadai) xi, **10b**
Wadāʾi (Wādāy, Čad) i, 98a, 910b, 1260a; ii, 123a, b, 124a; v, 357b; s, 164a, b, 165b, 166a
Wādāy → Wadāī
Wadd s, **820a**
al-Waḍḍāḥ → Djadhīma al-Abrash
al-Waḍḍāḥ s, 272b
Waḍḍāḥ al-Yaman (707) x, **13a,** 124b
Wad(d)ān ii, 575a, b; vi, 742b, 945b; vii, 623b
Wadhārī viii, 1030b; s, 176b
Wādī xi, **13b**
Wādīʿa xi, **21b**
Wādī ʿAbadān i, 767a; vi, 81a
Wādī ʾl-ʿAbīd vi, 340a, 742a; s, 223b
Wādī Abū Ḍabʿa s, 173b
Wādī Abū Raḳrāḳ viii, 506b (see also, *s.v.* Wād Bū Regreg)
Wādī ʾl-Abyaḍ i, 985b; v, 1156a, b; vii, 633a
Wādī Adhana (Dhana) vi, 559a, 560a, 561b, 562a, b, 564a, 565b; viii, 663a
Wādī al-Aḥḳāf vi, 81a
Wādī ʾl-ʿAḳīḳ → al-ʿAḳīḳ
Wādī ʿAḳl s, 159b
Wādī ʿAllāḳī → al-ʿAllāḳī, Wādī
Wādī ʿAmāḳīn xi, 302a
Wādī Ānā i, 242a, 489a; ix 14b
Wādī ʿĀra iii, 176 b; v, 799b
Wādī ʾl-ʿArab (Cyrenaica) i, 770a vi, 455b
Wādī ʿAraba (Jordan) i, **558b**; v, 897a; ix, 373a; s, 117a
Wādī Arīgha → Wādī Rīgh
Wādī Āsh (Guadix) vi, 575b; xi, **14b**; s, 399a
al-Wādī Āshī (1158) vi, 111a
al-Wādī Āshī, ibn al-Ḥaddād iii, **775b**
al-Wādīʾāshī, Shams al-Dīn Muḥammad (1348) xi, **15a**
Wādī Badr vi, 191a, b
Wādī Barhūt → Barhūt
Wādī al-Baṭn viii, 613b
Wādī Bayhān → Bayhān, wādī
Wādī Buṭnān → Buṭnān
Wādī Ḍahr vi, 191a; vii, 996a; xi, 271a
Wādī Damā s, 356a
Wādī Darʿa (Dra) vi, 134b; x, 170b
Wādī Dawʿan → Dawʿan
Wādī ʾl-Dawāsir i, 337a, 341a, 538a; ii, 177a; v, 62a; vii, 865a; xi, 41b
Wādī ʾl-Djarīr vii, 865b
Wādī Djayzān i, 109a; ii, **516a**
Wādī Duwayro i, 489a
Wādī Farsān vi, 167a

Wādī Fāṭima vi, 162b, 167a, 179b
Wādī Fāʾw ii, **867b**
Wādī Ḥadjar i, 538a; vii, 496b
Wādī Ḥaḍramawt i, 538a; iii, 51b, 52a; vi, 80a; x, 303a
Wādī Ḥalfa xi, **15b**
Wādī Ḥalfayn vi, 84b; xi, 47a
Wādī 'l-Ḥamḍ → Ḥamḍ, Wādī al-
Wādī Ḥanīfa i, 538b, 628b; ii, 92a; xi, **16a**
Wādī Ḥarīb → Ḥarīb
Wādī Ḥibawnā vi, 191a
Wādī 'l-Ḥidjāra xi, **16a**
Wādī Ibrāhīm vi, 179b
Wādī Ibro → Ibruh
Wādī Issīl vi, 589a
Wādī 'l-Kabīr i, 487b, 489a; iv, 116a; xi, **17b**
Wādī 'l-Khaznadār (battle of 1299) xi, **18a**
Wādī 'l-Ḳilt s, 173b
Wādī Ksob vi, 727b
Wādī 'l-Ḳurā v, 317b, 497b; vi, 344a, 875a; vii, 265a, 371b, 694a; xi, **18b**
Wādī Lakku s, **821b**
Wādī Madhhāb ii, 492a; vi, 436a; s, 505b
Wādī 'l-Madīna ii, 492a; vi, 220b
Wādī Madraka vi, 167a
Wādī 'l-Makhāzin i, 288b, 1058a; iii, 721a; v, 48b; vi, 894b
Wādī al-Masīla vi, 80a, 83a; x, 303a; s, 337a
Wādī Mellegue vi, 727a; x, 641b
Wādī Miskyana vi, 727a
Wādī Nabhān iv, 779b
Wādī Naʿmān i, 98a; vi, 179b
Wādī al-Naṭrūn → Naṭrūn; Dayr al-Suryānī
Wādī Nūl → Wādī Nūn
Wādī Nūn vi, 134a; xi, **19b**
Wādī Rādjil vii, 865a; viii, 757a
Wādī Rahyū vi, 404a
Wādī Ramāʾ vi, 80a
Wādī 'l-Raml v, 530a
Wādī Rīgh v, 1181b (see also, *s.v.* Maghrāwa. B.4)
Wādī Rimaʿ i, 1140b
Wādī 'l-Ruḳḳād xi, 290b, 291a
Wādī 'l-Rum(m)ah i, 538a, 1097b; vii, 865b; viii, 613a
Wādī Sabū v, 1185b, 1245a, b; vi, 741a
Wādī 'l-Sadīr → Wādī Tūmīlāt
Wādī al-Sahbāʾ i, 538b; ii, 92a, 1024b; iv, 1072b
Wādī Ṣaḥr vi, 727b
Wādī Salīṭ i, 991a; vii, 808a; x, 605a
Wādī Sarīr viii, 613a
Wādī Shaḳūra i, 489a; vii, 633a
Wādī Shalīf (Chélif) vi, 923b
Wādī Shanīl vi, 221b; xi, 18a
Wādī Sīdī Tūdjimān vii, 263a
Wādī Sirḥān i, 538a; vi, 490b; vii, 865a; ix, **673a**
Wādī Sūf ix, **763b**
Wādī Sūs vi, 742a; ix, 899a; x, 311a
Wādī Tadghat s, 132a
Wādī Tadjū i, 489a
Wādī Tansift iii, 69b, 300b; vi, 589a
Wādī 'l-Taym vi, 344a; ix, 435a
Wādī Thawba vi, 81a
Wādī Tifālfalt vi, 594b
Wādī al-Tīh ix, 912a; x, 480b
Wādī Tumīlāt i, 14b; v, 368a; x, 167b
Wādī Turaba i, 1299a; v, 62a; x, **670a**
Wādī Umm Rabīʿ ii, 873b; vi, 589a, 741a, b
Wādī Wargha s, 103a
Wādī Yāna (Āna) xi, **21b**
Wādī Zabīd i, 1140b; xi, 370a, b
Wādī 'l-Zāhir vi, 179b
Wādī Zīz ix, 545b; x, 82b
Wāḍiḥ (Ṭulayṭulā) (XI) i, 1044b; iii, 495b, 791a; viii, 880a; x, 605b
Wādīs (Tihāma) x, 482a
al-Wādiyāshī, Muḥammad b. Djābir ii, 744a; iv, 355b
Wadjd xi, **23a**
Wadjda (Oujda) i, 357b, 1281b; v, 1177a, 1187a; vi, 142b; viii, 440a; xi, **23b**
Wadjdī, Muḥammad Farīd (1954) i, 598a; iv, 159b, 720b; vi, 113b; vii, **439b**
Wadjdjādj b. Zallū (Zalw) (XI) vi, 744a; vii, 613a; s, 27a
Wadjh al-Ḳamar i, 280b
Wadjhī → Mathhawī.4
Wadjhī, Mullā ii, 865b; iii, 375b
Wādjib → Farḍ
Wādjid ʿAlī Khān (XIX) vi, 908b
Wādjid ʿAlī Shāh, Nawwāb (Awadh) (1856) i, 757b; ii, 7b, 73a; v, 635a, 961b; vi, 611b, 772b, 806a
Wadjīh al-Dīn Gudjarātī, Shaykh (XIV) i, 764b; vii, 440a
Wadjīh al-Dīn Masʿūd (Sabzawār) (1343) ix, 47b

Wadjīh al-Dīn Zangī b. al-Faryūmādī (1287) viii, 342b
Wadjīhids (ʿUmān) vii, 484b
al-Wādjikā → Abū Aḥmad ʿAbd al-Salām
Wadjnāʾ b. al-Rawwād al-Azdī (Tabrīz) (IX) vi, 499a; x, 42a
Wafā Ashrafī → Wafā, Mīrzā Mandī Ḳulī
Wafā, Abu ʾl-Ḳāsim Shīrāzī xi, **25b**
Wafā, Mīrzā Ḥasan ʿAlī Shīrāzī (1859) xi, **25a**
Wafā, Mīrzā Mahdī Ḳulī (XIX) xi, **25b**
Wafā, Mīrzā Muḥammad ʿAlī Kāshānī xi, **25b**
Wafā, Mīrzā Muḥammad ʿAlī Zawāraʾī (1829) xi, **25a**
Wafā, Mīrzā Sharaf al-Dīn ʿAlī Ḥusaynī (1785) xi, **25a**
Wafā, Muḥammad Amīn (1779) xi, **25a**
Wafā, Muḥammad Ḥusayn Farahānī (1794) xi, **25a**
Wafā, Shaykh Muḥammad Bākir Tammāmī (XIX) xi, **25a**
Wafāʾī → Aḥmad Ḥādjdjī Beg
al-Wafāʾī, ʿAbd al-ʿAzīz (1450) ix, 252b
Wafāʾiyya ix, 173a
Wafd ii, 467a, 934a; iii, 516a, 1069a; iv, 197b, 261a; vii, 904b, 905a; viii, 700a, b; s, 5b, 58a, 300b; xi, 219a
Wafd (Political Party) xi, **25b**
al-Wāfī, Shaykh Aḥmad (1921) viii, 449a
Wāfidiyya i, 946b, 1324b; xi, **26b**
Wafīk Pasha → Aḥmad Wafīk Pasha
Wāfir xi, **27b**
Wafḳ ii, 370a; v, 222b a; xi, **28a**
al-Wafrānī → al-Ifrānī
Wāḥa xi, **31a**
Waḥam xi, **32a**
al-Wāḥāt xi, **32b**
Wahb, Banū vii, 477a; viii, 535b; xi, **33a**
Wahb, al-Ḥusayn b. al-Ḳāsim (X) xi, **35b**
Wahb, Ḳāsim b. ʿUbayd Allāh Abu ʾl-Ḥusayb (902) xi, **33b**
Wahb Muḥammad b. al-Ḳāsim (X) xi, **33b**
Wahb Sulaymān b. Wahb, Abū Ayyūb (885) xi, **33a**
Wahb ʿUbayd Allāh b. Sulaymān (901) xi, **34a**
Wahb b. Baḳiyya i, 949a
Wahb b. al-Munabbih, Abū ʿAbd Allāh (728) ii, 363b; iii, 14a, 370a, 538a; iv, 212a, 369a; v, 811b; vii, 283b; viii, 478a; xi, **34a**; s, 88a, 116a
Wahbiyya → al-Ibāḍiyya
al-Wahbiyya ii, 459b, 460a; iii, 659a; vii, 893a
Waḥda xi, **36a**
Waḥdat al-Shuhūd xi, **37b**
Waḥdat al-Wudjūd → Waḥdat al-Shuhūd
Waḥdetī → Derwīsh Wāḥdetī
Wahhābī x, 943b
Wahhābiyya i, 38b, 98b, 106b, 166b, 233b, 277a, 528b, 554a, 628b, 748a, 1282a; ii, 10a, 63b, 254b, 517b, 572b, 625b, 783b; iii, 162b, 238a, 291b, 431a, 433a, 606a, 677b, 954b, 999a, 1064b; iv, 626a, 778a, 1073a; v, 62b, 507b, 808a, 997b, 998b; vi, 35a, 45b, 56b, 58b, 150b, 238a, 260a, 651b, 665a, 735b; vii, 425b; viii, 238a, 447a; xi, **39b**; s, 3b, 30b, 94b, 244b, 355b
– doctrine i, 188b, 259b, 416b, 714b, 1199b; iii, 679a; iv, 142b
– literature i, 796b; ii, 91b; iii, 773a
Wahhās b. Ghānim v, 1244b; x, 481b
Wahība, Āl xi, **47a**
Waḥīd → Yaḥyā-i Dārābī
Wahid Hasjim, K.H. (XX) vi, 731a, b
Wāḥidī (1535) iv, 472b, 473b; viii, 775b; xi, **47b**
al-Wāḥidī, Abu ʾl-Ḥasan (1076) v, 415b; vi, 476b, 913a; vii, 771a, b; xi, **48a**
Wāḥidī, Banū ii, 222b
Waḥīd-i Dastgardī iv, 71b
Wāḥidiyya i, 71a; iv, 668a; xi, 37a
Waḥidov → Nūr Waḥīdow
Wahm i, 112a; iii, 509b; xi, **48b**, 49a; s, **822b**
Wahrān (Oran) i, 270b; ii, 160b, 173a; vi, 592a; xi, **49b**; s, 376b
Wahrānī, Abū ʿAbd Allāh (1179) xi, **51b**
Wahrīz (ca. 575) ii, 190b, 193a; vii, 513b; xi, **52a**; s, 115b
Wahriz Boēs (Bōya) i, 102a, 102b; ii, 190a
Waḥsh xi, **52a**
Waḥshī (VII) iv, 68b; vii, 665a
Wahshī (1553) xi, 2a
Waḥshī (Bāfḳī) (Yazdī)(1583) viii, 775b; xi, **53a**
Waḥshī/Ḥūshī xi, **52b**
Wahsūdān (Rawwādī) (989) vii, 498a
Wahsūdān b. Djustān (IX) ii, 191a; iii, 245a; v, 602b

Wahsūdān b. Mamlān b. Abī 'l-Haydja (Rawwādī) (1054) iv, 347b, 453b; vi, 499b; viii, 470a; x, 42b
Wahsūdān b. Muḥammad (Musāfirid/ Sallārid) (957) iv, 662b; vii, 656b
Wahsūdānids ii, 192a; iv, 773a
Waḥy xi, **53b**
Wā'il → Bāhila; Bakr b. Wā'il
Wā'il, Banū i, 920b; vi, 649a
Wā'il b. Ḥadjr (VII) s, 337b
Wā'iẓ xi, **56a**
Wā'iẓ b. Isḥāḳ, 'Ubayd Allāh (XVIII) v, 1106a, b
Wakāla xi, **57b**
Waḳ'a-Nüwīs (Wāki'a nuwīs) i, 317a; ii, 338b; xi, **56a**
Waḳār, Mīrzā Aḥmad Shīrāzī (1881) vii, 478a; xi, **58b**
Waḳash vii, 773a; s, 236a
Waḳ'at al-Shi'b ii, 600b
Waḳf
– during the Umayyads and the 'Abbasids s, **823b**
– during the Fāṭimids and the Saldjūḳids s, **824a**
– during the Zangids and the Ayyūbids s, **825a**
– during the Mamlūks s, **825a**
– in classical islamic law xi, **59a**
– in the arab lands, Egypt xi, **63b**
– in Syria s, **823a**
– in north Africa to 1914 xi, **69a**
– in Muslim Spain xi, **75a**
– in the modern middle east and north Africa xi, **78b**
– in Persia xi, **81a**
– in the Ottoman empire to 1914 xi, **87b**; s, **826b**
– in central Asia xi, **92a**
– in Southeast Asia xi, **97a**
– in sub-saharan Africa xi, **99a**
Wakhān i, 223b; xi, **99b**
Wakhī i, 225a; ii, 31b
Wakhsh v, 75b; xi, **100b**; s, 125a
Wakhushtū Sulṭān (Georgia) (XVII) vii, 673b
Waḳī' i, 693b, 694a; s, 386b
Waḳī' Muḥammad b. Khalaf (918) x, 101a; xi, 101a
Waḳī' b. al-Djarrāḥ (812) i, 272b; vii, 607a; x, 29b; xi, **101a**
Wāḳi'a → al-Ḳur'ān
Wāḳi'a nuwīs → Waḳ'anuwīs
Wāḳid b. Djunaydib s, 177b
al-Wāḳidī, Abū 'Abd Allāh Muḥammad b. 'Umar (822) i, 140a; ii, 159a, 922bl; v, 1161b; vi, 262b, 263b, 411a; vii, 361a; viii, 515a; xi, **101b**; s, 263a
Wāḳif, Mollā Panāh i, 193b; ii, 217a
al-Wāḳifa (al-Wāḳifiyya, Shī'a) i, 275a; v, 1236a; vii, 647b; xi, **103a**
Wakīl → Wakāla
Wakīl al-Dawla, 'Abd al-Raḥīm v, 171a
Wakīl al-Ra'āyā, Ḥādjdjī (XX) vi, 485b
Wāḳim (al-Madīna) vii, 694a
Waḳḳās, Sayyid v, 771a
Waḳḳāṣ Biy (Mangit) (XV) vi, 417b
al-Waḳḳashī (al-Waḳshī), Abu 'l-Walīd (1096) i, 149a; vi, 606b; vii, 280b; xi, **103b**
Wakkom Muhammad Abdul Khader Maulavi (Mappila) (1932) vi, 462a
Wāḳ-wāḳ (Waḳwāḳ) v, 939b, 940a; vii, 245b; ix, 440b, 698b; xi, **103b**, 223b
Waḳt → Zamān
Walā' → Wilāya; Mawlā
Walad → Ṣaghīr
Walad Djalal (Zibane) vi, 364b
Walad al-Zarḳiyāl → al-Zarḳalī
Wālādjāh Muḥammad 'Alī Khān i, 937a
Walāsh → Adhur-Walāsh
Walasma' i, 763b; iii, 3b, 4a, 176a
Wālāta (Oualata, Mauritania) ii, 1002b; vii, 624b; xi, **109a**
al-Walātī, Muḥammad 'Abd Allāh (1805) vii, 625b
Walāya → Wilāya 2
Walba (Huelva) i, 6a, 155b; xi, **109a**
Walcott, Louis Eugene → Farrakhan
Wald 'Alī i, 483a
Wald Sulaymān (Bishr) i, 483a
Waldiyān vi, 504a
Wālī (Saint) xi, **109b**
Walī (Urdu Poet) (1707) x, **125b**
Walī al-'Ahd xi, **125b**
Walī Allāh al-Dihlawī → Dihlawī Shāh Walī Allāh
Walī Allāh (Farangī Maḥall) (1853) s, 292b
Walī, Amīr (Astarābādī) (XIV) ii, 401b
Walī Awrangābādī (1707) x, 878a
Walī Dakanī → Walī (Urdu Poet)

Walī Dasht-Bayāḍī (1592) viii, 775b; x, 439a
Walī al-Dīn (1342) i, 893a; iii, 24b
Walī al-Dīn Efendī iii, 158a
Walī al-Dīn Yakan iii, 593b
Walī Khān Bakash iii, 1106b; iv, 498b
Walī Mīrzā iv, 393a
Walī Muḥammad Khān ii, 638a
Walī, Shaykh (1549) i, 1284b
Walī Wēlūrī (XVIII) vi, 611a
Wāliba b. al-Ḥubāb (VIII) i, 107b, 143b; iv, 1003b; vii, 798b; viii, 884a; xi, **126b**
al-Walīd I b. ʿAbd al-Malik (Umayyad) (715) i, 45a, 58a, b, 77b, 196a, 305a, 381a, 493a, 610b, 612a, 761b, 787b, 1223a; ii, 198a, 280b, 304b, 788b, 956a, 957a; iii, 41a, 42a, 85b; iv, 712b, 742a, 973a; vi, 147a, 359b, 363b, 625a, 649b, 652a, 660b, 661a, 670a, 680b, 683b, 707b, 740a; xi, **127b**; s, 10a, 229a, 243a, 273a, b, 311a, b
al-Walīd II b. Yazīd (Umayyad) (744) i, 12b, 57b, 196b, 587a, 613a, 952b; ii, 198a, 427b; iii, 136a, 494b, 878a; iv, 1003a; v, 936b; vi, 139b, 623b, 624a, 740a; vii, 676a; xi, **128a**; s, 117a, 243a
al-Walīd b. ʿAbd al-Malik b. Zaydān (Saʿdid) (1636) vi, 595a
Walīd b. Hishām, Abu Rakwa (1007) xi, **129a**
al-Walīd b. al-Ḥusayn → al-Sharḳī b. al-Ḳuṭāmī
Wālid b. Khālunā (1798) vii, 614a, 622b
Walīd b. Khayzurān (X) vii, 248b
al-Walīd b. al-Mughīra (623) i, 115b; iii, 1017b; vi, 137b, 138a, 139a, 140a; viii, 1002b; xi, **129b**
al-Walīd b. Muslim (810) vii, 662b; s, 755b
al-Walīd b. Ṭarīf (795) ii, 524a; iii, 233b; xi, **129b**
al-Walīd b. ʿUḳba b. Abī Muʿayṭ (680) i, 382a; iii, 874a; vii, 497b; x, 166b; xi, **130a**
al-Walīd b. ʿUtba b. Abī Sufyān (VII) iii, 607b, 608a; vi, 621b, 622a; vii, 268b
al-Walīd b. al-Walīd b. al-Mughīra vi, 139a, b
al-Walīd b. Yazīd → al-Walīd II
al-Walīd al-ʿAbdī iii, 648b
al-Walīd al-Ḳurayshī, Āl s, 62a
Walīdād Khān i, 1300a
Wālide Ṣāliḥa Sulṭān (XVIII) vi, 55a, b; xi, **130a**
Wālide Sulṭān Bezm-i ʿAlem (XIX) i, 74b, 1226a; iv, 720a; v, 257a, 261b
Wālide Sulṭān Ṣafiyye → Ṣafiyye Sultān Baffa
Wālide Turkhān Khadīdje Sulṭān vi, 56b; x, **679a**
Wālihī, Aḥmed (Üsküb) (1599) xi, **132a**
Wālihī, Ḳurd-zāde (Edirne) (1586) xi, **131b**
Walikota i, 981a
Walīla/Walīlī (Volubilis) iii, 1031b, 1032a; vi, 889a, b; xi, **132b**; s, 103a
Walīma → ʿUrs
Walishān → Sībī
Wallachia → Eflāḳ
Wallāda bint Muḥammad III (Umayyad of Spain) (1078) xi, **133a**
Wallāda bint al-Mustakfī i, 601b; iii, 681b, 973b; vi, 751a
Walwal incident (1934) ix, 717b
Walwālīdj xi, **133b**
Wamānū, Banū vi, 427a
Wāmiḳ wa-ʿAdhrāʾ i, 1301a; xi, **134a**
Wān (Van) i, 627a, 634b, 637b, 638a, 644a, 1207a; ii, 34a; v, 441a, 442a, b; xi, **135a**; s, 130b
Wānā (Wazīristān) xi, 197b, 198a
Wanč i, 853b, 854a
Wandād-Hurmuzd (Ḳārinid) (780) iv, 645a; vi, 745b, 937b; ix, 392a
Wandād-Safān iv, 645a
Wandād Ummīd (Ḳarinid) (IX) vi, 745b
Wang Tai-yu (1657) x, 321b; xi, **136b**
Wangara iv, 548b, 773b; vi, 258b; xi, **137b**
wānḳulī, Meḥmed b. Muṣṭafā (1591) xi, **138a**
al-Wānī, Muḥammad b. Muṣṭafā i, 310a
al-Wanīsī, Ḥamdān (XX) v, 1029b; viii, 902a
Wansharīs (Ouarsenis) i, 371a, 372a; vi, 404a; xi, **138b**; s, 103a
al-Wansharīsī, Abu 'l-ʿAbbās Aḥmad (1508) i, 1341a; vii, 287a, 288b, 1052b; xi, **139b**; s, 27a, 403a
al-Wansharīsī, Shaykh al-Bashīr (1130) iii, 959b; vi, 592a
Wānūdīn b. Khazrūn b. Falfūl v, 1178a, b; s, 844b
Wanzamār, Banū v, 1174a, b, 1179a, 1180b

Wanzamār b. ʿArīf ii, 979a
Waraʿ xi, **141a**
Wara (Čad) i, 98a; xi, 11a; s, 164a
Wāra Dyābi (Takrūr) ix, 753b
Warād → Nagyvárad
Warād, Banū s, 350b
Waradīn (Petrocaradin/Peterwardein) xi, **142a**
Waraḳa b. Nawfal (VII) iii, 1206a; iv, 898b; vii, 363a; viii, 676a; xi, **142b**
Warāmīn xi, **143b**
Warangal v, 1216b; xi, **144a**
Warāwīnī → Marzbān-Nāma
Warayn, Banū vi, 815a; s, 145a
Ward (in Arabic literature) s, **828a**
Ward (Byzantin) (X) vi, 519b; xi, **144b**
Ward, Banū 'l- i, 1023b; iii, 386b
al-Ward al-Lak͟hmī i, 1023b
Warda → al-D̲j̲arādatānI
Wardak s, 367a
Wardān iii, 887a, 889a
al-Wardānī, Ibrāhīm Nāṣīf (1910) viii, 360a
Wardar (Vardar River) xi, **145a**
al-Wardī, ʿUmar b. Muẓaffar al-Maʿarrī Zayn al-Dīn (1348) iv, 864b; vi, 381b
Ward̲j̲ābī b. Rābīs vii, 584b
al-Wārd̲j̲alānī, Abū Yaʿḳūb Yūsuf b. Ibrāhīm (XI) x, 183a
Ward̲j̲lān → Wargla
al-Ward̲j̲lānī → Abū Zakariyyāʾ al-Ward̲j̲ lānī
Warfad̲j̲d̲j̲ūma, Banū i, 134b; v, 1164b; ix, 768a
Warg͟ha vi, 741a
al-Warg͟hī, Abū ʿAbd Allāh Muḥammad (1776) vi, 112b; xi, **145b**
Wargla iii, 656b, 657b, 1041a; xi, **145b**; s, 15b
Wariḳ xi, **147b**
Warīka, Banū vi, 742a; xi, **148a**
al-Wārit͟h b. Kaʿb al-K͟harūṣī (IX) iii, 652b; iv, 1085a; ix, 775a
Wārit͟h S͟hāh (1766) viii, 256b
Warithuddin Muhammad (Wallace Deen Muhammad) (XX) vii, 703a, b
Warḳāʾ al-Nak͟haʿī iv, 495a
Warḳāʾ b. ʿUmar (776) xi, **148a**
Wārkū, Banū iii, 1040b
Warna (Varna) xi, **148b**
Warrā, Banū v, 1178b, 1179a
Warrāḳ xi, **150a**
al-Warrāḳ, Abū ʿĪsā → Abū ʿĪsā
Warrāḳ, Ibn Sayyār → Ibn Sayyār
al-Warrāḳ Maḥmūd b. (al)-Ḥasan (845) xi, **151a**
al-Warrāḳ, Muḥammad b. Yūsuf (973) i, 156b; xi, **151a**
Warrū b. Saʿīd v, 1182a, b
Wars xi, **152a**
Wars͟h, ʿUt͟hmān b. Saʿīd (812) xi, **152a**
Warsheikh vi, 129a
Warsifān, Banū v, 1179a, b, 1183a
Wartadī, Banū vi, 1009a
al-Wart͟hīlānī (1779) ii, 161a; ix, 20b; s, 403a
Warwar/Varyara (Bosnia) xi, 152b
Warwari ʿAlī Pas͟ha (1648) xi, **152b**
Waryāg͟hal, Banū s, 377a
Warzamār, Banū → Wanzamār, Banū
Warzarāt vi, 590b
al-Wāsānī, Abu 'l-Ḳāsim (1003) xi, **153a**
Waṣf (in law) xi, **158b**
Waṣf (in poetry) xi, **153a**
Waṣfī (1971) xi, **159a**
Was͟hḳa (Huesca) i, 1057b; vi, 345a; xi, **159a**
al-Was͟hm (tattooing) xi, **160a**
– in older arab society s, **830b**
– in the recent arab society xi, **160a**
Was͟hmagīr b. Ziyār → Wus͟hm(a)gīr b. Ziyār (Ziyārid) (967)
al-Was͟hs͟hāʾ ii, 1032b; iii, 1263b; iv, 822b; v, 737a
al-Was͟hs͟hāʾ, Abu 'l-Ṭayyib Muḥammad (Ibn al-Was͟hs͟hāʾ) (937) xi, **160b**
Waṣī (in S͟hīʿism) xi, **161a**
Wāsiʿ Alīsī (Vasi Alîsi) (1543) iv, 505a; vi, 900a; xi, **162a**
Wāṣif, Aḥmed (1806) vi, 340b; xi, **162b**
Waṣīf b. Ṣuwārtigin al-K͟hazarī (amīr al-Ḥad̲j̲d̲j̲) (X) vii, 543a; s, 304b
Wāṣif Enderūnī (1824) xi, **163a**
Waṣīf al-Turkī (ḥād̲j̲ib) (IX) i, 271b, 273a, 789b; ii, 26b; vi, 900a; vii, 390a, 395a, 583a, 722b, 777b, 793b
Wāṣifī vii, 92b; s, 46b
al-Waṣīfī, Ibrāhīm b. Waṣīf S͟hān (X) xi, **163a**
Wāṣil, Banū viii, 866a
Wāṣil b. ʿAṭāʾ (748) i, 127b, 454a, 1080b; ii, 833b; iii, 985a, 1025b, 1142b; iv, 142a;

vi, 457b, 458a; vii, 260a, 783a; x, 440a; s, 225b, 227a; xi, **164a**
Wasīm-Awsīm vi, 411a
Wasīn, Banū → Wisyān, Banū
Wāsiṭ i, 77a, 103a, 132a, 867a, 949a, 1094b; ii, 248a, 319b; iii, 41a, 1252b, 1255a, 1267a; iv, 724b; vi, 119b, 247a, 270b, 335b, 345a, 427b, 613b, 661a, 679b, 691b, 740a; vii, 672a; xi, **165b**; s, 41a, 118a, 119a, 126b, 193a, 243a, 385a
Wāsiṭa ii, 857b; xi, **171a**
al-Wāsiṭī, Abū Bakr (931) (Khaṭīb) v, 332a; x, 314b, 377b; s, 785a
al-Wāsiṭī, Abu 'l-Fatḥ (1194) ii, 166b; vi, 354b
al-Wāsiṭī, Abū Ghālib Muḥammad b. ʿAlī (XI) vii, 270b
al-Wāsiṭī, Abu 'l-Ḳāsim ʿAlī b. Muḥammad (932) vi, 569b; vii, 312a; s, 13b
al-Wāsiṭī, Aḥmad b. Ibrāhīm (1311) iii, 954b
al-Wāsiṭī, Aḥmad b. Muḥammad, vizier (IX) v, 49a; s, 1a
al-Wāsiṭī, Djamāl al-Dīn (XIII) viii, 806a
al-Wāsiṭī, Ghāzī vii, 305a
Waṣiyya xi, **171b**
Waṣl xi, **172b**
Wasm xi, **173b**
Waṣṣāf al-Ḥadrat, ʿAbd Allāh b. Faḍl Allāh Shīrāzī (1334) iv, 67b; vi, 15b; vii, 343b, 481a; xi, **174a**
Wasūṭ iv, 1147a
Waṭan i, 64a; iv, 785b, 790b; xi, **174b**
Waṭaniyya iv, 784b, 785a; xi, **175a**
Wathaniyya xi, **176a**
al-Wāthiḳ bi-'llāh (ʿAbbāsid) (847) i, 10b, 18b, 271a, 551a, 1298b; ii, 188b, 198a, 236a; iii, 618a; iv, 138a; vi, 206a, 625b; vii, 4a, 279b, 518a, 776b, 777b; ix, 205b; xi, **178a**; s, 33a, 106a, 199a
al-Wāthiḳ (Almohad) → Abū Dabbūs
al-Wāthiḳ (Ḥafṣid) iii, 67a
Wathīḳa xi, **178b**
Wāthiḳī, Abū Muḥammad (XI) xi, **179a**
Wāthila b. al-Asḳaʿ i, 266b
Wathīma b. Mirsāl (IX) vii, 768b
Wathīma b. Mūsā al-Fasawī (851) xi, **179a**
Waththāb b. Sābiḳ al-Numayrī (1019) iii, 228a; xi, **180a**
Watid i, 670b, 671b, 674b; xi, **181b**
Waṭṭār, Ṭāhir al- v, 190a, 191a; s, 95a
Waṭṭās, Banū → Waṭṭāsids
Waṭṭāsids i, 706a, 1057b; ii, 463a, 510a, 819b; iv, 94a; v, 1190b, 1200a; vi, 134b, 248b, 574a, 741b, 1009a; vii, 37b; viii, 723a; ix, 507b; xi, **181b**
Waṭwāṭ → Rashīd al-Dīn
Waṭwāṭ (Bat) xi, **183a**
al-Waṭwāṭ, Djamāl al-Dīn (1318) ii, 900a; v, 1227a; vii, 897a; viii, 158b
Wāw xi, **183a**
al-Waʾwāʾ al-Dimashḳī, Abu 'l-Faradj (ca. 1000) ix, 55b; xi, **184a**
Wāwazgīt, Banū i, 161b; vi, 742a; s, 144b
Wayhind vi, 65b; xi, **184a**
Ways Khān iv, 512a
Ways Khān Zand v, 664a
Wāziʿ, Āl i, 1299a
Waẓīfa iv, 1055b; xi, **184a**
Wazīr (vizier) xi, **185a**
– during the ʿAbbāsids xi, **185a**
– during the Faṭimid Caliphate xi, **188a**
– during the Ayyūbids xi, **190a**
– in Muslim Spain xi, **191b**
– in Persia xi, **192b**
– in the Ottoman Empire xi, **194b**
Wazīr Begam → Çhoti Begam
Wazīr al-Dawla, Nawāb iv, 197a
Wazīr Ḥasan, Sayyid (XX) vi, 78a
Wazīr Khān (ʿIlm al-Dīn al-Anṣārī, Lāhawr, 1710) i, 914a; ii, 47b; v, 600a
Wazīr Khān Harawī i, 80b
al-Wazīr al-Maghribī (XI) vii, 651a
Wazīr Muḥammad Khān i, 1195b
al-Wazīr al-Ṣaghīr xi, **197b**
al-Wazīr al-Ṣāḥib Ṣafāʾ al-Dīn (XIII) vi, 111a
Wazīr Singh ii, 797b
Wazīra bint Munadjdjā (1316) viii, 156a
Wazīrābād ii, 47b, 258b; v, 888a
Wazīrīs / Wazīristān vi, 86a, b; xi, **197b;** s, 285a, 329b
Wazn xi, **198b**
Wazīrīstān → Wazīrīs
Wazzān (Morocco) i, 687b; vi, 356b, 890b; xi, **200b**; s, 404a
Wazzān, al-Hasan b. Muḥammad → Leo Africanus
al-Wazzānī, Muḥammad Ḥasa iii, 525a, b; s, 10a
Wazzāniyya xi, **201b**
Wēbi Shabēllā vi, 128b

Wed Bou Regreg → Wādī Abū Raḳrāḳ
Wedjīhī (1661) xi, **202a**
Wedjīhī Pasha ii, 636b
Wefā', Shaykh (1490) vii, 30b, 349a
Wehbī → Pīr Meḥmed
Wehbī, Sayyidī Ḥusayn (1736) vii, 839a; xi, **202a**
Welī Maḥmūd → Maḥmūd Pasha Welī
Welī Pasha i, 175a, 398b, 399a
Wenceslaus → Čeh
Wenedik (Venice) xi, **202b**
Werčikwār s, 158b
Weysī (1628) xi, **204b**
Wezī Köprü (Vezirköprü) xi, **205a**
Whēbyōt s, 339b
White Horde i, 1106b; ii, 44a, b, 571b; x, 511a; s, 459a
Wibisono, Jusuf vi, 731b
Widādī i, 193b
Widin (Vidin) iii, 628a, 629b; vi, 56a; viii, 284b, 287b; xi, **205b**
Widja' iv, 1088a, 1089b
Widjāda iii, 27b; s, 400b
al-Widyān i, 538b; xi, 13b
Wikāla ii, 148b; iv, 435a, b, 840b, 1015b
Wiḳār al-Mulk s, 74a
Wilāya xi, **208a**
Wilāyat 'Alī, Mawlawī (1853) vii, 291a; xi, 237a
Wilāyet → Eyālet
William of Rubruck vii, 230a; iv, 612b
Wīmā (Dunbāwand) vi, 744b
Wīrān, Ḥāfiẓ Ghulām ii, 222a
Wird ii, 224a; iv, 94b; xi, **209b**; s, 93a
Wīs u-Rāmīn ii, 1142b; xi, **210a**
Wiṣāl xi, **210b**
Wiṣāl, Kučak ii, 433b; iv, 69b
Wiṣāl, Mīrzā Muḥammad Shafī' (1845) s, **831a**
Wisām xi, **212a**
Wīsū i, 1305a, 1306a
Wisyān, Banū iii, 1041a; xi, 212a
al-Wisyānī xi, **212a**
al-Wisyānī, Abū Khazar Yaghlā b. Zaltaf (990) xi, **212a**
al-Wisyānī, Abū Mūsā Hārūn b. Abī 'Imrān al-Ḥammī (XI) iii, 657a; xi, **212b**
al-Wisyānī, Abū Rabī' Sulaymān b. 'Abd al-Salām (XII) xi, **212b**
al-Wisyānī, Shaykh Abū Khazar (X) vi, 947a
Witr (Watr) xi, **213a**
Witu Sultanate iv, 889a, b
Wizāra → Wazīr
Wize (Vize) xi, **213b**
Wizr b. Djābir Asad al-Rahīṣ i, 519a
Wodina (Vodina, Edessa, Macedonia) xi, **214a**
Wolof → Djolof; Senegal
Wolos → Ḳuluz
Woynuḳ xi, **214b**
Woywoda i, 1253a; iv, 1095b; xi, **215a**
Wu Ma (N.W. China) v, 844b; xi, **215b**
Wuchali, Treaty of vi, 643b
Wudjūd xi, **216a**
Wuḍū' xi, **218a**
Wufūd xi, **219a**
Wuhayb b. 'Abd Manāf i, 438b
Wuḥaydāt, Banū vii, 921a
Wuḳūf xi, **220b**
Wurukasha, lake iv, 400b
Wushm(a)gīr b. Ziyār (Ziyārid) (907) iii, 255a; iv, 23a, 100a, b; vi, 115b, 539a, b, 941b; viii, 597b; xi, **221b**
Wusun, Banū (E. Turkestan) xi, 224a
Wuthūḳ al-Dawla (1951) v, 24b; viii, 512a; xi, **221b**

X

Xanî, Ehmedê v, 482a
Xativa → Shāṭiba

Y

Yāʾ xi, **222a**
Yaʿāḳīb, Banū iii, 1004b
Yaʿāriba → Yaʿrubids
Yabāku (Yabaḳu), Banū viii, 160b; x, 689b
al-Yābānī (Japanese) xi, **223a**
Yabdar s, 402b
Yabg̲h̲u i, 420a, 661b, 852a; ii, 1107b; iv, 658b; x, 689b; xi, **224a**; s, 244b, 245a
Yābisa (Ibiza) xi, **224a**
Yabrīn (oasis) viii, 1048a; xi, **225a**
Yabrūḥ (man drake) xi, **225a**
Yābura (Evora) ix, 441a; xi, **225b**
Yaʿburī iii, 134a
Yacoub → Yaʿḳūb
Yada Tas̲h̲ xi, **226b**
Yadaʿʾil D̲h̲arīḥ b. Sumhuʿalī vi, 562a; ix, 675b
Yadaʿʾil Watar b. Sumhuʿalī Yanūf vi, 561a
Yadaʿʾil Yanūf vi, 559b
al-Yadālī (1753) xi, **227a**
Yadālī, S̲h̲ayk̲h̲ Muḥammad Saʿīd b. al-Muk̲h̲tār (1752) vii, 614a, 622b
Yaddar, Banū ii, 527a; vi, 743a
Yadd(u)ū b. Yaʿlā iii, 1042b, 1043b; v, 1177a; s, 843b, 844a
Yādgār xi, **228a**
Yādgār, Aḥmad s, 1b
Yādgār Nāṣir Mīrzā (XVI) iii, 633a
Yādigār Muḥammad (Astrakhan K̲h̲ān) (XVI) iv, 849b
Yādigār Muḥammad (Tīmūrid) (1470) i, 148b; vii, 928a
Yād̲j̲ūd̲j̲ Wa-Mād̲j̲ūd̲j̲ xi, **231a**
Yāfaʿ (sultanate) ii, 675b
Yāfā (Jaffa) vi, 32b, 322a; vii, 168b; xi, **234a**; s, 20b
Yāfiʿ, Banū (Yemen) iv, 745b; vii, 496a, 779a; ix, 235b; xi, **235b**; s, 338b
al-Yāfiʿī (1464) vi, 353a
al-Yāfiʿī, ʿAbd Allāh b. Asʿad al-Yamanī (1367) i, 255b; ii, 392a; vi, 354b; viii, 45a; xi, **236a**
Yāfit̲h̲ (Japhet) xi, **336b**
Yafran iii, 1039b, 1040a; vi, 435a
al-Yafranī, Hilāl b. Abī Ḳurra (1057) x, 144b
al-Yaftalī, Abu 'l-Fatḥ (951) i, 852a
Yaʿfur → Yuʿfir
Yaʿfūr ii, 624a; iii, 393b
Yaʿfurids → Yuʿfurids
Yag̲h̲amrāsan/Yag̲h̲murāsan (Zayyānid) (Tlemcen) (XIII) i, 92b; iii, 866a; v, 1180a; vi, 404a, 593a, 815b; vii, 722a
Yag̲h̲ī-basan b. G̲h̲āzī, Malik Niẓām al-Dīn (Dānishmendid) (1166) ii, 110b; viii, 36a; s, 154a
Yag̲h̲ı̊-bastı̊ (Īnd̲j̲ū) (XIV) iii, 1208b
Yāg̲h̲ı̊siyān, Amīr (Anṭakiya) (XI) i, 517a; v, 921b, 924a; viii, 947a
al-Yag̲h̲īsiyānī, Ṣalāḥ al-Dīn Muḥammad, (Amīr, Ḥamāt) (XII) vi, 870a; viii, 127b
Yāg̲h̲istān ii, 140a; xi, **237a**
Yag̲h̲lı̊kčı̊ Emīr iv, 193b
Yag̲h̲ma, Banū x, 689a; xi, **237b**
Yag̲h̲mā D̲j̲andaḳī, Abu 'l-Ḥasan (1859) iii, 355b; iv, 69b; vii, 754b; xi, **238a**
Yag̲h̲māʾī, Ḥabīb-i (1984) iv, 71b; xi, **235b**
Yag̲h̲murāsan b. Zayyān b. T̲h̲ābit (1283) xi, **239a**
al-Yag̲h̲mūrī, S̲h̲ihāb al-Dīn iv, 960a
Yag̲h̲nōbī Language s, 426a
Yag̲h̲ūt̲h̲ (idol) iii, 223a; vi, 651a; vii, 591b, 592a; s, **831a**
al-Yaḥīrī, Yaḥyā b. al-Ḥusayn s, 236a
Yaḥmad, Āl i, 813a; iv, 1084b; ix, 775a
Yaḥmūm vi, 653b
Yaḥṣib → Ils̲h̲araḥ Yaḥḍib
Yahūd (Jews) i, 264b, 265a, b, 491b, 546b, 565a, 1020-22, 1178a; ii, 85b, 145b, 229a, 230a, 563b, 620a, 725b, 835b, 859b, 912b, 913a, 1010a; iii, 80a, 147b, 324b, 326a; iv, 8a, 43b, 98b, 99a, 133b, 239a, 241b, 299a-313b, 603b, 824a, 1138a-1142a, 1174b; v, 326b, 334a, b, 337a, 436a, 668b, 994b; vi, 591b; xi, **239b**
Yahūdā b. Ḳuray̲s̲h̲ (900) viii, 1008a
al-Yahūdī → Māsard̲j̲awayh
Yahūdī, Yūsuf iv, 310a
al-Yahūdiyya (Afg̲h̲ānistān) vi, 915a
Yahūdiyya (Iṣfahān) iv, 98b, 106a
Yaḥyā (Banū G̲h̲āniya) (XIII) vi, 404a
Yaḥyā (John the Baptist) → Yaḥyā b. Zakariyyāʾ
Yaḥyā, Banū (Málaga) vi, 221a
Yaḥyā, Imām (Yemen) (1948) → Yaḥyā b. Muḥammad, al-Manṣūr al-Mutawakkil

Yaḥyā, Shaykh al-Islām (1644) viii, 215b; ix, 240a; s, **832a**
Yaḥyā I al-Muʿtalī (Ḥammūdid) (1036) i, 5b; iii, 147a; vi, 222a
Yaḥyā II b. Idrīs b. ʿAlī (Ḥammūdid) (1039) vi, 222a
Yaḥyā I (Idrīsid) iii, 1035b; iv, 632a
Yaḥyā II (Idrīsid) iii, 1035b
Yaḥyā III al-Miḳdām (Idrīsid) (905) iii, 1036a; vii, 641a
Yaḥyā IV (Idrīsid) (922) iii, 1036a; vi, 742b; vii, 641a; s, 132a
Yaḥyā b. ʿAbd Allāh (marabout) (Sūs) (XVII) vi, 594b
Yaḥyā b. ʿAbd Allāh b. al-Ḥasan (al-Daylamī) (803) i, 271b, 402b, 1034b; ii, 191a; iii, 233b, 616a, 617a; vii, 389a; xi, **242a**; s, 130a
Yaḥyā b. ʿAbd Allāh b. Saʿīd al-Ḥaḥī (XVII) s, 29a
Yaḥyā b. ʿAbd al-Aẓīm al-Djazzār (1270) x, 5a
Yaḥyā b. ʿAbd al-ʿAzīz iii, 138b; iv, 479b; v, 60b
Yaḥya b. ʿAbd al-Malik b. Makkī (1393) iv, 338a
Yaḥyā b. Abī Bakr b. Yūsuf b. Tāshufīn i, 389b; iii, 728a
Yaḥyā b. Abī Ḥafṣa Yazīd (VII) vi, 625a
Yaḥyā b. Abī Ḥāshid b. al-Ḍaḥḥāk s, 22a
Yaḥyā b. Abī Manṣūr al-Munadjdjim (830) iii, 8b, 1136b; vi, 599b, 600a
Yaḥyā b. Abī Ṭālib (ʿAzafī, Ceuta) (XIV) vii, 1023a; s, 112b
Yaḥyā b. Abī Yaḥyā, Shams al-Dīn s, 236a
Yaḥyā b. Ādam (818) iv, 1141b; x, 917b; xi, **243b**
Yaḥyā b. ʿAdī (974) i, 126b, 130a, 151b, 234b, 235a, 328a, 631b, 737a; ii, 779a; iii, 895b, 980a; v, 121a; vi, 204a, 637b, 845a; viii, 615a; xi, **245a**; s, 25a, 398b
Yaḥyā b. Aktham, Abū Muḥammad al-Marwazī (857) i, 271a, 273a; iii, 879a; vii, 778a; xi, **246a**
Yaḥyā b. ʿAlī → Munadjdjim, Banū 'l-.4
Yaḥyā b. ʿAlī b. Abī Ṭālib (VII) s, 92b
Yaḥyā b. ʿAlī b. Ghāniya (XII) i, 390a; ii, 1007a
Yaḥyā b. ʿAlī b. Ḥammūd → Yaḥyā I (Ḥammūdid)
Yaḥyā (Yuḥannā) b. al-Biṭrīḳ (XI) i, 235a, 589b, 736b; iii, 311b; xi, **246a**
Yaḥyā b. Ghāniya (1148) i, 165b; ii, 463b, 575a, 1007b; iii, 66b, 1039a; iv, 337b, 614b, 828a; viii, 763b
Yaḥyā b. al-Ḥakam (696) vi, 139a, 774b
Yaḥyā b. Ḥamdūn i, 1088a
Yaḥyā b. Ḥamza al-ʿAlawī (1344) iv, 252a; v, 901a; xi, **246b**
Yaḥyā b. al-Ḥārith al-Dhimārī iii, 704b
Yaḥyā b. Harthama i, 713a; iv, 100a
Yaḥyā b. al-Ḥasan b. Djaʿfar s, 401a
Yaḥyā b. Ḥātim Ipnā vi, 247a
Yaḥyā b. Hubayra → Ibn Hubayra, Yaḥyā
Yaḥyā b. Ḥurayth al-Djudhāmī (Mālaḳa) (747) vi, 221b
Yaḥyā b. al-Ḥusayn al-Hādī Ilā 'l-Ḥaḳḳ → al-Hādī Ilā 'l-Ḥaḳḳ Yaḥyā al-Rassī
Yaḥyā b. Ibrāhīm al-Gudālī (XI) ii, 1121b; v, 653b; vi, 744a; s, 27a
Yaḥyā b. Idrīs → Yaḥyā IV (Idrīsid)
Yaḥyā b. al-Ḳāsim → Yaḥyā III (Idrīsid)
Yaḥyā b. Ḳāsim (ʿIrāḳ) vii, 9b
Yaḥyā b. Ḳawām al-Dīn al-Marʿashī (XV) vi, 512b
Yaḥyā b. Ḳays al-Māribī vi, 566b
Yaḥyā b. Khaldūn → Ibn Khaldūn, Yaḥyā
Yaḥyā b. Khālid al-Barmakī (805) i, 936a, 1033a, 1034a, b, 1223a; ii, 79b, 305a; iii, 232b, 989a; iv, 16b, 119a, 1164a; v, 1238b; vi, 599b; vii, 215a, 646a; s, 48b, 225b, 393b
Yaḥyā b. Maḥmūd (XIII) vi, 199a; x, 904b
Yaḥya b. Maḥmūd al-Gudjarātī (1689) iv, 507a
Yaḥyā b. Maʿīn b. ʿAwn al-Murrī (847) viii, 515b; ix, 7b; xi, 102a, **247a**
Yaḥyā b. Manda s, 193a
Yaḥyā b. al-Manṣūr Ḥamīd al-Dīn (Zaydī) (Maḥmūd al-Mutawakkil ʿalā Allāh) (1948) v, 809a; vi, 192a, 262a
Yaḥyā b. Meḥmed ül-Kātib (XV) vii, 531b; viii, 544b
Yaḥyā b. Muʿādh → Bābak al-Khurramī
Yaḥyā b. Muʿādh (Nīshāpūr) (872) vi, 570a
Yaḥyā b. Muʿādh b. Muslim (Dhuhl; Banū) (IX) vi, 333a, 336b
Yaḥya b. Muḍar (al-Andalus) (IX) vi, 281a
Yaḥyā b. Muḥammad → Yaḥyā I (Idrīsid)

Yaḥyā b. Muḥammad Ḥamīd al-Dīn iv, 745b
Yaḥyā b. Muḥammad, Imām al-Manṣūr al-Mutawakkil (Yemen) (1948) vi, 262a; viii, 564a; xi, **247a**
Yaḥyā b. al-Mundhir iii, 743a
Yaḥyā b. al-Nāṣir b. al-Manṣūr al-Muʿtasim bi-'llāh (Almohad) (1229) v, 48b; vi, 339b, 592b
Yazyā b. Pīr ʿAlī → Newʿī
Yaḥyā b. Saʿdūn (1092) vi, 353b
Yaḥyā b. Saʿīd → al-Antākī
Yaḥyā b. Saʿīd (760) iii, 24b; vi, 263a, b; x, 29b
Yaḥyā b. Sāʿid (930) s, 400b
Yaḥyā b. Saʿīd (1034) vii, 115b
Yaḥyā b. Saʿīd al-Ḳaṭṭān → al-Ḳaṭṭān
Yaḥyā b. Sallām al-Baṣrī iv, 829b; x, 462b
Yaḥyā b. al-Samīna i, 600a
Yaḥyā b. Sarūr, Sharīf vi, 150b
Yaḥyā b. al-Shāṭir iii, 228a
Yaḥyā b. Sulaymān (875) vi, 900a
Yaḥyā b. Taʿfūft i, 689a
Yaḥyā b. Tamīm i, 149a
Yaḥyā b. ʿUmar (Almoravid) (1056) ii, 1002b, 1122a; iii, 288b; v, 653b, 654a, b; vii, 613a
Yaḥyā b. ʿUmar (Ifrīḳiya) (902) iii, 486a; viii, 844a; ix, 586b
Yaḥyā b. ʿUmar (Kūfa) (IX) vii, 390a
Yaḥyā b. ʿUmar al-Ṭālibī ii, 485a; iii, 908a, 1022b
Yaḥyā b. ʿUthmān b. Ṣāliḥ (895) viii, 895a
Yaḥyā b. Wasīnū ii, 1013a
Yaḥyā b. Yaghmūr (1150) vii, 37a; v, 586b
Yaḥyā b. Yaḥyā → Yaḥyā II (Idrīsid)
Yaḥyā b. Yaḥyā al-Laythī (Mālikī) (848) iv, 87a; vi, 744a; xi, **248a**
Yaḥyā b. Yaʿmar (ḳāḍī) vi, 670b
Yaḥyā b. Yaʿmur (Baṣra) iv, 731b
Yaḥyā b. Zakariyyāʾ (John the Baptist) ii, 279b, 281a; iii, 613b, 1175a, 1206a; iv, 724a, 912b; v, 421a; vi, 630a; vii, 551b; xi, **249a**
Yaḥyā b. Zayd b. ʿAlī b. al-Ḥusayn (743) i, 402b; ii, 608b, 1139b; iii, 1265b; iv, 446b; v, 3a, 230a; vii, 396a; ix, 433b; xi, **249b**
Yaḥyā b. Zikrawayh ii, 850b; iv, 493b, 660b; viii, 831a
Yaḥyā b. Ziyād al-Ḥārithī (VIII) ii, 806b; iv, 1003b; vii, 798b; ix, 387a
Yaḥyā al-Anṭakī (1065) vii, 164a; viii, 854b
Yaḥyā al-Aṭrash ii, 637b
Yaḥyā al-Barmākī → Yaḥyā b. Khālid
Yaḥyā Bey (Beg) → Tashlîdjalî Yaḥyā
Yaḥyā Efendī iv, 505a
Yaḥyā al-Ghazāl → al-Ghazāl
Yaḥyā al-Hādī ilā 'l-Ḥaḳḳ iv, 944b; s, **334b**, 557a
Yaḥyā Ḥaḳḳī (1992) vi, 91a; xi, **250b**
Yaḥyā Ḥamīd al-Dīn (Zaydī) (1904) vi, 192a; ix, 201b
Yaḥyā al-Ḳādir i, 446b, 986a; ii, 243a; s, 23a
Yaḥyā Karāwī (Sarbadār) (XIV) x, 552b
Yaḥyā al-Kātib iii, 1243a
Yaḥyā Kemāl Beyatlî (1958) v, 195a; xi, **251a**; s, 167b, 324b
Yaḥyā Khān (XX) iv, 177b; v, 1081b; viii, 242b, 999a
Yaḥyā al-Laythī i, 83a
Yaḥyā al-Maghribī → Abū Zakariyyāʾ al Maghribī
Yaḥyāal-Makkī, Abū ʿUthmān (IX) xi, **251b**
Yaḥyā Manērī, Shaykh (1291) vi, 410a, s, 571b, 577b
Yaḥyā al-Naḥwī (Johannes Grammaticus) (575) ii, 771b, 780b; xi, **251b**
Yaḥyā Nūrī, Mīrzā (Ṣubḥ-i Azal) (bābī) i, 809a, 833b, 847a, 911b; iv, 51b, 696a; viii, 114a; s, 53b
Yaḥyā Pasha (1566) x, 213b
Yaḥyā Pāshā-zāde Küčük Bālī Beg ii, 201b; iv, 657a
Yaḥyā-i Dārābī i, 833b, 847a
Yaḥyā-i Shirwanī ii, 1136b; iv, 991a, 992b; s, 208a
Yakan, ʿAldī (1933) xi, **253a**
Yakan, Muḥammad Walī al-Dīn (1921) xi, **253b**
Yakhshî Faḳīh (ca. 1413) xi, **253b**
Yakhshî Khān b. Maḥmūd Beg (Ḳaramān-oghullarî) (XIV) iv, 621b, 622a, b
Yakhshī Khān b. Ḳarasî (Bergama) (XIV) iv, 628a
Yakhshī b. Tīmurtash i, 1303a; ii, 611a
Yaḳīnī vii, 567b
Yaḳtan iv, 448a
Yaḳṭīn (tree) vi, 651a, 901a

Yaḳṭīn b. Mūsā s, 199a
Yaʿḳūb (Jacob) iii, 980a; xi, **254a**
Yaʿḳūb, Shaykh (Malāmī) (1581) vi, 228a, b
Yaʿḳūb, Sīdī vi, 591a
Yaʿḳūb I (Germiyān-oghlu) i, 346a, 510b; ii, 989a, b
Yaʿḳūb II (Germiyān-oghlu) (1428) i, 1118a; ii, 990a; vii, 644a; viii, 210b
Yaʿḳūb, Abū Yūsuf → Abū Yūsuf Yaʿḳūb
Yaʿkūb b. Aḥmad al-Kurdī (1078) vi, 913a
Yaʿḳūb b. ʿAlī Shīr → Yaʿḳūb I (Germiyān-oghlu)
Yaʿḳūb b. Dāʾūd → Abū ʿAbd Allāh Yaʿḳūb b. Dāʾūd
Yaʿḳūb b. Ḥumayd b. Kāsib (IX) vii, 409a
Yaʿḳūb b. Isḥāḳ b. al-Ward iv, 275b, 459b
Yaʿḳūb b. Killis → Ibn Killis
Yaʿḳūb b. al-Layth al-Ṣaffār (Ṣaffārid) (879) i, 145a, 452b, 1001a, 1008b, 1009b, 1294a, 1344b; ii, 196a, 553b, 812a, 978a, 1048b, 1082b, 1120a; iii, 195b, 245a; iv, 20b, 21a, b, 356b, 673a, 917b; v, 58a, 158a, 451b; vii, 410b, 413b, 777b, 794a, 801b; viii, 63a, 595b, 795b; ix, 683a; x, 105a; xi, **254b**; s, 125b, 127a
Yaʿḳūb b. Muḥammad al-Taʿāʾishī i, 49b; v, 1250b, 1251b, 1252b
Yaʿḳūb b. Nuʿmān al-Bulghārī i, 1307b
Yaʿḳūb b. Shayba (875) vii, 706a; viii, 860a
Yaʿḳūb b. Sulaymān → Yaʿḳūb II (Germiyān-oghlu)
Yaʿḳūb b. Sulṭān Shāh iv, 1159a
Yaʿḳūb b. Ṭāriḳ iii, 1136a
Yaʿḳūb b. Tāsh(u)fīn (Almoravid) (XI) vi, 134a
Yaʿḳūb al-ʿAwdāt (XX) vi, 307b
Yaʿḳūb Beg (Kāshghar) (1877) i, 314a, 733b; iii, 1120b; v, 30b, 364a; vi, 766a; viii, 240a; ix, 649b; x, 677a; xi, **255b**; s, 98a
Yaʿḳūb Beg b. Uzun Ḥasan (Aḳ Ḳoyunlu) (1490) i, 293a, 311b, 1019a, 1067a; ii, 884a, 1136b, iii, 316a; iv, 1048b; v, 54a, 243b, 492b; vi, 514a, 541a; vii, 104b, 173b; viii, 750a, 766b
Yaʿkūb Bey → Yaʿḳūb I (Germiyān-Oghlu)
Yaʿḳūb Čarkhī vii, 934a; s, 50b
Yaʿḳūb Čelebi → Germiyān Oghullarî
Yaʿḳūb al-Dibsī (XVIII) ii, 795a
Yaʿḳūb Efendi ii, 203b; ix, 199b
Yaʿḳūb Ḥanna, Muʿallim v, 93b, 94a
Yaʿḳūb Ḳadrī ʿOthmān-oghlu (Yakup Kadri Karaosmanoğlu) (1974) iv, 593b; v, 196a; vi, 95a; xi, **256b**
Yaʿḳūb Khān (Barakhzay) i, 87b, 232a, 796b b
Yaʿḳūb al-Mādjishūn (780) x, 32b
Yaʿḳūb al-Manṣūr (Almohad) → Abū Yūsuf Yaʿḳūb al-Manṣūr
Yaʿḳūb Pasha (1500) vi, 1025b; vii, 239a; xi, **257a**
Yaʿḳūb Pasha (Ḥekīm-Bashî) iii, 340a
Yaʿḳūb Pasha Ḳarā ʿOthmān-oghlu (XIX) iv, 593b
Yaʿḳūb Ṣanūʿ (XIX) vii, 438a
Yaʿḳūb Ṣanūʿ Abū Naḍḍāra → Abū Naḍḍāra, Yaʿḳūb b. Rafāʾīl Ṣanūʿ
Yaʿḳūb Ṣarfī, Shaykh iv, 709a; s, 167b
Yaʿḳūb Shāh Čak b. Yūsuf Shāh (Kashmīr) iv, 709a; s, 132a, 167a
Yaʿḳūb al-Tammār s, 25a
Yakūba (Yaʿḳūba) Sylla ii, 63b; iii, 107b, 180a; xi 469b
al-Yaʿḳūbī, Aḥmad b. Abī Yaʿḳūb (ca. 905) i, 591b; ii, 579b, 580a; iii, 1077b, 1206b; vi, 639b, 640a, 905a; xi, **257b**
Yaʿḳūbiyya (Jacobite) v, 121a, 896b
Yaʿḳūbiyyūn / Yaʿāḳiba / Yaʿḳūbiyya (Jacobites) xi, **258b**
Yakun, Walī al-Dīn i, 597a
Yakup Kadri Karaosmanoğlu (XX) → Yaʿḳūb Ḳadrī ʿOthmān-oghlu
Yāḳūt (Corundum) xi, **262a**
Yakut literature x, **732a**
Yāḳūt (Ḥādjib) (X) i, 1046b; iii, 46a, 197a, 1157a
Yāḳūt al-Ḥabshī → Djamāl al-Dīn Yaḳūt
Yāḳūṭ Khān iii, 15b; v, 1258a
Yāḳūṭ al-Mawṣilī ii, 496b
Yāḳūṭ al-Mursī i, 1070a
Yāḳūṭ al-Mustaʿṣimī Djamāl al-Dīn (1298) iii, 736b; iv, 1122b; viii, 805b, 806b; xi, **263b**
Yāḳūt al-Rūmī, Shihāb al-Dīn al-Ḥamawī (1229) i, 456b, 488a, 571a, 594b, 712b; ii, 585b; iii, 724a, 840a; iv, 131b, 132a, 223b; v, 1012a, 1019a, b; vi, 185b; xi, **264b**; s, 195a
Yāḳūtī (Artuḳid) (XII) i, 663a; vi, 540b
Yāḳūtī b. Čaghrî (XI) ii, 5a; viii 946a

Yaʿlā b. al-Futūḥ al-Azdādjī (Orania) (XI) vii, 942b
Yaʿlā b. Muḥammad al-Ifranī ii, 494b; iii, 1042a
Yaʿlā b. Muḥammad b. al-Khayr v, 1179a
Yaʿlā b. Munya iv, 1134b
Yalangtūsh Biy (Bī) (Alčīn) viii, 232b; s, 97a
Yalavač → Maḥmūd Yalawač
Yalbaḳ (X) vii, 414a
Yalbughā (Ylbughā) Nāṣirī Aḥmad (amīr) (XIV) i, 1050b; vi, 667b; vii, 170b; viii, 987b; ix, 154b; s, 409a
Yalbughā (Ylbughā) al-ʿUmarī (1366) i, 1050b; iii, 239b; vi, 231b, 323b; vii, 171a; ix, 154b; x, 612b
Yalbughā al-Yaḥyawī (Damascus) (XII) ix, 154b
Yalçin → Ḥusayn Djāhid
Yālī ii, 1119b
Yalī Köshku vi, 57a
Yalı̊ (Yalu) xi, **266b**
Yaliṭ vi, 562b
Yalowa (Yalova) xi, **267a**
Yaltakīn i, 824b
Yam (pass) vi, 504a
Yām xi, **267b**
Yām, Banū i, 545b; ii, 517b; iii, 179b, 259b, 327b; iv, 201a; vi, 190b, 191a, b, 566a; ix, 1b, 829a; xi, **268b**; s, 387b
Yām b. Nūḥ iv, 528b
Yamak (Yamaḳ) ii, 714b; iv, 322b
al-Yamāma i, 110b; ii, 126b, 569a; iv, 1072b; vi, 138b, 268a, 333b, 439a, 625b, 640b; xi, **269a**; s, 32a, 178a
al-Yamāmī, Muḥammad b. ʿAbd al-Waḥīd iv, 89b
Yaman (Yemen) i, 98b, 102a, 110b, 441a, 535a, 539a, 543b, 549a, 551b, 728a, 803b; ii, 660b; iii, 294a, 651b; iv, 198a, 199b, 448a, 519a, 745b, 834a, b, 902a; v, 807a, 895a, 1059a; vi, 9a, 35b, 40b, 45b, 72a, 74a, 84a, 118a, 137b, 138a, 140b, 141a, 144b, 145b, 149b, 151a, 178b, 190b, 191a, 221b, 266a, 280b, 293a, 320a, 321b, 334b, 337b, 345a, 371b, 436a, 473b, 559a, 561a, 720a, 911b; x, 94a, 481b; ix, 1a, 829a; xi, **269b**; s, 3b, 8b, 22a, 32b, 115b, 318a, 335a, 343b, 837a
– ethnography i, 39b, 194b; v, 346a, 953b
– literature ii, 441a; iii, 124b, 688b, 746b; iv, 1188b
– South v, 1059b
Yaman, Banū ii, 635a; iii, 233a; vi, 303a, 620b; s, 338a
Yamanī, ʿAbd Allāh (VII) vii, 472b
al-Yamanī, Ḥasan b. Aḥmad vi, 352a
Yaʿmar (Ḥazn) b. Zāʾida b. Laḳīṭ → Abū Nukhayla
Yāmid iii, 134a; s, 61b
Yamīn xi, **280a**
Yamīn al-Dawla → Maḥmūd b. Sebüktigin
Yamīniyān vi, 65a
Yamlūl, Banū ii, 463b; iv, 739b; x, 760a, b
Yamut, Banū iii, 1108a; vi, 495a
Yamūt b. al-Muzarraʿ al-ʿAbdī (ca. 915) xi, **280b**
Yanāltegīn i, 1130a
Yanbuʿ (Yanbo) iv, 748b; vi, 35a, 149a, 157a, 320a; ix, 908a, b; xi, **281a**; s, 383b
Yanbuḳ (Ḥaḍramawt) vi, 81a
Yangı̊ Kent (Dih-i Naw/al-Madīna al-Djadīda) x, 690a
Yang Dipertuan Agung vi, 238a; viii, 293a; s, 152a
Yanidj Beg ii, 984a
Yanina → Yanya
Yānis al-Rūmī, al-Amīr Abu 'l-Fatḥ Nāṣir (1132) i, 939a; ii, 858a; iii, 54b; viii, 831a; xi, **281b**
Yānis al-Mutaʿarrab ii, 234b, 237a
Yanko b. Dobrotič ii, 611a, 971b
Yannaḳo b. Yanniḳo iv, 713a
Yānnū b. ʿUmar al-Ḥādjdj (XI) vii, 587b
Yanosh → Sigismund, John
Yanova v, 258a, 259a
Yanya (Yanina) i, 398b; xi, **282a**
Yao (Bantu, Mozambique) vi, 203b; xi, **283a**
Yār Aḥmad Khūzānī → Nadjm-i Thānī
Yār Beg i, 853a
Yār Muḥammad (Kalhōra) (1718) ix, 440a
Yār Muḥammad Khān i, 231b, 282b, 1195a; ii, 185b, 186a; iv, 523b
Yarbay iv, 461b
Yarbūʿ, Banū vi, 267a, b, 268a; xi, **283b**
Yarbūʿ (Jerboa) xi, **283a**
Yardjūkh (Yārdjūkh) i, 278b; x, 617a
Yarghu vi, 482b; xi, **284b**
Yarī Beg i, 1068a
Yārī Mudhahhib i, 1211b, 1212a

Yārkand i, 46b; ix, 617b; xi, **286b**; s, 98a
Yārkandī Turks s, 327b
Yarkon (river) → Nahr Abi Fuṭrus
Yarli̊gh (Yarli̊ḳ) ii, 303b, 309a; xi, **288b**
Yarmūk xi, **290b**
Yarpūz (Yarpuz) ii, 503a, 693b; vi, 505b
Yaʿrūbī, Nāṣir b. Murshīd ix, 775b
Yaʿrubids i, 554a, 1282a; vi, 735a, 843a, 963a; vii, 227a; viii, 636a, 856b; xi, **292a**; s, 355a
Yārūkh ii, 483b
Yās, Banū i, 166a; ii, 557b, 618b, 619a; iv, 751b, 752a; v, 508b; vi, 961b; viii, 576b; xi, **292b**; s, 419a
Yāsā xi, **293a**
Yasaḳnāme → Ḳanūnnāme
Yāsamīn xi, **294a**
Yasār Abū Ḥasan al-Baṣrī (VII) vi, 920a
Yasārīzāde Muṣṭafā ʿIzzet iv, 1126a
Yasawī, Khwādja Aḥmad → Aḥmad Yasawī
Yasawiyya i, 299a; iii, 1115a; iv, 48a; x, 250a; xi, **294a**
Yash (Iasi/Jassy) s, **832b**
Yashbak al-Shaʿbānī ii, 781b; iv, 210a
Yashbak al-Ẓāhirī, Dawādār (Miṣr) (XV) vii, 173b, 174a, 175b
Yashdjub b. Yaʿrub vi, 565b
Yashīr i, 700a
al-Yashkūrī → Shirk
Yashkurī (Kaskar) s, 354b
Yashm xi, **296b**
Yashmut b. Hūlāgū (XIII) vi, 540b, 931b
Yashruṭiyya ix, 174a; xi, **298b**
al-Yaṣḥūbī, Muḥammad b. Yaḥyā (Labla) (XI) vii, 761a
Yasī → Turkistān
Yasi̊ (Ḥaḍrat, Kazakhistān/Turkistān) i, 147b, 299a; v, 859a; x, 250a; xi, 294a
Yāsīn (valley) ii, 30b; s, 158b, 327b
Yāsīn al-Hāshimi (XX) iii, 521b; viii, 445b
Yāsir ʿArafāt viii, 331b; s, 9a
Yaṣlitan → Īslitan
Yasrān (oasis) vi, 562a, b, 563a
Yassi̊ Čimen vi, 71a
Yatenga vii, 394a
Yathill (Yathill) vi, 88b; s, 821a
Yathrib (al-Madīna) i, 429a; iv, 824a, 835b; v, 436a, 994b; vi, 373b, 374a
Yāṭib s, 407b
Yatīm xi, **299a**
Yatīm Aḥmad vi, 610b
al-Yatīma (pearl) s, 253a
Yaʿūḳ vi, 651a; s, **834a**
Yaurawa (Nigeria) viii, 20b
Yavlaḳ Arslan → Muẓaffar al-Dīn Yavlaḳ
Yaw Ḥalīma → Ḥalīma
Yawm xi, **300b**
Yawm al-Djawnayn → Shiʿb Djabala
Yawm al-Liwā ix, 777a
Yawm al-Rashāʾ ix, 777a
Yawm Taḥlāḳ al-Limam x, 90a, 220a
Yawrawa (Nigeria) → Yaurawa
Yaxartes → Sīr Daryā
Yaya i, 348a; ii, 33a, 444b; xi, **301a**
Yayče v, 32a
Yayi̊ḳ (Ural river) xi, **301a**
Yaylaḳ v, 182b; xi, **301b**
Yazan, Banū xi, **302a**
Yazanīs iv, 541a
Yazbak ii, 444a
Yazd i, 3b; iii, 216a, 502a; iv, 7b, 465b, 466a, b; v, 152a, 171a, 871a, 1115b, 1116a, 1148b; vi, 366a, 494a, 627b; xi, **302a**; s, 54b, 61a, 73a, 115a, 139b, 342a, 386a
Yazdadjird I (Sāsānid) (420) ix, 75a
Yazdadjird II (Sāsānid) (457) v, 144b; ix, 76a
Yazdadjird III (Sāsānid) (651) iii, 571b, 586a; iv, 13b, 14b, 207b, 385a, b, 386a; v, 56b; vi, 620a, 745a; ix, 80a; xi, **309a**; s, 298a, 312a
Yazdān iii, 584a
Yazdānbukht (XI) (Manichaean) xi, 512a
Yazdānfādhār v, 370b; vi, 493a
Yazdānkhwāst → Māshāʾ Allāh b. Atharī
Yazdī → Madjd al-Mulk
al-Yazdī, ʿAbd Allāh (1573) viii, 778b
Yazdī, Djalāl al-Dīn Muḥammad (XVII) viii, 116a, 786a
Yazdī, Mrs. (XX) vi, 485b
Yazdī, Sayyid Kāẓim (XX) vi, 553a
Yazdī, Sharaf al-Dīn (1454) viii, 542b; s, 46b
Yazdigird → Yazdadjird
Yazīd I b. Muʿāwiya (Umayyad) (683) i, 5a, 40a, 45a, 50a, 54a, 55a, 109a, 453b, 550a, 920a, 1029b, 1152a; ii, 89b, 198a, 280b, 541a, 739b; iii, 226a, 227a, 270b, 607b, 620b, 645b, 976a; iv, 938b; v, 132a, 997a; vi, 140a, 147a, 216a, 379a, 505b, 622a, 634b, 640b; vii, 267b, 268a; viii,

119a; x, 841b; xi, **309b**; s, 10a, 26a, 230b, 231b
Yazīd II b. ʿAbd al-Malik (Umayyad) (724) i, 50a, 305a, 1149a; ii, 228b, 726b, 788b; iii, 2b, 42a, 650a, 802a; iv, 75b-76a; v, 590b; vi, 140b, 740a; vii, 359a; xi, **311a**; s, 10a, 52a, 243a
Yazīd III b. al-Walīd II (Umayyad) (744) i, 53b, 57a; iii, 224a, 990b; iv, 370b; vi, 623b; x, 842a; xi, **311b**
Yazīd, Banū iv, 345a, 347a, 348a
al-Yazīd, Mawlāy → al-Yazīd b. Muḥammad b. ʿAbd Allāh
Yazīd b. ʿAbd Allāh (Mālikī) vi, 263b
Yazīd b. ʿAbd al-Malik → Yazīd II
Yazīd b. Abī Anīsa iv, 1076b
Yazīd b. Abī Ḥabīb (746) v, 1124a; vi, 944b
Yazīd b. Abī Muslim (Dīnār) (721) i, 50a; ii, 145b; iii, 42a; xi, **312a**
Yazīd b. Abī Sufyān (639) i, 111a, 151b, 447a, 460b, 997b; ii, 280a, b, 535a, 911a; vii, 254a, 264a; ix, 99a, 263a, b; xi, **312b**
Yazīd b. Aḥmad iv, 346b
Yazīd b. Anīsa (Ibāḍī) viii, 112b
Yazīd b. Dīnār → Yazīd b. Abī Muslim
Yazīd b. D̲j̲ubayr vi, 774b
Yazīd b. Ḥammād b. Zayd s, 384b
Yazīd b. Hārūn ix, 492a; s, 89a
Yazīd b. Ḥātim b. Ḳabīsa b. al-Muhallabī (786) i, 18a, 125a; iii, 233a, 654b, 785a, 876a; iv, 336b, 827a, 829a; vi, 310b, 312a, 428a; vii, 160b, 189b, 229b, 360a; viii, 638b, 873b; ix, 901b
Yazīd Ibn Hubayra → Ibn Hubayra
Yazīd b. Ilyās iii, 1032a
Yazīd b. K̲h̲ālid al-Ḳasrī (745) vi, 624a
Yazīd b. Maysara i, 959b
Yazīd b. Mazyad al-S̲h̲aybānī (801) i, 149b; iii, 233b, 234a; iv, 645a; vi, 345a, 438a; vii, 694a; ix, 392a, 488a
Yazīd b. Miḳsam Ibn Ḍabba al-T̲h̲aḳafī (VIII) iv, 1003a, xi, **312b**
Yazīd b. Muʿāwiya (Umayyad) → Yazīd I b. Muʿāwiya (Umayyad)
Yazīd b. Mufarrig̲h̲ iv, 54b
Yazīd b. al-Muḥallab b. Abī Ṣufra (720) i, 12b, 77a, 550a, 720a; ii, 809a, 1141b; iii, 41a, 42a, 177a, 649b, 650a, 717b, 1255a; iv, 15a-b, 644b, 926b, 1098b; v, 157b; vi, 140b, 740a, 920b, 954b; vii, 357b, 359a, 777a; viii, 873b; ix, 821b; x, 429b, 821b, 844a; s, 41a, 299a, 350a
al-Yazīd b. Muḥammad b. ʿAbd Allāh, Mawlāy (ʿAlawid) (1792) i, 356b; ii, 510b, 835b; v, 1192a; vi, 595a; vii, 39a, 387a; s, 401b
Yazīd b. ʿUmar b. Hubayra (VIII) xi, 166b
Yazīd b. Usayd al-Sulamī i, 837a; iv, 344b, 578b, 1174a; ix, 488a
Yazīd b. al-Walīd → Yazīd III
Yazīd b. Yazīd b. al-Muhallab s, 41a
Yazīd b. Zurayʿ, Abū Muʿāwiya al-Baṣrī (798) iii, 838b; xi, **313a**
Yazīd al-Rāḍī iii, 748a
al-Yazīdī → Muḥammad b. al-ʿAbbās
Yazīdī, Abū ʿAlī (IX) vi, 821b
al-Yazīdī, Faḍl (IX) vii, 282a
al-Yazīdī, Abū Muḥammad Yahyā al-Baṣrī (817) ii, 293a; v, 174b; vii, 403b; xi, **316a**
Yazīdī, Yazīdiyya (sub-sect) i, 195b, 471b, 571a, 770b; ii, 16a, 184b, 459b, 526a, 1042a, 1070a; iii, 95b, 656a, b, 660a, 1040a, 1253b; iv, 1076b; v, 208b, 210b, 462a, 475b, 644a; vi, 201b; xi, **313a**
al-Yazīdī al-Naḥwī (925) vi, 352a
Yazīdī (Mazyadī) S̲h̲āhs vi, 201b; ix, 488a
Yazīdīs/Yazīdiyya (Shārwān) → Yazīd, Banū
al-Yāzid̲j̲ī, Ḥabīb (1870) xi, **318b**
al-Yāzid̲j̲ī, Ibrāhīm (1906) i, 572a, 596b; ii, 428a; iv, 967a; vi, 90b; xi, **318a**
al-Yāzid̲j̲ī, K̲h̲alīl (1889) xi, **318a**
al-Yāzid̲j̲ī, al-S̲h̲ayk̲h̲ Nāṣīf b. ʿAbdallāh (1871) i, 596b; ii, 428b; vi, 113a, 114b, 303b; vii, 901b; viii, 736a; xi, **317b**; s, 40a, 159b, 161a, b
al-Yāzid̲j̲ī, Warda (1924) xi, **318b**
al-Yazîd̲j̲î xi, **317a**
Yāzîd̲j̲î-og̲h̲lu Aḥmed → Bīdjān, Aḥmed
Yazîd̲j̲î-og̲h̲lu ʿAlī (XV) i, 21b, 419b; ii, 81a; iii, 738a; iv, 813a; viii, 163b
Yazîd̲j̲î-og̲h̲lu (Yazîd̲j̲î-zāde), Meḥmed Čelebi (1451) i, 1202a; ii, 985b; iii, 43b, 711a; ix, 62a; xi, **319a**
Yazîd̲j̲î Ṣalāḥ al-Dīn vi, 836a
Yazîd̲j̲î Ṣalīḥ b. Süleymān (XX) s, **834b**
Yazīr, Banū vi, 416a
al-Yāzūrī, Abū Muḥammad al-Ḥasan (1058) i, 533a, 1074a, b; ii, 495b, 856a,

858a, 860b; iii, 385b; v, 623b; vii, 730a, 731b; xi, **319b**
Yedi Adalar (seven Ionian islands) x, **835b**
Yedigey → Edigü
Yedikule iv, 225a, 233a, 617a, 900b, 901a
Yefet ben Eli → Japheth b. Eli
Yefremov, Filipp v, 29a
Yeğana, ʿAlī Münīf (1950) xi, **320b**
Yegen Meḥmed Pasha → Meḥmed Pasha Yegen
Yegen ʿOthmān Pasha → ʿOthmān Pasha Yegen
Yegen, Walī al-Dīn → Yakan, Muḥammad Walī al-Dīn
Yeha (Yeḥā) i, 883a; vi, 560a
Yeh-lü Ta-shih iv, 581a, b, 583a
Yehūdā ben Shlomo Ḥarīzī (1225) vi, 114b
Yemen → Yaman
Yemenlị Ḥasan Pasha (1604) iii, 252b; vi, 436b; s, **837a**
Yemishdji Ḥasan Pasha (1603) xi, **321b**
Yengikent → Djand
Yenibaghče iv, 232b
Yeñi Bāzār (Novi Pazar) xi, **321b**
Yeni-Čeri (Janissaries) i, 4a, 36a, 199a, 206b, 268b, 270b, 293b, 904a, 1061a, b, 1119a, 1120b, 1147b, 1162b, 1165a, 1256a, b, 1268a, 1277b; ii, 16a, 33b, 184b, 189b, 210b, 212a, 287a, 374a, 443a, 512b, 532b, 684a, 687a, 880b, 1086a, 1089b, 1135a; iii, 88a, 192a, b, 341b, 552b, 628b, 636a; iv, 237b, 242b, 867b; v, 32b, 275b, 359b, 642b, 643a; vi, 58a, 59a, 125a, 325a, 505a; viii, 176b, 178b, 182b, 193a, 196a, 198a, b; ix, 133a; xi, **322b**; s, 269b
Yeničeri Aghasị i, 658b, 687a, 838a, 1256a; ii, 34a, 212b, 723b; iv, 232a
Yeni Il i, 241a; ii, 724b
Yeni Djāmiʿ iv, 233b
Yeñi Ḳale (Crimea) iv, 892a; v, 140a, 141a; xi, **331b**
Yeni Kapị iv, 230b, 233a
Yeni Odalar iv, 228b, 229b
Yeñi Othmanlịlar i, 13b, 37b, 61b, 63b, 64a, 210a, 641b, 657a, 974b; ii, 430b, 642a, 643b, 728a, 876a; iii, 553b, 592a; iv, 872a; vi, 6b, 9a, b, 68b, 89b; xi, **331b**, 332b
Yeñi Shehir (Larissa) xi, **333a**
Yeñi Shehir (Yenisehir) xi, **332b**
Yeñishehirli ʿAbd Allāh Efendi, Shaykh al-Islām (1730) vi, 1004a; xi, 332b
Yeñishehirli ʿAwnī (XIX) s, 324b
Yeprim Khān iv, 862b
Yerāḳā, Afdah, Shabbethai iv, 607b
Yerliyya xi, **333b**
Yesḥaḳ (Ḥabash) (1429) ii, 545a; iii, 4a
Yeshbek (XV) iv, 463a; x, 966b
Yeshbum (ʿAwlaḳī) i, 767a
Yeshil Irmak (Yeşil Irmak) xi, **334a**
Yeshilköy (Ayastefanos) xi, **334b**
Yeșil Hisar iv, 580a, 622b
Yesü Möngke (Mongol, 1260) ii, 3a, b
Yesügei Abū Čingiz-Khān (1176) ii, 41b
Yesün-Toʾa i, 1311b; ii, 4a
Yeti Ṣu (Semirečye) ii, 43a; iii, 1120a; v, 858b; vi, 274a, 618b; vii, 218a; **xi, 335a**; ix, 659a; x, **335a**; s, 536b
Yetīm ʿAli Čelebi iv, 1158b
Yidghā ii, 31b
Yigit i, 322b
Yigit Pasha i, 1263a; v, 276b; x, 670b
Yịlandäräsi vi, 201a
Yịlanlị-oghlu ii, 207b
Yilbughā → Yalbughā
Yilbughā Nāṣirī (XIV) i, 1050b; ii, 285b, 286a
Yilbughā al-Sālimī iv, 437b
Yịldịz Köshkü → Yịldịz Sarāyị
Yịldịz Sarāyị (Palace) vi, 74b, 372b, 531b; xi, **336b**
Yịldịz, Tādj al-Dīn i, 64a, 393b, 855b; ii, 120a, 267a, 1049b, 1101b, 1103a; iii, 1155a; v, 501a, 546a; x, 60a; s, 360a
Yịltuwar i, 1305b
Yima → Djamshīd
Yimāk → Kipčak
Yināl → Ināl
Yintān b. ʿUmar iii, 959a
al-Yīnūḳ al-Farghānī vii, 191b
Yirmisekiz Meḥmed → Meḥmed Yirmisekiz
Yisḥāk (baḥr nagāš) vi, 642b
Ylbughā → Yalbugha/Yilbughā
Yithaʿʾamar Bayyin b. Sumhuʿalī Yanūf vi, 559b, 560a, 563a
Yithaʿʾamar Watar vi, 560b
Yoghurt xi, **337b**
Yogyakarta s, **837b**
Yoḳlama iv, 268a; v, 249b
Yol parasị i, 475b

Yola i, 180a; ii, 942b
Yomut, Banū s, **838a**
Yomut Türkmen iv, 1065a; v, 24a; s, 143b, 146b, 281a
Yorgan Ladîk → Lādhiḳ.2
Yoruba (Nigeria) iii, 646a; viii, 20b; xi, **337b**
Yörük (Yürük) x, 698a; xi, **338b**
Yōsēf ben Abraham → Yūsuf al-Baṣīr
Yotḳan v, 37a
Young Egypt Society → Djamʿiyyat Ittiḥād Miṣr al-Fatāt
Young Ottomans → Yeñi Ḳalʿe
Young Turks viii, 200a; xi, 332b
Youssi, Aït s, 145a
Yozgat xi, **341a**
Yubnā ii, 910b; v, 799b; vi, 652b
Yücel, Ḥasan ʿAlī (1961) iii, 1199b, 1200b; v, 281b, 282a, b; xi, **341b**; s, 42a, 283b
Yūdāsaf → Bilawhar wa-Yūdāsaf
Yūdghān iv, 96a, b, 603b
Yuʿfir, Āl s, 335a
Yuʿfir b. ʿAbd al-Raḥmān (Yuʿfirid(e)) (XI) xi, 272b, 342a
Yuʿfirid(e)s i, 551a, b; vi, 438b, 439a vii, 444b; viii, 706a; xi, **342a**
Yughrush (Title) xi, 224a
Yugoslavia i, 1275a; iv, 574a, b; v, 32a, 277a; xi, **342b**
Yuḥābir b. Madhḥidj vii, 591b
al-Yuḥānisī, Abū Marwān ʿAbd al-Malik b. Ibrāhīm al-Ḳaysī (XIII) vi, 356a
Yuḥannā (Ayla) vii, 373b
Yuḥannā b. Haylān ii, 778b
Yuḥannā b. Sarābiyūn (IX) i, 213b; xi, **343a**; s, 271b
Yuḥannā b. Yaʿḳūb b. Abkār iv, 130b
Yuḥannā b. Yūsuf (980) vii, 196b, 199b
Yuḥannā al-Kaṣīr v, 368a
Yük iii, 212b
Yukhārībāsh iv, 387b, 389b, 390b
Yuknakī → Aḥmad Yuknakī
Yulbars Khān (Uygur) (ca. 1975) v, 846a; xi, **343a**
Yuldash-oghlu Fazyl → Fāḍil Yuldash
Yulūḳ Arslān iii, 1119b
Yumgān iv, 199b; vii, 1006b
Yumugul-oghlu → Togan, Z.V.
Yūnān xi, **343b**
Yūnānī College (Delhi) i, 403b; vi, 488b
Yund Adalarî i, 792a
al-Yūnīnī, Ḳuṭb al-Dīn (1326) iii, 752b; vi, 354a; xi, **345a**; s, 400a
al-Yūnīnī, Sharaf al-Dīn iii, 861b
Yūnis b. Ḳurḳumāz Maʿn (XVII) vi, 343b
Yūnis Maʿn b. Fakhr al-Dīn ʿUthmān (1511) vi, 343a
Yunnan (Yünnan, China) v, 869a; viii, 259b; xi, **346b**
Yūnus (prophet) vi, 901a; viii, 51a
Yūnus, Ḳapudān iii, 1176b
Yūnus, Shaykh ii, 181b; iv, 428a
Yūnus b. ʿAbd al-Aʿlā (877) x, 4b
Yūnus b. ʿAbd Rabbih vi, 879a
Yūnus b. ʿAbd al-Raḥmān iii, 497b
Yūnus b. (Abī) Farwa (zindīḳ) vi, 829a
Yūnus b. ʿAlī Bey iii, 605a, 635b
Yūnus b. Bukayr (814) vii, 361a; ix, 661a
Yūnus b. Ḥabīb (798) i, 105b, 158a; vi, 625b, 821b; xi, **349a**
Yūnus b. Ilyās → Yūnus b. al-Yasaʿ
Yūnus b. Mattā (Jonaha) xi, **347b**
Yūnus b. al-Yasaʿ i, 1044a; v, 1160b; viii, 985b
Yūnus al-Aṣṭurlābī s, 267a, 372a
Yūnus Beg (Tardjumān) (1541) x, 237a
Yūnus al-Dawādār iv, 425b
Yūnus Emre (1320) iii, 1094a; iv, 812a; v, 264a, 677a, 681b; viii, 2b, 972b; xi, **349a**; s, 283a
Yūnus al-Kātib al-Mughannī (765) vii, 528a; xi, **350b**; s, 183a
Yūnus Khān i, 148a; ii, 45b, 622a
Yūnus Khōdja (Tashkent) (XIX) x, 349b, 681b
Yūnus Maʿn ii, 443b, 750b
Yūnus, Mongol Khān (1487) x, 349a
Yūnus Nādī (XX) ii, 475b; iii, 1117a; vi, 94b, 95b
Yūnus Pasha (1517) ii, 1042a; viii, 307b
Yūra viii, 160a
Yüregir-oghlu Ramaḍān i, 182b; ii, 38b
Yürkedj Pasha (XV) vii, 594b
Yurt → Khayma.iv
Yurtčî s, **838b**
Yürük i, 470b, 651b, 1302b; ii, 40b, 612b; iv, 563a; xi, **338b**
Yürün-Ḳüsh (XII) vii, 733b
Yūshā (Istanbul) vi, 57a
Yūshaʿ b. Nūn (Joshua) v, 926b; vi, 412b; xi, **351a**

al-Yūsī, Abū ʿAlī al-Ḥasan (1691) vi, 607a; viii, 671b; xi, **351b**; s, 28b, 223a
al-Yussāna i, 491b
Yūsuf (Ḥimyar) → Dhū Nuwās, Yūsuf Ashʿar
Yūsuf (Sādjid) (926) vii, 656a; xi, **355b**
Yūsuf I (Almohad) → Abū Yaʿḳūb Yūsuf
Yūsuf I al-Muʾayyad bi-ʾllāh, Abu ʾl-Ḥadjdjādj (Naṣrid) (1354) i, 1339b; ii, 115a, 1017a; iii, 835b; v, 1128a, 1149b; vii, 1020b, 1023b
Yūsuf II al-Mustaghnī bi-ʾllāh (Naṣrid) (1392) iii, 972b; vii, 1020b, 1025a
Yūsuf III al-Nāṣir li-Dīn Allāh, Abu ʾl-Ḥadjdjādj (Naṣrid) (1417) ii, 353a; vii, 1020b, 1025b
Yūsuf IV Abu ʾl-Ḥadjādjdj (Ibn al-Mawl/ Abenalmao) (Naṣrid) (1432) vii, 1020b, 1026a; s, 399a
Yūsuf V Ibn Aḥmad/Ibn Ismāʿīl (Aben Ismael) (Naṣrid) (1462) vii, 1020b, 1026a, b; s, 399a
Yūsuf I al-Malik al-Muẓaffar Shams al-Dīn (Rasūlid) (1295) i, 553a; v, 1241a; viii, 456a; s, 338b
Yūsuf, Abu ʾl-Ḳāsim (Sādjid) (928) vii, 656a; viii, 745b
Yūsuf, Abū Yaʿḳūb → Abū Yaʿḳūb Yūsuf
Yūsuf, ʿAlī (1913) ii, 466b; iii, 516a; viii, 699a; xi, **357a**; s, 121b
Yūsuf, Mawlāy → Mawlāy Yūsuf
Yūsuf b. al-Abbār iv, 338a
Yūsuf b. ʿAbd Allāh → Abu ʾl-Futūḥ Yūsuf
Yūsuf b. ʿAbd al-Hādī (1503) iii, 486b, 842b; vi, 350b, 353b; xi, **354a**
Yūsuf b. ʿAbd al-Muʾmin → Abū Yaʿḳūb Yūsuf
Yūsuf b. ʿAbd al-Raḥmān al-Fihrī (wālī al-Andalus) (759) i, 82a, 493b, 608b, 1079b; iv, 494b; v, 510b; vi, 221b, 568a; vii, 563b; ix, 870b; x, 848b; xi, **354b**; s, 81b
Yūsuf b. ʿAbd al-Wahhāb s, 11a
Yūsuf b. Abi ʾl-Sādj Dīwadād (928) i, 205a, 387a, 507a, 642b; ii, 191b, 453a, 679b; iii, 126b, 236a, 619b; iv, 22b; vii, 541b; xi, **355b**
Yūsuf b. Abī Saʿīd Muḥammad al-Marwanī (852) ii, 679a; vii, 666a
Yūsuf b. ʿĀbid al-Idrīsī (1584) xi, **355b**
Yūsuf b. Aḥmad → al-Muʾtamin, Yūsuf
Yūsuf b. ʿAlī Küčük i, 1160b; ii, 454a
Yūsuf b. Bābak i, 153b
Yūsuf b. Barsbāy ii, 6a
Yūsuf b. Dīwdād (Marāgha) (X) vi, 499a
Yūsuf b. Djihānshāh iv, 588a
Yūsuf b. al-Ḥasan b. Aḥmad "Shīrāzī" (Mombasa) (XVII) vii, 226a, b
Yūsuf b. al-Ḥasan (I), Mawlāy (1927) s, **839b**
Yūsuf b. Ḥasdāy i, 1091b
Yūsuf b. Ibrāhīm, Sulṭān ii, 124a
Yūsuf b. Ibrāhīm al-Dāya iii, 745b
Yūsuf b. Ḳādis iii, 1055b
Yūsuf b. Kaʿus i, 637a
Yūsuf b. Khalīl iv, 244b
Yūsuf b. Killis (Vizier) (X) x, 188a
Yūsuf b. Muḥammad (Harāt) (XVI) viii, 784b
Yūsuf b. Muḥammad Sharīf (Wadāī) (1898) xi, 11b
Yūsuf b. Muhammad b. Abī ʿIyāḍ b. ʿAbd al-Ḥakk (Marīnid) (XIV) vi, 593b
Yūsuf b. Muhammad b. Yūsuf Khurāsānī → Yūsufī
Yūsuf b. Nagralla i, 130b
Yūsuf b. Nūḥ iv, 605a
Yūsuf b. Saʿīd al-Ahansalī iii, 167a
Yūsuf b. al-Sarrādj, Abu ʾl-Ḥadjdjādj (1427) s, 399a
Yūsuf b. al-Sarrādj (1460) s, 399a
Yūsuf b. Sulaymān (dāʿī muṭlaḳ) s, 358b
Yūsuf b. Sulaymān (Gharnāṭa) ii, 1014a
Yūsuf b. Ṭāhir al-Khuwayyī (Khūwī) (1137) vi, 913b
Yūsuf b. Tāsh(u)fīn (Almoravid) (1106) i, 7a, 43b, 251a, 389b, 495a, 1148b, 1176a; ii, 525a, 818b, 821b, 874a, 1013a; iii, 138a, 542b, 771a, 904b, 977a; iv, 672b, 943a; v, 654b, 655a, 1178a, 1179a, 1189b; vi, 222b, 592a, 596a, 597a, 742b, 743b; vii, 585a, 589b, 613a, 721b, 767a, b; xi, **355b**
Yūsuf b. ʿUmar → Yūsuf I (Rasūlid)
Yūsuf b. ʿUmar al-Thaḳafī → al-Thaḳafī
Yūsuf b. Uzun Hasan → Ḳarā Yūsuf
Yūsuf b. Wadjīh (ʿUmān) (X) vii, 358a
Yūsuf b. Yaʿḳūb (Joseph, prophet) i, 1229b; ii, 873a; v, 193b, 233b, 423b; vi, 412b; xi, **352a**
Yūsuf b. Yaʿḳūb (Imāmī) s, 233a
Yūsuf (Sanūsī) s, 165a
Yūsuf ʿĀdil-Shāh (-Khān) (ʿĀdil-Shāh, Bīdjāpūr) (1510) i, 199a, 1202b; ii, 922b,

1084b; iii, 15a, 1159b; vi, 62b, 63a, b; vii, 459a
Yūsuf Āghā, (Rikābdār) (1646) iii, 623a, 983a, 1086a
Yūsuf Āghā Efendi (XVIII) vii, 276a
Yūsuf Akčura (Aḳčurin) (Simbirsk) (1935) vi, 584a; xi, **356b**; s, 47b
Yūsuf ʿAlī Khān i, 827b; ii, 83b
Yūsuf Amīrī (XV) vii, 567b
Yūsuf Asʿar → Dhū Nuwās
Yūsuf al-Athīr s, 159b, 161a, b
Yūsuf al-ʿAẓm (XX) vi, 918b
Yūsuf al-Badīʿī s, 362a, 652a
Yūsuf al-Barm (777) iv, 16b; v, 855a; xi, **358a**
Yūsuf al-Baṣīr (XI) iv, 305a, 306b, 605a; vii, 540a, 786a
Yūsuf Beg i, 354b
Yūsuf al-Bitrūdjī ii, 1009a; v, 586b
Yūsuf Buluggīn → Buluggīn b. Zīrī
Yūsuf Dāʿī (Yemen) (XI) vi, 436a, b
Yūsuf Ḍiyāʾ viii, 179a; s, 168a
Yūsuf Ḍiyā Pasha ii, 202a, 635b
Yūsuf al-Fihrī → Yūsuf b. ʿAbd al-Raḥmān
Yūsuf Hamadhānī, Shaykh (XII) i, 299a, 515b; ii, 1078a; ix, 4a
Yūsuf Ḥubaysh ii, 801a
Yūsuf Ḥusaynī (XIX) ii, 1114b; vii, 437a
Yūsuf ʿIzz al-Dīn (Ottoman) (XIX) vii, 525a
Yūsuf Ḳādir Khān b. Hārūn Bughra Khān (Ilek-khān) (1034) i, 662a; ii, 4b; iii, 347b, 1114a; v; 38b; vi, 557b, 853b; vii, 407a; viii, 236b; ix, 649a
Yūsuf Kāmil Pasha (1876) iii, 1199a; vi, 69b
Yūsuf Kāndhalawī Dihlawī Mawlānā (1965) xi, **358a**
Yūsuf Karam (1889) xi, **358b**
Yūsuf Ḳaramanli̊ ii, 161b; iv, 617b, 618a
Yūsuf Khān (Harāt) (XX) vi, 715a, b
Yūsuf Khān Čak (Kashmīr) (1586) → Yūsuf Shāh Čak
Yūsuf Khān Mustashār al-Dawla, Mīrzā (XIX) iv, 164a, 397b; vi, 291b; s, 71b, 109a
Yūsuf Khān Riḍwī (Raḍawī) Mīrzā (Kashmīr) (1601) iv, 709a; vii, 129b; xi, **359a**; s, 132a, 167b
Yūsuf Khāṣṣ Ḥādjib al-Balāsāghūnī (XI) i, 299a, 987a; iii, 1114a, 1116a; iv, 699a; v, 538a; ix, 239a; x, 368b; xi, **359a**
Yūsuf Khayl, Tatār Khān ii, 47b; s, 203a
Yūsuf Ḳurayshī, Shaykh iii, 633b, 634a
Yūsuf al-Makassarī (1699) x, 257a
Yūsuf al-Manṣūr (1105) vii, 501a
Yūsuf Muḥammad (1965) x, 38b
Yūsuf Mukhliṣ Pasha i, 992b
Yūsuf al-Muʾtamin i, 7a; iii, 542b, 706a
Yūsuf al-Muẓaffar v, 683a
Yūsuf Pasha (1646) → Yūsuf Agha
Yūsuf Pasha (1838) → Yūsuf Ḳaramānli̊
Yūsuf Pasha Khodja → Khodja Yūsuf Pasha
Yūsuf Pasha Sayfā (Sayf-oghlu) (1624) ii, 443b, 635a, 749b, 750b; vi, 345a, 580b
Yūsuf Shāh, Shams al-Dīn (Bengal) (1481) i, 1168a
Yūsuf Shāh I b. Alp Arghūn (Lur-i Buzurg) (XIII) v, 826b
Yūsuf Shāh II, Rukn al-Dīn (1340) v, 827a
Yūsuf Shāh Čak (Kashmīr) (1568) iv, 709a; s, 131b, 132a, 167a, 332b; 366b
Yūsuf Shams al-Dīn Tabrīzī, Shaykh vi, 245b
Yūsuf Shihāb i, 1078a; ii, 444a, 635b; s, 268b
Yūsuf al-Sibāʿī vi, 468b
Yūsuf Sinān b. ʿAlī b. Ḳayā Bey → Sunbuliyya
Yūsuf Sinān b. Yaʿḳūb Efendi (XVI) ii, 203b
Yūsuf al-Thaḳafī s, 354b
Yūsuf Wahbī (1981) ii, 39b; vi, 746b, 750b
Yūsuf Yāsīn, Shaykh (XX) vi, 172b, 176b
Yūsuf u Zalīkhā (Zulaykhā) iv, 62b; xi, **360a**; s, 65a
Yūsufī (Yūsuf b. Muḥammad b. Yūsuf Khurāsānī) (XVI) xi, **326b**
Yūsufzay, Banū xi, **362b**
Yūsufzays i, 218b, 220a, 229a, 229b, 769a, 864b; iv, 1102a; vi, 127a, 342b; vii, 220a
Yu-tʾien → Khotan
Yūz, Banū s, 46a
Yūz Āsaf i, 1217a
Yüzbashi̊ s, **840b**
Yuzbekī, ʿIzz al-Dīn Balban-i (1259) vi, 48a
Yuzbek-i Tughri̊l (Ḳi̊pčaḳ, Lakhnawti) (1257) vi, 48a
Yüzelli̊li̊kler xi, **363b**; s, 149b

Z

Zāʾ → Zāy
Ẓāʾ xi, **363a**
Zāb (pl. Zībān) (Algeria) i, 16a, 43a, 424a, 426b; ii, 249b; iii, 982a; iv, 1186b; v, 442a, 1180b; vi, 311b, 434b, 435a, 624b, 727a, b; xi, **364a**; s, 103a
al-Zāb al-Akbar (ʿIrāḳ) xi, **366a**
al-Zāb al-Aṣghar (ʿIrāḳ) xi, **366b**
al-Zabādī, ʿAbd al-Madjīd (1750) vi, 250a, 350a
al-Zabādī, Abu ʾl-Ḥasan al-Manālī s, 404a
Zābadj Zābidj, Zābag (Šrīvijayā) vi, 207b, 234a; xi, **367a**
al-Zabāniyya vi, 217a; xi, **369a**
Zabbā, Banū ix, 898b
al-Zabbāʾ (Zenobia) i, 450b, 548b; iv, 556b; vi, 468a; x, 79b; xi, **369a**
Zabbāl → Kannās
Zabbān b. Sayyār al-Fazārī i, 690a; iii, 23a
Zabīb xi, **369b**
Zabibē i, 525a
Zabīd ii, 91a, 996a; iii, 746a; iv, 1188b; v, 1244a, b; vi, 192a, 246a, 433a, 474b, 720a; vii, 270a, 514b, 579b; viii, 184a, 235b; x, 106b, 481b; xi, **370a**; s, 30b, 289a, 338a
al-Zabīdī (1791) viii, 458b
al-Zabīdī, Muḥammad Murtaḍā → Muḥammad Murtaḍā al-Zabīdī
al-Zabīdī, Muḥammad b. Yaḥyā (1160) vii, 546b
al-Zabīdī, Shaykh Abū ʿAbd Allāh → Ibn al-Daybaʿ
Zabi̊ta → Ḍābiṭ
Zābita Khān → Ḍābiṭa Khān
Zabtiyye → Ḍabṭiyya
Zābul / Zābulistān i, 86a, 147b, 226b; ii, 1048b; iii, 304a, 715b; iv, 356b; v, 1166b; vi, 65a; vii, 777a; viii, 67a; x, **371b**; s, 125b, 263a
Zabuls i, 226a
al-Zabūr i, 264a; xi, **372a**
Ẓabya (Ḳayna) s, 247a
Zacharias → Zakariyyāʾ
Zād al-Rākib ii, 785a; iv, 1143b
Zādawaih i, 451b
Zadjal i, 501b, 574b, 595b, 602a; ii, 1033a; iii, 849b, 851a; v, 1207a; vi, 248a; xi, **373a**
al-Zadjdjādj, Abū Isḥāḳ Ibrāhīm (923) iii, 838a; iv, 181b; viii, 14b; ix, 347a; x, 84b; xi, **377b**
al-Zadjdjādjī, Abu ʾl-Ḳāsim (949) iii, 597a, 838a, 1128a; x,15b; xi, **378a**
al-Zadjdjādjī, Abū ʿUmar (949) vi, 224a; vii, 279b, 914a
Zadjr → ʿIyāfa
Zafadola → Aḥmad III (Hūdid)
Ẓafār (Ḥimyar) xi, **379a**
Ẓafār (Oman) xi, **380a**
Ẓafar, Banū vi, 649a
Ẓafar ʿAlī Khān iii, 359a; s, 247b
Ẓafar Djang → Tadjammul Ḥusayn Khān
Ẓafar Khān (1663) viii, 851b
Ẓafar Khān (Bahmānid) → ʿAlāʿ al-Dīn Ḥasan Bahman
Ẓafar Khān (Gudjarāt) (1403) x, 593a
Ẓafar Khān (Kashmīr) (XVII) iv, 709a
Ẓafar Khān Ghāzī (Sātgāʿon) (XIII) ix, 83b; x, 574a
Ẓafar Khān Lodī II (Daryā Khān) (XIV) vi, 62a, 294a, 407b
Ẓafar Khān Malik Dīnār, nāẓim (Gudjarāt) (1319) ii, 1124a, b
Zafarabad ii, 498b, 499b
Zaʿfarān xi, **381a**
al-Zaʿfarānī, Mūsā → al-Tiflīsī, Abū ʿImrān
Zaʿfarāniyya vii, 868b
Zaʿfarānlū iii, 1104a, 1108a; v, 312a
al-Zafayān, ʿAṭaʾ b. Usayd (c. 700) viii, 377a; xi, **382a**
Ẓafīr → Ḍafīr
al-Ẓāfir Bi-Aʿdāʾ Allāh (Fāṭimid) (1154) i, 9a, 198b; iii, 868a; vii, 579a; x, 149b; xi, **382a**
Ẓāfir al-Ḥaddād (1134) xi, **383b**
Ẓāfir b. Sulaymān iv, 289b
al-Ẓafra i, 166a; ii, 557b; xi, **384a**
Zafrullah Khān i, 302a
Zaganos Pasha (1464) iv, 969a; vi, 70a; vii, 237a; xi, **384a**
Zagazig → al-Zaḳāzīḳ
Zaggan, Banū vi, 741a
al-Zaghall → Muḥammad XII (Naṣrid)
Zaghardji̊ Bashi̊ xi, **384b**
Zaghārī (dog) iv, 491a
Zaghāwa xi, **384b**; s, 190a, b

Zaghlūl → Saʿd Zaghlūl
Zaghra s, 330a
Zagros iii, 1253a; iv, 1a, 2b, 5a, b, 8a; v, 865b; vi, 200b; xi, **385b**; s, 147b
al-Zahāwī, Djamīl Ṣidķī (1936) i, 597b; iii, 1264b; iv, 145a, 720b; vi, 607a, 614a, 615a; xi, **386b**
Zahel → Sahl b. Bishr
Zāhid → Zuhd
Zāhid Gīlānī, Shaykh (1301) viii, 755a, 801a
Zāhid al-ʿUlamāʾ al-Fāriķī i, 1224a
Zāhida Khātūn (Shīrāz) (XII) vi, 482a; ix, 473b
Zāhidān xi, **387a**
Zāhidī, Faḍl Allāh (general) (XX) iv, 41b; vii, 447a, 655a; s, 675a
al-Zāhidī, Mukhtār b. Muḥammad (1260) viii, 893b
Zāhidiyya → Ṣafawids
Ẓahīr xi, **387b**
Ẓāhir xi, **388b**
al-Ẓāhir → Barķūķ, Baybars I
al-Ẓāhir (Mamlūk title) → under following name
al-Ẓāhir Bi-Amr Allāh (ʿAbbāsid) (1226) i, 198a, 227a; xi, **390b**
al-Ẓāhir Li-Iʿzāz Dīn Allāh (Fāṭimid) (1036) ii, 855a, b, 856a, 859a; iv, 514a; vi, 707b; vii, 162b, 482b; xi, **391a**
al-Ẓāhir (Yemen) vi, 433a
Zāhir Bouzrar (XX) vi, 754a
al-Ẓāhir Čaķmaķ → Čaķmaķ
Ẓāhir al-Dawla, ʿAlī Khān ii, 434a
Ẓahir al-Dawla Ibrāhīm (Ghaznawid) (1099) vi, 783a
Ẓahir al-Dīn b. al-ʿAṭṭār (XII) vii, 707a
Ẓahir al-Dīn b. Nāṣir al-Dīn (Marʿashī) (1489) vi, 513b, 514a, 516a; xi, **393b**; s, 363b
Ẓahir al-Dīn Muḥammad Bābur Pādishāh (Timūrid) (1530) i, 847b; vi, 768a
Ẓahir al-Dīn Mukhtār al-Manṣūrī (1316) viii, 158a
Ẓahīr-i Fāryābī (Ẓahīr al-Dīn Abu 'l-Faḍl) (1201) iv, 62a; xi, **392b**; s, 108a, 239b
al-Ẓāhir Ghāzī b. Ṣalāh al-Dīn, al-Malik (Ayyūbid, Aleppo) (1216) i, 197b, 798b, 803a, 989b, 996a, 1316b; ii, 37b, 353b, 556b; iii, 87b, 178a, 208b, 399b, 693b, 863a; iv, 482a; v, 924b; vi, 380b, 381a, 429a, b, 507a, 540b, 544a, 547b, 579a; xi, **392a**
Ẓāhir Hamdān (region) s, 22a
al-Ẓahīr Ķānsawh, al-Malik (Mamlūk) (1500) vi, 580b
Ẓahīr al-Kāzarūnī (1298) vi, 111a
Ẓāhir Shāh Bārakzay (XX) vii, 438b
Ẓāhir al-ʿUmar al-Zaydānī, Shaykh (ʿAkkā) (1776) i, 63a, 391b; ii, 534a, 635b, 912a; iii, 325a, 992a; vi, 325b; vii, 33a, 179a, 420b; viii, 738b; ix, 270a; xi, **393a**; s, 20b, 268a, b, 269a
al-Ẓāhir Wa'l-Bāṭin xi, **389a**
al-Ẓāhira (Oman) i, 1098a; iii, 1004b; xi, **394a**
al-Ẓāhirī → ʿAbd Allāh b. Ķāsim; Ibn Dāwūd; Ibn Ḥazm, ʿAlī
al-Ẓāhirī, Īnāl Bay b. Ķidjmās (XV) vi, 580b
al-Ẓāhirī, Khalīl b. Shāhīn → ibn Shāhīn
Ẓāhīrī Samarķandī (1161) x, 232a
al-Ẓāhirī, Sayf al-Dīn Baktimur Djillak (XV) vi, 580b
al-Ẓahirī, Sūdūn min ʿAlī Bak (amīr) (Ṭāz) (XV) iii, 239b; vi, 580b
Ẓāhiriyya i, 414a, 1325a; ii, 182b, 890a; iii, 308a, 744b, 790b, 1149a; iv, 46a; v, 73a; vi, 193b; vii, 271b, 570a; xi, **394a**; s, 386a, 396b
Zaḥla vi, 303a, 304a, b, 305a, 306a, b
al-Ẓahr s, 50a
Ẓahrān i, 73a, 811b; ii, 108b; iii, 363b; xi, **397a**
al-Zahrāwī, ʿAbd al-Ḥamīd (1916) viii, 908a; xi, **397a**
al-Zahrāwī, Abu 'l-Ķāsim (1009) i, 214a, 600b; ii, 482a, 901a; x, 454b; xi, **398a**; s, 271b, 272a;
Zahriyyāt xi, **399b**
Zaʿīm xi, **402b**
al-Zaʿīm, Ḥusnī (colonel) (1949) ii, 662a; v, 1047b; vi, 538a; xi, **403b**
Zaʿīm, Meḥmed → Meḥmed, Zaʿīm
al-Zaʿīm b. Yaḥyā (Zayyān, Banū) (XIII) vii, 722a
Zainuddin → Mappila
Zaʿīr (Zaër), Banū vi, 142b
Zaʿīrdja (Zaʿīradja) xi, **404a**
Zaïre iv, 749b; v, 176b
al-Zaʿīrī, Muḥammad b. Mubārik s, 28b
Zakandar v, 969a

Zākānī → ʿUbayd-i Zākānī
Zakarawayh vii, 192a
Zakarawayh b. Mihrawayh (907) xi, **405a**
Zakʿarids i, 507b, 508a
Zakariyyāʾ (Zacharias) vi, 630a; xi, **405b**; s, 402b
Zakariyyāʾ al-Anṣārī (1520) iii, 779a; viii, 425a; xi, **406a**
Zakariyyāʾ b. Mammatī → Ibn Mammātī, Muhadhdhab
Zakariyyā Aḥmad (1961) x, 144a
Zakariyyāʾ Kāndhalawī Sahāranpūrī (1982) xi, **406b**
Zakariyyā Khān v, 598b; vii, 457a
Zakariyyā Muḥyī al-Dīn s, 5b, 6a
Zakariyyāʾ Tāmir v, 193a; vi, 469a; x, 798a
Zakāt i, 968b, 1099b, 1142a, 1144a, 1146a; ii, 142b, 154a; iv, 485b, 1151b, 1152b; v, 424b, 1252a; xi, **406b**
al-Zaḳāzīḳ (Zagazig) xi, **422a**; s, 262b
Zakhir ʿAbd Allāh (1748) xi, **423a**
Zakhrafa xi, **423a**
Zākhū (Zākhō) xi, **425a**
Zakhūr Rāhib, Raphaël Anṭūn iii, 1245a
Zakī, Aḥmad → Abū Shādī
Zaki al-Dīn Muḥammad al-Birzālī i, 1238a
Zakī Nadjīb Maḥmūd (1993) x, 61b
al-Zākī Ṭamal ii, 828a
Zakī Ṭulaymāt (XX) vi, 750b, 751a
Zākiyā iii, 1039a, b; vi, 546a
al-Zakiyya, Muḥammad b. ʿAbd Allāh al-Nafs (762) vi, 441b
Zakka Khēls Afrīdī i, 238a, b; vii, 220b
al-Zaḳḳāḳ (1549) vi, 894a
al-Zaḳḳāḳ, ʿAlī b. al-Ḳāsim (1507) i, 428a; iii, 948b; xi, **425b**
Zaḳḳūm xi, **425b**
Zaklise (Zakynthos) xi, **426a**
Zakrī → Ibn Zakrī
Zakynthos → Zaklise
Zalīdj (Zallīdj) ii, 748a; xi, **426a**
Zalīkhā/Zulaykhā vi, 412b
Ẓālim b. al-Ṣaḥṣāḥ ii, 234a
Ẓālim Singh (fawdjdār) (1826) vi, 419b
Zallāḥ ix, 774b
al-Zallāḳa (Battle 1086) i, 7a, 43b, 242b; v, 1189b; vii, 553b, 590a, 775b, 778b; xi, **426b**
Zallīdj → Zalīdj
Zalzal, Manṣūr b. Djaʿfar (ca. 800) xi, **427b**
Zalzala/Zilzal xi, **428a**
Zām iv, 96b
Zamakhshar xi, **432b**
al-Zamakhsharī, Abu ʾl-Ḳāsim Maḥmūd (1144) i, 120a, 412a, 594a, 709a, 1129a; ii, 896a, 1079a; iii, 249a, 302a, 368b, 968a; iv, 524b, 525a, b, 527a, 615a; vi, 110b, 346b, 352b, 448b, 816a, 823b; vii, 469b, 914b; ix, 887a; x, 85a, 131b; xi, **432b**; s, 343a
– contributions to the fields of theology s, **840a**
Zamān xi, **434a**
Zamān, Mīr Muḥammad (XVI) viii, 783b
Zamān Khān (Kūh Gilūya) (XVII) vii, 674a
Zamān Shāh Durrānī (Durranī) (1800) i, 72b, 230b; ii, 838b; iii, 1158b; iv, 391b; v, 599a
Zamāna Beg → Mahābat Khān
Zamān-i Yazdī i, 1301a
Zamāniyya s, 325a
Zamfara (Nigeria) viii, 20a
Zāmil b. Djabr ii, 176a; s, 234a
Zamīndār ii, 158b, 784b; v, 686b; xi, **438b**
Zamīndārī → Zamīndār
Zamīndāwar i, 86a; ii, 1100b; iv, 536a, b; v, 691a; viii, 595b; xi, **439b**
Zamm xi, **440a**
Zammūr (Azemmour) (X) iii, 1043b; viii, 985a
Zammūr, Banū iv, 78a
Zamora → Sammūra
Zamorins (Calicut) iv, 547a; vi, 459a
Zamrāwa, Banū vi, 742a
Zamzam iv, 91b, 185a, 318a, 321a; vi, 144b, 151b, 165b, 166a, 167b, 171b, 665a, 666a, b, 676a, b, 677b, 708b; xi, **440a**
Zanādiḳa ii, 96a, 770b; xi, 510b
Ẓanāga → Ṣanhādja
Zanāna Rawḍa (Fatḥpur Sikrī) vi, 690a
Zanāra v, 695a, 697a
Zanāta, Banū i, 92a, 367a, 533a, 699b, 762b, 860a, 1174b, 1175b, 1177b, 1309a; ii, 818b, 821a, 852b; iii, 137b, 138a, 654a, 1036a, 1039a; v, 1174a, b, 1179a, 1182b; vi, 221b, 310b, 427a, 434b, 435b, 571a, b, 572a, 573b, 727a, 728a, b, 741a, 742b, 943b; vii, 802b, 994a; x, 100b; xi, 212a; s, 328b

al-Zanātī, Abū ʿAbd Allāh Muḥammad iv, 1129b
al-Zanātī, Khālid b. Ḥamīd/Ḥumayd (740) vi, 923b
al-Zanātī, Masʿūd b. Wānūdīn (XI) vii, 585a
Zand iii, 1102b; iv, 38a; v, 461b, 617a, 663b; xi, **443b**; s, 405b
Zanda Pīl → Aḥmad-i Djām
Zandādj (Zandāk), Banū v, 1181a; vi, 947b
Zandaḳa → Zindīḳ
Zanda-rūd → Zāyanda-rūd
Zandaward s, 354b
Zandj i, 18b, 23b, 33b, 36a, 73b, 133b, 388b, 551a, 921a, 937b, 1086a, 1096a; iii,880a; iv, 567a; v, 940b, 941b; vi, 606a, 920b; vii, 650a, 760a, 766a, 801b; ix, 698b; xi, **444b**; s, 49a
Zandj (ʿIrāḳ) xi, **445b**
Zandj, sea of → Baḥr al-Zandj
al-Zandj → ʿAlī b. Muḥammad
Zandjān vi, 498b, 502a; vii, 422b; xi, **446b**; s, 71a
al-Zandjānī, Abu ʾl-Ḥasan ʿAlī iii, 1071b
Zandjānī, Ṣadr al-Dīn Aḥmad Khālidī (XIII) ii, 982a; viii, 749b
al-Zandjānī, ʿIzz al-Dīn (XIII) s, **841b**
al-Zandjī, Muslim b. Khālid (795) ix, 182a
Zandjibār (Zanzibar) i, 36a, 554b, 1043b, 1282a, b; iv, 885b, 887b, 888a, 889a; v, 106b, 1030a; vi, 129a, 370a, 517a, 735b; vii, 53a; viii, 292b, 564a; ix, 699a; x, 194b, 622a; xi, **447a**; s, 351b
Zand (Irān) vi, 202b, 551a; xi, **443b**; s, 71a
Zangana, Banū iii, 1109a; v, 169b, 461a
Zangī Ātā (-Bābā) (1259) xi, **452a**
Zangī, Mullā i, 1121b
Zangī b. Mawdūd, Muẓaffar al-Dīn (Salghuri) (1146) viii, 978b; xi, **451a**
Zangids/Zankids i, 665b, 1161a; ii, 282b; vi, 327a; vii, 998b; ix, 597a; xi, **452b**; s, 205a
Zängimār (river) vi, 200b, 201a
Zankī, ʿImād al-Dīn b. Arslan Shāh I (Zangid) (Mosul) (XIII) v, 454b
Zankī, Nūr al-Dīn Maḥmūd (Zangid, Damascus/Aleppo, 1174) → Nūr al-Dīn Maḥmūd b. Zangī
Zankī b. Aḳ-Sunḳur, ʿImād al-Dīn (Zangid), Mosul) (1146) i, 314a, b, 426b, 466b, 664b, 797a, 971a, 1160b, 1358a; ii, 64b, 347b, 348b, 354b, 489a, 1082a; iii, 87a, 120a, 228b, 399a; v, 332a, 454a, b, 922a, 924b; vii, 578b, 733b, 734a
Zankī b. Čökermish (XII) vii, 408a
Zankids → Zangids
Ẓanna, Banū vi, 82b
Zante → Zaklise
Zanzibar x, 816b; xi, **447a**
Zār v, 676a; xi, **455b**
Zarādushtiyya → Madjūs
Zarāfa iii, 346b, 666a; xi, **457b**
Zarafshān (river) iii, 483a; v, 247a; vi, 419a, 619a; viii, 1031b; xi, **458a**; s, 97a
Zarah iii, 150a
Zarand(-g)(-dj)/Sidjistān v, 151a, 868a; vi, 368b, 633b, 667a; xi, **458b**
al-Zarānīḳ i, 1140b; xi, 248a
Zarda Kūh v, 826b; vi, 494b, 673b, 674a
Ẓarf **459b**
Zarhūn vi, 889a; s, 103a, 350b
Ẓarib vi, 562b
Zarībiyya iv, 668a
Ẓarīf xi, **460a**
Ẓarīfa vi, 564b
Zarīr(-ān) iii, 113a
al-Zarḳāʾ (Jordan) xi, **460b**
al-Zarḳāʾ, Sallāma (singer) iii, 682a; viii, **996b**; x, 885a
Zarḳāʾ bint al-Ḥasan al-Yamāma (VII) iii, 455a; v, 777b; ix, 565b; x, 359b; xi, **460b**
al-Zarḳalī Abū Isḥāḳ Ibrāhīm (Azarquiel) (1100) i, 600b, 725b, 726a, 727a; ii, 243b; iii, 1137a; vi, 543a, 601a; xi, **461a**
al-Zarḳālluh (XI) → al-Zarḳalī
al-Zarkashī, Abū Allāh (1392) ix, 887a; s, **842a**
al-Zarḳawī, Aḥmad Mūsā s, 153a
Zarmihr b. Sūkhrā (Ḳārinid) (VI) iv, 644a; vi, 745b; s, 298a
Zarmihrids v, 69b; vi, 745b; s, 298a
al-Zarnūdjī, Burhān al-Dīn (XIII) xi, **462b**
Zarrūḳ, Aḥmad b. Aḥmad al-Fāsī s, 404b
Zarrūḳ, Aḥmad b. Muḥammad al-Fāsī s, 44a, 403a
Zarrūḳī iv, 380a; ix, 173b, 174a
Zarrūḳiyya ix, 173a; x, 247b; xi, 184b
Zarūd ii, 92b; s, 198b
Zarwāl, Banū i, 84b; ii, 160a
Zarzā, Banū ix, 282b, 832b; x, 916b
Zātī → Dhātī
Zātī (Sulaymān) → Sulaymān Dhātī

Zattallī → Dja'far
Zāwa xi, **463a**
al-Zawāḥī, Sulaymān b. ʿAbd Allāh (XI) ix, 220b, 816a
Zawāḥids vi, 831b
al-Ẓawāhir i, 1313b, 1314a
Zawāḳīl xi, **463b**
Zarwāniyya → Madjūs
Zawāra xi, **464a**
al-Zawāwī → Ibn Muʿṭī
al-Zawāwī, Abu 'l-Ḳāsim (XVI) ix, 20b
al-Zawāwī, ʿAlī (XVII) iii, 720a
al-Zawāwī, ʿĪsā b. Maḥmūd (Mālikī) vi, 263a, b, 353a
al-Zawāwī, Muḥammad Saʿīd b. Aḥmad (XX) viii, 902a
al-Zāwayī, Ḳuṭb al-Dīn Haydar (1221) x, 251a
Zawda, Banū vi, 742b
Zawdj xi, **464b**
– usage in the dialects of the muslim east s, **842b**
Zāwī b. Zīrī (Zīrid) (1019) i, 84a; ii, 1012a; iii, 1110a; vii, 563b; ix, 18a; xi, **465a**
Zawīla ii, 875b; iii, 657b; iv, 567a; x, 789b; xi, **466a**
Zawīlat Ibn Khaṭṭāb (Zouila) vii, 186b
Zāwiya i, 139a, 290b, 1225a; iv, 380b, 383a, 433a; v, 1129b, 1201b, 1208b; xi, **466b**; s, 223a
al-Zawrāʾ i, 289b; vi, 676a, 1033a
al-Zawzan (Zūzan) iv, 910a; v, 450b; xi, **470a**
Zawzanī (980) vii, 772a
al-Zawzanī, Abū ʿAbd-Allāh al-Ḥusayn (1093) iv, 910a; s, 289b
al-Zawzanī, Abū Muḥammad ʿAbd Allāh al-ʿAbdalakānī (1030) vii, 527a
Zawzanī, Aṣīl al-Dīn s, 363a
Zawzanī, Ḥusayn iv, 525b
Zāy / Zāʾ xi, **471a**
Zāyanda-rūd iv, 98a, 674a; v, 869a, 872b, 873b, 874a; vi, 17b; xi, **472a**; s, 275a
al-Zayānī → al-Zayyānī
Zayānids → ʿAbd al-Wādids
Zayd, Sharīf (1666) vi, 150a
Zayd b. ʿAlī b. Ḥusayn (740) i, 402b; ii, 889a; iii, 493b, 617b, 1265b; iv, 371b, 446b, 1086b, 1161a; v, 3a; vi, 264a, 649b; vii, 396a, 662b; ix, 423a; x, 41b; xi, **166b, 473b**, s, 19a, 48b, 127a, 130a, 401a
Zayd b. ʿAmr b. Nufayl (VII) ii, 1060a; iii, 1206a; xi, **474b**
Zayd b. al-Djabal al-Ṭāʾī iv, 858b
Zayd b. Ḥammād (VI) i, 565a; vii, 568b
Zayd b. Ḥāritha al-Kalbī (Zayd al-Ḥibb) (629) i, 25a, 50b, 109b; ii, 275a, 372a, 573b, 842b, 873b; iv, 492b, 898b; vii, 364a, 372b, 374b, 756b; viii, 677a; xi, **475a**
Zayd b. Ḥusayn b. ʿAlī (1970) xi, **475b**
Zayd b. ʿĪsā s, 48b
Zayd b. Khālid vii, 187a; ix, 509b
Zayd b. Khalīfa i, 928b
Zayd b. al-Khaṭṭāb i, 1241b; ii, 569b; iv, 1131b
Zayd b. Mūsā al-Kāẓim (Ḥusaynid) (IX) vi, 334a
Zayd b. Rifāʿa (1010) i, 127a; iii, 1071b; vi, 823a
Zayd b. Thābit (622) ii, 540b, 886b; iii, 65a; v, 404b, 405a; xi, **476a**
Zayd b. Zāmil iv, 1072b
Zayd al-Khayl al-Ṭāʾī ii, 1005a; iii, 812a; iv, 832b; s, 304b
Zayd al-Khayr → Zayd al-Khayl al-Ṭāʾī
Zayd al-Nār (IX) vi, 334b
Zaydān, Djurdjī (1914) i, 597a; ii, 466b; v, 188a; vii, 900b, 902b; xi, **476b**; s, 161a, 263a
Zaydān b. Mawlāy Ismāʿīl (ʿAlawid) (1707) vi, 595a; vii, 38b
Zaydān al-Nāṣir b. Aḥmad al-Manṣūr, Mawlāy (Saʿdid) (1627) i, 280a; iii, 256b; iv, 970b; v, 1191b; vi, 594b; viii, 724b; s, 29a
Zaydāni → Saʿdid
al-Zaydī, al-Ḳāsim b. Ḥusayn (1003) vi, 436a
Zaydiyya i, 48b, 106b, 402b, 403a, 551b, 552a, 553b, 554a, 1350a, b; ii, 218a, 1111b; iii, 125b, 254a, 688b, 984b; iv, 44a, 46b, 944b; v, 1240b; vi, 36a, 149a, b, 150a, 334a, 338a, 433a, 435b; vii, 508b; ix, 423a, 507a; s, 13a, b, 19a, 25b, 32a, 48a, b, 129b, 334b, 338a, 343a, 356b, 363a, 401a
– doctrine i, 445b, 1113b; iii, 486b, 1166a, 1265b; iv, 183a, 944b; v, 1237b; xi, 273b, 246b, **477b**; s, 236a
Zāyid b. Khalīfa i, 166b; iv, 778a
Zāyid al-Malṭūm ii, 175b, 176a

Zāyid b. Sulṭān al-Nihayyān, Shaykh s, 418b
Zāyirdja → Zāʿirdja
Zaylaʿ (Zeila) i, 176b, 763b; iii, 3a, 5b; vi, 82b; vii, 515a; ix, 715a, b; xi, **481a**
al-Zaylaʿī (1342) iii, 163b; vii, 969b
al-Zaylāʿī, Shaykh ʿAbd al-Raḥmān (1882) ix, 722b
Zayn, Sultan Aḥmad b. Muḥammad (Patani) (1906) viii, 1042b
Zayn al-ʿĀbidīn b. Kaicil Gapi Baguna (Ternate) (1500) x, 419b
Zayn al-ʿĀbidīn (Shahī Khān b. Iskandar, Kashmīr) (1470) iii, 420a, 453a; iv, 707a, 708b; xi, **683b**; s, 131b, 167a
Zayn al-ʿĀbidīn, Marāghaʾī (1910) vi, 72a, 164b, 789a, xi, **683b**; s, 109b
Zayn al-ʿĀbidīn, Sayyid (Mīrzāpūr) vii, 132b
Zayn al-ʿĀbidīn Shīrwānbī (mast ʿAlī Shāh) (1837) xi, **484a**, b
Zayn al-ʿĀbidīn b. Ghiyāth al-Dīn al-Marʿashī (XV) vi, 513a
Zayn al-ʿĀbidīn b. Ismaʿīl i, 47b
Zayn al-ʿĀbidīn b. Mīr-i Buzurg (Marʿashī) (XV) vi, 512b, 514a, 516a
Zayn al-ʿĀbidīn ʿAlī b. al-Ḥusayn b. ʿAlī b. Abī Ṭālib (712) iii, 227b, 611b; iv, 277b; vi, 663a; vii, 398a; xi, 481b; xi, **481b**; s, 231b, 401a
Zayn al-ʿĀbidīn al-Kuntī v, 394a
Zayn al-ʿĀbidīn Pasha iv, 194a
Zayn al-ʿAbidīn Sharīf iv, 1123a
Zayn al-Aṣnām i, 359a
Zayn al-Dīn, Shaykh (XVII) iii, 588b
Zayn al-Dīn b. ʿAlī al-ʿĀmilī → al-Shahīd al-Thānī
Zayn al-Dīn b. Shaykh ʿAlī, Shaykh (Mappila) (1521) vi, 461b
Zayn al-Dīn ʿAbd al-Salām Kamūyī s, 414b
Zayn al-Dīn ʿAlī Kücük (XII) vi, 870b; viii, 129b
Zayn al-Dīn Barakāt → Barakāt b. Mūsā
Zayn al-Dīn Bashāra, Amīr-i Ākhūr (XIII) viii, 15b
Zayn al-Dīn Ḳaradja b. Dulḳādir (Dhu 'l-Ḳadr) (1353) ii, 239a; vi, 507b
Zayn al-Dīn Maʿn (XVI) vi, 343a
Zaynab (Zenobia) → al-Murābiṭūn
Zaynab Begum bint Ṭahmāsp (Ṣafawid) (XVI) vi, 483a; x, 110a
Zaynab bint ʿAbd Allāh iii, 616a
Zaynab bint ʿAbd Allāh al-Maḥḍ (VIII) xi, **484b**
Zaynab bint ʿAlī ii, 843a; iii, 609b; ix, 332a
Zaynab bint Djaḥsh (641) i, 44b; vi, 650b; xi, **484b**
Zaynab bint al-Hārith (VII) ix, 205b
Zaynab bint Isḥāḳ v, 654b, 1178b
Zaynab bint Khuzayma (Umm al-Masākīn) (625) xi, **485a**
Zaynab bint Maẓʿūn iii, 63b, 1017b
Zaynab bint Muḥammad (629) vii, 879a; xi, **485a**
Zaynab bint Ṭahmāsp iv, 977a; x, 110a
Zaynab bint Yaḥyā b. ʿAbd al-Salām (1334) viii, 156a
Zaynab al-Nafzāwiyya (XI) i, 251a, 389b; v, 654b, 655a; vi, 742b; vii, 585a; xi, 356a
Zaynābād i, 1331a
al-Zaynabī b. Ḳūla (VII) vi, 745a
al-Zaynabī, Abu 'l-Ḳāsim ʿAlī b. al-Ḥusayn (ḳāḍī al-ḳuḍāt) (1149) s, 193a
al-Zaynabī, Abu 'l-Ḳāsim ʿAlī b. Ṭarrād (Ṭirād) (vizier) (1144) iii, 327b; vii, 735a; viii, 356a; xi, **485b**
Zaynabī ʿAlawī (1031) vii, 19a
Zaynal Khān v, 33b
Zayniyya ix, 785a; x, 251a
Zayt xi, **485b**
Zaytūn (port) vii, 72a; xi, **487a**
Zaytūn (olive (tree)) xi, **486a**
Zaytūn/Zītūn (Chüʾan/Quanzhou) (China) xi, **487a**
Zaytūn/Zeitun Süleymanli (Town) xi, **487b**
Zaytūna, Djāmiʿ al-(698) xi, **488a**; s, 334a
al-Zayyādī, Nūr al-Dīn ʿAlī b. Yaḥyā (1615) viii, 425a
Zayyān, Banū → ʿAbd al-Wādids
Zayyān b. Mardanīsh iv, 673a; ix, 363b
al-Zayyānī, Abu 'l-Ḳāsim (1833) i, 315b, 593b; ii, 874b; iii, 806a; vi, 113a; vii, 387b; xi, **490a**; s, 401b
Zayyānids → ʿAbd al-Wādids
al-Zayyāt, Abū Ṭālib iii, 963b; vii, 203b
Zāzā, Banū ii, 193a, 1139b
Zāzā (Zāzākī) xi, **491a**
Zēbākī i, 225a, 854a

Zehrā Khanîm ii, 980a
Zeila → Zaylaʿ
Zekeriya Sertel (XX) vi, 95b
Zekariyyā-zāde Yaḥyā Efendi (XVII) iv, 884a; vii, 597b
Zekī Welīdī → Togan, Zekī
Zemmūr i, 84b, 171b; ii, 873b; s, 144b
Zenāga (Morocco) ii, 885a
Zenāga → Ṣanhādja
Zenāta → Zanāta
Zenātā, Banū x, 169b, 757b; xi, 236b
Zenghī b. Bursuḳ i, 1336b
Zengi ʿImād al-Dīn → Zankī
Zenkids → Zangids
Zenobia → al-Zabbāʾ
Zenta (Senta) (Battle, 1697) iii, 193b; xi, **492a**
Zerbadis (Zerbadees) (Burma) xi, **492b**
Zerdabi, Ḥasan Bey Melikov i, 193b; ii, 476b
Zərzāy iii, 139a
Zeybek (W. Anatolia) xi, **493b**
Zeyrek-zāde Rukn al-Dīn Efendi (XVI) vi, 967a
Zeytūn vi, 508b
Ẓḥa → Djuḥā
Zhana ii, 25a; iv, 178b
Zhōb (river/district) xi, **494b**; s, 329b
Zhouan-Zhouan (Juan-Juan) x, 687a
Zhukotin i, 1305b
Zhūpīn iii, 197a; s, 153a, 743a
Ziʿāmet xi, **495a**
Zia-ul Haqq, Muḥammad (1988) → Ẓiyāʾ al-Ḥaḳḳ
Zīb al-Nisāʾ Begum bint Awrangzīb → Makhfī
Ziʾbaḳ xi, **495b**
Zībān → Zāb
Zibane vi, 364b
Zibaṭra v, 1166b; vi, 231a, 505b, 775b; vii, 776a
Zibel → Djabala
al-Zibriḳān b. Badr (VII) i, 343b; iii, 641a; iv, 832b; xi, **496b**
Zīdj i, 393a, 1141a; ii, 504a, 578b, 584b, 586b; iii, 8b, 928b, 969b, 1136a, b, 1137b; iv, 517b; v, 47a; xi, **496b**
Zigana mountains i, 462b
Ziggurat vi, 365a; viii, 49a
Ziḥāf xi, **508a**
Ziḥāfāt i, 671b, 672a
Ẓihār iv, 688a; viii, 28a
Zikrawayh b. Mihrawayh i, 96a; iv, 198b, 660b, 661a; v, 1242b; viii, 922a; xi, **405a**
Zikrīs → Dhikrīs
Zilbīr → Zunūz
Ẓill al-Sulṭān, Mīrzā Masʿūd (XX) iv, 105a, 392a, 393b, 979a; viii, 1050b; s, 53a, 54b, 302a
Zimām ii, 324a, 325a; xi, **509a**
Ziml b. ʿAmr (VII) ix, 664b; x, 774a
Zimma i, 87b
Zināʾ i, 29b, 910b; ii, 551a; iii, 20b; xi, **509a**
Zinda Shāh Madār vi, 228b
Zinder (Sultanate) ix, 853b
Zindīḳ i, 11b, 17b, 127b; ii, 228a, 236b; iv, 16b, 771b, 1003b; v, 1238b; vi, 421b; x, 440b; xi, **540a**
Zindj i, 145a, 278b, 279a
Zindjibar Ḳalʿesi iv, 580b
Zindjirli (Zincirli) xi, **513b**
Zinnat Fathullin (XX) vi, 770b
Zirāʿa ii, 899a
Zīrak ii, 629a; s, 105b
Zīrbādh (island) s, 223a
Zīrī b. ʿAṭiyya (1001) i, 860a; iii, 819a, 1043a; v, 1176b, 1177a, b; vi, 431b, 728b; vii, 942b; xi, **236b**; s, **843a**
Zīrī b. Manād b. Manḳūs (X) i, 699a, 1309a; ii, 495a; iv, 459a; v, 1176a; vi, 728a; vii, 64b, 486a, 487a; ix, 18a
Zīrids i, 6a, 9a, 43b, 491b, 533a, 699b, 863a, 986b, 1148b, 1175b, 1204b, 1309a, 1341a; ii, 145b, 747b, 1012a, b, 1015a; iii, 137a, 138b, 324b, 386a; iv, 337a, 651a; v, 503b, 1182a, b; vi, 427a, 852a; vii, 162b, 563b; ix, 894b; x, 213a; xi, **513b**
Zirih (Zarah) (Lake) xi, **516a**
Zirīhgarān ii, 85b, 86b; iv, 343a; v, 285b
Ziryāb, Abu ʾl-Ḥasan ʿAlī (852) i, 83a, 600b; ii, 1072a; v, 743b; vi, 520b, 713a; ix, 231a; xi, **516b**
Zishtowa (Svistov) xi, **517a**
Zistova (treaty) (1791) ix, 671a
Ziwar Pasha → Aḥmad Ziwar Pasha
Ẓiyā Gökalp → Gökalp Ziyā
Ẓiyāʾ al-Ḥaḳḳ, Muḥammad (Zia ul-Hacq/ Zia-ul Haqq) (1988) v, 1082a; viii, 243a; xi, **518a**
Ẓiyā (Ḍiyāʾ) Pasha (1880) i, 62a, 630a; ii, 466a, 474a, 682b, 878a; iii, 357a, 1188a;

iv, 196a, 877a; vi, 92b, 759a, 826b; vii, 532a; ix, 737b; xi, **518b**; s, 324b
Ziyād b. ʿAbd Allāh b. ʿAdjlān al-Hamdānī s, 400b
Ziyād b. ʿAbd al-Ḥakam (Mālikī, al-Andalus) (VIII) vi, 281a
Ziyād b. Abīhi, Abu ʾl-Mughīra (Ziyād b. Abī Sufyān) (675) i, 3b, 86a, 107a, 111b, 195a, 385a, 1085b, 1313b, 1343b; ii, 232a, 323b, 480b, 788a; iii, 40b, 42a, 224b, 545a, 782a, 1254b, 1265b; iv, 14a, b, 222a, 491b, 755a; v, 346b, 1111a; vi, 193a, 336b, 362a, 477a, 620a, 622a, 653a, 660b, 662a, 669a, 680b, 828a; vii, 145b, 266a, 347b, 400b, 521b; x, 842b; s, 26a, 133b, 157a, xi, **519a**
Ziyād b. al-Aṣbaḥ (VII) vii, 843a
Ziyād b. Khalfūn iv, 829b
Ziyād b. Khaṣafa v, 19b
Ziyād b. Labīb al-Anṣārī viii, 97a; s, 337b
Ziyād b. Marwān al-Ḳandī (IX) vii, 647b
Ziyād b. Ṣāliḥ al-Ḥārithī → Ziyād b. Ṣāliḥ al Khuzāʿī
Ziyād b. Ṣāliḥ al Khuzāʿī (Ziyād b. Ṣāliḥ al-Ḥārithī) (752) i, 103b, 1294a; iv, 16a; v, 854b, 855a; x, 348b; xi, **522**
Ziyād b. Sumayya s, 354b
Ziyād al-Aʿdjam Ibn Salmā (718) i, 74a; xi, **522a**
Ziyādat Allāh I b. Ibrāhīm (Aghlabid) (838) i, 248a, 250a, 619b; iv, 822a, 827b, 829b; viii, 506a; ix, 584a
Ziyādat Allāh II b. Muḥammad (Aghlabid) (863) i, 250b
Ziyādat Allāh III b. ʿAbd Allāh (Aghlabid) (909) i, 104a, 249a, 250b; vi, 434b; ix, 396a
al-Ziyādī, Abū Ḥassān al-Ḥasan (856) xi, **523a**
Ziyādids i, 551a, 551b, 552a, 932a; v, 895b; vii, 861a; viii, 706a; ix, 439a; x, 481b; xi, 370a; **523b**; s, 338a
Ziyād-oghlu iv, 387b; iv, 389a
Ziyaeddin Fahri Findikoğlu → Fi̊ndi̊ḳoghlu
Ziyāniyya xi, **524a**
Ziyār (Iṣfahān) vi, 365b
Ziyāra xi, **524a**
Ziyārat (Fārs) vi, 384b
Ziyārat-nāma iii, 1170a; s, 95a
Ziyārids i, 1354b; ii, 192b; iv, 358a; vi, 66a, 115b, 193a, 433a, 539a, b; x, 553a; xi, **539b**; s, 235a, 363a
Zlās, Banū iv, 828b
Zlīṭen (Zalīṭan) s, 93a
Zmāla, Banū i, 67b; ii, 173a; xi, **540b**
Zodiac → Minṭaḳat al-Burūdj
Zog, King i, 657b; v, 285a
Zohāb ix, 64b
Zohra Nigar vi, 489b
Zolota ii, 119b
Zonguldak xi, **544b**
Zōrāwar Singh i, 1004b
Zoroaster iv, 12b; v, 1112b; x, 510b
Zoroastrians → Gabr; Madjūs
Zorṭalbī ii, 597b, 598a
Zoṭṭ → Zuṭṭ
Zouaves → Zwāwa
Zouila → Zawīla
Zraḳī, Banū v, 459b
Zsitvatorok xi, **545b**
Zuʿʿār xi, **546a**
Zuʿayr, Banū ii, 875a; vi, 741b
Zubāla, Ḳaṣr s, 198b, 199b
al-Zubāra (Ḳaṭar) ii, 177b; iv, 751a, 752a, 953b; vi, 358a; xi, **547a**
Zubayd, Banū i, 1096b
Zubayda bint Fatḥ ʿAlī Shāh (Ḳādjār) (XVIII) vi, 484a
Zubayda Khātūn bint Djaʿfar (831) i, 107b, 897a, 909b, 1233a; iv, 653a, 694b; vi, 179b, 331a, 332a; xi, **547b**s, 198b, 199a
Zubayda Khātūn umm Barkyārūḳ (Saldjūḳ) (1105) iv, 101b; vi, 275a, 482a; viii, 81b
al-Zubaydī (1488) vii, 537b
al-Zubaydī, Abū Bakr Muḥammad (989) x, 178a; xi, **548a**
al-Zubaydī al-Ishbīlī (X) i, 501b; iv, 501a; v, 606a, 608a; viii, 868b; s, 306a, 388a
al-Zubayr b. ʿAbd al-Muṭṭalib iii, 389b; s, 37a
al-Zubayr b. al-ʿAwwām (656) i, 1a, 43b, 109b, 152b, 308a, 381b, 382a, 383a, 451a, 482a, 713b, 738a; ii, 414b, 415b; iii, 209b, 1165b; iv, 521b; vi, 139a, b, 653b, 738b; vii, 364a, 649b; xi, **549a**; s, 44b, 89b, 267b
al-Zubayr b. Bakkār (870) i, 793b; ii, 1029b; iii, 757a, 820a, 878a; vi, 822a; vii, 649a, 967b; xi, **553a**
Zubayr b. al-Māhūẓ i, 810b
Zubayr al-Ḥasan b. Inʿām al-Ḥasan (1996) x, 38b

Zubayr Pasha (1874) viii, 356b; s, 164b
Zubayr Rāghī i, 852b
al-Zubayr Raḥma Manṣūr i, 49b, 929a, 962a, 1156b; ii, 123b; v, 1248b
al-Zubayrī (848) i, 591a
al-Zubayrī, Abū ʿAbd Allāh (929) viii, 840b
Zubayrids i, 1086a; vi, 139a, b, 140a, 546b, 622a, 623a
Zubda xi, **552a**
Zubdat al-Mulk → ʿUthmān Khān
Zudjādj (Zadjādj, Zidjādj) iv, 135a; v, 107a, 397b; xi, **552a**
Ẓufār i, 76b, 539b, 872b; v, 71a; vi, 80a, 82a, 83b, 84a, b, 433b, 561a, 563b; vii, 779a; viii, 914b; s, 22a, 234b, 338b, 339b
Zufar b. al Ḥārith al-Kilābī (VII) i, 76b; ii, 523b, 1023b; iii, 1175b; iv, 493a, 655a; v, 541a; vi, 545a
Zufar b. al-Hudhayl (775) i, 124a; iii, 163a; iv, 269b; vii, 758a
Zughār ii, 535a, 1024b; x, 884a
Zughārī → Zaghārī
Zughba, Banū i, 374a; iii, 137b, 386a; v, 1179a; vi, 728b
Zuhāb iv, 978b; v, 168a, 170a
Zuhāb (treaty) (1639) iii, 1257a; viii, 771b; ix, 368b
Zuhāk xi, **554b**
Zuḥal (Saturn) xi, **555a**; s, 153b
Zuhara (Venus) xi, **556a**; s, 153b
Zuhayr (ʿĀmirid) (1038) i, 1310a; vi, 576b; vii, 633a; xi, **559a**
Zuhayr b. Abī Sulmā Rabīʿa b. Rabāḥ (VI) ii, 1023a; iii, 641a; iv, 744b; vi, 107b, 344b, 625b, 817b; vii, 254b, 306a; xi, **556b**; s, 304b
Zuhayr b. Djadhīma al-ʿAbsī ii, 1023a; iii, 285b; s, 177a
Zuhayr b. Djanāb al-Kalbī ii, 1024a; iv, 421a, 492b; xi, **558b**
Zuhayr b. Ḥawiyya (VII) vii, 571a
Zuhayr b. al-Ḳayn al-Badjalī iii, 608b, 610a
Zuhayr b. Ḳays al-Balawī (695) ii, 160b; iii, 271a; iv, 403a; v, 518a, b; xi, **559a**
Zuhayr b. al-Musayyib b. Zuhayr al-Ḍabbī (IX) vi, 333a
Zuhayr b. ʿUrwa al-Sakb vi, 954b
Zuhayr al-Bahāʾ → Bahāʾ al-Dīn Zuhayr
al-Zuhayrī, Banū x, 91a
Zuhd x, 464b; xi, **559b**
Zühdī Pasha ii, 682b
Zuhdiyya xi, **562a**
Zuhra, Banū viii, 888a; ix, 38a; xi, **564b**
al-Zuhra, Muḥammad b. ʿĀli vi, 869b
Zuhra b. Ḥawiyya (VII) vii, 571a
Zuhra b. Kilāb, Banū iv, 896b; vi, 145a; s, 81b
Zuhra Bēgam i, 296a
al-Zuhrī, Abū Muṣʿab Aḥmad b. Abī Bakr (IX) vii, 409a
al-Zuhrī, al-Aswad b. ʿAbd Yaghūth vii, 32a
al-Zuhrī, Hārūn b. ʿAbd Allāh (846) vii, 4a; xi, **565a**
al-Zuhrī, Ibn Shihāb (742) vii, 33a; x, 81a; xi, **565a**
al-Zuhrī, Muḥammad b. Abī Bakr ii, 585a; iv, 383b, 1078a; xi, 566a
al-Zuhrī, Muḥammad b. al-Ashʿath (VIII) viii, 996b
al-Zuhrī, Muḥammad b. Muslim (741) ii, 888b; iii, 24a, 494b; v, 731a; vi, 263a, b, 278b; s, 310b, 311a, b, 358a, 386b
Zuhrī Aḥmed Efendi (1751) viii, 11a
al-Ẓuhūr iii, 658a
Ẓuhūr al-Dīn Ḥādjdjī Ḥudūr (XVI) vii, 440a
Ẓuhūri, Nūr al-Dīn Muḥammad Turshīzī (1616) i, 1203a; iv, 69a; vi, 271b; vii, 340b, 341a; xi, **566a**
Zūiya, Banū i, 763b
Zūḳ Mīkhāʾīl s, 33b
al-Zuḳur (island) i, 535b
Zula → Adulis
Zulālī (Khwānsār) (1615) iv, 69a; viii, 776a; xi, **567a**
Zülālī Ḥasan Efendi v, 642b, 643b
Zulātī, Abu ʾl-Ḥasan i, 780a
Zuldjū iv, 708a
Zulfiḳar Ali Bhutto → Bhutto, Zulfiḳar Ali
Ẓulla → Ṣuffa
Ẓulm xi, **567b**
Zumayl b. Rabīʿa (VII) vi, 545b
Zumurrud xi, **569b**
Zumurrud Khātūn bint Tīmurtash (Artuḳid) (1203) vi, 870b; xi, **571a**
Zumurrud Khātūn umm al-Nāṣir li-Dīn Allāh (ʿAbbāsid) (XII) vii, 997a
Zūn (Zhūn) xi, **571a**
Zunām (IX) vii, 207a

Zunayn (singer) vii, 390b
Zunbīl (Rutbīl) ii, 1048b; iii, 715b, 716a, 717b; iv, 356b, 536a; v, 541b; vi, 954b; vii, 777a; viii, 595b; ix, 683a; xi, 254b, 255a, 371b, **571b**; s, 125b
Zunghars s, 523b, 541a
Zunnār ii, 228a; iii, 77b; xi, **571b**
Zunūz (river) vi, 504a
Zunūz (town) vi, 505a
Zurʿa b. ʿĪsā b. Nasṭūrus ii, 858a
Zurʿa b. Tibbān Asʿad → Dhū Nuwās
Zurāʿa b. Awfā (ḳāḍī) (VII) vi, 670b
Zurāra b. Aʿyān (767) vii, 398b; viii, 387b
Zurayʿids (Aden) i, 181b, 552a, 1214b; iii, 125b, 134a; iv, 200b; v, 602a, 895b, 954b, 1244b; vii, 731a; xi, **572a**; s, 236a, 338a
Zurayḳ, Banū vi, 649a
Zurayḳ, Cōstī (Ḳusṭanṭīn) iv, 783a
al-Zurḳānī, Muḥammad b. ʿAbd al-Bāḳī (1710) vi, 264a, 279a; xi, **572b**
Zūrkhāna ii, 433a; iv, 8b; xi, **572b**
Zurna ii, 1027b; xi, **574a**
Zurvān ii, 95a; iv, 12b
Zuṭṭ (Djāt, Banū) i, 761b, 789b, 1005b, 1086a, 1094b, 1095a, 1096a, 1292b; ii, 36a, 40b, 456b; iii, 488a; iv, 534b, 1024b; v, 817b; vi, 336b, 338a, b, 774b, 968a; vii, 401a, 776a; viii, 138a; ix, 76a; s, 163a, 243a
al-Zuṭṭ xi, 168a, **574b**
al-Zuṭṭī, Abū Sālima (VII) ix, 98a
al-Zuṭṭī, al-Sarī b. al-Ḥakam b. Yūsuf (821) viii, 138b
Zuwāra x, 213b
Zuwārak vi, 539b
Zuwayla → Zawīla
Zvornik i, 1263b; vi, 71b, 227b; s, 506b
Zwāwa i, 1175a; iv, 362a, 478a; viii 795a
Zwāya (marabouts) vii, 616b